HISLOP'S

OFFICIAL INTERNATIONAL PRICE GUIDE TO FINE ART
2ND EDITION

Art Sales Index, Ltd.
Jodie Benson, Director
Ian Black, Office Manager
Eleonora Aveline, Assistant Editor
Esther Carter, Assistant Editor
Deborah Chubb, Assistant Editor
Lynette Davies, Assistant Editor
Margaret George, Assistant Editor
Bjorg Gough, Assistant Editor
Leslie Greenaway, Assistant Editor

LTB Media, Inc.
Robin Kamen, President, Artinfo.com
Lawrence Kaplan, President, LTB Media Sales & Marketing
Philippe Carlhammar, Director of Operations, Europe

LTB Holding, Parent Company
Louise Blouin MacBain, Chairman

HOUSE OF
COLLECTIBLES

House of Collectibles
New York, Toronto, London, Sydney, Auckland

This book is available at special discounts for bulk purchases for sales promotions or premiums. Special editions, including personalized covers, excerpts of existing books, and corporate imprints, can be created in large quantities for special needs. For more information, write to Special Markets/Premium Sales, 1745 Broadway, MD 6-2, New York, NY 10019 or e-mail specialmarkets@randomhouse.com.

Please address inquiries about electronic licensing of any products for use on a network, in software, or on CD-ROM to the Subsidiary Rights Department, Random House Information Group, fax 212-572-6003.

Visit the House of Collectibles Web site: www.houseofcollectibles.com

Printed in the United States of America

10 9 8 7 6 5 4 3 2 1

ISBN: 978-0-375-72214-1
ISSN: 1537-5889

Second Edition: March 2007

Front cover illustration courtesy of:
Estate of the Artist, the Susan Teller Gallery, New York, NY, and
Michael Rosenfeld Gallery, New York, NY

Georges Schreiber (1904-1977)
Late Light 1944
Oil on canvas, 29 1/8 x 40 inches, signed

CONTENTS

INTRODUCTION

Buying, collecting and selling artwork are activities that are not only exciting and interesting, but can be financially rewarding. Not that every purchase you make will be a winner; nearly everyone trading in artwork makes mistakes sometimes. The credo is "you win some and you lose some," and losing is probably superior to winning as a learning experience. As time goes on, the wins should increasingly exceed the losses.

Success depends on acquiring practical experience. This book is designed to help you make rapid progress toward your goal, whether it is to buy something beautiful or stimulating, to collect, to invest, or to trade profitably.

VALUE AND PRICE

Value is an interesting and complicated concept. The value of something may, for example, depend on scarcity, beauty, or usefulness. It may be psychologically valuable because it seems unobtainable. In contrast, when you have bought something, you sometimes wonder why you did so. John Updike put it starkly, "Possession diminishes perception of value immediately." Oscar Wilde makes a telling distinction between value and price In his definition of a cynic as "a man who knows the price of everything and the value of nothing."

There are many things that are priceless. A child's painting may be cherished by the parents, who would not part with it for anything. But in the more general run of things, Samuel Butler's precept that "For what is worth anything but so much money as it will bring" is a sensible guide. The price a piece of artwork commands depends on many factors. Robert Wraight has said: "A painting has no intrinsic worth. It is a luxury commodity for which a market is deliberately created and maintained by financially interested parties." This was illustrated by a charcoal drawing described as "English School, 18th Century" estimated to achieve at auction about $1,500. It was then discovered that the work was likely to be by Gainsborough, for which a considerable market has been created — a superb artist with a scarcity value based on the fact that an artist can paint only a limited number of pieces. When he is dead, there are no more. It actually sold for about $150,000. It was the same work with the same aesthetic value both before and after the discovery, but the highly marketable name made all the difference.

Similar striking differences in price arise when there are doubts as to whether a piece has actually been painted by the artist. There are two versions of what purport to be Vincent Van Gogh's painting "Sunflowers," one of which is claimed to be by the artist and one of which is not. It is known that his neighbor, Dr. Gachet, sometimes copied his paintings, and one might have been painted by him. Seen together, it is impossible for anyone other than an expert to tell the difference. The genuine one is worth $60 million while the other is worth perhaps ten thousand times less.

Pieces of artwork are commodities, and the prices they command are determined by supply and demand, fashion, and marketing. At serious prices, the name of the artist is what determines the price, which is why prices in this guide are listed by artist. It would be nice to believe that prices are somehow correlated with some sort of virtue, like the skill of the artist, the spiritual content, or a mind-blowing message. However, the millions of dollars paid for some sorts of modern art, which seem, to many observers, to be either rubbish or a joke or both, emphasizes the importance of fashion and marketing of names. Even when one can appreciate the qualities of a beautiful and inspiring painting, it is difficult to understand how it can be worth millions of dollars. But that is how the art industry works, and this book reflects how the market values the work of many artists.

Is there a "right" price?

If you are faced with having to give advice on the value of paintings by an unknown artist, what do you say? You can see that they might be priced at $150 each in a local art society exhibition, and some might sell at that price. However, put the same artwork into an auction, and they probably wouldn't sell at all.

Another item by a known artist is brought in for valuation. It looks genuine. The artist's name appears in the price guides, and his oil paintings have sold in the range $1,000 to $6,000. It is typical of the artist, skillfully painted, with convincing figures, horses and careful architectural depiction. It could well command upwards of $3,000 at auction. This argues for a price of $6,000 retail at the very least and probably a good deal more in a fashionable gallery. If the valuation is for insurance, then to be on the safe side one might argue for $7,500. All these ways of expressing price are used on the television program "The Antiques Road Show," which can cause confusion as to what is the "real" price.

Today, the auction price is considered the most dependable price. But even then, if you examine the prices that a particular popular artist has achieved over a year at auction, you will see a wide range. For example, Andy Warhol's works on paper vary in price from $450 for a watercolor to $15,750,000 for a silkscreen of Marilyn Monroe. Not only the name of the artist affects the price of an item, but so do other considerations such as size, subject, and the quality of the image.

The price of artwork can vary from one location to another, which is exploited by some art traders who will buy an item at one auction to sell at a profit at another. Prices can depend on the time of the year, the sentiment in the economy, and on who is actually at the auction. Regardless of all these factors, most auction houses manage to estimate the prices artwork will command with surprising accuracy. But they are not infallible. There are often negative surprises when pieces do not reach the estimated prices, and a few positive ones when the prices go way beyond the estimates. When estimating prices for artwork by known artists, the prices previously achieved, such as those given in this book, are the best guide.

Why do people buy artwork?

Some artwork is bought to furnish a room, when colors, shades, and brightness are important. The term "furnishing piece" is often used in a dismissive way to reduce expectations when an optimistic vendor brings a piece into an auction house for valuation. However, it is also a reasonable description of a wide range of artwork that is used to enhance a room. Another reason for buying is the appeal of the subject of the artwork. A number of these are recognized as being "commercial" in the trade. Examples are familiar landscapes or buildings, animals of any sort – wild, domestic, farm-cottages with children outside, seascapes, and beaches with children.

Many items are bought by collectors who want paintings by a particular artist or school or of specialist subjects — for example, hunting dogs, tabby cats, moonlit scenes, or Victorian sailing boats in difficulties. People may collect artwork as investments in the hope that, when they are ready to sell, the price of the item will have gone up. Then there is the trader who hopes to find a bargain and sell it again to make a quick profit.

The price that you are willing to pay for artwork depends on which of the above categories apply to you. If you are a furnishings piece buyer and you spot exactly the right item to set off your interior design, you will probably not be too concerned about the price. This is probably true of the "I like it, I want it" viewpoint of the buyer of an attractive or striking subject. These buyers accept the frequently given advice, "Buy what you like, what moves you, what appeals to you; back your own judgment."

This is not bad advice provided you are not concerned whether the price being paid is at least what you are likely to get back when you are ready to sell. The implication is that if it is worth it to you, the price is right. These buyers frequently buy from galleries and exhibitions and pay in the range of $100 to $50,000. They may say, "I have seen this artist fetching similar prices in galleries, and the price is fair." However, they have no way of knowing whether they are buying at the right price unless the work of the artist has an auction record (which it often doesn't). Nevertheless, from time to time an artist promoted by a gallery may become very successful, his or her exhibitions selling out at the private view and soon achieving an enviable auction performance. There are exceptions to every generality, so it is clearly a good idea to try to spot such artists.

Collectors are in a different category. They are generally well informed about their specialty, and they use price guides to check the prices they are prepared to pay. Sometimes the needs of the collection will override purely commercial considerations.

Investors and traders are very price conscious. The former in the long run, and the latter in the short run, aim to buy cheaply and sell dearly. They need to know the market price of what they want to buy and sell and what prospective purchasers will likely pay. The price guide is one of their essential tools.

How to Trade Profitably in the World of Art

One good piece of advice is to avoid trying to buy and sell everything. Be a specialist. Don't deal in "unknowns." Choose a niche. For example, focus on a very small number of artists, living or dead, of repute, whose artwork frequents auctions. Get to know the work of these artists — the subjects they have painted, the style, the way they apply paint, their history. There are other sorts of specialties — a particular "school" of painters or a type of painting. Choose what really interests you, so that any time you spend on research is not only valuable but enjoyable. Above all, buy items that other people are buying, so that you will find it easy to sell them.

Check the prices that are being asked or estimated, with the prices similar pieces have commanded at auctions, by using price guides. Check the artists' references in the various biographical books, such as *Davenport's Art Reference & Price Guide*, covering your chosen artists. Select the gallery or auction based on an opportunity to buy an item for a price that will enable you to make a profit when you are ready to sell it.

Market Trends

Broadly, the volume and value of the art market tend to follow the economic cycles. This can be seen in Fig.1, which shows the turnover in dollars (millions) and the number of lots sold in the International Art Auction Market from 1980 to 2006. There is a steady growth to 1986 and then a rapid buildup to the peak of 1990, which was fueled by the international boom at that time. This turnover was out of line with the longer-term trend from 1983. The fall after the boom showed the figures in 1992 resuming this longer-term trend. Subsequent years reflect the strength of the U.S. and international economies over the last few years with significant growth in the last three years.

Fig. 1

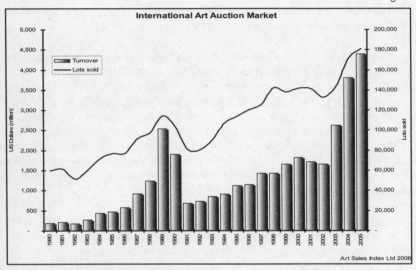

Those who can remember the fifties may recall artwork that could be bought then for a few hundred dollars, which now sells for a hundred thousand dollars or more. Some artwork purchased then is not worth much more now. In general, the experience has been that "good" art is a sound, long-term investment.

However, like the stock market, prices are sensitive to interest rates. While prices are going up, the interest cost of holding stock can be ignored. Conversely, if interest rates go up, people start to sell and prices can begin to tumble. The obvious, but often ignored, advice is to buy when the market is depressed and sell when it is buoyant.

Price Guides

A price guide, like this one, gives information on the results of art auctions. The price recorded here is the hammer price. This book lists the artists alphabetically. For an idea of what this book contains and how to use it, please see the section "About This Book" on page 33.

There are several other very good, in-depth pricing publications. The *2007 Art Sales Index* (available in book and CD formats) lists each lot sold by artist and provides information on over 175,000 works in oils, acrylic, tempera, gouache, watercolor, pastel, crayon, drawing, chalk, charcoal, prints, photography, sculpture, and miniatures. Other pricing guides (also available in book and CD formats) are the *Gordon's Print Price Annual* and the *Gordon's Photography Price Annual*, which report auction results for prints, posters, illustrated books, Picasso ceramics, and photographs (respectively). For an in-depth database of fine art pricing, the ArtInfo.com online database provides auction price results from 1970 through current sales with significant search and filtering capabilities. For further information on any of these price guides, visit www.gordonsart.com.

Using any of the above, you can compare prices obtained at auction with the estimates for artwork you are interested in purchasing. This will tell you what price you might expect to achieve for this piece at auction. For example, if the artist appears to command about $5,000 at auction for oil paintings of cows in the 20" by 30" size range, and you spot one of his paintings similar to these with an estimate of $1,500 in a provincial auction house, it looks like an opportunity to at least double your money.

Estimating a Price

You can estimate the price for an item using price guides. If you use this book, you will be able to get an idea of the range of prices and the median (see page 33). To refine the estimate, you will need to consult a more detailed price guide, such as the *Art Sales Index*, which will give you information regarding size and subject. Both show prices for various media, so you must be careful that you are not, for example, confusing oils with watercolors. Also bear in mind that there is a low value below which a piece will not appear in the list. In this guide, the low value is $1,000 for oils, watercolors, and miniatures, and $3,000 for prints and photographs. It is also important to note where an item was sold. A good price achieved in Germany may not be a good indicator of the price that might have been achieved had it been sold in the U.S. or the United Kingdom.

If you are going to buy at auction, most auctioneers will have estimated a "hammer" price, based on the auction house's experience and after consulting the price guides. However, you may discover that the auctioneer's estimate is well below what your research in the price guides suggest it ought to be. This may be because the auctioneer does not think it is a very good example of the artist's work; after all, artists do have "bad" days. It may also be a mistake or an intentionally low estimate to attract bidders.

There will always be some artwork that does not have a signature, or the signature is illegible and the artist is unknown. These are generally listed as "in the style of" some artist, or "School of painters," or as "American School," "English School," etc. Such items can be opportunities to buy if you recognize the style, the way it is painted, and hence can identify the artist. Sometimes there is an illegible signature that, again, you realize you have seen somewhere before, and you may have found a bargain.

RESEARCHING

The skill of spotting something that no one else has is cultivated by looking at many items and reading about them. You may become a specialist on a particular artist or niche or try to spread your expertise over a wide field. Either way, the more you see and learn, the more likely you are to spot the "sleeper" that no one else has seen (and the auctioneer has not realized is valuable), and obtain it for a bargain price.

The pricing publications are an initial guide as to what to pay for a piece. However, they need to be supplemented by further information. You may be drawn to an item at auction that is signed by an artist that does not appear in any of the price guides. It is very useful to be able to see what is known about him or her, and this is where Biographical Guides are necessary.

The Biographical Guides

These guides enable you to discover whether the artist has exhibited and what type of work he or she created. One that is widely used for little-known and hard-to-find artists is *Davenport's Art Reference & Price Guide* (available in book and CD formats). Here you'll find birth and death dates, nationality, sample auction results if available, type of work the artist is known for, where the artist studied, etc. for almost 300,000 artists.

The new ENGLISH version of *Benezit Dictionary of Artists* includes biographical entries on artists, descriptions of museums and galleries where the works of an artist can be found, graphics (including artist signatures, monograms and stamps of sale), auction records, and bibliographies of written works for over 170,000 artists.

A mention in either of the above is a reassurance that the artist actually existed, that the signature, if it is genuine, is of an artist of some substance, but not necessarily of value. For further information on these biographical guides, please visit www.gordonsart.com.

Galleries, Museums and Libraries

If you have decided to concentrate on one artist, or several, or even a school, you will want to do some research on them. A literature search can be done at most public libraries, and the relevant books can often be borrowed, or at least perused within the gallery library. The prodigious *Grove Dictionary of Art* in thirty-four volumes, published by the Grove Hale Press in 1996, and available in many good libraries, is a must for any serious student. This publication is now also available as an online database.

Another important source is the Archives of American Art, which is a bureau of the Smithsonian Institution that preserves original documents, diaries, letters and photographs of artists. The main offices are in Washington, D.C., with regional offices in New York City, Boston, Detroit and San Francisco.

Catalogue Subscriptions

Nearly all auction houses issue catalogues, ranging from plain photocopied sheets to the beautifully illustrated paperback books produced by the major houses such as Sotheby's and Christie's, which are of considerable value and cost. Most auction houses are eager for you to subscribe, so that catalogues are sent to you ahead of sales. If you are a good customer of an auction house, you may receive catalogues free. If you have artwork for sale at a particular auction, you will automatically be sent a catalogue for that sale. There is also a trade in old catalogues, which often appear in stalls at fairs. Finally, most auction houses now publish their catalogues at their websites for free. So, instead of paying a subscription fee, you can peruse the catalogue online at your leisure.

Many galleries, both private and public, issue catalogues for which a charge is usual. A catalogue issued in connection with a major exhibition may be a definitive document for a particular artist or group and well worth acquiring. Catalogues, particularly those with color illustrations, are good, relatively cheap sources of information, providing the opportunity to study many artists' works, note the subjects they painted, and note the colors they used, as well as being able to spot signatures and monograms.

The Internet

The Internet is the electronic doorway to museums, art galleries, and auction houses. Websites provide the opportunity to trawl the world for information about the art world, and to research specific artists and artwork.

To start your internet journey, enter "art galleries," "museums," or "auction houses" into the search box of any of the main search engines (such as Google or Ask). To narrow your search results, add a specific location, such as a city or state, or type of art. For example, you could search for "contemporary art galleries in New York City," or "art museums in London."

A very useful site is www.artinfo.com, which offers a comprehensive database of artists, artwork, museums, galleries, auction houses, and prices for works sold at auction. The site also covers news about art, and allows visitors to sign up for free email alerts about upcoming auctions and new artworks at galleries.

Internet Auctions

There are two main types of internet auctions. In one, the auction takes place over a period of a week or two. In the other, it is in real time, and it is as if you are in the auction room, able to bid. It takes a little perseverance to register and get into a position to bid or submit an item, but it is much more convenient and cost effective than traveling long distances.

Heffel.com is typical of the auctioneers who allow bidding to continue over a number of days. On its website, for each lot (item) you can see an illustration, estimate, the current bid, and the time remaining for you to bid. The hammer falls when the time runs out. The website also provides auction results for each sale, by lot number, with illustrations and details together with the price, including buyer's premium.

A major player in the online league is www.ebay.com. At any time there are over 100,000 artwork items for sale. Each piece has a description and illustration. Details can be enlarged, and often the reverse of the picture can be viewed. However, read the details closely as there are many reproductions offered for sale here. eBay has a very good system of rating the integrity and efficiency of sellers. This is based on purchasers' reports. Joining and bidding are free. As a seller, you will be charged a "seller's commission." As a buyer, you may be charged a "buyer's commission."

You are obligated to complete the transaction, whether buyer or seller, once the equivalent of the hammer has fallen. Each item has to be photographed (preferably front and back). Some familiarity with internet technology is desirable.

A recent lawsuit result suggests that eBay is legally considered to be a "service" rather than a "contents" provider, which means that a claim for compensation, after buying an item that subsequently turns out to be a fake, is likely to fail. It was also reported that three men had been charged with allegedly using more than forty user names to inflate bids on paintings in one case, again allegedly, from $0.35 to $135,505.

In the *Antique Trade Gazette* internet handbook, Jim Franses says that "buying and selling on eBay is a tactical game which takes a long time to learn." He also points out that the seller is known from the start of bidding and is available to the purchaser by e-mail so that it becomes possible to establish good relationships speedily.

Most of the conditions and considerations that apply to auctions in the physical world, and which are discussed later, apply to internet auctions. The auctioneers take very little, if any, legal responsibility for default by either seller or buyer. For example, eBay makes it clear that the "site acts as a venue." It is not involved in the actual transaction between buyer and seller and by implication takes no responsibility. Nevertheless, some internet auctioneers will provide condition reports, and the success of internet auctions depends on trust, integrity, and a good positive experience for clients.

If you make payments over the internet, it is usual to pay by credit card. There are a number of precautions that should be observed. The retailer's contact street address and ordinary telephone number should be available to you and should be noted. Use only companies that have an encryption certificate and use secure transaction technology. Make sure you are dealing with a legitimate business by telephoning the company. Keep copies of the trader's terms and conditions and returns policy. Never disclose your card's PIN number to anyone.

Buying on the internet also involves the matter of packing, delivery, and insurance. There are international couriers and professional packers that are used by many of the more important auction houses, who also arrange and charge for insurance.

DIFFERENT TYPES OF ARTWORK

As a collector, occasional trader, or full-time dealer, you may specialize in one of the categories briefly described here.

Oil Paintings

Oil paint consists of pigments mixed with oils, such as linseed oil or poppy oil. Pigment mixed with egg yolk is called tempera. The medium acrylic can be used as though it is a watercolor or an oil paint. It is an emulsion of pigments, water, and clear, non-yellowing acrylic resins, and it has the advantage that it dries quickly and does not darken with time.

Works On Paper

Drawings
Over the years, drawings have been done using a variety of materials: pencil, pen-and-ink, charcoal, chalks, and crayons. Pastels are drawn or painted with sticks of dry color.

Watercolors

Watercolors are painted with pigments, some of which are translucent and can be manipulated to some extent, and some of which dye the paper. Gouaches are painted with opaque pigments mixed with gum. Some watercolors are "heightened" with white gouache, and other colored gouaches may be used. The term "mixed media" covers combinations of the above.

Prints

Three elements are involved in making a print. These are: paper, an inked surface, and an image that is transferred from the inked surface onto the paper. The idea of printing is to make a number of copies, and this multiplicity of copies distinguishes a print from an original one-off. There are numerous printing processes with many variations, each of which is a specialty.

The most common prints are mechanical prints, which can be seen everywhere, from flea markets to prestigious stores. Many prints are of watercolors, and some are so good that it is easy to mistake them for the real thing, especially if they are under glass. Inspection with a magnifying glass will generally reveal the myriad of small dots of color. Some mechanical prints are numbered and signed by the artist and thereby assume some enhanced value.

There are other processes that can simulate oil paintings, so that you may think you can feel the paint. For example, oleographs (chromolithographs printed with oil paint on canvas in imitation of oil paintings), have been printed for more than a hundred years. You are most likely to be faced with the need to tell the difference between the real thing and a reproduction, at yard and garage sales, flea markets, junk stores, and antique shops. It can work both ways; you may be taken in, but it is just possible that you might buy a print for a few dollars and, either by luck or good judgment, discover that it is an original worth thousands of dollars. If, after doing your research, you think you have something of worth, the next step would be to have an appraiser value the item.

Silkscreen prints are often produced by contemporary artists in limited, numbered, and signed editions. They are made by using a finely meshed screen, often made of silk, and stencils to transfer the image to the paper. The artist generally supervises the printing, which may involve numerous colors, so there is some input into them apart from the original image, and they are to some extent one-offs.

Lithographs are prints, generally in color these days, although early ones were printed in black-and-white and colored by hand. Many famous artists have used lithography, and some of their work commands high prices. It is sometimes difficult to distinguish an original.

Wood and linocuts are produced from wooden blocks or pieces of lino and are known as relief or surface prints. Some are by famous artists such as Thomas Beckwith in the eighteenth century, and more recently, Kandinsky and Picasso.

Intaglio processes include line engraving, etching, aquatint, drypoint, and mezzotint. They involve incising a design into a metal plate, which is inked and pressed onto paper, forcing the paper into the incisions to take up the ink. The important thing to note is that the edge of the metal plate makes an indentation all around and close to the paper's edge. Not infrequently, prints are sold that are worthless mechanical prints of intaglio prints, which do not show the indentation. Many are framed and backed to look like old prints to deceive the buyer.

CONDITION, RESTORATION, FRAMING, AND FAKES

Condition

There are two parts to a picture, an image and a support. The most common supports are wood, fabric, and paper. Wood can split and become infested with wood-boring insects. Fabrics are treated with sizing materials that, with age, become brittle and can grow mold. Paper is made from cotton or linen rags or from ground-up wood fiber pulp, which can discolor and on which mold can grow.

It is sensible for the inexperienced to avoid pictures that are damaged or exhibit obvious blemishes. With prints, it is important to have a clear dense print and, if it is colored, for the color not to be faded. Prints may be torn, stained, or have spots of mold. They may be trimmed to fit into a frame. All such faults may make the print worthless or, at best, costly to restore. Similar considerations apply to drawings and watercolors. Oil paintings can suffer physical damage (often from careless handling and stacking), when the corner of a frame may press against the canvas of an adjoining picture. Paint can crack and come away from the canvas. Frames and stretchers can be riddled with woodworm. Wooden panels often warp and crack.

Restoration

Oil paintings

Often oil paintings have just accumulated dirt, which can be removed very carefully with water or proprietary liquids. Any such mild cleaning should be done very carefully, a little at a time, looking carefully for any signs of paint being removed. If this occurs, the procedure should be stopped immediately.

Restoration often involves removing varnish without damaging the original paint. Doing so can often transform a dark brown painting into a fresh-looking colored one. Frequently, acetone is used, diluted with white spirit. Tears can be repaired, and blemishes are often touched up. Where the paint is loose on canvas, the painting can be lined.

Problems occur when the artist has used too much linseed oil, which causes the paint to dry very slowly and become shriveled. The painting can never be fully restored to its original state but instead has to be retouched. Too much restoration can detract from the value of a painting, and the terms "original" condition or "unrestored" are often used to explain why an item has attracted competitive bidding at an auction.

Most prestigious galleries seem to clean oil paintings, so the colors are bright and fresh. It would appear that buyers like this, but insensitive cleaning can detract from the value of a painting.

If you intend to use a restorer, it is advisable to use someone recommended by a person or an institute that is professionally knowledgeable about restoration. Regrettably, a poor, unskilled, or inexperienced restorer can damage a painting irreparably. Good restorers are generally very busy, so they may hold an item for months. This is something to consider when you buy, if you want to sell the artwork quickly.

If you are buying from a dealer, you can inquire as to how much restoration has been carried out on the item you are considering. You can ask to use an ultraviolet lamp, which will show up recently applied paint. If there is much over painting, it may be a painting to avoid.

Watercolors
Foxed (stains caused by mold) watercolors can usually be restored satisfactorily. So-called "burn marks," tannin marks from wood that has been used as a backing, are more difficult to remove. Items with such marks should generally be avoided. Gouaches are also difficult to restore. Some restorers will touchup or paint over faded watercolors. When buying, this is something to watch for, because such retouching detracts from the originality of the painting.

Prints
Surface dirt can be removed with a soft eraser. Foxing requires expert treatment. A paper conservator, who is an expert in the structure of paper, should be consulted for the restoration of valuable prints.

Framing

A frame can often say something about the artwork it surrounds. Most amateur paintings are framed cheaply. An elaborate gold-leaf frame is often a good sign to corroborate the genuineness of an old painting. However, there are many reproduction pseudo gold frames, housing apparently old paintings with convincing craquelure, that were painted only yesterday. Sometimes, particularly at the lower end of the market, a frame may be worth more than the painting.

Forgeries

There are many unsigned paintings around, both amateur and professional. Some of these will acquire signatures, the effect of which is misleadingly to increase the conceived value of them. These are deliberate forgeries and are found everywhere, so it is necessary to be wary. The more famous forgeries were and still are painted specially to deceive, and there are many examples of these being bought by international museums for millions of dollars. See Christopher Wright's book "The Art of the Forger."

A "legal" deception is putting a name on a frame or mount to suggest that something is other than it actually is. Many examples of this occur in sale rooms. Fakes often seem to be too perfect. Tell-tale signs are whether the varnish has any crackle on the surface, whether the brushstrokes look right, or whether the signature of an oil painting is in a different color from any that have been used elsewhere in the painting.

When referencing the prices in this book (or any other pricing guide), it is essential to make sure that what seems a bargain is genuine. It is generally made clear at auction if there are doubts as to authenticity, and these need to be considered very carefully. Because a name means money, it is only too tempting to buy a signature. Authenticity requires many more clues, such as the subject, the way the paint is applied, the colors and paints used, the type of canvas, and so on.

BUYING AT AUCTION

Why buy at auction?

Many people buy at auction because they think that it will be cheaper than buying from a gallery. Additionally they think they may spot something that no one else has seen and so get a bargain. It is possible to see items that were sold at auction subsequently appearing in a gallery, with a massive markup. An example would be two pictures that were purchased at an auction for $1,100. They were then sold to a dealer for $1,900 who then sold them to a gallery for $2,800. The gallery showed and listed them for $7,800. You can compare gallery prices with the auction prices in this book to check the difference. There are also arguments in favor of buying from galleries, and these are discussed in a later section.

At auction, you are on your own. If you are not careful, you may pay too much, or buy a faded or damaged item or a forgery. You are competing with experts, and it is not unknown for dealers to bid you up to a price that is more than the item is worth. Nevertheless, there is the excitement of an auction, a wide choice of artwork to see, and the opportunity to buy a bargain. Provided you are aware of the many errors you can make and know how to avoid them, it is possible to buy and subsequently sell profitably. Above all, be clear why you are buying and how and where you are going to sell what you have bought.

The Catalogue

If you are going to buy at auction, the first thing to do is get a catalogue. This provides a list of what is for sale. Each item is numbered, and the sequence of numbers is the sequence in which the items (lots) will be sold. The sequence often seems to be arbitrary. There does not seem to be a sequence in terms of price, either. However, it is often the practice to put the important items at the end of the catalogue, and so, of the sale, presumably to ensure that as many buyers as possible stay to the end. Sometimes the catalogue separates prints, watercolors, and oils.

For each lot, the artist's name, if it is known, the title of the item, and often the size is given. In many catalogues, a range of prices is provided as a guide to what the piece is expected to fetch. Some catalogues have lavish illustrations, with every lot portrayed in color to emphasize the importance of the sale. Less prestigious sales may have photocopied lists with some illustrations. Others have no illustrations at all. It is useful to have the catalogue in advance of the sale. This may well happen if you are a regular buyer or seller at a particular auction and/or you subscribe. Many auction houses now have online notification services for upcoming auctions. ArtInfo.com provides a notification service for upcoming worldwide auctions based on a particular artist, auction house, or geographic area. These types of services are invaluable in today's world of overwhelming numbers of auctions.

One bonus of having an item for sale at auction is that you get the catalogue free. With a catalogue in advance, you are able to search through it to find any artists or subjects in whom you are interested, research prices and biographical details, and compare your idea of prices with the estimates.

In the auction catalogue, watch for the artist name "spelling mistake." This may be accidental or it may be a way of indicating that the item was not painted by the person whose signature is on the painting. Either way, if you are interested in buying this painting, it is essential to seek the auctioneer's understanding of the position before the sale and, if appropriate, to get the catalogue entry altered and signed.

Viewing

Viewing days are generally one or two days immediately before the sale, and many auction houses allow viewing on the day of the sale. The professionals frequently attend, and it can be quite busy, with dealers taking items off the wall to look at their backs and others moving steps around to look at high-up artwork. The occasional professional will even view an item while it is held up for sale, perhaps to demonstrate his expertise. If you can view on the day before the sale, it gives you ample time to check each item in which you are interested for the condition, signature, and the way it is painted. You also have time to check the price guides and consult the biographical books. You may finish up with twenty or thirty items that require more detailed scrutiny. You can then have a final look at any artwork you are not sure of, or you might see something you have missed. Some provincial sales do not have the estimates in the catalogue. However, they may have posted the list in the sale room, from which you can enter the estimates into your catalogue.

When you first enter the sale room, it is useful to have a preliminary look around to see if something immediately stands out. Is this one of the items you have already marked in the catalogue or something new? You may then review the pieces you have identified as being interesting. Finally, you should try to look at everything, especially the boxes of prints and folios of watercolors that seem to be of no account. Sometimes there is a treasure lurking there. Also pursue the ones you cannot find, which are generally in a cupboard or cabinet and which will be revealed by a porter or assistant on request. Follow the old adage "Leave no stone unturned."

Looking at artwork is a skill that can be developed with practice, but it is a lifelong learning process. It is best to be on one's own. Having a companion may seem to be advantageous in that you can get a second opinion, but the presence of someone else is distracting and reduces the ability to focus and carry on an intelligent conversation with oneself. By all means, when you have seen all you want to see, seek advice if you need to do so. However, it is important to be discreet. Otherwise you may draw attention to a possible bargain or "sleeper" that you have spotted and which you hope to purchase for significantly less than it is worth. Viewing is often an oscillation between looking at the catalogue and at the artwork. At the back of some catalogues there is an index of artists in alphabetical order, which is helpful if you are interested in only a few artists.

There will be some items that you like. You could see them on your wall. They would be pleasant to live with. Or they make a statement about you. This is all right if you are going to keep them. However, this is not a good criterion if you are hoping to sell them profitably. If you are buying to sell, you have to look through the eyes of your customers.

The Image

Examine the image carefully. Is it interesting, beautiful, arresting? Is it dark or light? Does it evoke pleasurable feelings? Is it of an important place — Venice, Paris, Valetta Harbor, for example? Is it well painted? Are there dull areas, where the artist has not taken much trouble? Is it technically correct, for example, as to perspective? Are the images ones that the public frequently buy? These include country scenes with animals or pretty girls. Images of children or young girls or boys are popular, but so are old folk with character. Most animals and some birds are eagerly sought after. People have nostalgia for the past — hay making, a village fair, and the seaside promenade. Pictures, often Victorian, that tell a story have a following.

On the negative side, many landscapes, although attractive at first sight, are often boring and "ten-a-penny." Be aware that some, if not many, of the items in an auction are there because they have been in a gallery for years and have not sold. These are clearly ones to avoid.

Size and Shape

There is a limited market for large pictures, which demand not only substantial wall space but a room big enough to allow the viewer to get far enough away from them to appreciate them properly. They also cause problems in transporting them to and from auctions if they do not sell. However, there is a market for them in places like boardrooms, churches, public art galleries, and museums. Very small items (miniatures) are a specialist market, but are very popular, not least of which because they take up so little space.

Most people can accommodate artwork up to about 20" by 30". Most are rectangular. When the vertical height is less than the horizontal, the picture is termed "landscape;" when the vertical height is greater than the horizontal, it is called "portrait." However, the portrait shape may fit modern wall spaces better than the landscape one. There are many other shapes (square, circular, semicircular, or lunette/oval) that fit in with most furnishing arrangements.

Condition

Not looking long and carefully is the reason many poor buying decisions are made.

Oil Paintings
Look for dirt, brown varnish, cracks, tears and "bloom" (a sort of mildew.) Is it on canvas, board, or wood panel? If the latter, look for cracks or badly filled-in cracks. Look at the back of the painting. Has it been lined? Look for over-painting; take the picture off the wall and look with your eye close to the canvas. At the same time, look for inscriptions and labels. Again, estimate the cost of cleaning and restoration.

Unless there is a very good reason to the contrary, it is best to buy paintings that are in good condition. Restoration is costly, especially when you take into account the cost of transporting the item to and from the restorer and the often long delay in getting the picture back (and therefore being able to sell it). However, if the painting is only dirty, a surreptitious smudge with a wetted finger end may reveal how bright the painting might be if cleaned properly.

Works on Paper
Look for foxing (brown circular mold marks), burn marks (which are usually vertical brown colored bands), scuffing (actual physical damage to the surface), fading, tears, creases, and where the work has been folded. If possible, estimate the cost of restoration.

Aesthetic Appeal and Commercial Value

Aesthetic appeal may be defined as the value placed on artwork for its own beauty. The problem with this definition is that "Beauty is in the eye of the beholder." It is a matter of taste. Whether this is an important consideration depends on the ultimate recipient of the work. What might seem exquisite to an older person may seem to be mundane to a younger one, and vice versa.

The commercial value may have little to do with aesthetics. This is certainly true of much highly priced modern art, where the main consideration seems to be on some notion of originality. With the right name an idea, however unexceptional, seems to be worth telephone numbers, even if the execution of the artwork is by someone else. This is a conventional phenomenon that may vaporize like some of the dotcoms have. Otherwise, commercially, the name is probably the most important consideration, so that the authenticity of an attribution is paramount.

The Frame

The frame may mislead. There is a market in old frames, and there are people who deal exclusively in them. If you have a genuine old painting that has been put into a modern frame, it may give the impression of not being quite right and therefore might not fetch the price it deserves. It would be sensible and legitimate to reframe it in an old frame where its integrity would be evident. However, note that oils recently painted in nineteenth century style and subject matter are also put into either genuine old frames or simulated old frames, and are often bought as genuine nineteenth century oils. With watercolors, it is often possible to see that the painting is in its original frame and that the nails and backing paper have not been disturbed. This is very reassuring. Even so, there is a market for old nails and old paper, and therefore a need for caution if the watercolor is expensive.

Attribution and Forgeries

At auction, the usual convention used in the catalogue to indicate that, in the opinion of the auction house, the artwork is by the artist stated, is to give the full recognized name of the artist, forenames as well as surname, and possibly the date of birth and death. An example would be "Samuel John Lamorna Birch (1855-1969)." Sometimes initials with following asterisk and the surname have the same implication. The term "signed" generally means the signature is that of the artist. The practical value of this is that if the artwork so designated subsequently turns out to be a deliberate forgery, then the sale is rescinded and the purchase price refunded.

There are generally time limits, which vary from one auction house to another, within which the auctioneer has to be informed in writing that the item is believed to be a forgery, and often a longer period within which the lot has to be returned. It has to be in the same condition as when it was bought, and the buyer has to produce evidence that the item is a forgery. This is an important safeguard, the terms of which are generally stated in the catalogue or otherwise in the auction room. They should be noted, in case advantage needs to be taken of them. Clearly you should try to avoid buying a forgery. However, if you buy an item by a well-known artist and have doubts as to its authenticity, perhaps because it was cheap and the trade did not seem to be bidding for it, take it to a gallery that specializes in the artist and check it out. As there are time limits to be observed, this should be done as expeditiously as possible.

If the forenames of the artist, or the initials with following asterisks and the surname, are not given, this indicates that in the opinion of the auction house there may be some degree of uncertainty as to whether the painting is the work of the named artist, and the degrees of increasing uncertainty are indicated by a series of phrases. "Attributed to" indicates that it is probably the work of the artist. The initials of the artist and surname can indicate that in the auctioneer's opinion, it is a work of the period of the artist, which may be wholly or partly his/her work. Just the surname of the artist implies that the work is unlikely to be by the artist, but is in his style and painted by a follower or a member of his school.

The word "after" associated with the name of the artist indicates a copy. "Bears signature" generally indicates doubt as to whether the signature is that of the artist. Similarly, "dated" usually means that the painting was painted at that date. "Bears a date" indicates some doubt as to the date. All these indications are "in the opinion of the auction house," and it is usually made clear in the small print that they should not be taken as statements or representations of fact. One of the ways money can be made is to have knowledge superior to that of the auctioneer, to be convinced that what he is unsure about is the real thing. One of the ways of losing money is to get this wrong.

It is essential to know whether the artwork is "right," whether the signature or monogram has been put on by the artist. There are so many unsigned items around that it is inevitable that some will acquire signatures. Viewing the artwork with the aid of an ultraviolet lamp may disclose additions to the item of a much later date than the original, including a signature. You can consult books of signatures and monograms, which are useful in identifying something the auctioneer has missed or which has been labeled "indistinctly signed." They may not help in spotting a forged signature, because the forger has access to the same books.

Provenance

A useful safeguard is to know where an item has come from. There is often such information in catalogues, and sometimes the back/bottom of the piece will provide a clue. Many galleries put a stock or exhibition label on the back of the piece or the frame, and some give stock numbers. Frame makers' labels are frequently to be found, and they may provide a starting point for research.

Estimates

Many catalogues give estimates for each lot as a lower and higher figure. These are estimates of the price range within which the auctioneers believe the artwork will sell. The question is whether the estimate is realistic. Most of them will have been based on the auction house's own records and examination of price data sources. Sometimes they will seem too low. There may be several possible reasons for this: the auctioneer has set it low to attract bargain hunters to the sale, it may be a private lot with no reserve, or the auctioneer has made a mistake. Sometimes it will seem too high. The item may be exceptional or it may be that the vendor who has put the piece in the sale has insisted on an unrealistically high price. If you compare the estimates with the prices actually achieved at any sale you attend, you will find that many prices fall within the estimates, but there will be a sizable number that do not reach the estimate and do not sell. There will also be a smaller number that sell well above the top estimate.

Check the price guides. Make sure the item you are considering is of the same type as that which appears in the price guides. If there are no entries, it may be that the artist's work has not been sold at auction for the period covered by the price data source or that it has not achieved the minimum price to be included in the price guide. Even if there are entries for the artist, it is possible that some, if not many, of his/her artwork has sold under the minimum price and therefore does not appear.

Reserves

The reserve is the lowest price at which the vendor has authorized the auctioneer to sell. This amount is generally discussed and agreed with the auctioneer, who does not want to waste time and money trying to sell an item with too high a reserve. It is sometimes argued that the artwork will achieve the right price if the reserve is too low, or even if there is no reserve at all. This is not necessarily true. Often there is only one bidder for a lot, and the sale is then made at the agreed reserve price. When this happens, the seller must wonder whether the reserve was set too low.

Some auction houses will consider that there is no reserve unless one has been agreed to in writing. Most indicate in their conditions of sale that the auctioneer has discretion to sell at 10% less than the agreed reserve. It is important, therefore, to decide whether you agree with this if you are the vendor, or whether you insist that the reserve is firm. If the reserve is not agreed upon with the auctioneer, your artwork may be sold too cheaply. Alternately, if you insisted on a too-high reserve and the artwork does not sell, there may be a considerable buy-in fee to pay.

The reserve may be the lower of the two estimates, but need not necessarily be so. The reserve is not known to the buyers at an auction, but is often guessed to be 10% below the lowest estimate, sometimes correctly. Some auction houses will not accept a reserve higher than the bottom estimate.

Commission Bids

A commission bid is a bid made by the auctioneer on your behalf. It is a way of buying if you cannot attend the sale. There is generally no charge made for this service. You make the bid on a form that the auction house provides, giving your personal details and the sale number and date, the lot number and the price you are prepared to have bid. Your bid will have to be at or above the reserve, which you do not know. The lowest figure for a commission bid will probably be the lowest of the estimates.

If you want to have a good chance of buying a lot, you will make your bid high. If the bidding on the day does not reach your bid, you should secure the item for whatever the next bid is, after all the other bidding has ceased. For example, your high commission bid is $1,000. On the day, the highest of all the other bids is $800. The next bid, which is yours, may be $850, and this is the price you will pay.

There is sometimes a problem, if you cannot attend the sale, when you spot a "sleeper" (a lot that you recognize as being valuable, but which has a very low estimate). For instance, you think it is worth $4,000, and the estimate in the catalogue is $200. Do you put in a low commission bid of, perhaps, $300, or a high one of $3,000? The low bid may be insufficient if someone else has spotted the sleeper. The high bid may seem to be safe enough if you do not mind paying $3,000, because if no one else is aware of the item's worth, you will get it for $200. However, your high bid might alert the auctioneer that he has underestimated the artwork, and he might revise the estimate, alerting others by so doing. Probably, the best compromise is to leave a bid that you think will not alert the auctioneer to revise the estimate.

When you leave a commission bid, it is best not to leave a round number, but the next bid up. This is because people often set a round number as their maximum bid. For example, if you want to leave $400, actually leave $420, which will outlast anyone who has decided to drop out at $400. You can also leave a commission bid even if you are going to attend the sale. You may wish to do this to avoid others seeing that you are bidding. If the bidding goes above your commission bid and you decide you want the item, you can then enter the bidding.

Telephone Bids

If you are undecided whether to bid after you have viewed, and then on the morning of the sale regret that you have not done so, you can generally telephone or e-mail a commission bid before the start of the sale. Alternatively, you can arrange for the auction house to telephone you while the auction is in progress, just before the lot you are interested in comes up. Someone at the auction house will let you know how the bidding is progressing and when the bidding stops. At this point you can decide whether to make a bid. This will not necessarily get you the artwork, as the previous bidder may bid again. However, with luck, he or she may give up once they hear there is another bidder.

THE DAY OF THE SALE

Make a note of the starting time of the sale. If the lot you wish to buy is going to be later in the sale, you can calculate when this is due, if you know how many lots per hour the auctioneer sells. Some auctioneers will sell sixty lots in an hour, others one hundred and twenty or more. You can generally find out the approximate rate when you view. It is sensible to add twenty minutes or so to your calculated time and check whether the lot numbers run consecutively, or whether there are some gaps that will affect your calculations.

Before the sale, you have to register. If you are going to settle with cash, there is no problem. But, if you intend to pay by check, you need to find out whether this is acceptable. Some auction houses may want to contact your bank before releasing your purchases. Credit cards are not accepted by some auction houses. Other houses charge a fee to accept credit cards. When you register, you will probably be given a number or a numbered paddle. However, some provincial houses just expect you to call out your name, and if you attend sales regularly, the auctioneer will have remembered it.

The Sale

The actual sale is a sort of theater. On exhibition are the works of many artists representing thousands of years of experience and effort. Attending the sale are many highly knowledgeable men and women. Decisions whether or not to buy have to be made in a matter of seconds. Although it is very exciting, most of the participants, who will be traders or gallery owners, display a laid-back nonchalance conveying that they are hardened professionals. If you are not one of these, you will find your heart beating faster as the lot you intend to bid for approaches.

If you attend the sale from the beginning, you can mark down the prices for each lot and compare them with the auctioneer's estimates or your own. You will have marked up your catalogue with the items you wish to buy and the price you are prepared to pay. Some lots will go beyond what you have marked as your buying price. Avoid the temptation to chase after them. It may be that one dealer buys all the items that you want. It requires discipline not to get so exasperated that you become determined to beat him or her. Such dealers are generally buying for prestigious retailers or private clients, who do not mind what they pay. If you beat them, you will probably pay too much. The same indiscretions can occur at provincial sales if the local trade tries to push you up or thwart your attempts to buy.

The auctioneer takes bids from the floor, but also bids on behalf of commission clients. He or she may also bid on behalf of the vendor, up to the reserve price. Doing so beyond the reserve price, sometimes referred to as "bidding off the wall," gives the false impression to the beginner that he is bidding against someone else in the room. This is clearly an illegitimate practice. The bidding for some lots does not reach the agreed reserve, and so they are unsold and are said to be "bought-in." In most auctions, at least 20-30% of the lots do not sell, and the percentage can be much higher. This will surprise you if you have not attended many auctions, because the auctioneer often tries to conceal the fact that there has not been a sale. It is often possible after the end of the sale to negotiate for some of the unsold lots.

Bidding prices go up in intervals, which are the custom and practice of the auction house. A familiar pattern is $5 intervals up to $50, $10 up to $200, and $20 and $30 intervals up to $500. For example, $220, $250, $280 — then $50 up to $1,000, $100 up to $2,000 and so on. It is useful to know the intervals so that you can work out when to enter the bidding to finish up with a final bid, which is the one beyond an even number. If your high bid is $320, you might enter the bidding at $220 so that the sequence will be: you $220, Miss Blank $250, you $280, Miss Blank $300, you $320.

Sleepers

A sleeper is a bargain, artwork whose true identity and value is unrecognized, except by the buyer. It is what everyone is looking for, and when found, it is hoped that no one else has spotted it. This search for the sleeper explains the noncommittal way the connoisseur examines the various lots, often commenting that "there is a lot of garbage about." Sleepers exist because of oversight or lack of knowledge. They are there at most auctions. Beware, however, of what appear to be sleepers, planted by the unscrupulous with "old" paper backs, nails, cracks, dirt, and dark varnish. One of the most famous sleepers was bought at auction for about $260, sold at another auction for $550,000, and allegedly subsequently sold to the Getty Foundation for approximately $9,000,000. This example is quoted in Philip Mould's book, "Sleepers: In Search of Lost Old Masters."

Buyer's Premium

Most auction houses charge a commission to the seller and buyer. Some major auction houses charge 15% up to $50,000 and 10% thereafter. There are exceptions where no buyer's premium is charged. It is important to take note of the buyer's premium when you decide to buy and also when you look at prices in the price guides, some of which exclude buyer's premium.

Taxes and Other Charges

It is important to be aware of the sales tax or any other tax — such as value-added tax in Europe — which may apply to the sales commission or buyer's premium. Also note other charges, such as insurance, storage, or delivery. These extra charges can make a significant difference to the profit you hope to realize when trading.

Withdrawals, Revised Descriptions, Estimates, and Extra Lots

These are all changes or corrections that occur from time to time. Their effect can vary from mild irritation to considerable waste of money and time if it means you have traveled a long way only to find that what you were hoping to buy has in some way been subject to alteration. For example, the sleeper you spotted has also been spotted by someone else, perhaps the vendor or the auctioneer's superiors, and has been withdrawn from the sale. The artwork catalogued as "attributed to XYZ" has the description revised to read "by XYZ." You knew it was "by XYZ" all the time but hoped no one else did. Of course, the estimate is then revised upward.

You do not know these bits of bad news until you turn up at the sale, excited at the thought of the bargain you are going to acquire. Clearly, auction houses do not like sleepers to occur, because it means that the vendor has been ill served and might sue.

Extra lots are new lots, not described in the catalogue, that present you with the temptation to make decisions without having had the opportunity to do necessary research. It is wise to treat these with caution.

Conditions of Sale

These are often set out in the catalogue or posted somewhere in the sale room. Most auction houses make it clear that their role is to act only as agents. They take no responsibility for any faults or defects. Everything they say are statements of opinion, not to be relied upon. They have absolute discretion to settle any dispute.

Once the hammer has fallen, the purchaser is completely responsible for the lot and is unlikely to be compensated for any subsequent damage. There is generally a time limit for payment after the sale, and if this is exceeded, storage charges may be incurred.

Although the conditions of sale may appear onerous and too much in the auctioneer's favor, it is generally the experience that if you make friends with the auctioneer's staff and do business with them, there is some flexibility in the application of the rules.

SELLING AT AUCTION

Why do you want to sell?

It may be that you wish to sell because you want something different on your walls. There is no urgency, and you are not too concerned with how much your artwork will fetch. Alternatively, you may want money urgently and as much of it as possible. You may be an investor who wants to see a good profit to cover the years of interest tied up, or you may be a trader looking for a quick profit.

To whom are you selling?

There are several possible potential customers for the artwork you put into auction: private parties looking for specific colors, artists, subjects etc.; gallery owners seeking examples of popular subjects that will sell; or dealers/runners looking for the same things as the gallery owners, but at a discount. It is largely a matter of luck who might buy your artwork. Ideally you hope for two private bidders with strong wills and plenty of money. However, most of the items at auction are bought by the trade.

If you are aiming for the private buyer, the artwork should be clean, in good condition, and in a good-quality and undamaged frame. These factors are also relevant to the gallery owner, but less so, as most galleries do framing and simple restoration. As long as the item is undamaged, condition is not so important to a gallery owner. If it is for the trade, do not bother to reframe or restore your artwork, don't even clean the glass. The private buyer is most probably unconcerned with the artist's name, but wants a nice piece. The gallery owner may be concerned with particular artists that his clients wish to buy. The trade mostly buys names and commercial subjects. The market is looking for artwork that is "fresh to the market" and "in unrestored condition." These would be genuine paintings or artwork in their original frames from a private source, which have not been restored.

Which Auction House?

There are a number of aspects to consider when deciding which auction house to use to sell your artwork. Not least is the auctioneer's advice as to the price the item will be expected to achieve. If you take a good piece to a number of auction houses and ask for estimates of what hammer price it is likely to achieve at a sale, you will be surprised at the wide range of figures you will be given. Some of the variation may be due to differences of opinion as to whether or not the item is by the artist whose signature is on it; some will be due to the differences of expertise and experience of those examining the item. If you appear to be a private seller (not of the trade) and apparently a novice, you may be persuaded that your artwork is of little value. It is therefore essential to get several opinions, unless you have enough experience to be fairly certain of the proper price at which to set the reserve.

It is clearly helpful if your artwork is by an artist listed in the price guides. It is not necessarily sensible to put the item with the auction house that gives you the highest estimate. You want to sell the artwork. However, it is costly in time, effort, and travel expenses to find that the bidding does not quite reach your reserve and therefore does not sell. Then, at the next auction, the artwork will not be fresh to the trade, and you will have to reduce the reserve. And again it might not sell. Better to agree on a reserve sufficiently low to get a sale, but not too low. The argument may be used that a low reserve and estimate will attract buyers, and the picture will find its true value from the bidding. However, you will often find that there is only one bidder interested in your artwork, and when the bidding reaches your reserve, your artwork is "knocked down" (term for sold referring to when the auction hammer falls).

When you agree on a reserve, it will probably be automatically subject to the "auctioneer's discretion," which means you give the auctioneer the right to sell at a percentage, usually 10%, below the agreed reserve. If you do not want to do this, you must insist that the reserve is firm and not subject to discretion. Be aware that most auction houses specify in their "conditions" that all goods are put up for sale without reserve, unless written instructions as to reserves are submitted before the sale.

Commissions and Charges

Sales commission is what the auctioneer charges you for selling your artwork. It is expressed as a percentage of the hammer price and can vary from about 7.5% to 20%. The charge is generally reduced for high-value items. Some auctioneers reduce the commission for members of the trade. Some make a minimum charge, and some make a handling charge of so much per item. Sometimes the charge includes insurance and an illustration charge. Away from the big auction houses, it is often possible to negotiate charges.

Insurance charges are levied as a matter of course, unless instructions are given to the contrary. They generally cover theft, but often with the proviso "following forcible entry," and fire and water damage, but not the ever-present possibility of accidental breakage or damage.

If your artwork does not sell, you may be charged for "buying-in." If you have agreed on the reserve price, then the buying-in charge should be modest. Often it is possible to negotiate that there will be no buying-in charge at all. If you have insisted on a reserve higher than the auctioneer agrees to, the buying-in charge may be severe, which is a good reason for avoiding this situation.

If your artwork has not sold, you may decide to remove it from the auctioneers. If so, make sure you do this quickly or you may incur storage charges. Most auction houses will propose to offer your bought-ins at another sale, possibly somewhere else, perhaps a little downmarket, and with a lower reserve. This may involve you in having to pay further selling commissions.

Many auctioneers stipulate that they have the right to illustrate any lot. It is important that you have a say in this. An illustration charge can be quite high, $80 to $300 or more for a color illustration. It is difficult to decide whether to agree to an illustration unless you can negotiate that only if the picture sells will you pay for the illustration. Otherwise you have to balance the illustration cost against the possible higher price it may generate. At the top end of the market, all pictures are illustrated.

Finally, read the small print, decide on all the above aspects, and put your intentions clearly in writing on the auctioneer's "instructions to sell" form.

BUYING FROM AND SELLING TO A GALLERY

It is a good idea to visit as many galleries as possible to see what is selling and what prices are being charged. Many galleries sell contemporary originals or prints by relatively unknown artists, and unless you like backing outsiders or are unaffected by mercenary considerations, it will be advisable not to buy. However, it is useful to note names and subjects, which may turn up at bargain prices at auction.

Quality, authenticity, framing, subject, image and the "name" are all important when buying from a gallery. At private views when the wine flows, there is an inferred pressure to buy, otherwise why would you be there? Reference may be made to an artist you are not familiar with, to the effect that similar artwork has been on sale elsewhere at much higher prices. It is difficult but essential not to be persuaded by sales talk, but to be hardheaded and objective.

Generally, it will cost more to buy the same artwork from a dealer than at auction. But this is only the beginning of the comparison. In doing so, you must have regard to the buyer's premium at auction and the retailer's sales tax. Also, the gallery artwork may have been reframed and restored or cleaned. The gallery takes responsibility for the condition and authenticity of the artwork so that you can return anything that is not quite right. There is also the convenience compared with attending an auction on a particular day that may not be convenient at a place that is possibly far away. The gallery may have financial arrangements that are helpful. Additionally, you may not be able to purchase artwork at auction as cheaply as the experienced gallery buyer can.

Be sure to get a detailed description, with the full name of the artist (forenames as well as surname) and "signed by," not "bears a signature" or "attributed to" and with no spelling mistakes, on the bill of sale accompanying your purchase. There is usually scope for negotiating the price downward. Many gallery owners have considerable expertise, and over a period of years, buying quality artwork from such a source can be very profitable.

Many of the galleries that sell "names" will be prepared to buy from you if everything is right, including the price. Most will not make an offer, but will ask you how much you want. Generally, they will not want to pay much more than the auction price. The profitability of a gallery depends on turning over stock as quickly as possible, so the price you are likely to achieve will depend on whether they believe that they can sell the artwork quickly. If you buy at auction with the intention of selling to a gallery, the hammer price needs to be considerably less than the gallery would expect it to be. You also need to step into the shoes of the gallery owner so that you buy the items he can readily sell. This means establishing a good relationship and gaining a good understanding of the way the gallery works.

Some galleries will take your artwork on a "sale or return" arrangement. Here the artwork is said to be "on consignment." If the item sells, you pay a commission, which will vary from about 20% to 50% or more. Theory is often better than reality here. However, a profitable arrangement can sometimes be established with a gallery that is short of funds and therefore unable to adequately finance stock.

OTHER PLACES TO BUY AND SELL ARTWORK

Fairs

There are numerous fairs varying widely in prestige and the quality of goods offered. At many of the run-of-the-mill fairs, much selling and buying seems to go on within the trade before the fair officially opens. Otherwise the customer is often an untutored member of the general public, who will buy on impulse with little regard to price or value. Having a stand at a fair is thus an alternative to having a gallery, with the possibility of dealing with less discerning buyers. It is also a way of developing a client list by persuading those visiting your stand to sign the visitors' book.

Antique Shops and Dealers

Many antique shops buy and sell artwork. The term "furnishing pieces" comes to mind, but there is always the possibility that there is an undiscovered gem waiting to be unearthed. There are also antique centers where a hundred or so dealers and units are gathered together; some are art dealers. You need to assess the expertise and integrity of the dealers in such places. Most are selling to the non-expert public who just want to buy something pleasing but not necessarily valuable. However, it is generally possible to pick out and make friends with dealers with knowledge on whom you can rely.

Shops with bric-a-brac or even "junk" may have something of interest. Some good finds have been made at such places. It is probably not worthwhile to make it a major activity to trawl such outlets, but as a diversion on holidays or weekends it can be fun.

Artwork is also bought and sold through advertisements in home-furnishing magazines and local papers by private people or dealers in disguise. Usually, most of what is offered is either overpriced or of little value. These outlets may be worthwhile to try if you have artwork to sell that is known to be popular in a particular geographic area.

Buying Directly From the Artist

Although most artists sell through galleries or agents, some do sell from their own studios. The advantage of buying directly from the artist is that you can discuss with him or her the range of work and can gain an understanding of how the artist paints. It is often possible that you can buy more cheaply this way.

An alternative is to become an agent for a new, and as yet, undiscovered artist. This can be interesting and exciting with the possibility of having set a genius on the road to fame. However, it can also be an expensive and financially unrewarding venture. The budding artist is generally penniless, and you may have to carry the cost of framing, arranging exhibitions, and even supplying materials. This can run into thousands of dollars. If you have found an artist of great promise, you might make a fortune, provided he or she repays you by staying with you.

TAKING CARE OF ARTWORK

It is amazing how artwork survives after being abandoned in lofts or roof spaces, only to be discovered a generation later, having appreciated substantially in value in the meantime.

Works on paper are more vulnerable than oils. Direct sunlight wreaks havoc. Unmounted works on paper can get creased or kinked. They should have a backing mount board made of pure rag fiber and be acid free. Archival quality boards should ideally be used with a pH level of not less than 8. The item should be framed with a glass front and a firm backing. Even framed watercolors can deteriorate in cold spaces where dampness is the enemy.

Oil paintings are quite durable, but are safer framed and under glass. However, dampness can encourage the growth of mold on oil paintings under glass.

The obvious necessity of having secure fixings on which to hang artwork is sometimes overlooked, and it is possible to wake in the morning to find the artwork on the floor with the frame and possibly the work damaged. Another source of damage is the rusting of what appears to be brass wire used for hanging.

Handling

Perhaps the best advice when handling artwork is to use two hands. This is especially true of unmounted watercolors or prints, which can so easily be kinked. But it is also true of the frames of oil paintings, evidence of which can be seen in many auction rooms. It is dangerous for the painting to put it on the floor and propped against a wall. This occurs frequently when someone is paying the bill after an auction.

Packing artwork is a job requiring skill and thought. For transport by car, it is best to wrap each of the items and separate them with cardboard or similar material. The stacking should ensure that there is no possibility of movement. Hooks and eyes should be removed. For transport by carrier or van, artwork should be wrapped in bubble wrap, and special precautions should be taken with the corners.

ABOUT THIS BOOK

Since 1968, Art Sales Index (ASI) has been reporting international auction prices for fine art. The ASI pricing results database includes over 3 million entries and covers oil paintings, miniatures, sculpture, prints, photographs and works on paper which cover a wide range of techniques from watercolor, drawings, gouache, chalk, charcoal, tempera, pen and ink.

This book contains the summarized prices for fine art that sold at public auction during August of 2005 through July of 2006. It covers over 158,000 works by over 28,000 artists and sculptors. The name of the artist is shown in full or as modified by the general usage of auctioneers. Information shown for each artist is:

a) full name
c) nationality

b) dates of birth, death (if known)
d) details of the median auction sale

The summarized price information for each artist is shown on separate lines for oil paintings, watercolors and drawings, and sculpture:

a) the number of works sold
c) average price

b) price range
d) median price

Median Price

No statistical device can fairly reflect the "value" of an artist's work, and that is not what we are trying to do in this publication. Rather it is our intent to show the current level of availability and demand as demonstrated by auction prices. ASI believes that the most satisfactory way to do this is to show the **median** price. The median is **not** an average but the middle figure of any range of figures. It comes close to being a "typical" price because it eliminates the freakish highest price and the freakish lowest price. For example, in the following range of numbers: 5, 12, 13, 18, 21, 27, 33, 37, 104 the middle one, "**21**" is the **median**.

If there is only one or an even number of entries for an artist, the lower of the two prices is shown. To assist the reader further, we have included the median auction sale for the artist. This shows the details of an actual auction sale event and should help to give a better idea of an artist's typical work.

Source of Information

The information is compiled from catalogues, price lists, and other details provided by auctioneers. ASI takes great care in extracting information accurately. However, ASI cannot be held responsible for errors unwittingly made, nor for unknowingly reproducing incorrect information. The price artwork reaches at auction can be influenced by many factors: condition, subject matter, and size are just a few. We recommend additional research when buying and selling fine art, such as consulting reference books and obtaining advice from experienced sources.

Media

ASI requires a minimum purchase price for each medium. Included media and their corresponding minimum starting prices are:

a) "oil" - oil paintings, including tempera and acrylic - $350
b) "wc/d" - watercolors and drawings, including collages, gouache, pen, pastel, crayon, pencil, charcoal, ink, and chalk - $350
c) "3D" – sculpture and three-dimensional works - $1,000

Price Recorded

The price recorded by ASI is the "hammer price," which is called out at auction and at which the lot is "knocked down" to the bidder. There may be occasions where a lot may consist of more than one item.

Many auctioneers levy an additional charge to the buyer. This is known as the "buyer's premium" and is **not** included in the price recorded by ASI. The seller must also expect deductions to be made to the hammer price to account for the auctioneer's commission.

Bought-in Artwork

Artwork offered for sale at auction usually has a "reserve" placed on it by the owner so that it is not sold at a price that the owner considers to be below its real value. This is not the same as the "estimate," which is provided by the auctioneer as a guide for the buyer. Items that do not reach the reserve are known as "bought-in." It is the policy of ASI to record only actual sales. "Bought-in" prices are not recorded.

THE $1,000,000 CLUB
for artists whose work has sold for over $1 million
from August 2005 to July 2006

AIVAZOVSKY, Ivan Konstantinovich (1817-1900) Russian

$1,000,000	£564,972	Moonlight. Apr 24, 2006 Christie's, NY
$1,324,400	£770,000	Mount Ararat. Dec 01, 2005 Sotheby's, London
$1,339,200	£720,000	Shipwreck off the Black Sea coast. May 31, 2006 Sotheby's, London
$1,376,000	£800,000	Fishing boat with a Russian merchant brig at anchor. Nov 30, 2005 Christie's, London
$2,883,000	£1,550,000	The Varangians on the Dnieper. May 31, 2006 Sotheby's, London
$14,778,083	£7,945,206	European fleet east of Crete in the Mediterranean. June 04, 2006 Uppsala Auktionskammare, Uppsala (Euro 11,600,000)

ANNIGONI, Pietro (1910-1988) Italian

$1,104,000	£600,000	Portrait of Princess Margaret. June 14, 2006 Christie's, London

ARP, Jean (1887-1966) French

$1,300,000	£730,337	Sculpture de silence, Corneille. Nov 01, 2005 Christie's, NY

BACON, Francis (1909-1992) British

$2,100,000	£1,206,897	Two figures. Nov 08, 2005 Christie's, NY
$4,048,000	£2,300,000	Two figures at a window. Feb 09, 2006 Sotheby's, London
$4,600,000	£2,643,678	Three studies of self-portrait. Nov 09, 2005 Sotheby's, NY
$6,290,000	£3,400,000	Self-portrait, three studies. June 22, 2006 Christie's, London
$8,096,000	£4,600,000	Self-portrait. Feb 08, 2006 Christie's, London
$8,096,000	£4,600,000	Portrait of Pope Innocent X. Feb 08, 2006 Christie's, London
$9,000,000	£5,172,414	Study for pope I. Nov 08, 2005 Christie's, NY

BAMBINI, Nicolo and TIEPOLO, Giovanni Battista (18th C) Italian

$6,497,260	£3,493,151	Coriolano. Tre Grazie. Ulisse e Achille. Apollo e Marsia. Ercole e Anteo. May 30, 2006 Sotheby's, Milan (Euro 5,100,000)

BARCELO, Miguel (1957-) Spanish

$1,008,642	£533,673	Bodegon. May 17, 2006 Tajan, Paris (Euro 784,500)

BARRY, James -18th C (1741-1806) British

$1,618,200	£870,000	King Lear weeping over the body of Cordelia. May 11, 2006 Sotheby's, London

BASCHENIS, Evaristo (1617-1677) Italian

$1,300,000	£751,445	Still life with musical instruments. Apr 06, 2006 Christie's, NY

BASELITZ, Georg (1938-) German

$1,000,000	£537,634	Hero. May 11, 2006 Phillips, NY
$1,936,000	£1,100,000	Ein Roter - The Communist. Feb 08, 2006 Christie's, London

BASQUIAT, Jean Michel (1960-1988) American

$1,150,500	£650,000	Leonardo and his five grotesque heads. Oct 25, 2005 Sotheby's, London
$1,200,000	£645,161	Ruffians. May 09, 2006 Christie's, NY
$1,212,556	£641,564	Marmaduke. May 17, 2006 Tajan, Paris (Euro 943,100)
$1,600,000	£919,540	Warrior. Nov 09, 2005 Sotheby's, NY
$1,665,000	£900,000	Negro period. June 22, 2006 Christie's, London
$2,200,000	£1,264,368	Untitled. Nov 08, 2005 Christie's, NY
$2,600,000	£1,397,850	M. May 09, 2006 Christie's, NY
$4,600,000	£2,643,678	The history of black people: the great show. Nov 09, 2005 Sotheby's, NY

BASQUIAT, Jean Michel and WARHOL, Andy (20th C) American

$1,202,500	£650,000	General electric. June 22, 2006 Christie's, London
$2,436,429	£1,289,116	Eiffel Tower. May 17, 2006 Tajan, Paris (Euro 1,895,000)

BECKMANN, Max (1884-1950) German
$1,320,000   £750,000   Still life of tulips with sea view. Feb 07, 2006 Sotheby's, London

BELLOTTO, Bernardo (1720-1780) Italian
$1,500,000   £852,273   The Grand Canal, looking north from the Palazzo Contarini dagli Scrigni.
                              Jan 26, 2006 Sotheby's, NY
$1,557,000   £900,000   The Bacino di San Marco, Venice. Dec 08, 2005 Christie's, London
$4,200,000   £2,386,364   The Piazza San Marco, Venice. Jan 26, 2006 Sotheby's, NY

BENTON, Thomas Hart (1889-1975) American
$1,600,000   £855,615   Keith Farm, Chilmark. May 24, 2006 Sotheby's, NY

BOCCIONI, Umberto (1882-1916) Italian
$1,284,830   £687,075   Portrait of Doctor Tian. May 23, 2006 Christie's, Milan (Euro 1,010,000)

BOGDANOFF-BJELSKI, Nikolai (1868-1945) Russian
$1,200,000   £674,157   Reading in the garden. Apr 26, 2006 Sotheby's, NY

BOGOMAZOV, Alexander (1880-1930) Russian
$1,118,000   £650,000   Abstract landscape. Dec 01, 2005 Sotheby's, London

BOMBERG, David (1890-1957) British
$1,549,800   £820,000   Ronda, in the Gorge of the Tajo. June 09, 2006 Christie's, London

BONNARD, Pierre (1867-1947) French
$1,196,000   £650,000   Au bord de la mer. June 19, 2006 Sotheby's, London
$1,387,500   £750,000   Nu au radiateur. June 20, 2006 Christie's, London
$1,800,000   £983,607   Paysage au toit rouge, le Cannet. May 02, 2006 Christie's, NY
$2,392,000   £1,300,000   Apres le dejeuner. June 19, 2006 Sotheby's, London
$4,400,000   £2,471,910   Paysage du Cannet. Nov 02, 2005 Sotheby's, NY
$6,100,000   £3,426,966   Compotiers et assiettes de fruits. Nov 01, 2005 Christie's, NY
$6,808,000   £3,700,000   Place Clichy. June 19, 2006 Sotheby's, London

BORISOV-MUSATOV, Viktor (1870-1905) Russian
$1,153,200   £620,000   The last day. May 31, 2006 Sotheby's, London

BOTERO, Fernando (1932-) Colombian
$1,350,000   £775,862   Musicians. Nov 16, 2005 Sotheby's, NY
$1,800,000   £962,567   Musicians. May 23, 2006 Christie's, NY
$1,800,000   £962,567   Cuatro musicos - Four musicians. May 24, 2006 Sotheby's, NY

BOUCHER, Francois (elder) (1703-1770) French
$1,850,000   £1,000,000   Sommeil de Venus. July 06, 2006 Christie's, London

BOUDIN, Eugene (1824-1898) French
$1,408,000   £800,000   Scene de plage a Trouville. Feb 07, 2006 Sotheby's, London

BOUGUEREAU, William Adolphe (1825-1905) French
$1,150,000   £646,067   Le gouter. Apr 25, 2006 Sotheby's, NY

BOURGEOIS, Louise (1911-) American/French
$2,700,000   £1,551,724   Spider. Nov 09, 2005 Sotheby's, NY

BRACK, Cecil John (1920-1999) Australian
$1,892,887   £1,087,866   The bar. Apr 11, 2006 Sotheby's, Melbourne (A.D 2,600,000)

BRANCUSI, Constantin (1876-1957) Rumanian
$3,200,000   £1,797,753   Le baiser. Nov 01, 2005 Christie's, NY

BRAQUE, Georges (1882-1963) French
$1,757,500   £950,000   Maisons a l'Estque. June 20, 2006 Christie's, London
$2,200,000   £1,202,186   Femme au pinceau. May 02, 2006 Christie's, NY
$2,389,500   £1,350,000   Eglise de Carrieres Saint-Denis. Feb 06, 2006 Christie's, London
$2,550,000   £1,393,443   Tasse. May 02, 2006 Christie's, NY
$4,944,494   £2,687,225   La terrasse. June 16, 2006 Kornfeld, Bern (S.FR 6,100,000)

BRUEGHEL, Pieter (younger) (1564-1637) Flemish
$1,017,500   £550,000   Peasants merrymaking outside inn. July 06, 2006 Christie's, London
$1,050,000   £596,591   L'auberge St. Michel. Jan 26, 2006 Sotheby's, NY
$1,124,500   £650,000   Winter landscape with the massacre of the innocents. Dec 07, 2005
                              Sotheby's, London
$2,400,000   £1,363,636   Peasant wedding procession. Jan 26, 2006 Sotheby's, NY
$8,510,001   £4,600,000   Procession to Calvary. July 05, 2006 Sotheby's, London

BRUSH, George de Forest (1855-1941) American
$2,300,000   £1,337,209   Council of the war party. Dec 01, 2005 Christie's, NY

BURRI, Alberto (1915-1995) Italian
| $1,062,000 | £600,000 | Sack. Oct 24, 2005 Sotheby's, London |
| $1,081,293 | £578,231 | Black, white and sack. May 27, 2006 Farsetti, Prato (Euro 850,000) |

CAILLEBOTTE, Gustave (1848-1894) French
| $1,400,000 | £765,027 | Roses jaunes dans un vase. May 02, 2006 Christie's, NY |
| $1,600,000 | £898,876 | Le parc de la propriete Caillebotte a Yerres. Nov 01, 2005 Christie's, NY |

CALDER, Alexander (1898-1976) American
$1,100,000	£632,184	Aux Shahn. Nov 09, 2005 Sotheby's, NY
$1,100,000	£591,398	Carousel. May 09, 2006 Christie's, NY
$1,200,000	£645,161	Three white dots and one yellow. May 10, 2006 Sotheby's, NY
$1,300,000	£747,126	Haverford monster. Nov 09, 2005 Sotheby's, NY
$1,600,000	£860,215	Untitled mobile. May 10, 2006 Sotheby's, NY
$2,150,000	£1,235,632	Brass in the sky. Nov 09, 2005 Sotheby's, NY
$5,000,000	£2,688,172	Flying dragon. May 10, 2006 Sotheby's, NY

CAMPENDONK, Heinrich (1889-1957) German
| $2,655,000 | £1,500,000 | Cow and calf. Feb 06, 2006 Christie's, London |

CANALETTO (1697-1768) Italian
| $2,183,000 | £1,180,000 | View of the Piazzetta looking North. July 05, 2006 Sotheby's, London |

CARO, Anthony (1924-) British
| $2,200,000 | £1,250,000 | Sculpture Two. Feb 09, 2006 Sotheby's, London |

CARRACCI, Lodovico (1555-1619) Italian
| $12,210,001 | £6,600,000 | Salmacis and Hermaphroditus. July 06, 2006 Christie's, London |

CASSATT, Mary (1844-1926) American
| $3,800,000 | £2,209,302 | Mother and two children. Dec 01, 2005 Christie's, NY |

CECCARELLI, Naddo (14th C) Italian
| $1,903,000 | £1,100,000 | The Madonna and Child. Dec 08, 2005 Christie's, London |

CEZANNE, Paul (1839-1906) French
| $6,845,000 | £3,700,000 | Maison dans la verdure. June 20, 2006 Christie's, London |
| $9,200,000 | £5,168,540 | Pommes et gateaux. Nov 01, 2005 Christie's, NY |

CHAGALL, Marc (1887-1985) French/Russian
$1,013,216	£550,661	Couple aux pivoines a Vence. June 16, 2006 Kornfeld, Bern (S.FR 1,250,000)
$1,053,745	£572,687	Femme et fleurs au foulard. June 16, 2006 Kornfeld, Bern (S.FR 1,300,000)
$1,094,273	£594,714	Les maries dans le ciel bleu du village. June 16, 2006 Kornfeld, Bern (S.FR 1,350,000)
$1,100,000	£617,978	Bouquet sur Vence, Nov 02, 2005 Sotheby's, NY
$1,144,000	£650,000	Self-portrait in profile. Feb 07, 2006 Sotheby's, London
$1,159,200	£630,000	Les amis. June 19, 2006 Sotheby's, London
$1,175,330	£638,767	La mariee au cirque. June 16, 2006 Kornfeld, Bern (S.FR 1,450,000)
$1,214,400	£660,000	Nuit enchantee. June 19, 2006 Sotheby's, London
$1,296,916	£704,846	Les fiances aux anemones. June 16, 2006 Kornfeld, Bern (S.FR 1,600,000)
$1,296,916	£704,846	Le couple dans le soileil. June 16, 2006 Kornfeld, Bern (S.FR 1,600,000)
$1,300,000	£730,337	Les musiciens. Nov 01, 2005 Christie's, NY
$1,320,000	£750,000	Le soir. Feb 07, 2006 Sotheby's, London
$1,337,445	£726,872	La famille aux deux bouquets dans la nuit. June 16, 2006 Kornfeld, Bern (S.FR 1,650,000)
$1,380,000	£750,000	Paysage a l'Isba. June 19, 2006 Sotheby's, London
$1,418,502	£770,925	Le bateau de l'Exode. June 16, 2006 Kornfeld, Bern (S.FR 1,750,000)
$1,500,000	£842,697	Le soir. Nov 02, 2005 Sotheby's, NY
$1,580,617	£859,031	Le coq-peintre a Paris. June 16, 2006 Kornfeld, Bern (S.FR 1,950,000)
$1,800,000	£983,607	Soldats. May 03, 2006 Sotheby's, NY
$1,864,317	£1,013,216	Le reve au cirque. June 16, 2006 Kornfeld, Bern (S.FR 2,300,000)
$1,985,903	£1,079,295	Le songe. June 16, 2006 Kornfeld, Bern (S.FR 2,450,000)
$2,200,000	£1,202,186	Couple. May 03, 2006 Sotheby's, NY
$2,220,000	£1,200,000	Famille. June 20, 2006 Christie's, London
$2,300,000	£1,256,831	Paradis. May 03, 2006 Sotheby's, NY
$2,500,000	£1,366,120	Grand cirque. May 03, 2006 Sotheby's, NY
$3,000,000	£1,639,344	Grand bouquet. May 03, 2006 Sotheby's, NY
$3,168,000	£1,800,000	Fleurs sur Saint-Jeannet. Feb 07, 2006 Sotheby's, London
$3,600,000	£2,022,472	Jongleur. Nov 02, 2005 Sotheby's, NY

CHANG YU SHU (1900-1966) Chinese
| $1,865,689 | £1,091,046 | Four nudes. Nov 27, 2005 Christie's, Hong Kong (HK.D 14,500,000) |

(cont'd) CHANG YU SHU (1900-1966) Chinese
$3,213,224   £1,857,355   Pink lotus. Apr 08, 2006 Sotheby's, Hong Kong (HK.D 25,000,000)

CHERNETSOV, Nikanor Grigorevich (1805-1879) Russian
$1,395,000   £750,000   View of Orianda on the southern shores of the Crimea. May 31, 2006
                 Sotheby's, London

CHILLIDA, Eduardo (1924-2002) Spanish
$1,936,000   £1,100,000   Elogia de la arquitectura XII - Praise of architecture XII. Feb 08, 2006
                 Christie's, London
$3,330,000   £1,800,000   Rumor de limites VI - Limit noise VI. June 22, 2006 Christie's, London

CHIRICO, Giorgio de (1888-1978) Italian
$1,157,619   £619,048   Mendiant de Thermopyles. May 23, 2006 Christie's, Milan (Euro 910,000)
$1,294,521   £684,932   Dioscuri con i campagni in riva al mare. June 07, 2006 Artcurial Briest, Paris
                 (Euro 1,000,000)
$1,947,000   £1,100,000   Sacred fish. Feb 06, 2006 Christie's, London

CHU TEH CHUN (1920-) Chinese
$2,964,163   £1,585,114   Rouge, la pluie de petales, blanc, le nuage au-dessus de la maison.
                 May 28, 2006 Christie's, Hong Kong (HK.D 23,000,000)

CLAUDEL, Camille (1864-1943) French
$1,500,000   £819,672   Abandon. May 04, 2006 Sotheby's, NY

COPLEY, John Singleton (1738-1815) American
$1,500,000   £802,139   Portrait of John Hancock. May 24, 2006 Sotheby's, NY
$3,000,000   £1,744,186   Mrs Theodore Atkinson, Jr. Nov 30, 2005 Sotheby's, NY

CRANACH, Lucas (elder) (1472-1553) German
$4,400,000   £2,543,353   Saint Barbara in wooded landscape. Apr 06, 2006 Christie's, NY

CROSS, Henri Edmond (1856-1910) French
$1,000,000   £546,448   Baigneuses. May 03, 2006 Sotheby's, NY

CUI RUZUO (1944-) Chinese
$1,675,396   £895,934   Snowy mountains. May 29, 2006 Christie's, Hong Kong (HK.D 13,000,000)

CULLEN, Maurice Galbraith (1866-1934) Canadian
$1,053,555   £616,114   The bird shop, St Lawrence Street. Nov 24, 2005 Heffel, Vancouver
                 (C.D 1,300,000)

CURTIS, Edward S (1868-1952) American
$1,250,000   £710,227   North American Indians. Oct 12, 2005 Christie's, NY

CUYP, Aelbert (1620-1691) Dutch
$1,730,000   £1,000,000   Landscape with a hunt and portrait of a youth with his tutor. Dec 07, 2005
                 Sotheby's, London

DALI, Salvador (1904-1989) Spanish
$2,100,000   £1,179,775   Echo nostalgique. Nov 02, 2005 Sotheby's, NY
$2,301,000   £1,300,000   Galatee. Feb 06, 2006 Christie's, London

DAVID, Jacques-Louis (1748-1825) French
$2,407,534   £1,301,370   Portrait de Jean-Pierre Delahaye. June 22, 2006 Christie's, Paris
                 (Euro 1,900,000)

DAVIS, Stuart (1894-1964) American
$2,800,000   £1,627,907   Still life with flowers. Dec 01, 2005 Christie's, NY
$4,000,000   £2,325,581   Rue de l'Echaude. Nov 30, 2005 Sotheby's, NY

DEGAS, Edgar (1834-1917) French
$3,363,000   £1,900,000   Pointes. Feb 06, 2006 Christie's, London
$11,040,001   £6,000,000   Sortie du bain. June 19, 2006 Sotheby's, London

DELACROIX, Eugene (1798-1863) French
$2,024,000   £1,100,000   Femmes a la fontaine. June 13, 2006 Sotheby's, London
$2,852,000   £1,550,000   Lion et lionne dans les montagnes. June 14, 2006 Christie's, London

DERAIN, Andre (1880-1954) French
$6,100,000   £3,333,333   Paysage a l'estaque. May 03, 2006 Sotheby's, NY

DEUTSCH, Ludwig (1855-1935) French
$1,450,000   £819,209   Palace guard. Apr 19, 2006 Christie's, NY
$1,472,000   £800,000   A gathering around the morning news, Cairo. June 14, 2006
                 Christie's, London

DEWING, Maria Richards Oakey (1845-1927) American
$1,800,000   £962,567   Rose garden. May 24, 2006 Sotheby's, NY

DOIG, Peter (1959-) British
$1,850,000   £1,000,000   Iron Hill. June 21, 2006 Sotheby's, London

DOMENICO DI MICHELINO (1417-1491) Italian
$1,500,000   £852,273   The triumph of fame, the triumph of time and the triumph of eternity.
Jan 26, 2006 Sotheby's, NY

DOMINGUEZ, Oscar (1906-1958) Spanish
$1,480,000   £800,000   Personnages surrealistes. June 20, 2006 Christie's, London

DONATELLO (1386-1466) Italian
$3,950,000   £2,244,318   The Madonna and Child. Jan 26, 2006 Sotheby's, NY

DONGEN, Kees van (1877-1968) French/Dutch
$1,500,000   £819,672   Venus. May 02, 2006 Christie's, NY
$2,000,000   £1,092,896   Nu au laurier. May 04, 2006 Sotheby's, NY
$2,024,000   £1,100,000   Carmen Vincente dansant. June 19, 2006 Sotheby's, London
$2,300,000   £1,292,135   Femme au grand chapeau. Nov 01, 2005 Christie's, NY
$3,515,000   £1,900,000   Espagnole. June 20, 2006 Christie's, London
$4,784,000   £2,600,000   Portrait de Fernande. June 19, 2006 Sotheby's, London

DOU, Gerard (1613-1675) Dutch
$1,100,000   £625,000   Bearded old man. Jan 26, 2006 Sotheby's, NY
$1,813,000   £980,000   Grocer's shop, herring seller and boy. July 06, 2006 Christie's, London

DREUX, Alfred de (1810-1860) French
$1,417,500   £750,000   An African groom holding a stallion, with a dog. May 19, 2006 Christie's,
London

DUBUFFET, Jean (1901-1985) French
$2,200,000   £1,182,796   Le tissu social. May 10, 2006 Sotheby's, NY
$4,600,000   £2,473,118   Trinite, Champs Elysees. May 10, 2006 Sotheby's, NY

DUFY, Raoul (1877-1953) French
$1,398,400   £760,000   Plage de Sainte-Adresse. June 19, 2006 Sotheby's, London

DUMAS, Marlene (1953-) Dutch
$1,050,000   £564,516   Feathered stola. May 09, 2006 Christie's, NY
$1,200,000   £689,655   Garden. Nov 08, 2005 Christie's, NY
$1,400,000   £752,688   Adult entertainment. May 11, 2006 Phillips, NY

DYCK, Sir Anthony van (1599-1641) Flemish
$1,350,000   £767,045   Adoration of the Shepherds. Jan 26, 2006 Sotheby's, NY

FALK, Robert Rafailovich (1886-1958) Russian
$1,548,000   £900,000   Woman with a pink fan. Nov 30, 2005 Christie's, London

FANTIN-LATOUR, Henri (1836-1904) French
$1,140,800   £620,000   Crysanthemes. June 19, 2006 Sotheby's, London

FEININGER, Lyonel (1871-1956) American/German
$1,056,000   £600,000   Normannisches dorf I. Feb 07, 2006 Sotheby's, London
$1,150,500   £650,000   Still life with apples. Feb 06, 2006 Christie's, London
$1,649,315   £958,904   Gelmeroda XI. Dec 03, 2005 Lempertz, Koln (Euro 1,400,000)
$6,808,000   £3,700,000   Angler mit blauem fisch II - Angler with blue fish II. June 19, 2006
Sotheby's, London

FELIXMULLER, Conrad (1897-1977) German
$1,000,000   £561,798   Clemens Braun. Nov 02, 2005 Sotheby's, NY

FILONOV, Pavel and PORET, Alicia (20th C) Russian
$1,300,000   £730,337   Poor people. Apr 26, 2006 Sotheby's, NY

FLEGEL, Georg (1563-1638) German
$3,600,000   £2,080,925   Still life of flowers. Apr 06, 2006 Christie's, NY

FONTANA, Lucio (1899-1968) Italian
$1,017,500   £550,000   Spatial concept. June 21, 2006 Sotheby's, London
$1,036,769   £554,422   Spatial concept, silver Venice. May 27, 2006 Farsetti, Prato (Euro 815,000)
$1,056,000   £600,000   Concetto spaziale, attese. Feb 09, 2006 Sotheby's, London
$2,400,000   £1,290,323   Coupure. May 09, 2006 Christie's, NY

FRAGONARD, Jean Honore (1732-1806) French
$1,470,500   £850,000   A young girl leaning on a window ledge. Dec 08, 2005 Christie's, London
$4,440,000   £2,400,000   Two girls on bed playing with their dogs. July 05, 2006 Sotheby's, London

FREUD, Lucian (1922-) British/German
$1,108,800   £630,000   Daffodils and celery. Feb 09, 2006 Sotheby's, London

(cont'd) FREUD, Lucian (1922-) British/German
$2,775,000	£1,500,000	John Deakin. June 21, 2006 Sotheby's, London
$5,100,000	£2,931,035	Naked girl perched on chair. Nov 08, 2005 Christie's, NY
$5,544,000	£3,150,000	Portrait of Bruce Bernard seated. Feb 09, 2006 Sotheby's, London
$6,512,000	£3,700,000	Man in a string chair. Feb 08, 2006 Christie's, London

FRIEDRICH, Caspar David (1774-1840) German
| $1,159,200 | £630,000 | Landscape with waterfall. June 13, 2006 Sotheby's, London |
| $1,840,000 | £1,000,000 | Sunset behind Dresden's Hofkirche. June 13, 2006 Sotheby's, London |

FRIESEKE, Frederick Carl (1874-1939) American
| $2,100,000 | £1,122,995 | Garden pool. May 25, 2006 Christie's, NY |

GALIZIA, Fede (1578-1630) Italian
| $1,110,000 | £600,000 | Peaches in pierced white faience basket. July 06, 2006 Christie's, London |
| $1,450,000 | £838,150 | Glass compote with peaches, jasmine flowers, quinces and grasshopper. Apr 06, 2006 Christie's, NY |

GAUGUIN, Paul (1848-1903) French
| $4,000,000 | £2,185,792 | Vase de fleurs et gourde. May 02, 2006 Christie's, NY |
| $19,360,000 | £11,000,000 | Deux femmes, la chevelure fleurie. Feb 07, 2006 Sotheby's, London |

GEROME, Jean Leon (1824-1904) French
$1,000,000	£564,972	Flag makers. Oct 25, 2005 Sotheby's, NY
$1,196,000	£650,000	Les pigeons. June 14, 2006 Christie's, London
$1,692,800	£920,000	La mosquee bleue. June 14, 2006 Christie's, London

GIACOMETTI, Alberto (1901-1966) Swiss
$1,000,000	£546,448	Bust. May 02, 2006 Christie's, NY
$1,017,500	£550,000	Composition cubiste, homme. June 20, 2006 Christie's, London
$1,100,000	£617,978	Nature morte aux pommes. Nov 01, 2005 Christie's, NY
$1,150,000	£628,415	Coin d'atelier avec poele et balai. May 02, 2006 Christie's, NY
$1,295,000	£700,000	Femme debout. June 20, 2006 Christie's, London
$1,350,000	£758,427	Sculptures dans l'atelier. Nov 01, 2005 Christie's, NY
$1,400,000	£752,688	Femme debout. Groupe de figures. May 09, 2006 Christie's, NY
$1,763,877	£969,163	Buste de Isaku Yanaihara. June 27, 2006 Christie's, Zurich (S.FR 2,200,000)
$2,208,000	£1,200,000	Cage, premiere version. June 19, 2006 Sotheby's, London
$2,700,000	£1,516,854	Figurine. Nov 02, 2005 Sotheby's, NY
$3,200,000	£1,797,753	Buste de Diego. Nov 01, 2005 Christie's, NY

GIACOMETTI, Giovanni (1868-1934) Swiss
| $1,468,421 | £789,474 | Monti di neve - Snow mountains. May 31, 2006 Sotheby's, Zurich (S.FR 1,800,000) |

GIAQUINTO, Corrado (c.1690-1765) Italian
| $1,200,000 | £681,818 | The Penitent Magdalene. Jan 26, 2006 Sotheby's, NY |

GOGH, Vincent van (1853-1890) Dutch
$3,700,000	£2,000,000	Still life of gladioli and lilacs in vase. June 20, 2006 Christie's, London
$4,200,000	£2,295,082	Les toits. May 03, 2006 Sotheby's, NY
$36,000,000	£19,672,130	Arlesienne, Madame Ginoux. May 02, 2006 Christie's, NY

GONTCHAROVA, Natalia (1881-1962) Russian
| $1,848,000 | £1,050,000 | Les rameurs. Feb 07, 2006 Christie's, London |

GRECO, El (1541-1614) Spanish
$1,059,592	£598,639	Saint James. Oct 05, 2005 Christie's, Madrid (Euro 880,000)
$1,276,327	£721,088	Saint Luke. Oct 05, 2005 Christie's, Madrid (Euro 1,060,000)
$1,572,500	£850,000	Espolio. July 06, 2006 Christie's, London

GREUZE, Jean-Baptiste (1725-1805) French
| $1,593,000 | £900,000 | Portraits of the artist's daughters. Feb 01, 2006 Dreweatt Neate, Newbury |

GRIS, Juan (1887-1927) Spanish
$1,000,000	£561,798	Nature morte avec bouteille et cigares. Nov 02, 2005 Sotheby's, NY
$2,035,000	£1,100,000	Nappe blanche. June 20, 2006 Christie's, London
$2,200,000	£1,235,955	Verre et carte a jouer. Nov 01, 2005 Christie's, NY

GROSZ, George (1893-1959) American/German
| $1,416,000 | £800,000 | Coffee bar. Feb 06, 2006 Christie's, London |

GRUNEWALD, Isaac (1889-1946) Swedish
| $1,248,493 | £671,233 | Circus scene, sea-lions doing tricks. June 02, 2006 Uppsala Auktionskammare, Uppsala (Euro 980,000) |

GUARDI, Francesco (1712-1793) Italian

$2,035,000	£1,100,000	Venice, view of the Lagoon. July 05, 2006 Sotheby's, London
$3,167,808	£1,712,329	View of the Grand Canal, Venice. June 22, 2006 Tajan, Paris (Euro 2,500,000)

GURSKY, Andreas (1955-) German

$2,000,000	£1,075,269	99 Cent. May 10, 2006 Sotheby's, NY

GUSTON, Philip (1913-1980) American

$2,800,000	£1,609,195	Mirror. Nov 08, 2005 Christie's, NY
$4,900,000	£2,816,092	Zone. Nov 08, 2005 Christie's, NY

HARRIS, Lawren Stewart (1885-1970) Canadian

$1,285,071	£687,204	Mount Lefroy. May 25, 2006 Heffel, Vancouver (C.D 1,450,000)

HARTLEY, Marsden (1877-1943) American

$1,000,000	£581,395	Red flowers and sailing boat. Dec 01, 2005 Christie's, NY
$2,000,000	£1,069,519	Storm down Pine Point Way, old orchard beach. May 24, 2006 Sotheby's, NY

HASSAM, Childe (1859-1935) American

$1,200,000	£697,674	Paris at twilight. Nov 30, 2005 Sotheby's, NY
$2,800,000	£1,497,326	Paris nocturne. May 24, 2006 Sotheby's, NY

HEADE, Martin Johnson (1819-1904) American

$1,200,000	£641,711	Orchid with amethyst woodstar. May 25, 2006 Christie's, NY

HECKEL, Erich (1883-1970) German

$1,320,000	£750,000	Houses near Rome. Landscape near Rome. Feb 07, 2006 Sotheby's, London

HEPWORTH, Dame Barbara (1903-1975) British

$1,300,000	£710,383	Three obliques: walk-in. May 03, 2006 Sotheby's, NY

HESSE, Eva (1936-1970) American

$2,000,000	£1,075,269	Ear in a pond. May 09, 2006 Christie's, NY

HEYDEN, Jan van der (1637-1712) Dutch

$1,150,000	£653,409	The Hofstede Wolf en Hoecke on the Purmer. Jan 26, 2006 Sotheby's, NY

HICKS, Edward (1780-1849) American

$2,800,000	£1,581,921	Peaceable Kingdom. Jan 20, 2006 Sotheby's, NY

HIRST, Damien (1965-) British

$1,100,000	£591,398	Never mind. May 10, 2006 Sotheby's, NY
$1,150,000	£660,920	The most beautiful thing in the world. Nov 09, 2005 Sotheby's, NY
$1,500,000	£806,452	Beauty and the beast. May 09, 2006 Christie's, NY
$3,000,000	£1,612,903	Away from the flock, divided. May 09, 2006 Christie's, NY

HOBBEMA, Meindert (1638-1709) Dutch

$3,500,000	£1,988,636	Wooded landscape with travellers on a track by a cottage. Jan 26, 2006 Sotheby's, NY

HOCKNEY, David (1937-) British

$3,200,000	£1,720,430	Neat lawn. May 09, 2006 Christie's, NY
$4,810,000	£2,600,000	Splash. June 21, 2006 Sotheby's, London

HODLER, Ferdinand (1853-1918) Swiss

$2,485,463	£1,365,639	Linienherrlichkeit - Beautiful outline, female nude. June 27, 2006 Christie's, Zurich (S.FR 3,100,000)
$3,272,567	£1,902,655	The Eiger, Monch and Jungfrau above a sea of cloud. Nov 29, 2005 Sotheby's, Zurich (S.FR 4,300,000)
$3,589,474	£1,929,825	Am Genfersee - Lake Geneva. May 31, 2006 Sotheby's, Zurich (S.FR 4,400,000)

HOFFMANN, Hans (c.1530-c.1591) German

$1,480,000	£800,000	Crouching cat. July 06, 2006 Christie's, London

HOFMANN, Hans (1880-1966) American/German

$1,400,000	£804,598	Stardust. Nov 08, 2005 Christie's, NY

HUYSUM, Jan van (1682-1749) Dutch

$2,590,000	£1,400,000	Festoon of flowers. July 06, 2006 Christie's, London
$5,365,000	£2,900,000	Still life of fruit on marble ledge. July 05, 2006 Sotheby's, London
$6,500,000	£3,693,182	Flowers in a terracotta vase on a marble ledge. Jan 26, 2006 Sotheby's, NY

IACOVLEFF, Alexandre (1887-1938) French/Russian

| $1,100,000 | £617,978 | General Ma-soo in the historical play ' Retreat of Kiai-Ting'. Apr 26, 2006 Sotheby's, NY |
| $1,600,000 | £898,876 | Kabuki dancer. Apr 26, 2006 Sotheby's, NY |

INDIANA, Robert (1928-) American

| $1,026,374 | £554,797 | Love, red and blue. June 26, 2006 Claude Aguttes, Neuilly (Euro 810,000) |
| $1,189,189 | £675,676 | Yield brother II, Hommage a Kennedy. Dec 19, 2005 Claude Aguttes, Neuilly (Euro 1,000,000) |

JAWLENSKY, Alexej von (1864-1941) Russian

$4,048,000	£2,200,000	Lola. June 19, 2006 Sotheby's, London
$4,600,000	£2,584,270	Sicilian woman with green shawl. Nov 02, 2005 Sotheby's, NY
$4,956,000	£2,800,000	Dark eyes. Feb 06, 2006 Christie's, London

JOHNS, Jasper (1930-) American

| $1,850,000 | £994,624 | Painting with two balls. May 09, 2006 Christie's, NY |

JORN, Asger (1914-1973) Danish

| $1,030,157 | £592,044 | Tristesse blanche - white sadness. Apr 03, 2006 Rasmussen, Copenhagen (D.KR 6,400,000) |

JUDD, Donald (1928-1994) American.

$1,700,000	£913,979	Bernstein. May 09, 2006 Christie's, NY.
$1,800,000	£967,742	Untitled. May 09, 2006 Christie's, NY
$2,200,000	£1,264,368	Untitled. Nov 09, 2005 Sotheby's, NY
$2,400,000	£1,290,323	Ballantine. May 09, 2006 Christie's, NY
$2,400,000	£1,290,323	Bernstein. May 09, 2006 Christie's, NY
$2,400,000	£1,290,323	Hernandez. May 09, 2006 Christie's, NY

KAHLO, Frida (1907-1954) Mexican

| $5,000,000 | £2,673,797 | Roots. May 24, 2006 Sotheby's, NY |

KANDINSKY, Wassily (1866-1944) Russian

$1,232,000	£700,000	Autumn near Murnau. Feb 07, 2006 Sotheby's, London
$2,090,754	£1,130,138	Coulant. June 26, 2006 Claude Aguttes, Neuilly (Euro 1,650,000)
$3,450,000	£1,885,246	Arrows. May 02, 2006 Christie's, NY

KENSETT, John Frederick (1816-1872) American

| $1,100,000 | £639,535 | Entrance to Newport Harbour. Dec 01, 2005 Christie's, NY |

KIEFER, Anselm (1945-) German

| $1,147,000 | £620,000 | Descent of the soul. June 21, 2006 Sotheby's, London |

KIRCHNER, Ernst Ludwig (1880-1938) German

$2,405,000	£1,300,000	Standing woman, Caryatides. June 20, 2006 Christie's, London
$3,363,000	£1,900,000	Street scene. Feb 06, 2006 Christie's, London
$7,788,000	£4,400,000	Portrait of woman in white. Adam and Eve. Feb 06, 2006 Christie's, London

KLEE, Paul (1879-1940) Swiss

| $2,800,000 | £1,573,034 | Young garden. Nov 02, 2005 Sotheby's, NY |

KLEIN, Yves (1928-1962) French

$1,056,000	£600,000	IKB 114. Feb 09, 2006 Sotheby's, London
$1,300,000	£698,925	MG20. May 09, 2006 Christie's, NY
$1,496,000	£850,000	IKB 92. Feb 09, 2006 Sotheby's, London
$1,584,000	£900,000	Ant 173. Feb 08, 2006 Christie's, London
$1,628,000	£880,000	IKB 234. June 22, 2006 Christie's, London
$3,600,000	£1,935,484	Ant 127. May 09, 2006 Christie's, NY
$4,200,000	£2,258,065	RE46. May 09, 2006 Christie's, NY

KLINE, Franz (1910-1962) American

$1,600,000	£919,540	Untitled. Nov 08, 2005 Christie's, NY
$1,700,000	£913,978	Giselle. May 10, 2006 Sotheby's, NY
$3,100,000	£1,781,609	Harley red. Nov 09, 2005 Sotheby's, NY
$4,850,000	£2,787,356	Painting in black and white color. Nov 08, 2005 Christie's, NY

KLODT VON JURGENSBURG, Michael (1832-1902) Russian

| $5,095,891 | £2,739,726 | Coastal landscape with beached fishing boats. June 04, 2006 Uppsala Auktionskammare, Uppsala (Euro 4,000,000) |

KOEKKOEK, Barend Cornelis (1803-1862) Dutch

| $1,106,250 | £625,000 | Wood-gatherers in a winter landscape. Apr 24, 2006 Sotheby's, Amsterdam (Euro 900,000) |
| $1,545,139 | £868,056 | Late afternoon with numerous skaters by a town. Apr 26, 2006 Christie's, Amsterdam (Euro 1,250,000) |

KOLBE, Georg (1877-1947) German
$1,150,500	£650,000	Dancer. Feb 06, 2006 Christie's, London

KONINCK, Philips de (1619-1688) Dutch
$1,500,000	£852,273	Panoramic river landscape. Jan 26, 2006 Sotheby's, NY

KOONING, Willem de (1904-1997) American/Dutch
$1,000,000	£537,634	Untitled composition no.18. May 10, 2006 Christie's, NY
$1,000,000	£574,713	Untitled 10. Nov 08, 2005 Christie's, NY
$1,100,000	£591,398	Woman IV. May 10, 2006 Sotheby's, NY
$1,150,000	£660,920	Untitled. Nov 08, 2005 Christie's, NY
$1,400,000	£752,688	Asheville I. May 09, 2006 Christie's, NY
$1,750,000	£1,005,747	Cross-legged figure. Nov 08, 2005 Christie's, NY
$2,500,000	£1,344,086	Garden in Delft. May 10, 2006 Sotheby's, NY
$2,775,000	£1,500,000	Untitled XXI. June 21, 2006 Sotheby's, London
$3,200,000	£1,839,081	Untitled. Nov 08, 2005 Christie's, NY
$5,100,000	£2,741,936	Study for Clamdigger, two women. May 09, 2006 Christie's, NY
$9,000,000	£4,838,710	Untitled. May 09, 2006 Christie's, NY
$9,500,000	£5,459,770	Untitled. Nov 08, 2005 Christie's, NY
$14,000,000	£7,526,881	Untitled XVI - Figural composition. May 10, 2006 Sotheby's, NY

KOONS, Jeff (1955-) American
$1,020,000	£586,207	Saint Benedict. Nov 08, 2005 Christie's, NY
$2,400,000	£1,290,323	Buster Keaton. May 11, 2006 Phillips, NY
$3,000,000	£1,724,138	Life boat. Nov 09, 2005 Sotheby's, NY
$3,500,000	£2,011,494	Self-portrait. Nov 08, 2005 Christie's, NY
$4,100,000	£2,204,301	Aqualung. May 09, 2006 Christie's, NY
$4,700,000	£2,526,882	New Hoover convertibles. May 10, 2006 Sotheby's, NY

KOROVINE, Constantin (1861-1939) Russian
$1,376,000	£800,000	Picnic. Dec 01, 2005 Sotheby's, London
$1,395,000	£750,000	Fishing on a sunny day. May 31, 2006 Sotheby's, London
$1,500,000	£842,697	Korovin's studio, Gurzuf. Crimea. Apr 26, 2006 Sotheby's, NY

KUHN, Walt (1877-1949) American
$1,000,000	£581,395	Chico in silk hat. Nov 30, 2005 Sotheby's, NY

KUSTODIEV, Boris (1878-1927) Russian
$2,580,000	£1,500,000	Odalisque. Nov 30, 2005 Christie's, London

LAM, Wilfredo (1902-1982) Cuban
$1,150,000	£614,973	Untitled. May 23, 2006 Christie's, NY

LANE, Fitz Hugh (1804-1865) American
$1,000,000	£534,759	Rafe's Chasm, Gloucester. May 25, 2006 Christie's, NY

LARIONOV, Mikhail (1881-1964) Russian
$1,302,000	£700,000	Sunset on the Black Sea. May 31, 2006 Sotheby's, London

LAURENS, Henri (1885-1954) French
$1,300,000	£730,337	Le matin. Nov 01, 2005 Christie's, NY

LAVERY, Sir John (1856-1941) British
$1,506,600	£810,000	Honeymoon. May 12, 2006 Christie's, London

LEGER, Fernand (1881-1955) French
$1,800,000	£983,607	Nature morte, le compas. May 03, 2006 Sotheby's, NY
$1,900,000	£1,067,416	La partie de cartes. Nov 01, 2005 Christie's, NY
$1,900,000	£1,038,251	Acrobate dans le cirque. May 02, 2006 Christie's, NY
$2,000,000	£1,092,896	Nature morte a la guitare. May 02, 2006 Christie's, NY
$2,850,000	£1,557,377	Nature morte, etat definitif. May 03, 2006 Sotheby's, NY
$4,300,000	£2,415,731	Le grand dejeuner. Nov 01, 2005 Christie's, NY
$4,800,000	£2,696,629	Constructeurs. Nov 02, 2005 Sotheby's, NY

LELY, Sir Peter (1618-1680) British
$1,606,500	£850,000	Portrait of Charles Dormer, 2nd Earl of Carnarvon. June 07, 2006 Sotheby's, London

LEMPICKA, Tamara de (1898-1980) Polish
$1,300,000	£730,337	Suzanne au bain. Nov 03, 2005 Sotheby's, NY
$2,800,000	£1,530,055	Groupe de quatre nus. May 02, 2006 Christie's, NY

LEVITAN, Isaac Ilyitch (1860-1900) Russian
$1,892,000	£1,100,000	Marsh at evening. Nov 30, 2005 Christie's, London

LIAO CHI-CHUN (1902-1976) Chinese
$1,933,150	£1,033,770	Garden. May 28, 2006 Christie's, Hong Kong (HK.D 15,000,000)

LICHTENSTEIN, Roy (1923-1997) American

$1,100,000	£632,184	Reflections on crash. Nov 10, 2005 Phillips, NY
$1,650,000	£948,276	Vick, I-I thought I heard your voice. Nov 08, 2005 Christie's, NY
$3,000,000	£1,612,903	Purist painting with pitcher, glass and classical column. May 10, 2006 Sotheby's, NY
$3,344,000	£1,900,000	Still life with a candy jar. Feb 09, 2006 Sotheby's, London
$14,000,000	£7,526,881	Sinking sun. May 10, 2006 Sotheby's, NY
$14,500,000	£8,333,334	In the car. Nov 08, 2005 Christie's, NY

LIEBERMANN, Max (1847-1935) German

| $3,344,000 | £1,900,000 | Flowers in front of the gardener's house. Feb 07, 2006 Sotheby's, London |

LIPCHITZ, Jacques (1891-1973) French

| $1,150,000 | £646,067 | Baigneuse. Nov 01, 2005 Christie's, NY |

LORENZO MONACO (c.1370-c.1425) Italian

| $1,557,000 | £900,000 | Saint Jerome in the Wilderness. Dec 07, 2005 Sotheby's, London |

LOUIS, Morris (1912-1962) American

| $1,600,000 | £860,215 | Floral V. May 09, 2006 Christie's, NY |

LOWRY, Laurence Stephen (1887-1976) British

| $1,795,500 | £950,000 | The Liver Buildings, Liverpool. June 09, 2006 Christie's, London |

LUTTICHUYS, Simon (1610-1662) Dutch

| $1,350,500 | £730,000 | Still life with pewter jug, glass of beer and walnuts. July 05, 2006 Sotheby's, London |

LYTRAS, Nikiforos (1832-1904) Greek

| $1,228,500 | £650,000 | Naughty grandchild. May 22, 2006 Sotheby's, London |

MAES, Nicolaes (1632-1693) Dutch

| $1,211,000 | £700,000 | Group portrait of a family in an Italianate garden with ornate fountain. Dec 08, 2005 Christie's, London |

MAGRITTE, Rene (1898-1967) Belgian

| $1,091,200 | £620,000 | Seducteur. Feb 07, 2006 Sotheby's, London |
| $2,200,000 | £1,202,186 | Idees claires. May 02, 2006 Christie's, NY |

MAILLOL, Aristide (1861-1944) French

| $2,000,000 | £1,092,896 | Montagne. May 03, 2006 Sotheby's, NY |
| $2,500,000 | £1,404,494 | La nuit. Nov 02, 2005 Sotheby's, NY |

MAKOVSKY, Konstantin (1839-1915) Russian

| $1,656,164 | £890,411 | A young beauty. June 04, 2006 Uppsala Auktionskammare, Uppsala (Euro 1,300,000) |

MAN-RAY (1890-1976) American

| $1,144,000 | £650,000 | Fortune II. Feb 07, 2006 Sotheby's, London |

MANET, Edouard (1832-1883) French

| $2,220,000 | £1,200,000 | Chanteuse de cafe-concert. June 20, 2006 Christie's, London |

MANZONI, Piero (1933-1963) Italian

| $1,097,400 | £620,000 | Achrome. Oct 24, 2005 Sotheby's, London |
| $1,700,000 | £913,979 | Achrome. May 09, 2006 Christie's, NY |

MARC, Franz (1880-1916) German

| $1,380,600 | £780,000 | Two nudes on red background. Feb 06, 2006 Christie's, London |

MARDEN, Brice (1938-) American

| $2,650,000 | £1,424,731 | Elements V. May 09, 2006 Christie's, NY |

MARIN, John (1870-1953) American

| $1,100,000 | £639,535 | Sailing boat, Brooklyn Bridge, NY skyline. Dec 01, 2005 Christie's, NY |

MARINI, Marino (1901-1980) Italian

| $1,416,000 | £800,000 | Little rider. Oct 24, 2005 Sotheby's, London |
| $1,593,000 | £900,000 | Rider. Oct 24, 2005 Sotheby's, London |

MARTIN, Agnes (1912-1999) American/Canadian

$1,200,000	£689,655	Untitled II. Nov 09, 2005 Sotheby's, NY
$1,350,000	£775,862	Untitled 0. Nov 08, 2005 Christie's, NY
$1,400,000	£752,688	UntitledIV. May 09, 2006 Christie's, NY
$1,550,000	£833,333	Untitled no.VIII. May 10, 2006 Sotheby's, NY

MASHKOV, Ilya (1881-1944) Russian

| $3,268,000 | £1,900,000 | Still life of flowers. Dec 01, 2005 Sotheby's, London |

MASSON, Andre (1896-1987) French
$1,593,000	£900,000	Vue emblematique de Tolede. Feb 06, 2006 Christie's, London

MATISSE, Henri (1869-1954) French
$1,000,000	£534,759	Beau matin d'ete, 1905. May 23, 2006 Doyle, NY
$1,300,000	£730,337	Grand nu accroupi, Olga. Nov 01, 2005 Christie's, NY
$3,768,282	£2,070,485	Les huitres. June 27, 2006 Christie's, Zurich (S.FR 4,700,000)
$9,750,000	£5,477,528	Robe jaune et robe Arlequin. Nov 02, 2005 Sotheby's, NY
$16,500,000	£9,016,394	Nu couche vu de dos. May 03, 2006 Sotheby's, NY

MATTA (1911-2002) Chilean
$1,200,000	£689,655	Water. Nov 16, 2005 Sotheby's, NY

MAZZOLA, Francesco (1503-1540) Italian
$1,295,000	£700,000	Portrait of bearded man in black hat and gold chain. July 06, 2006 Christie's, London

MEHTA, Tyeb (1925-) Indian
$1,100,000	£632,184	Falling figure with bird. Mar 29, 2006 Sotheby's, NY
$1,400,000	£777,778	Mahisasura. Sept 21, 2005 Christie's, NY

MEIDNER, Ludwig (1884-1966) German
$2,816,000	£1,600,000	Apocalyptic landscape. Landscape. Feb 07, 2006 Sotheby's, London

MENZEL, Adolph (1815-1905) German
$1,380,000	£750,000	View into little yard. June 13, 2006 Sotheby's, London

MIRO, Joan (1893-1983) Spanish
$1,050,000	£573,771	Personnage. May 03, 2006 Sotheby's, NY
$1,239,000	£700,000	Untitled. Feb 06, 2006 Christie's, London
$2,000,000	£1,123,596	Nature morte au raisin. Nov 01, 2005 Christie's, NY
$2,400,000	£1,348,315	Painting. Nov 01, 2005 Christie's, NY
$6,900,000	£3,876,405	Le soleil rouge ronge l'araignee. Nov 01, 2005 Christie's, NY
$8,096,000	£4,600,000	Oiseau au plumage deploye vole vers l'arbre argente. Feb 07, 2006 Sotheby's, London

MITCHELL, Joan (1926-1992) American
$1,350,000	£775,862	Sunflower V. Nov 08, 2005 Christie's, NY
$1,800,000	£967,742	Untitled. May 09, 2006 Christie's, NY
$1,900,000	£1,021,505	Gentian violet. May 10, 2006 Sotheby's, NY
$2,200,000	£1,264,368	Untitled. Nov 09, 2005 Sotheby's, NY

MODIGLIANI, Amedeo (1884-1920) Italian
$4,900,000	£2,752,809	Buste de Manuel Humbert. Nov 02, 2005 Sotheby's, NY
$5,000,000	£2,808,989	Moise Kisling seduto. Nov 01, 2005 Christie's, NY
$5,735,000	£3,100,000	Buste rouge, Cariatide. June 20, 2006 Christie's, London
$6,012,500	£3,250,000	Homme assis sur fond orange. June 20, 2006 Christie's, London
$26,864,000	£14,600,000	Jeanne Hebuterne au chapeau. June 19, 2006 Sotheby's, London

MONET, Claude (1840-1926) French
$1,200,000	£674,157	Le fjord, pres Christiania. Nov 02, 2005 Sotheby's, NY
$1,202,500	£650,000	Peches. June 20, 2006 Christie's, London
$1,250,000	£702,247	Maisons dans la neige, Norvege. Nov 02, 2005 Sotheby's, NY
$1,300,000	£730,337	Petit bras de la Seine a Argenteuil. Nov 02, 2005 Sotheby's, NY
$1,700,000	£955,056	Aiguille d'Etretat, maree basse. Nov 01, 2005 Christie's, NY
$1,700,000	£928,962	Azalees blanches en pot. May 03, 2006 Sotheby's, NY
$1,702,000	£920,000	Oliviers et palmiers, vallee de sasso. June 20, 2006 Christie's, London
$1,813,000	£980,000	Glacons, environs de Bennecourt. June 20, 2006 Christie's, London
$1,840,000	£1,000,000	Sandviken, Norvege, effet de neige. June 19, 2006 Sotheby's, London
$2,600,000	£1,460,674	Le panier de pommes. Nov 01, 2005 Christie's, NY.
$2,600,000	£1,420,765	La Seine a Bougival. May 02, 2006 Christie's, NY
$3,680,000	£2,000,000	Arbre en boule, Argenteuil. June 19, 2006 Sotheby's, London
$4,248,000	£2,400,000	La Seine a Vetheuil. Feb 06, 2006 Christie's, London
$4,500,000	£2,459,016	Pres de Monte-Carlo. May 03, 2006 Sotheby's, NY
$4,600,000	£2,584,270	Le pont japonais. Nov 02, 2005 Sotheby's, NY
$10,000,000	£5,464,481	Nympheas, temps gris. May 02, 2006 Christie's, NY
$11,500,000	£6,460,675	Grand Canal, Venise. Nov 02, 2005 Sotheby's, NY
$12,500,000	£7,022,472	Nympheas. Nov 01, 2005 Christie's, NY

MOORE, Henry O M (1898-1986) British
$1,634,000	£950,000	Mother and child. Nov 29, 2005 Bonhams, New Bond Street
$3,200,000	£1,748,634	Reclining figure. May 02, 2006 Christie's, NY
$4,500,000	£2,459,016	Large four piece reclining figure. May 02, 2006 Christie's, NY
$5,520,000	£3,000,000	Large four piece reclining figure. June 19, 2006 Sotheby's, London

MORAN, Thomas (1837-1926) American
$1,000,000	£546,448	On the Hance Trail, Grand Canyon of the Colorado River, Arizona. July 22, 2006 Coeur d'Alene, Hayden
$1,300,000	£755,814	Monterey coast. Nov 30, 2005 Sotheby's, NY
$1,700,000	£928,962	The eternal snows of Mt. Moran. July 22, 2006 Coeur d'Alene, Hayden

MORISOT, Berthe (1841-1895) French
| $2,220,000 | £1,200,000 | Interieur. June 20, 2006 Christie's, London |
| $4,600,000 | £2,584,270 | Cache-cache. Nov 02, 2005 Sotheby's, NY |

MORSE, Samuel F B (1791-1872) American
| $1,200,000 | £697,674 | Marquis de Lafayette. Nov 30, 2005 Sotheby's, NY |

MOTHERWELL, Robert (1915-1991) American
| $1,250,000 | £718,391 | New England elegy III. Nov 09, 2005 Sotheby's, NY |
| $1,900,000 | £1,091,954 | Elegy to the Spanish Republic 122. Nov 08, 2005 Christie's, NY |

MUNCH, Edvard (1863-1944) Norwegian
$1,020,800	£580,000	Ingeborg by the fjord. Feb 07, 2006 Sotheby's, London
$1,936,000	£1,100,000	Horses. Feb 07, 2006 Sotheby's, London
$2,288,000	£1,300,000	Generations. Feb 07, 2006 Sotheby's, London
$2,464,000	£1,400,000	Wave. Feb 07, 2006 Sotheby's, London
$2,640,000	£1,500,000	Self-portrait with Spanish flu. Feb 07, 2006 Sotheby's, London
$5,632,000	£3,200,000	Self-portrait against two colored backgrounds. Feb 07, 2006 Sotheby's, London
$9,680,001	£5,500,000	Summer day. Feb 07, 2006 Sotheby's, London

MUNNINGS, Sir Alfred (1878-1959) British
$1,795,500	£950,000	Tom and Luke Parsons on their ponies, Champagne and Squirrel, Exmoor. May 19, 2006 Christie's, London
$2,850,000	£1,656,977	Going out at Epsom. Dec 02, 2005 Sotheby's, NY
$3,650,000	£2,050,562	Gypsies on Epsom Downs, Derby week. Apr 25, 2006 Sotheby's, NY

MURAKAMI, Takashi (1962-) Japanese
| $1,000,000 | £537,634 | Nirvana. May 11, 2006 Sotheby's, NY |

MURILLO, Bartolome Esteban (1618-1682) Spanish
| $3,806,000 | £2,200,000 | Christ the Man of Sorrows. Dec 08, 2005 Christie's, London |

NETSCHER, Caspar (1639-1684) Dutch
| $1,650,000 | £937,500 | The seduction. Jan 26, 2006 Sotheby's, NY |

NOLDE, Emil (1867-1956) German
$1,239,000	£700,000	Lady in poppy garden. Feb 06, 2006 Christie's, London
$1,377,974	£748,899	Poppies and roses. June 16, 2006 Kornfeld, Bern (S.FR 1,700,000)
$1,465,069	£787,671	Farm house in an extensive landscape. June 03, 2006 Lempertz, Koln (Euro 1,150,000)
$1,672,000	£950,000	Sunflower. Feb 07, 2006 Sotheby's, London
$2,992,000	£1,700,000	Pansies. Feb 07, 2006 Sotheby's, London
$3,145,000	£1,700,000	Sonnenuntergang. June 20, 2006 Christie's, London
$3,422,500	£1,850,000	Rotblondes madchen. June 20, 2006 Christie's, London

O`KEEFFE, Georgia (1887-1986) American
| $1,200,000 | £697,674 | Corn no.III. Dec 01, 2005 Christie's, NY |

PAN YULIANG (1899-1977) Chinese
| $1,093,680 | £639,579 | Artist self portrait. Nov 27, 2005 Christie's, Hong Kong (HK.D 8,500,000) |

PARRISH, Maxfield (1870-1966) American
| $3,800,000 | £2,032,086 | Lantern bearers. May 25, 2006 Christie's, NY |
| $6,800,000 | £3,636,364 | Daybreak. May 25, 2006 Christie's, NY |

PASCALI, Pino (1935-1968) Italian
| $2,124,000 | £1,200,000 | Cannon Bella Ciao. Oct 24, 2005 Christie's, London |

PEALE, Charles Willson (1741-1827) American
| $19,000,000 | £10,734,464 | George Washington at Princeton. Jan 21, 2006 Christie's, NY |

PECHSTEIN, Max (1881-1955) German
| $1,043,129 | £557,823 | Houses by the sea. May 26, 2006 Villa Grisebach, Berlin (Euro 820,000) |

PICABIA, Francis (1878-1953) French
| $1,672,000 | £950,000 | Lunis. Feb 07, 2006 Sotheby's, London |

PICASSO, Pablo (1881-1973) Spanish
| $1,000,000 | £546,448 | Nu. May 03, 2006 Christie's, NY |
| $1,050,000 | £589,888 | Buste d'homme barbu. Nov 02, 2005 Christie's, NY |

(cont'd) PICASSO, Pablo (1881-1973) Spanish

$1,150,000	£628,415	Tete de femme. May 03, 2006 Christie's, NY
$1,202,500	£650,000	Nature morte a la bougie. June 20, 2006 Christie's, London
$1,267,200	£720,000	Buste de mousquetaire. Feb 07, 2006 Christie's, London
$1,520,000	£830,601	Peintre et modele. May 03, 2006 Sotheby's, NY
$1,734,600	£980,000	Chien dalmate. Feb 06, 2006 Christie's, London
$1,950,000	£1,095,506	Bouteille et verre. Nov 02, 2005 Sotheby's, NY
$2,000,000	£1,123,596	Femme assise au chapeau. Nov 01, 2005 Christie's, NY
$2,300,000	£1,292,135	L'atelier. Nov 01, 2005 Christie's, NY
$2,300,000	£1,250,000	Deux bustes de profil. June 19, 2006 Sotheby's, London
$2,500,000	£1,366,120	Enfants dessinant. May 03, 2006 Sotheby's, NY
$2,650,000	£1,488,764	Femme dans l'atelier. Nov 02, 2005 Sotheby's, NY
$2,775,000	£1,500,000	Portrait de femme. June 20, 2006 Christie's, London
$2,775,000	£1,500,000	Vase de fleurs et compotier. June 20, 2006 Christie's, London
$3,000,000	£1,685,393	Tete de femme. Nov 02, 2005 Sotheby's, NY
$3,000,000	£1,639,344	Femme se coiffant. May 02, 2006 Christie's, NY
$3,300,000	£1,853,933	Guitare, verre, bouteille de Vieux Marc. Nov 02, 2005 Sotheby's, NY
$4,100,000	£2,240,437	Sylvette. May 03, 2006 Sotheby's, NY
$4,232,000	£2,300,000	Courses a Auteuil. June 19, 2006 Sotheby's, London
$4,928,000	£2,800,000	Homme a la pipe. Feb 07, 2006 Sotheby's, London
$4,995,000	£2,700,000	Femme dans un fauteuil, bras croises, buste. June 20, 2006 Christie's, London
$5,000,000	£2,732,240	Tete de femme, Dora Maar. May 02, 2006 Christie's, NY
$5,600,000	£3,146,068	Buveuse accoudee. Nov 01, 2005 Christie's, NY
$5,735,000	£3,100,000	Tete d'homme. June 20, 2006 Christie's, London
$5,920,000	£3,200,000	Moulin Rouge, le divan japonais. June 20, 2006 Christie's, London
$6,000,000	£3,370,787	Buste de femme. Nov 01, 2005 Christie's, NY
$6,000,000	£3,278,689	Femme assise dans un fauteuil. May 03, 2006 Sotheby's, NY
$7,030,000	£3,800,000	Homme a la pipe assis et amour. June 20, 2006 Christie's, London
$7,200,000	£4,044,944	Sylvette au fauteuil vert. Nov 01, 2005 Christie's, NY
$9,000,000	£4,918,033	Arlequin au baton. May 03, 2006 Sotheby's, NY
$12,144,001	£6,600,000	Peintre et modele. June 19, 2006 Sotheby's, London
$12,250,000	£6,882,023	Nu jaune. Nov 02, 2005 Sotheby's, NY
$16,600,000	£9,071,039	Portrait de Germaine. May 02, 2006 Christie's, NY
$31,000,000	£16,939,890	Repos - Rest. May 02, 2006 Christie's, NY
$85,000,000	£46,448,088	Dora Maar au chat. May 03, 2006 Sotheby's, NY

PISSARRO, Camille (1830-1903) French

$1,050,000	£589,888	Le Louvre, soleil d'hiver, matin. Nov 02, 2005 Sotheby's, NY
$1,056,000	£600,000	Cours-la-Reine, cathedrale de Notre-Dame, Rouen. Feb 07, 2006 Sotheby's, London
$1,140,800	£620,000	Rue de l'Hermitage, Pontoise. June 19, 2006 Sotheby's, London
$1,239,000	£700,000	Neaufles-Saint-Martin, pres de Gisors. Feb 06, 2006 Christie's, London
$1,300,000	£730,337	Soleil couchant, autimne a Eragny. Nov 02, 2005 Sotheby's, NY
$1,500,000	£842,697	Petit pont sur la Viosne, Osny. Nov 02, 2005 Sotheby's, NY
$1,572,500	£850,000	Vallee de la Seine. June 20, 2006 Christie's, London
$1,650,000	£901,639	Etude de paysanne en plein air, bechant. May 02, 2006 Christie's, NY
$1,850,000	£1,000,000	Potager du manoir d'Ango, Varengeville, soleil couchant. June 20, 2006 Christie's, London
$2,000,000	£1,092,896	Eglise Saint-Jacques, Dieppe, matin, soleil. May 02, 2006 Christie's, NY
$2,124,000	£1,200,000	Fenaison a Eragny. Feb 06, 2006 Christie's, London
$2,590,000	£1,400,000	Pont Boieldieu. June 20, 2006 Christie's, London
$3,956,000	£2,150,000	Peupliers au matin, Eragny. June 19, 2006 Sotheby's, London
$4,600,000	£2,584,270	Paysage, la moisson, Pontoise. Nov 01, 2005 Christie's, NY

POLKE, Sigmar (1941-) German

$1,496,000	£850,000	Herr Kluncker - Mr. Kluncker. Feb 09, 2006 Sotheby's, London

POLLOCK, Jackson (1912-1956) American

$1,900,000	£1,021,505	The white angel. May 10, 2006 Sotheby's, NY

POTTER, Paulus (1625-1654) Dutch

$3,600,000	£2,045,454	Cattle in a field, with travellers in a wagon on a track beyond, rain storm approaching. Jan 26, 2006 Sotheby's, NY

PRENDERGAST, Charles E (1863-1948) American

$1,400,000	£813,954	Screen. Nov 30, 2005 Sotheby's, NY

PRINCE, Richard (1949-) Canadian

$1,100,000	£632,184	Untitled - Cowboy. Nov 08, 2005 Christie's, NY
$1,200,000	£645,161	Good news, bad news. May 09, 2006 Christie's, NY

RAUSCHENBERG, Robert (1925-) American
$1,200,000   £645,161   Cage. May 09, 2006 Christie's, NY

RAZA, Sayed Haider (1922-) Indian
$1,300,000   £747,126   Tapovan. Mar 29, 2006 Sotheby's, NY

REMBRANDT (1606-1669) Dutch
$3,800,000   £2,159,091   Study of an elderly woman in a white cap. Jan 26, 2006 Sotheby's, NY

REMINGTON, Frederic (1861-1909) American
$1,300,000   £710,383   An Apache. July 22, 2006 Coeur d'Alene, Hayden

RENOIR, Pierre Auge (1841-1919) French
$1,150,000   £628,415   Deux femmes dans le jardin de Cagnes. May 02, 2006 Christie's, NY
$1,300,000   £710,383   Laveuse. May 02, 2006 Christie's, NY
$2,500,000   £1,366,120   Fleurs et fruits. May 03, 2006 Sotheby's, NY
$3,000,000   £1,685,393   Dejeuner a Barneval. Nov 02, 2005 Sotheby's, NY
$3,186,000   £1,800,000   Portrait de Pierre Henri Renoir, le frere de l'artiste. Feb 06, 2006 Christie's, London
$6,290,000   £3,400,000   Ete: jeune femme dans un champ fleuri. June 20, 2006 Christie's, London
$8,096,000   £4,400,000   Femmes dans un jardin. June 19, 2006 Sotheby's, London

RICHTER, Gerhard (1932-) German
$1,017,500   £550,000   Sculptures for room by Palermo. June 22, 2006 Christie's, London
$1,050,000   £603,448   Abstract. Nov 09, 2005 Christie's, NY
$1,056,000   £600,000   A B Tower. Feb 08, 2006 Christie's, London
$1,144,898   £612,245   Landscape with cloud. May 26, 2006 Villa Grisebach, Berlin
                                                     (Euro 900,000)
$1,196,800   £680,000   Abstract. Feb 08, 2006 Christie's, London
$1,400,000   £804,598   Fairy. Nov 08, 2005 Christie's, NY
$1,650,000   £948,276   Abstract composition. Nov 08, 2005 Christie's, NY
$2,312,500   £1,250,000   Portrait of Lis Kertelge. June 21, 2006 Sotheby's, London
$3,515,000   £1,900,000   Tante Marianne - Aunt Marianne. June 21, 2006 Sotheby's, London
$4,312,000   £2,450,000   Untitled composition. Feb 09, 2006 Sotheby's, London

RILEY, Bridget (1931-) British
$1,942,500   £1,050,000   Diagonal curve. June 21, 2006 Sotheby's, London

RIVERA, Diego (1886-1957) Mexican
$1,100,000   £601,093   Flower seller in Xochimilco. July 22, 2006 Coeur d'Alene, Hayden

ROBERT, Hubert (1733-1808) French
$5,550,000   £3,000,000   Colonnade et jardins du Palais Medicis. Restes du palais du Pape Jules. July 06, 2006 Christie's, London

ROCKWELL, Norman (1894-1978) American
$1,200,000   £641,711   Hoodlum Street. May 24, 2006 Sotheby's, NY
$8,200,000   £4,385,027   Homecoming marine. May 24, 2006 Sotheby's, NY

RODIN, Auge (1840-1917) French
$1,144,000   £650,000   Eve. Feb 07, 2006 Sotheby's, London
$1,300,000   £730,337   La cathedrale. Nov 01, 2005 Christie's, NY
$2,112,000   £1,200,000   Faunesse a genoux. Feb 07, 2006 Sotheby's, London
$2,600,000   £1,420,765   Enfant prodigue. May 03, 2006 Sotheby's, NY

ROERICH, Nikolai Konstantinovitch (1874-1947) American/Russian
$1,100,000   £617,978   Confucius, the just one. Apr 26, 2006 Sotheby's, NY
$1,950,000   £1,095,506   Lao-Tze. Apr 26, 2006 Sotheby's, NY

ROSE, Guy (1867-1925) American
$1,700,000   £988,372   Owens River, Sierra Nevada, California. Nov 30, 2005 Sotheby's, NY

ROTHKO, Mark (1903-1970) American
$1,300,000   £747,126   Untitled. Nov 08, 2005 Christie's, NY
$2,250,000   £1,293,104   Untitled. Nov 08, 2005 Christie's, NY
$2,600,000   £1,397,850   Untitled composition. May 10, 2006 Sotheby's, NY
$3,700,000   £1,989,247   White, orange and yellow. May 10, 2006 Sotheby's, NY
$5,000,000   £2,873,563   Blue over red. Nov 08, 2005 Christie's, NY
$20,000,000   £11,494,254   Homage to Matisse. Nov 08, 2005 Christie's, NY

RUBENS, Sir Peter Paul (1577-1640) Flemish
$1,850,000   £1,000,000   Coronation of the Virgin by the Trinity. July 06, 2006 Christie's, London
$4,844,000   £2,800,000   Meleager and Atalanta hunting the Boar. Dec 08, 2005 Christie's, London

RUSCHA, Edward (1937-) American
$1,000,000   £537,634   Metro, petro, neuro, psycho. May 11, 2006 Sotheby's, NY

(cont'd) RUSCHA, Edward (1937-) American

$1,100,000	£591,398	Hell, heaven. May 10, 2006 Christie's, NY
$1,400,000	£804,598	Flag. Nov 08, 2005 Christie's, NY

RUSSELL, Charles M (1864-1926) American

$1,300,000	£755,814	Meat for the tribe. Dec 01, 2005 Christie's, NY

RYMAN, Robert (1930-) American

$1,800,000	£967,742	Meridian. May 10, 2006 Sotheby's, NY
$8,600,000	£4,623,656	Untitled composition. May 10, 2006 Sotheby's, NY

RYSSELBERGHE, Theo van (1862-1926) Belgian

$2,800,000	£1,573,034	Port de Cette, les tartanes. Nov 01, 2005 Christie's, NY

SAN-YU (1901-1966) Chinese

$2,409,993	£1,288,766	Flowers in a bright yellow vase. May 28, 2006 Christie's, Hong Kong (HK.D 18,700,000)

SARGENT, John Singer (1856-1925) British/American

$3,300,000	£1,918,605	The Rialto. Nov 30, 2005 Sotheby's, NY

SASSETTA, Stefano di Giovanni di (1392-c.1451) Italian

$1,000,000	£578,035	Saint Augine. Apr 06, 2006 Christie's, NY

SCHIELE, Egon (1890-1918) Austrian

$1,153,103	£655,172	Krumau - St Veit-church with houses. Oct 11, 2005 Wiener Kunst Auktionen, Vienna (Euro 950,000)
$1,232,000	£700,000	Girl in blue dress. Feb 07, 2006 Sotheby's, London
$1,702,000	£920,000	Hafen von Triest - Trieste harbour. June 20, 2006 Christie's, London
$1,770,000	£1,000,000	Reclining nude with black stockings. Feb 06, 2006 Christie's, London
$1,850,000	£1,000,000	Liegender akt. Sitzende frau. June 20, 2006 Christie's, London
$2,000,000	£1,123,596	Self-portrait as Saint Sebastian. Nov 02, 2005 Sotheby's, NY
$2,464,000	£1,400,000	Kneeling semi-nude. Feb 07, 2006 Sotheby's, London
$6,549,000	£3,700,000	Kniender weiblicher halbakt. Feb 06, 2006 Christie's, London
$19,425,000	£10,500,000	Herbstsonne - Autumn sun. June 20, 2006 Christie's, London

SCHLEMMER, Oskar (1888-1943) German

$2,200,000	£1,176,471	Rote Lieber, 1929. May 23, 2006 Doyle, NY

SEREBRIAKOVA, Zinaida (1884-1967) Russian

$1,250,000	£706,215	Sleeping nude. Apr 24, 2006 Christie's, NY

SHER-GIL, Amrita (1913-1941) Indian

$1,329,681	£747,012	Village scene. Mar 01, 2006 Osian, Mumbai (I.R 60,000,000)

SHISHKIN, Ivan Ivanovich (1832-1898) Russian

$1,118,000	£650,000	Forest clearing. Nov 30, 2005 Christie's, London

SIEMIRADZKI, Hendrik (1843-1902) Polish

$1,250,000	£706,215	The girl or the vase. Oct 25, 2005 Sotheby's, NY

SILVA, Francis Augus (1835-1886) American

$1,300,000	£695,187	On the Hudson, Nyack. May 24, 2006 Sotheby's, NY

SISLEY, Alfred (1839-1899) French

$1,416,000	£800,000	Promenade des maronniers. Feb 06, 2006 Christie's, London
$1,472,000	£800,000	La Seine a Saint-Mammes. June 19, 2006 Sotheby's, London
$1,500,000	£819,672	Canal du Loing. May 02, 2006 Christie's, NY
$1,600,000	£898,876	Bords de Seine a Port-Marly. Nov 01, 2005 Christie's, NY
$1,700,000	£928,962	Route de Hampton Court. May 02, 2006 Christie's, NY
$2,576,000	£1,400,000	Bords du Loing a Saint-Mammes. June 19, 2006 Sotheby's, London

SMITH, David -American (1906-1965) American

$1,800,000	£967,742	False peace spectre. May 09, 2006 Christie's, NY
$4,400,000	£2,528,736	Jurassic bird. Nov 08, 2005 Christie's, NY
$21,250,000	£12,212,645	Cubi XXVIII. Nov 09, 2005 Sotheby's, NY

SOMOV, Konstantin (1869-1939) Russian

$1,978,000	£1,150,000	Pierrot and a lady. Nov 30, 2005 Christie's, London

SOROLLA Y BASTIDA, Joaquin (1863-1923) Spanish

$1,380,000	£750,000	Ninos en el mar Playa de Valencia - Children by the sea, Valencia Beach. June 14, 2006 Christie's, London

SOULAGES, Pierre (1919-) French

$1,352,414	£731,034	Untitled - composition. July 06, 2006 Sotheby's, Paris (Euro 1,060,000)

SOUTINE, Chaim (1893-1943) Russian

$1,017,500	£550,000	Folle. June 20, 2006 Christie's, London
$1,435,200	£780,000	Femme en rouge sur fond bleu. June 19, 2006 Sotheby's, London
$2,035,000	£1,100,000	Arc-en-ciel, Cheret. June 20, 2006 Christie's, London
$2,500,000	£1,366,120	Femme en rouge appuyee a un fauteuil. May 03, 2006 Sotheby's, NY
$12,390,001	£7,000,000	Boeuf ecorche. Feb 06, 2006 Christie's, London

SOUZA, Francis Newton (1924-2002) British/Indian

$1,028,500	£550,000	Amsterdam landscape. May 23, 2006 Sotheby's, London
$1,288,860	£745,006	Lovers. Dec 06, 2005 Saffronart, Mumbai (I.R 59,444,000)

STAEL, Nicolas de (1914-1955) French

$1,017,500	£550,000	Composition. June 22, 2006 Christie's, London
$1,108,800	£630,000	Fleurs sur fond rouge. Feb 09, 2006 Sotheby's, London

STEEN, Jan (c.1626-1679) Dutch

$1,110,000	£600,000	Fair at Warmond. July 05, 2006 Sotheby's, London

STEICHEN, Edward J (1879-1973) American

$2,600,000	£1,494,253	Pond - moonlight. Feb 14, 2006 Sotheby's, NY

STELLA, Frank (1936-) American

$1,500,000	£806,452	Fortin de las flores. May 10, 2006 Sotheby's, NY
$1,500,000	£806,452	Pratfall. May 09, 2006 Christie's, NY

STIEGLITZ, Alfred (1864-1946) American

$1,200,000	£689,655	Georgia O'Keeffe, nude. Feb 14, 2006 Sotheby's, NY
$1,300,000	£747,126	Georgia O'Keeffe, hands. Feb 14, 2006 Sotheby's, NY

STILL, Clyfford (1904-1980) American

$2,400,000	£1,290,323	1955-K. May 09, 2006 Christie's, NY

STRUDWICK, John Melhuish (1849-1937) British

$1,320,000	£750,000	Summer songs. Dec 13, 2005 Sotheby's, London

STUART, Gilbert (1755-1828) American

$7,250,000	£4,215,116	George Washington. Nov 30, 2005 Sotheby's, NY

SVERTSCHKOFF, Nicolas Gregorovitch (1817-1898) Russian

$3,057,534	£1,643,836	Soldier on horseback. June 04, 2006 Uppsala Auktionskammare, Uppsala (Euro 2,400,000)
$3,567,123	£1,917,808	Soldier on horseback with figures. June 04, 2006 Uppsala Auktionskammare, Uppsala (Euro 2,800,000)

TAYLER, Albert Chevallier (1862-1925) British

$1,092,000	£600,000	Kent versus Lancashire, Canterbury. June 27, 2006 Sotheby's, London

TERPNING, Howard A (1927-) American

$1,300,000	£710,383	Search for the renegades. July 22, 2006 Coeur d'Alene, Hayden

THIEBAUD, Wayne (1920-) American

$1,800,000	£967,742	Seven candied apples. May 09, 2006 Christie's, NY

TISSOT, James Jacques Joseph (1836-1902) French

$2,835,000	£1,500,000	Preparing for the gala. June 08, 2006 Christie's, London

TOULOUSE-LAUTREC, Henri de (1864-1901) French

$1,200,000	£655,738	Madame Juliette Pascal. May 02, 2006 Christie's, NY
$20,000,000	£11,235,956	La blanchisseuse. Nov 01, 2005 Christie's, NY

TURNER, Joseph Mallord William (1775-1851) British

$9,672,001	£5,200,000	Blue Rigi, lake of Lucerne, sunrise. June 05, 2006 Christie's, London
$32,000,000	£18,497,110	Giudecca, Donna della Salute and San Giorgio, Venice. Apr 06, 2006 Christie's, NY

TWOMBLY, Cy (1928-) American

$7,100,000	£4,080,460	Untitled - Rome. Nov 09, 2005 Sotheby's, NY
$7,750,000	£4,454,023	Untitled -NY City. Nov 09, 2005 Sotheby's, NY

UYTEWAEL, Joachim (1566-1638) Dutch

$1,072,600	£620,000	The tribute money. Dec 07, 2005 Sotheby's, London

VALLOTTON, Felix (1865-1925) Swiss

$1,858,500	£1,050,000	En promenade. Feb 06, 2006 Christie's, London

VENETSIANOV, Alexei Gavrilovich (1780-1847) Russian

$4,331,507	£2,328,767	Portrait of young woman in national costume from Tver. June 04, 2006 Uppsala Auktionskammare, Uppsala (Euro 3,400,000)

VERETSHCHAGIN, Piotr (1836-1886) Russian
$1,300,000	£730,337	Nevsky Prospekt, Saint Petersburg. Apr 26, 2006 Sotheby's, NY

VLAMINCK, Maurice de (1876-1958) French
$1,295,000	£700,000	Portrait de jeune femme. June 20, 2006 Christie's, London
$1,416,000	£800,000	La Seine a Chatou. Feb 06, 2006 Christie's, London
$2,300,000	£1,256,831	Arbres sur la place. May 02, 2006 Christie's, NY
$2,552,000	£1,450,000	Pont de Chatou. Feb 07, 2006 Sotheby's, London
$3,864,000	£2,100,000	Verger. June 19, 2006 Sotheby's, London

VUILLARD, Edouard (1868-1940) French
$6,624,000	£3,600,000	Pot de gres. June 19, 2006 Sotheby's, London

WALDMULLER, Ferdinand Georg (1793-1865) Austrian
$1,295,890	£753,425	The interrupted pilgrimage. Nov 30, 2005 Dorotheum, Vienna (Euro 1,100,000)

WARHOL, Andy (1928-1987) American
$1,000,000	£537,634	Portrait of Nelson A Rockefeller no.3. May 10, 2006 Sotheby's, NY
$1,100,000	£632,184	One dollar bill. Nov 08, 2005 Christie's, NY
$1,100,000	£632,184	Boxes. Nov 09, 2005 Sotheby's, NY
$1,100,000	£632,184	Woman in blue. Nov 09, 2005 Christie's, NY
$1,150,000	£660,920	Dollar sign. Nov 08, 2005 Christie's, NY
$1,200,000	£689,655	Bald eagle. Nov 09, 2005 Sotheby's, NY
$1,200,000	£645,161	Four Jackies. May 09, 2006 Christie's, NY
$1,295,000	£700,000	Mick Jagger. June 21, 2006 Sotheby's, London
$1,300,000	£698,925	Self-portrait. May 10, 2006 Christie's, NY
$1,400,000	£804,598	Dollar sign. Nov 09, 2005 Sotheby's, NY
$1,408,000	£800,000	Self-portrait. Feb 09, 2006 Sotheby's, London
$1,500,000	£862,069	Mona Lisa four times. Nov 08, 2005 Christie's, NY
$1,572,500	£850,000	Flowers. June 21, 2006 Sotheby's, London
$1,600,000	£860,215	Self-portrait. May 10, 2006 Sotheby's, NY
$1,750,000	£1,005,747	Self-portrait. Nov 09, 2005 Sotheby's, NY
$1,850,000	£1,063,218	Black on black retrospective. Nov 10, 2005 Phillips, NY
$2,100,000	£1,129,032	Gun. May 10, 2006 Sotheby's, NY
$2,200,000	£1,264,368	Nine blue Marilyns, reversal series. Nov 09, 2005 Sotheby's, NY
$2,220,000	£1,200,000	Four multicolored Marilyns. June 21, 2006 Sotheby's, London
$2,288,000	£1,300,000	Mao no.7. Feb 09, 2006 Sotheby's, London
$2,405,000	£1,300,000	The scream. June 21, 2006 Sotheby's, London
$2,405,000	£1,300,000	American Indian Russell Means. June 22, 2006 Christie's, London
$2,700,000	£1,451,613	Brigitte Bardot. May 09, 2006 Christie's, NY
$2,900,000	£1,666,667	Self-portrait. Nov 08, 2005 Christie's, NY
$2,900,000	£1,559,140	Ladies and gentlemen. May 10, 2006 Sotheby's, NY
$3,500,000	£1,881,720	Flowers. May 09, 2006 Christie's, NY
$4,048,000	£2,300,000	Dollar sign. Feb 08, 2006 Christie's, London
$4,224,000	£2,400,000	Last Supper. Feb 08, 2006 Christie's, London
$4,600,000	£2,473,118	S and H green stamps. May 09, 2006 Christie's, NY
$6,000,000	£3,448,276	Flowers. Nov 09, 2005 Sotheby's, NY
$8,200,000	£4,712,644	Jackie Frieze. Nov 09, 2005 Sotheby's, NY
$10,500,000	£5,645,161	Small torn Campbell's soup can. May 09, 2006 Christie's, NY

WESSELMANN, Tom (1931-2004) American
$1,295,000	£700,000	Great American Nude 87. June 21, 2006 Sotheby's, London
$1,500,000	£806,452	Bedroom painting No.42. May 11, 2006 Phillips, NY

WILLIAMS, Frederick Ronald (1927-1982) Australian
$1,139,095	£658,436	Upwey landscape. Apr 10, 2006 Christie's, Melbourne (A.D 1,600,000)

WINTERHALTER, Franz Xavier (1806-1873) German
$1,748,000	£950,000	Queen Olga of Wurttemberg, Grand Duchess of Russia. June 14, 2006 Christie's, London

WITTEL, Gaspar van (1653-1736) Dutch
$1,656,164	£890,411	Veduta di Braccaiano, del lago e del Palazzo Odescalchi. May 30, 2006 Sotheby's, Milan (Euro 1,300,000)

WOOD, Grant (1892-1942) American
$6,200,000	£3,604,651	Spring ploughing. Nov 30, 2005 Sotheby's, NY

WOOL, Christopher (1955-) American
$1,100,000	£632,184	Untitled - Rundogrundogrun. Nov 08, 2005 Christie's, NY
$1,250,000	£672,043	Helter, helter. May 10, 2006 Sotheby's, NY

WU GUANZHONG (1919-) Chinese

$1,042,212   £609,481   Old pine in the Jingshan park in Beijing. Nov 27, 2005 Christie's, Hong Kong (HK.D 8,100,000)

WYETH, Andrew (1917-) American

$3,900,000   £2,085,561   South Cushing. May 24, 2006 Sotheby's, NY

ZHANG DAQIAN (1899-1983) Chinese

$1,808,759   £1,021,898   Snow capped mountains in Switzerland. Oct 24, 2005 Sotheby's, Hong Kong (HK.D 14,000,000)

ZUNIGA, Francisco (1913-1998) Costa Rican

$3,300,000   £1,764,706   Cuatro mujeres de pie - Four standing women. May 24, 2006 Sotheby's, NY

SUMMARIZED SALE RESULTS

**By Media for the Twelve Months
August 2005 to July 2006**

Name	No.	Price Range	Average	Median
AA, Dirk van der (1731-1809) Dutch				
oil	1	5,036	5,036	5,036
AABYE, Jorgen (1868-1959) Danish				
oil	1	1,690	1,690	1,690
AACHEN, Hans von (1552-1616) German				
oil	2	3,568-17,947	10,757	3,568
AAGAARD, C F (1833-1895) Danish				
oil	7	830-2,445	1,494	1,244
AAGAARD, Carl Frederic (1833-1895) Danish				
oil	6	2,064-15,000	6,801	3,982
AALTO, Alvar (20th C) Finnish				
wc/d	1	1,414	1,414	1,414
AALTO, Ilmari (1891-1934) Finnish				
oil	1	1,110	1,110	1,110
AALTONEN, Waino (1894-1966) Finnish				
oil	2	4,325-20,571	12,448	4,325
3D	3	2,443-6,171	3,685	2,443
AARON, Jessie (1887-1979) American				
3D	1	3,250	3,250	3,250
AARON, Joseph (1959-) American				
oil	2	1,200-1,600	1,400	1,200
AB THE FLAGMAN (1964-) American				
3D	1	6,800	6,800	6,800
ABA-NOVAK, Vilmos (1894-1941) Hungarian				
oil	1	42,411	42,411	42,411
wc/d	1	3,822	3,822	3,822
ABADES, Juan Martinez (1862-1920) Spanish				
oil	8	3,131-29,392	13,656	10,177
ABADIE, Jean (20th C) French				
oil	1	1,438	1,438	1,438
ABAKANOWICZ, Magdalena (1930-) Polish				
3D	3	10,000-380,000	145,833	47,500
ABARZUZA, Jose Felipe (20th C) Spanish				
oil	1	2,411	2,411	2,411
ABASCAL (19/20th C) Spanish				
oil	2	2,805-3,624	3,214	2,805
ABASCAL, Carlos (20th C) Spanish				
wc/d	2	832-1,427	1,129	832
ABATE, Alberto (1946-) Italian				
oil	1	3,024	3,024	3,024
wc/d	7	478-1,210	837	847
ABATE, Teonesto de (1898-1981) Italian				
oil	1	1,764	1,764	1,764
ABBATE, Niccolo dell' (1512-1571) Italian				
oil	1	24,596	24,596	24,596
ABBATI, Alberto (1923-) Italian				
wc/d	1	1,230	1,230	1,230
ABBATT, Agnes Dean (1847-1917) American				
oil	1	5,500	5,500	5,500
ABBEMA, Louise (1858-1927) French				
oil	2	1,176-41,760	21,468	1,176
ABBETT, Robert Kennedy (1926-) American				
oil	3	14,000-18,000	15,666	15,000
ABBIATI, Julius (19th C) Austrian?				
oil	1	3,063	3,063	3,063
ABBOTT, John White (1763-1851) British				
wc/d	8	2,422-59,520	16,045	8,304
ABBOTT, Lemuel Francis (1760-1803) British				
oil	5	2,250-460,200	147,476	14,742
ABBOTT, Yarnell (1870-1938) American				
oil	1	1,100	1,100	1,100
ABBOUD, Chafik (1926-) Lebanese				
oil	2	2,425-2,425	2,425	2,425
ABBRESCIA, Joe (1936-) American				
oil	2	6,500-16,000	11,250	6,500
ABD AL-JABAR (17th C) Persian				
wc/d	1	12,320	12,320	12,320
ABDELL, Doug (1947-) American				
3D	1	5,500	5,500	5,500
ABDULLAH, R Basoeki (1915-1993) Javanese				
oil	1	6,622	6,622	6,622

Name	No.	Price Range	Average	Median
ABDULLAH, Sudjono (1911-1991) Javanese				
oil	3	963-1,084	1,023	1,023
ABEDIN, Zainul (1917-1976) Indian				
wc/d	1	9,680	9,680	9,680
ABEELE, Albijn van den (1835-1918) Belgian				
oil	1	4,186	4,186	4,186
ABEELE, Remy van den (1918-1995) Belgian				
oil	8	1,178-3,131	2,227	1,870
ABEL, Ernst August (c.1720-c.1780) ?				
wc/d	1	5,048	5,048	5,048
ABEL, Joseph (1764-1818) Austrian				
oil	1	13,081	13,081	13,081
wc/d	2	425-425	425	425
ABEL-TRUCHET (1857-1918) French				
oil	8	500-35,716	7,243	2,100
ABELA, Eduardo (1891-1965) Cuban				
oil	2	14,000-16,000	15,000	14,000
ABELENDA, Manuel (1889-1957) Spanish				
oil	1	21,541	21,541	21,541
ABELS, Jacobus Theodorus (1803-1866) Dutch				
oil	3	1,463-7,224	3,789	2,682
ABERCROMBIE, Gertrude (1909-1977) American				
oil	8	2,800-15,000	6,968	6,500
ABERCROMBIE, John Brown (1843-1929) British				
oil	2	1,072-3,000	2,036	1,072
ABERDAM, Alfred (1894-1963) Polish				
oil	10	502-3,200	1,657	1,528
ABERG, Gunnar (1869-1894) Swedish				
oil	2	997-1,511	1,254	997
ABERG, Martin (1888-1946) Swedish				
oil	2	1,189-1,520	1,354	1,189
ABERG, Pelle (1909-1964) Swedish				
oil	22	524-30,575	4,908	3,944
wc/d	1	521	521	521
ABOUELOUAKAR, Mohamed (1946-) Moroccan				
wc/d	1	2,864	2,864	2,864
ABRAHAM, R (?) ?				
3D	1	2,028	2,028	2,028
ABRAHAMS, Ivor (1935-) British				
wc/d	2	743-1,332	1,037	743
3D	1	5,460	5,460	5,460
ABRAHAMSSON, Erik (1871-1907) Swedish				
oil	2	1,991-5,036	3,513	1,991
ABRAMOFSKY, Israel (1888-1975) American				
wc/d	1	1,300	1,300	1,300
ABRAMOVIC, Marina (1946-) Yugoslavian				
wc/d	1	22,500	22,500	22,500
ABRAMOVICH, Pinchas (1909-1986) Lithuanian				
oil	14	600-5,000	2,151	1,400
wc/d	2	400-450	425	400
ABRAMOWICZ, Leo (1889-1978) Russian				
oil	3	727-1,543	1,262	1,518
ABRATE, Angelo (1900-1985) Italian				
oil	3	1,640-4,013	2,444	1,679
ABREU BASTOS, Anton (1927-) Spanish				
oil	2	1,070-2,351	1,710	1,070
ABREU, Mario (1919-1993) Venezuelan				
oil	1	560	560	560
wc/d	3	650-1,860	1,176	1,020
3D	1	6,975	6,975	6,975
ABRIL Y BLASCO, Salvador (1862-1924) Spanish				
oil	2	1,320-10,130	5,725	1,320
ABRIL, Ben (1923-1995) American				
oil	1	1,700	1,700	1,700
ABRY, Léon Eugène (1857-1905) Belgian				
wc/d	1	1,335	1,335	1,335
ABSOLON, John (1815-1895) British				
wc/d	4	452-1,758	1,255	1,110
ABSOLON, Kurt (1925-1958) Austrian				
wc/d	2	2,910-6,370	4,640	2,910
ACAR, Kuzgun (1928-1976) Turkish				
3D	1	2,167	2,167	2,167

Name	No.	Price Range	Average	Median
ACCARDI, Carla (1924-) Italian				
oil	31	3,307-61,061	19,354	12,846
wc/d	9	1,399-8,604	3,597	3,236
3D	1	24,170	24,170	24,170
ACCATINO, Enrico (1920-) Italian				
oil	1	1,312	1,312	1,312
ACCHIARDI, Guido (1890-?) Italian				
oil	1	6,500	6,500	6,500
ACCIARI, Paul and CLEREN, Jean Paul (20th C) French				
wc/d	1	1,669	1,669	1,669
ACEVES, Jose (1909-1968) American				
oil	1	7,000	7,000	7,000
ACEVES, Tomas (19th C) Spanish				
oil	1	7,500	7,500	7,500
ACHARD, Jean Alexis (1807-1884) French				
oil	1	7,068	7,068	7,068
ACHEFF, William (1947-) American				
oil	15	3,900-51,000	19,426	13,000
ACHEN, Georg (1860-1912) Danish				
oil	1	11,180	11,180	11,180
ACHENBACH, Andreas (1815-1910) German				
oil	14	1,004-74,167	11,948	6,689
wc/d	1	467	467	467
ACHENBACH, Oswald (1827-1905) German				
oil	20	2,170-77,074	26,525	14,833
ACHILLOPOULO, Costa (20th C) British?				
3D	1	36,540	36,540	36,540
ACHINI, Angelo (1850-1930) Italian				
wc/d	4	904-5,437	2,693	1,900
ACHTERMANN, Theodor Wilhelm (1799-1884) German				
3D	1	5,670	5,670	5,670
ACHTSCHELLINCK, Lucas (1626-1699) Flemish				
oil	1	52,324	52,324	52,324
ACKE, J A G (1859-1924) Swedish				
oil	2	1,909-2,031	1,970	1,909
ACKE, Johan Axel Gustaf (1859-1924) Swedish				
oil	1	2,550	2,550	2,550
ACKEIN, Marcelle (1882-1952) French				
oil	1	135,479	135,479	135,479
wc/d	1	2,158	2,158	2,158
ACKERMAN, Paul (1908-1981) French				
oil	4	477-2,472	1,261	903
ACKERMANN, Franz (1963-) German				
oil	6	7,400-457,600	274,283	299,200
wc/d	2	2,870-40,000	21,435	2,870
ACKERMANN, Gerald (1876-1960) British				
wc/d	12	481-2,268	1,420	1,335
ACKERMANN, Max (1887-1975) German				
oil	17	1,178-30,575	12,254	12,103
wc/d	18	942-8,281	3,089	2,472
ACKERMANN, Peter (1934-) German				
oil	3	1,018-1,824	1,441	1,483
ACKERMANN, Rita (1968-) Hungarian				
wc/d	2	14,800-16,650	15,725	14,800
ACKRILL, Alfred (1907-1988) British				
oil	5	1,280-2,422	1,768	1,817
ACTON, William (1906-1945) British				
oil	1	26,460	26,460	26,460
ADAM, Albrecht (1786-1862) German				
oil	7	9,425-90,000	37,751	27,600
ADAM, Benno (1812-1892) German				
oil	3	7,297-35,910	18,962	13,680
ADAM, David Livingston (1883-1924) British				
oil	1	2,200	2,200	2,200
ADAM, Edmond Victor Charles (1868-1938) French				
oil	3	4,767-9,000	7,369	8,342
ADAM, Edouard (1847-1929) French				
oil	11	1,500-15,500	6,612	6,000
ADAM, Emil (1843-1924) German				
oil	5	7,655-27,280	17,004	14,175
ADAM, Eugen (1817-1880) German				
oil	1	3,138	3,138	3,138

Name	No.	Price Range	Average	Median
ADAM, Franz (1815-1886) German				
oil	1	4,519	4,519	4,519
ADAM, Heinrich (1787-1862) German				
oil	1	2,521	2,521	2,521
ADAM, Hippolyte (1808-1853) French				
oil	1	2,420	2,420	2,420
ADAM, Joseph Denovan (1842-1896) British				
oil	9	460-6,553	1,744	885
wc/d	1	800	800	800
ADAM, Joseph and Joseph Denovan (19th C) British				
oil	3	1,701-13,200	7,115	6,444
ADAM, Julius I (1826-1874) German				
oil	1	10,338	10,338	10,338
ADAM, Julius II (1852-1913) German				
oil	4	3,273-16,560	7,843	5,096
wc/d	1	690	690	690
ADAM, Otto (1901-1973) German				
oil	2	972-1,794	1,383	972
ADAM, Patrick William (1854-1929) British				
oil	7	824-26,550	8,922	3,440
wc/d	2	736-1,575	1,155	736
ADAM, Raoul (19/20th C) French				
oil	1	8,729	8,729	8,729
ADAM, Richard Benno (1873-1937) German				
oil	1	1,094	1,094	1,094
ADAM, Victor (1801-1866) French				
oil	1	12,603	12,603	12,603
ADAM, W (19th C) ?				
oil	1	3,480	3,480	3,480
ADAM, William (1846-1931) American				
oil	5	1,100-2,500	2,020	2,000
wc/d	1	700	700	700
ADAMI, Franco (1933-) Italian				
3D	1	6,780	6,780	6,780
ADAMI, Valerio (1935-) Italian				
oil	26	11,221-79,650	31,976	30,531
wc/d	20	467-10,763	4,333	2,957
ADAMS, Bernard (fl.1916-1939) British				
oil	1	1,611	1,611	1,611
ADAMS, Cassily (1843-1921) American				
oil	1	26,000	26,000	26,000
wc/d	3	1,500-2,250	1,916	2,000
ADAMS, Charles James (1857-1931) British				
oil	2	3,060-13,230	8,145	3,060
wc/d	7	558-3,150	1,469	979
ADAMS, Charles Partridge (1858-1942) American				
oil	4	3,650-11,000	6,537	5,500
wc/d	3	3,000-5,500	4,250	4,250
ADAMS, Douglas (1853-1920) British				
oil	1	2,262	2,262	2,262
ADAMS, Herbert (1858-1945) American				
3D	1	4,800	4,800	4,800
ADAMS, John Clayton (1840-1906) British				
oil	1	2,760	2,760	2,760
ADAMS, John Quincy (1874-1933) Austrian				
oil	3	2,400-10,541	5,380	3,200
ADAMS, John Wolcott (1874-1925) American				
wc/d	1	1,300	1,300	1,300
ADAMS, Mark (1925-) American				
oil	1	1,200	1,200	1,200
wc/d	1	800	800	800
ADAMS, Norman (1927-2005) British				
oil	1	641	641	641
wc/d	3	490-890	623	491
ADAMS, Peter (1950-) American				
oil	2	2,750-5,000	3,875	2,750
ADAMS, Robert (1917-1984) British				
3D	4	2,478-10,175	5,000	2,562
ADAMS, Wayman (1883-1959) American				
oil	1	1,800	1,800	1,800
ADAMSKI, Hans Peter (1947-) German?				
oil	1	2,297	2,297	2,297

Name	No.	Price Range	Average	Median
ADAMSON, Harry Curieux (1916-) American				
oil	2	8,000-12,000	10,000	8,000
ADAMSON, Sydney (fl.1892-1914) American				
oil	2	1,424-2,314	1,869	1,424
ADCOCK, Liliane (20th C) Belgian?				
oil	1	1,794	1,794	1,794
ADDAMS, Charles (1912-1988) American				
wc/d	4	2,000-9,500	7,000	8,000
ADEMOLLO, Luigi (1764-1849) Italian				
wc/d	1	12,098	12,098	12,098
ADENEY, Bernard (1878-1966) British				
oil	1	1,044	1,044	1,044
ADIE, Edith Helena (fl.1892-1930) British				
wc/d	1	2,100	2,100	2,100
ADIMOOLAM, K M (1938-) Indian				
oil	2	3,872-8,415	6,143	3,872
ADLEN, Michel (1899-1980) Russian				
oil	5	500-3,337	1,188	700
ADLER, Edmund (1871-1957) German				
oil	6	3,041-12,000	6,007	4,000
ADLER, Jankel (1895-1949) Polish				
oil	12	2,000-70,000	17,498	10,829
wc/d	11	600-33,966	5,552	1,350
ADLER, Karol (20th C) ?				
oil	1	1,730	1,730	1,730
ADLER, Oscar F (19/20th C) ?				
oil	1	3,800	3,800	3,800
ADLERSPARRE, Sophie (1808-1862) Swedish				
oil	1	3,365	3,365	3,365
ADLIVANKIN, Samuil Yakovlevich (1897-1966) Russian				
wc/d	3	3,640-16,829	8,036	3,640
ADNET, Françoise (1924-) French				
oil	6	548-2,028	1,019	630
ADOLFS, Gerard Pieter (1897-1968) Dutch				
oil	4	6,020-14,449	9,030	7,224
wc/d	1	1,293	1,293	1,293
ADOMEIT, George G (1879-1967) American				
oil	3	540-660	620	660
wc/d	1	900	900	900
ADRIAANS, Leon (1944-) Dutch				
oil	1	4,442	4,442	4,442
ADRIAENSSEN, Alexander (1587-1661) Flemish				
oil	1	31,552	31,552	31,552
ADRIAN-NILSSON, Gosta (1884-1965) Swedish				
oil	6	5,947-83,974	43,982	33,081
wc/d	18	1,018-73,890	15,837	7,888
ADRION, Lucien (1889-1953) French				
oil	30	1,788-53,650	11,758	7,875
ADSHEAD, Mary (1904-1995) British				
oil	6	4,872-19,140	12,267	10,092
ADUATZ, Fritz (1907-1994) Polish				
oil	1	12,857	12,857	12,857
ADZAK, Roy (1927-1987) British				
3D	4	3,153-8,758	5,300	3,854
AELST, Pieter Coecke van (1502-1550) Flemish				
oil	4	7,259-138,400	73,366	30,000
AELST, Willem van (1626-1683) Dutch				
oil	1	4,815	4,815	4,815
AERENS, Robert (1883-1969) Belgian				
oil	1	2,153	2,153	2,153
AERNI, Franz Theodor (1853-1918) German				
oil	4	1,332-16,000	8,810	8,458
AEROSOL, Jeff (20th C) ?				
oil	1	1,085	1,085	1,085
AERS, Marguerite (1918-1995) Belgian				
oil	7	509-2,195	1,158	1,030
AERTEBJERG, Kathrine (20th C) Danish				
oil	1	6,760	6,760	6,760
AESCHBACHER, Arthur (1923-) Swiss				
wc/d	9	956-4,326	1,872	1,332
AESCHBACHER, Hans (1906-) Swiss				
3D	2	2,875-6,450	4,662	2,875

Name	No.	Price Range	Average	Median
AESCHER, H (?) ?				
wc/d	1	2,106	2,106	2,106
AFFANDI (1907-1990) Indonesian				
wc/d	1	1,565	1,565	1,565
AFFLECK, William (1869-1909) British				
wc/d	3	550-3,696	2,002	1,760
AFRICANO, Nicholas (1948-) American				
oil	6	1,600-7,500	4,235	4,250
wc/d	1	400	400	400
3D	1	3,000	3,000	3,000
AFRO (1912-1976) Italian				
oil	8	18,446-254,422	105,442	51,429
wc/d	5	500-187,397	82,050	29,195
AFSARY, Cyrus (1940-) American				
oil	11	3,500-30,000	10,190	9,000
AGADATI, Baruch (20th C) ?				
wc/d	1	2,400	2,400	2,400
AGAFONOV, Evgeniy Andreievich (1879-c.1956) Russian				
wc/d	1	4,000	4,000	4,000
AGAM, Yaacov (1928-) Israeli				
oil	10	5,500-85,000	25,329	20,000
wc/d	1	3,507	3,507	3,507
3D	7	2,272-62,000	19,991	13,000
AGAR, Eileen (1899-1991) British				
oil	6	1,480-11,310	4,399	1,573
wc/d	11	1,408-6,612	2,826	2,580
AGARD, Charles (1866-1950) French				
oil	15	443-9,735	1,287	566
AGASSE, Jacques Laurent (1767-1849) Swiss				
oil	3	8,819-76,950	31,739	9,450
AGATIELLO, Mario Alberto (20th C) Argentinian				
oil	1	3,200	3,200	3,200
AGAZZI, Ermenegildo (1866-1945) Italian				
oil	1	2,604	2,604	2,604
AGAZZI, Rinaldo (1857-1939) Italian				
oil	2	6,062-6,705	6,383	6,062
wc/d	1	6,304	6,304	6,304
AGHAJANIAN, Sophie (20th C) Irish?				
wc/d	1	1,274	1,274	1,274
AGNEESENS, Edouard (1842-1885) Belgian				
oil	2	3,567-5,088	4,327	3,567
AGNER, Hans Peter (1933-1989) German				
oil	1	1,455	1,455	1,455
AGNETTI, Vincenzo (1926-1981) Italian				
wc/d	1	8,269	8,269	8,269
AGOPIAN, Simon (19/20th C) Armenian				
oil	2	3,186-9,672	6,429	3,186
AGOSTINI, Guido (19th C) Italian				
oil	3	1,100-2,460	1,797	1,832
wc/d	1	468	468	468
AGOSTINI, Max Michel (1914-1997) French				
oil	1	2,012	2,012	2,012
AGOSTINI, Tony (1916-1990) Italian				
oil	3	1,196-2,455	1,817	1,800
wc/d	1	658	658	658
AGOUST, Alfred (19/20th C) American				
oil	1	15,000	15,000	15,000
AGRASOT Y JUAN, Joaquim (1837-1919) Spanish				
oil	2	9,633-14,833	12,233	9,633
wc/d	1	500	500	500
AGREN, Marianne (?) Swedish?				
oil	1	3,607	3,607	3,607
AGREN, Olof (1874-1962) Swedish				
oil	1	1,057	1,057	1,057
AGRICOLA, Christoph Ludwig (1667-1719) German				
oil	1	766	766	766
wc/d	1	1,781	1,781	1,781
AGRICOLA, Eduard (1800-?) German				
oil	1	13,124	13,124	13,124
AGUADO, Tyrone (?) ?				
oil	1	1,052	1,052	1,052

Name	No.	Price Range	Average	Median
AGUAYO, Fermin (1926-1977) Spanish				
oil	1	21,857	21,857	21,857
AGUELI, Ivan (1869-1917) Swedish				
oil	4	8,226-109,897	61,641	18,545
AGUERO, Carlos (1942-1997) Argentinian				
oil	2	1,400-2,700	2,050	1,400
AGUERREGARAY, Charles Jean (20th C) French				
oil	1	1,918	1,918	1,918
AGUEZNAY, Malika (1934-) Moroccan				
oil	1	4,587	4,587	4,587
AGUIAR, Waldo (1930-2000) Spanish				
oil	1	1,018	1,018	1,018
AGUIARI, Tito (1834-1908) Italian				
wc/d	1	5,086	5,086	5,086
AGUILAR MORE, Ramon (1924-) Spanish				
oil	2	4,770-5,471	5,120	4,770
wc/d	1	1,136	1,136	1,136
AGUILAR, Mauricio (1919-) San Salvadorian				
oil	1	1,000	1,000	1,000
AHEARN, John (1951-) American				
wc/d	1	2,500	2,500	2,500
AHERDANE, Mahjoubi (1924-) Moroccan				
oil	1	7,463	7,463	7,463
AHGUPUK, George Twok Aden (1911-2001) North American				
wc/d	2	1,200-8,000	4,600	1,200
AHL, Henry Hammond (1869-1953) American				
oil	2	2,300-6,000	4,150	2,300
AHLBERG, Arvid Magnus (1851-1932) Swedish				
oil	2	3,020-3,116	3,068	3,020
AHLBERG, Ole (1949-) Danish				
oil	2	1,294-3,484	2,389	1,294
AHLBORN, August (1796-1857) German				
oil	1	3,854	3,854	3,854
AHLERS-HESTERMANN, Friedrich (1883-1973) German				
oil	5	1,288-35,400	11,666	4,698
AHLGREN, Lauri (1929-) Finnish				
oil	2	1,438-3,836	2,637	1,438
wc/d	2	479-819	649	479
AHLSTEDT, Fredrik (1839-1901) Finnish				
oil	2	1,636-3,390	2,513	1,636
AHMAD (19th C) Persian?				
oil	1	216,575	216,575	216,575
AHN SUNG-HA (1977-) Korean				
oil	1	19,000	19,000	19,000
AHRENDTS, Carl Eduard (1822-1898) Dutch				
oil	2	607-3,084	1,845	607
AHRENS, Max (1898-1967) German				
oil	1	1,377	1,377	1,377
AHTELA, H (1881-1968) Finnish				
oil	3	4,359-6,429	5,739	6,429
AI SHENG (20th C) Chinese				
wc/d	1	2,160	2,160	2,160
AI WEIWEI (1957-) Chinese				
3D	1	190,000	190,000	190,000
AI YINGXU (1973-) Chinese				
oil	2	4,393-6,904	5,648	4,393
AIGNER, Eduard (1903-1978) German				
oil	1	1,411	1,411	1,411
AIGNER, Fritz (1930-2005) Austrian				
oil	7	1,528-21,857	11,095	9,926
AIGNER, Robert (1901-1966) Austrian				
oil	1	1,030	1,030	1,030
AIKEN, Gayleen (20th C) American				
oil	1	1,300	1,300	1,300
wc/d	1	1,400	1,400	1,400
AIKEN, John Macdonald (1880-1961) British				
wc/d	1	4,416	4,416	4,416
AIKMAN, George W (1831-1906) British				
oil	3	835-1,376	1,056	957
AIKMAN, William (1682-1731) British				
oil	5	2,057-5,340	4,106	4,628
wc/d	1	606	606	606

Name	No.	Price Range	Average	Median
AILLAUD, Gilles (1928-) French				
oil	1	16,685	16,685	16,685
wc/d	1	717	717	717
AIMETTI, Carlo (1901-1980) Italian				
oil	3	642-1,894	1,067	667
AIMONE, Nino (1932-) Italian				
oil	1	2,336	2,336	2,336
AINI, Philippe (20th C) French				
wc/d	1	4,117	4,117	4,117
AINSLIE, Maud (1870-1960) American				
oil	1	1,900	1,900	1,900
AIRY, Anna (1882-1964) British				
oil	4	2,301-11,340	6,164	3,458
AISTROP, Edward (19/20th C) British				
oil	1	1,311	1,311	1,311
AIT YOUSSEF, Said (1920-1986) Moroccan				
wc/d	1	4,131	4,131	4,131
AITCHISON, Craigie (1926-) British				
oil	4	6,536-60,480	22,362	9,204
AITKEN, James (fl.1880-1935) British				
oil	1	2,046	2,046	2,046
wc/d	3	513-828	667	661
AITKEN, John Ernest (1881-1957) British				
wc/d	10	522-6,300	1,790	1,060
AIVAZOVSKY, Ivan Konstantinovich (1817-1900) Russian				
oil	61	18,602-14,778,083	598,341	297,634
wc/d	7	3,440-40,859	13,739	10,034
AIZELIN, Eugène (1821-1902) French				
3D	4	1,822-22,000	8,535	3,984
AIZENBERG, Roberto (1928-1996) Argentinian				
oil	3	26,000-87,000	52,666	45,000
AIZKORBE, Faustino (1948-) Spanish				
3D	2	3,012-4,703	3,857	3,012
AIZPIRI, Paul (1919-) French				
oil	26	3,894-31,320	12,785	12,884
wc/d	2	1,267-4,772	3,019	1,267
3D	1	3,356	3,356	3,356
AJDUKIEWICZ, Thaddeus von (1852-1916) Polish				
oil	2	15,653-20,602	18,127	15,653
AJMONE, Giuseppe (1923-2005) Italian				
oil	19	1,401-8,247	4,509	3,687
wc/d	6	486-1,070	842	732
AJMONE, Lidio (1884-1945) Italian				
oil	1	3,633	3,633	3,633
AKED, Aleen (1907-2003) Canadian				
oil	2	1,064-1,200	1,132	1,064
AKEEAKTASHUK (1898-1954) North American				
3D	1	2,362	2,362	2,362
AKELEY, Carl Ethan (1864-1926) American				
3D	1	20,000	20,000	20,000
AKERBLOM, Rudolf (1849-1925) Finnish				
oil	2	1,079-3,343	2,211	1,079
AKERS, Vivian Milner (1886-1966) American				
oil	3	1,600-13,000	6,200	4,000
AKERSLOOT-BERG, Betzij Rezora (1850-1922) Dutch				
oil	2	1,638-3,478	2,558	1,638
AKERSTROM, Jonas (1759-1795) Swedish				
oil	1	4,238	4,238	4,238
AKESUK, Latcholassie (1919-) North American				
3D	2	3,374-3,543	3,458	3,374
AKIN, Louis B (1868-1913) American				
oil	2	7,500-10,000	8,750	7,500
wc/d	1	6,000	6,000	6,000
AKKERINGA, Johannes Evert (younger) (1894-1983) Dutch				
oil	1	1,447	1,447	1,447
AKKERINGA, Johannes Evert Hendrik (1861-1942) Dutch				
oil	4	1,767-74,149	32,113	19,667
wc/d	2	477-4,005	2,241	477
AKKERMAN, Ben (1920-) Dutch				
oil	1	7,068	7,068	7,068
AKKERSDIJK, Jacob (1815-1862) Dutch				
oil	1	1,529	1,529	1,529

Name	No.	Price Range	Average	Median
AKOPIAN, Georges (1912-) Russian				
oil	5	1,260-2,397	1,523	1,318
AKPALIAPIK, Manasie (1955-) North American				
3D	5	1,687-5,568	3,037	1,940
AKRITHAKIS, Alexis (1939-) Greek				
oil	6	9,350-64,260	34,215	32,190
wc/d	2	1,870-12,180	7,025	1,870
3D	1	3,307	3,307	3,307
ALAJALOV, Constantin (1900-1987) American				
wc/d	1	5,500	5,500	5,500
ALANEN, Joseph (1885-1920) Finnish				
oil	1	2,038	2,038	2,038
ALAOUI, Moulay Ali (1924-2001) Moroccan				
oil	2	1,665-2,281	1,973	1,665
ALAPHILIPPE, Camille (20th C) French				
3D	1	4,459	4,459	4,459
ALARCON, Jose (19th C) Spanish				
oil	1	6,076	6,076	6,076
ALARCON-SUAREZ, Jose (19th C) Spanish				
oil	2	1,940-2,600	2,270	1,940
ALARIESTO, Andreas (1900-) Finnish				
oil	1	15,429	15,429	15,429
ALAUX, Gustave (1887-1965) French				
oil	4	1,004-17,500	5,964	2,238
ALAUX, Jean Pierre (1925-) French				
oil	5	523-2,108	1,100	851
ALBACETE, Alfonso (1950-) Spanish				
oil	4	2,993-10,776	5,685	3,831
ALBAN DE LESGALLERY, Jean Jacques (1808-?) French				
wc/d	1	16,473	16,473	16,473
ALBANI, Francesco (1578-1660) Italian				
oil	2	17,568-57,796	37,682	17,568
ALBEROLA, Jean Michel (1953-) French				
wc/d	1	8,415	8,415	8,415
ALBERS, Josef (1888-1976) American				
oil	36	14,960-720,000	234,868	190,000
wc/d	4	8,281-28,054	18,128	11,180
3D	1	7,500	7,500	7,500
ALBERT, Ernest (1857-1946) American				
oil	6	1,200-15,000	5,291	1,850
ALBERT, Gustaf (1866-1905) Swedish				
oil	2	810-2,976	1,893	810
ALBERT, Hans (1888-1979) German?				
oil	1	1,237	1,237	1,237
ALBERT, Hermann (20th C) ?				
oil	1	3,588	3,588	3,588
ALBERT, Jos (1886-1981) Belgian				
oil	7	693-22,048	4,187	884
ALBERT, Karl (1911-) American				
oil	2	2,750-3,250	3,000	2,750
ALBERTI, Carl (1800-?) German				
oil	1	19,265	19,265	19,265
ALBERTI, Durante (1538-1613) Italian				
wc/d	1	4,500	4,500	4,500
ALBERTI, Giuseppe Vizzotto (1862-1931) Italian				
oil	2	4,176-6,426	5,301	4,176
wc/d	5	2,848-4,531	3,580	3,625
ALBERTI, Rafael (1902-1999) Spanish				
wc/d	6	904-2,392	1,402	1,078
ALBERTINELLI, Mariotto (1474-1515) Italian				
oil	1	96,429	96,429	96,429
ALBERTINI, Luciano (1910-) Italian				
oil	1	1,145	1,145	1,145
ALBERTINI, Oreste (1887-1953) Italian				
oil	6	1,054-6,625	4,284	3,978
ALBERTIS, Sebastiano de (1828-1897) Italian				
oil	1	25,442	25,442	25,442
wc/d	4	10,356-15,459	12,845	11,892
ALBERTO, Pietro (1929-) Italian				
oil	2	1,816-1,844	1,830	1,816
wc/d	12	1,178-5,086	2,187	1,951

Name	No.	Price Range	Average	Median
ALBERTOLLI, Giocondo (1742-1839) Italian				
wc/d	2	1,036-10,000	5,518	1,036
ALBERTONI, Paolo (17th C) Italian				
oil	1	7,964	7,964	7,964
ALBERTS, Jacob (1860-1941) German				
oil	1	1,414	1,414	1,414
ALBERTS, Willem Jacobus (1912-1952) Dutch				
oil	1	1,585	1,585	1,585
ALBIERI, Gino (1881-1949) Italian				
oil	1	2,417	2,417	2,417
ALBIKER, Karl (1878-1961) German				
3D	1	3,027	3,027	3,027
ALBINO, Luca (1884-1952) Italian				
oil	3	1,900-5,733	4,073	4,586
ALBRECHTSEN, Michael (1962-) American				
oil	2	2,000-5,500	3,750	2,000
ALBRIER, Joseph (1791-1863) French				
oil	1	5,068	5,068	5,068
ALBRIGHT, Adam Emory (1862-1957) American				
oil	3	15,000-48,000	31,000	30,000
ALBRIGHT, Gertrude Partington (1883-1959) American				
oil	2	2,750-2,750	2,750	2,750
ALBRIGHT, Henry James (1887-1951) American				
oil	1	2,200	2,200	2,200
ALBRIGHT, Ivan le Lorraine (1897-1983) American				
wc/d	3	750-4,250	2,583	2,750
ALBY, Giuseppe (19th C) Italian				
oil	1	1,438	1,438	1,438
ALCALDE, Juan (1918-) Spanish				
oil	3	2,362-3,232	2,772	2,724
ALCANTARA, Antonio (1918-) Venezuelan				
oil	4	790-2,510	1,540	1,300
ALCARAZ, Julian (1863-1952) Spanish?				
oil	1	3,423	3,423	3,423
ALCAZAR Y RUIZ, Manuel (19th C) Spanish				
oil	1	1,521	1,521	1,521
ALCIATI, Evangelina Gemma (1883-1959) Italian				
oil	2	3,148-3,151	3,149	3,148
ALCORLO BARRERA, Manuel (1935-) Spanish				
oil	2	2,259-2,735	2,497	2,259
wc/d	3	729-843	783	777
ALDAZ Y SANCHO, Juan (19/20th C) Spanish				
oil	1	1,414	1,414	1,414
ALDERNAGHT, Maria (1902-1945) Belgian				
oil	1	2,356	2,356	2,356
ALDIN, Cecil (1870-1935) British				
oil	1	3,762	3,762	3,762
wc/d	18	531-5,040	1,433	1,126
ALDRICH, George Ames (1872-1941) American				
oil	11	2,144-22,500	6,694	6,000
ALDRIDGE, Frederick James (1850-1933) British				
oil	4	774-1,757	1,098	850
wc/d	19	484-2,405	1,238	1,292
ALDRIDGE, John Arthur Malcolm (1905-1984) British				
oil	9	567-2,832	1,713	1,682
wc/d	1	443	443	443
ALDROVANDINI, Pompeo (1677-1735) Italian				
wc/d	1	6,500	6,500	6,500
ALDUNATE, Carmen (1940-) Chilean				
wc/d	1	1,000	1,000	1,000
ALECHINSKY, Pierre (1927-) Belgian				
oil	28	8,035-202,400	57,066	38,532
wc/d	23	2,047-44,589	11,612	7,200
ALEF, Thorwald (1896-1974) Swedish				
oil	4	495-1,786	1,119	687
3D	6	3,434-5,495	4,052	3,709
ALEGRE, Agustin (1936-) Spanish				
oil	2	1,567-2,290	1,928	1,567
ALEGRE, Leon (1813-1884) French				
oil	1	3,168	3,168	3,168
ALENZA Y NIETO, Leonardo (1807-1845) Spanish				
oil	1	24,220	24,220	24,220

Name	No.	Price Range	Average	Median
ALESSANDRI, Lorenzo (1927-2000) Italian				
oil	3	561-1,051	739	607
wc/d	3	607-701	654	654
ALEXANCO, Jose Luis (1942-) Spanish				
oil	1	2,993	2,993	2,993
ALEXANDER, Alan (?) British				
oil	1	2,000	2,000	2,000
ALEXANDER, Douglas (1871-1945) British				
oil	3	1,637-3,507	2,611	2,689
wc/d	19	538-1,800	1,063	1,020
ALEXANDER, Edwin (1870-1926) British				
oil	1	433	433	433
wc/d	4	1,290-5,696	3,211	1,683
ALEXANDER, Francis (1800-1880) American				
oil	2	1,000-1,400	1,200	1,000
ALEXANDER, John (1945-) American				
oil	5	2,100-8,496	5,519	6,500
ALEXANDER, John White (1856-1915) American				
oil	2	5,470-10,000	7,735	5,470
ALEXANDER, Lena (fl.1905-1936) British				
wc/d	1	2,992	2,992	2,992
ALEXANDER, William (1767-1816) British				
wc/d	4	3,560-40,920	16,862	6,228
ALEXANDROVNA, Grand Duchess Olga (1882-1960) Russian				
oil	6	2,381-12,900	5,608	4,341
wc/d	16	652-140,137	14,048	1,581
ALEXANDROVSKY, Stepan Fedorovich (1842-1906) Russian				
wc/d	2	3,514-38,219	20,866	3,514
ALFANO, Carlo (1932-1990) Italian				
oil	3	4,057-10,132	6,428	5,096
wc/d	1	701	701	701
ALFARO HERNANDEZ, Andreu (1929-) Spanish				
3D	3	4,006-4,855	4,410	4,370
ALFELT, Else (1910-1975) Danish				
oil	3	6,466-28,973	16,642	14,487
ALFIERI, Antonio Vittorio (1938-) Italian				
oil	2	1,844-2,863	2,353	1,844
ALFIERI, C (19/20th C) Italian				
oil	1	1,533	1,533	1,533
ALFONS, Sven (1918-1996) Swedish				
oil	2	1,520-4,625	3,072	1,520
ALFORD, Leonard C (fl.1885-1904) British				
oil	1	1,840	1,840	1,840
ALFSEN, John Martin (1902-1971) Canadian				
oil	1	1,097	1,097	1,097
ALGARDI, Alessandro (1602-1654) Italian				
3D	1	85,135	85,135	85,135
ALHAZIAN, Ohannes (19/20th C) Turkish				
oil	1	27,520	27,520	27,520
ALI, Lutf (19th C) Persian				
oil	1	1,903	1,903	1,903
ALICE, Antonio (1886-1943) Argentinian				
oil	1	15,872	15,872	15,872
ALIKATUKTUK, Thomasie (1953-) Canadian				
3D	1	2,109	2,109	2,109
ALINARI, Luca (1943-) Italian				
oil	29	853-6,442	2,473	2,090
wc/d	8	488-11,712	3,569	1,060
ALIOTO, Massimiliano (1972-) Italian				
oil	7	914-1,942	1,474	1,427
ALISOV, Mikhail (1859-1933) Russian				
oil	3	2,368-5,505	3,472	2,544
ALIX, Yves (1890-1969) French				
oil	3	1,018-1,352	1,187	1,192
ALKARA, Ovadia (1939-) Israeli				
oil	1	4,000	4,000	4,000
ALKEN, Henry (jnr) (1810-1894) British				
oil	10	864-264,600	31,698	1,991
wc/d	1	600	600	600
ALKEN, Henry (snr) (1785-1851) British				
oil	13	1,040-132,000	26,920	20,000
wc/d	5	794-4,725	2,242	2,268

Name	No.	Price Range	Average	Median
ALKEN, Samuel (jnr) (1784-1825) British				
oil	1	22,680	22,680	22,680
ALKEN, Samuel (snr) (1756-1815) British				
oil	1	38,720	38,720	38,720
ALLAN, Archibald Russell Watson (1878-1959) British				
oil	4	1,947-24,780	11,009	7,632
wc/d	1	1,427	1,427	1,427
ALLAN, David (1744-1796) British				
oil	1	245,700	245,700	245,700
ALLAN, Robert Weir (1852-1942) British				
oil	3	8,850-15,664	12,650	13,436
wc/d	15	534-3,534	1,996	1,969
ALLAN, Sir Alexander (1764-1820) British				
wc/d	1	10,800	10,800	10,800
ALLARD-L'OLIVIER, Fernand (1883-1933) Belgian				
oil	7	1,638-42,411	11,368	3,116
wc/d	1	11,439	11,439	11,439
ALLASON, Silvio (1845-1912) Italian				
oil	1	1,332	1,332	1,332
ALLCOT, John (1888-1973) Australian				
oil	1	2,244	2,244	2,244
ALLEAUME, Ludovic (1859-?) French				
oil	1	2,548	2,548	2,548
ALLEGRAIN, Christophe Gabriel (1710-1795) French				
3D	1	3,456	3,456	3,456
ALLEGRAIN, Étienne (1653-1736) French				
oil	1	11,105	11,105	11,105
ALLEGRE, Raymond (1857-1933) French				
oil	3	4,250-9,699	6,261	4,834
ALLEGRINI, Francesco (1587-1663) Italian				
wc/d	5	771-1,823	1,150	972
ALLEN, Al (20th C) American				
oil	1	2,750	2,750	2,750
ALLEN, Harry Epworth (1894-1958) British				
oil	8	3,822-27,664	10,908	8,550
wc/d	5	712-11,628	3,760	2,455
ALLEN, Joseph (1770-1839) British				
oil	1	2,000	2,000	2,000
ALLEN, Joseph William (1803-1852) British				
oil	1	5,568	5,568	5,568
wc/d	1	463	463	463
ALLEN, Junius (1898-1962) American				
oil	1	1,900	1,900	1,900
ALLIEVI, Fernando (1954-) Argentinian				
wc/d	1	1,200	1,200	1,200
ALLIN, John (1934-1991) British				
oil	1	1,392	1,392	1,392
ALLINGHAM, Helen (1848-1926) British				
wc/d	17	1,157-37,200	14,257	13,650
ALLINSON, Adrian (1890-1959) British				
oil	2	1,325-3,000	2,162	1,325
3D	1	5,490	5,490	5,490
ALLIOT, Lucien Charles Edouard (1877-1967) French				
3D	1	1,815	1,815	1,815
ALLIS, C Harry (1876-1938) American				
oil	2	900-4,250	2,575	900
ALLISON OF SOUTHAMPTON, William (19th C) British				
wc/d	2	493-2,200	1,346	493
ALLOM, Thomas (1804-1872) British				
wc/d	6	864-10,620	4,180	1,674
ALLONGE, Auguste (1833-1898) French				
oil	1	839	839	839
wc/d	6	707-2,572	1,398	1,052
ALLOUARD, Henri (1844-1929) French				
3D	1	3,026	3,026	3,026
ALLSTON, Washington (1779-1843) American				
oil	1	40,000	40,000	40,000
ALLUAUD, Eugène (1866-1947) French				
oil	2	1,169-5,377	3,273	1,169
ALLWEIL, Arieh (1901-1967) Israeli				
oil	2	1,700-2,600	2,150	1,700

Name	No.	Price Range	Average	Median
ALMA, Peter (1886-1969) Dutch				
oil	2	5,724-8,905	7,314	5,724
ALMA-TADEMA, Sir Lawrence (1836-1912) British				
oil	6	32,986-170,000	80,684	55,000
wc/d	3	1,000-5,178	3,051	2,976
ALMANZOR, A B (?) ?				
3D	1	3,500	3,500	3,500
ALMAR, Agustin (19th C) Spanish				
oil	2	1,800-6,600	4,200	1,800
ALMARAZ, Carlos (1941-1989) ?				
oil	1	4,000	4,000	4,000
ALMAVIVA, Marco (1934-) Italian				
oil	2	1,640-2,035	1,837	1,640
ALMAZOV, N (19th C) Russian				
oil	1	45,863	45,863	45,863
ALMELKAR, Abdul Rahiman Appabhai (1920-1982) Indian				
oil	1	7,500	7,500	7,500
ALMON, Leroy (1938-1997) American				
3D	2	3,000-3,600	3,300	3,000
ALMQUIST, Anna (19th C) Swedish				
oil	1	1,123	1,123	1,123
ALMYDA, Joseph (20th C) American				
oil	1	1,000	1,000	1,000
ALOISE (1886-1964) Swiss				
wc/d	1	72,541	72,541	72,541
ALONSO, Carlos (1929-) Argentinian				
oil	4	2,800-14,000	9,200	10,000
wc/d	10	1,400-10,000	3,190	2,000
ALONSO, Raul (20th C) Argentinian				
wc/d	1	2,700	2,700	2,700
ALONSO, Saturio (1954-) Spanish				
3D	1	1,920	1,920	1,920
ALONSO-PEREZ, Carlos (19/20th C) Spanish				
oil	1	1,757	1,757	1,757
ALONSO-PEREZ, Mariano (1858-1914) Spanish				
oil	2	7,633-273,904	140,768	7,633
ALONZO, Angel (1923-1994) Spanish				
oil	1	1,014	1,014	1,014
ALONZO, Dominique de (19/20th C) French				
3D	2	2,675-2,735	2,705	2,675
ALOPHE, Marie Alexandre (1812-1883) French				
oil	2	1,236-1,318	1,277	1,236
ALORDA Y PEREZ, Ramon (1848-1899) Spanish				
oil	1	2,392	2,392	2,392
wc/d	1	2,112	2,112	2,112
ALOTT, Robert (1850-1910) Austrian				
oil	12	750-13,920	5,731	4,241
ALPUY, Julio (1919-) Uruguayan				
oil	3	2,500-9,000	4,916	3,250
wc/d	1	700	700	700
3D	1	19,000	19,000	19,000
ALSHEVSKI, Victor (1953-) Belarussian				
oil	2	801-1,701	1,251	801
ALSINA, Jose (19/20th C) ?				
oil	2	5,068-18,000	11,534	5,068
ALSLOOT, Denis van (c.1570-1628) Dutch				
oil	2	129,500-141,860	135,680	129,500
ALSLOOT, Denis van and CLERCK, Hendrick de (17th C) Dutch				
oil	2	26,615-26,700	26,657	26,615
ALSTON, Charles Henry (1907-1977) American				
oil	1	11,500	11,500	11,500
ALT, Franz (1821-1914) Austrian				
oil	3	658-2,500	1,391	1,017
wc/d	10	468-11,781	2,724	1,636
ALT, Jacob (1789-1872) German				
oil	1	26,703	26,703	26,703
wc/d	4	2,026-6,676	3,638	2,577
ALT, Otmar (1940-) German				
oil	4	1,915-3,770	2,494	2,068
wc/d	1	1,080	1,080	1,080
3D	1	4,477	4,477	4,477

Name	No.	Price Range	Average	Median
ALT, Rudolf von (1812-1905) Austrian				
oil	2	36,458-49,680	43,069	36,458
wc/d	24	760-111,267	26,678	8,469
ALTAF, Navjot (1949-) Indian				
oil	1	7,500	7,500	7,500
3D	1	3,800	3,800	3,800
ALTAMIRANO, Arturo Pacheco (1905-1978) Chilean				
oil	6	1,150-3,500	2,508	2,500
ALTAMURA (?) ?				
oil	1	43,200	43,200	43,200
ALTAMURA, Jean (1852-1878) Greek				
oil	1	1,581	1,581	1,581
wc/d	1	5,984	5,984	5,984
ALTEN, Mathias Joseph (1871-1938) German				
oil	2	3,250-18,000	10,625	3,250
wc/d	1	970	970	970
ALTENBOURG, Gerhard (1926-1989) German				
oil	1	11,466	11,466	11,466
wc/d	8	3,822-7,759	5,069	4,186
ALTENKIRCH, Otto (1875-1945) German				
oil	3	970-4,186	2,276	1,674
ALTHAUS, Fritz (fl.1881-1914) British				
oil	1	1,817	1,817	1,817
wc/d	1	487	487	487
ALTHEIDE, C Harvi (1874-1951) American				
oil	2	1,900-3,250	2,575	1,900
ALTHOFF, Kai (1966-) German				
wc/d	3	40,000-60,000	48,333	45,000
ALTINK, Jan (1885-1975) Dutch				
oil	10	4,267-57,329	21,992	11,466
wc/d	6	914-2,268	1,380	1,019
ALTMANN, Alexandre (1885-1950) Russian				
oil	38	3,273-65,000	19,945	17,000
ALTMANN, Gerard (1877-1940) Dutch				
oil	2	566-771	668	566
wc/d	2	845-968	906	845
ALTMANN, Gerard (1923-) French				
oil	1	1,081	1,081	1,081
ALTMANN, Nathan (1889-1970) Israeli				
oil	4	7,262-47,500	26,775	11,127
ALTOON, John (1925-1969) American				
oil	1	3,000	3,000	3,000
wc/d	2	1,131-2,000	1,565	1,131
ALTORF, J C (1876-1955) Dutch				
3D	1	3,562	3,562	3,562
ALTORF, Johan Coenraad (1876-1955) Dutch				
3D	2	1,764-17,010	9,387	1,764
ALTRUI, C (19th C) Italian				
oil	1	1,796	1,796	1,796
ALTSON, Abbey (1864-c.1949) British				
oil	2	3,024-12,744	7,884	3,024
ALVAR, Sunol (1935-) Spanish				
oil	2	8,246-24,739	16,492	8,246
3D	1	1,649	1,649	1,649
ALVARADO, Pedro Diego (1956-) Mexican				
oil	1	12,000	12,000	12,000
ALVAREZ AYLLON, Emilio (19/20th C) Spanish				
oil	4	654-3,575	1,843	847
ALVAREZ BASSO, Dario (1968-) Venezuelan				
oil	1	1,308	1,308	1,308
ALVAREZ CATALA, Luis (1836-1901) Spanish				
oil	2	60,000-83,425	71,712	60,000
ALVAREZ DIAZ, Emilio (1879-1952) Argentinian				
oil	2	1,492-4,638	3,065	1,492
ALVAREZ, Gonzalo (19/20th C) Spanish				
oil	1	2,378	2,378	2,378
ALVAREZ, Luis (19th C) Spanish				
oil	20	581-2,543	1,233	848
ALVAREZ, Mabel (1891-1985) American				
oil	6	750-20,000	5,925	1,900
ALVAREZ, Xavier (1949-) ?				
3D	1	4,795	4,795	4,795

Name	No.	Price Range	Average	Median
ALVAREZ-DUMONT, Eugenio (1864-1927) Spanish				
oil	1	1,654	1,654	1,654
ALVAREZ-SALA, Ventura (1869-1919) Spanish				
oil	1	4,186	4,186	4,186
ALVEAR, Gerardo de (1887-1964) Spanish				
oil	2	2,259-2,378	2,318	2,259
ALVES, Celestino (1913-1974) Portuguese				
oil	1	8,507	8,507	8,507
ALVIANI, Getulio (1939-) Italian				
oil	5	3,770-26,714	13,199	12,721
wc/d	2	971-18,154	9,562	971
3D	19	3,073-74,340	20,026	12,252
ALYS, Francis (1959-) Belgian				
oil	7	26,000-550,000	165,107	55,000
wc/d	2	6,750-17,000	11,875	6,750
AMADEUS-DIER, Erhard (1893-1969) Austrian				
oil	1	1,211	1,211	1,211
AMADIO, Giuseppe (1944-) Italian				
oil	11	1,008-3,196	1,979	1,942
wc/d	2	941-1,176	1,058	941
AMADIO, Vittorio (1934-) Italian				
oil	1	1,072	1,072	1,072
AMADO, Maria Fernanda (1924-) Portuguese				
oil	2	1,452-1,815	1,633	1,452
AMAL, Bachir (1954-) Moroccan				
wc/d	1	3,447	3,447	3,447
AMALFI, Carlo (18th C) Italian				
oil	2	15,000-30,575	22,787	15,000
AMAN-JEAN, Edmond François (1860-1935) French				
oil	1	9,513	9,513	9,513
AMARAL, Antonio Henrique (1935-) Brazilian				
oil	1	6,000	6,000	6,000
AMARSOTO, T (20th C) Asian				
oil	1	5,412	5,412	5,412
AMATO, Orazio (1884-1952) Italian				
oil	1	1,911	1,911	1,911
AMATO, Raphael (19th C) Italian				
oil	1	2,259	2,259	2,259
AMAYA, Armando (1935-) Mexican				
3D	1	6,114	6,114	6,114
AMBADAS (1922-) Indian				
oil	1	11,220	11,220	11,220
wc/d	2	2,768-4,844	3,806	2,768
AMBERG, Wilhelm (1822-1899) German				
oil	1	6,555	6,555	6,555
AMBROGIANI, Pierre (1907-1985) French				
oil	14	1,017-15,122	5,424	4,123
wc/d	7	605-1,090	915	1,065
AMBROSE, John (1931-) British				
oil	1	2,728	2,728	2,728
AMBROSI, Alfredo Gauro (1901-1945) Italian				
oil	1	6,442	6,442	6,442
AMBROSI, Gustinus (1893-1975) Austrian				
3D	3	3,137-11,348	8,293	10,395
AMEDEO DA PISTOIA (15th C) Italian				
oil	1	216,735	216,735	216,735
AMEGLIO, Mario (1897-1970) French				
oil	23	589-4,602	1,985	1,774
AMELIN, Albin (1902-1975) Swedish				
oil	9	1,951-114,658	23,338	12,469
wc/d	4	661-12,422	5,544	1,825
AMEN, Woody van (1936-) Dutch				
wc/d	1	2,544	2,544	2,544
AMER, Ghada (1963-) Egyptian				
oil	9	2,221-111,000	48,451	47,500
wc/d	2	4,602-19,138	11,870	4,602
AMERLING, Friedrich von (1803-1887) Austrian				
oil	7	608-20,027	4,940	3,041
wc/d	1	602	602	602
AMEROM, Hendrik Jan van (1777-1833) Dutch				
oil	1	3,387	3,387	3,387

Name	No.	Price Range	Average	Median
AMES, Ezra (1768-1836) American				
oil	2	3,250-3,500	3,375	3,250
AMES, Joseph Alexander (1816-1872) American				
oil	1	3,250	3,250	3,250
AMES, May (?-1946) American				
oil	2	660-3,275	1,967	660
AMES, Wally (1942-) American				
oil	3	675-5,000	2,141	750
AMEZAGA, Eduardo (1911-) Uruguayan				
oil	1	1,350	1,350	1,350
AMI, Ben (1897-?) Swiss				
oil	3	1,135-1,947	1,405	1,135
AMICIS, Cristoforo de (1902-1987) Italian				
oil	5	1,821-3,073	2,489	2,417
AMICK, Robert Wesley (1879-1969) American				
oil	1	4,750	4,750	4,750
wc/d	1	3,750	3,750	3,750
AMICONI, Bernardo (19th C) Italian				
oil	1	2,674	2,674	2,674
AMIET, Cuno (1868-1961) Swiss				
oil	35	2,293-440,969	69,516	30,467
wc/d	14	989-60,885	14,584	6,850
AMIGONI, Jacopo (1675-1752) Italian				
oil	4	16,071-480,000	233,177	156,640
wc/d	1	1,196	1,196	1,196
AMIGUET, Marcel (1891-1958) Swiss				
oil	1	27,476	27,476	27,476
AMIOT, Patrick (1960-) Canadian				
3D	1	3,732	3,732	3,732
AMIR OF KARRAYA, Shaikh Muhammad (fl.1820-1840) Indian				
wc/d	1	6,000	6,000	6,000
AMISANI, Giuseppe (1881-1941) Italian				
oil	5	1,288-18,185	9,423	7,027
AMITTU, Davidiluak Alasua (1910-1976) North American				
3D	2	4,218-4,724	4,471	4,218
AMMANN, Marguerite (1911-1962) Swiss				
oil	1	1,218	1,218	1,218
AMMIRATO, Domenico (1833-1890) Italian				
oil	1	1,095	1,095	1,095
AMORALES, Carlos (1970-) Mexican				
oil	1	19,000	19,000	19,000
AMORGASTI, Antonio (1880-1942) Italian				
3D	1	1,909	1,909	1,909
AMOROSI, Antonio (1660-1736) Italian				
oil	1	17,346	17,346	17,346
AMORSOLO, Fernando (1892-1972) Philippino				
oil	6	15,000-35,340	21,959	18,000
AMRANI, Aziz (20th C) Moroccan				
oil	2	4,712-4,712	4,712	4,712
AMUNDSON, Allyn (20th C) American				
oil	2	500-2,200	1,350	500
ANASTASI, Auguste (1820-1889) French				
oil	6	773-4,452	2,763	2,417
ANASTASI, William (1933-) American				
oil	1	1,200	1,200	1,200
ANATCHKOV (1941-1998) French				
3D	1	3,612	3,612	3,612
ANAUTA, Peter Ussuqi (1934-) North American				
3D	1	1,940	1,940	1,940
ANCHER, Anna (1859-1935) Danish				
oil	2	17,464-26,057	21,760	17,464
wc/d	9	474-2,055	874	711
ANCHER, Helga (1883-1964) Danish				
oil	1	6,821	6,821	6,821
ANCHER, Michael (1849-1927) Danish				
oil	46	1,218-381,022	34,230	12,160
wc/d	3	782-1,690	1,147	971
ANCIAUX, Germaine (?) ?				
oil	1	2,860	2,860	2,860
ANDENMATTEN, Leo (1922-1979) Swiss				
oil	7	1,518-22,842	6,277	4,079

Name	No.	Price Range	Average	Median
ANDER, Ture (1881-1959) Swedish				
oil	2	1,246-35,671	18,458	1,246
ANDERBERG, Niklas (1950-) Danish				
oil	1	1,683	1,683	1,683
ANDERBOUHR, Paul-Jean (1909-) French				
oil	5	502-5,104	1,811	1,004
ANDERLECHT, Engelbert van (1918-1961) Belgian				
oil	3	1,134-22,898	10,555	7,633
wc/d	2	892-2,803	1,847	892
ANDERMATT, Peter (1938-) Swiss				
oil	1	1,221	1,221	1,221
wc/d	1	458	458	458
ANDERMATT, Rita (1946-) Swiss				
wc/d	1	1,827	1,827	1,827
ANDERS, Ernst (1845-1911) German				
oil	3	832-2,646	1,556	1,192
ANDERSEN, Carl Christian (1849-1906) Danish				
oil	2	869-3,240	2,054	869
ANDERSEN, Cilius (1865-1913) Danish				
oil	3	500-3,301	2,004	2,213
ANDERSEN, Julius (19th C) Danish				
oil	1	2,055	2,055	2,055
ANDERSEN, Karin (1966-) German				
oil	1	1,296	1,296	1,296
ANDERSEN, Mogens (1916-2003) Danish				
oil	12	966-20,120	7,428	6,142
wc/d	2	865-2,910	1,887	865
ANDERSEN, Robin Christian (1890-1969) Austrian				
oil	1	6,429	6,429	6,429
wc/d	1	1,697	1,697	1,697
ANDERSEN, Roy H (1930-) American				
oil	7	14,000-45,000	27,857	23,000
ANDERSEN-LUNDBY, Anders (1841-1923) Danish				
oil	15	1,008-15,809	4,954	3,478
wc/d	1	1,890	1,890	1,890
ANDERSON, Clayton (1964-) Canadian				
oil	1	3,767	3,767	3,767
ANDERSON, Frank (1844-1891) American				
oil	1	185,000	185,000	185,000
ANDERSON, G (19th C) American				
wc/d	1	4,750	4,750	4,750
ANDERSON, Harold (1894-1973) American				
oil	2	9,000-14,000	11,500	9,000
ANDERSON, Harry (1906-1996) American				
oil	1	2,600	2,600	2,600
ANDERSON, John (19th C) British				
oil	1	1,201	1,201	1,201
ANDERSON, Ken (20th C) American				
wc/d	1	1,600	1,600	1,600
ANDERSON, Kjell (1937-) Swedish				
oil	1	2,643	2,643	2,643
ANDERSON, Lennart (1928-) American				
oil	1	7,000	7,000	7,000
ANDERSON, Oskar Leonard (1836-1868) Swedish				
oil	1	1,553	1,553	1,553
ANDERSON, Sophie (1823-1903) British				
oil	6	7,695-79,200	44,114	34,200
wc/d	1	2,784	2,784	2,784
ANDERSON, Stanley (1884-1966) British				
wc/d	3	531-2,576	1,894	2,576
ANDERSON, Victor C (1882-1937) American				
oil	3	1,500-3,500	2,381	2,144
ANDERSON, Walter (fl.1856-1886) British				
oil	1	17,000	17,000	17,000
ANDERSON, Walter Inglis (1903-1965) American				
oil	1	52,500	52,500	52,500
wc/d	8	2,000-35,000	10,187	5,750
ANDERSON, Will (fl.1880-1895) British				
oil	1	498	498	498
wc/d	1	1,400	1,400	1,400

Name	No.	Price Range	Average	Median
ANDERSON, William (1757-1837) British				
oil	3	3,740-7,480	5,457	5,152
wc/d	3	2,436-4,524	3,132	2,436
ANDERSSON, Karin Mamma (1962-) Swedish				
oil	3	5,814-42,287	19,511	10,433
ANDERSSON, Marten (1934-) Swedish				
wc/d	3	3,832-4,453	4,083	3,964
ANDERSSON, Nils (1817-1865) Swedish				
oil	1	1,179	1,179	1,179
ANDERSSON, Torsten (1926-) Swedish				
oil	7	3,436-32,376	9,014	4,835
wc/d	1	763	763	763
ANDOE, Joe (1955-) American				
oil	1	2,000	2,000	2,000
ANDRE, Albert (1869-1954) French				
oil	36	1,573-44,250	10,944	8,106
wc/d	4	486-7,262	2,316	608
ANDRE, Carl (1935-) American				
wc/d	4	16,000-110,000	66,500	65,000
3D	15	9,735-450,000	96,666	45,000
ANDRE, Jules (1807-1869) French				
oil	1	1,392	1,392	1,392
ANDRE, Paul (?) Canadian?				
oil	1	1,212	1,212	1,212
ANDREA, Cornelis (1914-) Dutch				
oil	4	648-1,767	1,119	1,001
ANDREA, John de (1941-) American				
3D	3	2,800-64,750	24,116	4,800
ANDREA, Pat (1942-) Dutch				
oil	2	1,192-4,442	2,817	1,192
wc/d	12	634-6,497	2,180	1,352
ANDREAS, Hans (1947-) Austrian				
oil	1	1,688	1,688	1,688
ANDREASEN, Signe (1853-1919) Danish				
oil	2	652-1,897	1,274	652
ANDREASSON, Folke (1902-1948) Swedish				
oil	1	3,436	3,436	3,436
ANDREENKO, Mikhail (1895-1982) Russian				
oil	3	1,216-1,918	1,632	1,764
wc/d	10	989-4,697	1,819	1,549
ANDREENKO-NECHITALYO, Mikhail (1894-1982) Russian				
oil	1	611	611	611
wc/d	1	1,679	1,679	1,679
ANDREEV, Ivan Petrovich (1847-1896) Russian				
wc/d	1	3,276	3,276	3,276
ANDREEV, P A (20th C) Dutch?				
oil	1	1,784	1,784	1,784
ANDREEW, Igor (1932-) Russian				
oil	1	3,720	3,720	3,720
ANDREIS, Alex de (fl.1880-1929) Belgian				
oil	7	780-3,828	1,693	1,155
ANDREN, Alvan (19th C) American				
wc/d	1	4,800	4,800	4,800
ANDREO-WOLF, Anne (20th C) French?				
3D	1	1,868	1,868	1,868
ANDREONI, Orazio (19th C) Italian				
3D	1	15,120	15,120	15,120
ANDREOTTI, Federico (1847-1930) Italian				
oil	3	2,832-49,685	28,525	33,060
wc/d	1	476	476	476
ANDREU, Mariano (1888-1976) Spanish				
wc/d	5	564-3,039	1,974	2,090
ANDREU, Teodoro (1870-1934) Spanish				
oil	1	1,028	1,028	1,028
ANDREWS, Benny (1930-) American				
wc/d	1	2,200	2,200	2,200
ANDREWS, C W (fl.1855-1865) British				
wc/d	1	2,958	2,958	2,958
ANDREWS, Charles W (fl.1855-1865) British				
wc/d	1	3,145	3,145	3,145
ANDREWS, George H (1816-1898) British				
wc/d	1	2,250	2,250	2,250

Name	No.	Price Range	Average	Median
ANDREWS, Henry (19th C) British				
oil	4	1,079-8,325	4,874	3,828
ANDREWS, J Winthrop (1879-?) American				
oil	1	2,250	2,250	2,250
ANDREWS, Michael (1928-1995) British				
oil	1	264,000	264,000	264,000
ANDREWS, Sybil (1898-1992) British				
oil	2	4,123-7,533	5,828	4,123
wc/d	1	506	506	506
ANDREY-PREVOST, Fernand (1890-1961) French				
oil	1	1,754	1,754	1,754
ANDRI, Ferdinand (1871-1956) Austrian				
oil	2	904-3,514	2,209	904
ANDRIEN, Mady (1941-) Belgian				
3D	1	21,405	21,405	21,405
ANDRIESSE, Erik (1957-1993) Dutch?				
oil	1	4,452	4,452	4,452
ANDRIESSEN, Anthony (1746-1813) Dutch				
wc/d	1	1,285	1,285	1,285
ANDRIESSEN, Mari Silvester (1897-1979) Dutch				
3D	1	2,417	2,417	2,417
ANDRISANO, Cosimo (1971-) Italian				
oil	1	1,018	1,018	1,018
wc/d	2	583-615	599	583
ANDROUET DU CERCEAU, Jacques (1510-c.1587) French				
wc/d	4	27,750-59,200	48,562	48,100
ANDROUSOW, Vadime (1895-1975) Russian				
3D	1	69,601	69,601	69,601
ANDRUS, Vera (1896-1979) American				
wc/d	1	1,200	1,200	1,200
ANDRYCHIEWICZ, Zygmunt (1861-1943) Polish				
oil	1	6,370	6,370	6,370
ANESI, Carlos (1945-) Argentinian				
oil	1	2,000	2,000	2,000
ANESI, Paolo (1697-1773) Italian				
oil	4	20,000-51,900	37,628	34,600
ANFRIE, Charles (1833-?) French				
3D	2	2,267-2,610	2,438	2,267
ANGE (?) ?				
oil	1	3,637	3,637	3,637
ANGE, Paul (20th C) Russian				
oil	1	1,500	1,500	1,500
ANGEL, Philip (1616-1683) Dutch				
oil	2	5,839-7,389	6,614	5,839
ANGELI, Eduard (1942-) Austrian				
oil	1	3,356	3,356	3,356
wc/d	1	701	701	701
ANGELI, Filippo (1600-1640) Italian				
oil	2	38,060-81,880	59,970	38,060
ANGELI, Franco (1935-1988) Italian				
oil	95	1,253-17,939	3,804	2,682
wc/d	11	727-14,500	3,149	1,767
ANGELI, Giuseppe (1709-1798) Italian				
oil	1	63,699	63,699	63,699
ANGELI, Heinrich von (1840-1924) Austrian				
oil	2	2,057-4,849	3,453	2,057
ANGELIS, Deiva de (1885-1925) Italian				
oil	1	1,029	1,029	1,029
ANGELL, Helen Cordelia (1847-1884) British				
wc/d	3	1,232-2,136	1,815	2,079
ANGERMAYER, Johann Adalbert (1674-c.1740) German				
oil	1	43,172	43,172	43,172
ANGEVIN (19th C) French				
3D	1	19,140	19,140	19,140
ANGHIK, Abraham Apakark (1951-) North American				
3D	1	1,687	1,687	1,687
ANGI, Alex (1965-) French				
3D	4	1,790-2,040	1,889	1,844
ANGIELSKI, Krol (?) Russian?				
oil	1	4,152	4,152	4,152
ANGILLIS, Pieter (1685-1734) Flemish				
oil	2	12,041-17,575	14,808	12,041

Name	No.	Price Range	Average	Median
ANGLADA-CAMARASA, Herman (1873-1959) Spanish				
oil	6	23,562-577,959	309,703	208,800
ANGLADA-PINTO, Luis (1873-1946) Spanish				
oil	3	1,432-2,667	2,080	2,141
ANGLADE, Andre (20th C) French				
oil	1	1,060	1,060	1,060
ANGLADE, Gaston (1854-1919) French				
oil	9	468-3,277	1,215	1,032
ANGLES, Joaquin (19/20th C) French				
3D	2	5,703-8,784	7,243	5,703
ANGNAYUINAK, Yaha (1907-1980) North American				
3D	1	1,518	1,518	1,518
ANGO, Robert (18th C) French				
wc/d	4	2,188-4,600	3,475	2,674
ANGQVIST, Olle (1922-) Swedish				
oil	2	1,336-1,909	1,622	1,336
ANIBAL, Miguel (1935-) ?				
oil	2	618-1,854	1,236	618
ANISFELD, Boris (1878-1973) Russian				
oil	12	18,000-948,600	240,900	45,000
wc/d	2	13,760-50,220	31,990	13,760
3D	1	12,000	12,000	12,000
ANIVITTI, Filippo (1876-1955) Italian				
oil	6	1,812-7,770	4,037	3,092
wc/d	6	1,980-5,568	2,876	2,293
ANJOS, Armando (?) ?				
oil	2	729-1,762	1,245	729
ANKARCRONA, Gustaf (1869-1933) Swedish				
oil	3	2,601-16,826	8,078	4,808
ANKARCRONA, Henrik (1831-1917) Swedish				
oil	2	3,988-6,182	5,085	3,988
ANKER, Albert (1831-1910) Swiss				
oil	10	1,216-571,053	192,462	37,990
wc/d	39	493-81,579	17,724	4,705
ANNENKOFF, Yuri (1889-1974) Russian				
oil	4	32,500-60,000	41,885	37,200
wc/d	6	1,360-136,800	42,726	5,952
ANNIGONI, Pietro (1910-1988) Italian				
oil	7	900-1,104,000	160,361	3,449
wc/d	29	460-6,732	2,204	1,848
ANNONI, Franco (1924-1992) Swiss				
3D	1	1,214	1,214	1,214
ANOUSH (1924-) Iranian				
oil	1	1,229	1,229	1,229
ANOWTALIK, Luke (1932-) North American				
3D	1	3,543	3,543	3,543
ANQUETIN, Louis (1861-1932) French				
oil	3	906-25,329	10,161	4,248
wc/d	8	486-370,000	50,297	1,113
ANREITER, Alois von (1803-1882) Austrian				
wc/d	2	1,940-2,990	2,465	1,940
ANSDELL, R (1815-1885) British				
oil	1	11,000	11,000	11,000
ANSDELL, Richard (1815-1885) British				
oil	14	5,500-195,800	52,142	32,500
ANSELMO, Giovanni (1921-) Italian				
wc/d	1	20,469	20,469	20,469
3D	1	385,306	385,306	385,306
ANSEN-HOFMANN, E (19/20th C) German				
oil	3	1,215-11,404	6,606	7,200
ANSHUTZ, Thomas Pollock (1851-1912) American				
oil	2	4,000-30,000	17,000	4,000
wc/d	1	4,000	4,000	4,000
ANSINGH, Lizzy (1875-1959) Dutch				
oil	6	1,627-33,486	11,830	2,472
wc/d	1	953	953	953
ANTCHER, Isaac (1899-1992) Rumanian				
oil	8	400-5,845	1,764	1,058
ANTES, Horst (1936-) German				
oil	3	12,945-101,918	44,657	19,110
wc/d	14	1,528-28,027	9,752	6,214
3D	13	1,903-11,003	5,418	5,096

Name	No.	Price Range	Average	Median
ANTHING, Johann Friedrich (1753-1805) Russian				
wc/d	1	34,724	34,724	34,724
ANTHONISSEN, Hendrick van (1606-?) Dutch				
oil	1	17,800	17,800	17,800
ANTHONY, Carol (1943-) American?				
oil	2	900-3,000	1,950	900
ANTIGNA, Marc (19/20th C) French				
oil	1	1,784	1,784	1,784
ANTOINE, Otto (1865-1951) German				
oil	8	450-15,265	3,992	803
ANTON, Bill (?) ?				
oil	11	2,600-40,000	12,054	5,500
wc/d	1	1,000	1,000	1,000
ANTONIANI, Paolo Maria (1735-1807) Italian				
oil	1	40,767	40,767	40,767
ANTONIO, Julio (1889-1919) Spanish				
3D	1	3,592	3,592	3,592
ANTONISSEN, Henri Joseph (1737-1794) Flemish				
oil	2	603-2,800	1,701	603
ANTONOV, Sergei Nikolaievich (1884-1956) Russian				
oil	1	4,713	4,713	4,713
wc/d	1	4,465	4,465	4,465
ANTRAL, Louis Robert (1895-1940) French				
oil	4	1,929-4,435	2,918	2,647
ANUSZKIEWICZ, Richard (1930-) American				
oil	4	9,500-27,500	17,750	14,000
ANZINGER, Siegfried (1953-) Austrian				
oil	7	1,205-16,562	5,868	1,808
wc/d	16	487-7,283	1,832	1,334
3D	1	10,924	10,924	10,924
APELLANIZ, Jesus (1898-1969) Spanish				
oil	1	1,089	1,089	1,089
APESTEGUIA, Efren Pelayo (1900-?) Peruvian				
oil	1	2,100	2,100	2,100
APOL, Armand-Adrien-Marie (1879-1950) Belgian				
oil	9	486-4,800	1,749	1,384
APOL, Louis (1850-1936) Dutch				
oil	18	890-74,167	23,284	9,568
wc/d	5	4,005-12,123	7,420	5,819
APOLLONIO, Marina (1940-) Italian				
oil	2	2,178-2,299	2,238	2,178
APOSTU, George (1934-) Rumanian				
3D	1	2,145	2,145	2,145
APPEL, Charles P (1857-1928) American				
oil	1	4,600	4,600	4,600
APPEL, Karel (1921-2006) Dutch				
oil	90	3,000-425,500	68,120	25,055
wc/d	39	425-64,795	15,559	11,350
3D	17	1,683-28,000	7,709	4,849
APPELMAN, Barend (1640-1686) Dutch				
oil	2	4,070-23,301	13,685	4,070
APPELT, Dieter (1935-) German				
wc/d	1	3,816	3,816	3,816
APPERLEY, George Owen Wynne (1884-1960) British				
oil	2	4,485-13,200	8,842	4,485
wc/d	10	900-18,600	5,214	1,701
APPERT, Eugène (1814-1867) French				
oil	2	2,493-2,742	2,617	2,493
APPERT, George (20th C) French				
oil	2	915-1,424	1,169	915
APPIA, Beatrice (20th C) Swiss				
oil	1	1,403	1,403	1,403
APPIA, Dominique (1926-) Swiss				
oil	1	1,046	1,046	1,046
APPIAN, Adolphe (1818-1898) French				
oil	9	1,210-5,828	2,531	2,420
APPIAN, Louis (1862-1896) French				
oil	1	1,458	1,458	1,458
APPIANI, Andrea (1754-1817) Italian				
oil	1	19,418	19,418	19,418
wc/d	4	1,600-13,368	5,554	2,071

Name	No.	Price Range	Average	Median
APPLEBEE, Leonard (1914-) British				
oil	2	630-711	670	630
3D	1	1,300	1,300	1,300
APPLEGATE, Frank (1882-1934) American				
wc/d	2	500-1,800	1,150	500
APPLEYARD, Frederick (1874-1963) British				
oil	4	588-49,140	13,865	1,211
APREA, Giuseppe (1879-?) Italian				
oil	1	1,823	1,823	1,823
APSHOVEN, Thomas van (1622-1664) Flemish				
oil	1	15,429	15,429	15,429
APSITIS, Aleksander Petrovic (1880-1944) Russian				
oil	1	6,880	6,880	6,880
AQIGAAQ, Mathew (1940-) North American				
3D	1	1,434	1,434	1,434
AQUINO, Luis (1895-1968) Argentinian				
oil	2	18,000-19,000	18,500	18,000
ARA, Krishna Hawlaji (1914-1985) Indian				
oil	3	6,160-8,500	7,386	7,500
wc/d	8	2,640-11,594	6,396	6,500
ARAD, Ron (20th C) American				
3D	1	50,000	50,000	50,000
ARAKKAL, Yusuf (1945-) Indian				
oil	1	10,000	10,000	10,000
wc/d	1	7,854	7,854	7,854
ARAMOFF, Serge (20th C) ?				
3D	1	5,000	5,000	5,000
ARANDA, J Z (19th C) Continental				
oil	1	32,500	32,500	32,500
ARANDA, Pedro de (20th C) ?				
oil	1	6,585	6,585	6,585
ARAPOFF, Alexis (1904-1948) Russian				
oil	2	3,507-12,900	8,203	3,507
ARATHOON, David (1959-) Canadian				
oil	1	1,237	1,237	1,237
ARATYM, Hubert (1926-2000) Austrian				
wc/d	2	1,520-1,520	1,520	1,520
ARAUJO Y RUANO, Joaquin (1851-1894) Spanish				
oil	1	4,800	4,800	4,800
ARBEY, Mathilde (1890-?) French				
oil	1	3,168	3,168	3,168
ARBORELIUS, Olof (1842-1915) Swedish				
oil	8	561-43,315	7,165	1,506
ARBOTONI, Bartolomeo (1594-1676) Italian				
oil	1	41,622	41,622	41,622
ARBUCKLE, George Franklin (1909-2001) Canadian				
oil	16	820-7,976	3,099	2,090
ARBUS, Andre (1903-1969) French				
wc/d	5	1,008-1,512	1,159	1,134
3D	1	5,856	5,856	5,856
ARBUS, Diane (1923-1971) American				
oil	1	13,230	13,230	13,230
ARCANGELO (1956-) Italian				
wc/d	4	549-6,062	4,222	4,580
ARCE, Marco (1968-) Mexican				
oil	1	7,000	7,000	7,000
ARCHER, James (1823-1904) British				
oil	2	4,800-51,300	28,050	4,800
ARCHIPENKO, Alexander (1887-1964) American/Russian				
oil	1	100,000	100,000	100,000
wc/d	4	6,000-123,200	35,942	7,068
3D	19	7,566-350,000	155,699	140,000
ARCHULETA, Felipe (1910-1991) American				
3D	1	4,300	4,300	4,300
ARCIDIACONO, Dario (1967-) Italian				
oil	1	1,991	1,991	1,991
ARDEN, Henri (1858-1917) Belgian				
oil	2	716-3,800	2,258	716
wc/d	1	2,860	2,860	2,860
ARDEN-QUIN, Carmelo (1913-) Uruguayan				
oil	7	1,424-15,000	5,853	4,531
wc/d	8	788-1,683	1,107	1,025

Name	No.	Price Range	Average	Median
ARDIA, Vincenzo (18th C) Italian				
3D	1	7,135	7,135	7,135
ARDISSONE, Yolande (1927-) French				
oil	21	708-4,500	2,097	1,800
wc/d	1	960	960	960
ARDIZZONE, Edward (1900-1979) British				
oil	1	4,524	4,524	4,524
wc/d	30	581-6,090	2,200	1,653
ARDON, Mordecai (1896-1992) Israeli				
oil	10	10,500-560,000	150,750	75,000
wc/d	2	4,800-6,000	5,400	4,800
ARDUINO, Nicola (1887-1974) Italian				
oil	1	1,211	1,211	1,211
ARDY, Bartolomeo (1821-1889) Italian				
oil	1	4,115	4,115	4,115
AREAL, Antonio (1934-1978) Portuguese				
wc/d	1	1,823	1,823	1,823
ARELLANO, Jose de (18th C) Spanish				
oil	1	72,245	72,245	72,245
ARELLANO, Juan de (1614-1676) Spanish				
oil	6	40,700-370,000	175,866	101,750
AREMSEN, C (20th C) ?				
oil	1	2,100	2,100	2,100
ARENDS, Karl Oskar (1863-1932) German				
oil	1	1,438	1,438	1,438
ARENDSEN, Arentina Hendrica (1836-1915) Dutch				
oil	1	7,040	7,040	7,040
ARENE, Jean (20th C) French				
oil	2	1,332-3,319	2,325	1,332
ARENTSZ, Arent (1586-1635) Dutch				
oil	1	84,081	84,081	84,081
ARENYS, Ricardo (1914-1977) Spanish				
oil	2	2,391-2,474	2,432	2,391
ARGELES, Rafael Escriche (1894-?) Spanish				
oil	1	2,288	2,288	2,288
ARGENTI, Antonio (19/20th C) Italian				
3D	1	32,040	32,040	32,040
ARGIMON, Daniel (1929-1996) Spanish				
oil	1	1,076	1,076	1,076
ARGOV, Michael (1920-) Israeli				
oil	3	500-4,000	2,333	2,500
wc/d	1	480	480	480
ARGUELLES, Julio Fernandez (1923-) Spanish				
oil	1	1,205	1,205	1,205
ARGYROS, Oumbertos (1877-1963) Greek				
oil	6	1,903-14,960	6,427	4,224
ARIAS, Francisco (1912-1977) Spanish				
oil	3	1,181-4,281	2,566	2,238
ARIAS, Jose (19th C) Spanish				
oil	1	1,707	1,707	1,707
ARIAS-MISSON, Alain (1938-) Belgian?				
3D	1	2,314	2,314	2,314
ARICO, Rodolfo (1930-2002) Italian				
oil	10	647-6,793	2,700	2,428
wc/d	5	509-3,279	1,427	1,092
ARIELI, Mordecai (1909-1993) Polish				
oil	4	380-3,400	1,332	600
ARIGLIANO, Giuseppe (1917-) Italian				
oil	1	1,776	1,776	1,776
ARIKHA, Avigdor (1929-) Israeli				
oil	5	7,000-74,000	31,500	12,000
wc/d	6	425-27,680	6,432	1,100
ARINBJARNAR, Snorri (1901-1958) Icelandic				
oil	1	3,556	3,556	3,556
ARKHIPOV, Abram (1862-1930) Russian				
oil	4	36,113-356,712	177,506	37,200
ARLE, Asmund (1918-1990) Swedish				
3D	2	2,417-2,977	2,697	2,417
ARLINGSSON, Erling (1904-1982) Swedish				
oil	3	1,184-1,711	1,461	1,488

Name	No.	Price Range	Average	Median
ARMAN, Fernandez (1928-2005) American/French				
oil	19	5,845-167,200	31,710	20,856
wc/d	25	596-165,701	19,960	8,918
3D	276	1,607-420,811	20,191	8,438
ARMAND-DELILLE, Ernest Émile (1843-1883) French				
oil	1	2,899	2,899	2,899
ARMAND-DUMARESQ, Edouard Charles (1826-1895) French				
oil	1	6,833	6,833	6,833
ARMANDO (1929-) Dutch				
oil	15	3,273-43,315	12,482	6,997
wc/d	8	942-4,909	2,484	2,104
3D	1	20,027	20,027	20,027
ARMANDO and PEETERS, Henk and SCHOONHOVEN, Jan (20th C) Dutch				
oil	1	73,782	73,782	73,782
ARMANI, Ernesto Giuliano (1898-) Italian				
wc/d	1	4,581	4,581	4,581
ARMAO, Angelo Maria (20th C) Italian				
oil	1	1,420	1,420	1,420
ARMAS, Enrico (1957-) Venezuelan				
oil	4	930-1,300	1,117	1,120
ARMENISE, Raffaello (1852-1925) Italian				
oil	2	4,043-8,919	6,481	4,043
ARMES, Thomas W (fl.1928-1933) British				
oil	1	1,384	1,384	1,384
ARMET Y PORTANEL, Jose (1843-1911) Spanish				
oil	2	1,796-8,476	5,136	1,796
ARMFIELD, Diana (1920-) British				
oil	4	1,085-3,762	1,926	1,357
wc/d	2	1,021-1,701	1,361	1,021
ARMFIELD, Edward (1817-1896) British				
oil	40	513-5,268	1,834	1,512
ARMFIELD, Edwin (19th C) British				
oil	1	1,914	1,914	1,914
ARMFIELD, G (fl.1840-1875) British				
oil	1	2,500	2,500	2,500
ARMFIELD, George (fl.1840-1875) British				
oil	35	578-7,500	2,264	1,800
ARMFIELD, Maxwell (1882-1972) British				
oil	17	1,969-30,240	7,234	5,236
wc/d	2	781-985	883	781
ARMFIELD, Stuart (1916-2000) British				
oil	2	1,131-1,204	1,167	1,131
wc/d	1	1,170	1,170	1,170
ARMINGTON, Caroline (1875-1939) American/Canadian				
oil	4	2,512-7,400	4,799	3,526
ARMINGTON, Frank Milton (1876-1941) Canadian				
oil	5	1,763-16,839	7,627	6,000
wc/d	3	742-4,123	2,144	1,567
ARMITAGE, Alfred (fl.1889-1905) British				
oil	2	696-8,188	4,442	696
ARMITAGE, H A (19/20th C) British				
oil	1	2,088	2,088	2,088
ARMITAGE, Kenneth (1916-2002) British				
wc/d	1	6,612	6,612	6,612
3D	10	26,550-115,050	55,018	49,560
ARMLEDER, John M (1948-) Swiss				
oil	3	3,000-25,479	12,537	9,133
wc/d	2	1,720-1,720	1,720	1,720
3D	1	3,250	3,250	3,250
ARMODIO (1938-) Italian				
wc/d	3	615-1,553	1,169	1,341
ARMOUR, Mary (1902-2000) British				
oil	19	1,566-10,680	5,725	5,370
wc/d	7	563-5,310	1,887	626
ARMS, John Taylor (1887-1953) American				
wc/d	2	2,200-2,200	2,200	2,200
ARMSTEAD, Henry Hugh (1828-1905) British				
3D	1	20,010	20,010	20,010
ARMSTRONG, Amos Lee (1899-?) American				
oil	1	1,000	1,000	1,000
ARMSTRONG, Arthur (1924-1996) Irish				
oil	15	1,800-14,531	5,684	4,836
wc/d	4	1,080-4,601	2,880	1,239

Name	No.	Price Range	Average	Median
ARMSTRONG, David Geoffrey (1928-) Canadian				
oil	1	1,244	1,244	1,244
ARMSTRONG, John (1893-1973) British				
oil	6	2,775-14,175	7,097	4,002
wc/d	1	3,330	3,330	3,330
ARMSTRONG, Rolf (1881-1960) American				
wc/d	1	19,000	19,000	19,000
ARMSTRONG, William (1822-1914) Canadian/Irish				
wc/d	10	725-14,986	5,108	2,645
ARNAL, François (1924-) French				
oil	7	849-3,840	2,586	2,572
ARNARSSON, Ingolfur (1956-) Icelandic				
wc/d	1	4,200	4,200	4,200
ARNASUNGAAQ, Barnabus (1924-) North American				
3D	7	1,518-12,654	3,386	1,940
ARNAUD, Marcel (1877-1956) French				
oil	2	1,767-2,919	2,343	1,767
ARND, Samuel (19th C) French?				
3D	1	13,352	13,352	13,352
ARNDT, Franz Gustav (1842-1905) German				
oil	1	7,613	7,613	7,613
ARNDT, Leo (1857-?) German				
oil	1	1,122	1,122	1,122
ARNEGGER, A (19/20th C) Austrian				
oil	2	2,121-2,213	2,167	2,121
ARNEGGER, Alois (1879-1967) Austrian				
oil	35	660-10,440	3,202	2,600
ARNEGGER, Alwin (1883-1916) Austrian				
oil	4	1,338-4,113	2,800	1,815
ARNEGGER, G (1905-) Austrian				
oil	1	3,649	3,649	3,649
ARNEL, Thomas (1922-) Danish				
oil	4	1,699-2,912	2,391	2,366
wc/d	1	1,294	1,294	1,294
ARNESEN, Vilhelm (1865-1948) Danish				
oil	28	715-17,371	3,143	1,737
ARNESON, Robert (1930-1992) American				
wc/d	3	400-6,500	3,466	3,500
ARNEZ, Helmut (20th C) Austrian?				
oil	1	12,857	12,857	12,857
ARNHEIM, Elly (1877-?) German				
oil	1	1,132	1,132	1,132
ARNING, Eddie (1898-1992) American				
oil	1	3,000	3,000	3,000
wc/d	5	2,250-3,100	2,710	2,600
ARNO, Peter (1904-1968) American				
wc/d	3	900-1,600	1,233	1,200
ARNOLD, Carl Johann (1829-1916) German				
oil	1	1,985	1,985	1,985
ARNOLD, Graham (1932-) British				
oil	1	1,593	1,593	1,593
ARNOLD, Josef (elder) (1788-1879) Austrian				
oil	2	1,757-1,937	1,847	1,757
ARNOLD, Karl (1883-1953) German				
oil	1	1,411	1,411	1,411
ARNOLDI, Charles (1946-) American				
oil	3	15,000-19,000	16,666	16,000
wc/d	1	3,750	3,750	3,750
ARNOLDI, Per (1941-) Danish				
oil	2	727-3,071	1,899	727
ARNOTT, James George McLellan (fl.1880-1902) British				
wc/d	1	1,100	1,100	1,100
ARNOULD, Reynold (1919-1980) French				
oil	6	531-4,613	1,640	934
ARNTZENIUS, Alida Margaretha Maria (1872-1954) Dutch				
oil	1	2,121	2,121	2,121
ARNTZENIUS, Elise Claudine (1902-1982) Dutch				
oil	1	1,767	1,767	1,767
wc/d	1	2,827	2,827	2,827
ARNTZENIUS, Floris (1864-1925) Dutch				
oil	9	2,090-80,347	25,240	13,155
wc/d	5	3,534-159,792	55,394	43,021

Name	No.	Price Range	Average	Median
ARNTZENIUS, Paul (1883-1965) Dutch				
oil	4	648-1,885	1,384	1,119
ARNUL, George (19th C) British				
oil	1	3,843	3,843	3,843
ARNZ, Albert (1832-1914) German				
oil	2	1,229-2,548	1,888	1,229
AROCH, Arieh (1908-1974) Russian				
oil	3	3,600-220,000	77,533	9,000
ARONSON, Boris (1900-1980) American/Russian				
oil	1	12,040	12,040	12,040
ARONSON, David (1923-) American				
oil	2	2,250-2,900	2,575	2,250
wc/d	1	2,000	2,000	2,000
3D	1	2,200	2,200	2,200
ARONSON, Naoum (1872-1943) Russian				
3D	4	6,230-32,000	18,432	9,500
ARONSON-LILJEGRAL, Martin (1869-?) Danish				
oil	1	1,511	1,511	1,511
AROSENIUS, Ivar (1878-1909) Swedish				
oil	2	23,681-99,710	61,695	23,681
wc/d	27	694-10,220	2,697	2,243
ARP, Carl (1867-1913) German				
oil	3	800-1,758	1,186	1,001
ARP, Jean (1887-1966) French				
oil	2	25,890-885,000	455,445	25,890
wc/d	17	2,182-111,920	15,881	9,000
3D	24	2,309-1,300,000	141,471	41,234
ARPA Y PEREA, Jose (1860-1952) Spanish				
oil	1	10,000	10,000	10,000
ARPA, J (1937-) Spanish?				
oil	1	1,885	1,885	1,885
ARPINO, Carlo (1866-1922) Italian				
oil	1	1,274	1,274	1,274
ARRANZ BRAVO, Eduard (1941-) Spanish				
oil	4	7,135-28,541	18,432	14,270
ARREDONDO Y CALMACHE, Ricardo (1850-1911) Spanish				
oil	5	10,541-38,733	19,812	15,226
wc/d	1	1,920	1,920	1,920
ARREGUI, Romana (1875-1932) French				
oil	2	836-1,944	1,390	836
ARRIETA, Jose Agustin (1802-1879) Mexican				
oil	2	70,000-70,000	70,000	70,000
ARROWSMITH, Sue (1968-) British				
oil	1	605	605	605
wc/d	1	605	605	605
ARROYO, Edouard (1937-) Spanish				
oil	10	6,997-28,603	16,786	15,840
wc/d	14	1,635-15,653	5,484	2,337
3D	4	1,549-3,576	2,506	1,784
ARRUE Y VALLE, Jose (1885-1977) Spanish				
wc/d	2	1,178-6,027	3,602	1,178
ARRUE, Ramiro (1892-1971) Spanish				
oil	3	972-10,082	4,163	1,435
wc/d	3	654-31,630	17,062	18,904
ARSENIUS, John (1818-1903) Swedish				
oil	7	871-5,733	2,327	1,441
wc/d	1	549	549	549
ARSENIUS, Karl Georg (1855-1908) Swedish				
oil	3	632-4,258	2,234	1,814
ART, Berthe (1857-1934) Belgian				
wc/d	6	501-2,754	1,429	983
ART-LANGUAGE (fl.1968) British				
oil	5	3,024-65,740	15,822	3,363
ARTAN, Louis (1837-1890) Belgian				
oil	13	486-11,747	3,818	3,185
wc/d	2	701-1,252	976	701
ARTENS, Peter von (1937-) Colombian				
oil	2	12,000-15,000	13,500	12,000
ARTER, Charles John (1860-1923) American				
oil	1	5,960	5,960	5,960
ARTER, Paul Julius (1797-1836) Swiss				
oil	1	1,446	1,446	1,446

Name	No.	Price Range	Average	Median
ARTETA Y ERRASTI, Felix (1890-1986) Spanish				
wc/d	2	1,196-1,686	1,441	1,196
ARTHURS, Stanley Massey (1877-1950) American				
oil	1	27,000	27,000	27,000
ARTSCHWAGER, Richard (1923-) American				
oil	6	22,000-750,000	247,413	130,000
wc/d	2	4,500-7,500	6,000	4,500
3D	6	4,000-35,000	19,553	13,000
ARTUS, Charles (1897-1978) French				
3D	1	10,524	10,524	10,524
ARTZ, Constant (1870-1951) Dutch				
oil	17	900-5,633	3,162	3,279
wc/d	1	3,287	3,287	3,287
ARTZ, David Adolf Constant (1837-1890) Dutch				
oil	7	2,503-22,125	6,046	3,330
wc/d	2	717-1,402	1,059	717
ASAM, Cosmas Damian (1686-1739) German				
oil	1	20,566	20,566	20,566
ASARTA, I (19th C) Spanish				
oil	1	2,634	2,634	2,634
ASCAIN, Robert (1932) French?				
oil	1	1,815	1,815	1,815
ASCH, Pieter Jansz van (1603-1678) Dutch				
oil	1	17,671	17,671	17,671
ASCHENBRENNER, Lennart (1943-) Swedish				
oil	2	662-15,268	7,965	662
ASCHER, Mary Goldman (1900-1988) American/British				
wc/d	1	1,000	1,000	1,000
ASDRUBALI, Gianni (1955-) Italian				
oil	5	760-3,236	2,210	2,330
wc/d	1	1,211	1,211	1,211
ASHBAUGH, Dennis (1946-) American				
oil	1	3,000	3,000	3,000
ASHBY, Steve (1904-1980) American				
oil	1	3,100	3,100	3,100
3D	4	2,500-5,500	4,325	4,200
ASHEVAK, Karoo (1940-1974) North American				
3D	4	2,868-14,341	10,346	11,521
ASHEVAK, Kenojuak (1927-) North American				
3D	3	1,687-2,531	2,193	2,362
ASHFORD, William (1746-1824) British				
oil	2	48,360-280,000	164,180	48,360
wc/d	1	900	900	900
ASHOONA, Kiawak (1933-) North American				
3D	1	3,374	3,374	3,374
ASHTON, Federico (1840-1904) Italian				
oil	2	2,182-5,342	3,762	2,182
wc/d	1	1,068	1,068	1,068
ASINS RODRIGUEZ, Elena (1940-) Spanish				
wc/d	3	1,437-3,592	2,463	2,362
ASIS, Antonio (1932-) Argentinian				
oil	2	3,012-5,648	4,330	3,012
3D	1	4,944	4,944	4,944
ASKENAZY, Maurice (1888-1961) American				
oil	3	900-20,000	10,633	11,000
ASKER, Curt (1930-) Swedish				
oil	2	1,272-1,454	1,363	1,272
3D	1	1,718	1,718	1,718
ASKEVOLD, Anders Monsen (1834-1900) Norwegian				
oil	7	4,060-12,880	7,516	7,755
ASLAN (20th C) French?				
3D	1	4,671	4,671	4,671
ASLUND, Acke (1881-1958) Swedish				
oil	5	1,057-16,562	8,098	6,594
wc/d	2	699-1,496	1,097	699
ASLUND, Kjell (1948-) Swedish				
wc/d	1	1,441	1,441	1,441
ASOMA, Tudashi (20th C) Japanese				
oil	1	3,500	3,500	3,500
ASPETTATI, Antonio Mario (1880-1949) Italian				
oil	3	757-15,000	7,590	7,014

Name	No.	Price Range	Average	Median
ASPEVIG, Clyde (1951-) American				
oil	7	5,000-45,000	27,857	34,000
ASPINALL, Sarah (1965-) British				
oil	1	1,512	1,512	1,512
ASPINWALL, Reginald (1858-1921) British				
oil	2	661-666	663	661
wc/d	2	487-865	676	487
ASSCHE, Henri van (1774-1841) Belgian				
oil	4	1,502-15,480	5,170	1,636
ASSCHE, Petrus van (1897-1974) Belgian				
oil	1	1,152	1,152	1,152
ASSELBERGS, Alphonse (1839-1916) Belgian				
oil	2	1,352-4,816	3,084	1,352
ASSELBERGS, Gustave (1938-1967) Dutch				
oil	1	9,425	9,425	9,425
wc/d	1	1,219	1,219	1,219
ASSELBERGS, Jan (1937-) Dutch				
oil	1	2,201	2,201	2,201
wc/d	2	626-1,627	1,126	626
ASSELIN, Maurice (1882-1947) French				
oil	2	3,716-3,766	3,741	3,716
ASSELYN, Jan (1610-1652) Dutch				
wc/d	2	2,102-17,517	9,809	2,102
ASSEMAT, Pierre (c.1945-) French				
oil	1	2,919	2,919	2,919
ASSIG, Martin (1959-) German				
oil	1	6,997	6,997	6,997
ASSTEYN, Bartholomeus (1607-?) Dutch				
oil	1	23,920	23,920	23,920
AST, Balthasar van der (1590-1656) Dutch				
oil	3	38,571-380,600	174,523	104,400
ASTERIADIS, Agenor (1898-1977) Greek				
oil	2	4,400-26,180	15,290	4,400
wc/d	3	2,805-5,280	3,941	3,740
ASTI, Angelo (1847-1903) French				
oil	2	979-2,200	1,589	979
ASTLES, Samuel (fl.1820-1850) British				
oil	1	10,726	10,726	10,726
ASTLEY, John (1730-1787) British				
oil	1	5,504	5,504	5,504
ASTOIN, Marie (1924-) French				
oil	3	2,297 4,338	3,448	3,709
ASTORE, Salvatore (1957-) Italian				
oil	1	2,356	2,356	2,356
3D	1	4,633	4,633	4,633
ASTORRI, Enrico (1859-1921) Italian				
3D	2	7,135-16,065	11,600	7,135
ASTROM, Werner (1885-1979) Finnish				
oil	1	2,057	2,057	2,057
ASTUDIN, Nicolai (1848-1925) German				
oil	7	1,374-5,721	2,714	2,662
ASVERI, Gianfranco (1948-) Italian				
wc/d	2	1,885-2,028	1,956	1,885
ATALAYA, Enrique (1851-1914) Spanish				
oil	2	3,600-8,500	6,050	3,600
ATAMIAN, Charles Garabed (1872-1947) Turkish				
oil	3	4,795-29,410	13,082	5,041
ATAR, Chaim (1902-1953) Israeli				
oil	1	1,600	1,600	1,600
ATCHEALAK, Davie (1947-) North American				
3D	1	7,171	7,171	7,171
ATCHISON, Joseph A (1895-1967) American				
3D	1	2,250	2,250	2,250
ATCHUGARRY, Pablo (1954-) Uruguayan				
3D	4	50,000-133,200	84,420	70,000
ATHERTON, Hope (1964-) American				
wc/d	1	5,500	5,500	5,500
ATHERTON, John (1900-1952) American				
oil	1	3,000	3,000	3,000
wc/d	1	435	435	435

Name	No.	Price Range	Average	Median
ATILA (1931-1987) French				
oil	11	433-1,518	1,110	1,168
wc/d	3	526-607	564	561
ATILA, Ede Kardy (1931-1987) French				
oil	1	1,204	1,204	1,204
wc/d	1	818	818	818
ATKINS, Samuel (fl.1787-1808) British				
wc/d	5	935-6,650	2,952	1,958
ATKINSON, George Mounsey Wheatley (1806-1884) British				
oil	2	72,000-74,400	73,200	72,000
ATKINSON, John (1863-1924) British				
oil	6	845-6,290	2,202	925
wc/d	17	752-6,300	2,128	1,432
ATKINSON, Terry (1939-) British				
oil	1	1,449	1,449	1,449
wc/d	1	1,213	1,213	1,213
ATKINSON, Thomas Witlam (1799-1861) British				
wc/d	1	17,200	17,200	17,200
ATKINSON, William Edwin (1862-1926) Canadian				
oil	2	620-978	799	620
wc/d	1	970	970	970
ATLAN, Jean (1913-1960) French				
oil	12	13,109-157,123	63,722	46,758
wc/d	11	5,739-22,125	10,978	9,352
ATTARDI, Massimo (1961-) Italian				
oil	2	1,219-1,424	1,321	1,219
ATTARDI, Thomas (1900-) American				
oil	1	6,500	6,500	6,500
ATTARDI, Ugo (1923-) Italian				
oil	6	4,350-12,945	9,225	9,425
wc/d	6	526-2,625	1,525	1,020
ATTERSEE, Christian Ludwig (1940-) Austrian				
oil	8	1,893-42,411	14,850	13,352
wc/d	5	588-3,045	1,692	1,293
ATTWELL, Mabel Lucie (1879-1964) British				
wc/d	4	2,035-4,810	3,098	2,405
ATWOOD, Thomas (18th C) British				
oil	1	6,545	6,545	6,545
AUBARET, Louis Gabriel Galderec (1825-1894) French				
wc/d	1	2,046	2,046	2,046
AUBE, Paul (1837-1916) French				
3D	1	3,250	3,250	3,250
AUBERJONOIS, René (1872-1957) Swiss				
oil	7	2,434-43,912	16,017	5,097
wc/d	7	458-2,061	1,112	984
AUBERLEN, Wilhelm (1860-?) German				
wc/d	1	468	468	468
3D	1	2,057	2,057	2,057
AUBERT, Jean Ernest (1824-1906) French				
wc/d	1	1,649	1,649	1,649
AUBERT, Louis (fl.1740-1780) French				
wc/d	2	5,724-11,545	8,634	5,724
AUBERTIN, Bernard (1934-) French				
oil	3	3,579-5,160	4,160	3,741
wc/d	10	951-3,708	1,762	1,272
AUBIN, Paul (19/20th C) French				
oil	1	14,400	14,400	14,400
AUBLET, Albert (1851-1938) French				
oil	2	3,045-113,100	58,072	3,045
AUBLET, Felix (1903-1978) French				
oil	1	1,437	1,437	1,437
wc/d	1	547	547	547
AUBRIET, Claude (c.1665-1742) French				
wc/d	1	9,370	9,370	9,370
AUBROECK, Karel (1894-1986) Belgian				
3D	1	2,637	2,637	2,637
AUBRY, Émile (1880-1964) French				
oil	2	480-4,795	2,637	480
AUBRY, Rene Marcel (20th C) French				
oil	2	546-2,217	1,381	546
AUBURTIN, Jean François (1866-1930) French				
wc/d	2	4,091-4,793	4,442	4,091

Name	No.	Price Range	Average	Median
AUDIBERT, Louis (1881-?) French				
oil	3	484-1,640	1,108	1,200
AUDIFFRED, Edouard (1818-1861) French				
oil	1	7,007	7,007	7,007
AUDRAT, Didier (20th C) French				
3D	1	3,503	3,503	3,503
AUDUBON, John James (1785-1851) American/French				
wc/d	1	70,000	70,000	70,000
AUDY, Jonny (19th C) French				
wc/d	8	513-1,693	1,058	716
AUERBACH, Arnold (1898-1978) British				
oil	2	696-5,610	3,153	696
wc/d	1	6,230	6,230	6,230
AUERBACH, Frank (1931-) British/German				
oil	16	73,920-740,000	384,779	334,400
wc/d	20	2,301-37,840	10,598	8,000
AUERBACH, Johann Gottfried (1697-1753) German				
oil	1	8,000	8,000	8,000
AUERBACH-LEVY, William (1889-1964) American				
oil	1	1,600	1,600	1,600
AUERSWALD, Heinz (1891-1974) German				
oil	1	1,455	1,455	1,455
AUFDENBLATTEN, Emil (1910-1958) Swiss				
oil	1	1,984	1,984	1,984
AUFFRAY, Alexandre (1869-1942) French				
oil	1	4,359	4,359	4,359
AUFRAY, Joseph (1836-?) French				
oil	1	2,500	2,500	2,500
AUGUIN, Louis Auguste (1824-1904) French				
oil	1	2,646	2,646	2,646
AUGUSTE, Henri (1759-1816) French				
wc/d	2	1,823-3,889	2,856	1,823
AUGUSTIN, Edgar (1936-1996) German				
wc/d	2	1,052-1,553	1,302	1,052
3D	2	1,800-4,676	3,238	1,800
AUGUSTIN, Ludwig (1882-1960) Austrian?				
oil	1	1,000	1,000	1,000
AUGUSTINCIC, Antun (1908-) Croatian?				
3D	1	4,437	4,437	4,437
AUGUSTINER, Werner (1922-1986) Austrian				
oil	1	1,553	1,553	1,553
wc/d	1	647	647	647
AUGUSTSON, Goran (1936-) Finnish				
oil	2	779-5,914	3,346	779
wc/d	1	1,671	1,671	1,671
AUJAME, Jean (1905-1965) French				
oil	1	951	951	951
wc/d	1	536	536	536
AULESTIA, Oswald (1946-) Spanish				
wc/d	1	2,577	2,577	2,577
AULIE, Reidar (1904-1977) Norwegian				
oil	1	1,272	1,272	1,272
AULT, George C (1891-1948) American				
oil	2	3,250-55,000	29,125	3,250
wc/d	1	1,100	1,100	1,100
AUMER, Franz (1896-1983) German				
oil	1	1,091	1,091	1,091
AUMONIER, James (1832-1911) British				
oil	8	450-3,330	1,622	941
wc/d	1	696	696	696
AUMONT, Louis (1805-1879) Danish				
oil	2	652-1,897	1,274	652
AURELI, Ramielo (1885-1975) Italian				
oil	1	1,288	1,288	1,288
AURIOL, Charles Joseph (1778-1834) Swiss				
oil	1	9,514	9,514	9,514
AURISICCHIO, Vincenzo (19th C) Italian				
3D	1	1,890	1,890	1,890
AUSLEGER, Rudolf (1897-1974) German				
oil	1	4,607	4,607	4,607
wc/d	1	946	946	946

Name	No.	Price Range	Average	Median
AUSTIN, Samuel (1796-1834) British				
wc/d	4	534-2,088	1,012	626
AUSTRIAN, Ben (1870-1921) American				
oil	14	1,600-36,000	13,400	12,000
AUTERE, Hannes (1888-1967) Finnish				
3D	1	1,757	1,757	1,757
AUTHOUART, Daniel (1943-) French				
oil	1	5,845	5,845	5,845
wc/d	3	803-1,462	1,222	1,403
AUTORINO, Anthony (1937-) American				
oil	1	2,250	2,250	2,250
AUZOU, Pauline (1775-1835) French				
oil	1	1,740	1,740	1,740
wc/d	1	535	535	535
AVAF (1968-) Brazilian				
3D	1	38,000	38,000	38,000
AVANZI, Vittorio (1850-1910) Italian				
oil	2	2,288-4,142	3,215	2,288
AVEDISIAN, Edward (1936-) American				
oil	3	700-1,900	1,200	1,000
AVENALI, Marcello (1912-1981) Italian				
oil	1	1,178	1,178	1,178
wc/d	3	934-2,071	1,320	957
AVENDANO, Serafin de (1838-1916) Spanish				
oil	3	1,920-24,170	10,703	6,019
wc/d	4	572-1,654	1,131	727
AVERY, Charles (20th C) British				
wc/d	1	8,500	8,500	8,500
AVERY, March (20th C) American				
oil	1	3,750	3,750	3,750
wc/d	1	700	700	700
AVERY, Milton (1885-1965) American				
oil	13	3,000-420,000	131,115	75,000
wc/d	12	1,900-240,000	51,325	26,000
AVERY, Sally Michel (1905-2003) American				
oil	2	3,500-5,000	4,250	3,500
AVILOV, Mikhual Ivanovitch (1882-1954) Russian				
oil	1	22,932	22,932	22,932
AVISSAR, Simon (1938-) Israeli				
oil	1	2,000	2,000	2,000
AVNER, Herve (1954-) French?				
wc/d	2	897-4,208	2,552	897
AVNI, Aaron (1906-1951) Israeli				
oil	2	1,100-3,000	2,050	1,100
AVONT, Pieter van and BRUEGHEL, Jan (younger) (17th C) Flemish				
oil	1	33,714	33,714	33,714
AVRAMIDIS, Joannis (1922-) Austrian				
oil	2	1,757-2,035	1,896	1,757
3D	5	2,104-93,699	49,653	55,834
AVRIL, Armand (20th C) French				
wc/d	1	1,097	1,097	1,097
AVY, Joseph (1871-?) French				
oil	1	1,784	1,784	1,784
AVY, M (19th C) ?				
oil	1	2,450	2,450	2,450
AXELL, Evelyne (1936-1972) Belgian				
oil	1	14,317	14,317	14,317
AYALA Y GALAN (20th C) Spanish				
oil	1	1,014	1,014	1,014
AYCOCK, Alice (1946-) American				
3D	1	1,900	1,900	1,900
AYERS, James (?) American?				
oil	3	2,500-4,600	3,533	3,500
AYLING, George (1887-1960) British				
oil	3	558-3,009	1,819	1,890
wc/d	2	920-1,232	1,076	920
AYLWARD, James de Vine (fl.1895-1917) British				
oil	3	1,869-2,941	2,256	1,958
AYME, Alix (1894-1989) French				
oil	1	1,984	1,984	1,984
wc/d	2	1,116-1,364	1,240	1,116

Name	No.	Price Range	Average	Median
AYOTTE, Leo (1909-1976) Canadian				
oil	2	1,386-2,038	1,712	1,386
AYRES, Gillian (1930-) British				
oil	8	6,475-32,220	13,540	11,000
wc/d	3	531-13,494	5,530	2,565
AYRTON, Michael (1921-1975) British				
oil	12	2,958-20,760	8,658	5,568
wc/d	14	534-12,580	3,070	1,246
3D	14	3,500-87,000	17,487	7,280
AYZANOA, Raul (20th C) Venezuelan				
oil	1	1,860	1,860	1,860
AZEMA, Ernest (20th C) French				
oil	2	1,656-4,370	3,013	1,656
AZEMA, Jacques (20th C) French?				
oil	1	18,551	18,551	18,551
wc/d	2	654-2,735	1,694	654
AZENE, Aryeh (1934-) Israeli				
oil	4	360-1,100	630	460
wc/d	1	405	405	405
AZPIROZ, Manuel de (1903-1953) Spanish				
oil	2	865-3,708	2,286	865
AZUMA, Kengiro (1926-) Japanese				
3D	1	2,163	2,163	2,163
AZZINARI, Franco (1949-) Italian				
oil	2	1,665-2,581	2,123	1,665
wc/d	1	610	610	610
BAADSGAARD, Alfrida (1839-1912) Danish				
oil	2	498-1,911	1,204	498
BAAGOE, Carl (1829-1902) Danish				
oil	2	2,134-16,599	9,366	2,134
BAANG, Johan August (1831-1912) Swedish				
oil	1	2,243	2,243	2,243
BAAR, Hugo (1873-1912) German?				
wc/d	1	4,576	4,576	4,576
BABA, Mirza (18/19th C) Persian				
wc/d	1	4,498	4,498	4,498
BABADIN, V (19/20th C) Russian				
oil	1	5,160	5,160	5,160
BABBERGER, Auguste (1885-1936) German				
wc/d	3	734-1,632	1,060	816
BABBERGER-TOBLER, Anna (1882-1935) Swiss				
wc/d	1	1,346	1,346	1,346
BAROULENE, Eugène (1905-1994) French				
oil	8	1,756-7,200	4,623	4,393
wc/d	1	2,700	2,700	2,700
BACARISAS, Gustavo (19/20th C) Spanish				
oil	1	1,210	1,210	1,210
wc/d	3	963-1,176	1,034	963
BACCARINI, Domenico (1882-1907) Italian				
oil	2	11,297-14,270	12,783	11,297
wc/d	2	595-892	743	595
BACCARINI, Lino (1893-1973) Italian				
oil	1	1,054	1,054	1,054
BACCI, Baccio Maria (1888-1974) Italian				
oil	3	3,185-21,626	9,486	3,648
BACCI, Edmondo (1913-) Italian				
wc/d	2	11,314-13,500	12,407	11,314
BACCI-VENUTI, Gualtiero de (19th C) Italian				
oil	1	2,500	2,500	2,500
BACH, Alois (1809-1893) German				
oil	2	1,272-1,432	1,352	1,272
BACH, Elvira (1951-) German				
oil	7	1,018-15,811	5,802	2,571
wc/d	4	585-2,675	1,468	729
BACH, Guido (1828-1905) German				
wc/d	2	1,305-7,392	4,348	1,305
BACH, Pierre (20th C) French				
oil	2	2,722-2,782	2,752	2,722
BACH, Robert (1859-?) Russian				
3D	1	6,500	6,500	6,500

Name	No.	Price Range	Average	Median
BACHE, Otto (1839-1927) Danish				
oil	16	485-15,000	3,642	1,690
wc/d	1	630	630	630
BACHER, Otto Henry (1856-1909) American				
oil	1	75,000	75,000	75,000
BACHMANN, Alfred (1863-1954) German				
oil	1	6,676	6,676	6,676
wc/d	2	1,212-1,435	1,323	1,212
BACHMANN, Hans (1852-1917) Swiss				
oil	5	1,010-3,729	2,038	1,619
BACHMANN, Karl (1874-1924) Hungarian				
oil	1	1,400	1,400	1,400
BACHMANN, Otto (1915-1996) Swiss				
oil	5	530-2,588	1,021	650
wc/d	1	419	419	419
BACHRACH-BAREE, Emmanuel (1863-1943) Austrian				
oil	1	1,100	1,100	1,100
BACHRACH-BAREE, Helmuth (1898-1964) German				
oil	2	1,217-1,255	1,236	1,217
BACHUR, Anthony (20th C) French				
oil	2	592-1,551	1,071	592
BACK, Admiral Sir George (1796-1878) British				
wc/d	1	5,292	5,292	5,292
BACKER, Adriaen (1635-1684) Dutch				
oil	1	72,660	72,660	72,660
BACKER, Jacob Adriaensz (1608-1651) Dutch				
oil	1	16,562	16,562	16,562
BACKER, Jacob de (1560-c.1590) Flemish				
oil	1	29,223	29,223	29,223
BACKLUND-CELSING, Elsa (1880-1974) Scandinavian				
oil	1	10,829	10,829	10,829
BACKMANN, Alfred (1863-1956) ?				
oil	2	2,299-2,541	2,420	2,299
BACKMANSSON, Hugo (1860-1953) Finnish				
oil	6	527-3,986	1,439	666
wc/d	5	851-5,377	2,019	1,169
BACKSTROM, Barbro (1939-1990) Swedish				
wc/d	1	1,189	1,189	1,189
3D	5	2,048-101,752	47,126	62,108
BACKUS, Albert (1906-1996) American				
oil	5	16,000-55,000	28,200	22,000
BACON, Charles Roswell (1868-1913) American				
oil	2	900-1,157	1,028	900
BACON, Francis (1909-1992) British				
oil	7	2,100,000-9,000,000	6,032,857	6,290,000
wc/d	2	1,850-647,500	324,675	1,850
BACON, John Henry Frederick (1868-1914) British				
oil	1	2,832	2,832	2,832
BACON, Peggy (1895-1987) American				
oil	3	1,200-1,800	1,500	1,500
wc/d	3	500-1,400	933	900
BACON, Randy (20th C) American				
oil	2	1,900-2,250	2,075	1,900
BADEL, Jules-Louis (1840-1869) Swiss				
oil	1	1,540	1,540	1,540
BADEN, Hans Jurriaens van (1604-1663) Dutch				
oil	6	1,500-14,013	7,464	4,214
BADGER, Samuel Finley Morse (1873-1919) American				
oil	4	8,500-16,000	12,125	9,000
BADI, Aquiles (1894-1976) Argentinian				
oil	11	1,800-13,000	5,191	4,050
BADII, Libero (1916-2001) Argentinian				
oil	1	1,200	1,200	1,200
3D	4	18,000-35,000	29,750	32,000
BADIN, Jules (19/20th C) French				
oil	2	11,400-14,720	13,060	11,400
BADIOLA, Txomin (1957-) Spanish				
3D	1	33,714	33,714	33,714
BADJOV, Stefan (1881-1953) Croatian				
oil	1	2,431	2,431	2,431
BADMIN, Stanley Roy (1906-1989) British				
wc/d	2	1,710-7,182	4,446	1,710

Name	No.	Price Range	Average	Median
BADODI, Arnaldo (1913-1942) Italian				
oil	1	6,473	6,473	6,473
BADOS, Angel (1945-) Spanish				
3D	1	8,159	8,159	8,159
BADUR, Frank (1944-) German				
oil	3	777-2,121	1,326	1,081
wc/d	1	7,658	7,658	7,658
BADURA, Ben and VANKA, Maximilian (20th C) Croatian/American				
oil	1	12,000	12,000	12,000
BAECHLER, Donald (1956-) American				
oil	13	6,640-52,800	22,461	17,700
wc/d	17	1,232-42,550	9,106	4,841
BAEDER, John (1938-) American				
oil	2	8,500-45,000	26,750	8,500
wc/d	1	17,000	17,000	17,000
BAEHR, Johann Karl (1801-1869) German				
oil	1	7,825	7,825	7,825
BAEN, Jan de (1633-1702) Dutch				
oil	1	3,200	3,200	3,200
BAER, Fritz (1850-1919) German				
oil	3	884-1,883	1,245	969
BAER, Martin (1894-1961) American				
oil	2	400-3,000	1,700	400
BAERT, Henri (19th C) Belgian				
oil	1	1,219	1,219	1,219
BAERTLING, Olle (1911-1981) Swedish				
oil	7	3,171-33,081	17,198	15,857
3D	1	16,518	16,518	16,518
BAERTSOEN, Albert (1866-1922) Belgian				
oil	1	1,084	1,084	1,084
BAERVOETS, C (19th C) ?				
wc/d	1	2,784	2,784	2,784
BAERWIND, Rudi (1910-1982) German				
oil	1	1,646	1,646	1,646
wc/d	1	505	505	505
BAES, E (?) Belgian				
oil	1	1,169	1,169	1,169
BAES, Émile (1879-1954) Belgian				
oil	10	590-3,277	1,487	1,197
wc/d	1	1,929	1,929	1,929
BAES, Firmin (1874-1945) Belgian				
oil	2	963-4,241	2,602	963
wc/d	17	630-3,884	1,867	1,767
BAES, Firmin and Henri (20th C) Belgian				
oil	1	3,131	3,131	3,131
BAES, Rachel (1912-1983) Belgian				
oil	7	636-5,780	2,090	1,794
BAETS, Marc (18th C) Flemish				
oil	2	2,500-11,678	7,089	2,500
BAEZA, Manuel (1915-1986) Spanish				
oil	2	2,534-4,017	3,275	2,534
BAGER, Johann Daniel (1734-1815) German				
oil	1	2,109	2,109	2,109
BAGG, Henry Howard (1852-1928) American				
oil	1	1,000	1,000	1,000
BAGGE, Dorothy (19/20th C) Australian?				
oil	1	1,216	1,216	1,216
BAGGE, Eva (1871-1964) Swedish				
oil	8	453-10,192	3,292	1,236
wc/d	2	403-777	590	403
BAGSHAWE, Joseph Richard (1870-1909) British				
oil	2	4,283-7,182	5,732	4,283
wc/d	6	1,062-5,133	2,448	2,124
BAHIEU, Jules G (19th C) Belgian				
oil	4	1,286-4,891	2,391	1,664
BAI YILUO (1968-) Chinese				
3D	1	10,000	10,000	10,000
BAIER, Jean (1932-) ?				
oil	5	794-5,675	3,488	4,918
BAIERL, Theodor (1881-1932) German				
oil	3	935-16,949	6,350	1,166
wc/d	2	2,104-5,856	3,980	2,104

Name	No.	Price Range	Average	Median
BAIKAS, Rafael (1956-) Greek				
oil	1	1,870	1,870	1,870
BAIL, Franck Antoine (1858-1924) French				
oil	1	5,394	5,394	5,394
BAIL, Joseph (1862-1921) French				
oil	9	1,223-66,840	20,414	20,880
BAILEY, Frederick Victor (20th C) British				
oil	4	630-7,000	2,355	748
BAILEY, G (19th C) ?				
oil	1	11,440	11,440	11,440
BAILEY, La Force (1893-1962) American				
wc/d	2	900-2,100	1,500	900
BAILEY, William (1930-) American				
oil	1	1,200	1,200	1,200
wc/d	1	9,000	9,000	9,000
BAILLIE, William (1905-?) British				
oil	1	1,288	1,288	1,288
BAILLY, Alice (1872-1938) Swiss				
oil	10	916-236,579	59,266	15,500
wc/d	2	4,377-40,789	22,583	4,377
BAIN, Donald (1904-1979) British				
oil	4	655-3,938	1,975	1,251
BAINBRIGGE, Philip James (1817-1881) British				
wc/d	1	9,000	9,000	9,000
BAINES, Thomas (1820-1875) British				
wc/d	1	2,232	2,232	2,232
BAIRD, Edward McEwan (1904-1949) British				
wc/d	1	3,717	3,717	3,717
BAIRD, Nathaniel Hughes (1865-c.1930) British				
oil	3	1,098-3,009	1,793	1,274
wc/d	1	657	657	657
BAIRD, W H (?) ?				
oil	1	4,248	4,248	4,248
BAIRD, William Baptiste (1847-1917) American				
oil	5	2,268-5,500	3,387	2,775
BAITLER, Zoma (1908-1994) Uruguayan				
oil	9	600-4,000	1,664	1,200
BAIZE, Wayne (1943-) American				
oil	1	12,500	12,500	12,500
wc/d	1	2,000	2,000	2,000
BAJ, Enrico (1924-2003) Italian				
oil	18	2,028-94,136	28,955	26,639
wc/d	31	608-84,960	13,835	4,451
3D	12	2,036-22,384	9,402	6,540
BAJ, Enrico and Andrea (20th C) Italian				
3D	1	2,577	2,577	2,577
BAJ, Enrico and KOSTABI, Mark (20th C) Italian/American				
wc/d	2	1,312-1,929	1,620	1,312
BAK, Samuel (1933-) Israeli				
oil	14	800-20,000	6,754	6,000
wc/d	8	600-2,571	1,131	800
BAKALEINIKOW, G (20th C) Russian				
oil	1	12,370	12,370	12,370
BAKALOWICZ, Ladislaus (1833-1904) Polish				
oil	7	1,750-22,080	7,947	3,116
BAKALOWICZ, Stephan Wladislawowitsch (1857-1947) Russian				
oil	2	1,800-102,300	52,050	1,800
wc/d	1	1,576	1,576	1,576
BAKELS, Reinier Sybrand (1873-1956) Dutch				
oil	2	1,688-3,687	2,687	1,688
BAKER OF LEAMINGTON, T (1809-1869) British				
oil	1	7,480	7,480	7,480
BAKER OF LEAMINGTON, Thomas (1809-1869) British				
oil	17	519-11,776	4,360	3,828
wc/d	9	440-1,653	994	1,009
BAKER, Arthur (19th C) British				
oil	1	2,500	2,500	2,500
BAKER, C N (?) American?				
oil	1	1,300	1,300	1,300
BAKER, Cyril Rigby (1895-1966) American				
oil	1	1,200	1,200	1,200

Name	No.	Price Range	Average	Median
BAKER, Elisha Taylor (1827-1890) American				
oil	6	1,072-25,000	11,470	8,000
BAKER, Ernest Hamlin (1889-1975) American				
wc/d	2	1,100-2,000	1,550	1,100
BAKER, George Herbert (1878-1943) American				
oil	2	1,100-1,200	1,150	1,100
BAKER, George O (1882-?) American				
oil	1	8,500	8,500	8,500
BAKER, Jennett Miller (1877-?) American				
oil	5	500-1,900	1,240	1,500
BAKER, Roger (1928-) American				
oil	1	3,250	3,250	3,250
BAKER, Samuel Henry (1824-1909) British				
oil	2	957-3,500	2,228	957
BAKHUYZEN, Alexandre H (1826-1878) Dutch				
oil	4	1,089-1,694	1,423	1,447
BAKHUYZEN, Gerardina Jacoba van de Sande (1826-1895) Dutch				
oil	2	32,139-117,431	74,785	32,139
BAKHUYZEN, Hendrick van de Sande (1795-1860) Dutch				
oil	2	6,429-20,331	13,380	6,429
BAKHUYZEN, Julius Jacobus van de Sande (1835-1925) Dutch				
oil	7	647-9,568	3,575	3,096
wc/d	1	3,956	3,956	3,956
BAKHUYZEN, Ludolf (1631-1708) Dutch				
oil	5	2,944-316,781	125,418	18,685
wc/d	1	3,737	3,737	3,737
BAKKER-KORFF, Alexander Hugo (1824-1882) Dutch				
oil	1	3,781	3,781	3,781
BAKOS, Jozef G (1891-1977) American				
oil	1	15,500	15,500	15,500
wc/d	1	3,250	3,250	3,250
BAKRE, Sadanand K (1920-) Indian				
oil	2	22,000-24,640	23,320	22,000
BAKSHEEV, Vasily (1862-1958) Russian				
oil	1	2,577	2,577	2,577
BAKST, Léon (1866-1924) Russian				
wc/d	26	1,189-591,429	34,229	8,496
BAKSTEEN, Dirk (1886-1971) Dutch				
oil	1	1,818	1,818	1,818
BAL, Gerardus Lodewyk Franciscus Jacobus (1872-1912) Belgian/Dutch				
oil	1	1,402	1,402	1,402
BALACA Y CANSECO, Eduardo (1840-1914) Spanish				
oil	1	3,014	3,014	3,014
BALAGUER, Doro (1931-) Spanish				
oil	1	4,895	4,895	4,895
BALANDE, Gaston (1880-1971) French				
oil	11	445-10,451	4,064	3,575
wc/d	1	642	642	642
BALASHOV, Piotr Ivanovich (c.1835-1888) Russian				
wc/d	2	32,244-44,645	38,444	32,244
BALCHEN, Bernt (1899-1973) American				
wc/d	1	2,250	2,250	2,250
BALCIAR, Gerald George (1942-) American				
3D	3	3,500-5,250	4,250	4,000
BALDAUF, J (19th C) Austrian?				
wc/d	1	7,730	7,730	7,730
BALDEN, Theo (1904-) ?				
3D	1	3,865	3,865	3,865
BALDERO (?) ?				
oil	1	3,395	3,395	3,395
BALDES Y ALBARCA, Ignacio (17th C) Latin American				
oil	1	3,568	3,568	3,568
BALDESSARI, John (1931-) American				
oil	1	26,550	26,550	26,550
BALDESSARI, Roberto Iras (1894-1965) Italian				
oil	17	586-67,932	6,641	1,073
wc/d	2	9,955-35,137	22,546	9,955
BALDI, Lazzaro (1624-1703) Italian				
wc/d	1	2,941	2,941	2,941
BALDOCK, Charles E (fl.1890-1905) British				
oil	1	3,850	3,850	3,850

Name	No.	Price Range	Average	Median
BALDOCK, James Walsham (c.1822-1898) British				
oil	2	3,312-3,420	3,366	3,312
BALDWIN, Michael (1945-) British				
wc/d	1	1,236	1,236	1,236
BALDWIN, W T (fl.1865) British				
oil	1	21,240	21,240	21,240
BALDWIN, William (fl.1830) American				
oil	1	3,000	3,000	3,000
BALDWYN, Charles H C (fl.1887-1912) British				
wc/d	2	1,026-1,218	1,122	1,026
BALE, C T (fl.1866-1875) British				
oil	1	1,874	1,874	1,874
BALE, Charles Thomas (fl.1866-1875) British				
oil	16	534-3,568	1,576	1,200
BALEN, Hendrik van and BRUEGHEL, Jan (younger) (17th C) Flemish				
oil	1	103,800	103,800	103,800
BALEN, Jan van (1611-1654) Flemish				
oil	2	11,689-72,000	41,844	11,689
BALESTRA, Antonio (1666-1740) Italian				
oil	1	26,639	26,639	26,639
BALESTRIERI, Lionello (1872-1958) Italian				
oil	2	1,192-1,512	1,352	1,192
wc/d	1	763	763	763
BALET, Jan (1913-) German				
oil	3	984-3,239	1,811	1,211
BALILI, Ahmed (1957-) Moroccan				
oil	2	4,131-4,587	4,359	4,131
BALINK, Hendricus (1882-1963) American				
oil	6	3,750-21,000	10,541	7,000
wc/d	1	6,000	6,000	6,000
BALJEU, Joost (1925-1991) Dutch				
wc/d	1	4,712	4,712	4,712
3D	1	15,315	15,315	15,315
BALKENHOL, Stephan (1957-) German				
wc/d	4	482-2,967	1,523	1,036
3D	5	16,493-63,699	32,500	27,750
BALL, Thomas (1819-1911) American				
3D	2	7,500-20,000	13,750	7,500
BALL, Wilfred Williams (1853-1917) British				
oil	1	1,211	1,211	1,211
wc/d	9	555-4,575	1,219	727
BALL-DEMONT, Adrienne (1886-?) French				
oil	1	1,215	1,215	1,215
BALLA, Elica (1914-1995) Italian				
oil	1	2,219	2,219	2,219
wc/d	1	954	954	954
BALLA, Giacomo (1871-1958) Italian				
oil	11	18,685-572,449	154,582	89,919
wc/d	18	1,293-275,240	70,835	23,425
BALLABENE, Rudolf Raimund (1890-1968) Austrian				
oil	3	994-2,877	1,929	1,918
BALLACHEY, Barbara (1949-) Canadian				
oil	2	656-1,576	1,116	656
BALLAGH, Robert (1943-) Irish				
oil	4	6,062-32,139	17,425	9,704
wc/d	1	2,268	2,268	2,268
BALLANTINI, Dario (1964-) Italian				
oil	1	1,106	1,106	1,106
wc/d	1	841	841	841
BALLANTYNE, Chris (1972-) American				
oil	1	9,000	9,000	9,000
BALLARD, Arthur Alexander (1915-1994) British				
oil	2	925-1,480	1,202	925
BALLARD, Brian (1943-) Irish				
oil	21	885-9,889	5,414	4,844
wc/d	1	496	496	496
BALLARIO, Matilde (1880-?) Italian				
oil	1	1,211	1,211	1,211
BALLAVOINE, Jules Frederic (1855-1901) French				
oil	5	622-8,507	4,656	3,707

Name	No.	Price Range	Average	Median
BALLE, Mogens (1921-1988) Danish				
oil	26	1,288-15,291	5,268	3,702
wc/d	4	727-1,455	909	727
BALLE, Mogens and DOTREMONT, Christian (20th C) Danish/Belgian				
wc/d	2	1,851-2,263	2,057	1,851
BALLENBERGER, Karl (1801-1860) German				
oil	1	1,790	1,790	1,790
wc/d	1	2,829	2,829	2,829
BALLENTYNE, Joyce (c.1920-) American				
wc/d	1	1,164	1,164	1,164
BALLERO, Antonio (1864-1932) Italian				
oil	1	1,529	1,529	1,529
wc/d	1	4,281	4,281	4,281
BALLESIO, Federico (19th C) Italian				
oil	1	5,394	5,394	5,394
wc/d	3	2,800-8,500	5,476	5,130
BALLESTRA, Evelyne (20th C) French				
oil	1	6,146	6,146	6,146
BALLEWYNS, Guillaume (1875-?) Belgian				
oil	1	1,200	1,200	1,200
BALLEYGUIER-DUCHATELET, Melanie (19/20th C) French				
wc/d	1	1,337	1,337	1,337
BALLIN, Auguste (1842-?) French				
oil	2	957-2,880	1,918	957
BALLINGALL, Alexander (fl.1880-1910) British				
wc/d	4	1,211-3,402	2,127	1,647
BALLINI, Gilles (1946-) French				
oil	27	485-2,607	929	727
wc/d	6	606-1,940	882	630
BALLOWE, Marcia (20th C) American				
oil	1	1,300	1,300	1,300
BALLUE, Pierre Ernest (1855-1928) French				
oil	2	720-1,649	1,184	720
BALLUF, Ernst (1921-) Austrian				
oil	1	1,029	1,029	1,029
wc/d	4	759-1,558	1,100	993
BALMER, George (1806-1846) British				
oil	1	1,080	1,080	1,080
BALMER, Joseph (1828-?) Swiss				
oil	1	1,142	1,142	1,142
BALMFORD, Hurst (1871-1950) British				
oil	6	522-2,670	1,418	1,232
BALSAMO, Salvatore (1894-1922) Italian				
oil	1	4,001	4,001	4,001
BALSAMO, Vincenzo (1935-) Italian				
oil	16	1,999-6,732	3,457	3,027
wc/d	2	549-2,201	1,375	549
BALSGAARD, Carl Vilhelm (1812-1893) Danish				
oil	2	3,822-10,219	7,020	3,822
BALTHUS (1908-2001) French				
oil	3	16,000-387,200	155,983	64,750
wc/d	2	3,394-4,257	3,825	3,394
BALUSCHEK, Hans (1870-1935) German				
wc/d	1	5,271	5,271	5,271
BALWE, Arnold (1898-1983) German				
oil	17	1,091-28,274	9,054	5,291
BALZE, Jean Paul Étienne (1815-1884) French				
oil	1	1,563	1,563	1,563
BAMA, James E (1926-) American				
oil	4	7,000-110,000	43,125	23,000
BAMBER, Bessie (fl.1900-1910) British				
oil	13	888-4,844	2,919	2,960
BAMBERGER, Fritz (1814-1873) German				
oil	2	3,299-26,711	15,005	3,299
BAMBINI, Nicolo (1651-1736) Italian				
oil	1	168,571	168,571	168,571
BAMBINI, Nicolo and TIEPOLO, Giovanni Battista (18th C) Italian				
oil	1	6,497,260	6,497,260	6,497,260
BAMFORD, T (19th C) Canadian?				
oil	1	2,852	2,852	2,852

Name	No.	Price Range	Average	Median
BAMFYLDE, Coplestone Warre (1719-1791) British				
oil	1	16,000	16,000	16,000
wc/d	1	888	888	888
BANCALARI, Ines (20th C) Argentinian				
oil	2	3,500-8,000	5,750	3,500
BANCEL, Louis (1926-1978) French				
3D	1	2,141	2,141	2,141
BANCHIERI, Giuseppe (1927-1994) Italian				
oil	23	773-4,198	2,157	2,057
wc/d	4	471-1,546	892	714
BANCILA, Octav (1872-1944) Rumanian				
oil	1	2,422	2,422	2,422
BANDEIRA, Antonio (1922-1967) Brazilian				
oil	2	12,858-50,000	31,429	12,858
wc/d	5	726-8,000	3,108	1,000
BANDINELLI, Baccio (1493-1560) Italian				
wc/d	1	10,000	10,000	10,000
BANDO, Toshio (1890-1973) Japanese				
oil	5	3,341-23,973	8,004	4,123
wc/d	1	2,238	2,238	2,238
BANGOR, J Dodd (19th C) British				
wc/d	1	1,246	1,246	1,246
BANKE, Hermann (1843-?) German				
oil	1	1,197	1,197	1,197
BANKS, J O (fl.1856-1873) British				
oil	1	1,288	1,288	1,288
BANKS, John O (fl.1856-1873) British				
oil	1	1,211	1,211	1,211
BANKS, Margo (1951-) Irish				
oil	1	2,189	2,189	2,189
BANKSY (1975-) British				
oil	5	9,680-33,300	19,045	13,875
BANNARD, Walter Darby (1931-) American				
oil	3	1,815-6,000	4,105	4,500
BANNARN, Henry Wilmer (1910-1965) American				
oil	1	7,500	7,500	7,500
BANNER, Alfred (fl.1878-1914) British				
oil	2	582-1,500	1,041	582
wc/d	1	519	519	519
BANNINGER, Otto Charles (1897-1973) Swiss				
3D	3	2,331-9,158	6,399	7,708
BANNISTER, Edward M (1833-1901) American				
oil	2	14,844-45,000	29,922	14,844
BANNISTER, Graham (20th C) British				
oil	1	2,832	2,832	2,832
BANOVICH, John E (1964-) American				
oil	1	45,000	45,000	45,000
BANTING, John (1902-1970) British				
oil	2	1,295-2,070	1,682	1,295
wc/d	3	700-1,496	1,107	1,125
BANTING, Sir Frederick Grant (1891-1941) Canadian				
oil	3	11,521-33,235	22,304	22,156
BANTZER, Carl (1857-1941) German				
oil	1	47,697	47,697	47,697
BANUELOS-THORNDIKE, Antonia (19/20th C) Spanish				
oil	1	10,000	10,000	10,000
BANUS, Tudor (1947-) Rumanian				
oil	1	2,131	2,131	2,131
BAPTISTA, Marciano Antonio (1826-1896) Portuguese				
wc/d	1	22,320	22,320	22,320
BAQUET, Jean Michel (1956-) French				
oil	1	11,712	11,712	11,712
BAQUIE, Richard (1952-) French				
wc/d	1	1,978	1,978	1,978
3D	1	7,169	7,169	7,169
BARABAS, Miklos (1810-1898) Hungarian				
oil	3	1,458-10,990	4,746	1,790
BARABINO, Angelo (1883-1950) Italian				
oil	1	17,671	17,671	17,671
BARANOFF-ROSSINE, Vladimir (1888-1942) Russian				
oil	5	48,360-533,200	392,472	430,000
wc/d	3	2,236-17,200	10,492	12,040

Name	No.	Price Range	Average	Median
BARATELLA, Paolo (1935-) Italian				
oil	16	647-3,562	1,419	1,178
wc/d	4	648-2,356	1,204	738
BARATTI, Filippo (19/20th C) Italian				
oil	2	18,400-350,000	184,200	18,400
BARB, Jean (1909-1989) French				
oil	1	1,204	1,204	1,204
BARBADILLO, Manuel (1929-2003) Spanish				
oil	2	2,362-6,654	4,508	2,362
BARBAIX, René (1909-1966) Belgian				
oil	3	680-3,039	1,941	2,104
BARBALONGA, Antonio (1600-1649) Italian				
oil	1	1,451	1,451	1,451
BARBARINI, Emil (1855-1930) Austrian				
oil	12	550-7,283	3,761	3,279
BARBARINI, Franz (1804-1873) Austrian				
oil	3	3,514-6,370	4,907	4,839
wc/d	2	1,654-3,748	2,701	1,654
BARBARINI, Gustav (1840-1909) Austrian				
oil	1	6,429	6,429	6,429
wc/d	1	420	420	420
BARBARO, Saverio (1924-) Italian				
oil	1	1,219	1,219	1,219
BARBASAN, Mariano (1864-1924) Spanish				
oil	7	2,822-55,680	16,661	7,655
BARBEAU, Marcel (1925-) Canadian				
oil	2	2,292-5,318	3,805	2,292
wc/d	1	2,624	2,624	2,624
BARBEDIENNE and ROUGELET (19/20th C) French				
3D	1	30,976	30,976	30,976
BARBEDIENNE, Ferdinand (1810-1892) French				
3D	2	1,844-4,772	3,308	1,844
BARBELLA, Giovanni Giacomo (1590-1656) Italian				
wc/d	1	1,942	1,942	1,942
BARBER, John (1898-1965) American				
oil	1	1,200	1,200	1,200
BARBER, Joseph Vincent (1788-1838) British				
oil	1	2,595	2,595	2,595
BARBER, Sam (1943-) American				
oil	6	1,900-8,200	4,350	3,000
BARBERA, Camilla Gioia (19th C) Italian				
oil	1	2,420	2,420	2,420
BARBERIS, Carlos (1861-1913) Italian				
oil	1	5,600	5,600	5,600
BARBETTI, Rinaldo (1830-1903) Italian				
wc/d	1	4,995	4,995	4,995
BARBIER, Andre (1883-1970) French				
oil	3	954-1,312	1,173	1,255
BARBIER, Georges (1882-1932) French				
wc/d	3	1,300-4,000	2,390	1,870
BARBIER, Jean Jacques le (1738-1826) French				
oil	1	12,215	12,215	12,215
wc/d	5	486-7,211	3,791	3,889
BARBIER, Louis le (17th C) French				
wc/d	1	2,922	2,922	2,922
BARBIERI, Contardo (1900-1960) Italian				
oil	1	4,863	4,863	4,863
BARBIERI, Eugenio (1927-) Italian				
oil	1	2,102	2,102	2,102
wc/d	1	538	538	538
BARBIERI, Jonathan (1955-) American				
oil	1	4,500	4,500	4,500
BARBIERS, Pieter (18/19th C) Dutch				
wc/d	1	2,102	2,102	2,102
BARBISAN, Giovanni (1914-1988) Italian				
oil	1	3,641	3,641	3,641
BARBONE, Guy (1927-) French				
oil	1	1,575	1,575	1,575
BARBOUD KOCH, Martha Elisabeth (fl.1890) ?				
oil	1	7,747	7,747	7,747
BARBOUR, Pat (20th C) American				
wc/d	3	950-2,200	1,716	2,000

Name	No.	Price Range	Average	Median
BARBOZA, Diego (1945-) Venezuelan				
wc/d	1	1,300	1,300	1,300
BARBUDO, Salvador Sanchez (1858-1917) Spanish				
oil	5	3,416-10,120	7,562	9,000
BARBUT-DAVRAY, Luc (1863-?) French				
oil	1	2,668	2,668	2,668
BARCAGLIA, Donato (1849-1930) Italian				
3D	1	2,460	2,460	2,460
BARCELO, Miguel (1957-) Spanish				
oil	11	38,060-1,008,642	243,031	129,500
wc/d	6	40,700-407,000	164,013	55,500
3D	1	55,500	55,500	55,500
BARCHENKOV, Nicolai (1918-) Italian				
oil	2	1,784-2,022	1,903	1,784
BARCHI, Annunzio (1869-1897) Italian				
oil	2	3,625-7,265	5,445	3,625
BARCHUS, Eliza R (1857-1959) American				
oil	2	1,600-5,000	3,300	1,600
BARCLAY, Edgar (1842-1913) British				
oil	3	4,550-10,395	6,827	5,536
BARCLAY, John Rankin (1884-1962) British				
oil	3	641-3,096	1,465	659
BARCLAY, McClelland (1891-1943) American				
oil	9	900-10,000	4,711	3,750
BARDASANO BAOS, Jose (1910-1979) Spanish				
oil	6	1,483-8,269	4,085	2,057
BARDELLINI, Pietro (1728-1806) Italian				
oil	1	25,950	25,950	25,950
BARDI, Luigi (19/20th C) Italian				
oil	1	3,675	3,675	3,675
BARDIN, Jean (1732-1809) French				
wc/d	1	3,330	3,330	3,330
BARDONE, Guy (1927-) French				
oil	16	467-5,005	1,775	1,200
wc/d	1	589	589	589
BARDWELL, Thomas (1704-1767) British				
oil	1	2,208	2,208	2,208
BAREL, Joav (1933-1977) Israeli?				
oil	1	5,000	5,000	5,000
BARENGER, James (jnr) (1780-1831) British				
oil	1	30,780	30,780	30,780
BARENTSZ, Dirck (1534-1592) Dutch				
oil	1	10,108	10,108	10,108
BARETTA, Michele (1916-1987) Italian				
oil	4	1,463-5,163	2,620	1,829
wc/d	1	954	954	954
BARGA, Pietro da (?) Italian				
3D	1	21,796	21,796	21,796
BARGELLINI, Giulio (1879-1936) Italian				
oil	1	1,692	1,692	1,692
BARGHEER, Eduard (1901-1979) German				
oil	8	1,623-35,619	13,616	9,271
wc/d	40	468-9,062	2,938	2,330
BARGIGGIA, Franco (1889-1966) Italian				
3D	1	4,789	4,789	4,789
BARGONI, Gian Carlo (1936-) Italian				
oil	3	643-2,386	1,706	2,090
wc/d	1	1,270	1,270	1,270
BARGUE, Charles (1826-1883) French				
oil	1	165,300	165,300	165,300
BARHAUG, Ty (1963-) American				
oil	1	5,000	5,000	5,000
BARICCHI, Mirko (1970-) Italian				
oil	2	1,296-2,071	1,683	1,296
wc/d	1	1,532	1,532	1,532
BARILLOT, Léon (1844-1929) French				
oil	5	2,221-7,102	4,593	5,066
BARISANI, Renato (1918-) Italian				
oil	1	2,704	2,704	2,704
wc/d	1	1,767	1,767	1,767
BARISON, Giuseppe (1853-1930) Italian				
oil	1	45,972	45,972	45,972

Name	No.	Price Range	Average	Median
BARJOLA, Juan (1919-2004) Spanish				
oil	3	8,199-37,655	23,312	24,082
BARJON, Victor (1845-?) French				
oil	1	1,237	1,237	1,237
BARKER OF BATH, Benjamin (1776-1838) British				
oil	1	1,740	1,740	1,740
wc/d	1	493	493	493
BARKER OF BATH, J (19th C) British				
oil	1	2,150	2,150	2,150
BARKER OF BATH, John Joseph (fl.1835-1866) British				
oil	3	887-2,000	1,535	1,720
BARKER OF BATH, Thomas (1769-1847) British				
oil	5	1,100-5,360	2,884	2,313
wc/d	1	880	880	880
BARKER, Benjamin (jnr) (1776-1838) British				
oil	1	1,012	1,012	1,012
BARKER, Clive (1940-) British				
oil	1	2,736	2,736	2,736
wc/d	2	748-1,870	1,309	748
3D	14	950-13,338	4,251	3,132
BARKER, John (1811-1886) British				
oil	5	665-7,120	2,206	1,062
BARKER, Thomas Jones (1815-1882) British				
oil	1	1,253	1,253	1,253
BARKER, Wright (1864-1941) British				
oil	6	1,914-55,000	16,596	9,396
BARKO, Diane (20th C) American				
oil	1	2,250	2,250	2,250
BARKOFF, Alexandre (1870-1942) Greek				
oil	1	9,152	9,152	9,152
wc/d	3	1,730-3,520	2,845	3,287
BARLACH, Ernst (1870-1938) German				
wc/d	7	3,884-12,945	6,772	5,563
3D	19	6,126-187,397	31,263	17,600
BARLOW, Francis (1626-1704) British				
oil	1	5,049	5,049	5,049
wc/d	1	9,515	9,515	9,515
BARLOW, John Noble (1861-1917) American/British				
oil	4	561-3,560	1,834	1,416
BARLOW, Myron (1873-1937) American				
oil	2	9,000-10,000	9,500	9,000
BARNABE, Duilio (1914-1961) Italian				
oil	7	1,574-7,283	4,008	3,330
wc/d	1	1,051	1,051	1,051
BARNARD, Emily (fl.1884-1911) British				
wc/d	1	1,032	1,032	1,032
BARNEKOW, Brita (1868-1936) Danish				
oil	2	1,000-2,201	1,600	1,000
BARNEKOW, Robert (1848-1931) Danish				
oil	1	8,550	8,550	8,550
BARNES, Archibald George (1887-1934) British				
oil	1	8,062	8,062	8,062
BARNES, Edward Charles (fl.1856-1882) British				
oil	5	859-10,000	3,374	2,124
BARNES, Ernest Harrison (1873-?) American				
oil	1	1,100	1,100	1,100
BARNES, John Pierce (1893-?) American				
oil	1	7,500	7,500	7,500
BARNES, Matthew (1880-1951) American				
oil	1	3,000	3,000	3,000
BARNET, Will (1911-) American				
oil	3	600-14,000	5,500	1,900
wc/d	1	19,000	19,000	19,000
BARNETT, Thomas P (1870-1929) American				
oil	1	2,500	2,500	2,500
BARNEY, Marian Greene (20th C) American				
oil	1	4,250	4,250	4,250
BARNEY, Matthew (1967-) American				
wc/d	2	18,000-40,000	29,000	18,000
3D	4	3,000-18,000	9,774	3,096

Name	No.	Price Range	Average	Median
BARNI, Roberto (1939-) Italian				
oil	3	3,579-4,961	4,270	4,272
wc/d	3	540-884	671	589
3D	1	5,400	5,400	5,400
BARNITZ, Harry Wilson (1864-?) American				
oil	1	13,000	13,000	13,000
BARNOIN, Henri Alphonse (1882-1935) French				
oil	14	1,080-17,542	8,499	7,902
wc/d	4	4,544-10,601	8,329	8,203
BARNS-GRAHAM, Wilhelmina (1912-2004) British				
oil	3	8,736-12,825	10,151	8,892
wc/d	5	1,068-67,860	19,674	5,220
BARNSLEY, James MacDonald (1861-1929) Canadian				
oil	2	1,205-1,558	1,381	1,205
wc/d	3	412-1,000	783	938
BAROCCI, Federico (1526-1612) Italian				
oil	2	50,000-57,857	53,928	50,000
wc/d	1	4,810	4,810	4,810
BAROJA, Ricardo (1871-1953) Spanish				
oil	2	14,270-14,984	14,627	14,270
BARON, Henri Charles Antoine (1816-1885) French				
oil	3	1,334-2,059	1,715	1,753
wc/d	1	522	522	522
BARON, Theodor (1840-1899) Belgian				
oil	9	482-4,171	1,700	927
BARON-RENOUARD, François (1918-) French				
oil	1	2,028	2,028	2,028
BAROYANTS, Mikhail (1925-) Russian				
oil	1	1,100	1,100	1,100
BARR, Roger (1921-) American				
oil	1	1,000	1,000	1,000
BARR, Timothy (1957-) American				
oil	1	2,000	2,000	2,000
BARR, William (1867-1933) American				
oil	7	400-6,000	2,215	1,600
BARRA, Didier (1590-1650) French				
oil	1	155,700	155,700	155,700
BARRABAND, Jacques (1767-1809) French				
wc/d	16	35,137-386,507	175,685	128,836
BARRADAS, Rafael (1890-1929) Uruguayan				
wc/d	2	1,500-1,646	1,573	1,500
BARRAGAN, Julio (1928-) Argentinian				
oil	4	800-5,200	2,925	1,500
BARRAGAN, Luis (20th C) South American				
oil	1	1,700	1,700	1,700
BARRATT OF STOCKBRIDGE, Thomas (fl.1852-1893) British				
oil	1	1,870	1,870	1,870
BARRATT, Reginald R (1861-1917) British				
wc/d	2	605-1,682	1,143	605
BARRAU, Laureano (1864-1957) Spanish				
oil	3	17,400-33,060	24,360	22,620
wc/d	1	2,145	2,145	2,145
BARRAUD, Aime (1902-1954) Swiss				
oil	8	916-12,899	4,429	1,998
BARRAUD, Aurele (1903-1969) Swiss				
oil	2	500-1,415	957	500
wc/d	2	749-833	791	749
BARRAUD, François (1899-1934) Swiss				
oil	1	4,242	4,242	4,242
BARRAUD, Gustave François (1883-1968) Swiss				
oil	2	856-1,526	1,191	856
wc/d	1	1,832	1,832	1,832
BARRAUD, Henry (1811-1874) British				
oil	7	3,132-58,590	20,319	17,010
BARRAUD, Henry and William (19th C) British				
oil	1	17,010	17,010	17,010
BARRAUD, Maurice (1889-1954) Swiss				
oil	11	2,428-18,969	9,442	7,566
wc/d	17	571-6,850	2,217	1,217
BARRAUD, William (1810-1850) British				
oil	5	5,292-24,360	12,445	6,960

Name	No.	Price Range	Average	Median
BARRE, Jean Auguste (1811-1896) French				
3D	2	3,057-15,565	9,311	3,057
BARRÉ, Martin (1924-1993) French				
oil	7	14,135-43,591	25,129	25,717
BARREDA, Enrique D (1880-1953) Peruvian				
oil	1	1,328	1,328	1,328
BARREDA, Ernesto (1927-) Chilean				
oil	2	1,200-2,750	1,975	1,200
BARREIRO, Jose Maria (1940-) Spanish				
oil	1	2,460	2,460	2,460
BARRENECHEA, Nestor (20th C) Spanish				
3D	1	1,806	1,806	1,806
BARRERA-BOSSI, Erma (1885-1960) Italian				
oil	1	64,795	64,795	64,795
BARRET, George (jnr) (1767-1842) British				
wc/d	6	491-3,186	1,289	660
BARRET, George (snr) (1728-1784) British				
wc/d	1	9,450	9,450	9,450
BARRET, Marius-Antoine (1865-1929) French				
oil	2	836-1,411	1,123	836
BARRETO, Luis (20th C) Venezuelan				
oil	1	1,535	1,535	1,535
BARRETO, Pedro (1935-) Venezuelan				
3D	1	2,100	2,100	2,100
BARRETT, Jerry (1824-1906) British				
oil	1	1,044	1,044	1,044
BARRETT, John (19th C) British				
oil	1	1,958	1,958	1,958
BARRETT, Joseph (1935 -) American				
oil	10	750-5,500	3,120	3,000
BARRETT, Max (1937-1997) British				
3D	1	1,760	1,760	1,760
BARRETT, Thomas Francis (fl.1906-1950) British				
oil	1	4,224	4,224	4,224
BARRETT, William S (1854-1927) American				
oil	1	650	650	650
wc/d	1	1,000	1,000	1,000
BARRETTE, Sacha (20th C) Canadian				
oil	1	1,234	1,234	1,234
BARRIAS, E (19/20th C) French				
3D	1	4,654	4,654	4,654
BARRIAS, Louis Ernest (1841-1905) French				
3D	6	2,297-17,810	8,945	7,560
BARRIE, Mardi (1931-2004) British				
oil	3	855-2,200	1,422	1,211
BARRIERE, Georges (1881-1944) French				
oil	1	1,438	1,438	1,438
BARRIGUES, Prosper de (1760-1850) Portuguese				
oil	1	3,168	3,168	3,168
BARRIOS, Armando (1920-) Venezuelan				
oil	2	7,200-28,140	17,670	7,200
wc/d	3	1,120-1,630	1,381	1,395
BARRIOT, C (?) ?				
oil	1	1,757	1,757	1,757
BARRON Y CARRILLO, Manuel (1814-1884) Spanish				
oil	1	30,102	30,102	30,102
BARRON, Howard (1900-1991) British				
oil	4	597-12,155	6,711	3,114
BARRON, Manuel (19th C) ?				
oil	3	3,887-130,500	50,015	15,660
BARROS, Augusto (1929-) Portuguese				
oil	1	1,276	1,276	1,276
BARROW, Thomas (1737-1822) British				
oil	7	875-1,313	1,070	1,050
BARRS, Lawrence (?) Canadian				
oil	2	587-1,426	1,006	587
BARRUETA-ASTENSIA, Benito (1873-1953) Spanish				
oil	1	4,460	4,460	4,460
BARRY, Claude-Francis (1883-1970) British				
oil	4	445-120,360	41,968	1,830

Name	No.	Price Range	Average	Median
BARRY, Edward Middleton (19th C) British				
wc/d	1	5,220	5,220	5,220
BARRY, James (1741-1806) British				
oil	1	1,618,200	1,618,200	1,618,200
BARRY, Jonathan (20th C) British				
oil	3	1,672-1,672	1,672	1,672
BARRY, Moyra A (1886-1960) Irish				
oil	2	3,307-4,477	3,892	3,307
wc/d	2	751-935	843	751
BARRY, Robert (1936-) American				
oil	2	800-10,000	5,400	800
wc/d	1	3,000	3,000	3,000
BARRY, Sir Charles (1795-1860) British				
wc/d	1	8,004	8,004	8,004
BARSANO, Ron (1945-) American				
oil	1	1,900	1,900	1,900
BARSE, George Randolph (jnr) (1861-1938) American				
wc/d	1	2,000	2,000	2,000
BARTA, Ladislas (1902-1961) Hungarian				
oil	1	2,008	2,008	2,008
BARTELS, Hans von (1856-1913) German				
oil	4	1,071-20,566	6,408	1,138
wc/d	2	1,946-10,338	6,142	1,946
BARTELS, Hermann (1928-) German				
oil	1	2,990	2,990	2,990
BARTELS, Karl (20th C) ?				
oil	1	705	705	705
wc/d	1	468	468	468
BARTELS, Wera von (1886-1922) German				
3D	2	1,944-8,357	5,150	1,944
BARTENBACH, Hans (1908-) German				
oil	1	1,000	1,000	1,000
BARTEZAGO, Enrico (19th C) Swiss				
oil	1	1,095	1,095	1,095
BARTH, Amade (1899-1926) Swiss				
oil	1	4,250	4,250	4,250
BARTH, Carl (1896-1976) German				
oil	3	1,649-2,425	1,964	1,818
BARTH, Guerard de la (18/19th C) ?				
wc/d	1	2,000	2,000	2,000
BARTH, Paul Basilius (1881-1955) Swiss				
oil	9	567-6,469	2,851	2,518
wc/d	1	1,135	1,135	1,135
BARTHALOT, Marius (1861-?) French				
oil	1	2,854	2,854	2,854
BARTHE, Richmond (1901-1989) American				
3D	1	70,000	70,000	70,000
BARTHEL, Friedrich (1775-1846) German				
oil	1	10,837	10,837	10,837
BARTHELEMY, Camille (1890-1961) Belgian				
oil	8	1,227-10,286	6,039	4,772
wc/d	1	823	823	823
BARTHELEMY, Catherine (20th C) French				
oil	1	2,400	2,400	2,400
BARTHELEMY, Gerard (1927-2003) French				
oil	2	477-2,141	1,309	477
BARTHELEMY, L (19/20th C) French				
3D	6	1,991-4,876	3,187	3,032
BARTHELME, Hugo (1822-1895) German				
oil	1	2,378	2,378	2,378
BARTHOLDI, Frederic Auguste (1834-1904) French				
wc/d	1	22,253	22,253	22,253
3D	2	2,057-2,600	2,328	2,057
BARTHOLOMEW, James H (1962-) British				
oil	2	5,310-5,610	5,460	5,310
BARTHOLOMEW, William Newton (1822-1898) American				
wc/d	1	1,000	1,000	1,000
BARTLETT (?) ?				
oil	1	5,531	5,531	5,531
BARTLETT, Dana (1878-1957) American				
oil	16	750-25,000	7,745	4,250

Name	No.	Price Range	Average	Median
BARTLETT, Frederic Clay (1873-1953) American				
oil	1	10,000	10,000	10,000
BARTLETT, Gray (1885-1951) American				
oil	2	7,500-10,000	8,750	7,500
BARTLETT, Jennifer (1941-) American				
oil	7	2,000-38,000	20,529	20,000
wc/d	7	3,000-28,000	10,064	4,200
BARTLETT, Paul Wayland (1881-1925) American				
3D	1	2,822	2,822	2,822
BARTLETT, William E (1960-) American				
oil	2	500-2,100	1,300	500
BARTLETT, William H (1858-1932) British				
oil	7	957-70,680	18,207	7,440
wc/d	1	4,927	4,927	4,927
BARTLETT, William Henry (1809-1854) British				
oil	1	878	878	878
wc/d	1	3,390	3,390	3,390
BARTO, Charles (?) ?				
wc/d	1	1,139	1,139	1,139
BARTOLENA, Cesare (1830-1903) Italian				
oil	1	39,435	39,435	39,435
BARTOLENA, Giovanni (1866-1942) Italian				
oil	9	1,295-19,082	8,878	8,247
BARTOLI, Amerigo (1890-1971) Italian				
oil	1	1,757	1,757	1,757
BARTOLINI, Giuseppe (1938-) Italian				
oil	1	9,136	9,136	9,136
BARTOLINI, Luciano (1948-1994) Italian				
oil	3	1,767-3,107	2,213	1,767
wc/d	4	648-1,907	1,214	776
BARTOLINI, Luigi (1892-1963) Italian				
oil	3	1,171-3,805	2,290	1,894
wc/d	1	597	597	597
BARTOLINI, Philippo (1861-1908) Italian				
wc/d	4	4,841-17,700	10,929	9,672
BARTOLINI, Ubaldo (1944-) Italian				
oil	13	726-3,073	1,876	1,885
BARTOLINI, Ugo Vittore (1906-1975) Italian				
oil	1	2,309	2,309	2,309
BARTOLO, Andrea di (fl.1389-1428) Italian				
oil	1	87,763	87,763	87,763
BARTOLOMEO DI DAVID (?-1544) Italian				
oil	1	14,400	14,400	14,400
BARTOLOMMEO DA BRESCIA-OLMO (1506-1579) Italian				
oil	1	144,490	144,490	144,490
BARTOLOMMEO, Fra (1472-1517) Italian				
wc/d	1	70,000	70,000	70,000
BARTOLOZZI, Francesco (1727-1815) Italian				
wc/d	1	4,500	4,500	4,500
BARTOLOZZI, Rafael Lozano (1943-) Spanish				
oil	1	2,299	2,299	2,299
wc/d	1	539	539	539
BARTON, Macena Alberta (1901-1986) American				
oil	1	1,700	1,700	1,700
BARTON, Mary (1861-1949) British				
wc/d	2	840-2,422	1,631	840
BARTON, Rose Maynard (1856-1929) British				
wc/d	5	651-16,530	10,093	10,440
BARTSCH, Reinhard (1925-1990) German				
oil	3	1,029-2,571	1,928	2,186
BARUCCI, Pietro (1845-1917) Italian				
oil	5	1,757-25,890	12,874	12,000
BARUCHELLO, Gianfranco (1924-) Italian				
oil	1	7,501	7,501	7,501
BARWE, Prabhakar (1936-1996) Indian				
oil	2	47,500-58,000	52,750	47,500
wc/d	2	6,000-8,000	7,000	6,000
BARWIG, Franz (1868-1931) Austrian				
3D	1	8,357	8,357	8,357
BARWOLF, Georges (1872-1935) Belgian				
oil	2	2,016-2,420	2,218	2,016

Name	No.	Price Range	Average	Median
BARYE (?) French				
3D	1	2,455	2,455	2,455
BARYE, A (19th C) French				
3D	1	4,947	4,947	4,947
BARYE, A-L (1796-1875) French				
3D	1	2,616	2,616	2,616
BARYE, Alfred (1839-1882) French				
3D	5	2,185-10,680	5,446	4,114
BARYE, Alfred and GUILLEMIN, Émile (19th C) French				
3D	1	9,122	9,122	9,122
BARYE, Antoine-Louis (1796-1875) French				
oil	3	2,000-5,468	3,664	3,524
wc/d	1	1,638	1,638	1,638
3D	75	1,557-41,760	8,477	5,500
BARZAGHI-CATTANEO, Antonio (1837-1922) Swiss				
oil	1	4,863	4,863	4,863
BARZAGLI, Massimo (1960-) Italian				
oil	7	530-5,856	1,543	934
wc/d	4	648-908	831	884
BARZANTI, Licinio (1857-1944) Italian				
oil	3	3,151-4,789	3,806	3,480
BARZANTI, Peter (19/20th C) Italian				
3D	3	2,835-13,124	6,736	4,250
BAS, Adrien (1884-1925) French				
oil	1	937	937	937
wc/d	2	1,140-1,440	1,290	1,140
BAS, Edward le (1904-1966) British				
oil	2	1,080-4,498	2,789	1,080
BAS, Hernan (1978-) American				
oil	3	16,000-75,000	38,666	25,000
BAS, Philip le (1925-) British				
oil	2	814-1,502	1,158	814
BASAGLIA, Vittorio (1936-2005) Italian				
oil	3	934-3,686	2,187	1,942
BASALDUA, Hector (1895-1976) Argentinian				
wc/d	2	1,800-3,000	2,400	1,800
BASCHENIS, Evaristo (1617-1677) Italian				
oil	1	1,300,000	1,300,000	1,300,000
BASCOULES, Jean Desire (1886-1976) French				
oil	5	759-5,069	3,849	4,676
wc/d	1	759	759	759
BASEBE, Henry (20th C) British				
oil	1	1,026	1,026	1,026
BASEDOW, Heinrich (1896-?) German				
oil	2	1,070-3,041	2,055	1,070
BASELEER, Richard (1867-1951) Belgian				
oil	1	510	510	510
wc/d	2	478-2,549	1,513	478
BASELITZ, Georg (1938-) German				
oil	8	75,000-1,936,000	553,037	325,000
wc/d	15	720-100,000	28,796	22,898
BASILETTI, Luigi (1780-1860) Italian				
wc/d	1	2,799	2,799	2,799
BASILEV, O (20th C) Russian				
oil	1	4,300	4,300	4,300
BASING, Charles (1865-1933) American				
oil	2	1,800-2,500	2,150	1,800
BASKE, Yamada (?-1934) American				
oil	1	1,200	1,200	1,200
wc/d	1	600	600	600
BASKERVILLE, Charles (1896-1994) American				
oil	2	400-500	450	400
wc/d	1	2,500	2,500	2,500
BASKIN, Leonard (1922-2000) American				
wc/d	8	1,000-5,000	2,637	1,500
3D	4	2,500-13,350	5,737	2,600
BASLOW, Michel (20th C) Belgian?				
wc/d	1	1,403	1,403	1,403
BASOLI, Antonio (1774-1848) Italian				
wc/d	1	1,018	1,018	1,018

Name	No.	Price Range	Average	Median
BASQUIAT, Jean Michel (1960-1988) American				
oil	30	20,000-4,600,000	788,799	450,000
wc/d	16	701-600,000	132,944	97,091
BASQUIAT, Jean Michel and WARHOL, Andy (20th C) American				
oil	7	200,000-2,436,429	784,147	462,500
wc/d	1	70,000	70,000	70,000
BASSANO, Francesco (younger) (1549-1592) Italian				
oil	2	43,592-56,960	50,276	43,592
BASSANO, Jacobo (1515-1592) Italian				
oil	3	6,541-70,000	38,065	37,655
BASSANO, Leandro (1557-1622) Italian				
oil	3	38,060-61,151	46,403	40,000
BASSEN, Bartholomeus van (1590-1652) Dutch				
oil	1	2,600	2,600	2,600
BASSETT, Reveau Mott (1897-1981) American				
oil	2	900-6,000	3,450	900
wc/d	2	600-1,500	1,050	600
BASSETTI, Marcantonio (1588-1630) Italian				
wc/d	1	2,552	2,552	2,552
BASSFORD, Wallace (1900-) American				
oil	1	1,100	1,100	1,100
BASTERT, Nicolaas (1854-1939) Dutch				
oil	2	1,808-11,959	6,883	1,808
wc/d	2	1,678-1,700	1,689	1,678
BASTET, Jean-Celestin (1858-1942) French				
oil	1	2,417	2,417	2,417
BASTGEN, Josef (19/20th C) German				
3D	1	2,153	2,153	2,153
BASTIEN LEPAGE, Jules (1848-1884) French				
oil	1	7,274	7,274	7,274
wc/d	1	2,057	2,057	2,057
3D	1	5,049	5,049	5,049
BASTIEN, Alfred (1873-1955) Belgian				
oil	40	514-7,224	1,245	836
wc/d	2	449-656	552	449
BASTIER, Jean-Joseph (1780-1845) French				
oil	1	3,058	3,058	3,058
BASTIN, Ernest (c.1870-?) Belgian				
3D	1	2,877	2,877	2,877
BATAIL, Jean (1930-) French				
oil	2	2,035-2,160	2,097	2,035
wc/d	1	1,054	1,054	1,054
BATCHELDER, Stephen (1849-1932) British				
wc/d	15	655-2,640	1,384	1,267
BATCHELLER, Frederick S (1837-1889) American				
oil	1	2,250	2,250	2,250
wc/d	1	1,900	1,900	1,900
BATCHELOR, Roland (1889-1990) British				
wc/d	4	549-2,188	1,134	845
BATEMAN, Henry Mayo (1887-1970) British				
wc/d	4	2,640-19,360	7,480	3,520
BATEMAN, Marianne (19th C) British				
oil	1	1,062	1,062	1,062
BATEMAN, Robert (1930-) Canadian				
oil	2	6,918-11,545	9,231	6,918
wc/d	2	2,000-9,896	5,948	2,000
BATES, David (1840-1921) British				
oil	18	888-18,700	4,262	1,663
wc/d	18	549-3,850	1,340	1,197
BATES, David (1952-) American				
oil	1	1,260	1,260	1,260
BATES, David (20th C) British				
oil	1	1,911	1,911	1,911
BATES, Frederic R (?-1879) American				
oil	2	525-3,250	1,887	525
BATES, Maxwell (1906-1980) Canadian				
oil	3	1,783-3,092	2,335	2,132
wc/d	4	1,319-4,431	2,597	1,687
BATIGNE, François Victor (fl.1907-1909) French				
oil	1	4,113	4,113	4,113
BATLLE PLANAS, Juan (1911-1966) Argentinian				
oil	3	3,200-22,000	10,400	6,000
wc/d	2	2,500-7,000	4,750	2,500

Name	No.	Price Range	Average	Median
BATO, Jozsef (1888-1966) Hungarian				
oil	3	2,249-3,879	3,133	3,273
BATONI, Pompeo (1708-1787) Italian				
oil	3	50,571-407,000	276,945	373,265
wc/d	5	1,125-55,500	15,321	6,479
BATS, Rex (20th C) British?				
wc/d	1	21,120	21,120	21,120
BATT, Arthur (1846-1911) British				
oil	3	727-2,975	1,586	1,056
BATTAGLIA, Carlo (1933-) Italian				
oil	2	829-2,299	1,564	829
wc/d	1	957	957	957
BATTAGLIA, Xante (1943-) Italian				
oil	7	471-2,201	1,002	766
wc/d	1	860	860	860
BATTAGLIOLI, Francesco (18th C) Italian				
oil	1	96,327	96,327	96,327
BATTAILLE, Eugène (1817-1875) French				
oil	1	9,000	9,000	9,000
BATTAILLE, Irene (1913-) Belgian				
oil	1	2,160	2,160	2,160
BATTAILLE, Jan (1808-1957) Belgian				
oil	1	1,083	1,083	1,083
BATTEM, Gerard van (1636-1684) Dutch				
oil	1	3,460	3,460	3,460
wc/d	2	17,572-66,857	42,214	17,572
BATTEN, John Dicksen (1860-1932) British				
oil	1	24,360	24,360	24,360
BATTHYANY, Gyula (1888-1959) Hungarian				
oil	2	22,750-43,295	33,022	22,750
BATTISTA, G (19th C) Italian				
oil	1	2,200	2,200	2,200
BATTISTA, Giovanni (1858-1925) Italian				
oil	3	1,529-2,180	1,859	1,870
wc/d	2	783-1,480	1,131	783
BATTISTUZZI, A (19th C) Italian				
oil	1	2,289	2,289	2,289
BATTY, Arthur (19th C) British				
oil	1	1,040	1,040	1,040
BATTY, Lt Col Robert (1789-1848) British				
wc/d	2	1,091-1,212	1,151	1,091
BATUCCHI, A (19/20th C) Italian				
3D	1	14,000	14,000	14,000
BAUCHANT, Andre (1873-1958) French				
oil	15	1,900-9,952	4,385	4,248
BAUDART, Johan (1961-) Belgian				
3D	1	5,096	5,096	5,096
BAUDE, François-Charles (1880-1953) French				
oil	1	1,550	1,550	1,550
BAUDESSON, Nicolas (1611-1680) French				
oil	1	25,205	25,205	25,205
BAUDIN, Joseph (c.1691-c.1753) British				
wc/d	1	72,917	72,917	72,917
BAUDIT, Amedee (1825-1890) French				
oil	3	496-3,520	2,506	3,503
BAUDIT, Louis (1870-1960) Swiss				
oil	3	1,138-4,355	2,747	2,749
wc/d	1	618	618	618
BAUDOIN, Jean François (1870-1961) French				
oil	1	30,625	30,625	30,625
BAUDRY, Leon Georges (1898-1978) French				
3D	1	2,117	2,117	2,117
BAUDRY, Paul (1828-1886) French				
oil	4	2,281-15,206	11,183	12,040
wc/d	1	1,155	1,155	1,155
BAUER, Auguste (1868-?) German				
3D	1	3,395	3,395	3,395
BAUER, Carl Franz (1879-1954) Austrian				
oil	3	996-2,182	1,658	1,798
wc/d	2	993-1,286	1,139	993

Name	No.	Price Range	Average	Median
BAUER, John (1882-1918) Swedish				
oil	2	1,321-2,243	1,782	1,321
wc/d	4	1,745-22,435	11,402	10,440
BAUER, Marius Alexander Jacques (1867-1932) Dutch				
wc/d	3	1,110-9,699	3,976	1,119
BAUER, Rudolf (1889-1953) Polish				
oil	2	18,849-33,486	26,167	18,849
wc/d	4	700-5,890	2,877	2,071
BAUER-STUMPF, Johanna (1873-1964) Dutch				
oil	1	1,678	1,678	1,678
BAUERLE, Carl Wilhelm Friedrich (1831-1912) German				
oil	1	7,500	7,500	7,500
BAUERMEISTER, Mary (1934-) German				
wc/d	1	1,600	1,600	1,600
3D	3	3,086-5,500	3,890	3,086
BAUERNFEIND, Gustav (1848-1904) Austrian				
oil	2	7,080-950,000	478,540	7,080
BAUFFE, Victor (1849-1921) Dutch				
oil	4	471-5,340	1,887	732
wc/d	4	475-1,000	808	850
BAUGNIET, Charles (1814-1886) Flemish				
oil	1	8,000	8,000	8,000
BAUGNIET, Marcel Louis (1896-1995) Belgian				
oil	3	828-935	865	834
wc/d	11	491-3,562	1,594	1,192
BAUGNOD, C (?) French?				
oil	1	4,052	4,052	4,052
BAUKNECHT, Philipp (1884-1933) German				
oil	2	16,228-33,123	24,675	16,228
BAUM (?) ?				
oil	1	19,000	19,000	19,000
BAUM, Mathias (20th C) German				
oil	1	1,151	1,151	1,151
BAUM, Paul (1859-1932) German				
oil	2	11,094-58,446	34,770	11,094
wc/d	2	1,274-5,351	3,312	1,274
BAUM, Walter Emerson (1884-1956) American				
oil	55	450-27,500	7,513	5,500
wc/d	5	800-2,250	1,550	1,800
BAUMAN, E (19th C) ?				
wc/d	1	2,747	2,747	2,747
BAUMANN, Fred (1947-) Swiss				
oil	1	1,045	1,045	1,045
BAUMANN, Gustave (1881-1971) American				
wc/d	1	8,100	8,100	8,100
BAUMANN, Julius (19th C) German				
oil	1	3,892	3,892	3,892
BAUMANN, Karl Herman (1911-1984) American				
oil	4	600-1,600	900	650
wc/d	4	400-500	443	425
BAUMBERGER, Otto (1889-1961) Swiss				
oil	1	2,518	2,518	2,518
wc/d	3	304-951	686	803
BAUMEISTER, Willi (1889-1955) German				
oil	13	3,507-268,250	110,687	105,500
wc/d	12	1,991-55,973	16,998	11,781
BAUMER, Eduard (1892-1977) German				
oil	1	4,243	4,243	4,243
BAUMER, Johan Ernst (1870-1919) Dutch				
oil	2	1,093-1,380	1,236	1,093
BAUMGARTEL, Tilo (1972-) German				
oil	4	16,000-28,000	22,410	21,000
BAUMGARTNER, Franz (1962-) German				
oil	1	2,073	2,073	2,073
BAUMGARTNER, Fritz (1929-) German				
oil	1	2,472	2,472	2,472
wc/d	1	2,569	2,569	2,569
BAUMGARTNER, J Jay (1865-1946) American				
wc/d	1	1,300	1,300	1,300
BAUMGARTNER, Peter (1834-1911) German				
oil	4	2,800-10,000	7,730	9,000

Name	No.	Price Range	Average	Median
BAUMGARTNER, Warren W (1894-1963) American				
oil	1	1,500	1,500	1,500
BAUMGRAS, Peter (1827-1904) American				
oil	1	28,000	28,000	28,000
BAUMHOFER, Walter M (1904-1986) American				
oil	2	1,400-2,400	1,900	1,400
BAUR, Johann Wilhelm (1607-c.1640) Austrian				
wc/d	1	4,625	4,625	4,625
BAURIEDL, Otto (1879-1956) German				
oil	3	791-1,286	1,098	1,218
wc/d	1	776	776	776
BAURSCHEIT, Jan Pieter van (elder) (1669-1728) Flemish				
3D	1	34,600	34,600	34,600
BAUX, B Raymond de (19th C) German				
oil	2	4,685-7,224	5,954	4,685
BAWA, Manjit (1941-) Indian				
oil	1	120,000	120,000	120,000
BAWDEN, Edward (1903-1989) British				
wc/d	8	5,292-27,300	12,713	7,700
BAXTER, Charles (1809-1879) British				
oil	1	2,001	2,001	2,001
BAXTER, Glen (1944-) British				
wc/d	1	1,200	1,200	1,200
BAXTER, Walter (?) British				
oil	1	1,176	1,176	1,176
BAYALIS, John A (jnr) (20th C) American				
wc/d	2	900-1,300	1,100	900
BAYARD, Émile Antoine (1837-1891) French				
wc/d	3	701-4,671	2,180	1,168
BAYENS, Han (1876-1945) Dutch				
oil	1	3,116	3,116	3,116
BAYENS, Hans (1924-) Dutch				
oil	1	844	844	844
3D	2	2,822-3,292	3,057	2,822
BAYER, August von (1803-1875) German				
oil	1	3,889	3,889	3,889
BAYER, Herbert (1900-1985) German				
oil	6	3,500-60,000	19,389	13,000
wc/d	5	1,700-36,247	9,884	3,273
BAYERLEIN, Fritz (1872-1955) German				
oil	2	935-2,028	1,481	935
BAYERN, Maria del Pilar von (1891-1978) German				
oil	1	2,057	2,057	2,057
BAYES, Alfred Walter (1832-1909) British				
oil	2	522-2,000	1,261	522
BAYES, Gilbert (1872-1953) British				
3D	1	3,164	3,164	3,164
BAYES, Walter (1869-1956) British				
oil	3	515-2,864	1,693	1,701
wc/d	1	479	479	479
BAYEU Y SUBIAS, Francisco (1734-1795) Spanish				
oil	2	17,014-250,000	133,507	17,014
BAYLISS, Margaret E (fl.1928-1938) British				
oil	1	2,752	2,752	2,752
BAYLY, Lancelot (1869-1952) Irish				
wc/d	1	2,145	2,145	2,145
BAYNES, Frederick Thomas (1824-1874) British				
oil	1	1,400	1,400	1,400
wc/d	5	623-1,315	893	885
BAYNES, Thomas Mann (1794-1854) British				
wc/d	1	1,131	1,131	1,131
BAYON SALADO, Juan (1903-1995) Spanish				
oil	2	1,250-5,890	3,570	1,250
BAYRLE, Thomas (1937-) German				
oil	1	17,082	17,082	17,082
BAYROS, Franz von (1866-1924) Austrian				
wc/d	3	751-15,660	5,916	1,338
BAZAINE, Jean (1904-1995) French				
oil	2	3,073-10,911	6,992	3,073
wc/d	10	654-5,777	2,457	2,378
BAZILE, Bernard (1952-) French				
3D	1	24,722	24,722	24,722

Name	No.	Price Range	Average	Median
BAZILE, Bernard and BUSTAMANTE, Jean Marc (1952-) French				
oil	1	16,069	16,069	16,069
BAZIOTES, William (1912-1963) American				
oil	6	700-180,000	113,450	130,000
wc/d	3	2,250-16,000	7,750	5,000
BAZZANI, Luigi (1836-1927) Italian				
wc/d	1	1,784	1,784	1,784
BAZZANTI, P (19/20th C) Italian				
3D	1	6,622	6,622	6,622
BAZZANTI, Pietro (19/20th C) Italian				
3D	2	36,540-65,000	50,770	36,540
BAZZARO, Ernesto (1859-1937) Italian				
3D	1	9,200	9,200	9,200
BAZZARO, Leonardo (1853-1937) Italian				
oil	6	2,425-24,247	11,319	9,122
3D	1	3,031	3,031	3,031
BAZZI, Giovanni Antonio (1477-1549) Italian				
wc/d	1	300,000	300,000	300,000
BAZZICALUVA, Ercole (17th C) Italian				
wc/d	1	1,752	1,752	1,752
BEACH, Thomas (1738-1806) British				
oil	2	2,992-11,100	7,046	2,992
BEAL, Gifford (1879-1956) American				
oil	45	350-60,000	5,878	625
wc/d	3	750-3,000	1,533	850
BEAL, Reynolds (1867-1951) American				
oil	2	425-1,800	1,112	425
wc/d	8	800-2,250	1,418	1,500
BEALE, Mary (1632-1697) British				
oil	1	9,450	9,450	9,450
BEALL, Cecil Calvert (1892-1967) American				
wc/d	1	3,250	3,250	3,250
BEAMAN, Mary Jane Fitch (1918-2004) American				
oil	1	1,000	1,000	1,000
BEAMENT, Thomas Harold (1898-1984) Canadian				
oil	7	529-6,559	2,391	1,410
BEANLAND, Frank (1936-) British				
oil	1	1,683	1,683	1,683
BEAR, Charlie (20th C) American				
wc/d	1	4,000	4,000	4,000
BEAR, George Telfer (1874-1973) British				
oil	1	1,232	1,232	1,232
BEARD, James Carter (1837-1913) American				
wc/d	1	2,000	2,000	2,000
BEARD, James Henry (1812-1893) American				
oil	5	2,500-8,000	5,350	5,500
BEARD, Peter (1938-) ?				
wc/d	1	90,000	90,000	90,000
BEARD, William Holbrook (1824-1900) American				
oil	7	2,500-250,000	40,928	6,500
BEARDEN, Romare (1914-1988) American				
oil	2	51,600-70,000	60,800	51,600
wc/d	7	4,200-95,000	58,814	90,000
BEARDMORE, William (fl.1822-1826) British				
oil	1	1,840	1,840	1,840
BEASLEY, Bruce (1939-) American				
3D	1	5,100	5,100	5,100
BEATON, Penelope (1886-1963) British				
oil	1	3,186	3,186	3,186
wc/d	1	1,777	1,777	1,777
BEATON, Sir Cecil (1904-1980) British				
oil	11	666-56,320	6,705	1,203
wc/d	16	410-9,150	2,102	1,200
BEATSON, Charles (19/20th C) British				
oil	1	1,715	1,715	1,715
BEATTIE, William (19th C) British				
3D	1	4,914	4,914	4,914
BEATTY, John William (1869-1941) Canadian				
oil	22	441-22,156	6,459	3,936
BEAU, Alcide le (1872-1943) French				
oil	2	4,442-19,911	12,176	4,442
wc/d	3	452-607	521	505

Name	No.	Price Range	Average	Median
BEAU, Henri (1863-1949) Canadian				
oil	4	1,312-3,116	2,048	1,821
BEAUCE, Andre (1911-) French				
oil	2	1,013-3,802	2,407	1,013
BEAUCHAMP, Robert (1923-1995) American				
oil	4	2,100-9,500	4,650	3,000
wc/d	3	900-4,000	2,066	1,300
BEAUDIN, Andre (1895-1979) French				
oil	7	2,225-14,055	6,257	4,493
wc/d	6	478-3,732	2,413	2,225
3D	1	5,622	5,622	5,622
BEAUDUIN, Jean (1851-1916) Belgian				
oil	1	3,000	3,000	3,000
BEAUFILS, Jean Luc (1953-) French				
wc/d	6	482-1,806	1,034	542
BEAUFRERE, Adolphe (1876-1960) French				
oil	16	1,403-11,923	4,040	3,390
wc/d	12	505-20,193	3,145	1,075
BEAULIEU, Henri de (1819-1884) French				
oil	2	2,158-3,527	2,842	2,158
BEAULIEU, Paul Vanier (1910-1995) Canadian				
oil	2	2,132-13,777	7,954	2,132
wc/d	7	837-3,374	1,714	1,265
BEAUME, Émile Marie (1888-1967) French				
oil	1	1,866	1,866	1,866
wc/d	1	2,408	2,408	2,408
BEAUME, Joseph (1796-1885) French				
oil	2	1,286-2,188	1,737	1,286
BEAUMONT, Arthur (?) American				
oil	1	4,000	4,000	4,000
BEAUMONT, Arthur Edwaine (1890-1978) American				
wc/d	4	2,000-4,250	3,187	2,250
BEAUMONT, Charles Edouard de (1812-1888) French				
oil	1	18,000	18,000	18,000
BEAUMONT, Claudio Francesco (1694-1766) Italian				
oil	1	3,330	3,330	3,330
wc/d	1	701	701	701
BEAUQUESNE, Wilfrid Constant (1847-1913) French				
oil	4	2,200-2,418	2,279	2,250
BEAUREGARD, Charles G (c.1856-d.1919) Canadian				
oil	1	1,800	1,800	1,800
BEAUREGARD, G Pierre (1847-1894) American?				
oil	1	11,000	11,000	11,000
BEAUVAIS, Lubin de (19/20th C) French				
oil	1	1,752	1,752	1,752
BEAUVAIS, Walter (1942-2004) British				
oil	9	460-3,500	1,265	586
BEAUVALLET, Nicole (20th C) French				
oil	1	1,790	1,790	1,790
BEAUVERIE, Charles Joseph (1839-1924) French				
oil	4	540-4,757	2,367	1,940
BEAUX, Cecilia (1855-1942) American				
oil	1	27,000	27,000	27,000
BEAVER, Fred (1911-1976) American				
oil	1	1,100	1,100	1,100
BEAVIS, Richard (1824-1896) British				
oil	9	941-8,750	3,690	3,219
wc/d	1	525	525	525
BEBB, Minnie Rosa (1857-?) British				
wc/d	1	2,921	2,921	2,921
BECCARIA, Angelo (1820-1897) Italian				
oil	1	3,875	3,875	3,875
BECERRA, Milton (1951-) Venezuelan				
3D	1	5,350	5,350	5,350
BECH, Poul Anker (1942-) Danish				
oil	2	7,112-8,048	7,580	7,112
wc/d	1	2,425	2,425	2,425
BECHER, Arthur Ernst (1877-1960) American				
oil	2	375-9,500	4,937	375
wc/d	2	800-800	800	800
BECHI, Luigi (1830-1919) Italian				
oil	1	23,534	23,534	23,534

Name	No.	Price Range	Average	Median
BECHTLE, Robert (1932-) American				
wc/d	1	50,000	50,000	50,000
BECHTOLD, Gottfried (1947-) Austrian				
3D	1	3,116	3,116	3,116
BECHTOLSHEIM, Gustav Freiherr von (1842-1924) German				
oil	4	484-3,579	1,942	1,029
BECK, Herbert (1920-) German				
wc/d	3	1,019-1,767	1,353	1,274
BECK, Jacob Samuel (1715-1778) German				
oil	1	6,429	6,429	6,429
BECK, Julia (1853-1935) Swedish				
oil	1	11,467	11,467	11,467
wc/d	1	1,374	1,374	1,374
BECK-ARNSTEIN, Manfred (1946-) German				
wc/d	1	1,054	1,054	1,054
BECKER, Albert (1830-1896) German				
oil	2	2,432-5,733	4,082	2,432
BECKER, August (1822-1887) German				
oil	4	1,459-3,933	2,580	2,253
BECKER, August and SCHMITZ, Adolf (19th C) German				
oil	1	6,020	6,020	6,020
BECKER, Benno (1860-?) German				
oil	1	2,169	2,169	2,169
BECKER, Carl (1862-?) German				
oil	3	1,021-1,710	1,469	1,678
BECKER, Carl Ludwig Friedrich (1820-1900) German				
oil	3	3,503-10,000	7,136	7,905
BECKER, Curt Georg (1904-1972) German				
wc/d	1	2,238	2,238	2,238
BECKER, Frederick W (1888-1974) American				
oil	2	400-3,000	1,700	400
BECKER, Friedrich (1808-?) German				
oil	1	2,314	2,314	2,314
BECKER, Jakob (1810-1872) German				
oil	1	15,799	15,799	15,799
wc/d	1	2,571	2,571	2,571
BECKER, Nicolas (20th C) Russian				
oil	2	4,143-15,547	9,845	4,143
BECKER, Walter (1893-1984) German				
wc/d	5	1,885-2,121	2,026	2,003
BECKERT, Josef Maria (1889-1962) German				
wc/d	1	1,237	1,237	1,237
BECKET, Maria A (?-1904) American				
oil	2	800-2,800	1,800	800
BECKETT, Charles E (1814-1867) American				
oil	1	7,500	7,500	7,500
BECKLY, E (18th C) ?				
oil	1	2,167	2,167	2,167
BECKMAN, Ford (1952-) American				
oil	7	1,300-4,000	2,412	2,342
BECKMANN (?) ?				
oil	1	3,027	3,027	3,027
BECKMANN, Hans (20th C) American				
oil	1	1,200	1,200	1,200
BECKMANN, Johann (1809-1882) German				
oil	1	1,907	1,907	1,907
BECKMANN, Max (1884-1950) German				
oil	6	50,884-1,320,000	448,480	120,000
wc/d	5	4,452-550,000	203,978	114,400
BECKWITH, James Carroll (1852-1917) American				
oil	2	4,800-5,000	4,900	4,800
BECQUEREL (19/20th C) French				
3D	1	2,784	2,784	2,784
BECQUEREL, Andre-Vincent (1893-1983) French				
3D	5	1,752-21,083	6,766	2,335
BEDA, Francesco (1840-1900) Italian				
oil	3	9,678-55,625	37,767	48,000
BEDA, Giulio (1879-1954) Italian				
oil	2	1,414-3,471	2,442	1,414
BEDIA, Jose (1959-) Cuban				
oil	3	15,000-35,000	26,666	30,000
wc/d	1	26,000	26,000	26,000

Name	No.	Price Range	Average	Median
BEDIKIAN, Krikor (1908-1981) Libyan				
oil	1	1,140	1,140	1,140
wc/d	1	583	583	583
BEDIL, Dewa Putu (1921-1999) Indonesian				
oil	2	2,890-3,612	3,251	2,890
BEDINI, Paolo (1844-1924) Italian				
oil	1	6,226	6,226	6,226
wc/d	1	874	874	874
BEDNOSHEI, Daniil Panteleevich (1924-) Russian				
oil	1	11,245	11,245	11,245
BEECH, John (1964-) American				
oil	1	3,200	3,200	3,200
BEECHAM, Greg A (1954-) American				
oil	2	1,500-9,000	5,250	1,500
BEECHEY, Captain Richard Brydges (1808-1895) British				
oil	1	34,800	34,800	34,800
BEECHEY, Sir William (1753-1839) British				
oil	3	817-292,950	99,922	6,000
BEECROFT, Vanessa (1969-) American				
oil	1	16,365	16,365	16,365
BEEK, Bernardus Antonie van (1875-1941) Dutch				
oil	2	2,577-3,687	3,132	2,577
BEEK, Harmsen van der (1897-1953) Dutch				
wc/d	4	433-2,288	1,296	1,232
BEEK, Jurrien (1879-1965) Dutch				
oil	5	375-1,929	1,236	1,463
BEEK, Randy van (20th C) American				
oil	2	5,000-7,500	6,250	5,000
BEEKMAN, Christiaan (1887-1964) Dutch				
oil	1	1,252	1,252	1,252
wc/d	2	877-5,845	3,361	877
BEELDEMAKER, Adriaen Cornelisz (c.1625-1709) Dutch				
oil	1	2,750	2,750	2,750
BEELER, Joe Neil (1931-) American				
oil	6	1,500-12,000	7,683	8,500
wc/d	4	500-3,500	2,000	1,000
3D	2	5,000-8,750	6,875	5,000
BEELT, Cornelis (fl.1660-1702) Dutch				
oil	2	37,000-48,411	42,705	37,000
BEEN (?) ?				
oil	1	2,150	2,150	2,150
BEER, Andrew (1862-1954) British				
oil	4	435-2,457	1,210	957
BEER, Dick (1893-1938) Swedish				
oil	1	25,479	25,479	25,479
BEER, Jan de (1475-1542) Flemish				
oil	1	186,846	186,846	186,846
BEER, Wilhelm Amandus (1837-1907) German				
oil	2	1,679-1,914	1,796	1,679
wc/d	1	2,827	2,827	2,827
BEERBOHM, Sir Max (1872-1956) British				
wc/d	6	1,780-10,230	4,706	2,775
BEERNAERT, Euphrosine (1831-1901) Flemish				
oil	2	2,073-3,039	2,556	2,073
BEERNS, C (19th C) ?				
oil	1	5,363	5,363	5,363
BEERS, Jan van (1852-1927) Belgian				
oil	4	636-3,562	1,875	693
BEERSTRATEN, Abraham (17th C) Dutch				
oil	2	56,960-69,200	63,080	56,960
BEERSTRATEN, Jan Abrahamsz (1622-1666) Dutch				
oil	3	16,435-32,040	23,278	21,360
BEERT, Osias I (c.1570-1624) Flemish				
oil	2	250,000-575,000	412,500	250,000
BEEST, Albertus van (1820-1860) Dutch				
oil	2	1,585-5,563	3,574	1,585
BEEVER, Emanuel Samson van (1876-1912) Dutch				
oil	1	5,486	5,486	5,486
BEFANI, Achille Formis (1832-1906) Italian				
oil	1	3,633	3,633	3,633
BEFANIO, Gennaro (1866-?) French				
oil	3	958-16,069	6,815	3,420

Name	No.	Price Range	Average	Median
BEGA, Cornelis Pietersz (1620-1664) Dutch				
oil	1	6,055	6,055	6,055
wc/d	1	1,†89	1,189	1,189
BEGAS, Adalbert (1836-1888) German				
oil	1	8,159	8,159	8,159
BEGAS, Karl-Joseph (1794-1854) German				
oil	1	11,517	11,517	11,517
wc/d	1	500	500	500
BEGAUD, Pierre Albert (1901-1966) French				
oil	1	1,942	1,942	1,942
BEGBIE, David (20th C) ?				
3D	1	1,907	1,907	1,907
BEGEYN, Abraham (1637-1697) Dutch				
oil	2	3,864-10,014	6,939	3,864
BEGGROF, Alexandre (1841-1914) Russian				
oil	3	2,934-39,261	21,919	23,563
BEGGROF, Alexandre and BENOIS, Albert Nikolaievitch (19th C) Russian				
wc/d	1	4,371	4,371	4,371
BEGUINE, Michel Leonard (1855-1929) French				
3D	2	2,400-4,449	3,424	2,400
BEGUION, S (fl.1880-1910) ?				
oil	1	3,520	3,520	3,520
BEHAEGHEL, Janine (1940-1993) Belgian				
3D	1	2,225	2,225	2,225
BEHAM, Barthel (1502-1540) German				
oil	1	37,369	37,369	37,369
BEHAN, John (1932-) Irish				
3D	10	2,432-5,721	4,117	3,888
BEHLER, Will (20th C) American				
oil	2	650-1,500	1,075	650
BEHN, Fritz (1878-1970) Austrian				
3D	4	2,622-8,230	5,541	4,886
BEHNES, William (1794-1864) British				
3D	1	3,612	3,612	3,612
BEHR, Carel Jacobus (1812-1895) Dutch				
oil	1	1,678	1,678	1,678
BEHR, Johann Philipp (?-1756) German				
oil	1	4,451	4,451	4,451
BEHRENDSEN, August (1819-1886) German				
oil	2	1,265-4,800	3,032	1,265
BEHRENS (?) ?				
oil	1	5,322	5,322	5,322
3D	1	11,439	11,439	11,439
BEHRENS, Ferdinand (1862-1925) German				
oil	1	1,991	1,991	1,991
BEHRENS, Howard (20th C) American				
oil	1	1,900	1,900	1,900
BEHRINGER, Ludwig (1824-1903) German				
oil	2	1,281-2,827	2,054	1,281
BEICH, Joachim Franz (1665-1748) German				
oil	3	3,041-9,790	5,835	4,676
BEINASCHI, Giovan Battista (1636-1688) Italian				
oil	2	6,336-40,700	23,518	6,336
wc/d	1	1,100	1,100	1,100
BEINKE, Fritz (1842-1907) German				
oil	8	1,458-3,048	2,378	2,356
BEJARANO, Alt Cobral (?) Spanish				
oil	1	1,885	1,885	1,885
BEJEMARK, K G (1922-) Swedish				
3D	4	1,982-17,177	6,707	3,308
BEKAERT, Piet (1939-2000) Belgian				
oil	7	1,781-4,204	3,072	3,816
3D	1	9,031	9,031	9,031
BEKIARI, Koula (1905-1992) Greek				
oil	2	7,854-8,800	8,327	7,854
BEL, Georges (19/20th C) French				
3D	1	7,543	7,543	7,543
BELAIR, Pierre de (1892-?) French				
oil	2	2,721-4,919	3,820	2,721
BELAMINE, Abdelkirm (1964-) Moroccan				
oil	1	4,131	4,131	4,131

Name	No.	Price Range	Average	Median
BELANGER, François Joseph (1744-1818) French				
wc/d	1	19,140	19,140	19,140
BELANGER, Louis (1736-1816) French				
oil	1	20,384	20,384	20,384
wc/d	2	4,253-14,800	9,526	4,253
BELARSKI, Rudolph (1900-1983) American				
oil	1	10,000	10,000	10,000
BELAY, Pierre de (1890-1947) French				
oil	16	3,281-31,200	10,302	7,320
wc/d	20	526-9,370	1,508	748
BELCASTRO, Alfredo (1893-1961) Italian				
oil	2	1,702-4,789	3,245	1,702
BELGRANO, Jose Denis (1844-1917) Spanish				
oil	1	5,986	5,986	5,986
BELINFANTE, Willy (1922-) Dutch				
oil	1	1,654	1,654	1,654
BELKAHIA, Farid (1934-) Moroccan				
3D	1	36,709	36,709	36,709
BELKNAP, Zedekiah (1781-1858) American				
oil	4	5,200-26,000	11,300	6,000
BELL, Alfred (1832-1895) British				
oil	2	11,960-11,960	11,960	11,960
BELL, Caroline M (?-1940) American				
oil	1	2,700	2,700	2,700
BELL, Charles (1935-1995) American				
wc/d	1	30,000	30,000	30,000
BELL, David C (1950-) British				
oil	1	3,028	3,028	3,028
BELL, Graham (1910-1943) British				
oil	1	6,475	6,475	6,475
BELL, Hamish (20th C) British				
oil	2	2,775-5,180	3,977	2,775
BELL, John (1823-1881) British				
oil	1	3,402	3,402	3,402
BELL, John (1812-1895) British				
oil	1	2,174	2,174	2,174
BELL, John Clement (19th C) British				
oil	2	4,446-7,120	5,783	4,446
BELL, Larry (1939-) American				
oil	3	1,500-2,250	1,916	2,000
wc/d	4	707-2,250	1,539	1,600
BELL, Robert Anning (1863-1933) British				
wc/d	2	1,203-10,010	5,606	1,203
BELL, Sandra (20th C) Irish?				
3D	1	9,425	9,425	9,425
BELL, Trevor (1930-) British				
oil	3	1,232-4,446	2,315	1,267
wc/d	3	510-5,130	3,362	4,446
BELL, Vanessa (1879-1961) British				
oil	3	8,188-113,400	45,749	15,660
wc/d	1	1,914	1,914	1,914
BELL-SMITH, Frederick Marlett (1846-1923) Canadian/British				
oil	9	853-22,957	6,294	5,360
wc/d	15	984-22,287	5,102	3,092
BELLA, Gabriele (18th C) Italian				
oil	2	10,703-222,000	116,351	10,703
BELLA, Gioppe di (1945-) Italian				
oil	7	1,553-2,238	1,843	1,829
BELLA, Stefano Della (1610-1664) Italian				
oil	1	5,920	5,920	5,920
wc/d	8	1,443-13,875	6,345	4,861
BELLA, Vincenzo la (1872-1954) Italian				
oil	1	1,911	1,911	1,911
BELLAMY, John Haley (1836-1914) American				
3D	2	8,000-10,750	9,375	8,000
BELLANDI, Ernesto (1842-?) Italian				
oil	1	1,262	1,262	1,262
BELLANDI, Giorgio (1930-) Italian				
oil	3	892-1,414	1,122	1,060
BELLANGER-ADHEMAR, Paul (1868-1925) French				
oil	1	2,500	2,500	2,500

Name	No.	Price Range	Average	Median
BELLANO, Bartolommeo (1434-1496) Italian				
3D	1	84,762	84,762	84,762
BELLANY, John (1942-) British				
oil	50	661-10,380	4,461	3,580
wc/d	10	1,056-4,048	2,249	1,947
BELLE, Alexis Simon (1674-1734) French				
oil	4	2,822-14,449	8,336	3,402
BELLE, Augustin Louis (1757-1841) French				
oil	1	32,730	32,730	32,730
BELLE, Charles Ernest de (1873-1939) Canadian/Hungarian				
oil	1	810	810	810
wc/d	8	427-2,997	974	690
BELLEFLEUR, Léon (1910-) Canadian				
wc/d	1	1,237	1,237	1,237
BELLEGARDE, Claude (1927-) French				
oil	7	969-2,631	1,647	1,545
wc/d	1	715	715	715
BELLEGHEM, Aime van (1922-1996) Belgian				
oil	2	1,697-4,540	3,118	1,697
BELLEGHEM, Roger van (1922-) Belgian				
oil	3	680-2,090	1,169	738
BELLEI, Gaetano (1857-1922) Italian				
oil	1	9,000	9,000	9,000
BELLEL, Jean-Joseph (1816-1898) French				
oil	1	3,620	3,620	3,620
BELLEMONT, Léon (1866-1961) French				
oil	1	3,625	3,625	3,625
BELLENGE, Michel Bruno (1726-1793) French				
oil	3	4,350-16,562	8,420	4,350
BELLERMANN, Ferdinand (1814-1889) German				
oil	3	22,188-70,800	41,829	32,500
wc/d	1	1,051	1,051	1,051
BELLEROCHE, William de (1912-1969) British				
wc/d	1	1,104	1,104	1,104
BELLEVOIS, Jacob Adriaensz (1621-1675) Dutch				
oil	2	12,857-40,767	26,812	12,857
BELLI, Carlo (1903-1991) Italian				
oil	2	4,834-7,633	6,233	4,834
BELLI, Domenico (1909-1983) Italian				
oil	1	4,099	4,099	4,099
BELLING, Rudolf (1866-1972) German				
3D	1	39,743	39,743	39,743
BELLINGEN, Jan van (c.1770-1828) Flemish				
oil	1	2,330	2,330	2,330
BELLINI, Emmanuel (1904-1989) French				
oil	2	1,491-1,605	1,548	1,491
BELLINI, Filippo (1550-1604) Italian				
wc/d	1	8,507	8,507	8,507
BELLIS, Hubert (1831-1902) Belgian				
oil	8	1,152-5,845	2,165	1,285
BELLMAN, J J (?) British?				
oil	1	2,600	2,600	2,600
BELLMER, Hans (1902-1975) French/Polish				
oil	2	47,027-81,420	64,223	47,027
wc/d	20	2,718-20,712	8,890	7,893
3D	1	69,694	69,694	69,694
BELLO PINEIRO, Felipe (1886-1953) Spanish				
oil	1	4,752	4,752	4,752
BELLO, Bruno di (1938-) Italian				
oil	1	776	776	776
wc/d	1	2,903	2,903	2,903
BELLO, Pietro (1830-1909) Turkish				
wc/d	1	1,683	1,683	1,683
BELLONI, Giorgio (1861-1944) Italian				
oil	1	2,803	2,803	2,803
BELLOTTO, Bernardo (1720-1780) Italian				
oil	4	190,300-4,200,000	1,861,825	1,500,000
wc/d	2	27,500-111,000	69,250	27,500
BELLOWS, Albert F (1829-1883) American				
oil	2	1,600-3,250	2,425	1,600

Name	No.	Price Range	Average	Median
BELLOWS, George (1882-1925) American				
oil	3	300,000-420,000	340,000	300,000
wc/d	3	2,000-30,000	11,583	2,750
BELLOY, Count (18th C) French?				
wc/d	1	3,600	3,600	3,600
BELLUCCI, Antonio (1654-1726) Italian				
oil	4	14,240-120,379	53,030	17,300
BELLY, Léon Adolphe Auguste (1827-1877) French				
oil	3	54,370-239,200	141,356	130,500
BELMON, Gaston (1907-1995) French				
oil	1	2,529	2,529	2,529
wc/d	1	903	903	903
BELMONDO, Paul (1898-1982) French?				
wc/d	11	738-3,356	1,373	1,215
BELOFF, Angelina (1884-1969) Russian				
oil	1	16,473	16,473	16,473
BELSKIE, Abraham (1907-1988) American?				
3D	1	4,000	4,000	4,000
BELSKY, Ivan (?) Russian				
oil	1	88,370	88,370	88,370
BELTON, Liam (20th C) Irish?				
oil	1	3,307	3,307	3,307
3D	1	2,035	2,035	2,035
BELTRAME, Achille (1871-1945) Italian				
oil	19	1,697-15,760	4,068	3,152
wc/d	27	485-34,398	3,181	1,940
BELTRAME, Alfredo (1901-1996) Austrian?				
oil	1	1,157	1,157	1,157
BELTRAN-MASSES, Frederico (1885-1949) Spanish				
oil	4	1,189-31,000	10,425	2,378
BELTSOV, Georgi Ivannovich (1920-) Russian				
oil	1	1,784	1,784	1,784
BELTZ, H (19th C) German				
oil	3	964-3,214	1,874	1,446
BELVEDERE, Andrea (1642-1732) Italian				
oil	1	30,568	30,568	30,568
BELVEDERE, Antinous du (17th C) French				
3D	1	21,875	21,875	21,875
BELZILE, Louis (1929-) Canadian				
oil	1	1,518	1,518	1,518
BEM, Elizaveta Merkurevna (1843-1914) Russian				
wc/d	1	1,318	1,318	1,318
BEMELMANS, Ludwig (1898-1963) American				
oil	7	1,600-5,000	2,764	2,500
wc/d	10	500-18,000	5,245	1,200
BEMMEL, Christoph von (1707-1783) German				
oil	1	2,073	2,073	2,073
BEMMEL, Georg Christoph Gottlieb von I (1738-1794) German				
wc/d	1	5,014	5,014	5,014
BEMMEL, Peter von (1685-1754) German				
oil	2	1,635-4,176	2,905	1,635
BEMMEL, Wilhelm von (1630-1708) Dutch				
oil	2	10,911-16,650	13,780	10,911
BEMPORAD, Franco (1926-) Italian				
oil	3	1,784-11,959	5,175	1,784
BEN (1935-) Swiss				
oil	31	1,285-18,703	5,183	3,612
wc/d	8	1,054-3,884	2,564	2,520
3D	22	2,102-12,858	4,676	3,737
BEN ALI R'BATI (1861-1939) Moroccan				
wc/d	3	4,091-59,935	37,392	48,151
BEN ALLAL, Mohamed (1928-1995) Moroccan				
oil	3	9,870-95,278	42,698	22,948
wc/d	3	2,795-5,740	3,776	2,795
BEN CHEFFAJ, Saad (1939-) Moroccan				
oil	3	12,760-14,914	14,045	14,462
wc/d	2	5,854-8,800	7,327	5,854
BEN DAHMAN, Abdelbassit (1952-) Moroccan				
oil	2	1,609-5,157	3,383	1,609
wc/d	2	1,837-2,065	1,951	1,837
BENADE, James Arthur (1823-1853) American				
oil	1	20,000	20,000	20,000

Name	No.	Price Range	Average	Median
BENAGLIA, Enrico (1938-) Italian				
oil	3	2,386-3,021	2,775	2,919
wc/d	1	707	707	707
BENAIM, Ricardo (20th C) South American				
wc/d	1	1,440	1,440	1,440
BENARD, Auguste Sebastien (1810-?) French				
oil	1	1,338	1,338	1,338
BENAROYA, Albert (1963-) French?				
oil	2	5,500-5,500	5,500	5,500
BENASSIT, Louis Émile (1833-1902) French				
oil	1	1,636	1,636	1,636
BENATI, Davide (1949-) Italian				
oil	3	1,635-4,548	2,722	1,985
BENAVIDES, Pablo (1918-) Venezuelan				
oil	8	700-13,950	2,808	1,025
BENAYOUN, Robert (20th C) ?				
wc/d	1	1,081	1,081	1,081
BENAZZI, Raffael (1933-) Swiss				
3D	1	2,921	2,921	2,921
BENCOVICH, Federico (1675-1753) Dalmatian				
oil	1	27,850	27,850	27,850
BENCZUR, Gyula Julius de (1844-1920) Hungarian				
oil	1	51,520	51,520	51,520
BENDA, Wladyslav T (1873-1948) American				
oil	1	2,000	2,000	2,000
BENDALL, Claude D (1891-1970) British/French				
oil	1	1,151	1,151	1,151
BENDEMANN, Eduard Julius Friedrich (1811-1889) German				
wc/d	1	3,857	3,857	3,857
BENDEMANN, Rudolf (1851-1884) German				
oil	1	3,080	3,080	3,080
BENDER, Bill (1920-) American				
oil	2	1,100-1,100	1,100	1,100
BENDER, Sarah E de Wolfe (1852-1935) American				
oil	2	4,000-4,000	4,000	4,000
BENDERSKY, Eduardo (20th C) Argentinian				
oil	3	2,500-3,000	2,766	2,800
BENDIEN, Jacob (1890-1933) Dutch				
oil	1	44,524	44,524	44,524
BENDRAT, Arthur (1872-?) German				
oil	1	1,826	1,826	1,826
BENDRE, Narayan Shridhar (1910-1992) Indian				
oil	2	19,000-120,000	69,500	19,000
wc/d	2	12,155-14,960	13,557	12,155
BENDTSEN, Folmer (1907-1993) Swedish				
oil	30	1,132-5,011	2,407	2,263
BENEDETTI, Andries (c.1615-?) Flemish				
oil	1	97,900	97,900	97,900
BENEDETTI, Renzo de (1904-1958) Italian				
oil	1	1,178	1,178	1,178
BENEDETTO, Enzo (1905-1993) Italian				
oil	1	2,400	2,400	2,400
BENEDETTO, Steve di (1958-) American?				
oil	1	39,000	39,000	39,000
BENEDINI, Gabriella (1932-) Italian				
wc/d	1	1,229	1,229	1,229
BENEDIT, Luis F (1937-) Argentinian				
oil	4	3,299-9,500	6,569	6,479
wc/d	1	1,500	1,500	1,500
BENEKER, Gerrit Albertus (1882-1934) American				
oil	15	1,000-15,000	5,830	2,900
BENES, Vlastimil (1919-1981) Czechoslovakian				
oil	1	2,504	2,504	2,504
BENET ESPUNY, Jose (1920-) Spanish				
oil	2	1,688-2,049	1,868	1,688
BENETTON, Simon (1933-) Italian				
3D	2	2,175-3,884	3,029	2,175
BENGLIS, Linda (1941-) American				
3D	4	2,200-30,000	12,550	3,000
BENGTS, Carl (1876-1934) Finnish				
oil	1	5,143	5,143	5,143

Name	No.	Price Range	Average	Median
BENGTSSON, Dick (1936-1989) Swedish				
wc/d	1	1,116	1,116	1,116
3D	1	5,286	5,286	5,286
BENHAM, Thomas C S (fl.1878-1922) British				
oil	1	3,132	3,132	3,132
BENINGFIELD, Gordon (1936-1998) British				
wc/d	2	510-1,602	1,056	510
BENJAMIN, A de (19th C) ?				
oil	1	10,837	10,837	10,837
BENK, Johannes (1844-1914) Austrian				
3D	1	2,500	2,500	2,500
BENLLIURE Y GIL, Jose (1855-1937) Spanish				
oil	5	7,775-61,250	36,829	33,250
wc/d	2	1,267-3,575	2,421	1,267
BENLLIURE Y GIL, Juan Antonio (19th C) Spanish				
oil	1	2,280	2,280	2,280
BENLLIURE Y GIL, Mariano (1862-1947) Spanish				
wc/d	2	1,430-5,382	3,406	1,430
BENLLIURE, Blas (1852-1936) Spanish				
oil	1	1,640	1,640	1,640
BENN (1905-1989) Polish				
oil	5	705-1,607	1,071	882
BENN, Ben (1884-1983) American				
oil	6	450-2,000	1,108	900
wc/d	1	400	400	400
BENNANI, Mohamed (1943-) Moroccan				
oil	1	9,402	9,402	9,402
BENNEKENSTEIN, Hermann (19th C) German				
oil	1	1,331	1,331	1,331
BENNER, Gerrit (1897-1981) Dutch				
oil	1	53,014	53,014	53,014
wc/d	7	3,741-9,555	6,307	6,361
BENNER, Henri (1776-c.1818) French				
wc/d	2	2,625-16,703	9,664	2,625
BENNER, Jean (1796-1849) French				
oil	1	1,334	1,334	1,334
BENNER, Jean (1836-1909) French				
oil	2	1,519-26,886	14,202	1,519
wc/d	1	608	608	608
BENNET, Baron Karl Stefan (1800-1878) Swedish				
oil	5	1,454-28,161	9,380	5,495
BENNETT, Andrew (20th C) Australian				
oil	4	785-1,309	1,038	842
wc/d	2	1,914-7,308	4,611	1,914
BENNETT, Frank Moss (1874-1953) British				
oil	18	661-45,240	8,886	4,536
BENNETT, Malcolm (1942-) British				
oil	2	1,116-1,209	1,162	1,116
BENNETT, Newton (1854-1914) British				
wc/d	2	605-1,418	1,011	605
BENNETT, William (1811-1871) British				
wc/d	6	440-15,000	3,081	493
BENNETTER, J J (1822-1904) Norwegian				
oil	1	1,523	1,523	1,523
BENOHOUD, Hicham (1968-) Moroccan				
wc/d	2	1,609-2,179	1,894	1,609
BENOIS, Albert (19/20th C) Russian				
wc/d	6	634-15,288	6,057	2,281
BENOIS, Albert Nikolaievitch (1852-1936) Russian				
wc/d	14	1,014-17,485	5,493	3,741
BENOIS, Alexander (1870-1960) Russian				
oil	1	17,755	17,755	17,755
wc/d	44	1,488-190,000	20,569	6,195
BENOIS, Nadia (1896-1975) Russian				
oil	5	445-1,638	1,134	1,218
wc/d	1	1,323	1,323	1,323
BENOIS, Nicola (1901-1988) Russian				
wc/d	5	1,767-10,320	6,306	7,500
BENOIS, Nicolas (19th C) Russian				
wc/d	1	24,928	24,928	24,928
BENOIS, Nikolaj Leontjewitsch (1813-1898) Russian				
wc/d	1	18,600	18,600	18,600

Name	No.	Price Range	Average	Median
BENOIT, Serge (1937-) French				
oil	6	600-1,077	884	892
3D	1	3,295	3,295	3,295
BENOIT-LEVY, Jules (1866-c.1925) French				
oil	1	3,583	3,583	3,583
BENOUVILLE, Jean-Achille (1815-1891) French				
oil	2	1,352-1,897	1,624	1,352
wc/d	3	514-3,176	2,247	3,053
BENRATH, Frederic (1930-) French				
oil	4	1,216-3,148	2,073	1,394
wc/d	1	514	514	514
BENSA, Alexander von (1820-1902) Austrian				
oil	3	832-1,788	1,398	1,576
BENSING, Frank C (1893-1983) American				
oil	2	400-3,500	1,950	400
BENSINGER, Amalie (1809-1889) German				
oil	1	11,439	11,439	11,439
BENSO, Giulio (1601-1668) Italian				
wc/d	1	2,680	2,680	2,680
BENSON, Ambrosius (1495-1550) Flemish				
oil	2	35,479-231,400	133,439	35,479
BENSON, Frank W (1862-1951) American				
oil	2	48,000-210,000	129,000	48,000
wc/d	3	26,000-55,000	42,833	47,500
BENSON, Ritchie (1941-1996) American				
wc/d	1	3,250	3,250	3,250
BENT, Jan van der (1650-1690) Dutch				
oil	5	2,649-12,460	7,719	7,576
BENTELE, Fidelis (1830-1901) German				
3D	1	2,422	2,422	2,422
BENTIVOGLIO, Cesare (1868-1952) Italian				
oil	4	1,006-12,429	5,134	2,131
BENTLEY, Charles (1806-1854) British				
wc/d	5	534-11,340	4,237	1,665
BENTLEY, Claude (1915-1990) American				
oil	1	880	880	880
wc/d	1	660	660	660
BENTLEY, John W (1880-1951) American				
oil	8	1,200-14,000	6,387	6,500
BENTON, Dwight (1834-?) American				
oil	1	7,000	7,000	7,000
BENTON, Thomas Hart (1889-1975) American				
oil	5	45,000-1,600,000	501,000	290,000
wc/d	6	850-200,000	63,825	2,500
3D	1	6,500	6,500	6,500
BENTUM, Rik van (1936-) Dutch				
wc/d	1	3,307	3,307	3,307
BENVENUTI, Benvenuto (1881-1959) Italian				
oil	1	17,810	17,810	17,810
BENVENUTI, Pietro (1769-1844) Italian				
oil	3	5,040-80,100	32,046	11,000
BENVENUTI, Robert (19/20th C) American				
oil	1	1,500	1,500	1,500
BENWELL, Joseph Austin (fl.1865-1886) British				
wc/d	2	3,560-26,000	14,780	3,560
BENYEI, Andrew (1949-) Canadian				
3D	1	1,230	1,230	1,230
BENZ, Severin (1834-1898) German				
oil	1	2,552	2,552	2,552
BENZIGER, August (1867-1955) Swiss				
oil	1	1,928	1,928	1,928
BENZONI, Giovanni Maria (1809-1873) Italian				
3D	2	13,920-38,000	25,960	13,920
BEOTHY, Étienne (1897-1961) Hungarian				
oil	8	2,160-8,880	3,395	2,400
wc/d	23	539-5,092	2,621	2,425
3D	1	5,143	5,143	5,143
BEOTHY-STEINER, Anna (1902-1985) Hungarian				
wc/d	1	3,460	3,460	3,460
BERAIN, Jean I and II (17/18th C) French				
wc/d	1	1,173	1,173	1,173

Name	No.	Price Range	Average	Median
BERALDO, Franco (1944-) Italian				
oil	16	589-4,056	1,501	1,296
BERANGER, Emmanuel (19th C) French				
oil	1	14,000	14,000	14,000
BERARD, Christian (1902-1949) French				
oil	6	5,006-47,000	21,731	8,834
wc/d	24	417-26,340	3,833	1,731
BERATON, Ferry (1860-1900) Austrian				
oil	1	20,000	20,000	20,000
BERAUD, Jean (1849-1936) French				
oil	7	7,875-368,000	161,764	139,200
wc/d	2	8,500-65,000	36,750	8,500
BERBER, Mersad (1940-) Yugoslavian				
oil	1	3,000	3,000	3,000
wc/d	2	531-11,066	5,798	531
BERBERIAN, Ovanes (1951-) American				
oil	2	400-2,750	1,575	400
BERBERICH, Fritz (1909-1990) German?				
oil	1	3,405	3,405	3,405
BERCHEM, Nicolaes (1620-1683) Dutch				
oil	4	13,793-692,000	193,170	31,783
wc/d	1	19,418	19,418	19,418
BERCHERE, Narcisse (1819-1891) French				
oil	5	2,973-34,213	12,840	9,370
wc/d	2	959-4,200	2,579	959
BERCHMANS, Sister Agnes (1879-1973) Canadian				
oil	2	1,500-2,900	2,200	1,500
BERCKAU, Heinrich (1660-1716) German				
oil	1	7,905	7,905	7,905
BERCOT, Paul (1898-1970) French				
oil	2	1,196-3,349	2,272	1,196
BERCOVITCH, Alexander (1892-1951) Canadian				
oil	1	1,712	1,712	1,712
BERDICH, Vera (1915-2003) American				
oil	3	400-600	500	500
wc/d	1	1,900	1,900	1,900
BERDYSZAK, Jan (1934-) Polish				
oil	2	1,520-1,784	1,652	1,520
BEREA, Demetre de (1908-1975) Rumanian				
oil	1	1,000	1,000	1,000
BERENDRECHT, Pieter Jansz van (1616-1662) Dutch				
oil	2	18,703-38,219	28,461	18,703
BERENY, Robert (1887-1953) Hungarian				
oil	2	5,000-63,699	34,349	5,000
BERESFORD, Frank Ernest (1881-1967) British				
oil	2	1,328-2,000	1,664	1,328
BERETTA, Petrus Augustus (1805-1866) Dutch				
oil	1	2,674	2,674	2,674
BERG, Adrian (1929-) British				
oil	4	915-3,420	1,878	1,566
BERG, Anna Carolina van den (1873-1942) Dutch				
oil	6	514-3,356	1,642	1,438
BERG, Christian (1893-1976) Swedish				
oil	1	622	622	622
3D	4	10,836-41,987	25,098	21,143
BERG, Else (1877-1942) Dutch				
wc/d	1	4,091	4,091	4,091
BERG, F van den (1918-) Dutch				
oil	2	1,092-3,884	2,488	1,092
BERG, Freek van den (1918-2000) Dutch				
oil	13	904-4,555	2,924	3,134
wc/d	1	1,199	1,199	1,199
BERG, Jacobus Everardus van den (1802-1861) Dutch				
oil	1	2,498	2,498	2,498
BERG, Jos van den (1905-1978) Dutch				
oil	3	589-2,799	1,591	1,386
BERG, Shlomo van der (1920-1986) Israeli				
oil	3	400-4,500	1,793	480
BERG, Siep van den (1913-) Dutch				
oil	3	1,829-3,534	2,763	2,926
BERG, Svante (1885-1946) Swedish				
oil	6	661-4,361	1,900	793

Name	No.	Price Range	Average	Median
BERG, Werner (1904-1981) Austrian				
oil	2	51,534-64,662	58,098	51,534
wc/d	1	820	820	820
BERG, Willem van den (1886-1970) Dutch				
oil	4	435-2,400	1,755	2,016
wc/d	2	1,127-1,999	1,563	1,127
BERGAGNA, Vittorio (1884-1965) Italian				
oil	1	3,986	3,986	3,986
BERGAMINI, Francesco (1815-1883) Italian				
oil	7	4,872-25,918	10,905	8,918
BERGE, Edward (1876-1924) American				
3D	2	2,400-30,000	16,200	2,400
BERGEL, Giyora (1963-) Israeli				
oil	2	1,000-1,000	1,000	1,000
BERGEN, C (19th C) German				
oil	1	1,193	1,193	1,193
BERGEN, Carl von (1853-1933) German				
oil	4	3,250-14,000	7,382	4,718
BERGEN, Claus (1885-1964) German				
oil	4	1,148-3,633	2,228	1,818
BERGEN, Dirck van (1645-1690) Dutch				
oil	2	3,770-4,257	4,013	3,770
BERGEN, Fritz (1857-?) German				
oil	1	1,065	1,065	1,065
wc/d	1	954	954	954
BERGENSTRAHLE, Marie Louise de Geer (1944-) Swedish				
oil	4	1,400-3,817	2,801	2,290
3D	1	3,304	3,304	3,304
BERGER, Ernst (1857-1919) Austrian				
oil	1	9,687	9,687	9,687
BERGER, F (19th C) Austrian				
oil	2	3,750-9,200	6,475	3,750
BERGER, Hans (1882-1977) Swiss				
oil	3	1,984-6,485	3,633	2,432
wc/d	2	811-1,135	973	811
BERGER, Jacques (1902-1977) Swiss				
oil	1	1,138	1,138	1,138
wc/d	2	653-3,100	1,876	653
BERGER, Jason (1923-) American				
oil	1	1,300	1,300	1,300
BERGER, Jenny (19th C) French				
oil	1	1,500	1,500	1,500
BERGERON, Henri (19th C) French				
oil	1	2,788	2,788	2,788
BERGES, Werner (1941-) German				
oil	2	3,041-7,389	5,215	3,041
wc/d	11	1,113-4,450	2,182	1,784
BERGEVIN, Edouard Edmond de (1861-1925) French				
oil	1	1,458	1,458	1,458
BERGH, Alphonse de (1844-1883) ?				
oil	1	1,752	1,752	1,752
BERGH, Andries van den (1817-1880) Dutch				
oil	1	3,134	3,134	3,134
BERGH, Edvard (1828-1880) Swedish				
oil	2	992-3,434	2,213	992
BERGH, Piet van den (1865-1950) Dutch				
oil	1	2,893	2,893	2,893
BERGH, Rickard (1858-1919) Swedish				
oil	1	1,057	1,057	1,057
BERGHE, Frits van den (1883-1939) Belgian				
oil	1	36,122	36,122	36,122
wc/d	5	899-5,274	2,814	2,803
BERGLER, Joseph (younger) (1753-1829) Austrian				
oil	1	15,459	15,459	15,459
wc/d	1	723	723	723
BERGMAN, Anna-Eva (1909-1987) Swedish/French				
oil	3	1,686-4,629	3,633	4,586
wc/d	1	1,073	1,073	1,073
BERGMAN, Franz (19/20th C) Austrian				
3D	4	2,768-4,325	3,693	3,633
BERGMAN, Franz Walter (1898-1977) American				
wc/d	1	10,000	10,000	10,000

Name	No.	Price Range	Average	Median
BERGMAN, Oskar (1879-1963) Swedish				
oil	4	962-16,562	5,823	2,747
wc/d	35	518-16,562	2,408	1,511
BERGMANN, Julius Hugo (1861-1940) German				
oil	2	779-3,579	2,179	779
BERGMANN, Max (1884-1955) German				
oil	5	484-1,753	1,113	1,091
BERGMANN-MICHEL, Ella (1896-1972) German				
wc/d	1	2,356	2,356	2,356
BERGMEISTER, Hermann (1869-1988) German				
oil	1	3,514	3,514	3,514
BERGNER, Yosl (1920-) Israeli				
oil	27	1,400-40,000	11,903	8,000
wc/d	6	380-850	553	420
BERGOLLI, Aldo (1916-1972) Italian				
oil	7	1,560-4,171	3,258	3,562
wc/d	1	595	595	595
BERGOO, Karin (1859-1928) Swedish				
oil	1	20,384	20,384	20,384
BERGSLIEN, Knud Larsen (1827-1908) Norwegian				
oil	1	60,720	60,720	60,720
BERGSLIEN, Nils (1853-1928) Norwegian				
wc/d	1	1,443	1,443	1,443
BERGUE, Tony Francis de (1820-1893) French				
oil	2	1,915-2,928	2,421	1,915
BERISTAYN, Jorge (1894-1964) Argentinian				
oil	2	3,700-6,500	5,100	3,700
BERJEAN, P (20th C) French?				
3D	1	2,572	2,572	2,572
BERJON, Antoine (1754-1843) French				
wc/d	3	467-20,000	7,218	1,189
BERK, Henrietta (1919-1993) American				
oil	1	2,250	2,250	2,250
BERKE, Ernest (1921-) American				
oil	1	1,200	1,200	1,200
BERKE, Hubert (1908-1979) German				
oil	2	3,534-3,822	3,678	3,534
wc/d	19	486-1,929	795	608
BERKES, Antal (1874-1938) Hungarian				
oil	4	447-1,800	1,011	700
BERKHEMER, Madeleine (1973-) Dutch				
wc/d	3	1,236-1,607	1,442	1,483
3D	1	3,214	3,214	3,214
BERKOWITZ, Leon (1919-) American				
oil	1	12,000	12,000	12,000
BERLANT, Tony (1941-) American				
3D	3	2,100-4,500	3,353	3,460
BERLIN, Dis (1959-) Spanish				
oil	2	7,603-45,755	26,679	7,603
BERLIN, Sven Paul (1911-2000) British				
oil	2	694-1,175	934	694
wc/d	1	961	961	961
BERLINGERI, Cesare (1948-) Italian				
oil	8	1,849-4,794	3,366	3,366
wc/d	8	471-10,171	3,338	610
3D	1	3,534	3,534	3,534
BERLIT, Rudiger (1883-1939) German				
oil	1	5,856	5,856	5,856
BERMAN, Eugene (1899-1972) American/Russian				
oil	4	2,200-5,550	3,800	2,250
wc/d	25	400-2,592	1,267	1,165
BERMAN, Leonid (1898-1976) Russian				
oil	1	1,942	1,942	1,942
BERMAN, Marieta (20th C) Venezuelan?				
wc/d	1	1,860	1,860	1,860
BERMANN, Cipri Adolf (1862-?) German				
3D	1	6,466	6,466	6,466
BERMANN, Franz (19/20th C) Austrian?				
3D	1	6,429	6,429	6,429
BERMUDEZ, Cundo (1914-) Cuban				
oil	2	26,000-55,000	40,500	26,000
wc/d	2	2,600-7,500	5,050	2,600

Name	No.	Price Range	Average	Median
BERMUDEZ, Federico-Gil (1867-?) Spanish				
oil	1	1,085	1,085	1,085
BERMUDEZ, Henry (20th C) ?				
oil	4	745-3,500	1,550	930
wc/d	1	930	930	930
BERMUDEZ, Salvador P (19/20th C) Continental				
oil	1	1,000	1,000	1,000
BERNAERTS, Nicasius (1620-1678) Flemish				
oil	1	4,450	4,450	4,450
BERNARD, Émile (1868-1941) French				
oil	16	962-440,137	62,021	3,766
wc/d	7	479-1,757	1,026	912
BERNARD, Jean Francois Armand Felix (1829-1894) French				
oil	1	12,109	12,109	12,109
BERNARD, Joseph (1864-1933) French				
wc/d	1	1,013	1,013	1,013
3D	2	25,442-36,201	30,821	25,442
BERNARD, Louis Michel (1885-1962) French				
wc/d	1	1,858	1,858	1,858
BERNARD, Valere (c.1860-1936) French				
oil	1	4,195	4,195	4,195
BERNARDI, Domenico de (1892-1963) Italian				
oil	3	2,038-14,055	7,958	7,782
BERNARDI, Joseph (1826-1907) German				
oil	2	817-2,658	1,737	817
BERNARDI, Romolo (1876-1956) Italian				
oil	2	605-7,054	3,829	605
BERNARDO, Mane (1913-1991) Argentinian				
oil	1	5,000	5,000	5,000
BERNASCONI, Pietro (1826-1891) Italian				
3D	1	13,230	13,230	13,230
BERNATZ, Johann Martin (1802-1878) German				
oil	1	4,839	4,839	4,839
BERNATZIK, Wilhelm (1853-1906) Austrian				
oil	1	12,083	12,083	12,083
BERNAY-THERIC, Sauveur (20th C) French				
oil	1	1,678	1,678	1,678
BERNDT, Bayard T (1908-1987) American				
oil	1	4,000	4,000	4,000
BERNE-BELLECOUR, Étienne Prosper (1838-1910) French				
oil	4	1,100-3,500	2,272	1,700
BERNE-BELLECOUR, Jean Jacques (1874-1939) French				
oil	1	1,900	1,900	1,900
BERNEKER, Louis Frederick (1876-1937) American				
oil	1	500	500	500
wc/d	1	1,200	1,200	1,200
BERNERS, Lord Gerald (1883-1950) British				
oil	1	6,265	6,265	6,265
BERNET, Roger (20th C) French				
oil	1	8,980	8,980	8,980
BERNHARD, Franz (1934-) German				
wc/d	1	1,152	1,152	1,152
3D	2	1,975-2,827	2,401	1,975
BERNHARD, Pieter Gerardus (1813-1880) Dutch				
oil	1	1,829	1,829	1,829
BERNHARDT, Franz (1800-1860) Swiss				
oil	1	16,493	16,493	16,493
BERNHARDT, Joseph (1805-1885) German				
oil	1	1,334	1,334	1,334
BERNI, Antonio (1905-1981) Argentinian				
oil	10	2,915-120,000	29,688	15,500
wc/d	3	4,800-15,000	9,100	7,500
BERNIER, Camille (1823-1903) French				
oil	1	2,422	2,422	2,422
BERNINGER, Edmund (1843-?) German				
oil	1	10,022	10,022	10,022
BERNINGER, John E (1897-1981) American				
oil	9	500-17,000	4,511	1,700
BERNINGHAUS, J Charles (1905-1988) American				
oil	1	1,600	1,600	1,600

Name	No.	Price Range	Average	Median
BERNINGHAUS, Oscar E (1874-1952) American				
oil	8	24,000-250,000	98,875	60,000
wc/d	4	8,000-16,500	11,625	10,000
BERNINI, Giovanni Lorenzo (1598-1680) Italian				
oil	1	259,500	259,500	259,500
3D	1	6,370	6,370	6,370
BERNSTEIN, Theresa F (1890-2002) American				
oil	1	9,000	9,000	9,000
wc/d	3	600-700	633	600
BERONNEAU, Andre (1896-1973) French				
oil	2	2,052-4,176	3,114	2,052
BEROUD, Louis (1852-1910) French				
oil	1	10,000	10,000	10,000
BERRE, Florent (1821-?) Belgian				
oil	1	2,950	2,950	2,950
BERRE, Jean Baptiste (1777-1838) Belgian				
oil	1	14,684	14,684	14,684
BERRESFORD, Virginia (1904-?) American				
wc/d	1	1,100	1,100	1,100
BERRICK, Andrew (20th C) American				
oil	1	2,000	2,000	2,000
BERROCAL, Miguel (1933-) Spanish				
wc/d	2	505-568	536	505
3D	36	1,401-24,196	5,097	3,000
BERROETA, Pierre de (1914-) French				
oil	3	642-4,055	1,803	714
BERRUTI, Valerio (1977-) Italian				
wc/d	1	1,551	1,551	1,551
BERRY, Philippe (1956-) French				
3D	3	3,818-7,398	5,329	4,772
BERSANI, Stefano (1872-1914) Italian				
oil	1	2,589	2,589	2,589
BERSERIK, Herman (1921-2002) Dutch				
oil	11	2,411-15,671	5,737	4,091
wc/d	3	518-1,447	1,075	1,260
BERSTAMM, Leopold Bernard (1859-1939) Russian				
3D	1	22,500	22,500	22,500
BERTALAN, Albert (1899-1957) Hungarian				
oil	1	1,071	1,071	1,071
BERTANI, Ernesto (20th C) Argentinian				
wc/d	1	8,500	8,500	8,500
BERTEAULT, Louis (fl.1891-1910) French				
wc/d	4	1,518-4,087	2,248	1,635
BERTEAUX, Hippolyte-Dominique (1843-1928) French				
oil	1	2,000	2,000	2,000
wc/d	2	2,775-4,938	3,856	2,775
BERTEL-NORDSTROM, Gustav Adolf Engelbert (1884-1967) Swedish				
oil	1	3,832	3,832	3,832
BERTELLI, Luigi (1832-1916) Italian				
oil	1	5,167	5,167	5,167
BERTELLI, Renato Guiseppe (1900-1974) Italian				
3D	2	5,553-13,469	9,511	5,553
BERTELLI, Santo (1840-1892) Italian				
wc/d	1	2,841	2,841	2,841
BERTELLO, Guido (1929-1993) Italian				
wc/d	1	1,091	1,091	1,091
BERTELSEN, Albert (1921-) Danish				
oil	18	1,213-28,726	9,759	8,449
wc/d	1	1,078	1,078	1,078
BERTELSMANN, Walter (1877-1963) Dutch				
oil	3	667-2,425	1,353	968
BERTEN, Hermann Hugo (1894-1959) Dutch				
oil	1	1,210	1,210	1,210
BERTHE, Louis Maurice (19/20th C) French				
oil	1	1,394	1,394	1,394
BERTHELEMY, Jean Simon (1743-1811) French				
wc/d	1	1,125	1,125	1,125
BERTHELON, Eugène (1829-1924) French				
oil	2	605-2,544	1,574	605
wc/d	1	3,741	3,741	3,741
BERTHELSEN, Christian (1839-1909) Danish				
oil	5	953-3,478	1,620	1,304

Name	No.	Price Range	Average	Median
BERTHELSEN, Johann (1883-1969) American				
oil	24	4,000-26,000	12,904	11,000
BERTHOLLE, Jean (1909-1996) French				
oil	7	1,435-11,308	4,951	4,559
wc/d	3	476-2,630	1,834	2,397
BERTHOLO, René (1935-) Portuguese				
wc/d	1	5,173	5,173	5,173
3D	1	1,908	1,908	1,908
BERTHOME-SAINT-ANDRE (1905-1977) French				
oil	1	537	537	537
wc/d	1	742	742	742
BERTHOME-SAINT-ANDRE, Louis (1905-1977) French				
oil	12	773-3,813	1,923	1,549
wc/d	2	579-608	593	579
BERTHON, Nicolas (1831-1888) French				
oil	1	2,565	2,565	2,565
BERTHOUD, Paul François (1870-?) French				
oil	1	2,395	2,395	2,395
BERTI, Antonio (1830-1912) Italian				
oil	1	1,308	1,308	1,308
wc/d	1	951	951	951
BERTI, Vinicio (1921-1991) Italian				
oil	18	1,029-4,302	2,069	1,638
wc/d	2	1,113-1,908	1,510	1,113
BERTIERI, Pilade (1874-?) British				
oil	1	1,750	1,750	1,750
BERTIN, Émile (1878-1957) French				
oil	1	1,890	1,890	1,890
BERTIN, Jean-Victor (1775-1842) French				
oil	7	1,903-43,250	21,452	15,000
BERTIN, Nicolas (1668-1736) French				
oil	1	27,351	27,351	27,351
BERTIN, Roger (1915-2003) French				
oil	8	840-1,866	1,373	1,320
BERTINI, Dante (1878-?) Italian				
oil	1	1,178	1,178	1,178
BERTINI, Gianni (1922-) Italian				
oil	18	1,555-23,378	8,286	6,797
wc/d	11	951-15,901	4,779	3,168
BERTINI, Giuseppe (1825-1898) Italian				
wc/d	2	304-6,429	3,366	304
BERTINI, L (?) Italian				
oil	2	2,342-2,447	2,394	2,342
BERTLE, Hans (1880-1943) German?				
oil	2	650-5,419	3,034	650
BERTLING, Carl (1835-1918) German				
oil	1	894	894	894
wc/d	1	471	471	471
BERTOCCI, Carlo (1946-) Italian				
oil	2	1,018-1,018	1,018	1,018
BERTOIA, Harry (1915-1978) American				
3D	50	6,500-150,000	36,403	26,000
BERTOLETTI, Nino (1890-1971) Italian				
oil	3	1,868-9,183	4,384	2,102
BERTOLI, Foscaro (18th C) Italian				
3D	1	23,189	23,189	23,189
BERTOLLA, Cesare (1845-1920) Italian				
oil	1	3,884	3,884	3,884
BERTON, Armand (1854-1927) French				
oil	2	1,832-9,503	5,667	1,832
BERTONI, Wander (1925-) Italian				
3D	2	2,425-60,690	31,557	2,425
BERTRAM, Abel (1871-1954) French				
oil	12	418-6,799	2,209	1,443
wc/d	3	486-836	627	561
BERTRAND, A C (?) ?				
oil	1	5,839	5,839	5,839
BERTRAND, Gaston (1910-1994) Belgian				
oil	2	7,658-9,541	8,599	7,658
wc/d	4	942-1,908	1,389	1,081

Name	No.	Price Range	Average	Median
BERTRAND, Huguette Aimee (1922-2005) French				
oil	4	723-7,856	4,610	2,008
wc/d	5	727-1,130	938	970
BERTRAND, Jean-Pierre (1937-) French				
oil	1	3,884	3,884	3,884
wc/d	1	11,003	11,003	11,003
BERTRAND, Pierre-Philippe (1884-1975) French				
oil	2	655-4,165	2,410	655
BERTRAND, Solange (1913-) French				
oil	26	485-3,395	1,107	727
wc/d	8	485-1,212	813	630
3D	1	10,440	10,440	10,440
BERTREUX, Edmond (1911-1991) French				
oil	4	596-725	646	608
wc/d	1	584	584	584
BERTUCHI NIETO, Mariano (1885-1955) Spanish				
oil	2	1,145-2,264	1,704	1,145
wc/d	1	542	542	542
BERTUZZI, Nicola (1710-1777) Italian				
oil	1	19,418	19,418	19,418
BERUETE, Aureliano de (1845-1911) Spanish				
oil	4	14,466-58,070	36,884	22,800
BERVOETS, Freddy (1941-) Belgian				
oil	4	1,403-5,980	3,986	2,719
wc/d	4	693-3,956	1,593	718
BERVOETS, Leo (1892-1978) Belgian				
oil	6	494-3,637	1,643	718
BESANA, Camillo (1887-1941) Italian?				
oil	1	6,469	6,469	6,469
BESANCENOT, Jean (1902-1992) French				
wc/d	1	3,279	3,279	3,279
BESANCON, Antoine (1734-1811) French				
oil	1	7,535	7,535	7,535
BESCHEY, Balthasar (1708-1776) Flemish				
oil	4	1,577-12,041	5,626	2,408
BESCHEY, Karel (1706-1776) Flemish				
oil	2	14,517-213,600	114,058	14,517
BESCO, Donald (1941-) Canadian				
oil	9	820-2,460	1,556	1,518
BESEDIN, Sergei (1901-1996) Russian				
oil	1	2,854	2,854	2,854
wc/d	1	1,189	1,189	1,189
BESKOW, Bo (1906-1989) Swedish				
oil	1	2,114	2,114	2,114
BESKOW, Elsa (1874-1953) Swedish				
wc/d	5	374-79,675	17,357	1,966
BESNARD, Albert (1849-1934) French				
oil	7	825-20,164	6,828	4,789
wc/d	6	1,199-7,947	4,756	3,150
BESNARD, Philippe (19/20th C) French				
3D	3	1,874-4,685	2,967	2,342
BESS, Forrest (1911-1977) American				
oil	5	20,000-70,000	47,000	48,000
BESSA, Pancrace (1772-1846) French				
wc/d	1	13,000	13,000	13,000
BESSET, Cyrille (1864-1902) French				
oil	1	5,980	5,980	5,980
BESSONOF, Boris (1862-1934) Russian				
oil	3	6,270-10,703	8,237	7,740
BESSOU, Pierre (20th C) French				
oil	1	1,168	1,168	1,168
BEST, Arthur W (1859-1935) American				
oil	4	1,000-1,900	1,450	1,200
BEST, Harry Cassie (1863-1936) American				
oil	3	1,800-8,000	5,266	6,000
BESTER, Willie (1956-) South African				
oil	2	942-1,090	1,016	942
BETAK, Alexandre de (20th C) French				
3D	3	15,226-20,497	16,983	15,226

Name	No.	Price Range	Average	Median
BETTENCOURT, Pierre (1917-) French				
oil	1	14,028	14,028	14,028
wc/d	1	11,651	11,651	11,651
3D	2	5,369-6,799	6,084	5,369
BETTI, Mathieu (19th C) Italian				
wc/d	1	1,050	1,050	1,050
BETTI, Niccolo (c.1550-1616) Italian				
oil	2	20,000-27,500	23,750	20,000
BETTINELLI, Mario (1880-1953) Italian				
oil	1	1,212	1,212	1,212
wc/d	1	1,401	1,401	1,401
BETTINGER, Gustave (20th C) French				
oil	1	2,848	2,848	2,848
wc/d	2	1,212-1,455	1,333	1,212
BETTINGER, Hoyland (1890-1950) American				
oil	1	1,700	1,700	1,700
BETTRIDGE and JENNENS (19th C) Canadian				
oil	1	1,100	1,100	1,100
BETTS, Harold H (1881-?) American				
oil	2	1,600-1,600	1,600	1,600
BETTS, Louis (1873-1961) American				
oil	2	2,000-9,000	5,500	2,000
BETZEN, Valerie von (20th C) American				
oil	2	800-2,000	1,400	800
BEUCKER, Pascal de (1861-1945) ?				
oil	3	2,008-7,827	4,449	3,514
BEUL, Bert de (1961-) Belgian				
oil	1	2,670	2,670	2,670
BEUL, Frans de (1849-1919) Belgian				
oil	7	1,219-4,529	2,291	2,000
BEUL, Henri de (1845-1900) Belgian				
oil	3	1,246-4,944	2,539	1,427
BEUL, Laurent de (1821-1872) Belgian				
oil	2	766-1,250	1,008	766
BEULAS, José (1921-) Spanish				
oil	17	1,929-14,449	4,798	3,816
wc/d	5	827-2,314	1,808	1,914
BEURDEN, Alfons van (jnr) (1878-1962) Belgian				
oil	1	9,555	9,555	9,555
BEURDEN, Alphonse van (snr) (1854-1938) Belgian				
3D	1	4,618	4,618	4,618
BEURMANN, Emil (1862-1951) Swiss				
oil	4	342-2,664	1,121	489
BEUYS, Joseph (1921-1986) German				
oil	6	1,914-92,500	49,629	27,750
wc/d	23	658-167,200	32,476	18,500
3D	35	680-555,000	66,096	9,555
BEUYS, Joseph and LUTHER, Adolf (20th C) German				
3D	1	8,247	8,247	8,247
BEVAN, Irvine (1852-1940) British				
wc/d	2	1,496-2,392	1,944	1,496
BEVAN, Robert (1865-1925) British				
oil	4	12,852-487,200	142,551	17,955
wc/d	1	3,515	3,515	3,515
BEVAN, Tony (1951-) British				
oil	4	9,250-38,720	24,535	20,571
wc/d	1	33,440	33,440	33,440
BEVERIDGE, Erskine (20th C) American				
oil	1	1,800	1,800	1,800
BEVERLEY, William Roxby (1811-1889) British				
wc/d	5	676-1,850	1,341	1,602
BEVILACQUA, Michael (1966-) American				
oil	1	14,000	14,000	14,000
BEWER, Clemens (1820-1884) German				
oil	1	14,137	14,137	14,137
BEWICK, Pauline (1935-) Irish				
oil	1	5,250	5,250	5,250
wc/d	11	973-9,773	4,602	5,041
BEYER, Jan de (1703-1780) Swiss				
wc/d	2	2,400-4,861	3,630	2,400
BEYER, Johan and Ludwig (?) ?				
wc/d	1	1,818	1,818	1,818

Name	No.	Price Range	Average	Median
BEYEREN, Abraham van (1620-1690) Dutch				
oil	2	24,523-90,000	57,261	24,523
BEYLE, Pierre Marie (1838-1902) French				
oil	2	1,132-1,620	1,376	1,132
BEYSCHLAG, Robert (1838-1903) German				
oil	2	1,286-2,510	1,898	1,286
BEZANIC, Nebojsa (1964-) Yugoslavian				
wc/d	1	26,460	26,460	26,460
BEZEM, Naphtali (1924-) Israeli				
oil	11	1,400-7,000	4,190	4,000
wc/d	4	460-800	640	550
BEZOMBES, Roger (1913-1994) French				
oil	16	2,425-63,700	10,578	6,370
wc/d	22	547-434,959	22,853	1,665
3D	8	1,911-4,084	2,872	2,722
BHATTACHARJEE, Bikash (1940-) Indian				
oil	3	35,000-80,000	53,333	45,000
BHATTACHARJEE, Chandra (1962-) Indian				
oil	1	10,380	10,380	10,380
BHAVSAR, Natvar (1934-) Indian				
wc/d	2	4,250-22,500	13,375	4,250
BIALINITSKI-BIROULIA, Vitold (1872-1957) Russian				
oil	4	9,460-57,414	21,994	10,260
BIAN SHOUMIN (18th C) Chinese				
wc/d	1	1,764	1,764	1,764
BIANCA, Dino La (1941-) Italian				
oil	1	1,200	1,200	1,200
BIANCHI, Alberto (1882-1969) Italian				
oil	1	1,344	1,344	1,344
BIANCHI, Domenico (1955-) Italian				
oil	3	4,676-10,177	6,859	5,724
wc/d	2	834-7,591	4,212	834
BIANCHI, Mose (1840-1904) Italian				
oil	1	21,875	21,875	21,875
wc/d	4	820-1,991	1,332	1,113
BIANCO, Armando dal (1899-?) Italian				
oil	1	8,174	8,174	8,174
BIANCO, Pieretto (1875-1937) Italian				
oil	3	1,424-2,973	2,322	2,571
wc/d	2	668-668	668	668
BIANCO, Remo (1922-1990) Italian				
oil	4	4,290-10,813	7,441	6,392
wc/d	9	732-6,214	3,363	3,196
3D	3	4,290-4,844	4,474	4,290
BIARD, François Auguste (1799-1882) French				
oil	2	11,900-44,350	28,125	11,900
BIASI DA TEULADA, Giuseppe (1885-1945) Italian				
oil	4	3,185-28,703	11,374	4,638
BIASI, Alberto (1937-) Italian				
oil	3	3,414-5,301	4,554	4,948
wc/d	15	1,018-9,709	5,318	4,917
3D	1	4,090	4,090	4,090
BIASI, Guido (1933-1984) Italian				
oil	8	724-3,505	1,536	1,054
wc/d	1	1,019	1,019	1,019
BIBIENA, Ferdinando Galli (1657-1743) Italian				
wc/d	1	9,500	9,500	9,500
BIBIENA, Francesco Galli (1659-1739) Italian				
wc/d	1	2,919	2,919	2,919
BIBIENA, Giuseppe Galli (1696-1756) Italian				
wc/d	1	11,100	11,100	11,100
BICCI DI LORENZO (1373-1452) Italian				
oil	4	70,000-140,000	99,521	84,286
BICCI, Neri di (1419-1491) Italian				
oil	3	50,000-85,100	68,366	70,000
BICKEL, Karl (1886-1982) Swiss				
oil	1	2,107	2,107	2,107
BICKERSTAFF, George (1893-1954) American				
oil	7	600-1,600	1,092	900
BICKERTON, Ashley (1959-) American				
3D	1	11,000	11,000	11,000

Name	No.	Price Range	Average	Median
BICKNELL, Frank Alfred (1866-1943) American				
oil	3	2,600-8,500	6,237	7,612
BICKNELL, John (1958-) British				
oil	1	3,204	3,204	3,204
BIDAULD, Jean Joseph Xavier (1758-1846) French				
oil	6	3,805-200,000	50,361	7,292
BIDDLE, George (1885-1973) American				
wc/d	2	1,800-2,000	1,900	1,800
BIDDLE, Laurence (1888-?) British				
oil	6	1,368-6,500	4,136	3,363
BIDDULPH, Sir Michael Anthony Schrapnel (1823-1904) British				
wc/d	1	4,248	4,248	4,248
BIDLO, Mike (1955-) American				
oil	3	4,500-42,000	19,166	11,000
wc/d	2	4,200-12,000	8,100	4,200
3D	1	4,000	4,000	4,000
BIDNER, Robert (1930-1983) American				
oil	1	2,000	2,000	2,000
BIE, Cornelis de (1621-1664) Dutch				
oil	2	4,466-10,837	7,651	4,466
BIE, Erasme de (1629-1675) Flemish				
oil	1	5,733	5,733	5,733
BIE, Eugène de (1914-1983) Belgian				
oil	1	1,060	1,060	1,060
BIEDERMAN, Charles (1906-2004) American				
oil	1	9,500	9,500	9,500
3D	2	16,000-17,000	16,500	16,000
BIEDERMAN, Jerome (1913-1996) American				
oil	1	1,500	1,500	1,500
BIEDERMANN, Johann Jakob (1763-1830) Swiss				
oil	5	17,027-60,204	34,710	21,648
wc/d	1	916	916	916
BIEGAS, Boleslas (1877-1954) Polish				
oil	2	3,687-8,011	5,849	3,687
3D	4	1,635-4,115	2,554	2,116
BIEGEL, Peter (1913-1988) British				
oil	8	622-13,176	2,955	1,098
wc/d	4	531-5,856	2,026	659
BIEHLE, August (1885-1979) American				
oil	1	5,000	5,000	5,000
wc/d	1	525	525	525
BIELER, André Charles (1896-1989) Canadian				
oil	6	902-22,919	5,325	1,312
wc/d	1	673	673	673
BIELER, Ernest (1863-1948) Swiss				
wc/d	10	759-213,097	45,370	10,623
BIELING, Hermann Friedrich (1887-1964) Dutch				
oil	9	771-5,063	2,557	2,163
3D	1	6,361	6,361	6,361
BIEMA, Carry van (1881-1942) German				
oil	1	4,622	4,622	4,622
BIENABE ARTIA, Bernardino (1889-1987) Spanish				
oil	1	3,616	3,616	3,616
BIENVETU, Gustav (19/20th C) French				
oil	1	2,253	2,253	2,253
BIERGE, Roland (1922-1991) French				
oil	5	463-2,038	1,180	989
wc/d	1	479	479	479
BIERK, David (1944-2001) Canadian				
oil	2	6,749-9,280	8,014	6,749
BIERLE, Rudolf (1920-) German				
oil	1	1,255	1,255	1,255
BIERMANN, Edouard (1803-1892) German				
oil	1	1,937	1,937	1,937
BIERNACKI, Andrzej (1958-) Polish				
oil	1	3,567	3,567	3,567
BIERSTADT, Albert (1830-1902) American/German				
oil	16	13,000-525,000	156,455	50,000
BIERTI, Francesco (1901-2000) Italian				
oil	2	1,401-1,870	1,635	1,401

Name	No.	Price Range	Average	Median
BIERUMA-OOSTING, Jeanne (1898-1995) Dutch				
oil	3	1,929-2,910	2,412	2,397
wc/d	1	707	707	707
BIESBROECK, Jean Baptiste van (1825-1878) Belgian				
oil	1	1,500	1,500	1,500
BIESE, Gerth (1901-1980) German				
oil	2	803-1,236	1,019	803
BIESE, Helmi (1867-1933) Finnish				
oil	4	4,114-9,900	6,399	5,143
wc/d	3	584-1,690	1,030	818
BIESEBROECK, Jules van (1873-1965) Belgian				
oil	11	468-4,052	1,321	876
wc/d	5	876-1,432	1,197	1,312
3D	1	3,366	3,366	3,366
BIESSY, Marie Gabriel (1854-1935) French				
oil	2	2,395-4,000	3,197	2,395
BIESZCZAD, Severin (1852-1923) European				
oil	1	2,450	2,450	2,450
BIGARI, Vittori (1692-1776) Italian				
wc/d	1	1,165	1,165	1,165
BIGATTI, Alfredo (?) Argentinian				
wc/d	1	1,500	1,500	1,500
3D	1	16,000	16,000	16,000
BIGATTI, Tommaso (18/19th C) Italian				
wc/d	1	4,625	4,625	4,625
BIGAUD, Wilson (1931-) Haitian				
oil	1	2,124	2,124	2,124
BIGAUX, Louis Felix (1850-?) French				
oil	1	1,386	1,386	1,386
BIGELOW, Daniel Folger (1823-1910) American				
oil	2	950-1,200	1,075	950
BIGELOW, Larry (20th C) Irish?				
oil	1	1,178	1,178	1,178
BIGGERS, John Thomas (1924-2001) American				
wc/d	1	15,000	15,000	15,000
BIGGI, Fausto (19th C) Italian				
3D	2	9,048-14,175	11,611	9,048
BIGGI, Felice Fortunato (17th C) Italian				
oil	1	17,858	17,858	17,858
BIGGI, Gastone (1925-) Italian				
oil	2	3,770-31,021	17,395	3,770
wc/d	4	1,885-3,652	2,542	2,316
BIGGS, Walter (1886-1968) American				
wc/d	1	1,000	1,000	1,000
BIGIOLI, Filippo (1798-1878) Italian				
wc/d	1	1,600	1,600	1,600
BIGOT, Georges (1860-1927) French				
oil	5	1,580-2,431	2,042	2,188
BIGOT, Raymond (1872-1953) French				
wc/d	6	760-2,281	1,360	1,192
BIGUM, Martin (1966-) Danish				
oil	1	8,048	8,048	8,048
BIHAN, Cyril le (20th C) French				
oil	1	1,113	1,113	1,113
BIHAN, D L (19th C) British				
oil	1	4,919	4,919	4,919
BIHAN, L (19th C) British				
oil	1	1,903	1,903	1,903
BILBAO Y MARTINEZ, Gonzalo (1860-1938) Spanish				
oil	1	21,600	21,600	21,600
BILBO, Jack (1907-1967) ?				
oil	3	855-2,478	1,642	1,593
BILCOQ, Marie Marc Antoine (1755-1838) French				
oil	1	15,130	15,130	15,130
BILDERS, Albertus Gerardus (1838-1865) Dutch				
oil	2	10,911-14,833	12,872	10,911
BILDERS, Johannes Wernardus (1811-1890) Dutch				
oil	5	1,454-8,653	3,971	1,794
BILDERS-BOSSE, Maria Philippina (1837-1900) Dutch				
oil	1	3,014	3,014	3,014

Name	No.	Price Range	Average	Median
BILIBIN, Ivan (1876-1942) Russian				
oil	1	100,000	100,000	100,000
wc/d	3	3,250-48,360	22,363	15,480
BILINSKY, Boris (1901-1948) Russian				
wc/d	1	3,045	3,045	3,045
BILL, Max (1908-1994) Swiss				
oil	9	1,073-42,240	28,416	25,965
wc/d	1	3,312	3,312	3,312
3D	4	12,000-350,000	98,425	14,000
BILLE, Carl (1815-1898) Danish				
oil	9	1,493-4,426	2,582	2,507
BILLE, Edmond (1878-1959) Swiss				
oil	4	2,203-31,000	12,851	5,303
wc/d	7	835-6,526	2,374	2,061
BILLE, Ejler (1910-) Danish				
oil	5	29,096-66,274	44,879	33,802
wc/d	3	3,058-4,024	3,433	3,219
BILLE, Vilhelm (1864-1908) Danish				
oil	5	652-6,730	2,602	1,423
BILLET, Étienne (1821-?) French				
oil	1	9,504	9,504	9,504
BILLET, Pierre (1837-1922) French				
oil	5	837-14,000	4,507	3,233
BILLGREN, Ernst (1957-) Swedish				
oil	6	3,181-58,528	18,320	5,550
wc/d	1	1,527	1,527	1,527
3D	8	2,775-51,537	11,596	7,125
BILLGREN, Helene (1952-) Swedish				
wc/d	2	954-1,321	1,137	954
BILLGREN, Ola (1940-2001) Swedish				
oil	18	2,799-303,935	55,377	38,322
wc/d	3	1,527-18,500	7,556	2,643
BILLIARD, Victor Marie Louis (1864-1952) French				
oil	1	2,520	2,520	2,520
BILLING, Anna (1849-1927) Swedish				
oil	1	1,168	1,168	1,168
wc/d	2	872-1,099	985	872
BILLING, Frederick W and MORAN, Peter and Thomas (19th C) American				
oil	1	80,000	80,000	80,000
BILLMYER, James Irwin (1897-?) American				
oil	2	500-1,100	800	500
wc/d	2	1,400-1,800	1,600	1,400
BILLOTEY, Louis Leon Eugene (1883-1940) French				
oil	12	1,204-38,014	7,154	2,534
wc/d	22	507-9,884	1,392	634
BILLOTTE, René (1846-1915) French				
oil	1	1,210	1,210	1,210
BILSECK, E Wolff (20th C) ?				
oil	1	1,958	1,958	1,958
BILSING, C (?) American				
oil	1	2,000	2,000	2,000
BILTIUS, Cornelis (17th C) Dutch				
oil	3	14,500-203,500	83,031	31,095
BILTIUS, Jacobus (1633-1681) Dutch				
oil	2	4,362-180,000	92,181	4,362
BIMBI, Bartolomeo (1648-1725) Italian				
oil	2	25,000-77,143	51,071	25,000
BIMMERMANN, Caesar (1821-1890) German				
oil	7	1,216-7,000	3,914	3,901
BIN, Émile J B (1825-1897) French				
oil	1	25,000	25,000	25,000
BINCKES, Henry Ashby (fl.1846-1880) British				
oil	1	3,828	3,828	3,828
BINDER, Avraham (1906-2001) American?				
oil	1	4,250	4,250	4,250
BINDER, Tony (1868-1944) British				
oil	14	788-5,021	2,427	2,008
wc/d	5	912-1,338	1,101	973
BINDESBOLL, Thorvald (1846-1908) Danish				
wc/d	1	2,586	2,586	2,586
BINEBINE, Mahi (1959-) Moroccan?				
oil	1	7,223	7,223	7,223
wc/d	1	13,676	13,676	13,676

Name	No.	Price Range	Average	Median
BINET, George (1865-1949) French				
oil	13	596-80,000	9,660	4,784
BINET, Victor Jean Baptiste Barthelemy (1849-1924) French				
oil	3	1,260-2,236	1,622	1,371
BINGHAM, George Caleb (1811-1879) American				
oil	1	1,100	1,100	1,100
BINGLEY, James George (1841-1920) British				
oil	2	957-1,750	1,353	957
wc/d	8	1,050-2,975	1,745	1,313
BINJE, Franz (1835-1900) Belgian				
oil	3	1,197-1,432	1,332	1,368
BINKS, Reuben Ward (fl.1924-1948) British				
wc/d	10	450-3,500	1,204	950
BINNING, Bertram Charles (1909-1976) Canadian				
oil	1	14,588	14,588	14,588
wc/d	1	2,097	2,097	2,097
BINOIT, Peter (17th C) German				
oil	2	92,500-198,523	145,511	92,500
BINZER, Carl von (1824-1904) German				
wc/d	1	1,632	1,632	1,632
BIONDA, Mario (1913-1985) Italian				
oil	5	1,054-5,088	2,450	2,028
wc/d	7	656-1,288	946	884
BIONDETTI, Andrea (1851-1946) Italian				
wc/d	3	839-1,331	1,070	1,040
BIONDI, Nicola (1866-1929) Italian				
oil	1	2,457	2,457	2,457
BIRCH, Samuel John Lamorna (1869-1955) British				
oil	28	1,346-15,570	5,417	4,176
wc/d	25	465-4,928	1,372	900
BIRCH, Thomas (1779-1851) American				
oil	5	3,750-40,000	15,950	15,000
BIRCK, Alphonse (1859-1942) French				
oil	1	6,204	6,204	6,204
wc/d	4	839-1,991	1,467	1,401
BIRD, Henry Richard (1909-2000) British				
oil	4	484-1,349	778	519
wc/d	1	554	554	554
BIRD, Margaret (1864-1948) British				
oil	1	2,100	2,100	2,100
BIRD, Mary Holden (fl.1923-1936) British				
wc/d	7	688-2,864	1,479	1,328
BIRD, Samuel C (19th C) British				
oil	1	2,750	2,750	2,750
BIRELINE, George Lee (1923-2002) American				
oil	2	1,700-3,250	2,475	1,700
BIRGER, Hugo (1854-1887) Swedish				
oil	5	872-49,855	13,623	4,986
wc/d	1	777	777	777
BIRGER-ERICSON, Birger (1904-1994) Swedish				
oil	6	372-4,708	1,485	712
BIRKEMOSE, Jens (1943-) Danish				
oil	13	1,605-8,082	4,380	4,041
wc/d	2	710-1,127	918	710
BIRKENRUTH, Adolphe (1863-?) German				
wc/d	1	2,249	2,249	2,249
BIRKHOLM, Jens (1869-1915) Danish				
oil	5	893-5,038	2,174	1,270
BIRKLE, Albert (1900-1986) Austrian/German				
oil	6	8,482-39,493	26,844	23,514
wc/d	3	1,914-7,304	4,042	2,910
BIRKNER, Thomas (1966-) American				
oil	2	644-6,090	3,367	644
BIRKS, Geoffrey W (1929-1993) British				
wc/d	1	1,744	1,744	1,744
BIRKS, J (19th C) ?				
oil	1	2,100	2,100	2,100
BIRLEY, Sir Oswald (1880-1952) British				
oil	1	12,975	12,975	12,975
BIRMANN, Peter (1758-1844) Swiss				
wc/d	3	2,748-16,650	8,167	5,104

Name	No.	Price Range	Average	Median
BIRMANN, Samuel (1793-1847) Swiss				
oil	2	584-9,159	4,871	584
BIRNEY, William Verplanck (1858-1909) American				
wc/d	1	1,700	1,700	1,700
BIROLLI, Renato (1906-1959) Italian				
oil	6	5,088-194,700	72,125	25,442
wc/d	10	820-6,997	2,433	1,585
BIRR, Jacques (1920-) French				
oil	1	1,815	1,815	1,815
BIRREN, Joseph Pierre (1865-1933) American				
oil	3	2,100-7,500	5,200	6,000
BIRSTINGER, Leopold (1903-1983) Austrian				
oil	1	2,910	2,910	2,910
BIRT, Colin (?) British?				
oil	1	2,745	2,745	2,745
BISCAINO, Bartolomeo (1632-1657) Italian				
wc/d	1	24,050	24,050	24,050
BISCARRA, Carlo Felice (1825-1894) Italian				
oil	1	6,562	6,562	6,562
wc/d	1	1,211	1,211	1,211
BISCARRA, Cesare (1866-1943) Italian				
oil	4	484-1,695	890	656
3D	2	1,818-2,700	2,259	1,818
BISCHOF, Anton (1877-?) German				
wc/d	1	1,211	1,211	1,211
BISCHOFBERGER, Bruno (1926-) Swiss				
oil	1	1,783	1,783	1,783
BISCHOFF, Elmer Nelson (1916-1991) American				
oil	1	490,000	490,000	490,000
wc/d	1	1,000	1,000	1,000
BISCHOFF, Franz A (1864-1929) American				
oil	15	2,250-110,000	23,250	17,000
wc/d	3	3,000-12,000	7,333	7,000
BISCHOFF, Henry (1882-1951) Swiss				
oil	1	1,374	1,374	1,374
BISCHOFF-CULM, Ernst (1870-?) German				
oil	1	4,973	4,973	4,973
BISCHOFFSHAUSEN, Hans (1927-1987) Austrian				
oil	2	6,442-14,786	10,614	6,442
wc/d	3	1,752-23,562	9,372	2,803
BISHOP, Isabel (1902-1988) American				
oil	2	2,000-37,500	19,750	2,000
wc/d	3	650-2,000	1,283	1,200
BISI, Fulvia (1818-1911) Italian				
oil	1	2,983	2,983	2,983
BISIAUX, Pierre (1924-) French				
oil	1	2,288	2,288	2,288
BISKINIS, Dimitrios (1891-1947) Greek				
oil	1	5,610	5,610	5,610
BISKY, Norbert (1970-) ?				
oil	8	9,425-60,000	28,426	22,000
wc/d	3	1,794-3,956	2,859	2,827
BISMOUTH, Maurice (1891-1965) French				
oil	3	507-1,036	806	876
wc/d	1	2,569	2,569	2,569
BISMUTH, Pierre (1963-) ?				
wc/d	1	3,236	3,236	3,236
BISON, Giuseppe Bernardino (1762-1844) Italian				
oil	7	3,366-155,700	59,657	54,781
wc/d	8	2,141-8,784	4,399	3,107
BISPHAM, Henry Collins (1841-1882) American				
oil	4	650-3,200	2,400	2,750
BISSCHOP, Abraham (1670-1731) Dutch				
oil	2	29,600-40,000	34,800	29,600
BISSCHOP, Christoffel (1828-1904) Dutch				
oil	1	3,588	3,588	3,588
wc/d	1	1,764	1,764	1,764
BISSCHOP, Jan de (1628-1671) Dutch				
wc/d	2	5,180-21,020	13,100	5,180
BISSCHOP, R (1840-1926) Dutch				
oil	1	1,558	1,558	1,558

Name	No.	Price Range	Average	Median
BISSCHOP-SWIFT, Kate (1834-1928) British				
oil	1	4,250	4,250	4,250
wc/d	1	2,158	2,158	2,158
BISSCHOPS, Charles (1894-1975) Belgian				
oil	5	536-1,697	1,065	850
BISSELL, Edgar Julien (1856-?) American				
oil	1	4,500	4,500	4,500
BISSIER, Jules (1893-1965) German				
oil	5	9,993-20,384	15,640	14,449
wc/d	15	1,767-15,133	7,670	8,000
BISSIERE, Roger (1884-1964) French				
oil	11	1,512-37,405	11,975	6,303
wc/d	1	2,829	2,829	2,829
BISSILL, George (1896-1973) British				
oil	2	460-3,250	1,855	460
wc/d	3	452-3,179	1,658	1,343
BISSON, Edouard (1856-?) French				
oil	1	6,500	6,500	6,500
BISTAGNE, Paul (1850-1886) French				
oil	1	4,550	4,550	4,550
BISTOLFI, Leonardo (1859-1933) Italian				
oil	2	1,940-2,863	2,401	1,940
3D	1	2,469	2,469	2,469
BISTTRAM, Emil (1895-1976) American				
oil	4	8,000-50,000	20,375	8,500
wc/d	9	1,800-15,000	4,544	2,200
BITRAN, Albert (1929-) French				
oil	8	1,054-3,718	2,238	2,027
wc/d	5	417-820	629	631
BITTAR, Antoine (1957-) Canadian				
oil	3	485-2,320	1,372	1,312
BITTAR, Pierre (1934-) French				
oil	2	2,500-4,498	3,499	2,500
BITTER, Ary (1883-1960) French				
3D	7	2,000-30,245	10,522	5,340
BITTER, Theo (1916-1994) Dutch				
oil	3	471-2,544	1,425	1,260
wc/d	1	801	801	801
BITTERLICH, Eduard (1834-1872) Austrian				
oil	1	2,577	2,577	2,577
BITTERLICH, Richard (1862-1940) Austrian				
oil	1	5,057	5,057	5,057
BIVA, Henri (1848-1928) French				
oil	7	2,957-25,000	8,277	5,890
wc/d	1	596	596	596
BIVA, Paul (1851-1900) French				
oil	1	1,438	1,438	1,438
BIXBEE, William Johnson (1850-1921) American				
oil	1	1,600	1,600	1,600
BIZER, Emil (1881-1957) German				
oil	3	973-2,408	1,786	1,978
BJAREBY, Alfred Gunnar (1899-?) American				
oil	1	1,200	1,200	1,200
BJERG, Johannes C (1886-1955) Danish				
3D	1	4,224	4,224	4,224
BJERKE-PETERSEN, Vilhelm (1909-1957) Danish				
oil	15	818-6,466	2,399	1,859
wc/d	2	661-1,690	1,175	661
BJORCK, Oscar (1860-1929) Swedish				
oil	3	1,218-2,493	1,695	1,374
wc/d	1	702	702	702
BJORKLUND, Frank (?) Scandinavian				
oil	1	1,626	1,626	1,626
BJORKLUND-RASMUSSEN, Poul (1909-1984) Danish				
oil	1	1,610	1,610	1,610
BJORNOE, T (19th C) Danish				
wc/d	1	1,088	1,088	1,088
BJULF, Soren Christian (1890-1958) Danish				
oil	5	963-3,132	1,727	1,436
BJURSTROM, Tor (1888-1966) Swedish				
oil	9	1,850-7,268	4,517	5,089

Name	No.	Price Range	Average	Median
BLAAS, Eugen von (1843-1932) Austrian				
oil	13	8,497-950,000	252,918	170,000
wc/d	1	3,250	3,250	3,250
BLAAS, Julius von (1845-1922) Austrian				
oil	10	725-15,653	4,165	3,099
wc/d	1	624	624	624
BLAAS, Karl von (1815-1894) Austrian				
oil	2	2,811-8,500	5,655	2,811
BLAAUW, Johannes de (?-1776) Dutch				
oil	1	17,534	17,534	17,534
BLACHE, Christian (1838-1920) Danish				
oil	15	601-6,821	2,811	2,608
BLACK, Andrew (1850-1916) British				
oil	5	525-11,440	4,600	1,557
BLACK, L F (?) American				
oil	1	9,000	9,000	9,000
BLACK, Laverne Nelson (1887-1938) American				
oil	4	40,000-460,000	167,500	85,000
wc/d	3	4,500-9,500	6,333	5,000
BLACK, Olive Parker (1868-1948) American				
oil	6	4,000-6,000	4,583	4,250
BLACKADDER, Elizabeth (1931-) British				
oil	6	5,568-13,350	8,337	5,907
wc/d	16	1,566-44,250	9,419	4,956
BLACKBURN, Arthur (19/20th C) British				
oil	2	735-1,353	1,044	735
BLACKBURN, Clarence (1914-1987) British				
oil	3	1,384-1,653	1,473	1,384
wc/d	2	460-460	460	460
BLACKBURN, David (1939-) British				
wc/d	1	1,480	1,480	1,480
BLACKBURN, Ed M (1940-) American				
oil	2	500-7,750	4,125	500
BLACKBURN, Robert (1920-2003) American				
wc/d	6	900-3,000	2,016	1,900
BLACKHAM, Dorothy Isobel (1896-1975) Irish				
oil	1	2,061	2,061	2,061
wc/d	1	811	811	811
BLACKLOCK, Thomas Bromley (1863-1903) British				
oil	3	1,558-4,450	2,694	2,076
BLACKLOCK, William Kay (1872-?) British				
oil	6	742-16,928	7,208	5,664
wc/d	2	487-2,816	1,651	487
BLACKMAN, Walter (1847-1928) American				
oil	2	2,088-3,500	2,794	2,088
BLACKMORE, Clive (1940-) British				
oil	1	1,110	1,110	1,110
BLACKSHAW, Basil (1932-) British				
oil	3	6,726-24,218	15,410	15,288
wc/d	3	6,195-32,870	18,272	15,753
BLACKWELL, Tom (1938-) American				
oil	1	83,959	83,959	83,959
BLACKWOOD, David L (1941-) Canadian				
wc/d	2	410-1,640	1,025	410
BLACKWOOD, Susan (20th C) American				
oil	1	7,000	7,000	7,000
BLAGONAVROV, Fedor P (c.1885-1961) Russian				
wc/d	1	8,281	8,281	8,281
BLAHAY, Henri (19th C) French				
oil	1	3,009	3,009	3,009
BLAINE, Julien (1942-) French				
oil	1	1,208	1,208	1,208
BLAINE, Mahlon (1894-1969) American				
oil	1	1,200	1,200	1,200
BLAINE, Nell (1922-1996) American				
oil	2	900-5,500	3,200	900
BLAIR, Charles Henry (19th C) British				
oil	1	3,250	3,250	3,250
BLAIR, John (1850-1934) British				
oil	1	2,024	2,024	2,024
wc/d	6	512-1,190	777	605

Name	No.	Price Range	Average	Median
BLAIR, Streeter (1888-1966) American				
oil	1	1,300	1,300	1,300
BLAIRAT, Marcel (1849-?) French				
oil	1	4,241	4,241	4,241
wc/d	4	467-2,288	1,343	820
BLAIS, Jean Charles (1956-) French				
oil	6	1,394-12,274	5,319	3,822
wc/d	10	1,434-9,425	4,888	3,884
BLAKE (?) ?				
wc/d	1	1,338	1,338	1,338
BLAKE, Benjamin (?-1830) British				
oil	4	2,052-4,900	3,064	2,500
BLAKE, Peter (1932-) British				
wc/d	8	522-25,950	8,661	4,440
BLAKE, Quentin (1932-) British				
wc/d	3	1,665-4,255	2,615	1,925
BLAKE, William (1757-1827) British				
wc/d	11	10,440-900,000	373,146	280,000
BLAKELOCK, Ralph Albert (1847-1919) American				
oil	14	1,000-19,000	8,825	9,000
BLAKELY, Corliss (20th C) American				
oil	1	3,500	3,500	3,500
BLAKESLEE, Frederic (1898-1973) American				
oil	2	1,500-3,000	2,250	1,500
BLAKESLEE, Sarah Jane (1912-2005) American				
oil	1	2,600	2,600	2,600
BLAMEY, Norman (1914-) British				
oil	1	5,916	5,916	5,916
BLAMPIED, Edmund (1886-1966) British				
oil	4	823-4,350	2,503	1,380
wc/d	6	888-3,720	2,694	2,405
BLANC, Celestin Joseph (1818-1888) French				
oil	2	2,182-4,561	3,371	2,182
BLANC, Louis-Ammy (1810-1885) German				
oil	4	7,224-33,714	17,937	15,051
BLANCH, Arnold (1896-1968) American				
oil	3	1,100-3,000	1,800	1,300
BLANCH, Lucille (1895-1981) American				
oil	1	1,500	1,500	1,500
BLANCHARD, Antoine (1910-1988) French				
oil	39	1,403-22,500	7,103	6,264
BLANCHARD, Antoine (jnr) (1930-) French				
oil	1	2,700	2,700	2,700
BLANCHARD, Evelyne (20th C) French				
oil	1	1,013	1,013	1,013
BLANCHARD, Henri Pierre Pharamond (1805-1873) French				
oil	1	25,479	25,479	25,479
BLANCHARD, Jacques (1600-1638) French				
oil	1	42,500	42,500	42,500
BLANCHARD, Maria (1881-1932) Spanish				
oil	5	78,871-249,750	139,437	95,408
wc/d	3	10,738-83,517	40,843	28,274
BLANCHARD, Nicole (20th C) French				
oil	6	1,200-1,800	1,483	1,400
BLANCHARD, Remy (1958-1993) French				
oil	3	2,101-4,438	3,128	2,847
wc/d	1	2,267	2,267	2,267
BLANCHE, Jacques Émile (1861-1942) French				
oil	16	1,512-60,000	14,338	4,435
wc/d	1	36,000	36,000	36,000
BLANCHET, Alexandre (1882-1961) Swiss				
oil	5	493-3,081	1,621	1,632
BLANCKENS, Barens van (17th C) Flemish?				
oil	1	2,213	2,213	2,213
BLANCO, Antonio Maria (1927-1999) American				
oil	1	12,041	12,041	12,041
BLANCO, Dionisio (1953-) Dominican				
oil	1	1,600	1,600	1,600
BLANCO, Venancio (20th C) Italian?				
3D	1	2,631	2,631	2,631
BLANCPAIN, Jules (1860-1914) Swiss				
oil	1	1,832	1,832	1,832

Name	No.	Price Range	Average	Median
BLANDIN, Étienne (1903-1991) French				
oil	5	507-3,142	1,825	1,571
wc/d	2	544-3,504	2,024	544
BLANES VIALE, Pedro (1879-1926) Uruguayan				
oil	3	26,500-64,500	43,000	38,000
BLANEY, Dwight (1865-1944) American				
oil	3	11,000-27,000	20,000	22,000
wc/d	1	550	550	550
BLANVILLAIN, Paul (1891-1965) French				
oil	3	2,306-3,763	2,832	2,428
BLARENBERGHE, Henri Desire van (1734-1812) French				
oil	1	4,229	4,229	4,229
BLARENBERGHE, Henri Joseph van (1741-1826) French				
oil	1	478	478	478
wc/d	1	35,677	35,677	35,677
BLARENBERGHE, Jacques Willem van (1669-1742) Dutch				
wc/d	1	1,883	1,883	1,883
BLARENBERGHE, Louis Nicolas van (1716-1794) French				
wc/d	5	1,000-72,917	16,243	1,649
BLASHFIELD, Edwin Howland (1848-1936) American				
oil	1	2,750	2,750	2,750
BLASSET, Nicolas (younger) (1600-1659) French				
3D	1	34,965	34,965	34,965
BLASZKO, Martin (1920-) Argentinian				
oil	1	26,000	26,000	26,000
wc/d	1	2,600	2,600	2,600
BLAT, Ismael (1901-1987) Spanish				
oil	1	1,060	1,060	1,060
wc/d	1	1,014	1,014	1,014
BLATAS, Arbit (1908-1999) American/Lithuanian				
oil	3	450-2,548	1,432	1,300
wc/d	1	2,750	2,750	2,750
BLATHERWICK, Lily (1854-1934) British				
oil	1	1,211	1,211	1,211
BLATTER, Bruno (19th C) German				
oil	2	764-3,220	1,992	764
BLATTERBAUER, Theodoor (1823-1906) German				
oil	1	1,401	1,401	1,401
BLAU, Tina (1845-1916) Austrian				
oil	3	7,755-84,685	35,264	13,352
BLAUENSTEINER, Leopold (1880-1947) Austrian				
oil	2	1,798-2,342	2,070	1,798
BLAUVELT, Charles F (1824-1900) American				
oil	1	1,750	1,750	1,750
BLAYLOCK, Thomas Todd (1876-1929) British				
oil	1	3,186	3,186	3,186
BLAYNEY, William A (1917-1986) American				
oil	1	6,600	6,600	6,600
BLAZEBY, J (19th C) British				
oil	1	11,900	11,900	11,900
BLAZEBY, James (19th C) British				
oil	1	4,500	4,500	4,500
BLECHEN, Karl (1798-1840) German				
oil	1	58,562	58,562	58,562
wc/d	2	9,425-17,671	13,548	9,425
BLECKMANN, Wilhelm Christiaan Constant (1853-1942) Dutch				
oil	2	2,167-2,425	2,296	2,167
BLECKNER, Ross (1949-) American				
oil	11	5,814-160,000	42,728	26,000
wc/d	4	700-3,500	1,681	1,262
BLEGER, Paul-Léon (1889-?) French				
oil	3	816-1,305	1,013	918
BLEIBTREU, Georg (1828-1892) German				
oil	2	2,400-19,110	10,755	2,400
BLEICH, Avi (1954-) Israeli				
oil	1	4,000	4,000	4,000
BLEIKER, Ulrich (1914-1994) Swiss				
3D	1	3,895	3,895	3,895
BLEIR, Jules (19th C) ?				
oil	1	1,900	1,900	1,900
BLEKER, Gerrit Claesz (fl.1625-1656) Dutch				
oil	1	8,174	8,174	8,174

Name	No.	Price Range	Average	Median
BLENNER, Carle J (1864-1952) American				
oil	4	1,600-5,250	3,900	3,750
BLES, David Joseph (1821-1899) Dutch				
oil	5	916-4,886	3,746	4,243
BLES, Joseph (1825-1875) Dutch				
oil	3	908-2,676	1,824	1,890
BLEULER, Johann Heinrich (1758-1823) Swiss				
wc/d	9	694-90,306	15,228	2,599
BLEULER, Johann Heinrich (younger) (1787-1857) Swiss				
wc/d	2	1,134-3,921	2,527	1,134
BLEULER, Johann Ludwig (1792-1850) Swiss				
wc/d	10	548-7,030	2,249	1,488
BLEY, Heinrich (1949-) German				
oil	1	2,667	2,667	2,667
BLEYENBERG, Karel (1913-) Dutch				
oil	2	884-1,355	1,119	884
BLIECK, Maurice (1876-1922) Belgian				
oil	5	716-4,401	2,050	1,636
BLIGNY, Albert (1849-1908) French				
oil	2	906-1,405	1,155	906
BLINKS, Thomas (1860-1912) British				
oil	8	8,736-140,000	57,196	20,000
wc/d	1	1,539	1,539	1,539
BLINOW, Nikoli Ossipovich (1868-1966) Russian				
oil	1	2,493	2,493	2,493
BLISS, Douglas Percy (1900-1984) British				
oil	1	6,840	6,840	6,840
BLISS, Robert R (1925-1981) American				
oil	13	950-11,000	6,292	7,000
BLOC, Andre (1896-1966) French				
wc/d	1	1,169	1,169	1,169
BLOCH, Albert (1882-1961) American				
oil	1	64,286	64,286	64,286
wc/d	1	19,000	19,000	19,000
BLOCH, Carl (1834-1890) Danish				
oil	1	34,743	34,743	34,743
BLOCH, Julius Thiengen (1888-1966) American				
oil	4	500-9,000	3,025	600
wc/d	2	500-950	725	500
BLOCH, Martin (1883-1956) German				
oil	2	1,850-3,828	2,839	1,850
wc/d	1	797	797	797
BLOCH, Pierrette (1928-) Swiss/French				
oil	1	1,236	1,236	1,236
BLOCK, Emanuel (1608-1688) German				
oil	1	5,648	5,648	5,648
BLOCK, Emiel de (1941-) Belgian				
3D	1	4,232	4,232	4,232
BLOCK, Eugène Francois de (1812-1893) Belgian				
oil	3	968-1,821	1,465	1,607
BLOCK, L (19th C) British				
wc/d	1	5,670	5,670	5,670
BLOEM, Matheus (17th C) Dutch				
oil	1	3,130	3,130	3,130
BLOEMAERT, Abraham (1564-1651) Dutch				
oil	5	7,899-95,548	41,972	30,405
wc/d	3	2,102-14,240	6,809	4,087
BLOEMAERT, Hendrick (1601-1672) Dutch				
oil	1	27,680	27,680	27,680
BLOEME, Herman Antonie de (1802-1867) Dutch				
oil	1	1,512	1,512	1,512
BLOEMEN, Jan Frans van (1662-1749) Flemish				
oil	6	20,000-42,500	28,201	20,712
wc/d	1	600	600	600
BLOEMEN, Jan Frans van and COSTANZI, Placido (18th C) Flemish/Italian				
oil	1	174,760	174,760	174,760
BLOEMEN, Pieter van (1657-1720) Flemish				
oil	7	1,573-21,020	8,382	6,370
wc/d	1	1,881	1,881	1,881
BLOEMERS, Arnoldus (c.1786-1844) Dutch				
oil	1	86,528	86,528	86,528

Name	No.	Price Range	Average	Median
BLOIS, François B de (1829-1913) Canadian				
oil	2	618-7,000	3,809	618
BLOMBERG, Stig (1901-1970) Swedish				
3D	1	4,097	4,097	4,097
BLOMMAERT, Maximilian (17/18th C) Flemish				
oil	1	2,492	2,492	2,492
BLOMMAERT, N C (18th C) Dutch				
oil	1	5,702	5,702	5,702
BLOMME, Alphonse-Joseph (1889-1979) Belgian				
oil	4	658-1,403	1,109	1,171
BLOMMERS, Bernardus Johannes (1845-1914) Dutch				
oil	7	708-90,711	26,701	5,839
wc/d	7	5,000-50,230	17,736	7,274
BLOMMESTEIN, Louise Alice (1882-1965) Dutch				
oil	1	1,638	1,638	1,638
BLOMSTEDT, Juhana (1937-) Finnish				
oil	2	1,221-1,274	1,247	1,221
BLOMSTEDT, Vaino (1871-1947) Finnish				
oil	5	2,314-14,027	7,282	7,262
BLOND, Maurice (1899-1974) French				
oil	8	433-1,798	1,056	959
BLONDAT, Max (1879-1926) French				
3D	40	1,816-12,109	3,500	2,906
BLONDEL, Émile (1893-1970) French				
oil	6	611-1,560	1,173	1,168
BLONDEL, George François (1730-1791) French				
wc/d	1	6,960	6,960	6,960
BLOOD, Brian (1962-) American				
oil	2	3,500-4,500	4,000	3,500
BLOOM, Hyman (1913-) American				
oil	1	6,000	6,000	6,000
BLOOMER, Hiram R (1845-1910) American				
oil	4	1,200-2,750	1,762	1,400
BLOORE, Ronald (1925-) Canadian				
oil	1	40,550	40,550	40,550
wc/d	5	422-539	467	456
BLOOT, Pieter de (1602-1658) Dutch				
oil	2	4,568-27,500	16,034	4,568
BLOS, Carl (1860-1941) German				
oil	2	553-1,790	1,171	553
BLOW, Sandra (1925-) British				
oil	16	435-41,760	9,450	7,832
wc/d	9	673-6,192	1,801	1,062
BLUEMNER, Oscar (1867-1938) American				
wc/d	12	750-150,000	20,575	1,700
BLUHM, Norman (1921-1999) American				
oil	9	3,800-90,000	36,866	16,000
wc/d	1	3,300	3,300	3,300
BLUHM, Oscar (1867-1912) German				
oil	7	643-1,753	1,244	1,169
wc/d	1	1,500	1,500	1,500
BLUM, Jerome S (1884-1956) American				
oil	2	2,000-10,000	6,000	2,000
BLUM, Ludwig (1891-1975) Israeli				
oil	12	4,600-40,000	12,289	8,500
BLUM, Maurice (1832-1909) French				
oil	4	800-3,737	1,660	828
BLUM, Robert Frederick (1857-1903) American				
wc/d	1	1,600	1,600	1,600
BLUME, Edmund (1844-?) German				
oil	1	1,800	1,800	1,800
BLUME, Peter (1906-1992) American/Russian				
oil	1	260,000	260,000	260,000
wc/d	2	500-750	625	500
BLUMENSCHEIN, Ernest L (1874-1960) American				
oil	5	2,200-390,000	97,840	30,000
BLUMENTHAL, Hermann (1905-1942) German				
3D	3	4,712-27,185	12,203	4,712
BLYHOOFT, Jacques Zacharias (17th C) Dutch				
oil	1	8,429	8,429	8,429
wc/d	1	2,431	2,431	2,431

Name	No.	Price Range	Average	Median
BLYK, Frans Jacobus van den (1806-1876) Dutch				
oil	1	1,543	1,543	1,543
BLYTH, Robert Henderson (1919-1970) British				
oil	1	7,785	7,785	7,785
wc/d	1	12,975	12,975	12,975
BLYTHE, David Gilmour (1815-1865) American				
oil	2	850-102,000	51,425	850
BO, Giacinto (1832-1912) Italian				
oil	11	555-6,054	2,965	2,910
BOARDMAN, William G (1815-1895) American				
oil	3	1,700-25,000	11,566	8,000
BOBAK, Bruno (1923-) Canadian				
oil	8	532-5,730	2,783	1,804
wc/d	1	768	768	768
BOBAK, Molly Lamb (1922-) Canadian				
oil	17	1,864-11,521	4,770	3,199
wc/d	4	576-1,319	1,023	1,054
BOBERG, Anna (1864-1935) Swedish				
wc/d	1	4,121	4,121	4,121
BOBERG, Ferdinand (1860-1946) Swedish				
wc/d	1	3,022	3,022	3,022
BOBERG, Jorgen (1940-) Swedish				
oil	3	2,263-4,872	3,842	4,393
BOBIES, Karl (1865-1897) Austrian				
oil	1	1,574	1,574	1,574
BOBROVSKY, Grigory Mikhailovich (1873-1942) Russian				
oil	3	1,940-5,092	3,758	4,243
BOCCACCI, Marcello (1914-1996) Italian				
oil	11	375-1,638	878	756
wc/d	1	568	568	568
BOCCHETTI, Gaetano (1888-1992) Italian				
oil	1	2,548	2,548	2,548
BOCCHI, Amedeo (1883-1976) Italian				
oil	1	1,180	1,180	1,180
BOCCHI, Faustino (1659-1742) Italian				
oil	2	59,200-112,450	85,825	59,200
BOCCIONI, Umberto (1882-1916) Italian				
oil	3	527,055-1,284,830	819,715	647,260
wc/d	3	2,799-44,507	18,529	8,281
BOCH, Anna (1848-1933) Belgian				
oil	8	1,927-14,556	5,488	2,166
wc/d	2	783-1,106	944	783
BOCHMANN, Gregor von (elder) (1850-1930) German				
oil	4	849-4,849	2,389	941
wc/d	3	944-2,803	1,854	1,815
BOCHNER, Mel (1940-) American				
wc/d	1	5,500	5,500	5,500
BOCION, François (1828-1890) Swiss				
oil	4	3,434-114,211	42,402	5,412
wc/d	10	496-1,550	978	759
BOCK, Adolf (1890-1968) Finnish				
oil	2	4,909-5,845	5,377	4,909
wc/d	7	479-3,343	2,063	1,543
BOCK, Arthur (1875-?) German				
3D	1	3,687	3,687	3,687
BOCK, John (1965-) German				
3D	3	35,000-50,000	41,666	40,000
BOCK, Ludwig (1886-1971) German				
oil	15	486-3,403	1,184	790
wc/d	4	547-851	729	729
BOCK, Theophile Emile Achille de (1851-1904) Dutch				
oil	13	586-4,756	1,840	1,200
wc/d	1	2,158	2,158	2,158
BOCKLIN, Arnold (1827-1901) Swiss				
oil	5	3,766-144,602	51,171	21,310
3D	1	122,850	122,850	122,850
BOCKSTIEGEL, Peter August (1889-1951) German				
wc/d	2	707-1,527	1,117	707
BODAAN, Johan Jacob (1881-1954) Dutch				
oil	1	1,341	1,341	1,341
BODARD, Pierre (1881-1937) French				
oil	2	509-1,394	951	509
wc/d	2	444-887	665	444

Name	No.	Price Range	Average	Median
BODAREWSKI, Nikolai (1850-1921) Russian				
oil	2	115,320-119,700	117,510	115,320
BODDIEN, Georg von (1850-?) German				
oil	1	3,633	3,633	3,633
BODDINGTON, Edwin H (1836-1905) British				
oil	6	788-2,392	1,683	1,730
BODDINGTON, H J (1811-1865) British				
oil	1	1,750	1,750	1,750
BODDINGTON, Henry John (1811-1865) British				
oil	6	2,262-38,850	10,668	6,000
BODECKER, Erich (1904-1971) German				
3D	2	2,432-4,077	3,254	2,432
BODECKER, Johann Friedrich (1658-1727) Dutch				
oil	1	3,695	3,695	3,695
BODELSON, Dan (1949-) American				
oil	2	1,000-2,500	1,750	1,000
wc/d	1	2,500	2,500	2,500
BODEMAN, Willem (1806-1880) Dutch				
oil	4	2,919-22,250	11,979	3,063
BODEMAN, Willem and VERBOECKHOVEN, Eugène (19th C) Dutch/Belgian				
oil	1	34,448	34,448	34,448
BODIFEE, Paul (1866-1938) Dutch				
oil	2	2,338-5,394	3,866	2,338
BODILY, Sheryl (20th C) American				
oil	4	475-2,500	1,431	750
BODINI, Floriano (1933-2005) Italian				
wc/d	1	2,225	2,225	2,225
BODINIER, Guillaume (1795-1872) French				
oil	1	24,075	24,075	24,075
wc/d	1	4,618	4,618	4,618
BODMER, Walter (1903-1973) Swiss				
oil	1	4,079	4,079	4,079
3D	1	26,105	26,105	26,105
BODOY, Ernest Alexandre (19th C) French				
oil	1	16,000	16,000	16,000
BOE, Frants Didrik (1820-1891) Norwegian				
oil	2	2,600-18,400	10,500	2,600
BOECHER, August (20th C) German				
oil	1	1,507	1,507	1,507
BOECK, Felix de (1898-1995) Belgian				
oil	18	764-8,372	3,095	2,166
BOECKHORST, Jan and BRUEGHEL, Jan (younger) (17th C) German/Flemish				
oil	1	51,652	51,652	51,652
BOECKL, Herbert (1894-1966) Austrian				
wc/d	5	9,000-22,898	16,611	17,173
BOEHLE, Fritz (1873-1916) German				
oil	1	3,637	3,637	3,637
BOEHM, Adolph (1844-?) German				
oil	1	3,273	3,273	3,273
BOEHM, Eduard (1830-1890) German/Austrian				
oil	10	1,145-3,148	2,029	1,903
BOEHM, Tuomas von (1916-2000) Finnish				
oil	2	1,054-1,757	1,405	1,054
BOEHME, Karl Theodor (1866-1939) German				
oil	5	2,910-3,503	3,275	3,360
BOEL, Pieter (1622-1674) Flemish				
oil	2	23,140-39,130	31,135	23,140
BOELTZIG, Richard (20th C) German				
3D	1	2,125	2,125	2,125
BOER, Hessel de (1921-2003) Dutch				
oil	2	884-2,003	1,443	884
BOER, Zoltan von (1924-1989) Swedish				
oil	1	1,982	1,982	1,982
BOEREWAARD, Door (1893-1972) Belgian				
oil	1	1,565	1,565	1,565
BOERMEESTER, Louis (1908-1992) Dutch				
wc/d	1	1,200	1,200	1,200
BOERO, Renata (1936-) Italian				
wc/d	3	1,874-5,088	3,133	2,438
BOERS, Frans Henri (1904-1988) Dutch				
oil	1	1,798	1,798	1,798

Name	No.	Price Range	Average	Median
BOERS, Sebastian Theodorus Voorn (1828-1893) Dutch				
oil	1	1,808	1,808	1,808
BOERS, Willy (1905-1978) Dutch				
oil	2	2,316-7,014	4,665	2,316
wc/d	1	4,267	4,267	4,267
BOESE, Henry (fl.1847-1863) American				
oil	1	3,250	3,250	3,250
BOESEN, Johannes (1847-1916) Danish				
oil	2	1,106-1,581	1,343	1,106
BOETTCHER, Christian Eduard (1818-1889) German				
oil	3	1,157-16,000	8,289	7,711
BOETTI, Alighiero e (1940-1994) Italian				
oil	2	10,177-13,548	11,862	10,177
wc/d	78	4,834-600,000	64,636	24,740
3D	2	58,562-672,600	365,581	58,562
BOETTI, Alighiero e and PALADINO, Mimmo (20th C) Italian				
wc/d	1	177,000	177,000	177,000
BOETTO, Giulio (1894-1967) Italian				
oil	5	908-9,993	5,256	3,404
BOEVER, Jean François de (1872-1949) Belgian				
wc/d	1	3,156	3,156	3,156
BOFFA TARLATTA, Luigi (1889-1965) Italian				
oil	1	1,212	1,212	1,212
BOFILL, Antoine (19/20th C) Spanish				
3D	1	1,911	1,911	1,911
BOGAARD, Willem Jacobus (1842-1891) Belgian?				
oil	1	1,200	1,200	1,200
BOGAERT, Andre (1920-1986) Belgian				
oil	2	668-2,277	1,472	668
wc/d	2	618-783	700	618
BOGAERT, Bram (1921-) Dutch				
oil	10	4,676-29,600	12,968	8,767
wc/d	27	566-22,276	5,249	4,586
3D	2	7,633-14,137	10,885	7,633
BOGAERT, Gaston (1918-) Belgian				
oil	5	959-3,349	2,074	1,636
BOGAERT, Hendrik (17th C) Dutch				
oil	1	5,920	5,920	5,920
BOGARDE, Dirk (20th C) British				
wc/d	1	1,840	1,840	1,840
BOGDANI, Jakob (1660-1724) Hungarian				
oil	1	60,550	60,550	60,550
BOGDANOFF-BJELSKI, Nikolai (1868-1945) Russian				
oil	15	10,320-1,200,000	143,041	40,000
BOGDANOVE, Abraham J (1888-1946) American				
oil	9	600-60,000	11,927	4,000
BOGDANOVITCH, George (20th C) American?				
oil	1	1,700	1,700	1,700
BOGERT, George H (1864-1944) American				
oil	8	450-4,250	2,296	1,900
BOGGIANI, Guido (1861-1902) Italian				
oil	2	6,629-16,397	11,513	6,629
BOGGIO, Emilio (1857-1920) French/Venezuelan				
oil	2	4,200-7,292	5,746	4,200
BOGGS, Frank Myers (1855-1926) French/American				
oil	10	2,486-25,000	9,370	7,573
wc/d	28	400-5,449	1,283	956
BOGHOSIAN, Varujan (1926-) American				
oil	1	1,300	1,300	1,300
BOGMAN, Hermanus Adrianus Charles (jnr) (1890-1975) Dutch				
oil	4	1,029-7,510	3,270	1,951
wc/d	1	471	471	471
BOGMAN, Hermanus Charles Christiaan (1861-1921) Dutch				
oil	5	700-1,808	1,062	1,045
BOGOLIUBOV, Alexei Petrovich (1824-1896) Russian				
oil	9	45,678-725,000	286,625	267,873
wc/d	3	4,243-8,486	5,778	4,607
BOGOMAZOV, Alexander (1880-1930) Russian				
oil	1	1,118,000	1,118,000	1,118,000
BOGOMOLOV, Oleg (1962-) Russian				
oil	4	930-2,976	1,911	1,780

Name	No.	Price Range	Average	Median
BOGUET, Didier (1755-1839) French				
wc/d	1	3,805	3,805	3,805
BOGUSLAWSKAJA, Xenia Puni (1892-1972) Russian				
oil	1	7,773	7,773	7,773
BOHATSCH, Erwin (1951-) Austrian				
oil	3	2,928-8,199	4,914	3,616
wc/d	2	599-659	629	599
BOHEMEN, Kees van (1928-1986) Dutch				
oil	4	8,918-12,959	11,072	9,555
wc/d	4	1,654-9,555	5,026	3,053
BOHLER, Joseph (?) American				
wc/d	2	6,000-6,500	6,250	6,000
BOHM, C Curry (1894-1972) American				
oil	3	1,100-7,000	4,200	4,500
BOHM, Hartmut (1938-) German				
3D	2	2,990-6,181	4,585	2,990
BOHM, Johann Georg (elder) (1673-1746) German				
oil	1	15,130	15,130	15,130
BOHM, Max (1868-1923) American				
oil	1	2,200	2,200	2,200
BOHM, Pal (1839-1905) Hungarian				
oil	2	2,600-3,766	3,183	2,600
BOHMER, Heinrich (1852-1930) German				
oil	4	688-6,336	3,214	2,432
BOHNDEL, Conrad Christian August (1779-1847) Danish				
oil	1	2,153	2,153	2,153
BOHNHORST, August (19th C) German				
oil	1	2,426	2,426	2,426
BOHRDT, Hans (1857-1945) German				
oil	2	1,987-2,629	2,308	1,987
wc/d	3	1,052-14,877	5,809	1,500
BOHRMANN, Karl (1928-1998) German				
oil	1	941	941	941
wc/d	6	608-2,121	1,413	1,169
BOHROD, Aaron (1907-1992) American				
oil	7	400-12,000	2,275	500
wc/d	10	425-6,500	1,932	1,000
BOILEAU, Philip (1864-1917) American				
oil	1	1,958	1,958	1,958
wc/d	1	16,000	16,000	16,000
BOILLE, Luigi (1926-) Italian				
oil	2	2,163-3,387	2,775	2,163
BOILLY, Jules (1796-1874) French				
wc/d	1	1,002	1,002	1,002
BOILLY, Louis Léopold (1761-1845) French				
oil	16	1,230-70,000	14,815	5,825
wc/d	5	3,504-11,181	6,349	5,143
BOISFREMONT, Charles Boulanger de (1773-1838) French				
oil	1	10,000	10,000	10,000
BOISJOLI, Dominique (1955-) Canadian				
oil	1	2,200	2,200	2,200
BOISROND, François (1959-) French				
oil	7	865-7,508	3,984	4,531
wc/d	2	667-3,387	2,027	667
BOISSEAU, Alfred (1823-1903) American				
oil	1	1,433	1,433	1,433
BOISSELIER, Émile (19/20th C) French				
wc/d	1	1,171	1,171	1,171
BOISSIEU, Jean Jacques de (1736-1810) French				
wc/d	9	595-7,730	3,051	2,059
BOIT, Robert A (20th C) American				
oil	1	1,900	1,900	1,900
BOITEL, Maurice (1919-) French				
oil	2	600-3,729	2,164	600
BOIX-VIVES, Anselme (1899-1969) French				
oil	2	911-7,598	4,254	911
wc/d	2	2,420-2,719	2,569	2,420
BOIZARD, C U (19/20th C) ?				
oil	1	2,400	2,400	2,400
BOIZOT, Simon Louis (1743-1809) French				
wc/d	1	10,712	10,712	10,712
3D	1	2,367	2,367	2,367

Name	No.	Price Range	Average	Median
BOJESEN, Kay (1886-1958) Danish				
3D	3	2,425-7,276	4,742	4,526
BOK, Hannes Vajn (1914-1964) American				
wc/d	1	3,500	3,500	3,500
BOKER, Carl (1836-1905) German				
oil	2	4,671-7,591	6,131	4,671
BOKKELEN, Lambert van (1809-?) German				
oil	1	2,356	2,356	2,356
BOKOBZA, Eliahou Eric (1963-) Israeli				
oil	1	3,000	3,000	3,000
BOKS, Martinus (1849-1895) Dutch				
oil	1	1,237	1,237	1,237
BOL, Ferdinand (1616-1680) Dutch				
oil	1	75,906	75,906	75,906
BOL, Hans (1534-1593) Dutch				
wc/d	1	40,000	40,000	40,000
BOLDING, Cornelis (1897-?) Dutch				
oil	1	1,567	1,567	1,567
BOLDINI, Giovanni (1842-1931) Italian				
oil	12	33,123-900,000	417,852	260,000
wc/d	15	654-56,959	11,706	5,143
BOLDUC, Blanche (1906-) Canadian				
oil	1	1,678	1,678	1,678
BOLGIANO, Ludwig (1866-?) German				
oil	1	2,057	2,057	2,057
BOLIN, Gustave (1920-1999) Swedish				
oil	10	467-4,229	1,997	1,113
BOLL, Reinholdt Fredrik (1825-1897) Norwegian				
oil	1	1,423	1,423	1,423
BOLLER, Louis Jakob (1862-1896) German				
oil	1	1,460	1,460	1,460
BOLLES, Enoch (1883-1976) American				
oil	1	9,000	9,000	9,000
BOLLFRAS, G (19/20th C) German				
oil	1	1,951	1,951	1,951
BOLLING, Sigrid (1853-1917) Norwegian				
oil	1	4,872	4,872	4,872
BOLLONGIER, Hans (1600-1644) Dutch				
oil	2	27,680-129,750	78,715	27,680
BOLOGNA, Domenico (1845-1885) Italian				
oil	1	3,633	3,633	3,633
BOLOGNE, Jean (?) Italian?				
3D	1	5,504	5,504	5,504
BOLOMEY, Roger Henry (1918-) American				
3D	1	2,250	2,250	2,250
BOLONACHI, Constantin (1837-1907) Greek				
oil	10	31,320-317,900	178,771	141,750
BOLOTOWSKY, Ilya (1907-1981) American/Russian				
oil	3	5,000-20,000	13,333	15,000
wc/d	1	2,200	2,200	2,200
BOLSTAD, E Melvin (?) American				
oil	1	1,600	1,600	1,600
BOLT, Johann Friedrich (1769-1836) German				
wc/d	1	1,649	1,649	1,649
BOLT, N P (1886-1965) Danish				
wc/d	1	1,429	1,429	1,429
BOLT, Ronald William (1938-) Canadian				
oil	7	829-7,493	4,006	3,936
BOLTANSKI, Christian (1944-) French				
3D	8	22,200-132,000	71,929	51,917
BOLTE, Adolf (1881-?) German				
oil	1	2,145	2,145	2,145
BOLTON, Hale William (1885-1920) American				
oil	1	18,000	18,000	18,000
wc/d	1	750	750	750
BOMAN, Lars Henning (c.1730-1799) Swedish				
oil	2	2,061-2,610	2,335	2,061
BOMANJI, Pestonji (1851-1938) Indian				
oil	1	7,000	7,000	7,000
BOMAR, Bill (1919-1991) American				
wc/d	1	1,100	1,100	1,100

Name	No.	Price Range	Average	Median
BOMBERG, David (1890-1957) British				
oil	10	20,760-1,549,800	228,171	54,810
wc/d	12	1,566-39,690	9,938	6,536
BOMBLED, Karel Frederik (1822-1902) Dutch				
oil	1	8,153	8,153	8,153
BOMBLED, Louis Charles (1862-1927) French				
oil	2	2,975-4,450	3,712	2,975
wc/d	1	1,113	1,113	1,113
BOMBOIS, Camille (1883-1970) French				
oil	24	2,000-18,500	7,418	6,000
BOMMEL, Elias Pieter van (1819-1890) Dutch				
oil	5	1,475-29,440	13,156	4,800
BOMMELS, Peter (1951-) German				
oil	2	1,529-9,555	5,542	1,529
BOMPARD, Maurice (1857-1936) French				
oil	5	764-3,292	1,795	1,176
BOMPIANI, Augusto (1851-1930) Italian				
oil	1	3,406	3,406	3,406
BOMPIANI, Roberto (1821-1908) Italian				
wc/d	1	2,293	2,293	2,293
BONAL, Jan (1927-) French				
oil	1	1,178	1,178	1,178
BONALUMI, Agostino (1935-) Italian				
oil	40	1,885-48,917	18,233	15,226
wc/d	13	1,252-39,875	8,642	6,473
3D	1	8,597	8,597	8,597
BONAMICI, Louis (1878-1966) Italian				
oil	1	1,328	1,328	1,328
BONAVIA, Carlo (fl.1740-1756) Italian				
oil	2	95,035-140,270	117,652	95,035
BONAVITA, Alfonso (1962-) Italian				
oil	1	1,894	1,894	1,894
BONAZZI, Jacopo Maria (18th C) Italian				
oil	1	2,500	2,500	2,500
BONCOMPAIN, Pierre (1938-) French				
oil	2	550-2,178	1,364	550
BOND, Marjory (20th C) British				
oil	1	1,170	1,170	1,170
BOND, Willard (1926-) American				
wc/d	2	1,800-1,800	1,800	1,800
BOND, William Joseph J C (1833-1926) British				
oil	11	552-5,075	2,008	2,208
wc/d	3	455-1,260	784	637
BONDE, Peter (1958-) Danish				
oil	8	740-2,748	2,139	2,263
BONDUEL, Roger (1930-) Belgian				
3D	1	1,806	1,806	1,806
BONDY, Walter (1880-1940) Czech/French				
oil	1	7,308	7,308	7,308
BONDY-GLASSOWA, Helene (1865-1935) Ukranian				
wc/d	1	1,757	1,757	1,757
BONE, Henry (1755-1834) British				
oil	1	3,078	3,078	3,078
BONE, Sir Muirhead (1876-1953) British				
oil	1	2,600	2,600	2,600
wc/d	13	475-2,835	960	788
BONE, Stephen (1904-1958) British				
oil	5	700-2,805	1,236	826
BONE, William Drummond (1907-1979) British				
wc/d	1	1,062	1,062	1,062
BONECHI, Lorenzo (1955-) Italian				
wc/d	2	796-1,911	1,353	796
BONEH, Schmuel (1930-) Israeli				
oil	2	700-2,000	1,350	700
BONETTI, Uberto (1909-1993) Italian				
wc/d	3	1,386-3,625	2,300	1,890
BONEVARDI, Marcelo (1929-1994) Argentinian				
oil	2	1,701-17,000	9,350	1,701
wc/d	3	2,000-17,000	7,000	2,000
3D	1	5,190	5,190	5,190
BONFANTE, Egidio (1922-) Italian				
oil	1	2,913	2,913	2,913

Name	No.	Price Range	Average	Median
BONFANTI, Arturo (1905-1978) Italian				
oil	2	5,280-6,760	6,020	5,280
BONFANTI, Emiliano (1944-) Italian				
oil	2	971-1,414	1,192	971
BONFANTINI, Sergio (1910-1989) Italian				
oil	2	1,890-4,905	3,397	1,890
BONFIELD, George R (1802-1898) American				
oil	1	2,250	2,250	2,250
BONFIGLI, Benedetto (1420-1496) Italian				
oil	1	180,000	180,000	180,000
BONFILS, Gaston (1855-1946) French				
oil	1	1,145	1,145	1,145
BONGART, Sergei R (1918-1985) American/Russian				
oil	1	6,000	6,000	6,000
BONHEUR, Auguste (1824-1884) French				
oil	6	1,455-59,200	18,989	4,240
BONHEUR, Ferdinand (19th C) French				
oil	2	5,351-5,455	5,403	5,351
BONHEUR, I (1827-1901) French				
3D	1	9,894	9,894	9,894
BONHEUR, Isidore (1827-1901) French				
3D	19	1,951-140,000	19,180	6,806
BONHEUR, Juliette Peyrol (1830-1891) French				
oil	2	1,199-8,352	4,775	1,199
BONHEUR, Rosa (1822-1899) French				
oil	10	1,837-139,200	21,384	6,000
wc/d	10	533-5,023	1,900	1,210
3D	2	1,868-3,250	2,559	1,868
BONHOMME, Léon (1870-1924) French				
wc/d	15	541-3,913	1,323	999
BONICHI, Claudio (1943-) Italian				
oil	3	1,300-1,400	1,350	1,352
BONIFACIO, Alfonso Gomez (1934-) Spanish				
oil	3	2,290-7,782	4,523	3,498
BONIFAZI, Adriano (1858-1914) Italian				
oil	3	1,663-7,308	3,798	2,425
BONINGTON, Richard Parkes (1802-1828) British				
oil	2	1,214-4,816	3,015	1,214
wc/d	6	836-59,160	20,940	6,055
BONINSEGNA, Michele (1826-1896) Italian				
3D	1	38,651	38,651	38,651
BONIS, Spiro de (20th C) ?				
oil	2	1,991-2,928	2,459	1,991
BONITO, Giuseppe (1705-1789) Italian				
oil	2	9,514-48,151	28,832	9,514
BONIVENTO, Eugenio (1880-1956) Italian				
oil	3	1,019-6,000	2,872	1,598
wc/d	1	1,308	1,308	1,308
BONJOUR, Jean-Baptiste (1801-1882) Swiss				
oil	1	2,498	2,498	2,498
BONNA, Alexander (?) Russian				
wc/d	1	1,083	1,083	1,083
BONNALLE, A F (18/19th C) French				
wc/d	1	2,600	2,600	2,600
BONNAR, James King (1885-1961) American				
oil	3	1,000-2,250	1,816	2,200
BONNARD, Pierre (1867-1947) French				
oil	26	46,020-6,808,000	1,165,789	400,000
wc/d	17	1,286-44,097	12,035	8,919
BONNARDEL, Alexandre François (1867-1942) French				
oil	4	1,060-2,610	2,011	1,798
BONNAT, Léon (1833-1922) French				
oil	4	6,000-42,812	15,802	6,880
BONNAUD, Pierre (1865-1930) French				
oil	1	2,457	2,457	2,457
BONNEAU, A (?) French				
3D	1	3,831	3,831	3,831
BONNEFOI, Christian (20th C) French?				
oil	1	1,854	1,854	1,854
BONNEFOIT, Alain (1939-) French				
oil	1	4,173	4,173	4,173
wc/d	3	597-900	732	700

Name	No.	Price Range	Average	Median
BONNEFOY, Henri-Arthur (1839-1917) French				
oil	1	5,220	5,220	5,220
BONNEN, Kaspar (1968-) Danish				
oil	3	3,219-4,364	3,869	4,024
BONNEN, Peter (1945-) Danish				
3D	2	3,219-4,829	4,024	3,219
BONNER, James King (?) American				
oil	1	3,000	3,000	3,000
BONNER, Jonathan (1947-) American				
3D	2	2,800-3,250	3,025	2,800
BONNESEN, Carl Johan (1868-1920) Danish				
3D	1	5,961	5,961	5,961
BONNET, Anne (1908-1960) Belgian				
oil	4	586-16,562	7,818	2,805
wc/d	4	742-4,326	2,595	1,607
BONNET, Leon (20th C) American				
oil	1	3,500	3,500	3,500
BONNET, Louis Marin (1736-1793) French				
wc/d	1	13,680	13,680	13,680
BONNET, Rudolf (1895-1978) Dutch				
wc/d	7	2,408-138,469	23,808	4,110
BONNETON, Germain Eugene (1874-1914) French				
oil	1	4,839	4,839	4,839
BONNICI, Giuseppe (1834-1900) Italian				
oil	1	1,500	1,500	1,500
BONNIE, Karen (20th C) American				
oil	1	3,000	3,000	3,000
BONNIER, Olle (1925-) Swedish				
oil	6	841-31,715	9,317	1,652
wc/d	8	388-2,643	1,277	925
BONNIN GUERIN, Francisco (1874-?) Spanish				
wc/d	1	4,822	4,822	4,822
BONNOPH, P (20th C) ?				
oil	1	15,555	15,555	15,555
BONS, Frederick (20th C) German				
oil	1	1,100	1,100	1,100
BONTJES VAN BEEK, Olga (1896-1995) German				
oil	6	665-2,572	1,285	1,028
BONVIN, François (1817-1887) French				
oil	5	2,165-22,455	12,850	14,137
wc/d	2	1,641-1,929	1,785	1,641
BONZAGNI, Aroldo (1887-1918) Italian				
oil	1	28,027	28,027	28,027
wc/d	1	9,136	9,136	9,136
BONZANIGO, Giuseppe Maria (1725-1820) Italian				
3D	1	3,762	3,762	3,762
BOOGAARD, Willem Jacobus (1842-1887) Dutch				
oil	1	1,500	1,500	1,500
BOOK, Harry Martin (1904-1971) American				
oil	3	475-2,500	1,258	800
BOOK, Max Mikael (1953-) Swedish				
oil	5	827-7,929	2,561	1,269
wc/d	8	727-2,672	1,727	1,850
BOOM, Charles (1858-1939) Belgian				
oil	4	1,215-6,712	4,067	3,814
BOOM, W (20th C) Belgian				
oil	1	3,637	3,637	3,637
BOOMER, Bob (1944-) American				
3D	1	2,500	2,500	2,500
BOON, Constantin (1830-1882) Dutch				
oil	1	1,900	1,900	1,900
BOON, Louis Paul (1912-1978) Dutch				
wc/d	1	2,392	2,392	2,392
BOONE, Elmer L (1881-1952) American				
oil	3	1,000-5,000	2,833	2,500
BOONEN, Arnold (1669-1729) Dutch				
oil	4	6,487-45,000	20,719	8,900
BOORM, Charles (19th C) ?				
oil	1	11,000	11,000	11,000
BOOS, Roman Anton (1733-1810) German				
3D	1	118,655	118,655	118,655

Name	No.	Price Range	Average	Median
BOOT, Henri F (1877-1963) Dutch				
oil	3	561-2,395	1,584	1,798
BOOT, William Henry James (1848-1918) British				
wc/d	1	1,632	1,632	1,632
BOOTH, George Warren (1917-1996) American				
wc/d	1	1,900	1,900	1,900
BOOTH, James W (1867-1953) British				
oil	1	4,872	4,872	4,872
wc/d	7	537-2,436	1,323	1,218
BOOTH, William (18/19th C) British				
wc/d	1	4,278	4,278	4,278
BOOTY, Frederick William (1840-1924) British				
oil	1	1,044	1,044	1,044
wc/d	11	452-3,500	1,893	2,052
BOOTZ, Frederic (1937-) French				
wc/d	1	1,824	1,824	1,824
BOQUET, Jean (1908-1976) Belgian				
oil	3	534-1,818	1,309	1,576
wc/d	1	890	890	890
BOR, Jan (1910-1994) Dutch				
oil	1	3,781	3,781	3,781
BORCHERS, Heinz (1898-1972) German				
oil	8	968-3,629	1,754	1,210
BORCHT, Pieter van der (16/17th C) Flemish				
oil	1	4,545	4,545	4,545
BORDAGE, Jean Claude (20th C) ?				
oil	1	1,649	1,649	1,649
BORDALO, Real (20th C) Portuguese				
oil	2	608-1,944	1,276	608
BORDARIER, Stephane (20th C) French				
oil	1	1,155	1,155	1,155
BORDERE, Marie (19th C) ?				
oil	1	15,000	15,000	15,000
BORDES, Coutisson des (?) French?				
oil	1	1,360	1,360	1,360
BORDES, Leonard (1898-1969) French				
oil	4	564-1,757	1,144	937
BORDIGNON, Noe (1841-1920) Italian				
oil	1	76,332	76,332	76,332
BORDONE, Paris (1500-1571) Italian				
oil	6	9,678-740,000	185,096	36,414
BORDONI, Enrico (1904-1969) Italian				
oil	1	1,308	1,308	1,308
wc/d	1	595	595	595
BORDUAS, Paul Emile (1905-1960) Canadian				
oil	4	90,711-186,398	138,981	132,938
wc/d	3	3,772-15,398	11,338	14,844
BOREEL, Wendela (1895-1985) British				
oil	1	1,479	1,479	1,479
BOREGAR, Vladimir Bolgarski (1913-) Russian				
oil	1	5,580	5,580	5,580
BOREIN, Edward (1872-1945) American				
wc/d	47	400-22,000	8,227	8,000
BORELLA, Rocco (1920-1994) Italian				
oil	4	983-1,874	1,334	1,210
BOREN, James (1921-1990) American				
oil	1	7,000	7,000	7,000
wc/d	5	1,000-16,000	4,770	2,000
BOREN, Nelson (1952-) American				
wc/d	5	4,000-12,000	8,150	8,000
BORENSTEIN, Samuel (1908-1969) Canadian				
oil	3	4,210-16,493	11,037	12,408
BORES, Francisco (1898-1972) Spanish				
oil	24	4,757-70,000	31,894	26,886
wc/d	29	830-9,924	3,719	3,507
BORG, Carl Oscar (1879-1947) American/Swedish				
oil	14	750-40,000	12,292	7,000
wc/d	12	800-18,000	4,512	1,900
BORGEAUD, Georges (1913-1997) Swiss				
oil	10	1,374-8,326	4,050	4,186
wc/d	1	455	455	455

Name	No.	Price Range	Average	Median
BORGEAUD, Marius (1861-1924) Swiss				
oil	1	22,832	22,832	22,832
BORGELLA, Frederic (19th C) French				
oil	5	500-2,572	1,581	1,402
BORGES, Jacobo (1931-) Venezuelan				
oil	2	8,840-13,720	11,280	8,840
BORGET, Auguste (1809-1877) French				
wc/d	1	2,124	2,124	2,124
BORGEY, Léon (1888-1959) French				
3D	1	7,000	7,000	7,000
BORGHESE, Franz (1941-2005) Italian				
oil	36	1,074-9,955	4,677	3,836
wc/d	21	471-1,849	885	825
3D	2	2,141-2,290	2,215	2,141
BORGHI, Alfonso (1944-) Italian				
oil	2	884-1,178	1,031	884
BORGHI, Ambrogio (1849-1887) Italian				
3D	1	128,800	128,800	128,800
BORGIA, Giancarlo (1958-) Italian				
oil	1	1,414	1,414	1,414
BORGLUM, Elisabeth Collins (1848-1922) American				
oil	1	2,500	2,500	2,500
BORGLUM, John Gutzon (1867-1941) American				
oil	1	2,750	2,750	2,750
wc/d	1	2,100	2,100	2,100
3D	1	120,000	120,000	120,000
BORGLUM, Solon Hannibal (1868-1922) American				
3D	1	8,500	8,500	8,500
BORGOGNONE, Ambrogio (1455-1530) Italian				
oil	1	290,350	290,350	290,350
BORGOGNONE, Francesco Ignazio (1724-?) Italian				
oil	1	12,945	12,945	12,945
BORIONE, Bernard Louis (1865-?) French				
oil	3	2,160-7,350	5,003	5,500
BORISENKOV, Vasily P (1924-) Russian				
oil	1	5,075	5,075	5,075
BORISOV, Aleksandr Alekseevich (1866-1934) Russian				
oil	1	1,095	1,095	1,095
BORISOV, L (20th C) Russian				
oil	1	3,440	3,440	3,440
BORISOV-MUSATOV, Viktor (1870-1905) Russian				
wc/d	1	1,153,200	1,153,200	1,153,200
BORISOVIC, Lakowsky Arnold (1880-1937) Russian				
oil	1	3,766	3,766	3,766
BORJE, Gideon (1891-1969) Swedish				
oil	3	595-3,832	1,874	1,195
wc/d	1	1,321	1,321	1,321
BORJESON, Agnes (1827-1900) Swedish				
oil	2	1,371-7,644	4,507	1,371
BORLA, Hector (1937-) Argentinian				
oil	3	1,790-17,000	7,596	4,000
BORMAN, Johannes (17th C) Dutch				
oil	1	17,517	17,517	17,517
BORNOY, Pepe (1942-) Spanish				
oil	1	1,447	1,447	1,447
BORNSTEIN, Eli (20th C) American				
3D	1	6,500	6,500	6,500
BOROFSKY, Jonathan (1942-) American				
oil	1	3,000	3,000	3,000
3D	1	8,000	8,000	8,000
BORONDA, Lester David (1886-1951) American				
oil	1	2,000	2,000	2,000
BOROWIKOFFSKI, Wladimir Lukitsch (1757-1825) Russian				
oil	1	44,720	44,720	44,720
BORRA, Pompeo (1898-1973) Italian				
oil	11	2,386-12,192	4,970	3,514
wc/d	4	471-1,054	681	589
BORRANI, Odoardo (1833-1905) Italian				
wc/d	1	2,356	2,356	2,356
BORRAS, Jorge (1952-) French				
3D	2	1,767-2,983	2,375	1,767

Name	No.	Price Range	Average	Median
BORRAS, Juan II (1947-) Spanish				
oil	1	2,035	2,035	2,035
BORRELL, Juli (1877-1957) Spanish				
oil	1	3,114	3,114	3,114
BORREMANS, Michael (1963-) Belgian				
oil	2	28,000-193,600	110,800	28,000
wc/d	1	18,000	18,000	18,000
BORRONI, Paolo (1749-1819) Italian				
oil	1	2,650	2,650	2,650
BORROW, William H (fl.1863-1893) British				
oil	5	1,058-9,100	4,389	1,925
BORSA, Emilio (1857-1931) Italian				
oil	1	8,247	8,247	8,247
wc/d	1	1,767	1,767	1,767
BORSA, Roberto (1880-1965) Italian				
oil	2	1,054-5,271	3,162	1,054
BORSATO, Renato (1927-) Italian				
oil	4	900-1,165	1,026	942
BORSSOM, Anthonie van (1630-1677) Dutch				
oil	1	4,597	4,597	4,597
wc/d	1	4,810	4,810	4,810
BORSTEL, Reginald Arthur (1875-1922) Australian				
oil	1	1,770	1,770	1,770
BORTHWICK, Alfred Edward (1871-1955) British				
wc/d	1	1,556	1,556	1,556
BORTIGNONI, Giuseppe (19/20th C) Italian				
oil	2	1,260-2,268	1,764	1,260
BORTNYIK, Sandor (1893-1976) Hungarian				
wc/d	1	9,555	9,555	9,555
BORTOLUZZI, Alfredo (1905-1995) Italian				
oil	1	3,579	3,579	3,579
BORTOLUZZI, Camillo (1868-1933) Italian				
oil	2	2,486-22,932	12,709	2,486
BORYSOWSKI, Stanislaw (1906-1988) Polish				
oil	1	2,003	2,003	2,003
BORZINO, Elda (1863-1927) Italian				
wc/d	2	1,070-1,189	1,129	1,070
BORZINO, Leopoldina Zanetti (1826-1902) Italian				
oil	1	1,546	1,546	1,546
wc/d	1	892	892	892
BOS, Henk (1901-1979) Dutch				
oil	5	1,286-2,754	1,748	1,400
BOSA, Eugenio (1807-1875) Italian				
oil	1	3,551	3,551	3,551
BOSA, Louis (1905-1981) American/Italian				
oil	5	1,000-17,000	4,890	2,000
wc/d	1	900	900	900
BOSAI, Kameda (1752-1826) Japanese				
wc/d	1	1,500	1,500	1,500
BOSBOOM, Johannes (1817-1891) Dutch				
oil	4	2,000-35,068	13,673	6,361
wc/d	12	630-27,507	6,086	4,075
BOSCH, Ernst (1834-?) German				
oil	1	15,000	15,000	15,000
BOSCH, J H (17th C) Dutch				
oil	1	16,937	16,937	16,937
BOSCH, Jacob Pieter van den (1868-1948) Dutch				
oil	1	4,703	4,703	4,703
BOSCH, Pieter van den (c.1613-1663) Dutch				
oil	2	5,255-12,038	8,646	5,255
BOSCHETTI, B (?) Italian				
3D	1	3,044	3,044	3,044
BOSCHI, Dino (1923-) Italian				
oil	1	1,844	1,844	1,844
wc/d	1	1,028	1,028	1,028
BOSCHI, Luigi (19th C) Italian				
oil	1	1,929	1,929	1,929
BOSELLI, Felice (1650-1732) Italian				
oil	1	27,680	27,680	27,680
BOSHART, Wilhelm (1815-1878) German				
oil	1	2,432	2,432	2,432

Name	No.	Price Range	Average	Median
BOSHIER, Derek (1937-) British				
oil	1	2,088	2,088	2,088
wc/d	1	1,134	1,134	1,134
BOSIA, Agostino (1886-1962) Italian				
oil	1	1,014	1,014	1,014
BOSIERS, René (1875-1927) Belgian				
oil	1	1,790	1,790	1,790
BOSILJ, Ilija Basicevic (1895-1972) Yugoslavian				
oil	1	1,297	1,297	1,297
wc/d	3	505-2,524	1,556	1,641
BOSKIN, Mihail Vasilievitch (1875-1930) Russian				
oil	1	7,904	7,904	7,904
BOSMA, Wim (1902-1985) Dutch				
oil	4	1,145-1,707	1,379	1,219
BOSMAN, Jacob (1901-1974) Dutch				
wc/d	2	1,465-1,465	1,465	1,465
BOSMAN, Richard (1944-) American				
oil	1	3,200	3,200	3,200
BOSQUET, Thierry (1937-) Belgian				
wc/d	1	1,250	1,250	1,250
BOSSCHAERT, Abraham (17th C) Flemish				
oil	2	38,060-70,068	54,064	38,060
BOSSCHAERT, Ambrosius (younger) (1609-1645) Dutch				
oil	3	34,600-337,203	146,533	67,797
BOSSCHAERT, Jean Baptiste (1667-1746) Flemish				
oil	7	4,364-85,000	31,448	15,288
BOSSCHE, Balthasar van den (1681-1715) Flemish				
oil	2	5,839-11,439	8,639	5,839
BOSSCHE, Hubert van den (1874-1957) Belgian				
oil	3	482-2,338	1,134	584
BOSSENROTH, Karl (1869-1935) German				
oil	2	1,878-3,655	2,766	1,878
BOSSHARD, Rodolphe-Theophile (1889-1960) Swiss				
oil	11	3,080-68,289	19,225	8,247
wc/d	4	607-999	789	775
BOSSLER, Hilding (1899-?) Swedish				
oil	1	1,145	1,145	1,145
BOSSO, Francesco (1864-1933) Italian				
oil	4	2,154-3,568	2,627	2,367
BOSSO, Renato di (1905-1982) French				
oil	1	15,265	15,265	15,265
BOSSOLI, Carlo (1815-1884) Italian				
oil	6	7,767-50,460	18,565	11,973
wc/d	5	423-41,760	11,367	909
BOSSUET, François Antoine (1798-1889) Belgian				
oil	4	1,549-91,176	27,396	6,259
wc/d	1	1,798	1,798	1,798
BOSTIER DE BEZ, Jean Joseph (1780-c.1845) French				
oil	1	1,391	1,391	1,391
BOSTON, Frederick James (1855-1932) American				
oil	2	550-20,000	10,275	550
BOSTON, Joseph H (1860-1954) American				
oil	5	2,750-16,000	7,200	5,000
BOSWELL, James (1906-1971) New Zealander				
oil	1	1,118	1,118	1,118
BOSWELL, Jessie (1881-1956) British?				
oil	1	8,192	8,192	8,192
BOTELLO, Angel (1913-1986) South American				
oil	17	5,500-50,000	23,352	20,000
3D	15	7,000-32,000	14,700	13,000
BOTERO, Fernando (1932-) Colombian				
oil	6	225,000-1,800,000	1,087,500	800,000
wc/d	19	3,507-175,000	56,293	38,531
3D	17	10,014-925,000	276,528	170,000
BOTH, Andries (1608-1650) Dutch				
wc/d	1	1,272	1,272	1,272
BOTH, Jan (1618-1652) Dutch				
oil	2	16,571-848,571	432,571	16,571
BOTKE, Jessie Arms (1883-1971) American				
oil	8	3,250-65,000	21,406	8,500

Name	No.	Price Range	Average	Median
BOTKIN, Henry Albert (1896-1983) American				
oil	1	450	450	450
wc/d	2	650-2,400	1,525	650
BOTKIN, Michael Petrovitch (1839-1914) Russian				
oil	1	9,342	9,342	9,342
BOTO, Martha (1925-2004) Argentinian				
3D	1	42,500	42,500	42,500
BOTT, Francis (1904-1998) German				
oil	14	811-4,442	2,272	1,942
wc/d	8	1,379-6,650	3,256	2,573
BOTT, Nicholas J (1941-) Canadian				
oil	1	1,426	1,426	1,426
BOTTA, Gregorio (1952-) Italian				
wc/d	1	5,856	5,856	5,856
3D	1	2,417	2,417	2,417
BOTTAI, Giovanni (1904-1978) Italian				
oil	1	2,131	2,131	2,131
BOTTANI, Giuseppe (1717-1784) Italian				
oil	1	6,764	6,764	6,764
BOTTET, Nicole (1942-) French				
oil	2	1,178-1,767	1,472	1,178
BOTTGER, Herbert (1898-1954) German				
oil	4	3,534-6,446	4,650	4,243
BOTTI, Francesco (17th C) Italian				
oil	2	6,049-95,150	50,599	6,049
BOTTI, Italo (1889-1974) Argentinian				
oil	6	2,500-5,500	3,933	3,600
BOTTICHER, Walter (1885-1916) German				
wc/d	1	3,162	3,162	3,162
BOTTICINI, Francesco (1446-1497) Italian				
oil	2	6,000-26,000	16,000	6,000
BOTTIGLIERI, Gennaro (19th C) Italian				
oil	2	1,440-1,440	1,440	1,440
BOTTINI, Georges (1873-1907) French				
wc/d	4	561-18,000	8,449	6,237
BOTTOMLEY, Ernest (1934-) British				
3D	1	1,890	1,890	1,890
BOTTOMLEY, John William (1816-1900) German				
oil	1	2,664	2,664	2,664
BOTTON, Jean Isy de (1898-1978) French				
oil	10	1,204-8,500	3,087	2,250
BOUCART, Gaston H (1878-1962) French				
oil	2	720-3,988	2,354	720
BOUCHARD (?) ?				
3D	1	4,077	4,077	4,077
BOUCHARD, Lorne Holland (1913-1978) Canadian				
oil	15	412-4,874	1,501	1,350
BOUCHARD, Marie Cecile (1920-) Canadian				
oil	2	529-2,292	1,410	529
BOUCHARD, Paul (1853-1937) French				
oil	1	54,948	54,948	54,948
BOUCHARD, Simone Mary (1912-1945) Canadian				
oil	1	1,410	1,410	1,410
BOUCHARDON, Edme (1698-1762) French				
wc/d	1	1,401	1,401	1,401
BOUCHAUD, Étienne (1898-1989) French				
oil	4	722-1,019	870	783
wc/d	8	482-1,505	818	719
BOUCHAUD, Jean (1891-1977) French				
oil	1	15,342	15,342	15,342
wc/d	5	1,204-3,652	2,268	2,185
BOUCHE, Georges (1874-1941) French				
oil	3	832-5,708	3,180	3,000
BOUCHE, Louis (1896-1969) American				
oil	3	550-2,750	1,500	1,200
BOUCHE, Louis Alexandre (1838-1911) French				
oil	3	1,565-4,335	3,190	3,672
BOUCHER, Alfred (1850-1934) French				
oil	1	1,270	1,270	1,270
3D	14	2,675-122,850	19,230	6,000

Name	No.	Price Range	Average	Median
BOUCHER, François (elder) (1703-1770) French				
oil	7	83,250-1,850,000	458,667	217,423
wc/d	12	1,243-130,813	35,439	14,449
BOUCHER, Jean (1870-1939) French				
3D	1	2,028	2,028	2,028
BOUCHER, Jean (1568-1633) French				
wc/d	1	18,373	18,373	18,373
BOUCHER-BEUG, Katherine (1947-) American				
wc/d	1	1,549	1,549	1,549
BOUCHERLE, Pierre (1894-1988) French/Tunisian				
oil	2	957-4,676	2,816	957
BOUCHET, Louis Andre Gabriel (1759-1842) French				
oil	1	1,883	1,883	1,883
BOUCHOR, Joseph Felix (1853-1937) French				
oil	6	1,502-10,520	4,525	3,631
BOUCHOT, François (1800-1842) French				
oil	1	2,000	2,000	2,000
BOUCLE, Pierre (1610-1673) Flemish				
oil	2	43,250-115,700	79,475	43,250
BOUDET, Pierre (1925-) French				
oil	9	518-3,270	1,532	1,132
BOUDEWYNS, Adriaen Frans (1644-1711) Flemish				
wc/d	1	5,000	5,000	5,000
BOUDEWYNS, Adriaen Frans (younger) (1673-1744) Flemish				
oil	1	4,671	4,671	4,671
BOUDEWYNS, Adriaen Frans and BOUT, Pieter (17/18th C) Flemish				
oil	2	7,120-11,571	9,345	7,120
BOUDEWYNS, Frans (18th C) Flemish				
wc/d	3	1,401-1,985	1,662	1,600
BOUDIN, Eugène (1824-1898) French				
oil	49	6,780-1,408,000	158,447	101,750
wc/d	28	773-132,000	14,889	5,081
BOUDON, Patrick (1944-) French				
oil	1	3,000	3,000	3,000
BOUDREAULT, Louis (20th C) French?				
oil	1	3,505	3,505	3,505
BOUDRY, Alois (1851-1938) Belgian				
oil	4	1,335-3,273	1,894	1,392
BOUGAIEV, Sergei (1966-) Russian				
wc/d	1	4,000	4,000	4,000
BOUGH, Sam (1822-1878) British				
oil	15	573-53,400	12,515	3,553
wc/d	10	528-7,134	2,224	972
BOUGHTON, George Henry (1833-1905) American/British				
oil	4	1,062-32,500	10,328	2,750
wc/d	3	750-1,665	1,238	1,300
BOUGOURD, Cecile (1857-1941) French				
oil	1	3,888	3,888	3,888
BOUGUEREAU, Elizabeth Gardner (1837-1922) American				
oil	1	9,341	9,341	9,341
BOUGUEREAU, William Adolphe (1825-1905) French				
oil	10	2,500-1,150,000	354,250	210,000
BOUILLARD, A (19th C) ?				
oil	1	1,821	1,821	1,821
BOUILLE, Christian (20th C) French				
oil	1	1,788	1,788	1,788
wc/d	1	715	715	715
BOUILLE, Etienne (1858-1933) French				
oil	2	626-2,104	1,365	626
BOUILLION, Michel de (17th C) Flemish				
oil	1	18,500	18,500	18,500
BOUILLIOT, Emile (1823-1905) Belgian				
oil	1	1,527	1,527	1,527
BOUILLON, François (1944-) French				
wc/d	1	2,071	2,071	2,071
BOUKERCHE, Miloud (?-1979) Algerian				
oil	3	2,616-3,884	3,335	3,507
BOUKHARI, Hassan (1965-) Moroccan				
oil	2	4,131-4,815	4,473	4,131
BOULANGER, François Jean Louis (1819-1873) Belgian				
oil	2	42,432-49,000	45,716	42,432

Name	No.	Price Range	Average	Median
BOULANGER, Graciela Rodo (1935-) Bolivian				
oil	1	2,277	2,277	2,277
3D	1	4,000	4,000	4,000
BOULANGER, Gustave Clarence Rodolphe (1824-1888) French				
oil	2	101,200-500,000	300,600	101,200
BOULANGER, Louis Vercelli (1806-1867) French				
oil	1	8,550	8,550	8,550
BOULARD, Auguste (1825-1897) French				
oil	2	836-1,523	1,179	836
BOULARD, Auguste (jnr) (1852-1927) French				
oil	1	1,900	1,900	1,900
BOULARD, Theodore (20th C) French				
oil	1	2,279	2,279	2,279
BOULAYE, Antoine de la (1849-?) French				
oil	3	1,209-4,094	2,303	1,607
wc/d	10	680-3,090	1,316	1,113
BOULBAR, Annick le (20th C) French				
oil	1	1,824	1,824	1,824
BOULENGER, Hippolyte (1837-1874) Belgian				
oil	2	2,277-3,090	2,683	2,277
BOULER, Andre (1924-1997) French				
oil	1	1,308	1,308	1,308
BOULET, Cyprien-Eugène (1877-1927) French				
oil	3	658-3,344	1,613	837
BOULIER, Lucien (1882-1963) French				
oil	7	535-1,458	997	1,073
wc/d	1	473	473	473
BOULLAIRE, Jacques (1893-1976) French				
wc/d	1	1,255	1,255	1,255
BOULLOGNE, Bon de (elder) (1649-1717) French				
wc/d	1	7,030	7,030	7,030
BOULLOGNE, Louis de (18th C) French				
oil	1	29,731	29,731	29,731
BOULLOGNE, Louis de (younger) (1654-1733) French				
wc/d	3	6,076-12,025	8,519	7,458
BOULOGNE, Valentin de (1591-1634) French				
oil	1	1,632	1,632	1,632
BOULT, Augustus S (fl.1815-1853) British				
oil	1	5,292	5,292	5,292
BOULT, Francis Cecil (fl.1877-1895) British				
oil	1	2,800	2,800	2,800
BOULTBEE, John (1745-1812) British				
oil	2	16,000-31,185	23,592	16,000
BOUMAN, Johannes (1602-c.1626) German				
oil	1	43,315	43,315	43,315
BOUNDY, J M (19th C) American?				
oil	1	2,500	2,500	2,500
BOUQUET, Michel (1807-1890) French				
wc/d	1	4,186	4,186	4,186
BOURAINE, M (20th C) French				
3D	1	7,658	7,658	7,658
BOURAINE, Marcel (20th C) French				
3D	4	1,911-79,714	21,818	2,038
BOURDELLE, Émile Antoine (1861-1929) French				
wc/d	7	539-3,200	2,130	2,155
3D	9	3,750-35,035	15,262	10,888
BOURDILLON, Frank (1851-1924) British				
oil	1	38,720	38,720	38,720
BOURDON, Sébastien (1616-1671) French				
oil	1	11,063	11,063	11,063
wc/d	1	5,068	5,068	5,068
BOURDONNAYE, Alain de la (1930-) French				
oil	3	1,291-3,512	2,381	2,341
BOURE, Ant Felix (19th C) Belgian				
3D	1	2,090	2,090	2,090
BOURGAIN, Jean Yves (20th C) ?				
oil	1	1,020	1,020	1,020
BOURGEAT, Jean Francois (20th C) French				
oil	7	550-5,000	2,221	2,750
BOURGEOIS du CASTELET, Constant (1767-1841) French				
wc/d	2	836-1,394	1,115	836

Name	No.	Price Range	Average	Median
BOURGEOIS du CASTELET, Constant and ZIX, Benjamin (18/19th C) French				
wc/d	2	2,661-3,801	3,231	2,661
BOURGEOIS, C (19th C) ?				
wc/d	2	1,521-9,123	5,322	1,521
BOURGEOIS, Charles Arthur (1838-1886) French				
3D	2	3,480-17,400	10,440	3,480
BOURGEOIS, E (19/20th C) French				
wc/d	1	4,435	4,435	4,435
BOURGEOIS, Eugène (1855-1909) French				
oil	2	1,139-2,265	1,702	1,139
BOURGEOIS, J (20th C) French				
oil	1	1,806	1,806	1,806
BOURGEOIS, Louise (1911-) American/French				
oil	1	160,000	160,000	160,000
wc/d	2	22,500-50,000	36,250	22,500
3D	8	45,760-2,700,000	738,845	550,000
BOURGES, Pauline Elise Leonide (1838-1910) French				
oil	1	1,253	1,253	1,253
BOURGOGNE, Pierre (1838-1904) French				
oil	1	2,799	2,799	2,799
BOURKE, Brian (1936-) Irish				
oil	1	3,387	3,387	3,387
wc/d	5	877-2,719	1,469	1,089
BOURLARD, Antoine Joseph (1826-1899) Belgian				
oil	1	2,622	2,622	2,622
BOURLIER, Marc (1947-) French				
3D	2	1,937-2,422	2,179	1,937
BOURNE, Gertrude Beals (1897-1962) American				
wc/d	2	500-2,600	1,550	500
BOURNE, James (1773-1854) British				
oil	2	696-2,104	1,400	696
wc/d	1	665	665	665
BOURNICHON, François Edouard (1816-1896) French				
oil	1	530	530	530
wc/d	1	1,520	1,520	1,520
BOUROTTE, Auguste (1853-?) Belgian				
oil	1	36,122	36,122	36,122
BOUSSARD, Jacques (20th C) French				
oil	1	1,500	1,500	1,500
BOUT, Pieter (1658-1719) Flemish				
oil	2	22,490-81,745	52,117	22,400
wc/d	1	1,752	1,752	1,752
BOUTELLE, De Witt Clinton (1817-1884) American				
oil	1	2,750	2,750	2,750
BOUTELLE, Flora Whitney Kemp (1866-1950) American				
oil	1	1,100	1,100	1,100
BOUTEN, Armand (1893-1965) Dutch				
oil	1	17,671	17,671	17,671
wc/d	1	964	964	964
BOUTER, Cornelis (1888-1966) Dutch				
oil	24	978-6,932	2,578	2,158
BOUTERWEK, Frederich (1806-1867) German				
oil	1	2,371	2,371	2,371
BOUTET DE MONVEL, Bernard (1884-1949) French				
oil	2	3,853-22,932	13,392	3,853
wc/d	1	662	662	662
BOUTHOORN, Willy Leo (1916-) Dutch				
oil	6	641-3,507	1,617	1,252
BOUTIBONNE, Charles-Edouard (1816-1897) Hungarian				
oil	1	5,557	5,557	5,557
wc/d	1	507	507	507
BOUTON, Charles Marie (1781-1853) French				
oil	4	1,812-3,801	2,501	2,008
BOUTTATS, Frederik (younger) (?-1676) Flemish				
oil	1	8,247	8,247	8,247
BOUTTATS, Jacob (17th C) Flemish				
oil	1	10,771	10,771	10,771
BOUTTON-PIERRIC (1944-) French?				
3D	1	2,534	2,534	2,534
BOUVAL, Maurice (1863-1920) French				
3D	2	1,800-2,610	2,205	1,800

Name	No.	Price Range	Average	Median
BOUVARD (19/20th C) French				
oil	8	4,004-29,580	13,300	7,562
BOUVARD, Antoine (1870-1956) French				
oil	33	3,402-48,720	16,976	15,033
BOUVARD, C (19th C) French				
oil	1	2,852	2,852	2,852
BOUVARD, Colette (19th C) French				
oil	2	3,036-5,220	4,128	3,036
BOUVARD, Joseph Antoine (1840-1920) French				
oil	4	10,845-36,540	18,552	12,886
BOUVARD, Noël (1912-1975) French				
oil	2	2,340-4,914	3,627	2,340
BOUVET, Henry (1859-1945) French				
oil	88	473-24,857	2,608	1,184
wc/d	37	473-7,694	1,543	1,089
BOUVIE, F A (20th C) Belgian				
oil	1	3,534	3,534	3,534
BOUVIER, Arthur (1837-1921) Belgian				
oil	5	756-4,410	2,408	1,940
BOUVIER, Augustus Jules (c.1827-1881) British				
oil	2	932-1,400	1,166	932
wc/d	8	534-3,500	1,238	875
BOUVIER, Pierre-Louis (1766-1836) Swiss				
oil	1	24,780	24,780	24,780
BOUVIER, Pietro (1839-1927) Italian				
oil	2	1,452-3,884	2,668	1,452
BOUVIOLLE, Maurice (1893-1971) French				
oil	4	1,171-2,589	1,910	1,752
wc/d	2	651-1,199	925	651
BOUYS, André (1656-1740) French				
oil	1	26,163	26,163	26,163
BOUYSSOU, Jacques (1926-1997) French				
oil	17	668-9,298	1,894	1,286
BOUZIANIS, Georgios (1885-1959) Greek				
oil	3	12,320-103,800	44,185	16,435
wc/d	1	28,050	28,050	28,050
BOVE, A (19th C) French				
oil	1	2,652	2,652	2,652
BOVET, Carl (19th C) French?				
wc/d	1	1,874	1,874	1,874
BOVIE, Felix (1812-1880) Belgian				
oil	1	1,414	1,414	1,414
BOVIN, Karl (1907-1985) Danish				
oil	4	727-2,101	1,254	889
BOWDOIN, Harriette (1880-1947) American				
oil	6	1,100-14,000	5,350	2,500
BOWEN, Denis (1921-) British				
oil	2	528-1,203	865	528
wc/d	1	1,300	1,300	1,300
BOWEN, Greta (1880-1981) Irish				
oil	2	2,301-3,720	3,010	2,301
wc/d	5	1,140-2,919	2,038	2,180
BOWEN, J R (19th C) American				
wc/d	1	4,600	4,600	4,600
BOWEN, Keith (1950-) British				
oil	2	1,593-3,240	2,416	1,593
wc/d	1	1,225	1,225	1,225
BOWEN, Owen (1873-1967) British				
oil	29	442-6,764	1,802	1,009
wc/d	4	655-1,044	855	713
BOWEN, Ralph (fl.1884-1915) British				
oil	1	2,250	2,250	2,250
BOWER, Alexander (1875-1952) American				
oil	3	400-7,000	4,300	5,500
wc/d	1	650	650	650
BOWER, Lucy Scott (1864-1934) American				
oil	1	2,425	2,425	2,425
BOWES, David (1957-) American				
oil	1	3,800	3,800	3,800
BOWETT, Druie (1924-) British				
oil	10	1,870-5,984	3,216	2,992

Name	No.	Price Range	Average	Median
BOWEY, Olwyn (1936-) British				
oil	3	552-2,088	1,157	833
BOWKETT, Jane Maria (1837-1891) British				
oil	1	7,266	7,266	7,266
BOWLING, Charles T (1891-1986) American				
oil	3	4,000-35,000	16,333	10,000
BOWLY, E (19th C) British				
oil	1	1,780	1,780	1,780
BOWMAN, John (1953-) American				
oil	3	650-1,656	1,279	1,531
BOWMAN, Richard (1918-2001) American				
oil	3	550-3,000	1,650	1,400
BOWYER, Robert (1758-1834) British				
wc/d	1	9,735	9,735	9,735
BOWYER, William (1926-) British				
oil	11	475-2,478	1,026	673
wc/d	1	875	875	875
BOX, Eden (1919-1988) British				
oil	2	885-1,505	1,195	885
BOXEL, Piet van (1912-2001) Dutch				
oil	2	500-2,500	1,500	500
BOYADJIAN, Micheline (1923-) Belgian				
oil	1	6,466	6,466	6,466
wc/d	1	4,849	4,849	4,849
BOYCE, William Thomas Nicholas (1857-1911) British				
wc/d	4	484-1,710	1,074	650
BOYCOTT-BROWN, Hugh (1909-1990) British				
oil	10	549-2,832	1,142	732
BOYD, Arthur Merric Bloomfield (1920-1999) Australian				
oil	1	12,900	12,900	12,900
BOYD, John (1937-) British				
oil	1	4,956	4,956	4,956
BOYD, John G (1940-2001) British				
oil	6	435-17,400	5,699	957
BOYD, Theodore Penleigh (1890-1923) Australian				
wc/d	1	3,762	3,762	3,762
BOYE, Abel Dominique (1864-1934) French				
oil	2	3,828-4,500	4,164	3,828
BOYLAN, Karen (20th C) American				
oil	1	5,000	5,000	5,000
BOYLE FAMILY (20th C) British				
oil	2	6,960-7,830	7,395	6,960
wc/d	3	4,123-10,014	7,265	7,658
3D	1	32,500	32,500	32,500
BOYLE, Alicia (1908-1997) Irish				
oil	2	1,192-2,903	2,047	1,192
wc/d	1	802	802	802
BOYLE, Allan (1967-) British?				
oil	2	2,500-3,500	3,000	2,500
BOYLE, Charles Wellington (1860-1925) American				
oil	1	17,000	17,000	17,000
BOYLE, Mark (1934-) British				
wc/d	1	5,000	5,000	5,000
BOYLE, Neil (1931-) American				
oil	2	3,000-5,000	4,000	3,000
BOYS, Thomas Shotter (1803-1874) British				
wc/d	1	15,390	15,390	15,390
BOZE, Honore (1830-1908) British				
oil	4	2,225-4,789	3,339	2,973
BOZE, Joseph (1744-1826) French				
wc/d	1	32,703	32,703	32,703
BOZNANSKA, Olga (1865-1945) Polish				
oil	1	4,700	4,700	4,700
BOZZATO, Attilio (19th C) Italian				
oil	1	1,556	1,556	1,556
wc/d	1	1,529	1,529	1,529
BOZZETTI, Francesco (1876-1949) Italian				
wc/d	1	1,234	1,234	1,234
BOZZOLINI, Silvano (1911-1998) Italian				
oil	13	553-7,880	3,943	4,676
wc/d	1	908	908	908

Name	No.	Price Range	Average	Median
BRAAKMAN, Anthonie (1811-1870) Dutch				
oil	1	5,007	5,007	5,007
BRAAM, Dirk Pieter (1908-1986) Dutch				
oil	2	701-1,781	1,241	701
BRAAQ (1951-1997) British				
oil	6	1,472-7,462	4,434	4,186
wc/d	4	773-2,800	1,710	1,380
BRABAZON, Hercules Brabazon (1821-1906) British				
wc/d	37	443-10,440	2,914	2,775
BRACCI, Pietro and RUSCONI, Camillo (18th C) Italian				
3D	1	550,000	550,000	550,000
BRACCIOLI, Mauro (1761-1810) Italian				
oil	1	7,644	7,644	7,644
BRACHO Y MURILLO, Jose Maria (1827-1882) Spanish				
oil	3	1,500-14,160	6,538	3,956
BRACHO, Gabriel (1915-1994) Venezuelan				
oil	7	465-2,370	902	510
wc/d	1	840	840	840
BRACHT, Eugen (1842-1921) Swiss				
oil	11	1,004-30,362	7,237	4,685
BRACK, Emil (1860-1905) German				
oil	1	15,641	15,641	15,641
BRACKETT, Walter M (1823-1919) American				
oil	4	4,000-12,000	8,437	8,250
BRACKLE, Jakob (1897-1987) German				
oil	20	618-10,603	2,708	1,881
BRACKMAN, Robert (1898-1980) American				
oil	6	750-5,000	1,766	800
wc/d	2	800-1,500	1,150	800
BRACQUEMOND, Émile Louis (20th C) French				
3D	2	3,120-3,159	3,139	3,120
BRACQUEMOND, Félix (1833-1914) French				
wc/d	1	2,000	2,000	2,000
BRACQUEMOND, Pierre (20th C) French				
oil	1	1,929	1,929	1,929
BRADBERRY, Georges (1878-1959) French				
wc/d	1	2,510	2,510	2,510
BRADBURY, Arthur Royce (1892-1977) British				
oil	1	6,668	6,668	6,668
BRADBURY, Bennett (1914-1991) American				
oil	15	800-15,000	3,260	2,750
BRADBURY, Gideon Elden (1833-1904) American				
oil	1	1,500	1,500	1,500
BRADFORD, William (1827-1892) American				
oil	5	25,000-410,000	110,800	45,000
wc/d	4	1,000-17,000	7,525	1,100
BRADLEY, Anne Cary (1884-?) American				
oil	3	450-2,000	1,100	850
BRADLEY, Basil (1842-1904) British				
wc/d	6	696-3,363	1,352	771
BRADLEY, Basil and TRAPPES, Francis M (19th C) British				
oil	1	6,264	6,264	6,264
BRADLEY, Helen (1900-1979) British				
oil	11	2,670-68,040	31,687	33,300
wc/d	4	496-5,550	1,977	496
BRADLEY, John (fl.1830-1874) American				
oil	1	12,000	12,000	12,000
BRADLEY, Martin (1931-) British				
oil	6	696-7,770	2,332	1,062
wc/d	3	586-1,914	1,200	1,100
BRADLEY, William (19/20th C) British				
oil	1	4,500	4,500	4,500
wc/d	2	1,840-1,936	1,888	1,840
BRADLEY, William (1801-1857) British				
oil	1	1,921	1,921	1,921
BRADSHAW, George Fagan (1887-1960) British				
oil	2	1,190-4,425	2,807	1,190
wc/d	1	616	616	616
BRADSHAW, Nell Mary (1904-) Canadian				
oil	3	1,518-8,389	3,907	1,814
BRADY, Charles (1926-1997) Irish/American				
oil	14	3,708-39,743	9,729	6,000

Name	No.	Price Range	Average	Median
BRAEKELEER, Adrien de (1818-1904) Belgian				
oil	5	1,989-11,063	5,359	3,492
BRAEKELEER, F de (19th C) Belgian				
oil	1	2,655	2,655	2,655
BRAEKELEER, Ferdinand de (19th C) Belgian				
oil	8	951-27,277	10,292	8,390
BRAEKELEER, Ferdinand de (elder) (1792-1883) Belgian				
oil	1	16,384	16,384	16,384
wc/d	1	1,890	1,890	1,890
BRAEKELEER, Ferdinand de (younger) (1828-1857) Belgian				
oil	1	1,276	1,276	1,276
BRAEKELEER, Henri de (1840-1888) Belgian				
oil	5	626-6,081	2,381	1,553
BRAESAS, Dimos (1882-1964) Greek				
oil	2	5,190-14,080	9,635	5,190
BRAGAGLIA, Alberto (1896-1985) Italian				
wc/d	2	1,119-1,551	1,335	1,119
BRAILOVSKY, Leonid Mikhailovich and Rimma (20th C) Russian				
oil	4	6,880-23,836	17,909	18,600
wc/d	1	13,760	13,760	13,760
BRAITH, Anton (1836-1905) German				
oil	8	1,060-17,897	7,978	5,845
BRAKENBURGH, Richard (1650-1702) Dutch				
oil	8	1,767-30,630	13,611	8,086
BRALEY, Clarence (1858-1925) American				
oil	1	2,700	2,700	2,700
BRAMBILLA, Ferdinando (1838-1921) Italian				
oil	2	1,210-3,627	2,418	1,210
BRAMER, Josef (1948-) Austrian				
oil	1	9,936	9,936	9,936
wc/d	1	1,893	1,893	1,893
BRAMER, Leonard (1596-1674) Dutch				
oil	4	7,598-55,000	21,342	11,094
wc/d	2	1,168-1,752	1,460	1,168
BRAMLEY, Frank (1857-1915) British				
oil	3	2,493-273,000	92,716	2,655
BRAMPTON, Herbert (19/20th C) British?				
wc/d	1	1,513	1,513	1,513
BRANCACCIO, Carlo (1861-1920) Italian				
oil	9	1,526-58,122	12,423	3,053
wc/d	1	1,414	1,414	1,414
BRANCACCIO, Giovanni (1903-1975) Italian				
oil	1	2,667	2,667	2,667
BRANCO, Francisco (1888-1958) Portuguese				
oil	1	1,823	1,823	1,823
BRANCUSI, Constantin (1876-1957) Rumanian				
3D	2	150,000-3,200,000	1,675,000	150,000
BRAND, Christian Hilfgott (1695-1756) Austrian				
oil	1	4,839	4,839	4,839
BRAND, Friedrich August (1755-1806) Austrian				
oil	1	3,624	3,624	3,624
wc/d	1	2,428	2,428	2,428
BRAND-PAGES, Ernst (1898-1983) German				
oil	2	2,870-4,001	3,435	2,870
BRANDANI, Enrico (1914-) Italian				
oil	2	1,927-2,860	2,393	1,927
BRANDARD, Robert (1805-1862) British				
wc/d	1	3,114	3,114	3,114
BRANDEIS, Antonietta (1849-1910) Hungarian				
oil	29	6,500-60,000	23,338	20,880
BRANDEIS, Johann (1818-1872) Czechoslovakian				
oil	1	5,220	5,220	5,220
BRANDENBURG, Martin (1870-?) German				
wc/d	1	3,109	3,109	3,109
BRANDENBURG, Wilhelm (1824-1901) German				
oil	4	726-4,616	1,737	742
BRANDES, Hans Heinrich Jurgen (1803-1868) German				
oil	1	15,500	15,500	15,500
BRANDES, Matthias (1950-) German				
oil	2	1,578-3,037	2,307	1,578

Name	No.	Price Range	Average	Median
BRANDES, Peter (1944-) Danish				
oil	6	2,736-13,682	6,449	4,024
wc/d	2	808-889	848	808
BRANDES, Willy (1876-1956) German				
oil	1	1,106	1,106	1,106
BRANDI, Domenico (1683-1736) Italian				
oil	2	3,503-5,946	4,724	3,503
BRANDIEN, Carl W (1886-1965) American				
oil	1	22,500	22,500	22,500
BRANDIS, August (1862-1947) German				
oil	5	825-2,662	1,630	1,752
BRANDL, Herbert (1959-) Austrian				
oil	2	5,394-30,575	17,984	5,394
wc/d	3	937-1,169	1,083	1,145
BRANDL, Peter (1668-1739) Czechoslovakian				
oil	1	6,000	6,000	6,000
BRANDNER, Karl (1898-1961) American				
oil	3	1,200-4,250	2,483	2,000
BRANDON, Jacques Émile Edouard (1831-1897) French				
oil	1	1,901	1,901	1,901
BRANDON-COX, Hugh (20th C) British				
wc/d	5	1,067-2,112	1,482	1,197
BRANDRIFF, George Kennedy (1890-1936) American				
oil	4	3,000-19,000	11,312	4,250
BRANDS, Eugène (1913-2002) Dutch				
oil	10	2,201-23,562	9,732	6,370
wc/d	25	1,003-6,106	1,978	1,767
BRANDT, Carl (1852-1930) Swedish				
oil	13	497-11,466	3,248	1,321
BRANDT, Edgar (1880-1960) French				
oil	1	2,548	2,548	2,548
wc/d	1	1,000	1,000	1,000
3D	2	4,224-13,000	8,612	4,224
BRANDT, Ernst V (1880-1957) Danish?				
oil	1	1,881	1,881	1,881
BRANDT, Federico (1878-1932) Venezuelan				
oil	2	1,675-6,980	4,327	1,675
BRANDT, Fritz (1853-1905) Canadian/German				
oil	1	1,874	1,874	1,874
wc/d	1	3,360	3,360	3,360
BRANDT, Johannes Herman (1850-1926) Danish				
oil	1	2,103	2,103	2,103
BRANDT, Josef von (1841-1915) Polish				
oil	1	146,476	146,476	146,476
BRANDT, Muriel (1909-1981) Irish				
wc/d	1	1,767	1,767	1,767
BRANDT, Rexford Elson (1914-2000) American				
wc/d	2	7,500-9,000	8,250	7,500
BRANDTNER, Fritz (1896-1969) Canadian				
oil	2	779-2,624	1,701	779
wc/d	14	486-2,468	1,111	938
BRANGWYN, Sir Frank (1867-1956) British				
oil	15	522-66,150	18,905	9,450
wc/d	16	552-13,950	3,244	1,472
BRANSOM, Paul (1885-1979) American				
oil	1	2,500	2,500	2,500
wc/d	2	475-2,500	1,487	475
BRANSON, Lloyd (1861-1925) American				
oil	1	7,000	7,000	7,000
BRANTS, Cynthia (1921-) American				
oil	1	1,200	1,200	1,200
wc/d	1	700	700	700
BRANTZKY, Franz (1856-1941) German				
oil	1	1,051	1,051	1,051
BRANWHITE, Charles Brooke (1851-1929) British				
oil	1	810	810	810
wc/d	2	440-648	544	440
BRAQUAVAL, Louis (1856-1919) French				
oil	2	6,429-7,130	6,779	6,429
BRAQUE, Georges (1882-1963) French				
oil	27	4,442-4,944,494	726,243	259,000
wc/d	7	5,674-49,950	20,975	13,000
3D	4	25,000-119,863	72,608	60,132

Name	No.	Price Range	Average	Median
BRASCASSAT, Jacques Raymond (1804-1867) French				
oil	4	1,874-32,945	11,569	2,937
BRASCH, Hans (1882-1973) German				
oil	2	2,827-4,841	3,834	2,827
wc/d	1	548	548	548
BRASCH, Wenzel Ignaz (?-1761) Czechoslovakian				
oil	1	6,090	6,090	6,090
BRASEN, Hans (1849-1930) Danish				
oil	5	1,737-104,228	31,283	6,636
BRASILIER, Andre (1929-2004) French				
oil	10	6,069-76,438	18,244	10,000
wc/d	1	1,900	1,900	1,900
BRASS, Hans (1885-1959) German				
oil	1	2,026	2,026	2,026
wc/d	1	530	530	530
BRASSAI (1899-1984) Hungarian/French				
wc/d	1	1,429	1,429	1,429
3D	1	1,638	1,638	1,638
BRASSAUW, Melchior (1709-1757) Flemish				
oil	1	6,020	6,020	6,020
BRASSCHAAT, Muller (?) Belgian?				
oil	1	3,514	3,514	3,514
BRASSEUR, Georges (1880-1950) Belgian				
oil	1	2,003	2,003	2,003
BRASSINGTON, Alan (1959-) British				
wc/d	5	592-5,040	2,111	756
BRASZ, Arnold Franz (1888-1966) American				
oil	1	26,000	26,000	26,000
BRATBY, John (1928-1992) British				
oil	34	708-28,350	6,555	4,550
wc/d	6	540-11,340	2,612	696
BRATE, Fanny (1861-1940) Swedish				
oil	3	655-1,698	1,177	1,179
BRATEAU, Jules (1844-1923) French				
3D	1	1,936	1,936	1,936
BRATKOWSKI, Roman (1869-1954) Polish				
oil	1	2,752	2,752	2,752
BRAUER, Erich (1929-) Austrian				
oil	5	4,855-35,342	19,803	21,658
wc/d	3	1,400-3,836	2,745	3,000
BRAUGHT, Ross Eugene (1898-1983) American				
oil	2	2,000-9,000	5,500	2,000
BRAULT, Prosper (19th C) American				
oil	1	1,600	1,600	1,600
BRAUN, Ludwig (1836-1916) German				
oil	4	766-4,010	2,650	2,827
BRAUN, Maurice (1877-1941) American				
oil	30	3,400-70,000	20,096	14,000
BRAUN, Oskar (1909-) German				
oil	1	1,285	1,285	1,285
BRAUN, Wilhelm (1873-1937) Austrian				
oil	1	3,356	3,356	3,356
BRAUNER, Victor (1903-1966) French/Rumanian				
oil	8	12,000-212,400	102,041	80,000
wc/d	23	986-64,726	14,987	7,400
BRAUNTUCH, Troy (1954-) American				
wc/d	1	19,265	19,265	19,265
BRAUSEWETTER, Otto (1835-1904) German				
oil	1	1,537	1,537	1,537
BRAVO, Claudio (1936-) Chilean				
oil	8	45,000-320,000	123,750	70,000
wc/d	2	14,514-90,000	52,257	14,514
BRAWLEY, Robert Julius (1937-) American				
oil	1	19,000	19,000	19,000
wc/d	3	500-1,600	1,066	1,100
BRAY, Alan (20th C) American				
wc/d	3	1,700-4,750	3,400	3,750
BRAY, Jan de (1627-1697) Dutch				
oil	1	8,544	8,544	8,544
wc/d	1	6,574	6,574	6,574

Name	No.	Price Range	Average	Median
BRAYER, Yves (1907-1990) French				
oil	32	2,917-23,555	8,274	6,442
wc/d	33	651-6,199	3,052	3,330
BRAZ, Osip Emmanuelovich (1873-1936) Russian				
oil	2	14,535-48,160	31,347	14,535
BREAKSPEARE, William A (1856-1914) British				
oil	5	945-4,498	2,422	2,188
BREANSKI, A de (snr) (1852-1928) British				
oil	2	1,211-10,380	5,795	1,211
BREANSKI, Alfred Fontville de (1877-1957) British				
oil	37	510-16,435	3,347	2,052
wc/d	1	463	463	463
BREANSKI, Alfred de (snr) (1852-1928) British				
oil	54	748-70,800	19,445	12,390
wc/d	2	800-2,445	1,622	800
BREANSKI, Gustave de (c.1856-1898) British				
oil	19	484-9,568	2,357	1,656
BREARD, Henri Georges (19/20th C) French				
wc/d	18	514-1,929	1,100	836
BREAUTE, Albert (1853-1939) French				
oil	1	3,382	3,382	3,382
BREBIETTE, Pierre (1598-1650) French				
wc/d	1	6,920	6,920	6,920
BRECHT, George (1926-) American				
wc/d	1	1,757	1,757	1,757
BRECHT, Jean Baptiste (19th C) ?				
wc/d	1	1,823	1,823	1,823
BRECHT, Theodore C (1839-1917) American				
oil	1	3,200	3,200	3,200
BRECK, John Leslie (1860-1899) American				
oil	1	200,000	200,000	200,000
BRECKENRIDGE, Hugh Henry (1870-1937) American				
wc/d	1	4,000	4,000	4,000
BREDA, Carl Fredrik von (1759-1818) Swedish				
oil	2	1,648-6,980	4,314	1,648
BREDAEL, Alexandre van (1663-1720) Flemish				
oil	1	29,739	29,739	29,739
BREDAEL, Jan Peter van (elder) (1654-1745) Flemish				
oil	1	37,116	37,116	37,116
BREDAEL, Joseph van (1688-1739) Flemish				
oil	6	44,500-178,356	91,290	75,000
BREDAEL, Peeter van (1629-1719) Flemish				
oil	1	31,450	31,450	31,450
BREDAL, Niels-Anders (1841-1888) Danish				
oil	3	1,300-2,608	1,829	1,581
wc/d	1	1,107	1,107	1,107
BREDOW, Albert (1828-1899) Russian				
oil	5	3,425-5,449	4,223	3,822
BREDOW, Rudolf (1909-1973) German				
wc/d	1	1,800	1,800	1,800
BREE, Anthony de (1856-1921) British				
oil	3	1,015-1,715	1,347	1,313
BREE, Philippe Jacques van (1786-1871) Flemish				
oil	5	1,551-18,229	6,213	4,224
BREE, Rev William (1754-1822) British				
wc/d	1	1,392	1,392	1,392
BREED, Dirk (1920-) Dutch				
oil	1	2,521	2,521	2,521
BREEDVELD, Hendrik (1918-) Dutch				
oil	1	2,992	2,992	2,992
BREEN, Cornelius (20th C) Irish				
3D	1	3,649	3,649	3,649
BREENBERG, Bartholomaus (1599-1659) Dutch				
oil	3	9,251-100,000	39,531	9,342
wc/d	2	714-2,600	1,657	714
BREETVELD, Dolf (1892-1975) Dutch				
3D	1	4,071	4,071	4,071
BREGNO, Jens Jacob (1877-1946) Danish				
3D	1	4,094	4,094	4,094
BREHMER, Emil (1822-1895) German				
oil	1	1,052	1,052	1,052

Name	No.	Price Range	Average	Median
BREIDENBRUCH, Frank and PENCK, A R (20th C) German				
oil	1	12,740	12,740	12,740
BREINLINGER, Hans (1888-1963) Swiss				
oil	6	608-2,311	1,064	730
wc/d	3	530-1,094	757	648
BREITNER, Georg Hendrik (1857-1923) Dutch				
oil	12	14,417-430,208	154,685	49,167
wc/d	7	1,798-42,432	13,056	9,833
BREITWIESER, Georg (1890-1938) German				
oil	1	2,121	2,121	2,121
BREITZ, Candice (1972-) American				
3D	1	20,000	20,000	20,000
BREKELENKAM, Quiryn Gerritsz van (1620-1668) Dutch				
oil	4	2,301-249,750	66,494	4,250
BREKER, Arno (1900-1991) German				
wc/d	2	680-1,435	1,057	680
3D	7	2,038-5,733	3,701	4,204
BRELING, Heinrich (1849-1914) German				
oil	8	727-4,186	1,689	1,000
BREM, Rolf (1926-) Swiss				
3D	3	2,666-7,493	4,353	2,900
BREMAN, Co (1865-1938) Dutch				
oil	1	12,274	12,274	12,274
BREMER, Anne Millay (1868-1923) American				
oil	1	10,000	10,000	10,000
BREMER, Uwe (1940-) German				
oil	1	1,885	1,885	1,885
BREMOND, Jean François (1807-1868) French				
oil	1	2,000	2,000	2,000
BRENDEKILDE, Hans Andersen (1857-1942) Danish				
oil	39	1,786-30,046	9,456	5,868
BRENDEL, Albert Heinrich (1827-1895) German				
oil	1	1,169	1,169	1,169
BRENET, Albert (1903-2005) French				
wc/d	11	530-19,640	4,493	2,492
BRENET, Nicolas (1728-1792) French				
oil	1	12,000	12,000	12,000
BRENNAN, Beverley (20th C) British				
oil	1	1,295	1,295	1,295
BRENNAN, J M (fl.1930-1950s) Irish?				
oil	1	1,636	1,636	1,636
BRENNEIS, Jo (1910-1994) German				
wc/d	5	820-1,911	1,181	1,060
BRENNER, Art (1924-) American				
oil	1	900	900	900
wc/d	1	1,582	1,582	1,582
BRENNER, Carl Christian (1838-1888) American				
oil	1	5,750	5,750	5,750
BRENTANO, Franz Anton (19th C) German				
oil	1	1,427	1,427	1,427
BRENTEL, Friedrich (1580-1651) German				
wc/d	2	8,000-22,490	15,245	8,000
BRERETON, James Joseph (1954-) British				
oil	2	2,500-5,310	3,905	2,500
BRESCIANI, Antonio (1902-1998) Italian				
oil	4	1,656-6,370	3,273	1,757
BRESCIANINO, Andrea del (1485-1525) Italian				
oil	1	49,479	49,479	49,479
BRESLAU, Marie-Louise-Catharine (1856-1928) Swiss				
oil	2	1,423-2,799	2,111	1,423
BRESSLER, Emile (1886-1966) Swiss				
oil	6	564-2,021	1,409	1,446
BRESSLERN-ROTH, Norbertine (1891-1978) Austrian				
oil	3	17,517-38,836	29,927	33,429
wc/d	3	1,812-5,394	3,135	2,201
BREST, Germain-Fabius (1823-1900) French				
oil	6	6,990-520,000	106,612	22,723
BRETEGNIER, Georges (1863-1892) French				
oil	1	25,342	25,342	25,342
BRETLAND, Thomas (1802-1874) British				
oil	2	13,000-17,955	15,477	13,000

Name	No.	Price Range	Average	Median
BRETON, Jules Adolphe (1827-1906) French				
oil	5	1,750-300,000	113,502	40,000
wc/d	1	19,082	19,082	19,082
BRETT, Dorothy (1883-1977) British/American				
oil	2	6,000-14,000	10,000	6,000
wc/d	1	1,600	1,600	1,600
BRETT, John (1831-1902) British				
oil	4	1,384-3,680	2,598	1,648
wc/d	1	1,780	1,780	1,780
BRETTE, Pierre (1905-1961) French				
wc/d	4	1,514-4,150	3,006	2,529
BREU, Max (?) German?				
oil	1	3,039	3,039	3,039
wc/d	1	638	638	638
BREUER, Henri Joseph (1860-1932) American				
oil	7	550-35,000	10,078	2,000
BREUER, Peter (1856-1930) German				
3D	1	2,722	2,722	2,722
BREUER-WEIL, David (1965-) British				
oil	5	4,914-19,470	10,901	11,100
BREUN, John Ernest (1862-1921) British				
wc/d	1	1,313	1,313	1,313
BREVEGLIERI, Cesare (1902-1948) Italian				
oil	2	2,225-2,225	2,225	2,225
wc/d	1	610	610	610
BREWER, Henry Charles (1866-1950) British				
wc/d	5	648-8,550	2,667	1,573
BREWERTON, George Douglas (1827-1901) American				
wc/d	6	700-1,700	1,166	1,000
BREWSTER, Anna Richards (1870-1952) American				
oil	5	700-15,000	5,580	2,700
BREWSTER, John (jnr) (1766-1854) American				
oil	2	500-10,000	5,250	500
BREWTNALL, Edward Frederick (1846-1902) British				
wc/d	1	52,800	52,800	52,800
BREYDEL, Frans (1679-1750) Flemish				
oil	1	8,429	8,429	8,429
BREYDEL, Karel (1678-1733) Flemish				
oil	8	4,204-14,466	7,753	5,455
BREYER, Robert (1866-1941) German				
oil	1	1,305	1,305	1,305
BRIANCHON, Maurice (1899-1979) French				
oil	10	3,500-175,551	37,185	9,541
wc/d	10	597-6,106	2,560	2,038
BRIANTE, Ezelino (1901-1970) Italian				
oil	19	541-5,153	2,074	1,414
BRIAS, Charles (1798-1884) Belgian				
oil	2	5,505-6,536	6,020	5,505
BRICARD, Xavier (19/20th C) French				
oil	1	2,431	2,431	2,431
BRICE, Edward Kington (1860-1948) British				
oil	1	3,000	3,000	3,000
BRICE, Freddie (20th C) American?				
oil	1	1,200	1,200	1,200
BRICE, William (1921-) American				
oil	1	2,000	2,000	2,000
BRICHER, A T (1837-1908) American				
oil	1	8,000	8,000	8,000
wc/d	1	3,200	3,200	3,200
BRICHER, Alfred Thompson (1837-1908) American				
oil	17	800-190,000	31,826	10,000
wc/d	16	800-18,000	4,903	2,600
BRICKDALE, Eleanor Fortesque (1871-1945) British				
wc/d	1	2,775	2,775	2,775
BRIDGES, Fidelia (1834-1923) American				
oil	2	1,700-15,000	8,350	1,700
wc/d	3	600-16,000	6,266	2,200
BRIDGES, John (19th C) British				
oil	1	3,200	3,200	3,200
BRIDGMAN, Charles (1841-1895) American				
oil	1	1,300	1,300	1,300

Name	No.	Price Range	Average	Median
BRIDGMAN, Frederick Arthur (1847-1928) American				
oil	18	1,521-487,200	71,504	16,000
wc/d	1	450	450	450
BRIEDE, Johan (1885-1980) Dutch				
oil	1	4,123	4,123	4,123
wc/d	1	1,260	1,260	1,260
BRIELMAN, Jacques-Alfred (?-1892) French				
oil	1	4,123	4,123	4,123
wc/d	1	509	509	509
BRIERLY, Sir Oswald Walter (1817-1894) British				
wc/d	2	2,288-4,675	3,481	2,288
BRIGANTI, Nicholas P (1895-1989) American				
oil	1	1,300	1,300	1,300
BRIGDEN, Frederick Henry (1871-1956) Canadian				
oil	3	774-2,531	1,454	1,058
wc/d	6	665-1,237	986	975
BRIGHT, Henry (1814-1873) British				
oil	3	2,832-32,130	16,079	13,275
wc/d	3	460-1,038	827	983
BRIGNOLI, Luigi (1881-1952) Italian				
oil	5	1,212-6,324	3,281	2,425
wc/d	1	788	788	788
BRIGNONI, Sergio (1903-2002) Swiss				
oil	8	455-6,661	3,084	2,081
wc/d	4	999-4,579	2,464	1,082
BRIL, Paul (1554-1626) Flemish				
oil	2	82,703-250,000	166,351	82,703
BRILL, Reginald C (1902-1974) British				
wc/d	3	595-14,500	5,491	1,380
BRILLIANTOV, Natascha (1973-) Israeli?				
oil	3	910-2,600	1,603	1,300
BRILLOUIN, Louis Georges (1817-1893) French				
oil	4	700-3,515	2,465	2,816
BRIN, Émile-Quentin (1863-?) French				
oil	1	1,352	1,352	1,352
BRINA, Francesco (16th C) Italian				
oil	2	2,000-18,147	10,073	2,000
BRINCKMANN, Enrique (1938-) Spanish				
oil	4	911-6,684	4,955	5,786
wc/d	5	957-5,747	2,080	1,017
BRINCKMANN, Philip Hieronymus (1709-1761) German				
oil	1	10,888	10,888	10,888
BRINDESI, J (19th C) ?				
wc/d	2	4,250-4,500	4,375	4,250
BRINDESI, Jean (19th C) ?				
wc/d	1	10,560	10,560	10,560
BRINDISI, Remo (1918-1996) Italian				
oil	60	514-14,750	3,019	2,422
wc/d	6	530-1,450	1,008	1,019
BRINTON, Edith D (fl.1885-1908) British				
oil	1	1,029	1,029	1,029
BRION, Gustave (1824-1877) French				
oil	1	2,577	2,577	2,577
BRIOSCHI, Athos (1910-2000) Italian				
oil	2	908-1,816	1,362	908
BRIOSCHI, Othmar (1854-1912) Austrian				
oil	1	1,192	1,192	1,192
BRISCOE, Arthur (1873-1943) British				
oil	2	1,040-4,077	2,558	1,040
wc/d	8	465-5,310	1,741	957
BRISCOE, Franklin D (1844-1903) American				
oil	5	1,300-16,000	6,270	3,750
wc/d	1	5,000	5,000	5,000
BRISGAND, Gustave (?-1950) French				
wc/d	2	751-2,718	1,734	751
BRISPOT, Henri (1846-1928) French				
2	3,629-4,844	4,236	3,629
BRISS, Sami (1930-) French				
oil	2	1,432-1,700	1,566	1,432
BRISSOT DE WARVILLE, Felix-Saturnin (1818-1892) French				
oil	5	2,288-7,000	3,666	2,851
wc/d	1	651	651	651

Name	No.	Price Range	Average	Median
BRISSOT, Franck (fl.1879) British				
oil	2	996-1,100	1,048	996
BRISTOL, John Bunyan (1826-1909) American				
oil	10	1,200-8,500	3,560	2,500
BRISTOW, Edmund (1787-1876) British				
oil	5	493-6,300	3,171	1,900
BRITT, Benjamin (19th C) American				
oil	1	1,250	1,250	1,250
BRITTAIN, Miller Gore (1912-1968) Canadian				
wc/d	4	1,687-4,948	2,628	1,898
BRITTAN, Charles Edward (snr) (1837-1888) British				
wc/d	3	375-3,249	1,979	2,314
BRITTEN, William Edward Frank (1848-1916) British				
oil	1	1,141	1,141	1,141
BRITTON, Grant H (20th C) Canadian				
oil	1	2,050	2,050	2,050
BRITTON, Harry (1878-1958) Canadian				
oil	13	539-5,318	1,945	1,630
wc/d	2	656-907	781	656
BRIULLOV, Karl Pavlovich (1799-1852) Russian				
oil	1	653,600	653,600	653,600
BRIZE, Cornelis (1622-1670) Dutch				
oil	1	230,000	230,000	230,000
BRIZIO, Francesco (1574-1623) Italian				
oil	1	100,000	100,000	100,000
BRIZZI, Ary (1930-) Argentinian				
oil	1	8,000	8,000	8,000
BRIZZOLARA, Luigi (1868-1937) Italian				
3D	1	2,431	2,431	2,431
BROADHURST, Christopher (1953-) Canadian				
oil	1	1,518	1,518	1,518
BROCAS, Samuel Frederick (1792-1847) Irish				
wc/d	1	24,218	24,218	24,218
BROCAS, William (?) British?				
wc/d	1	6,902	6,902	6,902
BROCH, Alois (20th C) German				
oil	1	2,046	2,046	2,046
BROCHART, Constant Joseph (1816-1899) French				
wc/d	3	1,800-5,040	3,696	4,250
BROCK, Charles Edmund (1870-1938) British				
wc/d	1	1,800	1,800	1,800
BROCK, Richard H (fl.1896-1925) British				
oil	2	680-2,405	1,542	680
BROCK, T van and VOGELS, Guillaume (19th C) Belgian				
oil	1	1,151	1,151	1,151
BROCKDORFF, Victor (1911-1992) Danish				
oil	3	889-2,586	1,496	1,014
BROCKER, Ernst (1893-1963) German				
oil	6	484-2,188	1,269	835
BROCKER, Karl (1903-1991) German				
oil	3	3,024-9,351	5,294	3,507
BROCKHURST, Gerald Leslie (1890-1978) British				
oil	2	8,208-10,829	9,518	8,208
BROCKHUSEN, Theo von (1882-1919) German				
oil	2	17,671-22,384	20,027	17,671
BROCKMANN, Gottfried (1903-1983) German				
wc/d	1	3,822	3,822	3,822
BROCQUY, Louis le (1916-) Irish				
oil	5	37,808-353,400	133,328	65,100
wc/d	21	13,705-120,900	38,014	34,164
BROCQUY, Melanie le (20th C) Irish				
3D	2	1,200-3,120	2,160	1,200
BROD, Fritzi (1900-1952) American				
wc/d	1	1,200	1,200	1,200
BRODERSON, Morris (1928-) American				
oil	1	4,250	4,250	4,250
BRODHEAD, Quita (1901-2002) American				
oil	2	3,500-4,750	4,125	3,500
BRODIE, William (1815-1881) British				
3D	2	2,784-3,363	3,073	2,784

Name	No.	Price Range	Average	Median
BRODSKY, Isaac Israelevitch (1883-1939) Russian				
oil	2	845-86,000	43,422	845
wc/d	1	1,029	1,029	1,029
BRODWOLF, Jurgen (1932-) Swiss				
wc/d	3	790-2,788	1,782	1,768
3D	1	1,821	1,821	1,821
BRODZSKY, Sandor (1819-1901) Hungarian				
oil	1	19,357	19,357	19,357
BROECK, Elias van den (1650-1708) Dutch				
oil	1	108,367	108,367	108,367
BROECKMAN, Anne Marinus (1874-1946) Dutch				
oil	1	1,788	1,788	1,788
BROEDELET, Andre Victor Leonard (1872-1936) Dutch				
oil	2	2,589-6,259	4,424	2,589
BROEK, Koen van den (1973-) Belgian				
oil	2	11,100-38,060	24,580	11,100
BROERMAN, Eugene (1861-1932) Belgian				
oil	1	1,019	1,019	1,019
BROET, Adolphe Felix (19/20th C) French				
oil	1	4,393	4,393	4,393
BROGE, Alfred (1870-1955) Danish				
oil	5	681-7,296	2,463	1,400
BROGER, Alfred (1922-) Swiss				
wc/d	2	1,217-2,596	1,906	1,217
BROGGER, Stig (1941-) Danish				
oil	1	1,374	1,374	1,374
BROMBO, Angelo (1893-1962) Italian				
oil	6	1,702-5,568	3,036	2,460
wc/d	1	1,459	1,459	1,459
BROMEIS, August (1813-1881) German				
oil	2	2,178-6,533	4,355	2,178
BROMLEY, John Mallard (1858-1939) British				
wc/d	3	563-6,764	2,677	704
BROMLEY, W (19th C) British				
oil	1	3,038	3,038	3,038
BROMLEY, William (19th C) British				
oil	6	764-5,888	2,442	1,298
BROMLEY, William III (fl.1843-1870) British				
oil	2	3,500-9,208	6,354	3,500
wc/d	1	1,203	1,203	1,203
BROMMER, Gerald F (1927-) American				
wc/d	1	3,500	3,500	3,500
BROMS, Birgit (1924-) Swedish				
oil	2	2,232-15,197	8,714	2,232
wc/d	1	2,290	2,290	2,290
BRONCKHORST, Jan Gerritsz van (1603-1677) Dutch				
oil	1	16,349	16,349	16,349
BRONCKHORST, Johannes (1648-1727) Dutch				
wc/d	1	11,678	11,678	11,678
BRONDY, Matteo (1866-1944) French				
oil	1	993	993	993
wc/d	3	647-1,274	1,030	1,169
BRONSON, Clark (1939-) American				
3D	1	1,900	1,900	1,900
BROOD, Herman (1946-2001) Dutch				
oil	4	1,260-3,053	2,287	2,316
BROODTHAERS, Marcel (1924-1976) Belgian				
wc/d	4	1,678-24,082	9,191	5,343
BROOK, Raymond Peter (1927-) British				
oil	6	1,125-2,275	1,832	1,911
BROOKE, Richard Norris (1847-1920) American				
oil	1	1,600	1,600	1,600
BROOKER, Bertram (1888-1955) Canadian				
oil	4	3,242-22,156	10,908	7,699
BROOKER, Harry (1848-1940) British				
oil	2	2,258-6,688	4,473	2,258
BROOKER, William (1918-1983) British				
oil	3	2,262-14,175	6,659	3,540
BROOKES, Samuel Marsden (1816-1892) American				
oil	2	3,000-3,750	3,375	3,000

Name	No.	Price Range	Average	Median
BROOKING, Charles (1723-1759) British				
oil	1	10,120	10,120	10,120
wc/d	2	522-7,560	4,041	522
BROOKS, Frank Leonard (1911-1989) Canadian				
oil	5	656-2,116	1,323	1,410
wc/d	2	378-573	475	378
BROOKS, James (1906-1992) American				
oil	7	7,500-65,000	34,428	32,000
wc/d	2	350-2,200	1,275	350
BROOKS, Jason (1968-) American				
oil	1	12,000	12,000	12,000
BROOKS, Kim (1936-) British				
oil	1	30,240	30,240	30,240
wc/d	2	473-550	511	473
BROOKS, Maria (1837-1912) British				
oil	1	4,839	4,839	4,839
BROOKS, Nicholas Alden (fl.1880-1914) American				
oil	5	1,200-48,000	15,690	7,000
BROOKS, Thomas (1818-1891) British				
oil	3	1,309-3,201	2,313	2,431
BROOME, William (1838-1892) British				
oil	5	870-1,701	1,281	1,302
BROOTA, Rameshwar (1941-) Indian				
oil	2	65,000-70,000	67,500	65,000
BROPHY, Elizabeth (20th C) Australian/Irish				
oil	12	1,091-5,482	2,289	1,946
BROSEN, Frederick (1954-) American				
wc/d	1	1,800	1,800	1,800
BROSNAN, Shaun (1961-) British				
3D	1	2,046	2,046	2,046
BROSSEK, M (20th C) ?				
oil	1	6,466	6,466	6,466
BROSTROM, Sverker (1938-1997) Swedish				
oil	1	1,982	1,982	1,982
BROTAT, Joan (1920-1990) Spanish				
oil	10	400-4,281	1,804	1,215
wc/d	3	479-595	522	494
BROTO, Jose Manuel (1949-) Spanish				
oil	5	4,079-38,531	15,520	5,014
wc/d	2	2,945-22,878	12,911	2,945
BROUGHTON, Emily J (fl.1878-1882) British				
oil	1	2,249	2,249	2,249
BROUILLARD, Eugène (1870-1950) French				
oil	2	960-3,514	2,237	960
BROUILLET, Pierre Andre (1857-1914) French				
oil	2	3,947-80,000	41,973	3,947
BROUSSE, Faube de (19th C) French				
3D	1	2,200	2,200	2,200
BROUTY, Charles (1897-1984) French				
wc/d	1	3,039	3,039	3,039
BROUWERS, Julius (1869-1955) Dutch				
oil	2	443-1,885	1,164	443
BROUWN, Stanley (1935-) German?				
wc/d	1	7,224	7,224	7,224
BROWERE, Albertus del Orient (1814-1887) American				
oil	3	4,000-8,500	6,166	6,000
BROWN, Alexander Kellock (1849-1922) British				
oil	2	1,007-5,500	3,253	1,007
BROWN, Annora (1899-1987) Canadian				
oil	1	2,062	2,062	2,062
wc/d	3	392-527	470	492
BROWN, Benjamin Chambers (1865-1942) American				
oil	6	5,500-50,000	29,125	25,000
BROWN, Bernard Will (1920-) Canadian				
oil	1	1,783	1,783	1,783
BROWN, Bolton (1865-1936) American				
wc/d	2	2,000-2,500	2,250	2,000
BROWN, Cecily (1969-) American?				
oil	6	10,208-850,000	249,451	85,000
BROWN, Christopher (20th C) American				
oil	1	8,000	8,000	8,000
3D	1	3,000	3,000	3,000

Name	No.	Price Range	Average	Median
BROWN, Delia (1969-) American				
oil	1	26,000	26,000	26,000
wc/d	2	9,000-9,500	9,250	9,000
BROWN, Dexter (1942-) British				
oil	1	1,549	1,549	1,549
BROWN, Don (1962-) British				
3D	1	5,632	5,632	5,632
BROWN, E (19th C) British				
oil	1	45,760	45,760	45,760
BROWN, F J (19/20th C) ?				
oil	1	3,750	3,750	3,750
BROWN, Ford Madox (1821-1893) British				
wc/d	1	9,625	9,625	9,625
BROWN, George Loring (1814-1889) American				
oil	3	2,000-350,000	119,083	5,250
wc/d	1	475	475	475
BROWN, Glenn (1966-) British				
oil	2	212,400-320,000	266,200	212,400
BROWN, Grafton Tyler (1841-1918) American				
oil	2	18,000-20,000	19,000	18,000
BROWN, Harley (1939-) Canadian				
wc/d	20	425-17,000	3,795	2,500
BROWN, Harrison B (1831-1915) American				
oil	9	750-6,000	3,366	3,000
BROWN, Henry Kirke (1814-1866) American				
3D	1	22,500	22,500	22,500
BROWN, Irving R (20th C) American				
oil	1	8,000	8,000	8,000
BROWN, J F (?) ?				
oil	1	1,400	1,400	1,400
BROWN, J Taylor (fl.1893-1940) British				
oil	2	1,062-2,443	1,752	1,062
BROWN, James (1951-) American				
oil	16	3,600-30,000	10,431	8,970
wc/d	7	2,000-10,000	5,096	4,928
3D	2	2,152-7,014	4,583	2,152
BROWN, James Francis (1862-1935) American				
oil	1	1,500	1,500	1,500
BROWN, Jean Louis (?-1930) French				
oil	1	1,197	1,197	1,197
BROWN, Joan (1938-1990) American				
oil	2	11,000-65,000	38,000	11,000
BROWN, Joe (1909-1985) American				
3D	1	3,000	3,000	3,000
BROWN, John (?) British				
oil	2	2,500-3,800	3,150	2,500
BROWN, John Appleton (1844-1902) American				
oil	3	1,100-5,000	2,766	2,200
wc/d	1	2,500	2,500	2,500
BROWN, John Arnesby (1866-1955) British				
oil	9	968-37,620	10,213	8,650
BROWN, John George (1831-1913) American				
oil	20	1,500-220,000	34,862	12,000
BROWN, John Lewis (1829-1890) French				
oil	9	1,138-8,750	3,645	3,000
wc/d	1	536	536	536
BROWN, Mather (1761-1831) British/American				
oil	1	6,840	6,840	6,840
wc/d	1	35,340	35,340	35,340
BROWN, May Marshall (1887-?) British				
oil	1	1,531	1,531	1,531
wc/d	1	696	696	696
BROWN, Michael (1854-1957) British				
wc/d	1	106,800	106,800	106,800
BROWN, Mozelle Rawson (20th C) American				
oil	2	1,500-2,400	1,950	1,500
BROWN, Peter (fl.1758-1799) British				
oil	1	1,300	1,300	1,300
BROWN, Peter (1967-) British				
oil	2	1,122-1,870	1,496	1,122

Name	No.	Price Range	Average	Median
BROWN, Ralph (1928-) British				
wc/d	1	1,110	1,110	1,110
3D	3	4,488-55,680	26,986	20,790
BROWN, Reynold (1917-1991) American				
oil	1	5,000	5,000	5,000
BROWN, Robert Woodley (19th C) British				
oil	1	1,585	1,585	1,585
BROWN, Roger (1941-1997) American				
oil	2	22,000-32,000	27,000	22,000
3D	1	19,000	19,000	19,000
BROWN, Roy (1879-1956) American				
oil	1	1,100	1,100	1,100
BROWN, Samuel Joseph (1907-1994) American				
oil	1	3,000	3,000	3,000
BROWN, Thomas Austen (1857-1924) British				
oil	3	727-33,630	12,144	2,076
wc/d	1	554	554	554
BROWN, Upfill (20th C) British?				
3D	1	2,394	2,394	2,394
BROWN, William Beattie (1831-1909) British				
oil	4	837-11,440	6,068	959
BROWN, William Marshall (1863-1936) British				
oil	9	3,078-29,370	13,070	11,570
wc/d	1	692	692	692
BROWN, William Mason (1828-1898) American				
oil	2	7,000-38,000	22,500	7,000
BROWN, William Theo (1919-) American				
oil	3	5,500-38,000	17,166	8,000
wc/d	2	1,000-2,500	1,750	1,000
BROWNE, Belmore (1880-1954) American/Canadian				
oil	1	13,000	13,000	13,000
BROWNE, Byron (1907-1961) American				
oil	7	550-8,500	3,221	3,000
wc/d	6	425-1,600	887	600
BROWNE, Charles Francis (1859-1920) American				
oil	3	1,200-8,000	4,650	4,750
BROWNE, E (19th C) British				
oil	1	3,060	3,060	3,060
BROWNE, George (1918-1958) American				
oil	3	7,000-22,500	12,500	8,000
BROWNE, George Elmer (1871-1946) American				
oil	6	3,500-11,000	7,750	8,000
BROWNE, Hablot K (1815-1892) British				
oil	1	9,072	9,072	9,072
wc/d	2	835-1,488	1,161	835
BROWNE, Joseph Archibald (1862-1948) Canadian				
oil	2	776-1,230	1,003	776
BROWNE, Madame Henriette (1829-1901) French				
oil	1	6,020	6,020	6,020
BROWNE, Robert Ives (1865-1956) Dutch				
oil	1	11,679	11,679	11,679
BROWNELL, Charles de Wolf (1822-1909) American				
oil	2	6,500-20,000	13,250	6,500
BROWNELL, Franklin (1856-1946) Canadian				
oil	7	1,956-36,682	11,317	7,976
wc/d	3	1,223-6,521	3,948	4,100
BROWNING, John Gaitha (1912-1992) American				
oil	1	1,900	1,900	1,900
BROWNING, Robert Barett (1846-1912) British				
3D	1	157,500	157,500	157,500
BROWNING, Steve (20th C) Irish?				
oil	1	1,459	1,459	1,459
BROWNLOW, George Washington (1835-1876) British				
oil	2	957-10,260	5,608	957
BROWNSCOMBE, Jennie (1850-1936) American				
oil	4	500-32,500	11,375	5,000
wc/d	1	400	400	400
BROZIK, Wenceslas (1851-1901) Bohemian				
oil	6	2,500-26,000	11,145	8,505
BRUANDET, Lazare (1755-1804) French				
wc/d	1	2,431	2,431	2,431

Name	No.	Price Range	Average	Median
BRUCE, Edward (1879-1943) American				
oil	2	600-9,500	5,050	600
BRUCE, Granville (1903-1989) American				
oil	1	4,000	4,000	4,000
BRUCE, Robert Donald (1911-1981) Canadian				
oil	2	330-2,062	1,196	330
wc/d	1	701	701	701
BRUCE, William (19/20th C) American				
oil	1	2,250	2,250	2,250
BRUCE, William Blair (1859-1906) Canadian				
oil	1	5,000	5,000	5,000
BRUCK, Lajos (1846-1910) Hungarian				
oil	2	3,529-11,382	7,455	3,529
BRUCKER, Edmund (1912-) American				
oil	1	2,200	2,200	2,200
BRUEGHEL, Abraham (1631-1690) Flemish				
oil	3	43,250-415,200	180,384	82,703
BRUEGHEL, Jan (elder) (1568-1625) Flemish				
oil	1	120,979	120,979	120,979
wc/d	2	17,575-33,300	25,437	17,575
BRUEGHEL, Jan (younger) (1601-1678) Flemish				
oil	8	46,711-203,500	100,466	91,216
BRUEGHEL, Jan (younger) and FRANCKEN, Frans (younger) (17th C) Flemish				
oil	1	35,600	35,600	35,600
BRUEGHEL, Jan (younger) and MOMPER, Joos de (17th C) Flemish				
oil	1	71,200	71,200	71,200
BRUEGHEL, Jan Pieter (1628-?) Flemish				
oil	1	6,764	6,764	6,764
BRUEGHEL, Pieter (younger) (1564-1637) Flemish				
oil	14	296,000-8,510,001	1,341,318	605,500
BRUEL, Willem van den (1871-1942) Belgian				
oil	2	597-2,431	1,514	597
BRUENCHENHEIN, Eugene von (1910-1983) American				
oil	1	3,600	3,600	3,600
BRUESTLE, Bertram G (1902-1968) American				
oil	1	1,250	1,250	1,250
BRUESTLE, George M (1871-1939) American				
oil	4	1,800-3,250	2,537	2,100
BRUGADA Y PANIZO, Ricardo (1867-1919) Spanish				
oil	2	17,019-34,934	25,976	17,019
BRUGAIROLLES, Victor (1869-1936) French				
oil	4	835-1,598	1,347	1,414
BRUGGER, Arnold (1888-1975) Swiss				
oil	3	1,068-2,137	1,679	1,832
BRUGHETTI, Faustino (1889-1974) Argentinian				
oil	2	6,000-11,000	8,500	6,000
BRUGNER, Colestin (1824-1887) German				
oil	7	582-1,539	1,072	1,091
BRUGNOLI, Emanuele (1859-1944) Italian				
oil	1	3,786	3,786	3,786
wc/d	7	1,000-5,096	2,738	2,604
BRUGUIERE, Fernand (19th C) French				
oil	1	1,695	1,695	1,695
BRUHS, Gunther (20th C) Swiss?				
wc/d	1	3,434	3,434	3,434
BRUIN, Cornelis de (1870-1940) Dutch				
oil	4	1,145-1,334	1,223	1,157
BRUKEN, Pieter van (18th C) Flemish				
oil	1	2,386	2,386	2,386
BRULE, Elmo A (1917-) American				
oil	1	3,214	3,214	3,214
BRULHARD, Ernest Hiram (1878-1947) Swiss				
oil	2	835-1,908	1,371	835
BRULOFF, Alexandre (1798-1877) Russian				
wc/d	1	3,478	3,478	3,478
BRUMATTI, Gianni (1901-1990) Italian				
oil	3	1,029-1,671	1,285	1,157
BRUMENT, Albert (19/20th C) French				
oil	1	1,506	1,506	1,506
BRUMIDI, Constantino (1805-1880) American				
oil	1	10,000	10,000	10,000

Name	No.	Price Range	Average	Median
BRUN, Alexandre (19th C) French				
oil	1	7,438	7,438	7,438
BRUN, Guillaume Charles (1825-1908) French				
oil	2	2,661-9,555	6,108	2,661
BRUN, Leon (19th C) French				
oil	1	1,100	1,100	1,100
BRUN, Louis le (20th C) ?				
oil	1	1,018	1,018	1,018
BRUNBERG, Hakan (1905-1978) Finnish				
oil	6	1,918-11,829	6,902	5,733
wc/d	5	605-8,031	2,959	2,277
BRUNDRIT, Reginald Grange (1883-1960) British				
oil	16	564-3,916	1,327	890
BRUNE (?) ?				
oil	1	2,188	2,188	2,188
BRUNE, Christian (1793-1849) French				
oil	1	4,243	4,243	4,243
BRUNE, Heinrich (1869-1945) German				
oil	2	1,532-1,532	1,532	1,532
BRUNE, Pierre (1887-1956) French				
oil	1	1,405	1,405	1,405
BRUNEAU, Odette (1891-1984) French				
oil	2	14,462-14,746	14,604	14,462
BRUNEL DE NEUVILLE (19/20th C) French				
oil	1	2,800	2,800	2,800
BRUNEL DE NEUVILLE, Alfred Arthur (1852-1941) French				
oil	35	400-8,500	3,072	2,750
BRUNELLESCHI, Umberto (1879-?) Italian				
oil	2	655-1,794	1,224	655
wc/d	8	600-3,416	1,089	600
BRUNERY, François (1849-1926) Italian				
oil	3	2,478-16,000	10,492	13,000
BRUNERY, Marcel (1893-1982) French				
oil	4	12,250-38,280	22,438	15,660
BRUNET, Fernanda (1964-) American?				
oil	1	15,000	15,000	15,000
BRUNET, Jean Marc (20th C) French				
oil	1	2,219	2,219	2,219
BRUNET-HOUARD, Pierre Auguste (1829-1922) French				
oil	2	2,213-5,322	3,767	2,213
BRUNETAUT, Jules (19/20th C) French				
oil	1	1,286	1,286	1,286
BRUNETTO, Silvio (1932-) Italian				
oil	1	1,211	1,211	1,211
BRUNI, Bruno (1935-) Italian				
oil	2	608-608	608	608
3D	7	1,940-2,827	2,333	2,356
BRUNIN, Charles (1841-1887) Belgian				
3D	1	2,860	2,860	2,860
BRUNIN, Léon (1861-1949) Belgian				
oil	6	1,512-4,724	2,502	1,907
wc/d	1	2,213	2,213	2,213
BRUNING, Peter (1929-1970) German				
wc/d	5	707-3,888	2,150	1,823
BRUNKER, Linda (20th C) Irish?				
3D	1	7,151	7,151	7,151
BRUNNER, F Sands (1886-1954) American				
oil	3	900-1,800	1,200	900
BRUNNER, Ferdinand (1870-1945) Austrian				
oil	5	5,455-27,917	18,266	19,082
BRUNNER, Georg (1804-1882) German				
wc/d	1	3,562	3,562	3,562
BRUNNER, Hans (1813-1888) German				
oil	1	1,909	1,909	1,909
BRUNNER, Leopold (19th C) Austrian				
oil	2	3,025-22,500	12,762	3,025
BRUNNER-LACOSTE, Émile Henri (1838-1881) French				
oil	1	2,521	2,521	2,521
BRUNONI, Serge (1930-) Canadian				
oil	15	727-3,988	2,034	1,649

Name	No.	Price Range	Average	Median
BRUNORI, Enzo (1924-1993) Italian				
oil	3	1,571-7,120	3,947	3,151
wc/d	4	589-1,399	1,096	1,178
BRUNSWICK MONOGRAMMIST (?) German				
oil	1	43,552	43,552	43,552
BRUS, Gunter (1938-) Austrian				
oil	1	7,068	7,068	7,068
wc/d	7	3,349-16,993	7,022	4,712
BRUSAFERRO, Girolamo (1700-1760) Italian				
oil	1	14,027	14,027	14,027
BRUSAFERRO, Girolamo and LAZZARINI, Gregorio (18th C) Italian				
oil	1	35,676	35,676	35,676
BRUSASORCI, Felice (1540-1605) Italian				
wc/d	1	5,469	5,469	5,469
BRUSENBAUCH, Arthur (1881-1957) German				
wc/d	1	1,171	1,171	1,171
BRUSEWITZ, Gunnar (1924-) Swedish				
oil	1	2,473	2,473	2,473
wc/d	1	2,610	2,610	2,610
BRUSEWITZ, Gustaf (1812-1899) Swedish				
oil	1	9,616	9,616	9,616
BRUSH, George de Forest (1855-1941) American				
oil	2	2,800-2,300,000	1,151,400	2,800
BRUSKIN, Grisha (1945-) Russian				
oil	1	53,940	53,940	53,940
BRUSSEL, Paul Theodore van (1754-1791) Dutch				
oil	2	6,846-60,000	33,423	6,846
BRUSSELMANS, Jean (1884-1953) Belgian				
oil	6	10,813-46,757	26,908	25,171
wc/d	5	1,296-11,387	6,240	8,269
BRUTT, Ferdinand (1849-1936) German				
oil	1	4,122	4,122	4,122
BRUUN, Henrik Buster (1929-) Danish				
oil	2	1,212-1,940	1,576	1,212
BRUYAS, Marc-Laurent (1821-1896) French				
oil	1	14,000	14,000	14,000
BRUYCKER, François Antoine de (1816-1882) Belgian				
oil	5	1,459-31,150	10,434	6,960
BRUYCKER, Jules de (1870-1945) Belgian				
wc/d	2	1,286-1,753	1,519	1,286
BRUYN, Barthel (elder) (1493-1555) German				
oil	1	222,000	222,000	222,000
BRUYN, Johannes Cornelis de (1800-1844) Dutch				
oil	1	10,730	10,730	10,730
BRUYNE, Dees de (1940-) Belgian				
oil	1	865	865	865
wc/d	2	598-600	599	598
BRUYNE, Gustaaf de (1914-1981) Belgian				
oil	3	963-15,582	5,916	1,204
BRUYNEEL, V (?) ?				
3D	1	2,000	2,000	2,000
BRUYNEEL, Victor (19th C) ?				
3D	1	2,544	2,544	2,544
BRUZZI, Stefano (1835-1911) Italian				
oil	8	3,781-152,877	44,775	28,479
BRYANT, A Moginie (19/20th C) British				
oil	1	1,300	1,300	1,300
BRYANT, Everett L (1864-1945) American				
oil	4	1,000-80,000	20,825	1,100
BRYANT, Henry C (fl.1860-1880) British				
oil	3	920-3,060	1,814	1,462
BRYANT, Maude Drein (1880-1946) American				
oil	3	2,400-4,250	3,483	3,800
BRYEN, Camille (1907-1977) French				
oil	6	3,236-320,582	57,939	4,685
wc/d	10	954-3,514	1,794	1,403
BRYERS, Duane (1911-) American				
oil	2	1,500-1,600	1,550	1,500
BRYMNER, William (1855-1925) Canadian				
oil	2	3,350-4,744	4,047	3,350
wc/d	2	495-5,289	2,892	495

Name	No.	Price Range	Average	Median
BRYULLOV, Pavel Aleksandrovich (1840-1914) Russian				
oil	1	1,870	1,870	1,870
wc/d	1	875	875	875
BRZOZOWSKI, Tadeusz (1918-1987) Polish				
oil	2	13,360-15,904	14,632	13,360
BUAL, Artur (1926-1999) Portuguese				
wc/d	1	2,552	2,552	2,552
BUBALI, Andrea (1869-1940) Italian				
oil	1	1,816	1,816	1,816
BUBARNIK, A Gyula (1936-) Hungarian				
oil	3	1,138-3,540	2,026	1,400
BUBLIKOW, Nikolaij (1871-1942) Russian				
oil	1	19,325	19,325	19,325
BUCCHI, Ermocrate (1842-1885) Italian				
oil	1	4,789	4,789	4,789
BUCCI, Anselmo (1887-1955) Italian				
oil	3	7,339-10,824	9,027	8,918
wc/d	1	1,193	1,193	1,193
BUCHANAN, Alexander Strachan (19/20th C) British				
oil	6	475-1,232	711	563
wc/d	3	620-735	658	620
BUCHANAN, Peter S (fl.1860-1911) British				
oil	2	1,100-1,739	1,419	1,100
BUCHE, Josef (1848-1917) Austrian				
oil	5	707-3,330	2,246	2,431
BUCHET, Gustave (1888-1963) Swiss				
oil	6	2,498-49,469	18,354	6,013
wc/d	3	2,245-13,630	7,789	7,493
BUCHHEISTER, Carl (1890-1964) German				
oil	4	4,091-9,351	6,599	4,676
wc/d	4	1,553-5,856	2,712	1,555
BUCHHOLZ, Erich (1891-1972) German				
wc/d	1	1,908	1,908	1,908
BUCHHOLZ, Karl (1849-1889) German				
oil	1	26,105	26,105	26,105
BUCHLER, Henri (18/19th C) German?				
wc/d	1	4,066	4,066	4,066
BUCHNER, Hans (1856-1941) German				
oil	3	1,193-7,000	3,388	1,973
BUCHNER, Johann (1815-1857) German				
oil	1	2,592	2,592	2,592
BUCHS, Raymond (1878-1958) Swiss				
oil	2	1,632-4,163	2,897	1,632
BUCHSEL, Elisabeth (1867-1957) German				
oil	2	1,229-1,455	1,342	1,229
BUCHSER, Frank (1828-1890) Swiss				
oil	4	6,118-40,088	21,422	16,652
BUCHTA, Alfred (1880-1952) Italian/Austrian				
oil	1	1,000	1,000	1,000
BUCHTA, Anthony (1896-1967) American				
oil	1	1,300	1,300	1,300
BUCHTGER, Robert (1862-1951) Russian				
oil	1	1,458	1,458	1,458
BUCK, Adam (1759-1833) British				
wc/d	5	848-4,208	2,589	3,162
BUCK, Evariste de (1892-1974) Belgian				
oil	2	2,293-5,890	4,091	2,293
BUCK, William H (1840-1888) American				
oil	4	1,900-90,000	36,350	7,500
BUCKEN, Peter (1831-1915) German				
oil	1	1,697	1,697	1,697
BUCKHAM, Lynn (1918-1982) American				
oil	1	2,300	2,300	2,300
BUCKLER, Charles E (1869-1953) American/Canadian				
oil	6	500-2,100	1,191	950
BUCKLER, John Chessel (1793-1894) British				
wc/d	1	1,203	1,203	1,203
BUCKLEY, John E (1820-1884) British				
wc/d	1	1,044	1,044	1,044
BUCKLEY, Stephen (1944-) British				
oil	4	473-3,916	2,045	1,479

Name	No.	Price Range	Average	Median
BUCKMASTER, Ernest (1897-1968) Australian				
oil	2	1,500-2,000	1,750	1,500
BUCKNALL, Ernest P (1861-?) British				
oil	1	4,628	4,628	4,628
BUCKNER, Richard (1812-1883) British				
oil	1	1,472	1,472	1,472
BUDD, David (20th C) American				
wc/d	1	1,951	1,951	1,951
BUDDENBERG, Wilhelm (1890-1967) German				
oil	2	935-1,067	1,001	935
BUDELOT, Philippe (18/19th C) French				
oil	4	644-11,372	5,263	3,461
BUDELOT, Philippe and DEMAY, Jean François (18/19th C) French				
oil	1	6,969	6,969	6,969
BUDTZ-MOLLER, Carl (1882-1953) Danish				
oil	11	667-3,794	1,698	1,304
BUDWORTH, William Sylvester (1861-1938) American				
wc/d	1	1,050	1,050	1,050
BUEHR, Karl Albert (1866-1952) American				
oil	2	525-12,000	6,262	525
BUELL, Alfred (1910-1996) American				
oil	1	2,500	2,500	2,500
BUENO FERRER, Pascual (1930-) Spanish				
oil	2	700-1,808	1,254	700
BUENO, Antonio (1918-1984) Italian				
oil	22	1,332-21,082	11,936	12,721
wc/d	5	1,176-6,096	2,497	1,546
BUENO, Pedro (1910-1993) Spanish				
oil	2	1,204-4,500	2,852	1,204
BUENO, Xavier (1915-1979) Spanish				
oil	31	9,092-99,892	19,851	16,714
wc/d	5	610-23,143	17,130	20,571
BUETTI, Daniele (1956-) American				
wc/d	1	5,500	5,500	5,500
3D	1	9,370	9,370	9,370
BUFANO, Beniamino (1898-1970) American				
3D	4	2,750-8,500	5,562	4,500
BUFF, Conrad (1886-1975) American				
oil	24	1,250-35,000	7,054	3,500
BUFF, Sebastian (1829-1880) Swiss				
oil	1	4,770	4,770	4,770
BUFFET, Bernard (1928-1999) French				
oil	54	5,115-290,000	73,790	55,000
wc/d	24	954-39,333	15,433	14,960
BUGATTI, Rembrandt (1885-1916) Italian				
wc/d	2	634-714	674	634
3D	9	3,390-504,110	176,057	106,027
BUGZESTER, Maxim (20th C) American?				
oil	1	1,200	1,200	1,200
BUHLER, Heinrich (1893-1986) German				
oil	1	1,147	1,147	1,147
BUHLER, Robert (1916-1989) British				
oil	3	522-1,500	1,116	1,328
wc/d	1	1,416	1,416	1,416
BUHLMANN, Johann Rudolf (1802-1890) Swiss				
oil	2	8,976-16,493	12,734	8,976
BUHOT, Felix (1847-1898) French				
oil	2	1,925-24,596	13,260	1,925
wc/d	7	970-20,634	8,423	7,032
BUHOT, Louis Charles Hippolyte (1815-1865) French				
3D	1	4,250	4,250	4,250
BUHRE, Leon Leonardovich (1887-1943) Russian				
oil	1	2,348	2,348	2,348
BUHRMANN, Gisela (1925-) German				
oil	1	1,076	1,076	1,076
BUI XUAN PHAI (1920-1988) Vietnamese				
oil	3	1,324-2,330	1,697	1,438
BUISSERET, Louis (1888-1956) Belgian				
oil	2	927-1,821	1,374	927
BUKOVAC, Vlacho (1855-1923) Yugoslavian				
oil	1	107,123	107,123	107,123

Name	No.	Price Range	Average	Median
BUKOVETSKY, Evgeniy Iosipovich (1866-1948) Russian				
oil	1	8,573	8,573	8,573
BULATOV, Erik (1933-1989) Russian				
wc/d	1	8,000	8,000	8,000
BULCKE, Émile (1875-1963) Belgian				
oil	1	435	435	435
wc/d	1	1,670	1,670	1,670
BULIO, Jean (1827-1911) French				
3D	1	3,387	3,387	3,387
BULLINGER, Johann-Balthazar (elder) (1713-1793) Swiss				
oil	1	4,142	4,142	4,142
BULMAN, Job (18th C) British?				
wc/d	1	1,018	1,018	1,018
BULMAN, Orville (1904-1978) American				
oil	5	5,500-30,000	15,500	13,000
BULMER, Lionel (1919-1992) British				
oil	3	440-1,593	1,061	1,151
BULVERA, S G (19th C) ?				
oil	1	1,800	1,800	1,800
BULZATTI, Aurelio (1954-) Italian				
oil	1	2,102	2,102	2,102
BUNBURY, Sir Henry E (18/19th C) British				
wc/d	1	1,539	1,539	1,539
BUNDEL, Willem van den (1577-1655) Dutch				
oil	2	25,950-35,000	30,475	25,950
BUNDEL, Willem van den and JORDAENS, Symon (16th C) Dutch				
oil	1	35,671	35,671	35,671
BUNDY, Edgar (1862-1922) British				
oil	3	1,665-8,700	5,097	4,927
wc/d	1	1,480	1,480	1,480
BUNDY, Horace (1814-1883) American				
oil	1	1,400	1,400	1,400
BUNDY, John Elwood (1853-1933) American				
oil	1	4,500	4,500	4,500
wc/d	3	900-2,250	1,416	1,100
BUNEL, Charles Eugène (1863-?) French				
oil	1	4,586	4,586	4,586
BUNK, Holger (1954-) German				
oil	1	8,918	8,918	8,918
wc/d	1	1,296	1,296	1,296
BUNKE, Franz (1857-1939) German				
oil	1	2,910	2,910	2,910
BUNN, George (fl.1885-1898) British				
oil	3	695-1,869	1,121	800
BUNNER, Andrew Fisher (1841-1897) American				
oil	1	2,500	2,500	2,500
BUNTZEN, Carl (19th C) Danish				
oil	1	1,475	1,475	1,475
BUONACCORSI, Pietro (1500-1547) Italian				
oil	1	10,192	10,192	10,192
wc/d	1	766	766	766
BUONO, Eugenio (1863-1954) Italian				
oil	1	5,271	5,271	5,271
BUONO, Léon Giuseppe (1888-1975) Italian				
oil	2	1,580-3,695	2,637	1,580
BUONTALENTI, Bernardo (1536-1608) Italian				
3D	1	24,218	24,218	24,218
BURAGLIO, Pierre (1939-) French				
oil	2	602-2,337	1,469	602
wc/d	1	1,285	1,285	1,285
BURAT, Fanny (1838-?) French				
oil	1	3,802	3,802	3,802
BURBANK, E A (1858-1949) American				
oil	1	1,500	1,500	1,500
BURBANK, Elbridge Ayer (1858-1949) American				
oil	7	400-10,000	4,307	3,750
wc/d	4	1,600-3,250	2,112	1,600
BURBURE, Louis de (1837-1911) Belgian				
oil	2	1,286-2,276	1,781	1,286
BURCA, Michael de (1913-1985) Irish?				
oil	1	16,365	16,365	16,365

Name	No.	Price Range	Average	Median
BURCH, Albertus van der (1672-1745) Dutch				
oil	1	15,760	15,760	15,760
BURCHARTZ, Max (1887-1961) German				
wc/d	1	1,054	1,054	1,054
BURCHFIELD, Charles (1893-1967) American				
oil	1	65,000	65,000	65,000
wc/d	19	600-90,000	21,671	4,750
BURCK, Paul (1878-?) German				
oil	1	1,878	1,878	1,878
BURCKHARDT, Ludwig August (1807-1878) Swiss				
oil	1	1,415	1,415	1,415
BURDEN, Chris (1946-) American				
3D	1	28,480	28,480	28,480
BURDICK, Horace Robbins (1844-1942) American				
oil	1	1,500	1,500	1,500
BURDICK, Scott Patrick (1967-) American				
oil	1	1,300	1,300	1,300
BURDY, Georges Henri (1871-1908) French				
oil	1	1,455	1,455	1,455
BUREAU, Léon (1866-1906) French				
3D	1	2,600	2,600	2,600
BUREN, Daniel (1938-) French				
oil	4	1,757-259,583	72,463	2,799
wc/d	1	1,070	1,070	1,070
BURFORD, Robert (1794-1861) British				
oil	1	3,916	3,916	3,916
BURGARITSKI, Joseph (1836-1890) Austrian				
oil	3	1,546-2,420	1,957	1,905
BURGDORFF, Ferdinand (1883-1975) American				
oil	6	500-4,500	1,916	1,300
BURGEL, Hugo (1853-1903) German				
oil	1	1,937	1,937	1,937
BURGER, A (19th C) ?				
oil	1	1,810	1,810	1,810
BURGER, Anton (1824-1905) German				
oil	4	819-36,486	10,804	1,824
wc/d	2	688-814	751	688
BURGER, Leopold (1861-1903) Austrian				
oil	1	5,000	5,000	5,000
BURGER, Walter (1923-) Swiss				
3D	1	6,073	6,073	6,073
BURGERS, Felix (1870-1934) German				
oil	2	546-2,432	1,489	546
BURGERS, Hendricus Jacobus (1834-1899) Dutch				
oil	4	1,897-9,500	4,494	2,580
BURGESS, Arthur James Wetherall (1879-1957) Australian				
oil	4	1,056-4,200	1,899	1,144
BURGESS, John Bagnold (1830-1897) British				
oil	4	1,092-30,245	13,069	5,822
BURGH, Hendrik Adam van der (1798-1877) Dutch				
oil	1	4,243	4,243	4,243
BURGH, Hendrik van der (1769-1858) Dutch				
oil	3	1,216-7,531	5,185	6,810
BURGHARDT, Gustav (1890-1970) German				
oil	5	766-2,073	1,263	1,296
BURGMEIER, Max (1881-1947) Swiss				
oil	4	811-1,218	1,074	1,054
BURI, Max (1868-1915) Swiss				
oil	2	10,605-15,889	13,247	10,605
BURI, Samuel (1935-) Swiss				
oil	1	2,434	2,434	2,434
BURIAN, Zdenek (1905-1981) Czechoslovakian				
oil	1	19,000	19,000	19,000
BURINI, Antonio (1656-1727) Italian				
wc/d	1	2,400	2,400	2,400
BURINSKAJA, Nina Feodorovna (19th C) Russian				
oil	1	1,246	1,246	1,246
BURK, Paul (1878-1947) German				
oil	1	1,212	1,212	1,212
BURKE, Augustus (c.1838-1891) British				
oil	2	4,707-5,444	5,075	4,707

Name	No.	Price Range	Average	Median
BURKEL, Heinrich (1802-1869) German				
oil	6	2,000-35,342	16,210	14,720
BURKHARDT, Fedor Karlovich (1854-1918) Russian				
oil	1	19,110	19,110	19,110
BURKHARDT, Rudy (20th C) American				
oil	1	1,000	1,000	1,000
BURLAKOV, Vsevolod Fedorovich (1919-1986) Russian				
oil	1	40,920	40,920	40,920
BURLEIGH, Charles H H (1875-1956) British				
oil	3	602-3,294	1,881	1,748
BURLING, Gilbert (1843-1875) American				
oil	1	10,000	10,000	10,000
BURLINS, A (19th C) ?				
oil	1	7,000	7,000	7,000
BURLIUK, David (1882-1967) American/Russian				
oil	80	1,000-85,000	13,868	11,000
wc/d	23	600-170,000	10,522	3,250
BURMAN, Jayasri (1960-) Indian				
oil	1	2,992	2,992	2,992
BURMAN, Sakti (1935-) Indian				
oil	19	5,708-65,534	32,659	32,500
wc/d	4	5,041-11,220	7,440	6,500
BURMANN, Fritz (1892-1945) German				
oil	1	3,270	3,270	3,270
BURMEISTER, Paul (1847-?) German				
oil	1	1,753	1,753	1,753
BURMESTER, Georg (1864-1936) German				
oil	1	1,786	1,786	1,786
wc/d	1	563	563	563
BURN, Howard Patrick (20th C) American				
oil	2	1,600-2,000	1,800	1,600
BURN, Rodney Joseph (1899-1984) British				
oil	1	1,110	1,110	1,110
BURNAND, Eugène (1850-1921) Swiss				
oil	1	5,311	5,311	5,311
wc/d	1	839	839	839
BURNE-JONES, Sir Edward Coley (1833-1898) British				
oil	1	2,288	2,288	2,288
wc/d	10	450-21,000	9,532	5,190
BURNE-JONES, Sir Philip (1861-1926) British				
oil	1	8,550	8,550	8,550
BURNHAM, Ruth W (20th C) American				
oil	1	1,600	1,600	1,600
BURNIER, Richard (1826-1884) Dutch				
oil	3	1,318-4,378	2,819	2,761
BURNITZ, Karl-Peter (1824-1886) German				
oil	9	479-4,256	1,599	1,127
BURNS, Alexander S (1911-1987) British				
oil	1	7,040	7,040	7,040
wc/d	1	3,344	3,344	3,344
BURNS, Colin W (1944-) British				
oil	26	1,505-34,020	9,531	7,059
wc/d	11	478-2,806	1,343	1,320
BURON, Henri Lucien Joseph (1880-1969) French				
oil	2	538-1,641	1,089	538
BURPEE, William P (1846-1940) American				
oil	1	8,500	8,500	8,500
wc/d	2	700-850	775	700
BURR, Alexander Hohenlohe (1837-1899) British				
oil	3	1,424-4,224	2,410	1,584
BURR, John (1831-1893) British				
oil	10	957-14,080	6,328	4,248
wc/d	1	791	791	791
BURRA, Edward (1905-1976) British				
wc/d	15	1,323-163,800	65,338	43,250
BURRI, Alberto (1915-1995) Italian				
oil	16	24,973-1,081,293	266,841	87,842
wc/d	2	177,000-407,100	292,050	177,000
BURRIDGE, C (19th C) British?				
oil	1	6,000	6,000	6,000
BURROUGHS, Bryson (1869-1934) American				
oil	1	4,250	4,250	4,250

Name	No.	Price Range	Average	Median
BURROWS, Robert (1810-1883) British				
oil	4	731-4,048	1,905	974
BURSSENS, Jan (1925-2002) Belgian				
oil	10	527-4,555	2,078	1,565
BURT, Charles Thomas (1823-1902) British				
oil	5	761-2,784	1,478	850
BURT, James (19th C) American				
oil	1	5,000	5,000	5,000
BURTON, Alice Mary (1893-?) British				
oil	1	1,079	1,079	1,079
BURTON, Dennis Eugène Norman (1933-) Canadian				
oil	2	4,509-9,019	6,764	4,509
BURTON, Richmond (1960-) American				
oil	2	2,200-8,500	5,350	2,200
wc/d	1	11,000	11,000	11,000
BURTON, Scott (1939-1989) American				
3D	2	24,000-100,000	62,000	24,000
BURTON, Sir Frederick William (1816-1900) British				
wc/d	1	26,885	26,885	26,885
BURTON, William Paton (1828-1883) British				
oil	1	836	836	836
wc/d	2	925-1,890	1,407	925
BURWOOD, G Vemply (19/20th C) British				
wc/d	1	2,567	2,567	2,567
BURY, Pol (1922-2005) Belgian				
wc/d	5	964-2,351	1,495	1,443
3D	11	3,534-32,730	17,568	19,872
BUSATO Y AMALIO FERNANDEZ, Jorge (19/20th C) Spanish				
wc/d	1	1,808	1,808	1,808
BUSCAGLIONE, Giuseppe (1868-1928) Italian				
oil	7	1,816-3,390	2,491	2,422
BUSCH, Peter Johan Valdemar (1861-1942) Danish				
oil	7	408-3,822	1,419	1,157
BUSCH, Walter (1898-1980) German				
oil	1	1,483	1,483	1,483
BUSCH, Wilhelm (1832-1908) German				
oil	11	6,167-25,442	14,159	14,595
wc/d	2	1,767-3,888	2,827	1,767
BUSCHELBERGER, Anton (1869-1934) German				
3D	1	2,384	2,384	2,384
BUSEYNE, G (?) ?				
3D	1	3,600	3,600	3,600
BUSH, Jack (1909-1977) Canadian				
oil	13	3,505-70,900	30,339	32,000
wc/d	2	984-1,319	1,151	984
BUSH, Norton (1834-1894) American				
oil	2	3,500-10,000	6,750	3,500
BUSHINSKY, Boris (?) ?				
wc/d	2	1,000-1,700	1,350	1,000
BUSI, Adolpho (1891-1977) Italian				
wc/d	2	1,260-1,449	1,354	1,260
BUSI, Luigi (1838-1884) Italian				
oil	1	12,600	12,600	12,600
BUSIERI, Giovanni Battista (1698-1757) Italian				
oil	1	31,140	31,140	31,140
wc/d	4	400-1,546	800	600
BUSNAGO, Giovanni da (19th C) Italian				
oil	1	1,676	1,676	1,676
BUSNEL, Robert Henri (1881-1957) French				
3D	1	3,695	3,695	3,695
BUSQUETS, Eusibi (20th C) Spanish				
oil	1	1,386	1,386	1,386
BUSSCHE, Joseph Emanuel van den (1837-1903) Belgian				
oil	1	1,455	1,455	1,455
BUSSE, Georg Heinrich (1810-1868) German				
wc/d	1	12,180	12,180	12,180
BUSSIERE, Gaston (1862-1929) French				
oil	1	21,541	21,541	21,541
BUSSOLINO, Vittorio (1853-1922) Italian				
oil	1	7,259	7,259	7,259

Name	No.	Price Range	Average	Median
BUSSON, Georges (1859-1933) French				
oil	1	37,800	37,800	37,800
wc/d	4	714-8,653	3,481	2,028
BUSSON, Marcel (1913-) French?				
oil	3	1,812-4,790	3,711	4,531
BUSSY, Simon (1869-1954) French				
wc/d	8	777-21,425	7,173	5,250
BUSUTTIL, Salvatore (1798-1854) Maltese				
wc/d	1	2,589	2,589	2,589
BUTHAUD, René (1886-1986) French				
wc/d	4	1,189-2,378	1,664	1,308
BUTHE, Michael (1944-1994) German				
oil	2	2,119-8,281	5,200	2,119
wc/d	3	1,401-5,184	2,709	1,542
BUTLAND, G W (fl.1831-1843) British				
oil	1	4,425	4,425	4,425
BUTLER, Antony (1927-) British				
oil	3	486-1,309	1,003	1,216
BUTLER, Charles Ernest (1864-c.1918) British				
oil	3	2,958-14,000	7,856	6,612
BUTLER, Edward Burgess (1853-1928) American				
oil	2	1,600-2,200	1,900	1,600
BUTLER, Edward Riche (1855-1916) American				
oil	1	4,477	4,477	4,477
BUTLER, Fray Guillermo (1880-1961) Argentinian				
oil	7	2,360-15,000	5,657	4,000
BUTLER, George Bernard (1838-1907) American				
oil	1	1,700	1,700	1,700
BUTLER, Herbert E (fl.1881-1921) British				
oil	1	1,416	1,416	1,416
wc/d	4	588-2,784	1,223	708
BUTLER, Horacio (1897-1983) Argentinian				
oil	7	4,200-74,000	24,610	15,000
BUTLER, Howard Russell (1856-1934) American				
oil	4	850-5,500	2,925	1,900
wc/d	1	500	500	500
BUTLER, James (1931-) British				
3D	2	2,268-5,472	3,870	2,268
BUTLER, Mary (1865-1946) American				
oil	6	1,000-2,800	1,700	1,500
BUTLER, Mildred Anne (1858-1941) British				
wc/d	11	900-24,740	7,206	4,560
BUTLER, Reg (1913-1981) British				
3D	12	2,121-71,820	22,054	13,650
BUTLER, Rozel Oertle (20th C) American				
oil	2	1,100-4,000	2,550	1,100
BUTLER, Theodore E (1861-1936) American				
oil	8	30,000-100,000	50,625	42,000
BUTMAN, Frederick A (1820-1871) American				
oil	1	2,250	2,250	2,250
BUTMAN, H R (?) American				
oil	1	4,500	4,500	4,500
BUTTERFIELD, Deborah (20th C) American				
3D	1	120,000	120,000	120,000
BUTTERSACK, Bernhard (1858-1925) German				
oil	4	1,100-1,900	1,608	1,632
BUTTERSWORTH, James E (1817-1894) American				
oil	9	35,000-470,000	131,666	70,000
BUTTERSWORTH, Thomas (1768-1842) British				
oil	13	1,780-160,650	34,229	14,352
wc/d	1	4,602	4,602	4,602
BUTTERSWORTH, Thomas (jnr) (19th C) British				
oil	1	16,530	16,530	16,530
BUTTERY, Thomas (?) British				
oil	1	2,625	2,625	2,625
BUTTGEN, Johann Peter (19th C) German				
oil	1	1,823	1,823	1,823
BUTTNER, Erich (1889-1936) German				
oil	2	1,196-1,196	1,196	1,196
BUTTNER, Werner (1954-) American				
oil	3	2,356-18,260	10,013	9,425
3D	1	4,241	4,241	4,241

Name	No.	Price Range	Average	Median
BUTTON, Albert Prentice (1872-?) American				
oil	1	2,900	2,900	2,900
wc/d	1	400	400	400
BUVELOT, Abram Louis (1814-1888) Swiss				
oil	1	6,652	6,652	6,652
BUXENSTEIN, C (20th C) German				
oil	1	4,586	4,586	4,586
BUYS, Cornelis (1746-1826) Dutch				
wc/d	1	1,337	1,337	1,337
BUZON, Marius de (1879-1958) French				
oil	2	4,435-4,534	4,484	4,435
BUZZI, Giuseppe (1794-?) Italian				
3D	1	2,076	2,076	2,076
BYARS, James Lee (1932-1997) American				
wc/d	5	5,610-17,000	11,351	10,596
BYE, Ranulph de Bayeux (1916-2003) American				
oil	2	3,750-8,500	6,125	3,750
wc/d	20	450-2,500	1,407	1,300
BYGRAVE, William (19th C) American				
oil	1	52,000	52,000	52,000
BYLANDT, Alfred Edouard van (1829-1890) Dutch				
oil	3	2,795-26,757	11,018	3,503
BYLERT, Jan van (1603-1671) Dutch				
oil	2	8,324-13,368	10,846	8,324
BYLERT, Jan van and ZWAERDECROON, Bernardus (17th C) Dutch				
oil	1	25,918	25,918	25,918
BYLES, William Hounsom (1872-c.1924) British				
oil	2	1,840-7,000	4,420	1,840
BYRON, Michael (1954-) American				
oil	1	1,200	1,200	1,200
BYSTROM, Johan Niklas (1783-1848) Swedish				
3D	1	47,362	47,362	47,362
BYTEBIER, Edgar (1875-1940) Belgian				
oil	1	1,788	1,788	1,788
BYWATERS, Jerry (1906-1989) American				
oil	2	3,500-26,000	14,750	3,500
BYZANTIOS, Constantin (1924-) Greek				
oil	3	2,805-7,560	5,060	4,816
CABAILLOT, Louis Simon (1810-?) French				
oil	2	1,800 2,000	1,945	1,800
CABALLERO, Jose Luis (1916-1991) Spanish				
oil	1	3,568	3,568	3,568
wc/d	6	479-2,928	1,851	1,794
CABALLERO, Luis (1943-1995) Colombian				
wc/d	5	1,054-7,500	4,774	5,104
CABANAS ERAUSQUIN, Juan (1907-1979) Spanish				
oil	1	6,533	6,533	6,533
CABANAS-OTEIZA, Angel (1875-1964) Spanish				
oil	1	2,973	2,973	2,973
wc/d	1	647	647	647
CABANE, Edouard (1857-?) French				
oil	2	5,293-16,340	10,816	5,293
CABANEL, Alexandre (1823-1889) French				
wc/d	4	1,411-3,664	2,353	1,929
CABANES, Louis François (1867-?) French				
oil	1	1,142	1,142	1,142
CABAT, Louis (1812-1893) French				
oil	4	654-5,501	2,647	1,017
CABEL, Adrian van der (c.1631-1705) Dutch				
oil	3	3,063-40,007	18,389	12,098
CABEZALERO, Juan Martin (1633-1673) Spanish				
oil	1	7,871	7,871	7,871
CABIANCA, Vincenzo (1827-1902) Italian				
oil	3	4,451-16,952	9,945	8,433
wc/d	2	1,274-4,685	2,979	1,274
CABIE, Louis Alexandre (1853-1939) French				
oil	8	505-1,984	1,251	1,399
CABOT, Edward Clark (1818-1901) American				
oil	1	2,600	2,600	2,600
CABRAL Y AGUADO, Manuel (1827-c.1890) Spanish				
oil	1	2,651	2,651	2,651

Name	No.	Price Range	Average	Median
CABRAL Y LLANO, Enrique (19th C) Spanish				
oil	1	9,500	9,500	9,500
CABRE, Manuel (1890-1983) Venezuelan				
oil	2	11,625-15,350	13,487	11,625
wc/d	1	4,420	4,420	4,420
CABRERA, Miguel (1695-1768) Mexican				
oil	1	25,000	25,000	25,000
CABRERA, Patricio (1958-) Spanish				
oil	2	1,272-5,627	3,449	1,272
CABUZEL, Auguste Hector (1836-?) French				
oil	1	2,342	2,342	2,342
CACCIA, Guglielmo (1568-1625) Italian				
oil	2	10,888-37,380	24,134	10,888
CACCIA, Ursola Maddalena (c.1596-1666) Italian				
oil	1	20,824	20,824	20,824
CACCIALI, Giuseppe (19th C) Italian				
oil	1	3,625	3,625	3,625
CACCIANIGA, Francesco (1700-1781) Italian				
oil	1	4,948	4,948	4,948
CACCIAPUOTI, Ettore (1860-?) Italian				
3D	1	1,999	1,999	1,999
CACCIAPUOTI, Guido (1892-1953) Italian				
3D	1	24,429	24,429	24,429
CACCIARELLI, Umberto (19/20th C) Italian				
wc/d	1	1,335	1,335	1,335
CACHOUD, François-Charles (1866-1943) French				
oil	2	2,761-3,000	2,880	2,761
CADEL, Eugène (1862-1942) French				
oil	1	1,500	1,500	1,500
CADELL, Francis Campbell Boileau (1883-1937) British				
oil	16	15,930-249,200	79,967	51,910
wc/d	11	1,850-18,795	11,438	12,180
CADENASSO, Giuseppe (1858-1918) American				
oil	3	1,800-4,000	2,600	2,000
wc/d	4	1,700-3,750	2,287	1,700
CADENHEAD, James (1858-1927) British				
oil	2	2,394-5,310	3,852	2,394
CADERE, Andre (1934-1978) Polish				
oil	1	2,503	2,503	2,503
3D	2	9,633-18,061	13,847	9,633
CADES, Giuseppe (1750-1799) Italian				
wc/d	2	5,041-7,500	6,270	5,041
CADMUS, Paul (1904-1999) American				
wc/d	9	3,000-14,000	7,411	7,500
CADORET, Michel (1912-1985) French				
oil	1	823	823	823
wc/d	1	536	536	536
CADRE, Pierre (19th C) French				
oil	1	5,507	5,507	5,507
CADWALLADER-GUILD, Emma Marie (1843-?) American				
3D	1	2,586	2,586	2,586
CADY, Walter Harrison (1877-1970) American				
wc/d	2	1,900-5,000	3,450	1,900
CAESAR, Doris (1892-1971) American				
3D	1	16,000	16,000	16,000
CAFFARO RORE, Mario (1910-2001) Italian				
oil	2	771-2,569	1,670	771
CAFFE, Nino (1909-1975) Spanish				
oil	16	1,100-8,750	4,081	3,273
wc/d	4	840-1,767	1,129	951
CAFFI, Ippolito (1809-1866) Italian				
oil	2	91,611-147,900	119,755	91,611
wc/d	1	4,839	4,839	4,839
CAFFI, Margherita (c.1650-1710) Italian				
oil	2	15,315-45,000	30,157	15,315
CAFFIERI, Hector (1847-1932) British				
wc/d	11	510-9,250	3,224	2,775
CAFFREY, Yona (20th C) Irish				
oil	3	1,296-2,071	1,811	2,068
CAFFYN, Walter Wallor (?-1898) British				
oil	5	1,131-26,100	7,095	3,287

Name	No.	Price Range	Average	Median
CAGE, John (1912-1992) American				
wc/d	4	6,372-14,000	9,478	6,922
3D	1	3,700	3,700	3,700
CAGLI, Corrado (1910-1976) Italian				
oil	6	2,417-12,721	6,510	3,770
wc/d	5	1,829-7,007	3,445	2,201
CAGNONE, Angelo (1941-) Italian				
oil	8	707-3,053	2,187	2,443
wc/d	3	1,885-2,420	2,137	2,108
CAHILL, Richard S (c.1827-1904) British				
oil	1	6,000	6,000	6,000
CAHN, Marcelle (1895-1981) French				
oil	2	3,520-7,920	5,720	3,520
wc/d	5	715-2,640	1,180	775
CAHOON, Charles D (1861-1951) American				
oil	3	1,548-3,400	2,416	2,300
CAHOON, Martha (1905-1999) American				
oil	1	3,250	3,250	3,250
CAHOON, Ralph (1910-1982) American				
oil	2	13,000-27,000	20,000	13,000
wc/d	1	3,250	3,250	3,250
CAHOURS, Henry Maurice (1889-1974) French				
oil	4	526-1,893	1,142	922
CAI GUO QIANG (1957-) Chinese				
wc/d	1	25,000	25,000	25,000
CAI JIA (c.1730-1782) Chinese				
wc/d	1	17,000	17,000	17,000
CAI JIN (1965-) Chinese				
oil	1	27,000	27,000	27,000
CAICEDO, Joaquin (1915-) Venezuelan				
oil	3	420-2,100	1,273	1,300
CAILLARD, Christian (1899-1985) French				
oil	5	496-12,396	3,692	1,641
wc/d	1	843	843	843
CAILLAUD, Aristide (1902-1990) French				
oil	2	841-1,320	1,080	841
wc/d	2	1,034-1,632	1,333	1,034
CAILLE, Léon Emile (1836-1907) French				
oil	7	1,197-6,650	3,149	2,270
CAILLEBOTTE, Gustave (1848-1894) French				
oil	9	51,745-1,600,000	585,821	478,400
CAILLET, Eulalie (19th C) French				
oil	1	4,772	4,772	4,772
CAIN, Auguste (1822-1894) French				
3D	6	1,940-10,395	5,774	4,055
CAIN, Georges (1856-1919) French				
oil	1	2,750	2,750	2,750
CAIRO, Francesco del (1607-1665) Italian				
oil	1	46,603	46,603	46,603
CAIZAC, A (19th C) French?				
wc/d	1	8,352	8,352	8,352
CAJAL GARRIGOS, Luis (1926-) Spanish				
oil	1	1,688	1,688	1,688
CAL, Giovanni de (19/20th C) Italian				
oil	1	2,207	2,207	2,207
CALABRIA, Ennio (1937-) Italian				
oil	7	1,571-5,966	3,851	3,631
CALAMATTA, Luigi (1802-1869) Italian				
wc/d	1	4,642	4,642	4,642
CALAME, Alexandre (1810-1864) Swiss				
oil	15	2,276-80,947	21,027	12,974
wc/d	6	530-2,498	1,458	1,217
CALAME, Alexandre and VERBOECKHOVEN, Eugène (19th C) Swiss/French				
oil	1	13,106	13,106	13,106
CALAME, Arthur (1843-1919) Swiss				
oil	6	571-2,518	1,414	1,297
CALANDRA, Edoardo (1852-1911) Italian				
oil	1	12,880	12,880	12,880
CALANDRI, Mario (1914-1993) Italian				
oil	1	4,671	4,671	4,671
wc/d	1	4,474	4,474	4,474

Name	No.	Price Range	Average	Median
CALBET, Antoine (1860-1944) French				
oil	5	769-2,854	1,670	1,512
wc/d	5	710-2,272	1,290	841
CALCAGNADORO, Antonino (1876-1935) Italian				
oil	3	1,979-17,836	7,346	2,225
CALCAGNO, Lawrence (1913-1993) American				
oil	3	900-2,400	1,766	2,000
wc/d	3	650-2,500	1,583	1,600
CALDER, Alexander (1898-1976) American				
oil	3	14,583-106,228	56,383	48,340
wc/d	78	2,500-200,000	29,839	28,000
3D	56	1,987-5,000,000	446,421	200,000
CALDER, Alexander Milne (1846-1923) American				
3D	1	6,250	6,250	6,250
CALDER, Alexander Stirling (1870-1945) American				
3D	1	3,500	3,500	3,500
CALDERARA, Antonio (1903-1978) Italian				
oil	7	3,818-22,723	8,285	5,966
wc/d	10	775-3,817	2,061	2,338
CALDERARA, Edoardo (1853-1928) Italian				
oil	1	1,065	1,065	1,065
CALDERINI, Luigi (1880-1973) Italian				
oil	2	555-1,452	1,003	555
CALDERINI, Marco (1850-c.1941) Italian				
oil	2	5,011-22,000	13,505	5,011
CALDERON, Charles-Clement (1870-1906) French				
oil	6	5,049-11,604	7,833	6,903
CALDERON, William Frank (1865-1943) British				
oil	1	6,000	6,000	6,000
wc/d	1	801	801	801
CALDWELL, Sam (1936-) American				
wc/d	1	2,000	2,000	2,000
CALES, Abbe Pierre (1870-1961) French				
oil	5	3,151-5,213	3,967	3,637
CALI (19th C) Italian				
3D	1	11,404	11,404	11,404
CALIARI, Carlo (1570-1596) Italian				
oil	3	38,836-52,297	44,186	41,425
CALIXTO DE JESUS, Benedicto (1853-1927) Brazilian				
oil	1	26,100	26,100	26,100
CALKINS, Larry (1955-) American				
3D	1	2,200	2,200	2,200
CALL, Jan van (elder) (1656-1703) Dutch				
wc/d	2	4,152-23,940	14,046	4,152
CALLAHAN, Kenneth L (1906-1986) American				
wc/d	1	1,600	1,600	1,600
CALLCOTT, Sir Augustus Wall (1779-1844) British				
oil	1	4,000	4,000	4,000
wc/d	1	1,860	1,860	1,860
CALLE, Paul (1928-) American				
oil	3	18,500-50,000	36,166	40,000
wc/d	3	475-5,500	3,741	5,250
CALLERY, Mary (20th C) American				
3D	1	13,000	13,000	13,000
CALLEWAERT, Charles René (1893-1936) Belgian				
oil	1	1,030	1,030	1,030
CALLIGAS, P (20th C) ?				
oil	1	1,649	1,649	1,649
CALLIYANNIS, Manolis (1926-) Greek				
oil	6	915-5,236	2,136	1,720
CALLMANDER, Carl Reinhold (1840-1922) Swedish				
oil	2	777-2,617	1,697	777
CALLOT, Anton von (1809-1880) Austrian				
oil	1	1,721	1,721	1,721
CALLOT, Henri Eugène (1875-1956) French				
oil	4	468-2,386	1,050	596
CALLOT, Jacques (1592-1635) French				
wc/d	1	16,650	16,650	16,650
CALLOW, E J (18th C) Continental				
oil	1	8,152	8,152	8,152
CALLOW, G (?) British				
oil	1	1,295	1,295	1,295

Name	No.	Price Range	Average	Median
CALLOW, George D (fl.1858-1873) British				
oil	2	1,513-2,035	1,774	1,513
wc/d	1	490	490	490
CALLOW, John (1822-1878) British				
oil	4	788-4,800	2,764	1,900
wc/d	6	598-3,500	1,706	1,131
CALLOW, William (1812-1908) British				
wc/d	20	661-16,245	3,904	2,088
CALMADY, Emily (19th C) ?				
wc/d	1	6,264	6,264	6,264
CALOUTSIS, Valerios (1927-) Greek				
oil	2	1,672-1,870	1,771	1,672
CALS, Adolphe Felix (1810-1880) French				
oil	26	753-20,710	6,495	4,644
wc/d	4	690-1,458	982	778
CALTHROP, Claude Andrew (1845-1893) British				
oil	1	1,038	1,038	1,038
CALVAERT, Dionisio (1540-1619) Flemish				
oil	1	203,836	203,836	203,836
wc/d	1	2,259	2,259	2,259
CALVERT, Frederick (c.1785-1845) British				
oil	8	1,566-19,580	5,961	2,992
CALVERT, Henry (1798-1869) British				
oil	1	2,750	2,750	2,750
CALVES, Léon Georges (1848-1924) French				
oil	2	2,367-3,000	2,683	2,367
CALVES, Marie (1883-1957) French				
oil	3	844-5,269	2,414	1,130
CALVI, Ercole (1824-1900) Italian				
oil	2	9,642-14,566	12,104	9,642
CALVI, Jacopo Alessandro (1740-1815) Italian				
wc/d	1	1,399	1,399	1,399
CALVI, Pietro (1833-1884) Italian				
3D	1	97,900	97,900	97,900
CALVO CARRION, Antonio (1921-1979) Spanish				
oil	1	1,178	1,178	1,178
CALVO, Carmen (1950-) Spanish				
wc/d	3	2,735-5,143	3,804	3,534
CALZA, Antonio (1653-1725) Italian				
oil	1	13,875	13,875	13,875
CALZOLARI, Pier Paolo (1943-) Italian				
oil	4	3,330-29,281	10,709	4,757
wc/d	6	3,748-7,000	5,371	4,839
3D	3	10,177-27,986	16,961	12,721
CAM, D V (?) ?				
3D	1	3,836	3,836	3,836
CAMACHO, Jorge (1934-) Cuban				
oil	3	1,018-7,516	3,837	2,979
wc/d	4	1,145-2,671	1,907	1,553
CAMARGO, Sergio de (1930-1990) Brazilian				
3D	5	40,000-75,000	50,100	43,264
CAMARLENCH, Ignacio Pinazo (1849-1916) Spanish				
oil	3	3,399-36,122	15,366	6,578
CAMARO, Alexander (1901-1992) German				
oil	2	1,054-1,911	1,482	1,054
CAMARROQUE, Charles (19th C) French				
oil	1	15,123	15,123	15,123
CAMAX-ZOEGGER, Marie Anne (19th C) French				
oil	1	1,337	1,337	1,337
CAMBI, Andrei (19th C) Italian				
3D	3	4,872-22,000	11,389	7,297
CAMBIASO, Domenico (1811-1894) Italian				
oil	1	6,747	6,747	6,747
CAMBIASO, Luca (1527-1585) Italian				
wc/d	4	4,359-17,000	10,566	7,030
CAMBIER, Guy (1923-) French				
oil	10	478-2,983	1,454	968
CAMBIER, Jules (?) Belgian				
oil	1	2,384	2,384	2,384
CAMBIER, Juliette (1879-1963) Belgian				
oil	4	716-3,884	1,558	751

Name	No.	Price Range	Average	Median
CAMBIER, Nestor (1879-1957) Belgian				
oil	1	1,076	1,076	1,076
CAMBOS, Jean Jules (1828-1917) French				
3D	1	5,500	5,500	5,500
CAMBOUR, Claude (?) French				
oil	1	1,000	1,000	1,000
CAMBRESIER, Jean (1856-1928) Belgian				
oil	2	756-832	794	756
wc/d	5	534-773	611	546
CAMENISCH, Paul (1893-1970) Swiss				
oil	3	3,450-7,216	5,159	4,811
wc/d	1	3,137	3,137	3,137
CAMERON, Duncan (1837-1916) British				
oil	5	1,183-9,790	3,305	1,496
CAMERON, Edgar Spier (1862-1944) American				
oil	1	2,800	2,800	2,800
CAMERON, Gordon Stewart (1916-1994) British				
oil	1	1,881	1,881	1,881
CAMERON, Hugh (1835-1918) British				
oil	1	20,570	20,570	20,570
wc/d	2	1,890-1,890	1,890	1,890
CAMERON, Katherine (1874-1965) British				
wc/d	7	515-9,048	2,366	1,619
CAMERON, Peter Caledonian (19th C) American				
wc/d	1	3,800	3,800	3,800
CAMERON, Shawn (1950-) American				
oil	1	8,000	8,000	8,000
CAMERON, Sir D Y (1865-1945) British				
oil	1	1,827	1,827	1,827
wc/d	2	731-1,705	1,218	731
CAMERON, Sir David Young (1865-1945) British				
oil	13	589-37,590	12,470	11,505
wc/d	6	1,125-3,026	1,673	1,211
CAMINADE, Alexandre François (1789-1862) French				
oil	1	10,200	10,200	10,200
CAMINATI, Aurelio (1924-) Italian				
oil	2	710-1,551	1,130	710
CAMINO, Augusto (1857-1937) Italian				
oil	1	1,260	1,260	1,260
CAMINO, Giuseppe (1818-1890) Italian				
oil	5	2,420-15,284	6,089	4,919
CAMLIN, James A (1918-1982) American				
wc/d	1	1,350	1,350	1,350
CAMMIDGE, George (1846-1916) British				
oil	5	770-4,104	2,086	2,223
CAMMILLIERI, Niccolo S (fl.1820-1855) Maltese				
wc/d	2	4,092-4,464	4,278	4,092
CAMOIN, Charles (1879-1965) French				
oil	38	900-227,500	27,443	12,283
wc/d	7	823-6,049	3,156	3,567
CAMP, Janie (20th C) American				
oil	1	4,000	4,000	4,000
CAMPA, Jean (1933-) French				
3D	2	3,185-3,185	3,185	3,185
CAMPAGNARI, Ottorino (1910-1981) Italian				
oil	6	450-2,655	1,254	1,030
CAMPANELLA, Vito (1932-) Argentinian				
oil	2	14,000-18,000	16,000	14,000
wc/d	1	2,500	2,500	2,500
CAMPANO, Miguel Angel (1948-) Spanish				
oil	7	1,916-14,449	7,111	6,541
CAMPBELL, Arthur M (1909-1994) Irish?				
wc/d	1	1,095	1,095	1,095
CAMPBELL, Duncan (19/20th C) American				
oil	1	1,500	1,500	1,500
CAMPBELL, George (1917-1979) British				
oil	27	1,400-52,080	15,287	10,946
wc/d	14	935-8,996	3,401	2,604
CAMPBELL, John Henry (1755-1828) Irish				
wc/d	5	885-5,679	2,548	1,395
CAMPBELL, Laurence (1911-1964) British				
wc/d	1	1,920	1,920	1,920

Name	No.	Price Range	Average	Median
CAMPBELL, Laurence A (1940-) American				
oil	3	2,100-28,000	13,366	10,000
CAMPBELL, R H (19/20th C) British				
oil	1	2,262	2,262	2,262
CAMPBELL, Raymond (20th C) British?				
oil	2	1,029-1,288	1,158	1,029
CAMPBELL, William Wright (1913-1992) British				
oil	1	4,248	4,248	4,248
CAMPENDONK, Heinrich (1889-1957) German				
oil	4	281,600-2,655,000	990,800	495,600
wc/d	2	5,262-55,500	30,381	5,262
CAMPHUYSEN, Govert Dircksz (1624-1672) Dutch				
oil	3	4,087-10,793	7,072	6,336
CAMPHUYSEN, Joachim Govertsz (1602-1659) Dutch				
oil	2	7,030-14,013	10,521	7,030
CAMPI, Bernardino (1522-1592) Italian				
wc/d	1	5,437	5,437	5,437
CAMPI, Galeazzo (16th C) Italian				
oil	1	29,774	29,774	29,774
CAMPI, Giulio (1502-1572) Italian				
wc/d	2	1,580-33,300	17,440	1,580
CAMPI, Vincenzo (1536-1591) Italian				
oil	1	80,000	80,000	80,000
CAMPIDOGLIO, Michele di (1610-1670) Italian				
oil	1	148,000	148,000	148,000
CAMPIGLI, Massimo (1895-1971) Italian				
oil	19	18,446-352,000	117,302	87,842
wc/d	6	3,053-27,840	12,778	13,993
CAMPION, George Bryant (1796-1870) British				
wc/d	2	1,015-1,750	1,382	1,015
CAMPION, John (1965-) Irish?				
oil	1	1,823	1,823	1,823
CAMPO, Federico del (1837-1923) Peruvian				
oil	7	22,620-270,000	99,120	73,080
CAMPO, Francesco del (?) Italian				
oil	1	31,483	31,483	31,483
CAMPOREALE, Sergio (1937-) Argentinian				
wc/d	1	5,000	5,000	5,000
CAMPOS, Florencio Molina (20th C) South American				
oil	1	1,900	1,900	1,900
wc/d	3	11,000-11,000	11,000	11,000
CAMPOTOSTO, Henry (1833-1910) Belgian				
oil	2	3,000-5,000	4,000	3,000
CAMPOTOSTO, Octavia (fl.1870-80) Belgian				
oil	2	920-1,325	1,122	920
CAMPRIANI, Alceste (1848-1933) Italian				
oil	3	1,800-12,740	7,300	7,360
CAMPRIANI, Giovanni (1880-?) Italian				
oil	2	1,529-3,366	2,447	1,529
CAMPROBIN, Pedro de (1605-1674) Spanish				
oil	2	94,054-95,150	94,602	94,054
CAMPS RIBERA, Francisco (1895-1949) Mexican/Spanish				
oil	1	4,186	4,186	4,186
CAMRADT, Johannes Ludvig (1779-1849) Danish				
oil	2	4,763-10,796	7,779	4,763
CAMUCCINI, Vincenzo (1773-1844) Italian				
oil	3	7,644-24,842	13,417	7,767
wc/d	1	2,571	2,571	2,571
CAMUS, Blanche (1881-1968) French				
oil	1	24,050	24,050	24,050
CAMUS, Gustave (1914-1984) Belgian				
oil	10	607-3,414	1,700	1,153
wc/d	1	1,812	1,812	1,812
CAMUS, Jacques (1937-) French				
oil	3	1,148-1,288	1,209	1,193
wc/d	1	761	761	761
CAMUS, Jean Marie (1877-1955) French				
3D	1	7,054	7,054	7,054
CAMUSSO, Catherine (20th C) French?				
wc/d	3	954-1,312	1,153	1,193
CANAL, Giambattista (1745-1825) Italian				
oil	1	38,919	38,919	38,919

Name	No.	Price Range	Average	Median
CANAL, Gilbert von (1849-1927) German				
oil	2	1,414-3,540	2,477	1,414
CANALETTO (1697-1768) Italian				
oil	2	32,040-2,183,000	1,107,520	32,040
CANALS Y LLAMBI, Ricardo (1876-1931) Spanish				
oil	1	39,000	39,000	39,000
wc/d	3	668-19,156	7,170	1,688
CANAS, Benjamin (1937-1987) Chilean				
oil	4	16,000-50,000	30,750	22,000
CANAS, Carlos (20th C) Argentinian				
oil	1	1,600	1,600	1,600
CANAVERAL Y PEREZ, Jose (19th C) Spanish				
oil	1	14,466	14,466	14,466
CANDIA, Domingo (1896-1976) Argentinian				
wc/d	1	5,000	5,000	5,000
CANDID, Peter (1548-1628) Flemish				
oil	1	50,000	50,000	50,000
wc/d	1	1,100	1,100	1,100
CANDIDO, Sal (19th C) Italian				
oil	2	16,200-19,140	17,670	16,200
CANDIOTI, Ana (20th C) Argentinian				
oil	1	2,000	2,000	2,000
CANE, Louis (1943-) French				
oil	13	1,321-6,062	3,077	2,797
wc/d	2	636-9,936	5,286	636
3D	8	2,455-7,767	4,634	3,468
CANEGALLO, Cesare Sexto (1892-1966) Italian				
wc/d	1	2,604	2,604	2,604
CANELLA, A (19th C) Italian				
oil	1	2,220	2,220	2,220
CANELLA, Giuseppe (1788-1847) Italian				
oil	12	1,816-117,808	26,303	11,297
CANESSA, Aurelio (1899-1973) Argentinian				
oil	2	2,200-4,200	3,200	2,200
CANET, Charles Emile (19/20th C) French				
oil	1	1,694	1,694	1,694
CANET, Marcel (1875-1959) French				
oil	1	719	719	719
wc/d	1	1,812	1,812	1,812
CANGEMI, Michael (20th C) American				
oil	1	1,100	1,100	1,100
CANGIULLO, Francesco (1884-1977) Italian				
oil	2	1,221-1,427	1,324	1,221
CANIARIS, Vlassis (1928-) Greek				
oil	2	11,220-13,090	12,155	11,220
wc/d	2	16,530-26,400	21,465	16,530
CANNAULT-UTZ, Micheline (?) French?				
oil	1	1,401	1,401	1,401
CANNAVACCIUOLO, Maurizio (1954-) Italian				
oil	1	2,945	2,945	2,945
CANNEEL, Eugène (1882-1966) Belgian				
3D	1	2,338	2,338	2,338
CANNEEL, Theodore (1817-1892) Belgian				
oil	1	7,603	7,603	7,603
CANNEY, Michael (1923-) British				
oil	5	1,100-2,805	2,072	2,288
wc/d	1	1,388	1,388	1,388
3D	2	2,244-2,958	2,601	2,244
CANNICCI, Nicolo (1846-1906) Italian				
oil	2	10,813-19,747	15,280	10,813
CANO, Jose Maria (1959-) American?				
wc/d	2	10,620-29,600	20,110	10,620
CANO, Pedro (1944-) Italian				
oil	1	1,571	1,571	1,571
CANOGAR, Rafael (1934-) Spanish				
oil	5	4,114-48,163	28,417	33,568
CANON, Hans (1829-1885) Austrian				
oil	2	834-1,189	1,011	834
wc/d	1	602	602	602
CANONICA, Pietro (1869-1959) Italian				
3D	1	5,996	5,996	5,996

Name	No.	Price Range	Average	Median
CANOVA, Antonio (1757-1822) Italian				
wc/d	1	38,163	38,163	38,163
3D	1	19,000	19,000	19,000
CANOVAS, Fernando (1960-) Argentinian				
oil	2	8,000-14,000	11,000	8,000
CANTA, Johannes Antonius (1816-1888) Dutch				
oil	1	2,682	2,682	2,682
CANTAGALLINA, Remigio (1582-1628) Italian				
wc/d	1	3,299	3,299	3,299
CANTARINI, Simone (1612-1648) Italian				
oil	1	350,000	350,000	350,000
wc/d	5	773-10,356	4,992	4,142
CANTATORE, Domenico (1906-1998) Italian				
oil	13	1,874-14,750	8,046	9,063
wc/d	5	610-5,890	2,693	2,700
CANTERO, M Lopez (19th C) Spanish				
oil	1	8,237	8,237	8,237
CANTONE, Francesco (?) Italian?				
oil	2	14,517-15,727	15,122	14,517
CANTRE, Jozef (1890-1957) Belgian				
3D	1	3,822	3,822	3,822
CANTU, Federico (1908-1989) Mexican				
oil	2	950-16,000	8,475	950
CANTZLER, Johan Oscar (1844-1921) Swedish				
oil	1	3,365	3,365	3,365
CANU, Yvonne (1921-) French				
oil	7	1,000-14,000	4,323	1,455
wc/d	1	630	630	630
CANUET, Louise (19th C) French				
oil	1	1,067	1,067	1,067
CANUTI, Domenico Maria (1620-1684) Italian				
wc/d	1	14,000	14,000	14,000
CANZIANI, Estella Louisa Michaela (1887-1964) British				
oil	1	2,024	2,024	2,024
wc/d	3	2,450-4,872	3,490	3,150
CAP, Constant (1842-1915) Belgian				
oil	2	764-2,145	1,454	764
CAPA, Joaquin (1941-) Spanish				
oil	1	1,823	1,823	1,823
CAPALDO, Rubens (1908-1997) French				
oil	1	1,274	1,274	1,274
CAPARNE, William John (fl.1882-1893) British				
wc/d	8	558-2,418	1,172	688
CAPDEVILLA PUIG, Genis (1860-1929) Spanish				
oil	1	1,132	1,132	1,132
CAPEINICK, Jean (1838-1890) Belgian				
oil	5	1,013-18,000	6,741	5,500
CAPELLA, Julia Gheli (19th C) Italian				
oil	1	4,450	4,450	4,450
CAPELLE, Jan van de (1624-1679) Dutch				
wc/d	1	4,197	4,197	4,197
CAPET, Marie Gabrielle (1761-1818) French				
wc/d	1	18,229	18,229	18,229
CAPOCCHINI, Ugo (1901-1980) Italian				
oil	8	849-12,000	4,600	3,152
CAPOGROSSI, Costanza Mennyey (20th C) Italian				
oil	1	3,854	3,854	3,854
CAPOGROSSI, Giuseppe (1900-1972) Italian				
oil	23	4,919-381,633	53,769	24,167
wc/d	6	6,646-20,350	12,772	12,083
CAPON, Georges Émile (1890-1980) French				
oil	3	637-3,039	1,519	882
CAPONE, Gaetano (1845-1920) Italian				
oil	3	700-1,100	916	950
wc/d	4	500-2,088	967	563
CAPORAEL, Suzanne (1946-) American				
wc/d	1	1,300	1,300	1,300
CAPPA-MARINETTI, Benedetta (1897-1977) Italian				
oil	1	1,211	1,211	1,211
CAPPELEN, August (1827-1852) Norwegian				
oil	2	3,416-55,200	29,308	3,416

Name	No.	Price Range	Average	Median
CAPPELLI, Giovanni (1923-1994) Italian				
oil	8	1,767-3,884	2,318	1,929
wc/d	4	572-1,798	1,062	584
CAPPELLI, Pietro (?-1724) Italian				
oil	1	5,068	5,068	5,068
CAPPIELLO, Leonetto (1875-1942) French				
oil	2	3,816-3,816	3,816	3,816
wc/d	2	839-2,315	1,577	839
CAPRILE, Vincenzo (1856-1936) Italian				
oil	6	3,514-22,007	10,993	7,027
wc/d	1	3,514	3,514	3,514
CAPRINI, Eugenio (1875-1932) Italian				
oil	1	1,308	1,308	1,308
CAPRISTO, Oscar (20th C) Argentinian				
oil	1	5,200	5,200	5,200
CAPRON, Jean Pierre (1921-1997) French				
oil	3	484-2,303	1,431	1,506
CAPSER, Mike (1952-) American				
3D	1	3,500	3,500	3,500
CAPULETTI, Jose Manuel (1925-1978) Spanish				
oil	1	4,200	4,200	4,200
wc/d	1	1,647	1,647	1,647
CAPUTO, Tonino (1933-) Italian				
oil	19	477-5,011	1,791	1,475
CARA, Ugo (1908-2004) Italian				
3D	1	1,815	1,815	1,815
CARABAIN, Jacques (1834-?) Belgian				
oil	16	6,078-60,616	21,254	15,000
CARABAIN, Victor (?-1942) Belgian				
oil	3	573-2,104	1,124	696
CARABIN, Rupert (1862-1932) French				
3D	1	11,712	11,712	11,712
CARACCIOLO, Giovanni Battista (1570-1637) Italian				
oil	1	235,616	235,616	235,616
CARACCIOLO, Niccolo d'Ardia (1941-1989) Italian				
oil	5	5,568-22,320	10,439	7,068
wc/d	3	849-3,871	2,506	2,799
CARADOSSI, Vittorio (1861-?) Italian				
3D	2	7,500-55,000	31,250	7,500
CARAS, Christos (1930-) Greek				
oil	3	5,049-34,600	16,116	8,700
CARASSO, Fred (1899-1969) Dutch				
3D	3	1,753-17,635	7,553	3,273
CARAUD, Joseph (1821-1905) French				
oil	4	2,236-42,000	16,809	10,000
CARAVIA-FLORA, Thalia (1871-1960) Greek				
oil	4	2,640-10,285	5,054	3,553
wc/d	3	1,936-7,920	4,532	3,740
CARAZO, Ramon (1896-1936) Spanish				
oil	1	5,000	5,000	5,000
CARBAAT, Jan (1866-1925) ?				
oil	2	485-1,576	1,030	485
CARBASIUS, Françoise Charlotte (1885-1984) Dutch				
3D	1	8,818	8,818	8,818
CARBONELL, Manuel (1918-) Cuban				
3D	4	2,000-19,000	7,062	3,000
CARBONELL, Santiago (1960-) Spanish				
oil	1	42,000	42,000	42,000
CARBONERO, Jose Moreno (1860-1942) Spanish				
oil	2	5,563-119,000	62,281	5,563
CARBONI, Luigi (1957-) Italian				
oil	2	1,527-1,767	1,647	1,527
wc/d	1	3,343	3,343	3,343
CARCANO, Filippo (1840-1910) Italian				
oil	1	16,397	16,397	16,397
CARDENAS, Augustin (1927-2001) Cuban				
wc/d	8	494-4,142	1,368	1,029
3D	14	3,300-130,000	31,266	20,000
CARDENAS, Juan (1939-) Colombian				
oil	1	22,000	22,000	22,000
CARDENAS, Marta (1944-) Spanish				
oil	1	5,741	5,741	5,741

Name	No.	Price Range	Average	Median
CARDENAS, Santiago (1937-) Colombian				
wc/d	2	2,700-3,180	2,940	2,700
CARDER, Malcolm (1936-) British				
wc/d	1	1,776	1,776	1,776
CARDINAL-SCHUBERT, Joanne (1942-) Canadian				
oil	2	492-656	574	492
wc/d	6	405-1,773	1,160	973
CARDINAUX, Emile (1877-1936) Swiss				
oil	6	3,434-11,421	6,657	3,816
wc/d	4	624-3,358	2,426	2,671
CARDON, Claude (fl.1892-1920) British				
oil	2	2,052-9,250	5,651	2,052
wc/d	2	712-1,638	1,175	712
CARDONA LLADOS, Juan (1877-1934) Spanish				
oil	2	963-9,644	5,303	963
CARDONA, Jose (19/20th C) Spanish				
3D	1	2,349	2,349	2,349
CARDONA, Juan (1877-c.1957) Spanish				
wc/d	5	1,085-7,312	4,570	5,394
CARDOZO, Eduardo (1965-) Uruguayan				
oil	1	1,400	1,400	1,400
CAREAGA, Enrique (20th C) Paraguayan				
oil	1	1,000	1,000	1,000
CARELLI, Achille (19th C) Italian				
wc/d	1	1,788	1,788	1,788
CARELLI, Augusto (19th C) Italian				
wc/d	1	1,784	1,784	1,784
CARELLI, C (?) Italian?				
oil	3	4,347-10,684	7,710	8,100
CARELLI, Consalve (1818-1900) Italian				
oil	4	6,062-38,537	18,665	7,767
wc/d	5	662-2,141	1,486	1,308
CARELLI, G (19th C) Italian				
oil	1	33,874	33,874	33,874
CARELLI, Gabrielli (1820-1900) Italian				
oil	1	4,142	4,142	4,142
wc/d	14	1,171-5,040	2,145	1,770
CARELLI, Giuseppe (1858-1921) Italian				
oil	8	3,872-12,686	6,515	4,849
CARENA, Antonio (1925-) Italian				
oil	2	1,295-1,752	1,523	1,295
CARENA, Felice (1879-1966) Italian				
oil	7	6,479-32,363	16,783	12,959
wc/d	3	464-835	627	584
CARESME, Jacques Philippe (1734-1796) French				
wc/d	3	1,308-5,827	3,012	1,903
CAREY, John W (19/20th C) British				
wc/d	1	3,562	3,562	3,562
CAREY, Joseph William (1859-1937) British				
wc/d	27	484-2,768	1,140	1,038
CAREY, Rockwell W (1882-1954) American				
oil	1	5,750	5,750	5,750
CARGALEIRO, Manuel (1927-) Portuguese				
oil	3	11,781-25,958	19,584	21,014
wc/d	6	1,234-8,900	2,903	1,411
CARGNEL, Vittore Antonio (1872-1931) Italian				
oil	4	3,330-18,163	8,197	3,637
CARIGIET, Alois (1902-1985) Swiss				
oil	2	7,303-41,097	24,200	7,303
wc/d	11	530-5,327	2,764	3,083
CARIOT, Gustave (1872-1950) French				
oil	13	2,044-31,860	10,723	6,479
CARISS, Henry T (1840-1903) American				
oil	1	8,000	8,000	8,000
CARL-ANGST, Albert (1875-1965) Swiss				
3D	1	3,794	3,794	3,794
CARL-ROSA, Mario (1855-1913) French				
oil	1	5,000	5,000	5,000
CARLANDI, Onorato (1848-1939) Italian				
oil	2	777-996	886	777
wc/d	5	425-3,107	1,369	878

Name	No.	Price Range	Average	Median
CARLAW, William (1847-1889) British				
wc/d	4	620-1,539	1,236	1,386
CARLBERG, Hugo (1880-1943) Swedish				
oil	1	3,000	3,000	3,000
CARLE, Anne de (18th C) British				
wc/d	1	1,580	1,580	1,580
CARLEBUR, François (19th C) Dutch				
wc/d	1	1,796	1,796	1,796
CARLEBUR, François II (1821-1893) Dutch				
wc/d	1	1,463	1,463	1,463
CARLES, Arthur B (1882-1952) American				
oil	2	1,800-6,000	3,900	1,800
wc/d	4	500-6,500	2,625	1,400
CARLES, Jean Antonin (1851-1919) French				
3D	1	2,517	2,517	2,517
CARLEVARIS, Luca (1665-1731) Italian				
oil	1	36,327	36,327	36,327
CARLIER, Emile François (1827-1879) French				
3D	1	42,500	42,500	42,500
CARLIER, Marie (1920-1986) Belgian				
oil	1	1,157	1,157	1,157
CARLIER, Max (1872-1938) Belgian				
oil	18	607-38,000	4,355	1,565
CARLIER, Modeste (1820-1878) Belgian				
oil	2	4,839-10,500	7,669	4,839
CARLIERI, Alberto (1672-1720) Italian				
oil	1	3,168	3,168	3,168
CARLIN, James (1909-) American				
oil	1	3,500	3,500	3,500
CARLINE, George (1855-1920) British				
oil	1	4,529	4,529	4,529
CARLO, Vittorio Maria di (1939-) Italian				
oil	34	471-3,000	1,010	884
CARLONE, Carlo (1686-1776) Italian				
oil	3	6,020-45,000	29,340	37,000
wc/d	3	703-11,500	5,001	2,800
CARLONE, Giovanni Andrea (1590-1630) Italian				
wc/d	3	1,800-9,500	6,571	8,414
CARLONI, Marco (1742-1796) Italian				
wc/d	1	7,778	7,778	7,778
CARLOTTI, Jean Albert (1909-2003) French				
oil	1	1,332	1,332	1,332
wc/d	1	820	820	820
CARLSEN, Carl (1855-1917) Danish				
oil	4	1,618-37,500	10,694	1,659
CARLSEN, Dines (1901-1966) American				
oil	1	12,000	12,000	12,000
CARLSEN, Emil (1853-1932) American/Danish				
oil	14	850-85,000	21,053	3,300
CARLSON, Arvid (1895-1962) Swedish				
oil	1	3,459	3,459	3,459
CARLSON, George (1940-) American				
wc/d	1	9,500	9,500	9,500
3D	1	4,250	4,250	4,250
CARLSON, John F (1875-1947) American				
oil	12	1,300-32,500	8,691	6,000
wc/d	3	3,500-6,500	5,166	5,500
CARLSON, Ken (1937-) American				
oil	5	11,000-37,500	26,000	32,500
wc/d	1	1,100	1,100	1,100
CARLSSON, Harry (c.1891-1968) Danish				
oil	2	483-24,247	12,365	483
CARLSTEDT, Birger (1907-1975) Finnish				
oil	2	1,260-1,671	1,465	1,260
wc/d	1	3,974	3,974	3,974
CARLSTROM, Gustaf (1896-1964) Swedish				
oil	3	997-2,198	1,646	1,745
CARLSUND, Otto (1897-1948) Swedish				
oil	2	36,340-87,791	62,065	36,340
CARLTON, Frederick (19th C) British				
oil	1	1,590	1,590	1,590

Name	No.	Price Range	Average	Median
CARLTON, William Tolman (1816-1888) American				
oil	1	40,000	40,000	40,000
CARLUS, Jean (1852-1930) French				
3D	1	1,321	1,321	1,321
CARLYLE, Florence (1864-1923) Canadian				
oil	1	3,199	3,199	3,199
CARMASSI, Arturo (1925-) Italian				
oil	10	1,295-9,370	4,606	4,833
wc/d	3	567-9,545	3,885	1,543
CARMELO DE ARZADUN (1888-1968) Uruguayan				
oil	1	2,000	2,000	2,000
CARMI, Eugenio (1920-) Italian				
oil	28	1,036-5,488	2,735	2,458
wc/d	3	455-569	505	493
CARMICHAEL, Franklin (1890-1945) Canadian				
oil	5	79,337-282,085	188,568	226,919
CARMICHAEL, Ida Barbour (1884-?) American				
oil	1	2,000	2,000	2,000
CARMICHAEL, J W (1800-1868) British				
wc/d	1	1,850	1,850	1,850
CARMICHAEL, John Wilson (1800-1868) British				
oil	24	770-139,200	29,114	9,735
wc/d	13	455-16,740	3,762	1,435
CARMIENCKE, Johan-Herman (1810-1867) Danish/American				
oil	4	1,200-55,000	15,169	1,630
CARMIGNANI, Guido (1838-1909) Italian				
oil	1	22,188	22,188	22,188
CARMINATI, Enrique (19th C) Spanish				
oil	1	3,629	3,629	3,629
CARMONTELLE, Louis Carrogis (1717-1806) French				
wc/d	5	1,070-18,500	10,650	13,125
CARNACINI, Ceferino (1888-1964) Argentinian				
oil	8	2,130-22,000	8,091	6,000
CARNEO, Antonio (1637-1692) Italian				
oil	2	42,324-50,959	46,641	42,324
CARNIELO, Rinaldo (1853-1910) Italian				
3D	1	5,533	5,533	5,533
CARNIER, H (?) ?				
oil	1	1,890	1,890	1,890
CARNOVALI, Giovanni (1806-1873) Italian				
oil	4	3,131-12,959	6,916	5,096
wc/d	1	2,425	2,425	2,425
CARNWATH, Squeak (1947-) American				
oil	1	19,000	19,000	19,000
CARO, Anthony (1924-) British				
oil	1	8,650	8,650	8,650
wc/d	1	3,806	3,806	3,806
3D	15	8,550-2,200,000	191,245	29,920
CARO, Baldassare de (1689-c.1755) Italian				
oil	6	3,107-44,265	19,395	11,100
CARO, Lorenzo de (18th C) Italian				
oil	1	9,515	9,515	9,515
CARO-DELVAILLE, Henri (1876-1926) French				
oil	4	5,592-22,500	15,773	13,000
CAROLIS, Adolfo de (1874-1928) Italian				
oil	1	1,985	1,985	1,985
CAROLUS, Jean (1814-1897) Belgian				
oil	4	2,407-14,000	6,513	3,646
CAROLUS-DURAN, Émile Auguste (1837-1917) French				
oil	8	1,008-37,500	8,750	4,000
CAROLUS-DURAN, Pauline Marie Charlotte (19th C) French				
wc/d	1	1,094	1,094	1,094
CARON, Alexandre-Auguste (1857-?) French				
3D	1	1,788	1,788	1,788
CARON, Henri Paul Edmond (1860-?) French				
oil	1	1,029	1,029	1,029
CARON, Marcel (1890-1961) Belgian				
oil	3	526-16,649	8,063	7,014
wc/d	1	595	595	595

Name	No.	Price Range	Average	Median
CARON, Paul Archibald (1874-1941) Canadian				
oil	2	529-6,204	3,366	529
wc/d	2	371-1,499	935	371
3D	1	2,986	2,986	2,986
CARPANETTO, Giovanni Battista (1863-1928) Italian				
oil	8	1,386-10,738	6,421	7,274
wc/d	1	4,411	4,411	4,411
CARPANI, Ricardo (?) Argentinian				
oil	1	26,000	26,000	26,000
CARPEAUX, J B (1827-1875) French				
3D	1	7,068	7,068	7,068
CARPEAUX, Jean Baptiste (1827-1875) French				
oil	3	3,034-8,416	5,689	5,619
wc/d	1	2,386	2,386	2,386
3D	22	2,378-37,800	10,290	8,421
CARPENDALE, William Henry (1830-1883) French				
wc/d	1	7,080	7,080	7,080
CARPENTER, Earl L (1931-) American				
oil	3	600-13,000	5,866	4,000
CARPENTER, G (19th C) British				
oil	1	9,790	9,790	9,790
CARPENTER, Margaret (1793-1872) British				
oil	2	3,740-16,065	9,902	3,740
CARPENTER, Percy (fl.1841-1858) British				
wc/d	1	1,784	1,784	1,784
CARPENTERO, Henri Joseph Gommarus (1820-1874) Belgian				
oil	4	775-10,141	3,317	1,166
CARPENTIER, Evariste (1845-1922) Belgian				
oil	4	1,018-19,418	12,342	12,932
CARPENTIER, Marguerite Jeanne (1886-1965) French				
oil	1	3,612	3,612	3,612
CARPENTIERS, Adrien (c.1713-1778) British				
oil	1	10,260	10,260	10,260
CARPI, Aldo (1886-1973) Italian				
oil	4	1,189-1,942	1,685	1,767
wc/d	5	486-1,916	870	647
CARPI, Girolamo da (1501-1556) Italian				
wc/d	2	6,000-15,000	10,500	6,000
CARPIONI, Giulio (1613-1679) Italian				
oil	3	3,700-53,167	22,008	9,158
CARR, David (19/20th C) British				
oil	2	3,078-3,740	3,409	3,078
wc/d	1	557	557	557
CARR, Emily M (1871-1945) Canadian				
oil	11	44,313-336,777	158,446	137,773
wc/d	5	28,803-84,194	55,824	64,834
CARR, Leslie (20th C) British				
oil	2	1,138-1,400	1,269	1,138
CARR, Lyle (1837-1908) American				
oil	1	10,000	10,000	10,000
CARR, Samuel S (1837-1908) American				
oil	2	5,000-7,000	6,000	5,000
CARR, Tom (1912-1977) British				
wc/d	2	623-4,488	2,555	623
CARR, Tom (1909-1999) British				
oil	4	5,208-36,000	19,587	5,520
wc/d	17	872-4,676	1,578	1,239
CARRA, Carlo (1881-1966) Italian				
oil	10	18,849-983,836	207,359	89,048
wc/d	7	2,497-10,924	5,403	4,757
CARRACCI, Annibale (1560-1609) Italian				
wc/d	1	2,141	2,141	2,141
CARRACCI, Lodovico (1555-1619) Italian				
oil	2	9,250-12,210,001	6,109,625	9,250
wc/d	3	2,180-50,000	19,193	5,400
CARRADE, Michel (1923-) French				
oil	1	1,844	1,844	1,844
CARRAND, Louis (1821-1899) French				
oil	3	1,360-2,577	1,918	1,818
CARRARESI, Eugenio (1893-1964) Italian				
oil	2	660-1,440	1,050	660

Name	No.	Price Range	Average	Median
CARRE, Ben (1883-1978) American				
oil	2	800-3,000	1,900	800
CARRE, Ketty (1882-1964) French				
wc/d	1	1,019	1,019	1,019
CARRE, Léon (1878-1942) French				
oil	1	2,675	2,675	2,675
wc/d	1	5,255	5,255	5,255
CARRE-SOUBIRAN, Victor (?-1897) French				
oil	1	5,130	5,130	5,130
CARREE, Michiel (1657-1747) Dutch				
oil	4	3,012-9,321	6,206	3,767
CARREGA, Ugo (1936-) Italian				
oil	1	494	494	494
wc/d	14	477-2,148	1,093	900
3D	1	2,057	2,057	2,057
CARRENO DE MIRANDA, Juan (1614-1685) Spanish				
oil	1	54,184	54,184	54,184
CARRENO, Anibal (1930-) Argentinian				
oil	1	2,500	2,500	2,500
CARRENO, Irene Sierra (1965-) Cuban				
oil	1	28,000	28,000	28,000
CARRENO, Mario (1913-1999) Cuban				
oil	3	19,000-55,000	41,333	50,000
wc/d	3	14,000-22,000	18,333	19,000
CARRENO, Omar (1927-) Venezuelan				
oil	3	745-2,790	1,565	1,160
CARRER, Guido (1902-1984) Italian				
oil	1	3,366	3,366	3,366
CARRERA, Augustin (1878-?) French				
oil	2	5,500-9,678	7,589	5,500
CARRERE, F Ouillon (20th C) ?				
3D	1	2,958	2,958	2,958
CARRESSE, Pierre (20th C) French				
oil	1	1,150	1,150	1,150
CARREY, Georges (1902-1953) French				
oil	3	1,168-1,491	1,303	1,252
CARRICK, Desmond (1930-) Irish				
oil	3	2,420-4,080	3,202	3,107
CARRICK, John Mulcaster (1833-1896) British				
oil	3	661-8,004	3,419	1,593
CARRICK, William (1879-1964) British				
oil	3	1,196-1,283	1,244	1,253
CARRIER-BELLEUSE (19/20th C) French				
3D	3	2,134-19,640	8,058	2,400
CARRIER-BELLEUSE, Albert (1824-1887) French				
3D	31	1,730-60,000	9,797	5,670
CARRIER-BELLEUSE, Louis (1848-1913) French				
oil	3	5,301-16,530	11,000	11,169
3D	1	2,914	2,914	2,914
CARRIER-BELLEUSE, Pierre (1851-1932) French				
oil	1	7,620	7,620	7,620
wc/d	14	1,204-46,980	8,187	3,568
CARRIERE, Eugène (1849-1906) French				
oil	13	2,356-51,302	14,171	8,500
wc/d	2	850-2,356	1,603	850
CARRIERE, R O (19/20th C) French				
wc/d	1	4,320	4,320	4,320
CARRIES, Jean (1855-1894) French				
3D	5	2,552-38,713	16,426	16,632
CARRINGTON, Dora (1893-1932) British				
oil	1	54,600	54,600	54,600
wc/d	1	885	885	885
CARRINGTON, James Yates (1857-1892) British				
oil	1	40,000	40,000	40,000
CARRINGTON, Leonora (1917-) British				
oil	6	65,000-480,000	169,166	110,000
wc/d	10	1,521-50,000	12,610	8,803
CARRINO, Nicola (1932-) Italian				
oil	1	2,983	2,983	2,983
wc/d	1	530	530	530
3D	1	4,500	4,500	4,500

Name	No.	Price Range	Average	Median
CARROL, Robert (1934-) American				
oil	6	1,060-1,942	1,486	1,312
wc/d	1	656	656	656
CARROLL, John (1892-1959) American				
oil	3	1,800-26,000	10,866	4,800
CARROLL, Lawrence (1954-) American				
3D	1	16,000	16,000	16,000
CARROLL, Pamela (1948-) American				
oil	1	1,000	1,000	1,000
CARSE, Alexander (c.1770-1843) British				
oil	1	10,560	10,560	10,560
CARSE, William (19th C) British				
oil	1	10,680	10,680	10,680
CARSON, Karen (1958-) American				
wc/d	1	2,000	2,000	2,000
CARSON, Robert Taylor (1919-) British				
oil	20	623-20,460	5,486	3,186
wc/d	4	554-1,239	867	588
CARSTAIRS, John Paddy (1916-1970) British				
wc/d	1	1,295	1,295	1,295
CARSTENSEN, Andreas Christian Riis (1844-1906) Danish				
oil	2	812-1,563	1,187	812
CARSTENSEN, Claus (1957-) Danish				
oil	1	805	805	805
wc/d	1	1,940	1,940	1,940
CARSTENSEN, Ebba (1885-1967) Danish				
oil	4	568-3,898	1,721	794
CARTE, Antoine (1886-1954) Belgian				
oil	6	3,131-190,816	36,475	4,789
wc/d	3	5,488-131,429	50,314	14,027
CARTER, Clarence Holbrook (1904-2000) American				
oil	4	510-9,500	3,065	1,000
wc/d	3	425-550	483	475
CARTER, Dennis Malone (1827-1881) American				
oil	2	1,300-27,500	14,400	1,300
CARTER, Frank Thomas (1853-1934) British				
oil	4	555-2,148	1,006	623
CARTER, Gary (1939-) American				
oil	3	1,250-39,000	14,750	4,000
CARTER, Henry Barlow (1803-1867) British				
oil	1	1,740	1,740	1,740
wc/d	6	582-4,628	1,678	735
CARTER, Howard (1873-1939) British				
wc/d	2	7,788-10,788	9,288	7,788
CARTER, Joseph Newington (1835-1871) British				
wc/d	2	821-1,251	1,036	821
CARTER, Poindexter Page (19/20th C) American				
oil	1	3,000	3,000	3,000
CARTER, Pruett A (1891-1955) American				
oil	4	900-22,000	7,575	1,400
CARTER, Richard Harry (1839-1911) British				
wc/d	3	800-2,848	1,564	1,044
CARTER, Samuel (19th C) British				
oil	1	2,941	2,941	2,941
CARTER, Samuel John (1835-1892) British				
oil	3	1,770-7,920	4,563	4,000
CARTER, Vernon P (20th C) Irish?				
oil	1	2,268	2,268	2,268
CARTER, William Sylvester (1909-) American				
oil	1	4,000	4,000	4,000
wc/d	1	700	700	700
CARTIER, A (19th C) ?				
3D	1	2,102	2,102	2,102
CARTIER, Eugene (1861-1943) French				
oil	11	479-7,432	1,691	959
CARTIER, Jacques (1907-2001) French				
oil	16	539-32,603	4,682	1,798
wc/d	14	535-2,803	947	662
3D	2	2,038-4,195	3,116	2,038
CARTIER, Max (20th C) French?				
3D	1	1,894	1,894	1,894

Name	No.	Price Range	Average	Median
CARTIER, Thomas (1879-1943) French				
3D	4	2,799-9,000	4,915	3,461
CARTON, Jean (1912-1988) French				
3D	1	19,140	19,140	19,140
CARTWRIGHT, Isabel Branson (1885-?) American				
oil	1	1,700	1,700	1,700
CARTWRIGHT, Joseph (1789-1829) British				
wc/d	1	2,595	2,595	2,595
CARTWRIGHT, W P (fl.1883-1896) British				
oil	1	1,211	1,211	1,211
CARTY, Ciaran (20th C) Irish				
wc/d	1	1,215	1,215	1,215
CARUELLE D'ALIGNY, Theodore (1798-1871) French				
wc/d	2	911-4,757	2,834	911
CARUS, Carl Gustav (1789-1869) German				
oil	3	31,808-77,143	48,415	36,294
CARUSO, Bruno (1927-) Italian				
oil	3	1,721-3,884	2,463	1,784
wc/d	7	420-1,401	1,027	1,018
CARUTTI, Augusto (1875-?) Italian				
oil	1	7,642	7,642	7,642
CARVALLO, Feliciano (1920-) Venezuelan				
oil	2	700-3,255	1,977	700
CARVEN, Luis Albert (20th C) Italian?				
3D	1	2,664	2,664	2,664
CARY, Evelyn Rumsey (1855-1924) American				
oil	1	1,500	1,500	1,500
CARY, William de la Montagne (1840-1922) American				
oil	2	25,000-40,000	32,500	25,000
wc/d	1	1,500	1,500	1,500
CARZOU, Jean (1907-2000) French				
oil	10	1,654-21,626	5,675	3,816
wc/d	11	500-2,385	1,336	1,452
CASADEMONT POU, Francesc d'Asis (1923-) Spanish				
oil	1	1,334	1,334	1,334
CASAGEMAS, Carlos (1881-1901) Spanish				
wc/d	1	3,240	3,240	3,240
CASAMADA, Alberto Rafols (1923-) Spanish				
oil	5	1,492-45,755	13,017	7,459
wc/d	3	1,381-2,141	1,634	1,381
CASANOVA Y ESTORACH, Antonio (1847-1896) Spanish				
oil	5	3,784-36,122	16,305	13,066
wc/d	1	2,411	2,411	2,411
CASANOVA, Agostino di (16th C) Italian				
oil	1	35,270	35,270	35,270
CASANOVA, Alexandre (1770-1844) French?				
oil	1	88,699	88,699	88,699
CASANOVA, Francesco Giuseppe (1727-1802) Italian				
oil	2	12,098-28,000	20,049	12,098
wc/d	2	476-2,917	1,696	476
CASANOVA, Jean (1887-1968) Swiss				
3D	2	2,447-3,100	2,773	2,447
CASCELLA, Basilio and Tommaso (20th C) Italian				
3D	1	2,945	2,945	2,945
CASCELLA, Michele (1892-1989) Italian				
oil	39	3,053-46,378	13,985	9,955
wc/d	13	2,000-23,143	8,616	7,000
CASCELLA, Pietro (1921-) Italian				
wc/d	1	934	934	934
3D	1	3,562	3,562	3,562
CASCELLA, Tommaso (1951-) Italian				
oil	3	502-2,356	1,432	1,438
wc/d	13	468-4,595	2,088	2,506
3D	2	1,885-3,102	2,493	1,885
CASCELLA, Tommaso (1890-1968) Italian				
oil	1	5,255	5,255	5,255
CASCIARO, Giuseppe (1861-1943) Italian				
oil	19	941-10,014	4,214	4,243
wc/d	35	1,054-9,425	3,383	2,589
CASCIARO, Guido (1900-1963) Italian				
oil	7	1,090-6,126	3,596	3,534

Name	No.	Price Range	Average	Median
CASE, Edmund E (1840-1919) American				
oil	2	1,400-3,750	2,575	1,400
CASEBIER, Cecil (1920-1996) American				
oil	1	1,900	1,900	1,900
CASELLI, Giuseppe (1893-1976) Italian				
oil	1	1,427	1,427	1,427
CASEMBROOT, Abraham (17th C) Dutch				
wc/d	1	3,000	3,000	3,000
CASENELLI, Victor (20th C) American				
wc/d	2	550-2,100	1,325	550
CASEY, Comhghall (1976-) Irish				
oil	2	2,338-2,432	2,385	2,338
CASHIN, Patrick (20th C) Irish				
oil	2	1,130-1,942	1,536	1,130
CASIA BIANCA (1864-1931) French?				
oil	1	4,435	4,435	4,435
CASILE, Alfred (1847-1909) French				
oil	1	2,805	2,805	2,805
CASILEAR, John W (1811-1893) American				
oil	2	3,500-4,250	3,875	3,500
CASISSA, Nicola (?-1730) Italian				
oil	2	36,122-36,990	36,556	36,122
CASNELLI, Victor (1867-1961) American				
wc/d	1	4,000	4,000	4,000
CASORATI, Felice (1883-1963) Italian				
oil	13	2,870-407,075	109,287	69,966
wc/d	9	3,034-30,247	14,305	9,103
3D	2	37,369-37,369	37,369	37,369
CASORATI, Francesco (1934-) Italian				
oil	2	895-1,226	1,060	895
CASPAR, Karl (1879-1956) German				
oil	1	13,597	13,597	13,597
CASPAR-FILSER, Maria (1878-1968) German				
oil	3	630-5,400	3,580	4,712
CASS, M L (19th C) American				
oil	1	4,500	4,500	4,500
CASSAIGNE, Joseph (1871-?) French				
3D	1	20,880	20,880	20,880
CASSANDRE, Adolphe (1901-1968) French				
wc/d	4	707-6,062	3,261	2,155
CASSAS, Louis-François (1756-1827) French				
wc/d	5	1,903-26,466	9,039	6,319
CASSATT, Mary (1844-1926) American				
oil	2	60,000-3,800,000	1,930,000	60,000
wc/d	9	7,250-600,000	193,694	120,000
CASSELLI, Henry (1946-) American				
wc/d	1	1,600	1,600	1,600
3D	1	8,750	8,750	8,750
CASSIDY, Ira Diamond Gerald (1879-1934) American				
oil	7	5,000-50,000	22,428	18,000
wc/d	1	12,000	12,000	12,000
CASSIE, James (1819-1879) British				
oil	3	7,392-11,570	9,168	8,544
wc/d	1	766	766	766
CASSIERS, Henry (1858-1944) Belgian				
oil	5	954-7,007	3,137	2,411
wc/d	5	655-4,917	1,988	1,502
CASSIGNEUL, Jean Pierre (1935-) French				
oil	14	7,500-140,000	45,347	33,000
CASSINARI, Bruno (1912-1992) Italian				
oil	25	1,821-67,315	17,925	12,945
wc/d	21	728-3,996	2,528	2,921
3D	1	2,071	2,071	2,071
CASSINETTO, Jack (1944-) American				
oil	1	2,750	2,750	2,750
CASSON, A J (1898-1992) Canadian				
oil	1	2,349	2,349	2,349
CASSON, Alfred Joseph (1898-1992) Canadian				
oil	32	6,647-81,043	24,114	18,235
wc/d	4	1,476-29,526	16,888	9,965
CASSON, Sir Hugh (1910-1999) British				
wc/d	36	592-2,958	1,507	1,392

Name	No.	Price Range	Average	Median
CASTAGNA, Blas (1935-) Argentinian				
oil	1	5,000	5,000	5,000
wc/d	1	14,000	14,000	14,000
3D	3	3,200-5,000	4,400	5,000
CASTAGNINO, Juan Carlos (1908-1972) Argentinian				
oil	7	9,000-25,000	14,285	13,500
wc/d	3	2,000-15,200	6,533	2,400
CASTAGNINO, Rodolfo (1893-1978) Italian				
3D	1	8,414	8,414	8,414
CASTAGNOLA, Gabriele (1828-1883) Italian				
oil	1	1,480	1,480	1,480
CASTAN, Gustave-Eugène (1823-1892) Swiss				
oil	13	973-17,947	5,163	3,053
CASTAN, Pierre Jean Edmond (1817-1892) French				
oil	1	3,270	3,270	3,270
CASTANEDA, Alfredo (1938-) Mexican				
oil	3	14,000-18,000	15,666	15,000
wc/d	1	7,000	7,000	7,000
CASTANEDA, Felipe (1933-) Mexican				
3D	6	3,000-47,500	12,845	6,000
CASTANO, Gabriel (20th C) Cuban				
wc/d	1	2,000	2,000	2,000
CASTEELS, Pauwel (17th C) Flemish				
oil	1	17,897	17,897	17,897
CASTEELS, Peter II (fl.1690-1699) Flemish				
oil	3	8,192-23,140	15,158	14,143
CASTEELS, Peter III (1684-1749) Flemish				
oil	6	5,092-85,000	27,330	14,800
CASTEL, Moshe (1909-1992) Israeli				
oil	19	2,000-80,000	21,710	15,000
wc/d	5	1,800-25,000	9,840	6,600
CASTELL, Anton (1810-1867) German				
oil	2	1,641-2,108	1,874	1,641
CASTELLAN, Paride (1911-1988) Italian				
oil	6	643-1,334	1,032	1,030
CASTELLANI, Charles (1838-1913) French				
oil	1	27,520	27,520	27,520
CASTELLANI, Enrico (1930-) Italian				
oil	17	9,204-247,800	64,719	49,192
wc/d	2	10,320-13,275	11,797	10,320
3D	2	11,127-175,808	93,467	11,127
CASTELLANOS, Andres (1956-) Spanish				
oil	2	596-2,225	1,410	596
CASTELLANOS, Julio (1905-1947) Mexican				
wc/d	1	11,000	11,000	11,000
CASTELLI, Alessandro (1809-1902) Italian				
oil	1	3,414	3,414	3,414
CASTELLI, Carmen Dede Bischoff (1936-) Swiss				
oil	1	11,656	11,656	11,656
CASTELLI, Luciano (1951-) Swiss				
oil	10	1,027-31,069	9,872	4,685
wc/d	6	2,855-22,898	9,365	2,945
CASTELLO, Giovanni Battista (1547-1637) Italian				
oil	1	14,887	14,887	14,887
wc/d	2	10,330-11,000	10,665	10,330
CASTELLON, Federico (1914-1971) American				
oil	1	32,500	32,500	32,500
wc/d	2	500-3,780	2,140	500
CASTELLS CAPURRO, Enrique (1913-1987) Uruguayan				
oil	1	2,400	2,400	2,400
wc/d	3	1,000-1,700	1,433	1,600
CASTEX-DEGRANGE, Adolphe Louis (1840-1918) French				
oil	2	2,000-3,000	2,500	2,000
CASTIGLIONE, Giovanni Benedetto (1616-1670) Italian				
wc/d	1	3,107	3,107	3,107
CASTIGLIONE, Giovanni Francesco (1641-1710) Italian				
oil	1	46,250	46,250	46,250
CASTIGLIONE, Giuseppe (1829-1908) Italian				
oil	3	3,156-30,000	12,218	3,500
CASTILLA, Marco (20th C) ?				
oil	2	1,169-3,612	2,390	1,169

Name	No.	Price Range	Average	Median
CASTILLO Y SAAVEDRA, Antonio del (1603-1667) Spanish				
wc/d	1	3,700	3,700	3,700
CASTILLO, Esteban (20th C) Colombian?				
oil	1	420	420	420
wc/d	1	1,630	1,630	1,630
CASTILLO, Jorge (1933-) Spanish				
oil	11	908-24,110	8,351	7,176
wc/d	7	538-2,631	1,206	718
CASTILLO, Marcos (1897-1966) Venezuelan				
oil	2	1,440-2,095	1,767	1,440
wc/d	1	605	605	605
CASTLE, Barry (20th C) British				
oil	1	2,422	2,422	2,422
CASTONGUAY, Gerard (1933-) Canadian				
oil	1	1,763	1,763	1,763
CASTRES, Edouard (1838-1902) Swiss				
oil	1	4,579	4,579	4,579
wc/d	1	1,296	1,296	1,296
CASTRES, Edouard Gaspard (1881-1964) Swiss				
oil	1	2,655	2,655	2,655
CASTRO CIRES, Raimundo (1894-1970) Spanish				
oil	1	1,430	1,430	1,430
CASTRO ORTEGA, Pedro (1956-) Spanish				
oil	3	1,308-2,616	1,744	1,308
wc/d	2	3,416-3,416	3,416	3,416
CASTRO, Bernardo Simonet (1914-) Spanish				
oil	1	1,600	1,600	1,600
CASTRO, Enrique (20th C) Argentinian				
oil	1	2,000	2,000	2,000
CASTRO, Fabian de (1868-?) Spanish				
oil	1	1,532	1,532	1,532
CASTRO, Laureys A (17th C) French				
oil	1	8,464	8,464	8,464
CASTRO, Leon Pedro (20th C) Venezuelan				
oil	2	1,160-1,720	1,440	1,160
CASTRO, Lorenzo (17th C) Spanish				
oil	1	55,000	55,000	55,000
CASTRO, Lourdes (1930-) Portuguese				
3D	2	5,437-62,909	34,173	5,437
CASTRO, Sergio de (1922-) Argentinian				
oil	7	974-12,361	3,702	2,160
wc/d	3	1,549-1,668	1,592	1,560
CAT, Roland (1943-) French				
wc/d	9	972-16,406	6,162	6,126
CATALA YUSTE, Jose (1959-) Spanish				
oil	1	2,735	2,735	2,735
CATALANI, Alessandro (1897-1942) Italian				
oil	1	1,784	1,784	1,784
CATALDI, Renato (20th C) Brazilian				
oil	1	1,062	1,062	1,062
CATANO, F (19th C) Italian				
wc/d	1	1,649	1,649	1,649
CATARSINI, Alfredo (1899-1993) Italian				
oil	12	537-2,744	1,089	825
CATEL, Franz Ludwig (1778-1856) German				
oil	1	19,268	19,268	19,268
CATERINA, Dario (1955-) Belgian				
oil	4	647-2,625	1,235	655
CATHELIN, Bernard (1919-2004) French				
oil	1	9,633	9,633	9,633
CATHERWOOD, Frederick (1799-1854) British				
wc/d	5	1,440-9,000	4,788	4,500
CATLIN, George (1796-1872) American				
wc/d	1	6,000	6,000	6,000
CATOIS, Gustave A (?) American?				
oil	1	1,000	1,000	1,000
CATS, Jacob (1741-1799) Dutch				
wc/d	2	1,527-6,055	3,791	1,527
CATTANEO, Achille (1872-1931) Italian				
oil	8	510-4,077	1,901	1,911

Name	No.	Price Range	Average	Median
CATTELAN, Maurizio (1960-) Italian				
oil	4	2,301-880,000	315,712	70,800
wc/d	8	1,850-129,500	31,988	3,009
3D	9	6,997-647,500	257,421	194,700
CATTI, Aurelio (1895-1966) Italian				
wc/d	1	3,879	3,879	3,879
CATTI, Michele (1855-1914) Italian				
oil	2	14,055-16,649	15,352	14,055
wc/d	1	1,942	1,942	1,942
CAUCHIE, Paul (1875-1952) Belgian				
wc/d	3	570-7,151	3,508	2,803
CAUCHOIS, Eugène-Henri (1850-1911) French				
oil	23	763-20,565	5,636	4,396
CAUER, Emil (19th C) German				
3D	1	7,441	7,441	7,441
CAUER, Robert (elder) (1831-1893) German				
3D	1	4,123	4,123	4,123
CAULA, Sigismondo (1637-1713) Italian				
wc/d	2	1,553-12,950	7,251	1,553
CAULFIELD, Patrick (1936-) British				
oil	2	556,800-850,500	703,650	556,800
CAULLERY, Louis de (16/17th C) French/Flemish				
oil	3	9,633-49,840	34,657	44,500
CAULLERY, Louis de and CLEVE, Hendrick van III (16th C) French/Flemish				
oil	1	8,304	8,304	8,304
CAULLET, Albert (1875-1950) Belgian				
oil	1	1,492	1,492	1,492
CAUR, Arpana (1954-) Indian				
oil	2	7,500-14,000	10,750	7,500
wc/d	1	7,000	7,000	7,000
CAUVIN, Louis Edouard Isidore (1816-1900) French				
wc/d	1	1,038	1,038	1,038
CAUVY, Léon (1874-1933) French				
oil	10	1,794-28,897	9,131	4,909
wc/d	6	2,589-9,062	4,907	3,884
CAUWER, Émile Pierre Joseph de (1828-1873) Belgian				
oil	2	4,285-10,510	7,397	4,285
CAVAEL, Rolf (1898-1979) German				
oil	12	540-17,199	6,720	5,088
wc/d	8	494-2,293	1,113	892
CAVAGLIERI, Mario (1887-1969) Italian				
oil	2	7,857-12,671	10,264	7,857
wc/d	1	3,025	3,025	3,025
CAVAGNA, Giovanni Paolo (1556-1627) Italian				
wc/d	1	3,884	3,884	3,884
CAVAILLES, Jules (1901-1977) French				
oil	11	3,540-42,000	15,054	12,000
wc/d	1	6,055	6,055	6,055
CAVALCANTI, Andrea di Lazzaro (1412-1462) Italian				
3D	1	36,308	36,308	36,308
CAVALCANTI, Emiliano di (1897-1976) Brazilian				
oil	5	35,000-410,000	129,000	70,000
wc/d	5	400-19,000	11,480	13,000
CAVALERI, Ludovico (1867-1942) Italian				
oil	3	1,019-11,781	4,691	1,274
CAVALIERE, Alik (1926-1998) Italian				
3D	4	3,588-13,185	7,556	4,451
CAVALIERE, Dan (1928-) American				
oil	1	4,500	4,500	4,500
CAVALLERI, Vittorio (1860-1938) Italian				
oil	4	1,816-5,966	3,217	2,182
CAVALLI, Emanuele (1904-1981) Italian				
oil	1	3,857	3,857	3,857
CAVALLON, Giorgio (1904-1989) American				
oil	2	12,000-26,000	19,000	12,000
wc/d	1	1,900	1,900	1,900
CAVALORI, Mirabello (c.1510-1572) Italian				
wc/d	2	5,301-18,500	11,900	5,301
CAVANAUGH, Tom Richard (1923-) American				
oil	1	1,500	1,500	1,500

Name	No.	Price Range	Average	Median
CAVE, Peter le (fl.1769-1810) British				
oil	2	1,298-1,770	1,534	1,298
wc/d	3	662-3,534	1,693	885
CAVEDONE, Giacomo (1577-1660) Italian				
wc/d	1	8,325	8,325	8,325
CAVELIER, Pierre Jules (1814-1896) French				
3D	1	17,800	17,800	17,800
CAVELLINI, Achille (1914-1990) Italian				
oil	1	3,857	3,857	3,857
wc/d	3	598-4,176	2,454	2,589
3D	1	3,625	3,625	3,625
CAVICCHIOLI, Fernando (1862-1941) Italian				
oil	1	1,011	1,011	1,011
CAVIEZEL, Ratus (1893-1980) Swiss				
oil	1	2,125	2,125	2,125
CAWDREY, Nancy Dunlop (1948-) American				
wc/d	2	4,000-4,000	4,000	4,000
CAWEN, Alvar (1886-1935) Finnish				
oil	1	89,178	89,178	89,178
CAWTHORNE, Christopher (20th C) British				
oil	1	1,940	1,940	1,940
CAWTHORNE, Neil (1936-) British				
oil	19	756-10,395	2,331	1,584
CAYLEY, Neville Henry Peniston (1853-1903) Australian				
wc/d	1	1,067	1,067	1,067
CAYON, Henri-Felix (1878-?) French				
oil	2	700-5,845	3,272	700
CAZIN, Jean Baptiste Louis (1782-1850) French				
oil	1	16,435	16,435	16,435
CAZIN, Jean Charles (1841-1901) French				
oil	6	2,342-5,724	4,192	4,000
CAZZANIGA, Carlo (1883-1936) Italian				
oil	1	3,625	3,625	3,625
CAZZANIGA, Giancarlo (1930-) Italian				
oil	20	671-5,696	2,347	2,314
wc/d	3	615-676	648	654
CECCARELLI, Naddo (14th C) Italian				
oil	1	1,903,000	1,903,000	1,903,000
CECCARINI, Alessandro (1825-1905) Italian				
oil	1	1,806	1,806	1,806
CECCHI, Adriano (1850-1936) Italian				
oil	2	1,200-5,041	3,120	1,200
CECCHI, Sergio (1921-1986) Italian				
oil	2	1,166-1,632	1,399	1,166
wc/d	1	800	800	800
CECCHINI, Antonio (1600-1680) Italian				
oil	1	1,796	1,796	1,796
CECCO di PIETRO (14th C) Italian				
oil	1	130,000	130,000	130,000
CECCOBELLI, Bruno (1952-) Italian				
oil	7	1,100-3,822	1,989	1,414
wc/d	54	418-9,555	2,746	1,784
3D	2	5,632-24,170	14,901	5,632
CECCONI, Alberto (1897-1971) Italian				
oil	2	1,030-1,455	1,242	1,030
CECCONI, Eugenio (1842-1903) Italian				
oil	5	1,908-7,767	5,214	4,685
wc/d	1	2,142	2,142	2,142
CECCONI, Niccolo (1835-?) Italian				
oil	1	1,946	1,946	1,946
CECCOTTI, Sergio (1935-) Italian				
oil	1	1,450	1,450	1,450
CECIONI, Adriano (1836-1886) Italian				
3D	1	6,000	6,000	6,000
CEDERGREN, Per Vilhelm (1823-1896) Swedish				
oil	1	1,371	1,371	1,371
wc/d	1	997	997	997
CEDERHOLM, Axel Fredrik (1780-1828) Swedish				
wc/d	1	1,123	1,123	1,123
CEDERSTROM, Eva (1909-1995) Finnish				
oil	6	1,753-6,078	2,880	2,038
wc/d	1	557	557	557

Name	No.	Price Range	Average	Median
CEDERSTROM, Gustaf (1845-1933) Swedish				
oil	2	5,733-140,137	72,935	5,733
CEDERSTROM, Ture Nikolaus (1843-1924) Swedish				
oil	3	744-9,500	3,913	1,496
CEDOR, Dieudonne L (1925-) Haitian				
oil	1	1,200	1,200	1,200
CELADA DA VIRGILIO, Ugo (1895-1995) Italian				
oil	8	1,676-9,062	4,775	4,438
wc/d	1	1,184	1,184	1,184
CELDRIN, Elizabeth (?) ?				
oil	1	3,403	3,403	3,403
CELEBRANO, Francesco (1729-1814) Italian				
oil	1	31,455	31,455	31,455
CELENTANO, Bernardo (1835-1863) Italian				
oil	1	1,958	1,958	1,958
CELENTANO, Daniel Ralph (1902-1980) American				
oil	1	10,000	10,000	10,000
wc/d	3	1,500-2,200	1,900	2,000
CELIBERTI, Giorgio (1929-) Italian				
oil	9	1,316-20,027	5,005	3,652
wc/d	8	1,178-3,937	1,919	1,360
CELLINI, Gaetano (1875-1957) Italian				
3D	1	2,577	2,577	2,577
CELMINS, Vija (1939-) American				
oil	1	500,000	500,000	500,000
CELOMMI, Pasquale (1860-1928) Italian				
oil	2	16,829-18,163	17,496	16,829
CELOMMI, Raffaello (19/20th C) Italian				
oil	2	3,045-6,442	4,743	3,045
CELOS, Julien (1884-?) Belgian				
oil	4	598-2,548	1,368	658
CENNI, Renato (1906-1977) Italian				
oil	1	1,598	1,598	1,598
wc/d	1	791	791	791
CENTURION, Emilio (1894-1970) Argentinian				
oil	6	1,800-40,000	14,350	4,000
CERACCHINI, Gisberto (1899-1982) Italian				
oil	4	819-4,671	2,023	967
wc/d	1	841	841	841
CERAMANO, Charles Ferdinand (1829-1909) Belgian				
oil	6	1,400-3,100	2,319	2,249
CERCONE, Ettore (1850-1896) Italian				
oil	3	611-2,917	1,728	1,657
CERETTI, Mino (1930-) Italian				
oil	1	1,457	1,457	1,457
wc/d	1	1,189	1,189	1,189
CERF, Ivan (1883-1963) Belgian				
oil	1	4,612	4,612	4,612
CERIA, Edmond (1884-1955) French				
oil	13	622-2,900	1,407	1,400
CERIEZ, Theodore (1832-1904) Belgian				
oil	2	3,371-8,342	5,856	3,371
CEROLI, Mario (1938-) Italian				
oil	1	4,057	4,057	4,057
wc/d	3	895-3,053	2,175	2,577
3D	9	2,016-8,604	5,270	5,256
CERONE, Giacinto (1957-2004) Italian				
3D	1	3,625	3,625	3,625
CERQUOZZI, Michelangelo and CODAZZI, Viviano (17th C) Italian				
oil	1	85,440	85,440	85,440
CERUTI, Giacomo (1698-1767) Italian				
oil	3	306,301-647,500	441,267	370,000
CERUTTI, Peter (20th C) ?				
oil	1	13,863	13,863	13,863
CERVELLI, Federico (1625-1700) Italian				
oil	2	21,626-39,705	30,665	21,626
CESAGE, Darain (?) American?				
oil	1	1,300	1,300	1,300
CESAR, Baldaccini (1921-1998) French				
oil	1	5,890	5,890	5,890
wc/d	19	608-62,183	10,553	6,450
3D	69	1,753-297,740	32,587	18,449

Name	No.	Price Range	Average	Median
CESARE, Ugo de (1950-) Italian				
oil	2	1,300-3,164	2,232	1,300
CESARI, Giuseppe (1568-1640) Italian				
wc/d	3	718-26,000	12,876	11,910
CESARI, Roberto (1949-) Italian				
oil	1	1,030	1,030	1,030
CESETTI, Giuseppe (1902-1990) Italian				
oil	17	2,658-11,781	6,247	6,049
wc/d	1	779	779	779
CESI, Bartolomeo (1556-1629) Italian				
wc/d	1	1,850	1,850	1,850
CEVAT, Nicolaas Frederick (1884-1955) Dutch				
oil	2	1,165-17,524	9,344	1,165
CEYTAIRE, Jean-Pierre (1946-) French				
oil	3	4,094-5,418	4,551	4,143
wc/d	1	506	506	506
3D	1	4,176	4,176	4,176
CEZANNE, Paul (1839-1906) French				
oil	3	109,120-9,200,000	5,384,706	6,845,000
wc/d	20	4,576-410,000	78,911	35,200
CHAB, Victor (1930-) Argentinian				
oil	7	1,500-12,000	5,585	4,800
CHABAA, Mohammed (1934-) Moroccan				
oil	2	5,740-6,310	6,025	5,740
CHABAL, Pierre Adrien (1819-1902) French				
wc/d	2	14,240-54,687	34,463	14,240
CHABANIAN, Arsene (1864-1949) French				
oil	5	732-3,397	1,722	1,079
wc/d	3	568-2,589	1,528	1,427
CHABAS, Maurice (1862-1947) French				
oil	4	613-10,356	3,367	1,071
wc/d	3	477-5,839	2,284	536
CHABAS, Paul (1869-1937) French				
oil	4	3,000-10,738	6,359	4,500
wc/d	1	3,801	3,801	3,801
CHABAUD, Auguste (1882-1955) French				
oil	14	559-12,397	3,803	2,625
wc/d	5	557-2,057	1,462	1,546
CHABOR, Moura (1905-1995) French				
oil	2	705-4,250	2,477	705
CHABOT, Hendrik (1894-1949) Dutch				
oil	1	30,575	30,575	30,575
3D	1	44,524	44,524	44,524
CHABRIER, G (?) ?				
oil	2	2,379-3,737	3,058	2,379
CHABRY, Leonce (1832-1883) French				
oil	1	3,461	3,461	3,461
CHACATON, Jean Nicolas Henri de (1813-?) French				
wc/d	1	1,286	1,286	1,286
CHACON, Sigfredo (20th C) South American?				
oil	1	3,720	3,720	3,720
wc/d	1	3,720	3,720	3,720
CHADWICK, Emma (1855-1932) Swedish				
oil	1	9,678	9,678	9,678
CHADWICK, Ernest Albert (1876-1955) British				
wc/d	2	1,600-6,726	4,163	1,600
CHADWICK, Lynn (1914-2003) British				
wc/d	6	1,740-5,664	3,453	2,457
3D	82	1,909-304,500	44,522	29,600
CHADWICK, William (1879-1962) American/British				
oil	2	2,500-8,000	5,250	2,500
CHAESE, Emilie (19th C) British?				
oil	1	1,600	1,600	1,600
CHAFFANEL, Eugène (19/20th C) French				
oil	1	1,098	1,098	1,098
CHAFFEE, Oliver N (1881-1944) American				
oil	2	800-2,100	1,450	800
CHAGALL, Marc (1887-1985) French/Russian				
oil	85	19,360-3,600,000	771,855	445,815
wc/d	105	2,400-1,800,000	128,257	49,192
CHAGOIT, R (19/20th C) French				
oil	1	3,600	3,600	3,600

Name	No.	Price Range	Average	Median
CHAHINE, Edgar (1874-1947) French				
oil	1	11,466	11,466	11,466
wc/d	1	1,230	1,230	1,230
CHAHNAZAR, Kouyoumdjian (20th C) Armenian				
oil	1	10,082	10,082	10,082
CHAIGNEAU, Jean Ferdinand (1830-1906) French				
oil	9	2,883-23,562	7,549	4,839
CHAIGNEAU, Paul (19/20th C) French				
oil	8	3,214-7,392	5,522	5,066
CHAILLOUX, Robert (1913-) French				
oil	13	900-3,128	1,794	1,616
CHAISSAC, Gaston (1910-1964) French				
oil	10	5,040-56,542	27,036	22,809
wc/d	16	1,214-50,396	7,496	3,996
3D	4	5,828-184,375	87,620	57,414
CHAKRAVARTY, Jayashri (1956-) Indian				
oil	1	8,500	8,500	8,500
CHALEYE, Jean (1878-1960) French				
oil	5	888-7,000	2,460	1,700
CHALFANT, Richard (1953-) American				
oil	1	1,500	1,500	1,500
CHALIAPIN, Boris (1904-1982) Russian				
oil	1	25,000	25,000	25,000
wc/d	2	3,461-17,480	10,470	3,461
CHALLE, Charles Michelange (1718-1778) French				
wc/d	1	1,580	1,580	1,580
CHALLENER, Frederick (1869-1959) Canadian				
oil	4	1,097-1,640	1,381	1,230
wc/d	1	369	369	369
CHALLIE, Jean Laurent (1880-1943) French				
oil	6	1,273-8,400	3,585	1,947
CHALLULAU, Marcel (20th C) French				
oil	2	1,000-1,221	1,110	1,000
CHALMERS, George Paul (1833-1878) British				
oil	5	846-6,195	2,323	1,435
CHALMERS, Hector (c.1849-1943) British				
oil	1	1,012	1,012	1,012
CHALMERS, John (19th C) British				
oil	2	2,562-3,500	3,031	2,562
CHALMERS, Victoria (1970-) British?				
oil	2	3,168-7,392	5,280	3,168
CHALON, Henry Bernard (1770-1849) British				
oil	2	64,750-71,820	68,285	64,750
CHALON, John James (1778-1854) British				
oil	1	2,000	2,000	2,000
wc/d	1	669	669	669
CHALON, Louis (1687-1741) Dutch				
oil	2	8,919-12,671	10,795	8,919
wc/d	1	2,400	2,400	2,400
CHALON, Louis (1866-1940) French				
3D	3	3,168-16,000	7,445	3,168
CHAMACO, Jorge (1954-) French?				
oil	1	2,827	2,827	2,827
CHAMAILLARD, Ernest (1862-1930) French				
oil	1	7,068	7,068	7,068
CHAMAROFF, Paul (20th C) French?				
oil	1	12,899	12,899	12,899
CHAMBARD, Louis Leopold (1811-1895) French				
3D	1	7,642	7,642	7,642
CHAMBAS, Jean Paul (1947-) French				
oil	3	950-2,525	1,591	1,300
wc/d	1	836	836	836
CHAMBERLAIN, Brenda (1912-1971) British				
oil	2	662-783	722	662
wc/d	1	1,638	1,638	1,638
CHAMBERLAIN, John (1927-) American				
oil	1	45,000	45,000	45,000
3D	20	6,000-900,000	166,670	100,000
CHAMBERLIN, Percy (19/20th C) British				
wc/d	1	1,147	1,147	1,147
CHAMBERS, C Bosseron (1882-1964) American				
oil	1	2,600	2,600	2,600

Name	No.	Price Range	Average	Median
CHAMBERS, George (jnr) (1830-?) British				
oil	3	592-6,228	2,850	1,730
wc/d	1	2,244	2,244	2,244
CHAMBERS, George (snr) (1803-1840) British				
oil	4	573-10,620	4,362	2,363
wc/d	1	6,574	6,574	6,574
CHAMBERS, George (19th C) British				
oil	1	1,740	1,740	1,740
CHAMBERS, Thomas (1808-1866) American				
oil	1	90,000	90,000	90,000
CHAMBERT, Eric (1902-1988) Swedish				
oil	1	1,272	1,272	1,272
CHAMBON, Emile François (1905-1993) Swiss				
oil	6	666-15,263	3,835	1,249
CHAMBRY, Pierre (?) French?				
wc/d	1	1,607	1,607	1,607
CHAMIZO, Didier (1951-) ?				
oil	1	21,359	21,359	21,359
CHAMPAGNE, Horace (1937-) Canadian				
wc/d	15	530-4,052	1,812	1,394
CHAMPIN, Amelie (19th C) French				
oil	1	1,138	1,138	1,138
CHAMPION, Theo (1887-1952) German				
oil	4	1,239-5,839	3,653	3,649
CHAMPNEY, Benjamin (1817-1907) American				
oil	5	650-28,000	8,750	5,500
wc/d	1	1,500	1,500	1,500
CHAMPNEY, James Wells (1843-1903) American				
oil	1	900	900	900
wc/d	3	375-1,300	875	950
CHANCEL, Benoit (1819-1891) French				
oil	1	1,420	1,420	1,420
CHANCO, Roland (1914-) French				
oil	2	1,790-2,552	2,171	1,790
wc/d	2	771-1,130	950	771
CHANCRIN, René (1920-1981) French				
oil	2	4,451-5,153	4,802	4,451
CHANDRA, Avinash (1931-) British				
oil	1	70,000	70,000	70,000
wc/d	14	2,464-22,880	8,935	6,055
CHANEY, Lester Joseph (1907-) American				
oil	3	1,000-2,700	2,066	2,500
CHANG YU SHU (1900-1966) Chinese				
oil	1	26,736	26,736	26,736
CHANTEREAU, Jerome François (?-1757) French				
wc/d	1	2,221	2,221	2,221
CHANTREY, Sir Francis (1781-1842) British				
3D	1	19,030	19,030	19,030
CHANTRON, Alexandre Jacques (1842-1918) French				
oil	3	2,670-4,734	3,468	3,000
CHANTRON, Antoine (1771-1842) French				
wc/d	1	4,601	4,601	4,601
CHAPAUD, Marc (1914-) French				
oil	1	1,000	1,000	1,000
CHAPELAIN-MIDY, Roger (1904-1992) French				
oil	9	605-4,835	2,507	1,874
wc/d	1	727	727	727
CHAPELET, Roger (1902-1995) French				
wc/d	2	1,870-9,276	5,573	1,870
CHAPELLE, David la (1960-) American				
wc/d	1	8,325	8,325	8,325
CHAPELLE, J (19th C) French				
oil	1	3,500	3,500	3,500
CHAPELLIER, Jose (1946-) Belgian				
oil	1	1,286	1,286	1,286
CHAPERON, Claude (fl.1692) French				
oil	1	12,000	12,000	12,000
CHAPERON, Eugène (1857-?) French				
oil	1	1,808	1,808	1,808
CHAPERON, Philippe Marie (1823-1907) French				
wc/d	1	1,285	1,285	1,285

Name	No.	Price Range	Average	Median
CHAPIN, Bryant (1859-1927) American				
oil	1	6,500	6,500	6,500
CHAPIN, C H (19th C) American				
oil	1	4,750	4,750	4,750
CHAPIN, Charles H (1830-1889) American				
oil	1	5,000	5,000	5,000
wc/d	1	4,500	4,500	4,500
CHAPIN, Francis (1899-1965) American				
oil	1	4,000	4,000	4,000
CHAPIRO, Jacques (1887-1972) Russian				
oil	11	1,420-10,014	4,128	3,078
wc/d	2	693-1,259	976	693
CHAPKIN, Mikhail Fedorovich (20th C) Russian				
oil	1	2,580	2,580	2,580
CHAPLIN, Arthur (1869-1935) French				
oil	1	2,408	2,408	2,408
CHAPLIN, Charles (1825-1891) French				
oil	8	2,476-70,000	16,090	4,861
CHAPLIN, Elisabeth (1890-1982) French				
oil	1	6,429	6,429	6,429
CHAPMAN, Carlton Theodore (1860-1925) American				
oil	1	1,600	1,600	1,600
CHAPMAN, Charles S (1879-1962) American				
oil	1	1,700	1,700	1,700
CHAPMAN, Conrad Wise (1842-1910) American				
oil	11	8,000-55,000	30,181	35,000
CHAPMAN, Dinos and Jake (20th C) British				
wc/d	1	22,880	22,880	22,880
3D	4	4,810-44,400	25,346	10,175
CHAPMAN, George (1908-1993) British				
oil	2	1,066-1,066	1,066	1,066
CHAPMAN, John Gadsby (1808-1889) American				
oil	3	1,800-23,000	15,600	22,000
CHAPMAN, John Watkins (1832-1903) British				
oil	2	905-2,700	1,802	905
CHAPMAN, Julie T (1963-) American				
oil	1	4,000	4,000	4,000
CHAPMAN, Margaret (20th C) British				
wc/d	1	2,457	2,457	2,457
CHAPOVAL, Youla (1919-1951) French/Russian				
oil	4	5,068-11,973	7,831	6,555
CHAPPEE, Julien (19/20th C) French				
oil	2	1,092-6,429	3,760	1,092
CHAPPELL, Reuben (1870-1940) British				
oil	2	2,300-6,747	4,523	2,300
wc/d	13	440-4,200	1,270	815
CHAPU, Henri Michel Antoine (1833-1891) French				
3D	1	2,336	2,336	2,336
CHARAVEL, Paul (1877-1961) French				
oil	2	1,171-2,160	1,665	1,171
CHARBONNEAU, Georges (19th C) French				
oil	1	1,823	1,823	1,823
CHARBONNIER, Alexis Ernest (1846-1932) French				
oil	1	1,169	1,169	1,169
CHARCHOUNE (1888-1975) Russian				
oil	1	9,301	9,301	9,301
wc/d	1	2,108	2,108	2,108
CHARCHOUNE, Serge (1888-1975) Russian				
oil	51	634-47,881	10,850	8,026
wc/d	10	454-10,138	2,671	1,079
CHARDIGNY, Jules (?-1892) French				
oil	1	2,548	2,548	2,548
CHARDIN, Jean Baptiste Simeon (1699-1779) French				
oil	2	21,082-580,000	300,541	21,082
CHARDIN, Paul Louis Leger (1833-?) French				
wc/d	1	1,056	1,056	1,056
CHARDON, Charles (1858-1929) French?				
oil	1	3,696	3,696	3,696
CHARETTE-DUVAL, François (1807-1895) Belgian				
oil	1	5,482	5,482	5,482
CHARIGNY, Andre Auguste (1902-2000) French				
oil	1	1,405	1,405	1,405

Name	No.	Price Range	Average	Median
CHARKAOUI, Abdelaziz (1963-) Moroccan				
oil	2	6,310-10,327	8,318	6,310
CHARLEMAGNE, Adolf-Jossifowitsch (1826-1901) Russian				
wc/d	1	9,918	9,918	9,918
CHARLEMAGNE, Iosef Iosefovich (1824-1870) Russian				
wc/d	1	20,640	20,640	20,640
CHARLEMONT, Eduard (1848-1906) Austrian				
oil	7	752-27,568	8,049	4,816
CHARLEMONT, Hugo (1850-1939) Austrian				
oil	3	4,601-21,750	13,468	14,055
wc/d	2	400-726	563	400
CHARLES, James (1851-1906) British				
oil	6	707-10,500	3,046	1,100
CHARLESWORTH, Rod (1955-) Canadian				
oil	11	665-1,476	1,033	851
CHARLET, Émile (1851-?) Belgian				
oil	3	705-4,359	2,039	1,054
CHARLET, Frans (1862-1928) Belgian				
oil	6	776-4,241	2,280	1,870
CHARLIER, Jacques (1720-1790) French				
wc/d	2	701-2,351	1,526	701
CHARLOT, Jean (1898-1979) Mexican/French				
oil	3	2,000-16,000	6,833	2,500
wc/d	2	530-2,500	1,515	530
CHARLOT, Louis (1878-1951) French				
oil	2	1,918-2,259	2,088	1,918
CHARLOT, Paul (1906-1985) French				
wc/d	1	1,288	1,288	1,288
CHARLTON, Alan (1948-) British				
oil	1	19,265	19,265	19,265
CHARLTON, George J (1899-1979) British				
oil	11	443-1,197	677	598
wc/d	4	636-1,392	928	636
CHARLTON, John (1849-1917) British				
oil	4	1,700-4,500	2,620	1,980
CHARLTON, Maria (20th C) Irish?				
oil	1	1,818	1,818	1,818
CHARMAISON, Raymond Louis (1876-1955) French				
oil	1	2,990	2,990	2,990
CHARMAN, Frederick Montague (1894-1921) American				
wc/d	1	1,100	1,100	1,100
CHARMY, Emilie (1877-1974) French				
oil	2	1,546-1,580	1,563	1,546
CHARON, Guy (1927-) French				
oil	1	7,500	7,500	7,500
CHAROUX, Siegfried (1896-1967) Austrian				
wc/d	1	478	478	478
3D	2	3,762-7,080	5,421	3,762
CHAROY, Bernard (1929-) French				
oil	1	1,520	1,520	1,520
CHARPENTIER, Alexandre (1856-1909) French				
3D	1	12,845	12,845	12,845
CHARPENTIER, Auguste (1813-1880) French				
oil	1	8,916	8,916	8,916
CHARPENTIER, Constance-Marie (1767-1849) French				
oil	1	2,592	2,592	2,592
CHARPENTIER, Eugène (1811-1890) French				
oil	1	3,200	3,200	3,200
CHARPENTIER, Felix (1858-1924) French				
3D	5	4,545-17,671	12,496	14,240
CHARPENTIER, Philippe (1949-) French				
oil	1	628	628	628
wc/d	3	589-1,824	1,306	1,506
CHARPENTIER-MIO, Maurice (1881-1976) French				
3D	6	2,035-3,831	2,713	2,634
CHARRETON, Victor (1864-1937) French				
oil	18	5,351-26,969	14,467	11,090
CHARRIER, Henri (1859-1950) French				
oil	1	1,752	1,752	1,752
CHARTIER, Alex Charles (1894-?) French				
oil	1	1,229	1,229	1,229

Name	No.	Price Range	Average	Median
CHARTRAN, Theobald (1849-1907) French				
oil	1	2,835	2,835	2,835
wc/d	1	2,464	2,464	2,464
CHARTRAND, Esteban (1824-1884) Cuban				
oil	2	35,000-150,000	92,500	35,000
CHARUVI, Samuel (1897-1965) Israeli				
oil	1	1,200	1,200	1,200
wc/d	3	850-1,200	1,050	1,100
CHASE, Harry (1853-1889) American				
oil	2	2,000-19,000	10,500	2,000
CHASE, William Merritt (1849-1916) American				
oil	9	7,500-500,000	128,388	30,000
wc/d	1	1,000	1,000	1,000
CHASHNIK, Ilya Grigorevich (1902-1929) Russian				
wc/d	2	18,602-21,541	20,071	18,602
CHASSAING, J (20th C) French				
wc/d	3	2,913-3,156	2,994	2,913
CHASSERIAU, Theodore (1819-1856) French				
oil	2	76,027-595,548	335,787	76,027
wc/d	2	2,674-3,858	3,266	2,674
CHASTEL, Roger (1897-1981) French				
oil	2	834-2,827	1,830	834
CHATAUD, Marc Alfred (1833-1908) French				
oil	1	2,973	2,973	2,973
CHATEIGNON, Ernest (1851-?) French				
oil	1	4,285	4,285	4,285
CHATELET, Claude Louis (1753-1794) French				
oil	1	10,738	10,738	10,738
wc/d	3	1,000-2,689	1,844	1,843
CHATER, Noureddine (1975-) Moroccan				
wc/d	1	3,333	3,333	3,333
CHATHAM, Russell (1940-) American				
oil	1	35,000	35,000	35,000
wc/d	1	550	550	550
CHATROUSSE, Émile (1829-1896) French				
3D	1	1,545	1,545	1,545
CHATTERTON, Clarence K (1880-1973) American				
oil	3	1,300-20,000	9,600	7,500
CHATZIS, Vasilios (1870-1915) Greek				
oil	3	4,114-160,650	105,321	151,200
CHAUDET, Georges (?-1899) French				
oil	1	1,455	1,455	1,455
CHAUDET, Jeanne Elisabeth (1767-1832) French				
oil	1	462,500	462,500	462,500
CHAURAY, Jean Claude (1934-) French				
oil	3	1,100-1,764	1,388	1,300
CHAUVEAU, Evrard (1660-1739) French				
oil	1	6,044	6,044	6,044
CHAUVIN, Jean (1889-1976) French				
wc/d	7	478-722	599	602
3D	3	7,500-18,000	12,723	12,671
CHAVANNES, Alfred (1836-1894) Swiss				
oil	1	8,158	8,158	8,158
CHAVAZ, Albert (1907-1990) Swiss				
oil	10	1,468-29,368	9,856	6,450
wc/d	3	493-1,518	835	496
CHAVDA, Shiavax (1914-1990) Indian				
oil	3	6,920-40,000	18,756	9,350
CHAVET, Victor Joseph (1822-1906) French				
oil	3	848-2,835	1,511	850
CHAVEZ LOPEZ, Gerardo (1937-) Peruvian				
oil	1	3,273	3,273	3,273
CHAYLLERY, Eugène Louis (fl.1894-1906) French				
oil	1	1,617	1,617	1,617
CHAZAL, Louis (20th C) French				
oil	1	1,262	1,262	1,262
CHAZAL, Malcolm de (1902-1981) French				
wc/d	14	1,147-4,281	2,125	1,903
CHEADLE, Henry (1852-1910) British				
oil	6	1,009-2,610	1,741	1,218

Name	No.	Price Range	Average	Median
CHECA Y SANZ, Ulpiano (1860-1916) Spanish				
oil	4	4,822-17,838	11,727	7,600
wc/d	2	722-722	722	722
CHECA, Felipe (1844-1907) Spanish				
oil	3	1,567-2,422	1,892	1,688
CHECA, Jose Luis (1950-) Spanish				
oil	14	603-1,506	1,022	1,029
CHECA, V (19th C) Spanish				
oil	1	5,425	5,425	5,425
CHEE, Benjamin Chee (1944-1977) Canadian				
wc/d	2	1,141-1,630	1,385	1,141
CHEESWRIGHT, Ethel S (1874-?) British				
oil	1	893	893	893
wc/d	16	654-1,462	1,005	1,023
CHELICAPELLA, Giulia (?-1915) Italian				
oil	1	1,526	1,526	1,526
CHELIUS, Adolf (1856-1923) German				
oil	1	1,914	1,914	1,914
CHELLINI, Silvano (19/20th C) Italian				
oil	1	1,000	1,000	1,000
CHELMINSKI, Jan van (1851-1925) Polish				
oil	6	2,450-15,765	5,413	2,450
CHELUSHKIN, Kirill (1968-) Russian				
wc/d	1	3,000	3,000	3,000
CHEMETOV, Boris (1908-1982) Russian				
oil	4	1,178-2,624	1,829	1,730
CHEMIAKIN, Mikhail (1943-) Russian				
oil	5	6,020-11,656	8,299	8,256
wc/d	25	586-33,480	6,936	5,531
3D	7	2,704-27,917	14,654	7,508
CHEMIN, Michel (1945-) Dutch				
oil	2	760-1,753	1,256	760
CHEN CHI (1912-) Chinese/American				
wc/d	1	1,000	1,000	1,000
CHEN DANQING (1953-) Chinese				
oil	1	55,000	55,000	55,000
CHEN WENBO (1969-) Chinese				
oil	1	28,000	28,000	28,000
CHEN WENXI (1906-1991) Chinese				
wc/d	1	1,100	1,100	1,100
CHEN YIFEI (1946-) Chinese				
oil	1	220,000	220,000	220,000
CHEN ZHEN (1955-2000) Chinese				
3D	7	11,000-110,000	56,924	60,000
CHEN, Hilo (1942-) American				
oil	1	6,500	6,500	6,500
CHENE DE VERE, H du (19th C) French				
oil	1	14,000	14,000	14,000
CHENEY, Harriet (1771-1848) British				
wc/d	5	2,112-24,640	8,096	4,224
CHENEY, Robert Henry (1801-1866) British				
wc/d	75	880-5,632	1,866	1,672
CHENEY, Russell (1881-1945) American				
oil	1	1,500	1,500	1,500
CHENG TSAI-TUNG (1953-) Chinese				
oil	1	25,000	25,000	25,000
CHENOWETH, Joseph G (fl.1920) American				
oil	1	1,100	1,100	1,100
CHENU, Didier (1956-) French				
oil	1	1,816	1,816	1,816
CHENU, Fleury (?) ?				
oil	1	6,000	6,000	6,000
CHENU, Lucien (20th C) French				
oil	1	1,164	1,164	1,164
CHEREMETEFF, Vassily (1830-?) Russian				
oil	1	9,600	9,600	9,600
CHEREPOV, George (1909-) American				
wc/d	1	1,600	1,600	1,600
CHERET, Jules (1836-1933) French				
oil	12	584-19,007	5,376	4,712
wc/d	28	518-26,610	4,497	1,829

Name	No.	Price Range	Average	Median
CHERICI, Angiolo (?) Italian				
oil	1	3,204	3,204	3,204
CHERIDNICHENKO, Anna Dmitriyevna (1917-) Russian				
oil	1	5,536	5,536	5,536
wc/d	1	684	684	684
CHERKAOUI, Ahmed (1934-1967) ?				
oil	1	31,157	31,157	31,157
wc/d	1	43,019	43,019	43,019
CHERKASSKY, Zoya (1976-) Russian				
3D	3	5,500-6,000	5,666	5,500
CHERMAYEFF, Serge (20th C) ?				
oil	2	1,100-2,300	1,700	1,100
CHERNETSOV, Nikanor Grigorevich (1805-1879) Russian				
oil	1	1,395,000	1,395,000	1,395,000
CHERNIKOV, Iakov (1889-1951) Russian				
wc/d	5	9,250-14,800	10,360	9,250
CHERON, Louis (1660-1715) French				
oil	1	34,600	34,600	34,600
wc/d	1	2,775	2,775	2,775
CHERRY, Emma Richardson (1859-1954) American				
oil	1	5,000	5,000	5,000
CHERRY, Kathryn (1871-1931) American				
oil	3	4,500-18,000	10,300	8,400
CHERRY-GARRARD, Apsley George Benet (1886-1959) British				
wc/d	1	2,457	2,457	2,457
CHERUBINI, Andrea (19th C) Italian				
oil	1	1,004	1,004	1,004
wc/d	1	726	726	726
CHERUBINI, Carlo (1890-1978) Italian				
oil	6	570-12,025	5,235	2,571
CHERUBINI, Giuseppe (1867-1960) Italian				
oil	1	1,432	1,432	1,432
wc/d	1	4,425	4,425	4,425
CHERVIN, Catalina (?) Argentinian				
wc/d	2	2,700-3,200	2,950	2,700
CHESSA, Gigi (1895-1935) Italian				
wc/d	1	2,219	2,219	2,219
CHESSA, Mauro (1933-) Italian				
oil	2	643-3,086	1,864	643
CHESTER, A (20th C) British				
wc/d	1	2,000	2,000	2,000
CHEVALIER, Adolf (1831-?) German				
oil	2	1,107-1,178	1,142	1,107
CHEVALIER, Ferdinand (19th C) Belgian				
oil	1	1,897	1,897	1,897
CHEVALIER, Jean (1913-2002) French				
oil	1	2,400	2,400	2,400
wc/d	1	703	703	703
CHEVALIER, Nicholas (1828-1902) Australian				
wc/d	1	1,144	1,144	1,144
CHEVALIER, Peter (1953-) German				
oil	4	797-4,653	1,987	1,211
CHEVALIER, Robert Magnus (fl.1876-1911) British				
oil	1	1,074	1,074	1,074
CHEVALLEY, Pierre (1926-) Swiss				
oil	1	2,121	2,121	2,121
CHEVALLIER, Hugues (20th C) French				
oil	2	1,432-1,790	1,611	1,432
CHEVIOT, Lilian (fl.1894-1930) British				
oil	6	692-12,000	5,574	3,500
CHEVOLLEAU, Jean (1924-1996) French				
oil	7	550-3,699	1,813	1,253
wc/d	1	504	504	504
CHEVRIER, Ferdinando (1920-) Italian				
oil	3	1,518-3,970	2,444	1,844
CHI PAI SHIH (20th C) Chinese				
wc/d	1	20,000	20,000	20,000
CHIA, Sandro (1946-) Italian				
oil	19	468-185,850	54,714	43,250
wc/d	29	957-37,500	8,683	5,773
3D	14	2,141-66,857	9,199	3,567

Name	No.	Price Range	Average	Median
CHIACIGH, Giuseppe (1895-1967) Italian				
oil	1	1,929	1,929	1,929
CHIALIVA, Luigi (1842-1914) Swiss				
oil	1	12,603	12,603	12,603
wc/d	5	908-5,733	2,844	1,683
CHIANCONE, Alberto (1904-1988) Italian				
oil	1	3,312	3,312	3,312
CHIANESE, Nicolo (1898-1971) Italian				
oil	5	710-2,604	1,266	888
CHIARI, Giuseppe (1926-) Italian				
oil	1	1,312	1,312	1,312
wc/d	43	471-6,269	1,001	756
3D	1	1,877	1,877	1,877
CHIARI, Giuseppe Bartolomeo (1654-1727) Italian				
wc/d	1	5,180	5,180	5,180
CHIAROTTINI, Francesco (1748-1796) Italian				
oil	1	71,200	71,200	71,200
CHICHESTER, Cecil (1891-1963) American				
oil	4	425-1,700	1,043	900
CHIERICI, Gaetano (1838-1920) Italian				
oil	1	64,228	64,228	64,228
wc/d	1	520	520	520
CHIESA, Pietro (1876-1959) Swiss				
oil	2	1,446-1,967	1,706	1,446
wc/d	3	661-1,832	1,082	753
CHIESA, Renato (1947-) Italian				
oil	2	778-6,340	3,559	778
wc/d	11	589-1,885	842	615
CHIESI, Andrea (1966-) Italian				
oil	2	1,189-1,767	1,478	1,189
CHIESI, Giorgio (1941-) Italian				
oil	8	471-1,193	760	712
wc/d	17	589-1,524	994	1,001
CHIEZO, Taro (1962-) American				
oil	1	2,752	2,752	2,752
CHIGHINE, Alfredo (1914-1974) Italian				
oil	3	7,375-22,253	17,084	21,626
wc/d	1	1,355	1,355	1,355
CHIGOT, Eugène (1860-1927) French				
oil	9	498-4,005	2,360	1,844
CHIKATOSHI, Enomoto (1898-1993) Japanese				
wc/d	1	9,500	9,500	9,500
CHIKUDEN, Tanomura (1777-1835) Japanese				
wc/d	1	2,400	2,400	2,400
CHIKUDO, Kishi (1826-1897) Japanese				
wc/d	1	4,000	4,000	4,000
CHILD, Charles (1902-1980) American				
oil	2	475-2,800	1,637	475
CHILDE, James Warren (c.1778-1862) British				
wc/d	1	1,392	1,392	1,392
CHILLIDA, Eduardo (1924-2002) Spanish				
oil	1	8,199	8,199	8,199
wc/d	4	17,700-100,974	47,183	20,350
3D	15	63,360-3,330,000	486,328	157,250
CHILTON, Alice (20th C) American				
oil	1	6,500	6,500	6,500
CHIMENTI, Jacopo (1554-1640) Italian				
oil	1	70,300	70,300	70,300
CHIMES, Thomas James (1921-) American				
oil	1	6,000	6,000	6,000
CHIMICOS, Paella (1962-) French				
oil	1	1,868	1,868	1,868
CHIMONAS, Nicholaos (1866-1929) Greek				
oil	2	3,520-17,400	10,460	3,520
CHIN, Hisiao (1935-) ?				
oil	1	2,028	2,028	2,028
wc/d	1	597	597	597
CHINARD, Joseph (1756-1813) French				
3D	2	13,368-34,028	23,698	13,368
CHINET, Charles (1891-1978) Swiss				
oil	3	1,526-5,342	3,434	3,434
wc/d	1	839	839	839

Name	No.	Price Range	Average	Median
CHING JANG YAO (1941-2000) Taiwanese				
oil	3	450-3,600	2,083	2,200
wc/d	1	1,518	1,518	1,518
CHING, Raymond (1939-) New Zealander				
oil	1	6,000	6,000	6,000
wc/d	3	4,200-4,500	4,300	4,200
CHINI, Galileo (1873-1956) Italian				
oil	3	2,658-5,343	3,843	3,529
CHINNERY, George (1774-1852) British				
oil	3	9,250-59,200	32,736	29,760
wc/d	20	528-536,500	32,043	3,806
CHINTREUIL, Antoine (1816-1873) French				
oil	11	1,246-8,870	4,160	4,033
CHIPARUS (1888-1950) Rumanian				
3D	1	7,274	7,274	7,274
CHIPARUS, D (1888-1950) Rumanian				
3D	3	1,908-40,912	15,523	3,750
CHIPARUS, Demetre (1888-1950) Rumanian				
3D	44	1,918-180,000	40,683	26,250
CHIRICO, Giorgio de (1888-1978) Italian				
oil	44	3,000-1,947,000	266,316	163,973
wc/d	15	2,592-82,000	23,934	23,425
3D	8	3,641-32,795	13,296	4,900
CHISTOVSKY, Lev (1902-1969) Russian				
oil	2	1,860-12,040	6,950	1,860
wc/d	6	7,440-48,160	16,526	7,740
CHITARIN, Traiano (1864-1935) Italian				
oil	1	1,334	1,334	1,334
CHITTENDEN, Alice B (1859-1944) American				
oil	5	800-5,500	2,910	2,500
CHITTUSSI, Anton (1847-1891) Czechoslovakian				
oil	1	6,192	6,192	6,192
CHIZMARICK, Steven (1898-?) American				
oil	5	1,000-2,750	1,590	1,400
CHLEBOWSKI, Stanislaus von (1835-1884) Polish				
oil	2	62,560-80,000	71,280	62,560
CHMAROFF, Paval (1874-1950) Russian				
oil	5	7,440-41,280	23,831	30,919
CHMIEL, Len (1942-) American				
oil	1	19,000	19,000	19,000
CHMIELINSKI, W T (1911-1979) Polish				
oil	2	664-3,474	2,069	664
CHMIELINSKI, Wladyslaw (1911-1979) Polish				
oil	8	1,270-4,750	2,499	1,784
wc/d	1	3,420	3,420	3,420
CHO YOUN-LYOUNG (1971-) Oriental				
3D	2	4,500-9,321	6,910	4,500
CHOCARNE-MOREAU, Paul Charles (1855-1931) French				
oil	2	5,327-10,346	7,836	5,327
CHODOWIECKI, Daniel (1726-1801) German				
wc/d	7	478-2,827	1,734	2,000
CHOI JEONG HWA (1961-) Korean				
3D	1	16,650	16,650	16,650
CHONG SON (1676-1759) Chinese				
wc/d	1	520,000	520,000	520,000
CHOQUET, René-Maxime (1860-1939) French				
oil	1	19,027	19,027	19,027
CHOSHUN, Miyagawa (1682-1752) Japanese				
oil	1	12,000	12,000	12,000
CHOULTSE, Ivan Fedorovich (1874-1939) Russian				
oil	24	11,160-90,000	46,767	50,000
CHOUMANOVITCH, Sawa (20th C) Yugoslavian				
oil	1	71,020	71,020	71,020
CHOWDHURY, Devi Prasad Roy (20th C) Indian				
wc/d	1	38,060	38,060	38,060
CHOWDHURY, Jogen (1939-) Indian				
oil	1	25,245	25,245	25,245
wc/d	11	3,750-80,000	24,290	15,000
CHOWNE, Gerard (1875-?) British				
oil	1	1,280	1,280	1,280
CHRETIEN, René Louis (1867-1942) French				
oil	6	1,311-8,500	4,061	2,275

Name	No.	Price Range	Average	Median
CHRIST, Fritz (1866-1906) German				
3D	2	4,200-6,261	5,230	4,200
CHRIST, Martin Alfred (1900-1979) Swiss				
oil	3	611-2,855	1,614	1,378
CHRISTEAUX, F (20th C) ?				
oil	1	2,003	2,003	2,003
CHRISTELER-MATTI, Jakob (1872-1950) Swiss				
oil	1	1,908	1,908	1,908
CHRISTENSEN, Antonore (1849-1926) Danish				
oil	9	632-5,691	2,046	1,624
CHRISTENSEN, Dan (1942-) American				
oil	2	1,288-1,500	1,394	1,288
CHRISTENSEN, Godfred (1845-1928) Danish				
oil	13	487-3,500	1,318	1,056
CHRISTENSEN, John (1896-1940) Danish				
oil	2	1,616-1,698	1,657	1,616
CHRISTENSEN, Kay (1899-1981) Danish				
oil	26	812-5,684	2,119	1,380
CHRISTENSEN, Scott L (1962-) American				
oil	3	8,000-17,000	13,666	16,000
CHRISTIAN, Anton (1940-) Austrian				
wc/d	1	1,093	1,093	1,093
CHRISTIANSEN, Jesper (1955-) Danish				
oil	2	1,932-2,093	2,012	1,932
CHRISTIANSEN, Niels (1873-1960) Danish				
oil	1	1,100	1,100	1,100
CHRISTIANSEN, Nils H (1850-1922) Danish				
oil	8	430-3,480	1,179	779
CHRISTIANSEN, Poul S (1855-1933) Danish				
oil	2	1,897-1,940	1,918	1,897
CHRISTIANSEN, Professor Hans (1866-1945) German				
oil	1	16,530	16,530	16,530
CHRISTIANSEN, Rasmus (1863-1940) Danish				
oil	1	2,858	2,858	2,858
CHRISTIANSEN, Ursula Reuter (1943-) Danish				
oil	2	2,274-2,923	2,598	2,274
CHRISTIDES, Achilleas (1959-) Greek				
oil	2	2,464-4,675	3,569	2,464
CHRISTIE, James Elder (1847-1914) British				
oil	4	637-38,219	12,276	2,249
CHRISTIE, Keith (1940-) American				
3D	1	3,000	3,000	3,000
CHRISTIE, Reid (1951-) American				
oil	1	11,000	11,000	11,000
CHRISTIE, Vera (fl.1893) British				
wc/d	1	1,144	1,144	1,144
CHRISTO (1935-) American/Bulgarian				
oil	7	21,082-194,250	62,632	26,885
wc/d	73	954-400,000	76,908	74,000
3D	7	2,671-88,500	19,725	5,814
CHRISTOFFEL, Anton (1871-1953) Swiss				
wc/d	1	1,979	1,979	1,979
CHRISTOFFERSEN, Frede (1919-1987) Danish				
oil	6	566-3,880	1,673	728
CHRISTOFFERSEN, Uffe (1947-) Danish				
oil	3	1,132-1,940	1,509	1,455
CHRISTOFIS, Alexandros (1882-1957) Greek				
wc/d	2	1,870-2,244	2,057	1,870
CHRISTOFOROU, John (1921-) British				
oil	29	443-9,709	3,642	2,635
wc/d	2	722-974	848	722
CHRISTOPHERSEN, Alejandro (1866-1946) Norwegian				
oil	3	4,490-21,205	13,898	16,000
CHRISTOU, Sandra (1959-) Greek				
oil	1	5,984	5,984	5,984
CHRISTY, Howard Chandler (1872-1952) American				
oil	1	5,000	5,000	5,000
wc/d	1	8,500	8,500	8,500
CHU TEH CHUN (1920-) Chinese				
oil	20	40,743-247,222	105,108	73,788
wc/d	9	13,457-27,243	21,117	22,801

Name	No.	Price Range	Average	Median
CHUANG CHE (1934-) Chinese				
oil	1	7,145	7,145	7,145
CHUBAC, Albert (1925-) Swiss				
3D	1	1,555	1,555	1,555
CHUGHTAI, Abdur Rahman (1894-1975) Indian				
oil	1	25,950	25,950	25,950
wc/d	7	1,384-96,800	34,274	22,440
CHULOVICH, Victor Nikolaevich (1922-1994) Russian				
oil	1	9,300	9,300	9,300
CHUMLEY, John (1928-1984) American				
wc/d	1	2,300	2,300	2,300
CHURBERG, Fanny Maria (1845-1892) Finnish				
oil	1	17,568	17,568	17,568
CHURCH, Charles (20th C) British				
oil	1	1,323	1,323	1,323
CHURCH, Frederick Stuart (1842-1923) American				
oil	2	5,500-6,000	5,750	5,500
wc/d	1	2,000	2,000	2,000
CHURCH, Katharine (1910-1999) British				
oil	1	1,454	1,454	1,454
CHURCHILL, John Spencer (1909-) British				
oil	1	1,044	1,044	1,044
CHURCHILL, Sir Winston (1874-1965) British				
oil	6	25,000-522,000	245,380	194,700
CHURCHILL, William W (1858-1926) American				
oil	2	6,000-18,000	12,000	6,000
CHURCHYARD, Thomas (1798-1865) British				
oil	2	1,531-4,625	3,078	1,531
wc/d	3	692-1,073	880	875
CHWALA, Adolf (1836-1900) Czechoslovakian				
oil	4	3,295-8,182	4,668	3,568
CIACELLI, Arturo (1883-1966) Italian				
oil	7	1,288-7,375	2,688	2,108
wc/d	3	1,074-2,577	1,724	1,523
CIAMBERLANI, Albert (1864-1956) Belgian				
oil	1	1,403	1,403	1,403
CIAMPI, Alimondo (1876-1939) Italian				
3D	3	2,395-25,767	10,647	3,781
CIANFANELLI, Nicola (1793-1848) Russian				
wc/d	1	4,332	4,332	4,332
CIANFARANI, Aristide Berto (1895-1960) American				
3D	1	2,100	2,100	2,100
CIANGOTTINI, Giovanni (1912-) Italian				
oil	1	1,093	1,093	1,093
wc/d	1	1,942	1,942	1,942
CIANI, Cesare (1854-1925) Italian				
oil	4	4,789-31,507	15,979	8,247
CIANI, Vittore A (1858-1908) Italian				
3D	1	4,000	4,000	4,000
CIAPPA, Giovanni (19th C) Italian				
oil	1	2,958	2,958	2,958
CIARDI, Beppe (1875-1932) Italian				
oil	8	4,000-70,000	14,325	5,856
CIARDI, Emma (1879-1933) Italian				
oil	5	3,038-10,000	5,611	5,986
CIARDI, Guglielmo (1842-1917) Italian				
oil	8	3,600-101,108	29,383	16,829
CIARDIELLO, Carmine (1871-?) Italian				
oil	2	2,460-9,687	6,073	2,460
CIARDIELLO, Michele (1839-?) Italian				
oil	1	5,363	5,363	5,363
CIARROCCHI, Arnoldo (1916-) Italian				
oil	1	6,525	6,525	6,525
CICCIA, Mauro (1961-) Italian				
oil	2	966-1,616	1,291	966
CICCOTELLI, Beniamino (1937-) Italian				
oil	10	615-1,598	1,122	1,106
CICERI, Eugène (1813-1890) French				
oil	1	2,997	2,997	2,997
wc/d	6	471-865	630	550
CICERI, Pierre Luc Charles (1782-1868) French				
wc/d	2	1,168-2,805	1,986	1,168

Name	No.	Price Range	Average	Median
CIENFUEGOS BROWN, Gonzalo (1949-) Chilean				
wc/d	1	2,300	2,300	2,300
CIFRONDI, Antonio (1657-1730) Italian				
oil	1	11,571	11,571	11,571
CIGNANI, Carlo (1628-1719) Italian				
wc/d	1	1,665	1,665	1,665
CIGNANI, Felice (1660-1724) Italian				
oil	1	5,341	5,341	5,341
CIGNAROLI, Giuseppe (1726-1796) Italian				
oil	1	121,088	121,088	121,088
CIGNAROLI, Vittorio Amedeo (c.1747-1793) Italian				
oil	1	17,838	17,838	17,838
CIKOVSKY, Nicolai (1894-1984) American				
oil	6	500-4,250	2,466	2,500
CILETTI, Nicola (1883-1967) Italian				
oil	1	2,293	2,293	2,293
CILFONE, Gianni (1908-1990) American/Italian				
oil	3	1,800-8,000	5,433	6,500
CILLIA, Enrico de (1910-1992) Italian				
oil	2	707-1,640	1,173	707
CIMA, Luigi (1860-1938) Italian				
oil	1	42,500	42,500	42,500
CIMAROLI, Giovanni Battista (17/18th C) Italian				
oil	1	24,196	24,196	24,196
CIMIOTTI, Gustave (1875-1969) American				
oil	5	425-9,500	2,865	800
CINALLI, Ricardo (1948-) Argentinian				
oil	1	8,188	8,188	8,188
wc/d	2	5,340-7,476	6,408	5,340
CINGANELLI, Michelangelo (c.1580-?) Italian				
wc/d	1	1,178	1,178	1,178
CINGOLANI, Marco (1961-) Italian				
oil	5	3,534-8,836	5,972	5,121
wc/d	1	647	647	647
CINTOLI, Claudio (1935-1978) Italian				
wc/d	1	3,867	3,867	3,867
CINTRACT, David (1970-) French				
oil	1	2,719	2,719	2,719
CIOBANU, Mircea (1950-) Russian				
oil	2	1,061-1,138	1,099	1,061
CIOCCHINI, Cleto (1899-1974) Argentinian				
oil	1	3,800	3,800	3,800
CIOCI, Antonio (18th C) Italian				
oil	1	85,000	85,000	85,000
CIOLINA, Gian Battista (1870-1955) Italian				
oil	1	1,019	1,019	1,019
CIOTTI, Giuseppe (1889-1991) Italian				
oil	5	1,171-1,757	1,639	1,757
CIPPER, Giacomo Francesco (c.1670-1738) Italian				
oil	7	6,042-70,685	34,578	41,233
CIPRA, C (?) French?				
wc/d	2	3,857-7,247	5,552	3,857
CIPRE, Stephane (1968-) French?				
3D	2	2,348-8,803	5,575	2,348
CIPRIANI, A (19th C) Italian				
3D	6	2,121-40,000	8,774	2,571
CIPRIANI, Ada (19/20th C) Italian?				
3D	1	2,200	2,200	2,200
CIPRIANI, Adolfo (19/20th C) Italian				
3D	1	11,500	11,500	11,500
CIPRIANI, Giovanni Battista (1727-1785) Italian				
wc/d	3	425-7,266	3,044	1,443
CIPRIANI, Nazzareno (1843-1925) Italian				
wc/d	3	1,211-1,600	1,405	1,405
CIRCIGNANI, Nicolo (1519-1591) Italian				
wc/d	1	3,160	3,160	3,160
CIRIA, Jose Manuel (1960-) British				
oil	3	838-3,629	2,007	1,555
wc/d	1	3,327	3,327	3,327
CIRINO, Antonio (1889-1983) American				
oil	2	2,300-13,000	7,650	2,300

Name	No.	Price Range	Average	Median
CIRY, Michel (1919-) French				
oil	1	2,225	2,225	2,225
wc/d	2	790-993	891	790
CISERI, Francois (19th C) Italian				
oil	2	1,008-4,971	2,989	1,008
wc/d	1	1,386	1,386	1,386
CITROEN, Paul (1896-1983) Dutch				
oil	1	2,026	2,026	2,026
wc/d	2	583-754	668	583
CITTADELLA, Bartolomeo (1636-1704) Italian				
oil	1	30,575	30,575	30,575
CITTADINI, Pier Francesco (1616-1681) Italian				
oil	2	85,000-96,006	90,503	85,000
wc/d	1	1,665	1,665	1,665
CITTADINI, Tito (1886-1960) Argentinian				
oil	1	1,985	1,985	1,985
CIUCA, Eugen (1913-) Italian				
3D	1	3,625	3,625	3,625
CIUCCI, Mario (1903-1968) Italian				
oil	1	1,065	1,065	1,065
CIVILETTI, Benoit (1846-1899) Italian				
3D	1	27,840	27,840	27,840
CIVITARESE, Goffredo (1938-) Italian				
oil	26	553-3,579	1,392	1,165
CLAASSEN, Tom (1964-) Dutch				
3D	1	8,630	8,630	8,630
CLAERHOUT, Jef (?) ?				
oil	1	2,225	2,225	2,225
CLAESZ, Pieter (1590-1661) Dutch				
oil	4	9,158-655,286	250,619	102,347
CLAEUW, Jacques Grief (?-1676) Dutch				
oil	1	33,300	33,300	33,300
CLAEYS, Albert (1889-1967) Belgian				
oil	4	742-3,113	1,983	1,532
CLAGHORN, Joseph C (1869-1947) American				
oil	1	3,000	3,000	3,000
wc/d	3	1,000-3,800	2,266	2,000
CLAIR, Charles (1860-1930) French				
oil	6	547-3,534	2,331	2,425
CLAIRIN, Georges (1843-1919) French				
oil	6	1,947-31,320	8,696	3,879
wc/d	5	500-2,455	1,298	1,132
CLAISSE, Genevieve (1935-) French				
oil	6	1,640-7,644	4,447	3,387
wc/d	6	546-1,675	881	759
3D	3	2,061-9,092	4,525	2,424
CLAPHAM, Peter (1924-) British				
3D	1	1,683	1,683	1,683
CLAPP, William H (1879-1954) Canadian				
oil	3	1,100-48,744	17,214	1,800
CLAPPERTON, Thomas John (1879-?) British				
3D	1	1,730	1,730	1,730
CLARA, Carlo (1830-1900) Italian				
oil	2	1,212-1,455	1,333	1,212
CLARA, Luigi (1875-1925) Italian				
oil	1	1,155	1,155	1,155
CLARAMUNT, Luis (1951-2000) Spanish				
oil	1	2,188	2,188	2,188
CLARANCE, Elizabeth M (19th C) British?				
wc/d	1	13,125	13,125	13,125
CLARE, G (1835-c.1890) British				
oil	1	1,012	1,012	1,012
CLARE, George (1835-c.1890) British				
oil	15	644-4,844	2,426	2,116
wc/d	1	1,376	1,376	1,376
CLARE, Oliver (1853-1927) British				
oil	29	623-7,308	2,451	1,903
CLARE, Vincent (1855-1930) British				
oil	19	465-4,750	1,777	1,471
wc/d	4	498-2,697	1,512	1,288
CLARENBACH, Max (1880-1952) German				
oil	15	650-19,852	6,086	4,671

Name	No.	Price Range	Average	Median
CLARET, Joan (1929-) Spanish				
oil	2	497-2,153	1,325	497
CLARET, Joaquin (1879-1965) Spanish				
3D	1	2,973	2,973	2,973
CLARK, A (19th C) British				
oil	1	4,375	4,375	4,375
CLARK, Albert (19th C) British				
oil	9	566-1,925	1,297	1,251
CLARK, Albert James (fl.1892-1909) British				
oil	1	2,138	2,138	2,138
CLARK, Alson Skinner (1876-1949) American				
oil	14	450-37,500	13,339	9,000
CLARK, Benton (1895-1964) American				
oil	3	4,000-4,250	4,083	4,000
CLARK, C Myron (1876-1925) American				
oil	6	450-1,700	1,191	1,100
CLARK, Christopher (1875-1942) British				
oil	2	8,550-22,230	15,390	8,550
CLARK, Claude L (19th C) British				
oil	1	1,133	1,133	1,133
CLARK, Dixon (1849-1944) British				
oil	4	1,343-14,240	4,912	1,740
CLARK, Eliot (1883-1980) American				
oil	6	700-2,600	1,900	1,700
CLARK, H V (19th C) ?				
oil	1	16,000	16,000	16,000
CLARK, James (fl.1858-1909) British				
oil	7	440-2,000	1,350	1,740
CLARK, James (1858-1943) British				
oil	3	750-4,968	2,826	2,760
wc/d	1	519	519	519
CLARK, James Lippitt (1883-1957) American				
3D	1	10,000	10,000	10,000
CLARK, John Cosmo (1897-1967) British				
oil	5	1,131-1,427	1,249	1,253
CLARK, Joseph (1834-1926) British				
oil	5	1,040-18,101	5,717	3,363
wc/d	3	531-974	690	566
CLARK, Joseph Benwell (1857-?) British				
oil	1	1,148	1,148	1,148
CLARK, Joyce (20th C) American?				
oil	2	1,800-2,250	2,025	1,800
CLARK, L Edgar (?) British				
oil	1	2,070	2,070	2,070
CLARK, Lygia (1920-1988) Brazilian				
3D	1	75,164	75,164	75,164
CLARK, Michael (1954-) British				
oil	3	10,912-73,920	44,704	49,280
wc/d	7	1,936-24,640	9,629	8,800
CLARK, Octavius T (1850-1921) British				
oil	5	885-1,653	1,186	1,107
CLARK, Paraskeva (1898-1986) Canadian				
oil	2	1,640-1,898	1,769	1,640
wc/d	2	1,155-1,567	1,361	1,155
CLARK, R (?) ?				
3D	1	5,382	5,382	5,382
CLARK, S Joseph (19th C) British				
oil	4	830-3,128	1,768	1,384
CLARK, Samuel James (19th C) British				
oil	2	2,036-5,632	3,834	2,036
CLARK, Samuel Joseph (snr) (?) British				
oil	1	2,992	2,992	2,992
CLARK, Sidney (19th C) British				
oil	1	1,062	1,062	1,062
CLARK, Stanley (1954-) American				
oil	1	1,075	1,075	1,075
CLARK, Thomas Brown (1895-1983) British				
oil	4	1,298-2,249	1,816	1,557
CLARK, W A (19/20th C) British				
oil	1	1,285	1,285	1,285
CLARK, Walter (1848-1917) American				
oil	2	825-2,800	1,812	825

Name	No.	Price Range	Average	Median
CLARK, William (19th C) American				
wc/d	1	3,000	3,000	3,000
CLARK, William (1803-1883) British				
oil	5	10,000-29,580	19,713	20,880
CLARK, William Albert (20th C) British				
oil	4	634-2,314	1,623	1,750
CLARKE, Carey (fl.1957-1979) Irish				
wc/d	1	1,403	1,403	1,403
CLARKE, David (20th C) Irish				
oil	1	2,622	2,622	2,622
CLARKE, Elizabeth (19th C) British				
wc/d	1	1,416	1,416	1,416
CLARKE, Geoffrey (1924-) British				
3D	4	2,275-22,750	10,764	5,292
CLARKE, Harry Harvey (1869-?) British				
oil	4	1,760-1,936	1,804	1,760
CLARKE, John Clem (1936-) American				
oil	1	2,500	2,500	2,500
CLARKE, Margaret (1888-1961) Irish				
oil	2	8,182-11,322	9,752	8,182
CLARKE, Samuel Barling (fl.1852-1872) British				
oil	1	4,070	4,070	4,070
CLARKSON, William H (1872-1944) British				
oil	1	5,568	5,568	5,568
CLARY, Jean Eugène (1856-1930) French				
oil	3	1,168-2,061	1,640	1,691
CLARY-BAROUX, Albert Adolphe (1865-1933) French				
oil	2	2,259-4,500	3,379	2,259
CLASEN, Karl (1812-1886) German				
oil	1	6,020	6,020	6,020
CLATWORTHY, Robert (1928-) British				
3D	4	4,104-27,435	12,044	7,434
CLAUDEL, Camille (1864-1943) French				
3D	8	5,400-1,500,000	222,645	22,384
CLAUDET, Max (1840-1893) French				
oil	1	3,884	3,884	3,884
3D	1	2,534	2,534	2,534
CLAUDI, Eugene (?) ?				
oil	1	1,000	1,000	1,000
CLAUDIUS, Wilhelm (1854-1942) German				
oil	1	5,721	5,721	5,721
CLAUDOT, Jean-Baptiste-Charles (1733-1805) French				
oil	4	4,043-39,373	19,310	15,123
CLAUDUS, Rodolfo (1893-c.1964) ?				
oil	1	1,767	1,767	1,767
CLAUS, Émile (1849-1924) Belgian				
oil	13	989-203,537	44,628	11,918
wc/d	1	1,854	1,854	1,854
CLAUS, William A J (1862-1926) American				
oil	1	7,000	7,000	7,000
CLAUSADES, Pierre de (1910-1976) French				
oil	19	534-5,500	2,433	2,309
CLAUSEN, Agnes (19th C) German				
wc/d	1	9,100	9,100	9,100
CLAUSEN, Christian (1862-1911) Danish				
oil	2	1,911-2,028	1,969	1,911
CLAUSEN, Franciska (1899-1986) Danish				
wc/d	7	600-8,082	4,052	4,041
CLAUSEN, Sir George (1852-1944) British				
oil	6	4,675-258,000	91,654	37,620
wc/d	15	515-20,880	2,605	1,079
CLAVAREAU, Pierre de (?-1776) French				
oil	1	7,240	7,240	7,240
CLAVE, Antoni (1913-2005) Spanish				
oil	26	1,784-154,514	40,548	22,878
wc/d	16	900-49,280	13,255	8,381
3D	2	7,576-31,514	19,545	7,576
CLAWSON, Rex (1933-) American				
oil	2	2,800-3,000	2,900	2,800
CLAXTON, Marshall (1812-1881) British				
oil	1	1,144	1,144	1,144

Name	No.	Price Range	Average	Median
CLAY, Elizabeth C Fisher (fl.1927-1938) American/British				
oil	3	438-2,000	1,046	700
CLAYES, Alice des (1890-?) Canadian				
wc/d	4	577-2,750	1,650	1,319
CLAYES, Berthe des (1877-1968) Canadian				
oil	4	1,804-4,863	3,041	2,645
wc/d	6	608-2,460	1,514	1,304
CLAYES, Gertrude des (1879-1949) Canadian				
oil	2	1,968-3,092	2,530	1,968
wc/d	1	1,484	1,484	1,484
CLAYS, Paul Jean (1819-1900) Belgian				
oil	12	647-4,900	2,061	1,800
wc/d	2	597-1,091	844	597
CLAYTON, Harold (1896-1979) British				
oil	9	3,828-32,130	16,448	17,100
CLAYTON, J Hughes (fl.1891-1929) British				
wc/d	15	531-1,903	1,218	1,404
CLAYTON, R (20th C) American				
oil	1	2,200	2,200	2,200
CLEARY, Shirley (1942-) American				
wc/d	1	3,000	3,000	3,000
CLEDAT DE LAVIGNERIE, Samuel (19th C) French				
oil	1	1,580	1,580	1,580
CLEEMPUT, Jean van (1881-?) Belgian				
oil	2	835-1,987	1,411	835
CLEENEWERCK, Henry (1818-1901) French				
oil	2	4,750-7,500	6,125	4,750
CLEM, Robert Verity (1933-) American				
wc/d	1	1,600	1,600	1,600
CLEMENCIN, François Andre (1878-?) French				
3D	1	2,486	2,486	2,486
CLEMENS, Curt (1911-1947) Swedish				
oil	3	684-4,580	2,518	2,290
CLEMENS, G A (1870-1918) Danish				
oil	4	556-1,859	1,121	929
CLEMENS, Gustaf Adolf (1870-1918) Danish				
oil	1	9,971	9,971	9,971
CLEMENS, Paul Lewis (1911-1992) American				
wc/d	1	6,500	6,500	6,500
CLEMENT, Charles (1889-1972) Swiss				
oil	5	1,221-2,039	1,623	1,526
CLEMENTE PEREZ, Salvador (1859-1909) Spanish				
oil	1	24,360	24,360	24,360
CLEMENTE, Francesco (1952-) Italian				
oil	3	65,000-194,700	113,233	80,000
wc/d	9	11,000-75,000	32,204	22,898
CLEMENTS, Gabrielle de Veaux (1858-1948) American				
	1	11,000	11,000	11,000
CLEMENTSCHITSCH, Arnold (1887-1970) Austrian				
oil	1	58,562	58,562	58,562
CLEMINSON, Robert (19th C) British				
oil	12	473-9,000	2,461	1,758
CLENNELL, Luke (1781-1840) British				
wc/d	2	588-7,308	3,948	588
CLERC, Oscar de (1892-1968) Belgian				
3D	1	73,200	73,200	73,200
CLERC, Yves (1947-) French				
oil	1	32,500	32,500	32,500
CLERCK, A de (fl.1880-1900) Dutch				
wc/d	1	1,914	1,914	1,914
CLERCK, Hendrick de (1570-1629) Flemish				
oil	1	25,950	25,950	25,950
CLERCK, Jan de (1881-1962) Belgian				
wc/d	2	1,565-2,114	1,839	1,565
CLERCQ, Alphonse de (1868-1945) Belgian				
oil	1	1,636	1,636	1,636
CLERCQ, Pieter Jan de (1891-1964) Belgian				
oil	2	684-1,051	867	684
wc/d	1	1,155	1,155	1,155
CLERICI, Fabrizio (1913-1993) Italian				
oil	2	3,514-4,108	3,811	3,514
wc/d	3	646-1,457	1,180	1,437

Name	No.	Price Range	Average	Median
CLERISSEAU, Charles Louis (1721-1820) French				
oil	1	7,184	7,184	7,184
wc/d	4	1,371-2,945	2,020	1,823
CLERK, Anton de (?) ?				
wc/d	1	3,366	3,366	3,366
CLERMONT, Auguste Henri Louis de (19th C) French				
oil	1	3,078	3,078	3,078
CLERSON, J (19th C) ?				
oil	2	1,060-2,071	1,565	1,060
CLERY, Meg Jean (1874-1960) French				
oil	1	2,228	2,228	2,228
CLESINGER, J B (1814-1883) French				
3D	2	3,625-3,866	3,745	3,625
CLESINGER, Jean Baptiste (1814-1883) French				
oil	1	1,942	1,942	1,942
3D	12	3,038-38,640	11,209	5,670
CLESSE, Louis (1889-1961) Belgian				
oil	20	514-7,766	2,286	1,565
CLEVE, Joos van (1485-1540) Dutch				
oil	1	25,132	25,132	25,132
CLEVE, Marten van (1527-1581) Flemish				
oil	2	120,250-224,900	172,575	120,250
CLEVE-JONAND, Agnes (1876-1951) Swedish				
oil	7	674-17,813	4,390	2,119
wc/d	1	997	997	997
CLEVELEY, John (18th C) British				
wc/d	1	24,570	24,570	24,570
CLEVELEY, John (jnr) (1747-1786) British				
wc/d	1	1,050	1,050	1,050
CLEVELEY, John (snr) (?-1792) British				
oil	2	80,000-111,360	95,680	80,000
wc/d	1	10,285	10,285	10,285
CLEVELEY, Robert (1747-1809) British				
wc/d	1	1,860	1,860	1,860
CLEVENBERGH, Charles-Antoine (c.1791-?) Flemish				
oil	1	3,214	3,214	3,214
CLIFFE, Henry (1919-1983) British				
oil	3	700-3,420	1,805	1,295
wc/d	7	728-1,366	1,127	1,116
3D	2	1,850-4,272	3,061	1,850
CLIFFORD, Edward (1844-1907) British				
wc/d	2	1,038-7,812	4,425	1,038
CLIME, Winfield Scott (1881-1958) American				
oil	2	1,100-4,250	2,675	1,100
CLIMENT, Elena (1955-) Mexican				
oil	1	8,500	8,500	8,500
CLINEDINST, Mary Spear (1887-1960) American				
oil	4	600-2,500	1,575	800
CLINT, George (1770-1854) British				
oil	1	6,000	6,000	6,000
CLIVETTE, Merton (1868-1931) American				
oil	2	850-1,200	1,025	850
CLOAR, Carroll (1913-1993) American				
oil	2	14,000-17,000	15,500	14,000
CLODION (1738-1814) French				
3D	2	2,486-2,950	2,718	2,486
CLOSE, Chuck (1940-) American				
wc/d	2	85,000-280,000	182,500	85,000
CLOSSON, William Baxter Palmer (1848-1926) American				
oil	2	9,000-12,000	10,500	9,000
CLOSTERMAN, Johann Baptist (1660-1713) German				
oil	2	30,240-45,360	37,800	30,240
CLOUARD, Albert (1866-1952) French				
oil	2	1,942-13,782	7,862	1,942
CLOUET, Pierre (1920-1991) Belgian				
oil	1	1,372	1,372	1,372
CLOUGH, George L (1824-1901) American				
oil	8	1,300-18,000	6,006	3,250
CLOUGH, Prunella (1919-2000) British				
oil	8	2,301-44,400	17,210	8,600
wc/d	5	1,443-7,400	3,282	1,770

Name	No.	Price Range	Average	Median
CLOUGH, Tom (1867-1943) British				
wc/d	4	1,203-2,288	1,861	1,780
CLOVER, Joseph (1779-1853) British				
oil	1	3,894	3,894	3,894
CLOVIO, Giulio (1498-1578) Italian				
oil	1	2,019	2,019	2,019
wc/d	2	65,000-70,300	67,650	65,000
CLOWES, Henry (1799-1871) British				
oil	1	1,229	1,229	1,229
CLUNIE, Robert (1895-1984) American				
oil	6	750-6,000	3,408	2,500
CLUSEAU-LANAUVE, Jean (1914-) French				
oil	2	586-2,207	1,396	586
CLUSMANN, William (1859-1927) American				
oil	3	800-2,400	1,533	1,400
wc/d	1	675	675	675
CLUSSERATH, August (1899-1966) German				
oil	2	636-727	681	636
wc/d	2	645-669	657	645
CLYMER, John Ford (1907-1989) American				
oil	8	2,600-550,000	85,405	11,645
COARDING, Gerald (20th C) American				
oil	2	7,880-8,000	7,940	7,880
COATES, D M (19th C) American				
oil	1	2,600	2,600	2,600
COATES, Edmund C (1816-1871) American				
oil	3	700-17,000	9,066	9,500
COATES, Tom (1941-) British				
oil	4	534-2,394	1,182	756
wc/d	2	1,735-1,800	1,767	1,735
COATS, Randolph (1891-?) American				
oil	2	1,100-7,000	4,050	1,100
COBBAERT, Jan (1909-1995) Belgian				
oil	6	584-2,675	1,634	1,674
wc/d	1	1,401	1,401	1,401
COBBETT, E J (1815-1899) British				
oil	1	3,312	3,312	3,312
COBBETT, Edward John (1815-1899) British				
oil	5	588-10,602	4,213	3,219
COBELLE, Charles (1902-1998) French				
oil	3	950-2,600	1,650	1,400
COBO BARQUERA, Juan Jose (1906-1984) Spanish				
oil	1	1,452	1,452	1,452
COBO, Chema (1952-) Spanish				
oil	3	2,114-3,750	3,021	3,200
wc/d	1	4,070	4,070	4,070
COBURN, Frank (1862-1938) American				
oil	2	2,500-3,200	2,850	2,500
COBURN, Frederick Simpson (1871-1960) Canadian				
oil	12	1,304-53,175	17,122	14,019
wc/d	4	448-1,621	771	487
COBURN, John (1925-) Australian				
oil	1	2,600	2,600	2,600
COCCETTI, Napoleon (1880-?) Italian				
oil	1	8,182	8,182	8,182
COCCHI, Mario (1898-1957) Italian				
oil	3	727-2,301	1,271	787
COCCO, Giuseppe Alberto (1879-1963) Italian				
oil	1	1,019	1,019	1,019
COCCORANTE, Leonardo (1680-1750) Italian				
oil	3	17,800-35,150	25,504	23,562
COCHET, Gustave (1894-1979) French				
oil	1	3,000	3,000	3,000
COCHIN, Charles-Nicolas (18th C) French				
wc/d	9	951-4,861	2,079	1,276
COCHIN, Charles-Nicolas (younger) (1715-1790) French				
wc/d	2	7,000-20,572	13,786	7,000
COCHRAN, Allen Dean (1888-1971) American				
oil	4	1,300-3,500	2,250	1,800
COCHRANE, Constance (1888-?) American				
oil	1	7,500	7,500	7,500

Name	No.	Price Range	Average	Median
COCK, Cesar de (1823-1904) Flemish				
oil	10	1,798-25,865	7,766	4,909
wc/d	1	2,686	2,686	2,686
COCK, Maarten de (17th C) Dutch				
wc/d	1	3,737	3,737	3,737
COCK, Oscar de (1823-1904) Belgian				
oil	1	2,572	2,572	2,572
COCKBURN, Major General James Pattison (1778-1847) British				
wc/d	1	1,200	1,200	1,200
COCKRILL, Maurice (1936-) British				
oil	21	478-10,920	2,351	1,890
wc/d	1	515	515	515
COCKS, John H (1850-1938) American				
oil	1	5,250	5,250	5,250
COCKX, Philibert (1879-1949) Belgian				
oil	4	738-5,643	3,067	2,788
COCLERS, Christian (?-1737) Belgian				
oil	1	45,189	45,189	45,189
COCTEAU, Jean (1889-1963) French				
oil	1	1,945	1,945	1,945
wc/d	82	643-14,720	2,524	1,800
3D	8	2,544-12,390	6,794	5,664
CODA ZABETTA, Roberto (1975-) Italian				
oil	8	707-7,068	2,681	1,296
wc/d	1	2,259	2,259	2,259
3D	1	2,134	2,134	2,134
CODAZZI, Niccolo (1648-1693) Italian				
oil	3	9,514-43,250	31,828	42,720
CODAZZI, Viviano (1603-1672) Italian				
oil	5	10,000-76,027	31,708	19,425
CODDE, Pieter (1599-1678) Dutch				
oil	4	16,650-320,000	106,142	21,673
wc/d	1	6,072	6,072	6,072
CODDRON, Oscar (1881-1960) Belgian				
oil	1	1,169	1,169	1,169
CODINA Y LANGLIN, Victoriano (1844-1911) Spanish				
oil	3	1,523-1,757	1,603	1,529
CODMAN, Charles (1800-1842) American				
oil	1	24,000	24,000	24,000
CODOVOZ, T (?) ?				
oil	1	2,288	2,288	2,288
COE, Ethel Louise (1880-1938) American				
oil	1	3,550	3,550	3,550
COENE, Isaac (1650-1713) Flemish				
oil	1	1,985	1,985	1,985
COENE, Jean Baptiste (1805-1850) Belgian				
oil	1	1,450	1,450	1,450
COENE, Jean Henri de (1798-1866) Flemish				
oil	4	2,338-8,182	5,118	2,455
COENE, Jozef de (1875-1950) Belgian				
oil	1	1,052	1,052	1,052
COENRAETS, Ferdinand (1860-1939) Belgian?				
wc/d	1	1,942	1,942	1,942
COESTER, Oskar (20th C) ?				
oil	1	1,171	1,171	1,171
wc/d	2	705-941	823	705
COETZEE, Christo (1929-2001) South African				
wc/d	1	1,435	1,435	1,435
COETZER, Willem H (1900-1983) South African				
oil	1	2,713	2,713	2,713
COFFIN, William A (1855-1925) American				
oil	1	13,000	13,000	13,000
COFFIN, William Haskell (1878-1941) American				
oil	3	500-1,600	1,233	1,600
wc/d	1	5,000	5,000	5,000
COFFRE, Benoit le (1671-1722) French				
oil	1	2,540	2,540	2,540
COGGHE, Remy (1854-1935) Belgian				
oil	1	10,320	10,320	10,320
COGHETTI, Francesco (1804-1875) Italian				
oil	1	7,102	7,102	7,102

Name	No.	Price Range	Average	Median
COGHUF (1905-1976) Swiss				
oil	3	761-2,283	1,396	1,145
COGHUF, Ernst Stocker (1905-1976) Swiss				
oil	2	2,914-3,035	2,974	2,914
wc/d	1	583	583	583
COGNATA, Giovanni la (1954-) Italian				
oil	2	2,386-3,962	3,174	2,386
COGNEE, Philippe (1957-) French				
oil	4	648-3,098	1,443	834
wc/d	2	2,225-5,845	4,035	2,225
3D	1	8,802	8,802	8,802
COGNIET, Léon (1794-1880) French				
oil	3	2,430-50,000	19,202	5,178
COGORNO, Felice (19th C) Italian				
wc/d	1	1,635	1,635	1,635
COGORNO, Santiago (1915-2001) Argentinian				
oil	2	2,500-4,000	3,250	2,500
wc/d	5	1,300-4,000	2,980	3,000
COHELEACH, Guy Joseph (1933-) American				
oil	2	18,000-22,500	20,250	18,000
COHEN, Alfred (1920-) American				
oil	5	531-1,196	775	695
wc/d	1	637	637	637
COHEN, Bernard (1933-) British				
oil	4	5,696-17,800	9,748	6,048
wc/d	6	428-3,249	1,115	592
COHEN, Bruce (1953-) American				
oil	1	16,000	16,000	16,000
COHEN, P (20th C) American				
oil	1	2,000	2,000	2,000
COHEN-GAN, Pinchas (1942-) Israeli				
oil	1	4,000	4,000	4,000
wc/d	1	3,000	3,000	3,000
COIGNARD, James (1925-1997) French				
oil	13	727-4,229	2,197	1,576
wc/d	12	531-6,616	1,782	1,110
COIGNARD, Louis (1810-1883) French				
oil	4	825-1,998	1,585	1,580
COIGNET, Jules Louis Philippe (1798-1860) French				
oil	2	4,815-6,441	5,628	4,815
COINER, Charles Toucey (1898-1989) American				
oil	2	1,000-1,300	1,150	1,000
COJOCARU, Miriam (1945-) Israeli				
oil	2	800-1,200	1,000	800
COKE, Lucretia (1917-) American				
wc/d	1	1,500	1,500	1,500
COKELBERGHS, Virgi (1893-1967) Belgian				
oil	2	909-1,212	1,060	909
COKER, Peter (1926-2004) British				
oil	2	5,728-18,200	11,964	5,728
wc/d	1	1,218	1,218	1,218
COL, Jan David (1822-1900) Belgian				
oil	3	1,286-20,350	7,855	1,929
COLACICCHI, Giovanni (1900-1993) Italian				
oil	2	2,342-5,800	4,071	2,342
COLACICCO, Salvatore (1935-) British/Italian				
oil	4	833-1,286	1,012	935
COLAHAN, Colin (1897-1987) Australian				
oil	1	1,914	1,914	1,914
COLAS, Pierre le (1930-) French				
oil	1	1,216	1,216	1,216
COLBURN, Elanor (1866-1939) American				
oil	1	6,000	6,000	6,000
COLBY, George E (1859-?) American				
oil	1	1,900	1,900	1,900
COLDSTREAM, Sir William (1908-1987) British				
oil	2	13,920-15,576	14,748	13,920
wc/d	1	1,593	1,593	1,593
COLE, Alfred Benjamin (1830-?) British				
oil	3	550-1,750	1,066	900
COLE, G (1810-1883) British				
oil	1	3,213	3,213	3,213

Name	No.	Price Range	Average	Median
COLE, George (1810-1883) British				
oil	4	519-16,625	7,043	589
wc/d	1	557	557	557
COLE, George Vicat (1833-1893) British				
oil	13	453-29,750	4,627	2,478
wc/d	1	579	579	579
COLE, James (19th C) British				
oil	2	997-1,683	1,340	997
COLE, James William (19th C) British				
oil	1	1,753	1,753	1,753
COLE, John Vicat (1903-1975) British				
oil	1	2,790	2,790	2,790
COLE, Joseph Foxcroft (1837-1892) American				
oil	4	1,400-2,800	1,975	1,600
COLE, Joseph Greenleaf (1803-1858) American				
oil	2	550-3,000	1,775	550
COLE, Leslie (1910-) British				
oil	1	1,758	1,758	1,758
COLE, Max (20th C) American				
wc/d	3	607-17,000	6,109	721
COLEMAN, Charles Caryl (1840-1928) American				
oil	4	6,500-600,000	163,625	8,000
wc/d	2	1,036-1,600	1,318	1,036
COLEMAN, Eamon (20th C) Irish?				
3D	1	2,003	2,003	2,003
COLEMAN, Edward (?-1867) British				
oil	1	2,016	2,016	2,016
COLEMAN, Enrico (1846-1911) Italian				
wc/d	8	3,500-15,812	8,285	7,830
COLEMAN, Francesco (1851-1918) Italian				
oil	1	7,750	7,750	7,750
wc/d	4	1,200-4,275	2,708	2,580
COLEMAN, Glenn O (1887-1932) American				
oil	1	12,000	12,000	12,000
COLEMAN, John (?) British				
3D	2	5,000-6,000	5,500	5,000
COLEMAN, Mary Dartes (1894-?) American				
oil	1	1,000	1,000	1,000
COLEMAN, Michael (1946-) American				
oil	11	850-32,000	12,622	9,500
wc/d	10	606-17,500	6,035	5,000
COLEMAN, Nicholas (1978-) American				
oil	7	700-6,000	3,921	4,000
COLEMAN, Simon (1916-) Irish				
oil	2	1,052-2,338	1,695	1,052
COLEMAN, William Stephen (1829-1904) British				
oil	1	19,030	19,030	19,030
wc/d	7	525-8,100	2,175	968
COLEN, Henri (?) Belgian				
oil	1	1,130	1,130	1,130
COLESCOTT, Robert (1925-) American				
oil	1	22,500	22,500	22,500
COLFER, John Thomas (20th C) American				
oil	2	2,350-5,500	3,925	2,350
COLIN DE LA BIOCHAYE, Christian Marie (1750-1816) French				
oil	1	120,000	120,000	120,000
COLIN, Alexandre Marie (1798-1873) French				
oil	2	2,827-6,301	4,564	2,827
COLIN, Gustave (1828-1910) French				
oil	6	527-13,548	4,897	2,259
COLIN, Paul (1892-1985) French				
oil	1	5,765	5,765	5,765
wc/d	5	937-5,500	2,293	1,638
COLINET, C J R (fl.1913-1945) French				
3D	1	2,550	2,550	2,550
COLINET, Claire Jeanne Roberte (fl.1913-1945) French				
3D	5	2,681-90,000	23,564	7,208
COLKETT, Samuel David (1806-1863) British				
oil	5	1,748-3,894	2,521	2,088
COLKETT, Victoria S (1840-1926) British				
oil	1	865	865	865
wc/d	1	438	438	438

Name	No.	Price Range	Average	Median
COLL, Francesc Pausas (1877-1942) Spanish				
oil	1	41,691	41,691	41,691
COLL, Pep (1959-) Spanish				
oil	1	2,259	2,259	2,259
COLLA, Ettore (1896-1968) Italian				
3D	1	76,327	76,327	76,327
COLLART, Marie (1842-1911) Belgian				
oil	1	2,600	2,600	2,600
COLLE, Gino de (19/20th C) Italian				
wc/d	1	1,141	1,141	1,141
COLLE, Michel-Auguste (1872-1949) French				
oil	5	1,227-3,737	2,304	2,186
COLLE, Raffaelino del (1490-1566) Italian				
oil	1	20,400	20,400	20,400
COLLEL, Jose (1912-) Spanish				
oil	1	1,492	1,492	1,492
COLLET, Edouard Louis (1876-?) Swiss				
3D	1	3,600	3,600	3,600
COLLEY, Andrew (19th C) British				
oil	2	1,288-5,520	3,404	1,288
COLLIANDER, Ina (1908-1985) Finnish				
oil	1	2,571	2,571	2,571
COLLIER, Alan Caswell (1911-1990) Canadian				
oil	20	820-10,720	2,408	1,558
wc/d	1	2,438	2,438	2,438
COLLIER, Evert (1640-1706) Dutch				
oil	5	4,696-48,440	16,664	10,380
COLLIER, The Hon John (1850-1934) British				
oil	3	2,610-18,900	9,185	6,045
wc/d	1	735	735	735
COLLIER, Thomas Frederick (fl.1848-1874) British				
wc/d	8	626-2,805	1,162	766
COLLIGNON, Georges (1923-2002) Belgian				
oil	5	2,141-15,196	7,775	5,845
wc/d	8	494-2,616	1,669	1,908
COLLIN DE VERMONT, Hyacinthe (1693-1761) French				
wc/d	1	8,000	8,000	8,000
COLLIN, Alberic (1886-1962) Belgian				
3D	5	2,805-19,178	10,152	8,718
COLLIN, Marcus (1882-1966) Finnish				
oil	6	703-3,974	1,696	996
wc/d	4	719-2,379	1,242	818
COLLINGS, Charles John (1848-1931) British				
oil	2	1,305-1,378	1,341	1,305
wc/d	1	2,100	2,100	2,100
COLLINGWOOD, William (1819-1903) British				
oil	1	1,050	1,050	1,050
COLLINI, P (19/20th C) Italian				
oil	1	5,959	5,959	5,959
COLLINS, Arthur George (1866-?) American				
oil	1	1,300	1,300	1,300
COLLINS, Cecil (1908-1989) British				
oil	2	3,894-7,938	5,916	3,894
wc/d	3	1,770-6,624	3,464	2,000
COLLINS, Charles (1851-1921) British				
oil	3	1,400-5,460	3,289	3,009
wc/d	1	925	925	925
COLLINS, Hugh (fl.1868-1892) British				
oil	5	750-8,342	2,482	1,074
COLLINS, Majella (1964-) Irish				
oil	1	2,182	2,182	2,182
COLLINS, Mary Susan (1880-?) American				
oil	1	2,850	2,850	2,850
COLLINS, Patrick (1911-1994) British				
oil	9	9,687-37,537	20,150	18,904
wc/d	1	1,038	1,038	1,038
COLLINS, William (1788-1847) British				
oil	2	1,979-2,760	2,369	1,979
COLLINS, William Wiehe (1862-1952) British				
oil	1	18,375	18,375	18,375
wc/d	1	570	570	570

Name	No.	Price Range	Average	Median
COLLINSON, James (1825-1881) British				
oil	1	12,528	12,528	12,528
COLLIS, Peter (1929-) Irish				
oil	22	994-10,171	4,969	3,840
COLLISHAW, Mat (1966-) British				
3D	3	1,665-5,310	3,471	3,440
COLLOMB, Fernand (1902-1981) French				
oil	11	722-3,733	2,045	1,940
COLLS, Ebenezer (1812-1887) British				
oil	4	1,739-5,220	2,746	1,947
COLLVER, Ethel Blanchard (1875-1955) American				
oil	1	1,438	1,438	1,438
COLLYER, Nora Frances Elisabeth (1898-1979) Canadian				
oil	4	4,123-70,521	21,527	4,457
COLMAN, Roi Clarkson (1884-1945) American				
oil	4	2,300-5,500	4,137	3,750
COLMAN, Samuel (1832-1920) American				
oil	9	500-55,000	12,533	3,500
wc/d	5	1,100-230,000	48,120	2,400
COLMEIRO, Manuel (1901-1999) Spanish				
wc/d	1	1,013	1,013	1,013
COLMENAREZ, Asdrubal (1936-) South American				
wc/d	1	3,720	3,720	3,720
COLMO, Giovanni (1867-1947) Italian				
oil	3	756-1,332	1,099	1,211
COLMORE, Nina (1889-1973) British				
oil	1	1,890	1,890	1,890
COLNOT, Arnout (1887-1983) Dutch				
oil	8	1,000-4,633	2,723	2,253
wc/d	1	1,808	1,808	1,808
COLOMBA, Giovanni Battista (1717-1801) Italian				
oil	1	10,684	10,684	10,684
COLOMBI, Plinio (1873-1951) Swiss				
oil	10	683-2,937	1,850	1,623
wc/d	3	541-1,459	964	892
COLOMBO, Gianni (1937-1993) Italian				
wc/d	1	23,425	23,425	23,425
3D	4	14,000-37,170	23,545	16,397
COLOMBO, Joe Cesare (1930-1971) Italian				
wc/d	4	2,521-4,285	3,340	2,521
COLOMBO, Virgilio (19th C) Italian				
wc/d	2	433-1,815	1,124	433
COLOMBOTTO ROSSO, Enrico (1925-) Italian				
oil	10	907-2,438	1,636	1,491
wc/d	7	471-1,133	682	615
COLOMBRES, Ignacio (?) Argentinian				
oil	1	3,000	3,000	3,000
COLOTTE, Aristide Nancy (1885-1959) French?				
3D	1	5,130	5,130	5,130
COLQUHOUN, Ithell (1906-1988) British				
oil	3	673-2,880	1,672	1,464
COLQUHOUN, Robert (1914-1962) British				
oil	2	968-147,900	74,434	968
wc/d	8	1,079-5,888	2,080	1,531
COLSON, Greg (1956-) American				
oil	1	1,300	1,300	1,300
COLSON, Jaime Antonio (20th C) Dominican				
oil	2	4,607-6,668	5,637	4,607
COLTHURST, Francis Edward (1874-1945) British				
oil	3	1,047-1,305	1,140	1,068
COLTMAN, Ora (20th C) American				
oil	1	3,250	3,250	3,250
COLTRO, Davide (1967-) Italian				
wc/d	1	1,881	1,881	1,881
COLUCCI, Gio (1892-1974) Italian				
oil	7	630-5,014	1,566	900
wc/d	1	632	632	632
3D	2	2,945-10,014	6,479	2,945
COLUNGA, Alejandro (1948-) Mexican				
wc/d	1	2,750	2,750	2,750
COLVILLE, Alex (1920-) Canadian				
oil	1	509,597	509,597	509,597

Name	No.	Price Range	Average	Median
COLVIN, Marta (1917-) Chilean				
wc/d	1	1,081	1,081	1,081
3D	1	2,408	2,408	2,408
COMAN, Charlotte Buell (1833-1925) American				
oil	1	2,000	2,000	2,000
COMBA, P (?-1934) French				
wc/d	2	1,196-2,392	1,794	1,196
COMBA, Pierre (1859-1934) French				
wc/d	6	865-2,751	1,352	989
COMBAS, Robert (1957-) French				
oil	60	895-49,601	12,898	9,370
wc/d	10	409-27,825	4,528	1,288
3D	5	1,752-7,899	3,343	2,201
COMBER, Melanie (1970-) British				
wc/d	1	7,280	7,280	7,280
COMBES, Simon (1940-) Kenyan				
oil	1	9,000	9,000	9,000
COMBET-DESCOMBES, Pierre (1885-1966) French				
oil	2	1,676-12,760	7,218	1,676
wc/d	9	660-2,710	1,563	1,576
COMELLI, Dante (1880-1958) Italian				
oil	2	2,068-3,649	2,858	2,068
COMENSOLI, Mario (1922-1993) Swiss/Italian				
oil	7	571-8,346	3,176	1,897
wc/d	9	527-12,938	2,944	2,119
COMERRE, Léon (1850-1916) French				
oil	11	876-90,000	25,968	9,000
wc/d	3	1,347-1,911	1,571	1,455
COMFORT, Charles Fraser (1900-1994) Canadian				
oil	7	1,968-14,588	7,054	3,879
wc/d	3	990-2,144	1,594	1,649
COMINETTI, Giuseppe (1882-1930) Italian				
oil	1	2,141	2,141	2,141
COMINS, Eben F (1875-1949) American				
oil	1	1,100	1,100	1,100
COMMENT, Jean-François (1919-2002) Swiss				
wc/d	1	1,518	1,518	1,518
COMMERE, Jean Yves (1920-1986) French				
oil	13	840-4,083	1,822	1,656
wc/d	1	1,119	1,119	1,119
COMMUNAL, Joseph (1876-1962) French				
oil	5	1,068-5,394	2,754	1,874
COMOLERA, Paul (1818-1897) French				
3D	1	5,220	5,220	5,220
COMOLLI, Gigi (1893-1976) Italian				
oil	5	788-3,637	2,345	2,395
COMOY, Marie Emmanuel Gustave (19th C) French				
oil	1	10,000	10,000	10,000
COMPAGNO, Scipione (1624-1685) Italian				
oil	1	12,740	12,740	12,740
COMPARD, Émile (1900-1977) French				
oil	6	584-1,641	1,089	760
COMPIGNE (18th C) French				
oil	4	2,008-26,359	11,375	2,071
COMPTE-CALIX, François Claudius (1813-1880) French				
oil	2	1,094-5,890	3,492	1,094
COMPTON, Charles (1828-1884) British				
oil	1	4,524	4,524	4,524
COMPTON, Edward (19th C) British				
wc/d	1	1,946	1,946	1,946
COMPTON, Edward Harrison (1881-1960) British				
oil	15	1,095-7,708	3,666	2,827
wc/d	14	544-2,397	1,214	1,178
COMPTON, Edward Theodore (1849-1921) British				
oil	1	2,498	2,498	2,498
wc/d	18	884-14,880	4,913	3,160
COMPTON, Edward Thomas (19/20th C) British				
oil	1	5,152	5,152	5,152
COMTE, Pierre Charles (1823-1895) French				
oil	5	6,125-40,000	15,315	9,735
COMTOIS, Ulysse (1931-) Canadian				
oil	3	770-2,281	1,362	1,037

Name	No.	Price Range	Average	Median
CONCA, Sebastiano (1676-1764) Italian				
oil	7	8,000-84,144	37,025	24,973
wc/d	2	1,029-1,414	1,221	1,029
CONCA, Sebastiano and LOCATELLI, Andrea (17/18th C) Italian				
oil	1	24,276	24,276	24,276
CONCONI, Luigi (1852-1917) Italian				
wc/d	1	7,120	7,120	7,120
CONDAMY, Charles Fernand de (1855-1913) French				
oil	1	1,151	1,151	1,151
wc/d	21	546-13,597	4,176	2,565
CONDE, Eleanore de (19th C) French				
oil	1	3,312	3,312	3,312
CONDE, Miguel (1939-) American				
wc/d	3	777-1,556	1,096	957
CONDE-GONZALEZ, Emile (?) Spanish?				
oil	1	2,356	2,356	2,356
CONDER, Charles (1868-1909) British				
oil	2	2,565-10,260	6,412	2,565
wc/d	1	777	777	777
CONDO, George (1957-) American				
oil	15	4,451-144,300	48,743	28,000
wc/d	4	954-4,000	2,213	1,900
CONDOPOULOS, Alecos (1905-1975) Greek				
wc/d	1	24,310	24,310	24,310
CONDOY, Honorio Garcia (1900-1953) Spanish				
3D	1	4,435	4,435	4,435
CONDY, Nicholas Matthew (1816-1851) British				
oil	7	974-11,310	6,501	7,728
CONE, Marvin D (1891-1964) American				
oil	2	30,000-48,000	39,000	30,000
CONEJO, Andres (1913-1994) Spanish				
oil	1	1,914	1,914	1,914
CONFORTINI, Jacopo (17th C) Italian				
wc/d	2	2,000-3,646	2,823	2,000
CONGNET, Gillis (1538-1599) Dutch				
oil	1	47,568	47,568	47,568
CONGNET, Michiel (fl.1640-1641) Flemish				
oil	1	7,707	7,707	7,707
CONGO THE CHIMP (1954-1964) British?				
oil	1	555	555	555
wc/d	2	2,832-5,664	4,248	2,832
CONINCK, Pierre Louis Joseph de (1828-1910) French				
oil	2	1,178-9,450	5,314	1,178
CONKLING, Mabel Viola Harris (1871-1966) American				
3D	1	3,250	3,250	3,250
CONNAWAY, Jay Hall (1893-1970) American				
oil	17	750-7,500	2,900	2,800
CONNELLY, Chuck (20th C) American				
oil	1	4,250	4,250	4,250
CONNELLY, Pierre Francis (1841-1902) American				
3D	1	3,000	3,000	3,000
CONNER, John Ramsey (1867-1952) American				
oil	2	650-2,900	1,775	650
CONNOR, Todd (1964-) American				
oil	1	13,000	13,000	13,000
CONOLLY, Ellen (fl.1873-1885) British				
oil	1	22,800	22,800	22,800
CONOR, William (1881-1968) Irish				
oil	2	7,266-43,784	25,525	7,266
wc/d	23	620-46,500	11,651	7,540
CONRAD, Albert (1837-1887) German				
oil	1	8,970	8,970	8,970
CONRAD, Bonnie (1947-) American				
oil	1	5,000	5,000	5,000
CONRADE, Alfred Charles (1863-1955) British				
wc/d	3	1,400-1,750	1,534	1,452
CONRADER, Georg (1838-1911) German				
oil	1	1,150	1,150	1,150
CONRADSEN, M (?) ?				
oil	1	4,442	4,442	4,442

Name	No.	Price Range	Average	Median
CONROY, Stephen (1964-) British				
oil	4	2,907-66,880	22,754	9,790
wc/d	1	15,840	15,840	15,840
CONSADORI, Silvio (1909-1996) Italian				
oil	8	1,036-4,794	2,167	1,210
CONSAGRA, Pietro (1920-2005) Italian				
wc/d	3	712-882	825	882
3D	19	1,767-122,143	16,630	2,544
CONSIGLIO, Mario (1968-) Italian				
wc/d	1	1,378	1,378	1,378
CONSOLAZIONE, Giovanni (1904-1964) Italian				
oil	1	1,874	1,874	1,874
CONSONNI, Vittorio (1956-) Italian				
wc/d	3	1,178-1,296	1,217	1,178
CONSTABLE, J (1776-1837) British				
oil	1	2,744	2,744	2,744
CONSTABLE, John (1776-1837) British				
oil	1	557,550	557,550	557,550
wc/d	7	2,400-112,450	32,429	13,020
CONSTANT (1920-2005) Dutch				
wc/d	18	1,649-35,342	11,236	9,351
3D	1	37,622	37,622	37,622
CONSTANT, Benjamin (1845-1902) French				
oil	7	756-532,911	85,940	2,160
CONSTANT, Joseph (1892-1969) French				
3D	6	1,868-14,013	4,745	2,336
CONSTANTIN, Ivan (1895-?) Russian				
oil	1	9,555	9,555	9,555
CONSTANTIN, Jean Antoine (1756-1844) French				
wc/d	3	668-8,758	3,992	2,552
CONSTANTIN, Marie (19th C) French				
oil	1	2,750	2,750	2,750
CONSTANTINE, G Hamilton (1875-1967) British				
wc/d	4	684-2,625	1,603	896
CONSTANTINE, George (20th C) ?				
oil	1	1,100	1,100	1,100
CONSTANTINI, Giuseppe (19th C) Italian				
oil	1	10,560	10,560	10,560
CONTE, Dante Mose (1885-1919) Italian				
oil	2	1,894-3,567	2,730	1,894
CONTE, Guillermo (1956-) Argentinian				
oil	1	7,000	7,000	7,000
CONTE, Meiffren (1630-1705) French				
oil	1	55,452	55,452	55,452
CONTE, Michelangelo (1913-1996) Italian				
wc/d	1	1,890	1,890	1,890
CONTE, Pino (1915-) Italian				
3D	1	6,361	6,361	6,361
CONTELL, R T (19th C) Italian				
oil	1	2,200	2,200	2,200
CONTENCIN, Charles Henry (1898-1955) French				
oil	2	2,398-3,503	2,950	2,398
CONTENT, Daniel (1902-1990) American				
oil	1	2,000	2,000	2,000
CONTESSE, Gaston Louis Joseph (1870-1946) French				
3D	1	2,108	2,108	2,108
CONTI, Primo (1900-1989) Italian				
oil	5	1,800-38,163	11,657	3,514
wc/d	3	598-3,816	1,748	832
CONTI, Tito (1842-1924) Italian				
oil	5	2,000-15,120	9,651	10,000
CONTI, William (1867-?) ?				
oil	1	1,214	1,214	1,214
CONTINI, Massimillano (1850-?) Italian				
3D	1	2,336	2,336	2,336
CONTRERAS, Jesus Fructuoso (1867-1902) Mexican				
3D	1	22,500	22,500	22,500
CONTWAY, Jay (20th C) American				
3D	1	2,663	2,663	2,663
CONWAY, John Severinus (1852-1925) American				
oil	1	1,191	1,191	1,191

Name	No.	Price Range	Average	Median
COOK OF PLYMOUTH, Samuel (1806-1859) British				
wc/d	3	963-1,496	1,167	1,044
COOK OF PLYMOUTH, William (fl.1870-1880) British				
oil	1	669	669	669
wc/d	1	555	555	555
COOK, Beryl (1926-) British				
oil	1	8,600	8,600	8,600
COOK, Charles Bailey (1865-1948) American				
oil	1	1,900	1,900	1,900
COOK, Charles W (20th C) American				
3D	1	2,800	2,800	2,800
COOK, Ebenezer Wake (1843-1926) British				
wc/d	8	458-2,353	1,257	1,147
COOK, Ebenezer Wake and GREGORY, Charles (19/20th C) British				
wc/d	1	1,073	1,073	1,073
COOK, Henry (1819-c.1890) British				
oil	1	2,057	2,057	2,057
COOK, Howard (1901-1980) American				
oil	2	2,750-5,500	4,125	2,750
wc/d	2	500-2,500	1,500	500
COOK, John A (1870-1936) American				
wc/d	2	650-1,400	1,025	650
COOK, Joshua (jnr) (fl.1852-1854) British				
oil	1	1,943	1,943	1,943
COOK, Margaret C (fl.1897-1913) British				
oil	1	1,044	1,044	1,044
COOK, Otis (1900-1980) American				
oil	8	1,900-5,000	3,312	3,200
COOK, Paul Rodda (1897-1972) American				
oil	1	1,300	1,300	1,300
COOK, Richard (1784-1857) British				
oil	1	2,646	2,646	2,646
COOKE, Barrie (1931-) British				
oil	9	2,121-29,667	9,911	6,076
wc/d	7	1,165-3,871	2,196	1,920
COOKE, E W (1811-1880) British				
oil	1	3,400	3,400	3,400
COOKE, Edward William (1811-1880) British				
oil	6	14,790-65,450	32,865	22,750
wc/d	4	445-4,498	1,844	956
COOKE, John Percy (20th C) British				
oil	1	1,593	1,593	1,593
COOKE, Roger (1941-) American				
oil	1	1,500	1,500	1,500
COOKE, William Edward (fl.1880-1886) British				
oil	2	925-3,240	2,082	925
COOKSEY, May Louise Greville (1878-1943) British				
oil	1	1,380	1,380	1,380
COOL, Gabriel de (1854-?) French				
oil	1	16,562	16,562	16,562
COOLE, Brian (19th C) British				
oil	3	632-1,450	1,060	1,100
COOLEY, Thomas (1795-1872) British				
wc/d	1	1,854	1,854	1,854
COOLIDGE, Cassius M (1844-1934) American				
oil	1	24,000	24,000	24,000
COOMANS, Auguste (19th C) Belgian				
oil	3	676-1,777	1,237	1,260
COOMANS, Pierre Olivier Joseph (1816-1889) Belgian				
oil	4	5,000-92,000	40,520	15,082
COONAN, Emily (1885-1971) Canadian				
oil	1	8,863	8,863	8,863
COONEY, Mary Wheeler (1866-1957) American				
oil	1	1,400	1,400	1,400
COOP, Hubert (1872-1953) British				
oil	1	1,216	1,216	1,216
wc/d	4	579-3,393	1,942	796
COOPER, Alexander Davis (fl.1837-1888) British				
oil	2	703-7,434	4,068	703
COOPER, Alfred Heaton (1864-1929) British				
oil	1	2,784	2,784	2,784
wc/d	8	592-3,784	1,811	1,080

Name	No.	Price Range	Average	Median
COOPER, Astley D M (1856-1924) American				
oil	3	650-2,000	1,416	1,600
COOPER, Colin Campbell (1856-1937) American				
oil	6	700-65,775	17,329	9,500
wc/d	6	750-6,750	3,858	3,250
COOPER, Douglas (20th C) American				
wc/d	3	1,000-1,000	1,000	1,000
COOPER, Edwin (1785-1833) British				
oil	3	2,336-4,844	3,986	4,779
COOPER, Eileen (1953-) British				
oil	1	1,343	1,343	1,343
COOPER, Forrest (20th C) American				
oil	1	1,300	1,300	1,300
COOPER, George Gordon Byron (?-1933) British				
oil	1	1,492	1,492	1,492
COOPER, Gerald (1898-1975) British				
oil	8	952-20,520	7,203	4,536
COOPER, J (?) British?				
oil	1	4,800	4,800	4,800
COOPER, Jessica (1967-) British				
oil	1	1,936	1,936	1,936
COOPER, John (1942-) British				
oil	1	2,784	2,784	2,784
COOPER, Margaret Miles (1874-1965) American				
oil	3	900-1,500	1,200	1,200
COOPER, T C (19th C) British				
oil	1	7,560	7,560	7,560
COOPER, T S (1803-1902) British				
oil	1	1,100	1,100	1,100
COOPER, Thomas Sidney (1803-1902) British				
oil	26	1,748-79,380	19,735	10,320
wc/d	4	522-7,560	4,383	2,610
COOPER, Thomas Sidney and OAKES, John Wright (19th C) British				
oil	1	6,301	6,301	6,301
COOPER, W Savage (fl.1880-1926) British				
oil	3	550-18,904	9,651	9,500
COOPER, William Heaton (1903-1995) British				
oil	1	500	500	500
wc/d	14	412-3,480	2,079	2,001
COOPER, William Sidney (1854-1927) British				
oil	8	1,026-14,964	5,638	2,784
wc/d	9	527-2,970	1,317	1,104
COOPSE, Pieter (?-1677) Dutch				
oil	1	9,251	9,251	9,251
wc/d	2	1,384-4,498	2,941	1,384
COORTE, Adriaen (fl.1685-1723) Dutch				
oil	1	814,000	814,000	814,000
COOSEMANS, Joseph (1828-1904) Belgian				
oil	3	1,646-4,660	3,420	3,956
COPCOPAN, J T (19th C) American				
oil	1	3,250	3,250	3,250
COPE, Charles West (1811-1890) British				
oil	1	34,800	34,800	34,800
COPE, Elizabeth (1952-) Irish				
oil	1	1,758	1,758	1,758
COPE, George (1855-1929) American				
oil	4	3,200-75,000	25,925	5,500
COPELAND, Alfred Bryant (1840-1909) American				
oil	2	3,800-4,500	4,150	3,800
COPELAND, Charles (1858-1945) American				
oil	1	3,000	3,000	3,000
COPLEY, John Singleton (1738-1815) American				
oil	5	75,000-3,000,000	1,064,000	425,000
COPLEY, William Nelson (1919-1996) American				
oil	7	2,400-40,767	14,743	5,250
wc/d	7	972-43,315	13,857	5,856
COPNALL, John (1928-) British				
oil	3	481-4,872	3,060	3,828
COPPARD, C Law (fl.1858-1891) British				
oil	1	1,288	1,288	1,288
COPPEDGE, Fern Isabel (1888-1951) American				
oil	11	20,000-160,000	57,818	55,000

Name	No.	Price Range	Average	Median
COPPENOLLE, E van (1846-1914) Belgian				
oil	1	2,311	2,311	2,311
COPPENOLLE, Edmon van (1846-1914) Belgian				
oil	3	3,156-19,000	9,006	4,863
COPPENOLLE, Jacques van (1878-1915) French				
oil	4	972-5,068	2,326	1,017
COPPENS, Frans (1895-1975) Belgian				
oil	3	959-1,318	1,138	1,139
COPPENS, Omer (1864-1926) Belgian				
oil	6	530-4,127	1,562	643
COPPING, Harold (1863-1932) British				
wc/d	1	15,000	15,000	15,000
COPPINI, Carlo (19th C) Italian				
oil	1	1,196	1,196	1,196
COPPINI, Fausto Eliseo (1870-1945) Italian				
oil	2	5,200-6,400	5,800	5,200
COPPOLA, A (?) Italian				
oil	1	4,500	4,500	4,500
COPPOLA, Antonio (1839-?) Italian				
oil	1	1,405	1,405	1,405
wc/d	3	784-4,071	1,911	880
COPPOLA-CASTALDO, Francesco (c.1845-1916) Italian				
oil	1	9,136	9,136	9,136
wc/d	1	1,295	1,295	1,295
COQUES, Gonzales (1614-1684) Flemish				
oil	1	20,350	20,350	20,350
wc/d	1	7,500	7,500	7,500
CORA, Sebastiano (1857-1930) Italian				
oil	1	1,641	1,641	1,641
CORASICK, William W (1907-) American				
oil	1	1,400	1,400	1,400
CORBELLA, Tito (1885-1966) Italian				
oil	1	3,352	3,352	3,352
wc/d	2	592-718	655	592
CORBELLI, Edgardo (1918-1989) Italian				
oil	2	545-1,767	1,156	545
CORBELLINI (?) ?				
oil	1	1,884	1,884	1,884
CORBELLINI, Luigi (1901-1968) French				
oil	10	500-1,929	1,065	900
CORBERO, Xavier (1935-) Spanish				
3D	2	15,000-24,082	19,541	15,000
CORBET, Matthew Ridley (1850-1902) British				
wc/d	1	1,925	1,925	1,925
CORBETT, Gail Sherman (1871-1952) American				
oil	1	2,750	2,750	2,750
CORBIN, Peter (20th C) ?				
oil	1	25,000	25,000	25,000
CORBINO, Jon (1905-1964) American				
oil	1	800	800	800
wc/d	1	350	350	350
CORBOULD, Alfred (fl.1831-1875) British				
oil	1	1,500	1,500	1,500
CORBOULD, Aster R C (1812-1882) British				
oil	2	2,288-10,680	6,484	2,288
CORBOULD, Edward Henry (1815-1905) British				
oil	2	15,390-30,000	22,695	15,390
wc/d	1	673	673	673
CORBUSIER, le (1887-1965) French				
oil	4	59,200-518,000	213,080	65,120
wc/d	31	3,816-60,000	21,984	18,771
CORCHON Y DIAQUE, Federico (19th C) Spanish				
oil	1	2,081	2,081	2,081
CORCOS, Vittorio (1859-1933) Italian				
oil	3	13,081-171,062	76,714	46,000
CORDEY, Frederic (1854-1911) French				
oil	3	1,318-7,955	3,571	1,440
CORDIER DE BONNEVILLE, Louis Joseph Ange (1766-1843) French				
wc/d	1	8,929	8,929	8,929
CORDIER, Charles Henri Joseph (1827-1905) French				
3D	6	10,092-82,800	58,045	56,000

Name	No.	Price Range	Average	Median
CORDIVIOLA, Luis Adolfo (1892-1967) Argentinian				
oil	3	7,200-15,000	10,400	9,000
CORDREY, John (fl.1765-1825) British				
oil	2	2,100-5,472	3,786	2,100
CORELLI, A (1853-1910) Italian				
oil	1	3,219	3,219	3,219
CORELLI, Augusto (1853-1910) Italian				
oil	1	1,636	1,636	1,636
wc/d	1	1,680	1,680	1,680
CORELLI, Giuseppe (19/20th C) Italian				
oil	1	1,900	1,900	1,900
COREY, Bernard (1914-2000) American				
oil	8	575-2,600	1,518	1,150
CORINTH, Lovis (1858-1925) German				
oil	10	4,568-267,568	100,006	83,959
wc/d	15	468-123,200	23,320	2,188
CORKOLE, Antoine (19th C) French				
oil	1	1,472	1,472	1,472
CORLIN, Gustave Auguste (1875-1970) French				
oil	1	1,947	1,947	1,947
CORNE, Michele Felice (1752-1832) American/Italian				
oil	1	8,500	8,500	8,500
CORNEAU, Eugène (1894-1976) French				
oil	6	800-2,420	1,639	1,414
CORNEILLE (1922-) Belgian				
oil	21	595-257,539	45,287	33,036
wc/d	32	1,230-17,208	6,141	4,477
3D	8	2,472-14,487	6,249	4,793
CORNEILLE DE LYON (?-1574) Flemish				
oil	1	55,500	55,500	55,500
CORNEILLE, Jean Baptiste (1649-1695) French				
oil	1	3,548	3,548	3,548
CORNEILLE, Michel (younger) (1642-1708) French				
oil	1	21,041	21,041	21,041
wc/d	4	900-24,050	8,080	2,616
CORNEJO, Francisco (?-1963) American?				
oil	2	500-2,250	1,375	500
wc/d	1	1,600	1,600	1,600
CORNELIANO, Francesco (1740-1815) Italian				
oil	1	15,459	15,459	15,459
CORNELISZ, Cornelis van Haarlem (1562-1638) Dutch				
oil	5	1,080-33,300	12,502	9,342
CORNELIUS, Jean Georges (1880-1963) French				
oil	3	1,874-3,912	2,747	2,455
CORNELL, Joseph (1903-1972) American				
wc/d	6	500-48,000	28,018	27,185
3D	5	170,000-520,000	288,000	260,000
CORNER, Philip (1933-) American				
wc/d	1	1,097	1,097	1,097
CORNIENTI, Cherubino (1816-1860) Italian				
oil	1	3,853	3,853	3,853
CORNILLIER, Pierre Emile (19th C) French				
oil	1	1,700	1,700	1,700
CORNILLON, Jean Baptiste (1821-?) French				
oil	1	1,197	1,197	1,197
CORNISH, Hubert (c.1770-1832) British				
wc/d	1	9,000	9,000	9,000
CORNISH, Norman (1919-) British				
wc/d	8	819-7,770	2,549	1,958
CORNOYER, Paul (1864-1923) American				
oil	3	400-3,750	1,816	1,300
CORNU, Jean Jean (1819-1876) French				
oil	1	6,500	6,500	6,500
CORNU, Pierre (1895-1996) French				
oil	6	1,491-3,461	2,038	1,757
wc/d	1	1,757	1,757	1,757
CORNU, Vital (1851-?) French				
3D	2	4,145-4,581	4,363	4,145
CORNWELL, Dean (1892-1960) American				
oil	8	600-65,000	21,625	6,000
wc/d	2	650-3,600	2,125	650

Name	No.	Price Range	Average	Median
COROMALDI, Umberto (1870-1948) Italian				
wc/d	2	1,523-3,374	2,448	1,523
CORONA, Poul (1872-1945) Danish				
oil	1	1,260	1,260	1,260
CORONA, Vittorio (1901-1966) Italian				
wc/d	1	23,425	23,425	23,425
CORONEL, Pedro (1923-1985) Mexican				
oil	4	37,500-140,000	76,875	50,000
CORONEL, Rafael (1932-) Mexican				
oil	11	1,900-55,000	14,650	7,000
wc/d	2	400-16,000	8,200	400
CORONELLI, G (19th C) Italian				
oil	1	2,200	2,200	2,200
COROT, Jean Baptiste Camille (1796-1875) French				
oil	33	15,000-700,000	126,008	75,000
wc/d	8	1,701-14,034	5,721	3,414
CORPET, Etienne (1877-?) French				
oil	3	486-6,969	4,808	6,969
CORPORA, Antonio (1909-2004) Italian				
oil	50	4,568-56,076	20,900	18,000
wc/d	50	2,234-42,719	5,084	3,699
CORRADI, Alfonso (1889-1972) Italian				
oil	2	1,796-2,189	1,992	1,796
CORRADI, Konrad (1813-1878) Swiss				
wc/d	4	549-1,565	1,087	784
CORRADINI, Mara (1880-1964) Swiss				
oil	1	7,611	7,611	7,611
CORRALES EGEA, Manuel (1910-1985) Spanish				
oil	1	1,270	1,270	1,270
CORREA DE VIVAR, Juan (fl.1550-1560) Spanish				
oil	1	44,551	44,551	44,551
CORREDOYRA DE CASTRO, Jesus Rodriguez (1889-1939) Spanish				
oil	1	5,400	5,400	5,400
CORREGGIO, Ludwig (1846-1920) German				
oil	3	647-2,104	1,188	814
CORRODI, Arnaldo (1846-1874) Italian				
wc/d	1	1,890	1,890	1,890
CORRODI, Hermann David Salomon (1844-1905) Italian				
oil	16	11,000-420,000	82,736	35,000
wc/d	1	10,293	10,293	10,293
CORRODI, Salomon (1810-1892) Swiss				
wc/d	9	5,708-24,050	15,318	15,534
CORSI DI BOSNASCO, Giacinto (1829-1909) Italian				
oil	1	1,386	1,386	1,386
wc/d	1	750	750	750
CORSI, Nicolas de (1882-1956) Italian				
oil	7	916-4,071	2,404	2,378
CORSI, Santi (19/20th C) Italian				
oil	2	7,964-15,811	11,887	7,964
CORSIA, Gilbert (1915-1985) French				
oil	1	1,073	1,073	1,073
CORSINI, Raffaele (19th C) Italian				
wc/d	1	4,450	4,450	4,450
CORTAZZO, Oreste (1836-?) Italian				
oil	2	4,834-6,000	5,417	4,834
CORTE, Gabriel de la (1648-1694) Spanish				
oil	1	37,500	37,500	37,500
CORTEGO, S de (?) ?				
oil	1	23,919	23,919	23,919
CORTEJARENA Y ALDEVO, Francisco Jose (1835-?) Spanish				
oil	2	953-1,192	1,072	953
CORTES BORRAS, Eva (20th C) Spanish				
oil	1	1,381	1,381	1,381
wc/d	1	1,059	1,059	1,059
CORTES Y AGUILAR, Andres (1810-1879) Spanish				
oil	1	2,945	2,945	2,945
CORTES Y CORDERO, Antonio (1826-1908) Spanish				
oil	2	1,416-1,770	1,593	1,416
CORTES, Andre (1815-1880) Spanish				
oil	3	2,121-4,380	3,193	3,078
CORTES, Antonio (19th C) Spanish				
oil	1	6,541	6,541	6,541

Name	No.	Price Range	Average	Median
CORTES, Daniel (19/20th C) Spanish				
oil	3	4,099-36,800	19,904	18,814
CORTES, Edouard (1882-1969) French				
oil	68	4,625-85,000	27,353	27,500
wc/d	6	4,821-15,000	7,836	6,600
CORTESE, Federico (1829-1913) Italian				
oil	1	3,292	3,292	3,292
CORTIELLO, Mario (1907-1982) Italian				
oil	7	942-2,063	1,389	1,214
CORTIER, Amedee (1921-1976) Belgian				
oil	3	701-4,256	2,938	3,857
CORTIJO, Francisco (1936-1996) Spanish				
oil	4	650-950	825	850
wc/d	3	482-506	490	482
CORTONA, Pietro da (1596-1669) Italian				
wc/d	3	843-138,750	48,513	5,946
CORTOR, Eldzier (1916-) American				
oil	1	32,500	32,500	32,500
CORTOT, Jean (1925-) French				
oil	3	742-1,854	1,149	851
CORVAYA, Salvatore (1872-1962) Italian				
oil	1	1,455	1,455	1,455
CORVINI, Giovanni (1820-1894) Italian				
oil	1	2,914	2,914	2,914
CORWIN, Charles Abel (1857-1938) American				
oil	4	525-8,000	3,206	1,300
CORZAS, Francisco (1936-1983) Mexican				
oil	1	21,000	21,000	21,000
COSENTINI, Maximo (20th C) ?				
oil	1	1,197	1,197	1,197
COSGROVE, Stanley Morel (1911-2002) Canadian				
oil	17	2,372-30,391	6,252	4,919
wc/d	4	738-4,218	1,795	990
COSMADOPOULOS, Georges (1899-?) Greek				
oil	3	3,200-5,236	4,557	5,236
COSOLA, Demetrio (1851-1895) Italian				
wc/d	2	969-1,514	1,241	969
COSSA, J (18th C) ?				
oil	1	11,125	11,125	11,125
COSSAAR, Jan (1874-1966) Dutch				
oil	4	515-12,603	3,580	539
COSSIAU, Jan Joost von (1660-1732) Dutch				
wc/d	1	1,018	1,018	1,018
COSSIERS, Jan (1600-1671) Flemish				
oil	1	37,000	37,000	37,000
COSSIO, Pancho (1898-1970) Spanish				
oil	1	39,000	39,000	39,000
wc/d	1	3,251	3,251	3,251
COSSON, Marcel (1878-1956) French				
oil	27	1,216-9,298	3,520	2,979
COSTA BEIRO, Alfonso (1943-) Spanish				
oil	2	2,682-3,086	2,884	2,682
COSTA VILLA, Jose (1953-) Spanish				
oil	1	1,646	1,646	1,646
COSTA, Angelo Maria (18th C) Italian				
oil	1	7,658	7,658	7,658
COSTA, Claudio (1942-) Italian				
oil	1	3,145	3,145	3,145
wc/d	11	605-3,937	2,348	2,342
3D	2	2,640-3,633	3,136	2,640
COSTA, Domingos (1867-1954) ?				
oil	1	1,944	1,944	1,944
COSTA, Emanuele (1833-1913) French/Italian				
oil	3	375-4,000	1,890	1,296
wc/d	10	899-7,911	3,103	2,441
COSTA, Giovanni (1833-1903) Italian				
oil	2	12,945-15,000	13,972	12,945
wc/d	2	597-2,800	1,698	597
COSTA, Giovanni Battista (1859-1938) Italian				
wc/d	1	2,188	2,188	2,188
COSTA, Nino Giovanni (1826-1903) Italian				
oil	1	10,829	10,829	10,829

Name	No.	Price Range	Average	Median
COSTA, Olga (1913-1993) Mexican/German				
oil	1	16,000	16,000	16,000
COSTA, Oreste (1851-?) Italian				
oil	1	5,500	5,500	5,500
COSTALONGA, Franco (1933-) Italian				
oil	10	884-3,292	2,018	1,909
wc/d	4	1,178-4,712	2,589	2,116
3D	7	1,790-5,178	3,650	3,341
COSTANTINI, Virgile (1882-1940) Italian				
oil	1	3,805	3,805	3,805
COSTANTINO, Massimo (1955-) Italian				
oil	2	648-884	766	648
wc/d	2	610-895	752	610
COSTETTI, Giovanni (1875-1949) Italian				
oil	2	8,836-9,578	9,207	8,836
wc/d	2	1,260-1,260	1,260	1,260
COSTIGAN, John E (1888-1972) American				
oil	4	600-10,000	4,925	2,100
wc/d	2	2,150-2,750	2,450	2,150
COSWAY, Richard (1742-1821) British				
wc/d	3	400-22,680	8,623	2,790
COSYNS, Gies (1920-1997) Belgian				
oil	3	504-1,520	1,072	1,193
COTANDA, Vicente Nicolau (1852-1898) Spanish				
oil	1	3,360	3,360	3,360
COTANI, Paolo (1940-) Italian				
oil	1	6,997	6,997	6,997
wc/d	2	1,214-3,629	2,421	1,214
COTE, Bruno (1940-) Canadian				
oil	4	902-1,950	1,468	1,208
COTER, Colijn de (1455-1540) Flemish				
oil	1	65,000	65,000	65,000
COTES, Francis (1726-1770) British				
oil	3	7,400-25,900	15,766	14,000
COTMAN, Frederick George (1850-1920) British				
oil	1	4,152	4,152	4,152
wc/d	3	484-796	670	731
COTMAN, John Joseph (1814-1878) British				
wc/d	7	779-3,540	2,265	2,422
COTMAN, John Sell (1782-1842) British				
wc/d	10	2,200-52,080	13,904	5,292
COTO, Luiz (1830-1891) Mexican				
oil	1	35,000	35,000	35,000
COTTAAR, Piet (1878-1950) Dutch				
oil	1	1,029	1,029	1,029
COTTAVOZ, Andre (1922-) French				
oil	35	500-16,182	2,669	1,798
wc/d	1	1,054	1,054	1,054
COTTET, Charles (1863-1924) French				
oil	4	662-17,334	8,723	7,598
COTTHEM, Michele van (1939-) Belgian?				
oil	2	1,800-2,040	1,920	1,800
COTTIN, Eugène (1840-1902) French				
oil	1	2,351	2,351	2,351
COTTINGHAM, Robert (1935-) American				
oil	1	25,000	25,000	25,000
COTTON, Alan (1936-) British				
oil	2	475-2,196	1,335	475
COTTON, Brent (20th C) American				
oil	1	40,000	40,000	40,000
COTTON, Will (1965-) American				
oil	1	30,000	30,000	30,000
COTTON, William (1880-1958) American				
oil	1	6,000	6,000	6,000
COTTRAU, Felix (1799-1852) French				
wc/d	1	12,671	12,671	12,671
COTTRELL, H S (fl.1840-1860) British				
oil	1	2,223	2,223	2,223
COTTRELL, Wellesley (fl.1882-1913) British				
oil	1	1,496	1,496	1,496
COTTS, Claire B (1964-) American				
oil	1	2,000	2,000	2,000

Name	No.	Price Range	Average	Median
COUBINE, Othon (1883-1969) Czechoslovakian				
oil	3	1,683-9,271	5,651	6,000
wc/d	1	906	906	906
COUCH, Shane (1963-) British				
oil	1	20,000	20,000	20,000
COUCHAUX, Marcel (1877-1939) French				
oil	2	3,152-3,637	3,394	3,152
COUDER, Alexandre (1808-1879) French				
oil	3	546-6,155	3,101	2,603
COUDER, Gustave-Émile (1845-1903) French				
oil	1	39,087	39,087	39,087
COUDRAY, B de (?) French				
oil	1	2,769	2,769	2,769
COUDRAY, Georges Charles (fl.1883-1903) French				
3D	2	6,969-7,007	6,988	6,969
COUGHTRIE, James Billington (fl.1881-1914) British				
wc/d	1	2,232	2,232	2,232
COUGHTRY, John Graham (1931-) Canadian				
oil	1	2,659	2,659	2,659
wc/d	1	1,410	1,410	1,410
COULAUD, Martin (?-1906) French				
oil	1	5,180	5,180	5,180
COULDERY, Horatio H (1832-1893) British				
oil	2	696-3,128	1,912	696
COULENTIANOS, Costas (1918-1995) French				
3D	4	1,647-2,534	1,964	1,774
COULET, Leon Gabriel Louis (1873-?) French				
oil	1	4,849	4,849	4,849
COULON, George D (1822-1904) American				
oil	1	2,600	2,600	2,600
COULON, Louis (19th C) ?				
oil	1	2,735	2,735	2,735
COULTER, William Alexander (1849-1936) American				
oil	7	1,900-70,000	15,700	4,000
COULTRE, Andree le (1917-1986) French				
oil	1	878	878	878
wc/d	1	780	780	780
COUMONT, Charles (1822-1889) Flemish				
oil	3	504-2,697	1,279	637
COUPER, William (1853-1942) American				
oil	1	1,200	1,200	1,200
COUR, Janus la (1837-1909) Danish				
oil	30	681-26,057	4,708	2,384
COURANT, Maurice (1847-1925) French				
oil	6	2,141-5,462	3,660	3,109
wc/d	1	1,788	1,788	1,788
COURBET, Gustave (1819-1877) French				
oil	18	7,135-260,000	58,785	26,886
COURBET, Gustave and PATA, Cherubino (19th C) French				
oil	1	4,553	4,553	4,553
COURDOUAN, Vincent-Joseph-François (1810-1893) French				
oil	1	17,622	17,622	17,622
wc/d	1	4,186	4,186	4,186
COURIARD, Pelagria P (1848-1898) Russian				
oil	1	2,200	2,200	2,200
COURMES, Alfred (1898-1993) French				
oil	2	2,919-67,799	35,359	2,919
COURNAULT, Étienne (1891-1948) French				
wc/d	4	817-6,000	2,302	1,168
COURREAU, Paul (19th C) French				
oil	1	2,258	2,258	2,258
COURT, Joseph-Desire (1797-1865) French				
oil	2	1,942-11,689	6,815	1,942
COURT, Lee Winslow (1903-1992) American				
oil	1	1,200	1,200	1,200
COURT, Martin de la (1640-1710) Flemish				
oil	4	2,392-16,937	8,914	5,500
COURTAIS, G (20th C) French				
oil	1	2,500	2,500	2,500
COURTEN, Comte Angelo de (1848-1925) Italian				
oil	2	477-40,480	20,478	477
wc/d	1	3,100	3,100	3,100

Name	No.	Price Range	Average	Median
COURTENS, Franz (1854-1943) Belgian				
oil	12	1,169-8,318	3,536	2,428
COURTENS, Hermann (1884-1956) Belgian				
oil	8	662-2,682	1,554	1,051
COURTICE, Rody Kenny (1895-?) Canadian				
oil	3	1,687-9,071	6,371	8,355
COURTIER, Marthe (?) French				
wc/d	1	1,911	1,911	1,911
COURTIER, Prosper le (1851-1924) French				
3D	1	2,336	2,336	2,336
COURTOIS DE BONNENCONTRE, Ernest (19/20th C) French				
oil	1	7,562	7,562	7,562
COURTOIS, Balthasar (17th C) Flemish				
oil	1	171,986	171,986	171,986
COURTOIS, Eugene (?) French?				
oil	1	1,178	1,178	1,178
COURTOIS, Guillaume (1628-1679) French				
wc/d	2	766-5,469	3,117	766
COURTOIS, Jacques (1621-1676) French				
oil	2	17,939-54,081	36,010	17,939
wc/d	3	1,110-3,500	2,170	1,900
COUSE, E Irving (1866-1936) American				
oil	29	6,000-190,000	71,534	65,000
wc/d	1	15,000	15,000	15,000
COUSIN, Charles (19/20th C) French				
oil	7	486-2,640	1,735	2,060
COUSIN, Charles Louis Auguste (1807-1887) French				
oil	1	5,010	5,010	5,010
COUSINS, Harold B (1916-1992) American				
3D	1	3,057	3,057	3,057
COUSTOU, Guillaume I (1677-1746) French				
3D	1	6,654	6,654	6,654
COUSTURIER, Lucie (1876-1925) French				
oil	4	2,460-16,000	8,239	2,848
wc/d	3	602-1,230	912	906
COUTAN, Jules Felix (1848-1939) French				
3D	3	4,743-16,065	10,401	10,395
COUTAUD, Lucien (1904-1977) French				
oil	9	584-6,684	2,736	1,512
wc/d	8	547-1,285	828	759
COUTTS, Alice Gray (1880-1973) American				
oil	2	2,000-2,500	2,250	2,000
COUTTS, Gordon (1868-1937) British/American				
oil	6	2,500-8,000	4,416	3,200
COUTURE, Thomas (1815-1879) French				
oil	4	4,531-5,495	4,917	4,642
wc/d	1	1,415	1,415	1,415
COUTURIER, Robert (1905-) French				
3D	3	15,470-21,541	17,596	15,779
COUTY, Jean (1907-1991) French				
oil	10	2,395-10,356	6,025	4,789
wc/d	1	2,040	2,040	2,040
COUTY, Jean Frederic (1829-1904) French				
oil	3	1,697-10,541	4,840	2,284
COUVER, Jan van (1836-1909) Dutch				
oil	7	727-4,250	2,409	2,001
wc/d	1	860	860	860
COUWENBERG, Christiaan van (1604-1667) Dutch				
oil	1	47,500	47,500	47,500
COUZENS, Fred (?) American				
oil	1	1,100	1,100	1,100
COVARRUBIAS, Miguel (1904-1957) Mexican				
oil	2	8,000-65,000	36,500	8,000
wc/d	4	2,800-7,500	5,212	4,750
COVENTRY, Gertrude Mary (1886-1964) British				
oil	1	1,300	1,300	1,300
COVENTRY, Keith (1958-) British				
oil	1	11,100	11,100	11,100
COVENTRY, Robert McGown (1855-1914) British				
oil	4	3,000-14,240	8,798	5,632
wc/d	5	1,548-4,300	2,967	3,114

Name	No.	Price Range	Average	Median
COWAN, John P (1920-) American				
wc/d	2	1,300-1,300	1,300	1,300
COWARD, Sir Noel (1899-1973) British				
oil	1	4,350	4,350	4,350
COWERN, Jenny (?) British				
oil	2	821-1,436	1,128	821
wc/d	1	684	684	684
COWIE, James (1886-1956) British				
oil	1	4,862	4,862	4,862
wc/d	2	835-2,864	1,849	835
COWLES, Maude Alice (1871-1905) American				
oil	1	2,300	2,300	2,300
COWLES, Russell (1887-1979) American				
oil	1	1,300	1,300	1,300
COX, Charles Brinton (1864-1905) American				
oil	3	425-3,250	1,625	1,200
COX, David (jnr) (1809-1885) British				
oil	1	865	865	865
wc/d	8	566-2,960	1,618	1,190
COX, David (1783-1859) British				
oil	7	1,720-29,750	7,179	2,958
wc/d	32	430-19,140	4,283	2,232
COX, Garstin (1892-1933) British				
oil	8	619-8,750	2,662	1,144
wc/d	1	522	522	522
COX, Jack (20th C) British				
oil	13	484-1,288	811	850
wc/d	5	478-761	553	513
COX, Jan (1919-1980) Belgian				
oil	1	35,793	35,793	35,793
COX, Kenyon C (1856-1919) American				
oil	7	1,254-12,540	4,984	3,500
COX, Neil (20th C) British				
oil	3	1,229-2,079	1,638	1,607
wc/d	8	1,710-3,402	2,314	2,052
COX, Stephen (1946-) British				
wc/d	1	2,220	2,220	2,220
COX, Walter I (1866-1930) American/British				
oil	1	3,000	3,000	3,000
COXCIE, Michiel I (1499-1592) Flemish				
oil	1	140,000	140,000	140,000
COXIE, Jan Anthonie (?-1720) Flemish				
oil	1	67,732	67,732	67,732
COYPEL, Antoine (1661-1722) French				
wc/d	2	1,900-31,758	16,829	1,900
COYPEL, Charles Antoine (1694-1752) French				
oil	1	10,082	10,082	10,082
COYPEL, Noel (1628-1707) French				
wc/d	1	3,805	3,805	3,805
COYPEL, Noel Nicolas (1690-1734) French				
wc/d	1	3,500	3,500	3,500
COZENS, Alexander (c.1717-1786) British				
wc/d	2	11,160-13,840	12,500	11,160
COZENS, John Robert (1752-1799) British				
wc/d	2	34,600-104,400	69,500	34,600
COZZENS, Frederick Schiller (1846-1928) American				
wc/d	8	550-3,600	1,618	1,500
CRABEELS, Florent (1829-1896) Flemish				
oil	1	13,110	13,110	13,110
CRACKING ART (20th C) Italian				
3D	1	5,271	5,271	5,271
CRACKNELL, Thomas C (fl.1853-1869) British				
oil	1	1,720	1,720	1,720
CRAECKE, Gaston Frank de (1899-1954) Belgian				
oil	1	2,356	2,356	2,356
CRAESBEECK, Joos van (1606-1654) Flemish				
oil	3	5,096-24,205	13,920	12,460
CRAFFONARA, Aurelio (1875-1945) Italian				
wc/d	4	710-5,108	3,111	1,657
CRAFT, Percy R (1856-1934) British				
oil	5	2,745-9,204	6,136	6,230

Name	No.	Price Range	Average	Median
CRAGG, Tony (1949-) British				
wc/d	1	3,822	3,822	3,822
3D	3	22,200-36,294	26,898	22,200
CRAIG, Ailsa (1895-1967) British				
oil	1	1,056	1,056	1,056
CRAIG, Charles (1846-1931) American				
oil	5	400-11,000	4,430	3,250
wc/d	1	4,250	4,250	4,250
CRAIG, Frank (1874-1918) British				
oil	1	3,500	3,500	3,500
wc/d	2	971-1,300	1,135	971
CRAIG, Henry Robertson (1916-1984) British				
oil	4	910-11,125	5,589	1,403
wc/d	4	480-1,920	957	624
CRAIG, J Humbert (1878-1944) Irish				
oil	31	550-51,432	11,906	8,938
CRAIG, James Stevenson (fl.1854-1870) British				
oil	2	1,100-9,000	5,050	1,100
CRAIG, T (20th C) Irish?				
oil	1	4,872	4,872	4,872
CRAIG, Thomas Bigelow (1849-1924) American				
oil	9	1,523-22,000	5,569	2,800
wc/d	1	800	800	800
CRAIG-MARTIN, Michael (1941-) Irish				
oil	1	28,000	28,000	28,000
3D	1	33,300	33,300	33,300
CRAIG-WALLACE, Robert (fl.1910-1914) British				
wc/d	1	2,076	2,076	2,076
CRALI, Tullio (1910-2000) Italian				
oil	6	2,983-67,932	17,009	5,143
wc/d	2	884-7,755	4,319	884
CRAMER, E (?) ?				
wc/d	1	1,985	1,985	1,985
CRAMER, Peter (1726-1782) Danish				
oil	3	734-1,588	1,100	978
CRAMM, Baroness Helga von (fl.1880-1901) British				
wc/d	1	3,084	3,084	3,084
CRAMPTON, William James Smith (1855-1935) British				
oil	1	1,085	1,085	1,085
CRANACH, Lucas (elder) (1472-1553) German				
oil	8	19,287-4,400,000	913,244	445,000
CRANACH, Lucas (younger) (1515-1586) German				
oil	1	60,000	60,000	60,000
CRANCH, John (1807-1891) American				
oil	1	1,000	1,000	1,000
CRANDALL, Vivi K (1944-2000) American				
oil	1	7,500	7,500	7,500
CRANDELL, Bradshaw (1896-1966) American				
wc/d	1	5,500	5,500	5,500
CRANE, Ann Brainerd (1881-1948) Danish				
oil	1	2,750	2,750	2,750
CRANE, Bruce (1857-1937) American				
oil	15	2,800-25,000	9,823	9,000
wc/d	1	1,000	1,000	1,000
CRANE, Walter (1845-1915) British				
wc/d	7	1,850-28,480	6,380	2,670
CRANFORD, Kenneth R (19th C) British				
oil	1	1,000	1,000	1,000
CRANSTON, Toller (1949-) Canadian				
oil	2	577-701	639	577
wc/d	1	612	612	612
CRAPELET, Louis-Amable (1822-1867) French				
oil	1	1,374	1,374	1,374
wc/d	3	1,004-2,900	1,681	1,140
CRAS, Monique (1910-) French				
oil	9	503-10,957	3,811	3,312
wc/d	23	479-843	627	602
CRAUK, Gustave Adolphe Desire (1827-1905) French				
3D	1	2,101	2,101	2,101
CRAUMER, Elda Hartman (20th C) American				
oil	1	1,700	1,700	1,700

Name	No.	Price Range	Average	Median
CRAVASSAC, Emmanuelle (20th C) French				
wc/d	1	1,790	1,790	1,790
CRAVEN, Edgar Malin (1891-?) American				
oil	2	700-2,000	1,350	700
CRAWFORD, Edmund Thornton (1806-1885) British				
oil	3	1,305-29,920	11,149	2,223
wc/d	1	773	773	773
CRAWFORD, Ralston (1906-1978) American				
oil	1	570,000	570,000	570,000
CRAWFORD, Robert C (1842-1924) British				
oil	1	1,238	1,238	1,238
CRAWFORD, Thomas (1813-1857) American				
3D	3	12,000-110,000	67,333	80,000
CRAWHALL, Joseph (1861-1913) British				
oil	2	2,148-13,148	7,648	2,148
wc/d	1	1,237	1,237	1,237
CRAWSHAW, Lionel Townsend (1864-1949) British				
oil	1	1,353	1,353	1,353
CRAXTON, John (1922-) British				
oil	4	6,475-46,980	22,671	18,200
wc/d	4	2,392-55,680	30,073	22,200
CREALOCK, Henry Hope (1831-1891) British				
wc/d	1	10,230	10,230	10,230
CREANEY, M Roze (19/20th C) ?				
oil	1	1,131	1,131	1,131
CREARA, Sante (1570-1630) Italian				
oil	1	38,713	38,713	38,713
CREEFT, Jose de (1884-1982) American/Spanish				
3D	1	14,000	14,000	14,000
CREFFIELD, Dennis (1931-) British				
wc/d	2	870-1,701	1,285	870
CREIXAMS, Pierre (1893-1965) Spanish				
oil	7	605-2,422	1,533	1,784
wc/d	3	478-1,498	837	537
CREMA, Giovanni Battista (1883-1964) Italian				
oil	3	1,029-12,714	5,596	3,045
wc/d	1	1,262	1,262	1,262
CREMER, Fritz (1906-1993) German				
3D	1	1,794	1,794	1,794
CREMER, Jan (1940-) Dutch				
oil	4	4,948-53,014	18,118	5,088
wc/d	3	4,948-9,425	7,250	7,378
CREMONA, Italo (1905-1979) Italian				
oil	5	2,458-7,375	4,533	3,236
CREMONINI, Leonardo (1925-) Italian				
oil	1	25,521	25,521	25,521
wc/d	1	835	835	835
CREMP, Erminio (20th C) Italian				
oil	1	5,950	5,950	5,950
wc/d	1	955	955	955
CREO, Leonard (19/20th C) ?				
oil	1	1,000	1,000	1,000
CREPAX, Guido (1933-2003) Italian				
oil	1	1,237	1,237	1,237
wc/d	2	764-1,147	955	764
CREPIN (?) French				
oil	1	1,942	1,942	1,942
CREPIN D'ORLEANS (18th C) French				
oil	1	1,999	1,999	1,999
CREPIN, Joseph (1875-1948) French				
oil	3	9,642-12,858	11,056	10,669
CREPIN, Louis Philippe (1772-1851) French				
oil	1	1,189	1,189	1,189
CRESPI, Daniele (1590-1630) Italian				
oil	1	170,000	170,000	170,000
wc/d	1	1,036	1,036	1,036
CRESPI, Giovanni Battista (1557-1633) Italian				
oil	2	4,281-20,274	12,277	4,281
CRESPI, Giuseppe Maria (1665-1747) Italian				
oil	1	832,500	832,500	832,500
CRESPI-LE-PRINCE, Charles Edouard (1784-?) French				
oil	1	42,811	42,811	42,811

Name	No.	Price Range	Average	Median
CRESPIN, Adolphe Louis Charles (1859-1944) Belgian				
oil	1	2,026	2,026	2,026
CRESSINI, Carlo (1864-1938) Italian				
oil	1	1,274	1,274	1,274
CRESSWELL, Alexander (1957-) British				
oil	1	1,138	1,138	1,138
wc/d	3	963-6,358	3,023	1,750
CRESTON, René Yves (20th C) French				
oil	2	3,221-4,417	3,819	3,221
wc/d	2	608-3,390	1,999	608
CRESWICK, Mortimer (?) British?				
wc/d	1	2,223	2,223	2,223
CRESWICK, Thomas (1811-1869) British				
oil	12	443-10,560	2,266	1,044
wc/d	1	680	680	680
CRETELLE, Georges (20th C) French				
wc/d	2	1,165-1,230	1,197	1,165
CRETEN, Victor (1878-1966) Belgian				
oil	1	1,204	1,204	1,204
CRETEN-GEORGES (1887-1966) Belgian				
oil	5	783-2,061	1,385	1,377
wc/d	3	637-1,812	1,055	716
CRETI, Donato (1671-1749) Italian				
wc/d	5	1,532-9,250	5,045	5,372
CRETIUS, Constantin (1814-1901) German				
oil	3	1,783-4,816	3,732	4,597
CREVECOEUR, Victorine (?) ?				
oil	1	3,099	3,099	3,099
CREVEL, René (20th C) French				
oil	1	11,000	11,000	11,000
CRIADO Y BACA, Manuel (1839-1899) Spanish				
oil	1	7,000	7,000	7,000
CRIPPA, Roberto (1921-1972) Italian				
oil	38	900-59,733	15,338	10,744
wc/d	44	971-36,891	8,100	6,042
3D	2	23,562-38,163	30,862	23,562
CRISCONIO, Luigi (1893-1946) Italian				
oil	3	3,822-4,459	4,101	4,024
CRISCUOLO, Renato (1954-) Italian				
oil	2	545-1,816	1,180	545
CRISS, Francis (1901-1973) American				
oil	1	14,000	14,000	14,000
CRISTALL, Joshua (1767-1847) British				
wc/d	6	1,068-3,828	2,122	1,400
CRISTESCO, Constantin (fl.1911) French				
3D	1	7,000	7,000	7,000
CRITE, Allan Rohan (1910-) American				
wc/d	1	5,600	5,600	5,600
CRIVELLI, Angelo Maria (17/18th C) Italian				
oil	2	10,000-16,650	13,325	10,000
CRIVELLI, Giovanni (?-1760) Italian				
oil	3	4,808-27,600	16,802	18,000
CROATTO, Bruno (1875-1945) Italian				
oil	1	9,062	9,062	9,062
wc/d	1	5,946	5,946	5,946
CROCE, Johann Nepomuk della (1736-1819) Austrian				
oil	2	1,251-3,102	2,176	1,251
CROCKER, Edna Earl (1873-1942) American				
oil	1	6,000	6,000	6,000
CROCKFORD, Duncan (1920-1991) Canadian				
oil	6	466-2,431	1,633	1,649
CROCKWELL, Spencer Douglas (1904-1968) American				
oil	1	3,750	3,750	3,750
CRODEL, Charles (1894-1973) French				
oil	4	803-5,023	2,293	1,196
wc/d	1	900	900	900
CRODEL, Paul Eduard (1862-1928) German				
oil	1	1,800	1,800	1,800
CROEGAERT, Georges (1848-1923) Belgian				
oil	4	4,487-18,400	8,627	5,000
wc/d	1	1,032	1,032	1,032

Name	No.	Price Range	Average	Median
CROFT, Richard (1935-) British				
oil	9	496-5,081	1,739	952
CROFTS, Ernest (1847-1911) British				
oil	3	2,288-17,858	7,666	2,853
CROIN, Joseph (1894-1949) Dutch				
oil	1	3,053	3,053	3,053
CROISSANT, Eugen (1898-1976) German				
3D	1	2,472	2,472	2,472
CROISSANT, Michael (1928-) German				
wc/d	3	518-608	570	586
3D	3	5,271-6,833	6,158	6,370
CROISY, Aristide-Onesime (1840-1899) French				
3D	1	3,200	3,200	3,200
CROLA, Georg Heinrich (1804-1879) German				
oil	1	19,286	19,286	19,286
CROLL, Carl Robert (1800-1842) German				
oil	1	2,102	2,102	2,102
CROME, John Berney (1794-1842) British				
oil	2	2,088-2,301	2,194	2,088
CROME, William Henry (1806-1873) British				
oil	3	2,301-3,250	2,831	2,944
CROMEK, Thomas Hartley (1809-1873) British				
wc/d	10	452-3,520	1,629	1,672
CROMWELL, Joane (1889-1966) American				
oil	7	600-14,000	2,828	900
CRONE, David (1937-) Irish				
wc/d	1	2,046	2,046	2,046
CRONQVIST, Lena (1938-) Swedish				
oil	15	2,417-574,833	61,948	10,836
wc/d	1	5,344	5,344	5,344
3D	3	3,944-33,697	18,053	16,518
CROOK, Don (1934-) American				
oil	3	3,000-6,000	4,333	4,000
CROOK, Pamela Jane (1945-) British				
oil	1	9,250	9,250	9,250
wc/d	2	7,560-15,930	11,745	7,560
CROOS, Anthony Jansz van der (1606-1662) Dutch				
oil	6	3,129-60,000	21,476	8,767
CROOS, Pieter van der (1610-1677) Dutch				
oil	1	53,400	53,400	53,400
CROPSEY, Jasper Francis (1823-1900) American				
oil	5	32,000-490,000	177,400	120,000
wc/d	3	9,500-35,000	22,333	22,500
CROSBIE, William (1915-1999) British				
oil	19	519-15,130	5,358	2,000
wc/d	4	589-2,904	1,864	1,131
CROSBY, William (1830-1910) British				
oil	2	1,012-1,557	1,284	1,012
CROSIO, Luigi (1835-1915) Italian				
oil	4	491-23,143	7,766	1,607
CROSS, Anson Kent (1862-1944) American				
oil	1	1,000	1,000	1,000
CROSS, Henri Edmond (1856-1910) French				
oil	6	8,500-1,000,000	397,087	160,000
wc/d	18	479-19,360	4,141	2,148
CROSS, Henry H (1837-1918) American				
oil	3	2,750-4,000	3,250	3,000
CROSSLAND, James Henry (1852-1939) British				
oil	3	740-1,777	1,103	794
CROSSMAN, Rod (20th C) American				
oil	1	1,100	1,100	1,100
CROTTI, Jean (1878-1958) French				
oil	8	2,750-34,551	10,803	4,544
wc/d	1	1,067	1,067	1,067
CROUCH, William (fl.1817-1850) British				
wc/d	5	644-3,312	1,502	1,056
CROWE, Eyre (1824-1910) British				
oil	4	581-4,675	2,780	1,440
CROWE, Victoria (1945-) British				
oil	3	774-3,045	1,609	1,009
wc/d	2	1,144-2,752	1,948	1,144

Name	No.	Price Range	Average	Median
CROWLEY, Donald (1926-) American				
oil	4	3,000-19,000	7,625	4,000
wc/d	1	3,500	3,500	3,500
CROWTHER, Henry (19/20th C) British				
oil	6	600-3,500	1,680	1,710
CROWTHER, John (fl.1876-1900) British				
wc/d	1	1,144	1,144	1,144
CROWTHER, Mollie (1867-1927) American				
oil	1	1,500	1,500	1,500
CROXFORD, Agnes McIntyre (19th C) British				
oil	1	1,455	1,455	1,455
CROZATIER, Charles (1795-1855) French				
3D	1	1,646	1,646	1,646
CROZIER, William (1930-) British				
oil	18	2,417-54,939	13,005	7,541
wc/d	3	4,325-8,000	6,719	7,832
CRUISE, Louis T (20th C) American				
oil	1	1,200	1,200	1,200
CRUM, D L (20th C) American				
oil	1	2,800	2,800	2,800
CRUMBO, Woodward (1912-1989) American				
wc/d	1	5,250	5,250	5,250
CRUMIERE, Victor (20th C) French				
oil	1	3,041	3,041	3,041
CRUYL, Lieven (c.1640-1720) Belgian				
wc/d	1	25,521	25,521	25,521
CRUZ HERRERA, Jose Herrerilla (1890-1972) Spanish				
oil	12	1,686-155,556	30,904	10,615
wc/d	1	2,854	2,854	2,854
CRUZ-DIEZ, Carlos (1923-) Venezuelan				
oil	6	33,300-89,048	48,122	37,500
wc/d	1	34,358	34,358	34,358
3D	3	8,380-84,082	38,820	24,000
CSABA, Markus (1953-) Hungarian				
wc/d	1	2,013	2,013	2,013
CSAKI-COPONY, Grete (1893-1990) Rumanian				
oil	2	5,066-5,184	5,125	5,066
CSAKY, Josef (1888-1971) French/Hungarian				
oil	1	500	500	500
3D	7	4,750-70,300	21,128	7,658
CSATO, Georges (1910-) Hungarian				
oil	5	531-14,160	4,800	4,071
CSERNA, Karoly (1867-1944) Hungarian				
oil	1	2,408	2,408	2,408
CSERNUS, Tibor (1927-) Hungarian				
oil	5	2,973-5,351	4,414	4,712
CUADRADO, A B (20th C) Spanish				
oil	2	4,498-4,849	4,673	4,498
CUBELLS Y RUIZ, Enrique Martinez (1874-1947) Spanish				
oil	8	2,055-130,500	29,012	7,135
CUBLEY, Henry Hadfield (fl.1882-1904) British				
oil	14	460-3,496	1,239	727
CUBLEY, William Harold (1816-1896) British				
oil	2	1,012-4,872	2,942	1,012
CUCCHI, Enzo (1949-) Italian				
oil	8	20,000-925,000	189,439	44,400
wc/d	22	3,924-108,129	19,981	8,000
3D	1	22,200	22,200	22,200
CUCUEL, Edward (1875-1951) American				
oil	4	23,562-68,250	47,153	36,800
wc/d	5	837-5,890	4,250	4,442
CUDENNEC, Patrice (1952-) French				
oil	4	467-2,572	1,156	477
CUDWORTH, Jack (1930-) British				
oil	5	606-3,299	1,533	766
wc/d	1	519	519	519
CUECO, Henri (1929-) French				
oil	6	1,554-13,593	5,076	2,541
wc/d	1	1,549	1,549	1,549
CUENI, August (1883-1966) Swiss				
oil	3	1,783-2,816	2,243	2,131

Name	No.	Price Range	Average	Median
CUEVAS, Jose Luis (1934-) Mexican				
wc/d	4	450-3,200	1,656	1,115
CUEVAS, Raymond (1932-) American				
oil	3	475-4,750	1,908	500
CUITT, George (elder) (1743-1818) British				
oil	1	13,230	13,230	13,230
CUIXART, Modest (1925-) Spanish				
oil	2	14,919-24,429	19,674	14,919
wc/d	2	932-12,982	6,957	932
CULHANE, Shamus (20th C) American				
wc/d	1	1,000	1,000	1,000
CULLBERG, Erland (1931-) Swedish				
oil	15	496-3,817	1,807	1,400
CULLEN, Maurice Galbraith (1866-1934) Canadian				
oil	17	12,370-1,053,555	121,188	24,597
CULLEN, Michael (1946-) Irish				
oil	2	2,664-5,449	4,056	2,664
wc/d	1	1,110	1,110	1,110
CULLEN, Stephen (1959) Irish				
oil	8	714-2,035	1,279	1,011
CULLIN, Isaac (fl.1881-1920) British				
oil	1	9,150	9,150	9,150
CULTRERA DE MONTALBANO, Armand (1901-) French				
wc/d	1	1,295	1,295	1,295
CULVER, Charles (1908-1967) American				
wc/d	11	500-3,250	1,195	850
CULVERHOUSE, Johann Mongels (1820-1892) Dutch				
oil	3	2,500-14,790	9,243	10,440
CUMAN, Fabio (1972-) Italian				
oil	2	707-707	707	707
wc/d	1	1,045	1,045	1,045
CUMBERWORTH, Charles (1811-1852) French				
3D	3	4,315-7,938	5,848	5,292
CUMELIN, Johan Peter (1764-1820) Swedish				
wc/d	1	1,511	1,511	1,511
CUMING, Beatrice (1903-1975) American				
wc/d	1	1,334	1,334	1,334
CUMING, Frederick G R (1930-) British				
oil	15	589-6,120	2,451	1,566
CUMMING, James (1922-1991) British				
oil	2	534-5,632	3,083	534
wc/d	4	692-5,310	2,101	783
CUMMINGS, George R (20th C) British				
oil	2	696-1,479	1,087	696
CUMMINGS, Vera (1891-1949) New Zealander				
oil	2	1,232-1,416	1,324	1,232
CUNAEUS, Conradyn (1828-1895) Dutch				
oil	2	1,576-12,000	6,788	1,576
CUNDALL, Charles (1890-1971) British				
oil	14	1,044-11,340	3,471	1,914
CUNEO, Jose (1887-1977) Uruguayan				
oil	2	2,800-9,000	5,900	2,800
wc/d	3	560-1,000	720	600
CUNEO, Rinaldo (1877-1935) American				
oil	1	2,250	2,250	2,250
CUNEO, Terence (1907-1996) British				
oil	6	4,498-121,940	32,086	12,006
wc/d	1	2,403	2,403	2,403
CUNHA, Candida (1927-) Portuguese				
oil	1	1,276	1,276	1,276
CUNNINGHAM, George (1924-1996) British				
oil	1	3,680	3,680	3,680
wc/d	3	805-3,128	1,689	1,135
CUNNINGHAM, John (1926-1999) British				
oil	12	1,197-13,806	7,206	6,444
CUNNINGHAM, William (?) British?				
oil	2	865-1,151	1,008	865
CUNZ, Martha (1876-1961) Swiss				
oil	6	1,082-4,021	2,075	1,214
wc/d	3	541-941	688	583
CURIE, Parvine (1936-) French?				
3D	1	2,661	2,661	2,661

Name	No.	Price Range	Average	Median
CURLING, Peter (1955-) Irish				
oil	5	8,767-102,300	54,315	54,490
wc/d	4	3,507-7,633	5,447	3,637
CURNET, F (19th C) American?				
oil	1	3,100	3,100	3,100
CURNOCK, James Jackson (1839-1891) British				
wc/d	3	662-2,760	1,610	1,408
CURNOE, Greg (1936-1992) Canadian				
wc/d	3	705-10,536	5,667	5,761
CURR, Tom (1887-1958) British				
oil	1	1,384	1,384	1,384
CURRADI, Francesco (1570-1661) Italian				
oil	2	6,764-43,315	25,039	6,764
wc/d	1	999	999	999
CURRAN, Charles Courtney (1861-1942) American				
oil	5	6,500-80,000	39,600	27,500
CURREN, Eleanor H (19th C) British				
wc/d	1	1,038	1,038	1,038
CURREY, Fanny W (1848-1917) British				
wc/d	2	1,937-2,338	2,137	1,937
CURRIE, J (19th C) British				
3D	1	1,750	1,750	1,750
CURRIE, Ken (1960-) British				
oil	4	19,315-40,710	27,883	19,315
wc/d	2	6,117-8,600	7,358	6,117
CURRIER, J Frank (1843-1909) American				
oil	1	2,500	2,500	2,500
CURRIN, John (1962-) American				
oil	1	150,000	150,000	150,000
wc/d	5	24,000-37,500	29,500	26,000
CURRY, Ethel Luella (1902-2000) Canadian				
oil	3	604-3,882	2,256	2,282
CURRY, John Steuart (1897-1946) American				
oil	3	10,000-34,000	20,666	18,000
CURRY, Robert F (1872-1945) American				
oil	11	500-5,103	1,522	942
wc/d	1	1,300	1,300	1,300
CURSITER, Stanley (1887-1976) British				
oil	5	1,730-105,600	27,909	12,460
wc/d	2	2,322-13,200	7,761	2,322
CURT, Xaver (19th C) ?				
oil	1	1,095	1,095	1,095
CURTIN, Maureen (20th C) Irish?				
oil	2	942-1,937	1,439	942
CURTIS, David Jan (1948-) British				
oil	1	1,513	1,513	1,513
CURTIS, Donker (19th C) British				
oil	1	1,500	1,500	1,500
CURTIS, George (19th C) American				
oil	1	60,000	60,000	60,000
CURTIS, James Waltham (1839-1901) Australian				
oil	1	1,900	1,900	1,900
CURTIS, Leland (1897-1989) American				
oil	3	5,000-55,000	22,500	7,500
CURTIS, Roger William (1910-2000) American				
oil	1	2,700	2,700	2,700
CURTOVICH, Ovide (1855-?) Turkish				
oil	1	5,304	5,304	5,304
CURTS, T (fl.1895-1930) Austrian				
3D	1	2,186	2,186	2,186
CURZON, Paul Alfred de (1820-1895) French				
oil	2	2,016-4,519	3,267	2,016
CUSHING, Howard Gardiner (1869-1915) American				
oil	1	5,000	5,000	5,000
CUSHING, Peter (1913-1994) British				
wc/d	2	1,672-1,760	1,716	1,672
CUSSOL, Beatrice (1970-) ?				
wc/d	1	3,395	3,395	3,395
CUSTER, Edward L (1837-1880) American				
oil	2	4,000-7,000	5,500	4,000

Name	No.	Price Range	Average	Median
CUTRONE, Ronnie (1948-) American				
oil	1	1,232	1,232	1,232
wc/d	2	703-1,274	988	703
CUTTING, Francis Harvey (1872-1964) American				
oil	2	700-1,300	1,000	700
CUVELIER, Pascale (20th C) French				
oil	2	1,868-3,041	2,454	1,868
CUYCK, Michel van (1797-1875) Belgian				
oil	1	1,878	1,878	1,878
CUYLENBORCH, Abraham van (1620-1658) Dutch				
oil	4	5,000-42,401	17,867	8,500
CUYP, Aelbert (1620-1691) Dutch				
oil	3	21,476-1,730,000	607,158	70,000
wc/d	1	2,400	2,400	2,400
CUYP, Benjamin Gerritsz (1612-1652) Dutch				
oil	3	4,625-13,430	7,929	5,733
CUYP, Jacob Gerritsz (1594-1651) Dutch				
oil	1	8,325	8,325	8,325
CUYPER, Floris de (1875-1965) Belgian				
3D	1	1,806	1,806	1,806
CYBIS, Jan (1897-1972) Polish				
oil	1	5,262	5,262	5,262
CYR, Georges (1880-1964) French				
oil	1	598	598	598
wc/d	1	1,147	1,147	1,147
CZACHORSKI, Ladislaus von (1850-1911) Polish				
oil	1	212,055	212,055	212,055
CZAWADZINSKI, Czeslaw (19/20th C) ?				
oil	1	1,215	1,215	1,215
CZECH, Emil (1862-1929) Austrian				
oil	1	2,178	2,178	2,178
wc/d	1	839	839	839
CZENCZ, Janos (19/20th C) Hungarian				
oil	1	4,511	4,511	4,511
CZERKAS, Victor (1914-2003) American				
oil	1	3,250	3,250	3,250
CZERNOTZKY, Ernst (1869-1939) Austrian				
oil	2	786-1,674	1,230	786
CZOBEL, Bela (1883-1974) Hungarian				
oil	2	9,000-38,060	23,530	9,000
wc/d	3	581-1,427	1,005	1,008
D'ACOSTA, Hy Walker (19th C) Spanish				
oil	1	7,000	7,000	7,000
D'AGAR, Charles (1669-1723) French				
oil	1	10,260	10,260	10,260
D'AGOSTINO, Gaetano (19th C) Italian				
oil	1	2,061	2,061	2,061
D'ALHEIM, Limosin (19th C) Russian				
oil	1	3,041	3,041	3,041
D'AMARO, Valentina (1966-) Italian				
oil	1	3,148	3,148	3,148
D'AMATO, Gennaro (1857-1949) Italian				
wc/d	2	1,752-6,423	4,087	1,752
D'AMATO, Raffaele (19th C) Italian				
oil	1	4,332	4,332	4,332
D'AMBROSSI, A (19th C) Italian				
oil	1	2,071	2,071	2,071
D'ANGELO, Soutz (20th C) French				
oil	1	7,200	7,200	7,200
D'ANNA, Alessandro (18th C) Italian				
oil	1	166,486	166,486	166,486
D'ANNA, Giulio (1908-1978) Italian				
oil	1	12,884	12,884	12,884
wc/d	2	10,813-16,537	13,675	10,813
D'APVRIL, Edouard (1843-1928) French				
oil	2	783-16,789	8,786	783
D'ARCANGELO, Allan (1930-) American				
oil	1	16,537	16,537	16,537
wc/d	1	375	375	375
D'ARIENZO, Miguel A (1950-) Argentinian				
oil	1	20,000	20,000	20,000

Name	No.	Price Range	Average	Median
D'ARTHOIS, Jacques (1613-1686) Flemish				
oil	4	11,000-67,640	25,414	11,447
D'ARTHOIS, Jacques and TENIERS, David (younger) (17th C) Flemish				
oil	1	63,699	63,699	63,699
D'ASSIA, Enrico (1927-2000) Italian				
oil	1	1,933	1,933	1,933
wc/d	1	2,392	2,392	2,392
D'ASTE, Joseph (20th C) Italian				
3D	5	1,823-3,612	2,385	2,153
D'AURIA, Vincenzo (1872-1939) Italian				
oil	1	1,200	1,200	1,200
D'AZEGLIO, Massimo (1798-1866) Italian				
oil	2	3,403-4,364	3,883	3,403
wc/d	1	1,816	1,816	1,816
DE, Biren (1926-) Indian				
oil	1	6,000	6,000	6,000
DEACON, Richard (1949-) British				
wc/d	1	6,000	6,000	6,000
DEAKIN, Edwin (1838-1923) American				
oil	3	750-2,750	1,966	2,400
DEAKIN, Peter (fl.1855-1879) British				
oil	1	1,505	1,505	1,505
DEAN, Frank (1865-1946) British				
oil	1	13,000	13,000	13,000
DEARDEN, Harold (1888-1969) British				
oil	5	792-3,872	1,459	888
DEARLE, John (19th C) British				
oil	1	4,048	4,048	4,048
DEARLE, John H (fl.1853-1891) British				
wc/d	1	1,665	1,665	1,665
DEARTH, Henry Golden (1864-1918) American				
oil	1	1,600	1,600	1,600
DEBAILLE, Maurice (1898-?) Belgian?				
oil	1	1,311	1,311	1,311
DEBAT-PONSAN, Edouard-Bernard (1847-1913) French				
oil	1	14,720	14,720	14,720
DEBAY, Caroline Louise Emma (1809-1832) French				
oil	2	558-3,854	2,206	558
DEBERDT, Francoise (1934-) French				
oil	1	2,800	2,800	2,800
DEBIASI, Giuseppe (1947-) Italian				
wc/d	2	1,209-1,272	1,240	1,209
DEBIENNE, Noemie (19/20th C) French				
3D	1	2,600	2,600	2,600
DEBON, Francois Hippolyte (1807-1872) French				
oil	2	5,878-7,135	6,506	5,878
DEBRE, Olivier (1920-1999) French				
oil	41	2,803-25,888	10,275	9,000
wc/d	15	482-6,241	1,582	1,019
3D	1	2,574	2,574	2,574
DEBRIE, Gustave Joseph (1842-1932) French				
3D	1	8,818	8,818	8,818
DEBRISSET, C (19th C) French?				
oil	1	3,625	3,625	3,625
DEBUCOURT, Philibert Louis (1755-1832) French				
oil	3	1,553-73,731	26,723	4,886
DEBUT, Jean-Didier (1824-1893) French				
3D	4	1,908-3,750	2,977	2,510
DEBUT, Marcel (1865-1933) French				
3D	2	2,000-3,892	2,946	2,000
DECAEN, Alfred (1820-?) French				
wc/d	1	2,188	2,188	2,188
DECAMP, Ralph Earll (1858-1936) American				
oil	2	6,000-10,000	8,000	6,000
DECAMPS, Alexandre Gabriel (1803-1860) French				
oil	1	2,300	2,300	2,300
wc/d	1	2,188	2,188	2,188
DECAMPS, Maurice (1892-1953) French				
oil	3	1,302-3,738	2,807	3,382
DECARIS, Albert (1901-1988) French				
wc/d	1	1,936	1,936	1,936

Name	No.	Price Range	Average	Median
DECHANT, Miles Boyer (1890-1942) American				
oil	1	7,500	7,500	7,500
DECKER, Cornelis Gerritsz (1625-1678) Dutch				
oil	1	19,110	19,110	19,110
DECKER, Jos de (1912-2000) Belgian				
3D	1	11,866	11,866	11,866
DECKER, Joseph (1853-1924) American				
oil	1	90,000	90,000	90,000
DECKERS, Émile (1885-1968) Belgian				
oil	6	1,967-15,288	8,381	7,027
wc/d	2	533-1,054	793	533
DEDECKER, Thomas (1951-) American				
oil	6	2,000-14,000	5,333	3,500
DEDIC, Drago (1937-) Yugoslavian				
wc/d	1	1,320	1,320	1,320
DEDINA, Jean (1870-1955) Czechoslovakian				
wc/d	2	2,335-4,321	3,328	2,335
DEEM, George (1932-) American				
oil	1	1,500	1,500	1,500
DEENY, Gillian (20th C) Irish				
oil	2	3,145-3,875	3,510	3,145
DEESE, Rupert T (1952-) American				
oil	1	3,500	3,500	3,500
DEFAUX, Alexandre (1826-1900) French				
oil	17	480-11,899	4,766	4,375
DEFEO, Charles (1892-1978) American				
oil	1	2,050	2,050	2,050
DEFESCHE, P (1921-1998) Dutch				
oil	1	2,397	2,397	2,397
wc/d	1	877	877	877
DEFESCHE, Pieter (1921-1998) Dutch				
oil	1	8,905	8,905	8,905
wc/d	2	715-1,286	1,000	715
DEFOREST, Lockwood (1850-1932) American				
oil	3	3,500-14,000	8,083	6,750
DEFOSSEZ, Alfred (1932-) French				
oil	3	1,014-2,028	1,451	1,312
DEFREES, T (19th C) American				
oil	1	2,500	2,500	2,500
DEFREGGER, Franz von (1835-1921) German				
oil	23	606-76,327	18,513	11,503
wc/d	3	850-2,662	1,695	1,573
DEFRESNE, Alice (19th C) ?				
oil	1	1,000	1,000	1,000
DEGAND, Eugène (1829-?) French				
oil	1	2,637	2,637	2,637
DEGAS, Edgar (1834-1917) French				
oil	11	34,347-3,363,000	389,750	81,400
wc/d	44	5,993-11,040,001	387,244	63,605
3D	10	8,000-650,000	172,694	75,000
DEGAUS, L (19th C) Belgian?				
3D	1	3,884	3,884	3,884
DEGNER, Artur (1887-1972) German				
oil	1	1,375	1,375	1,375
DEGODE, Wilhelm (1862-1931) German				
oil	3	814-1,818	1,477	1,800
DEGOTTEX, Jean (1918-1988) French				
oil	13	1,430-33,899	13,139	12,361
wc/d	9	742-9,678	3,585	1,558
3D	2	3,298-3,770	3,534	3,298
DEGOUVE DE NUNCQUES, William (1867-1935) Belgian				
oil	4	2,571-11,973	5,840	3,729
DEGREEF, Jean (1852-1894) Belgian				
oil	6	563-2,238	1,149	894
D'EGVILLE, James Herve (c.1810-1880) British				
oil	1	67,521	67,521	67,521
DEHAAN, Chuck (1933-) American				
oil	1	5,000	5,000	5,000
DEHAUSSY, Adele (1823-?) French				
oil	1	2,928	2,928	2,928

Name	No.	Price Range	Average	Median
DEHN, Adolf (1895-1968) American				
oil	2	1,100-2,000	1,550	1,100
wc/d	6	450-2,100	1,133	900
DEHNER, Dorothy (1901-1994) American				
wc/d	3	500-1,850	1,350	1,700
3D	2	2,000-22,000	12,000	2,000
DEHODENCQ, Alfred (1822-1882) French				
oil	2	4,232-22,932	13,582	4,232
wc/d	21	486-5,712	1,023	753
DEHOY, Charles (1872-1940) Belgian				
oil	2	1,236-2,572	1,904	1,236
DEIERLING, Heinrich Harry (1894-1989) German				
oil	3	837-3,214	1,649	897
DEIGHAN, Peter (20th C) British				
oil	3	952-1,784	1,378	1,399
DEIKER, Carl Friedrich (1836-1892) German				
oil	6	1,452-17,534	6,541	3,058
DEIKER, Johannes Christian (1822-1895) German				
oil	2	2,219-2,610	2,414	2,219
DEINEKA, Alexander (1899-1969) Russian				
oil	1	65,100	65,100	65,100
wc/d	1	26,040	26,040	26,040
DEIRA, Ernesto (1928-1986) Argentinian				
oil	1	25,000	25,000	25,000
DEISTLER, Michael (1949-) German				
oil	1	3,741	3,741	3,741
DEITERS, Heinrich (1840-1916) German				
oil	2	1,936-1,940	1,938	1,936
DEIX, Manfred (1949-) Austrian				
wc/d	1	1,918	1,918	1,918
DEJEAN, Louis (1872-1953) French				
3D	1	4,232	4,232	4,232
DEKEN, Albert de (1915-2003) Belgian				
oil	6	549-4,200	1,328	598
DEKEYSER, Danielle (1944-) French				
3D	1	2,152	2,152	2,152
DEKKER, Henk (1897-1974) Dutch				
oil	5	703-4,071	1,990	1,272
DEKKERS, Ad (1938-1974) Dutch				
oil	1	23,378	23,378	23,378
3D	2	5,293-8,192	6,742	5,293
DEKKERT, Eugène (1865-1956) German				
oil	7	656-9,027	2,782	1,584
DELABANO, Barney (1926-1997) American				
wc/d	2	1,000-2,000	1,500	1,000
DELABRIERE, P E (1829-1912) French				
3D	2	3,240-9,452	6,346	3,240
DELABRIERE, Paul Edouard (1829-1912) French				
3D	2	5,400-8,000	6,700	5,400
DELACOUR, William (18th C) French				
oil	1	60,520	60,520	60,520
DELACROIX, Auguste (1809-1868) French				
oil	1	5,323	5,323	5,323
DELACROIX, Eugène (1798-1863) French				
oil	4	140,000-2,024,000	654,442	140,971
wc/d	19	820-2,852,000	155,968	2,922
DELACROIX, Henry Eugène (1845-1929) French				
oil	2	935-5,271	3,103	935
DELAFOSSE, Jean Charles (1734-1789) French				
wc/d	2	2,066-10,137	6,101	2,066
DELAGRANGE, Léon Noel (1872-1910) French				
3D	2	3,649-7,223	5,436	3,649
DELAHAUT, Jo (1911-1992) Belgian				
oil	7	5,845-16,537	8,619	7,224
wc/d	1	4,295	4,295	4,295
3D	1	5,088	5,088	5,088
DELAHAYE, B (18th C) ?				
oil	1	4,099	4,099	4,099
DELAHOGUE, Alexis-Auguste (1867-1936) French				
oil	11	1,285-21,041	9,590	8,948
DELAHOGUE, Eugène Jules (1867-1934) French				
oil	2	4,772-9,709	7,240	4,772

Name	No.	Price Range	Average	Median
DELAIGUE, Victor Constantin (19/20th C) French				
3D	1	3,548	3,548	3,548
DELAMAIN, Paul (1821-1882) French				
oil	2	4,162-15,534	9,848	4,162
DELAMANE, H (19th C) French				
oil	1	9,500	9,500	9,500
DELAMONCE, Jean (1635-1708) French				
wc/d	1	1,337	1,337	1,337
DELAMOTTE, Jean François (17th C) French				
oil	1	22,000	22,000	22,000
DELAMOTTE, William (1775-1863) British				
oil	1	4,400	4,400	4,400
DELANEY, Arthur (1927-1987) British				
oil	33	531-22,695	9,550	8,880
DELANEY, Beauford (1901-1979) American				
oil	2	10,096-34,448	22,272	10,096
wc/d	1	2,750	2,750	2,750
DELANEY, Edward (1930-) Irish?				
wc/d	2	1,209-3,786	2,497	1,209
3D	6	3,585-22,717	7,885	4,844
DELANO, Gerard Curtis (1890-1972) American				
oil	10	2,000-120,000	46,650	19,000
wc/d	2	12,000-20,000	16,000	12,000
DELANOY, Jacques (1820-1890) French				
oil	2	1,272-3,750	2,511	1,272
DELAPLANCHE, Eugène (1836-1891) French				
3D	3	2,704-38,280	15,610	5,847
DELAPP, Terry (1934-) American				
oil	1	3,500	3,500	3,500
DELARIVA, Nicolas Louis Albert (1755-1818) French				
oil	2	920-5,696	3,308	920
DELAROCHE, Paul (1797-1856) French				
oil	1	17,390	17,390	17,390
wc/d	2	470-11,000	5,735	470
DELASALLE, Angele (1867-1938) French				
oil	1	4,712	4,712	4,712
DELATOUR, Mathilde (1852-1912) French?				
oil	1	2,136	2,136	2,136
DELATRE, Eugène (1864-?) French				
wc/d	1	1,542	1,542	1,542
DELATTRE, Henri (1801-1876) French				
oil	2	4,000-5,500	4,750	4,000
DELATTRE, Joseph (1858-1912) French				
oil	2	628-4,800	2,714	628
DELAUNAY, Robert (1885-1941) French				
oil	4	58,562-240,000	166,275	140,000
wc/d	1	158,400	158,400	158,400
DELAUNAY, Sonia (1885-1979) French/Russian				
oil	2	484,828-844,800	664,814	484,828
wc/d	30	527-68,000	15,698	8,372
DELAUNEY, Alfred Alexandre (1830-1894) French				
oil	1	1,414	1,414	1,414
DELAUNOIS, Albert (1895-1936) Belgian				
oil	1	1,636	1,636	1,636
DELAVALLEE, Henri (1862-1943) French				
oil	2	2,225-3,624	2,924	2,225
DELBOS, Julius (1879-1967) American				
wc/d	1	1,900	1,900	1,900
DELECLUSE, Auguste (1855-1928) French				
oil	1	1,879	1,879	1,879
DELECLUSE, Étienne Jean (1781-1863) French				
wc/d	1	3,805	3,805	3,805
DELECLUSE, Eugène (1882-?) French				
wc/d	7	468-1,991	1,092	703
DELEN, Dirk van (1605-1671) Dutch				
oil	3	80,000-380,000	230,000	230,000
DELEU, Arthur (1884-1966) Belgian				
oil	1	1,311	1,311	1,311
DELFF, Cornelis Jacobsz (1571-1643) Dutch				
oil	1	8,870	8,870	8,870
DELFF, Jacob Willemsz (younger) (1619-1661) Dutch				
oil	2	6,115-8,182	7,148	6,115

Name	No.	Price Range	Average	Median
DELFGAAUW, G J (1882-1947) Dutch				
oil	1	3,232	3,232	3,232
DELFGAAUW, Gerard Johannes (1882-1947) Dutch				
oil	22	693-8,762	2,716	2,121
DELFICO, Melchiorre (1825-1895) Italian				
wc/d	1	1,760	1,760	1,760
DELFOSSE, Eugène (1825-1865) Belgian				
oil	1	2,667	2,667	2,667
DELGADO RAMOS, Alvaro (1922-) Spanish				
oil	6	3,092-8,827	5,814	6,025
wc/d	2	1,113-1,337	1,225	1,113
DELGADO, Manuel Ignacio (20th C) South American				
oil	1	1,630	1,630	1,630
DELILLE, François (1817-?) French				
oil	1	1,200	1,200	1,200
DELIN, Nicolas Joseph (1741-1803) Flemish				
oil	1	1,311	1,311	1,311
DELIOTTI, Walter (1925-) Uruguayan				
oil	3	400-3,200	1,700	1,500
DELITALA, Mario (1887-?) Italian				
oil	1	1,019	1,019	1,019
DELIUS, Louis (19th C) American				
oil	1	3,000	3,000	3,000
DELL, G (19th C) British				
oil	1	7,106	7,106	7,106
DELL'ACQUA, Cesare Felix Georges (1821-1904) Italian				
oil	4	468-6,932	2,314	630
wc/d	3	934-2,521	1,942	2,371
DELLEANI, Lorenzo (1840-1908) Italian				
oil	4	3,514-88,290	28,961	11,931
DELLENBAUGH, Frederick Samuel (1853-1935) American				
oil	2	1,100-2,500	1,800	1,100
DELLEPIANE, David (1866-c.1932) French/Italian				
oil	1	3,155	3,155	3,155
DELL'ERA, Giovan Battista (1765-1798) Italian				
wc/d	1	4,531	4,531	4,531
DELMONTE, Alberto (1933-) Argentinian				
oil	1	1,400	1,400	1,400
DELMONTE, Simeon (1913-) Dutch				
oil	1	5,845	5,845	5,845
DELMOTTE, Marcel (1901-1984) Belgian				
oil	20	482-11,910	2,296	1,764
wc/d	2	727-1,641	1,184	727
DELOBBE, François Alfred (1835-1920) French				
oil	4	1,408-41,233	20,970	12,000
DELOBRE, Émile-Victor-Augustin (1873-1956) French				
oil	2	750-5,005	2,877	750
DELORME, Hubert E (19th C) French				
oil	1	2,800	2,800	2,800
DELORME, Pierre Claude François (1783-1857) French				
oil	1	2,788	2,788	2,788
DELORME, Raphael (1886-1962) French				
oil	2	2,930-7,027	4,978	2,930
DELORT, Charles Edouard (1841-1895) French				
oil	1	12,000	12,000	12,000
wc/d	1	565	565	565
DELPARD, Gaston (19/20th C) French				
oil	1	1,080	1,080	1,080
DELPIERRE, J B (?) French?				
oil	1	2,071	2,071	2,071
DELPY, Hippolyte Camille (1842-1910) French				
oil	20	989-38,000	10,050	7,000
DELPY, Jacques-Henry (1877-1957) French				
oil	3	2,594-3,500	2,921	2,671
DELPY, Lucien Victor (1898-1966) French				
oil	9	970-6,197	2,528	2,378
wc/d	1	1,767	1,767	1,767
DELTCHEV, Boris (20th C) ?				
wc/d	1	2,750	2,750	2,750
DELTIL, Jean Julien (1791-1863) French				
wc/d	1	48,333	48,333	48,333

Name	No.	Price Range	Average	Median
DELTOMBE, Paul (1878-1971) French				
oil	3	496-2,455	1,350	1,100
DELUERMOZ, Henri (1876-1943) French				
oil	1	7,373	7,373	7,373
DELVARRE, Henri Joseph (20th C) French				
oil	1	1,459	1,459	1,459
DELVAUX, Paul (1897-1994) Belgian				
oil	9	1,227-666,284	214,123	27,884
wc/d	21	818-620,000	39,435	7,774
DELVILLE, Jean (1867-1953) Belgian				
oil	1	10,177	10,177	10,177
DELVOYE, Wim (1965-) Dutch				
oil	1	5,845	5,845	5,845
wc/d	1	44,980	44,980	44,980
DEMACHY, Pierre Antoine (1723-1807) French				
oil	6	645-142,705	36,371	15,123
DEMANET, Victor (1895-1964) Belgian				
3D	1	2,378	2,378	2,378
DEMANGE, Adolphe (1857-1927) French				
oil	1	2,145	2,145	2,145
DEMARCO, Hugo Rodolfo (1932-1995) Argentinian				
3D	1	37,500	37,500	37,500
DEMARIA, Bernabe (1824-1910) Argentinian				
oil	2	14,000-24,000	19,000	14,000
DEMARMELS, Ludwig (1917-1992) Swiss				
oil	1	1,098	1,098	1,098
DEMARNE, Jean Louis (1744-1829) French				
oil	4	4,948-80,260	27,379	6,082
DEMENKO, Anatoli (20th C) Russian				
oil	16	576-1,647	1,001	915
DEMERS, Donald W (1956-) American				
oil	1	20,000	20,000	20,000
DEMETZ, Karl (1909-1986) German				
oil	4	480-2,735	1,100	577
DEMING, Edwin Willard (1860-1942) American				
oil	3	3,000-7,000	4,333	3,000
wc/d	3	650-1,300	966	950
DEMIRDJIAN, Yervant (1870-1938) ?				
oil	1	4,892	4,892	4,892
DEMIRGIAN, G (?) ?				
oil	1	14,118	14,118	14,118
DEMME, Paul (1866-1953) Swiss				
wc/d	1	19,000	19,000	19,000
DEMMEL, Willibald (1914-1989) German				
oil	5	729-1,824	1,203	1,337
DEMNATI, Amine (1942-1971) Moroccan				
oil	1	23,455	23,455	23,455
wc/d	1	7,778	7,778	7,778
DEMONT, Adrien (1851-1928) French				
oil	2	2,600-4,956	3,778	2,600
DEMONT-BRETON, Virginie (1859-1935) French				
oil	4	1,488-30,000	12,481	2,979
DEMOULIN, Jerome Rene (1758-1799) French				
oil	1	1,635	1,635	1,635
DEMPSEY, Michael (1966-) Irish?				
wc/d	1	2,141	2,141	2,141
DEMUTH, Charles (1883-1935) American				
wc/d	3	9,000-320,000	115,333	17,000
DENARIE, Paul (1859-1942) French				
oil	5	491-4,393	2,258	1,800
DENECHEAU, Seraphin (1831-1912) French				
3D	2	15,000-37,500	26,250	15,000
DENES, Agnes (20th C) ?				
wc/d	1	1,900	1,900	1,900
DENET-CLEMENT, Charles (1853-1939) French				
oil	1	6,500	6,500	6,500
DENEUX, Gabriel Charles (1856-?) French				
oil	1	3,469	3,469	3,469
DENGLER, Theodor (19/20th C) ?				
oil	1	3,969	3,969	3,969

Name	No.	Price Range	Average	Median
DENIS, Maurice (1870-1943) French				
oil	21	5,260-580,000	57,535	16,815
wc/d	6	1,169-56,712	12,647	2,303
DENIS, Simon Joseph Alexander Clement (1755-1813) Flemish				
oil	3	972-73,493	28,200	10,137
wc/d	5	851-26,736	7,121	2,674
DENMARK, James (20th C) American?				
wc/d	1	1,500	1,500	1,500
DENNEHY, Douglas Manson (1927-) Irish				
oil	1	1,753	1,753	1,753
DENNER, Balthasar (1685-1749) German				
oil	1	1,267	1,267	1,267
DENNERY, Gustave Lucien (1863-?) French				
oil	1	1,030	1,030	1,030
DENNING, Stephen (1795-1864) British				
oil	1	1,218	1,218	1,218
DENNIS, Jill (1957-) Irish/British				
oil	1	3,816	3,816	3,816
DENNIS, Roger Wilson (1902-1996) American				
oil	2	1,200-1,600	1,400	1,200
DENNY, Gideon Jacques (1830-1886) American				
oil	2	2,500-7,000	4,750	2,500
DENNY, Robin (1930-) British				
oil	3	3,000-21,750	10,686	7,308
wc/d	1	2,223	2,223	2,223
DENON, Vivant Dominique (1747-1825) French				
wc/d	2	2,134-3,480	2,807	2,134
DENONNE, Alexander (1879-1953) Belgian				
	7	556-7,151	1,772	1,076
DENT, David (1959-) British				
oil	2	946-1,098	1,022	946
wc/d	1	722	722	722
D'ENTRAYGUES, Charles Bertrand (1851-?) French				
oil	2	2,338-5,293	3,815	2,338
DENTZEL, Gustav A (fl.1890-1906) American				
3D	1	29,000	29,000	29,000
DENUNE, Peter (18th C) British				
oil	1	4,536	4,536	4,536
DEPERO, Fortunato (1892-1960) Italian				
oil	9	1,756-42,164	16,322	10,764
wc/d	30	650-35,137	3,974	1,209
DEPETRIS, Giovanni (1890-1940) Italian				
oil	3	1,211-10,911	4,767	2,180
D'EPINAY, Prosper (1830-1914) French				
3D	3	23,514-49,840	32,641	24,570
DEPRE, Marcel (1919-1990) French				
oil	4	850-3,034	1,669	850
wc/d	8	486-789	643	607
DERAIN, Andre (1880-1954) French				
oil	43	4,500-6,100,000	192,637	15,750
wc/d	84	452-520,000	15,713	1,168
3D	13	1,868-27,096	5,481	2,941
DERCHAIN, Philippe (1873-1947) Belgian				
wc/d	1	1,578	1,578	1,578
DEREL, Juliette (1918-) French				
3D	1	3,740	3,740	3,740
DEREUX, Philippe (1918-) French				
wc/d	2	6,062-6,473	6,267	6,062
DERICKX and SEVERDONCK, van (19th C) Belgian				
oil	1	4,500	4,500	4,500
DERKERT, Siri (1888-1973) Swedish				
oil	3	440-2,379	1,254	943
wc/d	3	828-2,036	1,378	1,272
DERNOVICH, Don (1942-) American				
oil	1	4,000	4,000	4,000
DEROME, Albert Thomas (1885-1959) American				
oil	3	3,250-7,000	4,750	4,000
DEROSSI, L (19th C) ?				
3D	1	2,134	2,134	2,134
DERPAPAS, Georgios (1937-) Greek				
oil	3	21,120-29,920	26,463	28,350

Name	No.	Price Range	Average	Median
DERUET, Claude (1588-1660) French				
oil	2	4,190-49,095	26,642	4,190
DESAINE, Henri (19th C) French				
oil	1	3,038	3,038	3,038
DESAMOIGNES, P Martin (19th C) French				
oil	1	14,137	14,137	14,137
DESAN, Charles (19th C) ?				
oil	1	1,296	1,296	1,296
DESANGES, Louis William (1822-1887) British				
oil	1	12,000	12,000	12,000
DESATNICK, Mike (1943-) American?				
oil	2	2,700-6,500	4,600	2,700
DESBOIS, Jules (1851-1935) French				
3D	4	1,890-4,789	2,847	2,268
DESCH, Frank H (1873-1934) American				
oil	1	6,500	6,500	6,500
DESCHAMPS, Camille (19th C) French				
oil	1	19,007	19,007	19,007
DESCHAMPS, Gabriel (1919-) French				
oil	7	566-2,581	1,612	1,522
DESCLABISSAC, Alexander (1868-?) German				
oil	1	1,074	1,074	1,074
DESCOMPS, J (1869-1950) French				
3D	1	2,805	2,805	2,805
DESCOMPS, Joe (1869-1950) French				
3D	6	2,336-10,000	4,750	3,151
DESEINE, Louis Pierre (1749-1822) French				
3D	1	3,822	3,822	3,822
DESGOFFE, Blaise (1830-1901) French				
oil	2	5,000-15,000	10,000	5,000
DESGOFFE, Jules (1864-?) French				
oil	1	1,151	1,151	1,151
DESGRANDCHAMPS, Marc (1960-) French				
oil	1	10,928	10,928	10,928
wc/d	1	1,236	1,236	1,236
DESHAYES, Charles Felix Edouard (1831-1895) French				
oil	4	588-6,184	2,437	1,076
DESHAYES, Eugène (1828-1890) French				
oil	8	1,058-11,127	5,207	4,094
wc/d	2	570-598	584	570
DESHAYES, Eugène Francois Adolphe (1868-1939) French				
oil	4	1,074-3,818	2,015	1,267
DESIATO, Giuseppe (1935-) Italian				
wc/d	1	2,421	2,421	2,421
DESIRE-LUCAS, Louis-Marie (1869-1949) French				
oil	5	1,210-7,247	3,720	3,853
DESMAREES, George (1697-1776) Swedish				
oil	1	16,743	16,743	16,743
DESMARQUAIS, Charles Hippolyte (1823-?) French				
oil	1	8,281	8,281	8,281
DESMIT, Alexandre Louis Benjamin (1812-1885) French				
oil	1	3,836	3,836	3,836
DESMOULINS, François Barthelemy Augustin (1788-1856) French				
oil	1	1,295	1,295	1,295
DESNOS, Ferdinand (1901-1958) French				
oil	6	480-2,631	1,222	720
DESNOYER, François (1894-1972) French				
oil	9	498-15,000	6,762	6,049
wc/d	2	608-776	692	608
D'ESPAGNAT, Georges (1870-1950) French				
oil	41	2,260-84,685	19,323	12,299
wc/d	4	1,067-2,997	1,917	1,344
DESPIAU, Charles (1874-1946) French				
wc/d	1	540	540	540
3D	7	2,800-58,390	14,823	5,000
DESPIERRE, Jacques (1912-1995) French				
oil	7	579-8,000	1,981	1,084
DESPORTES, Alexandre-François (1661-1743) French				
oil	7	50,000-259,000	143,329	160,000
DESPORTES, Andree Emma Felicite (1810-1869) French				
wc/d	1	3,403	3,403	3,403

Name	No.	Price Range	Average	Median
DESPORTES, Claude-François (1695-1774) French				
oil	1	18,904	18,904	18,904
DESPORTES, François (18th C) French				
oil	1	36,000	36,000	36,000
DESPORTES, Nicolas (1718-1787) French				
oil	1	16,649	16,649	16,649
DESPREZ, Louis Jean (1743-1804) French				
wc/d	3	855-4,861	3,324	4,258
DESRAIS, Claude Louis (1746-1816) French				
wc/d	6	547-81,096	16,879	1,000
DESROSIERS, Jean Guy (1934-) Canadian				
oil	1	1,072	1,072	1,072
DESRUELLES, Felix (1865-?) French				
3D	1	1,764	1,764	1,764
DESSERPRIT, Roger (1923-1985) French				
oil	2	1,901-3,152	2,526	1,901
3D	1	5,260	5,260	5,260
DESSI, Gianni (1955-) Italian				
oil	13	860-14,960	4,587	4,425
wc/d	2	662-17,810	9,236	662
DESSOULAVY, Thomas (fl.1839-1853) British				
oil	2	5,568-7,400	6,484	5,568
DESSY, Stanislao (1900-1986) Italian				
oil	1	2,386	2,386	2,386
D'ESTE, Antonio (1765-1827) Italian				
3D	1	6,473	6,473	6,473
D'ESTIENNE, Henri (1872-1949) French				
oil	1	28,110	28,110	28,110
wc/d	3	941-11,712	5,943	5,178
DESTOUCHES, Johanna von (1869-1956) German				
oil	5	687-3,341	1,915	1,885
DESTREE, Johannes Josephus (1827-1888) Belgian				
oil	1	4,243	4,243	4,243
DESVARREUX, Raymond (1876-1963) French				
oil	4	592-22,808	6,715	710
DESVARREUX-LARPENTEUR, James (1847-1937) American				
oil	1	2,160	2,160	2,160
DESVIGNES, Louis (20th C) French				
oil	1	1,192	1,192	1,192
DETAILLE, Charles (19th C) French				
wc/d	2	425-21,632	11,028	425
DETAILLE, Edouard (1848-1912) French				
oil	3	2,000-15,000	6,858	3,575
wc/d	5	486-5,568	1,733	806
DETANGER, Germain (1846-1902) French				
oil	1	1,211	1,211	1,211
DETILLEUX, Servais (1874-1940) Belgian				
oil	1	1,044	1,044	1,044
DETMOLD, Edward Julian (1883-1957) British				
wc/d	1	1,018	1,018	1,018
DETREVILLE, Richard (1864-1929) American				
oil	3	800-3,000	1,566	900
DETRIER, Pierre-Louis (1822-1897) French				
3D	1	4,241	4,241	4,241
DETROY, Léon (1857-1955) French				
oil	3	468-6,244	2,896	1,978
wc/d	2	533-777	655	533
DETRY, Arsene (1897-1981) Belgian				
oil	2	1,119-1,940	1,529	1,119
DETTHOW, Eve (20th C) Swedish				
oil	1	1,671	1,671	1,671
DETTI, Cesare Auguste (1847-1914) Italian				
oil	8	2,100-26,100	12,396	10,132
wc/d	3	584-1,424	881	637
DETTMANN, Ludwig Julius Christian (1865-1944) German				
wc/d	1	4,248	4,248	4,248
DEUCHERT, Heinrich (1840-?) German				
oil	1	3,027	3,027	3,027
DEUEL, Austin (1939-) American				
oil	1	850	850	850
wc/d	2	600-800	700	600

Name	No.	Price Range	Average	Median
DEULLY, Eugène Auguste Francois (1860-1933) French				
oil	1	1,285	1,285	1,285
DEURS, Caroline van (1860-1932) Danish				
oil	1	1,581	1,581	1,581
DEUSSER, August (1870-1942) German				
oil	1	1,526	1,526	1,526
DEUTMANN, Frans (1867-1915) Dutch				
oil	1	6,055	6,055	6,055
DEUTSCH, Ernst (1883-?) Austrian				
wc/d	3	839-1,286	1,078	1,110
DEUTSCH, Ludwig (1855-1935) French				
oil	6	5,437-1,472,000	788,386	870,000
DEUX, Fred (1924-) French				
wc/d	6	1,204-4,052	2,169	1,555
DEVADE, Marc (1943-1983) French				
oil	3	2,979-6,663	4,383	3,507
wc/d	2	2,145-3,508	2,826	2,145
DEVAL, Pierre (1897-1993) French				
oil	2	1,670-2,546	2,108	1,670
wc/d	2	1,901-3,341	2,621	1,901
DEVAMBEZ, Andre (1867-1943) French				
oil	5	1,065-6,049	3,987	4,872
DEVAS, Anthony (1911-1958) British				
oil	3	448-1,740	896	501
wc/d	1	2,223	2,223	2,223
DEVAUX, Jules Ernest (1837-?) French				
oil	1	2,922	2,922	2,922
DEVEDEUX, Louis (1820-1874) French				
oil	6	4,091-49,167	13,877	6,557
DEVELLY, Charles (1783-1849) French				
oil	1	7,498	7,498	7,498
DEVENTER, Jan Frederik van (1822-1886) Dutch				
oil	1	3,196	3,196	3,196
DEVENYNS, Steve (1953-) American				
oil	1	1,200	1,200	1,200
DEVERIA, Achille (1800-1857) French				
oil	2	1,400-2,199	1,799	1,400
wc/d	3	950-1,104	1,044	1,079
DEVERIA, Eugène (1808-1865) French				
oil	2	786-1,940	1,363	786
DEVETTA, Edoardo (1912-1993) Italian				
oil	1	1,478	1,478	1,478
DEVIS, Anthony (1729-1817) British				
wc/d	3	440-1,750	1,228	1,496
DEVIS, Arthur (1711-1787) British				
oil	4	7,560-113,400	68,160	38,280
DEVIS, Arthur William (1763-1822) British				
oil	1	270,000	270,000	270,000
DEVLAN, Francis Daniel (1835-1870) American				
oil	3	3,400-19,000	8,933	4,400
DEVLIN, George (1937-) British				
oil	2	3,401-7,740	5,570	3,401
wc/d	1	985	985	985
DEVOLDER, Roland (1938-) Belgian				
wc/d	1	2,158	2,158	2,158
DEVOLL, Frederick Usher (1873-1941) American				
oil	2	1,200-12,000	6,600	1,200
DEVOS, Albert (1868-1950) Belgian				
oil	1	1,565	1,565	1,565
DEVOS, Léon (1897-1974) Belgian				
oil	19	546-5,826	1,412	894
DEWASNE, Jean (1921-1999) French				
oil	5	7,068-28,160	14,035	12,643
wc/d	3	1,374-12,041	7,959	10,462
DEWEY, Charles Melville (1849-1937) American				
oil	2	600-5,500	3,050	600
wc/d	2	550-1,000	775	550
DEWHURST, Wynford (1864-1941) British				
oil	3	1,800-4,524	3,376	3,806
wc/d	1	1,392	1,392	1,392
DEWING, Maria Richards Oakey (1845-1927) American				
oil	1	1,800,000	1,800,000	1,800,000

Name	No.	Price Range	Average	Median
DEWING, Thomas W (1851-1938) American				
oil	1	11,000	11,000	11,000
DEWS, J Steven (1949-) British				
oil	10	2,047-120,000	45,837	45,000
wc/d	2	592-696	644	592
DEXEL, Walter (1890-1973) German				
oil	5	3,822-34,397	17,812	21,041
wc/d	5	1,656-5,096	3,115	2,760
DEY, John William (1912-1978) American				
oil	2	7,500-11,000	9,250	7,500
DEY, Manishi (20th C) Indian				
wc/d	1	1,408	1,408	1,408
DEYDIER, René (1882-1942) French				
oil	3	486-4,253	2,065	1,458
D'EYMAR, Rosalie (18th C) Swiss				
oil	1	6,336	6,336	6,336
DEYMONAZ, Gerard (20th C) French				
oil	1	1,029	1,029	1,029
DEYROLLE, Jean (1911-1967) French				
oil	11	2,046-7,773	4,134	3,565
DEYROLLE, Theophile-Louis (1844-1923) French				
oil	11	795-12,000	3,554	3,156
DEZAUNAY, Émile (1854-1940) French				
oil	2	2,221-2,678	2,449	2,221
wc/d	4	942-2,127	1,686	1,573
DEZEUZE, Daniel (1942-) French				
oil	1	1,636	1,636	1,636
wc/d	2	819-1,130	974	819
D'HAESE, Reinhoud (1928-) Belgian				
wc/d	1	903	903	903
3D	9	4,091-21,673	8,546	7,243
D'HAESE, Roel (1921-) Belgian				
3D	1	31,306	31,306	31,306
D'HARDWILLIER, Charles Achille (1795-?) French				
oil	2	4,488-8,228	6,358	4,488
DHAWAN, Rajendra (1936-) Indian				
oil	2	12,000-15,000	13,500	12,000
D'HONDT, Mieja (1948-) Belgian				
3D	1	13,245	13,245	13,245
D'HONT, Piet (1917-1997) Dutch				
3D	3	2,356-3,816	3,031	2,922
DHURANDHAR, Mahadev Viswanath (1867-1944) Indian				
wc/d	4	1,936-6,574	3,554	2,768
DIAL, Arthur (20th C) American				
wc/d	1	1,600	1,600	1,600
DIAL, Thornton (1928-) American				
oil	1	1,850	1,850	1,850
wc/d	1	2,600	2,600	2,600
DIAMANDOPOULOS, Diamantis (1914-1995) Greek				
oil	2	7,040-26,100	16,570	7,040
DIANO, Giacinto (1730-1803) Italian				
oil	1	67,640	67,640	67,640
DIANOV, Vladimir Aleksandrovich (1930-) Russian				
oil	2	2,022-2,141	2,081	2,022
DIAO, David (1943-) American				
oil	1	1,000	1,000	1,000
DIART, Frederic (20th C) French?				
wc/d	1	1,100	1,100	1,100
DIAS, Antonio (1944-) Brazilian				
wc/d	1	1,019	1,019	1,019
DIAZ CANEJA, Juan Manuel (1905-1988) Spanish				
oil	2	11,757-16,459	14,108	11,757
DIAZ CASTILLA, Luciano (1940-) Spanish				
oil	8	1,054-3,293	2,183	2,238
DIAZ DE LA PENA, Narcisse-Virgile (1807-1876) French				
oil	33	1,131-38,910	10,266	6,195
wc/d	2	2,000-5,920	3,960	2,000
DIAZ, F de P (19th C) Spanish				
oil	1	3,794	3,794	3,794
DIAZ, Jose (1930-2001) Spanish				
wc/d	1	1,196	1,196	1,196

Name	No.	Price Range	Average	Median
DIBDEN, Thomas Charles (19/20th C) British?				
wc/d	1	1,288	1,288	1,288
DIBDIN, Thomas Colman (1810-1893) British				
oil	1	5,984	5,984	5,984
wc/d	2	708-2,640	1,674	708
DIBLIK, Kantisek Xaver (20th C) Continental				
oil	1	2,500	2,500	2,500
DICERBO, Michael (1947-) American				
oil	1	1,800	1,800	1,800
DICHTL, Erich (1890-1955) Austrian				
oil	3	1,178-1,940	1,605	1,697
DICIERVO, Jorge (1947-) Argentinian				
oil	2	5,200-8,000	6,600	5,200
wc/d	1	1,600	1,600	1,600
DICK, George (1916-1978) American				
oil	3	700-1,700	1,200	1,200
DICK, Sir William Reid (1879-1961) British				
3D	2	13,230-14,175	13,702	13,230
DICKE, Karl Heinz H (1938-) German				
wc/d	1	1,885	1,885	1,885
DICKERHOF, Urs (1941-) Swiss				
oil	2	1,332-1,679	1,505	1,332
DICKINSON, Preston (1891-1930) American				
wc/d	3	8,000-60,000	30,666	24,000
DICKINSON, Ross Edward (1903-1978) American				
oil	2	1,700-2,250	1,975	1,700
DICKSEE, Frank (1853-1928) British				
wc/d	1	7,830	7,830	7,830
DICKSEE, Herbert (1862-1942) British				
oil	1	16,020	16,020	16,020
DICKSEE, John Robert (1817-1905) British				
oil	1	3,529	3,529	3,529
DICKSEE, Margaret Isabel (1808-1903) British				
oil	1	2,655	2,655	2,655
wc/d	1	1,044	1,044	1,044
DICKSEE, Thomas Francis (1819-1895) British				
oil	1	4,411	4,411	4,411
DICKSON, J (17th C) British				
oil	1	2,750	2,750	2,750
DICKSON, Mel (1960-) American				
oil	1	1,100	1,100	1,100
DICKSON, Tom (1949-) Canadian				
oil	2	2,659-3,545	3,102	2,659
DICKSON, William (fl.1881-1904) British				
oil	2	797-2,301	1,549	797
DIDAY, François (1802-1877) Swiss				
oil	2	493-11,421	5,957	493
DIDIER, Clovis François Auguste (1858-?) French				
oil	2	2,885-25,000	13,942	2,885
DIDIER, Jules (1831-1892) French				
oil	2	2,859-4,724	3,791	2,859
DIDIER, Luc (1954-) French				
oil	6	1,699-3,527	2,530	2,356
DIDIER-POUGET, William (1864-1959) French				
oil	4	606-2,125	1,307	1,000
DIDIONI, Francesco (1859-1895) Italian				
oil	1	12,103	12,103	12,103
DIDONNA, Henry (1932-) French				
oil	1	4,001	4,001	4,001
DIEBENKORN, Richard (1922-1993) American				
oil	3	750,000-780,000	770,000	780,000
wc/d	8	70,000-450,000	221,250	210,000
DIEDEREN, Jef (1920-) Dutch				
oil	1	3,562	3,562	3,562
DIEDERICHS, Peter (1923-1982) German				
3D	1	3,649	3,649	3,649
DIEFENBACH, Karl Wilhelm (1851-1931) German				
oil	3	3,805-10,946	7,117	6,600
DIEFFENBACH, Anton Heinrich (1831-1914) German				
oil	1	18,000	18,000	18,000
DIEGHEM, A van (19th C) Dutch				
oil	1	2,003	2,003	2,003

Name	No.	Price Range	Average	Median
DIEGHEM, Jacob van (19th C) Dutch				
oil	2	669-2,975	1,822	669
DIEGHEM, Joseph van (1843-1885) Belgian				
oil	5	900-2,682	1,984	2,464
DIEHL, Arthur (1870-1929) American				
oil	25	500-29,000	3,444	1,700
DIEHL, Fannie (20th C) American				
oil	1	2,600	2,600	2,600
DIEHL, Gosta (1899-1964) Finnish				
oil	1	1,221	1,221	1,221
wc/d	2	727-1,032	879	727
DIEHL, Guy (1949-) American				
oil	2	2,250-2,500	2,375	2,250
DIEHL, Randall (20th C) American				
wc/d	1	1,400	1,400	1,400
DIEHLE, Alwin (1854-?) German				
oil	3	568-2,154	1,341	1,302
DIELITZ, Konrad (1845-1933) German				
oil	1	1,452	1,452	1,452
DIELMAN, Frederick (1847-1935) German				
oil	1	1,600	1,600	1,600
DIEM, Johannes (1924-1991) Swiss				
oil	1	1,897	1,897	1,897
DIEMEN, Jan van (1954-) Dutch				
oil	1	2,757	2,757	2,757
DIEMER, Michael Zeno (1867-1939) German				
oil	7	2,425-8,663	5,026	3,279
wc/d	3	539-1,001	794	843
DIEPENBECK, Abraham van (1596-1675) Flemish				
wc/d	3	1,215-12,153	5,072	1,850
DIEPRAAM, Abraham (1622-1670) Dutch				
oil	2	2,378-13,320	7,849	2,378
DIERCKX, A R (?) ?				
oil	1	2,647	2,647	2,647
DIERSKE, Winfried (1934-) Danish				
oil	2	989-3,588	2,288	989
DIESNER, Gerhild (1915-1995) Austrian				
oil	1	21,848	21,848	21,848
DIESSL, A (19th C) German?				
3D	1	2,301	2,301	2,301
DIEST, Adriaen van (1655-1704) Dutch				
oil	1	7,612	7,612	7,612
DIEST, Frans van (19th C) Belgian				
oil	2	886-2,047	1,466	886
DIEST, Hieronymus van (1631-1673) Dutch				
oil	2	2,775-9,031	5,903	2,775
DIEST, Willem van (1610-1673) Dutch				
oil	3	8,590-32,143	16,461	8,650
DIETERLE, Marie (1856-1935) French				
oil	2	1,798-5,918	3,858	1,798
DIETERLE, Pierre Georges (1844-1937) French				
oil	2	4,789-21,425	13,107	4,789
DIETERLEN, Hans (1896-1973) German				
oil	2	1,168-1,285	1,226	1,168
DIETLER, Johann Friedrich (1804-1874) Swiss				
oil	3	531-3,092	1,707	1,499
DIETMANN, Erik (1937-2002) Swedish				
oil	1	3,540	3,540	3,540
wc/d	10	509-3,308	1,499	936
3D	2	3,186-14,536	8,861	3,186
DIETRICH, Adelheid (1827-?) German				
oil	3	16,000-100,000	51,940	39,822
DIETRICH, Adolf (1877-1957) Swiss				
oil	13	12,171-160,352	39,020	24,474
wc/d	2	3,246-7,841	5,543	3,246
DIETRICH, Christian Wilhelm Ernst (1712-1774) German				
oil	13	1,204-36,122	10,704	8,113
wc/d	2	1,527-3,330	2,428	1,527
DIETRICHSON, Mathilde (1837-1921) Norwegian				
oil	1	4,396	4,396	4,396
DIETZE, Bruno (1867-?) German				
oil	1	1,818	1,818	1,818

Name	No.	Price Range	Average	Median
DIETZSCH, Barbara Regina (1706-1783) German				
wc/d	2	6,069-22,200	14,134	6,069
DIETZSCH, Hans Hubert (1880-1926) German				
3D	1	2,681	2,681	2,681
DIETZSCH, Johann Christoph (1710-1769) German				
wc/d	2	2,804-2,804	2,804	2,804
DIETZSCH, Margareta Barbara (1716-1795) German				
wc/d	1	5,920	5,920	5,920
DIEU, Antoine (1662-1727) French				
wc/d	1	8,822	8,822	8,822
DIEUDONNE, Eugène Paul (1825-?) French				
oil	1	7,182	7,182	7,182
DIEUNDONNE, Emmanuel de (1845-1889) Swiss				
oil	1	90,000	90,000	90,000
DIEVENBACH, Hendricus Anthonius (1872-1946) Dutch				
oil	3	1,326-3,673	2,316	1,950
DIEZ, Julius (1870-1957) German				
oil	1	1,703	1,703	1,703
wc/d	1	666	666	666
DIEZ, Wilhelm von (1839-1907) German				
oil	2	994-3,073	2,033	994
DIEZLER, Jakob (1789-1855) German				
oil	7	6,533-8,743	7,127	6,533
DIGHTON, Phoebe (fl.1824-1835) British				
wc/d	3	561-2,590	1,545	1,484
DIGHTON, Robert (1752-1814) British				
wc/d	1	4,524	4,524	4,524
DIGNIMONT, Andre (1891-1965) French				
oil	1	1,798	1,798	1,798
wc/d	14	477-2,622	1,134	970
DIJSSELHOF, Gerrit Willem (1866-1924) Dutch				
oil	8	777-6,062	2,013	1,484
DIKE, Philip Latimer (1906-1990) American				
oil	4	13,000-50,000	32,625	27,500
wc/d	12	1,000-22,500	10,729	9,500
DILL, Laddie John (1943-) American				
oil	2	410-1,800	1,105	410
wc/d	4	500-3,000	1,225	500
DILL, Ludwig (1848-1940) German				
oil	19	597-13,308	2,853	2,057
wc/d	2	1,459-3,514	2,486	1,459
DILL, Otto (1884-1957) German				
oil	12	1,824-14,108	4,412	2,804
wc/d	7	525-3,109	1,582	1,073
DILLARD, Emily (1879-1968) American				
oil	1	1,250	1,250	1,250
DILLENS, Hendrick Joseph (1812-1872) Belgian				
oil	3	2,686-3,500	3,062	3,000
DILLENS, Henri (19th C) ?				
oil	1	13,124	13,124	13,124
DILLENS, Julien (1849-1904) Belgian				
3D	2	3,039-5,292	4,165	3,039
DILLER, Burgoyne (1906-1965) American				
oil	2	38,000-55,000	46,500	38,000
wc/d	4	1,700-14,000	5,675	3,000
DILLER, Richard (1890-) ?				
oil	1	1,285	1,285	1,285
DILLEY, Ramon (1933-) French				
oil	3	1,067-1,671	1,281	1,106
D'ILLIERS, Gaston (1876-1952) French				
3D	1	3,360	3,360	3,360
DILLIS, Cantius (1779-1856) German				
oil	1	22,384	22,384	22,384
DILLIS, Johann Georg von (1759-1841) German				
oil	3	1,703-34,714	13,148	3,029
wc/d	7	777-2,827	1,692	1,654
DILLON, Frank (1823-1909) British				
oil	2	2,747-4,750	3,748	2,747
DILLON, Gerard (1917-1971) Irish				
oil	24	2,232-115,200	49,918	47,123
wc/d	24	790-8,581	3,489	3,027
3D	1	2,432	2,432	2,432

Name	No.	Price Range	Average	Median
DILLON, Michael (1957-) Irish				
oil	1	1,674	1,674	1,674
DIMITRIADIS, Georgios (1889-?) Greek				
oil	1	2,640	2,640	2,640
DINE, Jim (1935-) American				
oil	9	9,000-115,050	53,227	47,500
wc/d	12	808-35,000	16,438	19,000
3D	1	75,000	75,000	75,000
DINET, Étienne (1861-1929) French				
oil	7	823-126,714	44,562	38,015
wc/d	8	1,911-17,740	5,190	3,802
DING YI (1962-) Chinese				
oil	1	22,000	22,000	22,000
DING YU (19th C) Chinese				
wc/d	1	1,566	1,566	1,566
DINGLINGER, Sophie Friederike (c.1739-1791) German				
wc/d	1	2,141	2,141	2,141
DINKEL, Markus (1762-1832) Swiss				
wc/d	1	2,447	2,447	2,447
DIODATI, Francesco Paolo (1864-?) Italian				
oil	2	2,600-10,603	6,601	2,600
DIOMEDE, Miguel (1902-1974) Argentinian				
oil	1	22,000	22,000	22,000
DION, Mark (1961-) American				
3D	1	9,889	9,889	9,889
DIONYSE, Carmen (1921-) Belgian				
3D	1	2,166	2,166	2,166
DIOS DEL VALLE, Juan de (1856-?) Spanish				
oil	1	1,070	1,070	1,070
DIRANIAN, Serkis (19th C) Turkish				
oil	1	2,400	2,400	2,400
DIRCKINCK-HOLMFELD, Helmuth (1835-1912) Danish				
oil	1	1,690	1,690	1,690
DIRCKX, Anton (1878-1927) Dutch				
oil	2	1,512-3,000	2,256	1,512
DIRKS, Andreas (1866-1922) German				
oil	1	1,067	1,067	1,067
DISCHLER, Hermann (1866-1935) German				
oil	5	1,767-10,041	5,815	6,668
wc/d	1	707	707	707
DISEN, Andreas (1845-1923) Norwegian				
oil	1	1,042	1,042	1,042
DISKA, Patricia (1924-) American				
3D	1	2,188	2,188	2,188
DISLER, Martin (1949-1996) Swiss				
oil	5	2,270-17,575	9,518	12,177
wc/d	17	644-6,897	2,742	2,405
DISTELBARTH, Friedrich (1768-1836) German				
3D	1	13,000	13,000	13,000
DISTLER, Rudolph (1946-) German				
oil	1	1,543	1,543	1,543
DITTMANN, Edmund (19th C) German				
oil	3	878-4,077	2,042	1,171
DIULGHEROFF, Nicolas (1901-1982) Italian/Bulgarian				
oil	2	2,108-3,279	2,693	2,108
wc/d	5	2,386-11,931	4,793	3,045
DIX, Otto (1891-1969) German				
oil	3	12,721-63,699	33,281	23,425
wc/d	29	586-299,200	47,413	14,500
DIXON, Anna (1873-1959) British				
wc/d	1	1,144	1,144	1,144
DIXON, Charles (fl.1748-1798) British				
wc/d	1	4,375	4,375	4,375
DIXON, Charles Edward (1872-1934) British				
wc/d	30	736-24,310	4,759	4,048
DIXON, Francis (?) ?				
oil	1	1,300	1,300	1,300
DIXON, Francis Stillwell (1872-1967) American				
oil	2	850-19,000	9,925	850
DIXON, James (1887-1970) British?				
oil	4	3,784-9,425	5,824	4,712

Name	No.	Price Range	Average	Median
DIXON, James Budd (1900-1967) American				
oil	3	5,381-41,859	17,939	6,578
DIXON, Maynard (1875-1946) American				
oil	9	10,000-650,000	172,055	47,500
wc/d	10	3,250-90,000	32,900	7,500
DIXON, William (18/19th C) British				
wc/d	1	8,000	8,000	8,000
DIZ, Juana Elena (20th C) American?				
oil	1	1,200	1,200	1,200
D'IZARNY, Francois (1952-) French				
oil	2	1,790-2,356	2,073	1,790
DIZIANI, Gaspare (1689-1767) Italian				
oil	4	14,108-175,000	59,727	14,800
wc/d	4	1,424-14,583	5,488	2,141
DJAYA, Otto (20th C) ?				
oil	1	1,806	1,806	1,806
DMITRIEF, G V (20th C) Russian				
wc/d	1	2,238	2,238	2,238
DMITRIENKO, Pierre (1925-1974) French				
oil	7	3,349-90,869	27,385	11,601
wc/d	2	2,249-2,990	2,619	2,249
DMITRIEV-ORENBURGSKY, Nikolai (1838-1898) Russian				
wc/d	1	3,402	3,402	3,402
DMITRIEVSKY, Lydia (1895-1967) Russian				
oil	2	10,192-110,000	60,096	10,192
DMOCHOWSKI, Vladislav (19th C) Polish				
oil	1	2,616	2,616	2,616
DOBASHI, Jun (1910-1975) Japanese				
oil	19	375-3,748	1,736	1,874
wc/d	4	469-586	528	473
DOBBIE, John (20th C) British				
oil	1	2,079	2,079	2,079
DOBBIN, Lady Kate (1868-1955) Irish				
wc/d	1	4,450	4,450	4,450
DOBOUJINSKY, Mstislav (1875-1957) Russian				
oil	18	1,909-99,558	29,746	23,426
wc/d	707	410-206,400	6,364	2,387
DOBRINSKY, Yitzhak (1891-1973) Russian				
oil	8	954-7,170	2,967	2,153
DOBROWSKY, Josef (1889-1964) Austrian				
oil	12	897-296,000	35,252	9,604
wc/d	14	550-4,364	2,143	1,985
DOBSON, Frank (1886-1963) British				
oil	1	3,420	3,420	3,420
wc/d	10	400-5,292	2,031	1,566
3D	2	26,460-601,800	314,130	26,460
DOBSON, Henry John (1858-1928) British				
oil	8	1,067-5,310	2,664	2,076
DOBSON, Margaret A (1888-1981) American				
oil	1	600	600	600
wc/d	1	4,500	4,500	4,500
DOBSON, Patricia (1947-) American				
oil	2	2,250-11,000	6,625	2,250
DOBSON, William Charles Thomas (1817-1898) British				
wc/d	1	1,044	1,044	1,044
DOCHARTY, A Brownlie (1862-1940) British				
oil	8	797-4,450	1,892	1,748
DOCHARTY, James (1829-1878) British				
oil	1	1,000	1,000	1,000
DOCTER, Marcia (20th C) American				
wc/d	1	1,400	1,400	1,400
DODD, Arthur Charles (fl.1878-1890) British				
oil	1	1,500	1,500	1,500
DODD, Howell (1910-2005) American				
wc/d	1	4,250	4,250	4,250
DODD, Louis (1943-) British				
oil	5	1,479-8,500	4,265	3,800
DODD, Robert (1748-1816) British				
oil	3	5,394-79,650	33,334	14,960
DODEIGNE, Eugène (1923-) French				
wc/d	8	1,169-3,131	1,881	1,403
3D	3	3,527-9,936	6,839	7,054

Name	No.	Price Range	Average	Median
DODERO, Pietro (1882-1967) Italian				
oil	3	947-2,959	2,170	2,604
DODGE, J T (19th C) ?				
wc/d	1	3,000	3,000	3,000
DODGE, John Wood (1807-1893) American				
wc/d	1	1,100	1,100	1,100
DODGE, William de Leftwich (1867-1935) American				
oil	5	800-4,800	2,770	3,000
DODIYA, Anju (1964-) Indian				
oil	1	90,000	90,000	90,000
wc/d	1	35,000	35,000	35,000
DODIYA, Atul (1959-) Indian				
oil	1	120,000	120,000	120,000
wc/d	4	19,000-160,000	92,250	40,000
DODSON, Tom (1910-1991) British				
oil	3	1,274-1,820	1,492	1,383
DOEMLING, John Carl (1892-?) American				
oil	1	1,300	1,300	1,300
DOERSTLING, Emil (1859-?) German				
oil	1	1,790	1,790	1,790
DOES, Simon van der (1653-1717) Dutch				
oil	2	1,753-6,020	3,886	1,753
DOES, Willem van der (1889-1966) Dutch				
oil	1	1,558	1,558	1,558
DOESBURGH, Elsa van (1875-1957) Dutch				
oil	2	2,061-6,592	4,326	2,061
DOEVE, Eppo (1907-) Dutch				
wc/d	1	1,025	1,025	1,025
DOFFO, Juan (20th C) Argentinian				
oil	2	3,200-4,000	3,600	3,200
DOGANCAY, Burhan (1929-2000) Turkish				
oil	4	13,000-74,400	38,956	19,007
wc/d	1	8,870	8,870	8,870
DOGARTH, Erich Josef (1927-) Austrian				
oil	1	4,562	4,562	4,562
DOGARTH, Oskar Robert (1898-1961) Austrian				
oil	4	455-1,929	1,220	708
DOHENY, Dennis M (1956-) American				
oil	3	7,500-13,000	9,500	8,000
DOHERTY, John (1949-) Irish				
oil	7	21,014-65,459	37,467	28,054
wc/d	1	5,611	5,611	5,611
DOHLMANN, Augusta (1847-1914) Austrian				
oil	2	1,294-2,432	1,863	1,294
DOIG, Peter (1959-) British				
oil	15	19,000-1,850,000	346,871	177,000
wc/d	3	13,200-46,250	27,833	24,050
DOIGNEAU, Edouard Edmond de (1865-1954) French				
oil	3	1,199-4,142	2,675	2,686
wc/d	18	468-1,827	791	526
DOK-HI KIM (20th C) Oriental				
oil	1	9,062	9,062	9,062
DOKOUPIL, Jiri Georg (1954-) Czechoslovakian				
oil	9	2,500-31,450	9,231	5,301
wc/d	3	584-7,120	3,213	1,936
DOLACK, Monte (20th C) American				
oil	1	6,000	6,000	6,000
DOLARD, Juvenal (1827-?) French				
oil	1	5,049	5,049	5,049
DOLBY, Joshua Edward A (fl.1837-1875) British				
wc/d	1	12,090	12,090	12,090
DOLCI, Carlo (1616-1686) Italian				
oil	4	75,000-260,000	200,400	207,600
DOLE, William (1917-1983) American				
wc/d	2	2,500-5,000	3,750	2,500
DOLICE, Leon (1892-1960) American				
oil	1	650	650	650
wc/d	3	375-1,600	891	700
DOLL, Anton (1826-1887) German				
oil	13	3,000-12,858	7,406	7,014
wc/d	5	708-4,442	1,826	1,337

Name	No.	Price Range	Average	Median
DOLL, Auguste (1871-1955) Austrian				
oil	1	2,682	2,682	2,682
DOLLA, Noel (1945-) French				
oil	8	656-3,975	2,067	1,462
wc/d	12	572-5,444	2,052	954
3D	1	2,744	2,744	2,744
DOLLOND, W Anstey (fl.1880-1911) British				
oil	1	828	828	828
wc/d	5	1,320-3,864	2,567	1,958
DOLPH, John Henry (1835-1903) American				
oil	2	2,500-18,000	10,250	2,500
DOLPHIN, Willem (1935-) Belgian				
oil	2	719-1,500	1,109	719
DOMBA, R (?) Italian?				
oil	1	7,560	7,560	7,560
DOMBROIS, E (19th C) French				
oil	1	4,872	4,872	4,872
DOMBROWSKI, Carl Ritter von (1872-1951) German				
oil	2	2,061-3,273	2,667	2,061
DOMBURG, Antoon (1882-1954) Dutch				
oil	1	2,500	2,500	2,500
DOMELA, A (19/20th C) Italian				
oil	1	3,960	3,960	3,960
DOMELA, Cesar (1900-1992) Dutch				
wc/d	3	954-6,997	3,804	3,461
3D	2	8,000-11,449	9,724	8,000
DOMENCHIN DE CHAVANNE, Pierre Salomon (1673-1744) French				
oil	1	1,702	1,702	1,702
DOMENICHINO (1581-1641) Italian				
oil	1	23,514	23,514	23,514
DOMENICI, Carlo (1898-1981) Italian				
oil	26	908-4,849	2,321	2,061
DOMENICO DI MICHELINO (1417-1491) Italian				
oil	1	1,500,000	1,500,000	1,500,000
DOMERGUE, Jean Gabriel (1889-1962) French				
oil	59	847-95,036	7,560	3,646
wc/d	5	611-3,828	2,333	3,131
DOMINGO Y FALLOLA, Roberto (1867-1956) Spanish				
oil	3	2,108-20,354	14,272	20,354
wc/d	15	545-9,644	2,362	892
DOMINGO Y MARQUES, Francisco (1842-1920) Spanish				
oil	6	3,240-33,000	15,039	11,712
wc/d	1	9,644	9,644	9,644
DOMINGO, Roberto (1883-1956) Spanish				
oil	1	2,431	2,431	2,431
wc/d	1	575	575	575
DOMINGUEZ BECQUER, Valeriano (1834-1870) Spanish				
oil	1	11,781	11,781	11,781
DOMINGUEZ NEIRA, Pedro (1894-1970) Argentinian				
oil	1	3,000	3,000	3,000
DOMINGUEZ, Nelson (1947-) Cuban				
oil	1	5,703	5,703	5,703
DOMINGUEZ, O (?) ?				
wc/d	1	4,195	4,195	4,195
DOMINGUEZ, Oscar (1906-1958) Spanish				
oil	20	3,138-1,480,000	205,139	44,402
wc/d	16	1,734-31,069	10,345	7,658
3D	3	13,000-531,000	216,533	105,600
DOMINICIS, Gino de (1947-1998) Italian				
oil	2	29,500-31,803	30,651	29,500
wc/d	1	7,591	7,591	7,591
DOMINIQUE, E (19th C) French				
oil	1	7,124	7,124	7,124
DOMMERSEN, Cornelis Christian (1842-1928) Dutch				
oil	4	800-15,547	5,445	2,438
DOMMERSEN, Pieter Christian (1834-1908) Dutch				
oil	19	1,740-19,778	6,682	4,479
DOMMERSEN, William (1850-1927) Dutch				
oil	22	774-6,370	2,444	2,002
DOMOTO, Hisao (1928-) Japanese				
oil	2	2,787-11,100	6,943	2,787

Name	No.	Price Range	Average	Median
DOMOTO, Insho (1891-1975) Japanese				
oil	1	3,700	3,700	3,700
wc/d	1	5,343	5,343	5,343
DOMPE, Hernan (20th C) Argentinian				
3D	2	2,500-5,500	4,000	2,500
DON, Martino del (19th C) Italian				
wc/d	1	6,076	6,076	6,076
DONALD, J Milne (fl.1888-1894) British				
oil	1	1,388	1,388	1,388
DONALDSON, David Abercrombie (1916-1996) British				
oil	1	3,480	3,480	3,480
wc/d	1	692	692	692
DONALDSON, Kim (1952-) Zimbabwean				
wc/d	3	907-3,780	2,822	3,780
DONALDSON, Marysia (20th C) British?				
oil	1	1,007	1,007	1,007
DONAS, Marthe (1885-1967) Belgian				
oil	4	3,879-55,000	18,724	6,429
wc/d	1	1,236	1,236	1,236
DONAT, Friederich Reginald (1830-1907) Belgian				
oil	3	916-1,883	1,450	1,551
DONATELLO (1386-1466) Italian				
3D	1	3,950,000	3,950,000	3,950,000
DONATI, Enrico (1909-) American/Italian				
oil	3	2,800-20,065	13,134	16,537
wc/d	4	5,946-25,000	14,371	6,541
DONCKER, Herman Mijnerts (17th C) Dutch				
oil	1	17,517	17,517	17,517
DONDUCCI, Giovanni Andrea (1575-1655) Italian				
oil	4	15,122-110,034	63,187	54,703
DONEUX, Alexandre (19th C) French				
oil	1	11,973	11,973	11,973
DONGE, J van (20th C) Dutch				
oil	1	2,003	2,003	2,003
DONGEN, Dionys van (1748-1819) Dutch				
oil	1	4,877	4,877	4,877
DONGEN, Iris van (1975-) Dutch				
wc/d	1	3,330	3,330	3,330
DONGEN, Kees van (1877-1968) French/Dutch				
oil	25	3,507-4,784,000	864,691	442,500
wc/d	20	1,483-188,368	40,161	11,918
3D	5	44,000-105,600	73,568	66,880
DONGHI, Antonio (1897-1963) Italian				
oil	3	28,110-41,980	32,733	28,110
DONNELLY, Anne (20th C) Irish				
oil	1	1,936	1,936	1,936
DONNER, P (19th C) ?				
oil	1	6,429	6,429	6,429
DONNINO DEL MAZZIERE, Antonio (1492-1529) Italian				
oil	1	16,435	16,435	16,435
DONNY, D (1798-1861) Flemish				
oil	1	4,176	4,176	4,176
DONNY, Desire (1798-1861) Flemish				
oil	1	11,743	11,743	11,743
DONOVAN, Phoebe (1902-1998) British				
oil	3	957-2,926	2,182	2,664
DONZEL, Charles (1824-1889) French				
oil	1	1,730	1,730	1,730
wc/d	3	588-764	705	764
DONZELLI, Bruno (1941-) Italian				
oil	23	610-8,352	2,246	1,767
wc/d	2	597-2,548	1,572	597
DOOLAARD, Cornelis Jans (1944-) Dutch				
oil	2	468-2,417	1,442	468
DOOMS, Vic (1912-1994) Belgian				
oil	11	716-2,392	1,163	1,019
DOOREN, A van (19th C) Dutch?				
oil	1	2,336	2,336	2,336
DOORN, Adriaan van (1825-1903) Dutch				
oil	1	3,588	3,588	3,588
DOORN, Tinus van (1905-1940) Dutch				
oil	2	1,403-5,455	3,429	1,403

Name	No.	Price Range	Average	Median
DOOYEWAARD, Jacob (1876-1969) Dutch				
oil	2	2,038-2,848	2,443	2,038
DOOYEWAARD, Willem (1892-1980) Dutch				
oil	3	1,688-4,219	2,772	2,411
wc/d	1	2,408	2,408	2,408
DORADO, Adrian (20th C) Argentinian				
wc/d	1	1,700	1,700	1,700
DORAZIO, Piero (1927-2005) Italian				
oil	58	1,058-154,289	22,283	11,651
wc/d	16	3,816-14,240	7,222	6,897
DORCHIN, Yaacov (1946-) Israeli				
oil	1	380	380	380
wc/d	2	500-530	515	500
3D	2	4,000-4,000	4,000	4,000
DORCHY, Henry (1920-) Belgian				
oil	1	1,147	1,147	1,147
DORE, Gustave (1832-1883) French				
oil	4	5,648-46,000	18,254	5,711
wc/d	9	550-85,000	11,781	1,450
3D	1	27,000	27,000	27,000
DORE, J (?) ?				
oil	1	1,823	1,823	1,823
DOREN, Émile van (1865-1949) Belgian				
oil	2	3,312-5,605	4,458	3,312
DORFLES, Gillo (1910-) Italian				
oil	1	4,685	4,685	4,685
D'ORGEIX, Christian (1927-) French				
3D	2	1,774-1,901	1,837	1,774
DORIE, Dominique (1958-) French				
oil	5	950-3,250	1,810	1,700
DORIGNAC, Georges (1879-1925) French				
oil	1	4,783	4,783	4,783
DORIGNY, Louis (1654-1742) French				
oil	1	23,301	23,301	23,301
DORING, Adam Lude (1925-) German				
oil	2	927-1,471	1,199	927
DORMAEL, Simone van (20th C) Belgian				
oil	1	3,625	3,625	3,625
DORMICE (20th C) ?				
oil	5	2,973-3,600	3,258	3,170
DORMOY, Maurice (1821-1895) French?				
wc/d	1	1,144	1,144	1,144
DORNE, Martin van (1736-1808) Flemish				
oil	1	4,023	4,023	4,023
DORNER, Helmut (1952-) German				
oil	1	1,100	1,100	1,100
DORNER, Johann Jakob (younger) (1775-1852) German				
oil	1	3,181	3,181	3,181
DOROKLOV, Konstantin Gavrilovich (1906-1960) Russian				
oil	1	5,190	5,190	5,190
DORPH, Bertha (1875-1960) Danish				
oil	2	809-1,630	1,219	809
DORR, Ferdinand (1880-1968) German				
oil	1	1,459	1,459	1,459
DORREE, Émile (1885-1959) French				
oil	1	2,428	2,428	2,428
DORRIES, Bernhard (1898-1978) German				
oil	1	2,531	2,531	2,531
DORSCH, Ferdinand (1875-1938) German				
oil	1	2,458	2,458	2,458
DORSEY, William (1942-) American				
oil	11	475-4,500	1,661	1,200
D'ORSI, Achille (1845-1929) Italian				
oil	1	400	400	400
3D	1	3,107	3,107	3,107
DORT, Willem van (snr) (1875-1949) Dutch				
wc/d	1	2,104	2,104	2,104
DOSAMANTES, Francisco (1911-) Mexican				
oil	2	12,000-20,000	16,000	12,000
DOSS, C J Antony (1933-) Indian				
oil	3	2,000-7,000	4,083	3,250

Name	No.	Price Range	Average	Median
DOSS, Inser Chunder (19th C) Indian				
wc/d	1	1,100	1,100	1,100
DOSSENA, Alceo (1878-1937) Italian				
3D	1	4,071	4,071	4,071
DOSSI, Battista (1474-1548) Italian				
oil	1	85,000	85,000	85,000
DOTREMONT, Christian (1922-1979) Belgian				
oil	1	38,795	38,795	38,795
wc/d	8	2,093-22,535	6,549	2,253
DOTTORI, Gerardo (1884-1977) Italian				
oil	6	8,269-44,524	27,571	25,375
wc/d	4	3,156-6,054	5,092	5,271
DOU, Gerard (1613-1675) Dutch				
oil	3	411,429-1,813,000	1,108,143	1,100,000
DOUCET, Jacques (1924-1994) French				
oil	13	2,544-29,223	12,488	11,959
wc/d	14	473-14,137	2,675	1,672
DOUFFET, Gerard (1594-1660) Flemish				
oil	1	207,600	207,600	207,600
DOUGHERTY, Paul (1877-1947) American				
oil	18	950-10,000	3,091	2,400
DOUGHTY, Thomas (1793-1856) American				
oil	3	7,500-85,000	43,333	37,500
DOUGHTY, William (?-1782) British				
oil	2	2,576-4,301	3,438	2,576
DOUGLAS, A (19th C) British				
wc/d	1	1,925	1,925	1,925
DOUGLAS, Aaron (1898-1979) American				
wc/d	1	5,500	5,500	5,500
DOUGLAS, Edward Algernon Stuart (1850-c.1920) British				
oil	4	2,081-30,240	12,350	2,081
wc/d	1	549	549	549
DOUGLAS, Edwin (1848-1914) British				
oil	4	1,038-59,840	27,819	1,780
DOUGLAS, Jean Harmon (20th C) American?				
wc/d	4	600-1,900	1,037	800
DOUGLAS, Rose (?) British				
oil	1	1,197	1,197	1,197
DOUGLAS, Sir William Fettes (1822-1891) British				
oil	4	1,864-6,688	4,568	4,795
DOUGLAS, Walter (1864-?) American				
oil	2	500-1,000	750	500
wc/d	1	750	750	750
DOUKAS, Hector (1885-1969) Greek				
oil	5	2,464-8,996	4,932	4,400
DOUKE, Daniel (1943-) American				
oil	1	1,100	1,100	1,100
DOUMAS, Haralambos (1910-1991) Greek				
oil	1	3,168	3,168	3,168
DOUMET, Zacharie Felix (1761-1818) French				
wc/d	2	2,832-11,570	7,201	2,832
DOUTHWAITE, Patricia (1939-2002) British				
wc/d	52	435-3,843	1,449	1,320
DOUTRELEAU, Pierre (1938-) French				
oil	4	1,196-3,250	2,158	1,998
wc/d	1	973	973	973
DOUVEN, Jan Frans van (1656-1727) German				
oil	2	6,934-9,633	8,283	6,934
DOUW, Simon Johannes van (1630-1677) Flemish				
oil	4	7,591-17,300	10,761	8,544
DOUZETTE, Louis (1834-1924) German				
oil	11	1,415-6,090	3,028	2,983
DOVA, Gianni (1925-1991) Italian				
oil	42	1,986-28,274	9,944	9,541
wc/d	18	1,168-19,286	5,253	2,945
DOVASTON, Margaret (1884-1955) British				
oil	4	895-8,352	2,942	1,131
DOVE, Arthur G (1880-1946) American				
wc/d	8	850-48,000	34,856	40,000
DOVERA, Achille (1838-1895) Italian				
oil	1	6,475	6,475	6,475

Name	No.	Price Range	Average	Median
DOVIANE, Auguste (1825-1887) Swiss				
oil	2	1,400-2,671	2,035	1,400
DOW, Arthur W (1857-1922) American				
oil	4	2,500-60,000	29,000	3,500
DOWD, John (1960-) American				
oil	4	2,300-3,400	2,750	2,500
DOWELL, Charles R (?-1935) British				
oil	1	3,806	3,806	3,806
DOWERAKER, A M (fl.1920-1940) British				
wc/d	1	2,784	2,784	2,784
DOWLING, Dan (?) British				
wc/d	1	1,328	1,328	1,328
DOWLING, Robert (1827-1886) British				
oil	1	6,324	6,324	6,324
wc/d	1	605	605	605
DOWNARD, Ebeneezer Newman (fl.1849-1889) British				
oil	1	3,969	3,969	3,969
DOWNES, Rackstraw (1939-) American				
oil	1	3,250	3,250	3,250
wc/d	3	4,250-9,000	6,750	7,000
DOWNIE, Patrick (1854-1945) British				
oil	6	526-13,275	4,958	2,523
wc/d	3	481-3,828	1,813	1,131
DOWNING, Delapoer (fl.1886-1902) British				
oil	1	9,450	9,450	9,450
DOWNING, Joe (1925-) American				
oil	2	2,525-3,818	3,171	2,525
wc/d	1	989	989	989
DOWNING, Thomas (1928-) American				
oil	1	4,250	4,250	4,250
DOWNMAN, John (1750-1824) British				
wc/d	11	435-6,090	2,134	1,750
DOWS, Olin (1904-1981) American				
oil	2	3,000-3,000	3,000	3,000
wc/d	1	2,750	2,750	2,750
DOYEN, Gabriel François (1726-1806) French				
wc/d	1	10,082	10,082	10,082
DOYEN, Louis Marie (1864-1943) French				
oil	1	7,000	7,000	7,000
DOYER, Jacobus Schoemaker (1792-1867) Dutch				
wc/d	1	6,000	6,000	6,000
DOYLE, Charles Altamont (1832-1893) British				
wc/d	2	777-2,835	1,806	777
DOYLE, Hastings (19th C) British				
wc/d	1	1,200	1,200	1,200
DOYLE, Richard (1824-1883) British				
wc/d	2	1,566-6,498	4,032	1,566
DOYLE, Sam (1906-1985) American				
oil	3	2,100-5,500	3,866	4,000
D'OYLY, Sir Charles (1781-1845) British				
oil	1	10,620	10,620	10,620
wc/d	2	500-1,682	1,091	500
DOZIER, Otis (1904-1987) American				
oil	1	12,500	12,500	12,500
wc/d	4	1,500-2,000	1,750	1,500
DRACHMANN, Holger (1846-1908) Danish				
oil	4	2,654-5,691	4,046	3,397
DRAHONET, Alexandre Jean Dubois (1791-1834) French				
oil	1	2,637	2,637	2,637
wc/d	1	2,571	2,571	2,571
DRAIJER, Rein (1899-1986) Dutch				
oil	6	707-3,299	1,727	1,060
DRAPER, Herbert James (1864-1920) British				
oil	2	8,822-21,498	15,160	8,822
DRAPPIER, Edmond (19th C) French				
3D	1	7,642	7,642	7,642
DRATZ, Jean (1905-1967) Belgian				
	3	742-1,461	1,026	876
DRAYTON, Grace G (1877-1936) American				
wc/d	1	2,000	2,000	2,000
DRECHSLER, Johann Baptist (1756-1811) Austrian				
oil	1	30,260	30,260	30,260

Name	No.	Price Range	Average	Median
DREHER, K (19th C) American				
oil	1	10,000	10,000	10,000
DREI, Ercole (1886-1973) Italian				
oil	2	2,378-3,748	3,063	2,378
DREIBHOLZ, Cristiaan Lodewyck Willem (1799-1874) Dutch				
oil	3	1,296-3,687	2,580	2,757
wc/d	1	1,001	1,001	1,001
DREISBACH, Clarence I (1903-) American				
oil	2	1,200-5,000	3,100	1,200
DRENKHAHN, Reinhard (20th C) German				
oil	1	5,040	5,040	5,040
DREONI, Arrigo (1911-1987) Italian				
oil	1	1,262	1,262	1,262
DRESCHER, Arno (1882-1971) German				
oil	1	1,196	1,196	1,196
DRESSLER, Adolph (1814-1868) German				
3D	1	2,436	2,436	2,436
DRESSLER, August Wilhelm (1886-1970) German				
oil	2	532-1,060	796	532
wc/d	2	636-1,018	827	636
DRESSLER, Franz (1918-) Austrian				
oil	1	4,208	4,208	4,208
wc/d	1	663	663	663
DRESSLER, Friedrich Wilhelm Albert (1822-1897) German				
oil	2	915-1,127	1,021	915
DREUX, Alfred de (1810-1860) French				
oil	4	24,360-1,417,500	389,315	26,703
wc/d	1	24,189	24,189	24,189
DREVEN, Maarten A van (1941-2001) Dutch				
wc/d	1	1,296	1,296	1,296
DREVET, Paul (19th C) French				
oil	1	4,241	4,241	4,241
DREVIN, Alexander (1889-1938) Russian				
oil	1	25,800	25,800	25,800
DREW, Clement (1806-1889) American				
oil	11	850-10,000	4,222	4,000
DREW, George W (1875-1968) American				
oil	8	650-3,250	1,393	1,200
DREW, Mary (fl.1881-1901) British				
oil	1	3,456	3,456	3,456
DREWES, Werner (1899-1985) American				
oil	4	4,500-50,000	24,604	8,918
wc/d	4	1,200-1,800	1,551	1,600
DREXEL, Francis Martin (1792-1863) American				
oil	2	6,250-8,000	7,125	6,250
DREYER, Dankvart (1816-1852) Danish				
oil	2	5,211-6,520	5,865	5,211
DRIAN, Étienne (1885-1961) French				
oil	4	3,805-40,260	18,630	5,014
wc/d	2	2,141-3,805	2,973	2,141
DRIBEN, Peter (c.1903-1968) American				
oil	1	11,000	11,000	11,000
DRIES, Jean (1905-1973) French				
oil	1	1,569	1,569	1,569
DRIESCH, Johannes (1901-1930) German				
oil	1	9,425	9,425	9,425
DRIESTEN, Arend Jan van (1878-1969) Dutch				
wc/d	1	1,878	1,878	1,878
DRIESTEN, Joseph Emmanuel van (1853-?) French				
wc/d	1	4,400	4,400	4,400
DRINKARD, David (1948-) American				
oil	3	4,000-4,000	4,000	4,000
DRISCOLL, Robert (?) ?				
oil	1	4,680	4,680	4,680
DRISSI, Mohamed (1946-2003) Moroccan				
wc/d	2	1,140-1,381	1,260	1,140
DRIVIER, Leon-Ernest (1878-1951) French				
3D	1	18,811	18,811	18,811
DROCCO, Guido and MELLO, Franco (20th C) Italian				
3D	1	4,451	4,451	4,451

Name	No.	Price Range	Average	Median
DROESE, Felix (1950-) German				
oil	1	6,126	6,126	6,126
wc/d	2	972-3,884	2,428	972
DROLLING, Michel Martin (1786-1851) French				
oil	4	1,211-278,767	98,344	5,696
DRONSART, Alexandre (19th C) French				
oil	1	1,499	1,499	1,499
DROOCHSLOOT, Cornelis (1630-1673) Dutch				
oil	1	3,737	3,737	3,737
DROOCHSLOOT, Joost Cornelisz (1586-1666) Dutch				
oil	12	9,515-60,000	25,660	24,050
DROSSIS, Leonidas (1834-1882) Greek				
3D	1	55,680	55,680	55,680
DROUAIS, François Hubert (1727-1775) French				
wc/d	1	1,636	1,636	1,636
DROUET-CORDIER, Suzanne (1885-1973) French				
oil	1	12,041	12,041	12,041
DROUNGAS, Achilleas (1940-) Greek				
wc/d	2	7,480-8,448	7,964	7,480
DROUOT, E (1859-1945) French				
3D	2	1,522-3,268	2,395	1,522
DROUOT, Edouard (1859-1945) French				
3D	11	2,142-6,081	3,901	3,380
DROWN, William Staples (1856-1915) American				
oil	2	8,000-31,000	19,500	8,000
wc/d	1	3,400	3,400	3,400
DROZHDIN, Petr Semenovich (c.1745-1805) Russian				
oil	1	29,410	29,410	29,410
DRUMAUX, Angelina (1881-1959) Luxembourger				
oil	3	2,267-9,351	4,744	2,616
DRUMMOND, Arthur (1871-1951) British				
oil	5	5,235-28,000	13,326	9,000
DRUMMOND, Malcolm (1880-1945) British				
oil	2	1,575-15,660	8,617	1,575
DRUMMOND, Norah (20th C) British				
oil	1	3,979	3,979	3,979
DRUPSTEEN, Wilhelmina Cornelia (1880-1966) Dutch				
oil	1	3,409	3,409	3,409
DRURY, Alfred (1856-1944) British				
3D	1	2,670	2,670	2,670
DRYANDER, Johann-Friedrich (1756-1812) German				
oil	1	7,415	7,415	7,415
DRYER, Moira (1957-1992) American				
wc/d	2	2,000-2,400	2,200	2,000
DRYSDALE, Alexander John (1870-1934) American				
oil	9	1,300-5,000	3,111	3,200
wc/d	1	3,250	3,250	3,250
DU YINGQIANG (1939-) Chinese				
wc/d	1	5,255	5,255	5,255
DUBASTY, Adolphe Henri (1814-1884) French				
oil	1	2,517	2,517	2,517
DUBAUT, Pierre (1886-1968) French				
wc/d	17	484-2,661	1,134	786
DUBBELS, Hendrik (1620-1676) Dutch				
oil	2	30,260-69,200	49,730	30,260
DUBE, Mathie (1861-?) American				
oil	1	3,800	3,800	3,800
DUBIEL, Evelyn S (c.1922-) American				
oil	1	1,300	1,300	1,300
wc/d	4	450-600	518	500
DUBOIS, Adolphe (1826-1862) German/Swiss				
3D	1	1,446	1,446	1,446
DUBOIS, Ambroise (1543-1614) French				
wc/d	1	30,000	30,000	30,000
DUBOIS, Charles-Edouard (1847-1885) French				
oil	1	725	725	725
wc/d	1	655	655	655
DUBOIS, Ernest (1863-1931) French				
3D	1	5,372	5,372	5,372
DUBOIS, François (1790-1871) French				
oil	2	4,350-110,000	57,175	4,350

Name	No.	Price Range	Average	Median
DUBOIS, Guillam (1620-1680) Dutch				
oil	2	9,031-35,150	22,090	9,031
DUBOIS, Henri Pierre Hippolyte (1837-1909) French				
oil	1	27,986	27,986	27,986
DUBOIS, Jean (1789-1849) Swiss				
wc/d	1	1,526	1,526	1,526
DUBOIS, Louis (1830-1880) Belgian				
oil	6	668-5,298	2,332	1,636
DUBOIS, Paul (1858-1938) Belgian				
3D	1	3,387	3,387	3,387
DUBOIS, Paul (1829-1905) French				
3D	12	1,790-13,179	5,293	4,000
DUBOIS, Paul-Elie (1886-1949) French				
oil	15	779-76,439	7,712	3,116
wc/d	5	599-5,732	3,064	2,997
DUBOIS, Raphael (1888-?) Belgian				
oil	5	935-2,195	1,475	1,094
DUBOIS, Simon (1632-1708) Dutch				
oil	1	1,932	1,932	1,932
DUBOIS-PILLET, Albert (1845-1890) French				
oil	1	9,250	9,250	9,250
DUBORD, Jean Pierre (1949-) French				
oil	18	595-3,500	1,160	1,000
DUBOSSARSKY, Vladimir and VINOGRADOV, Alexandre (20th C) Russian				
oil	1	8,562	8,562	8,562
DUBOURG, Louis Alexandre (c.1825-1891) French				
oil	3	2,351-4,757	3,270	2,704
DUBOURG, Louis Fabricius (1693-1775) Dutch				
wc/d	1	1,987	1,987	1,987
DUBOVSKOY, Nicolay Nikanorovich (1859-1918) Russian				
oil	3	44,720-65,360	52,502	47,426
DUBOY, Paul (1830-c.1887) French				
3D	1	3,831	3,831	3,831
DUBREUIL, Marie (1852-?) French				
oil	1	2,958	2,958	2,958
DUBREUIL, Victor (19th C) French				
oil	1	14,000	14,000	14,000
DUBSKY, Mario (1939-1985) British				
oil	8	673-3,540	1,389	885
wc/d	3	797-3,540	2,507	3,186
DUBUC, Roland (1924-1998) Swiss				
oil	10	1,178-3,974	2,161	1,821
wc/d	5	718-1,014	844	834
DUBUCAND, A (1828-1894) French				
3D	1	3,063	3,063	3,063
DUBUCAND, Alfred (1828-1894) French				
3D	9	1,740-28,000	7,378	3,440
DUBUFE, Edouard Louis (1820-1883) French				
oil	4	1,989-86,949	31,957	5,890
DUBUFE, Edouard Marie Guillaume (1853-1909) French				
oil	3	19,622-25,713	21,888	20,331
wc/d	1	2,268	2,268	2,268
DUBUFFET, Jean (1901-1985) French				
oil	37	19,779-4,600,000	330,134	85,000
wc/d	45	5,000-420,000	38,046	22,000
3D	3	101,750-280,000	197,250	210,000
DUBUIS, Fernand (1908-1991) Swiss				
oil	3	1,973-3,916	3,227	3,794
DUBUISSON, Alexandre (1805-1870) French				
oil	3	2,309-18,814	8,145	3,314
wc/d	1	1,337	1,337	1,337
DUC, Edmond Eugène (1856-1949) French				
oil	1	1,149	1,149	1,149
DUCAIRE, Maryse (20th C) French				
oil	1	1,100	1,100	1,100
DUCHAMP, Marcel (1887-1968) French				
oil	1	11,781	11,781	11,781
wc/d	4	21,240-106,200	48,195	26,400
3D	5	5,351-778,800	193,786	12,740
DUCHATEAU, Hugo (1938-) Belgian				
oil	1	2,637	2,637	2,637

Name	No.	Price Range	Average	Median
DUCHEIN, Paul (20th C) French?				
3D	1	4,435	4,435	4,435
DUCHESS AGNES OF SAXE-ALTENBURG (19th C) German?				
oil	1	6,622	6,622	6,622
DUCHOW, Achim (1948-) German				
oil	1	1,234	1,234	1,234
DUCIS, Louis (1775-1847) French				
oil	1	1,942	1,942	1,942
DUCK, Jacob (1600-1660) Dutch				
oil	3	34,600-170,000	106,419	114,658
DUCKER, Eugène Gustav (1841-1916) German				
oil	2	3,503-3,854	3,678	3,503
DUCKWORTH, Ruth (1919-) British				
3D	1	2,124	2,124	2,124
DUCLAUX, Jean Antoine (1783-1868) French				
oil	3	606-6,336	2,708	1,184
DUCLERE, Teodoro (1816-1867) Italian				
oil	2	5,890-11,712	8,801	5,890
wc/d	1	510	510	510
DUCLUZEAU, Marie Adelaide (1787-1849) French				
oil	1	2,788	2,788	2,788
DUCMELIC, Zdravko (1923-) Argentinian				
oil	1	3,600	3,600	3,600
wc/d	3	1,200-3,500	2,500	2,800
3D	1	10,000	10,000	10,000
DUCOMMUN, Jean Felix (1920-1958) Swiss				
oil	2	1,459-4,996	3,227	1,459
DUCOS DE LA HAILLE, Pierre Henri (1889-1972) French				
wc/d	1	4,114	4,114	4,114
DUCROS, Abraham Louis Rodolphe (1748-1810) Swiss				
wc/d	4	5,342-9,515	6,899	6,370
DUCROS, Abraham Louis Rodolphe and VOLPATO, Giovanni (18th C) Swiss/Italian				
wc/d	3	5,208-6,067	5,643	5,655
DUDIN, Samuel Martinovich (1863-1929) Russian				
oil	1	12,884	12,884	12,884
DUDLEY, Charles (19/20th C) British				
oil	2	1,300-1,305	1,302	1,300
DUDLEY, Frank V (1868-1957) American				
oil	4	5,000-10,000	8,250	8,500
DUDLEY, Robert (fl.1880-1893) British				
oil	1	1,607	1,607	1,607
DUDOVICH, Marcello (1878-1962) Italian				
oil	2	1,171-4,671	2,921	1,171
wc/d	8	589-1,701	826	607
DUDREVILLE, Leonardo (1885-1974) Italian				
oil	2	2,577-6,218	4,397	2,577
wc/d	1	1,178	1,178	1,178
DUDZINSKI, A (20th C) ?				
oil	1	9,436	9,436	9,436
DUESBURY, Horace (1851-1904) American				
oil	2	400-1,600	1,000	400
DUESSEL, Henry A (19th C) American/German				
oil	2	700-2,000	1,350	700
DUEZ, Ernest Ange (1846-1896) French				
wc/d	2	2,803-3,503	3,153	2,803
DUFAU, Evelyne (20th C) French				
oil	1	22,500	22,500	22,500
DUFAU, Helene (1869-1937) French				
oil	3	650-10,000	6,883	10,000
DUFAUX, Frederic II (1852-1943) Swiss				
oil	7	382-2,997	1,800	1,249
DUFES, Jeanne (19th C) French?				
oil	1	2,486	2,486	2,486
DUFEU, Edouard (1840-1900) French				
oil	3	1,998-3,000	2,556	2,671
DUFF, John Robert Keitley (1862-1938) British				
oil	1	7,392	7,392	7,392
DUFF, Sir Charles G (fl.1898-1903) British				
wc/d	2	1,232-1,936	1,584	1,232
DUFFIELD, William (1816-1863) British				
oil	4	1,701-5,520	3,289	2,457

Name	No.	Price Range	Average	Median
DUFFY, Rita (1959-) British				
oil	1	1,770	1,770	1,770
wc/d	2	1,298-3,287	2,292	1,298
DUFNER, Edward (1872-1957) American				
oil	4	1,300-60,000	27,950	23,000
DUFOUR, Bernard (1922-) French				
oil	3	1,294-2,145	1,658	1,535
DUFOUR, Camille (1841-1931) French				
oil	2	718-13,000	6,859	718
DUFRENE, François (1930-1992) French				
wc/d	14	3,872-92,040	15,209	6,984
DUFRESNE, Charles (1876-1938) French				
oil	4	1,267-8,000	3,663	2,124
wc/d	4	1,212-4,079	2,229	1,794
DUFRESNE, Francois (1930-1982) French				
wc/d	1	1,901	1,901	1,901
DUFWA, Torgny (1876-?) Swedish				
oil	1	1,717	1,717	1,717
DUFY, Jean (1888-1964) French				
oil	35	1,500-120,000	37,910	38,000
wc/d	63	510-46,250	11,049	7,265
DUFY, Raoul (1877-1953) French				
oil	43	1,405-1,398,400	224,047	166,500
wc/d	229	476-460,000	23,430	1,656
3D	1	20,000	20,000	20,000
DUGDALE, Thomas Cantrell (1880-1952) British				
oil	1	14,514	14,514	14,514
DUGGINS, James Edward (1881-1968) British				
oil	1	2,390	2,390	2,390
DUGHET, Gaspard (1615-1675) French				
oil	1	6,230	6,230	6,230
DUGMORE, Arthur Radclyffe (1870-1955) American				
oil	1	4,000	4,000	4,000
DUGUET, Madeleine (1909-1974) Belgian				
oil	1	1,991	1,991	1,991
DUHAMEL, Gaston Pierre (20th C) French				
oil	1	4,248	4,248	4,248
DUIJN, Alexandrine van (20th C) ?				
oil	1	9,351	9,351	9,351
DUJARDIN, John (19th C) British				
oil	1	1,740	1,740	1,740
DUJARDIN, Karel (1622-1678) Dutch				
oil	1	5,438	5,438	5,438
DUJARDIN, Rene Marie (1913-) Belgian				
oil	1	2,521	2,521	2,521
DUJARDIN, Simone (20th C) Belgian				
wc/d	3	606-2,667	1,616	1,576
DUKE, Peder (1938-2003) Swedish				
oil	4	2,163-2,926	2,472	2,290
DULAC, Edmund (1882-1953) British/French				
wc/d	6	905-28,000	7,878	1,780
DULIEU, René (20th C) French				
oil	2	1,335-1,727	1,531	1,335
DULMEN KRUMPELMAN, Erasmus Bernhard van (1897-1987) Dutch				
oil	2	3,781-7,120	5,450	3,781
wc/d	3	894-2,877	2,008	2,253
DUMAIGE, Étienne-Henri (1830-1888) French				
3D	3	1,550-5,364	2,889	1,753
DUMAS, Marlene (1953-) Dutch				
oil	6	73,920-1,400,000	661,861	150,450
wc/d	21	2,003-101,750	29,607	19,360
DUMBLETON, Bertram (1896-1966) ?				
oil	1	1,015	1,015	1,015
DUMINI, L (19th C) ?				
oil	1	2,076	2,076	2,076
DUMITRESCO, Natalie (1915-1997) French				
oil	49	579-8,500	2,053	1,671
wc/d	8	579-1,029	786	771
DUMMER, H Boylston (1878-1945) American				
oil	1	1,000	1,000	1,000
DUMOND, Frank Vincent (1865-1951) American				
oil	3	3,500-13,000	7,518	6,054

Name	No.	Price Range	Average	Median
DUMONT, Alfred (1828-1894) Swiss				
oil	3	611-8,486	4,711	5,037
DUMONT, Cesar Alvarez (19th C) Spanish				
oil	1	6,600	6,600	6,600
DUMONT, François (1850-?) Belgian				
oil	1	1,574	1,574	1,574
DUMONT, Frans (19/20th C) Belgian				
oil	1	3,099	3,099	3,099
DUMONT, Jean (1701-1781) French				
oil	1	42,752	42,752	42,752
wc/d	1	3,741	3,741	3,741
DUMONT, Maurice (19th C) French				
wc/d	1	3,737	3,737	3,737
DUMONT, Pierre (1884-1936) French				
oil	6	1,818-7,200	3,100	1,854
DUMOUCHEL, L (?) French				
3D	1	2,589	2,589	2,589
DUMOULIN, Romeo (1883-1944) Belgian				
oil	4	467-5,092	1,760	606
wc/d	4	963-4,114	2,301	1,627
DUN, Nicholas François (1764-1832) French				
wc/d	1	1,152	1,152	1,152
DUNAND, Jean (1877-1942) Swiss				
oil	3	8,199-31,678	23,851	31,678
3D	1	32,698	32,698	32,698
DUNAND, Jean and LAMBERT-RUCKI, Jean (20th C) Swiss/French				
oil	1	164,934	164,934	164,934
DUNAND, Jean and Pierre (20th C) Swiss/French				
oil	1	10,235	10,235	10,235
DUNAND, Jean and SCHMIED, Francois Louis (20th C) Swiss				
oil	1	105,413	105,413	105,413
DUNANT, Jacques (1825-1870) Swiss				
oil	1	2,748	2,748	2,748
DUNANT-VALLIER, Jean Marc (1818-1888) Swiss				
wc/d	2	833-1,680	1,256	833
DUNBAR, George (1927-) American				
oil	2	2,200-3,000	2,600	2,200
wc/d	2	900-1,400	1,150	900
DUNBAR, Harold (1882-1953) American				
oil	5	900-2,500	1,480	1,500
DUNBAR, Patrick (?) ?				
oil	1	1,200	1,200	1,200
DUNCAN, Darwin (1905-) American				
oil	2	600-1,500	1,050	600
DUNCAN, Edward (1803-1882) British				
wc/d	7	626-8,996	3,303	1,740
DUNCAN, James D (1806-1881) Canadian				
wc/d	2	7,989-9,749	8,869	7,989
DUNCAN, John (1866-1945) British				
oil	1	25,060	25,060	25,060
DUNCAN, John McKirdy (1866-1945) British				
oil	1	7,120	7,120	7,120
DUNCAN, Joseph (1920-) British				
oil	1	1,372	1,372	1,372
DUNCAN, Mary (1885-1964) British				
oil	3	1,169-2,189	1,509	1,169
DUNCAN, Robert (1952-) American				
oil	1	70,000	70,000	70,000
DUNCAN, Stephen (1952-) British				
3D	1	4,500	4,500	4,500
DUNCAN, Thomas (1807-1845) British				
oil	1	1,197	1,197	1,197
DUNCAN, Walter (fl.1880-c.1910) British				
oil	1	540	540	540
wc/d	1	1,218	1,218	1,218
DUNCANSON, Robert S (1821-1872) American				
oil	1	250,000	250,000	250,000
DUNDAS, Agnes (19th C) British				
wc/d	1	1,138	1,138	1,138
DUNHAM, Carroll (1949-) American				
oil	1	2,293	2,293	2,293
wc/d	3	3,822-85,000	31,306	5,096

Name	No.	Price Range	Average	Median
DUNHAM, David R (19th C) American				
oil	4	1,600-3,800	2,575	1,800
DUNHAM, George E (19th C) American				
wc/d	1	25,000	25,000	25,000
DUNINGTON, Albert (1860-c.1928) British				
oil	2	740-824	782	740
wc/d	1	450	450	450
DUNKELBERGER, Ralph D (1894-1965) American				
wc/d	1	1,100	1,100	1,100
D'UNKER, Carl (1829-1866) Swedish				
oil	1	4,945	4,945	4,945
DUNKER, Philip-Heinrich (1780-1836) German				
wc/d	1	2,163	2,163	2,163
DUNLAP, Helena (1876-1955) American				
oil	2	1,000-13,000	7,000	1,000
DUNLOP, Ronald Ossory (1894-1973) British				
oil	39	465-10,447	2,910	2,088
wc/d	2	1,451-2,262	1,856	1,451
DUNN, Harvey (1884-1952) American				
oil	3	4,123-80,000	38,874	32,500
DUNNE, George (20th C) Irish				
oil	8	606-2,311	1,202	849
DUNNING, John R (fl.1892-1914) British				
oil	1	1,056	1,056	1,056
DUNNING, Robert Spear (1829-1905) American				
oil	1	25,000	25,000	25,000
DUNOUY, Alexandre Hyacinthe (1757-1841) French				
oil	4	8,500-35,677	25,649	27,500
DUNOYER DE SEGONZAC, Andre (1884-1974) French				
oil	9	1,753-7,378	4,847	5,500
wc/d	32	400-40,000	5,299	2,153
DUNSMORE, John Ward (1856-1945) British				
oil	2	500-1,500	1,000	500
DUNSMORE, Lord Alfred (?) American				
wc/d	1	7,000	7,000	7,000
DUNSTAN, Bernard (1920-) British				
oil	26	1,131-5,472	2,674	2,400
wc/d	2	2,223-2,223	2,223	2,223
DUNTON, W Herbert (1878-1936) American				
oil	10	6,500-260,000	61,400	20,000
DUNTZE, Johannes Bertholomaus (1823-1895) German				
oil	7	3,480-15,123	9,946	9,991
DUNZENDORFER, Albrecht (1907-1980) Austrian				
oil	9	701-3,086	2,132	2,057
wc/d	2	584-642	613	584
DUONG, Anh (1960-) ?				
wc/d	1	2,152	2,152	2,152
DUPAGNE, Arthur (1895-1961) Belgian				
3D	4	4,451-18,849	8,305	4,671
DUPAS, Jean (1882-1964) French				
oil	4	2,704-9,000	6,376	6,600
wc/d	4	2,047-17,568	7,528	5,000
DUPERREUX, Alexandre Louis Robert Millin (1764-1843) French				
oil	1	2,452	2,452	2,452
DUPLESSI-BERTAUX, Jean (1747-1819) French				
oil	2	2,917-4,350	3,633	2,917
wc/d	2	1,665-1,901	1,783	1,665
DUPLESSIS, Joseph Siffrede (1725-1802) French				
oil	1	13,976	13,976	13,976
DUPLESSIS, Marc Antoine Michel Hamon (18th C) French				
oil	1	4,986	4,986	4,986
DUPLESSIS, Michel (18th C) French				
oil	3	1,605-16,435	11,054	15,123
DUPON, Josue (1864-1935) Belgian				
3D	9	2,221-25,000	9,662	7,014
DUPONT, Ernest (1825-?) French				
oil	1	3,022	3,022	3,022
DUPONT, Frederick George (19th C) French?				
oil	1	2,805	2,805	2,805
DUPONT, Gainsborough (1755-1797) British				
oil	2	42,143-204,694	123,418	42,143
wc/d	1	708	708	708

Name	No.	Price Range	Average	Median
DUPONT, Jacques (1909-1978) French				
oil	1	1,767	1,767	1,767
DUPONT, Pieter (1870-1911) Dutch				
wc/d	1	2,142	2,142	2,142
DUPRAT, Albert Ferdinand (1882-?) Italian				
oil	8	649-4,545	2,405	1,900
wc/d	1	4,663	4,663	4,663
DUPRAY, Henry-Louis (1841-1909) French				
oil	6	700-2,690	1,853	1,800
wc/d	1	947	947	947
DUPRE, Daniel (1752-1817) Dutch				
wc/d	2	1,527-2,335	1,931	1,527
DUPRE, Georges (1807-1853) French				
oil	1	7,500	7,500	7,500
DUPRE, Henri (20th C) French				
oil	1	1,600	1,600	1,600
DUPRE, J (19th C) French				
oil	1	2,945	2,945	2,945
DUPRE, Jules (1811-1889) French				
oil	17	2,997-15,419	6,300	5,000
wc/d	1	653	653	653
DUPRE, Julien (1851-1910) French				
oil	7	6,250-155,000	66,601	60,000
wc/d	3	2,922-15,000	7,039	3,196
DUPRE, Louis (1789-1837) French				
wc/d	1	6,602	6,602	6,602
DUPRE, Victor (1816-1879) French				
oil	11	700-7,500	4,009	3,794
DUPUIS, Georges (1875-?) French				
wc/d	1	1,025	1,025	1,025
DUPUIS, Pierre (1610-1682) French				
oil	1	86,811	86,811	86,811
DUPUIS, Pierre (1833-?) French				
oil	1	1,019	1,019	1,019
DUPUIS, Toon (1877-1937) Belgian				
3D	1	5,878	5,878	5,878
DUPUY, L (19th C) French				
oil	3	602-2,290	1,188	673
DUPUY, Louis (1854-1941) French				
oil	4	1,451-5,918	3,702	1,757
DUPUY, Paul Michel (1869-1949) French				
oil	9	1,627-15,000	5,646	4,712
DUQUE, Adonay (20th C) ?				
oil	1	1,070	1,070	1,070
DUQUESNOY, François (1594-1643) Flemish				
3D	1	15,284	15,284	15,284
DURA GISBERT, Guillermo (1943-) Spanish				
oil	1	1,549	1,549	1,549
DURAMEAU, Louis Jean (1733-1796) French				
wc/d	1	3,700	3,700	3,700
DURAN, Santa (1909-) American				
oil	1	3,500	3,500	3,500
DURANCAMPS, Rafael (1891-1979) Spanish				
oil	6	8,400-23,486	13,425	12,041
DURAND, A (20th C) British				
oil	1	2,121	2,121	2,121
DURAND, Asher Brown (1796-1886) American				
oil	2	42,000-95,000	68,500	42,000
DURAND, Louis (1817-1890) Swiss				
oil	1	1,984	1,984	1,984
DURAND, Lucien (20th C) French				
oil	2	1,300-2,100	1,700	1,300
DURAND, Simon (1838-1896) Swiss				
oil	1	3,805	3,805	3,805
DURAND-BRAGER, Jean Baptiste Henri (1814-1879) French				
oil	4	1,741-8,678	5,125	2,520
DURAND-HENRIOT, Jacques (1922-1997) French				
wc/d	1	1,106	1,106	1,106
DURAND-ROSE, Auguste (1887-1964) French				
oil	2	684-1,427	1,055	684
DURANTE, Domenico Maria (1879-1944) Italian				
oil	1	4,653	4,653	4,653

Name	No.	Price Range	Average	Median
DURANTI, Fortunato (1787-1863) Italian				
wc/d	4	1,308-19,418	13,596	16,829
DURANTON, Jeanne (19/20th C) French				
oil	1	1,300	1,300	1,300
DURCK, Friedrich (1809-1884) German				
oil	2	2,510-2,531	2,520	2,510
DUREAU, George (1930-) American				
wc/d	1	1,200	1,200	1,200
DUREL, Gaston (1879-1954) French				
oil	2	2,552-8,872	5,712	2,552
DURENNE, Eugène Antoine (1860-1944) French				
oil	5	945-4,451	2,930	2,571
DURER, Albrecht (1471-1528) German				
oil	1	4,472	4,472	4,472
DURET, Francisque-Joseph (1804-1864) French				
3D	3	2,000-3,113	2,582	2,634
DURET-DUJARRIC, Isabelle (1949-) French				
oil	1	38,060	38,060	38,060
wc/d	1	7,080	7,080	7,080
DUREUIL, Michel (1929-) French				
oil	2	650-2,750	1,700	650
DURHAM, Joseph (1814-1877) British				
3D	1	11,340	11,340	11,340
DURIEUX, Emile (?) French				
oil	1	1,670	1,670	1,670
DURIEUX, Rene Auguste (19th C) French				
oil	7	484-2,420	1,270	1,210
DURINI, Giulio (1966-) Italian				
oil	1	23,425	23,425	23,425
DUROSE, Edward (20th C) American				
oil	1	10,500	10,500	10,500
DUROT, Louis (20th C) French				
3D	1	2,170	2,170	2,170
DURR, Johann Sebastian (18/19th C) German				
wc/d	2	5,418-5,418	5,418	5,418
DURR, Louis (1896-1973) Swiss				
oil	11	534-4,197	1,555	1,415
DURRANT, Roy Turner (1925-1998) British				
oil	2	428-2,262	1,345	428
wc/d	19	463-4,488	1,831	1,539
DURRENMATT, Friedrich (1921-1990) Swiss				
wc/d	4	999-1,526	1,231	1,068
DURRIE, George Henry (1820-1863) American				
oil	1	65,000	65,000	65,000
DURSTON, Arthur (1897-1938) American				
oil	1	19,000	19,000	19,000
DURY-VASSELON, Hortense (19th C) French				
oil	2	1,679-4,241	2,960	1,679
DUSART, Cornelis (1660-1704) Dutch				
oil	2	4,816-12,460	8,638	4,816
DUSAULCHOY, Charles (1781-1852) French				
oil	1	7,200	7,200	7,200
DUSCHEK, Geza (19th C) German?				
wc/d	1	1,216	1,216	1,216
DUSI, Carlo (1917-1995) Italian				
oil	1	1,219	1,219	1,219
wc/d	1	2,438	2,438	2,438
DUSSEUIL, Leonie (1843-1912) French				
oil	1	3,884	3,884	3,884
DUTHOIT, Paul (1858-?) French				
oil	1	2,800	2,800	2,800
DUTRIEU, Michel (1910-) Belgian				
oil	1	1,318	1,318	1,318
DUTTLER, Herbert (1948-) German				
oil	5	561-2,101	1,069	701
DUTTON, Thomas G (c.1819-1891) British				
oil	1	9,000	9,000	9,000
wc/d	1	1,073	1,073	1,073
DUTZSCHOLD, Henri (1841-1891) French				
oil	1	1,139	1,139	1,139
DUVAL, E (19/20th C) ?				
oil	1	3,405	3,405	3,405

Name	No.	Price Range	Average	Median
DUVAL, Eustace François (fl.1784-1836) French				
oil	1	5,702	5,702	5,702
DUVAL, Francois (1869-1937) Swiss?				
oil	1	1,468	1,468	1,468
DUVAL, Victor (19th C) French				
oil	1	3,344	3,344	3,344
DUVAL-GOZLAN (1853-1941) French				
oil	2	1,311-3,099	2,205	1,311
DUVAL-GOZLAN, Léon (1853-1941) French				
oil	1	3,214	3,214	3,214
DUVAL-LECAMUS, J (19th C) French				
oil	1	3,116	3,116	3,116
DUVAL-LECAMUS, Jules Alexandre (1814-1878) French				
oil	1	7,434	7,434	7,434
DUVAL-LECAMUS, Pierre (1790-1854) French				
oil	1	27,840	27,840	27,840
DUVALL, John (1816-1892) British				
oil	6	554-4,248	1,978	1,840
DUVANNES, Albert (1881-1962) American				
oil	1	3,500	3,500	3,500
DUVAUX, Jules Antoine (1818-1884) French				
oil	1	2,750	2,750	2,750
DUVENECK, Frank (1848-1919) American				
oil	3	1,300-6,500	4,016	4,250
wc/d	1	4,000	4,000	4,000
DUVENT, Charles Jules (1867-1940) French				
oil	1	1,325	1,325	1,325
DUVERGER, Alec (1888-?) Belgian				
3D	1	2,300	2,300	2,300
DUVERGER, Theophile Emmanuel (1821-1886) French				
oil	7	4,479-23,920	12,177	6,880
DUVIEUX, Henri (1855-?) French				
oil	9	1,100-7,349	4,372	4,210
wc/d	1	2,342	2,342	2,342
DUVILLIER, René (1919-2002) French				
oil	14	537-2,843	1,424	1,174
DUVOISIN, Henri (1877-1959) Swiss				
oil	1	1,755	1,755	1,755
DUWE, Harald (1926-1984) German				
oil	1	1,052	1,052	1,052
DUYCK, Francois (19/20th C) Belgian?				
oil	1	3,625	3,625	3,625
DUYK, Frans (19/20th C) Belgian				
oil	1	1,483	1,483	1,483
DUYTS, Gustave den (1850-1897) Belgian				
oil	1	23,108	23,108	23,108
wc/d	2	700-1,453	1,076	700
DVORAK, Franz (1862-1927) Austrian				
oil	1	29,580	29,580	29,580
DWYER, Nancy (1954-) American				
3D	1	3,500	3,500	3,500
DYBRIS, Freddie (1922-1993) Danish				
oil	1	1,218	1,218	1,218
DYCK, Abraham van (1635-1672) Dutch				
oil	1	25,691	25,691	25,691
DYCK, Albert van (1902-1951) Belgian				
oil	1	2,225	2,225	2,225
DYCK, Sir Anthony van (1599-1641) Flemish				
oil	7	15,123-1,350,000	458,242	320,000
wc/d	3	3,568-4,757	4,202	4,281
DYCKMANS, Josephus Laurentius (1811-1888) Flemish				
oil	3	1,574-4,033	2,702	2,500
DYDYSCHKO, Konstantin (1876-1932) ?				
oil	2	5,160-27,520	16,340	5,160
wc/d	1	1,467	1,467	1,467
DYE, Charlie (1906-1972) American				
oil	4	7,000-47,500	28,625	20,000
wc/d	1	2,300	2,300	2,300
DYE, Clarkson (1869-1955) American				
oil	2	2,750-11,500	7,125	2,750
DYER, Alfred Henry (fl.1905-1940) British				
oil	2	3,591-10,395	6,993	3,591

Name	No.	Price Range	Average	Median
DYER, Brian (19th C) American				
oil	1	2,800	2,800	2,800
DYER, Charles Gifford (1846-1912) American				
oil	2	11,000-29,580	20,290	11,000
DYER, Jimmy (1956-) American				
oil	1	1,300	1,300	1,300
DYF (1899-1985) French				
oil	2	2,137-3,816	2,976	2,137
DYF, Marcel (1899-1985) French				
oil	58	1,700-40,000	11,455	10,000
wc/d	1	537	537	537
DYKE, S P (19th C) American				
oil	1	3,300	3,300	3,300
DYKEN, Derk van (1945-) Dutch?				
oil	1	1,219	1,219	1,219
DYKSTRA, Johan (1896-1978) Dutch				
oil	4	15,196-24,170	20,654	21,041
wc/d	4	1,942-47,123	14,534	3,814
DYNELEY, Amelia Frederica (1830-?) Canadian				
wc/d	1	6,171	6,171	6,171
DYONNET, Edmond (1859-1954) Canadian				
oil	1	1,518	1,518	1,518
DZAMA, Marcel (1974-) American				
wc/d	7	5,000-30,000	9,643	6,500
DZBANSKI, Sixtus von (1874-1938) Polish				
oil	3	816-1,907	1,194	860
DZIGURSKI, Alex (1911-1995) American				
oil	16	800-2,777	1,731	1,800
DZUBAS, Friedel (1915-1994) American/German				
oil	9	4,750-45,000	20,861	18,000
EADIE, Robert (1877-1954) British				
wc/d	2	946-1,634	1,290	946
EADIE, William (fl.1880-1894) British				
oil	3	1,056-2,848	1,800	1,496
EAGLES, Edmund (fl.1851-1877) British				
oil	1	5,985	5,985	5,985
EAKINS, Susan (1851-1938) American				
oil	1	2,200	2,200	2,200
EAKINS, Thomas (1844-1916) American				
oil	1	15,000	15,000	15,000
EANDI, Fernando (1926-) Italian				
oil	1	1,868	1,868	1,868
EARDLEY, Joan (1921-1963) British				
oil	6	8,496-60,520	18,865	8,900
wc/d	7	3,580-37,840	13,607	10,560
EARL, George (1824-1908) British				
oil	6	1,418-16,000	7,685	4,644
EARL, Maud (1863-1943) British				
oil	3	5,000-122,850	53,956	34,020
wc/d	1	1,800	1,800	1,800
EARL, Ralph (1751-1801) American				
oil	1	4,275	4,275	4,275
EARL, Thomas William (1815-1885) British				
oil	3	1,777-8,570	6,115	8,000
EARLE, Eyvind (1916-2000) American				
oil	1	1,000	1,000	1,000
wc/d	2	1,600-4,250	2,925	1,600
EARLE, Paul Barnard (1872-1955) Canadian				
oil	2	697-1,558	1,127	697
EARLEY, Leo (1925-2001) Irish				
oil	1	2,689	2,689	2,689
EARLY, Miles J (1886-1957) American				
oil	1	1,900	1,900	1,900
EARP, Henry (19th C) British				
wc/d	1	1,550	1,550	1,550
EARP, Henry (snr) (1831-1914) British				
oil	2	672-8,352	4,512	672
wc/d	16	567-2,288	1,101	900
EAST, Sir Alfred (1849-1913) British				
oil	4	531-4,600	2,337	1,564
wc/d	5	482-2,139	1,304	1,663

Name	No.	Price Range	Average	Median
EASTLAKE, Charles Herbert (fl.1889-1927) British				
oil	1	2,208	2,208	2,208
EASTLAKE, Mary Alexandra (1864-1951) Canadian				
wc/d	2	907-3,458	2,182	907
EASTMAN, Harrison (1823-1886) American				
wc/d	1	2,600	2,600	2,600
EASTMAN, Mary (20th C) British				
oil	1	4,464	4,464	4,464
EATON, Charles Harry (1850-1901) American				
oil	6	1,200-7,000	4,166	3,800
wc/d	1	408	408	408
EATON, Charles Warren (1857-1937) American				
oil	20	1,000-80,000	10,746	4,800
wc/d	2	5,500-9,500	7,500	5,500
EBBE, Axel (1868-1941) Swedish				
3D	1	1,692	1,692	1,692
EBBESEN, Johannes P (1897-1950) Danish				
oil	3	575-1,267	839	676
wc/d	4	439-1,521	870	676
EBEL, Fritz Carl Werner (1835-1895) German				
oil	1	8,174	8,174	8,174
EBERHARD, Heinrich (1884-1973) German				
oil	2	3,063-4,477	3,770	3,063
EBERHARD, Konrad (1768-1859) German				
wc/d	1	3,063	3,063	3,063
EBERL, François (1887-1962) French				
oil	13	1,405-6,442	2,639	2,631
EBERLE, Abastenia St Leger (1878-1942) American				
3D	1	6,000	6,000	6,000
EBERLE, Adolf (1843-1914) German				
oil	3	9,158-50,000	23,615	11,689
EBERLE, Richard (1918-2001) German				
oil	2	849-2,303	1,576	849
EBERLE, Robert (1815-1860) Swiss				
oil	1	4,419	4,419	4,419
EBERSBACH, Hartwig (1940-) German				
oil	2	1,885-2,870	2,377	1,885
EBERT, Albert (1906-1976) German				
oil	13	622-5,023	2,590	2,870
EBERT, Anton (1845-1896) German				
oil	5	788-2,534	1,591	1,416
EBERT, Carl (1821-1885) German				
oil	3	624-2,926	1,738	1,665
EBERT, Charles H (1873-1959) American				
oil	2	1,100-20,000	10,550	1,100
EBERZ, Josef (1880-1942) German				
oil	4	900-31,219	13,331	8,247
EBICHE, Eugene (?) French?				
oil	2	4,115-7,310	5,712	4,115
EBIHARA, Kinosuke (1904-1970) Japanese				
oil	2	13,155-13,155	13,155	13,155
EBNER, Ludwig (19th C) German				
oil	1	1,070	1,070	1,070
EBNETH, Lajos von (1902-1982) Hungarian				
oil	1	14,055	14,055	14,055
EBNOTHER, Josef (1937-) Swiss				
oil	2	1,411-1,568	1,489	1,411
EBSTER, Manfred (1941-) Austrian				
oil	2	723-2,805	1,764	723
EBY, Kerr (1889-1946) American				
wc/d	1	1,400	1,400	1,400
ECHAURREN, Pablo (1951-) Italian				
oil	3	477-2,569	1,413	1,193
wc/d	2	1,752-4,204	2,978	1,752
ECHAURRI, Miguel Angel (1927-) Spanish				
oil	1	7,603	7,603	7,603
ECHEVARRIA, Giosvany (1968-) Cuban				
oil	1	8,000	8,000	8,000
ECHEVERRIA, Federico de (1911-2004) Spanish?				
oil	2	2,167-5,088	3,627	2,167
ECHTER, Michael (1812-1879) German				
oil	2	4,083-4,083	4,083	4,083

Name	No.	Price Range	Average	Median
ECHTLER, Adolf (1843-1914) German				
oil	2	8,918-9,730	9,324	8,918
ECK, Francis (20th C) French				
oil	1	1,767	1,767	1,767
ECKARDT, Christian (1832-1914) Danish				
oil	8	487-5,500	2,284	1,352
ECKART, Charles (1935-) American				
oil	1	1,500	1,500	1,500
ECKART, Christian (1959-) Canadian				
oil	1	3,717	3,717	3,717
ECKELL, Ana (1947-) Argentinian				
oil	1	2,800	2,800	2,800
ECKENBRECHER, Themistocles von (1842-1921) German				
oil	9	1,453-14,720	5,299	4,712
wc/d	7	643-2,244	1,130	835
ECKENFELDER, Friedrich (1861-1938) German				
oil	8	1,883-4,800	3,154	2,866
ECKERLER, Karl (19th C) German				
oil	1	1,694	1,694	1,694
ECKERMANN, Karl (19th C) ?				
oil	1	5,351	5,351	5,351
ECKERSBERG, C W (1783-1853) Danish				
oil	3	11,907-238,139	107,062	71,140
wc/d	1	1,920	1,920	1,920
ECKERSBERG, Hansine (1826-1860) Danish				
oil	1	1,774	1,774	1,774
ECKERSBERG, Johan Fredrik (1822-1870) Norwegian				
oil	2	13,040-16,530	14,785	13,040
ECKERSLEY, Tom and LOMBERS, Eric (20th C) British				
wc/d	1	3,132	3,132	3,132
ECKL, Vilma (1892-1982) Austrian				
wc/d	1	2,277	2,277	2,277
ECONOMIDI, Penelope (1885-1967) Greek				
oil	1	4,400	4,400	4,400
ECONOMOS, Michael (1937-) Greek				
oil	1	83,520	83,520	83,520
ECONOMOU, Ioannis (1860-1931) Greek				
oil	1	6,688	6,688	6,688
ECONOMOU, Michalis (1888-1933) Greek				
oil	2	84,480-160,650	122,565	84,480
EDDLER, Adolf (19th C) Austrian				
oil	1	17,000	17,000	17,000
EDE, Basil (1931-) British				
wc/d	2	4,928-5,000	4,964	4,928
EDE, Frederick Charles Vipond (1865-1943) American				
oil	3	3,960-7,000	5,218	4,696
EDEFALK, Cecilia (1954-) Swedish				
oil	3	2,799-51,537	20,355	6,730
EDELFELT, Albert (1854-1905) Finnish				
oil	6	13,500-97,714	41,465	19,942
wc/d	5	659-63,191	15,206	4,500
EDELMANN, Albert (1886-1963) Swiss				
oil	1	3,137	3,137	3,137
EDELMANN, Charles Auguste (1879-1950) French				
oil	1	1,109	1,109	1,109
wc/d	1	2,667	2,667	2,667
EDELMANN, Yrjo (1941-) Swedish				
oil	6	2,162-43,315	11,634	6,607
wc/d	1	730	730	730
3D	1	2,545	2,545	2,545
EDEN, William (1849-1915) British				
oil	2	576-5,916	3,246	576
EDER, Martin (1968-) German				
oil	3	5,088-150,000	82,529	92,500
wc/d	20	3,000-30,525	12,576	8,784
EDER, Otto (1924-1982) Austrian				
3D	1	7,791	7,791	7,791
EDGAR, Norman (1943-) British				
oil	2	1,038-1,665	1,351	1,038
EDGAR, W (?) British				
oil	1	4,416	4,416	4,416

Name	No.	Price Range	Average	Median
EDLICH, Stephen (1944-) American				
oil	2	9,500-14,000	11,750	9,500
EDMONDSON, Machiko (1965-) British?				
oil	1	15,930	15,930	15,930
EDMONDSON, William (1874-1951) American				
3D	1	42,000	42,000	42,000
EDRIDGE, Henry (1769-1821) British				
oil	1	12,390	12,390	12,390
wc/d	3	1,026-4,698	2,309	1,203
EDSBERG, Knud (1911-2003) Danish				
oil	1	1,098	1,098	1,098
EDSON, Allan (1846-1888) Canadian				
oil	3	853-22,287	8,830	3,350
wc/d	1	853	853	853
EDWARDS, George Henry (fl.1883-1910) British				
wc/d	1	1,288	1,288	1,288
EDWARDS, Lionel (1878-1966) British				
oil	3	6,020-56,960	35,826	44,500
wc/d	20	528-30,780	6,144	2,618
EDWARDS, Malcolm (?) British				
wc/d	1	1,106	1,106	1,106
EDWARDS, Melvin (1937-) American				
3D	1	7,500	7,500	7,500
EDWARDS, Peter (1955-) British				
oil	2	1,157-3,026	2,091	1,157
wc/d	2	1,246-20,470	10,858	1,246
EDY-LEGRAND (1892-1970) French				
wc/d	1	4,459	4,459	4,459
EDY-LEGRAND, Edouard Léon Louis (1892-1970) French				
oil	4	1,806-141,514	74,840	61,250
wc/d	3	1,686-44,714	16,895	4,285
EDZARD, Dietz (1893-1963) German				
oil	20	700-20,027	8,226	7,000
EECKHOUDT, Jean van den (1875-1946) Belgian				
oil	1	38,574	38,574	38,574
EECKHOUT, Gerbrand van den (1621-1674) Dutch				
oil	1	7,007	7,007	7,007
wc/d	2	6,290-10,175	8,232	6,290
EECKHOUT, Jakob Joseph (1793-1861) Flemish				
oil	2	5,394-6,540	5,967	5,394
EECKHOUT, Victor (1821-1879) Flemish				
oil	2	3,894-43,315	23,604	3,894
EEKELEN, Leo Theodor van (1900-1974) Dutch				
oil	1	3,170	3,170	3,170
EEKMAN, Nicolaas (1889-1973) Belgian				
oil	3	1,512-4,586	2,656	1,870
wc/d	3	561-1,656	926	561
EERELMAN, Otto (1839-1926) Dutch				
oil	4	64,581-215,270	120,171	65,625
wc/d	3	4,425-11,361	7,484	6,668
EFIMOVA, Olga Aleksandrova (1934-) Russian				
oil	1	2,259	2,259	2,259
EGAN, Felim (1952-) British?				
oil	4	876-6,663	4,273	4,459
wc/d	4	974-2,141	1,265	974
EGAN, Joseph (1906-1962) Swiss				
wc/d	1	1,055	1,055	1,055
EGEA LOPEZ, Alberto (1901-1958) Venezuelan				
oil	1	1,115	1,115	1,115
wc/d	1	465	465	465
EGEBJERG, Jens Jensen (1848-1922) Danish				
oil	1	1,390	1,390	1,390
EGERLAND, Arnold William (20th C) American				
oil	1	1,000	1,000	1,000
EGERSDORFER, Andreas (1866-?) German				
oil	1	1,060	1,060	1,060
EGGENHOFER, Nick (1897-1985) American				
oil	3	1,100-12,500	7,200	8,000
wc/d	23	500-25,000	4,795	2,750
EGGENSCHWILER, Franz (1930-) Swiss				
oil	1	4,186	4,186	4,186

Name	No.	Price Range	Average	Median
EGGER, Ernst (1938-) ?				
oil	1	1,582	1,582	1,582
EGGER, Jean (1897-1934) Austrian				
wc/d	1	2,102	2,102	2,102
EGGER-LIENZ, Albin (1868-1926) Austrian				
oil	4	8,523-968,219	264,912	28,286
wc/d	1	1,311	1,311	1,311
EGGINTON, Frank (1908-1990) British				
oil	5	2,108-6,597	4,579	4,767
wc/d	70	612-10,912	3,371	2,544
EGGINTON, Robert (?) British?				
oil	1	609	609	609
wc/d	3	673-1,328	1,009	1,027
EGGINTON, Wycliffe (1875-1951) British				
wc/d	21	452-3,306	1,160	974
EGGLESTON, Benjamin (1867-1937) American				
oil	1	4,000	4,000	4,000
EGGLI, Johann Jakob (1812-1880) Swiss				
oil	1	1,936	1,936	1,936
EGLAU, Max (1825-1900) American				
oil	1	4,000	4,000	4,000
EGNER, John (1940-) American				
oil	1	1,700	1,700	1,700
EGNER, Marie (1850-1940) Austrian				
oil	4	4,622-23,562	14,669	7,068
wc/d	9	1,084-24,196	5,012	2,662
EGTER VAN WISSEKERKE, Anna (1872-1969) Dutch				
oil	1	1,199	1,199	1,199
EGUIA, Fermin (1942-) Argentinian				
wc/d	1	1,500	1,500	1,500
EGUSQUIZA, Rogelio (1845-1913) Spanish				
oil	1	84,640	84,640	84,640
EHLINGER, Maurice Ambrose (1896-1981) French				
oil	6	1,036-3,695	2,427	2,182
EHMSEN, Heinrich (1886-1964) German				
wc/d	1	2,544	2,544	2,544
EHNINGER, John W (1827-1889) American				
oil	1	20,000	20,000	20,000
EHREN, Julius von (1864-?) German				
oil	1	9,678	9,678	9,678
EHRENBERG, Wilhelm von (1630-1676) Dutch				
oil	1	10,380	10,380	10,380
EHRENSTRAHL, Anna Maria Klocker von (1666-1729) Swedish				
oil	1	8,242	8,242	8,242
EHRENSTRAHL, David Klocker von (1629-1698) German				
oil	1	24,082	24,082	24,082
EHRENSVARD, Carl August (1745-1800) Swedish				
wc/d	7	549-13,087	3,057	1,374
EHRET, Georg Dyonis (1710-1770) British				
wc/d	4	18,600-74,400	41,850	37,200
EHRHARDT, Curt (1895-1972) Swiss				
oil	4	3,534-10,829	7,083	5,724
EHRIG, William Columbus (1892-1969) American				
oil	2	1,150-1,700	1,425	1,150
EHRKE, Julius (1837-1890) German				
oil	1	1,914	1,914	1,914
EHRLICH, Felix (1866-1931) German				
wc/d	1	1,452	1,452	1,452
EIBACH, J (19th C) ?				
oil	1	6,105	6,105	6,105
EIBL, Ludwig (1842-1918) Austrian				
oil	2	1,219-4,586	2,902	1,219
EIBNER, Friedrich (1825-1877) German				
oil	2	3,214-10,829	7,021	3,214
wc/d	1	969	969	969
EICHENBERG, Fritz (1901-1990) American				
wc/d	1	1,200	1,200	1,200
EICHENS, Friedrich Eduard (1804-1877) German				
wc/d	1	25,442	25,442	25,442
EICHHOLTZ, Jacob (1776-1842) American				
oil	3	2,400-5,000	3,466	3,000

Name	No.	Price Range	Average	Median
EICHHORST, Franz (1885-1948) German				
oil	2	1,094-1,286	1,190	1,094
EICHINGER, Erwin (1892-1950) Austrian				
oil	6	701-3,414	1,515	1,164
EICHINGER, Otto (1922-) Austrian				
oil	2	781-2,457	1,619	781
EICHLER, Johann Conrad (1668-1748) German				
oil	13	2,408-126,429	26,668	12,041
EICHLER, Julian (1712-1748) German				
oil	1	1,844	1,844	1,844
EICHLER, Reinhold Max (1872-1947) German				
oil	5	846-11,757	3,884	2,829
EICHLER, Theodor Karl (1868-1946) German				
3D	2	1,829-2,979	2,404	1,829
EICHSTAEDT, Rudolf (1857-c.1924) German				
oil	1	1,113	1,113	1,113
EICKELBERG, Willem Hendrik (1845-1920) Dutch				
oil	3	623-2,750	1,724	1,800
EICKEN, Elisabeth von (1862-1940) German				
oil	2	3,733-4,411	4,072	3,733
EICKHOFF, Gottfred (1902-?) Danish				
3D	1	14,487	14,487	14,487
EIDENBERGER, Josef (20th C) Austrian				
oil	2	6,049-7,233	6,641	6,049
EIDENSCHER, Yaacov (20th C) American?				
oil	1	6,500	6,500	6,500
EIELSON, Jorge (1924-) Peruvian				
oil	1	3,884	3,884	3,884
EILERSEN, Eiler Rasmussen (1827-1912) Danish				
oil	2	2,265-3,175	2,720	2,265
EILSHEMIUS, Louis M (1864-1941) American				
oil	14	650-4,750	1,846	1,600
wc/d	1	1,200	1,200	1,200
EINARSSON, Gudmundur (1895-1963) Icelandic				
oil	1	1,778	1,778	1,778
EINBECK, Walter (1890-?) German				
oil	1	1,360	1,360	1,360
EINHOFF, Friedrich G (1901-1988) German				
oil	1	3,299	3,299	3,299
EINSLE, Anton (1801-1871) Austrian				
oil	2	1,267-3,534	2,400	1,267
EISEN, Charles-Dominique-Joseph (1720-1778) French				
oil	1	14,517	14,517	14,517
wc/d	2	972-1,427	1,199	972
EISEN, François (1695-1778) Flemish				
oil	1	2,047	2,047	2,047
EISENBERG, Yaacov (1897-1966) Israeli				
oil	8	700-2,500	1,475	1,400
wc/d	1	500	500	500
EISENBERGER, E (19/20th C) German				
3D	1	2,860	2,860	2,860
EISENDIECK, Suzanne (1908-1998) German				
oil	9	759-18,000	4,235	2,600
wc/d	1	6,500	6,500	6,500
EISENHUT, Ferencz (1857-1903) Hungarian				
oil	1	55,000	55,000	55,000
EISENLOHR, Edward G (1872-1961) American				
wc/d	5	1,050-2,750	2,140	2,500
EISENMAN, Nicole (1963-) American				
wc/d	1	1,600	1,600	1,600
EISENSCHER, Yaacov (1896-1980) Israeli				
oil	8	700-8,500	2,625	1,500
wc/d	4	500-3,600	1,400	600
EISENSCHITZ, Willy (1889-1974) French				
oil	2	19,421-25,479	22,450	19,421
wc/d	4	628-3,813	1,676	687
EISLER, Georg (1928-1998) Austrian				
oil	4	1,200-5,786	2,833	1,438
wc/d	2	546-723	634	546
EISNER, Jeppe (1952-) Danish				
oil	7	676-2,750	1,199	845

Name	No.	Price Range	Average	Median
EISNER, Will (1917-2005) American				
wc/d	1	1,700	1,700	1,700
EISUKE, Miyao (19/20th C) Japanese				
3D	1	4,176	4,176	4,176
EITEL, Tim (1971-) German?				
oil	7	16,000-177,000	71,934	48,100
EITNER, Ernst (1867-1955) German				
oil	15	688-19,357	5,910	3,992
wc/d	1	605	605	605
EJSMOND, Franz von (1859-1931) Polish				
oil	1	4,477	4,477	4,477
EKAGINA, Peggy (1919-) North American				
3D	1	3,881	3,881	3,881
EKBLAD, Felix (19th C) American				
oil	1	1,500	1,500	1,500
EKEGARDH, Hans (1891-1962) Swedish				
oil	4	759-1,527	1,238	1,148
EKELS, Jan (elder) (1724-1781) Dutch				
oil	1	61,151	61,151	61,151
EKELS, Jan (younger) (1759-1793) Dutch				
oil	1	12,950	12,950	12,950
EKELUND, Poul (1920-1976) Danish				
oil	10	453-2,704	1,334	890
EKELUND, Ragnar (1892-1960) Finnish				
oil	4	659-1,991	1,022	719
EKLUND, Anders (1734-1802) Swedish				
oil	1	6,232	6,232	6,232
EKLUND, Sten (1942-) Swedish				
oil	1	1,994	1,994	1,994
wc/d	1	382	382	382
EKLUNDH, Claes (1944-) Swedish				
oil	3	1,850-3,436	2,775	3,039
EKMAN, Emil (1880-1951) Swedish				
oil	3	838-4,403	2,418	2,013
EKMAN, Robert Wilhelm (1808-1873) Finnish				
oil	2	6,090-7,329	6,709	6,090
wc/d	1	1,029	1,029	1,029
EKMAN, Stina (1950-) Swedish				
3D	1	2,545	2,545	2,545
EKSTROM, Per (1844-1935) Swedish				
oil	29	603-25,479	6,261	5,220
EKSTROM, Thea (1920-1988) Swedish				
oil	1	705	705	705
wc/d	1	1,388	1,388	1,388
EKVALL, Emma (1838-1925) Swedish				
oil	2	497-10,440	5,468	497
EKVALL, Knut (1843-1912) Swedish				
oil	5	2,387-4,726	3,549	3,739
EL AHARAH, Taoufa (1950-) Moroccan				
oil	3	1,140-1,495	1,300	1,267
EL ANZAOUI, Mohamed (1964-) Moroccan				
oil	1	1,140	1,140	1,140
EL BEKAY, Khalid (1966-) Moroccan				
wc/d	1	2,876	2,876	2,876
EL MOURABITI, Mohamed (1968-) Moroccan				
oil	1	1,901	1,901	1,901
EL-GLAOUI, Hassan (1924-) French				
oil	1	5,170	5,170	5,170
wc/d	6	2,646-28,105	15,098	12,038
EL-HANANI, Jacob (1947-) American				
wc/d	1	1,700	1,700	1,700
ELAND, Leonardus Joseph (1884-1952) Dutch				
oil	3	1,324-2,289	1,692	1,463
ELANDER, Kristina A (1952-) Swedish				
wc/d	2	793-1,652	1,222	793
ELDH, Carl (1873-1955) Swedish				
3D	4	2,335-8,475	4,146	2,617
ELDRED, Lemeul D (1848-1921) American				
oil	5	1,500-14,000	4,540	2,200
ELDRED, Thomas Brownell (1903-1993) American				
wc/d	1	1,300	1,300	1,300

Name	No.	Price Range	Average	Median
ELDRIDGE, Mildred E (1909-1991) British				
wc/d	1	3,560	3,560	3,560
ELESZKIEWICZ, Stanislas (1900-1963) Polish				
oil	5	719-9,589	4,474	5,562
ELEUNER, Carle (?) American?				
oil	1	2,000	2,000	2,000
ELFORD, Victor (1912-) British				
oil	1	1,175	1,175	1,175
ELFVEN, Erik (1921-) Swedish				
oil	1	2,643	2,643	2,643
ELHANANI, Jacob (1947-) Israeli?				
wc/d	3	2,572-2,806	2,650	2,572
ELIAS, Étienne (1936-) Belgian				
oil	3	1,071-3,116	2,369	2,922
ELIASSON, Olafur (1967-) Danish				
oil	4	8,853-42,027	19,075	9,257
3D	1	1,771	1,771	1,771
ELIM, Frank (20th C) French				
oil	1	1,500	1,500	1,500
ELIOT, Maurice (1864-?) French				
oil	1	2,848	2,848	2,848
ELIOTT, Harry (1882-1959) ?				
oil	1	858	858	858
wc/d	1	2,022	2,022	2,022
ELISCU, Frank (1912-1996) American				
3D	1	190,000	190,000	190,000
ELK, Gerard Pieter van (1941-) Dutch				
oil	5	2,392-12,858	8,160	8,429
3D	1	15,653	15,653	15,653
ELKINS, Henry Arthur (1847-1884) American				
oil	4	500-3,250	1,737	1,300
ELLE, Edouard (1854-1911) Belgian				
oil	2	667-1,551	1,109	667
ELLE, Louis (elder) (1612-1689) French				
oil	1	20,469	20,469	20,469
ELLENRIEDER, Maria (1791-1863) Swiss				
oil	3	912-2,892	1,739	1,414
wc/d	2	470-941	705	470
ELLENSHAW, Peter (1913-) American/British				
oil	4	2,000-11,000	5,500	3,500
ELLIGER, Ottmar (17/18th C) Swedish				
oil	1	17,635	17,635	17,635
ELLINGER, David (1913-2003) American				
oil	12	1,100-8,000	3,816	3,200
wc/d	10	1,300-2,400	1,810	1,600
ELLIOT, H (?) ?				
oil	1	5,750	5,750	5,750
ELLIOT, J (1858-1925) American				
oil	1	2,293	2,293	2,293
ELLIOTT, Emily Louise Orr (1867-1952) Canadian				
oil	2	1,060-1,148	1,104	1,060
ELLIOTT, Josh (1973-) American				
oil	1	15,000	15,000	15,000
ELLIS, Edwin (1841-1895) British				
oil	3	736-1,701	1,145	1,000
wc/d	2	478-712	595	478
ELLIS, Fremont F (1897-1985) American				
oil	14	4,400-28,000	14,510	13,000
wc/d	1	4,250	4,250	4,250
ELLIS, Gordon (1920-1978) British				
oil	1	648	648	648
wc/d	2	470-470	470	470
ELLIS, Paul H (fl.1882-1908) British				
oil	1	1,638	1,638	1,638
ELLIS, Ray G (1921-) American				
oil	3	700-5,750	2,416	800
ELLIS, Tristram (1844-1922) British				
wc/d	11	787-11,160	3,936	2,683
ELLRICK, A J M (20th C) American				
oil	1	3,000	3,000	3,000
ELLSWORTH, Clarence (1885-1961) American				
oil	5	1,000-9,500	5,350	5,000

Name	No.	Price Range	Average	Median
ELLYS, John (1700-1757) British				
oil	1	3,828	3,828	3,828
ELMER, Stephen (1717-1796) British				
oil	3	7,500-30,240	17,305	14,175
ELMHIRST, Charles Cutts (fl.1897-1912) British				
oil	1	5,152	5,152	5,152
ELMORE, Alfred (1815-1881) British				
oil	1	1,165	1,165	1,165
ELMQVIST, Hugo (1862-1930) Swedish				
3D	1	1,659	1,659	1,659
ELROD, Jeff (1966-) American				
oil	1	20,000	20,000	20,000
ELSAM, Richard (fl.1797-1807) British				
wc/d	1	2,249	2,249	2,249
ELSASSER, Friedrich August (1810-1845) German				
oil	2	9,643-19,852	14,747	9,643
ELSHEIMER, Adam (1574-1620) German				
oil	1	7,694	7,694	7,694
ELSHOECHT, Jean Jacques Marie Carl Vital (1797-1856) French				
3D	1	16,949	16,949	16,949
ELSHOLTZ, Ludwig (1805-1850) German				
oil	1	30,102	30,102	30,102
ELSLEY, Arthur John (1861-1952) British				
oil	3	140,000-780,000	383,333	230,000
ELSNER, Franz (1898-1977) Austrian				
oil	1	2,425	2,425	2,425
ELSNER, Otto (20th C) German?				
wc/d	2	714-2,903	1,808	714
ELSNER, Slawomir (1976-) Polish				
oil	1	8,500	8,500	8,500
ELSTROM, Harry (1906-1993) Belgian				
3D	1	1,907	1,907	1,907
ELTEN, H D Kruseman van (1829-1904) Dutch				
oil	1	1,300	1,300	1,300
ELTEN, Hendrik Dirk Kruseman van (1829-1904) Dutch				
oil	3	3,000-16,000	7,533	3,600
wc/d	3	800-1,600	1,300	1,500
ELWELL, Frederick William (1870-1958) British				
oil	10	522-8,004	2,860	1,388
ELWELL, Robert Farrington (1874-1962) American				
oil	6	1,300-9,500	5,258	4,500
wc/d	1	1,700	1,700	1,700
ELWELL, William (18/19th C) American				
oil	1	2,500	2,500	2,500
ELWES, Luke (1961-) British				
oil	3	448-1,611	1,163	1,432
ELWYN, John (1916-1997) British				
oil	1	920	920	920
wc/d	5	1,592-4,325	3,584	3,979
EMBLEMA, Salvatore (1929-) Italian				
oil	12	2,336-7,767	4,631	3,818
wc/d	4	549-10,325	3,881	766
EMERSON, Charles Chase (?-1922) American				
oil	2	550-4,000	2,275	550
EMERSON, William C (1865-?) American				
oil	1	1,500	1,500	1,500
EMERY, James (19th C) American				
oil	1	6,500	6,500	6,500
EMETT, Rowland (1906-1990) British				
wc/d	1	1,068	1,068	1,068
EMIN, Tracey (1963-) British				
wc/d	4	3,872-56,640	39,950	44,250
3D	3	13,840-38,720	28,853	34,000
EMM, J (20th C) ?				
oil	1	7,120	7,120	7,120
EMMENEGGER, Hans (1866-1940) Swiss				
oil	3	2,359-7,493	5,636	7,057
EMMERIK, Govert van (1808-1882) Dutch				
oil	9	2,170-26,490	5,868	3,254
EMMERSON, Henry H (1831-1895) British				
oil	3	4,968-6,920	5,712	5,250
wc/d	1	1,144	1,144	1,144

Name	No.	Price Range	Average	Median
EMMS, John (1843-1912) British				
oil	28	810-760,000	67,209	22,125
EMMS, John and KING, Henry John Yeend (19/20th C) British				
oil	1	13,200	13,200	13,200
EMOND, Martin (1895-1965) Swedish				
oil	59	391-4,432	958	652
wc/d	6	391-1,173	601	417
EMPI, Maurice (1932-) ?				
oil	8	524-2,303	1,061	800
wc/d	3	480-2,458	1,217	713
EMSLIE, Alfred Edward (1848-1918) British				
oil	2	2,088-2,457	2,272	2,088
wc/d	2	647-792	719	647
ENCKELL, Magnus (1870-1925) Finnish				
oil	3	3,857-16,714	9,857	9,000
wc/d	1	545	545	545
ENDE, Edgar (1901-1965) German				
oil	1	19,286	19,286	19,286
wc/d	1	828	828	828
ENDE, Hans am (1864-1918) German				
oil	3	20,384-31,455	26,151	26,615
wc/d	1	1,119	1,119	1,119
ENDER, Eduard (1822-1883) Austrian				
oil	2	790-1,405	1,097	790
ENDER, Johann Nepomuk (1793-1854) Austrian				
oil	1	5,189	5,189	5,189
wc/d	1	1,455	1,455	1,455
ENDER, Thomas (1793-1875) Austrian				
oil	5	3,514-42,343	16,165	9,900
wc/d	7	1,324-14,449	7,060	6,049
ENDERBY, Samuel G (1860-1921) British				
oil	1	6,615	6,615	6,615
ENDLICHTER, Theresia (18/19th C) Swiss				
wc/d	1	2,410	2,410	2,410
ENDO, Choei (1913-) Japanese				
3D	1	11,100	11,100	11,100
ENDRES, Louis John (1896-1989) American				
oil	4	3,507-29,807	11,825	3,889
wc/d	1	537	537	537
ENEHIELM, Cris af (1954-) Finnish				
wc/d	1	1,558	1,558	1,558
ENFANTIN, Augustin (1793-1827) French				
oil	2	2,169-2,521	2,345	2,169
ENFIELD, Henry (1849-1908) British				
oil	6	505-2,880	1,502	1,452
ENGALIERE, Marius (1824-1857) French				
oil	1	1,262	1,262	1,262
ENGBERG, Gabriel Karl (1872-1953) Finnish				
oil	4	787-2,637	1,337	848
ENGEL, Adolphe Charles Maximilien (1801-1833) Belgian				
oil	1	2,121	2,121	2,121
ENGEL, Frederick (1872-1958) Dutch				
oil	1	1,829	1,829	1,829
ENGEL, Otto Heinrich (1866-1949) German				
oil	1	2,272	2,272	2,272
wc/d	1	1,914	1,914	1,914
ENGELBRECHTSZ, Cornelisz (1468-1533) Dutch				
oil	1	120,000	120,000	120,000
ENGELEN, Piet van (1863-1923) Belgian				
oil	6	701-6,171	2,599	1,200
ENGELHARDT, Baron Hermann (1853-?) German				
oil	1	1,929	1,929	1,929
ENGELHARDT, Georg (1823-1883) German				
oil	3	1,331-3,500	2,233	1,868
ENGELHARDT, Georg-Hermann (1855-?) German				
oil	3	1,138-5,605	2,937	2,068
ENGELHART, Josef (1864-1941) Austrian				
3D	1	2,003	2,003	2,003
ENGELMANN, Johann H (19th C) Austrian				
oil	1	5,063	5,063	5,063

Name	No.	Price Range	Average	Median
ENGELS, Lisl (1916-) Austrian				
oil	2	959-3,395	2,177	959
wc/d	3	1,029-1,543	1,364	1,520
ENGELSBERG, Léon (1908-1999) Israeli				
oil	1	9,000	9,000	9,000
ENGELSTEIN, Sharon (1965-) Canadian				
3D	1	3,200	3,200	3,200
ENGELUND, Svend (1908-) Danish				
oil	11	970-9,378	2,977	1,940
ENGL, Hugo (1852-?) Austrian				
oil	2	4,204-5,856	5,030	4,204
ENGLAND, E S (19/20th C) ?				
oil	2	560-22,750	11,655	560
ENGLARD, Yehudit (20th C) Israeli				
oil	2	1,300-1,400	1,350	1,300
ENGLEHART, John Joseph (1867-1915) American				
oil	5	800-2,800	1,640	1,600
ENGLEHEART, Evelyn L (fl.1906-1921) British				
wc/d	2	452-2,604	1,528	452
ENGLISH, Frank F (1854-1922) American				
oil	1	700	700	700
wc/d	13	950-2,500	1,773	1,900
ENGLISH, Kim (1957-) American				
oil	2	1,750-2,800	2,275	1,750
ENGLISH, Simon (1959-) British				
oil	1	2,220	2,220	2,220
ENGLISH, Thomas (20th C) American				
oil	1	4,500	4,500	4,500
ENGLUND, Lars (1933-) Swedish				
oil	3	2,545-4,453	3,393	3,181
wc/d	4	397-5,947	1,856	509
3D	5	1,909-19,085	7,287	3,817
ENGMAN, Harald (1903-1968) Danish				
oil	9	1,616-6,466	3,332	1,932
ENGONOPOULOS, Nikos (1910-1985) Greek				
oil	1	59,840	59,840	59,840
wc/d	2	12,672-44,880	28,776	12,672
ENGSTROM, Albert (1869-1940) Swedish				
oil	1	616	616	616
wc/d	4	424-478	449	448
ENGSTROM, Leander (1886-1927) Swedish				
oil	7	7,136-165,616	42,311	19,161
wc/d	1	2,114	2,114	2,114
ENGSTROM, Martin (1952-) Swedish				
oil	1	1,388	1,388	1,388
ENGUIDANOS, Juan (20th C) Spanish?				
oil	1	3,092	3,092	3,092
ENHUBER, Karl von (1811-1867) German				
oil	3	3,063-9,158	5,602	4,586
ENJOLRAS, Delphin (1857-1945) French				
oil	15	7,289-70,575	24,260	20,000
wc/d	5	2,186-29,440	9,928	4,576
ENKAOUA, Daniel (1962-) Israeli				
oil	1	10,000	10,000	10,000
ENNEKING, John J (1841-1916) American				
oil	25	1,000-30,000	6,712	3,750
wc/d	2	475-3,000	1,737	475
ENNEKING, Joseph Elliot (1881-1942) American				
oil	4	1,200-1,800	1,550	1,500
ENNESS, Augustus William (1876-1948) British				
oil	10	460-2,941	1,024	622
ENNIS, George Pearse (1884-1936) American				
oil	5	775-8,000	4,075	4,250
wc/d	2	1,000-1,000	1,000	1,000
ENNS, Maureen (1943-) Canadian				
oil	2	533-2,437	1,485	533
wc/d	2	615-738	676	615
ENNUTSIAK (1896-1967) North American				
3D	2	12,654-14,341	13,497	12,654
ENOCH, Dina (1946-) Israeli				
oil	2	1,900-2,400	2,150	1,900

Name	No.	Price Range	Average	Median
ENOCK, Arthur Henry (fl.1869-1910) British				
wc/d	4	555-2,576	1,341	669
ENOTRIO (1920-1989) Argentinian				
oil	12	478-2,675	1,236	955
ENRIQUEZ, Carlos (1900-1957) Cuban				
oil	1	95,000	95,000	95,000
ENRIQUEZ, Nicolas (fl.1738-1770) Mexican				
oil	1	1,414	1,414	1,414
ENROTH, Erik (1917-1975) Finnish				
oil	5	719-3,748	1,970	1,991
ENSELING, Josef (1886-1957) German				
3D	3	2,003-3,299	2,632	2,596
ENSOR, James (1860-1949) Belgian				
oil	5	5,250-221,250	68,657	51,426
wc/d	14	1,147-84,480	13,517	5,633
ENTZ, Loren (1949-) American				
oil	2	2,100-10,000	6,050	2,100
wc/d	1	1,100	1,100	1,100
ENWRIGHT, J J (1905-) American				
oil	6	1,700-2,900	2,458	2,650
EPP, Rudolf (1834-1910) German				
oil	6	1,832-12,000	5,244	2,719
EPPER, Ignaz (1892-1969) Swiss				
oil	1	2,276	2,276	2,276
wc/d	10	611-6,161	2,181	1,297
EPPLE, Emil (1877-?) German				
3D	1	3,000	3,000	3,000
EPSTEIN, Henri (1892-1944) Polish/French				
oil	8	2,887-9,161	5,616	4,014
wc/d	3	1,255-1,788	1,591	1,731
EPSTEIN, Jehudo (1870-1946) Polish				
oil	2	893-1,750	1,321	893
EPSTEIN, Sir Jacob (1880-1959) British/American				
wc/d	19	875-8,142	3,392	2,835
3D	25	1,870-121,800	22,502	13,090
EPSTEIN-HEFTER, Elisabeth (1879-1956) Swiss				
oil	2	1,600-2,945	2,272	1,600
EQUIPO CRONICA (20th C) Spanish				
oil	2	59,143-71,837	65,490	59,143
3D	1	14,865	14,865	14,865
ERBA, Carlo (1884-1917) Italian				
wc/d	1	1,829	1,829	1,829
ERBACH, Alois (1880-1972) German				
oil	1	2,121	2,121	2,121
ERBE, Joan (20th C) American				
oil	4	550-1,000	737	700
wc/d	1	550	550	550
ERBEN, Ulrich (1940-) German				
oil	8	533-10,838	4,976	3,058
ERDMANN, Ludwig (1820-?) German				
oil	1	2,919	2,919	2,919
EREDI, Oscar (1901-?) Italian				
oil	1	2,983	2,983	2,983
ERFMANN, Ferdinand (1901-1968) Dutch				
oil	1	22,898	22,898	22,898
ERGO, Ronald (1936-) Belgian				
oil	1	1,013	1,013	1,013
ERHARDT, Georg Friedrich (1825-1881) German				
oil	1	9,122	9,122	9,122
ERICSON, Johan (1849-1925) Swedish				
oil	9	1,246-10,578	4,042	2,620
ERIKSSON, Christian (1858-1935) Swedish				
3D	6	1,617-3,984	3,073	3,022
ERIKSSON, Ernst Elis (1906-2006) Swedish				
oil	3	1,189-13,875	5,946	2,775
wc/d	5	661-1,454	925	859
3D	1	5,947	5,947	5,947
ERIKSSON, Liss (1919-2000) Swedish				
3D	2	2,227-2,545	2,386	2,227
ERISTOFF-KAZAK, Princess Marie (19/20th C) Russian				
oil	1	10,177	10,177	10,177
wc/d	1	24,080	24,080	24,080

Name	No.	Price Range	Average	Median
ERIXSON, Sven (1899-1970) Swedish				
oil	29	1,157-19,161	5,292	3,964
wc/d	8	547-4,625	1,598	1,321
ERLEBACHER, Martha Mayer (1937-) American				
oil	2	1,000-1,000	1,000	1,000
ERLER, Fritz (1868-1940) German				
oil	2	653-39,333	19,993	653
ERMELTRAUT, Franz Anton (1717-1767) German				
oil	1	3,063	3,063	3,063
ERMILOV, Vassily (1894-1968) Russian				
3D	1	8,500	8,500	8,500
ERNI, Hans (1909-) Swiss				
oil	8	3,083-15,221	7,110	4,961
wc/d	12	916-10,605	3,507	2,831
ERNST, Emil von (fl.1860-1880) German				
oil	1	1,829	1,829	1,829
ERNST, Gustav (1858-1945) German				
oil	1	1,453	1,453	1,453
ERNST, Helge (1916-1990) Danish				
oil	15	487-4,829	1,874	1,455
ERNST, Jimmy (1920-1984) American/German				
oil	7	425-18,000	8,503	9,000
wc/d	1	1,900	1,900	1,900
ERNST, Max (1891-1976) German				
oil	25	7,591-850,000	245,092	150,000
wc/d	22	1,414-198,590	55,944	42,719
3D	11	7,000-240,000	55,301	13,357
ERNST, Max and CAUQUIL-PRINCE, Yvette (20th C) German/French				
wc/d	1	30,000	30,000	30,000
ERNST, Rudolph (1854-1932) Austrian				
oil	13	1,286-322,000	168,513	150,000
ERRO, Gudmundur (1932-) Icelandic				
oil	39	1,286-84,145	13,419	8,357
wc/d	20	716-17,534	3,701	2,337
ERTE, Romain de Tirtoff (1892-1990) Russian				
wc/d	65	557-5,160	2,158	1,875
3D	19	1,500-5,500	3,290	3,200
ERWIN, Jack (1920-) American				
oil	3	1,200-2,500	1,900	2,000
ESBENS, Emile Étienne (1821-?) French				
oil	1	1,798	1,798	1,798
ESBRAT, Raymond Noel (1809-1856) French				
oil	1	1,874	1,874	1,874
ESBROECK, Eduard van (1869-1949) Belgian				
oil	1	1,073	1,073	1,073
ESCHBACH, Paul Andre Jean (1881-1961) French				
oil	8	606-3,912	1,463	825
ESCHKE, Richard-Hermann (1859-1944) German				
oil	3	922-2,534	1,491	1,018
ESCHWEGE, Elmar von (1856-1935) German				
oil	1	19,265	19,265	19,265
ESCUDIER, Charles-Jean-Auguste (1848-?) French				
oil	1	1,870	1,870	1,870
ESKILSON, Per (1820-1872) Swedish				
oil	1	1,165	1,165	1,165
ESKRIDGE, Robert Lee (1891-1975) American				
wc/d	2	1,900-6,000	3,950	1,900
ESMEIN, Maurice Marcel Marie (1888-1918) French				
oil	1	1,636	1,636	1,636
ESPALIU, Pepe (1955-1993) Spanish				
oil	1	2,076	2,076	2,076
3D	1	2,481	2,481	2,481
ESPINA Y CAPO, Juan (1848-1933) Spanish				
oil	3	478-5,596	2,660	1,907
wc/d	2	595-1,343	969	595
ESPINOSA, Antonio de (17th C) Spanish				
oil	1	133,500	133,500	133,500
ESPINOSA, Jacinto Raymundo de (1631-1707) Spanish				
oil	1	2,870	2,870	2,870
ESPINOSA, Jeronimo Jacinto (1600-1680) Spanish				
oil	2	22,200-22,200	22,200	22,200

Name	No.	Price Range	Average	Median
ESPINOSA, Manuel (?) Argentinian				
oil	4	1,929-13,000	7,407	6,200
ESPINOZA, Eugenio (20th C) ?				
oil	1	2,880	2,880	2,880
ESPOSITO, Cesare (1886-1943) Italian				
wc/d	1	1,911	1,911	1,911
ESPOSITO, Enzo (1946-) Italian				
oil	1	3,366	3,366	3,366
wc/d	3	984-3,356	1,845	1,197
ESPOSITO, Gaetano (1858-1911) Italian				
oil	3	985-4,714	2,685	2,356
wc/d	2	666-2,356	1,511	666
ESPOSITO, Vincenzo (fl.1890-1920) Maltese				
wc/d	5	495-2,760	1,227	900
ESPOY, Angel (1879-1963) American				
oil	6	1,600-10,000	5,683	5,500
ESQUERRE, Laurent (1967-) French?				
3D	1	1,632	1,632	1,632
ESQUIVEL, Antonio Maria de (1806-1857) Spanish				
oil	1	9,514	9,514	9,514
ESSELENS, Jacob (1626-1687) Dutch				
oil	1	15,925	15,925	15,925
wc/d	1	3,460	3,460	3,460
ESSEN, Cornelis van (17/18th C) Dutch				
oil	3	5,550-20,470	10,636	5,890
ESSEN, Johannes Cornelis (1854-1936) Dutch				
oil	2	2,521-5,633	4,077	2,521
ESSENHIGH, Inka (1969-) American				
oil	4	10,560-42,000	32,390	35,000
ESSER, Vincent Pieter Semeyn (1914-2004) Dutch				
3D	1	4,468	4,468	4,468
ESSFELD, Alexander (20th C) German				
oil	1	1,375	1,375	1,375
ESSIG, George E (1838-1926) American				
wc/d	3	500-3,000	1,383	650
ESSIG, Gustav (19/20th C) German?				
oil	1	1,520	1,520	1,520
ESTES, Richard (1932-) American				
oil	2	135,000-185,000	160,000	135,000
wc/d	4	1,000-95,408	55,352	40,000
ESTEVAN, Enrique (1849-1927) Spanish				
oil	1	1,085	1,085	1,085
ESTEVE, Maurice (1904-2001) French				
oil	15	20,713-271,944	84,048	58,690
wc/d	19	5,103-42,028	20,174	17,862
ESTEVEZ, Antonio (1910-1983) American				
oil	1	3,000	3,000	3,000
ESTILL, Gerard G (20th C) American				
oil	1	2,000	2,000	2,000
ESTRUGA, Oscar (1933-) Spanish				
oil	1	1,903	1,903	1,903
ETCHEVERRY, Denis (1867-1950) French				
oil	1	3,036	3,036	3,036
ETIDLOOIE, Etidlooie (1911-1981) North American				
3D	1	1,518	1,518	1,518
ETIENNE (19th C) French				
3D	2	14,897-19,135	17,016	14,897
ETIENNE-MARTIN (1913-1995) French				
3D	4	4,703-12,485	7,231	5,658
ETNIER, Stephen (1903-1984) American				
oil	7	8,000-27,500	15,785	13,000
ETROG, Sorel (1933-) Canadian/Rumanian				
3D	4	2,742-19,498	7,860	4,200
ETTING, Emlen (1905-1992) American				
oil	2	1,500-2,900	2,200	1,500
ETTINGER, Josef Carl (1805-1860) German				
oil	1	5,523	5,523	5,523
ETTY, William (1787-1849) British				
oil	15	522-16,245	4,260	2,750
wc/d	2	554-800	677	554
ETUNGAT, Abraham (1911-) ?				
3D	3	2,278-5,062	3,965	4,555

Name	No.	Price Range	Average	Median
EUGEN (1865-1947) Swedish				
oil	9	3,434-382,192	48,642	5,495
wc/d	6	687-2,885	2,065	2,198
EULER, Pierre Nicolas (1846-1915) French				
oil	1	3,156	3,156	3,156
EURICH, Richard (1903-1992) British				
oil	18	1,122-20,880	7,145	3,740
EUSCHEN, Heiderun (20th C) German				
oil	2	2,432-2,504	2,468	2,432
wc/d	4	1,669-2,125	1,897	1,897
EVA and ADELE (20th C) ?				
wc/d	1	1,212	1,212	1,212
EVALUARDJUK, Henry (1923-) North American				
3D	3	1,687-4,218	3,318	4,049
EVANS, Captain Andrew F (18/19th C) American?				
wc/d	1	2,100	2,100	2,100
EVANS, Cerith Wyn (1959-) British				
3D	1	8,000	8,000	8,000
EVANS, Charles (1907-) American				
oil	1	900	900	900
wc/d	1	5,250	5,250	5,250
EVANS, David (1942-) British				
oil	1	2,013	2,013	2,013
EVANS, De Scott (1847-1898) American				
oil	2	14,000-16,000	15,000	14,000
wc/d	1	1,000	1,000	1,000
EVANS, Donald (1945-1977) American				
wc/d	2	4,459-7,007	5,733	4,459
EVANS, Frank MacNamara (?) British				
wc/d	2	493-1,549	1,021	493
EVANS, Frederick M (1859-1929) British				
oil	1	3,690	3,690	3,690
wc/d	9	522-2,464	1,304	1,121
EVANS, Jessie Benton (1866-1954) American				
oil	2	3,500-4,250	3,875	3,500
EVANS, Merlyn (1910-1973) British				
oil	1	1,151	1,151	1,151
EVANS, Minnie (1892-1987) American				
wc/d	11	425-3,600	1,886	1,600
EVANS, Richard (1784-1871) British				
oil	1	24,780	24,780	24,780
EVANS, Will (fl.1935-1940) British				
wc/d	1	1,012	1,012	1,012
EVANS, William E (fl.1889-1897) British				
wc/d	1	1,400	1,400	1,400
EVE, Jean (1900-1968) French				
oil	2	3,575-4,607	4,091	3,575
EVEN, Andre (1918-) French				
oil	6	510-1,073	679	530
wc/d	1	514	514	514
EVENEPOEL, Henri (1872-1899) Belgian				
oil	4	2,264-132,000	38,940	8,342
wc/d	1	643	643	643
EVENO, Edouard (fl.1930) French				
oil	1	3,033	3,033	3,033
wc/d	1	3,507	3,507	3,507
EVERBROECK, Frans van (17th C) Flemish				
oil	1	11,105	11,105	11,105
EVERDINGEN, Allart (1621-1675) Dutch				
oil	3	5,364-41,520	21,961	19,000
wc/d	3	1,795-4,905	3,502	3,806
EVERETT, Ethel Fanny (fl.1900-1939) British				
oil	1	18,810	18,810	18,810
EVERETT, Raymond (1885-1940) American				
oil	1	4,000	4,000	4,000
EVERETT, Robert Emerson (?-1994) Canadian				
oil	1	1,064	1,064	1,064
EVERETT, Walter Hunt (1880-1946) American				
oil	1	7,000	7,000	7,000
EVERGOOD, Phillip (1901-1973) American				
oil	3	1,400-8,000	3,766	1,900
wc/d	1	550	550	550

Name	No.	Price Range	Average	Median
EVERLEY, Cecil (20th C) American				
oil	2	1,100-1,600	1,350	1,100
EVERS, John (1797-1884) American				
oil	1	3,500	3,500	3,500
EVERSDYCK, Cornelis Willemsz (1590-1644) Dutch				
oil	1	3,514	3,514	3,514
EVERSDYCK, Willem (?-1671) Dutch				
oil	1	6,081	6,081	6,081
EVERSEN, Adrianus (1818-1897) Dutch				
oil	16	2,301-45,446	17,075	15,660
wc/d	2	2,458-2,569	2,513	2,458
EVERSEN, Johannes Hendrik (1906-1995) Dutch				
oil	7	4,712-30,240	14,361	12,285
EVERTAEN, A (19th C) Dutch				
oil	1	3,889	3,889	3,889
EVES, Reginald Grenville (1876-1941) British				
oil	4	1,272-28,480	8,806	1,914
EVRARD, Victor (1807-1877) French				
3D	1	5,310	5,310	5,310
EWALD, Louis (1891-?) American				
oil	1	2,259	2,259	2,259
EWEN, William Paterson (1925-2002) Canadian				
oil	2	48,000-60,000	54,000	48,000
wc/d	1	7,052	7,052	7,052
EWER, Louis C (19/20th C) American				
oil	1	4,750	4,750	4,750
EWERS, Heindrich (1817-1885) German				
oil	3	1,991-9,342	6,830	9,159
EWING, Giulio (19th C) ?				
wc/d	2	6,000-24,000	15,000	6,000
EXNER, Julius (1825-1910) Danish				
oil	7	1,294-7,272	3,596	2,718
wc/d	1	453	453	453
EXNER, Karl (20th C) Austrian				
oil	1	1,387	1,387	1,387
EXPORT, Valie (1940-) Austrian				
wc/d	2	24,000-32,000	28,000	24,000
EXTER, Alexandra (1882-1949) Russian				
oil	12	9,100-777,000	135,973	68,800
wc/d	20	1,767-42,780	15,510	11,689
EXTER, Dirk den (1903-1953) Dutch				
oil	1	1,127	1,127	1,127
EXTER, Julius (1863-1939) German				
oil	2	1,531-4,740	3,135	1,531
EYBERGEN, Hans von (19th C) Dutch				
oil	1	1,400	1,400	1,400
EYBL, Franz (1806-1880) Austrian				
oil	4	1,216-6,442	2,687	1,546
wc/d	1	1,152	1,152	1,152
EYCK, Caspar van (1613-1673) Flemish				
oil	2	9,405-16,886	13,145	9,405
EYCK, Charles (1897-1983) Dutch				
oil	2	1,502-1,520	1,511	1,502
wc/d	2	1,252-1,752	1,502	1,252
EYCK, Nicolaas van I (1617-1679) Flemish				
oil	1	10,694	10,694	10,694
EYCKEN, Charles van den (19th C) Belgian				
oil	2	1,929-7,759	4,844	1,929
EYCKEN, Charles van den (jnr) (1859-1923) Belgian				
oil	9	2,800-50,363	17,380	16,743
EYER, Gustav (1887-?) German				
oil	1	1,313	1,313	1,313
EYMER, Arnoldus Johannes (1803-1863) Dutch				
oil	2	1,760-6,429	4,094	1,760
EYNARD-CHATELAIN, Charles (1807-1876) Swiss				
oil	1	1,145	1,145	1,145
EZEKIEL, Moses (1844-1917) American				
3D	1	2,400	2,400	2,400
FA RUOZHEN (1613-1696) Chinese				
wc/d	1	55,000	55,000	55,000
FABARIUS, Friedrich Wilhelm (1815-1900) German				
oil	2	2,421-4,849	3,635	2,421

Name	No.	Price Range	Average	Median
FABBI, Alberto (1858-1906) Italian				
wc/d	1	1,894	1,894	1,894
FABBI, Fabio (1861-1946) Italian				
oil	12	4,757-310,000	67,090	46,000
wc/d	5	895-19,778	6,545	5,180
FABBIANI, Juan Vicente (1910-) Venezuelan				
oil	6	605-2,790	1,357	700
FABBRI, Agenore (1911-1998) Italian				
oil	6	549-10,177	3,200	1,145
wc/d	5	561-3,534	1,523	1,018
3D	6	2,544-9,833	5,367	4,452
FABELO, Roberto (1950-) Cuban				
oil	1	15,000	15,000	15,000
FABER DU FAUR, Hans von (1863-1949) German				
oil	2	610-1,707	1,158	610
wc/d	3	488-1,158	873	975
FABER DU FAUR, Otto von (1828-1901) German				
oil	3	1,074-5,473	3,236	3,162
FABER, Arthur (1908-) American				
wc/d	1	1,200	1,200	1,200
FABER, Josephine Margaretha (1891-1984) Dutch				
oil	1	2,049	2,049	2,049
FABER, Karl Gottfried Traugott (1786-1863) German				
oil	1	18,061	18,061	18,061
FABER, Will (1901-1987) German/Spanish				
oil	1	1,166	1,166	1,166
FABIAN, Brigitte (20th C) Swiss				
wc/d	1	1,526	1,526	1,526
FABIAN, Felix (20th C) British				
wc/d	1	5,520	5,520	5,520
FABIAN, Gottfried (1905-) German				
oil	1	3,036	3,036	3,036
FABIEN, Louis (1924-) Belgian				
oil	2	475-1,750	1,112	475
FABIJANSKI, Erasmus Rudolph (1829-1891) Polish				
oil	1	1,171	1,171	1,171
FABIJANSKI, Stanislas Poraj (1865-1947) Polish				
oil	1	1,023	1,023	1,023
FABLO, Serge (1937-) Canadian				
oil	1	2,296	2,296	2,296
FABRE, François-Xavier (1766-1837) French				
wc/d	1	2,378	2,378	2,378
FABRE, Helene (19th C) French				
oil	1	1,265	1,265	1,265
FABRE, Jan (1958-) Belgian				
wc/d	4	2,408-2,649	2,588	2,649
3D	1	19,872	19,872	19,872
FABRES Y COSTA, Antonio (1854-1936) Spanish				
wc/d	1	18,000	18,000	18,000
FABRETTI, Quirina Alippi (19th C) Italian				
oil	1	1,700	1,700	1,700
FABRIS, Jacobo (1689-1761) Italian				
oil	2	51,081-64,750	57,915	51,081
FABRIS, Pietro (18th C) Italian				
oil	1	18,123	18,123	18,123
FABRITIUS DE TENGNAGEL, F M E (1781-1849) Danish				
oil	2	3,423-3,822	3,622	3,423
FABRO, Luciano (1936-) Italian				
3D	5	15,045-421,429	178,961	200,000
FABRY, Elisee (1882-1949) Belgian				
oil	9	714-3,092	1,915	2,259
FABRY, Émile (1865-1966) Belgian				
oil	11	482-3,884	1,442	1,260
wc/d	4	900-1,192	1,088	1,074
FACCINCANI, Athos (1951-) Italian				
oil	28	937-5,178	2,806	2,543
wc/d	3	853-1,036	916	860
FACHE, Rene (19th C) French				
3D	1	2,338	2,338	2,338
FADER, Fernando (1882-1935) Argentinian				
oil	2	29,000-53,000	41,000	29,000
wc/d	1	22,000	22,000	22,000

Name	No.	Price Range	Average	Median
FAED, James (snr) (1821-1911) British				
oil	1	1,548	1,548	1,548
FAED, John (1820-1902) British				
oil	3	783-3,250	1,866	1,566
FAED, Thomas (1826-1900) British				
oil	8	3,828-110,360	29,682	12,460
wc/d	4	2,494-22,880	8,006	3,132
FAES, Pieter (1750-1814) Belgian				
oil	1	46,124	46,124	46,124
FAFARD, Joseph (1942-) Canadian				
3D	5	1,587-17,318	6,569	2,531
FAGAN, Robert (1745-1816) British				
oil	1	3,709	3,709	3,709
FAGEL, Léon (1851-1913) French				
3D	1	3,828	3,828	3,828
FAGERLIN, Ferdinand (1825-1907) Swedish				
oil	2	806-1,992	1,399	806
FAGGIOLI, Juan Carlos (19/20th C) Argentinian				
oil	2	1,200-1,300	1,250	1,200
FAGIOLI, G (?) Italian				
3D	1	2,284	2,284	2,284
FAGUAYS, Pierre le (1892-1935) French				
3D	3	2,102-4,250	3,007	2,670
FAHERTY, Evelyn A (1919-) American				
oil	1	1,000	1,000	1,000
FAHEY, Edward Henry (1844-1907) British				
oil	1	673	673	673
wc/d	1	1,068	1,068	1,068
FAHLCRANTZ, Axel-Erik-Valerius (1851-1925) Swedish				
oil	3	440-5,495	2,193	646
FAHLSTROM, Oyvind (1928-1976) Swedish				
wc/d	2	3,435-21,143	12,289	3,435
FAHND, T (19th C) ?				
oil	1	13,000	13,000	13,000
FAHNLE, Hans (1903-1968) German				
oil	2	971-1,865	1,418	971
FAHRBACH, Carl Ludwig (1835-1902) German				
oil	3	2,272-3,152	2,614	2,420
wc/d	1	1,035	1,035	1,035
FAHRINGER, Carl (1874-1952) Austrian				
oil	4	3,281-12,237	6,789	5,048
wc/d	2	3,214-4,393	3,803	3,214
FAHRNER, Kurt (1932-1977) Swiss				
oil	1	1,062	1,062	1,062
FAIRBAIRN, Thomas (1820-1884) British				
wc/d	1	1,104	1,104	1,104
FAIRBANKS, John Leo (1878-1946) American				
oil	1	1,900	1,900	1,900
FAIRHURST, Angus (1966-) British				
oil	2	6,020-6,020	6,020	6,020
FAIRLEY, Barker (1887-1986) Canadian				
oil	6	1,968-5,118	3,358	2,821
FAIRMAN, Frances C (1836-1923) British				
oil	3	1,600-2,730	2,325	2,646
wc/d	2	1,700-1,903	1,801	1,700
FAIRMAN, James (1826-1904) American				
oil	6	640-20,000	6,801	4,250
FAISTAUER, Anton (1887-1930) Austrian				
wc/d	2	3,770-3,865	3,817	3,770
FAISTENBERGER, Anton (1663-1708) Austrian				
oil	1	11,439	11,439	11,439
FAISTENBERGER, Simon Benedikt (1695-1759) Austrian				
oil	1	6,049	6,049	6,049
FAIT, Camillo (1935-) Italian				
oil	3	605-1,767	1,085	884
FAIVRE, Jules-Abel (1867-1945) French				
oil	1	9,469	9,469	9,469
wc/d	1	1,184	1,184	1,184
FAJARDO, Jose Luis (1941-) Spanish				
3D	1	1,796	1,796	1,796
FALAT, Julian (1853-1929) Polish				
oil	1	8,000	8,000	8,000

Name	No.	Price Range	Average	Median
FALBE, Joachim Martin (1709-1782) German				
oil	1	11,689	11,689	11,689
FALCHETTI, A (1878-1952) Italian				
oil	1	4,024	4,024	4,024
FALCHETTI, Alberto (1878-1952) Italian				
oil	3	669-3,633	1,657	669
FALCHETTI, Giuseppe (1843-1918) Italian				
oil	8	2,342-7,755	3,945	3,162
FALCO PUJOL, Joaquim (1958-) Spanish				
oil	3	825-2,356	1,367	922
FALCONER, Douglas (?) British				
oil	5	554-2,478	1,082	835
FALCUCCI, Robert (1900-1982) ?				
oil	1	1,124	1,124	1,124
FALENS, Carel van (1683-1733) Dutch				
oil	1	16,650	16,650	16,650
FALERO, Luis Riccardo (1851-1896) Spanish				
oil	4	10,000-22,080	15,054	10,137
FALES, Douglas (1929-) Canadian				
oil	2	1,230-1,237	1,233	1,230
FALGUIERE, A (1831-1900) French				
3D	1	5,191	5,191	5,191
FALGUIERE, Alexandre (1831-1900) French				
3D	7	2,000-6,000	4,123	4,872
FALK, George D (20th C) American				
oil	2	800-1,200	1,000	800
FALK, Hans (1918-2002) Swiss				
oil	2	1,135-11,728	6,431	1,135
wc/d	6	855-12,863	4,494	1,947
FALK, Hjalmar (1856-1938) Swedish				
oil	1	21,658	21,658	21,658
wc/d	1	3,434	3,434	3,434
FALK, Lars-Erik (1922-) Swedish				
wc/d	2	529-793	661	529
3D	1	4,229	4,229	4,229
FALK, Robert Rafailovich (1886-1958) Russian				
oil	5	11,743-1,548,000	559,948	375,000
wc/d	1	50,220	50,220	50,220
FALKENSTEIN, Claire (1908-1997) American				
wc/d	1	5,980	5,980	5,980
3D	4	4,000-15,000	9,625	9,500
FALKNER, Fanny (19/20th C) Swedish				
wc/d	1	4,258	4,258	4,258
FALL, George (c.1848-1925) British				
oil	1	3,078	3,078	3,078
wc/d	12	443-1,471	714	547
FALLANT, Constanza (19th C) ?				
oil	1	4,238	4,238	4,238
FALLON, Conor (1939-) Irish?				
wc/d	1	629	629	629
3D	3	5,323-14,014	8,409	5,890
FALTER, John P (1910-1982) American				
oil	3	2,800-13,000	7,766	7,500
wc/d	1	2,000	2,000	2,000
FALTER, Marcel (1866-?) French				
oil	2	2,203-2,447	2,325	2,203
FALTERMEIER, Heinrich (1909-) German				
3D	1	6,370	6,370	6,370
FALTIN, Margarete (1865-?) German				
oil	1	3,507	3,507	3,507
FALTRARD, H W (19th C) British				
oil	1	2,288	2,288	2,288
FAN ZENG (1938-) Chinese				
wc/d	1	1,286	1,286	1,286
FANELLI, Francesco (c.1590-c.1661) Italian				
3D	3	32,870-188,898	93,656	59,200
FANELLI, Francesco (1863-1924) Italian				
oil	1	8,650	8,650	8,650
FANG LIJUN (1963-) Chinese?				
oil	3	60,000-230,000	133,333	110,000
FANGE, Jens (1965-) Swedish				
oil	2	2,672-6,607	4,639	2,672

Name	No.	Price Range	Average	Median
FANGH, Desiderius (1876-?) Austrian				
oil	1	1,520	1,520	1,520
wc/d	1	968	968	968
FANGOR, Wojciech (1922-) Polish				
oil	2	25,000-60,000	42,500	25,000
FANNEN, John (fl.1890-1900) British				
oil	1	5,310	5,310	5,310
FANTACCHIOTTI, Odoardo (1809-1877) Italian				
3D	1	41,760	41,760	41,760
FANTIN-LATOUR, Henri (1836-1904) French				
oil	14	9,570-1,140,800	240,059	84,480
wc/d	2	888-2,366	1,627	888
FANTUZZI, Eliano (1909-1987) Italian				
oil	14	586-3,092	1,161	954
FARA, Teresio (1929-1986) Argentinian				
oil	6	2,130-17,000	7,438	3,500
FARALLA, Richard (1916-1996) American				
3D	2	3,000-3,500	3,250	3,000
FARALLI, Gianpaolo (1955-) Italian				
oil	7	597-1,890	1,050	707
FARAONI, Enzo (1920-) Italian				
oil	3	693-1,920	1,255	1,152
FARASYN, Edgard (1858-1938) Belgian				
oil	6	596-1,945	968	727
wc/d	1	1,396	1,396	1,396
FARCY, Victor Marius (1858-1942) French				
oil	1	1,253	1,253	1,253
FARDON, Pierre Jean Jacques (1873-1930) Dutch				
oil	1	1,021	1,021	1,021
FAREY, Cyril A (1888-1954) British				
wc/d	2	3,114-3,600	3,357	3,114
FARFA (1881-1964) Italian				
oil	3	2,926-9,535	6,082	5,786
wc/d	2	647-1,790	1,218	647
FARGE, L (?) ?				
oil	1	1,145	1,145	1,145
FARGUE, Paulus Constantin la (1732-1782) Dutch				
wc/d	1	1,700	1,700	1,700
FARHI, Jean Claude (1940-) French				
3D	1	3,349	3,349	3,349
FARINA, Ernesto (1912-) Argentinian				
oil	1	2,000	2,000	2,000
FARINATI, Orazio (1559-c.1616) Italian				
wc/d	1	2,589	2,589	2,589
FARINATI, Paolo (1524-1606) Italian				
wc/d	1	83,250	83,250	83,250
FARINGTON, Joseph (1747-1821) British				
oil	1	11,245	11,245	11,245
wc/d	3	529-2,450	1,391	1,196
FARKASHAZY, Nicolas (1895-1964) Hungarian				
wc/d	1	5,482	5,482	5,482
FARLEY, Richard Blossom (1875-1951) American				
oil	1	5,500	5,500	5,500
FARM, Gerald (1935-) American				
oil	1	1,300	1,300	1,300
FARMER, Josephus (1894-?) American				
3D	2	3,500-6,500	5,000	3,500
FARMER, Walter (1870-1947) British				
oil	1	5,280	5,280	5,280
FARNBOROUGH, Lady Amelia Long (1762-1837) British				
oil	1	4,214	4,214	4,214
FARNDON, Walter (1876-1964) American				
oil	14	2,250-22,000	6,589	4,250
FARNHAM, Alexander (1926-) American				
oil	3	1,500-4,500	3,333	4,000
FARNHAM, Sally James (1876-1943) American				
3D	1	17,000	17,000	17,000
FARNSWORTH, Jerry (1895-1982) American				
oil	2	3,100-4,500	3,800	3,100
FARNY, Henry F (1847-1916) American				
oil	2	1,405-6,500	3,952	1,405
wc/d	4	40,000-250,000	119,375	47,500

Name	No.	Price Range	Average	Median
FARQUHARSON, David (1839-1907) British				
oil	11	1,218-19,360	6,530	3,588
FARQUHARSON, Giles (20th C) British				
oil	1	1,564	1,564	1,564
FARQUHARSON, Joseph (1846-1935) British				
oil	12	1,196-480,600	61,227	14,160
FARR, Charles Griffin (1908-) American				
oil	3	4,500-9,000	6,166	5,000
FARR, Ellen B (1840-1907) American				
oil	2	2,000-3,500	2,750	2,000
FARRE, Henri (1871-1934) American				
oil	1	7,000	7,000	7,000
FARRELL, J A (19/20th C) Irish?				
3D	1	4,833	4,833	4,833
FARRELL, Micheal (1945-2000) Irish				
oil	3	763-31,808	13,606	8,247
wc/d	1	2,843	2,843	2,843
FARREN, Robert (1832-?) British				
oil	1	2,503	2,503	2,503
FARRER, Henry (1843-1903) American/British				
wc/d	4	500-3,500	1,450	600
FARRERAS, Francisco (1927-) Spanish				
oil	1	2,829	2,829	2,829
wc/d	3	2,973-3,468	3,193	3,138
FARRIER, Robert (1796-1879) British				
oil	2	3,740-6,264	5,002	3,740
FARSKY, Otto (19/20th C) American				
oil	1	1,150	1,150	1,150
FARUFFINI, Federico (1831-1869) Italian				
oil	2	1,030-9,710	5,370	1,030
FARULLI, Fernando (1923-1997) Italian				
oil	2	882-1,262	1,072	882
wc/d	1	584	584	584
FASANOTTI, Gaetano (1831-1882) Italian				
oil	2	5,445-6,090	5,767	5,445
FASINI, Alexandre (1892-1982) Russian				
oil	2	5,634-7,598	6,616	5,634
FASSBENDER, Josef (1903-1974) German				
oil	1	2,121	2,121	2,121
FASSIANOS, Alecos (1935-) Greek				
oil	14	786-52,920	17,934	11,340
wc/d	5	1,415-2,595	2,017	2,244
FASSIN, Nicholas de (1728-1811) Flemish				
oil	1	9,000	9,000	9,000
FATHI, Hassan (1957-) Egyptian				
oil	7	647-1,659	1,130	1,229
wc/d	7	1,230-2,704	1,948	1,829
FATHWINTER (1906-) German				
wc/d	1	1,483	1,483	1,483
FATORI (?) ?				
3D	1	6,105	6,105	6,105
FATTORI, Giovanni (1825-1908) Italian				
oil	3	19,418-216,678	87,146	25,342
wc/d	4	667-4,123	2,681	2,400
FATTORINI, Eliseo Tuderte (1830-1887) Italian				
wc/d	2	979-1,056	1,017	979
FAUBERT, Jean (1946-) French				
oil	2	887-947	917	887
wc/d	3	553-599	575	575
FAUCON, Jean Claude (1939-) French				
wc/d	6	1,014-2,534	1,943	2,281
FAUCONNET, Pierre (1882-1920) French				
oil	1	22,680	22,680	22,680
FAUCONNIER, Henri le (1881-1946) French				
oil	2	760-3,816	2,288	760
wc/d	1	3,507	3,507	3,507
FAUERHOLDT, Viggo (1832-1883) Danish				
oil	2	1,488-3,739	2,613	1,488
FAUGINET, Jacques Auguste and MAROCHETTI, Baron Charles (19th C) French				
3D	1	3,884	3,884	3,884
FAULDS, James (fl.1896-1938) British				
oil	1	4,844	4,844	4,844

Name	No.	Price Range	Average	Median
FAULKNER, Henry Lawrence (1924-1981) American				
oil	2	1,700-3,500	2,600	1,700
FAULKNER, John (c.1830-1888) British				
wc/d	12	1,100-8,396	2,943	2,280
FAULKNER, Richard (1917-1988) British				
oil	4	433-2,124	1,145	433
FAURE, Amandus (1874-1931) German				
oil	2	1,500-2,101	1,800	1,500
FAURET, Léon (1863-1955) French				
oil	1	9,450	9,450	9,450
FAUST, Joseph (1868-?) French				
oil	2	1,262-42,500	21,881	1,262
FAUSTMAN, Mollie (1883-1966) Swedish				
oil	3	388-13,875	4,885	393
wc/d	1	399	399	399
FAUTRIER, Jean (1898-1964) French				
oil	13	3,155-184,800	73,336	61,716
wc/d	22	701-16,459	4,938	3,155
3D	3	10,560-175,341	69,108	21,425
FAUVELET, Jean Baptiste (1819-1883) French				
oil	2	1,433-2,265	1,849	1,433
FAUX-FROIDURE, Eugenie-Juliette (1886-?) French				
wc/d	3	656-2,581	1,675	1,790
FAVAI, Gennaro (1882-?) Italian?				
oil	1	2,589	2,589	2,589
wc/d	1	2,577	2,577	2,577
FAVEN, Antti (1882-1948) Finnish				
oil	2	801-1,318	1,059	801
wc/d	2	748-1,414	1,081	748
FAVEROT, Joseph (1862-?) French				
oil	1	2,395	2,395	2,395
FAVIER, Philippe (1957-) French				
oil	1	4,816	4,816	4,816
wc/d	3	2,189-4,816	3,130	2,387
FAVIER, Victor (1824-?) French				
oil	1	3,168	3,168	3,168
FAVILLE, William Baker (1866-1947) American				
wc/d	1	2,750	2,750	2,750
FAVORIN, Ellen (1853-1919) Finnish				
oil	6	2,057-4,442	3,315	3,086
FAVORY, Andre (1888-1937) French				
oil	6	479-2,385	1,065	705
FAVRAY, Antoine de (1706-1791) French				
oil	1	35,510	35,510	35,510
FAVRE, Valerie (1959-) ?				
oil	1	2,977	2,977	2,977
FAVRETTO, G (1849-1887) Italian				
wc/d	3	7,027-7,027	7,027	7,027
FAVRETTO, Giacomo (1849-1887) Italian				
wc/d	2	2,548-5,825	4,186	2,548
FAWCETT, Clarence Calhoun (1902-1988) American				
oil	1	1,500	1,500	1,500
FAWCETT, John (1952-) American				
oil	3	2,000-7,500	5,416	6,750
wc/d	2	3,300-3,750	3,525	3,300
FAWCETT, Robert (1903-1967) American				
wc/d	2	1,900-2,200	2,050	1,900
FAXON, Richard (19th C) French				
oil	1	1,901	1,901	1,901
FAY, Arlene Hooker (1937-) American				
wc/d	1	2,000	2,000	2,000
FAZIO, R di (20th C) Italian				
oil	2	1,942-2,330	2,136	1,942
FAZZINI, Pericle (1913-1987) Italian				
oil	1	454	454	454
wc/d	4	442-2,336	1,074	694
3D	6	5,500-18,101	10,516	8,000
FEARING, Kelly (1918-) American				
oil	1	5,500	5,500	5,500
wc/d	1	2,250	2,250	2,250

Name	No.	Price Range	Average	Median
FEARNLEY, Thomas (1802-1842) Norwegian				
oil	3	14,720-52,500	38,353	47,840
wc/d	1	27,600	27,600	27,600
FEARON, Hilda (1878-1917) British				
oil	1	22,680	22,680	22,680
FEBRARI (?) ?				
3D	1	13,884	13,884	13,884
FEBVRE, Edouard (20th C) French				
oil	11	565-2,552	1,164	800
wc/d	1	668	668	668
FECHIN, Nicolai (1881-1955) American/Russian				
oil	4	5,000-400,000	211,250	180,000
wc/d	2	5,500-5,500	5,500	5,500
FECTEAU, Marcel (1927-) Canadian				
oil	1	1,621	1,621	1,621
FEDDEN, Mary (1915-) British				
oil	43	4,816-49,140	13,947	12,040
wc/d	37	1,246-19,140	5,859	4,524
FEDDER, Otto (1873-1919) German				
oil	1	1,532	1,532	1,532
FEDDERSEN, Hans Peter (younger) (1848-1941) Danish				
oil	3	1,920-11,315	5,368	2,870
FEDELER, Carl Justus Harmen (1799-1858) German				
oil	1	33,714	33,714	33,714
FEDER, Adolphe (1886-1940) French				
oil	10	839-77,672	21,164	5,600
FEDERICO, Cavalier Michele (1884-1966) Italian				
oil	11	482-3,534	1,249	1,000
FEDI, Pio (1816-1892) Italian				
3D	1	40,000	40,000	40,000
FEDIER, Franz (1922-) Swiss				
oil	5	811-4,463	1,922	1,526
wc/d	6	763-1,783	1,274	1,145
FEDOROV, Simeon Fedorovich (1867-1910) Russian				
oil	1	22,435	22,435	22,435
FEDOROVA, Maria (1859-1934) Russian				
oil	4	756-2,700	1,860	1,414
FEDOROVITCH, Vladimir (1871-?) Russian				
oil	1	14,055	14,055	14,055
FEDOTOV, Pavel Andreevich (1815-1852) Russian				
oil	1	13,807	13,807	13,807
wc/d	1	127,397	127,397	127,397
FEENEY, Jacinta (20th C) Irish?				
oil	2	1,392-3,875	2,633	1,392
FEHDMER, Richard (1860-?) German				
oil	1	1,127	1,127	1,127
wc/d	1	557	557	557
FEHER, Laszlo (1953-) Hungarian				
oil	1	1,656	1,656	1,656
FEHER, Tony (1956-) American				
3D	1	26,000	26,000	26,000
FEHR, Bartholome (1747-1811) Swiss				
wc/d	1	4,162	4,162	4,162
FEHR, Friedrich (1862-1927) German				
oil	2	1,286-6,775	4,030	1,286
FEHR, Henri (1888-1974) Swiss				
oil	1	1,145	1,145	1,145
wc/d	2	1,582-3,330	2,456	1,582
FEHRLE, Jakob Wilhelm (1884-1974) German				
3D	2	4,253-4,944	4,598	4,253
FEIBUSCH, Hans (1898-1998) German				
oil	2	1,044-2,754	1,899	1,044
wc/d	2	743-1,860	1,301	743
FEID, Josef (1806-1870) Austrian				
oil	1	1,394	1,394	1,394
FEIERTAG, Karl (1874-1944) German				
oil	1	3,507	3,507	3,507
FEIGIN, Dov (1907-2000) Israeli?				
3D	1	5,000	5,000	5,000

Name	No.	Price Range	Average	Median
FEILER, Paul (1918-) British				
oil	8	14,620-160,080	67,977	54,870
wc/d	5	1,056-12,285	6,857	6,960
3D	1	9,968	9,968	9,968
FEININGER, Lyonel (1871-1956) American/German				
oil	10	74,000-6,808,000	1,282,871	706,849
wc/d	67	764-149,956	22,782	15,840
FEIST, Andreas (20th C) German				
oil	1	1,832	1,832	1,832
FEIST, Harold (20th C) ?				
oil	1	2,296	2,296	2,296
FEITH, Gustav (1875-1951) Austrian				
wc/d	3	1,210-4,839	2,500	1,452
FEITO, Luis (1929-) Spanish				
oil	15	1,414-60,000	17,785	12,214
wc/d	13	825-38,531	8,689	4,302
FELBER, Carl (1880-1932) Swiss				
oil	2	1,145-2,443	1,794	1,145
FELDBAUER, Max (1869-1948) German				
oil	2	5,291-8,818	7,054	5,291
FELDERHOFF, Reinhold (1865-1919) German				
3D	1	2,026	2,026	2,026
FELDHUTTER, Ferdinand (1842-1898) German				
oil	5	719-2,510	1,414	1,189
FELEZ, Mariano (1883-1942) Spanish				
oil	1	2,116	2,116	2,116
FELICE, Aurelio de (1915-) ?				
3D	1	2,108	2,108	2,108
FELIPE, Antonio de (1965-) Spanish				
oil	1	4,000	4,000	4,000
FELISARI, Enrico (1897-1981) Italian				
oil	5	550-5,444	2,790	2,330
FELIXMULLER, Conrad (1897-1977) German				
oil	4	8,500-1,000,000	268,795	9,351
wc/d	3	1,987-5,806	4,312	5,143
FELL, Sheila (1931-1979) British				
oil	13	9,200-49,000	18,757	13,050
FELLOWS, Deborah (1945-) American				
3D	1	5,500	5,500	5,500
FELLOWS, Fred (1934-) American				
oil	5	2,600-8,500	4,880	4,000
3D	5	2,000-42,500	10,800	3,000
FENASSE, Paul (1899-1976) French				
oil	2	647-2,225	1,436	647
FENDI, Peter (1796-1842) Austrian				
wc/d	3	605-2,356	1,713	2,178
FENDT, René (1948-) Swiss				
oil	1	2,110	2,110	2,110
wc/d	1	568	568	568
FENETTY, F M (1854-1915) American/Italian				
oil	1	1,700	1,700	1,700
FENETTY, Frederick M (1854-1915) American/Italian				
oil	1	3,000	3,000	3,000
FENG MENGBO (1966-) Chinese				
oil	1	40,000	40,000	40,000
FENG ZHENGJIE (1968-) Chinese				
oil	2	30,903-80,000	55,451	30,903
FENG ZIKAI (1898-1975) Chinese				
wc/d	1	1,168	1,168	1,168
FENIMORE, Thomas J (19th C) American				
oil	1	1,700	1,700	1,700
FENNER-BEHMER, Herman (1866-1913) German				
oil	2	4,821-13,676	9,248	4,821
FENOSA, Apelles (1899-1989) Spanish				
3D	3	2,260-3,795	3,262	3,732
FENSON, Robert (19/20th C) British				
oil	4	450-1,416	1,016	900
wc/d	1	1,114	1,114	1,114
FENSTERMACHER, Henry (?) American				
oil	1	3,250	3,250	3,250
FENTON, Beatrice (1887-1983) American				
3D	1	6,500	6,500	6,500

Name	No.	Price Range	Average	Median
FENTON, Hallie Champlin (1880-1935) American				
oil	1	1,500	1,500	1,500
FENYES, Adolphe (1867-1945) Hungarian				
oil	1	4,123	4,123	4,123
FENZONI, Ferrau (1562-1645) Italian				
wc/d	2	7,767-15,725	11,746	7,767
FEODOROVA, Maria Alekseevna (1859-1916) Russian				
oil	3	611-2,038	1,342	1,377
FERAT, Serge (1881-1958) Russian				
oil	7	4,600-38,014	21,084	15,206
wc/d	1	4,783	4,783	4,783
FERAU Y ALSINA, Enrique (1825-1887) Spanish				
wc/d	1	1,060	1,060	1,060
FERAUD, Albert (1921-) French				
wc/d	7	471-825	664	684
3D	17	1,674-19,667	4,394	3,236
FERBER, Herbert (1906-1991) American				
oil	2	1,200-1,532	1,366	1,200
3D	1	20,000	20,000	20,000
FERET, Alain (20th C) French				
wc/d	1	2,919	2,919	2,919
FERG, Franz de Paula (1689-1740) Austrian				
oil	5	9,753-162,800	75,554	24,196
FERGOLA, Francesco (19th C) Italian				
wc/d	2	1,068-18,400	9,734	1,068
FERGOLA, Sergio (1936-) Italian				
oil	1	1,656	1,656	1,656
FERGUSON, Elizabeth (1884-1925) American				
oil	1	1,300	1,300	1,300
FERGUSON, Henry Augustus (1842-1911) American				
oil	3	3,000-6,000	4,833	5,500
FERGUSON, Nancy Maybin (1872-1967) American				
oil	3	3,250-75,000	30,750	14,000
FERGUSON, William Gowe (1632-1695) British				
oil	2	7,644-12,567	10,105	7,644
FERGUSSON, John Duncan (1874-1961) British				
oil	4	12,155-196,900	104,116	56,960
wc/d	30	1,309-88,500	8,595	5,310
FERLOTTI, G (19th C) Italian				
3D	1	3,400	3,400	3,400
FERMARIELLO, Sergio (1961-) Italian				
oil	1	7,014	7,014	7,014
wc/d	1	4,071	4,071	4,071
FERMEUS, Victor (1894-1963) Belgian				
oil	1	2,803	2,803	2,803
FERMIN, Pedro Luis (20th C) Venezuelan?				
oil	2	630-750	690	630
wc/d	2	420-560	490	420
FERNANDEZ ALVARADO, Jose (1875-1935) Spanish				
oil	1	2,225	2,225	2,225
FERNANDEZ ARIAS, Cesar (1952-) Venezuelan				
oil	1	1,078	1,078	1,078
FERNANDEZ CUEVAS, Antonio (1835-1909) Spanish				
oil	1	1,565	1,565	1,565
FERNANDEZ CUEVAS, Telesforo (1849-1934) Spanish				
oil	3	2,186-4,886	3,300	2,829
FERNANDEZ DE VILLASANTE, Julio Moises (1888-1968) Spanish				
oil	1	1,326	1,326	1,326
FERNANDEZ MAR, Nicasio (1916-1979) Argentinian				
3D	1	6,000	6,000	6,000
FERNANDEZ MARTIN, Trinidad (1937-) Spanish				
oil	1	2,119	2,119	2,119
FERNANDEZ, Alejandro (1969-) Peruvian				
wc/d	1	2,201	2,201	2,201
FERNANDEZ, Antonio (1882-1970) Spanish				
oil	1	3,801	3,801	3,801
FERNANDEZ, Francisco (1897-?) Venezuelan				
oil	1	2,790	2,790	2,790
FERNELEY, Claude Lorraine (1822-1892) British				
oil	5	756-5,000	2,336	1,500
FERNELEY, John (19th C) British				
oil	1	2,000	2,000	2,000

Name	No.	Price Range	Average	Median
FERNELEY, John (jnr) (1815-1862) British				
oil	7	3,515-22,000	14,048	15,000
FERNELEY, John (snr) (1781-1860) British				
oil	9	22,680-567,000	196,528	114,400
FERNHOUT, Edgar (1912-1976) Dutch				
oil	4	10,829-101,918	37,604	15,288
FERNIER, Robert (1895-1977) French				
oil	4	2,057-3,663	2,599	2,165
FERNKORN, Anton Dominik von (1813-1878) Austrian				
3D	1	13,050	13,050	13,050
FERNSTROM, Linn (1974-) Swedish				
oil	1	16,518	16,518	16,518
wc/d	3	1,209-3,039	2,221	2,417
FERON, Eloi Firmin (1802-1876) French				
oil	1	1,411	1,411	1,411
FERON, Julien Hippolyte (1864-1944) French				
oil	2	989-1,686	1,337	989
FERON, William (1858-1894) Swedish				
oil	3	1,870-6,213	4,388	5,083
FERRANDIZ Y BADENES, Bernardo (1835-1890) Spanish				
oil	3	723-55,000	18,976	1,205
FERRANDO, Augustin (1880-1957) Algerian				
oil	8	1,168-3,236	2,008	1,752
FERRANO, William (19th C) ?				
3D	1	5,046	5,046	5,046
FERRANT Y FISCHERMANS, Alejandro (1843-1917) Spanish				
oil	1	1,946	1,946	1,946
FERRANT, Angel (1891-1961) Spanish				
3D	2	6,684-8,703	7,693	6,684
FERRANTE, E (?) ?				
oil	1	3,733	3,733	3,733
FERRANTI, Carlo (19th C) Italian				
oil	1	2,500	2,500	2,500
FERRARI, A (19/20th C) Italian				
oil	1	1,940	1,940	1,940
FERRARI, Adolfo de (1898-1978) Argentinian				
oil	2	1,100-1,500	1,300	1,100
FERRARI, Agostino (1938-) Italian				
oil	8	1,045-2,589	2,157	2,301
wc/d	3	549-1,618	1,095	1,119
FERRARI, Arturo (1861-1932) Italian				
oil	1	4,685	4,685	4,685
wc/d	1	1,011	1,011	1,011
FERRARI, Berto (1887-1965) Italian				
oil	9	669-4,261	2,229	2,486
FERRARI, Defendente (1490-c.1535) Italian				
oil	2	22,000-314,545	168,272	22,000
FERRARI, Enea (1908-1980) Italian				
oil	1	11,192	11,192	11,192
wc/d	1	597	597	597
FERRARI, Ettore (1849-1929) Italian				
wc/d	2	2,141-3,279	2,710	2,141
FERRARI, G (?) Italian				
3D	1	1,927	1,927	1,927
FERRARI, Giovanni Battista (1829-1906) Italian				
oil	1	45,308	45,308	45,308
FERRARI, Giuseppe (1840-1905) Italian				
oil	2	2,022-7,633	4,827	2,022
FERRARI, Gregorio de (1647-1726) Italian				
oil	1	6,370	6,370	6,370
FERRARI, Leon (1920-) Argentinian				
wc/d	1	16,000	16,000	16,000
3D	2	15,000-50,000	32,500	15,000
FERRARI, Luca (1605-1654) Italian				
oil	1	22,490	22,490	22,490
FERRARI, Orazio de (1605-1657) Italian				
oil	1	111,000	111,000	111,000
FERRARI, Teodoro Wolf (1876-1945) Italian				
oil	1	20,610	20,610	20,610
wc/d	1	23,347	23,347	23,347
FERRARI, Vincenzo (1941-) Italian				
wc/d	3	2,035-3,307	2,873	3,279

Name	No.	Price Range	Average	Median
FERRARINI, E (19th C) ?				
3D	1	2,112	2,112	2,112
FERRARIS, Arthur (1856-1936) Hungarian				
oil	2	26,970-163,862	95,416	26,970
FERRARIS, Serafino (1903-) Italian				
oil	1	1,940	1,940	1,940
FERRAZZI, Ferruccio (1891-1978) Italian				
oil	2	30,452-40,993	35,722	30,452
FERREN, John (1905-1970) American				
oil	4	3,800-11,000	7,450	6,500
FERRER Y CORRIOL, Antonio (1849-1909) Spanish				
oil	1	2,033	2,033	2,033
FERRER, Anne (20th C) French?				
wc/d	1	628	628	628
3D	1	5,363	5,363	5,363
FERRER, Joaquin (1929-) Cuban				
oil	2	1,903-2,472	2,187	1,903
wc/d	1	790	790	790
FERRER, Rafael (1933-) American				
oil	2	3,500-6,000	4,750	3,500
FERRERO, Alberto (1883-1963) Italian				
oil	1	1,332	1,332	1,332
FERRERS, Benjamin (?-1732) British				
oil	4	2,322-3,096	2,623	2,322
FERRI DECLER, Ludmisia (20th C) ?				
oil	1	1,512	1,512	1,512
FERRI, Augusto (1829-1895) Italian				
oil	3	1,239-7,071	3,436	1,998
FERRI, Cesare (1864-1936) Italian				
oil	2	1,823-2,309	2,066	1,823
FERRI, Ciro (1634-1689) Italian				
oil	1	11,192	11,192	11,192
wc/d	1	25,950	25,950	25,950
FERRIER, Dick (1929-) Canadian				
oil	2	1,804-3,116	2,460	1,804
FERRIER, Gabriel (1847-1914) French				
oil	1	4,757	4,757	4,757
wc/d	1	643	643	643
FERRIERES, Jacques Martin (1893-1972) French				
oil	8	3,000-29,000	9,391	6,000
FERRIGNO, Antonio (1863-1940) Italian				
oil	3	1,784-35,676	13,293	2,420
FERRIN, Douglas (1959-) American				
oil	2	900-1,800	1,350	900
FERRINI, Alberto (?) Italian				
oil	2	3,850-8,050	5,950	3,850
FERRIS, Jean Leon Jerome (1863-1930) American				
wc/d	1	2,000	2,000	2,000
FERRIS, Stephen James (1835-?) ?				
oil	1	3,250	3,250	3,250
FERRON, Marcelle (1924-2001) Canadian				
oil	4	1,630-37,666	14,698	8,419
wc/d	2	1,012-3,465	2,238	1,012
FERRONI, Egisto (1835-1912) Italian				
oil	3	1,100-31,200	11,292	1,576
FERRONI, Gianfranco (1927-2001) Italian				
oil	4	3,092-33,075	12,765	7,283
wc/d	15	595-11,010	1,963	892
FERROT, E (?) ?				
oil	1	2,200	2,200	2,200
FERRU, Odette (1915-) French?				
oil	1	1,800	1,800	1,800
FERRUCCI, Francesco di Simone da Fiesole (1437-1493) Italian				
3D	1	103,378	103,378	103,378
FERRUCCI, Giovanni Domenico (1619-?) Italian				
oil	1	7,644	7,644	7,644
FERTBAUER, Leopold (1802-1875) Austrian				
oil	3	2,253-8,836	6,641	8,836
FERTIG, David (20th C) American				
oil	2	900-9,000	4,950	900
FERVILLE-SUAN, Charles (19th C) French				
3D	1	3,181	3,181	3,181

Name	No.	Price Range	Average	Median
FERY, John (1859-1934) American/Hungarian				
oil	6	4,250-50,000	19,625	15,000
FESSLER, Adolf Ivanovich (1826-1885) German/Russian				
oil	1	65,100	65,100	65,100
FESTA, Tano (1938-1988) Italian				
oil	82	442-35,400	6,045	5,255
wc/d	10	589-5,724	2,791	1,571
3D	4	1,674-89,048	26,853	4,800
FETTERMAN, Alan (20th C) American				
oil	4	600-1,400	1,025	700
FETTING, Rainer (1949-) German				
oil	28	5,190-105,600	30,633	28,973
wc/d	5	417-3,408	2,088	2,544
FEUBURE, Ferdinand le (1815-1898) German				
wc/d	1	11,781	11,781	11,781
FEUCHT, Theodore (1867-1944) German				
oil	1	6,301	6,301	6,301
FEUDEL, Arthur (1857-1929) Dutch				
oil	3	526-1,875	1,078	834
FEUERBACH, Anselm (1829-1880) German				
oil	2	4,712-8,522	6,617	4,712
wc/d	3	530-6,325	3,395	3,330
FEUERLEIN, Johann Peter (1668-1728) German				
oil	1	3,612	3,612	3,612
FEUERMAN, Carole Jeane (1945-) American				
3D	1	6,000	6,000	6,000
FEUGER, G (20th C) Danish				
oil	1	1,720	1,720	1,720
FEUILLATTE, Raymond (1901-1971) French				
oil	1	2,650	2,650	2,650
FEURE, Georges de (1868-1943) French				
oil	1	10,542	10,542	10,542
wc/d	1	3,741	3,741	3,741
FEVOLA, Felix Pascal (1882-1953) French				
3D	1	1,890	1,890	1,890
FEYEN, Eugene (1815-1908) French				
oil	5	1,300-7,265	4,098	3,000
FEYEN-PERRIN, François Nicolas Augustin (1826-1888) French				
oil	3	2,500-7,603	5,754	7,159
FEYERABEND, Franz (1755-1800) Swiss				
oil	1	4,540	4,540	4,540
FIAMMINGO, Giusto (17th C) Italian				
oil	1	291,310	291,310	291,310
FIAMMINGO, Paolo (1540-1596) Flemish				
oil	1	36,000	36,000	36,000
FIASCHI, E (19th C) Italian				
3D	1	1,700	1,700	1,700
FIASCHI, Emilio (1858-1941) Italian				
3D	1	3,600	3,600	3,600
FIASCHI, P C E (19/20th C) Italian				
3D	1	11,000	11,000	11,000
FIASCHI, P E (19/20th C) Italian				
3D	1	3,366	3,366	3,366
FIAULT, Catherine (20th C) French				
wc/d	1	2,219	2,219	2,219
FICARA, Franz (1926-1994) Italian				
oil	4	884-1,790	1,201	954
FICHARD, Baron Maximilien de (1836-?) Polish				
oil	1	1,745	1,745	1,745
FICHEFET, Georges (1864-1954) Belgian				
oil	1	1,927	1,927	1,927
FICHEL, Benjamin Eugène (1826-1895) French				
oil	2	4,625-4,872	4,748	4,625
FICHEL, Eugène (19th C) French				
oil	1	1,832	1,832	1,832
FICHEL, L M (19th C) Continental				
oil	1	3,540	3,540	3,540
FICHERELLI, Felice (1605-1660) Italian				
oil	2	7,339-22,878	15,108	7,339
FICHET, Pierre (1927-) French				
oil	7	877-5,825	2,151	1,688

Name	No.	Price Range	Average	Median
FICKERT VAN DER MEER, Albert (19th C) ?				
oil	1	6,865	6,865	6,865
FICO, Ettore (1917-2004) Italian				
oil	4	1,868-2,647	2,073	1,890
wc/d	1	525	525	525
FIDAKIS, Panos (1956-2003) Greek				
oil	5	3,460-11,220	6,601	4,576
FIDANZA, Francesco (1747-1819) Italian				
oil	1	87,669	87,669	87,669
FIDDES, Christopher (20th C) British				
oil	2	1,592-8,192	4,892	1,592
FIDLER, Harry (1856-1935) British				
oil	11	1,075-8,142	4,248	3,168
FIEBIG, Frederic (1885-1953) Russian				
wc/d	1	1,372	1,372	1,372
FIEDLER, Arnold (1900-1985) German				
oil	3	1,165-2,979	1,774	1,178
wc/d	1	1,017	1,017	1,017
FIEDLER, Bernhard (1816-1904) German				
oil	2	1,125-3,294	2,209	1,125
FIEDLER, Herbert (1891-1962) Dutch				
oil	2	756-4,442	2,599	756
FIEDLER, Johann Christian (1697-1765) German				
oil	1	10,946	10,946	10,946
FIELD, E Loyal (1856-1914) American				
oil	10	750-4,000	1,850	1,300
FIELD, Erastus Salisbury (1805-1900) American				
oil	3	4,000-12,000	9,333	12,000
FIELD, Maurice (1905-1988) British				
oil	1	2,124	2,124	2,124
FIELD, Sabra (1935-) American				
wc/d	1	1,000	1,000	1,000
FIELDING, Anthony Vandyke Copley (1787-1855) British				
oil	6	433-8,938	2,423	1,200
wc/d	24	473-7,965	2,346	1,566
FIENE, Ernest (1894-1965) American/German				
oil	4	1,600-4,500	3,062	2,900
wc/d	1	950	950	950
FIERAVINO, Francesco (17th C) Italian				
oil	1	53,507	53,507	53,507
FIESCHI, Giannetto (1921-) Italian				
oil	2	1,649-4,024	2,836	1,649
FIEVRE, Yolande (1907-1983) French				
wc/d	1	2,319	2,319	2,319
3D	1	6,062	6,062	6,062
FIGARELLA, Dominique (1966-) French				
oil	1	3,579	3,579	3,579
FIGARES, Matias (20th C) Spanish				
oil	1	1,654	1,654	1,654
FIGARI, Andrea (1858-1945) Italian				
oil	7	947-56,816	17,657	10,061
FIGARI, Pedro (1861-1938) Uruguayan				
oil	10	2,100-40,000	18,410	12,000
wc/d	4	800-1,200	1,000	800
FIGUEIROA, Jose Luis (1925-) Portuguese				
oil	1	1,823	1,823	1,823
FIKS, Albert (20th C) ?				
oil	1	1,678	1,678	1,678
FILARSKI, Dirk Herman Willem (1885-1964) Belgian				
oil	18	2,521-21,205	7,062	4,676
wc/d	1	2,195	2,195	2,195
FILDES, Denis Quintin (1899-?) British				
oil	1	1,044	1,044	1,044
FILDES, Sir Luke (1843-1927) British				
oil	1	5,610	5,610	5,610
wc/d	2	2,112-4,576	3,344	2,112
FILIBERTI, Georges Guido (1881-1970) French				
oil	1	1,331	1,331	1,331
FILIGER, Charles (1863-1928) French				
wc/d	1	15,310	15,310	15,310
FILIPKIEWICZ, Stefan (1879-1944) Polish				
oil	1	1,064	1,064	1,064

Name	No.	Price Range	Average	Median
FILIPOV, Konstantin Nikolaivich (1830-1878) Russian				
oil	1	52,200	52,200	52,200
FILIPOVIC, Augustin (1931-) ?				
3D	1	2,680	2,680	2,680
FILIPPELLI, Cafiero (1889-1973) Italian				
oil	12	1,171-5,096	2,891	2,773
FILIPPI, Fernando de (1940-) Italian				
oil	9	579-1,767	1,043	1,014
wc/d	3	589-1,748	978	597
FILIPPI, Leonida de (1969-) Italian				
oil	1	1,295	1,295	1,295
FILIPPINI, Francesco (1853-1895) Italian				
wc/d	1	3,567	3,567	3,567
FILIPPOV, Andrei (1959-) Russian				
oil	1	52,080	52,080	52,080
FILKUKA, Anton (1888-1957) Austrian				
oil	3	876-7,803	4,350	4,371
FILLA, Emil (1882-1953) Czechoslovakian				
oil	1	178,396	178,396	178,396
wc/d	4	840-12,945	4,194	1,171
3D	1	7,068	7,068	7,068
FILLEAU, Emery A (1855-1935) American				
oil	1	2,700	2,700	2,700
FILLERUP, Mel (1924-) American				
oil	1	3,500	3,500	3,500
FILLIA (1904-1936) Italian				
oil	4	33,658-96,536	58,952	35,343
FILLIARD, Ernest (1868-1933) French				
wc/d	4	610-3,196	1,682	670
FILLIOU, Robert (1926-1987) French				
wc/d	2	1,518-5,655	3,586	1,518
3D	1	4,477	4,477	4,477
FILLIPOV, L (19th C) Russian				
oil	1	1,710	1,710	1,710
FILLON, Arthur (1900-1974) French				
oil	4	850-2,293	1,492	879
wc/d	1	1,214	1,214	1,214
FILOCAMO, Luigi (1906-1988) Italian				
oil	1	1,178	1,178	1,178
FILONOV, Pavel and PORET, Alicia (20th C) Russian				
oil	1	1,300,000	1,300,000	1,300,000
FILOPOULOU, Maria (1964-) Greek				
oil	2	7,040-8,800	7,920	7,040
FIMA (1916-2005) Israeli				
oil	1	1,400	1,400	1,400
wc/d	1	600	600	600
FIN, Jose (1916-1969) Spanish				
oil	1	9,568	9,568	9,568
FINALE, Moises (1957-) Cuban				
oil	4	1,683-2,589	2,168	2,201
FINART, Noel Dieudonne (1797-1852) French				
wc/d	1	1,694	1,694	1,694
FINAZZER, Flori (1896-1960) Italian				
oil	1	1,539	1,539	1,539
FINCH, Alfred William (1854-1930) Belgian				
oil	4	1,008-18,703	7,843	1,378
FINCH, E E (19th C) American				
oil	1	3,750	3,750	3,750
FINCH, Heneage (1751-1812) British				
wc/d	2	3,720-10,034	6,877	3,720
FIND, Ludvig (1869-1945) Danish				
oil	1	2,535	2,535	2,535
FINE, Judd (1944-) American				
wc/d	1	1,100	1,100	1,100
FINGESTEN, Michel (1884-1943) German?				
oil	2	907-1,435	1,171	907
wc/d	1	478	478	478
FINI, Leonor (1908-1996) Italian				
oil	9	5,351-122,979	38,054	15,315
wc/d	30	410-7,159	1,440	1,082
FINK, Carl W E (1814-?) German				
oil	1	10,235	10,235	10,235

Name	No.	Price Range	Average	Median
FINK, Waldemar (1893-1948) Swiss				
oil	5	500-1,984	1,017	763
wc/d	1	1,446	1,446	1,446
FINKE, Heinrich Jonathan (1816-1868) German				
oil	1	7,827	7,827	7,827
FINKENZELLER, Xaver (19th C) Swiss				
wc/d	1	1,051	1,051	1,051
FINLAYSON, Alfred (19th C) British				
oil	1	9,000	9,000	9,000
FINLEY, Chris (1976-) American				
oil	1	2,500	2,500	2,500
FINNEY, Harry (19th C) ?				
oil	2	6,500-16,000	11,250	6,500
FINNEY, Virginia L (fl.1887-1896) British				
oil	1	5,000	5,000	5,000
FINNIN, Martin (1968-) Irish				
oil	2	3,892-5,005	4,448	3,892
FINOT, Alfred (1874-1947) French				
3D	1	1,936	1,936	1,936
FINOT, Jules Baron (1826-1906) French				
wc/d	8	605-3,151	1,764	1,757
FINSTER, Howard (1916-2001) American				
oil	6	1,300-6,500	3,450	2,800
wc/d	1	1,700	1,700	1,700
FINSTERLIN, Hermann (1887-1973) German				
wc/d	1	2,068	2,068	2,068
FINZI, Ennio (1931-) Italian				
oil	47	825-5,486	2,482	2,267
wc/d	20	488-2,589	1,012	738
FIORENTINO, Paolo (1965-) Italian				
wc/d	1	3,579	3,579	3,579
FIORENZO DI LORENZO (c.1445-1525) Italian				
oil	1	95,548	95,548	95,548
FIORONI, Giosetta (1932-) Italian				
oil	6	1,178-7,755	3,442	2,356
wc/d	6	1,193-2,007	1,536	1,527
FIORUCCI, Luciano (?) Italian				
oil	1	2,736	2,736	2,736
FIOT, Maximilien Louis (1886-1953) French				
3D	4	2,520-8,604	4,300	2,692
FIRFIRES, Nicholas S (1917-1990) American				
oil	6	650-8,000	2,983	1,500
FIRLE, Walter (1859-1929) German				
oil	6	849-9,568	3,897	2,979
FIRMENICH, Josef (1821-1891) German				
oil	1	2,200	2,200	2,200
FIRMIN, Claude (1864-1944) French				
oil	9	969-4,917	2,242	2,090
wc/d	3	529-751	636	630
FIRTH, Richard M (20th C) British				
oil	3	9,000-18,000	12,422	10,266
FISCHBACH, Johann (1797-1871) Austrian				
oil	2	1,290-3,148	2,219	1,290
wc/d	1	1,178	1,178	1,178
FISCHER, Anton Otto (1882-1962) American				
oil	7	1,000-16,000	5,571	4,000
FISCHER, August (1854-1921) Danish				
oil	11	611-5,702	2,051	1,205
FISCHER, Carl (1887-1962) Danish				
oil	2	731-2,000	1,365	731
FISCHER, Carl (1888-1987) Swiss				
3D	1	7,632	7,632	7,632
FISCHER, Edmund (?-1944) Danish				
oil	1	1,107	1,107	1,107
FISCHER, Ernst Albert (1853-1932) German				
oil	2	2,750-4,110	3,430	2,750
FISCHER, Ernst Maria (1907-1939) German				
oil	1	2,213	2,213	2,213
FISCHER, Franz (1900-) Czechoslovakian				
3D	1	5,211	5,211	5,211
FISCHER, Hans Christian (1849-1886) Danish				
oil	1	1,352	1,352	1,352

Name	No.	Price Range	Average	Median
FISCHER, Heinrich (1820-1886) Swiss				
oil	1	1,908	1,908	1,908
wc/d	1	2,595	2,595	2,595
FISCHER, Joel (1947-) American				
3D	1	1,730	1,730	1,730
FISCHER, Johann Georg Paul (1786-1875) German				
wc/d	2	1,033-4,472	2,752	1,033
FISCHER, Johannes (1888-1955) Austrian				
oil	1	2,277	2,277	2,277
FISCHER, Lothar (1933-) German				
wc/d	1	468	468	468
3D	7	1,794-12,959	5,296	4,305
FISCHER, Ludwig Hans (1848-1915) German				
oil	2	1,937-9,955	5,946	1,937
wc/d	3	968-5,011	2,734	2,225
FISCHER, Oskar (1892-1955) German				
oil	1	2,589	2,589	2,589
wc/d	1	1,553	1,553	1,553
FISCHER, Paul (1860-1934) Danish				
oil	34	680-146,449	29,454	17,390
wc/d	5	626-1,581	1,078	949
FISCHER, Rob (1968-) American				
wc/d	1	3,000	3,000	3,000
FISCHER, Vincenz (1729-1810) Austrian				
oil	1	24,276	24,276	24,276
FISCHER-DERENBURG, Friedrich Wilhelm (1882-1973) German				
oil	1	1,089	1,089	1,089
FISCHETTI, Fedele (1734-1789) Italian				
oil	1	57,329	57,329	57,329
wc/d	2	1,100-5,000	3,050	1,100
FISCHHOF, Georg (1859-1914) Austrian				
oil	9	556-3,306	1,588	1,452
FISCHINGER, Oskar (1900-1967) American				
oil	1	3,000	3,000	3,000
FISCHL, Eric (1948-) American				
oil	8	20,000-450,000	162,937	95,000
wc/d	7	4,000-30,393	13,951	9,000
FISCHLI, Peter and WEISS, David (20th C) Swiss				
3D	1	31,860	31,860	31,860
FISH, George Drummond (1876-1938) Irish				
wc/d	5	463-3,600	1,812	1,574
FISH, Janet (1938-) American				
oil	3	6,000-32,500	18,166	16,000
wc/d	3	1,500-6,500	4,166	4,500
FISHER, Alvan (1792-1863) American				
oil	2	13,000-16,000	14,500	13,000
FISHER, Anna S (1873-1942) American				
oil	1	1,100	1,100	1,100
FISHER, Harrison (1875-1934) American				
wc/d	2	400-1,700	1,050	400
FISHER, Hugo Antoine (1854-1916) American				
oil	3	1,500-32,500	12,500	3,500
wc/d	5	500-2,300	1,064	672
FISHER, Percy Harland (1867-1944) British				
oil	3	1,665-13,230	6,965	6,000
wc/d	2	519-865	692	519
FISHER, Rowland (1885-1969) British				
oil	3	739-3,460	1,708	925
FISHER, Vernon (1943-) American				
oil	1	3,200	3,200	3,200
FISHER, W C (19th C) British				
oil	1	2,694	2,694	2,694
FISHER, William Mark (1841-1923) British/American				
oil	5	700-8,505	3,405	2,314
FISHMAN, Louise (1939-) American				
oil	1	8,500	8,500	8,500
FISHWICK, Clifford (1923-1997) British				
oil	5	524-4,114	1,908	1,566
wc/d	1	524	524	524
FISKE, Gertrude (1879-1961) American				
oil	1	2,100	2,100	2,100

Name	No.	Price Range	Average	Median
FISSETTE, Leopold (1814-1889) German				
oil	1	1,784	1,784	1,784
FISSORE, Daniele (1947-) Italian				
oil	17	518-2,569	1,250	1,001
FITCH, Gladys Kelley (1896-1971) American				
oil	1	3,000	3,000	3,000
FITCH, Thomas (19/20th C) American				
oil	1	1,200	1,200	1,200
FITTON, James (1899-1982) British				
wc/d	4	1,800-5,220	3,250	2,500
FITZGERALD, Florence (?-1927) British				
oil	1	3,402	3,402	3,402
FITZGERALD, James (1899-1971) American				
oil	1	3,000	3,000	3,000
wc/d	5	550-20,000	6,910	4,500
FITZGERALD, John Austen (1832-1906) British				
wc/d	1	44,000	44,000	44,000
FITZGERALD, Joseph (fl.1878-1894) Irish				
oil	1	2,264	2,264	2,264
FITZGERALD, Lionel Lemoine (1890-1956) Canadian				
oil	5	2,836-34,443	11,046	4,408
wc/d	14	533-3,711	1,625	1,402
FITZGERALD, Lloyd (1941-) Canadian				
oil	1	1,148	1,148	1,148
FITZHARRIS, Mike (1952-) Irish				
oil	1	2,338	2,338	2,338
FITZI, Johann Ulrich (1798-1855) Swiss				
wc/d	1	5,668	5,668	5,668
FITZPATRICK, Fred (19/20th C) Irish				
oil	1	3,287	3,287	3,287
FIUME, Salvatore (1915-1997) Italian				
oil	16	3,160-30,630	14,455	12,192
wc/d	7	2,290-3,805	2,822	2,586
FIX-MASSEAU, Pierre-Felix (1869-1937) French				
3D	2	3,504-4,000	3,752	3,504
FJAESTAD, Gustaf (1868-1948) Swedish				
oil	4	10,594-35,716	17,768	11,677
wc/d	1	4,113	4,113	4,113
FJELLBOE, Paul (1873-1948) American				
oil	1	2,250	2,250	2,250
FLAGG, H Peabody (1859-1937) American				
oil	2	550-700	625	550
wc/d	1	750	750	750
FLAGG, James Montgomery (1877-1960) American				
oil	1	70,000	70,000	70,000
wc/d	5	2,900-4,750	3,930	3,750
FLAIG, Waldemar (1892-1932) German				
oil	1	2,033	2,033	2,033
FLAMENG, François (1856-1923) French				
oil	2	2,600-19,000	10,800	2,600
FLAMENG, Marie Auguste (1843-1893) French				
oil	2	1,252-1,475	1,363	1,252
FLAMING, Jon (20th C) American				
oil	1	1,750	1,750	1,750
FLAMM, Albert (1823-1906) German				
oil	5	1,901-14,013	6,058	4,545
FLANAGAN, Barry (1941-) British				
wc/d	1	3,131	3,131	3,131
3D	19	2,297-370,001	69,306	12,110
FLANAGAN, Fergal (?) British?				
oil	1	1,573	1,573	1,573
FLANAGAN, Terence P (1929-) British				
oil	6	2,921-8,767	4,778	4,077
wc/d	6	1,520-6,674	3,358	2,945
FLANDIN, Eugène Napoleon (1803-1876) French				
oil	3	2,586-20,846	14,180	19,110
wc/d	3	1,445-3,038	2,056	1,686
FLANDRIN, Jean Hippolyte (1809-1864) French				
oil	1	7,940	7,940	7,940
wc/d	1	2,829	2,829	2,829
FLANDRIN, Jules (1871-1947) French				
oil	5	642-16,562	5,835	3,063

Name	No.	Price Range	Average	Median
FLANDRIN, Paul Jean (1811-1902) French				
oil	2	4,182-13,863	9,022	4,182
FLANNAGAN, John B (1895-1942) American				
3D	1	4,250	4,250	4,250
FLANNERY, Vaughn (1898-1955) American				
oil	1	3,000	3,000	3,000
FLANNIGAN, Moyna (1963-) American				
oil	1	2,000	2,000	2,000
FLASSCHOEN, Gustave (1868-1940) Belgian				
oil	11	591-5,696	2,758	2,116
FLAVELLE, Geoff H (19th C) American				
wc/d	1	1,440	1,440	1,440
FLAVIN, Dan (1933-1996) American				
3D	10	55,000-600,000	241,500	220,000
FLAXMAN, John (1755-1826) British				
wc/d	7	800-28,350	9,066	3,500
FLECK, Joseph A (1892-1977) Austrian				
oil	2	2,000-13,000	7,500	2,000
wc/d	1	2,500	2,500	2,500
FLECK, Karl Anton (1928-1983) Austrian				
oil	2	2,928-5,856	4,392	2,928
wc/d	7	1,405-4,099	2,442	2,524
FLECK, Ralph (1951-) German				
oil	4	1,296-5,143	2,432	1,411
FLEETWOOD-WALKER, Bernard (1893-1969) British				
oil	3	1,505-8,892	3,978	1,539
wc/d	1	555	555	555
FLEGE, Ernst (1898-1965) German				
oil	1	3,073	3,073	3,073
FLEGEL, Georg (1563-1638) German				
oil	2	60,490-3,600,000	1,830,245	60,490
FLEISCHMANN, Adolf (1892-1969) German				
oil	6	10,829-35,619	26,109	22,384
wc/d	5	2,822-8,465	4,515	3,534
FLEISCHMANN, August (19/20th C) German				
wc/d	1	5,184	5,184	5,184
FLEISCHMANN, Emil (20th C) Austrian				
oil	1	1,316	1,316	1,316
FLEMING, Frank (1940-) American				
3D	1	3,250	3,250	3,250
FLEMING, Ian (1906-1994) British				
wc/d	2	445-2,262	1,353	445
FLEMING, John (1792-1845) British				
oil	1	2,685	2,685	2,685
FLENSBURG, Anette Harboe (1961-) Danish				
oil	4	1,610-5,853	3,681	2,736
FLERS, Camille (1802-1868) French				
oil	1	6,997	6,997	6,997
wc/d	1	1,011	1,011	1,011
FLETCHER, Edwin (1857-1945) British				
oil	14	490-4,524	1,652	883
wc/d	1	443	443	443
FLETCHER, William Blandford (1858-1936) British				
oil	3	1,800-2,200	2,036	2,108
FLEURY, Antoine Claude (18th C) French				
oil	1	1,455	1,455	1,455
FLEURY, J Vivien de (19th C) British				
oil	2	1,770-11,040	6,405	1,770
FLEURY, Leon Francois Antoine (1804-1858) French				
oil	3	1,781-14,027	6,795	4,579
FLEURY, Lucien (1928-) French				
oil	1	2,033	2,033	2,033
FLEURY, Mme Fanny (1848-?) French				
oil	3	1,764-2,788	2,296	2,338
FLEURY, Pierre (1900-1985) French				
oil	1	2,228	2,228	2,228
FLEURY, Sylvie (1961-) French				
oil	1	6,020	6,020	6,020
3D	4	1,519-25,800	15,931	11,000
FLEXOR, Samson (1907-1971) French				
oil	1	2,760	2,760	2,760
wc/d	1	1,800	1,800	1,800

Name	No.	Price Range	Average	Median
FLICKEL, Paul Franz (1852-1903) German				
oil	2	1,940-8,227	5,083	1,940
FLIEHER, Karl (1881-1958) Austrian				
oil	2	887-1,632	1,259	887
wc/d	5	486-2,903	1,149	760
FLIGHT, Claude (1881-1955) British				
oil	1	12,974	12,974	12,974
wc/d	1	1,456	1,456	1,456
FLINCK, Govaert (1615-1660) Dutch				
oil	3	50,000-284,800	154,418	128,456
wc/d	3	3,036-4,905	4,098	4,355
FLINT, Sir William Russell (1880-1969) British				
oil	2	34,200-50,000	42,100	34,200
wc/d	65	350-74,340	15,869	9,200
FLINTE, Fritz (1876-1963) German				
oil	2	1,674-2,338	2,006	1,674
FLOCH, Josef (1895-1977) American/Austrian				
oil	9	5,500-46,124	24,349	18,740
wc/d	1	608	608	608
FLOCH, Lionel (1895-1972) French				
oil	2	1,010-4,208	2,609	1,010
FLOCKENHAUS, Heinz (1856-1919) German				
oil	2	1,800-2,057	1,928	1,800
FLOOD, Daro (20th C) American				
3D	1	2,500	2,500	2,500
FLOOD, Mark (1957-) American				
oil	1	5,500	5,500	5,500
FLOQUET, Christian (1961-) Swiss				
oil	1	1,461	1,461	1,461
FLORA, Paul (1922-) Austrian				
oil	1	1,168	1,168	1,168
wc/d	17	701-3,534	1,852	1,800
FLOREANI, Roberto (1956-) Italian				
oil	3	1,573-2,829	2,052	1,754
wc/d	1	1,210	1,210	1,210
FLORES KAPEROTXIPI, Mauricio (1901-1997) Argentinian				
oil	6	2,351-13,000	6,147	4,784
wc/d	1	837	837	837
FLORES, Pedro (1897-1967) Spanish				
oil	3	618-15,429	8,123	8,324
wc/d	2	1,794-8,159	4,976	1,794
FLORIAN, Maximilian (1901-1982) Austrian				
oil	1	6,027	6,027	6,027
FLORIDO BERNILS, Enrique (1873-1929) Spanish				
oil	1	1,381	1,381	1,381
FLORIDO, Enrique (19th C) Spanish				
oil	1	3,024	3,024	3,024
FLORIS, Carmelo (1891-1960) Italian				
oil	1	11,712	11,712	11,712
FLORIS, Frans (16/17th C) Flemish				
oil	1	19,027	19,027	19,027
wc/d	1	3,551	3,551	3,551
FLORIS, Frans (elder) (1516-1570) Flemish				
wc/d	1	4,995	4,995	4,995
FLOUQUET, Pierre Louis (1900-1967) Belgian				
wc/d	3	1,236-2,877	2,010	1,918
FLOUTIER, Louis (20th C) French				
oil	5	2,152-22,986	8,831	6,932
FLOYD, Donald H (1892-1965) British				
oil	5	739-1,628	1,090	1,012
FLUCK, Johann Peter (1902-1954) Swiss				
oil	3	1,068-2,429	1,609	1,332
FLUCK, Martin Peter (1935-) Swiss				
oil	1	2,137	2,137	2,137
FLUGGEN, Hans (1875-1942) German				
oil	1	1,459	1,459	1,459
FLUMIANI, Ugo (1876-1938) Italian				
oil	2	4,243-13,053	8,648	4,243
FLURY, Burckhardt (1862-1928) Swiss				
oil	3	583-2,124	1,457	1,665
wc/d	2	486-1,621	1,053	486

Name	No.	Price Range	Average	Median
FLURY, Johannes Christian (1804-1880) Swiss				
wc/d	1	1,135	1,135	1,135
FOA, A (fl.c.1900) ?				
wc/d	3	1,518-2,335	1,985	2,102
FOCARDI, Piero (1889-1945) Italian				
oil	2	1,215-2,870	2,042	1,215
FOCARDI, Ruggero (1864-1934) Italian				
oil	5	1,197-22,150	6,107	1,522
FOCHT, Frederic (1879-?) French				
3D	1	2,038	2,038	2,038
FOCK, Geradus Hubertus von Brucken (1859-1935) Dutch				
oil	1	1,030	1,030	1,030
FOGELIN, Anders (1933-1982) Swedish				
oil	1	2,775	2,775	2,775
FOGELQUIST, Jorgen (1927-) Swedish				
oil	3	590-1,982	1,121	793
wc/d	1	661	661	661
FOGGIA, Mario Moretti (1882-1954) Italian				
oil	4	2,676-5,988	4,008	2,919
FOGGIE, David (1878-1948) British				
oil	2	2,124-9,790	5,957	2,124
wc/d	3	463-1,373	876	792
FOGGINI, Giovanni Battista (1652-1725) Italian				
wc/d	2	3,330-33,300	18,315	3,330
FOHR, Karl Philipp (1795-1818) German				
wc/d	2	20,027-50,000	35,013	20,027
FOKAS, Odysseus (1865-1946) Greek				
oil	1	3,806	3,806	3,806
FOLCHI, Ferdinand (1822-1883) Italian				
wc/d	1	1,392	1,392	1,392
FOLCHI, Paulo (19th C) Italian				
wc/d	1	3,540	3,540	3,540
FOLDES, Peter (1924-) Hungarian				
oil	2	542-953	747	542
wc/d	1	420	420	420
FOLEY, John Henry (1818-1874) British				
3D	4	2,580-20,616	11,581	4,968
FOLINSBEE, John F (1892-1972) American				
oil	13	650-250,000	34,096	10,000
wc/d	1	1,500	1,500	1,500
FOLKARD, Charles (1878-1963) British				
wc/d	2	525-3,872	2,198	525
FOLKERTS, Poppe (1875-1943) German				
oil	4	2,910-15,760	7,846	5,455
FOLLAK, Alex (1915-) Russian				
oil	2	937-1,536	1,236	937
FOLLINI, Carlo (1848-1938) Italian				
oil	10	3,507-20,164	8,030	5,966
FOLMER, Georges (1895-1977) French				
oil	6	2,071-6,304	3,978	3,575
wc/d	2	1,818-3,637	2,727	1,818
FOLON, Jean Michel (1934-2005) Belgian				
wc/d	10	1,581-8,281	5,205	5,514
3D	1	128,571	128,571	128,571
FOLTYN, Frantisek (1891-1976) Czechoslovakian				
oil	1	17,341	17,341	17,341
wc/d	1	1,518	1,518	1,518
FOLTZ, Philipp von (1805-1877) German				
wc/d	2	879-1,885	1,382	879
FOMENOK, Stanislav (1941-) Russian				
oil	7	660-1,925	1,124	1,138
FOMEZ, Antonio (1937-) Italian				
oil	1	1,230	1,230	1,230
FON, Jade (1911-1983) American				
wc/d	2	6,500-8,500	7,500	6,500
FONDA, Enrico (1892-1929) Italian				
oil	1	2,443	2,443	2,443
FONECHE, Andre (20th C) French				
oil	1	1,686	1,686	1,686
FONSECA, Caio (1958-) American				
oil	4	19,000-38,000	24,750	20,000

Name	No.	Price Range	Average	Median
FONSECA, Gonzalo (1922-1997) Uruguayan				
oil	3	3,500-6,500	5,066	5,200
wc/d	1	647	647	647
3D	1	75,000	75,000	75,000
FONSECA, Reynaldo (1925-) Brazilian				
oil	1	21,000	21,000	21,000
FONT, Constantin (1890-1954) French				
oil	4	817-2,625	1,557	1,352
FONTAINE, Alexandre Victor (1815-?) French				
oil	2	4,750-8,000	6,375	4,750
FONTAINE, L (19th C) ?				
oil	1	4,052	4,052	4,052
FONTAINE, Pierre François Leonard (1762-1853) French				
wc/d	3	51,042-115,451	74,942	58,333
FONTAINE, Thomas Sherwood la (1915-) British				
oil	2	15,000-26,000	20,500	15,000
FONTAN, Leo (1884-1965) French				
oil	2	974-1,236	1,105	974
FONTANA, Ernesto (1837-1918) Italian				
oil	1	7,229	7,229	7,229
FONTANA, Lavinia (1552-1614) Italian				
oil	2	69,200-70,067	69,633	69,200
FONTANA, Lucio (1899-1968) Italian				
oil	18	5,915-2,400,000	456,780	264,000
wc/d	78	1,427-1,056,000	169,679	37,479
3D	73	1,753-920,400	89,241	42,480
FONTANA, Roberto (1844-1907) Italian				
oil	5	1,197-3,534	2,266	1,796
wc/d	1	3,884	3,884	3,884
FONTANAROSA, Lucien (1912-1975) French				
oil	2	800-820	810	800
wc/d	1	2,293	2,293	2,293
FONTANESI, Antonio (1818-1882) Italian				
oil	1	32,363	32,363	32,363
FONTEBASSO, Francesco (1709-1769) Italian				
oil	4	6,473-242,200	76,043	18,000
wc/d	7	892-4,000	2,758	3,970
FONTENAY, Jean Baptiste Belin de (1653-1715) French				
oil	2	29,410-42,000	35,705	29,410
FONTENAY, Jean Baptiste Belin de (younger) (1688-1730) French				
oil	1	11,892	11,892	11,892
FONTENE, Robert (1892-1980) French				
oil	90	477-4,534	1,252	954
wc/d	3	477-1,670	1,053	1,014
FONTIROSSI, Roberto (1940-) Italian				
oil	6	648-971	843	825
wc/d	1	799	799	799
FONTOFF, N (20th C) Russian?				
oil	1	1,305	1,305	1,305
FONVILLE, Horace-Antoine (1832-1910) French				
oil	6	527-3,484	1,439	527
FONVILLE, Nicolas Victor (1805-1856) French				
oil	3	596-3,330	1,962	1,962
FOO FAT, Dulcie (1946-) Canadian?				
oil	2	620-5,329	2,974	620
FOOTE, Will Howe (1874-1965) American				
oil	2	2,500-6,000	4,250	2,500
FOPPIANI, Gustavo (1925-1986) Italian				
oil	2	1,300-7,633	4,466	1,300
wc/d	3	1,029-3,500	2,143	1,900
FORAIN, Jean Louis (1852-1931) French				
oil	9	3,039-12,950	6,882	6,372
wc/d	18	480-53,650	4,970	750
FORBES, Bart John (1939-) American				
oil	1	2,250	2,250	2,250
wc/d	1	550	550	550
FORBES, Charles Stuart (1856-1926) American				
oil	1	14,865	14,865	14,865
FORBES, Edwin Austin (1839-1895) American				
oil	1	7,000	7,000	7,000
FORBES, Elizabeth Adela (1859-1912) British				
wc/d	1	14,080	14,080	14,080

Name	No.	Price Range	Average	Median
FORBES, Michael (1968-) British				
oil	5	870-4,048	1,632	968
FORBES, Robert (1948-) American				
oil	1	2,500	2,500	2,500
FORBES, Stanhope Alexander (1857-1947) British				
oil	7	1,760-88,920	35,227	32,130
FORD, Henry Chapman (1828-1894) American				
oil	6	2,000-35,000	12,208	5,000
FORD, Henry Justice (1860-1941) British				
oil	1	1,593	1,593	1,593
wc/d	2	1,320-2,816	2,068	1,320
FORD, K Doyle (1910-1993) American				
oil	1	1,000	1,000	1,000
FORD, Marcus (1914-) British				
oil	7	435-1,496	932	1,044
wc/d	1	452	452	452
FOREAU, Louis Henri (1866-1938) French				
oil	6	510-4,200	1,336	771
FOREST, E (19th C) Continental				
oil	1	2,860	2,860	2,860
FOREST, Roy de (1930-) American				
wc/d	3	2,500-12,000	6,083	3,750
FORESTIER, Adolphe (1801-1885) French				
oil	1	1,000	1,000	1,000
FORESTIER, Étienne (19/20th C) French				
3D	1	2,595	2,595	2,595
FORESTIER, Henri-Claude (1875-1922) Swiss				
wc/d	1	2,546	2,546	2,546
FORET, Eugene la (20th C) American?				
oil	1	3,000	3,000	3,000
FORETAY, Alfred (1861-1944) Swiss				
oil	3	731-3,505	1,967	1,665
FORG, Gunther (1952-) German				
oil	10	4,779-31,680	15,595	14,000
wc/d	13	468-16,365	3,651	1,529
3D	5	2,827-8,000	5,062	5,160
FORGIOLI, Attilio (1933-) Italian				
oil	3	589-1,784	1,195	1,214
wc/d	1	409	409	409
FORKUN, Roy (20th C) American				
oil	1	1,000	1,000	1,000
FORNARA, Carlo (1871-1968) Italian				
oil	1	45,000	45,000	45,000
FORNER, Raquel (1902-1990) Argentinian				
oil	5	5,000-90,000	42,800	36,000
FORNEROD, Rodolphe (1877-1953) Swiss				
wc/d	2	701-5,260	2,980	701
FORNES ISERN, Pablo (1930-) Spanish				
oil	1	1,796	1,796	1,796
FORNS BADA, Carlos (1956-) French				
oil	2	1,078-3,038	2,058	1,078
wc/d	1	1,189	1,189	1,189
FORRESTALL, Thomas de Vany (1936-) Canadian				
oil	1	5,033	5,033	5,033
wc/d	3	410-1,394	763	485
FORSBERG, Carl Johan (1868-1938) Swedish				
wc/d	2	802-1,521	1,161	802
FORSSELL, Victor (1846-1931) Swedish				
oil	2	927-1,887	1,407	927
FORSTEN, Lennart (1817-1886) Finnish				
oil	1	1,286	1,286	1,286
FORSTER, George (1817-1896) American				
oil	1	55,000	55,000	55,000
FORSTER, George E (19th C) American				
oil	1	6,000	6,000	6,000
FORSTER, Noel (1932-) British				
oil	1	1,701	1,701	1,701
wc/d	1	473	473	473
FORSTER, Paul (20th C) American				
oil	1	1,000	1,000	1,000
FORSTERLING, Otto (1843-?) German				
oil	1	1,900	1,900	1,900

Name	No.	Price Range	Average	Median
FORSYTHE, Victor Clyde (1885-1962) American				
oil	4	1,500-7,500	3,562	2,000
FORT, Jean Antoine Simeon (1793-1861) French				
wc/d	2	1,286-3,600	2,443	1,286
FORT, Theodore (19th C) French				
oil	2	2,336-2,719	2,527	2,336
wc/d	1	714	714	714
FORTE, Luca (fl.1625-c.1670) Italian				
oil	2	13,000-783,200	398,100	13,000
FORTE, Vicente (1912-1980) Argentinian				
oil	7	1,800-9,000	4,222	2,915
FORTESCUE, Henrietta Anne (c.1765-1841) British				
wc/d	1	1,000	1,000	1,000
FORTESCUE, William B (1850-1924) British				
oil	7	1,335-189,000	33,010	9,256
FORTI, Ettore (19th C) Italian				
oil	3	1,405-80,000	32,468	16,000
FORTIN, Charles (1815-1865) French				
oil	1	1,870	1,870	1,870
wc/d	1	16,209	16,209	16,209
FORTIN, Marc-Aurele (1888-1970) Canadian				
oil	25	4,509-164,929	39,718	19,941
wc/d	9	1,783-31,019	9,755	7,090
FORTIN, Therese (20th C) French				
oil	1	4,671	4,671	4,671
FORTUNATO, Franco (1946-) Italian				
oil	10	895-2,458	1,457	1,230
FORTUNEY (1878-1950) French				
wc/d	5	771-3,211	1,637	1,401
FORTUNEY, Louis (1878-1950) French				
oil	1	535	535	535
wc/d	1	2,928	2,928	2,928
FORTUNSKI, Leo von (19th C) ?				
oil	1	2,314	2,314	2,314
FORTUNY Y CARBO, Mariano (1838-1874) Spanish				
oil	5	1,500-110,400	34,013	21,500
wc/d	5	654-15,640	6,466	2,580
FORTUNY Y MADRAZO, Mariano (1871-1949) Spanish				
oil	4	2,552-6,578	5,039	5,068
FORUP, Carl Christian (1883-1939) Danish				
oil	2	487-1,897	1,192	487
FOSCHI, Francesco (?-1780) Italian				
oil	3	43,552-70,000	52,953	45,308
FOSCHI, Pier Francesco (1502-1567) Italian				
oil	1	80,000	80,000	80,000
FOSIE, Johanna (1726-1764) Danish				
wc/d	1	4,585	4,585	4,585
FOSS, Peder Nielsen (1821-1882) Danish				
oil	1	1,588	1,588	1,588
FOSSATI, Andrea (1844-?) Italian				
oil	2	8,653-22,000	15,326	8,653
FOSSATI, Enrico (?) Italian?				
oil	1	1,100	1,100	1,100
FOSSOUX, Claude (1946-) French				
oil	3	518-2,443	1,311	972
FOSTER, Ben (1852-1926) American				
oil	4	450-12,000	4,037	500
FOSTER, Gilbert (?) British				
oil	1	2,685	2,685	2,685
wc/d	1	4,849	4,849	4,849
FOSTER, Hal (1892-1982) American				
wc/d	1	1,600	1,600	1,600
FOSTER, John (1908-1989) American				
oil	4	1,200-9,500	3,937	1,800
FOSTER, John Ernest (1877-1965) British				
oil	1	2,610	2,610	2,610
FOSTER, Myles Birket (1825-1899) British				
oil	1	3,933	3,933	3,933
wc/d	42	450-45,240	11,208	6,612
FOSTER, Viola (20th C) American?				
oil	1	1,200	1,200	1,200

Name	No.	Price Range	Average	Median
FOSTER, William Gilbert (1855-1906) British				
oil	1	8,352	8,352	8,352
wc/d	1	522	522	522
FOSTER, William Harden (1886-1941) American				
oil	2	2,800-3,250	3,025	2,800
FOTHERGILL, Charles (19/20th C) British				
wc/d	1	1,392	1,392	1,392
FOTINSKY, Serge (1897-1971) Russian				
oil	7	726-2,757	1,905	2,277
wc/d	6	479-850	650	615
FOTOPOULOS, Dionyssis (1943-) Greek				
wc/d	1	1,584	1,584	1,584
FOUACE, Guillaume Romain (1827-1895) French				
oil	6	2,253-30,000	14,097	9,710
wc/d	1	5,583	5,583	5,583
FOUGERON, Andre (1913-) French				
oil	1	1,315	1,315	1,315
FOUGEROUSSE, Claude (20th C) French				
oil	1	3,284	3,284	3,284
FOUILLE, Georges (1909-1994) French				
wc/d	1	1,320	1,320	1,320
FOUJITA (1886-1968) French/Japanese				
wc/d	1	3,884	3,884	3,884
FOUJITA, Tsuguharu (1886-1968) French/Japanese				
oil	21	4,600-185,000	82,672	79,200
wc/d	57	1,178-118,400	23,444	18,000
FOULKES, Lynn (1934-) American				
oil	1	6,500	6,500	6,500
FOUQUERAY, Charles (1872-1956) French				
oil	5	526-15,000	6,463	2,694
wc/d	10	477-3,236	1,311	703
FOUQUIER, Jacques (1580-1659) French				
oil	3	14,833-28,480	20,652	18,643
FOURMOIS, Theodore (1814-1871) Belgian				
oil	5	468-6,562	3,198	1,849
FOURNIALS, J Marguerite (20th C) French				
oil	1	2,959	2,959	2,959
FOURNIER, Alain (1931-1983) French				
oil	4	1,193-2,386	1,671	1,196
FOURNIER, Alexis Jean (1865-1948) American				
oil	1	8,500	8,500	8,500
FOURNIER, Charles (1803-1854) French				
oil	1	4,435	4,435	4,435
FOURNIER, Paul (1939-) Canadian				
oil	1	1,493	1,493	1,493
FOURNIER, Victor Alfred (1872-1924) French				
oil	2	700-2,342	1,521	700
FOWERAKER, A Moulton (1873-1942) British				
oil	1	2,196	2,196	2,196
wc/d	17	854-4,450	2,190	1,850
FOWLER, Daniel (1810-1894) British?				
wc/d	3	512-2,460	1,161	512
FOWLER, F Ron (1946-) American				
oil	2	900-1,500	1,200	900
FOWLER, Graham (1952-) Canadian				
oil	1	2,531	2,531	2,531
FOWLER, Robert (1853-1926) British				
oil	9	452-6,228	1,494	920
FOWLES, Arthur W (c.1815-1878) British				
oil	5	2,392-14,025	6,902	6,960
FOX, Charles James (1860-?) British				
wc/d	1	2,941	2,941	2,941
FOX, E M (19th C) British				
oil	1	1,030	1,030	1,030
FOX, Edwin M (19th C) British				
oil	1	1,496	1,496	1,496
FOX, Emanuel Phillips (1865-1915) Australian				
oil	1	22,125	22,125	22,125
FOX, John R (1927-) Canadian				
oil	5	697-9,384	3,422	1,621
wc/d	1	1,312	1,312	1,312

Name	No.	Price Range	Average	Median
FOX, Kathleen (1880-1963) British				
oil	1	4,325	4,325	4,325
wc/d	2	1,560-2,121	1,840	1,560
FOX, R Atkinson (1860-c.1927) American/Canadian				
oil	6	1,300-6,000	2,950	1,900
FOX, William Edward (1872-?) British				
oil	1	1,479	1,479	1,479
FRAASS, Erich (1893-1974) German				
oil	2	1,076-4,697	2,886	1,076
FRACCAROLI, Innocenzo (1805-1882) Italian				
3D	1	20,274	20,274	20,274
FRAGIACOMO, Pietro (1856-1922) Italian				
oil	8	1,796-67,890	17,744	2,356
wc/d	1	1,757	1,757	1,757
FRAGONARD, Alexandre Evariste (1780-1850) French				
wc/d	5	579-4,519	3,095	3,480
FRAGONARD, Jean Honore (1732-1806) French				
oil	6	3,270-4,440,000	1,051,797	70,000
wc/d	9	2,066-83,244	20,783	7,000
FRAGSTEIN, Marie von (1870-1954) German				
oil	1	1,178	1,178	1,178
FRAI, Felicita (1914-) Czechoslovakian				
oil	1	1,070	1,070	1,070
FRAILE, Alfonso (1930-1988) Spanish				
oil	1	5,363	5,363	5,363
wc/d	3	2,829-9,105	4,982	3,012
FRAME, Robert Aaron (1924-1999) American				
oil	3	2,200-3,000	2,733	3,000
FRAMPTON, Edward Reginald (1872-1923) British				
oil	2	920-18,900	9,910	920
FRAN-BARO (1926-2000) French				
oil	8	477-3,575	1,256	729
FRANC-LAMY, Pierre (1855-1919) French				
oil	1	2,580	2,580	2,580
FRANCAIS, Anne (1909-1995) French				
oil	5	1,483-2,990	2,302	2,264
FRANCAIS, François Louis (1814-1897) French				
oil	2	900-937	918	900
wc/d	2	486-2,571	1,528	486
FRANCE, Charles (19th C) British				
oil	1	1,313	1,313	1,313
FRANCES Y PASCUAL, Placido (1840-?) Spanish				
wc/d	1	1,907	1,907	1,907
FRANCES, Juana (1926-1990) Spanish				
oil	1	3,315	3,315	3,315
FRANCESCHI, M de (1849-1896) Italian				
wc/d	1	1,200	1,200	1,200
FRANCESCHI, Mariano de (1849-1896) Italian				
oil	2	5,825-9,555	7,690	5,825
wc/d	1	1,089	1,089	1,089
FRANCESCHINI, Baldassare (1611-1689) Italian				
wc/d	4	1,400-2,259	1,927	1,800
FRANCESCHINI, Edoardo (1928-) Italian				
oil	9	738-1,781	1,352	1,457
wc/d	3	1,145-2,799	1,719	1,214
FRANCESCHINI, Marco Antonio (1648-1729) Italian				
oil	2	111,000-420,000	265,500	111,000
wc/d	1	4,861	4,861	4,861
FRANCESCHINI, Vincenzo (1812-1885) Italian				
oil	1	6,049	6,049	6,049
FRANCESCO DA VOLTERRA (14th C) Italian				
oil	1	420,000	420,000	420,000
FRANCESCO, Benjamino de (?-1869) Italian				
oil	1	12,123	12,123	12,123
FRANCESE, Franco (1920-1996) Italian				
oil	3	2,185-5,890	3,720	3,086
wc/d	2	2,744-2,829	2,786	2,744
FRANCHERE, Joseph-Charles (1866-1921) Canadian				
oil	4	530-3,526	1,917	1,144
FRANCHI, Pietro (19th C) Italian				
3D	1	14,449	14,449	14,449

Name	No.	Price Range	Average	Median
FRANCHI, Rossello di Jacopo (1377-1456) Italian				
oil	1	85,000	85,000	85,000
FRANCHINO, Telesforo (1892-1964) Italian				
oil	1	1,551	1,551	1,551
FRANCIA, Alexandre T (1820-1884) French				
wc/d	5	1,204-5,068	2,833	1,944
FRANCIA, Camillo (1955-) Italian				
oil	23	530-4,056	1,702	1,585
FRANCIA, Francesco di Marco (1450-1517) Italian				
oil	1	15,000	15,000	15,000
FRANCIA, François Louis Thomas (1772-1839) French				
wc/d	1	20,760	20,760	20,760
FRANCIA, Giacomo (1486-1557) Italian				
oil	1	10,680	10,680	10,680
FRANCIA, Giulio and Giacomo (16th C) Italian				
oil	1	31,808	31,808	31,808
FRANCIABIGIO (1482-1525) Italian				
oil	1	580,000	580,000	580,000
FRANCILLON, René (1876-1973) Swiss				
oil	1	1,293	1,293	1,293
FRANCIS, John F (1808-1886) American				
oil	1	60,000	60,000	60,000
FRANCIS, Mark (1962-) British				
oil	8	1,740-12,900	7,366	7,068
FRANCIS, Sam (1923-1994) American				
oil	104	3,408-600,000	40,640	20,000
wc/d	37	3,200-240,500	39,697	17,022
FRANCIS, Victor (1854-?) Belgian				
oil	1	3,853	3,853	3,853
FRANCISCO, J Bond (1863-1931) American				
oil	2	1,000-4,000	2,500	1,000
FRANCISCO, Pietro de (1873-1969) Italian				
oil	3	5,271-18,740	13,859	17,568
wc/d	1	954	954	954
FRANCK, Albert Jacques (1899-1973) Canadian				
oil	3	573-4,408	2,072	1,237
wc/d	4	1,066-3,608	2,134	1,476
FRANCK, Frederick S (1909-) American				
oil	2	1,100-1,400	1,250	1,100
FRANCK, Hector (1961-) Cuban				
oil	3	576-1,560	1,012	900
FRANCK, Philipp (1860-1944) German				
oil	6	11,449-37,479	19,807	15,265
wc/d	1	3,816	3,816	3,816
FRANCKE, Bernhard Christoph (?-1729) German				
oil	4	3,612-90,306	31,607	6,020
FRANCKE-NAUTSCHUTZ, Rudolf (1860-?) German				
oil	1	1,940	1,940	1,940
FRANCKEN, Frans II (1581-1642) Flemish				
oil	8	2,281-369,452	92,197	7,068
FRANCKEN, Frans II and NEEFFS, Pieter (younger) (16/17th C) Flemish				
oil	1	19,030	19,030	19,030
FRANCO Y CORDERO, Jose (19th C) Spanish				
oil	4	1,823-5,786	3,532	2,420
FRANCO, Giovanni Battista (c.1498-1580) Italian				
wc/d	3	3,330-10,000	5,910	4,400
FRANCOIS, Ange (1800-?) Flemish				
oil	1	3,053	3,053	3,053
FRANCOIS, Charles Émile (1821-?) French				
oil	1	4,308	4,308	4,308
FRANCOIS, Georges (1880-1968) French				
oil	4	1,079-5,394	3,337	1,818
wc/d	2	482-719	600	482
FRANCOIS, Joseph Charles (1851-1940) Belgian				
oil	11	561-45,796	6,098	953
FRANCOIS, Pierre Joseph C (1759-1851) Flemish				
oil	4	480-2,625	1,134	584
FRANCUCCI, Innocenzo (1494-1550) Italian				
oil	1	181,633	181,633	181,633
FRANDSEN, Emile Theodore (1902-1969) ?				
oil	2	1,437-2,514	1,975	1,437

Name	No.	Price Range	Average	Median
FRANDSEN, Erik A (1957-) Danish				
oil	6	2,425-6,438	4,117	2,910
wc/d	3	808-4,849	2,155	808
3D	1	5,634	5,634	5,634
FRANDZEN, Eugene M (1893-1972) American				
oil	1	1,900	1,900	1,900
FRANGELLA, Luis (1944-1990) Argentinian				
oil	1	1,078	1,078	1,078
FRANGI, Giovanni (1959-) Italian				
oil	13	2,973-16,829	6,739	4,359
wc/d	7	637-5,825	2,674	1,942
FRANGIAMORE, Salvatore (1853-1915) Italian				
oil	3	3,514-12,603	8,792	10,260
FRANGIPANE, Niccolo (1555-1600) Italian				
oil	1	62,300	62,300	62,300
FRANK WILL (1900-1951) French				
oil	9	1,100-4,560	2,884	3,090
wc/d	35	626-6,630	2,050	1,638
FRANK, Franz (1897-1986) German				
oil	7	1,821-4,560	3,046	2,631
wc/d	1	727	727	727
FRANK, Franz Friedrich (1627-1687) German				
oil	1	10,235	10,235	10,235
FRANK, Friedrich (1871-1945) Austrian				
wc/d	8	727-7,124	3,541	2,420
FRANK, Frigyes (1890-1976) Hungarian				
oil	1	7,965	7,965	7,965
FRANK, Hans (1884-1948) Austrian				
oil	4	1,818-4,796	3,226	2,170
wc/d	1	1,940	1,940	1,940
FRANK, Jean Michel (1893-1941) French				
3D	1	2,100	2,100	2,100
FRANK, Johan Willem (1720-1761) Dutch				
oil	1	2,592	2,592	2,592
FRANK, Leo (1884-1959) Austrian				
oil	1	4,795	4,795	4,795
FRANK, Lucien (1857-1920) Belgian				
oil	17	598-28,603	5,869	3,575
wc/d	6	939-3,884	2,669	2,460
FRANK, Magda (20th C) Argentinian				
3D	6	6,000-32,000	15,916	12,000
FRANK, Mary (1933-) American				
oil	1	4,000	4,000	4,000
FRANK, Raoul (1867-1939) Austrian				
oil	1	2,572	2,572	2,572
FRANK-KRAUSS, Robert (1893-1950) German				
oil	6	558-2,386	1,282	1,178
FRANKE, Albert (1860-1924) German				
oil	3	1,720-30,000	11,327	2,262
FRANKEN, Paul von (1818-1884) German				
oil	2	19,842-46,711	33,276	19,842
FRANKENTHALER, Helen (1928-) American				
oil	6	55,000-600,000	195,000	60,000
FRANKL, Adolf (1903-1983) Austrian				
oil	1	3,596	3,596	3,596
FRANKL, Franz (1881-1940) German				
oil	1	1,168	1,168	1,168
FRANKL, Gerhart (1901-1965) Austrian				
wc/d	2	1,514-16,714	9,114	1,514
FRANQUELIN, Jean Augustin (1798-1839) French				
oil	2	5,860-9,790	7,825	5,860
FRANQUINET, Eugene Pierre (1875-1940) American				
oil	1	1,600	1,600	1,600
FRANSIOLI, Thomas Adrian (1906-) American				
oil	1	2,750	2,750	2,750
FRANZ, Ettore Roesler (1845-1907) Italian				
wc/d	5	6,372-18,585	9,717	7,560
FRANZEN, John E (1942-) Swedish				
oil	1	15,857	15,857	15,857
FRANZEN, Werner (1928-) German				
3D	1	1,937	1,937	1,937

Name	No.	Price Range	Average	Median
FRAPPA, Jose (1854-1904) French				
oil	1	1,070	1,070	1,070
FRARY, Michael (1918-) American				
oil	1	8,000	8,000	8,000
wc/d	3	700-1,300	1,033	1,100
FRASCA, Nato (1931-) Italian				
wc/d	1	1,001	1,001	1,001
FRASER, A (19th C) British				
oil	1	1,691	1,691	1,691
FRASER, Alexander (jnr) (1828-1899) British				
oil	4	560-2,422	1,252	845
FRASER, Alexander (snr) (1786-1865) British				
oil	3	1,281-22,880	9,963	5,728
FRASER, Alexander (19th C) British				
oil	1	1,796	1,796	1,796
FRASER, Alexander (1940-) British				
oil	1	1,056	1,056	1,056
FRASER, Alexander Anderson (fl.1884-1885) British				
wc/d	1	1,229	1,229	1,229
FRASER, Calum (1956-) French				
wc/d	1	1,549	1,549	1,549
FRASER, Charles (1782-1860) American				
wc/d	1	1,750	1,750	1,750
FRASER, Claude Lovat (1890-1921) British				
wc/d	3	661-2,275	1,326	1,044
FRASER, Donald Hamilton (1929-) British				
oil	13	500-12,000	5,525	4,500
wc/d	2	4,301-10,000	7,150	4,301
FRASER, James Earle (1876-1953) American				
3D	2	2,500-11,000	6,750	2,500
FRASER, John (1858-1927) British				
wc/d	3	961-2,610	1,987	2,392
FRASER, John Arthur (1839-1898) Canadian/British				
wc/d	4	750-1,763	1,090	825
FRASER, Valerie (20th C) British				
wc/d	1	1,479	1,479	1,479
FRASSATI, Dominique (1896-1947) French				
oil	2	2,959-3,669	3,314	2,959
FRASSON, Tonio (1922-) Swiss				
oil	1	1,468	1,468	1,468
FRATERMAN, Pieter (1910-1969) Dutch				
oil	1	1,134	1,134	1,134
FRATES, William E (1896-1969) American				
oil	3	500-900	733	800
wc/d	1	500	500	500
FRATIN, Christopher (1800-1864) French				
3D	6	2,200-7,134	3,868	2,997
FRAU, Greta (1942-) German?				
oil	1	1,911	1,911	1,911
FRAU, Jose (1898-1976) Spanish				
oil	1	23,919	23,919	23,919
wc/d	4	573-1,058	731	573
FRAYE, Andre (1888-1963) French				
oil	2	477-1,262	869	477
wc/d	1	820	820	820
FRAZER, Andrew (?) ?				
oil	1	2,700	2,700	2,700
FRAZER, William Miller (1864-1961) British				
oil	17	950-10,285	3,831	3,179
FRAZIER, Kenneth (1867-1949) American				
oil	3	1,200-3,000	2,000	1,800
FRAZIER, Luke (20th C) American				
oil	5	5,000-18,000	11,900	15,000
FRECHKOP, Leonid (1897-1982) Belgian				
oil	2	1,401-2,640	2,020	1,401
wc/d	1	486	486	486
FRECHON, Charles (1856-1929) French				
oil	3	668-11,297	5,930	5,827
FREDDIE, Wilhelm (1909-1995) Danish				
oil	9	1,779-8,370	4,300	4,849
wc/d	2	590-4,507	2,548	590

Name	No.	Price Range	Average	Median
FREDERIC, Léon (1856-1940) Belgian				
oil	11	732-8,604	3,312	2,803
wc/d	2	505-505	505	505
FREDERICH, Eduard (1811-1864) German				
oil	2	10,235-15,653	12,944	10,235
FREDERICK, Frank Forest (1866-?) American				
oil	1	1,100	1,100	1,100
FREDERICK, Rod (20th C) American				
oil	1	6,500	6,500	6,500
FREDERICKS, Alfred (19/20th C) American				
oil	1	1,223	1,223	1,223
FREDERICKS, Marshall Maynard (1908-1998) American				
3D	3	2,750-3,250	2,916	2,750
FREDOU, Jean Martial (1711-1795) French				
oil	1	1,701	1,701	1,701
FREDRIKS, Johannes Hendrik (1751-1822) Dutch				
oil	1	8,500	8,500	8,500
FREE, J A (19/20th C) ?				
oil	1	16,815	16,815	16,815
FREE, John D (1929-) American				
oil	1	3,000	3,000	3,000
FREEDMAN, Maurice (1904-?) American				
oil	1	2,750	2,750	2,750
FREEMAN, Dick (1932-1991) Canadian				
oil	3	533-1,886	1,103	891
FREEMAN, Don (1908-1978) American				
oil	1	2,000	2,000	2,000
FREEMAN, Kathryn (1956-) American				
oil	1	1,000	1,000	1,000
FREEMAN, T C (19th C) British				
oil	1	3,000	3,000	3,000
FREEMAN, William Philip Barnes (1813-1897) British				
oil	1	1,027	1,027	1,027
FREEZOR, George Augustus (fl.1861-1879) British				
oil	2	438-10,500	5,469	438
FREGEVIZE, Frederic (1770-1849) Swiss				
oil	1	21,096	21,096	21,096
FREILICHER, Jane (1924-) American				
oil	1	15,000	15,000	15,000
FREIMANN, Christoph (1940-) German				
3D	1	2,121	2,121	2,121
FREIRE, Luciano (1864-1935) Portuguese				
oil	1	1,215	1,215	1,215
FREIST, Greta (1904-1993) Austrian				
oil	3	760-28,027	9,898	909
FREITAG, Conrad (?-1894) American				
oil	2	17,000-32,500	24,750	17,000
FREIXANES, Jose (1953-) Spanish				
oil	2	3,214-3,449	3,331	3,214
wc/d	1	2,472	2,472	2,472
FREMIET, Emmanuel (1824-1910) French				
3D	26	1,978-20,000	4,814	3,277
FREMOND, Andre (20th C) French				
oil	1	2,922	2,922	2,922
FREMY, Zoe (19th C) American?				
oil	1	2,900	2,900	2,900
FRENCH, Annie (1872-1965) British				
wc/d	9	3,452-33,630	9,934	4,450
FRENCH, Daniel Chester (1850-1931) American				
3D	3	2,500-4,000	3,166	3,000
FRENCH, Frank (1850-1933) American				
oil	1	8,000	8,000	8,000
FRENCH, Frederick (19/20th C) British				
oil	3	650-3,150	1,576	930
FRENCH, Jared (1905-1987) American				
wc/d	3	4,200-8,000	6,233	6,500
FRENCH, Michael (1951-) Canadian				
oil	1	4,123	4,123	4,123
wc/d	3	882-3,444	1,742	902
FRENCH, P (1854-1920) Irish				
wc/d	1	5,550	5,550	5,550

Name	No.	Price Range	Average	Median
FRENCH, Percy (1854-1920) Irish				
oil	1	7,027	7,027	7,027
wc/d	29	3,695-53,514	10,321	8,160
FRENKEL, Itzhak (1900-1981) Israeli				
oil	14	400-3,800	1,553	700
wc/d	1	400	400	400
FRENNET, Lucien (1838-?) Belgian				
oil	4	524-5,482	2,158	837
FRERE, Charles Edouard (1837-1894) French				
oil	4	3,800-27,600	13,622	7,562
FRERE, Charles Theodore (1814-1888) French				
oil	10	534-43,000	11,984	7,603
wc/d	10	1,424-7,767	3,731	2,686
FRERE, Edouard (1819-1886) French				
oil	3	13,572-104,400	45,457	18,400
FRERE, Michel (1961-) Belgian				
oil	1	1,178	1,178	1,178
FRERICHS, William C A (1829-1905) American				
oil	8	2,800-22,000	9,381	6,750
FRESNAYE, Roger de la (1885-1925) French				
oil	3	3,000-52,800	22,641	12,123
wc/d	9	1,200-42,000	13,245	7,000
FREUD, Lucian (1922-) British/German				
oil	7	616,000-6,512,000	3,194,257	2,775,000
wc/d	5	10,920-45,000	25,792	27,750
FREUDENBERG, Jacobus (1818-1873) Dutch				
oil	3	1,204-8,100	5,006	5,716
FREUDENBERGER, Sigmund (1745-1801) Swiss				
wc/d	3	530-2,348	1,742	2,348
FREUDENTHAL, Peter (1938-) Swedish				
oil	5	1,048-16,562	4,560	1,654
FREUND, Harry Louis (1905-1979) American				
oil	1	1,500	1,500	1,500
FREUNDLICH, Jeanne (1892-1966) Austrian?				
wc/d	1	1,229	1,229	1,229
FREUNDLICH, Otto (1878-1943) German				
wc/d	2	6,195-21,658	13,926	6,195
FREY, Alice (1895-1981) Belgian				
oil	5	567-3,371	1,847	1,987
FREY, Eugène (1864-1930) French				
oil	1	979	979	979
wc/d	1	482	482	482
FREY, Johann Jakob (1813-1865) Swiss				
oil	3	3,514-48,720	19,845	7,303
FREY, Joseph F (1892-1977) American				
oil	3	1,100-1,500	1,300	1,300
FREY-MOOCK, Adolf (1881-1954) German				
oil	7	628-5,103	2,220	2,342
FREY-SURBECK, Marguerite (1886-1981) Swiss				
oil	4	666-3,497	2,040	1,499
FREYDANCK, Carl Daniel (1811-1887) German				
oil	1	33,429	33,429	33,429
FREYMUTH, Alphons (1940-) Dutch				
oil	1	1,438	1,438	1,438
FRIANT, Émile (1863-1932) French				
oil	4	594-440,000	131,146	10,911
FRIAS Y ESCALANTI, Juan Antonio de (1630-1670) Spanish				
oil	1	43,397	43,397	43,397
FRIBERG, Roj (1934-) Swedish				
wc/d	2	502-2,672	1,587	502
FRIBOULET, Jef (1919-2003) French				
oil	11	530-4,171	2,000	1,909
FRICART, Marianne (19th C) German?				
oil	1	2,238	2,238	2,238
FRICERO, Joseph (1807-1870) French				
wc/d	4	825-2,153	1,347	1,156
FRICH, Joachim (1810-1858) Norwegian				
oil	1	25,043	25,043	25,043
FRICK, Paul de (1864-1935) French				
oil	1	3,534	3,534	3,534

Name	No.	Price Range	Average	Median
FRIDELL, Axel (1894-1935) Swedish				
oil	1	20,384	20,384	20,384
wc/d	3	927-2,335	1,591	1,511
FRIDMAN, Karl Sholomovich (1926-) Russian				
oil	1	99,760	99,760	99,760
FRIE, Peter (1947-) Swedish				
oil	5	1,781-28,411	12,932	4,199
FRIEBERG, Ryno (1920-) Swedish				
oil	1	1,265	1,265	1,265
FRIED, Heinrich Jakob (1802-1870) German				
oil	1	4,257	4,257	4,257
FRIED, Pal (1893-1976) Hungarian/American				
oil	30	627-4,750	2,357	2,309
wc/d	5	720-3,000	1,483	1,262
FRIEDBICHLER, Franz (1854-1880) German				
oil	1	2,392	2,392	2,392
FRIEDEBERG, Pedro (1937-) Italian				
oil	2	600-9,500	5,050	600
3D	2	2,800-18,000	10,400	2,800
FRIEDENBERG, Wilhelm (1845-1911) German				
oil	1	4,077	4,077	4,077
FRIEDENSON, Arthur (1872-1955) British				
oil	10	539-6,408	2,034	1,770
FRIEDLAND, Howard (20th C) American				
oil	1	4,500	4,500	4,500
FRIEDLANDER, Camilla (1856-1928) Austrian				
oil	2	3,646-5,500	4,573	3,646
FRIEDLANDER, Friedrich (1825-1901) Austrian				
oil	7	1,205-16,800	5,295	4,712
FRIEDLANDER, Hedwig (1863-1916) Austrian				
oil	1	3,770	3,770	3,770
FRIEDLANDER, Johnny (1912-1992) French				
wc/d	1	2,121	2,121	2,121
FRIEDLANDER, Julius (1810-1861) Danish				
oil	2	2,223-4,864	3,543	2,223
FRIEDMAN, Irene (20th C) American/Canadian				
wc/d	1	1,100	1,100	1,100
FRIEDMAN, Tom (1965-) American				
wc/d	2	175,000-270,000	222,500	175,000
3D	5	55,000-230,000	173,000	190,000
FRIEDRICH, Caspar David (1774-1840) German				
oil	1	1,840,000	1,840,000	1,840,000
wc/d	3	72,587-1,159,200	437,211	79,846
FRIEDRICH, Johann Nepomuk (1817-1895) Austrian				
wc/d	1	2,420	2,420	2,420
FRIEDRICH, Nicolaus (1865-?) German				
3D	1	15,284	15,284	15,284
FRIEDRICH, Otto (1862-1937) Austrian				
wc/d	1	4,099	4,099	4,099
FRIEDRICH, Waldemar (1846-1910) German				
wc/d	1	2,163	2,163	2,163
FRIEND, Donald Stuart Leslie (1915-1989) Australian				
wc/d	1	2,565	2,565	2,565
FRIEND, Washington F (1820-1886) British				
wc/d	4	890-7,533	3,514	1,100
FRIES, Anna Susanna (1827-1901) Swiss				
oil	1	1,818	1,818	1,818
FRIES, Charles Arthur (1854-1940) American				
oil	8	1,900-17,000	7,800	7,000
FRIES, Ernst (1801-1833) German				
wc/d	1	1,145	1,145	1,145
FRIES, Hanny (1918-) Swiss				
oil	2	1,522-2,566	2,044	1,522
FRIES, Karl Friedrich (1831-1871) German				
oil	1	4,208	4,208	4,208
FRIES, Pia (1955-) Swiss				
oil	1	1,556	1,556	1,556
FRIESE, Richard (1854-1918) German				
oil	4	2,592-12,370	6,647	3,748
wc/d	5	893-3,854	1,923	1,414
FRIESEKE, Frederick Carl (1874-1939) American				
oil	5	36,000-2,100,000	625,200	310,000

Name	No.	Price Range	Average	Median
FRIESS, Leopold (1841-1919) Austrian				
oil	1	2,420	2,420	2,420
FRIESZ, Émile Othon (1879-1949) French				
oil	39	2,124-570,000	32,442	9,233
wc/d	26	471-29,920	2,594	950
FRIEWALD, Till (1963-) German				
wc/d	1	4,200	4,200	4,200
FRIGOLI, Marlene (20th C) Italian?				
oil	1	2,160	2,160	2,160
FRIIS, Hans Gabriel (1838-1892) Danish				
oil	3	1,593-4,075	2,867	2,934
FRINK, Elizabeth (1930-1993) British				
oil	1	2,088	2,088	2,088
wc/d	19	1,110-30,960	11,224	9,620
3D	28	4,275-623,700	97,990	52,200
FRIPP, Alfred Downing (1822-1895) British				
wc/d	3	1,740-4,158	2,737	2,314
FRIPP, Charles Edwin (1854-1906) British				
wc/d	1	1,225	1,225	1,225
FRIPP, George Arthur (1813-1896) British				
wc/d	9	845-10,395	4,289	3,872
FRIPP, Thomas William (1864-1931) Canadian/British				
wc/d	3	1,012-1,329	1,164	1,152
FRISCH, Johann Christoph (1738-1815) German				
oil	1	29,600	29,600	29,600
FRISCH, John Didrik (1835-1867) Danish				
oil	2	3,898-4,075	3,986	3,898
FRISCHE, Heinrich Ludwig (1831-1901) German				
oil	2	7,224-8,429	7,826	7,224
FRISCHKNECHT, Fritz (1893-1983) Swiss				
oil	2	4,868-6,478	5,673	4,868
FRISHMUTH, Harriet Whitney (1880-1980) American				
3D	8	5,000-550,000	105,592	17,740
FRISON, Jehan (1882-1961) Belgian				
oil	9	656-4,948	2,456	2,586
FRISON-FABRICE, Lucienne (1889-?) French				
wc/d	1	3,737	3,737	3,737
FRISONI, Davide (1965-) Italian				
oil	1	1,193	1,193	1,193
FRISTROM, Oscar (1856-1918) Swedish/Australian				
oil	2	1,191-1,191	1,191	1,191
FRITH, William Powell (1819-1909) British				
oil	5	1,414-129,882	30,938	6,612
FRITSCH, Elizabeth (1940-) British				
3D	1	18,900	18,900	18,900
FRITSCH, Ernst (1892-1965) German				
oil	1	3,534	3,534	3,534
wc/d	1	2,338	2,338	2,338
FRITSCH, Katarina (1956-) American?				
3D	6	5,890-238,950	49,941	8,836
FRITSCH, Melchior (1825-1889) Austrian				
oil	3	824-2,592	1,423	853
FRITZ, Andreas (1828-1906) Danish				
oil	1	1,161	1,161	1,161
FRITZ, Charles (20th C) American				
oil	3	6,500-10,000	8,166	8,000
FRITZ, Emmett (1917-1975) American				
oil	3	1,300-8,500	4,266	3,000
wc/d	1	1,900	1,900	1,900
FRITZ, Henry Eugene (1875-1956) American				
oil	1	2,500	2,500	2,500
FRITZ, Max (1849-?) German				
oil	2	900-1,657	1,278	900
FRITZ, Otto (?-1903) German				
oil	1	3,575	3,575	3,575
FRITZSCHE, H (?) German				
oil	1	1,790	1,790	1,790
FRIX, Jean (19/20th C) ?				
oil	1	2,180	2,180	2,180
FRIZE, Bernard (1949-) French				
oil	1	8,183	8,183	8,183

Name	No.	Price Range	Average	Median
FROBERG, Maria (1886-1962) Swedish				
oil	1	2,747	2,747	2,747
FRODMAN-CLUZEL, Boris (1878-?) Swedish/Russian				
3D	1	7,423	7,423	7,423
FROELICH, Maren M (1870-1921) American				
oil	2	500-5,000	2,750	500
FROHLICH, Bernard (1823-1885) Austrian				
oil	1	2,863	2,863	2,863
FROHLICH, Fritz (1910-) Austrian				
oil	2	2,392-2,877	2,634	2,392
wc/d	6	467-642	603	642
FROHNER, Adolf (1934-) German				
oil	1	5,558	5,558	5,558
wc/d	5	719-2,928	1,537	1,514
FROLICH, Lorenz (1820-1908) Danish				
oil	7	921-7,498	3,378	3,636
wc/d	2	511-585	548	511
FROLICHER, Otto (1840-1890) Swiss				
oil	6	666-9,251	3,989	2,900
FROMAN, Ramon Mitchell (1908-1980) American				
oil	2	1,600-6,000	3,800	1,600
wc/d	2	650-900	775	650
FROMANGER, Gerard (1939-) French				
oil	1	7,013	7,013	7,013
wc/d	1	1,236	1,236	1,236
FROMANTIOU, Hendrik de (1633-c.1700) German				
oil	1	290,000	290,000	290,000
FROMEL, Gerde (1931-1975) Irish				
3D	1	11,503	11,503	11,503
FROMENT-MEURICE, Jacques Charles (1864-1948) French				
wc/d	2	561-1,427	994	561
3D	2	1,821-15,288	8,554	1,821
FROMENTIN, Eugène (1820-1876) French				
oil	9	1,600-142,397	30,440	10,440
wc/d	10	473-3,160	1,350	1,196
FROMME, Ludwig (19/20th C) ?				
oil	1	1,403	1,403	1,403
wc/d	1	1,134	1,134	1,134
FROMMEL, Carl Ludwig (1789-1863) German				
oil	1	6,563	6,563	6,563
wc/d	2	1,036-1,100	1,068	1,036
FROMUTH, Charles Henry (1861-1937) American				
wc/d	4	935-7,000	3,993	1,600
FRONGIA, Lino (1958-) Italian				
oil	2	8,758-15,122	11,940	8,758
FRONIUS, Hans (1903-1988) Austrian				
oil	2	10,286-15,315	12,800	10,286
wc/d	4	599-820	667	606
FRONT, Yehoshua (1946-) Israeli				
oil	1	1,400	1,400	1,400
FROOT, Harry D (19/20th C) ?				
oil	2	550-4,000	2,275	550
FROST, A B (1851-1928) American				
oil	1	1,300	1,300	1,300
FROST, Anthony (1951-) British				
oil	6	880-2,275	1,272	1,056
FROST, Arthur Burdett (1851-1928) American				
oil	3	1,800-21,000	9,433	5,500
wc/d	3	500-4,400	1,966	1,000
FROST, John (1890-1937) American				
oil	2	1,300-65,000	33,150	1,300
FROST, John Orne Johnson (1852-1928) American				
oil	1	50,000	50,000	50,000
FROST, Terry (1915-2003) British				
oil	34	1,056-144,300	21,929	11,505
wc/d	36	722-10,380	3,413	2,478
FROST, William Edward (1810-1877) British				
oil	4	811-8,918	3,523	1,218
wc/d	2	493-1,575	1,034	493
FROSTERUS-SALTIN, Alexandra (1837-1916) Finnish				
oil	1	1,405	1,405	1,405
FROWD, Thomas T J (19th C) British				
oil	1	1,170	1,170	1,170

Name	No.	Price Range	Average	Median
FROY, Martin (1926-) British				
oil	1	1,323	1,323	1,323
FRUHBECK, Franz Josef (1795-?) Austrian				
wc/d	5	530-3,063	1,548	1,414
FRUHMANN, Johann (1928-1985) Austrian				
oil	2	6,310-14,143	10,226	6,310
FRUHTRUNK, Gunther (1923-1983) German				
oil	9	7,071-34,164	18,499	17,671
FRY, Anthony (1927-) British				
oil	2	1,320-8,950	5,135	1,320
FRY, Roger (1866-1934) British				
oil	5	2,975-51,900	16,324	5,310
wc/d	1	586	586	586
FRYE, Thomas (1710-1762) British				
wc/d	2	17,670-38,748	28,209	17,670
FU BAOSHI (1904-1965) Chinese				
wc/d	2	8,500-82,297	45,398	8,500
FU HONG (1946-) ?				
oil	1	20,000	20,000	20,000
FUCHS, Bernard (1932-) American				
oil	1	2,500	2,500	2,500
wc/d	1	7,500	7,500	7,500
FUCHS, Ernst (1930-2000) Austrian				
oil	1	14,373	14,373	14,373
wc/d	4	2,170-3,748	2,999	2,338
3D	7	1,808-2,652	2,093	2,121
FUCHS, Franz Xaver (1868-1944) Austrian				
oil	1	1,576	1,576	1,576
FUCHS, Herbert (1954-) Austrian				
oil	1	1,678	1,678	1,678
FUCHS, Karl (1836-1886) German				
oil	1	1,139	1,139	1,139
FUCHS, Richard (1852-?) German				
oil	1	5,351	5,351	5,351
FUCHS, Rudolf (1868-1918) Austrian				
oil	1	1,311	1,311	1,311
FUCHSEL, Hermann (1833-1915) American				
oil	2	2,073-8,342	5,207	2,073
FUEGER, Friedrich Heinrich (1751-1818) German				
oil	1	7,224	7,224	7,224
wc/d	1	1,885	1,885	1,885
FUERTES, Louis Agassiz (1874-1927) American				
oil	1	20,000	20,000	20,000
wc/d	3	2,200-8,000	5,900	7,500
FUGAI, Ekun (1568-1650) Japanese				
wc/d	2	12,000-26,000	19,000	12,000
FUHR, Franz Xaver (1898-1973) German				
oil	5	4,529-53,075	15,435	7,068
wc/d	5	960-2,640	1,538	1,212
FUHRICH, Josef von (1800-1876) Austrian				
wc/d	3	531-1,815	1,020	714
FUHRMANN, Arend (1918-1984) Swiss?				
oil	2	1,135-1,135	1,135	1,135
FUJITA, Gajin (1972-) American				
oil	1	9,500	9,500	9,500
FUKUDA, Suiko (1895-1973) Japanese				
wc/d	1	8,000	8,000	8,000
FUKUI, Ryonosuke (1924-1986) Japanese				
oil	2	4,000-4,861	4,430	4,000
FUKUSHIMA, Tikashi (1920-2001) Brazilian/Japanese				
oil	1	4,650	4,650	4,650
FULCHER, Charles (1959-) American				
oil	1	2,500	2,500	2,500
FULDE, Edward (19/20th C) American				
oil	1	1,042	1,042	1,042
FULLARTON, James (1946-) British				
oil	4	4,450-10,266	6,591	5,664
FULLER, Alfred (1899-1990) American				
oil	2	500-1,700	1,100	500
wc/d	1	650	650	650
FULLER, Arthur Davenport (1889-1967) American				
wc/d	1	1,300	1,300	1,300

Name	No.	Price Range	Average	Median
FULLER, Edmund G (fl.1888-1916) British				
oil	3	534-1,395	1,009	1,100
wc/d	2	581-1,357	969	581
FULLER, George (1822-1884) American				
oil	2	700-1,400	1,050	700
FULLEYLOVE, John (1845-1908) British				
oil	1	500	500	500
wc/d	8	521-2,610	1,464	1,056
FULOP, Karoly (1893-1963) American				
wc/d	3	800-3,000	2,066	2,400
FULTON, Fitch Burt (1879-1955) American				
oil	1	6,000	6,000	6,000
FULTON, Samuel (1855-1941) British				
oil	10	880-16,910	5,961	3,828
FUNCH, Edgar (1915-1995) Danish				
3D	2	1,778-2,182	1,980	1,778
FUNG MING-CHIP (1951-) Chinese				
wc/d	1	5,000	5,000	5,000
FUNI, Achille (1890-1972) Italian				
oil	4	2,386-22,669	10,577	4,295
wc/d	2	1,551-6,479	4,015	1,551
FUNKE, Helene (1869-1957) Austrian				
oil	1	12,000	12,000	12,000
FUR, L Silva le (20th C) French				
oil	1	1,100	1,100	1,100
FUREDI, Lily (1901-1969) American				
oil	1	1,100	1,100	1,100
wc/d	1	600	600	600
FURET, François (1842-1919) Swiss				
oil	1	7,632	7,632	7,632
FURINI, Francesco (1604-1646) Italian				
oil	2	56,960-72,000	64,480	56,960
FURLOW, Malcolm (20th C) American				
oil	1	1,500	1,500	1,500
FURNAS, Barnaby (1973-) American?				
oil	1	340,000	340,000	340,000
wc/d	4	19,000-75,000	45,500	38,000
FURSE, Charles Wellington (1868-1904) British				
wc/d	1	1,796	1,796	1,796
FURT, Leonce (19/20th C) French				
oil	1	5,706	5,706	5,706
FUSARO, Jean (1925-) French				
oil	14	3,587-10,307	6,041	5,000
FUSI, Walter (1924-) Italian				
oil	13	471-1,708	791	647
wc/d	8	504-884	586	504
FUSSELL, Charles Lewis (1840-1909) American				
wc/d	1	3,600	3,600	3,600
FUSSELL, Frederick Ralph (fl.1843-1858) British				
oil	1	2,436	2,436	2,436
FUSSELL, Michael (1927-1974) British				
oil	1	1,505	1,505	1,505
FUSSLI, Johann Heinrich (1741-1825) Swiss				
wc/d	2	1,214-4,788	3,001	1,214
FUSSLI, Johann Melchior (1677-1736) Swiss				
wc/d	1	1,138	1,138	1,138
FUSSMANN, Klaus (1938-) German				
oil	15	2,990-11,192	6,457	7,007
wc/d	26	1,018-10,603	3,712	3,507
FUSTER, Miguel Roca (1942-) Spanish				
oil	1	891	891	891
wc/d	1	5,761	5,761	5,761
FYFE, Samuel H (19th C) British				
oil	1	5,220	5,220	5,220
FYFE, William (1836-1882) British				
oil	1	26,550	26,550	26,550
FYT, Jan (1611-1661) Flemish				
oil	4	8,174-35,000	23,531	25,000
GAAL, Ignacz (1820-1880) Austrian				
wc/d	2	4,757-6,500	5,628	4,757
GABANI, Giuseppe (1846-1900) Italian				
wc/d	1	5,583	5,583	5,583

Name	No.	Price Range	Average	Median
GABBRIELLI, Donatello (20th C) Italian				
3D	1	2,200	2,200	2,200
GABE, Eugene (19th C) French?				
oil	1	1,881	1,881	1,881
GABINO (1928-) Spanish				
oil	1	2,259	2,259	2,259
GABINO, Amadeo (1922-2004) Spanish				
oil	1	2,188	2,188	2,188
wc/d	2	838-1,078	958	838
3D	2	2,392-2,631	2,511	2,392
GABLE, John (1944-) American				
wc/d	1	2,000	2,000	2,000
GABORIAUD, Josue (1883-1955) French				
oil	1	2,030	2,030	2,030
GABRIEL, François (?-1993) French				
oil	3	1,463-2,000	1,687	1,600
GABRIEL, Isabelle (1902-1990) French				
oil	1	1,300	1,300	1,300
GABRIEL, Paul Joseph Constantin (1828-1903) Dutch				
oil	8	2,472-46,972	21,137	8,372
wc/d	5	696-1,752	1,033	909
GABRIELSE, Johan (1881-1945) Dutch				
oil	1	2,571	2,571	2,571
wc/d	1	1,678	1,678	1,678
GABRINI, Pietro (1865-1926) Italian				
oil	5	1,752-11,342	7,643	8,192
wc/d	2	600-700	650	600
GABRON, Guilliam (1619-1678) Belgian				
oil	2	14,137-19,421	16,779	14,137
GADAN, Antoine (1854-1934) French				
oil	4	4,200-11,334	7,762	5,377
GADBOIS, Louis (?-1826) French				
wc/d	1	3,152	3,152	3,152
GADBOIS, Louise (1896-1985) Canadian				
oil	1	1,234	1,234	1,234
GADDI, Taddeo (?-1366) Italian				
oil	1	520,000	520,000	520,000
GADE, Hari Ambados (1917-2001) Indian				
oil	2	12,000-15,000	13,500	12,000
wc/d	3	2,500-6,920	4,020	2,640
GADEGAARD, Paul (1920-1996) Danish				
oil	4	3,233-10,830	5,654	4,024
GADSBY, William H (1844-1924) British				
oil	1	2,478	2,478	2,478
GAEL, Barent (c.1620-1703) Dutch				
oil	6	2,800-35,150	14,210	6,622
GAERTNER, Johann Philipp Eduard (1801-1877) German				
oil	1	240,000	240,000	240,000
wc/d	1	2,417	2,417	2,417
GAG, Wanda (1893-1946) American				
wc/d	1	4,000	4,000	4,000
GAGEN, Robert Ford (1847-1926) Canadian				
wc/d	6	412-1,814	1,098	608
GAGLIARDINI, Julien Gustave (1846-1927) French				
oil	3	558-6,125	2,466	716
GAGNEUX, Paul (?-1892) French				
oil	1	2,035	2,035	2,035
GAGNON, Clarence A (1881-1942) Canadian				
oil	9	4,919-53,175	22,663	22,156
wc/d	19	410-30,924	9,466	4,692
GAHAGAN, Lawrence (18/19th C) British				
3D	1	53,100	53,100	53,100
GAIDAN, Louis (1847-1925) French				
oil	1	3,801	3,801	3,801
GAIGHER, Horazio (1870-1938) ?				
oil	8	546-1,318	811	719
wc/d	5	546-1,139	797	727
GAIL, Wilhelm (1804-1890) German				
oil	1	4,208	4,208	4,208
GAILLARD, Andre (20th C) French				
3D	1	2,736	2,736	2,736

Name	No.	Price Range	Average	Median
GAILLARDOT, Pierre (1910-2002) French				
oil	7	643-1,907	1,111	1,073
wc/d	6	596-1,330	813	615
GAILLIARD, Franz (1861-1932) Belgian				
oil	3	5,550-105,600	43,834	20,354
GAILLIARD, Jean Jacques (1890-1976) Belgian				
oil	7	662-26,703	5,739	2,356
wc/d	3	578-1,144	853	837
GAIMARI, Enrique (1911-1999) Argentinian				
3D	4	1,800-10,000	5,325	4,500
GAINSBOROUGH, Thomas (1727-1788) British				
oil	14	18,347-557,550	163,524	66,150
wc/d	8	11,764-84,000	44,833	40,920
GAISSER, Jakob Emmanuel (1825-1899) German				
oil	12	599-4,534	2,679	2,303
GAISSER, Max (1857-1922) German				
oil	2	1,695-3,514	2,604	1,695
GAITIS, Yannis (1923-1984) Greek				
oil	16	5,536-68,040	25,648	18,900
wc/d	1	4,224	4,224	4,224
3D	4	2,387-20,570	14,135	14,449
GAITONDE, Vasudeo S (1924-2001) Indian				
oil	2	80,000-200,000	140,000	80,000
wc/d	2	12,000-16,000	14,000	12,000
GAJIC, Philippe (20th C) French				
wc/d	1	2,336	2,336	2,336
GAL, Menchu (1923-) Spanish				
oil	1	44,349	44,349	44,349
wc/d	1	5,388	5,388	5,388
GALAN, Julio (1958-) Mexican				
oil	2	9,500-10,000	9,750	9,500
wc/d	2	1,100-8,000	4,550	1,100
GALAND, Léon (1872-1960) French				
oil	1	1,500	1,500	1,500
GALANIS, Demetrius (1882-1966) French				
oil	4	4,660-187,000	71,642	7,480
wc/d	1	5,280	5,280	5,280
GALANTE, Francesco (1884-1972) Italian				
oil	1	1,427	1,427	1,427
GALANTE, Nicola (1883-1969) Italian				
oil	1	7,755	7,755	7,755
wc/d	2	610-1,071	840	610
GALBUSERA, Giovacchino (1871-1944) Italian				
oil	3	2,283-9,159	4,671	2,571
wc/d	1	1,145	1,145	1,145
GALE, Martin (1949-) British				
oil	9	3,629-17,896	10,034	10,603
wc/d	1	2,384	2,384	2,384
GALE, William (1823-1909) British				
oil	2	1,408-12,025	6,716	1,408
wc/d	1	925	925	925
GALEA, Luigi M (1847-1917) Maltese				
oil	6	2,976-22,932	8,169	4,725
wc/d	2	1,244-7,080	4,162	1,244
GALEAZZI, Gaetano (1870-?) Italian				
oil	2	1,414-3,864	2,639	1,414
GALEOTA-RUSSO, Leopoldo (1868-1938) Italian				
oil	2	1,818-7,658	4,738	1,818
GALEOTTI, Sebastiano (1676-1746) Italian				
wc/d	2	3,107-4,531	3,819	3,107
GALEY, Jean Fabien (1877-?) French				
oil	2	909-3,031	1,970	909
GALI, Zvi (1921-1962) ?				
oil	1	1,200	1,200	1,200
GALIEN-LALOUE (1854-1941) French				
oil	1	3,031	3,031	3,031
GALIEN-LALOUE, E (1854-1941) French				
oil	1	4,607	4,607	4,607
GALIEN-LALOUE, Eugène (1854-1941) French				
oil	50	701-22,360	5,335	3,612
wc/d	75	1,903-85,000	19,666	17,000
GALIMARD, Nicolas Auguste (1813-1880) French				
oil	1	1,337	1,337	1,337

Name	No.	Price Range	Average	Median
GALIMBERTI, Dario (20th C) Italian				
oil	4	1,453-2,059	1,665	1,453
GALIZIA, Fede (1578-1630) Italian				
oil	2	1,110,000-1,450,000	1,280,000	1,110,000
GALL, François (1912-1987) French/Hungarian				
oil	99	1,255-19,110	5,782	4,835
wc/d	5	680-3,850	1,763	1,569
GALLACE, Maureen (1960-) American				
oil	1	22,000	22,000	22,000
GALLAGHER, Ellen (1967-) American				
oil	1	120,000	120,000	120,000
GALLAGHER, Mary (1952-) British				
oil	3	605-7,965	3,721	2,595
GALLAND, Andre Charles (1886-1965) French				
wc/d	1	1,518	1,518	1,518
GALLAND, Gilbert (1870-?) French				
oil	1	3,387	3,387	3,387
wc/d	1	467	467	467
GALLAND, Pierre Victor (1822-1892) French				
oil	1	2,822	2,822	2,822
GALLARD, Michel de (1921-) French				
oil	3	744-2,500	1,566	1,455
GALLARD-LEPINAY, Paul Charles Emmanuel (1842-1885) French				
oil	5	3,507-13,000	5,688	4,000
GALLAY-CHARBONNEL, Nina (19/20th C) French				
wc/d	1	1,430	1,430	1,430
GALLE, Émile (1846-1904) French				
3D	1	66,600	66,600	66,600
GALLEGOS Y ARNOSA, Jose (1859-1917) Spanish				
oil	4	12,109-104,400	41,714	19,027
GALLELLI, Massimiliano (1863-1956) Italian				
oil	1	4,734	4,734	4,734
GALLEN-KALLELA, Akseli Valdemar (1865-1931) Finnish				
oil	9	3,514-112,110	47,692	46,286
GALLI, Angelo (1870-1933) Italian				
oil	2	728-1,894	1,311	728
GALLI, Eduardo (1854-?) Italian				
oil	2	1,078-1,505	1,291	1,078
GALLI, Fortunato (?-1918) Italian				
3D	1	60,000	60,000	60,000
GALLI, G (?) Italian				
oil	2	6,475-8,205	7,340	6,475
GALLI, Giuseppe (1866-1953) Italian				
oil	1	1,036	1,036	1,036
GALLI, Pietro (1804-1877) Italian				
3D	1	34,000	34,000	34,000
GALLI, Riccardo (1869-1944) Italian				
oil	3	2,188-4,132	3,236	3,390
GALLIAC, Louis (1849-1931) French				
oil	2	4,839-8,767	6,803	4,839
GALLIAN, Octave (1855-?) French				
oil	1	1,929	1,929	1,929
GALLIANI, Omar (1954-) Italian				
oil	12	1,171-9,833	5,337	4,595
wc/d	15	847-9,000	4,571	3,888
GALLIANO, Daniele (1961-) Italian				
oil	1	1,929	1,929	1,929
GALLIARI, Bernardino (1707-1794) Italian				
oil	1	10,816	10,816	10,816
wc/d	1	3,500	3,500	3,500
GALLIARI, Gaspare (1761-1823) Italian				
wc/d	1	1,500	1,500	1,500
GALLIBERT, Genevieve (1888-1978) French				
oil	1	10,770	10,770	10,770
GALLINA, Lodovico (1752-1787) Italian				
oil	1	45,000	45,000	45,000
GALLINA, Pietro (1937-) Italian				
3D	1	1,936	1,936	1,936
GALLIZIO, Piergiorgio (1935-2000) Italian				
oil	7	471-1,036	723	744
wc/d	3	471-1,001	647	471

Name	No.	Price Range	Average	Median
GALLIZIO, Pinot (1902-1964) Italian				
oil	2	16,384-22,188	19,286	16,384
wc/d	6	1,285-21,360	9,335	4,272
GALLO, Giuseppe (1954-) Italian				
oil	4	2,422-8,247	4,617	2,983
wc/d	1	2,589	2,589	2,589
3D	1	5,890	5,890	5,890
GALLO, Luciana (1963-) Italian				
oil	8	589-4,272	2,860	2,945
GALLON, Robert (1845-1925) British				
oil	11	817-6,090	3,689	4,000
GALLOTTI, Alessandro (1879-1961) Italian				
oil	1	2,330	2,330	2,330
GALLOWAY, Steve (1952-) American				
wc/d	1	3,250	3,250	3,250
GALMUZZI, Antonio (19th C) Italian				
3D	2	2,664-10,395	6,529	2,664
GALOFRE SURIS, Francisco (1900-1986) Spanish				
oil	1	6,636	6,636	6,636
GALOFRE Y GIMENEZ, Baldomero (1849-1902) Spanish				
oil	3	8,433-25,716	15,716	13,000
GALOYER, Francois (1944-) French				
3D	2	1,844-2,959	2,401	1,844
GALSCHIOT, Jens (1954-) Danish				
3D	3	2,111-3,152	2,473	2,157
GALSWORTHY, Frank (1863-1927) British				
wc/d	1	8,500	8,500	8,500
GALT, Cameron (1964-) British?				
wc/d	1	1,229	1,229	1,229
GALVANO, Albino (1907-1991) Italian				
oil	17	589-5,777	2,180	1,829
GALVEZ, Juan (1774-1847) Spanish				
oil	1	28,800	28,800	28,800
GAMAIN, Louis Honore Frederic (1803-1871) French				
oil	1	1,134	1,134	1,134
GAMARRA, Jose (1934-) Uruguayan				
oil	2	2,500-2,643	2,571	2,500
GAMBARDELLA, Julia (19/20th C) Italian				
oil	1	1,145	1,145	1,145
GAMBARTES, Leonidas (1909-1963) Argentinian				
wc/d	2	6,000-35,000	20,500	6,000
GAMBINO, Giuseppe (1928-1997) Italian				
oil	3	1,000-2,141	1,602	1,665
GAMBLE, John M (1863-1957) American				
oil	12	6,000-160,000	60,083	42,000
GAMBOGI, Giuseppe (19/20th C) Italian				
3D	1	38,000	38,000	38,000
GAMBONE, Francesco (19th C) Italian				
oil	1	1,149	1,149	1,149
GAMBONI, Domenico (18th C) ?				
oil	1	19,986	19,986	19,986
GAMBORG, Knud (1828-1900) Danish				
oil	1	1,386	1,386	1,386
GAMELIN, Jacques (1738-1803) French				
oil	1	2,342	2,342	2,342
GAMP, Botho von (1894-1977) German				
oil	1	1,459	1,459	1,459
GAMPERT, Otto (1842-1924) Swiss				
oil	6	541-1,788	1,056	811
GAMREKELI, Irakli (1894-1943) Russian				
oil	1	1,918	1,918	1,918
GANA, F (19th C) Continental				
3D	1	13,000	13,000	13,000
GANDARA, Antonio de la (1862-1917) French				
oil	1	2,016	2,016	2,016
GANDOLFI, Gaetano (1734-1802) Italian				
oil	2	45,308-519,000	282,154	45,308
wc/d	7	3,800-148,000	43,632	14,270
GANDOLFI, Mauro (1764-1834) Italian				
oil	1	147,050	147,050	147,050
GANDOLFI, Paola (1949-) Italian				
oil	1	1,767	1,767	1,767

Name	No.	Price Range	Average	Median
GANDOLFI, Ubaldo (1728-1781) Italian				
wc/d	2	4,142-9,709	6,925	4,142
GANDY, Herbert (?-1920) British				
oil	1	9,350	9,350	9,350
GANDY, Joseph Michael (1771-1843) British				
wc/d	1	1,100	1,100	1,100
GANLY, Rose Brigid (1934-2002) Irish				
oil	3	605-5,108	2,469	1,695
wc/d	1	935	935	935
GANMAR, Georg (1916-1978) Swedish				
3D	1	6,663	6,663	6,663
GANNE, Yves (1931-) French				
oil	1	1,272	1,272	1,272
GANO, Cara (1971-) French				
oil	1	6,429	6,429	6,429
GANS, Heinrich (1904-1966) German				
oil	1	3,403	3,403	3,403
GANS, Paula (1883-1941) Czechoslovakian				
wc/d	2	648-3,063	1,855	648
GANSO, Emil (1895-1941) American				
oil	1	2,000	2,000	2,000
wc/d	1	1,100	1,100	1,100
GANTAI, Kishi (1785-1865) Japanese				
wc/d	1	1,800	1,800	1,800
GANTNER, Bernard (1928-) French				
oil	4	984-5,271	2,285	1,190
wc/d	1	1,286	1,286	1,286
GANTZ, John (18/19th C) British				
wc/d	1	6,475	6,475	6,475
GANUCCI, Ugolino (18th C) Italian				
wc/d	1	9,722	9,722	9,722
GANZ, Edwin (1871-1948) Swiss				
oil	2	1,168-1,427	1,297	1,168
GAO QIFENG (1889-1933) Chinese				
wc/d	1	4,500	4,500	4,500
GAO XINGJIAN (1940-) Chinese				
wc/d	1	30,000	30,000	30,000
GARABETIAN, Cricor (1908-) Rumanian				
oil	1	1,080	1,080	1,080
GARACHE, Claude (1930-) French				
oil	1	1,913	1,913	1,913
GARATE Y CLAVERO, Juan Jose (1870-1939) Spanish				
oil	2	4,392-13,807	9,099	4,392
GARAU, Augusto (1923-) Italian				
oil	1	1,335	1,335	1,335
GARAU, Salvatore (1953-) Italian				
oil	1	6,361	6,361	6,361
GARAUD, Gustave Cesaire (1847-1914) French				
oil	1	1,740	1,740	1,740
GARAY Y AREVALO, Manuel (19th C) Spanish				
oil	2	1,171-1,267	1,219	1,171
GARAY, Marie de (19th C) French				
oil	1	6,000	6,000	6,000
GARBE, Richard (1876-1957) British				
3D	2	7,938-13,920	10,929	7,938
GARBELL, Alexandre (1903-1970) Latvian				
oil	7	500-5,023	1,689	1,100
GARBER, Daniel (1880-1958) American				
oil	2	60,000-130,000	95,000	60,000
wc/d	1	3,750	3,750	3,750
GARBIERI, Lorenzo (1580-1654) Italian				
oil	1	15,653	15,653	15,653
GARBUZ, Yair (1945-) Israeli				
oil	1	4,000	4,000	4,000
wc/d	1	1,500	1,500	1,500
GARCERA, Javier (1967-) Spanish				
wc/d	1	1,085	1,085	1,085
GARCIA BARRENA, Carmelo (1926-) Spanish				
oil	3	820-5,088	3,275	3,918
GARCIA BENITO, Eduardo (1891-1981) Spanish				
oil	1	3,801	3,801	3,801

Name	No.	Price Range	Average	Median
GARCIA DONAIRE, Joaquin (1926-2003) Spanish				
oil	1	2,392	2,392	2,392
GARCIA GUERRERO, Luis (1921-) Mexican				
oil	2	8,000-14,000	11,000	8,000
GARCIA LARA, Juan (19th C) Spanish				
wc/d	1	2,945	2,945	2,945
GARCIA LORCA, Gloria (1945-) American				
oil	1	2,155	2,155	2,155
GARCIA OCHOA, Luis (1920-) Spanish				
oil	1	7,054	7,054	7,054
wc/d	2	542-1,543	1,042	542
GARCIA REINO, Oscar (1910-1993) Uruguayan				
oil	1	1,900	1,900	1,900
GARCIA SAENZ, Santiago (20th C) Argentinian				
oil	1	3,200	3,200	3,200
GARCIA Y RAMOS, Jose (1852-1912) Spanish				
oil	3	5,878-11,310	9,341	10,837
wc/d	1	707	707	707
GARCIA Y RODRIGUEZ, Manuel (1863-1925) Spanish				
oil	10	5,878-69,600	26,938	23,591
wc/d	4	1,018-3,485	1,752	1,100
GARCIA Y VALDEMORO, Juan (19th C) Spanish				
oil	1	2,600	2,600	2,600
GARCIA, Daniel (1958-) Argentinian				
oil	1	8,500	8,500	8,500
GARCIA, J (19th C) ?				
oil	1	1,767	1,767	1,767
GARCIA, Juan Gil (1879-1931) Cuban				
oil	1	1,900	1,900	1,900
GARCIA-ROSSI, Horacio (1929-) Argentinian				
oil	8	2,386-10,356	5,486	4,948
GARCIA-SEVILLA, Ferran (1949-) Spanish				
oil	2	3,600-3,600	3,600	3,600
GARDAIR, Christian (1938-) French				
oil	1	1,788	1,788	1,788
GARDELL-ERICSON, Anna (1853-1939) Swedish				
wc/d	14	449-6,370	2,444	1,870
GARDEN, William Fraser (1856-1921) British				
wc/d	5	920-11,718	4,651	2,960
GARDET, Georges (1863-1939) French				
3D	4	2,200-8,500	4,243	3,032
GARDIER, Raoul du (1871-1952) French				
oil	6	1,475-51,781	21,699	15,727
GARDINER, Stanley (1888-1952) British				
oil	4	531-1,701	1,179	1,062
GARDNER, Daniel (1750-1805) British				
oil	1	8,550	8,550	8,550
wc/d	3	1,480-4,275	2,910	2,976
GARDNER, Derek George Montague (1914-) British				
wc/d	2	531-5,236	2,883	531
GARDNER, Fred (1880-1952) American				
oil	1	8,000	8,000	8,000
GARDNER, Stanley Horace (?) British				
oil	1	1,320	1,320	1,320
GARDNER, Violet Dunn (19th C) French				
oil	1	1,400	1,400	1,400
GAREL, Philippe (1945-) French				
oil	1	19,872	19,872	19,872
wc/d	1	701	701	701
GARELLI, Franco (1909-) Italian				
3D	1	1,909	1,909	1,909
GAREMYN, Jan Anton (1712-1799) Flemish				
wc/d	1	2,153	2,153	2,153
GARF, Salomon (1879-1943) Dutch				
wc/d	7	488-15,493	3,839	900
GARFINKIEL, David (1902-1970) Polish				
oil	1	1,788	1,788	1,788
GARFIT, William (1944-) British				
oil	1	1,488	1,488	1,488
GARGALLO, Pablo (1881-1934) Spanish				
3D	1	45,678	45,678	45,678

Name	No.	Price Range	Average	Median
GARGIULIO, Domenico (1612-1679) Italian				
wc/d	2	1,200-1,757	1,478	1,200
GARIAZZO, Piero Antonio (1879-1963) Italian				
oil	7	705-1,670	1,016	970
wc/d	1	667	667	667
GARIBALDI, Gariani (1861-1930) Italian				
oil	1	7,500	7,500	7,500
GARIBALDI, Joseph (1863-1941) French				
oil	2	30,000-220,548	125,274	30,000
GARIN, Louis (1888-1959) French				
oil	5	818-4,712	3,116	3,770
GARINEI, Giuseppe (fl.1887) Italian				
oil	2	1,459-2,667	2,063	1,459
GARINEI, Michele (1871-1960) Italian				
oil	2	496-2,293	1,394	496
GARINO, Angelo (1860-?) Italian				
oil	3	1,211-9,545	4,752	3,500
GARLAND, Charles Trevor (1851-1906) British				
oil	1	4,250	4,250	4,250
GARLAND, H (19th C) British				
3D	1	19,110	19,110	19,110
GARLAND, Henry (fl.1854-1900) British				
oil	5	3,496-8,800	6,592	7,400
GARLAND, Valentine Thomas (1868-1914) British				
oil	2	1,418-3,500	2,459	1,418
GARLAND, William (?-1882) British				
oil	1	1,760	1,760	1,760
GARNELO Y ALDA, Jose (1866-1945) Spanish				
oil	2	568-9,644	5,106	568
GARNERAY, Ambroise Louis (1783-1857) French				
oil	1	111,507	111,507	111,507
wc/d	2	2,571-16,815	9,693	2,571
GARNERAY, Auguste (1785-1824) French				
wc/d	1	1,014	1,014	1,014
GARNERAY, Jean François (1755-1837) French				
oil	1	11,892	11,892	11,892
wc/d	1	1,531	1,531	1,531
GARNIER, Jean (1820-1895) French				
3D	1	4,568	4,568	4,568
GARNIER, Jean (1853-1910) French				
3D	1	6,600	6,600	6,600
GARNIER, Jules Arsene (1847-1889) French				
oil	2	2,500-3,000	2,750	2,500
GARNIER, Marie (fl.1750s) ?				
wc/d	1	1,414	1,414	1,414
GARNIER, Michel (18th C) French				
oil	1	81,918	81,918	81,918
GARNIER, P (?) ?				
3D	1	5,500	5,500	5,500
GARNIER, Pierre (1847-1937) French				
oil	2	1,440-6,107	3,773	1,440
GARNIER, Pierre (1928-) French				
3D	1	4,638	4,638	4,638
GAROFALINI, Giacinto (1666-1723) Italian				
oil	1	8,834	8,834	8,834
GAROUSTE, Gerard (1946-) French				
oil	4	4,909-50,571	22,052	15,196
wc/d	4	1,640-4,816	3,384	2,267
3D	2	10,207-12,041	11,124	10,207
GARRARD, George (1760-1826) British				
oil	1	23,940	23,940	23,940
GARRAUD, Léon (1877-1961) French				
oil	1	1,080	1,080	1,080
GARREAU, G (20th C) French				
3D	1	1,826	1,826	1,826
GARRETT, Edmund (1853-1929) American				
oil	3	500-2,250	1,133	650
GARRIDO, Eduardo Léon (1856-1949) Spanish				
oil	11	1,697-59,589	18,186	5,700
GARRIDO, Louis Edouard (1893-1982) French				
oil	9	620-4,127	2,001	1,680

Name	No.	Price Range	Average	Median
GARRONE, Francesco (1858-1924) Italian				
oil	1	3,148	3,148	3,148
GARROS, Catherine (1954-) French				
oil	1	2,250	2,250	2,250
GARRY, Charley (1891-) French				
oil	1	16,000	16,000	16,000
GARSIDE, Oswald (1879-1942) British				
oil	1	519	519	519
wc/d	5	540-2,079	1,213	1,068
GARSIDE, Thomas H (1906-1980) Canadian				
oil	6	713-19,498	4,280	1,230
GARSTIN, Alethea (1894-1978) British				
wc/d	2	1,663-4,071	2,867	1,663
GARSTIN, Norman (1847-1926) British/Irish				
wc/d	2	690-1,479	1,084	690
GARTHWAITE, William (1821-1889) British				
oil	1	4,813	4,813	4,813
GARTMAN, German Eduard (20th C) German				
wc/d	1	1,240	1,240	1,240
GARTNER, Fritz (1882-?) German				
oil	1	2,803	2,803	2,803
GARTNER, L (19/20th C) ?				
oil	1	1,800	1,800	1,800
GARTNER, Louis (19/20th C) ?				
oil	1	1,593	1,593	1,593
GARUTTI, Alberto (1948-) Italian				
3D	1	4,685	4,685	4,685
GARWOOD, Audrey (1927-2004) Canadian				
oil	1	1,493	1,493	1,493
GARZOLINI, Giuseppe (1850-1938) Italian				
oil	3	843-1,286	1,031	964
GARZONI, Giovanna (1600-1670) Italian				
oil	2	43,347-48,163	45,755	43,347
wc/d	1	320,000	320,000	320,000
GASCAR (1635-1701) French				
oil	1	6,020	6,020	6,020
GASCAR, Henri (1635-1701) French				
oil	2	17,010-70,000	43,505	17,010
GASIOROWSKI, Gerard (1930-1986) French				
oll	2	1,909-7,130	4,519	1,909
wc/d	2	2,128-2,472	2,300	2,128
GASKIN, Arthur Joseph (1862-1928) British				
oil	1	4,176	4,176	4,176
GASPARD, Léon (1882-1964) French				
oil	13	900-42,500	16,453	12,000
wc/d	3	4,000-25,000	18,000	25,000
GASPARI, Luciano (1913-) Italian				
oil	2	819-1,286	1,052	819
GASPARINI, Bruna (1937-) Italian				
oil	1	1,790	1,790	1,790
GASPARINI, Luigi (1779-?) Italian				
wc/d	1	3,131	3,131	3,131
GASPARO, Oronzo Vito (1903-1969) American/Italian				
oil	1	1,334	1,334	1,334
GASPART, Alfred (1900-1993) French				
oil	1	18,828	18,828	18,828
wc/d	1	690	690	690
GASPERI, Filippo de (1928-) Italian				
oil	2	471-1,532	1,001	471
GASPERONI, Walter (20th C) Italian				
oil	1	1,178	1,178	1,178
GASQ, Paul Jean Baptiste (1860-1944) French				
3D	1	1,797	1,797	1,797
GASQUET, Gerard (1945-) French				
oil	2	1,054-1,054	1,054	1,054
GASSER, Henry (1909-1981) American				
oil	3	8,000-12,000	9,333	8,000
wc/d	8	700-8,000	3,895	2,100
GASSIES, Jean Baptiste Georges (1829-1919) French				
oil	1	1,249	1,249	1,249
wc/d	1	716	716	716

Name	No.	Price Range	Average	Median
GASTALDI, Andrea (1826-1889) Italian				
oil	1	1,210	1,210	1,210
GASTE, Constant Georges (1869-1910) French				
oil	2	3,250-6,656	4,953	3,250
GASTEIGER, Anna Sophie (1878-1954) German				
oil	2	1,686-1,806	1,746	1,686
GASTEIGER, Jacob (1953-) Austrian				
oil	4	3,514-13,352	9,198	7,071
GASTEMANS, Émile (1883-1956) Belgian				
oil	2	3,131-5,192	4,161	3,131
wc/d	1	506	506	506
GASTINEAU, Henry (1791-1876) British				
wc/d	1	5,460	5,460	5,460
GASTINEAU, Maria G (1824-1890) British				
wc/d	2	1,332-1,388	1,360	1,332
GASTINI, Marco (1938-) Italian				
oil	1	1,074	1,074	1,074
wc/d	3	597-2,335	1,409	1,295
GAT, Eliahu (1919-1987) Israeli				
oil	2	2,000-3,000	2,500	2,000
GATCH, Lee (1902-1968) American				
oil	3	2,200-4,000	3,066	3,000
GATES, Robert Franklin (1906-) American				
oil	1	2,800	2,800	2,800
GATIN, Sergei Zakharovich (1923-) Russian				
oil	1	4,602	4,602	4,602
GATT, Ferdinand (1847-1909) Austrian				
wc/d	2	1,030-1,030	1,030	1,030
GATTA, Saverio della (?-1829) Italian				
wc/d	6	3,150-8,414	5,015	3,480
GATTESCHI, Roberto Pio (1872-1958) Italian				
oil	1	1,453	1,453	1,453
GATTI DOURA, Juan (1948-1983) ?				
oil	2	1,100-1,300	1,200	1,100
GATTI, Annibale (1828-1909) Italian				
oil	1	5,041	5,041	5,041
GATTI, Antoine (19th C) French				
oil	1	1,176	1,176	1,176
GATTI, G (19th C) Italian?				
3D	1	18,000	18,000	18,000
GATTI, Giuseppe (1807-1880) Italian				
wc/d	1	4,839	4,839	4,839
GATTIKER, Hermann (1865-1950) Swiss				
oil	1	1,290	1,290	1,290
GATTO, Domingo (20th C) Argentinian				
oil	1	7,000	7,000	7,000
GATTO, Victor Joseph (1893-1965) American				
oil	10	425-3,500	1,675	700
GAUCHER, Yves (1933-) Canadian				
oil	1	9,896	9,896	9,896
GAUD, Léon (1844-1908) Swiss				
oil	1	2,900	2,900	2,900
GAUDEFROY, Alphonse (1845-1936) French				
oil	2	789-1,908	1,348	789
GAUDENZI, Enrico (1912-) Italian				
oil	1	2,811	2,811	2,811
GAUDENZI, Pietro (1880-1955) Italian				
oil	1	12,298	12,298	12,298
wc/d	1	1,405	1,405	1,405
GAUDEZ, Adrien Étienne (1845-1902) French				
3D	9	1,920-16,000	5,024	3,403
GAUDIER-BRZESKA, Henri (1891-1915) French				
wc/d	16	925-28,350	9,737	7,770
3D	2	29,580-32,130	30,855	29,580
GAUDION, Georges (1885-1942) French				
wc/d	1	2,022	2,022	2,022
GAUER, Bernhard (1882-1955) German				
oil	1	1,210	1,210	1,210
GAUERMANN, Friedrich (1807-1862) Austrian				
oil	7	4,685-145,175	37,715	23,562
wc/d	1	542	542	542

Name	No.	Price Range	Average	Median
GAUFFRIAUX, Emile (1877-1957) French				
oil	2	656-720	688	656
wc/d	2	530-631	580	530
GAUGAIN, Thomas (1748-1812) French				
oil	1	3,150	3,150	3,150
GAUGUIN, Paul (1848-1903) French				
oil	4	650,000-19,360,000	6,187,500	740,000
wc/d	9	4,519-444,000	73,275	26,000
3D	4	3,461-25,716	12,726	6,301
GAUL, Arrah Lee (1888-1980) American				
oil	3	500-3,000	2,000	2,500
GAUL, August (1869-1921) German				
wc/d	1	707	707	707
3D	16	1,978-63,243	11,676	7,633
GAUL, Gilbert (1855-1919) American				
oil	7	3,000-110,000	34,392	26,000
GAUL, Winfred (1928-) German				
oil	3	1,757-4,712	3,596	4,320
wc/d	4	419-1,274	860	548
GAULD, David (1865-1936) British				
oil	7	6,444-30,000	11,691	9,204
GAULEY, Robert David (1875-1943) American				
oil	1	2,200	2,200	2,200
GAULI, Piero (1916-) Italian				
oil	3	597-3,658	1,752	1,001
GAULLI, Giovanni Battista (1639-1709) Italian				
oil	1	22,200	22,200	22,200
wc/d	1	1,500	1,500	1,500
GAULT, Alfred de (19th C) French?				
oil	1	6,473	6,473	6,473
GAUME, Henri René (1834-?) French				
oil	1	6,500	6,500	6,500
GAUPILLAT, Henry (19th C) French				
oil	1	2,541	2,541	2,541
GAUPP, Gustav Adolf (1844-1918) German				
oil	1	2,038	2,038	2,038
GAUSE, Wilhelm (1853-1916) German				
oil	1	11,125	11,125	11,125
GAUSSEN, Adolphe-Louis (1871-1954) French				
oil	3	1,062-4,595	2,292	1,219
GAUSSON, Leo (1860-1944) French				
oil	6	613-15,793	4,930	1,600
wc/d	1	2,979	2,979	2,979
GAUTHERIN, Jacques (1929-1997) French				
oil	1	1,157	1,157	1,157
GAUTHERIN, Jean (1840-1890) French				
3D	1	3,534	3,534	3,534
GAUTHIER, Joachim (1897-1988) Canadian				
oil	6	487-4,100	1,461	856
wc/d	1	451	451	451
GAUTHIER, Léon Ambroise (1822-1880) French				
oil	1	7,500	7,500	7,500
GAUTHIER, Oscar (1921-) French				
oil	11	1,286-12,945	4,406	3,000
wc/d	2	494-1,401	947	494
GAUTIER D'AGOTY, Jean Baptiste (1740-1786) French				
oil	1	12,671	12,671	12,671
GAUTIER, Jacques (1831-?) French				
3D	1	20,790	20,790	20,790
GAUTIER, Jean Fabien (1747-?) French				
oil	1	1,176	1,176	1,176
GAUTSCHI, Joseph (1900-1977) Swiss				
oil	1	1,142	1,142	1,142
GAUVRIT, Jean Jacques (1948-) French?				
oil	1	1,800	1,800	1,800
GAVIN, Robert (1827-1883) British				
oil	3	2,422-17,600	7,612	2,816
GAVRILKEVICH, Yevgeny (1929-) Russian				
oil	1	1,400	1,400	1,400
GAVRILOV, Vladimir Nikolaevich (1923-1970) Russian				
oil	1	1,567	1,567	1,567

Name	No.	Price Range	Average	Median
GAW, William Alexander (1891-1973) American				
oil	2	3,500-5,500	4,500	3,500
GAWELL, Oskar (1888-1955) Austrian				
oil	1	3,600	3,600	3,600
wc/d	5	1,028-2,160	1,489	1,414
GAWNE, John C (1952-) American				
oil	1	5,000	5,000	5,000
GAY, Edward (1837-1928) American				
oil	4	2,000-3,500	2,612	2,250
GAY, François (1940-) Swiss				
oil	3	571-1,513	1,157	1,387
GAY, Jacques Louis (1851-1925) French				
oil	1	8,281	8,281	8,281
GAY, Walter (1856-1937) American				
oil	5	2,000-47,500	15,002	10,000
wc/d	4	6,500-10,000	8,375	8,000
GAYA, Ramon (1910-2005) Spanish				
oil	1	28,286	28,286	28,286
wc/d	3	7,714-21,699	13,019	9,644
GAYLOR, Adelaide L (1889-1986) American				
oil	1	1,300	1,300	1,300
GAYLOR, Samuel Wood (1883-1957) American				
wc/d	1	1,200	1,200	1,200
GAYRARD, Joseph Raymond Paul (1807-1855) French				
3D	2	7,000-18,900	12,950	7,000
GAYS, Eugenio (1861-1938) Italian				
wc/d	2	1,210-1,816	1,513	1,210
GAZE, Harold (20th C) American				
wc/d	1	2,900	2,900	2,900
GAZI (1900-1975) French?				
oil	1	1,062	1,062	1,062
GAZZERA, Romano (1908-1985) Italian				
oil	1	7,767	7,767	7,767
GBOURI, Fatna (1924-) Moroccan				
oil	3	798-14,914	5,503	798
GE XIANGLAN (1904-1964) Chinese				
wc/d	1	1,518	1,518	1,518
GEAR, William (1915-1997) British				
oil	12	841-20,880	8,508	5,104
wc/d	9	800-7,080	3,062	2,775
GEARY, Kevin (1952-) Irish?				
oil	5	2,384-4,580	3,167	2,919
GEBAUER, Christian David (1777-1831) German				
oil	1	6,324	6,324	6,324
GEBHARD, Albert (1869-1937) Finnish				
oil	1	3,086	3,086	3,086
GEBHARDT, Eduard K F von (1838-1925) German				
oil	5	491-4,400	1,693	1,169
wc/d	1	730	730	730
GEBHARDT, Ludwig (1830-1908) German				
oil	3	468-20,384	7,437	1,459
GEBLER, Otto Friedrich (1838-1917) German				
oil	3	1,824-9,414	5,694	5,845
wc/d	1	1,388	1,388	1,388
GECELLI, Johannes (1925-) German				
oil	4	2,121-8,905	4,296	2,338
GECHTER, Jean François Theodore (1796-1844) French				
3D	2	3,540-5,702	4,621	3,540
GECHTOFF, Leonid (1883-1941) American				
oil	3	365-800	605	650
wc/d	1	443	443	443
GEDDES, Andrew (1783-1844) British				
oil	2	2,832-9,680	6,256	2,832
GEDDES, Norman Bel (1893-1958) American				
wc/d	1	1,600	1,600	1,600
GEDDES, William (1841-1884) British				
oil	1	2,000	2,000	2,000
GEDLEK, Ludwig (1847-1904) Austrian				
oil	2	7,500-16,562	12,031	7,500
GEEFS, Fanny (1814-1883) Belgian				
oil	2	1,788-9,092	5,440	1,788

Name	No.	Price Range	Average	Median
GEEL, Jacob Jacobsz van (1585-1638) Dutch				
oil	1	34,600	34,600	34,600
GEEL, Joost van (1631-1698) Dutch				
oil	1	14,240	14,240	14,240
GEER, Carl Johan de (1938-) Swedish				
oil	1	5,286	5,286	5,286
GEERTSEN, Ib (1919-) Danish				
oil	2	1,493-2,495	1,994	1,493
3D	1	1,610	1,610	1,610
GEEST, Wybrand-Simonsz de (elder) (1592-1659) Dutch				
oil	1	29,035	29,035	29,035
GEETERE, Frans de (20th C) Belgian				
wc/d	1	1,818	1,818	1,818
GEETS, Willem (1838-1919) Belgian				
oil	3	1,555-20,331	8,378	3,250
wc/d	1	2,028	2,028	2,028
GEFELDT, E (19th C) Danish				
oil	1	3,281	3,281	3,281
GEGERFELT, Wilhelm von (1844-1920) Swedish				
oil	12	373-8,101	3,633	3,022
wc/d	2	1,301-2,610	1,955	1,301
GEHMAN, Mildred S (20th C) American				
oil	32	350-5,750	1,460	1,000
GEHR, Ferdinand (1896-1996) Swiss				
oil	6	3,921-16,195	8,057	5,489
wc/d	10	941-10,978	5,209	3,830
GEHRI, Franz (1882-1960) Swiss				
oil	1	1,082	1,082	1,082
GEHRI, Hermann (1879-1944) German				
wc/d	1	3,010	3,010	3,010
GEHRIG, Jakob (1846-1922) German				
oil	1	2,486	2,486	2,486
GEHRTS, Carl (1853-1898) German				
oil	1	10,885	10,885	10,885
GEHRY, Frank (1929-) American				
3D	1	7,000	7,000	7,000
GEIDEL, Gerhard (1925-) German				
oil	1	2,268	2,268	2,268
GEIGER, Caspar Augustin (1847-1924) German				
oil	2	1,312-6,969	4,140	1,312
GEIGER, Ernst (1876-1965) Swiss				
oil	6	1,526-58,282	13,018	4,186
GEIGER, Philip (1956-) American				
oil	1	2,600	2,600	2,600
GEIGER, Richard (1870-1945) Austrian				
oil	4	525-3,279	1,476	1,000
GEIGER, Rupprecht (1908-) German				
oil	10	5,845-56,055	31,315	30,575
wc/d	2	505-3,762	2,133	505
GEIGER, Willi (1878-1971) German				
oil	2	941-3,534	2,237	941
wc/d	1	1,671	1,671	1,671
GEIRNAERT, Jozef (1791-1859) Belgian				
oil	1	2,655	2,655	2,655
GEISER, Karl (1898-1957) Swiss				
wc/d	2	500-757	628	500
3D	5	4,540-10,548	6,637	5,612
GEISER, O (19th C) German				
oil	1	2,400	2,400	2,400
GEISSBUHLER, Domenic Karl (1932-) Swiss				
oil	1	1,945	1,945	1,945
GEISSER, Johann Josef (1824-1894) Swiss				
oil	5	622-8,018	3,195	2,748
GEISSLER, Paul (1881-1965) German				
oil	1	2,028	2,028	2,028
GEITLINGER, Ernst (1895-1972) German				
oil	1	2,121	2,121	2,121
wc/d	1	413	413	413
GELDER, Aert de (1645-1727) Dutch				
oil	1	11,892	11,892	11,892
GELDER, Lucia Mathilde von (1865-1899) German				
oil	1	11,000	11,000	11,000

Name	No.	Price Range	Average	Median
GELDER, Steve van (20th C) American?				
oil	1	1,000	1,000	1,000
GELDEREN, Simon van (1905-1986) Belgian				
oil	1	1,085	1,085	1,085
GELDORP, Gortzius (1553-1618) Flemish				
oil	4	800-14,000	6,871	2,400
GELENG, Giuliano (1949-) Italian				
oil	1	1,260	1,260	1,260
GELENG, Otto (19th C) German				
oil	2	1,947-10,000	5,973	1,947
GELHAAR, Emil (1862-1934) American				
oil	1	3,000	3,000	3,000
GELHAY, Edouard (1856-?) French				
oil	2	3,781-6,020	4,900	3,781
GELIBERT, Gaston and Jules Bertrand (19/20th C) French				
wc/d	1	1,546	1,546	1,546
GELIBERT, Jules-Bertrand (1834-1916) French				
oil	8	849-14,000	5,268	3,754
wc/d	3	1,204-37,083	16,264	10,507
GELISSEN, Maximilien Lambert (1786-1867) Belgian				
oil	3	1,447-6,049	4,133	4,905
GELLEE, Claude (c.1600-1682) French				
oil	2	20,571-677,315	348,943	20,571
GELLER, Johann Nepomuk (1860-1954) Austrian				
oil	1	7,007	7,007	7,007
wc/d	3	1,149-3,816	2,800	3,435
GELLI, Odoardo (1852-1933) Italian				
oil	1	8,653	8,653	8,653
GELMO, Marianne (19th C) Austrian				
oil	1	2,534	2,534	2,534
GELY, Gabriel (1924-) Canadian?				
oil	2	897-1,304	1,100	897
GEMIGNANI, Sineo (1917-1973) Italian				
oil	1	1,512	1,512	1,512
GEMITO, Vincenzo (1852-1929) Italian				
wc/d	1	3,637	3,637	3,637
3D	20	1,776-37,800	8,847	4,142
GEMMELL, Michael (1950-) Irish				
oil	5	484-3,781	2,019	1,505
GEMPT, Bernard de (1826-1879) Dutch				
oil	2	3,871-10,130	7,000	3,871
GEN-PAUL (1895-1975) French				
oil	28	753-38,877	15,044	11,689
wc/d	63	468-7,767	2,616	2,124
GENBERG, Anton (1862-1939) Swedish				
oil	16	647-25,479	3,742	1,994
GENDRON, Annick (20th C) French?				
wc/d	1	1,073	1,073	1,073
GENEGEN, Jos van (1857-1936) Belgian				
oil	6	584-2,863	1,681	1,214
GENELLI, Bonaventura (1798-1868) German				
wc/d	2	1,286-5,890	3,588	1,286
GENENGER, Theodor (19th C) Dutch				
oil	2	1,027-1,260	1,143	1,027
GENERAL IDEA (20th C) Canadian				
oil	1	12,098	12,098	12,098
GENET, Paulette (c.1890-?) French				
oil	1	1,523	1,523	1,523
GENGA, Girolamo (1476-1551) Italian				
oil	1	66,892	66,892	66,892
GENICOT, Robert Albert (1890-1981) French				
oil	1	10,356	10,356	10,356
GENIN, Lucien (1894-1958) French				
oil	11	941-18,500	6,873	6,304
wc/d	35	547-8,919	1,976	1,420
GENIS, René (1922-2004) French				
oil	14	500-3,816	1,789	1,256
GENISSON, Jules Victor (1805-1860) Belgian				
oil	4	1,403-51,625	14,399	2,059
GENN, Robert (1936-) Canadian				
oil	19	453-5,730	1,411	923

Name	No.	Price Range	Average	Median
GENNARELLI, Amedeo (20th C) Italian				
3D	3	2,400-4,033	3,159	3,045
GENNARI, Cesare (1637-1688) Italian				
oil	1	138,750	138,750	138,750
GENOD, Michel Philebert (1795-1862) French				
oil	2	4,173-8,870	6,521	4,173
GENOVES, Juan (1930-) Spanish				
oil	2	24,429-77,736	51,082	24,429
wc/d	1	3,854	3,854	3,854
GENTH, Lillian (1876-1953) American				
oil	4	2,500-8,000	4,550	2,900
GENTILESCHI, Artemisia (1597-1651) Italian				
oil	1	45,000	45,000	45,000
GENTILINI, Franco (1909-1981) Italian				
oil	8	12,687-69,966	43,760	42,164
wc/d	3	1,208-9,908	4,490	2,356
GENTILS, Vic (1919-1997) Belgian				
wc/d	1	3,507	3,507	3,507
3D	6	2,163-10,520	5,073	3,956
GENTLEMAN, David (1930-) British				
oil	1	1,914	1,914	1,914
GENTRY (20th C) ?				
oil	1	2,736	2,736	2,736
GENTRY, Herbert (1921-) ?				
oil	1	1,940	1,940	1,940
GENTY, Emmanuel (1830-1904) French				
oil	1	2,432	2,432	2,432
GENTZ, Karl Wilhelm (1822-1890) German				
oil	1	6,270	6,270	6,270
GENUTAT, Fritz (1876-?) German				
oil	1	1,776	1,776	1,776
GENZKEN, Isa (1948-) German?				
3D	1	10,000	10,000	10,000
GENZMER, Berthold (1858-?) German				
oil	1	4,671	4,671	4,671
GEOFFROY, Henry Jules Jean (1853-1924) French				
oil	1	27,000	27,000	27,000
wc/d	1	1,005	1,005	1,005
GEOGHEGAN, Trevor (1946-) Irish				
oil	5	1,336-5,611	3,309	2,667
GEORGAS, Michalis (1947-) Greek				
oil	1	11,220	11,220	11,220
GEORGE, Herbert (19th C) British?				
oil	1	1,147	1,147	1,147
GEORGE-JULLIARD, Jean Philippe (1818-1888) Swiss				
oil	9	569-6,578	1,878	763
GEORGE-LEGRAND, Louis (1801-1883) Swiss				
oil	1	2,089	2,089	2,089
GEORGES, Claude (1929-1988) French				
oil	3	742-1,455	1,136	1,212
GEORGI, Friedrich Otto (1819-1874) German				
oil	1	5,874	5,874	5,874
wc/d	1	3,363	3,363	3,363
GEORGIOU, Kostis (1956-) Greek				
oil	5	2,076-9,680	6,783	9,350
GERADA, C (?) Italian				
oil	1	2,000	2,000	2,000
GERAEDTS, Pieter (1911-) Dutch				
oil	1	1,800	1,800	1,800
GERAETS, Michel (1829-1908) Belgian?				
oil	1	1,707	1,707	1,707
GERALIS, Apostolos (1886-1983) Greek				
oil	7	5,236-22,680	15,693	17,010
wc/d	1	5,610	5,610	5,610
GERALIS, Loucas (1875-1958) Greek				
oil	7	4,675-10,912	7,364	7,266
GERANIOTIS, Dimitrios (1871-1966) Greek				
oil	1	5,984	5,984	5,984
GERARD, Baron François (1770-1837) French				
oil	4	705-975,000	396,426	300,000
wc/d	51	419-4,549	1,251	839

Name	No.	Price Range	Average	Median
GERARD, E (19th C) French				
oil	1	1,145	1,145	1,145
GERARD, L (?) ?				
oil	1	4,000	4,000	4,000
GERARD, Louis Auguste (1782-1862) French				
oil	1	5,146	5,146	5,146
GERARD, Lucien (1852-1935) Belgian				
oil	3	743-4,272	1,971	900
GERARD, Marguerite (1761-1837) French				
oil	1	2,338	2,338	2,338
GERARD, Theodore (1829-1895) Belgian				
oil	5	927-21,205	7,501	5,005
GERASCH, August (1822-1908) Austrian				
oil	1	1,949	1,949	1,949
GERASIMOV, Sergei Vassilievich (1885-1964) Russian				
oil	2	1,745-1,757	1,751	1,745
wc/d	1	3,031	3,031	3,031
GERASIMOVICH, Iosif (1893-1982) Russian				
wc/d	1	5,500	5,500	5,500
GERAUD, Marguerite (1879-1969) French				
wc/d	1	38,571	38,571	38,571
GERBINO, Rosario Urbino (1900-1972) American				
oil	2	1,100-7,500	4,300	1,100
GERCHMAN, Rubens (1942-) Brazilian				
oil	1	13,000	13,000	13,000
wc/d	1	2,500	2,500	2,500
GERDES, Friedrich (fl.1880-1920) German				
oil	1	4,743	4,743	4,743
GERE, Charles M (1869-1957) British				
oil	1	1,018	1,018	1,018
wc/d	2	570-692	631	570
GERECHTER, Siegmund (1850-1902) German				
oil	1	3,579	3,579	3,579
GERELL, Greta (1898-1982) Swedish				
oil	2	1,165-2,294	1,729	1,165
wc/d	1	2,493	2,493	2,493
GERGELY, Imre (1868-1914) Hungarian				
oil	2	2,061-6,500	4,280	2,061
GERHARDINGER, Constantin (1888-1970) German				
oil	4	1,312-8,027	3,919	1,453
GERHARDT, Christophe (19th C) French				
wc/d	1	1,903	1,903	1,903
GERHARDT, Eduard K F von (1813-1888) German				
wc/d	2	1,008-1,527	1,267	1,008
GERHART, Charles J (20th C) American				
oil	1	6,500	6,500	6,500
GERHARTZ, Dan (1965-) American				
oil	4	1,900-13,500	5,475	3,000
GERHOLD, Mel (1928-) American				
oil	1	1,400	1,400	1,400
GERI, G (19th C) ?				
oil	1	37,500	37,500	37,500
GERICAULT, Theodore (1791-1824) French				
wc/d	7	3,200-270,000	54,001	14,000
GERINI, Niccolo di Pietro (?-1415) Italian				
oil	1	177,397	177,397	177,397
GERLACH, Georg (1874-1962) German				
wc/d	1	1,210	1,210	1,210
GERLACH, Otto (1862-1908) German				
wc/d	1	1,288	1,288	1,288
GERMAIN, Jacques (1915-2001) French				
oil	92	473-23,836	3,335	2,622
wc/d	19	454-2,293	856	634
GERMAIN, Marie Louise (?) French?				
oil	1	2,000	2,000	2,000
GERMAIN-THILL (1873-1925) French				
oil	1	3,888	3,888	3,888
GERMAIN-THILL, Alphonse Leon Antoine (1873-1925) French				
oil	3	701-8,767	3,623	1,403
GERMANA, Mimmo (1944-1992) Italian				
oil	20	786-10,898	4,778	4,099
wc/d	3	900-1,967	1,399	1,331

Name	No.	Price Range	Average	Median
GERMASCHEFF, Michail (1868-1930) Russian				
oil	1	7,200	7,200	7,200
GERMENIS, Vasilis (1896-1966) Greek				
oil	11	3,366-13,230	7,095	5,632
wc/d	1	7,040	7,040	7,040
GERMIAS, Yiannis (1954-) Greek				
oil	1	1,760	1,760	1,760
GERNANDT, Wilhelm (1863-1920) Swedish				
oil	1	1,099	1,099	1,099
GERNES, Poul (1925-1996) Danish				
oil	3	4,185-4,829	4,614	4,829
GERNEZ, Paul Elie (1888-1948) French				
oil	1	6,027	6,027	6,027
wc/d	5	1,381-7,603	3,812	3,366
GEROME, François (1895-?) French				
oil	12	600-2,250	1,123	1,100
GEROME, Jean Léon (1824-1904) French				
oil	13	1,795-1,692,800	355,563	47,840
wc/d	3	935-20,000	7,406	1,285
3D	4	3,540-15,660	6,724	3,600
GEROS, Dimitris (1948-) Greek				
oil	2	4,498-5,236	4,867	4,498
GERRITS, Gerrit Jacobus (1893-1965) Dutch				
oil	1	2,290	2,290	2,290
GERRITZ, Frank (1964-) German				
wc/d	1	2,200	2,200	2,200
GERRY, Samuel Lancaster (1813-1891) American				
oil	5	1,500-5,250	3,450	3,000
GERSHUNI, Moshe (1936-) Israeli				
oil	3	4,500-10,000	7,333	7,500
wc/d	4	1,500-16,000	5,525	1,800
GERSTNER, Karl (c.1930-) Swiss				
oil	1	2,750	2,750	2,750
wc/d	1	4,079	4,079	4,079
3D	1	4,463	4,463	4,463
GERTLER, Mark (1891-1939) British				
oil	2	30,240-31,320	30,780	30,240
wc/d	2	845-1,007	926	845
GERTNER, Johan Vilhelm (1818-1871) Danish				
oil	2	852-1,581	1,216	852
GERTNER, Peter (16th C) German				
oil	1	24,082	24,082	24,082
wc/d	1	480,000	480,000	480,000
GERVAIS, Lise (1933-1998) Canadian				
oil	7	2,773-13,777	8,520	9,071
GERVEX, Henri (1852-1929) French				
oil	7	1,375-48,720	12,824	5,255
wc/d	1	3,263	3,263	3,263
GERWEN, Abraham van (17th C) Dutch?				
oil	1	16,910	16,910	16,910
GERZ, Jochen (1940-) German				
wc/d	1	6,622	6,622	6,622
GERZSO, Gunther (1915-2000) Mexican				
oil	2	30,000-110,000	70,000	30,000
wc/d	1	60,000	60,000	60,000
3D	1	27,000	27,000	27,000
GESELSCHAP, Eduard (1814-1878) Dutch				
oil	3	1,870-6,622	4,102	3,816
GESELSCHAP, Friedrich (1835-1898) German/Italian				
oil	1	1,381	1,381	1,381
GESSA Y ARIAS, Sebastian (1840-1920) Spanish				
oil	4	1,140-14,270	5,910	2,851
GESSNER, Richard (1894-1988) German				
oil	1	1,401	1,401	1,401
GESSNER, Robert S (1908-1982) Swiss				
oil	4	487-2,921	1,249	605
wc/d	1	1,058	1,058	1,058
GESTEL, Leo (1881-1941) Dutch				
oil	5	12,721-241,701	63,879	20,384
wc/d	20	935-87,669	8,312	2,145
GEUDENS, Albert (1869-1949) Belgian				
oil	2	1,392-1,654	1,523	1,392

Name	No.	Price Range	Average	Median
GEVA, Tzibi (1951-) Israeli?				
oil	2	4,000-10,000	7,000	4,000
GEVAERT, Arthur (1902-?) Belgian				
oil	1	1,215	1,215	1,215
GEVERS, Helene (19th C) Belgian				
oil	1	5,011	5,011	5,011
GEYER, Alexius (1816-1883) German				
oil	1	1,752	1,752	1,752
GEYER, Fritz (1875-1947) German				
oil	5	492-2,128	1,640	1,824
GEYER, Georg (1823-1912) Austrian				
oil	3	2,431-4,290	3,216	2,928
wc/d	1	903	903	903
GEYER, Wilhelm (1900-1968) German				
oil	2	486-2,670	1,578	486
GEYGER, Ernst Moritz (1861-1941) German				
3D	2	3,516-9,200	6,358	3,516
GEYLING, Carl (1814-1880) Austrian				
oil	1	1,178	1,178	1,178
GEYLING, Remigius (19/20th C) ?				
wc/d	2	1,144-1,360	1,252	1,144
GEYNET, Jacques (20th C) French				
oil	1	1,868	1,868	1,868
GEYP, Adriaan Marinus (1855-1926) Dutch				
oil	5	492-2,682	1,356	1,400
GHAFARI, Abul Hasan (19th C) Persian				
wc/d	1	8,650	8,650	8,650
GHARBAOUI, Jilali (1930-1971) French				
oil	2	17,865-33,237	25,551	17,865
GHEDUZZI, Cesare (1894-1944) Italian				
oil	11	1,197-6,054	2,847	2,182
GHEDUZZI, Giuseppe (1889-1957) Italian				
oil	13	1,940-12,109	4,566	3,879
GHEDUZZI, Mario (1891-1970) Italian				
oil	5	1,193-2,667	1,843	1,756
GHEDUZZI, Ugo (1853-1925) Italian				
oil	2	2,425-4,033	3,229	2,425
GHERARDI, Giuseppe (19th C) Italian				
oil	1	32,500	32,500	32,500
GHERARDINI, Stephane (1696-1756) Italian				
oil	1	48,952	48,952	48,952
GHERMANDI, Quinto (1916-) Italian				
3D	1	4,071	4,071	4,071
GHEYN, Jacob de (younger) (1565-1629) Dutch				
oil	1	1,558	1,558	1,558
wc/d	1	276,800	276,800	276,800
GHEYNST, Berroni van der (1876-1946) Belgian				
oil	2	656-9,955	5,305	656
GHEZZI, Giuseppe (1634-1721) Italian				
oil	2	23,759-92,500	58,129	23,759
GHEZZI, Pier Leone (1674-1755) Italian				
wc/d	7	2,590-7,767	5,619	5,500
GHIGLIA, Paulo (1905-1979) Italian				
oil	1	16,762	16,762	16,762
GHIGLIA, Valentino (1903-1960) Italian				
oil	3	950-1,940	1,359	1,189
GHIKA, Nicolas (1906-1994) Greek				
oil	3	22,620-39,690	30,220	28,350
wc/d	3	3,553-11,340	6,489	4,576
3D	2	9,350-10,285	9,817	9,350
GHILARDI, Olindo (1848-1930) Italian				
oil	1	1,334	1,334	1,334
GHIRARDELLI, Vincenzo (1894-1967) Italian				
oil	7	1,405-4,531	2,627	2,201
GHOBERT, Jules (1881-1971) Belgian				
oil	2	876-1,285	1,080	876
GHURAYYA, Seema (1964-) Indian				
oil	1	9,350	9,350	9,350
GIACHI, E (19th C) Italian				
oil	1	12,180	12,180	12,180
GIACOMELLI, Vincenzo (1841-1890) Italian				
oil	1	9,840	9,840	9,840

Name	No.	Price Range	Average	Median
GIACOMETTI, Alberto (1901-1966) Swiss				
oil	5	824,658-1,350,000	1,064,931	1,100,000
wc/d	27	6,850-1,400,000	106,499	42,412
3D	21	22,500-3,200,000	793,477	320,000
GIACOMETTI, Alberto and Diego (20th C) Swiss				
3D	13	22,000-200,000	98,479	91,520
GIACOMETTI, Augusto (1877-1947) Swiss				
oil	7	69,342-799,115	281,597	150,110
wc/d	17	3,434-84,185	28,112	13,780
GIACOMETTI, Diego (1902-1985) Swiss				
3D	73	6,897-369,600	69,105	47,568
GIACOMETTI, Giovanni (1868-1934) Swiss				
oil	15	6,018-1,468,421	318,860	204,868
wc/d	7	3,783-53,274	25,037	19,788
GIACOMOTTI, Felix Henri (1828-1909) French/Italian				
oil	1	10,000	10,000	10,000
GIALLINA, Angelos (1857-1939) Greek				
wc/d	23	400-23,375	6,718	5,984
GIAMBIAGI, Carlos (1887-1965) Argentinian				
wc/d	2	1,200-1,400	1,300	1,200
GIAMPEDI, Giuseppe (18th C) Italian				
wc/d	1	37,000	37,000	37,000
GIANFAGNA, Charles (20th C) American				
wc/d	1	1,700	1,700	1,700
GIANI, Felice (1760-1823) Italian				
oil	1	7,782	7,782	7,782
wc/d	2	1,424-7,400	4,412	1,424
GIANI, Giovanni (1866-1937) Italian				
oil	3	892-22,253	9,229	4,543
GIANNACCINI, Ilio (1897-1968) Italian				
oil	2	430-2,134	1,282	430
GIANNETTI, Raffaele (1832-1916) Italian				
oil	1	13,840	13,840	13,840
wc/d	1	1,850	1,850	1,850
GIANNI, G (19th C) Italian				
oil	1	3,894	3,894	3,894
wc/d	1	8,400	8,400	8,400
GIANNI, Gerolamo (1837-1887) Italian				
oil	4	3,268-12,600	6,913	3,460
wc/d	3	1,274-9,735	4,141	1,416
GIANNI, Gian (19th C) Italian				
oil	1	19,470	19,470	19,470
wc/d	1	1,823	1,823	1,823
GIANNI, M (19th C) Italian				
oil	1	2,548	2,548	2,548
wc/d	4	1,500-4,900	2,956	2,100
GIANNI, Maria (19th C) Italian				
wc/d	2	800-1,936	1,368	800
GIANOLI, Damiano (1946-) Swiss				
oil	1	1,526	1,526	1,526
GIANPIETRINO (1493-1540) Italian				
oil	1	57,130	57,130	57,130
GIANQUINTO, Alberto (1929-2002) Italian				
oil	6	890-10,286	5,395	2,003
wc/d	1	1,168	1,168	1,168
GIANVIELLO, G (20th C) Italian				
oil	1	2,848	2,848	2,848
GIAQUINTO, Corrado (c.1690-1765) Italian				
oil	2	95,000-1,200,000	647,500	95,000
wc/d	1	832	832	832
GIARDELLO, Giovanni (19/20th C) Italian				
oil	1	2,284	2,284	2,284
GIARDIELLO, G (?) Italian				
oil	1	3,078	3,078	3,078
GIARDIELLO, Giuseppe (19/20th C) Italian				
oil	4	1,900-3,213	2,627	2,332
GIARUSSO (20th C) French				
3D	1	6,425	6,425	6,425
GIAUQUE, Fernand (1895-1973) Swiss				
oil	3	1,499-2,107	1,729	1,582
GIBB, H W Phelan (1870-1948) British				
oil	4	400-11,505	3,706	1,328

Name	No.	Price Range	Average	Median
GIBB, Robert (elder) (1801-1837) British				
oil	1	6,726	6,726	6,726
GIBB, William Menzies (1859-1931) New Zealander				
oil	1	1,097	1,097	1,097
wc/d	1	708	708	708
GIBBONS, J (?) ?				
wc/d	1	1,246	1,246	1,246
GIBBONS, William (19th C) British				
oil	1	2,076	2,076	2,076
GIBBS, Anthony (1951-) British				
wc/d	1	3,640	3,640	3,640
GIBBS, Ewan (1973-) American				
wc/d	1	5,000	5,000	5,000
GIBBS, Henry (19th C) British				
oil	5	531-15,120	4,232	885
GIBBS, Len (1929-) Canadian				
oil	3	412-1,687	920	661
wc/d	1	492	492	492
GIBBS, Timothy (1923-) Italian				
wc/d	1	1,320	1,320	1,320
GIBERT, L (1904-1988) French				
3D	1	1,720	1,720	1,720
GIBERT, Lucien (1904-1988) French				
3D	5	1,911-12,298	4,871	2,631
GIBON, Sengai (1750-1837) Japanese				
wc/d	1	4,500	4,500	4,500
GIBSON, Charles Dana (1867-1944) American				
oil	1	4,000	4,000	4,000
wc/d	5	400-4,500	2,290	1,700
GIBSON, Colin (1948-) British				
oil	6	522-1,302	1,056	1,209
GIBSON, Joseph Vincent (fl.1861-1898) British				
oil	4	1,850-4,872	3,153	2,775
GIBSON, Patrick (1782-1829) British				
oil	1	3,000	3,000	3,000
GIBSON, William Alfred (1866-1931) British				
oil	11	865-3,654	2,186	2,088
GIDDING, Jaap (1887-1955) Dutch				
oil	2	1,008-1,764	1,386	1,008
GIDE, François Theophile Etienne (1822-1890) French				
wc/d	1	2,385	2,385	2,385
GIEBERICH, Oscar H (1886-?) American				
oil	1	3,600	3,600	3,600
GIEHLER, Torben (1973-) German				
oil	2	10,000-16,000	13,000	10,000
GIERSING, Harald (1881-1927) Danish				
oil	2	3,233-3,233	3,233	3,233
GIES, Joseph W (1860-1935) American				
oil	7	500-1,300	967	1,100
wc/d	1	650	650	650
GIESECKE, Wilhelm (1854-1917) Austrian				
3D	1	4,200	4,200	4,200
GIESEL, Hermann (1847-1906) Rumanian				
oil	1	12,138	12,138	12,138
GIESEL, Johann Ludwig (1747-1814) German				
oil	1	1,717	1,717	1,717
GIESSMANN, Friedrich (1810-1847) German				
oil	1	1,218	1,218	1,218
GIETL, Josua von (1847-1922) German				
oil	2	537-1,883	1,210	537
GIFFORD, Charles H (1839-1904) American				
oil	3	3,400-8,000	5,066	3,800
GIFFORD, John (19th C) British				
oil	5	7,120-13,000	9,260	8,500
GIFFORD, R Swain (1840-1905) American				
oil	3	1,600-1,900	1,800	1,900
GIFFORD, Sanford Robinson (1823-1880) American				
oil	4	20,000-220,000	88,875	38,000
GIFFORD, Virginia Mason (1907-2003) American				
wc/d	1	1,500	1,500	1,500

Name	No.	Price Range	Average	Median
GIGANTE, Giacinto (1806-1876) Italian				
oil	1	2,038	2,038	2,038
wc/d	2	8,836-15,925	12,380	8,836
GIGER, Hans-Rudolf (1940-) Swiss				
oil	2	1,785-4,057	2,921	1,785
wc/d	1	2,270	2,270	2,270
GIGNOUS, Eugenio (1850-1906) Italian				
oil	2	7,847-7,880	7,863	7,847
GIGNOUS, Lorenzo (1862-c.1954) Italian				
oil	3	486-15,534	6,590	3,750
GIGNOUX, François Regis (1816-1882) American/French				
oil	1	3,500	3,500	3,500
GIGOUX, Jean (1806-1894) French				
oil	1	1,070	1,070	1,070
GIHON, Albert Dakin (1866-?) American				
oil	4	400-1,600	1,025	501
GIHON, Clarence M (1871-1929) American				
oil	1	2,400	2,400	2,400
GIKOW, Ruth (1913-1982) American/Ukranian				
oil	2	600-1,600	1,100	600
GIL SALA, Ignacio (1912-) Spanish				
oil	4	1,189-14,301	7,647	6,600
GIL, Ignacio (1913-) Spanish				
oil	2	5,000-7,603	6,301	5,000
GILADI, Aharon (1907-1993) Israeli				
oil	3	900-1,200	1,033	1,000
GILARDI, Pier Celestino (1837-1905) Italian				
oil	1	2,000	2,000	2,000
GILARDI, Piero (1942-) Italian				
oil	1	4,452	4,452	4,452
3D	21	1,523-46,849	8,980	6,361
GILARDI, Silvano (1933-) Italian				
oil	1	1,890	1,890	1,890
GILBERT (?) ?				
oil	1	1,214	1,214	1,214
GILBERT and GEORGE (20th C) British				
oil	1	88,500	88,500	88,500
wc/d	6	1,204-26,000	11,170	4,000
GILBERT, A (19/20th C) ?				
3D	1	2,104	2,104	2,104
GILBERT, Alfred (1854-1934) British				
3D	4	7,938-68,040	39,312	32,130
GILBERT, Arthur (1819-1895) British				
oil	6	1,012-3,540	2,061	1,740
GILBERT, Arthur Hill (1894-1970) American				
oil	9	2,700-85,000	20,855	5,500
wc/d	1	450	450	450
GILBERT, C Ivar (1882-1972) American				
oil	2	1,700-10,192	5,946	1,700
GILBERT, Kate (1843-?) British				
oil	1	4,000	4,000	4,000
GILBERT, Sir John (1817-1897) British				
oil	2	475-814	644	475
wc/d	1	1,100	1,100	1,100
GILBERT, Stephen (1910-) British				
oil	2	6,438-7,938	7,188	6,438
wc/d	1	1,671	1,671	1,671
3D	1	4,829	4,829	4,829
GILBERT, Victor (1847-1933) French				
oil	17	1,138-85,000	22,191	14,548
wc/d	4	4,625-7,782	6,447	5,643
GILBERY, Michael (1913-2000) British				
oil	3	957-5,040	2,431	1,296
GILBOA, Nahum (1917-) Bulgarian				
wc/d	1	2,400	2,400	2,400
GILBOY, Margaretta (1943-) American				
wc/d	1	1,700	1,700	1,700
GILCHREST, Joan (1918-) British				
oil	19	549-16,830	4,236	2,992
GILDER, Robert Fletcher (1856-1940) American				
oil	2	550-2,050	1,300	550

Name	No.	Price Range	Average	Median
GILDEWART, Friedrich Vordemberge (1899-1962) Dutch				
wc/d	1	4,712	4,712	4,712
GILE, Selden Connor (1877-1947) American				
oil	6	3,500-90,000	35,416	15,000
wc/d	2	1,000-4,500	2,750	1,000
GILES, Carl (1916-1995) British				
wc/d	3	1,850-4,152	2,859	2,576
GILES, Geoffrey Douglas (1857-1941) British				
oil	2	2,112-34,020	18,066	2,112
GILES, James William (1801-1870) British				
oil	1	2,610	2,610	2,610
wc/d	2	534-3,204	1,869	534
GILFRANCO, V (20th C) ?				
oil	1	2,197	2,197	2,197
GILHOOLY, David (1943-) Canadian				
wc/d	1	1,000	1,000	1,000
GILIOLI, Émile (1911-1977) French				
wc/d	22	467-5,611	1,604	1,178
3D	22	2,000-54,184	14,576	7,767
GILL, DeLancey (1859-1940) American				
oil	1	1,500	1,500	1,500
wc/d	1	1,200	1,200	1,200
GILL, Edmund (1820-1894) British				
oil	3	490-3,828	1,759	961
GILL, Edmund Ward (fl.1843-1868) British				
oil	1	1,911	1,911	1,911
wc/d	1	3,750	3,750	3,750
GILL, Eric (1882-1940) British				
wc/d	7	1,408-4,300	2,303	2,220
3D	3	5,550-22,680	14,023	13,840
GILL, Mariquita (1865-1915) American				
oil	1	6,000	6,000	6,000
GILLAR, Rob (19th C) Continental				
oil	1	20,000	20,000	20,000
GILLARD, Henri Vincent (1902-1980) ?				
oil	1	1,427	1,427	1,427
GILLBERG, Jacob Axel (1769-1845) Swedish				
wc/d	1	3,572	3,572	3,572
GILLE, Christian Friedrich (1805-1899) German				
oil	5	1,168-11,781	5,469	2,153
GILLEMANS, Jan Pauwel (elder) (1618-1675) Flemish				
oil	5	16,714-43,943	28,877	29,410
GILLEMANS, Jan Pauwel (younger) (1651-1704) Flemish				
oil	3	12,460-56,108	41,003	54,441
GILLEON, R Thomas (1942-) American				
oil	2	35,000-35,000	35,000	35,000
GILLES, Piet (1908-) Dutch				
oil	4	818-1,403	1,057	972
GILLES, Werner (1894-1961) German				
oil	4	3,748-12,721	7,706	3,816
wc/d	8	527-11,781	3,670	2,928
GILLESPIE, George K (1924-1996) British				
oil	21	2,478-17,671	6,298	5,088
GILLESPIE, Ken (1948-) Canadian				
oil	1	1,054	1,054	1,054
GILLESPIE, Rowan (1953-) Irish?				
wc/d	1	3,387	3,387	3,387
3D	8	6,126-27,900	10,390	7,259
GILLET, Roger Edgar (1924-2003) French				
oil	15	658-6,082	2,955	2,919
wc/d	5	597-2,008	1,233	837
GILLI, Claude (1938-) French				
oil	1	1,229	1,229	1,229
wc/d	3	1,052-1,518	1,294	1,312
3D	6	1,758-7,826	4,057	2,919
GILLIAM, Sam (1933-) American				
oil	3	4,250-13,000	8,416	8,000
3D	1	13,000	13,000	13,000
GILLIARD, Eugène (1861-1921) Swiss				
oil	2	3,414-3,414	3,414	3,414
GILLIES, Sir William George (1898-1973) British				
oil	8	1,757-38,720	17,953	15,045
wc/d	24	1,068-7,876	3,666	3,287

Name	No.	Price Range	Average	Median
GILLIG, Jacob (1636-1701) Dutch				
oil	5	2,253-27,680	13,501	8,650
GILLION, Fernand (?-1950) Belgian				
oil	1	608	608	608
wc/d	1	584	584	584
GILLOT, Eugène Louis (1868-1925) French				
wc/d	1	1,133	1,133	1,133
GILMAN, Benjamin Ferris (1856-1934) American				
oil	2	1,700-1,800	1,750	1,700
GILOT, Françoise (1921-1986) French				
oil	5	3,500-32,500	15,180	9,000
GILPIN, Sawrey (1733-1807) British				
oil	1	5,500	5,500	5,500
GILROY, John William (1868-1944) British				
oil	3	501-4,325	1,954	1,036
wc/d	1	661	661	661
GILS, Fritz (1901-1957) German				
oil	2	2,356-3,770	3,063	2,356
GILSOUL, Leon (1884-1961) Belgian				
oil	1	1,029	1,029	1,029
GILSOUL, Victor (1867-1939) Belgian				
oil	12	468-4,479	1,265	599
GIMEL, Georges (1898-1962) French				
oil	2	1,521-2,783	2,152	1,521
GIMENO Y ARASA, Francisco (1858-1927) Spanish				
oil	1	14,466	14,466	14,466
wc/d	2	2,893-3,024	2,958	2,893
GIMENO, Andres (1879-1927) Spanish				
oil	1	701	701	701
wc/d	1	1,137	1,137	1,137
GIMIGNANI, Giacinto (1611-1681) Italian				
oil	1	40,000	40,000	40,000
GIMMI, Wilhelm (1886-1965) Swiss				
oil	24	648-70,771	6,050	2,997
wc/d	4	454-1,374	989	833
GIMOND, Marcel (1891-1961) French				
3D	2	6,429-20,990	13,709	6,429
GINAIN, Louis Eugène (1818-1886) French				
oil	1	2,038	2,038	2,038
GINDERTAEL, Roger van (1899-1982) Belgian				
oil	3	477-2,035	1,161	971
wc/d	1	8,918	8,918	8,918
GINE, Alexander Vasilievitsch (1830-1880) Russian				
oil	1	38,795	38,795	38,795
GINGELEN, Jacques van (1801-1864) Flemish				
oil	2	850-2,016	1,433	850
GINKEL, Paul van (1960-) Canadian				
oil	3	770-1,418	1,143	1,241
GINNER, Charles (1878-1952) British				
oil	2	4,486-41,580	23,033	4,486
GINNETT, Louis (1875-1946) British				
oil	3	1,091-1,496	1,277	1,246
GINORI, Giacomo (19th C) Italian				
3D	1	4,844	4,844	4,844
GINOTTI, Giacomo (1837-1897) Italian				
3D	1	2,249	2,249	2,249
GINOVSZKY, Joseph (1800-1857) Austrian				
oil	1	5,702	5,702	5,702
GINSBOURG, Ilya (1854-?) Russian				
3D	1	9,460	9,460	9,460
GINSBURG, Max (1931-) American				
oil	1	1,200	1,200	1,200
GIOBEL-OYLER, Elsa (1882-1979) Swedish				
oil	1	1,371	1,371	1,371
GIOJA, Belisario (1829-1906) Italian				
wc/d	2	1,800-3,000	2,400	1,800
GIOJA, Edoardo (1862-1937) Italian				
oil	2	2,722-6,500	4,611	2,722
GIOLDASIS, Dimitrios (1897-1993) Greek				
oil	1	3,366	3,366	3,366

Name	No.	Price Range	Average	Median
GIOLI, Francesco (1849-1922) Italian				
oil	4	1,308-10,911	5,810	2,777
wc/d	1	4,325	4,325	4,325
GIOLI, Luigi (1854-1947) Italian				
oil	5	3,000-38,163	14,040	3,879
GIORDANI, Giulio (1875-1948) Italian				
oil	1	1,090	1,090	1,090
GIORDANI, Italo (1882-?) Italian				
oil	9	485-2,761	1,668	2,289
GIORDANO DI PALMA (1886-?) Italian				
oil	1	2,288	2,288	2,288
GIORDANO DI PALMA, Léon Jean (1886-?) French				
oil	1	3,818	3,818	3,818
GIORDANO, Felice (1880-1964) Italian				
oil	18	898-10,197	3,823	2,750
GIORDANO, Luca (1632-1705) Italian				
oil	8	15,653-80,000	44,721	31,455
wc/d	5	1,300-3,932	2,545	2,800
GIORGINI, Andrea (19th C) Italian				
oil	1	4,550	4,550	4,550
GIORGIO, Vincenzo di (1945-) Italian				
oil	2	1,106-2,028	1,567	1,106
GIORGIS, Renato de (1923-1955) Italian?				
oil	2	2,338-2,338	2,338	2,338
GIOTTI, G (?) Italian?				
wc/d	1	2,736	2,736	2,736
GIOVACCHINI, Ulderico (1890-1965) Italian				
oil	1	1,455	1,455	1,455
GIOVAGNOLI, Luca (1963-) Italian				
wc/d	1	1,119	1,119	1,119
GIOVANNI DI PAOLO (1403-1483) Italian				
oil	1	70,000	70,000	70,000
GIOVANNI FRANCESCO DA RIMINI (15th C) Italian				
oil	1	550,000	550,000	550,000
GIOVANNINI, Vincenzo (1816-1868) Italian				
oil	2	1,474-28,603	15,038	1,474
GIOVANNONI, Alessandra (1954-) Italian				
oil	1	6,442	6,442	6,442
GIRALDEZ Y PENALVER, Adolfo (c.1840-1920) Spanish				
oil	1	1,532	1,532	1,532
GIRANIANI (19th C) Italian				
oil	1	20,460	20,460	20,460
GIRARD, Alexandre (19/20th C) French				
oil	1	1,376	1,376	1,376
GIRARD, Ernest (1813-1898) French				
wc/d	1	2,870	2,870	2,870
GIRARD, Marie Firmin (1838-1921) French				
oil	5	700-121,622	28,713	7,436
GIRARD, Pascal (20th C) French				
oil	1	1,199	1,199	1,199
GIRARDET, Eugène Alexis (1853-1907) French				
oil	7	4,302-19,140	10,148	7,014
wc/d	1	6,541	6,541	6,541
GIRARDET, Jules (1856-1946) French/Swiss				
oil	2	12,000-13,200	12,600	12,000
wc/d	1	1,168	1,168	1,168
GIRARDET, Karl (1813-1871) Swiss				
oil	8	624-12,740	5,235	2,432
GIRARDET, Leopold Henri (1848-1904) Swiss				
oil	1	4,079	4,079	4,079
GIRARDIN, Frank J (1856-1945) American				
oil	1	1,100	1,100	1,100
GIRARDOT, Alexandre Antoine (1815-?) French				
oil	1	3,211	3,211	3,211
GIRARDOT, Ernest Gustave (fl.1860-1893) British				
oil	3	880-5,278	2,574	1,564
GIRARDOT, Georges Marie Julien (?-1914) French				
oil	1	1,000	1,000	1,000
GIRARDOT, Louis Auguste (1858-1933) French				
oil	2	10,938-29,282	20,110	10,938
GIRAUD, Byng (19th C) ?				
wc/d	1	1,246	1,246	1,246

Name	No.	Price Range	Average	Median
GIRAUD, Henri Émile (1825-1892) French				
oil	1	3,397	3,397	3,397
GIRAUD, Pierre Francois Eugène (1806-1881) French				
oil	2	25,342-110,000	67,671	25,342
wc/d	1	9,570	9,570	9,570
GIRAUD, Sebastien Charles (1819-1892) French				
oil	1	8,182	8,182	8,182
GIRAULT, Gaston (20th C) French?				
oil	1	1,032	1,032	1,032
GIRBAU, Jorge (1958-) Spanish				
3D	1	3,514	3,514	3,514
GIRIER, Jean-Aime (1837-1912) French				
oil	1	1,200	1,200	1,200
GIRIEUD, Pierre (1876-1940) French				
wc/d	1	1,296	1,296	1,296
GIRIN, David Eugène (1848-1917) French				
oil	4	720-3,273	1,844	840
GIRKE, Raimund (1930-2002) German				
oil	8	1,411-17,199	6,449	3,185
wc/d	5	1,753-3,600	2,362	2,293
GIRODET DE ROUCY TRIOSON, Anne Louis (1767-1824) French				
oil	1	60,690	60,690	60,690
wc/d	5	643-56,860	16,201	7,500
GIROLAMI (19th C) ?				
3D	1	3,631	3,631	3,631
GIRONA, Maria (1923-) Spanish				
oil	2	2,510-2,616	2,563	2,510
GIRONCOLI, Bruno (1936-) Austrian				
wc/d	2	5,786-8,497	7,141	5,786
3D	1	18,207	18,207	18,207
GIRONELLA, Alberto (1929-1999) Mexican				
wc/d	1	11,404	11,404	11,404
GIROUX, Andre (1801-1879) French				
oil	5	701-7,014	3,386	2,521
GIRTIN, Thomas (1775-1802) British				
wc/d	4	4,914-22,680	14,439	9,405
GIRV, Alfred Aleksandrovich (19/20th C) Russian				
oil	1	5,418	5,418	5,418
GISCHIA, Léon (1903-1991) French				
oil	11	1,038-4,295	2,740	2,577
GISCLARD, Stephane (1966-) French				
oil	2	1,079-2,667	1,873	1,079
GISSEL, Mogens (1941-) Danish				
oil	1	1,132	1,132	1,132
GISSING, Roland (1895-1967) Canadian				
oil	14	489-4,714	2,223	1,886
wc/d	2	810-3,102	1,956	810
GISSON, Andre (1928-2003) American				
oil	35	700-9,000	2,847	2,600
GIUDICE, Marcello lo (1955-) Italian				
wc/d	1	647	647	647
3D	1	16,685	16,685	16,685
GIUDICI, Reinaldo (1853-1921) Argentinian				
oil	1	5,200	5,200	5,200
GIUFFRIDA, Antonino (1861-1940) Italian				
oil	1	6,184	6,184	6,184
GIULI, Franco (1934-) Italian				
oil	1	1,051	1,051	1,051
GIULIANO, Bartolomeo (1829-1909) Italian				
oil	2	4,500-12,740	8,620	4,500
GIULIO DA MILANO (1895-1990) Italian				
oil	11	860-4,905	2,636	2,458
wc/d	3	934-1,197	1,098	1,165
GIUNTA, Joseph (1911-2001) Canadian				
oil	8	566-2,292	1,091	827
GIUSTI, Guglielmo (1824-1916) Italian				
oil	2	1,639-3,330	2,484	1,639
wc/d	7	1,683-4,531	3,219	3,357
GIUSTO, Faust (1867-1941) Italian				
oil	5	1,214-6,869	3,457	3,505
GJERDEVIK, Niels Erik (1962-) Norwegian				
oil	6	808-1,940	1,360	1,288

Name	No.	Price Range	Average	Median
GLACKENS, William (1870-1938) American				
oil	6	40,000-175,000	101,666	80,000
wc/d	6	1,200-6,500	3,275	2,750
GLADSTONE, Gerald (1929-) Canadian				
oil	1	907	907	907
3D	1	1,402	1,402	1,402
GLAESER, Gotthelf Leberecht (1784-1851) German				
wc/d	1	3,534	3,534	3,534
GLAIZE, Auguste Barthelemy (1807-1893) French				
oil	1	3,913	3,913	3,913
GLANSDORFF, Hubert (1877-1964) Belgian				
oil	11	506-7,292	1,914	1,144
GLAOUI, Hassan el (1924-) Moroccan				
oil	2	4,043-15,222	9,632	4,043
wc/d	4	4,043-8,550	5,830	5,260
GLARNER, Fritz (1899-1972) American/Swiss				
wc/d	1	12,237	12,237	12,237
GLASCO, Joseph (1925-) American				
oil	1	2,736	2,736	2,736
wc/d	1	2,000	2,000	2,000
GLASS, Giorgio (19th C) Italian				
wc/d	1	24,421	24,421	24,421
GLASS, Margaret (1950-) British				
oil	1	630	630	630
wc/d	3	493-613	565	589
GLASS, William Mervyn (1885-1965) British				
oil	4	1,840-5,568	4,210	4,602
GLATTFELDER, Hansjorg (1939-) Swiss				
oil	2	1,600-7,633	4,616	1,600
3D	1	2,750	2,750	2,750
GLATZ, Oszkar (1872-1958) Hungarian				
oil	2	2,200-3,000	2,600	2,200
GLAUBACHER, Franz (1896-1974) Yugoslavian				
oil	1	2,057	2,057	2,057
GLAUBER, Johannes (1646-1726) Dutch				
wc/d	1	2,784	2,784	2,784
GLAZUNOV, Ilya (1930-) Russian				
oil	8	500-44,720	20,418	15,480
GLEASON, Joe Duncan (1881-1959) American				
oil	3	750-29,000	14,583	14,000
wc/d	1	2,000	2,000	2,000
GLEESON, Gerald (1915-1986) American				
wc/d	1	2,250	2,250	2,250
GLEHN, Oswald von (1858-?) German				
oil	1	63,360	63,360	63,360
GLEHN, Wilfred Gabriel de (1870-1951) British				
oil	8	1,100-49,140	14,819	9,460
wc/d	2	522-692	607	522
GLEICH, John (1879-?) German				
oil	6	1,947-8,449	5,173	4,816
GLEICHEN-RUSSWURM, Heinrich Ludwig von (1836-1901) German				
oil	1	3,405	3,405	3,405
wc/d	1	727	727	727
GLEICHMANN, Otto (1887-1963) German				
wc/d	2	763-16,397	8,580	763
GLEIZES, Albert (1881-1953) French				
oil	10	12,274-210,405	76,068	46,250
wc/d	22	486-123,200	24,721	9,425
GLENAVY, Lady Beatrice (1883-1970) British				
oil	1	1,573	1,573	1,573
GLENDENING, A A (19th C) British				
oil	1	9,261	9,261	9,261
GLENDENING, Alfred (19th C) British				
wc/d	1	3,186	3,186	3,186
GLENDENING, Alfred Augustus (19th C) British				
oil	6	1,018-16,192	6,471	3,000
GLENDENING, Alfred Augustus (jnr) (1861-1907) British				
oil	6	1,947-24,640	12,700	9,452
wc/d	4	400-7,040	4,797	4,750
GLENDENING, Alfred Augustus (snr) (?-c.1910) British				
oil	6	2,500-13,000	7,091	5,500

Name	No.	Price Range	Average	Median
GLEYRE, Charles (1806-1874) Swiss				
wc/d	1	32,813	32,813	32,813
GLIBERT, Albert (1832-1917) Belgian				
oil	2	3,490-4,625	4,057	3,490
GLIGOROV, Robert (1960-) ?				
oil	1	1,781	1,781	1,781
GLIKSBERG, Haim (1904-1970) Israeli				
oil	2	6,000-7,000	6,500	6,000
GLINDONI, Henry Gillard (1852-1913) British				
oil	4	1,131-9,204	4,876	1,612
wc/d	1	794	794	794
GLINK, Franz Xaver (1795-1873) German				
oil	1	2,238	2,238	2,238
GLINTENKAMP, Hendrik (1887-1946) American				
oil	3	940-1,700	1,321	1,325
GLINZ, Theo (1890-1962) Swiss				
oil	9	486-4,313	2,223	1,725
GLISENTI, Achille (1848-1906) Italian				
oil	1	11,000	11,000	11,000
GLOCKNER (18th C) German?				
wc/d	1	4,253	4,253	4,253
GLOCKNER, Hermann (1889-1987) German				
oil	15	618-8,406	2,262	1,136
wc/d	10	494-18,542	5,068	2,631
GLOSSOP, Allerley (1870-1955) South African				
oil	1	1,593	1,593	1,593
GLOUTCHENKO, Nicholai Petrovitch (1902-1977) Russian				
oil	2	3,174-7,800	5,487	3,174
GLOVER, John (1767-1849) British				
oil	3	1,251-49,140	29,130	37,000
wc/d	5	592-5,307	1,574	662
GLOVER, William (c.1791-?) British				
wc/d	1	1,131	1,131	1,131
GLUCK (?) ?				
oil	1	5,250	5,250	5,250
GLUCK, Anselm (1950-) Austrian				
oil	1	7,283	7,283	7,283
wc/d	1	1,091	1,091	1,091
GLUCK, Eugène (1820-1898) French				
oil	2	757-22,809	11,783	757
GLUCKERT, Johannes (1868-?) German				
oil	1	1,506	1,506	1,506
GLUCKLICH, Simon (1863-1943) German				
oil	3	1,473-12,103	5,153	1,883
GLUCKMANN, Grigory (1898-1973) American/Russian				
oil	8	3,889-35,340	20,578	19,000
wc/d	3	1,558-3,250	2,519	2,750
GLUCKSTEIN, Hannah (1895-1976) British				
oil	2	5,130-5,310	5,220	5,130
GLYDE, Henry George (1906-1998) Canadian				
oil	11	2,482-10,635	5,010	4,874
wc/d	5	574-8,104	2,228	793
GMELIN, Felix (1962-) Swedish				
oil	1	1,916	1,916	1,916
GMELIN, Friedrich Wilhelm (1760-1820) German				
wc/d	4	1,674-6,479	3,951	2,631
GNIEWEK, Robert (1951-) American				
oil	2	1,700-5,000	3,350	1,700
GNOLI, Domenico (1933-1970) Italian				
oil	4	15,265-601,800	287,016	247,800
wc/d	2	12,361-13,000	12,680	12,361
3D	1	93,699	93,699	93,699
GNOZZI, Roberto (1947-) Italian				
3D	1	3,503	3,503	3,503
GOBAILLE, Jean (?) French?				
oil	3	539-2,474	1,318	942
GOBAUT, Gaspard (1814-1882) French				
wc/d	5	766-4,334	2,188	1,033
GOBER, Robert (1954-) American				
3D	5	19,000-90,000	44,800	26,000
GOBERT, Pierre (1662-1744) French				
oil	2	9,103-19,418	14,260	9,103

Name	No.	Price Range	Average	Median
GOBI, A (19th C) Italian?				
oil	1	7,700	7,700	7,700
GOBI, Antonio (?) Italian?				
oil	1	1,780	1,780	1,780
GOBILLARD, Paule (1869-1946) French				
oil	3	937-7,027	3,410	2,267
GOBL, Camilla (1871-1965) Austrian				
oil	7	527-2,102	1,164	964
GOBO, Georges (1876-1958) French				
oil	9	533-1,480	815	710
wc/d	2	473-592	532	473
GODARD, A (19/20th C) French				
3D	1	3,822	3,822	3,822
GODARD, Armand (19th C) French				
3D	2	5,882-7,612	6,747	5,882
GODARD, Gabriel (1933-) ?				
oil	12	800-5,500	1,966	1,051
GODBOLD, Samuel Barry (fl.1842-1875) British				
oil	1	2,474	2,474	2,474
GODCHAUX (?) ?				
oil	3	2,061-18,163	7,657	2,748
GODCHAUX, Alfred (1835-1895) French				
oil	4	2,788-3,637	3,235	3,152
GODCHAUX, Emil (1860-1938) French				
oil	14	458-8,486	1,798	701
GODCHAUX, Roger (1878-1958) French				
oil	1	13,436	13,436	13,436
3D	1	5,096	5,096	5,096
GODDARD, J Bedloe (fl.1880-1894) British				
wc/d	1	2,478	2,478	2,478
GODDERIS, Jack (1916-1971) Belgian				
oil	3	445-1,607	1,112	1,286
GODERIS, Hans (17th C) Dutch				
oil	2	7,555-25,691	16,623	7,555
GODET, Henri (1863-1937) French				
3D	1	1,557	1,557	1,557
GODFREY, Michael (1958-) American/German				
oil	1	4,500	4,500	4,500
GODFREY, O (19th C) ?				
oil	1	2,057	2,057	2,057
GODFRINON, Ernest (1878-1927) Belgian				
oil	2	1,885-18,703	10,294	1,885
GODIEN, Adrien (1873-1949) French				
oil	4	527-8,505	2,779	996
wc/d	2	468-586	527	468
GODLEVSKY, Ivan (1908-1998) Russian				
oil	3	2,249-5,160	3,354	2,655
GODWARD, John William (1858-1922) British				
oil	4	44,110-393,300	209,352	180,000
GODWIN, Edward (19/20th C) British				
3D	1	3,024	3,024	3,024
GODWIN, Karl (1893-?) American				
oil	1	1,500	1,500	1,500
GODWIN, Ted (1933-) Canadian				
oil	3	1,216-3,074	2,294	2,593
wc/d	1	973	973	973
GOEBEL, Carl (1824-1899) Austrian				
wc/d	7	648-2,336	1,300	1,051
GOEBEL, Karl Peter (1793-1823) Austrian				
oil	1	2,455	2,455	2,455
GOEBEL, Rod (1946-1993) American				
oil	4	2,000-5,000	2,937	2,250
GOEDE, Kees de (1954-) Dutch				
wc/d	2	1,169-2,338	1,753	1,169
GOEDE, Leo de (1958-) Dutch?				
oil	1	5,504	5,504	5,504
GOEJE, Pieter de (1779-1859) Dutch				
oil	1	3,025	3,025	3,025
GOENEUTTE, Norbert (1854-1894) French				
oil	4	1,776-11,744	7,383	5,343
wc/d	1	1,415	1,415	1,415

Name	No.	Price Range	Average	Median
GOEPFERT, Hermann (1926-1982) German				
oil	1	2,803	2,803	2,803
3D	1	3,822	3,822	3,822
GOEPP, Albert (19/20th C) French				
oil	1	5,400	5,400	5,400
GOERG, Edouard (1893-1969) French				
oil	15	1,420-8,397	4,257	3,822
GOERING, Christian Anton (1836-1905) German				
wc/d	1	8,000	8,000	8,000
GOERITZ, Mathias (1915-1990) Mexican/German				
oil	1	290,000	290,000	290,000
wc/d	2	57,500-65,000	61,250	57,500
3D	5	18,000-75,000	51,000	45,000
GOETSCH, Gustave (1877-1969) American				
oil	3	650-1,800	1,316	1,500
wc/d	1	900	900	900
GOETSCH, Joseph (1728-1793) German				
3D	1	3,063	3,063	3,063
GOETZ, A (?) ?				
oil	1	3,000	3,000	3,000
GOETZ, Henri (1909-1989) French				
oil	15	1,560-9,710	3,267	2,675
wc/d	26	584-3,801	1,503	1,200
GOETZE, M (1865-?) German				
3D	1	1,522	1,522	1,522
GOEY, Walter (20th C) French?				
oil	1	1,019	1,019	1,019
GOFF, Frederick E J (1855-1931) British				
wc/d	11	561-7,000	2,681	2,832
GOFF, Lloyd Lozes (1917-1982) American				
oil	2	3,000-13,000	8,000	3,000
GOFFINON, Aristide (1881-1952) Belgian				
oil	2	814-1,795	1,304	814
GOGARTEN, Heinrich (1850-1911) German				
oil	7	573-3,299	1,739	1,312
GOGH, Vincent van (1853-1890) Dutch				
oil	2	3,700,000-36,000,000	19,850,000	3,700,000
wc/d	2	334,400-4,200,000	2,267,200	334,400
GOGO, Felix (1872-1953) Belgian				
oil	4	728-10,188	3,371	1,260
wc/d	2	605-953	779	605
GOHLER, H (?) German?				
oil	1	3,039	3,039	3,039
GOHLER, Hermann (1874-?) German				
oil	3	934-1,940	1,378	1,262
GOINGS, Ralph (1928-) American				
oil	1	50,000	50,000	50,000
wc/d	2	18,000-19,000	18,500	18,000
GOLA, Emilio (1852-1923) Italian				
oil	3	4,001-68,329	42,959	56,548
wc/d	1	1,911	1,911	1,911
GOLD, Albert (1906-) American				
oil	1	650	650	650
wc/d	1	475	475	475
GOLD, Ferdinand Karl (1882-1981) Austrian				
oil	1	4,099	4,099	4,099
GOLD, Josef (1840-1922) Austrian				
oil	1	1,054	1,054	1,054
GOLDBERG, Arnold (1947-) Israeli				
oil	1	1,100	1,100	1,100
GOLDBERG, Michael (1924-) American				
wc/d	1	2,900	2,900	2,900
GOLDBERG, Rube (1883-1970) American				
wc/d	1	2,200	2,200	2,200
GOLDEN, Rolland (1931-) American				
oil	1	1,500	1,500	1,500
wc/d	1	1,000	1,000	1,000
GOLDFARB, Walter (1964-) Brazilian				
oil	1	22,000	22,000	22,000
GOLDIE, Charles Frederick (1870-1947) New Zealander				
oil	1	34,200	34,200	34,200

Name	No.	Price Range	Average	Median
GOLDING, Tomás (1909-) Venezuelan				
oil	11	880-4,280	2,477	2,700
GOLDMAN, Robert (1955-) German?				
oil	1	1,800	1,800	1,800
GOLDSCHEIDER (19/20th C) Austrian				
3D	1	1,760	1,760	1,760
GOLDSCHEIDER, Friedrich (1845-1897) Austrian/French				
3D	6	2,386-9,109	5,103	3,600
GOLDSCHMIDT, Gertrudis (1912-1994) Venezuelan				
3D	1	290,000	290,000	290,000
GOLDSMITH, Callander (19th C) British				
oil	2	650-1,539	1,094	650
GOLDSTEIN, Jack (1946-2003) Canadian				
oil	1	34,600	34,600	34,600
GOLDSWORTHY, Andy (1956-) British				
wc/d	3	3,888-3,888	3,888	3,888
3D	2	7,400-28,160	17,780	7,400
GOLIA, G (20th C) Italian				
oil	1	2,610	2,610	2,610
GOLLER, Bruno (1901-) German				
oil	1	4,685	4,685	4,685
GOLLINGS, William Elling (1878-1932) American				
oil	4	35,000-110,000	67,500	60,000
wc/d	1	9,000	9,000	9,000
GOLOVIN, Aleksandr (1863-1930) Russian				
oil	1	6,903	6,903	6,903
wc/d	3	3,000-5,000	3,833	3,500
GOLTZ, Alexander Demetrius (1857-1944) Austrian				
oil	2	1,574-1,582	1,578	1,574
GOLTZ, Walter (1875-1956) American				
oil	1	3,750	3,750	3,750
GOLTZIUS, Hendrik (1558-1616) Dutch				
wc/d	1	31,622	31,622	31,622
GOMEZ ABAD, Jose (20th C) Spanish				
oil	1	1,113	1,113	1,113
GOMEZ CAMPUZANO, Ricardo (1891-1981) Colombian				
oil	1	1,700	1,700	1,700
GOMEZ MIR, Eugenio (19/20th C) Spanish				
oil	1	2,280	2,280	2,280
wc/d	1	729	729	729
GOMEZ Y GIL, Guillermo (1862-1942) Spanish				
oil	3	1,435-10,938	6,279	6,466
GOMEZ, Marco Antonio (1910-1972) American/Mexican				
oil	2	400-3,000	1,700	400
GOMEZ, Susy (1964-) Spanish				
wc/d	2	4,214-5,780	4,997	4,214
GOMMAERTS, Fernand (1894-?) Belgian				
oil	2	607-1,639	1,123	607
GONAZ, Francois (19th C) French				
oil	1	10,000	10,000	10,000
GONG XIAN (1599-1689) Chinese				
wc/d	1	45,000	45,000	45,000
GONIN, Francesco (1808-1889) Italian				
oil	1	12,098	12,098	12,098
wc/d	1	1,211	1,211	1,211
GONIN, Jacques Ferdinand (1883-?) French				
oil	3	595-2,250	1,344	1,189
GONNE, Christian F (1813-1906) German				
oil	1	9,589	9,589	9,589
GONSKE, Walt (1942-) American				
oil	1	2,900	2,900	2,900
GONTARD, Moris (1940-) French				
oil	1	3,996	3,996	3,996
GONTCHAROVA, Natalia (1881-1962) Russian				
oil	9	8,357-1,848,000	257,186	45,370
wc/d	37	1,113-61,600	14,308	9,873
3D	1	27,694	27,694	27,694
GONTIER, Clement (19th C) French				
oil	2	1,200-1,800	1,500	1,200
GONZAGA, Giovanfrancesco (1921-) Italian				
oil	34	1,152-12,945	5,989	5,655

Name	No.	Price Range	Average	Median
GONZAGA, Pietro di Gottardo (1751-1831) Italian				
wc/d	1	10,175	10,175	10,175
GONZALES, J (?) ?				
oil	1	9,000	9,000	9,000
GONZALES, Paul (1856-?) French				
3D	1	1,646	1,646	1,646
GONZALES, Robert (1939-1981) American				
wc/d	1	1,000	1,000	1,000
GONZALES, Roberta (1909-1976) French				
wc/d	1	1,200	1,200	1,200
GONZALEZ ALACREU, Juan (1937-) Spanish				
oil	1	3,514	3,514	3,514
GONZALEZ BOGEN, Carlos (20th C) South American				
oil	2	560-1,675	1,117	560
GONZALEZ BRAVO, Justo (1944-) Spanish				
wc/d	1	2,803	2,803	2,803
GONZALEZ DE AGREDA, Manuel (19/20th C) Spanish				
oil	1	1,414	1,414	1,414
GONZALEZ POBLETE, Daniel (1944-) Spanish				
oil	2	1,204-1,267	1,235	1,204
GONZALEZ PRIETO, Fermin (1900-1987) Spanish				
oil	7	599-2,035	1,185	1,211
GONZALEZ VELAZQUEZ, Antonio (1723-1793) Spanish				
oil	2	60,204-101,750	80,977	60,204
GONZALEZ VELAZQUEZ, Zacarias (1763-1834) Spanish				
oil	2	40,939-121,100	81,019	40,939
GONZALEZ, Bartolome (1564-1627) Spanish				
oil	1	114,041	114,041	114,041
GONZALEZ, Beatriz (1936-) Colombian				
oil	1	11,000	11,000	11,000
GONZALEZ, Damian (1967-) Cuban				
oil	1	13,000	13,000	13,000
GONZALEZ, Joan (c.1868-1908) Spanish				
wc/d	1	2,408	2,408	2,408
GONZALEZ, Julio (1876-1942) Spanish				
oil	1	38,485	38,485	38,485
wc/d	9	7,730-26,401	13,110	11,125
3D	3	22,000-780,000	350,666	250,000
GONZALEZ, Pedro Angel (1901-1981) Venezuelan				
oil	3	745-5,770	3,878	5,120
wc/d	3	440-465	456	465
GONZALEZ, Rafael Ramón (1894-1975) Portuguese				
oil	2	1,625-3,255	2,440	1,625
GONZALEZ, Roberto (1930-1999) Argentinian				
oil	1	1,500	1,500	1,500
wc/d	3	1,800-3,800	3,066	3,600
GONZALEZ, Zacarias (1923-2003) Spanish				
oil	1	1,197	1,197	1,197
wc/d	1	771	771	771
GONZALEZ-TORRES, Felix (1957-1996) Cuban				
wc/d	1	18,000	18,000	18,000
GOOCH, Gerald (1933-) American				
oil	1	2,250	2,250	2,250
GOOCH, Thomas (1750-1802) British				
oil	1	2,835	2,835	2,835
GOOD, John Willis (1845-1879) British				
3D	2	5,916-6,510	6,213	5,916
GOOD, Samuel S (1808-1885) American?				
oil	2	3,200-3,200	3,200	3,200
GOODACRE, Glenna (20th C) American				
3D	3	6,000-35,000	15,666	6,000
GOODALL, Edward Alfred (1819-1908) British				
oil	2	1,170-75,000	38,085	1,170
wc/d	5	634-9,072	5,063	6,230
GOODALL, Frederick (1822-1904) British				
oil	14	400-36,800	8,341	1,777
wc/d	1	1,800	1,800	1,800
GOODALL, Thomas F (1856-1944) British				
oil	1	4,325	4,325	4,325
GOODALL, Walter (1830-1889) British				
oil	1	10,192	10,192	10,192
wc/d	1	1,860	1,860	1,860

Name	No.	Price Range	Average	Median
GOODAN, Tillman Parker (1896-1958) American				
oil	2	5,000-9,500	7,250	5,000
wc/d	2	3,000-3,250	3,125	3,000
GOODE, Joe (1937-) American				
oil	3	7,500-8,800	8,266	8,500
3D	1	12,000	12,000	12,000
GOODE, John (19th C) British				
oil	1	2,958	2,958	2,958
GOODE, Tom (19th C) British				
oil	1	11,340	11,340	11,340
GOODIN, Walter (1907-1992) British				
oil	7	518-4,446	2,081	2,124
GOODING, Maria Simonds (1938-) Irish				
oil	1	1,636	1,636	1,636
wc/d	1	1,987	1,987	1,987
GOODMAN, Maude (1860-1938) British				
oil	1	5,220	5,220	5,220
GOODNOUGH, Robert (1917-) American				
oil	4	712-7,000	3,853	1,500
GOODRICH, William Wells (19th C) American				
oil	1	1,000	1,000	1,000
GOODWIN, Albert (1845-1932) British				
oil	5	3,680-160,000	39,479	10,395
wc/d	19	493-13,000	3,152	2,464
GOODWIN, Arthur C (1866-1929) American				
oil	9	1,900-47,500	11,166	8,000
wc/d	9	500-13,000	5,610	4,000
GOODWIN, Hamilton (19th C) British				
oil	1	3,294	3,294	3,294
GOODWIN, Phillip R (1882-1935) American				
oil	6	4,000-90,000	41,416	22,500
wc/d	1	12,000	12,000	12,000
GOODWIN, Richard Labarre (1840-1910) American				
oil	3	4,750-420,000	143,183	4,800
GOODWIN, Robin (20th C) British				
oil	1	1,204	1,204	1,204
GOOL, Andries Johannes Jacobus van (1901-) Dutch				
oil	1	3,562	3,562	3,562
GOOL, Jan van (1685-1763) Dutch				
oil	1	21,658	21,658	21,658
GOOSEN, Frits J (1943-) Dutch				
oil	2	1,036-1,593	1,314	1,036
GOOSEY, G Turland (?) British				
oil	4	528-2,112	1,426	1,175
GOOSSENS, Josse (1876-1929) German				
wc/d	1	1,411	1,411	1,411
GOOSSENS, Simon (1893-?) ?				
3D	1	3,312	3,312	3,312
GOOZEE, Dan (1943-) American				
oil	1	20,000	20,000	20,000
GORANSSON, Ake (1902-1942) Swedish				
oil	7	5,471-34,989	20,049	18,449
GORBAN, Michel (?) Israeli?				
oil	2	2,200-3,600	2,900	2,200
GORBATOFF, Konstantin (1876-1945) Russian				
oil	20	1,649-326,800	81,063	51,429
wc/d	7	6,696-130,200	37,520	25,800
GORDER, Luther Emerson van (1861-1931) American				
oil	1	18,000	18,000	18,000
GORDIGIANI, Edoardo (1866-1961) Italian				
oil	5	592-2,016	1,204	909
GORDIGIANI, Michele (1835-1909) Italian				
oil	1	8,726	8,726	8,726
GORDILLO, Luis (1939-) Spanish				
oil	2	5,029-42,270	23,649	5,029
wc/d	19	592-7,224	1,797	1,573
GORDIN, Sidney (1918-) American				
3D	2	3,500-24,000	13,750	3,500
GORDINE, Dora (1906-1991) British				
3D	1	6,000	6,000	6,000
GORDON, Arthur (19th C) British				
oil	2	2,457-3,287	2,872	2,457

Name	No.	Price Range	Average	Median
GORDON, Douglas (1966-) British				
wc/d	1	22,000	22,000	22,000
GORDON, Hortense Mattice (1889-1961) Canadian				
oil	2	410-3,711	2,060	410
GORDON, Sir John Watson (1788-1864) British				
oil	3	920-14,960	7,715	7,266
GORDON-CUMMING, Constance Frederika (1837-1924) British				
wc/d	1	1,295	1,295	1,295
GORDY, Robert (20th C) American				
oil	1	1,600	1,600	1,600
wc/d	1	750	750	750
GORDYN, Hermanus Gerardus (1932-) Dutch				
oil	1	4,948	4,948	4,948
GORE, Frederick (1913-) British				
oil	10	4,872-24,360	9,739	8,880
GORE, Hon Charles (1729-1807) British				
wc/d	9	1,125-3,806	2,371	2,249
GORE, Spencer (1878-1914) British				
oil	1	18,585	18,585	18,585
GORE, William Crampton (1871-1946) Irish				
oil	1	19,200	19,200	19,200
GORE, William Henry (fl.1880-1916) British				
oil	1	2,436	2,436	2,436
GORE-BOOTH, Constance (1868-1927) British				
oil	1	7,750	7,750	7,750
wc/d	3	5,419-11,479	7,928	6,887
GORELOV, Gavriil Nikitich (1880-1966) Russian				
oil	1	16,435	16,435	16,435
GOREY, Edward (1929-) American				
wc/d	1	1,200	1,200	1,200
GORGUET, Auguste (1862-1927) French				
oil	1	3,762	3,762	3,762
GORI, Affortunato (19/20th C) Italian				
3D	1	34,984	34,984	34,984
GORI, G (20th C) French				
3D	1	4,234	4,234	4,234
GORI, Giorgio (1910-) French				
oil	1	790	790	790
3D	1	6,980	6,980	6,980
GORIN, Jean (1899-1981) French				
oil	2	700-12,041	6,370	700
3D	3	6,382-22,000	13,070	10,829
GORIUSHKIN-SOROKOVPUDOV, Ivan (1873-1954) Russian				
wc/d	2	23,000-37,200	30,100	23,000
GORKA, Paul (20th C) American				
oil	3	550-1,800	1,150	1,100
GORKY, Arshile (1904-1948) American				
oil	1	90,000	90,000	90,000
wc/d	12	7,741-235,344	68,164	16,000
GORLOV, Nikolai Nikolaievitch (1917-1987) Russian				
oil	2	910-1,730	1,320	910
GORMAN, R C (1932-) American				
wc/d	2	750-4,000	2,375	750
GORMAN, Richard Borthwick (1935-) Canadian				
oil	5	825-3,711	2,534	2,292
GORMLEY, Anthony (1950-) British				
wc/d	5	4,602-11,781	6,441	4,995
3D	8	47,520-314,500	184,277	140,000
GORNIK, April (1953-) American				
oil	1	9,515	9,515	9,515
GOROKHOVSKY, Eduard (1929-2004) Ukranian				
oil	1	279,000	279,000	279,000
GORP, Henri Nicolas van (1756-1819) French				
oil	3	951-5,351	3,361	3,781
GORRA, Giulio (1832-1884) Italian				
oil	4	1,392-21,214	10,738	4,919
GORRIARENA, Carlos (20th C) Argentinian				
wc/d	1	1,800	1,800	1,800
GORSON, Aaron Henry (1872-1933) American				
oil	1	11,000	11,000	11,000
GORTER, A M (1866-1933) Dutch				
oil	2	4,216-4,250	4,233	4,216

Name	No.	Price Range	Average	Median
GORTER, Arnold Marc (1866-1933) Dutch				
oil	7	2,000-14,833	6,070	4,411
wc/d	1	700	700	700
GORUS, Jaak (1901-1981) Belgian				
oil	2	680-2,472	1,576	680
GORUS, Pieter (1881-1941) Belgian				
oil	3	668-16,857	6,720	2,637
GORY, A (19th C) French				
3D	2	2,800-6,162	4,481	2,800
GORY, Affortunato (fl.1895-1925) Italian				
3D	4	5,400-17,700	10,942	8,000
GOS, Albert (1852-1942) Swiss				
oil	12	763-15,263	4,530	3,263
wc/d	1	496	496	496
GOS, François (1880-1975) Swiss				
oil	10	541-12,645	2,456	1,290
wc/d	2	446-816	631	446
GOSCHEL, Eberhard (1943-) German				
oil	2	1,089-4,452	2,770	1,089
GOSCHL, Roland (1932-) Austrian				
3D	1	7,644	7,644	7,644
GOSLING, William (1824-1883) British				
oil	1	1,009	1,009	1,009
GOSSE, Sylvia (1881-1968) British				
oil	8	528-24,220	6,180	2,175
wc/d	1	484	484	484
GOSSIN, F (19th C) French				
3D	1	24,722	24,722	24,722
GOTCH, Thomas Cooper (1854-1931) British				
oil	3	528-54,870	20,113	4,941
wc/d	6	531-3,168	1,219	549
GOTCLIFFE, Sid (1899-1969) American				
oil	1	3,750	3,750	3,750
GOTH, Moricz (1873-1944) Hungarian				
oil	1	4,425	4,425	4,425
GOTSCH, Friedrich Karl (1900-1984) Danish				
oil	2	6,960-23,919	15,439	6,960
wc/d	4	761-2,425	1,609	1,440
GOTT, Joseph (1785-1860) British				
3D	2	18,000-29,295	23,647	18,000
GOTTBERG, Susanne (1964-) Finnish				
oil	1	3,343	3,343	3,343
GOTTLIEB, Adolph (1903-1974) American				
oil	8	60,000-800,000	284,214	170,000
wc/d	2	11,000-37,500	24,250	11,000
GOTTLIEB, Leopold (1883-1934) Polish				
oil	1	8,500	8,500	8,500
GOTTLIEB, Moritz (1856-1879) Polish				
oil	1	110,000	110,000	110,000
GOTTWALD, Frederick C (1860-1941) American				
oil	1	3,300	3,300	3,300
GOTZ, J (?) German?				
oil	1	2,474	2,474	2,474
GOTZ, Karl Otto (1914-) German				
oil	1	18,185	18,185	18,185
wc/d	15	600-26,753	7,566	3,816
GOTZE, Moritz (1964-) German				
oil	1	3,312	3,312	3,312
GOTZL, Willi (1907-1978) Austrian				
oil	1	1,168	1,168	1,168
GOTZLOFF, Carl (1799-1866) German				
wc/d	1	2,003	2,003	2,003
GOU, Georges (?) ?				
3D	1	2,220	2,220	2,220
GOUBERT, Lucien Georges (1887-1964) French				
wc/d	1	3,520	3,520	3,520
GOUBIE, Jean Richard (1842-1899) French				
oil	2	41,580-45,000	43,290	41,580
GOUD, Laxma (1940-) Indian				
wc/d	6	6,500-11,000	8,391	8,000

Name	No.	Price Range	Average	Median
GOUDIE, Alexander (1933-) British				
oil	4	2,249-11,036	6,342	3,186
wc/d	1	515	515	515
GOUGIS, Jacqueline (1926-) French				
oil	1	2,625	2,625	2,625
GOULANDRIS, Leonidas (1927-) ?				
oil	1	25,000	25,000	25,000
GOULDING, Tim (1945-) Irish				
oil	1	1,034	1,034	1,034
wc/d	1	867	867	867
GOULET, Yann Renard (1914-1999) Irish/French				
wc/d	1	6,106	6,106	6,106
GOUNAROPOULOS, Georges (1889-1977) Greek				
oil	3	8,700-22,680	15,390	14,790
GOUPIL, Ernest (1814-1841) French				
oil	1	1,637	1,637	1,637
GOUPIL, Jules Adolphe (1839-1883) French				
oil	1	2,944	2,944	2,944
GOUPIL, Léon (1834-1890) French				
oil	1	3,575	3,575	3,575
GOURDET, Pierre Eugène (?-1889) French				
oil	1	3,024	3,024	3,024
GOURDON, Jean Paul (20th C) French				
3D	1	7,233	7,233	7,233
GOURDON, René (1855-?) French				
oil	1	1,500	1,500	1,500
GOURLIER, Paul Dominique (1813-1869) French				
oil	1	5,671	5,671	5,671
GOUSSET, Eugene (19/20th C) French				
oil	1	2,250	2,250	2,250
GOUVERNEUR, Simon (20th C) American				
oil	1	2,000	2,000	2,000
GOUWE, Adriaan Herman (1875-1965) Dutch				
oil	2	6,479-18,849	12,664	6,479
GOUWELOOS, Jean (1868-1943) Belgian				
oil	9	975-23,836	11,631	13,521
GOVAERTS, Abraham (1589-1626) Flemish				
oil	4	19,852-66,538	36,296	22,595
GOVAERTS, Jan Baptist (1701-1746) Flemish				
oil	1	5,260	5,260	5,260
GOW, Andrew Carrick (1848-1920) British				
oil	2	478-10,620	5,549	478
GOW, Mary L (1851-1929) British				
oil	1	20,520	20,520	20,520
GOWING, Lawrence (1918-1991) British				
oil	3	1,881-4,622	3,301	3,401
GOYA Y LUCIENTES, Francisco Jose de (1746-1828) Spanish				
wc/d	1	300,000	300,000	300,000
GOYEN, A van (18th C) Flemish				
oil	1	3,038	3,038	3,038
GOYEN, Jan van (1596-1656) Dutch				
oil	12	27,680-333,000	136,856	120,000
wc/d	12	2,336-22,200	12,885	11,245
GOZZARD, J Walter (1888-1950) British				
oil	1	800	800	800
wc/d	1	905	905	905
GRAADT VAN ROGGEN, Johannes Mattheus (1867-1959) Dutch				
oil	2	975-5,088	3,031	975
GRAAFLAND, Robert Archibald Antonius Joan (1875-1940) Dutch				
oil	2	9,452-53,940	31,696	9,452
GRAAT, Barend (1628-1709) Flemish				
oil	1	16,473	16,473	16,473
GRAB, Walter (1927-1989) Swiss				
oil	6	454-2,434	1,032	530
GRABACH, John R (1886-1981) American				
oil	14	700-40,000	8,162	3,750
wc/d	1	650	650	650
GRABAR, Igor (1872-1960) Russian				
oil	1	39,130	39,130	39,130
GRABEL, Frans (19/20th C) ?				
oil	1	10,888	10,888	10,888

Name	No.	Price Range	Average	Median
GRABMAYER, Franz (1927-) German				
oil	2	10,014-27,917	18,965	10,014
wc/d	1	1,405	1,405	1,405
GRABONE, Arnold (1896-1981) German				
oil	15	400-1,463	614	546
wc/d	1	808	808	808
GRABOWSKI, Jerzy (1933-) Polish				
oil	1	1,057	1,057	1,057
GRABOWSKI, Stanislas (1901-1957) Polish				
wc/d	1	1,438	1,438	1,438
GRACE, A F (1844-1903) British				
wc/d	1	1,740	1,740	1,740
GRACE, A L (19th C) British				
oil	1	2,494	2,494	2,494
GRACE, Alfred Fitzwalter (1844-1903) British				
oil	1	1,079	1,079	1,079
wc/d	2	499-756	627	499
GRACE, James Edward (1851-1908) British				
oil	2	783-1,740	1,261	783
wc/d	1	855	855	855
GRACEY, Theodore J (1895-1959) British				
oil	1	952	952	952
wc/d	4	519-1,668	910	727
GRACHEV (19th C) Russian				
3D	5	5,200-200,000	47,912	11,180
GRACHT, Jakob van der (1593-1652) Dutch				
oil	1	6,992	6,992	6,992
GRACIA, Manuel de (1937-) Spanish				
oil	1	2,735	2,735	2,735
GRADA, Raffaele de (1885-1957) Italian				
oil	12	1,032-13,081	4,918	3,281
wc/d	2	509-1,295	902	509
GRADL, Hermann (1883-1964) German				
oil	7	589-2,635	1,219	1,060
GRADY, Napoleone (1860-1949) Italian				
oil	2	970-1,401	1,185	970
GRAEF, Gustav (1821-1895) German				
oil	1	5,285	5,285	5,285
GRAEFF, Werner (1901-1964) German				
oil	1	1,674	1,674	1,674
GRAEME, Colin (fl.1858-1910) British				
oil	21	806-7,120	3,266	3,213
GRAESER, Camille (1892-1980) Swiss				
oil	4	648-40,000	14,786	648
GRAF, Erich (1947-) German				
oil	1	2,145	2,145	2,145
GRAF, F (19/20th C) German				
oil	1	10,200	10,200	10,200
GRAF, Franz (1954-) Austrian				
wc/d	2	2,293-6,429	4,361	2,293
GRAF, Gerhard (1883-1960) German				
oil	5	684-1,514	1,209	1,454
GRAF, Johann (1653-1710) Austrian				
oil	1	88,699	88,699	88,699
GRAF, Ludwig (1838-1894) Austrian				
oil	1	19,421	19,421	19,421
GRAF, Oskar (1870-1958) German				
oil	4	766-2,297	1,371	893
GRAF, Philip (1874-?) German				
oil	4	584-2,431	1,266	835
GRAF, S (?) ?				
oil	1	2,167	2,167	2,167
GRAF-PFAFF, Cacilie (1862-1939) German				
oil	1	1,786	1,786	1,786
GRAFF, Anton (1736-1813) German/Swiss				
oil	2	9,730-15,082	12,406	9,730
GRAFTON, Robert W (1876-1936) American				
oil	3	1,800-66,000	35,933	40,000
GRAHAM, Dan (1942-) American				
wc/d	1	3,214	3,214	3,214
3D	2	4,250-23,562	13,906	4,250

Name	No.	Price Range	Average	Median
GRAHAM, Dan and WALL, Jeff (20th C) American/Canadian				
wc/d	6	1,051-3,461	1,720	1,360
GRAHAM, Dorothy Young (1922-2002) American				
oil	1	1,600	1,600	1,600
wc/d	1	900	900	900
GRAHAM, George (1881-1949) British				
oil	4	748-2,436	1,505	957
wc/d	1	452	452	452
GRAHAM, James Lillie (1873-1965) Canadian				
oil	4	978-3,668	2,224	1,956
GRAHAM, John D (c.1881-1961) American/Russian				
oil	3	16,000-110,000	57,000	45,000
wc/d	7	3,000-18,000	6,964	5,500
GRAHAM, Patrick (20th C) Irish				
wc/d	1	2,311	2,311	2,311
GRAHAM, Peter (1836-1921) British				
oil	16	2,109-28,160	8,992	5,610
GRAHAM, Robert (1938-) American				
3D	2	3,000-4,750	3,875	3,000
GRAHAM, Robert Macdonald (jnr) (1919-) American				
oil	1	3,500	3,500	3,500
wc/d	1	550	550	550
GRAHAM, Rodney (1949-) Canadian				
3D	1	20,000	20,000	20,000
GRAHAM, Stanley (19/20th C) British				
oil	1	1,424	1,424	1,424
GRAHN, Hjalmar (1882-1949) Swedish				
oil	5	655-2,511	1,410	763
GRAILLY, Victor de (1804-1889) French				
oil	2	1,500-1,815	1,657	1,500
GRAM, Andrea (1853-1927) Norwegian				
oil	1	2,610	2,610	2,610
GRAMAJO GUTIERREZ, Alfredo (1893-1961) Argentinian				
oil	4	6,000-36,000	14,050	6,200
GRAMATKY, Hardie (1907-1979) American				
wc/d	2	2,250-3,500	2,875	2,250
GRAMATTE, Walter (19/20th C) ?				
wc/d	1	3,366	3,366	3,366
GRAMMATICA, Antiveduto (1571-1626) Italian				
oil	1	59,595	59,595	59,595
GRAN, Enrique (1928-1999) Spanish				
oil	2	3,766-6,622	5,194	3,766
GRANATA, L (19/20th C) French				
oil	1	3,185	3,185	3,185
GRANATA, Louis (19/20th C) French				
oil	3	578-9,031	3,785	1,746
GRANBERG, C I (19th C) ?				
oil	1	1,496	1,496	1,496
GRANDARA, I (?) French?				
oil	1	3,010	3,010	3,010
GRANDAUER, Josef (1822-1897) Austrian				
oil	1	2,119	2,119	2,119
GRANDEE, Joe (1929-1976) American				
oil	2	1,000-2,000	1,500	1,000
wc/d	1	2,600	2,600	2,600
GRANDGERARD, Lucien Henri (1880-1965) French				
oil	3	606-4,048	2,229	2,035
GRANDHOMME, Paul (fl.1874-1898) French				
oil	1	8,469	8,469	8,469
GRANDI, Francesco (1831-1891) Italian				
oil	2	473-947	710	473
wc/d	2	710-829	769	710
GRANDI, Francesco de (1968-) Italian				
oil	3	1,414-6,096	3,048	1,635
GRANDI, Mario Dario (1918-1971) Argentinian				
oil	1	3,200	3,200	3,200
GRANDIN, Eugène (1833-1919) French				
wc/d	4	1,100-3,010	2,137	1,438
GRANDIO, Constantino (1923-1977) Spanish				
oil	2	6,442-18,542	12,492	6,442
wc/d	1	1,029	1,029	1,029

Name	No.	Price Range	Average	Median
GRANDMAISON, Nickola de (1892-1978) Canadian/Russian				
oil	2	4,100-5,673	4,886	4,100
wc/d	7	1,230-17,218	9,507	9,778
GRANDMAISON, Oreste de (1932-1985) Canadian				
oil	12	443-2,593	1,085	770
GRANDVILLE, Jean Ignace (1803-1847) French				
wc/d	5	714-21,405	9,302	3,637
GRANELL, Eugenio F (1912-2001) Spanish				
oil	4	11,959-42,240	30,662	31,450
wc/d	2	2,000-9,568	5,784	2,000
GRANER Y ARRUFI, Luis (1863-1929) Spanish				
oil	11	1,437-69,600	15,433	10,440
GRANER, Ernst (1865-1943) Austrian				
wc/d	9	584-6,799	2,167	1,936
GRANERI, Giovanni Michele (18th C) Italian				
oil	1	22,878	22,878	22,878
GRANET, François Marius (1775-1849) French				
oil	1	13,000	13,000	13,000
wc/d	2	2,268-5,500	3,884	2,268
GRANFELT, Erik (1919-1990) Finnish				
oil	3	1,029-3,039	1,901	1,636
GRANOVSKI, Sam (1889-?) Russian				
oil	1	599	599	599
wc/d	2	954-27,900	14,427	954
GRANQVIST, Karin (1965-) Swedish				
oil	1	1,850	1,850	1,850
GRANSTEDT, Hilda (1841-1932) Finnish				
oil	2	959-1,543	1,251	959
GRANT, Blanche (1874-1948) American				
oil	1	3,000	3,000	3,000
GRANT, Carleton (fl.1885-1899) British				
oil	1	460	460	460
wc/d	2	592-1,730	1,161	592
GRANT, Donald (1942-) British				
	14	1,548-24,000	7,377	5,500
GRANT, Duncan (1885-1978) British				
oil	24	3,500-83,520	19,711	11,340
wc/d	15	496-12,000	3,173	2,394
GRANT, Frederick M (1886-1959) American				
oil	2	2,000-9,000	5,500	2,000
GRANT, Gordon (1875-1962) American				
oil	6	1,800-10,500	5,125	3,200
wc/d	8	425-5,500	2,049	1,200
GRANT, J Jeffrey (1883-1960) American				
oil	1	3,000	3,000	3,000
wc/d	1	2,100	2,100	2,100
GRANT, Mimi (20th C) American				
oil	1	3,500	3,500	3,500
GRANT, Sir Francis (1810-1878) British				
oil	3	400-5,130	2,698	2,565
GRAPHITO, Speedy (1961-) ?				
oil	3	707-1,567	1,069	935
wc/d	2	1,798-4,195	2,996	1,798
GRASHOF, Otto (1812-1876) German				
oil	1	3,629	3,629	3,629
GRASS, Carl Gottlob (1767-1814) Balkan/Italian				
oil	1	4,163	4,163	4,163
GRASSEL, Franz (1861-1948) German				
oil	4	7,135-23,378	13,488	11,192
GRASSET, Eugène (1841-1917) Swiss				
wc/d	2	6,233-11,678	8,955	6,233
GRASSI, Alfonso (1919-2002) Italian				
wc/d	1	1,019	1,019	1,019
GRASSI, Nicola (1662-1748) Italian				
oil	3	3,514-31,450	20,566	26,736
GRASSON, Jean Pierre (18th C) French				
wc/d	1	2,417	2,417	2,417
GRATALOUP, Guy Rachel (20th C) French?				
wc/d	1	9,926	9,926	9,926
GRATCHEFF, A P (1780-1850) Russian				
3D	1	12,959	12,959	12,959

Name	No.	Price Range	Average	Median
GRATCHEFF, Alexei Petrovitch (1780-1850) Russian				
3D	3	4,487-25,055	13,154	9,921
GRATCHEV (?) Russian				
3D	1	40,767	40,767	40,767
GRATCHEV, Vassily (1831-1905) Russian				
3D	4	10,796-356,712	101,097	15,798
GRATE, Eric (1896-1983) Swedish				
3D	1	2,290	2,290	2,290
GRATZ, Theodor (1859-1947) German				
oil	1	1,403	1,403	1,403
GRAU GARRIGA, Josep (1929-) Spanish				
oil	1	2,378	2,378	2,378
GRAU SANTOS, Julian (1937-) Spanish				
oil	11	1,176-5,986	2,882	2,939
wc/d	2	506-1,113	809	506
GRAU-SALA (1911-1975) Spanish				
oil	1	55,500	55,500	55,500
GRAU-SALA, Emile (1911-1975) Spanish				
oil	32	3,534-61,600	26,298	23,000
wc/d	46	556-14,013	2,377	1,236
GRAUBNER, Gotthard (1930-) German				
oil	5	5,260-40,055	20,374	10,192
wc/d	6	729-11,781	7,170	9,425
3D	1	12,370	12,370	12,370
GRAUER, William C (1896-1985) American				
oil	1	900	900	900
wc/d	1	480	480	480
GRAUSS, Geert (1882-1929) Dutch				
oil	1	1,145	1,145	1,145
wc/d	1	1,062	1,062	1,062
GRAVELY, Percy (fl.1886-1904) British				
oil	2	1,197-7,000	4,098	1,197
GRAVES, Abbott Fuller (1859-1936) American				
oil	14	1,200-175,000	42,242	17,000
wc/d	2	4,500-5,500	5,000	4,500
GRAVES, Mike (20th C) American				
oil	3	850-1,800	1,383	1,500
GRAVES, Morris (1910-2001) American				
oil	3	6,500-30,000	16,500	13,000
wc/d	2	37,500-40,000	38,750	37,500
GRAVES, Nancy (1940-1995) American				
oil	1	12,000	12,000	12,000
wc/d	1	4,000	4,000	4,000
3D	1	30,000	30,000	30,000
GRAY, A (?) ?				
oil	1	1,298	1,298	1,298
GRAY, Cedric (fl.1880) British				
oil	1	2,100	2,100	2,100
GRAY, Cleve (1918-) American				
oil	3	700-5,000	2,650	2,250
GRAY, Douglas Stannus (1890-1959) British				
oil	2	1,239-2,590	1,914	1,239
GRAY, Henry Percy (1869-1952) American				
oil	2	19,000-37,500	28,250	19,000
wc/d	15	2,500-42,500	20,411	18,555
GRAY, Henry Peters (1819-1877) American				
oil	1	7,500	7,500	7,500
GRAY, Jack L (1927-1981) American				
oil	7	7,336-90,000	42,976	38,000
wc/d	4	1,100-2,400	1,675	1,200
GRAY, Lucy (19th C) British				
oil	1	1,092	1,092	1,092
GRAY, Luke (1961-) American				
oil	1	1,000	1,000	1,000
GRAY, Monica F (fl.1898-1919) British				
oil	1	855	855	855
wc/d	1	8,850	8,850	8,850
GRAZI, Lionello (19th C) Italian				
oil	1	4,524	4,524	4,524
GRAZIANI, A (20th C) Italian				
oil	1	1,374	1,374	1,374
GRAZIANI, Alfio Paolo (1900-?) Italian				
oil	2	847-4,435	2,641	847

Name	No.	Price Range	Average	Median
GRAZIANI, Ercole (younger) (1688-1765) Italian				
oil	1	33,714	33,714	33,714
GRAZIANI, Francesco (17th C) Italian				
oil	6	3,588-18,643	10,715	7,856
GREACEN, Edmund William (1877-1949) American				
oil	6	3,500-65,000	18,985	9,500
GREAUME, Laurent (1960-) French				
oil	1	2,249	2,249	2,249
GREAVES, Derrick (1927-) British				
oil	3	9,250-24,780	15,590	12,740
wc/d	3	743-2,832	1,623	1,295
GREAVES, Walter (1846-1930) British				
oil	7	641-14,175	3,736	1,758
wc/d	6	589-4,628	1,631	895
GREBBER, Pieter de (1600-c.1655) Dutch				
wc/d	1	2,102	2,102	2,102
GREBENNICK, Vitali Sergeevich (1928-) Russian				
oil	1	5,190	5,190	5,190
GREBER, Henri Léon (1855-1941) French				
3D	1	16,020	16,020	16,020
GREBESTEIN, Ferdinand (1883-1974) German?				
oil	1	2,188	2,188	2,188
GRECO, Alberto (1931-1965) Argentinian				
wc/d	4	2,529-16,000	7,062	4,451
GRECO, El (1541-1614) Spanish				
oil	3	1,059,592-1,572,500	1,302,806	1,276,327
GRECO, Emilio (1913-1995) Italian				
oil	3	623-1,665	1,229	1,400
wc/d	7	477-5,364	2,012	1,555
3D	5	12,000-35,042	19,024	15,000
GRECO, Emilio (1932-) Italian				
oil	2	885-1,400	1,142	885
GRECO, Gennaro (1663-1714) Italian				
oil	1	7,120	7,120	7,120
GRECO, James (20th C) American				
3D	1	3,000	3,000	3,000
GREEN, Alan (1932-) British				
oil	2	1,298-5,301	3,299	1,298
wc/d	2	636-1,850	1,243	636
GREEN, Anthony (1939-) British				
oil	1	4,500	4,500	4,500
GREEN, Charles (1840-1898) British				
wc/d	1	2,088	2,088	2,088
GREEN, Charles Lewis (1844-1915) American				
oil	4	3,500-12,000	6,750	5,000
GREEN, Edward Frederick (c.1767-1851) British				
oil	1	20,384	20,384	20,384
GREEN, Frank Russell (1856-1940) British				
oil	3	863-5,500	2,904	2,350
GREEN, Jasper (1829-1910) American				
oil	1	1,100	1,100	1,100
GREEN, Madelaine (1884-1947) British				
oil	1	6,018	6,018	6,018
GREEN, Margaret (1925-2003) British				
oil	5	525-14,790	5,225	2,436
GREEN, Nathaniel Everett (fl.1880-1896) British				
wc/d	2	460-3,132	1,796	460
GREEN, William (1760-1823) British				
wc/d	3	560-3,402	1,550	688
GREENAWAY, Kate (1846-1901) British				
wc/d	2	736-6,475	3,605	736
GREENBAUM, Dorothea (1893-1986) American				
oil	1	550	550	550
3D	1	7,000	7,000	7,000
GREENBAUM, Joseph David (1864-1940) American				
oil	4	750-7,000	3,237	1,700
GREENBLAT, Rodney Alan (1960-) American				
oil	1	1,600	1,600	1,600
GREENE, Albert van Nesse (1887-1971) American				
oil	1	700	700	700
wc/d	4	850-1,700	1,312	1,100

Name	No.	Price Range	Average	Median
GREENE, Balcomb (1904-1990) American				
wc/d	1	1,200	1,200	1,200
GREENE, Bruce (1953-) American				
3D	2	3,800-5,000	4,400	3,800
GREENE, Catherine (?) Irish?				
3D	1	4,359	4,359	4,359
GREENE, Elmer Westley (jnr) (1907-1964) American				
oil	1	4,250	4,250	4,250
GREENE, George Sears (1908-1985) American				
oil	1	1,000	1,000	1,000
GREENE, Leroy E (1893-1974) American				
oil	1	2,500	2,500	2,500
GREENE, Mark (1916-1986) American				
oil	1	3,000	3,000	3,000
GREENE, Matt (1971-) American				
oil	1	26,000	26,000	26,000
GREENE, Millie (20th C) American				
oil	6	1,400-4,250	2,583	2,250
GREENFIELD-SANDERS, Isca (1978-) American				
wc/d	1	1,401	1,401	1,401
GREENHAM, Peter (1909-1992) British				
oil	2	2,262-4,810	3,536	2,262
GREENHAM, Robert Duckworth (1906-1975) British				
oil	5	696-4,576	2,300	1,584
GREENLEAF, Benjamin (1786-1864) American				
oil	1	3,500	3,500	3,500
GREENOUGH, Horatio (1805-1852) American				
3D	1	6,115	6,115	6,115
GREENWOOD, Ethan Allen (1779-1856) American				
oil	1	2,000	2,000	2,000
GREENWOOD, George Parker (fl.1870-1904) British				
oil	1	2,208	2,208	2,208
GREENWOOD, Joseph H (1857-1927) American				
oil	2	375-2,300	1,337	375
GREENWOOD, Orlando (1892-1989) British				
oil	3	528-2,478	1,181	537
GREENWOOD, Parker (fl.1880-c.1904) British				
oil	1	2,112	2,112	2,112
GREER, A D (1904-1998) American				
oil	6	3,800-17,500	8,716	5,500
GREEVES, Richard (1925-) American				
3D	1	3,250	3,250	3,250
GREFERATH, Johannes (1872-1946) German				
oil	1	1,178	1,178	1,178
GREGOIRE, Émile (19th C) French				
3D	1	2,336	2,336	2,336
GREGOIRE, Jan (1887-1960) Dutch				
oil	1	4,142	4,142	4,142
GREGOIRE, Jean-Louis (1840-1890) French				
3D	1	30,000	30,000	30,000
GREGOIRE, Paul (19/20th C) French				
oil	3	1,753-3,390	2,480	2,297
wc/d	1	757	757	757
GREGOOR, Gillis Smak (1770-1843) Dutch				
oil	1	4,142	4,142	4,142
GREGOR, Harold (1929-) American				
oil	1	1,000	1,000	1,000
GREGORIO, Marco de (1829-1876) Italian				
oil	2	592-9,425	5,008	592
GREGORY, Arthur V (1867-1957) Australian				
wc/d	1	1,350	1,350	1,350
GREGORY, Charles (1850-1920) British				
wc/d	1	2,464	2,464	2,464
GREGORY, George (1849-1938) British				
oil	4	1,416-7,480	4,275	3,480
wc/d	1	1,032	1,032	1,032
GREGORY, Michael (20th C) American				
oil	1	1,100	1,100	1,100
GREIFFENHAGEN, Maurice (1862-1931) British				
oil	2	4,475-9,750	7,112	4,475

Name	No.	Price Range	Average	Median
GREIG, Donald (1916-) British				
oil	2	531-766	648	531
wc/d	1	525	525	525
GREIL, Alois (1841-1902) Austrian				
wc/d	2	963-1,210	1,086	963
GREINER, Otto (1869-1916) German				
oil	1	10,603	10,603	10,603
wc/d	4	884-25,918	8,702	1,527
GREIS, Otto (1913-2001) German				
oil	3	1,874-4,216	3,302	3,816
wc/d	1	3,514	3,514	3,514
GREIVE, Johan Conrad (jnr) (1837-1891) Dutch				
oil	2	1,911-3,836	2,873	1,911
GREKOV, Mitrofan Borisovich (1882-1934) Russian				
wc/d	1	9,722	9,722	9,722
GRELA, Juan (1914-1992) Argentinian				
oil	3	1,800-6,500	3,700	2,800
wc/d	1	4,000	4,000	4,000
GRELLE, Martin (1954-) American				
oil	10	6,250-230,000	56,025	18,000
GREMLICH, Adolf (1915-1971) German				
oil	2	648-4,454	2,551	648
GRENET DE JOIGNY, Dominique Adolphe (1821-1885) French				
oil	1	1,106	1,106	1,106
GRENET, Edward (1857-?) French				
oil	1	2,400	2,400	2,400
GRENIER DE SAINT-MARTIN, Francisque Martin François (1793-1867) French				
oil	1	7,644	7,644	7,644
GRENNESS, Johannes (1875-1963) Danish				
oil	2	2,529-5,059	3,794	2,529
GRENVILLE, Hugo (20th C) British				
oil	1	1,000	1,000	1,000
wc/d	1	870	870	870
GRES, Serge Czerefkow (1899-1970) French				
oil	1	1,918	1,918	1,918
wc/d	1	2,277	2,277	2,277
GRESLEY, Frank (1855-1936) British				
oil	2	460-1,693	1,076	460
wc/d	12	623-1,748	1,171	1,211
GRESLEY, Harold (1892-1967) British				
oil	1	1,740	1,740	1,740
wc/d	6	1,903-2,422	2,054	1,925
GRESLEY, James S (1829-1908) British				
oil	1	1,313	1,313	1,313
wc/d	4	589-1,120	898	810
GRETZNER, Harold (1902-1977) American				
wc/d	4	1,700-4,250	2,525	1,900
GREUZE, Jean-Baptiste (1725-1805) French				
oil	7	1,250-1,593,000	293,529	76,027
wc/d	6	8,507-140,270	50,908	29,223
GREVE, Hedwige (1850-?) German				
oil	1	1,260	1,260	1,260
GREVE, Rudolf (1883-?) German				
oil	1	1,260	1,260	1,260
GREVENBROECK, Jan II (1731-1807) Italian				
oil	1	7,135	7,135	7,135
GREVENBROECK, Orazio (17/18th C) Dutch				
oil	2	6,659-15,000	10,829	6,659
GREVILLE, Charles Francis (1749-1809) British				
oil	1	3,092	3,092	3,092
GREVIN, Alfred and BEER, Friedrich (19th C) French				
3D	1	2,918	2,918	2,918
GREY, Alfred (1845-1926) British				
oil	6	1,695-4,676	3,206	2,338
GREY, Gregor (fl.1880-1911) British				
oil	2	1,473-2,338	1,905	1,473
GREY, Roger de (1918-) British				
oil	1	3,366	3,366	3,366
GREYTAK, Don (20th C) American				
wc/d	1	2,500	2,500	2,500

Name	No.	Price Range	Average	Median
GRIBBLE, Bernard Finegan (1873-1962) British				
oil	5	1,216-19,000	7,963	5,500
wc/d	2	732-1,584	1,158	732
GRIBBLE, Kenneth (1925-) British				
oil	2	870-1,357	1,113	870
GRIBBLE, Paul S (1938-) British				
oil	1	7,182	7,182	7,182
GRIEKEN, Jef van (1950-) Belgian				
oil	2	1,335-1,335	1,335	1,335
wc/d	2	955-1,790	1,372	955
GRIENT, Cornelis de (1691-1783) Dutch				
wc/d	1	1,125	1,125	1,125
GRIERSON, Charles MacIver (1864-1939) British				
wc/d	1	1,313	1,313	1,313
GRIERSON, Mary (20th C) British				
wc/d	1	2,220	2,220	2,220
GRIESHABER, Helmut A P (1909-1981) German				
oil	2	694-1,051	872	694
wc/d	5	971-2,104	1,439	1,236
GRIFFA, Giorgio (1936-) Italian				
oil	14	2,330-10,813	6,941	7,633
wc/d	1	1,473	1,473	1,473
GRIFFEN, Davenport (1894-?) American				
oil	1	2,300	2,300	2,300
GRIFFIER, Jan (elder) (1652-1718) Dutch				
oil	1	7,224	7,224	7,224
GRIFFIER, Robert (1688-1750) British				
oil	2	17,300-370,000	193,650	17,300
GRIFFIN, Charles Gerald (1864-1945) American				
oil	1	1,600	1,600	1,600
GRIFFIN, Keith Alastair (1927-) British				
oil	2	1,151-1,566	1,358	1,151
GRIFFIN, Nina Kickbusch (1894-) American				
oil	1	4,000	4,000	4,000
GRIFFIN, Thomas Bailey (1858-1918) American				
oil	7	750-3,000	1,357	1,200
GRIFFIN, Walter (1861-1935) American				
oil	2	1,300-15,000	8,150	1,300
GRIFFING, Robert (1940-) American				
oil	4	3,800-75,000	33,325	9,500
GRIFFITH, Marie Osthaus (1855-1927) American/German				
oil	1	2,500	2,500	2,500
GRIFFITH, William Alexander (1866-1940) American				
oil	3	1,700-3,000	2,233	2,000
GRIFFITHS, David (1939-) British				
oil	1	2,079	2,079	2,079
GRIFFITHS, James (1825-1896) Canadian				
wc/d	1	1,763	1,763	1,763
GRIGGS, Samuel W (1827-1898) American				
oil	2	1,300-5,000	3,150	1,300
GRIGNANI, Franco (1908-1999) Italian				
oil	1	3,562	3,562	3,562
GRIGORESCO, Nicolas (1838-1907) Rumanian				
oil	2	15,000-20,000	17,500	15,000
GRIGORIEV, Boris (1886-1939) Russian				
oil	8	34,400-705,200	305,802	189,200
wc/d	19	1,822-84,145	14,999	8,600
GRIGORYEV, Vitally (1957-) Russian				
oil	3	1,600-1,800	1,716	1,750
GRILL, Oswald (1878-1969) Austrian				
oil	1	3,974	3,974	3,974
wc/d	1	1,210	1,210	1,210
GRILLO, John (1917-) American				
oil	1	3,000	3,000	3,000
GRILLON, Roger-Maurice (1881-1938) French				
oil	2	623-2,595	1,609	623
GRILO, Sarah (1921-) Argentinian				
oil	3	1,701-22,000	13,067	15,500
wc/d	1	4,000	4,000	4,000
GRIM, Maurice (1890-1968) French				
oil	1	1,200	1,200	1,200

Name	No.	Price Range	Average	Median
GRIMALDI, Alessandro (1630-1663) Italian				
wc/d	1	3,145	3,145	3,145
GRIMALDI, Giovanni Francesco (1606-1680) Italian				
wc/d	1	5,365	5,365	5,365
GRIMALT, Ramon (1937-) French				
oil	20	478-2,153	934	718
wc/d	8	478-1,076	671	538
GRIMANI, Guido (1871-1933) Italian				
oil	3	781-7,714	4,979	6,442
GRIMELUND, Johannes Martin (1842-1917) Norwegian				
oil	5	621-7,360	2,908	1,620
GRIMM, Arthur (1883-1948) German				
oil	1	3,405	3,405	3,405
GRIMM, Constantine von (19th C) ?				
wc/d	1	4,400	4,400	4,400
GRIMM, Paul (1892-1974) American				
oil	22	1,300-7,500	3,895	3,500
GRIMM, Samuel Hieronymus (1733-1794) Swiss				
wc/d	2	1,509-9,100	5,304	1,509
GRIMM, Stanley (1891-1966) British				
oil	3	1,110-4,956	2,422	1,200
GRIMM, Vincenz (19th C) German?				
oil	1	2,803	2,803	2,803
GRIMM, Willem (1904-1986) German				
oil	1	2,990	2,990	2,990
wc/d	6	468-2,178	1,045	544
GRIMMER, Abel (1573-1619) Flemish				
oil	1	35,150	35,150	35,150
GRIMMER, Jacob (1526-1589) Flemish				
oil	3	64,726-124,600	92,708	88,800
GRIMONT, Therese (1901-?) French				
oil	1	6,336	6,336	6,336
GRIMOU, Alexis (1680-1740) French				
oil	1	7,329	7,329	7,329
GRIMSHAW, Atkinson (1836-1893) British				
oil	20	41,580-434,700	211,186	188,100
wc/d	1	78,120	78,120	78,120
GRIMSHAW, Louis (1870-1943) British				
oil	3	14,535-64,980	35,205	26,100
GRINNELL, Roy (1934-) American				
oil	1	1,814	1,814	1,814
GRINSHPON, Alexander (1949-) Israeli				
oil	1	3,600	3,600	3,600
GRIPENHOLM, Ulf (1943-) Swedish				
oil	3	821-20,357	8,160	3,304
GRIPPO, Carlos (1946-) Uruguayan				
oil	1	1,295	1,295	1,295
GRIS, Juan (1887-1927) Spanish				
oil	5	129,500-2,200,000	1,014,639	543,699
wc/d	6	11,959-1,000,000	261,640	22,880
GRISCHENKO, Alexei Vasilievich (1883-1967) Russian				
oil	1	12,090	12,090	12,090
GRISENKO, Nikolas (1856-1900) Russian				
oil	1	18,920	18,920	18,920
GRISET, Ernest (1844-1907) French				
wc/d	1	1,665	1,665	1,665
GRISMER, Dennis (20th C) American				
oil	1	1,250	1,250	1,250
GRISON, François Adolphe (1845-1914) French				
oil	5	3,000-45,000	17,816	10,000
wc/d	3	466-750	596	572
GRISOT, Pierre (1911-1995) French				
oil	27	605-3,102	1,530	1,505
GRISWOLD, Casimir Clayton (1834-1918) American				
oil	2	400-2,700	1,550	400
GRISWOLD, Victor Moreau (1819-1872) American				
oil	1	1,700	1,700	1,700
GRITCHENKO, Alexis (1883-1977) Russian				
oil	13	1,018-16,384	5,937	4,795
wc/d	1	1,798	1,798	1,798
GRIVAS, Lambros (1890-1956) Greek				
oil	2	3,740-8,448	6,094	3,740

Name	No.	Price Range	Average	Median
GRIVAZ, Eugène (1852-1915) Swiss				
oil	1	5,220	5,220	5,220
GRIVEAU, Lucien (1858-?) Italian				
oil	1	1,288	1,288	1,288
GRIVOLAS, Antoine (1843-1902) French				
oil	1	1,106	1,106	1,106
GRIXONI, Mario (19/20th C) ?				
wc/d	1	1,418	1,418	1,418
GROB, Konrad (1828-1904) Swiss				
oil	2	1,221-34,342	17,781	1,221
GROBE, German (1857-1938) German				
oil	14	628-4,135	1,688	1,452
GROEBER, Hermann (1865-1935) German				
oil	1	3,854	3,854	3,854
GROENEWEGEN, Adrianus Johannes (1874-1963) Dutch				
oil	4	390-2,474	1,337	927
wc/d	4	666-2,003	1,433	1,252
GROENEWEGEN, Pieter Anthonisz van (?-1658) Dutch				
oil	1	22,188	22,188	22,188
GROHE, Glenn (1912-1956) American				
wc/d	1	1,500	1,500	1,500
GROISEILLIEZ, Marcelin de (1837-1880) French				
oil	1	5,021	5,021	5,021
GROLIG, Curt Victor Clemens (1805-1863) German				
oil	2	2,919-3,802	3,360	2,919
GROLL, Andreas (1850-1907) Austrian				
oil	1	4,961	4,961	4,961
GROLL, Henriette (20th C) French?				
oil	1	1,260	1,260	1,260
GROLL, Theodor (1857-1913) German				
oil	3	2,704-7,071	4,309	3,153
GROLLERON, Paul Louis Narcisse (1848-1901) French				
oil	3	1,200-8,000	3,643	1,730
GROMAIRE, Marcel (1892-1971) French				
oil	12	8,400-58,690	23,852	21,476
wc/d	44	662-32,733	3,576	1,854
GROMME, Owen J (1896-1991) American				
oil	1	15,000	15,000	15,000
GRONLAND, Nelius (1859-?) French				
oil	1	1,065	1,065	1,065
GRONLAND, Theude (1817-1876) German				
oil	2	8,000-27,125	17,562	8,000
GROOMS, Red (1937-) American				
oil	1	14,000	14,000	14,000
wc/d	7	850-16,000	4,500	2,250
3D	3	10,000-25,000	18,333	20,000
GROOT, Frans Arnold Breuhaus de (1824-1872) Belgian				
oil	2	1,168-6,630	3,899	1,168
GROOT, Frans Breuhaus de (1796-1875) Dutch				
oil	2	1,090-22,200	11,645	1,090
GROOT, Nanno de (20th C) American				
oil	2	1,500-3,500	2,500	1,500
GROOTH, George Christoph (1716-1749) Russian				
oil	1	129,000	129,000	129,000
GROPPER, William (1897-1977) American				
oil	3	1,400-4,000	2,800	3,000
wc/d	3	800-1,250	1,016	1,000
GROS, Achille (19th C) French				
oil	1	2,425	2,425	2,425
GROS, Antoine Jean (1771-1835) French				
oil	1	630,137	630,137	630,137
wc/d	1	82,639	82,639	82,639
GROS, Lucien Alphonse (1845-1913) French				
oil	2	2,338-4,359	3,348	2,338
GROSE, Daniel C (1838-1890) American				
oil	3	531-1,900	1,046	708
GROSS, Anthony (1905-1984) British				
oil	3	447-5,236	2,052	475
wc/d	4	1,404-2,832	2,287	2,436
GROSS, Chaim (1904-1991) American				
wc/d	9	400-1,400	677	700
3D	7	3,250-55,000	18,521	9,500

Name	No.	Price Range	Average	Median
GROSS, Michael (1920-) Israeli				
oil	7	2,600-170,000	42,014	15,000
wc/d	2	2,100-2,600	2,350	2,100
GROSS, Milt (1895-1953) American				
wc/d	1	3,000	3,000	3,000
GROSS, Oskar (1871-?) American				
oil	1	7,000	7,000	7,000
GROSS, Peter Alfred (1849-1914) American				
oil	2	475-2,000	1,237	475
GROSSBACH, Peter (1934-1988) German				
3D	1	4,948	4,948	4,948
GROSSBARD, Yehushua (1902-1992) Israeli				
oil	2	450-1,700	1,075	450
GROSSBERG, Carl (1894-1940) German				
wc/d	1	4,841	4,841	4,841
GROSSE, Katherina (1961-) German				
oil	1	15,000	15,000	15,000
GROSSMAN, Joseph (1889-?) American				
oil	5	750-2,200	1,290	1,100
GROSSMAN, Nancy (1940-) American				
oil	1	2,000	2,000	2,000
wc/d	2	400-2,000	1,200	400
GROSSMANN, Rudolf (1882-1941) German				
oil	1	1,236	1,236	1,236
wc/d	3	644-1,119	802	644
GROSSMANN, Wilhelm (fl.1878-1886) German				
oil	1	13,807	13,807	13,807
GROSSO, Alfonso (1893-1983) Spanish				
oil	4	5,500-12,552	8,837	6,000
GROSSO, Giacomo (1860-1938) Italian				
oil	2	1,911-2,425	2,168	1,911
GROSZ, George (1893-1959) American/German				
oil	6	11,712-1,416,000	259,875	24,050
wc/d	70	750-457,600	23,198	10,000
GROTEMEYER, Fritz (1864-?) German				
oil	1	22,680	22,680	22,680
GROTH, Vilhelm (1842-1899) Danish				
oil	4	632-1,746	1,079	809
GROUARD, John E (1859-?) ?				
oil	1	9,000	9,000	9,000
GROULT, Andre and ZADKINE, Ossip (20th C) French				
oil	1	135,000	135,000	135,000
GROUMELLEC, Loic le (1958-) French				
oil	3	877-3,507	2,540	3,236
GROUNAUER, Lucien (1906-1997) Swiss				
oil	1	1,582	1,582	1,582
GROUSINSKY, Peter (1837-1892) Russian				
oil	1	44,720	44,720	44,720
GROUX, Charles de (1825-1870) Belgian				
oil	2	1,001-9,710	5,355	1,001
wc/d	1	1,806	1,806	1,806
GROVE, Nordahl (1822-1885) Danish				
oil	6	489-3,700	1,683	949
GROVES, John (?) British?				
wc/d	1	1,740	1,740	1,740
GROVES, Naomi Jackson (1910-2001) Canadian				
oil	2	560-1,553	1,056	560
GROVES, Paula (1969-) British				
3D	1	2,835	2,835	2,835
GRUAU, René (1910-2004) Italian				
oil	1	6,686	6,686	6,686
wc/d	9	579-3,536	1,788	1,665
GRUBACS, Carlo (19th C) Italian				
oil	5	16,493-34,969	22,840	22,080
wc/d	2	3,717-45,000	24,358	3,717
GRUBACS, Giovanni (1829-1919) Italian				
oil	2	8,182-42,381	25,281	8,182
GRUBAS, Marco (1839-1910) Italian				
oil	6	1,946-5,984	3,357	2,145
GRUBE, Gunleif (1947-) Danish				
oil	1	2,586	2,586	2,586

Name	No.	Price Range	Average	Median
GRUBER, Francis (1912-1948) French				
oil	1	17,810	17,810	17,810
GRUBER, Franz Xaver (1801-1862) Austrian				
oil	1	16,560	16,560	16,560
GRUBER, Hannes (1928-) Swiss				
oil	1	6,086	6,086	6,086
GRUBER, Jacques (1870-1933) French				
oil	1	2,662	2,662	2,662
GRUBHOFER, Toni (1855-1935) Austrian				
wc/d	1	1,030	1,030	1,030
GRUELLE, Richard Buckner (1851-1914) American				
oil	1	7,000	7,000	7,000
GRUN, Jules Alexandre (1868-1934) French				
oil	6	600-6,668	2,596	1,911
wc/d	3	562-1,067	785	726
GRUN, Maurice (1869-1947) French				
oil	4	877-2,997	1,583	1,199
GRUND, Johann (1808-1887) Austrian				
oil	2	850-2,945	1,897	850
GRUND, Norbert Joseph Carl (1717-1767) Czechoslovakian				
oil	1	17,858	17,858	17,858
GRUNDMANN, B (1726-1798) German				
3D	1	3,513	3,513	3,513
GRUNDMANN, Basilius (1726-1798) German				
oil	1	2,040	2,040	2,040
GRUNENWALD, Jakob (1822-1896) German				
oil	2	17,027-21,000	19,013	17,027
GRUNEWALD, Gustav Johann (1805-1878) German				
oil	1	5,500	5,500	5,500
GRUNEWALD, Isaac (1889-1946) Swedish				
oil	43	2,363-1,248,493	80,752	17,840
wc/d	24	529-21,143	4,551	2,926
GRUNFELD, Thomas (1956-) German				
3D	6	1,854-38,940	15,960	6,799
GRUNWALD, Bela Ivanyi (1867-1940) Hungarian				
oil	1	2,671	2,671	2,671
GRUNWALD, Carl (1907-1968) German				
oil	1	1,757	1,757	1,757
wc/d	2	876-1,120	998	876
GRUPPE, Charles C (1928-) American				
oil	8	375-2,600	1,037	850
GRUPPE, Charles Paul (1860-1940) American				
oil	13	1,001-10,000	4,347	3,000
wc/d	3	700-900	783	750
GRUPPE, Emile A (1896-1978) American				
oil	64	1,000-44,000	10,943	9,000
wc/d	5	700-2,200	1,380	1,300
GRUPPE, Robert C (20th C) American				
oil	14	1,300-4,100	2,275	2,100
GRUPPO N (20th C) Italian				
wc/d	1	12,103	12,103	12,103
GRUPPO STRUM (20th C) Italian				
3D	1	3,250	3,250	3,250
GRUTZKE, Johannes (1937-) German				
oil	6	1,512-35,619	14,979	4,243
wc/d	7	684-5,786	2,323	1,929
GRUTZNER, Eduard von (1846-1925) German				
oil	13	2,392-17,568	10,303	11,924
wc/d	8	509-753	632	608
GRUYER-BRIELMANN, Eugenie Claire (1837-1921) French				
oil	1	1,496	1,496	1,496
GRUYTER, Jacob de (1630-1681) Dutch				
oil	1	3,637	3,637	3,637
GRUYTER, Willem (jnr) (1817-1880) Dutch				
oil	3	2,757-8,486	5,416	5,007
GRYEFF, Adriaen de (1670-1715) Flemish				
oil	4	4,862-7,785	6,957	7,474
GRZIMEK, Waldemar (1918-1984) Polish				
3D	1	3,741	3,741	3,741
GSCHOSMANN, Ludwig (c.1901-1988) German				
oil	7	494-4,600	1,354	948

Name	No.	Price Range	Average	Median
GSELL, Laurent (1860-1944) French				
oil	3	818-1,636	1,189	1,113
wc/d	2	722-903	812	722
GU WENDA (1956-) Chinese				
wc/d	3	17,000-85,000	42,000	24,000
GUAEDULIEG, Casel Max Gerlach Anton (c.1823-1874) Italian				
oil	1	55,000	55,000	55,000
GUAITAMACCHI, Jonathan (1961-) British/Italian				
oil	3	1,695-14,531	7,129	5,163
wc/d	6	2,003-8,784	4,476	4,272
GUALA, Pier Francesco (1698-1757) Italian				
oil	1	46,250	46,250	46,250
GUALLINO (20th C) French				
wc/d	1	2,919	2,919	2,919
GUAN LIANG (1899-1985) Chinese				
wc/d	1	6,686	6,686	6,686
GUAN WEI (1957-) Australian/Chinese				
oil	1	25,000	25,000	25,000
GUANSE, Antonio (1926-) Spanish				
oil	3	705-1,914	1,132	778
GUARDABASSI, Guerrino (1841-?) Italian				
oil	1	3,250	3,250	3,250
GUARDI, Francesco (1712-1793) Italian				
oil	12	38,060-3,167,808	527,688	102,857
wc/d	2	17,635-29,600	23,617	17,635
GUARDI, Giacomo (1764-1835) Italian				
oil	4	11,757-72,587	28,547	12,211
wc/d	11	1,646-18,500	11,095	11,297
GUARDI, Giovanni Antonio (1698-1760) Italian				
oil	1	173,000	173,000	173,000
wc/d	2	2,141-16,000	9,070	2,141
GUARIENTI, Carlo (1923-) Italian				
oil	2	2,040-2,400	2,220	2,040
wc/d	1	2,259	2,259	2,259
GUARINO, Luigi (19th C) Italian				
oil	1	1,416	1,416	1,416
GUARLOTTI, Giovanni (1869-1954) Italian				
oil	2	1,784-3,390	2,587	1,784
GUARNIERI, Riccardo (1933-) Italian				
oil	1	630	630	630
wc/d	2	1,032-2,063	1,547	1,032
GUAY, Gabriel (1848-?) French				
oil	1	2,221	2,221	2,221
GUAYASAMIN, Oswaldo (1919-1999) Ecuadorian				
oil	5	16,743-75,000	38,251	36,000
GUBAREV, Valentin (1948-) Belarussian				
oil	2	859-3,401	2,130	859
GUBARGU, Mick (c.1925-) Australian				
wc/d	1	1,000	1,000	1,000
GUBBELS, Klaas (1934-) Dutch				
oil	5	1,036-3,273	1,906	1,987
GUBELLINI, Alcides (1900-1957) Argentinian				
oil	1	1,500	1,500	1,500
GUBLER, Eduard (1891-1971) Swiss				
oil	4	605-1,967	1,361	1,249
GUBLER, Ernst (1895-1958) Swiss				
oil	2	522-2,666	1,594	522
wc/d	1	2,196	2,196	2,196
3D	1	2,611	2,611	2,611
GUBLER, Max (1898-1973) Swiss				
oil	13	6,053-52,633	20,918	20,388
wc/d	3	771-1,362	1,040	989
3D	1	4,487	4,487	4,487
GUCCIONE, Piero (1925-) Italian				
oil	2	11,781-29,730	20,755	11,781
wc/d	5	477-5,856	2,165	1,640
GUDDEN, Rudolf (1863-1935) German				
oil	1	2,121	2,121	2,121
GUDE, Hans Fredrik (1825-1903) Norwegian				
oil	5	1,545-17,068	10,731	14,720
GUDEY, Catherine B (fl.1908-1928) British				
wc/d	1	1,218	1,218	1,218

Name	No.	Price Range	Average	Median
GUDGEON, Ralston (1910-1984) British				
oil	1	801	801	801
wc/d	19	458-905	667	695
GUDIN, Fidel (19th C) French				
oil	2	819-15,000	7,909	819
GUDIN, Henriette (1825-?) French				
oil	13	1,060-4,240	2,498	2,259
GUDIN, Theodore (1802-1880) French				
oil	9	832-41,280	8,565	3,004
wc/d	10	602-3,218	1,155	722
GUDIOL, Montserrat (1933-) Spanish				
oil	1	21,551	21,551	21,551
GUDNASON, Svavar (1909-1988) Icelandic				
oil	4	4,507-25,863	15,660	13,682
wc/d	4	1,207-1,690	1,408	1,288
GUDNI, Georg (1961-) Icelandic				
oil	1	13,215	13,215	13,215
wc/d	1	1,018	1,018	1,018
GUELDRY, Ferdinand Joseph (1858-1945) French				
oil	1	21,857	21,857	21,857
GUERARD, Charles-Jean (1790-?) French				
oil	1	10,082	10,082	10,082
GUERARD, Eugène Charles Francois (1821-1866) French				
wc/d	1	1,823	1,823	1,823
GUERAULT, H (19th C) French				
oil	1	12,600	12,600	12,600
GUERCINO (1591-1666) Italian				
wc/d	5	9,250-51,800	19,507	11,245
GUERCINO, Giovanni Francesco (1591-1666) Italian				
oil	4	90,734-573,500	230,691	102,832
wc/d	9	705-222,000	60,368	25,132
GUERESCHI, Giuseppo (20th C) Italian				
oil	1	1,000	1,000	1,000
GUERIN, A (19th C) ?				
3D	1	83,710	83,710	83,710
GUERIN, Charles (1875-1939) French				
oil	6	450-4,411	1,429	693
GUERIN, Ernest (1887-1952) French				
oil	2	1,987-7,175	4,581	1,987
wc/d	18	643-18,904	3,835	2,981
GUERIN, François (?-1791) French				
oil	1	2,572	2,572	2,572
GUERIN, Gabriel (1869-1916) French				
oil	1	1,500	1,500	1,500
GUERIN, Jean Urbain (1760-1836) French				
wc/d	3	1,512-19,911	8,757	4,849
GUERIN, Pierre Narcisse (1774-1833) French				
wc/d	1	3,000	3,000	3,000
GUERMACHEV, Mikhail Mikhailovich (1867-1930) Russian				
oil	5	5,504-18,316	10,338	8,370
GUERMONPREZ, Daniel (1933-) French				
oil	2	1,790-2,983	2,386	1,790
GUERNIER, Louis du II (1677-1716) French				
wc/d	1	3,515	3,515	3,515
GUERRA, Achille (1832-1903) Italian				
oil	1	5,351	5,351	5,351
GUERRA, Evaristo (1942-) Spanish				
oil	1	3,633	3,633	3,633
GUERRA, Indio (20th C) South American				
oil	1	2,700	2,700	2,700
GUERREIRO, Miguel Angel (1957-) Argentinian				
oil	2	1,236-1,236	1,236	1,236
GUERRERO GALVAN, Jesus (1910-1973) Mexican				
oil	3	20,000-32,000	24,666	22,000
wc/d	4	850-7,500	3,837	3,000
GUERRERO MALAGON, Cecilio (1909-1996) Spanish				
wc/d	1	1,326	1,326	1,326
GUERRERO, Jose (1914-1992) Spanish				
oil	3	17,939-132,449	81,796	95,000
GUERRESCHI, Giuseppe (1929-1985) Italian				
oil	5	2,059-9,342	4,965	4,370
wc/d	9	450-1,942	783	547

Name	No.	Price Range	Average	Median
GUERRIER, Raymond (1920-2002) French				
oil	26	565-5,500	1,378	1,100
wc/d	1	1,582	1,582	1,582
GUERRIERI, Giovanni Francesco (1589-1655) Italian				
oil	1	258,904	258,904	258,904
GUERY, Armand (1850-1912) French				
oil	5	941-11,470	4,956	3,100
GUERZONI, Franco (1948-) Italian				
oil	3	504-946	777	882
wc/d	1	1,386	1,386	1,386
GUES, Alfred François (1837-?) French				
oil	1	2,827	2,827	2,827
GUET, Charlemagne Oscar (1801-1871) French				
oil	1	7,007	7,007	7,007
GUEUDET, Alain (20th C) French				
oil	1	3,041	3,041	3,041
GUEVARA MORENO, Luis (1926-) Spanish				
oil	7	440-5,120	1,628	930
wc/d	1	1,350	1,350	1,350
GUEYTON (19th C) French				
3D	1	4,855	4,855	4,855
GUEYTON, G (?) French?				
3D	1	2,221	2,221	2,221
GUFFENS, Godfried (1823-1901) Belgian				
oil	2	1,030-1,600	1,315	1,030
GUGGI (1959-) Irish				
oil	1	5,351	5,351	5,351
GUGLIELMI, Luigi (19th C) Italian				
3D	1	24,000	24,000	24,000
GUGLIELMI, O Louis (1906-1956) American				
oil	1	50,000	50,000	50,000
wc/d	1	1,200	1,200	1,200
GUIBERT, Eugene (19th C) French				
oil	1	14,583	14,583	14,583
GUIDA, Federico (1969-) Italian				
oil	2	2,415-2,710	2,562	2,415
wc/d	2	4,712-6,597	5,654	4,712
GUIDA, Giovanni (1837-?) Italian				
oil	1	1,827	1,827	1,827
GUIDI, Guido (1901-1998) Italian				
oil	1	2,548	2,548	2,548
GUIDI, Virgilio (1892-1984) Italian				
oil	95	1,812-35,034	11,633	9,469
wc/d	19	604-3,551	1,474	1,295
GUIDOBONO, Bartolomeo (1657-1709) Italian				
oil	1	106,800	106,800	106,800
wc/d	1	4,519	4,519	4,519
GUIETTE, René (1893-1976) Belgian				
oil	2	970-1,558	1,264	970
wc/d	8	953-8,938	2,312	1,335
GUIGI (20th C) French				
wc/d	1	1,824	1,824	1,824
GUIGNARD, Alexandre Gaston (1848-1922) French				
oil	1	19,007	19,007	19,007
GUIGON, Charles-Louis (1807-1882) Swiss				
oil	3	734-2,281	1,383	1,135
GUIGONI, Eugenio (1864-1934) Italian				
oil	1	13,320	13,320	13,320
GUIGOU, Paul (1834-1871) French				
oil	7	19,007-133,966	78,977	78,871
GUIJARRO, Antonio (1923-) Spanish				
oil	3	878-2,290	1,563	1,523
GUILBERT (?) French				
oil	1	6,541	6,541	6,541
GUILBERT, Ernest Charles Demosthene (1848-?) French				
3D	1	4,685	4,685	4,685
GUILLABERT, Alex (?) ?				
3D	1	1,885	1,885	1,885
GUILLAIN, Marthe (1890-1974) Belgian				
oil	3	878-1,794	1,203	937
wc/d	1	471	471	471

Name	No.	Price Range	Average	Median
GUILLAUBEY, Christiane (1946-) French				
3D	1	3,748	3,748	3,748
GUILLAUME, Albert (1873-1942) French				
oil	1	8,948	8,948	8,948
GUILLAUME, Paul (20th C) French				
oil	1	17,644	17,644	17,644
GUILLAUMET, Gustave (1840-1887) French				
oil	7	989-25,890	9,730	4,253
wc/d	1	1,222	1,222	1,222
GUILLAUMIN, Armand (1841-1927) French				
oil	45	4,200-160,000	48,228	36,750
wc/d	7	2,506-25,442	9,040	6,659
GUILLE, Captain J D (20th C) British				
oil	1	2,290	2,290	2,290
GUILLEMET, C (19th C) French?				
oil	1	2,250	2,250	2,250
GUILLEMET, Jean Baptiste Antoine (1843-1918) French				
oil	10	2,000-15,640	5,197	3,840
GUILLEMIN, Alexandre Marie (1817-1880) French				
oil	3	1,818-10,507	5,667	4,676
GUILLEMIN, Émile Coriolan Hippolyte (1841-1907) French				
3D	1	54,000	54,000	54,000
GUILLEMINET, Antoine (19th C) French				
oil	1	3,400	3,400	3,400
GUILLEMINET, Claude (1821-1860) French				
oil	4	1,291-2,546	1,910	1,312
GUILLERMO, Juan (1916-1968) Spanish				
oil	1	4,816	4,816	4,816
GUILLERY, Etienne (20th C) Belgian				
oil	1	2,704	2,704	2,704
GUILLERY, Franz (1863-1933) German				
oil	1	3,162	3,162	3,162
GUILLON, Adolphe-Irenee (1829-1896) French				
oil	1	3,156	3,156	3,156
GUILLON, Eugène Antoine (1834-1869) French				
oil	1	12,000	12,000	12,000
GUILLONNET, Octave Denis Victor (1872-1967) French				
oil	4	2,141-3,416	2,824	2,392
wc/d	1	467	467	467
GUILLOU, Alfred (1844-1926) French				
oil	5	561-26,885	9,711	5,238
GUILLOUX, Albert Gaston (1871-1952) French				
3D	1	9,555	9,555	9,555
GUILLOUX, Charles Victor (1866-1946) French				
oil	5	968-6,997	2,590	1,543
wc/d	2	526-964	745	526
GUILLOUZO, Thierry (20th C) French				
oil	1	2,919	2,919	2,919
GUIMARAES, Jose de (1939-) Portuguese				
oil	1	2,719	2,719	2,719
wc/d	7	2,863-10,485	7,600	8,132
3D	2	16,857-18,663	17,760	16,857
GUIMARD, Louise de (1827-?) French				
oil	1	2,000	2,000	2,000
GUIMARES, Jose de (19/20th C) ?				
wc/d	1	7,068	7,068	7,068
GUINART-CANDELICH, Francisco (1888-?) Spanish				
oil	2	1,495-1,529	1,512	1,495
GUINEGAULT, Georges P (1893-?) French				
oil	2	1,214-3,092	2,153	1,214
wc/d	1	1,210	1,210	1,210
GUINGAND, Pierre de (19/20th C) French				
wc/d	1	2,408	2,408	2,408
GUINIER, Henri Jules (1867-1927) French				
oil	1	2,130	2,130	2,130
GUINNESS, Lindy (1941-) British				
oil	1	1,110	1,110	1,110
GUINNESS, May (1863-1955) British				
oil	2	5,143-8,406	6,774	5,143
GUINO, Michel (20th C) ?				
3D	3	2,035-3,036	2,447	2,272

Name	No.	Price Range	Average	Median
GUINO, Richard (1890-1973) French				
wc/d	1	1,019	1,019	1,019
3D	2	2,000-4,204	3,102	2,000
GUINO, Richard and RENOIR, Pierre Auguste (20th C) French				
3D	5	5,000-34,486	24,514	28,160
GUINOVART, Jose (1927-) Spanish				
oil	2	932-4,757	2,844	932
wc/d	3	773-6,654	4,001	4,576
GUINTHER, Eleonore (?) Dutch				
oil	1	1,000	1,000	1,000
GUINZO, Miguel (20th C) Venezuelan?				
3D	1	1,680	1,680	1,680
GUIRAMAND, Paul (1926-) French				
oil	5	1,400-2,385	1,783	1,632
wc/d	1	1,074	1,074	1,074
GUIRAND DE SCEVOLA, Lucien (1871-1950) French				
oil	5	1,168-9,570	3,354	2,166
wc/d	10	668-13,050	4,498	1,168
GUIRAUD, L Raoul (1888-?) French				
oil	1	97,200	97,200	97,200
GUIRAUD-RIVIERE, Maurice (1881-?) French				
3D	2	15,429-16,470	15,949	15,429
GUISE, Pieter Jan (1814-1859) Dutch				
oil	1	1,827	1,827	1,827
GUITERAS DE SOTO, Jose (1885-1950) Spanish				
oil	1	3,131	3,131	3,131
GUITET, James (1925-) French				
oil	3	1,335-6,037	3,039	1,746
wc/d	2	588-5,130	2,859	588
GUITRY, Sacha (1885-1957) ?				
wc/d	2	617-2,919	1,768	617
GUIZEL, F (19th C) ?				
oil	1	2,108	2,108	2,108
GUIZOT, A (?) ?				
oil	1	7,500	7,500	7,500
GUJRAL, Satish (1929-) Indian				
oil	4	18,000-42,500	33,750	37,000
wc/d	1	4,000	4,000	4,000
3D	2	6,100-7,800	6,950	6,100
GULBRANSSON, Olaf (1873-1958) Norwegian				
oil	1	1,293	1,293	1,293
wc/d	2	494-1,940	1,217	494
GULICK, Henry Thomas (1872-1964) American				
oil	5	750-6,500	2,870	2,500
GULIK, Franciscus Lodewijk van (1841-1899) Dutch				
oil	1	3,857	3,857	3,857
GULLY, John (1819-1888) New Zealander				
wc/d	1	10,416	10,416	10,416
GULUCHE, Joseph le (1849-?) French				
3D	1	1,933	1,933	1,933
GUMMELT, Sam (1944-) American				
wc/d	1	1,000	1,000	1,000
GUNARSA, Nyoman (1944-) Indonesian				
oil	2	963-4,576	2,769	963
GUNDELACH, Matthaeus (1566-1653) German				
oil	1	32,698	32,698	32,698
GUNN, Herbert James (1893-1964) British				
oil	4	3,460-88,500	39,475	28,320
wc/d	1	8,544	8,544	8,544
GUNSAM, Karl Joseph (1900-1972) Austrian				
wc/d	1	2,398	2,398	2,398
GUNSTON, Audley (fl.1903-1935) British				
wc/d	1	1,496	1,496	1,496
GUNTHER, Erwin (1864-1927) German				
oil	10	746-3,250	1,375	970
GUNTHER, Herta (1934-) German				
wc/d	2	1,607-2,153	1,880	1,607
GUNTHER, Kurt (1893-1955) German				
oil	1	4,944	4,944	4,944
GUNTHER, Theodor (19/20th C) German				
oil	1	1,134	1,134	1,134

Name	No.	Price Range	Average	Median
GUNTNER, Anna (1932-) Polish				
oil	1	3,171	3,171	3,171
GUNZ, Engelbert (1908-) Swiss				
oil	1	1,674	1,674	1,674
GUO JIN (1964-) Chinese				
oil	3	13,000-22,594	16,198	13,000
GUO WEI (1960-) Chinese				
oil	4	16,365-31,450	22,089	18,542
GUPTA, Subodh (1964-) Indian				
oil	3	5,000-42,500	20,166	13,000
GUREVICH, Joseph Michiallovich (20th C) Russian				
oil	1	17,000	17,000	17,000
GUREVICH, Mikhail (1904-1943) Russian				
oil	1	5,500	5,500	5,500
GURLITT, Louis (1812-1897) German				
oil	5	2,238-30,102	10,713	8,758
GURSCHNER, Herbert (1901-1975) Austrian				
oil	2	7,612-72,000	39,806	7,612
GURTNER, L (20th C) ?				
oil	1	2,200	2,200	2,200
GURVICH, Iosif (1907-1992) Russian				
oil	3	4,844-7,135	5,988	5,985
GURVICH, Jose (1927-1974) Lithuanian				
oil	3	1,350-12,000	8,116	11,000
wc/d	2	1,255-17,500	9,377	1,255
GUSSONI, Vittorio (1893-1968) Italian				
oil	12	510-7,613	2,395	1,529
GUSSOW, Bernard (1881-1957) American				
oil	1	2,500	2,500	2,500
wc/d	1	500	500	500
GUSTAVSSON, Mats (1951-) Swedish				
wc/d	1	1,400	1,400	1,400
GUSTIN, Paul M (1886-?) American				
oil	1	1,500	1,500	1,500
GUSTON, Philip (1913-1980) American				
oil	10	22,000-4,900,000	943,700	300,000
wc/d	6	12,000-200,000	95,666	42,000
GUTENSOHN, Johann Gottfried (1792-1851) German				
wc/d	1	4,253	4,253	4,253
GUTERSLOH, Albert Paris (1887-1973) Austrian				
wc/d	2	844-1,885	1,364	844
GUTFREUND, Otto (1889-1927) Czechoslovakian				
wc/d	4	1,165-5,959	4,015	4,171
3D	4	4,712-20,027	8,936	5,400
GUTH, Jean Baptiste (fl.1883-1921) French				
wc/d	3	1,408-2,640	2,229	2,640
GUTHRIE, James (1859-1930) British				
oil	1	1,424	1,424	1,424
GUTIERREZ DE LA VEGA, Jose (?-1865) Spanish				
oil	1	11,452	11,452	11,452
GUTIERREZ MONTIEL, Juan (1934-) Spanish				
oil	1	1,427	1,427	1,427
GUTIERREZ, Juan Simon (c.1644-1718) Spanish				
oil	1	13,840	13,840	13,840
GUTMAN, Nachum (1898-1978) Israeli				
oil	10	643-90,000	30,240	18,000
wc/d	15	467-11,000	4,839	3,800
GUTMANN, Adam (fl.1612-1637) Austrian				
wc/d	1	11,100	11,100	11,100
GUTMANN, Bernhard (1869-1936) American				
oil	4	850-6,500	2,887	1,700
GUTTER, Piet (1944-) Dutch				
oil	1	2,073	2,073	2,073
GUTTERO, Alfredo (1882-1932) Argentinian				
oil	6	7,000-75,000	30,666	12,000
GUTTUSO, Renato (1912-1987) Italian				
oil	30	3,884-203,537	53,747	39,822
wc/d	59	1,193-21,425	5,472	4,023
GUY, Alexander (1962-) British				
oil	1	1,780	1,780	1,780
GUY, Francis (1760-1820) American				
oil	1	900,000	900,000	900,000

Name	No.	Price Range	Average	Median
GUY, Jean Baptiste Louis (1824-1888) Italian				
oil	1	1,527	1,527	1,527
wc/d	1	1,730	1,730	1,730
GUY, Seymour (1824-1910) American				
oil	3	1,200-55,000	22,733	12,000
GUYOMARD, Gerard (1936-) French				
oil	5	2,102-5,438	3,582	3,579
wc/d	2	2,225-4,442	3,333	2,225
GUYON, Maximilienne (1868-1903) French				
wc/d	2	900-2,102	1,501	900
GUYOT, Georges Lucien (1885-1973) French				
oil	3	527-12,945	4,749	777
wc/d	6	1,157-17,518	5,235	3,236
3D	6	2,200-19,357	12,006	11,781
GUYS, Constantin (1802-1892) French				
wc/d	21	450-7,516	1,619	1,208
GUZHAVIN, Mikhail Markelovich (1888-1931) Russian				
wc/d	1	29,760	29,760	29,760
GUZMAN, Federico (1964-) Spanish				
oil	1	8,650	8,650	8,650
GUZMAN, Juan Bautista de (19th C) Spanish				
oil	3	2,225-3,717	2,761	2,342
GUZZI, Beppe (1902-1982) Italian				
oil	6	630-2,589	1,126	756
GUZZI, Virgilio (1902-1978) Italian				
oil	2	1,514-1,933	1,723	1,514
GUZZONE, Sebastiano (1856-1890) Italian				
oil	1	4,077	4,077	4,077
GWYNNE-JONES, Allan (1892-1982) British				
oil	2	1,589-10,846	6,217	1,589
GYANINY, Geo (20th C) ?				
oil	2	1,070-1,109	1,089	1,070
GYBORSON, Indiana (20th C) American				
oil	2	1,600-1,800	1,700	1,600
GYLLENHAMMAR, Charlotte (1963-) Swedish?				
wc/d	1	2,141	2,141	2,141
GYNGELL, Albert (fl.1873-1892) British				
oil	3	475-1,564	1,146	1,400
GYOKUDO, Uragami (1745-1820) Japanese				
wc/d	1	40,000	40,000	40,000
GYSBRECHTS, Franciscus (17th C) Dutch				
oil	1	8,802	8,802	8,802
GYSELINCKX, Joseph (1845-?) Belgian				
oil	1	1,100	1,100	1,100
GYSELS, Philips (fl.1650) Dutch				
oil	1	28,027	28,027	28,027
GYSELS, Pieter (1621-1690) Flemish				
oil	3	21,360-138,750	60,870	22,500
GYSELS, Pieter and IMMENRAET, Philips Augustyn (17th C) Flemish				
oil	1	8,767	8,767	8,767
GYSIN, Brion (1916-1986) French				
oil	4	1,200-1,647	1,472	1,394
wc/d	16	634-2,408	1,180	887
GYSIS, Nicolas (1842-1901) Greek				
oil	8	5,984-280,500	77,285	44,000
wc/d	3	10,285-21,505	14,025	10,285
HA SANG-LIM (1961-) Korean				
wc/d	1	7,000	7,000	7,000
HAAG, Carl (1820-1915) German				
wc/d	6	1,249-34,200	12,308	7,259
HAAG, Jean Paul (19th C) French				
oil	1	1,350	1,350	1,350
HAAG, Johann (19th C) Austrian				
oil	1	9,271	9,271	9,271
HAAG, Tethart Philip Christiaan (1737-1812) German				
wc/d	1	1,401	1,401	1,401
HAAGEN, Joris van der (c.1615-1669) Dutch				
oil	1	7,030	7,030	7,030
wc/d	2	2,595-5,536	4,065	2,595
HAALAND, Lars Laurits (1855-1938) Norwegian				
oil	1	1,747	1,747	1,747

Name	No.	Price Range	Average	Median
HAAN, Franciscus Antonius de (1823-1873) Dutch				
oil	1	1,023	1,023	1,023
HAAN, Jurjen de (1936-) Dutch				
oil	3	1,001-1,708	1,452	1,649
HAAN, Willem Jacob de (1913-1967) Dutch				
oil	1	6,370	6,370	6,370
HAANEN, Adriana (1814-1895) Dutch				
oil	5	7,135-67,986	25,051	15,582
HAANEN, Casparis (1778-1849) Dutch				
oil	1	2,313	2,313	2,313
HAANEN, Cecil van (1844-1914) Dutch				
oil	1	13,155	13,155	13,155
HAANEN, Elisabeth Alida (1809-1845) Dutch				
oil	1	10,507	10,507	10,507
HAANEN, Georg Gillis van (1807-1876) Dutch				
oil	3	2,386-4,555	3,772	4,375
HAANEN, Remi van (1812-1894) Dutch				
oil	8	1,868-30,308	9,801	4,932
HAAPANEN, John Nichols (1891-?) American				
oil	3	1,000-1,500	1,200	1,100
HAARDT, Georges van (1907-) Polish				
oil	4	477-1,013	655	536
wc/d	3	477-834	675	715
HAAREN, Dirk Johannes van (1878-1953) Dutch				
oil	1	1,205	1,205	1,205
wc/d	1	542	542	542
HAARTMAN, Axel (1877-1969) Finnish				
oil	5	2,057-6,195	3,560	2,443
HAAS, Aad de (1920-1972) Dutch				
oil	1	12,740	12,740	12,740
HAAS, Gaston (1852-1899) German				
oil	1	3,150	3,150	3,150
HAAS, Gordon (20th C) American				
oil	1	3,000	3,000	3,000
HAAS, Hermann (1878-?) German				
oil	1	3,024	3,024	3,024
HAAS, Johannes Hubertus Leonardus de (1832-1908) Flemish				
oil	7	1,023-8,786	5,670	6,668
HAAS, Louis (19/20th C) German?				
oil	1	1,453	1,453	1,453
HAAS, Mauritz F H de (1832-1895) Dutch				
oil	12	3,250-44,500	13,573	9,000
wc/d	1	1,700	1,700	1,700
HAAS, William F de (1830-1880) Dutch				
oil	1	45,000	45,000	45,000
HAASE, Hermann Georg (1864-1912) German				
3D	1	4,001	4,001	4,001
HAASE, Ove (1894-1989) Danish				
oil	1	1,493	1,493	1,493
HAAXMAN, Pieter Alardus (1814-1887) Dutch				
oil	1	7,747	7,747	7,747
HABERLE, John (1856-1933) American				
oil	1	300,000	300,000	300,000
HABERMANN, Hugo von (1849-1929) German				
oil	1	1,332	1,332	1,332
wc/d	1	973	973	973
HABERT, Eugène (?-1916) French				
oil	1	1,686	1,686	1,686
HABERT-DYS, Jules Auguste (1850-1924) French				
wc/d	2	876-2,569	1,722	876
HABLIK, Wenzel (1881-1934) German				
oil	1	3,266	3,266	3,266
HACKAERT, Jan (1629-1699) Dutch				
wc/d	1	18,165	18,165	18,165
HACKE, Rudolf (1881-?) German				
oil	1	2,474	2,474	2,474
HACKENSOLLNER, Camillo (19th C) Austrian				
oil	1	1,566	1,566	1,566
HACKER, Arthur (1858-1919) British				
oil	2	1,638-5,000	3,319	1,638
wc/d	1	1,575	1,575	1,575

Name	No.	Price Range	Average	Median
HACKER, Dieter (1942-) German				
oil	1	1,274	1,274	1,274
HACKERT, Jacob Philippe (1737-1807) German				
oil	6	24,000-758,500	255,669	47,320
wc/d	7	2,590-17,517	9,135	7,176
HACKETT, Mary (1906-1989) American				
oil	1	3,750	3,750	3,750
HACKL, Gabriel von (1843-1926) German				
oil	1	6,553	6,553	6,553
wc/d	1	707	707	707
HADDEN, Nellie (fl.1885-1920) British				
wc/d	1	1,584	1,584	1,584
HADDON, R (19th C) British				
oil	1	1,575	1,575	1,575
HADDON, Trevor (1864-1941) British				
oil	11	554-5,220	2,248	2,400
wc/d	2	463-823	643	463
HADER, Elmer Stanley (1889-1973) American				
oil	1	800	800	800
wc/d	1	500	500	500
HADJI-MINACHE, Genia (20th C) ?				
wc/d	1	11,160	11,160	11,160
HADJIMICHAIL, Theofilos (1871-1933) Greek				
oil	1	99,110	99,110	99,110
HADJIMICHALI, Angeliki (1895-1965) Greek				
oil	1	1,122	1,122	1,122
HADZI, Dimitri (1921-) American				
3D	3	2,000-4,000	3,333	4,000
HAECKEL, Ernst (1834-1919) German				
wc/d	4	1,204-1,445	1,294	1,204
HAEFLIGER, Leopold (1929-1989) Swiss				
oil	11	510-10,824	3,755	2,892
wc/d	6	624-1,176	806	666
HAEN, Abraham de II (1707-1748) Dutch				
wc/d	1	1,109	1,109	1,109
HAEN, Antony de (1640-?) Dutch				
oil	1	36,122	36,122	36,122
HAEN, David de (1602-1659) Dutch				
oil	1	48,440	48,440	48,440
HAEN, J de (?) Belgian				
oil	1	2,250	2,250	2,250
HAENEN, Frederic de (1853-1928) French				
wc/d	2	1,285-2,102	1,693	1,285
HAERDE, Joseph van (19th C) Flemish				
oil	1	1,890	1,890	1,890
HAERNING, August (1874-1961) Danish				
oil	2	1,216-3,162	2,189	1,216
HAES, Carlos de (1829-1898) Spanish				
oil	10	6,622-38,531	18,238	13,245
wc/d	1	2,022	2,022	2,022
HAESE, Gunter (1924-) German				
3D	2	10,829-15,925	13,377	10,829
HAESEKER, Alexandra (20th C) Canadian				
oil	1	2,144	2,144	2,144
wc/d	1	412	412	412
HAEVEN (?) ?				
oil	1	3,596	3,596	3,596
HAFELFINGER, Eugen (1898-1979) Swiss				
wc/d	1	1,795	1,795	1,795
HAFFNER, P (20th C) ?				
oil	1	1,823	1,823	1,823
HAFIF, Marcia (1929-) American				
oil	2	4,000-6,500	5,250	4,000
HAFNER, Carl (1814-1873) German				
oil	1	1,824	1,824	1,824
HAFNER, Thomas (16th C) Swiss				
oil	1	1,531	1,531	1,531
HAFSTROM, Jan (1937-) Swedish				
oil	9	763-22,465	5,612	3,964
wc/d	9	422-5,089	2,040	1,057
HAGAN, Carol (?) American				
oil	1	15,000	15,000	15,000

Name	No.	Price Range	Average	Median
HAGARTY, Clara (1871-1958) Canadian				
oil	2	2,624-2,645	2,634	2,624
HAGAY, Sara (1939-) Israeli				
oil	1	1,500	1,500	1,500
HAGBORG, August (1852-1925) Swedish				
oil	10	1,116-14,957	5,251	4,258
HAGEDORN, Friedrich (1814-1889) German				
wc/d	1	16,200	16,200	16,200
HAGEDORN, Karl (1889-1969) British				
oil	2	1,000-1,464	1,232	1,000
wc/d	1	783	783	783
HAGEL, Frank (1933-) American				
oil	1	12,000	12,000	12,000
HAGEMAN, Victor (1868-1938) Belgian				
oil	2	1,214-2,166	1,690	1,214
HAGEMANS, Maurice (1852-1917) Belgian				
oil	3	468-567	513	504
wc/d	11	485-2,649	1,455	1,286
HAGEMEISTER, Karl (1848-1933) German				
oil	4	8,081-18,260	12,165	10,541
wc/d	6	996-6,361	2,827	1,679
HAGEN, Jakobus van der (1657-1715) Dutch				
oil	1	3,700	3,700	3,700
HAGEN, Soren (?) ?				
oil	4	487-1,786	1,305	1,410
HAGEN, Theodor (1842-1919) German				
oil	7	667-3,637	1,738	1,703
HAGENAUER (20th C) Austrian				
3D	1	18,000	18,000	18,000
HAGENAUER, Franz (1906-1986) Austrian				
3D	13	2,293-27,000	8,399	6,479
HAGENAUER, Karl (1898-1956) Austrian				
3D	5	2,827-6,442	5,097	5,733
HAGER, Albert (1857-1940) Belgian				
oil	1	2,074	2,074	2,074
HAGERBAUMER, David (1921-) American				
wc/d	5	1,220-5,000	3,164	3,500
HAGERUP, Nels (1864-1922) American				
oil	18	700-4,500	1,975	1,700
HAGG, Herman (1884-1966) Swedish				
oil	1	2,747	2,747	2,747
HAGG, Jacob (1839-1931) Swedish				
wc/d	1	4,986	4,986	4,986
HAGHE, Louis (1806-1885) Belgian				
wc/d	4	700-3,168	1,494	979
HAGN, Richard von (1850-c.1890) German				
wc/d	1	1,034	1,034	1,034
HAGUE, E (?) British?				
oil	1	2,832	2,832	2,832
HAGUE, J Houghton (1842-?) British				
oil	3	1,325-3,496	2,216	1,827
wc/d	1	607	607	607
HAGUE, Louis (19th C) ?				
wc/d	1	8,182	8,182	8,182
HAHN, David (?) American				
oil	6	650-4,000	1,333	750
HAHN, Friedemann (1949-) German				
oil	1	486	486	486
wc/d	1	1,052	1,052	1,052
HAHN, Gustav Adolphe (1811-1872) German				
oil	1	4,500	4,500	4,500
HAHN, Karl Wilhelm (1829-1887) German				
oil	3	2,200-110,000	38,483	3,250
HAHN, William (1840-1890) American?				
oil	3	52,500-190,000	114,166	100,000
HAHNISCH, Anton (1817-1897) Austrian				
wc/d	1	1,113	1,113	1,113
HAHS, Erwin (1887-1970) German				
oil	1	2,827	2,827	2,827
HAIDA, Abderrahmane (1968-) Moroccan				
oil	2	507-1,495	1,001	507

Name	No.	Price Range	Average	Median
HAIER, Joseph (1816-1891) Austrian				
oil	3	900-4,000	2,489	2,569
HAIG, Earl (20th C) British				
oil	4	883-1,870	1,268	940
HAIGH, Alfred Grenfell (1870-1963) British				
oil	3	865-3,000	1,729	1,323
HAIGH, Peter (1914-1994) British				
oil	4	797-2,595	1,576	1,400
HAINES, Frederick Stanley (1879-1960) Canadian				
oil	15	648-4,408	2,220	2,109
HAINES, Richard (1906-1984) American				
oil	1	1,500	1,500	1,500
HAINES, William Henry (1812-1884) British				
oil	1	1,144	1,144	1,144
wc/d	1	496	496	496
HAINS, Raymond (1926-) French				
wc/d	12	1,312-88,500	29,822	16,938
3D	7	11,712-129,945	35,795	24,196
HAINZ, Georg (17th C) German				
oil	1	10,380	10,380	10,380
HAIR, Alfred (1941-1970) American				
oil	1	1,500	1,500	1,500
HAIVAOJA, Heikki (1929-) Finnish				
3D	1	5,034	5,034	5,034
HAJDU, Étienne (1907-1996) French				
wc/d	2	1,641-4,817	3,229	1,641
3D	8	3,732-33,658	9,752	4,817
HAJEK, Otto Herbert (1927-) Czechoslovakian				
oil	1	3,214	3,214	3,214
wc/d	2	1,036-1,272	1,154	1,036
3D	5	1,874-38,219	12,842	3,770
HAJERI, Ahmed (1948-) Tunisian				
oil	1	9,709	9,709	9,709
HAKA, Janusz (1951-) ?				
oil	4	882-2,148	1,297	951
HAKE, Otto Eugene (1876-?) American				
oil	3	800-1,300	1,033	1,000
HAKES, J A (fl.1870-1880) British				
oil	1	1,697	1,697	1,697
HAKKAART, Fer (1941-) Dutch				
oil	1	1,654	1,654	1,654
HAKSE, Jerre (1937-) Dutch				
oil	1	877	877	877
wc/d	1	760	760	760
HAKUIN, Ekaku (1685-1768) Japanese				
wc/d	4	14,000-100,000	40,250	17,000
HALAUSKA, Ludwig (1827-1882) German				
oil	3	492-4,234	2,424	2,548
wc/d	1	726	726	726
HALBACH, David Allen (1931-) American				
wc/d	9	1,500-6,500	2,972	2,500
HALBERG-KRAUSS, Fritz (1874-1951) German				
oil	27	602-8,182	2,055	1,752
HALDAR, Asit Kumar (1890-1964) Indian				
oil	1	8,686	8,686	8,686
HALE, John Howard (1863-1955) British				
oil	1	1,044	1,044	1,044
HALE, Kathleen (1898-) British				
oil	2	5,310-9,735	7,522	5,310
HALE, Lilian Westcott (1881-1963) American				
oil	1	64,000	64,000	64,000
HALE, Philip L (1865-1931) American				
oil	3	12,000-20,000	15,000	13,000
wc/d	1	22,500	22,500	22,500
HALE, Scott (?) American				
oil	1	2,000	2,000	2,000
HALE-SANDERS, T (19/20th C) British				
wc/d	1	1,602	1,602	1,602
HALEY, John C (1905-1991) American				
oil	1	400	400	400
wc/d	1	4,500	4,500	4,500

Name	No.	Price Range	Average	Median
HALICKA, Alice (1895-1975) Polish				
oil	2	4,922-24,220	14,571	4,922
wc/d	1	1,793	1,793	1,793
HALIL-BEY (1859-c.1940) Turkish				
oil	2	7,068-8,370	7,719	7,068
HALKETT, François (1856-1921) Belgian				
oil	1	4,917	4,917	4,917
HALKO, Joe (1940-) American				
3D	1	4,000	4,000	4,000
HALL, Carlos (1928-1997) American				
oil	1	1,000	1,000	1,000
HALL, Clifford (1904-1973) British				
oil	5	478-2,760	1,355	761
HALL, Doug (20th C) American				
oil	4	3,000-8,000	5,050	4,200
HALL, Frederick (1860-1948) British				
oil	9	851-45,240	7,838	2,174
HALL, George Henry (1825-1913) American				
oil	6	2,500-13,000	7,666	7,500
HALL, George Lothian (1825-1888) British				
wc/d	2	1,110-2,275	1,692	1,110
HALL, Harald R (1866-1902) British				
oil	2	890-3,186	2,038	890
HALL, Harry (1814-1882) British				
oil	3	3,894-80,000	31,136	9,516
HALL, Henry R (19th C) British				
oil	6	1,200-4,725	2,351	1,710
HALL, John Scott (20th C) Canadian?				
oil	1	1,640	1,640	1,640
HALL, Kenneth (1913-1946) British				
oil	2	7,812-7,920	7,866	7,812
HALL, Nigel (1943-) British/Australian				
oil	1	850	850	850
wc/d	3	501-1,850	1,400	1,850
HALL, Patrick (1935-) Irish				
oil	1	2,616	2,616	2,616
wc/d	1	644	644	644
HALL, Richard (20th C) American				
oil	1	3,250	3,250	3,250
HALL, Thomas P (fl.1837-1867) British				
oil	5	650-22,230	6,661	2,500
HALLAM, Joseph Sydney (1898-1953) Canadian				
oil	2	1,155-11,545	6,350	1,155
HALLATZ, Emil (1837-1888) German				
oil	2	1,868-6,654	4,261	1,868
HALLBERG, Carl Peter (1809-1879) Swedish				
oil	1	1,171	1,171	1,171
HALLE, Albert (1844-1896) German				
oil	2	1,057-1,776	1,416	1,057
HALLE, Charles Edward (1846-1914) British				
oil	2	445-45,360	22,902	445
HALLER, Michael (19th C) Austrian				
oil	1	1,090	1,090	1,090
HALLER, Tony (1907-1944) Austrian				
oil	1	1,204	1,204	1,204
HALLET, Andre (1890-1959) Belgian				
oil	20	486-4,425	2,022	1,951
HALLETT, Dorothy S (fl.1913-30) British				
wc/d	1	1,100	1,100	1,100
HALLEY, Peter (1953-) American				
oil	13	2,928-85,000	53,618	60,000
wc/d	1	2,928	2,928	2,928
HALLFORS-SIPILA, Greta (20th C) Finnish				
wc/d	1	4,208	4,208	4,208
HALLOWELL, George Hawley (1871-1926) American				
wc/d	3	450-8,199	3,199	950
HALLSTROM, Christian (19th C) Swedish				
oil	1	1,100	1,100	1,100
HALLSTROM, Eric (1893-1946) Swedish				
oil	12	930-30,393	5,782	2,799
wc/d	5	397-8,281	2,743	1,454

Name	No.	Price Range	Average	Median
HALLSTROM, Staffan (1914-1976) Swedish				
oil	6	744-14,536	5,684	3,668
wc/d	6	403-6,607	2,039	636
HALMI, Arthur (1866-1939) Hungarian				
oil	1	8,832	8,832	8,832
HALOI, Ganesh (1936-) Indian				
wc/d	4	12,155-50,000	25,538	14,000
HALONEN, Arttu (1885-1965) Finnish				
3D	1	1,757	1,757	1,757
HALONEN, Emil (1875-1950) Finnish				
3D	3	1,753-21,857	8,704	2,503
HALONEN, Pekka (1865-1933) Finnish				
oil	16	1,618-39,743	18,953	12,884
HALOZAN, Bertha A (20th C) American				
oil	1	1,200	1,200	1,200
HALPERT, Samuel (1884-1930) American				
oil	2	2,600-19,000	10,800	2,600
HALPIN, M N (20th C) American				
oil	1	2,200	2,200	2,200
HALS, Dirck (1591-1656) Dutch				
oil	3	45,863-173,000	110,437	112,450
HALS, F (16/17th C) Dutch				
oil	1	5,758	5,758	5,758
HALS, Harmen (1611-1669) Dutch				
oil	1	3,287	3,287	3,287
HALSEY, J B (19th C) American				
oil	1	1,500	1,500	1,500
HALSWELLE, Keeley (1832-1891) British				
oil	6	748-51,900	10,941	1,770
HALSZEL, Johann Baptist (1710-1777) German				
oil	2	7,259-15,652	11,455	7,259
HALTER, Jean H (1916-1981) American				
oil	2	1,300-3,500	2,400	1,300
HAM JIN (1978-) Korean				
3D	1	17,000	17,000	17,000
HAMALAINEN, Vaino (1876-1940) Finnish				
oil	12	776-43,714	6,755	2,629
wc/d	1	5,143	5,143	5,143
HAMBACH, Johann Michael (17th C) German				
oil	1	25,714	25,714	25,714
HAMBLETON, Richard (1954-) American				
oil	4	500-2,000	1,212	650
HAMBLING, Maggi (1945-) British				
oil	3	1,328-6,960	3,866	3,312
wc/d	1	3,186	3,186	3,186
HAMBOURG, Andre (1909-1999) French				
oil	41	1,072-39,555	10,528	8,325
wc/d	15	613-1,800	1,201	1,079
HAMBUCHEN, Georg (1901-1971) German				
oil	2	957-1,573	1,265	957
HAMBUCHEN, Wilhelm (1869-1939) German				
oil	16	726-9,122	2,740	1,581
HAMDY-BEY, Osman (1842-1910) Turkish				
wc/d	1	1,200	1,200	1,200
HAMEL, Otto (1866-1950) German				
oil	10	484-3,063	1,302	954
HAMILL, Francis (?) British?				
oil	1	1,332	1,332	1,332
HAMILTON, Augustus Terrick (19th C) Canadian?				
wc/d	2	3,988-6,647	5,317	3,988
HAMILTON, Carl Wilhelm de (1668-1754) Austrian				
oil	1	8,357	8,357	8,357
HAMILTON, Elaine (1920-) American				
oil	1	1,929	1,929	1,929
HAMILTON, Eva H (1876-1960) British				
oil	2	2,061-6,054	4,057	2,061
HAMILTON, Gavin (1723-1798) British				
oil	2	8,000-442,500	225,250	8,000
HAMILTON, Hamilton (1847-1928) American/British				
oil	2	6,000-15,000	10,500	6,000
wc/d	1	2,200	2,200	2,200

Name	No.	Price Range	Average	Median
HAMILTON, Hugh Douglas (1739-1808) British				
wc/d	12	1,298-29,061	12,368	9,929
HAMILTON, James (1819-1878) American				
oil	7	1,000-18,000	6,407	5,500
HAMILTON, James (1853-1894) British				
oil	2	1,190-17,000	9,095	1,190
HAMILTON, James Whitelaw (1860-1932) British				
oil	7	1,203-4,498	2,630	2,670
HAMILTON, Johann Georg de (1672-1737) Flemish				
oil	1	10,137	10,137	10,137
HAMILTON, Ken (20th C) Irish				
oil	3	2,595-6,055	4,452	4,707
wc/d	1	678	678	678
HAMILTON, Letitia (1878-1964) British				
oil	20	4,676-39,556	16,176	14,027
wc/d	1	6,115	6,115	6,115
HAMILTON, Philipp Ferdinand de (1664-1750) Flemish				
oil	5	9,250-62,900	35,385	29,600
HAMILTON, Richard (1922-) British				
wc/d	1	774,400	774,400	774,400
3D	1	65,740	65,740	65,740
HAMILTON, Tom G (20th C) American				
oil	1	1,750	1,750	1,750
HAMILTON, William (1751-1801) British				
oil	1	80,000	80,000	80,000
wc/d	1	3,680	3,680	3,680
HAMILTON-RENWICK, Lionel (1919-) British				
oil	2	1,012-6,615	3,813	1,012
HAMMAN, Edouard-Michel-Ferdinand (1850-?) French				
oil	1	1,330	1,330	1,330
HAMMER, Hans Jorgen (1815-1882) Danish				
oil	1	8,088	8,088	8,088
HAMMER, Trygve (1878-1947) American/Norwegian				
oil	1	1,100	1,100	1,100
HAMMERSCHLAG, Alice Berger (1917-1969) Irish/Austrian				
oil	2	630-952	791	630
wc/d	1	1,298	1,298	1,298
HAMMERSHOI, Svend (1873-1948) Danish				
oil	6	711-1,793	1,332	1,303
HAMMERSHOI, Vilhelm (1864-1916) Danish				
oil	4	19,051-956,800	310,164	106,720
HAMMERSTIEL, Robert (1933-) ?				
oil	2	2,061-2,939	2,500	2,061
HAMMOND, Arthur Henry Knighton (1875-1970) British				
oil	2	554-870	712	554
wc/d	2	552-623	587	552
HAMMOND, Hermione Francis (1910-2005) British				
oil	11	1,029-5,236	2,388	1,683
wc/d	3	1,683-2,618	2,119	2,057
HAMMOND, John A (1843-1939) Canadian				
oil	11	1,209-17,725	6,509	4,055
HAMMOND, R J (fl.1882-1911) British				
oil	1	5,040	5,040	5,040
HAMMOND, Robert John (fl.1882-1911) British				
oil	4	1,131-2,220	1,498	1,244
HAMMOND, William Oxenden (fl.1860-1920) British				
wc/d	1	5,550	5,550	5,550
HAMMONS, David (1943-) American				
wc/d	1	60,000	60,000	60,000
HAMNETT, Nina (1890-1956) British				
oil	1	4,872	4,872	4,872
wc/d	2	1,488-2,610	2,049	1,488
HAMON, Jean Louis (1821-1874) French				
oil	1	1,200	1,200	1,200
HAMONET, Leon (1877-1953) French				
wc/d	3	2,003-2,718	2,319	2,238
HAMPE, E (19th C) ?				
oil	1	8,758	8,758	8,758
HAMPE, G (1839-1902) German				
oil	1	1,119	1,119	1,119
HAMPE, Guido (1839-1902) German				
oil	2	1,062-7,644	4,353	1,062

Name	No.	Price Range	Average	Median
HAMPSON, Roger (1925-1996) British				
oil	13	925-1,914	1,226	1,131
HAMPTON, John Wade (1918-2000) American				
oil	3	5,000-12,000	8,333	8,000
wc/d	1	1,500	1,500	1,500
3D	1	15,000	15,000	15,000
HAMRI, Mohamed (1932-2000) Moroccan				
oil	2	8,262-10,213	9,237	8,262
HAMZA, Hans (1879-1945) Austrian				
oil	2	2,447-2,486	2,466	2,447
HAMZA, Johann (1850-1927) German				
oil	7	7,658-21,205	14,638	16,000
HAN HSIANG-NING (1938-) Chinese				
oil	1	10,000	10,000	10,000
HAN, Hsiang Ning (1939-) American				
oil	1	4,173	4,173	4,173
HANAK, Anton (1875-1934) Austrian				
wc/d	2	757-1,262	1,009	757
HANCOCK, Charles (1795-1868) British				
oil	2	854-1,584	1,219	854
HANDLER, Richard (1932-) Austrian				
oil	1	1,543	1,543	1,543
HANDMANN, Emanuel (1718-1781) Swiss				
wc/d	1	2,331	2,331	2,331
HANGER, Max (1874-1955) German				
oil	21	455-1,767	1,055	975
HANICOTTE, Augustin (1870-1957) French				
wc/d	27	468-11,572	1,192	620
HANKINS, Abraham (1903-1963) American				
oil	4	650-2,500	1,262	900
HANLEY, Edgar (fl.1878-1883) British				
oil	1	3,850	3,850	3,850
HANLON, Father Jack (1913-1968) Irish				
oil	9	4,622-24,547	10,415	8,653
wc/d	13	1,740-4,800	2,890	2,422
HANMANN, Inger (20th C) Danish				
oil	1	1,288	1,288	1,288
HANNA-BARBERA STUDIO (20th C) American				
wc/d	1	1,000	1,000	1,000
HANNAOUI, Abdelmajid (1951-) Moroccan				
wc/d	1	9,174	9,174	9,174
HANNAUX, Emmanuel (1855-1934) French				
3D	2	3,781-5,878	4,829	3,781
HANNAUX, Paul (1899-1954) French				
oil	1	10,520	10,520	10,520
HANNEMAN, Adriaen (1601-1671) Dutch				
oil	1	133,500	133,500	133,500
HANNERT (20th C) American				
oil	1	2,400	2,400	2,400
HANNOCK, Stephen (20th C) American?				
oil	1	6,500	6,500	6,500
HANRATTY, Alice (1939-) Irish				
oil	1	2,503	2,503	2,503
HANS, Josefus Gerardus (1826-1891) Dutch				
oil	3	5,092-8,762	6,620	6,008
wc/d	1	607	607	607
HANS, Rolf (1938-1996) German				
oil	1	2,003	2,003	2,003
wc/d	1	1,296	1,296	1,296
HANSCH, Anton (1813-1876) Austrian				
oil	4	715-4,579	2,994	2,863
HANSCH, Johannes (1875-1945) German				
oil	1	1,452	1,452	1,452
HANSELAERE, Pieter van (1786-1862) Flemish				
oil	1	10,137	10,137	10,137
HANSEN, Al (1927-1995) American				
oil	1	5,733	5,733	5,733
wc/d	1	510	510	510
HANSEN, Armin Carl (1886-1957) American				
oil	2	42,500-45,000	43,750	42,500
HANSEN, Constantin (1804-1880) Danish				
oil	4	711-3,260	1,852	1,699

Name	No.	Price Range	Average	Median
HANSEN, Hans Jacob (1859-1942) Danish				
wc/d	3	1,914-5,340	4,188	5,310
HANSEN, Heinrich (1821-1890) Danish				
oil	5	953-15,660	6,524	4,872
HANSEN, Herman Wendelborg (1854-1924) American				
oil	1	7,000	7,000	7,000
wc/d	6	1,600-60,000	24,933	21,000
HANSEN, J T (1848-1912) Danish				
oil	2	1,618-1,941	1,779	1,618
HANSEN, James (1951-1977) American				
oil	1	1,100	1,100	1,100
HANSEN, James Lee (1925-) American				
3D	1	5,500	5,500	5,500
HANSEN, Job (1899-1960) Dutch				
oil	1	6,370	6,370	6,370
HANSEN, Jorgen Teik (1947-) Danish				
oil	1	1,697	1,697	1,697
HANSEN, Josef Theodor (1848-1912) Danish				
oil	1	6,650	6,650	6,650
HANSEN, Knut (1876-1926) Danish				
oil	1	1,757	1,757	1,757
HANSEN, Niels Christian (1834-1922) Danish				
oil	3	940-5,705	2,794	1,737
HANSEN, Osmund (1908-1995) Danish				
oil	1	1,374	1,374	1,374
HANSEN, Peter (1868-1928) Danish				
oil	4	1,742-4,426	2,743	2,371
wc/d	2	614-1,703	1,158	614
HANSEN, Sigvard (1859-1938) Danish				
oil	7	439-6,350	2,783	1,270
HANSEN-JACOBSEN, Niels (1861-1941) Danish				
3D	1	2,265	2,265	2,265
HANSEN-REISTRUP, Karl (1863-1929) Danish				
oil	3	747-1,161	912	830
wc/d	1	597	597	597
HANSON, Duane (1925-1996) American				
3D	2	180,000-190,000	185,000	180,000
HANSON, Rolf (1953-) Swedish				
oil	6	4,625-26,719	13,351	10,688
wc/d	2	636-1,209	922	636
HANSTEEN, Nils (1855-1912) Norwegian				
oil	3	1,192-8,959	4,519	3,406
HANTAI, Simon (1922-) French				
oil	14	8,281-572,770	133,037	80,347
wc/d	3	4,968-17,534	12,857	16,069
HANTMAN, Carl (1935-) American				
oil	2	1,700-12,000	6,850	1,700
wc/d	1	1,000	1,000	1,000
HANZ, Ivan (17th C) ?				
oil	1	4,214	4,214	4,214
HANZEN, Aleksei Vasilievich (1876-1937) Russian				
oil	6	1,720-40,920	17,023	13,950
HAPPEL, Carl (1819-1914) German				
oil	1	3,031	3,031	3,031
HAQUETTE, Georges Jean Marie (1854-1906) French				
oil	4	496-3,250	2,249	2,500
HARA, Katsuro (1889-1966) Japanese				
oil	1	3,822	3,822	3,822
HARARI, Hananiah (1912-) American				
wc/d	1	2,200	2,200	2,200
HARDER, J (?) ?				
oil	1	1,267	1,267	1,267
HARDERS, Johannes (1871-1950) German				
oil	4	605-1,907	1,325	1,204
HARDIE, Charles Martin (1858-1916) British				
oil	2	1,471-3,660	2,565	1,471
HARDIE, Eldridge (1940-) American				
oil	1	11,000	11,000	11,000
HARDIME, Simon (1672-1737) Flemish				
oil	1	5,000	5,000	5,000
HARDING, Alexis (1973-) British				
oil	4	1,062-3,894	2,787	2,655

Name	No.	Price Range	Average	Median
HARDING, James Duffield (1798-1863) British				
oil	2	1,923-4,000	2,961	1,923
wc/d	2	892-1,392	1,142	892
HARDING, John (18th C) British				
oil	1	4,000	4,000	4,000
wc/d	1	493	493	493
HARDING, Ly Stellar (20th C) American				
oil	1	1,200	1,200	1,200
HARDMAN, J (19th C) British				
oil	1	4,000	4,000	4,000
HARDRICK, John W (1891-1968) American				
oil	3	1,900-4,200	2,800	2,300
HARDT, Ernst (1869-1917) German				
oil	1	1,920	1,920	1,920
HARDWICK, Melbourne H (1857-1916) American				
oil	3	650-42,500	19,716	16,000
HARDWICK, William Noble (1805-1865) British				
oil	1	3,000	3,000	3,000
HARDY, Anna Eliza (1839-1934) American				
oil	2	5,500-6,000	5,750	5,500
HARDY, David (fl.1855-1870) British				
oil	1	969	969	969
wc/d	2	447-2,610	1,528	447
HARDY, Dudley (1865-1922) British				
oil	3	1,122-6,920	3,854	3,520
wc/d	9	481-5,096	1,706	1,200
HARDY, Evelyn Stuart (1866-1935) British				
wc/d	1	1,056	1,056	1,056
HARDY, Frederick Daniel (1826-1911) British				
oil	6	1,305-11,776	4,968	3,022
HARDY, Greg (1950-) Canadian				
oil	1	2,132	2,132	2,132
HARDY, Heywood (1843-1933) British				
oil	17	3,000-50,000	21,628	19,580
HARDY, Heywood and James (jnr) (19th C) British				
oil	1	3,335	3,335	3,335
HARDY, Heywood and SYER, John (19th C) British				
oil	1	2,687	2,687	2,687
HARDY, James (19th C) British				
oil	15	567-2,992	1,270	1,190
wc/d	1	498	498	498
HARDY, James (jnr) (1832-1889) British				
oil	6	1,110-103,950	36,778	4,500
wc/d	4	1,104-12,460	6,745	3,024
HARDY, Janes (20th C) British				
oil	1	2,000	2,000	2,000
HARDY, Jean Michel (20th C) French?				
oil	1	3,600	3,600	3,600
HARDY, Jeremiah Pearson (1800-1888) American				
oil	2	1,700-40,000	20,850	1,700
HARDY, Kaspar Bernhard (1726-1819) German				
3D	1	6,081	6,081	6,081
HARDY, Robert (1952-) British				
oil	2	1,062-1,335	1,198	1,062
HARDY, Thomas (1757-1805) British				
oil	1	1,200	1,200	1,200
HARDY, Thomas Bush (1842-1897) British				
oil	1	6,156	6,156	6,156
wc/d	50	498-10,092	2,258	1,462
HARDY, W J (fl.1845-1856) British				
oil	2	2,141-2,141	2,141	2,141
HARE, Channing (1899-1976) American				
oil	1	1,700	1,700	1,700
HARE, John (1908-1978) American				
oil	7	1,425-6,200	2,675	1,900
wc/d	12	375-4,500	1,244	575
HARE, Julius (1859-1932) British				
oil	1	1,416	1,416	1,416
HARE, St George (1857-1933) British				
oil	1	6,000	6,000	6,000
HARGENS, Charles W (jnr) (1893-1996) American				
oil	2	1,200-2,800	2,000	1,200

Name	No.	Price Range	Average	Median
HARGITT, Edward (1835-1895) British				
oil	6	373-4,784	2,229	1,416
wc/d	2	493-566	529	493
HARING, Keith (1958-1990) American				
oil	18	8,980-480,000	168,879	100,000
wc/d	63	742-70,300	15,914	10,829
3D	13	5,377-300,000	104,285	84,480
HARING, Keith and LA2 (20th C) American				
oil	6	750-32,375	20,506	17,575
wc/d	5	4,451-11,195	7,204	5,724
HARITONOFF, Nicholas Basil (1880-1944) American				
oil	1	1,600	1,600	1,600
HARKINS, John (19/20th C) American				
oil	1	5,500	5,500	5,500
HARKNESS, Hilary (1971-) American				
oil	1	35,000	35,000	35,000
HARLAMOFF, Alexis (1842-1915) Russian				
oil	16	870-525,000	118,750	61,920
wc/d	3	2,600-17,010	8,944	7,224
HARLEY, Richard (1836-1884) British				
oil	1	1,100	1,100	1,100
HARLOFF, Guy (1933-1991) French				
oil	1	2,386	2,386	2,386
wc/d	7	656-3,579	1,745	1,427
HARLOW, George Henry (1787-1819) British				
oil	3	1,500-20,000	8,166	3,000
wc/d	1	8,000	8,000	8,000
HARMAN, Fred (jnr) (1902-1982) American				
oil	1	6,000	6,000	6,000
HARMAN, Jean C (1897-?) American				
oil	1	1,200	1,200	1,200
HARMON, Annie (1855-1930) American				
oil	3	1,200-4,750	2,483	1,500
HARMON, Charles (1859-1936) American				
oil	9	550-15,000	3,405	2,000
wc/d	1	650	650	650
HARMS, Anton Friedrich (1695-1745) German				
oil	1	18,125	18,125	18,125
HARNEST, Fritz (1905-) German				
oil	5	2,548-3,822	3,312	3,822
HARNETT, William Michael (1848-1892) American				
oil	2	1,300-22,428	11,864	1,300
HARNEY, Paul E (1850-1915) American				
oil	5	500-3,750	1,610	1,300
HARNISCH, Albert Ernest (1843-?) American				
3D	1	7,500	7,500	7,500
HAROS, Manolis (1960-) Greek				
oil	2	4,114-5,280	4,697	4,114
HARPER, Adolf Friedrich (1725-1806) German				
oil	2	2,238-19,028	10,633	2,238
HARPER, Charles (1943-) Irish				
oil	1	5,797	5,797	5,797
wc/d	2	632-1,091	861	632
HARPER, Henry Andrew (1835-1900) British				
wc/d	2	937-1,796	1,366	937
HARPER, Thomas (1820-1889) British				
oil	1	3,132	3,132	3,132
HARPER, William (19th C) British				
wc/d	1	2,000	2,000	2,000
HARPIGNIES, Henri (1819-1916) French				
oil	26	468-20,000	5,690	3,600
wc/d	38	476-28,000	4,611	2,378
HARPLEY, Sydney (1927-1992) British				
3D	3	2,378-12,155	8,324	10,440
HARRADEN, Richard Bankes (1778-1862) British				
oil	2	6,020-122,850	64,435	6,020
wc/d	1	4,806	4,806	4,806
HARRER, Hugo Paul (1836-1876) German				
oil	1	7,200	7,200	7,200
HARRI, Juhani (1939-2003) Finnish				
wc/d	3	701-5,529	3,521	4,334

Name	No.	Price Range	Average	Median
HARRINGTON, R (1800-1882) British				
oil	1	1,539	1,539	1,539
HARRIS, Bess (20th C) Canadian?				
oil	1	3,881	3,881	3,881
HARRIS, Charles X (1856-?) American				
oil	1	20,000	20,000	20,000
HARRIS, Edwin (1855-1906) British				
oil	2	7,182-8,550	7,866	7,182
HARRIS, Henry (1852-1926) British				
oil	10	629-5,075	1,381	748
HARRIS, James (1810-1887) British				
oil	2	2,800-85,050	43,925	2,800
HARRIS, Lawren Stewart (1885-1970) Canadian				
oil	20	13,194-1,285,071	301,446	137,773
wc/d	13	2,659-28,803	8,398	5,062
HARRIS, Mabel Rollins (20th C) American				
wc/d	1	3,500	3,500	3,500
HARRIS, Pat (20th C) Irish?				
oil	1	17,644	17,644	17,644
HARRIS, Robert (1849-1919) Canadian				
oil	3	2,132-3,250	2,558	2,292
wc/d	1	660	660	660
HARRIS, Robert G (1911-) American				
oil	2	4,500-12,000	8,250	4,500
HARRIS, Sam Hyde (1889-1977) American				
oil	17	1,947-22,500	7,320	5,000
HARRIS, William E (1856-1929) British				
oil	3	890-7,000	3,065	1,305
HARRIS-ROBERTS, Hugh (1942-) British				
3D	2	3,024-3,969	3,496	3,024
HARRISON, Birge (1854-1929) American				
oil	9	5,500-38,000	15,638	16,000
HARRISON, Charles Harmony (1842-1902) British				
wc/d	11	400-4,248	1,623	1,232
HARRISON, Claude (1922-) British				
oil	4	1,565-3,111	2,181	1,750
HARRISON, Clifford (20th C) British				
oil	4	821-2,379	1,559	878
HARRISON, Emma Florence (fl.1871-1891) British				
wc/d	1	1,480	1,480	1,480
HARRISON, F C (20th C) British				
oil	1	1,770	1,770	1,770
HARRISON, George (19/20th C) British				
oil	1	788	788	788
wc/d	1	696	696	696
HARRISON, John Cyril (1898-1985) British				
wc/d	22	460-10,024	2,356	2,000
HARRISON, Ted (1926-) Canadian				
oil	3	2,296-7,592	5,469	6,519
HARRISON, Thomas Alexander (1853-1930) American				
oil	4	2,262-35,000	12,065	3,000
HARROWING, Walter (fl.1877-1904) British				
oil	2	500-3,402	1,951	500
HART, Alfred A (1816-1906) American				
oil	1	4,500	4,500	4,500
HART, C H (19th C) British				
oil	1	5,670	5,670	5,670
HART, Elizabeth (fl.1898-1912) British				
oil	1	1,914	1,914	1,914
HART, Frederick (1943-1999) American				
3D	3	2,400-4,200	3,493	3,880
HART, George Overbury (1868-1933) American				
wc/d	1	1,100	1,100	1,100
HART, James (?) British				
oil	1	3,750	3,750	3,750
HART, James MacDougal (1828-1901) American				
oil	16	650-18,000	6,515	5,500
HART, Roger (20th C) French				
oil	1	4,411	4,411	4,411
HART, Thomas (?-1886) British				
wc/d	1	1,122	1,122	1,122

Name	No.	Price Range	Average	Median
HART, Thomas (1830-1916) British				
wc/d	3	704-10,044	3,875	878
HART, William Howard (1863-?) American				
oil	1	3,000	3,000	3,000
HART, William MacDougal (1823-1894) American				
oil	13	1,125-22,000	11,156	10,000
HARTA, Felix Albrecht (1884-1970) Hungarian/Austrian				
oil	1	10,286	10,286	10,286
wc/d	1	970	970	970
HARTELL, John (1902-?) American				
oil	1	2,750	2,750	2,750
HARTENKAMPF, Gottlieb Theodor Kempf von (1871-1964) Austrian				
oil	2	3,514-4,849	4,181	3,514
HARTIGAN, Grace (1922-) American				
oil	1	55,000	55,000	55,000
wc/d	1	2,000	2,000	2,000
HARTING, Lloyd (1901-1976) American				
wc/d	7	500-4,000	1,642	850
HARTLAND, Henry Albert (1840-1893) Irish				
wc/d	2	877-1,574	1,225	877
HARTLEY, Alfred (1855-1933) British				
wc/d	1	1,172	1,172	1,172
HARTLEY, Ben (c.1930-) British				
wc/d	2	985-1,164	1,074	985
HARTLEY, Jonathan Scott (1845-1912) American				
3D	1	2,700	2,700	2,700
HARTLEY, Marsden (1877-1943) American				
oil	11	38,000-2,000,000	516,636	310,000
wc/d	6	1,000-20,000	5,750	2,000
HARTMAN, John (1950-) ?				
oil	1	2,292	2,292	2,292
wc/d	1	1,640	1,640	1,640
HARTMANN, Bertram (1882-1960) American				
oil	1	700	700	700
wc/d	1	9,450	9,450	9,450
HARTMANN, Hugo Friedrich (1870-1960) German				
oil	3	1,132-1,788	1,458	1,455
HARTMANN, Johann Jacob (1680-1730) Czechoslovakian				
oil	2	60,490-132,449	96,469	60,490
HARTMANN, Johann Joseph (1753-1830) German				
wc/d	1	1,636	1,636	1,636
HARTMANN, Joseph (1812-1885) German				
oil	1	2,841	2,841	2,841
wc/d	1	486	486	486
HARTMANN, Ludwig (1835-1902) German				
oil	5	2,121-13,721	8,862	10,000
HARTMANN, Paul (20th C) German				
wc/d	1	1,674	1,674	1,674
HARTMANN, Peter (19th C) Austrian?				
wc/d	1	1,908	1,908	1,908
HARTSON, Walter C (1866-?) British				
oil	2	500-5,500	3,000	500
HARTUNG, Hans (1904-1989) French/German				
oil	42	7,598-222,000	57,824	46,849
wc/d	37	1,907-77,295	24,681	21,600
3D	1	34,397	34,397	34,397
HARTUNG, Heinrich (1851-1919) German				
oil	1	1,679	1,679	1,679
HARTUNG, J (19th C) German				
oil	3	1,784-4,772	3,198	3,038
HARTUNG, Karl (1908-1967) German				
wc/d	3	518-1,178	838	820
3D	4	3,092-20,634	11,470	5,696
HARTWICK, George Gunther (?-1899) American				
oil	5	2,100-8,000	5,160	6,500
HARTWIG, Heinie (1937-) American				
oil	32	400-5,500	1,505	1,000
HARTZ, Lauritz (1903-1987) Danish				
oil	5	1,327-8,370	4,587	4,203
HARTZ, Louis (1869-1935) Dutch				
oil	1	1,252	1,252	1,252

Name	No.	Price Range	Average	Median
HARUMI, Tateishi (1908-1994) Japanese				
wc/d	3	1,600-5,000	3,200	3,000
HARVENG, Carl Friedrich (1832-1874) German				
oil	2	1,051-11,192	6,121	1,051
HARVEY, Charles W (1895-1970) British				
oil	3	739-2,719	2,016	2,592
HARVEY, Eli (1860-1957) American				
3D	2	5,000-8,000	6,500	5,000
HARVEY, G (1933-) American				
oil	10	3,480-190,000	37,629	10,500
3D	1	2,500	2,500	2,500
HARVEY, George Wainwright (1855-1930) American				
oil	2	800-1,500	1,150	800
wc/d	1	750	750	750
HARVEY, Gerald (1933-) American				
oil	2	5,500-60,000	32,750	5,500
HARVEY, Harold (1874-1941) British				
oil	11	8,496-149,600	37,699	22,200
HARVEY, John Rabone (1862-1933) British				
oil	4	455-5,250	1,842	744
HARVEY, Marcus (1963-) British				
oil	1	22,500	22,500	22,500
HARVEY, Marion Roger Hamilton (1886-1971) British				
oil	1	4,725	4,725	4,725
wc/d	2	626-1,032	829	626
HARVEY, Quatman (1937-2002) Swedish				
oil	1	2,290	2,290	2,290
HARVEY, Sir George (1806-1876) British				
oil	1	732	732	732
wc/d	1	528	528	528
HARZE, Leopold (1831-1893) Belgian				
3D	1	1,829	1,829	1,829
HASCH, Carl (1834-1897) Austrian				
oil	4	3,041-7,007	4,897	4,241
HASCH, Victor (1945-) ?				
oil	1	1,460	1,460	1,460
HASEGAWA, Kiyoshi (1891-1980) Japanese				
wc/d	1	2,775	2,775	2,775
HASEGAWA, Shoichi (1929-) Japanese				
wc/d	1	1,297	1,297	1,297
HASELTINE, Herbert (1877-1962) American				
3D	2	27,500-30,000	28,750	27,500
HASELTINE, William Stanley (1835-1900) American				
oil	3	4,400-19,000	9,466	5,000
HASEMANN, Wilhelm Gustav Friederich (1850-1913) German				
oil	4	596-12,237	5,105	1,914
HASENCLEVER, Johann Peter (1810-1853) German				
oil	2	935-5,000	2,967	935
HASHMI, Zarina (1937-) Indian				
3D	1	10,000	10,000	10,000
HASIOR, Wladyslaw (1928-1999) Polish				
wc/d	1	15,288	15,288	15,288
HASKINS, John (1938-) British?				
oil	2	1,148-1,435	1,291	1,148
HASSAM, Childe (1859-1935) American				
oil	17	27,500-2,800,000	380,735	100,000
wc/d	10	1,075-600,000	109,742	26,000
HASSAN EL FAROUJ, Fatima (1945-) Moroccan				
oil	7	2,281-10,573	4,509	4,017
HASSANI, Saad (1948-) Moroccan				
wc/d	2	1,837-4,017	2,927	1,837
HASSEBRAUK, Ernst (1905-1974) German				
oil	5	3,214-6,370	5,157	5,439
wc/d	1	1,581	1,581	1,581
HASSELBERG, Per (1850-1894) Swedish				
3D	3	2,867-9,971	5,733	4,362
HASSELL, Hilton Macdonald (1910-1980) Canadian				
oil	4	656-1,649	1,089	907
HASSENTEUFEL, Hans (1887-1943) German				
oil	5	843-15,226	4,573	1,874

Name	No.	Price Range	Average	Median
HASSLER, Carl von (1887-1962) American				
oil	1	4,500	4,500	4,500
wc/d	1	9,000	9,000	9,000
HASSOUN, Ali (1964-) Lebanese				
oil	1	1,193	1,193	1,193
HASTINGS, Edward (fl.1804-1827) British				
oil	1	3,293	3,293	3,293
HASTINGS, Matthew (1834-1919) American				
oil	1	2,500	2,500	2,500
HASTINGS, Thomas (fl.1804-1831) British				
wc/d	1	1,068	1,068	1,068
HASUI, Kawase (1883-1957) Japanese				
wc/d	4	1,900-2,100	1,975	1,900
HATFIELD, Joseph Henry (1863-?) Canadian				
oil	1	3,250	3,250	3,250
HATHAWAY, George M (1852-1903) American				
oil	7	650-5,500	1,792	1,100
wc/d	1	1,400	1,400	1,400
HATHAWAY, Rufus (1770-1822) American				
oil	1	380,000	380,000	380,000
HATOUM, Mona (1952-) Palestinian				
wc/d	1	1,800	1,800	1,800
3D	2	56,320-96,800	76,560	56,320
HATZ, Felix (1904-1999) Swedish				
oil	1	1,654	1,654	1,654
HAU, Eduard (1807-1870) Russian				
wc/d	1	33,480	33,480	33,480
HAU, Woldemar (1816-1895) Russian				
wc/d	1	2,088	2,088	2,088
HAUBENSAK, Pierre (1935-) Swiss				
wc/d	1	1,461	1,461	1,461
HAUBTMANN, Michael (1843-1921) German/Czech				
oil	3	608-1,496	1,186	1,455
HAUCK, Augustus Christianus (1742-1801) German				
oil	1	6,936	6,936	6,936
HAUDEBOURT-LESCOT, Antoinette (1784-1845) French				
wc/d	1	1,457	1,457	1,457
HAUEISEN, Albert (1872-1954) German				
oil	1	1,457	1,457	1,457
HAUER, Christa (1925-) Austrian				
oil	1	8,357	8,357	8,357
HAUER, Leopold (1896-1984) Austrian				
oil	2	2,158-8,357	5,257	2,158
HAUGEN-SORENSEN, Arne (1932-) Danish				
oil	5	1,616-25,754	9,087	6,438
HAUN, August C (1815-1894) German				
wc/d	1	5,048	5,048	5,048
HAUPT, Matti (1912-1999) Finnish				
wc/d	2	479-503	491	479
3D	2	8,357-21,214	14,785	8,357
HAUPTMANN, Ivo (1886-1973) German				
oil	8	1,052-18,849	8,025	4,364
wc/d	19	590-2,521	1,331	1,067
HAUPTMANN, Karl (1880-1947) German				
oil	9	1,151-14,449	5,165	4,005
HAUPTMANN, P (20th C) German?				
oil	1	1,940	1,940	1,940
HAUPTMANN, Sven (1911-1984) Danish				
wc/d	1	1,616	1,616	1,616
HAUS, Hendrik Manfried (1803-1843) Dutch				
oil	1	9,031	9,031	9,031
HAUSDORF, Georg (20th C) German				
oil	1	2,100	2,100	2,100
HAUSE, Rudolf (1877-1961) German				
oil	1	1,090	1,090	1,090
HAUSER, Carry (1895-1985) Austrian				
oil	1	7,598	7,598	7,598
wc/d	1	2,108	2,108	2,108
HAUSER, Eric (1930-) German				
3D	6	2,283-27,194	11,472	9,889
HAUSER, Johann (1926-1996) German				
wc/d	7	757-4,039	1,844	1,514

Name	No.	Price Range	Average	Median
HAUSER, John (1859-1918) American				
oil	1	3,000	3,000	3,000
wc/d	5	900-30,000	10,630	9,000
HAUSFELDT, Hans (1902-1977) German				
oil	4	630-1,885	1,384	1,475
HAUSHOFER, Alfred (1872-1943) German				
wc/d	1	3,162	3,162	3,162
HAUSMANN, Gustav (1827-1899) German				
oil	2	3,371-12,041	7,706	3,371
HAUSMANN, Raoul (1886-1971) Austrian				
oil	1	87,809	87,809	87,809
wc/d	2	3,236-5,178	4,207	3,236
HAUSMANN, Wilhelm (1906-1980) German				
oil	1	3,836	3,836	3,836
HAUSNER, Rudolf (1914-) Austrian				
oil	1	47,123	47,123	47,123
HAUSNER, Xenia (1951-) Austrian				
oil	1	18,849	18,849	18,849
HAVARD, James (1937-) American				
oil	4	1,800-3,750	2,572	1,909
HAVE, Henrik (1946-) Danish				
oil	1	1,616	1,616	1,616
HAVEKOST, Eberhard (1967-) American				
oil	12	50,000-193,600	110,779	90,000
HAVELL, Alfred C (1855-1928) British				
oil	2	704-7,392	4,048	704
HAVELL, Alfred C and HOPKINS, William H (1855-1928) British				
oil	1	3,780	3,780	3,780
HAVELL, Edmund (jnr) (1819-1894) British				
oil	1	7,500	7,500	7,500
HAVELL, Robert (jnr) (1793-1878) British				
oil	12	650-140,000	37,720	15,000
wc/d	3	4,750-110,000	49,916	35,000
HAVELL, William (1782-1857) British				
oil	3	504-21,824	7,761	957
wc/d	2	1,575-4,347	2,961	1,575
HAVEN, Franklin de (1856-1934) American				
oil	6	700-4,250	2,491	2,000
HAVERMANN, Hendrik Johannes (1857-1928) Dutch				
oil	2	1,925-2,822	2,373	1,925
wc/d	2	565-1,134	849	565
HAVERTY, Joseph Patrick (1794-1864) British				
oil	1	74,400	74,400	74,400
HAVSTEEN-MIKKELSEN, Sven (1912-1999) Danish				
oil	5	2,535-9,054	5,669	6,438
HAWAY, Georges (1941-) Belgian				
oil	2	1,189-1,649	1,419	1,189
HAWEIS, Stephen (19/20th C) British				
oil	1	1,197	1,197	1,197
HAWKINS, Edward Mack Curtis (1877-?) American				
oil	1	2,500	2,500	2,500
HAWKINS, Louis Welden (1849-1910) British				
oil	3	7,800-167,263	61,387	9,100
HAWKINS, William (1895-1990) American				
oil	1	12,000	12,000	12,000
HAWKINSON, Tim (1960-) American				
wc/d	2	17,000-18,000	17,500	17,000
HAWKSLEY, Dorothy Webster (1884-1970) British				
wc/d	2	2,816-26,100	14,458	2,816
HAWORTH, Bobs Cogill (1904-1988) Canadian				
oil	3	1,010-3,526	1,914	1,208
wc/d	5	485-1,499	1,065	1,155
HAWORTH, Peter (1889-1986) Canadian				
oil	3	536-2,531	1,569	1,640
wc/d	1	1,476	1,476	1,476
HAWTHORNE, Charles W (1872-1930) American				
oil	9	2,500-95,000	23,611	12,000
HAWTHORNE, Marion C (1870-1945) American				
oil	1	2,500	2,500	2,500
HAY, Bernard (1864-?) British/Italian				
oil	4	850-13,308	7,361	6,069

Name	No.	Price Range	Average	Median
HAY, George (1831-1913) British				
oil	2	985-2,805	1,895	985
HAY, J (19th C) ?				
oil	1	3,349	3,349	3,349
HAY, William M (fl.1852-1881) British				
oil	1	17,010	17,010	17,010
HAYCOCK, Maurice Hall (1900-1988) Canadian				
oil	2	775-2,320	1,547	775
HAYDEN, Charles Henry (1856-1901) American				
oil	1	4,250	4,250	4,250
HAYDEN, Curt (1936-) Austrian				
oil	1	1,506	1,506	1,506
HAYDEN, Edward Parker (1858-1922) American				
oil	1	2,750	2,750	2,750
HAYDEN, Henri (1883-1970) French				
oil	26	1,074-92,500	9,687	2,503
wc/d	6	2,027-8,767	4,255	2,822
HAYDEN, Palmer (1890-1973) American				
oil	1	30,000	30,000	30,000
HAYDON, Benjamin Robert (1786-1846) British				
wc/d	1	4,272	4,272	4,272
HAYE, Reinier de la (1640-1684) Dutch				
oil	2	1,589-8,480	5,034	1,589
HAYER, Arthur (?) German				
oil	2	1,458-2,200	1,829	1,458
HAYES, Claude (1852-1922) British				
oil	3	731-4,927	2,773	2,661
wc/d	10	487-4,025	973	589
HAYES, Edward (1797-1864) British				
wc/d	3	626-1,453	1,064	1,113
HAYES, Edwin (1820-1904) British				
oil	17	490-76,438	13,099	8,416
wc/d	9	716-7,134	2,421	1,695
HAYES, Ernest (1914-1978) British				
oil	2	1,152-1,200	1,176	1,152
HAYES, John (1786-1866) British				
oil	1	1,131	1,131	1,131
HAYES, Lee (1854-1946) American				
oil	1	2,750	2,750	2,750
HAYES, Michael Angelo (1820-1877) British				
wc/d	5	1,262-8,505	3,775	2,417
HAYET, Louis (1854-1940) French				
oil	3	1,212-4,607	2,546	1,819
HAYEZ, Francesco (1791-1882) Italian				
oil	2	52,068-113,918	82,993	52,068
HAYLLAR, Edith (1860-1948) British				
oil	1	10,620	10,620	10,620
HAYLLAR, James (1829-1920) British				
oil	3	616-15,120	5,506	783
wc/d	2	736-13,920	7,328	736
HAYLLAR, Kate (fl.1883-1898) British				
wc/d	1	32,040	32,040	32,040
HAYMAN, Patrick (1915-1988) British				
oil	4	2,457-6,048	4,229	3,401
wc/d	1	552	552	552
HAYNES, John (1857-1945) British				
oil	1	1,471	1,471	1,471
HAYNES, John William (fl.1852-1882) British				
oil	3	1,512-8,325	4,323	3,132
HAYS, Barton S (1826-1914) American				
oil	3	1,300-10,500	6,433	7,500
HAYS, George Arthur (1854-1945) American				
oil	3	850-1,900	1,383	1,400
wc/d	1	900	900	900
HAYS, William Jacob (snr) (1830-1875) American				
oil	2	1,100-11,000	6,050	1,100
HAYTER, Sir George (1792-1871) British				
oil	5	549-5,280	2,375	2,392
HAYTER, Stanley William (1901-1988) British				
oil	6	550-14,560	5,497	3,250
wc/d	4	859-5,000	2,815	2,153

Name	No.	Price Range	Average	Median
HAYWARD, Alfred Frederick William (1856-1939) British				
oil	6	609-1,592	1,072	785
HAYWARD, Arthur (1889-1971) British				
oil	3	609-6,475	2,717	1,068
HAZARD, Arthur Merton (1872-1930) American				
oil	2	750-3,500	2,125	750
HAZELHUST, Ernest William (1866-1949) British				
wc/d	2	662-2,800	1,731	662
HAZLEDINE, Alfred (1876-1954) Belgian				
oil	4	970-5,845	2,955	1,430
HBICHA, Said (1964-) Moroccan				
oil	1	1,837	1,837	1,837
HE JIAYING (1957-) Chinese				
wc/d	1	1,029	1,029	1,029
HE SEN (1968-) Chinese				
oil	1	32,000	32,000	32,000
HE SENG (?) Chinese				
wc/d	1	1,366	1,366	1,366
HE TIANJIAN (1893-1974) Chinese				
wc/d	2	771-6,500	3,635	771
HEADE, Martin Johnson (1819-1904) American				
oil	6	100,000-1,200,000	398,333	250,000
HEALY, George Peter Alexander (1813-1894) American				
oil	6	400-4,250	1,525	700
HEALY, Henry (1909-1985) Irish?				
oil	6	1,753-4,080	2,666	2,290
HEALY, Laura (20th C) American				
oil	1	21,575	21,575	21,575
HEALY, Michael (1873-1941) British				
oil	4	509-1,029	672	509
wc/d	3	605-3,741	2,189	2,221
HEANEY, Charles Edward (1897-1981) American				
oil	1	4,540	4,540	4,540
HEARD, Isaac (1804-1869) British				
oil	1	15,000	15,000	15,000
HEARD, Joseph (1799-1859) British				
oil	5	10,440-22,620	14,313	13,050
HEARNE, Thomas (1744-1817) British				
wc/d	2	666-30,240	15,453	666
HEASLIP, William (1898-1970) Canadian				
oil	1	5,000	5,000	5,000
HEATH, Adrian (1920-1992) British				
oil	1	1,770	1,770	1,770
wc/d	2	951-1,936	1,443	951
HEATH, Frank Gascoigne (1873-1936) British				
oil	3	889-7,192	3,515	2,464
HEATH, Frank Lucien (1857-1921) American				
oil	1	5,000	5,000	5,000
HEATON, E (?) British				
oil	1	1,840	1,840	1,840
HEBBAR, Kattingeri Krishna (1911-1996) Indian				
oil	2	37,500-60,550	49,025	37,500
wc/d	2	885-2,552	1,718	885
HEBENSTREIT, Manfred (1957-) German?				
oil	2	1,987-2,038	2,012	1,987
HEBERER, Charles (1868-1951) American				
oil	4	750-3,250	1,775	1,100
HEBERT, Adrien (1890-1967) Canadian				
wc/d	1	1,244	1,244	1,244
HEBERT, Jules (1812-1897) French				
oil	2	1,526-9,158	5,342	1,526
HEBERT, Pierre Eugène Emile (1828-1893) French				
3D	2	2,939-10,000	6,469	2,939
HEBERT, Rene (1932-) Canadian				
oil	1	2,026	2,026	2,026
HEBRO, Leon (1850-1897) French				
oil	1	4,000	4,000	4,000
HECHELMANN, Friedrich (1948-) German				
wc/d	2	865-1,332	1,098	865
HECHT, Hendrick van der (1841-1901) Belgian				
oil	2	953-1,764	1,358	953

Name	No.	Price Range	Average	Median
HECHT, Joseph (1891-1951) Polish				
oil	1	1,612	1,612	1,612
HECK, Georg (1897-1982) German				
oil	1	3,349	3,349	3,349
wc/d	1	777	777	777
HECKE, Willem van (1893-1976) Belgian				
oil	5	486-2,754	1,530	1,656
HECKEL, Erich (1883-1970) German				
oil	10	9,864-1,320,000	186,849	50,884
wc/d	37	3,514-44,767	13,454	9,709
HECKEN, Abraham van den (17th C) Dutch				
oil	1	3,814	3,814	3,814
HECKEN, Samuel van den (17th C) Flemish				
oil	1	14,143	14,143	14,143
HECKENDORF, Franz (1888-1962) German				
oil	5	1,818-7,644	4,524	3,273
wc/d	3	1,298-3,414	2,056	1,458
HECKER, Franz (1870-1944) German				
oil	2	6,689-11,678	9,183	6,689
HECKERT-FECHNER, Maria (1880-?) German				
oil	1	1,590	1,590	1,590
HECKMAN, R Frederick (20th C) American				
oil	1	6,000	6,000	6,000
HECQ, Émile (1924-) French				
oil	1	1,052	1,052	1,052
HEDA, Willem Claesz (1594-1680) Dutch				
oil	4	39,735-218,483	134,619	72,660
HEDLEY, Ralph (c.1851-1913) British				
oil	37	450-109,200	8,285	2,595
wc/d	2	554-1,038	796	554
HEDOUIN, Edmond (1820-1889) French				
oil	2	2,848-6,062	4,455	2,848
HEDQVIST, Tage (1909-) Swedish				
oil	1	1,988	1,988	1,988
HEEL, Jan van (1898-1991) Dutch				
oil	9	1,764-8,650	4,872	4,005
wc/d	6	942-3,529	2,054	1,512
HEEM, Cornelis de (1631-1695) Dutch				
oil	5	32,870-203,478	80,591	57,819
HEEM, Jan Davidsz de (1606-1684) Dutch				
oil	3	128,456-222,095	176,302	178,356
HEEMSKERK, Egbert van (17/18th C) Dutch				
oil	3	4,500-17,300	8,895	4,886
HEEMSKERK, Egbert van (elder) (1610-1680) Dutch				
oil	1	3,254	3,254	3,254
HEEMSKERK, Egbert van (younger) (1634-1704) Dutch				
oil	4	2,186-40,000	16,299	8,010
HEEMSKERK, Jacob Eduard van Beest (1828-1894) Dutch				
oil	2	790-4,697	2,743	790
HEEMSKERK, Jacoba Berendina van Beest (1876-1923) Dutch				
oil	2	9,425-13,993	11,709	9,425
wc/d	1	4,091	4,091	4,091
HEENCK, Jabez (1752-1782) French				
wc/d	1	1,401	1,401	1,401
HEEREMANS, Thomas (fl.1660-1697) Dutch				
oil	10	7,120-38,014	18,395	10,929
HEEREN, Minna (1823-1898) German				
oil	2	5,296-7,188	6,242	5,296
HEERICH, Erwin (1922-) German				
3D	1	5,733	5,733	5,733
HEERUP, Henry (1907-1993) Danish				
oil	22	812-22,812	7,437	6,117
wc/d	5	885-10,507	3,325	1,616
3D	17	2,897-49,898	9,018	6,438
HEES, Gustav Adolf van (1862-?) German				
oil	1	29,500	29,500	29,500
HEFFEN, Jean Baptiste van (1840-?) Belgian				
3D	1	18,300	18,300	18,300
HEFFNER, Karl (1849-1925) German				
oil	18	455-5,838	2,122	1,764
wc/d	1	820	820	820

Name	No.	Price Range	Average	Median
HEGENBARTH, Josef (1884-1962) German				
oil	3	3,588-8,836	6,201	6,181
wc/d	17	468-5,933	2,087	1,403
HEGER, Heinrich Anton (1832-1888) German				
oil	1	9,926	9,926	9,926
HEGETHORN, Bengt (1925-) Swedish				
oil	1	2,114	2,114	2,114
HEICKE, Franz (19th C) Austrian				
oil	1	1,670	1,670	1,670
HEICKE, Joseph (1811-1861) Austrian				
oil	1	1,500	1,500	1,500
HEIDNER, Heinrich (1876-1951) German				
oil	2	718-3,600	2,159	718
HEIDRICH, Eckard (1930-) German				
oil	2	1,414-1,543	1,478	1,414
HEIJKOOP, Willem (?) Dutch				
oil	1	1,324	1,324	1,324
HEIKKA, Earle E (1910-1941) American				
3D	12	2,100-7,400	3,875	2,750
HEIL, Daniel van (1604-1662) Flemish				
oil	4	5,633-155,700	48,317	12,083
HEILBUTH, Ferdinand (1826-1889) French				
oil	3	1,549-9,360	5,236	4,800
wc/d	1	1,600	1,600	1,600
HEILEMANN, Ernst (1870-?) German				
oil	2	2,957-3,405	3,181	2,957
HEILIGER, Bernhard (1915-1995) German				
wc/d	4	478-851	640	574
3D	2	3,816-8,905	6,360	3,816
HEILMAN, Mary (1940-) American				
oil	1	26,000	26,000	26,000
HEILMANN, Flora (1872-1944) Danish				
oil	1	2,529	2,529	2,529
HEILMANN, Gerhard (1859-1946) Danish				
oil	1	1,352	1,352	1,352
HEIM, François Joseph (1787-1865) French				
oil	1	4,886	4,886	4,886
wc/d	2	600-9,955	5,277	600
HEIMBACH, Christian Wolfgang (1613-1678) German				
oil	1	2,788	2,788	2,788
HEIMERDINGER, Friedrich (1817-1882) Italian/German				
oil	1	1,634	1,634	1,634
HEIMERL, Josef (19/20th C) Austrian				
oil	4	478-1,750	1,164	1,134
HEIMIG, Walter (1881-1955) German				
oil	5	571-2,249	1,181	847
HEIN, H E (?) German				
oil	1	3,330	3,330	3,330
HEIN, Hendrik Jan (1822-1866) Dutch				
oil	1	42,000	42,000	42,000
HEINE, Friedrich Wilhelm (1845-1921) German				
oil	3	1,627-12,041	6,763	6,622
HEINE, Johann Adalbert (1850-?) German				
oil	4	970-1,678	1,226	970
HEINE, Thomas Theodor (1867-1948) German				
oil	2	2,493-12,721	7,607	2,493
wc/d	7	421-3,534	1,475	1,196
HEINEFETTER, Johann (1815-1902) German				
oil	2	912-3,440	2,176	912
HEINISCH, Karl Adam (1847-1923) German				
oil	5	689-2,259	1,305	1,021
HEINRICH, Otto (1891-?) German				
oil	1	15,660	15,660	15,660
HEINRICH-HANSEN, Adolf (1859-1925) Danish				
oil	1	1,905	1,905	1,905
HEINSEN, Hein (1935-) Danish				
3D	1	1,610	1,610	1,610
HEINSIUS, Johann Ernst (1740-1812) German				
oil	2	7,507-9,000	8,253	7,507
HEINTZ, Johann (17th C) ?				
wc/d	1	2,544	2,544	2,544

Name	No.	Price Range	Average	Median
HEINTZ, Joseph (elder) (1564-1609) Swiss				
oil	1	17,755	17,755	17,755
wc/d	1	1,600	1,600	1,600
HEINTZ, Richard (1871-1929) Belgian				
oil	13	1,018-8,357	2,883	1,942
HEINZ, Wolfgang (?) German				
oil	1	1,090	1,090	1,090
HEINZE, Adolph (1887-1958) American				
oil	2	4,500-10,000	7,250	4,500
HEINZMAN, Louis (1905-1982) American				
oil	1	1,300	1,300	1,300
HEISIG, Bernhard (1925-) Polish				
oil	5	17,306-27,986	21,307	20,384
wc/d	1	622	622	622
HEISKA, Joonas (1873-1937) Finnish				
oil	5	1,318-2,464	1,793	1,695
HEISS, Johann (1640-1704) German				
oil	3	12,153-43,347	24,081	16,743
HEISTER, Hans Siebert von (1888-1967) German				
oil	1	8,918	8,918	8,918
HEITER, Guillermo (1915-) Czechoslovakian				
oil	2	840-1,400	1,120	840
HEITMULLER, August (1873-1935) German				
oil	4	1,060-4,595	2,223	1,355
HEKKING, Willem (1796-1862) Dutch				
oil	1	2,400	2,400	2,400
HEKKING, William M (1885-1970) American				
oil	1	1,700	1,700	1,700
HEKMAN, Joop (1921-) Dutch				
3D	1	2,586	2,586	2,586
HELAND, Marten Rudolf (1765-1814) Swedish				
wc/d	1	6,869	6,869	6,869
HELBING, Ferenc (1870-1958) Hungarian				
oil	1	6,500	6,500	6,500
HELCK, Peter (1893-1988) American				
oil	1	2,100	2,100	2,100
wc/d	1	720	720	720
HELCKE, Arnold (fl.1865-1911) British				
oil	1	1,730	1,730	1,730
HELD, Al (1928-2005) American				
oil	3	5,500-42,500	26,000	30,000
wc/d	3	12,000-16,000	14,333	15,000
HELD, Alma M (1898-1988) American				
oil	1	2,100	2,100	2,100
HELD, Georg (18th C) German				
oil	1	7,591	7,591	7,591
HELD, John (jnr) (1889-1958) American				
wc/d	3	900-1,500	1,133	1,000
HELDER, Johannes (1842-1913) Dutch				
oil	3	732-3,000	1,496	756
HELDNER, Collette Pope (1902-1996) American				
oil	3	500-4,000	1,733	700
HELDNER, Knute (1884-1952) American				
oil	5	3,200-7,500	4,900	3,500
HELDT, Werner (1904-1954) German				
oil	1	21,082	21,082	21,082
wc/d	8	1,640-8,784	4,376	2,342
HELENIUS, Ester (1875-1955) Finnish				
oil	6	1,157-1,757	1,453	1,453
wc/d	2	539-605	572	539
HELIKER, John Edward (1909-2000) American				
oil	3	1,500-2,400	1,800	1,500
HELION, Jean (1904-1987) French				
oil	16	3,190-120,000	18,805	10,911
wc/d	45	1,636-15,780	6,842	5,702
HELL, Friedrich (1869-1957) Austrian				
oil	1	5,993	5,993	5,993
HELL, Johan van (1889-1952) Dutch				
oil	3	41,980-82,687	66,998	76,327
HELLEMANS, Pierre (1787-1845) Belgian				
oil	1	5,539	5,539	5,539

Name	No.	Price Range	Average	Median
HELLESEN, Hanne (1801-1844) Danish				
oil	3	10,000-23,814	17,595	18,971
HELLEU, Jean (1894-1985) French				
oil	4	832-5,774	2,407	995
HELLEU, Paul-Cesar (1859-1927) French				
oil	1	1,500	1,500	1,500
wc/d	12	905-35,617	8,916	7,135
HELLGREWE, Rudolf (1860-1935) German				
oil	7	468-20,384	4,790	1,355
wc/d	1	2,035	2,035	2,035
HELLQVIST, Carl Gustav (1851-1890) Swedish				
wc/d	1	1,191	1,191	1,191
HELLWAG, Rudolf (1867-1942) German				
oil	3	983-1,647	1,409	1,598
HELMAN, Robert (1910-1990) French				
oil	2	791-1,455	1,123	791
HELMANTEL, Henk (1945-) Dutch				
oil	1	17,534	17,534	17,534
HELMBERGER, Adolf (1885-1967) Austrian				
oil	3	1,091-2,950	2,226	2,637
HELMBREKER, Theodor (1633-1696) Flemish				
oil	1	18,502	18,502	18,502
HELMERT, Herbert (1924-1997) German				
oil	8	807-2,160	1,614	1,560
HELMICK, Howard (1845-1907) American				
oil	4	878-24,360	7,587	1,838
HELMONT, Jan van II (1650-1714) Flemish				
oil	1	3,277	3,277	3,277
HELMONT, Matheus van (1623-1679) Flemish				
oil	5	4,253-63,699	30,043	29,301
HELNWEIN, Gottfried (1948-) Austrian				
wc/d	1	2,637	2,637	2,637
HELPS, Francis (1890-1972) British				
oil	1	1,800	1,800	1,800
HELSBY, Alfredo (1862-1933) Chilean				
oil	2	1,488-4,750	3,119	1,488
HELST, Bartholomeus van der (1613-1670) Dutch				
oil	1	18,000	18,000	18,000
HELST, Lodewyck van der (1642-1680) Dutch				
oil	1	6,475	6,475	6,475
HELSTED, Axel (1847-1907) Danish				
oil	3	1,132-5,080	3,552	4,445
HELSTED, Vigo (1861-1926) Danish				
oil	2	468-1,549	1,008	468
HELT, C A (?) ?				
oil	1	6,750	6,750	6,750
HELWIG, Arthur Louis (1899-1976) American				
oil	1	1,000	1,000	1,000
HEM, Louise de (1866-1922) Belgian				
wc/d	1	1,812	1,812	1,812
HEM, Piet van der (1885-1961) Dutch				
oil	5	2,277-14,137	5,951	4,712
wc/d	12	834-46,757	11,150	6,370
HEMCHE, Abdelhalim (1906-1979) Algerian				
oil	3	2,817-9,503	5,220	3,341
HEMING, Arthur (1870-1940) Canadian				
oil	4	2,468-15,867	10,946	12,156
wc/d	1	793	793	793
HEMINGWAY, Andrew (1955-) British				
oil	1	1,134	1,134	1,134
HEMKEN, Willem de Haas (1831-1911) Dutch				
oil	1	12,858	12,858	12,858
HEMPFING, Wilhelm (1886-1951) German				
oil	6	947-4,839	1,883	1,317
HEMSLEY, William (1819-1906) British				
oil	7	669-2,944	1,795	1,500
HEMY, Bernard Benedict (1845-1913) British				
oil	12	500-4,833	1,308	1,009
wc/d	2	1,147-2,848	1,997	1,147
HEMY, Charles Napier (1841-1917) British				
oil	6	1,200-32,130	11,586	7,080
wc/d	11	605-8,850	4,109	2,775

Name	No.	Price Range	Average	Median
HEMY, Thomas Marie (1852-1937) British				
oil	3	797-2,700	1,609	1,332
wc/d	4	835-2,685	2,021	2,100
HENAULT, Jean-Pierre (1942-) French				
oil	1	2,460	2,460	2,460
HENDERIKSE, Jan Jozias (1937-) Dutch				
oil	1	2,125	2,125	2,125
wc/d	1	1,781	1,781	1,781
HENDERSON, Charles Cooper (1803-1877) British				
oil	2	3,402-27,500	15,451	3,402
wc/d	1	945	945	945
HENDERSON, James (1871-1951) Canadian				
oil	3	478-2,800	1,972	2,639
HENDERSON, John (1860-1924) British				
oil	3	626-5,916	3,302	3,366
HENDERSON, Joseph (1832-1908) British				
oil	15	835-14,240	4,023	2,941
HENDERSON, Joseph Morris (1863-1936) British				
oil	12	761-14,000	3,481	1,416
HENDRICH, Hermann (1856-1931) German				
oil	1	3,680	3,680	3,680
HENDRICKX, Michel (1847-1906) Dutch				
oil	1	1,134	1,134	1,134
HENDRIKS, Gerardus (1804-1859) Dutch				
oil	2	1,326-2,503	1,914	1,326
HENDRIKS, Willem (1828-1891) Dutch				
oil	1	1,990	1,990	1,990
HENDRIKS, Wybrand (1744-1831) Dutch				
oil	1	438	438	438
wc/d	1	1,145	1,145	1,145
HENDRY, Frank (1863-1939) American				
oil	1	1,900	1,900	1,900
HENEL, Edwin (1883-1953) German				
oil	1	2,422	2,422	2,422
HENG, Auguste (1891-1968) Swiss				
3D	1	76,575	76,575	76,575
HENGELER, Adolf (1863-1927) German				
oil	4	1,054-3,273	1,912	1,506
HENGER, B (19th C) ?				
oil	1	2,356	2,356	2,356
HENGSBACH, Franz (1814-1883) German				
oil	3	879-1,767	1,266	1,152
HENGST, Jan den (1904-1983) Dutch				
oil	4	491-1,567	1,186	1,169
HENLEY, Henry W (fl.1871-1895) British				
oil	2	2,088-2,268	2,178	2,088
HENNEBICQ, Andre (1836-1904) Belgian				
oil	2	2,301-3,099	2,700	2,301
HENNELL, Thomas (1903-1945) British				
wc/d	1	4,275	4,275	4,275
HENNEQUIN, Philippe Auguste (1762-1833) French				
oil	1	1,879	1,879	1,879
HENNER, Jean Jacques (1829-1905) French				
oil	17	425-7,007	3,342	2,997
wc/d	3	535-1,215	785	605
HENNESSEY, Frank Charles (1893-1941) Canadian				
wc/d	3	1,319-3,882	2,174	1,322
HENNESSY, Patrick (1915-1980) Irish				
oil	15	2,472-34,164	10,879	9,642
HENNESSY, William John (1839-1917) British				
oil	9	1,100-78,120	35,148	29,760
HENNIG, Anton (1964-) German				
oil	1	1,821	1,821	1,821
HENNIGS, Gosta von (1866-1941) Swedish				
oil	2	1,923-4,353	3,138	1,923
HENNING, A S (19th C) British				
oil	1	14,000	14,000	14,000
HENNING, Adolf (1809-1900) German				
oil	1	9,687	9,687	9,687
HENNING, Anton (1964-) ?				
oil	2	8,000-53,100	30,550	8,000

Name	No.	Price Range	Average	Median
HENNING, Ester Matilda (1887-1985) Swedish				
oil	1	1,018	1,018	1,018
wc/d	1	541	541	541
HENNING, Gerhard (1880-1967) Swedish				
3D	6	3,863-14,225	7,598	4,385
HENNINGER, Manfred (1894-1986) German				
oil	11	973-9,997	3,037	2,428
wc/d	3	668-2,811	1,940	2,342
HENNINGS, Ernest Martin (1886-1956) American				
oil	7	50,000-350,000	205,857	250,000
HENNINGS, Johann Friedrich (1838-1899) German				
oil	5	1,060-7,899	3,669	2,919
HENNINGSEN, Erik (1855-1930) Danish				
oil	5	1,304-34,743	11,665	7,904
wc/d	3	552-2,085	1,249	1,111
HENNINGSEN, Frants (1850-1908) Danish				
oil	3	564-5,946	2,978	2,426
wc/d	2	596-4,901	2,748	596
HENRI, Robert (1865-1929) American				
oil	10	9,000-290,000	78,600	20,000
wc/d	11	400-85,000	9,875	3,000
HENRICHSEN, Carsten (1824-1897) Danish				
oil	5	571-3,074	1,717	1,460
HENRICKSEN, Ralf Christian (1907-1975) American				
wc/d	1	3,000	3,000	3,000
HENRIET, Henk (1903-1945) Dutch				
oil	1	3,562	3,562	3,562
HENRIKSEN, William (1880-1964) Danish				
oil	2	3,500-4,200	3,850	3,500
HENRION, Armand (1875-?) Belgian				
oil	4	1,584-5,310	3,396	2,267
HENRION, Joseph (1936-1983) Belgian				
3D	1	10,286	10,286	10,286
HENRY D'ARLES, Jean (1734-1784) French				
oil	4	8,500-213,596	90,372	22,500
HENRY, E L (1841-1919) American				
oil	1	20,000	20,000	20,000
HENRY, Edward Lamson (1841-1919) American				
oil	6	8,000-60,000	24,500	19,000
wc/d	2	1,200-2,300	1,750	1,200
HENRY, George (1859-1943) British				
oil	4	3,114-69,200	23,074	8,477
wc/d	2	14,960-22,880	18,920	14,960
HENRY, Grace (1868-1953) British				
oil	4	3,299-17,014	7,802	4,944
wc/d	1	1,683	1,683	1,683
HENRY, James Levin (1855-?) British				
oil	3	1,328-7,785	4,306	3,806
wc/d	1	557	557	557
HENRY, Marjorie (1900-1974) British?				
oil	4	657-6,126	2,361	1,280
wc/d	1	606	606	606
HENRY, Michel (1928-) French				
oil	2	527-2,400	1,463	527
HENRY, Olive (1902-1989) British				
oil	1	2,622	2,622	2,622
wc/d	3	443-643	509	443
HENRY, Paul (1876-1958) Irish				
oil	20	22,973-390,600	94,453	61,260
wc/d	4	19,872-53,514	30,236	23,378
HENSCHE, Ada Rayner (1901-1984) American				
oil	2	1,125-1,400	1,262	1,125
HENSCHE, Henry (1901-1992) American				
oil	3	2,000-9,100	5,433	5,200
HENSCHEL, George (1850-1934) British				
wc/d	1	1,890	1,890	1,890
HENSEL, Stephen Hopkins (1921-1979) American				
oil	1	1,000	1,000	1,000
HENSELER, Ernst (1852-1940) German				
oil	1	712	712	712
wc/d	1	565	565	565
HENSELER, Josef (19th C) ?				
oil	2	1,818-1,940	1,879	1,818

Name	No.	Price Range	Average	Median
HENSHALL, John Henry (1856-1928) British				
wc/d	4	2,093-3,750	2,889	2,175
HENSHAW, Frederick Henry (1807-1891) British				
oil	2	865-4,654	2,759	865
wc/d	1	440	440	440
HENSHAW, Glenn Cooper (1881-1946) American				
oil	1	22,000	22,000	22,000
HENZE, Sara (?) ?				
oil	1	1,199	1,199	1,199
HENZE-DESSAU, Max (1889-1952) German				
oil	1	2,397	2,397	2,397
HENZELL, Isaac (1815-1876) British				
oil	1	1,295	1,295	1,295
HEPPER, George (1839-1868) British				
oil	1	2,408	2,408	2,408
HEPPLE, Robert Norman (1908-1994) British				
oil	7	623-3,204	1,758	1,239
HEPPLE, Wilson (1853-1937) British				
oil	2	1,709-50,000	25,854	1,709
wc/d	3	592-1,967	1,087	704
HEPWORTH, Dame Barbara (1903-1975) British				
oil	3	69,930-79,380	75,600	77,490
wc/d	2	17,010-60,480	38,745	17,010
3D	8	78,300-1,300,000	467,300	238,950
HERALD, James Watterson (1859-1914) British				
wc/d	5	4,956-9,735	7,186	7,080
HERBERG, Marianne (1901-1991) German				
oil	1	1,060	1,060	1,060
HERBERT, Alfred (?-1861) British				
wc/d	2	835-2,832	1,833	835
HERBERT, Emile (19th C) ?				
3D	1	2,175	2,175	2,175
HERBERT, John Rogers (1810-1890) British				
oil	2	665-35,150	17,907	665
HERBERTE, Edward Benjamin (fl.1860-1893) British				
oil	2	1,050-2,262	1,656	1,050
HERBIG, Otto (1889-1971) German				
oil	1	1,800	1,800	1,800
wc/d	3	837-1,200	1,077	1,196
HERBIN, Auguste (1882-1960) French				
oil	33	17,199-570,000	78,175	50,000
wc/d	15	3,515-38,796	12,565	11,003
HERBO, Fernand (1905-1995) French				
oil	15	705-5,021	2,529	2,750
wc/d	7	718-3,162	1,565	1,364
HERBO, Léon (1850-1907) Belgian				
oil	21	834-40,480	8,687	4,750
HERBST, Adolf (1909-1983) Swiss				
oil	16	627-4,162	2,036	1,623
wc/d	7	457-1,490	924	835
HERBST, Rene (1891-1982) French				
3D	1	8,183	8,183	8,183
HERBST, Thomas (1848-1915) German				
oil	20	794-7,658	3,442	3,299
wc/d	2	501-546	523	501
HERBSTOFFER, Peter Rudolf Karl (1821-1876) French				
oil	1	3,405	3,405	3,405
HERDEG, Christian (1942-) Swiss				
wc/d	1	1,055	1,055	1,055
3D	1	7,303	7,303	7,303
HERDLE, George Linton (1868-1922) American				
wc/d	1	1,500	1,500	1,500
HERDMAN, Robert (1828-1888) British				
oil	9	990-27,680	8,221	5,907
HEREDIA, Alberto (20th C) Argentinian				
3D	2	2,600-14,000	8,300	2,600
HERETAKIS, Alexandros (1959-) Greek				
oil	1	1,870	1,870	1,870
HERGENRODER, Georg Heinrich (1736-1794) German				
oil	1	6,078	6,078	6,078
HERING, Georg Wilhelm Richard (1884-1936) Dutch				
oil	1	10,141	10,141	10,141

Name	No.	Price Range	Average	Median
HERING, George Edwards (1805-1879) British				
oil	5	1,062-9,515	6,165	6,708
HERIOT, George (1766-1844) Canadian				
wc/d	1	4,498	4,498	4,498
HERKENRATH, Peter (1900-1992) German				
oil	14	486-8,836	3,544	2,116
wc/d	2	764-1,581	1,172	764
HERKOMER, Hubert von (1849-1914) British				
oil	2	2,076-3,500	2,788	2,076
wc/d	3	1,424-2,342	1,848	1,780
HERLAND, Emma (1856-1947) French				
oil	2	1,427-2,398	1,912	1,427
wc/d	1	912	912	912
HERMAN, Hermine (1857-?) Austrian				
oil	1	2,595	2,595	2,595
HERMAN, John (20th C) British?				
oil	1	1,246	1,246	1,246
HERMAN, Josef (1911-1999) British				
oil	17	637-14,025	5,577	4,758
wc/d	30	478-1,740	1,078	957
HERMANJAT, Abraham (1862-1932) Swiss				
oil	3	1,752-2,855	2,345	2,428
wc/d	2	2,121-2,656	2,388	2,121
HERMANN, Franz Georg (younger) (1692-1768) German				
oil	1	11,439	11,439	11,439
HERMANN, Franz Ludwig (1710-1791) German				
wc/d	1	1,649	1,649	1,649
HERMANN, Hans (1813-1890) German				
oil	1	13,155	13,155	13,155
HERMANN, Heiko (1953-) German				
oil	2	1,127-1,207	1,167	1,127
HERMANN, L (19th C) ?				
oil	1	4,023	4,023	4,023
HERMANN, Leo (19th C) French				
oil	3	727-3,500	1,697	865
HERMANN, Ludwig (1812-1881) German				
oil	8	1,000-13,125	5,376	3,503
HERMANN, Woldemar (1807-1878) German				
wc/d	1	1,272	1,272	1,272
HERMANN-PAUL (1874-1940) French				
wc/d	1	1,991	1,991	1,991
HERMANNES, Carl (1874-1955) German				
oil	1	1,079	1,079	1,079
HERMANNS, Heinrich (1862-1942) German				
oil	14	870-8,511	2,486	1,670
wc/d	1	912	912	912
HERMANS, Charles (1839-1924) Belgian				
oil	5	760-55,000	14,803	5,068
wc/d	1	2,047	2,047	2,047
HERMANS, Toon (1916-2000) Dutch				
oil	1	1,296	1,296	1,296
HERMANSEN, O A (1849-1897) Danish				
oil	1	1,390	1,390	1,390
HERMANSEN, Olaf August (1849-1897) Danish				
oil	3	2,426-4,110	3,419	3,721
HERMANUS, Paul (1859-1911) Belgian				
oil	2	1,907-5,369	3,638	1,907
wc/d	1	727	727	727
HERMELIN, Olof (1827-1913) Swedish				
oil	15	590-4,258	2,139	2,293
HERMOSO, Eugenio (1883-1963) Spanish				
oil	2	19,140-26,815	22,977	19,140
HERNANDEZ MOMPO, Manuel (1927-1992) Spanish				
oil	5	18,811-75,310	35,756	32,108
wc/d	4	960-26,490	8,884	3,592
3D	5	21,673-33,714	27,538	26,000
HERNANDEZ PIJUAN, Juan (1931-) Spanish				
oil	3	4,995-20,354	11,664	9,643
wc/d	1	3,168	3,168	3,168
HERNANDEZ, Antonio Sistere de (1854-?) Spanish				
oil	1	8,159	8,159	8,159

Name	No.	Price Range	Average	Median
HERNANDEZ, Caesar A (1909-1996) American				
wc/d	1	1,000	1,000	1,000
HERNANDEZ, Daniel (1856-1932) Peruvian				
oil	3	1,555-20,815	9,956	7,500
HERNANDEZ, Jose (1944-) Spanish				
oil	1	21,673	21,673	21,673
wc/d	2	1,255-1,401	1,328	1,255
HERNANDEZ, Mateo (1885-1949) Spanish				
wc/d	1	1,229	1,229	1,229
3D	2	7,375-9,678	8,526	7,375
HERNANDEZ, Sergio (1957-) Mexican				
oil	3	20,000-35,000	28,333	30,000
3D	1	24,000	24,000	24,000
HEROLD, Frank (?-1929) American				
oil	1	5,000	5,000	5,000
HEROLD, Georg (1947-) German				
wc/d	2	26,000-42,240	34,120	26,000
3D	2	10,014-10,208	10,111	10,014
HEROLD, Jacques (1910-1987) Rumanian				
oil	3	1,445-5,069	2,756	1,754
wc/d	3	537-715	631	643
HEROLD, James (20th C) British				
wc/d	1	12,110	12,110	12,110
HERON, Hilary (1923-) Irish				
3D	1	11,427	11,427	11,427
HERON, Luc (20th C) French				
oil	1	3,284	3,284	3,284
HERON, Patrick (1920-1999) British				
oil	5	31,140-518,700	141,860	46,980
wc/d	12	6,048-52,920	20,139	14,160
HERON, William (fl.1883-1896) British				
wc/d	1	1,860	1,860	1,860
HERP, Willem van (elder) (1614-1677) Flemish				
oil	2	6,336-12,950	9,643	6,336
HERPFER, Carl (1836-1897) German				
oil	4	2,906-32,000	13,732	7,500
HERPIN, Léon (1841-1880) French				
oil	1	6,896	6,896	6,896
HERREGOUTS, Hendrik (1633-c.1704) Flemish				
oil	1	9,576	9,576	9,576
HERREMANS, Lievin (1858-1921) Belgian				
oil	5	1,260-10,603	4,392	2,609
HERRER, Cesar de (1868-1919) Spanish				
oil	2	1,336-1,415	1,375	1,336
HERRERA, Arturo (1959-) Venezuelan				
wc/d	1	6,000	6,000	6,000
3D	1	4,750	4,750	4,750
HERRERA, Carlos Maria (1875-1914) Uruguayan				
wc/d	1	3,200	3,200	3,200
HERRERO, Federico (1978-) Costa Rican				
oil	1	4,500	4,500	4,500
HERREROS GALAN, Jose (20th C) Spanish				
oil	1	1,317	1,317	1,317
HERREROS, Enrique (1903-1977) Spanish				
oil	1	1,236	1,236	1,236
HERRFELDT, Marcel René von (1890-1965) French				
oil	3	1,403-2,761	2,303	2,747
HERRIMAN, George (1880-1944) American				
wc/d	12	2,800-7,000	4,608	3,000
HERRING, Benjamin (jnr) (1830-1871) British				
oil	3	735-4,200	2,555	2,730
HERRING, Frank Stanley (1894-) American				
oil	8	400-2,800	1,362	600
wc/d	18	400-2,600	883	750
HERRING, John Frederick (19/20th C) British				
oil	2	8,500-8,836	8,668	8,500
HERRING, John Frederick (jnr) (1815-1907) British				
oil	21	3,211-32,760	14,337	11,340
HERRING, John Frederick (snr) (1795-1865) British				
oil	32	985-680,000	79,677	24,000

Name	No.	Price Range	Average	Median
HERRIOT, Alan Beattie (20th C) British				
oil	2	12,144-18,480	15,312	12,144
3D	1	2,288	2,288	2,288
HERRLEIN, Johann Andreas (1720-1796) German				
oil	1	6,081	6,081	6,081
HERRMANN, Carl Gustav (1857-?) German				
oil	1	1,030	1,030	1,030
HERRMANN, Curt (1854-1929) German				
oil	4	6,069-35,619	17,525	10,603
HERRMANN, Hans (1858-1942) German				
oil	5	775-8,767	5,992	7,297
HERRMANN, Peter (1937-) German				
oil	1	2,472	2,472	2,472
wc/d	1	718	718	718
HERRMANN-LEON, Charles (1838-1908) French				
oil	1	13,942	13,942	13,942
HERSCHEL, Otto (1871-1937) German				
oil	3	1,178-14,143	5,584	1,433
HERSENT, Louis (1777-1860) French				
wc/d	1	3,200	3,200	3,200
HERSON, Emile Antoine François (1805-?) French				
wc/d	1	2,464	2,464	2,464
HERTEL, Albert (1843-1912) German				
oil	2	552-1,551	1,051	552
HERTER, Adele (1869-1946) American				
oil	2	1,100-7,500	4,300	1,100
HERTER, Albert (1871-1950) American				
oil	4	9,500-45,000	23,078	15,315
wc/d	1	65,000	65,000	65,000
HERTERICH, Ludwig Ritter von (1856-1932) German				
oil	2	1,155-1,946	1,550	1,155
HERTZ, Mogens (1909-1990) Danish				
oil	13	1,212-5,819	2,423	1,778
HERVE, Jules R (1887-1981) French				
oil	70	618-19,000	4,743	3,750
HERVE-MATHE, Jules Alfred (1868-1953) French				
oil	4	486-6,732	2,305	665
HERVENS, Jacques (1890-1928) Belgian				
oil	2	932-1,130	1,031	932
HERVIEU, Louise (1878-1954) French				
wc/d	4	502-3,858	1,698	1,052
HERWERDEN, Jacob Dirk van (1806-1879) Dutch				
oil	1	3,879	3,879	3,879
HERWIJNEN, Jan van (1889-1965) Dutch				
oil	3	1,512-3,356	2,232	1,829
HERZIG, Heinrich (1887-1964) Swiss				
oil	4	698-3,077	1,683	763
HERZIG, Wolfgang (1941-) German				
wc/d	1	3,822	3,822	3,822
HERZMANOVSKY-ORLANDO, Fritz von (1877-1954) Austrian				
wc/d	3	485-2,121	1,151	849
HERZOG, August (1885-1959) German				
oil	2	2,039-3,921	2,980	2,039
HERZOG, Hermann (1832-1932) American/German				
oil	28	1,500-150,000	22,105	9,500
HESELDIN, James (1887-?) British				
wc/d	1	1,050	1,050	1,050
HESELTINE, Arthur (fl.1879-1884) British				
oil	1	1,322	1,322	1,322
HESEMANN, Heinrich (1814-1856) German				
3D	1	1,927	1,927	1,927
HESS, Hieronymus (1799-1850) Swiss				
wc/d	2	5,301-19,000	12,150	5,301
HESS, John N (19th C) American				
oil	1	1,283	1,283	1,283
HESS, Ludwig (1760-1800) Swiss				
oil	1	6,868	6,868	6,868
HESS, Peter von (1792-1871) German				
wc/d	1	1,199	1,199	1,199
HESSE, Alexandre (1806-1879) French				
oil	1	9,503	9,503	9,503

Name	No.	Price Range	Average	Median
HESSE, Bruno (1905-) Swiss				
oil	3	1,621-2,748	2,023	1,702
HESSE, Eva (1936-1970) American				
oil	1	260,000	260,000	260,000
wc/d	2	18,000-230,000	124,000	18,000
3D	2	300,000-2,000,000	1,150,000	300,000
HESSE, Hermann (1877-1962) German				
wc/d	17	530-32,423	6,981	2,967
HESSELBOM, Otto (1848-1913) Swedish				
oil	1	9,891	9,891	9,891
HESSING, Gustav (1909-1981) Rumanian				
oil	1	1,678	1,678	1,678
wc/d	4	841-2,038	1,501	1,438
HESSLER, Otto (1858-?) German				
oil	2	1,335-2,436	1,885	1,335
HETZ, Carl (1828-1899) German				
oil	1	1,432	1,432	1,432
HETZEL, George (1826-1899) American				
oil	2	6,500-14,000	10,250	6,500
HEUDEBERT, Raymonde (1905-) French				
oil	3	963-1,565	1,324	1,445
wc/d	1	506	506	506
HEUKELOM, Frans van (1812-1872) Dutch				
oil	1	1,463	1,463	1,463
HEUMANN, Augustinus (1885-1919) German				
oil	1	1,001	1,001	1,001
HEURTAUX, Andre Gaston (1898-1983) French				
oil	1	6,871	6,871	6,871
HEUSCH, Jacob de (1657-1701) Dutch				
oil	1	16,829	16,829	16,829
HEUSER, Carl (19th C) German				
oil	1	1,384	1,384	1,384
HEUSSER, Heinrich (1886-1943) Swiss?				
oil	1	2,922	2,922	2,922
HEUVEL, Theodore Bernard de (1817-1906) Flemish				
oil	2	3,402-3,709	3,555	3,402
HEWARD, Prudence (1896-1947) Canadian				
oil	4	4,076-19,450	8,962	4,076
HEWITT, P (?) British?				
oil	1	2,100	2,100	2,100
HEWLETT, Allan B (fl.1930-1953) British				
oil	1	1,388	1,388	1,388
HEWTON, Randolph Stanley (1888-1960) Canadian				
oil	7	6,171-15,668	11,201	12,156
HEY, Paul (1867-1952) German				
oil	4	1,918-3,770	2,940	2,569
wc/d	6	1,109-3,063	2,300	2,676
HEYBOER, Anton (1924-2005) Dutch				
oil	10	477-9,425	3,659	1,312
wc/d	10	583-1,438	815	700
HEYDEN, Carl (1845-1933) German				
oil	2	911-1,576	1,243	911
HEYDEN, J C J van der (1928-) Dutch				
oil	2	5,845-21,041	13,443	5,845
HEYDEN, Jan van der (1637-1712) Dutch				
oil	3	55,500-1,150,000	440,901	117,205
HEYDENDAHL, Friedrich Joseph Nicolai (1844-1906) German				
oil	6	589-2,104	1,267	1,060
HEYENBROCK, Johan Coenrad Hermann (1871-1948) Dutch				
oil	2	1,627-8,136	4,881	1,627
wc/d	2	2,128-2,378	2,253	2,128
HEYER, Arthur (1872-1931) German				
oil	16	558-6,555	2,338	1,951
HEYERDAHL, Hans Olaf (1857-1913) Norwegian				
oil	3	2,500-5,500	3,666	3,000
HEYLIGERS, Antoon François (1828-1897) Dutch				
oil	1	69,600	69,600	69,600
HEYLIGERS, Hendrik (1877-1967) Dutch				
oil	1	5,200	5,200	5,200
HEYMAN, Charles (1881-1915) French				
wc/d	1	8,500	8,500	8,500

Name	No.	Price Range	Average	Median
HEYMAN, Hilda Frederika (1872-1955) Danish				
oil	1	1,137	1,137	1,137
HEYMANS, Adriaan Josef (1839-1921) Flemish				
oil	6	478-9,993	3,074	1,445
HEYMANS, Jan Hendrik (1806-1888) Dutch				
oil	1	1,212	1,212	1,212
HEYN, Auguste (1837-1920) German				
oil	1	6,880	6,880	6,880
HEYN, Heinrich Eduard (19th C) German				
oil	2	892-1,665	1,278	892
HEYRAULT, Louis Robert (19th C) French				
oil	1	7,560	7,560	7,560
HEYRMAN, Hugo (1942-) Belgian				
oil	1	5,966	5,966	5,966
HEYSEN, Sir Hans (1877-1968) Australian				
wc/d	1	4,232	4,232	4,232
HEYWORTH, Alfred (1926-1976) British				
oil	2	708-1,305	1,006	708
HIBBARD, A T (1886-1972) American				
oil	2	7,000-10,000	8,500	7,000
HIBBARD, Aldro Thompson (1886-1972) American				
oil	20	4,000-50,000	11,865	9,000
HIBI, Hisako (1907-1991) American/Japanese				
oil	1	1,800	1,800	1,800
HICK, Jacqueline (1920-) Australian				
oil	1	1,593	1,593	1,593
HICKEY, Desmond (20th C) British?				
oil	2	2,249-2,378	2,313	2,249
HICKEY, Patrick (1927-1999) Irish				
oil	3	4,378-7,184	5,870	6,049
wc/d	2	3,741-4,841	4,291	3,741
HICKS, Edward (1780-1849) American				
oil	1	2,800,000	2,800,000	2,800,000
HICKS, George Elgar (1824-1914) British				
oil	5	609-35,000	9,070	3,312
HICKS, Nicola (1960-) British				
wc/d	4	1,134-4,524	2,680	1,325
3D	2	3,680-91,000	47,340	3,680
HICKS, Thomas (1823-1890) American				
oil	1	1,300	1,300	1,300
HIDALGO DE CAVIEDES, Hipolito (1902-1996) Spanish				
oil	5	887-6,600	3,222	3,527
wc/d	2	502-1,411	956	502
HIDALGO DE CAVIEDES, Rafael (1864-1950) Spanish				
oil	2	2,116-7,642	4,879	2,116
HIDALGO Y PADILLA, Felix Resurreccion (1853-1913) Spanish				
wc/d	1	1,267	1,267	1,267
HIDDEMANN, Friedrich Peter (1829-1892) German				
oil	1	5,786	5,786	5,786
HIER, J van (20th C) ?				
oil	1	2,158	2,158	2,158
HIETANEN, Reino (1932-) Finnish				
oil	2	1,403-2,571	1,987	1,403
HIGGINS, George F (1850-1884) American				
oil	4	500-4,250	2,750	2,500
HIGGINS, Victor (1884-1949) American				
oil	4	9,000-160,000	102,250	110,000
HIGGS, Thomas (19th C) British				
oil	1	3,312	3,312	3,312
HIGHAM, Thomas B (20th C) American				
oil	3	1,200-1,400	1,300	1,300
HIGUERO, Enrique Marin (1876-?) Spanish				
oil	1	4,500	4,500	4,500
wc/d	10	569-2,652	1,411	1,145
HIGUET, Georges (1892-1956) Belgian				
oil	1	722	722	722
wc/d	1	586	586	586
HIIRONEN, Eero (1938-) Finnish				
oil	1	1,139	1,139	1,139
HIKOSAKA, Naoyoshi (1946-) Japanese				
oil	1	6,500	6,500	6,500
3D	1	7,000	7,000	7,000

Name	No.	Price Range	Average	Median
HILAIRE, Camille (1916-2004) French				
oil	28	1,864-13,886	5,313	4,772
wc/d	9	608-1,993	1,364	1,414
HILDEBRANDT, Eduard (1818-1869) German				
oil	4	4,545-89,440	26,857	5,845
wc/d	1	2,500	2,500	2,500
HILDEBRANDT, Friedrich Fritz (1819-1885) German				
oil	2	1,518-6,799	4,158	1,518
HILDEBRANDT, Howard Logan (1872-1958) American				
oil	4	425-4,500	1,668	850
HILDER, Richard (1813-1852) British				
oil	2	1,221-2,618	1,919	1,221
HILDER, Rowland (1905-1993) British				
oil	3	957-5,490	2,759	1,830
wc/d	14	491-2,835	1,869	1,700
HILDING, Tommy (1954-) Swedish?				
oil	2	3,563-4,962	4,262	3,563
HILDITCH, George (1803-1857) British				
oil	1	8,550	8,550	8,550
HILGEMANN, Ewerdt (1938-) German				
3D	1	2,121	2,121	2,121
HILGERS, Adolf (1896-1959) German				
oil	1	1,229	1,229	1,229
HILGERS, Carl (1818-1890) German				
oil	12	1,694-11,678	4,993	3,270
HILGERS, Georg (1879-1944) German				
oil	1	1,052	1,052	1,052
HILL, Adrian (1897-1977) British				
oil	2	512-1,030	771	512
wc/d	1	1,870	1,870	1,870
HILL, Anthony (1930-) British				
3D	2	7,280-15,130	11,205	7,280
HILL, Arthur (19th C) British				
oil	5	574-2,750	1,413	1,282
HILL, Berrisford (19/20th C) British				
oil	1	1,750	1,750	1,750
wc/d	1	840	840	840
HILL, Carl Frederik (1849-1911) Swedish				
oil	3	10,990-35,716	25,760	30,575
wc/d	21	529-15,111	4,181	3,614
HILL, David Octavius (1802-1870) British				
oil	1	1,061	1,061	1,061
HILL, Derek (1916-2000) British				
oil	8	2,088-11,160	6,012	3,390
wc/d	1	1,091	1,091	1,091
HILL, Edward (1843-1923) American				
oil	1	1,300	1,300	1,300
HILL, Edward Rufus (1852-c.1908) American				
oil	1	2,100	2,100	2,100
HILL, George Snow (1898-1969) American				
oil	1	1,800	1,800	1,800
HILL, Howard (19th C) American				
oil	3	2,600-5,500	4,533	5,500
HILL, James John (1811-1882) British				
oil	5	1,947-14,000	5,879	4,675
HILL, John Henry (1839-1922) American/British				
wc/d	2	1,200-4,000	2,600	1,200
HILL, John William (1812-1879) American				
wc/d	2	4,000-19,000	11,500	4,000
HILL, Rowland (1915-1979) British				
oil	6	779-3,058	1,664	1,148
wc/d	1	796	796	796
HILL, Rowland Henry (1873-1952) British				
oil	3	963-4,524	2,220	1,175
wc/d	11	696-5,428	2,177	1,619
HILL, Thomas (1829-1908) American				
oil	14	13,000-280,000	44,821	20,000
HILLARD, William H (1888-1951) American				
oil	2	1,600-2,000	1,800	1,600
HILLEGAERT, Pauwels van (c.1596-1640) Dutch				
wc/d	1	2,071	2,071	2,071

Name	No.	Price Range	Average	Median
HILLEMACHER, Eugène Ernest (1818-1887) French				
oil	1	37,699	37,699	37,699
HILLENIUS, Jaap (1934-1999) Dutch				
oil	5	1,512-4,676	2,600	2,356
wc/d	1	596	596	596
HILLER, Heinrich (19th C) German				
oil	5	697-5,096	2,041	1,453
HILLER, Karol (1891-1939) Polish				
wc/d	1	5,890	5,890	5,890
HILLER, Susan (1940-) American				
wc/d	1	4,000	4,000	4,000
HILLERN FLINSCH, Wilhelm von (1884-1986) German				
oil	1	618	618	618
wc/d	2	648-1,060	854	648
HILLERSBERG, Lars (1937-) Swedish				
oil	1	2,417	2,417	2,417
wc/d	2	891-3,436	2,163	891
HILLESTROM, Carl Peter (1760-1812) Swedish				
oil	1	2,493	2,493	2,493
wc/d	1	8,918	8,918	8,918
HILLESTROM, Per (1733-1816) Swedish				
oil	5	9,616-369,452	89,056	26,100
HILLIARD, William Henry (1836-1905) American				
oil	12	950-14,000	2,706	1,500
HILLIER, H Deacon (19th C) British				
oil	2	4,350-8,142	6,246	4,350
wc/d	1	588	588	588
HILLIER, Tristram (1905-1983) British				
oil	5	6,954-38,060	21,946	18,130
HILLINGFORD, Robert Alexander (1825-1904) British				
oil	3	1,052-2,112	1,495	1,323
HILLS, Anna A (1882-1930) American				
oil	12	1,800-32,500	10,691	5,000
wc/d	3	1,200-2,750	1,783	1,400
HILLS, Laura Coombs (1859-1952) American				
wc/d	8	4,500-30,000	10,343	7,000
HILLS, Robert (1769-1844) British				
wc/d	3	525-2,832	1,365	740
HILLYARD, J W (19th C) British				
oil	1	6,438	6,438	6,438
HILMAR, Jiri (1937-) Czechoslovakian				
wc/d	1	1,272	1,272	1,272
HILTON, John William (1904-1983) American				
oil	8	2,250-4,250	3,000	2,750
HILTON, Roger (1911-1975) British				
oil	5	1,056-29,240	9,890	7,500
wc/d	19	452-35,910	4,190	1,830
HILTON, Rose (1931-) British				
oil	11	616-9,256	2,339	1,218
HILTUNEN, Eila (1922-2003) Finnish				
3D	3	3,273-32,795	15,346	9,971
HILVERDINK, Eduard Alexander (1846-1891) Dutch				
oil	3	2,411-12,123	7,935	9,271
HILVERDINK, Johannes (1813-1902) Dutch				
oil	1	3,747	3,747	3,747
HILZ, Sepp (20th C) German				
oil	3	2,180-4,844	3,275	2,803
wc/d	3	1,168-2,336	1,635	1,401
HINCKLEY, Thomas H (1813-1896) American				
oil	2	4,250-8,000	6,125	4,250
HIND, Frank (fl.1884-1904) British				
oil	1	1,800	1,800	1,800
HIND, William George Richardson (1833-1888) Canadian				
wc/d	1	1,814	1,814	1,814
HINDLIP, Lord (1940-) British				
wc/d	1	3,680	3,680	3,680
HINDS, Will (20th C) American				
oil	3	815-2,500	1,905	2,400
HINE, Henry George (1811-1895) British				
wc/d	4	1,012-2,775	2,053	2,213
HINES, Jack (20th C) American				
oil	1	8,000	8,000	8,000

Name	No.	Price Range	Average	Median
HINES, Theodore (fl.1876-1889) British				
oil	10	455-3,600	1,335	800
HINKLE, Clarence Keiser (1880-1960) American				
oil	3	4,000-65,000	24,600	4,800
wc/d	1	7,000	7,000	7,000
HINMAN, Charles (1932-) American				
oil	1	2,200	2,200	2,200
HINTERMEISTER, Henry (1897-1972) American				
oil	6	496-7,250	3,774	3,500
HINTERREITER, Hans (1902-1989) Swiss				
oil	2	8,158-12,177	10,167	8,158
wc/d	1	2,664	2,664	2,664
HINTNER, Cornelius (19/20th C) German?				
oil	1	5,482	5,482	5,482
HINTZ, Julius (1805-1862) German				
oil	1	3,503	3,503	3,503
HINZ, Johann Georg (1630-1688) German				
oil	4	20,566-31,140	25,225	24,196
HINZ, Volker (1947-) German				
oil	1	3,307	3,307	3,307
HIOLLE, Ernest Eugène (1834-1886) French				
3D	1	9,450	9,450	9,450
HIOS, Theo (1910-) American				
oil	2	1,870-2,400	2,135	1,870
HIPS, Phil (fl.1910-1940) British				
oil	1	1,380	1,380	1,380
HIQUILY, Philippe (1925-) French				
wc/d	1	716	716	716
3D	6	9,074-34,028	22,028	18,123
HIRAKAWA, Isamu (1921-) Japanese				
oil	7	760-3,933	2,149	2,281
HIREMY-HIRSCHL, Adolph (1860-1933) Hungarian				
oil	1	1,274	1,274	1,274
HIRN, Jean Georges (1777-1839) French				
oil	1	15,811	15,811	15,811
HIRNBRAND (19th C) ?				
oil	1	18,061	18,061	18,061
HIROSHIGE and HOKUSAI (19th C) Japanese				
wc/d	1	1,665	1,665	1,665
HIRSCH, Alphonse (1843-1884) French				
oil	1	9,500	9,500	9,500
wc/d	1	650	650	650
HIRSCH, Auguste Alexandre (1833-1912) French				
oil	2	27,351-73,600	50,475	27,351
HIRSCH, Joseph (1910-1981) American				
oil	2	1,800-6,079	3,939	1,800
wc/d	4	400-850	537	400
HIRSCH, Stefan (1899-1964) American				
oil	1	100,000	100,000	100,000
HIRSCHBERG, Carl (1854-1923) American				
oil	1	1,530	1,530	1,530
HIRSCHEL, Caspar (1698-1743) German				
oil	1	9,926	9,926	9,926
HIRSCHENAUER, Max (1885-1955) Austrian				
oil	4	934-1,671	1,322	1,051
HIRSCHFELD, Al (1903-2003) American				
wc/d	11	800-10,000	4,554	3,400
HIRSCHHORN, Thomas (1957-) Swiss				
3D	3	2,800-42,000	16,066	3,400
HIRSCHMANN, Johann Leonhard (1672-1750) German				
oil	1	12,041	12,041	12,041
HIRSCHMANN, Sophie (1871-1937) Dutch				
oil	1	4,500	4,500	4,500
HIRSCHVOGEL (1966-) German				
wc/d	2	2,356-2,827	2,591	2,356
HIRSHFIELD, Morris (1872-1946) American				
oil	1	50,000	50,000	50,000
HIRST, Claude Raguet (1855-1942) American				
oil	2	30,000-40,000	35,000	30,000

Name	No.	Price Range	Average	Median
HIRST, Damien (1965-) British				
oil	28	3,949-1,500,000	297,870	210,000
wc/d	5	1,062-28,000	12,020	8,496
3D	6	280,000-3,000,000	1,012,583	570,000
HIRT, Friedrich Wilhelm (1721-1772) German				
oil	2	1,920-9,576	5,748	1,920
HIRT, Heinrich (1841-1902) German				
oil	1	8,500	8,500	8,500
HIRT, Marthe (1890-1985) Swiss				
oil	5	546-1,549	1,161	1,311
HIRT, Michael Conrad (c.1615-1695) German				
oil	1	21,052	21,052	21,052
HIRTH DU FRENES, Rudolf (1846-1916) German				
oil	5	885-2,983	1,951	2,028
wc/d	2	605-1,013	809	605
HIRTZ, Lucien (1864-1928) French				
oil	1	16,470	16,470	16,470
HIS, René Charles Edmond (1877-1960) French				
oil	10	603-8,256	4,247	4,472
HISCHEN, Ernst (fl.1886-1901) German				
3D	1	2,675	2,675	2,675
HISCOCK, Keith (20th C) Canadian				
oil	7	456-3,164	1,345	1,012
HISCOX, George (1840-1909) British				
oil	1	2,478	2,478	2,478
HISLOP, Margaret Ross (1894-1972) British				
oil	4	865-2,768	1,772	1,211
wc/d	1	637	637	637
HITCHCOCK, D Howard (1861-1943) American				
oil	3	17,000-70,000	35,666	20,000
HITCHCOCK, George (1850-1913) American				
wc/d	4	400-1,740	1,072	850
HITCHCOCK, Harold (1914-) British				
oil	1	684	684	684
wc/d	3	557-1,218	823	696
HITCHENS, Ivon (1893-1979) British				
oil	27	20,350-166,320	66,469	56,700
wc/d	2	498-1,239	868	498
HITCHENS, John (1940-) British				
oil	5	460-2,992	1,162	801
wc/d	1	534	534	534
HITCHENS, Joseph (1838-1893) American				
oil	1	4,750	4,750	4,750
HITTELL, Charles Joseph (1861-1938) American				
oil	1	3,750	3,750	3,750
HITZLER, Franz (1946-) German				
oil	8	588-3,343	1,284	707
wc/d	2	648-1,532	1,090	648
HITZLER, Franz and STURM, Helmut (20th C) German				
oil	1	1,549	1,549	1,549
HIXON, James Thompson (1636-1868) British				
oil	1	3,480	3,480	3,480
HJELM, Fanny (1858-1944) Swedish				
oil	1	2,243	2,243	2,243
HJERTEN, Sigrid (1885-1948) Swedish				
oil	20	2,926-254,795	58,138	27,991
wc/d	5	396-5,344	2,887	2,379
HJORTH, Bror (1894-1968) Swedish				
oil	2	52,166-145,360	98,763	52,166
wc/d	3	449-6,607	2,586	702
3D	5	1,718-4,757	2,748	1,718
HJORTH-NIELSEN, Soren (1901-1983) Danish				
oil	9	415-9,014	3,306	2,323
HJORTZBERG, Olle (1872-1959) Swedish				
oil	21	520-83,796	14,695	5,195
wc/d	11	390-3,572	1,247	1,171
HLAVACEK, Anton (1842-1926) Austrian				
oil	2	832-2,906	1,869	832
wc/d	1	963	963	963
HLINA, Ladislav (1947-) German				
3D	1	5,462	5,462	5,462
HLITO, Alfredo (1923-1993) Argentinian				
oil	1	17,000	17,000	17,000

Name	No.	Price Range	Average	Median
HOAD, Jeremiah (1924-1999) Irish?				
oil	1	1,091	1,091	1,091
HOAR, Steve (20th C) Canadian				
3D	1	3,464	3,464	3,464
HOARE, William (1706-1799) British				
oil	1	6,372	6,372	6,372
HOBART, Clark (1868-1948) American				
oil	2	3,250-16,000	9,625	3,250
HOBBEMA, Meindert (1638-1709) Dutch				
oil	3	69,200-3,500,000	1,216,099	79,097
HOBBS, George T (1846-1929) American				
oil	1	1,000	1,000	1,000
HOBBY, Jess (20th C) American				
oil	2	3,250-4,250	3,750	3,250
HOBDELL, Roy (1911-1961) British				
oil	2	920-1,288	1,104	920
wc/d	7	773-1,472	1,085	1,012
HOBERMAN, Nicky (1967-) South African				
oil	4	2,580-7,040	4,491	3,872
HOBSON, Henry E (fl.1857-1866) British				
oil	1	3,460	3,460	3,460
wc/d	1	696	696	696
HOCH, Franz Xaver (1869-1916) German				
oil	1	1,432	1,432	1,432
HOCH, Hannah (1889-1979) German				
oil	5	4,320-21,082	13,430	14,651
wc/d	18	742-8,247	3,369	2,544
HOCH, Johann Jakob (1750-1829) German				
wc/d	1	1,440	1,440	1,440
HOCHARD, Gaston (1863-1913) French				
oil	1	1,500	1,500	1,500
HOCHECKER, Franz (1730-1782) German				
oil	2	9,678-10,888	10,283	9,678
HOCK, Daniel (1858-1934) Austrian				
oil	1	4,500	4,500	4,500
HOCKELMANN, Antonius (1937-) German				
oil	4	1,885-18,849	7,222	2,421
wc/d	6	547-7,644	2,691	547
3D	4	1,911-7,068	4,169	3,695
HOCKNER, Rudolf (1864-1942) German				
oil	12	504-6,049	1,900	1,440
HOCKNEY, David (1937-) British				
oil	8	37,620-4,810,000	1,176,277	194,700
wc/d	32	1,197-350,000	53,154	22,000
3D	1	25,000	25,000	25,000
HOD, Edmund (fl.1871-1886) Austrian				
oil	1	1,818	1,818	1,818
HOD, Nir (1970-) Israeli				
oil	1	40,000	40,000	40,000
HODE, Pierre (1889-1942) French				
oil	6	5,397-46,124	16,432	5,828
HODGES, Jim (1957-) American				
wc/d	2	8,000-50,000	29,000	8,000
HODGES, William (1744-1797) British				
oil	1	17,100	17,100	17,100
HODGES, William Merrett (fl.1896-1938) British				
oil	1	1,392	1,392	1,392
HODGKIN, Eliot (1905-1987) British				
oil	12	830-22,490	8,906	9,450
wc/d	1	696	696	696
HODGKIN, Howard (1932-) British				
oil	4	102,080-350,000	205,520	111,000
wc/d	3	5,605-11,100	7,726	6,475
HODGKINS, Frances (1869-1947) New Zealander				
wc/d	1	10,620	10,620	10,620
HODGSON, John Evan (1831-1895) British				
oil	1	27,600	27,600	27,600
wc/d	1	498	498	498
HODICKE, Karl Horst (1938-) German				
oil	1	34,397	34,397	34,397

Name	No.	Price Range	Average	Median
HODIENER, Hugo (1886-c.1935) German				
oil	2	1,033-3,200	2,116	1,033
wc/d	1	1,440	1,440	1,440
HODINOS, Emile Josome (1853-1905) ?				
wc/d	13	1,029-6,171	3,423	3,270
HODLER, Ferdinand (1853-1918) Swiss				
oil	11	608-3,589,474	961,000	114,159
wc/d	35	568-28,833	5,287	3,671
HODSON, John (1945-) British				
3D	1	3,906	3,906	3,906
HODSON, Samuel John (1836-1908) British				
wc/d	2	1,168-4,070	2,619	1,168
HOEBER, Arthur (1854-1915) American				
oil	2	850-8,500	4,675	850
wc/d	1	1,400	1,400	1,400
HOECKE, Caspar van den (1595-1648) Flemish				
oil	1	2,338	2,338	2,338
HOECKE, Robert van den (1622-1668) Flemish				
oil	1	10,581	10,581	10,581
HOECKER, Paul (1854-1910) German				
oil	1	1,708	1,708	1,708
HOEF, A van der (17th C) Dutch				
oil	1	5,839	5,839	5,839
HOEF, Abraham van der (fl.1613-1649) Dutch				
oil	2	11,094-12,740	11,917	11,094
HOEFFLER, Adolf (1826-1898) German				
oil	1	3,750	3,750	3,750
HOEGEL, Mina (1849-1929) Austrian				
oil	1	1,296	1,296	1,296
HOEGG, Joseph (1826-?) German				
oil	1	9,633	9,633	9,633
HOEHME, Gerhard (1920-1990) German				
oil	10	1,320-166,315	27,815	8,905
wc/d	14	1,060-6,479	2,454	2,003
HOEHN, Alfred (1875-?) German				
oil	2	606-2,027	1,316	606
HOEHN, Georg (1812-1879) German				
oil	1	16,857	16,857	16,857
HOEK, Hans van (1947-) Dutch				
wc/d	1	1,178	1,178	1,178
HOENIGSMANN, Rela (1865-?) German				
oil	2	1,632-1,909	1,770	1,632
wc/d	1	477	477	477
HOERLE, Heinrich (1895-1936) German				
oil	1	12,740	12,740	12,740
wc/d	3	1,978-2,592	2,372	2,548
HOERMAN, Carl (1885-1955) American				
oil	5	1,000-4,500	2,680	2,750
HOESE, Jean de la (1846-1917) Belgian				
oil	2	1,204-1,890	1,547	1,204
HOET, Gerard (elder) (1648-1733) Dutch				
oil	2	12,460-22,200	17,330	12,460
wc/d	1	2,102	2,102	2,102
HOET, Gerard (younger) (1698-1760) Dutch				
oil	1	10,175	10,175	10,175
HOETERICKX, Émile (1858-1923) Belgian				
wc/d	1	1,432	1,432	1,432
HOETGER, Bernhard (1874-1949) German				
wc/d	1	825	825	825
3D	7	1,753-9,405	5,437	4,938
HOEVENAAR, Cornelis Willem (elder) (1802-1873) Dutch				
oil	1	1,640	1,640	1,640
HOEYDONCK, Paul van (1925-) Belgian				
oil	3	718-5,980	2,671	1,316
wc/d	5	897-1,850	1,179	989
3D	4	1,908-3,973	2,487	2,035
HOFER, August (1899-1981) Austrian				
oil	4	2,297-3,038	2,650	2,458
HOFER, Heinrich (1825-1878) German				
oil	1	2,724	2,724	2,724

Name	No.	Price Range	Average	Median
HOFER, Karl (1878-1955) German				
oil	29	7,493-157,250	49,862	38,163
wc/d	14	1,414-16,537	5,276	3,000
HOFF, Adrianus Johannes van (1893-1939) Dutch				
oil	3	667-2,061	1,172	788
wc/d	2	546-1,030	788	546
HOFF, Carl Heinrich (elder) (1838-1890) German				
oil	1	28,000	28,000	28,000
HOFF, Margo (1912-) American				
oil	1	2,100	2,100	2,100
wc/d	1	2,000	2,000	2,000
HOFF, Syd (1912-) American				
wc/d	1	1,100	1,100	1,100
HOFFBAUER, Charles (1875-1957) French				
oil	4	2,200-95,000	49,925	22,500
wc/d	1	1,000	1,000	1,000
HOFFMAN, Frank B (1888-1958) American				
oil	12	1,000-47,500	12,691	7,500
HOFFMAN, Harry Leslie (1871-1964) American				
oil	2	1,600-5,000	3,300	1,600
HOFFMAN, Malvina (1887-1966) American				
3D	18	1,700-38,000	7,335	4,200
HOFFMANN (?) ?				
oil	1	2,432	2,432	2,432
HOFFMANN, Anker (1904-1985) Danish				
3D	4	1,699-1,812	1,765	1,771
HOFFMANN, Anton (1863-1938) German				
oil	3	643-1,414	1,017	995
wc/d	1	545	545	545
HOFFMANN, Eduardo (1957-) Argentinian				
oil	1	22,000	22,000	22,000
HOFFMANN, Hans (?-c.1591) German				
wc/d	1	1,480,000	1,480,000	1,480,000
HOFFMANN, Heinrich (19th C) German				
oil	1	1,824	1,824	1,824
HOFFMANN, Hubert (20th C) ?				
wc/d	1	10,000	10,000	10,000
HOFFMANN, J F (19th C) ?				
oil	1	6,042	6,042	6,042
HOFFMANN, Josef (1831-1904) Austrian				
oil	1	1,665	1,665	1,665
wc/d	1	2,088	2,088	2,088
HOFFMANN, Nicolaus (1740-1823) German				
wc/d	1	1,094	1,094	1,094
HOFFMANN, O (20th C) ?				
3D	1	8,269	8,269	8,269
HOFFMANN, Oskar Adolfovitch (1851-1913) Russian				
oil	4	2,027-18,696	8,565	4,055
HOFFMANN, Otto (1885-1915) German				
3D	1	1,844	1,844	1,844
HOFFMANN, Samuel (1592-1648) Swiss				
oil	1	2,548	2,548	2,548
HOFFMEISTER, C L (19th C) Austrian				
oil	2	15,205-33,123	24,164	15,205
HOFKER, Willem Gerard (1902-1981) Dutch				
wc/d	5	454-2,288	1,451	1,528
HOFKUNST, Alfred (1942-2004) Austrian				
oil	1	10,548	10,548	10,548
wc/d	3	1,010-4,169	2,808	3,246
HOFLAND, Thomas Richard (1816-1876) British				
oil	1	4,675	4,675	4,675
HOFLEHNER, Rudolf (1916-1995) Austrian				
wc/d	1	1,753	1,753	1,753
HOFMAN, A (20th C) Dutch?				
oil	1	2,569	2,569	2,569
HOFMANN, Hans (1880-1966) American/German				
oil	9	19,000-1,400,000	376,531	160,000
wc/d	12	6,000-33,123	22,176	19,000
HOFMANN, Johann Michael F H (1824-1911) German				
oil	1	10,510	10,510	10,510

Name	No.	Price Range	Average	Median
HOFMANN, Ludwig von (1861-1945) German				
oil	6	884-69,920	33,797	11,192
wc/d	9	478-46,000	6,497	841
HOFMEISTER, Johannes (1914-1990) Danish				
oil	12	1,699-8,370	3,544	2,986
HOFNER, Johann Baptist (1832-1913) German				
oil	1	2,827	2,827	2,827
HOGART, George H (19th C) American				
oil	1	2,300	2,300	2,300
HOGARTH, Burne (20th C) American				
wc/d	1	2,200	2,200	2,200
HOGE, Oscar (20th C) ?				
wc/d	1	1,818	1,818	1,818
HOGENDORPS JACOB, Adrienne Jacqueline van (1857-1920) Dutch				
oil	1	1,951	1,951	1,951
HOGER, Rudolf A (1877-1930) Austrian				
oil	2	3,138-9,159	6,148	3,138
HOGERWAARD, Frans (1882-1921) Dutch				
oil	1	2,303	2,303	2,303
HOGFELDT, Robert (1894-1986) Swedish				
oil	2	1,648-2,061	1,854	1,648
wc/d	7	496-5,632	3,254	3,241
HOGFORD, A (19th C) British?				
oil	1	2,250	2,250	2,250
HOGGAN, Jack (20th C) British				
oil	8	1,190-7,120	3,892	1,601
HOGGATT, William (1880-1961) British				
oil	3	1,730-6,300	3,426	2,249
wc/d	3	835-3,201	1,751	1,218
HOGLER, Franz (1802-1855) Austrian				
3D	1	16,473	16,473	16,473
HOGUE, Alexandre (1898-1994) American				
oil	1	3,250	3,250	3,250
HOGUET, Charles (1821-1870) French				
oil	1	4,123	4,123	4,123
HOGUET, Louis (1825-?) German				
oil	1	2,040	2,040	2,040
HOHENBERG, Rosa (19/20th C) German				
oil	1	5,959	5,959	5,959
HOHENBERGER, Enrico (1843-1897) Italian				
oil	3	1,757-4,114	3,242	3,857
HOHERMANN, Alice (1902-1943) Polish				
wc/d	2	630-1,449	1,039	630
HOHLENBERG, Johannes Edouard (1881-1960) Danish				
oil	1	2,606	2,606	2,606
HOHNSTEDT, Peter Lanz (1872-1957) American				
oil	8	550-5,000	2,206	2,000
HOIN, Claude (1750-1817) French				
wc/d	1	1,308	1,308	1,308
HOKE, Giselbert (1927-) Austrian				
wc/d	5	1,757-7,071	5,379	5,856
HOKUSAI, Katsushika (1760-1849) Japanese				
wc/d	1	37,000	37,000	37,000
HOLBECH, N P (1804-1889) Danish				
oil	2	1,448-1,533	1,490	1,448
HOLCK, Julius (1845-1911) Norwegian				
oil	1	1,868	1,868	1,868
HOLD, Abel (1815-1891) British				
oil	3	865-1,424	1,068	915
HOLD, B L (?) ?				
oil	1	1,376	1,376	1,376
HOLD, Tom (19th C) British				
oil	2	1,305-2,408	1,856	1,305
HOLDER, Edward Henry (fl.1864-1917) British				
oil	10	552-2,392	1,290	1,012
HOLDER, Edwin (fl.1856-1864) British				
oil	1	4,900	4,900	4,900
HOLDER, Henry Wharrey (19th C) British				
oil	1	2,852	2,852	2,852
HOLDER, William (20th C) Canadian				
wc/d	1	1,013	1,013	1,013

Name	No.	Price Range	Average	Median
HOLDING, Henry James (1833-1872) British				
oil	1	8,304	8,304	8,304
wc/d	1	528	528	528
HOLDREDGE, Ransome G (1836-1899) American				
oil	9	425-12,000	4,497	3,500
HOLDSTOCK, Alfred Worsley (1820-1901) Canadian				
wc/d	2	1,322-5,289	3,305	1,322
HOLE, William B (1846-1917) British				
oil	1	33,440	33,440	33,440
HOLENSTEIN, Werner (1932-) Swiss				
oil	1	2,918	2,918	2,918
HOLGATE, Edwin Headley (1892-1977) Canadian				
oil	4	882-44,313	18,998	14,588
wc/d	6	577-33,235	7,979	1,956
HOLGATE, Thomas W (fl.1899-1910) British				
oil	1	3,366	3,366	3,366
HOLIDAY, Gilbert (1879-1937) British				
oil	1	4,440	4,440	4,440
wc/d	1	648	648	648
HOLIDAY, Henry (1839-1927) British				
wc/d	2	1,044-4,002	2,523	1,044
HOLL, Frank (1845-1888) British				
oil	2	1,672-29,580	15,626	1,672
HOLL, Werner (1898-1984) German				
oil	1	1,060	1,060	1,060
HOLLAENDER, Alphons (1845-1923) German				
oil	3	1,903-10,813	4,918	2,040
HOLLAMS, F M (1877-1963) British				
oil	2	1,323-1,691	1,507	1,323
HOLLAMS, F Mabel (1877-1963) British				
oil	16	865-12,285	2,830	2,079
wc/d	1	496	496	496
HOLLAND, Harry (1941-) British				
oil	2	2,941-3,806	3,373	2,941
HOLLAND, J (18/19th C) British				
oil	1	2,944	2,944	2,944
HOLLAND, James (1800-1870) British				
oil	5	775-4,597	2,278	2,208
wc/d	11	550-7,785	3,088	2,236
HOLLAND, John (18/19th C) British				
oil	1	700	700	700
wc/d	1	1,134	1,134	1,134
HOLLAND, John (snr) (fl.1831-1879) British				
oil	3	1,380-30,000	11,148	2,064
HOLLAND, Sebastopol Samuel (fl.1877-1911) British				
oil	3	534-3,969	2,114	1,840
HOLLAND, Sylvia (20th C) American				
wc/d	1	1,500	1,500	1,500
HOLLANDER, Hendrik (1823-1884) Dutch				
oil	2	1,500-2,788	2,144	1,500
HOLLAR, Wencelaus (1606-1677) Hungarian				
wc/d	1	8,370	8,370	8,370
HOLLEBEKE, Karin (20th C) American				
oil	1	5,000	5,000	5,000
HOLLEGHA, Wolfgang (1929-) Austrian				
oil	2	19,421-36,000	27,710	19,421
wc/d	1	849	849	849
HOLLENBERG, Felix (1868-1946) German				
oil	1	7,014	7,014	7,014
HOLLENSTEIN, Stephanie (1886-1944) Austrian				
oil	1	5,856	5,856	5,856
HOLLESTELLE, Jacob (1858-1920) Dutch				
oil	1	1,145	1,145	1,145
wc/d	1	1,134	1,134	1,134
HOLLINGSWORTH, Alvin Carl (1928-1000) American				
oil	2	1,900-2,400	2,150	1,900
wc/d	1	4,000	4,000	4,000
HOLLINGSWORTH, William R (1910-1944) American				
wc/d	2	4,500-7,500	6,000	4,500
HOLLOWAY, Charles Edward (1838-1897) British				
oil	1	1,288	1,288	1,288

Name	No.	Price Range	Average	Median
HOLLOWAY, Edward Stratton (?-1939) American				
oil	1	4,750	4,750	4,750
HOLLYER, Eva (1865-1948) British				
oil	1	1,440	1,440	1,440
HOLLYER, W P (1834-1922) British				
oil	3	1,000-2,510	1,552	1,148
HOLM, Anders (1770-1828) Swedish				
oil	4	1,496-3,988	2,531	1,620
HOLM, Frederik (1882-?) Danish				
oil	1	1,052	1,052	1,052
HOLM, H G F (1803-1861) Danish				
wc/d	1	5,715	5,715	5,715
HOLM, P C and PETERSEN, H (19th C) Danish/German				
oil	1	2,747	2,747	2,747
HOLM, Peder (1798-1875) Danish				
oil	1	1,056	1,056	1,056
HOLM, Per Daniel (1835-1903) Swedish				
oil	4	756-2,612	1,497	859
HOLM, Peter Christian and PETERSEN, Lorenz (19th C) Danish/German				
oil	1	3,086	3,086	3,086
HOLMAN, Arthur Stearns (1926-) American				
oil	1	4,750	4,750	4,750
HOLMAN, Francis (1729-1790) British				
oil	2	49,140-70,000	59,570	49,140
HOLMBERG, August (1851-1911) German				
oil	1	1,574	1,574	1,574
HOLMBOE, Thorolf (1866-1935) Norwegian				
oil	2	1,068-2,200	1,634	1,068
HOLMES, B (?) ?				
oil	1	2,640	2,640	2,640
HOLMES, Dwight (1900-1988) American				
oil	7	500-3,000	1,735	1,600
HOLMES, Frank (1938-) American				
oil	1	3,000	3,000	3,000
HOLMES, John J (20th C) British				
oil	4	657-2,431	1,613	1,309
HOLMES, Kenneth (1902-) British				
wc/d	2	1,144-1,575	1,359	1,144
HOLMES, Ralph (1876-1963) American				
oil	11	400-4,750	2,254	2,500
HOLMES, Walter (20th C) European				
oil	1	481	481	481
wc/d	2	1,073-1,702	1,387	1,073
HOLMLUND, Josephina (1827-1905) Swedish				
oil	14	522-2,991	1,808	2,013
HOLMSTEDT, J (19/20th C) Scandinavian				
oil	1	1,824	1,824	1,824
HOLMSTEDT, Johann (1851-1929) Swedish				
oil	4	964-5,160	2,637	1,189
HOLMSTRAND, Cajsa (1951-) Swedish				
oil	2	777-1,527	1,152	777
HOLMSTRÖM, Tora Vega (1880-1967) Swedish				
oil	4	1,145-2,239	1,656	1,586
wc/d	1	529	529	529
HOLROYD, Newman (fl.1906-1914) British				
oil	1	3,696	3,696	3,696
HOLSBEEK, Albert van (1877-1948) Belgian				
oil	1	1,110	1,110	1,110
HOLSCHER, Constantin (1861-1921) German				
oil	1	13,357	13,357	13,357
HOLSCHER, Theo (1895-?) German				
oil	1	3,534	3,534	3,534
HOLSOE, Carl (1863-1935) Danish				
oil	24	1,618-229,315	30,086	16,503
HOLSOE, Niels (1865-1928) Danish				
oil	3	815-3,480	2,029	1,793
HOLST, Johan Gustaf von (1841-1917) Swedish				
oil	5	608-8,475	2,952	1,371
HOLST, Johannes (1880-1965) German				
oil	13	937-11,342	5,956	5,797

Name	No.	Price Range	Average	Median
HOLST, Laurits (1848-1934) Danish				
oil	2	865-1,757	1,311	865
HOLST, Theodore von (1810-1844) British				
oil	1	8,280	8,280	8,280
HOLSTAYN, Josef (20th C) German				
oil	2	12,740-15,653	14,196	12,740
HOLSTEIN, Bent (1942-) Danish				
oil	3	1,051-1,051	1,051	1,051
HOLSTEIN, Gustav (1876-?) Russian				
oil	1	1,106	1,106	1,106
HOLSTER, Jacoba Wilhelmina (1818-1891) Dutch				
wc/d	1	1,147	1,147	1,147
HOLSTEYN, Cornelis (1618-1658) Dutch				
oil	1	9,342	9,342	9,342
HOLSTEYN, Pieter (elder) (1580-1662) Dutch				
wc/d	1	1,514	1,514	1,514
HOLSTEYN, Pieter (younger) (1614-1687) Flemish				
wc/d	6	1,518-25,691	8,489	3,970
HOLT, Edwin Frederick (fl.1864-1897) British				
oil	6	875-40,000	8,100	1,401
HOLTY, Carl (1900-1973) American				
oil	4	2,050-7,500	5,200	4,750
wc/d	1	450	450	450
HOLTZMANN, Carl Friedrich (1740-1811) German				
wc/d	1	1,540	1,540	1,540
HOLWECK, Oskar (1924-) German				
3D	1	4,560	4,560	4,560
HOLY, Adrien (1898-1978) Swiss				
oil	7	516-1,518	984	811
wc/d	1	833	833	833
HOLZ, Albert (1884-1954) German				
oil	2	937-1,089	1,013	937
HOLZ, Johann Daniel (1867-1945) German				
oil	6	502-2,188	1,413	1,219
HOLZ, Paul (1883-1938) German				
wc/d	1	1,908	1,908	1,908
HOLZEL, Adolf (1853-1934) German				
oil	1	29,281	29,281	29,281
wc/d	11	2,719-20,354	8,325	6,584
HOLZER, Adi (1936-) Austrian?				
oil	1	6,630	6,630	6,630
HOLZER, Brigitte (?) German				
oil	1	1,824	1,824	1,824
HOLZER, Jenny (1950-) American				
oil	1	8,000	8,000	8,000
3D	7	5,920-60,000	31,912	35,000
HOLZHANDLER, Dora (1928-) British/French				
oil	1	609	609	609
wc/d	1	522	522	522
HOLZHAUER, Emil Eugen (1887-1986) American				
oil	1	5,000	5,000	5,000
wc/d	1	1,600	1,600	1,600
HOLZMAN, Shimshon (1907-1986) Israeli				
oil	8	480-6,500	1,438	500
wc/d	1	450	450	450
HOLZMEISTER, Clemens (1886-1983) Austrian				
wc/d	1	4,442	4,442	4,442
HOM, Poul (1905-1994) Danish				
oil	2	2,197-3,248	2,722	2,197
HOME, Robert (1752-1834) British				
oil	1	11,382	11,382	11,382
HOMITZKY, Peter (20th C) ?				
oil	1	1,200	1,200	1,200
HOMMET, Raimond (20th C) French				
oil	1	2,386	2,386	2,386
HONDECOETER, Gillis Claesz de (1570-1638) Dutch				
oil	6	3,560-31,140	13,371	7,049
HONDECOETER, Gysbert Gillisz de (1604-1653) Dutch				
oil	1	92,500	92,500	92,500
HONDECOETER, Melchior de (1636-1695) Dutch				
oil	3	56,108-350,000	158,702	70,000

Name	No.	Price Range	Average	Median
HONDIUS, Abraham (1625-1695) Dutch				
oil	5	1,438-101,750	30,873	17,208
HONDT, Lambert de (17th C) Flemish				
oil	1	10,208	10,208	10,208
HONE, David (20th C) British				
oil	4	1,296-8,482	4,692	3,629
HONE, Evie (1894-1955) Irish				
wc/d	14	872-35,288	6,356	4,241
HONE, Nathaniel I (1718-1784) British				
oil	1	12,090	12,090	12,090
HONE, Nathaniel II (1831-1917) Irish				
oil	14	4,712-89,280	23,610	12,744
wc/d	10	484-2,805	1,168	1,020
HONEDER, Walter (1906-) Austrian				
oil	2	1,757-2,061	1,909	1,757
wc/d	2	1,030-1,940	1,485	1,030
HONEGGER, Gottfried (1917-) Swiss				
oil	6	1,967-22,449	11,310	10,423
wc/d	1	1,435	1,435	1,435
3D	2	2,119-4,463	3,291	2,119
HONG JI-YEUN (20th C) Korean				
oil	2	6,000-7,500	6,750	6,000
HONG KYONG TACK (1968-) Korean				
oil	1	35,000	35,000	35,000
HONICH, Heinrich (1875-1957) German				
oil	1	1,832	1,832	1,832
HONIGBERGER, Ernst (1885-1976) German				
oil	3	2,299-3,273	2,839	2,945
wc/d	1	942	942	942
HONNORAT, Ernest (19/20th C) French				
oil	1	1,390	1,390	1,390
HONOLD, Konrad (1918-) German				
oil	1	3,296	3,296	3,296
HONTA, Renée (1894-1955) Irish				
oil	1	2,249	2,249	2,249
HONTHORST, Gerrit van (1590-1656) Dutch				
oil	2	38,531-205,214	121,872	38,531
HOOCH, Charles Cornelisz de (?-1638) Dutch				
oil	1	9,342	9,342	9,342
HOOCH, Horatius de (17th C) Dutch				
oil	1	20,000	20,000	20,000
HOOCH, Pieter de (1629-1681) Dutch				
oil	1	157,250	157,250	157,250
HOOD, John (18th C) British				
wc/d	1	1,914	1,914	1,914
HOODLESS, Harry (1913-1997) British				
oil	1	4,070	4,070	4,070
HOOG, Bernard de (1867-1943) Dutch				
oil	10	1,682-16,069	6,879	4,872
HOOG, Birger (1899-1929) Swedish				
oil	2	1,404-3,563	2,483	1,404
HOOGERHEYDEN, Engel (1740-1809) German				
oil	1	4,822	4,822	4,822
HOOGSTEYNS, Jan (1935-) Belgian				
oil	1	1,656	1,656	1,656
HOOGSTRATEN, Samuel van (1627-1678) Flemish				
oil	2	14,013-44,376	29,194	14,013
HOOK, George van (20th C) American				
oil	1	2,600	2,600	2,600
HOOK, James Clarke (1819-1907) British				
oil	1	12,603	12,603	12,603
HOOK, Walter (1919-1989) American				
oil	1	6,000	6,000	6,000
HOOM, van (19/20th C) Dutch				
oil	1	1,600	1,600	1,600
HOOPER, John Horace (fl.1877-1899) British				
oil	6	595-6,090	2,654	2,050
HOOPLE, Warner (20th C) American				
wc/d	1	10,000	10,000	10,000
HOOPSTAD, Elisabeth Iosetta (1787-1847) Dutch				
oil	1	1,844	1,844	1,844

Name	No.	Price Range	Average	Median
HOORDE, Gustave van (19/20th C) Belgian				
oil	1	2,000 ·	2,000	2,000
HOOWY, Jan (1907-1987) Dutch				
oil	2	606-667	636	606
wc/d	1	606	606	606
HOPE, James (1818-1892) American				
oil	2	3,500-3,800	3,650	3,500
HOPE, Robert (1869-1936) British				
oil	4	589-7,120	3,474	1,141
HOPFGARTEN, August Ferdinand (1807-1896) German				
wc/d	1	1,145	1,145	1,145
HOPKIN, Robert (1832-1909) American				
oil	4	650-3,250	1,787	850
wc/d	1	1,200	1,200	1,200
HOPKINS, Arthur (1848-1930) British				
wc/d	5	1,424-5,000	2,675	2,500
HOPKINS, Eric (20th C) American				
wc/d	2	2,500-2,600	2,550	2,500
HOPKINS, Frances Anne (1838-1919) British				
oil	1	1,216	1,216	1,216
wc/d	3	2,301-24,780	11,188	6,483
HOPKINS, William H (?-1892) British				
oil	2	510-52,920	26,715	510
HOPPE, Erik (1897-1968) Danish				
oil	3	5,658-9,699	7,284	6,496
HOPPE, Georg (fl.1844-1860) German				
oil	2	827-3,822	2,324	827
HOPPENBROUWERS, Johannes Franciscus (1819-1866) Dutch				
oil	3	1,308-4,932	2,679	1,798
HOPPER, Edward (1882-1967) American				
wc/d	10	2,500-85,000	15,725	3,250
HOPPNER, John (1758-1810) British				
oil	3	6,000-71,820	29,273	10,000
wc/d	1	5,568	5,568	5,568
HOPS, Johann Baptist (elder) (1681-1728) German				
3D	1	21,892	21,892	21,892
HOPS, Tom (1906-1976) German				
oil	2	1,067-2,316	1,691	1,067
wc/d	3	555-732	627	596
HOPWOOD, Henry Silkstone (1860-1914) British				
wc/d	2	1,656-4,928	3,292	1,656
HORBERG, Pehr (1746-1816) Swedish				
oil	3	518-2,061	1,275	1,246
HORBIGER, Alfred (1891-1945) Austrian?				
oil	1	2,572	2,572	2,572
HOREJC, Frantisek (1885-?) Czechoslovakian				
oil	1	1,890	1,890	1,890
HOREMANS, Jan Josef (18th C) Flemish				
oil	1	9,000	9,000	9,000
HOREMANS, Jan Josef (elder) (1682-1759) Flemish				
oil	3	2,775-7,027	4,853	4,757
wc/d	3	1,635-3,000	2,093	1,646
HOREMANS, Jan Josef (younger) (1714-1790) Flemish				
oil	3	7,200-22,200	14,116	12,950
HOREMANS, Peter Jacob (1700-1776) Flemish				
oil	3	6,903-9,633	8,635	9,370
HORENBANT, Joseph (1863-1956) Belgian				
oil	3	538-5,605	2,371	970
HORGNIES, Norbert Joseph (19th C) Belgian				
oil	1	1,668	1,668	1,668
HORIUCHI, Paul (1906-1999) Japanese/American				
oil	1	8,000	8,000	8,000
HORL, Ottmar (1950-) German				
3D	1	3,045	3,045	3,045
HORLOR, George W (fl.1849-1891) British				
oil	3	2,124-30,000	11,752	3,132
HORMANN, Theodor von (1840-1895) Austrian				
oil	12	1,665-96,783	24,028	4,712
HORN, Harry (1901-1982) American				
oil	2	550-8,000	4,275	550
HORN, Karen (20th C) American				
wc/d	1	4,000	4,000	4,000

Name	No.	Price Range	Average	Median
HORN, Rebecca (1944-) German				
wc/d	2	2,315-9,515	5,915	2,315
3D	6	2,064-26,000	11,861	4,325
HORN, Roni (1955-) American				
wc/d	1	35,000	35,000	35,000
3D	1	70,000	70,000	70,000
HORNE, Sir William van (1843-1915) Canadian				
oil	1	12,299	12,299	12,299
HORNEL, Edward Atkinson (1864-1933) British				
oil	16	12,460-149,600	44,559	28,050
HORNEMANN, Friedrich Adolf (1813-1890) German				
oil	1	87,862	87,862	87,862
HORNEMANN, Hans Adolf (1866-1916) German				
oil	1	6,442	6,442	6,442
HORNER, Friedrich (1800-1864) Swiss				
wc/d	1	5,724	5,724	5,724
HORNER, Johan (1711-1763) Danish				
oil	2	2,529-6,520	4,524	2,529
HORNSLETH, Kristian (1963-) British				
oil	1	2,253	2,253	2,253
wc/d	1	1,778	1,778	1,778
HORNSTAIN, Gabriel (17th C) German				
wc/d	1	3,737	3,737	3,737
HORNUNG, Emile (1883-1956) Swiss				
oil	3	1,138-2,039	1,603	1,632
HORNUNG, Preben (1919-1989) Danish				
oil	13	420-20,205	4,950	3,557
HORNUNG-JENSEN, C (1882-1960) Danish				
oil	2	487-1,537	1,012	487
HORNUNG-JENSEN, Carl (1882-1960) Danish				
oil	1	1,739	1,739	1,739
HORNYANSKY, Nicholas (1896-1965) Canadian				
wc/d	1	1,772	1,772	1,772
HOROWITZ, Eleanor (1965-) Israeli				
oil	2	650-1,400	1,025	650
HORSCHELT, Theodor (1829-1871) German				
wc/d	3	1,209-6,880	3,142	1,338
HORSLEY, Walter Charles (c.1855-1921) British				
wc/d	1	1,607	1,607	1,607
HORST, Gerrit Willemsz (1612-1652) Dutch				
oil	1	4,833	4,833	4,833
HORSTOK, Johannes Petrus van (1745-1825) Dutch				
oil	1	9,926	9,926	9,926
HORT, E (19/20th C) ?				
oil	1	2,625	2,625	2,625
HORTON, Etty (fl.1882-1905) British				
oil	3	766-1,556	1,100	978
HORTON, George (1859-1950) British				
oil	2	850-1,183	1,016	850
wc/d	5	554-1,315	873	890
HORTON, William Samuel (1865-1936) American				
oil	5	2,600-16,000	8,420	7,500
wc/d	3	950-4,500	2,316	1,500
HORVATH, Pal (1936-) Hungarian				
wc/d	1	556	556	556
3D	1	1,987	1,987	1,987
HORY, Elmyr de (1905-1978) French				
oil	2	2,378-11,000	6,689	2,378
HOSCH, Hans (1855-1902) German				
oil	1	2,040	2,040	2,040
HOSCHEDE-MONET, Blanche (1865-1947) French				
oil	9	1,211-31,507	15,677	17,195
HOSENDO (19th C) Japanese				
3D	1	10,440	10,440	10,440
HOSIASSON, Philippe (1898-1978) French				
oil	1	2,991	2,991	2,991
HOSKIN, John (1921-1992) British				
3D	1	9,100	9,100	9,100
HOSKINS, Gayle Porter (1887-1962) American				
oil	6	450-13,000	2,704	600
HOSLET, Jean Joseph (1899-1981) Belgian				
oil	1	1,091	1,091	1,091

Name	No.	Price Range	Average	Median
HOSOTTE, Georges (1936-) French				
oil	2	7,767-13,981	10,874	7,767
HOST, Oluf (1884-1966) Danish				
oil	21	4,527-53,342	21,398	18,589
HOSTEIN, Edouard (1804-1889) French				
oil	3	2,422-7,658	4,459	3,299
HOTTENROTH, Edmond (1804-1889) Austrian				
oil	1	17,000	17,000	17,000
HOTTOT, Louis (1834-1905) French				
3D	3	3,762-9,555	5,856	4,253
HOTZENDORFF, Theodor von (1898-1974) German				
oil	8	771-3,481	1,517	1,094
HOU, Axel (1860-1948) Danish				
oil	1	1,779	1,779	1,779
HOUBEN, Charles (1871-1931) Belgian				
oil	2	953-5,343	3,148	953
HOUBEN, H (1858-1931) Belgian				
oil	1	4,973	4,973	4,973
HOUBEN, Henri (1858-1931) Belgian				
oil	3	1,500-4,861	2,915	2,386
HOUBRAKEN, Arnold (1660-1719) Dutch				
oil	1	22,500	22,500	22,500
wc/d	1	1,168	1,168	1,168
HOUBRAKEN, Niccolino van (1660-1723) Italian				
oil	1	19,200	19,200	19,200
HOUBRON, Frederic Anatole (1851-1908) French				
wc/d	2	572-3,306	1,939	572
HOUCKGEEST, Gerard (1600-1661) Dutch				
oil	1	12,857	12,857	12,857
HOUDON, Jean Antoine (1741-1828) French				
3D	4	18,229-180,000	65,660	29,333
HOUEL, Jean Pierre (1735-1813) French				
oil	1	2,430	2,430	2,430
wc/d	2	714-1,500	1,107	714
HOUGH, William (fl.1857-1894) British				
wc/d	5	505-2,000	1,307	1,225
HOUGUE, Jean de la (1874-1959) French				
oil	1	2,811	2,811	2,811
HOUMAINE, Mahjoub (1966-) Moroccan				
oil	1	3,675	3,675	3,675
HOUSE, Gordon (1932-) British				
oil	1	1,416	1,416	1,416
HOUSER, Allan C (1915-1994) American				
3D	11	2,750-32,000	12,431	12,000
HOUSMAN, Laurence (1865-1959) British				
wc/d	1	1,424	1,424	1,424
HOUSSER, Bess (1890-1969) Canadian				
oil	1	2,216	2,216	2,216
HOUSSER, Yvonne McKague (1898-1996) Canadian				
oil	6	2,132-14,180	6,692	4,948
wc/d	2	839-3,775	2,307	839
HOUSTON, George (1869-1947) British				
oil	32	779-22,880	5,292	3,591
wc/d	2	510-5,280	2,895	510
HOUSTON, Ian (1934-) British				
oil	5	493-3,024	1,108	696
wc/d	1	1,018	1,018	1,018
HOUSTON, John (1930-) British				
oil	15	961-8,950	4,171	3,366
wc/d	6	463-1,990	1,090	1,032
HOUSTON, John R (1856-1932) British				
oil	1	915	915	915
wc/d	1	915	915	915
HOUSTON, Robert (1891-1942) British				
oil	4	516-3,186	2,218	2,076
HOUT, Pieter (1879-1965) Dutch				
oil	4	736-1,500	1,096	771
HOUTEN, Barbara van (1862-1950) Dutch				
oil	1	5,933	5,933	5,933
HOUTMAN, Sipke Cornelis (1871-1945) Dutch				
oil	3	1,018-2,417	1,611	1,399

Name	No.	Price Range	Average	Median
HOUYOUX, Léon (1856-?) Belgian				
oil	1	703	703	703
wc/d	1	728	728	728
HOVE, Bartholomeus Johannes van (1790-1880) Dutch				
oil	2	9,219-9,568	9,393	9,219
HOVE, Franz van den (19/20th C) Belgian				
oil	2	1,736-4,114	2,925	1,736
HOVE, Hubertus van (1814-1865) Dutch				
oil	5	759-7,774	3,644	4,145
HOVENDEN, Thomas (1840-1895) American/Irish				
oil	1	20,000	20,000	20,000
HOW, Beatrice (1867-1932) British				
wc/d	1	1,318	1,318	1,318
HOW, Walter Ernest (1884-1972) British				
wc/d	1	5,773	5,773	5,773
HOWARD, Henry (1769-1847) British				
oil	1	4,000	4,000	4,000
HOWARD, Humbert (1905-1990) American				
oil	1	4,750	4,750	4,750
HOWARD, Jessie (20th C) American				
oil	1	2,500	2,500	2,500
HOWARD, Ken (1932-) British				
oil	41	810-27,840	5,271	3,420
wc/d	12	498-2,268	1,050	855
HOWARD, W (17th C) British				
oil	1	4,872	4,872	4,872
HOWARD, William (17th C) British				
oil	2	2,208-6,726	4,467	2,208
HOWARTH, Derek (20th C) British				
3D	1	11,340	11,340	11,340
HOWD, Douglas van (20th C) American				
3D	1	19,000	19,000	19,000
HOWE, L van (19th C) Dutch				
oil	1	3,027	3,027	3,027
HOWE, William Henry (1846-1929) American				
oil	4	1,950-5,000	3,412	2,500
HOWELL, Edward A (1848-1924) American				
oil	1	6,500	6,500	6,500
HOWELL, Felicie (1897-1968) American				
oil	2	3,000-6,000	4,500	3,000
wc/d	2	12,000-15,000	13,500	12,000
HOWELL, Frank (20th C) American				
oil	1	1,200	1,200	1,200
HOWELL, Henry (17/18th C) British				
oil	1	1,145	1,145	1,145
HOWELL, Peter (1932-) British				
oil	2	534-6,500	3,517	534
HOWELL, Raymond (1927-) American				
oil	1	3,250	3,250	3,250
HOWELL-SICKLES, Donna (20th C) American				
wc/d	2	1,100-5,000	3,050	1,100
HOWES, Jerome (20th C) American				
oil	1	1,400	1,400	1,400
HOWET, Marie (1897-1984) Belgian				
oil	7	597-3,349	1,527	1,311
wc/d	2	546-1,424	985	546
HOWEY, John William (1873-1938) British				
oil	2	736-2,136	1,436	736
HOWEY, Robert Leslie (1900-1981) British				
oil	3	1,218-4,524	2,386	1,416
wc/d	8	487-4,002	1,103	592
HOWIE, B A (fl.1844-1857) British				
oil	1	2,523	2,523	2,523
HOWITT, John Newton (1885-1958) American				
oil	1	6,000	6,000	6,000
HOWITT, Samuel (1765-1822) British				
wc/d	4	599-9,100	4,272	703
HOWLAND, John D (1843-1914) American				
oil	2	1,400-5,500	3,450	1,400
HOWLETT, Ray (1940-) American				
3D	1	4,500	4,500	4,500

Name	No.	Price Range	Average	Median
HOWSON, Peter (1958-) British				
oil	23	1,328-155,000	12,878	5,500
wc/d	19	440-5,310	1,751	1,211
HOYLAND, John (1934-) British				
oil	12	3,633-9,658	6,295	5,220
wc/d	6	661-3,600	2,549	2,351
HOYOS, Anna Mercedes (1942-) Colombian				
oil	4	4,650-26,000	11,482	7,000
HOYTE, John Barr Clarke (1835-1913) New Zealander				
wc/d	1	3,720	3,720	3,720
HOYTON, Inez E (1903-1983) British				
oil	1	1,683	1,683	1,683
wc/d	1	1,062	1,062	1,062
HRDLICKA, Alfred (1928-) Austrian				
wc/d	6	1,152-5,733	3,554	2,637
3D	4	1,794-3,947	3,040	2,592
HRUBY, Sergius (1869-1943) Austrian				
wc/d	1	1,060	1,060	1,060
HSIA-LING TSAI (1936-) Chinese				
oil	1	2,799	2,799	2,799
HSIAO CHIN (1935-) Chinese				
oil	11	1,189-5,856	3,627	3,600
wc/d	9	583-2,336	1,287	1,189
HSU PEI HUNG (1895-1953) Chinese				
wc/d	1	16,000	16,000	16,000
HUANG BINHONG (1864-1955) Chinese				
wc/d	2	45,000-90,000	67,500	45,000
HUANG YONG PING (1954-) Chinese				
3D	1	140,000	140,000	140,000
HUANG YONGYU (1924-) Chinese				
wc/d	1	15,000	15,000	15,000
HUANG ZHOU (1925-1997) Chinese				
wc/d	1	3,250	3,250	3,250
HUARD, D (?) French				
oil	1	2,367	2,367	2,367
HUART, Claude (20th C) French				
oil	1	1,753	1,753	1,753
HUBACEK, William (1871-1958) American				
oil	3	750-4,000	2,583	3,000
HUBACHER, Hermann (1885-1976) Swiss				
3D	1	10,423	10,423	10,423
HUBBARD, Bennett (1806-1870) British				
oil	1	2,816	2,816	2,816
HUBBARD, Richard William (1817-1888) American				
oil	2	9,800-30,000	19,900	9,800
HUBBARD, Whitney Myron (1875-1965) American				
oil	1	5,500	5,500	5,500
HUBBELL, Henry Salem (1870-1949) American				
oil	2	8,000-8,486	8,243	8,000
HUBBUCH, Karl (1891-1979) German				
oil	3	659-63,605	26,681	15,780
wc/d	21	479-10,560	1,510	865
HUBEEK, Abraham Frederik (1884-1952) Dutch				
oil	1	1,200	1,200	1,200
HUBER, Carl Rudolf (1839-1896) Austrian				
oil	2	2,057-2,975	2,516	2,057
HUBER, Conrad (1752-1830) German				
oil	2	3,299-4,203	3,751	3,299
HUBER, Ernst (1895-1960) Austrian				
oil	9	2,877-19,138	7,617	7,890
wc/d	23	1,052-5,845	1,901	1,293
HUBER, Hermann (1888-1968) Swiss				
oil	4	486-1,214	767	683
wc/d	1	607	607	607
HUBER, Jean (1721-1786) Swiss				
oil	1	6,049	6,049	6,049
HUBER, Léon (1858-1928) French				
oil	3	598-2,744	1,663	1,649
HUBER, Max Emanuel (1903-) Swiss				
oil	1	1,082	1,082	1,082
HUBER, Monika (1959-) German				
oil	1	1,499	1,499	1,499

Name	No.	Price Range	Average	Median
HUBER, Richard (1903-) German				
oil	1	15,062	15,062	15,062
HUBER, Thomas (1700-1779) German				
oil	1	5,890	5,890	5,890
wc/d	1	3,534	3,534	3,534
HUBER, Wilhelm (1787-1871) German				
wc/d	2	1,812-1,823	1,817	1,812
HUBER-AUDORF, Eduard (1877-1965) German				
oil	4	531-3,434	2,169	2,289
HUBER-SULZEMOOS, Hans (1873-1951) German				
oil	5	608-1,483	837	608
wc/d	2	884-1,113	998	884
HUBERT, Edgar (1906-1985) British				
oil	3	692-1,125	951	1,038
wc/d	16	519-5,190	1,953	1,557
HUBERT-WURZBURGER, F (?) ?				
oil	1	2,057	2,057	2,057
HUBERTI, Antonio (Pseudonym) (1907-2000) French				
oil	1	3,460	3,460	3,460
wc/d	10	1,074-3,114	1,754	1,318
HUBLIN, Émile Auguste (1830-?) French				
oil	3	26,610-50,000	40,536	45,000
HUBNER, Carl Wilhelm (1814-1879) German				
oil	7	577-6,622	2,840	2,569
HUBNER, Ferdinand (fl.1832-1860) German				
oil	1	1,341	1,341	1,341
HUBNER, Heinrich (1869-1945) German				
oil	1	1,304	1,304	1,304
HUBNER, Ulrich (1872-1932) German				
oil	4	1,337-7,905	3,478	2,128
HUBRECHT, Amalda (1855-1913) Dutch				
wc/d	1	1,627	1,627	1,627
HUCHET, Urbain (1930-) French				
oil	1	1,092	1,092	1,092
HUCHTENBURG, Jacob van (1639-1675) Dutch				
oil	1	12,335	12,335	12,335
HUCHTENBURGH, Jan van (1647-1733) Dutch				
oil	3	6,830-38,015	22,741	23,378
wc/d	1	1,500	1,500	1,500
HUDDLE, Nannie Zenobia (1860-1951) American				
oil	1	8,000	8,000	8,000
HUDON, Normand (1929-1997) Canadian				
oil	2	611-11,460	6,035	611
HUDSON, Charles Bradford (1865-1938) American				
oil	1	1,200	1,200	1,200
HUDSON, Eric (1864-1932) American				
oil	3	1,200-7,000	3,233	1,500
HUDSON, Gertrude (1878-1958) British				
oil	2	1,139-1,317	1,228	1,139
HUDSON, Grace Carpenter (1865-1937) American				
oil	8	1,400-23,000	9,143	2,500
wc/d	2	700-3,000	1,850	700
HUDSON, Robert (jnr) (?-1884) British				
oil	1	1,602	1,602	1,602
HUDSON, Thomas (1701-1779) British				
oil	4	13,000-44,376	25,211	20,790
HUDSON, Willis (fl.1922-1934) British				
oil	1	1,740	1,740	1,740
HUE, Jean François (1751-1823) French				
oil	2	2,182-17,244	9,713	2,182
wc/d	1	2,922	2,922	2,922
HUEBER, A (19/20th C) ?				
oil	1	2,761	2,761	2,761
HUEBNER, Mentor (1917-2001) American				
oil	1	4,844	4,844	4,844
HUECK, Georges de (1904-1964) Russian				
oil	1	1,323	1,323	1,323
HUET, Christophe (1694-1759) French				
oil	1	13,520	13,520	13,520
HUET, Jean Baptiste (1745-1811) French				
oil	4	4,000-92,500	37,443	15,275
wc/d	11	1,011-7,770	3,369	2,141

Name	No.	Price Range	Average	Median
HUET, Paul (1803-1869) French				
oil	6	479-6,343	2,935	1,512
wc/d	4	1,337-2,188	1,591	1,415
HUETOS, Domingo (1928-) Spanish				
oil	1	1,796	1,796	1,796
HUG, Charles (1899-1979) Swiss				
oil	6	648-3,450	1,541	973
HUG, Fritz Rudolf (1921-1989) Swiss				
oil	9	986-6,088	2,148	1,214
HUGARD DE LA TOUR, Claude-Sebastian (1818-1886) French				
oil	1	2,276	2,276	2,276
HUGARD, Claude S (1861-?) French				
oil	1	14,000	14,000	14,000
HUGENTOBLER, Ivan Edwin (1886-1972) Swiss				
oil	2	645-1,795	1,220	645
wc/d	2	567-882	724	567
HUGENTOBLER, Johannes (1897-1955) Swiss				
oil	1	3,450	3,450	3,450
HUGGINS, William (1820-1884) British				
oil	5	504-16,245	7,439	6,840
HUGGINS, William John (1781-1845) British				
oil	5	945-92,040	25,309	7,200
HUGHES (?) ?				
oil	1	1,701	1,701	1,701
HUGHES, Arthur (1832-1915) British				
oil	5	1,104-2,208	1,656	1,656
wc/d	1	6,370	6,370	6,370
HUGHES, Arthur Ford (1856-1934) British				
wc/d	2	549-9,680	5,114	549
HUGHES, Bill (1932-1992) American				
oil	10	400-7,000	2,430	2,000
HUGHES, Daisy Marguerite (1883-1968) American				
oil	3	400-3,250	2,216	3,000
HUGHES, Edward (1832-1908) British				
oil	4	612-1,800	1,175	810
HUGHES, Edward John (1913-) Canadian				
oil	9	4,457-221,564	93,101	79,763
wc/d	7	810-34,443	7,257	1,459
HUGHES, Edward Robert (1851-1914) British				
oil	1	3,366	3,366	3,366
wc/d	4	1,553-20,460	8,264	5,280
HUGHES, George E (1907-1990) American				
oil	1	11,000	11,000	11,000
HUGHES, George Hart (1839-1921) Canadian				
oil	2	1,386-2,218	1,802	1,386
HUGHES, Patrick (1939-) British				
oil	2	2,035-29,410	15,722	2,035
wc/d	2	669-1,200	934	669
3D	1	23,010	23,010	23,010
HUGHES, Ronnie (1965-) British				
oil	1	1,398	1,398	1,398
HUGHES, Talbot (1869-1942) British				
oil	2	2,800-3,434	3,117	2,800
HUGHES, William (1842-1901) British				
oil	6	792-3,045	1,415	979
HUGHES-STANTON, Blair (1902-) British				
oil	1	4,275	4,275	4,275
HUGHES-STANTON, Sir Herbert (1870-1937) British				
oil	4	692-4,114	1,700	700
wc/d	2	1,157-3,872	2,514	1,157
HUGNET, Georges (1906-1974) French				
wc/d	2	707-14,786	7,746	707
HUGO, Jean (1894-1984) French				
oil	7	3,442-10,286	6,177	6,952
wc/d	5	526-5,890	2,556	1,734
HUGO, Valentine (1890-1968) French				
oil	5	2,383-35,847	12,365	2,979
wc/d	33	476-54,823	4,189	1,920
3D	1	7,150	7,150	7,150
HUGO, Victor Marie (1802-1885) French				
wc/d	2	4,114-20,456	12,285	4,114

Name	No.	Price Range	Average	Median
HUGUENIN, Viretaux-Henri-Edouard (1878-1958) Swiss				
oil	4	457-3,916	1,482	725
HUGUENIN-LASSANGUETTE, Fritz Eduard (1842-1926) Swiss				
oil	3	725-2,518	1,489	1,224
HUGUES, Jean (20th C) French?				
3D	1	2,281	2,281	2,281
HUGUES, Paul Jean (1891-?) French				
oil	1	2,335	2,335	2,335
HUGUES, Victor Louis (1827-?) French				
oil	1	1,500	1,500	1,500
HUGUET, Victor Pierre (1835-1902) French				
oil	2	2,200-24,549	13,374	2,200
HUHTAMO, Kari (1943-) Finnish				
3D	2	2,757-3,600	3,178	2,757
HUHTHOFF, Jaeger (?) French?				
3D	1	6,684	6,684	6,684
HUIDOBRO LAPLANA, Luis (1870-1936) Spanish				
oil	1	1,929	1,929	1,929
HUILLIOT, Pierre Nicolas (1674-1751) French				
oil	1	25,950	25,950	25,950
HULBERT, Katherine Allmond (?-1937) American				
oil	2	800-2,400	1,600	800
HULDAH, Cherry Jeffe (1901-2001) American				
3D	3	3,000-3,750	3,416	3,500
HULETT, Ralph (19/20th C) American				
oil	1	5,000	5,000	5,000
HULINGS, Clark (1922-) American				
oil	12	6,000-172,500	67,125	55,000
HULK, A (jnr) (1851-1922) British				
oil	1	1,764	1,764	1,764
HULK, Abraham (19th C) Dutch				
oil	3	6,336-11,392	8,551	7,925
HULK, Abraham (jnr) (1851-1922) British				
oil	13	396-10,041	2,147	774
HULK, Abraham (snr) (1813-1897) Dutch				
oil	21	1,200-32,680	9,235	5,933
wc/d	1	6,156	6,156	6,156
HULK, Hendrik (1842-1937) Dutch				
oil	5	1,566-3,781	2,138	1,707
HULK, John Frederick (jnr) (1855-1913) Dutch				
wc/d	2	1,697-16,983	9,340	1,697
HULK, John Frederick (snr) (1829-1911) Dutch				
oil	3	1,929-12,123	5,550	2,600
HULK, William F (1852-1906) British				
oil	7	654-1,566	1,007	1,050
HULL, Marie (1890-1980) American				
oil	2	7,500-8,750	8,125	7,500
wc/d	1	2,500	2,500	2,500
HULLGREN, Oscar (1869-1948) Swedish				
oil	5	560-2,379	1,315	1,496
HULME, Frederick William (1816-1884) British				
oil	3	974-3,268	1,766	1,058
HULSDONCK, Jacob van (1582-1647) Flemish				
oil	1	111,000	111,000	111,000
HULSER, Joseph (1819-1850) German				
oil	1	2,102	2,102	2,102
HULSMAN, Howard (19th C) American				
oil	1	1,200	1,200	1,200
HULSMAN, Johann (17th C) German				
oil	3	16,937-54,441	32,622	26,490
HULST, Frans de (1610-1661) Flemish				
oil	1	28,027	28,027	28,027
HULST, Maerten Frans van der (17th C) Dutch				
oil	1	24,220	24,220	24,220
HULSTEYN, Johan van (1860-1894) Dutch				
oil	1	1,463	1,463	1,463
HULTBERG, Charles Evald (1874-1948) American/Swedish				
wc/d	1	1,000	1,000	1,000
HULTBERG, John (1922-2005) American				
oil	4	900-1,250	1,062	1,000

Name	No.	Price Range	Average	Median
HULTEN, Bo (1945-) Swedish				
3D	1	2,672	2,672	2,672
HULTEN, Carl Otto (1916-) Swedish				
oil	2	1,321-1,400	1,360	1,321
wc/d	2	1,321-2,907	2,114	1,321
HULTGREN, Lars Huck (1931-) Swedish				
oil	1	1,255	1,255	1,255
HUMBERT-VIGNOT, Leonie (1878-1960) French				
oil	2	615-1,757	1,186	615
HUMBLOT, Robert (1907-1962) French				
oil	6	530-2,631	1,851	1,794
HUMBORG, Adolf (1847-1913) Austrian				
oil	2	3,000-20,027	11,513	3,000
HUME, Edith (fl.1862-1906) British				
oil	3	1,653-5,600	3,801	4,152
HUME, Gary (1962-) British				
oil	7	9,500-150,450	87,710	91,520
wc/d	1	1,740	1,740	1,740
HUMMEL, Carl (1821-1907) German				
oil	3	1,295-3,299	2,025	1,483
wc/d	2	658-1,018	838	658
HUMMEL, Theodor (1864-1939) German				
oil	1	1,090	1,090	1,090
HUMPHREY, Edward J (fl.1872-1889) British				
oil	1	1,223	1,223	1,223
HUMPHREY, Jack Weldon (1901-1967) Canadian				
oil	2	820-882	851	820
wc/d	9	369-1,434	682	597
HUMPHREY, Ozias (1742-1810) British				
oil	1	605	605	605
wc/d	1	750	750	750
HUMPHREY, Ralph (1932-1990) American				
oil	2	2,200-6,000	4,100	2,200
HUMPHREY, Walter Beach (1892-1966) American				
oil	1	4,000	4,000	4,000
HUMPHRIES, Geoffrey (20th C) British?				
oil	2	3,500-4,617	4,058	3,500
HUMPHRISS, Charles Henry (1867-1934) British				
3D	1	1,900	1,900	1,900
HUNAEUS, Andreas (1814-1866) Danish				
oil	1	1,299	1,299	1,299
HUNDERTWASSER, Friedrich (1928-2000) Austrian				
oil	2	2,571-5,955	4,263	2,571
wc/d	4	14,055-129,500	59,081	18,849
HUNG, Francisco (1937-) Chinese				
oil	11	840-5,580	3,065	2,790
HUNN, T (19/20th C) British				
wc/d	1	1,033	1,033	1,033
HUNNEMANN (?) ?				
oil	1	24,082	24,082	24,082
HUNT, Alfred William (1830-1896) British				
wc/d	5	688-5,664	2,633	1,770
HUNT, Bryan (1947-) American				
3D	2	12,000-16,000	14,000	12,000
HUNT, C M (?) American?				
oil	1	2,000	2,000	2,000
HUNT, Charles (jnr) (1829-1900) British				
oil	3	1,760-3,168	2,532	2,670
HUNT, Charles (snr) (1803-1877) British				
oil	3	475-5,856	2,494	1,151
HUNT, Charles (19th C) British				
oil	1	3,806	3,806	3,806
HUNT, Charles D (1840-1914) American				
oil	5	765-11,000	3,513	1,700
HUNT, Claude (1863-1949) British				
oil	1	5,882	5,882	5,882
HUNT, Edgar (1876-1953) British				
oil	13	5,478-60,180	29,624	27,520
HUNT, Edward Aubrey (1855-1922) British				
oil	7	885-3,179	1,821	1,780
wc/d	1	460	460	460

Name	No.	Price Range	Average	Median
HUNT, Lynn Bogue (1878-1960) American				
oil	1	12,000	12,000	12,000
wc/d	1	1,400	1,400	1,400
HUNT, Millson (fl.1875-1900) British				
oil	2	1,089-1,326	1,207	1,089
HUNT, Thomas (1854-1929) British				
wc/d	3	487-1,796	1,131	1,110
HUNT, Thomas Lorraine (1882-1938) American				
oil	2	3,250-3,500	3,375	3,250
HUNT, Walter (1861-1941) British				
oil	8	9,000-88,000	28,472	14,560
HUNT, William Henry (1790-1864) British				
wc/d	11	468-8,700	4,015	3,850
HUNT, William Holman (1827-1910) British				
oil	2	11,830-42,750	27,290	11,830
wc/d	4	519-106,020	37,018	16,740
HUNT, William Morris (1824-1879) American				
oil	1	340,000	340,000	340,000
wc/d	3	2,000-3,200	2,533	2,400
HUNTEN, Emil Johann (1827-1902) German				
oil	1	6,668	6,668	6,668
HUNTEN, Franz Johann Wilhelm (1822-1887) German				
oil	3	605-1,697	1,247	1,440
HUNTER, Clementine (1887-1988) American				
oil	20	1,500-18,000	5,012	4,600
HUNTER, Colin (1841-1904) British				
oil	7	425-21,120	3,822	968
HUNTER, George Leslie (1877-1931) British				
oil	18	19,895-284,800	77,796	60,180
wc/d	6	4,425-23,270	10,183	7,080
HUNTER, George Sherwood (1846-1919) British				
oil	1	2,450	2,450	2,450
HUNTER, John (?) British?				
oil	2	1,636-1,947	1,791	1,636
HUNTER, Leslie (1877-1931) British				
oil	2	84,480-105,600	95,040	84,480
HUNTER, Russell Vernon (1900-1955) American				
wc/d	1	15,500	15,500	15,500
HUNTER, William (c.1890-1967) British				
oil	1	7,920	7,920	7,920
HUNTINGTON, Anna Hyatt (1876-1973) American				
3D	3	6,500-120,000	45,333	9,500
HUNTINGTON, Chris (1938-) American				
oil	3	1,000-3,000	1,800	1,400
HUNTINGTON, Dwight W (1860-1906) American				
wc/d	2	3,200-7,000	5,100	3,200
HUNZIKER, Max (1901-1976) Swiss				
wc/d	1	1,979	1,979	1,979
HURARD, Joseph Marius (1887-1956) French				
oil	2	1,680-1,991	1,835	1,680
HURD, Peter (1904-1984) American				
oil	1	12,000	12,000	12,000
wc/d	4	1,100-1,700	1,425	1,300
HURLEY, Wilson (1924-) American				
oil	4	4,750-30,000	17,937	15,000
HURRY, Leslie (1909-1978) British				
oil	1	2,013	2,013	2,013
wc/d	6	509-4,446	1,981	1,122
HURT, Louis B (1856-1929) British				
oil	20	830-115,050	30,893	19,791
wc/d	1	4,000	4,000	4,000
HURTADO, Angel (1927-) Venezuelan				
oil	1	3,720	3,720	3,720
HURTADO, Jesus M (20th C) Venezuelan?				
oil	1	2,100	2,100	2,100
HURTEN, Carl Ferdinand (1818-?) German				
oil	1	1,015	1,015	1,015
HURTUBISE, Jacques (1939-) Canadian				
oil	1	7,834	7,834	7,834
wc/d	1	4,210	4,210	4,210

Name	No.	Price Range	Average	Median
HUSAIN, Maqbool Fida (1915-) Indian				
oil	40	7,000-420,000	120,907	120,000
wc/d	16	5,000-110,000	34,835	30,000
HUSAIN, Owais (1967-) Indian				
oil	1	5,000	5,000	5,000
HUSAIN, Shamshad (1946-) Indian				
oil	1	4,500	4,500	4,500
HUSON, Thomas (1844-1920) British				
oil	2	650-1,388	1,019	650
HUSS, Judson (1942-) American				
oil	1	1,400	1,400	1,400
HUSSEIN, Ibrahim (1936-) Malaysian				
oil	1	2,640	2,640	2,640
HUSSEM, Willem (1900-1974) Dutch				
oil	15	1,767-10,829	5,527	4,712
wc/d	1	2,290	2,290	2,290
HUSSMANN, Albert Heinrich (1874-1946) German				
3D	6	2,432-17,955	7,359	4,451
HUSSON-DUMOUTIER, Alain (c.1939-) French				
oil	1	2,647	2,647	2,647
HUSTON, William (19th C) American				
oil	1	5,000	5,000	5,000
HUSTWICK, Francis (18/19th C) British				
oil	1	1,218	1,218	1,218
HUSZAR, Vilmos (1884-1960) Dutch				
oil	3	1,008-8,767	3,660	1,205
HUTCHENS, Frank Townsend (1869-1937) American				
oil	2	1,200-50,000	25,600	1,200
HUTCHINSON, Eugenia M (1868-1904) American				
oil	1	16,000	16,000	16,000
HUTCHINSON, Leonard (1896-1980) Canadian				
oil	1	1,058	1,058	1,058
HUTCHINSON, Marieluise (1947-) American				
oil	3	1,100-2,800	1,733	1,300
HUTCHINSON, Nick Hely (1955-) Irish				
oil	4	722-2,349	1,569	1,044
wc/d	3	666-1,110	962	1,110
HUTCHISON, Frederick William (1871-1953) Canadian				
oil	2	2,559-3,280	2,919	2,559
wc/d	1	3,444	3,444	3,444
HUTCHISON, Robert Gemmeli (1855-1936) British				
oil	31	1,298-193,600	28,489	15,570
wc/d	4	3,132-6,612	5,064	4,475
HUTCHISON, William Oliphant (1889-c.1971) British				
oil	1	2,262	2,262	2,262
HUTEAU, Marie (19/20th C) French?				
oil	1	1,929	1,929	1,929
HUTH, Franz (1876-?) German				
oil	1	947	947	947
wc/d	4	536-1,302	825	586
HUTH, Julius (1838-1892) German				
oil	1	2,182	2,182	2,182
HUTH, Willy Robert (1890-1977) German				
wc/d	1	1,295	1,295	1,295
HUTHER, Julius (1881-1954) German				
oil	4	1,492-1,764	1,639	1,543
wc/d	1	1,414	1,414	1,414
HUTIN, Charles-François (1715-1776) French				
oil	1	53,407	53,407	53,407
HUTSON, Laurence Burgess (20th C) Irish?				
oil	3	714-3,039	1,568	951
HUTSON, Marshall C (1903-2001) British				
oil	7	892-2,572	1,851	2,022
wc/d	4	856-1,169	1,007	951
HUTTENLOCHER, Britta (1962-) Dutch?				
wc/d	1	2,338	2,338	2,338
HUTTER, Schang (1934-) Swiss				
3D	1	16,228	16,228	16,228
HUTTER, Wolfgang (1928-) Austrian				
wc/d	1	5,890	5,890	5,890

Name	No.	Price Range	Average	Median
HUTTON, Thomas S (c.1865-1935) British				
oil	1	680	680	680
wc/d	20	515-1,765	903	779
HUTTY, Alfred (1877-1954) American				
oil	4	7,500-22,500	13,750	11,000
wc/d	2	11,000-27,000	19,000	11,000
HUXLEY, Paul (1938-) British				
oil	1	2,750	2,750	2,750
HUYGENS, François Joseph (1820-1908) Belgian				
oil	4	486-4,176	2,296	959
HUYS, Modeste (1875-1932) Belgian				
oil	5	4,555-37,405	12,394	7,658
wc/d	1	3,567	3,567	3,567
HUYSMANS, Cornelis (1648-1727) Flemish				
oil	1	11,100	11,100	11,100
HUYSMANS, Jan Baptist (1826-1906) Belgian				
oil	4	7,500-70,068	31,865	13,092
HUYSUM, Jan van (1682-1749) Dutch				
oil	7	2,337-6,500,000	2,070,461	16,562
wc/d	2	993-65,000	32,996	993
HUYSUM, Justus van I (1659-1716) Dutch				
oil	1	59,200	59,200	59,200
HUZE, Guy (?) ?				
wc/d	1	3,010	3,010	3,010
HYBERT, Fabrice (1961-) French				
oil	2	5,980-10,763	8,371	5,980
wc/d	6	934-29,899	10,626	6,429
3D	4	3,156-12,041	5,741	3,884
HYDE, Doug (1946-) American				
3D	3	4,000-7,000	5,916	6,750
HYDE, Frank (fl.1872-1916) British				
oil	1	1,496	1,496	1,496
HYDE, Helen (?) American				
wc/d	1	2,500	2,500	2,500
HYDE-POWNALL, George (1876-1932) British				
oil	1	4,900	4,900	4,900
HYDMAN-VALLIEN, Ulrika (1938-) Swedish				
oil	2	945-2,016	1,480	945
HYER, Florine (1868-1936) American				
oil	1	2,200	2,200	2,200
HYLANDER, Einar (1913-1989) Swedish				
wc/d	2	1,520-3,039	2,279	1,520
HYLANDER, W (?) Scandinavian				
oil	1	1,057	1,057	1,057
HYNAIS, Voytech (1854-1925) Czechoslovakian				
oil	1	10,192	10,192	10,192
HYNCKES, Raoul (1893-1973) Dutch				
oil	3	2,544-14,000	6,683	3,507
HYNCKES-ZAHN, Marguerite (1897-1978) Dutch				
oil	1	1,520	1,520	1,520
HYNDMAN, Arnold (fl.1921-1932) British				
oil	1	2,436	2,436	2,436
HYON, Georges Louis (1855-?) French				
oil	2	750-1,901	1,325	750
IACCHETTI, Paolo (1953-) Italian				
oil	1	1,331	1,331	1,331
IACOVLEFF, Alexandre (1887-1938) French/Russian				
oil	8	5,500-1,600,000	507,867	150,000
wc/d	21	1,757-427,800	37,051	13,760
IACURTO, Francesco (1908-2001) Canadian				
oil	1	4,402	4,402	4,402
IAKUNCHIKOVA, Maria Vasilevna (20th C) Russian				
oil	7	14,620-68,800	35,505	30,960
wc/d	2	5,160-18,920	12,040	5,160
IASNOVSKII, Fedor Ivanovich (1833-1902) Russian				
oil	1	4,872	4,872	4,872
IBANEZ, Manuel Ramirez (20th C) Mexican?				
oil	1	60,000	60,000	60,000
IBARROLA, Agustin (20th C) ?				
wc/d	1	7,531	7,531	7,531
IBBETSON, Denzil (1775-1857) British				
oil	1	6,726	6,726	6,726

Name	No.	Price Range	Average	Median
IBBETSON, Julius Caesar (1759-1817) British				
oil	3	2,803-113,400	39,720	2,958
IBORRA, Casimiro Lino (1857-1935) Spanish				
oil	1	1,445	1,445	1,445
IBSEN, Henrik (1828-1906) Norwegian				
wc/d	1	34,343	34,343	34,343
ICARO, Paolo (1936-) Italian				
3D	2	3,625-5,373	4,499	3,625
ICART, Louis (1888-1950) French				
oil	9	2,571-16,714	7,085	6,546
wc/d	3	599-1,305	907	818
IEPEREN, Johan Hendrik van (1909-1995) Dutch				
oil	1	2,356	2,356	2,356
wc/d	3	884-1,296	1,021	884
IGLESIAS SANZ, Antonio (1935-) Spanish				
oil	2	1,171-1,447	1,309	1,171
IGLESIAS, Cristina (1956-) ?				
3D	2	13,000-42,143	27,571	13,000
IHLEE, Rudolph (1883-1968) British				
oil	1	1,710	1,710	1,710
IHLENFELD, Klaus (20th C) American?				
3D	2	2,000-4,500	3,250	2,000
IHRAN, Manne (1877-1917) Swedish				
oil	1	1,122	1,122	1,122
IIDA, Yoshikuni (1923-) Japanese				
3D	1	4,000	4,000	4,000
IKE NO TAIGA (1723-1776) Japanese				
wc/d	2	12,000-24,000	18,000	12,000
IKEMURA, Leiko (1951-) ?				
oil	2	1,529-4,531	3,030	1,529
IKKEI, Hanabusa and KUNISADA, Utagawa (19th C) Japanese				
wc/d	1	2,775	2,775	2,775
IKUTAAQ, David (1929-1984) North American				
3D	4	2,446-16,028	7,149	4,218
ILIOPOULOS, George (1947-) Greek				
oil	1	3,179	3,179	3,179
ILIOPOULOU, Irene (1950-) Greek				
oil	2	2,244-13,200	7,722	2,244
ILISITUK, Tivi (1933-) North American				
3D	1	1,518	1,518	1,518
ILLE, Eduard (1823-1900) German				
wc/d	1	4,186	4,186	4,186
ILMONI, Einar (1880-1946) Finnish				
oil	1	1,695	1,695	1,695
ILSTED, Peter Vilhelm (1861-1933) Danish				
oil	9	2,055-101,062	25,653	6,350
wc/d	1	869	869	869
IMAI, Toshimitau (1928-) Japanese				
oil	1	1,335	1,335	1,335
wc/d	1	1,519	1,519	1,519
IMANDT, Willem (1882-1967) Dutch				
oil	1	1,565	1,565	1,565
IMBERT, M L (?) French				
oil	1	1,701	1,701	1,701
IMER, Edouard Auguste (1820-1881) French				
oil	1	4,477	4,477	4,477
IMHOF, Heinrich Maximilian (1798-1869) Swiss				
3D	1	5,322	5,322	5,322
IMHOF, Joseph A (1871-1955) American				
oil	4	1,750-8,000	5,500	4,250
wc/d	1	1,500	1,500	1,500
IMKAMP, Wilhelm (1906-1990) German				
oil	3	1,927-2,670	2,421	2,667
wc/d	2	1,019-1,147	1,083	1,019
IMMENDORF, Jorg (1945-) German				
oil	14	2,827-53,014	22,861	18,811
wc/d	21	1,178-24,151	12,063	12,016
3D	8	3,822-203,550	37,364	12,959
IMMENKAMP, Wilhelm (1870-1931) German				
oil	1	1,082	1,082	1,082
IMMENRAEDT, Philip Augustyn (1627-1679) Flemish				
oil	1	3,263	3,263	3,263

Name	No.	Price Range	Average	Median
IMMERZEEL, Christiaan (1806-1886) Dutch				
oil	3	1,260-4,302	2,477	1,870
IMPENS, Josse (1840-1905) Belgian				
oil	4	493-10,771	3,159	666
IMPERIALE, Francisco Jose Osvaldo (1913-1977) Argentinian				
oil	5	2,100-14,000	9,560	12,000
IMPERIALI, Francesco (18th C) Italian				
oil	1	21,625	21,625	21,625
IMPIGLIA, Giancarlo (1940-) American/Italian				
oil	1	5,500	5,500	5,500
IMSCHOOT, Jules van (1821-1884) Flemish				
oil	2	1,297-4,676	2,986	1,297
INCHBOLD, John William (1830-1888) British				
wc/d	2	1,118-2,848	1,983	1,118
INCHBOLD, Stanley (1856-?) British				
wc/d	1	3,363	3,363	3,363
INDENBAUM, Léon (1892-1980) Russian				
3D	2	3,822-7,013	5,417	3,822
INDERMAUR, Robert (1947-) Swiss				
oil	1	4,540	4,540	4,540
wc/d	1	984	984	984
INDIANA, Robert (1928-) American				
oil	8	35,000-1,189,189	435,596	314,500
wc/d	5	3,784-11,100	6,361	5,550
3D	9	22,000-1,026,374	248,630	170,000
INDONI, Filippo (1800-1884) Italian				
oil	1	12,000	12,000	12,000
wc/d	4	450-1,600	1,149	972
INDONI, Filippo (jnr) (1842-1908) Italian				
wc/d	1	2,220	2,220	2,220
INDUNI, Eduardo (19/20th C) Argentinian				
oil	2	3,200-7,000	5,100	3,200
INDUNO, Domenico (1815-1878) Italian				
oil	1	92,000	92,000	92,000
wc/d	2	667-727	697	667
INDUNO, Gerolamo (1827-1890) Italian				
oil	5	15,315-636,986	196,345	78,000
INFANTE-ARANA, Francisco (1943-) Russian				
oil	1	17,670	17,670	17,670
wc/d	2	37,200-223,200	130,200	37,200
INGALL, John Spence (1850-1936) British				
wc/d	5	552-2,171	1,046	854
INGANNI, Angelo (1807-1880) Italian				
oil	1	72,917	72,917	72,917
wc/d	1	4,262	4,262	4,262
INGELS, Domien (1881-1946) Belgian				
3D	1	2,342	2,342	2,342
INGEMANN, Lucie (1792-1868) Danish				
oil	1	2,104	2,104	2,104
INGENMEY, Franz Maria (1830-1878) German				
oil	1	4,750	4,750	4,750
INGERLE, Rudolph (1879-1950) American				
oil	1	3,300	3,300	3,300
INGHAM, Bryan (1936-1997) British				
oil	1	10,320	10,320	10,320
wc/d	4	626-7,830	3,588	1,740
INGLEFIELD, Admiral Sir Edward Augustus (1820-1894) British				
wc/d	2	2,088-16,740	9,414	2,088
INGRAM, Charles (20th C) American				
oil	1	1,100	1,100	1,100
INGRAM, William Ayerst (1855-1913) British				
oil	2	1,649-7,422	4,535	1,649
wc/d	2	529-920	724	529
INGRES, Jean Auguste Dominique (1780-1867) French				
oil	1	114,041	114,041	114,041
wc/d	5	6,920-50,411	19,886	15,000
INGUIMBERTY, Joseph (1896-1971) French				
oil	4	1,288-19,794	6,585	1,288
INGVARSSON, Jarl (1955-) Swedish				
oil	1	7,136	7,136	7,136
wc/d	1	5,286	5,286	5,286

Name	No.	Price Range	Average	Median
INLANDER, Henry (1925-1983) British				
oil	2	1,151-1,200	1,175	1,151
INNANEN, Martti (?) Finnish				
oil	1	1,918	1,918	1,918
INNES, Alice Amelia (1890-1970) Canadian				
oil	2	1,968-2,624	2,296	1,968
INNES, Callum (1962-) British				
oil	3	1,932-9,658	6,199	7,007
INNES, James Dickson (1887-1914) British				
oil	1	12,950	12,950	12,950
wc/d	1	9,100	9,100	9,100
INNES, John (1863-1941) Canadian				
oil	1	2,132	2,132	2,132
INNESS, George (1825-1894) American				
oil	17	3,500-100,000	35,676	17,500
INNESS, George (jnr) (1853-1926) American				
oil	5	2,295-10,000	5,159	4,000
INNOCENT, Ferenc (1859-1934) Hungarian				
oil	2	1,427-3,637	2,532	1,427
INNOCENT, Franck (1912-1983) French?				
oil	5	482-2,957	1,305	995
INNOCENTI, Camillo (1871-1961) Italian				
oil	7	850-28,274	8,792	2,021
INSHAW, David (1943-) British				
oil	1	5,400	5,400	5,400
INSLEY, Albert (1842-1937) American				
oil	6	900-8,000	2,591	1,200
INSOLL, Christopher (1956-) British				
oil	1	2,136	2,136	2,136
INUKPUK, Johnny (1911-) North American				
3D	1	11,346	11,346	11,346
IOKI, Bunsai (1863-1906) Japanese				
wc/d	1	5,550	5,550	5,550
IOMMI, Enio (1926-) Argentinian				
3D	3	9,500-27,000	15,833	11,000
IOMMI, Raffaele (1953-) Italian				
oil	1	1,908	1,908	1,908
IPEELEE, Osuitok (1923-) North American				
3D	3	2,193-5,905	4,105	4,218
IPOLYI-MERZ, Sigrid von (1920-) German				
3D	1	3,565	3,565	3,565
IPOUSTEGUY, Jean (1920-) French				
oil	1	1,071	1,071	1,071
wc/d	1	834	834	834
3D	1	22,000	22,000	22,000
IPPOLITO, Angelo (1922-2002) American				
oil	1	1,600	1,600	1,600
IPSEN, Poul Janus (1936-) Danish				
oil	2	647-1,449	1,048	647
IRANNA, G R (1970-) Indian				
oil	1	12,000	12,000	12,000
IRAZU, Pello (1963-) Spanish				
oil	1	1,796	1,796	1,796
IRIARTE, Ignacio de (1621-1685) Spanish				
oil	1	23,784	23,784	23,784
IRMER, Carl (1834-1900) German				
oil	2	771-2,303	1,537	771
IROLLI, Vincenzo (1860-1949) Italian				
oil	14	5,023-99,555	28,307	9,687
wc/d	1	7,644	7,644	7,644
IRONSIDE, Robin (1912-1965) British				
oil	1	1,000	1,000	1,000
wc/d	1	473	473	473
IRVIN, Albert (1922-) British				
oil	3	1,947-4,186	2,870	2,478
wc/d	2	650-1,305	977	650
IRVIN, Rea (1881-1972) American				
wc/d	1	11,000	11,000	11,000
IRVINE, Wilson (1869-1936) American				
oil	8	8,500-60,000	21,937	17,000
wc/d	1	1,100	1,100	1,100

Name	No.	Price Range	Average	Median
IRVING, William C (1866-1943) British				
oil	1	10,024	10,024	10,024
IRWIN, Benoni (1840-1896) American				
oil	2	2,800-4,500	3,650	2,800
IRWIN, Gwyther (1931-) British				
wc/d	2	740-10,380	5,560	740
IRWIN, Robert (1928-) American				
oil	1	380,000	380,000	380,000
ISAAC, Jeffrey (1956-) American				
oil	1	1,527	1,527	1,527
ISAAKSZ, Isaac (17th C) Dutch				
oil	1	9,000	9,000	9,000
ISABEY, Eugène (1803-1886) French				
oil	16	651-22,080	8,962	8,496
wc/d	9	515-3,889	1,983	2,066
ISABEY, Jean Baptiste (1767-1855) French				
oil	2	1,070-1,753	1,411	1,070
wc/d	7	400-3,168	1,068	654
ISAKSON, Karl (1878-1922) Swedish				
oil	11	997-42,027	12,211	7,929
ISBRAND, Victor (1897-1989) Danish				
oil	1	1,449	1,449	1,449
ISCAN, Ferit (1931-1986) French				
oil	3	720-1,800	1,120	840
ISELI, Rolf (1934-) Swiss				
oil	1	2,548	2,548	2,548
wc/d	8	1,060-8,018	3,473	2,356
ISELIN, Christoph (1910-1987) Swiss				
oil	1	1,090	1,090	1,090
ISENBART, Marie Victor Émile (1846-1921) French				
oil	1	8,497	8,497	8,497
ISENBRANDT, Adriaen (1490-1551) Flemish				
oil	1	157,250	157,250	157,250
ISER, Heinrich (1881-1932) ?				
oil	1	3,000	3,000	3,000
ISGRO, Emilio (1936-) Spanish				
oil	1	10,813	10,813	10,813
wc/d	8	823-11,712	4,262	1,058
ISHIKAWA, Kinichiro (1871-1945) Japanese				
wc/d	3	1,744-2,225	2,064	2,225
ISIK, Levent (1961-) American				
oil	3	525-1,600	1,041	1,000
ISKOWITZ, Gershon (1921-1988) Canadian				
oil	2	8,419-10,635	9,527	8,419
wc/d	3	1,155-1,410	1,276	1,265
ISNARD, Vivien (1946-) French?				
wc/d	2	1,936-3,872	2,904	1,936
ISOLA, Maija (1927-) Finnish?				
oil	1	2,225	2,225	2,225
ISOM, Graham (1945-) British				
oil	2	1,003-1,298	1,150	1,003
ISRAEL, Daniel (1859-1901) Austrian				
oil	2	9,570-10,137	9,853	9,570
ISRAELS, Isaac (1865-1934) Dutch				
oil	18	3,514-394,007	113,551	107,635
wc/d	12	1,374-71,292	17,664	7,990
ISRAELS, J (1824-1911) Dutch				
oil	1	1,119	1,119	1,119
ISRAELS, Josef (1824-1911) Dutch				
oil	13	6,760-65,972	21,537	17,000
wc/d	10	450-38,795	7,949	1,700
ISSAIEV, Nicolas (1891-1977) French/Russian				
oil	19	630-2,979	1,825	1,675
wc/d	2	470-834	652	470
ISSELSTEYN, Adrianus van (?-1684) Dutch				
oil	1	13,875	13,875	13,875
ISSTOMIN, Konstantin (1887-1942) Russian				
oil	1	8,342	8,342	8,342
ISSUPOFF, Alessio (1889-1957) Russian				
oil	22	2,301-55,040	12,447	7,200
wc/d	2	777-906	841	777

Name	No.	Price Range	Average	Median
ISTLER, Josef (1919-) Czechoslovakian				
wc/d	5	539-8,326	2,471	1,079
ISTRATI, Alexandre (1915-1991) Rumanian				
oil	66	419-6,557	2,138	1,793
wc/d	6	530-1,767	838	579
ISTVANFFY, Gabrielle Rainer (1877-1964) Hungarian				
oil	1	1,096	1,096	1,096
ITAYA, Foussa (1919-) French				
oil	4	400-1,825	1,100	650
ITEN, Hans (1874-1930) Swiss/British				
oil	3	2,003-8,469	5,061	4,712
ITHAKISIOS, Vasilis (1878-1977) Greek				
oil	3	7,560-34,020	24,880	33,060
ITO, Okyu (fl.1920-1940s) Japanese				
oil	1	1,388	1,388	1,388
ITTAR, Henryk (1773-1850) Polish				
3D	1	77,850	77,850	77,850
ITTEN, Johannes (1888-1967) Swiss				
wc/d	5	2,125-4,066	2,870	2,625
ITTENBACH, Franz (1813-1879) German				
oil	3	4,370-7,827	5,992	5,780
ITTMAN, Hans (1914-1972) Dutch				
oil	2	844-1,870	1,357	844
ITURRIA, Ignacio de (1949-) Uruguayan				
oil	5	3,100-24,000	15,420	16,000
ITURRINO, Francisco de (1864-1924) Spanish				
wc/d	1	4,757	4,757	4,757
IUPPA, G (20th C) ?				
wc/d	1	6,473	6,473	6,473
IVACKOVIC, Djoka (1930-) Balkan				
oil	2	409-1,394	901	409
wc/d	1	835	835	835
IVANOFF, L (19/20th C) Russian				
oil	1	2,289	2,289	2,289
IVANOFF, Serge (1893-1983) Bulgarian				
wc/d	1	5,500	5,500	5,500
IVANOFF, Vassil (1897-1973) Russian?				
3D	2	2,922-4,676	3,799	2,922
IVANOV, A (20th C) Russian				
oil	1	1,169	1,169	1,169
IVANOV, Alexander Andreavitch (1806-1858) Russian				
oil	1	17,071,232	17,071,232	17,071,232
IVANOV-SAKACHEV, Ivan Stepanovich (1926-1980) Russian				
oil	1	5,580	5,580	5,580
IVANYI, N H (19th C) Hungarian				
oil	1	4,750	4,750	4,750
IVARSON, Ivan (1900-1939) Swedish				
oil	13	3,988-198,218	43,929	33,036
wc/d	1	2,481	2,481	2,481
IVERSEN, Kraesten (1886-1955) Danish				
oil	4	1,051-3,233	2,121	1,778
IVES, Chauncey Bradley (1810-1894) American				
3D	3	2,250-5,500	4,416	5,500
IVES, H S (20th C) American?				
oil	1	1,750	1,750	1,750
IVES, Halsey Cooley (1847-1911) American				
oil	1	3,200	3,200	3,200
IVES, Lewis Thomas (1833-1894) American				
oil	1	1,000	1,000	1,000
IVES, Percy (1864-1928) American				
oil	2	1,100-2,250	1,675	1,100
IWILL, Joseph (1850-1923) French				
oil	3	4,959-8,880	6,662	6,148
wc/d	3	1,381-8,174	4,698	4,540
IYAITUK, Matiusie (1950-) North American				
3D	1	2,868	2,868	2,868
IZQUIERDO VIVAS, Mariano (?) Spanish				
oil	1	2,351	2,351	2,351
JAAKOLA, Alpo (1929-1997) Finnish				
oil	4	2,180-3,857	2,891	2,186
JABONNEAU, E J (?) ?				
wc/d	1	1,812	1,812	1,812

Name	No.	Price Range	Average	Median
JACCARD, Christian (1939-) French				
oil	1	1,870	1,870	1,870
JACHWAK, William (20th C) American				
oil	13	375-1,900	1,032	850
JACK, John (19/20th C) British				
oil	2	1,373-4,675	3,024	1,373
JACK, Richard (1866-1952) Canadian/British				
oil	5	528-9,019	3,858	3,793
JACKLIN, Bill (1943-) British				
oil	2	28,320-36,294	32,307	28,320
wc/d	1	513	513	513
JACKSON, Alexander Young (1882-1974) Canadian				
oil	39	7,533-70,095	25,115	20,616
wc/d	6	2,292-35,261	8,512	2,624
JACKSON, Elbert McGran (1896-1962) American				
oil	3	750-8,000	3,916	3,000
JACKSON, Frederick William (1859-1918) British				
oil	7	1,204-8,448	4,237	2,403
wc/d	3	531-2,236	1,131	626
JACKSON, Geneva A (20th C) Canadian				
oil	3	474-1,940	1,022	652
JACKSON, George (19th C) British				
oil	2	5,250-8,550	6,900	5,250
JACKSON, Gerald Goddard (fl.1907-1936) British				
oil	1	10,560	10,560	10,560
JACKSON, H Sinclair (fl.1887-1896) British				
oil	1	2,832	2,832	2,832
JACKSON, Harry (1924-) American				
3D	9	1,800-12,500	8,055	8,200
JACKSON, Helen (?-1911) British				
wc/d	1	1,472	1,472	1,472
JACKSON, Kurt (1961-) British				
oil	3	1,480-4,048	2,391	1,647
wc/d	13	669-4,625	1,695	1,135
JACKSON, Lesley Elizabeth (1866-1958) American				
oil	1	1,800	1,800	1,800
JACKSON, Martin (1919-1986) American				
oil	4	600-3,500	1,337	600
JACKSON, Mary (1936-) British				
oil	1	1,663	1,663	1,663
JACKSON, Michael (1961-) British				
oil	1	1,850	1,850	1,850
JACKSON, Robert C (1964-) American				
oil	1	1,100	1,100	1,100
JACKSON, Samuel (1794-1869) British				
wc/d	3	623-5,220	3,339	4,176
JACKSON, Samuel Phillips (1830-1904) British				
wc/d	6	673-2,670	1,266	1,104
JACKSON, William Franklin (1850-1936) American				
oil	4	2,500-20,000	8,500	5,000
JACOB, Alexandre (1876-1972) French				
oil	5	715-10,620	4,428	2,655
JACOB, Alice (?) ?				
oil	1	1,987	1,987	1,987
JACOB, Jean Germain (20th C) French				
oil	1	4,224	4,224	4,224
JACOB, Johann (19th C) ?				
oil	1	1,621	1,621	1,621
JACOB, Julius (elder) (1811-1882) German				
wc/d	1	2,569	2,569	2,569
JACOB, Julius (younger) (1842-1929) German				
oil	1	1,781	1,781	1,781
wc/d	1	13,993	13,993	13,993
JACOB, Max (1876-1944) French				
oil	3	697-2,879	1,581	1,169
wc/d	14	558-4,281	1,841	1,411
JACOB, Ned (1938-) American				
wc/d	4	400-4,000	1,725	1,200
JACOB, Stephen (1846-?) French				
oil	2	906-5,600	3,253	906
JACOBBER, Moise (1786-1863) French				
oil	2	2,351-26,885	14,618	2,351

Name	No.	Price Range	Average	Median
JACOBI, J (19/20th C) ?				
oil	1	14,228	14,228	14,228
JACOBI, Otto Reinhard (1812-1901) German/Canadian				
oil	2	738-6,969	3,853	738
wc/d	3	682-970	846	886
JACOBS, A Rodolphe (?) Belgian				
oil	2	1,458-1,580	1,519	1,458
JACOBS, Adolphe (1859-1940) Belgian				
oil	2	848-7,151	3,999	848
JACOBS, Gerard (1865-1958) Belgian				
oil	3	1,320-1,911	1,524	1,341
JACOBS, H (19/20th C) Belgian				
3D	1	3,200	3,200	3,200
JACOBS, Hobart B (1851-1935) American				
oil	1	7,500	7,500	7,500
JACOBS, Jacob Albertus Michael (1812-1879) Belgian				
oil	3	1,760-7,500	4,333	3,741
JACOBS, Louis Adolphe (1855-1929) Belgian				
oil	2	701-1,870	1,285	701
JACOBSEN, A (19th C) ?				
oil	8	507-3,810	1,790	1,543
JACOBSEN, Anton (1879-?) Danish				
oil	1	1,001	1,001	1,001
JACOBSEN, Antonio (1850-1921) American				
oil	42	5,000-60,000	18,533	16,000
JACOBSEN, August (1868-1955) Norwegian				
oil	5	1,521-6,846	2,876	2,213
JACOBSEN, David (1821-1871) Danish				
oil	4	766-1,581	1,067	873
JACOBSEN, Egill (1910-1998) Danish				
oil	14	1,207-132,548	32,639	14,548
wc/d	6	1,293-6,438	2,871	1,932
JACOBSEN, Georg (1887-1976) Danish				
oil	4	1,288-6,466	3,309	2,586
JACOBSEN, Jurian (1624-1685) German				
oil	1	11,192	11,192	11,192
JACOBSEN, Ludvig (1890-1957) Danish				
oil	2	731-1,659	1,195	731
JACOBSEN, Robert (1912-1993) Danish				
oil	4	950-2,649	1,989	1,771
wc/d	11	837-2,803	1,444	1,436
3D	13	3,395-75,981	16,379	8,445
JACOBSEN, Sophus (1833-1912) Norwegian				
oil	5	1,152-6,429	3,399	3,750
JACOBSON, Oscar Brousse (1882-1966) American				
oil	1	4,000	4,000	4,000
JACOBY, Valeri Ivanovitch (1836-1909) Russian				
oil	1	2,290	2,290	2,290
JACOMB-HOOD, George Percy (1857-1937) British				
oil	2	5,472-11,447	8,459	5,472
JACOMIN, Jean Marie (1789-1858) French				
oil	1	3,928	3,928	3,928
JACOMIN, Marie Ferdinand (1843-1902) French				
oil	1	3,000	3,000	3,000
JACOULET, Paul (1902-1960) French				
wc/d	1	5,500	5,500	5,500
JACQUAND, Claudius (1804-1878) French				
oil	3	4,071-6,869	5,461	5,444
JACQUE, Charles Émile (1813-1894) French				
oil	25	626-40,000	7,265	4,142
wc/d	4	471-2,577	1,099	533
JACQUE, Émile (1848-1912) French				
oil	4	629-2,431	1,580	1,496
JACQUEMART, Alfred (1824-1896) French				
3D	1	1,446	1,446	1,446
JACQUEMON, Pierre (1936-2002) French				
oil	3	707-1,640	1,022	720
JACQUES, Charles (20th C) French				
oil	3	2,142-6,000	4,130	4,250
JACQUES, Jean Pierre (1913-) Swiss				
oil	1	1,748	1,748	1,748

Name	No.	Price Range	Average	Median
JACQUET, Alain (1939-) French				
oil	4	2,806-16,829	7,696	5,103
wc/d	2	1,081-9,936	5,508	1,081
JACQUET, Gustave-Jean (1846-1909) French				
oil	7	3,587-69,692	17,754	10,000
wc/d	1	1,600	1,600	1,600
JACQUETTE, Yvonne (1934-) American				
oil	1	11,000	11,000	11,000
JACQUIER, Henry (1878-1921) French				
oil	1	3,025	3,025	3,025
JAECKEL, Henry (19th C) German				
oil	2	2,504-2,571	2,537	2,504
JAECKEL, Willy (1888-1944) German				
oil	2	3,588-6,840	5,214	3,588
wc/d	4	618-1,405	935	761
JAEGER, Wilhelm (1941-) German				
oil	1	6,218	6,218	6,218
JAEKEL, Joseph (1907-1985) German				
3D	1	2,548	2,548	2,548
JAENISCH, Hans (1907-1989) German				
oil	4	665-1,794	995	761
wc/d	3	494-1,272	961	1,119
JAFURY DA PALERMO, R (19/20th C) Italian?				
oil	1	6,944	6,944	6,944
JAGER, Gerke Jans de (c.1748-1822) Dutch				
oil	1	120,250	120,250	120,250
JAGGER, Charles Sargeant (1885-1934) British				
3D	1	699,300	699,300	699,300
JAGGER, David (fl.1917-1940) British				
oil	4	1,860-69,600	20,318	4,450
JAGGI, Luc (1887-1976) Swiss				
3D	1	8,324	8,324	8,324
JAGOUPOVA, Maria Markovna (?-1967) Russian				
oil	1	1,764	1,764	1,764
JAGUTTIS, Emden Martin (20th C) Belgian				
oil	1	1,551	1,551	1,551
JAHL, Wladyslaw Adam Alojzy (1886-1953) Polish				
oil	2	693-2,584	1,638	693
JAHNS, Rudolf (1896-1983) German				
wc/d	1	12,721	12,721	12,721
JAIMAL, Har (18th C) Indian				
wc/d	1	19,800	19,800	19,800
JAIMES SANCHEZ, Humberto (1930-) South American				
oil	3	560-3,250	2,200	2,790
wc/d	2	440-840	640	440
JAKIMOV, Igor von (1885-1962) German				
oil	1	8,514	8,514	8,514
JAKOBIDES, Georg (1853-1932) Greek				
oil	3	40,020-151,200	82,640	56,700
wc/d	1	2,917	2,917	2,917
3D	1	17,400	17,400	17,400
JAKOBSSON, Fritz (1940-) Finnish				
oil	2	4,099-13,500	8,799	4,099
JAKOWLEFF, Michael (1880-1942) Russian				
wc/d	1	3,132	3,132	3,132
JAKUCHU, Ito (1716-1800) Japanese				
wc/d	2	35,000-380,000	207,500	35,000
JAKUPSSON, Bardur (?) Icelandic				
oil	1	1,293	1,293	1,293
JALLAND, G H (19/20th C) British				
wc/d	1	14,080	14,080	14,080
JALLIER DE SAVAULT, Claude Jean-Baptiste (1738-1806) French				
wc/d	1	1,288	1,288	1,288
JAMAR, Armand (1870-1946) Belgian				
oil	12	572-3,181	1,301	1,064
wc/d	1	1,020	1,020	1,020
JAMBERS, Theodorus (1804-?) Belgian				
oil	1	3,527	3,527	3,527
JAMBOR, Louis (1884-1955) American				
oil	1	37,500	37,500	37,500
JAMES, B T (fl.1870-1880) British?				
oil	1	9,735	9,735	9,735

Name	No.	Price Range	Average	Median
JAMES, David (fl.1881-1898) British				
oil	16	859-42,480	12,844	7,120
JAMES, Frederick (1857-1932) American				
oil	2	1,100-25,000	13,050	1,100
JAMES, John Wells (1873-?) American				
oil	2	9,000-11,000	10,000	9,000
JAMES, Roy Walter (1897-?) American				
oil	1	2,500	2,500	2,500
JAMES, Will (1892-1942) American				
wc/d	8	3,000-11,000	5,531	4,500
JAMES, William (fl.1754-1771) British				
oil	1	74,340	74,340	74,340
JAMESON, James Arthur Henry (fl.1883-1923) British				
oil	1	763	763	763
wc/d	1	1,080	1,080	1,080
JAMESON, John (1842-1864) American				
oil	1	135,000	135,000	135,000
JAMIESON, Alexander (1873-1937) British				
oil	2	1,128-1,870	1,499	1,128
JAMIESON, F E (1895-1950) British				
oil	1	1,288	1,288	1,288
JAMIESON, Florence (20th C) British?				
wc/d	2	622-1,505	1,063	622
JAMIN, Leon (1872-1944) Belgian				
oil	2	1,432-1,649	1,540	1,432
JAMMES, Louis (20th C) French?				
oil	1	2,281	2,281	2,281
JAN, Elvire (1904-1996) French/Bulgarian				
oil	6	2,154-5,381	4,277	4,735
wc/d	5	837-3,675	1,559	1,136
JANAK, Heinz (1942-1998) Austrian				
oil	1	2,572	2,572	2,572
JANCO, Marcel (1895-1984) Israeli/Rumanian				
oil	20	2,400-38,000	14,498	8,000
wc/d	16	360-3,200	1,052	700
JANCZAK, Jan (1938-) Polish				
oil	9	571-1,973	1,018	835
JANEBE (1907-2000) Swiss				
oil	2	1,374-6,868	4,121	1,374
JANENSCH, Gerhard Adolf (1860-1933) German				
3D	1	1,776	1,776	1,776
JANES, Alfred (1911-1999) British				
oil	1	4,498	4,498	4,498
JANIN, Louise (1893-1996) French				
wc/d	1	2,674	2,674	2,674
JANK, Angelo (1868-1940) German				
oil	6	471-3,312	1,580	714
JANKOWSKI, J Wilhelm (fl.1825-1861) Austrian				
oil	2	775-4,600	2,687	775
JANKOWSKY, N (19th C) Austrian?				
oil	1	2,606	2,606	2,606
JANMOT, Anne François Louis (1814-1892) French				
wc/d	3	468-3,524	1,630	900
JANN, C (?) ?				
oil	1	2,577	2,577	2,577
JANNECK, Franz Christoph (1703-1761) Austrian				
oil	3	12,041-22,986	16,422	14,240
JANNIOT, Alfred Auguste (1889-1969) French				
wc/d	1	3,497	3,497	3,497
3D	9	3,185-27,096	12,108	11,244
JANNY, Georg (1864-1946) Austrian				
wc/d	1	1,324	1,324	1,324
JANOGE, Jeanne (1890-?) French?				
oil	1	1,445	1,445	1,445
JANOWITZ, P (20th C) German				
oil	1	6,370	6,370	6,370
JANOWSKI, Georg (19th C) Austrian?				
oil	1	2,281	2,281	2,281
JANS, Edouard de and NEUHUYS, Jan Antoon (19th C) Belgian				
oil	1	2,057	2,057	2,057
JANSCHA, Lorenz (1749-1812) Austrian				
wc/d	1	2,661	2,661	2,661

Name	No.	Price Range	Average	Median
JANSEM (1920-1990) French				
wc/d	1	1,100	1,100	1,100
JANSEM, Jean (1920-1990) French				
oil	15	1,546-27,500	11,370	9,500
wc/d	15	480-2,812	1,835	1,991
JANSEN, Egbert A (1877-1957) Dutch				
oil	1	2,400	2,400	2,400
JANSEN, Franz Maria (1885-1958) German				
oil	1	1,176	1,176	1,176
JANSEN, Hendrik Willebrord (1855-1908) Dutch				
oil	1	1,808	1,808	1,808
JANSEN, Johannes Maurisz (1812-1857) Dutch				
oil	2	1,627-2,290	1,958	1,627
JANSEN, Joseph (1829-1905) German				
oil	1	2,182	2,182	2,182
JANSEN, Willem George Frederick (1871-1949) Dutch				
oil	13	978-21,875	5,383	3,687
wc/d	1	1,200	1,200	1,200
JANSON, Johannes (1729-1784) Dutch				
oil	6	1,286-8,429	4,918	3,884
JANSON, Jonathan (1950-) American				
oil	1	3,625	3,625	3,625
wc/d	1	530	530	530
JANSON, Marc (1930-) French				
oil	4	586-2,154	1,142	877
wc/d	1	608	608	608
JANSSAUD, Mathurin (1857-1940) French				
oil	4	2,922-4,676	3,886	3,624
wc/d	4	600-4,793	2,657	2,431
JANSSEN, Horst (1929-1995) German				
wc/d	50	608-39,493	5,743	3,242
3D	1	3,884	3,884	3,884
JANSSEN, Jacob (19th C) ?				
wc/d	2	19,250-22,750	21,000	19,250
JANSSEN, Peter Johann Theodor (1844-1908) German				
oil	1	2,569	2,569	2,569
JANSSEN, Willem (1950-) Dutch				
oil	1	1,286	1,286	1,286
JANSSENS, Ann Veronica (1956-) Belgian				
3D	1	18,920	18,920	18,920
JANSSENS, Hieronymus (1624-1693) Flemish				
oil	2	10,680-12,460	11,570	10,680
JANSSENS, Pieter Elinga (17th C) Dutch				
oil	1	64,291	64,291	64,291
JANSSENS, Victor Honore (1658-1736) Flemish				
oil	1	14,087	14,087	14,087
JANSSON, Alfred (1863-1931) American/Swedish				
oil	4	1,000-1,700	1,300	1,000
JANSSON, Eugène (1862-1915) Swedish				
oil	1	13,737	13,737	13,737
wc/d	2	1,209-2,742	1,975	1,209
JANSSON, Rune (1918-) Swedish				
oil	17	382-6,211	1,931	1,590
JANSSON, Tove (1914-2001) Finnish				
oil	6	2,186-4,685	3,469	3,397
wc/d	9	484-21,857	4,948	995
JANSSON, Viktor (1886-1958) Finnish				
3D	1	2,314	2,314	2,314
JANVIER, Alex (1935-) Canadian				
oil	2	866-2,755	1,810	866
wc/d	1	1,072	1,072	1,072
JANZ, Franz (1946-) Austrian				
wc/d	3	849-4,555	2,084	849
JAPY, Louis Aime (1840-1916) French				
oil	10	1,500-15,315	5,304	4,000
wc/d	2	772-1,168	970	772
JAQUES, Francis Lee (1887-?) American				
oil	1	20,000	20,000	20,000
JAQUET, Jacques (1830-1898) Belgian				
3D	1	104,386	104,386	104,386
JAQUET, Jan Jozef (1822-1898) Belgian				
3D	1	4,872	4,872	4,872

Name	No.	Price Range	Average	Median
JARAMILLO, Jorge (20th C) Colombian?				
wc/d	1	4,650	4,650	4,650
JARDINES, Jose Maria (1862-?) Spanish				
oil	6	718-4,595	2,297	1,089
JARITZ, Jozsa (1893-1986) Hungarian				
oil	1	9,709	9,709	9,709
JARNEFELT, Eero (1863-1937) Finnish				
oil	2	28,286-50,363	39,324	28,286
wc/d	8	1,678-16,365	5,218	3,471
JARNEFELT, Kasper (1859-1941) Finnish				
oil	3	1,414-3,600	2,228	1,671
JARRY, Gaston (1889-1974) Argentinian				
oil	1	2,700	2,700	2,700
JARRY, Henri (19th C) Belgian				
oil	1	4,002	4,002	4,002
JARVIS, Don (1923-2001) Canadian				
oil	1	1,066	1,066	1,066
JARVIS, Georgia (1944-1990) Canadian				
oil	3	1,595-5,096	3,633	4,210
JARVIS, John Wesley (1780-1840) American				
oil	1	2,250	2,250	2,250
JASINSKI, Zdzislaw (1863-1932) Polish				
oil	1	5,400	5,400	5,400
JAUDON, Valerie (1945-) American				
oil	1	3,500	3,500	3,500
wc/d	1	7,500	7,500	7,500
JAUMANN, Rudolf Alfred (1859-?) German				
oil	1	1,091	1,091	1,091
JAUNBERSIN, J (?) ?				
oil	1	68,800	68,800	68,800
JAWLENSKY, Alexej von (1864-1941) Russian				
oil	23	36,247-4,956,000	795,565	200,274
wc/d	5	1,854-15,925	6,628	5,536
JAWLENSKY, Andreas (1902-1984) Polish				
oil	3	1,785-4,057	2,840	2,678
wc/d	1	6,090	6,090	6,090
JAY, Florence (fl.1905-1920) British				
oil	2	641-4,914	2,777	641
wc/d	1	740	740	740
JAY, William Samuel (1843-1933) British				
oil	3	842-3,363	2,181	2,338
JAZET, Paul-Léon (1848-?) French				
oil	1	32,000	32,000	32,000
JEAN, Marcel (1900-1994) French				
oil	1	6,970	6,970	6,970
3D	1	25,343	25,343	25,343
JEAN-HAFFEN, Yvonne (1895-1993) French				
oil	1	3,383	3,383	3,383
wc/d	1	825	825	825
JEAN-JACQUES, Carlo (1943-1990) Haitian				
oil	1	1,005	1,005	1,005
JEANCLOS, Georges (1933-1997) French				
3D	5	12,361-27,310	17,575	13,597
JEANMAIRE, Edouard (1847-1916) Swiss				
oil	5	1,065-7,611	3,583	2,854
JEANNERET, Gustave (1847-1927) Swiss				
oil	2	1,328-2,656	1,992	1,328
JEANNIN, Georges (1841-1925) French				
oil	7	1,697-9,730	4,856	4,948
JEANNIOT, Pierre Georges (1848-1934) French				
oil	1	2,000	2,000	2,000
wc/d	1	1,140	1,140	1,140
JEAURAT, Étienne (1699-1789) French				
oil	1	7,200	7,200	7,200
JEBRANE, Moulay Driss (1968-) Moroccan				
oil	2	1,723-2,864	2,293	1,723
JECT-KEY, David Wu (1890-1968) Chinese				
oil	4	1,600-5,250	2,812	2,200
JEFFERSON, Jack (1921-2000) American				
wc/d	1	4,000	4,000	4,000
JEFFERSON, Joseph (1829-1905) American				
oil	3	865-3,800	2,107	1,656

Name	No.	Price Range	Average	Median
JEFFERYS, Arthur B (1892-1970) American				
oil	2	2,500-4,000	3,250	2,500
JEFFERYS, Charles William (1869-1951) Canadian				
wc/d	1	1,168	1,168	1,168
JEFFERYS, Marcel (1872-1924) Belgian				
oil	5	1,001-16,272	10,186	11,265
wc/d	1	1,424	1,424	1,424
JEFFREYS, Arthur Bishop (1892-?) American				
oil	1	1,300	1,300	1,300
JEHAN, Christophe (1961-) French				
oil	9	893-1,659	1,122	957
JEJER, Anatoli (1937-) Russian				
oil	1	1,455	1,455	1,455
JELINEK, Rudolf (1880-1958) Austrian				
oil	2	1,178-1,400	1,289	1,178
JELLETT, Mainie (1897-1944) Irish				
oil	4	17,534-130,200	50,647	23,007
wc/d	9	3,348-31,808	12,032	9,896
JELLEY, James Valentine (fl.1878-1942) British				
oil	1	3,916	3,916	3,916
wc/d	2	1,098-3,009	2,053	1,098
JENDRASSIK, Jeno (1860-1919) Hungarian				
oil	1	1,640	1,640	1,640
JENKINS, Arthur H (1871-?) British				
oil	1	1,104	1,104	1,104
JENKINS, F Lynn (1870-1927) American/British				
3D	1	3,000	3,000	3,000
JENKINS, George (1920-) Canadian				
oil	2	446-2,181	1,313	446
JENKINS, John Eliot (1868-1937) American				
oil	3	900-6,500	3,966	4,500
JENKINS, Joseph John (1811-1885) British				
wc/d	2	905-1,672	1,288	905
JENKINS, Lincoln Pugh (1901-1988) British				
wc/d	1	1,780	1,780	1,780
JENKINS, Paul (1923-) American				
oil	44	1,800-26,000	11,788	10,929
wc/d	23	596-9,500	3,298	3,000
JENKINS, Wilfred (fl.1875-1888) British				
oil	5	1,472-14,000	4,525	2,200
JENNER, Isaac Walter (1836-1901) Australian/British				
oil	1	1,505	1,505	1,505
JENNEWEIN, Carl Paul (1890-1978) American				
3D	3	10,720-35,000	25,240	30,000
JENNEY, Neil (1945-) American				
oil	2	46,020-100,000	73,010	46,020
JENNINGS, Humphrey (1907-1950) British				
oil	19	740-4,440	1,816	1,480
wc/d	10	481-7,400	1,940	703
JENNINGS, James Harold (1931-) American				
3D	1	2,050	2,050	2,050
JENNINGS, William George (18/19th C) British				
oil	1	957	957	957
wc/d	3	696-1,131	899	870
JENNY, Arnold (1831-1881) Swiss				
oil	1	1,218	1,218	1,218
JENSEN, Alfred (1903-1981) American				
oil	5	820-22,000	7,412	2,928
wc/d	1	12,000	12,000	12,000
JENSEN, Alfred (1859-1935) Danish				
oil	19	582-3,529	1,548	1,403
JENSEN, Alfred V (19/20th C) Danish				
oil	6	502-2,213	1,209	676
JENSEN, Arup (1906-) Danish				
oil	2	1,000-2,688	1,844	1,000
JENSEN, C A (1792-1870) Danish				
oil	1	1,956	1,956	1,956
JENSEN, Christian Albrecht (1792-1870) Danish				
oil	3	11,689-17,534	15,585	17,534
JENSEN, E M (1822-1915) Danish				
oil	1	1,304	1,304	1,304

Name	No.	Price Range	Average	Median
JENSEN, George (1878-?) American				
oil	3	700-7,000	3,983	4,250
JENSEN, H (19th C) Danish?				
oil	1	2,890	2,890	2,890
JENSEN, Hans Christian (1836-1903) Danish				
oil	1	5,780	5,780	5,780
JENSEN, Holger J (1900-1966) Danish				
oil	2	808-1,700	1,254	808
JENSEN, J-L (1800-1856) Danish				
oil	3	2,489-5,705	3,684	2,858
JENSEN, Johan-Laurents (1800-1856) Danish				
oil	24	700-96,160	12,866	6,350
JENSEN, Johannes (1818-1874) Danish				
oil	1	1,111	1,111	1,111
JENSEN, Karl (1851-1933) Danish				
oil	2	1,270-1,956	1,613	1,270
JENSEN, Louis Isak Napolean (1858-1908) Danish				
oil	3	1,022-1,300	1,124	1,051
JENSEN, Soren Georg (1917-1982) Danish				
3D	3	1,851-5,658	3,365	2,586
JENSON, Ivan (1962-) American				
oil	1	4,000	4,000	4,000
JENSSEN, Olav Christopher (1954-) Norwegian				
oil	1	1,654	1,654	1,654
wc/d	2	1,272-1,718	1,495	1,272
JENTZEN, Friedrich (1815-1901) German				
oil	1	12,846	12,846	12,846
JENTZSCH, Johann Moritz Gottfried (1759-1826) German				
wc/d	1	1,001	1,001	1,001
JENTZSCH, Johannes Gabriel (1862-?) German				
oil	1	1,985	1,985	1,985
JEPPERSON, Samuel (1855-1931) American				
oil	1	1,200	1,200	1,200
JEPSON, Kenneth (?) British?				
oil	1	1,550	1,550	1,550
JEQUIER, Jules (1834-1898) Swiss				
oil	3	3,916-5,711	4,938	5,189
JERACE, Gaetano (1860-1940) Italian				
oil	1	1,401	1,401	1,401
JERANIAN, Richard (1928-) ?				
oil	2	1,008-1,432	1,220	1,008
JERDON, Thomas Claverhill (1811-1872) British				
wc/d	2	44,400-77,700	61,050	44,400
JERICHAU, Harald Adolf Nikolai (1851-1878) Danish				
oil	1	26,057	26,057	26,057
JERICHAU, Holger H (1861-1900) Danish				
oil	9	727-4,075	1,848	1,588
wc/d	1	1,414	1,414	1,414
JERICHAU, Jens Adolf (1890-1916) Danish				
oil	1	61,425	61,425	61,425
JERICHAU-BAUMANN, Elisabeth (1819-1881) Danish				
oil	5	1,375-7,904	5,330	4,743
JERKEN, Erik (1898-1947) Swedish				
oil	2	879-2,163	1,521	879
JERNBERG, August (1826-1896) Swedish				
oil	6	1,246-19,110	9,861	4,986
JERNBERG, Olof (1855-1935) Swedish				
oil	4	748-4,612	2,878	1,620
JERSILD, Julius (1846-1920) Danish				
oil	2	2,445-4,864	3,654	2,445
JERVAS, Charles (1675-1739) British				
oil	5	2,958-30,780	16,602	16,065
JESPERS, Floris (1889-1965) Belgian				
oil	64	536-144,490	11,801	3,273
wc/d	15	598-31,561	4,652	2,631
JESPERS, Oscar (1887-1970) Belgian				
3D	1	2,572	2,572	2,572
JESPERSEN, Eline Hertz (1879-1958) Danish				
oil	1	3,211	3,211	3,211
JESPERSEN, Henrik (1853-1936) Danish				
oil	4	1,429-3,586	2,429	2,085

Name	No.	Price Range	Average	Median
JESSUP, Frederick (1920-) Australian				
oil	4	700-2,200	1,220	880
JESSUP, Robert (20th C) American				
oil	1	6,500	6,500	6,500
JESSURUN DE MESQUITA, Samuel (1868-1944) Dutch				
wc/d	3	760-1,808	1,322	1,399
JETTEL, Eugen (1845-1901) Austrian				
oil	2	12,000-24,276	18,138	12,000
JETTMAR, Rudolf (1869-1939) Austrian				
oil	1	7,632	7,632	7,632
JEUNE, Elizabeth le (20th C) Irish?				
3D	1	2,178	2,178	2,178
JEUNE, Henry le (1820-1904) British				
oil	5	750-5,742	2,587	2,478
JEUNE, James le (1910-1983) Irish				
oil	11	5,005-33,905	12,057	9,585
wc/d	1	2,400	2,400	2,400
JEVEREN, G V (1918-) ?				
oil	1	2,420	2,420	2,420
JEWETT, Frederick Stiles (1819-1864) American				
oil	1	8,000	8,000	8,000
JEWETT, William and WALDO, Samuel Lovett (19th C) American				
oil	1	4,000	4,000	4,000
JEX, Garnet W (1895-1979) American				
oil	1	9,000	9,000	9,000
JI DACHUN (1968-) Chinese				
oil	3	10,000-26,000	19,867	23,601
wc/d	1	7,400	7,400	7,400
JIA YOUFU (1943-) Chinese				
wc/d	1	5,000	5,000	5,000
JIANG HONGWEI (1957-) Chinese				
wc/d	1	3,036	3,036	3,036
JIANG JIE (19th C) Chinese				
wc/d	1	10,000	10,000	10,000
JIANG TINGXI (1669-1732) Chinese				
wc/d	2	600-4,671	2,635	600
JIANGUO SUI (1956-) Chinese				
3D	8	2,616-80,000	12,832	2,735
JILEK, Karel (1896-1983) Czechoslovakian				
oil	1	1,286	1,286	1,286
JIMENEZ DEREDIA, Jorge (1954-) Costa Rican				
3D	1	24,000	24,000	24,000
JIMENEZ Y ARANDA, Jose (1837-1903) Spanish				
oil	2	16,493-108,980	62,736	16,493
wc/d	2	825-4,418	2,621	825
JIMENEZ Y ARANDA, Luis (1845-1928) Spanish				
oil	6	1,546-18,400	6,739	1,649
wc/d	1	2,751	2,751	2,751
JIMENEZ Y FERNANDEZ, Federico (1841-?) Spanish				
oil	1	2,510	2,510	2,510
JIMENEZ Y MARTIN, Juan (1858-1901) Spanish				
oil	3	1,800-31,500	19,766	26,000
wc/d	2	1,288-2,027	1,657	1,288
JIMENEZ, Carlos (1833-1896) Spanish				
oil	1	5,648	5,648	5,648
JIMENEZ, Patricio (1949-) Chilean				
oil	1	7,500	7,500	7,500
JIRLOW, Lennart (1936-) Swedish				
oil	16	2,417-76,438	16,234	8,722
wc/d	9	1,909-9,514	5,175	4,071
JOANOVITCH, Paul (1859-1957) Austrian				
oil	4	5,342-42,411	24,378	12,959
JOBBE-DUVAL, Felix Armand Marie (1821-1889) French				
oil	1	2,517	2,517	2,517
JOBBE-DUVAL, Gaston (1856-1929) French				
oil	1	2,299	2,299	2,299
JOBERT, Fernand (19th C) French				
wc/d	1	1,199	1,199	1,199
JOBLING, Isa (1850-1926) British				
oil	1	9,016	9,016	9,016

Name	No.	Price Range	Average	Median
JOBLING, Robert (1841-1923) British				
oil	15	623-22,750	9,824	9,853
wc/d	2	552-1,110	831	552
JOBSON, John (1941-) British				
oil	7	589-2,790	1,306	1,210
JOCHAMS, Hyacinth (19th C) Belgian				
oil	1	2,104	2,104	2,104
JOCHEMS, Frans (1880-1949) Belgian				
3D	1	3,279	3,279	3,279
JOCHIMS, Reimer (1934-) German				
oil	1	3,822	3,822	3,822
wc/d	1	636	636	636
JOCHMUS, Harry (1855-1915) German				
oil	1	24,000	24,000	24,000
JODE, Peeter de I (1570-1634) Flemish				
wc/d	2	2,592-2,795	2,693	2,592
JODELET, Emmanuel (1883-1969) French				
oil	4	484-838	683	599
wc/d	1	719	719	719
JODL, Ferdinand (1805-1882) German				
oil	1	1,731	1,731	1,731
JOE, Oreland C (1958-) American				
3D	2	3,400-5,000	4,200	3,400
JOENSEN-MIKINES, Samuel (1906-1979) Danish				
oil	6	3,718-10,668	7,725	7,726
JOFFE, Chantal (1969-) British				
wc/d	1	11,244	11,244	11,244
JOFRE, Rafael (1960-) Spanish				
oil	1	2,059	2,059	2,059
JOHANNOT, Tony (1803-1852) French				
oil	1	4,048	4,048	4,048
JOHANNSEN, Albert (1890-1975) German				
oil	2	1,219-1,844	1,531	1,219
JOHANSEN, Fridolin (1868-1908) Danish				
oil	2	2,895-4,864	3,879	2,895
JOHANSEN, Jan (1938-) American				
oil	1	2,500	2,500	2,500
JOHANSEN, Svend (1890-1970) Danish				
oil	2	4,024-8,405	6,214	4,024
JOHANSEN, Victor (1888-?) Danish				
oil	1	1,500	1,500	1,500
JOHANSEN, Viggo (1851-1935) Danish				
oil	16	534-34,231	5,093	2,157
JOHANSON, Chris (1968-) American				
oil	1	4,200	4,200	4,200
JOHANSON-THOR, Emil (1889-1958) Swedish				
oil	2	435-3,435	1,935	435
JOHANSSON VON COLN, Anders (1663-1716) Swedish				
oil	1	2,119	2,119	2,119
JOHANSSON, Albert (1926-1998) Swedish				
oil	9	1,095-3,700	2,062	2,114
wc/d	4	2,163-2,799	2,529	2,379
JOHANSSON, Arvid (1862-1923) Swedish				
oil	5	448-2,752	1,263	787
JOHANSSON, Carl (1863-1944) Swedish				
oil	13	590-4,808	1,965	1,580
JOHANSSON, Johan (1879-1951) Swedish				
oil	4	1,189-6,998	3,050	1,652
JOHANSSON, Stefan (1876-1955) Swedish				
oil	1	51,520	51,520	51,520
wc/d	1	3,116	3,116	3,116
JOHANSSON, Sven-Erik (1925-) Swedish				
oil	1	2,178	2,178	2,178
JOHFRA (1919-) Dutch				
oil	1	1,146	1,146	1,146
JOHN, Augustus (1878-1961) British				
oil	10	566-113,100	39,026	37,800
wc/d	24	537-124,560	8,113	2,088
3D	1	3,560	3,560	3,560
JOHN, Grace Spaulding (1890-1972) American				
oil	1	8,000	8,000	8,000

Name	No.	Price Range	Average	Median
JOHN, Gwen (1876-1939) British				
wc/d	8	3,740-25,800	10,529	8,600
JOHNS, Jasper (1930-) American				
oil	1	8,433	8,433	8,433
wc/d	3	80,000-1,850,000	960,000	950,000
3D	3	48,000-65,000	57,666	60,000
JOHNSON, A Hale (?) American				
oil	2	1,200-3,200	2,200	1,200
JOHNSON, Alfred (fl.1881-1887) British				
oil	1	2,418	2,418	2,418
JOHNSON, Cecile (20th C) American				
wc/d	1	3,750	3,750	3,750
JOHNSON, Charles Edward (1832-1913) British				
oil	6	692-5,236	2,182	1,100
JOHNSON, Clarence R (1894-1981) American				
oil	1	15,000	15,000	15,000
JOHNSON, David (1827-1908) American				
oil	11	8,000-240,000	44,363	14,000
wc/d	2	750-1,000	875	750
JOHNSON, Eastman (1824-1906) American				
oil	8	2,000-210,000	65,187	20,000
wc/d	1	3,000	3,000	3,000
JOHNSON, Edward (1911-) American				
oil	1	2,700	2,700	2,700
wc/d	1	2,300	2,300	2,300
JOHNSON, Frank Tenney (1874-1939) American				
oil	15	5,000-320,000	107,800	80,000
wc/d	4	1,400-37,500	10,862	1,800
JOHNSON, Harry John (1826-1884) British				
oil	1	9,570	9,570	9,570
wc/d	5	534-2,238	1,231	1,203
JOHNSON, Harvey W (1920-) American				
oil	2	8,750-15,000	11,875	8,750
wc/d	1	600	600	600
JOHNSON, J Seward (jnr) (1930-) American				
3D	1	30,000	30,000	30,000
JOHNSON, Joshua (1765-1830) American				
oil	2	6,500-8,500	7,500	6,500
JOHNSON, Lester (1919-) American				
oil	2	1,800-7,000	4,400	1,800
JOHNSON, Marshall (1850-1921) American				
oil	6	900-10,000	2,800	1,400
JOHNSON, Minnie Wolaver (1874-1954) American				
oil	1	1,400	1,400	1,400
JOHNSON, Neville (1911-1999) British				
oil	3	3,348-8,892	5,508	4,285
JOHNSON, Ray (1927-1995) American				
oil	1	15,000	15,000	15,000
wc/d	10	1,940-10,200	3,703	2,586
JOHNSON, Robert (1890-1964) Australian				
oil	2	1,584-2,500	2,042	1,584
JOHNSON, Samuel Yates (19/20th C) British?				
oil	1	5,103	5,103	5,103
JOHNSTON, Alexander (1815-1891) British				
oil	1	1,800	1,800	1,800
JOHNSTON, David (1946-) British				
oil	2	1,328-4,248	2,788	1,328
JOHNSTON, David Claypoole (1797-1865) American				
wc/d	4	500-3,200	1,262	650
JOHNSTON, Francis (1760-1829) British				
wc/d	4	8,834-40,386	20,193	15,145
JOHNSTON, Frank Hans (1888-1949) Canadian				
oil	33	1,979-49,479	13,912	10,635
wc/d	2	1,725-2,292	2,008	1,725
JOHNSTON, Henrietta (?-c.1728) American				
wc/d	1	45,000	45,000	45,000
JOHNSTON, John Bernard (1847-1886) American				
oil	2	1,000-1,800	1,400	1,000
JOHNSTON, R (?) British				
oil	1	3,000	3,000	3,000

Name	No.	Price Range	Average	Median
JOHNSTON, Reuben le Grand (1850-1919) American				
oil	2	1,000-3,872	2,436	1,000
wc/d	1	1,200	1,200	1,200
JOHNSTONE, Henry James (1835-1907) British				
wc/d	1	3,828	3,828	3,828
JOHNSTONE, John Young (1887-1930) Canadian				
oil	4	3,242-7,379	4,782	3,242
JOHNSTONE, Robert J (20th C) American				
oil	2	1,300-1,360	1,330	1,300
JOHNSTONE, William (1897-1981) British				
oil	8	957-14,268	5,491	4,602
wc/d	2	452-870	661	452
JOLI, Antonio (1700-1770) Italian				
oil	6	185,000-777,000	444,416	370,000
JOLIN, Einar (1890-1976) Swedish				
oil	27	786-20,384	4,622	3,436
wc/d	11	435-8,986	2,927	2,202
JOLLAIN, Nicolas René (younger) (1732-1804) French				
wc/d	2	2,552-2,775	2,663	2,552
JOLLY, F R Auguste (1782-c.1840) French?				
oil	1	11,000	11,000	11,000
JOLLY, Henri Jean Baptist (1812-1853) Belgian				
oil	1	4,944	4,944	4,944
JOLY, Julia (19th C) French				
oil	5	530-1,473	1,083	1,060
JON ONE (20th C) French				
oil	1	5,011	5,011	5,011
JON-AND, John (1889-1941) Swedish				
oil	1	2,417	2,417	2,417
JONAS, John (20th C) British				
oil	1	1,044	1,044	1,044
JONAS, Josef (1805-1863) Austrian				
oil	1	1,937	1,937	1,937
JONAS, Lucien (1880-1947) French				
oil	4	811-25,900	12,575	4,585
wc/d	1	2,102	2,102	2,102
JONCHERE, Evariste (1892-?) French				
oil	2	3,534-3,596	3,565	3,534
3D	2	9,425-14,384	11,904	9,425
JONCIERES, Leonce J V de (1871-1947) French				
oil	2	3,010-4,560	3,785	3,010
JONCKHEER, Jacobus de (fl.1668-1684) Dutch				
oil	1	5,500	5,500	5,500
JONES, A R (?) ?				
oil	1	3,979	3,979	3,979
JONES, Adrian (1845-1938) British				
oil	3	2,464-5,490	3,631	2,941
JONES, Allen (1937-) British				
oil	3	27,750-48,411	38,127	38,220
wc/d	7	522-66,150	14,486	3,292
3D	5	1,653-8,505	5,952	7,400
JONES, Aneurin M (20th C) British				
oil	2	952-2,937	1,944	952
JONES, Arne (1914-1976) Swedish				
3D	3	2,114-19,110	7,923	2,545
JONES, Arthur (20th C) American				
oil	1	2,500	2,500	2,500
JONES, Barbara (1912-1978) British				
wc/d	1	9,204	9,204	9,204
JONES, Bayard (1869-?) American				
wc/d	1	1,200	1,200	1,200
JONES, Brian J (19/20th C) British				
oil	5	5,504-10,440	7,503	6,612
JONES, Charles (1836-1892) British				
oil	7	756-14,080	4,220	2,646
JONES, Chuck (20th C) American				
wc/d	1	6,000	6,000	6,000
JONES, Daniel Adolphe Robert (1806-1874) Belgian				
oil	2	2,111-15,582	8,846	2,111
JONES, David (1895-1974) British				
wc/d	1	28,350	28,350	28,350

Name	No.	Price Range	Average	Median
JONES, F Eastman (19th C) American				
oil	2	1,900-5,000	3,450	1,900
JONES, Frank (1900-1969) American				
wc/d	1	3,800	3,800	3,800
JONES, Fred Cecil (1891-1956) British				
wc/d	1	1,710	1,710	1,710
JONES, Frederick D (1914-) American				
wc/d	1	2,600	2,600	2,600
JONES, Hugh Bolton (1848-1927) American				
oil	10	5,000-30,000	12,624	8,500
JONES, J (?) ?				
3D	1	3,857	3,857	3,857
JONES, Jack (1922-1993) British				
oil	1	650	650	650
wc/d	2	1,098-1,208	1,153	1,098
JONES, Joe (1909-1963) American				
oil	4	450-80,000	20,637	900
JONES, Leon Foster (1871-1934) American				
oil	1	18,000	18,000	18,000
JONES, Lois Mailou (1905-1998) American				
oil	8	4,200-24,000	10,587	6,500
wc/d	10	2,000-7,000	3,485	2,600
JONES, Lucy (1955-) British				
oil	2	522-2,327	1,424	522
JONES, Paul (1921-1998) Australian				
wc/d	5	531-1,581	1,278	1,488
JONES, Paul (19th C) British				
oil	12	519-6,372	1,962	1,400
JONES, Samuel John Egbert (fl.1820-1855) British				
oil	5	708-18,000	6,582	5,500
JONES, Thomas (1742-1803) British				
oil	1	350,550	350,550	350,550
JONES, Tom (?) British				
wc/d	1	1,328	1,328	1,328
JONES, William E (19th C) British				
oil	1	1,400	1,400	1,400
JONG, Hens de (1927-2003) Dutch				
oil	3	514-7,304	2,881	825
JONG, Pieter Josselin de (1861-1906) Dutch				
wc/d	1	10,603	10,603	10,603
JONGE, Johan Antonio de (1864-1927) Dutch				
oil	2	500-7,375	3,937	500
wc/d	1	16,685	16,685	16,685
JONGELINGHS, Karel (?) Belgian				
oil	1	1,215	1,215	1,215
JONGENELIS, Hewald (1962-) Dutch				
oil	1	1,908	1,908	1,908
JONGERE, A van (18/19th C) Dutch?				
oil	1	8,900	8,900	8,900
JONGERE, M de (1912-1978) Dutch				
oil	1	1,832	1,832	1,832
JONGERE, Marinus de (1912-1978) Dutch				
oil	8	717-3,982	2,706	3,000
wc/d	4	492-1,688	844	492
JONGH, Ludolf de (1616-1679) Dutch				
oil	1	11,892	11,892	11,892
JONGH, Oene Romkes de (1812-1896) Dutch				
oil	6	1,818-5,293	3,948	3,886
JONGH, Tinus de (1885-1942) Dutch				
oil	2	1,505-1,567	1,536	1,505
JONGHE, Gustave de (1829-1893) Belgian				
oil	2	3,960-25,000	14,480	3,960
JONGHE, Jan Baptiste de and VERBOECKHOVEN, Eugène (19th C) Flemish				
oil	1	38,014	38,014	38,014
JONGKIND, Johan Barthold (1819-1891) Dutch				
oil	13	1,581-120,377	49,667	43,500
wc/d	28	589-27,951	5,774	2,510
JONK, Nic (1928-1994) Dutch				
3D	6	1,908-8,818	4,424	3,562
JONNEVOLD, Carl Henrik (1856-1955) American				
oil	8	700-7,000	1,950	1,100

Name	No.	Price Range	Average	Median
JONSDOTTIR, Kristin (1888-1958) Icelandic				
oil	1	2,667	2,667	2,667
JONSON, Cornelis (1593-1664) Dutch				
oil	3	5,520-20,000	10,880	7,120
JONSON, Raymond (1891-1982) American				
oil	4	3,750-45,000	24,187	18,000
wc/d	1	7,000	7,000	7,000
JONSON, Sven (1902-1981) Danish				
oil	18	2,036-67,434	14,943	6,234
wc/d	1	2,672	2,672	2,672
JONSSON, Anders (1883-1963) Swedish				
3D	1	10,139	10,139	10,139
JONSSON, Erik (1893-1950) Swedish				
oil	2	1,057-2,048	1,552	1,057
JONSSON, Kers Erik (19th C) Swedish				
oil	1	1,040	1,040	1,040
JONSSON, Lars (1952-) Swedish				
wc/d	1	4,493	4,493	4,493
JONSSON, Ragnar (1956-) Icelandic				
wc/d	2	808-1,212	1,010	808
JONXIS, Pieter Hendrik Lodewyk (1815-1852) Dutch				
oil	1	5,396	5,396	5,396
JONZEN, Hadar (1885-1977) Swedish				
oil	1	1,586	1,586	1,586
JONZEN, Karin (1914-1998) British				
oil	1	448	448	448
3D	2	1,870-4,816	3,343	1,870
JOOP, Wolfgang (20th C) German				
wc/d	1	9,589	9,589	9,589
JOOS, Hildegard and SCHENKER, Harold (20th C) Austrian				
oil	1	8,918	8,918	8,918
JOOSTEN, Dirk Jan Hendrik (1818-1882) Dutch				
oil	2	2,503-19,778	11,140	2,503
JOOSTENS, Paul (1889-1960) Belgian				
oil	10	718-4,944	2,461	1,878
wc/d	6	575-3,371	1,918	1,360
JORBA, Cristoforo Monserrat (1869-1938) Spanish				
oil	1	2,535	2,535	2,535
JORDAENS, Hans (elder) (1539-1630) Flemish				
oil	1	16,571	16,571	16,571
JORDAENS, Hans III (1595-1643) Flemish				
oil	3	6,479-21,776	11,760	7,027
JORDAENS, Jacob (1593-1678) Flemish				
oil	3	16,000-31,679	21,942	18,147
wc/d	4	4,438-25,691	13,082	11,100
JORDAN, Eithne (20th C) Irish?				
oil	1	4,529	4,529	4,529
JORGENSEN, Aksel (1883-1957) Danish				
oil	1	879	879	879
wc/d	1	1,690	1,690	1,690
JORGENSEN, Christian (1860-1935) American				
oil	4	4,000-15,500	8,500	5,000
wc/d	11	1,200-4,250	2,609	2,500
JORGENSEN, Willer (20th C) Danish				
oil	2	1,956-6,125	4,040	1,956
JORGENSON, Patricia (1936-) Irish				
wc/d	3	1,018-2,432	1,520	1,110
JORI, Marcello (1951-) Italian				
oil	8	941-6,146	2,966	2,438
wc/d	1	7,027	7,027	7,027
JORIS, Edgar (1885-1916) Belgian				
3D	1	11,387	11,387	11,387
JORIS, Pio (1843-1921) Italian				
wc/d	4	1,197-2,928	1,755	1,295
JORISSEN, Willem (1871-1910) Dutch				
oil	1	4,756	4,756	4,756
JORN, Asger (1914-1973) Danish				
oil	39	1,001-1,030,157	115,130	42,671
wc/d	19	1,527-30,712	9,249	6,117
3D	3	11,315-56,337	33,546	32,986
JORON, Maurice Paul (1883-1937) French				
oil	1	1,700	1,700	1,700

Name	No.	Price Range	Average	Median
JORSTEDT, Kjell (1943-) Swedish?				
oil	1	3,039	3,039	3,039
JOSEPH (1965-2003) French				
wc/d	1	1,193	1,193	1,193
JOSEPH, George Francis (1764-1846) British				
oil	1	4,524	4,524	4,524
JOSEPH, Joseph (?-2003) French				
oil	1	2,392	2,392	2,392
wc/d	1	1,075	1,075	1,075
JOSEPH, Julian (1882-1964) American				
oil	1	1,000	1,000	1,000
JOSEPH, Philip (20th C) American				
oil	1	1,250	1,250	1,250
JOSEPHSON, Ernst (1851-1906) Swedish				
oil	1	796,750	796,750	796,750
wc/d	25	715-137,371	13,451	3,614
JOSEPHSON, Hans (1920-) Swiss				
3D	1	9,789	9,789	9,789
JOST, Joseph (1888-?) Austrian				
oil	2	2,314-3,480	2,897	2,314
JOTTI, Carlo (1826-1905) Italian				
oil	1	1,916	1,916	1,916
JOUAS, Charles (1866-1942) French				
wc/d	2	526-25,918	13,222	526
JOUBERT, Andree (19th C) French				
oil	2	1,784-3,312	2,548	1,784
JOUBERT, Léon (19th C) French				
oil	1	5,394	5,394	5,394
JOUCLARD, Adrienne (1882-1971) French				
oil	5	592-3,270	1,640	1,401
wc/d	1	960	960	960
JOUENNE, Michel (1933-) French				
oil	8	1,068-7,017	4,243	3,992
wc/d	1	757	757	757
JOUETT, Matthew Harris (1788-1827) American				
oil	1	16,000	16,000	16,000
JOUHAUD, Léon (c.1874-1950) French				
oil	1	2,854	2,854	2,854
JOUKOVSKI, Stanislav (1873-1944) Russian				
oil	5	5,878-407,671	106,092	37,391
JOULIN, Lucien (1842-?) French				
oil	1	7,549	7,549	7,549
JOULLIN, Amadee (1862-1917) American				
oil	1	5,500	5,500	5,500
wc/d	1	800	800	800
JOURAVLOV, Mikael (1952-) Russian				
oil	2	803-1,204	1,003	803
JOURDAN, Émile (1860-1931) French				
oil	3	450-20,083	9,064	6,660
JOURDAN, Theodore (1833-?) French				
oil	1	7,014	7,014	7,014
JOURDEUIL, Louis-Adrien (1849-1907) Russian/French				
oil	1	1,390	1,390	1,390
JOURNIAC, Michel (1943-) French				
wc/d	1	660	660	660
3D	1	2,529	2,529	2,529
JOUSSET, Claude (c.1935-) French				
oil	2	740-3,292	2,016	740
JOUVE, Paul (1880-1973) French				
oil	2	11,449-18,099	14,774	11,449
wc/d	7	624-6,429	4,294	5,036
JOUVENET, Jean Baptiste (1644-1717) French				
wc/d	1	12,153	12,153	12,153
JOUVENET, Noel (?-1698) French				
oil	1	3,010	3,010	3,010
JOVANOVIC, E (19th C) Serbian				
oil	1	25,103	25,103	25,103
JOWETT, Frank B (fl.1915-1938) British				
oil	1	1,313	1,313	1,313
JOWSEY, John Wilson (1884-1963) British				
oil	1	1,566	1,566	1,566

Name	No.	Price Range	Average	Median
JOY, George William (1844-1925) British				
oil	3	15,045-35,910	25,175	24,570
JOY, Thomas Musgrave (1812-1866) British				
oil	1	9,350	9,350	9,350
JOY, William (1803-1867) British				
oil	1	12,180	12,180	12,180
wc/d	2	957-5,610	3,283	957
JOYA, Jose (1931-1995) Philippino				
oil	1	1,400	1,400	1,400
JOYANT, Jules Romain (1803-1854) French				
wc/d	2	714-3,396	2,055	714
JOYCE, Jeff (1956-) American				
oil	2	800-3,000	1,900	800
JOYCE, Stewart (20th C) British				
oil	2	935-1,216	1,075	935
JOYNER, Tim (1966-) American				
oil	1	4,500	4,500	4,500
JOYNT, Dick (1938-2003) Irish				
oil	1	2,104	2,104	2,104
3D	2	2,356-3,063	2,709	2,356
JU MING (1938-) Chinese				
3D	1	130,000	130,000	130,000
JUAN, Ronaldo de (1930-) Argentinian				
oil	1	11,000	11,000	11,000
JUAREZ, Roberto (20th C) ?				
oil	1	16,000	16,000	16,000
JUBIN (?) French?				
oil	1	13,676	13,676	13,676
JUCHSER, Hans (1894-1977) ?				
oil	4	969-6,799	3,976	1,539
wc/d	2	989-1,076	1,032	989
JUDD, Donald (1928-1994) American				
wc/d	6	9,500-800,000	163,429	18,500
3D	59	4,250-2,400,000	547,815	420,000
JUDOWIN, Solomon Borissovitch (c.1892-1955) Russian				
oil	1	54,000	54,000	54,000
JUDSON, William Lees (1842-1928) American				
oil	1	3,750	3,750	3,750
wc/d	1	1,400	1,400	1,400
JUEL, Jens (1745-1802) Danish				
oil	6	13,028-31,752	25,058	28,456
JUILLERAT, Clotilde (1806-1904) French				
oil	1	9,452	9,452	9,452
JUILLERAT, Jacques-Henri (1770-1860) Swiss				
wc/d	3	761-1,458	1,044	913
JUINVILLE, E (19th C) ?				
oil	1	2,816	2,816	2,816
JULIAN, Paul Hull (1914-1995) American				
oil	1	3,500	3,500	3,500
JULIANA Y ALBERT, Jose (1844-1890) Spanish				
wc/d	4	806-4,099	2,189	907
JULIEN, Jean Pierre (1888-?) French				
oil	1	1,940	1,940	1,940
JULIEN, Pierre (1731-1804) French				
3D	1	17,014	17,014	17,014
JULIEN, René (1937-) Belgian				
oil	1	1,335	1,335	1,335
3D	1	1,753	1,753	1,753
JULIEN, Simon (1735-1798) French				
wc/d	1	1,285	1,285	1,285
JULIENNE, Eugène (c.1800-1874) French				
wc/d	1	3,646	3,646	3,646
JULIN, Johan Fredrik (1798-1843) Swedish				
wc/d	2	1,496-9,066	5,281	1,496
JULIUS, Per (1951-) Swedish				
oil	1	943	943	943
wc/d	4	679-2,368	1,311	1,099
JULIUS, Victor (1882-?) American				
oil	1	1,400	1,400	1,400
JULLIAN, Philippe (1919-1977) French				
wc/d	1	1,058	1,058	1,058

Name	No.	Price Range	Average	Median
JULYAN, Mary (fl.1880-1911) British				
oil	1	1,472	1,472	1,472
JUNCKER, Franz (1899-1980) German?				
oil	1	1,155	1,155	1,155
JUNCKER, Hermann Theophil (1929-) German				
oil	1	1,338	1,338	1,338
JUNCKER, Justus (1703-1767) German				
oil	5	2,189-50,000	16,685	9,472
JUNDT, Gustave (1830-1884) French				
oil	1	22,000	22,000	22,000
JUNG, Charles Jacob (?) ?				
oil	1	28,000	28,000	28,000
JUNG, Georg (1899-1957) Austrian				
oil	4	3,857-18,000	7,403	3,879
wc/d	1	2,667	2,667	2,667
JUNGBLUT, Johann (1860-1912) German				
oil	24	486-3,629	1,523	1,401
JUNGHANNS, Julius Paul (1876-1958) Austrian				
oil	2	778-2,057	1,417	778
JUNGHANS, Fritz (1909-1975) German				
oil	1	9,425	9,425	9,425
JUNGHEIM, Carl (1803-1886) German				
oil	1	3,250	3,250	3,250
JUNGMANN, Nico W (1872-1935) British/Dutch				
oil	1	1,548	1,548	1,548
wc/d	2	1,548-2,000	1,774	1,548
JUNGNICKEL, Ludwig Heinrich (1881-1965) German				
oil	2	9,000-15,145	12,072	9,000
wc/d	24	505-7,192	1,830	1,139
JUNGSTEDT, Kurt (1894-1963) Swedish				
oil	4	991-7,441	2,762	1,027
JUNGWIRTH, Martha (1940-) Austrian				
oil	1	9,103	9,103	9,103
wc/d	2	1,403-3,279	2,341	1,403
JURRES, Johannes Hendricus (1875-1946) Dutch				
oil	1	1,800	1,800	1,800
JURY, Anne P (1907-1995) Irish				
oil	4	1,703-4,498	2,761	2,249
JUSELIUS, Erik (1891-1948) Finnish				
oil	3	580-1,678	1,193	1,323
JUSTICE, Jack T (1941-1995) American				
oil	4	970-1,576	1,333	1,334
JUSTYNE, Percy William (1812-1883) British				
oil	1	4,500	4,500	4,500
JUSZCZYK, James (1943-) American				
oil	1	1,654	1,654	1,654
JUTZ, Carl (elder) (1838-1916) German				
oil	10	1,500-39,684	16,131	10,510
JUTZ, Carl (younger) (1873-1915) German				
oil	1	3,534	3,534	3,534
JUUEL, Andreas (1817-1868) Danish				
oil	5	1,141-5,211	2,168	1,537
JUUL, Ole (1852-1927) Norwegian				
oil	3	1,236-2,198	1,781	1,911
JUVA, Kari (1939-) Finnish				
oil	1	3,162	3,162	3,162
JUVENELL, Paul (elder) (1579-1643) German				
oil	1	23,356	23,356	23,356
KABAKOV, Ilya (1933-) Russian				
wc/d	3	3,200-409,200	139,133	5,000
3D	1	70,000	70,000	70,000
KACIMI, Mohamed (1942-2003) Moroccan				
oil	1	5,727	5,727	5,727
KADAR, Bela (1877-1955) Hungarian				
oil	1	1,500	1,500	1,500
wc/d	54	538-32,000	5,776	4,200
KADISHMAN, Menashe (1932-) Israeli				
oil	18	900-10,000	3,587	2,130
3D	4	4,200-30,000	16,550	12,000
KAELIN, Charles Salis (1858-1929) American				
wc/d	2	1,020-2,300	1,660	1,020

Name	No.	Price Range	Average	Median
KAEMMERER, Frederik Hendrik (1839-1902) Dutch				
oil	6	1,987-35,000	16,357	14,720
KAEMMERER, Johan Hendrik (1894-1970) Dutch				
oil	1	1,295	1,295	1,295
KAFANOV, Vasily (1952-) Russian				
oil	2	1,189-8,870	5,029	1,189
wc/d	1	29,730	29,730	29,730
3D	1	7,849	7,849	7,849
KAFKA, Bohumil (1878-?) Czechoslovakian				
3D	1	42,324	42,324	42,324
KAHANA, Aharon (1905-1967) Israeli				
oil	8	460-16,000	7,457	5,000
KAHLER, Carl (1855-?) Austrian				
oil	1	2,400	2,400	2,400
KAHLER, Eugen von (1882-1911) Czechoslovakian				
oil	1	4,123	4,123	4,123
KAHLHAMER, Brad (1956-) American?				
wc/d	2	6,000-20,000	13,000	6,000
KAHLO, Frida (1907-1954) Mexican				
oil	1	5,000,000	5,000,000	5,000,000
KAHN, Susan B (1924-) American				
oil	2	400-3,500	1,950	400
KAHN, Wolf (1927-) American				
oil	8	5,500-25,000	18,937	20,000
wc/d	6	600-4,250	2,658	2,750
KAHRER, Max (1878-1937) Rumanian				
oil	2	1,558-2,148	1,853	1,558
KAIGORODOV, Anatole Dmitrevich (1878-1945) Russian				
oil	2	6,840-7,200	7,020	6,840
KAIN, Thomas (1886-1948) Irish				
oil	1	2,900	2,900	2,900
KAIPIAINEN, Birger (1915-1988) Finnish				
oil	1	3,273	3,273	3,273
KAIRA, Alice (1913-) Finnish				
oil	1	3,343	3,343	3,343
KAISER, C (18th C) German				
oil	1	1,885	1,885	1,885
KAISER, Friedrich (1815-1889) German				
oil	1	1,911	1,911	1,911
KAISER, Fritz (1891-1974) German				
oil	5	542-4,576	2,061	2,104
KAISER, Joseph (1763-1820) German				
3D	1	2,145	2,145	2,145
KAISER, Leander (1947-) Austrian				
oil	1	3,408	3,408	3,408
KAIVANTO, Kimmo (1932-) Finnish				
wc/d	1	1,286	1,286	1,286
KAKABADZE, David (1889-1952) Russian				
oil	1	65,000	65,000	65,000
KAKS, Olle (1941-2003) Swedish				
oil	1	1,018	1,018	1,018
wc/d	1	382	382	382
3D	1	15,904	15,904	15,904
KALAEF, Alexei (1902-1978) Russian				
oil	1	4,886	4,886	4,886
KALCKREUTH, Karl Walter Leopold von (1855-1928) German				
oil	3	1,452-6,540	4,691	6,081
KALCKREUTH, P von (1892-1970) German				
oil	1	2,027	2,027	2,027
KALCKREUTH, Patrick von (1892-1970) German				
oil	21	584-2,142	1,089	877
wc/d	1	730	730	730
KALCKREUTH, Stanislas von (1821-1894) German				
oil	1	7,007	7,007	7,007
KALF, Willem (1619-1693) Dutch				
oil	1	36,330	36,330	36,330
KALININ, Vyacheslav Vasilevich (1939-) Russian				
oil	2	5,580-7,440	6,510	5,580
KALINOWSKI, Horst Egon (1924-) German				
wc/d	2	485-573	529	485
3D	1	2,990	2,990	2,990

Name	No.	Price Range	Average	Median
KALISH, Max (1891-1945) American				
3D	1	4,400	4,400	4,400
KALKAR, Isidor (19/20th C) ?				
oil	1	3,004	3,004	3,004
KALLAT, Jitish (1973-) Indian				
wc/d	2	16,000-35,000	25,500	16,000
KALLAT, Reena Saini (1973-) Indian				
oil	1	32,500	32,500	32,500
wc/d	1	5,236	5,236	5,236
KALLMORGEN, Friedrich (1856-1924) German				
oil	5	4,200-9,555	6,326	4,917
KALLOS, Paul (1928-2002) French				
oil	9	983-4,817	2,283	1,774
wc/d	1	825	825	825
KALLOUDIS, Alexandros (1853-1923) Greek				
oil	1	5,280	5,280	5,280
KALLSTENIUS, Gottfried (1861-1943) Swedish				
oil	20	451-45,332	6,303	1,994
KALMAKOFF, Nicolas (1873-1955) Russian				
oil	3	27,096-121,100	69,309	59,733
wc/d	2	48,360-111,600	79,980	48,360
KALMAR, Georg (1913-1994) Austrian				
oil	1	3,514	3,514	3,514
KALOGEROPOULOS, Leon (1928-2002) Greek				
oil	2	4,928-5,610	5,269	4,928
KALOGEROPOULOS, Nicholaos (1889-1957) Greek				
oil	3	3,740-10,560	7,883	9,350
KALTENMOSER, Kaspar (1806-1867) German				
oil	1	2,474	2,474	2,474
KAMAHIRA, Ben (20th C) American				
oil	1	12,000	12,000	12,000
KAMEKE, Otto von (1826-1899) German				
oil	4	780-2,510	1,571	1,374
KAMENEV, Valerian Konstantinovich (1823-1874) Russian				
oil	1	31,620	31,620	31,620
KAMI, Y Z (1962-) ?				
oil	1	30,000	30,000	30,000
KAMINSKI, Max G (1938-) German				
oil	2	1,767-2,945	2,356	1,767
KAMINSKI, Stan (1952-) British				
oil	1	3,591	3,591	3,591
wc/d	13	448-1,157	774	756
KAMPF, Arthur (1864-1950) German				
oil	2	850-2,788	1,819	850
wc/d	1	350	350	350
KAMPF, Eugen (1861-1933) German				
oil	4	934-2,057	1,535	1,334
KAMPF, Max (1912-1982) Swiss				
oil	2	3,358-5,828	4,593	3,358
wc/d	1	1,068	1,068	1,068
KAMPHUIS, Gerrit (fl.1761-1772) Dutch				
wc/d	1	1,752	1,752	1,752
KAMPMAN, Jack (1914-1989) Danish				
oil	5	995-2,253	1,528	1,455
KAMPMANN, Walter (1887-1945) German				
oil	1	7,027	7,027	7,027
KAMPPURI, Vaino (1891-1972) Finnish				
oil	4	839-3,086	1,560	1,029
KAMROWSKI, Gerome (1914-) American				
oil	1	3,750	3,750	3,750
KAN KIT-KEUNG (1943-) Chinese				
wc/d	1	30,000	30,000	30,000
KANAS, Antonis (1915-) Greek				
oil	4	3,520-5,236	4,586	4,400
KANDELIN, Ole (1920-1947) Finnish				
oil	1	5,657	5,657	5,657
KANDINSKY, Wassily (1866-1944) Russian				
oil	5	157,250-3,450,000	1,506,000	1,232,000
wc/d	8	8,500-647,500	225,279	107,300
KANDYLIS, Michalis (1909-) Greek				
oil	1	1,408	1,408	1,408

Name	No.	Price Range	Average	Median
KANE, Michael (20th C) Irish?				
oil	1	2,735	2,735	2,735
KANELBA, Raymond (1897-1960) Polish				
oil	3	2,038-4,197	3,037	2,877
KANELLIS, Orestis (1910-1979) Greek				
oil	1	1,903	1,903	1,903
KANEMITSU, Matsumi (20th C) ?				
oil	1	8,487	8,487	8,487
KANNE, Philippus Anthonius Alexander (1833-1872) Dutch				
oil	1	1,573	1,573	1,573
KANNEMANS, Christian Cornelis (1812-1884) Dutch				
oil	3	2,081-13,521	6,354	3,461
KANNIK, Frans (1949-) Danish				
wc/d	1	1,293	1,293	1,293
KANO, Tsunenobu (1636-1713) Japanese				
wc/d	1	4,750	4,750	4,750
KANOLDT, Alexander (1881-1939) German				
oil	3	19,110-50,264	36,869	41,233
KANOLDT, Edmund (1845-1904) German				
oil	7	546-8,247	3,055	1,573
wc/d	5	518-1,683	1,126	1,212
KANTERS, Hans (1947-) Dutch				
oil	3	1,767-3,356	2,807	3,299
KANTOR, Morris (1896-1974) American				
oil	1	50,000	50,000	50,000
wc/d	2	450-1,000	725	450
KANTOR, Tadeus (1915-1990) Polish				
oil	5	8,949-20,357	14,543	15,000
wc/d	7	661-40,550	9,579	3,802
KANTOUR, Tibari (1954-) Moroccan				
wc/d	1	4,587	4,587	4,587
KANTSEROV, Alexander Grigorievitch (1877-?) Russian				
wc/d	1	10,320	10,320	10,320
KAO CHI PEI (1672-1734) Chinese				
wc/d	1	3,130	3,130	3,130
KAPELL, P (1876-1943) German				
oil	1	1,690	1,690	1,690
KAPELL, Paul (1876-1943) German				
oil	4	912-5,500	2,386	1,335
KAPLAN, Anatoli (1903-1980) Israeli/Russian				
wc/d	3	1,199-1,539	1,425	1,539
KAPLAN, Hubert (1940-) German				
oil	12	1,084-6,546	3,071	3,012
KAPLAN, Joseph (1900-1980) American				
oil	2	475-800	637	475
wc/d	1	500	500	500
KAPOOR, Anish (1954-) British/Indian				
oil	1	11,968	11,968	11,968
wc/d	5	7,400-49,280	28,054	25,900
3D	5	92,500-740,000	377,300	407,000
KAPOOR, Bhagwan (20th C) Indian				
wc/d	1	2,944	2,944	2,944
KAPP, Gary (1942-) American				
oil	5	2,900-7,000	5,670	6,250
KAPPIS, Albert (1836-1914) German				
oil	5	1,181-17,897	5,017	1,455
KAPPL, Franko (1962-) Austrian				
oil	3	586-4,500	1,968	820
wc/d	2	771-771	771	771
KARAHALIOS, Constantin (1923-) ?				
oil	1	1,212	1,212	1,212
wc/d	2	596-834	715	596
KARAS, Christos (1930-) Greek				
oil	1	29,920	29,920	29,920
KARASIN, Nikolai (1842-1908) Russian				
oil	1	3,343	3,343	3,343
wc/d	3	1,168-8,600	5,570	6,943
KARAVOUSIS, Sarandis (1938-) Greek				
oil	6	954-5,984	1,979	1,074
KARBOWSKY, Adrien (1855-?) French				
oil	1	3,514	3,514	3,514

Name	No.	Price Range	Average	Median
KARCHER, Amalie (19th C) German				
oil	1	1,911	1,911	1,911
KARDIN, V (?) ?				
oil	1	1,854	1,854	1,854
KARDORFF, Konrad von (1877-1945) German				
oil	2	1,399-1,532	1,465	1,399
KARDOVSKAIA, Olga della von (1875-1952) Russian				
oil	1	186,000	186,000	186,000
KARDOVSKY, Dmitry Nikolaevich (1866-1943) Russian				
wc/d	1	14,880	14,880	14,880
KARELLA, Marina (1940-) American				
3D	1	1,730	1,730	1,730
KARFIOL, Bernard (1886-1952) American				
oil	14	600-17,000	3,892	2,900
KARGEL, Axel (1896-1971) Swedish				
oil	9	2,162-5,022	3,268	3,171
KARGER, Karl (1848-1913) Austrian				
oil	1	5,444	5,444	5,444
KARGL, Franz (1834-?) Austrian				
oil	1	1,060	1,060	1,060
KARLOVSKY, Bertalan de (1858-c.1938) Hungarian				
oil	3	599-1,374	1,007	1,050
KARLOWSKA, Stanislawa (1876-1952) Polish				
oil	3	2,262-2,268	2,266	2,268
KARLSSON, C Goran (1944-) Swedish				
oil	5	925-5,598	2,454	1,982
KARNEC, Jean Etienne (1865-1934) Austrian				
oil	1	1,332	1,332	1,332
wc/d	1	1,818	1,818	1,818
KAROLY, G (20th C) Continental				
oil	1	2,264	2,264	2,264
KAROLY, Gerna (1867-1944) Hungarian				
oil	1	2,622	2,622	2,622
KARPINSKI, Alfons (1875-1961) Polish				
oil	1	13,821	13,821	13,821
KARPOFF, Ivan (1898-1970) Russian				
oil	5	623-2,386	1,144	1,018
KARPPANEN, Matti (1873-1953) Finnish				
oil	3	2,571-9,643	4,950	2,637
KARS, Georges (1882-1945) Czechoslovakian				
oil	5	665-7,054	4,059	4,665
KARSCH, Joachim (1897-1945) German				
3D	4	1,757-2,577	2,143	2,003
KARSEN, Jan Eduard (1860-1941) Dutch				
oil	4	1,200-4,219	2,254	1,205
KARSEN, Kaspar (1810-1896) Dutch				
oil	6	4,524-24,722	13,513	9,833
KARSKAYA, Ida (1905-1990) French				
oil	5	715-2,860	1,585	1,312
wc/d	3	715-1,013	893	953
KARSSEN, Anton (1945-) Dutch				
oil	2	825-2,503	1,664	825
KARTSCH, Marie (1848-?) Austrian				
oil	1	1,430	1,430	1,430
KASAKOV, Boris (1937-) Belarussian				
oil	2	708-1,343	1,025	708
KASATKIN, Nikolai Alexeievich (1859-1930) Russian				
oil	1	10,320	10,320	10,320
KASHINA, Nina Vasilievna (1903-?) Russian				
oil	1	10,192	10,192	10,192
KASIMIR, Luigi (1881-1962) Austrian				
oil	1	1,286	1,286	1,286
wc/d	4	935-1,403	1,139	1,052
KASPAR, Paul (1891-1953) Austrian				
oil	1	599	599	599
wc/d	6	602-1,600	1,042	968
KASPARIDES, Edouard (1858-1926) Austrian				
oil	5	5,260-10,188	8,232	9,643
KASPRAZAK, Stephan (1889-?) Russian				
oil	1	1,740	1,740	1,740
KASSAK, Lajos (1887-1967) Hungarian				
wc/d	4	4,087-27,812	13,121	5,860

Name	No.	Price Range	Average	Median
KASYN, John (1926-) Canadian				
oil	5	3,600-13,118	7,305	6,204
wc/d	8	1,312-2,109	1,684	1,687
KAT, Anne-Pierre de (1881-1968) Belgian				
oil	6	477-7,014	2,232	1,023
KAT, Otto Boudewijn de (1907-1995) Dutch				
oil	8	1,527-7,233	4,456	3,781
KATCHADOURIAN, Sarkis (20th C) Iranian				
wc/d	1	1,080	1,080	1,080
KATH, Eske (1975-) Danish				
oil	1	4,507	4,507	4,507
KATO, Hajime (1925-) Japanese				
oil	1	2,616	2,616	2,616
KATZ, Alex (1927-) American				
oil	28	11,000-297,297	78,670	24,000
wc/d	2	450-13,000	6,725	450
3D	1	17,000	17,000	17,000
KATZ, Michele (1936-) French				
wc/d	1	1,155	1,155	1,155
KATZENBERGER, Balthasar (fl.1602-1613) German?				
wc/d	1	7,591	7,591	7,591
KATZENSTEIN, Louis (1822-1907) German				
oil	1	2,958	2,958	2,958
KATZGRABER, Franz (1926-) Austrian				
3D	1	1,753	1,753	1,753
KATZIANNER, T (?) Belgian?				
oil	2	1,753-2,301	2,027	1,753
KATZKE, Gunter (?-1944) German				
wc/d	1	1,414	1,414	1,414
KAUBA, Carl (1865-1922) Austrian/American				
3D	7	2,000-50,000	9,785	2,800
KAUFFER, Edward McKnight (1890-1954) American				
oil	2	6,264-7,308	6,786	6,264
wc/d	2	619-3,024	1,821	619
KAUFFMANN, Angelica (1741-1807) Swiss				
oil	7	37,800-200,000	99,628	60,000
wc/d	1	6,055	6,055	6,055
KAUFFMANN, Craig (1932-) American				
3D	3	13,000-50,000	33,666	38,000
KAUFFMANN, Hermann (elder) (1808-1889) German				
oil	1	3,730	3,730	3,730
wc/d	1	1,403	1,403	1,403
KAUFFMANN, Hugo Wilhelm (1844-1915) German				
oil	16	547-62,000	15,165	7,644
wc/d	4	849-1,757	1,190	1,065
KAUFMANN (19/20th C) ?				
oil	1	2,050	2,050	2,050
KAUFMANN, Adolf (1848-1916) Austrian				
oil	9	650-38,219	6,863	3,178
KAUFMANN, Arthur (1888-1971) German/Argentinian				
oil	1	9,370	9,370	9,370
wc/d	1	507	507	507
KAUFMANN, Ferdinand (1864-1942) German				
oil	11	2,000-10,000	4,818	5,500
KAUFMANN, Hugo (1868-1919) German				
3D	1	1,920	1,920	1,920
KAUFMANN, Isidor (1853-1921) Austrian				
oil	6	23,920-430,000	178,986	110,000
KAUFMANN, Joseph Clemens (1867-1925) Swiss				
oil	1	1,224	1,224	1,224
KAUFMANN, Karl (1843-1901) Austrian				
oil	31	526-24,596	2,991	1,697
KAUFMANN, Massimo (1963-) Italian				
oil	1	2,592	2,592	2,592
KAUFMANN, Wilhelm (1895-1975) Austrian				
oil	9	727-3,343	1,611	1,274
wc/d	1	784	784	784
KAUL, A (20th C) German				
oil	1	2,041	2,041	2,041
KAULA, William J (1871-1952) American				
oil	6	1,900-10,000	7,241	7,250
wc/d	1	500	500	500

Name	No.	Price Range	Average	Median
KAULBACH, Anton (1864-1930) German				
oil	3	565-727	664	701
wc/d	1	907	907	907
KAULBACH, Friedrich (1822-1903) German				
oil	2	7,827-8,429	8,128	7,827
wc/d	1	701	701	701
KAULBACH, Friedrich August von (1850-1920) German				
oil	11	707-10,603	4,039	4,204
wc/d	4	608-3,534	1,533	973
KAULBACH, Hermann (1846-1909) German				
oil	6	892-6,360	2,877	2,040
KAULBACH, Wilhelm von (1805-1874) German				
wc/d	1	1,272	1,272	1,272
KAULUM, Haakon Jensen (1863-1933) Norwegian				
oil	1	1,022	1,022	1,022
KAUPPI, Lea (1917-) Finnish				
oil	1	2,314	2,314	2,314
KAUS, Max (1891-1977) German				
oil	5	2,928-17,568	8,836	4,834
wc/d	4	1,375-4,452	2,865	1,818
KAUTZKY, Ted (?-1953) American/Hungarian				
oil	1	3,750	3,750	3,750
KAUW, Albrecht (1621-1681) Swiss				
oil	1	133,500	133,500	133,500
KAUZMANN, Paul (1874-1951) German				
oil	3	2,592-12,123	6,182	3,832
KAVANAGH, Joseph Malachy (1856-1918) Irish				
oil	5	700-29,452	15,299	11,427
KAVANAGH, Mark (1977-) Irish				
oil	1	1,295	1,295	1,295
KAVIK, John (1897-1993) North American				
wc/d	2	3,037-5,736	4,386	3,037
3D	9	1,603-4,387	2,310	2,193
KAVLI, Arne Texnes (1878-1970) Norwegian				
oil	2	4,250-25,760	15,005	4,250
KAWABATA, Ryushi (1885-1966) Japanese				
wc/d	1	2,500	2,500	2,500
KAWARA, On (1933-) Japanese				
wc/d	8	40,700-545,600	276,581	240,000
KAY, Archibald (1860-1935) British				
oil	6	878-9,790	3,596	1,211
KAY, James (1858-1942) British				
oil	13	974-15,930	7,529	5,340
wc/d	12	496-11,180	2,272	1,451
KAYE, Otis (1885-1974) American				
oil	3	8,000-12,000	9,333	8,000
KAYSER, Conrad (1880-?) German				
oil	1	1,459	1,459	1,459
KCHAOUDOFF, Jeantimir (1941-) French				
oil	1	760	760	760
wc/d	2	1,193-1,752	1,472	1,193
KCHO (1970-) Cuban				
wc/d	2	8,500-12,000	10,250	8,500
KEABLE, William (c.1714-1774) British				
oil	1	16,000	16,000	16,000
KEANE, John (1954-) British				
oil	3	4,984-10,620	7,694	7,480
KEANE, Margaret (1927-) American				
oil	1	750	750	750
wc/d	1	1,800	1,800	1,800
KEANE, Paul (20th C) American				
oil	1	2,200	2,200	2,200
KEARNEY, John (1924-) American				
3D	1	2,000	2,000	2,000
KEARNS, Stapleton (1952-) American				
oil	1	1,200	1,200	1,200
KEAST, Susette Schultz (?-1932) American				
oil	1	2,600	2,600	2,600
KEATING, Sean (1889-1978) Irish				
oil	7	14,880-194,384	92,490	96,417
wc/d	9	3,720-28,431	12,418	11,676

Name	No.	Price Range	Average	Median
KEATS, Cecil Jack (?) British				
wc/d	1	1,505	1,505	1,505
KECIR, Bohomil (1904-1987) Austrian				
oil	3	1,678-2,910	2,128	1,798
KECK, Otto (1873-1948) German				
oil	4	1,216-3,273	2,040	1,455
KEDL, Rudolf (1928-1991) Austrian?				
3D	2	7,598-24,276	15,937	7,598
KEELHOFF, Frans (1820-1893) Belgian				
oil	1	3,741	3,741	3,741
KEELING, William Knight (1807-1886) British				
oil	1	3,828	3,828	3,828
KEENE, Charles Samuel (1823-1891) British				
wc/d	2	1,860-2,232	2,046	1,860
KEENEESIAK (20th C) North American				
3D	1	3,206	3,206	3,206
KEEP, Alice Leavitt (19/20th C) American				
oil	1	1,600	1,600	1,600
KEHREN, C (19th C) German				
oil	1	11,959	11,959	11,959
KEIJZER, Rob (1958-) Dutch				
oil	1	2,799	2,799	2,799
KEIL, Bernhard (1624-1687) Danish				
oil	4	4,861-90,000	45,215	26,000
KEIL, Christian (1826-1890) German				
3D	1	15,205	15,205	15,205
KEIL, Edouard (20th C) French				
oil	1	4,629	4,629	4,629
KEIL, G F (19th C) American				
oil	1	14,000	14,000	14,000
KEINANEN, Sigfrid August (1841-1914) Finnish				
oil	4	2,928-6,312	4,152	3,514
KEIRINCX, Alexander (1600-1652) Flemish				
oil	1	8,918	8,918	8,918
KEISERMANN, Franz (1765-1833) Swiss				
wc/d	11	1,942-29,600	10,610	5,412
KEITH, William (1839-1911) American				
oil	19	1,500-170,000	15,505	4,750
wc/d	3	1,200-3,800	2,466	2,400
KEIZO, Morishita (1944-) Japanese				
oil	1	1,272	1,272	1,272
KELDER, Toon (1894-1973) Dutch				
oil	7	1,272-28,027	8,328	5,852
wc/d	1	1,878	1,878	1,878
KELETY, Alexander (20th C) French				
3D	4	1,878-70,275	20,775	3,236
KELL, Laurence (1974-) British				
oil	1	1,274	1,274	1,274
KELLEN, David van der (19th C) Dutch				
oil	1	2,090	2,090	2,090
KELLEN, David van der III (1827-1895) Dutch				
oil	1	3,507	3,507	3,507
KELLEN, Hendrika Wilhelmina van der (1846-1903) Dutch				
oil	3	630-2,503	1,687	1,929
KELLER, A (?) ?				
wc/d	1	2,831	2,831	2,831
KELLER, Albert von (1844-1920) Swiss				
oil	9	912-3,649	2,319	1,987
KELLER, Arthur (?) German?				
oil	1	3,480	3,480	3,480
KELLER, Arthur I (1866-1925) American				
wc/d	2	1,000-1,500	1,250	1,000
KELLER, Clyde Leon (1872-1962) American				
oil	4	850-1,600	1,125	850
KELLER, Edgar Martin (1868-1932) American				
oil	2	1,900-3,500	2,700	1,900
KELLER, F (19th C) West Indian				
oil	1	2,264	2,264	2,264
KELLER, Ferdinand (1842-1922) German				
oil	2	8,818-77,280	43,049	8,818

Name	No.	Price Range	Average	Median
KELLER, Friedrich von (1840-1914) German				
oil	11	1,492-13,200	3,830	2,572
KELLER, G W (19th C) American				
oil	1	2,710	2,710	2,710
KELLER, Henry George (1870-1949) American				
oil	1	800	800	800
wc/d	2	400-730	565	400
KELLER, Johann Heinrich (1692-1765) Swiss				
oil	1	6,910	6,910	6,910
KELLER-REUTLINGEN, Paul Wilhelm (1854-1920) German				
oil	4	1,414-7,259	5,483	6,000
wc/d	1	1,548	1,548	1,548
KELLEY, Mike (1954-) American				
oil	5	12,000-360,000	92,900	30,000
wc/d	8	10,000-390,000	116,125	40,000
3D	7	20,027-400,000	166,003	170,000
KELLEY, Ramon (1939-) American				
oil	7	600-7,000	2,871	2,250
wc/d	7	400-4,000	2,321	2,400
KELLUM, Hayden Charles (1894-1953) American				
oil	1	1,500	1,500	1,500
KELLY, Ellsworth (1923-) American				
wc/d	2	90,000-140,000	115,000	90,000
KELLY, Felix (1916-1994) New Zealander				
oil	3	4,350-19,140	12,390	13,680
wc/d	1	450	450	450
KELLY, John (1932-) Irish				
wc/d	1	2,121	2,121	2,121
KELLY, John Melville (1879-1962) American				
oil	1	50,000	50,000	50,000
KELLY, Leon (1901-1982) American				
oil	6	2,224-4,994	3,344	2,848
wc/d	15	648-3,625	1,742	1,424
KELLY, Oisin (?) British?				
oil	1	681	681	681
3D	3	2,664-12,016	7,834	8,822
KELLY, Paul (1968-) Irish				
oil	3	726-3,218	1,910	1,788
KELLY, Peter (20th C) British				
oil	1	1,229	1,229	1,229
KELLY, Richard Barrett Talbot (1896-1971) British				
wc/d	5	718-1,932	1,262	1,128
KELLY, Robert George Talbot (1861-1934) British				
wc/d	7	516-5,952	1,998	1,110
KELLY, Sir Gerald (1879-1972) British				
oil	11	659-74,760	15,016	2,418
KELPE, Paul (1902-1985) German				
wc/d	1	26,000	26,000	26,000
KELS, Franz (1828-1893) German				
oil	1	14,500	14,500	14,500
KELSEY, Greg (?) American				
3D	1	9,000	9,000	9,000
KELSEY, Robert (1949-) British				
oil	1	2,160	2,160	2,160
KEMBLE, Kenneth (1912-1998) Argentinian				
oil	2	25,000-28,000	26,500	25,000
wc/d	1	2,000	2,000	2,000
KEMENY, Kalman (1896-1994) Hungarian				
oil	1	1,539	1,539	1,539
KEMENY, Zoltan (1907-1965) Swiss				
3D	1	9,737	9,737	9,737
KEMM, Robert (fl.1874-1885) British				
oil	6	2,119-10,082	6,065	6,612
KEMNITZ, Ludwig von (19th C) German				
oil	1	1,985	1,985	1,985
KEMP, Jeka (1876-1967) British				
wc/d	2	1,253-3,553	2,403	1,253
KEMP, Louise (?) American?				
oil	1	1,000	1,000	1,000
KEMP, Oliver (1887-1934) American				
oil	1	13,000	13,000	13,000

Name	No.	Price Range	Average	Median
KEMP-WELCH, Lucy (1869-1958) British				
oil	3	1,131-15,652	6,087	1,480
wc/d	8	718-19,845	5,714	3,654
KENDE, Geza (1889-1952) American				
oil	2	1,200-9,000	5,100	1,200
KENDRICK, Mel (1949-) American				
3D	2	2,250-4,200	3,225	2,250
KENDRICK, Sydney (1874-1955) British				
oil	1	4,375	4,375	4,375
KENNEDY, Cecil (1905-1997) British				
oil	14	657-59,840	20,466	11,895
KENNEDY, Joseph (fl.1861-1888) British				
oil	1	1,225	1,225	1,225
KENNEDY, Maurice (?) American				
oil	1	1,100	1,100	1,100
KENNEDY, William (1860-1918) British				
oil	3	4,618-6,222	5,197	4,752
KENNEDY, William W (1818-1871) American				
oil	2	4,000-6,000	5,000	4,000
KENNEY, John Theodore Eardley (1911-1972) British				
oil	2	6,500-6,500	6,500	6,500
KENNINGTON, Eric (1888-1960) British				
wc/d	2	9,405-14,160	11,782	9,405
KENNINGTON, Thomas Benjamin (1856-1916) British				
oil	2	90,000-90,720	90,360	90,000
KENNY, Desmond (1956-) Irish				
oil	1	1,070	1,070	1,070
KENNY, Michael (1941-2000) British				
wc/d	2	885-1,480	1,182	885
KENSETT, John Frederick (1816-1872) American				
oil	7	2,250-1,100,000	184,964	15,000
wc/d	1	1,800	1,800	1,800
KENT, Rockwell (1882-1971) American				
oil	4	15,000-90,000	65,000	70,000
wc/d	9	400-9,000	2,511	1,700
KENTRIDGE, William (1955-) South African				
wc/d	2	26,400-35,000	30,700	26,400
KENWORTHY, John Dalzell (1858-1954) British				
oil	1	2,852	2,852	2,852
KENZLER, Carl (20th C) German				
oil	1	1,381	1,381	1,381
KEOGH, Tom (1921-1980) American/Irish				
wc/d	1	4,190	4,190	4,190
KEPES, Gyorgy (1906-2001) American/Hungarian				
oil	4	475-2,500	1,803	2,040
wc/d	1	5,000	5,000	5,000
KER, Dorian (1948-) British				
wc/d	1	5,000	5,000	5,000
KERANEN, Veikko (1935-) Finnish				
3D	1	2,048	2,048	2,048
KERELS, Henri (1896-1956) Belgian				
oil	4	715-5,959	2,531	1,697
KERKAM, Earl C (1890-1965) American				
oil	1	1,000	1,000	1,000
wc/d	1	375	375	375
KERKHOFF, Maurits van den (1830-1908) Dutch				
oil	1	2,277	2,277	2,277
KERKOVIUS, Ida (1879-1970) German				
oil	4	1,623-12,103	6,108	5,143
wc/d	16	445-10,813	3,695	2,428
KERMADEC, Eugène Nestor le (1899-1976) French				
oil	6	2,655-6,903	4,697	4,685
wc/d	2	1,057-1,288	1,172	1,057
KERMAN, E (?) ?				
oil	1	1,840	1,840	1,840
KERMARREC, Joel (1939-) French				
oil	4	1,286-5,959	3,761	3,625
wc/d	3	486-1,788	1,252	1,483
KERN, Hermann (1839-1912) Hungarian				
oil	18	1,073-8,281	4,394	3,933
KERN, Josef (20th C) ?				
oil	1	4,586	4,586	4,586

Name	No.	Price Range	Average	Median
KERNN-LARSEN, Rita (1904-1998) Danish				
oil	2	566-3,541	2,053	566
wc/d	3	483-515	493	483
KERNOFF, Harry Aaron (1900-1974) British				
oil	9	1,979-96,603	25,112	15,811
wc/d	16	1,740-25,027	6,468	3,708
KERR, Blanche Weyburn (1872-1955) American				
oil	1	1,900	1,900	1,900
KERR, George Cochrane (c.1825-1907) British				
oil	4	563-26,100	7,386	968
KERR, Henry Wright (1857-1936) British				
oil	1	1,286	1,286	1,286
wc/d	9	412-3,096	1,304	1,062
KERR, Illingsworth Holey (1905-1988) Canadian				
oil	21	746-23,621	4,393	2,803
wc/d	4	410-643	562	574
KERR, Tiko (1953-) Canadian?				
oil	1	8,863	8,863	8,863
KERR-LAWSON, James (1865-1939) British				
oil	2	487-4,848	2,667	487
KERSCHENSTEINER, Joseph (1864-1936) German				
oil	2	485-1,826	1,155	485
KERSEY, Laurie (20th C) American				
oil	1	3,750	3,750	3,750
KERSHAW, J Franklin (20th C) British				
oil	1	3,490	3,490	3,490
KERSTING, Georg Friedrich (1785-1847) Danish				
oil	1	26,482	26,482	26,482
KESSANLIS, Nikos (1930-2004) Greek				
oil	5	12,155-54,230	38,291	40,020
wc/d	3	8,650-24,360	13,886	8,650
KESSEL, Jan van I (1626-1679) Flemish				
oil	6	43,250-130,000	72,805	51,800
KESSEL, Jan van II (1654-1708) Flemish				
oil	1	55,373	55,373	55,373
KESSEL, Willem van (18th C) Flemish				
oil	1	2,919	2,919	2,919
KESSLER, August (1826-1906) German				
oil	3	1,518-13,110	8,411	10,605
KESSLER, Carl (1876-1968) German				
oil	2	589-665	627	589
wc/d	5	514-1,757	1,040	909
KESSLER, David (1950-) American				
oil	2	3,250-4,000	3,625	3,250
KESSLER, Jon (1957-) American				
3D	1	1,730	1,730	1,730
KESSLER, Stephan (1622-1700) Austrian				
oil	1	24,196	24,196	24,196
KESTING, Edmund (1892-1970) German				
wc/d	7	538-4,919	1,960	1,674
KET, Dick (1902-1940) Dutch				
wc/d	1	3,507	3,507	3,507
KETTEMANN, Erwin (1897-1971) German				
oil	10	608-3,403	1,527	1,073
wc/d	1	779	779	779
KETTER, Clay (1961-) Swedish				
oil	3	1,784-11,000	5,928	5,000
KETTLE, Tilly (1735-1786) British				
oil	5	9,000-85,000	30,704	20,520
KEULEN, Simon van (1926-) Dutch				
3D	1	2,290	2,290	2,290
KEULEYAN-LAFON, Jean (1886-1973) French				
oil	3	507-3,569	1,621	787
KEULTJES, Gerrit Laurens (1786-?) Dutch				
oil	1	2,281	2,281	2,281
KEVER, Jacob Simon Hendrik (1854-1922) Dutch				
oil	7	1,400-4,944	2,973	2,411
wc/d	3	1,100-11,677	7,847	10,764
KEVILLE LEGROS, James (20th C) ?				
wc/d	2	3,579-12,528	8,053	3,579
KEVORKIAN, Jean (1933-) French?				
oil	1	2,822	2,822	2,822

Name	No.	Price Range	Average	Median
KEY, Geoffrey (1946-) British				
oil	10	487-8,883	2,883	1,770
wc/d	16	487-1,131	697	623
KEY, John Ross (1837-1920) American				
oil	1	5,500	5,500	5,500
KEY-AABERG, Elisif (1899-1982) Swedish				
oil	1	2,163	2,163	2,163
KEYL, Friedrich Wilhelm (1823-1871) German				
oil	2	3,828-5,292	4,560	3,828
KEYMEULEN, Émile (1840-1882) Belgian				
oil	1	1,032	1,032	1,032
KEYSER, Adrien de (1914-1950) French?				
oil	2	518-1,665	1,091	518
KEYSER, Albert de (1829-1890) Belgian				
oil	1	2,697	2,697	2,697
KEYSER, Elisabeth (1851-1898) Swedish				
oil	2	1,745-10,220	5,982	1,745
KEYSER, Ephraim (1850-1937) American				
3D	1	4,250	4,250	4,250
KEYSER, Hendrick de (elder) (1565-1621) Dutch				
3D	1	25,950	25,950	25,950
KEYSER, Jean Baptiste de (1857-?) Belgian				
3D	1	10,000	10,000	10,000
KEYSER, Nicaise de (1813-1887) Flemish				
oil	1	4,536	4,536	4,536
KEYSER, Ragnhild (1889-1943) Norwegian				
oil	1	1,293	1,293	1,293
KEYSER, Raoul de (1933-) Belgian				
oil	3	4,500-7,007	5,449	4,841
wc/d	4	2,500-5,096	3,746	3,567
KEYSER, Thomas de (1596-1667) Dutch				
oil	1	24,205	24,205	24,205
KEYT, George (1901-1993) Indian				
oil	15	7,500-89,760	23,021	19,360
wc/d	6	2,112-20,000	9,700	4,928
KHAIMOV, Iakov (1914-1991) Russian				
oil	1	24,780	24,780	24,780
KHAKKAR, Bhupen (1934-2003) Indian				
wc/d	2	7,000-9,500	8,250	7,000
KHAN, Ghulam Murtaza (19th C) Indian				
wc/d	2	13,500-25,200	19,350	13,500
KHANNA, Balraj (1940-) Indian				
oil	9	1,038-37,400	10,656	3,168
KHANNA, Krishen (1925-) Indian				
oil	8	12,110-75,000	40,032	28,050
wc/d	4	7,500-13,000	10,625	11,000
KHARITONOV, Nikolai Vasilievich (1880-1944) Russian				
oil	2	4,350-13,000	8,675	4,350
KHASTGIR, Sudhir Ranjan (1907-1974) Indian				
wc/d	1	2,525	2,525	2,525
KHIDEKEL, Lazar Markovich (1904-1986) Russian				
wc/d	1	2,976	2,976	2,976
KHITROVA, Tamara (20th C) Russian				
oil	1	3,092	3,092	3,092
KHMELUK, Vassyl (1903-) Russian				
oil	22	1,506-17,200	5,066	3,766
wc/d	10	504-3,529	1,634	1,008
KHNOPFF, Fernand (1858-1921) Belgian				
wc/d	6	2,795-147,900	47,037	17,524
KHODASEVICH, Valentina (1894-1970) Russian				
wc/d	2	10,000-16,368	13,184	10,000
KHOLODOVSKY, Mikhail Ivanovich (1855-1925) Russian				
oil	3	6,821-56,700	28,614	22,323
KHOOR, Jozsef (1817-?) Hungarian				
oil	1	1,192	1,192	1,192
KHOURY, Michael (1950-) Canadian				
oil	1	1,148	1,148	1,148
KHRUSTALYOVA, Sophia Ivanovna (1915-) Russian				
oil	1	2,500	2,500	2,500
KIAERSKOU, F (1805-1891) Danish				
oil	5	538-2,197	1,116	869

Name	No.	Price Range	Average	Median
KIAERSKOU, Frederik (1805-1891) Danish				
oil	4	2,085-10,829	4,516	2,258
KICCO (1969-) Italian				
oil	1	2,003	2,003	2,003
wc/d	2	1,909-2,160	2,034	1,909
3D	2	1,844-1,942	1,893	1,844
KICK, Cornelis (1635-1681) Dutch				
oil	1	95,000	95,000	95,000
KIDD, Joseph Bartholomew (1806-1889) British				
oil	2	3,449-45,000	24,224	3,449
KIDD, Niall (1951-) Irish?				
oil	1	1,100	1,100	1,100
KIDD, Richard (1917-) British				
wc/d	1	1,593	1,593	1,593
KIDD, William (1790-1863) British				
oil	1	2,108	2,108	2,108
KIEFER, Anselm (1945-) German				
oil	7	8,182-1,147,000	390,697	277,500
wc/d	4	19,000-130,000	79,312	83,250
KIELDRUP, A E (1826-1869) Danish				
oil	2	1,078-2,432	1,755	1,078
KIELDRUP, Anton Edvard (1826-1869) Danish				
oil	1	4,385	4,385	4,385
KIELHOLZ, Heinrich (1942-) Swiss				
wc/d	4	457-1,598	1,217	1,370
KIEN, Josef (1903-1985) German				
oil	3	1,212-5,291	2,725	1,674
wc/d	3	529-1,060	883	1,060
KIENBUSCH, William (1914-1980) American				
oil	1	6,000	6,000	6,000
wc/d	3	800-4,500	2,333	1,700
KIENHOLZ, Edward (1927-1994) American				
oil	1	3,000	3,000	3,000
wc/d	2	1,845-1,972	1,908	1,845
3D	2	1,982-3,884	2,933	1,982
KIENHOLZ, Edward and Nancy (20th C) American				
3D	3	3,500-11,712	6,737	5,000
KIENINGER, Vinzenz Georg (1768-1851) Austrian?				
wc/d	1	4,944	4,944	4,944
KIENMAYER, Franz (20th C) German				
oil	2	1,030-4,087	2,558	1,030
KIERS, George Laurens (1838-1916) Dutch				
oil	2	1,334-5,257	3,295	1,334
KIERS, Petrus (1807-1875) Dutch				
oil	1	1,808	1,808	1,808
KIERZKOWSKI, Bronislaw (1924-1993) Polish				
oil	1	1,244	1,244	1,244
KIESEL, Conrad (1846-1921) German				
oil	4	964-17,000	8,802	1,697
KIESEWETTER, August Wilhelm (1811-1865) German				
oil	1	2,534	2,534	2,534
KIESLER, Frederic (1896-?) American				
3D	1	2,400	2,400	2,400
KIEWE, Chaim (1912-1983) Israeli				
oil	2	1,200-1,500	1,350	1,200
KIFF, Ken (1935-2001) British				
oil	1	14,800	14,800	14,800
wc/d	2	1,947-2,924	2,435	1,947
KIHLEN, Ides (20th C) Argentinian				
wc/d	1	1,460	1,460	1,460
KIJNO, Ladislas (1921-) French				
oil	45	887-22,966	3,074	1,786
wc/d	43	418-5,208	1,914	1,816
3D	1	4,676	4,676	4,676
KIKOINE, Michel (1892-1968) Russian				
oil	25	3,186-19,622	9,426	7,875
wc/d	8	420-3,306	1,168	717
KIKUCHI, Yosai (1788-1878) Japanese				
wc/d	1	4,671	4,671	4,671
KILBURNE, George Goodwin (1839-1924) British				
oil	8	1,283-7,830	3,976	2,590
wc/d	22	626-18,600	3,919	3,000

Name	No.	Price Range	Average	Median
KILBURNE, George Goodwin (jnr) (1863-1938) British				
wc/d	1	4,092	4,092	4,092
KILIMNICK, Karen (1955-) American				
oil	4	46,000-230,000	138,000	111,000
wc/d	6	7,392-35,000	20,348	17,700
KILLEN, Robert T (?) British?				
oil	1	3,892	3,892	3,892
KILPACK, Sarah Louise (1839-1909) British				
oil	16	500-5,022	2,057	2,200
wc/d	1	465	465	465
KILPATRICK, Aaron Edward (1872-1953) American				
oil	1	1,000	1,000	1,000
KIM EN JOONG (1940-) Korean				
wc/d	2	1,075-1,075	1,075	1,075
KIM KANG-YONG (1950-) Korean				
wc/d	1	18,000	18,000	18,000
KIM KIRA (1950-) Korean				
3D	1	12,950	12,950	12,950
KIM SOOJA (1957-) Korean				
3D	1	18,000	18,000	18,000
KIM TSCHANG-YEUL (1929-) Korean				
oil	4	17,019-42,000	28,060	24,000
KIM, Minjung (1962-) Korean				
wc/d	2	12,000-15,000	13,500	12,000
KIMBALL, Charles Frederick (1835-1903) American				
oil	3	800-2,500	1,400	900
KIMBALL, Eliot (20th C) American				
oil	1	2,500	2,500	2,500
KIMMEL, Cornelis (1804-1877) British				
oil	3	1,205-7,192	3,305	1,518
KINABLE, Joseph Dieudonne (18/19th C) ?				
3D	1	1,790	1,790	1,790
KINCH, Agnete Helvig (1872-1956) Danish				
oil	1	2,223	2,223	2,223
KINDBORG, Johan (1861-1907) Swedish				
oil	4	590-5,400	3,304	1,994
KINDERMANN, Dominik (1739-1817) Czechoslovakian				
wc/d	1	1,927	1,927	1,927
KINDERMANS, Jean-Baptiste (c.1822-1876) Belgian				
oil	1	3,741	3,741	3,741
KINDLEBERGER, David (fl.1900-1905) American				
oil	1	17,000	17,000	17,000
KINDLER, Albert (1833-1876) German				
oil	2	536-2,000	1,268	536
KINDT, Adele (1804-1884) Belgian				
oil	1	7,526	7,526	7,526
KINDT, Max (?-1970) German				
oil	1	1,640	1,640	1,640
KING CARL XV OF SWEDEN (1826-1872) Swedish				
oil	1	4,121	4,121	4,121
KING, Albert F (1854-1945) American				
oil	4	1,096-7,500	4,711	4,750
KING, Brian (20th C) Irish?				
3D	1	6,539	6,539	6,539
KING, Captain John Duncan (1789-1863) British				
oil	1	5,952	5,952	5,952
KING, Cecil (1921-1986) Irish				
oil	16	707-5,207	2,278	1,453
wc/d	5	1,155-3,330	1,757	1,520
KING, Charles Bird (1785-1862) American				
oil	1	1,000	1,000	1,000
KING, Edward (1863-?) British				
oil	6	1,009-3,500	2,270	2,100
KING, Elizabeth Thomson (1848-1914) British				
oil	1	609	609	609
wc/d	1	487	487	487
KING, Gordon (?) British				
oil	1	2,590	2,590	2,590
wc/d	4	673-4,200	1,778	952
KING, Haynes (1831-1904) British				
oil	8	1,400-12,320	4,763	3,480

Name	No.	Price Range	Average	Median
KING, Henry John Yeend (1855-1924) British				
oil	22	400-11,340	3,953	3,480
wc/d	7	463-1,890	1,236	1,209
KING, James S (1852-1925) American				
oil	1	3,000	3,000	3,000
KING, Jessie M (1875-1949) British				
wc/d	8	463-4,956	1,234	534
KING, John Baragwanath (1864-1939) British				
oil	2	845-1,295	1,070	845
wc/d	2	692-708	700	692
KING, John Gregory (1929-) British				
wc/d	2	821-2,600	1,710	821
KING, May V (19/20th C) American				
oil	1	1,200	1,200	1,200
KING, Paul (1867-1947) American				
oil	5	1,800-26,000	11,510	4,750
KING, Phillip (1934-) British				
3D	2	4,000-12,950	8,475	4,000
KING, Robert (1936-) British				
oil	4	711-1,691	1,248	990
KING, Thomas W (19th C) British				
oil	2	1,400-1,607	1,503	1,400
KING, W Gunning (1859-1940) British				
oil	6	865-1,607	1,113	915
KING-HARMAN, Ann Stafford (1919-1979) Irish				
oil	1	1,210	1,210	1,210
wc/d	1	570	570	570
KINGERLEE, John (1936-) Irish?				
oil	30	970-93,000	9,797	3,816
wc/d	11	966-3,185	1,469	1,089
KINGILIK, Dominic (1939-1990) North American				
3D	1	2,531	2,531	2,531
KINGMAN, Dong (1911-2000) American				
wc/d	6	450-10,000	4,283	2,750
KINGMAN, Eduardo (1913-1997) Ecuadorian				
oil	2	8,500-8,500	8,500	8,500
KINGSTON, Jennifer (20th C) Irish				
oil	2	1,060-1,697	1,378	1,060
KINGSTON, Richard (1922-2003) British				
oil	13	1,165-12,109	6,189	5,760
KININGER, Vincenz Georg (1767-1851) German				
wc/d	1	1,580	1,580	1,580
KINKADE, Thomas (20th C) American				
oil	1	30,000	30,000	30,000
KINLEY, Peter (1926-1988) British				
oil	4	6,726-24,000	14,015	9,405
wc/d	1	1,038	1,038	1,038
KINNAIRD, Frederick Gerald (19th C) British				
oil	2	1,460-2,317	1,888	1,460
KINNAIRD, Henry J (fl.1880-1908) British				
oil	4	1,500-5,704	3,838	3,150
wc/d	24	673-4,524	1,531	1,232
KINNEY, Desmond (1934-) British				
oil	2	1,107-1,818	1,462	1,107
wc/d	1	2,425	2,425	2,425
KINSELLA, Lucy (1960-) British				
3D	1	52,920	52,920	52,920
KINSEY, Alberta (1875-1955) American				
oil	5	1,700-14,000	4,620	2,400
KINSON, François Joseph (1771-1839) Flemish				
wc/d	1	8,236	8,236	8,236
KINZEL, Josef (1852-1925) Austrian				
oil	5	1,526-6,105	2,660	2,027
KINZEL, Liesl (1886-1961) Austrian				
oil	1	1,998	1,998	1,998
wc/d	1	1,414	1,414	1,414
KIOERBOE, Carl Fredrik (1799-1876) Swedish				
	3	1,447-4,500	2,478	1,488
KIPPENBERGER, Martin (1953-1997) German				
oil	26	8,767-777,000	174,080	94,247
wc/d	15	2,797-50,000	12,517	7,965
3D	5	3,500-28,000	15,967	17,300

Name	No.	Price Range	Average	Median
KIPPENBERGER, Martin and OEHLEN, Albert (20th C) German				
oil	1	180,000	180,000	180,000
KIPRENSKY, Oreste (c.1778-1836) Russian				
wc/d	1	2,472	2,472	2,472
KIPS, Erich (1869-?) German				
oil	6	665-4,855	1,943	1,311
KIRBERG, Otto (1850-1926) German				
oil	4	605-3,045	1,805	1,255
KIRBY, John (1949-) British				
oil	2	8,850-24,975	16,912	8,850
KIRCHNER, Albert Emil (1813-1885) German				
oil	1	10,507	10,507	10,507
KIRCHNER, Ernst Ludwig (1880-1938) German				
oil	5	8,132-7,788,000	2,477,357	725,102
wc/d	64	1,671-220,000	24,466	13,000
3D	1	2,405,000	2,405,000	2,405,000
KIRCHNER, Raphael (1867-1917) Austrian				
wc/d	1	1,513	1,513	1,513
KIRCHOFF, Thorsten (1960-) ?				
oil	1	6,361	6,361	6,361
KIRCHSBERG, Ernestine von (1857-1924) Austrian				
oil	3	584-1,635	992	759
wc/d	3	526-712	588	526
KIRICHECK, Yakov (1925-2000) Russian				
oil	1	2,000	2,000	2,000
KIRK, Eve (1900-1969) British				
oil	3	885-2,903	1,823	1,682
KIRKEBY, Per (1938-) Danish				
oil	11	4,829-93,699	41,257	43,460
wc/d	16	480-25,863	5,167	3,200
3D	1	97,350	97,350	97,350
KIRKEGAARD, Anders (1946-) Danish				
oil	1	1,212	1,212	1,212
KIRKMAN, Jay Boyd (1958-) British				
wc/d	2	2,565-11,340	6,952	2,565
KIRKPATRICK, Joseph (1872-c.1930) British				
oil	1	1,729	1,729	1,729
wc/d	2	531-1,653	1,092	531
KIRKPATRICK, William Arber Brown (1880-?) British/American				
oil	1	5,000	5,000	5,000
KIRMSE, Marguerite (1885-1954) American/British				
oil	1	1,800	1,800	1,800
wc/d	1	1,400	1,400	1,400
KIROUAC, Louise Lecor (1939-) Canadian				
oil	7	574-1,804	1,234	1,230
KIRSCH (?) ?				
oil	1	4,800	4,800	4,800
KIRSCH, Johanna (1856-?) German				
oil	1	3,573	3,573	3,573
KIRSCHENBAUM, Jules (1930-) American				
oil	1	3,200	3,200	3,200
wc/d	1	6,500	6,500	6,500
KIRSCHL, Wilfried (1930-) Austrian				
wc/d	1	1,403	1,403	1,403
KIRSZENBAUM, Jecheskiel D (1900-1954) Polish				
oil	1	1,318	1,318	1,318
KISHI, Masatoyo (1924-) American				
oil	3	1,700-2,000	1,866	1,900
KISLING, Moise (1891-1953) French				
oil	34	15,000-240,000	60,113	45,796
wc/d	4	3,162-12,000	6,194	3,637
KISS, Andrew (1946-) Canadian				
oil	1	3,767	3,767	3,767
KISSEL, Gernot (1939-) German				
oil	2	979-1,795	1,387	979
KISSELEOV, Alexandre Alexandrovitch (1838-1911) Russian				
oil	4	20,640-382,192	128,208	25,000
KISSLING, Richard (1848-1919) Swiss				
3D	1	33,386	33,386	33,386
KITAGAWA, Tamiji (1894-1989) Japanese				
wc/d	1	8,000	8,000	8,000

Name	No.	Price Range	Average	Median
KITAGAWA, Toshiharu (20th C) Japanese?				
3D	1	3,250	3,250	3,250
KITAJ, R B (1932-) American				
oil	4	44,000-62,280	54,520	51,600
wc/d	1	4,712	4,712	4,712
KITCHELL, Hudson Mindell (1862-1944) American				
oil	9	650-3,500	2,038	2,000
KITO, Akira (1925-) Japanese				
oil	2	1,632-1,778	1,705	1,632
KITT, Ferdinand (1897-1962) Austrian				
oil	1	10,448	10,448	10,448
wc/d	1	1,514	1,514	1,514
KITTELSEN, Theodor (1857-1914) Norwegian				
wc/d	1	75,680	75,680	75,680
KITTLESON, John Henry (1930-) American				
3D	2	2,100-2,500	2,300	2,100
KITTON, R (19th C) British				
wc/d	1	17,670	17,670	17,670
KIWSCHENKO, Alexei Danilovtich (1851-1895) Russian				
oil	1	165,616	165,616	165,616
KJAER, Kirsten (20th C) Danish				
oil	1	1,169	1,169	1,169
KJARGAARD, John Ingvard (1902-?) Danish				
oil	1	2,500	2,500	2,500
KJELDBAEK, Bentemarie (1952-) Danish				
oil	1	1,375	1,375	1,375
KJERNER, Esther (1873-1952) Swedish				
oil	18	547-6,319	3,174	2,747
KLAGMANN, Jean Baptiste Jules (1810-1867) French				
3D	1	4,442	4,442	4,442
KLAMMER, Mariska (1873-?) Hungarian				
oil	1	1,267	1,267	1,267
KLAMROTH, Anton (1860-1929) Russian				
oil	1	1,028	1,028	1,028
KLAPHECK, Konrad (1935-) German				
oil	4	56,219-159,247	88,174	60,905
KLAPISH, Liliane (1933-) Israeli				
oil	2	9,000-13,000	11,000	9,000
wc/d	1	600	600	600
KLARWEIN, Mati (20th C) ?				
oil	1	3,534	3,534	3,534
KLASEN, Peter (1935-) German				
oil	46	1,942-31,069	9,567	7,432
wc/d	4	2,979-5,825	4,060	3,263
KLASS, Friedrich Christian (1752-1827) German				
oil	1	3,649	3,649	3,649
KLATT, Albert (1892-1970) German				
wc/d	1	1,157	1,157	1,157
KLATT, Hans (1876-1936) German				
oil	2	960-1,532	1,246	960
KLAUKE, Jurgen (1943-) German				
oil	1	703	703	703
wc/d	1	585	585	585
KLAUS, Joseph (19th C) Belgian				
oil	2	1,052-1,286	1,169	1,052
KLAUSNER, R (?) ?				
oil	1	2,408	2,408	2,408
KLAVDIOS (1958-) Greek				
oil	1	1,730	1,730	1,730
wc/d	1	1,760	1,760	1,760
KLECZKOWSKI, S (20th C) Polish				
wc/d	1	3,312	3,312	3,312
KLEE, Paul (1879-1940) Swiss				
oil	4	303,509-2,800,000	970,877	380,000
wc/d	35	8,767-420,000	90,445	40,993
KLEEHAAS, Theodor (1854-1929) German				
oil	3	1,929-5,000	3,776	4,400
KLEEMANN, J J (18th C) German				
oil	1	3,646	3,646	3,646
KLEFF, van (19th C) Dutch?				
oil	1	11,781	11,781	11,781

Name	No.	Price Range	Average	Median
KLEH, Janos (19th C) ?				
oil	1	1,500	1,500	1,500
KLEIMA, Ekke Abel (1899-1958) Dutch				
oil	2	11,003-12,959	11,981	11,003
KLEIN VON DIEPOLD, Julian (1868-1947) German				
oil	1	8,767	8,767	8,767
wc/d	1	726	726	726
KLEIN, Cesar (1876-1954) German				
oil	1	3,916	3,916	3,916
wc/d	2	475-1,414	944	475
KLEIN, Friedrich Franz (1898-1990) Dutch				
oil	5	655-11,689	5,227	4,834
wc/d	1	1,127	1,127	1,127
KLEIN, Johann Adam (1792-1875) German				
oil	3	10,603-27,474	20,939	24,740
wc/d	6	588-1,656	1,203	1,176
KLEIN, Jurgen (1904-1978) German				
3D	1	2,592	2,592	2,592
KLEIN, Medard P (1905-2000) American				
oil	1	12,000	12,000	12,000
KLEIN, Stephanie (20th C) American				
3D	1	22,500	22,500	22,500
KLEIN, William (1926-) American				
oil	1	2,306	2,306	2,306
KLEIN, Yves (1928-1962) French				
oil	4	25,182-1,300,000	368,022	25,768
wc/d	15	993-4,200,000	1,028,387	600,000
3D	28	3,983-125,322	38,792	32,794
KLEINEH, Oskar (1846-1919) Finnish				
oil	7	11,571-46,286	25,472	20,571
wc/d	2	533-1,211	872	533
KLEINENBROICH, Wilhelm (1814-1897) German				
oil	1	1,080	1,080	1,080
KLEINSCHMIDT, Paul (1883-1949) German				
oil	2	12,884-49,612	31,248	12,884
wc/d	2	1,060-7,644	4,352	1,060
KLEINT, Boris (1903-) German				
oil	2	1,649-6,668	4,158	1,649
KLEITSCH, Joseph (1885-1931) American				
oil	9	16,000-150,000	63,722	32,500
KLEMENSIEWICZ, Piotr (1957-) Polish				
oil	2	707-3,813	2,260	707
KLEMT, Agathon (1830-1889) Czechoslovakian				
oil	1	48,392	48,392	48,392
KLENGEL, Johan Christian (1751-1824) German				
oil	2	4,895-7,422	6,158	4,895
wc/d	2	589-763	676	589
KLEPPER, Frank (1890-1955) American				
oil	6	900-8,500	4,500	3,000
KLERK, Willem de (1800-1876) Dutch				
oil	3	3,063-8,290	5,120	4,007
KLERX, Zilia (fl.c.1900) Dutch				
oil	1	2,003	2,003	2,003
KLESTOVA, Irene (1908-1989) British?				
oil	7	898-8,600	4,830	4,472
KLEVER, Julius Sergius von (1850-1924) Russian				
oil	22	2,829-840,822	67,202	21,082
wc/d	2	731-2,835	1,783	731
KLEVER, Julius Sergius von and VLADIMIROFF, Ivan A (19/20th C) Russian				
oil	1	26,370	26,370	26,370
KLEVER, Julius Sergius von and Yuli Yulievich (younger) (19/20th C) Russian				
oil	1	68,208	68,208	68,208
KLEVER, Yuli Yulievich (younger) (1882-1942) Russian				
oil	3	7,500-159,247	59,022	10,320
KLEY, Heinrich (1863-1945) German				
oil	1	589	589	589
wc/d	4	669-2,297	1,186	823
KLEYDORFF, Freiherr Eberhard von (1900-) German				
oil	1	2,392	2,392	2,392
KLEYN, Lodewyk Johannes (1817-1897) Dutch				
oil	10	1,212-49,167	15,562	8,035

Name	No.	Price Range	Average	Median
KLEYN, Pieter Rudolph (1785-1816) Dutch				
wc/d	1	2,827	2,827	2,827
KLEYN, Reinhardt Willem (1828-1889) Dutch				
oil	1	1,688	1,688	1,688
KLIE, Zoltan (1897-1992) Hungarian				
oil	1	3,000	3,000	3,000
KLIEMANN, Carl Heinz (1924-) German				
oil	2	2,608-4,099	3,353	2,608
KLIEN, Erika Giovanna (1900-1957) German				
wc/d	1	14,566	14,566	14,566
KLIMEK, Ludwig (1912-1992) Polish				
oil	2	1,189-1,197	1,193	1,189
KLIMSCH, Fritz (1870-1960) German				
3D	19	2,392-67,986	17,143	10,829
KLIMT, Ernst (1864-1892) Austrian				
wc/d	1	1,169	1,169	1,169
KLIMT, Gustav (1862-1918) Austrian				
oil	1	15,904	15,904	15,904
wc/d	45	3,822-277,500	41,145	21,848
KLINCKENBERG, Eugen (1858-?) Dutch				
oil	2	935-3,572	2,253	935
KLINE, Franz (1910-1962) American				
oil	13	10,000-4,850,000	941,652	170,000
wc/d	10	12,500-400,000	113,397	70,000
KLINGBEIL, Karsten (1925-) German				
3D	2	41,452-45,110	43,281	41,452
KLINGER, Max (1857-1920) German				
oil	2	14,000-16,562	15,281	14,000
wc/d	5	1,704-7,027	3,265	2,822
3D	2	4,855-34,095	19,475	4,855
KLINGHOFFER, Clara (1900-1972) British				
oil	1	990	990	990
wc/d	2	504-531	517	504
KLINGSPOR, Fredrik Philip (1761-1832) Swedish				
wc/d	1	1,648	1,648	1,648
KLINKAN, Alfred (1950-) Austrian				
oil	1	14,143	14,143	14,143
wc/d	1	1,085	1,085	1,085
KLINKENBERG, Johannes Christiaan Karel (1852-1924) Dutch				
oil	7	4,219-275,068	77,659	55,625
wc/d	4	2,182-19,507	10,702	2,682
KLINKOSCH, J C (19/20th C) Austrian				
3D	3	2,314-6,181	4,315	4,450
KLIOUNE, Ivan (1870-1942) Russian				
wc/d	2	7,603-12,671	10,137	7,603
KLITGAARD, Georgina (1893-?) American				
oil	1	1,000	1,000	1,000
KLITGAARD-MAY, Christiane Brix (1876-1954) British				
oil	1	2,250	2,250	2,250
KLITSCH, Peter (1934-) Austrian				
oil	1	818	818	818
wc/d	1	1,403	1,403	1,403
KLITZ, Tony (1917-2000) Irish/British				
oil	27	460-4,601	1,309	797
wc/d	1	803	803	803
KLIUN, Ivan (1873-1943) Russian				
oil	3	8,236-43,680	20,189	8,653
wc/d	4	3,583-36,945	18,365	7,166
KLODT VON JURGENSBURG, Baron Petr Karlovich (1805-1867) Russian				
3D	1	74,400	74,400	74,400
KLODT VON JURGENSBURG, Michael (1832-1902) Russian				
oil	1	5,095,891	5,095,891	5,095,891
KLODT, Nikolai Aleksandrovich (1865-1918) Russian				
oil	1	178,356	178,356	178,356
KLOMBEEK, Johann Bernard (1815-1893) Dutch				
oil	5	9,425-74,167	48,471	45,972
KLOMBEEK, Johann Bernard and VERBOECKHOVEN, Eugène (19th C) Dutch				
oil	2	79,896-95,700	87,798	79,896
KLOMP, Aelbert (1618-1688) Dutch				
oil	2	3,755-6,764	5,259	3,755
KLOPPER, Johan (1610-1734) Swedish				
wc/d	1	1,683	1,683	1,683

Name	No.	Price Range	Average	Median
KLOSE, Friedrich Wilhelm (1804-1863) German				
oil	1	1,210	1,210	1,210
wc/d	1	763	763	763
KLOSE, P (19th C) American				
oil	1	3,500	3,500	3,500
KLOSE, Paul (20th C) German				
oil	3	1,720-2,230	2,016	2,100
KLOSE, Walter (1921-2004) German				
wc/d	1	1,531	1,531	1,531
KLOSS, Friedrich Theodore (1802-1876) German				
oil	1	4,268	4,268	4,268
KLOSS, Gene (1903-1996) American				
wc/d	2	6,000-6,500	6,250	6,000
KLOSSOWSKI, Erich (1875-?) German				
oil	1	1,528	1,528	1,528
KLOSSOWSKI, Pierre (1905-2001) French				
wc/d	3	22,209-29,224	26,209	27,195
KLOTS, Trafford (20th C) American				
oil	3	600-15,000	5,633	1,300
KLOTZ, Barend (17th C) Dutch				
wc/d	1	1,401	1,401	1,401
KLOTZ, Caspar Gerhard (c.1774-1847) German				
wc/d	1	2,529	2,529	2,529
KLOTZ, Lenz (1925-) Swiss				
oil	3	5,274-6,086	5,680	5,680
KLUGE, Constantine (1912-2003) French				
oil	25	2,000-12,000	5,475	5,000
KLUGE, Gustav (1947-) German				
oil	1	7,068	7,068	7,068
KLUGE, Kurt (1886-1940) German				
3D	1	5,088	5,088	5,088
KLUMPKE, Anna (1856-1942) American				
oil	1	8,000	8,000	8,000
KLUMPP, Gustav (1902-1980) American				
oil	1	5,000	5,000	5,000
KLUNDER, Harold (1943-) Canadian				
oil	2	4,100-7,976	6,038	4,100
KLUSKA, Johann (1904-c.1973) German				
oil	2	1,255-1,255	1,255	1,255
KLUTSIS, Gustav Gustavovich (1895-1944) Russian				
wc/d	1	18,602	18,602	18,602
KLUYVER, Pieter Lodewijk Francisco (1816-1900) Dutch				
oil	9	2,797-29,500	11,987	12,292
KNAB, Ferdinand (1834-1902) German				
oil	2	4,135-10,669	7,402	4,135
KNAB, Frederick (1873-1918) American				
oil	1	1,100	1,100	1,100
KNAP, Jan (1949-) Czechoslovakian				
wc/d	2	1,929-3,924	2,926	1,929
KNAP, Joseph D (1875-?) American				
wc/d	1	1,900	1,900	1,900
KNAPP, Charles W (1822-1900) American				
oil	5	2,500-9,000	5,200	5,000
KNAPP, Stephan (1921-) British				
oil	2	1,496-1,600	1,548	1,496
KNAPP-FISHER, John (1931-) British				
wc/d	4	720-2,208	1,232	810
KNATHS, Karl (1891-1971) American				
oil	3	7,000-10,000	8,666	9,000
KNAUS, Eugen (1900-1976) German				
oil	1	6,668	6,668	6,668
KNAUS, Ludwig (1829-1910) German				
oil	5	500-250,000	54,364	6,000
wc/d	1	1,334	1,334	1,334
KNAUS, Robert (1910-) Austrian				
oil	1	4,250	4,250	4,250
KNECHT, Fred E (1934-) Swiss				
oil	1	1,526	1,526	1,526
KNECHT, Hermann (1893-1978) Swiss				
oil	2	543-4,049	2,296	543

Name	No.	Price Range	Average	Median
KNECHTLI, Johann Ulrich (1845-1923) Swiss				
oil	1	7,632	7,632	7,632
KNEFFEL, Karin (1957-) German				
oil	1	24,205	24,205	24,205
KNEIPP, Georg (1793-1862) German				
oil	1	1,455	1,455	1,455
KNEIPP, Johann (1818-1868) German				
oil	1	1,119	1,119	1,119
KNELL, Adolphus (fl.1860-1890) British				
oil	12	493-5,664	2,124	1,385
KNELL, W C (1830-1876) British				
oil	1	2,436	2,436	2,436
KNELL, William Adolphus (1805-1875) British				
oil	6	510-2,262	1,020	557
wc/d	1	2,000	2,000	2,000
KNELL, William Callcott (1830-1876) British				
oil	13	513-19,000	4,136	2,784
wc/d	1	1,044	1,044	1,044
KNELLER, Sir Godfrey (1646-1723) British				
oil	6	10,719-650,204	127,003	24,570
wc/d	1	875	875	875
KNEZOVIC, Radivoje (1923-) ?				
3D	1	4,321	4,321	4,321
KNIBBERGEN, François van (17th C) Dutch				
oil	1	11,564	11,564	11,564
KNIE, Rolf (jnr) (1949-) Swiss				
wc/d	1	4,579	4,579	4,579
3D	1	1,518	1,518	1,518
KNIGHT, A Roland (19th C) British				
oil	9	470-7,134	1,880	1,328
KNIGHT, Charles (19/20th C) British				
oil	1	4,140	4,140	4,140
wc/d	4	810-1,656	1,129	1,012
KNIGHT, Charles Robert (1874-1953) American				
oil	3	2,800-20,000	12,933	16,000
wc/d	1	2,800	2,800	2,800
3D	1	15,000	15,000	15,000
KNIGHT, Dame Laura (1877-1970) British				
oil	5	502-37,840	25,342	30,940
wc/d	44	448-52,800	3,112	1,368
KNIGHT, Daniel Ridgway (1839-1924) American				
oil	8	18,000-270,000	149,125	150,000
wc/d	7	1,700-30,000	12,707	5,500
KNIGHT, George (19th C) British				
oil	3	405-3,098	1,930	2,288
wc/d	1	842	842	842
KNIGHT, Harold (1874-1961) British				
oil	4	1,557-16,720	8,551	2,697
wc/d	3	1,138-5,580	3,172	2,800
KNIGHT, John Buxton (1843-1908) British				
oil	7	534-1,038	774	779
wc/d	1	756	756	756
KNIGHT, Joseph (1837-1909) British				
wc/d	1	2,112	2,112	2,112
KNIGHT, Louis Aston (1873-1948) American				
oil	18	550-90,000	19,554	15,000
KNIGHT, P (19th C) British				
oil	2	2,436-3,600	3,018	2,436
KNIGHT, William Henry (1823-1863) British				
oil	3	3,460-10,962	7,657	8,550
KNIKKER, Aris (1887-1962) Dutch				
oil	12	589-3,879	1,511	1,008
KNIKKER, Jan (jnr) (1911-1990) Dutch				
oil	10	784-1,473	1,173	1,119
KNIKKER, Jan (snr) (1889-1957) Dutch				
oil	6	549-3,755	1,749	1,260
KNILLE, Otto (1832-1898) German				
oil	2	7,224-21,673	14,448	7,224
KNIP, August (1819-?) Dutch				
oil	3	2,219-11,721	5,500	2,560
KNIP, Henri (1819-1897) Dutch				
wc/d	6	671-5,382	2,823	2,724

Name	No.	Price Range	Average	Median
KNIP, Henriette G (1783-1842) Dutch				
oil	2	15,872-19,778	17,825	15,872
wc/d	1	7,373	7,373	7,373
KNIP, Josephus Augustus (1777-1847) Dutch				
wc/d	2	4,671-5,180	4,925	4,671
KNIP, Matthys Dirk (1785-1845) Dutch				
wc/d	1	7,007	7,007	7,007
KNIP, Pauline de (1781-1851) French				
wc/d	1	14,000	14,000	14,000
KNIP, Willem (1883-1967) Dutch				
oil	5	1,512-9,534	4,209	3,616
KNIPPEL, Wilhelm August (1806-1861) Danish				
wc/d	1	2,400	2,400	2,400
KNOBLOCH, Gertrud (1867-?) German				
oil	1	1,092	1,092	1,092
KNOEBEL, Imi (1940-) German				
oil	13	3,562-35,671	13,197	6,370
3D	2	2,121-18,967	10,544	2,121
KNOLLER, Martin (1725-1804) Austrian				
oil	1	5,550	5,550	5,550
KNOOP, A (1856-1900) German				
oil	1	1,909	1,909	1,909
KNOOP, August (1856-1900) German				
oil	3	1,978-20,384	12,671	15,652
KNOOP, Guiton (20th C) French?				
oil	2	537-1,555	1,046	537
KNOP, Naum (20th C) Argentinian				
3D	6	2,000-6,500	3,816	3,200
KNOPF, Herman (1870-1928) Austrian				
oil	2	1,693-2,182	1,937	1,693
KNOPFER, Otto (?) German				
wc/d	1	1,091	1,091	1,091
KNOPP, Axel (1942-) German				
oil	1	1,532	1,532	1,532
KNOPPEL, Arvid (1893-1970) Swedish				
3D	2	1,683-3,739	2,711	1,683
KNORR, Hugo (1834-1904) German				
oil	1	1,844	1,844	1,844
KNOWLES, Bill (20th C) American?				
oil	1	1,900	1,900	1,900
KNOWLES, Davidson (fl.1879-1902) British				
oil	2	1,015-9,515	5,265	1,015
KNOWLES, Dorothy (1927-) Canadian				
oil	3	4,123-28,365	14,355	10,578
wc/d	6	620-1,230	1,032	1,058
KNOWLES, Elizabeth McGillivray (1886-1929) Canadian				
oil	3	738-1,968	1,313	1,234
wc/d	1	574	574	574
KNOWLES, Farquhar McGillivray (1859-1932) Canadian				
oil	7	591-3,879	1,419	820
KNOWLES, Fred J (1874-?) British				
oil	3	570-1,752	1,326	1,656
wc/d	2	566-592	579	566
KNOWLES, Gareth P (1965-) Irish				
3D	1	2,400	2,400	2,400
KNOWLES, George Sheridan (1863-1931) British				
oil	6	2,000-26,000	10,440	4,000
wc/d	1	3,500	3,500	3,500
KNOWLTON, Helen Mary (1832-1918) American				
oil	1	1,400	1,400	1,400
KNOX, Archibald (1864-1933) British				
wc/d	1	1,295	1,295	1,295
KNOX, Jack (1936-) British				
oil	4	493-2,376	1,506	835
KNOX, John (1778-1845) British				
oil	1	7,392	7,392	7,392
KNOX, Susan Ricker (1875-1959) American				
oil	2	375-3,000	1,687	375
KNOX, Wilfred (1884-1966) British				
wc/d	4	549-2,697	1,255	557
KNUDSEN, Borge L (1911-1994) Danish				
oil	1	6,325	6,325	6,325

Name	No.	Price Range	Average	Median
KNUDSEN, Jesper (20th C) Danish				
oil	1	2,897	2,897	2,897
wc/d	1	3,395	3,395	3,395
KNUDSEN, Mark (20th C) American				
oil	1	9,500	9,500	9,500
KNUDSEN, Peder (1868-1944) Danish				
oil	8	550-9,485	2,142	812
KNUPFER, Benes (1848-1910) Czechoslovakian				
oil	1	13,053	13,053	13,053
KNUPFER, Jean Charles (1925-1997) Swiss				
oil	1	4,079	4,079	4,079
KNUPFER, Nicolaus (1603-1660) German				
wc/d	1	1,113	1,113	1,113
KNUTSON, Johan (1816-1899) Finnish				
oil	4	1,171-5,377	3,309	2,572
KNUTSON-TZARA, Greta (1899-1983) Swedish				
oil	1	2,036	2,036	2,036
wc/d	1	960	960	960
KNUTTEL, Graham (1954-) Irish				
oil	15	1,272-8,905	4,168	3,800
wc/d	2	1,908-1,908	1,908	1,908
KNYFF, Chevalier Alfred de (1819-1885) Belgian				
oil	1	2,950	2,950	2,950
KNYFF, Wouter (1607-1693) Dutch				
oil	1	14,270	14,270	14,270
KO, Young-Hoon (1952-) Korean				
oil	1	30,000	30,000	30,000
KOBAYASHI, Ryusho (20th C) Japanese				
wc/d	1	16,000	16,000	16,000
KOBE, Martin (1973-) American				
oil	1	35,000	35,000	35,000
KOBEL, Georg (1807-1894) German				
oil	1	3,442	3,442	3,442
KOBELL, Ferdinand (1740-1799) German				
oil	1	11,447	11,447	11,447
wc/d	2	972-2,625	1,798	972
KOBELL, Franz (1749-1822) German				
wc/d	8	850-1,514	1,232	1,237
KOBELL, Jan (1756-1833) Dutch				
oil	1	1,488	1,488	1,488
KOBELL, Jan Baptist (1778-1814) Dutch				
oil	2	1,885-3,180	2,532	1,885
KOBELL, Wilhelm von (1766-1855) German				
oil	2	13,124-40,066	26,595	13,124
wc/d	4	1,083-35,342	10,231	1,824
KOBERLING, Bernd (1938-) German				
oil	7	486-16,537	7,961	9,955
wc/d	3	1,272-1,607	1,404	1,335
KOBERSTEIN, Hans (1864-?) German				
oil	1	1,106	1,106	1,106
KOBKE, Christen (1810-1848) Danish				
oil	2	17,371-71,140	44,255	17,371
wc/d	1	2,846	2,846	2,846
KOBUKE, Kentaro (1975-) Japanese				
wc/d	1	2,500	2,500	2,500
KOCH, François (1944-) South African				
oil	4	732-55,000	16,326	1,575
KOCH, Georg (1857-1926) German				
oil	3	1,341-6,370	4,099	4,586
wc/d	1	471	471	471
KOCH, Jakob (fl.1900-1920) ?				
wc/d	1	1,300	1,300	1,300
KOCH, John (1909-1978) American				
oil	5	5,000-525,000	117,200	9,000
KOCH, Josef Anton (1768-1839) Austrian				
wc/d	2	11,781-14,000	12,890	11,781
KOCH, Ludwig (1866-1934) Austrian				
oil	4	1,221-3,507	2,150	1,455
wc/d	2	1,368-1,678	1,523	1,368
KOCH, Pyke (1901-1991) Dutch				
oil	1	111,918	111,918	111,918

Name	No.	Price Range	Average	Median
KOCH, Walther (1875-1915) German				
wc/d	1	1,522	1,522	1,522
KOCH-GOTHA, Fritz (1877-1956) German				
oil	1	1,420	1,420	1,420
wc/d	1	544	544	544
KOCHANOWSKY, Roman (1856-1945) Polish				
oil	3	725-2,417	1,696	1,946
KOCHERSCHEIDT, Kurt (1943-1992) Austrian				
oil	3	12,138-18,000	16,046	18,000
KODRA, Ibrahim (1918-2006) Israeli?				
oil	8	1,312-5,900	2,574	2,175
wc/d	5	825-1,908	1,170	1,018
KOECHL, Manfred (1956-) Austrian				
oil	1	2,338	2,338	2,338
KOECHLIN, Alfred Eugene (1845-1878) French				
oil	1	1,034	1,034	1,034
KOEHL, Anton (18/19th C) German				
wc/d	5	598-4,545	2,344	2,272
KOEHLER, Henry (1927-) American				
oil	9	1,040-12,000	6,837	6,000
wc/d	3	425-7,000	3,102	1,881
KOEHLER, Paul R (c.1866-1909) American				
oil	1	1,500	1,500	1,500
wc/d	2	571-1,600	1,085	571
KOEK-KOEK, Stephen Roberto (1887-1934) Argentinian				
oil	16	1,091-66,000	11,988	8,000
KOEKKOEK, Barend Cornelis (1803-1862) Dutch				
oil	5	104,400-1,545,139	643,445	257,600
wc/d	4	3,073-5,419	4,523	4,219
KOEKKOEK, Gerard (1871-1956) Dutch				
oil	2	1,364-2,990	2,177	1,364
KOEKKOEK, H (jnr) (1836-1909) Dutch				
oil	1	1,700	1,700	1,700
KOEKKOEK, Hendrik Barend (1849-1909) Dutch				
oil	5	973-7,375	3,636	2,800
KOEKKOEK, Hendrik Pieter (1843-1890) Dutch				
oil	6	1,567-15,045	6,964	5,733
KOEKKOEK, Hermanus (1815-1882) Dutch				
oil	15	3,196-154,000	36,869	22,986
KOEKKOEK, Hermanus (jnr) (1836-1909) Dutch				
oil	3	1,392-25,115	9,982	3,440
wc/d	2	652-1,025	838	652
KOEKKOEK, Hermanus Willem (1867-1929) Dutch				
oil	3	6,500-26,311	14,439	10,507
KOEKKOEK, J H B (1840-1912) Dutch				
oil	1	6,712	6,712	6,712
KOEKKOEK, Jan Hermanus (1778-1851) Dutch				
oil	8	5,423-172,083	29,745	8,486
KOEKKOEK, Jan Hermanus Barend (1840-1912) Dutch				
oil	14	2,436-66,678	15,816	5,741
KOEKKOEK, Johannes (1811-1831) Dutch				
oil	1	4,204	4,204	4,204
KOEKKOEK, Marinus Adrianus I (1807-1870) Dutch				
oil	11	2,182-69,920	21,008	6,833
KOEKKOEK, Willem (1839-1895) Dutch				
oil	8	5,250-266,800	96,516	75,164
KOENE, Isaac (1640-1713) Dutch				
oil	1	3,568	3,568	3,568
KOENIG, John Franklin (1924-) American				
oil	1	2,622	2,622	2,622
wc/d	2	471-753	612	471
KOENIGER, Walter (1881-1945) American				
oil	5	700-13,000	4,990	4,250
KOEPF, Werner (1909-) American				
oil	1	3,500	3,500	3,500
KOERLE, Pancraz (1823-1875) German				
oil	1	5,113	5,113	5,113
KOERNER, Ernst Karl Eugen (1846-1927) German				
oil	4	606-40,480	19,007	9,600
wc/d	1	2,066	2,066	2,066
KOERNER, Henry (1915-1991) American				
oil	1	280,000	280,000	280,000

Name	No.	Price Range	Average	Median
KOERNER, W H D (1878-1938) American				
oil	5	7,500-50,000	21,000	13,000
KOERNER, William Henry Dethlef (1878-1938) American				
oil	8	5,000-80,000	32,312	8,500
KOESTER, Alexander (1864-1932) German				
oil	20	3,299-62,640	18,735	12,138
wc/d	7	716-9,122	2,641	1,200
KOETS, Roelof (elder) (1592-1655) Dutch				
oil	1	7,709	7,709	7,709
KOETSCHET, Achille (1862-1895) Swiss				
oil	2	475-2,900	1,687	475
KOFOED, Herman (1743-1815) Danish				
oil	2	2,282-4,286	3,284	2,282
KOGAN, Moissey (1879-1942) Russian				
wc/d	5	655-2,166	1,149	1,001
3D	2	3,741-8,836	6,288	3,741
KOGAN, Nina (1887-1942) Russian				
wc/d	17	2,422-20,274	9,031	9,504
KOGELNIK, Kiki (1935-1997) Austrian				
oil	1	58,562	58,562	58,562
3D	5	12,857-30,575	18,692	15,315
KOGEVINAS, Lykourgos (1887-1940) Greek				
oil	1	5,280	5,280	5,280
KOGL, Benedict (1892-1969) German				
oil	13	495-2,928	1,377	1,148
KOGLER, Peter (1959-) Austrian				
oil	3	3,514-10,188	7,601	9,103
KOGLSPERGER, Adolf (1891-?) German				
oil	1	4,948	4,948	4,948
KOHARI, Masood (1939-) Indian				
oil	1	4,500	4,500	4,500
KOHL, Hans (1897-1990) German				
oil	1	3,152	3,152	3,152
KOHL, Pierre-Ernest (1897-1987) French				
oil	1	2,431	2,431	2,431
KOHL, Robert (1891-1944) German				
oil	1	19,110	19,110	19,110
KOHLBRENNER, Beat (20th C) Swiss?				
3D	1	2,434	2,434	2,434
KOHLER, Christian (1809-1861) German				
oil	2	21,673-30,102	25,887	21,673
KOHLER, Fritz (1887-1971) German				
oil	2	934-1,800	1,367	934
KOHLER, Hans Michael (1956-) German				
oil	1	2,458	2,458	2,458
KOHLER, Julius (19th C) Continental				
oil	1	10,000	10,000	10,000
KOHLER, Maxim (1908-1959) German				
oil	1	1,030	1,030	1,030
KOHLER, Mela (1885-1960) Austrian				
wc/d	1	1,139	1,139	1,139
KOHLHOFF, Walter (1906-1981) German				
oil	2	509-718	613	509
wc/d	1	1,399	1,399	1,399
KOHLHOFF, Wilhelm (1893-1971) German				
oil	1	3,708	3,708	3,708
wc/d	1	1,216	1,216	1,216
KOHLMANN, Ejnar (1888-1968) Finnish				
oil	11	666-3,982	1,741	1,288
KOHLMEYER, Ida (1912-1997) American				
oil	4	5,250-19,500	14,437	16,000
KOHN, Gabriel (1910-1975) American				
3D	1	3,250	3,250	3,250
KOHN, William Roth (1931-) American				
oil	1	2,600	2,600	2,600
KOHNHOLZ, Johann Wilhelm Julius (1839-1925) German				
oil	1	1,618	1,618	1,618
KOHTZ, L (19/20th C) German				
oil	1	2,667	2,667	2,667
KOHUT, N (20th C) American				
oil	1	2,200	2,200	2,200

Name	No.	Price Range	Average	Median
KOISTINEN, Unto (1917-1994) Finnish				
oil	17	1,438-14,055	4,474	3,982
wc/d	3	643-2,571	1,772	2,104
KOIVU, Rudolf (1890-1946) Finnish				
oil	2	1,558-3,273	2,415	1,558
wc/d	2	575-3,039	1,807	575
KOIVUSALO, Jussi (1929-2000) Finnish				
3D	1	4,114	4,114	4,114
KOKEN, Edmund (1814-1872) German				
oil	1	12,643	12,643	12,643
KOKEN, Paul (1853-?) German				
oil	2	2,057-5,786	3,921	2,057
KOKIAN (1971-) French				
oil	2	1,812-3,341	2,576	1,812
KOKKEN, Henry (1860-1941) Belgian				
oil	2	1,816-2,741	2,278	1,816
KOKKORIS, Dimitrios (1914-) Greek				
oil	3	6,920-11,310	9,536	10,380
KOKO, Demeter (1891-1929) Austrian				
oil	1	8,758	8,758	8,758
KOKOSCHKA, Oskar (1886-1980) Austrian				
oil	2	23,425-294,521	158,973	23,425
wc/d	25	1,113-108,288	25,113	10,010
KOKS, Endel (1912-1983) Estonian				
wc/d	1	1,157	1,157	1,157
KOLAR, Jiri (1914-2002) Czechoslovakian				
oil	3	701-1,189	863	701
wc/d	29	648-6,479	2,416	1,699
KOLARE, Nils (1930-) Swedish				
oil	2	1,018-1,189	1,103	1,018
KOLBE, Carl Wilhelm (younger) (1781-1853) German				
oil	1	1,065	1,065	1,065
KOLBE, Georg (1877-1947) German				
wc/d	10	750-5,611	3,157	2,827
3D	13	3,186-1,150,500	146,800	45,789
KOLBL, Alois (1820-1871) German				
oil	1	1,420	1,420	1,420
KOLDEWAY, Bernard Marie (1859-1898) Dutch				
oil	2	945-1,829	1,387	945
KOLESNIKOFF, Sergei (1889-1947) Russian				
oil	2	18,000-35,000	26,500	18,000
wc/d	2	2,598-3,750	3,174	2,598
KOLESNIKOFF, Stepan (1879-1955) Russian				
oil	2	17,100-35,340	26,220	17,100
wc/d	1	2,002	2,002	2,002
KOLESOV, Aleksei Mikhailovich (1834-1902) Russian				
oil	1	2,903	2,903	2,903
KOLIG, Cornelius (1942-) Austrian?				
3D	1	2,170	2,170	2,170
KOLIN, Peter (1947-) Austrian				
oil	1	2,221	2,221	2,221
KOLKOUTINE, Andrej (20th C) Russian?				
oil	1	1,697	1,697	1,697
KOLL, A (19th C) Italian				
oil	1	2,747	2,747	2,747
KOLLE, Claus Anton (1827-1872) Danish				
oil	1	1,375	1,375	1,375
KOLLE, Helmut (1899-1931) German				
oil	1	24,205	24,205	24,205
KOLLER, Johann Caspar (1808-1887) Swiss				
oil	1	12,138	12,138	12,138
KOLLER, Konrad (1916-2001) Austrian				
oil	1	1,168	1,168	1,168
KOLLER, Oskar (1925-2004) German				
oil	5	1,414-2,225	1,709	1,656
wc/d	2	764-764	764	764
KOLLER, Rudolf (1828-1905) Swiss				
oil	13	1,221-25,441	9,034	8,550
wc/d	1	3,178	3,178	3,178
KOLLER, Wilhelm (1829-1884) Austrian				
wc/d	1	1,907	1,907	1,907

Name	No.	Price Range	Average	Median
KOLLER-PINELL, Broncia (1863-1934) Austrian				
oil	3	486-4,364	1,919	909
KOLLMANN, Carl Ivanovich (1788-1846) Russian				
wc/d	2	9,300-12,900	11,100	9,300
KOLLREIDER, Oswald (1922-) Austrian				
oil	1	1,318	1,318	1,318
KOLLWITZ, Kathe (1867-1945) German				
oil	1	43,252	43,252	43,252
wc/d	7	3,507-122,979	31,202	9,727
3D	8	5,296-141,600	40,268	17,836
KOLNIK, Arthur (1890-1972) Israeli				
oil	4	567-2,000	1,056	599
KOLOSVARY, Sigismund (1899-1983) Hungarian				
oil	3	668-1,199	980	1,074
wc/d	1	1,774	1,774	1,774
KOLSCHBACH, Joseph (1892-?) German				
oil	1	12,103	12,103	12,103
KOLTE, Prabharkar (1946-) Indian				
oil	1	10,000	10,000	10,000
wc/d	1	22,500	22,500	22,500
KOLTHOFF, Mark (1901-1993) Dutch				
oil	3	1,272-7,633	3,519	1,654
wc/d	1	1,018	1,018	1,018
KOLUJNI, Dmitri (20th C) Russian				
oil	1	1,098	1,098	1,098
KOMAR and MELAMID (20th C) American/Russian				
oil	1	32,500	32,500	32,500
KOMLOSY, Irma (1850-?) Austrian				
oil	1	2,674	2,674	2,674
KONARSKY, Josef (1850-1918) Polish				
oil	3	2,428-4,267	3,167	2,807
KONCHALOVSKY, Piotr Petrovich (1876-1956) Russian				
oil	12	22,763-619,200	217,748	146,200
wc/d	1	20,000	20,000	20,000
KONDOS, Gregory (1923-) American				
oil	1	9,500	9,500	9,500
KONDRATENKO, Gavril (1854-1924) Russian				
oil	3	13,680-39,060	30,600	39,060
KONER, Sophie (1855-1929) British				
oil	1	42,143	42,143	42,143
KONIG, Fritz (1924-) German				
wc/d	3	960-2,400	1,760	1,920
3D	9	2,250-14,696	7,948	7,247
KONIG, G (20th C) German				
oil	2	1,767-2,121	1,944	1,767
KONIG, Hugo (1856-1899) German				
oil	1	1,062	1,062	1,062
KONIG, Johann (1586-1642) German				
oil	3	6,423-380,600	154,957	77,850
wc/d	1	3,500	3,500	3,500
KONIG, Leo von (1871-1944) German				
oil	1	16,397	16,397	16,397
KONIGSBRUNN, Hermann von (1823-1907) Austrian				
wc/d	1	10,603	10,603	10,603
KONIJNENBURG, Willem A van (1868-1943) Dutch				
oil	3	839-1,260	1,075	1,127
wc/d	1	471	471	471
KONINCK, Daniel de (1668-c.1720) Dutch				
oil	1	20,676	20,676	20,676
KONINCK, Philips de (1619-1688) Dutch				
oil	3	51,900-1,500,000	541,966	74,000
KONINGH, Leendert de (elder) (1777-1849) Dutch				
oil	1	1,816	1,816	1,816
wc/d	1	486	486	486
KONINGH, Leonard de (younger) (1810-1887) Dutch				
oil	1	3,440	3,440	3,440
KONO, Micao (1900-1979) Japanese				
oil	1	4,435	4,435	4,435
wc/d	1	1,215	1,215	1,215
KONOLEI, Manya (20th C) American?				
3D	1	4,500	4,500	4,500

Name	No.	Price Range	Average	Median
KONOPATZKY, Eugène (19/20th C) Russian				
oil	1	1,338	1,338	1,338
KONOPKA, Joseph (1932-) American				
oil	1	1,500	1,500	1,500
KONOVALOV, Viktor (1912-1995) Russian				
oil	1	1,205	1,205	1,205
KONSTANTINOVA, Maria (1953-) Russian				
oil	2	7,000-8,600	7,800	7,000
KONTOGLOU, Fotis (1895-1965) German				
wc/d	1	16,720	16,720	16,720
KONTULY, Bela (1904-1983) Belgian?				
oil	5	610-6,000	1,962	1,075
KOOL, Sipke (1836-1902) Dutch				
oil	1	2,500	2,500	2,500
KOOL, Willem (1608-1666) Dutch				
oil	2	5,096-20,384	12,740	5,096
KOONING, Elaine de (1920-1989) American				
oil	9	1,600-16,000	6,533	4,500
wc/d	12	850-3,250	1,841	1,500
KOONING, Willem de (1904-1997) American/Dutch				
oil	42	9,500-14,000,000	1,379,284	200,000
wc/d	33	4,500-1,000,000	110,093	40,000
3D	5	16,000-1,750,000	555,200	350,000
KOONS, Jeff (1955-) American				
oil	2	350,000-1,020,000	685,000	350,000
3D	17	1,698-4,700,000	1,193,798	400,000
KOOPMAN, Augustus (1869-1914) American				
oil	1	3,000	3,000	3,000
KOORNSTRA, Metten (1912-1978) Dutch				
oil	1	1,781	1,781	1,781
KOPAC, Slavko (1913-) Yugoslavian				
oil	1	2,805	2,805	2,805
wc/d	4	2,349-3,507	3,100	3,039
KOPCKE, Arthur (1928-1977) Danish				
oil	2	2,093-8,884	5,488	2,093
wc/d	3	1,288-2,093	1,610	1,449
KOPFERMANN, Sigrid (1923-) German				
oil	2	1,942-2,592	2,267	1,942
KOPMAN, Benjamin (1887-1965) American				
oil	2	1,600-2,500	2,050	1,600
KOPP, Wolfgang (1738-1807) Austrian				
oil	1	7,560	7,560	7,560
KOPPAY, Joszi Arpad Baron von Dretoma (1859-?) Hungarian				
oil	1	2,000	2,000	2,000
KOPPENOL, Cornelis (1865-1946) Dutch				
oil	4	896-1,500	1,206	1,210
KOPSIDIS, Rallis (1929-) Greek				
wc/d	1	1,029	1,029	1,029
KOPYSTIANSKAYA, Svetlana (1950-) Russian				
oil	1	9,460	9,460	9,460
wc/d	1	7,740	7,740	7,740
KOPYSTIANSKY, Igor (1954-) Russian				
oil	1	27,900	27,900	27,900
KORAB, Karl (1937-) Austrian				
oil	2	3,514-5,180	4,347	3,514
wc/d	11	643-5,993	1,607	1,152
KORBY, Sol (20th C) American				
oil	1	2,300	2,300	2,300
KORDA, Henry (1957-) British				
oil	1	14,960	14,960	14,960
KORMAN, Harriet (1947-) American				
oil	1	5,000	5,000	5,000
KORN, Johan Philip (1728-1796) Swedish				
oil	3	997-7,418	4,636	5,495
KORNBECK, Julius (1839-1920) German				
oil	7	522-2,238	1,099	1,090
KORNBECK, Peter (1837-1894) Danish				
oil	3	1,581-5,533	3,127	2,268
KORNER, John (1967-) Danish				
oil	3	2,912-12,877	7,409	6,438
KORNERUP, Jacob (1825-1913) Danish				
oil	1	6,949	6,949	6,949

Name	No.	Price Range	Average	Median
KORNERUP, Valdemar (1865-1924) Danish				
oil	3	1,111-2,323	1,531	1,161
KOROCHANSKY, Michel (1866-1925) Russian				
oil	9	1,028-9,993	3,624	2,351
KOROLKOFF, Serge (20th C) Russian				
wc/d	1	1,767	1,767	1,767
KOROMPAY, Duilio (1876-1952) Italian				
oil	2	1,674-2,342	2,008	1,674
KOROVINE, Alexei Konstantinovitch (1897-1950) Russian				
wc/d	1	6,536	6,536	6,536
KOROVINE, Constantin (1861-1939) Russian				
oil	57	2,600-1,500,000	152,599	30,308
wc/d	8	1,555-29,760	12,005	11,000
KORSCHMANN, Charles (1872-?) Czechoslovakian				
3D	1	2,548	2,548	2,548
KORT, Arnold Willem (1881-) Dutch				
oil	1	3,625	3,625	3,625
KORTHALS, J (1916-1972) Dutch				
oil	1	1,821	1,821	1,821
KORTHALS, Johannes (1916-1972) Dutch				
oil	7	707-4,381	2,603	2,395
KORTHAUS, Carl A (1879-1956) German				
oil	1	1,019	1,019	1,019
KORTMAN, Johan E (1858-1923) Finnish				
oil	2	1,438-4,442	2,940	1,438
KORWAN, Franz (1865-?) German				
oil	1	1,788	1,788	1,788
KORZOUKHIN, Alexei Ivanovich (1835-1894) Russian				
oil	1	9,071	9,071	9,071
KOSA, Emil (jnr) (1903-1968) American				
oil	6	2,750-15,000	7,583	6,500
wc/d	11	900-8,500	5,013	4,750
KOSA, Emil (snr) (1876-1955) American				
oil	1	4,000	4,000	4,000
KOSHELEV, Nikolaij Andreevitch (1840-1918) Russian				
oil	1	9,370	9,370	9,370
KOSHEVOI, Victor (1924-) Russian				
oil	10	516-6,372	1,407	860
KOSICE, Gyula (1924-) Argentinian				
3D	6	3,500-17,500	7,403	5,000
KOSKULL, Anders Gustaf (1831-1904) Swedish				
oil	3	780-1,288	1,079	1,171
KOSLER, Franz Xavier (1864-1905) Austrian				
oil	3	3,312-15,315	7,483	3,822
KOSLOW, Howard (?) American				
oil	1	1,000	1,000	1,000
KOSMADOPOULOS, Georgios (1895-1967) Greek				
oil	1	6,160	6,160	6,160
KOSNICK-KLOSS, Jeanne (1892-1955) German				
oil	1	5,178	5,178	5,178
wc/d	5	647-2,356	1,437	1,532
KOSOLAPOV, Alexander (1943-) Russian				
oil	2	4,750-20,000	12,375	4,750
KOSORAK, Michael J (20th C) American				
oil	1	3,000	3,000	3,000
KOSSAK, Jerzy (1890-1963) Polish				
oil	6	650-3,464	1,864	1,067
KOSSAK, Julius (1824-1899) Polish				
wc/d	1	1,316	1,316	1,316
KOSSJAKOFF, Georgis Antonowitsch (1872-?) Russian				
wc/d	1	3,096	3,096	3,096
KOSSOFF, Léon (1926-) British				
oil	1	127,400	127,400	127,400
wc/d	3	2,327-60,480	22,954	6,055
KOSSONOGI, Joseph (1908-1981) ?				
oil	3	1,700-2,800	2,133	1,900
wc/d	11	380-1,200	695	650
KOSSOVSKY, Avinoam (1949-) Israeli				
oil	2	550-1,800	1,175	550
KOSSOWSKI, Henryk (younger) (1855-1921) Polish				
3D	2	2,188-2,534	2,361	2,188

Name	No.	Price Range	Average	Median
KOSTA, Alex (1925-) Swiss?				
wc/d	1	1,531	1,531	1,531
3D	1	4,500	4,500	4,500
KOSTABI, Mark (1961-) American				
oil	64	950-13,275	5,772	4,703
wc/d	3	549-3,816	1,792	1,011
3D	1	1,903	1,903	1,903
KOSTABI, Paul (1962-) American				
oil	12	1,119-2,827	1,799	1,491
KOSTABI, Paul and SOLIS, Micael (20th C) American				
oil	1	1,001	1,001	1,001
KOSTANDI, Kiriak (1853-1921) Russian				
wc/d	1	5,580	5,580	5,580
KOSTER, Antonie L (1859-1937) Dutch				
oil	2	2,443-7,990	5,216	2,443
KOSTER, Everhardus (1817-1892) Dutch				
oil	1	9,889	9,889	9,889
KOSTER, Jo (1869-1944) Dutch				
oil	1	3,879	3,879	3,879
KOSTER, Paul (1855-1946) German				
oil	6	605-1,757	1,111	849
KOSTIN, Mikhail Alekseevich (1918-1972) Russian				
oil	1	1,665	1,665	1,665
KOSTOMOLOTSKY, Alexander (1897-1975) Russian				
wc/d	1	3,560	3,560	3,560
KOSUTH, Joseph (1945-) American				
3D	1	141,600	141,600	141,600
KOSZKOL, Jeno (1868-1935) Hungarian				
wc/d	1	2,047	2,047	2,047
KOTARBINSKI, Wilhelm Aleksandrovich (1849-1921) Polish				
oil	7	35,959-447,200	200,183	163,680
wc/d	1	10,703	10,703	10,703
KOTCHAR, Meline (20th C) French?				
oil	5	476-1,430	1,096	1,192
wc/d	4	476-2,548	1,378	892
KOTHE, Fritz (1916-) German				
oil	3	3,562-4,849	3,991	3,562
wc/d	2	1,033-1,288	1,160	1,033
KOTIK, Jan (1916-) Czechoslovakian				
oil	1	8,767	8,767	8,767
KOTIK, Pravoslav (1889-1970) Czechoslovakian				
oil	1	3,356	3,356	3,356
KOTIN, Albert (1907-1980) American				
wc/d	1	1,100	1,100	1,100
KOTLYAROV, Leo (1925-) Russian				
oil	1	5,310	5,310	5,310
KOTONDO, Torii (1900-1976) Japanese				
wc/d	1	8,325	8,325	8,325
KOTSCH, Theodor (1818-1884) German				
oil	1	2,182	2,182	2,182
KOTSCHAU, Georg (1889-?) German				
oil	1	1,405	1,405	1,405
KOTSCHENREITER, Hugo (1854-1908) German				
oil	3	972-1,210	1,121	1,183
KOTTIS, Yannis (1949-) Greek				
oil	8	5,280-17,010	10,477	7,920
wc/d	1	13,920	13,920	13,920
KOTTULA, Dominik (18/19th C) Czechoslovakian				
oil	1	1,730	1,730	1,730
KOTZEBUE, August Alexander von (1815-1889) Russian				
oil	1	33,480	33,480	33,480
wc/d	1	506	506	506
KOUGIOUMTZIS, Pavlos (1945-) Greek				
3D	1	13,464	13,464	13,464
KOUNELLIS, Jannis (1936-) Greek				
oil	8	8,500-796,500	197,388	20,879
wc/d	9	586-616,000	78,423	5,733
3D	6	9,370-296,000	141,124	90,000
KOUPETZIAN, Aram (1928-) Russian				
oil	9	602-3,801	1,378	838
KOUSNETZOFF, Constantin (1863-1936) Russian				
oil	15	486-4,800	1,926	1,403

Name	No.	Price Range	Average	Median
KOUWENBERGH, Philips van (1671-1729) Dutch				
oil	1	24,220	24,220	24,220
KOUZNETSOV, Nikolai (1850-1930) Russian				
oil	1	15,480	15,480	15,480
KOVACEVIC, Stassa (1888-1945) Turkish				
wc/d	1	1,054	1,054	1,054
KOVACS, Attila (1938-) Hungarian				
oil	1	637	637	637
wc/d	1	1,911	1,911	1,911
KOVACS, Francois (1920-) Hungarian				
3D	1	1,987	1,987	1,987
KOVATS, Z (19/20th C) ?				
3D	1	2,803	2,803	2,803
KOVNER, Michael (1948-) ?				
oil	1	12,000	12,000	12,000
KOVSHENKOV, Ivan Fedorovich (1824-1898) Russian				
3D	1	100,000	100,000	100,000
KOWALCZEWSKI, Paul Ludwig (1865-1910) German				
3D	1	2,100	2,100	2,100
KOWALEWSKY, Pawel Ossipovitch (1843-1903) Russian				
oil	1	10,320	10,320	10,320
KOWALSKI, Ivan Ivanovitch (20th C) Russian				
oil	4	470-1,998	1,025	500
wc/d	5	487-3,000	1,485	1,274
KOWALSKI, Piotr (1927-) ?				
3D	3	4,452-14,435	8,633	7,013
KOWALSKY, Leopold Franz (1856-1931) Russian/French				
oil	5	546-22,000	10,037	6,950
KOWANZ, Brigitte (1957-) Austrian				
wc/d	1	568	568	568
3D	1	4,099	4,099	4,099
KOWSKI, Uwe (1963-) German				
oil	1	32,870	32,870	32,870
KOYANAGUI, Sei (1896-1948) Japanese				
oil	4	400-2,000	1,160	800
KOZELL, Mikhael (1911-) Russian				
oil	1	1,120	1,120	1,120
KOZHUKH, Vladimir (1953-) Belarussian				
oil	1	1,328	1,328	1,328
KOZLOFF, Joyce (1942-) American				
wc/d	1	3,750	3,750	3,750
KOZLOWSKI, Julius (20th C) American				
oil	1	1,200	1,200	1,200
KRAA, Kirsten (20th C) American				
oil	1	1,600	1,600	1,600
KRABBE, Hendrik Maarten (1868-1931) Dutch				
oil	3	1,341-4,849	2,772	2,128
wc/d	2	1,091-2,244	1,667	1,091
KRAEMER, Peter (jnr) (1857-1941) German				
oil	1	932	932	932
wc/d	8	726-3,649	1,800	941
KRAEMER, Peter (snr) (1823-1907) German				
oil	2	1,607-2,136	1,871	1,607
wc/d	1	3,827	3,827	3,827
KRAFFT, Albert (19th C) German				
oil	2	4,816-6,705	5,760	4,816
KRAFFT, Carl R (1884-1938) American				
oil	10	800-20,000	6,020	3,000
KRAFFT, Per (elder) (1724-1793) Swedish				
oil	1	8,475	8,475	8,475
KRAFFT, Per (younger) (1777-1863) Swedish				
oil	1	4,564	4,564	4,564
KRAFT, Frederik (1823-1854) Danish				
oil	1	7,303	7,303	7,303
KRAGH, Johannes (1870-1946) Danish				
oil	1	1,897	1,897	1,897
KRAJCBERG, Frans (1921-) Brazilian/Polish				
wc/d	1	1,543	1,543	1,543
KRAJICEK, Jindrich Duchoslav (1867-1944) Czechoslovakian				
oil	1	1,374	1,374	1,374
KRAKAUER, Leopold (1890-1954) Israeli				
wc/d	3	1,400-3,000	1,933	1,400

Name	No.	Price Range	Average	Median
KRALINGEN, Joop van (1916-2001) Dutch				
3D	1	5,878	5,878	5,878
KRAMER, Jacob (1892-1962) British				
oil	4	676-12,528	6,607	1,914
wc/d	6	498-1,776	893	570
KRAMER, James (1927-) American				
wc/d	1	2,000	2,000	2,000
KRAMER, Johann Victor (1861-1949) Austrian				
oil	1	2,141	2,141	2,141
wc/d	2	907-1,452	1,179	907
KRAMMER, Franz (1797-1834) Austrian				
oil	1	4,241	4,241	4,241
KRAMSZTYK, Roman (1885-1942) Polish				
wc/d	1	1,411	1,411	1,411
KRANTZ, F (19/20th C) ?				
oil	1	1,764	1,764	1,764
KRANZ, Albert (?) German?				
oil	1	2,061	2,061	2,061
KRAPIVNITSKY, Evgeny (1893-1979) Russian				
wc/d	1	2,790	2,790	2,790
KRASNER, Lee (1908-1984) American				
oil	3	90,000-720,000	453,333	550,000
wc/d	4	25,000-210,000	79,375	32,500
KRASNOPEVTSEV, Dimitri (1925-1998) Russian				
oil	7	9,300-837,000	158,937	48,160
KRASNY, Yuri (1925-) Russian				
wc/d	5	1,543-2,571	2,180	2,108
KRATSCHOWSKI, Jossif (1854-1914) Russian				
oil	3	7,379-99,370	50,955	46,116
KRAUEL, Bruno (1911-) German				
oil	2	1,062-2,276	1,669	1,062
KRAUL, Fritz (1862-1935) German				
oil	2	553-4,500	2,526	553
KRAUS, August (1852-1917) German				
oil	2	1,368-2,000	1,684	1,368
KRAUS, Eva Templeton (?) ?				
oil	1	4,700	4,700	4,700
KRAUS, Friedrich (1826-1894) German				
oil	1	2,000	2,000	2,000
KRAUS, Georg Melchior (1737-1806) German				
oil	2	3,100-3,884	3,492	3,100
KRAUSE, Emil (1871-1945) Danish				
oil	2	1,475-4,743	3,109	1,475
wc/d	1	613	613	613
KRAUSE, Emil A (fl.1891-1914) British				
oil	2	1,581-2,055	1,818	1,581
wc/d	2	630-2,924	1,777	630
KRAUSE, Franz Emil (1836-1900) German				
oil	2	1,405-8,026	4,715	1,405
KRAUSE, Heinrich (1885-1985) Austrian				
oil	1	1,212	1,212	1,212
KRAUSE, Wilhelm August (1803-1864) German				
oil	2	2,057-2,259	2,158	2,057
KRAUSKOPF, Bruno (1892-1960) German				
oil	6	1,473-4,425	2,967	2,870
wc/d	6	407-2,548	1,119	584
KRAUSZ, Wilhelm Viktor (1878-1959) Hungarian				
oil	2	759-6,536	3,647	759
KRAWAGNER, Peter (1937-) German				
oil	2	934-7,591	4,262	934
KRAWIEC, Harriet (1894-1968) American				
oil	1	1,300	1,300	1,300
KRAWIEC, Walter (1889-?) American				
wc/d	1	2,675	2,675	2,675
KREBEPZ, Honig (19th C) ?				
oil	1	1,368	1,368	1,368
KREBS, Fritz (1914-1995) Swiss				
oil	4	544-835	729	721
wc/d	1	567	567	567
KREBS, Walter (1900-1965) Swiss				
oil	2	458-2,442	1,450	458

Name	No.	Price Range	Average	Median
KREBS, Xavier (1923-) French				
oil	1	1,193	1,193	1,193
KREGCZY, Edmund (1855-?) Austrian				
oil	1	3,000	3,000	3,000
KREGTEN, Fedor van (1871-1937) Dutch				
oil	6	512-2,397	1,138	844
KREHBIEL, Albert H (20th C) American				
oil	1	6,500	6,500	6,500
KREIBICH, Vilem (1884-1955) Czechoslovakian				
oil	1	3,600	3,600	3,600
KREIDOLF, Ernst Konrad Theophil (1863-1956) Swiss				
oil	3	1,332-2,747	1,970	1,832
wc/d	6	1,145-2,498	1,592	1,249
KREITZ, Willy (1903-1982) Belgian				
3D	2	4,529-21,162	12,845	4,529
KREMEGNE, Pinchus (1890-1981) Russian				
oil	38	500-38,283	6,303	4,500
KREMER, Alex (1966-) Israeli				
oil	1	11,000	11,000	11,000
KREMER, Petrus (1801-1888) Flemish				
oil	2	1,480-3,974	2,727	1,480
KREMP, Erminio (20th C) Italian				
oil	1	6,668	6,668	6,668
KRENEK, Carl (1880-1948) Austrian				
wc/d	1	5,143	5,143	5,143
KREPP, Friedrich (19th C) Austrian				
oil	1	8,653	8,653	8,653
KRESTIN, Lazar (1868-1938) Russian				
oil	1	5,000	5,000	5,000
KRETSCHMER, Wilhelm (1806-1897) German				
wc/d	1	5,839	5,839	5,839
KRETZSCHMAR, Bernhard (1889-1972) German				
oil	1	16,317	16,317	16,317
wc/d	1	1,174	1,174	1,174
KRETZSCHMER, Johann Hermann (1811-1890) German				
oil	2	1,296-7,633	4,464	1,296
KREUDER, Loni (1940-) German				
3D	1	3,111	3,111	3,111
KREUGER, Nils (1858-1930) Swedish				
oil	14	2,747-41,130	12,664	6,730
wc/d	5	496-15,288	3,782	1,119
KREUL, Johann Lorenz (1765-1840) German				
wc/d	1	1,204	1,204	1,204
KREUTZ, Heinz (1923-) German				
oil	5	1,483-14,726	4,624	2,225
wc/d	14	468-4,114	1,262	820
KREUTZFELDER, Joachim Georg (1622-1702) German				
oil	1	15,000	15,000	15,000
KREUTZMANN, Johannes (1862-1940) Danish				
3D	1	10,595	10,595	10,595
KREUZER, Vinzenz (1809-1888) Austrian				
oil	3	8,247-26,100	14,685	9,710
KREYDER, Alexis (1839-1912) French				
oil	7	1,800-8,514	5,932	6,250
KREYHER, Otto (1836-1905) German				
oil	1	6,559	6,559	6,559
KRICHATSKI, V (20th C) Russian?				
oil	1	1,612	1,612	1,612
KRICHELDORF, Carl (1863-?) German				
oil	1	1,296	1,296	1,296
KRIEG, Dieter (1937-) German?				
oil	3	2,544-10,911	7,877	10,177
wc/d	2	851-3,516	2,183	851
KRIEGER, Johanna Carolina (1802-1884) German				
oil	1	1,430	1,430	1,430
KRIEGHOFF, Cornelius (1815-1872) Canadian				
oil	16	10,659-288,626	73,432	60,782
wc/d	1	9,019	9,019	9,019
KRIEHUBER, Josef (1800-1876) Austrian				
wc/d	7	662-5,444	1,988	1,565
KRIFLA, Ahmed (1936-) Moroccan				
oil	1	5,740	5,740	5,740

Name	No.	Price Range	Average	Median
KRIGE, François (1913-1994) South African				
oil	1	4,498	4,498	4,498
KRIKI (1965-) French				
oil	3	1,196-2,387	1,830	1,907
KRISHNAMACHARI, Bose (1962-) Indian				
oil	1	22,500	22,500	22,500
KRISTIANS, Antonius Johannes (1883-1957) Dutch				
wc/d	1	1,558	1,558	1,558
KRISTIANSEN, Joannis (1918-1988) Danish				
oil	1	2,680	2,680	2,680
KRISTO, Bela de (1920-) ?				
oil	6	2,425-6,319	4,529	4,500
KRISTUPAS, R David (1954-) British				
oil	1	1,229	1,229	1,229
wc/d	1	756	756	756
KRITIKOS, Spyros (1960-) Greek				
oil	1	5,280	5,280	5,280
KRIZE, Yehiel (1909-1968) Israeli				
oil	1	1,400	1,400	1,400
wc/d	1	1,100	1,100	1,100
KRODEL, Wolfgang (elder) (1500-?) German				
oil	1	17,517	17,517	17,517
KROG, Arnold (1856-1931) Danish				
oil	1	1,051	1,051	1,051
KROHA, Ladislav (20th C) ?				
oil	3	935-1,654	1,369	1,520
KROHG, Christian (1852-1925) Norwegian				
oil	5	6,324-101,200	31,998	17,390
KROHG, Per (1889-1965) Norwegian				
oil	2	966-23,125	12,045	966
KROHN, Inari (1945-) Finnish				
oil	1	580	580	580
wc/d	1	1,323	1,323	1,323
KROJER, Tom (1942-) Danish				
oil	5	1,212-5,795	2,533	1,537
wc/d	1	485	485	485
KROKHONYATKIN, Pyotre (1929-) Russian				
oil	3	6,055-12,390	8,743	7,785
KROLL, Leon (1884-1974) American				
oil	13	1,000-110,000	35,357	8,000
wc/d	3	550-800	683	700
KROMBACH, Paul Peter (1867-1947) German				
oil	1	2,189	2,189	2,189
KROMKA, Frederico (1890-1942) Czechoslovakian				
wc/d	2	3,236-5,178	4,207	3,236
KRON, Paul (1869-1936) French				
oil	2	536-2,959	1,747	536
KRONBERG, Julius (1850-1921) Swedish				
oil	7	983-32,337	11,291	7,478
wc/d	1	959	959	959
KRONBERG, Louis (1872-1965) American				
oil	9	1,900-20,000	8,372	5,000
wc/d	3	2,000-8,500	5,333	5,500
KRONBERGER, Carl (1841-1921) Austrian				
oil	5	2,500-4,295	3,222	3,063
KRONER, Christian (1838-1911) German				
oil	2	742-1,523	1,132	742
wc/d	4	304-1,210	706	522
KROP, Hildo (1884-1970) Dutch				
3D	2	2,116-7,642	4,879	2,116
KROPFF, Joop (1892-1979) Dutch				
oil	6	589-1,104	852	900
wc/d	2	647-884	765	647
KROPIVNITSKAYA, Valentina (1924-) Russian				
wc/d	2	6,880-6,880	6,880	6,880
KROPIVNITSKY, Lev (1922-1995) Russian				
wc/d	1	6,500	6,500	6,500
KROTOV, Youri (1964-) Russian				
oil	1	2,975	2,975	2,975
KROUTHEN, Johan (1858-1932) Swedish				
oil	29	1,545-118,566	11,573	6,716

Name	No.	Price Range	Average	Median
KROYER, Peder Severin (1851-1909) Danish				
oil	18	6,324-165,028	45,010	26,544
wc/d	4	1,107-13,279	4,900	2,529
KRUCHEN, Julius (1845-1912) German				
oil	1	3,058	3,058	3,058
KRUEGER, E (19/20th C) American				
oil	1	2,250	2,250	2,250
KRUEGER, H J (19/20th C) ?				
oil	1	3,000	3,000	3,000
KRUGER, Barbara (1945-) American				
oil	1	24,000	24,000	24,000
KRUGER, Franz (1797-1857) German				
oil	4	50,571-74,653	60,914	52,211
wc/d	2	1,000-3,053	2,026	1,000
KRUGER, Hermann (1823-1909) German				
oil	1	1,649	1,649	1,649
KRUGER, Richard (1880-?) American				
oil	1	1,200	1,200	1,200
KRUGLIKOVA, Elizaveta Sergeevna (1865-1941) Russian				
wc/d	1	4,816	4,816	4,816
KRUIF, Henri Gilbert de (1882-1944) American				
oil	1	1,000	1,000	1,000
KRUIS, Ferdinand (1869-1944) Austrian				
wc/d	1	1,936	1,936	1,936
KRUMLINDE, Olof (1856-1945) Swedish				
oil	9	373-12,740	2,580	1,305
KRUMMACHER, Karl (1867-1955) German				
oil	3	2,910-3,637	3,271	3,266
KRUSE, Christian (1876-1953) Swedish				
oil	1	871	871	871
wc/d	1	661	661	661
KRUSEMAN, Frederik Marianus (1817-1882) Dutch				
oil	7	4,224-95,676	32,445	9,219
KRUSEMAN, Jan Adam (1804-1862) Dutch				
wc/d	1	3,755	3,755	3,755
KRUSEMAN, Jan Theodor (1835-1895) Dutch				
oil	2	2,917-5,425	4,171	2,917
KRUSHENICK, Nicholas (1929-) American				
oil	1	3,800	3,800	3,800
KRUSI, Hans (1920-1995) Swiss				
oil	1	1,366	1,366	1,366
wc/d	2	609-759	684	609
KRUYDER, Herman (1881-1935) Dutch				
oil	1	47,123	47,123	47,123
KRUYSEN, Antoon (1898-1977) Dutch				
oil	5	593-8,247	3,179	2,163
KRUYSEN, Johannes (1874-1938) Dutch				
oil	2	1,638-16,384	9,011	1,638
KRYGER, Preben (?) Danish?				
3D	1	2,193	2,193	2,193
KRYMOV, Nikolai Petrovich (1884-1958) Russian				
oil	2	3,880-32,680	18,280	3,880
KRYSTALLIS, Andreas (1901-1951) Greek				
oil	1	2,768	2,768	2,768
wc/d	2	968-1,936	1,452	968
KRYSTUFEK, Elke (1970-) Austrian				
oil	2	13,000-20,384	16,692	13,000
wc/d	3	2,290-6,429	4,093	3,562
KRYZHITSKY, Constantin (1858-1911) Russian				
oil	4	1,403-130,215	40,558	1,520
wc/d	1	2,752	2,752	2,752
KRZYSKO, Roman (1933-) ?				
oil	1	1,080	1,080	1,080
KUBART, Reinhold (1879-?) German				
3D	1	1,815	1,815	1,815
KUBIERSCHKY, Erich (1854-1944) German				
oil	5	638-4,905	1,845	1,060
KUBIN, Alfred (1877-1959) Austrian				
oil	1	8,486	8,486	8,486
wc/d	48	608-40,529	7,131	3,816
KUBIN, Karoline (1870-1942) Czechoslovakian				
oil	1	2,637	2,637	2,637

Name	No.	Price Range	Average	Median
KUBISTA, Bohumil (1884-1918) Czechoslovakian				
oil	1	14,270	14,270	14,270
KUCHEL, Theodor (1819-1885) German				
oil	1	1,122	1,122	1,122
KUCHLER, Albert (1803-1886) Danish				
oil	2	790-28,577	14,683	790
KUCHLER, Rudolf (1867-?) Austrian				
3D	1	6,426	6,426	6,426
KUCHUMOV, Vasili Nikitich (1888-1959) Russian				
oil	1	2,342	2,342	2,342
KUCKEI, Peter (1938-) German				
oil	1	3,461	3,461	3,461
KUCZEWSKI, Hartmut (1949-) German				
wc/d	1	3,181	3,181	3,181
KUDALLUR, Achutan (1945-) Indian				
oil	1	1,496	1,496	1,496
KUDO, Tetsumi (1935-1990) Japanese				
3D	5	2,263-14,672	8,764	11,689
KUDRIASHEV, Ivan (1896-1972) Russian				
wc/d	1	6,020	6,020	6,020
KUEHL, Gotthardt Johann (1850-1915) German				
oil	2	1,696-5,633	3,664	1,696
KUEHNE, Max (1880-c.1968) American				
oil	15	750-12,000	3,296	2,400
wc/d	6	850-2,750	1,275	950
KUGACH, Mikhail Yurevich (1939-) Russian				
oil	1	11,245	11,245	11,245
KUGELGEN, Wilhelm von (1802-1867) German				
oil	1	1,004	1,004	1,004
KUHFELD, Peter (1952-) British				
oil	2	2,244-3,458	2,851	2,244
KUHFUSS, Paul (1883-1960) German				
oil	4	718-1,236	961	837
wc/d	4	954-1,703	1,173	1,017
KUHLSTRUNK, Franz (1861-1944) Austrian				
oil	1	546	546	546
wc/d	1	1,318	1,318	1,318
KUHN, Bob (1920-) American				
oil	10	15,000-190,000	87,250	85,000
wc/d	2	3,500-4,158	3,829	3,500
3D	1	4,000	4,000	4,000
KUHN, Friedrich (1926-1972) Swiss				
wc/d	5	530-2,596	1,264	730
3D	1	4,868	4,868	4,868
KUHN, Ludwig (1859-?) German				
oil	1	1,670	1,670	1,670
KUHN, Max (1838-1888) German				
oil	2	1,334-9,000	5,167	1,334
KUHN, Walt (1877-1949) American				
oil	6	2,750-1,000,000	193,296	3,027
wc/d	6	750-7,000	2,375	1,700
KUHNEN, Pieter Lodewyk (1812-1877) Belgian				
oil	1	2,267	2,267	2,267
KUHNERT, Wilhelm (1865-1926) German				
oil	11	3,900-140,000	42,972	17,992
wc/d	4	589-10,775	3,901	1,414
KUHSTOSS, Paul (1870-1898) Belgian				
oil	2	1,878-3,371	2,624	1,878
KUINDJI, Arkhip Ivanovitch (1842-1910) Russian				
oil	2	120,400-146,200	133,300	120,400
KUITCA, Guillermo (1961-) Argentinian				
oil	11	32,000-130,000	60,876	52,800
wc/d	2	55,000-70,000	62,500	55,000
KUJASALO, Matti (1946-) Finnish				
oil	12	584-2,928	1,868	1,586
KUKKONEN, Pertti (1954-) Finnish				
3D	2	2,038-2,342	2,190	2,038
KULBIN, Nikolai (1868-1917) Russian				
oil	1	27,900	27,900	27,900
KULICKE, Robert (1924-) American				
oil	1	4,250	4,250	4,250

Name	No.	Price Range	Average	Median
KULKARNI, Krishna Shamrao (1916-1996) Indian				
oil	1	7,480	7,480	7,480
KULMALA, George Arthur (1896-1940) Canadian				
oil	3	487-4,948	2,261	1,350
KUMALO, Sidney (1935-) South African				
3D	1	6,216	6,216	6,216
KUMAR, Ram (1924-) Indian				
oil	14	15,895-470,000	147,372	90,000
wc/d	7	10,000-75,000	29,131	24,000
KUMMER, Karl Robert (1810-1889) German				
oil	4	2,625-4,417	3,510	3,341
wc/d	1	1,010	1,010	1,010
KUMPF, Gottfried (1930-) Austrian				
oil	1	14,548	14,548	14,548
3D	9	1,818-7,192	3,137	2,524
KUNA, Henri (1885-?) Polish				
3D	1	2,500	2,500	2,500
KUNC, Milan (1944-) Czechoslovakian				
oil	3	2,250-3,816	2,938	2,750
wc/d	1	1,527	1,527	1,527
KUNDIG, Reinhold (1888-1984) Swiss				
oil	17	341-6,105	2,133	1,960
KUNERT, Ove (20th C) ?				
oil	1	1,157	1,157	1,157
KUNILIUSEE, Paulosee (1927-) North American				
3D	1	7,592	7,592	7,592
KUNIYOSHI, Yasuo (1893-1953) American				
oil	2	17,000-170,000	93,500	17,000
wc/d	7	1,100-80,000	29,300	15,000
KUNL, Wilhelm (1811-?) Austrian?				
oil	1	1,453	1,453	1,453
KUNST, Berend (1794-1881) Dutch				
wc/d	1	1,134	1,134	1,134
KUNSTLER, Mort (1931-) American				
oil	1	1,000	1,000	1,000
wc/d	1	2,400	2,400	2,400
KUNTZ, Carl (1770-1830) German				
oil	1	3,405	3,405	3,405
KUNTZ, Roger (1926-1975) American				
oil	3	9,000-14,000	10,666	9,000
KUNZ, Karl (1905-1971) German				
oil	1	8,325	8,325	8,325
KUNZ, Ludwig Adam (1857-1929) Austrian				
oil	2	510-2,297	1,403	510
KUNZLI, David (20th C) ?				
oil	2	539-710	624	539
wc/d	1	716	716	716
KUPELWIESER, Hans (1948-) Austrian				
oil	1	2,524	2,524	2,524
KUPELWIESER, Leopold (1796-1862) Austrian				
wc/d	1	1,204	1,204	1,204
KUPER, Yuri (1940-) Russian				
oil	6	1,657-13,124	7,823	7,994
wc/d	3	1,942-6,681	3,673	2,398
KUPFERMAN, David (20th C) American				
oil	2	620-673	646	620
wc/d	1	750	750	750
KUPFERMAN, Moshe (1926-2003) Israeli				
oil	8	500-37,500	11,776	4,200
wc/d	4	580-2,400	1,295	700
KUPFERSCHMID, Hermann (1885-1975) German				
oil	1	1,885	1,885	1,885
KUPHAL, Walter (1890-?) German				
oil	3	750-1,334	1,045	1,052
KUPKA, Frank (1871-1957) Czechoslovakian				
oil	1	200,000	200,000	200,000
wc/d	20	1,215-55,500	18,871	11,712
KUPRIN, Aleksandr Vasilievich (1880-1960) Russian				
oil	1	3,640	3,640	3,640
KURELEK, William (1927-1977) Canadian				
oil	3	16,839-33,235	24,937	24,739
wc/d	16	529-61,706	12,095	7,090

Name	No.	Price Range	Average	Median
KURFISS, Gottlieb (20th C) ?				
oil	1	1,244	1,244	1,244
KURODA, Aki (1944-) ?				
oil	2	934-1,403	1,168	934
KURON, Herbert (1888-?) German				
oil	1	1,398	1,398	1,398
KURTZ, Carl von (1817-1887) Italian				
oil	1	2,510	2,510	2,510
KUSAMA, Yayoi (1929-) Japanese				
oil	28	2,409-800,000	85,957	13,000
wc/d	13	3,562-55,000	17,033	11,180
3D	7	6,688-50,000	22,348	13,000
KUSHNER, Robert (1949-) American				
wc/d	2	750-1,400	1,075	750
KUSS, Ferdinand (1800-1886) Austrian				
oil	1	5,260	5,260	5,260
KUSTNER, Carl (1861-1934) German				
oil	4	707-1,918	1,371	942
KUSTODIEV, Boris (1878-1927) Russian				
oil	2	41,280-2,580,000	1,310,640	41,280
wc/d	7	15,000-60,000	31,142	30,000
KUTCHAKA, Timothy (1924-) North American				
3D	1	7,171	7,171	7,171
KUTTNER, Fritz (1897-?) German				
oil	1	1,030	1,030	1,030
KUWAHARA, Masahiko (1959-) Japanese				
wc/d	1	1,430	1,430	1,430
KUWASSEG, Charles Euphrasie (1838-1904) French				
oil	14	468-24,247	6,754	3,780
wc/d	1	954	954	954
KUWASSEG, Karl-Josef (1802-1877) French				
oil	1	5,351	5,351	5,351
KUWAYAMA, Tadaaki (1932-) Japanese				
oil	2	1,300-4,712	3,006	1,300
KUYCK, Frans van (1852-1915) Belgian				
oil	3	1,193-1,701	1,520	1,668
KUYL, Gerard van (1604-1673) Dutch				
oil	1	420,000	420,000	420,000
KUYPERS, Cornelis (1864-1932) Dutch				
oil	6	732-6,049	2,771	1,553
KUYPERS, Gaston (?) French?				
oil	1	1,800	1,800	1,800
KUYTEN, Harrie (1883-1952) Dutch				
oil	3	2,877-19,110	10,470	9,425
wc/d	1	964	964	964
KUYTENBROUWER, Martinus Antonius (18/19th C) Dutch				
oil	1	2,967	2,967	2,967
KUZNETSOV, Pavel (1878-1968) Russian				
oil	1	78,120	78,120	78,120
KVAPIL, Charles (1884-1958) Belgian				
oil	28	1,084-12,250	4,120	3,053
KVIUM, Michael (1955-) Danish				
oil	7	2,021-37,021	7,860	3,219
wc/d	3	1,127-2,495	2,012	2,414
KWIATKOWSKI, Teofil (1809-1891) Polish				
wc/d	1	5,340	5,340	5,340
KWONG-SANG (19th C) Chinese				
oil	1	4,576	4,576	4,576
KYHN, Vilhelm (1819-1903) Danish				
oil	22	518-4,977	2,574	2,230
KYLBERG, Carl (1878-1952) Swedish				
oil	19	1,205-216,297	53,929	20,483
wc/d	2	503-1,586	1,044	503
KYLE, Georgina Moutray (1865-1950) British				
oil	3	885-4,135	2,458	2,356
KYNWITZ, A (20th C) ?				
wc/d	1	3,010	3,010	3,010
KYOSAI, Kawanabe (1831-1899) Japanese				
wc/d	1	3,515	3,515	3,515
KYYHKYNEN, Juho (1875-1909) Finnish				
oil	2	6,429-9,000	7,714	6,429

Name	No.	Price Range	Average	Median
LAAN, Gerard van der (1844-1915) Dutch				
oil	1	2,016	2,016	2,016
LAANEN, Jasper van der (1592-1626) Flemish				
oil	2	4,014-25,950	14,982	4,014
LAAR, Bernardus and Jan Hendrik van de (19th C) Dutch				
oil	1	4,267	4,267	4,267
LAAR, Bernardus van de (1804-1872) Dutch				
oil	2	2,926-5,096	4,011	2,926
LABANDA, Jordi (1968-) Uruguayan				
wc/d	1	6,969	6,969	6,969
LABARQUE, Werner (20th C) Belgian				
oil	1	1,019	1,019	1,019
LABAS, Alexandre Arkadevich (1900-1983) Russian				
oil	1	89,910	89,910	89,910
LABAUDT, Lucien Adolphe (1880-1943) American				
oil	2	2,250-15,000	8,625	2,250
LABHARDT, Emanuel (1810-1874) Swiss				
wc/d	1	1,757	1,757	1,757
LABIED, Miloud (1939-) Moroccan				
oil	2	3,092-5,626	4,359	3,092
wc/d	1	3,269	3,269	3,269
LABILLE-GUIARD, Madame Adelaide (1749-1803) French				
oil	1	7,000	7,000	7,000
LABISSE, Felix (1905-1982) French				
oil	11	718-17,810	5,803	3,770
wc/d	10	719-8,400	2,737	1,794
LABO, Savinio (1899-1976) Italian				
oil	6	707-5,966	2,618	1,317
LABORDE, Chas (1886-1941) French				
oil	1	1,276	1,276	1,276
wc/d	3	595-1,066	851	892
LABORNE, Edme Émile (1837-1913) French				
oil	2	3,096-4,629	3,862	3,096
wc/d	4	492-1,752	842	539
LABOUCHERE, Pierre Antoine (1807-1873) French				
wc/d	1	2,604	2,604	2,604
LABOULAYE, Paul de (19th C) French				
oil	1	12,883	12,883	12,883
LABOUREUR, Jean Émile (1877-1943) French				
wc/d	3	654-4,281	2,675	3,092
LABRA, Jose Maria de (1925-) Spanish				
wc/d	1	2,694	2,694	2,694
LABROUCHE, Pierre (fl.1905-1921) French				
oil	1	2,577	2,577	2,577
LABRUZZI, Carlo (1748-1818) Italian				
wc/d	2	4,099-12,975	8,537	4,099
LACALMONTIE, Jean-François (1947-) French				
oil	1	1,315	1,315	1,315
LACAMERA, Fortunato (1887-1951) Argentinian				
oil	4	6,000-33,000	21,500	16,000
LACASSE, Joseph (1894-1975) Belgian				
oil	5	1,707-11,440	6,298	4,607
wc/d	3	555-5,800	3,482	4,091
LACAZE, Germaine (1908-1994) French				
oil	2	1,337-3,317	2,327	1,337
LACEY, Bruce (1927-) British				
3D	1	15,470	15,470	15,470
LACH, Andreas (1817-1882) Austrian				
oil	1	3,648	3,648	3,648
LACHAISE, Gaston (1882-1935) American/French				
wc/d	5	550-5,000	3,360	4,000
3D	2	3,840-55,000	29,420	3,840
LACHIEZE-REY, Henri (1927-1974) French				
oil	5	3,750-13,260	9,741	10,000
LACHMAN, Harry (1886-1974) American/French				
oil	3	850-5,500	2,983	2,600
LACINA, Josef (1899-?) Czechoslovakian				
oil	3	600-3,637	2,347	2,805
LACKERBAUER, René (1861-1934) French				
oil	3	546-1,674	1,043	911
LACOM, Wayne (1922-) American				
wc/d	1	2,000	2,000	2,000

Name	No.	Price Range	Average	Median
LACOMA, Francisco Jose Pablo (1784-1849) Spanish				
oil	1	3,568	3,568	3,568
LACOMBE, Georges (1868-1916) French				
oil	1	9,466	9,466	9,466
LACOSTE, Charles (1870-1959) French				
oil	1	1,427	1,427	1,427
LACOSTE, Eugène (19th C) French				
oil	2	900-3,729	2,314	900
LACOSTE, Jules (19th C) French				
oil	1	1,901	1,901	1,901
LACOSTE, Pierre Eugene (1818-1908) French				
wc/d	1	2,661	2,661	2,661
LACOUR, Charles (1863-1941) French				
oil	2	624-5,096	2,860	624
LACROIX DE MARSEILLE, Charles François (1720-c.1782) French				
oil	12	30,411-177,397	71,688	65,000
wc/d	1	1,701	1,701	1,701
LACROIX, Gaspard Jean (1810-1878) French				
oil	1	3,534	3,534	3,534
LACROIX, Paul (fl.1858-1869) French?				
oil	1	9,500	9,500	9,500
LACROIX, Richard (1939-) Canadian				
oil	1	2,548	2,548	2,548
LACY, Charles J de (1860-1936) British				
oil	3	750-1,840	1,213	1,050
wc/d	1	696	696	696
LADBROOKE, John Berney (1803-1879) British				
oil	12	952-41,580	8,015	3,312
LADDAGA, Angel (1911-) Argentinian				
oil	1	1,800	1,800	1,800
LADELL, Edward (1821-1886) British				
oil	12	9,936-56,320	29,501	28,160
LADELL, Ellen (fl.1886-1898) British				
oil	2	4,725-6,612	5,668	4,725
LAEISZ, Carl (1803-1864) German				
wc/d	1	4,976	4,976	4,976
LAENEN, Jan (1881-1965) Belgian?				
oil	1	1,460	1,460	1,460
LAER, Alexander T van (1857-1920) American				
oil	1	2,600	2,600	2,600
LAERMANS, Eugène (1864-1940) Belgian				
oil	5	1,133-44,524	16,654	11,689
wc/d	1	5,400	5,400	5,400
LAESSOE, Thorald (1816-1878) Danish				
oil	5	1,132-26,875	8,643	3,952
wc/d	1	3,810	3,810	3,810
LAEVENS, A (19/20th C) ?				
oil	1	1,674	1,674	1,674
LAEZZA, Giuseppe (?-1905) Italian				
oil	3	13,000-17,014	14,934	14,790
LAFABRIQUE, Nicolas (1649-1733) Flemish				
oil	1	3,000	3,000	3,000
LAFAGE, Raymond (1656-1690) French				
wc/d	3	783-6,500	3,361	2,800
LAFARGE, John (1835-1910) American				
oil	2	15,000-55,000	35,000	15,000
wc/d	3	12,500-22,500	16,666	15,000
LAFFON, Carmen (1934-) Spanish				
oil	1	23,919	23,919	23,919
wc/d	1	1,883	1,883	1,883
LAFITE, Ernst (1826-1885) Austrian				
oil	1	3,612	3,612	3,612
LAFON, François (19th C) French				
oil	2	2,500-30,000	16,250	2,500
LAFOND, Charles Nicolas Rafael (1774-1835) French				
oil	1	8,182	8,182	8,182
LAFOSSE, Cecile (19th C) French				
wc/d	1	3,053	3,053	3,053
LAFOSSE, Charles de (1636-1716) French				
oil	1	34,201	34,201	34,201
wc/d	14	906-20,065	7,785	5,825

Name	No.	Price Range	Average	Median
LAGAGE, Pierre (1911-1977) French				
oil	2	900-1,200	1,050	900
wc/d	1	535	535	535
LAGAR, Celso (1891-1966) Spanish				
oil	9	3,399-21,021	14,327	17,836
wc/d	18	478-6,475	2,000	1,326
LAGARE, Eugene (19th C) French				
3D	1	1,528	1,528	1,528
LAGERSTAM, Berndt (1868-1930) Finnish				
oil	1	3,507	3,507	3,507
LAGET, Denis (c.1958-) French				
oil	2	1,152-5,727	3,439	1,152
wc/d	1	1,001	1,001	1,001
LAGNEAU, Nicolas (16/17th C) French				
wc/d	1	6,290	6,290	6,290
LAGO RIVERA, Antonio (1916-1990) Spanish				
oil	3	2,571-3,211	2,965	3,113
wc/d	1	654	654	654
LAGODICH, Simeon (1954) American				
oil	1	1,100	1,100	1,100
wc/d	1	1,200	1,200	1,200
LAGONI, Luigi (19/20th C) Italian				
oil	1	1,000	1,000	1,000
LAGOOR, Jan van (17th C) Dutch				
oil	1	16,650	16,650	16,650
LAGORIO, Antonio (17th C) Italian				
oil	3	64,726-88,356	72,602	64,726
LAGORIO, Lev Feliksovich (1827-1905) Russian				
oil	4	5,059-240,000	119,896	96,926
wc/d	4	1,496-5,856	3,242	2,571
LAGORIO, Maria (1893-1979) Polish				
oil	1	9,300	9,300	9,300
LAGRANGE, Andre (1889-?) French				
oil	1	1,414	1,414	1,414
LAGRANGE, Jacques (1917-1995) French				
oil	5	972-4,795	2,637	2,500
LAGRENEE, Jean Jacques (1739-1821) French				
oil	2	11,689-40,000	25,844	11,689
LAGRENEE, Louis Jean François (1725-1805) French				
oil	5	7,335-138,069	61,075	38,836
LAGRIFFOUL, Henri Albert (1907-1981) French				
3D	1	7,516	7,516	7,516
LAGRU, Dominique (1873-1960) French				
oil	1	1,081	1,081	1,081
LAGRUE, Jean Pierre (1939-) French				
oil	1	1,260	1,260	1,260
LAGYE, Victor (1825-1896) Belgian				
oil	7	800-25,918	9,643	7,644
LAHLOU, Taieb (1919-1972) Moroccan				
oil	6	2,864-18,361	7,254	4,844
LAHNER, Émile (1893-1980) French				
oil	4	565-994	838	851
wc/d	1	503	503	503
LAHS, Curt (1893-1958) German				
oil	1	1,288	1,288	1,288
LAHUERTA, Genaro (1905-1985) Spanish				
oil	2	479-9,503	4,991	479
LAI FONG (fl.1890-1910) Chinese				
oil	5	2,805-17,000	6,881	4,114
LAI SUNG (fl.1850-1885) Chinese				
oil	1	2,100	2,100	2,100
LAINE, Olavi (1922-) Finnish				
oil	16	668-1,800	1,081	1,029
LAING, Gerald (1936-) British				
oil	1	69,200	69,200	69,200
LAING, Tomson (fl.1890-1904) British				
oil	5	835-1,468	1,201	1,246
LAING, William Wardlaw (fl.1873-98) British				
oil	1	3,366	3,366	3,366
wc/d	1	1,672	1,672	1,672

Name	No.	Price Range	Average	Median
LAIRESSE, Gerard de (1641-1711) Flemish				
oil	1	98,836	98,836	98,836
wc/d	3	509-3,036	1,585	1,211
LAISSEMENT, Henri Adolphe (?-1921) French				
oil	2	1,212-1,490	1,351	1,212
LAJOUE, Jacques de (1687-1761) French				
oil	2	7,280-63,014	35,147	7,280
wc/d	1	7,329	7,329	7,329
LAKHOVSKY, Arnold Borisovich (1880-1937) Russian				
oil	3	8,600-12,040	10,213	10,000
LAKNER, Laszlo (1936-) Hungarian				
oil	1	11,466	11,466	11,466
LALAISSE, François Hippolyte (1812-1884) French				
oil	1	2,188	2,188	2,188
wc/d	2	534-1,578	1,056	534
LALANDE, Louise (1834-1890) French				
oil	2	2,834-8,505	5,669	2,834
LALANNE, Claude (1927-) French				
3D	1	2,225	2,225	2,225
LALANNE, François-Xavier (1924-) French				
3D	8	3,090-327,297	59,187	14,028
LALAUZE, Alphonse (1872-?) French				
oil	1	876	876	876
wc/d	1	1,521	1,521	1,521
LALIBERTE, Alfred (1878-1953) Canadian				
3D	6	1,804-33,235	13,891	8,199
LALIQUE, René J (1860-1945) French				
wc/d	1	1,330	1,330	1,330
LALIQUE, Suzanne (1899-?) French				
oil	4	840-2,040	1,185	900
LALL, Oscar de (1903-1971) Canadian				
oil	5	530-1,265	840	656
wc/d	1	793	793	793
L'ALLEMAND, Conrad (1809-1880) German				
oil	2	4,576-6,622	5,599	4,576
L'ALLEMAND, Fritz (1812-1866) Austrian				
oil	1	1,518	1,518	1,518
LALLEMAND, Henri (1810-?) Belgian				
oil	2	1,496-4,822	3,159	1,496
LALLEMAND, Jean Baptiste (1710-1805) French				
wc/d	8	1,914-8,507	4,882	4,500
LALOY, Yves (1920-1999) French				
oil	3	4,772-5,322	5,058	5,081
LAM QUA (19th C) Chinese				
oil	1	2,000	2,000	2,000
LAM, Wilfredo (1902-1982) Cuban				
oil	12	8,500-170,000	52,903	24,276
wc/d	17	3,180-1,150,000	83,586	17,840
3D	5	5,000-21,000	10,123	5,500
LAMART, Cyrille (20th C) French				
wc/d	1	3,579	3,579	3,579
LAMAZARES, Anton (1954-) Spanish				
oil	7	3,038-9,643	5,151	4,393
wc/d	1	10,837	10,837	10,837
LAMB, Charles Vincent (1893-1964) Irish				
oil	20	2,919-42,219	10,033	7,068
LAMB, F Mortimer (1861-1936) American				
oil	5	400-1,700	1,100	1,300
wc/d	3	500-1,700	1,133	1,200
LAMB, Helen Adelaide (1889-1981) British				
oil	1	1,636	1,636	1,636
LAMB, Henry (1883-1960) British				
oil	4	2,379-113,400	30,984	2,958
wc/d	2	3,366-6,615	4,990	3,366
LAMB, Jim (1946-) American				
oil	1	3,000	3,000	3,000
LAMB, Lynton (1907-) British				
oil	1	1,495	1,495	1,495
LAMB, Matt (20th C) American				
oil	1	1,018	1,018	1,018
LAMBDIN, George Cochran (1830-1896) American				
wc/d	1	4,000	4,000	4,000

Name	No.	Price Range	Average	Median
LAMBEAUX, Jef (1852-1908) Belgian				
3D	18	1,987-11,439	3,784	3,053
LAMBERT, A (?) ?				
wc/d	1	5,021	5,021	5,021
LAMBERT, Antoine Eugène (1824-1903) French				
oil	1	1,125	1,125	1,125
LAMBERT, Camille Nicholas (1876-?) Belgian				
oil	4	1,211-6,300	3,024	1,214
LAMBERT, Clement (c.1855-1925) British				
wc/d	1	1,152	1,152	1,152
LAMBERT, Elie (20th C) French				
oil	2	1,040-2,835	1,937	1,040
LAMBERT, Eugène (1825-1900) French				
oil	2	3,240-4,500	3,870	3,240
wc/d	1	1,092	1,092	1,092
LAMBERT, Fernand-Alexis (1868-?) French				
oil	2	900-1,458	1,179	900
LAMBERT, George (1700-1765) British				
oil	1	307,800	307,800	307,800
LAMBERT, Georges (1919-) French				
oil	2	890-1,392	1,141	890
LAMBERT, Isabel (1912-1992) British				
oil	1	2,366	2,366	2,366
LAMBERT, Maurice (1901-1964) French				
3D	1	7,854	7,854	7,854
LAMBERT, Maurice Walter Edmond de (1873-?) French				
oil	1	530	530	530
wc/d	1	1,752	1,752	1,752
LAMBERT, Ted R (1905-1960) American				
oil	2	3,000-9,500	6,250	3,000
LAMBERT-RUCKI, Jean (1888-1967) French				
oil	3	6,181-9,991	8,123	8,199
wc/d	2	561-731	646	561
3D	7	2,959-10,500	6,779	6,969
LAMBIE, Jim (1964-) British				
oil	1	7,000	7,000	7,000
3D	2	8,000-13,000	10,500	8,000
LAMBINET, Émile (1815-1877) French				
oil	9	911-5,940	3,875	4,359
LAMBORDI (19th C) ?				
oil	1	4,320	4,320	4,320
LAMBOURNE, Alfred (1850-1926) American				
oil	1	19,000	19,000	19,000
LAMBRE, Sylvain (1889-1958) Belgian				
oil	4	486-2,306	1,026	584
LAMBRECHT, William Alphonse (1876-1940) French				
oil	1	3,507	3,507	3,507
LAMBRECHTS, Jan Baptist (1680-1731) Flemish				
oil	9	1,147-10,703	5,081	4,094
LAMBRICHS, Edmond Alfonse Charles (1830-1887) Belgian				
oil	1	3,196	3,196	3,196
LAMBRICHS-HAARDT, Gabrielle (1917-2004) Belgian				
wc/d	1	2,027	2,027	2,027
LAMBRON DES PILTIERES, Albert (1836-?) French				
oil	1	7,120	7,120	7,120
LAMEN, Christoffel Jacobsz van der (c.1606-1651) Flemish				
oil	2	3,979-13,612	8,795	3,979
LAMERS, Kiki (1964-) Dutch				
oil	1	14,000	14,000	14,000
LAMESI, Temistocle A (1870-1957) Italian				
oil	2	906-2,736	1,821	906
LAMEYER, T N (19th C) Continental				
oil	1	6,323	6,323	6,323
LAMI, Eugène Louis (1800-1890) French				
oil	1	11,404	11,404	11,404
wc/d	10	400-3,986	1,703	1,551
LAMM, Albert (1873-?) German				
oil	1	2,314	2,314	2,314
LAMM, Erich Albert (1880-1934) Austrian				
oil	1	3,132	3,132	3,132
LAMMEYER, Ferdinand (1899-?) German				
oil	1	1,578	1,578	1,578

Name	No.	Price Range	Average	Median
LAMMI, Ilkka (1976-2000) Finnish				
oil	6	43,714-99,000	59,413	51,429
LAMOND, William B (1857-1924) British				
oil	7	669-6,195	3,021	1,936
LAMORINIERE, Jean Pierre François (1828-1911) Belgian				
oil	5	649-4,697	2,757	2,428
LAMOTHE, Geo (20th C) French				
oil	1	2,268	2,268	2,268
LAMOTTE, Bernard (1903-1983) French				
oil	4	700-1,300	1,000	800
LAMOURDEIEU, Raoul (1877-1963) French				
3D	1	4,789	4,789	4,789
LAMPA, Gunnar (1873-1952) Swedish				
oil	1	2,368	2,368	2,368
LAMPART, P (?) ?				
oil	1	3,108	3,108	3,108
LAMPE, A (19/20th C) German				
oil	1	3,042	3,042	3,042
LAMPI, Francesco (1782-1852) Italian				
oil	1	4,248	4,248	4,248
LAMPI, Johann Baptist (18/19th C) Italian				
oil	1	102,300	102,300	102,300
LAMPI, Johann Baptist (elder) (1751-1830) Italian				
oil	3	15,196-59,200	37,656	38,574
LAMPI, Johann Baptist (younger) (1775-1837) Italian				
oil	1	35,895	35,895	35,895
LAMPI, Vilho (1898-1936) Finnish				
oil	1	2,829	2,829	2,829
LAMPIT, Ronald (1906-) British				
wc/d	1	1,300	1,300	1,300
LAMPLOUGH, A O (1877-1930) British				
wc/d	1	2,313	2,313	2,313
LAMPLOUGH, Augustus Osborne (1877-1930) British				
wc/d	14	946-6,650	2,163	1,584
LAMPRECHT, Anton (1901-1984) German				
oil	1	1,818	1,818	1,818
LAMY (?) French				
wc/d	1	9,625	9,625	9,625
LAN BAR (1912-1987) Polish/French				
oil	4	1,000-1,079	1,023	1,008
LAN-BAR, David (1912-1987) Israeli				
oil	1	1,051	1,051	1,051
LANBY, R (20th C) ?				
oil	1	2,225	2,225	2,225
LANCASTER, Mark (1938-) British				
oil	1	1,044	1,044	1,044
LANCASTER, Percy (1878-1951) British				
oil	1	5,160	5,160	5,160
wc/d	3	537-870	722	759
LANCE, George (1802-1864) British				
oil	3	2,013-13,233	6,348	3,800
LANCERAY (19/20th C) Russian				
3D	1	9,460	9,460	9,460
LANCERAY, Eugène Alexandro (1848-1886) Russian				
3D	29	3,162-103,200	39,915	37,840
LANCERAY, Yevgeni (1875-1946) Russian				
wc/d	3	950-13,081	5,931	3,762
LANCEROTTO, Egisto (1848-1916) Italian				
oil	3	5,327-62,319	37,048	43,500
wc/d	1	521	521	521
LANCKOW, Ludwig (19th C) German				
oil	1	1,095	1,095	1,095
LANCRET, Nicolas (1690-1743) French				
oil	1	20,000	20,000	20,000
wc/d	4	700-14,572	8,277	4,757
LAND, Ernest Albert (20th C) American				
oil	3	400-1,800	1,133	1,200
LANDALUZE, Victor Patricio (1828-1889) Cuban/Spanish				
oil	1	16,000	16,000	16,000
LANDAU, Zygmunt (1898-1962) Polish				
oil	3	1,890-2,757	2,254	2,116
wc/d	2	600-850	725	600

Name	No.	Price Range	Average	Median
LANDEAU, Sandor L (1864-1924) French				
oil	1	2,604	2,604	2,604
LANDELLE, Charles Zacharie (1812-1908) French				
oil	3	688-22,007	9,329	5,292
LANDER, Benjamin (19th C) American				
oil	3	565-1,584	1,031	946
LANDER, John St Helier (1869-1944) British				
oil	1	1,760	1,760	1,760
LANDERS, Sean (1962-) German				
oil	2	50,000-52,000	51,000	50,000
3D	1	2,750	2,750	2,750
LANDERSET, Joseph de (1753-1824) German				
wc/d	1	1,480	1,480	1,480
LANDES, Marie Louise (20th C) French				
oil	1	1,946	1,946	1,946
LANDI, Angelo (1879-1944) Italian				
oil	1	3,152	3,152	3,152
LANDI, Bruno (1941-) Italian				
oil	44	471-5,890	1,867	1,826
LANDI, Edoardo (1937-) Italian				
oil	2	1,829-4,056	2,942	1,829
wc/d	1	1,767	1,767	1,767
LANDI, Ricardo Verdugo (1871-1930) Spanish				
oil	2	1,796-2,225	2,010	1,796
LANDOLT, Salomon (1741-1818) Swiss				
wc/d	1	1,973	1,973	1,973
LANDOWSKI, Paul Maximilien (1875-1961) French				
3D	4	2,592-42,324	17,290	10,137
LANDRE, Louise Amelie (1852-?) French				
oil	1	12,000	12,000	12,000
LANDSEER, Sir Edwin (1802-1873) British				
oil	3	7,297-102,600	40,132	10,500
wc/d	4	2,655-44,250	13,685	2,835
LANDSEER, Thomas (1795-1880) British				
wc/d	1	1,125	1,125	1,125
LANDT, Frants (1885-1976) Danish				
oil	2	509-1,897	1,203	509
LANDUYT, Octave (1922-) Belgian				
oil	1	3,442	3,442	3,442
LANDWEHR, Curt A (1920-1988) ?				
oil	1	1,184	1,184	1,184
LANDY, Michael (1963-) British?				
wc/d	1	24,050	24,050	24,050
3D	1	13,875	13,875	13,875
LANE, Fitz Hugh (1804-1865) American				
oil	3	825,000-1,000,000	883,333	825,000
LANE, Leonard C (c.1910-1978) Canadian?				
oil	1	2,000	2,000	2,000
LANE, Lois (1948-) American				
oil	1	1,100	1,100	1,100
LANE, Samuel (1780-1859) British				
oil	1	70,800	70,800	70,800
LANFANT DE METZ, François Louis (1814-1892) French				
oil	7	2,026-13,077	5,698	3,600
LANFRANCO, Giovanni (1582-1647) Italian				
oil	1	129,750	129,750	129,750
wc/d	1	800	800	800
LANG (?) ?				
oil	1	6,054	6,054	6,054
LANG SHINING (1688-1766) Chinese/Italian				
wc/d	1	9,910	9,910	9,910
LANG, Albert (1847-1933) German				
oil	3	825-2,267	1,329	895
wc/d	1	907	907	907
LANG, Hans (1898-1971) Austrian				
oil	2	1,178-1,178	1,178	1,178
LANG, Hermann (1856-1899) German				
oil	1	6,932	6,932	6,932
LANG, Josef Adolf (1873-1936) Austrian				
oil	1	1,021	1,021	1,021
LANG, Louis (1814-1893) German				
oil	1	4,000	4,000	4,000

Name	No.	Price Range	Average	Median
LANG, Richard (1861-?) German				
oil	1	2,213	2,213	2,213
LANG, Steven (1944-) American				
oil	2	3,000-4,000	3,500	3,000
LANG-LARIS, Hermine (1842-?) Austrian				
oil	1	2,622	2,622	2,622
LANGASKENS, Maurice (1884-1946) Belgian				
oil	3	9,405-14,317	11,519	10,837
LANGE, Augusto (20th C) Latin American				
3D	1	2,370	2,370	2,370
LANGE, Fritz (1851-1922) German				
oil	2	1,506-3,827	2,666	1,506
LANGE, Helene (1875-?) German				
wc/d	1	2,068	2,068	2,068
LANGE, Johann Gustav (1811-1887) German				
oil	4	727-3,633	2,119	1,549
LANGE, Julius (1817-1878) German				
oil	6	1,767-6,312	3,683	3,275
LANGE, Maar Julius (1897-1979) Danish				
oil	3	1,051-3,380	2,177	2,101
LANGE, Richard W (20th C) British?				
3D	1	3,114	3,114	3,114
LANGENDYK, Dirk (1748-1805) Dutch				
wc/d	3	1,051-1,635	1,362	1,401
LANGENDYK, Jan Anthonie (1780-1818) Dutch				
wc/d	1	10,703	10,703	10,703
LANGER, Viggo (1860-1942) Danish				
oil	12	443-184,726	16,205	890
LANGERER, Freddie (1899-1948) Dutch				
oil	1	7,510	7,510	7,510
LANGETTI, Giovanni Battista (1625-1676) Italian				
oil	3	9,709-36,000	21,114	17,635
LANGEVELD, Frans (1877-1939) Dutch				
oil	1	26,521	26,521	26,521
LANGEVIN, Claude (1942-) Canadian				
oil	14	529-3,728	1,656	1,640
LANGEWEG, Ger (1891-1970) Dutch				
wc/d	1	1,430	1,430	1,430
LANGHAMMER, Walter (1905-1977) Austrian				
oil	1	4,928	4,928	4,928
LANGKER, Sir Erik (1898-1982) Australian				
oil	1	1,600	1,600	1,600
LANGKO, Dietrich (1819-1896) German				
oil	1	2,104	2,104	2,104
LANGLAIS, Bernard (1921-1977) American				
oil	2	10,000-20,000	15,000	10,000
3D	2	2,200-3,500	2,850	2,200
LANGLAIS, Xavier de (1906-1975) French				
oil	1	1,927	1,927	1,927
LANGLANDS and BELL (20th C) British				
3D	1	4,326	4,326	4,326
LANGLEY, Walter (1852-1922) British				
oil	4	460-25,800	11,008	673
wc/d	12	828-29,370	8,942	5,280
LANGLOIS, C de (18/19th C) French				
oil	1	1,832	1,832	1,832
LANGLOIS, J (19th C) British				
oil	2	1,890-4,844	3,367	1,890
LANGLOIS, Mark W (fl.1862-1873) British				
oil	9	497-2,400	1,085	957
LANGS, Leo (19th C) Austrian				
wc/d	1	1,933	1,933	1,933
LANIAU, Jean (1931-) French				
3D	2	2,472-3,637	3,054	2,472
LANINO, Bernardino (1510-1578) Italian				
oil	1	29,410	29,410	29,410
LANNES, Mario (1900-1983) Italian				
oil	1	1,144	1,144	1,144
LANOE, Alphonse (1926-) Swiss				
oil	2	1,045-1,621	1,333	1,045
wc/d	2	759-803	781	759

Name	No.	Price Range	Average	Median
LANOEL, Juan Alejandro (1919-1985) Argentinian				
wc/d	1	1,200	1,200	1,200
LANOOY, Chris (1881-1948) Dutch				
oil	1	5,724	5,724	5,724
LANOS, Henri (19th C) French				
wc/d	2	4,671-6,423	5,547	4,671
LANOUX, B (19th C) French?				
oil	2	975-1,646	1,310	975
LANSAC, François-Emile de (1803-1890) French				
oil	1	3,356	3,356	3,356
LANSDOWNE, James Fenwick (1937-) Canadian				
wc/d	2	2,132-2,531	2,331	2,132
LANSIL, Walter Franklin (1846-1925) American				
oil	5	550-2,200	1,270	1,200
LANSKOY, Andre (1902-1976) French/Russian				
oil	60	833-187,027	38,081	29,774
wc/d	54	1,200-48,020	8,971	7,764
LANSON, Alfred Desire (1851-1898) French				
3D	1	32,130	32,130	32,130
L'ANSON, Mark (20th C) British				
wc/d	1	1,091	1,091	1,091
LANSYER, Emmanuel (1835-1893) French				
oil	3	3,273-6,008	4,712	4,855
wc/d	1	530	530	530
LANTERI, Alberto Remo Carlo (1955-) Italian				
oil	2	1,229-3,460	2,344	1,229
LANTOINE, F (1876-c.1955) French				
oil	1	2,910	2,910	2,910
LANTOINE, Fernand (1876-c.1955) French				
oil	13	482-65,891	6,501	1,145
LANTZ, Paul (1908-2000) American				
oil	2	1,100-1,800	1,450	1,100
LANTZ, Walter (20th C) American				
oil	1	1,298	1,298	1,298
LANYON, Deborah (1958-) British				
wc/d	2	1,793-1,793	1,793	1,793
LANYON, Peter (1918-1964) British				
oil	3	6,000-263,900	136,366	139,200
wc/d	4	7,958-36,400	17,917	11,245
LANZA, Giovanni (1827-1889) Italian				
wc/d	4	2,618-9,514	5,723	3,279
LANZA, Luigi (19th C) Italian				
oil	1	973	973	973
wc/d	4	1,036-1,942	1,650	1,812
LANZA, Vicenzo (1822-1902) Italian				
oil	1	9,350	9,350	9,350
LANZANI, Polidoro (1515-1565) Italian				
oil	1	16,649	16,649	16,649
LAP, Jan Willemsz (17th C) Dutch				
wc/d	1	1,401	1,401	1,401
LAPASSOUZE, Emma (20th C) French				
oil	1	1,790	1,790	1,790
LAPAYESE BRUNA, Jose (1899-1982) Spanish				
oil	1	7,714	7,714	7,714
LAPAYESE DEL RIO, Jose (1926-2000) Spanish				
oil	4	900-3,000	1,788	1,567
LAPCHINE, Georges (1885-1951) Russian				
oil	17	3,096-93,207	31,521	25,205
wc/d	3	1,376-4,836	3,466	4,186
LAPICQUE, Charles (1898-1988) French				
oil	20	1,514-63,115	14,995	9,630
wc/d	26	521-10,207	1,854	1,178
3D	1	2,637	2,637	2,637
LAPINE, Andreas Christian Gottfried (1868-1952) Canadian				
oil	4	1,146-4,218	2,083	1,265
wc/d	2	441-2,460	1,450	441
LAPINI, Cesare (1848-?) Italian				
3D	5	4,612-18,900	9,858	10,000
LAPIRA, Pasquale (?) Italian				
wc/d	1	1,695	1,695	1,695
LAPIS, Hieronymus (1723-1798) Italian				
oil	2	1,373-1,513	1,443	1,373

Name	No.	Price Range	Average	Median
LAPITO, Louis Auguste (1803-1874) French				
oil	1	4,325	4,325	4,325
wc/d	2	876-1,403	1,139	876
LAPORTE, Emile (1858-1907) French				
3D	2	2,350-5,096	3,723	2,350
LAPORTE, George Henry (1799-1873) German				
oil	4	2,928-58,080	21,822	3,402
wc/d	1	1,325	1,325	1,325
LAPORTE, Georges (1926-2000) French				
oil	17	543-3,644	1,643	1,374
LAPORTE, John (1761-1839) British				
oil	1	10,380	10,380	10,380
LAPORTE, Marcellin (1839-1906) French				
oil	2	4,500-6,750	5,625	4,500
LAPORTE-BLAIRSY, Leo (1865-1923) French				
3D	1	3,200	3,200	3,200
LAPOSTOLET, Charles (1824-1890) French				
oil	3	1,326-3,395	2,688	3,343
LAPOUJADE, Robert (1921-) French				
oil	2	1,094-1,320	1,207	1,094
LAPRA, Paul (19th C) French				
oil	1	2,221	2,221	2,221
LAPRADE, Pierre (1875-1932) French				
oil	12	1,215-28,431	5,851	3,092
wc/d	4	565-1,546	1,086	968
LAQUY, Willem Joseph (1738-1798) German				
oil	1	30,908	30,908	30,908
LARA, Edwina (19th C) British				
oil	2	1,750-1,848	1,799	1,750
LARA, Georgina (fl.1862-1871) British				
oil	5	956-5,632	2,240	1,408
LARCHE, Raoul (1860-1912) French				
3D	7	2,351-38,280	20,116	17,671
LARCHER, Jules (1849-1920) French				
oil	1	1,312	1,312	1,312
L'ARCHEVEQUE, Andre (1923-) Canadian				
oil	1	4,919	4,919	4,919
LARCO, Jorge (1897-1967) Argentinian				
wc/d	1	2,800	2,800	2,800
LARDERA, Berto (1911-) French				
wc/d	2	485-1,000	742	485
3D	1	26,714	26,714	26,714
LARGE, George (1936-) British				
wc/d	1	1,435	1,435	1,435
LARGILLIERE, Nicolas de (1656-1746) French				
oil	8	10,000-175,750	65,953	48,100
LARIONOV, Mikhail (1881-1964) Russian				
oil	5	15,175-1,302,000	302,613	34,200
wc/d	18	766-25,800	8,551	7,434
LARIVE-GODEFROY, Pierre Louis de (1735-1817) Swiss				
wc/d	4	1,214-2,572	1,892	1,679
LARNER, Liz (?) American?				
3D	1	12,000	12,000	12,000
LAROCHE, Armand (1826-1903) French				
oil	1	6,612	6,612	6,612
LARONZE, Jean (1852-1937) French				
oil	1	4,000	4,000	4,000
LAROON, Marcellus (jnr) (1679-1774) British				
oil	1	1,472	1,472	1,472
LARRAMENDI, Juan (1917-) Spanish				
oil	1	3,646	3,646	3,646
LARRANAGA, Enrique de (1900-1956) Argentinian				
oil	2	3,708-11,200	7,454	3,708
LARRAVIDE, Manuel (1871-1910) Uruguayan				
oil	1	9,000	9,000	9,000
wc/d	1	9,000	9,000	9,000
LARRAZ, Julio (1944-) Cuban				
oil	5	55,000-140,000	83,000	60,000
LARROUX, Antonin (1859-1913) French				
3D	1	4,849	4,849	4,849
LARRUE, Guillaume (1851-?) French				
oil	2	1,548-3,801	2,674	1,548

Name	No.	Price Range	Average	Median
LARSEN, Emanuel (1823-1859) Danish				
oil	7	809-3,794	2,664	2,846
LARSEN, Hugo Valdemar (1875-1950) Danish				
oil	2	650-2,699	1,674	650
LARSEN, Johannes (1867-1961) Danish				
oil	8	1,030-16,241	6,518	4,393
wc/d	5	841-3,982	2,100	1,327
LARSEN, Knud (1865-1922) Danish				
oil	2	3,380-3,380	3,380	3,380
LARSEN, Oscar (1882-1972) Austrian				
oil	5	530-1,697	1,094	975
wc/d	6	485-1,844	1,140	727
LARSEN, Thorvald (1881-1947) Scandinavian				
oil	1	1,051	1,051	1,051
LARSEN-SAERSLOV, Fredrik (1870-1942) Danish				
oil	1	5,500	5,500	5,500
LARSSEN, Johan (1853-1920) Norwegian				
oil	1	2,300	2,300	2,300
LARSSON, Bo (1945-) Swedish				
oil	2	5,344-8,722	7,033	5,344
wc/d	1	764	764	764
LARSSON, Carl (1853-1919) Swedish				
oil	1	62,319	62,319	62,319
wc/d	19	997-441,600	84,258	16,562
LARSSON, Marcus (1825-1864) Swedish				
oil	11	1,132-12,464	6,114	6,481
LARTIGUE, Guy (1927-) French				
3D	1	4,401	4,401	4,401
LARUS, Eliane (1944-) French				
oil	3	656-2,543	1,610	1,632
wc/d	3	702-3,996	1,929	1,090
LARWIN, Johann (1873-1938) Austrian				
oil	2	2,524-10,520	6,522	2,524
LASALLE, Charles (1894-1958) American				
oil	1	7,500	7,500	7,500
wc/d	1	425	425	425
LASALLE, Jean (?) ?				
	1	1,800	1,800	1,800
LASCANO, Juan (1947-) Argentinian				
oil	1	27,000	27,000	27,000
LASCAUX, Elie (1888-1969) French				
oil	10	605-5,444	1,919	1,210
wc/d	1	605	605	605
LASEK, Andrej (1945-) Polish				
oil	1	1,119	1,119	1,119
LASERSTEIN, Lotte (1898-1993) Swedish				
oil	1	1,062	1,062	1,062
wc/d	1	2,114	2,114	2,114
LASINSKY, Johann Adolf (1808-1871) German				
oil	1	3,649	3,649	3,649
wc/d	1	680	680	680
LASITHIOTAKIS, Yannis (1956-) Greek				
wc/d	2	2,992-3,872	3,432	2,992
LASKARIDOU, Sophia (1882-1965) Greek?				
oil	3	3,740-7,560	5,013	3,740
LASKE, Oskar (1874-1951) Austrian				
wc/d	5	1,757-11,348	6,592	6,027
LASKER, Jonathan (1948-) American				
oil	2	51,800-60,000	55,900	51,800
wc/d	4	2,672-5,089	3,672	2,832
LASSAW, Ibram (1913-) American/Egyptian				
3D	2	3,750-15,000	9,375	3,750
LASSEN, Hans August (1857-1938) German				
oil	3	1,265-2,213	1,748	1,768
LASSNIG, Maria (1919-) Austrian				
oil	4	46,124-135,000	78,273	59,143
wc/d	7	2,577-15,429	6,158	4,000
LASSONDE, Omer (1903-1980) American				
oil	2	1,576-2,600	2,088	1,576
LASZLO DE LOMBOS, Philip Alexius de (1869-1937) British				
oil	6	2,288-34,020	19,403	14,800

Name	No.	Price Range	Average	Median
LATAPIE, Louis (1891-1972) French				
oil	18	714-5,648	2,732	2,698
wc/d	7	693-1,518	965	887
LATASTER, Ger (1920-) Dutch				
oil	5	2,572-6,997	4,714	3,822
wc/d	1	712	712	712
LATHAM, John (1921-) British				
oil	1	21,625	21,625	21,625
LATHAM, Molly M (c.1900-1987) British				
oil	3	600-3,460	2,109	2,268
wc/d	1	609	609	609
LATHANGUE, Henry Herbert (1859-1929) British				
oil	5	9,625-160,650	63,087	47,880
LATHROP, William Langson (1859-1938) American				
oil	4	4,500-22,500	14,000	14,000
wc/d	1	500	500	500
LATIMER, Lorenzo Palmer (1857-1941) American				
wc/d	2	1,000-3,750	2,375	1,000
LATOIX, Gaspard (fl.1882-1903) British				
oil	1	1,592	1,592	1,592
LATORRE RODRIGO, Federico (19/20th C) Spanish				
oil	1	1,080	1,080	1,080
LATOUCHE, Claude Gaston (20th C) French				
wc/d	1	1,978	1,978	1,978
LATOUCHE, Gaston de (1854-1913) French				
oil	14	2,464-170,000	41,477	16,000
wc/d	1	3,387	3,387	3,387
LATOUR, Maurice Quentin de (1704-1788) French				
wc/d	1	12,038	12,038	12,038
LATOUR, René (?) ?				
oil	1	51,520	51,520	51,520
LATRI, Mikhail Pelopidovich (1875-1942) Russian				
oil	1	12,485	12,485	12,485
wc/d	1	43,315	43,315	43,315
LATTRY, Michel (1875-1941) French/Russian				
wc/d	2	1,334-1,818	1,576	1,334
LAU CHUN (1942-) ?				
oil	1	1,225	1,225	1,225
LAUBER, Joseph (19/20th C) American?				
oil	1	4,800	4,800	4,800
LAUBIES, René (1924-) French				
oil	4	1,276-4,182	2,288	1,754
wc/d	2	1,002-1,818	1,410	1,002
LAUBIN, Carl (1947-) American				
oil	1	1,589	1,589	1,589
L'AUBINIERE, Georgina M de (1848-1930) British				
oil	1	1,500	1,500	1,500
wc/d	1	1,282	1,282	1,282
LAUCHERT, Richard (1823-1869) German				
oil	1	10,014	10,014	10,014
LAUDER, Charles James (1841-1920) British				
wc/d	5	592-2,088	1,090	788
LAUDER, Robert Scott (1803-1869) British				
oil	2	1,740-45,760	23,750	1,740
LAUDY, Jean (1877-1956) Belgian				
oil	13	642-9,555	2,331	1,332
wc/d	1	775	775	775
LAUENSTEIN, Paul (1898-1980) German				
oil	2	643-1,757	1,200	643
LAUER, Josef (1818-1881) Austrian				
oil	2	19,638-70,435	45,036	19,638
LAUGE, Achille (1861-1944) French				
oil	9	18,703-153,154	63,668	49,950
wc/d	1	1,184	1,184	1,184
LAUGEE, Desire (1823-1896) French				
oil	1	1,074	1,074	1,074
LAUGEE, Georges (1853-?) French				
oil	4	1,500-14,000	7,125	6,000
LAUNAY, Fernand de (19th C) French				
oil	1	3,503	3,503	3,503
LAUNOIS, Jean (1898-1942) French				
wc/d	12	701-7,767	1,869	1,403

Name	No.	Price Range	Average	Median
LAUR, Marie Yvonne (1879-1943) French				
oil	1	2,636	2,636	2,636
LAURENCE, Sydney Mortimer (1865-1940) American				
oil	12	8,400-120,000	26,408	17,000
LAURENCIN, Marie (1885-1956) French				
oil	23	11,000-270,000	75,143	60,000
wc/d	27	714-35,000	7,483	3,540
LAURENS, Henri (1885-1954) French				
wc/d	4	7,135-221,747	67,549	7,875
3D	11	38,000-1,300,000	219,420	55,000
LAURENS, Jean Paul (1838-1921) French				
wc/d	2	1,168-1,226	1,197	1,168
LAURENS, Nicolas Auguste (1829-1908) French				
oil	1	15,000	15,000	15,000
LAURENS, Paul Albert (1870-1934) French				
oil	2	1,465-2,167	1,816	1,465
LAURENT, Bruno Émile (1928-) French				
oil	4	597-1,432	1,005	893
wc/d	2	482-506	494	482
LAURENT, Ernest Joseph (1859-1929) French				
oil	1	15,500	15,500	15,500
wc/d	3	506-589	555	570
LAURENT, Eugène (1832-1898) French				
3D	3	1,621-2,803	2,408	2,800
LAURENT, Jean (1906-) French				
oil	7	580-4,983	2,826	2,200
LAURENT, Jean Émile (1906-) French				
oil	3	4,400-5,130	4,789	4,839
LAURENT, Jean Michel (1898-1988) ?				
oil	3	750-2,400	1,716	2,000
LAURENT, Marcel (1892-1948) French				
oil	2	876-1,987	1,431	876
LAURENT, Robert (1890-1970) American				
3D	1	2,500	2,500	2,500
LAURENT-GSELL, Lucien (1860-1944) French				
oil	1	1,956	1,956	1,956
LAURENTI, Cesare (1854-1937) Italian				
oil	1	32,500	32,500	32,500
wc/d	1	28,664	28,664	28,664
LAUREUS, Alexander (1783-1823) Swedish				
oil	1	7,027	7,027	7,027
LAURI, Filippo (1623-1694) Italian				
oil	2	5,301-24,050	14,675	5,301
LAURIOZ, Patrice (1959-) French				
oil	6	1,683-9,936	4,747	2,922
LAURITZ, Paul (1889-1975) American				
oil	12	1,900-13,000	5,070	4,000
LAUSEN, Uwe (1941-1970) German?				
oil	3	2,263-16,459	8,632	7,176
wc/d	1	4,115	4,115	4,115
LAUTERBURG, Martin (1891-1960) Swiss				
oil	3	522-2,997	1,681	1,526
LAUTREC, Lucien (1909-1991) French				
oil	2	2,021-2,910	2,465	2,021
LAUVERGNE, Barthelemy (1805-1871) French				
oil	2	2,503-17,740	10,121	2,503
LAUVRAY, Abel (1870-1950) French				
oil	9	835-4,375	1,888	1,455
LAUX, August (1847-1921) American				
oil	4	1,400-4,500	2,375	1,600
LAVAGNINO, Pier Luigi (1933-1999) Italian				
oil	2	2,238-3,352	2,795	2,238
wc/d	1	492	492	492
LAVALLEE-POUSSIN, Étienne de (1733-1793) French				
wc/d	3	942-1,878	1,256	950
LAVAULT, Albert Tibule Furcy de (19th C) French				
oil	1	8,000	8,000	8,000
LAVERENNE, Nicolas (?) ?				
3D	2	1,780-2,848	2,314	1,780
LAVERGNE (?) ?				
oil	1	4,579	4,579	4,579

Name	No.	Price Range	Average	Median
LAVERGNE, Claudius (1814-1887) French				
oil	1	1,600	1,600	1,600
LAVERNE, Philip Kelvin (20th C) American				
3D	1	2,100	2,100	2,100
LAVERY, Sir John (1856-1941) British				
oil	23	1,720-1,506,600	177,584	50,411
wc/d	1	22,932	22,932	22,932
LAVEZZARI, A (19th C) ?				
wc/d	1	2,208	2,208	2,208
LAVIEILLE, Eugène (1820-1889) French				
oil	5	4,123-9,873	7,009	5,828
wc/d	1	851	851	851
LAVIER, Bertrand (1949-) French				
oil	4	676-14,449	10,091	12,041
wc/d	1	2,983	2,983	2,983
3D	3	7,655-16,857	12,014	11,531
LAVOINE, L P Robert (1916-1999) French				
oil	2	834-835	834	834
wc/d	3	473-1,073	721	618
LAVONEN, Ahti (1928-1970) Finnish				
oil	1	3,514	3,514	3,514
LAVONEN, Kuutti (1960-) Finnish				
wc/d	1	1,543	1,543	1,543
LAVROFF, G (1895-?) Russian				
3D	1	6,361	6,361	6,361
LAVROFF, Georges (1895-?) Russian				
3D	4	2,640-6,361	3,830	3,151
LAW, Andrew (fl.1895-1940) British				
oil	1	1,288	1,288	1,288
LAW, Bob (1934-) British				
wc/d	1	770	770	770
3D	1	3,078	3,078	3,078
LAW, David (1831-1901) British				
oil	1	880	880	880
wc/d	1	470	470	470
LAW, Denys (1907-1981) British				
oil	6	1,211-4,071	2,110	1,770
LAWES, Harold (fl.1890`s) British				
wc/d	1	1,209	1,209	1,209
LAWLESS, Carl (1894-1934) American				
oil	1	4,000	4,000	4,000
LAWLEY, Douglas (1906-1971) Canadian				
oil	3	697-2,624	1,557	1,350
LAWRENCE, Edith Mary (1890-1973) British				
oil	1	1,296	1,296	1,296
LAWRENCE, George (c.1758-1802) British				
wc/d	1	3,600	3,600	3,600
LAWRENCE, Jacob (1917-2000) American				
wc/d	1	42,500	42,500	42,500
LAWRENCE, Marguerite E (fl.1903-1919) British				
oil	1	1,908	1,908	1,908
LAWRENCE, R (?) ?				
oil	1	2,013	2,013	2,013
LAWRENCE, Sir Thomas (1769-1830) British				
oil	7	7,000-130,000	35,768	18,900
wc/d	3	2,220-34,800	13,390	3,150
LAWRENCE, William Goadby (1913-2002) American				
oil	1	5,000	5,000	5,000
LAWRIE, Alexander (1828-1917) American				
oil	2	719-8,000	4,359	719
LAWRIE, Hamish (1919-1987) British				
oil	4	626-3,344	1,448	905
wc/d	2	557-592	574	557
LAWRIE, Lee (1877-1963) American				
3D	1	11,000	11,000	11,000
LAWS, Thomas B (20th C) British?				
wc/d	1	2,262	2,262	2,262
LAWSHE, Hank (1935-1993) American				
oil	1	3,000	3,000	3,000
LAWSON, Alexander (fl.1890-1903) British				
oil	1	1,183	1,183	1,183

Name	No.	Price Range	Average	Median
LAWSON, Cecil Gordon (1851-1882) British				
oil	1	3,114	3,114	3,114
LAWSON, Ernest (1873-1939) American				
oil	18	500-95,000	44,083	35,000
LAWSON, George Anderson (1832-1904) British				
3D	1	22,500	22,500	22,500
LAWSON, Robert (1892-1967) American				
wc/d	1	24,000	24,000	24,000
LAWSON, Sonia (1934-) British				
oil	1	1,700	1,700	1,700
LAWSON, Tim Allen (1963-) American				
oil	1	10,000	10,000	10,000
LAYCOCK, Brent R (1947-) Canadian				
oil	1	793	793	793
wc/d	3	495-729	573	495
LAYRAUD, Joseph-Fortune (1834-1912) French				
oil	1	1,013	1,013	1,013
LAZARE-LEVY (1867-1933) ?				
oil	2	1,312-5,369	3,340	1,312
LAZAREV, Sergei (20th C) Russian				
oil	1	10,380	10,380	10,380
LAZAREV, Vladimir (20th C) Russian				
oil	2	700-2,600	1,650	700
LAZARIS, Theodoros (1885-1958) Greek				
oil	4	4,224-17,400	9,943	8,700
LAZERGES, Jean Raymond Hippolyte (1817-1887) French				
oil	5	1,215-7,134	4,332	5,098
LAZERGES, Paul Jean Baptiste (1845-1902) French				
oil	3	11,478-19,418	15,632	16,000
LAZZARI, Alfredo (1871-1949) Argentinian				
oil	1	2,800	2,800	2,800
LAZZARI, Bice (1900-1981) Italian				
oil	2	4,401-9,955	7,178	4,401
wc/d	2	3,816-4,452	4,134	3,816
LAZZARINI, Gregorio (1655-1730) Italian				
oil	1	15,459	15,459	15,459
LAZZARINI, Robert (1965-) American				
3D	1	17,000	17,000	17,000
LAZZARO, Walter (1914-1989) Italian				
oil	4	5,643-9,425	7,989	8,414
LAZZOLO, Vasco (20th C) ?				
oil	1	1,151	1,151	1,151
LE PHO (1907-2001) Vietnamese				
oil	35	4,500-63,793	21,497	18,000
wc/d	10	1,885-136,757	42,358	23,591
LE THI LUU (1911-1988) Vietnamese				
oil	2	3,568-4,162	3,865	3,568
wc/d	1	22,500	22,500	22,500
LE-TAN, Pierre (1950-) French				
oil	1	15,904	15,904	15,904
wc/d	24	471-4,948	1,678	1,414
LEA, Tom (1907-2001) American				
oil	2	32,000-90,000	61,000	32,000
wc/d	1	47,500	47,500	47,500
LEACH, Ely (fl.1790s) Central American				
wc/d	1	2,790	2,790	2,790
LEADER, B W (1831-1923) British				
oil	1	2,400	2,400	2,400
LEADER, Benjamin Williams (1831-1923) British				
oil	37	440-37,800	10,842	7,000
LEADER, Charles (19th C) British				
oil	4	676-1,454	1,089	1,038
LEADER, Walton (1877-1966) American				
oil	1	1,700	1,700	1,700
LEAH (20th C) North American				
3D	1	2,025	2,025	2,025
LEAH, Frank (20th C) Irish				
wc/d	1	6,362	6,362	6,362
LEAHY, Ramie (20th C) Irish				
oil	1	7,767	7,767	7,767
wc/d	1	595	595	595

Name	No.	Price Range	Average	Median
LEAKE, Gerald (1885-1975) American				
oil	1	1,250	1,250	1,250
LEAKEY, James (1775-1865) British				
oil	2	1,122-1,682	1,402	1,122
LEANDRE, Charles (1862-1930) French				
wc/d	2	605-1,758	1,181	605
LEAR, Edward (1812-1888) British				
oil	1	240,000	240,000	240,000
wc/d	45	600-102,300	11,495	6,574
LEARNED, Harry (1842-?) American				
oil	1	1,500	1,500	1,500
LEAVER, Charles (19th C) British				
oil	5	2,816-7,955	4,985	4,440
LEAVER, Noel Harry (1889-1951) British				
wc/d	33	560-7,000	2,655	2,150
LEAVERS, Lucy A (fl.1887-1898) British				
oil	1	1,638	1,638	1,638
LEAVITT, Edward C (1842-1904) American				
oil	5	850-4,000	2,870	3,000
LEBADANG (1922-) French/Vietnamese				
oil	1	2,000	2,000	2,000
wc/d	1	475	475	475
LEBARON-DESVES, Augusta (1804-?) French				
oil	1	2,303	2,303	2,303
LEBAS, Gabriel-Hippolyte (1812-1880) French				
oil	3	1,499-4,971	2,745	1,767
wc/d	2	547-628	587	547
LEBASQUE, Henri (1865-1937) French				
oil	29	2,800-750,000	104,893	65,000
wc/d	31	375-17,575	4,574	2,458
LEBASQUE, Pierre (1912-) French				
3D	1	1,786	1,786	1,786
LEBDUSKA, Lawrence (1894-1966) American				
oil	11	400-5,000	2,118	2,000
wc/d	1	450	450	450
LEBEDEV, Vladimir V (1891-1967) Russian				
wc/d	3	753-1,730	1,314	1,459
LEBEDJEV, Klawdij (1852-1916) Russian				
oil	4	11,127-94,600	35,926	12,180
wc/d	1	1,800	1,800	1,800
LEBEL, Antoine (1705-1793) French				
oil	1	1,649	1,649	1,649
LEBEL, Jean Jacques (1936-) French				
oil	1	2,651	2,651	2,651
wc/d	5	510-3,884	1,326	764
LEBENSTEIN, Jan (1930-1999) Polish/French				
oil	1	5,000	5,000	5,000
wc/d	4	3,371-6,184	4,568	3,709
LEBLANC, Walter (1932-1986) Belgian				
oil	1	6,429	6,429	6,429
wc/d	6	1,400-20,384	7,719	4,077
LEBOURG, Albert (1849-1928) French				
oil	50	1,218-50,959	16,534	15,265
wc/d	29	544-2,977	1,335	1,021
LEBRET, Frans (1820-1909) Dutch				
oil	1	7,500	7,500	7,500
LEBRETON, Constant (1895-1985) French				
oil	3	879-5,068	2,526	1,632
LEBRON, Robert (1928-) American				
oil	2	2,250-2,500	2,375	2,250
LEBRUN, Andre Jean (1737-1811) French				
wc/d	1	1,929	1,929	1,929
LEBRUN, C (1619-1690) French				
oil	1	2,700	2,700	2,700
LEBRUN, Charles (1619-1690) French				
wc/d	1	18,703	18,703	18,703
LEBRUN, Christopher (1951-) British				
oil	2	1,710-2,958	2,334	1,710
LEBRUN, Marc Eugène (1867-?) French				
oil	1	8,237	8,237	8,237
LEBRUN, Marcel (19/20th C) French?				
oil	2	3,690-12,000	7,845	3,690

Name	No.	Price Range	Average	Median
LEBRUN, Rico (1900-1964) American/Italian				
wc/d	4	450-4,000	1,562	600
LEBSCHE, Karl-August (1800-1877) Polish				
wc/d	1	1,178	1,178	1,178
LECCIA, Ange (1952-) French				
wc/d	1	4,171	4,171	4,171
LECHNER, Ferdinand (1855-?) German				
wc/d	2	668-1,654	1,161	668
LECHNER, Karl Max (1890-1974) German				
oil	1	1,105	1,105	1,105
LECHNER, R (19/20th C) ?				
oil	1	1,967	1,967	1,967
LECHTER, Melchior (1865-1936) German?				
oil	1	2,870	2,870	2,870
LECK, Bart van der (1876-1958) Dutch				
oil	2	35,342-37,405	36,373	35,342
wc/d	3	2,945-3,025	2,971	2,945
3D	1	14,137	14,137	14,137
LECLERC DES GOBELINS, Sebastian (1734-1785) French				
oil	2	900-12,130	6,515	900
wc/d	1	941	941	941
LECLERC, Sebastien (younger) (1676-1763) French				
wc/d	1	2,188	2,188	2,188
LECLERCQ, Leopold (1911-1977) Belgian				
oil	3	1,940-4,849	2,909	1,940
LECLERCQ, Lucien (1895-1955) Belgian				
oil	1	3,099	3,099	3,099
LECLERCQ, Victor (1896-1944) Belgian				
oil	1	3,025	3,025	3,025
LECOINTE, Charles Joseph (1824-1886) French				
oil	1	1,649	1,649	1,649
LECOMTE DU NOUY, Jean Jules Antoine (1842-1923) French				
oil	1	2,497	2,497	2,497
LECOMTE, Etienne Cherubin (1766-c.1806) French				
wc/d	1	6,960	6,960	6,960
LECOMTE, Hippolyte (1781-1857) French				
oil	1	6,676	6,676	6,676
LECOMTE, Paul (1842-1920) French				
oil	5	530-3,548	2,137	2,279
wc/d	3	444-1,311	884	897
LECOMTE, Paul Émile (1877-1950) French				
oil	12	1,331-15,459	3,901	2,124
wc/d	2	643-2,268	1,455	643
LECOMTE-VERNET, Charles Émile (1821-1900) French				
oil	1	16,000	16,000	16,000
LECOQUE, Alois (1891-1981) Czechoslovakian				
oil	2	885-2,100	1,492	885
LECOSTY, J (fl.1890s) Belgian				
oil	1	3,399	3,399	3,399
LECOURT, Raymond (1882-1946) French				
oil	8	1,401-3,758	2,512	2,428
LECOURTIER, Prosper (1855-1924) French				
3D	4	4,956-13,000	7,488	5,520
LECUONA, Juan (20th C) Argentinian				
wc/d	1	3,700	3,700	3,700
LECURIEUX, Jacques Joseph (1801-1867) French				
wc/d	1	1,890	1,890	1,890
LEDANNOIS, Jean Marie (20th C) French				
oil	1	2,460	2,460	2,460
LEDDA, Carlos Jose (1932-) Argentinian				
oil	1	2,071	2,071	2,071
LEDERER, Hugo (1871-?) German				
3D	1	5,088	5,088	5,088
LEDFORD, Freda Widder (1904-) American				
oil	1	1,200	1,200	1,200
LEDGER, Janet (20th C) British				
oil	1	1,305	1,305	1,305
LEDRAY, Charles (1960-) American				
3D	1	65,000	65,000	65,000
LEDRU, Auguste (1860-1902) French				
3D	1	4,566	4,566	4,566

Name	No.	Price Range	Average	Median
LEDUC, Arthur Jacques (1848-1918) French				
3D	1	13,230	13,230	13,230
LEDUC, Charles (1831-1911) French				
oil	1	10,510	10,510	10,510
LEDUC, Fernand (1916-) Canadian				
oil	1	6,149	6,149	6,149
wc/d	3	749-2,132	1,375	1,244
LEDUC, Paul (1876-1943) Belgian				
oil	11	1,445-8,390	4,039	2,917
LEDWARD, Gilbert (1886-1960) British				
wc/d	1	915	915	915
3D	1	41,280	41,280	41,280
LEE DONGI (1967-) Korean				
oil	1	13,000	13,000	13,000
LEE U-FAN (1936-) Korean				
oil	1	140,000	140,000	140,000
LEE YONG-DEOK (1956-) Korean				
3D	1	20,000	20,000	20,000
LEE, Bertha Stringer (1873-1937) American				
oil	1	1,800	1,800	1,800
LEE, Bob (1933-) American				
oil	1	2,800	2,800	2,800
LEE, Doris (1905-1983) American				
oil	1	3,800	3,800	3,800
wc/d	1	2,500	2,500	2,500
LEE, Frederick Richard (1798-1879) British				
oil	3	963-32,130	16,731	17,100
LEE, Jake (1915-1992) American				
wc/d	4	950-6,500	2,837	1,400
LEE, Joseph (1780-1859) British				
oil	1	25,000	25,000	25,000
LEE, Marjorie Johnson (1911-1997) American				
oil	1	1,200	1,200	1,200
LEE, Robert J (1921-1994) American				
oil	1	1,300	1,300	1,300
LEE, Won (20th C) ?				
3D	2	9,000-9,000	9,000	9,000
LEE-HANKEY, William (1869-1952) British				
oil	18	1,134-13,090	7,146	5,985
wc/d	6	1,028-10,092	4,173	2,436
LEE-SMITH, Hughie (1915-1999) American				
oil	2	16,000-20,000	18,000	16,000
LEECH, John (1817-1864) British				
oil	2	764-2,124	1,444	764
LEECH, William John (1881-1968) Irish				
oil	5	12,351-478,904	132,640	24,722
wc/d	1	26,757	26,757	26,757
LEEKE, Ferdinand (1859-1923) German				
oil	6	2,253-4,671	2,975	2,625
LEEMPOELS, Jef (1867-1935) Belgian				
oil	1	5,419	5,419	5,419
LEEMPUT, Remi van (1607-1675) Flemish				
oil	1	5,839	5,839	5,839
LEEMPUTTEN, Cornelis van (1841-1902) Belgian				
oil	9	643-10,000	3,528	3,000
LEEMPUTTEN, Frans van (1850-1914) Belgian				
oil	9	1,054-4,914	2,472	2,548
LEEMPUTTEN, Jean Baptiste Leopold van (1831-1924) Belgian				
oil	3	1,300-1,800	1,504	1,414
LEEMPUTTEN, Jef Louis van (1865-1948) Belgian				
oil	19	526-7,007	1,466	764
LEEN, Willem van (1753-1825) Dutch				
oil	2	12,000-31,455	21,727	12,000
LEEN, Willem van and LELIE, Adriaen de (18/19th C) Dutch				
oil	1	8,230	8,230	8,230
LEENE, Jules van de (1887-1962) Belgian				
oil	4	1,808-3,822	2,882	2,338
wc/d	1	1,812	1,812	1,812
LEEPE, van der (17th C) Flemish				
oil	1	7,298	7,298	7,298
LEERMANS, Pieter (1655-1706) Dutch				
oil	1	2,248	2,248	2,248

Name	No.	Price Range	Average	Median
LEES, Derwent (1885-1931) British				
oil	2	5,220-21,735	13,477	5,220
wc/d	1	900	900	900
LEEUW, Alexis de (fl.1848-1883) Belgian				
oil	6	1,298-7,071	3,821	2,100
LEEUWEN, Henk van (1890-1972) Dutch				
oil	3	565-2,003	1,122	800
LEEWENS, Will (1923-1987) Dutch				
oil	3	707-2,356	1,610	1,767
wc/d	3	2,003-2,592	2,277	2,238
LEFAKIS, Christos (1906-1968) Greek				
oil	1	14,960	14,960	14,960
LEFEBRE, Wilhelm (1873-1974) German				
oil	2	701-1,627	1,164	701
LEFEBVRE, Jules Joseph (1836-1911) French				
oil	2	2,750-25,000	13,875	2,750
LEFEBVRE, Madeleine (19/20th C) ?				
oil	3	727-1,455	1,050	970
LEFEBVRE, Maurice Jean (1873-1954) Belgian				
oil	1	2,704	2,704	2,704
LEFEBVRE, Valentin (c.1642-1680) Flemish				
wc/d	3	1,008-1,752	1,356	1,308
LEFEVRE, Charles (19th C) French				
oil	4	537-2,330	1,354	880
LEFEVRE, Robert Jacques François (1755-1830) French				
oil	6	3,828-126,712	36,880	15,660
LEFEVRE, Robert Jacques François and VERNET, Carle (18th C) French				
oil	1	32,000	32,000	32,000
LEFFEL, David (1931-) American				
oil	2	8,500-24,000	16,250	8,500
LEFKOCHIR, Costa (1952-) Belgian?				
oil	1	4,537	4,537	4,537
LEFLER, Heinrich (1863-1919) Austrian				
wc/d	2	1,512-1,512	1,512	1,512
LEFORT, Alex (1908-1954) French				
oil	2	500-3,026	1,763	500
LEFORT, Jean (1875-1954) French				
oil	3	582-1,500	1,194	1,500
wc/d	1	484	484	484
LEFORTIER, Henri Jean (1819-1886) French				
oil	1	1,401	1,401	1,401
LEFRANC, Jules (1887-1972) French				
oil	3	1,700-7,270	5,390	7,200
LEFRANC, Roland (1931-2000) French				
oil	1	1,005	1,005	1,005
LEGA, Achille (1899-1934) Italian				
oil	1	4,800	4,800	4,800
LEGA, Silvestro (1826-1895) Italian				
oil	2	57,245-174,760	116,002	57,245
wc/d	1	851	851	851
LEGANGER, Nicolay Tysland (1832-1894) American				
oil	2	2,400-10,000	6,200	2,400
LEGASPI, Cesar (1917-1994) Philippino				
wc/d	1	3,720	3,720	3,720
LEGAT, Léon (1829-?) French				
oil	2	17,000-35,910	26,455	17,000
LEGENDRE, Léon (19th C) French				
oil	1	1,133	1,133	1,133
LEGENTILE, Louis Victor (1815-1889) French				
oil	1	3,397	3,397	3,397
LEGER, Fernand (1881-1955) French				
oil	22	89,310-4,800,000	1,183,568	471,233
wc/d	70	2,225-492,800	82,657	46,250
3D	6	3,500-250,000	78,166	25,000
LEGGETT, Alexander (1828-1884) British				
oil	5	1,400-3,872	2,446	1,914
LEGGETT, Lucile (1896-?) American				
oil	1	2,000	2,000	2,000
LEGNANI, Stefano Maria (1660-1715) Italian				
oil	1	11,439	11,439	11,439

Name	No.	Price Range	Average	Median
LEGOUT-GERARD, Fernand (1856-1924) French				
oil	10	2,671-29,301	10,057	5,021
wc/d	5	620-10,000	3,193	1,640
LEGRAND, Louis Auguste Mathieu (1863-1951) French				
wc/d	3	895-3,928	1,950	1,029
LEGRAND, Pierre Nicolas (1758-1829) Swiss				
oil	3	5,351-26,163	12,883	7,135
LEGRAND, Rene (1953-) British				
oil	1	1,015	1,015	1,015
LEGRAND, René (1923-) French				
oil	2	769-2,351	1,560	769
LEGRAS, Auguste J F (1864-1915) Dutch				
oil	2	1,558-1,890	1,724	1,558
LEGREW, James (1803-1857) British				
3D	1	5,780	5,780	5,780
LEGRIP, Frederic (19th C) ?				
oil	1	1,073	1,073	1,073
LEGROS, Alphonse (1837-1911) French				
wc/d	3	1,305-1,944	1,634	1,653
LEHERB, Helmut (1933-1997) Austrian				
wc/d	3	719-1,818	1,165	959
LEHMANN, Alfred (1899-1979) German				
wc/d	1	1,328	1,328	1,328
LEHMANN, Edvard (1815-1892) Danish				
oil	4	489-7,938	3,443	1,870
LEHMANN, Henri (1814-1882) French				
oil	2	3,500-11,658	7,579	3,500
wc/d	2	526-634	580	526
LEHMANN, Herbert (1890-?) German				
oil	1	1,074	1,074	1,074
LEHMBRUCK, Wilhelm (1881-1919) German				
wc/d	1	2,460	2,460	2,460
3D	7	3,363-763,767	135,637	10,978
LEHMDEN, Anton (1929-) Austrian				
oil	3	14,629-21,848	17,264	15,315
wc/d	3	1,870-3,786	3,017	3,395
LEHNER, Tobias (1974-) German				
oil	1	14,000	14,000	14,000
LEHOCZKY, Gyorgy (1901-1979) Hungarian				
oil	2	954-1,178	1,066	954
LEHOUX, Pierre François (1803-1892) French				
oil	1	31,320	31,320	31,320
LEHR, Adam (1853-1924) American				
oil	2	1,020-1,500	1,260	1,020
LEHTINEN, Kauko (1925-) Finnish				
wc/d	1	1,157	1,157	1,157
LEIBERG, Helge (1954-) German				
oil	1	8,918	8,918	8,918
wc/d	1	1,196	1,196	1,196
LEIBL, Wilhelm (1844-1900) German				
oil	5	2,008-70,274	26,379	7,360
wc/d	1	2,121	2,121	2,121
LEIBOVITCH, Moni (1946-) Israeli				
oil	1	5,000	5,000	5,000
LEICKAERT, J (19th C) Dutch				
oil	1	5,655	5,655	5,655
LEICKERT, Charles (1818-1907) Belgian				
oil	29	1,341-141,354	30,628	15,315
wc/d	1	3,048	3,048	3,048
LEIDI, Pietro (1892-?) Italian				
oil	1	8,507	8,507	8,507
LEIER, Grant (1956-) American				
wc/d	3	618-1,418	1,138	1,378
LEIGH, Roger (1925-1997) British				
3D	1	16,380	16,380	16,380
LEIGH, Rosa J (1853-1925) Belgian				
oil	2	775-3,575	2,175	775
LEIGH, William R (1866-1955) American				
oil	7	1,200-240,000	76,628	26,000
wc/d	4	8,000-160,000	54,500	14,000

Name	No.	Price Range	Average	Median
LEIGHTON, Alfred Crocker (1901-1965) British				
oil	1	1,402	1,402	1,402
wc/d	9	371-5,539	1,238	798
LEIGHTON, Edmund Blair (1853-1922) British				
oil	1	460,200	460,200	460,200
LEIGHTON, Kathryn Woodman (1876-1952) American				
oil	5	425-30,000	10,885	6,000
LEIGHTON, Lord Frederic (1830-1896) British				
oil	1	20,790	20,790	20,790
wc/d	3	1,740-9,672	4,860	3,168
3D	4	24,570-28,350	26,115	24,570
LEIGHTON, Scott (1849-1898) American				
oil	6	800-20,000	4,672	1,300
LEIMANIS, Andris (1938-) Canadian				
oil	2	529-1,804	1,166	529
LEINECKER, Franz (1825-1917) German				
oil	2	1,091-2,425	1,758	1,091
LEIPOLD, Karl (1864-1943) German				
oil	1	3,277	3,277	3,277
LEIRO, Francisco (1957-) Spanish				
3D	2	11,297-66,224	38,760	11,297
LEISSLER, Arnold (20th C) German				
oil	1	1,060	1,060	1,060
LEIST, Frederick William (1878-1945) Australian				
wc/d	1	2,330	2,330	2,330
LEISTIKOW, Walter (1865-1908) Russian				
oil	7	3,039-90,000	18,863	4,685
wc/d	3	1,527-3,514	2,308	1,883
LEISZ, Mary B (?-1931) American				
oil	2	550-16,000	8,275	550
LEITAO, Pedro (20th C) Portuguese				
oil	1	1,197	1,197	1,197
LEITCH, William Leighton (1804-1883) British				
oil	1	68,400	68,400	68,400
wc/d	21	455-11,375	1,661	925
LEITH-ROSS, Harry (1886-1973) American				
oil	13	4,500-140,000	29,346	14,000
wc/d	8	1,200-9,315	3,439	2,750
LEITNER, Heinrich (1842-1913) Austrian				
oil	2	996-1,013	1,004	996
LEITNER, Thomas (1876-1948) Austrian				
oil	3	899-3,879	1,905	937
LEJEUNE, Eugène (1818-1897) French				
oil	3	805-4,800	2,951	3,250
LEK, Hans van der (1936-2001) Dutch				
oil	1	1,590	1,590	1,590
LEKAKIS, Michael (1907-1998) American				
oil	1	2,431	2,431	2,431
LEKLETI, Mohamed (?) ?				
oil	1	1,816	1,816	1,816
LELEUX, Adolphe (1812-1891) French				
oil	2	1,665-75,000	38,332	1,665
LELIE, Adriaen de (1755-1820) Dutch				
oil	1	32,500	32,500	32,500
LELIENBERGH, Cornelis van (1626-c.1676) Dutch				
oil	2	10,793-44,980	27,886	10,793
LELLI, Giovan Battista (1828-1887) Italian				
oil	3	3,592-28,926	19,394	25,665
LELLOUCHE, Jules (1903-1963) French				
oil	12	514-3,567	1,874	1,686
LELLOUCHE, Ofer (1947-) Israeli				
oil	4	4,000-9,500	6,650	6,100
wc/d	1	500	500	500
LELOIR, Alexandre Louis (1843-1884) French				
oil	1	80,000	80,000	80,000
wc/d	1	1,750	1,750	1,750
LELOIR, Heloise Suzanne (1820-1873) French				
wc/d	1	37,699	37,699	37,699
LELOIR, Jean Baptiste Auguste (1809-1892) French				
oil	1	18,814	18,814	18,814

Name	No.	Price Range	Average	Median
LELOIR, Maurice (1853-1940) French				
oil	1	3,562	3,562	3,562
wc/d	2	1,030-1,823	1,426	1,030
LELONG, Paul (19th C) French				
wc/d	3	8,160-18,432	12,197	10,000
LELONG, Pierre (1908-1984) French				
oil	3	595-1,790	1,095	900
LELONG, René (19th C) French?				
wc/d	1	4,087	4,087	4,087
LELOUP, Antoine (1730-?) Belgian				
wc/d	1	1,168	1,168	1,168
LELOUP, Olivier (1951-) Belgian?				
3D	1	3,131	3,131	3,131
LELY, Sir Peter (1618-1680) British				
oil	5	1,500-1,606,500	347,448	34,020
LEMAIRE, Casimir (19/20th C) French				
oil	1	15,000	15,000	15,000
LEMAIRE, Henri (1879-1949) Belgian				
wc/d	2	1,697-1,800	1,748	1,697
LEMAIRE, Jean (1598-1659) French				
oil	1	111,000	111,000	111,000
LEMAIRE, Joseph (1891-1972) Belgian				
oil	2	894-4,290	2,592	894
LEMAIRE, Madeleine (1845-1928) French				
wc/d	5	584-5,702	2,457	1,169
LEMAITRE, Adrien (1863-?) French				
oil	2	1,051-1,823	1,437	1,051
LEMAITRE, Albert (1886-1975) Belgian				
oil	4	514-1,909	1,259	951
LEMAITRE, Gustave (19th C) French				
oil	1	3,390	3,390	3,390
LEMAITRE, Léon (1850-1905) French				
oil	1	10,911	10,911	10,911
LEMAITRE, Maurice (1929-) French				
oil	11	561-2,939	2,209	2,397
LEMAITRE, Nathanael (1831-1897) French				
oil	1	3,053	3,053	3,053
LEMAN, Robert (1799-1863) British				
wc/d	1	3,162	3,162	3,162
LEMARQUIER, Charles Paul Alfred (19th C) French				
3D	1	2,234	2,234	2,234
LEMASLE, Louis Nicolas (1788-1870) French				
oil	1	76,560	76,560	76,560
LEMEE, Leontine (19th C) French				
oil	1	11,100	11,100	11,100
LEMERCIER, Charles Nicolas (1797-1859) French				
oil	1	1,646	1,646	1,646
LEMIEUX, Clement (1946-) Canadian				
3D	3	1,640-3,164	2,189	1,763
LEMIEUX, Jean Paul (1904-1990) Canadian				
oil	14	2,600-336,777	81,448	48,744
wc/d	3	4,408-4,948	4,758	4,919
LEMIRE, Sophie (1785-?) French				
wc/d	1	2,661	2,661	2,661
LEMKE, Johann Philip (1631-1711) German				
oil	1	8,514	8,514	8,514
LEMMEN, Georges (1865-1916) Belgian				
oil	15	3,955-44,419	18,869	15,196
wc/d	9	596-5,000	1,851	1,731
LEMMENS, E (19th C) French				
oil	1	4,425	4,425	4,425
LEMMENS, Theophile Victor Émile (1821-1867) French				
oil	2	1,405-4,182	2,793	1,405
LEMMERS, Georges (1871-1944) Belgian				
oil	4	602-5,643	2,412	1,236
LEMMERZ, Christian (1959-) German				
oil	1	5,634	5,634	5,634
LEMOHN, J (18th C) ?				
oil	1	1,757	1,757	1,757
LEMOINE, Jacques (1751-1824) French				
wc/d	3	663-4,500	2,583	2,586

Name	No.	Price Range	Average	Median
LEMOINE, Marie Victoire (1754-1820) French				
oil	2	4,000-23,562	13,781	4,000
LEMONNIER, Anicet Charles Gabriel (1743-1824) French				
wc/d	2	486-2,674	1,580	486
LEMORDANT, Jean Julien (1882-1968) French				
oil	1	12,741	12,741	12,741
wc/d	6	608-2,877	1,677	1,438
LEMOYNE, François (1688-1737) French				
wc/d	2	3,281-32,813	18,047	3,281
LEMPEREUR, Henri Jules (1890-?) Belgian				
oil	1	1,627	1,627	1,627
LEMPEREUR-HAUT, Marcel (1898-1986) Belgian				
oil	1	2,506	2,506	2,506
wc/d	1	909	909	909
LEMPICKA, Tamara de (1898-1980) Polish				
oil	6	29,899-2,800,000	789,789	210,000
wc/d	3	9,000-17,000	13,771	15,313
LENAGHAN, Brenda (1941-) British				
wc/d	1	1,488	1,488	1,488
LENAIN, Louis (1593-1648) French				
oil	1	118,919	118,919	118,919
LENBACH, Franz von (1836-1904) German				
oil	8	2,919-22,898	8,261	7,068
LENDORFF, Hans (1863-1946) Swiss				
oil	1	1,581	1,581	1,581
LENG MEI (18th C) Chinese				
wc/d	1	1,000	1,000	1,000
LENGELLE, Paul (20th C) French				
wc/d	2	1,414-1,929	1,671	1,414
LENGO Y MARTINEZ, Horacio (1840-1890) Spanish				
oil	3	570-6,500	3,534	3,534
LENK, Franz (1898-1968) German				
oil	1	11,781	11,781	11,781
wc/d	3	2,472-3,109	2,737	2,631
LENKIEWICZ, R O (1941-2002) British/Jewish				
oil	13	4,425-44,980	12,400	9,744
wc/d	8	531-5,310	1,914	1,044
LENKIEWICZ, Robert O (1941-2002) British/Jewish				
oil	27	1,827-35,600	11,146	10,500
wc/d	5	1,021-8,352	3,105	1,683
LENN, Misha (1962-) Russian				
wc/d	2	1,600-1,600	1,600	1,600
LENNON, Paddy (1955-) Irish				
wc/d	1	3,277	3,277	3,277
LENOIR, A (?) French				
oil	1	1,929	1,929	1,929
LENOIR, Charles Amable (1861-1940) French				
oil	1	17,000	17,000	17,000
LENOIR, Maurice (20th C) French				
oil	1	6,500	6,500	6,500
LENOIR, Pierre (1879-?) French				
3D	1	1,584	1,584	1,584
LENORDEZ, Pierre (1815-1892) French				
3D	6	2,914-8,529	5,435	5,400
LENORMAND (20th C) French				
3D	1	2,950	2,950	2,950
LENS, Bernard (17/18th C) British				
wc/d	1	1,032	1,032	1,032
LENS, Bernard III (1682-1740) British				
wc/d	1	6,090	6,090	6,090
LENTREIN, Jules (1875-1943) Belgian				
oil	2	876-3,884	2,380	876
LENTZ, Jance (20th C) American				
oil	1	1,900	1,900	1,900
LENZ, Alfred David (1872-1926) American				
3D	1	3,250	3,250	3,250
LENZ, Maximilien (1860-1948) Austrian				
oil	2	3,500-234,900	119,200	3,500
LEO, Francis J (?) German?				
oil	1	1,074	1,074	1,074
LEON Y ESCOSURA, Ignacio de (1834-1901) Spanish				
oil	3	4,000-17,568	9,045	5,568

Name	No.	Price Range	Average	Median
LEON, Jean (20th C) French				
oil	2	1,260-1,260	1,260	1,260
LEON, Jose de (1958-) Spanish				
oil	1	1,435	1,435	1,435
LEONARD, Agathan (1841-1923) French				
3D	4	9,653-31,500	20,736	12,041
LEONARD, Maurice (1899-1971) French				
oil	8	561-1,191	858	724
wc/d	7	505-732	604	631
LEONARD, Patrick (1918-2005) Irish				
oil	154	1,113-25,958	4,740	3,214
wc/d	129	477-49,444	3,438	2,145
LEONARDO DA PISTOIA (fl.1516-1540) Italian				
oil	1	36,724	36,724	36,724
LEONARDO DA VINCI (1452-1519) Italian				
oil	1	24,082	24,082	24,082
LEONARDO, Paolo (1973-) Italian				
wc/d	1	3,435	3,435	3,435
LEONCILLO (1915-1968) Italian				
oil	1	2,417	2,417	2,417
wc/d	3	2,116-10,177	4,976	2,637
3D	1	12,298	12,298	12,298
LEONE, John (1929-) American				
oil	2	1,800-6,500	4,150	1,800
LEONE, Romolo (19th C) French				
oil	6	687-4,919	2,309	898
LEONESSA, Enrico della (1865-1921) Italian				
oil	1	15,760	15,760	15,760
LEONHARD, Johannes (1858-1913) German				
oil	1	75,000	75,000	75,000
LEONI, Ottavio (1587-1630) Italian				
oil	1	3,857	3,857	3,857
LEONORI, R G L (fl.1847-1848) American				
oil	1	2,500	2,500	2,500
LEOPOLD-LEVY (1882-1966) French				
oil	1	1,199	1,199	1,199
LEPAGE, Celine (1882-1928) French				
3D	3	4,250-19,109	9,296	4,531
LEPAPE, George (1887-1971) French				
wc/d	2	458-4,000	2,229	458
LEPAULLE, François Gabriel (1804-1886) French				
oil	2	8,486-9,425	8,955	8,486
LEPERE, Auguste (1849-1918) French				
oil	2	2,057-4,232	3,144	2,057
wc/d	2	2,046-3,631	2,838	2,046
LEPIC, Ludovic Napoleon (1839-1890) French				
oil	2	5,671-8,550	7,110	5,671
LEPICIE, Michel Nicolas Bernard (1735-1784) French				
wc/d	1	2,775	2,775	2,775
LEPIE, Ferdinand (1824-1883) Czechoslovakian				
oil	6	2,000-4,250	2,630	2,288
LEPINE, Joseph Louis Francois (1867-1943) French				
oil	1	2,141	2,141	2,141
LEPINE, L (?) Continental				
oil	1	2,719	2,719	2,719
LEPINE, Stanislas (1835-1892) French				
oil	6	1,914-57,021	21,799	12,390
LEPLAE, Charles (1903-1961) Belgian				
3D	3	2,472-12,085	5,676	2,472
L'EPLATTENIER, Charles (1874-1946) Swiss				
oil	7	2,289-29,974	10,199	4,579
wc/d	4	763-1,145	876	763
3D	1	2,892	2,892	2,892
LEPOITTEVIN, Eugène (1806-1870) French				
oil	1	9,699	9,699	9,699
LEPOITTEVIN, Louis (1847-1909) French				
oil	2	6,969-50,000	28,484	6,969
LEPPER, Robert Lewis (1906-1991) American				
wc/d	1	7,014	7,014	7,014
LEPPIEN, Jean (1910-1991) German				
oil	9	2,356-7,270	4,096	3,732
wc/d	15	455-2,534	1,206	1,077

Name	No.	Price Range	Average	Median
LEPREUX, Albert (1898-1959) French				
wc/d	1	1,518	1,518	1,518
LEPRI, Stanislao (1905-1980) Italian				
oil	4	570-10,878	4,325	1,168
LEPRIN, Marcel (1891-1933) French				
oil	9	468-20,384	8,020	9,000
wc/d	1	586	586	586
LEPRINCE, Auguste Xavier (1799-1826) French				
oil	1	5,856	5,856	5,856
wc/d	2	706-1,796	1,251	706
LEPRINCE, Jean Baptiste (1734-1781) French				
oil	3	27,750-277,500	112,583	32,500
wc/d	3	697-5,369	2,323	905
LEPRINCE, Robert Leopold (1800-1847) French				
oil	2	3,341-7,591	5,466	3,341
LEQUESNE, Eugène L (1815-1887) French				
3D	1	5,986	5,986	5,986
LERAY, Prudent Louis (1820-1879) French				
oil	3	851-6,062	2,871	1,700
LERCHE, Freddie A (1937-) Danish				
oil	1	2,265	2,265	2,265
LERCHE, Vincent Stoltenberg (1837-1892) Norwegian				
oil	1	1,488	1,488	1,488
LERFELDT, Hans Henrik (1946-1990) Danish				
oil	2	3,380-16,096	9,738	3,380
wc/d	5	1,449-17,053	7,117	7,146
LERGAARD, Niels (1893-1982) Danish				
oil	7	1,940-7,243	4,976	5,473
LERICHE (18/19th C) ?				
oil	1	3,568	3,568	3,568
LERIN, Lars (20th C) ?				
wc/d	2	1,586-3,365	2,475	1,586
LERMAN, Leonid (1953-) American/Ukranian				
3D	1	6,000	6,000	6,000
LERMITE, Jean Pierre (1920-1977) French				
wc/d	2	763-2,498	1,630	763
LERMONTOFFE, E (19th C) Russian				
oil	2	40,000-40,000	40,000	40,000
LERNIA, Francesco di (1966-) Italian				
oil	3	1,045-2,073	1,432	1,178
LEROLLE, Henry (1848-1929) French				
oil	2	1,100-1,900	1,500	1,100
LEROUX, Auguste (1871-1954) French				
oil	4	700-7,308	3,483	2,500
LEROUX, Gaston (1854-1942) French				
3D	3	10,829-37,582	20,994	14,572
LEROUX, Georges (1877-1957) French				
oil	1	1,028	1,028	1,028
wc/d	2	922-1,386	1,154	922
LEROUX, Henri (1872-1942) Belgian				
oil	2	934-3,596	2,265	934
LEROY DE LIANCOURT, François (1741-1835) French				
oil	1	2,041	2,041	2,041
LEROY, C (19th C) ?				
oil	1	6,264	6,264	6,264
LEROY, Camille (1905-1995) French?				
oil	2	539-1,259	899	539
wc/d	2	1,259-1,318	1,288	1,259
LEROY, Eugène (1910-2000) French				
oil	4	16,365-31,860	23,679	22,932
wc/d	1	5,096	5,096	5,096
LEROY, Hippolite (1857-1943) Belgian				
oil	1	4,834	4,834	4,834
LEROY, Jules (1833-1865) French				
oil	1	4,500	4,500	4,500
LEROY, Jules (1856-1921) French				
oil	5	2,397-3,720	2,941	2,866
LEROY, Paul Alexandre Alfred (1860-1942) French				
oil	4	888-6,750	2,947	1,403
LERSY, Roger (1920-) French				
oil	3	1,443-1,753	1,649	1,753

Name	No.	Price Range	Average	Median
LERVEN, Henri van (1875-1954) Dutch				
oil	1	1,543	1,543	1,543
LESAGE, Augustin (1876-1954) French				
oil	1	39,743	39,743	39,743
LESAINT, Charles Louis (1795-?) French				
oil	1	2,195	2,195	2,195
LESBROS, Alfred (1873-1940) French				
oil	117	510-2,803	899	764
wc/d	1	605	605	605
LESBROUSSART, Genny (19th C) Belgian				
oil	1	1,892	1,892	1,892
LESIEUR, Pierre (1922-) French				
oil	8	450-11,483	3,896	1,300
LESIRE, Paulus (1611-?) Dutch				
oil	1	8,000	8,000	8,000
LESLIE, Alfred (1927-) American				
oil	3	8,500-60,000	29,500	20,000
wc/d	1	3,000	3,000	3,000
LESLIE, Charles (1835-1890) British				
oil	11	443-4,498	1,216	1,055
LESLIE, Charles Robert (1794-1859) British				
oil	2	10,000-11,115	10,557	10,000
wc/d	2	2,349-46,280	24,314	2,349
LESLIE, George Dunlop (1835-1921) British				
oil	1	182,700	182,700	182,700
LESNE, Camille (1908-) French				
oil	1	2,239	2,239	2,239
LESOURD-BEAUREGARD, Ange Louis Guillaume (1800-1885) French				
oil	1	5,400	5,400	5,400
LESPAGNOL, Madeleine (20th C) French				
oil	1	2,125	2,125	2,125
LESPINASSE, Theodore (19th C) French				
oil	2	728-1,320	1,024	728
LESREL, Adolphe Alexandre (1839-1929) French				
oil	6	9,251-100,000	43,432	27,000
LESSARD, Real (1939-) ?				
oil	1	5,845	5,845	5,845
LESSI, Giovanni (1852-1922) Italian				
oil	1	20,712	20,712	20,712
LESSI, Tito (1858-1917) Italian				
oil	1	7,613	7,613	7,613
LESSING, Karl Friedrich (1808-1880) German				
oil	3	3,299-15,000	8,819	8,159
LESSING, Konrad Ludwig (1852-1916) German				
oil	1	3,330	3,330	3,330
LESTER, Leonard (1876-?) American/British				
oil	2	800-2,400	1,600	800
LESTER, William Lewis (1910-1991) American				
wc/d	3	400-9,000	4,466	4,000
LESUEUR, Pierre Étienne (18th C) French				
oil	1	3,503	3,503	3,503
LESUR, Henri Victor (1863-1900) French				
oil	2	2,500-18,000	10,250	2,500
LESY, Desire (1806-1859) Belgian				
oil	2	643-1,418	1,030	643
LETENDRE, Rita (1928-) Canadian				
oil	6	1,877-7,052	3,731	2,531
LETH, Harald (1899-1986) Danish				
oil	7	1,132-2,586	1,600	1,374
LETHIERE, Guillaume-Guillon (1760-1832) French				
oil	1	46,980	46,980	46,980
LETO, Antonino (1844-1913) Italian				
oil	2	8,229-19,747	13,988	8,229
LETSCH, Louis (1856-?) German				
oil	5	1,546-4,560	2,707	2,158
LETYANIN, Viktor F (1921-) Russian				
oil	1	1,665	1,665	1,665
LEU, August Wilhelm (1819-1897) German				
oil	4	2,180-14,013	5,688	2,667
LEU, Oscar (1864-1942) German				
oil	5	500-2,431	1,272	1,205

Name	No.	Price Range	Average	Median
LEU, Otto (1855-1922) German				
oil	1	1,674	1,674	1,674
LEUENBERGER, Ernst Otto (1856-1937) Swiss				
oil	1	1,145	1,145	1,145
LEUFERT, Gerd (1914-1998) Lithuanian				
wc/d	1	9,000	9,000	9,000
LEUPIN, Herbert (1916-) Swiss?				
oil	1	3,330	3,330	3,330
LEUPPI, Leo Peter (1893-1972) Swiss				
oil	3	5,675-11,348	7,957	6,850
wc/d	2	1,522-1,674	1,598	1,522
LEURS, Johannes Karel (1865-1938) Dutch				
oil	5	539-2,886	1,329	1,204
LEUSDEN, Willem van (1886-?) Dutch				
oil	1	5,096	5,096	5,096
wc/d	3	2,121-3,534	2,670	2,356
LEUUS, Jesus (1931-) Mexican				
oil	3	2,200-3,500	2,666	2,300
LEUW, Friedrich August de (1817-1888) German				
oil	1	3,116	3,116	3,116
LEV, Etty (20th C) Israeli				
oil	5	800-2,400	1,410	1,000
LEVACK, John (fl.1851-1857) British				
oil	1	4,158	4,158	4,158
LEVANON, Mordechai (1901-1968) Israeli				
oil	5	1,400-20,000	8,660	9,000
wc/d	19	350-1,400	638	510
LEVASSEUR, Henri (1853-1934) French				
3D	1	1,824	1,824	1,824
LEVASTI, Filli (1883-1966) Italian				
oil	1	5,812	5,812	5,812
LEVCHENKO, Petr Alekseevich (1859-1917) Russian				
oil	1	41,280	41,280	41,280
LEVEDAG, Fritz (1899-1951) German				
oil	1	803	803	803
wc/d	1	1,110	1,110	1,110
LEVEE, John (1924-) American				
oil	3	650-1,131	947	1,062
wc/d	1	708	708	708
LEVEILLE, Andre (1880-1963) French				
oil	2	3,181-8,346	5,763	3,181
wc/d	1	553	553	553
LEVENE, Ben (1938-) British				
oil	6	516-6,880	3,207	2,088
LEVEQUE, Cathy (20th C) French				
oil	1	1,332	1,332	1,332
LEVEQUE, Edmund Louis Auguste (1814-1875) French				
3D	1	6,799	6,799	6,799
LEVER, Richard Hayley (1876-1958) American				
oil	40	650-40,000	6,262	3,500
wc/d	8	750-2,500	1,456	1,000
LEVI, Basil (1878-1954) Russian				
oil	10	703-114,658	15,092	1,246
LEVI, Carlo (1902-1975) Italian				
oil	12	1,790-7,144	4,450	4,685
wc/d	4	530-1,674	887	589
LEVI, L (20th C) French?				
oil	1	8,357	8,357	8,357
LEVI, Lia (1931-) Italian				
oil	2	1,089-1,573	1,331	1,089
LEVIER, Adolfo (1873-1953) Italian				
oil	2	2,186-3,857	3,021	2,186
wc/d	1	1,929	1,929	1,929
LEVIER, Charles (1920-2003) French				
oil	11	450-3,150	1,445	1,100
LEVIGNE, Theodore (1848-1912) French				
oil	7	375-11,881	3,376	2,160
LEVIN, Evgeni Nissalovitch (1922-1989) Russian				
oil	1	1,189	1,189	1,189
LEVIN, Julo (1901-1943) ?				
wc/d	1	1,784	1,784	1,784

Name	No.	Price Range	Average	Median
LEVINE, David (20th C) American				
oil	1	850	850	850
wc/d	2	1,600-4,250	2,925	1,600
LEVINE, Jack (1915-) American				
oil	4	750-32,000	14,862	1,700
wc/d	2	650-4,000	2,325	650
LEVINE, Sherrie (1947-) American				
oil	1	64,750	64,750	64,750
wc/d	1	48,000	48,000	48,000
LEVINI, Salvatore (1956-) Italian				
wc/d	1	1,874	1,874	1,874
LEVIS, Giuseppe Augusto (1873-1926) Italian				
oil	4	920-1,818	1,465	1,453
LEVIS, Maurice (1860-1940) French				
oil	13	1,249-10,120	3,997	2,610
LEVITAN, Adoljeff Iljitsch (20th C) Israeli?				
oil	1	22,000	22,000	22,000
LEVITAN, Isaac Ilyitch (1860-1900) Russian				
oil	7	8,114-1,892,000	430,086	43,405
LEVOLI, Nicola (1730-1801) Italian				
oil	1	7,224	7,224	7,224
LEVRAC-TOURNIERES, Robert (1667-1752) French				
oil	2	5,863-16,459	11,161	5,863
LEVREL, René (1900-1981) French				
oil	1	1,676	1,676	1,676
LEVRERO, Beppe (1901-1986) Italian				
oil	1	1,008	1,008	1,008
LEVY, Alexander (1881-1947) American				
oil	3	800-1,800	1,150	850
LEVY, Charles-Octave (?-1899) French				
3D	1	2,958	2,958	2,958
LEVY, Edgar (1907-1975) American				
oil	1	1,700	1,700	1,700
LEVY, Émile (1826-1890) French				
oil	1	1,236	1,236	1,236
wc/d	1	689	689	689
LEVY, Emmanuel (1900-) British				
oil	1	2,655	2,655	2,655
LEVY, Henri Leopold (1840-1904) French				
oil	2	522-6,214	3,368	522
wc/d	1	911	911	911
LEVY, Maya Cohen (1955-) Israeli				
oil	1	4,000	4,000	4,000
LEVY, Moses (1885-1968) Italian				
oil	5	845-9,342	5,174	6,171
wc/d	3	580-1,073	771	660
LEVY, Ra'anan (1954-) Israeli				
wc/d	1	2,000	2,000	2,000
LEVY-DHURMER (1865-1953) French				
wc/d	1	1,184	1,184	1,184
LEVY-DHURMER, Lucien (1865-1953) French				
oil	3	3,567-120,000	47,813	19,872
wc/d	16	701-149,243	36,026	4,411
LEWAN, Dennis (1943-) American				
oil	1	1,200	1,200	1,200
LEWIN, James Morgan (1836-1877) American				
oil	1	1,100	1,100	1,100
LEWIN, Stephen (fl.1890-1910) British				
oil	3	693-6,500	3,044	1,940
LEWIS, Arthur James (1824-1901) British				
oil	1	2,208	2,208	2,208
LEWIS, C J (1830-1892) British				
oil	1	1,443	1,443	1,443
wc/d	1	2,760	2,760	2,760
LEWIS, Charles James (1830-1892) British				
oil	3	851-2,960	1,847	1,730
wc/d	1	1,566	1,566	1,566
LEWIS, Earl (20th C) Canadian				
3D	1	3,057	3,057	3,057
LEWIS, Edmund Darch (1835-1910) American				
oil	14	2,200-50,000	11,282	7,500
wc/d	25	400-5,600	1,640	1,000

Name	No.	Price Range	Average	Median
LEWIS, Edward Morland (1903-1943) British				
oil	2	513-1,881	1,197	513
LEWIS, Emerson (20th C) American				
oil	1	1,100	1,100	1,100
LEWIS, John Frederick (1805-1876) British				
wc/d	5	7,830-20,520	11,771	10,440
LEWIS, L (19th C) British				
wc/d	2	1,800-2,100	1,950	1,800
LEWIS, Mary (?) ?				
oil	1	1,800	1,800	1,800
LEWIS, Maud (1903-1970) Canadian				
oil	23	2,116-8,915	4,921	4,891
LEWIS, Neville (1895-1972) South African				
oil	1	2,590	2,590	2,590
LEWIS, Norman Wilfred (1909-1979) American				
oil	2	9,000-22,000	15,500	9,000
wc/d	1	19,000	19,000	19,000
LEWIS, Paul (20th C) American				
3D	2	6,300-7,560	6,930	6,300
LEWIS, Percy Wyndham (1882-1957) British				
wc/d	5	6,264-33,060	20,868	26,000
LEWIS, Shelton (fl.1875-1880) British				
wc/d	1	1,512	1,512	1,512
LEWIS, Thomas (19th C) American				
oil	1	1,500	1,500	1,500
LEWIS-BROWN, John (1829-1890) British				
oil	3	1,985-20,561	9,329	5,443
wc/d	1	484	484	484
LEWITT, Sol (1928-) American				
oil	1	75,000	75,000	75,000
wc/d	51	788-90,000	12,090	6,896
3D	6	4,712-190,000	66,522	40,000
LEWY, Kurt (1898-1963) Belgian				
oil	2	4,576-10,188	7,382	4,576
wc/d	1	1,147	1,147	1,147
LEXMON, Ake (?) Swedish?				
oil	1	1,555	1,555	1,555
LEY, S van der (19th C) Dutch				
oil	1	5,293	5,293	5,293
LEYDE, Otto (1835-1897) German				
wc/d	2	796-3,894	2,345	796
LEYDEN, Ernest van (1892-1969) Dutch				
oil	2	1,169-7,151	4,160	1,169
LEYDEN, Karin van (1906-1977) German				
oil	4	766-6,062	4,131	3,879
LEYDET, Louis (1873-1944) French				
oil	1	8,535	8,535	8,535
LEYDET, Victor (1861-1904) French				
oil	1	2,752	2,752	2,752
LEYENDECKER, Frank Xavier (1877-1924) American				
oil	1	30,000	30,000	30,000
LEYENDECKER, J C (1874-1951) American				
oil	1	4,750	4,750	4,750
LEYENDECKER, Joseph C (1874-1951) American				
oil	7	500-180,000	47,785	25,000
wc/d	3	8,000-22,500	16,833	20,000
LEYINE, Jack (20th C) ?				
oil	1	1,134	1,134	1,134
LEYKIN, Nickolai (20th C) Ukranian				
oil	2	1,225-5,490	3,357	1,225
LEYPOLD, Karl Julius von (1806-1874) German				
oil	1	5,807	5,807	5,807
LEYRITZ, Léon Albert Marie de (1888-1976) French				
3D	1	12,600	12,600	12,600
LEYS, Baron Hendrik (1815-1869) Belgian				
oil	6	2,290-7,375	3,868	2,336
LEYSING, Piet (1885-1933) German				
oil	1	1,001	1,001	1,001
LEYSTER, Judith (1600-1660) Dutch				
oil	1	111,000	111,000	111,000
LEYVA, Ruben (1953-) Mexican				
oil	2	9,000-11,000	10,000	9,000

Name	No.	Price Range	Average	Median
LHARDY Y GARRIGUES, Agustin (1848-1918) Spanish				
oil	2	954-1,914	1,434	954
L'HAY, Michele-Eudes de (19th C) French				
oil	1	2,249	2,249	2,249
LHERMITTE, Léon (1844-1925) French				
oil	7	2,063-280,000	111,041	85,000
wc/d	12	4,685-32,000	16,343	15,000
LHOMME, Victor (1870-1957) French				
oil	1	3,389	3,389	3,389
LHOTE, Andre (1885-1962) French				
oil	34	983-120,408	40,159	27,750
wc/d	41	475-41,462	5,000	2,997
LHOTELLIER, Henry (1908-) French				
oil	1	1,216	1,216	1,216
L'HUILLIER, Jacques (1867-?) French				
oil	1	1,320	1,320	1,320
LI DAFANG (1971-) Chinese				
oil	3	5,021-24,000	17,007	22,000
LI JIKAI (1975-) Chinese				
oil	1	13,000	13,000	13,000
LI KERAN (1907-1989) Chinese				
oil	1	58,784	58,784	58,784
wc/d	2	7,500-55,000	31,250	7,500
LI KUCHAN (1898-1983) Chinese				
wc/d	3	1,196-9,993	6,081	7,054
LI SHAN (1942-) Chinese				
oil	3	22,000-105,000	52,374	30,124
LI SHUANG (1957-) Chinese				
oil	2	10,042-15,000	12,521	10,042
LI TIANBING (1974-) Chinese				
oil	1	12,025	12,025	12,025
LI ZHANYANG (1969-) Chinese				
3D	1	8,000	8,000	8,000
LIANG, Calvin (1960-) American/Chinese				
oil	1	5,500	5,500	5,500
LIANG, Weizhen (20th C) American				
oil	1	2,000	2,000	2,000
LIAUSU, Camille (1894-1975) French				
oil	1	20,000	20,000	20,000
LIBANO, Cesare (1884-1969) Italian				
oil	1	1,574	1,574	1,574
LIBBY, F Orville (1883-1961) American				
oil	1	3,500	3,500	3,500
LIBERI, Pietro (1614-1687) Italian				
oil	1	70,068	70,068	70,068
LIBERICH, Nicolai Ivanovich (1828-1883) Russian				
3D	5	12,098-55,000	35,911	30,960
LIBERMAN, Alexander (1912-1999) American				
oil	4	3,000-18,000	7,750	4,000
3D	3	3,500-15,000	7,566	4,200
LIBERT, Amalie Betzy (1862-1927) Danish				
oil	1	1,624	1,624	1,624
LIBERT, Georg Emil (1820-1908) Danish				
oil	10	476-8,449	2,459	1,042
LIBERTS, Ludolfs (1895-1959) Russian				
oil	5	3,708-9,889	5,391	4,079
LIBESSART, Christian (1958-) French?				
oil	3	7,120-12,298	8,888	7,247
LICATA, Riccardo (1929-) Italian				
oil	33	1,106-21,476	4,847	4,371
wc/d	24	549-5,419	1,819	1,286
3D	2	2,945-4,241	3,593	2,945
LICHT, Hans (1876-1935) German				
oil	3	732-1,878	1,121	753
LICHTENSTEIN, Roy (1923-1997) American				
oil	14	16,715-14,500,000	2,766,872	450,000
wc/d	11	3,045-1,100,000	308,092	140,000
3D	6	3,395-320,000	62,953	7,000
LICHTNER-AIX, Werner (1939-) German				
oil	1	2,272	2,272	2,272

Name	No.	Price Range	Average	Median
LICINI, Osvaldo (1894-1958) Italian				
oil	5	43,252-85,500	68,747	69,966
wc/d	5	3,816-5,852	4,447	4,099
LICINIO, Bernardino (1489-1565) Italian				
oil	2	35,068-128,571	81,819	35,068
LIDBERG, Sven (1929-1985) Swedish				
oil	3	622-1,325	922	821
wc/d	1	547	547	547
LIDDERDALE, Charles Sillem (1831-1895) British				
oil	3	3,168-5,160	4,409	4,900
wc/d	3	525-3,480	1,531	589
LIE, Jonas (1880-1940) American				
oil	1	75,000	75,000	75,000
LIEBENWEIN, Maximilian (1869-1926) Austrian				
wc/d	2	1,703-8,400	5,051	1,703
LIEBER, Tom (1949-) American				
oil	1	2,750	2,750	2,750
LIEBERMAN, Harry (1876-1983) American				
oil	1	3,500	3,500	3,500
LIEBERMANN, Ernst (1869-1960) German				
oil	5	710-4,629	2,193	1,885
LIEBERMANN, Ferdinand (1883-1941) German				
3D	2	2,422-7,899	5,160	2,422
LIEBERMANN, M (1847-1935) German				
oil	1	107,753	107,753	107,753
LIEBERMANN, Max (1847-1935) German				
oil	48	4,361-3,344,000	244,112	88,000
wc/d	81	851-304,054	19,618	4,865
LIEBERMANN, Thaddaeus (19th C) Austrian				
wc/d	1	1,200	1,200	1,200
LIEBICH, Curt (1868-1937) German				
oil	1	21,892	21,892	21,892
LIECK, Joseph (1849-?) French				
oil	1	2,108	2,108	2,108
LIEDER, Franz (1780-1859) Austrian				
oil	2	1,221-19,140	10,180	1,221
LIEGI, Ulvi (1860-1939) Italian				
oil	10	2,431-41,648	18,103	12,571
LIENDER, Paul van (1731-1797) Dutch				
wc/d	3	1,401-3,500	2,295	1,985
LIENDER, Pieter Jan van (1727-1779) Dutch				
wc/d	1	1,868	1,868	1,868
LIER, Adolf (1826-1882) German				
oil	7	1,018-14,317	3,962	2,984
LIES, Jozef H (1821-1865) Belgian				
oil	3	911-5,502	3,169	3,094
LIESEGANG, Helmut (1858-1945) German				
oil	3	791-2,676	1,448	877
LIESHOUT, Joep van (1963-) ?				
3D	2	3,507-5,825	4,666	3,507
LIESTE, Cornelis (1817-1861) Dutch				
oil	4	4,789-21,575	11,784	4,795
LIEVENS, Jan (1607-1674) Dutch				
wc/d	1	9,000	9,000	9,000
LIEVIN, Jacques (1850-?) French				
oil	1	1,095	1,095	1,095
LIEZEN-MAYER, Alexander von (1839-1898) Hungarian				
oil	1	5,040	5,040	5,040
LIFSHITZ, Uri (1936-) Israeli				
oil	2	8,000-16,000	12,000	8,000
wc/d	4	400-650	537	500
LIGABUE, Antonio (1899-1965) Italian				
oil	1	202,828	202,828	202,828
LIGARI, Enrico (1899-?) Italian				
3D	1	3,884	3,884	3,884
LIGER HIDALGO, F (19/20th C) Spanish				
oil	1	2,281	2,281	2,281
LIGHT, Joe Louis (1934-) American				
oil	1	1,100	1,100	1,100
LIGHTMAN, Jean G (20th C) American				
oil	1	1,100	1,100	1,100

Name	No.	Price Range	Average	Median
LIGNY, Charles (1812-1889) Belgian				
oil	1	1,212	1,212	1,212
LIGON, Glenn (1960-) American				
oil	1	24,000	24,000	24,000
LIGOZZI, Jacopo (1547-1632) Italian				
oil	2	190,000-203,500	196,750	190,000
LIGTELIJN, Evert Jan (1893-1977) Dutch				
oil	3	596-2,438	1,568	1,670
LIISBERG, Carl Hugo (1896-1958) Danish				
3D	1	3,556	3,556	3,556
LILANGA DI NYAMA, Georges (1934-2005) African				
oil	14	1,260-9,092	3,260	2,422
wc/d	2	1,784-1,812	1,798	1,784
3D	1	1,790	1,790	1,790
LILJEFORS, Bruno (1860-1939) Swedish				
oil	49	1,885-382,192	39,385	23,681
wc/d	10	561-20,384	5,399	2,751
3D	2	1,994-2,198	2,096	1,994
LILJEFORS, Lindorm (1909-1985) Swedish				
oil	29	414-25,479	3,028	1,114
LILJELUND, Arvid (1844-1899) Finnish				
oil	3	2,517-10,286	6,688	7,262
LILJESTROM, Gustave (1882-1958) American				
oil	4	900-2,500	1,675	1,500
wc/d	1	425	425	425
LILLONI, Umberto (1898-1980) Italian				
oil	24	4,005-40,130	12,385	11,449
wc/d	3	951-2,443	1,795	1,991
LILLY, Marjorie (1891-1980) British				
oil	1	4,488	4,488	4,488
LILLYWHITE, Raphael (1891-1958) American				
oil	1	5,000	5,000	5,000
LIM, H H (1954-) ?				
oil	2	1,812-1,933	1,872	1,812
LIM, Kim (1936-) British				
3D	1	20,930	20,930	20,930
LIMA CRUZ, Maria Adelaide (1878-1963) Portuguese				
oil	1	1,519	1,519	1,519
LIMA, Yuye de (20th C) Venezuelan				
oil	1	1,300	1,300	1,300
LIMBACH, Hans Jorg (1928-1990) Swiss				
3D	1	5,708	5,708	5,708
LIMBURG STIRUM, Eldina Aldegonda Rinsina van (1855-1941) Dutch				
oil	1	1,052	1,052	1,052
LIMOUSE, Roger (1894-1990) French				
oil	8	1,200-33,890	8,433	2,259
LIN FENGMIAN (1900-1991) Chinese				
wc/d	8	10,439-210,000	43,303	14,000
LIN, Maya (1959-) American				
3D	1	7,000	7,000	7,000
LIN, Richard (1933-) British				
oil	7	1,683-17,400	6,248	2,655
wc/d	1	5,236	5,236	5,236
LINCE, Marcel de (1886-?) Belgian				
oil	1	1,286	1,286	1,286
LINCK, Jean Antoine (1766-1843) Swiss				
wc/d	3	1,526-12,974	8,754	11,764
LIND, Andreas (1815-1885) Norwegian				
wc/d	1	4,602	4,602	4,602
LINDAU, Dietrich Wilhelm (1799-1862) German				
oil	1	11,656	11,656	11,656
LINDBERG DE GEER, Marianne (1946-) Swedish				
oil	1	2,379	2,379	2,379
wc/d	1	4,071	4,071	4,071
LINDBERG, Alf (1905-1990) Swedish				
oil	8	794-6,343	3,127	2,907
LINDBERG, Frans (1858-1944) Swedish				
wc/d	1	1,182	1,182	1,182
LINDBERG, Harald (1901-1976) Swedish				
oil	5	414-4,326	2,078	1,612
LINDBERG, Maria (1958-) Swedish				
oil	2	1,272-2,545	1,908	1,272

Name	No.	Price Range	Average	Median
LINDBLOM, Sivert (1931-) Swedish				
wc/d	1	1,590	1,590	1,590
LINDE, Johan van de (1887-1956) Dutch				
oil	1	1,573	1,573	1,573
LINDE, Wladimir (1862-?) Russian				
oil	1	2,386	2,386	2,386
LINDE-WALTHER, Heinrich Eduard (1868-1939) German				
oil	4	786-3,162	1,935	1,573
LINDELL, Lage (1920-1980) Swedish				
oil	3	3,817-19,085	9,500	5,598
wc/d	5	414-3,171	1,167	854
LINDEMANN, Kai (1931-) Danish				
oil	2	2,157-4,688	3,422	2,157
LINDEMANN-FROMMEL, Karl (1819-1891) German				
wc/d	1	3,770	3,770	3,770
LINDEN, Helge (1897-1971) Swedish				
oil	4	1,432-4,071	2,789	1,691
LINDENAU, Martin (20th C) French				
oil	3	2,662-4,660	3,328	2,662
LINDENEG, Thor (1941-) Danish				
oil	4	1,616-2,323	1,863	1,742
LINDENMUTH, Tod (1885-1976) American				
oil	4	550-4,500	2,537	1,100
LINDENSCHMIT, Hermann (1857-1939) German				
oil	2	1,088-1,911	1,499	1,088
LINDENSCHMIT, Wilhelm von (19th C) German				
oil	1	1,936	1,936	1,936
LINDER, Alf (1944-) Swedish				
oil	1	382	382	382
wc/d	1	1,654	1,654	1,654
LINDER, Lambert (1841-1889) German				
oil	1	4,359	4,359	4,359
LINDER, Philippe Jacques (19th C) French				
wc/d	1	1,432	1,432	1,432
LINDERMAN, Earl William (1931-) American				
oil	1	2,500	2,500	2,500
LINDERUM, Richard (1851-?) German				
oil	3	1,212-4,789	3,112	3,337
LINDFORS, Kent (1938-) Swedish				
wc/d	1	1,718	1,718	1,718
LINDH, Bror (1877-1941) Swedish				
oil	1	1,364	1,364	1,364
LINDHBERG, Per (1785-1868) Swedish				
wc/d	2	1,020-1,618	1,319	1,020
LINDHOLM, Berndt (1841-1914) Finnish				
oil	13	3,330-61,714	18,111	10,929
LINDHOLM, Lorenz August (1819-1854) Swedish				
oil	1	1,147	1,147	1,147
LINDLAR, Johann Wilhelm (1816-1896) German				
oil	4	727-3,330	2,129	1,300
LINDMAN, Axel (1848-1930) Swedish				
oil	8	518-52,201	8,732	2,282
LINDNER, Carl (1840-1883) Austrian?				
oil	1	1,054	1,054	1,054
LINDNER, Ernest (1897-1988) Canadian				
wc/d	5	405-23,090	8,761	7,090
LINDNER, Richard (1901-1978) American/German				
wc/d	6	4,500-102,347	36,020	21,776
3D	1	3,587	3,587	3,587
LINDNER, Theodor (1882-1956) German				
oil	1	1,331	1,331	1,331
LINDO, F (18th C) British				
oil	1	2,052	2,052	2,052
LINDQVIST, Axel Hjalmar (1843-1917) Swedish				
oil	1	2,811	2,811	2,811
LINDQVIST, Herman (1868-1923) Swedish				
oil	1	7,693	7,693	7,693
LINDSAY, Thomas Corwin (1845-1907) American				
oil	1	2,900	2,900	2,900
LINDSTROM, Arvid Mauritz (1849-1923) Swedish				
oil	13	1,114-8,725	2,936	2,493

Name	No.	Price Range	Average	Median
LINDSTROM, Bengt (1925-) Swedish				
oil	95	1,018-216,575	15,792	7,598
wc/d	21	411-5,890	2,075	1,400
LINDSTROM, Fritz (1874-1962) Swedish				
oil	3	1,786-5,472	3,285	2,598
LINDSTROM, Rikard (1882-1943) Swedish				
oil	5	435-5,897	3,208	3,600
LINDTMAYER, Daniel (younger) (1552-1607) Swiss				
wc/d	1	5,839	5,839	5,839
LINE JAGOT (1920-2001) French				
oil	4	482-784	678	723
wc/d	1	603	603	603
LINER, Carl (1914-1997) Swiss				
oil	57	818-22,673	6,021	4,705
wc/d	18	492-5,263	1,780	1,458
LINER, Carl August (1871-1946) Swiss				
oil	18	1,176-27,445	8,873	5,724
wc/d	1	1,461	1,461	1,461
LINES, Henry H (1800-1889) British				
oil	2	963-1,315	1,139	963
wc/d	1	783	783	783
LINFORD, Charles (1846-1897) American				
oil	3	1,500-8,035	4,845	5,000
LING JIAN (1963-) Chinese				
oil	4	7,007-28,000	17,501	15,000
LING, Dolores (1932-1999) French				
oil	1	2,979	2,979	2,979
wc/d	6	501-3,575	1,094	560
LINGELBACH, Johannes (1622-1674) Dutch				
oil	4	1,979-37,000	16,299	2,356
LINGELBACH, Johannes and WYNANTS, Jan (17th C) Dutch				
oil	1	21,360	21,360	21,360
LINGNER, Otto (1856-?) German				
oil	2	1,700-3,263	2,481	1,700
LINGQUIST, Arthur (20th C) American				
oil	1	1,400	1,400	1,400
LINKE, J Conrad (1892-1995) American				
oil	1	2,100	2,100	2,100
LINKE, Paul Rudolf (1844-1917) German				
oil	1	6,479	6,479	6,479
LINKE, Simon (1958-) American				
oil	1	7,500	7,500	7,500
LINKER, Tom (20th C) American				
oil	1	2,500	2,500	2,500
wc/d	1	600	600	600
LINNANE, Anna (1965-) Irish				
3D	1	1,800	1,800	1,800
LINNELL, James Thomas (1826-1905) British				
oil	1	3,496	3,496	3,496
wc/d	1	1,298	1,298	1,298
LINNELL, John (1792-1882) British				
oil	10	1,232-246,400	43,857	11,340
wc/d	4	926-4,152	2,098	1,424
LINNELL, William (1826-1910) British				
oil	1	9,072	9,072	9,072
wc/d	2	661-777	719	661
LINNIG, E (1821-1860) Belgian				
oil	1	10,639	10,639	10,639
LINNIG, Egidius (1821-1860) Belgian				
oil	2	1,334-11,959	6,646	1,334
LINNIG, Jan Theodor Joseph (1815-1891) Belgian				
oil	1	5,396	5,396	5,396
LINNOVAARA, Juhani (1934-) Finnish				
oil	1	9,000	9,000	9,000
wc/d	4	2,572-3,397	3,060	2,928
LINNQVIST, Hilding (1891-1984) Swedish				
oil	14	2,643-68,706	20,135	13,215
wc/d	7	520-8,143	2,845	1,057
LINO, Gustave (1893-1961) French				
oil	9	956-3,827	2,212	1,903
wc/d	1	4,435	4,435	4,435
LINO, Silva (1911-1984) Portuguese				
oil	2	1,823-2,188	2,005	1,823

Name	No.	Price Range	Average	Median
LINOIS, Alexandre (20th C) French?				
wc/d	1	1,243	1,243	1,243
LINS, Adolf (1856-1927) German				
oil	5	746-3,503	2,225	2,541
LINT, Hendrik van (1684-1763) Flemish				
oil	4	10,680-138,400	78,342	60,490
LINT, Louis van (1909-1986) Belgian				
oil	4	1,636-25,442	9,837	5,257
wc/d	3	1,193-3,592	2,443	2,544
LINT, Peter van (1609-1690) Flemish				
oil	2	4,070-142,608	73,339	4,070
wc/d	1	22,200	22,200	22,200
LINTHORST, Jacobus (1745-1815) Dutch				
oil	1	116,779	116,779	116,779
LINTON, Sir James Dromgole (1840-1916) British				
oil	2	746-1,523	1,134	746
wc/d	4	522-700	643	661
LINTON, William (1791-1876) British				
oil	2	606-17,100	8,853	606
LINTON, William Evans (1878-?) British				
oil	1	4,602	4,602	4,602
LINTOTT, Edward Bernard (1875-1951) British				
oil	1	2,500	2,500	2,500
LINVILLE, Marlin (1950-) American				
oil	3	1,000-1,600	1,200	1,000
LION, Alexander (1823-1852) Belgian				
oil	1	2,411	2,411	2,411
LIOT, Paul (1855-1902) French				
oil	1	1,859	1,859	1,859
LIOTARD, Jean-Étienne (1702-1789) Swiss				
wc/d	1	4,272	4,272	4,272
LIPA (1907-1976) French				
3D	1	2,640	2,640	2,640
LIPCHITZ, Jacques (1891-1973) French				
wc/d	10	750-12,320	4,023	2,800
3D	24	4,000-1,150,000	223,576	25,890
LIPHART, Ernest Friedrich von (1847-1934) Russian				
oil	3	4,464-471,255	172,162	40,767
wc/d	1	1,072	1,072	1,072
LIPOT, Herman (1884-1972) Hungarian				
oil	3	425-1,455	1,060	1,300
wc/d	1	450	450	450
LIPPI, Lorenzo (1606-1665) Italian				
oil	2	130,502-182,016	156,259	130,502
LIPPINCOTT, William H (1849-1920) American				
oil	3	3,000-19,000	10,533	9,600
LIPPO D'ANDREA (1377-?) Italian				
oil	2	80,000-155,700	117,850	80,000
LIPSKI, Donald (20th C) American?				
3D	1	2,400	2,400	2,400
LIRA, Armando (1903-1959) Chilean				
oil	1	1,490	1,490	1,490
LIRA, Benjamin (1950-) Chilean				
oil	1	1,200	1,200	1,200
LISA, Esteban (1895-1983) Argentinian				
oil	1	11,000	11,000	11,000
wc/d	1	1,300	1,300	1,300
LISA, Mario (1908-1992) Italian				
oil	2	1,211-1,332	1,271	1,211
LISENKOV, Valentin Aleksandrovich (1938-) Russian				
oil	1	1,000	1,000	1,000
LISIEWSKA, Anna Rosina (1716-1783) German				
oil	4	7,224-24,082	16,857	18,061
LISIO, Arnaldo de (1869-1949) Italian				
oil	1	1,700	1,700	1,700
wc/d	3	900-1,900	1,250	950
LISMANN, Hermann (1878-1943) German				
oil	1	2,336	2,336	2,336
LISMER, Arthur (1885-1969) Canadian				
oil	22	7,699-38,495	18,948	15,578
wc/d	17	574-7,493	1,734	1,234

Name	No.	Price Range	Average	Median
LISS, Jan (c.1595-1629) Dutch				
oil	1	535,069	535,069	535,069
LISSAC, Pierre (1878-?) French				
oil	1	1,338	1,338	1,338
wc/d	25	486-2,718	960	730
LISSE, Dirck van der (1607-1669) Dutch				
oil	2	4,671-13,877	9,274	4,671
LISSIM, Simon (1900-1981) Russian				
wc/d	2	1,100-5,160	3,130	1,100
LISSITZKY, El (1890-1941) Russian				
oil	1	209,330	209,330	209,330
wc/d	2	32,246-46,849	39,547	32,246
LIST, Wilhelm (1864-1918) Austrian				
oil	3	2,472-644,000	230,830	46,020
LISTERE, A de (18th C) French				
oil	1	3,568	3,568	3,568
LISZEWSKI, Georg (1674-1750) Polish				
oil	1	8,000	8,000	8,000
LISZT, Maria Veronica (1902-1992) American				
oil	1	1,600	1,600	1,600
LITSAS, Dimitrios (1883-1952) Greek				
oil	1	8,800	8,800	8,800
LITTERINI, Bartolommeo (1669-1745) Italian				
oil	1	12,486	12,486	12,486
LITTLE, Dennis G (1884-1963) British				
wc/d	1	3,420	3,420	3,420
LITTLE, Graham (1972-) American				
wc/d	1	35,000	35,000	35,000
LITTLE, Howard John (1883-1965) American				
oil	2	650-1,400	1,025	650
LITTLE, John (1907-1984) American				
oil	1	7,000	7,000	7,000
LITTLE, John C (1928-) Canadian				
oil	10	3,702-17,725	8,823	8,246
LITTLE, Philip (1857-1942) American				
oil	2	1,000-6,500	3,750	1,000
wc/d	1	850	850	850
LITTLE, Robert (1854-1944) British				
oil	2	522-10,024	5,273	522
wc/d	1	851	851	851
LITTROW, Leo von (1860-1914) Austrian				
oil	3	4,757-8,918	6,469	5,733
LITVINOV, B (20th C) Russian				
wc/d	1	2,784	2,784	2,784
LITVINOVSKY, Pinchas (1894-1985) Israeli				
oil	10	500-15,000	5,860	4,500
wc/d	3	370-18,000	6,490	1,100
LITWAK, Israel (1868-1960) Russian				
oil	1	8,035	8,035	8,035
LITZINGER, Dorothea M (1889-1925) American				
oil	1	1,600	1,600	1,600
LIU DAHONG (1962-) Chinese				
oil	1	35,000	35,000	35,000
LIU DAN (1953-) Chinese				
wc/d	1	95,000	95,000	95,000
LIU GUANDAO (?) Chinese				
wc/d	1	45,240	45,240	45,240
LIU GUOSONG (1932-) Chinese				
wc/d	1	120,000	120,000	120,000
LIU HUIHAN (1952-) Chinese				
oil	1	9,000	9,000	9,000
LIU JIYOU (1918-1983) Chinese				
wc/d	1	3,828	3,828	3,828
LIU KUILING (1885-1968) Chinese				
wc/d	1	2,500	2,500	2,500
LIU MING (1957-) Chinese				
oil	1	4,393	4,393	4,393
wc/d	1	12,138	12,138	12,138
LIU WEI (1965-) Chinese				
oil	1	80,000	80,000	80,000
LIU XIAODONG (1963-) Chinese				
oil	2	75,000-255,000	165,000	75,000

Name	No.	Price Range	Average	Median
LIU ZIJIAN (1956-) Chinese				
wc/d	1	20,000	20,000	20,000
LIVEMONT, Franz (19th C) Belgian				
oil	1	1,014	1,014	1,014
LIVEMONT, Privat (1861-1936) Belgian				
oil	3	1,189-1,881	1,471	1,344
wc/d	2	927-18,000	9,463	927
LIVENS, Henry (19th C) British				
oil	2	1,151-1,151	1,151	1,151
LIVENS, Horace Mann (1862-1936) British				
oil	3	850-2,846	1,606	1,122
wc/d	5	515-704	600	595
LIVERSEEGE, Henry (1803-1832) British				
oil	1	1,211	1,211	1,211
LIVESAY, Richard (1753-1823) British				
oil	1	2,100	2,100	2,100
LIVEZEY, Dale (1957-) American				
oil	1	2,500	2,500	2,500
LIZCANO Y ESTEBAN, Angel (1846-1929) Spanish				
oil	4	1,171-3,816	2,454	2,178
LJUBA (1934-) Yugoslavian				
oil	4	480-12,959	5,148	600
wc/d	6	518-2,945	1,237	776
LJUNGBERG, Sven (1913-) Swedish				
oil	2	452-2,290	1,371	452
LJUNGGREN, Reinhold (1920-) Swedish				
oil	5	1,586-4,493	3,045	3,241
LJUNGQUIST, Birger (1898-1965) Swedish				
oil	1	1,454	1,454	1,454
LLANECES, Jose (1863-1919) Spanish				
oil	3	2,400-3,575	3,058	3,200
LLANOS, Fernando (fl.1504-1530) Spanish				
oil	1	117,640	117,640	117,640
LLEWELLYN, Sir William (1858-1941) British				
oil	1	2,784	2,784	2,784
LLIMOS, Robert (1943-) Spanish				
oil	2	3,357-6,585	4,971	3,357
LLORENS ARTIGAS, Josep and MIRO, Joan (20th C) Spanish				
3D	1	25,656	25,656	25,656
LLORENS Y DIAZ, Francisco (1874-1948) Spanish				
oil	2	1,500-12,000	6,750	1,500
LLOVERAS, Federico (1912-1983) Spanish				
oil	2	846-1,668	1,257	846
wc/d	1	507	507	507
LLOYD, Edward (19th C) British				
oil	1	6,222	6,222	6,222
LLOYD, Frank Edward (?-1945) American				
wc/d	1	1,100	1,100	1,100
LLOYD, James (1905-1974) British				
wc/d	2	1,283-2,960	2,121	1,283
LLOYD, Llewelyn (1879-1950) Italian				
oil	4	7,135-23,568	13,398	7,767
LLOYD, Reg J (1926-) British				
oil	1	1,151	1,151	1,151
LLOYD, T Ivester (1873-1942) British				
oil	3	522-1,914	1,190	1,134
wc/d	3	550-1,200	866	850
LLOYD, Thomas James (1849-1910) British				
wc/d	8	440-5,113	2,357	1,556
LLOYD, W Stuart (fl.1875-1929) British				
oil	2	3,250-5,000	4,125	3,250
wc/d	15	458-3,553	1,253	1,131
LLULL, Jose Pinelo (1861-1922) Spanish				
oil	1	8,836	8,836	8,836
LO A NJOE, Guillaume Theodor (1937-) Dutch				
oil	1	1,145	1,145	1,145
LOAN, Dorothy van (1904-1999) American				
oil	4	500-2,250	1,187	800
wc/d	1	1,000	1,000	1,000
LOBBEDEZ, Charles-Auguste-Romain (1825-1882) French				
oil	1	5,327	5,327	5,327

Name	No.	Price Range	Average	Median
LOBDELL, Frank (1921-) American				
oil	2	23,919-38,271	31,095	23,919
LOBEL-RICHE, Almery (1880-1950) French				
oil	1	1,145	1,145	1,145
LOBO, Balthazar (1910-1993) Spanish				
wc/d	2	2,108-4,071	3,089	2,108
3D	6	6,000-83,572	26,653	10,669
LOBRE, Maurice (1862-1951) French				
oil	1	42,750	42,750	42,750
LOBRICHON, Timoleon Marie (1831-1914) French				
oil	1	12,517	12,517	12,517
LOCASO, Ruben (20th C) Argentinian				
3D	1	3,000	3,000	3,000
LOCATELLI, Achille (1864-1948) Italian				
oil	1	1,455	1,455	1,455
LOCATELLI, Andrea (1693-1741) Italian				
oil	4	32,986-124,274	68,441	46,603
wc/d	1	5,833	5,833	5,833
LOCATELLI, Antonio (1895-1936) Italian				
oil	1	2,811	2,811	2,811
LOCHER, Carl (1851-1915) Danish				
oil	22	974-14,228	5,036	4,075
LOCHER, Jens (1825-1869) Danish				
oil	4	415-3,100	1,535	1,192
LOCHER, Thomas (1956-) American				
oil	1	6,181	6,181	6,181
LOCHHEAD, Kenneth (1926-) Canadian				
oil	4	1,078-11,019	5,137	2,969
wc/d	3	738-1,476	1,011	820
LOCHORE, Brad (1960-) New Zealander				
oil	1	3,168	3,168	3,168
LOCKARD, Robert Ivan (1905-1974) American				
wc/d	1	1,000	1,000	1,000
LOCKETT, Milo (20th C) American				
oil	1	3,000	3,000	3,000
LOCKHART, Tom (1950-) American				
oil	1	5,000	5,000	5,000
LOCKHART, William Ewart (1846-1900) British				
oil	2	3,128-5,610	4,369	3,128
wc/d	1	4,117	4,117	4,117
LOCKWOOD, John Ward (1894-1963) American				
oil	1	4,750	4,750	4,750
LODER OF BATH, Edwin (1827-1885) British				
oil	4	750-2,394	1,565	1,229
LODER OF BATH, James (1784-1860) British				
oil	7	2,300-14,000	6,320	6,000
LODER, Matthaus (1781-1828) Austrian				
wc/d	1	13,875	13,875	13,875
LODGE, George Edward (1860-1954) British				
oil	4	730-2,646	1,393	1,062
wc/d	14	531-12,460	3,998	1,800
LODOLA, Marco (1955-) Italian				
oil	45	530-7,714	1,380	1,178
wc/d	9	471-1,196	684	648
3D	24	1,790-4,917	3,338	3,625
LOEB, Damien (1970-) American				
oil	2	17,000-65,000	41,000	17,000
LOEBER, Lou (1894-1983) Dutch				
oil	3	3,562-7,633	5,134	4,208
LOEDING, Harmen (1637-1673) Dutch				
oil	1	48,440	48,440	48,440
LOEFFLER, Gisella (1900-) American/Austrian				
oil	1	3,250	3,250	3,250
LOELD, Lars Olof (1930-) Swedish				
oil	1	1,018	1,018	1,018
LOEMANS, Alexander François (c.1816-1898) Canadian/French				
oil	5	1,380-26,000	7,021	2,216
LOEVY, Edward (1857-1911) Polish				
wc/d	2	1,051-2,385	1,718	1,051

Name	No.	Price Range	Average	Median
LOFDAHL, Eva (1953-) Swedish				
oil	1	636	636	636
wc/d	1	529	529	529
3D	1	2,907	2,907	2,907
LOFER, Andre (20th C) French?				
oil	1	5,400	5,400	5,400
LOFFLER, August (1822-1866) German				
oil	3	2,595-3,472	2,951	2,788
wc/d	1	484	484	484
LOFFLER, Bertold (1874-1960) Austrian				
oil	1	6,370	6,370	6,370
LOFFLER, Franz Karl (1875-1955) German				
oil	2	707-811	759	707
wc/d	1	1,532	1,532	1,532
LOFFLER, Hugo (1859-1935) German				
oil	1	3,330	3,330	3,330
LOFFLER, Richard (1956-) American				
3D	1	6,500	6,500	6,500
LOFFLER-RADYMNO, Leopold (1827-1898) Austrian				
oil	1	15,727	15,727	15,727
LOFFREDO, Silvio (1920-) Italian				
oil	5	471-2,142	1,103	788
wc/d	3	530-1,800	1,160	1,152
LOFGREN, Hans (19/20th C) Danish?				
oil	1	1,267	1,267	1,267
LOGAN, Maurice (1886-1977) American				
oil	3	5,500-32,500	18,000	16,000
wc/d	4	700-3,250	1,937	1,300
LOGAN, Robert Henry (1874-1942) American				
oil	5	475-900	715	800
wc/d	1	1,204	1,204	1,204
LOGELAIN, Henri (1889-1968) Belgian				
oil	4	596-1,286	792	630
wc/d	1	3,625	3,625	3,625
LOGHI, Kimon (1871-?) Yugoslavian				
oil	2	2,757-3,637	3,197	2,757
LOGOZZO, Jack (1948-) American				
3D	1	4,500	4,500	4,500
LOGSDAIL, William (1859-1944) British				
oil	3	592-13,230	6,440	5,500
LOGSDON, Richard (20th C) American				
oil	1	3,000	3,000	3,000
LOHAN, Mary (20th C) Irish?				
oil	6	1,427-12,603	5,092	3,390
LOHMANN, A (20th C) German				
oil	2	2,386-3,405	2,895	2,386
LOHMANN, Adolf (1928-) German				
oil	5	535-1,468	1,014	916
LOHR, August (1843-1919) German				
oil	6	12,000-55,000	31,000	25,000
wc/d	2	7,478-7,555	7,516	7,478
LOHR, Emil Ludwig (1809-1876) German				
oil	3	1,903-4,355	3,457	4,113
LOHSE, Carl (20th C) German				
oil	3	1,483-15,315	7,288	5,066
LOHSE, Richard Paul (1902-1988) Swiss				
oil	4	18,740-114,490	51,998	36,711
LOIR, Luigi (1845-1916) French				
oil	3	1,698-19,135	9,258	6,943
wc/d	4	547-18,596	8,270	3,497
LOISEAU, Gustave (1865-1935) French				
oil	65	4,476-135,000	49,848	50,000
wc/d	28	486-2,979	1,275	972
LOIZOU, Renos (20th C) ?				
oil	1	6,188	6,188	6,188
wc/d	1	1,424	1,424	1,424
LOJACONO, Francesco (1841-1915) Italian				
oil	2	38,219-178,356	108,287	38,219
LOKHORST, Dirk Pieter van (1848-?) Dutch				
oil	1	1,585	1,585	1,585
LOKHORST, Dirk van (1818-1893) Dutch				
oil	1	1,518	1,518	1,518

Name	No.	Price Range	Average	Median
LOKHORST, Jan van (1837-1874) Dutch				
oil	1	2,290	2,290	2,290
LOKI, Bunsai (?) ?				
wc/d	1	19,000	19,000	19,000
LOL (1958-) French?				
wc/d	2	2,338-2,649	2,493	2,338
LOMAKIN, Oleg (1924-) Russian				
oil	1	1,448	1,448	1,448
LOMAX, John Arthur (1857-1923) British				
oil	4	2,958-13,920	8,554	6,960
LOMBARD, Alfred (1884-1973) French				
oil	1	1,196	1,196	1,196
LOMBARDI, Enrico (1958-) Italian				
oil	1	2,071	2,071	2,071
LOMBARDI, Giovanni Battista (1823-c.1880) Italian				
3D	1	85,000	85,000	85,000
LOMBARDI, Giovanni Domenico (1682-1752) Italian				
oil	1	30,102	30,102	30,102
LOMBARDO, Sergio (1939-) Italian				
oil	1	1,178	1,178	1,178
LOMEDICO, Thomas Gaetano (1904-1985) American				
3D	1	2,200	2,200	2,200
LOMI, Giovanni (1889-1969) Italian				
oil	15	1,100-4,165	2,661	2,548
LOMIKINE, Konstantin (1924-1992) Russian				
oil	17	951-7,373	3,095	2,141
wc/d	17	654-8,324	2,925	2,170
LOMMEN, Wilhelm (1838-1895) German				
oil	2	1,956-2,420	2,188	1,956
LONBERG, Lorens (1726-1811) Swedish				
oil	1	1,870	1,870	1,870
LONDONIO, Francesco (1723-1783) Italian				
oil	1	5,364	5,364	5,364
wc/d	1	1,424	1,424	1,424
LONE WOLF (1882-1970) American				
oil	3	2,250-5,500	3,416	2,500
LONG, A (?) ?				
oil	1	1,911	1,911	1,911
LONG, Edwin (1829-1891) British				
oil	3	1,218-200,000	67,603	1,591
LONG, Lieutenant (19th C) ?				
oil	1	3,871	3,871	3,871
LONG, Marion (1882-1970) Canadian				
oil	5	853-18,967	5,318	2,645
LONG, Richard (1945-) British				
wc/d	5	1,073-19,360	8,912	3,800
3D	6	60,000-120,000	87,013	80,000
LONG, Sydney (1871-1955) Australian				
wc/d	4	1,860-3,162	2,557	2,232
LONG, Ted (1933-) American				
oil	1	2,750	2,750	2,750
LONG, Woodie (20th C) American				
oil	1	1,600	1,600	1,600
LONGA, Louis Anselme (1809-1869) French				
oil	1	3,168	3,168	3,168
LONGABOUGH, Charles Oglesby (1885-1944) American				
wc/d	1	1,800	1,800	1,800
LONGARETTI, Trento (1916-) Italian				
oil	25	1,432-9,709	4,254	3,416
wc/d	5	488-1,158	732	571
LONGCHAMP, Gaston (19/20th C) French				
wc/d	1	2,400	2,400	2,400
LONGEPIED, Leon Eugene (1849-1888) French				
3D	1	1,999	1,999	1,999
LONGHI, Alessandro (1733-1813) Italian				
oil	1	39,790	39,790	39,790
LONGHI, Barbara (1552-1638) Italian				
oil	1	28,804	28,804	28,804
LONGHI, Pietro (1702-1785) Italian				
oil	1	38,219	38,219	38,219
LONGHURST, Joseph (?-1922) British				
oil	1	1,625	1,625	1,625

Name	No.	Price Range	Average	Median
LONGMAN, Joanna (1918-1973) British				
oil	1	1,309	1,309	1,309
LONGO, Robert (1953-) American				
oil	4	4,000-110,000	35,478	13,913
wc/d	7	2,000-85,000	31,546	18,062
3D	2	7,000-30,000	18,500	7,000
LONGOBARDI, Nino (1953-) Italian				
wc/d	1	859	859	859
3D	2	3,312-31,849	17,580	3,312
LONGONI, Emilio (1859-1933) Italian				
oil	1	169,829	169,829	169,829
LONGPRE, Paul de (1855-1911) American/French				
oil	5	3,000-20,000	8,500	6,500
wc/d	7	2,250-26,000	15,292	15,000
LONGPRE, Raoul de (1859-1920) French				
wc/d	8	1,200-10,000	4,593	3,750
LONGSTAFF, Sir John (1861-1941) Australian				
oil	2	2,600-4,464	3,532	2,600
LONGUET, Alexandre Marie (?-1850) French				
oil	1	2,155	2,155	2,155
LONNBERG, William (1887-1949) Finnish				
oil	4	799-1,929	1,319	1,199
LONNROTH, Arvid Fredrik (1823-1880) Swedish				
oil	1	1,870	1,870	1,870
LONSDALE, James (1777-1839) British				
oil	1	1,472	1,472	1,472
LONSKY, G (19th C) German				
oil	1	2,880	2,880	2,880
LOO, Carle van (1705-1765) French				
oil	2	16,054-45,000	30,527	16,054
wc/d	2	999-13,863	7,431	999
LOO, Jacob van (1614-1670) Dutch				
oil	2	21,020-103,800	62,410	21,020
LOO, Jean Baptiste van (1684-1745) French				
oil	2	7,182-13,728	10,455	7,182
LOO, Louis-Michel van (1707-1771) French				
oil	2	6,000-30,000	18,000	6,000
LOO, Pieter van (1600-1660) Flemish				
wc/d	1	1,636	1,636	1,636
LOO, Pieter van (1731-1784) Dutch				
wc/d	1	15,459	15,459	15,459
LOOMIS, Manchus C (20th C) American				
oil	1	1,000	1,000	1,000
LOON, Theodoor van (c.1585-c.1667) Flemish				
oil	1	251,074	251,074	251,074
LOOS, Friedrich (1797-1890) Austrian				
wc/d	1	3,857	3,857	3,857
LOOS, John F (19th C) Belgian				
oil	1	3,500	3,500	3,500
LOOSCHEN, Hermann (elder) (1807-1873) German				
oil	1	5,577	5,577	5,577
LOOTZ, Eva (1940-) Austrian				
oil	1	4,071	4,071	4,071
LOOY, Jacobus van (1855-1930) Dutch				
oil	3	935-14,351	6,485	4,171
wc/d	1	589	589	589
LOPEZ ARMENTIA, Gustavo (1949-) Argentinian				
oil	2	3,200-12,000	7,600	3,200
wc/d	1	6,500	6,500	6,500
LOPEZ GARCIA, Antonio (1936-) Spanish				
oil	1	299,200	299,200	299,200
wc/d	2	22,338-22,338	22,338	22,338
3D	1	722,449	722,449	722,449
LOPEZ GARCIA, Juan Luis (1894-1978) Spanish				
oil	1	1,556	1,556	1,556
LOPEZ LEAO DE LAGUNA, Baruch (1864-1943) Dutch				
oil	1	1,199	1,199	1,199
wc/d	1	1,073	1,073	1,073
LOPEZ MENDEZ, Luis Alfredo (1901-?) Venezuelan				
oil	16	1,300-6,280	3,396	2,680
LOPEZ MEZQUITA, Jose Maria (1883-1954) Spanish				
oil	1	1,440	1,440	1,440

Name	No.	Price Range	Average	Median
LOPEZ MORELLO, Ramon (1903-?) Spanish				
oil	1	1,560	1,560	1,560
LOPEZ TAJES, Agustin (1938-) Spanish				
oil	10	536-2,259	1,412	1,447
LOPEZ Y PORTANA, Vicente (1772-1850) Spanish				
wc/d	1	1,936	1,936	1,936
LOPEZ, C V (20th C) Philippino				
oil	1	1,216	1,216	1,216
LOPEZ, Gasparo (1650-1732) Italian				
oil	1	15,459	15,459	15,459
LOPEZ-CABRERA, Ricardo (1866-1950) Spanish				
oil	5	1,920-8,970	5,692	6,027
LOPEZ-CURVAL, Catherine (1954-) French				
oil	4	879-6,473	2,387	1,004
wc/d	1	3,766	3,766	3,766
LOPEZ-MONTOYA, Esperanza (1926-) Spanish				
3D	2	2,672-2,907	2,789	2,672
LOPP, Harry Leonard (1888-1974) American				
oil	1	4,000	4,000	4,000
LOPPE, Gabriel (1825-1913) French				
oil	3	2,289-10,813	7,567	9,600
LORAINE, Nevison Arthur (fl.1889-1908) British				
oil	1	8,400	8,400	8,400
LORAN, Erle (1905-1999) American				
oil	2	1,500-2,500	2,000	1,500
wc/d	4	400-750	625	650
LORCHER, Alfred (1875-1962) ?				
wc/d	3	588-840	691	647
3D	2	2,883-8,026	5,454	2,883
LORCK, Karl Julius (1829-1882) Norwegian				
oil	1	17,306	17,306	17,306
LORENTSON, Waldemar (1899-1982) Swedish				
oil	17	1,272-44,929	8,231	2,313
wc/d	1	10,688	10,688	10,688
LORENTZEN, C A (1746-1828) Danish				
oil	2	1,267-5,559	3,413	1,267
LORENTZEN, Carl Friedrich Adolph (1801-1880) German				
oil	1	3,004	3,004	3,004
LORENTZEN, Christian August (1746-1828) Danish				
oil	2	6,802-8,088	7,445	6,802
LORENZ, Ernest (1872-?) German				
oil	1	4,559	4,559	4,559
wc/d	1	843	843	843
LORENZ, Richard (1858-1915) German				
oil	6	800-150,000	56,800	42,000
LORENZ, Willi (1901-1981) German				
oil	6	584-2,180	1,079	790
LORENZ-MUROWANA, Ernst Hugo (1872-?) German				
oil	1	1,110	1,110	1,110
LORENZL, Josef (1892-1950) Austrian				
3D	8	2,250-5,536	3,803	4,002
LORENZO MONACO (c.1370-c.1425) Italian				
oil	2	647,500-1,557,000	1,102,250	647,500
LORENZO, Antonio (1932-) Spanish				
oil	3	1,100-2,057	1,585	1,600
LORENZO, Matilde (19th C) Spanish?				
oil	1	1,808	1,808	1,808
LORENZO, Myriam di (20th C) ?				
oil	1	2,983	2,983	2,983
LORIA, Vincenzo (1850-?) Italian				
oil	2	500-5,226	2,863	500
wc/d	4	541-3,096	1,702	592
LORIMER, John Henry (1856-1936) British				
oil	1	115,050	115,050	115,050
LORING, William Cushing (1879-?) American				
oil	1	5,000	5,000	5,000
LORJOU, Bernard (1908-1986) French				
oil	15	1,133-20,760	5,957	5,000
wc/d	7	851-4,000	2,042	1,424
LORME, Anthonie de (1610-1673) Dutch				
oil	1	9,250	9,250	9,250

Name	No.	Price Range	Average	Median
LORME, Anthonie de and PALAMEDES, Anthonie (17th C) Dutch				
oil	1	75,000	75,000	75,000
LORMIER, J (?) French				
3D	2	2,400-2,760	2,580	2,400
LORRAIN, Louis Joseph le (1715-1759) French				
oil	1	60,822	60,822	60,822
wc/d	1	41,319	41,319	41,319
LORTEL, Leberecht (c.1818-1901) French				
oil	3	1,576-20,354	7,870	1,680
LORY, Gabriel Ludwig (1763-1840) Swiss				
wc/d	2	2,740-3,913	3,326	2,740
LOS CARPINTEROS (20th C) Cuban				
wc/d	3	5,000-35,000	16,500	9,500
3D	1	30,000	30,000	30,000
LOSADA, Manuel (1865-1949) Spanish				
wc/d	1	3,356	3,356	3,356
LOSCHKIN, A (19/20th C) Russian				
wc/d	1	1,111	1,111	1,111
LOSSOW, Heinrich (1843-1897) German				
oil	6	969-7,555	4,560	4,014
LOSTE, Patrick (1955-) French				
oil	1	1,812	1,812	1,812
LOT, Hendrik (1821-1878) Dutch				
oil	1	8,836	8,836	8,836
LOTH, Johann Karl (1632-1698) German				
oil	2	4,487-35,000	19,743	4,487
wc/d	1	3,200	3,200	3,200
LOTH, Wilhelm (1920-1993) German				
wc/d	1	1,555	1,555	1,555
3D	1	5,955	5,955	5,955
LOTIRON, Robert (1886-1966) French				
oil	6	753-3,091	1,683	1,529
LOTTI, Ludovico (1860-1928) Italian				
oil	1	1,815	1,815	1,815
LOTTIER, Louis (1815-1892) French				
oil	1	3,039	3,039	3,039
LOTZ, Marie (1871-1970) Swiss				
oil	2	726-3,138	1,932	726
LOTZ, Mathilde (1858-1923) American				
oil	2	1,418-5,000	3,209	1,418
LOU, Liza (1969-) American				
3D	5	5,500-48,000	21,400	19,000
LOUARDIRI, Ahmed (1928-1974) Moroccan				
oil	4	7,611-42,413	26,422	13,774
LOUBCHANSKY, Marcelle (1917-1988) French				
oil	8	628-1,607	1,159	1,094
wc/d	1	507	507	507
LOUBON, Émile Charles Joseph (1809-1863) French				
oil	1	2,027	2,027	2,027
LOUCHE, Constant (19/20th C) French				
oil	3	1,134-3,390	2,618	3,330
LOUCHET, Paul-François (1854-1936) French				
oil	4	495-5,655	1,969	827
LOUD, Richard K (1942-) American				
oil	1	12,000	12,000	12,000
LOUDERBACK, Walt (1887-1941) American				
oil	1	3,500	3,500	3,500
LOUGHEED, Robert Elmer (1910-1982) Canadian				
oil	13	2,997-37,500	12,294	9,500
wc/d	3	3,000-25,000	17,000	23,000
LOUGUININE-WOLKONSKY, Maria (1875-1960) Russian				
oil	1	1,176	1,176	1,176
LOUIS, Jean Marc (20th C) Belgian				
wc/d	1	3,200	3,200	3,200
LOUIS, Morris (1912-1962) American				
oil	6	123,900-1,600,000	535,650	240,000
LOUKIDIS, Tasos (1884-1972) Greek				
oil	2	1,760-3,740	2,750	1,760
wc/d	1	1,408	1,408	1,408
LOUND, Thomas (1802-1861) British				
oil	1	15,120	15,120	15,120
wc/d	4	531-1,151	809	743

Name	No.	Price Range	Average	Median
LOUP, Eugène (1867-1948) French				
wc/d	1	1,868	1,868	1,868
LOUPPE, Leo (1869-?) French				
oil	1	7,068	7,068	7,068
LOUREIRO, Arthur Jose de Souza (1853-1932) Portuguese				
oil	1	15,799	15,799	15,799
LOUSTAS, Costas (1933-) Greek?				
oil	2	3,460-10,912	7,186	3,460
LOUTHERBOURG, Jacques Philippe de II (1740-1812) French				
oil	2	10,139-22,490	16,314	10,139
wc/d	1	8,650	8,650	8,650
LOUVRIER, Maurice (1878-1954) French				
oil	3	2,281-4,248	2,971	2,386
LOUYOT, Edmond (1861-1909) German				
oil	1	1,215	1,215	1,215
wc/d	1	3,365	3,365	3,365
LOVATTI, August (1852-1921) Italian				
oil	1	19,000	19,000	19,000
LOVATTI, Matteo (1861-?) Italian				
wc/d	1	2,024	2,024	2,024
LOVE, Mary Adams (19/20th C) American				
oil	1	1,600	1,600	1,600
LOVE, Ralph (1907-) American				
oil	8	1,300-5,000	3,012	3,000
LOVEGROVE, W (20th C) British				
3D	1	2,408	2,408	2,408
LOVELL, Tom (1909-1997) American				
oil	4	4,500-375,000	139,500	8,500
wc/d	4	7,500-20,000	11,875	9,000
LOVER, Samuel (1797-1868) British				
wc/d	2	684-1,800	1,242	684
LOVERIDGE, Clinton (19th C) American				
oil	3	500-3,000	1,833	2,000
LOVEROFF, Frederick Nicholas (1894-1959) Canadian				
oil	5	2,870-6,171	4,290	3,796
wc/d	2	410-495	452	410
LOVET-LORSKI, Boris (1894-1973) Russian/American				
oil	1	850	850	850
3D	1	3,750	3,750	3,750
LOVMAND, Christine Marie (1803-1872) Danish				
oil	1	9,554	9,554	9,554
LOW, Sir David (1891-1963) British				
wc/d	4	854-1,157	1,014	979
LOW, Will Hicock (1853-1932) American				
oil	1	3,800	3,800	3,800
LOWE, George (20th C) American				
wc/d	1	1,400	1,400	1,400
LOWE, Stephen (1938-) Canadian				
wc/d	1	1,342	1,342	1,342
LOWELL, Milton H (1848-1927) American				
oil	6	650-1,500	1,108	1,100
wc/d	2	650-700	675	650
LOWELL, Orson Byron (1871-1956) American				
oil	2	4,750-5,000	4,875	4,750
LOWENGARD, Kurt (1895-1940) German				
wc/d	1	1,052	1,052	1,052
LOWENSBERG, Verena (1912-1986) Swiss				
oil	4	9,000-23,658	17,055	12,721
LOWGREN, Torsten (1903-?) Swedish				
oil	1	1,757	1,757	1,757
LOWITH, Wilhelm (1861-1932) Austrian				
oil	2	3,930-7,297	5,613	3,930
LOWNDES, Alan (1921-1978) British				
oil	19	870-14,025	7,152	7,182
wc/d	6	452-1,100	672	557
LOWRY, Laurence Stephen (1887-1976) British				
oil	25	25,800-1,795,500	279,484	147,200
wc/d	40	2,595-118,320	20,787	13,050
LOXTON, John S (1903-1971) Australian				
wc/d	2	1,302-1,674	1,488	1,302
LOY, Mina (1882-1966) American				
wc/d	3	1,942-24,596	10,572	5,178

Name	No.	Price Range	Average	Median
LOYER, Stanislas Auguste (1797-c.1870) French				
oil	1	3,440	3,440	3,440
LOZA, Ricardo Z (1967-) Colombian				
oil	2	1,000-2,750	1,875	1,000
wc/d	1	400	400	400
LOZANO SANCHIS, Francisco (1912-2000) Spanish				
oil	4	7,827-38,571	22,122	13,807
wc/d	1	1,200	1,200	1,200
LOZANO, Lazaro (?) ?				
oil	1	4,000	4,000	4,000
LOZZA, Raul (20th C) Argentinian				
oil	3	2,800-22,000	10,933	8,000
LU HAO (1969-) Chinese				
oil	1	8,880	8,880	8,880
3D	1	30,000	30,000	30,000
LU JI (c.1475-1503) Chinese				
wc/d	1	12,000	12,000	12,000
LU SHENG ZHONG (1952-) Chinese				
3D	1	25,000	25,000	25,000
LUBBERS, Adriaan (1892-1954) Dutch				
oil	6	6,361-48,340	29,523	28,274
wc/d	4	1,908-3,099	2,428	1,908
LUBBERS, Holger (1850-1931) Danish				
oil	15	812-4,517	2,184	1,746
LUBICH, Fernand (19th C) German				
oil	1	1,940	1,940	1,940
LUBIENIECKI, Bogdan Theodor (1653-1726) Polish				
oil	2	2,314-5,143	3,728	2,314
LUBIENIECKI, Christofel (1660-1728) Polish				
oil	1	60,550	60,550	60,550
LUBIN, Arieh (1897-1980) Israeli				
oil	4	1,300-10,000	4,375	3,000
wc/d	8	350-3,200	1,375	1,000
LUBITCH, Ossip (1896-1986) French				
oil	11	440-4,676	1,752	1,512
wc/d	1	887	887	887
LUCA, A de (?) ?				
3D	1	3,588	3,588	3,588
LUCA, Ferdinando de (19/20th C) Italian?				
3D	1	3,166	3,166	3,166
LUCA, Santolo de (1960-) Italian				
oil	1	1,784	1,784	1,784
LUCANDER, Anitra (1918-2000) Finnish				
oil	11	2,277-14,523	6,267	5,143
LUCANDER, Robert (20th C) Finnish				
oil	1	1,123	1,123	1,123
wc/d	1	3,000	3,000	3,000
LUCANO, Pietro (1878-1972) Italian				
oil	2	843-2,408	1,625	843
LUCAS Y VILLAAMIL, Eugenio (1858-1918) Spanish				
oil	9	1,574-24,082	8,977	7,747
wc/d	1	2,649	2,649	2,649
LUCAS, Albert Durer (1828-1918) British				
oil	5	1,701-7,480	4,459	4,275
LUCAS, Albert Pike (1862-1945) American				
oil	1	2,400	2,400	2,400
LUCAS, Edward George Handel (1861-1936) British				
oil	5	634-4,400	2,299	1,384
LUCAS, George (19th C) British				
oil	1	5,664	5,664	5,664
LUCAS, Henry Frederick Lucas (c.1848-1943) British				
oil	10	445-35,910	5,078	1,134
LUCAS, Jean (1823-?) French				
oil	1	45,760	45,760	45,760
LUCAS, John Seymour (1849-1923) British				
oil	2	2,301-2,910	2,605	2,301
LUCAS, John Templeton (1836-1880) British				
oil	2	979-1,086	1,032	979
LUCAS, N (20th C) ?				
oil	1	2,548	2,548	2,548

Name	No.	Price Range	Average	Median
LUCAS, Sarah (1962-) British				
wc/d	1	53,100	53,100	53,100
3D	3	5,833-148,000	87,944	110,000
LUCAS, Seymour (19th C) British				
oil	1	1,384	1,384	1,384
LUCAS, Wilhelm (1884-1918) German				
oil	4	1,753-6,171	3,164	1,815
LUCAS, William (1840-1895) British				
oil	1	1,131	1,131	1,131
LUCAS-ROBIQUET, Marie Aimee (1858-1959) French				
oil	1	2,293	2,293	2,293
LUCASSEN, Reinier (1939-) Dutch				
oil	4	5,260-10,520	6,935	5,845
LUCCA, Flaminio (19th C) Italian				
3D	1	3,540	3,540	3,540
LUCCHESI, Bruno (1926-) American				
wc/d	1	6,000	6,000	6,000
LUCCHESI, Giorgio (1855-1941) Italian				
oil	2	15,000-18,000	16,500	15,000
LUCCHINI, Cesare (1941-) Swiss				
oil	1	1,864	1,864	1,864
LUCE (?) ?				
3D	1	4,281	4,281	4,281
LUCE, Maximilien (1858-1941) French				
oil	121	1,753-528,000	29,761	13,000
wc/d	60	486-7,972	1,423	1,070
LUCE, Molly (1896-1986) American				
oil	3	750-11,000	5,750	5,500
LUCEBERT (1924-1994) Dutch				
oil	14	2,003-37,699	10,848	5,856
wc/d	24	691-7,243	2,663	2,093
LUCERO, Michael (1953-) American?				
3D	1	6,000	6,000	6,000
LUCHIAN, Stefan (1868-1916) Rumanian				
wc/d	2	9,921-32,632	21,276	9,921
LUCI, F (19th C) Italian				
3D	1	6,500	6,500	6,500
LUCIANI, Ascanio (1621-1706) Italian				
oil	1	3,625	3,625	3,625
LUCIONI, Luigi (1900-1988) American				
oil	17	2,000-70,000	12,338	7,500
wc/d	2	500-4,250	2,375	500
LUCKEROTH, Jupp (1919-1993) German				
oil	1	1,019	1,019	1,019
LUCKX, Frans (1802-1849) Belgian				
oil	3	3,282-26,311	13,053	9,568
LUDECKE, Albert Bogislav (19th C) German				
oil	1	4,973	4,973	4,973
LUDECKE-CLEVE, August (1868-1957) German				
oil	3	600-3,579	1,860	1,401
LUDERS, David (1710-1759) German				
oil	2	10,488-66,224	38,356	10,488
LUDINS, Eugene David (1904-1996) American				
oil	1	4,000	4,000	4,000
LUDOVICI, Albert (1820-1894) British				
oil	6	1,000-6,498	3,600	1,611
wc/d	1	627	627	627
LUDOVICI, Albert (jnr) (1852-1932) British				
oil	3	837-4,810	2,165	850
wc/d	1	673	673	673
LUDOVICI, Marguerite (19/20th C) British				
oil	1	1,600	1,600	1,600
LUDUENA PEPA, Jorge Mario (1927-) Argentinian				
oil	1	1,361	1,361	1,361
LUDWIG, Auguste (1834-c.1900) German				
oil	1	2,599	2,599	2,599
LUDWIG, Friedrich (1891-1970) German				
oil	1	4,241	4,241	4,241
wc/d	1	3,534	3,534	3,534
LUDWIG, Karl Julius Emil (1839-1901) German				
oil	3	1,531-2,854	2,090	1,885

Name	No.	Price Range	Average	Median
LUDWIG, Wolfgang (1923-) German				
oil	1	1,978	1,978	1,978
LUEDERS, Jimmy (1927-1994) American				
oil	4	600-1,800	1,075	800
LUEGER, Michael (1804-1883) German				
oil	1	4,241	4,241	4,241
LUERZER, Friderick (1858-1917) German				
oil	1	1,691	1,691	1,691
LUETHI, Rolf (1933-) Swiss				
3D	1	8,018	8,018	8,018
LUGARDON, Albert (1827-1909) French				
oil	6	1,138-6,487	3,236	1,915
LUGARDON, Jean-Leonard (1801-1884) Swiss				
oil	1	1,054	1,054	1,054
LUGERTH, Ferdinand (fl.1885-1915) Dutch?				
3D	1	2,145	2,145	2,145
LUGLI, S (?) Italian?				
3D	1	3,036	3,036	3,036
LUGRIS VADILLO, Urbano (1942-) Spanish				
oil	2	2,153-3,588	2,870	2,153
LUIGGI, P (19/20th C) Italian?				
oil	1	5,858	5,858	5,858
LUIGI, Mario de (1908-1978) Italian				
oil	1	4,919	4,919	4,919
LUIGINI, Ferdinand-Jean (1870-1943) French				
oil	1	1,281	1,281	1,281
wc/d	1	1,044	1,044	1,044
LUINI, Aurelio (1530-1593) Italian				
wc/d	1	10,694	10,694	10,694
LUISE, Diana (20th C) American				
oil	1	1,400	1,400	1,400
LUISE, Enrico de (1840-1915) Italian				
oil	1	1,800	1,800	1,800
LUISI, Nicholas J (1894-1977) American				
oil	2	550-2,500	1,525	550
LUIZ, Eduardo (1932-) Portuguese				
oil	1	4,830	4,830	4,830
wc/d	1	10,249	10,249	10,249
LUIZADA, Avigdor Renzo (1905-1987) Israeli				
oil	4	1,000-3,800	3,000	3,400
LUKA, Madeleine (1900-1989) French				
oil	3	485-1,506	1,155	1,475
wc/d	2	508-895	701	508
LUKACS, Attila Richard (1962-) Canadian				
wc/d	3	9,896-15,066	11,619	9,896
LUKE, Alexandra (1901-1967) Canadian				
oil	2	454-3,917	2,185	454
wc/d	1	2,116	2,116	2,116
LUKE, John (1906-1975) British				
oil	1	74,400	74,400	74,400
wc/d	1	4,241	4,241	4,241
LUKENS, Jim (1959-) American				
oil	2	1,200-3,500	2,350	1,200
LUKER, William (jnr) (1867-1951) British				
oil	1	1,134	1,134	1,134
LUKER, William (1828-1905) British				
oil	5	1,890-28,000	9,615	3,150
LUKIN, Sven (1934-) American				
oil	1	1,038	1,038	1,038
LUKITS, Theodore Nikolai (1897-1992) American				
oil	2	4,250-4,750	4,500	4,250
LUKOMSKI, George (1884-1954) Russian				
wc/d	4	875-6,324	2,897	1,260
LUKS, George (1867-1933) American				
oil	7	4,000-180,000	60,214	32,000
wc/d	8	450-40,000	5,940	800
LUMERMAN, Juana (1905-1982) Argentinian				
oil	1	2,997	2,997	2,997
LUMLEY, Augustus Savile (fl.1880-1899) British				
oil	1	1,700	1,700	1,700
LUMSDEN, Ernest Stephen (1883-1948) British				
oil	1	1,225	1,225	1,225

Name	No.	Price Range	Average	Median
LUMSDEN, J (fl.1820-1830) British				
oil	1	1,760	1,760	1,760
LUNA, Antonio Rodriguez (1910-1985) Spanish				
oil	2	650-2,500	1,575	650
LUNA, Carlos (1969-) Cuban				
oil	1	16,000	16,000	16,000
LUNAR, Emerio Dario (1940-1990) Venezuelan				
oil	1	2,420	2,420	2,420
LUND, F C (1826-1901) Danish				
oil	3	1,267-2,725	2,177	2,540
LUND, Frederik Christian (1826-1901) Danish				
oil	4	792-15,634	5,096	1,588
wc/d	1	7,817	7,817	7,817
LUND, Henrik (1879-1935) Norwegian				
oil	2	2,157-10,184	6,170	2,157
LUND, Soren (1852-1933) Danish				
oil	1	1,137	1,137	1,137
LUND, Troels (1802-1867) Danish				
oil	1	1,265	1,265	1,265
LUNDAHL, Amelie (1850-1914) Finnish				
oil	1	4,371	4,371	4,371
wc/d	4	1,260-2,342	1,671	1,414
LUNDAHL, Nadine (1958-) Finnish				
oil	4	2,443-4,442	3,416	2,571
LUNDBERG, Mikael (1952-) Swedish				
3D	1	1,781	1,781	1,781
LUNDBERG, Robert (1861-1903) Swedish				
oil	1	9,066	9,066	9,066
LUNDBERG, Theodor (1852-1925) Swedish				
3D	2	1,923-5,550	3,736	1,923
LUNDBOHM, Sixten (1895-1982) Swedish				
oil	1	859	859	859
wc/d	2	445-679	562	445
LUNDBYE, Johan Thomas (1818-1848) Danish				
oil	1	86,949	86,949	86,949
wc/d	4	635-11,321	3,542	1,028
LUNDE, Anders (1809-1886) Danish				
oil	1	2,540	2,540	2,540
LUNDEEN, George W (1948-) American				
3D	1	1,800	1,800	1,800
LUNDEGARD, Justus (1860-1924) Swedish				
oil	3	661-4,403	1,936	746
LUNDENS, Gerrit (1622-c.1683) Dutch				
oil	2	8,325-9,405	8,865	8,325
LUNDGREN, Charles (19/20th C) American				
oil	2	550-2,500	1,525	550
LUNDGREN, Egron Sillif (1815-1875) Swedish				
oil	1	1,427	1,427	1,427
wc/d	11	399-3,529	979	702
LUNDGREN, Johan Erik (1822-1895) Swedish				
oil	1	8,929	8,929	8,929
LUNDGREN, Tyra (1897-1979) Swedish				
3D	2	2,182-5,455	3,818	2,182
LUNDH, J (19th C) ?				
oil	1	3,248	3,248	3,248
LUNDH, Theodor (1812-1896) Swedish				
oil	2	1,496-1,994	1,745	1,496
LUNDMARK, Leon (1875-1942) American				
oil	10	650-3,500	1,097	850
LUNDQUIST, Evert (1904-1994) Swedish				
oil	25	411-69,979	7,285	2,368
LUNDQVIST, Rita (1953-) Swedish?				
oil	2	5,947-7,888	6,917	5,947
LUNDSTROM, Vilhelm (1893-1950) Danish				
oil	5	23,920-113,151	47,948	34,762
wc/d	3	1,293-4,948	2,915	2,505
LUNGKWITZ, Hermann (1813-1890) German				
oil	1	135,000	135,000	135,000
wc/d	2	800-10,500	5,650	800
LUNINA-JUNG, Elena (1960-) French/Russian				
oil	1	3,221	3,221	3,221

Name	No.	Price Range	Average	Median
LUNTESCHUTZ, Jules (1822-1893) French				
oil	1	1,745	1,745	1,745
LUNY, Thomas (1759-1837) British				
oil	22	3,250-115,050	22,106	7,500
LUO BROTHERS (1963-) Chinese				
wc/d	3	22,000-50,000	34,000	30,000
LUPERTZ, Markus (1941-) Czechoslovakian				
oil	24	4,545-146,507	36,677	27,096
wc/d	24	636-22,932	3,350	2,068
3D	7	4,685-111,000	28,868	15,417
LUPIANEZ Y CARRASCO, Jose (1864-1933) Spanish				
oil	3	1,204-1,567	1,333	1,230
LUPO, Alessandro (1876-1953) Italian				
oil	9	1,455-18,558	7,612	3,781
LUPORINI, Sandro (1930-) Italian				
oil	1	1,386	1,386	1,386
wc/d	1	958	958	958
LUPU, Zehava (1948-) Israeli				
oil	1	1,100	1,100	1,100
LUQUE, Manuel (1854-?) Spanish				
oil	1	1,080	1,080	1,080
LURCAT, Jean (1892-1966) French				
oil	6	4,587-19,000	8,403	6,336
wc/d	11	701-8,000	3,010	2,428
LURCZYNSKI, Mieczyslaw (1908-) French				
oil	1	1,512	1,512	1,512
LUSCHER, Ingeborg (1936-) German				
oil	1	1,461	1,461	1,461
LUSCOMBE, Henry A (1820-?) British				
oil	1	9,204	9,204	9,204
wc/d	1	630	630	630
LUSHANSKY, Jacob (20th C) Israeli?				
3D	1	1,800	1,800	1,800
LUSSANET, Paul de (1940-) Dutch				
oil	1	1,942	1,942	1,942
LUSTY, Otto (19th C) ?				
oil	1	1,299	1,299	1,299
LUTHANDER, Carl (1879-1967) Swedish				
oil	1	1,081	1,081	1,081
LUTHER, Adolf (1912-1990) German				
oil	1	11,466	11,466	11,466
wc/d	3	3,395-6,115	4,884	5,143
3D	17	2,799-15,315	6,793	6,361
LUTHI, Urs (1947-) Swiss				
oil	3	2,827-6,897	4,240	2,997
LUTHY, Oskar Wilhelm (1882-1945) Swiss				
oil	9	487-22,763	5,681	3,425
wc/d	2	611-1,945	1,278	611
LUTI, Benedetto (1666-1724) Italian				
oil	1	1,286	1,286	1,286
LUTKEN, Mathias (1841-1905) Danish				
oil	3	1,327-1,874	1,600	1,600
LUTSCHER, Fernand (19th C) French				
oil	1	1,438	1,438	1,438
LUTTERELL, Edward (1650-1710) British				
wc/d	1	1,566	1,566	1,566
LUTTEROTH, Ascan (1842-1923) German				
oil	7	1,403-18,849	4,641	1,985
wc/d	1	1,452	1,452	1,452
LUTTICHUYS, Simon (1610-1662) Dutch				
oil	1	1,350,500	1,350,500	1,350,500
LUTTRINGSHAUSEN, Johann Heinrich (1783-1857) German				
wc/d	1	3,277	3,277	3,277
LUTYENS, Charles Augustus Henry (1829-1915) British				
oil	3	1,056-2,275	1,693	1,750
LUTZ, Anton (1894-1992) Austrian				
oil	6	4,671-9,351	7,394	7,192
LUYKEN, Jan (1649-1712) Dutch				
wc/d	1	2,102	2,102	2,102
LUYKX, Christiaan (1623-c.1653) Flemish				
oil	3	55,500-170,000	130,666	166,500

Name	No.	Price Range	Average	Median
LUYT, Arie Marthinus (1879-1951) Dutch				
oil	1	2,652	2,652	2,652
LUYTEN, Henri (1859-1945) Belgian				
oil	2	3,299-5,382	4,340	3,299
LUZANOWSKY, Lydia (1899-?) Russian				
wc/d	2	1,267-1,394	1,330	1,267
3D	1	3,168	3,168	3,168
LUZURIAGA, Juan Ramon (1938-) Spanish				
oil	2	1,381-1,427	1,404	1,381
LUZZATI, Emanuele (1921-) Italian				
oil	1	2,682	2,682	2,682
wc/d	2	914-1,386	1,150	914
3D	1	2,316	2,316	2,316
LUZZI, Cleto (19/20th C) Italian				
oil	4	3,196-6,747	4,478	3,600
LVOV, Piotr Ivanovich (1882-1944) Russian				
oil	4	841-3,360	1,917	1,070
LYALL, Laura Adeline (1860-1930) Canadian				
oil	3	3,988-22,678	16,274	22,156
wc/d	2	2,886-8,815	5,850	2,886
LYAPKALO, Viktor (1956-) Russian				
oil	5	915-1,947	1,455	1,424
LYBAERT, Theophile Marie Françoise (1848-1927) Belgian				
oil	1	7,644	7,644	7,644
LYDEN, Edvin (1879-1956) Finnish				
oil	3	1,870-2,221	2,065	2,104
LYDIS, Mariette (1890-1970) Austrian				
oil	5	500-10,000	4,012	3,330
wc/d	1	1,020	1,020	1,020
LYFORD, Philip (20th C) American				
oil	1	2,500	2,500	2,500
LYLE, Thomas Byron (fl.1880-1890) British				
oil	1	2,668	2,668	2,668
LYMAN, Harry (1856-1933) American				
oil	2	1,100-2,384	1,742	1,100
LYMAN, John Goodwin (1886-1967) Canadian				
oil	4	2,026-5,673	3,762	2,431
wc/d	4	492-1,223	766	529
LYMAN, Joseph (jnr) (1843-1913) American				
oil	2	600-2,700	1,650	600
LYMAN, Stephen (1957-1996) American				
wc/d	1	4,500	4,500	4,500
LYNCH, Albert (1851-?) Peruvian				
oil	4	5,180-36,800	18,342	7,389
wc/d	1	421	421	421
LYNCH, Justo (1870-1953) Argentinian				
oil	4	3,400-39,000	23,132	15,130
LYNCH, Padraig (1940-) Irish				
oil	3	818-1,581	1,275	1,427
LYNDSAY, Roy (1945-) Irish?				
oil	2	9,600-10,395	9,997	9,600
LYNE, Michael (1912-1989) British				
oil	5	2,457-10,395	6,047	4,550
wc/d	1	1,283	1,283	1,283
LYNEN, Amedee (1852-1938) Belgian				
oil	1	882	882	882
wc/d	5	602-1,064	884	1,019
LYNEN, Armand (20th C) Belgian				
oil	1	537	537	537
wc/d	2	477-1,985	1,231	477
LYNGE-AHLBERG, Einar (1913-1980) Swedish				
oil	2	1,018-2,511	1,764	1,018
LYNN, John (fl.1826-1838) British				
oil	3	3,236-9,570	5,577	3,927
LYON, Harold (1930-) Canadian				
oil	1	1,621	1,621	1,621
LYON, John Howard (?-1921) British				
oil	2	3,500-7,667	5,583	3,500
LYON, Thomas Bonar (1873-1955) British				
oil	2	3,132-4,248	3,690	3,132
LYRE, Adolphe la (1850-1935) French				
oil	3	484-2,625	1,314	835

Name	No.	Price Range	Average	Median
LYS, Maurice (20th C) French				
wc/d	1	4,872	4,872	4,872
LYTH, Harald (1937-) Swedish				
oil	1	2,775	2,775	2,775
LYTRAS, Maria (1899-1975) Greek				
oil	1	9,570	9,570	9,570
LYTRAS, Nikiforos (1832-1904) Greek				
oil	1	1,228,500	1,228,500	1,228,500
wc/d	3	1,384-3,366	2,522	2,816
LYTRAS, Pericles (1888-1940) Greek				
oil	1	34,800	34,800	34,800
LYTZEN, N A (1826-1890) Danish				
oil	1	2,157	2,157	2,157
M R (?) ?				
oil	1	7,500	7,500	7,500
3D	4	4,928-27,000	13,640	5,632
MA HAN (1968-) Chinese				
3D	1	40,000	40,000	40,000
MA JIN (1900-1971) Chinese				
wc/d	1	5,143	5,143	5,143
MA LIUMING (1969-) Chinese				
oil	3	35,145-59,003	44,716	40,000
3D	1	18,828	18,828	18,828
MAAR, Dora (1909-1997) French				
oil	11	476-6,500	2,764	1,885
wc/d	1	1,029	1,029	1,029
MAAREL, Marinus van der (1857-1921) Dutch				
oil	1	4,877	4,877	4,877
MAARNI, Elvi (1907-) Finnish				
oil	4	1,678-4,216	3,550	4,099
wc/d	11	920-2,700	1,904	1,929
MAAS, Ernst (1904-1971) Swiss				
oil	1	2,611	2,611	2,611
MAAS, Harry (1906-1982) Dutch				
oil	3	1,502-3,755	2,753	3,004
MAAS, Lorenz Johann (1845-1882) German				
oil	2	993-4,882	2,937	993
MAAS, Paul (1890-1962) Belgian				
oil	9	643-3,109	1,389	1,314
MAASDIJK, Alexander Henri Robert van (1856-1931) Dutch				
oil	1	1,447	1,447	1,447
MAASS, David (20th C) American				
oil	1	22,500	22,500	22,500
MAASS, Ferdinand (1837-1902) Austrian				
oil	1	3,625	3,625	3,625
MAATEN, Jacob Jan van der (1820-1879) Dutch				
oil	2	6,250-8,486	7,368	6,250
MAATSCH, Thilo (1900-1983) German				
oil	3	2,038-2,592	2,392	2,548
wc/d	2	707-1,911	1,309	707
MABE, Manabu (1924-1997) Brazilian/Japanese				
oil	3	15,000-16,000	15,666	16,000
MABREY, Ken (20th C) American				
oil	1	2,110	2,110	2,110
MAC, Luz (20th C) French?				
wc/d	1	4,371	4,371	4,371
McAFEE, Ila Mae (1897-1995) American				
oil	5	1,500-9,000	4,000	3,000
MACAIONE, Tommy (1907-1992) American				
oil	1	1,500	1,500	1,500
McALEER, Clement (1949-) Irish				
oil	1	561	561	561
wc/d	1	1,527	1,527	1,527
McALLISTER, Ian (20th C) Irish				
oil	2	877-1,211	1,044	877
MACALLUM, Hamilton (1841-1896) British				
oil	3	731-7,854	4,361	4,498
MACARA, Andrew (1944-) British				
oil	23	655-2,394	1,350	1,313
MACARRON, Ricardo (1926-) Spanish				
oil	3	1,176-1,556	1,386	1,427

Name	No.	Price Range	Average	Median
MACARTHUR, Blanche (fl.1870-1903) British				
oil	1	4,725	4,725	4,725
McAULEY, Charles (1910-1999) British				
oil	26	1,682-16,688	4,098	3,460
MACAULEY, Kate (fl.1880-1896) British				
wc/d	1	1,116	1,116	1,116
McAULEY, Michael (20th C) Irish?				
wc/d	1	1,824	1,824	1,824
McAULIFFE, James J (1848-1921) American				
oil	1	4,000	4,000	4,000
MACAVOY, Edouard (1905-1991) French				
oil	5	634-3,956	1,985	858
wc/d	1	2,431	2,431	2,431
MACAYA, Miguel (1964-) Spanish				
oil	1	1,800	1,800	1,800
MACBETH, Robert Walker (1848-1910) British				
oil	2	2,088-3,240	2,664	2,088
McBEY, James (1883-1959) British				
oil	2	2,805-15,930	9,367	2,805
wc/d	9	1,134-5,520	2,532	1,964
MacBRIDE, William (1856-1913) British				
oil	1	2,309	2,309	2,309
MACCABE, Gladys (1918-) Irish				
oil	25	1,557-16,800	4,076	3,186
wc/d	2	850-7,297	4,073	850
McCAFFERTY, Jay David (1948-) American				
oil	1	3,250	3,250	3,250
McCAIN, Buck (20th C) American				
oil	1	800	800	800
3D	1	5,000	5,000	5,000
McCALL, Charles (1907-1989) British				
oil	6	712-1,392	1,082	1,062
McCALLUM, Andrew (1821-1902) British				
wc/d	2	518-11,340	5,929	518
McCALLUM, P (19th C) British				
oil	1	1,125	1,125	1,125
McCANCE, William (1894-1970) British				
oil	1	56,760	56,760	56,760
wc/d	1	1,342	1,342	1,342
MACCARI, Mino (1898-1989) Italian				
oil	56	572-19,667	5,398	4,411
wc/d	39	467-2,803	1,117	900
3D	2	4,772-4,772	4,772	4,772
McCARTER, Henry (1866-1947) American				
oil	1	2,500	2,500	2,500
McCARTHY, Doris Jean (1910-) Canadian				
oil	4	2,886-10,635	6,071	3,173
wc/d	8	1,394-5,483	2,918	2,604
McCARTHY, Frank (1924-2002) American				
oil	26	3,500-85,000	29,721	27,500
wc/d	2	5,500-5,700	5,600	5,500
McCARTHY, Justin (1892-1977) American				
oil	5	475-2,600	1,105	800
wc/d	1	400	400	400
McCARTHY, Paul (1945-) American				
wc/d	2	18,000-29,000	23,500	18,000
3D	4	26,000-492,800	319,700	380,000
McCAW, Dan (1942-) American				
oil	2	2,500-4,000	3,250	2,500
McCAW, Terence (1913-1979) South African				
oil	1	4,425	4,425	4,425
McCAY, Winsor (1869-1934) American				
wc/d	1	24,000	24,000	24,000
McCHESNEY, Clara Taggart (1860-1928) American				
oil	3	850-1,800	1,216	1,000
MACCIO, Gerard di (1948-) French				
oil	4	1,293-4,302	2,097	1,293
wc/d	1	2,213	2,213	2,213
MACCIO, Romulo (1931-) Argentinian				
oil	3	1,944-9,500	6,314	7,500
wc/d	1	26,900	26,900	26,900
McCLELLAND, Robert John (1906-1977) American				
oil	1	2,000	2,000	2,000

Name	No.	Price Range	Average	Median
McCLOSKEY, William J (1859-1941) American				
oil	1	100,000	100,000	100,000
McCLOY, Samuel (1831-1904) British				
oil	1	4,203	4,203	4,203
wc/d	2	4,600-6,429	5,514	4,600
McCLUNG, Florence (1896-1992) American				
oil	2	5,000-21,000	13,000	5,000
McCLURE, Daphne (1930-) British				
oil	3	498-1,021	752	739
wc/d	5	528-1,032	737	773
McCLURE, Darrell (1903-1987) American				
wc/d	1	1,800	1,800	1,800
McCLURE, David (1926-1998) British				
oil	13	900-16,020	5,840	4,325
wc/d	3	1,557-4,524	2,554	1,582
MACCO, Georg (1863-1933) German				
oil	16	440-40,000	6,744	2,625
wc/d	12	669-6,562	2,786	2,288
McCOLLUM, Allan (1944-) American				
oil	2	1,400-55,000	28,200	1,400
3D	6	6,000-35,200	19,386	16,500
McCOMAS, Francis (1874-1938) American				
oil	1	10,000	10,000	10,000
wc/d	5	2,250-22,500	9,750	8,500
McCOMB, Leonard (1930-) British				
oil	1	4,440	4,440	4,440
MACCONNEL, Kim (1946-) American				
oil	1	2,000	2,000	2,000
wc/d	5	1,000-2,250	1,310	1,100
McCORD, George (1848-1909) American				
oil	12	500-12,000	4,904	3,500
McCORD, Jake (20th C) American				
oil	3	800-1,600	1,233	1,300
MACCORD, Mary Nicholena (1864-1955) American				
oil	1	2,000	2,000	2,000
McCORMICK, Harry (1942-) American				
oil	4	1,200-1,700	1,425	1,350
McCORMICK, M Evelyn (1869-1948) American				
oil	1	22,500	22,500	22,500
McCORMICK, N E (19th C) American?				
oil	1	2,750	2,750	2,750
McCOUBREY, Sarah (1956-) American				
oil	2	1,200-2,900	2,050	1,200
McCOY, Wilton Guy (1902-1986) American				
oil	2	1,250-1,900	1,575	1,250
McCRACKEN, James (20th C) American				
oil	1	3,250	3,250	3,250
McCRACKEN, John (1934-) American				
oil	1	65,000	65,000	65,000
wc/d	1	984	984	984
3D	3	60,000-100,000	85,000	95,000
McCULLOCH, Horatio (1805-1867) British				
oil	2	495-28,160	14,327	495
McDERMOTT and McGOUGH (20th C) American				
oil	2	2,250-4,750	3,500	2,250
McDERMOTT, John R (1919-1977) American				
oil	1	1,500	1,500	1,500
MACDONALD, Alexander (1839-1921) British				
oil	1	4,232	4,232	4,232
MacDONALD, Arthur (fl.1897-1940) British				
oil	2	1,830-5,220	3,525	1,830
MACDONALD, Frances E (1874-1921) British				
wc/d	1	102,300	102,300	102,300
MACDONALD, Grant (1944-) American				
oil	2	2,000-6,500	4,250	2,000
MACDONALD, Grant Kenneth (1909-) Canadian				
oil	1	1,322	1,322	1,322
MACDONALD, James Edward Hervey (1873-1932) Canadian				
oil	9	21,318-688,863	170,689	72,938
wc/d	3	1,230-2,116	1,775	1,979
MACDONALD, James W G (1897-1960) Canadian				
oil	1	37,109	37,109	37,109

Name	No.	Price Range	Average	Median
MACDONALD, John Blake (1829-1901) British				
oil	3	622-50,120	17,493	1,739
MACDONALD, Manly Edward (1889-1971) Canadian				
oil	22	693-10,635	4,367	3,936
MACDONALD, Murray (fl.1889-1910) British				
oil	1	1,522	1,522	1,522
MACDONALD, W Alister (1861-c.1948) British				
wc/d	3	522-2,775	1,532	1,300
MACDONALD-WRIGHT, Stanton (1890-1973) American				
oil	6	3,250-31,000	10,698	6,000
wc/d	5	1,100-6,000	3,756	3,250
McDONNELL, Hector (1947-) British				
oil	5	1,097-30,245	11,530	1,903
McDOUGAL, John (?-1941) British				
wc/d	7	510-2,340	1,244	794
McDOWELL, William John Patton (1888-1950) British				
wc/d	1	2,838	2,838	2,838
McDUFF, Frederick H (1931-) American				
oil	3	650-3,186	1,945	2,000
MACE, Edward Churchill (1863-1928) South African				
oil	1	2,036	2,036	2,036
McELCHERAN, William (1927-1999) Canadian				
3D	6	3,175-28,000	13,386	9,019
McENTAGGART, Brett (1939-) Irish?				
oil	1	2,163	2,163	2,163
wc/d	1	1,018	1,018	1,018
McENTEE, Jervis (1828-1891) American				
oil	4	5,000-105,000	38,525	6,600
MACENTYRE, Eduardo (1929-) Argentinian				
oil	5	2,400-20,000	8,580	5,000
McEVOY, Ambrose (1878-1927) British				
oil	2	5,236-14,535	9,885	5,236
wc/d	5	600-2,301	1,053	859
McEVOY, Henry Nesbitt (1828-1914) Canadian				
oil	1	1,488	1,488	1,488
McEWEN, Jean (1923-1999) Canadian				
oil	13	3,732-49,479	20,721	21,270
wc/d	1	2,073	2,073	2,073
McEWEN, Walter (1860-1943) American				
oil	2	7,500-40,000	23,750	7,500
McFADYEN, Ron (1943-) Canadian				
oil	1	1,861	1,861	1,861
McFARLANE, Duncan (fl.1834-1871) British				
oil	1	22,000	22,000	22,000
McFARLANE, R (19th C) American				
oil	1	4,500	4,500	4,500
McFEE, Henry Lee (1886-1953) American				
oil	1	5,960	5,960	5,960
wc/d	1	600	600	600
McGARY, Dave (1958-) American				
3D	4	1,500-6,500	3,575	3,100
McGEE, Barry (1966-) American				
oil	1	15,500	15,500	15,500
wc/d	3	6,500-19,000	11,000	7,500
3D	4	3,000-10,000	5,812	4,750
MacGEORGE, William Stewart (1861-1931) British				
oil	4	7,480-14,080	10,386	8,352
McGHIE, John (1867-1952) British				
oil	13	792-22,125	10,102	8,996
McGILL, Eloise Polk (1868-1939) American				
oil	2	2,100-2,500	2,300	2,100
MACGINNIS, Henry R (1874-1962) American				
oil	1	2,100	2,100	2,100
MACGINNIS, Robert E (1926-) American				
oil	4	5,500-16,000	8,625	5,500
McGLYNN, Thomas A (1878-1966) American				
oil	1	5,500	5,500	5,500
McGONIGAL, Maurice (1900-1979) British				
oil	8	900-28,863	15,634	13,020
wc/d	1	666	666	666
McGOOGAN, Archibald (20th C) British				
wc/d	1	2,040	2,040	2,040

Name	No.	Price Range	Average	Median
McGORAN, Kieran (1932-1990) British				
wc/d	8	1,239-5,190	3,247	2,249
MACGOUN, Hannah C Preston (1864-1913) British				
oil	1	5,220	5,220	5,220
wc/d	1	8,900	8,900	8,900
McGRATH, Clarence (20th C) American				
oil	2	600-1,400	1,000	600
McGRATH, Raymond (1903-1977) Irish				
wc/d	3	554-3,180	1,490	737
McGREGOR, Robert (1848-1922) British				
oil	18	750-40,767	7,626	4,248
McGREW, Ralph Brownell (1916-1994) American				
oil	9	2,300-170,000	33,144	10,000
wc/d	2	6,500-11,000	8,750	6,500
3D	1	11,000	11,000	11,000
McGUINNESS, Norah (1903-1980) British				
oil	10	7,200-267,534	48,004	22,685
wc/d	8	763-17,877	6,394	4,005
McGUINNESS, Tom (20th C) British				
oil	3	2,775-10,726	5,526	3,078
wc/d	5	709-2,595	1,361	1,110
McGUINNESS, William Bingham (1849-1928) British				
wc/d	23	369-3,649	1,424	1,272
McGUIRE, Edward (1932-1986) Irish				
oil	2	17,671-40,329	29,000	17,671
McGURL, Joseph (1958-) American				
oil	1	10,000	10,000	10,000
MACH, David (1956-) British				
wc/d	2	7,958-8,850	8,404	7,958
3D	2	5,143-10,380	7,761	5,143
MACHADO, Juares (1941-) South American				
oil	1	23,356	23,356	23,356
MACHADO, Rico (20th C) ?				
oil	2	840-1,160	1,000	840
MACHAIN, Paul (20th C) French				
oil	1	1,200	1,200	1,200
MACHELL, R (fl.1881-1900) British				
oil	1	2,500	2,500	2,500
MACHELL, Reginald (fl.1881-1900) British				
oil	2	1,817-10,813	6,315	1,817
MACHETANZ, Fred (1908-2002) American				
oil	1	8,000	8,000	8,000
MACHIN (?) ?				
oil	1	3,041	3,041	3,041
McILHENNY, Charles Morgan (1858-c.1908) American				
oil	1	15,000	15,000	15,000
McINNES, Alex (19th C) British				
oil	1	1,700	1,700	1,700
McINNIS, Robert (1942-) Canadian				
oil	5	798-4,055	2,115	2,050
McINTOSH, Archibald Dunbar (1936-) British				
oil	2	708-1,505	1,106	708
McINTOSH, Dwight (20th C) American?				
oil	1	1,900	1,900	1,900
wc/d	3	2,400-3,300	2,800	2,700
McINTOSH, Newton (19th C) American?				
oil	1	3,400	3,400	3,400
McINTYRE, Donald (1923-) British				
oil	65	1,062-10,620	3,344	2,992
wc/d	4	1,203-2,523	1,726	1,440
MACINTYRE, James (1926-) British				
oil	4	1,730-7,501	4,172	2,503
wc/d	3	673-2,076	1,340	1,272
McINTYRE, Joseph Wrightson (fl.1866-1888) British				
oil	5	874-4,928	2,820	2,941
MACK, Bill (1949-) American				
3D	1	1,325	1,325	1,325
MACK, Heinz (1931-) German				
oil	7	3,312-21,658	9,180	7,655
wc/d	5	10,829-27,096	21,585	22,898
3D	12	2,293-33,123	11,763	7,658

Name	No.	Price Range	Average	Median
MACK, Leal (1892-1962) American				
oil	3	700-4,800	2,300	1,400
McKAIN, Bruce (1900-1990) American				
oil	3	1,500-5,000	3,066	2,700
McKAY, Arthur Fortesque (1926-) Canadian				
oil	1	3,767	3,767	3,767
wc/d	1	8,246	8,246	8,246
McKAY, Frances H (1880-?) American				
oil	2	600-2,250	1,425	600
MACKAY, James M (19/20th C) British				
oil	1	1,462	1,462	1,462
wc/d	1	3,382	3,382	3,382
MACKAY, Thomas (19/20th C) British				
wc/d	6	473-3,186	1,403	1,388
McKAY, William Darling (1844-1924) British				
oil	6	783-29,920	5,992	1,131
MACKE, August (1887-1914) German				
oil	6	73,920-668,800	211,524	106,200
wc/d	13	1,440-55,000	19,645	21,795
MACKE, Helmuth (1891-1936) German				
wc/d	2	2,182-2,719	2,450	2,182
McKEAN, Graham (20th C) British				
oil	1	1,131	1,131	1,131
McKEEVER, Ian (1946-) British				
oil	1	5,984	5,984	5,984
wc/d	1	3,520	3,520	3,520
MACKELDEY, Karl Bernhard (1826-1890) German				
oil	1	2,803	2,803	2,803
McKELL, James (1885-1956) American				
oil	1	1,300	1,300	1,300
McKELLAR, Jerry (20th C) American				
3D	1	8,000	8,000	8,000
McKELVEY, Frank (1895-1974) Irish				
oil	13	6,324-120,164	27,393	16,069
wc/d	9	531-24,205	10,449	8,938
MACKEN, Marc (1913-1977) Belgian				
3D	1	2,890	2,890	2,890
McKENNA, Stephen (1939-) Irish?				
oil	1	7,068	7,068	7,068
MACKENNAL, Sir Edgar Bertram (1863-1931) Australian				
3D	1	34,020	34,020	34,020
MACKENSEN, Fritz (1866-1953) German				
oil	2	2,186-3,390	2,788	2,186
MACKENZIE, Alexander (1923-2002) British				
oil	5	3,560-25,480	11,108	6,920
MACKENZIE, Frederick (1787-1854) British				
wc/d	1	1,019	1,019	1,019
MACKENZIE, Hugh Seaforth (1928-) Canadian				
oil	1	2,474	2,474	2,474
McKENZIE, James Wilson (fl.1888-1890) British				
oil	1	1,496	1,496	1,496
MACKENZIE, John (fl.1924-1971) British				
3D	1	1,903	1,903	1,903
MACKENZIE, Marie Henrie (1878-1961) Dutch				
oil	8	882-5,425	3,249	3,254
MACKENZIE, William Gibbes (1857-1924) British				
oil	3	850-2,422	1,857	2,301
McKENZIE, Winifred (1905-?) British				
oil	1	1,110	1,110	1,110
MACKEOWN, James (1961-) British				
oil	2	3,717-4,767	4,242	3,717
MACKEPRANG, Adolf (1833-1911) Danish				
oil	11	635-5,946	2,521	2,022
McKERAN, David (1963-) British				
oil	1	1,850	1,850	1,850
MACKEY, Kim (20th C) American				
oil	7	1,100-5,500	3,142	3,000
MACKIE, Charles H (1862-1920) British				
oil	4	500-1,253	1,010	1,044
wc/d	1	2,744	2,744	2,744

Name	No.	Price Range	Average	Median
MACKIE, John (1953-) British				
oil	4	452-1,740	847	589
wc/d	6	661-1,539	975	821
MACKIE, Peter R M (1867-1959) British				
oil	1	1,373	1,373	1,373
McKIE, Todd (20th C) American?				
oil	2	1,200-1,300	1,250	1,200
wc/d	1	425	425	425
McKIM, Charles C (1872-1939) American				
oil	2	5,000-12,000	8,500	5,000
MACKINNON (19/20th C) British				
oil	1	3,766	3,766	3,766
MACKINNON, Hugh (1925-) British				
oil	2	1,203-1,295	1,249	1,203
MACKINNON, Sine (1901-1997) British				
oil	1	2,232	2,232	2,232
McKINSTRY, Cherith (1928-2004) British				
oil	1	5,086	5,086	5,086
MACKINTOSH, Charles Rennie (1868-1928) British				
wc/d	2	4,248-9,204	6,726	4,248
MACKINTOSH, Margaret MacDonald (1864-1933) British				
wc/d	1	23,010	23,010	23,010
MACKLIN, Thomas Eyre (1867-1943) British				
oil	2	1,427-10,000	5,713	1,427
MACKNIGHT, Dodge (1860-1950) American				
wc/d	3	1,800-3,750	3,016	3,500
McKNIGHT, Robert Johnson (1905-1989) American				
3D	1	1,900	1,900	1,900
MACKOWIAK, Erwin (1926-) Belgian				
oil	3	707-2,625	1,595	1,455
MACKRILL, Martyn (1961-) British				
oil	3	8,700-20,570	13,756	12,000
wc/d	4	1,870-4,675	2,625	1,870
McLANE, Kelly (1968-) American				
oil	1	8,500	8,500	8,500
McLANE, Myrtle Jean (1878-1964) American				
oil	5	3,250-30,000	14,350	16,000
McLAREN, Charlotte G (fl.1895-1932) British				
oil	1	1,158	1,158	1,158
McLAREN, Peter (20th C) British				
oil	1	1,392	1,392	1,392
wc/d	2	895-957	926	895
McLARNON, Samuel (1911-) British				
oil	4	673-797	717	692
wc/d	1	433	433	433
McLAUGHLIN, Gerald (1925-) American				
oil	2	1,200-2,200	1,700	1,200
McLAUGHLIN, John (1898-1976) American				
oil	1	28,000	28,000	28,000
McLAUGHLIN, Nancy (1932-1984) American				
wc/d	1	9,000	9,000	9,000
McLAUGHLIN, Robert Samuel (20th C) Canadian				
oil	1	1,939	1,939	1,939
McLEA, John Watson (19th C) British				
oil	2	1,214-1,647	1,430	1,214
McLEAN, Bruce (1942-) British				
oil	4	985-3,043	1,717	1,343
wc/d	3	2,314-5,096	4,012	4,628
McLEAN, John (1939-) British				
oil	4	555-2,478	1,410	740
wc/d	1	487	487	487
McLEAN, Richard (1934-) American				
wc/d	1	7,000	7,000	7,000
McLEAN, Thomas Wesley (1881-1951) Canadian				
oil	1	4,250	4,250	4,250
MacLEAN, Will (1941-) British				
3D	1	6,265	6,265	6,265
MACLEAN, William T (20th C) British				
oil	1	1,104	1,104	1,104
McLEOD, John (19th C) British				
oil	2	577-8,448	4,512	577

Name	No.	Price Range	Average	Median
MACLET, Elisee (1881-1962) French				
oil	63	894-9,219	4,003	3,387
wc/d	34	425-2,330	924	777
MACLET, Maurice (1860-1940) French				
oil	1	2,510	2,510	2,510
MACLISE, Daniel (1806-1870) British/Irish				
oil	1	2,024	2,024	2,024
wc/d	2	2,797-7,068	4,932	2,797
McLOUGHLIN, Rosemary (20th C) Irish?				
oil	3	1,030-2,906	1,917	1,815
McMANAWAY, David (1927-) American				
oil	1	2,100	2,100	2,100
McMASTER, James (1856-1913) British				
wc/d	6	588-6,195	2,858	1,211
MACMIADHACHAIN, Padraig (1929-) Irish				
oil	16	833-3,363	1,619	1,401
wc/d	2	1,116-1,328	1,222	1,116
MACMONNIES, Frederick William (1863-1937) American				
3D	5	8,000-24,000	17,400	21,000
MACMONNIES, Mary Fairchild (1858-1946) American				
oil	3	1,300-15,000	6,850	4,250
McNAIRN, Caroline (1955-) British				
oil	1	1,408	1,408	1,408
wc/d	2	573-589	581	573
McNAMARA, Desmond (1916-) Irish				
3D	1	2,338	2,338	2,338
MACNAUGHTON, John H (?) Canadian?				
wc/d	2	1,640-1,814	1,727	1,640
MACNEE, Robert Russell (1880-1952) British				
oil	7	512-10,680	3,561	915
McNEIL, George (1908-1995) American				
oil	3	1,700-2,750	2,150	2,000
wc/d	1	4,000	4,000	4,000
McNELLIS, Laura Craig (1957-) American				
oil	1	650	650	650
wc/d	1	1,100	1,100	1,100
McNICOLL, Helen Galloway (1879-1915) Canadian				
oil	2	145,877-210,711	178,294	145,877
McPHAIL, Roger (1953-) British				
wc/d	1	5,160	5,160	5,160
MACPHERSON, Earl (1910-1993) American				
wc/d	1	3,750	3,750	3,750
MACPHERSON, John (fl.1865-1884) British				
wc/d	3	491-3,780	1,644	661
MACPHERSON, Kevin (1956-) American				
oil	3	750-4,500	2,183	1,300
MACPHERSON, R T (19th C) British				
wc/d	1	3,560	3,560	3,560
MACPHERSON, Sophie (1957-) British				
oil	1	1,138	1,138	1,138
MACQUOID, Percy (1852-1925) British				
oil	1	4,956	4,956	4,956
MACRAE, Elmer (1875-1953) American				
oil	6	2,500-70,000	18,583	4,750
wc/d	1	1,000	1,000	1,000
MACREAU, Michel (1935-1995) French				
oil	6	454-6,780	3,244	2,571
wc/d	2	1,942-2,201	2,071	1,942
MACRUM, George (1888-?) American				
oil	2	1,000-1,100	1,050	1,000
MACS, Yan (1933-1993) Latvian				
oil	1	1,000	1,000	1,000
McSWEENEY, Sean (1935-) Irish				
oil	16	1,590-15,315	5,449	4,117
wc/d	1	3,708	3,708	3,708
McSWINEY, Eugène (1866-1936) British				
oil	1	5,933	5,933	5,933
MacTAGGART, Sir William (1903-1981) British				
oil	10	595-38,940	10,655	4,325
wc/d	2	800-800	800	800

Name	No.	Price Range	Average	Median
McTAGGART, William (1835-1910) British				
oil	17	2,150-158,400	39,034	31,680
wc/d	7	1,238-8,850	4,642	5,190
McVICKER, Jesse Jay (1911-) American				
oil	4	700-1,000	925	1,000
wc/d	3	700-2,500	1,566	1,500
MacWHIRTER, John (1839-1911) British				
oil	14	484-44,000	6,562	2,379
wc/d	7	460-3,168	1,243	833
McWILLIAM, Frederick Edward (1909-1992) British				
wc/d	7	885-4,909	1,965	1,753
3D	11	4,750-55,800	24,673	27,900
McWILLIAMS, Joe (1938-) Irish				
wc/d	1	1,947	1,947	1,947
MACY, William Ferdinand (1852-1901) American				
oil	1	19,000	19,000	19,000
MACZNIK, Jacob (1905-1945) Polish				
oil	1	1,430	1,430	1,430
MADDALENA, Salvatore (1875-1957) Italian				
oil	1	5,825	5,825	5,825
MADDEN, Anne (1932-) British				
oil	1	5,096	5,096	5,096
MADDERSON, Arthur K (20th C) Irish?				
oil	1	7,304	7,304	7,304
wc/d	1	7,068	7,068	7,068
MADDOX, Conroy (1912-2004) British				
oil	4	900-4,176	2,345	1,500
wc/d	6	1,068-1,881	1,418	1,239
MADELAIN, Gustave (1867-1944) French				
oil	11	941-5,437	2,765	2,788
MADELINE, Paul (1863-1920) French				
oil	16	1,240-35,150	9,553	7,613
wc/d	1	837	837	837
MADERSON, Arthur (1942-) British				
oil	16	443-12,714	4,701	3,307
wc/d	1	727	727	727
MADIAI, Mario (1944-) Italian				
oil	8	630-2,386	1,230	1,134
MADIOL, Adrien Jean (1845-1892) Dutch				
oil	2	2,546-3,687	3,116	2,546
MADLENER, Josef (1881-1967) German				
oil	1	1,360	1,360	1,360
MADONINI, Giovanni (1915-) Italian				
oil	1	1,300	1,300	1,300
MADOU, Jean Baptiste (1796-1877) Belgian				
oil	2	584-6,301	3,442	584
wc/d	10	993-2,805	1,459	1,286
MADRASSI, Luca (1848-1919) Italian				
3D	2	4,077-15,288	9,682	4,077
MADRASSI, Ludovic Lucien (1881-1956) French				
wc/d	1	1,678	1,678	1,678
MADRAZO Y GARRETA, Raimundo de (1841-1920) Spanish				
oil	6	4,243-170,000	36,962	8,784
MADRAZO Y KUNTZ, don Federigo de (1815-1894) Spanish				
oil	3	4,469-7,658	5,537	4,485
wc/d	2	1,665-1,783	1,724	1,665
MADRIGALI, Olynthe (1887-1950) Moroccan?				
oil	1	1,438	1,438	1,438
MADRITSCH, Karl (1908-1986) Swiss				
oil	1	855	855	855
wc/d	2	624-1,218	921	624
MADSEN, Alfred (20th C) Danish				
oil	2	809-1,462	1,135	809
wc/d	1	974	974	974
MADSEN, Andreas Peter (1822-1911) Danish				
oil	1	3,816	3,816	3,816
MADSEN, Karl (1855-1938) Danish				
oil	1	1,630	1,630	1,630
MADSEN, Sophie (1829-1856) Danish				
oil	2	1,452-8,150	4,801	1,452
MADURA, Jean (19/20th C) Italian				
oil	1	2,917	2,917	2,917

Name	No.	Price Range	Average	Median
MADYOL, Jacques (1874-1950) Belgian				
oil	8	643-1,907	1,048	835
MAEDA, Josaku (1926-) Japanese				
oil	2	1,499-4,500	2,999	1,499
MAEGT, Johan de (?) Belgian				
3D	1	2,253	2,253	2,253
MAENPAA, Arvid (1899-1976) Finnish				
oil	2	855-1,171	1,013	855
wc/d	1	1,260	1,260	1,260
MAENTEL, Jacob (1763-1863) American				
wc/d	2	3,250-400,855	202,052	3,250
MAEROFF, Adam (20th C) American				
	2	800-1,700	1,250	800
MAERTELAERE, Edmond de (1876-1938) Belgian				
oil	1	5,611	5,611	5,611
MAERTENS, Medard (1875-1946) Belgian				
oil	4	501-10,639	3,219	722
MAES, Agnes (1942-) Belgian				
oil	1	3,612	3,612	3,612
MAES, Eugène Remy (1849-1931) Belgian				
oil	7	1,668-25,479	9,199	7,000
MAES, Godfried (1649-1700) Flemish				
wc/d	1	1,635	1,635	1,635
MAES, Jacques (1905-1968) Belgian				
oil	3	1,076-3,579	2,029	1,432
MAES, Nicolaes (1632-1693) Dutch				
oil	10	5,000-1,211,000	150,413	28,027
MAES, Pieter van (17th C) Dutch				
oil	1	27,500	27,500	27,500
MAESTOSI, Fortunato (19th C) Italian				
oil	1	24,974	24,974	24,974
MAESTRI, Michelangelo (?-1812) Italian				
wc/d	5	2,200-16,473	8,461	7,159
MAET, Marc (1955-) Belgian				
oil	3	927-3,596	1,858	1,051
MAETZEL, Emil (1877-1955) German				
oil	2	2,160-4,607	3,383	2,160
wc/d	5	505-1,111	727	589
MAETZEL-JOHANNSEN, Dorothea (1886-1930) German				
wc/d	2	509-2,548	1,528	509
MAEXMONTAN, Frans (1847-1901) Finnish				
oil	1	4,195	4,195	4,195
MAEYENS, Mil (1882-1952) Belgian				
oil	1	1,193	1,193	1,193
MAEYER, Marcel (1920-) Belgian				
oil	1	1,806	1,806	1,806
MAEZTU, Gustavo de (1887-1947) Spanish				
oil	1	11,127	11,127	11,127
wc/d	1	3,315	3,315	3,315
MAFAI, Antonietta Raphael (1900-1975) Italian				
3D	1	7,707	7,707	7,707
MAFAI, Mario (1902-1965) Italian				
oil	3	5,856-33,075	21,154	24,531
MAFFEI, Francesco (1620-1660) Italian				
wc/d	1	4,070	4,070	4,070
MAFFEI, Guido von (1838-1924) German				
oil	1	5,611	5,611	5,611
MAFFEI, Ricardo (1953-) Latin American				
oil	2	3,891-5,000	4,445	3,891
MAFLI, Walter (1915-) Swiss				
oil	6	419-6,079	1,882	567
wc/d	1	571	571	571
MAGAFAN, Ethel (1916-) American				
oil	2	500-2,600	1,550	500
MAGANZA, Alessandro (1556-1630) Italian				
oil	1	10,656	10,656	10,656
wc/d	2	800-14,000	7,400	800
MAGATTI, Pietro Antonio (1687-1768) Italian				
oil	1	21,857	21,857	21,857
MAGAUD, Dominique (1817-1899) French				
oil	1	1,883	1,883	1,883

Name	No.	Price Range	Average	Median
MAGAZZINI, Salvatore (1955-) Italian				
oil	38	502-2,059	1,107	983
MAGEE, Alan (1947-) American				
oil	2	12,000-75,000	43,500	12,000
wc/d	3	3,000-6,500	4,466	3,900
MAGGI, Cesare (1881-1961) Italian				
oil	10	2,395-96,680	24,856	14,531
MAGGI, Lorenzo (19/20th C) Italian?				
oil	1	13,521	13,521	13,521
MAGGIONE, Piero (1931-1995) Italian				
oil	6	707-2,718	1,978	1,920
wc/d	4	1,295-6,361	4,061	2,589
MAGGIOTTO, Domenico (1713-1794) Italian				
oil	2	7,400-24,196	15,798	7,400
MAGGS, John Charles (1819-1896) British				
oil	5	1,900-7,568	3,688	3,000
MAGHETTI, Giovanni (19th C) Italian				
oil	1	10,776	10,776	10,776
MAGIASSIS, Vassilis (1880-1926) Greek				
oil	2	3,872-14,080	8,976	3,872
MAGILL, Elizabeth (1959-) British				
oil	1	1,328	1,328	1,328
MAGILL, R C (1881-1950) American				
oil	1	3,750	3,750	3,750
MAGILL, Roscoe Clarence (1881-1950) American				
oil	1	7,000	7,000	7,000
MAGINI, Carlo (1720-1806) Italian				
oil	2	50,363-138,400	94,381	50,363
MAGNASCO, Alessandro (1667-1749) Italian				
oil	3	9,105-127,397	60,500	45,000
wc/d	2	1,557-5,104	3,330	1,557
MAGNE, Desire Alfred (1855-1936) French				
oil	1	4,350	4,350	4,350
MAGNELLI, Alberto (1888-1971) Italian				
oil	8	10,130-174,000	64,782	45,796
wc/d	8	756-7,274	2,665	1,752
MAGNI, Giuseppe (1869-1956) Italian				
oil	11	480-22,000	4,952	780
MAGNUS, Camille (1850-?) French				
oil	3	1,094-5,184	2,678	1,757
MAGNUSSON, Ragnvald (1904-1984) Swedish				
oil	3	2,036-3,436	2,550	2,180
MAGRITTE, René (1898-1967) Belgian				
oil	6	222,534-2,200,000	741,189	470,000
wc/d	19	5,724-1,091,200	292,198	75,000
MAGROTTI, Ercole (1890-1958) Italian				
oil	5	559-1,940	1,210	1,147
MAGUIRE, Cecil (1930-) British				
oil	17	1,557-21,014	8,792	7,866
MAGUIRE, Gerard (20th C) British				
oil	2	1,038-1,211	1,124	1,038
MAGUIRE, Robert (1921-2005) American				
oil	1	2,700	2,700	2,700
MAHAFFEY, Josephine (1903-1982) American				
oil	2	600-2,500	1,550	600
wc/d	7	500-2,000	985	800
MAHAFFEY, Merrill (1937-) American				
oil	1	16,000	16,000	16,000
MAHE, Joseph (20th C) French				
oil	1	2,689	2,689	2,689
MAHLKNECHT, Edmund (1820-1903) Austrian				
oil	7	3,024-15,811	6,801	5,890
MAHONEY, James (1816-1879) Irish				
wc/d	1	1,131	1,131	1,131
MAHRINGER, Anton (1902-1974) German				
oil	1	57,048	57,048	57,048
wc/d	1	3,514	3,514	3,514
MAHU, Cornelis (1613-1689) Flemish				
oil	5	5,633-69,600	25,524	16,650
MAHU, Victor (?-1700) Flemish				
oil	1	11,302	11,302	11,302

Name	No.	Price Range	Average	Median
MAHY, Émile (1903-) Belgian				
oil	3	760-2,421	1,839	2,338
MAI THU (1906-1980) Vietnamese				
oil	5	7,438-12,123	8,760	7,810
wc/d	5	2,016-19,456	12,005	17,976
MAIDMENT, Henry (19/20th C) British				
oil	4	630-3,238	1,569	845
wc/d	1	676	676	676
MAIER, John (1819-1877) American				
oil	1	1,800	1,800	1,800
MAIGNAN, Albert Pierre René (1845-1908) French				
wc/d	1	1,445	1,445	1,445
MAIGRET, Jacobus Adrianus (1812-1893) Dutch				
oil	1	1,036	1,036	1,036
MAILE, Ben (1900-) British				
oil	9	463-1,602	958	974
wc/d	1	974	974	974
MAILICK, Alfred (1869-?) German?				
oil	1	1,452	1,452	1,452
MAILLARD, Émile (1846-1926) French				
oil	1	1,695	1,695	1,695
MAILLART, Diogene Ulysse Napoleon (1840-1926) French				
oil	1	28,000	28,000	28,000
MAILLART, Jean Denis (1913-) French				
oil	1	1,374	1,374	1,374
MAILLAUD, Fernand (1863-1948) French				
oil	11	1,721-14,875	4,491	3,038
wc/d	1	6,037	6,037	6,037
MAILLOL, Aristide (1861-1944) French				
oil	1	37,808	37,808	37,808
wc/d	24	1,414-26,610	6,531	3,540
3D	14	46,849-2,500,000	639,307	220,000
MAIN, Irene Lesley (20th C) British				
oil	1	1,418	1,418	1,418
MAINARDI, Sebastiano (1460-1513) Italian				
oil	1	80,000	80,000	80,000
MAINDRON, Hippolyte (1801-1884) French				
3D	1	2,674	2,674	2,674
MAINELLA, Raffaele (1858-1907) Italian				
wc/d	9	589-6,473	2,194	1,991
MAINGAUD, Martin (17th C) French				
oil	3	9,633-15,653	11,639	9,633
MAINOLFI, Luigi (1948-) Italian				
wc/d	6	1,219-5,696	2,758	2,195
3D	9	2,926-14,630	7,740	8,247
MAINSSIEUX, Lucien (1885-1958) French				
oil	5	790-3,397	1,421	1,014
wc/d	1	518	518	518
MAIOLO, Francesco (1940-) Italian				
oil	1	1,133	1,133	1,133
MAIPAS, Themos (1936-1996) Greek				
oil	1	3,740	3,740	3,740
MAIR, Cornelius de (1944-) Dutch				
oil	1	6,429	6,429	6,429
MAIRE, Andre (1898-1985) French				
oil	13	2,225-8,429	5,315	4,712
wc/d	54	468-6,743	2,298	1,686
MAIRE, Ferdinand Henri (1901-1963) Swiss				
oil	2	458-2,331	1,394	458
MAIRHOFER, H (19th C) ?				
oil	1	3,575	3,575	3,575
MAIROVICH, Zvi (1911-1973) Israeli				
oil	12	850-4,000	2,300	1,800
wc/d	5	400-4,500	1,614	550
MAIRWOGER, Gottfried (1951-) Austrian				
oil	1	1,499	1,499	1,499
MAISONNEUVE, Louis (?-1926) French				
oil	1	1,911	1,911	1,911
MAISSEN, Fernand (1873-?) French				
wc/d	1	1,236	1,236	1,236
MAISTRE, Xavier de (1763-1852) French				
oil	1	19,110	19,110	19,110

Name	No.	Price Range	Average	Median
MAITLAND, Paul (1869-1909) British				
oil	4	983-3,660	2,348	1,620
MAITY, Paresh (1965-) Indian				
oil	1	25,000	25,000	25,000
wc/d	1	27,500	27,500	27,500
MAJERUS, Michel (1967-2002) American?				
oil	3	38,219-59,200	46,039	40,700
MAJEWICZ, George (1897-1965) German?				
oil	3	995-3,096	2,395	3,096
MAJOR, Theodore (1908-1999) British				
oil	16	3,132-42,525	12,786	8,496
wc/d	9	661-3,540	1,462	1,239
MAJORELLE, Jacques (1886-1962) French				
oil	19	1,832-217,292	47,792	7,940
wc/d	12	3,045-187,397	84,414	103,906
MAJORES, Rosso H (1911-1996) German				
oil	1	1,113	1,113	1,113
MAK, Paul (1891-1967) Russian				
wc/d	10	1,260-8,136	3,121	2,827
MAKAROV, Ivan Kozmich (1822-1897) Russian				
oil	2	27,900-343,973	185,936	27,900
MAKAROV, Nikolai (1952-) Russian				
wc/d	1	4,995	4,995	4,995
MAKART, Hans (1840-1884) Austrian				
oil	6	1,881-223,836	44,214	8,247
MAKI (20th C) ?				
oil	1	5,845	5,845	5,845
MAKILA, Otto (1904-1955) Finnish				
oil	5	719-95,548	20,491	2,342
MAKK, Americo (1927-) American/Hungarian				
oil	1	2,000	2,000	2,000
MAKOKIAN, Vartan (1869-1937) Armenian				
oil	2	7,714-19,530	13,622	7,714
MAKOVSKAIA, Aleksandra Egorovna (1837-1915) Russian				
oil	2	4,325-197,466	100,895	4,325
MAKOVSKY, Konstantin (1839-1915) Russian				
oil	21	6,000-1,656,164	238,591	47,880
wc/d	11	558-17,362	4,925	2,232
MAKOVSKY, Vladimir (1846-1920) Russian				
oil	9	10,703-360,000	120,875	86,000
wc/d	10	3,420-82,808	29,899	19,007
MAKOWSKI, Alexander W (1869-1924) Russian				
oil	6	7,224-199,420	82,165	25,826
wc/d	1	1,740	1,740	1,740
MAKOWSKI, Tade (1882-1932) Polish				
oil	1	24,276	24,276	24,276
wc/d	1	6,574	6,574	6,574
MAKOWSKI, Zbigniew (1930-) Polish				
wc/d	1	2,800	2,800	2,800
MAKROULAKIS, Michalis (1940-) Greek				
oil	2	3,344-32,130	17,737	3,344
MAKROZHITSKY, Viktor (1924-) Russian				
oil	1	17,700	17,700	17,700
MAKS, Cornelis Johannes (1876-1967) Dutch				
oil	6	4,477-280,541	68,855	19,082
MAKSIMENKO, Taras Nikitiyevich (1884-1972) Russian				
oil	1	4,162	4,162	4,162
MAKULA, Angelo (1959-) Austrian				
oil	1	1,808	1,808	1,808
MALACARNE, Claudio (1956-) Italian				
oil	3	1,081-1,411	1,270	1,318
MALAGODI, Giuseppe (1890-1968) Italian				
oil	3	778-1,641	1,118	937
MALANCA, Jose (1897-1967) Argentinian				
oil	5	4,900-20,000	10,880	8,500
MALANGA, Gerard and WARHOL, Andy (20th C) American				
wc/d	1	68,800	68,800	68,800
MALANI, Nalini (1946-) Indian				
oil	2	8,500-18,000	13,250	8,500
wc/d	3	4,000-10,000	6,166	4,500
MALASSIS, Edmond (19/20th C) French?				
wc/d	2	1,110-1,169	1,139	1,110

Name	No.	Price Range	Average	Median
MALATESTA, Adeodato (1806-1891) Italian				
oil	1	7,339	7,339	7,339
MALATESTA, Narciso (1835-?) Italian				
oil	2	1,400-9,062	5,231	1,400
MALAVAL, Robert (1937-1980) French				
oil	4	12,884-38,104	22,743	19,325
wc/d	2	935-937	936	935
3D	2	3,709-35,068	19,388	3,709
MALDARELLI, Federico (1826-1893) Italian				
oil	4	764-13,230	5,359	2,945
MALDARELLI, Oronzio (1892-1963) American/Italian				
3D	1	15,000	15,000	15,000
MALDEREN, Jan van (1883-?) Belgian				
oil	1	2,160	2,160	2,160
MALDONADO, Alexander (1901-1989) American				
oil	2	1,500-1,500	1,500	1,500
MALDURA, Giovanni (?-1849) Italian				
oil	1	9,158	9,158	9,158
MALEAS, Constantine (1879-1928) Greek				
oil	4	43,500-78,540	62,300	63,580
wc/d	1	54,810	54,810	54,810
MALEMPRE, Leo (fl.1887-1901) British				
oil	1	2,062	2,062	2,062
MALESPINA, Louis Ferdinand (1874-1940) French				
oil	2	1,427-1,519	1,473	1,427
wc/d	1	1,229	1,229	1,229
MALET, Albert (1905-1986) French				
oil	4	1,084-2,577	1,897	1,780
MALEVICH, Kasimir (1878-1935) Russian				
wc/d	4	10,010-70,686	49,037	44,767
MALEWSKY, S de (1905-1973) Russian				
oil	1	2,027	2,027	2,027
MALFAIT, Hubert (1898-1971) Belgian				
oil	4	1,870-21,575	12,078	5,733
wc/d	1	1,784	1,784	1,784
MALFRAY, Charles Alexandre (1887-1940) French				
3D	1	6,195	6,195	6,195
MALFROY (19/20th C) French				
oil	1	2,664	2,664	2,664
MALFROY, Charles (1862-1918) French				
oil	2	4,200-6,300	5,250	4,200
MALFROY, Henry (1895-1944) French				
oil	13	1,036-8,182	4,516	4,607
MALHARRO, Martin (1865-1911) Argentinian				
oil	1	14,000	14,000	14,000
MALHERBE, William (1884-1951) French				
oil	5	700-2,930	1,529	1,100
MALHOTRA, K K (20th C) Indian?				
oil	1	1,400	1,400	1,400
MALI, Christian (1832-1906) German				
oil	5	1,273-8,767	3,547	2,700
MALIAVINE, Philippe (1869-1940) Russian				
oil	12	17,362-464,400	156,033	94,600
wc/d	8	561-6,880	2,816	2,580
MALICOAT, Philip Cecil (1908-1981) American				
oil	1	2,200	2,200	2,200
wc/d	1	700	700	700
MALINCONICO, Nicola (1654-1721) Italian				
oil	1	27,185	27,185	27,185
MALINOVSKY, Anton Vladislavovich (1856-?) Russian				
oil	2	18,920-65,100	42,010	18,920
MALINOWSKI, Arno (?) ?				
3D	2	7,114-9,378	8,246	7,114
MALINOWSKY, Lise (1957-) Danish				
oil	8	2,897-7,243	4,753	4,185
MALINVERNI, Angelo (1877-1947) Italian				
oil	1	1,203	1,203	1,203
MALINVERNO, Atilio (1890-1936) Argentinian				
oil	3	1,350-9,200	4,080	1,690
MALIOUTIN, Serge (1859-1937) Russian				
wc/d	2	832-2,141	1,486	832

Name	No.	Price Range	Average	Median
MALISSARD, Georges (1877-1942) French				
3D	1	19,287	19,287	19,287
MALKOV, Kirill (20th C) Russian				
oil	2	805-1,657	1,231	805
MALLE, Charles (1935-) French				
oil	13	1,246-3,073	1,948	1,786
wc/d	1	834	834	834
MALLEBRANCHE, Louis-Claude (1790-1838) French				
oil	4	2,815-13,938	9,415	9,000
MALLET, Jean Baptiste (1759-1835) French				
wc/d	4	911-47,500	22,427	20,217
MALLINA, Erich (1873-1954) Austrian				
wc/d	1	1,262	1,262	1,262
MALLO, Cristino (1905-1987) Spanish				
wc/d	6	541-999	672	586
3D	2	5,648-17,014	11,331	5,648
MALLOL SUAZO, Josep M (1910-1986) Spanish				
oil	2	5,986-5,986	5,986	5,986
MALMSTROM, August (1829-1901) Swedish				
oil	5	806-86,000	18,620	1,572
MALNOVITZER, Zvi (1945-) Israeli				
oil	5	2,200-16,000	9,880	12,000
MALONEY, Robert (20th C) ?				
wc/d	1	1,649	1,649	1,649
MALSKAT, Lothar (1913-1988) German				
oil	1	1,520	1,520	1,520
wc/d	4	643-2,443	1,495	1,030
MALTESTE, Louis (1862-1928) French				
wc/d	2	1,285-1,401	1,343	1,285
MALTEZOS, Yannis (1915-1987) Greek				
wc/d	1	4,114	4,114	4,114
MALTINO, Francis (?) Italian				
oil	1	5,236	5,236	5,236
MALTON, Thomas (jnr) (1748-1804) British				
wc/d	1	13,050	13,050	13,050
MALVANO, Ugo (1878-1952) Italian				
oil	1	1,625	1,625	1,625
MALY, August Ritter von (1835-?) Austrian				
oil	2	62,612-72,245	67,428	62,612
MALYSHEV, Nikolai Tarasievich (1851-?) Russian				
oil	1	32,680	32,680	32,680
MALZAHN, Jerry (1946-) American				
oil	1	2,000	2,000	2,000
MAMBOR, Renato (1936-) Italian				
oil	10	1,694-21,604	4,959	2,299
wc/d	10	1,767-14,317	4,692	2,682
MAMBOUR, Auguste (1896-1968) Belgian				
oil	6	4,325-15,948	11,526	12,858
wc/d	6	514-7,730	3,380	1,401
MAMMEN, Jeanne (1890-1976) German				
oil	1	2,592	2,592	2,592
wc/d	5	892-4,697	2,071	1,649
3D	1	2,945	2,945	2,945
MAMPASO, Manuel (1924-) Spanish				
oil	1	3,472	3,472	3,472
wc/d	1	1,676	1,676	1,676
MAN, Cornelis de (1621-1706) Dutch				
oil	2	9,751-13,000	11,375	9,751
MAN-COLLOT (1903-1962) French				
oil	1	1,084	1,084	1,084
MAN-RAY (1890-1976) American				
oil	11	8,237-1,144,000	167,175	14,000
wc/d	19	1,500-29,145	10,253	8,870
3D	29	1,654-101,918	19,174	11,689
MANAGO, Vincent (1880-1936) French				
oil	4	1,520-2,178	1,846	1,753
MANAURE, Mateo (1926-) Venezuelan				
oil	10	465-3,250	1,650	1,395
wc/d	1	1,210	1,210	1,210
3D	1	6,745	6,745	6,745
MANCA, Mauro (1913-1969) Italian				
oil	5	1,674-3,588	2,439	2,392
3D	1	2,033	2,033	2,033

Name	No.	Price Range	Average	Median
MANCHADO PASCUAL, Faustino (1951-) Spanish				
oil	1	1,171	1,171	1,171
wc/d	1	1,808	1,808	1,808
MANCINI, Antonio (1852-1930) Italian				
oil	9	1,145-77,671	23,730	19,911
wc/d	3	1,295-4,216	3,045	3,625
MANCINI, Carlo (1829-1910) Italian				
oil	3	1,437-10,938	4,731	1,818
MANCINI, Francesco (1829-1905) Italian				
oil	2	12,085-12,721	12,403	12,085
wc/d	1	5,698	5,698	5,698
MANCINI, Francesco Longo (1880-1954) Italian				
oil	2	2,640-8,256	5,448	2,640
MANCINI, John (1925-) American				
oil	1	2,500	2,500	2,500
MANCOBA, Sonja Ferlov (1911-1984) Danish				
3D	5	3,219-77,262	23,822	12,877
MANDELBERG, Johan Edvard (1730-1786) Danish				
oil	1	1,870	1,870	1,870
MANDELLI, Pompilio (1912-) Italian				
oil	3	712-2,335	1,274	777
MANDER, Karel van I (1548-1606) Dutch				
oil	1	6,684	6,684	6,684
MANDER, Karel van III (1610-1672) Dutch				
oil	1	23,814	23,814	23,814
wc/d	1	14,800	14,800	14,800
MANDER, William Henry (1850-1922) British				
oil	15	473-8,725	2,331	1,620
MANDERS, Jos (20th C) Dutch				
3D	1	2,003	2,003	2,003
MANDIN, Richard (1909-) French				
oil	2	908-1,210	1,059	908
MANDLICK, Auguste (1860-?) Austrian				
wc/d	1	3,469	3,469	3,469
MANE KATZ (1894-1962) French				
oil	36	3,200-90,000	20,448	13,000
wc/d	24	502-9,500	2,479	1,701
3D	2	1,546-4,500	3,023	1,546
MANERA, Enrico (1947-) Italian				
oil	65	471-5,285	1,242	971
wc/d	8	485-900	659	597
MANES, Josef (1820-1871) Czechoslovakian				
oil	1	5,359	5,359	5,359
MANESSIER, Alfred (1911-1993) French				
oil	17	2,299-61,838	18,384	15,459
wc/d	13	1,300-7,767	4,702	5,040
MANET, Edouard (1832-1883) French				
oil	3	13,737-2,220,000	991,245	740,000
wc/d	4	11,404-250,000	82,337	12,945
MANETAS, Miltos (1964-) Greek				
oil	1	4,071	4,071	4,071
MANETTI, Antonio (?) Italian				
3D	1	3,567	3,567	3,567
MANETTI, Rutilio (1571-1639) Italian				
oil	1	229,315	229,315	229,315
MANFREDI, Alberto (1930-2001) Italian				
oil	6	1,929-6,090	4,289	4,534
wc/d	5	703-2,379	1,318	878
MANG, Hans (1892-?) German				
oil	1	4,839	4,839	4,839
MANGANELLI, Ferucci (1883-?) Italian				
oil	1	3,996	3,996	3,996
MANGIN, August (19th C) French				
oil	1	28,000	28,000	28,000
MANGOLD, Josef (1884-1942) German				
oil	4	1,459-10,603	7,251	7,389
wc/d	2	764-892	828	764
MANGOLD, Robert (1937-) American				
oil	6	20,000-195,000	61,333	32,500
wc/d	3	18,000-30,000	22,666	20,000
MANGOLD, Sylvia (1938-) American				
oil	2	18,000-20,000	19,000	18,000

Name	No.	Price Range	Average	Median
MANGUIN, Henri (1874-1949) French				
oil	24	2,422-386,507	49,959	16,649
wc/d	7	1,694-14,629	6,117	5,250
MANHART, Eduard (1880-1945) Austrian				
oil	1	1,883	1,883	1,883
wc/d	3	584-1,752	1,323	1,635
MANIATTY, Stephen G (1910-) American				
oil	5	400-4,600	2,390	2,800
MANIEVITCH, Abraham (1883-1942) American/Russian				
	13	8,000-223,200	43,115	25,800
MANIGAULT, Edward Middleton (1887-1922) American				
oil	8	1,500-11,000	6,125	4,800
wc/d	1	2,200	2,200	2,200
MANIQUET, Frederic Marius (1833-1896) French				
oil	2	1,092-1,701	1,396	1,092
MANKES, Jan (1889-1920) Dutch				
oil	2	64,795-259,178	161,986	64,795
MANLY, Charles MacDonald (1855-1924) Canadian				
oil	1	1,476	1,476	1,476
wc/d	2	577-742	659	577
MANN, Alexander (1853-1908) British				
oil	7	534-11,340	5,688	4,914
MANN, David (1948-) American				
oil	12	4,000-20,500	11,000	9,000
MANN, Harrington (1864-1937) British				
oil	1	5,742	5,742	5,742
MANN, Joshua Hargrave Sams (?-1886) British				
oil	1	1,575	1,575	1,575
MANNERS, William (fl.1885-c.1910) British				
oil	6	582-1,903	1,094	696
wc/d	12	455-3,916	1,222	700
MANNHEIM, Jean (1863-1945) American/German				
oil	7	850-12,000	5,814	5,000
MANNING, Eliza F (fl.1879-1889) British				
wc/d	1	1,151	1,151	1,151
MANNING, James (?) ?				
wc/d	1	1,211	1,211	1,211
MANNUCCI, Cipriano (1882-1970) Italian				
oil	5	1,665-13,676	6,974	4,757
MANNUCCI, Edgardo (1904-1986) Italian				
3D	2	4,285-4,789	4,537	4,285
MANOLIDIS, Theodoros (1940-) Greek				
oil	2	7,040-9,515	8,277	7,040
MANOLO (1872-1945) Spanish				
3D	4	4,889-11,451	7,333	5,063
MANOUKIAN, Sarah (20th C) American?				
oil	1	2,395	2,395	2,395
MANQUE, A B (19th C) Belgian				
oil	1	1,832	1,832	1,832
MANRIQUE, Cesar (1920-1992) Spanish				
oil	2	4,712-7,658	6,185	4,712
wc/d	2	1,916-2,700	2,308	1,916
MANRIQUE, Maria Eugenia (20th C) Venezuelan?				
oil	1	1,190	1,190	1,190
MANSER, Albert (1937-) Swiss				
oil	3	3,529-7,057	5,283	5,263
MANSER, Josef (20th C) German				
oil	1	6,478	6,478	6,478
MANSFELD, Heinrich August (1816-1901) Austrian				
oil	2	1,549-2,262	1,905	1,549
MANSFELD, Josef (1819-1894) Austrian				
oil	3	1,178-4,375	3,184	4,000
MANSFELD, Moritz (fl.1850-1890) Austrian				
oil	2	1,098-2,761	1,929	1,098
MANSFIELD, Louise (1876-?) American				
oil	6	510-2,124	1,267	952
MANSHIP, John Paul (1927-2000) American				
oil	2	800-1,000	900	800
wc/d	1	400	400	400
MANSHIP, Paul Howard (1885-1966) American				
3D	8	2,400-160,000	56,562	35,000

Name	No.	Price Range	Average	Median
MANSKIRSCH, Jacob (18th C) German				
oil	1	5,786	5,786	5,786
MANSO, Leo (1914-1993) American				
oil	2	750-1,300	1,025	750
wc/d	2	1,000-1,200	1,100	1,000
MANSON, James Bolivar (1879-1945) British				
oil	4	800-5,130	2,201	1,388
wc/d	1	491	491	491
MANSOUROFF, Paul (1896-1983) French				
oil	5	6,106-15,196	11,255	11,712
wc/d	3	579-1,073	805	764
MANSSON, Per (1896-1949) Swedish				
oil	1	1,116	1,116	1,116
MANSSON, Theodore Henri (1811-1850) French				
wc/d	2	960-1,403	1,181	960
MANTEGAZZA, Giacomo (1853-1920) Italian				
oil	1	8,507	8,507	8,507
MANTEL, Jean Gaston (1914-1995) ?				
oil	10	6,541-89,201	29,102	18,789
wc/d	6	499-4,876	1,817	547
MANTELET, Albert Goguet (1858-?) French				
oil	1	2,137	2,137	2,137
MANTOVANI, Alessandro (1814-1892) Italian				
oil	2	6,062-8,500	7,281	6,062
wc/d	1	16,562	16,562	16,562
MANTOVANI, Luigi (1880-1957) Italian				
oil	3	667-4,919	2,672	2,431
MANTYNEN, Jussi (1886-1978) Finnish				
3D	9	2,395-7,730	5,154	5,143
MANTZAVINOS, Tasos (1958-) Greek				
oil	2	2,816-5,610	4,213	2,816
MANUEL, David (1940-) American				
3D	2	12,000-12,000	12,000	12,000
MANUEL, Victor (1897-1969) Cuban				
oil	8	3,355-38,000	21,595	19,007
wc/d	1	1,426	1,426	1,426
MANUYO, V (19th C) ?				
oil	1	2,611	2,611	2,611
MANZANA-PISSARRO (1871-1961) French				
oil	1	6,681	6,681	6,681
MANZANA-PISSARRO, Georges (1871-1961) French				
oil	12	2,108-26,000	13,348	13,305
wc/d	9	5,250-42,000	17,901	17,500
MANZELLI, Margherita (1968-) Italian				
wc/d	1	3,888	3,888	3,888
MANZONE, Giuseppe (1887-1983) Italian				
oil	1	3,737	3,737	3,737
wc/d	1	1,211	1,211	1,211
MANZONI, Piero (1933-1963) Italian				
wc/d	15	4,057-1,700,000	405,938	325,600
3D	5	14,055-107,753	49,034	35,400
MANZONI, Ridolfo (1675-1743) Italian				
oil	1	157,250	157,250	157,250
MANZU, Giacomo (1908-1991) Italian				
wc/d	10	971-4,127	2,538	2,544
3D	19	3,021-370,000	115,751	92,500
MANZUOLI, Egisto (19th C) Italian?				
oil	1	3,186	3,186	3,186
MAO XUHUI (1956-) Chinese				
oil	1	27,000	27,000	27,000
MAO YAN (1968-) Chinese				
oil	1	28,000	28,000	28,000
MAOUS, M (19th C) Belgian?				
oil	1	1,933	1,933	1,933
MAPLESTONE, Henry (1819-1884) British				
wc/d	1	2,958	2,958	2,958
MAPPLETHORPE, Robert (1946-1989) American				
wc/d	1	12,000	12,000	12,000
MARA, Antonio (1680-1750) Italian				
oil	1	21,162	21,162	21,162

Name	No.	Price Range	Average	Median
MARA, Pol (1920-1998) Belgian				
oil	6	2,392-9,633	5,751	4,944
wc/d	22	530-2,649	1,336	1,264
MARACEK, Bohumil (1884-?) Czechoslovakian				
oil	1	7,308	7,308	7,308
MARAGALL, Julio (1936-) Latin American				
3D	1	3,255	3,255	3,255
MARAINI, Otto (1904-1968) Italian				
oil	1	2,521	2,521	2,521
MARAIS, Adolphe Charles (1856-1940) French				
oil	2	992-9,450	5,221	992
MARAIS, Jean (1914-1998) French				
3D	1	4,772	4,772	4,772
MARAIS-MILTON, Victor (1872-1948) French				
oil	6	1,890-18,375	7,150	4,524
MARANGOPOULOU, Koula (1913-1997) Greek				
wc/d	1	1,496	1,496	1,496
MARANIELLO, Giuseppe (1945-) Italian				
oil	2	7,120-7,658	7,389	7,120
wc/d	1	6,146	6,146	6,146
3D	2	3,503-7,633	5,568	3,503
MARASCO, Antonio (1886-1975) Italian				
oil	5	2,238-4,855	3,578	3,625
wc/d	8	725-2,803	1,252	1,015
MARATTA, Carlo (1625-1713) Italian				
oil	1	726,600	726,600	726,600
wc/d	4	830-6,000	4,112	4,625
MARC, Franz (1880-1916) German				
oil	1	1,380,600	1,380,600	1,380,600
wc/d	2	4,703-25,442	15,072	4,703
MARC, Robert (1943-1993) French				
oil	4	556-5,664	2,605	742
MARC, Wilhelm (1839-1907) German				
oil	2	4,500-18,147	11,323	4,500
MARCA-RELLI, Conrad (1913-2000) American				
oil	13	1,700-65,000	20,862	12,000
wc/d	10	1,018-20,384	9,048	7,500
3D	1	29,000	29,000	29,000
MARCACCIO, Fabian (1963-) Argentinian				
oil	3	10,179-24,000	14,917	10,572
MARCE, Marta (1972-) Spanish				
oil	1	2,035	2,035	2,035
MARCED FURIO, Jose (1896-?) Spanish				
oil	1	1,916	1,916	1,916
MARCEL-BERONNEAU, Pierre Amedee (1869-1937) French				
oil	1	1,376	1,376	1,376
wc/d	1	1,752	1,752	1,752
MARCEL-CLEMENT, Amedee Julien (1873-?) French				
oil	2	3,637-5,068	4,352	3,637
wc/d	1	3,750	3,750	3,750
MARCEL-LENOIR, Jules (1872-1931) French				
oil	4	833-4,835	2,861	1,082
wc/d	1	547	547	547
MARCETTE, Alexandre (1853-1929) Belgian				
oil	3	586-5,094	2,313	1,260
wc/d	2	1,001-3,514	2,257	1,001
MARCETTE, Henri (1824-1890) Belgian				
oil	3	501-3,254	1,427	526
MARCH, Giovanni (1894-1974) Tunisian				
oil	2	3,281-6,553	4,917	3,281
MARCH, Horacio (1899-1978) Argentinian				
oil	2	2,600-2,800	2,700	2,600
wc/d	2	1,100-4,000	2,550	1,100
MARCH, Sidney (1875-1968) British				
3D	1	2,958	2,958	2,958
MARCH, Vicente (1859-1914) Spanish				
oil	1	55,200	55,200	55,200
MARCHAIS, Pierre Antoine (1864-1889) French				
oil	2	2,309-2,447	2,378	2,309
MARCHAND, Andre (1907-1998) French				
oil	6	1,424-9,469	4,141	2,959
wc/d	2	546-790	668	546

Name	No.	Price Range	Average	Median
MARCHAND, Andre (1877-1951) French				
oil	3	1,153-2,552	2,045	2,431
wc/d	1	790	790	790
MARCHAND, C (19th C) Austrian?				
oil	1	3,514	3,514	3,514
MARCHAND, Jean Hippolyte (1883-1940) French				
oil	2	760-16,397	8,578	760
MARCHAND, Phillipe (20th C) French				
oil	3	450-2,500	1,266	850
MARCHANT, Alfons (19th C) Belgian				
oil	2	644-3,982	2,313	644
MARCHE, Ernest Gaston (1864-1932) French				
oil	1	4,644	4,644	4,644
MARCHEGIANI, Elio (1929-) Italian				
oil	1	2,417	2,417	2,417
wc/d	2	1,665-1,790	1,727	1,665
MARCHENKO, Viacheslav (1952-) Russian?				
oil	1	1,929	1,929	1,929
MARCHETTI, Ludovico (1853-1909) Italian				
oil	2	539-2,867	1,703	539
wc/d	8	927-5,839	3,523	3,737
MARCHI, Mario Vellani (1895-1979) Italian				
oil	1	3,045	3,045	3,045
wc/d	1	910	910	910
MARCHI, Virgilio (1895-1960) Italian				
wc/d	1	7,350	7,350	7,350
MARCHIG, Giannino (1897-1983) Italian				
oil	3	1,218-12,110	8,479	12,110
wc/d	3	1,038-1,471	1,240	1,211
MARCHIS, Alessio de (1684-1752) Italian				
oil	1	7,373	7,373	7,373
wc/d	1	1,942	1,942	1,942
MARCHISIO, Andrea (1850-1927) Italian				
oil	3	1,735-2,057	1,869	1,816
MARCHOU, Georges (1898-1984) French				
oil	5	514-2,378	1,090	697
MARCIL, René (1917-1993) Canadian				
oil	4	1,072-2,952	2,051	1,536
wc/d	1	2,000	2,000	2,000
MARCKE DE LUMMEN, Jean van (1875-1918) French				
oil	1	14,000	14,000	14,000
MARCKS, Gerhard (1889-1981) German				
oil	1	3,822	3,822	3,822
wc/d	3	673-2,293	1,222	700
3D	16	3,063-169,829	23,698	10,192
MARCLAY, Christian (20th C) American				
wc/d	1	18,000	18,000	18,000
MARCO, Andrea di (1970-) Italian				
oil	1	5,271	5,271	5,271
MARCOLA, Marco (1740-1793) Italian				
oil	2	9,514-21,796	15,655	9,514
wc/d	2	584-3,515	2,049	584
MARCONI (16th C) Italian				
oil	1	55,000	55,000	55,000
MARCONI, Rocco (?-1529) Italian				
oil	1	19,265	19,265	19,265
MARCOTTE, Marie Antoinette (1869-1929) French				
oil	2	554-1,638	1,096	554
MARCOUSSIS, Louis (1883-1941) French				
oil	5	23,035-56,000	36,935	35,479
wc/d	2	21,475-150,000	85,737	21,475
MARCUCCI, Mario (1910-1992) Italian				
oil	17	969-8,486	2,962	2,335
wc/d	2	610-1,576	1,093	610
MARCUEYZ, P (20th C) French?				
oil	1	3,449	3,449	3,449
MARCUSE, Rudolf (1878-?) German				
3D	2	3,058-6,276	4,667	3,058
MARDEN, Brice (1938-) American				
oil	2	900,000-2,650,000	1,775,000	900,000
wc/d	2	30,000-70,000	50,000	30,000
MARE, Georges le (1866-1942) French				
oil	2	3,390-7,283	5,336	3,390

Name	No.	Price Range	Average	Median
MARECHAL, Charles (1865-?) French				
oil	1	2,604	2,604	2,604
MARECHAL, Jean Baptiste (18th C) French				
wc/d	1	14,271	14,271	14,271
MARECHAL, Victor (1879-?) French				
oil	1	4,849	4,849	4,849
MAREELS, Maurice (1893-1975) Belgian				
oil	1	4,250	4,250	4,250
MAREES, Albert de (19th C) German				
oil	1	2,081	2,081	2,081
MAREVNA, Marie (1892-1984) Russian				
oil	7	7,755-190,000	42,137	18,600
wc/d	7	1,384-17,300	4,851	2,941
MARFAING, Andre (1925-1987) French				
oil	11	2,789-11,105	6,296	5,947
wc/d	2	1,937-2,914	2,425	1,937
MARFFY, Odon (1878-1959) Hungarian				
oil	1	9,000	9,000	9,000
MARGAT, Andre (1903-1999) French				
oil	1	6,361	6,361	6,361
wc/d	1	502	502	502
MARGETSON, William Henry (1861-1940) British				
wc/d	2	3,850-5,340	4,595	3,850
MARGETTS, Mary (fl.1841-1886) British				
wc/d	1	1,027	1,027	1,027
MARGO, Boris (1902-1995) American/Russian				
wc/d	1	2,000	2,000	2,000
MARGUERAY, Michel (1938-) French				
oil	2	1,973-3,588	2,780	1,973
MARIA, Mario de (1853-1924) Italian				
oil	1	2,038	2,038	2,038
MARIA, Nicola de (1954-) Italian				
oil	12	2,979-250,552	41,756	27,986
wc/d	7	1,788-28,628	9,354	6,090
MARIA, Walter de (1935-) American				
3D	1	200,000	200,000	200,000
MARIANI, Carlo Maria (1931-) Italian				
oil	2	38,000-38,163	38,081	38,000
MARIANI, Elio (1943-) Italian				
oil	1	3,562	3,562	3,562
wc/d	1	2,035	2,035	2,035
MARIANI, Francisco (1883-1953) Argentinian				
oil	1	2,700	2,700	2,700
MARIANI, Pompeo (1857-1927) Italian				
oil	12	3,162-64,726	18,276	9,699
wc/d	6	592-3,788	1,605	975
MARIANI, Umberto (1936-) Italian				
oil	11	589-2,102	1,203	1,029
wc/d	2	589-1,211	900	589
MARIE, Adrien Emmanuel (1848-1891) French				
oil	1	6,563	6,563	6,563
wc/d	2	584-935	759	584
MARIEN, Marcel (1920-1993) Belgian				
3D	1	6,429	6,429	6,429
MARIENHOF, Jan (1610-1650) Dutch				
oil	1	142,866	142,866	142,866
MARIESCHI, Michele (1696-1743) Italian				
oil	2	340,000-684,500	512,250	340,000
MARIL, Herman (1908-1986) American				
oil	2	482-2,400	1,441	482
MARILHAT, Prosper (1811-1847) French				
oil	2	4,920-36,875	20,897	4,920
wc/d	3	1,318-12,858	5,898	3,520
MARIN CARES, Isidoro (1863-1926) Spanish				
wc/d	2	4,490-4,789	4,639	4,490
MARIN MARIE (1901-1987) French				
wc/d	2	1,200-28,863	15,031	1,200
MARIN SEVILLA, Enrique (1876-1940) Spanish				
wc/d	2	1,414-2,420	1,917	1,414
MARIN, Emanuel (1942-) Spanish				
3D	5	1,978-9,534	5,101	4,326

Name	No.	Price Range	Average	Median
MARIN, Javier (1962-) Mexican				
3D	4	4,250-27,000	13,687	10,500
MARIN, John (1870-1953) American				
oil	8	55,000-1,100,000	321,875	120,000
wc/d	26	4,500-140,000	23,957	16,000
MARIN, Joseph Charles (1759-1834) French				
3D	1	27,951	27,951	27,951
MARIN, Marie (?) French?				
wc/d	2	4,208-8,942	6,575	4,208
MARINALI, Orazio (1643-1720) Italian				
3D	1	21,284	21,284	21,284
MARINELLI, Mario (1906-) Italian				
oil	2	1,193-1,312	1,252	1,193
MARINELLI, Vincenzo (1820-1892) Italian				
oil	1	11,712	11,712	11,712
MARINI, Antonio (1788-1861) Italian				
oil	1	59,548	59,548	59,548
MARINI, Benedetto (c.1590-c.1627) Italian				
wc/d	1	4,440	4,440	4,440
MARINI, Marino (1901-1980) Italian				
oil	8	12,000-644,178	177,949	80,000
wc/d	15	2,600-110,000	22,130	10,541
3D	12	12,000-1,593,000	341,875	105,000
MARINKO, George (1908-1989) American				
oil	1	1,500	1,500	1,500
MARINKOV, Evgeney (1963-) Russian				
oil	1	1,313	1,313	1,313
MARINO, Francesco di (1892-1954) Italian				
oil	4	1,070-1,911	1,340	1,171
MARINONI, Antonio (1796-1871) Italian				
oil	1	10,192	10,192	10,192
MARINSKY, Harry (1909-) American				
3D	1	2,200	2,200	2,200
MARINUS, Ferdinand Joseph Bernard (1808-1890) Belgian				
oil	2	2,521-8,905	5,713	2,521
MARIONI, Joseph (1943-) American				
oil	2	42,041-50,959	46,500	42,041
MARIOTON, Eugène (1854-1925) French				
3D	2	2,610-3,250	2,930	2,610
MARIOTTI, Leopoldo (1848-1916) Italian				
wc/d	3	650-1,500	1,216	1,500
MARIS, Ferdinand Johannes Jacobus (1873-1935) Dutch				
oil	1	1,025	1,025	1,025
MARIS, Jacob (1837-1899) Dutch				
oil	8	1,171-30,903	9,549	5,563
wc/d	2	2,425-18,147	10,286	2,425
MARIS, Simon (1873-1935) Dutch				
oil	2	723-1,707	1,215	723
MARIS, Willem (1844-1910) Dutch				
oil	4	1,296-12,370	6,891	3,596
wc/d	4	1,073-10,620	4,749	2,142
MARISALDI, Elena Falco (1902-1986) Italian				
oil	2	954-1,212	1,083	954
MARITON, Eugene (1854-1933) French?				
3D	1	1,741	1,741	1,741
MARK, Lajos (1867-1942) Hungarian				
oil	3	400-1,818	1,064	974
MARKETTIS, Ericos (19th C) Greek				
oil	1	17,400	17,400	17,400
MARKHAM, Kyra (1891-1967) American				
oil	2	2,200-30,000	16,100	2,200
MARKIEWICS, Comte Kasimir Dunin (1874-1932) Polish				
oil	1	19,110	19,110	19,110
MARKKULA, Mauno (1905-1959) Finnish				
oil	7	900-1,987	1,390	1,403
MARKLE, Robert Nelson (1936-) Canadian				
wc/d	1	2,886	2,886	2,886
MARKLUND, Bror (1907-1977) Swedish				
3D	2	1,909-2,313	2,111	1,909
MARKO, Andreas (1824-1895) Austrian				
oil	8	1,500-11,447	7,793	8,247

Name	No.	Price Range	Average	Median
MARKO, Henry (1855-1921) Italian				
oil	4	763-2,795	1,965	1,816
MARKO, Karl (younger) (1822-1891) Hungarian				
oil	4	1,951-8,324	4,781	3,894
MARKOS, Lajos (1917-1993) American/Rumanian				
oil	5	500-7,000	3,200	1,900
MARKOWICZ, Arthur (1872-1934) Polish				
wc/d	1	2,500	2,500	2,500
MARKS, Barnett Samuel (1827-1916) British				
oil	1	5,610	5,610	5,610
MARKS, Claude (fl.1899-1915) British				
oil	1	800	800	800
wc/d	2	595-673	634	595
MARKS, George (fl.1876-1922) British				
oil	1	1,800	1,800	1,800
wc/d	2	875-3,132	2,003	875
MARKUS, Ans (1947-) Dutch				
oil	2	7,644-8,918	8,281	7,644
MARLE, Felix del (1889-1952) French				
wc/d	3	6,473-10,235	8,019	7,350
MARLET, Jean Henri (1771-1847) French				
oil	1	13,920	13,920	13,920
MARLIER, Philippe de (c.1573-1668) Flemish				
oil	1	8,357	8,357	8,357
MARLINOVSKA, Olga de (19/20th C) ?				
oil	1	4,735	4,735	4,735
MARLOW, William (1740-1813) British				
oil	2	44,460-623,700	334,080	44,460
MARMA, Rodolfo (1923-1997) Italian				
oil	10	533-1,030	779	756
wc/d	3	630-819	756	819
MARNEFFE, Ernest (1866-1921) Belgian				
oil	6	1,344-14,317	6,428	4,295
MARNY, Paul (1829-1914) British				
oil	3	470-870	702	766
wc/d	9	445-2,697	1,319	1,157
MAROCCO, Armando (1939-) Italian				
oil	2	1,229-2,422	1,825	1,229
wc/d	2	3,236-3,579	3,407	3,236
MAROCHETTI, Baron Charles (1805-1867) French				
3D	3	7,308-12,138	9,672	9,570
MARON, Anton von (1733-1808) Austrian				
oil	3	14,517-94,500	47,679	34,020
MARONIEZ, Georges Philibert Charles (1865-1933) French				
oil	10	505-3,314	1,740	1,288
MAROT, François (1666-1719) French				
oil	4	17,000-50,000	33,500	22,000
MAROTO, Julian (1962-) Spanish				
wc/d	1	2,349	2,349	2,349
MAROTTA, Gino (1935-) Italian				
oil	2	1,196-2,428	1,812	1,196
3D	4	2,521-4,855	3,613	3,514
MARPICATI, Iros (?) Italian?				
oil	1	1,649	1,649	1,649
MARPLE, William (1827-1910) American				
oil	1	3,000	3,000	3,000
MARQUANT, Peter (1956-) Austrian				
wc/d	1	2,338	2,338	2,338
MARQUE, Albert (1872-?) French				
3D	1	2,200	2,200	2,200
MARQUES, Guilherme d'Oliveira (1887-?) ?				
oil	2	514-1,798	1,156	514
MARQUESTE, Laurent Honore (1848-1920) French				
3D	2	3,500-38,280	20,890	3,500
MARQUET, Albert (1875-1947) French				
oil	36	13,000-520,000	98,410	69,200
wc/d	27	489-19,470	4,649	2,655
MARQUET, Alix (1875-?) French				
3D	1	18,685	18,685	18,685
MARQUET, Gaston (1848-?) French				
oil	2	2,468-3,770	3,119	2,468

Name	No.	Price Range	Average	Median
MARQUIS, J Richard (?-1885) British				
oil	4	3,312-6,256	4,723	4,524
MARR, Carl Ritter von (1858-1936) German/American				
oil	1	2,443	2,443	2,443
wc/d	1	937	937	937
MARR, J W Hamilton (1846-?) British				
oil	1	1,500	1,500	1,500
MARR, Joseph Heinrich Ludwig (1807-1871) German				
oil	1	62,909	62,909	62,909
MARREL, Jacob (1614-1681) Dutch				
oil	4	53,400-157,250	108,174	111,000
MARRIOTT, Richard (1902-1942) British				
oil	1	1,400	1,400	1,400
MARS, Ethel (1876-1956) American				
wc/d	1	2,200	2,200	2,200
MARS, Peter Joseph Lawrence (1874-1949) American				
oil	1	1,000	1,000	1,000
MARSACANI, A (19th C) ?				
oil	1	1,767	1,767	1,767
MARSAL, Edouard Antoine (1845-?) French				
oil	1	9,000	9,000	9,000
MARSCHALL, Ken (20th C) American				
oil	1	5,500	5,500	5,500
MARSDEN, Theodore (fl.1860-1890) Australian				
oil	1	1,100	1,100	1,100
MARSDEN, W (19/20th C) British				
oil	1	1,937	1,937	1,937
MARSH, John (19th C) British?				
oil	1	2,076	2,076	2,076
MARSH, Reginald (1898-1954) American				
oil	6	6,500-42,500	24,166	20,000
wc/d	20	672-30,000	10,656	8,500
MARSHALL, Ben (1767-1835) British				
oil	1	111,150	111,150	111,150
MARSHALL, Francis (1946-) French				
oil	2	994-1,052	1,023	994
MARSHALL, Herbert Menzies (1841-1913) British				
wc/d	4	455-2,975	1,649	905
MARSHALL, John Fitz (1859-1932) British				
oil	7	1,573-3,168	2,215	2,100
MARSHALL, Kerry James (1955-) American				
oil	3	45,000-90,000	71,666	80,000
MARSHALL, Richard (1943-) British				
oil	2	1,218-2,436	1,827	1,218
wc/d	1	534	534	534
MARSHALL, Roberto Angelo Kittermaster (1849-c.1923) British				
wc/d	4	788-5,600	2,651	1,740
MARSHALL, Thomas Falcon (1818-1878) British				
oil	1	4,498	4,498	4,498
MARSHALL, Thomas William (1875-1914) British				
oil	2	2,104-2,338	2,221	2,104
MARSHENNIKOV, Sergei (1971-) Russian				
oil	9	3,480-15,555	7,923	5,696
MARSTBOOM, Antoon (1905-1960) Belgian				
3D	1	1,854	1,854	1,854
MARSTON, George Edward (1882-1940) British				
oil	1	14,400	14,400	14,400
MARSTON, Reginald St Clair (1886-1943) British				
oil	1	1,479	1,479	1,479
MARSTRAND, Wilhelm (1810-1873) Danish				
oil	7	978-60,328	10,749	2,858
wc/d	1	443	443	443
MARTCHENKO, Tatiana (1918-) Russian				
oil	1	1,427	1,427	1,427
MARTEL, Jan and Joel (1896-1966) French				
wc/d	2	1,911-2,293	2,102	1,911
3D	18	1,911-315,302	32,840	11,678
MARTEL, Joel (1896-1966) French				
3D	1	2,854	2,854	2,854
MARTELLANGE, Étienne de (16th C) French				
oil	1	27,877	27,877	27,877

Name	No.	Price Range	Average	Median
MARTEN, Dimitrij E (1860-1918) Russian				
oil	1	22,320	22,320	22,320
MARTENS, Gysbert George (1894-1979) Dutch				
oil	1	10,177	10,177	10,177
wc/d	1	723	723	723
MARTENS, Henry (?-1860) British				
wc/d	2	1,147-1,369	1,258	1,147
MARTENS, Max (1887-1970) German				
oil	4	486-1,034	805	791
wc/d	3	884-1,546	1,109	899
MARTENS, Theodor (1822-1884) German				
oil	1	2,541	2,541	2,541
MARTHAS, Takis (1905-1965) Greek				
oil	1	13,090	13,090	13,090
MARTI Y AGUILO, Ricardo (1868-1936) Spanish				
oil	1	5,641	5,641	5,641
MARTI Y ALSINA, Ramon (1826-1894) Spanish				
oil	2	644-15,265	7,954	644
wc/d	1	766	766	766
MARTI, Agostino (1485-c.1537) Italian				
oil	1	16,000	16,000	16,000
MARTIN REBOLLO, Tomas (1858-1919) Spanish				
oil	3	722-4,545	2,355	1,800
MARTIN, Agnes (1912-1999) American/Canadian				
oil	6	260,000-1,550,000	1,093,333	1,200,000
wc/d	3	70,400-200,000	143,466	160,000
MARTIN, Alex Louis (1887-1954) Belgian				
oil	3	700-2,028	1,287	1,133
MARTIN, Annie D (fl.1884-1906) Canadian				
oil	1	3,444	3,444	3,444
MARTIN, Cameron (1970-) American?				
oil	1	25,000	25,000	25,000
MARTIN, Cimane (19th C) Italian				
oil	1	7,508	7,508	7,508
MARTIN, David (1736-1798) British				
oil	1	14,535	14,535	14,535
MARTIN, David (fl.1887-1935) British				
oil	1	1,061	1,061	1,061
wc/d	1	515	515	515
MARTIN, David McLeod (1922-) British				
oil	6	1,239-6,195	2,881	2,275
wc/d	1	1,164	1,164	1,164
MARTIN, Elias (1739-1818) Swedish				
oil	2	6,357-10,303	8,330	6,357
wc/d	4	1,099-3,984	2,764	2,404
MARTIN, F (?) ?				
oil	1	5,500	5,500	5,500
MARTIN, Fletcher (1904-1979) American				
oil	2	3,000-70,000	36,500	3,000
wc/d	2	900-1,200	1,050	900
MARTIN, François (19th C) French				
wc/d	2	3,780-4,158	3,969	3,780
MARTIN, François (1945-) French				
oil	1	1,073	1,073	1,073
wc/d	1	1,073	1,073	1,073
MARTIN, Henri (1860-1943) French				
oil	40	5,260-869,500	158,822	70,000
MARTIN, Henriette (19th C) French?				
wc/d	1	3,507	3,507	3,507
MARTIN, Henry (1835-1908) British				
oil	2	525-704	614	525
wc/d	1	505	505	505
MARTIN, Homer D (1836-1897) American				
oil	3	4,000-8,500	6,833	8,000
MARTIN, Jacques (1844-1919) French				
oil	2	1,169-10,938	6,053	1,169
MARTIN, Jason (1970-) British				
oil	12	14,620-82,560	43,401	32,000
MARTIN, Johan Fredrik (1755-1816) Swedish				
wc/d	1	7,728	7,728	7,728
MARTIN, John (1789-1854) British				
wc/d	1	20,395	20,395	20,395

Name	No.	Price Range	Average	Median
MARTIN, John Blennerhassett (1797-1857) American				
oil	1	9,000	9,000	9,000
MARTIN, Kenneth (1905-1984) British				
oil	4	531-3,828	1,466	736
3D	1	3,560	3,560	3,560
MARTIN, Mary (1907-1969) British				
oil	2	1,032-1,335	1,183	1,032
MARTIN, Milo (1893-1970) Swiss				
3D	1	2,061	2,061	2,061
MARTIN, Paul (1821-1901) German				
oil	1	1,274	1,274	1,274
MARTIN, Philip (1927-) British				
oil	2	1,014-2,163	1,588	1,014
MARTIN, René (1891-) ?				
oil	1	8,236	8,236	8,236
wc/d	1	2,930	2,930	2,930
MARTIN, Ronald Albert (1943-) Canadian				
oil	1	12,370	12,370	12,370
MARTIN, Sylvester (fl.1856-1906) British				
oil	3	957-5,760	2,637	1,196
MARTIN, Thomas Mower (1838-1934) Canadian				
oil	3	443-3,102	1,466	853
wc/d	5	574-2,109	916	620
MARTIN, William A K (1817-1867) American				
oil	1	1,400	1,400	1,400
MARTIN-FERRIERES, Jac (1893-1972) French				
oil	12	1,784-15,265	6,726	5,820
wc/d	1	1,430	1,430	1,430
MARTIN-KAVEL, François (1861-1931) French				
oil	7	1,824-10,000	4,744	3,107
MARTINDALE, Thomas (19th C) British				
oil	1	1,881	1,881	1,881
MARTINEAU, Edith (1842-1909) British				
wc/d	2	699-3,150	1,924	699
MARTINETTI, Maria (1864-?) Italian				
wc/d	3	1,580-18,920	8,131	3,894
MARTINEZ CELAYA, Enrique (1964-) Mexican				
3D	1	22,500	22,500	22,500
MARTINEZ DE ESPINOZA, Juan Jose (1826-1902) Spanish				
wc/d	1	1,197	1,197	1,197
MARTINEZ DE LA VEGA, Joaquin (1846-1905) Spanish				
wc/d	1	2,635	2,635	2,635
MARTINEZ DIAZ, Rafael (1915-1991) Spanish				
oil	1	1,211	1,211	1,211
MARTINEZ HOWARD, Julio (1932-1999) Spanish				
wc/d	5	500-2,600	1,330	800
MARTINEZ NOVILLO, Cirilo (1921-) Spanish				
oil	2	3,498-3,816	3,657	3,498
wc/d	1	2,163	2,163	2,163
MARTINEZ PEDRO, Luis (1910-1990) Cuban				
wc/d	1	4,000	4,000	4,000
MARTINEZ TARRASSO, Casimiro (1900-1980) Spanish				
oil	1	1,137	1,137	1,137
MARTINEZ VAZQUEZ, Eduardo (1886-1971) Spanish				
oil	1	2,342	2,342	2,342
MARTINEZ VILLAFINEZ, Lino (1892-1960) Spanish				
oil	1	3,092	3,092	3,092
MARTINEZ, Alfredo Ramos (1872-1946) Mexican				
oil	1	15,000	15,000	15,000
wc/d	8	3,000-150,000	30,968	10,000
MARTINEZ, Coque (?) ?				
oil	1	3,500	3,500	3,500
MARTINEZ, Pedro Antonio (1886-?) Spanish				
oil	1	10,100	10,100	10,100
MARTINEZ, Raoul (1876-1973) Dutch/Cuban				
oil	4	1,008-2,158	1,401	1,036
MARTINEZ, Raymond (20th C) French				
oil	2	1,014-1,019	1,016	1,014
MARTINEZ, Raymundo (1938-) Mexican				
oil	1	10,000	10,000	10,000
MARTINEZ, Ricardo (1918-) Mexican				
oil	4	5,374-25,000	17,343	18,000

Name	No.	Price Range	Average	Median
MARTINEZ, Xavier (1869-1943) American				
oil	1	4,000	4,000	4,000
MARTINI, Alberto (1876-1954) Italian				
oil	2	3,330-3,805	3,567	3,330
wc/d	5	4,229-22,958	8,990	6,256
MARTINI, Arturo (1889-1947) Italian				
oil	1	2,670	2,670	2,670
wc/d	4	2,829-4,243	3,600	3,600
3D	5	3,884-57,245	29,559	22,898
MARTINI, Gaetano de (1845-1917) Italian				
oil	2	8,000-8,000	8,000	8,000
MARTINI, Quinto (1908-1990) Italian				
3D	1	3,078	3,078	3,078
MARTINI, Sandro (1941-) Italian				
oil	1	5,178	5,178	5,178
MARTINKOVA, Marie (1886-?) Czechoslovakian				
oil	1	2,610	2,610	2,610
MARTINO di Bartolomeo di Biagio (?-1434) Italian				
oil	1	190,000	190,000	190,000
MARTINO, Antonio Pietro (1902-1989) American				
oil	17	1,000-70,000	13,597	8,000
wc/d	3	800-2,750	1,516	1,000
MARTINO, Edoardo (1838-1912) Italian				
oil	3	5,000-18,000	9,406	5,220
wc/d	2	1,000-1,683	1,341	1,000
MARTINO, Giovanni (1908-1998) American				
oil	7	1,200-7,500	3,700	2,500
wc/d	1	425	425	425
MARTINOTTI, Ugo (1905-?) Italian				
oil	1	1,212	1,212	1,212
MARTINS, Maria (1900-1973) Brazilian				
3D	1	200,000	200,000	200,000
MARTORELL, Maria (20th C) Argentinian				
oil	2	3,500-4,200	3,850	3,500
MARTOS, Rufino (1912-1993) Spanish				
oil	1	1,210	1,210	1,210
MARTOUGEN, Stanislas (1873-?) ?				
oil	1	8,182	8,182	8,182
MARTSEN, Jan (younger) (1609-c.1647) Flemish				
oil	1	14,014	14,014	14,014
MARTTINEN, Veikko (1917-2003) Finnish				
oil	3	2,397-2,997	2,612	2,443
MARTY, David (?) American				
oil	1	4,000	4,000	4,000
MARTY, G (?) French?				
oil	1	3,514	3,514	3,514
MARUSIC, Zivko (1944-) Balkan				
3D	1	5,271	5,271	5,271
MARUSSIG, Anton (1868-1925) Austrian				
oil	3	1,034-2,314	1,887	2,314
MARUSSIG, Piero (1879-1937) Italian				
oil	6	1,844-46,849	17,167	8,199
wc/d	2	820-1,585	1,202	820
MARUSSO, Vittorio (?) Italian				
wc/d	1	1,295	1,295	1,295
MARVAL (19th C) ?				
oil	1	18,900	18,900	18,900
MARVAL, Jacqueline (1866-1932) French				
oil	4	3,534-9,830	6,717	5,260
MARWAN (1934-) Syrian				
oil	1	5,088	5,088	5,088
MARX, Gustav (1855-1928) German				
oil	1	1,967	1,967	1,967
MARX, Johann (1866-1837) German				
oil	2	1,139-2,057	1,598	1,139
MARX, Marsha (20th C) American				
oil	1	1,600	1,600	1,600
MARX, Maurice Roger (1872-?) French				
3D	1	2,054	2,054	2,054
MARXER, Alfred (1876-1945) Swiss				
oil	4	567-9,159	3,022	1,068

Name	No.	Price Range	Average	Median
MARYAN (1927-1977) American				
oil	5	1,073-14,302	5,187	3,600
wc/d	3	834-2,719	1,555	1,113
MARYAN, Burstein Pinchas (1927-1977) American				
oil	7	560-18,493	4,760	2,301
wc/d	1	450	450	450
MARZIANI, Hugo de (1941-) Latin American				
oil	4	2,000-6,000	3,600	2,400
MARZIN, Alfred (20th C) French				
oil	1	2,104	2,104	2,104
MARZOTTO CAOTORTA, Franco (20th C) Italian				
3D	1	9,828	9,828	9,828
MAS Y FONDEVILA, Arcadio (1852-1934) Spanish				
oil	1	20,880	20,880	20,880
MAS, Felix (20th C) Spanish				
oil	1	4,057	4,057	4,057
MASCARDI, Angelo (1857-1940) Italian				
oil	1	2,959	2,959	2,959
MASCART, Gustave (1834-1914) French				
oil	20	953-11,342	3,421	2,719
MASCART, Paul (1874-1958) French				
oil	4	648-1,987	1,316	1,316
wc/d	3	584-718	633	598
MASCART, Pierre (1875-c.1931) French				
oil	1	4,017	4,017	4,017
MASCHEK, Karoline (1857-1938) Austrian				
wc/d	1	15,000	15,000	15,000
MASCHERINI, Marcello (1906-1983) Italian				
3D	2	2,631-10,286	6,458	2,631
MASCRE, Emile (fl.1870-1890) Belgian				
oil	1	1,700	1,700	1,700
MASE, Pieter van (c.1650-1703) Dutch				
oil	1	12,846	12,846	12,846
MASELLI, Titina (1924-2005) Italian				
oil	7	2,033-59,557	18,758	10,875
MASEREEL, Frans (1889-1972) Belgian				
oil	24	1,036-12,959	3,393	1,940
wc/d	14	484-1,553	932	854
MASHKOV, Ilya (1881-1944) Russian				
oil	6	1,265-3,268,000	616,043	18,211
MASI, Roberto (1940-) Italian				
oil	4	630-3,073	1,575	1,197
MASIDE, Carlos (1897-1958) Spanish				
oil	1	6,585	6,585	6,585
MASJUTIN, Wassilij N (1884-1957) Russian				
wc/d	2	1,180-1,180	1,180	1,180
MASLENNIKOV, Pavel (1916-) Russian				
oil	1	2,616	2,616	2,616
MASOLLE, Helmer (1884-1969) Swedish				
oil	2	3,434-11,795	7,614	3,434
MASON, Barry (1927-) British				
oil	2	736-7,728	4,232	736
MASON, Bateson (1910-1977) British				
oil	2	525-3,894	2,209	525
MASON, Dick (1951-1993) American				
oil	1	1,050	1,050	1,050
MASON, Emily Florence (1870-?) British				
oil	1	1,003	1,003	1,003
wc/d	1	700	700	700
MASON, Frank H (1876-1965) British				
oil	17	561-10,120	2,252	1,672
wc/d	29	470-3,306	1,560	1,638
MASON, Frank Herbert (1921-) American				
oil	1	700	700	700
wc/d	1	550	550	550
MASON, George Finch (1850-1915) British				
wc/d	6	510-2,268	1,324	1,100
MASON, John (1868-?) American				
oil	1	2,400	2,400	2,400
MASON, Maud Mary (1867-1956) American				
oil	1	1,000	1,000	1,000

Name	No.	Price Range	Average	Median
MASON, Roy M (1886-1972) American				
oil	1	1,200	1,200	1,200
wc/d	1	3,250	3,250	3,250
MASON, William Sanford (1824-1864) American				
oil	2	1,300-7,000	4,150	1,300
MASQUERIER, John James (1778-1855) British				
oil	2	5,985-10,260	8,122	5,985
MASRELIEZ, Louis (1748-1810) Swedish				
wc/d	1	2,885	2,885	2,885
MASRIERA Y MANOVENS, Francisco (1842-1902) Spanish				
oil	3	845-24,080	8,901	1,780
wc/d	1	2,392	2,392	2,392
MASRIERA Y MANOVENS, Jose (1841-1912) Spanish				
oil	1	5,664	5,664	5,664
MASRIERA Y ROSES, Luis (1872-1958) Spanish				
oil	2	833-16,800	8,816	833
MASSANI, Pompeo (1850-1920) Italian				
oil	5	592-4,995	2,770	3,551
MASSE, Emmanuel Auguste (1818-1881) French				
oil	1	7,259	7,259	7,259
MASSE, Jean Eugène Julien (1856-1950) French				
oil	3	953-2,384	1,609	1,492
wc/d	1	1,013	1,013	1,013
MASSERIA, Francisco (1927-) Argentinian				
oil	1	1,500	1,500	1,500
MASSEY, Rod (1949-) American				
oil	3	1,000-1,300	1,133	1,100
MASSIER, Clement (19/20th C) French				
3D	1	3,111	3,111	3,111
MASSION, Michele (20th C) French				
oil	1	2,919	2,919	2,919
MASSIRONI, Manfredo (1937-) Italian				
oil	1	4,272	4,272	4,272
wc/d	1	4,295	4,295	4,295
3D	1	4,241	4,241	4,241
MASSMANN, Carl (1859-1929) Austrian				
oil	1	1,140	1,140	1,140
MASSMANN, Hans (1887-1973) Rumanian				
oil	3	1,918-2,637	2,281	2,290
wc/d	1	603	603	603
MASSON, Andre (1896-1987) French				
oil	26	9,328-1,593,000	125,617	48,000
wc/d	61	884-135,000	12,158	4,697
MASSON, Benedict (1819-1893) French				
oil	2	1,147-3,548	2,347	1,147
MASSON, Clovis (1838-1913) French				
3D	1	2,803	2,803	2,803
MASSON, Edouard (1881-1950) Belgian				
oil	3	486-1,551	862	549
wc/d	1	654	654	654
MASSON, F (?) ?				
wc/d	1	9,271	9,271	9,271
MASSON, Georges Armand (1892-1977) French				
wc/d	1	1,073	1,073	1,073
MASSON, Henri Jacques (1908-1995) French				
oil	3	1,064-1,241	1,152	1,152
MASSON, Henri L (1907-1996) Canadian				
oil	30	978-14,844	3,849	2,645
wc/d	10	369-1,237	745	656
MASSON, Jules-Edmond (1871-1932) French				
3D	3	2,000-4,855	3,777	4,477
MASSONET, Armand (1892-1979) Belgian				
oil	3	701-2,529	1,633	1,671
MASSONI, Egisto (fl.1880-1885) Italian				
oil	1	3,107	3,107	3,107
MASSOT, Firmin (1766-1849) Swiss				
oil	1	3,739	3,739	3,739
MASTENBROEK, Johann Hendrik van (1875-1945) Dutch				
oil	11	4,917-26,311	14,463	14,351
wc/d	4	884-12,123	5,604	3,879
MASTER B G (17th C) German?				
3D	1	225,000	225,000	225,000

Name	No.	Price Range	Average	Median
MASTER OF 1518 (16th C) Flemish				
oil	1	53,400	53,400	53,400
MASTER OF ALL (15th C) Spanish				
oil	1	37,000	37,000	37,000
MASTER OF GROSSGMAIN (fl.1480-1499) German				
oil	1	259,500	259,500	259,500
MASTER OF HOOGSTRAETEN (16th C) Flemish				
oil	1	37,500	37,500	37,500
MASTER OF LATHROP TONDO (15/16th C) Italian				
oil	1	216,259	216,259	216,259
MASTER OF MONTE OLIVETO (14th C) Italian				
oil	1	730,000	730,000	730,000
MASTER OF SAINT IVO (14th C) Italian				
oil	1	46,849	46,849	46,849
MASTER OF SAINT JOHN ON PATMOS (16th C) ?				
oil	1	150,621	150,621	150,621
MASTER OF THE ASHMOLEAN PREDELLA (15th C) Italian				
oil	1	14,000	14,000	14,000
MASTER OF THE BARBERINO (14th C) Italian				
oil	1	135,000	135,000	135,000
MASTER OF THE BIGALLO CRUCIFIX (fl.1225-1255) Italian				
oil	1	415,200	415,200	415,200
MASTER OF THE CARNATIONS (15th C) Italian				
oil	1	85,000	85,000	85,000
MASTER OF THE DEMI FIGURE (?) ?				
oil	1	94,138	94,138	94,138
MASTER OF THE FEMALE HALF LENGTHS (16th C) Flemish				
oil	3	85,440-130,000	105,730	101,750
MASTER OF THE FERTILITY OF THE EGG (17th C) Italian				
oil	1	9,425	9,425	9,425
MASTER OF THE INCREDULITY OF SAINT THOMAS (16th C) Italian				
oil	1	15,570	15,570	15,570
MASTER OF THE LANGMATT FOUNDATION VIEW (fl.1740-1770) Italian				
oil	6	12,000-157,250	75,893	56,959
MASTER OF THE LEGEND OF SAINT URSULA (15th C) German				
oil	1	100,340	100,340	100,340
MASTER OF THE LOMBARD FRUIT BOWL (17th C) Spanish				
oil	1	950,000	950,000	950,000
MASTER OF THE LUNEBURG BENEDIKT PANELS (15th C) German?				
oil	1	12,846	12,846	12,846
MASTER OF THE MADONNA LAZZARONE (15th C) Italian				
oil	1	70,000	70,000	70,000
MASTER OF THE PARROT (16th C) Flemish				
oil	1	55,360	55,360	55,360
MASTER OF THE PRODIGAL SON (16th C) Flemish				
oil	2	53,842-57,618	55,730	53,842
MASTER OF THE SEMINARY MADONNA (fl.1315-1330) Italian				
oil	1	112,450	112,450	112,450
MASTER OF VELLETRI (15th C) Italian?				
oil	1	38,163	38,163	38,163
MASTER OF VIRGOLETTA (15th C) Italian				
3D	1	24,218	24,218	24,218
MASTERKOVA, Lydia (1927-) Russian				
oil	1	90,000	90,000	90,000
MASTERS, E (19th C) British				
oil	2	3,330-3,515	3,422	3,330
MASTERS, Edward (19th C) British				
oil	1	1,218	1,218	1,218
MASTERS, Edwin (19th C) British				
oil	3	770-5,340	2,348	935
MASTROIANNI, Umberto (1910-1998) Italian				
oil	16	1,285-3,658	2,457	2,102
wc/d	19	477-2,945	1,357	1,168
3D	16	1,752-12,528	4,387	3,151
MASUI, Paul Auguste (1888-1981) Luxembourger				
oil	3	705-5,257	2,416	1,286
MASURE, Georges Paul (19/20th C) French?				
oil	1	1,070	1,070	1,070
MASUTTI, Carlo (1873-1953) Italian				
oil	1	1,452	1,452	1,452

Name	No.	Price Range	Average	Median
MATANIA, Fortunino (1881-1963) Italian				
oil	4	592-13,230	6,223	3,762
wc/d	1	1,512	1,512	1,512
MATARE, Ewald (1887-1965) German				
wc/d	3	3,534-6,479	5,301	5,890
3D	16	5,655-135,479	43,435	30,630
MATAWOWSKA, Jadwega (20th C) Polish				
oil	1	33,945	33,945	33,945
wc/d	1	1,091	1,091	1,091
MATEOS, Francisco (1894-1976) Spanish				
oil	5	5,021-14,270	9,576	9,807
wc/d	1	1,130	1,130	1,130
MATHAUSER, Josef (1846-1917) Czechoslovakian				
oil	1	1,267	1,267	1,267
MATHE, Jules Herve (1868-?) French				
oil	1	6,650	6,650	6,650
MATHESON, Ivar John (?-1963) American				
oil	1	1,200	1,200	1,200
MATHEU, Leonel (1967-) Cuban				
oil	1	1,200	1,200	1,200
MATHEWS, John Chester (fl.1884-1912) British				
oil	1	1,500	1,500	1,500
MATHEWSON, Frank Convers (1862-1941) American				
oil	1	2,750	2,750	2,750
wc/d	3	650-1,200	850	700
MATHEY, Jacques (1883-1973) French				
oil	1	1,757	1,757	1,757
MATHEY, Paul (1844-1929) French				
oil	1	8,000	8,000	8,000
MATHIESEN, Egon (1907-1976) Danish				
oil	4	647-3,071	1,576	808
MATHIEU, Cornelius (17th C) Dutch				
oil	2	16,365-21,020	18,692	16,365
MATHIEU, Georges (1921-) French				
oil	35	8,035-153,646	58,002	48,333
wc/d	37	540-17,224	6,499	5,702
MATHIEU, Paul (1872-1932) Belgian				
oil	12	656-10,286	3,473	2,356
MATHIOPOULOS, Pavlos (1876-1956) Greek				
wc/d	1	4,152	4,152	4,152
MATHIS, Leonie (1883-1952) Argentinian				
wc/d	4	800-22,500	13,325	8,000
MATHYS, Albert François (1885-1956) Belgian				
oil	2	1,193-2,860	2,026	1,193
MATIFAS, Louis Remy (1847-1896) French				
oil	2	700-1,914	1,307	700
MATIGNON, Albert (1869-?) French				
oil	1	954	954	954
wc/d	1	1,285	1,285	1,285
MATILLA Y MARINA, Segundo (1862-1937) Spanish				
wc/d	1	5,351	5,351	5,351
MATINO, Vittorio (1943-) Italian				
oil	1	3,301	3,301	3,301
MATISSE, Henri (1869-1954) French				
oil	7	148,000-16,500,000	4,515,183	1,000,000
wc/d	42	5,750-814,000	125,133	65,000
3D	4	48,000-1,300,000	449,500	100,000
MATIUSHIN, Mikhail V (1861-1934) Russian				
wc/d	1	17,200	17,200	17,200
MATOUT, Louis (1811-1888) French				
wc/d	1	1,671	1,671	1,671
MATSCHINSKY-DENNINGHOFF, Brigitte and Martin (20th C) German				
3D	4	7,598-48,301	21,322	10,541
MATT, Annemarie von (1905-1967) Swiss				
oil	1	11,416	11,416	11,416
MATTA (1911-2002) Chilean				
oil	39	7,027-1,200,000	121,535	58,000
wc/d	29	820-36,247	7,807	5,000
3D	7	2,534-23,000	9,576	5,462
MATTAS, Ake (1920-1962) Finnish				
wc/d	1	1,870	1,870	1,870

Name	No.	Price Range	Average	Median
MATTEIS, Francesco de (1852-?) Italian				
3D	1	5,565	5,565	5,565
MATTEIS, Paolo de (1662-1728) Italian				
oil	3	16,816-175,750	74,976	32,363
wc/d	1	5,000	5,000	5,000
MATTERN, Walter (20th C) American				
oil	1	3,750	3,750	3,750
MATTESON, Tompkins Harrison (1813-1884) American				
oil	1	9,000	9,000	9,000
MATTHEUER, Wolfgang (1927-2004) German				
oil	2	8,269-9,370	8,819	8,269
wc/d	3	7,415-13,993	10,259	9,370
MATTHEWS, James (19th C) British				
wc/d	2	497-2,088	1,292	497
MATTHEWS, Maggie (20th C) British				
oil	1	1,320	1,320	1,320
MATTHEWS, Marmaduke (1837-1913) Canadian				
oil	1	1,804	1,804	1,804
wc/d	6	597-1,319	997	825
MATTHEWS, William F (1878-1966) American				
wc/d	2	5,000-8,000	6,500	5,000
MATTHEY, Gill Julien (1889-1956) French?				
oil	1	2,062	2,062	2,062
wc/d	1	1,752	1,752	1,752
MATTHIESEN, Oscar Adam Otto (1861-1957) German				
oil	2	425-5,040	2,732	425
MATTHIEU, Georg David (1737-1776) German				
oil	1	5,466	5,466	5,466
MATTHISON, William (fl.1883-1923) British				
oil	2	637-957	797	637
wc/d	2	1,479-1,750	1,614	1,479
MATTHYS, Thomas (19/20th C) Belgian				
oil	1	2,600	2,600	2,600
MATTHYSEN, Jan Ryk (1816-1850) Dutch				
oil	1	2,662	2,662	2,662
MATTI, Luca (1964-) Italian				
oil	1	4,205	4,205	4,205
MATTIA, Gianluigi (1940-) Italian				
oil	1	2,919	2,919	2,919
MATTIACCI, Eliseo (1940-) Italian				
wc/d	4	1,145-3,515	2,275	2,220
3D	4	14,055-37,479	24,576	16,537
MATTINEN, Seppo (1930-) Finnish				
oil	2	1,455-1,456	1,455	1,455
MATTIOLI, Carlo (1911-1994) Italian				
oil	7	4,607-27,185	17,149	15,429
wc/d	6	1,571-6,705	3,897	3,514
MATTIS-TEUTSCH, Janos (1884-1960) Bohemian				
wc/d	2	989-17,671	9,330	989
3D	1	19,747	19,747	19,747
MATTO, Francisco (1911-1995) Uruguayan				
wc/d	1	1,300	1,300	1,300
MATTON, Arsene (1873-1933) Belgian				
3D	2	4,714-7,827	6,270	4,714
MATTON, Charles (1933-) French				
wc/d	1	1,360	1,360	1,360
3D	1	13,500	13,500	13,500
MATTONI DE LA FUENTE, Virgilio (1842-1923) Spanish				
oil	1	4,234	4,234	4,234
MATTSON, Henry Elis (1887-1971) American				
oil	1	2,200	2,200	2,200
MATULKA, Jan (1890-1972) American				
oil	9	1,000-29,000	11,083	8,000
MATUSHEVSKI, Yuri (1930-1999) Russian				
oil	6	2,124-3,850	2,612	2,450
MATVEYEV, Gerasim Ivanov (19th C) Russian				
oil	1	24,000	24,000	24,000
MATZOW, Frederick (19/20th C) American				
oil	1	1,000	1,000	1,000
MAUBERT, James (1666-1746) British				
oil	2	9,450-24,180	16,815	9,450

Name	No.	Price Range	Average	Median
MAUCH, Richard (1874-1921) Austrian				
oil	1	3,375	3,375	3,375
MAUFRA, Maxime (1861-1918) French				
oil	13	500-77,700	21,950	18,118
wc/d	6	479-3,403	1,557	750
MAUGERI, Concetto (1919-1951) Italian				
oil	1	2,336	2,336	2,336
MAULBERTSCH, Franz Anton (1724-1796) Austrian				
3D	1	5,153	5,153	5,153
MAUNY, Jacques (1893-1962) French				
oil	1	3,000	3,000	3,000
MAURER, Alfred H (1868-1932) American				
oil	3	37,500-120,000	79,166	80,000
wc/d	1	14,000	14,000	14,000
MAURER, Ingo (1932-) German				
3D	6	14,055-35,138	24,750	18,740
MAURER, Sidney Randolph (1926-) American				
wc/d	1	3,250	3,250	3,250
MAURI, Fabio (1926-) Italian				
wc/d	3	3,505-11,678	6,350	3,867
3D	1	12,603	12,603	12,603
MAURIER, Georges du (1834-1896) French				
oil	1	1,214	1,214	1,214
MAURIN, Charles (1856-1914) French				
wc/d	7	719-2,546	1,160	959
MAURUS, Hans (1901-1942) German				
oil	9	816-3,317	1,459	1,067
MAURY, F (1861-1933) French				
oil	1	2,500	2,500	2,500
MAUTORT, Alfred de (19th C) German				
oil	1	1,312	1,312	1,312
MAUVE, Anton (1838-1888) Dutch				
oil	6	1,036-42,500	10,078	1,740
wc/d	11	471-29,096	6,701	4,000
MAUZAISSE, Jean Baptiste (1784-1844) French				
oil	1	4,176	4,176	4,176
wc/d	1	8,236	8,236	8,236
MAUZAN, Achille (1883-1952) Italian/French				
oil	1	1,752	1,752	1,752
MAUZEY, Merritt (1898-1973) American				
oil	1	800	800	800
wc/d	2	2,200-4,250	3,225	2,200
MAVRO, Mania (1889-1969) Russian				
oil	4	479-1,176	823	695
wc/d	1	535	535	535
MAVROGORDATO, Alexander James (fl.1892-1933) British				
oil	1	4,617	4,617	4,617
wc/d	3	493-1,424	810	515
MAVROIDIS, Giorgios (1913-2003) Greek				
oil	1	5,536	5,536	5,536
MAVROS, Haris (1953-) Greek				
oil	1	5,610	5,610	5,610
MAX, Gabriel von (1840-1915) Czechoslovakian				
oil	5	1,312-7,071	3,078	2,572
MAX, Heinrich (1847-1900) Czechoslovakian				
oil	1	3,440	3,440	3,440
MAX, Peter (1937-) American/German				
oil	3	2,200-3,400	2,866	3,000
MAX-EHRLER, Louise (1850-?) Italian				
wc/d	1	27,351	27,351	27,351
MAXENCE, Edgard (1871-1954) French				
oil	11	656-210,000	31,891	7,007
wc/d	2	5,504-8,784	7,144	5,504
MAXFIELD, C P (19th C) British?				
oil	1	5,000	5,000	5,000
MAXIMOUCHKINA, Vera (1923-) Russian				
oil	1	4,055	4,055	4,055
MAXWELL, Hamilton (1830-1923) British				
oil	1	1,107	1,107	1,107
MAXWELL, John (1905-1962) British				
oil	1	8,304	8,304	8,304
wc/d	2	528-1,110	819	528

Name	No.	Price Range	Average	Median
MAXWELL, Paul (1926-) American				
oil	3	550-1,500	1,016	1,000
wc/d	1	650	650	650
MAY, Heinz (1878-1954) German				
oil	1	3,652	3,652	3,652
MAY, Henrietta Mabel (1884-1971) Canadian				
oil	12	2,320-265,877	31,860	7,332
MAY, Olivier le (1734-1797) French				
oil	3	2,195-25,342	10,891	5,138
wc/d	4	654-6,473	2,832	1,635
MAY, Phil (1864-1903) British				
wc/d	2	952-1,112	1,032	952
MAYA CORTES, Antonio (1950-) Spanish				
oil	1	1,414	1,414	1,414
wc/d	1	1,816	1,816	1,816
MAYBURGER, Josef (1813-1908) Austrian				
oil	3	3,892-8,247	6,463	7,250
MAYDELL, Baron Ernst von (1888-?) German				
wc/d	3	1,900-4,500	2,833	2,100
MAYER, A (?) ?				
oil	1	2,141	2,141	2,141
MAYER, August Georg (1834-1889) Austrian				
oil	1	4,750	4,750	4,750
MAYER, Constant (1832-1911) French				
oil	2	800-7,500	4,150	800
MAYER, Frank Blackwell (1827-1899) American				
oil	1	8,000	8,000	8,000
MAYER, Friedrich Carl (1824-1903) German				
oil	1	3,010	3,010	3,010
MAYER, Gustav (1847-1900) German				
oil	1	1,459	1,459	1,459
MAYER, L (?) ?				
oil	1	2,420	2,420	2,420
MAYER, Louis (1791-1843) German				
oil	1	1,548	1,548	1,548
MAYER, Martin (1931-) German				
3D	1	11,466	11,466	11,466
MAYER, Peter Bela (1888-1954) American				
oil	1	1,300	1,300	1,300
MAYER-FELICE, Felix (1876-?) German				
oil	1	2,121	2,121	2,121
MAYER-FRANKEN, Georg (1870-1926) German				
oil	1	1,423	1,423	1,423
MAYER-MARTON, Georg (1897-?) Hungarian				
oil	1	9,000	9,000	9,000
MAYEUR, Jean le (1880-1958) Belgian				
oil	19	716-374,795	33,028	4,290
wc/d	11	655-25,286	8,563	7,151
MAYHEW, Richard (1924-) American				
oil	1	10,000	10,000	10,000
MAYNARD, Guy (20th C) French				
oil	1	10,170	10,170	10,170
MAYNARD, Richard Field (1875-1952) American				
oil	2	1,903-2,000	1,951	1,903
MAYNE, C L (19th C) ?				
oil	1	2,640	2,640	2,640
MAYNE, Jean (1850-1905) Belgian				
oil	2	501-1,791	1,146	501
MAYO, Antoine Malliarakis (1905-1990) French/Egyptian				
oil	7	742-3,179	1,761	1,632
wc/d	1	879	879	879
MAYO, Drummond (fl.1980) British				
oil	1	800	800	800
wc/d	1	1,044	1,044	1,044
MAYODON, Jean (1893-1967) French				
oil	1	860	860	860
wc/d	2	440-1,021	730	440
3D	1	33,600	33,600	33,600
MAYOR, Fred (1868-1916) British				
oil	1	7,000	7,000	7,000
wc/d	2	926-1,332	1,129	926

Name	No.	Price Range	Average	Median
MAYOR, Hannah (1871-1947) British				
wc/d	1	1,656	1,656	1,656
MAYR, Christian (1805-1851) American/German				
oil	1	4,750	4,750	4,750
MAYR, Josef (1829-1865) Austrian				
oil	2	820-5,890	3,355	820
MAYR, Peter (1758-1836) German				
wc/d	1	10,738	10,738	10,738
MAYR-GRAZ, Karl (1850-1929) German				
oil	1	1,338	1,338	1,338
MAYRSHOFER, Max (1875-1950) German				
oil	5	546-1,414	824	727
wc/d	3	964-1,580	1,233	1,157
MAZAL, Ricardo (1950-) Mexican				
oil	1	21,000	21,000	21,000
MAZE, Paul (1887-1979) French				
oil	12	743-12,285	3,676	2,500
wc/d	62	443-18,000	2,669	1,653
MAZEROLLE, Alexis Joseph (1826-1889) French				
oil	3	3,750-20,000	9,166	3,750
wc/d	2	1,094-4,253	2,673	1,094
MAZINI, Ciro (20th C) Italian				
wc/d	1	1,500	1,500	1,500
MAZLIAH, Tal (1961-) Israeli				
oil	1	10,000	10,000	10,000
MAZO, Maurice (1901-) Algerian				
oil	1	1,157	1,157	1,157
MAZUMDAR, Chittrovanu (1956-) Indian				
oil	5	6,500-60,000	38,700	35,000
MAZUR, Michael (1935-) American				
wc/d	1	2,800	2,800	2,800
MAZUROWSKI, Wiktor (1859-1944) Polish				
oil	1	5,081	5,081	5,081
MAZY, Emile T (20th C) American				
oil	1	2,750	2,750	2,750
MAZZA, Giuseppe (1817-1884) Italian				
oil	1	23,946	23,946	23,946
MAZZA, Horacio Blas (1933-) Argentinian				
oil	1	2,000	2,000	2,000
MAZZA, Salvatore (1819-1886) Italian				
oil	3	1,816-16,562	11,222	15,288
MAZZANOVICH, Lawrence (1872-1946) American				
oil	1	4,000	4,000	4,000
MAZZELLA, J (19th C) French				
oil	1	1,359	1,359	1,359
MAZZETTA, J (19th C) Italian				
oil	1	2,832	2,832	2,832
MAZZETTI, Emo (1870-1955) Italian				
oil	2	3,024-3,857	3,440	3,024
MAZZOLA, Francesco (1503-1540) Italian				
oil	1	1,295,000	1,295,000	1,295,000
wc/d	1	70,300	70,300	70,300
MAZZOLA, Giuseppe (1748-1838) Italian				
wc/d	1	6,319	6,319	6,319
MAZZOLANI, Enrico (1876-1967) Italian				
oil	3	951-4,550	2,472	1,916
MAZZOLANI, Giuseppe (1842-1916) Italian				
oil	1	6,880	6,880	6,880
MAZZOLINI, Giuseppe (1806-1876) Italian				
oil	4	2,518-5,632	3,387	2,700
MAZZON, Galliano (1896-1978) Italian				
oil	4	771-2,163	1,268	951
wc/d	1	647	647	647
MAZZONI, Antonella (1975-) Italian				
oil	1	1,414	1,414	1,414
MAZZONI, Sebastiano (c.1611-1678) Italian				
oil	1	38,060	38,060	38,060
MAZZOTTA, Federico (19th C) Italian				
oil	2	4,816-40,767	22,791	4,816
MAZZUCHELLI, Pietro Francesco (1571-1626) Italian				
oil	1	15,226	15,226	15,226

Name	No.	Price Range	Average	Median
McCAIG, Norman J (1929-2001) Irish				
oil	20	1,239-8,469	3,651	3,053
McCORMACK, Selma (20th C) Irish				
oil	7	519-1,471	878	779
wc/d	2	559-1,295	927	559
3D	1	1,817	1,817	1,817
McCROSSAN, Mary (?-1934) British				
oil	2	1,464-3,520	2,492	1,464
McEWAN, Tom (1846-1914) British				
oil	9	576-8,850	2,959	2,595
wc/d	1	2,262	2,262	2,262
MEACCI, Ricciardo (1856-?) Italian				
wc/d	4	550-8,280	3,576	1,251
MEAD, Ray John (1921-1998) Canadian				
oil	3	5,318-9,071	7,012	6,647
MEAD, Rose (fl.1896-1899) British				
oil	2	865-1,211	1,038	865
MEADE, Arthur (1863-1948) British				
oil	1	1,990	1,990	1,990
MEADMORE, Clement (1929-2005) American/Australian				
3D	1	18,000	18,000	18,000
MEADOR, Joshua (1911-1965) American				
oil	5	750-2,250	1,420	1,400
MEADOWS, Arthur Joseph (1843-1907) British				
oil	14	774-13,200	6,196	4,176
MEADOWS, Bernard (1915-2005) British				
wc/d	2	2,958-3,132	3,045	2,958
3D	10	3,500-47,500	16,414	10,920
MEADOWS, Gordon Arthur (1868-?) British				
oil	2	898-1,602	1,250	898
MEADOWS, James (snr) (1798-1864) British				
oil	1	2,750	2,750	2,750
MEADOWS, James Edwin (1828-1888) British				
oil	8	1,980-8,246	3,987	2,835
MEADOWS, William (fl.1870-1895) British				
oil	8	1,914-5,600	3,464	3,287
MEAKIN, Lewis Henry (1853-1917) American				
oil	3	1,250-6,500	3,750	3,500
MEANS, Jamie (20th C) American				
wc/d	1	3,500	3,500	3,500
MEARS, Henrietta Dunn (1877-?) American				
oil	1	2,200	2,200	2,200
MEASHAM, Henry (1844-1922) British				
oil	1	1,309	1,309	1,309
MECATI, Dario (1909-1976) Italian				
oil	2	5,845-9,118	7,481	5,845
MECHAU, Frank (1904-1946) American				
wc/d	1	5,000	5,000	5,000
MECHMACHA, Omar (20th C) Moroccan				
oil	1	7,778	7,778	7,778
MECKLENBURG-STRELIZ, Marie von (19th C) German				
oil	1	1,686	1,686	1,686
MECRAY, John (1939-) American				
wc/d	1	11,000	11,000	11,000
MEDARD, Jules Ferdinand (c.1853-1927) French				
oil	2	3,352-13,436	8,394	3,352
MEDCALF, William J (fl.1901-1930) British				
oil	1	1,739	1,739	1,739
MEDEARIS, Roger (1920-2001) American				
wc/d	4	550-3,250	1,512	650
3D	1	2,600	2,600	2,600
MEDICI DEL VASCELLO, Osvaldo (1902-1978) Italian				
oil	1	3,889	3,889	3,889
wc/d	2	840-1,140	990	840
MEDINA SERRANO, Antonio (1944-) Spanish				
oil	1	3,575	3,575	3,575
MEDINA, Angel (1924-) Spanish				
oil	1	1,326	1,326	1,326
MEDINA, Sir John (1659-1710) British				
oil	1	3,096	3,096	3,096
MEDIZ-PELIKAN, Emilie (1861-1908) Austrian				
oil	1	1,703	1,703	1,703

Name	No.	Price Range	Average	Median
MEDLEY, Robert (1905-1994) British				
oil	3	1,239-6,090	3,376	2,800
wc/d	1	460	460	460
MEDNYANSZKY, Laszlo von (1852-1919) Hungarian				
oil	3	3,400-8,500	5,948	5,946
MEDOVIKOVA, Mascha (1952-) Russian				
oil	1	1,210	1,210	1,210
MEEGAN, Harry (19/20th C) British				
oil	2	460-2,262	1,361	460
MEEGAN, Walter (1859-1944) British				
oil	8	728-4,536	1,773	1,288
wc/d	1	5,220	5,220	5,220
MEEGEREN, Han van (1889-1947) Dutch				
oil	4	959-9,452	3,745	1,890
wc/d	4	800-3,129	1,585	951
MEEKER, Dean (1920-2002) American				
3D	1	1,700	1,700	1,700
MEEKER, Joseph R (1827-1889) American				
oil	7	1,200-110,000	28,242	15,000
MEERBERGEN, Rudolf (1908-1987) Belgian				
oil	3	701-5,096	2,224	877
MEERHOUD, Jan (?-1677) Dutch				
oil	1	2,331	2,331	2,331
MEERMAN, Bas (1970-) Dutch				
oil	2	1,870-8,182	5,026	1,870
MEERT, Joseph (1905-) American				
oil	1	2,000	2,000	2,000
MEERTS, Frans (1836-1896) Belgian				
oil	4	550-1,453	1,158	1,272
MEESE, Jonathan (1970-) German?				
oil	5	6,429-45,000	17,308	10,500
MEESER, Lillian B (1864-1942) American				
oil	2	750-1,700	1,225	750
MEESTER DE BETZENBROECK, Raymond de (1904-1995) Belgian				
3D	14	1,753-17,534	4,667	3,754
MEETEREN BROUWER, Menno van (1882-1974) Dutch				
oil	1	3,612	3,612	3,612
MEGAIDES, Herve (1951-) French				
oil	2	1,004-1,073	1,038	1,004
MEGE, Henri (1909-1984) ?				
oil	1	1,438	1,438	1,438
MEGERT, Christian (1937-) Swiss				
oil	1	2,803	2,803	2,803
3D	3	1,940-6,370	4,893	6,370
MEGGESON, J T (fl.1860-1871) British				
oil	1	18,000	18,000	18,000
MEHEUT, François (?) French				
3D	1	4,401	4,401	4,401
MEHEUT, Mathurin (1882-1958) French				
oil	4	3,349-16,949	8,682	3,912
wc/d	36	588-11,548	2,400	1,514
MEHRA, Rolf (20th C) German				
oil	1	1,332	1,332	1,332
MEHRETU, Julie (1970-) American				
wc/d	3	32,000-55,000	42,333	40,000
MEHTA, Tyeb (1925-) Indian				
oil	5	216,250-1,400,000	664,050	374,000
3D	1	110,000	110,000	110,000
MEI, Paolo (19th C) Italian				
oil	1	7,500	7,500	7,500
MEIDNER, Ludwig (1884-1966) German				
oil	6	4,241-2,816,000	475,382	7,658
wc/d	18	598-88,000	13,737	4,452
MEIER, Theo (1908-1982) Swiss				
oil	5	5,274-22,699	12,649	14,460
MEIERHANS, Joseph (1890-1980) Swiss				
oil	20	350-7,500	1,642	850
wc/d	2	1,400-3,250	2,325	1,400
MEIFREN Y ROIG, Eliseo (1859-1940) Spanish				
oil	12	3,130-457,551	86,063	52,200
MEIJER, Cristoffel (1776-1813) Dutch				
wc/d	1	1,764	1,764	1,764

Name	No.	Price Range	Average	Median
MEILINGER, Lothar Rudolf (1887-1935) German				
oil	2	766-2,600	1,683	766
MEINEL, Johann Philipp (1806-1893) German				
oil	1	5,364	5,364	5,364
MEINERI, Guido (1869-1944) Italian				
oil	1	1,894	1,894	1,894
MEINERS, Piet (1857-1903) Dutch				
oil	1	1,196	1,196	1,196
MEINZOLT, Georg (1863-1945) German				
oil	1	3,155	3,155	3,155
MEIRAGHE, V (19th C) ?				
wc/d	1	2,474	2,474	2,474
MEIRELES, Cildo (1948-) Brazilian				
wc/d	1	8,000	8,000	8,000
3D	1	70,000	70,000	70,000
MEIREN, Jan Baptist van der (1664-1708) Flemish				
oil	3	1,780-19,110	13,333	19,110
MEISCHKE-SMITH (19/20th C) ?				
oil	1	2,400	2,400	2,400
MEISSER, Leonhard (1902-1977) Swiss				
oil	2	835-1,211	1,023	835
MEISSNER, Adolf Ernst (1837-1902) German				
oil	3	3,330-3,816	3,591	3,629
MEISSNER, Gustav (1830-?) German				
oil	1	1,200	1,200	1,200
MEISSNER, Leo John (1895-?) American				
oil	3	900-5,750	2,550	1,000
MEISSNER, Paul (1907-1982) Austrian				
oil	1	1,697	1,697	1,697
MEISSONIER, Jean Louis Ernest (1815-1891) French				
oil	13	700-40,000	8,507	4,364
wc/d	7	570-3,700	1,610	1,560
3D	1	6,804	6,804	6,804
MEISSONNIER, Joseph (1864-1943) French				
oil	2	1,095-9,082	5,088	1,095
MEISTER, Willi (1918-) Swiss				
oil	1	1,513	1,513	1,513
MEISTERMANN, Georg (1911-1990) German				
oil	5	2,225-45,863	11,568	3,063
wc/d	7	486-2,803	1,345	912
MEJO, Oscar de (20th C) ?				
oil	5	800-2,800	1,620	1,600
MEJOCA, Alice (20th C) ?				
oil	1	1,318	1,318	1,318
MELAMUD, Shaya Noevich (1911-) Russian				
oil	1	14,705	14,705	14,705
MELANI, S (20th C) ?				
3D	1	2,000	2,000	2,000
MELBYE, Anton (1818-1875) Danish				
oil	8	929-14,160	4,845	3,042
MELBYE, Wilhelm (1824-1882) Danish				
oil	20	1,107-12,155	4,122	2,800
MELCARTH, Edward (1914-) American				
oil	1	400	400	400
3D	2	3,000-3,750	3,375	3,000
MELCHER-TILMES, Jan Hermanus (1847-1920) Dutch				
oil	3	550-1,523	1,191	1,502
MELCHERS, Gari (1860-1932) American				
oil	1	1,800	1,800	1,800
wc/d	1	2,600	2,600	2,600
MELCHIOR, Wilhelm (1817-1860) German				
oil	2	848-2,400	1,624	848
MELCHIORI, Giovanni (1664-1745) Italian				
oil	1	23,759	23,759	23,759
MELE, Juan (1923-) Argentinian				
oil	2	1,267-7,000	4,133	1,267
wc/d	1	634	634	634
MELEHI, Mohammed (1936-) Moroccan				
oil	2	2,978-6,880	4,929	2,978
MELEZET, du (17th C) ?				
oil	1	380,000	380,000	380,000

Name	No.	Price Range	Average	Median
MELGAARD, Bjarne (1967-) Norwegian				
wc/d	1	3,832	3,832	3,832
MELGERS, Henk (20th C) Dutch				
oil	1	6,096	6,096	6,096
wc/d	3	1,386-4,477	2,543	1,767
MELIDA Y ALINARI, Don Enrique (1834-1892) Spanish				
oil	1	6,960	6,960	6,960
MELIES, Georges (1861-1938) French				
wc/d	1	1,987	1,987	1,987
MELIKOFF-LORIS, Athanase (19/20th C) French?				
oil	1	6,336	6,336	6,336
MELIS MARINI, Felice (1871-1953) Italian				
oil	1	3,221	3,221	3,221
MELISSENT, Maurice (?) French				
wc/d	2	957-1,549	1,253	957
MELKA, Vinzenz (1834-1911) Rumanian				
oil	1	1,928	1,928	1,928
MELL, Ed (1942-) American				
oil	1	53,000	53,000	53,000
MELLE (1908-1976) Dutch				
oil	1	6,479	6,479	6,479
MELLEN, Mary (1817-?) American				
oil	1	30,000	30,000	30,000
MELLER, Ingo (1955-) German				
oil	1	1,784	1,784	1,784
MELLER, Reijo (1944-) Finnish				
oil	2	887-1,858	1,372	887
MELLER, Vadim (1884-1962) Russian				
wc/d	1	27,900	27,900	27,900
MELLERUP, Tage (1910-1988) Danish				
oil	1	7,146	7,146	7,146
MELLERY, Xavier (1845-1921) Belgian				
oil	3	903-2,548	1,739	1,767
wc/d	5	1,204-14,657	5,028	3,131
MELLI, Roberto (1885-1958) Italian				
oil	1	9,541	9,541	9,541
MELLIN, Charles (c.1597-1647) French				
wc/d	1	8,264	8,264	8,264
MELLING, Caspar (18th C) German				
oil	1	1,640	1,640	1,640
MELLON, Campbell (1876-1955) British				
oil	18	662-21,735	6,511	3,219
MELLOR, Everett W (1878-1965) British				
oil	4	1,175-5,160	2,852	1,317
MELLOR, Joseph (fl.1850-1885) British				
oil	6	552-4,446	2,117	1,038
MELLOR, William (1851-1931) British				
oil	53	510-16,376	5,966	5,709
wc/d	3	1,890-6,960	5,230	6,840
MELLYN, Sean (1965-) American				
oil	1	3,500	3,500	3,500
MELONI, Gino (1905-1989) Italian				
oil	5	1,784-3,156	2,323	2,185
wc/d	1	707	707	707
MELOTTE, Antoine Marie (1722-1795) Flemish				
3D	1	19,140	19,140	19,140
MELOTTI, Fausto (1901-1986) Italian				
oil	4	3,279-42,480	16,517	5,086
wc/d	4	2,342-3,562	2,904	2,544
3D	17	3,562-203,550	39,706	14,602
MELROSE, Andrew (1836-1901) American				
oil	8	2,000-85,000	14,306	3,500
MELS, Rene (1909-1977) Belgian				
oil	4	643-2,338	1,506	818
MELSEN, Marten (1870-1947) Belgian				
oil	2	1,435-14,351	7,893	1,435
MELTSNER, Paul R (1905-1966) American				
oil	2	1,000-1,600	1,300	1,000
MELTZER, Arthur (1893-1989) American				
oil	13	500-65,000	14,550	5,500
wc/d	1	400	400	400

Name	No.	Price Range	Average	Median
MELVILLE, Arthur (1858-1904) British				
oil	1	3,927	3,927	3,927
wc/d	4	5,220-92,560	49,235	45,760
MELVILLE, John (1902-1986) British				
oil	4	552-1,044	728	563
wc/d	2	522-648	585	522
MELZER, Moritz (1877-1966) German				
oil	1	1,236	1,236	1,236
MENA, Juan de Dios (1897-1954) Argentinian				
3D	3	10,000-15,000	12,333	12,000
MENABONI, Athos (1895-1990) American/Italian				
wc/d	1	3,500	3,500	3,500
MENAGO, V (?) ?				
oil	1	1,710	1,710	1,710
MENARD, Emile René (1862-1930) French				
oil	3	1,500-5,955	3,851	4,099
wc/d	7	584-7,123	2,532	1,401
MENARD, René-Joseph (1827-1887) French				
oil	3	1,539-9,452	6,604	8,822
MENARDEAU, Maurice (1897-1977) French				
oil	7	800-2,152	1,495	1,514
wc/d	3	526-2,635	1,264	631
MENCHERO, Jose (1956-) Spanish?				
oil	1	1,580	1,580	1,580
MENCIA, Antoine Garcia (19th C) Italian				
oil	1	31,000	31,000	31,000
MENDELSON, Marc (1915-) Belgian				
oil	1	1,908	1,908	1,908
MENDEZ OSUNA, Elbano (20th C) Venezuelan				
oil	2	1,070-1,150	1,110	1,070
MENDEZ, Manuel Gonzales (fl.1880-1900) Spanish				
oil	1	11,000	11,000	11,000
MENDHAM, Edith (1888-1911) British				
wc/d	1	2,958	2,958	2,958
MENDIVE, Manuel (1944-) Cuban				
oil	1	10,703	10,703	10,703
MENDJISKY, Maurice (1889-1951) Polish				
oil	5	1,985-19,986	7,466	4,663
MENDJISKY, Serge (1929-) French				
oil	9	665-2,472	1,550	1,674
wc/d	4	1,014-4,261	2,518	2,303
MENDOZA, C G (19/20th C) Cuban				
oil	1	2,301	2,301	2,301
MENDOZA, Jonidel (20th C) Venezuelan				
3D	1	1,930	1,930	1,930
MENDOZA, June (20th C) British/Australian				
oil	1	4,400	4,400	4,400
MENDOZA, Philip (c.1899-?) ?				
wc/d	1	5,280	5,280	5,280
MENDOZA, Ryan (1971-) American				
oil	1	4,198	4,198	4,198
MENE, P J (1810-1879) French				
3D	7	1,790-10,800	3,969	2,910
MENE, Pierre Jules (1810-1879) French				
3D	62	1,780-37,699	7,879	3,924
MENEGAZZI, Carlo (19/20th C) Italian				
wc/d	2	454-1,942	1,198	454
MENENDEZ PIDAL, Luis (1864-1932) Spanish				
oil	2	1,316-8,400	4,858	1,316
MENESES, Jesus (?) Spanish				
wc/d	1	2,411	2,411	2,411
MENG FU (?) Chinese				
wc/d	1	5,220	5,220	5,220
MENGE, Charles (1920-) Swiss				
oil	3	897-9,789	4,921	4,079
MENGHI, Jose Luis (1904-1985) Argentinian				
oil	2	750-4,000	2,375	750
MENGIN, Paul Eugène (1853-1937) French				
3D	1	6,370	6,370	6,370
MENGS, Anton Raphael (1728-1779) German				
oil	2	968-40,939	20,953	968
wc/d	1	2,330	2,330	2,330

Name	No.	Price Range	Average	Median
MENGUY, Frederic (1927-) French				
oil	30	609-4,305	1,848	1,815
wc/d	1	606	606	606
MENINSKY, Bernard (1891-1950) British				
oil	11	828-8,505	3,259	2,784
wc/d	25	696-12,087	2,226	1,539
MENKES, Zygmunt (1896-1986) Polish				
oil	9	3,250-15,904	5,876	4,750
wc/d	3	650-3,500	2,183	2,400
MENN, Barthelemy (1815-1893) Swiss				
oil	2	1,224-5,274	3,249	1,224
MENNERET, Charles Louis (1876-1946) French				
oil	2	1,312-1,757	1,534	1,312
MENNYEY, Francesco (1889-1950) Italian				
oil	4	605-2,422	1,210	908
MENON, Anjolie Ela (1940-) Indian				
oil	10	6,500-55,000	28,300	15,000
MENPES, Mortimer L (1860-1938) British				
oil	10	1,368-29,600	5,223	2,301
wc/d	2	1,770-2,992	2,381	1,770
MENRIQUE, Cesar (20th C) French				
wc/d	1	12,621	12,621	12,621
MENS, Isidorus Maria Cornelis van (1890-1985) Belgian				
oil	3	3,612-8,784	5,722	4,772
wc/d	10	477-2,154	1,252	1,165
MENSA, Manuel (1875-?) Spanish				
oil	3	475-1,688	1,054	1,000
MENSAQUE Y ALVARADO, Antonio (19th C) Spanish				
oil	1	5,890	5,890	5,890
MENSE, Carlo (1886-1965) German				
oil	7	2,803-15,288	9,009	8,281
wc/d	3	1,147-2,710	1,851	1,697
MENSHAUSEN-LABRIOLA, Frieda (1861-?) German				
wc/d	3	666-1,300	1,022	1,100
MENSION, Cornelis Jan (1882-1950) Dutch				
oil	2	841-1,890	1,365	841
MENTAULT, Marie Louise (19th C) Swiss				
oil	1	6,829	6,829	6,829
MENTESSI, Giuseppe (1857-1931) Italian				
oil	1	1,295	1,295	1,295
MENTOR, Blasco (1918-2003) Spanish				
oil	2	1,403-2,338	1,870	1,403
wc/d	1	584	584	584
MENZEL, Adolph (1815-1905) German				
wc/d	20	450-1,380,000	114,258	18,500
MENZIO, Francesco (1899-1979) Italian				
oil	7	3,221-25,691	9,796	6,562
wc/d	1	1,985	1,985	1,985
MENZLER, Wilhelm (1846-1926) German				
oil	1	3,780	3,780	3,780
MERCADANTE, Biagio (1893-1971) Italian				
oil	1	3,312	3,312	3,312
MERCADE, Jaime (1889-1967) Spanish				
oil	1	2,272	2,272	2,272
MERCADE, Jordi (1923-) Spanish				
oil	1	1,085	1,085	1,085
MERCATALI, F (fl.1890-1913) Italian				
oil	1	5,000	5,000	5,000
MERCHI, Gaetano (1747-1823) Italian				
3D	1	6,552	6,552	6,552
MERCIE, Marius Jean Antonin (1845-1916) French				
3D	15	3,600-42,000	11,652	8,000
MERCIER, Jean A (1899-1995) French				
oil	2	1,029-2,057	1,543	1,029
wc/d	92	514-6,429	1,590	900
MERCIER, Philippe (1689-1760) French				
oil	1	100,000	100,000	100,000
MERCK, Jacob Franz van der (1610-1664) Dutch				
oil	1	4,849	4,849	4,849
MERCKER, Erich (1891-1973) German				
oil	14	544-3,857	1,441	1,007

Name	No.	Price Range	Average	Median
MERCULIANO, Giacomo (1859-1935) French				
3D	2	2,500-5,462	3,981	2,500
MERDY, Jean le (1928-) French				
oil	3	1,598-3,912	3,056	3,660
MEREDITH, Alice (1905-?) American				
oil	1	1,600	1,600	1,600
MEREDITH, John (1933-2000) Canadian				
wc/d	2	1,750-2,997	2,373	1,750
MERELLO, Rubaldo (1872-1922) Italian				
oil	1	125,714	125,714	125,714
MERGIER, Paul Louis (1891-?) French				
3D	1	52,500	52,500	52,500
MERIDA, Carlos (1891-1984) Guatemalan				
oil	5	17,000-95,000	50,000	50,000
wc/d	4	25,000-55,000	38,750	30,000
MERIEL-BUSSY, Andre (1902-1985) French				
oil	2	490-701	595	490
wc/d	2	909-1,649	1,279	909
MERIENNE, Nancy (1792-1860) Swiss				
wc/d	1	3,889	3,889	3,889
MERIMEE, Jean Francois Leonor (1757-1836) French				
wc/d	1	4,200	4,200	4,200
MERINO, Daniel (1941-) Spanish				
oil	1	1,316	1,316	1,316
MERITE, Edouard Paul (1867-1941) French				
oil	11	1,014-3,568	1,894	1,565
wc/d	8	631-2,148	1,294	1,193
3D	1	5,655	5,655	5,655
MERKEL, Georg (1881-1976) Austrian				
oil	6	2,104-12,138	4,753	3,029
MERLE, Hughes (1823-1881) French				
oil	3	10,669-105,000	50,823	36,800
MERLIN, Daniel (1861-1933) French				
oil	4	2,694-5,670	3,619	2,803
MERLINO, Silvio (1952-) American				
wc/d	1	3,266	3,266	3,266
MERLO, Camillo (1856-1931) Italian				
oil	6	666-1,998	1,380	908
MERLO, Metello (1886-1964) Italian				
oil	4	605-2,016	973	605
wc/d	1	873	873	873
MERME, Charles (19th C) French				
oil	1	5,605	5,605	5,605
MERODACK-JEANNEAU, Alexis (1873-1919) French				
oil	1	2,979	2,979	2,979
wc/d	3	775-2,777	1,780	1,788
MERODE, Carl von (1853-1909) Austrian				
oil	1	7,068	7,068	7,068
MERODIO, Carlos (1944-) Spanish				
oil	1	1,025	1,025	1,025
MERON, C (19th C) ?				
oil	1	3,434	3,434	3,434
MERRICK, James Kirk (1905-1985) American				
wc/d	1	1,900	1,900	1,900
MERRIFIELD, Tom (1932-) Australian				
wc/d	1	1,044	1,044	1,044
3D	2	10,320-13,920	12,120	10,320
MERRILD, Knud (1894-1954) Danish				
wc/d	2	2,500-6,500	4,500	2,500
MERRILL, Christine Herman (20th C) American				
oil	1	4,000	4,000	4,000
MERRIOTT, Jack (1901-1968) British				
wc/d	3	525-3,675	1,664	794
MERRITT, Anna Lea (1844-1930) British				
oil	2	1,200-45,360	23,280	1,200
MERSON, Luc-Olivier (1846-1920) French				
wc/d	3	484-6,171	2,456	714
MERSSEMAN, Auguste Joseph Marie de (1808-1879) French				
oil	1	2,431	2,431	2,431
MERTENS, Adrien (1910-1968) Belgian				
3D	1	4,332	4,332	4,332

Name	No.	Price Range	Average	Median
MERTENS, Charles (1865-1919) Belgian				
oil	2	1,784-4,127	2,955	1,784
wc/d	2	637-637	637	637
MERTENS, Hedi (1893-1982) Swiss				
oil	2	1,000-1,000	1,000	1,000
MERTENS, Jan Frans Josef (18th C) Flemish				
oil	1	3,579	3,579	3,579
MERTENS, Wouter (17th C) Flemish				
oil	1	330,000	330,000	330,000
MERTES-FRADY, Gudrun (1939-) German				
	2	1,414-2,121	1,767	1,414
MERTZ, Albert (1920-1990) Danish				
oil	2	970-1,132	1,051	970
MERTZ, Johann Cornelius (1819-1891) Dutch				
oil	1	4,607	4,607	4,607
MERWIN, Antoinette de Forrest (1861-1941) American				
oil	1	1,900	1,900	1,900
MERY, Alfred Émile (1824-1896) French				
wc/d	2	2,405-2,592	2,498	2,405
MERZ, Albert (1942-) Swiss				
wc/d	1	530	530	530
3D	2	2,029-2,191	2,110	2,029
MERZ, Gerhard (1947-) German				
oil	1	7,040	7,040	7,040
3D	1	30,000	30,000	30,000
MERZ, Juliana (20th C) American				
oil	1	1,900	1,900	1,900
MERZ, Mario (1925-2003) Italian				
oil	4	13,155-96,327	42,680	18,740
wc/d	10	692-61,950	22,872	15,653
3D	2	144,490-265,500	204,995	144,490
MESCHERSKY, Arsenii Ivanovich (1834-1902) Russian				
oil	1	28,000	28,000	28,000
MESCIULAM, Plinio (1926-) Italian				
oil	2	983-3,687	2,335	983
wc/d	2	1,903-2,022	1,962	1,903
MESDAG VAN HOUTEN, Sientje (1834-1909) Dutch				
oil	2	1,576-9,889	5,732	1,576
MESDAG, H W (1831-1915) Dutch				
wc/d	1	4,195	4,195	4,195
MESDAG, Hendrik-Willem (1831-1915) Dutch				
oil	6	55,625-295,000	151,727	109,110
wc/d	7	1,878-28,000	11,530	8,604
MESENS, Edouard Léon Theodore (1903-1971) British				
oil	1	2,057	2,057	2,057
wc/d	3	1,654-2,983	2,221	2,028
MESGRINY, Claude François Auguste de (1836-1884) French				
oil	3	1,486-13,000	7,769	8,822
MESLY, David (1918-) ?				
3D	4	2,546-4,903	3,472	2,741
MESMER, Gustav (1865-?) German				
oil	1	2,188	2,188	2,188
MESNAGER, Jerome (1961-) French				
oil	12	565-4,438	1,490	1,051
wc/d	4	701-3,134	1,905	1,808
MESS, George J (1898-1962) American				
oil	1	1,800	1,800	1,800
MESSAC, Ivan (1948-) French				
oil	4	973-4,671	2,680	1,192
wc/d	1	2,460	2,460	2,460
MESSAGER, Annette (1943-) French				
oil	1	12,040	12,040	12,040
wc/d	1	2,102	2,102	2,102
MESSAGIER, Jean (1920-1999) French				
oil	8	1,767-10,357	5,979	6,681
wc/d	9	654-3,273	1,684	1,192
MESSEG, Aharon (1942-) Israeli				
oil	1	2,800	2,800	2,800
MESSEL, Oliver (1904-1978) British				
oil	1	6,992	6,992	6,992
wc/d	4	443-6,440	3,422	1,288

Name	No.	Price Range	Average	Median
MESSENSEE, Jurgen (1937-) Austrian				
oil	3	1,286-2,019	1,586	1,455
wc/d	4	1,091-2,637	1,966	1,567
MESSER, Peter (1954-) British				
oil	1	2,408	2,408	2,408
MESSER, Sam (1955-) American				
oil	1	3,879	3,879	3,879
MESSERLI, Paul Pierre (1899-1987) Swiss				
oil	2	734-2,121	1,427	734
MESSERSCHMITT, Pius Ferdinand (1858-1915) German				
wc/d	4	589-2,003	1,332	1,156
MESSINA, Francesco (1900-1995) Italian				
3D	7	1,929-59,655	15,325	7,611
MESSINA, Salvatore (1916-1982) Italian				
3D	1	25,767	25,767	25,767
MESSMANN, Carl Ludvig Ferd (1826-1893) Danish				
oil	1	1,405	1,405	1,405
MESTROVIC, Ivan (1883-1962) American/Yugoslavian				
3D	1	3,099	3,099	3,099
METCALF, Conger (1914-1998) American				
wc/d	8	550-3,500	1,700	1,300
METCALF, Willard Leroy (1858-1925) American				
oil	2	150,000-825,000	487,500	150,000
wc/d	1	6,000	6,000	6,000
METCALFE, Gerald Fenwick (fl.1894-1929) British				
oil	1	18,811	18,811	18,811
METEYARD, Thomas B (1865-1928) American				
wc/d	1	2,100	2,100	2,100
METS, Pieter de (1880-1965) Belgian?				
oil	1	1,113	1,113	1,113
METSYS, Jan (c.1509-1575) Flemish				
oil	2	7,598-39,130	23,364	7,598
METTENLEITER, Johann Jakob (1750-1825) German				
oil	1	46,757	46,757	46,757
METZ, Caesar (1823-1895) German				
oil	1	3,337	3,337	3,337
METZ, Conrad Martin (1749-1827) British				
wc/d	2	2,000-17,000	9,500	2,000
METZ, Gustav (1817-1853) German				
oil	1	45,755	45,755	45,755
METZENER, Alfred (1833-1905) Swiss				
oil	2	719-6,526	3,622	719
METZGER, Ige (19th C) German				
wc/d	1	1,095	1,095	1,095
METZINGER, Jean (1883-1956) French				
oil	14	13,548-230,000	72,761	40,411
wc/d	7	1,020-38,170	11,344	5,000
METZKER, M (19/20th C) German				
oil	1	1,816	1,816	1,816
METZKES, Harald (1929-) German				
oil	2	3,507-5,262	4,384	3,507
METZLER, Kurt Laurenz (1941-) Swiss				
wc/d	1	3,246	3,246	3,246
3D	5	2,272-9,737	5,660	4,868
METZMACHER, Émile Pierre (19th C) French				
oil	2	12,000-23,220	17,610	12,000
METZOLDT, Max (1859-?) German				
oil	1	7,054	7,054	7,054
MEUCCI, Anthony (fl.1818-1827) American/Italian				
wc/d	2	11,000-25,000	18,000	11,000
MEUCCI, Michelangelo (19th C) Italian				
oil	11	525-3,390	1,743	1,764
MEULEN, Adam Frans van der (1632-1690) Flemish				
oil	1	6,042	6,042	6,042
wc/d	4	700-23,784	13,716	8,507
MEULEN, Dirk van de (1945-) German				
oil	1	718	718	718
wc/d	1	494	494	494
MEULENAERE, Edmond de (1884-1963) Belgian				
oil	1	1,528	1,528	1,528
MEULENER, Pieter (1602-1654) Dutch				
oil	2	4,757-50,571	27,664	4,757

Name	No.	Price Range	Average	Median
MEUNIER, Constantin (1831-1905) Belgian				
oil	3	688-9,425	4,647	3,828
3D	8	1,764-17,979	4,754	2,803
MEUNIER, Georgette (1859-1951) Belgian				
oil	1	2,460	2,460	2,460
MEUNIER, Jean Baptiste (1786-1858) French				
wc/d	1	1,405	1,405	1,405
MEUNIER, Mark (1949-) American				
oil	2	1,100-1,500	1,300	1,100
MEURICE, Jean Michel (1938-) French				
oil	1	2,589	2,589	2,589
wc/d	1	1,294	1,294	1,294
MEURIS, Emmanuel (1894-1969) Italian				
wc/d	1	1,500	1,500	1,500
MEURON, Albert de (1823-1897) Swiss				
oil	1	1,415	1,415	1,415
MEURON, Louis de (1868-1949) Swiss				
oil	1	1,054	1,054	1,054
MEURS, Harmen (1891-1964) Dutch				
oil	2	1,001-1,260	1,130	1,001
MEUSEL, E (20th C) ?				
3D	1	2,314	2,314	2,314
MEUSER (1947-) ?				
oil	1	5,890	5,890	5,890
3D	1	3,700	3,700	3,700
MEVIUS, Hermann (1820-1864) German				
oil	4	1,368-15,979	5,283	1,573
MEXIA DE ARRIABAS, Fernanda Frances (1862-1938) Spanish				
oil	1	1,145	1,145	1,145
MEY, Jos de (1928-) Belgian				
oil	1	1,686	1,686	1,686
MEYER AM RHYN, Jost (1834-1898) Swiss				
oil	3	687-3,053	1,501	763
MEYER DE HAAN, Isaac Jacob (1852-1895) Dutch				
oil	1	4,579	4,579	4,579
MEYER VON BREMEN, Johann Georg (1813-1886) German				
oil	7	3,250-55,680	21,087	8,000
wc/d	1	3,390	3,390	3,390
MEYER, A (19/20th C) ?				
oil	1	6,622	6,622	6,622
MEYER, Auguste (19th C) French				
oil	2	4,214-7,224	5,719	4,214
MEYER, C (19/20th C) German				
oil	1	3,409	3,409	3,409
MEYER, Charles Louis (1882-1980) French				
oil	1	1,602	1,602	1,602
MEYER, Claus (1856-1919) German				
oil	4	839-2,386	1,673	1,300
MEYER, Conrad (1618-1689) Swiss				
wc/d	1	21,205	21,205	21,205
MEYER, Edgar (1853-1925) Austrian				
oil	1	8,784	8,784	8,784
wc/d	1	2,066	2,066	2,066
MEYER, Elias (1763-1809) Danish				
oil	1	4,901	4,901	4,901
MEYER, Émile (19th C) French				
oil	2	7,500-9,000	8,250	7,500
MEYER, Ernst (1796-1861) Danish				
oil	2	3,474-5,211	4,342	3,474
wc/d	1	1,226	1,226	1,226
MEYER, G (?) ?				
oil	1	1,213	1,213	1,213
MEYER, Hendrik de (17/18th C) Dutch				
oil	2	2,979-6,423	4,701	2,979
MEYER, Hendrik de I (1600-1690) Dutch				
oil	3	10,451-41,520	26,573	27,750
MEYER, Jan (1927-1995) Dutch				
oil	2	908-1,403	1,155	908
wc/d	1	1,127	1,127	1,127
MEYER, Johan (1885-1970) Dutch				
oil	5	814-6,592	2,175	1,006

Name	No.	Price Range	Average	Median
MEYER, Johan Hendrik Louis (1809-1866) Dutch				
oil	1	6,578	6,578	6,578
MEYER, Johann Crescenz (1735-1824) Swiss				
oil	2	2,039-3,916	2,977	2,039
MEYER, Johann Jakob (1787-1858) Swiss				
wc/d	1	2,313	2,313	2,313
MEYER, L (19th C) ?				
oil	1	65,000	65,000	65,000
MEYER, Ludwig (1705-1785) Swiss				
oil	1	8,803	8,803	8,803
MEYER, Otto (1839-?) German				
oil	1	1,816	1,816	1,816
MEYER, Rudolph Theodor (1605-1638) Swiss				
wc/d	1	2,960	2,960	2,960
MEYER, Sal (1877-1965) Dutch				
oil	10	1,199-12,658	4,801	2,397
MEYER-AMDEN, Otto (1885-1933) Swiss				
wc/d	2	1,362-3,497	2,429	1,362
MEYER-BELART, Emil Eugen (1891-1940) Swiss				
oil	1	5,612	5,612	5,612
MEYER-MAINZ, Paul (1864-1909) German				
oil	1	5,220	5,220	5,220
MEYER-WALDECK, Kunz (1859-1953) German				
oil	4	1,296-3,152	2,176	1,991
MEYER-WIEGAND, Rolf Dieter (1929-) German				
oil	1	1,752	1,752	1,752
MEYERHEIM, Friedrich Edouard (1808-1879) German				
oil	1	19,079	19,079	19,079
MEYERHEIM, Hermann (1840-1880) German				
oil	3	8,000-9,500	8,614	8,342
MEYERHEIM, Paul Friedrich (1842-1915) German				
oil	6	522-6,479	2,524	993
wc/d	1	1,455	1,455	1,455
MEYERHEIM, Wilhelm Alexander (1815-1882) German				
oil	5	2,928-6,020	4,295	4,171
MEYEROWITZ, William (1898-1981) American				
oil	1	5,000	5,000	5,000
wc/d	1	1,500	1,500	1,500
MEYERS, Isidore (1836-1917) Belgian				
oil	7	482-1,870	1,005	959
MEYERS, Ralph (1885-1948) American				
oil	1	4,000	4,000	4,000
MEYERS, Robert (1919-1970) American				
oil	1	4,000	4,000	4,000
MEYLAN, Henry (1895-?) Swiss				
oil	2	687-1,679	1,183	687
MEYNART, Maurice (1894-1976) Belgian				
oil	3	1,000-7,151	3,384	2,003
MEYNIER, Jules Joseph (1826-c.1903) French				
oil	2	1,384-4,171	2,777	1,384
wc/d	1	1,211	1,211	1,211
MEYS, Louis (1902-1995) Dutch				
oil	3	1,649-18,000	7,192	1,929
MEZA, Guillermo (1917-) Mexican				
oil	2	8,000-13,000	10,500	8,000
wc/d	1	500	500	500
MEZGER, Caroline (1787-1843) Swiss				
wc/d	1	2,039	2,039	2,039
MEZGER, Johann Heinrich (1845-1891) Swiss				
wc/d	1	1,632	1,632	1,632
MEZIANE, Meriem (1930-) Moroccan				
oil	2	16,771-45,895	31,333	16,771
MEZIAT, Renato (1952-) Brazilian				
oil	3	20,000-50,000	35,833	37,500
MEZZADRI, Antonio (fl.c.1688) Italian				
oil	1	48,649	48,649	48,649
MEZZERA, Rosa (1791-1826) Italian				
oil	1	5,828	5,828	5,828
MIALHE, Federico (1800-1868) French				
oil	1	37,500	37,500	37,500
MIASOYEDOV, Grigori Grigorievich (1834-1911) Russian				
oil	2	20,880-311,594	166,237	20,880

Name	No.	Price Range	Average	Median
MICAELLES, Ruggero (1898-1976) Italian				
oil	1	2,301	2,301	2,301
MICCINI, Eugenio (1925-) Italian				
wc/d	3	694-1,635	1,280	1,512
MICH, Jean T (1871-1919) Luxembourger				
3D	1	2,890	2,890	2,890
MICHA, Maurice Jean (1890-1969) Belgian				
oil	1	3,625	3,625	3,625
MICHAEL, H (?) ?				
oil	1	2,384	2,384	2,384
MICHAELEDES, Michael (1927-) Italian				
oil	1	6,442	6,442	6,442
MICHAHELLES, Ernesto (1893-1959) Italian				
wc/d	3	1,590-2,417	1,908	1,717
MICHAILOV, D (20th C) Russian				
oil	1	7,000	7,000	7,000
MICHAILOW, Nikola (1876-1960) Bulgarian				
oil	1	3,781	3,781	3,781
MICHALEK, Ludwig (1859-?) Austrian				
oil	1	9,889	9,889	9,889
MICHALLON, Achille Etna (1796-1822) French				
oil	4	10,000-110,000	47,143	15,062
MICHALOVSKI, Piotr (1801-1855) Polish				
oil	4	5,068-21,240	11,321	5,702
MICHAU, Theobald (1676-1765) Flemish				
oil	3	10,703-138,840	53,861	12,041
MICHAUT, E K (?) ?				
oil	1	3,507	3,507	3,507
MICHAUX, Henri (1899-1984) Belgian				
oil	16	1,767-21,240	6,965	5,023
wc/d	48	2,392-40,828	11,056	7,080
MICHAUX, John (1876-1956) Belgian				
oil	5	485-3,879	1,369	514
MICHEL, Alfonso (1897-1957) Mexican				
oil	2	22,000-40,000	31,000	22,000
MICHEL, Charles (1874-1940) Belgian				
oil	2	400-4,071	2,235	400
MICHEL, Georges (1763-1843) French				
oil	11	1,757-22,000	12,028	10,603
wc/d	1	850	850	850
MICHEL, Georges and SWEBACH, Edouard (19th C) French				
oil	1	5,702	5,702	5,702
MICHEL, Gustave Frederic (1851-1924) French				
3D	1	6,283	6,283	6,283
MICHEL, Robert (1897-1983) German				
wc/d	4	2,548-31,808	11,127	4,200
MICHEL-HENRY (1928-) French				
oil	5	600-4,500	1,900	1,500
MICHEL-LEVY, Henri (1845-1914) French				
oil	1	10,200	10,200	10,200
MICHELACCI, Luigi (1879-1959) Italian				
oil	2	1,091-2,395	1,743	1,091
MICHELENA, Arturo (1863-1898) Venezuelan				
oil	1	75,000	75,000	75,000
MICHELETTI, Mario (1892-1975) Italian				
oil	6	605-1,752	1,063	847
MICHELI, Alberto (1870-?) Italian				
oil	1	1,796	1,796	1,796
wc/d	1	1,008	1,008	1,008
MICHELI, Gioxe de (1947-) Italian				
oil	3	1,071-1,638	1,260	1,071
MICHELI, Guglielmo (1866-1926) Italian				
oil	12	1,527-17,810	5,617	4,580
MICHELIDAKIS, Fidias (c.1895-?) Greek				
oil	1	1,870	1,870	1,870
MICHELIS, Alexander (1823-1868) German				
oil	1	1,166	1,166	1,166
MICHELOZZI, Corrado (1883-1965) Italian				
oil	1	1,260	1,260	1,260
MICHELSON, Leo (1887-1978) Russian				
oil	1	1,113	1,113	1,113
wc/d	1	1,000	1,000	1,000

Name	No.	Price Range	Average	Median
MICHETTI, Francesco Paolo (1851-1929) Italian				
oil	4	788-27,185	13,298	6,479
wc/d	9	892-9,514	4,296	4,712
MICHIE, David (1928-) British				
oil	2	574-2,768	1,671	574
MICHIE, James Coutts (1861-1919) British				
oil	2	546-2,682	1,614	546
MICHIELI, Andrea dei (1542-1617) Italian				
wc/d	1	1,832	1,832	1,832
MICHIS, Pietro (1836-1903) Italian				
oil	1	2,625	2,625	2,625
MICHON, Guy (1925-) Canadian				
oil	1	1,078	1,078	1,078
MICHONZE, Gregoire (1902-1982) French				
oil	10	420-4,268	1,688	1,632
wc/d	4	989-5,664	2,264	1,192
MICKER, Jan Christiansz (1600-1664) Dutch				
oil	2	4,325-6,370	5,347	4,325
MIDAVAINE, Louis (1888-1979) French?				
oil	1	5,089	5,089	5,089
MIDDEL, Maurits van (1886-?) Belgian				
oil	1	1,806	1,806	1,806
MIDDENDORF, Helmut (1953-) German				
oil	10	2,428-17,836	7,295	4,576
wc/d	8	648-4,070	1,934	1,136
MIDDLEDITCH, Edward (1923-1987) British				
oil	1	14,560	14,560	14,560
wc/d	2	531-2,024	1,277	531
MIDDLETON, Colin (1910-1983) British				
oil	19	12,103-198,716	54,961	38,219
wc/d	37	496-5,096	1,492	1,211
MIDDLETON, J (1828-1856) British				
oil	1	1,740	1,740	1,740
MIDDLETON, James Godsell (fl.1826-1872) British				
oil	1	1,870	1,870	1,870
MIDDLETON, Janet (1922-) Canadian				
wc/d	1	1,216	1,216	1,216
MIDDLETON, John (1828-1856) British				
oil	1	7,965	7,965	7,965
MIDLER, Viktor Markovich (1888-1979) Russian				
oil	2	5,580-5,580	5,580	5,580
MIDWOOD, William Henry (fl.1867-1871) British				
oil	4	1,122-18,375	6,335	2,835
MIEDUCH, Dan (1947-) American				
oil	3	11,500-20,000	16,000	16,500
MIEGHEM, Eugène van (1875-1930) Belgian				
oil	3	6,684-24,276	14,521	12,603
wc/d	19	468-14,949	3,120	1,483
MIELDS, Rune (1935-) German				
oil	2	2,548-2,827	2,687	2,548
wc/d	2	548-3,058	1,803	548
MIELICH, Alfons Leopold (1863-1929) Austrian				
oil	4	894-23,919	10,587	5,400
MIELLE, Elise (19th C) French				
wc/d	1	1,174	1,174	1,174
MIENVILLE, C (20th C) French				
oil	1	4,618	4,618	4,618
MIEREVELT, Michiel Jans van (1567-1641) Dutch				
oil	3	7,071-27,500	18,748	21,673
MIERIS, Frans van (17/18th C) Dutch				
oil	1	2,616	2,616	2,616
MIERIS, Frans van (younger) (1689-1763) Dutch				
oil	2	10,770-32,919	21,844	10,770
MIERIS, Willem van (1662-1747) Dutch				
oil	3	16,993-111,000	49,864	21,600
wc/d	1	62,300	62,300	62,300
MIES, J (20th C) ?				
oil	1	6,000	6,000	6,000
MIESTCHANINOFF, Oscar (1886-1956) Russian				
3D	2	4,468-8,160	6,314	4,468
MIGADIS, Yannis (1926-) Greek				
oil	1	4,400	4,400	4,400

Name	No.	Price Range	Average	Median
MIGLIARA, Giovanni (1785-1837) Italian				
wc/d	1	4,844	4,844	4,844
MIGLIARO, Vincenzo (1858-1938) Italian				
oil	5	2,356-8,918	5,517	6,000
MIGLIOZZI, Gianfranco (1941-) Italian				
wc/d	1	2,351	2,351	2,351
MIGNARD, Nicolas (1606-1668) French				
wc/d	1	2,250	2,250	2,250
MIGNARD, Paul (c.1638-1691) French				
oil	1	9,585	9,585	9,585
MIGNARD, Pierre (17/18th C) French				
oil	2	103,800-112,450	108,125	103,800
MIGNARD, Pierre I (1612-1695) French				
oil	2	13,443-39,735	26,589	13,443
MIGNECO, Giuseppe (1908-1997) Italian				
oil	15	1,790-29,281	11,488	8,642
wc/d	21	651-9,955	3,084	2,506
MIGNERY, Herb (1937-) American				
3D	3	4,500-7,000	5,833	6,000
MIGNON, Léon (1847-1898) Belgian				
3D	2	2,116-2,378	2,247	2,116
MIGNON, Lucien (1865-1944) French				
oil	9	840-8,324	3,097	2,049
MIGONNEY, Jules (1876-1929) French				
oil	2	2,694-45,972	24,333	2,694
MIHALOVITS, Miklos (1888-1960) Hungarian				
oil	5	850-2,085	1,311	900
MIKESHIN, Boris Mikhailovich (1873-1937) Russian				
3D	1	28,603	28,603	28,603
MIKHAILOV, Grigori Karpovich (1814-1867) Russian				
oil	1	37,200	37,200	37,200
MIKHNOV-VOITENKO, Evgeny (1932-1988) Russian				
wc/d	1	1,900	1,900	1,900
MIKI, Andy (1918-1983) North American				
3D	8	1,518-17,716	5,040	3,206
MIKI, Tomio (1937-1937) American				
3D	3	5,000-19,000	13,000	15,000
MIKL, Josef (1929-) Austrian				
oil	5	2,572-54,621	22,073	4,315
wc/d	4	1,079-4,841	3,103	2,928
MIKLOS, Gustave (1888-1967) French				
oil	1	28,479	28,479	28,479
wc/d	1	17,568	17,568	17,568
MIKOLA, Nandor (1911-2006) Finnish				
oil	2	779-1,558	1,168	779
wc/d	10	484-1,199	826	899
MILANI, Aureliano (1675-1749) Italian				
oil	1	44,767	44,767	44,767
wc/d	1	8,155	8,155	8,155
MILANI, Umberto (1912-1969) Italian				
oil	3	452-5,088	3,404	4,673
wc/d	2	486-1,272	879	486
MILCENDEAU, Charles (1872-1919) French				
wc/d	2	1,647-5,890	3,768	1,647
MILES, Leonidas Clint (fl.1858-1883) British				
oil	2	1,218-2,784	2,001	1,218
MILES, Thomas Rose (fl.1869-1906) British				
oil	12	623-8,464	4,274	3,689
MILESI, Alessandro (1856-1945) Italian				
oil	6	2,121-5,878	4,417	4,586
MILHAZES, Beatriz (1960-) Brazilian				
oil	4	90,000-238,950	159,850	150,450
MILIADIS, Stelios (1881-1965) Greek				
oil	1	3,740	3,740	3,740
MILIAN, Raul (1914-1986) Cuban				
wc/d	7	900-2,571	1,507	1,157
MILICI, Reynard F (1942-) American				
oil	2	2,600-4,000	3,300	2,600
MILIOTI, Nikolai Dimitrievich (1874-1962) Russian				
oil	2	4,250-27,900	16,075	4,250

Name	No.	Price Range	Average	Median
MILLAIS, Raoul (1901-1999) British				
oil	9	920-7,695	3,365	2,941
wc/d	4	557-3,784	1,680	1,056
MILLAIS, Sir John Everett (1829-1896) British				
oil	2	11,505-684,000	347,752	11,505
wc/d	4	487-12,528	4,083	1,134
MILLAIS, William Henry (1828-1899) British				
wc/d	3	1,125-3,500	2,121	1,740
MILLAR, Addison T (1860-1913) American				
oil	5	1,100-6,000	3,088	3,503
MILLAR, Alexander (1960-) British				
oil	3	4,375-36,750	17,716	12,025
wc/d	1	1,480	1,480	1,480
MILLAR, James (18th C) British				
oil	3	3,306-45,360	18,888	8,000
MILLARES, Manolo (1926-1972) Spanish				
wc/d	6	6,027-333,000	103,413	37,001
MILLER, Alfred Jacob (1810-1874) American				
oil	2	3,000-4,750	3,875	3,000
wc/d	8	900-120,000	31,812	20,000
MILLER, Archibald Elliot Haswell (1887-1979) British				
oil	2	493-7,080	3,786	493
MILLER, Barse (1904-1973) American				
oil	1	12,000	12,000	12,000
wc/d	2	1,800-3,000	2,400	1,800
MILLER, Carol (1933-) American/Mexican				
3D	1	2,800	2,800	2,800
MILLER, Charles Henry (1842-1922) American				
oil	6	600-3,250	1,975	2,100
MILLER, Charles Keith (19th C) British				
oil	5	870-19,250	9,356	8,400
MILLER, F (?) American				
oil	1	4,750	4,750	4,750
MILLER, Franklin H (1843-1911) American				
oil	2	2,600-3,250	2,925	2,600
MILLER, Frederick (19th C) British				
wc/d	1	3,186	3,186	3,186
MILLER, Harriette G (1892-1971) American				
3D	1	2,500	2,500	2,500
MILLER, Henry (1891-1980) American				
oil	1	650	650	650
wc/d	5	1,440-2,939	2,069	1,800
MILLER, Henry and SOUZA, F N (20th C) American/British				
wc/d	1	16,000	16,000	16,000
MILLER, Jack Lawrence (20th C) British				
oil	1	880	880	880
wc/d	2	783-1,392	1,087	783
MILLER, James (fl.1773-1791) British				
oil	1	29,070	29,070	29,070
wc/d	1	13,920	13,920	13,920
MILLER, Janet (?) British?				
wc/d	1	1,139	1,139	1,139
MILLER, John (1911-1975) British				
oil	1	1,610	1,610	1,610
MILLER, John (1953-) American				
3D	2	3,200-5,500	4,350	3,200
MILLER, John (fl.1876-1890) British				
oil	1	3,334	3,334	3,334
MILLER, John (1931-2002) British				
oil	11	528-7,476	2,785	2,088
wc/d	6	885-1,947	1,488	1,345
MILLER, Joseph (19th C) German				
oil	1	6,171	6,171	6,171
MILLER, Kenneth Hayes (1876-1952) American				
oil	1	1,300	1,300	1,300
MILLER, Laura (20th C) American				
oil	2	1,000-2,000	1,500	1,000
MILLER, Mildred Bunting (1892-1964) American				
oil	8	900-13,000	5,256	2,750
MILLER, Nick (20th C) British				
oil	3	2,145-2,420	2,288	2,301
wc/d	1	969	969	969

Name	No.	Price Range	Average	Median
MILLER, R A D (20th C) American				
oil	1	18,000	18,000	18,000
MILLER, Ralph Davison (1858-1946) American				
oil	6	650-7,000	2,484	1,300
MILLER, Richard E (1875-1943) American				
oil	5	5,000-480,000	142,000	35,000
MILLER, Richard McDermott (1922-2004) American				
3D	1	15,000	15,000	15,000
MILLER, Roy (1938-) British				
oil	4	549-2,639	1,349	586
MILLER, William G (fl.1891-1908) British				
wc/d	1	2,244	2,244	2,244
MILLER, William Rickarby (1818-1893) American				
oil	5	2,800-8,500	6,040	7,000
wc/d	1	800	800	800
MILLES, Carl (1875-1955) Swedish/American				
3D	12	2,460-216,359	31,650	5,983
MILLES, Ruth (1873-1941) Swedish				
3D	4	1,798-3,297	2,402	2,061
MILLESON, Royal Hill (1849-1926) American				
oil	1	3,200	3,200	3,200
wc/d	1	350	350	350
MILLET, Aime (1819-1891) French				
3D	1	2,432	2,432	2,432
MILLET, Clarence (1897-1959) American				
oil	3	11,000-24,000	17,333	17,000
MILLET, Francis Davis (1846-1912) American				
oil	1	5,500	5,500	5,500
MILLET, Francisque II (1666-1723) French				
oil	1	15,123	15,123	15,123
MILLET, Jean Baptiste (1831-1906) French				
wc/d	2	1,097-1,665	1,381	1,097
MILLET, Jean François (1814-1875) French				
oil	1	73,600	73,600	73,600
wc/d	26	1,077-250,000	26,198	4,200
MILLIER, Arthur (1893-1975) American/British				
wc/d	1	1,500	1,500	1,500
MILLIERE, Maurice (1871-1946) French				
oil	4	1,212-7,000	3,458	1,790
wc/d	2	537-727	632	537
MILLIKEN, Robert W (1920-) British				
oil	1	2,301	2,301	2,301
wc/d	10	475-2,301	880	695
MILLIOTTI, Nicolai (1874-?) Russian				
oil	1	3,503	3,503	3,503
MILLNER, Karl (1825-1894) German				
oil	4	2,552-22,500	9,346	4,680
MILLNER, William Edward (1849-1885) British				
oil	2	591-3,132	1,861	591
MILNE, David Brown (1882-1953) Canadian				
oil	2	48,626-194,976	121,801	48,626
wc/d	18	7,294-97,488	32,522	19,791
MILNE, Joe (fl.1905-1908) British				
oil	7	1,200-11,440	4,159	1,830
MILNE, John E (1931-1978) British				
3D	5	1,683-5,797	3,149	3,009
MILNE, John Maclaughlan (1885-1957) British				
oil	14	2,595-54,870	16,303	7,434
wc/d	14	1,038-13,728	6,223	4,425
MILNE, Joseph (1861-1911) British				
oil	6	974-8,996	3,203	1,471
wc/d	1	554	554	554
MILNE, William (19/20th C) British				
oil	1	1,300	1,300	1,300
MILNE, William Watt (fl.1900-1915) British				
oil	11	602-6,802	3,060	3,026
wc/d	1	676	676	676
MILNER, Allan (?) ?				
oil	1	1,656	1,656	1,656
MILNER-GULLAND, Alison (20th C) British				
oil	1	2,196	2,196	2,196

Name	No.	Price Range	Average	Median
MILO, Christie (20th C) French				
oil	1	2,750	2,750	2,750
MILO, Jean (1906-1993) Belgian				
oil	7	478-6,615	2,662	643
wc/d	3	509-742	607	572
MILOCH, Henri (20th C) French				
oil	1	1,558	1,558	1,558
MILON, Joseph (1868-1947) French				
oil	1	2,937	2,937	2,937
MILONADIS, Konstantin (20th C) American				
3D	1	3,200	3,200	3,200
MILONE, Antonio (?-1920) Italian				
oil	2	900-2,915	1,907	900
MILOUDI, Houssein (1945-) Moroccan				
wc/d	1	8,718	8,718	8,718
MILOVITCH, Tanasko (1900-?) American/Yugoslavian				
oil	1	2,400	2,400	2,400
MILROY, Lisa (1959-) Canadian				
oil	1	7,785	7,785	7,785
MILTON-JENSEN, C (1855-1928) Danish				
oil	1	1,630	1,630	1,630
MILTON-JENSEN, Carl (1855-1928) Danish				
oil	1	1,400	1,400	1,400
MIMNAUGH, Terry (20th C) American				
oil	3	500-27,000	15,500	19,000
MIN, Jaap (1914-1987) Dutch				
oil	2	3,507-3,741	3,624	3,507
wc/d	2	1,145-1,205	1,175	1,145
MINARTZ, Tony (1873-1944) French				
oil	1	1,980	1,980	1,980
wc/d	1	8,880	8,880	8,880
MINASI, A (?) Italian				
3D	1	1,806	1,806	1,806
MINASSIAN, Leone (1905-1978) Turkish/Italian				
oil	1	2,366	2,366	2,366
MINAUX, Andre (1923-1988) French				
oil	4	650-3,717	2,092	1,401
wc/d	1	2,590	2,590	2,590
MINDEN, Robert van (20th C) ?				
wc/d	1	1,199	1,199	1,199
MING DYNASTY, 16th C (16th C) Chinese				
oil	1	35,000	35,000	35,000
MING DYNASTY, 17th C (17th C) Chinese				
wc/d	1	16,000	16,000	16,000
MINGUILLON, Julia (1907-1965) Spanish				
wc/d	1	1,916	1,916	1,916
MINGUZZI, Luciano (1911-2004) Italian				
wc/d	6	832-1,414	1,093	1,058
3D	1	1,929	1,929	1,929
MINKOWSKI, Maurice (1881-1930) Polish				
oil	4	3,600-53,000	22,525	9,500
wc/d	5	1,000-8,000	2,900	1,600
MINNE, G (1866-1941) Belgian				
3D	1	2,221	2,221	2,221
MINNE, George (1866-1941) Belgian				
wc/d	2	1,656-9,936	5,796	1,656
3D	13	2,102-64,291	8,827	3,387
MINNE, Joris (1897-1988) Belgian				
wc/d	1	504	504	504
3D	1	3,029	3,029	3,029
MINNER, Herman (1924-1981) Belgian				
oil	1	2,922	2,922	2,922
MINNIGERODE, Ludwig (1847-?) Austrian				
wc/d	1	1,796	1,796	1,796
MINOLI, Paolo (1942-) Italian				
oil	1	2,452	2,452	2,452
MINOR, Robert Crannell (1839-1904) American				
oil	3	650-2,900	1,750	1,700
MINTCHINE, Abraham (1898-1931) Russian				
oil	2	5,500-9,300	7,400	5,500
wc/d	3	2,121-9,625	5,775	5,580

Name	No.	Price Range	Average	Median
MINTER, Marilyn (1948-) American				
oil	1	18,000	18,000	18,000
MINTON, John (1917-1957) British				
oil	3	6,264-9,570	7,498	6,660
wc/d	14	435-18,500	4,448	1,505
MINTZ, Raymond (1925-) American				
oil	1	3,273	3,273	3,273
MINUJIN, Marta (20th C) ?				
wc/d	1	7,000	7,000	7,000
MINYAEV, Vasily Aleksandrovich (1903-1993) Russian				
oil	1	25,800	25,800	25,800
MIODUSZEVSKI, Jan Ostoja (1831-?) Czechoslovakian				
oil	1	3,314	3,314	3,314
MIOLEE, Adrianus (1879-1961) Dutch				
oil	1	1,025	1,025	1,025
MIOTTE, Jean (1926-) French				
oil	2	7,159-7,767	7,463	7,159
wc/d	3	500-1,788	929	500
MIR Y TRINXET, Joaquin (1873-1940) Spanish				
oil	3	24,360-121,800	57,469	26,248
MIRA, Alfred S (1900-1981) American				
oil	2	1,000-3,000	2,000	1,000
MIRA, Victor (1949-2003) Spanish				
oil	13	1,414-5,774	2,481	1,865
wc/d	2	941-958	949	941
MIRABELLA, Mario (1870-1931) Italian				
oil	1	2,589	2,589	2,589
MIRAGLIA, Juan Carlos (1900-1983) Argentinian				
oil	1	1,100	1,100	1,100
MIRALDA, Antoni (1942-) Spanish				
wc/d	3	1,081-16,949	6,543	1,600
3D	1	4,453	4,453	4,453
MIRALDA, Antoni and SELZ, Dorothee (20th C) Spanish/French				
3D	1	2,926	2,926	2,926
MIRALLES DARMANIN, Enrique (1855-1900) Spanish				
oil	1	4,800	4,800	4,800
MIRALLES DARMANIN, Jose (1851-1900) Spanish				
oil	1	5,000	5,000	5,000
wc/d	3	1,665-1,665	1,665	1,665
MIRALLES, F (19/20th C) ?				
oil	1	4,670	4,670	4,670
MIRALLES, Francisco (1848-1901) Spanish				
oil	7	1,100-243,600	45,950	6,475
wc/d	1	1,200	1,200	1,200
MIRAZOVIC, Filip (?) ?				
oil	2	3,612-4,335	3,973	3,612
MIRER, Rudolf (1937-) Swiss				
oil	1	2,588	2,588	2,588
MIRKO (1910-1969) Italian				
oil	1	3,816	3,816	3,816
wc/d	8	586-10,813	3,011	1,171
3D	1	11,712	11,712	11,712
MIRO LLEO, Gaspar (1859-1930) Spanish				
oil	3	2,432-5,000	3,361	2,651
MIRO, Joachim (1875-1941) Spanish				
oil	7	1,700-9,360	4,746	4,629
MIRO, Joan (1893-1983) Spanish				
oil	12	88,800-8,096,000	1,855,501	420,000
wc/d	53	6,370-1,239,000	133,010	65,000
3D	11	33,630-1,050,000	192,070	81,140
MIROU, Antoine (1583-1669) Flemish				
oil	2	29,410-65,740	47,575	29,410
MISCH, R (18th C) ?				
wc/d	1	1,885	1,885	1,885
MISCHELING, Jean (1623-1695) ?				
oil	1	90,306	90,306	90,306
MISKEY, Julian de (20th C) American				
wc/d	1	11,000	11,000	11,000
MISTI-MIFLIEZ, Ferdinand (1865-1923) French				
wc/d	1	1,750	1,750	1,750

Name	No.	Price Range	Average	Median
MISTRY, Dhruva (1957-) Indian				
wc/d	2	2,112-2,464	2,288	2,112
3D	1	18,000	18,000	18,000
MITA, Georges (1871-1904) French				
oil	3	1,205-6,125	3,553	3,330
MITARAS, Dimitris (1934-) Greek				
oil	6	7,480-34,595	15,040	9,350
wc/d	5	3,740-15,895	7,627	4,928
MITCHELL, Alfred (19/20th C) British				
oil	1	2,500	2,500	2,500
MITCHELL, Alfred R (1888-1972) American				
oil	13	3,250-180,000	22,557	7,000
MITCHELL, Denis (1912-1993) British				
oil	1	4,524	4,524	4,524
3D	13	2,379-17,200	9,922	12,390
MITCHELL, Edith (1864-1944) American				
oil	2	950-4,800	2,875	950
MITCHELL, Flora H (1890-1973) Irish				
wc/d	4	2,046-8,961	4,577	3,534
MITCHELL, Gladys Vinson (1894-1968) American				
oil	1	5,500	5,500	5,500
MITCHELL, J (?) ?				
wc/d	1	1,603	1,603	1,603
MITCHELL, Jackie (20th C) Irish?				
oil	3	690-1,683	1,167	1,130
MITCHELL, James Edgar (1871-1922) British				
oil	1	1,332	1,332	1,332
MITCHELL, Janet (1912-1998) Canadian				
wc/d	9	825-4,948	1,746	1,230
MITCHELL, Joan (1926-1992) American				
oil	22	20,000-2,200,000	552,770	180,000
MITCHELL, John Campbell (1862-1922) British				
oil	5	452-3,979	2,215	2,013
MITCHELL, Lewis (1932-) British				
oil	1	1,056	1,056	1,056
MITCHELL, M (19th C) ?				
oil	1	1,786	1,786	1,786
MITCHELL, Madge Young (fl.1930-1938) British				
oil	1	2,225	2,225	2,225
MITCHELL, Madison Fred (1923-) American				
oil	1	8,500	8,500	8,500
MITCHELL, Philip (1814-1896) British				
wc/d	1	2,805	2,805	2,805
MITCHELL, Ray (1944-) American				
oil	1	8,000	8,000	8,000
MITCHELL, Robert (20th C) British?				
3D	1	3,894	3,894	3,894
MITCHELL, Rosemary (1943-) British				
oil	1	2,544	2,544	2,544
MITCHELL, Thomas John (1875-?) American				
oil	1	1,500	1,500	1,500
MITELLI, Giuseppe Maria (1634-1718) Italian				
oil	1	42,324	42,324	42,324
wc/d	1	1,812	1,812	1,812
MITILIAS, Vassilis (19th C) Greek				
oil	1	13,840	13,840	13,840
MITORAJ, Igor (1944-) German				
3D	12	1,854-12,858	5,066	3,034
MITROKHIN, Dimitri Isidorovich (1883-1973) Russian				
wc/d	1	5,952	5,952	5,952
MITSCHKE COLLANDE, Constantin von (1884-?) German				
oil	1	6,078	6,078	6,078
MITTAG, Bill (20th C) American				
oil	3	2,000-3,000	2,583	2,750
MITTENHOFF, Albert Frederic Alexandre (19th C) French				
oil	1	26,400	26,400	26,400
MIVILLE, Jakob Christoph (1786-1836) Swiss				
wc/d	1	3,330	3,330	3,330
MIYAJIMA, Tatsuo (1957-) Japanese				
3D	1	120,000	120,000	120,000
MIYAKE, Shintaro (1970-) Japanese				
wc/d	2	7,392-10,208	8,800	7,392

Name	No.	Price Range	Average	Median
MIYAO (?) Japanese				
3D	1	8,352	8,352	8,352
MLENEK, Hannes (1956-) Austrian				
oil	1	1,411	1,411	1,411
MNGUNI, Simoni (1885-1956) South African				
wc/d	1	4,450	4,450	4,450
MO JINGDAOREN (?) Chinese				
wc/d	1	14,400	14,400	14,400
MO, Carlo (1923-2004) French				
3D	1	2,186	2,186	2,186
MOAL, Jean le (1909-) French				
oil	11	1,152-19,007	6,949	4,562
MOBIUS, Karl (1876-?) German				
3D	1	1,920	1,920	1,920
MOCCI, Jean Pierre (1952-) French?				
oil	1	2,425	2,425	2,425
MODERSOHN, Otto (1865-1943) German				
oil	30	2,967-39,493	14,224	10,888
MODERSOHN-BECKER, Paula (1876-1907) German				
oil	8	10,541-267,143	103,762	89,048
wc/d	2	1,937-10,874	6,405	1,937
MODESITT, John (1955-) American				
oil	5	750-5,500	3,260	4,000
MODIGLIANI, Amedeo (1884-1920) Italian				
oil	7	32,986-26,864,000	6,987,783	5,000,000
wc/d	24	8,000-400,000	106,101	68,402
3D	3	27,441-74,356	58,137	72,616
MOE, Carl (1889-1942) Norwegian				
oil	1	1,588	1,588	1,588
MOE, Louis (1859-1945) Norwegian				
oil	1	2,085	2,085	2,085
wc/d	1	608	608	608
MOELLER, Arnold (1886-1963) German				
oil	2	1,014-1,532	1,273	1,014
MOELLER, Louis C (1855-1930) American				
oil	2	10,000-67,500	38,750	10,000
MOENCH, Charles (1784-1867) French				
oil	1	3,500	3,500	3,500
MOER, Jean Baptiste van (1819-1884) Belgian				
oil	2	10,141-36,370	23,255	10,141
MOERENHOUT, Joseph Jodocus (1801-1874) Belgian				
oil	2	4,767-8,758	6,762	4,767
MOERMAN, Johannes Lodewyk (1850-1896) Belgian				
oil	3	2,666-7,134	4,444	3,534
MOEYAERT, Nicolaes Cornelisz (1592-1655) Dutch				
wc/d	2	2,336-3,970	3,153	2,336
MOFCHUM, Gerald (20th C) American				
oil	1	2,300	2,300	2,300
MOFFAT, Donald (1955-) ?				
oil	1	16,000	16,000	16,000
MOFFAT, Sandy (20th C) British				
oil	1	1,848	1,848	1,848
MOFFETT, Donald (?) American?				
oil	1	10,000	10,000	10,000
MOFFETT, Ross E (1888-1971) American				
oil	3	1,800-16,000	6,866	2,800
wc/d	1	450	450	450
MOGET, Piet (1928-) Dutch				
oil	2	1,793-4,537	3,165	1,793
MOGFORD, John (1821-1885) British				
oil	3	813-3,901	2,345	2,322
wc/d	6	841-4,788	2,332	1,958
MOHOLY-NAGY, Laszlo (1895-1946) American/Hungarian				
oil	1	185,000	185,000	185,000
wc/d	4	1,900-101,322	33,055	4,000
MOHR, Albert (20th C) German				
oil	2	2,250-2,250	2,250	2,250
MOHR, Johann Georg (1864-1943) German				
oil	2	719-1,377	1,048	719
MOHRMANN, John Henry (1857-1916) American				
oil	1	3,128	3,128	3,128

Name	No.	Price Range	Average	Median
MOHSAN, Mir (17th C) Persian				
wc/d	1	8,800	8,800	8,800
MOHWALD, Otto (1933-) German				
oil	1	2,153	2,153	2,153
MOIGNE, Andre le (1898-1987) French				
oil	1	6,668	6,668	6,668
MOIGNIEZ, Jules (1835-1894) French				
3D	19	2,008-27,524	6,819	4,550
MOILLIET, Louis (1880-1962) Swiss				
oil	1	3,080	3,080	3,080
wc/d	3	3,408-6,088	4,840	5,026
MOILLON, Louise (1609-1696) French				
oil	2	101,500-173,000	137,250	101,500
MOINE, Antonin Marie (1796-1849) French				
wc/d	1	1,731	1,731	1,731
MOIRAGHI, Anacleto (1880-1943) Italian				
oil	2	550-1,553	1,051	550
MOISE, Joseph Thony (20th C) Haitian				
oil	1	1,000	1,000	1,000
MOISO, Giorgio (1942-) Italian				
oil	1	648	648	648
wc/d	1	1,291	1,291	1,291
MOISSET, Maurice (1860-1946) French				
oil	3	505-2,750	1,272	561
MOITROUX, Alfred (1886-1938) Belgian				
oil	1	6,171	6,171	6,171
MOITTE, Jean Guillaume (1746-1810) French				
wc/d	1	7,000	7,000	7,000
MOJA, Frederico (1802-1885) Italian				
wc/d	1	1,553	1,553	1,553
MOKADY, Moshe (1902-1975) Israeli				
oil	9	1,000-16,000	5,372	4,400
wc/d	1	600	600	600
MOL, Leo (1915-) Canadian				
3D	1	2,460	2,460	2,460
MOL, Pieter Laurens (1946-) Dutch				
wc/d	1	2,544	2,544	2,544
3D	1	5,890	5,890	5,890
MOLA, Pier Francesco (1612-1666) Italian				
oil	1	9,526	9,526	9,526
wc/d	4	1,200-37,500	17,188	2,104
MOLANUS, Mattheus (?-1645) Dutch				
oil	1	21,848	21,848	21,848
MOLARSKY, Abraham (c.1883-?) Russian/American				
oil	1	2,900	2,900	2,900
MOLARSKY, Maurice (1885-1950) American				
oil	1	1,500	1,500	1,500
MOLDOVAN, Kurt (1918-1977) Austrian				
wc/d	6	1,029-7,572	3,066	1,286
MOLDOVAN, Sacha (1901-1982) American/Russian				
oil	4	7,000-10,000	8,750	8,000
MOLE, John Henry (1814-1886) British				
wc/d	6	546-2,088	1,227	739
MOLEIRO, Raul (1903-?) Venezuelan				
oil	2	1,025-1,860	1,442	1,025
MOLENAAR, Johannes Petrus (1914-1989) Dutch				
oil	5	562-3,004	1,674	1,523
MOLENAER, Bartholomeus (1612-1650) Dutch				
oil	1	14,108	14,108	14,108
MOLENAER, Jan Jacobz (1654-?) Dutch				
oil	1	2,997	2,997	2,997
MOLENAER, Jan Miense (1610-1668) Dutch				
oil	10	5,550-180,000	49,203	9,425
MOLENAER, Klaes (1630-1676) Dutch				
oil	15	3,036-152,877	26,375	12,600
MOLENKAMP, Nico (1920-1998) Dutch				
oil	2	703-1,567	1,135	703
MOLEZUN SUAREZ, Manuel (1920-) Spanish				
oil	1	1,701	1,701	1,701
wc/d	1	654	654	654
MOLFENTER, Hans (1884-1979) German				
oil	1	1,296	1,296	1,296

Name	No.	Price Range	Average	Median
MOLIN, Johan Peter (1814-1873) Swedish				
3D	2	4,258-9,450	6,854	4,258
MOLIN, Lei (1927-1990) Dutch				
wc/d	3	1,209-2,421	1,634	1,274
MOLIN, Oreste da (1856-1921) Italian				
oil	1	14,865	14,865	14,865
MOLINA CAMPOS, Florencio (1891-1959) Argentinian				
oil	6	4,500-80,000	28,323	16,000
wc/d	6	5,298-25,000	13,549	12,000
MOLINA MONTERO, Francisco (1962-) Spanish				
oil	1	3,221	3,221	3,221
MOLINA SANCHEZ, Jose Antonio (1918-) Spanish				
oil	1	12,055	12,055	12,055
MOLINA, Fernando (19/20th C) Spanish				
oil	1	4,944	4,944	4,944
MOLINARI, Guido (1933-2004) Canadian				
oil	3	7,422-21,270	13,995	13,294
wc/d	1	701	701	701
MOLINARY, Andre (1847-1915) American				
oil	1	82,500	82,500	82,500
MOLINS, H (?) ?				
3D	1	3,284	3,284	3,284
MOLITOR, Martin von (1759-1812) Austrian				
oil	1	1,500	1,500	1,500
MOLITOR, Mathieu (1873-1929) German				
3D	1	9,534	9,534	9,534
MOLK, Josef Adam (1714-1794) Austrian				
oil	1	6,336	6,336	6,336
MOLL, Carl (1861-1945) Austrian				
oil	2	133,517-160,714	147,115	133,517
MOLL, Evert (1878-1955) Dutch				
oil	24	643-11,891	2,555	1,764
wc/d	1	701	701	701
MOLL, Oskar (1875-1947) German				
oil	6	3,035-23,378	9,672	5,096
wc/d	2	3,822-9,425	6,623	3,822
MOLL, Petra (1921-1989) German				
oil	1	1,212	1,212	1,212
MOLLARI, Mario Miguel (1930-) Argentinian				
oil	5	4,000-12,000	8,200	8,000
wc/d	1	19,000	19,000	19,000
MOLLENHAUER, Ernst (1892-1963) German				
oil	1	21,205	21,205	21,205
wc/d	2	3,534-8,836	6,185	3,534
MOLLER, Andreas (1684-1758) Danish				
oil	3	8,429-12,041	10,435	10,837
MOLLER, Hans (1905-) American				
oil	1	3,265	3,265	3,265
MOLLER, J P (1783-1854) Danish				
oil	1	2,282	2,282	2,282
wc/d	1	1,022	1,022	1,022
MOLLER, Jens Peter (1783-1854) Danish				
oil	1	2,028	2,028	2,028
MOLLER, Olivia Holm (1875-1970) Danish				
oil	1	1,779	1,779	1,779
MOLLER, Otto (1883-1964) German				
oil	2	618-6,466	3,542	618
MOLLER, Reinhold von (1847-1918) German				
oil	2	3,041-3,801	3,421	3,041
MOLLER, Rudolf (1881-1964) German				
oil	3	937-3,416	2,040	1,767
wc/d	1	729	729	729
MOLLER, Sigurd (1895-1984) Swedish				
oil	2	1,400-2,379	1,889	1,400
MOLLERBERG, Nils (1892-1954) Swedish				
3D	1	4,238	4,238	4,238
MOLLES, Andrew (1907-) American				
oil	1	8,357	8,357	8,357
MOLLINGER, Alexander (1836-1867) Dutch				
oil	1	5,274	5,274	5,274
MOLLINGER, Louis Gerard Constant (1825-1860) Dutch				
oil	1	1,883	1,883	1,883

Name	No.	Price Range	Average	Median
MOLLINO, Carlo (1905-1973) Italian				
wc/d	1	35,138	35,138	35,138
MOLNAR, George (1953-) American				
oil	1	7,000	7,000	7,000
MOLNAR, L Reizes (1903-) Hungarian				
oil	1	1,000	1,000	1,000
MOLS, Florent (19th C) Belgian				
oil	1	1,064	1,064	1,064
MOLS, N P (1859-1921) Danish				
oil	5	652-2,323	1,457	1,690
MOLS, Robert (1848-1903) Belgian				
oil	5	1,000-3,836	1,980	1,553
MOLSTED, Chr (1862-1930) Danish				
oil	6	2,064-102,660	22,344	4,401
wc/d	2	974-5,309	3,141	974
MOLTENI, Giovanni (1898-1967) Italian				
oil	1	18,771	18,771	18,771
MOLTENI, Giuseppe (1800-1867) Italian				
oil	1	102,826	102,826	102,826
MOLTINO, Francis (1818-1874) British				
oil	3	736-5,610	2,655	1,619
MOLTKE, Harald (1871-1960) Danish				
oil	5	650-4,110	1,809	1,221
MOLYN, Petrus Marius (1819-1849) Belgian				
oil	1	41,858	41,858	41,858
MOLYN, Pieter (1595-1661) Dutch				
oil	4	12,552-32,040	20,628	13,840
wc/d	2	888-5,536	3,212	888
MOLZAHN, Johannes (1892-1965) German				
wc/d	1	5,955	5,955	5,955
MOMEN, Karl (1935-) Swedish				
oil	3	1,053-3,944	2,514	2,545
MOMMERS, Hendrik (1623-1693) Dutch				
oil	3	7,329-24,075	13,377	8,729
MOMPER, Frans de (1603-1660) Flemish				
oil	2	24,360-95,548	59,954	24,360
MOMPER, Joos de (1564-1635) Flemish				
oil	7	20,000-164,350	61,761	43,250
wc/d	1	7,500	7,500	7,500
MOMPER, Philips de (elder) (1598-1634) Flemish				
oil	1	58,333	58,333	58,333
MOMPOU, Joseph (1888-1969) Spanish				
oil	2	4,114-8,438	6,276	4,114
MONACA, Alberto la (1862-1936) Italian				
wc/d	1	1,566	1,566	1,566
MONACHESI, Sante (1910-1991) Italian				
oil	16	766-4,123	2,299	2,438
wc/d	2	525-773	649	525
MONACO, Primaldo (20th C) Argentinian				
oil	1	25,000	25,000	25,000
MONAHAN, Hugh (1914-1970) Irish				
oil	4	648-2,221	1,458	1,380
MONALDI, Paolo (18th C) Italian				
oil	3	12,945-25,479	18,479	17,014
MONAMY, Peter (1689-1749) British				
oil	4	5,610-52,360	23,806	9,256
MONARD, Louis de (1873-?) French				
3D	1	7,182	7,182	7,182
MONASTERIOS, Rafael (1884-1961) Venezuelan				
oil	1	6,975	6,975	6,975
wc/d	1	3,020	3,020	3,020
MONCADA, Ignazio (1932-) Italian				
oil	4	1,767-2,945	2,140	1,909
wc/d	4	1,937-2,458	2,297	2,356
MONCHABLON, Alphonse (1835-1907) French				
oil	1	5,104	5,104	5,104
MONCHABLON, Jean Ferdinand (1855-1904) French				
oil	5	1,815-32,500	15,024	12,000
MONDAL, Rabin (20th C) Indian				
oil	1	55,000	55,000	55,000

Name	No.	Price Range	Average	Median
MONDINO, Aldo (1939-2005) Italian				
oil	32	1,527-17,568	5,816	3,854
wc/d	7	1,189-11,973	4,320	3,399
3D	2	5,256-20,726	12,991	5,256
MONDO, Domenico (1717-1806) Italian				
oil	1	6,423	6,423	6,423
wc/d	1	600	600	600
MONDRIAAN, Frits (1853-1932) Dutch				
oil	1	1,260	1,260	1,260
MONDRIAN, Piet (1872-1944) Dutch				
oil	5	52,800-270,000	146,060	92,500
wc/d	6	15,000-343,469	109,303	69,966
MONDRUS, Martin (20th C) American				
oil	2	600-3,000	1,800	600
MONDZAIN, Simon François Stanislas (1890-1979) French				
oil	2	2,142-4,091	3,116	2,142
MONEDERO, Manuel (1925-) Spanish				
oil	1	11,178	11,178	11,178
MONET, Claude (1840-1926) French				
oil	24	48,002-12,500,000	3,038,249	1,700,000
wc/d	3	13,200-211,200	80,960	18,480
MONFALLET, Adolphe François (1816-1900) French				
oil	1	18,400	18,400	18,400
MONFORT, Octavianus (17th C) Italian				
oil	1	8,919	8,919	8,919
MONFREID, Georges Daniel de (1856-1929) French				
oil	1	5,036	5,036	5,036
wc/d	1	28,000	28,000	28,000
MONFREID, Henry de (1879-1974) French				
wc/d	1	3,211	3,211	3,211
MONGE, Jules (1855-?) French				
oil	2	1,100-1,911	1,505	1,100
MONGINOT, Charles (1825-1900) French				
oil	1	2,744	2,744	2,744
MONGODIN, Victor (1819-?) French				
oil	1	1,368	1,368	1,368
MONGRELL Y TORRENT, Jose (1870-1934) Spanish				
oil	3	4,995-208,800	89,326	54,184
MONGRELL, Bartolome (1882-1938) Spanish				
oil	1	3,471	3,471	3,471
MONI, Louis de (1698-1771) Dutch				
oil	1	37,380	37,380	37,380
MONIER (?) ?				
oil	1	1,479	1,479	1,479
MONINOT, Bernard (20th C) French				
oil	1	10,130	10,130	10,130
wc/d	1	1,030	1,030	1,030
MONK, E van (fl.1832-1840) British				
oil	1	4,752	4,752	4,752
MONK, William (1863-1937) British				
wc/d	1	1,023	1,023	1,023
MONLEON Y TORRES, Raphael (1847-1900) Spanish				
oil	1	1,492	1,492	1,492
MONNICKENDAM, Martin (1874-1943) Dutch				
oil	2	4,789-14,108	9,448	4,789
wc/d	1	1,567	1,567	1,567
MONNIER, Charles (1925-) Swiss				
oil	1	1,332	1,332	1,332
MONNINI, Alvaro (1922-1987) Italian				
oil	2	4,099-5,856	4,977	4,099
MONNOT, Maurice Louis (1869-1937) French				
oil	4	953-4,123	1,994	1,400
MONNOYER, Antoine (1670-1747) French				
oil	2	17,000-130,000	73,500	17,000
MONNOYER, Jean Baptiste (1636-1699) French				
oil	4	29,600-158,792	80,481	60,493
MONOGRAMMIST A B (?) ?				
oil	3	3,889-14,508	10,304	12,517
MONOGRAMMIST A C (?) ?				
3D	1	6,000	6,000	6,000
MONOGRAMMIST A E D (?) ?				
oil	1	1,390	1,390	1,390

Name	No.	Price Range	Average	Median
MONOGRAMMIST A E S (?) ?				
oil	1	1,414	1,414	1,414
MONOGRAMMIST A L (?) ?				
oil	2	1,088-1,135	1,111	1,088
MONOGRAMMIST A R (?) ?				
oil	5	650-18,061	4,980	2,188
MONOGRAMMIST A S (?) ?				
oil	1	1,332	1,332	1,332
MONOGRAMMIST A W (?) ?				
wc/d	1	4,944	4,944	4,944
MONOGRAMMIST B C K (?) ?				
oil	1	4,131	4,131	4,131
MONOGRAMMIST B H I C (?) ?				
oil	1	1,920	1,920	1,920
MONOGRAMMIST B V K (?) ?				
oil	2	4,393-4,393	4,393	4,393
MONOGRAMMIST B X (?) ?				
oil	1	1,051	1,051	1,051
MONOGRAMMIST C A V (?) ?				
oil	1	11,466	11,466	11,466
MONOGRAMMIST C B (?) ?				
oil	1	776	776	776
wc/d	1	937	937	937
MONOGRAMMIST C D (?) ?				
oil	1	4,364	4,364	4,364
MONOGRAMMIST C D H (?) ?				
oil	1	14,013	14,013	14,013
MONOGRAMMIST C F L (?) ?				
oil	1	7,007	7,007	7,007
MONOGRAMMIST C H (?) ?				
oil	1	5,733	5,733	5,733
MONOGRAMMIST C K P (?) ?				
oil	1	4,743	4,743	4,743
MONOGRAMMIST C M (?) ?				
3D	1	1,218	1,218	1,218
MONOGRAMMIST C M C (?) ?				
oil	1	4,545	4,545	4,545
MONOGRAMMIST C R G (?) ?				
oil	1	3,086	3,086	3,086
MONOGRAMMIST D E (?) ?				
oil	1	4,848	4,848	4,848
MONOGRAMMIST D T (?) ?				
oil	1	1,142	1,142	1,142
MONOGRAMMIST D V H (?) ?				
oil	1	7,591	7,591	7,591
MONOGRAMMIST D Z (?) ?				
oil	1	3,482	3,482	3,482
MONOGRAMMIST E C P (?) ?				
oil	1	1,178	1,178	1,178
MONOGRAMMIST E W (?) ?				
oil	1	1,127	1,127	1,127
MONOGRAMMIST F B (?) ?				
oil	3	471-9,600	3,606	749
MONOGRAMMIST F G (?) ?				
oil	1	2,145	2,145	2,145
MONOGRAMMIST F H (?) ?				
oil	1	2,221	2,221	2,221
MONOGRAMMIST F J (?) ?				
wc/d	1	1,196	1,196	1,196
MONOGRAMMIST F K (?) ?				
oil	1	4,622	4,622	4,622
MONOGRAMMIST F M (?) ?				
oil	1	609	609	609
wc/d	1	400	400	400
MONOGRAMMIST F R (?) ?				
oil	1	964	964	964
wc/d	1	1,027	1,027	1,027
MONOGRAMMIST F V (?) ?				
oil	1	1,130	1,130	1,130
MONOGRAMMIST F W V (?) ?				
oil	1	3,387	3,387	3,387

Name	No.	Price Range	Average	Median
MONOGRAMMIST F Z (?) ? oil	1	2,178	2,178	2,178
MONOGRAMMIST G A E (?) ? oil	1	55,500	55,500	55,500
MONOGRAMMIST G B (?) ? oil	1	1,060	1,060	1,060
MONOGRAMMIST G H (?) ? oil	1	28,274	28,274	28,274
MONOGRAMMIST G R (?) ? oil	2	1,878-30,362	16,120	1,878
MONOGRAMMIST G S (?) ? oil	1	1,403	1,403	1,403
MONOGRAMMIST G W (?) ? oil	2	586-2,548	1,567	586
MONOGRAMMIST H A (?) ? oil	1	4,476	4,476	4,476
MONOGRAMMIST H B (?) ? oil	4	502-16,857	5,201	935
MONOGRAMMIST H D (?) ? wc/d	1	1,984	1,984	1,984
MONOGRAMMIST H I S (?) ? oil	1	3,148	3,148	3,148
MONOGRAMMIST H K (?) ? oil	1	730	730	730
3D	1	7,750	7,750	7,750
MONOGRAMMIST H M (?) ? oil	1	1,460	1,460	1,460
MONOGRAMMIST H W (?) ? oil	1	1,573	1,573	1,573
MONOGRAMMIST I H (?) ? wc/d	1	1,414	1,414	1,414
MONOGRAMMIST I P (?) ? oil	1	1,052	1,052	1,052
MONOGRAMMIST I S G B (?) ? oil	1	2,903	2,903	2,903
MONOGRAMMIST J B (?) ? oil	2	1,463-7,007	4,235	1,463
wc/d	1	1,142	1,142	1,142
MONOGRAMMIST J C (?) ? oil	1	2,378	2,378	2,378
MONOGRAMMIST J F M (?) ? oil	1	3,575	3,575	3,575
MONOGRAMMIST J G (?) ? oil	1	1,030	1,030	1,030
MONOGRAMMIST J V G (?) ? oil	1	1,649	1,649	1,649
MONOGRAMMIST K (?) ? oil	1	6,126	6,126	6,126
MONOGRAMMIST K R (?) ? oil	2	471-1,649	1,060	471
MONOGRAMMIST L I S (?) ? oil	1	1,255	1,255	1,255
MONOGRAMMIST L M (?) ? oil	1	26,700	26,700	26,700
MONOGRAMMIST M F (?) ? 3D	1	4,224	4,224	4,224
MONOGRAMMIST M S (?) ? oil	2	589-701	645	589
wc/d	1	2,303	2,303	2,303
MONOGRAMMIST P (?) ? wc/d	1	3,299	3,299	3,299
MONOGRAMMIST P A V H (?) ? oil	1	20,760	20,760	20,760
MONOGRAMMIST P L (?) ? oil	3	1,312-5,066	2,711	1,757
MONOGRAMMIST P O (?) ? oil	2	565-15,263	7,914	565
MONOGRAMMIST P S (?) ? oil	1	4,131	4,131	4,131
MONOGRAMMIST P V B (?) ? oil	1	140,137	140,137	140,137

Name	No.	Price Range	Average	Median
MONOGRAMMIST R D (?) ?				
oil	1	1,500	1,500	1,500
MONOGRAMMIST R H (?) ?				
oil	2	839-1,440	1,139	839
MONOGRAMMIST R R (?) ?				
oil	1	1,632	1,632	1,632
MONOGRAMMIST S C K (?) ?				
oil	1	3,012	3,012	3,012
MONOGRAMMIST S L V (?) ?				
oil	1	1,216	1,216	1,216
MONOGRAMMIST S N (?) ?				
oil	1	2,926	2,926	2,926
MONOGRAMMIST S R (?) ?				
oil	1	6,081	6,081	6,081
MONOGRAMMIST T H (?) ?				
oil	2	2,356-3,365	2,860	2,356
MONOGRAMMIST T P (?) ?				
wc/d	1	2,858	2,858	2,858
MONOGRAMMIST T R (?) ?				
oil	1	1,052	1,052	1,052
MONOGRAMMIST V D H (?) ?				
oil	1	1,089	1,089	1,089
MONOGRAMMIST W H (?) ?				
oil	1	5,469	5,469	5,469
MONOGRAMMIST W L (?) ?				
oil	1	1,868	1,868	1,868
MONOGRAMMIST W R (?) ?				
oil	1	4,712	4,712	4,712
MONOGRAMMIST W S H (?) ?				
oil	1	1,297	1,297	1,297
MONORY, Jacques (1924-) French				
oil	5	8,653-34,612	19,035	17,306
wc/d	3	1,119-2,038	1,477	1,274
MONRO, Nicholas (1936-) British				
3D	2	2,394-8,208	5,301	2,394
MONROE, Lanford (1950-2000) American				
oil	10	1,200-32,500	10,595	10,000
MONSTED, Peder (1859-1941) Danish				
oil	90	873-130,000	15,770	8,686
wc/d	2	597-7,904	4,250	597
MONTAGNA, Bartolommeo (1450-1523) Italian				
wc/d	1	100,000	100,000	100,000
MONTAGNE, Harry la (20th C) ?				
3D	1	12,858	12,858	12,858
MONTAGNE, Louis (1879-1960) French				
oil	11	492-6,023	2,526	2,356
wc/d	6	593-1,475	1,106	848
MONTAGNIER, E (?) French?				
oil	1	2,577	2,577	2,577
MONTAGUE, Alfred (fl.1832-1883) British				
oil	14	566-5,250	2,846	2,992
MONTAGUE, Clifford (fl.1883-1900) British				
oil	2	1,104-3,225	2,164	1,104
MONTAGUE, Lilian Amy (20th C) American				
oil	1	5,000	5,000	5,000
MONTALAND, F de (19/20th C) French				
oil	1	4,248	4,248	4,248
MONTALANT, Julius O (19th C) French?				
oil	1	21,000	21,000	21,000
MONTALD, Constant (1862-1944) Belgian				
oil	2	529-1,699	1,114	529
wc/d	2	1,399-1,808	1,603	1,399
MONTAN, Anders (1846-1917) Swedish				
oil	4	715-6,324	2,969	1,405
MONTANARI, Giuseppe (1889-1970) Italian				
oil	6	448-8,916	4,708	1,621
wc/d	1	567	567	567
MONTANARINI, Luigi (1906-1998) Italian				
oil	11	430-5,301	1,810	1,359
wc/d	7	615-1,106	828	882
MONTANELLA, Evasio (1878-1940) Italian				
oil	1	2,722	2,722	2,722

Name	No.	Price Range	Average	Median
MONTANER, Miguel (20th C) ?				
oil	1	1,285	1,285	1,285
MONTANIER, Francis (1895-1974) French				
oil	1	848	848	848
wc/d	1	1,130	1,130	1,130
MONTE, Ira (1918-) Spanish				
oil	2	900-3,200	2,050	900
MONTEFORTE, Eduardo (1849-1933) Italian				
oil	2	1,009-12,429	6,719	1,009
MONTEIL, Jacques (1800-?) French				
oil	1	1,500	1,500	1,500
MONTEMEZZO, Antonio (1841-1898) German				
oil	3	484-8,000	3,111	851
MONTEN, Dietrich (1799-1843) German				
oil	2	700-38,531	19,615	700
MONTENARD, Frederic (1849-1926) French				
oil	3	1,721-7,192	3,657	2,059
MONTENEGRO CAPELL, Jose (1855-1924) Spanish				
oil	1	1,686	1,686	1,686
MONTENEGRO, Roberto (1885-1968) Mexican				
oil	2	3,000-8,000	5,500	3,000
MONTES LENGUAS, Jose (1929-2001) Uruguayan?				
oil	2	1,250-2,000	1,625	1,250
MONTESANO, Gian Marco (1949-) Italian				
oil	13	908-3,534	2,355	2,290
wc/d	1	1,463	1,463	1,463
MONTESINOS, M (19th C) Spanish				
oil	1	1,700	1,700	1,700
MONTET, Maurice (1905-) French				
oil	1	3,720	3,720	3,720
MONTEZEMOLO, Guido (1878-1941) Italian				
oil	3	1,816-6,054	3,633	3,031
MONTEZIN, Pierre Eugène (1874-1946) French				
oil	41	4,800-352,000	32,274	16,397
wc/d	7	651-47,500	14,320	3,062
MONTFORT, Franz van (1889-1980) Belgian				
oil	1	716	716	716
wc/d	1	1,153	1,153	1,153
MONTGOMERY, Alfred (1857-1922) American				
oil	6	950-13,000	4,958	2,600
MONTGOMERY, Gladys Eleanor (fl.1950s) Canadian				
oil	1	2,309	2,309	2,309
MONTHOLON, François de (1856-1940) French				
oil	2	850-1,519	1,184	850
MONTI, Cesare (1891-1952) Italian				
oil	2	2,577-4,971	3,774	2,577
MONTI, Francesco (1646-1712) Italian				
oil	1	25,950	25,950	25,950
MONTI, Vincenzo (20th C) Italian				
oil	1	1,200	1,200	1,200
MONTICELLI, Adolphe (1824-1886) French				
oil	15	3,000-27,877	14,124	12,335
MONTIEL, Jonio (1924-1986) South American				
oil	1	1,600	1,600	1,600
MONTIEL, Jose Justo (1822-1899) Mexican				
oil	1	10,000	10,000	10,000
MONTIGNY, Jenny (1875-1937) Belgian				
oil	1	15,196	15,196	15,196
MONTIGNY, Jules Léon (1847-1899) Belgian				
oil	4	1,013-12,959	5,021	1,607
MONTINI, Giovanni (fl.1650) Italian				
oil	1	12,740	12,740	12,740
MONTINI, Umberto (1897-1978) Italian				
oil	2	734-3,107	1,920	734
MONTOYA, Gustavo (1905-) Mexican				
oil	6	2,000-15,000	7,583	3,500
MONTOYA, Mariano (?) Spanish				
oil	1	1,171	1,171	1,171
MONTPEZAT, Henri d'Ainecy Comte de (1817-1859) French				
oil	3	8,000-9,000	8,666	9,000
wc/d	1	2,640	2,640	2,640

Name	No.	Price Range	Average	Median
MONTZAIGLE, Edgard (1867-?) French				
wc/d	1	1,784	1,784	1,784
MONVOISIN, Raymond Auguste Quinsac de (1794-1870) French				
oil	1	1,580	1,580	1,580
MONVOISIN, Solange (1911-1985) French				
oil	2	1,757-4,435	3,096	1,757
MONZON RELOVA, Rene (1966-) Cuban				
oil	4	720-1,665	1,163	1,073
MOODIE, Donald (1892-1963) British				
oil	2	1,914-2,390	2,152	1,914
MOODY, A (?) British?				
oil	1	1,925	1,925	1,925
MOOG, Peter (1932-) Dutch				
wc/d	1	3,514	3,514	3,514
MOON, Carl (1878-1948) American				
oil	2	1,600-7,000	4,300	1,600
MOON, Henry George (1857-1905) British				
oil	2	673-2,816	1,744	673
MOONEY, Edward Hartley (c.1878-1938) British				
oil	2	515-1,558	1,036	515
MOONEY, Martin (1960-) British				
oil	9	1,674-40,767	11,271	5,580
MOONY, Robert James Enraght (1879-1946) British				
oil	3	1,052-3,148	2,368	2,906
wc/d	1	1,574	1,574	1,574
MOOR, Carel de (1656-1738) Dutch				
oil	1	3,080	3,080	3,080
MOOR, Christian de (1899-1981) Dutch				
oil	4	630-1,885	1,181	825
wc/d	5	527-1,874	1,010	942
MOOR, Henrik (1876-1942) German				
oil	1	1,091	1,091	1,091
MOOR, Karel de (1695-?) Dutch				
oil	1	3,712	3,712	3,712
MOORE OF IPSWICH, John (1820-1902) British				
oil	13	974-10,620	4,113	2,301
MOORE, A Harvey (?-1905) British				
oil	1	3,872	3,872	3,872
MOORE, Barlow (fl.1863-1891) British				
wc/d	2	696-2,088	1,392	696
MOORE, Benson Bond (1882-1974) American				
oil	18	750-23,000	6,425	1,750
MOORE, Claude T S (1853-1901) British				
oil	3	3,717-10,440	6,090	4,114
MOORE, Edward (19/20th C) British				
oil	2	802-1,298	1,050	802
MOORE, Edwin Augustus (1858-1925) American				
oil	1	3,400	3,400	3,400
MOORE, Frank Montague (1877-1967) American/British				
oil	8	950-3,250	1,687	1,100
MOORE, H O M (1898-1986) British				
wc/d	1	5,190	5,190	5,190
MOORE, Harry Humphrey (1844-1926) American				
oil	2	1,200-2,300	1,750	1,200
MOORE, Henry O M (1898-1986) British				
wc/d	30	7,000-314,500	44,198	21,240
3D	80	1,870-5,520,000	304,434	72,150
MOORE, Henry R A (1831-1895) British				
oil	12	513-13,050	5,147	4,872
wc/d	3	2,581-8,352	5,786	6,426
MOORE, J (?) British				
oil	1	1,890	1,890	1,890
MOORE, Nelson Augustus (1823-1902) American				
oil	2	1,000-3,750	2,375	1,000
wc/d	1	1,200	1,200	1,200
MOORE, R H (19th C) British				
oil	1	2,013	2,013	2,013
MOORE, Robert (1905-?) British				
oil	7	1,740-8,352	5,406	4,675
MOORE, Robert C (1957-) American				
oil	1	14,000	14,000	14,000

Name	No.	Price Range	Average	Median
MOORE, William (snr) (1790-1851) British				
oil	1	1,368	1,368	1,368
wc/d	1	3,382	3,382	3,382
MOORE, Yvonne (20th C) Irish				
oil	6	763-5,655	3,619	2,710
MOORMANS, Franz (1832-1893) Dutch				
oil	4	969-1,900	1,259	1,019
MOOS, Max von (1903-1979) Swiss				
oil	12	571-19,474	6,421	2,666
wc/d	3	588-1,499	1,047	1,055
MOOS, Rudolf von (1858-1885) Swiss				
oil	1	1,450	1,450	1,450
MOPOPE, Stephen (1898-1974) American				
oil	1	1,100	1,100	1,100
wc/d	3	1,400-5,000	3,383	3,750
MORA, Francis Luis (1874-1940) American				
oil	6	800-8,500	3,966	3,000
MORA, Lita (1958-) Spanish				
oil	4	1,078-1,580	1,221	1,089
MORADO, Jose Chavez (1909-) Mexican				
oil	1	24,000	24,000	24,000
MORALES, Armando (1927-) Nicaraguan				
oil	8	3,000-150,000	59,183	7,166
wc/d	1	18,000	18,000	18,000
MORALES, Eduardo (c.1869-1938) Cuban				
oil	1	2,500	2,500	2,500
MORALES, Francisco (19th C) Mexican?				
wc/d	1	2,000	2,000	2,000
MORALES, Rodolfo (1925-2001) Mexican				
oil	7	24,000-180,000	61,142	38,000
MORALIS, Yannis (1916-) Greek				
oil	2	196,350-316,800	256,575	196,350
MORALT, Willy (1884-1947) German				
oil	13	1,192-10,338	4,595	4,257
wc/d	2	1,453-1,703	1,578	1,453
MORAN, Cythnia (20th C) Irish				
3D	1	4,243	4,243	4,243
MORAN, E Percy (1862-1935) American				
oil	3	1,000-2,600	1,933	2,200
wc/d	1	850	850	850
MORAN, Earl (1893-1984) American				
oil	1	5,000	5,000	5,000
MORAN, Edward (1829-1901) American				
oil	10	3,250-52,000	20,956	11,000
wc/d	1	1,500	1,500	1,500
MORAN, H Marcus (1877-1960) American				
oil	1	1,000	1,000	1,000
MORAN, Leon (1864-1941) American				
wc/d	3	550-2,100	1,133	750
MORAN, Paul Nimmo (1864-1907) American				
oil	1	2,000	2,000	2,000
MORAN, Percy (1862-?) American				
oil	1	13,000	13,000	13,000
MORAN, Peter (1841-1914) American				
oil	3	2,000-3,750	3,000	3,250
wc/d	3	1,000-5,500	2,700	1,600
MORAN, Thomas (1837-1926) American				
oil	6	2,600-1,700,000	683,433	70,000
wc/d	3	35,000-480,000	191,666	60,000
MORAN, Thomas Sydney (19/20th C) American				
oil	1	2,600	2,600	2,600
MORAND, Georges (?) French?				
oil	1	2,950	2,950	2,950
MORANDELL, Peter Paul (1907-) Italian				
oil	1	1,818	1,818	1,818
MORANDI, Giorgio (1890-1964) Italian				
oil	10	216,259-708,000	393,408	374,795
wc/d	15	4,767-69,200	32,230	21,476
MORANDINI, Marcello (1940-) Italian				
oil	3	1,149-7,613	4,691	5,311
wc/d	1	1,697	1,697	1,697
3D	3	8,905-13,993	10,756	9,370

Name	No.	Price Range	Average	Median
MORANDO, Pietro (1892-1980) Italian				
oil	12	1,890-8,230	3,953	3,495
wc/d	11	549-2,356	1,391	1,193
MORANG, Alfred (1901-1958) American				
oil	10	2,000-15,000	5,875	4,000
MORANG, Dorothy (1906-) American				
oil	1	800	800	800
wc/d	2	650-750	700	650
MORAS, Bruno (19/20th C) German				
oil	3	497-3,503	1,629	888
MORAS, Walter (1856-1925) German				
oil	11	484-14,014	3,572	1,649
MORBELLI, Angelo (1853-1919) Italian				
oil	1	58,904	58,904	58,904
MORBELLI, Gigi (1900-1980) Italian				
oil	1	2,521	2,521	2,521
wc/d	3	970-5,334	2,546	1,334
MORCH, Aksel (1883-1960) Danish				
oil	1	1,000	1,000	1,000
MORCHAIN, Paul Bernard (1876-1939) French				
oil	9	638-6,789	2,328	1,870
MORE, Jacob (1740-1793) British				
oil	1	160,650	160,650	160,650
MORE, Paul le (1863-1914) French				
oil	3	1,209-2,200	1,615	1,438
MOREAU DE TOURS, Georges (1848-1901) French				
oil	1	1,153	1,153	1,153
MOREAU, Adrien (1843-1906) French				
oil	2	1,001-8,286	4,643	1,001
wc/d	1	1,936	1,936	1,936
MOREAU, Auguste (1834-1917) French				
oil	1	280,274	280,274	280,274
3D	13	1,821-7,249	3,967	3,857
MOREAU, Charles (1830-?) French				
oil	2	3,762-8,000	5,881	3,762
MOREAU, Gustave (1826-1898) French				
oil	1	644,000	644,000	644,000
wc/d	2	20,000-25,890	22,945	20,000
MOREAU, H F (19/20th C) American				
3D	1	3,236	3,236	3,236
MOREAU, Hippolite (19th C) French				
3D	5	2,306-11,639	5,315	3,646
MOREAU, Hippolyte François (1832-1927) French				
3D	1	1,816	1,816	1,816
MOREAU, Jacques Gaston (1903-1994) French				
oil	1	1,514	1,514	1,514
MOREAU, Jean Michel (younger) (1741-1814) French				
wc/d	5	1,094-176,215	37,903	3,600
MOREAU, Louis (?) French				
wc/d	1	2,330	2,330	2,330
3D	1	2,104	2,104	2,104
MOREAU, Louis-Auguste (1855-1919) French				
3D	1	2,922	2,922	2,922
MOREAU, Mathurin (1822-1912) French				
3D	21	1,522-75,000	9,090	3,933
MOREAU, Max (1902-1992) Belgian				
oil	3	517-17,877	6,778	1,940
MOREAU, Nicolas (19th C) French				
oil	1	3,708	3,708	3,708
MOREAU-NELATON, Étienne (1859-1927) French				
oil	1	2,158	2,158	2,158
MOREAU-VAUTHIER, Edme Augustin Jean (1831-1893) French				
3D	1	8,153	8,153	8,153
MOREAU-VAUTHIER, Paul (1871-1936) French				
3D	2	2,225-6,370	4,297	2,225
MOREELSE, Paulus (1571-1638) Dutch				
oil	4	8,650-65,329	29,059	12,000
MOREL FATIO, Antoine Léon (1810-1871) French				
oil	3	3,132-18,373	10,206	9,115
wc/d	1	486	486	486
MOREL, Casparus Johannes (1798-1861) Dutch				
oil	4	3,170-20,896	10,969	8,750

Name	No.	Price Range	Average	Median
MOREL, Jan Evert I (1769-1808) Flemish				
oil	2	2,910-5,500	4,205	2,910
MOREL, Jan Evert II (1835-1905) Dutch				
oil	13	1,219-12,292	4,353	3,200
MOREL, Louise (?) ?				
oil	1	2,336	2,336	2,336
MOREL, Willem F A I Vaarzon (1868-1955) Dutch				
oil	3	7,990-24,583	14,463	10,817
wc/d	3	536-3,196	2,309	3,196
MORELAND, Marylee (20th C) American				
oil	1	2,500	2,500	2,500
MORELL BELLET, Fausto (1851-1928) Spanish				
oil	1	8,818	8,818	8,818
MORELLET, François (1926-) French				
oil	3	16,586-38,276	24,307	18,061
wc/d	2	4,576-25,767	15,171	4,576
3D	3	9,226-114,388	48,830	22,878
MORELLI Y SANCHEZ GIL, Victor (1860-1936) Spanish				
oil	1	3,485	3,485	3,485
MORELLI, Domenico (1826-1901) Italian				
oil	4	1,582-13,275	7,347	4,722
wc/d	3	589-3,366	2,336	3,053
MORELLI, Luigi (19th C) Italian				
oil	1	2,800	2,800	2,800
MORELLO, Federico (19/20th C) Italian				
oil	1	1,676	1,676	1,676
MORENI, Mattia (1920-1999) Italian				
oil	9	3,884-58,562	34,275	38,163
MORENO, Michel (1945-) French				
oil	2	1,416-2,301	1,858	1,416
wc/d	1	501	501	501
MORENO, Rafael (1887-1955) Spanish				
oil	1	32,500	32,500	32,500
MORENO-GIMENO, Manuel (c.1900-?) Spanish				
oil	1	1,070	1,070	1,070
MORERA Y GALICIA, Jaime (1854-1927) Spanish				
oil	1	1,633	1,633	1,633
MORERE, Louis (20th C) French				
oil	1	2,722	2,722	2,722
MORET, Henry (1856-1913) French				
oil	16	23,562-180,000	65,304	58,562
wc/d	3	1,325-2,973	2,309	2,630
MORETH, J (18th C) French				
wc/d	1	1,145	1,145	1,145
MORETTI, Alberto (1922-) Italian				
oil	1	4,906	4,906	4,906
wc/d	4	630-882	693	630
MORETTI, Francesco (1833-1917) Italian				
wc/d	1	1,427	1,427	1,427
MORETTI, Lucien Philippe (1922-2000) French				
oil	2	832-2,324	1,578	832
wc/d	2	820-1,113	966	820
MORETTI, Luigi (1884-?) Italian				
oil	5	572-1,260	948	1,134
wc/d	1	3,107	3,107	3,107
MORETTI, Raymond (1931-2005) French				
oil	2	835-972	903	835
wc/d	3	475-1,106	819	876
MORFF, Gottlob Wilhelm (1771-1857) German				
oil	1	1,632	1,632	1,632
MORGAN, Cole (1950-) Dutch				
oil	1	10,177	10,177	10,177
wc/d	5	4,459-14,014	8,884	7,007
MORGAN, Frederick (1847-1927) British				
oil	3	6,438-20,355	14,931	18,000
wc/d	1	29,580	29,580	29,580
MORGAN, Gertrude (1900-1980) American				
wc/d	1	2,800	2,800	2,800
MORGAN, Howard (1949-) British				
oil	4	2,262-6,125	3,401	2,610
wc/d	2	696-696	696	696
MORGAN, John (1823-1886) British				
oil	5	2,141-27,300	10,935	7,562

Name	No.	Price Range	Average	Median
MORGAN, Mary Vernon (1871-1927) Canadian				
oil	1	1,835	1,835	1,835
MORGAN, Mary de Neale (1868-1948) American				
oil	6	3,250-15,000	7,791	7,000
wc/d	1	1,000	1,000	1,000
MORGAN, R F (1929-) American				
oil	4	3,000-4,500	3,862	3,700
MORGAN, Sister Gertrude (1900-1980) American				
oil	1	6,000	6,000	6,000
wc/d	3	1,400-17,000	7,366	3,700
MORGAN, William (1826-1900) American				
oil	2	2,250-4,250	3,250	2,250
MORGENSTERN, Friedrich Ernst (1853-1919) German				
oil	4	957-5,845	3,166	1,168
MORGENSTERN, Johann Friedrich (1777-1844) German				
oil	1	2,588	2,588	2,588
MORGENSTERN, Johann Ludwig Ernst (1738-1819) German				
oil	6	3,854-34,600	18,488	11,678
wc/d	1	5,679	5,679	5,679
MORGENSTERN, Karl (1811-1893) German				
oil	4	5,523-69,289	26,151	8,136
MORGENSTERNE MUNTHE, G (1875-1927) Dutch				
oil	1	3,596	3,596	3,596
MORGENSTERNE MUNTHE, Gerhard (1875-1927) Dutch				
oil	7	1,260-34,417	11,749	5,394
MORGENTHALER, Ernst (1887-1962) Swiss				
oil	8	569-16,743	3,556	1,366
wc/d	3	458-1,297	814	687
MORGNER, Michael (1942-) German?				
oil	1	1,703	1,703	1,703
wc/d	1	973	973	973
MORGNER, Wilhelm (1891-1917) German				
wc/d	3	791-7,644	3,597	2,356
MORI, Mariko (1967-) American				
3D	1	6,000	6,000	6,000
MORIANI, A (?) ?				
wc/d	1	2,250	2,250	2,250
MORIANI, Giuseppe (fl.1709-1739) Italian				
oil	1	4,200	4,200	4,200
MORIGI, Giorgio (1908-1941) Italian				
3D	3	2,268-2,268	2,268	2,268
MORILLON, Étienne (20th C) French				
oil	2	660-720	690	660
wc/d	1	527	527	527
MORIMURA, Yasumasa (1951-) Japanese				
wc/d	1	3,700	3,700	3,700
MORIN, A (?) ?				
oil	1	3,389	3,389	3,389
MORIN, Adolphe (1841-?) French				
oil	1	2,000	2,000	2,000
MORIN, Edmond (1824-1882) French				
wc/d	1	2,003	2,003	2,003
MORIN, Georges (1874-1928) German				
3D	2	2,443-4,393	3,418	2,443
MORINORI, Kano (18/19th C) Japanese				
wc/d	1	15,000	15,000	15,000
MORIS, Louis Marie (1818-1883) French				
3D	1	6,078	6,078	6,078
MORISOT, Berthe (1841-1895) French				
oil	2	2,220,000-4,600,000	3,410,000	2,220,000
wc/d	4	4,600-28,986	13,386	5,388
MORISOT, Edma (1839-1921) French				
oil	3	763-2,662	1,421	839
MORISSET, Andre (1876-1954) French				
oil	1	1,914	1,914	1,914
MORISSET, François Henri (1870-?) French				
oil	1	4,506	4,506	4,506
MORITA, Hideharu (20th C) Japanese				
wc/d	1	7,000	7,000	7,000
MORITZ, Friedrich Wilhelm (1783-1855) Swiss				
wc/d	4	1,366-3,044	1,909	1,488

Name	No.	Price Range	Average	Median
MORITZ, Louis (1773-1850) Dutch				
oil	1	2,548	2,548	2,548
MORIZOT, Edma (fl.1864-1868) French?				
oil	1	1,414	1,414	1,414
MORLAND, G (1763-1804) British				
oil	1	2,646	2,646	2,646
MORLAND, George (1763-1804) British				
oil	12	2,992-47,880	11,644	6,500
wc/d	4	475-1,890	895	519
MORLAND, Henry Robert (c.1719-1797) British				
oil	1	2,610	2,610	2,610
MORLE, Stuart (1960-) British				
oil	7	2,945-5,852	4,020	3,162
MORLEY, Harry (1881-1943) British				
oil	2	599-2,223	1,411	599
wc/d	1	531	531	531
MORLEY, Malcolm (1931-) British				
oil	2	8,106-22,500	15,303	8,106
wc/d	6	1,300-5,500	3,568	3,500
MORLEY, Robert (1857-1941) British				
oil	1	1,566	1,566	1,566
MORLOTTI, Ennio (1910-1992) Italian				
oil	9	4,834-42,292	22,630	21,020
wc/d	13	1,649-6,990	3,839	3,658
MORMILE, Gaetano (1839-1890) Italian				
oil	1	2,264	2,264	2,264
MORNER, Axel Otto (1774-1852) Swedish				
oil	1	2,747	2,747	2,747
MORNER, Hjalmar (1794-1837) Swedish				
oil	1	2,445	2,445	2,445
MORNER, Stellan (1896-1979) Swedish				
oil	25	673-25,108	3,827	2,368
wc/d	3	459-871	616	518
MORNEWICK, Charles Augustus (19th C) British				
oil	1	7,308	7,308	7,308
MORO, Ferruccio (1859-?) Italian				
oil	1	849	849	849
wc/d	2	550-618	584	550
MORO, Gino (1901-1977) Italian				
oil	1	1,296	1,296	1,296
MORODER, Josef Theodor (1846-1939) Austrian				
oil	1	4,021	4,021	4,021
wc/d	1	730	730	730
MORONEY, Ken (1949-) British				
oil	14	460-3,884	1,160	883
MOROT, Aime (1850-1913) French				
oil	2	1,293-9,000	5,146	1,293
MOROT-SIR, Gerard (1931-2003) French				
3D	1	2,141	2,141	2,141
MOROTTI, E (19/20th C) Italian?				
oil	1	1,815	1,815	1,815
MOROZ, Mihal (1904-1992) Ukranian				
oil	1	3,404	3,404	3,404
MOROZOV, Aleksandr Ivanovich (1835-1904) Russian				
oil	1	4,200	4,200	4,200
MOROZOV, Nikolai (1882-1956) Russian				
oil	1	4,732	4,732	4,732
MORPHESIS, Jim (20th C) American				
oil	2	500-1,600	1,050	500
wc/d	1	1,100	1,100	1,100
MORRELL, Wayne (1923-) American				
oil	13	375-2,500	1,390	1,300
MORREN, Georges (1868-1941) Belgian				
wc/d	1	1,987	1,987	1,987
MORRICE, James Wilson (1865-1924) Canadian				
oil	8	5,730-163,981	56,269	19,678
wc/d	3	2,474-4,848	3,471	3,092
MORRIEN, Johann Hendrik (1819-1878) Dutch				
oil	1	2,754	2,754	2,754
MORRIS, A (?) British/American				
oil	1	3,281	3,281	3,281

Name	No.	Price Range	Average	Median
MORRIS, Alfred (19th C) British				
oil	3	1,557-3,741	2,632	2,600
MORRIS, Carl (1911-1993) American				
oil	1	5,750	5,750	5,750
MORRIS, Cedric (1889-1982) British				
oil	7	2,500-40,020	14,088	9,558
MORRIS, Edmund Montague (1871-1913) Canadian				
oil	4	574-2,229	1,601	1,706
wc/d	2	574-574	574	574
MORRIS, Franklin E (1938-) American				
oil	2	2,500-4,000	3,250	2,500
MORRIS, George Ford (1873-1960) American				
oil	1	28,000	28,000	28,000
MORRIS, George L K (1905-1975) American				
oil	4	6,000-75,000	33,692	26,885
MORRIS, Gloria (20th C) ?				
3D	1	2,452	2,452	2,452
MORRIS, John (19th C) British				
oil	13	400-21,441	5,181	3,107
MORRIS, John Floyd (20th C) American?				
oil	1	1,000	1,000	1,000
MORRIS, John W (19th C) British				
oil	1	2,595	2,595	2,595
MORRIS, Kathleen (1893-1986) Canadian				
oil	5	12,967-230,427	99,882	97,488
MORRIS, Margaret (1891-1980) British				
oil	1	5,220	5,220	5,220
MORRIS, Philip Richard (1838-1902) British				
oil	9	589-38,000	7,223	4,224
MORRIS, Richard Allen (1933-) American				
oil	1	4,500	4,500	4,500
MORRIS, Robert (1931-) American				
3D	2	9,031-30,000	19,515	9,031
MORRIS, Sarah (1967-) American				
oil	1	38,000	38,000	38,000
MORRIS, William Bright (1844-?) British				
wc/d	1	3,026	3,026	3,026
MORRISEAU (20th C) Canadian				
oil	1	2,531	2,531	2,531
MORRISON, James (1932-) British				
oil	7	1,611-5,753	3,819	3,460
MORRISON, John Lowrie (1948-) British				
oil	3	2,610-10,440	7,830	10,440
MORRISON, Paul (1966-) British				
oil	3	23,125-46,250	36,691	40,700
MORRISON, Robert Boyd (1896-?) British				
oil	1	2,544	2,544	2,544
MORRISSEAU, Norval (1932-) Canadian				
oil	7	1,459-8,104	3,347	2,241
wc/d	1	1,100	1,100	1,100
MORRO-HENZE, Ingfried Paul (1925-1972) German				
oil	1	5,250	5,250	5,250
MORROCCO, Alberto (1917-1998) British				
oil	7	9,500-30,090	18,867	19,470
wc/d	1	522	522	522
MORROCCO, Léon (1942-) Australian				
oil	2	2,928-15,930	9,429	2,928
wc/d	3	856-7,080	3,286	1,922
MORSE, C Roy (20th C) American				
oil	1	1,900	1,900	1,900
MORSE, Henry D (1826-1888) American				
oil	2	1,100-3,700	2,400	1,100
MORSE, Jonathan Bradley (1834-1898) American				
oil	1	2,200	2,200	2,200
MORSE, Samuel F B (1791-1872) American				
oil	3	2,000-1,200,000	402,066	4,200
MORSING, Ivar (1919-) Swedish				
oil	5	764-3,181	1,338	917
MORTARAKOS, Kyriakos (1948-) Greek				
oil	1	1,760	1,760	1,760
MORTEL, Jan (1650-1719) Dutch				
oil	2	166,500-173,000	169,750	166,500

Name	No.	Price Range	Average	Median
MORTELMANS, Edward (20th C) ?				
oil	1	1,653	1,653	1,653
MORTELMANS, Frans (1865-c.1936) Belgian				
oil	10	2,338-29,131	12,581	7,151
wc/d	1	1,784	1,784	1,784
MORTENSEN, Richard (1910-1994) Danish				
oil	12	1,207-88,529	31,382	13,682
wc/d	11	644-4,527	2,007	1,368
3D	2	2,511-2,748	2,629	2,511
MORTIER, Antoine (1908-1998) Belgian				
wc/d	3	700-5,597	3,777	5,034
MORTON, H (19th C) ?				
oil	1	3,503	3,503	3,503
MORTON-JOHNSON, Francis (1878-1931) French				
oil	1	2,529	2,529	2,529
MOSBACHER, Alois (1954-) Austrian				
oil	6	524-4,712	2,272	1,514
wc/d	7	471-1,171	693	603
MOSCA, Ivan (1913-) Italian?				
oil	1	1,600	1,600	1,600
MOSCARDO, Jose (1953-) Spanish				
oil	1	1,221	1,221	1,221
MOSCONI, Lodovico (1928-1987) Italian				
oil	1	2,428	2,428	2,428
MOSEE, Carl (1860-?) Austrian				
wc/d	1	1,113	1,113	1,113
MOSENGEL, Adolf (1837-1885) German				
oil	1	1,049	1,049	1,049
MOSER, Jurg (1950-) Swiss				
3D	1	2,110	2,110	2,110
MOSER, Kolo (1868-1918) Austrian				
oil	4	35,619-242,055	138,149	46,124
wc/d	2	1,893-3,786	2,839	1,893
MOSER, Nikolaus (1956-) Austrian				
oil	3	2,581-3,503	2,888	2,581
MOSER, Richard (1874-?) Austrian				
wc/d	2	2,751-7,224	4,987	2,751
MOSER, Vinzenz Franz Maria (1831-?) German?				
wc/d	1	1,017	1,017	1,017
MOSER, Wilfried (1914-1997) Swiss				
oil	6	2,270-13,699	4,861	2,806
wc/d	1	419	419	419
MOSES, Anna Mary Robertson (Grandma) (1860-1961) American				
oil	16	3,000-520,000	79,812	45,000
MOSES, Ed (1926-) American				
oil	4	3,250-11,000	6,562	5,000
MOSES, Forrest K (1893-1974) American				
oil	1	1,600	1,600	1,600
MOSES, Forrest Lee (jnr) (1934-) American				
oil	3	750-2,000	1,283	1,100
MOSES, Thomas Palmer (1808-1881) American				
oil	1	6,000	6,000	6,000
MOSES, Walter Farrington (1874-?) ?				
oil	1	1,400	1,400	1,400
MOSHER, Donald Allen (1945-) American				
oil	1	1,450	1,450	1,450
wc/d	1	1,900	1,900	1,900
MOSKO and ASSOCIATES (20th C) ?				
wc/d	1	1,447	1,447	1,447
MOSKOVITZ OF SAFED, Shalom (1885-1980) Israeli				
wc/d	2	1,300-1,400	1,350	1,300
MOSKOWITZ, Robert (1935-) American				
oil	3	800-7,500	3,366	1,800
MOSLER, Henry (1841-1920) American				
oil	4	1,286-9,000	3,543	1,665
MOSNER, Ricardo (1948-) Argentinian				
oil	1	1,168	1,168	1,168
MOSNIER, Jean Laurent (1743-1808) French				
oil	3	15,120-171,713	89,957	83,040
MOSNY, Henri (19th C) French				
oil	2	903-3,600	2,251	903

Name	No.	Price Range	Average	Median
MOSQUERA, Luis (1899-1987) Spanish				
oil	2	2,694-7,265	4,979	2,694
MOSS, Irene (20th C) American				
oil	1	1,200	1,200	1,200
MOSSA, Alexis (1844-1926) French				
wc/d	6	718-3,270	1,601	1,017
MOSSA, Gustave Adolf (1883-1971) French				
oil	1	530	530	530
wc/d	12	707-15,000	2,697	927
MOSSCHER, Jacob van (16/17th C) Dutch				
oil	1	24,220	24,220	24,220
MOSSDORF, Karl (1823-1891) German				
oil	1	1,145	1,145	1,145
MOSSEL, Julius (1871-?) German				
oil	6	2,000-5,000	3,958	3,750
wc/d	4	2,250-2,750	2,625	2,750
MOSSET, Olivier (1944-) Swiss				
oil	2	22,007-26,793	24,400	22,007
MOSSMER, Joseph (1780-1845) Austrian				
oil	1	2,057	2,057	2,057
MOSTEIRO, Mario (?) Argentinian				
oil	1	1,500	1,500	1,500
MOSTYN, Tom (1864-1930) British				
oil	9	502-17,480	6,372	5,888
MOSWITZER, Gerhard (1940-) Austrian				
3D	1	3,273	3,273	3,273
MOTA Y MORALES, Vicente (19/20th C) Spanish				
oil	1	1,686	1,686	1,686
MOTE, Alden (1840-1917) American				
oil	1	1,100	1,100	1,100
MOTE, George William (1832-1909) British				
oil	4	1,320-2,595	1,690	1,328
MOTELEY, Jules Georges (1865-1923) French				
oil	5	695-2,670	1,755	1,788
MOTHERWELL, Robert (1915-1991) American				
oil	25	18,500-1,900,000	277,568	93,514
wc/d	8	7,000-110,000	35,150	24,000
MOTLEY, Archibald John (jnr) (1891-1981) American				
oil	1	15,000	15,000	15,000
MOTTA, Raffaellino (1550-1578) Italian				
wc/d	1	2,431	2,431	2,431
MOTTET, Yvonne (1906-1968) French				
oil	4	792-3,109	1,933	1,360
MOTTRAM, Charles Sim (fl.1880-1919) British				
oil	1	537	537	537
wc/d	5	618-2,088	1,049	696
MOUALLA, Fikret (1903-1967) Turkish				
oil	5	1,883-24,196	7,908	4,186
wc/d	36	588-30,000	8,205	3,766
MOUCHERON, Frederic de (1633-1686) Dutch				
oil	2	6,920-24,920	15,920	6,920
wc/d	1	6,126	6,126	6,126
MOUCHERON, Isaac de (1667-1744) Dutch				
oil	2	8,507-27,792	18,149	8,507
wc/d	3	1,427-7,007	3,644	2,500
MOUCHOT, Louis Claude (1830-1891) French				
oil	3	971-2,600	1,712	1,565
MOUGINS, Pierre de (1966-) French				
oil	1	1,929	1,929	1,929
wc/d	1	893	893	893
MOULD, John (20th C) British				
oil	7	623-2,576	1,339	1,104
wc/d	1	661	661	661
MOULIN, Charles Lucien (19th C) French				
wc/d	1	1,903	1,903	1,903
MOULT, Christian le (1941-) Belgian				
oil	1	688	688	688
wc/d	1	894	894	894
MOULTRAY, James Douglas (fl.1860-1880s) British				
oil	1	1,373	1,373	1,373

Name	No.	Price Range	Average	Median
MOULY, Marcel (1920-) French				
oil	8	2,600-22,000	8,944	4,500
wc/d	1	7,603	7,603	7,603
MOUNCEY, William (1852-1901) British				
oil	2	1,990-2,422	2,206	1,990
MOUNT, Rita (1888-1967) Canadian				
oil	6	820-8,863	3,764	1,499
MOUNT, William Sidney (1807-1868) American				
oil	2	1,000-13,000	7,000	1,000
MOURIER-PETERSEN, Christian (1858-1945) Danish				
oil	1	3,397	3,397	3,397
MOUSSEAU, Jean Paul (1927-1991) Canadian				
oil	2	10,635-24,597	17,616	10,635
wc/d	1	2,468	2,468	2,468
MOUTON, Antoine (c.1765-?) French				
3D	2	4,435-126,714	65,574	4,435
MOUTTE, Jean Joseph Marie Alphonse (1840-1913) French				
oil	1	5,750	5,750	5,750
MOYA Y CALVO, Victor (1884-1972) Spanish				
oil	1	2,116	2,116	2,116
MOYA, Patrick (1955-) French				
oil	3	1,052-1,883	1,340	1,085
MOYERS, John (1958-) American				
oil	16	1,000-56,000	12,025	5,500
MOYERS, Terri Kelly (1953-) American				
oil	1	5,000	5,000	5,000
MOYERS, William (1916-1976) American				
oil	2	4,000-6,000	5,000	4,000
wc/d	1	500	500	500
MOYNAN, Richard Thomas (1856-1906) British				
oil	1	343,973	343,973	343,973
MOYNIHAN, Rodrigo (1910-1991) British				
oil	6	573-5,310	2,145	840
wc/d	1	1,138	1,138	1,138
MOYSE, Edouard (1827-1908) French				
oil	1	3,138	3,138	3,138
wc/d	2	1,300-1,752	1,526	1,300
MOZIN, Charles Louis (1806-1862) French				
oil	2	2,975-7,686	5,330	2,975
wc/d	1	3,155	3,155	3,155
MOZLEY, Charles (1914-1991) British				
oil	1	880	880	880
wc/d	3	561-2,262	1,173	696
MOZLEY, Loren Norman (1905-1989) American				
oil	1	30,000	30,000	30,000
wc/d	1	1,100	1,100	1,100
MOZOS, Pedro (1915-1983) Spanish				
oil	1	6,838	6,838	6,838
wc/d	1	655	655	655
MR (1969-) Japanese				
oil	2	10,000-20,000	15,000	10,000
3D	1	2,279	2,279	2,279
MRKVICKA, Jan V (1856-?) Bulgarian				
oil	1	4,000	4,000	4,000
MUBAYI, Sylvester (1942-) Zimbabwean				
3D	1	2,528	2,528	2,528
MUBIN, Orhon (1924-1981) Turkish				
oil	6	819-13,233	4,100	1,440
MUCCINI, Marcello (1926-1978) Italian				
oil	3	835-1,985	1,338	1,196
MUCHA, Alphonse (1860-1939) Czechoslovakian				
oil	1	53,360	53,360	53,360
wc/d	11	1,400-31,280	9,351	3,600
MUCHA, Paul (1856-?) ?				
oil	1	19,357	19,357	19,357
MUCKE, Carl Emil (1847-1923) German				
oil	3	1,036-2,003	1,537	1,573
MUCKLEY, Louis Fairfax (fl.1887-1901) British				
wc/d	2	463-6,336	3,399	463
MUDHARAT, C (?) Egyptian?				
oil	1	1,764	1,764	1,764

Name	No.	Price Range	Average	Median
MUE, Maurice August del (1875-1955) American/French				
oil	3	1,800-7,500	5,100	6,000
MUEBACH, Dieter Diedrich (1825-1911) German				
wc/d	1	1,400	1,400	1,400
MUECK, Ron (1958-) Australian				
3D	1	58,000	58,000	58,000
MUEHLHAUS, Daniel (1907-1981) Dutch				
oil	1	1,414	1,414	1,414
MUENCH, Charles (20th C) American				
oil	2	1,100-1,200	1,150	1,100
MUENIER, Jules Alexis (1863-1942) French				
oil	1	30,000	30,000	30,000
wc/d	1	2,634	2,634	2,634
MUFF, Orla (1903-1984) Danish				
oil	3	1,618-3,074	2,426	2,588
MUGGE, Berthold (1896-1970) German				
oil	1	1,414	1,414	1,414
MUHE, Philip (?) ?				
oil	1	13,680	13,680	13,680
MUHL, Otto (1924-) Austrian				
oil	11	1,514-22,384	7,489	3,836
wc/d	5	647-2,272	1,244	1,109
MUHL, Roger (1929-) French				
oil	19	524-10,192	5,533	6,000
wc/d	2	3,200-4,083	3,641	3,200
MUHLE, Hermann (1822-?) German				
oil	1	1,212	1,212	1,212
MUHLEN, Hermann (1886-1964) German				
oil	2	742-3,299	2,020	742
MUHLEN-SCHMID, Josephine (1888-1960) German?				
oil	1	2,631	2,631	2,631
MUHLENEN, Max von (1903-1971) Swiss				
oil	3	666-1,378	1,097	1,249
MUHLENFELD, Otto (1871-1907) American				
oil	1	20,000	20,000	20,000
MUHLENHAUPT, Kurt (1921-) German				
oil	6	1,145-2,631	1,620	1,360
MUHLIG, Bernard (1829-1910) German				
oil	4	565-3,314	1,675	1,205
MUHLIG, Hugo (1854-1929) German				
oll	8	2,061-23,848	7,460	4,579
wc/d	2	1,109-1,401	1,255	1,109
MUHLSTOCK, Louis (1904-2001) Canadian				
oil	3	1,649-3,711	2,419	1,898
wc/d	4	1,237-1,507	1,363	1,244
MUHRMANN, Ludwig (1886-?) German				
oil	2	1,138-1,794	1,466	1,138
MUIJSENBERG, Toon van den (1901-1967) Dutch				
oil	1	2,417	2,417	2,417
MUIR, Anne Davidson (?-1951) British				
oil	1	1,419	1,419	1,419
wc/d	2	546-783	664	546
MUIR, Emily (1904-2004) American				
oil	3	750-3,000	2,216	2,900
MUIR, Jack W (20th C) American				
3D	1	11,000	11,000	11,000
MUKHERJEE, Robin (20th C) Indian				
oil	1	10,000	10,000	10,000
MULCAHY, Jeremiah Hodges (?-1889) British				
oil	1	66,960	66,960	66,960
MULCAHY, Michael (1952-) Irish				
oil	7	547-3,507	1,862	2,022
wc/d	2	608-969	788	608
MULDER, Jan (1897-1962) Dutch				
oil	2	1,798-4,937	3,367	1,798
MULDERS, Camille van (1868-1949) Belgian				
oil	4	486-3,010	1,646	1,204
MULDERS, Jean (1913-) Belgian				
oil	1	1,152	1,152	1,152
MULDERS, Marc (1958-) Dutch				
oil	3	2,803-19,110	9,837	7,598

Name	No.	Price Range	Average	Median
MULET-CLAVER, Vincent (1895-1945) Spanish				
oil	2	1,874-9,570	5,722	1,874
MULHAUPT, Frederick J (1871-1938) American				
oil	8	4,000-60,000	22,125	15,500
MULHOLLAND, S A (19th C) British				
oil	1	2,323	2,323	2,323
MULIER, Pieter (17th C) Dutch				
wc/d	1	3,503	3,503	3,503
MULIER, Pieter (elder) (1615-1670) Dutch				
oil	3	14,014-34,600	26,008	29,410
MULIER, Pieter (younger) (1637-1701) Dutch				
oil	2	3,092-39,160	21,126	3,092
MULLARD, Joseph Albert (1868-?) British				
oil	1	1,100	1,100	1,100
MULLER VON SIEL, Georg Bernhard (19/20th C) German				
oil	1	2,303	2,303	2,303
MULLER, Albert (1897-1926) Swiss				
oil	2	3,358-36,476	19,917	3,358
wc/d	16	568-12,321	2,377	1,332
MULLER, Alfredo (1869-1940) Italian				
oil	2	6,869-8,486	7,677	6,869
MULLER, August (1836-1885) German				
oil	2	788-2,510	1,649	788
MULLER, Carl Wilhelm (1839-1904) German				
oil	2	1,400-4,796	3,098	1,400
MULLER, Dave (1964-) American				
wc/d	1	4,500	4,500	4,500
MULLER, E G (fl.1836-1871) British				
oil	1	1,914	1,914	1,914
MULLER, Eduard (19/20th C) Swiss				
oil	1	4,197	4,197	4,197
MULLER, Eduard Josef (1851-1922) German				
oil	4	1,130-1,798	1,462	1,285
MULLER, Emil (1924-) Swiss				
oil	1	2,596	2,596	2,596
MULLER, Emma von (1859-1925) Austrian				
oil	4	818-1,868	1,416	1,430
MULLER, Erich Martin (1888-1972) German				
oil	3	701-7,315	3,685	3,041
MULLER, Franz Adolf Christian (1841-1903) Swiss				
oil	1	6,105	6,105	6,105
MULLER, Friedrich Wilhelm (18/19th C) German				
oil	1	4,816	4,816	4,816
MULLER, G (?) ?				
oil	1	3,700	3,700	3,700
MULLER, Gerard (1861-1929) Dutch				
oil	1	1,543	1,543	1,543
wc/d	1	719	719	719
MULLER, Heinrich (1903-1978) Swiss				
oil	6	687-4,553	2,729	2,732
MULLER, Heinz (1872-?) German				
3D	1	2,421	2,421	2,421
MULLER, Jacques (1930-1997) Belgian				
oil	6	958-1,490	1,161	1,157
MULLER, Jan Harmensz (c.1571-1628) Dutch				
oil	1	7,297	7,297	7,297
MULLER, Johan (19th C) ?				
oil	1	2,450	2,450	2,450
MULLER, Johann Georg (1913-1986) German				
oil	9	5,856-356,712	91,793	47,571
wc/d	9	1,543-19,286	8,376	5,890
MULLER, Julie (19th C) German				
wc/d	1	2,870	2,870	2,870
MULLER, Karl (1818-1893) German				
oil	2	2,000-3,000	2,500	2,000
3D	1	1,907	1,907	1,907
MULLER, Karl Josef (1865-1942) German				
oil	1	23,568	23,568	23,568
MULLER, Leopold Carl (1834-1892) German				
oil	5	950-14,055	5,378	3,960
wc/d	1	1,936	1,936	1,936

Name	No.	Price Range	Average	Median
MULLER, Maria (1847-?) Austrian				
oil	1	1,073	1,073	1,073
MULLER, Moritz (jnr) (20th C) German				
oil	2	606-1,824	1,215	606
MULLER, Moritz (snr) (1841-1899) German				
oil	2	730-1,659	1,194	730
MULLER, Otto (1874-1930) German				
wc/d	9	777-777,000	122,041	14,833
3D	2	1,366-14,432	7,899	1,366
MULLER, Peter Gottlieb (1766-1804) German?				
oil	1	1,800	1,800	1,800
MULLER, Richard (1874-1954) Austrian				
oil	5	999-122,368	27,332	2,631
wc/d	2	1,145-1,890	1,517	1,145
MULLER, Rosa (19th C) German				
oil	1	2,835	2,835	2,835
wc/d	1	748	748	748
MULLER, Rudolf (1907-1969) German				
oil	1	3,481	3,481	3,481
MULLER, Rudolph (1802-1885) Swiss				
wc/d	5	1,418-8,269	3,601	2,589
MULLER, Rudolph Gustav (1858-1888) German				
oil	1	1,914	1,914	1,914
MULLER, William James (1812-1845) British				
oil	4	696-3,500	1,818	1,229
wc/d	6	555-8,316	2,862	1,903
MULLER-BAUMGARTEN, Carl (1879-1946) German				
oil	6	544-1,632	1,003	973
MULLER-BRITTNAU, Willy (1938-) Swiss				
oil	4	837-1,522	1,163	837
MULLER-CORNELIUS, Ludwig (1864-1946) German				
oil	9	510-2,592	1,430	1,432
MULLER-GOSSEN, Franz (1871-1946) German				
oil	4	816-3,653	1,810	1,091
MULLER-HUFSCHMID, Willi (1890-1966) German				
oil	1	2,827	2,827	2,827
MULLER-KAEMPFF, Paul (1861-1941) German				
oil	10	983-21,822	4,696	3,503
MULLER-LINGKE, Albert (1844-?) German				
oil	4	970-1,918	1,460	1,308
MULLER-LINOW, Bruno (1909-1997) German				
oil	1	989	989	989
wc/d	2	865-865	865	865
MULLER-MUNSTER, Franz (1867-?) German				
oil	1	1,255	1,255	1,255
MULLER-SAMERBERG, Karl Hermann (1869-1946) German				
oil	1	3,284	3,284	3,284
wc/d	1	1,883	1,883	1,883
MULLER-SCHEESEL, Ernst (1863-1936) German				
wc/d	1	1,212	1,212	1,212
MULLER-WISCHIN, Anton (1865-1949) German				
oil	5	727-2,827	1,539	1,212
MULLEY, Oskar (1891-1949) Austrian				
oil	13	993-12,552	7,624	10,305
MULLICAN, Matt (1951-) American				
oil	3	5,500-38,000	16,833	7,000
3D	1	6,000	6,000	6,000
MULREADY, Augustus E (fl.1863-1905) British				
oil	7	613-23,660	6,000	2,301
MULREADY, William (1786-1863) British				
oil	3	2,640-3,500	2,991	2,835
MUMFORD, Elizabeth (20th C) American				
oil	3	1,000-3,200	2,166	2,300
MUMPRECHT, Walter Rudolf (1918-) Swiss				
oil	1	648	648	648
wc/d	4	725-4,163	2,387	1,166
MUNAKATA, Shiko (1903-1975) Japanese				
wc/d	1	8,000	8,000	8,000
MUNARI, Bruno (1907-1998) Italian				
oil	3	5,088-8,905	7,006	7,027
wc/d	9	1,229-4,788	2,287	1,649

Name	No.	Price Range	Average	Median
MUNCASTER, Claude (1903-1974) British				
oil	3	606-1,040	767	657
wc/d	4	515-885	628	555
MUNCH, Axel (1918-1974) Danish				
oil	2	2,157-2,323	2,240	2,157
MUNCH, Edvard (1863-1944) Norwegian				
oil	10	257,600-9,680,001	2,740,960	1,936,000
wc/d	2	26,000-123,200	74,600	26,000
MUNCH, Horst (1951-) German				
oil	1	1,694	1,694	1,694
MUNDARAY, Ismael (1952-) Venezuelan				
oil	1	1,440	1,440	1,440
MUNDO, Ignasi (1918-) Spanish				
oil	1	2,035	2,035	2,035
MUNDT, Caroline Emilie (1849-1922) Danish				
oil	4	647-15,876	4,750	946
MUNGER, Gilbert (1837-1903) American				
oil	4	598-150,000	39,196	2,436
MUNIE, J L (19/20th C) ?				
oil	1	2,600	2,600	2,600
MUNIER, Émile (1840-1895) French				
oil	3	120,000-208,800	159,600	150,000
MUNIZ, Vik (1961-) Brazilian				
oil	1	19,000	19,000	19,000
MUNK, Jacob (c.1810-1885) German				
oil	2	1,430-25,286	13,358	1,430
MUNKACSY, Mihaly Lieb (1844-1900) Hungarian				
wc/d	4	1,565-3,130	1,956	1,565
MUNN, Paul Sandby (1773-1845) British				
wc/d	6	445-3,132	1,080	570
MUNNINGHOFF, Xeno (1873-1944) Dutch				
oil	1	1,341	1,341	1,341
MUNNINGS, Sir Alfred (1878-1959) British				
oil	33	13,200-3,650,000	497,516	230,000
wc/d	18	602-470,000	54,727	4,158
MUNNS, Henry Turner (1832-1898) British				
oil	1	3,480	3,480	3,480
MUNOZ BARBERAN, Manuel (1921-) Spanish				
oil	2	2,431-4,500	3,465	2,431
wc/d	2	668-1,337	1,002	668
MUNOZ RUBIO, Antonio (19th C) Spanish				
wc/d	1	1,573	1,573	1,573
MUNOZ RUBIO, Ramon (19th C) Spanish				
oil	3	7,613-9,000	8,075	7,613
MUNOZ Y CUESTA, Domingo (1850-1912) Spanish				
oil	1	1,205	1,205	1,205
MUNOZ, Bartolome Mongrell (1890-1038) Spanish				
oil	1	4,123	4,123	4,123
MUNOZ, Godofredo Ortega (1905-1982) Spanish				
oil	4	10,200-119,728	44,315	20,994
MUNOZ, Juan (1953-2001) Spanish				
oil	1	47,500	47,500	47,500
3D	8	29,000-211,200	73,478	55,625
MUNOZ, Lucio (1929-1998) Spanish				
oil	1	33,714	33,714	33,714
wc/d	2	30,102-49,378	39,740	30,102
MUNOZ, M (?) Spanish				
oil	1	28,000	28,000	28,000
MUNOZ, Rafael (1897-1981) Argentinian				
oil	1	1,200	1,200	1,200
MUNOZ-DEGRAIN, Antoine (1843-1924) French				
oil	1	7,176	7,176	7,176
MUNOZ-VERA, Guillermo (1956-) Chilean				
oil	5	2,543-85,000	33,564	27,000
MUNRO, Alexander (1825-1871) British				
3D	1	75,600	75,600	75,600
MUNRO, Peter (1954-) British				
oil	4	567-2,394	1,194	870
MUNROE, Sarah Sewell (1870-1946) American				
oil	1	18,000	18,000	18,000
MUNSCH, Eric (20th C) ?				
oil	1	2,336	2,336	2,336

Name	No.	Price Range	Average	Median
MUNSCH, Josef (1832-1896) Austrian				
oil	1	9,000	9,000	9,000
MUNSCH, Leopold (1826-1888) Austrian				
oil	3	1,823-8,836	5,320	5,301
MUNSTERHJELM, Ali (1873-1944) Finnish				
oil	11	1,318-6,686	3,206	2,397
MUNSTERHJELM, Hjalmar (1840-1905) Finnish				
oil	8	5,143-28,848	14,076	14,055
wc/d	1	719	719	719
MUNTANE MUNS, Luis (1899-1987) Spanish				
oil	1	1,492	1,492	1,492
MUNTEAN, Markus and ROSENBLUM, Adi (1962-) Austrian/Israeli				
oil	5	10,175-14,080	11,691	12,000
wc/d	1	4,928	4,928	4,928
MUNTER, David Heinrich (1816-1879) German				
oil	1	89,178	89,178	89,178
MUNTER, Gabriele (1877-1962) German				
oil	20	15,288-518,000	78,730	38,219
wc/d	4	8,778-24,170	15,237	10,603
MUNTHE, Gerhard Peter Franz Vilhelm (1849-1929) Norwegian				
oil	6	4,243-13,336	9,548	9,456
MUNTHE, Ludvig (1841-1896) Norwegian				
oil	3	872-3,737	2,081	1,636
MUNTHE-NORSTEDT, Anna (1854-1936) Swedish				
oil	3	1,371-5,220	3,443	3,739
MUNTZ, Johann Heinrich (1727-1798) German				
oil	1	3,330	3,330	3,330
MUNZER, Adolf (1870-1952) German				
wc/d	2	567-1,591	1,079	567
MUNZER-NEUMANN, Kathe (1877-?) German				
oil	1	3,829	3,829	3,829
MURA, Francesco de (1696-1782) Italian				
oil	1	9,251	9,251	9,251
wc/d	1	5,000	5,000	5,000
MURAKAMI, Takashi (1962-) Japanese				
oil	7	14,160-1,000,000	212,808	110,000
wc/d	3	2,752-25,000	12,917	11,000
3D	3	3,156-330,000	113,052	6,000
MURATON, Euphemie (1840-?) French				
oil	1	1,694	1,694	1,694
MURATORI, Teresa (1662-1708) Italian				
wc/d	1	1,189	1,189	1,189
MURAVYOV, Count Vladimir Leonidovich (1861-1931) Russian				
oil	2	30,405-48,080	39,242	30,405
wc/d	4	8,600-89,178	49,786	21,600
MURCH, Henry (fl.1850-1851) British				
oil	1	7,229	7,229	7,229
MURCH, Walter (1907-1967) American/Canadian				
wc/d	1	1,800	1,800	1,800
MURDAY, J (19th C) British				
oil	1	10,000	10,000	10,000
MURER, Augusto (1922-1985) Italian				
wc/d	1	1,432	1,432	1,432
MURER, Christoph (1558-1614) Swiss				
wc/d	1	10,938	10,938	10,938
MURGIA DE CASTRO, Ovidio (1871-1900) Spanish				
oil	2	5,100-8,230	6,665	5,100
MURGUIA, Ovidio (19th C) Spanish				
oil	2	1,044-1,914	1,479	1,044
MURILLO BRACHO, Jose Maria (1827-1882) Spanish				
oil	3	2,281-9,041	6,586	8,438
MURILLO, Bartolome Esteban (1618-1682) Spanish				
oil	5	760-3,806,000	887,878	187,632
wc/d	1	18,229	18,229	18,229
MURPHY, Herman Dudley (1867-1945) American				
oil	5	7,500-47,500	20,700	8,500
MURPHY, J Francis (1853-1921) American				
oil	12	710-5,960	2,835	2,000
wc/d	2	1,000-1,300	1,150	1,000
MURRAY, Archibald (fl.1920-1950) British				
oil	1	1,540	1,540	1,540

Name	No.	Price Range	Average	Median
MURRAY, Elizabeth (1940-) American				
oil	1	55,000	55,000	55,000
wc/d	4	1,488-5,952	3,406	2,400
MURRAY, George (fl.1883-1922) British				
wc/d	1	1,460	1,460	1,460
MURRAY, James and THOMAS, George Housman (19th C) British				
wc/d	1	1,408	1,408	1,408
MURRAY, John Reid (1861-1906) British				
oil	1	2,960	2,960	2,960
MURRAY, Sir David (1849-1933) British				
oil	8	552-8,800	2,664	1,012
MURRAY, Tatyana (1971-) American				
3D	1	3,700	3,700	3,700
MURRY, J B (?) American?				
wc/d	2	3,500-4,250	3,875	3,500
MURTIC, Edo (1921-) Yugoslavian				
oil	5	970-9,000	5,263	5,691
wc/d	1	1,200	1,200	1,200
MURUA, Mario (1952-) Chilean				
oil	1	2,750	2,750	2,750
MUS, Italo (1892-1967) Italian				
oil	1	6,668	6,668	6,668
MUSANTE, Francesco (1950-) Italian				
oil	2	1,649-1,708	1,678	1,649
wc/d	10	716-3,534	1,786	1,463
MUSCHAMP, F Sydney (1851-1929) British				
oil	4	828-9,450	3,924	1,305
MUSE, John F (19/20th C) British				
wc/d	1	1,158	1,158	1,158
MUSGRAVE, Arthur Franklyn (1880-?) American				
wc/d	1	1,500	1,500	1,500
MUSIC, Zoran (1909-2005) Italian				
oil	19	9,425-117,123	50,719	38,877
wc/d	32	1,671-13,155	6,573	5,819
MUSIN, Auguste (1852-1920) Belgian				
oil	3	1,911-13,495	7,628	7,478
wc/d	2	1,512-1,818	1,665	1,512
MUSIN, François Etienne (1820-1888) Belgian				
oil	13	2,822-30,308	12,177	9,889
wc/d	1	883	883	883
MUSIN, Maurice (1939-) Belgian				
oil	5	477-3,025	1,374	1,134
MUSIN, P (20th C) Belgian				
oil	1	4,956	4,956	4,956
MUSIN, Paul (20th C) ?				
oil	9	465-2,275	1,046	963
MUSITELLI, Giulio Vito (1901-1990) Italian				
oil	1	1,134	1,134	1,134
MUSLIN, Joseph (1911-) French?				
oil	3	1,000-3,949	2,449	2,400
MUSS-ARNOLT, Gustav (1858-1927) American				
oil	3	1,827-37,500	15,942	8,500
MUSSCHER, Michiel van (1645-1705) Dutch				
oil	1	45,026	45,026	45,026
MUSSILL, William (19th C) Austrian?				
wc/d	1	2,848	2,848	2,848
MUSSO, Carlo (1907-1968) Italian				
oil	11	909-3,996	2,404	2,543
MUTER, Mela (1886-1967) French				
oil	9	865-50,000	13,776	8,500
wc/d	2	2,000-2,400	2,200	2,000
MUTHSPIEL, Agnes (1914-1968) Austrian				
oil	3	2,910-5,394	3,899	3,395
MUTRIE, Annie Feray (1826-1893) British				
oil	1	9,452	9,452	9,452
MUTRIE, Martha Darley (1824-1885) British				
oil	1	1,044	1,044	1,044
MUUKKA, Elias (1853-1938) Finnish				
oil	4	1,008-3,507	2,051	1,377
MUXEL, Josef Anton (1786-1842) German				
oil	1	1,998	1,998	1,998

Name	No.	Price Range	Average	Median
MUYDEN, Alfred van (1818-1898) Swiss				
oil	4	1,665-5,724	3,703	3,263
wc/d	3	683-2,284	1,261	816
MUZIKA, Frantisek (1900-1974) Czechoslovakian				
oil	1	2,829	2,829	2,829
MUZZIOLI, Giovanni (1854-1894) Italian				
oil	3	5,000-80,000	41,666	40,000
MY, Hieronymus van der (1687-1761) Dutch				
oil	1	13,840	13,840	13,840
MYERS, Forrest Warden (1941-) American				
3D	1	5,500	5,500	5,500
MYERS, Frank Harmon (1899-1956) American				
oil	7	1,000-14,000	4,750	3,000
MYERS, Jerome (1867-1940) American				
oil	2	5,500-13,000	9,250	5,500
wc/d	2	450-750	600	450
MYERS, Mark Richard (1945-) British/American				
wc/d	1	2,057	2,057	2,057
MYERS, Philip H (20th C) American				
oil	1	1,100	1,100	1,100
MYLDORFER, Franz August (18th C) German				
wc/d	1	2,356	2,356	2,356
MYLES, John (19th C) British				
oil	1	1,075	1,075	1,075
MYN, Francis van der (1719-1783) Dutch				
oil	1	2,392	2,392	2,392
MYNTTI, Eemu (1890-1943) Finnish				
oil	4	1,288-3,273	2,279	1,753
wc/d	1	779	779	779
MYRAH, Newman (1921-) Canadian				
oil	6	950-8,500	5,625	6,000
MYTENS, Jan (1614-1670) Dutch				
oil	3	5,733-39,160	17,335	7,114
MYTTEIS, Victor (1874-1936) Hungarian				
oil	2	1,109-1,518	1,313	1,109
NAAGER, Franz (1870-1942) German				
oil	2	608-3,857	2,232	608
NABASQUE, Gerard le (1948-) French				
oil	1	1,029	1,029	1,029
NABERT, Wilhelm (1830-1904) German				
oil	1	1,405	1,405	1,405
NABILI, Mohammed (1952-) Moroccan				
wc/d	2	2,065-2,065	2,065	2,065
NACIRI, Mohamed (1943-) Moroccan				
wc/d	1	2,179	2,179	2,179
NADAL FARRERAS, Carlos (1918-1998) Spanish?				
oil	1	7,027	7,027	7,027
wc/d	3	556-1,316	936	937
NADAL, Carlos (1917-1998) Spanish				
oil	25	1,770-74,000	17,607	13,275
wc/d	7	1,274-5,190	2,699	2,124
NADELMAN, Elie (1882-1946) American/Polish				
wc/d	3	1,100-5,000	2,966	2,800
3D	3	65,000-250,000	130,000	75,000
NADER (19th C) ?				
oil	1	6,500	6,500	6,500
NAEGELE, Charles Frederick (1857-1944) American				
oil	1	2,250	2,250	2,250
NAEKE, Gustav Heinrich (1786-1835) German				
wc/d	1	4,241	4,241	4,241
NAEL, Hanna (1959-) British				
wc/d	1	5,310	5,310	5,310
NAFTEL, Paul Jacob (1817-1891) British				
oil	1	605	605	605
wc/d	13	574-14,104	2,224	1,032
NAGANO, Shozo (20th C) American?				
oil	1	1,300	1,300	1,300
NAGARE, Masayuki (1923-) Japanese				
3D	2	3,250-4,250	3,750	3,250
NAGEL, Andres (1947-) Spanish				
oil	1	13,170	13,170	13,170
wc/d	1	4,757	4,757	4,757

Name	No.	Price Range	Average	Median
NAGEL, Johann Friedrich (1765-1825) German				
wc/d	1	7,572	7,572	7,572
NAGEL, Otto (1894-1967) German				
oil	1	8,199	8,199	8,199
wc/d	3	3,279-7,027	4,528	3,279
NAGELE, Reinhold (1884-1972) German				
oil	1	6,799	6,799	6,799
wc/d	1	7,803	7,803	7,803
NAGORNOV, Vladislav (1974-) Russian				
oil	6	763-3,150	1,896	1,750
NAGTEGAAL, Jan (1920-2000) Dutch				
oil	3	647-2,503	1,759	2,128
NAGY, Vilmos (1874-1953) Hungarian				
oil	2	1,100-1,500	1,300	1,100
NAHAULAITUQ, Samuel (1923-) North American				
3D	1	1,603	1,603	1,603
NAHER, Christa (1947-) German				
wc/d	1	1,532	1,532	1,532
NAHL, Charles C (1818-1878) American				
wc/d	1	7,000	7,000	7,000
NAHT, F (19th C) ?				
oil	1	3,148	3,148	3,148
NAIDA, Dmitri (1969-) Russian				
oil	1	1,212	1,212	1,212
NAIDITCH, Vladimir (1903-1980) Russian				
oil	10	898-2,397	1,663	1,459
NAIMO, Nicola (1951-) Italian				
oil	1	1,229	1,229	1,229
NAIR, Surendran (1956-) Indian				
oil	1	40,000	40,000	40,000
wc/d	2	14,000-60,000	37,000	14,000
NAISH, Richard E (1912-1988) British				
oil	1	3,480	3,480	3,480
NAKAMURA, Kazuo (1926-2002) Canadian/Japanese				
oil	3	10,536-24,682	15,251	10,536
wc/d	2	1,350-3,585	2,467	1,350
NAKAMURA, Nakiko (20th C) Japanese?				
oil	1	2,420	2,420	2,420
NAKAMURA, Naondo (1905-1981) Japanese				
wc/d	1	5,528	5,528	5,528
NAKHALOV, Boris (1925-) Russian				
oil	4	468-3,092	1,175	540
NAKHOVA, Irina (1955-) Russian				
wc/d	1	10,000	10,000	10,000
NAKIAN, Reuben (1897-1986) American				
wc/d	2	400-950	675	400
3D	3	3,500-5,000	4,250	4,250
NAKKEN, Willem Carel (1835-1926) Dutch				
oil	12	3,031-32,040	9,151	4,453
NALBANDIAN, Dmitri A (1906-1993) Russian				
oil	1	25,000	25,000	25,000
NALDINI, Giovan Battista (1537-1591) Italian				
oil	1	70,000	70,000	70,000
NALL (20th C) ?				
wc/d	2	4,071-26,736	15,403	4,071
NALLARD, Louis (1918-) French				
oil	2	1,890-3,010	2,450	1,890
NAM KWAN (1911-1990) Korean				
oil	1	9,000	9,000	9,000
NAM, Jacques (1881-1974) French				
oil	5	1,255-11,211	3,638	2,104
wc/d	17	504-7,014	1,579	941
NAMCHEONG (19th C) Chinese				
oil	2	1,295-8,370	4,832	1,295
NAMUR, Franz (1877-?) French				
oil	1	3,148	3,148	3,148
NANDIN, Edmond (19th C) French				
oil	1	3,871	3,871	3,871
NANGERONI, Carlo (1922-) American				
oil	6	1,432-4,653	3,014	2,848
NANI, Giacomo (1701-1770) Italian				
oil	1	7,767	7,767	7,767

Name	No.	Price Range	Average	Median
NANNEY, Chuck (1958-) French				
oil	4	887-1,267	1,124	1,140
wc/d	1	1,014	1,014	1,014
NANNI, Mario (1922-) Italian				
oil	1	1,001	1,001	1,001
NANNINGA, Jaap (1904-1962) Dutch				
oil	1	6,361	6,361	6,361
wc/d	4	760-3,741	2,012	1,767
NANNINI, Raphael (fl.1870-1895) Italian				
3D	1	2,330	2,330	2,330
NANNUCCI, Maurizio (1939-) Italian				
3D	1	7,259	7,259	7,259
NANTEUIL, Robert (1623-1678) French				
wc/d	2	1,200-4,114	2,657	1,200
NAONOBU, Kano (1607-1650) Japanese				
wc/d	1	3,515	3,515	3,515
NAPIER, Jason (1973-) American				
3D	1	2,250	2,250	2,250
NAPIER, William Henry Edward (1829-1894) Canadian				
wc/d	2	825-3,173	1,999	825
NAPPER, John (1916-) British				
oil	1	855	855	855
wc/d	1	555	555	555
NAPS (19th C) ?				
3D	1	14,000	14,000	14,000
NAPS, E (19th C) ?				
3D	2	2,432-248,425	125,428	2,432
NAPS, Jevgeni (19th C) Russian				
3D	1	13,020	13,020	13,020
NAPS, L (19th C) Russian				
3D	1	14,882	14,882	14,882
NAQSH, Jamil (1938-) Indian				
oil	6	5,190-24,000	12,370	7,920
wc/d	6	3,168-6,336	5,236	5,280
NARA, Yoshimoto (1959-) American				
oil	18	7,434-950,000	188,851	129,500
wc/d	23	1,286-260,000	26,313	7,500
3D	4	1,940-100,000	39,785	13,200
NARA, Yoshimoto and SUGITO, Hiroshi (20th C) American/Japanese				
wc/d	2	3,330 5,280	4,305	3,330
NARA, Yoshitomo (1959-) American				
oil	3	22,000-150,000	67,333	30,000
wc/d	2	8,000-8,500	8,250	8,000
NARAHA, Takashi (1930-) Japanese				
3D	3	2,163-4,757	3,748	4,326
NARAYAN, Badri (1929-) Indian				
wc/d	3	6,055-27,500	14,613	10,285
NARAYANAN, Akkitham (1939-) ?				
wc/d	1	4,114	4,114	4,114
NARBONA BELTRAN, Francisco (1860-1926) Spanish				
oil	1	1,600	1,600	1,600
wc/d	1	1,440	1,440	1,440
NARBONNE, Eugène (1885-?) French				
oil	1	2,392	2,392	2,392
NARDI, Enrico (1864-1947) Italian				
wc/d	4	1,942-18,400	6,250	2,071
NARDI, J (?) ?				
oil	2	9,514-11,892	10,703	9,514
NARES, James (1953-) American				
oil	1	40,000	40,000	40,000
NAREZO, Jose Garcia (20th C) Mexican				
oil	1	1,100	1,100	1,100
NARJOT, Ernest (1826-1898) American				
oil	1	1,300	1,300	1,300
NARVAEZ, Francisco (1905-1982) Venezuelan				
oil	2	5,500-14,880	10,190	5,500
wc/d	2	2,100-2,100	2,100	2,100
3D	3	4,190-10,000	7,523	8,380
NASH, David (1945-) British				
3D	1	12,900	12,900	12,900
NASH, Frederick (1782-1856) British				
wc/d	5	1,018-4,070	2,414	1,665

Name	No.	Price Range	Average	Median
NASH, John (1893-1977) British				
oil	1	15,120	15,120	15,120
wc/d	14	463-3,828	1,246	925
NASH, Jorgen (1920-) Danish				
oil	1	4,041	4,041	4,041
NASH, Joseph (1808-1878) British				
wc/d	3	963-11,160	4,398	1,073
NASH, Paul (1889-1946) British				
wc/d	15	3,240-66,150	13,791	8,850
NASMYTH, Alexander (1758-1840) British				
oil	8	8,010-158,400	45,123	16,720
wc/d	3	722-9,680	3,765	894
NASMYTH, Charlotte (1804-1884) British				
oil	1	35,200	35,200	35,200
NASMYTH, Jane (1788-1867) British				
oil	2	3,894-21,120	12,507	3,894
NASMYTH, Patrick (1787-1831) British				
oil	7	1,730-10,560	3,414	2,076
wc/d	1	2,992	2,992	2,992
NASON, Gertrude (1890-1969) American				
oil	1	2,000	2,000	2,000
NASON, Pieter (1612-1688) Dutch				
oil	2	19,030-22,000	20,515	19,030
NASSAU, William (20th C) British?				
oil	2	659-1,464	1,061	659
NASSY, Joseph (1904-1976) Dutch				
oil	1	2,186	2,186	2,186
NAST, Gustave Louis (1826-?) French				
3D	1	23,973	23,973	23,973
NASTAPOKA, Sarah (1925-) North American				
3D	2	2,868-3,037	2,952	2,868
NAT, Willem Hendrik van der (1864-1929) Dutch				
wc/d	2	1,205-1,752	1,478	1,205
NATALI, A (19th C) ?				
3D	1	12,000	12,000	12,000
NATALI, Renato (1883-1979) Italian				
oil	21	557-10,356	3,462	2,973
wc/d	1	707	707	707
NATESAN, Shibu (1966-) Indian				
wc/d	1	9,350	9,350	9,350
NATH, Friedrich (1859-?) German				
oil	3	816-5,301	2,334	887
NATHAN, Max (1880-1952) Danish				
oil	1	1,141	1,141	1,141
NATHE, Christoph (1753-1806) German				
wc/d	1	1,944	1,944	1,944
NATIVI, Gualtiero (1921-1997) Italian				
oil	17	2,121-8,905	4,631	4,425
wc/d	7	504-5,597	2,266	1,018
NATKIN, Robert (1930-) American				
oil	5	2,250-16,000	6,550	4,750
wc/d	1	3,200	3,200	3,200
NATOIRE, Charles-Joseph (1700-1777) French				
oil	2	43,250-51,302	47,276	43,250
wc/d	6	851-8,000	4,798	5,833
NATON, Avraham (1906-1959) Israeli				
wc/d	1	1,800	1,800	1,800
NATORP, Gustav (1836-?) German				
3D	1	3,560	3,560	3,560
NATTERO, Louis (19/20th C) French				
oil	6	507-6,276	2,416	1,767
NATTES, John Claude (1765-1822) British				
wc/d	1	1,573	1,573	1,573
NATTIER, Jean Marc (1685-1766) French				
wc/d	2	2,750-12,418	7,584	2,750
NATTINI, Amos (1892-?) Italian				
oil	3	1,401-7,007	4,359	4,671
NAUEN, Heinrich (1880-1941) German				
oil	2	17,836-19,110	18,473	17,836
wc/d	1	912	912	912
NAUJOKS, Heino (1937-) German				
wc/d	1	1,532	1,532	1,532

Name	No.	Price Range	Average	Median
NAULITUK, Mattiusi (1904-1984) North American				
3D	1	1,518	1,518	1,518
NAUMAN, Bruce (1941-) American				
wc/d	1	115,000	115,000	115,000
3D	5	4,500-460,200	166,940	150,000
NAUMANN, Hermann (1930-) German				
oil	1	1,360	1,360	1,360
wc/d	1	593	593	593
NAUMER, Helmuth (1907-1989) American				
oil	1	3,500	3,500	3,500
wc/d	1	2,750	2,750	2,750
NAVARRA, Pietro (17/18th C) Italian				
oil	1	55,000	55,000	55,000
NAVARRETE Y FOS, Ricardo (1834-1910) Spanish				
oil	1	17,838	17,838	17,838
NAVARRO LLORENS, Jose (1867-1923) Spanish				
oil	4	4,281-36,800	12,979	4,576
wc/d	1	11,210	11,210	11,210
NAVARRO, Miquel (1945-) Spanish				
wc/d	1	2,408	2,408	2,408
NAVASCUES, Jose Maria (1944-) Spanish				
3D	1	8,919	8,919	8,919
NAVEZ, Arthur (1881-1931) Belgian				
oil	3	1,806-11,700	5,837	4,005
NAVEZ, François Joseph (1787-1869) Belgian				
oil	2	1,052-8,910	4,981	1,052
wc/d	1	927	927	927
NAVEZ, Léon (1900-1967) Belgian				
oil	9	547-8,352	2,042	972
NAVIASKY, Philip (1894-1983) British				
oil	10	463-1,044	685	641
wc/d	1	650	650	650
NAVRATIL, Walter (1950-) Austrian				
oil	2	3,312-6,676	4,994	3,312
NAY, Ernst Wilhelm (1902-1968) German				
oil	5	20,384-210,405	86,460	58,904
wc/d	18	2,342-33,123	14,932	14,014
NAZON, François-Henri (1821-1902) French				
oil	1	1,870	1,870	1,870
NAZZARI, Bartolommeo (1699-1758) Italian				
oil	1	10,829	10,829	10,829
NEAGLE, John (1796-1865) American				
oil	3	800-11,000	4,683	2,250
NEAGU, Octavian (1965-) Rumanian				
oil	1	1,288	1,288	1,288
NEAL, David (1837-1915) American				
oil	1	1,453	1,453	1,453
NEAL, James (1918-) British				
oil	1	1,018	1,018	1,018
NEALE, Andrew (1958-) British				
3D	1	5,280	5,280	5,280
NEAME, Austin (fl.c.1832-?) British				
oil	1	7,350	7,350	7,350
NEBBIA, Cesare (1536-1614) Italian				
wc/d	1	2,500	2,500	2,500
NEBEKER, Bill (1942-) American				
3D	1	5,000	5,000	5,000
NEBEL. Carlos (1805-1855) German				
oil	2	74,400-78,120	76,260	74,400
NEBEL, Friedrich Joseph Adolf (1818-1892) German				
oil	1	1,908	1,908	1,908
NEBEL, Otto (1892-1975) German				
oil	1	1,500	1,500	1,500
wc/d	8	973-5,711	2,925	2,331
NEBEL, P (19/20th C) German?				
3D	1	12,938	12,938	12,938
NEBESIKHIN, Sergey (1964-) Russian				
oil	3	1,225-1,750	1,429	1,313
NEBOT, Balthasar (18th C) British				
oil	1	32,490	32,490	32,490
NECK, Jan van (1635-1714) Dutch				
oil	2	4,243-20,713	12,478	4,243

Name	No.	Price Range	Average	Median
NEDELJKOVIC, Dragan (1957-) Russian				
wc/d	1	2,400	2,400	2,400
NEDER, Johann Michael (1807-1882) Austrian				
oil	2	3,646-9,722	6,684	3,646
NEEDELL, Philip Gregory (1886-1974) British				
oil	1	1,285	1,285	1,285
NEEFFS, Pieter (elder) (1578-1658) Flemish				
oil	4	6,423-71,200	28,475	10,510
NEEFFS, Pieter (younger) (1620-1675) Flemish				
oil	3	7,007-30,000	20,121	23,356
NEEL, Alice (1900-1984) American				
oil	2	55,000-350,000	202,500	55,000
NEELMEYER, Ludwig (1814-1870) German				
oil	1	1,254	1,254	1,254
NEER, Aert van der (1603-1677) Dutch				
oil	7	20,044-54,184	31,436	30,531
NEER, Eglon Hendrik van der (1634-1703) Dutch				
oil	2	17,000-800,000	408,500	17,000
NEFF, Edith (20th C) American				
oil	1	1,400	1,400	1,400
wc/d	1	700	700	700
NEFF, Janet (20th C) American				
wc/d	1	1,000	1,000	1,000
NEFF, Sibylle (1929-) Swiss				
oil	3	8,097-12,546	10,279	10,194
NEGELE, Julius (1935-) German				
oil	3	1,169-2,425	1,714	1,549
NEGRE, Dominique Alphonse (19th C) French				
oil	2	1,360-2,198	1,779	1,360
NEGRET, Edgar (1920-) Colombian				
3D	2	6,000-13,000	9,500	6,000
NEGRI, Mario (1916-1987) Italian				
3D	2	4,000-5,088	4,544	4,000
NEGRI, Nina (1909-1981) French?				
oil	1	1,130	1,130	1,130
NEHER, Michael (1798-1876) German				
oil	1	19,135	19,135	19,135
wc/d	1	560	560	560
NEHLIG, Victor (1830-1910) American				
oil	2	5,000-14,000	9,500	5,000
NEHMER, Rudolf (1912-1983) German				
oil	1	17,306	17,306	17,306
NEILL, Henry Echlin (1888-1981) British				
oil	2	484-2,640	1,562	484
NEILLOT, Louis (1898-1973) French				
oil	15	878-10,763	3,429	2,719
NEILSON, Lilian (1938-) British				
oil	2	1,021-1,091	1,056	1,021
NEILSON, Raymond Perry Rodgers (1881-1964) American				
oil	1	60,000	60,000	60,000
NEIMAN, Leroy (1926-) American				
oil	6	6,500-67,500	27,416	14,500
wc/d	5	600-6,635	3,367	3,000
NEITHARDT, Johann Matthias (1816-1886) Swiss				
oil	1	9,159	9,159	9,159
NEIZVESTNY, Ernst (1926-) Russian				
3D	3	1,770-5,000	3,456	3,600
NEJAD, Mehmed (1923-1994) Turkish				
oil	3	7,120-30,000	16,558	12,555
wc/d	2	5,438-7,200	6,319	5,438
NELIDOV (19th C) Russian				
oil	1	5,504	5,504	5,504
NELIMARKKA, Eero (1891-1977) Finnish				
oil	23	810-3,865	1,846	1,738
wc/d	1	920	920	920
NELLENS, Roger (1937-) Belgian				
oil	2	2,356-2,421	2,388	2,356
NELSON, Edmund (1911-) British				
oil	1	10,680	10,680	10,680
NELSON, Edward D (19th C) American				
oil	1	32,000	32,000	32,000

Name	No.	Price Range	Average	Median
NELSON, George Laurence (1887-1978) American				
oil	1	3,000	3,000	3,000
NELSON, Leonard L (1912-1993) American				
oil	3	1,600-3,500	2,500	2,400
NELSON, W J (19th C) British?				
oil	1	5,500	5,500	5,500
NELSON, William (20th C) American				
oil	1	1,000	1,000	1,000
NEME, Clarel (1926-) Uruguayan				
oil	1	2,250	2,250	2,250
NEMES, Endre (1909-1985) Hungarian				
oil	9	1,057-16,518	7,071	6,343
wc/d	4	1,000-2,379	1,799	1,781
NEMETHY, Albert (1920-) American				
oil	8	1,150-4,300	2,143	2,200
NEMOURS, Aurelie (1910-2005) French				
oil	11	3,783-56,572	20,785	21,186
wc/d	1	6,936	6,936	6,936
NEMUKHIN, Vladimir (1925-) Russian				
oil	1	17,199	17,199	17,199
wc/d	10	4,010-200,000	48,121	22,360
NENONEN, Anna Kaarina (1961-) Finnish				
oil	1	1,991	1,991	1,991
NEOGRADY, Antal (1861-1942) Hungarian				
oil	3	1,000-2,700	1,590	1,072
NEOGRADY, Laszlo (1896-1962) Hungarian				
oil	16	450-4,200	1,615	950
NEPO, Ernst (1895-1971) Austrian				
wc/d	3	727-1,455	1,010	849
NERI, Manuel (1930-) American				
wc/d	2	1,600-13,000	7,300	1,600
3D	1	1,700	1,700	1,700
NERI, Marco (1968-) Italian				
oil	1	2,059	2,059	2,059
NERI, Paul (1910-1966) Italian?				
oil	1	1,903	1,903	1,903
wc/d	1	1,285	1,285	1,285
NERLI, Marchese Girolamo Ballatti (1860-1926) Italian				
oil	2	1,894-8,878	5,386	1,894
NERLY, Friedrich (elder) (1807-1878) Italian/Austrian				
oil	4	25,918-560,000	198,020	87,842
NERLY, Friedrich (younger) (1824-1919) Italian				
oil	1	13,920	13,920	13,920
NERMAN, Einar (1888-1983) Swedish				
oil	1	1,941	1,941	1,941
NERUD, Josef Karl (1900-1982) German				
oil	1	3,299	3,299	3,299
wc/d	2	1,002-1,528	1,265	1,002
NES, Adi (1966-) Israeli				
oil	3	8,000-20,000	12,500	9,500
NESBITT, Frances E (1864-1934) British				
oil	1	1,418	1,418	1,418
NESBITT, Jackson Lee (1913-) American				
wc/d	1	1,100	1,100	1,100
NESBITT, John (1831-1904) British				
oil	3	814-4,788	3,193	3,979
NESBITT, Lowell (1933-1993) American				
oil	6	500-3,500	1,841	1,600
wc/d	1	621	621	621
NESCH, Rolf (1893-1975) Norwegian				
wc/d	4	720-49,444	13,703	1,435
NESFIELD, William Andrews (1793-1881) British				
wc/d	2	2,124-2,816	2,470	2,124
NESHAT, Shirin (1957-) American				
oil	1	42,240	42,240	42,240
wc/d	3	5,724-51,040	28,308	28,160
NESPOLO, Ugo (1941-) Italian				
oil	40	315-9,425	3,970	3,686
wc/d	10	825-4,248	2,040	1,427
3D	2	3,024-3,279	3,151	3,024
NESS, Albert Kenneth (1903-2001) American				
oil	1	1,000	1,000	1,000

Name	No.	Price Range	Average	Median
NESS, Beatrice Whitney van (1888-1981) American				
oil	2	1,410-4,000	2,705	1,410
NESSIM, Suzanne (1944-) Swedish				
oil	3	700-2,672	1,392	806
NESSLER, Walter H (1912-) British/German				
oil	1	1,000	1,000	1,000
NESTE, Alfred Joseph Auguste van (1874-1969) Belgian				
oil	4	1,165-1,686	1,361	1,193
NESTEROV, Mikhail Vasilievich (1862-1942) Russian				
oil	2	24,080-27,520	25,800	24,080
NESTEROVA, Natalia (1944-) Russian				
oil	3	9,500-40,920	23,686	20,640
NETHERWOOD, Arthur (1864-1930) British				
oil	2	650-1,593	1,121	650
wc/d	1	2,646	2,646	2,646
NETO, Ernesto (1964-) Brazilian				
wc/d	1	3,000	3,000	3,000
3D	1	8,000	8,000	8,000
NETSCHER, Caspar (1639-1684) Dutch				
oil	2	7,304-1,650,000	828,652	7,304
NETSCHER, Constantyn (1668-1723) Dutch				
oil	1	21,673	21,673	21,673
NETTI, Francesco (1834-1894) Italian				
oil	1	1,885	1,885	1,885
NETZER, Hubert (1865-?) German				
3D	1	2,234	2,234	2,234
NEUBER, Herman (19th C) German				
oil	1	3,616	3,616	3,616
NEUBERG, Carl (?) German				
oil	1	1,090	1,090	1,090
NEUBERT, Ludwig (1846-1892) German				
oil	2	485-2,797	1,641	485
NEUBOCK, Max (1893-1960) Austrian				
oil	2	1,576-2,577	2,076	1,576
NEUFCHATEL, Nicolas (1527-1590) Flemish				
oil	1	46,256	46,256	46,256
NEUHAUS, Fritz (1852-?) German				
oil	1	4,099	4,099	4,099
NEUHAUS, Fritz Berthold (1882-?) German				
oil	1	1,844	1,844	1,844
NEUHAUS, Werner (1897-1934) Swiss				
oil	2	2,498-16,652	9,575	2,498
wc/d	1	624	624	624
NEUHUYS, Albert (1844-1914) Dutch				
oil	5	1,951-8,700	5,121	6,062
wc/d	1	2,268	2,268	2,268
NEUJEAN, Nat (1923-) Belgian				
3D	1	5,007	5,007	5,007
NEUKIRCH, Josef (1896-1953) Austrian				
oil	2	817-876	846	817
wc/d	2	701-1,401	1,051	701
NEUMANN, Carl (1833-1891) Danish				
oil	6	978-11,857	5,148	2,953
NEUMANN, Johan (1860-1940) Danish				
oil	9	382-5,069	1,588	845
NEUMANN, Johann Heinrich Engelbert (1801-1879) German				
oil	2	4,816-46,500	25,658	4,816
NEUMANN, Juul (1919-1997) Dutch				
oil	2	1,403-3,299	2,351	1,403
NEUMANN, Max (1949-) German				
oil	2	701-7,007	3,854	701
wc/d	8	547-2,870	1,495	1,272
NEUMONT, Maurice Louis Henri (1868-1930) French				
oil	1	1,665	1,665	1,665
NEUQUELMAN, Lucien (1909-1988) French				
oil	5	599-2,548	1,553	1,680
wc/d	1	2,016	2,016	2,016
NEUREUTHER, Ludwig (fl.1830-1854) German				
wc/d	1	2,356	2,356	2,356
NEUSCHUL, Ernest (1895-1968) Austrian				
oil	1	4,241	4,241	4,241
wc/d	1	1,800	1,800	1,800

Name	No.	Price Range	Average	Median
NEUSTEIN, Joshua (1940-) Israeli				
oil	3	600-1,600	1,166	1,300
wc/d	1	3,000	3,000	3,000
NEUVILLE, Alphonse Marie de (1835-1885) French				
oil	6	412-26,000	9,283	7,020
NEVELSON, Louise (1899-1988) American				
oil	2	2,400-4,500	3,450	2,400
wc/d	5	475-2,545	1,430	1,500
3D	22	2,800-150,000	39,342	30,000
NEVILLE, Barbara (1943-) American				
oil	1	3,000	3,000	3,000
NEVILLE-CUMMING, Richard Henry (19/20th C) British				
wc/d	3	9,350-10,285	9,661	9,350
NEVINSON, Christopher Richard Wynne (1889-1946) British				
oil	8	12,180-207,600	68,418	24,360
wc/d	3	4,872-17,765	9,309	5,292
NEWBERY, Mary (1892-1985) British				
wc/d	1	1,416	1,416	1,416
NEWCOMB, Marie Guise (1865-?) American				
oil	1	3,500	3,500	3,500
NEWCOMB, Mary (1922-) British				
oil	10	11,180-49,560	27,942	20,880
wc/d	3	435-1,080	679	522
NEWCOMBE, William John Bertram (1907-1969) Canadian				
oil	2	882-1,146	1,014	882
wc/d	2	529-529	529	529
NEWELL, George Glenn (1870-1947) American				
oil	3	1,900-3,000	2,633	3,000
NEWELL, Hugh (1830-?) British				
oil	2	650-4,250	2,450	650
NEWELL, John Perry (1831-1898) American				
wc/d	1	3,000	3,000	3,000
NEWELL, Peter Shead Hersey (1862-1924) American				
wc/d	2	1,800-8,500	5,150	1,800
NEWELL, Robert R (19th C) American				
wc/d	1	4,300	4,300	4,300
NEWENHAM, Frederick (1807-1859) British				
oil	1	20,350	20,350	20,350
NEWMAN, Barnett (1905-1970) American				
wc/d	1	25,717	25,717	25,717
NEWMAN, Benjamin Tupper (1859-1940) American				
oil	1	1,300	1,300	1,300
NEWMAN, Elias (1903-1999) American				
wc/d	1	1,100	1,100	1,100
NEWMAN, George Adolph (1875-1965) American				
oil	1	2,600	2,600	2,600
NEWMAN, Henry Roderick (c.1833-1918) American				
wc/d	1	14,000	14,000	14,000
NEWMAN, Joseph (1890-1979) American				
oil	4	1,600-5,500	2,887	1,700
wc/d	1	400	400	400
NEWMAN, Robert Loftin (1827-1912) American				
oil	1	1,700	1,700	1,700
NEWTON, Algernon (1880-1968) British				
oil	4	1,218-22,360	7,703	3,520
wc/d	1	5,220	5,220	5,220
NEWTON, Harold (20th C) American				
oil	1	1,600	1,600	1,600
NEWTON, Kenneth (20th C) British				
oil	1	2,697	2,697	2,697
NEWTON, Lilias Torrance (1896-1980) Canadian				
oil	1	1,898	1,898	1,898
wc/d	1	2,144	2,144	2,144
NEY, Alexander (1939-) Russian				
3D	1	13,000	13,000	13,000
NEY, Lancelot (1900-1965) Hungarian				
oil	8	425-3,099	1,495	1,200
NEY, Lloyd Raymond (1893-1964) American				
oil	1	38,000	38,000	38,000
wc/d	9	900-8,500	2,438	1,800
NEYMARK, Gustave (1850-?) French				
oil	1	1,996	1,996	1,996

Name	No.	Price Range	Average	Median
NEYN, Pieter de (1597-1639) Dutch				
oil	1	18,643	18,643	18,643
NEYTS, Gillis (1623-1687) Flemish				
oil	4	2,944-42,244	15,259	7,603
wc/d	3	531-4,000	1,977	1,401
NGUYEN GIA TRI (1908-1993) Vietnamese				
wc/d	1	8,429	8,429	8,429
N'GUYEN PHAN CHANH (1892-1984) Vietnamese				
oil	1	8,486	8,486	8,486
wc/d	2	10,111-11,757	10,934	10,111
NGUYEN VAN TY (1917-1997) Vietnamese				
oil	1	2,303	2,303	2,303
NIBBRIG, Ferdinand Hart (1866-1915) Dutch				
oil	4	5,363-64,291	26,960	15,288
NIBBS, Richard Henry (1816-1893) British				
oil	2	6,624-11,310	8,967	6,624
wc/d	5	484-3,312	1,718	1,100
NIBLETT, Gary (1943-) American				
oil	8	700-25,000	6,962	4,000
NICHOLAS, Peter William (1934-) British				
3D	1	2,670	2,670	2,670
NICHOLAS, Thomas (20th C) American				
oil	1	3,750	3,750	3,750
NICHOLAS, Thomas Andrew (1934-) American				
oil	1	1,800	1,800	1,800
NICHOLL, Andrew (1804-1886) British				
wc/d	9	566-19,872	7,924	5,400
NICHOLLS, Bertram (1883-1974) British				
oil	2	696-3,026	1,861	696
wc/d	1	1,085	1,085	1,085
NICHOLLS, Burr H (1848-1915) American				
oil	2	1,600-1,900	1,750	1,600
NICHOLLS, Charles Wynne (1831-1903) British				
oil	2	4,914-4,914	4,914	4,914
NICHOLLS, John E (fl.1922-1955) British				
oil	1	1,903	1,903	1,903
NICHOLS, Dale (1904-1995) American				
oil	3	18,000-28,000	22,833	22,500
wc/d	2	800-800	800	800
NICHOLS, Frederick (20th C) American				
oil	1	1,900	1,900	1,900
NICHOLS, Henry Hobart (1869-1962) American				
oil	5	1,950-5,000	3,488	3,500
wc/d	1	550	550	550
NICHOLS, Perry (1911-1992) American				
oil	3	2,000-20,000	8,033	2,100
NICHOLS, Roy (20th C) American				
oil	1	4,250	4,250	4,250
NICHOLS, Spencer B (1875-1950) American				
wc/d	1	1,000	1,000	1,000
NICHOLSON, Ben (1894-1982) British				
oil	21	10,092-654,900	126,832	75,600
wc/d	20	2,057-60,480	20,264	12,155
3D	1	68,289	68,289	68,289
NICHOLSON, Elizabeth (1833-1926) American				
oil	1	1,500	1,500	1,500
NICHOLSON, F (1753-1844) British				
wc/d	1	1,537	1,537	1,537
NICHOLSON, Francis (1753-1844) British				
wc/d	8	522-6,960	2,209	1,479
NICHOLSON, George W (1832-1912) American				
oil	11	750-7,000	2,740	2,000
NICHOLSON, Lillie May (1884-1964) American				
oil	2	1,100-5,500	3,300	1,100
NICHOLSON, Sir William (1872-1949) British				
oil	6	19,360-147,050	87,105	71,820
NICHOLSON, Winifred (1893-1981) British				
oil	2	53,100-54,600	53,850	53,100
NICK, George (1927-) American				
oil	1	1,600	1,600	1,600
NICKISCH, Alfred (1872-?) German				
oil	1	1,168	1,168	1,168

Name	No.	Price Range	Average	Median
NICKLE, Lawrence (?) Canadian				
oil	1	2,680	2,680	2,680
NICKLIN, Tim (20th C) Kenyan				
3D	2	15,593-30,260	22,926	15,593
NICKOL, Adolf (1824-1905) German				
oil	1	3,471	3,471	3,471
NICKSON, Graham (1946-) American				
oil	1	2,500	2,500	2,500
NICOL, Erskine (1825-1904) British				
oil	11	2,478-38,335	14,423	13,020
wc/d	3	1,110-15,840	6,376	2,178
NICOL, Erskine E (1868-1926) British				
oil	1	1,305	1,305	1,305
NICOL, John Watson (?-1926) British				
oil	3	531-7,000	3,064	1,663
NICOLA, Francesco de (1882-1958) Italian				
oil	4	595-7,274	3,591	2,675
NICOLAI, Carsten (1965-) ?				
oil	2	7,500-9,500	8,500	7,500
NICOLAI, Paul (1876-1948) ?				
oil	4	732-1,551	1,155	1,139
NICOLAISEN, Peter (1894-1989) Danish				
oil	3	879-1,462	1,118	1,014
NICOLAS, Frances (c.1400-1468) Spanish				
oil	1	276,800	276,800	276,800
NICOLAS, Marie (19th C) French				
oil	1	1,900	1,900	1,900
NICOLAS, Paul Harris (c.1790-1860) British				
wc/d	1	30,090	30,090	30,090
NICOLAY, Helen (1866-1954) American				
oil	1	1,700	1,700	1,700
NICOLETTI, V (20th C) Italian?				
oil	2	2,604-11,245	6,924	2,604
NICOLI, Claudio (1958-) Italian				
3D	3	2,148-2,803	2,429	2,336
NICOLIE, Josephus Christianus (1791-1854) Belgian				
oil	2	2,775-7,375	5,075	2,775
NICOLL, James Craig (1846-1918) American				
oil	1	4,800	4,800	4,800
NICOLL, Marion Florence (1909-1985) Canadian				
oil	2	2,474-3,299	2,886	2,474
wc/d	1	618	618	618
NICOLLE, Victor Jean (1754-1826) French				
wc/d	25	400-23,786	6,644	4,435
NICOT, François (20th C) French				
oil	1	3,810	3,810	3,810
NICZKY, Edouard (1850-1919) German				
oil	3	606-8,500	3,921	2,658
NIDO, Davide (1966-) Italian				
oil	1	8,905	8,905	8,905
wc/d	1	4,685	4,685	4,685
NIEDECKEN, George Mann (1878-1945) American				
oil	1	8,000	8,000	8,000
NIEDERHAUSERN, François Louis Fritz de (1828-1888) Swiss				
oil	2	1,221-4,163	2,692	1,221
wc/d	1	2,330	2,330	2,330
NIEDERHAUSERN-RODO (1863-1913) Swiss				
3D	1	11,757	11,757	11,757
NIEDMANN, August Heinrich (1826-1910) German				
oil	1	5,057	5,057	5,057
NIEHAUS, Kaspar (1889-1974) Dutch				
oil	1	1,818	1,818	1,818
NIEKERK, Maurits (1871-1940) Dutch				
oil	1	3,956	3,956	3,956
NIELSEN, Ejnar (1872-1956) Danish				
oil	3	971-1,536	1,266	1,293
NIELSEN, Jais (1885-1961) Danish				
oil	3	1,616-25,863	9,752	1,778
NIELSEN, Kai (1882-1924) Danish				
oil	2	1,771-2,101	1,936	1,771
3D	1	3,882	3,882	3,882

Name	No.	Price Range	Average	Median
NIELSEN, Kay (1886-1957) Danish				
wc/d	3	9,644-45,000	23,214	15,000
NIELSEN, Kehnet (1947-) Danish				
oil	4	1,610-9,980	6,292	6,789
wc/d	1	614	614	614
NIELSEN, Knud (1916-) Danish				
oil	16	644-10,022	3,329	2,414
NIELSEN, Peter (1873-1965) American/Danish				
oil	2	1,000-3,000	2,000	1,000
NIELSEN, Poul (1920-1998) Danish				
oil	14	520-2,897	1,561	1,637
NIELSON, Peter (20th C) American				
oil	1	2,750	2,750	2,750
NIEMANN, Edmund John (1813-1876) British				
oil	26	500-11,594	3,472	2,288
NIEMANN, Edmund John (jnr) (19th C) British				
oil	3	1,691-2,625	2,038	1,800
NIEMANN, Edward H (fl.1863-1887) British				
oil	15	452-6,055	2,049	1,211
NIEMANN, Hennie (1941-) South African				
oil	1	1,151	1,151	1,151
NIEMEYER, Jo (1946-) German				
oil	1	2,119	2,119	2,119
NIEMEYER-HOLSTEIN, Otto (1896-1984) German				
oil	2	1,598-2,225	1,911	1,598
wc/d	2	478-989	733	478
NIEPOLD, Frank (1890-?) American				
oil	1	8,000	8,000	8,000
NIERMAN, Leonardo (1932-) Mexican				
oil	26	750-6,000	1,858	1,300
wc/d	1	500	500	500
NIESTLE, Henry (1876-1966) Swiss				
oil	1	1,528	1,528	1,528
NIESTLE, Jean Bloe (1884-1942) German				
oil	1	47,137	47,137	47,137
NIETO, Anselmo Miguel (1881-1964) Spanish				
oil	3	2,275-3,130	2,753	2,854
wc/d	1	3,057	3,057	3,057
NIETO, Hector Sixto (1917-) Argentinian				
3D	1	4,000	4,000	4,000
NIETO, Rodolfo (1936-1988) Mexican				
oil	3	3,567-28,000	17,855	22,000
wc/d	1	19,000	19,000	19,000
NIETSCHE, Paul (1885-1950) British				
oil	3	1,302-4,779	2,980	2,860
wc/d	1	1,520	1,520	1,520
NIEULANDT, Adriaen van (16/17th C) Flemish/Dutch				
oil	2	23,425-27,351	25,388	23,425
NIEULANDT, Willem van II (1584-1635) Flemish				
oil	2	31,450-97,900	64,675	31,450
NIEUWENHUYS, Johannes (1922-1986) Dutch				
oil	1	2,586	2,586	2,586
NIEWEG, Jaap (1877-1955) Dutch				
oil	2	6,361-7,642	7,001	6,361
NIGHTINGALE, Basil (1864-1940) British				
oil	3	974-13,680	5,342	1,373
wc/d	16	574-2,928	1,320	1,218
NIGHTINGALE, Robert (1815-1895) British				
oil	1	6,804	6,804	6,804
NIGRIS, Giuseppe de (1832-1903) Italian				
oil	2	2,750-4,722	3,736	2,750
NIGRO, Adolfo (1942-) Argentinian				
oil	8	580-33,000	12,371	5,800
wc/d	2	700-4,800	2,750	700
NIGRO, Mario (1917-1992) Italian				
oil	15	2,071-16,493	7,102	5,966
wc/d	7	761-3,996	1,773	1,331
NIIZUMA, Minoru (1930-1998) Japanese				
3D	2	2,000-3,000	2,500	2,000
NIJHOFF, Eliza Agnetus Emilius (1826-1903) Dutch				
oil	1	10,000	10,000	10,000

Name	No.	Price Range	Average	Median
NIJLAND, Dirk (1881-1955) Dutch				
oil	2	1,343-8,269	4,806	1,343
NIKEL, Lea (1918-2005) Israeli				
oil	27	950-38,000	10,913	8,000
wc/d	2	700-800	750	700
3D	1	7,000	7,000	7,000
NIKIFOR (1895-1968) Polish				
wc/d	2	818-1,320	1,069	818
NIKITIN, S (19/20th C) Russian				
oil	1	5,160	5,160	5,160
NIKODEM, Artur (1870-1940) Austrian				
oil	1	21,658	21,658	21,658
wc/d	2	1,052-2,410	1,731	1,052
NIKOLAEV, Kuzma Vasilevich (1890-1972) Russian				
oil	1	7,080	7,080	7,080
NIKOLAOU, Nikos (1909-1986) Greek				
wc/d	1	5,280	5,280	5,280
NIKUTOWSKI, Erich (1872-1921) German				
oil	3	628-3,048	1,548	968
NILOUSS, Piotr Alexandrovitch (1869-1943) Russian				
oil	4	7,531-57,500	31,494	13,320
NILSON, K G (1942-) Swedish				
oil	2	763-3,308	2,035	763
NILSON, Karl Gustaf (1942-) Swedish				
oil	3	654-1,781	1,213	1,205
NILSON, Severin (1846-1918) Swedish				
oil	25	505-17,171	3,280	1,990
NILSSON, Axel (1889-1981) Swedish				
oil	11	1,189-6,107	2,693	2,379
wc/d	1	2,290	2,290	2,290
NILSSON, Bert Johnny (1934-) Swedish				
oil	1	1,812	1,812	1,812
NILSSON, Lars (1956-) Swedish				
oil	1	9,670	9,670	9,670
NILSSON, Nils (1901-1949) Swedish				
oil	3	1,561-8,589	3,962	1,736
NILSSON, Olof (1868-1956) Swedish				
oil	2	544-1,561	1,052	544
NILSSON, Vera (1888-1979) Swedish				
oil	8	1,916-52,858	10,364	3,700
wc/d	2	859-1,057	958	859
NILSSON, Wiven (1897-1974) Swedish				
3D	1	3,109	3,109	3,109
NIMPTSH, Uli (1897-) German				
3D	1	1,881	1,881	1,881
NINAS, Paul (1903-1964) American				
wc/d	1	4,600	4,600	4,600
NINO, Carmelo (20th C) South American				
oil	1	4,500	4,500	4,500
NINVILLE, J de (?) ?				
oil	1	3,982	3,982	3,982
NISBET, John (20th C) British?				
oil	1	1,200	1,200	1,200
wc/d	1	557	557	557
NISBET, Peter (1948-) American				
oil	1	1,800	1,800	1,800
NISBET, Pollock (1848-1922) British				
oil	7	487-2,013	1,033	935
wc/d	1	496	496	496
NISBET, Robert Buchan (1857-1942) British				
oil	4	481-3,132	1,312	748
wc/d	2	496-692	594	496
NISBET, Robert H (1879-1961) American				
oil	2	1,600-7,500	4,550	1,600
NISBET, Tom (1909-2001) Irish				
oil	1	2,311	2,311	2,311
wc/d	9	484-2,290	1,036	971
NISHIMURA, Keiou (1909-2000) Japanese				
oil	1	2,313	2,313	2,313
NISS, Thorvald (1842-1905) Danish				
oil	12	790-16,562	3,986	1,423

Name	No.	Price Range	Average	Median
NISSKY, Georgiy Grigorievich (1903-1957) Russian				
oil	1	25,000	25,000	25,000
NISSL, Rudolf (1870-1955) Austrian				
oil	4	1,918-2,510	2,200	1,940
NITKOWISI, Stani (1949-2001) ?				
oil	2	4,942-5,531	5,236	4,942
wc/d	1	628	628	628
NITSCH, Hermann (1938-) Austrian				
oil	28	1,152-102,660	22,652	12,884
wc/d	14	485-19,747	6,034	2,035
3D	3	9,514-20,384	13,137	9,514
NITSCH, Richard (1866-1945) German				
oil	5	492-1,602	1,081	1,270
NITSCHE, Frank (1964-) German?				
oil	4	18,000-60,000	34,545	26,550
NITSCHKE, Detlev (1935-) German				
oil	4	2,788-4,529	3,899	3,822
NITTIS, Giuseppe de (1846-1884) Italian				
oil	3	31,483-208,800	92,608	37,541
wc/d	1	135,479	135,479	135,479
NIVELON, Anne Baptiste (18th C) French				
oil	1	11,410	11,410	11,410
NIVELT, Roger (1899-1962) French				
oil	1	3,116	3,116	3,116
wc/d	2	2,038-2,890	2,464	2,038
NIVERVILLE, Louis de (1933-) Canadian				
oil	1	1,410	1,410	1,410
wc/d	3	410-2,460	1,667	2,132
NIVINSKI, Ignati Ignatievich (1881-1933) Russian				
wc/d	1	1,132	1,132	1,132
NIVOLA, Costantino (1911-1988) Italian				
wc/d	1	2,028	2,028	2,028
NIXON, John (1760-1818) British				
wc/d	3	1,512-4,104	3,032	3,480
NIXON, Mima (fl.1894-1918) British				
wc/d	2	1,200-1,695	1,447	1,200
NIXON, Nils (1912-1998) Swedish				
oil	1	1,454	1,454	1,454
NO, Michel (20th C) ?				
oil	1	1,029	1,029	1,029
NOACK, Astrid (1888-?) Swedish?				
3D	1	1,859	1,859	1,859
NOAILLY, Francisque (1855-1942) French?				
oil	2	818-4,435	2,626	818
NOBBE, Jacob (1850-1919) Danish				
oil	1	1,267	1,267	1,267
wc/d	1	504	504	504
NOBELE, Henri de (c.1820-1870) Belgian				
oil	1	1,936	1,936	1,936
NOBILI, Elena (1833-1900) Italian				
oil	1	1,377	1,377	1,377
NOBLE, J (19/20th C) British				
oil	1	1,903	1,903	1,903
NOBLE, James (1919-1989) British				
oil	7	623-3,238	1,378	874
NOBLE, John Sargeant (1848-1896) British				
oil	4	7,500-62,300	28,501	19,000
NOBLE, Robert (1857-1917) British				
oil	7	458-7,120	3,039	2,506
NOBLE, Thomas Satterwhite (1835-1907) American				
oil	1	24,000	24,000	24,000
NOBLE, Tim and WEBSTER, Sue (20th C) American				
3D	4	26,550-100,000	60,387	50,000
NOCI, Arturo (1875-1953) Italian				
oil	1	9,000	9,000	9,000
NOCKOLDS, Roy (1911-1979) British				
oil	2	570-9,396	4,983	570
wc/d	2	748-3,515	2,131	748
NODE, Charles (1811-1886) French				
oil	1	36,644	36,644	36,644
NOE, Luis Felipe (1933-) Argentinian				
wc/d	1	10,000	10,000	10,000

Name	No.	Price Range	Average	Median
NOEL, Alexandre Jean (1752-1834) French				
wc/d	2	2,922-7,014	4,968	2,922
NOEL, Georges (1924-) French				
oil	2	1,267-3,817	2,542	1,267
wc/d	4	500-3,155	1,478	819
NOEL, John Bates (fl.1893-1909) British				
oil	3	696-2,223	1,263	870
wc/d	1	496	496	496
NOEL, Jules (1815-1881) French				
oil	11	3,471-108,384	17,351	8,182
wc/d	3	467-1,300	764	526
NOEL, Martin (1956-) German				
3D	1	3,312	3,312	3,312
NOERR, Julius (1827-1897) German				
oil	2	3,440-4,056	3,748	3,440
NOGUCHI, Isamu (1904-1988) American				
wc/d	2	3,237-120,000	61,618	3,237
3D	8	24,000-550,000	173,375	70,000
NOGUE MASSO, Jose (1880-1973) Spanish				
oil	1	1,512	1,512	1,512
NOH SANG KYOON (1958-) Chinese				
3D	1	28,000	28,000	28,000
NOIRE, Maxime (1861-1927) French				
oil	9	1,065-8,026	3,941	4,531
NOIRET, Joseph (1927-) British?				
oil	1	1,484	1,484	1,484
NOIROT, Émile (1853-1924) French				
oil	5	942-2,760	1,849	1,621
wc/d	2	1,920-2,400	2,160	1,920
NOJECHOWIZ, Noe (1929-1998) Argentinian				
oil	1	3,500	3,500	3,500
wc/d	1	4,000	4,000	4,000
NOLAN, Sidney (1917-1992) Australian				
oil	2	4,070-13,050	8,560	4,070
NOLAND, Cady (1956-) American				
wc/d	1	55,000	55,000	55,000
NOLAND, Kenneth (1924-) American				
oil	15	13,993-575,000	111,028	75,000
wc/d	1	4,000	4,000	4,000
NOLDE, Emil (1867-1956) German				
oil	13	24,740-3,422,500	1,322,424	1,239,000
wc/d	55	7,642-333,000	96,398	84,480
NOLF, John Thomas (1872-1955) American				
oil	1	1,600	1,600	1,600
NOLHAC, Henri Girault de (1884-1948) French				
oil	1	2,338	2,338	2,338
NOLKEN, Franz (1884-1918) German				
oil	1	18,185	18,185	18,185
wc/d	1	9,062	9,062	9,062
NOLL, Alexandre (1890-1970) French				
3D	3	6,000-140,000	66,666	54,000
NOLLEKENS, Joseph (1737-1823) British				
3D	2	4,601-60,550	32,575	4,601
NOLTEE, Cornelis (1903-1967) Dutch				
oil	14	605-9,568	2,383	1,618
NOME, François de (1593-c.1640) French				
oil	4	24,218-129,750	82,287	55,180
NOMEIER, Alfred (1939-) German				
oil	1	1,212	1,212	1,212
NOMELLINI, Plinio (1866-1943) Italian				
oil	3	30,452-76,130	48,130	37,808
NOMMIK, Juhan (20th C) Spanish				
oil	2	2,571-3,471	3,021	2,571
NONAS, Richard (1936-) American				
oil	1	1,145	1,145	1,145
wc/d	2	450-600	525	450
NONELL Y MONTURIOL, Isidro (1873-1911) Spanish				
oil	2	457,551-765,600	611,575	457,551
wc/d	3	1,798-22,595	9,010	2,637
NONN, Carl (1876-1949) German				
oil	1	1,405	1,405	1,405

Name	No.	Price Range	Average	Median
NONNI, Francesco (1885-1964) Italian				
oil	2	595-1,546	1,070	595
wc/d	1	595	595	595
3D	1	29,730	29,730	29,730
NONNIS, Giovanni (1930-) Italian				
oil	2	954-2,863	1,908	954
NONNOTTE, Donat (1708-1785) French				
oil	1	3,204	3,204	3,204
NONO, Luigi (1850-1918) Italian				
oil	1	24,247	24,247	24,247
NOOMS, Reinier (1623-1667) Dutch				
oil	1	3,560	3,560	3,560
NOORDE, Cornelis van (1731-1795) Dutch				
wc/d	1	1,401	1,401	1,401
NOORT, Gijsbert Nonus Op (1821-1870) Dutch				
oil	1	2,351	2,351	2,351
NOORT, Jan van (16/18th C) Dutch				
oil	2	4,671-6,541	5,606	4,671
NOORT, Pieter van (1602-1648) Dutch				
oil	4	518-58,603	17,399	3,000
NOOTEBOOM, Jacobus Hendricus Johannes (1811-1878) Dutch				
oil	1	1,229	1,229	1,229
NOPSANEN, Aarne (1907-1990) Finnish				
oil	1	8,767	8,767	8,767
NORBERTO (1927-) Italian				
oil	4	5,317-14,055	7,673	5,400
NORCROSS, Grace (1899-?) American				
oil	1	3,200	3,200	3,200
NORDELL, Emma Parker (1876-1956) American				
wc/d	2	450-3,000	1,725	450
NORDENBERG, Bengt (1822-1902) Swedish				
oil	6	6,481-33,123	13,130	9,066
NORDENBERG, Hendrick (1857-1928) Swedish				
oil	3	1,496-7,017	3,587	2,250
NORDFELDT, B J O (1878-1955) American				
oil	1	22,500	22,500	22,500
NORDFELDT, Bror Julius Olsson (1878-1955) American				
oil	4	6,000-16,000	10,875	9,500
NORDLIEN, Olaf (1864-1919) Norwegian				
oil	1	1,618	1,618	1,618
NORDLING, Adolf (1840-1888) Swedish				
oil	1	1,510	1,510	1,510
NORDLUND, Elin (1861-1941) Finnish				
oil	2	581-2,572	1,576	581
NORDMANN, Germaine (20th C) French				
oil	1	1,288	1,288	1,288
NORDOY, Amariel (20th C) Danish?				
oil	1	1,932	1,932	1,932
NORDSTRAND, Nathalie Johnson (1932-) American				
oil	1	1,500	1,500	1,500
wc/d	2	450-900	675	450
NORDSTROM, Carl Harold (1876-1965) American				
oil	4	750-1,600	1,087	800
NORDSTROM, Jockum (1963-) Swedish				
oil	3	33,081-45,804	40,390	42,287
wc/d	4	10,043-35,679	19,095	10,836
NORDSTROM, Karl (1855-1923) Swedish				
oil	2	4,396-6,869	5,632	4,396
wc/d	4	496-1,127	706	521
NORDSTROM, Lars Gunnar (1924-) Finnish				
oil	1	4,371	4,371	4,371
wc/d	2	1,918-3,086	2,502	1,918
NOREN, Bertil (1889-1934) Swedish				
oil	1	8,475	8,475	8,475
NORGAARD, Bjorn (1947-) Danish				
3D	2	2,575-3,219	2,897	2,575
NORGARD, Lars (1956-) Danish				
oil	5	2,263-4,041	3,160	3,219
NORIE, Orlando (1832-1901) British				
wc/d	12	448-2,128	1,243	1,073
NORIERI, Auguste (1860-1898) American				
oil	1	42,500	42,500	42,500

Name	No.	Price Range	Average	Median
NORLIND, Ernst (1877-1952) Swedish				
oil	2	684-1,866	1,275	684
NORMAN, Wilmina Maclean de (1803-1863) British				
wc/d	1	6,336	6,336	6,336
NORMANN, Adelsteen (1848-1918) Norwegian				
oil	13	2,301-38,640	14,175	11,000
NORRIS, Joe (1924-) Canadian				
oil	2	2,836-3,504	3,170	2,836
NORRMAN, Gunnar (1912-) Swedish				
wc/d	1	1,057	1,057	1,057
NORRMAN, Herman (1864-1906) Swedish				
oil	1	6,107	6,107	6,107
NORRMAN, Lars (1915-1979) Swedish				
oil	1	1,321	1,321	1,321
NORSELIUS, Erik (1874-1956) Swedish				
oil	1	5,946	5,946	5,946
NORTH, John William (1842-1924) British				
oil	1	1,074	1,074	1,074
wc/d	1	4,806	4,806	4,806
NORTHCOTE, Henry B (19th C) American				
oil	1	1,000	1,000	1,000
NORTHCOTE, James (1746-1831) British				
oil	1	15,120	15,120	15,120
NORTHEN, Adolf (1828-1876) German				
oil	2	6,479-54,184	30,331	6,479
NORTON, Benjamin Cam (1835-1900) British				
oil	5	1,232-13,000	5,005	3,522
NORTON, Jim C (1953-) American				
oil	9	2,750-37,000	19,972	16,000
NORTON, William Edward (1843-1916) American				
oil	11	900-12,000	4,150	3,750
NORWELL, Graham Noble (1901-1967) Canadian				
oil	7	591-7,379	3,186	1,558
NOST, Alain le (1934-) French?				
oil	1	1,964	1,964	1,964
NOTEN, Jean van (1903-1982) Belgian				
oil	1	1,505	1,505	1,505
wc/d	1	1,335	1,335	1,335
NOTER, David de (1825-1875) Belgian				
oil	4	1,260-16,000	8,965	6,479
NOTER, Pierre François de (1779-1843) Belgian				
oil	1	11,757	11,757	11,757
NOTERMAN, Emmanuel (1808-1863) Flemish				
oil	5	501-23,400	5,443	1,093
NOTERMAN, Zacharias (1820-1890) German				
oil	7	1,085-5,250	2,643	2,016
NOTHNAGEL, August Friedrich Wilhelm (1822-1899) German				
oil	1	3,507	3,507	3,507
NOTMAN, Howard (1881-1964) American				
oil	1	3,000	3,000	3,000
NOTT, Raymond (1888-1948) American				
wc/d	2	600-2,000	1,300	600
NOTTE, Emilio (1891-1982) Italian				
oil	6	2,735-13,676	6,371	3,514
wc/d	2	1,274-13,377	7,325	1,274
NOUVEAU, Henri (1901-1959) Hungarian				
oil	12	1,767-3,770	2,670	2,356
wc/d	11	1,680-10,507	4,367	3,822
NOVATI, Marco (1895-1975) Italian				
oil	2	2,314-3,600	2,957	2,314
NOVELLI, Gastone (1925-1968) Italian				
oil	4	4,099-62,075	37,400	40,707
wc/d	5	1,790-169,829	59,384	38,163
3D	1	5,856	5,856	5,856
NOVELLI, Pietro Antonio (1729-1804) Italian				
wc/d	7	800-8,199	4,472	4,919
NOVO, Stefano (1862-1902) Italian				
oil	2	8,000-41,858	24,929	8,000
NOVOA, Gustavo (1941-) Chilean				
oil	3	700-2,500	1,383	950

Name	No.	Price Range	Average	Median
NOVOA, Leopoldo (1929-) Uruguayan				
oil	3	2,141-2,616	2,378	2,378
wc/d	2	500-1,094	797	500
NOVOTNY, Elmer L (1909-1997) American				
oil	1	1,025	1,025	1,025
NOWAK, Ernst (1853-1919) Austrian				
oil	3	972-4,099	2,500	2,431
NOWAK, Franz (1885-1973) Austrian				
oil	1	1,145	1,145	1,145
NOWELL, Arthur Trevithan (1862-1940) British				
oil	1	1,479	1,479	1,479
NOYER, Philippe (1917-1985) French				
oil	2	1,200-2,200	1,700	1,200
NOYES (?) ?				
oil	1	3,000	3,000	3,000
NOYES, George L (1864-1954) Canadian				
oil	9	650-48,000	11,716	4,250
NOZAL, Alexandre (1852-1929) French				
oil	3	589-4,800	3,306	4,531
wc/d	1	3,029	3,029	3,029
NUBANI, Ibrahim (1961-) Israeli				
oil	1	3,000	3,000	3,000
NUCARA, Renzo (1948-) Italian				
oil	1	1,816	1,816	1,816
NUDERSCHER, Frank (1880-1959) American				
oil	4	550-3,200	1,987	1,800
NUESCH, Johann Jakob (1845-1895) Swiss				
oil	1	1,725	1,725	1,725
NUGENT, Bob (1947-) American				
oil	1	1,000	1,000	1,000
NUILAALIK, Josiah (1928-) North American				
3D	4	1,518-2,531	1,834	1,603
NUNAMAKER, Alfred R (1915-1988) American				
oil	3	8,500-12,000	10,166	10,000
NUNAMAKER, Kenneth R (1890-1957) American				
oil	4	24,000-140,000	74,750	60,000
NUNEZ DEL PRADO, Marina (1911-1995) Bolivian				
3D	1	2,200	2,200	2,200
NUNEZ LOSADA, Francisco (1889-1973) Spanish				
oil	1	2,761	2,761	2,761
NUNEZ, Benicio (1924-1992) Argentinian				
oil	1	2,200	2,200	2,200
NUNZIANTE, Antonio (1956-) Italian				
oil	22	3,063-10,603	5,286	5,066
NUNZIO (1954-) American				
wc/d	5	1,767-12,298	4,143	2,342
3D	3	8,352-17,671	11,854	9,541
NUSE, Roy Cleveland (1885-1975) American				
oil	9	3,250-70,000	17,722	11,000
NUSS, Fritz (20th C) German?				
3D	3	2,063-5,968	4,326	4,948
NUSSBAUM, Felix (1904-1944) German				
oil	2	28,054-60,000	44,027	28,054
wc/d	3	7,068-31,849	18,470	16,493
NUSSBAUM, Walter (1913-1984) Swiss				
oil	1	3,053	3,053	3,053
NUSSI, Arnaldo (1906-) Italian				
oil	1	1,764	1,764	1,764
NUSSIO, Oscar (1899-1976) Swiss				
oil	8	457-2,747	1,048	687
NUTARALUK, Elizabeth Aulatjut (1914-2002) North American				
3D	1	4,218	4,218	4,218
NUTI, Mario (1923-) Italian				
oil	1	6,106	6,106	6,106
NUTT, Elizabeth Styring (1870-1946) British				
oil	1	1,141	1,141	1,141
NUTT, Jim (1938-) American				
wc/d	1	9,000	9,000	9,000
NUVOLONE, Carlo Francesco (1608-1665) Italian				
oil	2	25,865-28,480	27,172	25,865
NUVOLONE, Carlo Francesco and Giuseppe (17th C) Italian				
oil	1	44,014	44,014	44,014

Name	No.	Price Range	Average	Median
NUYEN, Wijbrand Johannes Josephus (1813-1839) Dutch				
oil	4	3,596-18,703	10,229	5,096
wc/d	1	1,094	1,094	1,094
NUZZI, Mario (1603-1673) Italian				
oil	4	5,369-185,000	78,389	25,890
NYBOE, Friis (1869-1929) Danish				
oil	2	1,304-1,659	1,481	1,304
NYE, Edgar (1879-1943) American				
oil	4	750-4,250	1,775	900
NYGAARD, Kaare (1903-) ?				
3D	1	5,500	5,500	5,500
NYL, M (20th C) ?				
oil	1	2,797	2,797	2,797
NYL-FROSCH, Marie (1857-1914) German				
oil	1	1,459	1,459	1,459
NYMAN, Olle (1909-1999) Swedish				
oil	10	769-12,103	2,681	1,553
wc/d	1	780	780	780
3D	5	1,718-3,054	2,562	2,604
NYMAN-EGBERT, Gote Peter (1879-1957) Swedish				
oil	1	3,964	3,964	3,964
NYMEGEN, Elias van (1667-1755) Dutch				
wc/d	1	1,635	1,635	1,635
NYSTROM, Jenny (1854-1946) Swedish				
oil	2	448-14,424	7,436	448
wc/d	30	373-19,568	4,257	3,864
O-CHI-YAI (20th C) Oriental				
wc/d	1	47,000	47,000	47,000
OAKLEY, Charles (1925-) British				
oil	1	3,348	3,348	3,348
wc/d	1	534	534	534
OATES, Bennett (1928-) British				
oil	6	1,400-7,544	3,007	2,200
3D	1	2,655	2,655	2,655
OBATA, Chiura (1885-1975) American				
wc/d	4	475-2,500	1,443	1,400
OBERHAUSER, Emanuel (19/20th C) Austrian				
oil	2	11,000-29,000	20,000	11,000
OBERHUBER, Oswald (1931-) Austrian				
wc/d	9	631-2,293	1,120	849
OBERLE, Jean (1900-1961) French				
oil	1	2,145	2,145	2,145
OBERMUELLNER, Adolf (1833-1898) Austrian				
oil	1	2,145	2,145	2,145
OBERMULLER, Franz (1869-1917) Austrian				
oil	1	2,854	2,854	2,854
OBERNITZ, Walter von (20th C) German?				
oil	1	1,405	1,405	1,405
OBERSTEINER, Ludwig (1857-?) Austrian				
oil	1	2,740	2,740	2,740
OBERTEUFFER, George (1878-1940) American				
oil	1	16,000	16,000	16,000
OBERTHUER, Joseph (1872-1956) ?				
wc/d	3	716-3,708	1,755	843
OBOZNENKO, Dimitri (1930-) Russian				
oil	1	1,657	1,657	1,657
OBREGON, Alejandro (1920-1992) Colombian				
wc/d	1	5,000	5,000	5,000
O'BRIEN, Dermod (1865-1945) British				
oil	4	1,455-33,375	10,402	1,937
O'BRIEN, Geraldine (1922-) Irish				
oil	2	2,264-2,622	2,443	2,264
O'BRIEN, Kitty Wilmer (1910-1982) British				
oil	3	1,520-13,705	6,096	3,063
wc/d	3	1,399-7,985	3,751	1,870
O'BRIEN, Lucius Richard (1832-1899) Canadian				
oil	1	42,313	42,313	42,313
wc/d	2	1,402-3,092	2,247	1,402
O'BRIEN, Robert (fl.1848-1863) American				
oil	1	1,000	1,000	1,000

Name	No.	Price Range	Average	Median
OCAMPO, Miguel (1922-) Argentinian				
oil	2	4,000-16,000	10,000	4,000
wc/d	1	3,800	3,800	3,800
O'CASEY, Breon (1928-) British				
oil	5	1,232-7,812	3,422	2,418
wc/d	2	1,815-2,976	2,395	1,815
3D	5	4,092-7,440	6,212	6,510
O'CEALLACHAIN, Diarmuid (1915-1993) Irish				
oil	1	1,169	1,169	1,169
OCEAN, Humphrey (1951-) British				
wc/d	1	4,628	4,628	4,628
OCHAGAVIA, Carlos (1913-) Argentinian				
oil	1	1,000	1,000	1,000
OCHIAI, Tam (1967-) American?				
wc/d	1	4,500	4,500	4,500
OCHOA Y MADRAZO, Raphael de (1858-?) Spanish				
oil	1	2,411	2,411	2,411
OCHSE, Louise (19th C) Belgian				
3D	1	3,292	3,292	3,292
OCHTMAN, Leonard (1854-1934) American				
oil	2	850-10,000	5,425	850
OCHTMAN, Mina Funda (1862-1924) American				
oil	2	750-2,300	1,525	750
OCKEL, Eduard (1834-1910) German				
oil	1	1,636	1,636	1,636
O'COLMAIN, Seamus (1925-1990) Irish				
oil	5	648-4,800	2,286	1,695
OCON TORIBIO, Adolfo (1863-?) Spanish				
oil	1	3,327	3,327	3,327
O'CONNELL, Madame Frederique Emile Auguste (1823-1885) German				
wc/d	2	904-4,498	2,701	904
O'CONNOR, J A (1792-1841) British				
oil	1	2,460	2,460	2,460
O'CONNOR, James Arthur (1792-1841) British				
oil	4	3,200-66,628	24,735	3,633
wc/d	1	555	555	555
O'CONNOR, John (1913-) British				
oil	2	673-985	829	673
wc/d	2	531-708	619	531
O'CONNOR, Roderic (1860-1940) Irish				
oil	1	19,357	19,357	19,357
wc/d	1	3,107	3,107	3,107
O'CONOR, R (1860-1940) Irish				
oil	1	5,565	5,565	5,565
O'CONOR, Roderic (1860-1940) Irish				
oil	9	15,904-372,000	146,950	138,630
wc/d	6	4,944-14,880	8,644	5,580
ODDE, Knud (1955-) Danish				
oil	2	3,233-4,829	4,031	3,233
ODDIE, Walter M (1808-1865) American				
oil	1	2,750	2,750	2,750
O'DEA, Michael (1958-) Irish				
oil	2	867-3,162	2,014	867
ODEKERKEN, Willem van (?-1677) Dutch				
oil	1	21,205	21,205	21,205
ODELMARK, F W (1849-1937) Swedish				
oil	1	5,207	5,207	5,207
ODELMARK, Frans Wilhelm (1849-1937) Swedish				
oil	15	497-18,971	4,105	1,786
wc/d	2	1,757-8,281	5,019	1,757
ODERMATT, Josef Maria (1934-) Swiss				
3D	1	2,434	2,434	2,434
ODEVAERE, Joseph Denis (1778-1830) Belgian				
oil	2	4,219-100,000	52,109	4,219
ODIER, Jacques (1853-1930) Swiss				
oil	2	1,061-2,442	1,751	1,061
ODIERNO, Guido (1913-1991) Italian				
oil	10	572-2,548	1,234	849
wc/d	1	1,130	1,130	1,130
ODIN, Blanche (1865-1957) French				
wc/d	5	1,288-3,174	2,386	2,268

Name	No.	Price Range	Average	Median
ODJIG, Daphne (1928-) Canadian				
oil	1	4,948	4,948	4,948
O'DOHERTY, David (1935-) Irish				
oil	2	1,132-1,311	1,221	1,132
O'DOHERTY, Eamon (20th C) Irish				
3D	3	4,531-12,000	7,159	4,948
O'DONOGHUE, Hughie (1953-) British				
oil	5	8,476-30,247	18,394	21,796
O'DOWD, Gwen (?) ?				
oil	1	2,182	2,182	2,182
OEDER, Georg (1846-1931) German				
oil	1	1,168	1,168	1,168
OEHLEN, Albert (1954-) German				
oil	12	4,005-388,500	213,581	170,000
wc/d	6	1,274-19,425	6,080	3,299
OEHME, Ernst Ferdinand (1797-1855) German				
wc/d	2	1,585-25,918	13,751	1,585
OEHMICHEN, Hugo (1843-1933) German				
oil	7	1,211-14,684	5,473	3,730
OEHRING, Hedwig (1855-?) German				
oil	4	547-1,897	1,396	1,560
OELZE, Don (1965-) American				
oil	1	6,000	6,000	6,000
OELZE, Richard (1900-1980) German				
oil	1	53,429	53,429	53,429
wc/d	1	27,986	27,986	27,986
OELZNER, Rudolf (1906-1985) German				
3D	1	1,654	1,654	1,654
OEPTS, Willem Anthonie (1904-1988) Dutch				
oil	4	2,637-17,534	11,780	12,959
OER, Theobald Reinhold von (1807-1885) German				
oil	1	7,572	7,572	7,572
wc/d	1	1,543	1,543	1,543
OERDER, Frans (1866-1944) Dutch				
oil	3	1,097-3,292	1,910	1,341
OERTEL, Johannes Adam Simon (1823-1909) German				
oil	1	8,000	8,000	8,000
OESER, Auguste (1821-?) German				
oil	1	3,766	3,766	3,766
OESTERLEY, Carl August Heinrich Ferdinand (1839-1930) German				
oil	5	479-2,934	1,696	1,332
OESTERLEY, Carl Wilhelm Friedrich (1805-1891) German				
oil	3	4,816-13,245	7,947	5,780
OFEK, Avraham (1935-1990) Israeli				
oil	3	950-3,600	2,583	3,200
wc/d	2	360-400	380	360
OFFER, Frank Rawlings (1847-1932) British				
oil	1	1,044	1,044	1,044
OFFERMANS, Anthony Jacob (1796-1872) Dutch				
oil	1	3,000	3,000	3,000
OFFERMANS, Tony Lodewyk George (1854-1911) Dutch				
oil	1	847	847	847
wc/d	1	701	701	701
OFILI, Chris (1968-) British				
oil	1	531,000	531,000	531,000
wc/d	10	5,280-155,760	36,094	12,103
OGE, Pierre Marie François (1849-1913) French				
3D	2	1,914-17,400	9,657	1,914
OGGIONO, Marco (1470-1530) Italian				
oil	1	29,739	29,739	29,739
OGIER, Marie Louise (1912-) French				
oil	1	1,500	1,500	1,500
OGILVIE, William Abernethy (1901-1989) Canadian				
oil	2	536-825	680	536
wc/d	1	1,058	1,058	1,058
O'GORMAN, Juan (1905-1982) Mexican				
oil	1	105,000	105,000	105,000
wc/d	2	12,000-38,000	25,000	12,000
OGUISS, Takanari (1901-1986) Japanese				
oil	16	2,761-115,000	51,048	47,926
wc/d	3	1,506-9,503	6,217	7,644

Name	No.	Price Range	Average	Median
O'HAGAN, Harriet Osborne (fl.1854-1880) Irish				
oil	1	4,442	4,442	4,442
O'HALLORAN, Fogarty (20th C) Irish				
oil	1	1,062	1,062	1,062
wc/d	1	620	620	620
O'HALLORAN, James (1955-) Irish				
oil	1	1,788	1,788	1,788
OHASHI, Yutaka (1923-) American/Japanese				
oil	1	1,900	1,900	1,900
O'HIGGINS, Pablo (1904-1983) Mexican				
oil	1	1,200	1,200	1,200
wc/d	1	1,900	1,900	1,900
OHL, Fritz (1904-1976) Dutch				
oil	9	819-3,612	2,055	2,167
OHLSEN, Jeppe Madsen (1891-1948) Danish				
oil	3	3,235-5,473	4,196	3,882
OHLSEN, Theodor (1855-1913) German				
oil	1	1,100	1,100	1,100
OHLSON, Alfred (1868-1940) Swedish				
3D	2	1,620-8,182	4,901	1,620
OHLUND, Bertil (1923-) Swedish				
oil	2	554-1,586	1,070	554
OHM, August (1943-) German				
oil	1	3,947	3,947	3,947
wc/d	1	1,440	1,440	1,440
OHMITT, Mary Ann (20th C) American				
oil	1	1,500	1,500	1,500
OHRSTROM, Alma (1897-1987) Swedish				
oil	1	1,123	1,123	1,123
OHRSTROM, Edvin (1906-) Scandinavian				
3D	1	1,745	1,745	1,745
OIESTAD, H Steven (20th C) American				
wc/d	1	3,500	3,500	3,500
OINONEN, Mikko (1883-1956) Finnish				
oil	5	839-3,086	1,920	1,543
OJA, Onni (1909-2004) Finnish				
oil	11	819-3,986	2,690	3,027
OKADA, Kenzo (1902-1982) American/Japanese				
oil	11	1,900-35,000	16,081	16,000
OKADA, Saburosuke (1869-1939) Japanese				
oil	1	1,374	1,374	1,374
OKAMOTO, Yajiro (1891-1963) American/Japanese				
oil	1	1,400	1,400	1,400
OKAMURA, Arthur (1932-) American				
oil	3	800-3,000	1,766	1,500
wc/d	2	650-700	675	650
O'KANE, Elizabeth (20th C) Irish				
3D	1	2,330	2,330	2,330
OKASHY, Avshalom (1916-1980) Israeli				
oil	3	900-6,000	2,633	1,000
wc/d	1	490	490	490
O'KEEFFE, Georgia (1887-1986) American				
oil	9	170,000-1,200,000	457,777	360,000
wc/d	3	38,000-825,000	361,000	220,000
O'KELLY, Aloysius (1853-1929) Irish				
oil	8	13,020-40,920	21,350	19,110
wc/d	1	15,810	15,810	15,810
O'KELLY, Mattie Lou (1907-1997) American				
wc/d	1	2,200	2,200	2,200
OKOKTOK, Vital (1912-) North American				
3D	1	1,856	1,856	1,856
OKOLOWITSCH, Nikolai Andrejewitsch (1876-?) Russian				
oil	1	1,320	1,320	1,320
OKUBO, Mine (1912-2001) American				
oil	2	1,700-2,000	1,850	1,700
wc/d	2	1,400-1,800	1,600	1,400
OKUN, Edward (1872-1945) Polish				
oil	2	10,938-11,545	11,241	10,938
OLAFSSON, Trygvi (1940-) Icelandic				
oil	1	1,618	1,618	1,618
OLASAGASTI, Jesus de (1907-1955) Spanish				
oil	1	1,903	1,903	1,903

Name	No.	Price Range	Average	Median
OLATUNDE, Asiru (1918-1993) Nigerian				
3D	1	4,425	4,425	4,425
OLDENBURG, Claes (1929-) American				
oil	1	22,000	22,000	22,000
wc/d	14	2,816-410,000	60,842	9,541
3D	15	4,091-720,000	129,000	11,000
OLDFIELD, Fred (20th C) American				
oil	2	425-2,500	1,462	425
OLDFIELD, Otis (1890-1969) American				
oil	1	1,600	1,600	1,600
OLEA CERVAN, Jose Luis (1921-) Spanish				
oil	1	1,567	1,567	1,567
OLEFFE, Auguste (1867-1931) Belgian				
oil	2	2,548-6,562	4,555	2,548
wc/d	2	1,013-1,527	1,270	1,013
OLIN, Nahui (1893-1978) Mexican				
oil	1	15,000	15,000	15,000
OLINSKY, Ivan G (1878-1962) American				
oil	2	5,000-20,000	12,500	5,000
wc/d	1	1,300	1,300	1,300
OLIS, Jan (1610-1676) Dutch				
oil	3	2,698-9,250	5,681	5,096
OLITSKI, Jules (1922-) American/Russian				
oil	4	11,000-120,000	49,071	15,727
OLIVA Y RODRIGO, Eugenio (1854-1925) Spanish				
oil	1	1,113	1,113	1,113
OLIVARI, Eugenio (c.1883-1917) Italian				
oil	1	23,640	23,640	23,640
OLIVE DES MARTIGUES, Henri (1898-1980) French				
oil	3	1,210-5,351	2,590	1,210
OLIVE, Ceferi (1907-1995) Spanish				
wc/d	7	832-2,059	1,488	1,574
OLIVE, Jacint (1896-1967) French?				
oil	3	766-1,427	1,050	958
OLIVE, Jean Baptiste (1848-1936) French				
oil	8	10,924-52,068	31,149	27,600
OLIVEIRA VIEITEZ, Juan (1929-) Spanish				
3D	1	7,775	7,775	7,775
OLIVEIRA, Nathan (1928-) American				
oil	1	47,500	47,500	47,500
wc/d	5	3,750-6,750	5,800	6,000
OLIVER, Archer James (1774-1842) British				
oil	1	1,653	1,653	1,653
OLIVER, Emma Sophie (1819-1885) British				
oil	2	1,408-6,932	4,170	1,408
OLIVER, Isaac (c.1550-1617) British				
wc/d	1	2,827	2,827	2,827
OLIVER, Julie Ford (20th C) British/American				
oil	3	500-3,400	1,566	800
OLIVER, T Clark (1827-1893) American				
oil	1	1,100	1,100	1,100
OLIVER, W (19th C) British				
oil	1	4,600	4,600	4,600
OLIVER, William (1805-1853) British				
oil	1	4,675	4,675	4,675
OLIVER, William (fl.1865-1897) British				
oil	6	1,000-4,325	2,751	1,914
OLIVERI, P (20th C) Italian				
3D	1	7,938	7,938	7,938
OLIVERIO, Alessandro (1500-c.1544) Italian				
oil	1	20,634	20,634	20,634
OLIVERO, Matteo (1879-1932) Italian				
oil	1	1,218	1,218	1,218
OLIVIE-BON, Léon (1863-1901) French				
oil	1	2,589	2,589	2,589
OLIVIER, Ferdinand (1873-1957) French				
oil	1	1,523	1,523	1,523
OLIVIER, Ferdinand Johann Heinrich von (1785-1841) German				
wc/d	1	4,005	4,005	4,005
OLIVIER, Friedrich (1791-1859) German				
wc/d	1	14,317	14,317	14,317

Name	No.	Price Range	Average	Median
OLIVIER, Herbert Arnould (1861-1952) British				
oil	3	744-4,500	2,306	1,674
OLIVIER, Michel Barthelemy (1712-1784) French				
oil	1	44,349	44,349	44,349
OLIVIERI (?) Italian				
3D	1	9,000	9,000	9,000
OLIVIERI, Claudio (1934-) Italian				
oil	5	835-2,945	1,721	1,574
OLIVIETTI, Salvatore (1833-1902) Italian				
oil	1	4,159	4,159	4,159
OLLER, Francisco (1833-1917) Puerto Rican				
oil	1	85,000	85,000	85,000
OLLEROS Y QUINTANA, Blas (1851-1919) Italian				
oil	1	1,200	1,200	1,200
OLLEY, Margaret Hannah (1923-) Australian				
wc/d	1	1,531	1,531	1,531
OLLEY, Robert (20th C) British				
oil	1	1,074	1,074	1,074
OLLILA, Yrjo (1887-1932) Finnish				
oil	4	484-12,740	4,780	1,008
wc/d	2	630-651	640	630
OLMES, Mildred Young (1906-) American				
oil	1	2,400	2,400	2,400
OLRIK, Lisbeth (1936-) Danish				
oil	1	1,299	1,299	1,299
OLSANSKY, Klement (c.1909-1963) Canadian				
oil	1	1,499	1,499	1,499
OLSEN, Carl (1818-1878) Danish				
oil	4	1,793-4,948	3,008	1,818
OLSEN, Chr Benjamin (1873-1935) Danish				
oil	16	443-4,890	1,374	937
OLSEN, Gudmund (1913-1985) Danish				
oil	5	1,007-1,860	1,299	1,288
OLSEN, Hans (1902-1983) Danish?				
3D	1	3,880	3,880	3,880
OLSEN, Herb (1905-1973) American				
wc/d	1	3,250	3,250	3,250
OLSEN, Torbjorn (1956-) Danish				
oil	1	2,575	2,575	2,575
OLSEN, William Skotte (1945-2005) Danish				
oil	10	1,778-6,791	3,422	2,586
wc/d	2	3,219-5,015	4,117	3,219
OLSOMMER, Charles Clos (1883-1966) Swiss				
oil	1	6,934	6,934	6,934
wc/d	11	531-6,118	2,827	2,724
OLSON, Axel (1899-1986) Swedish				
oil	23	734-6,362	2,721	2,327
wc/d	9	1,404-7,929	2,812	1,527
OLSON, Eric H (1909-1996) Swedish				
oil	1	1,916	1,916	1,916
3D	9	2,511-8,457	4,622	4,199
OLSON, Erik (1901-1986) Swedish				
oil	28	519-87,216	15,056	4,229
wc/d	1	16,518	16,518	16,518
OLSSON, Julius (1864-1942) British				
oil	10	835-5,888	3,643	3,784
OLSSON-HAGALUND, Olle (1904-1972) Swedish				
oil	9	744-522,329	90,871	50,215
wc/d	2	1,781-11,451	6,616	1,781
OLSTED, P (1824-1887) Danish				
oil	1	1,270	1,270	1,270
OLSTED, Peter (1824-1887) Danish				
oil	1	7,824	7,824	7,824
OLTMANNS, Willi (1905-1979) German				
oil	1	1,936	1,936	1,936
O'LYNCH OF TOWN, Karl (1869-1942) German				
oil	6	878-4,241	1,913	1,074
O'MALLEY, Jane (1944-) Irish				
oil	2	1,211-3,633	2,422	1,211
wc/d	1	704	704	704
O'MALLEY, Michael Augustine Power (1878-1946) Irish				
oil	1	1,800	1,800	1,800

Name	No.	Price Range	Average	Median
O'MALLEY, Tony (1913-2003) British/Irish				
oil	15	4,320-84,162	30,859	18,163
wc/d	24	2,262-17,534	6,946	5,812
OMAN, Valentin (1935-) Austrian				
oil	2	3,214-4,114	3,664	3,214
wc/d	1	2,928	2,928	2,928
OMCIKOUS, Pierre (1926-) French/Yugoslavian				
oil	1	3,548	3,548	3,548
OMERTH, Georges (fl.1895-1925) French				
3D	1	5,733	5,733	5,733
OMICCIOLI, Giovanni (1901-1975) Italian				
oil	15	829-17,173	3,529	1,991
wc/d	2	589-657	623	589
OMMEGANCK, Balthasar Paul (1755-1826) Flemish				
oil	7	1,192-12,098	4,853	3,631
wc/d	1	1,532	1,532	1,532
ONDERBERG, Pieter Jan (1821-1890) Dutch				
oil	1	1,459	1,459	1,459
ONDERDONK, Julian (1882-1922) American				
oil	11	6,500-120,000	27,636	16,000
wc/d	3	2,750-21,000	9,666	5,250
O'NEILL, Daniel (1920-1974) British				
oil	41	2,249-145,080	36,694	18,849
wc/d	1	1,574	1,574	1,574
O'NEILL, Henry (1798-1880) British				
oil	1	246,400	246,400	246,400
O'NEILL, Henry Nelson (1817-1880) British				
oil	1	13,230	13,230	13,230
O'NEILL, Hugh (1784-1824) British				
wc/d	1	3,348	3,348	3,348
O'NEILL, Liam (20th C) Irish				
oil	4	3,162-9,351	5,896	5,088
O'NEILL, Mark (1963-) Irish				
oil	89	3,058-27,194	9,044	7,280
O'NEILL, Michael (20th C) Irish?				
oil	1	1,334	1,334	1,334
O'NEILL, Rose (1875-1944) American				
wc/d	2	1,700-2,000	1,850	1,700
ONGANIA, Umberto (19th C) Italian				
wc/d	3	605-1,980	1,184	968
ONGARO, Athos (1947-) Italian				
oil	1	3,770	3,770	3,770
wc/d	3	665-1,028	907	1,028
ONGLEY, William (1836-1890) American?				
oil	1	3,000	3,000	3,000
ONISHI, Shigeru (1928-) Japanese				
wc/d	5	1,169-3,349	2,406	2,750
ONKEN, Karl (1846-1934) German				
oil	1	4,000	4,000	4,000
ONLEY, Toni (1928-2004) Canadian				
oil	7	902-9,280	3,176	2,309
wc/d	9	577-2,320	926	749
ONNES, Harm Henrick Kamerlingh (1893-1985) Dutch				
oil	22	1,219-11,582	4,797	3,901
wc/d	16	549-2,438	1,403	1,199
ONOFRI, Crescenzio (1632-1698) Italian				
wc/d	1	1,903	1,903	1,903
ONOSATO, Toshinobu (1912-1986) Japanese				
oil	2	8,000-8,500	8,250	8,000
ONSERING, Kim (20th C) British				
oil	1	1,032	1,032	1,032
ONSLOW (?) British				
oil	2	3,884-3,884	3,884	3,884
ONSLOW-FORD, Edward (1852-1901) British				
3D	1	4,703	4,703	4,703
ONSLOW-FORD, Gordon (1912-2003) British				
oil	5	9,500-17,000	11,900	9,500
wc/d	2	7,500-8,000	7,750	7,500
ONSTAD, Albert Bernhard (1895-1981) Swedish				
oil	1	1,321	1,321	1,321
ONTANI, Luigi (1943-) Italian				
wc/d	9	4,633-15,459	11,078	11,651

Name	No.	Price Range	Average	Median
OONARK, Jessie (1906-1985) North American				
wc/d	1	1,350	1,350	1,350
OORDT, Willem van (fl.1635-1655) Dutch				
wc/d	1	2,686	2,686	2,686
OOST, Jacques van (17th C) Belgian				
oil	1	88,699	88,699	88,699
OOST, Jacques van (elder) (1601-1671) Belgian				
oil	1	27,750	27,750	27,750
OOST, Jacques van (younger) (1637-1713) Flemish				
oil	1	39,600	39,600	39,600
OOSTEN, Izaack van (1613-1661) Flemish				
oil	5	68,097-333,000	129,089	77,850
OOSTSANEN, Jacob Cornelisz van (1477-1533) Dutch				
oil	1	778,500	778,500	778,500
OPALKA, Roman (1931-) Polish				
oil	2	92,500-111,000	101,750	92,500
wc/d	1	16,000	16,000	16,000
OPAZO, Rodolfo (1925-) Chilean				
oil	3	500-35,000	12,300	1,400
OPDENHOFF, George Willem (1807-1873) Dutch				
oil	12	3,004-20,331	10,004	6,062
wc/d	1	1,030	1,030	1,030
OPERTI, Albert Jasper (1852-1927) Italian				
wc/d	1	1,000	1,000	1,000
OPFERMANN, Karl (1891-) German				
3D	1	15,901	15,901	15,901
OPHEY, Walter (1882-1930) German				
oil	2	3,828-4,500	4,164	3,828
wc/d	1	3,649	3,649	3,649
OPIE, John (1761-1807) British				
oil	2	4,114-5,340	4,727	4,114
OPIE, Julian (1958-) British				
oil	4	4,070-55,500	24,225	7,920
3D	4	8,850-45,000	23,912	14,800
OPISSO SALA, Ricardo (1880-1966) Spanish				
oil	1	1,600	1,600	1,600
wc/d	6	824-1,394	1,104	1,014
OPITZ, Georg Emanuel (1775-1841) German				
wc/d	3	1,017-1,414	1,149	1,017
OPIZ, G (19th C) German				
oil	1	3,480	3,480	3,480
OPPEL, Lisel (1897-1960) German				
oil	3	2,572-3,637	3,121	3,156
OPPELT, Eduard (19th C) Austrian				
oil	1	4,241	4,241	4,241
OPPENHEIM, Dennis (1938-) American				
oil	2	2,250-5,786	4,018	2,250
wc/d	9	2,600-11,743	6,902	6,423
3D	2	4,087-5,180	4,633	4,087
OPPENHEIM, Meret (1913-1986) Swiss				
oil	4	6,485-14,460	10,099	8,106
wc/d	10	708-8,237	3,717	3,481
3D	2	2,744-6,160	4,452	2,744
OPPENHEIM, Yves (1948-) French				
oil	1	4,816	4,816	4,816
OPPENHEIMER, Charles (1875-1961) British				
wc/d	2	1,239-1,556	1,397	1,239
OPPENHEIMER, Jonny (1923-) Swedish				
oil	4	484-2,738	1,320	516
OPPENHEIMER, Max (1885-1954) Austrian				
oil	5	5,856-17,568	8,664	6,429
wc/d	2	535-3,279	1,907	535
OPPENOORTH, Willem (1847-1905) Dutch				
oil	3	975-3,616	2,684	3,461
wc/d	1	2,268	2,268	2,268
OPPER, John (1908-) American				
oil	1	2,500	2,500	2,500
OPPI, Ubaldo (1889-1942) Italian				
wc/d	2	763-1,463	1,113	763
OPPITZ, Wilhelm (1874-?) Bohemian				
oil	1	2,910	2,910	2,910

Name	No.	Price Range	Average	Median
OPRANDI, Giorgio (1883-1963) Italian				
oil	1	2,848	2,848	2,848
OPSOMER, Isidore (1878-1967) Belgian				
oil	9	751-11,677	2,698	1,332
ORAM, Ann (1956-) British				
oil	1	1,176	1,176	1,176
wc/d	1	2,816	2,816	2,816
ORAMAS, Alirio (1924-) Venezuelan				
oil	3	1,860-2,790	2,185	1,905
ORANGE, Maurice Henri (1868-1916) French				
oil	1	16,145	16,145	16,145
ORANT, Marthe (1874-1953) French				
oil	5	656-1,758	1,293	1,455
ORCHARDSON, Sir William Quiller (1832-1910) British				
oil	5	1,122-28,160	15,884	17,600
wc/d	2	2,112-2,816	2,464	2,112
ORD, Joseph Biays (1805-1865) American				
oil	1	9,500	9,500	9,500
ORDNER, Paul (1900-1969) French?				
oil	1	3,131	3,131	3,131
ORDWAY, Alfred (1819-1897) American				
oil	1	3,250	3,250	3,250
ORECK, Sandra Zahn (1940-) American				
3D	1	1,800	1,800	1,800
O'REILLY, Bart (1975-) Irish				
wc/d	2	788-1,212	1,000	788
O'REILLY, Patrick (1957-) Irish				
oil	1	1,169	1,169	1,169
3D	6	2,783-8,822	5,095	3,633
ORESKOVA, Petra (1941-) Czechoslovakian				
oil	1	1,074	1,074	1,074
ORFEI, Orfeo (1836-1915) Italian				
oil	2	1,800-11,781	6,790	1,800
ORGAN, Bryan (1935-) British				
wc/d	1	1,468	1,468	1,468
ORI, Luciano (1928-) Italian				
wc/d	1	2,458	2,458	2,458
ORIANI, Pippo (1909-1972) Italian				
oil	22	1,196-20,354	5,334	4,712
wc/d	12	589-2,827	1,499	1,288
ORLAI, Soma Samuel (1822-1880) Hungarian				
oil	2	2,384-2,622	2,503	2,384
ORLANDINI, Antoine (1886-1956) French				
3D	1	1,649	1,649	1,649
ORLIK, Emil (1870-1932) Czechoslovakian				
oil	2	993-1,018	1,005	993
wc/d	4	825-2,572	1,756	1,210
ORLOFF, Alexander (1899-1979) Polish				
oil	12	588-3,832	1,585	1,352
3D	2	3,822-6,370	5,096	3,822
ORLOFF, Chana (1878-1968) French				
3D	15	2,827-63,357	29,181	27,000
ORLOV, Alexandr Grigorievich (1868-?) Russian				
oil	1	2,186	2,186	2,186
ORLOV, Nikolai Vasilievich (1863-1924) Russian				
oil	1	6,049	6,049	6,049
ORLOVA, Elena (1953-) Russian				
oil	1	4,750	4,750	4,750
ORLOWSKI, Vladimir (1842-1914) Russian				
oil	2	23,949-400,000	211,974	23,949
ORMENESE, Benito (1935-) Italian				
wc/d	2	1,556-1,844	1,700	1,556
OROQUIETA, Famuceno Bonifacio (1901-?) Argentinian				
oil	1	2,500	2,500	2,500
OROZCO, Jose Clemente (1883-1949) Mexican				
oil	1	7,531	7,531	7,531
wc/d	3	12,000-47,500	26,500	20,000
ORPEN, Bea (1913-1980) British				
oil	1	1,978	1,978	1,978
wc/d	5	1,130-2,843	2,013	2,101

Name	No.	Price Range	Average	Median
ORPEN, Sir William (1878-1931) Irish				
oil	8	25,479-390,600	141,662	70,680
wc/d	9	1,081-61,600	10,675	2,088
ORR, Eric (1939-1998) American				
oil	1	16,000	16,000	16,000
ORR, Joseph (1949-) American				
oil	1	2,000	2,000	2,000
ORRENTE, Pedro (1570-1644) Spanish				
oil	1	25,865	25,865	25,865
ORROCK, James (1829-1913) British				
oil	3	448-6,264	2,616	1,138
wc/d	4	473-666	540	478
ORSEL, Victor (1795-1850) French				
oil	1	55,680	55,680	55,680
ORSELLI, Arturo (19th C) Italian				
oil	1	5,568	5,568	5,568
ORSI, Lelio (1511-1587) Italian				
wc/d	2	3,000-7,266	5,133	3,000
ORTEGA, Jose (1880-1955) Spanish				
oil	2	1,168-1,498	1,333	1,168
ORTEGA, Jose (1921-1991) Spanish				
oil	1	1,052	1,052	1,052
wc/d	3	590-2,799	2,004	2,625
ORTEGA, Juan Jose (20th C) Spanish				
oil	1	2,059	2,059	2,059
ORTEGA, Pelayo (1956-) Spanish				
oil	1	2,022	2,022	2,022
ORTH, Willy (1889-1976) American/German				
oil	3	1,700-3,600	2,566	2,400
ORTIZ DE ZARATE, Manuel (1886-1946) French				
oil	3	1,885-20,000	8,044	2,249
wc/d	1	7,136	7,136	7,136
ORTIZ, Angel (1967-) American				
wc/d	1	700	700	700
3D	1	3,250	3,250	3,250
ORTIZ, Manuel Angeles (1895-1984) Spanish				
oil	5	1,316-5,708	2,696	2,288
wc/d	4	1,674-2,392	1,886	1,674
ORTLIEB, Friedrich (1839-1909) German				
oil	1	2,510	2,510	2,510
ORTLIP, Aimee E (1888-?) American				
oil	1	7,000	7,000	7,000
ORTLIP, Paul Daniel (1926-) American				
oil	1	5,500	5,500	5,500
ORTMANN, Theo (1902-1941) German/Dutch				
oil	1	3,107	3,107	3,107
ORTMANS, François-Auguste (1827-1884) French				
oil	1	1,584	1,584	1,584
ORTOLANI, Enrico (1883-1972) Italian				
oil	1	1,295	1,295	1,295
ORTUNO, Pancho (1950-) Spanish				
oil	1	1,078	1,078	1,078
ORTVAD, Erik (1917-) Danish				
oil	8	1,779-20,925	9,665	5,658
ORTWED, Kirsten (1948-) Danish				
3D	1	1,616	1,616	1,616
ORUP, Bengt (1916-1996) Swedish				
oil	1	1,654	1,654	1,654
O'RYAN, Fergus (1911-1989) Irish				
oil	15	1,018-10,712	3,304	2,338
wc/d	4	637-2,068	1,116	827
OS, Georgius Jacobus Johannes van (1782-1861) Dutch				
oil	10	608-328,700	105,635	20,331
OS, J van (1744-1808) Dutch				
oil	1	3,204	3,204	3,204
OS, Jan van (1744-1808) Dutch				
oil	4	2,800-80,100	49,650	40,700
OS, Maria Margrita van (1780-1862) Dutch				
oil	1	5,363	5,363	5,363
OS, P G van (1776-1839) Dutch				
oil	1	2,320	2,320	2,320

Name	No.	Price Range	Average	Median
OS, Pieter Gerardus van (1776-1839) Dutch				
oil	6	1,153-3,341	2,367	2,158
wc/d	2	825-2,101	1,463	825
OSBERT, Alphonse (1857-1939) French				
oil	3	518-3,568	2,279	2,752
wc/d	1	870	870	870
OSBORNE, Elizabeth (20th C) American				
oil	1	1,700	1,700	1,700
OSBORNE, Louise Brettner (1889-1968) American				
oil	1	1,700	1,700	1,700
OSBORNE, Walter (1859-1903) Irish				
oil	8	1,656-50,959	24,290	23,945
wc/d	2	1,560-14,880	8,220	1,560
OSCARSSON, Bernhard (1894-1971) Swedish				
oil	4	401-2,368	1,121	780
OSGOOD, Charles (1809-1890) American				
oil	1	2,600	2,600	2,600
OSGOOD, Harry Haviland (1875-?) American				
oil	1	1,500	1,500	1,500
O'SICKEY, Joseph B (1918-) American				
oil	2	1,600-5,000	3,300	1,600
OSIPOW, Paul (1937-) Finnish				
oil	1	3,600	3,600	3,600
OSMOLOVSKY, Anatoly (1969-) Russian				
3D	1	2,000	2,000	2,000
OSNAGHI, Josefine (fl.1890-1920) Austrian				
oil	2	832-3,266	2,049	832
OSOUF, Jean (1898-1996) French				
3D	3	2,044-3,563	2,597	2,185
OSSLUND, Helmer (1866-1938) Swedish				
oil	50	620-348,986	18,157	4,986
wc/d	2	622-7,478	4,050	622
OSSOLA, Giancarlo (1935-) Italian				
oil	1	1,178	1,178	1,178
OSSORIO, Alfonso (1916-1990) American				
oil	1	35,000	35,000	35,000
OSSOVSKI, Piotr (1925-) Russian				
oil	5	476-2,912	1,224	595
OST, Alfred (1884-1945) Belgian				
oil	1	1,520	1,520	1,520
wc/d	4	510-1,196	948	1,008
OSTADE, Adriaen van (1610-1684) Dutch				
oil	7	17,838-415,200	189,410	133,200
wc/d	2	5,878-7,007	6,442	5,878
OSTADE, Isaac van (1621-1649) Dutch				
oil	5	11,986-185,000	50,338	16,349
OSTENDORFER, Michael (c.1490-1559) German				
oil	1	22,200	22,200	22,200
OSTERLIN, Anders (1926-) Swedish				
oil	2	793-2,163	1,478	793
OSTERLIND, Allan (1855-1938) Swedish				
oil	2	1,511-4,945	3,228	1,511
wc/d	2	520-1,786	1,153	520
OSTERLIND, Anders (1887-1960) French				
oil	9	817-2,397	1,464	1,459
OSTERMILLER, Dan (1956-) American				
3D	1	3,500	3,500	3,500
OSTERSETZER, Carl (1865-1914) Austrian				
oil	8	547-3,295	1,698	908
OSTERWALD, George (1803-1884) German				
wc/d	1	7,292	7,292	7,292
OSTHAUS, Edmund H (1858-1928) American				
oil	9	9,000-90,000	51,555	50,000
wc/d	15	1,045-20,000	12,323	15,000
OSTLIHN, Barbro (1930-1995) Swedish				
oil	2	2,036-4,580	3,308	2,036
OSTMAR, Tommy (1934-) Swedish				
oil	3	1,781-3,436	2,532	2,379
OSTUNI, Peter (20th C) American?				
oil	3	750-1,700	1,316	1,500

Name	No.	Price Range	Average	Median
O'SULLIVAN, Sean (1906-1964) British				
oil	2	12,858-20,460	16,659	12,858
wc/d	4	606-1,937	1,312	1,173
OSUNA, Justo (20th C) Venezuelan?				
3D	1	1,440	1,440	1,440
OSVER, Arthur (20th C) American				
oil	2	2,200-5,000	3,600	2,200
OSWALD, C W (fl.1892) British				
oil	1	1,335	1,335	1,335
OSWALD, Charles W (19th C) British				
oil	3	514-1,600	1,117	1,239
OTERO ABELEDO LAXEIRO, Jose (1908-1996) Spanish				
oil	1	14,500	14,500	14,500
wc/d	3	969-1,137	1,065	1,090
OTERO, Alejandro (1921-1990) Venezuelan				
oil	1	65,000	65,000	65,000
OTERO, Camilo (20th C) ?				
3D	1	2,458	2,458	2,458
OTERO, Carlos (1886-1977) Venezuelan				
oil	3	1,540-2,750	2,220	2,370
OTERO, Juan (?) Argentinian?				
oil	1	2,600	2,600	2,600
OTERO, Mariano (1942-) Spanish				
wc/d	1	2,151	2,151	2,151
OTHONEOS, Nicholaos (1877-1950) Greek				
oil	1	2,076	2,076	2,076
OTHONIEL, Jean Michel (1964-) French				
3D	2	1,853-6,473	4,163	1,853
OTIS, Bass (1784-1861) American				
oil	1	1,800	1,800	1,800
OTIS, George Demont (1877-1962) American				
oil	7	1,200-14,000	5,950	5,500
OTTE, William Louis (1871-1957) American				
oil	2	5,000-6,000	5,500	5,000
wc/d	1	8,000	8,000	8,000
OTTENFELD, Rudolf Ritter von (1856-1913) Italian				
oil	3	688-8,000	4,770	5,622
OTTERBEEK, Jacobus Hermanus (1839-1902) Dutch				
oil	1	1,707	1,707	1,707
OTTERNESS, Tom (1952-) American				
3D	1	28,000	28,000	28,000
OTTERSTEDT, Alexander (1848-1909) Russian				
oil	2	1,051-2,039	1,545	1,051
OTTESEN, Johannes (1875-1936) Danish				
oil	1	1,932	1,932	1,932
OTTESEN, Otto Didrik (1816-1892) Danish				
oil	2	3,156-7,824	5,490	3,156
wc/d	1	500	500	500
OTTEVAERE, Henri (1870-1940) Belgian				
oil	3	643-1,967	1,376	1,520
OTTINGER, George Martin (1833-1917) American				
oil	4	1,600-4,750	3,775	4,250
wc/d	1	6,500	6,500	6,500
OTTINI, Pasquale (1580-1630) Italian				
oil	2	9,503-41,520	25,511	9,503
OTTMANN, Henri (1877-1927) French				
oil	8	1,197-6,125	3,545	3,758
wc/d	2	485-738	611	485
OTTO, Johann Heinrich (fl.1762-1797) American				
wc/d	1	2,000	2,000	2,000
OTTO, Ludwig (1850-1920) German				
oil	1	8,000	8,000	8,000
OUBORG, Piet (1893-1956) Dutch				
oil	1	1,084	1,084	1,084
wc/d	5	1,590-2,922	2,218	2,104
OUDART, Paul Louis (1796-1850) French				
wc/d	1	1,757	1,757	1,757
OUDENDYCK, Evert (17th C) Dutch				
oil	1	20,384	20,384	20,384
OUDERRA, Clothildis van der (19/20th C) Belgian				
oil	2	1,205-1,757	1,481	1,205

Name	No.	Price Range	Average	Median
OUDERRA, Pierre van der (1841-1915) Belgian				
oil	3	701-29,571	10,757	2,000
OUDINOT, Achille (1820-1891) Flemish				
oil	2	1,700-3,739	2,719	1,700
OUDOT, R (1897-1981) French				
oil	1	1,694	1,694	1,694
OUDOT, Roland (1897-1981) French				
oil	16	616-7,017	2,449	2,000
wc/d	1	1,196	1,196	1,196
OUDRY, Jean Baptiste (1686-1755) French				
wc/d	4	1,701-21,875	12,196	4,861
OUDSHOORN, Albert Jan (1877-1930) Dutch				
oil	2	841-1,757	1,299	841
OUELLETTE, Tom (1954-) American				
oil	1	1,500	1,500	1,500
OULESS, Philip J (1817-1885) British				
oil	1	46,980	46,980	46,980
OULINE (20th C) ?				
3D	1	2,548	2,548	2,548
OULTON, Therese (1953-) British				
oil	3	1,479-4,070	2,911	3,186
OUREN, Karl (1882-1934) American/Norwegian				
oil	2	375-1,649	1,012	375
OURSLER, Tony (1957-) American				
3D	2	35,000-65,000	50,000	35,000
OUSLEY, William (1866-1953) American				
oil	5	675-1,600	1,005	900
OUTER, Nestor (1865-1923) Belgian				
wc/d	1	1,192	1,192	1,192
OUTERBRIDGE, Paul (jnr) (1896-1958) American				
wc/d	1	3,185	3,185	3,185
OUTEZ, Constant (?) ?				
oil	1	1,513	1,513	1,513
OUTIN, Pierre (1840-1899) French				
oil	1	42,320	42,320	42,320
OUVRIE, Justin (1806-1879) French				
oil	3	1,286-11,781	7,328	8,918
wc/d	3	784-8,247	3,537	1,580
OUWATER, Isaak (1750-1793) Dutch				
oil	1	138,750	138,750	138,750
wc/d	1	2,336	2,336	2,336
OVADYAHU, Samuel (1892-1963) Israeli				
oil	5	400-3,400	1,305	777
wc/d	1	1,100	1,100	1,100
OVCHINNIKOV, Nikolai (1958-) Russian				
oil	1	18,600	18,600	18,600
OVENDEN, F W (fl.1834-1843) British				
oil	2	6,498-17,010	11,754	6,498
OVENDEN, Graham (1943-) British				
oil	6	1,710-42,750	9,612	2,745
wc/d	3	855-3,420	1,909	1,454
OVERBECK, Fritz (1869-1909) German				
oil	2	8,182-31,455	19,818	8,182
OVERBECK, Johann Friedrich (1789-1869) German				
wc/d	2	1,178-98,441	49,809	1,178
OVERBEEK, Gijsbertus Johannes van (1882-1947) Dutch				
oil	3	878-2,400	1,457	1,093
wc/d	2	566-566	566	566
OVERBERGHE, Cel (1937-) Belgian				
oil	1	1,752	1,752	1,752
OVERPECK, Ray (1933-) American				
oil	12	1,400-4,750	2,704	2,250
wc/d	1	400	400	400
OVTCHINNIKOV, Vladimir (1941-) Russian				
oil	2	3,440-14,620	9,030	3,440
OWEN, Bill (1942-) American				
oil	2	1,300-4,500	2,900	1,300
OWEN, Chris (20th C) American				
wc/d	2	9,000-12,000	10,500	9,000
OWEN, George (19th C) American				
oil	1	3,404	3,404	3,404

Name	No.	Price Range	Average	Median
OWEN, George O (19/20th C) British				
wc/d	1	2,136	2,136	2,136
OWEN, Robert Emmett (1878-1957) American				
oil	10	850-7,500	3,310	2,750
OWEN, Samuel (1768-1857) British				
wc/d	3	2,076-3,009	2,391	2,088
OWENS, Laura (1970-) American				
oil	2	15,000-26,000	20,500	15,000
OYENS, David (1842-1902) Flemish				
oil	3	823-12,103	4,932	1,870
wc/d	1	1,455	1,455	1,455
OYENS, Pierre (1842-1894) Flemish				
oil	1	9,568	9,568	9,568
OZENFANT, Amedee (1886-1966) French				
oil	4	9,699-29,920	18,742	17,500
wc/d	4	2,038-5,733	3,885	3,312
OZERI, Yigal (1958-) Israeli				
oil	2	10,000-22,500	16,250	10,000
wc/d	1	7,000	7,000	7,000
PAALEN, Wolfgang (1905-1959) Austrian				
oil	4	11,000-50,000	27,921	19,008
PAAR, Ernst (1906-) Austrian				
oil	1	5,394	5,394	5,394
PAAVOLA, Antero (1956-) Finnish				
wc/d	1	1,029	1,029	1,029
PABLO BARCIA, Maximo de (1930-) Spanish				
oil	2	1,430-1,523	1,476	1,430
PABST, Charles H (1950-) American				
oil	1	1,100	1,100	1,100
PACE, Achille (1923-) Italian				
oil	29	471-5,178	1,772	1,450
PACE, Giovanni Battista (17th C) Italian				
oil	1	15,727	15,727	15,727
PACE, Ranieri del (1681-1738) Italian				
oil	1	6,020	6,020	6,020
PACENZA, Onofrio (1904-1971) Argentinian				
oil	6	3,500-18,000	6,483	3,900
wc/d	1	2,700	2,700	2,700
PACETTI, Ivos (1901-1970) Italian				
3D	1	7,007	7,007	7,007
PACHT, Wilhelm (1843-1912) Danish				
oil	2	492-711	601	492
wc/d	1	830	830	830
PACKARD, Ann (20th C) American				
oil	12	550-12,000	3,720	3,250
PACKARD, Cynthia (20th C) American				
oil	3	950-2,100	1,383	1,100
PADAMSEE, Akbar (1928-) Indian				
oil	10	8,500-625,000	211,253	90,000
wc/d	13	5,984-60,000	17,177	12,000
PADDOCK, Josephine (1885-1964) American				
oil	1	23,000	23,000	23,000
PADUA, Paul Matthias (1903-1981) Austrian				
oil	7	941-17,572	4,322	1,435
wc/d	1	1,440	1,440	1,440
PADUANO, Alexander (?-1596) Italian				
wc/d	1	1,458	1,458	1,458
PAEDE, Paul (1868-1929) German				
oil	10	1,074-4,796	3,048	3,343
PAEFFGEN, C O (1933-) German				
oil	5	1,234-20,027	12,300	15,288
wc/d	2	564-564	564	564
PAELINCK, Joseph (1781-1839) Belgian				
oil	2	3,330-60,000	31,665	3,330
PAEP, Thomas (1628-1670) Flemish				
oil	1	28,898	28,898	28,898
PAERELS, Willem (1878-1962) Belgian/Dutch				
oil	7	2,035-58,904	12,215	4,909
wc/d	4	471-1,532	1,029	910
PAESCHKE, Paul (1875-1943) German				
oil	1	7,633	7,633	7,633
wc/d	2	834-1,018	926	834

Name	No.	Price Range	Average	Median
PAEZ VILARO, Jorge (1922-) Uruguayan				
wc/d	1	3,700	3,700	3,700
PAEZ, Jose de (1720-?) Mexican				
oil	2	8,280-18,000	13,140	8,280
PAGAN, Luigi (1907-1980) Italian				
oil	1	2,227	2,227	2,227
PAGE, Edward A (1850-1928) American				
oil	1	1,900	1,900	1,900
wc/d	1	750	750	750
PAGE, Florence W (fl.1920s) British				
oil	1	3,000	3,000	3,000
PAGE, Henry Maurice (fl.1878-1890) British				
oil	1	3,200	3,200	3,200
PAGE, J Wilton (19th C) American?				
oil	1	1,600	1,600	1,600
PAGE, Marie Danforth (1869-1940) American				
oil	1	5,500	5,500	5,500
PAGE, William (1811-1885) American				
wc/d	1	4,152	4,152	4,152
PAGELS, Hermann Joachim (1876-?) German				
3D	1	2,033	2,033	2,033
PAGES, Aimee (1803-1886) French				
oil	1	3,095	3,095	3,095
PAGES, Jules Eugene (1867-1946) American				
oil	5	2,400-30,000	11,080	6,000
PAGES, Mariano (20th C) Argentinian				
3D	2	6,700-15,000	10,850	6,700
PAGET, Sidney (1861-1908) British				
oil	1	4,350	4,350	4,350
wc/d	2	525-1,649	1,087	525
PAGGI, Giovanni Battista (1554-1627) Italian				
wc/d	3	1,300-5,550	3,530	3,741
PAGLIACCI, Aldo (1913-) Italian				
oil	2	951-1,200	1,075	951
PAGLIACCI, Mirko (1959-) Swiss				
oil	1	3,092	3,092	3,092
PAGLIANO, Eleuterio (1826-1903) Italian				
oil	4	1,272-8,001	4,288	3,145
PAGNI, Ferruccio (1866-1935) Italian				
oil	1	18,446	18,446	18,446
PAGOWSKA, Teresa (1926-) Polish				
oil	1	76,438	76,438	76,438
PAGUENAUD, Jean-Louis (1876-1952) French				
oil	4	504-5,400	2,825	700
PAHISSA LAPORTA, Jaime (1846-1928) Spanish				
oil	1	5,425	5,425	5,425
PAI, Laxman (1926-) Indian				
oil	1	15,895	15,895	15,895
wc/d	1	9,350	9,350	9,350
PAICE, George (1854-1925) British				
oil	13	476-4,000	1,146	756
PAIK, Nam June (1932-) American/Korean				
oil	2	742-8,000	4,371	742
wc/d	1	5,890	5,890	5,890
3D	9	2,803-99,517	40,806	42,028
PAIL, Edouard (1851-1916) French				
oil	2	1,600-1,649	1,624	1,600
PAILES, Isaac (1895-1978) French				
oil	9	588-5,000	2,588	2,917
PAILLARD, Henri (1844-1912) French				
oil	1	3,014	3,014	3,014
wc/d	1	1,147	1,147	1,147
PAILLER, Henri (1876-1954) French				
oil	2	2,735-16,054	9,394	2,735
PAILLET, Charles (1871-1937) French				
3D	1	4,450	4,450	4,450
PAILOS, Manuel (1917-2005) Uruguayan				
oil	2	7,500-40,000	23,750	7,500
wc/d	4	1,200-5,000	2,700	1,400
PAILTHORPE, Grace (1883-1971) British				
wc/d	7	500-4,524	1,777	1,456

Name	No.	Price Range	Average	Median
PAIN, Thomas (19th C) British				
oil	1	1,323	1,323	1,323
PAINE, Joseph Polley (1912-) American				
wc/d	1	3,200	3,200	3,200
PAINE, Roxy (1966-) American				
3D	1	4,224	4,224	4,224
PAJETTA, Guido (1898-1987) Italian				
oil	6	2,686-9,833	4,491	2,913
wc/d	1	2,356	2,356	2,356
PAJETTA, Pietro (1845-1911) Italian				
oil	1	34,164	34,164	34,164
PAJOT, Émile Paul (1870-1930) French				
wc/d	1	6,897	6,897	6,897
PAJOT, Gilbert (?) French				
wc/d	2	1,520-1,870	1,695	1,520
PAJOU, Augustin (1730-1809) French				
wc/d	5	1,070-5,727	3,006	2,022
PAJOU, Jacques Augustin Catherine (1766-1828) French				
oil	1	19,000	19,000	19,000
wc/d	1	14,696	14,696	14,696
PAL, Fried (1914-) Hungarian				
oil	10	584-7,000	2,376	1,300
PALA, Eliseo (20th C) Spanish				
oil	1	1,171	1,171	1,171
PALACIOS, Joaquin Vaquero (1900-1998) Spanish				
oil	2	11,892-16,000	13,946	11,892
PALADINI, Filippo (17th C) Italian				
wc/d	1	2,616	2,616	2,616
PALADINI, Vinicio (1902-1971) Italian				
3D	1	15,930	15,930	15,930
PALADINO, Mimmo (1948-) Italian				
oil	19	2,631-247,800	63,610	53,877
wc/d	34	999-40,055	9,572	6,429
3D	6	6,578-148,000	59,814	33,986
PALAGI, Pelagio (1775-1860) Italian				
wc/d	1	6,214	6,214	6,214
PALAMEDES, Anthonie (1601-1673) Dutch				
oil	8	2,768-138,840	29,473	7,709
PALAMEDES, Palamedesz I (1607-1638) Dutch				
oil	1	19,852	19,852	19,852
PALANTI, Giuseppe (1881-1946) Italian				
oil	2	2,577-2,675	2,626	2,577
PALATKO, Dimitri (20th C) Russian				
oil	1	2,604	2,604	2,604
PALAZUELO, Pablo (1916-) Spanish				
oil	1	144,490	144,490	144,490
wc/d	1	9,414	9,414	9,414
PALAZZI, Bernardino (1907-1987) Italian				
oil	3	1,405-3,504	2,608	2,917
PALDI, Israel (1892-1979) Israeli				
oil	4	1,300-23,000	7,575	2,000
wc/d	1	2,400	2,400	2,400
PALENCIA, Benjamin (1894-1980) Spanish				
oil	8	2,040-73,080	28,965	22,723
wc/d	17	658-3,951	1,427	1,204
PALERMO, Blinky (1943-1977) German				
oil	2	140,000-700,000	420,000	140,000
PALESTINE, Charlemagne (1947-) American				
3D	1	1,815	1,815	1,815
PALEY, Albert (1944-) American				
3D	2	5,500-19,000	12,250	5,500
PALEZIEUX, Gerard (1919-) Swiss				
oil	2	3,053-7,342	5,197	3,053
wc/d	1	2,289	2,289	2,289
PALIN, William Mainwaring (1862-1947) British				
oil	5	1,104-2,024	1,558	1,531
PALIZZI, Filippo (1818-1899) Italian				
oil	5	533-12,507	5,082	5,351
wc/d	1	3,185	3,185	3,185
PALIZZI, Giuseppe (1812-1888) Italian				
oil	6	1,647-26,671	9,257	7,686
wc/d	1	1,424	1,424	1,424

Name	No.	Price Range	Average	Median
PALLADY, Theodor (1871-1956) Rumanian				
oil	1	11,181	11,181	11,181
PALLANDT, Charlotte van (1898-1997) Dutch				
3D	1	4,938	4,938	4,938
PALLARES Y ALLUSTANTE, Joaquin (1853-1935) Spanish				
oil	1	11,449	11,449	11,449
wc/d	1	5,304	5,304	5,304
PALLIERE, Armand Julien (1784-1862) French				
oil	1	29,000	29,000	29,000
PALLIK, Bela (1845-1908) Hungarian				
oil	1	1,246	1,246	1,246
PALLMANN, Gotz (1908-1966) German				
oil	3	1,987-4,253	2,910	2,492
PALLMANN, Kurt (1886-?) German				
oil	1	2,417	2,417	2,417
PALLUQ, Qaunaq (1936-) North American				
3D	1	2,531	2,531	2,531
PALM, Anna (1859-1924) Swedish				
wc/d	18	568-22,932	4,358	2,293
PALM, Gustaf Wilhelm (1810-1890) Swedish				
oil	11	2,055-82,808	17,692	8,226
wc/d	1	2,371	2,371	2,371
PALM, Olaf (1935-2000) American				
oil	9	425-3,000	1,008	650
PALM, Torsten (1875-1934) Swedish				
oil	1	1,264	1,264	1,264
PALMA, Jacopo (16/17th C) Italian				
oil	1	14,137	14,137	14,137
wc/d	1	1,649	1,649	1,649
PALMA, Jacopo (il Giovane) (1544-1628) Italian				
oil	7	30,000-180,000	84,351	59,143
wc/d	10	916-51,800	7,854	3,000
PALMA, Jacopo (il Vecchio) (1480-1528) Italian				
oil	2	18,500-380,000	199,250	18,500
PALMAI, C (1850-?) Hungarian				
oil	1	3,651	3,651	3,651
PALMAROLI Y GONZALEZ, Vicente (1834-1896) Spanish				
oil	2	6,500-32,000	19,250	6,500
PALME, Carl (1879-1960) Swedish				
oil	1	1,272	1,272	1,272
PALMEIRO, Jose (1903-1984) Spanish				
oil	22	600-3,600	1,625	1,270
wc/d	1	1,070	1,070	1,070
PALMENBERG, Emilie von (1864-1931) ?				
oil	1	1,001	1,001	1,001
PALMER (?) ?				
oil	3	1,097-1,687	1,406	1,434
3D	1	46,000	46,000	46,000
PALMER, Adelaide (1851-1938) American				
oil	2	2,700-2,750	2,725	2,700
PALMER, Clement (1857-1952) ?				
wc/d	1	1,239	1,239	1,239
PALMER, F L (19th C) American				
oil	1	10,000	10,000	10,000
PALMER, Franklin (1921-1990) Canadian				
oil	3	633-1,484	972	801
wc/d	1	309	309	309
PALMER, Harry Sutton (1854-1933) British				
oil	1	3,480	3,480	3,480
wc/d	12	453-4,375	2,001	1,602
PALMER, Herbert Sidney (1881-1970) Canadian				
oil	11	388-6,559	2,074	1,230
PALMER, James Lynwood (1868-1941) British				
oil	1	8,000	8,000	8,000
PALMER, Pauline (1867-1938) American				
oil	12	1,200-14,000	6,658	4,600
wc/d	1	1,400	1,400	1,400
PALMER, Samuel (1805-1881) British				
wc/d	6	12,090-148,800	53,605	33,480
PALMER, Simon (1956-) British				
wc/d	4	3,382-4,248	3,770	3,382

Name	No.	Price Range	Average	Median
PALMER, Sir James (1584-1657) British				
oil	1	4,498	4,498	4,498
PALMER, Walter L (1854-1932) American				
oil	5	5,500-85,000	24,800	11,000
wc/d	3	8,500-14,000	11,833	13,000
PALMEZZANO, Marco (1458-1539) Italian				
oil	2	23,356-140,000	81,678	23,356
PALMIE, Charles (1863-1911) German				
oil	3	608-12,899	6,336	5,501
PALMIERI, Giuseppe (1677-1740) Italian				
wc/d	1	2,983	2,983	2,983
PALMIERI, Pietro Giacomo (?-c.1819) Italian				
wc/d	2	1,298-2,431	1,864	1,298
PALMROOS, Elin Maria (1866-?) Finnish?				
oil	1	1,109	1,109	1,109
PALMU, Jan (1945-1995) Finnish				
oil	1	1,449	1,449	1,449
PALSA, Kalervo (1947-1987) Finnish				
wc/d	1	4,757	4,757	4,757
PALTRINIERI, Oreste (1873-?) Italian				
oil	7	838-7,910	4,252	3,830
PALTRONIERI, Pietro (1673-1741) Italian				
oil	1	30,000	30,000	30,000
PALUE, Pierre (1920-) French				
oil	1	1,700	1,700	1,700
PALUMBO, Alphonse (1890-1947) American				
oil	2	770-1,830	1,300	770
PALUMBO, Eduardo (1932-) Italian				
oil	6	1,767-3,687	2,695	2,589
PALUMBO, Michele (1874-?) Italian				
oil	2	1,267-1,267	1,267	1,267
PALYART, Jacques (19/20th C) French				
oil	1	2,442	2,442	2,442
PAMBOUJIAN, Gerard (1941-) French				
oil	3	1,157-2,442	1,806	1,820
PAMPALONI, Luigi (1791-1847) Italian				
3D	3	2,293-7,423	5,139	5,702
PAN SIMU (1756-c.1843) Chinese				
wc/d	1	1,008	1,008	1,008
PAN ZHENYONG (1852-1921) Chinese				
wc/d	1	2,336	2,336	2,336
PANABAKER, Frank S (1904-1992) Canadian				
oil	12	978-11,810	3,539	2,742
PANAMARENKO (1940-) Belgian				
wc/d	2	2,631-4,685	3,658	2,631
3D	2	8,352-19,778	14,065	8,352
PANAYOTOU, Angelos (1943-) Greek				
oil	2	18,700-40,020	29,360	18,700
PANCERA, Enrico (19/20th C) Italian				
3D	1	2,420	2,420	2,420
PANCHAL, Shanti (1951-) Indian				
wc/d	1	2,640	2,640	2,640
PANCOAST, Clara C (1873-1959) American				
oil	3	800-4,000	2,266	2,000
wc/d	2	1,200-1,500	1,350	1,200
PANCOAST, Morris Hall (1877-1963) American				
oil	4	800-1,640	1,185	1,100
PANCRAZI, Luca (1961-) Italian				
oil	1	1,111	1,111	1,111
PANDA, Jagannath (1970-) Indian				
wc/d	1	5,500	5,500	5,500
PANDURO, Henny (1863-1930) Danish				
oil	1	1,270	1,270	1,270
PANE, Gina (1939-1999) Italian				
wc/d	1	1,752	1,752	1,752
PANERAI, Ruggero (1862-1923) Italian				
oil	5	3,063-49,192	17,255	7,767
PANGNARK, John (1920-1980) North American				
3D	9	1,687-9,280	3,946	3,121
PANINI, Ferdinando (18th C) Italian				
oil	1	7,291	7,291	7,291

Name	No.	Price Range	Average	Median
PANINI, Francesco (18th C) Italian				
wc/d	1	4,200	4,200	4,200
PANINI, Giovanni Paolo (1691-1765) Italian				
oil	2	60,544-176,712	118,628	60,544
wc/d	2	12,298-38,850	25,574	12,298
PANITZSCH, Robert (1879-1949) German/Danish				
oil	3	1,216-3,127	1,871	1,272
PANKIEWICZ, Jozef (1866-1940) Polish				
oil	1	8,465	8,465	8,465
PANKOK, Otto (1893-1966) German				
wc/d	1	5,184	5,184	5,184
3D	1	4,359	4,359	4,359
PANN, Abel (1883-1963) Israeli/Latvian				
oil	3	4,579-15,000	9,693	9,500
wc/d	19	547-46,000	15,760	13,000
PANNETT, Juliet (1911-2005) British				
wc/d	17	496-2,136	1,026	890
PANOMAREVA, Natalia (1905-1942) Russian				
oil	1	4,849	4,849	4,849
PANSART, Guy (1939-) French				
oil	1	1,403	1,403	1,403
PANSART, Robert (1909-1973) French?				
oil	2	3,822-8,280	6,051	3,822
PANSERA, Malek (1940-) Italian				
oil	1	2,330	2,330	2,330
3D	1	1,937	1,937	1,937
PANSING, Fred (19th C) American				
oil	3	12,884-38,000	21,761	14,400
wc/d	1	600	600	600
PANT, Theresia van der (1924-) Dutch				
3D	1	2,572	2,572	2,572
PANTA, Egisto da (19th C) Italian				
3D	1	9,699	9,699	9,699
PANTALEON, Theodoros (1945-) Greek				
oil	2	3,520-11,968	7,744	3,520
PANTALEONI, Ideo (1904-1993) Italian				
oil	3	2,342-5,139	3,754	3,781
PANTAZIS, Pericles (1849-1884) Greek				
oil	7	26,219-113,400	53,292	43,500
PANTELAKIS, Pavlos (1914-1973) Greek				
oil	1	4,862	4,862	4,862
PANTON, Lawrence Arthur Colley (1894-1954) Canadian				
oil	7	512-5,739	2,911	1,587
wc/d	3	392-882	595	512
PANZA, Giovanni (1894-1989) Italian				
oil	6	2,945-7,644	4,784	4,841
PANZER, Hans (fl.1613-1617) German				
wc/d	1	8,905	8,905	8,905
PAOLETTI, Antonio (1834-1912) Italian				
oil	6	1,576-49,680	20,358	7,200
PAOLETTI, Paolo (1671-c.1735) Italian				
oil	1	65,740	65,740	65,740
PAOLETTI, Pietro (1801-1847) Italian				
oil	1	2,178	2,178	2,178
PAOLETTI, Rodolfo (1866-1940) Italian				
oil	3	1,211-1,816	1,473	1,393
PAOLILLO, Luigi (1864-?) Italian				
oil	3	500-5,081	2,723	2,589
PAOLINI, Giulio (1940-) Italian				
wc/d	12	3,576-156,531	34,343	10,541
3D	2	45,796-150,450	98,123	45,796
PAOLINI, Pietro (1603-1681) Italian				
oil	1	5,327	5,327	5,327
PAOLINO, Fra Paolo (1490-1547) Italian				
oil	1	25,000	25,000	25,000
PAOLOZZI, Eduardo (1924-2005) British				
wc/d	7	546-14,320	3,219	1,366
3D	22	1,453-75,600	18,986	15,725
PAOLUCCI, Flavio (1934-) Swiss				
wc/d	2	1,785-1,947	1,866	1,785
PAP, Emil (1884-?) Hungarian				
oil	2	2,800-3,781	3,290	2,800

Name	No.	Price Range	Average	Median
PAP, Gyala (1899-1984) Hungarian				
wc/d	2	1,058-5,878	3,468	1,058
PAPADIA, Daniela (1963-) Italian				
oil	1	1,757	1,757	1,757
PAPALOUCAS, Spyros (1892-1957) Greek				
oil	6	5,882-89,760	46,826	31,320
PAPALUCA, L (20th C) Italian				
wc/d	2	3,211-8,976	6,093	3,211
PAPALUCA, Louis (1890-1934) Italian				
oil	4	400-600	500	500
wc/d	2	950-3,306	2,128	950
PAPANAGIOTOU, Stavros (1885-1955) Greek				
oil	1	4,576	4,576	4,576
PAPANELOPOULOS, Yiannis (1936-) Greek				
oil	4	2,992-5,984	4,303	3,740
PAPANICOLAOU, Spyros (1906-1986) Greek				
oil	2	2,288-4,928	3,608	2,288
PAPART, Max (1911-1994) French				
oil	26	494-17,000	4,517	4,190
wc/d	12	526-2,843	1,619	1,294
PAPASAVVAS, Stavros (1928-) Greek				
oil	2	1,200-4,071	2,635	1,200
wc/d	1	4,071	4,071	4,071
PAPAZOFF, Georges (1894-1972) Bulgarian				
oil	7	6,969-25,976	10,345	7,416
wc/d	1	1,521	1,521	1,521
PAPE, Abraham de (1620-1666) Dutch				
oil	1	20,760	20,760	20,760
PAPE, Eduard (1817-1905) German				
oil	2	2,145-3,155	2,650	2,145
PAPE, Eric (1870-1938) American				
wc/d	1	1,500	1,500	1,500
PAPE, Frank Cheyne (1878-1972) American				
wc/d	1	15,725	15,725	15,725
PAPE, Friedrich Eduard (1817-1905) German				
oil	1	1,640	1,640	1,640
PAPENDRECHT, Jan Hoynck van (1858-1933) Dutch				
oil	1	12,390	12,390	12,390
wc/d	1	3,099	3,099	3,099
PAPESCH, Paul (19/20th C) German?				
wc/d	2	1,139-1,139	1,139	1,139
PAPETTI, Alessandro (1958-) Italian				
oil	9	4,162-11,405	6,736	6,592
PAPIKYAN, Albert (1926-) Russian				
oil	2	1,907-1,929	1,918	1,907
PAPPERITZ, Fritz Georg (1846-1918) German				
oil	3	869-3,507	2,426	2,903
PAQUIN, Pauline (1952-) Canadian				
oil	8	529-3,191	1,322	973
PARACHINI, Achille (1888-1970) Italian				
oil	1	1,176	1,176	1,176
PARADIES, Herman Cornelis Adolf (1883-1966) Dutch				
oil	2	2,170-2,877	2,523	2,170
wc/d	1	3,514	3,514	3,514
PARADISE, Philip Herschel (1905-1997) American				
wc/d	3	5,500-32,500	15,000	7,000
PARANT, Jean Luc (1943-) French				
wc/d	5	903-1,790	1,368	1,230
PARANT, Titi (1947-) French				
wc/d	1	1,236	1,236	1,236
PARAVANO, Dino (1935-) South African				
wc/d	1	1,229	1,229	1,229
PARC, Julio le (1928-) Argentinian				
oil	8	2,827-38,000	11,150	7,184
wc/d	3	850-1,909	1,214	884
3D	1	37,500	37,500	37,500
PARCELL, Malcolm S (1896-1987) American				
oil	1	2,000	2,000	2,000
PARDI, Gian Franco (1933-) Italian				
oil	3	3,279-5,605	4,445	4,451
wc/d	1	860	860	860

Name	No.	Price Range	Average	Median
PARDO, Jorge (1963-) German				
oil	1	5,500	5,500	5,500
wc/d	3	2,464-11,000	7,438	8,850
PARDON, James (fl.1800-1850) British				
oil	1	5,180	5,180	5,180
PAREDES, Vicente Garcia de (1845-1903) Spanish				
oil	2	5,504-15,660	10,582	5,504
wc/d	1	1,688	1,688	1,688
PAREDIS, Gustave (1897-1963) Belgian				
oil	2	486-1,940	1,213	486
PAREJA, Miguel Angel (1908-1984) Uruguayan				
oil	1	1,100	1,100	1,100
PAREKH, Manu (1942-) Indian				
oil	5	5,000-14,000	8,471	5,360
wc/d	1	9,500	9,500	9,500
PARENT, Claude (1923-) French				
wc/d	2	1,325-1,565	1,445	1,325
PARENT, J (19th C) French				
wc/d	1	1,321	1,321	1,321
PARENT, Léon (1869-?) French				
oil	1	4,757	4,757	4,757
PARENT, Mimi (1925-2005) Canadian				
oil	1	4,629	4,629	4,629
3D	2	4,055-8,905	6,480	4,055
PARENT, Roger (1881-1963) French				
oil	2	584-927	755	584
wc/d	1	927	927	927
PARENTANI, Antonino (16/17th C) Italian				
wc/d	1	1,295	1,295	1,295
PARENTE, G (19th C) Italian				
3D	1	1,929	1,929	1,929
PARESCE, Renato (1886-1937) Italian				
oil	4	29,259-44,524	36,891	30,531
wc/d	5	468-1,757	1,300	1,464
PARESSANT, Jules (?) French				
oil	1	2,587	2,587	2,587
PARIN, Gino (1876-1944) Italian				
oil	3	722-15,429	6,883	4,500
PARIS, Camille Adrien (1834-1901) French				
oil	1	1,176	1,176	1,176
PARIS, Enrico T de (1960-) Italian				
oil	1	4,876	4,876	4,876
PARIS, Harold (1925-1979) American				
wc/d	1	800	800	800
3D	1	3,500	3,500	3,500
PARIS, Maurice (1903-1969) French				
oil	1	1,210	1,210	1,210
PARIS, René (1881-1970) French				
3D	1	1,940	1,940	1,940
PARIS, Roland (1894-?) French				
3D	4	1,718-3,527	2,362	1,868
PARIS, Walter (1842-1906) American/British				
wc/d	3	1,100-1,600	1,400	1,500
PARISI, Francisco Paolo (1857-1948) Italian				
oil	2	6,160-38,000	22,080	6,160
PARISOD, Charles (20th C) Swiss				
oil	1	1,249	1,249	1,249
PARISON, Gaston (1889-?) French				
oil	2	718-6,473	3,595	718
PARISOT, Adriano (1912-) Italian				
oil	2	1,553-3,770	2,661	1,553
wc/d	1	1,295	1,295	1,295
PARK JAI YOUG (1957-) Korean				
oil	1	3,857	3,857	3,857
PARK SUNG-TAE (1960-) Korean				
3D	1	19,000	19,000	19,000
PARK, David (1911-1960) American				
oil	1	820,000	820,000	820,000
wc/d	2	11,000-14,000	12,500	11,000
PARK, John Anthony (1880-1962) British				
oil	20	528-19,030	3,947	2,775

Name	No.	Price Range	Average	Median
PARK, Stuart (1862-1933) British				
oil	27	865-16,856	4,648	3,000
PARKE, Jessie Burns (1889-?) American				
oil	1	1,200	1,200	1,200
PARKER, Agnes Miller (1895-?) British				
oil	1	41,170	41,170	41,170
PARKER, Charles S (1860-1930) American				
oil	1	1,740	1,740	1,740
PARKER, Cornelia (1956-) British?				
wc/d	1	4,800	4,800	4,800
PARKER, Daniel (20th C) American				
3D	1	6,000	6,000	6,000
PARKER, Erik (1968-) American				
oil	3	14,000-35,000	25,000	26,000
wc/d	1	8,000	8,000	8,000
3D	1	6,500	6,500	6,500
PARKER, Henry H (1858-1930) British				
oil	13	1,840-26,460	6,625	3,128
wc/d	3	740-1,890	1,315	1,317
PARKER, Henry Perlee (1795-1873) British				
oil	3	3,460-8,004	5,372	4,654
PARKER, Lawton S (1868-1954) American				
oil	2	450-2,500	1,475	450
PARKER, Ray (1922-1990) American				
oil	3	1,800-6,000	3,350	2,250
PARKER, Richard Henry (1881-1930) British				
oil	1	6,813	6,813	6,813
PARKER, Robert Andrew (1927-) American				
wc/d	2	506-4,250	2,378	506
PARKES, Michael (1944-) American				
oil	4	6,370-15,315	12,784	14,137
PARKMAN, Alfred Edward (1852-?) British				
wc/d	1	1,044	1,044	1,044
PARKS, Bob (1948-) American				
3D	1	2,250	2,250	2,250
PARLEVLIET, Hans (1953-) Dutch				
oil	1	8,247	8,247	8,247
PARLOW, Robert (?) ?				
oil	1	1,260	1,260	1,260
PARLOW, Roland (20th C) German				
oil	1	3,974	3,974	3,974
PARMEGGIANI, Romano (1931-) Italian				
oil	2	1,208-3,588	2,398	1,208
PARMENTIER, Felix (1821-?) French				
oil	1	1,416	1,416	1,416
PARMENTIER, Jacques (1658-1730) French				
oil	1	2,618	2,618	2,618
PARMENTIER, Michel (1938-2000) French				
oil	1	43,347	43,347	43,347
PARMENTIER, Pol (20th C) Belgian				
oil	1	1,753	1,753	1,753
PARMIGGIANI, Claudio (1943-) Italian				
wc/d	4	2,293-42,143	12,446	2,548
3D	4	2,342-57,796	34,299	31,306
PAROLARI, Bruno (?) Italian				
oil	1	1,091	1,091	1,091
PAROUBEC, Jana (1940-1987) Czechoslovakian				
3D	1	4,477	4,477	4,477
PARPAGNOLI, Gaetano (?) ?				
oil	1	1,100	1,100	1,100
PARPAN, Ferdinand (1902-) French				
3D	58	1,790-27,500	4,618	2,625
PARR (1893-1969) North American				
wc/d	1	4,555	4,555	4,555
PARR, James Wingate (20th C) American				
oil	1	800	800	800
wc/d	1	550	550	550
PARR, Nuna (1949-) North American				
3D	2	4,640-7,090	5,865	4,640
PARRA, Gines (1895-1960) Spanish				
oil	5	1,447-5,959	4,182	4,500

Name	No.	Price Range	Average	Median
PARRENS, Louis (1904-) French				
oil	2	1,052-1,461	1,256	1,052
PARRINO, Steven (1958-) American				
oil	1	15,000	15,000	15,000
PARRIS, Edmond Thomas (1793-1873) British				
wc/d	2	700-1,313	1,006	700
PARRISH, M (20th C) American				
oil	1	8,000	8,000	8,000
PARRISH, Maxfield (1870-1966) American				
oil	6	2,000-6,800,000	1,901,166	115,000
PARRISH, Stephen (1846-1938) American				
oil	2	1,000-1,200	1,100	1,000
wc/d	2	650-750	700	650
PARROCEL, Charles (1688-1752) French				
oil	1	19,622	19,622	19,622
wc/d	2	1,823-2,500	2,161	1,823
PARROCEL, Joseph (1646-1704) French				
oil	3	10,536-35,042	20,233	15,123
PARROCEL, Joseph François (1704-1781) French				
wc/d	3	595-1,665	1,037	851
PARROT, William Samuel (1844-1915) American				
oil	3	3,000-9,500	5,500	4,000
PARROT-LECOMTE, Philippe (19th C) French				
oil	1	110,000	110,000	110,000
PARROTT, William (1813-1869) British				
oil	4	4,500-59,850	24,910	5,292
PARROW, Karin (1900-1986) Swedish				
oil	1	1,035	1,035	1,035
PARSHALL, Dewitt (1864-1956) American				
oil	1	1,600	1,600	1,600
PARSHALL, Douglas (1899-1990) American				
oil	3	2,250-42,000	16,583	5,500
wc/d	1	600	600	600
PARSONS, Alfred William (1847-1920) British				
oil	4	1,232-6,992	3,575	2,790
wc/d	3	435-3,186	1,407	600
PARSONS, Arthur Wilde (1854-1931) British				
oil	8	558-2,160	1,147	1,023
wc/d	9	460-2,013	1,098	1,151
PARSONS, Beatrice (1870-1955) British				
wc/d	9	516-12,648	3,288	2,275
PARSONS, Charles (1821-1910) American				
wc/d	1	12,000	12,000	12,000
PARSONS, Edith Baretto (1878-1956) American				
3D	1	25,000	25,000	25,000
PARSONS, Leon (20th C) American				
oil	1	2,000	2,000	2,000
PARSONS, Orrin Sheldon (1866-1943) American				
oil	2	7,500-35,000	21,250	7,500
PARSONS, Sheldon (?) American?				
oil	4	5,500-22,000	13,250	6,500
PARTENHEIMER, Jurgen (1947-) German				
wc/d	4	1,296-2,121	1,826	1,767
PARTHAN, Baiju (1956-) Indian				
oil	2	11,000-17,000	14,000	11,000
PARTHENIS, Constantine (1878-1967) Greek				
oil	3	24,640-400,200	156,573	44,880
wc/d	1	1,384	1,384	1,384
PARTIGLIONE, S (19th C) Italian				
oil	1	5,916	5,916	5,916
PARTIKEL, Alfred (1888-1946) German				
oil	1	3,312	3,312	3,312
wc/d	1	727	727	727
PARTINGTON, Richard Langtry (1868-1929) American/British				
oil	2	1,800-3,500	2,650	1,800
PARTON, Arthur (1842-1914) American				
oil	4	2,900-8,000	5,600	5,500
PARTON, Ernest (1845-1933) British				
oil	9	1,300-10,500	3,746	2,600
wc/d	1	900	900	900
PARTON, Henry Woodbridge (1858-1933) American				
oil	1	1,400	1,400	1,400

Name	No.	Price Range	Average	Median
PARTRIDGE, Alfred (19th C) British				
oil	2	783-1,700	1,241	783
PARTRIDGE, Bernard (1861-1945) British				
wc/d	1	1,557	1,557	1,557
PARVEZ, Ahmed (1926-1979) Indian				
oil	2	2,640-3,520	3,080	2,640
PARYS, Ad (19th C) French				
wc/d	2	2,928-3,737	3,332	2,928
PARYS, H S (19/20th C) French				
wc/d	1	3,504	3,504	3,504
PAS, Wilfried (1940-) Belgian				
3D	1	2,744	2,744	2,744
PASCAL, A (19th C) ?				
wc/d	1	2,910	2,910	2,910
PASCAL, Antoine (1803-1859) French				
oil	1	6,500	6,500	6,500
PASCAL, Paul (1832-1903) French				
wc/d	12	742-3,341	1,688	1,378
PASCALE, Ricardo (1942-) Uruguayan				
3D	1	17,000	17,000	17,000
PASCALI, Pino (1935-1968) Italian				
oil	1	8,199	8,199	8,199
wc/d	21	1,219-12,884	4,753	3,884
3D	2	842,857-2,124,000	1,483,428	842,857
PASCH, Lorens (elder) (1702-1776) Swedish				
oil	1	1,245	1,245	1,245
PASCH, Lorens (younger) (1733-1805) Swedish				
oil	2	2,061-15,580	8,820	2,061
PASCH, Ulrika (1735-1796) Swedish				
oil	1	45,332	45,332	45,332
PASCHETTA, Mario (1949-) Italian				
oil	20	488-1,551	866	884
wc/d	1	471	471	471
PASCHKE, Ed (1939-2004) American				
oil	1	8,000	8,000	8,000
PASCIN, Jules (1885-1930) American/Bulgarian				
oil	14	15,000-150,000	50,856	45,796
wc/d	55	400-32,179	2,185	1,200
PASCIUTI, Antonio (1937-) Italian				
oil	6	1,178-2,950	1,918	1,229
PASCU, Nelu (20th C) Rumanian				
oil	1	2,040	2,040	2,040
PASCUA CAMARA, Lorenzo (1937-) Spanish				
oil	1	2,160	2,160	2,160
PASCUAL I SAMARANCH, Josep Luis (1947-) Spanish				
3D	2	2,141-3,588	2,864	2,141
PASCUAL RODES, Ivo (1883-1949) Spanish				
oil	1	2,411	2,411	2,411
PASCUAL TEJERINA, Sebastian (?) Spanish				
oil	1	1,073	1,073	1,073
PASETTI, O (?) ?				
oil	1	2,177	2,177	2,177
PASINELLI, Lorenzo (1629-1700) Italian				
oil	1	14,597	14,597	14,597
PASINI, Alberto (1826-1899) Italian				
oil	9	1,823-143,520	46,889	40,775
wc/d	5	3,287-27,600	11,482	6,000
PASINI, Lazzaro (1861-1949) Italian				
oil	4	600-2,068	1,385	962
PASINI, Ludwig (1832-1903) Austrian				
wc/d	3	975-3,520	1,942	1,331
PASKELL, William (1866-1951) American				
oil	2	450-800	625	450
wc/d	1	400	400	400
PASMORE, Frederick George (jnr) (fl.1875-1884) British				
oil	2	1,416-2,200	1,808	1,416
PASMORE, John (fl.1830-1845) British				
oil	1	3,569	3,569	3,569
PASMORE, John F (1820-1871) British				
oil	3	2,616-4,425	3,573	3,680

Name	No.	Price Range	Average	Median
PASMORE, Victor (1908-1998) British				
oil	14	1,874-48,440	23,445	22,620
wc/d	4	2,394-18,500	8,892	3,366
3D	2	39,690-76,560	58,125	39,690
PASQUA, Philippe (1965-) French				
oil	3	1,790-11,125	6,247	5,826
wc/d	6	1,401-8,175	3,756	2,338
PASQUAROSA (1896-1973) Italian				
oil	1	3,142	3,142	3,142
PASSAGE, Comte Arthur Marie Gabriel du (1838-1909) French				
3D	2	6,500-7,400	6,950	6,500
PASSANI, Pierre (20th C) French?				
oil	1	2,919	2,919	2,919
PASSAROTTI, Bartolomeo (1529-1592) Italian				
oil	1	21,162	21,162	21,162
wc/d	3	3,471-8,325	5,319	4,162
PASSERI, Giuseppe (1654-1714) Italian				
oil	2	23,759-35,000	29,379	23,759
wc/d	5	773-48,100	17,274	13,000
PASSEY, Charles H (fl.1870-1885) British				
oil	3	1,281-1,305	1,291	1,288
PASSIGLI, Carlo (1881-1953) Italian				
oil	3	960-5,178	2,490	1,332
PASTEGA, Luigi (1858-1927) Italian				
oil	5	2,917-51,101	23,861	25,800
wc/d	1	5,096	5,096	5,096
PASTERNAK, Leonid Ossipowitsch (1862-1945) Russian				
oil	2	146,200-322,437	234,318	146,200
wc/d	1	59,527	59,527	59,527
PASTINA, Giuseppe (1863-1942) Italian				
oil	2	11,003-12,298	11,650	11,003
PASTOR CALPENA, Vicente (1918-1993) Spanish				
wc/d	2	904-1,607	1,255	904
PASTOR, Conrad (19th C) ?				
oil	1	1,585	1,585	1,585
PASTORE, Angelo (19th C) Italian				
oil	1	1,058	1,058	1,058
PASTORIO, Ezio (1911-) Italian				
oil	6	589-2,431	1,635	1,951
PASTOUKHOFF, Boris (1894-1974) Russian				
oil	9	524-3,567	1,485	1,176
PASTOUR, Louis (1876-1948) French				
oil	4	1,109-1,347	1,259	1,236
PASZKIEWISZ, Marjan (20th C) Polish				
oil	1	1,694	1,694	1,694
PAT, Andrea (1942-) ?				
wc/d	1	2,201	2,201	2,201
PATA, Cherubino (1827-1899) French				
oil	4	6,500-38,015	16,134	6,688
PATAKY VON SOSPATAK, Laszlo (1857-1912) Hungarian				
oil	1	7,068	7,068	7,068
PATCH, J V D (19/20th C) American				
oil	1	2,500	2,500	2,500
PATCH, Thomas (1720-1782) British				
oil	2	302,400-327,945	315,172	302,400
PATEL, Antoine Pierre (younger) (1648-1707) French				
oil	2	37,380-39,838	38,609	37,380
wc/d	1	3,507	3,507	3,507
PATEL, Gieve (1940-) Indian				
oil	1	26,000	26,000	26,000
PATEL, Homi B (1928-2004) Indian				
oil	1	10,000	10,000	10,000
PATEL, Pierre (elder) (1605-1676) French				
oil	2	30,837-164,350	97,593	30,837
PATELLA, Luca (1934-) Italian				
oil	1	1,272	1,272	1,272
wc/d	1	1,208	1,208	1,208
PATELLIERE, Amedee de la (1890-1932) French				
oil	4	608-2,589	1,815	1,646
wc/d	2	547-764	655	547

Name	No.	Price Range	Average	Median
PATER, Jean Baptiste (1695-1736) French				
oil	4	29,131-279,730	136,900	109,241
wc/d	2	1,215-11,090	6,152	1,215
PATERNOSTO, Cesar (1931-) Argentinian				
oil	1	16,000	16,000	16,000
PATERNOTTE, M (20th C) ?				
oil	1	4,214	4,214	4,214
PATERSON, Caroline (1856-1911) British				
wc/d	2	10,440-16,740	13,590	10,440
PATERSON, James (1854-1932) British				
oil	7	885-8,950	4,286	4,176
wc/d	12	1,044-6,265	3,322	2,610
PATERSON, Mary Viola (1899-1982) British				
oil	1	1,392	1,392	1,392
PATERSON, Viola (1899-1981) British				
oil	2	619-2,208	1,413	619
PATERSSON, Benjamin (c.1748-1815) Swedish				
oil	1	94,600	94,600	94,600
PATINI, Teofilo (1840-1906) Italian				
oil	2	7,773-111,329	59,551	7,773
PATINO, Anton (1957-) Spanish				
oil	1	4,895	4,895	4,895
PATKIN, Itzar (1955-) American				
oil	3	500-2,500	1,500	1,500
PATKO, Karoly (1895-1941) Hungarian				
wc/d	2	842-3,540	2,191	842
PATON, Hubert (19/20th C) British?				
oil	1	4,675	4,675	4,675
PATON, Sir Joseph Noel (1821-1901) British				
oil	3	1,748-14,160	8,547	9,735
wc/d	2	555-865	710	555
PATON, Waller Hugh (1828-1895) British				
oil	1	2,494	2,494	2,494
wc/d	17	452-4,928	2,065	1,190
PATOUX, Émile (1893-1985) Belgian				
oil	3	526-1,940	1,424	1,806
PATRIARCA, Amato (1945-) Italian				
oil	3	610-2,306	1,608	1,909
PATRICALAKIS, Faidon (1935-) Greek				
oil	1	3,872	3,872	3,872
PATRICK, Emily (?) British?				
oil	1	3,306	3,306	3,306
PATRICK, James McIntosh (1907-1998) British				
oil	9	5,916-28,480	19,934	21,360
wc/d	8	1,204-7,434	3,571	2,697
PATRISSE, Albert (1892-?) French				
3D	1	1,901	1,901	1,901
PATROGOS, Pan (20th C) Greek				
oil	1	5,486	5,486	5,486
PATROIS, Isidore (1815-1884) French				
oil	1	1,897	1,897	1,897
PATRU, Émile (1877-1940) Swiss				
oil	2	1,370-1,370	1,370	1,370
PATRY, Edward (1856-1940) British				
oil	1	5,236	5,236	5,236
PATTEIN, Cesar (1850-1931) French				
oil	1	10,000	10,000	10,000
PATTEN, Alfred Fowler (1829-1888) British				
oil	3	613-49,140	27,924	34,020
PATTEN, William (jnr) (?-1843) British				
oil	1	2,548	2,548	2,548
PATTERSON, Ben (1934-) American?				
wc/d	1	1,196	1,196	1,196
PATTERSON, Charles Robert (1878-?) American				
oil	3	750-5,000	2,250	1,000
PATTERSON, F (?) ?				
wc/d	1	2,219	2,219	2,219
PATTERSON, Margaret Jordan (1867-1950) American				
oil	1	2,384	2,384	2,384
wc/d	1	1,700	1,700	1,700
PATTERSON, Neil (1947-) Canadian				
oil	3	1,155-2,250	1,729	1,783

Name	No.	Price Range	Average	Median
PATTI, Stefano (20th C) ?				
3D	1	10,092	10,092	10,092
PATTISON, Robert J (1838-1903) American				
wc/d	1	2,000	2,000	2,000
PATTISON, Thomas William (1894-1983) British				
wc/d	1	1,038	1,038	1,038
PATTON, Eric (1925-2004) Irish				
oil	3	877-1,674	1,168	954
PATTON, John (20th C) Irish				
wc/d	1	1,403	1,403	1,403
PATURSSON, Trondur (20th C) Danish				
oil	1	1,132	1,132	1,132
PATWARDHAN, Sudhir (1949-) Indian				
wc/d	1	7,106	7,106	7,106
PATZELT, Andreas (1896-1980) Austrian				
oil	3	545-2,022	1,171	947
PAU DE SAINT MARTIN, Alexandre (18th C) French				
oil	1	16,280	16,280	16,280
PAU DE SAINT MARTIN, Pierre Alexandre (18/19th C) French				
oil	1	3,480	3,480	3,480
PAUDISS, Christoph (1618-1666) German				
oil	1	28,898	28,898	28,898
PAUL, John (19th C) British				
oil	2	1,566-5,985	3,775	1,566
PAUL, Joseph (1804-1887) British				
oil	4	1,211-2,301	1,707	1,548
PAUL, Maurice (1889-1965) Dutch				
oil	1	3,151	3,151	3,151
PAUL, P (1977-) American				
wc/d	1	5,500	5,500	5,500
PAULET, Constantin (1917-) Rumanian				
oil	1	3,766	3,766	3,766
PAULI, Georg (1855-1935) Swedish				
oil	12	696-24,928	4,598	1,803
wc/d	4	440-2,198	1,709	2,036
PAULI, Hanna (1864-1940) Swedish				
oil	6	893-3,614	2,318	1,923
wc/d	1	1,030	1,030	1,030
PAULIN, Paul (19/20th C) French				
3D	1	66,150	66,150	66,150
PAULMAN, Joseph (19th C) British				
oil	4	1,300-1,800	1,447	1,300
PAULSEN, Ingwer (1883-1943) German				
oil	1	1,150	1,150	1,150
PAULSEN, Julius (1860-1940) Danish				
oil	27	507-9,463	2,172	1,410
PAULUCCI, Enrico (1901-1999) Italian				
oil	33	1,034-14,630	5,599	4,772
wc/d	20	492-2,299	1,133	860
PAULUS, Leonhard (?) ?				
oil	2	1,084-4,234	2,659	1,084
PAULUS, Paul (1915-) German				
oil	9	1,432-2,863	1,909	1,790
PAULUS, Pierre (1881-1959) Belgian				
oil	6	1,295-21,551	9,315	6,615
PAULY, Erich Bogdanffy (1869-1918) German				
oil	2	1,144-5,952	3,548	1,144
PAUS, Herbert Andrew (1880-1946) American				
wc/d	1	5,500	5,500	5,500
PAUSER, Sergius (1896-1970) Austrian				
oil	1	19,421	19,421	19,421
wc/d	4	1,405-15,288	5,203	1,543
PAUSINGER, Franz von (1839-1915) German				
oil	4	820-9,667	4,400	2,900
wc/d	2	688-725	706	688
PAUTEX, Louis (1841-1916) Swiss				
oil	1	2,517	2,517	2,517
PAUVERT, Odette Marie (1903-1966) French				
oil	2	2,718-10,356	6,537	2,718
PAUW, J J (19th C) ?				
wc/d	1	5,537	5,537	5,537

Name	No.	Price Range	Average	Median
PAUW, Jef de (1888-1930) Belgian				
oil	5	760-5,753	2,187	1,212
PAUWELS, Henri Jules (1903-1987) Belgian				
oil	2	1,305-1,914	1,609	1,305
PAVAN, Angelo (1893-1945) Italian				
oil	11	1,821-20,712	5,045	3,152
PAVELIC, Myfanwy Spencer (1916-) Canadian				
oil	1	671	671	671
wc/d	1	7,422	7,422	7,422
PAVIL, Elie Anatole (1873-1948) French				
oil	14	608-35,000	8,157	4,676
wc/d	1	1,008	1,008	1,008
PAVILLON, Isidore Pean du (1790-1856) French				
oil	1	62,640	62,640	62,640
PAVLIKEVICH, J (19/20th C) Russian				
wc/d	1	2,046	2,046	2,046
PAVLISHAK, Josif Andreevich (1923-) Russian				
oil	1	1,903	1,903	1,903
PAVLOPOULOS, Tasos (1955-) Greek				
oil	1	8,976	8,976	8,976
PAVLOS (1930-) Greek				
oil	1	16,065	16,065	16,065
wc/d	9	4,203-27,840	13,738	13,090
3D	6	7,890-36,122	16,340	13,377
PAVLOVSKY, Vladmir (1884-1944) American				
oil	2	850-2,500	1,675	850
wc/d	1	1,100	1,100	1,100
PAVLOWSKY, Jacqueline (20th C) Russian				
oil	1	1,788	1,788	1,788
PAVONI, Y (20th C) Italian				
oil	1	2,000	2,000	2,000
PAVY, Eugène (19th C) French				
oil	2	1,674-3,780	2,727	1,674
PAVY, Philippe (1860-?) French				
oil	1	1,611	1,611	1,611
PAWLOWSKI, Jan (20th C) American				
oil	1	1,218	1,218	1,218
PAXSON, Edgar S (1852-1919) American				
oil	2	19,000-32,500	25,750	19,000
wc/d	8	1,700-15,000	7,337	7,500
PAXTON, William McGregor (1869-1941) American				
oil	4	900-65,000	29,225	8,500
PAYE, Richard Morton (?-1821) British				
oil	1	4,446	4,446	4,446
PAYNE, Charles Johnson (1884-1967) British				
oil	1	2,340	2,340	2,340
wc/d	14	539-23,000	4,116	1,392
PAYNE, David (19th C) British				
oil	2	2,992-3,374	3,183	2,992
PAYNE, Edgar (1882-1947) American				
oil	49	1,080-280,000	53,491	27,000
PAYNE, William (1760-1830) British				
oil	1	550	550	550
wc/d	12	418-6,048	1,853	1,050
PAYRO, Anita (1897-1980) Argentinian				
oil	1	2,500	2,500	2,500
PAYZANT, Charles (1898-1980) American/Canadian				
wc/d	3	3,000-4,250	3,750	4,000
PAZ JIMENEZ, Maria (1909-1975) Spanish				
oil	1	2,486	2,486	2,486
PAZERO, Stefano (fl.1661-1665) Italian				
oil	1	3,330	3,330	3,330
PAZOTTI (19/20th C) ?				
oil	2	5,092-5,980	5,536	5,092
PAZZINI, Romeo (1852-1942) Italian				
3D	1	3,025	3,025	3,025
PEACOCK, Ralph (1868-1946) British				
oil	1	7,920	7,920	7,920
PEAK, Bob (1928-1992) American				
oil	1	3,500	3,500	3,500
PEAKE, Mervyn (1911-1968) British				
wc/d	6	1,770-3,894	2,334	1,947

Name	No.	Price Range	Average	Median
PEALE, Charles Willson (1741-1827) American				
oil	4	4,000-19,000,000	4,759,250	16,000
PEALE, James (elder) (1749-1831) American				
oil	4	2,200-460,000	130,425	22,000
PEALE, Rembrandt (1778-1860) American				
oil	8	1,600-150,000	43,293	10,000
PEALE, Sarah Miriam (1800-1885) American				
oil	2	3,000-7,000	5,000	3,000
PEALE, Titian Ramsay (1799-1885) American				
oil	2	20,000-25,000	22,500	20,000
PEAN, René (1875-1956) French				
wc/d	1	1,100	1,100	1,100
PEARCE, Bryan (1929-) British				
oil	9	7,920-22,880	11,680	10,788
wc/d	4	1,068-3,330	2,467	2,478
PEARCE, Charles Sprague (1851-1914) American				
oil	4	605-5,774	3,896	3,640
PEARCE, Leonard John (1932-) British				
oil	2	3,800-4,500	4,150	3,800
PEARCE, Stephen (1819-1904) British				
wc/d	1	18,522	18,522	18,522
PEARCE, William Houghton Sprague (1864-1935) American				
oil	3	1,100-1,600	1,333	1,300
PEARLMAN, Burnam (20th C) American				
oil	1	2,250	2,250	2,250
PEARLSTEIN, Philip (1924-) American				
oil	2	25,000-150,000	87,500	25,000
wc/d	5	2,000-12,000	4,280	2,200
PEARS, Charles (1873-1958) British				
oil	8	748-11,960	4,298	2,784
wc/d	1	522	522	522
PEARS, Dion (20th C) British?				
oil	1	2,024	2,024	2,024
PEARSON, Cornelius and WAINEWRIGHT, Thomas Francis (19th C) British				
wc/d	1	1,320	1,320	1,320
PEARSON, John (19th C) British				
oil	1	1,800	1,800	1,800
PEARSON, Marguerite S (1898-1978) American				
oil	6	600-9,500	3,946	1,230
PEARSON, Peter (20th C) Irish				
oil	1	4,355	4,355	4,355
PEASE, Alonzo (1820-1881) ?				
oil	1	16,000	16,000	16,000
PEASE, Ray (1908-) American				
oil	5	450-1,400	750	550
wc/d	1	1,100	1,100	1,100
PECHAUBES, Eugène (1890-1967) French				
oil	11	835-3,870	1,587	1,281
wc/d	1	1,004	1,004	1,004
PECHEUX, Laurent (1729-1821) French				
oil	1	31,597	31,597	31,597
PECHSTEIN, Max (1881-1955) German				
oil	18	2,472-849,600	172,824	100,000
wc/d	25	1,523-53,877	15,430	12,959
PECK, Sheldon (1797-1868) American				
oil	1	35,000	35,000	35,000
PECORARO, Antonio (1938-) Spanish				
oil	2	1,013-2,119	1,566	1,013
PECRUS, C (1826-1907) French				
oil	1	4,375	4,375	4,375
PECRUS, Charles (1826-1907) French				
oil	4	2,455-6,379	4,043	2,479
PECZELY, Anton (1891-?) Hungarian				
oil	4	550-2,700	1,368	825
wc/d	1	647	647	647
PEDDER, John (1850-1929) British				
wc/d	1	2,832	2,832	2,832
PEDERSEN, Carl-Henning (1913-1993) Danish				
oil	15	13,967-193,154	42,827	32,192
wc/d	4	1,859-5,819	3,177	2,121
PEDERSEN, Finn (1944-) Danish				
oil	11	837-4,834	1,949	1,610

Name	No.	Price Range	Average	Median
PEDERSEN, Hugo Vilfred (1870-1959) Danish				
oil	10	425-8,088	2,476	1,620
PEDERSEN, Viggo (1854-1926) Danish				
oil	22	489-23,000	3,937	1,304
PEDERSEN, Vilhelm (1820-1859) Danish				
oil	1	5,824	5,824	5,824
PEDON, Bartolomeo (1665-1732) Italian				
oil	1	18,000	18,000	18,000
PEDRETTI, Antonio (1950-) Italian				
oil	6	1,295-3,579	2,514	2,356
wc/d	2	1,812-2,438	2,125	1,812
PEDRETTI, Turo (1896-1964) Swiss				
oil	5	5,327-13,699	7,762	6,088
wc/d	6	908-4,947	2,436	1,827
PEDRIELLE, Charles (19th C) ?				
oil	1	13,305	13,305	13,305
PEDRINI, Domenico (1728-1800) Italian				
wc/d	1	2,330	2,330	2,330
PEDRONO, Alain (1951-) French				
	1	3,086	3,086	3,086
PEEL, James (1811-1906) British				
oil	5	748-2,422	1,430	1,098
PEEL, Paul (1861-1892) Canadian				
oil	6	3,772-141,801	33,435	9,839
PEELE, John Thomas (1822-1897) British				
oil	2	2,200-6,000	4,100	2,200
PEETERS, Bonaventura (17th C) Flemish				
oil	2	10,380-31,140	20,760	10,380
PEETERS, Bonaventura I (1614-1652) Flemish				
oil	6	3,260-12,000	8,968	9,250
PEETERS, Henk (1925-) Dutch				
oil	1	8,269	8,269	8,269
wc/d	4	1,753-7,633	4,307	1,987
PEETERS, Jacob (17/18th C) Flemish				
oil	1	3,129	3,129	3,129
PEETERS, Jan (1624-1680) Flemish				
oil	2	10,192-40,767	25,479	10,192
PEGOT-OGIER, Jean Bertrand (1877-1915) French				
oil	8	2,922-12,262	5,608	4,417
wc/d	5	505-1,514	797	643
PEGRUM, E F (?) ?				
oil	1	1,388	1,388	1,388
PEGURIER, Auguste (1856-1936) French				
oil	12	500-7,730	2,861	1,565
wc/d	5	485-1,593	1,099	1,082
PEHRSON, Karl Axel (1921-) Swedish				
oil	11	777-13,614	4,511	3,054
3D	1	4,835	4,835	4,835
PEICHL, Gustav (20th C) Austrian				
wc/d	2	705-1,753	1,229	705
PEIFFER, Auguste Joseph (1832-c.1879) French				
3D	1	2,351	2,351	2,351
PEIFFER-WATENPHUL, Max (1896-1976) German				
oil	3	9,730-29,301	20,864	23,562
wc/d	6	1,942-12,370	5,478	3,770
PEINADO, Francisco (1941-) Spanish				
oil	2	2,903-5,347	4,125	2,903
wc/d	1	1,546	1,546	1,546
PEINADO, Joaquin (1898-1975) Spanish				
oil	5	21,699-90,816	40,263	26,353
wc/d	9	527-4,669	1,525	775
PEINTE, Henri (1845-1912) French				
3D	2	2,000-3,529	2,764	2,000
PEIRCE, Waldo (1884-1970) American				
oil	7	750-4,000	2,078	1,800
PEIRE, Luc (1916-1994) Belgian				
oil	11	1,555-25,479	7,857	7,224
wc/d	1	1,210	1,210	1,210
PEISER, Kurt (1887-1962) Belgian				
oil	15	478-7,283	2,310	1,788
wc/d	1	1,084	1,084	1,084

Name	No.	Price Range	Average	Median
PEITHNER VON LICHTENFELS, Eduard (1833-1913) Austrian				
oil	2	1,897-2,281	2,089	1,897
PEIZEL, Bart (1887-1974) Dutch				
wc/d	1	1,079	1,079	1,079
PEKARY, Istvan (1905-1981) Hungarian				
oil	4	600-2,250	1,562	1,400
PEKER, Elya (?) ?				
oil	1	1,800	1,800	1,800
PELAEZ, Amelia (1897-1968) Cuban				
oil	2	5,500-6,000	5,750	5,500
wc/d	1	14,270	14,270	14,270
PELAEZ, Juan (1881-1937) Argentinian				
oil	3	2,300-7,400	4,900	5,000
PELAEZ, Mariano (1920-) Spanish				
oil	5	509-1,640	1,073	1,076
PELAYO FERNANDEZ, Eduardo (c.1850-?) Spanish				
oil	1	1,440	1,440	1,440
PELAYO, Orlando (1920-1990) Spanish				
oil	4	1,669-9,271	4,230	1,731
wc/d	4	518-2,967	1,368	775
PELC, Antonin (1895-1967) Czechoslovakian				
oil	1	1,500	1,500	1,500
PELECASSIS, Spiridon (1843-1916) Greek				
oil	1	9,450	9,450	9,450
PELEGRY, Arsene (1813-?) French				
oil	3	2,289-2,378	2,318	2,289
PELESKA-LUNARD (20th C) German?				
3D	1	4,005	4,005	4,005
PELEZ, Fernand (1843-1913) French				
oil	1	6,540	6,540	6,540
PELHAM, Thomas Kent (fl.1860-1891) British				
oil	6	554-12,180	4,043	2,747
PELLAN, Alfred (1906-1988) Canadian				
oil	1	14,180	14,180	14,180
wc/d	5	815-6,611	3,569	3,280
PELLAR, Hanns (1886-1971) Austrian				
oil	5	1,212-4,917	2,304	1,908
wc/d	2	968-2,275	1,621	968
PELLEGRIN, Honore (1800-1870) French				
wc/d	4	3,503-15,000	8,428	5,664
PELLEGRIN, Louis (19th C) French				
wc/d	2	1,500-2,781	2,140	1,500
PELLEGRINI, Alfred Heinrich (1881-1958) Swiss				
oil	2	777-5,708	3,242	777
wc/d	2	519-878	698	519
PELLEGRINI, Carlo (1839-1889) Italian				
wc/d	12	1,232-5,696	2,616	2,112
PELLEGRINI, Riccardo (1863-1934) Italian				
oil	9	938-10,829	4,097	2,367
PELLEGRINO DI MARIANO (?-1492) Italian				
oil	1	60,000	60,000	60,000
PELLEGRINO, Oscar (1947-) Venezuelan				
wc/d	1	2,325	2,325	2,325
PELLEKAAN, Rachel Fernhout (1905-1989) Dutch				
oil	2	2,290-8,905	5,597	2,290
PELLERIER, Maurice (1875-?) French				
oil	1	4,291	4,291	4,291
PELLETIER, Auguste (fl.1800-1847) French				
wc/d	8	29,281-58,562	43,921	46,849
PELLETIER, Pierre-Jacques (1869-1931) French				
oil	1	525	525	525
wc/d	1	2,788	2,788	2,788
PELLICCIOTTI, Tito (1872-1943) Italian				
oil	8	1,818-4,844	3,020	2,993
PELLIER, Pierre Edme Louis (18/19th C) French				
oil	1	110,000	110,000	110,000
PELLIS, Giovanni Napoleone (1888-1962) Italian				
oil	1	6,429	6,429	6,429
PELLIZZA DA VOLPEDO, Giuseppe (1868-1907) Italian				
oil	1	28,479	28,479	28,479

Name	No.	Price Range	Average	Median
PELLON, Gina (1925-) Cuban				
oil	2	3,211-5,956	4,583	3,211
wc/d	1	628	628	628
PELLOUX, Pierre (20th C) French				
oil	2	1,405-1,405	1,405	1,405
PELOUSE, Léon Germain (1838-1891) French				
oil	5	1,199-6,861	4,250	4,350
PELS, Albert (1910-1998) American				
oil	3	1,050-1,700	1,350	1,300
PELTON, Agnes (1881-1961) American				
oil	2	2,000-2,700	2,350	2,000
PELUSO, Francesco (1836-?) Italian				
oil	3	1,414-4,519	2,963	2,958
PELUZZI, Eso (1894-1985) Italian				
oil	8	2,131-7,159	3,780	2,858
wc/d	3	1,034-2,148	1,736	2,028
PELVO, Paavo (1947-) Finnish				
oil	1	1,286	1,286	1,286
PEMBERTON, John (20th C) British				
oil	1	1,083	1,083	1,083
PENA Y MUNOZ, Maximino (1863-1940) Spanish				
wc/d	5	542-3,289	1,589	1,237
PENA, Alfonso X (1903-) Mexican				
wc/d	1	15,000	15,000	15,000
PENA, Angel (1949-) Venezuelan				
oil	1	2,745	2,745	2,745
PENA, Tonita (1895-1949) American				
wc/d	2	900-1,700	1,300	900
PENALBA, Alicia (1918-1982) Argentinian				
wc/d	3	2,636-2,979	2,792	2,761
3D	9	6,500-50,000	14,235	8,500
PENALVA, Joao (20th C) ?				
wc/d	1	1,296	1,296	1,296
PENCK, A R (1939-) German				
oil	37	4,712-175,750	31,680	15,315
wc/d	18	494-60,180	9,727	2,270
3D	8	1,881-16,537	7,941	3,822
PENCO, Palmiro (19th C) Italian				
oil	1	1,078	1,078	1,078
PENCREACH, Stephane (1970-) French?				
wc/d	1	1,359	1,359	1,359
PENDER, Jack (1918-1998) British				
oil	6	669-7,308	2,250	1,338
wc/d	1	1,496	1,496	1,496
PENDL, Erwin (1875-1945) Austrian				
wc/d	4	1,204-3,150	2,279	2,221
PENE DU BOIS, Guy (1884-1958) American				
oil	13	2,000-230,000	34,295	7,000
wc/d	2	500-1,400	950	500
PENFIELD, Edward (1866-1925) American				
wc/d	2	4,250-8,500	6,375	4,250
PENG WEI (1974-) Chinese				
wc/d	2	8,000-17,000	12,500	8,000
PENG YANG (19th C) Chinese				
wc/d	1	3,857	3,857	3,857
PENHALL, Ross (1959-) Canadian				
oil	1	5,062	5,062	5,062
PENKOAT, Pierre (1945-) French				
oil	3	607-727	657	637
wc/d	5	570-2,569	1,151	710
PENLEY, Aaron Edwin (1807-1870) British				
wc/d	3	662-1,760	1,109	905
PENN, Irving (1917-) American				
oil	1	49,140	49,140	49,140
wc/d	1	40,000	40,000	40,000
PENN, William Charles (1877-1968) British				
oil	3	522-5,670	2,388	974
PENNASILICO, Giuseppe (1861-1940) Italian				
oil	3	600-7,120	3,932	4,077
PENNE, Olivier de (1831-1897) French				
oil	9	1,200-86,528	17,916	6,681
wc/d	12	742-39,556	14,760	12,979

Name	No.	Price Range	Average	Median
PENNEFATHER, Dorothea (19th C) Irish				
wc/d	1	1,150	1,150	1,150
PENNELL, Joseph (1860-1926) American				
wc/d	2	550-2,500	1,525	550
PENNY, Edwin (1930-) British				
wc/d	7	814-5,000	3,551	4,250
PENNY, J C (19th C) British				
oil	1	1,914	1,914	1,914
PENNY, William Daniel (1834-1924) British				
oil	4	888-1,416	1,071	962
PENONE, Giuseppe (1947-) Italian				
oil	1	204,694	204,694	204,694
wc/d	4	5,852-69,103	25,963	14,449
3D	3	10,235-33,714	18,392	11,228
PENOT, Albert Joseph (19th C) French				
oil	2	1,901-2,661	2,281	1,901
PENROSE, Sir Roland (1900-1984) British				
oil	1	18,200	18,200	18,200
wc/d	1	1,440	1,440	1,440
PEPE, Lorenzo (1916-1984) Italian				
3D	1	3,292	3,292	3,292
PEPE, Valentine (19/20th C) French				
oil	1	6,000	6,000	6,000
PEPLOE, Denis (1914-1993) British				
oil	2	2,745-10,620	6,682	2,745
PEPLOE, Samuel John (1871-1935) British				
oil	16	26,550-814,200	328,326	265,500
wc/d	3	1,131-6,764	4,123	4,475
PEPPER, Beverly (1924-) American				
3D	2	4,750-60,000	32,375	4,750
PEPPER, Charles Hovey (1864-1950) American				
oil	1	1,000	1,000	1,000
wc/d	1	1,100	1,100	1,100
PEPPER, George Douglas (1903-1962) Canadian				
oil	7	820-28,863	6,435	2,460
PEPPER, Mark (20th C) Irish?				
oil	1	2,016	2,016	2,016
PEPPERCORN, Arthur Douglas (1847-1924) British				
oil	2	400-1,632	1,016	400
PEPPERSTEIN, Pavel (1966-) Russian				
wc/d	1	1,200	1,200	1,200
PEPYN, Marten (1575-1642) Flemish				
oil	1	13,430	13,430	13,430
PEPYN, Marten and UTRECHT, Adriaen van (17th C) Flemish				
oil	1	40,135	40,135	40,135
PERAHIM, Jules (20th C) French				
oil	1	1,316	1,316	1,316
PERBOYRE, Paul Emile Léon (c.1826-1907) French				
oil	5	850-2,549	1,628	1,511
PERCEVAL, Don Louis (1908-1979) American				
oil	1	1,600	1,600	1,600
PERCIER, Charles (1764-1838) French				
wc/d	2	1,403-7,856	4,629	1,403
PERCIVAL, Harold (1868-1914) British				
wc/d	1	1,200	1,200	1,200
PERCIVAL, Phyllis M (20th C) Canadian				
oil	1	1,208	1,208	1,208
PERCY, Arthur (1886-1976) Swedish				
oil	6	925-38,219	8,503	3,181
PERCY, Sidney Richard (1821-1886) British				
oil	16	1,300-107,730	34,490	26,460
PERDISCH, Adolf (1806-?) German				
oil	1	2,167	2,167	2,167
PERDOMO, Felix (1956-) Venezuelan				
wc/d	1	2,100	2,100	2,100
PERDRIAT, Helene Marie Marguerite (1894-1969) French				
oil	5	510-4,917	1,565	634
PEREGO, Eugenio (1845-1923) Italian				
oil	1	1,432	1,432	1,432
wc/d	1	656	656	656
PEREHUDOFF, William (1919-) Canadian				
oil	4	697-4,431	3,150	3,702

Name	No.	Price Range	Average	Median
PEREJAUME (1957-) Spanish				
oil	3	2,155-9,633	4,882	2,859
PERELLON, Celedonio (1926-) Spanish				
oil	1	996	996	996
wc/d	3	545-2,303	1,272	969
PERELMAGNE, Vladimir (c.1870-1922) Russian				
3D	1	3,151	3,151	3,151
PERENY, Madeline S (1896-1970) American				
oil	4	600-4,700	1,825	850
wc/d	3	600-950	733	650
PERETTI, Matteo (1975-) Italian				
wc/d	1	1,933	1,933	1,933
3D	1	3,503	3,503	3,503
PEREZ CELIS (1939-) Argentinian				
wc/d	1	5,000	5,000	5,000
PEREZ DE VILLAAMIL, Genaro (1807-1854) Spanish				
wc/d	1	4,519	4,519	4,519
PEREZ GIL, Jose (1918-1998) Spanish				
oil	3	3,588-11,322	6,360	4,171
wc/d	1	1,189	1,189	1,189
PEREZ MARTINEZ, Jose Francisco (1907-) Spanish				
oil	2	957-2,035	1,496	957
PEREZ MOLINA, Francisco (1941-1993) Spanish				
oil	2	1,414-1,936	1,675	1,414
wc/d	1	622	622	622
PEREZ ORUE, Ernesto (1897-1927) Spanish				
oil	1	8,438	8,438	8,438
PEREZ RUBIO, Antonio (1822-1888) Spanish				
oil	1	3,800	3,800	3,800
PEREZ VILLALTA, Guillermo (1948-) Spanish				
oil	3	8,980-48,163	22,258	9,633
wc/d	1	2,945	2,945	2,945
PEREZ Y VILLAGROSSA, Mariano Alonso (1857-1930) Spanish				
wc/d	1	2,178	2,178	2,178
PEREZ, Alonzo (fl.1893-1914) Spanish				
oil	3	1,473-4,000	2,491	2,000
PEREZ, Enoc (1967-) Puerto Rican				
oil	1	37,000	37,000	37,000
wc/d	2	8,000-26,000	17,000	8,000
PEREZ, Jose (1929-) American				
oil	4	900-1,700	1,250	1,100
PEREZ, Manuel (20th C) South American				
oil	1	1,300	1,300	1,300
PEREZ, Mario (1960-) Argentinian				
oil	1	13,000	13,000	13,000
PEREZ, Raphael (1938-) Swiss/Venezuelan				
wc/d	1	2,325	2,325	2,325
PEREZ-ARAD, Esther (?) ?				
oil	2	800-1,600	1,200	800
PERFETTI, Giorgio (20th C) Italian?				
oil	1	1,209	1,209	1,209
PERGAY, Maria (1937-) French				
3D	1	16,983	16,983	16,983
PERI, Lazslo (1889-1967) Hungarian				
wc/d	1	6,574	6,574	6,574
PERICOLI, Tullio (1936-) Italian				
wc/d	3	453-4,321	1,850	777
PERIES, Ivan (1921-1988) Indian				
oil	5	4,114-12,000	6,926	6,732
wc/d	1	11,000	11,000	11,000
PERIGAL, Arthur (jnr) (1816-1884) British				
oil	2	448-4,048	2,248	448
wc/d	1	828	828	828
PERIGNON, Alexis Joseph (1806-1882) French				
oil	1	17,400	17,400	17,400
PERIGNON, Alexis Nicolas (elder) (1726-1782) French				
wc/d	1	1,801	1,801	1,801
PERILLI, Achille (1927-) Italian				
oil	14	2,577-46,849	17,037	15,000
wc/d	37	1,199-31,803	10,025	6,951
PERIN-SALBREUX, Lie Louis (1753-1817) French				
oil	1	19,007	19,007	19,007

Name	No.	Price Range	Average	Median
PERINO and VELE (20th C) Italian				
3D	1	8,199	8,199	8,199
PERIS BRELL, Julio (1866-1944) Spanish				
oil	1	2,472	2,472	2,472
PERIZI, Nino (1917-1994) Italian				
wc/d	1	1,694	1,694	1,694
PERIZI, Tiziano (1895-1975) Italian				
oil	2	502-2,314	1,408	502
PERKINS, B F (20th C) American				
oil	1	2,400	2,400	2,400
PERKINS, Granville (1830-1895) American				
oil	4	1,500-3,000	2,237	2,200
wc/d	2	1,300-2,100	1,700	1,300
PERKINS, Harley (1883-1964) American				
oil	1	1,800	1,800	1,800
PERLBERG, Christian (1806-1884) German				
oil	1	35,793	35,793	35,793
PERLBERG, Friedrich (1848-1921) German				
wc/d	6	774-5,696	2,867	2,631
PERLIN, Bernard (1918-) American				
wc/d	1	2,800	2,800	2,800
PERLMUTTER, Isaac (1866-1932) Czechoslovakian				
oil	1	1,300	1,300	1,300
PERLOTTI, Luis (1890-1969) Argentinian				
3D	2	4,500-8,500	6,500	4,500
PERMEKE, Constant (1886-1952) Belgian				
oil	11	5,753-46,757	13,588	9,568
wc/d	9	3,131-18,061	7,150	4,335
3D	1	21,041	21,041	21,041
PERMEKE, Paul (1918-1990) Belgian				
oil	22	618-3,292	1,532	1,091
PERNA, Claudio (20th C) South American				
oil	1	8,370	8,370	8,370
PERNES, Leo (?-1960) ?				
oil	2	1,094-1,169	1,131	1,094
PERNET, Jean Henry Alexandre (1763-?) French				
wc/d	4	1,011-2,275	1,565	1,033
PERNHARDT, Marcus (1828-1871) Austrian				
oil	1	84,966	84,966	84,966
PERNOT, Henri (19th C) French				
3D	1	3,200	3,200	3,200
PERON, Pierre (1905-1988) French?				
oil	2	643-1,540	1,091	643
PEROV, Vasili (1833-1882) Russian				
oil	3	7,644-47,426	23,499	15,429
PERRACHON, Andre (1827-1909) French				
oil	1	19,156	19,156	19,156
PERRACHON, Joseph (20th C) French				
oil	1	1,286	1,286	1,286
PERRACHON, L (?) French				
oil	1	8,750	8,750	8,750
PERRAUDIN, Paul (1907-1993) French				
wc/d	2	727-1,403	1,065	727
PERRAULT, Léon (1832-1908) French				
oil	2	8,000-26,000	17,000	8,000
PERRET, Aime (1847-1927) French				
oil	2	4,442-13,000	8,721	4,442
PERRETT, Galen Joseph (1875-1949) American				
oil	2	550-11,000	5,775	550
PERRETT, S (19th C) British				
oil	1	1,000	1,000	1,000
PERRIN, Dan (1963-) Swedish				
oil	2	2,672-3,054	2,863	2,672
PERRIN, Émile Cesar Victor (1814-1885) French				
oil	1	2,498	2,498	2,498
PERRIN-LEMAITRE, Em (19th C) French?				
oil	1	6,429	6,429	6,429
PERRIN-MAXENCE, Henri (1872-1944) French				
oil	1	1,394	1,394	1,394
PERRINE, Van Dearing (1869-1955) American				
oil	1	5,500	5,500	5,500

Name	No.	Price Range	Average	Median
PERRON, Charles Clement Francis (1893-1958) French				
oil	10	596-3,894	1,811	1,227
PERRONEAU, Jean Baptiste (1715-1783) French				
oil	2	6,920-15,753	11,336	6,920
wc/d	1	8,948	8,948	8,948
PERROT, Ferdinand (1808-1841) French				
oil	2	1,212-4,500	2,856	1,212
PERRY, Adelaide (1891-1973) Australian				
oil	1	1,600	1,600	1,600
PERRY, Arthur W (fl.1908-1939) British				
wc/d	2	1,295-1,479	1,387	1,295
PERRY, Enoch Wood (1831-1915) American				
oil	1	20,000	20,000	20,000
PERRY, Frank Chester (1859-?) American				
oil	1	1,200	1,200	1,200
PERRY, Grayson (1960-) British				
3D	8	8,650-77,700	34,218	26,400
PERRY, John S (1895-1980) Canadian				
wc/d	1	1,979	1,979	1,979
PERRY, Lilla Cabot (1848-1933) American				
oil	1	5,500	5,500	5,500
wc/d	1	1,700	1,700	1,700
PERSEUS, Edward (1841-1890) Swedish				
oil	2	629-1,496	1,062	629
PERSICO, Mario (1930-) Italian				
oil	2	1,214-2,022	1,618	1,214
wc/d	2	1,578-2,141	1,859	1,578
PERSOGLIA, Franz von (1852-1912) Austrian				
oil	1	2,379	2,379	2,379
PERSON, Henri (1876-1926) French				
oil	1	2,104	2,104	2,104
PERSSON, Ragnar (1905-1993) Swedish				
oil	27	414-9,555	2,183	1,769
PERTILE, Livia (1968-) Italian				
oil	2	1,295-2,581	1,938	1,295
PERTOSSI, Paolo (19th C) Italian				
oil	1	1,571	1,571	1,571
PERUGINI, Charles Edward (1839-1918) British				
oil	3	23,660-63,700	49,653	61,600
PERUZZI, Osvaldo (1907-2004) Italian				
oil	3	1,757-3,935	2,756	2,577
PERUZZINI, Antonio Francesco (1668-?) Italian				
oil	1	9,678	9,678	9,678
PERVOLARAKIS, Othon (1887-1974) Greek				
oil	1	12,320	12,320	12,320
PESA, Giuseppe (1928-1992) Italian				
oil	1	1,019	1,019	1,019
PESCE, Gaetano (1939-) Italian				
3D	1	3,500	3,500	3,500
PESCHEL, Carl Gottlieb (1798-1879) German				
wc/d	1	5,890	5,890	5,890
PESCHKA, Anton (1885-1940) Austrian				
oil	1	485	485	485
wc/d	2	1,274-1,929	1,601	1,274
PESCHKE, Christian (1946-) German				
oil	2	486-486	486	486
wc/d	1	870	870	870
3D	1	2,342	2,342	2,342
PESCI, Girolamo (1684-1759) Italian				
oil	2	23,759-24,196	23,977	23,759
PESCI, Ottilio (1877-?) Italian				
3D	1	1,854	1,854	1,854
PESER, O (20th C) German?				
3D	1	3,027	3,027	3,027
PESKE, Geza (1859-1934) Hungarian				
oil	2	1,000-1,700	1,350	1,000
PESKE, Jean (1870-1949) French				
oil	16	760-9,405	4,398	3,246
wc/d	17	584-16,066	2,989	1,193
PESNE, Antoine (1683-1757) French				
oil	4	8,247-72,245	38,273	30,102

Name	No.	Price Range	Average	Median
PESSINA, Carlo (1836-1884) Italian				
3D	1	40,000	40,000	40,000
PESSLER, Ernst (1838-1900) Austrian				
wc/d	1	5,260	5,260	5,260
PETER, Emanuel (1799-1873) Austrian				
wc/d	1	1,089	1,089	1,089
PETER, Wenzel Johann (1742-1829) Austrian				
oil	1	3,200	3,200	3,200
PETERDI, Gabor (1915-2001) American/Hungarian				
oil	2	800-5,000	2,900	800
wc/d	2	960-1,000	980	960
PETERELLE, Adolphe (1874-1947) French				
oil	4	1,414-2,710	1,941	1,638
PETERS, Anna (1843-1926) German				
oil	10	600-14,400	3,906	960
wc/d	2	870-2,438	1,654	870
PETERS, Carl W (1897-1980) American				
oil	15	550-9,000	5,140	4,600
PETERS, Charles Rollo (1862-1928) American				
oil	5	1,200-15,000	6,490	5,500
PETERS, F (?) ?				
oil	1	11,310	11,310	11,310
PETERS, Joseph (?) ?				
wc/d	1	1,453	1,453	1,453
PETERS, Matthew William (1742-1814) British				
oil	2	3,460-5,500	4,480	3,460
wc/d	1	2,595	2,595	2,595
PETERS, Nikolai (1766-1825) Danish				
oil	2	4,426-6,846	5,636	4,426
PETERS, Pieter Francis (1818-1903) Dutch				
oil	3	900-4,676	3,261	4,208
wc/d	1	484	484	484
PETERS, Pietronella (1848-1924) German				
oil	1	6,903	6,903	6,903
PETERS, Robert (1960-) American				
oil	1	4,000	4,000	4,000
PETERS, Udo (1884-1964) German				
oil	5	2,221-5,611	3,886	4,091
PETERS, Wilhelm Otto (1851-1935) Norwegian				
oil	2	2,445-34,899	18,672	2,445
PETERSEN, Albert (1875-1957) Danish				
oil	3	556-2,157	1,283	1,137
PETERSEN, Armand (1891-1969) Swiss/French				
3D	3	7,949-12,740	10,403	10,520
PETERSEN, Carl Ludvig (1824-?) Danish				
oil	1	17,742	17,742	17,742
PETERSEN, Edvard (1841-1911) Danish				
oil	14	711-37,175	8,727	2,282
PETERSEN, Emmanuel Aage (1894-1948) Danish				
oil	18	714-4,517	2,216	1,624
PETERSEN, Fritz (1816-1900) Danish				
oil	2	815-15,097	7,956	815
PETERSEN, Hans Gyde (1862-1943) Danish				
oil	2	1,618-2,608	2,113	1,618
PETERSEN, Hans Ritter von (1850-1914) German				
oil	1	1,286	1,286	1,286
PETERSEN, Heinrich Andreas (1834-1916) German				
oil	1	6,000	6,000	6,000
PETERSEN, Julius (1851-1911) Danish				
oil	1	5,080	5,080	5,080
PETERSEN, Lorenz (1803-1870) German				
oil	2	2,986-6,640	4,813	2,986
PETERSEN, Olaf (20th C) Norwegian				
oil	1	2,748	2,748	2,748
PETERSEN, Olivia (19th C) Danish				
oil	1	6,471	6,471	6,471
PETERSEN, Roland (1926-) American				
oil	3	55,000-100,000	80,000	85,000
PETERSEN, Vilhelm (1812-1880) Danish				
oil	11	1,265-14,228	4,658	2,688
PETERSEN, Walter (1862-1950) German				
wc/d	2	865-1,750	1,307	865

Name	No.	Price Range	Average	Median
PETERSEN-ANGELN, Heinrich (1850-1906) German				
oil	1	1,908	1,908	1,908
PETERSEN-FLENSBURG, Heinrich (1861-1908) German				
oil	2	1,212-1,452	1,332	1,212
PETERSON, Jane (1876-1965) American				
oil	27	375-180,000	18,113	8,000
wc/d	31	500-22,000	4,625	2,600
PETERSON, Robert Baard (1943-) American				
oil	1	1,000	1,000	1,000
PETERSSEN, Eilif (1852-1928) Norwegian				
oil	3	14,720-110,400	54,880	39,522
PETERSSON, Axel (1868-1925) Swedish				
3D	17	1,745-63,699	12,435	6,869
PETERZANO, Simone (c.1590-?) Italian				
wc/d	1	4,844	4,844	4,844
PETHER, Abraham (1756-1812) British				
oil	6	1,427-6,545	3,750	2,941
PETHER, Henry (fl.1828-1865) British				
oil	1	1,062	1,062	1,062
PETHER, Sebastian (1790-1844) British				
oil	5	528-10,395	3,386	2,400
PETHYBRIDGE, J Ley (fl.1885-1893) British				
oil	1	12,629	12,629	12,629
PETILLION, Jules (1845-1899) French				
oil	2	1,911-2,805	2,358	1,911
PETIT, Eugène (1839-1886) French				
oil	7	1,036-8,700	3,645	3,000
PETIT, Pierre Joseph (1768-1825) French				
oil	1	4,555	4,555	4,555
PETITI, Filiberto (1845-1924) Italian				
oil	3	1,033-5,946	3,362	3,107
wc/d	1	729	729	729
PETITJEAN, Edmond (1844-1925) French				
oil	27	1,296-15,000	6,129	4,960
PETITJEAN, Hippolyte (1854-1929) French				
oil	6	1,386-38,795	10,766	6,000
wc/d	3	509-4,142	2,268	2,153
PETITPAS, Sophie (20th C) French				
oil	1	7,416	7,416	7,416
wc/d	5	888-8,358	5,298	5,780
PETLEY, Roy (1951-) British				
oil	13	620-3,145	1,523	1,239
wc/d	2	531-1,628	1,079	531
PETLEY-JONES, Llewellyn (1908-1986) Canadian				
oil	4	820-2,880	1,335	820
wc/d	5	460-496	481	496
PETO, John F (1854-1907) American				
oil	2	21,000-32,500	26,750	21,000
PETRAVICH, Nicholai (20th C) Russian				
oil	1	1,239	1,239	1,239
PETRAZZI, Astolfo (1579-1665) Italian				
oil	1	11,000	11,000	11,000
PETRELLA DA BOLOGNA, Vittorio (1886-1951) Italian				
oil	2	1,512-1,529	1,520	1,512
PETRENKO, V (19/20th C) Ukranian				
oil	1	4,043	4,043	4,043
PETRIDES, Konrad (1863-1943) Austrian				
oil	5	485-2,038	1,168	1,215
PETRIE, Ferdinand Ralph (1925-) American				
wc/d	1	1,100	1,100	1,100
PETRIE, George (1790-1866) British				
oil	1	9,466	9,466	9,466
PETRILLI, Professor A (19th C) Italian				
3D	1	6,500	6,500	6,500
PETRITSKY, Anatoli (1895-1964) Russian				
wc/d	6	1,215-37,200	16,195	5,144
PETROCELLI, Achille (1861-?) Italian				
oil	1	1,044	1,044	1,044
PETROCELLI, Arturo (1856-?) Italian				
oil	1	1,500	1,500	1,500
PETROFF, Andre (1893-1975) Russian				
oil	1	1,890	1,890	1,890

Name	No.	Price Range	Average	Median
PETROFF, Vassili Petrovitch (c.1770-1811) Russian				
oil	1	78,000	78,000	78,000
PETROFF, Wladimir (20th C) French/Russian				
oil	3	1,390-1,947	1,588	1,429
PETROV, Arkadi (1940-) Russian				
oil	1	14,000	14,000	14,000
3D	1	3,250	3,250	3,250
PETROV-VODKIN, Kuzma (1878-1939) Russian				
wc/d	4	4,017-41,280	14,803	5,096
PETROVICHEV, Piotr Ivanovich (1874-1947) Russian				
oil	2	31,620-94,600	63,110	31,620
PETROVSKY, Ivan (1913-) Hungarian				
wc/d	1	2,140	2,140	2,140
PETRUOLO, Salvatore (1857-1946) Italian				
oil	3	970-16,008	9,339	11,040
wc/d	1	900	900	900
PETRUS, Marco (1960-) Italian				
oil	4	597-14,317	5,684	3,816
wc/d	1	1,312	1,312	1,312
PETRY, Victor (1903-) American				
oil	1	1,800	1,800	1,800
PETTENKOFEN, August von (1822-1889) Austrian				
oil	6	3,646-30,630	15,127	8,469
wc/d	2	783-4,355	2,569	783
PETTER, Franz Xaver (1791-1866) Austrian				
oil	6	5,271-82,500	32,620	23,140
wc/d	5	884-7,000	3,211	2,500
PETTERSSON, Joel (1892-1937) Finnish				
oil	1	5,856	5,856	5,856
PETTERSSON, Primus Mortimer (1895-1975) Swedish				
oil	6	496-1,527	1,101	1,189
PETTIBON, Raymond (1957-) American				
oil	2	30,000-650,000	340,000	30,000
wc/d	28	3,250-51,330	12,903	10,000
PETTIBONE, Richard (1938-) American				
oil	26	5,500-65,000	22,115	18,480
wc/d	13	7,000-140,000	28,384	24,000
PETTIE, John (1839-1893) British				
oil	5	974-5,280	2,614	1,796
PETTITT, Charles (19th C) British				
oil	2	2,565-3,591	3,078	2,565
PETTITT, Joseph Paul (1812-1882) British				
oil	4	961-5,310	2,803	2,366
PETTITT, Wilfred Stanley (1904-1978) British				
oil	2	797-1,776	1,286	797
PETTORUTI, Emilio (1892-1971) Argentinian				
oil	4	12,500-130,000	63,625	47,000
PETTY, Roy F (20th C) American				
oil	1	1,050	1,050	1,050
PETUEL, Rudolf (1870-1937) German				
oil	2	1,030-1,580	1,305	1,030
PETZET, Hermann (1860-?) German				
oil	1	1,252	1,252	1,252
PETZHOLDT, Fritz (1805-1838) Danish				
oil	1	6,324	6,324	6,324
PETZL, Joseph (1803-1871) German				
oil	1	5,838	5,838	5,838
PETZOLD, Werner (20th C) German?				
oil	1	2,116	2,116	2,116
PEUKER, Wolfgang (1945-2001) German				
oil	1	5,216	5,216	5,216
PEUTEMAN, Pieter (?-1692) Dutch				
oil	1	3,337	3,337	3,337
PEVERELLI, Cesare (1922-2000) Italian				
oil	15	588-5,363	2,275	2,040
wc/d	6	884-2,625	1,766	1,920
3D	1	2,928	2,928	2,928
PEVERNAGIE, Erik (1939-) Belgian				
oil	2	15,000-15,000	15,000	15,000
wc/d	3	8,429-9,568	8,989	8,970

Name	No.	Price Range	Average	Median
PEVSNER, Antoine (1886-1962) Russian				
oil	1	223,600	223,600	223,600
wc/d	1	2,939	2,939	2,939
PEYNOT, Émile Edmond (1850-1932) French				
3D	3	3,612-26,000	15,537	17,000
PEYRAUD, Frank Charles (1858-1948) American				
oil	2	1,200-2,000	1,600	1,200
PEYRE, Raphael (1872-1949) French				
3D	1	13,000	13,000	13,000
PEYRISSAC, Jean (1895-1974) French				
wc/d	1	2,356	2,356	2,356
3D	2	15,206-20,275	17,740	15,206
PEYRO-URREA, Juan (1847-1924) Spanish				
oil	1	4,500	4,500	4,500
PEYROL, François Auguste Hippolyte (1856-1929) French				
3D	1	10,962	10,962	10,962
PEYRON, Guido (1898-1960) Italian				
oil	4	1,940-10,800	6,020	5,280
PEYROTTE, Alexis (1699-1769) French				
wc/d	2	925-7,000	3,962	925
PEYTON, Bertha S Menzler (1871-1950) American				
oil	1	3,300	3,300	3,300
PEYTON, Elizabeth (1965-) American				
oil	8	110,000-750,000	353,750	260,000
wc/d	13	13,000-37,000	23,209	22,000
PEZANT, Aymar (1846-1916) French				
oil	1	1,458	1,458	1,458
PEZOLT, Georg (1810-1878) Austrian				
wc/d	1	1,084	1,084	1,084
PEZOUS, Jean (1815-1885) French				
oil	1	3,637	3,637	3,637
PEZZO, Lucio del (1933-) Italian				
oil	10	644-18,473	6,631	4,844
wc/d	17	467-7,633	4,582	5,014
3D	2	4,585-7,633	6,109	4,585
PFAFF, Jean (1945-) Swiss				
oil	1	3,027	3,027	3,027
PFAFF, Judy (1946-) American/British				
wc/d	3	650-3,800	1,883	1,200
PFAHLER, Karl Georg (1926-2002) German				
oil	6	1,316-7,068	4,778	5,563
wc/d	1	1,991	1,991	1,991
PFEFFERKORN, Felix Samuel (1945-) German				
oil	4	1,080-4,200	2,180	1,405
PFEIFFER, Fred (1940-1995) American				
oil	1	3,250	3,250	3,250
PFEIFFER, Harry R (1874-1960) American				
oil	2	800-1,500	1,150	800
PFEIFFER, Paul (1966-) American?				
3D	3	85,000-130,000	111,666	120,000
PFEILER, Maximilian (18th C) German				
oil	1	10,014	10,014	10,014
PFENNINGER, Heinrich (1749-1815) Swiss				
oil	1	1,832	1,832	1,832
PFEUFFER, Helmut (1933-) German?				
oil	3	3,857-9,643	6,043	4,629
wc/d	7	586-2,057	1,026	900
PFISTER, A (1884-?) Swiss				
oil	1	1,442	1,442	1,442
PFISTER, Albert (1884-1978) Swiss				
oil	6	839-2,855	2,286	2,359
PFISTER, Emile (19/20th C) French				
3D	1	1,794	1,794	1,794
PFISTER, Jean Jacques (1878-1949) American				
oil	3	1,100-2,500	1,861	1,985
PFLUG, Johan Baptist (1785-1866) German				
wc/d	1	21,476	21,476	21,476
PFLUMM, Daniel (1968-) Swiss				
3D	1	6,000	6,000	6,000
PFORR, Johann Georg (1745-1798) German				
oil	1	3,442	3,442	3,442

Name	No.	Price Range	Average	Median
PFUND, Roger (1943-) Swiss				
oil	2	1,068-1,499	1,283	1,068
PFYFFER, Jacques (19th C) Swiss				
wc/d	1	1,783	1,783	1,783
PHELAN, Charles T (1840-?) American				
oil	1	3,000	3,000	3,000
PHELAN, Ellen (1943-) American				
oil	1	900	900	900
wc/d	1	2,750	2,750	2,750
PHELAN, Pat (20th C) Irish?				
wc/d	1	3,273	3,273	3,273
PHELPS, Helen Watson (1859-1944) American				
oil	2	2,750-2,750	2,750	2,750
PHELPS, Nan (1904-1990) American				
oil	1	1,000	1,000	1,000
PHELPS, William Preston (1848-1923) American				
oil	2	4,000-4,200	4,100	4,000
PHIDIAS (20th C) Greek				
oil	1	6,960	6,960	6,960
PHILIPP, Robert (1895-1981) American				
oil	19	600-11,000	3,276	2,000
wc/d	1	950	950	950
PHILIPPE (?) French				
3D	1	3,168	3,168	3,168
PHILIPPE, Jules (19th C) French				
wc/d	1	1,138	1,138	1,138
PHILIPPE, P (19/20th C) French				
3D	1	3,579	3,579	3,579
PHILIPPE, Paul (fl.1920-1929) French				
3D	2	2,611-3,503	3,057	2,611
PHILIPPEAU, Karel Frans (1825-1897) Dutch				
oil	2	10,507-14,137	12,322	10,507
PHILIPPOTEAUX, Henri Felix Emmanuel (1815-1884) French				
oil	2	3,168-46,020	24,594	3,168
PHILIPS-WEBER, Marie (19/20th C) German				
oil	1	2,384	2,384	2,384
PHILIPSEN, Theodor (1840-1920) Danish				
oil	10	845-48,640	10,254	3,493
PHILIPSON, Robin (1916-1992) British				
oil	17	2,076-35,600	13,168	12,460
wc/d	12	534-15,045	5,699	4,844
PHILLIP, John (1817-1867) British				
oil	7	490-22,000	6,632	2,079
PHILLIPS, A E (?) American?				
oil	1	4,000	4,000	4,000
PHILLIPS, Ammi (1787-1865) American				
oil	5	3,250-15,000	7,250	6,500
PHILLIPS, Bert G (1868-1956) American				
oil	4	2,700-85,000	31,675	18,000
wc/d	1	1,750	1,750	1,750
PHILLIPS, Gordon (1927-) American				
oil	2	2,600-11,000	6,800	2,600
wc/d	1	2,000	2,000	2,000
3D	1	2,100	2,100	2,100
PHILLIPS, Henry Wyndham (1820-1868) British				
oil	1	3,135	3,135	3,135
PHILLIPS, James (?) ?				
oil	1	1,300	1,300	1,300
PHILLIPS, Jay C (1954-1987) American				
3D	1	3,000	3,000	3,000
PHILLIPS, Joel (1960-) American				
oil	2	2,500-7,000	4,750	2,500
PHILLIPS, Peter (1939-) British				
oil	2	9,735-11,505	10,620	9,735
wc/d	1	19,425	19,425	19,425
PHILLIPS, Richard (1963-) American				
wc/d	1	10,000	10,000	10,000
PHILLIPS, Samuel George (c.1890-1965) American				
oil	2	11,000-18,000	14,500	11,000
PHILLIPS, T (1770-1845) British				
oil	1	7,392	7,392	7,392

Name	No.	Price Range	Average	Median
PHILLIPS, Thomas (1770-1845) British				
oil	5	1,044-8,010	4,139	2,944
PHILLIPS, Tom (1937-) British				
wc/d	3	1,112-8,010	3,516	1,427
PHILLIPS, W J (1884-1963) American/Canadian				
wc/d	1	6,327	6,327	6,327
PHILLIPS, Walter Joseph (1884-1963) American/Canadian				
wc/d	9	3,280-16,209	7,847	4,874
PHILLOTT, Constance (1842-1931) British				
wc/d	1	1,144	1,144	1,144
PHILP, James George (1816-1885) British				
oil	1	1,848	1,848	1,848
PHILPOT, Glyn (1884-1937) British				
oil	3	8,505-45,240	23,581	17,000
wc/d	3	1,225-11,340	5,116	2,784
3D	1	10,395	10,395	10,395
PHIPPEN, George (1916-1966) American				
oil	1	12,500	12,500	12,500
wc/d	2	1,700-3,500	2,600	1,700
3D	1	4,000	4,000	4,000
PHOENIX, George (1863-1935) British				
oil	1	762	762	762
wc/d	1	528	528	528
PHOTIADES, Vassily (1900-1975) Greek				
oil	1	10,440	10,440	10,440
PHYSICK, Robert (fl.1859-1866) British				
oil	1	7,308	7,308	7,308
PIACENTINO, Gianni (1945-) Italian				
wc/d	2	2,057-3,037	2,547	2,057
3D	7	7,315-37,286	15,981	9,643
PIACENZA, Carlo (1814-1887) Italian				
oil	2	882-3,000	1,941	882
PIACESI, Walter (1929-) Italian				
oil	13	707-3,625	2,269	2,581
wc/d	3	1,230-1,877	1,568	1,598
PIAMONTE, Giovanni di (fl.1459) Italian				
oil	1	99,932	99,932	99,932
PIAN, Antonio de (1784-1851) Italian				
oil	1	4,253	4,253	4,253
PIANA, Giuseppe Ferdinando (1864-1958) Italian				
oil	1	2,367	2,367	2,367
wc/d	1	1,427	1,427	1,427
PIANCA, Giuseppe Antonio (1703-1757) Italian				
oil	2	7,224-24,196	15,710	7,224
PIANON, Alessandro (20th C) Italian				
3D	1	3,031	3,031	3,031
PIAT, Frederic Eugène (1827-1903) French				
3D	1	3,767	3,767	3,767
PIATTELLA, Oscar (1932-) Italian				
oil	3	597-2,544	1,285	716
PIATTI, Celestino (1922-) Swiss				
wc/d	1	3,921	3,921	3,921
PIAUBERT, Jean (1900-2001) French				
oil	4	477-1,801	924	584
wc/d	8	851-3,857	2,266	1,753
PIAZZA, A (?) Italian				
3D	3	5,500-20,000	13,166	14,000
PIAZZA, Calisto (1505-1561) Italian				
oil	1	129,324	129,324	129,324
PIAZZA, Martino (?-c.1527) Italian				
oil	1	30,382	30,382	30,382
PIAZZETTA, Giambattista (1682-1754) Italian				
oil	1	45,000	45,000	45,000
wc/d	2	13,368-17,622	15,495	13,368
PIAZZONI, Gottardo (1872-1945) American/Swiss				
oil	2	9,500-42,500	26,000	9,500
PICABIA, Francis (1878-1953) French				
oil	26	9,120-1,672,000	211,403	65,000
wc/d	34	1,054-480,000	37,586	12,121
PICANET, Emile Louis (1833-1915) French				
3D	1	2,422	2,422	2,422

Name	No.	Price Range	Average	Median
PICARD, Biddy (?) British				
oil	3	440-1,848	1,046	850
PICARD, Georges (1857-?) French?				
oil	1	14,720	14,720	14,720
PICART LE DOUX, Charles (1881-1959) French				
oil	5	573-6,000	2,375	1,288
wc/d	1	1,169	1,169	1,169
PICART LEDOUX, Jean (1902-1982) French				
oil	1	2,500	2,500	2,500
wc/d	2	2,718-8,836	5,777	2,718
PICART, Bernard (1673-1733) French				
wc/d	1	2,455	2,455	2,455
PICART, Jean Michel (1600-1682) Flemish				
oil	2	27,952-40,789	34,370	27,952
PICASSO (20th C) Spanish				
wc/d	1	1,500	1,500	1,500
PICASSO, Pablo (1881-1973) Spanish				
oil	42	440,000-85,000,000	6,092,897	2,650,000
wc/d	162	1,455-12,250,000	207,238	80,960
3D	467	1,978-300,000	10,311	6,000
PICAULT, C E (19/20th C) French				
oil	1	5,000	5,000	5,000
PICAULT, Émile (1839-1915) French				
3D	14	1,821-95,000	12,463	2,803
PICCINNI, Gennaro (1933-) Italian				
wc/d	1	1,355	1,355	1,355
PICCOLI, Sergio (1946-) Italian				
oil	1	1,081	1,081	1,081
wc/d	2	529-1,018	773	529
PICHETTE, James (1920-1996) French				
oil	16	667-3,822	2,114	1,555
wc/d	9	433-3,041	1,318	912
PICHHADZE, Meir (1955-) Israeli				
oil	6	1,600-10,000	5,183	3,000
PICHLER, Luigi (1773-1854) Austrian?				
3D	1	31,140	31,140	31,140
PICHLER, Walter (1936-) Austrian				
wc/d	3	823-5,733	3,119	2,803
PICHOT, Ramon (1924-1996) Spanish				
oil	1	2,200	2,200	2,200
PICINI, Andrea (1935-2003) Italian				
oil	1	4,179	4,179	4,179
3D	1	3,073	3,073	3,073
PICK, Anton (1840-1905) Austrian				
oil	2	1,680-1,907	1,793	1,680
PICK-MORINO, Edmund (1877-1958) Belgian				
oil	1	1,543	1,543	1,543
PICKARD, Louise (c.1865-1928) British				
oil	1	4,048	4,048	4,048
PICKERING, Joseph Langsdale (1845-1912) British				
oil	5	764-26,100	6,115	1,100
PICKERSGILL, Frederick Richard (1820-1900) British				
oil	1	18,200	18,200	18,200
PICKING, John (1939-) British				
oil	6	589-1,475	1,063	1,045
PICKNELL, William Lamb (1854-1897) American				
oil	2	10,000-37,500	23,750	10,000
PICO RIBERA, Hernan (1911-) Spanish				
oil	1	1,176	1,176	1,176
PICO, Jose (1904-1991) Spanish				
oil	1	1,447	1,447	1,447
PICOT, François (1786-1868) French				
oil	1	8,158	8,158	8,158
wc/d	1	766	766	766
PICOU, Henri Pierre (1824-1895) French				
oil	6	5,021-24,167	11,565	5,828
PICQUE, Charles (1799-1869) Belgian				
oil	2	1,399-4,290	2,844	1,399
PIDDOCK, David (1960-) British				
oil	1	2,618	2,618	2,618
PIECHAUD, Guillaume (20th C) French?				
3D	1	4,794	4,794	4,794

Name	No.	Price Range	Average	Median
PIECK, Adri (1894-1982) Dutch				
oil	1	2,253	2,253	2,253
PIECK, Anton (1895-1987) Dutch				
oil	1	3,048	3,048	3,048
wc/d	1	12,292	12,292	12,292
PIEK, Anton (19th C) German?				
oil	1	1,697	1,697	1,697
PIELER, Franz Xaver (1879-1952) Austrian				
oil	7	531-6,764	3,412	3,038
PIEMONTI, Lorenzo (1935-) Italian				
oil	11	589-2,827	1,682	1,670
wc/d	2	518-1,189	853	518
PIENE, Otto (1928-) German				
oil	15	1,414-35,671	13,866	10,367
wc/d	10	937-6,370	3,099	3,162
3D	2	5,890-20,384	13,137	5,890
PIENEMAN, Johanna (1889-?) Dutch				
oil	1	1,158	1,158	1,158
PIENEMAN, Nicolaas (elder) (1809-1860) Dutch				
oil	1	1,878	1,878	1,878
PIEPENHAGEN, August (1791-1868) Polish				
oil	2	400-1,816	1,108	400
PIERATTI, Domenico (1656-?) Italian				
3D	1	328,700	328,700	328,700
PIERCE, Charles Drew (19th C) American?				
oil	1	1,000	1,000	1,000
PIERCE, Charles Franklin (1844-1920) American				
oil	5	475-1,000	705	700
wc/d	1	600	600	600
PIERCE, Herman Winthrop (1850-1935) American				
oil	1	2,200	2,200	2,200
PIERCE, Joseph W (19th C) American				
wc/d	1	6,000	6,000	6,000
PIERCE, R E (?) American?				
oil	2	4,000-5,500	4,750	4,000
PIERCY, Rob (20th C) British				
wc/d	2	1,035-5,400	3,217	1,035
PIERECK, F (19th C) ?				
oil	1	3,053	3,053	3,053
PIERI, D (16th C) Italian				
3D	1	36,486	36,486	36,486
PIERO DI COSIMO (1462-1521) Italian				
oil	1	340,000	340,000	340,000
PIERRAKOS, Alkis (1920-) ?				
oil	2	3,092-6,920	5,006	3,092
PIERRE, A (19/20th C) ?				
oil	1	5,500	5,500	5,500
PIERRE, Jean Baptiste Marie (1713-1789) French				
oil	2	30,000-151,233	90,616	30,000
PIERRON, Charles (19/20th C) ?				
wc/d	1	1,686	1,686	1,686
PIERS, Leontine (?) Belgian?				
oil	1	2,338	2,338	2,338
PIERSON, Alden (1874-1921) American				
oil	1	1,630	1,630	1,630
PIERSON, Jack (1960-) American				
oil	1	8,500	8,500	8,500
3D	10	5,190-180,000	79,859	60,000
PIET, Fernand (1869-1942) French				
oil	2	1,074-14,135	7,604	1,074
PIETERCELIE, Alfred (1879-1955) Belgian				
oil	4	600-1,683	1,175	1,032
PIETERS, Evert (1856-1932) Dutch				
oil	5	1,770-94,865	21,949	4,877
wc/d	1	2,026	2,026	2,026
PIETRI, Pietro Antonio de (1663-1716) Italian				
wc/d	2	1,400-3,700	2,550	1,400
PIETTE, Ludovic (1826-1877) French				
oil	1	4,091	4,091	4,091
PIETTNER, J C B (19th C) ?				
oil	1	26,490	26,490	26,490

Name	No.	Price Range	Average	Median
PIFFARD, Harold (fl.1895-1899) British				
oil	1	3,145	3,145	3,145
PIFFARETTI, Bernard (1955-) French				
oil	2	2,383-5,063	3,723	2,383
PIGATO, Orazio (1896-1966) Italian				
oil	1	2,330	2,330	2,330
PIGEON, Maurice (1883-1944) French?				
oil	1	3,399	3,399	3,399
wc/d	2	1,874-2,428	2,151	1,874
PIGGELEN, H J van (1889-1961) Dutch				
wc/d	1	3,152	3,152	3,152
PIGHLEIN, Elimar Ulrich Bruno (1848-1894) German				
oil	1	2,311	2,311	2,311
PIGNATELLI, Ercole (1935-) Italian				
oil	27	1,045-6,361	2,610	1,929
wc/d	7	471-3,053	1,858	1,999
PIGNATELLI, Luca (1962-) Italian				
oil	13	3,514-26,938	11,433	9,955
wc/d	17	1,951-25,890	7,255	2,863
PIGNOLAT, Pierre (1838-1913) Swiss				
oil	2	2,061-4,789	3,425	2,061
PIGNON, Edouard (1905-1993) French				
oil	17	2,189-29,223	7,809	6,082
wc/d	29	471-5,049	1,894	1,695
PIGNON-ERNEST, Ernest (1942-) French				
wc/d	4	4,442-6,555	5,877	5,959
PIGNONI, Simone (1614-1698) Italian				
oil	1	35,000	35,000	35,000
PIGOTT, William Henry (1833-1901) British				
oil	1	4,450	4,450	4,450
wc/d	2	563-736	649	563
PIGUET, Rodolphe (1840-1915) Swiss				
oil	1	2,919	2,919	2,919
PIIRTO, Tapani (?) Finnish				
oil	1	1,798	1,798	1,798
PIKE, W H (1846-1908) British				
oil	1	2,436	2,436	2,436
PIKE, William H (1846-1908) British				
oil	5	589-3,185	1,617	1,496
PILET, Léon (1839-1916) French				
3D	1	6,000	6,000	6,000
PILICHOWSKI, Leopold (c.1864-1934) Polish				
wc/d	1	5,257	5,257	5,257
PILLARD, Elizabeth (19th C) French?				
oil	1	22,080	22,080	22,080
PILLEMENT, Jean (1728-1808) French				
oil	6	17,300-77,298	42,900	34,027
wc/d	14	1,903-10,000	4,348	4,393
PILLET, Edgar (1912-1996) French				
oil	26	477-7,730	2,023	1,432
wc/d	7	536-4,176	1,772	776
3D	8	1,790-4,653	2,803	2,386
PILLHOFER, Josef (1921-) Austrian				
oil	1	2,829	2,829	2,829
wc/d	1	1,169	1,169	1,169
3D	2	2,221-17,568	9,894	2,221
PILLIN, Polia (1909-1992) American				
oil	1	1,600	1,600	1,600
PILNY, Otto (1866-1936) Swiss				
oil	6	471-100,000	30,301	8,395
wc/d	1	955	955	955
PILO, Carl Gustaf (1712-1792) Swedish				
oil	1	28,456	28,456	28,456
PILO, Jons (1707-?) Swedish				
oil	2	15,288-25,479	20,383	15,288
PILOT, Albert (1922-) French				
oil	1	1,784	1,784	1,784
PILOT, Robert Wakeham (1898-1967) Canadian				
oil	33	3,545-115,213	21,709	12,299
wc/d	1	597	597	597
PILOTY, Ferdinand (1828-1895) German				
oil	1	9,388	9,388	9,388

Name	No.	Price Range	Average	Median
PILOTY, Karl Theodor von (1824-1886) German				
oil	1	4,000	4,000	4,000
PILS, Edouard Aime (1823-1850) French				
oil	1	7,603	7,603	7,603
PILS, Isidore (1813-1875) French				
oil	1	1,200	1,200	1,200
wc/d	3	486-4,000	2,028	1,600
PILSBURY, Wilmot (1840-1908) British				
wc/d	4	740-1,510	1,189	1,203
PILTERS, Joseph (1877-1957) German				
oil	1	3,708	3,708	3,708
PIMENOV, Valeri (1920-) Russian?				
oil	1	1,274	1,274	1,274
PIMM, L (19th C) British?				
oil	1	2,852	2,852	2,852
PIMONENKO, Nikolai Kornilovich (1862-1912) Russian				
oil	4	9,971-36,747	19,588	14,434
PINA, Alfredo (1887-1966) Italian				
3D	12	1,649-30,240	11,507	7,830
PINAL, Fernand (1881-1958) French				
oil	2	1,598-2,805	2,201	1,598
PINCEMIN, Jean-Pierre (1944-) French				
oil	24	654-38,837	19,101	19,867
wc/d	1	18,147	18,147	18,147
PINCHART, Émile Auguste (1842-1924) French				
oil	4	3,000-22,480	9,800	3,800
wc/d	1	572	572	572
PINCHERLE, Adriana (1906-1992) Italian				
oil	6	537-5,255	2,726	1,455
PINCHON, Robert Antoine (1886-1943) French				
oil	7	2,592-28,710	11,601	8,490
wc/d	1	480	480	480
PINCHUK, Mikhail (20th C) Russian				
oil	1	2,928	2,928	2,928
PINE, Robert Edge (1742-1788) British				
oil	1	9,405	9,405	9,405
PINEDA, Jose (1837-1907) Spanish				
wc/d	8	750-3,000	1,966	2,154
PINEDA-MONTON, Miguel (?) Spanish				
oil	1	11,095	11,095	11,095
PINEDO (19th C) French				
3D	1	3,360	3,360	3,360
PINEDO, Émile (1840-1916) French				
3D	3	1,790-4,498	2,936	2,521
PINEL DE GRANDCHAMP, Louis-Émile (1831-1894) French				
oil	1	38,000	38,000	38,000
PINELLI, Pino (1938-) Italian				
oil	3	530-2,148	1,270	1,133
wc/d	3	648-3,534	1,760	1,100
3D	1	3,024	3,024	3,024
PINGGERA, Heinz (1900-?) Italian				
wc/d	1	2,167	2,167	2,167
PINGRET, Edouard Henri Theophile (1788-1875) French				
oil	4	3,794-75,310	22,175	4,378
wc/d	1	1,267	1,267	1,267
PINHEIRO, Costa (1932-) Portuguese				
wc/d	1	2,188	2,188	2,188
PINK, Lutka (1916-) ?				
oil	2	1,434-1,793	1,613	1,434
PINKETT, Neil (1958-) British				
oil	1	1,144	1,144	1,144
PINKOFSKY, Silke (1972- 1972-) German				
oil	1	1,076	1,076	1,076
PINKUS, Sara M (20th C) American				
oil	1	2,200	2,200	2,200
PINNEY, Eunice (1770-1849) American				
wc/d	3	3,000-5,000	3,800	3,400
PINO, Giuseppe Dangelico (1939-) American				
oil	1	33,000	33,000	33,000
PINO, Marco da (1525-1588) Italian				
oil	1	60,811	60,811	60,811

Name	No.	Price Range	Average	Median
PINOLE Y RODRIGUEZ, Nicanor (1877-1978) Spanish				
wc/d	6	482-4,685	1,855	1,113
PINOS, Juan (1862-1910) Spanish				
oil	2	2,411-6,720	4,565	2,411
PINOT, Albert (1875-1962) Belgian				
oil	7	599-4,203	1,877	1,134
PINOTTI, G (19/20th C) Italian				
wc/d	1	2,890	2,890	2,890
PINSON, Isabelle (18th C) French				
oil	1	2,552	2,552	2,552
PINTALDI, Cristiano (1970-) Italian				
wc/d	1	1,219	1,219	1,219
PINTO, Abdon (20th C) Venezuelan				
oil	1	2,790	2,790	2,790
PINTO, M T (?) ?				
3D	1	3,854	3,854	3,854
PINWELL, George John (1842-1875) British				
wc/d	1	13,920	13,920	13,920
PIOLA, Domenico (elder) (1627-1703) Italian				
wc/d	3	3,390-12,298	6,768	4,618
PIOMBANTI AMMANNATI, Giuseppe (1898-1996) Italian				
oil	2	2,219-3,036	2,627	2,219
wc/d	8	514-954	733	656
PIOMBINO, Umberto (?) Italian				
oil	1	1,649	1,649	1,649
PIOMBO, Sebastiano del (1485-1547) Italian				
oil	1	1,700	1,700	1,700
PIOT, Adolphe (1850-1910) French				
oil	3	6,000-30,000	16,666	14,000
PIOTROWSKI, A (20th C) Polish				
oil	1	8,000	8,000	8,000
PIOTROWSKI, Antoni (1853-1924) Polish				
oil	1	4,000	4,000	4,000
PIPER, Edward (1938-1990) British				
oil	1	1,770	1,770	1,770
wc/d	1	531	531	531
PIPER, Jane (20th C) British				
oil	2	2,300-2,800	2,550	2,300
PIPER, John (1903-1992) British				
oil	6	1,566-148,680	73,901	49,140
wc/d	64	1,653-72,800	12,033	7,854
PIPPAL, Hans Robert (1915-1999) Austrian				
wc/d	3	964-2,805	1,618	1,085
PIPPEL, Otto (1878-1960) German				
oil	50	816-12,041	3,294	2,336
PIPPICH, Carl (1862-1932) Austrian				
wc/d	2	1,445-2,880	2,162	1,445
PIPPIN, Horace (1888-1946) American				
oil	1	130,000	130,000	130,000
PIQTOUKUN, David Ruben (1950-) North American				
3D	3	1,856-4,640	3,641	4,429
PIQUARD, Robert (20th C) French				
oil	1	2,797	2,797	2,797
PIQUET DE BRIENNE, Auguste (1789-?) French				
oil	1	2,337	2,337	2,337
PIRA, Gioacchino la (19th C) Italian				
wc/d	2	6,880-9,900	8,390	6,880
PIRANDELLO, Fausto (1899-1975) Italian				
oil	2	67,260-140,548	103,904	67,260
wc/d	9	2,704-45,796	8,044	3,107
PIRANESI, Giovan Battista (1720-1778) Italian				
wc/d	3	3,500-42,000	17,333	6,500
PIRAS, Luigi (20th C) Italian				
oil	2	954-1,193	1,073	954
PIRATZKI, Karl Karlovitch (1815-1871) Russian				
wc/d	2	31,004-34,724	32,864	31,004
PIRE, Ferdinand (1943-) Belgian				
oil	1	2,314	2,314	2,314
PIRE, Marcel (1913-1981) Belgian				
oil	3	1,414-1,929	1,750	1,908
wc/d	1	2,829	2,829	2,829

Name	No.	Price Range	Average	Median
PIRES, Yves (1958-) French				
3D	1	6,379	6,379	6,379
PIRIA, Maria Olga (1927-) Uruguayan				
oil	1	1,200	1,200	1,200
PIRIE, Sir George (1863-1946) British				
oil	5	1,313-3,629	2,611	2,565
PIRKER, Johann (1823-1891) Austrian				
oil	1	1,518	1,518	1,518
PIRNIE, Larry (1940-) American				
oil	1	6,500	6,500	6,500
PIROGOV, Nikolai Vasilievich (1872-1913) Russian				
oil	1	3,720	3,720	3,720
PIRON, Léon (1899-1962) Belgian				
oil	1	8,390	8,390	8,390
PISA, Alberto (1864-1931) Italian				
wc/d	2	974-3,583	2,278	974
PISANI, Louis (18/19th C) Italian?				
oil	1	2,760	2,760	2,760
PISANI, Vettor (1938-) Italian				
wc/d	2	2,108-3,579	2,843	2,108
PISANO, Edouardo (1912-) Spanish				
oil	4	932-2,016	1,445	1,157
PISANO, Giovanni (1875-1954) Italian				
oil	3	970-4,844	2,281	1,029
PISANO, Gustavo (1877-?) Italian				
oil	7	1,274-4,459	2,751	2,548
PISANTE, Francesco (19th C) Italian				
wc/d	4	1,640-3,480	2,802	3,045
PISCHINGER, Carl (1823-1886) Austrian				
oil	1	2,182	2,182	2,182
PISCO, Fr (19th C) German				
oil	1	1,951	1,951	1,951
PISECKI, Josef (1878-1954) Czechoslovakian				
oil	1	1,800	1,800	1,800
PISIS, Filippo de (1896-1956) Italian				
oil	47	3,440-203,311	49,744	29,828
wc/d	10	1,829-13,233	4,950	3,307
PISSARRO, Camille (1830-1903) French				
oil	31	5,220-4,600,000	1,084,238	846,400
wc/d	82	1,079-247,800	17,355	6,000
PISSARRO, Claude (1935-) French				
oil	5	7,000-10,000	8,700	8,500
wc/d	7	1,615-3,500	2,516	2,655
PISSARRO, Lucien (1863-1944) British/French				
oil	2	34,800-37,800	36,300	34,800
wc/d	3	2,300-4,524	3,328	3,160
PISSARRO, Ludovic Rodo (1878-1952) French				
oil	3	953-2,610	2,037	2,549
wc/d	13	608-1,722	953	837
PISSARRO, Orovida (1893-1968) British				
oil	2	3,480-7,308	5,394	3,480
wc/d	2	4,872-6,264	5,568	4,872
PISSARRO, Paul Émile (1884-1972) French				
oil	16	1,119-11,000	5,008	4,091
wc/d	9	501-3,200	1,569	1,500
PISSARRO, Victor (1891-1937) Argentinian				
oil	1	1,600	1,600	1,600
PISTOLETTO, Michelangelo (1933-) Italian				
oil	9	4,772-460,200	102,826	16,829
wc/d	4	8,416-79,650	31,894	15,429
3D	1	123,900	123,900	123,900
PISTOR, Hermann (1832-?) German				
oil	1	1,243	1,243	1,243
PISTOR, Oskar von (1865-1920) Austrian				
oil	2	1,168-1,168	1,168	1,168
PISTORIUS, Eduard (1796-1862) German				
oil	1	14,880	14,880	14,880
PISTRUCCI, Benedetto (1784-1855) Italian				
3D	1	37,000	37,000	37,000
PITA, Gerardo (1950-) ?				
wc/d	1	5,000	5,000	5,000

Name	No.	Price Range	Average	Median
PITHAWALLA, Manchershaw (1872-1937) Indian				
oil	1	12,000	12,000	12,000
PITLOO, Antonio Sminck (1791-1837) Dutch				
oil	1	19,747	19,747	19,747
wc/d	2	727-7,562	4,144	727
PITOCCHI, Matteo de (17th C) Italian				
oil	1	2,676	2,676	2,676
PITRA, Margot (?) ?				
3D	1	6,214	6,214	6,214
PITT, James Lynn (?-1921) British				
oil	2	1,408-1,584	1,496	1,408
PITT, William (19th C) British				
oil	7	478-7,134	2,483	1,218
wc/d	1	460	460	460
PITTARA, Carlo (1836-1890) Italian				
oil	2	2,983-11,503	7,243	2,983
PITTMAN, Hobson (1900-1972) American				
oil	8	500-18,000	7,350	6,000
wc/d	2	2,800-3,750	3,275	2,800
PITTMAN, Lari (1952-) American				
oil	1	45,000	45,000	45,000
PITTO, Guiseppe (1857-1928) Italian				
oil	3	1,484-5,394	2,866	1,720
PITTONI, Giovanni Battista (younger) (1687-1767) Italian				
oil	3	49,946-182,069	99,512	66,522
PITTS, Elizabeth McCord (1880-1963) American				
oil	1	1,700	1,700	1,700
PITZNER, Max Joseph (1855-1912) German				
oil	3	650-6,081	3,814	4,712
PIUMATI, Giovanni (1850-1915) Italian				
oil	1	1,885	1,885	1,885
PIVI, Paola (1971-) Italian				
3D	1	26,000	26,000	26,000
PIVOVAROV, Nikolai Vladimirovich (1957-) Russian				
oil	1	5,580	5,580	5,580
PIXIS, Theodor (1831-1907) German				
oil	1	1,818	1,818	1,818
PIZA, Arthur (1928-) Brazilian				
wc/d	2	2,121-2,863	2,492	2,121
PIZZI CANNELLA, Piero (1955-) Italian				
oil	9	3,269-10,510	7,174	7,767
wc/d	9	1,176-4,595	2,659	2,577
PIZZINATO, Armando (1910-2004) Italian				
oil	3	5,500-17,671	9,597	5,622
PIZZIRANI, Guglielmo (1886-1971) Italian				
oil	2	1,135-2,289	1,712	1,135
PIZZO, Giovanni (1934-) Italian				
oil	1	1,316	1,316	1,316
PIZZUTO, Albachiara (1972-) Italian				
wc/d	1	1,208	1,208	1,208
PLA Y GALLARDO, Cecilio (1860-1934) Spanish				
oil	1	48,720	48,720	48,720
wc/d	4	486-1,204	863	832
PLA Y RUBIO, Alberto (1867-1929) Spanish				
oil	3	4,163-10,650	6,537	4,800
PLAGNOL, Serge (1951-) French				
oil	1	947	947	947
wc/d	1	486	486	486
PLAKHOV, Lavr Kuzmich (1821-1881) Russian				
oil	1	67,521	67,521	67,521
PLANDING, Otto (1887-?) Canadian				
oil	1	1,208	1,208	1,208
PLANELLS, Angel (1902-1989) Spanish				
oil	1	1,197	1,197	1,197
PLANQUETTE, Felix (1873-1964) French				
oil	5	628-2,498	1,735	2,178
PLANSON, Andre (1898-1981) French				
oil	15	502-6,654	2,615	1,670
wc/d	7	618-2,297	1,732	1,913
PLANTE, Daniel (1958-) Canadian				
oil	2	485-1,804	1,144	485

Name	No.	Price Range	Average	Median
PLANTEY, Madeleine (19/20th C) French				
oil	1	1,204	1,204	1,204
PLAS, Nicholaas van der (1954-) Dutch				
oil	15	643-3,250	1,444	1,300
PLAS, Pieter (1810-1853) Dutch				
oil	2	1,512-8,372	4,942	1,512
PLASENCIA, Casto (1846-1890) Spanish				
oil	3	2,160-4,752	3,495	3,575
PLASKETT, Joe (1918-) Canadian				
oil	9	1,265-9,697	4,496	4,218
wc/d	7	371-1,024	651	647
PLASSAN, Antoine-Émile (1817-1903) French				
oil	3	3,025-5,000	3,993	3,956
PLASSE, Georges (1878-?) French				
oil	1	1,800	1,800	1,800
PLATH, Sylvia (1932-1963) British				
wc/d	6	1,388-40,940	8,827	1,757
PLATONOV, Charitan Platonovitch (1842-1907) Russian				
oil	1	44,460	44,460	44,460
PLATSCHEK, Hans (1923-) German				
oil	2	2,898-9,555	6,226	2,898
PLATT, John Edgar (1886-1967) British				
oil	1	1,682	1,682	1,682
PLATTE, Ewald (1894-?) German				
wc/d	2	1,944-2,188	2,066	1,944
PLATTNER, Karl (1919-1987) Austrian				
oil	6	8,919-45,544	21,629	12,486
PLATZ, Ernst Heinrich (1867-1940) German				
oil	2	608-1,783	1,195	608
wc/d	2	1,174-1,360	1,267	1,174
PLATZER, Johann Georg (1704-1761) Austrian				
oil	3	20,760-195,740	93,247	63,243
PLATZODER, Ludwig (1898-1976) German				
oil	1	1,091	1,091	1,091
PLAVINSKY, Dimitri (1937-) Russian				
oil	2	31,620-68,800	50,210	31,620
wc/d	1	27,000	27,000	27,000
PLAZZOTTA, Enzo (1921-1981) Italian				
wc/d	1	537	537	537
3D	6	4,956-15,555	8,105	6,715
PLE, Henri Honore (1853-1922) French				
3D	2	40,480-65,000	52,740	40,480
PLEISSNER, Ogden M (1905-1983) American				
oil	1	29,000	29,000	29,000
wc/d	11	3,000-70,000	29,590	23,000
PLENSA, Jaume (1955-) Spanish				
wc/d	4	666-28,431	11,230	7,644
3D	5	24,548-46,758	36,633	36,122
PLERICO, Silvio (20th C) Italian				
oil	1	1,796	1,796	1,796
PLESSEN, Magnus von (1967-) German				
oil	1	26,000	26,000	26,000
PLESSEN, Victor von (1900-1980) ?				
oil	1	1,445	1,445	1,445
PLESSI, Fabrizio (1940-) Italian				
oil	5	2,163-6,361	4,261	4,272
wc/d	4	1,635-3,102	2,198	1,790
PLETKA, Paul (1946-) American				
oil	2	12,000-16,000	14,000	12,000
PLEUER, Hermann (1863-1911) German				
oil	5	572-5,648	2,468	2,061
PLEYSIER, Ary (1809-1879) Dutch				
oil	2	1,029-3,402	2,215	1,029
PLOCK, K (?) German?				
oil	1	1,199	1,199	1,199
PLOCKHORST, Bernhard (1825-1907) German				
oil	1	1,762	1,762	1,762
PLOLL, Victor (?) ?				
oil	1	1,523	1,523	1,523
PLOMTEUX, Leopold (1920-) Belgian				
oil	1	1,136	1,136	1,136
wc/d	2	501-654	577	501

Name	No.	Price Range	Average	Median
PLONTKE, Anna (1890-1930) German				
oil	1	1,065	1,065	1,065
PLOOS VAN AMSTEL, Cornelis (1726-1798) Dutch				
wc/d	1	4,198	4,198	4,198
PLOQUIN, Gaston (?) ?				
oil	1	4,350	4,350	4,350
PLOSKY, Jonas (1940-) British				
oil	6	528-3,078	1,301	870
PLOWMAN, Frederik Prussia (?-1820) Irish				
oil	1	3,232	3,232	3,232
PLUMB, John (1927-) British				
oil	1	1,914	1,914	1,914
PLUYMS, Louis (1814-1880) Belgian				
oil	1	7,747	7,747	7,747
PO, Giacomo del (1652-1726) Italian				
oil	1	18,849	18,849	18,849
POCCETTI, Bernardino (1542-1612) Italian				
wc/d	1	1,683	1,683	1,683
POCCI, Franz Graf von (1807-1876) German				
wc/d	1	3,534	3,534	3,534
POCHERO, Peter Charlie (1895-1962) American				
oil	1	9,500	9,500	9,500
POCHINI, V (20th C) Italian?				
3D	1	2,066	2,066	2,066
POCHITONOV, Ivan Pavlovitch (1850-1923) Russian				
oil	16	8,000-180,000	62,062	50,000
POCOCK, Nicholas (1740-1821) British				
wc/d	5	484-2,975	2,034	2,432
PODCHERNIKOFF, Alexis M (1886-1933) American/Russian				
oil	15	1,000-18,000	4,691	3,250
PODESTA, Giampiero (1943-) Italian				
oil	1	4,707	4,707	4,707
PODKOWINSKI, Wladyslaw (1866-1895) Polish				
oil	1	23,945	23,945	23,945
POEL, Adriaen Lievensz van der (1626-1685) Dutch				
oil	1	81,745	81,745	81,745
POEL, Egbert van der (1621-1664) Dutch				
oil	7	4,497-84,857	32,321	14,000
POELENBURGH, Cornelis van (1586-1667) Dutch				
oil	9	3,857-55,500	23,025	20,027
wc/d	1	2,674	2,674	2,674
POELS, Albert (1903-1984) Belgian				
3D	3	1,560-4,132	3,086	3,567
POERTZEL, Otto (1876-1963) German				
3D	7	1,967-18,000	7,073	4,671
POETZELBERGER, Oswald (1893-1966) German				
oil	2	730-2,338	1,534	730
POETZELBERGER, Robert (1856-1930) Austrian				
oil	1	2,225	2,225	2,225
POETZSCH, Paul (1858-1936) German				
oil	1	1,030	1,030	1,030
POGANY, Willy (1882-1956) American				
wc/d	1	1,760	1,760	1,760
POGEDAIEFF, George (1899-1971) Russian				
oil	12	878-14,620	6,055	4,425
wc/d	4	3,784-44,640	20,058	15,810
POGGENBEEK, Geo (1853-1903) Dutch				
oil	5	1,001-4,607	2,595	2,178
wc/d	4	1,678-5,852	2,790	1,752
POGZEBA, Wolfgang (1936-) American				
oil	3	1,100-10,000	4,533	2,500
POHL, Edward Henry (1874-1956) American				
wc/d	1	4,250	4,250	4,250
POHL, Hugo David (1878-1960) American				
oil	3	1,000-1,500	1,333	1,500
POHLE, Hermann (1831-1901) German				
oil	2	1,455-10,014	5,734	1,455
POHLE, Léon (1841-1908) German				
oil	1	1,214	1,214	1,214
POIGNANT, Lucien (20th C) French				
oil	1	2,259	2,259	2,259

Name	No.	Price Range	Average	Median
POIJARVI, Annikki (1931-) Finnish				
oil	1	2,314	2,314	2,314
POINGDESTRE, Charles H (?-1905) British				
oil	1	1,880	1,880	1,880
POINT, Armand (1860-1932) French				
oil	4	2,572-9,514	5,178	3,317
wc/d	4	701-6,197	3,303	2,835
POINTNER, Rudolf (1907-1991) Austrian				
wc/d	3	667-1,424	1,047	1,051
POIRIER, Anne and Patrick (20th C) French				
wc/d	1	1,764	1,764	1,764
POIRIER, Charles (19th C) French				
oil	1	1,051	1,051	1,051
POISSON, Louverture (1914-1985) Haitian				
oil	3	800-1,600	1,100	900
POISSON, Pierre Marie (1876-1953) French				
3D	1	4,455	4,455	4,455
POITEVIN, E (19th C) French				
oil	1	4,071	4,071	4,071
POITRAS, Jane Ash (1951-) Canadian				
oil	2	618-1,237	927	618
wc/d	7	815-4,231	2,009	1,968
POIVRET, Jean-Luc (1950-) French				
oil	1	1,196	1,196	1,196
POKITONOV, Ivan (1850-1923) Russian				
oil	3	10,541-49,144	33,879	41,952
POKORNY, Richard (1907-) Austrian				
wc/d	4	722-1,806	1,295	1,324
POL, Christiaen van (1752-1813) Dutch				
oil	1	60,000	60,000	60,000
wc/d	1	3,928	3,928	3,928
POLA, Hendrick (1676-1748) Dutch				
oil	1	4,241	4,241	4,241
POLARI, B (18th C) Italian?				
3D	1	3,440	3,440	3,440
POLAROLI, Adolfo (1862-1952) Italian				
oil	2	1,937-7,027	4,482	1,937
POLE, C L (19th C) British?				
oil	1	1,892	1,892	1,892
POLEDNE, Franz (1873-1932) Austrian				
wc/d	4	661-1,445	1,003	708
POLENOV, Vassili (1844-1927) Russian				
oil	5	17,390-584,800	280,933	334,839
POLEO, Hector (1918-) Venezuelan				
oil	1	11,630	11,630	11,630
wc/d	1	7,070	7,070	7,070
POLESELLO, Rogelio (1939-) Argentinian				
oil	8	3,160-16,000	7,914	7,500
3D	3	1,860-20,000	8,020	2,200
POLGE, Denis (1972-) French				
oil	1	1,767	1,767	1,767
wc/d	1	825	825	825
POLI, Gherardo (1676-1739) Italian				
oil	3	24,000-26,700	25,471	25,714
POLI, Jacques (1938-) French				
oil	5	1,721-4,171	2,763	2,719
POLIAKOFF, Nicolas (1899-1976) Russian				
oil	4	596-5,041	2,417	1,360
POLIAKOFF, Serge (1906-1969) Russian				
oil	36	18,819-492,800	188,239	172,480
wc/d	29	6,732-101,081	41,141	38,720
POLICASTRO, Enrique (1898-1971) Argentinian				
oil	2	8,000-20,000	14,000	8,000
wc/d	1	3,800	3,800	3,800
POLIDORO DA CARAVAGGIO (1492-1543) Italian				
oil	1	19,421	19,421	19,421
wc/d	1	720	720	720
POLITTI, Leo (1908-) American				
wc/d	1	3,500	3,500	3,500
POLITZER, Michel (1933-) French?				
3D	1	4,855	4,855	4,855

Name	No.	Price Range	Average	Median
POLK, Frank Frederick (1908-2000) American				
3D	1	2,498	2,498	2,498
POLK, Naomi (1892-1984) American				
wc/d	1	1,500	1,500	1,500
POLKE, Sigmar (1941-) German				
oil	11	12,110-850,000	163,558	91,177
wc/d	25	834-1,496,000	92,435	16,365
POLL, J (20th C) ?				
oil	1	2,520	2,520	2,520
POLLAK, August (1838-?) Austrian				
oil	1	1,784	1,784	1,784
POLLAK, Julius (1845-?) Austrian				
oil	1	1,784	1,784	1,784
POLLAK, Wilhelm (1802-1860) Austrian				
oil	1	3,099	3,099	3,099
POLLARD, James (1797-1867) British				
oil	3	12,000-90,000	54,000	60,000
POLLEN, John Hungerford (1820-1902) British				
oil	1	3,382	3,382	3,382
POLLENTINE, Alfred (fl.1861-1880) British				
oil	22	445-10,560	4,318	3,096
wc/d	1	2,262	2,262	2,262
POLLES (?) ?				
3D	1	3,449	3,449	3,449
POLLET, Joseph Michel-Ange (1814-1870) French				
3D	1	2,076	2,076	2,076
POLLOCK, Jackson (1912-1956) American				
oil	2	120,000-1,900,000	1,010,000	120,000
wc/d	3	60,084-800,000	353,361	200,000
POLLONERA, Carlo (c.1849-1923) Italian				
oil	2	2,521-44,980	23,750	2,521
POLSKY, Cynthia (1939-) American				
oil	1	4,000	4,000	4,000
POLYAKOV, Valentin Ivanovich (1915-1977) Russian				
oil	1	2,378	2,378	2,378
POLYKOV, Sergei (20th C) Russian				
oil	1	2,450	2,450	2,450
POLYKRATIS, Georgios (1931-) Greek				
oil	1	1,408	1,408	1,408
POMA, Silvio (1840-1932) Italian				
oil	8	2,249-60,616	14,357	5,178
POMMEREULLE, Daniel (1937-) French				
3D	1	3,576	3,576	3,576
POMODORO, Arnaldo (1926-) Italian				
oil	1	5,088	5,088	5,088
wc/d	1	17,000	17,000	17,000
3D	41	2,016-316,233	54,052	13,760
POMODORO, Gio (1930-2002) Italian				
wc/d	8	595-3,102	1,690	1,308
3D	10	2,983-53,100	18,989	9,514
POMPA, Gaetano (1933-1998) Italian				
oil	1	2,000	2,000	2,000
wc/d	2	1,109-1,767	1,438	1,109
POMPIGNOLI, Luigi (19th C) Italian				
oil	1	2,750	2,750	2,750
POMPON, François (1855-1933) French				
3D	15	9,062-141,370	40,822	34,714
PONC, Joan (1927-1984) Spanish				
oil	1	3,403	3,403	3,403
wc/d	5	4,995-11,297	7,291	7,400
PONCE DE LEON, Fidelio (1896-1957) Cuban				
oil	2	16,000-16,000	16,000	16,000
PONCE, Jorge (20th C) Argentinian				
oil	2	3,000-4,500	3,750	3,000
PONCE-CAMUS, Marie Nicolas (1778-1839) French				
oil	1	8,286	8,286	8,286
PONCELET, Thierry (1946-) Belgian				
oil	1	3,250	3,250	3,250
PONCET, Antoine (1928-) Swiss				
3D	11	2,000-13,000	7,830	8,000
PONCET, Francois Marie (1736-1797) French				
3D	1	375,411	375,411	375,411

Name	No.	Price Range	Average	Median
PONDICK, Rona (1952-) American				
3D	1	9,500	9,500	9,500
PONGRATZ, Peter (1940-) German				
oil	1	14,566	14,566	14,566
PONOMAREW, Serge (20th C) Russian				
oil	1	643	643	643
wc/d	1	514	514	514
3D	1	1,784	1,784	1,784
PONS, Jean (1913-) French				
oil	2	502-2,238	1,370	502
PONS-ARNAU, Francisco (1886-1955) Spanish				
oil	1	1,686	1,686	1,686
PONSEN, Tunis (1891-1968) American				
oil	3	600-2,700	1,800	2,100
PONSIOEN, Johannes Bernardus (1900-1969) Dutch				
oil	2	2,049-14,027	8,038	2,049
PONSON, Luc Raphael (1835-1904) French				
oil	1	5,568	5,568	5,568
PONSONBY, Sarah (1943-) British				
oil	1	2,035	2,035	2,035
PONSTINGL, Frank (1927-1988) American?				
oil	3	1,000-2,300	1,666	1,700
PONT VERGES, Pedro (20th C) Argentinian?				
wc/d	1	2,500	2,500	2,500
PONTE, R (19th C) ?				
oil	1	3,312	3,312	3,312
PONTHUS-CINIER, Antoine (1812-1885) French				
oil	1	3,568	3,568	3,568
wc/d	1	583	583	583
PONTI, Gio (1891-1979) Italian				
oil	1	6,920	6,920	6,920
wc/d	1	759	759	759
PONTOY, Henri Jean (1888-1968) French				
oil	47	829-78,988	19,777	8,872
wc/d	15	2,919-10,346	5,318	4,435
PONTRELLI, Tino (20th C) American?				
wc/d	1	3,000	3,000	3,000
PONZA, Giuseppe (20th C) Italian				
oil	1	10,440	10,440	10,440
POOL, Juriaen II (1665-1745) Dutch				
oil	1	5,190	5,190	5,190
POOLE, Paul Falconer (1807-1879) British				
oil	4	438-13,200	3,796	681
POONS, Larry (1937-) American				
oil	1	66,628	66,628	66,628
POORE, Henry Rankin (1859-1940) American				
oil	1	32,000	32,000	32,000
POORTEN, Jacobus Johannes van (1841-1914) German				
oil	6	1,178-3,503	2,267	1,844
POORTENAAR, Jan (1886-1958) Dutch				
oil	1	2,303	2,303	2,303
POORTVLIET, Rien (1932-1995) Dutch				
oil	2	4,195-5,394	4,794	4,195
wc/d	2	1,252-1,252	1,252	1,252
POOSCH, Max von (1872-1960) Austrian				
oil	1	2,182	2,182	2,182
POPE, Alexander (1849-1924) American				
oil	7	3,500-90,000	23,357	10,000
POPE, Gustav (19th C) British				
oil	1	41,580	41,580	41,580
POPE, Nicholas (1949-) British				
3D	1	6,764	6,764	6,764
POPE, Perpetua (1916-) British				
oil	3	433-2,784	1,449	1,131
POPE, Thomas Benjamin (?-1891) American				
oil	1	1,100	1,100	1,100
POPEA, Elena (1885-1942) Rumanian				
oil	1	2,700	2,700	2,700
POPELS, Jan (17th C) Dutch				
oil	1	9,633	9,633	9,633
POPHAM, M (?) ?				
oil	1	1,890	1,890	1,890

Name	No.	Price Range	Average	Median
POPIELARCZYK, W K (20th C) ?				
oil	1	2,500	2,500	2,500
POPINEAU, Emile (20th C) French				
3D	1	5,856	5,856	5,856
POPKOV, Viktor Efimovich (1932-) Russian				
oil	1	48,160	48,160	48,160
POPOFF, Alexander (20th C) Russian				
oil	1	1,600	1,600	1,600
POPOFF, Georges (20th C) Russian?				
oil	1	3,312	3,312	3,312
POPOV, Alexander Nikolaevich (19/20th C) Russian				
oil	1	1,900	1,900	1,900
POPOVA, Liubov (1889-1924) Russian				
oil	2	13,500-19,007	16,253	13,500
wc/d	3	3,480-4,849	3,936	3,480
POPP, Jon (1862-?) German				
oil	2	701-1,338	1,019	701
POPPLETON, Chad (?) American				
oil	1	5,000	5,000	5,000
PORAY, Stanislaus (1888-1948) American				
oil	2	900-2,250	1,575	900
PORBUCHRAI, Yehuda (1949-) Israeli				
oil	1	5,000	5,000	5,000
PORCAR RIPOLLES, Juan Bautista (1888-1974) Spanish				
oil	2	1,916-22,800	12,358	1,916
PORCELLIS, Jan (16/17th C) Dutch				
oil	1	31,450	31,450	31,450
PORCHER, Albert (1834-1895) French				
oil	1	1,694	1,694	1,694
POREAU, Oswald (1877-1955) Belgian				
oil	10	494-5,244	1,489	834
PORET, Xavier de (1894-1975) Swiss				
wc/d	12	531-41,421	5,479	1,784
PORGES, Clara (1879-1963) Swiss				
oil	1	7,642	7,642	7,642
wc/d	2	1,582-1,998	1,790	1,582
PORSCHE, Otto Maria (1858-1931) German				
oil	4	468-3,279	1,244	527
PORSET MARTINEZ, Emilio (19th C) Spanish				
oil	1	1,076	1,076	1,076
PORTA, Guglielmo della (c.1514-1577) Italian				
3D	2	23,514-101,769	62,641	23,514
PORTAELS, Jean François (1818-1895) Belgian				
oil	9	486-128,800	21,914	8,269
wc/d	2	900-910	905	900
PORTER, Bruce (1865-1953) American				
oil	2	3,250-9,500	6,375	3,250
PORTER, Charles E (1847-1923) American				
oil	3	6,000-27,500	17,166	18,000
PORTER, Fairfield (1907-1975) American				
oil	2	75,000-210,000	142,500	75,000
wc/d	1	3,750	3,750	3,750
PORTER, George Edward (1916-) American				
oil	1	1,200	1,200	1,200
PORTER, Ralph (1942-) North American				
3D	1	1,434	1,434	1,434
PORTIELJE, Edward Antoon (1861-1949) Belgian				
oil	18	1,458-37,083	14,292	12,274
PORTIELJE, Gerard (1856-1929) Belgian				
oil	10	5,500-40,000	24,360	25,055
wc/d	5	468-701	561	468
PORTIELJE, Gerard and BOOGAARD, Willem Jacobus (19th C) Belgian				
oil	1	8,000	8,000	8,000
PORTIELJE, Jon Frederik Pieter (1829-1908) Belgian/Dutch				
oil	14	4,203-32,000	14,120	13,185
PORTINARI, Candido (1903-1962) Brazilian				
oil	6	160,000-825,000	447,500	390,000
wc/d	4	17,000-120,000	55,875	24,000
PORTO, Raul (20th C) Venezuelan				
oil	1	2,325	2,325	2,325

Name	No.	Price Range	Average	Median
PORTOCARRERO, René (1912-1986) Cuban				
oil	3	30,000-140,000	76,883	60,649
wc/d	16	707-32,000	10,181	5,500
PORTWAY, Douglas (1922-1993) South African				
oil	3	1,556-3,916	2,759	2,805
wc/d	2	1,388-1,566	1,477	1,388
PORWOLL, Hans (20th C) German?				
oil	2	655-1,951	1,303	655
PORZANO, Giacomo (1925-) Italian				
oil	1	8,758	8,758	8,758
POSCHINGER, Richard von (1839-1915) German				
oil	4	547-4,622	2,557	969
POSE, Eduard Wilhelm (1812-1878) German				
oil	1	12,671	12,671	12,671
POSEN, Leonid (1849-1921) Russian				
3D	4	6,000-80,000	39,020	18,000
POSKAS, Peter (1939-) American				
oil	1	9,000	9,000	9,000
POSPOLITAKI, Yevgeni (1852-1910) Russian				
oil	1	1,376	1,376	1,376
POSSART, Felix (1837-1928) German				
oil	3	763-2,588	1,450	1,000
wc/d	1	820	820	820
POSSENTI, Antonio (1933-) Italian				
oil	43	595-6,297	2,272	1,885
wc/d	12	589-1,767	1,017	1,001
POSSIN, Rudolf (1861-1922) German				
wc/d	1	1,764	1,764	1,764
POSSOZ, Milly (1889-1967) Portuguese				
wc/d	1	2,674	2,674	2,674
POST, George (1906-1997) American				
wc/d	11	2,250-6,000	3,795	3,750
POST, William Merritt (1856-1935) American				
oil	6	2,200-5,000	3,950	4,500
wc/d	2	550-1,700	1,125	550
POSTEL, Jules (1867-1955) Belgian				
oil	9	482-1,827	1,015	942
POSTHUMA, Simon (1939-) Dutch				
oil	1	2,104	2,104	2,104
POSTIGLIANI (?) ?				
oil	1	4,152	4,152	4,152
POSTIGLIONE, Luca (1876-1936) Italian				
oil	4	1,500-12,103	6,476	4,536
POSTMA, Cornelius (1903-1977) Dutch				
oil	5	647-1,573	1,209	1,210
wc/d	1	844	844	844
POSTMA, Gerrit (1819-1894) Dutch				
oil	1	5,408	5,408	5,408
POTAGE, Michel (1949-) French				
oil	1	1,794	1,794	1,794
wc/d	1	829	829	829
POTAMIANOS, Haralambos (1909-1958) Greek				
oil	1	2,914	2,914	2,914
POTENZA, Primo (?) Italian				
oil	1	2,330	2,330	2,330
POTHAST, Bernard (1882-1966) Dutch/Belgian				
oil	12	8,000-27,840	15,851	15,582
POTRONAT, Lucien (1889-?) French				
oil	6	597-1,750	1,018	900
POTT, Laslett John (1837-1898) British				
oil	1	9,204	9,204	9,204
POTTER, Beatrix (1866-1943) British				
wc/d	5	748-18,500	6,612	4,984
POTTER, George (1941-) Irish				
oil	2	2,180-5,959	4,069	2,180
wc/d	1	667	667	667
POTTER, Ken (1926-) American				
wc/d	2	2,500-3,500	3,000	2,500
POTTER, Louis McClellan (1873-1912) American				
3D	1	16,000	16,000	16,000

Name	No.	Price Range	Average	Median
POTTER, Mary (1900-1981) British				
oil	9	4,425-36,330	16,620	18,900
wc/d	4	662-1,151	940	974
POTTER, Paulus (1625-1654) Dutch				
oil	3	4,023-3,600,000	1,202,926	4,757
POTTER, Pieter Symonsz (1597-1652) Dutch				
oil	3	5,758-31,306	17,238	14,651
POTTER, Raymond (20th C) British				
oil	1	1,480	1,480	1,480
POTTER, Sydney (fl.1883-1889) British				
oil	1	4,400	4,400	4,400
POTTER, William J (1883-1964) American				
oil	3	400-1,500	833	600
wc/d	1	1,045	1,045	1,045
POTTHAST, Edward Henry (1857-1927) American				
oil	8	1,475-240,000	103,121	42,500
wc/d	4	1,000-22,000	10,150	1,600
POTTHOF, Hans (1911-2003) Swiss				
oil	4	2,331-8,106	4,442	3,137
wc/d	4	649-4,487	1,971	1,249
POTWOROWSKI, Peter (1898-1962) Polish				
oil	1	18,165	18,165	18,165
POUGET, Marcel (1923-) French				
oil	1	1,255	1,255	1,255
POUGHEON, Eugène Robert (1886-1955) French				
oil	1	7,000	7,000	7,000
wc/d	1	10,541	10,541	10,541
POUGNY, Jean (1894-1956) French/Russian				
oil	29	3,062-46,284	16,699	12,599
wc/d	7	479-39,060	6,772	1,350
POUJOL, Pierre Louis Marius (1858-?) French				
oil	1	17,000	17,000	17,000
POULAIN, Jean (20th C) French				
oil	2	742-1,798	1,270	742
wc/d	11	556-3,116	1,681	1,678
POULSEN, M C (1953-) American				
oil	1	45,000	45,000	45,000
POULSON, Ernest (19th C) British				
oil	1	4,675	4,675	4,675
POUMEYROL, Jean-Marie (1945-) French				
oil	1	4,143	4,143	4,143
wc/d	1	1,942	1,942	1,942
POURBUS, Frans (elder) (1545-1581) Flemish				
oil	1	25,000	25,000	25,000
POURTAU, Léon (1868-1898) French				
oil	3	7,598-10,850	9,232	9,250
POUSETTE-DART, Richard (1916-1992) American				
oil	2	32,500-47,500	40,000	32,500
POUWELSEN, Willem (1801-1873) Dutch				
oil	1	3,312	3,312	3,312
POVORINA-AHLERS-HESTERMANN, Alexandra (1888-1963) Russian				
oil	1	3,750	3,750	3,750
POWELL, Ace (1912-1978) American				
oil	10	3,750-18,000	7,655	5,000
POWELL, Charles Martin (1775-1824) British				
oil	6	537-11,505	4,798	2,687
POWELL, Dave (1954-) American				
oil	1	5,500	5,500	5,500
wc/d	1	492	492	492
POWELL, Joseph (1780-1834) British				
wc/d	1	1,000	1,000	1,000
POWELL, Lucien Whiting (1846-1930) American				
oil	1	3,400	3,400	3,400
wc/d	3	400-750	533	450
POWELL, W E (19/20th C) British				
wc/d	1	1,104	1,104	1,104
POWER, Arthur (20th C) Irish?				
3D	1	2,175	2,175	2,175
POWER, Harold Septimus (1878-1951) New Zealander				
oil	1	29,600	29,600	29,600
POWERS, Asahel (1813-1843) American				
oil	2	8,000-20,000	14,000	8,000

Name	No.	Price Range	Average	Median
POWERS, Hiram (1805-1873) American				
3D	2	75,000-95,000	85,000	75,000
POWERS, Marion (20th C) American				
oil	1	2,250	2,250	2,250
POWNALL, George Hyde (c.1876-1932) Australian				
oil	2	2,928-2,958	2,943	2,928
POY DALMAU, Emilio (1876-1933) Spanish				
oil	4	1,399-4,469	2,581	1,447
POYNTER, Sir Edward John (1836-1919) British				
oil	1	68,040	68,040	68,040
wc/d	5	1,730-12,110	5,322	3,440
POZHEDAEV, Georgy Anatolevich (1897-1971) Russian				
oil	1	13,760	13,760	13,760
POZIER, Jacinte (1844-1915) French				
oil	1	2,386	2,386	2,386
POZZATI, Concetto (1935-) Italian				
oil	23	1,178-12,857	4,178	3,588
wc/d	13	766-6,732	2,976	2,589
POZZATO, Paride (1899-1971) Italian				
oil	3	1,455-4,243	2,465	1,697
POZZI, F (20th C) Italian				
3D	2	1,881-1,942	1,911	1,881
POZZI, Walter (1911-1989) Italian				
oil	5	700-2,848	1,412	1,312
POZZO, Ugo (1900-1981) Italian				
oil	1	4,371	4,371	4,371
PRABHA, B (1933-2001) Indian				
oil	8	8,500-52,800	32,312	27,680
wc/d	4	5,500-20,000	11,470	6,358
PRACHENSKY, Markus (1932-) Austrian				
oil	13	9,710-67,932	30,632	29,131
wc/d	9	3,857-8,281	5,849	5,733
PRACHENSKY, Wilhelm Nikolaus (1898-1956) Austrian				
oil	4	7,572-38,571	16,611	9,699
wc/d	1	1,635	1,635	1,635
PRADA, Carlo (1884-1960) Italian				
oil	3	3,160-18,791	8,849	4,597
PRADAL, Carlos (1932-1988) Spanish				
oil	1	3,138	3,138	3,138
PRADES, Alfred F de (fl.1844-1883) British				
oil	3	1,313-13,090	6,710	5,728
wc/d	1	1,702	1,702	1,702
PRADIER, Jean Jacques (1792-1852) French/Swiss				
wc/d	1	8,880	8,880	8,880
3D	7	2,572-21,875	8,021	5,220
PRADILLA Y ORTIZ, Francisco (1848-1921) Spanish				
oil	4	2,514-15,660	6,551	3,640
wc/d	1	1,936	1,936	1,936
PRADILLA, Francisco (1840-1921) Spanish				
oil	2	121,800-139,200	130,500	121,800
wc/d	2	714-714	714	714
PRAM-HENNINGSEN, Christian (1846-1892) Danish				
oil	2	1,897-2,779	2,338	1,897
PRAMPOLINI, Enrico (1894-1956) Italian				
oil	11	3,086-152,260	39,752	25,442
wc/d	7	996-3,349	1,991	1,767
PRANGENBERG, Norbert (1949-) German				
oil	1	825	825	825
wc/d	1	4,077	4,077	4,077
PRANISHNIKOFF, Ivan (1841-1910) Russian				
oil	2	20,640-37,840	29,240	20,640
PRANTL, Karl (1923-) Austrian				
3D	1	64,286	64,286	64,286
PRASAD, Devi (20th C) Indian				
wc/d	1	1,705	1,705	1,705
PRASSINOS, Mario (1916-1985) Turkish				
oil	12	983-24,310	10,523	8,650
wc/d	5	1,229-4,393	2,716	3,031
PRATELLA, Attilio (1856-1949) Italian				
oil	31	1,274-40,480	13,288	10,166
PRATELLA, Fausto (1888-1964) Italian				
oil	13	1,155-14,240	4,634	3,366
wc/d	1	2,460	2,460	2,460

Name	No.	Price Range	Average	Median
PRATERE, Edmond Joseph de (1826-1888) Belgian				
oil	3	2,572-4,676	3,838	4,268
PRATI, E (19/20th C) Italian				
3D	1	5,600	5,600	5,600
PRATI, Eugenio (1842-1907) Italian				
oil	1	1,890	1,890	1,890
PRATI, Franz (20th C) Italian?				
oil	1	1,057	1,057	1,057
PRATT, Claude (1860-c.1935) British				
oil	1	5,190	5,190	5,190
PRATT, Colonel Charles (1789-1869) Irish				
wc/d	3	1,911-6,370	4,204	4,332
PRATT, Douglas Fieldew (1900-1972) Australian				
oil	2	842-1,936	1,389	842
wc/d	1	465	465	465
PRATT, Henry Lark (1805-1873) British				
oil	1	1,700	1,700	1,700
PRATT, Hugo (20th C) ?				
wc/d	1	1,193	1,193	1,193
PRATT, Jonathan (1835-1911) British				
oil	1	2,035	2,035	2,035
PRATT, Mary Frances (1935-) Canadian				
oil	1	8,863	8,863	8,863
wc/d	1	2,952	2,952	2,952
PRATT, William (1855-1936) British				
oil	3	655-32,040	11,186	865
PRAX, Valentine (1899-1981) French				
oil	11	2,033-12,274	6,190	5,041
wc/d	4	1,400-3,155	2,416	2,525
PREAUX, Michel (20th C) French				
oil	1	1,178	1,178	1,178
PREDA, Ambrogio (1839-1906) Italian				
oil	2	2,284-4,863	3,573	2,284
PREDESCU-MELZER, Alina (1948-) Swiss				
3D	1	3,329	3,329	3,329
PREDONZANI, Dino (1914-1994) Italian				
oil	2	1,210-1,331	1,270	1,210
PREECE, Patricia (1900-1971) British				
oil	1	1,392	1,392	1,392
PREEN, Hugo von (1854-?) Austrian				
oil	1	1,093	1,093	1,093
PREGEN, N (19th C) ?				
oil	1	2,595	2,595	2,595
PREGNIARD, C Martin (20th C) ?				
oil	1	2,832	2,832	2,832
PREGO, Manuel (1915-1986) Spanish				
oil	1	3,131	3,131	3,131
wc/d	3	823-2,586	1,782	1,937
PREISS, Ferdinand (1882-1943) German				
wc/d	2	425-950	687	425
3D	24	1,806-51,240	10,308	4,586
PREISSLER, Daniel (1627-1665) German				
oil	1	2,616	2,616	2,616
PREKAS, Paris (1926-1999) Greek				
oil	5	11,220-44,880	30,380	29,580
PRELL, Hermann (1854-1922) German				
3D	1	7,890	7,890	7,890
PRELLER, Alexis (1911-1975) South African				
oil	2	10,720-13,194	11,957	10,720
PRELLER, Friedrich Johann Christian Ernst (1804-1878) German				
oil	2	1,100-6,563	3,831	1,100
wc/d	4	732-3,770	1,798	763
PRELLER, Louis Friedrich (1838-1901) German				
oil	1	12,162	12,162	12,162
PRELOG, Drago J (1939-) Yugoslavian				
oil	1	7,283	7,283	7,283
wc/d	3	1,052-1,171	1,102	1,083
PREM, Heimrad (1934-1978) German				
oil	5	1,527-11,712	7,062	8,818
wc/d	2	885-10,829	5,857	885
PRENCIPE, Umberto (1879-1962) Italian				
oil	4	973-1,459	1,221	1,155

Name	No.	Price Range	Average	Median
PRENDERGAST, Charles E (1863-1948) American				
oil	1	1,400,000	1,400,000	1,400,000
wc/d	1	11,000	11,000	11,000
3D	2	37,500-37,500	37,500	37,500
PRENDERGAST, Maurice (1859-1924) American				
oil	4	90,000-300,000	207,500	140,000
wc/d	4	8,500-400,000	150,875	55,000
PRENTICE, Bruce (1921-1985) American				
wc/d	2	2,000-2,750	2,375	2,000
PRENTICE, Levi Wells (1851-1935) American				
oil	8	3,000-30,000	12,368	9,000
PRENTZEL, Hans (1880-1956) German				
oil	1	2,385	2,385	2,385
PRESAS, Leopoldo (1915-) Argentinian				
oil	10	2,500-30,000	11,230	4,500
PRESCOTT, Charles Barrow (1870-1932) British				
oil	1	1,607	1,607	1,607
PRESS, Otto (19th C) German				
oil	1	2,289	2,289	2,289
PRESSLER, Gene (20th C) American				
wc/d	1	6,500	6,500	6,500
PRESSMANE, Joseph (1904-1967) French				
oil	11	717-6,000	2,946	3,057
PRESTEL, Johann Erdmann Gottlieb (younger) (1804-1885) German				
oil	1	11,125	11,125	11,125
PRESTILEO, Enzo (1957-) Italian				
oil	2	5,605-8,174	6,889	5,605
PRESTON, Chloe (20th C) British?				
wc/d	1	1,300	1,300	1,300
PRESTON, May Wilson (1873-1949) American				
oil	1	4,200	4,200	4,200
PRETE, Danilo di (1911-1985) Brazilian				
oil	1	1,720	1,720	1,720
PRETE, Juan del (1897-1987) Argentinian				
oil	7	4,500-30,000	12,857	11,000
wc/d	1	10,000	10,000	10,000
PRETI, Gregorio (1603-1672) Italian				
oil	1	64,726	64,726	64,726
PRETI, Mattia (1613-1699) Italian				
oil	1	117,205	117,205	117,205
PREUSS, Emil (19th C) German				
oil	1	14,000	14,000	14,000
PREUSS, Rudolf (1879-?) Austrian				
wc/d	1	2,178	2,178	2,178
PREVERAUD DE SONNEVILLE, Georges (1889-1978) French				
oil	2	989-1,174	1,081	989
PREVERT, Jacques (1900-1977) French				
wc/d	6	2,769-5,786	4,318	4,500
PREVIATI, Gaetano (1852-1920) Italian				
oil	1	16,026	16,026	16,026
wc/d	3	4,531-22,384	11,560	7,767
PREVOST, Antoine (1930-) Canadian				
oil	2	1,394-2,886	2,140	1,394
wc/d	1	615	615	615
PREVOST, Jean Louis (1760-1810) French				
oil	3	5,143-26,859	16,613	17,837
PREVOT-VALERI, Andre (1890-1930) French				
oil	3	492-1,874	1,084	887
PREVOT-VALERI, Auguste (1857-1930) French				
oil	2	850-3,138	1,994	850
PREY, Juan de (1904-1962) Puerto Rican				
oil	1	3,300	3,300	3,300
PREYER, Emilie (1849-1930) German				
oil	2	11,342-33,652	22,497	11,342
PREYER, Johann Wilhelm (1803-1889) German				
oil	2	74,167-89,737	81,952	74,167
wc/d	1	522	522	522
PREYER, Paul (1847-1931) German				
oil	1	1,459	1,459	1,459
PREZIOSI, Amadeo (1816-1882) Italian				
wc/d	16	2,232-78,120	23,591	7,007

Name	No.	Price Range	Average	Median
PRIANICHNIKOFF, Ilarion Michailovitch (1840-1894) Russian				
oil	1	11,478	11,478	11,478
PRIANICHNIKOFF, Ivan (1841-1909) Russian				
wc/d	1	8,600	8,600	8,600
PRICA, Zlatko (1916-2003) Croatian				
oil	1	803	803	803
wc/d	1	600	600	600
PRICE, Alan (1926-2002) American				
oil	1	1,400	1,400	1,400
PRICE, Clark Kelly (1945-) American				
oil	1	4,000	4,000	4,000
PRICE, Clayton Sumner (1874-1950) American				
oil	3	11,000-47,500	25,166	17,000
PRICE, Edna Pattison (19th C) American				
oil	1	2,750	2,750	2,750
PRICE, James (fl.1842-1876) British				
oil	1	1,701	1,701	1,701
wc/d	2	435-673	554	435
PRICE, Ken (1935-) American				
3D	1	105,000	105,000	105,000
PRICE, Mary Elizabeth (1875-1960) American				
wc/d	1	3,250	3,250	3,250
PRICE, Norman Mills (1877-1951) American				
oil	1	4,250	4,250	4,250
wc/d	1	450	450	450
PRICE, Winchell Addison (1907-) Canadian				
oil	5	427-3,936	1,607	1,304
PRIEBE, Karl (1914-1976) American				
wc/d	1	3,500	3,500	3,500
PRIECHENFRIED, Alois (1867-1953) German				
oil	7	1,300-17,200	5,994	2,525
PRIEST, Henry (19th C) British				
oil	1	3,872	3,872	3,872
PRIESTMAN, Bertram (1868-1951) British				
oil	22	522-5,310	1,699	1,144
PRIETO ANGUITA, Miguel (1907-1956) Spanish				
oil	1	2,422	2,422	2,422
PRIETO, Gregorio (1899-1992) Spanish				
oil	1	2,238	2,238	2,238
wc/d	2	1,916-7,774	4,845	1,916
PRIETO, Manuel Jimenez (1849-?) Spanish				
oil	1	15,660	15,660	15,660
PRIETO, Monique (1962-) American				
oil	1	13,000	13,000	13,000
PRIEUR, Georges Étienne (19th C) French				
oil	1	2,637	2,637	2,637
PRIEUR-BARDIN, François L (1870-1939) French				
oil	3	950-19,287	7,955	3,629
PRIKING, Franz (1927-1979) French				
oil	14	1,285-11,192	3,677	2,507
wc/d	9	648-1,969	1,229	1,350
PRIMATICCIO, Francesco (1504-1570) French				
wc/d	1	1,295	1,295	1,295
PRIMI, Italo (1983-1983) Italian				
oil	1	1,210	1,210	1,210
PRINA, Carla (1911-) Italian				
oil	1	1,229	1,229	1,229
PRINCE NICHOLAS OF GREECE (20th C) Greek				
oil	1	3,460	3,460	3,460
PRINCE, Richard (1949-) Canadian				
oil	16	32,000-1,200,000	336,500	200,000
wc/d	7	6,000-185,850	63,592	52,800
3D	2	100,000-150,000	125,000	100,000
PRINCE, William Meade (1893-1951) American				
oil	1	4,000	4,000	4,000
PRINCESS GAGARINE STOURZA (19th C) Russian				
oil	1	3,000	3,000	3,000
PRINCESS LEROFF PARLAGHY (19/20th C) ?				
oil	1	1,000	1,000	1,000
PRINCESS LUISE HOLLANDINE (1622-1709) German				
oil	1	12,041	12,041	12,041

Name	No.	Price Range	Average	Median
PRINCETEAU, René (1844-1914) French				
oil	1	13,592	13,592	13,592
PRINET, René-Xavier (1861-1946) French				
oil	3	703-2,424	1,471	1,286
PRINGLE, John Quinton (1864-1925) British				
oil	1	22,880	22,880	22,880
PRINGLE, William J (fl.1834-1858) British				
oil	1	1,328	1,328	1,328
PRINI, Emilio (1943-) Italian				
wc/d	1	3,750	3,750	3,750
PRINS, Benjamin (1860-1934) Dutch				
oil	1	1,169	1,169	1,169
PRINS, Johannes Huibert (1757-1806) Dutch				
wc/d	1	4,438	4,438	4,438
PRINS, Pierre (1838-1913) French				
oil	8	715-8,850	3,146	1,665
wc/d	31	419-4,171	1,230	957
PRINSEP, James (1799-1840) British				
wc/d	1	23,400	23,400	23,400
PRINSEP, Valentine Cameron (1838-1904) British				
oil	1	14,875	14,875	14,875
wc/d	1	478	478	478
PRINSEP, William (1794-1874) British				
wc/d	2	3,740-4,680	4,210	3,740
PRINZ, Christian August (1819-1867) Norwegian				
oil	2	1,423-2,747	2,085	1,423
PRINZ, Karl Ludwig (1875-1944) Austrian				
oil	2	561-1,200	880	561
wc/d	2	433-740	586	433
PRIOR, William Matthew (1806-1873) American				
oil	4	1,900-4,600	2,737	2,200
PRIOU, Louis (1845-?) French				
oil	1	1,300	1,300	1,300
PRITCHARD, G Thompson (1878-1962) American				
oil	8	660-6,500	2,176	1,400
PRITCHARD, Gwilym (1931-) British				
oil	7	440-3,680	1,786	1,416
PRITCHARD, Wilfred (20th C) British				
3D	1	9,450	9,450	9,450
PRITCHETT, Edward (fl.1828-1864) British				
oil	4	3,500-20,880	9,962	3,500
wc/d	2	3,480-6,300	4,890	3,480
PRITCHETT, Robert Taylor (1828-1907) British				
oil	1	6,660	6,660	6,660
PRIVAT, Gilbert Auguste (1892-1969) French				
3D	2	5,089-6,612	5,850	5,089
PROBST, Annick (20th C) French				
oil	1	3,041	3,041	3,041
PROBST, Carl (1854-1924) Austrian				
oil	1	5,180	5,180	5,180
PROBST, Joachim (1913-) American				
oil	2	650-3,200	1,925	650
PROBST, Thorwald (1886-1948) American				
oil	4	800-4,750	2,187	1,300
PROBSTHAYN, Carl (1770-1818) Danish				
oil	1	4,710	4,710	4,710
PROCACCINI, Camillo (1546-1629) Italian				
oil	1	89,178	89,178	89,178
wc/d	1	14,800	14,800	14,800
PROCACCINI, Ercole (16/17th C) Italian				
wc/d	1	3,107	3,107	3,107
PROCACCINI, Ercole (younger) (1596-1676) Italian				
oil	1	1,922	1,922	1,922
wc/d	1	10,938	10,938	10,938
PROCHAZKA, Antonin (1882-1945) Czechoslovakian				
wc/d	1	1,471	1,471	1,471
PROCKTOR, Patrick (1936-2003) British				
oil	8	1,760-12,975	5,276	3,186
wc/d	11	599-4,956	1,862	1,701
PROCOPIO, Pino (1954-) Italian				
oil	3	1,708-2,213	1,976	2,007

Name	No.	Price Range	Average	Median
PROCTER, Burt (1901-1980) American				
oil	7	4,250-15,000	7,492	7,000
PROCTER, Dod (1892-1972) British				
oil	4	3,806-71,820	31,191	22,680
wc/d	3	561-1,183	793	636
PROCTER, Ernest (1886-1935) British				
oil	1	3,186	3,186	3,186
PROCTOR, Alexander Phimister (1862-1950) American				
3D	3	5,500-17,000	11,833	13,000
PROIETTI, Norberto (1927-) Italian				
oil	5	922-7,315	3,868	4,315
PROKOFIEFF, Dimitrij (1870-1944) Russian				
oil	1	5,160	5,160	5,160
PROKOFIEV, Oleg (1928-) Russian				
3D	1	70,680	70,680	70,680
PROKOPENKO, Alexei Andreyevich (1926-) Russian				
oil	1	1,070	1,070	1,070
PROKSCH, Peter (1935-) Austrian?				
oil	2	2,200-2,800	2,500	2,200
PROLSS, Friedrich Anton Otto (1855-?) German				
oil	2	1,621-7,233	4,427	1,621
PRONSATO, Domingo (1881-1971) Argentinian				
oil	1	4,000	4,000	4,000
PROOM, Al (1933-) American				
oil	2	1,000-1,000	1,000	1,000
PROOST, Frans (1866-1941) Belgian				
oil	3	1,800-3,360	2,840	3,360
PROOYEN, Albert Jurardus van (1834-1898) Dutch				
oil	9	580-7,000	1,874	1,318
PROPER, Ida Sedgwick (1876-1957) American				
oil	1	9,000	9,000	9,000
PROPPES, Moshe (20th C) Israeli				
oil	1	3,400	3,400	3,400
PROSALENTIS, Emilios (1859-1926) Greek				
oil	4	4,675-54,810	21,291	10,560
wc/d	5	3,460-7,920	4,968	4,114
PROSALENTIS, Spyros (19/20th C) Greek				
oil	3	1,870-11,220	8,103	11,220
PROSDOCINI, Alberto (1852-1925) Italian				
oil	1	1,083	1,083	1,083
wc/d	12	814-7,880	4,157	2,945
PROSPERI, Liberio (19/20th C) British				
wc/d	4	1,760-2,112	1,892	1,760
PROST, Maurice (1894-1967) French				
oil	1	3,299	3,299	3,299
wc/d	1	506	506	506
3D	4	4,841-11,449	8,206	7,632
PROTAIS, Paul Alexandre (1826-1890) French				
oil	1	4,000	4,000	4,000
PROTHEAU, Francois (1823-1865) French				
3D	1	2,040	2,040	2,040
PROTOPATSIS, Antonis (1897-1942) Greek				
wc/d	1	1,408	1,408	1,408
PROTOPOPOV, Nikolai Adrianovich (1876-1960) Russian				
oil	1	3,781	3,781	3,781
PROUT, Margaret Fisher (1875-1963) British				
oil	3	1,044-1,793	1,476	1,593
PROUT, Samuel (1783-1852) British				
wc/d	18	400-34,020	4,946	1,229
PROVERBIO, Luciano (1936-) Italian				
oil	3	707-968	794	707
wc/d	1	701	701	701
PROVINO, Salvatore (1943-) Italian				
oil	18	676-12,945	3,480	2,589
PROVIS, Alfred (19th C) British				
oil	4	627-2,625	1,775	1,750
PROZOR, Safet Zec (?) ?				
wc/d	1	1,573	1,573	1,573
PRUCHA, G (1875-1952) Austrian				
oil	1	1,558	1,558	1,558
PRUCHA, Gustav (1875-1952) Austrian				
oil	4	911-3,306	1,655	973

Name	No.	Price Range	Average	Median
PRUCKENDORFER, Hans (1518-?) German				
oil	1	5,143	5,143	5,143
PRUDHON, Pierre Paul (1758-1823) French				
wc/d	2	5,000-13,592	9,296	5,000
PRULHIERE, Edouard (20th C) French				
oil	2	716-1,551	1,133	716
3D	1	1,551	1,551	1,551
PRUNA, Pedro (1904-1977) Spanish				
oil	4	6,630-33,753	14,008	7,233
wc/d	4	4,886-15,671	8,048	5,611
PRUTSCHER, Otto (1880-1949) Austrian				
wc/d	3	2,003-4,241	3,102	3,063
PRYDE, James (1869-1941) British				
oil	1	24,920	24,920	24,920
PRYN, Harald (1891-1968) Danish				
oil	20	575-27,600	5,766	1,850
PRYOR, Yvonne (1885-1962) American				
oil	1	4,000	4,000	4,000
PSAIER, Pietro (1939-) American				
oil	8	744-4,836	2,053	791
wc/d	5	479-1,209	894	832
PSEUDO FARDELLA (17th C) Italian				
oil	1	40,993	40,993	40,993
PSEUDO GRANACCI (15/16th C) Italian				
oil	1	320,000	320,000	320,000
PSEUDO GUARDI (18th C) Italian				
oil	1	57,090	57,090	57,090
PSEUDO PIER FRANCESCO FIORENTINO (fl.c.1460-1500) Italian				
oil	1	43,250	43,250	43,250
PSEUDO ROESTRAETEN (17th C) ?				
oil	1	7,644	7,644	7,644
PSEUDO SALINI (fl.1633-1655) Italian				
oil	1	92,500	92,500	92,500
PSYCHOPEDIS, Yiannis (1945-) Greek				
oil	1	4,224	4,224	4,224
3D	1	4,114	4,114	4,114
PU HUA (1830-1911) Chinese				
wc/d	1	7,642	7,642	7,642
PU RU (1896-1963) Chinese				
wc/d	2	3,600-4,243	3,921	3,600
PUCCI, Silvio (1892-1961) Italian				
oil	2	694-1,388	1,041	694
PUCCIARELLI, Mario (1928-) Argentinian				
oil	6	4,500-16,000	8,333	5,000
PUCCINI, Mario (1869-1920) Italian				
oil	2	23,007-29,730	26,368	23,007
PUCHINGER, Erwin (1876-1944) Austrian				
oil	2	847-1,455	1,151	847
wc/d	9	584-1,929	1,034	725
PUCHLER, Johann Michael (fl.1680-1702) German				
wc/d	1	3,299	3,299	3,299
PUDLICH, Robert (1905-1962) German				
oil	2	750-1,649	1,199	750
wc/d	3	509-840	729	840
PUECH, Denis (1854-1942) French				
3D	2	26,100-30,000	28,050	26,100
PUGH, Clifton Ernest (1924-1990) Australian				
oil	1	2,200	2,200	2,200
PUGH, David (1946-1994) Canadian				
oil	7	486-2,659	1,017	820
PUGI (19th C) Italian				
3D	2	2,246-5,993	4,119	2,246
PUGI, G (19th C) Italian				
3D	1	12,460	12,460	12,460
PUGLISI, Giuseppe (1965-) Italian				
oil	1	1,868	1,868	1,868
PUIFORCAT, Jean (1897-1945) French				
3D	1	4,077	4,077	4,077
PUIG BENLLOCH, Ramon (20th C) Spanish				
oil	1	3,978	3,978	3,978
PUIG, Vicente (1882-1965) Argentinian				
wc/d	1	1,800	1,800	1,800

Name	No.	Price Range	Average	Median
PUIG-RODA, Gabriel (1865-1919) Spanish				
oil	3	3,827-15,480	8,269	5,500
wc/d	4	3,500-16,857	11,540	9,041
PUIGAUDEAU, Fernand du (1866-1930) French				
oil	11	2,973-28,320	16,311	18,500
wc/d	2	595-1,824	1,209	595
PUIGDENGOLAS BARELLA, Jose (1906-1987) Spanish				
oil	2	11,743-17,306	14,524	11,743
PUJIA, Antonio (1929-) Argentinian				
3D	2	1,800-4,200	3,000	1,800
PUJOL DE GUASTAVINO, Clement (1850-1905) French				
wc/d	1	15,225	15,225	15,225
PUJOL, Adrian (20th C) South American				
wc/d	1	1,440	1,440	1,440
PUJOL, Ernesto (c.1961-) Cuban				
oil	1	9,000	9,000	9,000
PUJOS, Andre (1738-1788) French				
wc/d	1	1,033	1,033	1,033
PULEO, Stefano (1950-) Italian				
oil	1	1,178	1,178	1,178
PULGA, Bruno (1922-) Italian				
oil	4	700-9,062	3,363	971
PULHAM, Peter Rose (1910-1956) British				
oil	2	1,435-2,124	1,779	1,435
PULIGO, Domenico (1492-1527) Italian				
oil	1	92,500	92,500	92,500
PULINCKX, Louis (1843-1910) Belgian				
oil	2	1,218-1,218	1,218	1,218
PULLER, John Anthony (fl.1821-1867) British				
oil	2	4,789-10,620	7,704	4,789
PULZONE, Scipione (1550-1598) Italian				
oil	1	116,507	116,507	116,507
PUMMIL, Robert (1936-) American				
oil	1	6,500	6,500	6,500
PUMPIN, Fritz (1901-1972) Swiss				
oil	6	761-6,105	2,644	1,415
PUPINI, Biagio (16th C) Italian				
oil	2	5,500-50,000	27,750	5,500
wc/d	3	841-37,500	14,603	5,469
PUQIQNAK, Uriash (1946-) North American				
3D	2	2,953-5,736	4,344	2,953
PURIFICATO, Domenico (1915-1984) Italian				
oil	2	5,163-9,062	7,112	5,163
wc/d	3	604-3,401	1,538	610
PURRMANN, Hans (1880-1966) German				
oil	9	17,851-129,945	66,569	51,800
wc/d	7	3,181-12,162	6,779	5,178
PURSCHKE, Walther (1924-) German				
oil	2	550-1,500	1,025	550
PURSER, Sarah (1848-1943) British				
oil	3	14,014-114,274	56,351	40,767
wc/d	2	1,296-2,710	2,003	1,296
PURSER, William (c.1790-c.1852) British				
wc/d	2	930-4,928	2,929	930
PURUGGANAN, Ricarte (1912-1998) Philippino				
oil	1	4,454	4,454	4,454
PURVIS, T G (fl.1900-1910) British				
oil	3	2,153-2,580	2,437	2,580
PURYEAR, Martin (1941-) American				
3D	1	500,000	500,000	500,000
PURYGIN, Leonid (1951-1995) Russian				
oil	5	8,370-55,800	26,832	26,040
wc/d	1	65,000	65,000	65,000
3D	1	35,000	35,000	35,000
PUSA, Unto (1913-1973) Finnish				
oil	2	969-11,105	6,037	969
PUSHMAN, Hovsep (1877-1966) American				
oil	8	28,000-95,000	48,812	40,000
PUSOLE, Pierluigi (1963-) Italian				
oil	10	2,625-7,767	3,877	3,073
wc/d	5	1,229-2,822	1,841	1,764

Name	No.	Price Range	Average	Median
PUTEANI, Friedrich von (1849-1917) German				
oil	2	748-11,100	5,924	748
PUTEUS, Domenico Maria (17th C) Italian				
oil	1	8,286	8,286	8,286
PUTHOD, Dolores (1934-) Italian				
oil	2	895-1,598	1,246	895
PUTHUFF, Hanson Duvall (1875-1972) American				
oil	11	4,000-70,000	21,163	14,000
PUTNAM, Arthur (1873-1930) American				
3D	5	5,000-35,000	12,887	7,500
PUTSAGE, Marguerite (1868-1946) Belgian				
wc/d	1	3,671	3,671	3,671
PUTTEMANS, Auguste (1866-1927) Belgian				
3D	1	2,877	2,877	2,877
PUTTER, Pieter de (1600-1659) Dutch				
oil	2	11,094-22,490	16,792	11,094
PUTTMAN, Donald (1926-) American				
oil	2	750-9,500	5,125	750
wc/d	1	1,000	1,000	1,000
PUTTNER, Josef Carl Berthold (1821-1881) Austrian				
oil	3	1,580-3,579	2,530	2,432
PUTTNER, Walther (1872-1953) German				
oil	1	1,218	1,218	1,218
PUTZ, Leo (1869-1940) German				
oil	11	753-591,429	100,698	33,966
wc/d	2	2,153-4,757	3,455	2,153
PUTZHOFEN-HAMBUCHEN, Paul (19/20th C) German				
oil	1	1,576	1,576	1,576
PUVIS DE CHAVANNES, Pierre (1824-1898) French				
wc/d	2	1,452-4,253	2,852	1,452
PUVREZ, Henri (1893-1971) Belgian				
3D	1	2,741	2,741	2,741
PUY, Jean (1876-1960) French				
oil	17	2,104-59,459	14,602	8,371
wc/d	4	482-2,342	1,040	486
PUYBAREAU, Annie (1955-) French				
oil	12	550-6,000	1,983	1,500
PUYET, Jose (1922-2004) Spanish				
oil	9	837-8,710	3,323	2,761
PUYROCHE-WAGNER, Elise (1828-1895) German				
oil	1	6,107	6,107	6,107
PYATKOV, D M (?) Russian				
oil	1	1,546	1,546	1,546
PYCKE, François (1890-1960) Belgian				
oil	1	3,879	3,879	3,879
PYE, Patrick (1929-) Irish				
oil	1	1,576	1,576	1,576
PYE, William (1938-) British				
3D	2	1,776-9,460	5,618	1,776
PYK, Madeleine (1934-) Swedish				
oil	25	705-8,457	3,355	2,545
wc/d	1	730	730	730
PYLE, Howard (1853-1911) American				
oil	1	25,000	25,000	25,000
wc/d	1	11,000	11,000	11,000
PYLYPCHUK, Jon (1972) Canadian				
wc/d	1	16,000	16,000	16,000
PYNACKER, Adam (1622-1673) Dutch				
oil	2	12,335-30,837	21,586	12,335
PYNAS, Jacob (1585-1648) Dutch				
oil	1	39,160	39,160	39,160
PYNE, Ganesh (1937-) Indian				
wc/d	3	10,000-18,000	14,000	14,000
PYNE, James Baker (1800-1870) British				
oil	11	696-5,000	2,961	3,312
wc/d	5	560-4,788	2,226	1,427
PYNE, Kartik Chandra (1931-) Indian				
oil	2	7,480-8,500	7,990	7,480
PYNE, Robert Lorraine (19th C) American				
oil	1	7,500	7,500	7,500
PYRA, Greg (20th C) Canadian				
oil	1	1,152	1,152	1,152

Name	No.	Price Range	Average	Median
PYYKONEN, Kimmo (20th C) Finnish				
oil	1	1,211	1,211	1,211
wc/d	1	727	727	727
QADRI, Sohan (1932-) Indian				
oil	2	18,000-54,230	36,115	18,000
QI BAISHI (1863-1957) Chinese				
wc/d	18	2,250-210,000	30,963	12,858
QI LIANGCHI (1921-) Chinese				
wc/d	1	1,100	1,100	1,100
QI ZHILONG (1962-) Chinese				
oil	2	58,000-170,000	114,000	58,000
QIAN HUIAN (1833-1911) Chinese				
wc/d	3	600-3,000	1,550	1,051
QIAN SONGYAN (1898-1985) Chinese				
wc/d	1	42,324	42,324	42,324
QIATSUK, Lukta (1928-2004) North American				
3D	1	3,374	3,374	3,374
QIN FENG (1961-) Chinese				
wc/d	1	19,000	19,000	19,000
QING DYNASTY (?) Chinese				
oil	1	536,500	536,500	536,500
QING DYNASTY, 18th C (18th C) Chinese				
wc/d	1	10,000	10,000	10,000
QING DYNASTY, 18th/19th C (18th/19th C) Chinese				
oil	1	12,000	12,000	12,000
QIU ANXIONG (1972-) Chinese				
oil	1	7,000	7,000	7,000
QIU SHIHUA (1940-) Chinese				
oil	1	38,000	38,000	38,000
QIU TING (1971-) Chinese				
wc/d	1	6,000	6,000	6,000
QIU YING (c.1510-1551) Chinese				
wc/d	2	1,200-12,500	6,850	1,200
QODAID, Said (1968-) Moroccan				
oil	1	1,609	1,609	1,609
QU GUANGCI (1969-) Chinese				
3D	1	17,000	17,000	17,000
QUADAL, Martin Ferdinand (1736-1811) Austrian				
oil	2	1,200-11,570	6,385	1,200
QUADRONE, Giovanni Battista (1844-1898) Italian				
oil	1	22,500	22,500	22,500
wc/d	1	4,712	4,712	4,712
QUAEDVLIEG, Carel Max Gerlach Anton (1823-1874) Dutch				
oil	1	45,000	45,000	45,000
QUAGLIA, Carlo (1907-1970) Italian				
oil	7	837-4,438	2,112	2,035
QUAGLIA, Ferdinando (1780-1853) Italian				
wc/d	1	3,612	3,612	3,612
QUAGLINO, Massimo (1899-1982) Italian				
oil	5	1,868-2,521	2,192	2,142
wc/d	1	656	656	656
QUAGLIO, Domenico (younger) (1787-1837) German				
oil	1	11,040	11,040	11,040
QUAGLIO, Franz (1844-1920) German				
oil	5	850-5,741	2,350	1,790
QUAGLIO, Lorenzo II (1793-1869) German				
oil	1	21,205	21,205	21,205
QUANNE, Michael (1941-) British				
oil	3	1,197-1,625	1,418	1,432
QUARENGHI, Federico (1858-1940) Italian				
oil	1	2,592	2,592	2,592
QUARENGHI, Giacomo (1744-1817) Italian				
oil	1	72,240	72,240	72,240
wc/d	10	2,616-86,000	32,977	18,920
QUARTLEY, Arthur (1839-1886) American				
oil	1	2,000	2,000	2,000
QUARTO, Andrea (1959-) Italian				
oil	8	712-1,942	1,111	942
QUARTREMAIN, William Wells (fl.1906-1908) British				
wc/d	5	525-2,436	1,462	1,305

Name	No.	Price Range	Average	Median
QUAST, Pieter (1606-1647) Dutch				
oil	3	3,434-22,000	13,668	15,570
wc/d	4	1,051-1,752	1,372	1,051
QUEEN OF DENMARK, Louise (1817-1898) Danish				
oil	1	8,449	8,449	8,449
QUEEN OF GREECE, Olga (1851-1926) Greek				
wc/d	1	2,057	2,057	2,057
QUEJIDO, Manuel (1946-) Spanish				
oil	4	6,276-26,162	12,119	7,531
QUELLINUS, Erasmus II and VERBRUGGEN, Gaspar Pieter (17th C) Flemish				
oil	1	15,226	15,226	15,226
QUELLINUS, Jan Erasmus (1634-1715) Flemish				
oil	2	4,626-16,562	10,594	4,626
QUELVEE, François Albert (1884-1967) French				
oil	4	935-2,167	1,390	1,028
QUENCE, Raymond (1932-) French				
oil	1	1,700	1,700	1,700
QUENNELL, Marjorie (1884-1972) British				
wc/d	1	1,068	1,068	1,068
QUENTIN, Bernard (1923-) French				
oil	10	611-2,510	1,413	1,205
wc/d	16	413-3,767	772	586
QUERCIA, Federico (19th C) Italian				
oil	1	6,160	6,160	6,160
QUERE, René (1932-) French				
oil	1	2,272	2,272	2,272
QUERENA, Luigi (1820-c.1890) Italian				
oil	1	26,757	26,757	26,757
QUERFURT, August (1696-1761) German				
oil	4	3,102-10,356	5,814	4,450
wc/d	1	942	942	942
QUERFURT, Tobias (elder) (fl.1689-1730) German				
oil	1	10,837	10,837	10,837
QUERNER, Curt (1904-1976) German				
oil	1	1,674	1,674	1,674
wc/d	8	598-9,271	2,996	1,731
QUERO, Jose (1932-) Spanish				
oil	1	1,025	1,025	1,025
QUERRIERE, Gaston de la (1926-1987) French				
wc/d	1	1,215	1,215	1,215
QUERVAIN, Daniel de (1937-) Swiss				
oil	1	2,518	2,518	2,518
QUESADA PORTO, Antonio (1932-) Spanish				
oil	1	28,510	28,510	28,510
QUIGLEY, Edward B (1895-1986) American				
oil	3	425-8,000	3,441	1,900
wc/d	2	425-450	437	425
QUIGNON, Fernand Just (1854-1941) French				
oil	2	903-1,405	1,154	903
QUILICI, Pancho (1954-) Venezuelan				
oil	1	16,750	16,750	16,750
QUILLIER, Cesaire (19th C) French				
oil	1	1,100	1,100	1,100
QUILLINAN, Maurice (1961-) Irish				
oil	2	1,395-1,674	1,534	1,395
QUILLIVIC, René (1879-1969) French				
oil	3	701-5,040	3,313	4,200
3D	1	6,663	6,663	6,663
QUINET, Charles Henri (1830-1912) French				
oil	1	4,685	4,685	4,685
QUINN, Marc (1964-) British				
3D	8	2,640-168,150	57,605	43,250
QUINQUAND, Anna (1890-1984) French				
3D	1	8,536	8,536	8,536
QUINQUELA MARTIN, Benito (1890-1977) Argentinian				
oil	6	15,000-200,000	81,500	50,000
wc/d	1	2,600	2,600	2,600
QUINSA, Giovanni (17th C) Italian				
oil	1	9,425	9,425	9,425
QUINSAC, Paul François (1858-?) French				
oil	3	820-40,000	15,606	6,000

Name	No.	Price Range	Average	Median
QUINTAINE, Roger (20th C) French				
oil	2	1,193-2,572	1,882	1,193
QUINTANA CASTILLO, Manuel (1928-) Venezuelan				
oil	8	930-6,280	2,383	1,720
wc/d	2	835-11,630	6,232	835
QUINTANA, George (20th C) American				
wc/d	1	4,500	4,500	4,500
QUINTAVALLE, Noel (1893-1975) Italian				
oil	4	701-16,163	5,630	2,460
QUINTE, Lothar (1923-2000) German				
oil	1	3,461	3,461	3,461
QUINTERO, Daniel (1940-) Spanish				
oil	1	10,703	10,703	10,703
wc/d	3	1,028-14,919	5,719	1,210
QUIROS, Antonio (1918-1984) Spanish				
oil	2	2,047-15,000	8,523	2,047
wc/d	1	1,360	1,360	1,360
QUIROS, Cesareo Bernaldo (1881-1968) Argentinian				
oil	6	13,450-130,000	72,408	50,000
QUIRT, Walter (1902-1968) American				
oil	1	8,158	8,158	8,158
QUISPEL, Matthys (1805-1858) Dutch				
oil	1	1,447	1,447	1,447
QUISTDORFF, Victor (1883-1953) Danish				
oil	10	630-3,534	1,128	790
QUISTGAARD, Johan Valdemar (1877-1962) Danish				
oil	1	2,431	2,431	2,431
QUITON, Eugene (19th C) French?				
3D	1	2,636	2,636	2,636
QUITTNER, Rudolf (1872-1910) Austrian				
oil	1	1,796	1,796	1,796
QUIVIERES, Augustin Marcotte de (1854-1907) French				
oil	2	2,884-13,000	7,942	2,884
QUIZET, Alphonse (1885-1955) French				
oil	10	550-6,500	2,847	1,942
wc/d	1	558	558	558
QUMALUK, Levi (1919-) North American				
3D	1	2,109	2,109	2,109
QUOST, Ernest (1844-1931) French				
oil	3	510-6,300	3,689	4,258
RAADAL, Erik (1905-1941) Danish				
oil	2	1,991-3,718	2,854	1,991
RAADSIG, Peter (1806-1882) Danish				
oil	11	971-7,817	2,834	1,932
RAADT, Marja de (1950-) Dutch				
oil	1	1,299	1,299	1,299
RAAPHORST, C (1875-1954) Dutch				
oil	1	6,078	6,078	6,078
RAAPHORST, Cornelis (1875-1954) Dutch				
oil	5	2,726-7,621	4,829	4,849
RAATIKAINEN, Orvo (1914-2000) Finnish				
oil	4	731-1,453	1,085	899
RABARAMA (1969-) Italian				
oil	4	3,955-8,718	5,800	4,359
3D	7	2,458-12,214	6,747	5,727
RABBONI, Marco (17th C) Italian				
oil	1	12,950	12,950	12,950
RABE, Otto (1841-?) German				
oil	1	1,168	1,168	1,168
RABES, Max (1868-1944) Austrian				
oil	9	650-55,000	8,610	2,057
RABI, Abdelkbir (1944-) Moroccan				
oil	1	9,174	9,174	9,174
RABINE, Oskar (1928-) Russian				
oil	6	5,708-93,000	35,348	18,000
wc/d	4	2,736-85,000	31,809	5,500
RABINOVITCH, Isaac (1894-1961) Russian				
wc/d	1	3,420	3,420	3,420
RABUZIN, Ivan (1919-) Yugoslavian				
oil	4	2,640-6,360	3,930	3,120

Name	No.	Price Range	Average	Median
RACCAGNI, Andrea (1921-2005) Italian				
oil	3	840-6,473	3,585	3,442
wc/d	8	615-1,440	960	884
3D	1	2,314	2,314	2,314
RACE, George (1872-1957) British				
oil	1	1,267	1,267	1,267
RACITI, Mario (1934-) Italian				
oil	2	2,386-2,458	2,422	2,386
wc/d	4	615-3,180	1,871	1,119
RACKHAM, Arthur (1867-1939) British				
wc/d	7	3,894-69,600	28,769	21,750
RADECKER, John (1885-1956) Dutch				
wc/d	4	1,764-3,299	2,177	1,764
3D	4	2,238-21,162	7,468	2,945
RADEMACHER, N G (1812-1885) Danish				
oil	2	869-2,055	1,462	869
RADEMACHER, Niels Gronbeck (1812-1885) Danish				
wc/d	1	4,087	4,087	4,087
RADEMAKER, Abraham (1675-1735) Dutch				
wc/d	5	570-2,102	1,476	1,752
RADERSCHEIDT, Anton (1892-1970) German				
oil	2	825-825	825	825
wc/d	4	1,019-8,918	3,183	1,216
RADFORD, Edward (1831-1920) British				
oil	1	3,969	3,969	3,969
wc/d	1	2,668	2,668	2,668
RADICE, Mario (1900-1987) Italian				
oil	6	1,178-19,082	9,876	10,177
wc/d	4	1,145-5,724	2,687	1,291
RADIMSKY, Vaclav (1867-1946) Czechoslovakian				
oil	2	2,384-23,920	13,152	2,384
RADL, Anton (1774-1852) German				
wc/d	1	1,029	1,029	1,029
RADLER, Josef Karl (19/20th C) Austrian				
wc/d	2	2,548-3,058	2,803	2,548
RADLER, Max (1904-1971) German				
oil	2	1,764-3,214	2,489	1,764
wc/d	1	837	837	837
RADY, Elsa (1943-) American				
3D	1	2,750	2,750	2,750
RADZIWILL, Franz (1895-1983) German				
oil	4	14,400-50,884	30,862	17,173
wc/d	5	1,455-12,945	5,953	1,812
RAE, Barbara (1943-) British				
oil	1	10,740	10,740	10,740
wc/d	4	2,001-3,186	2,598	2,076
RAE, Fiona (1963-) British				
oil	2	17,600-47,790	32,695	17,600
RAEBURN, Sir Henry (1756-1823) British				
oil	8	3,500-50,000	18,945	13,962
RAEDECKER, Michael (1963-) American				
oil	1	148,000	148,000	148,000
RAETZ, Markus (1941-) Swiss				
oil	3	10,132-36,476	24,992	28,370
wc/d	3	1,370-16,211	6,888	3,083
RAFAY, I (?) ?				
oil	1	3,250	3,250	3,250
RAFFAEL, Joseph (1933-) American				
wc/d	1	2,000	2,000	2,000
RAFFAELE, Ambrogio (1860-1928) Italian				
oil	3	477-3,341	1,670	1,193
RAFFAELLI, Jean François (1850-1924) French				
oil	13	9,466-85,000	40,023	37,000
wc/d	6	935-6,500	3,531	3,515
RAFFAELLO (?) Italian				
wc/d	1	83,250	83,250	83,250
RAFFET, Auguste-Marie (1804-1860) French				
wc/d	5	425-2,076	1,388	1,546
RAFFINI, Martine (20th C) French?				
oil	1	3,041	3,041	3,041
RAFFORT, Étienne (1802-1885) French				
wc/d	1	1,147	1,147	1,147

Name	No.	Price Range	Average	Median
RAFTERY, Ted (1938-) Canadian				
oil	1	2,188	2,188	2,188
RAGGIO, Giuseppe (1823-1916) Italian				
oil	2	4,143-15,315	9,729	4,143
RAGIONE, Raffaele (1851-1925) Italian				
oil	3	16,562-24,842	20,596	20,384
RAGN-JENSEN, Leif (1911-1993) Danish				
oil	2	1,056-1,493	1,274	1,056
RAGOT, Jules (19th C) French				
oil	4	536-5,310	2,108	1,211
RAGUENEAU, Abraham (c.1623-?) Dutch				
oil	1	7,071	7,071	7,071
RAGUENET, Nicolas (18th C) French				
oil	2	101,083-154,597	127,840	101,083
RAGUSA, Eleonora (1861-1939) Italian				
oil	1	5,856	5,856	5,856
RAHL, Carl (1812-1865) Austrian				
oil	1	1,994	1,994	1,994
RAHMING, Norris (1886-1959) American				
oil	1	2,500	2,500	2,500
RAHNEN, Johann Friedrich (18th C) German				
oil	1	3,371	3,371	3,371
RAHO, Alessandro (1971-) British?				
oil	2	10,912-11,000	10,956	10,912
RAHON, Alice (1916-1987) French				
oil	3	500-4,006	2,050	1,646
wc/d	1	2,500	2,500	2,500
RAHOULE, Abderrahman (1944-) Moroccan				
oil	2	4,017-4,017	4,017	4,017
RAIMONDI, Aldo (1902-1998) Italian				
wc/d	4	958-1,665	1,311	1,197
RAIMONDI, Elviro (1867-?) French				
oil	1	8,066	8,066	8,066
RAINALDI, Oliviero (1956-) Italian				
wc/d	1	2,175	2,175	2,175
RAINBERGER, F (?) ?				
oil	1	1,800	1,800	1,800
RAINE, Jean (1927-1986) Belgian				
wc/d	1	1,521	1,521	1,521
RAINER, Arnulf (1929-) Austrian				
oil	29	2,029-77,700	16,580	10,192
wc/d	28	1,757-32,456	7,060	4,500
3D	1	12,857	12,857	12,857
RAINER, Arnulf and ROTH, Dieter (20th C) Austrian/German				
oil	1	8,918	8,918	8,918
wc/d	4	1,870-7,658	4,557	4,115
RAINERI, Carlo Antonio and Vittorio (18/19th C) Italian				
oil	1	19,397	19,397	19,397
RAINS, Malcolm (1947-) Canadian				
oil	2	3,796-10,635	7,215	3,796
RAIX, David (20th C) British?				
3D	1	3,780	3,780	3,780
RAKOCI, Dubravka (20th C) Croatian				
oil	1	1,700	1,700	1,700
RAKOCZI, Basil (1908-1979) British				
oil	9	1,318-22,055	9,341	5,419
wc/d	9	1,098-6,081	3,000	2,790
RAKOFF, Rastislaw (1904-1982) Russian				
oil	4	600-4,472	2,043	1,500
RALEIGH, Charles Sidney (1830-1925) American				
oil	2	20,000-25,000	22,500	20,000
RALEIGH, Henry Patrick (1880-1944) American				
wc/d	3	1,600-2,800	2,100	1,900
RALLI, Theodore Jacques (1852-1909) Greek				
oil	6	2,244-79,380	26,861	11,340
RAMA, Carol (1918-) Italian?				
oil	2	8,352-10,744	9,548	8,352
wc/d	10	647-6,553	2,531	1,890
RAMACHANDRAN, A (1935-) Indian				
wc/d	1	14,000	14,000	14,000
RAMAH, Henri (1887-1947) Belgian				
oil	3	969-1,483	1,172	1,064

Name	No.	Price Range	Average	Median
RAMAUGE, Roberto (1890-1973) French/Argentinian				
oil	4	714-2,500	1,247	834
RAMBALDI, Emanuele (1903-1968) Italian				
oil	3	3,996-10,738	6,816	5,716
RAMBAUD, Bernard (19/20th C) Swiss?				
wc/d	1	1,868	1,868	1,868
RAMBAUDI, Piero (1906-1991) Italian				
oil	2	467-1,230	848	467
wc/d	1	1,590	1,590	1,590
RAMBELLI, Domenico (1886-1972) Italian				
wc/d	2	536-2,142	1,339	536
RAMET, Jules (1842-1915) French				
oil	2	1,632-2,290	1,961	1,632
RAMETTE, Philippe (1961-) French				
wc/d	2	537-819	678	537
3D	3	3,507-10,521	6,624	5,845
RAMGOPAL (20th C) Indian				
wc/d	1	7,920	7,920	7,920
RAMIREZ, Martin (1895-1963) Mexican				
wc/d	1	42,000	42,000	42,000
RAMIREZ-IBANEZ, Manuel (1856-1925) Spanish				
oil	2	1,927-34,020	17,973	1,927
RAMOS ARTAL, Manuel (1855-1900) Spanish				
oil	5	904-9,031	2,694	1,243
wc/d	1	568	568	568
RAMOS, Carlos (1912-1983) Portuguese?				
oil	1	6,684	6,684	6,684
RAMOS, F (?) ?				
oil	1	3,680	3,680	3,680
RAMOS, Mel (1935-) American				
oil	1	135,000	135,000	135,000
wc/d	7	17,534-51,800	33,359	35,400
RAMOS, Patricio (?) South American				
oil	2	28,000-45,000	36,500	28,000
RAMOS, Rodolfo (1937-) Argentinian				
wc/d	1	6,000	6,000	6,000
RAMOS, Tod (1956-) British				
oil	1	1,283	1,283	1,283
RAMOS, Willy (1954-) Colombian				
oil	1	4,978	4,978	4,978
RAMPASO, Luciano (1936-) Italian				
oil	15	425-3,250	1,178	1,000
RAMPIN, Saverio (1930-1992) Italian				
oil	2	1,014-1,308	1,161	1,014
RAMSAY, Allan (1713-1784) British				
oil	1	52,920	52,920	52,920
wc/d	2	2,076-72,660	37,368	2,076
RAMSAY, Allan (fl.1880-1920) British				
oil	4	644-1,730	1,156	952
RAMSAY, James (1786-1854) British				
oil	1	6,592	6,592	6,592
RAMSEY, Milne (1847-1915) American				
oil	7	2,750-45,000	13,058	7,500
RAMSTONEV (?) ?				
wc/d	1	3,750	3,750	3,750
RAMUS, Joseph Marius (1805-1888) French				
3D	1	2,675	2,675	2,675
RANC, Jean (1674-1735) French				
oil	2	13,840-70,541	42,190	13,840
RANCILLAC, Bernard (1931-) French				
oil	5	4,919-14,914	7,790	5,178
wc/d	1	1,942	1,942	1,942
RANCILLAC, Jean Jules Paul (1934-) French				
3D	2	4,533-5,702	5,117	4,533
RANCOULET, Ernest (19th C) French				
3D	5	1,866-7,531	4,337	4,000
RAND, Henry (1886-?) American				
oil	4	2,500-47,500	16,500	3,000
RANDAL, Frank (fl.1887-1901) British				
wc/d	1	3,213	3,213	3,213

Name	No.	Price Range	Average	Median
RANDAVEL, Louis (1869-1947) French				
oil	1	584	584	584
wc/d	2	954-1,656	1,305	954
RANDONI, Carlo (18th C) Italian				
wc/d	1	7,030	7,030	7,030
RANFT, Richard (1862-1931) Swiss				
oil	1	4,841	4,841	4,841
RANFTL, Johann Matthias (1805-1854) Austrian				
oil	1	3,938	3,938	3,938
wc/d	1	722	722	722
RANGER, Henry Ward (1858-1916) American				
oil	9	2,400-13,000	5,916	4,250
wc/d	1	650	650	650
RANK, William (20th C) American				
wc/d	1	2,100	2,100	2,100
RANKIN, Andrew Scott (1868-1942) British				
oil	1	2,670	2,670	2,670
wc/d	2	458-669	563	458
RANSMAYR, Johann (19th C) Austrian				
wc/d	1	1,445	1,445	1,445
RANSON, Paul (1864-1909) French				
oil	2	138,750-140,800	139,775	138,750
wc/d	1	4,544	4,544	4,544
RANSONNETTE, Charles (1793-1877) French				
wc/d	1	1,566	1,566	1,566
RANSY, Jean (1910-1991) Belgian				
oil	6	841-2,356	1,679	1,543
RANTANEN, Silja (1955-) Finnish				
wc/d	1	1,113	1,113	1,113
RANUCCI, Lucio (1924-) Italian				
oil	5	1,178-5,178	3,121	2,950
RANVIER-CHARTIER, Lucie (1867-1932) French				
oil	1	1,532	1,532	1,532
RANZONI, Daniele (1843-1889) Italian				
oil	3	4,849-23,562	13,803	13,000
RANZONI, Gustav (1826-1900) Austrian				
oil	2	1,815-5,271	3,543	1,815
RANZONI, Hans (elder) (1868-1956) Austrian				
oil	2	750-2,662	1,706	750
RAOUX, Albert (19th C) French				
oil	1	3,254	3,254	3,254
wc/d	1	495	495	495
RAOUX, Jean (1677-1734) French				
oil	2	46,710-78,137	62,423	46,710
RAPACKI, Jozef (1871-1929) Polish				
oil	1	8,507	8,507	8,507
RAPAIRE, Georges (20th C) French				
oil	2	5,419-9,031	7,225	5,419
RAPHAEL, Joseph (1869-1950) American				
oil	5	8,247-27,500	18,059	16,000
wc/d	3	1,000-2,500	1,666	1,500
RAPHAEL, William (1833-1914) Prussian/Canadian				
oil	3	6,000-26,801	13,888	8,863
wc/d	1	815	815	815
RAPOUS, Michele Antonio (1733-1819) Italian				
oil	2	25,890-35,270	30,580	25,890
RAPPARLIER, C (20th C) French				
oil	1	1,818	1,818	1,818
RAPPINI, Vittorio (1877-1939) Italian				
wc/d	3	1,203-4,092	2,414	1,947
RASCH, Heinrich (1840-1913) German				
oil	6	995-4,882	2,666	2,503
RASCHEN, Henry (1854-1937) German/American				
oil	4	599-15,000	8,899	7,000
RASELL, Robert (fl.1868-1880) British				
oil	2	885-1,424	1,154	885
RASER, J Heyl (1824-1901) American				
oil	2	4,600-5,000	4,800	4,600
RASETTI, Georges (elder) (1851-1931) French				
oil	1	5,980	5,980	5,980
RASIM, Otto (1878-1936) Austrian				
oil	2	839-2,860	1,849	839

Name	No.	Price Range	Average	Median
RASMUSSEN, Carl (1831-1903) Danish				
oil	2	2,860-21,188	12,024	2,860
RASMUSSEN, Eli Sigvard (1915-) Danish				
oil	1	1,288	1,288	1,288
RASMUSSEN, Georg Anton (1842-1914) Norwegian				
oil	12	751-15,181	4,763	2,761
RASMUSSEN, I E C (1841-1893) Danish				
oil	4	1,699-15,082	6,040	3,411
RASMUSSEN, Jens Erik Carl (1841-1893) Danish				
oil	5	3,586-39,121	13,091	8,686
RASPAY, Jean Pierre (1748-1825) French				
oil	1	4,861	4,861	4,861
RASSENFOSSE, Armand (1862-1934) Belgian				
oil	1	3,034	3,034	3,034
wc/d	12	722-7,598	2,586	1,764
RATCLIFFE, William (1870-1955) British				
oil	1	35,400	35,400	35,400
RATEAU, Armand Albert (1882-1938) French				
3D	1	8,269	8,269	8,269
RATH, Hildegard (1909-) American/German				
oil	2	1,300-2,500	1,900	1,300
RATHBONE, Harold (1858-?) British				
wc/d	1	3,500	3,500	3,500
RATHBONE, John (1750-1807) British				
oil	2	3,816-11,970	7,893	3,816
RATTERMAN, Walter G (1887-1944) American				
oil	1	1,300	1,300	1,300
RATTIGAN, James Henry (19/20th C) American				
oil	1	1,200	1,200	1,200
RATTNER, Abraham (1895-1978) American				
oil	2	4,000-17,000	10,500	4,000
wc/d	2	500-650	575	500
RATTRAY, Alexander Wellwood (1849-1902) American				
oil	1	1,665	1,665	1,665
RATY, Albert (1889-1970) Belgian				
oil	18	1,155-19,622	4,762	2,417
wc/d	1	951	951	951
RAU, Emil (1858-1937) German				
oil	5	2,676-16,562	5,895	3,405
RAU, Woldemar Heinrich (1827-1889) German				
wc/d	1	2,447	2,447	2,447
RAUCH, Christian (1777-1857) German				
3D	4	8,938-204,694	70,265	24,082
RAUCH, Johann Nepomuk (1804-1847) Austrian				
oil	1	5,029	5,029	5,029
RAUCH, Neo (1960-) German				
oil	15	14,014-740,000	139,570	31,140
wc/d	2	21,240-70,000	45,620	21,240
RAUCHWERGER, Jan (1942-) Israeli				
oil	1	1,200	1,200	1,200
RAUGHT, John Willard (1857-1931) American				
oil	2	1,000-2,000	1,500	1,000
RAULIN, Alexandre (19th C) French				
oil	2	11,404-14,790	13,097	11,404
RAUPP, Friedrich (1871-1949) German				
oil	1	3,387	3,387	3,387
RAUPP, Karl (1837-1918) German				
oil	2	9,699-18,400	14,049	9,699
RAUSCH, Leonhard (1813-1895) German				
oil	3	1,985-19,265	8,145	3,186
RAUSCHENBERG, Robert (1925-) American				
oil	6	55,000-308,000	152,725	103,051
wc/d	15	2,166-1,200,000	294,608	130,000
3D	4	4,097-550,000	154,774	5,000
RAVAL, Rasik Durgashanker (1928-1980) Indian				
oil	1	15,000	15,000	15,000
RAVANNE, Léon Gustave (1854-1904) French				
oil	2	6,233-6,592	6,412	6,233
RAVEEL, Roger (1921-) Belgian				
oil	4	4,555-38,531	16,484	5,993
wc/d	3	839-5,301	3,410	4,091

Name	No.	Price Range	Average	Median
RAVEL, Edouard-John E (1847-1920) Swiss				
oil	3	2,061-16,530	7,230	3,100
wc/d	1	6,000	6,000	6,000
RAVEL, Jules (1826-1898) French				
oil	1	3,330	3,330	3,330
RAVEN, Ernst von (1816-1890) German				
oil	2	2,858-2,906	2,882	2,858
RAVEN, Samuel (1775-1847) British				
oil	2	600-2,268	1,434	600
RAVENSTEIN, Paul von (1854-1938) German				
oil	1	2,676	2,676	2,676
RAVENSWAAY, Jan van (1789-1869) Dutch				
oil	1	3,156	3,156	3,156
wc/d	2	589-766	677	589
RAVENSWAAY, Johannes van (younger) (1815-1849) Dutch				
oil	2	14,640-172,083	93,361	14,640
RAVESTEYN, Dirck de Quade van (fl.1589-1619) Dutch				
oil	1	61,151	61,151	61,151
RAVESTEYN, Hubert van (1638-1691) Dutch				
oil	1	38,219	38,219	38,219
RAVESTEYN, Jan Anthonisz van (1570-1657) Dutch				
oil	4	16,349-76,438	46,663	17,838
RAVESTEYN, Nicolas van II (1661-1750) Dutch				
oil	1	2,473	2,473	2,473
RAVET, Victor (1840-1895) Belgian				
oil	2	1,171-2,003	1,587	1,171
RAVIER, Auguste François (1814-1895) French				
oil	6	583-5,088	2,245	1,815
wc/d	13	468-5,068	2,174	1,523
RAVILIOUS, Eric (1903-1942) British				
wc/d	2	132,240-154,800	143,520	132,240
RAVLIN, Grace (1885-1956) American				
oil	1	3,500	3,500	3,500
RAVN, Lars (1959-) Danish				
oil	1	1,288	1,288	1,288
RAWAL, Yogesh (20th C) Indian				
wc/d	2	4,500-7,500	6,000	4,500
RAWLINS, Violet (fl.1904-1912) British				
oil	1	1,302	1,302	1,302
RAWSON, Albert Leighton (1829-1902) American				
oil	1	2,000	2,000	2,000
RAWSON, Carl W (1884-1970) American				
oil	1	1,700	1,700	1,700
RAY, Carl (1943-1978) Canadian				
wc/d	1	1,548	1,548	1,548
RAY, Charles (1953-) American				
3D	1	580,000	580,000	580,000
RAY, Jules le (19/20th C) French				
oil	2	1,671-2,163	1,917	1,671
RAY, Shyamal Dutta (1934-2005) Indian				
wc/d	3	4,250-6,000	5,083	5,000
RAYA-SORKINE (1936-) French				
oil	5	1,844-4,302	2,992	2,747
wc/d	2	1,909-4,176	3,042	1,909
RAYEN, James (1935-) American				
oil	1	2,600	2,600	2,600
RAYMOND, H (?) ?				
oil	1	3,000	3,000	3,000
RAYMOND, Lodovico (1825-1898) Italian				
oil	1	4,844	4,844	4,844
RAYMOND, Marie (1908-1988) French				
oil	4	490-2,378	1,762	1,901
wc/d	4	950-1,647	1,284	1,140
RAYNAUD, Auguste (19th C) French				
oil	2	2,272-12,395	7,333	2,272
RAYNAUD, Jean Pierre (1939-) French				
wc/d	2	3,600-23,378	13,489	3,600
3D	10	1,577-32,364	11,912	5,178
RAYNAUD, Tatiana (20th C) French?				
oil	1	1,703	1,703	1,703
RAYNER, Henry Hewitt (1903-1957) Australian				
wc/d	1	2,314	2,314	2,314

Name	No.	Price Range	Average	Median
RAYNER, Louise (1832-1924) British				
wc/d	5	800-61,600	31,158	28,350
RAYNES, Sidney (1907-) American				
oil	1	1,300	1,300	1,300
RAYSSE, Martial (1936-) French				
oil	1	241,958	241,958	241,958
wc/d	4	848-17,862	7,628	5,381
3D	2	10,520-20,566	15,543	10,520
RAZA, Sayed Haider (1922-) Indian				
oil	56	15,535-1,300,000	113,987	74,168
wc/d	4	32,000-210,139	82,019	33,440
RAZIS, Angelos (1943-) Greek				
oil	1	5,610	5,610	5,610
RAZUMOV, Konstantin (1974-) Russian				
oil	51	477-4,900	1,565	1,313
RAZUMOVSKAYA, Yulia Vasilevna (1896-1987) Russian				
oil	1	60,000	60,000	60,000
wc/d	1	18,600	18,600	18,600
RE, Guglielmo da (1867-?) Italian				
oil	1	1,455	1,455	1,455
RE, Marco del (1950-) French?				
oil	1	4,544	4,544	4,544
REA, Cecil W (1861-1935) British				
oil	1	1,557	1,557	1,557
REA, Constance (19/20th C) British				
oil	1	6,615	6,615	6,615
REA, Remo (?) ?				
oil	1	1,140	1,140	1,140
wc/d	2	600-600	600	600
READ, Thomas Buchanan (1822-1872) American				
oil	2	1,900-5,088	3,494	1,900
READSHAW, Emily S (19th C) British				
oil	1	1,000	1,000	1,000
REAL DEL SARTE, Maxime (1888-1954) French				
3D	1	4,411	4,411	4,411
REAL, Charles (1898-1979) French				
oil	2	7,500-10,000	8,750	7,500
REALFONSO, Tommaso (18th C) Italian				
oil	1	31,552	31,552	31,552
REAM, Carducius Plantagenet (1837-1917) American				
oil	10	950-19,000	7,290	6,500
REASON, Florence (fl.1883-1903) British				
oil	1	2,436	2,436	2,436
wc/d	1	748	748	748
REAUGH, Charles Franklin (1860-1945) American				
wc/d	4	7,500-15,000	11,625	11,000
REBAY, Hilla (1890-1967) American/French				
wc/d	2	764-1,400	1,082	764
REBELL, Joseph (1787-1828) Austrian				
oil	2	16,560-76,316	46,438	16,560
wc/d	1	7,120	7,120	7,120
REBEYROLLE, Paul (1926-2005) French				
oil	18	2,337-66,857	21,618	12,730
wc/d	4	825-31,521	16,366	7,880
REBOUSSIN, Roger Andre Fernand (1881-1965) French				
wc/d	2	479-1,665	1,072	479
REBRY, Gaston (1933-) Canadian				
oil	13	441-2,788	1,440	1,216
RECALCATI, Antonio (1938-) Italian				
oil	7	1,000-21,452	6,568	3,045
wc/d	2	676-1,475	1,075	676
RECCO, Elena (17th C) Italian				
oil	1	20,710	20,710	20,710
RECCO, Giovan Battista (1630-1675) Italian				
oil	1	703,000	703,000	703,000
RECCO, Giuseppe (1634-1695) Italian				
oil	4	38,060-157,250	86,530	45,000
RECHLIN, Karl (1804-1882) German				
oil	1	12,041	12,041	12,041
RECIPON, Georges (1860-1920) French				
3D	1	1,914	1,914	1,914

Name	No.	Price Range	Average	Median
RECK, Hermine von (1833-1906) German				
oil	1	3,891	3,891	3,891
RECKELBUS, Louis (1864-1958) Belgian				
oil	1	1,314	1,314	1,314
wc/d	1	3,733	3,733	3,733
RECKEWITZ, Wilfried (1925-) German				
oil	1	1,296	1,296	1,296
RECKHARD, Gardner Arnold (1858-1908) American				
oil	2	2,500-3,000	2,750	2,500
RECKITT, Rachel (fl.1930-1950) British				
oil	1	1,343	1,343	1,343
RECKLESS, Stanley Lawrence (1892-?) American				
oil	1	1,500	1,500	1,500
RECKNAGEL, John (19/20th C) German				
oil	1	1,458	1,458	1,458
wc/d	1	3,624	3,624	3,624
RECKNAGL, Theodor (19th C) German				
oil	2	1,100-1,573	1,336	1,100
REDEL, Eike (1951-) German				
oil	2	975-2,142	1,558	975
REDER, Bernard (1897-1963) Israeli				
3D	1	1,800	1,800	1,800
REDER-BROILI, Franz (1854-1918) German				
oil	1	1,311	1,311	1,311
REDERER, Franz J (1899-1965) Swiss				
oil	6	572-9,921	3,075	1,725
REDFIELD, Edward (1869-1965) American				
oil	11	2,250-650,000	203,613	130,000
wc/d	1	2,500	2,500	2,500
REDGATE, Arthur W (fl.1880-1906) British				
oil	6	496-5,280	2,241	684
REDIG, Laurent Herman (1822-1861) Dutch				
oil	1	5,121	5,121	5,121
REDING, Leon (19th C) Belgian				
oil	1	3,750	3,750	3,750
REDL, Erwin (1963-) American				
wc/d	1	3,400	3,400	3,400
REDMOND, Granville (1871-1935) American				
oil	14	6,000-230,000	78,642	40,000
REDMORE, Edward King (1860-1941) British				
oil	3	900-4,872	2,297	1,119
REDMORE, Henry (1820-1887) British				
oil	15	2,301-24,310	10,255	10,120
REDON, Georges (19/20th C) French				
oil	1	1,052	1,052	1,052
REDON, Odilon (1840-1916) French				
oil	6	42,500-832,500	323,197	130,000
wc/d	6	6,726-800,000	251,110	115,000
REDONDELA, Agustin (1922-) Spanish				
oil	4	5,856-13,993	9,083	8,159
REDOUTE, Pierre Joseph (1759-1840) French				
wc/d	2	527-17,000	8,763	527
REDPATH, Anne (1895-1965) British				
oil	12	31,140-155,760	72,904	53,400
wc/d	9	1,190-15,045	8,341	8,900
REEB, David (1952-) Israeli				
oil	9	850-57,500	9,355	3,200
REED (20th C) American				
oil	1	4,986	4,986	4,986
REED, David (1946-) American				
oil	5	2,076-62,000	22,509	9,555
REED, Doel (1894-1985) American				
oil	1	14,000	14,000	14,000
REED, Joseph (1822-1877) British				
wc/d	2	915-1,480	1,197	915
REED, L E (19th C) British				
oil	1	3,560	3,560	3,560
REED, Marjorie (1915-1997) American				
oil	7	1,000-8,000	4,642	5,000
REED, Peter Fishe (1817-1887) American				
oil	1	3,750	3,750	3,750

Name	No.	Price Range	Average	Median
REED, Robert (1938-) American				
wc/d	1	1,000	1,000	1,000
REED, William E (1903-1989) American				
oil	1	2,200	2,200	2,200
REEDER, Dixon (1912-1970) American				
wc/d	1	1,500	1,500	1,500
REEDY, Leonard Howard (1899-1956) American				
oil	1	1,400	1,400	1,400
wc/d	34	500-4,000	1,765	1,500
REEKERS, Hendrik (1815-1854) Dutch				
oil	1	148,333	148,333	148,333
REEKERS, Johannes (jnr) (1824-1895) Dutch				
oil	1	4,944	4,944	4,944
REES, Otto van (1884-1957) Dutch				
oil	4	6,500-37,405	19,451	16,365
wc/d	1	1,403	1,403	1,403
REESE, Dorothy V (1899-1989) American				
oil	1	2,100	2,100	2,100
REESE, Marx C E (1881-1960) Danish				
oil	1	1,299	1,299	1,299
REEVE, Russell Sidney (1895-1970) British				
oil	1	1,581	1,581	1,581
REEVE-FOWKES, Amy C (1886-1968) British				
wc/d	1	1,392	1,392	1,392
REEVES, Claude (fl.1900) British				
oil	2	4,171-4,171	4,171	4,171
REEVES, Joseph Mason (jnr) (1898-1974) American				
oil	3	900-2,250	1,450	1,200
REEVES, Richard Stone (1921-) American				
oil	2	7,422-14,000	10,711	7,422
REGAGNON, Albert (1874-1961) French				
oil	1	6,195	6,195	6,195
REGAMEY, Felix Elie (1844-1907) French				
wc/d	1	3,270	3,270	3,270
REGEMORTER, Ignatius Josephus van (1785-1873) Flemish				
oil	2	1,824-11,678	6,751	1,824
REGEMORTER, Petrus Johannes van (1755-1830) Flemish				
oil	1	3,004	3,004	3,004
REGGI, Emanuel de (1957-) Italian				
3D	1	5,342	5,342	5,342
REGGIANI, Mauro (1897-1980) Italian				
oil	21	2,499-55,973	14,367	8,247
wc/d	8	922-8,497	3,390	2,647
REGGIANINI, Vittorio (1858-1939) Italian				
oil	1	100,973	100,973	100,973
REGILD, Carsten (1941-1992) Swedish				
oil	2	1,620-2,114	1,867	1,620
wc/d	2	954-5,853	3,403	954
REGIMBAL, James (1949-) American				
3D	2	1,800-1,800	1,800	1,800
REGNAULT, Baron Jean Baptiste (1754-1829) French				
oil	1	14,500	14,500	14,500
wc/d	2	4,500-10,137	7,318	4,500
REGNAULT, Henri (1843-1871) French				
oil	2	1,654-2,362	2,008	1,654
wc/d	3	620-24,078	9,803	4,712
REGNIER, Nicolas (1590-1667) Flemish				
oil	1	70,067	70,067	70,067
REGO MONTEIRO, Vicente do (1899-1970) Brazilian				
wc/d	2	6,897-8,000	7,448	6,897
REGO, Paula (1935-) Portuguese				
oil	1	74,340	74,340	74,340
wc/d	1	316,800	316,800	316,800
3D	1	10,620	10,620	10,620
REGOS, Polykleitos (1903-1984) Greek				
oil	8	8,996-21,505	12,302	10,208
wc/d	1	4,576	4,576	4,576
REGRAGUI, Fquih (20th C) French?				
oil	6	1,381-22,948	10,911	6,065
REGSCHEK, Kurt (1923-) Austrian				
oil	1	1,326	1,326	1,326
wc/d	1	573	573	573

Name	No.	Price Range	Average	Median
REGTEREN ALTENA, Marie E van (1868-1958) Dutch				
oil	4	975-5,192	2,683	1,152
REGTERS, T (1710-1768) Dutch				
oil	1	22,253	22,253	22,253
REHBERGER, Tobias (1966-) ?				
oil	1	3,000	3,000	3,000
REHDER, Julius Christian (1861-1955) German				
oil	1	1,040	1,040	1,040
REHN, Frank Knox Morton (1848-1914) American				
oil	5	800-3,000	1,470	1,000
wc/d	2	500-2,400	1,450	500
REHNBERG, Hakan (1953-) Swedish				
oil	2	1,454-1,586	1,520	1,454
REICH, Adolf (1887-1963) Austrian				
oil	2	1,940-3,363	2,651	1,940
REICH, Anton (20th C) Austrian?				
oil	1	1,155	1,155	1,155
REICHEL, Hans (1892-1958) German				
oil	3	2,225-35,200	17,995	16,562
wc/d	6	2,799-19,718	8,704	5,088
REICHEL, Karl Anton (1874-?) German				
oil	1	4,600	4,600	4,600
REICHEL, Valesca (1833-?) German				
oil	1	1,051	1,051	1,051
REICHERT, Carl (1836-1918) Austrian				
oil	11	3,646-25,000	10,058	6,070
REICHERT, Franz Heinrich (19th C) Austrian				
oil	1	3,750	3,750	3,750
REICHLE, Paul (1900-1981) German				
oil	3	637-1,401	1,019	1,019
REID, Allen (?) British				
oil	2	1,305-1,530	1,417	1,305
REID, George Agnew (1860-1947) Canadian				
oil	12	529-141,043	25,496	5,739
REID, George Ogilvy (1851-1928) British				
oil	7	552-15,840	6,045	3,675
wc/d	1	1,392	1,392	1,392
REID, Irene Hoffar (1908-1994) Canadian				
oil	1	2,512	2,512	2,512
REID, James Eadie (19/20th C) British				
oil	1	1,000	1,000	1,000
REID, John Robertson (1851-1926) British				
oil	3	1,062-3,480	2,036	1,566
wc/d	1	870	870	870
REID, Mary Augusta Hiester (1854-1921) Canadian				
oil	2	4,200-15,867	10,033	4,200
REID, Nano (1900-1981) Irish				
oil	2	12,351-17,671	15,011	12,351
wc/d	4	2,622-5,419	3,593	2,799
REID, Robert (1862-1929) American				
oil	4	4,250-35,000	17,062	12,000
REID, Robert Payton (1859-1945) British				
oil	3	5,310-6,802	6,053	6,048
REID, Stephen (1873-1948) British				
oil	2	1,663-2,391	2,027	1,663
REID, William Ronald (1920-1998) Canadian				
3D	3	13,294-105,355	56,536	50,960
REID-HENRY, David M (1919-1977) British				
wc/d	2	1,068-1,424	1,246	1,068
REIDY, Lorna Wilson (20th C) American				
oil	1	1,500	1,500	1,500
REIFF, Franz (1835-1902) German				
oil	1	4,581	4,581	4,581
REIFFEL, Charles (1862-1942) American				
oil	2	17,000-42,500	29,750	17,000
REIFFENSTEIN, Leo (1856-?) Austrian				
oil	2	1,812-4,696	3,254	1,812
REIHILL, Zita (20th C) Irish				
oil	1	1,694	1,694	1,694
REILLE, Karl (1886-1975) French				
oil	11	1,784-8,653	6,268	6,799
wc/d	40	951-19,160	6,887	5,563

Name	No.	Price Range	Average	Median
REILLY, James (1956-) American				
oil	1	27,520	27,520	27,520
REILLY, John Lewis (19th C) British				
oil	1	3,363	3,363	3,363
REIMPRE, Thibault de (1949-) French				
oil	2	507-1,854	1,180	507
REINA, Miela (1935-1972) Italian				
wc/d	1	1,573	1,573	1,573
REINAGLE, Philip (1749-1833) British				
oil	2	797-22,680	11,738	797
REINERMANN, Friedrich Christian (1764-1835) German				
oil	2	2,272-9,926	6,099	2,272
wc/d	1	1,136	1,136	1,136
REINHARD, Josef (1749-1824) Swiss				
oil	4	775-4,079	1,974	1,366
REINHARDT, Ad (1913-1967) American				
oil	4	35,342-380,000	193,835	160,000
REINHARDT, August Friedrich (1831-1915) German				
oil	1	1,649	1,649	1,649
REINHARDT, Louis (1849-1870) German				
oil	2	1,951-4,238	3,094	1,951
REINHARDT, Siegfried (1925-1984) American				
wc/d	1	1,100	1,100	1,100
REINHART, Benjamin Franklin (1829-1885) American				
oil	1	2,800	2,800	2,800
REINHART, Johann Christian (1761-1847) German				
wc/d	2	589-3,770	2,179	589
REINHOLD, Bernhard (1824-1892) German				
oil	1	24,842	24,842	24,842
REINHOLD, Franz (1816-1893) Austrian				
oil	1	1,296	1,296	1,296
REINHOLD, Friedrich Philipp (1779-1840) German				
oil	1	12,873	12,873	12,873
REINHOLD, Heinrich (1788-1825) Austrian				
wc/d	3	705-5,890	2,905	2,121
REINHOLD, Thomas (1953-) Austrian				
oil	2	1,199-2,342	1,770	1,199
REINICKE, René (1860-1926) German				
oil	1	727	727	727
wc/d	1	1,323	1,323	1,323
REINIGER, Otto (1863-1909) German				
oil	5	486-2,432	1,421	1,636
REINIKE, Charles Henry (1906-1983) American				
wc/d	4	1,000-1,200	1,150	1,200
REINKEN, Clara (1855-?) German				
oil	1	1,940	1,940	1,940
REINOSO, Pablo (1955-) Argentinian				
3D	1	3,279	3,279	3,279
REIS PEREIRA, Julio (1902-1983) Portuguese				
wc/d	1	1,944	1,944	1,944
REIS, Joao (1899-1982) Portuguese				
oil	1	7,535	7,535	7,535
REISER, Carl (1877-1950) German				
oil	2	668-1,940	1,304	668
wc/d	1	3,857	3,857	3,857
REISMAN, Ori (1924-1991) Israeli				
oil	1	5,000	5,000	5,000
REISMAN, Philip (1904-1992) American				
oil	1	3,200	3,200	3,200
REISS, Fritz (1857-1916) German				
oil	1	1,697	1,697	1,697
wc/d	1	1,806	1,806	1,806
REISS, Fritz Winold (1886-1953) American/German				
wc/d	2	1,300-3,000	2,150	1,300
REITER, Erwin (1933-) Austrian				
3D	1	4,005	4,005	4,005
REITER, Johann Baptist (1813-1890) Austrian				
oil	2	6,370-14,517	10,443	6,370
REITTEFER, Rety (19th C) ?				
oil	1	1,214	1,214	1,214
REJLANDER, Oscar Gustav (1813-1875) British				
wc/d	1	1,780	1,780	1,780

Name	No.	Price Range	Average	Median
RELANDER, E (1877-1937) Finnish				
oil	2	1,618-3,248	2,433	1,618
REMBRANDT (1606-1669) Dutch				
oil	1	3,800,000	3,800,000	3,800,000
wc/d	2	65,000-210,000	137,500	65,000
REMFRY, David (1942-) British				
wc/d	1	1,157	1,157	1,157
REMIENS, Adrianus (1890-1972) Dutch				
oil	1	3,562	3,562	3,562
REMINGTAM, Frederik (19/20th C) American				
oil	1	3,992	3,992	3,992
REMINGTON, Frederic (1861-1909) American				
oil	4	47,500-1,300,000	504,375	290,000
wc/d	7	1,250-65,000	27,035	28,000
3D	14	2,000-450,000	135,222	75,000
REMOND, J (?) French				
oil	1	2,121	2,121	2,121
REMOND, Jean Charles Joseph (1795-1875) French				
oil	3	1,757-6,184	4,344	5,092
REMSEY, Jeno (1885-1960) Hungarian				
oil	2	510-2,200	1,355	510
REN, Chuck (1941-1995) American				
oil	2	3,750-4,750	4,250	3,750
RENARD, A Constantin (19th C) French				
oil	2	1,573-2,057	1,815	1,573
RENARD, Fredericus Theodorus (1778-?) Dutch				
oil	1	8,000	8,000	8,000
RENARD, Stephen J (1947-) British				
oil	9	2,057-35,000	13,045	11,000
RENAUD, Francis (1887-?) French				
3D	1	10,065	10,065	10,065
RENAUDIN, Alfred (1866-1944) French				
oil	5	2,061-4,411	3,382	3,500
RENAUDOT, Paul (1871-1920) French				
oil	1	2,647	2,647	2,647
RENAULT, Gaston (1855-?) French				
oil	1	65,000	65,000	65,000
RENAULT, Luigi P (1845-c.1910) Italian				
wc/d	1	2,121	2,121	2,121
RENDON, Manuel (1894-1980) Ecuadorian/French				
oil	2	12,000-35,000	23,500	12,000
RENE, Jean Jacques (1943-) French				
oil	6	835-3,625	2,069	1,555
wc/d	4	477-596	536	501
RENEH, I (1910-1976) Balinese				
wc/d	1	1,204	1,204	1,204
RENESON, Chet (1934-) American				
wc/d	2	1,800-2,600	2,200	1,800
RENGIFO, Cesar (1915-1980) Venezuelan				
oil	2	2,790-17,440	10,115	2,790
wc/d	4	740-3,500	2,042	1,955
RENI, Guido (1575-1642) Italian				
oil	1	126,863	126,863	126,863
wc/d	5	2,589-97,500	36,297	29,600
RENNIE, George Melvin (1874-1953) British				
oil	5	1,012-2,610	1,681	1,548
RENNINGER, Katharine Steele (1925-) American				
wc/d	1	1,800	1,800	1,800
RENNINGER, Wilmer Brunner (1909-1935) American				
oil	1	2,200	2,200	2,200
RENNY, James (20th C) British				
wc/d	1	1,196	1,196	1,196
RENOIR, Pierre Auguste (1841-1919) French				
oil	68	26,400-8,096,000	634,523	296,000
wc/d	10	11,651-420,000	99,975	32,000
3D	8	6,475-50,000	17,774	9,680
RENOIR, Pierre Auguste and GUINO, Richard (19/20th C) French				
3D	3	11,000-25,000	16,333	13,000
RENOUF, Edda (1943-) ?				
oil	3	450-8,035	3,695	2,600
wc/d	4	701-9,500	4,800	4,500

Name	No.	Price Range	Average	Median
RENOUX, Andre (1939-) French				
oil	2	850-1,386	1,118	850
RENOUX, Charles (1795-1846) French				
oil	5	1,068-27,500	7,437	3,168
wc/d	1	659	659	659
RENOUX, Jules Ernest (1863-1932) French				
oil	3	1,212-1,556	1,386	1,392
RENQVIST, Torsten (1924-) Swedish				
oil	4	1,527-3,436	2,449	2,290
3D	2	1,654-3,563	2,608	1,654
RENTERIA, Horacio (1912-1972) Mexican				
oil	2	7,500-8,500	8,000	7,500
RENTINCK, Arnold (1712-1774) Dutch				
oil	1	4,048	4,048	4,048
RENTZELL, August von and TRIEBEL, Carl (19th C) German				
oil	1	1,459	1,459	1,459
RENUCCI, Renuccio (1880-1947) Italian				
oil	8	509-4,452	2,014	1,638
RENVALL, Ben (1903-1979) Finnish				
3D	1	2,314	2,314	2,314
RENVALL, Essi (1911-1979) Finnish				
3D	1	5,400	5,400	5,400
RENZ, Alfred (1877-1930) German				
oil	3	607-1,295	1,007	1,119
RENZI, Clement (20th C) American				
3D	1	2,000	2,000	2,000
REPETTO, Armando E (1893-1968) Argentinian				
oil	10	1,300-5,800	2,700	2,500
wc/d	1	6,000	6,000	6,000
REPIN, Ilia (1844-1930) Russian				
oil	12	3,748-764,384	150,808	37,840
wc/d	31	1,171-50,959	7,361	3,241
REPIN, Yuri Ilich (1877-1954) Russian				
oil	1	1,286	1,286	1,286
REPPEN, Jack (20th C) Canadian				
oil	1	1,148	1,148	1,148
REPPEN, John Richard (1933-1964) Canadian				
wc/d	1	3,879	3,879	3,879
REQUICHOT, Bernard (1929-1961) French				
oil	1	7,730	7,730	7,730
wc/d	1	9,514	9,514	9,514
RERBERG, Fedor Ivanovich (1865-1938) Russian				
oil	1	210,205	210,205	210,205
RESCALLI, Don Angelo (1884-c.1956) Italian				
oil	3	898-8,850	3,653	1,211
RESCHI, Pandolfo (1643-1699) Polish				
oil	3	7,400-24,596	15,627	14,887
RESCHREITER, Rudolf (1868-?) German				
oil	1	2,827	2,827	2,827
wc/d	4	1,216-2,667	1,834	1,273
RESIKA, Paul (20th C) American				
oil	6	1,600-20,000	7,175	3,000
RESIO, Raffaele (1854-1927) Italian				
oil	1	1,311	1,311	1,311
wc/d	1	769	769	769
RESNICK, Milton (1917-2004) American				
oil	3	7,000-60,000	27,666	16,000
wc/d	1	6,000	6,000	6,000
RESTELLINI, Giampiero (1895-?) Italian				
oil	4	568-9,699	2,861	589
RESTOUT, Jean (younger) (1692-1768) French				
oil	1	11,570	11,570	11,570
RESTOUT, Jean Bernard (1732-1797) French				
oil	1	9,000	9,000	9,000
wc/d	1	1,815	1,815	1,815
RETH, Alfred (1884-1966) French				
oil	14	1,403-29,774	10,747	7,714
wc/d	8	1,014-5,825	2,764	2,100
RETIF, Maurice (19/20th C) French				
oil	2	608-1,641	1,124	608

Name	No.	Price Range	Average	Median
RETS, Jean (1910-1998) Belgian				
oil	9	1,032-8,192	3,030	2,637
wc/d	3	476-1,014	695	597
RETTICH, Karl Lorenz (1841-1904) German				
oil	1	5,363	5,363	5,363
RETZLAFF, Ernst Carl Walter (1898-1976) German				
oil	1	1,171	1,171	1,171
REUET, Simone (20th C) French				
oil	1	6,668	6,668	6,668
REUMERT, Niels (1949-) Danish				
oil	4	1,127-2,587	1,777	1,455
REUSCH, Erich (1925-) Swiss?				
wc/d	1	2,293	2,293	2,293
3D	1	7,644	7,644	7,644
REUSCH, Joseph (1887-1976) German				
oil	1	1,907	1,907	1,907
wc/d	3	2,420-3,854	2,978	2,662
REUSS, Albert (1889-1976) ?				
oil	3	708-1,760	1,353	1,593
REUTER, Erich Fritz (1911-1997) German				
3D	1	1,654	1,654	1,654
REUTERSWARD, Carl Fredrik (1934-) Swedish				
oil	11	1,703-67,521	11,567	5,418
wc/d	8	529-2,146	1,250	932
3D	1	6,079	6,079	6,079
REUTERSWARD, Oscar (1915-2002) Swedish				
3D	2	1,718-2,545	2,131	1,718
REUTHER, Wolf (1917-) ?				
oil	1	1,091	1,091	1,091
REVEL, Gabriel (1642-1712) French				
oil	1	15,284	15,284	15,284
REVERON, Armando (1889-1954) Venezuelan				
oil	3	95,000-190,000	138,333	130,000
wc/d	1	8,600	8,600	8,600
REVESZ, Imre (1859-1945) Hungarian				
oil	1	8,256	8,256	8,256
REVILLA RUBIO, Justo (1940-) Spanish				
oil	2	603-2,108	1,355	603
REVILLA, Carlos (1940-) Peruvian				
oil	2	824-3,390	2,107	824
REVILLE, H Whittaker (fl.1881-1903) British				
oil	1	1,744	1,744	1,744
REVOIL, Pierre (1776-1842) French				
wc/d	1	3,403	3,403	3,403
REVOL, Jean (1929-) French				
oil	1	1,255	1,255	1,255
REX, Oskar (1857-1929) Austrian				
oil	3	7,027-23,425	14,054	11,712
REY SANTIAGO, Gabino (1928-) Spanish				
oil	2	1,796-1,796	1,796	1,796
REY, Philippe (18th C) French				
oil	1	18,123	18,123	18,123
REY-MILLET, Constant (1905-) French				
wc/d	1	1,332	1,332	1,332
REYCEND, Enrico (1855-1928) Italian				
oil	3	14,317-15,152	14,864	15,123
REYES FERREIRA, Jesus (1882-1977) Mexican				
oil	1	500	500	500
wc/d	2	800-2,200	1,500	800
REYES MEZA, Jose (1924-) Mexican				
oil	1	1,000	1,000	1,000
REYL-HANISCH, Herbert von (1898-1937) Austrian				
oil	1	12,932	12,932	12,932
REYLANDER-BOHME, Ottilie (1882-1965) German				
oil	1	2,243	2,243	2,243
REYMOND, Carlos (1884-1970) French				
oil	3	851-7,254	4,793	6,276
REYMOND, Casimir (1893-1969) Swiss				
oil	1	2,283	2,283	2,283
REYNA, Antonio Maria de (1859-1937) Spanish				
oil	10	3,514-39,959	19,889	17,014

Name	No.	Price Range	Average	Median
REYNAUD, François (1825-1909) French				
oil	1	3,156	3,156	3,156
REYNAULT, E (19th C) ?				
oil	1	6,600	6,600	6,600
REYNEAU, Betsy Graves (1888-1964) American				
oil	1	11,000	11,000	11,000
REYNEK, Bohuslav (1892-1971) Czechoslovakian				
wc/d	3	677-1,518	1,237	1,518
REYNI, Ingalvur av (1920-) Icelandic				
oil	2	5,309-6,636	5,972	5,309
REYNOLDS, Alan (1926-) British				
oil	4	5,000-85,540	43,452	15,930
wc/d	5	5,568-17,400	9,981	9,204
REYNOLDS, Charles H (1902-1963) American				
oil	4	850-6,000	2,537	1,000
REYNOLDS, James (1926-) American				
oil	7	5,000-25,000	16,785	17,000
REYNOLDS, Sir Joshua (1723-1792) British				
oil	8	28,350-778,500	255,305	94,050
wc/d	2	3,086-3,343	3,214	3,086
REYNOLDS, Wellington Jarard (1869-?) American				
oil	3	1,100-2,500	1,633	1,300
REYNTJENS, Henrich Engelbert (1817-1900) Dutch				
oil	3	2,863-4,671	3,974	4,389
REYON, A (?) ?				
oil	1	7,744	7,744	7,744
REYPENS, Laurent (1954-) Belgian				
oil	1	1,019	1,019	1,019
REYSSCHOOT, Peter Jan van (1702-1772) Flemish				
oil	1	29,195	29,195	29,195
REZES-MOLNAR, Lajos (1896-1989) Hungarian				
oil	1	1,070	1,070	1,070
REZIA, Felice A (fl.1866-1902) British				
oil	5	491-2,100	1,339	1,326
RHEAM, Henry Meynell (1859-1920) British				
wc/d	6	684-4,625	2,771	2,937
RHEINER, Louis (1863-1924) Swiss				
oil	1	1,632	1,632	1,632
wc/d	1	761	761	761
RHO, Manlio (1901-1957) Italian				
oil	2	18,154-30,531	24,342	18,154
wc/d	1	7,990	7,990	7,990
RHODES, Carol (1959-) British				
oil	1	2,112	2,112	2,112
RHODES, Zandra (1940-) British				
wc/d	1	1,114	1,114	1,114
RHYS, Oliver (fl.1876-1895) British				
oil	3	1,496-16,000	7,218	4,158
RIAB, Boris (1898-1975) American/Russian				
wc/d	3	539-4,300	2,261	1,946
RIABOUCHINSKY, Nicholai (1876-1951) Russian				
3D	1	16,000	16,000	16,000
RIBA-ROVIRA, François (1913-) Spanish				
oil	2	2,272-4,351	3,311	2,272
RIBAK, Louis (1902-1979) American				
oil	2	550-1,500	1,025	550
wc/d	1	2,600	2,600	2,600
RIBAS SICILIA, Maryan (?) Spanish				
oil	1	1,781	1,781	1,781
RIBAUPIERRE, François de (1886-1981) Swiss				
oil	3	531-986	764	775
wc/d	2	531-12,237	6,384	531
RIBCOWSKY, Dey de (1880-1936) American/Bulgarian				
oil	10	1,100-6,000	3,040	2,400
RIBEIRO, Lance (1933-) ?				
oil	2	2,640-3,168	2,904	2,640
RIBEMONT-DESSAIGNES, Georges (1884-1974) French				
wc/d	1	1,193	1,193	1,193
RIBERA GOMEZ, Francisco (20th C) Spanish				
oil	1	4,099	4,099	4,099
RIBERA, Francisco (1907-1990) Spanish				
oil	1	5,143	5,143	5,143

Name	No.	Price Range	Average	Median
RIBERA, Jusepe de (1588-1656) Spanish				
oil	4	166,500-481,000	325,250	203,500
wc/d	1	10,000	10,000	10,000
RIBERA, Pierre (1867-1932) French				
oil	1	3,155	3,155	3,155
wc/d	1	1,637	1,637	1,637
RIBERA, Roman (1848-1935) Spanish				
oil	3	12,041-80,000	34,694	12,041
RIBOT, Jules (19/20th C) French				
oil	1	1,004	1,004	1,004
RIBOT, Theodule (1823-1891) French				
oil	3	726-8,000	4,548	4,919
RIBOULET, Jeff (1919-) French				
oil	1	1,551	1,551	1,551
RICARD-CORDINGLEY, Georges (1873-1939) French				
oil	5	605-3,947	2,181	1,505
RICARDO, P (?) Italian?				
oil	1	3,078	3,078	3,078
RICCARDI, Gemma (20th C) Italian				
oil	1	1,985	1,985	1,985
RICCHI, Pietro (1605-1675) Italian				
oil	2	11,651-18,123	14,887	11,651
RICCI, Arturo (1854-1919) Italian				
oil	2	130,000-239,200	184,600	130,000
RICCI, Francisco (1608-1685) Spanish				
oil	1	41,149	41,149	41,149
RICCI, Guido (1836-1897) Italian				
oil	1	6,090	6,090	6,090
RICCI, Marco (1676-1729) Italian				
oil	1	16,365	16,365	16,365
wc/d	4	24,220-37,000	30,892	27,750
RICCI, Pio (?-1919) Italian				
oil	6	6,500-25,800	11,507	7,000
RICCI, Sebastiano (1659-1734) Italian				
oil	2	108,973-138,400	123,686	108,973
wc/d	1	1,200	1,200	1,200
RICCIARDI, Oscar (1864-1935) Italian				
oil	19	725-7,120	2,956	2,330
RICCIARDI, V (20th C) Italian				
oil	1	2,124	2,124	2,124
RICCIO, Andrea (1470-1532) Italian				
3D	1	38,748	38,748	38,748
RICCIOLINI, Michelangelo (1654-1715) Italian				
oil	1	4,770	4,770	4,770
RICCIOLINI, Niccolo (1687-?) Italian				
wc/d	1	1,295	1,295	1,295
RICE, Anne Estelle (1879-1959) American				
oil	2	35,600-54,870	45,235	35,600
RICE, Henry Webster (1853-1934) American				
wc/d	1	1,200	1,200	1,200
RICE, Jessica (20th C) American				
oil	1	7,000	7,000	7,000
RICE, Lucy (1874-1963) American				
oil	1	2,000	2,000	2,000
RICE, Noreen (20th C) British				
oil	1	880	880	880
wc/d	4	618-2,906	1,205	618
RICE, William Morton Jackson (1854-1922) American				
oil	1	1,168	1,168	1,168
RICE-PEREIRA, Irene (1907-1971) American				
oil	2	6,500-40,000	23,250	6,500
wc/d	5	700-38,000	9,300	1,800
RICH, Jason (1970-) American				
oil	2	8,000-10,000	9,000	8,000
RICHARD, Alexandre Louis Marie Theodore (1782-1859) French				
oil	1	1,304	1,304	1,304
RICHARD, Durando Togo (1910-) ?				
oil	1	1,944	1,944	1,944
RICHARD, E (?) ?				
oil	2	5,250-36,122	20,686	5,250
RICHARD, F (19/20th C) ?				
oil	1	3,500	3,500	3,500

Name	No.	Price Range	Average	Median
RICHARD, Fleury François (1777-1852) French				
oil	1	2,201	2,201	2,201
RICHARD, Otto (19/20th C) German				
oil	2	1,090-1,193	1,141	1,090
RICHARD, René (1895-1982) Canadian				
oil	15	656-4,457	2,388	2,292
wc/d	1	617	617	617
RICHARD, Ruth (1937-) French				
3D	1	7,039	7,039	7,039
RICHARD, T (19th C) Swiss				
oil	1	1,790	1,790	1,790
RICHARDE, Ludvig (1862-1929) Swedish				
oil	6	1,119-26,174	5,832	1,648
RICHARDS (?) ?				
oil	1	1,200	1,200	1,200
RICHARDS, Ceri (1903-1971) British				
oil	3	5,310-160,080	60,930	17,400
wc/d	7	1,197-23,660	8,210	6,615
RICHARDS, David (19/20th C) American				
oil	1	3,250	3,250	3,250
RICHARDS, Frederick de Berg (1822-1903) American				
oil	2	2,800-4,750	3,775	2,800
RICHARDS, Henry (19th C) British				
oil	1	1,221	1,221	1,221
RICHARDS, John Inigo (1731-1810) British				
oil	2	870-3,150	2,010	870
RICHARDS, Thomas Addison (1820-1900) American				
oil	3	1,500-6,000	3,500	3,000
RICHARDS, W T (1833-1905) American				
wc/d	1	7,300	7,300	7,300
RICHARDS, William Trost (1833-1905) American				
oil	18	4,250-300,000	61,541	14,500
wc/d	12	1,956-44,000	10,636	5,500
RICHARDSON (?) ?				
wc/d	1	1,432	1,432	1,432
RICHARDSON, Edward (1810-1874) British				
wc/d	4	570-4,756	1,685	703
RICHARDSON, H Linley (1878-1947) New Zealander				
wc/d	1	1,674	1,674	1,674
RICHARDSON, Harry Oliver (19th C) British				
oil	1	1,456	1,456	1,456
RICHARDSON, Jonathan (snr) (1665-1745) British				
oil	4	7,400-60,000	28,795	15,653
RICHARDSON, Margaret Foster (1881-c.1945) American				
wc/d	1	1,300	1,300	1,300
RICHARDSON, Mary Curtis (1848-1931) American				
oil	1	8,000	8,000	8,000
RICHARDSON, R Esdaile (fl.1890s) British				
wc/d	1	5,250	5,250	5,250
RICHARDSON, Ray (1964-) British				
oil	2	1,611-3,222	2,416	1,611
RICHARDSON, Theodore J (1855-1914) American				
wc/d	1	2,200	2,200	2,200
RICHARDSON, Thomas Miles (jnr) (1813-1890) British				
wc/d	20	448-16,720	3,382	1,134
RICHARDSON, Thomas Miles (snr) (1784-1848) British				
wc/d	5	582-20,125	5,609	2,327
RICHARDSON, Volney A (1880-1950) American				
oil	1	3,132	3,132	3,132
RICHARDT, Ferdinand (1819-1895) Danish				
oil	9	1,991-44,453	11,049	7,938
RICHE, Louis (1877-1949) French				
3D	3	2,158-3,279	2,771	2,877
RICHEMONT, Alfred Paul Marie Panon Desbassayna de (1857-1911) French				
oil	1	1,260	1,260	1,260
RICHET, Léon (1847-1907) French				
oil	22	647-21,246	5,813	4,320
wc/d	1	450	450	450
RICHEVILLAIN, Henri (19/20th C) ?				
oil	3	1,243-2,803	1,773	1,274
RICHIER, Germaine (1904-1959) French				
3D	23	2,837-457,600	85,489	45,526

Name	No.	Price Range	Average	Median
RICHIR, Herman (1866-1942) Belgian				
oil	8	492-55,680	8,972	903
wc/d	2	827-1,549	1,188	827
RICHLY, Rudolf (1886-1975) Austrian				
wc/d	2	883-1,136	1,009	883
RICHMAN, Anders Reinhold (1786-1862) Swedish				
oil	1	3,614	3,614	3,614
RICHMOND, Agnes M (1870-1964) American				
oil	1	2,670	2,670	2,670
RICHMOND, George (1809-1896) British				
wc/d	3	487-3,393	1,537	731
RICHMOND, Leonard (1889-1965) British				
oil	2	602-992	797	602
wc/d	1	699	699	699
RICHMOND, Sir William Blake (1842-1921) British				
oil	4	1,408-10,150	4,333	1,619
wc/d	1	1,392	1,392	1,392
RICHTER, Albert (1845-1898) German				
oil	1	2,165	2,165	2,165
RICHTER, August (1801-1873) German				
wc/d	2	700-1,697	1,198	700
RICHTER, Aurel (1870-1957) Hungarian				
oil	4	2,276-6,450	4,222	3,912
wc/d	3	1,767-2,732	2,105	1,816
RICHTER, Christian (elder) (?-1667) German				
wc/d	1	8,905	8,905	8,905
RICHTER, Daniel (1962-) German				
oil	6	95,000-388,500	189,156	138,750
RICHTER, Edouard Frederic Wilhelm (1844-1913) French				
oil	2	5,260-22,620	13,940	5,260
RICHTER, Gerhard (1932-) German				
oil	57	2,040-4,312,000	441,462	88,500
wc/d	5	2,290-88,800	43,091	53,877
3D	2	220,000-1,017,500	618,750	220,000
RICHTER, Gottfried (1904-) German				
oil	1	927	927	927
wc/d	1	608	608	608
RICHTER, Hans (1888-1975) German				
oil	2	15,570-25,950	20,760	15,570
wc/d	2	3,986-12,945	8,465	3,986
RICHTER, Hans Theo (1902-1969) German				
oil	1	4,784	4,784	4,784
wc/d	5	598-4,784	1,591	884
RICHTER, Helene (19th C) German				
oil	1	6,062	6,062	6,062
RICHTER, Herbert Davis (1874-1955) British				
oil	15	500-10,120	2,762	1,859
wc/d	2	519-552	535	519
RICHTER, Johan Anton (1665-1745) Swedish				
oil	4	32,000-148,000	81,250	65,000
RICHTER, Ludwig Adrian (1803-1884) German				
wc/d	15	579-22,384	5,572	4,477
RICHTER, Otto (1867-?) German				
3D	1	15,120	15,120	15,120
RICHTER, Robert (1860-?) German				
oil	1	1,331	1,331	1,331
RICHTER, Wilmer Siegfried (1891-?) American				
oil	1	2,500	2,500	2,500
RICHTER-JOHANNSEN, Hans (20th C) ?				
oil	1	1,066	1,066	1,066
RICHTERS, Bernard (1888-1966) Dutch				
3D	1	1,881	1,881	1,881
RICHTERS, Marius (1878-1955) Dutch				
oil	2	1,523-1,543	1,533	1,523
RICKARDS, Robert L (?) American				
oil	1	6,000	6,000	6,000
RICKEL, Carmelo (20th C) Venezuelan?				
3D	1	4,190	4,190	4,190
RICKETTS, Charles de Sousy (1866-1931) British				
oil	1	42,750	42,750	42,750
RICKEY, George (1907-2002) American				
3D	21	2,478-240,000	61,172	38,000

Name	No.	Price Range	Average	Median
RICKLUND, Folke (1900-1986) Swedish				
oil	1	1,404	1,404	1,404
RICKMAN, Philip (1891-1982) British				
wc/d	6	600-3,784	1,752	1,229
RICKS, Douglas (1954-) American				
oil	3	2,000-3,250	2,716	2,900
RICO Y ORTEGA, Martin (1833-1908) Spanish				
oil	10	1,196-115,000	44,112	14,055
wc/d	2	3,315-6,000	4,657	3,315
RICOIS, François Edme (1795-1881) French				
wc/d	2	880-4,099	2,489	880
RICQUIER, Louis (1792-1884) Belgian				
oil	1	1,204	1,204	1,204
RIDDEL, James (1858-1928) British				
oil	1	1,216	1,216	1,216
RIDDER, J de (?) ?				
3D	1	3,637	3,637	3,637
RIDEOUT, Philip H (fl.1880-1912) British				
oil	3	433-2,165	1,299	1,300
RIDER, Arthur G (1886-1975) American				
oil	4	3,250-42,000	14,937	5,000
wc/d	1	3,000	3,000	3,000
RIDER, H Orne (1860-?) American				
oil	3	600-4,200	1,900	900
RIDINGER, Johann Elias (1698-1767) German				
wc/d	2	1,178-4,186	2,682	1,178
RIDLEY, Janice (20th C) ?				
3D	1	5,400	5,400	5,400
RIECKE, George (1848-1924) ?				
oil	1	3,100	3,100	3,100
RIEDEL, August (1799-1883) German				
oil	3	5,750-6,578	6,109	6,000
RIEDEL, Helene (20th C) ?				
oil	1	3,250	3,250	3,250
RIEDER, Marcel (1852-1942) French				
oil	1	4,815	4,815	4,815
RIEDMULLER, Franz Xaver (1829-1901) German				
oil	1	2,008	2,008	2,008
RIEGEN, Nicolaas (1827-1889) Dutch				
oil	10	626-9,041	5,199	3,933
RIEGER, Albert (1834-1905) Austrian				
oil	9	501-46,000	7,060	2,455
RIEGER, August (1886-1941) Austrian				
oil	1	1,769	1,769	1,769
RIELLO, Antonio (1958-) Italian				
3D	1	2,863	2,863	2,863
RIELLY, James (1956-) ?				
oil	2	11,505-12,390	11,947	11,505
RIENACKER, Gustav (1861-?) German				
oil	2	974-1,697	1,335	974
RIEPENHAUSEN, Johann (1788-1860) German				
oil	2	19,265-33,714	26,489	19,265
RIERA Y ARAGO, Jose M (1954-) Spanish				
oil	3	702-5,346	2,888	2,616
wc/d	1	1,669	1,669	1,669
RIERA, Javier (1964-) Spanish				
oil	1	1,029	1,029	1,029
RIESENBERG, Sidney (1885-1962) American				
oil	1	1,600	1,600	1,600
RIESENBERGER, Johann Moritz (elder) (?-1708) German				
wc/d	1	12,621	12,621	12,621
RIESENER, Henri François (1767-1828) French				
oil	3	2,580-38,060	16,013	7,400
RIESENER, Léon (1808-1878) French				
oil	1	3,857	3,857	3,857
wc/d	2	1,870-2,735	2,302	1,870
RIESS, Paul (1857-1933) German				
wc/d	1	4,087	4,087	4,087
RIESS, Wilhelm (1856-1919) American				
oil	2	2,100-2,700	2,400	2,100
RIESTRA, Adolfo (1944-1989) Mexican				
oil	1	1,100	1,100	1,100

Name	No.	Price Range	Average	Median
RIET, Jan van (1948-) Belgian				
oil	1	1,083	1,083	1,083
RIETH, Paul (1871-1925) German				
oil	1	3,708	3,708	3,708
RIETSCHOOF, Hendrik (1687-1746) Dutch				
wc/d	1	2,803	2,803	2,803
RIETVELD, Gerrit (1888-1964) Dutch				
3D	2	14,027-35,068	24,547	14,027
RIGAUD, Hyacinthe (1659-1743) French				
oil	2	29,144-164,595	96,869	29,144
RIGAUD, Jacques (1681-1754) French				
wc/d	3	29,167-36,458	33,217	34,028
RIGAUD, Jean (1912-1999) French				
oil	4	1,080-5,462	2,426	1,405
wc/d	1	2,792	2,792	2,792
RIGAUD, John Francis (1742-1810) British				
oil	1	12,880	12,880	12,880
RIGAUD, Pierre Gaston (1874-?) French				
oil	3	714-2,993	1,742	1,521
RIGAUX, Louis (1887-1954) Belgian				
oil	2	835-1,293	1,064	835
RIGET, Karl Age (1933-2001) Danish				
oil	3	1,183-2,586	1,795	1,616
RIGG, Ernest Higgins (1868-1947) British				
oil	10	463-38,280	8,191	2,200
RIGG, Jack (1927-) British				
oil	10	515-1,183	896	870
wc/d	2	479-870	674	479
RIGGS, Robert (1896-1970) American				
oil	8	400-170,000	29,300	7,000
wc/d	3	550-3,750	1,966	1,600
RIGHETTI, Francesco (1738-1819) Italian				
3D	1	26,340	26,340	26,340
RIGHETTI, Guido (1875-1958) Italian				
3D	5	1,918-3,567	2,785	2,922
RIGHETTI, Renato (1916-) Italian				
wc/d	1	1,212	1,212	1,212
RIGHINI, Sigismund (1870-1937) German				
oil	4	1,960-3,805	2,995	3,081
RIGL, Vitus Felix (18th C) German				
wc/d	1	2,400	2,400	2,400
RIGLEY, Frederick Wildermuth (1914-) American				
oil	1	2,000	2,000	2,000
RIGOLOT, Albert (1862-1932) French				
oil	8	1,082-100,000	15,853	4,099
RIGOT, G (?) French				
3D	1	3,729	3,729	3,729
RIHA, Josef (19/20th C) Czechoslovakian				
3D	1	2,773	2,773	2,773
RIJK, James de (1806-1882) Dutch				
oil	1	1,638	1,638	1,638
wc/d	1	10,175	10,175	10,175
RIJKELIJKHUYSEN, Hermanus Jan Hendrik (1813-1883) Dutch				
oil	3	1,229-2,356	1,661	1,400
RIKET, Léon (1876-1938) Belgian				
oil	1	1,638	1,638	1,638
RIKIZO (1946-) Japanese				
oil	7	809-2,111	1,538	1,456
RILEY, Bridget (1931-) British				
oil	3	193,600-721,600	388,683	250,850
wc/d	8	15,480-1,942,500	313,726	35,000
RILEY, Harold (1934-) British				
oil	10	779-5,916	3,119	2,784
wc/d	22	522-6,612	1,705	1,328
RILEY, Harry Arthur (19/20th C) British				
wc/d	1	1,197	1,197	1,197
RILEY, John (1646-1691) British				
oil	3	3,762-22,000	10,120	4,600
RILEY, Kenneth (1919-) American				
oil	6	3,750-75,000	31,208	17,000
wc/d	3	5,300-6,000	5,600	5,500

Name	No.	Price Range	Average	Median
RIMBEZ, Zacharie (?) French?				
3D	1	10,000	10,000	10,000
RIMBOECK, Max (1890-?) German				
oil	3	1,200-4,822	3,614	4,821
RIMMER, Itzu (1948-) Israeli				
oil	11	550-3,000	1,365	1,200
RINALDI, Claudio (19th C) Italian				
oil	3	1,750-15,000	8,528	8,836
RINALDO, Antonio (19th C) Italian				
oil	1	9,699	9,699	9,699
RINAS, Vangelis (1966-) Greek				
oil	1	14,025	14,025	14,025
RINCK, Adolph D (1810-?) French				
oil	3	9,250-23,000	14,416	11,000
RINCK, Helene (1855-?) German				
oil	1	1,018	1,018	1,018
RINCON, Serafin Martinez del (1840-1892) Spanish				
oil	2	2,170-2,170	2,170	2,170
RINEHART, William Henry (1825-1874) American				
3D	1	40,000	40,000	40,000
RING, Laurits Andersen (1854-1933) Danish				
oil	16	845-34,927	8,606	4,426
RING, Ole (1902-1972) Danish				
oil	19	711-8,280	3,542	2,381
RINGEISEN, Josef (fl.1905) German				
oil	1	3,041	3,041	3,041
RINGEL D'ILLZACH, Jean Desire (1847-1916) French				
3D	1	3,366	3,366	3,366
RINGEL, Franz (1940-) Austrian				
oil	3	2,805-15,226	8,759	8,247
wc/d	5	701-5,425	2,856	3,600
RINGEL, Frederic (19th C) Belgian				
oil	1	1,439	1,439	1,439
RINGEL, Maximilien Victor (1859-?) French				
3D	1	3,857	3,857	3,857
RINGER, Oton (20th C) Argentinian				
oil	7	1,500-3,300	2,585	2,700
RINK, Paulus Philippus (1861-1903) Dutch				
wc/d	1	2,997	2,997	2,997
RINSEMA, Thijs (1877-1947) Dutch				
wc/d	1	3,273	3,273	3,273
RINTEL, Theo van (1936-) Belgian				
oil	1	1,455	1,455	1,455
wc/d	1	837	837	837
RIO, Paul del (20th C) ?				
oil	2	1,020-1,300	1,160	1,020
RIOPELLE, Jean-Paul (1923-2002) Canadian				
oil	48	12,370-550,000	116,508	61,706
wc/d	9	6,185-40,000	16,644	13,938
3D	2	13,194-18,142	15,668	13,194
RIOS, Ricardo de los (1846-1929) Spanish				
oil	3	1,326-3,268	2,198	2,000
RIOU, Louis (1893-1958) French				
oil	4	934-2,338	1,498	1,293
RIP, Willem C (1856-1922) Dutch				
oil	6	1,204-4,784	2,823	2,769
wc/d	1	942	942	942
RIPAMONTE, Carlos Pablo (1874-1968) Argentinian				
oil	4	2,400-3,600	2,925	2,700
RIPE, W (19th C) German				
oil	1	5,418	5,418	5,418
RIPERTI DI CANALE, Michelangelo (?) Italian?				
wc/d	1	2,848	2,848	2,848
RIPLEY, Aiden Lassell (1896-1969) American				
oil	2	4,250-11,000	7,625	4,250
wc/d	6	600-47,500	15,516	4,000
RIPOLLES, Juan (1932-) Spanish				
oil	1	1,458	1,458	1,458
RIPPEL, Morris (b.1930) American				
wc/d	1	7,000	7,000	7,000
RIPPINGILLE, Edward Villiers (1798-1859) British				
oil	3	1,012-5,130	3,262	3,646

Name	No.	Price Range	Average	Median
RIPPL-RONAI, Jozsef (1861-1927) Hungarian				
oil	1	492,000	492,000	492,000
wc/d	2	6,500-23,895	15,197	6,500
RISHELL, Robert (1917-1976) American				
oil	3	450-6,000	3,233	3,250
RISLEY, John (20th C) American				
3D	1	2,262	2,262	2,262
RISS, Thomas (1871-1959) Austrian				
oil	1	2,524	2,524	2,524
RISSANEN, Juho (1873-1950) Finnish				
oil	4	3,356-16,714	7,620	3,982
wc/d	2	1,019-16,484	8,751	1,019
RIST, Johann Christoph (1790-1876) German				
wc/d	1	5,301	5,301	5,301
RIST, Pipilotti (1962-) German				
3D	2	1,718-33,300	17,509	1,718
RISUENO, Joaquin (1957-) Spanish				
oil	1	1,796	1,796	1,796
RIT, Gaston (1882-1943) Brazilian				
oil	1	1,352	1,352	1,352
RITCHIE, John (fl.1841-1875) British				
oil	1	31,680	31,680	31,680
RITCHIE, Matthew (1964-) American?				
oil	2	56,000-170,000	113,000	56,000
wc/d	2	1,520-13,000	7,260	1,520
RITMAN, Louis (1889-1963) American/Russian				
oil	18	1,000-210,000	30,961	2,800
RITSCHEL, William (1864-1949) American				
oil	9	4,250-95,000	50,583	52,500
wc/d	1	2,000	2,000	2,000
RITSCHL, Otto (1885-1976) German				
oil	6	2,572-7,658	5,043	4,477
wc/d	1	2,967	2,967	2,967
RITSEMA, Coba (1876-1961) Dutch				
oil	2	3,827-7,644	5,735	3,827
RITSEMA, Jacob Coenraad (1869-1943) Dutch				
oil	4	792-1,438	1,089	964
RITTER, Caspar (1861-1923) German				
oil	2	609-12,956	6,782	609
RITTER, Eduard (1808-1853) Austrian				
oil	2	2,625-9,678	6,151	2,625
RITTER, Henry (1816-1853) Canadian				
oil	1	1,752	1,752	1,752
RITZ, Raphael (1829-1894) Swiss				
oil	5	6,070-19,842	11,654	6,526
wc/d	3	763-4,895	2,267	1,145
RITZBERGER, Albert (1853-1915) German				
oil	1	3,629	3,629	3,629
RITZENHOFEN, Hubert (1879-1961) Dutch				
oil	1	1,438	1,438	1,438
RITZOW, Charlotte (1971-) German				
oil	1	604	604	604
wc/d	2	777-1,260	1,018	777
RIVA, Giuseppe (19th C) Italian				
wc/d	1	2,200	2,200	2,200
RIVAROLI, Giuseppe (1885-1943) Italian				
oil	7	970-14,137	6,022	3,748
RIVAS Y OLIVER, Antonio (19th C) Spanish				
wc/d	1	2,586	2,586	2,586
RIVAS, Antonio (19th C) Italian				
oil	1	1,740	1,740	1,740
RIVERA, Diego (1886-1957) Mexican				
oil	2	150,000-1,100,000	625,000	150,000
wc/d	24	1,500-240,000	40,583	27,500
RIVERA, Manuel (1927-1995) Spanish				
oil	2	18,061-29,281	23,671	18,061
wc/d	1	6,660	6,660	6,660
RIVERO SANAVRIA, Carlos (1864-1915) Venezuelan				
oil	1	4,560	4,560	4,560
RIVERS, Elizabeth (1903-1964) British				
oil	3	1,286-4,601	2,745	2,349
wc/d	1	4,005	4,005	4,005

Name	No.	Price Range	Average	Median
RIVERS, Larry (1923-2002) American				
oil	10	3,000-300,000	87,901	50,000
wc/d	4	550-11,000	4,137	2,400
RIVERS, Leopold (1852-1905) British				
oil	7	443-1,740	1,005	732
wc/d	1	550	550	550
RIVIER, Louis (1885-1963) Swiss				
oil	3	3,900-21,648	10,147	4,895
RIVIERE, Adriaan de la (1857-1941) Dutch				
oil	3	514-1,405	875	707
wc/d	1	1,104	1,104	1,104
RIVIERE, Briton (1840-1920) British				
oil	2	12,000-125,280	68,640	12,000
RIVIERE, Henri (1864-1951) French				
wc/d	14	507-3,281	1,928	1,521
RIVIERE, Henry Parsons (1811-1888) British				
wc/d	5	433-4,685	2,167	1,760
RIVIERE, Joseph (1912-) French				
3D	1	5,000	5,000	5,000
RIVIERE, Theodore (1857-1912) French				
3D	5	3,044-41,580	14,190	4,099
RIVOIRE, Raymond (1884-1966) French				
3D	2	9,123-9,884	9,503	9,123
RIX, Julian (1850-1903) American				
oil	8	700-45,000	12,650	5,500
RIXENS, Jean Andre (1846-1924) French				
oil	1	10,426	10,426	10,426
RIXENS, Paul Emile (19/20th C) French				
oil	1	7,508	7,508	7,508
RIZEK, Emil (1901-1988) Austrian				
oil	1	1,010	1,010	1,010
wc/d	1	663	663	663
RIZNISCHENKO, Feodor Petrovich (1865-1922) Russian				
oil	2	2,689-280,274	141,481	2,689
RIZZETTI, Carlo (1969-) Italian				
wc/d	2	1,818-2,160	1,989	1,818
RIZZETTO, Ezio (20th C) Italian				
oil	1	1,036	1,036	1,036
RIZZI, Antonio (1869-1940) Italian				
oil	1	1,078	1,078	1,078
RIZZI, Emilio (1881-1952) Italian				
oil	1	9,514	9,514	9,514
RIZZI, James (1950-) American				
oil	1	1,296	1,296	1,296
wc/d	2	480-485	482	480
RIZZONI, Alexandre (1836-1902) Russian				
oil	2	4,961-9,300	7,130	4,961
ROA, Francisco (1963-) Spanish				
wc/d	1	1,089	1,089	1,089
ROASIO, Maurizio (1946-) Italian				
oil	7	3,416-5,408	4,100	3,937
wc/d	11	5,727-14,317	8,534	7,304
ROBATTO, Giovanni Stefano (1649-1733) Italian				
oil	1	42,720	42,720	42,720
ROBB, William George (1872-1940) British				
oil	5	668-3,675	1,655	974
ROBBE, Henri (1807-1899) Belgian				
oil	2	1,145-1,700	1,422	1,145
ROBBE, Louis (1806-1887) Belgian				
oil	18	387-15,196	3,974	2,622
ROBBE, Manuel (1872-1936) French				
wc/d	1	9,250	9,250	9,250
ROBBIA, Andrea and Giovanni della (15th C) Italian				
3D	1	91,510	91,510	91,510
ROBBIA, Giovanni della (fl.1510-1520) Italian				
3D	1	97,297	97,297	97,297
ROBBINS, H (19th C) British				
oil	1	3,213	3,213	3,213
ROBELLAZ, Emile (1844-1882) Swiss				
oil	1	3,212	3,212	3,212
ROBER, George (1893-1969) Dutch				
oil	1	2,338	2,338	2,338

Name	No.	Price Range	Average	Median
ROBERT, Aurele (1805-1871) Swiss				
oil	2	8,086-31,639	19,862	8,086
wc/d	1	5,180	5,180	5,180
ROBERT, H (?) French/Belgian				
oil	1	1,832	1,832	1,832
ROBERT, Henry (1881-1961) French				
oil	4	507-1,027	697	628
wc/d	1	604	604	604
ROBERT, Hubert (1733-1808) French				
oil	17	11,100-5,550,000	454,205	87,669
wc/d	30	654-121,528	16,262	3,092
ROBERT, Leopold-Louis (1794-1835) French				
oil	1	2,148	2,148	2,148
wc/d	1	999	999	999
ROBERT, Marius Hubert (19/20th C) French				
oil	4	631-1,680	1,162	935
ROBERT, Maurice (1909-) Swiss				
oil	1	1,366	1,366	1,366
ROBERT, Nicolas (1614-1685) French				
wc/d	15	4,099-23,425	8,901	5,856
ROBERT, Philippe (1881-1930) Swiss				
oil	4	1,374-8,381	3,791	2,498
wc/d	3	833-1,984	1,383	1,332
ROBERT, Steven Paul (1896-1985) Swiss				
oil	5	708-5,303	1,695	816
ROBERT, Theophile (1879-1954) Swiss				
oil	2	1,333-3,137	2,235	1,333
wc/d	2	833-2,914	1,873	833
ROBERT, W (?) ?				
oil	1	2,137	2,137	2,137
ROBERTI, Domenico (1642-1707) Italian				
oil	1	22,338	22,338	22,338
ROBERTO, Ernest (fl.1882-1912) Italian				
wc/d	1	2,400	2,400	2,400
ROBERTO, Luigi (1845-1910) Italian				
wc/d	2	4,241-6,054	5,147	4,241
ROBERTS, David (1796-1864) British				
oil	5	818-70,400	16,122	2,394
wc/d	19	2,422-95,150	21,504	13,840
ROBERTS, Edwin (1840-1917) British				
oil	4	4,524-17,100	8,622	5,984
ROBERTS, Erling (1902-?) American				
oil	1	1,800	1,800	1,800
ROBERTS, Gary Lynn (1953-) American				
oil	5	1,600-37,500	13,120	7,500
ROBERTS, I L (19th C) British				
oil	1	2,405	2,405	2,405
ROBERTS, James (19th C) French				
wc/d	1	6,718	6,718	6,718
ROBERTS, Joe Rader (20th C) American				
oil	1	3,500	3,500	3,500
ROBERTS, Julie (1963-) American				
oil	1	4,772	4,772	4,772
ROBERTS, Thomas (1748-1778) Irish				
oil	1	307,800	307,800	307,800
ROBERTS, Thomas Keith (1909-1998) Canadian				
oil	13	793-2,320	1,477	1,194
wc/d	1	742	742	742
ROBERTS, Wilf (20th C) British?				
oil	6	1,593-5,040	3,860	3,960
ROBERTS, Will (1910-2000) British				
oil	5	2,478-5,124	3,142	2,682
wc/d	4	519-1,318	874	623
ROBERTS, William (1895-1980) British				
wc/d	5	2,262-14,790	7,795	4,872
ROBERTS, William Goodridge (1904-1974) Canadian				
oil	19	2,645-48,626	10,588	8,915
wc/d	4	705-1,655	1,120	734
ROBERTS-JONES, Ivor (1916-1966) British				
wc/d	4	1,112-2,052	1,453	1,112
3D	12	1,710-162,450	27,156	3,762

Name	No.	Price Range	Average	Median
ROBERTSON, Charles (1844-1891) British				
wc/d	3	712-24,780	9,054	1,672
ROBERTSON, Henry (1848-1930) British				
wc/d	12	648-2,035	1,310	1,388
ROBERTSON, J B (20th C) British				
oil	1	1,903	1,903	1,903
ROBERTSON, James Downie (1931-) British				
oil	1	1,408	1,408	1,408
wc/d	3	692-5,310	2,243	728
ROBERTSON, Percy (1868-?) British				
wc/d	2	885-1,767	1,326	885
ROBERTSON, Royal (1936-) American				
oil	2	500-2,500	1,500	500
wc/d	1	400	400	400
ROBERTSON, S (1856-1922) Dutch				
oil	1	1,798	1,798	1,798
ROBERTSON, Sarah Margaret (1891-1948) Canadian				
oil	1	4,728	4,728	4,728
ROBERTSON, Suze (1856-1922) Dutch				
oil	5	1,197-9,568	4,312	1,854
ROBERTSON, Tom (1850-1947) British				
oil	5	915-2,405	1,520	946
ROBIE, Jean Baptiste (1821-1910) Belgian				
oil	9	1,093-109,459	22,297	2,860
ROBIN, Georges (19/20th C) French				
oil	1	6,125	6,125	6,125
ROBINS, H (19th C) British				
oil	1	3,150	3,150	3,150
ROBINS, Luke (18/19th C) American				
wc/d	1	4,000	4,000	4,000
ROBINS, Thomas (elder) (1715-1770) British				
wc/d	1	34,020	34,020	34,020
ROBINS, Thomas (younger) (1745-1806) British				
wc/d	2	8,550-8,550	8,550	8,550
ROBINS, Thomas Sewell (1814-1880) British				
wc/d	11	555-14,352	4,577	3,132
ROBINSON, Albert Henry (1881-1956) Canadian				
oil	7	3,092-17,725	10,776	10,536
ROBINSON, Alexander (1867-1952) American				
oil	1	2,061	2,061	2,061
wc/d	3	400-600	500	500
ROBINSON, Cayley (19th C) ?				
oil	1	1,204	1,204	1,204
ROBINSON, Chas Dorman (1847-1933) American				
oil	7	1,500-6,000	3,164	2,500
ROBINSON, Frederick Cayley (1862-1927) British				
oil	1	8,497	8,497	8,497
wc/d	1	8,800	8,800	8,800
ROBINSON, Gregory (fl.1907-1934) British				
wc/d	2	531-1,620	1,075	531
ROBINSON, Hal (1875-1933) American				
oil	8	700-4,500	1,925	1,700
ROBINSON, J H (19th C) British				
oil	1	3,750	3,750	3,750
ROBINSON, John (19/20th C) British				
oil	1	3,480	3,480	3,480
ROBINSON, John Henry (1796-1871) British				
oil	1	1,079	1,079	1,079
ROBINSON, Markey (1918-1999) Irish				
oil	41	1,125-26,040	6,685	4,844
wc/d	54	531-8,342	2,530	1,987
3D	2	1,908-2,967	2,437	1,908
ROBINSON, Matthias (fl.1856-1885) British				
oil	2	925-1,505	1,215	925
ROBINSON, Theodore (1852-1896) American				
oil	7	11,000-300,000	86,285	45,000
wc/d	4	800-25,000	7,450	1,600
ROBINSON, William Heath (1872-1944) British				
wc/d	9	915-5,500	2,682	2,457
ROBINSON, William R (19th C) British				
oil	2	641-2,076	1,358	641

Name	No.	Price Range	Average	Median
ROBINSON, William S (1861-1945) American				
oil	5	2,000-10,500	4,710	3,300
ROBIROSA, Josefina (1932-) Argentinian				
oil	3	2,500-10,108	7,469	9,800
wc/d	2	2,800-9,500	6,150	2,800
ROBJENT, Richard (1937-) British				
wc/d	9	491-5,292	2,870	3,591
ROBSON, George Fennel (1788-1833) British				
wc/d	7	497-10,560	2,787	1,122
ROBSON, William (1868-1952) British				
oil	1	3,740	3,740	3,740
ROBUS, Hugo (1885-1964) American				
3D	2	4,250-16,000	10,125	4,250
ROC ROUSSEY, Jean Pierre (20th C) French				
oil	1	22,794	22,794	22,794
ROCA DELPECH COSTA, Santiago (20th C) Spanish				
oil	1	1,337	1,337	1,337
ROCCA, Ketty la (1938-1976) Italian				
wc/d	1	13,993	13,993	13,993
ROCCA, Michele (1670-1751) Italian				
oil	3	8,900-21,857	14,289	12,110
ROCCATAGLIATA, Niccolo (16/17th C) Italian				
3D	1	48,435	48,435	48,435
ROCCHI, Francesco de (1902-1978) Italian				
oil	3	3,810-9,425	6,655	6,732
ROCHA, Joaquim Manoel da (1727-1786) Portuguese				
oil	1	34,600	34,600	34,600
ROCHARD, Irenee (1906-1984) French				
3D	2	2,625-3,387	3,006	2,625
ROCHAT, Willy (1920-) Swiss				
wc/d	4	833-3,319	2,446	2,392
ROCHE RABELL, Arnaldo (1955-) Puerto Rican				
oil	3	19,000-27,000	21,666	19,000
ROCHE, Alexander (1861-1921) British				
oil	2	1,701-2,148	1,924	1,701
ROCHE, Charles Ferdinand de la (19th C) French				
wc/d	1	1,253	1,253	1,253
ROCHE, Oisin (1973-) Irish				
oil	1	3,884	3,884	3,884
ROCHEFOUCAULD, Antoine de la (1862-1960) French				
oil	1	3,025	3,025	3,025
ROCHEGROSSE, Georges (1859-1938) French				
oil	5	1,197-2,811	1,944	1,942
ROCHELT AMANN, Juan Jose (1881-1953) Spanish				
oil	1	24,110	24,110	24,110
ROCHER, Ernest (1871-1938) French				
oil	1	1,430	1,430	1,430
ROCHER, Maurice (1918-) French				
oil	6	727-2,225	1,299	1,004
ROCHER, Miriam (1886-1971) French				
oil	1	2,498	2,498	2,498
ROCHFORT, I D (19th C) British				
oil	1	5,377	5,377	5,377
ROCHLING, Carl (1855-1920) German				
oil	3	1,526-15,419	6,804	3,468
ROCHUSSEN, Charles (1814-1894) Dutch				
oil	2	492-7,375	3,933	492
wc/d	2	1,463-1,678	1,570	1,463
ROCK, G (1923-2000) Canadian				
oil	1	1,265	1,265	1,265
ROCK, Geoffrey (1923-2000) Canadian				
oil	4	512-5,318	1,775	615
ROCKBURNE, Dorothea (1934-) Canadian				
oil	1	15,000	15,000	15,000
wc/d	1	3,000	3,000	3,000
ROCKENSCHAUB, Gerwald (1952-) Austrian				
oil	3	6,625-32,870	15,925	8,281
3D	1	7,644	7,644	7,644
ROCKLINE, Vera (1896-1934) American				
oil	10	11,757-309,600	77,557	38,015
wc/d	2	1,394-1,901	1,647	1,394

Name	No.	Price Range	Average	Median
ROCKMAN, Alexis (1962-) American				
oil	2	1,600-5,500	3,550	1,600
wc/d	1	20,760	20,760	20,760
ROCKMORE, Noel (1928-1995) American				
oil	3	700-2,750	1,550	1,200
wc/d	1	1,600	1,600	1,600
ROCKWELL, Cleveland (1837-1907) American				
oil	1	3,750	3,750	3,750
ROCKWELL, Norman (1894-1978) American				
oil	13	19,000-8,200,000	877,346	95,000
wc/d	21	400-110,000	23,248	16,000
RODA, Leonardo (1868-1933) Italian				
oil	18	425-14,317	4,343	3,534
RODCHENKO, Alexander (1891-1956) Russian				
oil	1	440,000	440,000	440,000
wc/d	4	32,143-41,622	37,945	38,015
RODDE, Karl Gustav (1830-1906) German				
oil	4	1,553-7,135	3,105	1,865
RODET, Alphonse (1890-1975) French				
oil	1	1,640	1,640	1,640
RODEWALD, Otto (1891-1960) German				
wc/d	1	1,455	1,455	1,455
RODGER, Willie (1930-) British				
oil	1	1,638	1,638	1,638
RODGERS, Roy (20th C) British				
oil	1	1,392	1,392	1,392
RODHE, Lennart (1916-) Swedish				
oil	5	3,563-45,168	14,107	7,929
wc/d	9	509-1,454	858	705
RODIN, Auguste (1840-1917) French				
wc/d	16	2,330-32,363	13,026	9,000
3D	70	2,182-2,600,000	185,210	45,863
RODOCANACHI, Paolo (1891-1955) Italian?				
oil	5	1,835-10,938	6,002	4,772
RODON, Francisco (1934-) Puerto Rican				
oil	1	30,000	30,000	30,000
RODRIGO, Eugenio Oliva (1857-1925) Spanish				
oil	1	3,600	3,600	3,600
RODRIGUE, George (1944-) American				
oil	2	5,262-9,000	7,131	5,262
RODRIGUEZ CASTELAO, Alfonso (1886-1950) Spanish				
wc/d	1	2,349	2,349	2,349
RODRIGUEZ DE LOSADA, Jose Maria (1826-1896) Spanish				
oil	1	1,686	1,686	1,686
RODRIGUEZ ETCHART, Severo (1864-?) South American				
oil	2	18,000-20,000	19,000	18,000
RODRIGUEZ LOZANO, Manuel (1896-1974) Mexican				
oil	1	22,000	22,000	22,000
RODRIGUEZ MOREY, Antonio (1874-1930) Cuban				
oil	1	3,500	3,500	3,500
RODRIGUEZ SAN CLEMENT, Francisco (1861-1956) Spanish				
oil	2	1,200-1,500	1,350	1,200
RODRIGUEZ SANCHEZ CLEMENT, Francisco (1893-1968) Spanish				
oil	4	2,635-10,898	5,207	3,134
RODRIGUEZ, Alfredo (1954-) American				
oil	2	1,250-8,000	4,625	1,250
RODRIGUEZ, Alirio (1934-) Venezuelan				
oil	4	1,395-8,370	4,476	1,630
RODRIGUEZ, Mariano (1912-1990) Cuban				
oil	1	24,000	24,000	24,000
wc/d	5	1,000-9,500	5,384	5,500
RODRIGUEZ, Rodrigo (20th C) Venezuelan?				
wc/d	1	1,675	1,675	1,675
RODRIGUEZ, Victor (1970-) Mexican				
oil	3	12,000-16,000	13,666	13,000
RODUIT, Michel (20th C) Swiss				
oil	1	775	775	775
wc/d	1	1,224	1,224	1,224
RODWITTIYA, Rekha (1958-) Indian				
oil	1	6,000	6,000	6,000
wc/d	1	30,000	30,000	30,000

Name	No.	Price Range	Average	Median
ROE, Clarence (1850-1909) British				
oil	13	505-2,805	1,011	810
ROE, Robert Ernest (fl.1860-1880) British				
oil	1	1,925	1,925	1,925
wc/d	3	481-1,593	905	641
ROE, Walter Herbert (fl.1882-1893) British				
oil	1	6,020	6,020	6,020
ROED, Holger Peter (1846-1874) Danish				
oil	1	1,132	1,132	1,132
ROEDE, Jan (1914-) Dutch				
oil	7	1,908-6,429	5,025	5,845
wc/d	2	766-3,816	2,291	766
ROEDER, Emy (1890-1971) German				
3D	1	14,143	14,143	14,143
ROEDER, John (1877-1964) American				
oil	1	3,000	3,000	3,000
ROEDER, Max (1866-1947) German				
oil	1	3,000	3,000	3,000
ROEDERSTEIN, Ottilie Wilhelmine (1859-1937) Swiss				
oil	2	1,374-1,374	1,374	1,374
ROEDIG, Johann Christian (1751-1802) Dutch				
oil	2	34,600-293,014	163,807	34,600
ROEGGE, Wilhelm (jnr) (1870-1947) German				
oil	2	2,057-4,087	3,072	2,057
ROEGGE, Wilhelm (snr) (1829-1908) German				
oil	5	468-3,500	2,145	2,761
ROEHN, Adolphe Eugène Gabriel (1780-1867) French				
oil	2	7,000-9,772	8,386	7,000
ROEHN, Jean Alphonse (1799-1864) French				
oil	2	951-12,215	6,583	951
ROEHR, Peter (1944-1968) German				
wc/d	1	14,651	14,651	14,651
ROEKENS, Paulette van (1896-?) American				
oil	5	4,000-9,500	6,050	4,750
wc/d	2	650-2,000	1,325	650
ROELOFS, Albert (1877-1920) Dutch				
oil	2	1,018-3,273	2,145	1,018
wc/d	1	19,778	19,778	19,778
ROELOFS, Willem (1822-1897) Dutch				
oil	14	909-32,139	11,713	7,283
wc/d	4	1,752-10,764	6,035	2,408
ROELOFS, Willem Elisa (1874-1940) Dutch				
oil	3	788-1,414	1,028	882
ROELZ, L (19th C) Belgian?				
oil	1	7,260	7,260	7,260
ROERICH, Nikolai Konstantinovitch (1874-1947) American/Russian				
oil	16	55,040-1,950,000	421,497	206,400
wc/d	4	17,200-190,000	69,840	27,520
ROERICH, Svetoslav (1904-1993) Russian				
oil	2	12,090-83,700	47,895	12,090
wc/d	2	3,096-3,748	3,422	3,096
ROESEN, Severin (fl.1848-1872) American/German				
oil	7	9,500-80,000	48,000	55,000
ROESSINGH, Louis Albert (1873-1951) Dutch/Belgian				
oil	5	701-8,918	3,161	2,253
ROESSLER, Georg (1861-1925) German				
oil	1	2,600	2,600	2,600
ROESTRATEN, Pieter Gerritsz van (1630-1700) Dutch				
oil	3	19,000-60,000	43,511	51,534
ROFFIAEN, Jean François (1820-1898) Belgian				
oil	7	1,385-5,845	3,644	3,762
ROGANEAU, François-Maurice (1883-1974) French				
oil	1	3,190	3,190	3,190
ROGER Y ALBA, Jose (19th C) Spanish				
oil	2	837-2,027	1,432	837
ROGER, Eugène (1807-1840) French				
oil	1	6,775	6,775	6,775
ROGER, Suzanne (1898-1986) French				
oil	1	2,225	2,225	2,225
ROGERS, A Lee (fl.1871-1894) Canadian				
oil	1	3,242	3,242	3,242

Name	No.	Price Range	Average	Median
ROGERS, C P (20th C) American				
oil	1	3,250	3,250	3,250
ROGERS, Charles Herbert (fl.1970s) British				
oil	1	1,073	1,073	1,073
ROGERS, Claude (1907-1979) British				
oil	2	662-1,593	1,127	662
ROGERS, Florence M (fl.1877-1897) Canadian				
oil	1	2,773	2,773	2,773
ROGERS, Frank Whiting (1854-?) American				
oil	2	10,000-12,000	11,000	10,000
ROGERS, Howard (1932-) American				
oil	5	1,000-5,220	2,704	2,500
3D	1	2,000	2,000	2,000
ROGERS, Hubert (1898-1982) American?				
oil	1	2,000	2,000	2,000
ROGERS, J (snr) (19th C) British				
oil	1	7,728	7,728	7,728
ROGERS, John (1829-1904) American				
3D	1	3,750	3,750	3,750
ROGERS, Les (1966-) American				
oil	1	22,000	22,000	22,000
ROGERS, Otto Donald (1935-) Canadian				
oil	5	738-5,329	3,005	2,952
wc/d	1	5,360	5,360	5,360
ROGERS, P (19th C) American				
oil	1	4,815	4,815	4,815
ROGERS, Randolph (1825-1892) American				
3D	1	20,000	20,000	20,000
ROGERS, Raymond M (?) ?				
oil	2	950-1,300	1,125	950
ROGERS, Robert B (20th C) American				
oil	1	2,200	2,200	2,200
ROGERS, Scott Howard (1922-1982) American				
oil	1	2,250	2,250	2,250
ROGERS, Wendell (20th C) American				
oil	1	1,400	1,400	1,400
ROGERS, William (19th C) British				
oil	1	2,457	2,457	2,457
ROGERS, William P (fl.1842-1872) British				
oil	1	3,312	3,312	3,312
ROGGE, Adalbert (1861-?) German				
oil	1	3,343	3,343	3,343
ROGIER, Camille (19th C) French				
wc/d	1	2,000	2,000	2,000
ROGNIAT, R (20th C) ?				
oil	1	3,631	3,631	3,631
ROGNONI, Franco (1913-1999) Italian				
oil	11	853-17,208	7,670	4,877
wc/d	12	527-2,616	1,122	707
ROGUIN, Louis (19th C) French				
wc/d	1	1,222	1,222	1,222
ROGY, Georges (1897-1981) Belgian				
oil	4	566-1,987	1,024	643
ROH, Franz (1890-1965) German				
wc/d	1	1,019	1,019	1,019
ROHDE, Fredrik (1816-1886) Danish				
oil	4	1,189-1,991	1,616	1,549
ROHL, Karl Peter (1890-1975) German				
wc/d	3	1,908-9,045	5,592	5,825
ROHL-SMITH, Carl Wilhelm Daniel (1848-1900) Danish				
3D	1	50,000	50,000	50,000
ROHLFS, Christian (1849-1938) German				
oil	25	2,575-81,057	31,474	27,096
wc/d	19	544-53,507	14,930	11,712
ROHLING, Carl (1849-1922) German				
oil	1	2,189	2,189	2,189
ROHNER, Georges (1913-2000) French				
oil	4	2,000-7,849	4,351	3,014
wc/d	1	502	502	502
ROHR, Max (1960-) Italian				
oil	2	942-7,027	3,984	942

Name	No.	Price Range	Average	Median
ROIG Y SOLER, Juan (1852-1909) Spanish				
oil	1	1,076	1,076	1,076
wc/d	1	5,819	5,819	5,819
ROIG, Jean (1926-) Belgian				
oil	1	1,334	1,334	1,334
ROIG, Jose (1898-1968) Argentinian				
oil	1	2,000	2,000	2,000
ROILOS, Georgios (1867-1928) Greek				
oil	3	1,760-8,700	5,356	5,610
ROJAS, Antonio (1962-) Spanish				
oil	3	659-1,796	1,038	659
ROJAS, Carlos (1933-) Colombian				
wc/d	1	3,815	3,815	3,815
ROJE, Arsen (20th C) Yugoslavian				
oil	1	1,000	1,000	1,000
ROJKA, Fritz (1878-1939) Austrian				
oil	1	5,679	5,679	5,679
ROLAND DE LA PORTE, Henri Horace (1724-1793) French				
oil	1	15,000	15,000	15,000
ROLAND, Jacques Francois Joseph (1757-1804) French				
oil	1	10,644	10,644	10,644
ROLAND, Rolli Luke (fl.1940s-1950s) Swiss				
oil	2	2,338-2,572	2,455	2,338
ROLDAN, Enrique (19th C) Spanish				
oil	3	1,558-2,400	2,012	2,079
ROLFE, Alexander F (fl.1839-1873) British				
oil	1	1,496	1,496	1,496
ROLFE, Henry Leonidas (fl.1847-1881) British				
oil	5	2,935-9,308	6,053	7,007
ROLL, Fritz (1879-?) German				
3D	1	4,340	4,340	4,340
ROLLA, Adolfo Giuseppe (1899-1967) Italian				
oil	2	1,670-3,996	2,833	1,670
ROLLAND, Auguste (1797-1859) French				
wc/d	1	2,371	2,371	2,371
ROLLIN, J (19th C) French				
oil	1	1,978	1,978	1,978
ROLLIN, Louis Arthur (1831-1861) French				
oil	2	1,267-1,415	1,341	1,267
ROLLINS, Tim and K O S (20th C) American				
oil	1	8,000	8,000	8,000
wc/d	2	1,000-3,800	2,400	1,000
ROLLINS, Warren E (1861-1962) American				
oil	1	9,000	9,000	9,000
wc/d	2	1,250-2,500	1,875	1,250
ROLLMANN, Julius (1827-1865) German				
oil	1	3,941	3,941	3,941
ROLSHOVEN, Julius (1858-1930) American				
oil	1	5,500	5,500	5,500
wc/d	2	400-4,000	2,200	400
ROLT, Charles (19th C) British				
oil	1	2,768	2,768	2,768
ROMA, Gianni (1901-1993) Italian				
oil	1	643	643	643
wc/d	1	514	514	514
ROMAGNOLI, Angiolo (19th C) Italian				
oil	2	893-1,558	1,225	893
ROMAGNONI, Bepi (1930-1964) Italian				
oil	1	5,521	5,521	5,521
wc/d	5	486-714	629	656
ROMAKO, Anton (1832-1889) Austrian				
oil	2	6,780-11,781	9,280	6,780
wc/d	2	2,178-14,517	8,347	2,178
ROMAN, Max Wilhelm (1849-1910) German				
oil	1	1,295	1,295	1,295
ROMANDON, Gedeon (1667-1697) Italian				
oil	1	7,224	7,224	7,224
ROMANELLI, C (20th C) Italian				
3D	1	5,000	5,000	5,000
ROMANELLI, Giovanni Francesco (1610-1662) Italian				
oil	2	33,658-116,541	75,099	33,658

Name	No.	Price Range	Average	Median
ROMANELLI, Pasquale (1812-1887) Italian				
3D	7	5,500-47,500	20,693	17,000
ROMANIDIS, Konstantin (1884-1972) Greek				
oil	5	9,570-14,960	11,746	10,440
ROMANINI, Fanny (c.1795-1854) Italian				
wc/d	1	4,123	4,123	4,123
ROMANO, Antoniazzo (fl.1460-1508) Italian				
oil	1	200,000	200,000	200,000
ROMANO, Elio (1906-1996) Italian				
oil	1	1,312	1,312	1,312
ROMANO, Emanuel Glicen (1897-1984) American/Italian				
oil	2	1,200-2,000	1,600	1,200
ROMANO, Giulio (1499-1546) Italian				
wc/d	2	4,250-9,250	6,750	4,250
ROMANOVA, Maria Pavlovna (1890-1958) Russian				
oil	1	1,984	1,984	1,984
ROMANOVSKY, Dimitri (1886-1971) American				
oil	1	4,640	4,640	4,640
ROMANY, Adele (1769-1846) French				
oil	2	20,880-34,800	27,840	20,880
ROMBAUX, Egide (1865-1942) Belgian				
3D	3	2,104-5,160	3,590	3,507
ROMBERG DE VAUCORBEIL, Maurice (1862-1943) French				
oil	2	5,026-20,384	12,705	5,026
wc/d	1	3,857	3,857	3,857
ROMBOUTS, Adriaen (17th C) Dutch?				
oil	1	6,764	6,764	6,764
ROMBOUTS, Salomon (1652-c.1702) Dutch				
oil	2	5,396-6,115	5,755	5,396
ROMERO DE TORRES, Julio (1879-1930) Spanish				
oil	1	577,959	577,959	577,959
ROMERO FERNANDEZ, Juan (1932-1996) Spanish				
oil	1	1,025	1,025	1,025
ROMERO RESSENDI, Baldomero (1922-1977) Spanish				
oil	5	4,541-20,566	9,552	7,836
ROMERO, Carlos Orozco (1898-1984) Mexican				
oil	3	1,800-11,000	7,600	10,000
ROMERO, Juan (1932-) Spanish				
wc/d	1	2,356	2,356	2,356
ROMERO, Vicente (1956-) Spanish				
wc/d	1	2,928	2,928	2,928
ROMEYN, Willem (1624-1694) Dutch				
oil	4	1,077-9,678	4,885	2,141
ROMITI, Gino (1881-1967) Italian				
oil	15	1,523-4,789	2,820	2,425
ROMITI, Romano (1906-1951) Italian				
oil	2	1,823-2,188	2,005	1,823
ROMITI, Sergio (1928-2000) Italian				
oil	4	7,943-12,884	10,386	10,177
wc/d	1	3,534	3,534	3,534
ROMNEY, George (1734-1802) British				
oil	11	16,065-130,000	60,150	40,000
wc/d	6	484-20,010	8,359	4,278
ROMPAEY, Oscar van (1898-1997) Belgian				
oil	3	955-1,821	1,330	1,214
RONA, Jesse (20th C) British				
oil	1	1,253	1,253	1,253
RONALD, William S (1926-1998) Canadian				
oil	7	492-6,647	3,331	3,711
wc/d	3	800-1,499	1,068	907
RONCOURT, Jean de (20th C) ?				
3D	2	1,763-2,197	1,980	1,763
RONDA, Omar (1947-) Italian				
oil	3	4,359-9,600	7,794	9,425
wc/d	4	2,667-8,784	6,016	4,414
3D	6	6,008-19,418	9,286	6,146
RONDAS, Willi (1907-1975) British/Belgian				
oil	1	1,305	1,305	1,305
RONDEL, Frederick (1826-1892) American				
oil	6	1,000-300,000	53,450	3,000
wc/d	2	1,400-1,600	1,500	1,400

Name	No.	Price Range	Average	Median
RONDELLI, Giuseppe (1665-1745) Italian				
oil	1	7,071	7,071	7,071
RONDINONE, Ugo (1963-) French				
oil	1	60,000	60,000	60,000
3D	2	50,000-260,000	155,000	50,000
RONEY, Harold (1899-1986) American				
oil	4	700-3,250	1,500	750
RONG RONG (1968-) Chinese				
oil	1	15,725	15,725	15,725
RONMY, Guillaume Frederic (1786-1854) French				
oil	1	4,815	4,815	4,815
RONNE, Svend (1868-1938) Danish				
oil	1	1,326	1,326	1,326
RONNER, Henriette (1821-1909) Dutch				
oil	22	477-75,000	27,507	14,833
wc/d	4	1,502-6,799	3,804	3,337
RONTINI, Alessandro (1854-?) Italian				
oil	1	7,613	7,613	7,613
RONTINI, Ferruccio (1893-1964) Italian				
oil	9	1,189-3,395	2,287	2,395
RONZONI, Pietro (1780-1862) Italian				
oil	1	11,781	11,781	11,781
ROOBJEE, Pjeroo (1945-) Belgian				
oil	2	1,076-2,392	1,734	1,076
ROOKE, Thomas Matthew (1842-1942) British				
oil	1	150,000	150,000	150,000
wc/d	1	458	458	458
ROOKER, Michael Angelo (1743-1801) British				
oil	1	2,760	2,760	2,760
wc/d	2	1,144-14,880	8,012	1,144
ROONEY, Mick (1944-) British				
oil	1	3,132	3,132	3,132
wc/d	1	736	736	736
ROOS, Cajetan (1690-1770) Italian				
oil	2	3,596-35,145	19,370	3,596
ROOS, Evert (1876-1933) Finnish				
oil	1	1,054	1,054	1,054
ROOS, H (18th C) ?				
oil	1	2,604	2,604	2,604
ROOS, Johann Melchior (1659-1731) German				
oil	4	1,374-7,714	5,959	7,104
ROOS, Nina (1956-) Finnish				
oil	1	4,962	4,962	4,962
ROOS, Philipp Peter (1657-1706) German				
oil	12	1,308-29,600	10,885	7,135
ROOSDORP, Frederik (1839-1865) Dutch				
oil	1	1,125	1,125	1,125
ROOSE, Aage Valdemar Larsen (1880-1970) Danish				
oil	1	2,258	2,258	2,258
ROOSE, Charles van (1883-1960) Belgian				
oil	1	3,562	3,562	3,562
ROOSENBOOM, A (19th C) Belgian				
oil	1	14,583	14,583	14,583
ROOSENBOOM, Albert (1845-1875) Belgian				
oil	4	705-4,770	2,448	2,160
ROOSENBOOM, Margaretha (1843-1896) Dutch				
wc/d	1	38,000	38,000	38,000
ROOSENBOOM, Nicolaas Johannes (1805-1880) Dutch				
oil	8	1,639-60,848	19,181	7,233
ROOSENBOOM, Nicolaas Johannes and VERBOECKHOVEN, Eugène (19th C) Dutch				
oil	1	58,192	58,192	58,192
ROOSKENS, Anton (1906-1976) Dutch				
oil	12	4,712-33,802	16,239	15,265
wc/d	9	1,341-11,466	4,875	3,534
ROOSVAAL-KALLSTENIUS, Gerda (1864-1939) Swedish				
oil	1	8,475	8,475	8,475
ROPE, George Thomas (1846-1929) British				
oil	2	1,328-1,451	1,389	1,328
ROPELE, Walter (1934-) Swiss				
oil	2	1,908-2,289	2,098	1,908
ROPP, Roy M (1888-1974) American				
oil	1	1,100	1,100	1,100

Name	No.	Price Range	Average	Median
ROPS, Felicien (1833-1898) Belgian				
oil	4	7,014-19,135	13,093	13,081
wc/d	8	714-15,196	6,335	3,039
ROQUE GAMEIRO, Alfredo (1864-1935) Portuguese				
wc/d	1	1,398	1,398	1,398
ROQUEPLAN, Camille (1803-1855) French				
oil	7	845-13,368	5,912	3,592
wc/d	2	1,286-2,784	2,035	1,286
RORBYE, Martinus (1803-1848) Danish				
oil	5	3,788-95,542	40,027	40,000
wc/d	2	897-6,812	3,854	897
ROS Y GUELL, Antonio (1873-1957) Spanish				
oil	2	665-1,405	1,035	665
ROS, J F (?) ?				
oil	1	2,431	2,431	2,431
ROSA, Herve di (1959-) French				
oil	16	500-11,918	4,134	3,507
wc/d	6	1,285-7,120	3,215	2,919
ROSA, Luigi (1850-?) Italian				
oil	1	2,914	2,914	2,914
ROSA, Manuel de la (?) ?				
oil	1	1,914	1,914	1,914
ROSA, Martin la (1972-) Argentinian				
oil	1	45,000	45,000	45,000
ROSA, Raffaele de (1940-) Italian				
oil	5	895-1,885	1,210	1,178
ROSA, Richard di (1963-) French				
wc/d	2	518-583	550	518
3D	6	1,774-16,857	5,454	2,688
ROSA, Salvator (1615-1673) Italian				
oil	6	3,084-117,568	43,766	7,014
wc/d	5	951-35,000	9,126	3,500
ROSADO DEL VALLE, Julio (1922-) Puerto Rican				
oil	2	12,000-28,000	20,000	12,000
ROSAI, Ottone (1895-1957) Italian				
oil	25	8,177-127,211	38,317	21,750
wc/d	9	1,093-22,800	5,260	2,428
ROSAIRE, Arthur Dominique (1879-1922) Canadian				
oil	4	820-3,526	1,867	1,558
ROSALES, Eduardo (1836-1873) Spanish				
oil	3	941-11,493	6,126	5,946
ROSATI, Albert (19th C) Italian				
wc/d	1	4,750	4,750	4,750
ROSATI, Giulio (1858-1917) Italian				
oil	1	80,000	80,000	80,000
wc/d	5	9,500-32,000	16,199	13,498
ROSCH, Carl (1884-?) German				
oil	4	3,239-12,956	8,399	4,858
ROSCH, Ludwig (1865-1936) Austrian				
wc/d	1	1,084	1,084	1,084
ROSCOE, F H (19th C) ?				
oil	1	9,450	9,450	9,450
ROSE, A (?) ?				
oil	1	1,502	1,502	1,502
ROSE, Gerard de (1918-1987) British				
oil	2	600-1,400	1,000	600
ROSE, Guy (1867-1925) American				
oil	2	380,000-1,700,000	1,040,000	380,000
ROSE, Iver (1899-1972) American				
oil	1	1,000	1,000	1,000
wc/d	1	3,500	3,500	3,500
ROSE, Julius (1828-1911) German				
oil	3	1,450-1,674	1,591	1,649
ROSE, William S (1810-1873) British				
oil	2	1,682-9,391	5,536	1,682
ROSELAND, Harry (1868-1950) American				
oil	14	650-17,000	5,107	2,500
ROSELL, Alexander (1859-1922) British				
oil	3	613-2,301	1,427	1,368
ROSELLI, Carlo (1939-) Italian				
oil	15	766-3,884	1,651	1,295

Name	No.	Price Range	Average	Median
ROSEMAN, Bill (20th C) American				
oil	1	1,300	1,300	1,300
ROSEMAN, Isa (1877-?) French				
oil	1	1,293	1,293	1,293
ROSEN (20th C) ?				
oil	1	6,054	6,054	6,054
ROSEN, Jan (1854-1936) Polish				
wc/d	1	1,879	1,879	1,879
ROSEN, Kay (20th C) American?				
oil	4	2,800-4,200	3,675	3,500
ROSENBERG, Edward (1858-1934) Swedish				
oil	4	672-1,994	1,101	746
ROSENBERG, Friedrich (1758-1833) Swiss				
oil	1	17,517	17,517	17,517
ROSENBERG, Henry M (1858-1947) American				
wc/d	1	1,700	1,700	1,700
ROSENBORG, Ralph (1913-1992) American				
oil	2	650-6,000	3,325	650
wc/d	1	375	375	375
ROSENFELD, Eugen (1870-1953) German				
oil	1	2,155	2,155	2,155
ROSENHAUER, Theodor (1901-1996) German				
wc/d	1	2,719	2,719	2,719
ROSENHOF, Franz Rosel von (1626-1700) Austrian				
oil	1	21,673	21,673	21,673
ROSENKRANTZ, Arild (1870-1964) Danish				
wc/d	2	1,293-1,374	1,333	1,293
ROSENQUIST, James (1933-) American				
oil	12	60,000-481,000	267,941	270,000
wc/d	2	10,000-85,000	47,500	10,000
3D	2	7,500-800,000	403,750	7,500
ROSENSTAND, Vilhelm (1838-1915) Danish				
oil	2	6,636-8,338	7,487	6,636
ROSENSTOCK, Isidore (1880-1956) French				
oil	1	716	716	716
wc/d	3	707-2,208	1,305	1,001
ROSENTHAL, Albert (1863-1939) American				
oil	1	1,900	1,900	1,900
ROSENTHAL, Toby Edward (1849-1917) American				
oil	1	1,844	1,844	1,844
ROSENTHAL, Tony (1914-) American				
3D	1	2,500	2,500	2,500
ROSIER, Amedee (1831-1898) French				
oil	5	5,323-17,671	12,064	13,077
wc/d	2	1,936-1,936	1,936	1,936
ROSIERSE, Johannes (1818-1901) Dutch				
oil	1	1,627	1,627	1,627
ROSIGNANO, Livio (1924-) Italian				
oil	1	1,286	1,286	1,286
ROSIN, Dino (1948-) American?				
3D	1	2,655	2,655	2,655
ROSLER, Louise (1907-1993) German				
oil	1	1,874	1,874	1,874
ROSLER, Waldemar (19/20th C) German				
oil	1	6,070	6,070	6,070
ROSMARIN, Susie (20th C) American				
oil	1	5,500	5,500	5,500
ROSNAY, Gaetan de (1914-) French				
oil	1	2,104	2,104	2,104
ROSOFSKY, Seymour (1925-1981) American				
oil	3	900-4,750	2,750	2,600
ROSOMAN, Leonard (1913-) British				
wc/d	2	1,203-1,758	1,480	1,203
ROSS, Christian Meyer (1843-1904) Norwegian				
oil	1	23,895	23,895	23,895
ROSS, James (18/19th C) British				
oil	1	27,000	27,000	27,000
ROSS, Janet (?) ?				
oil	1	1,600	1,600	1,600
ROSS, Mary Herrick (20th C) American				
oil	1	3,750	3,750	3,750

Name	No.	Price Range	Average	Median
ROSS, Sanford (1907-1954) American				
wc/d	2	400-4,000	2,200	400
ROSS, Sir William Charles (1794-1860) British				
oil	1	1,840	1,840	1,840
ROSSANO, Federico (1835-1912) Italian				
oil	9	3,568-75,000	21,106	7,135
ROSSE, Franz (1858-1900) German				
3D	2	2,548-2,829	2,688	2,548
ROSSEAU, Percival (1859-1937) American				
oil	7	9,000-120,000	47,642	47,500
ROSSEL DE CERCY, Auguste Louis (1736-1804) French				
oil	1	7,017	7,017	7,017
ROSSELL, Peter (1964-) Danish				
oil	2	2,253-4,849	3,551	2,253
ROSSELLI, Bernardo di Stefano (1450-1526) Italian?				
oil	1	52,500	52,500	52,500
ROSSELLO, Mario (1927-2000) Italian				
oil	5	832-2,544	1,803	2,145
ROSSERT, Paul (1851-1918) French				
oil	1	2,062	2,062	2,062
wc/d	1	478	478	478
ROSSET, Joseph (c.1703-1786) French				
3D	1	11,881	11,881	11,881
ROSSETTI, Dante Gabriel (1828-1882) British				
oil	1	54,600	54,600	54,600
wc/d	5	21,840-324,900	91,076	34,200
ROSSI, Alberto (1858-1936) Italian				
oil	1	5,143	5,143	5,143
wc/d	2	630-3,818	2,224	630
ROSSI, Alberto Maria (1879-1965) Argentinian				
oil	2	2,800-7,700	5,250	2,800
ROSSI, Alexander M (fl.1870-1905) British				
oil	1	530	530	530
wc/d	1	900	900	900
ROSSI, Barbara (1940-) American				
wc/d	1	2,200	2,200	2,200
ROSSI, Carlo (1921-) British				
oil	3	1,350-1,800	1,647	1,793
ROSSI, E (19th C) Italian				
3D	1	2,835	2,835	2,835
ROSSI, Gino (1884-1947) Italian				
oil	1	281,096	281,096	281,096
wc/d	1	8,199	8,199	8,199
ROSSI, Giovan Battista (fl.1749-1782) Italian				
oil	1	12,153	12,153	12,153
ROSSI, Giuseppe (19th C) Italian				
oil	1	1,068	1,068	1,068
ROSSI, Joseph (1892-1930) French				
oil	4	1,757-3,138	2,541	2,385
wc/d	2	816-941	878	816
ROSSI, Lucius (1846-1913) French				
oil	1	42,320	42,320	42,320
wc/d	3	700-3,637	2,658	3,637
ROSSI, Luigi (1853-1923) Swiss				
oil	2	8,199-51,781	29,990	8,199
wc/d	1	2,061	2,061	2,061
ROSSI, Mariano (1731-1807) Italian				
oil	1	18,740	18,740	18,740
ROSSI, Roberto (1896-1957) Argentinian				
oil	2	1,800-2,500	2,150	1,800
ROSSITER, Thomas Pritchard (1817-1871) American				
oil	2	2,750-30,000	16,375	2,750
ROSSLER-HERMES, Mary (1876-1944) British				
oil	1	1,455	1,455	1,455
ROSSO, Jose D (1898-1958) Argentinian				
oil	1	2,800	2,800	2,800
ROSSO, Lina (1888-?) Italian				
oil	1	2,166	2,166	2,166
ROSSO, Medardo (1858-1928) Italian				
3D	1	2,722	2,722	2,722

Name	No.	Price Range	Average	Median
ROSSO, Mino (1904-1963) Italian				
oil	1	2,919	2,919	2,919
wc/d	1	693	693	693
ROSSUM DU CHATTEL, Fredericus Jacobus van (1856-1917) Dutch				
oil	4	1,794-23,973	8,272	2,500
wc/d	3	1,500-3,442	2,148	1,502
ROSTRUP-BOYESEN, P (1882-1952) Danish				
oil	1	1,277	1,277	1,277
ROSTRUP-BOYESEN, Peter (1882-1952) Danish				
oil	2	589-1,532	1,060	589
ROSZAK, Theodore (1907-1981) American				
oil	1	16,000	16,000	16,000
wc/d	1	425	425	425
3D	1	70,000	70,000	70,000
ROTA, Giuseppe (1777-1821) Italian				
oil	1	2,000	2,000	2,000
ROTACH, Johannes (1892-1981) Swiss				
oil	1	3,137	3,137	3,137
ROTAR, Robert (1926-1999) German				
oil	2	2,038-5,890	3,964	2,038
ROTARI, Pietro (1707-1762) Italian				
oil	1	85,000	85,000	85,000
ROTELLA, Mimmo (1918-2006) Italian				
oil	12	2,735-84,770	23,954	13,124
wc/d	57	1,308-279,864	32,268	13,910
3D	1	2,400	2,400	2,400
ROTEN-CALPINI, Berthe (1873-1962) Swiss				
oil	1	2,855	2,855	2,855
ROTERS, Carl (1890-1989) American?				
wc/d	1	16,000	16,000	16,000
ROTH, August (1864-1952) Austrian				
oil	1	1,500	1,500	1,500
ROTH, Dieter (1930-1998) German				
oil	3	937-3,299	2,511	3,299
wc/d	15	649-33,630	5,539	3,045
3D	6	2,822-7,644	5,381	5,605
ROTH, Frederick George Richard (1872-1944) American				
3D	2	2,500-4,000	3,250	2,500
ROTH, Leo (1910-) Israeli				
oil	8	950-2,200	1,718	1,600
ROTH, Philipp (1841-1921) German				
oil	3	700-1,581	1,132	1,116
wc/d	2	707-1,978	1,342	707
ROTHAUG, Alexander (1870-1946) Austrian				
wc/d	2	1,199-1,438	1,318	1,199
ROTHBORT, Samuel (1882-1971) American				
oil	1	1,100	1,100	1,100
ROTHENBERG, Susan (1945-) American				
oil	1	480,000	480,000	480,000
wc/d	1	8,500	8,500	8,500
ROTHENBURGH, Otto (1893-1992) American				
oil	1	2,600	2,600	2,600
ROTHENSTEIN, Sir William (1872-1945) British				
oil	1	7,308	7,308	7,308
wc/d	5	486-2,610	1,134	900
ROTHKO, Mark (1903-1970) American				
oil	8	700,000-20,000,000	4,556,250	2,250,000
ROTHMEYER, Johann Jacob Ludwig (18th C) German				
wc/d	2	2,790-9,300	6,045	2,790
ROTHSTEIN, Irma (1896-1971) American/Russian				
3D	1	1,937	1,937	1,937
ROTHSTEN, Carl Abraham (1826-1877) Swedish				
oil	6	586-7,830	2,412	935
ROTIG, Georges Frederic (1873-1961) French				
oil	24	1,909-19,360	6,281	4,909
wc/d	9	717-13,597	4,202	1,451
ROTKY, Carl (1891-1977) Austrian				
oil	1	2,219	2,219	2,219
wc/d	1	971	971	971
ROTTENHAMMER, Johann (1564-1625) German				
oil	1	277,500	277,500	277,500
ROTTERMAN, Mozart (1874-) ?				
oil	1	2,625	2,625	2,625

Name	No.	Price Range	Average	Median
ROTTMANN, Carl (1798-1850) German				
oil	1	50,207	50,207	50,207
wc/d	3	954-1,401	1,213	1,285
ROTTMANN, Leopold (1812-1881) German				
wc/d	2	2,827-5,890	4,358	2,827
ROTTMANN, Mozart (1874-?) Hungarian				
oil	5	443-80,000	17,290	1,017
ROTTMAYR, Johann Michael (1654-1730) Austrian				
oil	1	12,098	12,098	12,098
ROUAN, François (1943-) French				
oil	2	60,822-85,438	73,130	60,822
wc/d	4	10,837-18,469	13,346	11,222
ROUAULT, Georges (1871-1958) French				
oil	30	9,699-368,912	107,747	60,000
wc/d	16	482-37,500	12,532	5,845
ROUAULT, Georges Dominique (1904-) French				
oil	2	837-897	867	837
wc/d	1	584	584	584
ROUBAL, Franz (1889-1967) Austrian				
oil	14	518-3,737	1,168	906
wc/d	6	518-1,295	808	642
ROUBAUD, A (20th C) French?				
oil	1	2,039	2,039	2,039
ROUBAUD, Franz (1856-1928) Russian				
oil	31	3,216-361,200	50,434	20,896
wc/d	7	849-8,600	4,584	4,534
ROUBAUD, Jean Baptiste (1871-?) French				
oil	1	1,890	1,890	1,890
ROUBAUDO, Georges (1898-1999) French				
oil	1	1,030	1,030	1,030
ROUBTZOFF, Alexandre (1884-1949) Russian				
oil	8	3,273-8,681	5,546	5,270
wc/d	2	1,942-5,671	3,806	1,942
ROUBY, Alfred (1849-1909) French				
oil	5	683-4,800	2,242	1,099
ROUDINE, Noelle (?) French?				
oil	1	3,168	3,168	3,168
ROUGE, Frederic (1867-1950) Swiss				
oil	2	916-5,724	3,320	916
wc/d	1	816	816	816
ROUGELET, Benedict (1834-1894) French				
3D	1	14,175	14,175	14,175
ROUGEMONT, Guy de (1935-) French				
oil	2	2,890-4,653	3,771	2,890
3D	3	2,336-24,196	9,732	2,664
ROUGET, Elaine (20th C) French?				
wc/d	2	1,084-1,455	1,269	1,084
ROUGET, Georges (1784-1869) French				
oil	1	9,790	9,790	9,790
ROUKHIN, Evgeny (1943-1976) Russian				
wc/d	2	23,000-50,000	36,500	23,000
ROULET, Henry (1915-1995) Swiss				
oil	7	1,518-6,526	3,085	2,692
ROULIN, Louis François Marie (19th C) French				
wc/d	1	1,100	1,100	1,100
ROULLEAU, Jules Pierre (1855-1895) French				
3D	1	3,801	3,801	3,801
ROULLET, Gaston (1847-1925) French				
oil	5	755-4,816	2,549	2,378
ROUNTREE, Harry (1878-1950) British				
wc/d	1	1,644	1,644	1,644
ROURA, Lluis (1943-) Spanish				
oil	5	1,914-3,160	2,555	2,571
ROUSSEAU, Adrien (19th C) French				
oil	2	1,366-2,671	2,018	1,366
ROUSSEAU, Albert (1908-1982) Canadian				
oil	2	571-1,466	1,018	571
wc/d	1	530	530	530
ROUSSEAU, Helen (1896-1992) American				
oil	2	5,500-10,000	7,750	5,500

Name	No.	Price Range	Average	Median
ROUSSEAU, Henri Emilien (1875-1933) French				
oil	11	1,701-40,768	7,670	4,500
wc/d	1	6,479	6,479	6,479
ROUSSEAU, Henri Julien Felix (1844-1910) French				
oil	3	5,104-42,412	22,323	19,454
ROUSSEAU, Jean Felix (1807-1836) Dutch				
oil	1	1,366	1,366	1,366
ROUSSEAU, Jean Simeon (1747-?) French				
wc/d	1	1,458	1,458	1,458
ROUSSEAU, Philippe (1816-1887) French				
oil	5	1,816-50,685	17,012	2,917
ROUSSEAU, T (1812-1867) French				
oil	1	4,000	4,000	4,000
ROUSSEAU, Theodore (1812-1867) French				
oil	9	2,474-100,822	19,775	8,575
wc/d	12	611-15,123	3,621	1,635
ROUSSEAU, Victor (1865-1954) Belgian				
3D	14	1,800-16,272	5,877	4,241
ROUSSEL, Charles-Emanuel-Joseph (1861-1936) French				
oil	3	2,474-5,092	4,054	4,597
ROUSSEL, Ker Xavier (1867-1944) French				
oil	4	2,950-9,632	5,962	4,793
wc/d	14	379-40,000	7,042	3,700
ROUSSEL, Pierre (1927-1995) French				
oil	4	476-3,507	1,881	504
ROUSSET, Jules (1840-?) French				
oil	1	1,134	1,134	1,134
ROUSSIN, Victor (1812-c.1900) French				
oil	2	1,893-3,156	2,524	1,893
ROUX, Antoine (younger) (1799-1872) French				
oil	1	2,535	2,535	2,535
wc/d	4	4,800-17,897	11,341	9,545
ROUX, Constant (1865-1929) French				
3D	1	6,466	6,466	6,466
ROUX, Constantin le (?-1909) French				
oil	1	1,991	1,991	1,991
ROUX, Émile (19th C) French				
oil	1	1,526	1,526	1,526
ROUX, François Geoffroy (1811-1882) French				
wc/d	1	2,760	2,760	2,760
ROUX, Frederic (1805-1874) French				
wc/d	1	7,500	7,500	7,500
ROUX, Gaston Louis (1904-1988) French				
wc/d	1	1,098	1,098	1,098
ROUX, Joseph Ange Antoine (1765-1835) French				
wc/d	5	1,740-11,678	4,020	2,408
ROUX, Louis Francois Prosper (1817-1903) French				
wc/d	3	3,500-5,255	4,251	4,000
ROUX, Marcel (1878-1922) French				
wc/d	4	1,140-1,620	1,350	1,260
ROUX, Rene (1891-1952) French?				
oil	1	3,805	3,805	3,805
ROUX, Vincent (1928-) French				
oil	1	3,395	3,395	3,395
ROVERE, Giovanni Battista della (1561-c.1630) Italian				
oil	1	33,300	33,300	33,300
ROWBOTHAM, Charles (1856-1921) British				
wc/d	28	510-7,000	2,163	1,500
ROWBOTHAM, Mark (1959-) British				
oil	1	1,029	1,029	1,029
wc/d	2	435-1,281	858	435
ROWBOTHAM, Thomas Charles Leeson (1823-1875) British				
wc/d	16	455-18,900	3,906	1,091
ROWBOTHAM, Thomas Leeson (snr) (1783-1853) British				
wc/d	1	1,246	1,246	1,246
ROWE, E Arthur (1863-1922) British				
wc/d	11	792-22,320	4,111	1,740
ROWE, George James (?-1883) British				
oil	1	8,550	8,550	8,550
ROWE, Nellie Mae (1900-1982) American				
wc/d	4	600-3,000	1,375	600

Name	No.	Price Range	Average	Median
ROWE, Sydney Grant (1861-1928) British				
oil	1	3,344	3,344	3,344
ROWLANDSON, George Derville (1861-1928) British				
oil	2	5,000-8,000	6,500	5,000
wc/d	1	684	684	684
ROWLANDSON, Thomas (1756-1827) British				
oil	1	2,093	2,093	2,093
wc/d	61	440-20,760	3,936	2,262
ROWNTREE, Harry (1878-1950) British				
wc/d	1	2,220	2,220	2,220
ROWORTH, Edward (1880-1964) British				
oil	1	1,302	1,302	1,302
ROY, A (?) ?				
oil	1	3,400	3,400	3,400
ROY, Jamini (1887-1972) Indian				
oil	39	3,114-51,900	17,293	16,720
wc/d	13	761-17,000	8,517	7,500
ROY, Jean Baptiste de (1759-1839) Belgian				
oil	3	2,841-5,605	4,148	4,000
ROY, Pierre (1880-1950) Italian				
oil	7	15,000-69,966	35,170	23,143
wc/d	1	718	718	718
ROYAL, Stanley (?) British?				
wc/d	1	2,394	2,394	2,394
ROYBET, Ferdinand (1840-1920) French				
oil	19	900-22,750	4,614	3,162
ROYC, Mitja (20th C) Yugoslavian				
oil	1	2,883	2,883	2,883
ROYDS, Lieutenant Charles Rawson (1879-1931) British				
wc/d	1	3,600	3,600	3,600
ROYER, Henri (1869-1938) French				
oil	1	1,074	1,074	1,074
wc/d	1	894	894	894
ROYER, Lionel-Noel (1852-1926) French				
oil	2	5,622-11,000	8,311	5,622
ROYLE, Herbert (1870-1958) British				
oil	22	961-16,020	5,303	4,272
ROYLE, Stanley (1888-1961) British				
oil	3	7,120-22,784	12,427	7,379
ROYO, Neus Martin (1968-) Spanish				
oil	1	1,874	1,874	1,874
ROYON, Louis (1882-1968) Belgian				
oil	4	626-5,418	1,879	656
ROZANOVA, Olga (1886-1918) Russian				
wc/d	1	13,200	13,200	13,200
ROZEN, Jerome George (1895-1987) American				
oil	1	3,750	3,750	3,750
ROZHANKOVSKY, P (19/20th C) Russian				
wc/d	1	1,710	1,710	1,710
ROZHENKOV, Anatoly Konstantinovich (1925-) Russian				
oil	1	11,160	11,160	11,160
ROZIER, Jules (1821-1882) French				
oil	7	606-17,671	3,499	1,060
ROZMAINSKY, Vladimir (1885-1943) Russian				
oil	1	2,521	2,521	2,521
RUBCZAK, Jan (1884-1949) Polish				
oil	1	23,822	23,822	23,822
RUBEN, Franz Leo (1842-1920) German				
oil	1	5,702	5,702	5,702
RUBEN, Richards (1925-1998) American				
oil	1	7,000	7,000	7,000
RUBENS, Sir Peter Paul (1577-1640) Flemish				
oil	9	3,568-4,844,000	816,890	106,800
wc/d	1	222,000	222,000	222,000
RUBIN, Reuven (1893-1974) Israeli				
oil	34	16,000-380,000	88,030	60,000
wc/d	17	2,866-17,000	7,918	6,500
3D	1	1,600	1,600	1,600
RUBINCAM, Barclay Lawrence Jacob (1920-1978) American				
oil	8	1,000-38,000	14,062	5,500
wc/d	5	1,200-4,000	2,220	2,000

Name	No.	Price Range	Average	Median
RUBINSTEIN, Gerti (1945-2002) Israeli				
oil	1	1,200	1,200	1,200
RUCCIBA, P (19/20th C) Italian				
oil	1	5,220	5,220	5,220
RUCKER, Robert (1932-2000) American				
oil	1	2,300	2,300	2,300
wc/d	2	2,200-2,600	2,400	2,200
RUCKHABERLE, Christoph (1972-) German				
oil	1	14,000	14,000	14,000
RUCKRIEM, Ulrich (1938-) German				
wc/d	1	458	458	458
3D	1	25,479	25,479	25,479
RUCKSTUHL, Xaver (1911-1979) German				
3D	1	3,100	3,100	3,100
RUCKTESCHELL, Walter von (1882-1941) German				
oil	1	1,286	1,286	1,286
RUDA, Gunnar (1887-1948) Swedish				
wc/d	1	1,850	1,850	1,850
RUDAKOV, Konstantin Ivanovich (1891-1949) Russian				
wc/d	10	779-12,401	2,114	933
RUDBERG, Gustav (1915-1994) Swedish				
oil	27	622-9,514	3,827	2,926
RUDE, François (1784-1855) French				
3D	4	3,000-17,800	8,517	3,270
RUDE, Olaf (1886-1957) Danish				
oil	16	1,293-24,247	5,819	4,041
wc/d	1	808	808	808
RUDELL, Carl (1852-1920) German				
wc/d	12	606-7,297	2,853	1,752
RUDELL, Peter Edward (1854-1899) American				
oil	1	3,250	3,250	3,250
RUDHARDT, Claude Charles (1829-1895) Swiss				
oil	1	7,027	7,027	7,027
RUDISUHLI, Eduard (1875-1938) Swiss				
oil	3	583-1,800	1,137	1,030
RUDISUHLI, Hermann (1864-1944) Swiss				
oil	8	569-3,503	1,669	1,506
RUDOLF, Paul (1877-?) German				
oil	1	1,874	1,874	1,874
RUDOLPH, Harold (1850-1884) American				
oil	1	14,000	14,000	14,000
RUDOLPH, Wilhelm (1889-?) German				
oil	1	2,928	2,928	2,928
wc/d	2	1,018-1,316	1,167	1,018
RUE, Louis-Felix de la (1731-c.1765) French				
wc/d	4	945-1,701	1,442	1,458
RUEDA, Gerardo (1926-1996) Spanish				
oil	3	1,368-3,946	2,881	3,330
wc/d	3	3,471-11,297	6,728	5,418
3D	1	4,839	4,839	4,839
RUEFF, M (19th C) German				
oil	1	3,507	3,507	3,507
RUEGG, Ernst Georg (1883-1948) Swiss				
oil	5	417-1,669	1,146	1,518
RUELAS, Julio (1870-1907) Mexican				
oil	1	310,000	310,000	310,000
RUETER, Georg (1875-1966) Dutch				
oil	3	1,528-3,836	2,672	2,652
RUFFALO, Carlos Roberto (?) Uruguayan				
oil	1	2,000	2,000	2,000
RUFS, F (20th C) ?				
oil	1	7,500	7,500	7,500
RUGENDAS, Georg Philipp I (1666-1742) German				
oil	1	120,408	120,408	120,408
RUGENDAS, Johann Moritz (1802-1858) German				
oil	2	1,196-55,000	28,098	1,196
wc/d	1	643	643	643
RUGGERI, Piero (1930-) Italian				
oil	21	584-14,240	4,502	4,057
wc/d	14	467-3,529	1,508	1,168

Name	No.	Price Range	Average	Median
RUGGIERO, Carmine di (1934-) Italian				
oil	1	1,210	1,210	1,210
wc/d	1	701	701	701
RUGGIERO, Leopold (20th C) Italian				
oil	1	1,200	1,200	1,200
RUGGIERO, Pasquale (1851-1916) Italian				
oil	5	1,512-6,500	3,603	3,235
RUGGLES, Edward (19th C) American				
oil	1	2,750	2,750	2,750
RUGIER, P (17/18th C) ?				
oil	1	7,135	7,135	7,135
RUHLE, Rutjer (1939-) German				
oil	1	2,250	2,250	2,250
RUIPEREZ, Luis (1832-1867) Spanish				
oil	1	12,852	12,852	12,852
RUITH, Horace van (1839-1923) British				
oil	1	1,151	1,151	1,151
wc/d	2	850-1,134	992	850
RUIZ PULIDO, Cristobal (1881-1962) Spanish				
oil	1	3,801	3,801	3,801
RUIZ, Antonio (1897-1964) Mexican				
wc/d	1	16,000	16,000	16,000
RUIZ, B Yamero (fl.1890-1910) American				
oil	2	1,100-1,400	1,250	1,100
RUIZ, Juan (18th C) Spanish				
oil	1	24,220	24,220	24,220
RUIZ, Tomasso (18th C) Spanish				
oil	1	129,750	129,750	129,750
RUIZ-PIPO, Manolo (1929-1998) Spanish				
oil	4	1,200-3,884	2,177	1,437
wc/d	5	922-2,581	1,435	1,229
RULE, Nicolas (1956-) American				
oil	2	760-1,754	1,257	760
RUMEAU, Jean Claude (18/19th C) French				
wc/d	1	16,145	16,145	16,145
RUMOROSO, Enrique (19th C) Spanish				
wc/d	1	1,767	1,767	1,767
RUMPF, Philipp (1821-1896) German				
oil	1	1,671	1,671	1,671
RUMPLER, Franz (1848-1922) Austrian				
oil	3	1,574-4,839	3,489	4,055
RUMSEY, Charles Cary (1879-1922) American				
3D	1	20,000	20,000	20,000
RUNACRES, Frank (1904-1974) British				
oil	2	486-2,000	1,243	486
RUNDALIZEV, Mikhail Viktorovich (1871-1935) Russian				
oil	1	9,000	9,000	9,000
RUNDMANN, G (20th C) ?				
3D	1	3,063	3,063	3,063
RUNDSTEDT, S von (19th C) ?				
oil	1	6,622	6,622	6,622
RUNEBERG, Walter (1838-1920) Finnish				
3D	1	30,392	30,392	30,392
RUNGIUS, Carl (1869-1959) American/German				
oil	11	40,000-850,000	155,681	65,000
RUOKOKOSKI, Jalmari (1886-1936) Finnish				
oil	5	959-2,928	1,589	1,211
RUOPPOLO, Gian Battista (1629-1693) Italian				
oil	4	32,694-110,034	68,386	38,060
RUOPPOLO, Giuseppe (1639-1710) Italian				
oil	1	9,514	9,514	9,514
RUPP, Walter (1902-?) German				
3D	1	2,160	2,160	2,160
RUPPERSBERG, Allen (1944-) American				
wc/d	2	5,000-37,500	21,250	5,000
RUPPERT, Otto von (1841-?) German				
oil	4	2,922-9,991	5,198	3,086
RUSCA, Carlo Francesco (1696-1769) Swiss				
oil	2	19,265-20,469	19,867	19,265
RUSCHA, Edward (1937-) American				
oil	19	30,000-1,400,000	408,880	190,000
wc/d	13	4,200-480,000	151,092	150,000

Name	No.	Price Range	Average	Median
RUSCHI, Francesco (17th C) Italian				
oil	2	7,014-18,147	12,580	7,014
RUSHBURY, Sir Henry (1889-1968) British				
wc/d	5	557-2,232	1,208	875
RUSHTON, George Robert (1869-1947) British				
wc/d	2	797-2,775	1,786	797
RUSINOL, Santiago (1861-1931) Spanish				
oil	3	60,900-330,600	173,433	128,800
wc/d	1	1,171	1,171	1,171
RUSKIN, John (1819-1900) British				
wc/d	1	1,750	1,750	1,750
RUSS, Franz (younger) (1844-1906) Austrian				
oil	3	3,086-6,555	4,501	3,864
RUSS, Robert (1847-1922) Austrian				
oil	4	4,676-29,452	15,564	11,192
wc/d	3	605-1,573	1,207	1,445
RUSSELL (?) ?				
oil	1	6,033	6,033	6,033
RUSSELL, Charles (1852-1910) British				
oil	1	1,600	1,600	1,600
RUSSELL, Charles M (1864-1926) American				
oil	5	120,000-1,300,000	458,000	340,000
wc/d	21	13,000-600,000	146,976	75,000
3D	11	6,000-120,000	30,045	8,000
RUSSELL, E J (1835-1906) American				
wc/d	1	1,750	1,750	1,750
RUSSELL, George (1867-1935) Irish				
oil	14	5,086-29,667	17,332	17,534
RUSSELL, George Horne (1861-1933) Canadian				
oil	8	615-3,323	1,716	1,209
wc/d	2	441-970	705	441
RUSSELL, Gyrth (1892-1970) Canadian				
oil	8	487-3,460	1,302	576
RUSSELL, John (1745-1806) British				
wc/d	3	9,300-46,500	22,380	11,340
RUSSELL, John Bucknell (1819-1893) British				
oil	1	22,250	22,250	22,250
RUSSELL, John Wentworth (1879-1959) Canadian				
oil	1	1,400	1,400	1,400
RUSSELL, Morgan (1886-1953) American				
oil	1	1,500	1,500	1,500
RUSSELL, Shirley (1886-?) American				
oil	2	750-16,000	8,375	750
RUSSELL, Sir Walter Westley (1867-1949) British				
oil	2	2,394-20,000	11,197	2,394
RUSSELL, Walter (1871-1946) American				
oil	4	850-1,800	1,225	950
RUSSMAN, Felix (1888-1962) American				
oil	2	1,600-4,250	2,925	1,600
RUSSO, Enzo (20th C) European				
oil	1	1,300	1,300	1,300
RUSSO, Gaetano (20th C) Italian				
3D	1	160,000	160,000	160,000
RUSSO, Nicola Maria (1647-1702) Italian				
oil	1	15,226	15,226	15,226
RUSSO, Raul (1912-1984) Argentinian				
oil	2	2,600-14,500	8,550	2,600
RUSSO, Silvio (20th C) Italian				
oil	1	3,633	3,633	3,633
RUSSOLO, Luigi (1885-1947) Italian				
wc/d	1	5,088	5,088	5,088
RUST, Johan Adolph (1828-1915) Dutch				
oil	4	2,000-7,233	4,407	2,832
RUSTIN, Jean (1928-) French				
oil	3	5,173-30,137	14,242	7,417
wc/d	4	588-1,381	1,069	1,023
RUSZKOWSKI, Zdzislaw (1907-1990) Polish				
oil	3	1,575-3,420	2,540	2,625
RUTAULT, Claude (20th C) French				
wc/d	1	1,463	1,463	1,463
RUTHART, Karl Andreas (1630-1703) German				
oil	1	25,342	25,342	25,342

Name	No.	Price Range	Average	Median
RUTHENBECK, Reiner (1937-) German				
wc/d	1	777	777	777
3D	2	1,927-10,014	5,970	1,927
RUTHERFORD, G L (19th C) American				
oil	1	4,500	4,500	4,500
RUTHERFURD, Georgette (20th C) American				
oil	1	1,400	1,400	1,400
RUTHS, Amelie (1871-1956) German				
oil	1	1,008	1,008	1,008
RUTHS, Valentin (1825-1905) German				
oil	6	492-3,687	1,455	1,076
wc/d	2	485-676	580	485
RUTHVEN, Jerry (1947-) American				
oil	1	1,400	1,400	1,400
RUTLEDGE, June (20th C) American				
oil	1	2,000	2,000	2,000
RUTS, F (19th C) German				
oil	1	4,576	4,576	4,576
RUTZ, Andreas (19/20th C) German				
wc/d	1	1,221	1,221	1,221
RUVIALE, Francesco (fl.1527-1560) Italian				
oil	1	36,122	36,122	36,122
RUYSCH, Rachel (1664-1750) Dutch				
oil	3	70,135-400,000	193,727	111,047
RUYSDAEL, Jacob Salomonsz van (1630-1681) Dutch				
oil	3	22,200-53,400	42,500	51,900
RUYSDAEL, Jacob van (1628-1682) Dutch				
oil	2	320,000-550,000	435,000	320,000
RUYSDAEL, Salomon van (1600-1670) Dutch				
oil	13	7,866-990,000	150,413	74,000
RUYTER, Lisa (1968-) German?				
oil	8	20,000-42,000	29,390	26,000
RUYTINX, Alfred (1871-?) Belgian				
oil	1	2,253	2,253	2,253
RUZHEINIKOV, P (20th C) Russian				
oil	1	2,378	2,378	2,378
RUZICKA, Othmar (1877-1962) Austrian				
oil	1	535	535	535
wc/d	1	1,686	1,686	1,686
RUZICKA-LAUTENSCHLAGER, Hans (1862-1933) Austrian				
oil	1	2,489	2,489	2,489
RYABUSHKIN, Andrei Petrovich (1861-1904) Russian				
oil	1	65,000	65,000	65,000
RYAN, Anne (1889-1954) American				
wc/d	3	3,500-8,000	5,166	4,000
RYAN, Thomas (1929-) Irish				
oil	4	4,014-7,664	5,013	4,171
wc/d	2	1,403-2,432	1,917	1,403
RYAN, Tom (1922-) American				
oil	2	6,500-8,000	7,250	6,500
wc/d	3	4,000-12,000	7,000	5,000
RYBACK, Issachar (1897-1935) Russian				
oil	14	2,160-35,000	10,757	7,440
wc/d	13	600-9,600	3,251	3,000
3D	1	2,000	2,000	2,000
RYBERG, Elis (1919-1985) Swedish				
oil	1	1,014	1,014	1,014
RYCK, Pieter Cornelisz van (1568-c.1628) Dutch				
oil	1	16,473	16,473	16,473
RYCKAERT, David (younger) (1586-1642) Flemish				
oil	1	9,000	9,000	9,000
RYCKAERT, David III (1612-1661) Flemish				
oil	6	5,838-14,449	9,321	8,352
RYCKAERT, Marten (1587-1631) Flemish				
oil	5	5,878-129,750	61,993	58,820
RYCKHALS, Frans (1600-1647) Dutch				
oil	3	552-8,429	4,550	4,671
RYDBERG, Gustaf (1835-1933) Swedish				
oil	9	419-8,974	3,256	2,747
RYDER, Albert Pinkham (1847-1917) American				
oil	2	30,000-45,000	37,500	30,000

Name	No.	Price Range	Average	Median
RYDER, Chauncey F (1868-1949) American				
oil	15	3,500-17,000	8,567	7,000
wc/d	2	350-650	500	350
RYDER, Jack van (1898-1968) American				
oil	5	1,700-5,000	3,090	2,600
RYDER, Platt Powell (1821-1896) American				
oil	4	400-2,000	1,450	1,600
RYDER, Sophie (1963-) British				
3D	2	6,000-10,920	8,460	6,000
RYDER, Susan (1944-) British				
wc/d	1	4,872	4,872	4,872
RYDHOLM, Sven Leonard (1821-1885) Swedish				
oil	1	118,479	118,479	118,479
RYLAARSDAM, Jan (1911-) Dutch				
oil	5	1,025-4,315	2,468	1,908
wc/d	6	914-3,250	2,277	1,752
RYLAND, Henry (1856-1924) British				
wc/d	9	519-8,505	3,050	2,088
RYLAND, Robert K (1873-1951) American				
oil	1	1,000	1,000	1,000
RYLANDER, Hans Chr (1939-) Danish				
wc/d	2	970-1,212	1,091	970
RYLEY, Charles Reuben (1752-1798) British				
wc/d	1	16,435	16,435	16,435
RYLOV (19/20th C) Russian				
wc/d	1	2,177	2,177	2,177
RYMAN, Robert (1930-) American				
oil	6	35,000-8,600,000	1,900,000	400,000
RYN, Nico van (1887-1962) Dutch				
oil	3	659-3,299	2,183	2,592
RYSBRACK, Jean Michel (1693-1770) Flemish				
3D	1	242,200	242,200	242,200
RYSBRACK, Pieter (1655-1729) Flemish				
oil	1	11,689	11,689	11,689
RYSER, Fritz (1910-1990) Swiss				
oil	2	839-1,249	1,044	839
RYSSELBERGHE, Theo van (1862-1926) Belgian				
oil	5	4,057-2,800,000	572,733	7,400
wc/d	10	964-64,291	14,429	4,625
RYSWYCK, Jan van (?) ?				
oil	1	2,314	2,314	2,314
3D	1	1,878	1,878	1,878
RYSWYCK, Theodor van (1811-1849) Belgian				
3D	1	7,007	7,007	7,007
SAABYE, Carl Anton (1807-1878) Danish				
oil	1	27,500	27,500	27,500
SAABYE, Svend (1913-2004) Danish				
oil	8	487-3,650	1,424	1,183
SAAF, Erik (1856-1934) Swedish				
oil	1	1,870	1,870	1,870
SAAL, Georg (1818-1870) German				
oil	2	5,838-16,703	11,270	5,838
SAALBORN, Louis (1890-1957) Dutch				
oil	3	1,158-1,463	1,293	1,260
SAARBYE, Eveline (19th C) Danish				
oil	1	2,338	2,338	2,338
SAARINEN, Yrjo (1899-1958) Finnish				
oil	2	5,400-14,027	9,713	5,400
SABATER, Daniel (1888-1951) Spanish				
oil	6	571-15,671	4,276	1,054
SABATINI, I (19th C) Italian				
oil	1	18,000	18,000	18,000
SABATINI, Luigi (19th C) Italian				
oil	1	4,961	4,961	4,961
SABATTIER, Louis (19th C) French				
oil	3	450-20,000	9,193	7,129
wc/d	16	1,168-8,758	3,379	2,919
SABAVALA, Jehangir (1922-) Indian				
oil	3	21,000-145,000	88,452	99,358
SABBAGH, Georges (1887-1951) French				
oil	4	949-9,709	3,597	1,221

Name	No.	Price Range	Average	Median
SABINO, Marius Ernest (1878-1961) ?				
3D	1	4,855	4,855	4,855
SABLET, François Jean (1745-1819) French/Swiss				
oil	1	51,302	51,302	51,302
SABLET, Jacques Henri (1749-1803) Swiss				
oil	1	12,237	12,237	12,237
wc/d	1	2,521	2,521	2,521
SABOURAUD, Émile (1900-1996) French				
oil	6	400-4,079	2,050	1,274
SABY, Bernard (1925-1975) French				
oil	2	2,592-4,948	3,770	2,592
wc/d	1	526	526	526
SACCARO, John (1913-1981) American				
oil	1	32,500	32,500	32,500
SACCHETTI, Giotto (1877-1950) Italian				
oil	1	1,171	1,171	1,171
SACCOROTTI, Oscar (1898-) Italian				
oil	1	3,551	3,551	3,551
SACHAROFF, Olga (1889-1969) Russian				
wc/d	1	4,017	4,017	4,017
SACHERI, Giuseppe (1863-1950) Italian				
oil	5	1,455-6,465	3,383	3,263
SACHS, Tom (1966-) American				
wc/d	2	6,500-6,500	6,500	6,500
3D	9	13,000-129,500	37,222	25,000
SACHY, Henri Émile de (19th C) French				
oil	1	1,800	1,800	1,800
SACKLARIAN, Stephen (1889-1983) American				
oil	1	1,000	1,000	1,000
wc/d	1	1,800	1,800	1,800
SACKS, Joseph (1887-1974) American				
oil	4	550-2,250	1,275	1,100
SACRE, Émile (1844-1882) Belgian				
oil	1	11,918	11,918	11,918
SADEE, Philippe (1837-1904) Dutch				
oil	5	1,205-63,360	16,155	4,200
SADEQUAIN (1930-1987) Indian				
oil	14	10,380-38,720	23,454	20,760
wc/d	3	4,498-15,000	8,259	5,280
SADIQ, Muhammad (18th C) Persian				
oil	1	52,800	52,800	52,800
SADKOWSKI, Alex (1934-) Swiss				
oil	1	3,816	3,816	3,816
wc/d	1	757	757	757
SADKOWSKI, Eugen H von (20th C) German?				
oil	1	2,577	2,577	2,577
SADLER, T (?) ?				
oil	1	2,340	2,340	2,340
SADLER, Walter Dendy (1854-1923) British				
oil	3	2,338-11,310	6,266	5,152
SADLER, William (jnr) (1782-1839) British				
oil	5	4,676-19,872	8,734	6,663
SADOUK, Abdellah (1950-) Moroccan				
oil	2	1,267-1,381	1,324	1,267
SADUN, Piero (1919-1974) Italian				
oil	5	2,028-4,451	2,679	2,386
SAEDELEER, Valerius de (1867-1941) Belgian				
oil	1	2,649	2,649	2,649
wc/d	1	3,955	3,955	3,955
SAENE, Maurice van (1919-2000) Belgian				
oil	2	897-1,147	1,022	897
wc/d	1	1,401	1,401	1,401
SAENZ DE LA CALZADA, Luis (1910-1994) Spanish				
wc/d	1	1,437	1,437	1,437
SAENZ, Joaquin (1931-) Spanish				
oil	1	7,603	7,603	7,603
SAETTI, Bruno (1902-1984) Italian				
oil	9	2,903-28,110	11,286	9,600
wc/d	7	522-9,342	3,677	1,985
SAEZ, Luis (1925-) Spanish				
oil	1	3,279	3,279	3,279

Name	No.	Price Range	Average	Median
SAEZ, Manuel (1961-) Spanish				
oil	1	1,556	1,556	1,556
SAFFARO, Lucio (1929-) Italian				
oil	1	1,573	1,573	1,573
SAFFER, Hans Konrad (1860-1940) German				
oil	2	521-1,894	1,207	521
SAFTLEVEN, Cornelis (1607-1681) Dutch				
oil	4	19,110-26,982	22,828	19,273
SAFTLEVEN, Herman (1609-1685) Dutch				
oil	10	10,235-80,000	38,204	25,950
wc/d	5	2,076-9,425	4,456	3,343
SAGEWKA, Ernst (1883-1959) German				
oil	1	4,123	4,123	4,123
SAGGIAK, Kumakuluk (1944-) North American				
3D	3	1,687-6,116	3,191	1,772
SAHLER, Helen G (1877-1950) American				
3D	1	3,750	3,750	3,750
SAHLSTEN, Anna (1859-1931) Finnish				
oil	3	479-5,914	2,918	2,361
SAHRAOUI, Schems Eddine (1948-) Tunisian				
oil	1	3,236	3,236	3,236
wc/d	1	1,343	1,343	1,343
SAIETZ, Gunnar (1936-) Danish				
oil	1	1,127	1,127	1,127
SAILA, Pauta (1916-) North American				
3D	4	2,868-7,171	5,563	5,972
SAIN, Edouard Alexandre (1830-1910) French				
oil	4	2,521-21,000	10,273	4,343
SAIN, Paul Étienne (1904-?) French				
oil	6	486-15,266	5,938	3,527
SAIN, Paul Jean Marie (1853-1908) French				
oil	4	1,019-6,600	3,748	2,700
SAINT CLAIR, Norman (1863-1912) American				
wc/d	2	1,700-2,750	2,225	1,700
ST JOHN, Edwin (19th C) British				
wc/d	1	1,133	1,133	1,133
ST JOHN-JONES, Herbert (fl.1905-1923) British				
oil	7	1,305-28,000	8,540	5,340
SAINT, Louise Anne (1865-?) French				
oil	1	1,013	1,013	1,013
SAINT-ANDRE, Simon Renard de (1614-1677) French				
oil	1	77,850	77,850	77,850
SAINT-AUBIN, Gabriel de (1724-1780) French				
wc/d	1	13,863	13,863	13,863
SAINT-DELIS, Henri de (1878-1949) French				
oil	4	3,349-6,219	4,313	3,595
wc/d	6	1,890-4,919	2,955	2,264
SAINT-DELIS, René de (1877-1958) French				
oil	3	1,311-2,026	1,610	1,495
wc/d	2	894-1,132	1,013	894
SAINT-EDME, Ludovic Alfred de (1820-?) French				
oil	1	16,703	16,703	16,703
SAINT-GAUDENS, Augustus (1848-1907) American				
3D	2	2,000-4,800	3,400	2,000
SAINT-GERANS, A de (19/20th C) ?				
oil	1	3,534	3,534	3,534
SAINT-GERMIER, Joseph (1860-1925) French				
oil	1	3,306	3,306	3,306
SAINT-JEAN, Marcel (1914-1994) French				
oil	1	1,796	1,796	1,796
SAINT-JEAN, Simon (1808-1860) French				
oil	5	2,000-210,000	52,324	10,137
wc/d	1	5,500	5,500	5,500
SAINT-MARCEAUX, René (1845-1915) French				
3D	3	1,767-4,703	3,131	2,924
SAINT-MARCEL, Émile Normand (1840-?) French				
oil	1	2,117	2,117	2,117
SAINT-NON, L'Abbe de (1727-1791) French				
wc/d	1	2,188	2,188	2,188
SAINT-PHALLE, Niki de (1930-2002) French				
wc/d	16	763-9,074	3,557	2,596
3D	62	1,703-409,388	42,826	26,550

Name	No.	Price Range	Average	Median
SAINT-PHALLE, Niki de and TINGUELY, Jean (20th C) French/Swiss				
wc/d	1	5,890	5,890	5,890
3D	3	23,378-25,442	24,290	24,050
SAINT-PIERRE, Gaston Casimir (1833-1916) French				
oil	2	6,336-22,080	14,208	6,336
SAINT-QUENTIN, Jacques Philippe Jos de (1783-?) French				
wc/d	2	1,903-3,655	2,779	1,903
SAINTIN, Henri (1846-1899) French				
oil	4	1,076-4,012	2,189	1,168
SAINTIN, Jules Émile (1829-1894) French				
oil	3	900-47,840	17,942	5,088
SAINZ Y SAINZ, Casimiro (1853-1898) Spanish				
oil	3	1,883-8,159	5,005	4,973
SAITO, Kikuo (20th C) Japanese				
oil	1	1,500	1,500	1,500
SAKAI, Kazuya (1927-2001) Argentinian				
oil	3	2,500-9,000	6,166	7,000
wc/d	2	2,800-3,800	3,300	2,800
SAKAYAN, Edouardos (1957-) Greek				
oil	1	7,040	7,040	7,040
SAKELLARIDIS, Dimitris (1912-1999) Greek				
oil	1	1,870	1,870	1,870
SAKLIKOVSKAYA, Sofia (1899-1975) Russian				
oil	1	267,534	267,534	267,534
SALA Y FRANCES, Emilio (1850-1910) Spanish				
oil	4	890-107,880	29,839	2,750
SALA, Eugène de (1899-1987) Danish				
oil	4	1,127-3,233	2,178	1,455
SALA, Juan (1867-1918) Spanish				
oil	1	155,646	155,646	155,646
SALA, Paolo (1859-1929) Italian				
oil	2	2,760-4,033	3,396	2,760
wc/d	5	1,621-17,671	8,130	3,164
SALABERRY, A de (?) ?				
wc/d	1	6,799	6,799	6,799
SALABET, Jean (20th C) French				
oil	6	700-1,900	1,190	1,200
SALADI, Abbes (1950-1992) Moroccan				
wc/d	1	10,327	10,327	10,327
SALADIN, Alphonse (1879-?) French				
3D	1	3,292	3,292	3,292
SALAS, Tito (1888-1974) Venezuelan				
oil	1	5,350	5,350	5,350
wc/d	6	560-1,025	760	745
SALATHE, Friedrich (1793-1860) French				
wc/d	3	992-6,301	3,782	4,053
SALAZAR, Luis (1956-) ?				
oil	2	1,790-3,568	2,679	1,790
SALCEDO, Bernardo (1939-) American?				
3D	1	2,250	2,250	2,250
SALCEDO, Doris (1958-) Colombian				
3D	2	50,000-410,000	230,000	50,000
SALCES Y GUTIERREZ, Manuel (1861-1932) Spanish				
oil	3	644-1,453	992	879
wc/d	1	522	522	522
SALDIVAR, Jaime (1926-1974) Mexican				
oil	1	22,000	22,000	22,000
SALEH, Raden (c.1814-1880) Javanese				
oil	2	21,673-770,738	396,205	21,673
SALEM, Aly Ben (1910-2001) Swedish				
wc/d	5	373-1,940	1,264	1,616
SALEMME, Attilio (1911-1955) American				
oil	2	1,300-3,000	2,150	1,300
SALENDRE, Georges (20th C) French				
3D	1	6,597	6,597	6,597
SALENTIN, Hubert (1822-1910) German				
oil	1	20,000	20,000	20,000
SALES ROVIRALTA, Francesco (1904-1977) Spanish				
oil	5	1,492-1,616	1,566	1,616
SALGADO COSME, Demetrio (1915-) Spanish				
oil	1	1,054	1,054	1,054

Name	No.	Price Range	Average	Median
SALGADO, Veloso (1864-1945) Portuguese				
oil	1	7,292	7,292	7,292
SALICATH, Jenny (1867-1944) Danish				
wc/d	1	1,048	1,048	1,048
SALIETTI, Alberto (1892-1961) Italian				
oil	2	5,825-15,753	10,789	5,825
SALIGER, Ivo (1894-1987) Austrian				
oil	7	934-3,012	1,669	1,514
SALIGO, Charles Louis (1804-1874) Belgian				
oil	1	4,285	4,285	4,285
SALIMBENI, Arcangelo (16th C) Italian				
oil	1	5,040	5,040	5,040
SALIMBENI, Raffaello Arcangelo (1914-1991) Italian				
oil	1	4,165	4,165	4,165
SALINAS, Pablo (1871-1946) Spanish				
oil	6	714-174,000	49,722	24,000
SALINAS, Porfirio (1910-1972) American				
oil	11	3,750-25,000	11,931	11,500
SALIOLA, Antonio (1939-) Italian				
oil	4	1,635-11,167	7,388	5,826
SALIS-SOGLIO, Carl Albert von (1886-1941) Swiss				
oil	1	8,106	8,106	8,106
SALISBURY, Frank O (1874-1962) British				
oil	4	736-144,000	36,847	1,098
wc/d	1	12,880	12,880	12,880
SALKELD, Cecil (1908-1968) British				
oil	1	5,984	5,984	5,984
SALKIN, Fernand (1862-?) French				
oil	1	1,192	1,192	1,192
SALLAERT, Anthonie (1590-1657) Flemish				
oil	1	25,950	25,950	25,950
SALLE, Andre Augustin (1891-?) French				
3D	1	2,003	2,003	2,003
SALLE, David (1952-) American				
oil	13	20,000-500,000	149,473	125,000
wc/d	5	2,500-11,000	7,044	6,500
3D	1	180,000	180,000	180,000
SALLEO, Carmelo (1892-1963) Italian				
oil	1	3,341	3,341	3,341
SALLES, Pierre Alexandre (1867-1915) French				
oil	1	3,102	3,102	3,102
SALLES-WAGNER, Adelaide (1825-1890) German				
oil	1	5,760	5,760	5,760
SALLINEN, Tyko (1879-1955) Finnish				
oil	1	1,127	1,127	1,127
wc/d	5	479-1,139	672	605
SALM, Adriaan (fl.1708-1720) Dutch				
wc/d	2	59,200-89,178	74,189	59,200
SALM, Reynier van (17/18th C) Dutch				
wc/d	1	46,250	46,250	46,250
SALMI, Max (1931-1995) Finnish				
oil	10	1,405-2,829	2,321	2,397
SALMON, Robert (1775-1844) American				
oil	7	9,000-240,000	90,205	80,000
SALMONES, Victor (1937-1989) Mexican				
3D	4	3,000-4,500	3,875	4,000
SALMSON, Hugo (1844-1894) Swedish				
oil	3	1,923-3,988	2,611	1,923
wc/d	1	1,648	1,648	1,648
SALMSON, Jean Jules (1823-1902) French				
3D	2	3,323-12,740	8,031	3,323
SALO, W (19/20th C) Finnish?				
oil	1	2,757	2,757	2,757
SALOKIVI, Santeri (1886-1940) Finnish				
oil	18	819-20,384	6,148	4,629
SALOME (1954-) German				
oil	13	3,884-17,568	8,244	7,068
wc/d	3	618-1,237	872	763
SALOMON (?) ?				
oil	1	5,388	5,388	5,388
SALOMONI, Tito (20th C) American				
oil	1	1,300	1,300	1,300

Name	No.	Price Range	Average	Median
SALOSMAA, Aarno (1941-) Finnish				
oil	2	937-1,929	1,433	937
wc/d	1	1,286	1,286	1,286
SALT, James (19th C) British				
oil	6	534-2,600	1,474	1,472
SALT, John (1937-) British				
oil	1	8,767	8,767	8,767
wc/d	1	11,000	11,000	11,000
SALTER, William (1804-1875) British				
oil	1	19,470	19,470	19,470
SALTI, Giulio (1899-1984) Italian				
oil	3	673-13,863	5,937	3,277
SALTINI, Pietro (1839-1908) Italian				
oil	1	40,000	40,000	40,000
SALTO, Axel (1889-1961) Danish				
oil	3	1,778-11,267	6,395	6,142
wc/d	2	550-1,293	921	550
SALTO, Kamma (1890-?) Danish				
oil	1	1,586	1,586	1,586
SALTZMANN, Carl (1847-1923) German				
oil	2	730-7,000	3,865	730
SALTZMANN, Henri Gustave (1811-1872) Swiss				
oil	2	500-1,532	1,016	500
SALUCCI, Alessandro (17th C) Italian				
oil	1	58,904	58,904	58,904
SALUSTRI, Piero (1957-) Italian				
oil	1	1,229	1,229	1,229
SALVADO, Jacinto (1892-1983) Spanish				
oil	2	1,176-3,663	2,419	1,176
SALVAT, Beatrice (20th C) French				
wc/d	1	2,028	2,028	2,028
SALVAT, François (1892-1976) French				
oil	23	504-3,781	912	630
wc/d	7	527-1,145	777	756
SALVATORE, Nino di (1924-) Italian				
oil	1	8,481	8,481	8,481
SALVATORI, Giuseppe (1955-) Italian				
oil	1	1,219	1,219	1,219
wc/d	1	1,640	1,640	1,640
SALVESTRINI, Bartolomeo (?-c.1630) Italian				
wc/d	1	3,281	3,281	3,281
SALVIATI, Francesco (1510-1563) Italian				
wc/d	1	48,100	48,100	48,100
SALVIATI, Giovanni (1881-1950) Italian				
oil	4	937-4,816	2,915	2,803
SALVIATI, Giuseppe Porta (c.1520-1573) Italian				
wc/d	1	4,995	4,995	4,995
SALVIN, M de (19/20th C) French?				
oil	1	2,076	2,076	2,076
SALVINO, Andrea (1969-) Italian				
oil	1	3,503	3,503	3,503
SALVO (1947-) Italian				
oil	33	1,414-53,100	13,556	11,781
wc/d	6	705-2,356	1,464	1,106
3D	3	3,010-3,181	3,107	3,131
SALY, Jacques François Joseph (1717-1776) French				
3D	1	121,599	121,599	121,599
SALZER, Liesel (20th C) Austrian				
oil	1	3,514	3,514	3,514
SALZMANN, Gottfried (1943-) Austrian				
wc/d	4	849-2,146	1,579	1,567
SAMACCHINI, Orazio (1532-1577) Italian				
oil	1	24,000	24,000	24,000
wc/d	1	10,380	10,380	10,380
SAMANT, Mohan B (1926-) Indian				
oil	1	35,000	35,000	35,000
SAMARAS, Lucas (1936-) American/Greek				
oil	2	5,500-65,000	35,250	5,500
3D	2	37,840-50,000	43,920	37,840
SAMBA, Cheri (1956-) Zairean				
oil	4	6,936-13,939	10,534	7,414

Name	No.	Price Range	Average	Median
SAMBERGER, Leo (1861-1949) German				
wc/d	1	2,180	2,180	2,180
SAMBONET, Roberto (1924-1995) Italian				
wc/d	1	1,214	1,214	1,214
SAMIOS, Paulos (1948-) ?				
oil	1	4,400	4,400	4,400
SAMMER, Otto (20th C) Polish?				
oil	1	1,200	1,200	1,200
SAMMONS, Carl (1888-1968) American				
oil	17	1,600-10,000	4,020	3,750
wc/d	8	650-1,700	1,006	900
SAMOKHVALOV, Alexandre (1894-1971) Russian				
oil	2	34,400-53,750	44,075	34,400
SAMOKICH, Nicolai (1860-1944) Russian				
oil	4	9,604-89,280	38,576	27,520
wc/d	1	43,315	43,315	43,315
SAMPLE, Paul (1896-1974) American				
oil	3	12,000-95,000	40,000	13,000
wc/d	7	475-8,500	2,646	1,100
SAMSON, Eddy (1914-1981) Dutch				
oil	1	1,455	1,455	1,455
SAMSONOV, Igor (1963-) Russian				
oil	1	2,500	2,500	2,500
SAMUELSON, Ulrik (1935-) Swedish				
oil	7	1,123-58,144	12,692	3,436
wc/d	1	11,451	11,451	11,451
3D	2	10,815-28,628	19,721	10,815
SAN JOSE, Francisco (1919-1981) Spanish				
oil	3	1,774-3,612	2,524	2,186
wc/d	3	572-2,351	1,192	654
SAN MARTIN, Benigno (19th C) Spanish				
oil	2	1,978-1,978	1,978	1,978
SAN-YU (1901-1966) Chinese				
wc/d	4	8,507-18,837	11,545	8,507
SANCHEZ (?) Spanish				
oil	1	6,969	6,969	6,969
SANCHEZ CARRALERO, Jose (1942-) Spanish				
oil	4	1,145-2,290	1,691	1,523
SANCHEZ COELLO, Alonso (c.1531-1588) Spanish				
oil	2	129,750-231,250	180,500	129,750
SANCHEZ ENTRALLA, Jose ('?) Spanish				
oil	1	2,003	2,003	2,003
SANCHEZ SOLA, Eduardo (1869-1949) Spanish				
oil	3	697-6,890	3,413	2,652
SANCHEZ, Edgar (1940-) Venezuelan				
oil	2	1,670-6,980	4,325	1,670
SANCHEZ, Juan Manuel (20th C) Spanish				
oil	1	3,400	3,400	3,400
SANCHEZ, Pepi (1932-) Spanish				
oil	5	400-2,040	1,066	783
SANCHEZ, Tomas (1948-) Cuban				
oil	6	60,000-310,000	158,333	140,000
wc/d	3	9,000-42,500	26,166	27,000
SANCHEZ-PERRIER, Emilio (1855-1907) Spanish				
oil	6	12,000-52,200	26,466	18,000
SANCTIS, Giuseppe de (1858-1924) Italian				
oil	3	2,293-11,211	5,364	2,589
SAND, George (1804-1876) French				
wc/d	3	3,360-7,349	5,028	4,375
SAND, Lennart (1946-) Swedish				
oil	4	744-6,601	2,660	1,191
SANDBACK, Fred (1943-2003) American				
oil	1	45,000	45,000	45,000
wc/d	6	2,992-13,000	7,389	7,500
SANDBERG, Hjalmar (1847-1888) Swedish				
oil	2	1,179-2,742	1,960	1,179
SANDBERG, Ragnar (1902-1972) Swedish				
oil	22	3,700-132,146	29,699	22,465
wc/d	12	396-27,751	4,848	1,255
SANDBY, Paul (1730-1809) British				
wc/d	17	600-15,660	4,295	2,450

Name	No.	Price Range	Average	Median
SANDELS, Gosta (1877-1919) Swedish				
oil	3	4,229-36,898	16,762	9,161
SANDER, Karin (1957-) German				
oil	1	2,800	2,800	2,800
SANDER, Ludwig (1906-1975) American				
oil	5	2,750-14,000	6,250	4,750
SANDER, Sherry Salari (1941-) American				
3D	3	6,000-15,000	9,000	6,000
SANDER, Tom (1938-) American				
oil	1	2,000	2,000	2,000
wc/d	1	2,000	2,000	2,000
SANDER-PLUMP, Agnes (1888-1980) German				
oil	1	4,559	4,559	4,559
SANDERS, Christopher (1905-1991) British				
oil	4	455-1,925	1,162	560
SANDERS, Hedwyn (1885-1971) American				
oil	1	1,400	1,400	1,400
SANDERS, John (jnr) (1750-1825) British				
wc/d	1	2,220	2,220	2,220
SANDERS, Walter G (fl.1882-1892) British				
oil	2	1,300-1,419	1,359	1,300
SANDERSON, Julia (fl.1870-1880) British				
oil	1	1,392	1,392	1,392
SANDERSON-WELLS, John (1872-1955) British				
oil	7	1,246-12,250	4,264	3,000
wc/d	2	525-1,381	953	525
SANDHAM, Henry (1842-1910) Canadian				
oil	1	1,300	1,300	1,300
wc/d	1	9,500	9,500	9,500
SANDIG, Jacobus Nicolaus (1876-1933) Dutch				
3D	1	2,385	2,385	2,385
SANDLE, Michael (1936-) British/German				
wc/d	2	895-1,711	1,303	895
3D	1	6,498	6,498	6,498
SANDONA, Matteo (1881-1964) American				
wc/d	1	3,500	3,500	3,500
SANDORFI, Istvan (1948-) French				
oil	5	3,514-30,285	11,032	6,555
SANDOWSKI, Moshe (1931-) Israeli				
3D	1	3,400	3,400	3,400
SANDOZ, Edouard-Marcel (1881-1971) Swiss				
oil	1	2,338	2,338	2,338
3D	9	2,700-150,000	31,656	7,007
SANDRART, Auguste von (19th C) German				
oil	1	2,662	2,662	2,662
SANDRART, Joachim von (younger) (1668-1691) German				
wc/d	1	3,758	3,758	3,758
SANDRI, Gino (1892-1959) Italian				
wc/d	1	2,054	2,054	2,054
SANDROCK, Leonhard (1867-1945) German				
oil	7	1,145-3,214	2,384	2,153
SANDYS, Frederick (1832-1904) British				
wc/d	3	3,806-13,572	8,432	7,920
SANDYS-LUMSDAINE, Leesa (1936-) British				
oil	1	2,300	2,300	2,300
SANDZEN, Birger (1871-1954) American/Swedish				
oil	15	10,000-100,000	43,571	35,000
SANEJOUAND, Jean Michel (1934-) French				
oil	7	468-18,703	10,039	12,098
SANFILIPPO, Antonio (1923-1980) Italian				
oil	12	1,300-24,080	12,845	12,945
wc/d	5	2,458-25,442	12,036	5,184
SANFOURCHE, Jean Joseph (1929-) French?				
oil	1	450	450	450
wc/d	1	2,520	2,520	2,520
SANGBERG, Monica (20th C) ?				
oil	2	486-4,868	2,677	486
SANI, Alessandro (19/20th C) Italian				
oil	6	500-4,800	2,622	1,337
SANIN, Jurij (1912-) ?				
oil	1	1,060	1,060	1,060

Name	No.	Price Range	Average	Median
SANKOWSKI, T W (19th C) ?				
oil	1	2,182	2,182	2,182
SANMARTINO, Giuseppe (1720-1793) Italian				
3D	1	37,500	37,500	37,500
SANNUY, Juan (1850-1908) South American?				
wc/d	2	1,000-1,000	1,000	1,000
SANSEAU, Christian (20th C) French				
oil	1	1,229	1,229	1,229
SANSON, Justin Chrysostome (1833-1910) French				
3D	1	2,356	2,356	2,356
SANT, James (1820-1916) British				
oil	6	510-141,750	28,375	6,233
SANTA, Claude (1925-1979) French				
3D	1	1,788	1,788	1,788
SANTACROCE, Girolamo da (16th C) Italian				
oil	1	9,968	9,968	9,968
SANTAFEDE, Fabrizio (1559-c.1634) Italian				
oil	1	28,541	28,541	28,541
SANTAGOSTINO, Agostino (1635-1706) Italian				
oil	1	88,027	88,027	88,027
SANTALA, E (?) Finnish				
oil	1	1,816	1,816	1,816
SANTHOSH, T V (1968-) Indian				
oil	2	11,000-14,000	12,500	11,000
SANTI, Giuseppe (?-1825) Italian				
oil	1	25,865	25,865	25,865
SANTIESTEBAN, Carlos (1928-) Spanish				
wc/d	1	1,694	1,694	1,694
SANTO, Patsy (1893-1975) American				
oil	1	5,000	5,000	5,000
SANTOLONI, Felice (?) Italian				
wc/d	2	6,615-12,285	9,450	6,615
SANTOMASO, Giuseppe (1907-1990) Italian				
oil	10	5,400-234,247	79,955	39,822
wc/d	25	3,178-78,897	12,966	9,105
SANTORO, Rubens (1859-1942) Italian				
oil	13	4,248-168,150	61,705	33,123
wc/d	1	22,932	22,932	22,932
SANTOSH, Gulam Rasool (1929-1997) Indian				
oil	10	4,000-47,500	15,873	10,000
SANTVOORT, Dirck van (1610-1680) Dutch				
oil	2	10,380-30,260	20,320	10,380
SANTVOORT, Philipp van (18th C) Flemish				
oil	2	4,712-5,501	5,106	4,712
SANYAL, Bhabesh C (1904-2003) Indian				
wc/d	1	1,760	1,760	1,760
SAPORETTI, Edgardo (1865-1909) Italian				
oil	1	4,459	4,459	4,459
SAPORETTI, F (?) Italian				
wc/d	1	3,637	3,637	3,637
SAPP, Allen (1929-) Canadian				
oil	22	620-5,318	2,299	1,898
SAPP, George Kitt (1887-?) American				
oil	1	2,200	2,200	2,200
SAPUNOV, Nikolai Nikolaievich (1880-1912) Russian				
oil	1	82,560	82,560	82,560
SARAZIN DE BELMONT, Louise Josephine (1790-1870) French				
oil	3	3,273-18,000	8,989	5,696
SARDA LADICO, Francisco (1877-1912) Spanish				
oil	1	14,000	14,000	14,000
SARDA, Enrique (1923-) Venezuelan				
oil	1	2,325	2,325	2,325
SARESTONIEMI, Reidar (1925-1981) Finnish				
oil	5	6,429-51,429	27,892	31,159
wc/d	2	1,246-2,571	1,908	1,246
SARGENT, John Singer (1856-1925) British/American				
oil	5	100,000-3,300,000	954,000	600,000
wc/d	10	3,600-190,000	57,800	9,000
3D	1	18,900	18,900	18,900
SARGENT, Paul Turner (1880-1946) American				
oil	3	800-3,000	1,900	1,900

Name	No.	Price Range	Average	Median
SARGHINI, Mohamed (1923-) Moroccan				
oil	1	28,688	28,688	28,688
SARIAN, Martiros (1880-1972) Armenian				
oil	6	40,000-160,000	74,173	55,040
wc/d	3	2,356-39,456	15,270	4,000
SARKA, Charles Nicolas (1879-1960) American				
wc/d	2	800-2,000	1,400	800
SARKIS (1938-) ?				
wc/d	1	1,168	1,168	1,168
SARKISIAN, Sarkis (1909-1977) American				
oil	1	2,000	2,000	2,000
SARLUIS, Leonard (1874-1949) French				
oil	2	823-2,975	1,899	823
wc/d	1	4,375	4,375	4,375
SARMENTO, Juliao (1948-) Portuguese				
oil	3	3,000-18,130	12,043	15,000
wc/d	1	3,895	3,895	3,895
SARONI, Sergio (1935-1991) Italian				
oil	2	1,555-11,094	6,324	1,555
SARRI, Sergio (1938-) Italian				
oil	8	922-2,148	1,462	1,424
SARSONY, Robert (1938-) American				
oil	2	650-1,900	1,275	650
SARTANI, Arie (1920-) Israeli				
oil	1	2,600	2,600	2,600
SARTHOU, Maurice (1911-2000) French				
oil	3	760-900	826	818
wc/d	1	541	541	541
SARTORE, Hugo (1935-) Uruguayan				
oil	2	800-2,000	1,400	800
SARTORELLI, Francesco (1856-1939) Italian				
oil	2	1,576-6,370	3,973	1,576
SARTORI, Augusto (1880-1957) Swiss				
oil	2	4,811-16,035	10,423	4,811
SARTORI, Federico (1865-1938) Italian				
oil	1	1,458	1,458	1,458
SARTORI, Johann Conrad (fl.1637-?) Italian				
wc/d	1	2,290	2,290	2,290
SARTORIO, Giulio Aristide (1861-1932) Italian				
oil	1	9,555	9,555	9,555
wc/d	2	3,279-25,767	14,523	3,279
SARTORIUS, Francis (elder) (1734-1804) British				
oil	3	6,475-18,000	11,938	11,340
SARTORIUS, Francis (younger) (1777-?) British				
oil	1	3,000	3,000	3,000
SARTORIUS, John Francis (c.1775-1831) British				
oil	4	2,991-132,000	38,872	4,500
SARTORIUS, John Nott (1759-1828) British				
oil	10	3,402-84,480	19,570	9,500
SARTORIUS, William (18th C) British				
oil	4	2,289-59,459	24,359	3,560
SASNAL, Wilhelm (1972-) ?				
oil	11	10,000-170,000	70,430	77,700
wc/d	5	6,200-10,000	8,540	9,500
SASPORTAS, Yehudit (1969-) Israeli				
oil	1	5,500	5,500	5,500
SASSENBROUCK, Achille van (1886-1979) Belgian				
oil	8	693-3,337	1,591	1,210
wc/d	1	479	479	479
SASSETTA, Stefano di Giovanni di (1392-c.1451) Italian				
oil	1	1,000,000	1,000,000	1,000,000
SASSO, Antonio (19th C) Italian				
oil	1	4,250	4,250	4,250
SASSOFERRATO (1609-1685) Italian				
oil	7	25,243-328,700	88,404	48,411
SASSONE, Marco (1942-) Italian				
oil	1	1,000	1,000	1,000
SASSU, Aligi (1912-2000) Italian				
oil	25	1,551-45,308	13,359	8,919
wc/d	16	922-28,634	4,563	2,827
SATO, Key (1906-1978) Japanese				
oil	4	717-4,770	2,490	1,308

Name	No.	Price Range	Average	Median
SATOMI, Munetsugu (20th C) Japanese				
oil	1	5,597	5,597	5,597
SATOR, Isa (20th C) French				
wc/d	1	2,189	2,189	2,189
SATTERLEE, Walter (1844-1908) American				
oil	1	1,000	1,000	1,000
SATTERTHWAITE, Cliff (20th C) American				
oil	2	1,900-2,400	2,150	1,900
SATTLER, Hermann (1892-1945) German				
oil	1	1,334	1,334	1,334
SATTLER, Hubert (1817-1904) Austrian				
oil	3	841-1,784	1,180	916
SAUBERLI, Michelle (20th C) ?				
oil	1	3,503	3,503	3,503
SAUBERT, Tom (1950-) American				
oil	1	2,000	2,000	2,000
SAUBIDET, Tito (1891-1953) Argentinian				
oil	5	1,120-2,460	1,967	2,015
wc/d	8	1,790-14,000	5,970	3,140
SAUER, Walter (1889-1927) Belgian				
wc/d	10	882-15,288	8,433	9,031
SAUERBRUCH, Hans (1910-) German				
wc/d	2	1,034-3,405	2,219	1,034
SAUERWEIN, Frank P (1871-1910) American				
oil	1	1,000	1,000	1,000
SAUGER, Amelie (?-1951) French				
wc/d	1	2,185	2,185	2,185
SAUGY, Louis (1863-?) French				
oil	1	4,052	4,052	4,052
SAUL, F (19th C) ?				
3D	2	4,500-12,000	8,250	4,500
SAUL, Peter (1934-) American				
oil	1	28,703	28,703	28,703
wc/d	3	9,500-20,713	14,854	14,351
SAULO, Georges Ernest (1865-?) French				
3D	1	2,784	2,784	2,784
SAUNDERS, Ann (19th C) British				
oil	1	1,505	1,505	1,505
SAUNDERS, S M (20th C) American				
oil	1	3,250	3,250	3,250
SAURA, Antonio (1930-1998) Spanish				
oil	15	29,224-246,400	101,781	70,800
wc/d	6	7,714-58,820	21,103	9,414
SAURFELT, Leonard (1840-?) French				
oil	4	1,286-4,524	3,022	2,435
SAUTER, H (?) ?				
oil	1	2,768	2,768	2,768
SAUTS, Dirck (17th C) Dutch				
oil	1	72,616	72,616	72,616
SAUVAGE, François Phillippe (19th C) French				
oil	1	2,385	2,385	2,385
SAUVAGE, Philippe François (19th C) French				
oil	2	400-6,500	3,450	400
SAUVAIGE, Marcel Louis (?-1927) French				
oil	1	3,600	3,600	3,600
SAUVAIGO, Martin (19/20th C) ?				
oil	1	1,757	1,757	1,757
SAUX, J le (?) ?				
oil	1	1,860	1,860	1,860
SAUZAY, Adrien Jacques (1841-1928) French				
oil	1	4,712	4,712	4,712
SAVAGE, Anne (1896-1971) Canadian				
oil	3	7,934-26,237	14,186	8,389
SAVAGE, Augusta Christine (1900-1962) American				
3D	1	10,000	10,000	10,000
SAVAL, Alex (20th C) French				
oil	1	1,200	1,200	1,200
SAVATER, Juan Carlos (1953-) Spanish				
oil	1	1,414	1,414	1,414
SAVELLI, Angelo (1911-1995) Italian				
oil	1	3,500	3,500	3,500
wc/d	1	937	937	937

Name	No.	Price Range	Average	Median
SAVERY, Roeland (1576-1639) Dutch				
oil	3	14,317-119,230	64,699	60,550
SAVERYS, Albert (1886-1964) Belgian				
oil	22	1,052-27,441	8,258	6,115
wc/d	3	602-2,873	1,876	2,153
SAVIADJUK, Mathewsie (1950-) North American				
3D	1	1,687	1,687	1,687
SAVIGNY, Paul (20th C) French				
oil	1	5,075	5,075	5,075
SAVILLE, Jenny (1970-) British				
oil	2	45,760-111,000	78,380	45,760
SAVIN, Maurice (1894-1973) French				
oil	8	476-6,674	2,306	1,315
SAVINIO, Alberto (1891-1952) Italian				
oil	2	8,269-737,823	373,046	8,269
wc/d	1	108,129	108,129	108,129
SAVINIO, Ruggero (1934-) Italian				
oil	1	6,361	6,361	6,361
SAVINOV, Yuri Alexandrovich (1929-1997) Russian				
oil	1	2,790	2,790	2,790
SAVIO, Francesco Lo (1935-1963) Italian				
oil	1	192,370	192,370	192,370
3D	1	150,450	150,450	150,450
SAVITSKY, Georgy Konstantinovich (1887-1949) Russian				
oil	1	93,000	93,000	93,000
SAVITSKY, Jack (1910-1991) American				
oil	5	800-2,400	1,470	1,500
wc/d	3	400-600	491	475
SAVRASOV, Aleksei Kondratievitch (1830-1897) Russian				
oil	2	86,000-613,800	349,900	86,000
SAVRY, Hendrick (1823-1907) Dutch				
oil	4	1,878-3,607	2,621	1,998
SAVY, Max (1918-) French?				
oil	3	850-2,038	1,442	1,438
SAWERT, Karl (1888-?) German				
oil	1	1,196	1,196	1,196
SAWREY, Hugh (1923-1999) Australian				
oil	1	1,454	1,454	1,454
SAWYER, Clifton Howard (1896-1966) American				
oil	1	2,500	2,500	2,500
SAWYER, Helen (1900-1999) American				
oil	1	2,900	2,900	2,900
SAY, Frederick Richard (c.1827-1860) British				
oil	1	1,322	1,322	1,322
SAYRE, Fred Grayson (1879-1938) American				
oil	4	2,750-6,500	4,187	3,250
SCACCABAROZZI, Antonio (1936-) Italian				
oil	3	1,432-2,028	1,750	1,790
wc/d	2	1,821-2,063	1,942	1,821
SCACCIATI, Andrea (1642-1704) Italian				
oil	2	15,000-41,520	28,260	15,000
SCAFFAI, Luigi (1837-?) Italian				
oil	2	9,000-24,000	16,500	9,000
SCAGLIA, Cesare (1866-1944) Italian				
oil	1	12,103	12,103	12,103
SCAGLIA, Michele (1859-1918) Italian				
oil	1	1,211	1,211	1,211
SCAGLIONE, Raffaele (1945-) Italian				
oil	1	1,176	1,176	1,176
SCALCO, Giorgio (1929-) Italian				
oil	1	4,595	4,595	4,595
SCANAVINO, Emilio (1922-1986) Italian				
oil	42	1,908-53,429	16,635	11,712
wc/d	20	492-19,667	4,069	2,108
3D	4	2,035-7,633	5,996	7,159
SCANLAN, Robert Richard (c.1801-1876) Irish				
wc/d	6	550-7,068	1,895	740
SCARABELLO, Angelo (1711-1795) Italian				
3D	1	20,585	20,585	20,585
SCARBOROUGH, Joe (1938-) British				
oil	4	1,748-4,600	3,202	2,800
wc/d	1	736	736	736

Name	No.	Price Range	Average	Median
SCARBROUGH, Frank William (fl.1896-1939) British				
wc/d	13	850-17,765	5,194	3,872
SCARCELLINO, Ippolito (1551-1620) Italian				
oil	4	5,622-64,216	29,308	19,110
SCARLETT, Rolph (1889-1984) American				
oil	1	22,000	22,000	22,000
wc/d	3	850-1,600	1,216	1,200
SCARPITTA, Salvatore (1919-) American				
oil	6	17,897-168,150	52,492	25,442
wc/d	2	186,633-267,143	226,888	186,633
3D	4	48,340-150,000	80,385	52,800
SCARVELLI, Spyridon (1868-1942) Greek				
oil	1	8,996	8,996	8,996
wc/d	8	750-10,034	4,271	2,805
SCATIZZI, Sergio (1918-) Italian				
oil	52	476-4,243	1,351	1,058
wc/d	2	485-615	550	485
SCATTOLA, Ferruccio (1873-1950) Italian				
oil	2	1,784-5,178	3,481	1,784
SCAUFLAIRE, Edgar (1893-1960) Belgian				
oil	12	656-15,534	3,906	1,130
wc/d	8	567-3,092	1,327	882
SCEMA, Viviane (20th C) French?				
wc/d	1	1,215	1,215	1,215
SCHAAP, Hendrik (1878-1955) Dutch				
oil	1	2,003	2,003	2,003
SCHABELITZ, Rudolph Frederick (1884-1959) American				
oil	1	1,600	1,600	1,600
SCHACHINGER, Gabriel (1850-1912) German				
oil	2	19,942-30,729	25,335	19,942
SCHACHNER, Therese (1890-c.1930) Austrian				
oil	1	1,549	1,549	1,549
wc/d	1	722	722	722
SCHACHT, Rudolf (1900-1974) German				
oil	2	1,252-1,312	1,282	1,252
SCHAD, Christian (1894-1982) German				
oil	4	41,732-740,000	276,284	146,404
wc/d	3	6,485-407,000	149,150	33,966
SCHAD, Robert (1953-) German				
3D	1	2,945	2,945	2,945
SCHADE, Karl Martin (1862-1954) Austrian				
oil	1	1,543	1,543	1,543
SCHADOW, Wilhelm von (1788-1862) German				
oil	2	90,306-156,400	123,353	90,306
SCHAEFELS, Hendrik Frans (1827-1904) Belgian				
oil	1	3,507	3,507	3,507
wc/d	1	1,338	1,338	1,338
SCHAEFER, Carl Fellman (1903-1995) Canadian				
oil	5	978-56,730	18,504	15,398
wc/d	7	705-2,821	1,587	1,297
SCHAEFFER, August (1833-1916) Austrian				
oil	2	2,752-8,000	5,376	2,752
wc/d	1	1,210	1,210	1,210
SCHAEFFER, Henri (1900-1975) French				
oil	1	1,386	1,386	1,386
SCHAEFFER, Mead (1898-1980) American				
wc/d	1	18,000	18,000	18,000
SCHAEFFLER, Franz Matthias (?-1757) German				
wc/d	1	8,836	8,836	8,836
SCHAEFLER, Fritz (1888-1954) German				
wc/d	5	837-4,685	2,117	1,414
SCHAEP, Aime (19th C) Belgian?				
oil	1	6,592	6,592	6,592
SCHAEP, Henri Adolphe (1826-1870) Dutch				
oil	2	1,800-20,880	11,340	1,800
wc/d	1	2,534	2,534	2,534
SCHAEPKENS, Theodor (1810-1883) Dutch				
oil	1	1,232	1,232	1,232
SCHAFER, Dirk (1864-1941) Dutch				
wc/d	1	1,576	1,576	1,576
SCHAFER, F F (1839-1927) American				
oil	1	2,531	2,531	2,531

Name	No.	Price Range	Average	Median
SCHAFER, Frederick Ferdinand (1839-1927) American				
oil	13	850-22,500	6,816	4,000
SCHAFER, Henri (?-c.1900) French?				
oil	3	1,575-4,255	2,742	2,397
SCHAFER, Henry Thomas (1854-1915) British				
oil	12	455-5,000	1,894	1,309
wc/d	4	696-1,600	1,327	1,447
SCHAFER, Philipp Otto (1868-?) German				
oil	1	4,597	4,597	4,597
SCHAFFER, Carolyn (20th C) American				
oil	1	1,100	1,100	1,100
SCHAFFER, Hans (?-1881) ?				
oil	1	3,312	3,312	3,312
SCHAGEN, Gerbrand Frederik van (1880-1968) Dutch				
oil	4	586-2,521	1,724	1,352
SCHAIK, Willem Henri van (1876-1938) Dutch				
oil	1	1,334	1,334	1,334
SCHALCK, Heinrich Franz (1791-1832) German				
wc/d	1	1,697	1,697	1,697
SCHALCKE, Cornelis Simonsz van der (1611-1671) Dutch				
oil	2	5,500-14,143	9,821	5,500
SCHALCKEN, Godfried (1643-1706) Dutch				
oil	2	1,576-14,013	7,794	1,576
SCHALIN, Greta (1897-1993) Finnish				
oil	3	2,225-3,279	2,615	2,342
SCHALL, Jean Frederic (1752-1825) French				
oil	4	3,884-17,300	9,211	6,473
SCHAMPHELEER, Edmond de (1824-1899) Belgian				
oil	3	760-4,208	1,979	971
SCHANTZ, Francis (20th C) American				
oil	1	1,300	1,300	1,300
SCHANTZ, Philip von (1928-1998) Swedish				
oil	1	3,490	3,490	3,490
wc/d	4	2,246-5,598	3,158	2,246
SCHAPER, Friedrich (1869-1956) German				
oil	11	1,127-6,392	2,363	1,764
SCHARER, Hans (1927-1997) Swiss				
oil	1	784	784	784
wc/d	4	534-6,088	3,010	1,255
SCHARF, Kenny (1958-) American				
oil	18	5,845-130,000	47,001	32,500
wc/d	1	4,800	4,800	4,800
SCHARFENBERG, Emanuel (1932-) German				
3D	1	6,181	6,181	6,181
SCHARFF, Erwin (1887-1955) German				
oil	1	466	466	466
wc/d	1	1,018	1,018	1,018
SCHARFF, William (1886-1959) Danish				
oil	6	566-4,526	2,556	1,132
wc/d	1	647	647	647
SCHARL, Josef (1896-1954) German				
wc/d	4	1,010-3,299	1,828	1,113
SCHARY, Saul (1904-1978) American				
oil	1	1,500	1,500	1,500
SCHATZ, Bezalel (1912-1978) Israeli				
oil	1	5,000	5,000	5,000
SCHATZ, Manfred (1925-) German				
oil	10	1,636-8,469	4,464	3,600
SCHATZ, Otto Rudolf (1901-1961) Austrian				
oil	1	11,571	11,571	11,571
wc/d	5	1,576-9,173	3,665	2,303
SCHAUMAN, Sigrid (1877-1979) Finnish				
oil	1	4,216	4,216	4,216
SCHAUMBURG, Jules (1839-1886) Belgian				
oil	1	59,840	59,840	59,840
SCHAUSS, Ferdinand (1832-1916) German				
oil	1	20,000	20,000	20,000
SCHAWINSKY, Xanti (1904-1979) Italian				
oil	3	2,679-4,676	3,359	2,724
SCHEDRIN, Sylvester Feodosievich (1791-1830) Russian				
oil	1	394,354	394,354	394,354

Name	No.	Price Range	Average	Median
SCHEERBOOM, Andries (1832-1891) Dutch				
oil	1	12,000	12,000	12,000
SCHEERES, Hendricus Johannes (1829-1864) Dutch				
oil	1	2,049	2,049	2,049
SCHEFFER VON LEONHARTSHOFF, Johann (1795-1822) Austrian				
wc/d	1	2,649	2,649	2,649
SCHEFFER, Ary (1795-1858) French				
oil	3	1,492-33,123	13,889	7,054
wc/d	1	790	790	790
SCHEFFER, Jean Gabriel (1797-1876) Swiss				
oil	1	3,816	3,816	3,816
SCHEGGI, Paolo (1940-1971) Italian				
oil	4	15,226-40,993	23,866	18,163
3D	6	14,630-34,600	20,861	19,418
SCHEIB, Hans (1949-) German				
3D	1	6,799	6,799	6,799
SCHEIBE, Edgar (1899-1977) German				
wc/d	1	2,438	2,438	2,438
SCHEIBE, Richard (1879-1964) German				
3D	11	2,421-28,027	9,903	6,615
SCHEIBEL, Greg (?) American				
oil	1	1,750	1,750	1,750
SCHEIBER, Hugo (1873-1950) Hungarian				
oil	5	1,671-69,200	16,193	2,272
wc/d	18	715-9,000	4,465	4,305
SCHEIBITZ, Thomas (1968-) German				
oil	10	16,000-260,000	106,170	70,000
wc/d	2	6,195-14,800	10,497	6,195
SCHEIBL, Hubert (1951-) Austrian				
oil	7	4,099-21,848	7,493	5,143
wc/d	1	844	844	844
SCHEIBNER, Vira B McIlrath (1889-1956) American				
oil	1	2,250	2,250	2,250
SCHEIDL, Franz Anton von (1731-1801) Austrian				
wc/d	3	436-8,325	4,770	5,550
SCHEIDL, Roman (1949-) Austrian				
oil	3	1,117-25,714	11,047	6,310
SCHEINS, Karl Ludwig (1808-1879) German				
oil	1	2,792	2,792	2,792
SCHEIWE, Walter (1892-1971) German				
oil	1	1,518	1,518	1,518
SCHELCK, Maurice (1906-1978) Belgian				
oil	7	783-3,827	2,162	2,472
SCHELENZ, Walter (1903-1987) German				
3D	1	2,827	2,827	2,827
SCHELFHOUT, A (1787-1870) Dutch				
oil	2	24,000-86,671	55,335	24,000
SCHELFHOUT, Andreas (1787-1870) Dutch				
oil	21	5,000-212,158	62,258	49,167
wc/d	2	1,060-1,171	1,115	1,060
SCHELL, Ludwig (1833-1913) German?				
oil	1	1,000	1,000	1,000
SCHELL, Susan Gertrude (1891-1970) American				
oil	2	2,600-5,000	3,800	2,600
SCHELLEIN, Karl (1820-1888) Austrian				
oil	1	2,431	2,431	2,431
SCHELLINKS, Willem (1627-1678) Dutch				
oil	2	2,959-15,419	9,189	2,959
SCHELOUMOFF, Athanasei (1912-1976) Russian				
oil	1	2,145	2,145	2,145
SCHELOUMOV, Athanas (1892-1983) Russian				
oil	10	450-3,053	1,474	1,285
SCHELVER, August Franz (1805-1844) German				
oil	2	54,184-120,408	87,296	54,184
SCHENCK, Bill (1947-) American				
oil	1	8,000	8,000	8,000
SCHENCK, P (18th C) German				
oil	1	10,283	10,283	10,283
SCHENDEL, Mira (1919-1988) Brazilian				
oil	1	240,000	240,000	240,000
wc/d	1	13,000	13,000	13,000

Name	No.	Price Range	Average	Median
SCHENDEL, Petrus van (1806-1870) Belgian				
oil	13	849-437,500	138,476	110,000
SCHENK, Christoph Daniel (1633-1691) German				
3D	2	43,250-180,000	111,625	43,250
SCHENK, Karl (1905-1973) Swiss				
oil	10	1,499-4,579	2,982	2,498
SCHENKER, Jacques Matthias (1854-1927) German				
oil	1	3,565	3,565	3,565
SCHENONE PUIG, Dolcey (1896-1952) Uruguayan?				
oil	1	2,900	2,900	2,900
SCHEPENS, Edmond (19/20th C) French?				
oil	1	13,993	13,993	13,993
SCHERER, Hermann (1893-1927) Swiss				
oil	1	304,425	304,425	304,425
SCHERFIG, Hans (1905-1979) Danish				
oil	3	6,083-15,754	10,605	9,980
wc/d	1	3,879	3,879	3,879
SCHERG, Gisele (20th C) French?				
wc/d	1	1,253	1,253	1,253
SCHERMAN, Tony (1950-) Canadian				
oil	2	14,000-16,000	15,000	14,000
wc/d	3	6,115-8,199	7,367	7,789
SCHERREWITZ, Johan (1868-1951) Dutch				
oil	11	1,918-21,194	9,344	6,799
wc/d	1	3,031	3,031	3,031
SCHERTEL, Josef (1810-1869) German				
oil	3	727-5,351	2,742	2,148
SCHETKY, John Christian (1778-1874) British				
oil	2	595-13,760	7,177	595
wc/d	3	515-1,566	957	792
SCHEUCHZER, Wilhelm (1803-1866) Swiss				
oil	1	6,370	6,370	6,370
wc/d	1	1,757	1,757	1,757
SCHEUERER, Julius (1859-1913) German				
oil	7	715-6,081	2,129	1,798
SCHEUERLEIN, Th (19th C) ?				
oil	1	1,555	1,555	1,555
SCHEUERMANN, Carl Georg (1803-1859) Danish				
oil	1	3,397	3,397	3,397
SCHEUREN, Caspar Johann Nepomuk (1810-1887) German				
oil	4	649-11,439	5,101	1,168
wc/d	1	2,795	2,795	2,795
SCHEURENBERG, Joseph (1846-1914) German				
oil	1	1,134	1,134	1,134
SCHIANCHI, Federico (1858-1919) Italian				
wc/d	3	1,295-2,088	1,724	1,790
SCHIAVINATO, Enrico (20th C) Italian				
oil	1	1,427	1,427	1,427
SCHIAVIO, Vincenzo (1888-1954) Italian				
oil	1	2,548	2,548	2,548
SCHIAVONE, Andrea (1522-c.1563) Italian				
oil	1	100,000	100,000	100,000
SCHIAVONI, Augusto (1893-1942) Argentinian				
oil	1	6,500	6,500	6,500
SCHIAVONI, Natale (1777-1858) Italian				
oil	2	5,845-30,102	17,973	5,845
wc/d	1	970	970	970
SCHICK, Rudolf (1840-1887) German				
oil	1	4,077	4,077	4,077
SCHIEDGES, Peter Paulus (elder) (1812-1876) Dutch				
oil	4	2,411-9,644	5,102	4,033
SCHIEDGES, Peter Paulus (younger) (1860-1922) Dutch				
oil	3	518-3,687	1,617	647
SCHIELE, Egon (1890-1918) Austrian				
oil	5	88,800-19,425,000	4,536,680	1,153,103
wc/d	38	14,640-6,549,000	657,240	200,276
3D	1	2,928	2,928	2,928
SCHIELE, H (?) ?				
oil	1	1,588	1,588	1,588
SCHIERENBERG, Tai Shan (1962-) British				
oil	3	4,488-12,744	7,278	4,602

Name	No.	Price Range	Average	Median
SCHIESS, Ernst Traugott (1872-1919) Swiss				
oil	2	916-1,998	1,457	916
SCHIESS, Hans Rudolf (1904-1978) Swiss				
oil	1	1,221	1,221	1,221
SCHIESS, Traugott (1834-1869) Swiss				
oil	2	1,294-5,097	3,195	1,294
SCHIESTL, Matthaus (1869-1939) German				
oil	2	2,498-3,395	2,946	2,498
SCHIESTL-ARDING, Albert (20th C) ?				
oil	3	847-1,452	1,237	1,414
SCHIETZOLD, Rudolph (1842-1908) German				
oil	1	7,905	7,905	7,905
SCHIEVELKAMP, Helmuth (1849-?) German				
3D	1	3,395	3,395	3,395
SCHIFANO, Mario (1934-1998) Italian				
oil	110	1,767-167,034	19,482	9,062
wc/d	47	478-353,425	11,225	2,121
3D	2	2,760-7,283	5,021	2,760
SCHIFFER, Anton (1811-1876) Austrian				
oil	3	820-16,397	9,555	11,449
SCHIFFERLE, Claudia (1955-) Swiss				
oil	1	1,062	1,062	1,062
SCHIFFNER, T (20th C) German				
3D	1	5,500	5,500	5,500
SCHILBACH, Johann Heinrich (1798-1851) German				
wc/d	1	5,890	5,890	5,890
SCHILCHER, Hans (1879-?) German				
oil	1	817	817	817
wc/d	1	1,458	1,458	1,458
SCHILDER, Andrei Nikolaevich (1861-1919) Russian				
oil	4	13,000-118,479	41,121	14,087
SCHILDKNECHT, Georg (1850-1939) German				
oil	1	1,014	1,014	1,014
SCHILDT, Gary (1938-) American				
oil	3	600-10,000	5,366	5,500
3D	1	2,500	2,500	2,500
SCHILKING, Heinrich (1815-1895) German				
oil	1	1,581	1,581	1,581
SCHILL, Emil (1870-1958) Swiss				
oil	6	395-2,498	1,215	941
SCHILLE, Alice (1969-1955) American				
wc/d	5	5,500-20,000	9,080	6,400
SCHILLER, Andreas (1963-) German				
oil	1	3,343	3,343	3,343
SCHILLER, Charlotte von (19th C) ?				
wc/d	1	1,459	1,459	1,459
SCHILLER, Frits (1886-1971) Dutch				
oil	1	8,136	8,136	8,136
SCHILLMARK, Nils (1745-1804) Finnish				
oil	1	5,914	5,914	5,914
SCHILT, Martinus (1867-1921) Dutch				
oil	3	386-4,581	2,993	4,014
SCHIMMEL, Wilhelm (1817-1890) American/German				
3D	3	7,500-11,000	9,333	9,500
SCHINDLER, Carl (1821-1842) Austrian				
wc/d	1	1,767	1,767	1,767
SCHINDLER, Emil Jakob (1842-1892) Austrian				
oil	3	4,158-16,993	12,310	15,779
SCHINNERER, Adolf (1876-1949) German				
oil	1	1,929	1,929	1,929
SCHIOLER, Inge (1908-1971) Swedish				
oil	21	3,308-127,397	28,610	15,268
wc/d	16	622-3,304	1,513	1,463
SCHIOTT, August (1823-1895) Danish				
oil	1	1,746	1,746	1,746
SCHIOTTZ-JENSEN, N F (1855-1941) Danish				
oil	10	1,265-3,474	2,010	1,956
SCHIOTTZ-JENSEN, Niels F (1855-1941) Danish				
oil	4	1,800-34,779	11,199	4,110
SCHIPPERS, Joseph (1868-1950) Belgian				
oil	3	729-4,973	2,696	2,386

Name	No.	Price Range	Average	Median
SCHIPPERUS, Pieter Adrianus (1840-1929) Dutch				
oil	2	1,688-4,633	3,160	1,688
wc/d	2	876-900	888	876
SCHIRMER, August Wilhelm (1802-1866) German				
oil	1	3,137	3,137	3,137
SCHIRMER, Johann Wilhelm (1807-1863) German				
oil	1	2,666	2,666	2,666
wc/d	3	1,073-4,477	2,481	1,893
SCHIRREN, Ferdinand (1872-1944) Belgian				
oil	1	14,027	14,027	14,027
wc/d	14	1,051-5,611	3,152	3,131
SCHITZ, Jules Nicolas (1817-1871) French				
oil	1	1,415	1,415	1,415
SCHIVE, Jacob Oxholm (1847-1912) Norwegian				
oil	1	9,000	9,000	9,000
SCHIVERT, Victor (1863-?) Rumanian				
oil	4	596-3,810	1,503	600
SCHIWETZ, Edward M (1898-1984) American				
wc/d	4	950-5,000	2,862	2,000
SCHJERFBECK, Helene (1862-1946) Finnish				
oil	2	15,429-202,400	108,914	15,429
wc/d	4	6,115-82,808	26,936	8,281
SCHLANKHWEIN, Johann (17th C) German				
wc/d	1	1,401	1,401	1,401
SCHLATER, Alexander Georg (1834-1879) German				
oil	1	11,125	11,125	11,125
SCHLATTER, Ernst Emil (1883-1954) Swiss				
oil	2	2,105-2,591	2,348	2,105
SCHLAWING, Adolf (1888-?) German				
oil	2	586-1,757	1,171	586
SCHLECHTA, Adalbert (18th C) Bohemian				
oil	1	1,001	1,001	1,001
SCHLEGEL, Friedrich (1865-1935) German				
oil	1	1,994	1,994	1,994
SCHLEICH, August (1814-1865) German				
oil	1	4,770	4,770	4,770
SCHLEICH, Eduard (19th C) German				
oil	2	2,121-2,472	2,296	2,121
SCHLEICH, Eduard (elder) (1812-1874) German				
oil	6	4,001-14,137	7,499	5,724
SCHLEICH, Eduard (younger) (1853-1893) German				
oil	2	2,311-18,828	10,569	2,311
SCHLEICH, Robert (1845-1934) German				
oil	4	730-3,263	1,724	1,004
wc/d	1	608	608	608
SCHLEICHER, Carl (19th C) Austrian				
oil	7	643-11,340	4,193	4,238
SCHLEIME, Cornelia (1953-) ?				
wc/d	8	1,178-17,671	4,408	2,342
SCHLEMM, Betty Lou (1934-) American				
oil	2	500-1,400	950	500
wc/d	1	900	900	900
SCHLEMMER, Oskar (1888-1943) German				
oil	6	12,000-2,200,000	567,933	78,871
wc/d	3	1,335-17,568	10,205	11,712
SCHLESINGER, Adam Johan (1759-1829) German				
oil	1	1,130	1,130	1,130
SCHLESINGER, Felix (1833-1910) German				
oil	3	3,750-22,500	13,101	13,053
wc/d	1	3,747	3,747	3,747
SCHLESINGER, Henri-Guillaume (1814-1893) French				
oil	3	12,489-35,959	22,529	19,140
SCHLESINGER, Samuel (1896-1986) Israeli				
oil	2	4,800-9,500	7,150	4,800
wc/d	1	900	900	900
SCHLICHTEN, Jan Philipp van (1681-1745) Dutch				
oil	1	1,827	1,827	1,827
SCHLICHTER, Rudolf (1890-1955) German				
wc/d	10	717-21,120	8,730	8,096
SCHLICHTING CARLSEN, Carl (1852-1903) Danish				
oil	2	1,549-2,200	1,874	1,549

Name	No.	Price Range	Average	Median
SCHLICHTKRULL, J C (1866-1945) Danish				
oil	1	3,175	3,175	3,175
SCHLICK, Benst (19th C) Italian				
oil	1	1,295	1,295	1,295
SCHLIECKER, August Eduard (1833-1911) German				
oil	1	5,408	5,408	5,408
SCHLIEF, Heinrich (1894-1974) German				
oil	1	4,712	4,712	4,712
SCHLIESSER, Thomas (20th C) ?				
wc/d	1	1,414	1,414	1,414
SCHLIPF, Eugen (1869-?) German				
3D	1	5,092	5,092	5,092
SCHLIPPE, Alexey von (1915-1988) Russian				
oil	1	3,527	3,527	3,527
SCHLITT, Heinrich (1849-1923) German				
oil	7	974-12,979	5,718	4,568
wc/d	1	787	787	787
SCHLITZ, J (20th C) ?				
3D	1	8,000	8,000	8,000
SCHLOBACH, Willy (1865-1951) Belgian				
oil	2	52,800-237,600	145,200	52,800
SCHLOGL, Josef von (1851-1913) Austrian				
oil	3	1,089-3,737	2,600	2,975
SCHLOSSER, Gerard (1931-) French				
oil	10	8,949-32,364	17,348	15,969
wc/d	6	777-2,420	1,396	1,169
SCHLOSSER-WEITZ, Irene (1922-) German				
oil	1	6,833	6,833	6,833
SCHMALIX, Hubert (1952-) Austrian				
oil	13	1,199-18,643	5,699	3,395
wc/d	8	400-2,548	1,312	1,169
SCHMALZ, Carl Nelson (1926-) American				
wc/d	1	1,400	1,400	1,400
SCHMALZ, Herbert Gustave (1856-1935) British				
oil	2	9,405-24,310	16,857	9,405
SCHMALZIGAUG, Ferdinand (1847-1902) German				
oil	1	3,567	3,567	3,567
SCHMALZIGAUG, Jules (1882-1917) Belgian				
oil	1	1,401	1,401	1,401
wc/d	2	602-2,517	1,559	602
SCHMERLING, Oskar (1863-1938) Russian				
oil	1	17,517	17,517	17,517
SCHMETZ, Wilhelm (1890-?) German				
oil	1	1,084	1,084	1,084
SCHMID, David Alois (1791-1861) Swiss				
wc/d	2	2,352-2,352	2,352	2,352
SCHMID, Emil (1891-1978) Swiss				
oil	1	1,619	1,619	1,619
SCHMID, Erich (1908-1984) Austrian				
oil	2	1,085-1,440	1,262	1,085
SCHMID, Johann (19th C) ?				
wc/d	1	1,014	1,014	1,014
SCHMID, Julius (1854-1935) Austrian				
oil	3	4,197-19,079	13,092	16,000
SCHMID, Mathias (1835-1923) Austrian				
oil	3	968-12,959	8,535	11,678
SCHMID, Richard (1934-) American				
oil	6	3,500-40,000	15,500	4,500
SCHMID, Wilhelm (1892-1971) Swiss				
oil	4	1,903-8,819	4,158	2,108
wc/d	2	457-495	476	457
SCHMIDLIN, Adolf (1868-?) German				
oil	1	1,276	1,276	1,276
SCHMIDT (?) ?				
oil	1	3,330	3,330	3,330
SCHMIDT, A P (19/20th C) ?				
oil	2	1,081-1,521	1,301	1,081
SCHMIDT, Albert (1883-1970) Swiss				
oil	5	2,498-16,743	7,482	3,747
wc/d	1	4,947	4,947	4,947

Name	No.	Price Range	Average	Median
SCHMIDT, Anton Karl (1887-1974) Austrian				
oil	1	818	818	818
wc/d	1	847	847	847
SCHMIDT, Bernhard (1712-1782) Austrian				
oil	1	3,514	3,514	3,514
SCHMIDT, Carl (1885-1969) American				
oil	3	375-3,000	1,425	900
SCHMIDT, Christian (1835-?) German				
oil	1	6,500	6,500	6,500
SCHMIDT, Eduard (1806-1862) German				
oil	1	1,200	1,200	1,200
SCHMIDT, George (1944-) American				
oil	1	1,000	1,000	1,000
SCHMIDT, Hans W (1859-1950) German				
oil	1	5,080	5,080	5,080
wc/d	1	584	584	584
SCHMIDT, Harold von (1893-1982) American				
oil	1	13,000	13,000	13,000
SCHMIDT, Izaak Riewert (1781-1826) Dutch				
wc/d	1	1,272	1,272	1,272
SCHMIDT, Jay (1929-) American				
oil	1	4,750	4,750	4,750
SCHMIDT, Johann Heinrich (1749-1829) German				
wc/d	1	3,560	3,560	3,560
SCHMIDT, Johann Martin (1718-1801) German				
oil	4	2,378-40,432	17,884	4,450
SCHMIDT, Karl (1890-1962) American				
oil	6	650-100,000	18,900	3,250
wc/d	1	600	600	600
SCHMIDT, Mary Jane (20th C) American				
oil	1	1,500	1,500	1,500
SCHMIDT, Olle (1960-) Swedish				
oil	1	1,850	1,850	1,850
SCHMIDT, Theodor (1855-?) German				
oil	1	1,200	1,200	1,200
SCHMIDT, Tim (20th C) American?				
oil	1	1,900	1,900	1,900
SCHMIDT, Werner (1888-1964) German				
oil	1	1,236	1,236	1,236
SCHMIDT, Willem Hendrik (1809-1849) Dutch				
oil	1	3,012	3,012	3,012
SCHMIDT-HAMBURG, Richard (20th C) German				
oil	1	1,936	1,936	1,936
SCHMIDT-HOFER, Otto (19/20th C) German				
3D	1	2,667	2,667	2,667
SCHMIDT-KESTNER, Erich (1877-?) German				
3D	1	15,120	15,120	15,120
SCHMIDT-PEDERSEN, Lene (20th C) Danish?				
oil	1	1,137	1,137	1,137
SCHMIDT-ROTTLUFF, Karl (1884-1976) German				
oil	1	95,408	95,408	95,408
wc/d	35	4,000-234,247	30,766	19,082
SCHMIDT-WEHRLIN, Emile (19/20th C) ?				
oil	1	36,000	36,000	36,000
SCHMIECHEN (19th C) German?				
oil	1	2,422	2,422	2,422
SCHMIED, François Louis (1873-1941) Swiss				
oil	1	173,571	173,571	173,571
SCHMIEGELOW, Pedro Ernst Johann (1863-1943) German				
oil	1	1,901	1,901	1,901
SCHMIEL, Julius (fl.1838-1842) German				
oil	1	3,534	3,534	3,534
SCHMIT, J H (?) ?				
3D	1	3,884	3,884	3,884
SCHMITSON, Teutwart (1830-1863) German				
oil	1	7,531	7,531	7,531
SCHMITT, Oskar (19/20th C) German				
oil	2	787-1,267	1,027	787
SCHMITZ, A (1825-1894) German				
oil	1	2,008	2,008	2,008
SCHMITZ, Anton (1855-?) German				
oil	1	1,946	1,946	1,946

Name	No.	Price Range	Average	Median
SCHMITZ, C L (19th C) German				
oil	1	1,907	1,907	1,907
SCHMITZ, Hans (1886-1977) German				
3D	2	3,416-3,534	3,475	3,416
SCHMITZ-PLEIS, Carl (?) ?				
oil	1	11,781	11,781	11,781
SCHMITZBERGER, Josef (1851-?) German				
oil	2	6,589-12,103	9,346	6,589
SCHMOLL, Ferdinand (20th C) ?				
oil	1	1,000	1,000	1,000
SCHMUTZLER, Leopold (1864-1941) German				
oil	9	850-4,176	2,148	1,900
SCHNABEL, Julian (1951-) American				
oil	13	4,000-170,000	58,148	45,000
3D	1	170,000	170,000	170,000
SCHNACKENBERG, Walter (1880-1961) German				
wc/d	3	955-2,457	1,682	1,636
SCHNAEBLE, J B (18th C) ?				
oil	1	3,162	3,162	3,162
SCHNARRENBERGER, Wilhelm (1892-?) German				
oil	4	3,090-4,673	3,980	3,708
SCHNARS-ALQUIST, Hugo (1855-1939) German				
oil	2	1,767-27,000	14,383	1,767
SCHNAUDER, Reinhard (1856-1923) German				
3D	1	1,780	1,780	1,780
SCHNAUDER, Richard George (1886-1956) German				
3D	1	2,769	2,769	2,769
SCHNEIDAU, Christian von (1893-1976) American				
oil	4	2,600-7,500	5,900	6,500
SCHNEIDER, Alexander (1870-1927) Russian				
oil	1	94,500	94,500	94,500
wc/d	1	1,089	1,089	1,089
SCHNEIDER, Amable (1824-1884) French				
oil	1	5,271	5,271	5,271
SCHNEIDER, Arthur (1866-1942) American				
oil	1	3,750	3,750	3,750
SCHNEIDER, Caspar (1753-1839) German				
oil	1	2,656	2,656	2,656
SCHNEIDER, Georg (1759-1842) German				
oil	1	2,504	2,504	2,504
SCHNEIDER, Gerard (1896-1986) Swiss				
oil	24	1,670-61,953	15,518	9,833
wc/d	19	683-13,938	5,068	2,581
SCHNEIDER, Herbert (1924-1984) German				
oil	1	2,160	2,160	2,160
SCHNEIDER, Otto Henry (1865-1950) American				
oil	1	4,000	4,000	4,000
SCHNEIDER, Theophile (1872-1960) American				
oil	1	1,900	1,900	1,900
SCHNEIDT, Max (1858-1937) German				
oil	1	1,350	1,350	1,350
SCHNELL, David (1971-) German				
oil	1	120,000	120,000	120,000
SCHNIDER, Adolf (1890-1961) Swiss				
oil	1	1,145	1,145	1,145
SCHNIER, Jacques (1898-1988) American				
3D	1	30,000	30,000	30,000
SCHNITZLER, Christa von (1922-) German				
3D	1	3,045	3,045	3,045
SCHNORR VON CAROLSFELD, Julius (1794-1872) German				
wc/d	14	707-22,384	7,047	3,700
SCHNORR VON CAROLSFELD, Julius and Ludwig (19th C) German				
wc/d	1	11,781	11,781	11,781
SCHNYDER, Albert (1898-1989) German				
oil	9	1,221-13,322	6,322	6,244
wc/d	5	534-3,035	1,630	1,166
SCHOBEL, Georg (1860-1941) German				
oil	1	4,671	4,671	4,671
wc/d	1	636	636	636
SCHOBINGER, Karl Friedrich (1879-1951) Swiss				
oil	1	2,081	2,081	2,081
wc/d	1	470	470	470

Name	No.	Price Range	Average	Median
SCHODL, Max (1834-1921) Austrian				
oil	3	2,384-12,055	6,237	4,274
SCHOEFF, Johannes (1608-1666) Dutch				
oil	3	9,391-19,273	14,225	14,013
SCHOELLER, Johann Christian (1782-1851) Austrian				
wc/d	2	1,334-1,576	1,455	1,334
SCHOELLHORN, Hans Karl (1892-1983) Swiss				
oil	10	495-1,598	813	734
wc/d	1	624	624	624
SCHOEVAERDTS, Mathys (c.1665-1723) Flemish				
oil	4	20,566-200,000	67,864	24,975
SCHOFFER, Nicolas (1912-) French				
oil	1	1,529	1,529	1,529
3D	5	2,589-35,084	10,705	3,576
SCHOFIELD, Dan (20th C) American				
wc/d	1	1,200	1,200	1,200
SCHOFIELD, E H (19th C) American				
oil	1	2,800	2,800	2,800
SCHOFIELD, John William (1865-1944) British				
wc/d	1	1,225	1,225	1,225
SCHOFIELD, Walter Elmer (1867-1944) American				
oil	6	7,000-30,000	18,691	11,651
SCHOLANDER, Fredrik (1816-1881) Swedish				
wc/d	1	1,745	1,745	1,745
SCHOLDER, Fritz (1937-2005) American				
oil	7	3,500-13,000	7,857	8,000
SCHOLL, John (1827-1916) American				
3D	1	170,000	170,000	170,000
SCHOLTEN, Frederik Carl Emil von (1786-1873) Danish				
wc/d	1	15,000	15,000	15,000
SCHOLZ, Georg (1890-1945) German				
oil	1	148,000	148,000	148,000
SCHOLZ, Heinrich Karl (1880-?) Austrian				
3D	1	1,909	1,909	1,909
SCHOLZ, Werner (1898-1982) German				
oil	4	2,356-11,712	6,153	4,685
SCHON, Friedrich Wilhelm (1810-1868) German				
oil	1	4,411	4,411	4,411
SCHONBERGER, Alfred Karl Julius Otto von (1845-?) German				
oil	4	1,420-2,827	2,249	2,277
SCHONBERGER, Armand (1885-1974) Hungarian				
wc/d	1	1,090	1,090	1,090
SCHONBERGER, Lorenz Adolf (1768-1847) German				
oil	1	5,021	5,021	5,021
SCHONEBECK, Eugen (1936-) German				
wc/d	1	10,813	10,813	10,813
SCHONFELD, Johann Heinrich (1609-1682) German				
oil	1	1,958	1,958	1,958
SCHONIAN, Alfred (1856-1936) German				
oil	2	942-1,703	1,322	942
SCHONING, Dietrich (1931-) German				
3D	1	3,527	3,527	3,527
SCHONK, Jan (1889-1976) Dutch				
3D	1	2,116	2,116	2,116
SCHONLEBER, Gustav (1851-1917) German				
oil	5	1,790-39,130	10,965	4,519
wc/d	1	1,034	1,034	1,034
SCHONN, Alois (1826-1897) Austrian				
oil	2	18,000-25,479	21,739	18,000
SCHONREITHER, Georg (19th C) Austrian				
oil	1	4,633	4,633	4,633
SCHONROCK, Julius (1835-?) German				
oil	1	1,184	1,184	1,184
SCHONZEIT, Ben (1942-) American				
oil	1	26,714	26,714	26,714
SCHOOFS, Rudolf (1932-) German				
oil	1	2,392	2,392	2,392
wc/d	1	607	607	607
SCHOONHOVEN VAN BEURDEN, Alexander Franciscus van (1883-1963) Dutch				
oil	1	1,199	1,199	1,199

Name	No.	Price Range	Average	Median
SCHOONHOVEN, Jan J (1914-1994) Dutch				
oil	1	48,301	48,301	48,301
wc/d	17	1,767-93,514	11,407	3,534
3D	1	127,397	127,397	127,397
SCHOONOVER, Frank E (1877-1972) American				
oil	8	1,500-50,000	22,625	12,000
SCHOOTEN, Floris van (1590-1657) Dutch				
oil	2	7,621-35,671	21,646	7,621
SCHOPIN, Frederic Henri (1804-1880) French				
oil	1	3,341	3,341	3,341
SCHOPPE, Julius (elder) (1795-1868) German				
wc/d	1	1,000	1,000	1,000
SCHORER, Hans Friedrich (17th C) German				
wc/d	1	2,417	2,417	2,417
SCHOTEL, Anthonie Pieter (1890-1958) Dutch				
oil	3	1,707-4,849	3,307	3,366
wc/d	1	4,506	4,506	4,506
SCHOTEL, Jan Christianus (1787-1838) Dutch				
oil	4	7,493-43,021	16,934	8,372
SCHOTEL, Petrus Jan (1808-1865) Dutch				
oil	4	673-36,875	11,637	3,514
SCHOTH, Anton (1859-1906) Austrian				
oil	4	696-2,580	1,283	870
SCHOTT, Karl Albert von (1840-1911) German				
oil	1	825	825	825
wc/d	1	801	801	801
SCHOU, Sigurd (1875-1944) Danish				
oil	2	452-6,000	3,226	452
SCHOUMAN, Aert (1710-1792) Dutch				
oil	2	2,548-6,228	4,388	2,548
wc/d	4	1,401-13,350	6,986	4,438
SCHOUMAN, Martinus (1770-1848) Dutch				
oil	1	38,713	38,713	38,713
wc/d	1	6,167	6,167	6,167
SCHOUTEN, Henry (1864-1927) Belgian				
oil	50	470-9,722	2,274	1,576
SCHOVELIN, Axel Thorsen (1827-1893) Danish				
oil	6	1,265-6,076	2,910	1,588
SCHOYERER, Josef (1844-1923) German				
oil	6	592-5,890	2,571	1,060
SCHRADER, Julius Friedrich Anton (1815-1900) German				
oil	2	682-5,611	3,146	682
SCHRADER-VELGEN, Carl Hans (1876-1945) German				
oil	2	1,341-1,435	1,388	1,341
SCHRAG, Karl (1912-1995) American/German				
wc/d	1	1,200	1,200	1,200
SCHRAM, Alois Hans (1864-1919) Austrian				
oil	5	1,720-11,700	5,376	3,039
SCHRAM, Wouter Jorinus (1895-1987) Dutch				
oil	1	2,637	2,637	2,637
SCHRAMM, Viktor (1865-1929) Rumanian				
oil	1	6,903	6,903	6,903
SCHRAMM-ZITTAU, Rudolf (1874-1950) German				
oil	8	816-16,349	4,128	2,213
SCHRANZ, Anton (1769-1839) Austrian				
oil	2	19,140-21,390	20,265	19,140
SCHRANZ, John (1794-1882) Maltese				
wc/d	1	1,860	1,860	1,860
SCHRAUDOLPH, Claudius von (younger) (1843-1891) German				
oil	1	81,486	81,486	81,486
SCHRECKENGOST, Victor (1906-) American				
wc/d	1	3,000	3,000	3,000
SCHREIBER, Charles Baptiste (1845-1903) French				
oil	4	1,638-4,000	2,807	1,956
SCHREIBER, Charlotte Mount Brook Morrell (1834-1922) Canadian				
oil	1	4,848	4,848	4,848
SCHREIBER, Conrad Peter (1816-1894) German				
oil	1	7,591	7,591	7,591
SCHREIBER, Hugo (19/20th C) ?				
wc/d	1	2,724	2,724	2,724
SCHREIBER, Paul (19th C) Austrian				
oil	1	1,635	1,635	1,635

Name	No.	Price Range	Average	Median
SCHREINER, Friedrich Wilhelm (1836-?) German				
oil	1	1,824	1,824	1,824
SCHRETER, Zygmunt (c.1896-1977) French				
oil	10	667-1,430	1,039	1,050
wc/d	1	494	494	494
SCHREUDER VAN DE COOLWIJK, Jan W H (1868-1962) Dutch				
oil	1	8,822	8,822	8,822
SCHREUDER, Jan Hendrik (1904-1964) Dutch				
oil	1	1,313	1,313	1,313
SCHREUER, Wilhelm (1866-1933) German				
oil	7	1,403-19,459	5,748	3,041
wc/d	5	1,985-5,081	3,220	2,336
SCHREYER, Adolf (1828-1899) German				
oil	15	1,164-190,000	58,946	31,304
wc/d	2	817-1,033	925	817
SCHREYER, Franz (1858-?) German				
oil	1	2,293	2,293	2,293
SCHREYVOGEL, Charles (1861-1912) American				
oil	1	6,000	6,000	6,000
3D	1	60,000	60,000	60,000
SCHRIEBER, Ludwig Gabriel (1907-1973) German				
3D	1	2,811	2,811	2,811
SCHRIECK, Otto Marseus van (1619-1678) Dutch				
oil	4	7,120-18,147	13,587	13,877
SCHRIJNDER, Joseph Alphons (1894-1968) Dutch				
oil	1	4,005	4,005	4,005
SCHRIKKEL, Louis (1902-1995) Dutch				
oil	1	1,286	1,286	1,286
SCHRIMPF, Georg (1889-1938) German				
oil	1	37,479	37,479	37,479
SCHRODER, Carl Julius Hermann (1802-1867) German				
oil	1	3,271	3,271	3,271
SCHRODER, Heinrich (1881-1941) German				
oil	1	7,145	7,145	7,145
SCHRODER, Johann Heinrich (1757-1812) German				
wc/d	2	9,633-12,041	10,837	9,633
SCHRODER, Poul (1894-1957) Danish				
oil	7	1,051-3,235	1,976	1,462
SCHRODER, Sierk (1903-2002) Dutch				
oil	2	1,134-5,786	3,460	1,134
wc/d	1	596	596	596
SCHRODER-SONNENSTERN, F (1892-1982) German				
wc/d	2	2,509-3,625	3,067	2,509
SCHRODER-SONNENSTERN, Friedrich (1892-1982) German				
oil	2	3,000-3,832	3,416	3,000
wc/d	18	548-7,150	2,798	2,990
SCHRODL, Anton (1823-1906) Austrian				
oil	4	833-2,860	1,919	1,237
SCHRODL, Norbert (1842-1912) Austrian				
oil	1	2,397	2,397	2,397
SCHROEDER, J H (19th C) German?				
oil	1	7,224	7,224	7,224
SCHROEDER-WIBORG, Bernhard (1892-?) German				
oil	1	4,712	4,712	4,712
SCHROM, Ernst (1902-1969) Austrian				
oil	2	1,079-2,108	1,593	1,079
wc/d	2	1,388-1,388	1,388	1,388
SCHROTER, Annette (1956-) German				
oil	2	2,185-3,399	2,792	2,185
SCHROTER, Wilhelm (1849-1904) German				
oil	2	1,520-12,250	6,885	1,520
SCHROTTER, Alfred von (1856-1935) Austrian				
oil	1	2,039	2,039	2,039
SCHROTZBERG, Franz (1811-1889) Austrian				
oil	4	3,349-24,082	10,004	4,944
SCHUBACK, Emil Gottlieb (1820-1902) German				
oil	1	4,553	4,553	4,553
SCHUCKER, James (20th C) American				
wc/d	1	2,800	2,800	2,800
SCHUELER, Jon R (1916-1992) American				
oil	2	1,932-3,219	2,575	1,932
wc/d	1	850	850	850

Name	No.	Price Range	Average	Median
SCHUERR, Aaron (20th C) American				
oil	1	1,500	1,500	1,500
SCHUFFENECKER, Claude Émile (1851-1934) French				
oil	2	21,875-200,000	110,937	21,875
wc/d	5	647-3,215	1,329	779
SCHUFRIED, Dominik (1810-?) Austrian				
oil	2	3,045-3,045	3,045	3,045
SCHUHMACHER, Immanuel Friedrich (1754-1824) German				
oil	1	4,375	4,375	4,375
SCHUHMACHER, Wim (1894-1986) Dutch				
oil	1	11,449	11,449	11,449
wc/d	2	723-2,799	1,761	723
SCHULDT, Fritiof (1891-1978) Swedish				
oil	2	570-4,757	2,663	570
SCHULER, Hans (1874-?) German				
3D	1	13,230	13,230	13,230
SCHULER, Jean (1914-) German				
oil	1	730	730	730
wc/d	1	608	608	608
SCHULMAN, David (1881-1966) Dutch				
oil	11	1,000-6,884	3,244	2,250
wc/d	2	1,134-3,414	2,274	1,134
SCHULMAN, Lion (1851-1943) Dutch				
oil	2	929-1,165	1,047	929
SCHULMANN, Jean (?) Belgian?				
oil	1	1,520	1,520	1,520
SCHULT, Hans Jurgen (1939-) German				
3D	1	5,643	5,643	5,643
SCHULTE, Auguste von (1800-?) German				
oil	1	6,020	6,020	6,020
SCHULTEN, Arnold (1809-1874) German				
oil	4	1,413-4,517	3,142	3,270
SCHULTEN, Curtius (1893-1967) German				
oil	1	1,255	1,255	1,255
SCHULTHEISS, Natalie (1865-1952) Austrian				
oil	2	1,427-2,827	2,127	1,427
SCHULTZ, George F (1869-1934) American				
oil	3	550-4,600	2,216	1,500
wc/d	1	900	900	900
SCHULTZ, Harry (1874-?) German				
oil	3	1,752-9,753	5,091	3,770
SCHULTZBERG, Anshelm (1862-1945) Swedish				
oil	26	397-40,767	5,653	2,861
SCHULTZE, Bernard (1915-2005) German				
oil	13	1,212-22,384	7,612	2,803
wc/d	27	510-20,384	3,105	2,342
SCHULTZE, Robert (1828-1919) German				
oil	3	2,400-5,000	3,611	3,434
SCHULZ, Adrien (1851-1931) French				
oil	3	1,004-1,130	1,075	1,091
SCHULZ, Carl (19th C) German				
oil	1	1,004	1,004	1,004
SCHULZ, Charles M (1922-2000) American				
wc/d	3	11,000-14,000	12,333	12,000
SCHULZ, H (?) German				
oil	3	4,816-18,061	9,311	5,057
SCHULZ, J H (19th C) German				
wc/d	1	1,272	1,272	1,272
SCHULZ, Karl Friedrich (1796-1866) German				
oil	1	12,237	12,237	12,237
SCHULZ-GOLDAP, Lothar (1924-) German				
oil	1	2,420	2,420	2,420
SCHULZ-MATAN, Walter (1889-1965) German				
oil	2	1,080-4,712	2,896	1,080
SCHULZ-RUMPOLD, Volkmar (1956-) German				
wc/d	1	2,434	2,434	2,434
SCHULZ-STRADTMANN, Otto (1892-1960) German				
oil	3	484-3,442	1,581	819
SCHULZE, Andreas (1955-) German				
oil	1	2,038	2,038	2,038
wc/d	1	5,500	5,500	5,500

Name	No.	Price Range	Average	Median
SCHUMACHER, Carl Georg (1797-1869) German				
oil	2	20,000-20,000	20,000	20,000
SCHUMACHER, Emil (1912-1999) German				
oil	13	660-164,932	49,729	34,164
wc/d	6	960-152,877	32,193	6,668
SCHUMACHER, Ernst (1905-1963) German				
oil	4	1,018-4,685	2,761	1,272
wc/d	1	1,145	1,145	1,145
SCHUMACHER, Harald (1836-1912) Danish				
oil	3	474-1,956	1,180	1,111
SCHUMACHER, Hugo (1939-) Swiss				
wc/d	2	1,217-3,816	2,516	1,217
SCHUMACHER, Mathias (20th C) German				
oil	1	4,355	4,355	4,355
SCHUMANN, Christian (1970-) American				
oil	4	5,000-22,500	12,250	5,500
SCHUMANN, Paul (1876-1946) American				
oil	1	2,500	2,500	2,500
SCHUPPEN, Jacob van (1670-1751) Dutch				
oil	1	13,245	13,245	13,245
wc/d	1	2,500	2,500	2,500
SCHURCH, Johann Robert (1895-1941) Swiss				
oil	2	1,166-1,582	1,374	1,166
wc/d	9	486-3,044	1,011	690
SCHURJIN, Raul (1907-1983) Argentinian				
oil	1	2,500	2,500	2,500
SCHURR, Claude (1920-) French				
oil	14	450-5,959	1,734	1,130
wc/d	3	547-1,192	829	748
SCHUSSLER, Alfred von (1820-1849) German				
oil	1	10,320	10,320	10,320
SCHUSTER, Donna (1883-1953) American				
oil	5	3,500-14,000	6,400	4,000
wc/d	1	1,900	1,900	1,900
SCHUSTER, Josef (1812-1890) Austrian				
oil	1	3,816	3,816	3,816
SCHUSTER, Karl Maria (1871-1953) Austrian				
oil	2	2,425-3,099	2,762	2,425
wc/d	1	1,405	1,405	1,405
SCHUSTER-WOLDAN, Raffael (1870-1951) German				
oil	2	1,054-1,815	1,434	1,054
SCHUT, Cornelis (17th C) Flemish				
oil	1	3,646	3,646	3,646
SCHUT, Cornelis (elder) (1597-1655) Flemish				
oil	1	146,507	146,507	146,507
SCHUTTE, Thomas (1954-) German				
oil	2	8,653-18,000	13,326	8,653
wc/d	5	2,803-22,200	14,128	16,000
3D	4	3,000-260,000	102,225	25,900
SCHUTZ, Carl (1745-1800) Austrian				
wc/d	1	16,857	16,857	16,857
SCHUTZ, Christian Georg (18/19th C) German				
oil	2	7,642-26,982	17,312	7,642
SCHUTZ, Christian Georg I (1718-1791) German				
oil	5	7,259-48,440	23,232	16,493
SCHUTZ, Christian Georg II (1758-1823) German				
oil	3	2,922-40,940	16,744	6,370
SCHUTZ, Dana (1976-) American				
oil	1	80,000	80,000	80,000
SCHUTZ, Franz (1751-1781) German				
oil	1	1,433	1,433	1,433
SCHUTZ, Herbert (1903-1964) Austrian				
oil	1	2,158	2,158	2,158
SCHUTZ, Jan Frederik (1817-1888) Dutch				
oil	5	1,260-4,914	3,330	4,186
SCHUTZ, Johannes (20th C) Swiss				
oil	2	1,582-2,829	2,205	1,582
SCHUTZE, Wilhelm (1840-1898) German				
oil	4	550-28,000	8,209	1,626
SCHUYFF, Peter (1958-) Dutch				
oil	7	2,600-16,000	7,187	3,800

Name	No.	Price Range	Average	Median
SCHUYLER, Remington (1887-1953) American				
oil	6	2,000-4,500	3,208	3,000
wc/d	1	500	500	500
SCHUZ, Theodor (1830-1900) German				
oil	1	3,405	3,405	3,405
SCHVARTZ, Marcia (1955-) Argentinian				
oil	2	1,000-10,500	5,750	1,000
SCHWABACHER, Ethel K (1903-1984) American				
wc/d	1	8,000	8,000	8,000
SCHWABE, Carlos (1866-1926) Swiss				
oil	1	46,020	46,020	46,020
wc/d	6	1,770-60,900	12,903	1,890
SCHWABE, Emil (1856-?) German				
oil	1	3,794	3,794	3,794
SCHWABEDA, Johann Michael (1734-1794) German				
oil	1	2,676	2,676	2,676
SCHWAIGER, Rudolf (1924-1979) Austrian				
wc/d	1	1,438	1,438	1,438
3D	3	1,798-2,277	1,964	1,818
SCHWALBE, Ole (1929-1990) Danish				
oil	3	971-5,819	3,121	2,575
SCHWANFELDER, Charles Henry (1774-1837) British				
oil	1	3,024	3,024	3,024
SCHWANTHALER, Johann Peter (elder) (1720-1795) German				
3D	1	13,179	13,179	13,179
SCHWARTZ, Andrew T (1867-1942) American				
oil	1	1,800	1,800	1,800
SCHWARTZ, Avi (1938-) Israeli				
oil	1	1,200	1,200	1,200
SCHWARTZ, Davis F (1879-1969) American				
oil	4	650-3,000	1,425	650
wc/d	1	1,200	1,200	1,200
SCHWARTZ, Ernst (1883-1932) German				
oil	1	4,267	4,267	4,267
SCHWARTZ, Frans (1850-1917) Danish				
oil	4	421-3,004	1,473	809
SCHWARTZ, Henry (1927-) American				
oil	3	800-1,800	1,366	1,500
SCHWARTZ, Johann Christian A (1756-1814) German				
wc/d	2	4,816-11,439	8,127	4,816
SCHWARTZ, Mommie (1876-1942) Dutch				
oil	1	4,219	4,219	4,219
wc/d	1	1,649	1,649	1,649
SCHWARTZ, Walter (1889-1958) Danish				
oil	1	1,042	1,042	1,042
SCHWARTZ, William S (1896-1977) American				
oil	4	3,000-28,000	11,062	4,250
wc/d	3	1,800-7,000	4,350	4,250
SCHWARZ, Hans (1922-2003) British/Austrian				
oil	1	1,029	1,029	1,029
wc/d	2	700-1,029	864	700
SCHWARZ, Rudolf (19th C) German				
3D	1	2,180	2,180	2,180
SCHWARZENBACH, Hans (1911-1983) Swiss				
oil	2	1,332-1,415	1,373	1,332
SCHWARZER, Ludwig (1912-1989) Austrian				
wc/d	1	1,212	1,212	1,212
SCHWATSCHKE, John (1943-) Irish				
oil	6	1,212-3,053	2,269	2,071
SCHWEBEL, Ivan (1932-) Israeli				
oil	4	600-8,000	2,625	700
wc/d	2	480-2,000	1,240	480
SCHWEGLER, Xaver (1832-1902) Swiss				
oil	4	1,224-21,368	11,358	3,816
SCHWEIG, Suzanne (1918-) American				
oil	1	2,200	2,200	2,200
SCHWEITZER, Cajetan (1844-1913) German				
wc/d	1	1,145	1,145	1,145
SCHWEITZER, Reinhold (1876-1940) German				
oil	1	2,422	2,422	2,422
SCHWENINGER, Carl (elder) (1818-1887) Austrian				
oil	2	2,000-2,616	2,308	2,000

Name	No.	Price Range	Average	Median
SCHWENINGER, Carl (younger) (1854-1903) Austrian				
oil	4	6,562-32,500	16,200	12,740
SCHWENINGER, Wilhelm (?) German				
oil	1	1,427	1,427	1,427
SCHWERDGEBURTH, Charlotte Amalia (1795-1831) German				
wc/d	2	3,307-5,343	4,325	3,307
SCHWERIN, Amelie von (1819-1897) Swedish				
oil	2	1,505-1,615	1,560	1,505
SCHWERING, Conrad (?) American?				
oil	1	3,250	3,250	3,250
SCHWETZ, Franz (1910-) Austrian				
oil	1	1,818	1,818	1,818
SCHWEYEN, Brian (1968-) American				
oil	1	2,000	2,000	2,000
SCHWICHTENBERG, Martel (1896-1945) German				
wc/d	3	1,753-2,221	2,026	2,104
SCHWIERING, Conrad (1916-1986) American				
oil	3	7,000-16,000	10,666	9,000
SCHWIMMER, Max (1895-1960) German				
oil	2	2,518-3,349	2,933	2,518
wc/d	10	547-3,349	1,393	1,095
SCHWIND, Moritz von (1804-1871) Austrian				
oil	1	6,000	6,000	6,000
wc/d	5	919-349,600	71,845	2,061
SCHWINGE, Friedrich Wilhelm (1852-1913) German				
oil	5	550-970	808	837
wc/d	2	598-600	599	598
SCHWITTERS, Kurt (1887-1948) German				
oil	5	6,362-36,247	14,953	10,035
wc/d	11	2,589-333,000	64,631	31,069
SCHWIZGEBEL, Robert (?-1950) Swiss				
wc/d	2	1,908-1,908	1,908	1,908
SCHYL, Jules (1893-1977) Swedish				
oil	8	727-3,832	1,744	1,462
wc/d	1	3,054	3,054	3,054
SCIACCA, Antonio (1957-) Italian				
oil	8	1,178-2,744	1,590	1,229
SCIALOJA, Toti (1914-1998) Italian				
oil	5	4,905-47,068	15,337	7,068
wc/d	6	1,168-12,083	6,579	6,090
SCIFONI, Anatolio (1841-1884) Italian				
oil	1	22,620	22,620	22,620
SCILTIAN, Gregorio (1900-1985) Russian				
oil	4	2,990-43,697	16,547	9,546
wc/d	3	658-3,562	1,990	1,752
SCIOLA, Pinuccio (1942-) Italian				
3D	1	8,199	8,199	8,199
SCIPIONE (1904-1933) Italian				
oil	1	50,055	50,055	50,055
SCIUTI, Giuseppi (1834-1911) Italian				
oil	1	6,668	6,668	6,668
SCIVER, Pearl Aiman van (1896-1966) American				
oil	3	650-900	783	800
wc/d	1	425	425	425
SCKELL, Ludwig (1833-1912) German				
oil	6	1,215-3,514	2,218	1,883
SCOGNAMIGLIO, Edwardo (19th C) Italian				
oil	2	350-1,929	1,139	350
SCOPPA, Giuseppe Gustavo (1856-?) Italian				
wc/d	2	6,426-7,007	6,716	6,426
SCOPPA, Raimondo (1820-?) Italian				
oil	2	1,821-3,185	2,503	1,821
SCOPPETTA, Pietro (1863-1920) Italian				
oil	7	3,828-8,026	5,649	5,021
SCORZA, Sinibaldo (1589-1631) Italian				
wc/d	1	7,730	7,730	7,730
SCORZELLI, Eugenio (1890-1958) Italian				
oil	4	2,735-8,203	4,551	2,910
SCOTT, Adam Sherriff (1887-1980) Canadian				
oil	5	675-5,329	2,931	2,292
SCOTT, Alfred T (19th C) American				
oil	1	1,800	1,800	1,800

Name	No.	Price Range	Average	Median
SCOTT, Anthony (20th C) Irish?				
3D	1	2,007	2,007	2,007
SCOTT, Bill (1956-) American				
oil	2	3,250-5,000	4,125	3,250
SCOTT, Clyde Eugene (1884-1959) American				
oil	4	1,400-17,000	7,225	5,000
SCOTT, David (1806-1849) British				
oil	2	2,200-2,220	2,210	2,200
SCOTT, Frank (20th C) British				
wc/d	1	1,068	1,068	1,068
SCOTT, Georges (1907-?) French?				
wc/d	1	2,367	2,367	2,367
SCOTT, Georges Bertin (1873-1942) French				
oil	2	1,265-75,000	38,132	1,265
wc/d	18	553-12,262	2,665	1,532
SCOTT, Harold Winfield (1899-1977) American				
oil	1	2,500	2,500	2,500
SCOTT, Henry (1911-1966) British				
oil	12	609-30,000	11,811	9,000
SCOTT, Johan (1953-) Swedish				
oil	2	1,454-2,926	2,190	1,454
wc/d	1	1,321	1,321	1,321
SCOTT, John (1907-1987) American				
oil	3	4,000-19,000	14,000	19,000
SCOTT, John (1849-1919) British				
oil	1	3,700	3,700	3,700
wc/d	1	1,068	1,068	1,068
SCOTT, John (1802-1885) British				
oil	2	5,190-5,897	5,543	5,190
SCOTT, John W A (1815-1907) American				
oil	2	3,000-9,000	6,000	3,000
SCOTT, Jonathan (1914-) American				
wc/d	1	1,000	1,000	1,000
SCOTT, Julian (1846-1901) American				
oil	3	1,700-9,500	5,900	6,500
wc/d	1	1,700	1,700	1,700
SCOTT, Lady Caroline Lucy (?) British?				
wc/d	1	1,232	1,232	1,232
SCOTT, Malcolm (1935-) British				
oil	1	1,218	1,218	1,218
SCOTT, Marian Dale (1906-1993) Canadian				
oil	4	882-1,244	1,063	882
SCOTT, Michael (20th C) American?				
oil	4	688-7,120	3,128	900
SCOTT, Patrick (1921-) Irish				
oil	1	6,081	6,081	6,081
wc/d	3	2,544-4,844	3,397	2,805
SCOTT, Ralph C (1896-?) American				
oil	1	1,200	1,200	1,200
SCOTT, Samuel (1703-1772) British				
oil	2	28,215-230,000	129,107	28,215
SCOTT, Septimus Edwin (1879-c.1952) British				
oil	1	1,665	1,665	1,665
SCOTT, Sir Peter (1909-1989) British				
oil	6	1,869-10,440	4,710	2,600
wc/d	1	2,300	2,300	2,300
SCOTT, Thomas (1771-1841) British				
wc/d	1	2,249	2,249	2,249
SCOTT, Tom (1854-1927) British				
oil	2	458-985	721	458
wc/d	15	739-22,375	4,977	2,301
SCOTT, William (1913-1989) British				
oil	21	28,350-604,800	195,443	152,653
wc/d	12	3,500-78,318	31,181	29,240
SCOTT, William Bell (1811-1890) British				
oil	1	2,928	2,928	2,928
wc/d	3	890-5,280	2,611	1,665
SCOTT, William Edouard (1884-1964) American				
oil	2	4,800-5,600	5,200	4,800
SCOTT, William Henry Stothard (1783-1850) British				
wc/d	1	1,320	1,320	1,320

Name	No.	Price Range	Average	Median
SCOTT-MILLER, Melissa (1959-) British				
oil	1	1,665	1,665	1,665
SCOTT-STEWART, Beatrice (20th C) Irish?				
3D	1	3,405	3,405	3,405
SCOTTI, Ernesto Mariano (1901-1957) Argentinian				
oil	1	3,400	3,400	3,400
SCOUEZEC, Maurice le (1881-1940) French				
oil	9	1,752-9,351	5,456	5,301
wc/d	2	1,168-5,494	3,331	1,168
SCOUFLAIRE, Fernand (1885-?) Belgian				
oil	1	2,124	2,124	2,124
SCRINZI, Giovan Battista (18th C) Italian				
wc/d	1	4,438	4,438	4,438
SCRIVER, Robert Macfie (1914-1999) American				
3D	12	1,900-18,000	6,512	4,500
SCROPPO, Filippo (1910-1993) Italian				
oil	3	615-5,139	2,716	2,395
SCUDDER, James Long (1836-1881) American				
oil	1	1,000	1,000	1,000
SCUDDER, Janet (1873-1940) American				
3D	1	6,000	6,000	6,000
SCUFFI, Marcello (1948-) Italian				
oil	20	1,355-5,066	2,760	2,506
SCULLY, Harry (?-1935) British				
wc/d	1	2,832	2,832	2,832
SCULLY, Sean (1946-) American/Irish				
oil	7	61,920-800,000	350,224	231,250
wc/d	5	10,829-59,520	36,109	37,500
3D	1	4,537	4,537	4,537
SCULTHORPE, Peter (1948-) American				
wc/d	1	2,600	2,600	2,600
SDRUSCIA, Achille (1910-1994) Italian				
oil	2	846-1,635	1,240	846
SEABROOKE, Elliott (1886-1950) British				
oil	3	1,218-4,628	3,076	3,382
SEAGO, Edward (1910-1974) British				
oil	84	748-145,000	30,592	24,640
wc/d	22	806-18,500	8,691	7,525
SEALY, Colin (1891-1964) British				
wc/d	1	2,088	2,088	2,088
SEARLE, Ronald (1920-) British				
wc/d	51	833-31,790	4,085	3,700
SEARLE, Terry (1936-) British				
oil	1	2,417	2,417	2,417
SEARS, Ronald (1919-1941) British				
wc/d	1	5,152	5,152	5,152
SEASSARO, Saverio (1917-) Italian				
oil	1	1,302	1,302	1,302
SEATH, Ethel (1879-1963) Canadian				
oil	2	9,749-9,896	9,822	9,749
wc/d	3	2,474-5,360	4,162	4,653
SEAVEY, George W (1841-1916) American				
oil	1	1,900	1,900	1,900
SEBA, Sigfried Shalom (1897-1975) Israeli				
oil	2	4,600-16,000	10,300	4,600
wc/d	1	900	900	900
SEBIRE, Gaston (1920-2001) French				
oil	10	400-5,000	2,271	2,000
SEBOY, Ole Johnson (?-c.1845) Norwegian				
wc/d	1	3,588	3,588	3,588
SEBREE, Charles (1912-) American				
oil	2	6,000-10,000	8,000	6,000
wc/d	3	700-6,500	4,233	5,500
SEBRON, Hippolyte Victor Valentin (1801-1879) French				
oil	2	2,297-5,507	3,902	2,297
SECCHI, Silvio (19/20th C) Italian				
oil	1	1,296	1,296	1,296
SECHAS, Alain (1955-) French				
wc/d	1	1,424	1,424	1,424
SECKHAM, Violet Thorne (fl.1909-1923) British				
oil	1	2,500	2,500	2,500

Name	No.	Price Range	Average	Median
SEDGLEY, Peter (1930-) British				
oil	2	1,870-4,200	3,035	1,870
SEDGWICK, Francis Mintorn (1904-1967) American				
oil	1	1,700	1,700	1,700
SEDLACEK, Joseph Anton (1789-1845) Austrian				
oil	1	14,790	14,790	14,790
SEDLACEK, Stephan (1868-1936) Czechoslovakian				
oil	2	759-3,646	2,202	759
SEDLAK, Gunter Silva (1941-) Austrian				
oil	1	2,893	2,893	2,893
SEDRAC, S (1878-1974) Russian				
oil	1	1,204	1,204	1,204
SEDRAC, Serge (1878-1974) Russian				
oil	7	959-5,209	2,781	2,728
SEEBACH, Lothar von (1853-1930) German				
oil	1	3,880	3,880	3,880
SEEBOLD, Marie M (1866-1948) American				
oil	1	5,000	5,000	5,000
SEEGER, Hermann (1857-1920) German				
oil	1	14,800	14,800	14,800
SEEGER, Leon (?) Belgian?				
oil	1	1,316	1,316	1,316
SEEHAUS, Paul Adolf (1891-1919) German				
oil	1	30,575	30,575	30,575
SEEKATZ, Johann Conrad (1719-1768) German				
oil	1	4,865	4,865	4,865
SEEL, Adolf (1829-1907) German				
oil	1	17,000	17,000	17,000
SEELOS, Gottfried (1829-1900) Austrian				
oil	3	1,757-5,595	3,483	3,099
SEELOS, Gustav (1831-1911) Austrian				
oil	1	3,805	3,805	3,805
SEELY, Walter Fredrick (1886-1959) American				
oil	1	1,700	1,700	1,700
SEEMAN, Enoch (17/18th C) German/Polish				
oil	1	4,114	4,114	4,114
SEEVAGEN, Lucien (1887-1959) French				
oil	4	716-1,686	1,035	771
SEEWALD, Richard Josef (1889-1976) German				
oil	1	18,740	18,740	18,740
SEFARBI, Harry (1917-) American				
oil	1	2,600	2,600	2,600
SEFTON, Alfred (?) British				
oil	1	1,750	1,750	1,750
SEGAER, Pieter (?-1650) Belgian				
oil	1	10,120	10,120	10,120
SEGAL, Arthur (1875-1944) Rumanian				
oil	7	2,918-113,480	21,776	6,195
SEGAL, George (1924-2000) American				
wc/d	2	1,650-3,250	2,450	1,650
3D	6	3,562-42,500	18,593	9,500
SEGAL, Simon (1898-1969) French				
oil	6	400-2,750	1,143	756
SEGALL, Lasar (1891-1957) Brazilian/Lithuanian				
oil	1	910	910	910
wc/d	6	400-1,032	600	400
SEGALMAN, Richard (1934-) American				
oil	1	2,000	2,000	2,000
wc/d	1	450	450	450
SEGANTINI, Giovanni (1858-1899) Italian				
oil	4	32,363-289,204	126,493	72,159
wc/d	2	2,577-52,115	27,346	2,577
SEGANTINI, Gottardo (1882-1974) Italian				
oil	19	10,548-310,000	65,323	37,939
SEGANTINI, Mario (1885-1916) Italian				
oil	1	9,894	9,894	9,894
SEGARD, Raymond (20th C) American				
oil	1	1,600	1,600	1,600
SEGARRA CHIAS, Pablo (1945-) Spanish				
oil	1	4,610	4,610	4,610

Name	No.	Price Range	Average	Median
SEGE, Alexandre (1818-1885) French				
oil	2	707-1,568	1,137	707
wc/d	3	3,403-8,264	5,023	3,403
SEGER, Ernst (1868-1939) German				
3D	3	2,425-7,040	4,322	3,503
SEGERS, Adrien (1876-1950) Belgian				
oil	2	586-19,286	9,936	586
SEGERSTRAHLE, Lennart (1892-1975) Finnish				
oil	10	719-11,314	4,183	4,216
wc/d	6	484-787	567	503
SEGHERS, Daniel (1590-1661) Flemish				
oil	1	121,100	121,100	121,100
SEGOFFIN, Victor (1867-1925) French				
3D	2	3,600-7,642	5,621	3,600
SEGOVIA, Andres (c.1929-) Spanish				
oil	1	1,000	1,000	1,000
SEGRELLES, Eustaquio (1936-) Spanish				
oil	2	1,916-2,635	2,275	1,916
wc/d	1	539	539	539
SEGUI, Antonio (1934-) Argentinian				
oil	12	4,783-55,000	24,238	20,000
wc/d	4	1,600-13,000	7,070	1,680
SEGUIN, Jocelyne (1921-1999) French				
oil	2	950-3,434	2,192	950
SEGUIN-BERTAULT, Paul (1869-1964) French				
oil	1	3,503	3,503	3,503
SEGURA IGLESIAS, Agustin (1900-1988) Spanish				
oil	1	2,121	2,121	2,121
SEHMER, Ludowika J C (1848-1929) Danish				
oil	1	1,829	1,829	1,829
SEIBELS, Carl (1844-1877) German				
oil	2	2,000-4,087	3,043	2,000
SEIBNER, H (?) Canadian				
wc/d	1	4,134	4,134	4,134
SEIBOLD, Christian (1697-1768) German				
oil	3	12,041-57,500	28,947	17,300
SEIBOLD, Maxim (19/20th C) American				
wc/d	2	950-2,000	1,475	950
SEIDEL, August (1820-1904) German				
oil	6	484-3,507	1,730	1,091
SEIDEL, Emory P (1881-?) American				
3D	1	2,000	2,000	2,000
SEIDENBEUTEL, Efraim (1903-1945) Polish				
oil	1	3,200	3,200	3,200
SEIFERT, Alfred (1850-1901) Czechoslovakian				
oil	3	825-24,000	8,771	1,488
SEIFERT, David (1896-?) Polish				
oil	2	1,483-1,483	1,483	1,483
SEIFERT, Victor Heinrich (1870-1953) German				
3D	2	2,827-3,279	3,053	2,827
SEIFFERT, Paul (1874-?) German				
oil	1	4,602	4,602	4,602
SEIGNAC, Guillaume (1870-1924) French				
oil	6	2,121-115,000	27,936	7,728
wc/d	1	5,733	5,733	5,733
SEIGNAC, Paul (1826-1904) French				
oil	6	3,096-21,750	11,789	6,442
SEIGNEURGENS, Ernest Louis Augustin (1820-1904) French				
oil	1	2,356	2,356	2,356
SEIGNOL, Claudius (20th C) French				
oil	1	2,760	2,760	2,760
SEIJO Y RUBIO, Jose (1881-1970) Spanish				
oil	1	3,092	3,092	3,092
wc/d	1	969	969	969
SEILER, Carl Wilhelm Anton (1846-1921) German				
oil	3	1,074-13,875	6,085	3,306
SEILER, Hans (1907-1986) Swiss				
oil	2	2,152-2,221	2,186	2,152
wc/d	3	1,067-1,987	1,491	1,420
SEITEI, Watanabe (1851-1918) Japanese				
wc/d	2	925-2,600	1,762	925

Name	No.	Price Range	Average	Median
SEITZ, Alexander Maximilian (1811-1888) German				
oil	1	8,500	8,500	8,500
SEITZ, Anton (1829-1900) German				
oil	2	643-14,833	7,738	643
SEITZ, Georg (1810-1870) German				
oil	3	5,068-5,364	5,244	5,301
SEITZ, Gustav (1906-1969) German				
oil	1	1,171	1,171	1,171
wc/d	1	837	837	837
3D	6	3,273-18,446	8,498	4,459
SEIWERT, Franz Wilhelm (1894-1933) German				
oil	1	323,973	323,973	323,973
SEIXAS, Cruzeiro (1920-) Portuguese				
wc/d	3	2,188-3,038	2,592	2,552
SEIYA, Genryusai (19th C) Japanese				
3D	1	24,360	24,360	24,360
SEKOTO, Gerard (1913-1993) South African				
oil	3	17,405-186,000	73,691	17,670
wc/d	1	31,620	31,620	31,620
SEKULA, Sonja (1918-1963) American/Swiss				
wc/d	5	800-2,588	1,523	1,297
SEKULIC, Sava (20th C) ?				
oil	1	1,785	1,785	1,785
SELANI SANDRI, Mario (?) Italian?				
wc/d	1	1,065	1,065	1,065
SELBY, Joe (1893-1960) American				
oil	1	3,000	3,000	3,000
wc/d	1	1,700	1,700	1,700
SELDEN, Roger (1945-) American				
oil	1	1,316	1,316	1,316
SELDRON, Elisabeth (18th C) French?				
oil	1	10,082	10,082	10,082
SELENIN, Andrej (1976-) Russian				
oil	1	1,337	1,337	1,337
SELF, Colin (1941-) British				
wc/d	6	684-6,840	2,507	1,002
SELIGER, Max (1865-1920) German				
oil	1	3,762	3,762	3,762
SELIGMAN, Adalbert Franz (1862-1945) Austrian				
oil	2	1,800-15,708	8,754	1,800
SELIGMANN, Kurt (1900-1962) American/Swiss				
oil	2	3,748-55,000	29,374	3,748
wc/d	1	2,800	2,800	2,800
SELL, Christian (elder) (1831-1883) German				
oil	8	1,697-2,640	2,096	2,003
SELLA, Tancredi (1852-1918) Italian				
oil	1	605	605	605
wc/d	1	787	787	787
SELLAER, Vincent (16th C) Flemish				
oil	2	46,710-74,760	60,735	46,710
SELLAIO, Jacopo del (1441-1493) Italian				
oil	1	750,000	750,000	750,000
SELLENY, Josef (1824-1875) Austrian				
wc/d	3	1,204-3,955	2,281	1,686
SELMYHR, Conrad (1877-1944) Norwegian				
oil	4	350-3,800	1,666	937
SELOUS, Henry Courtney (1811-1890) British				
oil	1	6,438	6,438	6,438
SELTZER, Olaf C (1877-1957) American				
oil	10	4,250-100,000	46,425	40,000
wc/d	4	10,000-60,000	29,000	11,000
SELTZER, Otto (1854-1891) German				
oil	1	1,331	1,331	1,331
SELTZER, William Steve (1955-) American				
oil	3	2,750-13,000	9,250	12,000
wc/d	1	2,000	2,000	2,000
SELVATICO, Lino (1872-1924) Italian				
oil	1	7,120	7,120	7,120
SELWYN, William (1933-) British				
oil	2	1,380-2,655	2,017	1,380
wc/d	17	974-4,248	1,753	1,350

Name	No.	Price Range	Average	Median
SEM (1863-1934) French				
oil	50	482-9,031	1,172	662
wc/d	5	482-2,569	1,312	1,133
SEMEGHINI, Pio (1878-1964) Italian				
oil	4	1,800-12,959	6,790	4,789
wc/d	2	1,578-1,812	1,695	1,578
SEMENOFF, Boris (1938-) Belgian				
oil	2	1,800-3,579	2,689	1,800
SEMENOWSKY, Eisman (1857-1911) French				
oil	10	1,854-14,880	4,867	2,863
SEMENOWSKY, Sigman (20th C) ?				
oil	4	5,610-11,220	7,573	5,610
SEMERANO, Antonio (20th C) Spanish?				
oil	2	1,229-1,844	1,536	1,229
SEMERTZIDES, Valias (1911-1983) Greek				
oil	1	10,285	10,285	10,285
SEMMES, Beverly (1952-) American				
3D	1	3,200	3,200	3,200
SEMPE, Jean Jacques (1932-) French				
wc/d	1	1,800	1,800	1,800
SEMPERE, Eusebio (1924-) Spanish				
wc/d	6	4,861-9,236	7,880	8,357
SEMPLE, Joseph (fl.1863-1878) British				
oil	1	4,488	4,488	4,488
SEN, Paritosh (1918-) Indian				
oil	3	7,854-14,960	10,604	9,000
wc/d	5	7,480-14,025	9,784	9,000
SENAPE, Antonio (?-1842) Italian				
wc/d	6	1,306-46,250	10,249	2,330
SENAT, Prosper L (1852-1925) American				
wc/d	3	1,019-4,500	2,773	2,800
SENAVE, Jacques Albert (1758-1829) Belgian				
oil	1	7,508	7,508	7,508
SENDAK, Maurice (1928-) American				
wc/d	1	20,000	20,000	20,000
SENE, Henry (1889-1961) French				
oil	1	15,206	15,206	15,206
SENECHAL DE KERDREORET, Gustave Edouard le (1840-1920) French				
oil	3	935-6,600	4,011	4,498
SENET, Rafael (1856-1926) Spanish				
oil	2	2,667-30,000	16,333	2,667
wc/d	3	1,192-5,761	3,214	2,691
SENFF, Adolf (1785-1863) German				
oil	3	6,668-12,085	9,855	10,813
wc/d	3	1,697-2,667	2,141	2,061
SENIOR, Mark (1864-1927) British				
oil	5	609-33,464	13,961	10,440
wc/d	1	1,368	1,368	1,368
SENISE, Daniel (1955-) Brazilian				
oil	1	3,853	3,853	3,853
wc/d	1	5,363	5,363	5,363
SENN, Traugott (1877-1955) Swiss				
oil	4	419-1,082	621	457
wc/d	1	304	304	304
SENNHAUSER, John (1907-1978) American/Swiss				
oil	1	1,200	1,200	1,200
SENNO, Pietro (1831-1904) Italian				
oil	2	2,640-3,748	3,194	2,640
SEO-BO PARK (1931-) Korean				
oil	1	28,000	28,000	28,000
SEOANE, Luis (1910-1979) Argentinian				
oil	4	1,117-21,000	7,515	3,900
wc/d	6	1,176-2,000	1,489	1,316
SEON, Alexandre (1855-1917) French				
wc/d	1	3,403	3,403	3,403
SEPESHY, Zoltan L (1898-1974) American				
oil	4	850-2,300	1,712	1,500
wc/d	2	650-1,000	825	650
SERADOUR, Guy (1922-) French				
oil	4	1,171-4,243	2,116	1,178
SERAFINI, Eric (1962-) Italian				
wc/d	1	1,018	1,018	1,018

Name	No.	Price Range	Average	Median
SERAPHINE DE SENLIS (1864-1942) French				
oil	1	2,400	2,400	2,400
SERBAROLI, Hector (1881-1951) American				
oil	1	3,500	3,500	3,500
SEREBRIAKOV, Alexander (1907-1994) Russian				
oil	1	14,000	14,000	14,000
wc/d	3	2,378-7,812	5,002	4,816
SEREBRIAKOVA, Ekaterina Borissevna (fl.1945-1970) Russian				
wc/d	1	1,134	1,134	1,134
SEREBRIAKOVA, Zinaida (1884-1967) Russian				
oil	4	130,000-1,250,000	443,100	186,000
wc/d	10	3,078-163,400	84,034	69,693
SERGEANT, Emma (1959-) British				
oil	2	2,262-2,960	2,611	2,262
SERGEL, Johan Tobias (1740-1814) Swedish				
wc/d	1	2,867	2,867	2,867
SERGENT, Lucien Pierre (1849-1904) French				
oil	2	2,128-3,781	2,954	2,128
SERGENT, René (20th C) Belgian				
oil	1	1,338	1,338	1,338
SERGER, Frederick B (1889-1965) American				
oil	2	1,100-2,500	1,800	1,100
SERGEYEV, Nikolai Alexandrovich (1855-1919) Russian				
oil	1	73,890	73,890	73,890
SERGOULOPOULOS, Ioannis (1920-2002) Greek				
oil	2	2,805-4,488	3,646	2,805
SERJAKOV, Jakob (1818-1869) Russian				
3D	1	159,247	159,247	159,247
SERL, Jon (1894-?) American				
oil	3	1,700-2,900	2,100	1,700
SERNA, Ismael de la (1897-1968) Spanish				
oil	8	2,012-37,500	20,314	25,918
wc/d	15	714-21,875	5,163	1,521
SERNE, Adrianus (1773-1853) Dutch				
oil	1	1,130	1,130	1,130
SERNEELS, Clement (1912-1991) Belgian				
oil	5	602-4,122	1,921	1,697
SERNY, Ricardo (1908-1995) Spanish				
oil	1	1,646	1,646	1,646
SEROV, Valentin Alexandrovitch (1865-1911) Russian				
oil	2	10,138-60,000	35,069	10,138
wc/d	1	310,000	310,000	310,000
SERPAN, Jaroslav (1922-1976) Czechoslovakian				
oil	2	500-3,507	2,003	500
wc/d	6	634-6,578	2,759	2,392
SERRA SANTA, Jose (1916-1998) Spanish/Argentinian				
oil	1	2,108	2,108	2,108
SERRA Y AUQUE, Enrico (1859-1918) Spanish				
oil	8	1,060-5,655	3,551	3,053
SERRA Y PORSON, Jose (1824-1910) Spanish				
oil	2	1,463-4,919	3,191	1,463
SERRA, Richard (1953-) American				
oil	1	120,000	120,000	120,000
SERRA, Richard (1939-) American				
oil	12	1,430-120,000	62,288	70,000
wc/d	2	1,073-180,000	90,536	1,073
SERRA, Rosa (1944-) Dutch				
3D	8	2,922-7,054	3,875	3,185
SERRALUNGA, Luigi (1880-1940) Italian				
wc/d	1	1,015	1,015	1,015
SERRANO RUEDA, Santiago (1942-) Spanish				
oil	1	4,351	4,351	4,351
SERRANO, Manuel Ignacio (20th C) Venezuelan?				
wc/d	2	1,720-1,800	1,760	1,720
SERRANO, Pablo (1910-1985) Spanish				
3D	5	2,314-5,262	3,621	3,766
SERRASANTA, Jose (1916-2000) Argentinian				
oil	2	2,101-3,536	2,818	2,101
SERRE, Georges (1889-1956) French				
3D	2	2,225-7,964	5,094	2,225
SERRES, Antony (1828-1898) French				
oil	2	577-8,475	4,526	577

Name	No.	Price Range	Average	Median
SERRES, Dominic (1722-1793) British				
oil	6	6,090-264,600	112,283	38,280
SERRES, John Thomas (1759-1825) British				
oil	2	12,180-15,312	13,746	12,180
wc/d	2	2,249-2,958	2,603	2,249
SERRI, Alfredo (1897-1972) Italian				
oil	2	1,100-2,400	1,750	1,100
SERRUR, Henri Auguste Calixte Cesar (1794-1865) French				
oil	2	3,240-5,178	4,209	3,240
SERRURE, Auguste (1825-1903) Flemish				
oil	2	971-1,380	1,175	971
SERT Y BADIA, Jose Maria (1876-1945) Spanish				
oil	1	29,392	29,392	29,392
SERT, Henri (1938-1964) French				
oil	2	1,400-2,910	2,155	1,400
wc/d	1	941	941	941
SERUSIER, Marguerite Gabrielle (1885-1950) French				
oil	1	2,104	2,104	2,104
SERUSIER, Paul (1863-1927) French				
oil	11	9,370-76,027	45,527	48,151
wc/d	8	1,168-7,120	3,367	2,221
SERVAES, Albert (1883-1966) Belgian				
oil	4	1,784-14,395	6,195	3,505
wc/d	3	994-1,274	1,145	1,169
SERVEAU, Clement (1886-1972) French				
oil	14	514-10,177	3,675	2,945
wc/d	2	890-1,701	1,295	890
SERVI, Giovanni (19th C) Italian				
oil	1	4,877	4,877	4,877
SERVRANCKX, Victor (1897-1965) Belgian				
oil	2	3,053-12,945	7,999	3,053
wc/d	2	486-680	583	486
3D	1	15,760	15,760	15,760
SESEMANN, Elga (1922-) Finnish				
oil	3	944-1,438	1,217	1,271
wc/d	1	779	779	779
SESSIONS, James (1882-1962) American				
wc/d	6	600-2,600	1,533	1,200
SETELIK, Jaroslav (1881-1955) Polish				
oil	1	1,736	1,736	1,736
SETHER, Gulbrand (1869-1910) American/Norwegian				
oil	1	1,200	1,200	1,200
SETSUKO, Mitsuhashi (1939-1975) Japanese				
wc/d	1	4,500	4,500	4,500
SETTARI, Wilhelm Anton Maria (1841-1905) German				
wc/d	3	690-2,008	1,213	941
SETTEI, Hasegawa (1819-1882) Japanese				
wc/d	1	2,400	2,400	2,400
SETTLE, William F (1821-1897) British				
oil	1	12,210	12,210	12,210
wc/d	1	524	524	524
SEUPHOR, Michel (1901-1999) Belgian				
wc/d	9	849-2,640	1,796	1,901
SEURAT, Georges (1859-1891) French				
wc/d	3	7,262-425,500	280,628	409,122
SEUSS, Dr (1904-1991) American				
wc/d	1	26,000	26,000	26,000
SEVAISTRE, Pierre (1879-?) French				
oil	1	677	677	677
wc/d	1	608	608	608
SEVELLEC, Jim (1897-1971) French				
oil	3	584-3,624	1,909	1,520
wc/d	1	1,388	1,388	1,388
SEVERDONCK, Franz van (1809-1889) Belgian				
oil	14	1,090-7,747	3,137	2,538
SEVERDONCK, Jan van (19th C) ?				
oil	1	1,564	1,564	1,564
SEVERDONCK, Joseph van (1819-1905) Belgian				
oil	1	2,860	2,860	2,860
SEVERI, Aldo (1876-1956) Italian				
oil	1	4,500	4,500	4,500

Name	No.	Price Range	Average	Median
SEVERINI, Gino (1883-1966) Italian				
oil	6	4,480-76,327	37,396	36,308
wc/d	27	1,649-885,000	50,834	6,676
3D	2	3,982-7,633	5,807	3,982
SEVERN, Joseph (1793-1879) British				
oil	2	5,036-32,040	18,538	5,036
SEVERN, Joseph Arthur Palliser (1842-1931) British				
wc/d	6	452-7,000	1,907	731
SEVERN, Walter (1830-1904) British				
wc/d	3	1,050-2,655	1,997	2,288
SEVESO, Pompilio (1877-1949) Italian				
oil	2	972-1,215	1,093	972
SEVIER, Michael (1886-?) British				
oil	1	1,556	1,556	1,556
SEVILLANO, Angel (1942-1994) Spanish				
oil	6	1,929-6,442	3,861	3,801
SEWELL, Amos (1901-1983) American				
oil	2	1,800-2,500	2,150	1,800
wc/d	1	1,600	1,600	1,600
SEWELL, Robert van Vorst (1860-1924) American				
oil	1	6,000	6,000	6,000
SEWOHL, Waldemar (1887-1967) German				
oil	3	509-2,000	1,420	1,752
wc/d	1	510	510	510
SEXTON, Leo Lloyd (jnr) (1912-1990) American				
oil	4	18,000-42,500	33,250	32,500
SEXTON, Ray (1959-1996) American				
oil	3	2,000-6,000	3,500	2,500
SEYDEL, Eduard (1822-1881) Luxembourger				
oil	1	12,437	12,437	12,437
SEYLBERGH, Jacques van den (1884-1960) Belgian				
oil	2	715-1,405	1,060	715
SEYLER, Julius (1873-1958) German				
oil	20	486-3,503	1,413	999
SEYMOUR, James (1702-1752) British				
oil	4	16,470-141,750	79,245	26,460
SEYMOUR, Tom (19th C) British				
oil	3	514-9,396	3,590	860
SEYSSAUD, René (1867-1952) French				
oil	8	907-6,550	3,851	4,117
wc/d	1	786	786	786
SEYSSES, Auguste (1862-?) French				
3D	2	3,596-3,746	3,671	3,596
SFORZA, Pietro C (1967-) Italian				
oil	1	1,176	1,176	1,176
SGAN-COHEN, Michael (1944-) Israeli				
oil	2	4,000-5,000	4,500	4,000
SGOUROS, Stefanos (1924-) Greek				
wc/d	2	2,618-4,928	3,773	2,618
SHAA, Aqjangajuk (1937-) Canadian				
3D	2	4,874-5,905	5,389	4,874
SHABBAT, Ozer (1901-1978) Israeli				
oil	1	1,200	1,200	1,200
SHACKLETON, Keith (1923-) British				
oil	11	534-9,500	2,742	2,079
SHACKLETON, William (1872-1933) British				
oil	1	1,008	1,008	1,008
SHADBOLT, Jack (1909-1998) Canadian				
oil	12	1,237-37,666	9,198	6,171
wc/d	9	577-5,761	2,887	2,460
SHADE, K (20th C) ?				
oil	1	1,897	1,897	1,897
SHAFFER, Mary (20th C) American				
3D	1	8,500	8,500	8,500
SHAFIK, Medhat (1956-) Egyptian				
wc/d	8	776-7,422	3,207	3,341
SHAH, Himmat (1933-) Indian				
3D	1	19,000	19,000	19,000
SHAHABUDDIN (1950-) Indian				
oil	1	6,500	6,500	6,500

Name	No.	Price Range	Average	Median
SHAHN, Ben (1898-1969) American				
oil	1	55,000	55,000	55,000
wc/d	16	800-26,000	3,665	1,900
SHALDERS, George (1826-1873) British				
oil	1	1,443	1,443	1,443
wc/d	2	1,392-3,096	2,244	1,392
SHANAHAN, Sean (1960-) Irish				
oil	1	2,903	2,903	2,903
SHANE, Frederick (1907-1992) American				
wc/d	1	2,800	2,800	2,800
SHANKLIN, Barbara K (20th C) Danish				
3D	1	2,425	2,425	2,425
SHANKS, Duncan F (1937-) British				
oil	1	1,566	1,566	1,566
wc/d	2	661-6,726	3,693	661
SHANKS, William Somerville (1864-1951) British				
oil	4	531-2,249	1,346	1,086
SHANNON, Sir James Jebusa (1862-1923) British/American				
oil	1	31,860	31,860	31,860
SHAO FAN (1964-) Chinese				
3D	1	10,175	10,175	10,175
SHAO SHAOYI and SHAO YOUXUAN (20th C) Chinese				
wc/d	1	1,500	1,500	1,500
SHAPIRO, Joel (1941-) American				
wc/d	4	10,000-45,000	20,000	12,000
3D	4	20,000-100,000	68,750	60,000
SHAPLEIGH, Frank Henry (1842-1906) American				
oil	10	1,600-75,000	11,200	3,250
wc/d	2	650-800	725	650
SHAPOVALOV, Anatoli (1949-) Russian				
oil	10	1,182-7,440	2,738	1,750
SHAQU, Mannumi (1917-) North American				
3D	1	1,603	1,603	1,603
SHARADIN, Henry William (1872-1966) American				
oil	4	650-1,400	1,050	850
SHARER, William (1934-) American?				
oil	4	3,000-6,000	4,187	3,250
SHARF, Kenny (20th C) ?				
oil	1	7,863	7,863	7,863
SHARKEY, Kevin (1961-) Irish?				
oil	1	1,169	1,169	1,169
SHARMA, Ashim (20th C) Indian				
oil	1	2,750	2,750	2,750
SHARMA, Natraj (1958-) Indian				
wc/d	1	3,250	3,250	3,250
SHARMA, Om Prakash (1932-) Indian				
oil	1	3,000	3,000	3,000
SHARMA, R Binod (1964-) Indian				
oil	1	10,000	10,000	10,000
SHARMAN, John (20th C) Australian				
oil	1	32,000	32,000	32,000
SHARP, Dorothea (1874-1955) British				
oil	28	3,520-118,300	28,815	19,140
SHARP, John O Robert (1911-1955) American				
oil	1	1,000	1,000	1,000
SHARP, John T (1944-) American				
3D	1	2,700	2,700	2,700
SHARP, Joseph Henry (1859-1953) American				
oil	37	15,000-775,000	120,039	87,000
wc/d	1	3,500	3,500	3,500
SHARP, William (fl.1839-1885) American				
oil	1	1,500	1,500	1,500
SHARPE, George (1802-1877) Irish				
oil	1	247,222	247,222	247,222
SHARPLES, James (1752-1811) American				
wc/d	2	4,000-9,000	6,500	4,000
SHART (1927-) French?				
oil	1	1,753	1,753	1,753
SHATTUCK, Aaron Draper (1832-1928) American				
oil	5	3,500-9,000	6,200	6,000
SHAW, Charles (19th C) British				
oil	1	4,000	4,000	4,000

Name	No.	Price Range	Average	Median
SHAW, Charles Green (1892-1974) American				
oil	7	2,400-15,000	7,371	7,000
wc/d	3	1,825-2,300	2,041	2,000
SHAW, Charles L (19th C) British				
oil	1	2,288	2,288	2,288
SHAW, George (1966-) British				
oil	1	1,496	1,496	1,496
SHAW, Harry Hutchinson (1897-?) American				
oil	1	5,500	5,500	5,500
SHAW, Jim (1952-) American				
oil	3	28,431-42,000	33,477	30,000
wc/d	7	3,440-34,953	15,553	14,000
SHAW, John Byam (1872-1919) British				
oil	2	8,000-10,000	9,000	8,000
SHAW, Joshua (1776-1860) American/British				
oil	3	2,137-11,000	7,045	8,000
SHAW, Raqib (1974-) British/Indian				
oil	2	42,500-60,000	51,250	42,500
SHAW, Robert (20th C) Canadian				
oil	1	22,000	22,000	22,000
SHAW, Walter (1851-1933) British				
oil	2	1,332-1,575	1,453	1,332
SHAWCROSS, Neal (1940-) British				
oil	1	5,686	5,686	5,686
wc/d	16	797-7,785	3,927	3,337
SHAYER, Henry (c.1825-1864) British				
oil	1	2,436	2,436	2,436
SHAYER, Henry and Charles (19th C) British				
oil	4	4,872-13,680	10,088	10,800
SHAYER, T (19th C) British				
oil	1	2,457	2,457	2,457
SHAYER, W J (1811-1892) British				
oil	1	3,660	3,660	3,660
SHAYER, William (snr) (1787-1879) British				
oil	30	550-33,060	9,685	6,650
SHAYER, William (19th C) British				
oil	1	1,325	1,325	1,325
SHAYER, William J (1811-1892) British				
oil	6	1,300-17,000	6,511	3,078
SHCHEKOTIKHINA-POTOTSKAYA, Aleksandra Vasilievna (1892-1967) Russian				
oil	1	23,563	23,563	23,563
SHCHERBOV, Pavel Egorovich (1866-1938) Russian				
wc/d	1	1,392	1,392	1,392
SHEARBON, Andrew (fl.1860s) British				
oil	1	1,334	1,334	1,334
SHEARER, Christopher H (1840-1926) American				
oil	23	1,000-5,500	3,004	3,000
SHEARER, Edmund Leaf (1851-1935) American				
oil	1	3,200	3,200	3,200
SHEARER, Georgia Bard (20th C) American				
oil	1	1,300	1,300	1,300
SHEARER, Rosa L (fl.1899-1912) British				
oil	1	3,306	3,306	3,306
SHEARER, Victor (20th C) American				
oil	5	550-3,200	1,290	800
SHEE, Sir Martin Archer (1769-1850) British				
oil	6	3,000-23,355	8,373	5,180
SHEELER, Charles (1883-1965) American				
oil	2	95,000-180,000	137,500	95,000
wc/d	3	55,000-130,000	101,666	120,000
SHEETS, Millard (1907-1989) American				
oil	1	20,000	20,000	20,000
wc/d	18	800-17,000	7,766	7,000
SHEFFIELD, Isaac (1798-1845) American				
oil	1	5,600	5,600	5,600
SHEIKH, Gulam (1937-) Indian				
wc/d	1	9,500	9,500	9,500
SHELBOURNE, Anita (1938-) Irish?				
oil	5	1,126-3,180	2,296	2,417
wc/d	1	1,053	1,053	1,053
SHELDON-WILLIAMS, Inglis (1870-1940) Canadian				
wc/d	1	2,604	2,604	2,604

Name	No.	Price Range	Average	Median
SHELESNYAK, Henry (1938-1980) Israeli				
oil	3	7,000-16,000	10,666	9,000
SHELLEY, Samuel (c.1750-1808) British				
wc/d	2	773-2,700	1,736	773
SHELTON, Alphonse Joseph (1905-1976) American				
oil	2	500-5,250	2,875	500
SHELTON, Margaret D (1915-1984) Canadian				
oil	1	825	825	825
wc/d	9	353-753	448	405
SHELTON, Peter (1951-) American				
3D	2	12,000-36,000	24,000	12,000
SHEMI, Menachem (1896-1951) Israeli				
oil	5	3,450-30,000	10,440	5,000
SHEMI, Yehiel (1922-2003) Israeli				
3D	2	3,000-5,500	4,250	3,000
SHENSTONE, Clare (1948-) British				
oil	1	21,120	21,120	21,120
SHEPARD, E H (1879-1976) British				
wc/d	2	14,080-49,280	31,680	14,080
SHEPARD, Ernest Howard (1879-1976) British				
wc/d	8	731-46,020	11,433	1,566
SHEPHARD, Rupert (1909-1992) British				
oil	1	1,593	1,593	1,593
SHEPHERD, David (1931-) British				
oil	25	4,114-110,000	26,691	20,000
wc/d	2	2,124-3,132	2,628	2,124
SHEPHERD, George Sydney (1784-c.1858) British				
wc/d	2	433-7,308	3,870	433
SHEPHERD, J Clinton (1888-1963) American				
oil	1	2,800	2,800	2,800
SHEPHERD, Kate (1961-) American				
oil	1	19,000	19,000	19,000
SHEPHERD, S Horne (1909-1993) British				
wc/d	1	1,092	1,092	1,092
SHEPHERD, Thomas Hosmer (1792-1864) British				
wc/d	2	1,480-1,740	1,610	1,480
SHEPPARD, Michael (20th C) British				
oil	1	1,584	1,584	1,584
SHEPPARD, Peter Clapham (1882-1965) Canadian				
oil	28	422-23,090	4,022	1,322
SHEPPARD, Warren W (1858-1937) American				
oil	17	1,000-40,000	8,061	6,000
wc/d	1	1,200	1,200	1,200
SHERIDAN, Noel (1936-) Irish				
oil	11	972-6,799	3,048	3,053
SHERINGHAM, George (1884-1937) British				
wc/d	2	1,100-2,262	1,681	1,100
SHERLOCK, Marjorie (1897-1973) British				
oil	1	1,382	1,382	1,382
SHERLOCK, William P (1780-?) British				
oil	3	1,600-18,032	7,351	2,422
SHERMAN, Cindy (1954-) American				
wc/d	1	62,000	62,000	62,000
SHERRIN, Daniel (1868-1940) British				
oil	26	452-7,656	1,591	1,100
SHERRIN, John (1819-1896) British				
wc/d	4	1,110-2,610	1,914	1,636
SHEVCHUK, Alexander (1960-) Ukranian				
oil	1	1,098	1,098	1,098
SHIBUSAWA, Kei (1949-) Japanese				
wc/d	1	10,141	10,141	10,141
SHIELDS, Irion (1895-1983) American				
oil	1	4,250	4,250	4,250
SHIELDS, Mark (20th C) Irish?				
oil	2	2,076-2,249	2,162	2,076
SHIELS, William (1785-1857) British				
oil	1	16,720	16,720	16,720
SHIGEKO, Ishida (20th C) Japanese				
wc/d	1	5,500	5,500	5,500
SHIH-FU CHIU YING (?) Chinese				
wc/d	1	8,870	8,870	8,870

Name	No.	Price Range	Average	Median
SHIKLER, Aaron (1922-) American				
oil	4	2,250-70,000	20,762	3,800
wc/d	3	5,000-50,000	21,500	9,500
SHILEY, S B (fl.1893-1905) American				
oil	1	3,130	3,130	3,130
SHILLING, Arthur (1941-1986) Canadian				
oil	7	1,237-8,374	3,498	1,706
SHILSTONE, Arthur (1922-) American				
wc/d	1	5,500	5,500	5,500
SHILTSOV, Pavel Savvich (1820-1893) Russian				
oil	1	13,863	13,863	13,863
SHIMOMOURA, Izan (1865-1949) Japanese				
wc/d	1	1,850	1,850	1,850
SHIN SUNG-HY (1948-) Korean				
oil	1	15,000	15,000	15,000
SHINABARGER, Tim (1966-) American				
3D	1	3,500	3,500	3,500
SHINDE, Vijay (20th C) Indian				
oil	1	4,000	4,000	4,000
SHINN, Everett (1876-1953) American				
oil	3	1,600-55,000	33,866	45,000
wc/d	13	600-100,000	10,357	2,500
SHINNORS, John (1950-) Irish				
oil	15	4,477-43,264	16,872	13,986
SHINODA, Toko (1913-) Japanese				
wc/d	1	5,700	5,700	5,700
SHINSHIKI, Kosen (20th C) Japanese				
oil	1	13,875	13,875	13,875
SHIRAGA, Kazuo (1924-) Japanese				
oil	3	10,000-16,537	14,179	16,000
SHIRLAW, Walter (1838-1909) American				
oil	1	800	800	800
wc/d	2	850-3,000	1,925	850
SHIRLEY, Charlotte (19th C) British				
wc/d	1	1,564	1,564	1,564
SHIROKOV, Andrei (1960-) Russian				
oil	1	1,080	1,080	1,080
SHISHKIN, Ivan Ivanovich (1832-1898) Russian				
oil	11	7,730-1,118,000	367,802	223,200
SHKURKIN, Vladimir Pavlovich (1900-1990) American				
oil	1	4,250	4,250	4,250
SHOEI, Asami (1886-1969) Japanese				
wc/d	4	2,000-5,000	3,800	4,000
SHOESMITH, Kenneth Denton (1890-1939) British				
wc/d	3	694-3,916	2,193	1,971
SHOKADO, Shojo (1584-1939) Japanese				
wc/d	1	7,000	7,000	7,000
SHONBORN, John Lewis (1852-1931) Hungarian				
oil	3	467-3,039	1,967	2,397
SHORE, Henrietta (1880-1963) American				
oil	3	4,000-45,000	20,000	11,000
SHORT, Obadiah (1803-1886) British				
oil	1	2,595	2,595	2,595
SHORT, Richard (1841-1916) British				
oil	1	808	808	808
wc/d	1	549	549	549
SHRADY, Henry M (1871-1922) American				
3D	1	2,000	2,000	2,000
SHRAPNEL, Edward Scrope (1847-1920) British/Canadian				
oil	1	3,526	3,526	3,526
wc/d	1	660	660	660
SHREIBER, Vasili Ivanovich (1850-?) Russian				
oil	1	14,882	14,882	14,882
SHRESHTHA, Laxman (1939-) Indian				
oil	1	30,000	30,000	30,000
SHRIGLEY, David (1968-) ?				
wc/d	1	3,000	3,000	3,000
SHTANGE, Irina (1906-1992) Russian				
oil	1	55,800	55,800	55,800
SHTERENBERG, David (1881-1948) Russian				
oil	1	525,000	525,000	525,000

Name	No.	Price Range	Average	Median
SHU BE HONG (20th C) Chinese				
wc/d	1	11,000	11,000	11,000
SHUGRIN, Anatoly (1906-) Russian				
oil	1	7,440	7,440	7,440
SHUKHAEV, Vasili (1887-1973) Russian				
oil	2	71,308-99,760	85,534	71,308
SHUKI, Okamoto (c.1807-1862) Japanese				
wc/d	1	2,800	2,800	2,800
SHULGA, Ivan (1889-1956) Russian				
oil	2	2,259-2,378	2,318	2,259
SHULZ, Ada Walter (1870-1928) American				
oil	1	12,000	12,000	12,000
SHULZ, G R (20th C) ?				
oil	1	9,000	9,000	9,000
SHUNKO, Saeki (1909-1942) Japanese				
wc/d	1	4,800	4,800	4,800
SHURBOOM, Andrew (fl.1870s) British				
oil	1	1,144	1,144	1,144
SHURTLEFF, Roswell Morse (1838-1915) American				
oil	4	1,200-2,900	1,775	1,500
SI CHEN YUAN (1912-1974) ?				
oil	1	19,000	19,000	19,000
SIBARI, A (19th C) Italian?				
oil	1	3,185	3,185	3,185
SIBER, Johann Baptist (1802-?) German				
oil	1	1,649	1,649	1,649
SIBERDT, Eugène (1851-1931) Belgian				
oil	3	746-1,286	1,059	1,147
SIBERECHTS, Jan (1627-1703) Flemish				
oil	2	30,000-49,840	39,920	30,000
SICARD, Francois Léon (1862-1934) French				
3D	2	7,054-12,285	9,669	7,054
SICARD, Pierre (1900-1980) French				
oil	36	505-2,398	799	631
wc/d	1	631	631	631
SICHEL, Harold (1881-1948) American				
oil	2	600-4,000	2,300	600
SICHEL, Nathaniel (1843-1907) German				
oil	1	1,089	1,089	1,089
SICHELKOW, Valdemar (19th C) Danish				
oil	1	1,132	1,132	1,132
SICILIA, Jose Maria (1954-) Spanish				
oil	7	5,946-38,720	16,811	13,081
wc/d	2	4,200-24,548	14,374	4,200
SICKERT, Walter Richard (1860-1942) British				
oil	8	17,010-81,900	43,468	38,940
wc/d	14	519-22,680	6,721	5,220
SICKLES, Donna Howell (20th C) American				
oil	1	7,000	7,000	7,000
SIDANER, Henri le (1862-1939) French				
oil	26	7,730-647,500	182,480	58,254
wc/d	5	1,401-19,007	7,291	3,319
SIDNEY, Herbert (1858-1923) British				
oil	1	1,883	1,883	1,883
SIDNEY, Thomas (19th C) British				
oil	1	1,384	1,384	1,384
wc/d	2	854-1,184	1,019	854
SIDOLI, Nazzareno (1879-1970) Italian				
oil	3	788-1,697	1,353	1,576
SIDOROVICZ (19th C) ?				
oil	1	2,362	2,362	2,362
SIDOROVICZ, Sigmund (1846-1881) Austrian				
oil	2	4,466-4,848	4,657	4,466
SIEBEL, N (?) ?				
oil	1	11,127	11,127	11,127
SIEBELIST, Arthur (1870-1945) ?				
oil	1	14,240	14,240	14,240
SIEBER, Friedrich (1925-) German				
oil	1	1,236	1,236	1,236
SIEBERT, Hermann (19th C) German?				
wc/d	1	1,147	1,147	1,147

Name	No.	Price Range	Average	Median
SIEBNER, Herbert Johannes Joseph (1925-) Canadian				
oil	4	853-5,360	2,711	2,144
wc/d	2	454-3,021	1,737	454
SIECK, Rudolf (1877-1957) German				
oil	4	1,562-5,377	3,286	2,351
wc/d	1	790	790	790
SIEFFERT, Paul (1874-1957) French				
oil	9	2,893-24,975	12,849	12,180
SIEGEN, August (19th C) German				
oil	14	661-6,500	3,613	3,031
SIEGERT, August Friedrich (1820-1883) German				
oil	2	7,728-26,490	17,109	7,728
SIEGFRIED, Arne (1893-1985) Swiss				
oil	1	1,260	1,260	1,260
SIEGFRIED, Edwin C (1889-1955) American				
wc/d	4	450-1,500	1,187	1,300
SIEGMUND, Johann Jakob (1807-1881) Swiss				
oil	1	10,829	10,829	10,829
SIEGRIEST, Louis Bassi (1899-1989) American				
oil	6	1,600-11,000	4,200	1,900
SIEGRIEST, Lundy (1925-1985) American				
oil	1	1,100	1,100	1,100
wc/d	1	1,000	1,000	1,000
SIEHERT, P (?) ?				
oil	1	2,829	2,829	2,829
SIEMIRADZKI, Hendrik (1843-1902) Polish				
oil	4	130,500-1,250,000	536,705	133,920
SIENA, James (20th C) ?				
oil	1	15,000	15,000	15,000
SIEPMANN, Heinrich (1904-) German				
oil	4	937-10,192	4,948	3,822
SIERHUIS, Jan (1928-) Dutch				
oil	4	900-3,039	1,468	964
wc/d	1	591	591	591
SIERRA, Paul (20th C) Cuban				
oil	1	1,100	1,100	1,100
SIES, Walter (19th C) American				
oil	2	2,100-3,250	2,675	2,100
SIETSEMA, Paul (1968-) American				
wc/d	1	6,000	6,000	6,000
SIEVANEN, Jaakko (1932-) Finnish				
oil	1	3,982	3,982	3,982
wc/d	1	2,277	2,277	2,277
SIEWERT, Feliciano (1942-) Dutch				
wc/d	1	1,808	1,808	1,808
SIGARD, Eliahu (1901-1975) Israeli				
oil	2	600-950	775	600
wc/d	3	350-500	403	360
SIGG, Hermann-Alfred (1924-) Swiss				
oil	4	2,283-3,246	2,772	2,518
SIGHICELLI, Elisa (1968-) Italian				
3D	1	6,726	6,726	6,726
SIGMUND, Benjamin D (fl.1880-1904) British				
wc/d	2	979-1,305	1,142	979
SIGNAC, Ginette (1913-1980) French				
oil	1	1,514	1,514	1,514
SIGNAC, Paul (1863-1935) French				
oil	5	113,496-193,600	145,144	140,000
wc/d	42	2,616-60,000	17,969	13,275
SIGNER, G (20th C) ?				
oil	1	1,798	1,798	1,798
SIGNORELLI, Luca (1441-1523) Italian				
oil	1	99,211	99,211	99,211
SIGNORET-LEDIEU, Lucie (1858-1904) French				
3D	1	2,003	2,003	2,003
SIGNORI, Carlo Sergio (c.1906-) Italian				
3D	3	2,800-3,827	3,142	2,800
SIGNORINI, Giovanni (1808-1864) Italian				
oil	1	31,280	31,280	31,280
SIGNORINI, Giuseppe (1857-1932) Italian				
wc/d	2	571-7,000	3,785	571

Name	No.	Price Range	Average	Median
SIGNORINI, Telemaco (1835-1901) Italian				
oil	7	9,062-152,260	57,746	33,658
SIGRIST, Franz (18/19th C) Austrian				
oil	2	15,727-20,274	18,000	15,727
SIGRIST, Franz I (1727-1803) Austrian				
oil	1	1,427	1,427	1,427
SIGRISTE, Guido (1864-1915) Swiss				
oil	1	2,165	2,165	2,165
SIIKAMAKI, Arvo (1943-) Finnish				
3D	1	2,108	2,108	2,108
SIKANDER, Shahzia (1969-) Pakistani				
oil	1	25,000	25,000	25,000
SIKELIOTIS, Giorgos (1917-1984) Greek				
oil	1	14,080	14,080	14,080
wc/d	3	5,610-8,800	6,680	5,632
SIKSTROM, Cecilia (1962-) Swedish				
oil	2	2,799-3,171	2,985	2,799
SILBERT, Ben (1893-1940) Russian				
oil	2	851-1,215	1,033	851
SILERI, T (?) Italian?				
oil	1	1,894	1,894	1,894
SILFVERSTRALE, Gustaf (1748-1816) Swedish				
wc/d	1	2,747	2,747	2,747
SILHOUETTE, Guy (20th C) French				
wc/d	1	1,414	1,414	1,414
SILLEN, Herman (1857-1908) Swedish				
oil	4	8,517-64,812	30,712	24,040
SILLETT, James (1764-1840) British				
wc/d	1	7,440	7,440	7,440
SILLMAN, Amy (1966-) American				
oil	2	1,500-18,000	9,750	1,500
wc/d	2	1,600-6,000	3,800	1,600
SILO, Adam (1674-1772) Dutch				
oil	3	5,438-85,440	34,292	12,000
SILVA BRUHNS, Ivan da (1881-1980) French				
wc/d	1	1,200	1,200	1,200
SILVA, Carlos (1930-1987) Argentinian				
oil	1	3,400	3,400	3,400
wc/d	5	1,200-4,200	2,600	3,000
SILVA, Francis Augustus (1835-1886) American				
oil	3	5,500-1,300,000	685,166	750,000
wc/d	2	5,000-11,000	8,000	5,000
SILVA, Joao Cristino da (1820-1877) Portuguese				
oil	1	3,038	3,038	3,038
SILVA, William P (1859-1948) American				
oil	29	600-32,500	7,063	4,000
SILVAIN, Christian (1950-) Belgian				
3D	1	1,870	1,870	1,870
SILVANI, Ferdinando (1823-1899) Italian				
oil	4	817-3,646	2,386	2,178
SILVEN, Jakob (1851-1924) Swedish				
oil	3	702-3,406	1,718	1,048
SILVERMAN, Burton (1928-) American				
wc/d	6	500-2,800	1,175	500
SILVESTRE, Albert (1869-1954) Swiss				
oil	1	1,679	1,679	1,679
SILVESTRE, Israel (younger) (1621-1691) French				
wc/d	1	4,253	4,253	4,253
SILVESTRE, Louis (younger) (1675-1760) French				
wc/d	1	2,188	2,188	2,188
SILVESTRE, Paul (1884-?) French				
3D	4	1,967-9,048	4,139	2,264
SILVESTRI, Giovanni Battista (1796-1873) Italian				
wc/d	1	3,180	3,180	3,180
SILVESTRI, Oreste (1858-1936) Italian				
oil	1	1,816	1,816	1,816
SIMA, Joseph (1891-1971) Czechoslovakian				
oil	3	15,315-45,479	28,057	23,378
wc/d	14	540-8,035	2,959	2,337
SIMARD, Claude A (1943-) Canadian				
oil	1	1,793	1,793	1,793

Name	No.	Price Range	Average	Median
SIMARD, Marie Louise (?) French				
3D	1	47,500	47,500	47,500
SIMBARI, Nicola (1927-) Italian				
oil	18	700-22,490	7,194	6,000
SIMBERG, Hugo (1873-1917) Finnish				
oil	5	3,407-23,143	10,915	3,857
wc/d	1	1,929	1,929	1,929
SIMETI, Turi (1929-) Italian				
oil	20	589-16,703	4,627	3,633
wc/d	1	846	846	846
SIMI, Filadelfo (1849-1923) Italian				
oil	1	2,421	2,421	2,421
SIMIL, Emilcar (1944-) Canadian				
oil	1	1,188	1,188	1,188
SIMKHOVITCH, Simka (1893-1949) Russian				
oil	2	4,250-5,000	4,625	4,250
SIMKINS, Martha (20th C) American				
oil	1	3,400	3,400	3,400
SIMMEN, Henri (20th C) ?				
3D	1	15,811	15,811	15,811
SIMMONS, Edward Emerson (1852-1931) American				
oil	2	3,500-17,000	10,250	3,500
SIMMONS, Freeman Willis (?-1926) American				
oil	1	3,000	3,000	3,000
SIMMONS, Gary (1964-) American				
wc/d	1	27,500	27,500	27,500
SIMMS, G H (fl.1864-1865) British				
oil	1	3,016	3,016	3,016
SIMON, Andree (1896-1981) French				
oil	3	1,455-6,062	3,394	2,667
SIMON, Émile (1890-1976) French				
oil	4	536-4,034	2,136	1,403
wc/d	2	1,029-1,073	1,051	1,029
SIMON, Franz (?) Belgian				
oil	1	3,099	3,099	3,099
SIMON, Henry (1910-1987) French				
oil	2	867-1,124	995	867
wc/d	1	3,624	3,624	3,624
SIMON, Hermann Gustave (1846-1895) American				
oil	4	1,600-7,000	3,962	2,500
SIMON, Lucien (1861-1945) French				
oil	7	2,572-33,600	10,365	5,845
wc/d	8	1,262-13,793	7,542	7,949
SIMON, Maurice (20th C) French				
oil	1	1,200	1,200	1,200
SIMON, Yohanan (1905-1976) Israeli				
oil	25	1,900-42,000	10,376	8,000
wc/d	6	1,800-12,000	6,783	6,500
SIMONDO, Pietro (1928-) Italian				
oil	10	610-2,195	1,010	884
wc/d	2	549-1,231	890	549
SIMONE, A de (19/20th C) Italian				
wc/d	11	1,216-7,106	3,010	2,610
SIMONE, Giuliano di (?) ?				
oil	1	90,000	90,000	90,000
SIMONE, Michele de (19/20th C) Italian				
oil	3	484-3,279	2,015	2,283
SIMONE, Nicolo de (17th C) Italian				
oil	1	51,800	51,800	51,800
SIMONE, Tommaso de (19th C) Italian				
oil	3	4,200-13,572	7,757	5,500
wc/d	11	1,500-7,830	4,595	4,048
SIMONE, de (19/20th C) Italian				
oil	1	4,005	4,005	4,005
wc/d	5	1,178-4,241	3,082	3,299
SIMONELLI, Giuseppe (1650-1710) Italian				
oil	2	21,875-26,938	24,406	21,875
SIMONET, Enrique (1898-1978) Spanish				
oil	2	878-2,674	1,776	878
SIMONETTI, A (19/20th C) Italian				
oil	1	3,780	3,780	3,780

Name	No.	Price Range	Average	Median
SIMONETTI, Alfonso (1840-1892) Italian				
oil	1	4,094	4,094	4,094
SIMONETTI, Amedeo (1874-1922) Italian				
wc/d	2	1,008-2,000	1,504	1,008
SIMONETTI, Attilio (1843-1925) Italian				
oil	1	1,000	1,000	1,000
wc/d	1	726	726	726
SIMONETTI, Gianni Emilio (1940-) Italian				
oil	2	425-1,985	1,205	425
wc/d	1	1,811	1,811	1,811
SIMONETTI, Luigi (19th C) Italian				
3D	1	5,500	5,500	5,500
SIMONETTI, R (19/20th C) Italian				
oil	1	2,314	2,314	2,314
SIMONI, Gustavo (1846-1926) Italian				
oil	2	1,171-14,055	7,613	1,171
wc/d	9	2,000-20,003	7,518	7,434
SIMONI, Scipione (19/20th C) Italian				
oil	1	3,000	3,000	3,000
wc/d	4	1,405-18,185	6,027	2,000
SIMONIN, Julien (20th C) French				
oil	1	3,579	3,579	3,579
SIMONIN, Victor (1877-1946) Belgian				
oil	3	877-1,008	961	1,000
wc/d	1	839	839	839
SIMONINI, Francesco (1686-1753) Italian				
oil	6	4,815-217,500	57,701	26,000
SIMONS, Franz (1855-1919) Belgian				
oil	3	1,386-2,114	1,752	1,757
SIMONS, Michiel (?-1673) Dutch				
oil	3	40,000-121,100	91,933	114,700
SIMONSEN, Niels (1807-1885) Danish				
oil	4	1,737-8,112	4,097	3,162
SIMONSEN, Simon (1841-1928) Danish				
oil	12	632-8,853	3,461	2,507
SIMONSSON, Birger (1883-1938) Swedish				
oil	2	1,043-1,321	1,182	1,043
SIMONT-GUILLEN, Jose (1875-1968) Spanish				
wc/d	12	1,752-8,175	4,593	4,671
SIMONY, Stefan (1860-1950) Austrian				
oil	2	3,534-8,199	5,866	3,534
wc/d	1	4,123	4,123	4,123
SIMPSON, Charles Walter (1885-1971) British				
oil	8	616-9,250	4,926	5,130
wc/d	6	756-3,500	1,779	1,295
SIMPSON, Charles Walter (1878-1942) Canadian				
oil	3	984-3,702	2,278	2,150
wc/d	1	451	451	451
SIMPSON, David (1928-) American				
oil	5	600-3,500	2,225	2,428
SIMPSON, Jane (1965-) British				
3D	1	2,464	2,464	2,464
SIMPSON, John (1782-1847) British				
oil	1	6,840	6,840	6,840
SIMPSON, W H (19/20th C) British				
oil	1	4,248	4,248	4,248
SIMPSON, William (1823-1899) British				
wc/d	12	958-18,000	6,456	5,180
SIMS, Charles (1873-1926) British				
oil	3	531-6,125	2,468	748
SIMS, William Percy (19th C) British				
oil	1	1,239	1,239	1,239
SIMSON, William (1800-1847) British				
oil	1	2,805	2,805	2,805
wc/d	2	641-3,344	1,992	641
SINCLAIR, Deborah Lougheed (1953-) Canadian				
oil	2	1,152-3,545	2,348	1,152
SINCLAIR, Gerrit van W (1890-1955) American				
oil	1	2,900	2,900	2,900
SINCLAIR, Irving (1895-1969) American				
oil	1	3,900	3,900	3,900
wc/d	1	400	400	400

Name	No.	Price Range	Average	Median
SINCLAIR, Max (fl.1890-1910) British				
oil	3	716-4,810	2,168	978
SINDING, Otto Ludvig (1842-1909) Norwegian				
oil	2	647-4,332	2,489	647
SINDING, Stephan (1846-1922) Norwegian				
3D	3	4,841-10,395	7,050	5,916
SINEMUS, Willem Frederik (1903-1987) Dutch				
oil	1	4,071	4,071	4,071
wc/d	5	648-1,654	1,131	942
SING, Johann Kaspar (1651-1729) German				
oil	1	13,000	13,000	13,000
SINGENDONCK, Diederik Jan (1784-1833) Dutch				
oil	1	10,448	10,448	10,448
SINGER, Albert (1869-1922) German				
oil	1	1,815	1,815	1,815
SINGER, Burr (1912-) American				
oil	1	9,000	9,000	9,000
SINGER, Clyde (1908-1999) American				
oil	8	660-4,800	1,606	1,080
wc/d	1	3,000	3,000	3,000
SINGER, Jeremie (19th C) German?				
oil	1	2,803	2,803	2,803
SINGER, William Henry (jnr) (1868-1943) American				
wc/d	1	2,600	2,600	2,600
SINGH, Anjum (1967-) Indian				
oil	1	3,750	3,750	3,750
SINGH, Arpita (1937-) Indian				
oil	1	150,000	150,000	150,000
wc/d	1	9,000	9,000	9,000
SINGH, Gurcharan (20th C) Indian				
oil	1	9,000	9,000	9,000
SINGH, Maharana Bhim (1778-1828) Indian				
wc/d	1	1,566	1,566	1,566
SINGH, Paramjit (1935-) Indian				
oil	2	11,000-11,000	11,000	11,000
SINGIER, Gustave (1909-1985) French				
oil	5	3,850-35,000	15,250	11,784
wc/d	8	717-3,600	2,264	2,225
SINGLETON, Henry (1766-1839) British				
oil	1	26,550	26,550	26,550
SINHA, Satish (1893-1965) Indian				
oil	1	2,800	2,800	2,800
SINIBALDI, G (19/20th C) Italian				
oil	1	3,080	3,080	3,080
SINIBALDI, Jean Paul (1857-1909) French				
oil	1	1,701	1,701	1,701
SINKEL, Heinrich Johann (1835-1908) Dutch				
oil	1	1,332	1,332	1,332
SINOCHKIN, Andrei (1950-) Russian				
oil	1	1,587	1,587	1,587
SINTENIS, Renée (1888-1965) German				
oil	1	4,944	4,944	4,944
wc/d	2	618-718	668	618
3D	35	1,757-204,561	19,606	9,541
SION, Peeter (1649-1695) Flemish				
oil	2	5,959-5,959	5,959	5,959
SIPILA, Sulho (1895-1945) Finnish				
oil	3	479-3,982	1,810	969
SIPKES, Joseph (1787-1852) Dutch				
oil	1	2,667	2,667	2,667
SIPORIN, Mitchell (20th C) American				
oil	1	1,400	1,400	1,400
SIQUEIROS, David (1896-1974) Mexican				
oil	9	6,000-110,000	43,722	40,000
SIRAG, Karel H (1948-) Dutch				
oil	2	1,808-2,652	2,230	1,808
SIRAK, Carol (1906-1976) American				
oil	3	1,700-16,000	6,650	2,250
SIRANI, Elisabetta (1638-1665) Italian				
wc/d	2	2,592-5,724	4,158	2,592

Name	No.	Price Range	Average	Median
SIRONI, Mario (1885-1961) Italian				
oil	32	3,986-890,476	80,271	18,849
wc/d	56	1,288-44,507	6,590	4,892
SIROTTI, Raimondi (1934-) Italian				
oil	1	1,967	1,967	1,967
SISLEY, Alfred (1839-1899) French				
oil	21	75,000-2,576,000	865,828	672,600
SISS, W (20th C) ?				
oil	1	2,420	2,420	2,420
SISSON, Laurence P (1928-) American				
oil	4	1,800-6,000	3,700	3,500
wc/d	3	700-1,000	900	1,000
SITE, Mino delle (1914-1996) Italian				
oil	4	3,867-8,269	5,975	5,724
SITNIKOV, Alexander (1945-) Russian				
oil	1	40,000	40,000	40,000
SITTE, Willi (1921-) German?				
oil	3	1,295-39,556	15,677	6,181
SITU MIAN (1953-) Chinese				
oil	9	3,000-190,000	43,163	17,000
SITU, W Jason (20th C) American				
oil	1	4,000	4,000	4,000
SIVELL, Robert (1888-1958) British				
oil	1	5,190	5,190	5,190
SIVERTSEN, Jan (1951-) Danish				
oil	1	1,293	1,293	1,293
SIVIERO, Carlo (1882-1953) Italian				
oil	4	1,529-3,279	2,345	2,259
SIVORI, Edouardo (1847-1918) Argentinian				
oil	1	10,200	10,200	10,200
SIVUARAPIK, Thomassiapik (1941-) North American				
3D	1	1,772	1,772	1,772
SJAMAAR, Pieter Geerard (1819-1876) Dutch				
oil	3	770-2,854	1,958	2,250
SJOBERG, Axel (1866-1950) Swedish				
oil	3	1,923-5,495	3,302	2,489
wc/d	1	1,305	1,305	1,305
SJOSTRAND, Carl Eneas (1828-1906) Finnish				
3D	1	2,221	2,221	2,221
SJOSTRAND, Helmi (1864-1956) Finnish				
oil	2	581-3,982	2,281	581
SJOSTROM, Lars Petter (1820-1896) Swedish				
wc/d	5	759-1,984	1,392	1,426
SJOSTROM, Tyra (1875-1928) Finnish				
oil	1	1,008	1,008	1,008
SJOSTROM, Vilho (1873-1944) Finnish				
oil	7	584-4,909	2,707	3,045
SKAALE, J A (20th C) Danish?				
oil	1	1,288	1,288	1,288
SKALA, Robert (1874-1945) Austrian				
oil	1	1,648	1,648	1,648
SKANBERG, Carl (1850-1883) Swedish				
oil	9	786-13,737	3,897	1,870
SKARBINA, Franz (1849-1910) German				
oil	3	1,824-17,480	9,781	10,041
wc/d	10	496-4,580	1,717	1,243
SKEAPING, John (1901-1980) British				
wc/d	14	703-4,576	2,666	2,805
SKEATS, Leonard Frank (1874-1943) British				
oil	1	1,018	1,018	1,018
SKEELE, Anna Katharine (1896-1963) American				
oil	1	13,000	13,000	13,000
SKELTON, John (1923-1999) Irish/British				
oil	5	531-11,322	4,756	3,633
wc/d	2	714-1,272	993	714
SKELTON, John (1924-) Irish				
oil	1	2,930	2,930	2,930
wc/d	1	2,178	2,178	2,178
SKERRETT, Palm (19/20th C) Irish?				
oil	1	7,250	7,250	7,250
SKINNER, Charlotte B (1879-1963) American				
oil	1	1,700	1,700	1,700

Name	No.	Price Range	Average	Median
SKIPWORTH, Frank Markham (1854-1929) British				
oil	1	5,550	5,550	5,550
SKIRA, Pierre (1938-) French				
wc/d	4	1,200-2,640	1,680	1,320
SKITALTSEV, Evgeni Nikolaevich (1918-1927) Russian				
oil	1	4,602	4,602	4,602
SKLAR, Dorothy (20th C) American				
wc/d	3	650-3,250	1,566	800
SKLAVOS (1927-1967) Greek				
3D	5	8,486-14,400	10,162	8,919
SKLAVOS, Yerassimos (1927-1967) Greek				
wc/d	1	2,769	2,769	2,769
3D	5	4,077-28,160	13,099	10,829
SKODA, Vladimir (1942-) ?				
3D	1	2,128	2,128	2,128
SKODLERRAK, Horst (1920-) German				
oil	4	1,638-3,299	2,494	1,764
SKOLD, Otte (1894-1958) Swedish				
oil	8	842-10,836	2,580	1,272
wc/d	2	509-1,718	1,113	509
SKORODUMOVA, Tayssiya Nikolayevna (1928-) Russian				
wc/d	1	1,665	1,665	1,665
SKOTNES, Cecil (1926-) South African				
oil	1	3,540	3,540	3,540
SKOULAKIS, Dimos (1939-) Greek				
oil	1	7,392	7,392	7,392
SKOVGAARD, Joakim (1856-1933) Danish				
oil	2	1,048-1,141	1,094	1,048
SKOVGAARD, Niels (1858-1938) Danish				
oil	2	1,178-1,218	1,198	1,178
SKOVGAARD, P C (1817-1875) Danish				
oil	1	2,282	2,282	2,282
SKOVGAARD, Peter Christian (1817-1875) Danish				
oil	8	3,162-46,849	10,819	4,864
SKRAMSTAD, Ludwig (1855-1912) Norwegian				
oil	3	1,390-1,496	1,460	1,496
SKREBER, Dirk (1961-) German				
oil	14	19,000-430,000	125,955	105,600
wc/d	2	2,392-3,109	2,750	2,392
SKRETA, Karl (1610-1674) Czechoslovakian				
oil	1	7,474	7,474	7,474
wc/d	1	7,000	7,000	7,000
SKULASON, Thorvaldur (1906-1984) Icelandic				
oil	1	28,973	28,973	28,973
SKULME, Uga (1895-1963) Russian				
oil	1	2,700	2,700	2,700
SKUM, Nils Nilsson (1872-1951) Swedish				
wc/d	14	756-2,867	1,493	1,195
3D	1	3,241	3,241	3,241
SKURJENI, Matija (1888-1978) Hungarian				
oil	1	3,240	3,240	3,240
SKUTEZKY, Dominik (1850-1921) Hungarian				
oil	1	8,324	8,324	8,324
SLABBINCK, Frank (1942-) Belgian				
oil	2	556-865	710	556
wc/d	1	1,091	1,091	1,091
SLABBINCK, Rik (1914-1991) Belgian				
oil	18	892-10,764	3,707	2,637
wc/d	1	989	989	989
SLADE, Caleb Arnold (1882-1961) American				
oil	3	700-3,300	1,800	1,400
SLAGER, Frederic François (1876-1953) Dutch				
oil	2	1,512-9,041	5,276	1,512
SLAGER, Tom (1918-1994) Dutch				
oil	1	1,914	1,914	1,914
SLATER, John Falconar (1857-1937) British				
oil	38	458-6,612	1,312	900
wc/d	4	452-1,114	784	666
SLAUGHTER, William A (1923-) American				
oil	2	1,500-4,500	3,000	1,500
SLAVICEK, Jan (1900-) Czechoslovakian				
oil	1	1,145	1,145	1,145

Name	No.	Price Range	Average	Median
SLAVONA, Maria (1865-1931) German				
oil	1	5,088	5,088	5,088
SLEATOR, James Sinton (1889-1950) British				
oil	3	969-42,028	15,024	2,076
SLEEBE, Ferdinand Joseph (1907-1994) Dutch				
oil	5	530-2,290	1,075	932
wc/d	1	1,296	1,296	1,296
SLEESWYK, Alexander Cornelis (1870-1945) Dutch				
oil	1	1,377	1,377	1,377
SLEETH MILLER, Lola (1860-1951) American				
oil	1	2,400	2,400	2,400
SLEIGH, Bernard (1872-1954) British				
oil	1	33,120	33,120	33,120
SLEPYSHEV, Anatoli (1932-) Russian				
oil	3	7,440-27,900	14,260	7,440
SLETTEMARK, Kjartan (1932-) Swedish				
wc/d	2	1,057-2,114	1,585	1,057
SLEVOGT, Max (1868-1932) German				
oil	12	4,712-270,959	47,228	20,240
SLIND, Stuart (1951-) American				
oil	1	1,719	1,719	1,719
SLINGELANDT, Pieter van (1640-1691) Dutch				
oil	1	166,500	166,500	166,500
SLOAN, Diane Wiener (1940-) American				
oil	1	1,200	1,200	1,200
SLOAN, Helen Farr (1911-2005) American				
oil	2	750-4,500	2,625	750
SLOAN, John (1871-1951) American				
oil	6	4,000-190,000	56,125	11,000
wc/d	5	1,300-14,000	5,060	3,000
SLOAN, Junius R (1827-1900) American				
oil	1	9,750	9,750	9,750
wc/d	1	350	350	350
SLOANE, Eric (1910-1985) American				
oil	21	1,600-28,000	11,657	12,000
wc/d	1	425	425	425
SLOANE, George (1864-1942) American				
oil	2	2,000-2,650	2,325	2,000
SLOANE, Marian Parkhurst (1876-c.1954) American				
oil	3	1,300-3,500	2,060	1,380
SLOANE, Mary Anne (1889-1961) British				
wc/d	1	1,903	1,903	1,903
SLOANE, Sandi (20th C) American				
oil	1	2,400	2,400	2,400
SLOBODKINA, Esphyr (1908-) American				
oil	1	5,500	5,500	5,500
SLOCOMBE, Edward (1850-?) British				
wc/d	1	1,232	1,232	1,232
SLODKI, Marceli (?) Italian?				
oil	2	3,090-3,273	3,181	3,090
SLOM, Andre (?-1909) French/Polish				
wc/d	2	1,051-3,737	2,394	1,051
SLOMINSKI, Andreas (1959-) German				
3D	1	12,320	12,320	12,320
SLONIM, David (?) American				
oil	1	3,000	3,000	3,000
SLOT, John Van't (1946-) Dutch				
oil	1	2,170	2,170	2,170
SLOTT-MOLLER, Harald (1864-1937) Danish				
oil	11	714-64,211	9,527	3,066
SLOUN, Frank van (1879-1938) American				
oil	3	1,200-4,250	2,416	1,800
wc/d	1	1,000	1,000	1,000
SLUGLEJT, Iegosua Moiseevic (19/20th C) Russian?				
oil	1	9,414	9,414	9,414
SLUIS, Peter (1929-) Irish/Dutch				
oil	2	546-3,875	2,210	546
wc/d	1	814	814	814
SLUITER, Willy (1873-1949) Dutch				
oil	5	1,165-16,069	7,500	4,789
wc/d	7	890-9,452	3,080	2,682

Name	No.	Price Range	Average	Median
SLUSSER, Jean Paul (1886-?) American				
oil	1	9,500	9,500	9,500
SLUYS, Jacob van der (1660-1732) Dutch				
oil	1	4,325	4,325	4,325
SLUYTER, Anna (1866-1931) Dutch				
oil	2	3,816-8,269	6,042	3,816
SLUYTERMANN VON LANGEWEYDE, Georg (1903-1978) German				
oil	1	1,752	1,752	1,752
SLUYTERS, Jan (1881-1957) Dutch				
oil	9	3,616-233,784	57,225	25,918
wc/d	17	643-15,288	5,474	3,180
SLUYTERS, Jan (jnr) (1914-2005) Dutch				
oil	9	630-98,836	13,049	2,395
SLUYTERS, Lous (1908-1981) Dutch				
oil	1	1,169	1,169	1,169
SLYPER, Hendrik Johannes (1922-) Belgian				
oil	1	1,447	1,447	1,447
wc/d	1	777	777	777
SMAJIC, Peter (1910-) Yugoslavian				
3D	1	3,029	3,029	3,029
SMART, Edgar Rowley (1887-1934) British				
oil	2	487-2,262	1,374	487
SMART, Edmund Hodgson (1873-1942) British				
oil	2	1,750-3,560	2,655	1,750
SMART, John (1838-1899) British				
oil	2	606-2,805	1,705	606
wc/d	1	740	740	740
SMEDLEY, William Thomas (1858-1920) American				
wc/d	1	2,200	2,200	2,200
SMEERS, Frans (1873-1960) Belgian				
oil	15	718-12,858	3,847	1,940
SMEETS, Richard (1955-) Dutch				
oil	2	971-1,699	1,335	971
SMET, Gustave de (1877-1943) Belgian				
oil	5	2,637-88,000	23,238	8,247
wc/d	1	229,655	229,655	229,655
SMET, Henri de (1865-1940) Belgian				
oil	1	3,156	3,156	3,156
SMET, Léon de (1881-1966) Belgian				
oil	12	10,764-167,200	43,289	31,849
wc/d	1	2,637	2,637	2,637
SMETAK, T (19th C) ?				
oil	1	1,885	1,885	1,885
SMETHAM-JONES, G W (fl.1887-1893) British				
wc/d	2	679-3,420	2,049	679
SMETS, Louis (1840-1896) Belgian				
oil	2	1,373-4,000	2,686	1,373
SMIDT, Emil Leonhard (1878-1954) German				
oil	2	1,649-2,356	2,002	1,649
SMIDTH, Hans (1839-1917) Danish				
oil	13	1,352-3,301	1,982	1,699
wc/d	1	942	942	942
SMILLER, Francesca Volo (17th C) Italian				
oil	1	24,689	24,689	24,689
SMILLIE, George H (1840-1921) American				
oil	6	2,500-8,500	4,250	3,250
wc/d	1	3,000	3,000	3,000
SMILLIE, James David (1833-1909) American				
oil	1	4,250	4,250	4,250
SMIRKE, Mary (1789-1853) British				
wc/d	1	1,890	1,890	1,890
SMIRKE, Robert (1752-1845) British				
oil	1	1,014	1,014	1,014
SMIRSCH, Johann (1801-1869) Austrian				
oil	1	1,892	1,892	1,892
SMISSEN, Jacob (1735-1813) German				
wc/d	1	1,200	1,200	1,200
SMIT, Arie (1916-) Dutch				
oil	1	5,890	5,890	5,890
wc/d	1	2,890	2,890	2,890
SMIT, Derk (20th C) Dutch/American				
oil	1	1,300	1,300	1,300

Name	No.	Price Range	Average	Median
SMITH OF CHICHESTER, George (1714-1776) British				
oil	5	2,944-28,350	9,651	5,130
SMITH OF CHICHESTER, George and John (18th C) British				
oil	1	16,245	16,245	16,245
SMITH, Alexander R (19th C) British				
wc/d	1	1,056	1,056	1,056
SMITH, Alexis (1949-) American				
oil	1	13,000	13,000	13,000
SMITH, Alfred (1853-1946) French				
oil	3	753-3,028	1,705	1,334
SMITH, Alice Ravenel Huger (1876-1945) American				
wc/d	2	20,000-50,000	35,000	20,000
SMITH, Archibald Cary (1837-1911) American				
oil	1	80,000	80,000	80,000
SMITH, Arthur Reginald (1871-1934) British				
oil	1	1,602	1,602	1,602
wc/d	13	481-1,653	889	855
SMITH, B (19th C) British				
oil	1	1,171	1,171	1,171
SMITH, Brantley (20th C) American				
oil	1	1,500	1,500	1,500
wc/d	1	1,500	1,500	1,500
SMITH, Brett (1958-) American				
oil	2	10,000-12,500	11,250	10,000
SMITH, Brett James (1958-) American				
oil	3	10,000-13,000	11,333	11,000
SMITH, Carlton A (1853-1946) British				
oil	1	7,182	7,182	7,182
wc/d	8	1,097-23,250	7,187	3,500
SMITH, Charles (1749-1824) British				
oil	1	25,900	25,900	25,900
SMITH, Charles (fl.1857-1908) British				
oil	1	1,300	1,300	1,300
SMITH, Charles Hamilton (1776-1859) British				
wc/d	2	436-34,020	17,228	436
SMITH, Colvin (1795-1875) British				
oil	2	5,160-8,900	7,030	5,160
SMITH, Dan (?) ?				
oil	1	9,500	9,500	9,500
SMITH, David (1906-1965) American				
oil	2	60,000-420,000	240,000	60,000
wc/d	4	15,000-52,000	35,625	28,000
3D	4	475,000-21,250,000	6,981,250	1,800,000
SMITH, Decost (1864-1939) American				
wc/d	1	4,500	4,500	4,500
SMITH, Drew (20th C) American				
oil	1	2,000	2,000	2,000
SMITH, E Boyd (1860-1943) American				
oil	2	1,100-12,000	6,550	1,100
SMITH, Edward (19/20th C) British				
oil	1	10,395	10,395	10,395
SMITH, Ernest Browning (1866-1951) American				
oil	3	500-3,000	1,433	800
SMITH, Francis (1881-1961) Portuguese				
oil	8	11,100-50,400	33,641	31,450
wc/d	5	605-24,459	9,834	6,577
SMITH, Francis Hopkinson (1838-1915) American				
wc/d	4	600-22,500	6,700	700
SMITH, Frank Hill (1841-1904) American				
oil	3	2,200-3,500	2,766	2,600
SMITH, Frank Vining (1879-1967) American				
oil	8	1,250-20,000	13,193	13,500
SMITH, Frederick Carl (1868-1955) American				
oil	3	550-15,000	6,116	2,800
SMITH, Garden Grant (1860-1913) British				
oil	1	1,548	1,548	1,548
SMITH, Gary Ernest (1942-) American				
oil	10	1,400-19,000	6,985	6,000
SMITH, George (1829-1901) British				
oil	1	16,065	16,065	16,065
wc/d	2	463-2,128	1,295	463

Name	No.	Price Range	Average	Median
SMITH, George (1870-1934) British				
oil	15	828-5,191	3,054	2,992
SMITH, Gladys Nelson (19/20th C) American				
oil	4	500-4,000	1,962	550
SMITH, Gordon Appelby (1919-) Canadian				
oil	10	717-14,019	4,848	3,796
wc/d	1	923	923	923
SMITH, Grace Cossington (1892-1984) Australian				
oil	1	5,160	5,160	5,160
SMITH, Harry Knox (20th C) American				
wc/d	1	1,700	1,700	1,700
SMITH, Hassel (1915-) American				
oil	1	6,000	6,000	6,000
SMITH, Hely Augustus Morton (1862-1941) British				
oil	2	531-3,060	1,795	531
wc/d	1	700	700	700
SMITH, Henry Pember (1854-1907) American				
oil	14	950-22,000	5,517	3,750
wc/d	1	900	900	900
SMITH, Hobbe (1862-1942) Dutch				
oil	6	1,576-19,135	6,755	2,682
wc/d	1	3,031	3,031	3,031
SMITH, Howard E (1885-1970) American				
oil	1	1,300	1,300	1,300
SMITH, J Henry (19th C) American				
oil	1	2,000	2,000	2,000
SMITH, Jack (1928-) British				
wc/d	1	4,070	4,070	4,070
SMITH, Jack W (1873-1949) American				
oil	12	605-67,500	18,171	16,000
SMITH, Jacob Getlar (1898-1958) American				
oil	1	9,000	9,000	9,000
SMITH, James Burrell (1824-1897) British				
oil	3	2,595-3,580	3,218	3,480
wc/d	13	458-10,680	1,844	870
SMITH, Jesse Willcox (1863-1935) American				
oil	1	70,000	70,000	70,000
wc/d	7	7,000-170,000	63,785	60,000
SMITH, John Brandon (fl.1859-1884) British				
oil	8	875-5,670	2,639	1,720
SMITH, John Raphael (1752-1812) British				
oil	1	1,325	1,325	1,325
wc/d	1	4,176	4,176	4,176
SMITH, John Rubens (1775-1849) British/American				
oil	1	9,000	9,000	9,000
SMITH, John S (20th C) British				
oil	1	2,805	2,805	2,805
SMITH, John Warwick (1749-1831) British				
wc/d	6	797-12,090	4,993	2,975
SMITH, Jori (1907-2005) Canadian				
oil	4	441-3,775	1,799	1,322
SMITH, Joseph B (1798-1876) American				
oil	1	110,000	110,000	110,000
SMITH, Joseph Lindon (1863-1950) American				
oil	2	9,500-11,000	10,250	9,500
SMITH, Jules Andre (1880-1959) American				
oil	1	800	800	800
wc/d	1	700	700	700
SMITH, K A (19th C) British				
oil	1	2,855	2,855	2,855
SMITH, Kiki (1954-) American				
3D	5	22,490-250,000	136,498	95,000
SMITH, Kimber (1922-1981) American				
oil	1	3,888	3,888	3,888
wc/d	5	589-1,500	865	707
SMITH, Leon Polk (1906-1996) American				
oil	1	35,000	35,000	35,000
wc/d	2	800-1,288	1,044	800
SMITH, Lilian Wilhelm (1882-1971) American				
oil	1	1,300	1,300	1,300
SMITH, Lowell Ellsworth (1924-) American				
wc/d	2	1,600-1,750	1,675	1,600

Name	No.	Price Range	Average	Median
SMITH, Marcella (1887-1963) British				
oil	2	1,104-1,380	1,242	1,104
wc/d	1	531	531	531
SMITH, Marius (1868-1938) American				
oil	1	4,000	4,000	4,000
SMITH, Mary (1842-1878) American				
oil	4	1,500-7,500	5,750	6,500
SMITH, Mary P (19th C) American				
oil	1	1,500	1,500	1,500
SMITH, Mary Tillman (1904-1995) American				
oil	6	700-1,850	1,175	900
SMITH, Ray (1959-) American				
oil	4	5,286-13,875	9,155	8,000
SMITH, Richard (1931-) British				
oil	3	970-11,284	4,838	2,262
wc/d	1	3,382	3,382	3,382
SMITH, Robin Artine (1903-1992) American				
oil	1	2,100	2,100	2,100
SMITH, Russell (1812-1896) American				
oil	8	1,900-10,000	5,762	4,500
SMITH, Sir Matthew (1879-1959) British				
oil	10	500-87,360	34,397	27,840
wc/d	4	1,740-11,764	5,567	3,096
SMITH, Spence (?) ?				
oil	2	3,740-8,096	5,918	3,740
SMITH, Stephen Catterson (elder) (1806-1872) British				
oil	2	1,023-17,670	9,346	1,023
SMITH, Tony (1912-1980) American				
3D	4	16,000-120,000	58,250	42,000
SMITH, Tucker (20th C) American				
oil	1	52,500	52,500	52,500
SMITH, Vernon B (1894-?) American				
oil	1	3,750	3,750	3,750
SMITH, Vivian (19/20th C) British				
oil	1	1,376	1,376	1,376
SMITH, Walter Granville (1870-1938) American				
oil	3	6,000-20,000	10,666	6,000
wc/d	1	1,850	1,850	1,850
SMITH, Wilhelm (1867-1949) Swedish				
oil	2	4,212-18,545	11,378	4,212
SMITH, William Collingwood (1815-1887) British				
oil	1	1,639	1,639	1,639
wc/d	2	435-2,288	1,361	435
SMITH, William H (fl.1863-1880) British				
oil	1	1,357	1,357	1,357
SMITH, Xanthus (1838-1929) American				
oil	2	1,400-2,400	1,900	1,400
SMITH-HALD (19/20th C) Norwegian				
oil	1	6,910	6,910	6,910
SMITH-HALD, Frithjof (1846-1903) Norwegian				
oil	4	791-14,720	8,181	5,000
SMITHSON, Robert (1938-1973) American				
wc/d	2	14,000-90,000	52,000	14,000
3D	2	320,000-620,000	470,000	320,000
SMITS, Jakob (1856-1928) Belgian				
oil	4	658-7,774	2,866	1,457
wc/d	7	927-19,178	7,297	3,956
SMITS, Louis (19th C) Belgian				
oil	1	4,142	4,142	4,142
SMITSEN, Franciscus (?) ?				
oil	1	2,625	2,625	2,625
SMITZ, Gaspar (1635-1707) Dutch				
oil	1	15,000	15,000	15,000
SMOLDERS, Pol (1921-1997) Belgian				
oil	1	1,483	1,483	1,483
wc/d	1	1,674	1,674	1,674
SMOORENBERG, Dirk (1883-1960) Dutch				
oil	11	5,088-25,442	10,780	7,658
SMOUKROVITCH, Piotr (1928-) Russian				
oil	1	2,750	2,750	2,750
SMUGLEVITZ, Franciszek (1745-1807) Polish				
wc/d	1	10,000	10,000	10,000

Name	No.	Price Range	Average	Median
SMULDERS, Paul (1962-) Dutch				
oil	2	1,636-2,805	2,220	1,636
SMYTH, Brian (1974-) Irish				
oil	1	1,036	1,036	1,036
SMYTH, Norman (20th C) Irish				
oil	2	1,730-1,903	1,816	1,730
SMYTHE, Edward Robert (1810-1899) British				
oil	6	968-15,045	3,749	1,274
wc/d	1	1,479	1,479	1,479
SMYTHE, Leslie (19th C) British				
oil	1	1,200	1,200	1,200
SMYTHE, Thomas (1825-1906) British				
oil	19	1,246-25,665	6,399	4,600
wc/d	1	1,770	1,770	1,770
SNAPHAEN, Abraham (1651-1691) Dutch				
oil	1	1,012	1,012	1,012
SNAPP, Frank (20th C) American				
wc/d	1	2,250	2,250	2,250
SNEBUR (1964-) Italian				
oil	1	2,108	2,108	2,108
SNEL, Han (1925-1998) Dutch				
oil	1	6,020	6,020	6,020
SNELGROVE, Walter (1924-) American				
oil	2	750-1,500	1,125	750
SNELL, Henry Bayley (1858-1943) American				
oil	11	1,400-30,000	7,200	3,500
wc/d	1	2,000	2,000	2,000
SNELL, James Herbert (1861-1935) British				
oil	6	490-3,560	1,333	601
SNELL, Rosie (1971-) British				
oil	1	3,894	3,894	3,894
SNELLINCK, Cornelis (?-1669) Dutch				
oil	1	40,000	40,000	40,000
SNELLMAN, Anna (1884-1962) Finnish				
oil	8	504-2,314	979	727
wc/d	2	533-702	617	533
SNELLMAN, Christina (1928-) Finnish				
oil	7	599-3,600	1,381	1,079
SNICK, Jozef van (1860-1945) Belgian				
oil	1	18,437	18,437	18,437
SNIDOW, Gordon (1936-) British				
wc/d	1	50,000	50,000	50,000
SNOW, Francis W (19th C) American				
oil	2	700-2,000	1,350	700
SNOW, John Harold Thomas (1911-2004) Canadian				
oil	3	833-2,460	1,675	1,732
SNOW, Michael (1929-) Canadian				
oil	1	68,886	68,886	68,886
wc/d	2	9,896-12,370	11,133	9,896
SNYDER, Annie M (1852-1927) American				
oil	1	7,500	7,500	7,500
SNYDER, William McKendree (1848-1930) American				
oil	3	1,750-2,000	1,850	1,800
SNYDERS, Frans (1579-1657) Dutch				
oil	3	70,135-115,714	86,169	72,660
SNYERS, Pieter (1681-1752) Flemish				
oil	4	6,920-38,060	22,182	17,800
SOANE, Sir John (1753-1837) British				
wc/d	1	4,524	4,524	4,524
SOAVE, Mario (1955-) Italian				
oil	2	825-1,414	1,119	825
SOBIESKI, W L D (20th C) Polish				
oil	1	2,250	2,250	2,250
SOBRADO, Pedro (1936-) Spanish				
oil	13	1,113-2,275	1,677	1,674
wc/d	3	507-784	631	603
SOBRINO BUHIGAS, Carlos (1885-1978) Spanish				
wc/d	1	25,865	25,865	25,865
SOBRINO, Francisco (1932-) Spanish				
3D	1	1,799	1,799	1,799

Name	No.	Price Range	Average	Median
SOCRATE, Carlo (1889-1967) Italian				
oil	1	3,279	3,279	3,279
wc/d	1	4,568	4,568	4,568
SODERBERG, Ernst (1889-?) Swedish				
oil	1	1,718	1,718	1,718
SODERBERG, Yngve Edward (1896-1971) American				
wc/d	1	2,000	2,000	2,000
SODERGREN, Johanna Sophia (1847-1923) Swedish				
oil	1	1,288	1,288	1,288
SODRING, Frederik (1809-1862) Danish				
oil	3	518-4,241	2,673	3,260
SOEHENE, Charles F (?) ?				
wc/d	1	48,100	48,100	48,100
SOEHNEE, Charles Frederic (1789-1878) French?				
wc/d	1	24,075	24,075	24,075
SOELEN, Theodore van (1890-1964) American				
oil	1	35,000	35,000	35,000
SOERJOSOEBROTO, Abdullah (1879-1941) Indonesian				
oil	1	1,701	1,701	1,701
SOEST, Louis W van (1867-1948) Dutch				
oil	1	2,158	2,158	2,158
SOEST, Pierre Gerardus Cornelis van (1930-2001) Dutch				
oil	1	1,447	1,447	1,447
SOETE, Pierre de (20th C) Belgian				
3D	1	2,503	2,503	2,503
SOETERIK, Theodoor (1810-1883) Dutch				
oil	1	5,341	5,341	5,341
SOFFIANTINO, Giacomo (1929-) Italian				
oil	3	492-1,909	995	584
wc/d	3	467-525	502	514
SOFFICI, Ardengo (1879-1964) Italian				
oil	14	10,541-175,685	59,609	37,479
wc/d	6	3,053-12,945	8,506	8,562
SOFRONOVA, Antonina (1892-1966) Russian				
wc/d	5	1,411-10,138	6,041	7,603
SOHN, Carl Rudolf (1845-1908) German				
oil	2	2,400-55,200	28,800	2,400
SOHN, Wilhelm (?) German?				
oil	1	1,004	1,004	1,004
SOISALO, Juha (1941-) Finnish				
oil	6	479-2,460	1,444	1,288
SOKOLOFF, Alexander Petrovitch (1829-1913) Russian				
oil	1	12,000	12,000	12,000
wc/d	1	1,052	1,052	1,052
SOKOLOFF, Anatolio (1891-1971) Russian				
oil	1	18,810	18,810	18,810
SOKOLOFF, Piotr Fiodorovitch (c.1791-1847) Russian				
wc/d	1	22,320	22,320	22,320
SOKOLOFF, Piotr Petrovitch (1821-1899) Russian				
oil	1	39,060	39,060	39,060
wc/d	1	10,320	10,320	10,320
SOKOLOV, Pavel Petrovich (1899-1961) Russian				
oil	2	38,060-70,680	54,370	38,060
SOLANO, Susana (1946-) Spanish				
3D	2	24,082-36,122	30,102	24,082
SOLAVAGGIONE, Piero (1899-1979) Italian				
oil	1	1,197	1,197	1,197
SOLDAN-BROFELDT, Venny (1863-1945) Finnish				
oil	19	727-35,068	5,678	4,451
wc/d	2	727-4,909	2,818	727
SOLDANI, Massimiliano (1658-1740) Italian				
3D	1	50,857	50,857	50,857
SOLDATI, Atanasio (1896-1953) Italian				
oil	6	1,288-22,898	10,966	9,534
wc/d	12	876-4,919	3,127	2,829
SOLDATI, Massimo (1959-) Italian				
oil	2	2,544-2,577	2,560	2,544
SOLDERA, Emilio (1874-1955) Italian				
oil	1	2,330	2,330	2,330
SOLDI, Émile (1846-1906) French				
3D	2	4,554-6,612	5,583	4,554

Name	No.	Price Range	Average	Median
SOLDI, Raul (1905-1994) Argentinian				
oil	11	1,000-46,000	11,015	6,000
wc/d	4	3,000-9,000	5,750	5,000
SOLDWEDEL, Frederic (1886-1957) American				
wc/d	1	6,000	6,000	6,000
SOLENGHI, Giuseppe (1879-1944) Italian				
oil	9	606-3,269	1,699	1,274
SOLER GILL, Domingo (1871-1951) Spanish				
oil	1	1,017	1,017	1,017
wc/d	1	589	589	589
SOLER PUIG, Juan (1906-1984) Spanish				
oil	1	1,134	1,134	1,134
SOLER, J (20th C) ?				
oil	1	2,411	2,411	2,411
SOLER, Juan (1941-) Spanish				
oil	13	600-2,655	1,554	1,464
SOLERI-BRANCALEONI, Giuseppe (?-1806) Italian				
oil	1	2,141	2,141	2,141
wc/d	1	425	425	425
SOLERO, Pio (1881-?) Italian				
oil	4	3,857-13,500	7,296	5,400
SOLIMENA, Francesco (1657-1747) Italian				
oil	6	12,884-224,900	74,951	40,767
wc/d	2	1,200-16,829	9,014	1,200
SOLIN, Timo (1947-) Swedish				
wc/d	1	1,123	1,123	1,123
3D	2	1,691-3,563	2,627	1,691
SOLIS, Francisco de (1620-1684) Spanish				
oil	1	65,740	65,740	65,740
SOLIS, Virgil (elder) (1514-1562) German				
wc/d	2	40,707-54,701	47,704	40,707
SOLLIDAY, Tim (1952-) American				
oil	3	5,500-41,000	19,666	12,500
wc/d	2	1,000-2,200	1,600	1,000
SOLLIER, Henri Alexandre (1886-?) French				
oil	1	1,109	1,109	1,109
SOLMAN, Joseph (1909-) American				
oil	4	1,600-3,600	2,675	2,700
wc/d	3	1,200-2,400	1,833	1,900
SOLNTSEV, S (20th C) ?				
oil	1	1,860	1,860	1,860
SOLODOVNIKOV, Alexei Pavlovitch (1928-) Russian				
oil	1	15,930	15,930	15,930
SOLOMKO, Sergei (1859-1926) Russian				
wc/d	3	7,120-11,180	9,253	9,460
SOLOMON, Abraham (1824-1862) British				
oil	2	3,480-8,550	6,015	3,480
wc/d	1	648	648	648
SOLOMON, Daniel (20th C) Canadian?				
oil	1	1,109	1,109	1,109
SOLOMON, Hyde (1911-1982) American				
oil	2	1,000-6,000	3,500	1,000
SOLOMON, Lance Vaiben (1913-1989) Australian				
oil	1	3,344	3,344	3,344
SOLOMON, Simeon (1840-1905) British				
oil	1	32,760	32,760	32,760
wc/d	3	1,104-6,612	3,822	3,750
SOLOMON, Solomon J (1860-1927) British				
oil	4	490-13,000	5,685	3,700
SOLOMONS, Estella Frances (1882-1968) Irish				
oil	10	1,110-11,981	3,440	2,264
SOLON, Leon Victor (1872-?) American/British				
oil	1	11,000	11,000	11,000
wc/d	1	2,958	2,958	2,958
SOLONEN, Jouko (1920-) Finnish				
oil	1	1,054	1,054	1,054
SOLOTAIRE, Robert (20th C) American				
oil	1	1,000	1,000	1,000
SOLOVIOV, A (20th C) Russian				
oil	1	4,000	4,000	4,000
SOMER, Hendrik van (1615-1685) Dutch				
oil	1	84,857	84,857	84,857

Name	No.	Price Range	Average	Median
SOMERS, Louis (1813-1880) Belgian				
oil	1	6,562	6,562	6,562
SOMERSCALES, Thomas (1842-1927) British				
oil	4	3,740-40,480	19,565	10,120
SOMERVILLE, Edith Oenone (1858-1949) British				
oil	1	2,472	2,472	2,472
wc/d	1	1,440	1,440	1,440
SOMERVILLE, Peggy (1918-1975) British				
oil	2	1,408-2,036	1,722	1,408
wc/d	5	531-2,301	1,009	743
SOMERVILLE, Stuart (1908-1983) British				
oil	9	473-2,301	1,119	1,044
SOMM, Henry (1844-1907) French				
wc/d	10	425-10,541	3,937	3,514
SOMME, Theophile (1871-1952) French				
3D	1	6,000	6,000	6,000
SOMMER, Carl August (1829-?) German				
oil	1	4,849	4,849	4,849
SOMMER, Ferdinand (1822-1901) Swiss				
oil	3	916-1,832	1,491	1,725
SOMMER, G (20th C) ?				
3D	1	2,580	2,580	2,580
SOMMER, J (19/20th C) German?				
oil	1	4,000	4,000	4,000
SOMMER, R (1866-?) German?				
oil	1	15,136	15,136	15,136
SOMMER, Richard (1866-1939) German?				
oil	2	16,397-26,219	21,308	16,397
SOMMER, William (1867-1949) American				
wc/d	9	1,000-6,000	2,944	2,400
SOMMYEVRE, Bernard de (19th C) French				
oil	1	1,229	1,229	1,229
SOMOGYI, Daniel (1837-1890) Hungarian				
oil	1	1,168	1,168	1,168
SOMOV, Konstantin (1869-1939) Russian				
oil	1	1,978,000	1,978,000	1,978,000
wc/d	5	19,325-361,200	105,305	48,160
SOMVILLE, Roger (1923-) Belgian				
oil	9	1,435-15,925	7,803	7,265
wc/d	9	509-3,152	1,276	860
SON, Joris van (1623-1667) Flemish				
oil	7	9,073-74,000	39,668	38,571
SONDERBORG, Kurt R H (1923-) Danish				
oil	7	6,361-19,110	12,806	12,740
wc/d	9	1,414-7,771	3,120	2,631
SONDERGAARD, Jens (1895-1957) Danish				
oil	17	2,910-16,164	7,000	6,496
wc/d	3	582-711	646	647
3D	1	1,859	1,859	1,859
SONDERMANN, Hermann (1832-1901) German				
oil	1	2,068	2,068	2,068
SONG WENZHI (1918-1999) Chinese				
wc/d	1	1,093	1,093	1,093
SONG YONG HONG (1966-) Chinese				
oil	1	37,654	37,654	37,654
SONIN, V (19th C) Russian				
oil	1	22,932	22,932	22,932
SONJE, Jan Gabrielsz (1625-1707) Dutch				
oil	2	9,342-9,350	9,346	9,342
SONNE, Jorgen Valentin (1801-1890) Danish				
oil	2	1,111-17,390	9,250	1,111
SONNEGA, Auke (1910-1963) Dutch				
oil	3	7,827-16,540	11,430	9,924
SONNEMAN (18th C) ?				
oil	2	9,080-14,000	11,540	9,080
SONNENSCHEIN, Eliezer (1967-) Israeli				
oil	1	11,000	11,000	11,000
SONNIER, Keith (1941-) American				
wc/d	1	1,649	1,649	1,649
3D	1	4,248	4,248	4,248
SONNIUS, Hendrik (?-1662) Dutch				
oil	1	8,247	8,247	8,247

Name	No.	Price Range	Average	Median
SONNTAG, William L (1822-1900) American				
oil	15	2,500-35,000	14,350	14,000
wc/d	2	3,250-4,250	3,750	3,250
SONNTAG, William L (jnr) (1869-1898) American				
wc/d	3	2,750-7,500	4,583	3,500
SONREL, Elisabeth (1874-1953) French				
wc/d	2	1,184-20,217	10,700	1,184
SOOLMAKER, Jan Frans (1635-1685) Flemish				
oil	3	4,628-12,335	9,114	10,380
SOONIUS, Louis (1883-1956) Dutch				
oil	10	650-20,726	5,934	3,400
SOPER, George (1870-1942) British				
wc/d	1	1,190	1,190	1,190
SORBI, Giulio (1883-1975) Italian				
oil	1	1,767	1,767	1,767
SORBI, Raffaello (1844-1931) Italian				
oil	14	957-150,000	17,039	5,301
wc/d	1	1,496	1,496	1,496
SORDET, Eugène Etienne (1836-1915) Swiss				
oil	2	554-3,273	1,913	554
SORDINI, Ettore (1934-) Italian				
wc/d	5	584-1,986	1,294	1,401
SORDO (20th C) Moroccan				
oil	3	2,022-4,995	3,766	4,281
SOREAU, Isaak (1604-?) Dutch				
oil	2	79,486-92,511	85,998	79,486
SORENSEN, C F (1818-1879) Danish				
oil	2	1,098-1,161	1,129	1,098
wc/d	1	711	711	711
SORENSEN, Carl Frederick (1818-1879) Danish				
oil	16	373-9,485	4,363	3,211
SORENSEN, David (1937-) Canadian?				
oil	1	2,132	2,132	2,132
SORENSEN, Henrik (1882-1962) Norwegian				
oil	1	2,473	2,473	2,473
wc/d	1	423	423	423
SORENSEN, Jens Flemming (1933-) Danish				
3D	1	4,990	4,990	4,990
SORESSI, Alfredo (1897-?) Italian				
oil	3	1,815-5,812	3,349	2,420
SORGE, Peter (1937-) German				
oil	1	1,119	1,119	1,119
SORGH, Hendrik Martensz (1611-1670) Dutch				
oil	5	565-43,250	14,540	11,439
SORIANO, Elvira (?) European				
oil	1	3,500	3,500	3,500
SORIANO, Juan (1920-) Mexican				
oil	2	11,000-16,000	13,500	11,000
wc/d	1	15,000	15,000	15,000
SORINE, Saveli (1878-1953) Russian				
oil	1	19,778	19,778	19,778
wc/d	3	8,132-60,200	42,844	60,200
SORIO, Enrico (1838-1909) Italian				
oil	2	608-3,366	1,987	608
SORKAU, Albert (1874-?) French				
oil	1	2,221	2,221	2,221
SOROKALETOV, Gavril (1913-) Russian				
oil	1	2,141	2,141	2,141
SOROLLA Y BASTIDA, Joaquin (1863-1923) Spanish				
oil	20	7,782-1,380,000	232,711	119,600
wc/d	2	3,449-19,357	11,403	3,449
SORONGAS, Sotiris (1936-) Greek				
oil	1	4,675	4,675	4,675
SOROUJOUN, Sultana (20th C) ?				
oil	3	420-8,000	3,240	1,300
SORTET, Paul (1905-1966) Belgian				
oil	1	2,182	2,182	2,182
SORUSILUK, Mary Irqiquq (1941-) North American				
3D	1	3,543	3,543	3,543
SOSSON, L (20th C) French				
3D	1	3,058	3,058	3,058

Name	No.	Price Range	Average	Median
SOSSON, Louis (20th C) French				
3D	2	2,422-3,086	2,754	2,422
SOTO, Jesus Rafael (1923-2005) Venezuelan				
oil	3	64,291-259,000	150,930	129,500
wc/d	4	4,650-88,219	35,128	10,700
3D	40	1,757-360,000	76,981	49,367
SOTOMAYOR Y ZARAGOZA, Fernando (1875-1960) Spanish				
oil	3	3,762-21,857	11,161	7,864
SOTOMAYOR, Juan (1956-) ?				
oil	1	1,784	1,784	1,784
SOTTER, George William (1879-1953) American				
oil	18	1,300-200,000	67,669	34,000
SOTTOCORNOLA, Giovanni (1855-1917) Italian				
oil	1	2,275	2,275	2,275
wc/d	5	2,589-36,247	12,220	6,732
SOTTSASS, Ettore (1917-) Austrian				
3D	2	5,377-7,633	6,505	5,377
SOUBRE, Charles (1821-1895) Belgian				
oil	1	7,418	7,418	7,418
SOUCH, John (c.1593-1645) British				
oil	1	56,700	56,700	56,700
SOUDAN, Octaaf (1872-1948) Belgian				
oil	5	1,013-1,312	1,168	1,192
SOUDBINNIE, Seraphin (1870-1944) Russian?				
3D	1	22,320	22,320	22,320
SOUDEIKINE, Sergei (1883-1946) Russian				
oil	2	20,000-27,500	23,750	20,000
wc/d	5	14,000-70,000	41,000	36,000
SOUKOP, Willi (1907-1995) British				
3D	1	2,035	2,035	2,035
SOUKUP, Frantisek Ladislaw (1888-1954) ?				
oil	1	1,500	1,500	1,500
SOULACROIX, Frederic (1825-1879) French				
oil	9	9,500-210,000	65,637	27,500
SOULAGES, Pierre (1919-) French				
oil	10	53,100-1,352,414	447,612	323,750
wc/d	7	3,307-98,889	43,381	32,945
SOULEN, Henry James (1888-1965) American				
oil	1	11,000	11,000	11,000
wc/d	1	500	500	500
SOULIE, Tony (1955-) French				
oil	2	821-2,719	1,770	821
wc/d	4	1,075-1,978	1,474	1,360
SOULIKIAS, Paul (1926-) Canadian				
oil	1	2,320	2,320	2,320
SOUNGOUROFF, Antonin Ivanovitch (1894-?) Russian				
oil	1	2,395	2,395	2,395
SOUPER, Charles Edward (1842-?) British				
wc/d	1	1,573	1,573	1,573
SOUTER, Camille (1929-) British				
oil	3	5,890-19,374	12,622	12,603
SOUTER, Georges (19th C) ?				
oil	1	2,384	2,384	2,384
SOUTER, John Bulloch (1890-1972) British				
oil	5	637-3,806	1,970	1,032
SOUTHALL, Joseph Edward (1861-1944) British				
wc/d	1	3,078	3,078	3,078
SOUTHERN, C (?) ?				
oil	1	1,056	1,056	1,056
SOUTHGATE, Frank (1872-1916) British				
oil	1	652	652	652
wc/d	14	403-4,071	1,808	1,216
SOUTHWARD, Vernon (1911-1981) British				
oil	2	736-1,564	1,150	736
SOUTINE, Chaim (1893-1943) Russian				
oil	15	110,000-12,390,001	1,625,766	680,000
wc/d	3	9,568-12,740	11,682	12,740
SOUTMAN, Pieter Claesz (1580-1657) Dutch				
wc/d	1	1,874	1,874	1,874
SOUTO, Arturo (1901-1964) Spanish				
oil	1	14,449	14,449	14,449

Name	No.	Price Range	Average	Median
SOUTTER, Louis (1871-1942) Swiss				
oil	3	8,106-89,163	39,448	21,075
wc/d	11	734-218,855	71,597	56,740
SOUVERBIE, Jean (1891-1981) French				
oil	7	8,000-120,000	49,698	44,014
wc/d	2	773-17,107	8,940	773
SOUZA, Francis Newton (1924-2002) British/Indian				
oil	58	10,000-1,028,500	146,143	110,000
wc/d	37	1,144-27,500	11,105	11,000
SOUZA-PINTO, Alberto Carlos (1861-1939) Portuguese				
oil	2	3,534-3,534	3,534	3,534
SOUZA-PINTO, Jose Giulio (1856-1939) Portuguese				
oil	12	4,113-32,986	13,245	7,120
wc/d	4	9,092-9,699	9,547	9,699
SOWERBY, John G (1850-1914) British				
oil	1	1,104	1,104	1,104
SOWERBY, Kate (fl.1883-1900) British				
oil	1	1,575	1,575	1,575
SOYER, Moses (1899-1974) American				
oil	13	1,344-14,000	3,572	2,400
wc/d	2	750-1,400	1,075	750
SOYER, Paul Constant (1823-1903) French				
oil	1	2,165	2,165	2,165
SOYER, Raphael (1899-1987) American				
oil	10	1,500-26,000	6,800	3,250
wc/d	11	400-1,600	725	675
SPACAL, Luigi (1907-2000) Italian				
oil	1	4,757	4,757	4,757
SPACKMAN, Isaac (?-1771) British				
wc/d	5	1,969-3,938	3,101	3,133
SPACKMAN, Sarah (1958-) British				
oil	2	1,090-1,286	1,188	1,090
SPADA, Costantino (20th C) Italian				
oil	1	3,221	3,221	3,221
SPADA, Lionello (1576-1622) Italian				
oil	1	59,548	59,548	59,548
SPADA, Valerio (1613-1688) Italian				
wc/d	1	4,750	4,750	4,750
SPADARI, Gian Giacomo (1938-1997) Italian				
oil	5	884-2,330	1,382	1,145
SPADINI, Armando (1883-1925) Italian				
oil	1	3,600	3,600	3,600
SPADINO, Giovanni Paolo (17th C) Italian				
oil	1	58,378	58,378	58,378
SPAENDONCK, Cornelis van (1756-1840) French				
oil	5	1,178-46,124	13,595	6,833
wc/d	1	21,586	21,586	21,586
SPAENDONCK, Gerard van (1746-1822) French				
oil	1	80,000	80,000	80,000
wc/d	2	9,515-11,245	10,380	9,515
SPAEY, M van (18th C) Dutch				
oil	1	19,580	19,580	19,580
SPAGNULO, Giuseppe (1936-) Italian				
oil	1	1,272	1,272	1,272
wc/d	4	1,764-5,890	3,066	1,764
3D	7	2,571-22,839	10,129	7,633
SPAIN, Mary (20th C) American				
oil	1	1,920	1,920	1,920
SPALLETTI, Ettore (1940-) Italian				
oil	1	10,541	10,541	10,541
wc/d	1	35,400	35,400	35,400
SPALMACHI, O (?) Italian?				
3D	1	40,000	40,000	40,000
SPAMPINATO, Clemente (1912-) American				
3D	1	4,948	4,948	4,948
SPANELL, Hans (19/20th C) German				
3D	1	6,562	6,562	6,562
SPANG, Frederick A (1834-1891) American				
oil	3	700-10,000	4,366	2,400
SPANGENBERG, Louis (1824-1893) German				
oil	1	3,579	3,579	3,579

Name	No.	Price Range	Average	Median
SPANO, Raffaello (1817-?) Italian				
oil	2	1,052-1,300	1,176	1,052
SPANYI, Bela von (1852-1914) Hungarian				
oil	3	1,424-4,712	3,212	3,500
SPARE, Austin Osman (1888-1956) British				
wc/d	7	655-4,536	2,564	2,013
SPARKS, Will (1862-1937) American				
oil	7	2,500-11,000	6,528	6,500
SPARRE, Emma (1851-1913) Swedish				
oil	1	2,867	2,867	2,867
SPARRE, Louis (1863-1964) Finnish/Swedish				
oil	10	727-25,414	4,627	1,800
SPARROW, Geoffrey (?) British?				
wc/d	3	445-2,580	1,305	890
SPARROW, Simon (1914-2000) American				
wc/d	1	4,000	4,000	4,000
SPAT, Gabriel (1890-1967) French				
oil	7	750-1,600	1,130	1,007
wc/d	1	650	650	650
SPAUN, Paul von (1876-1932) Austrian				
oil	4	497-3,279	1,722	1,178
SPAZZAPAN, Luigi (1890-1958) Italian				
oil	7	3,495-11,211	6,197	6,096
wc/d	3	2,268-2,521	2,375	2,336
SPEAR, Ruskin (1911-1990) British				
oil	14	522-37,800	13,327	11,100
wc/d	2	1,914-4,176	3,045	1,914
SPEARS, Ethel (1903-1974) American				
oil	1	1,300	1,300	1,300
wc/d	1	4,500	4,500	4,500
SPEARS, Gregg (20th C) American				
oil	1	2,700	2,700	2,700
SPECHT, Friedrich (1839-1909) German				
oil	1	1,870	1,870	1,870
SPECK, Loran (1944-) American				
oil	2	5,000-12,000	8,500	5,000
SPECKAERT, Hans (?-c.1577) Flemish				
wc/d	1	75,000	75,000	75,000
SPEECHLEY, Sir William (c.1740-1826) British				
wc/d	1	1,400	1,400	1,400
SPEECKAERT, Michel Joseph (1748-1838) Belgian				
oil	2	6,674-7,770	7,222	6,674
SPEED, Grant (1930-) American				
3D	1	4,000	4,000	4,000
SPEED, Lancelot (1860-1931) British				
oil	1	6,055	6,055	6,055
SPEED, Ulysses Grant (1930-) American				
3D	2	4,750-5,000	4,875	4,750
SPEEDY GRAPHITO (1961-) French				
oil	2	1,670-1,909	1,789	1,670
wc/d	1	1,229	1,229	1,229
SPEICHER, Eugene (1883-1962) American				
oil	9	350-4,500	2,588	2,500
wc/d	3	700-1,000	816	750
SPELLMAN, Coreen (1905-1978) American				
oil	1	6,000	6,000	6,000
wc/d	1	500	500	500
SPELMAN, John A (1880-1941) American				
oil	3	1,500-3,250	2,383	2,400
SPELMAN, Tom (?) Irish?				
oil	1	1,130	1,130	1,130
SPENCE, Harry (1860-1928) British				
oil	1	2,088	2,088	2,088
SPENCELAYH, Charles (1865-1958) British				
oil	12	1,566-434,700	85,310	34,905
wc/d	5	968-16,740	7,461	6,090
SPENCER, Fred (fl.1891-1924) British				
wc/d	1	1,881	1,881	1,881
SPENCER, George (?) British				
oil	1	1,288	1,288	1,288

Name	No.	Price Range	Average	Median
SPENCER, Gilbert (1892-1979) British				
oil	4	2,992-26,460	9,918	4,550
wc/d	2	531-2,163	1,347	531
SPENCER, John Clinton (1861-1919) American				
oil	2	500-1,800	1,150	500
SPENCER, Liam (1964-) British				
oil	1	4,176	4,176	4,176
SPENCER, Niles (1893-1952) American				
oil	2	6,000-19,000	12,500	6,000
SPENCER, R B (fl.1840-1870) British				
oil	1	1,740	1,740	1,740
SPENCER, Richard B (fl.1840-1870) British				
oil	8	4,500-17,000	10,372	8,550
SPENCER, Robert (1879-1931) American				
oil	3	7,500-310,000	116,500	32,000
SPENCER, Sir Stanley (1891-1959) British				
oil	4	20,790-519,750	153,075	22,620
wc/d	10	557-38,940	8,738	4,872
SPENCER, Vera (1926-) British				
oil	1	1,368	1,368	1,368
SPENCER, William Barnett (19th C) British				
oil	2	1,496-3,894	2,695	1,496
SPENDER, Humphrey (1910-2005) British				
oil	1	850	850	850
wc/d	1	830	830	830
SPENLOVE, Frank Spenlove (1868-1933) British				
oil	1	662	662	662
wc/d	1	970	970	970
SPERANTZAS, Vassilis (1938-) Greek				
oil	3	2,618-13,920	8,446	8,800
wc/d	2	3,872-5,280	4,576	3,872
SPERL, Johann (1840-1914) German				
oil	3	2,104-12,552	5,919	3,102
SPERLI, Johann Jakob (1770-1841) Swiss				
wc/d	1	3,102	3,102	3,102
SPERLICH, Sophie (1863-1906) German				
oil	5	835-1,720	1,083	953
SPERLING, Heinrich (1844-1924) German				
oil	4	611-7,827	3,313	1,158
wc/d	1	968	968	968
SPESCHA, Mathias (1925-) Swiss				
oil	1	2,276	2,276	2,276
wc/d	1	3,946	3,946	3,946
SPEYBROUCK, Edouard von (20th C) Belgian?				
oil	1	1,826	1,826	1,826
SPICER-SIMSON, Theodore (1871-1959) British				
3D	1	3,204	3,204	3,204
SPICUZZA, Francesco J (1883-1962) American				
oil	16	400-6,000	1,123	750
wc/d	3	450-1,134	761	700
SPIEGEL, Natan (1890-c.1943) Polish				
oil	1	1,321	1,321	1,321
SPIEGLER, Franz Josef (1691-1757) German				
oil	1	3,041	3,041	3,041
SPIELMANN, Max (1906-1984) Austrian				
wc/d	2	1,152-1,576	1,364	1,152
SPIELMANN, Oscar (1901-1974) Austrian				
oil	2	1,023-2,158	1,590	1,023
SPIELTER, Carl Johann (1851-1922) German				
oil	3	8,338-16,203	12,310	12,390
SPIESS, Walter (1895-1942) Russian				
wc/d	6	2,600-3,200	2,833	2,600
SPIESS-FERRIS, Eleanor (1941-) American				
oil	1	1,500	1,500	1,500
wc/d	1	500	500	500
SPILIMBERGO, Adriano (1908-1975) Italian				
oil	8	3,366-8,743	5,647	5,178
SPILIMBERGO, Lino Eneas (1896-1964) Argentinian				
oil	1	12,000	12,000	12,000
wc/d	1	4,000	4,000	4,000
SPILLIAERT, L (1881-1946) Belgian				
wc/d	1	4,914	4,914	4,914

Name	No.	Price Range	Average	Median
SPILLIAERT, Léon (1881-1946) Belgian				
wc/d	21	1,199-101,769	16,400	9,568
SPIN, Jacob (1806-1875) Dutch				
oil	1	3,160	3,160	3,160
wc/d	1	957	957	957
SPINDLER, Hans (1585-1650) Austrian				
3D	1	19,265	19,265	19,265
SPINETTI, Mario (19/20th C) Italian				
wc/d	2	1,000-2,300	1,650	1,000
SPINKS, Thomas (19th C) British				
oil	4	1,178-2,800	1,920	1,496
SPINOSA, Domenico (1916-) Italian				
wc/d	1	1,427	1,427	1,427
SPINOSA, E (?) ?				
wc/d	1	4,932	4,932	4,932
SPIRIDON, Ignace (fl.1869-1900) Italian				
oil	4	546-10,000	5,449	4,750
SPIRO, Eugen (1874-1972) German				
oil	5	500-19,459	7,823	4,056
wc/d	1	937	937	937
SPIRO, Georges (1909-1994) French				
oil	21	649-5,853	1,683	1,334
SPITZER, Emanuel (1844-1919) German				
oil	1	5,000	5,000	5,000
SPITZER, Walter (1927-) Polish				
oil	6	1,070-1,793	1,556	1,555
wc/d	1	643	643	643
3D	1	2,238	2,238	2,238
SPITZWEG, Carl (1808-1885) German				
oil	13	5,184-424,110	96,337	36,800
wc/d	21	341-4,005	1,603	1,312
SPLITGERBER, August (1844-1918) German				
oil	9	713-2,431	1,277	1,051
SPODE, Samuel (19th C) British				
oil	3	1,176-6,018	3,131	2,200
SPOERER, Eduard (1841-1898) German				
oil	1	2,432	2,432	2,432
SPOERRI, Daniel (1930-) Swiss				
wc/d	14	707-30,393	5,929	2,803
3D	31	1,987-97,350	14,847	9,735
SPOHLER, J J (1811-1866) Dutch				
oil	1	7,007	7,007	7,007
SPOHLER, J P (19th C) Dutch				
oil	1	2,606	2,606	2,606
SPOHLER, Jan Jacob (1811-1866) Dutch				
oil	9	2,910-160,694	43,582	26,671
SPOHLER, Jan Jacob Coenraad (1837-1923) Dutch				
oil	14	1,796-31,521	11,890	7,274
SPOHLER, Johannes Franciscus (1853-1894) Dutch				
oil	8	6,475-62,189	27,046	18,082
SPONGBERG, Grace (1906-) American				
wc/d	1	1,200	1,200	1,200
SPOONER, Arthur (1873-1962) British				
oil	8	504-4,712	1,978	1,566
SPORIKHINE, Boris (1927-) Russian				
oil	1	19,030	19,030	19,030
SPORRER, Philipp (1829-1899) German				
wc/d	1	1,002	1,002	1,002
SPORRI, Eduard (1901-1995) Swiss				
3D	1	3,080	3,080	3,080
SPRANGER, Bartholomaeus (1546-1611) Flemish				
oil	1	693,833	693,833	693,833
SPREAFICO, Leonardo (1907-1974) Italian				
oil	2	884-1,844	1,364	884
SPREEUWEN, Jacob van (1611-?) Dutch				
oil	1	2,158	2,158	2,158
SPRENG, Sebastian (1956-) Latin American				
oil	1	3,200	3,200	3,200
SPRIET, Louis Charles Alexandre (1864-1913) French				
oil	1	1,414	1,414	1,414

Name	No.	Price Range	Average	Median
SPRINCHORN, Carl (1887-1971) American				
oil	2	6,000-9,500	7,750	6,000
wc/d	5	400-2,500	1,380	1,400
SPRING, Alfons (1843-1908) German				
oil	1	1,500	1,500	1,500
SPRING, J J (19th C) Swiss				
oil	1	2,061	2,061	2,061
SPRINGER, Carl (1874-1935) American				
oil	1	1,300	1,300	1,300
SPRINGER, Cornelis (1817-1891) Dutch				
oil	6	3,073-766,389	301,616	157,603
wc/d	4	4,784-9,568	6,109	5,023
SPRONKEN, Arthur (1930-) Dutch				
3D	2	11,757-29,452	20,604	11,757
SPROTTE, Siegward (1913-) German				
oil	9	606-5,819	2,472	1,967
wc/d	5	478-4,529	1,848	1,136
SPRUCE, Everett (1908-) American				
oil	2	27,000-40,000	33,500	27,000
SPRUYT, E (18th C) ?				
oil	1	2,805	2,805	2,805
SPURLING, Jack (1870-1933) British				
oil	1	1,626	1,626	1,626
wc/d	2	4,176-10,285	7,230	4,176
SPURRIER, Steven (1878-1961) British				
oil	1	4,914	4,914	4,914
SPYROPOULOS, Jannis (1912-1990) Greek				
oil	9	3,600-53,940	16,925	10,878
wc/d	1	50,460	50,460	50,460
SQUARCINA, Giovanni (1825-1891) Italian				
oil	1	1,944	1,944	1,944
SQUIER, Jack Leslie (1927-) American				
3D	1	2,000	2,000	2,000
SQUILLANTINI, Remo (1920-1996) Italian				
oil	21	1,665-10,000	5,728	6,392
wc/d	5	592-3,884	2,467	2,458
SQUIRE, Geoffrey (1923-) British				
oil	1	1,548	1,548	1,548
SQUIRRELL, Leonard (1893-1979) British				
wc/d	14	797-5,180	2,332	2,220
SQUITIERI, Italo (1907-1994) Italian				
oil	1	1,021	1,021	1,021
SREDIN, Alexander (1872-1934) Russian				
oil	1	30,575	30,575	30,575
SRKALOVIC, Lalo (1948-) Austrian?				
oil	1	1,012	1,012	1,012
ST CLAIR, Linda (1952-) American				
oil	2	3,500-4,000	3,750	3,500
ST GILLES (1956-) Canadian				
oil	1	618	618	618
wc/d	1	536	536	536
STAACKMAN, Heinrich Maria (1852-1940) German				
oil	1	16,537	16,537	16,537
STAATEN, Louis van (1836-1909) Dutch				
oil	2	974-1,211	1,092	974
wc/d	11	468-1,474	683	574
STABLER, Phoebe (?-1955) British				
3D	1	2,314	2,314	2,314
STABLI, Adolf (1842-1901) Swiss				
oil	4	816-6,665	2,976	1,499
STACEY, Anna Lee (1871-1943) American				
oil	3	1,700-3,000	2,483	2,750
STACEY, John F (1859-1941) American				
oil	3	2,000-11,000	6,000	5,000
wc/d	1	7,000	7,000	7,000
STACHOWSKI, Wladyslaw von (1852-1932) Polish				
oil	2	588-1,767	1,177	588
STACK, Josef Magnus (1812-1868) Swedish				
oil	4	618-7,728	3,154	997
STACK, Michael (1947-) American				
oil	10	2,000-14,000	4,880	3,800

Name	No.	Price Range	Average	Median
STACKHOUSE, Robert (1942-) American?				
wc/d	1	5,000	5,000	5,000
STACKS, William Leon (1928-1991) American				
oil	1	1,100	1,100	1,100
STADELHOFER, H (?) German				
oil	1	2,667	2,667	2,667
STADEMANN, Adolf (1824-1895) German				
oil	23	849-11,094	3,326	2,662
STADLER, J (19th C) ?				
oil	1	3,500	3,500	3,500
STADLER, Martin (1792-1841) Austrian				
oil	1	1,933	1,933	1,933
STADLER, Toni (1888-1982) German				
oil	1	589	589	589
wc/d	3	504-851	667	647
3D	5	2,945-94,247	23,253	5,419
STAEGER, Ferdinand (1880-1975) German				
oil	1	1,566	1,566	1,566
STAEL, Nicolas de (1914-1955) French				
oil	10	17,740-1,108,800	472,662	260,000
wc/d	8	5,104-40,000	15,375	11,000
STAEMPFLI, George W (1910-1999) American				
wc/d	1	2,100	2,100	2,100
STAFFORD, Simeon (1956-) British				
oil	4	606-1,479	1,149	1,216
STAGE, Ruth (1969-) British				
wc/d	2	979-1,925	1,452	979
STAGER, Balz (1861-1937) Swiss				
oil	4	916-12,146	5,127	1,374
STAGURA, Albert (1866-1947) German				
oil	2	1,302-4,500	2,901	1,302
wc/d	6	1,368-4,839	2,533	1,989
STAHL, Benjamin F (1932-) American				
oil	1	1,200	1,200	1,200
STAHL, Franz Xaver (1901-) German				
oil	1	12,959	12,959	12,959
STAHL, Friedrich (1863-1940) German				
oil	3	2,611-21,041	14,739	20,566
STAHLE, Ugo (20th C) Italian?				
oil	1	1,401	1,401	1,401
STAHLI-RYCHEN, Gottfried (1822-1901) Austrian				
oil	1	1,157	1,157	1,157
STAHLY, François (1911-) French				
3D	2	3,613-27,877	15,745	3,613
STAIGER, Paul (?) ?				
oil	1	1,100	1,100	1,100
STAINTON, George (fl.1860-1890) British				
oil	4	1,197-6,300	2,968	1,914
STAITE, Harriet (fl.1895-1903) British				
oil	1	1,044	1,044	1,044
STALBEMT, Adriaen van (1580-1662) Flemish				
oil	2	77,700-92,500	85,100	77,700
wc/d	1	5,920	5,920	5,920
STALLENBERGH, Theodore Wynant (1738-?) Belgian				
oil	1	11,571	11,571	11,571
STAMOS, Theodoros (1922-1997) American				
oil	20	3,366-70,715	27,360	21,908
wc/d	1	6,000	6,000	6,000
STAMPART, Frans van (1675-1750) Flemish				
oil	1	26,490	26,490	26,490
STAMPFLI, Peter (1937-) Swiss				
wc/d	1	19,082	19,082	19,082
STANCHI, Giovanni (c.1645-?) Italian				
oil	1	11,757	11,757	11,757
STANCHI, Nicolo (1623-1690) Italian				
oil	1	27,753	27,753	27,753
STANCLIFF, J W (1814-1879) American				
oil	1	3,250	3,250	3,250
STANCZAK, Julian (1928-) American/Polish				
oil	5	2,500-8,500	5,700	5,000
STANDING, H W (19/20th C) British				
wc/d	1	1,012	1,012	1,012

Name	No.	Price Range	Average	Median
STANDING, William (1904-1951) American				
oil	2	2,000-10,000	6,000	2,000
STANFIELD, Clarkson (1793-1867) British				
oil	5	430-6,018	2,912	2,400
wc/d	6	400-7,440	3,504	1,295
STANFIELD, George Clarkson (1828-1878) British				
oil	3	5,152-7,224	6,039	5,742
wc/d	2	655-1,044	849	655
STANGELBERGER, Rudolf (20th C) Austrian				
oil	1	1,255	1,255	1,255
STANGL, Heinz (1942-) Austrian				
oil	1	1,688	1,688	1,688
wc/d	2	849-1,052	950	849
STANGL, Reinhard (1950-) German				
oil	1	1,196	1,196	1,196
STANISLAWSKI, Jan (1860-1907) Polish				
oil	2	3,781-4,350	4,065	3,781
STANKIEWICZ, Richard (1922-) American				
3D	1	8,000	8,000	8,000
STANKOWSKI, Anton (1906-1998) German				
oil	1	3,641	3,641	3,641
STANLEY, Bob (1932-) American				
oil	1	10,177	10,177	10,177
STANLEY, Caleb Robert (1795-1868) British				
oil	1	4,176	4,176	4,176
STANLEY, John Mix (1814-1872) American				
oil	2	80,000-110,000	95,000	80,000
STANLEY, Shaun (1958-) Irish				
wc/d	1	1,654	1,654	1,654
STANNARD OF NORWICH, Emily (1803-1885) British				
oil	1	13,230	13,230	13,230
STANNARD, Alfred (1806-1889) British				
oil	9	1,025-10,726	4,261	3,460
STANNARD, Eloise Harriet (c.1828-1915) British				
oil	6	1,328-34,020	10,334	3,500
STANNARD, Henry Sylvester (1870-1951) British				
wc/d	50	481-6,160	2,020	1,400
STANNARD, Joseph (1797-1830) British				
oil	3	3,460-33,630	17,968	16,815
wc/d	1	1,097	1,097	1,097
STANNARD, Lilian (1877-1944) British				
wc/d	6	692-3,780	2,199	2,112
STANNUS, Anthony Carey (fl.1862-1910) British				
wc/d	2	968-14,000	7,484	968
STANWOOD, Franklin (1856-1888) American				
oil	1	5,500	5,500	5,500
STANZANI, Emilio (1906-1977) Swiss				
3D	1	2,270	2,270	2,270
STANZIONE, Massimo (1585-1656) Italian				
oil	2	57,329-220,068	138,698	57,329
STAPERT, Fokke (17/18th C) Dutch				
oil	1	7,714	7,714	7,714
STAPLES, Owen (1866-1949) British				
oil	1	1,476	1,476	1,476
STAPPEN, Charles van der (1843-1910) Belgian				
3D	1	33,370	33,370	33,370
STAPPERS, Julien (1875-1960) Belgian				
oil	6	715-4,335	1,644	1,023
STAPRANS, Raymond (1926-) American				
oil	3	600-6,000	3,292	3,276
STARCK, Jean (1948-) French?				
oil	1	835	835	835
wc/d	1	542	542	542
STARCK, Julien Josephus Gaspard (1814-1884) Belgian				
oil	1	8,100	8,100	8,100
STARCK, Philippe (1949-) French				
3D	1	3,560	3,560	3,560
STARING, Willem Constantijn (1847-1916) Dutch				
wc/d	2	732-4,917	2,824	732
STARITSKY, Anna (1908-1981) French				
oil	3	3,251-14,620	8,501	7,633
wc/d	2	682-729	705	682

Name	No.	Price Range	Average	Median
STARK, Arthur James (1831-1902) British				
oil	4	561-952	762	600
wc/d	1	555	555	555
STARK, James (1794-1859) British				
oil	12	1,218-37,800	12,713	4,956
wc/d	2	460-496	478	460
STARK, Karl (1921-) Austrian				
oil	6	3,970-10,286	5,687	5,143
wc/d	3	1,893-5,048	3,438	3,375
STARK, Melville F (1904-1987) American				
oil	5	500-5,000	3,170	3,750
wc/d	1	1,200	1,200	1,200
STARKE, Phil (1957-) American				
oil	1	6,500	6,500	6,500
STARKENBORGH, Jacobus Nicolas Tjarda van (1822-1895) Dutch				
oil	1	17,517	17,517	17,517
STARKENBORGH, Willem Tjarda van (1823-1885) Dutch				
oil	1	7,658	7,658	7,658
STARKER, Erwin (1872-1938) German				
oil	3	766-2,356	1,455	1,243
wc/d	1	622	622	622
STARKWEATHER, William Edward (1879-1969) American				
oil	2	1,000-4,200	2,600	1,000
STARLING, Albert (fl.1878-1922) British				
oil	2	452-6,336	3,394	452
STARN TWINS (1961-) American				
wc/d	1	17,000	17,000	17,000
STARR, Louisa (1845-1909) British				
oil	1	696	696	696
wc/d	1	8,004	8,004	8,004
STARREVELD, Pieter (1911-1989) Dutch?				
3D	2	2,922-3,039	2,980	2,922
STASEK, F (20th C) ?				
oil	1	8,818	8,818	8,818
STASI, Paolo Emilio (19th C) Italian				
oil	1	1,767	1,767	1,767
STASIO, Stefano di (1948-) Italian				
oil	1	1,767	1,767	1,767
wc/d	2	2,213-2,452	2,332	2,213
STATHOPOULOS, George (1944-) Greek				
oil	2	2,595-3,179	2,887	2,595
STATTLER, Fritz (1867-?) Austrian				
oil	1	1,430	1,430	1,430
STAUB, Erich (20th C) Swiss				
oil	1	1,526	1,526	1,526
STAUB, Josef (1931-) Swiss				
oil	1	2,434	2,434	2,434
3D	1	44,868	44,868	44,868
STAUDACHER, Hans (1923-) Swiss				
oil	11	5,753-38,841	15,641	14,137
wc/d	34	584-3,356	1,935	1,940
STAUDACHER, Vitus (1850-1925) German				
oil	4	814-2,160	1,545	1,324
STAUFFER, Fred (1892-1980) Swiss				
oil	9	913-3,027	1,348	1,082
wc/d	5	320-916	599	687
STAUFFER-BERN, Karl (1857-1891) Swiss				
wc/d	1	1,832	1,832	1,832
STAVEREN, Jan van (1625-1668) Dutch				
oil	2	8,325-8,919	8,622	8,325
STAVERNUS, Petrus (1634-1654) Dutch				
oil	2	37,369-38,060	37,714	37,369
STAVROWSKY, Oleg (1927-) American				
oil	5	850-30,000	11,670	10,500
STAZEWSKI, Henryk (1894-1988) Polish				
oil	1	10,701	10,701	10,701
wc/d	1	6,701	6,701	6,701
3D	1	36,000	36,000	36,000
STEAD, Fred (1863-1940) British				
oil	3	455-7,400	3,389	2,314
STEADMAN, Ralph Idris (1936-) British				
oil	1	1,295	1,295	1,295
wc/d	2	880-1,335	1,107	880

Name	No.	Price Range	Average	Median
STEEL, John (1770-1807) American/British				
wc/d	1	2,400	2,400	2,400
STEELE, Louis John (1843-1918) New Zealander				
oil	1	18,000	18,000	18,000
STEELE, Theodore Clement (1847-1926) American				
oil	3	15,000-50,000	28,000	19,000
STEELE, Zulma (1881-1979) American				
oil	2	2,500-2,500	2,500	2,500
wc/d	2	1,800-3,700	2,750	1,800
STEELINK, Willem (1826-1913) Dutch				
oil	3	870-4,053	1,968	983
wc/d	2	550-1,740	1,145	550
STEELINK, Willem (jnr) (1856-1928) Dutch				
wc/d	1	1,818	1,818	1,818
STEELL, Gourlay (1819-1894) British				
oil	2	800-10,560	5,680	800
wc/d	2	2,750-5,500	4,125	2,750
STEELL, Sir John Robert (1804-1891) British				
3D	2	5,728-8,413	7,070	5,728
STEEN, A van der (18th C) ?				
wc/d	1	10,175	10,175	10,175
STEEN, H (19th C) ?				
oil	1	2,405	2,405	2,405
STEEN, Heinrich (1907-) German				
oil	1	1,106	1,106	1,106
STEEN, Jan (c.1626-1679) Dutch				
oil	5	7,658-1,110,000	406,118	340,000
STEENBAULT, A de (19th C) ?				
oil	1	7,342	7,342	7,342
STEENBERGEN, Albert (1814-1900) Dutch				
oil	2	2,000-3,402	2,701	2,000
wc/d	1	8,500	8,500	8,500
STEENE, Augustus van den (1803-1870) Belgian				
oil	1	3,781	3,781	3,781
STEENWYCK, Harmen van (1612-1656) Dutch				
oil	3	12,600-48,440	27,266	20,760
STEENWYCK, Hendrik van (17th C) Dutch				
oil	1	32,986	32,986	32,986
STEER, Philip Wilson (1860-1942) British				
oil	4	592-473,200	121,942	2,076
wc/d	9	478-2,610	1,153	1,062
STEFAN, Ross (1934-1999) American				
oil	10	2,000-10,500	5,685	4,250
STEFANONI, Tino (1937-) Italian				
oil	14	1,272-3,236	2,494	2,577
wc/d	1	1,942	1,942	1,942
STEFANOU, Nikos (1933-) Greek				
oil	2	6,160-6,160	6,160	6,160
STEFANSSEN, Jon (1881-1962) Icelandic				
oil	4	14,548-24,247	20,019	19,315
STEFFAN, Johann Gottfried (1815-1905) Swiss				
oil	24	839-48,947	10,583	5,011
STEFFANI, Luigi (1827-1898) Italian				
oil	2	756-25,000	12,878	756
STEFFEK, Carl (1818-1890) German				
oil	3	1,109-8,290	4,286	3,461
STEFFELAAR, Nicolaas (1852-1918) Dutch				
oil	1	2,500	2,500	2,500
STEFFEN, Walter Arnold (1924-1982) Swiss				
oil	21	454-2,656	1,070	759
STEFFENINI, Ottavio (1889-1971) Italian				
oil	1	484	484	484
wc/d	1	2,238	2,238	2,238
STEFFENS, Wilhelm (19/20th C) German				
oil	1	2,182	2,182	2,182
STEFFENSEN, Hans Voigt (1941-) Danish				
oil	6	566-5,795	3,639	4,041
STEFFENSEN, Poul (1866-1923) Danish				
oil	11	489-10,595	2,160	1,659
STEFFERL, Bartholomaus (19/20th C) Austrian				
oil	2	876-1,165	1,020	876

Name	No.	Price Range	Average	Median
STEFULA, Giorgio (1913-) German				
oil	1	1,298	1,298	1,298
STEGEMANN, Heinrich (1888-1945) German				
oil	1	2,213	2,213	2,213
STEGER, Milly (1881-1948) German				
3D	2	2,356-4,123	3,239	2,356
STEGGLES, Walter James (1910-1997) British				
oil	1	1,062	1,062	1,062
STEGMAIER, German (1959-) German				
oil	2	941-1,176	1,058	941
STEGMANN, Franz (1831-1892) German				
oil	1	3,270	3,270	3,270
STEIB, Josef (1898-1957) German				
oil	2	666-1,455	1,060	666
STEIG, William (1907-) American				
wc/d	1	8,000	8,000	8,000
STEIGER, Robert von (1856-1941) Swiss				
oil	1	3,162	3,162	3,162
STEIGER, William (20th C) American				
oil	2	1,000-5,000	3,000	1,000
STEIN, Georges (1870-?) French				
oil	6	1,394-6,876	3,741	3,190
wc/d	3	1,573-3,529	2,401	2,101
STEIN, Joel (1926-) French				
oil	1	3,592	3,592	3,592
STEIN, Walter (1924-) ?				
oil	1	11,712	11,712	11,712
STEINACH, Anton Victor Alexander (1819-1891) German				
oil	1	4,400	4,400	4,400
STEINACKER, Alfred (1838-1914) Austrian				
oil	6	703-1,671	1,221	1,140
STEINBACH, Eduard (1878-?) German				
oil	2	1,430-1,844	1,637	1,430
STEINBACH, Haim (1944-) American				
3D	1	39,556	39,556	39,556
STEINBERG, Edward (1937-) Russian				
oil	1	186,000	186,000	186,000
wc/d	2	27,900-44,640	36,270	27,900
STEINBERG, Saul (1914-1999) American				
wc/d	19	1,000-45,000	14,513	12,000
3D	1	37,500	37,500	37,500
STEINBERGER (20th C) ?				
oil	1	3,000	3,000	3,000
STEINBRENNER, Hans (1928-) German				
3D	6	1,757-9,370	4,275	2,811
STEINEL, Johann Paul (1878-?) German				
3D	1	2,939	2,939	2,939
STEINER, Bernd (1884-1933) Austrian				
oil	1	1,929	1,929	1,929
STEINER, Clement Leopold (1853-1899) French				
3D	1	4,458	4,458	4,458
STEINER, Josef Kamenitzky (1910-1981) Austrian				
oil	1	3,330	3,330	3,330
STEINFELD, Wilhelm (1816-1854) Austrian				
oil	3	908-4,332	2,070	970
STEINGOLD, Meir (?) ?				
oil	1	1,100	1,100	1,100
STEINHARDT, Jakob (1887-1968) Israeli				
oil	5	3,000-9,500	6,400	8,000
wc/d	3	800-5,000	2,216	850
STEINHAUSEN, Wilhelm (1846-1924) German				
oil	1	2,102	2,102	2,102
STEINIKE, Heinrich (1825-1909) German				
oil	1	2,384	2,384	2,384
STEINKE, Bettina (1913-1999) American				
oil	2	4,500-8,000	6,250	4,500
STEINLE, Edward Jakob von (1810-1886) Austrian/German				
wc/d	3	800-2,035	1,470	1,576
STEINLEN, Aime Daniel (1923-) French				
oil	1	1,133	1,133	1,133

Name	No.	Price Range	Average	Median
STEINLEN, Theophile Alexandre (1859-1923) Swiss				
wc/d	54	504-24,524	3,174	1,680
3D	3	2,800-19,200	11,463	12,390
STEINMETZ, Fritz (1860-1937) German				
oil	1	4,971	4,971	4,971
STEINWORTH, Skip (1950-) American				
wc/d	1	3,250	3,250	3,250
STEIR, Pat (1940-) American				
oil	2	5,664-11,000	8,332	5,664
wc/d	1	13,000	13,000	13,000
STELLA, Andrea (1950-) Italian				
oil	1	2,880	2,880	2,880
STELLA, Frank (1936-) American				
oil	7	9,500-1,500,000	599,554	170,000
wc/d	4	3,000-180,000	59,054	15,000
3D	6	3,800-160,000	46,735	9,000
STELLA, G (19th C) Italian				
oil	1	2,331	2,331	2,331
STELLA, Jacques de (1596-1657) French				
oil	1	8,544	8,544	8,544
wc/d	2	3,342-37,000	20,171	3,342
STELLA, Joseph (1879-1946) American/Italian				
oil	2	4,250-10,440	7,345	4,250
wc/d	11	450-140,000	15,247	1,600
STELLETSKY, Dimitri (1875-1947) Russian				
wc/d	5	25,800-59,520	43,552	48,160
STELLWAGEN, Captain Henry Schreiner (?-1866) American				
wc/d	21	450-6,000	1,492	1,200
STEMATSKY, Avigdor (1908-1989) Israeli				
oil	6	4,000-28,000	14,166	9,500
wc/d	5	800-2,400	1,480	1,400
STENBERG, Georgiy and Vladimir (20th C) Russian				
wc/d	4	2,939-26,040	13,522	12,090
STENGEL, Stephan von (1750-1822) German				
wc/d	2	555-1,641	1,098	555
STENGELIN, Alphonse (1852-1938) French				
oil	1	1,560	1,560	1,560
STENIUS, Per (1922-) Finnish				
oil	7	959-3,086	2,111	1,991
STENN, Henri (20th C) ?				
oil	4	800-2,090	1,240	973
STENNER, Hermann (1891-1914) German				
oil	1	6,676	6,676	6,676
STENVERT, Curt (1920-1994) Austrian				
wc/d	1	788	788	788
3D	1	3,363	3,363	3,363
STEPANOV, Alexander Nikolavich (1843-1911) Russian				
oil	1	89,178	89,178	89,178
wc/d	1	7,478	7,478	7,478
STEPANOV, Claude (1858-1923) Russian				
oil	1	96,000	96,000	96,000
STEPANOV, Klawdi Petrovitch (1854-1910) Russian				
oil	1	4,849	4,849	4,849
STEPHAN, J (18th C) ?				
oil	1	39,160	39,160	39,160
STEPHAN, Joseph (1709-1786) German				
oil	1	16,473	16,473	16,473
STEPHAN, Leopold (1826-1890) Czechoslovakian				
oil	1	3,279	3,279	3,279
STEPHENS, Alfred (19/20th C) British?				
3D	1	5,670	5,670	5,670
STEPHENS, Alice Barber (1858-1932) American				
oil	1	7,000	7,000	7,000
wc/d	1	24,000	24,000	24,000
STEPHENS, Daniel Owen (1893-1937) American				
oil	1	2,200	2,200	2,200
STEPHENS, Elizabeth (?) American				
wc/d	1	3,250	3,250	3,250
STEPHENS, Thomas Edgar (1888-1966) American				
oil	1	1,100	1,100	1,100
STEPHENSON, Desmond (1922-1964) Irish				
oil	1	2,264	2,264	2,264

Name	No.	Price Range	Average	Median
STEPHENSON, John Cecil (1889-1965) British				
oil	1	2,124	2,124	2,124
wc/d	2	915-8,700	4,807	915
STEPHENSON, Lionel Macdonald (1854-1907) Canadian				
oil	3	427-1,939	1,228	1,319
STEPPE, Romain (1859-1927) Belgian				
oil	32	477-2,408	1,037	777
STERIS, Gerasimos (1895-1985) Greek				
oil	2	20,790-71,060	45,925	20,790
wc/d	3	452-5,536	2,619	1,870
STERL, Robert Hermann (1867-1932) German				
oil	1	12,237	12,237	12,237
STERLING, Marc (1898-1976) Russian				
oil	4	669-4,945	2,015	1,113
wc/d	3	715-1,632	1,020	715
STERN, Bernhard (1920-2002) American				
oil	2	657-1,104	880	657
wc/d	1	440	440	440
STERN, Ignaz (1680-1748) German				
oil	2	1,557-10,581	6,069	1,557
STERN, Irma (1894-1966) South African				
wc/d	1	7,009	7,009	7,009
STERNE, Maurice (1878-1957) American				
oil	5	1,200-12,000	4,210	3,000
wc/d	2	425-1,000	712	425
STERNER, Albert Edward (1863-1946) American				
oil	3	700-3,500	1,733	1,000
wc/d	3	350-1,800	866	450
STERNSCHUSS, Moshe (1903-1992) Israeli				
3D	1	4,000	4,000	4,000
STERRER, Franz (1818-1901) ?				
oil	1	1,021	1,021	1,021
STETBAY, Gloria (20th C) French				
wc/d	1	3,649	3,649	3,649
STETSON, Charles Walter (1858-1911) American				
oil	4	1,100-2,750	2,109	1,900
STEUERWALDT, Wilhelm II (1815-1871) German				
oil	1	4,498	4,498	4,498
STEVAN, Jean (1896-1962) Belgian				
oil	2	983-1,479	1,231	983
STEVEN, Fernand (1895-1955) Belgian				
oil	1	1,311	1,311	1,311
wc/d	1	546	546	546
STEVENS, Agapit (1849-1917) Belgian				
oil	5	526-14,240	4,613	3,109
STEVENS, Albert George (1863-1925) British				
wc/d	1	2,784	2,784	2,784
STEVENS, Alfred (1823-1906) Belgian				
oil	14	555-37,622	9,593	7,135
wc/d	1	1,518	1,518	1,518
STEVENS, Alfred George (1817-1875) British				
wc/d	2	800-1,584	1,192	800
STEVENS, Edward John (jnr) (1923-1988) American				
wc/d	1	1,200	1,200	1,200
STEVENS, Gustav Max (1871-1946) German				
oil	5	1,293-15,284	4,806	2,234
wc/d	1	659	659	659
STEVENS, Joseph (1819-1892) Belgian				
oil	4	1,636-4,332	2,789	2,384
STEVENS, Will Henry (1881-1949) American				
wc/d	1	2,700	2,700	2,700
STEVENS, William Lester (1888-1969) American				
oil	21	1,200-20,000	6,061	4,400
wc/d	11	700-1,900	1,211	1,000
STEVENSON, James (?-1844) British				
wc/d	1	1,780	1,780	1,780
STEVENSON, Jeannie G (19th C) British				
oil	2	515-1,803	1,159	515
STEVENSON, Robert Macaulay (1860-1952) British				
oil	3	661-1,496	1,124	1,216
STEVENSON, Ruth Rolston (20th C) American				
oil	1	3,750	3,750	3,750

Name	No.	Price Range	Average	Median
STEVENSON, Wendy L (1950-2003) British				
oil	4	455-1,138	695	525
wc/d	1	788	788	788
STEVICK, Richard (20th C) American				
oil	1	3,200	3,200	3,200
STEVNS, Niels Larsen (1864-1941) Danish				
oil	1	4,024	4,024	4,024
wc/d	1	1,940	1,940	1,940
STEWARD, Aleta (20th C) American				
oil	1	1,600	1,600	1,600
STEWART, A (?) ?				
oil	1	2,500	2,500	2,500
STEWART, Hannah (20th C) British				
3D	1	3,477	3,477	3,477
STEWART, James Lawson (fl.1883-1889) British				
wc/d	4	600-1,681	1,127	854
STEWART, John (19/20th C) British				
wc/d	2	4,200-5,500	4,850	4,200
STEWART, John A (1951-) British				
wc/d	3	1,305-1,392	1,334	1,305
STEWART, Julius L (1855-1919) American				
oil	3	5,670-280,000	113,556	55,000
STEWART, N Neale (19th C) American				
oil	1	1,000	1,000	1,000
STEWART, Robert (19/20th C) American				
oil	1	6,750	6,750	6,750
STEYN, Stella (1907-1987) British/Irish				
oil	20	511-10,603	3,287	3,337
wc/d	1	662	662	662
STIACCINI, R (?) Italian				
3D	1	41,622	41,622	41,622
STIACCINI, U (19/20th C) Italian				
3D	2	1,956-4,238	3,097	1,956
STICK, Frank (1884-1966) American				
oil	6	17,000-32,500	22,750	19,000
STICKS, George Blackie (1843-1938) British				
oil	17	522-5,610	1,616	1,253
wc/d	1	2,436	2,436	2,436
STIDHAM, Michael (20th C) American				
oil	1	3,000	3,000	3,000
STIEFEL, Eduard (1875-1968) Swiss				
oil	1	1,370	1,370	1,370
STIELER, Joseph Karl (1781-1858) German				
wc/d	2	1,452-6,276	3,864	1,452
STIENTJES, Staf (1883-1974) Belgian				
oil	1	2,425	2,425	2,425
STIEPEVICH, Vincent G (1841-1910) Russian				
oil	3	18,000-40,000	26,000	20,000
STIERHOF, Ernst (1918-) German				
oil	1	2,008	2,008	2,008
STIFTER, Moritz (1857-1905) Austrian				
oil	4	1,100-13,124	4,635	1,255
STIHA, Vladan (1908-1992) American				
oil	2	1,000-1,250	1,125	1,000
STILL, Clyfford (1904-1980) American				
oil	2	950,000-2,400,000	1,675,000	950,000
STILLMAN, Eleanor (1928-) American				
3D	1	11,346	11,346	11,346
STILLMAN, Marie Spartali (1844-1927) British				
wc/d	2	5,208-90,000	47,604	5,208
STINGEL, Rudolf (1956-) Austrian				
oil	5	19,470-45,863	35,166	38,000
wc/d	1	12,000	12,000	12,000
3D	1	5,000	5,000	5,000
STINTON, James (1870-1961) British				
wc/d	1	1,573	1,573	1,573
STIPHOUT, Theo (1913-) Dutch				
oil	8	959-4,712	1,663	959
STIRLING, David (1889-1971) American				
oil	4	400-2,000	1,043	475
STIRLING-BROWN, A E D G (19/20th C) British				
oil	3	926-2,464	1,735	1,817

Name	No.	Price Range	Average	Median
STIRNBRAND, Franz Seraph (1788-1882) Austrian				
oil	1	37,405	37,405	37,405
STIRNER, Karl (1882-1943) German				
oil	3	668-4,079	2,818	3,708
STITT, Hobart D (1880-1943) American				
oil	1	2,500	2,500	2,500
STIVERS, Don (20th C) American				
oil	1	4,000	4,000	4,000
STOBART, John (1929-) British				
oil	7	2,576-10,672	7,254	7,728
STOBBAERTS, Marcel (c.1899-1979) Belgian				
oil	11	494-10,837	2,383	1,555
STOCK, Henry John (1853-1930) British				
oil	1	6,440	6,440	6,440
STOCK, Ignatius van der (17th C) Dutch				
oil	1	9,425	9,425	9,425
STOCK, Johann Friedrich (?-1866) German				
oil	1	2,163	2,163	2,163
STOCK, Joseph Whiting (1815-1855) American				
oil	6	6,000-16,000	12,000	13,000
STOCKEL, I (19th C) Austrian?				
3D	1	40,000	40,000	40,000
STOCKER, Ernst (1905-1976) Swiss				
wc/d	1	2,351	2,351	2,351
STOCKHOLDER, Jessica (1959-) American				
wc/d	1	3,500	3,500	3,500
3D	2	10,000-13,000	11,500	10,000
STOCKLEIN, Christian (1741-1795) Swiss				
oil	1	7,224	7,224	7,224
STOCKLI, Simon (20th C) ?				
oil	2	1,394-2,155	1,774	1,394
STOCKMANN, Hermann (1867-1939) German				
oil	3	1,014-3,507	2,134	1,883
STOCKS, Arthur (1846-1889) British				
oil	1	140,000	140,000	140,000
STOCKTON, Pansy Cornelia (1895-1972) American				
wc/d	1	2,250	2,250	2,250
STOCKUM, Hilda van (1908-) Dutch				
oil	4	7,032-9,177	7,980	7,598
STOCQUART, Ildephonse (1819-1889) Belgian				
oil	2	2,492-2,734	2,613	2,492
STODDARD, Alice Kent (1893-1976) American				
oil	5	800-4,000	2,410	2,400
STOEBEL, Edgar (1909-2001) French				
oil	11	502-14,914	4,146	1,883
STOECKLI, Paul (1906-1992) Swiss				
oil	4	496-3,330	2,088	1,362
wc/d	9	470-1,582	734	643
STOECKLIN, Niklaus (1896-1982) Swiss				
oil	7	4,049-57,105	20,034	6,088
wc/d	6	457-4,858	1,537	913
STOEGMANN-BOHRN, Irene (1864-?) Austrian				
oil	1	2,687	2,687	2,687
STOFFE, Jan van der (1611-1682) Dutch				
oil	1	4,048	4,048	4,048
STOHR, Johann Heinrich (1745-?) Swiss				
oil	1	1,415	1,415	1,415
STÖHRER, Walter (1937-2000) German				
oil	6	2,548-21,658	11,793	4,241
wc/d	9	803-24,205	5,531	3,279
STOILOFF, C (1850-1924) Austrian/Russian				
oil	2	2,919-7,292	5,105	2,919
STOILOFF, Constantin (1850-1924) Austrian/Russian				
oil	37	529-15,288	4,976	3,792
STOISA, Luigi (1958-) Italian				
oil	1	1,585	1,585	1,585
wc/d	1	934	934	934
STOITZNER, Constantin (1863-1934) Austrian				
oil	6	1,018-2,928	1,900	1,815
STOITZNER, Josef (1884-1951) Austrian				
oil	6	8,486-18,207	13,269	12,123

Name	No.	Price Range	Average	Median
STOITZNER, Siegfried (1892-1976) Austrian				
oil	3	1,688-10,849	5,977	5,394
STOITZNER, Walter (1890-1921) Austrian				
oil	2	1,286-2,342	1,814	1,286
STOJANOW, Pjotr (fl.1887-1894) Russian				
oil	2	6,114-6,500	6,307	6,114
STOJAROV, Vladimir (1926-1973) Russian				
oil	3	2,893-16,016	7,402	3,299
STOK, Jacobus van der (1795-1864) Dutch				
oil	2	9,073-15,979	12,526	9,073
STOKELD, James (1827-1877) British				
oil	3	650-1,672	1,057	851
STOKES, Adrian (1854-1935) British				
oil	2	1,001-1,740	1,370	1,001
STOKES, George Vernon (1873-1954) British				
oil	1	1,674	1,674	1,674
wc/d	4	549-1,656	1,041	814
STOLKER, Jan (1724-1785) Dutch				
wc/d	3	823-2,219	1,714	2,102
STOLL, Artur (1947-) ?				
oil	2	999-3,762	2,380	999
STOLL, Josef (20th C) Austrian				
oil	1	2,314	2,314	2,314
STOLL, Leopold (1792-1850) German				
oil	4	1,942-36,000	10,871	2,384
STOLTENBERG, Fritz (1855-1921) German				
oil	1	4,066	4,066	4,066
STOLZ, Erwin (1896-1987) Austrian				
oil	1	800	800	800
wc/d	3	425-800	550	425
STOM, Antonio (18th C) Italian				
oil	2	6,969-43,784	25,376	6,969
STOMER, Matthias I (c.1600-c.1650) Flemish				
oil	1	250,000	250,000	250,000
STOMER, Matthias II (1649-1702) Flemish				
oil	1	12,109	12,109	12,109
STONE, Don (1929-) American				
oil	4	900-2,000	1,425	1,300
STONE, G P (19/20th C) American?				
oil	1	3,500	3,500	3,500
STONE, Louis K (1902-1984) American				
wc/d	1	1,700	1,700	1,700
STONE, Marcus (1840-1921) British				
oil	2	1,566-12,600	7,083	1,566
wc/d	1	555	555	555
STONE, Robert (fl.1900) British?				
oil	4	941-13,000	8,227	7,000
STONE, Rudolf (19/20th C) British				
oil	3	3,857-5,292	4,624	4,725
STONE, Sarah (18th C) ?				
wc/d	1	25,515	25,515	25,515
STONE, Thomas Albert (1897-1978) Canadian				
oil	2	1,630-3,526	2,578	1,630
STONE, W R (19/20th C) British				
oil	2	1,299-2,606	1,952	1,299
STONE, William (19/20th C) British				
oil	6	623-1,512	1,082	968
STONE, William R (19th C) British				
oil	1	1,100	1,100	1,100
STONEHOUSE, Fred (20th C) American				
oil	1	2,750	2,750	2,750
STONER, Tim (1970-) British				
oil	2	5,550-12,390	8,970	5,550
STONHAM, Frederick Henry (1924-2003) British				
oil	12	1,505-9,735	5,317	3,894
STOOP, Dirk (1618-1681) Dutch				
oil	1	12,041	12,041	12,041
STOOP, Maerten (1620-1647) Dutch				
oil	1	35,105	35,105	35,105
STOOPENDAAL, Georg (1866-1953) Swedish				
oil	2	719-1,426	1,072	719

Name	No.	Price Range	Average	Median
STOOPENDAAL, Mosse (1901-1948) Swedish				
oil	23	372-76,438	6,060	1,887
wc/d	2	755-3,022	1,888	755
STOOPS, Herbert Morton (1887-1948) American				
oil	1	2,300	2,300	2,300
STOPFORD, Robert Lowe (1813-1898) British				
wc/d	1	12,621	12,621	12,621
STORCH, Frederik (1805-1883) Danish				
oil	3	1,132-24,265	12,033	10,703
STORCH, Karl (elder) (1864-1954) German				
oil	2	1,854-4,622	3,238	1,854
STORCK, Abraham (c.1635-c.1710) Dutch				
oil	4	21,586-151,027	60,795	32,510
wc/d	3	952-14,143	6,415	4,152
STORCK, Jacob (1641-1687) Dutch				
wc/d	1	10,520	10,520	10,520
STORER, Charles (1817-1907) American				
oil	2	1,000-11,000	6,000	1,000
STOREY, David (1948-) American				
wc/d	1	2,000	2,000	2,000
STOREY, George Adolphus (1834-1919) British				
oil	1	1,239	1,239	1,239
STORM, Juan (1927-1995) Uruguayan				
oil	2	2,500-4,300	3,400	2,500
STORRS, John (1885-1956) American				
3D	1	85,000	85,000	85,000
STORTENBEKER, Cornelis Samuel (1838-1885) Dutch				
oil	1	2,065	2,065	2,065
STORTENBEKER, Pieter (1828-1898) Dutch				
oil	2	1,311-6,000	3,655	1,311
STORY, George H (1835-1923) American				
oil	1	6,000	6,000	6,000
STORY, Julian Russell (1850-1919) American				
oil	1	3,738	3,738	3,738
STORY, Waldo Thomas (1855-1915) British				
3D	3	4,000-140,000	49,500	4,500
STOTHARD, Thomas (1755-1834) British				
oil	2	644-1,408	1,026	644
STOTZ, Fritz (1884-1920) German				
wc/d	1	1,225	1,225	1,225
STOUT, Myron (1908-1987) American				
oil	1	3,750	3,750	3,750
STOVER, Dieter (1922-1984) German				
oil	1	1,176	1,176	1,176
STOWARD, F (19th C) ?				
oil	2	7,000-8,750	7,875	7,000
STOWELL, Flaxney (19/20th C) ?				
wc/d	1	1,152	1,152	1,152
STOWER, Willy (1864-1931) German				
oil	2	1,435-3,588	2,511	1,435
wc/d	3	2,049-3,099	2,565	2,548
STRACCA, Guglielmo (1889-1971) Italian				
oil	2	1,414-1,671	1,542	1,414
STRACHAN, Claude (1865-1929) British				
oil	1	828	828	828
wc/d	19	490-7,182	3,017	3,114
STRACK, Ludwig Philipp (1761-1836) German				
oil	1	23,356	23,356	23,356
STRADONE, Giovanni (1911-1981) Italian				
oil	4	860-2,803	1,675	1,253
STRAET, Jan van der (1523-1605) Flemish				
wc/d	2	17,000-50,000	33,500	17,000
STRAETEN, George van der (1856-1928) Belgian				
3D	1	2,744	2,744	2,744
STRAGLIATI, Carlo (1868-1925) Italian				
wc/d	1	2,832	2,832	2,832
STRAHALM, Franz (1879-1935) American/Austrian				
oil	3	700-7,250	4,016	4,100
STRAHN, Peter Josef (1904-) German				
oil	1	1,903	1,903	1,903

Name	No.	Price Range	Average	Median
STRAIN, John Paul (1955-) American				
oil	1	3,000	3,000	3,000
wc/d	5	700-4,000	1,800	1,500
STRAKA, Josef (1864-1946) Austrian				
oil	1	5,351	5,351	5,351
STRANG, Ray C (1893-1957) American				
oil	2	3,500-7,500	5,500	3,500
STRANG, William (1859-1921) British				
wc/d	1	1,218	1,218	1,218
STRASSER, Arthur (1854-1927) Austrian				
3D	2	2,188-2,342	2,265	2,188
STRASSER, Ernst (1905-?) Belgian				
oil	1	2,384	2,384	2,384
STRASSER, Jakob (1896-1978) Swiss				
oil	2	381-1,674	1,027	381
wc/d	2	304-533	418	304
STRASSER, Roland (1892-1974) Austrian				
oil	4	4,816-64,286	21,703	5,057
wc/d	1	1,686	1,686	1,686
STRATHMANN, Carl (1866-1939) German				
oil	1	1,746	1,746	1,746
STRAUBE, William (1871-1954) German				
oil	5	1,532-5,856	3,296	2,356
wc/d	3	816-3,534	1,895	1,335
STRAUCH, Lorenz (1554-1630) German				
oil	1	11,918	11,918	11,918
STRAUS, Meyer (1831-1905) American/German				
oil	4	700-65,000	16,925	800
STRAUSS, Andre (1885-1971) French				
oil	1	2,200	2,200	2,200
STRAUSS, Hugo (1872-1944) Swiss				
oil	1	1,061	1,061	1,061
STRAWINSKY, Theodore (1907-1989) Russian				
oil	3	811-3,348	1,664	833
STRAZZA, Guido (1922-) Italian				
oil	3	3,142-5,800	4,620	4,919
wc/d	2	510-799	654	510
STREBELL, F J (18th C) German				
oil	1	4,379	4,379	4,379
STRECKENBACH, Max T (1865-1936) German				
oil	6	800-3,650	2,316	2,119
STRECKER, Emil (1841-1925) German				
oil	1	4,257	4,257	4,257
STRECKER, Paul (1900-1950) German				
oil	1	2,342	2,342	2,342
STREECK, Jurriaen van (1632-1687) Dutch				
oil	5	21,857-61,151	38,355	28,286
STREET, Robert (1796-1865) American				
oil	2	550-4,000	2,275	550
STREICHMAN, Yehezkel (1906-1993) Israeli				
oil	3	34,000-120,000	65,666	43,000
wc/d	7	1,100-3,000	2,242	2,600
STREIGHT, Howard A (1836-1912) American				
oil	1	1,000	1,000	1,000
STREIT, Robert (1883-1957) Austrian				
oil	1	1,334	1,334	1,334
STREITT, Franciszek (1839-1890) Polish				
oil	1	6,450	6,450	6,450
STREMPEL, Horst (1904-1975) German				
oil	1	1,316	1,316	1,316
STRENG, Johan Joachim (1703-1763) Swedish				
oil	1	1,620	1,620	1,620
STRETTON, Philip Eustace (fl.1884-1919) British				
oil	3	3,132-16,000	9,044	8,000
wc/d	3	589-1,295	994	1,100
STREVENS, John (1902-1990) British				
oil	4	957-3,060	1,727	1,056
STRICCOLI, Carlo (1897-?) Italian				
oil	1	1,523	1,523	1,523
STRICH-CHAPELL, Walter (1877-1960) German				
oil	10	471-1,989	1,108	1,113

Name	No.	Price Range	Average	Median
STRID, Hardy (1921-) Swedish				
oil	6	464-1,419	838	645
wc/d	2	489-725	607	489
STRIEFFLER, Heinrich (1872-1949) German				
oil	2	2,137-3,786	2,961	2,137
STRIGEL, Bernhard (1460-1528) German				
oil	1	18,207	18,207	18,207
STRINDBERG, August (1849-1912) Swedish				
oil	1	760,290	760,290	760,290
STRINGER, Francis (18th C) British				
oil	1	6,408	6,408	6,408
STRINGER, Thomas (1722-1790) British				
oil	1	94,050	94,050	94,050
STRISIK, Paul (1918-1998) American				
oil	7	1,400-6,200	4,042	4,500
STROBEL, Bartholomaus (younger) (1591-1644) Polish				
wc/d	1	10,813	10,813	10,813
STROBEL, C (19th C) ?				
oil	1	2,068	2,068	2,068
STROBENTZ, Fritz (1856-1929) German				
oil	1	1,401	1,401	1,401
STROEBEL, Johann Anthonie Balthasar (1821-1905) Dutch				
oil	4	1,496-9,388	4,515	1,796
STROHER, Friedrich Karl (1876-1925) German				
oil	1	8,952	8,952	8,952
wc/d	1	649	649	649
STROMAN, J (19th C) American				
oil	1	42,000	42,000	42,000
STROMBERG, Henrik (1880-1956) Danish				
oil	1	1,746	1,746	1,746
STROMBERG, Julia (1851-1920) Swedish				
oil	1	1,150	1,150	1,150
STROMEYER, Helene Marie (1834-1924) German				
oil	1	1,818	1,818	1,818
STRONCEK, Lee (1952-) American				
oil	1	2,500	2,500	2,500
STRONG, Elizabeth (1855-1941) American				
oil	1	6,000	6,000	6,000
STRONG, Ray Stanford (1905-) American				
oil	2	2,250-3,500	2,875	2,250
STROOBANT, François (1819-1916) Belgian				
oil	1	2,104	2,104	2,104
STROUD, Clara (1890-?) American				
oil	1	2,200	2,200	2,200
STROUDLEY, James (1906-1985) British				
oil	1	1,850	1,850	1,850
STROUT, C (?) ?				
oil	1	2,492	2,492	2,492
STROZZI, Bernardo (1581-1644) Italian				
oil	3	48,857-164,350	121,416	151,042
STRUBE, Adolf (1881-?) German				
oil	2	2,121-2,238	2,179	2,121
wc/d	2	468-643	555	468
STRUBE, Jan (20th C) Dutch				
oil	1	16,384	16,384	16,384
STRUBIN, Robert (1897-1965) Swiss				
wc/d	1	2,914	2,914	2,914
STRUCK, Herman (1887-1954) American				
oil	1	3,000	3,000	3,000
STRUDWICK, John Melhuish (1849-1937) British				
oil	2	123,200-1,320,000	721,600	123,200
STRUPLER, Hans Rudolf (1935-) Swiss				
wc/d	3	341-3,434	1,589	992
STRUTH, Thomas (1954-) German				
oil	1	52,800	52,800	52,800
STRUTT, Alfred William (1856-1924) British				
oil	2	3,979-15,660	9,819	3,979
STRUTT, William (1826-1915) British				
oil	1	12,600	12,600	12,600
wc/d	1	5,160	5,160	5,160
STRUTZEL, Otto (1855-1930) German				
oil	5	1,620-8,182	3,777	3,022

Name	No.	Price Range	Average	Median
STRUYK, Nicolas (18th C) ?				
wc/d	2	865-1,800	1,332	865
STRUYKEN, Peter (1939-) Dutch				
oil	1	3,012	3,012	3,012
wc/d	1	1,885	1,885	1,885
STRY, Abraham van (elder) (1753-1826) Dutch				
oil	3	10,175-54,948	28,182	19,425
wc/d	2	993-1,927	1,460	993
STRY, Jacob van (1756-1815) Dutch				
oil	4	3,700-16,562	8,221	4,622
wc/d	4	490-4,800	1,703	560
STRYDONCK, Guillaume van (1861-1937) Belgian				
oil	3	497-5,900	2,972	2,521
STUART, Alexander Charles (1831-1898) American				
oil	2	1,300-6,000	3,650	1,300
STUART, Charles (19th C) British				
oil	8	895-7,920	2,335	1,575
STUART, Gilbert (1755-1828) American				
oil	10	11,160-7,250,000	790,740	35,000
STUART, Gordon (20th C) British				
wc/d	1	4,628	4,628	4,628
STUART, James Everett (1852-1941) American				
oil	23	400-24,000	3,031	1,400
STUART, James Reeve (1834-1915) American				
oil	1	40,000	40,000	40,000
STUART, Jane (1816-1888) American				
oil	2	1,500-3,250	2,375	1,500
STUART, Michelle (1940-) American				
wc/d	1	1,018	1,018	1,018
STUART, William (19th C) British				
oil	1	5,533	5,533	5,533
STUART-HILL, A (20th C) British				
oil	1	5,130	5,130	5,130
STUBBENDORF, A (?) ?				
oil	1	2,662	2,662	2,662
STUBBS, George (1724-1806) British				
oil	1	529,200	529,200	529,200
STUBBS, Ralph Reuben (1820-1879) British				
oil	2	1,628-2,400	2,014	1,628
STUBBS, W P (1842-1909) American				
oil	1	8,100	8,100	8,100
STUBBS, William P (1842-1909) American				
oil	12	3,500-14,000	8,416	7,500
STUBER, Dedrick B (1878-1954) American				
oil	7	2,000-9,041	3,970	3,250
STUCK, Franz von (1863-1928) German				
oil	6	5,890-69,920	27,558	19,000
wc/d	5	1,914-15,925	5,714	3,857
3D	7	10,192-32,500	17,324	13,230
STUCKELBERG, Ernst (1831-1903) Swiss				
oil	1	1,216	1,216	1,216
STUDDY, George Ernest (1878-1948) British				
wc/d	3	1,038-1,750	1,484	1,665
STUDER, Johann Rudolf (1700-?) Swiss				
oil	1	4,579	4,579	4,579
STUHLMULLER, Karl (1858-1930) German				
oil	12	817-73,890	19,158	8,836
STUIVENBERG, Pieter Antonie van (1901-1988) Dutch				
3D	1	2,939	2,939	2,939
STULINK, Wilhelm (19th C) German				
oil	1	1,455	1,455	1,455
STULL, Henry (1851-1913) American				
oil	9	2,600-75,000	15,900	8,500
STULTUS, Dyalma (1902-1977) Italian				
oil	3	2,057-4,114	3,385	3,986
STUNDL, Theodor (1875-1934) Austrian				
3D	1	1,740	1,740	1,740
STUPAR, Marko (1936-) ?				
oil	3	953-6,473	3,875	4,200
wc/d	1	637	637	637
STURGEON, Eric (1920-2001) British				
wc/d	1	1,850	1,850	1,850

Name	No.	Price Range	Average	Median
STURGESS, John (fl.1869-1903) British				
oil	4	801-2,000	1,397	1,134
STURM, Helmut (1932-) German				
oil	3	1,616-10,829	5,039	2,672
wc/d	1	900	900	900
STURSA, Jan (1880-1925) Czechoslovakian				
3D	2	3,287-12,932	8,109	3,287
STURTEVANT, Elaine (1926-) American				
oil	2	30,000-36,237	33,118	30,000
wc/d	2	50,000-460,000	255,000	50,000
3D	1	120,000	120,000	120,000
STURTEVANT, Helena (1872-1946) American				
oil	1	2,100	2,100	2,100
STURZENEGGER, Hans (1875-1943) Swiss				
oil	3	1,142-1,542	1,283	1,166
STUTTERHEIM, Lodewyk Philippus (1873-1943) Dutch				
oil	2	488-1,598	1,043	488
STUTTERHEIM, Robert (1878-1961) Dutch				
oil	2	851-7,308	4,079	851
STUTZER, Alwin (1889-?) German				
wc/d	1	2,003	2,003	2,003
STUVEN, Ernst (1660-1712) German				
oil	1	21,020	21,020	21,020
STYKA, Adam (1890-1959) French				
oil	9	10,603-76,439	38,298	34,855
STYLIANIDIS, Argyris (1909-1998) Greek				
oil	4	5,632-9,152	7,202	6,545
STYRSKY, Jindrich (1899-1942) Czechoslovakian				
wc/d	3	1,784-5,825	4,176	4,920
SU XINPING (1960-) Oriental				
oil	2	27,750-170,000	98,875	27,750
wc/d	1	18,500	18,500	18,500
SUAREZ, Antonio (1923-) Spanish				
oil	4	838-3,750	1,713	851
SUBERO, Oswaldo (1934-) Venezuelan				
oil	1	3,250	3,250	3,250
wc/d	3	840-1,500	1,090	930
SUBIRACHS, Jose Maria (1927-) Spanish				
3D	1	5,400	5,400	5,400
SUBLEYRAS, Pierre (1699-1749) French				
oil	1	70,541	70,541	70,541
SUBRAMANYAN, K G (1924-) Indian				
oil	6	8,000-35,000	13,662	9,000
wc/d	2	6,000-7,000	6,500	6,000
SUCH, William T (fl.1847-1857) British				
oil	1	1,750	1,750	1,750
SUCHODOLSKA, Lisbeth von (1844-?) German				
oil	1	1,850	1,850	1,850
SUDAI, Ezer (1976-) Israeli				
oil	1	1,900	1,900	1,900
SUDDABY, Rowland (1912-1973) British				
oil	2	840-1,416	1,128	840
wc/d	5	766-2,784	1,606	1,197
SUDDUTH, Jimmy Lee (1910-) American				
oil	17	500-2,000	1,008	800
wc/d	1	4,800	4,800	4,800
SUDEIKIN, Sergei Yurievich (1882-1946) Russian				
oil	3	11,712-86,000	41,744	27,520
wc/d	4	2,262-129,454	39,653	2,301
SUDKOVSKY, Rufin (1850-1885) Russian				
oil	3	9,300-21,822	15,517	15,429
SUETIN, Nikolai Mikhailovich (1897-1954) Russian				
oil	2	1,001-32,005	16,503	1,001
wc/d	5	5,068-51,900	16,448	7,603
SUEUR, Eustache le (1617-1655) French				
oil	1	119,726	119,726	119,726
SUGAI, Kumi (1919-1996) Japanese				
oil	3	1,767-15,315	8,050	7,068
wc/d	2	879-3,360	2,119	879
SUGHI, Alberto (1928-) Italian				
oil	17	3,073-12,528	7,743	7,767
wc/d	14	471-3,262	1,427	853

Name	No.	Price Range	Average	Median
SUGITO, Hiroshi (1970-) Japanese?				
oil	17	4,500-61,950	29,031	22,000
SUHRLANDT, Carl (1828-1919) German				
oil	5	1,518-5,500	3,273	3,102
SUHRLANDT, Johann Heinrich (1742-1827) German				
oil	1	10,680	10,680	10,680
SUHRLANDT, Rudolf (1781-1862) German				
oil	1	2,928	2,928	2,928
wc/d	1	4,477	4,477	4,477
SUISSE, Gaston (1896-1988) French				
oil	4	4,562-182,603	54,425	10,510
wc/d	23	1,168-23,302	3,103	1,890
SUKADA, Made (1945-1982) Indonesian				
oil	1	3,853	3,853	3,853
SUKHODOLSKY, Pyotr Alexandrovich (1835-1903) Russian				
oil	1	3,740	3,740	3,740
SUKKERT, Adolf (19th C) German				
oil	2	29,795-92,000	60,897	29,795
SULLIVAN, Billy (1946-) American				
wc/d	1	7,000	7,000	7,000
SULLIVAN, Charles (1794-1867) American				
oil	1	2,000	2,000	2,000
SULLY, Alfred (1820-1879) American				
wc/d	1	15,000	15,000	15,000
SULLY, Thomas (1783-1872) American/British				
oil	12	885-70,000	13,988	5,500
SULTAN, Charles (?) American				
oil	4	1,250-3,700	2,012	1,500
SULTAN, Donald (1951-) American				
oil	5	6,920-55,000	19,098	8,304
wc/d	9	5,000-17,000	8,971	8,000
SULZER, Julius von (1818-1889) Swiss				
oil	1	1,027	1,027	1,027
SUMMERS, Robert (1940-) American				
oil	3	1,800-9,000	4,466	2,600
3D	2	4,400-4,750	4,575	4,400
SUMNER, Maud (1902-1985) South African				
wc/d	1	1,454	1,454	1,454
SUNAGE, Sterk (20th C) American				
wc/d	1	1,000	1,000	1,000
SUNDARAM, Vivan (1943-) Indian				
oil	1	42,500	42,500	42,500
SUNDBLOM, Haddon Hubbard (1899-1976) American				
oil	1	5,000	5,000	5,000
SUNDELL, Thure (1864-1924) Finnish				
oil	4	1,171-8,767	4,554	2,422
SUNESSON, Stina (1925-1998) Swedish				
wc/d	4	1,932-24,205	8,285	2,198
SUNG NAKHEE (1971-) Korean				
wc/d	1	8,000	8,000	8,000
SUNQUA (19th C) Chinese				
oil	1	25,000	25,000	25,000
wc/d	2	8,500-40,000	24,250	8,500
SUNYER, Joachim (1875-1956) Spanish				
oil	6	12,162-85,260	37,797	26,815
wc/d	2	1,205-5,500	3,352	1,205
SUOMI, Risto (1951-) Finnish				
oil	1	3,955	3,955	3,955
wc/d	1	815	815	815
SUPERSTUDIO (20th C) Italian				
wc/d	1	1,578	1,578	1,578
SUPISICHE, Ricardo (1912-1992) Argentinian				
oil	2	3,800-5,000	4,400	3,800
SUPONO, Ogeng Huru (1937-1991) Javanese				
oil	1	2,047	2,047	2,047
SUPPANTSCHITSCH, Max (1865-1953) Austrian				
wc/d	1	1,936	1,936	1,936
SUPPIN, Lucas (1911-1998) Austrian				
oil	1	2,397	2,397	2,397
SURAND, Gustave (1860-1937) French				
oil	1	3,390	3,390	3,390
wc/d	2	2,397-2,397	2,397	2,397

Name	No.	Price Range	Average	Median
SURBEK, Victor (1885-1975) Swiss				
oil	4	500-15,819	5,105	1,832
SURDI, Luigi (1897-1959) Italian				
oil	2	444-3,142	1,793	444
SUREAU (20th C) French				
oil	1	6,261	6,261	6,261
SUREDA, Andre (1872-1930) French				
oil	2	651-651	651	651
wc/d	6	583-1,445	1,004	779
SURIAN, Christiane (1942-) French				
oil	1	3,341	3,341	3,341
SURIKOV, Vasilii Ivanovich (1848-1916) Russian				
oil	1	20,640	20,640	20,640
wc/d	1	37,200	37,200	37,200
SURLS, James (1943-) American				
3D	2	6,500-19,000	12,750	6,500
SUROVTSEVA, Daria (20th C) Russian?				
3D	1	15,181	15,181	15,181
SURREY, Philip Henry (1910-1990) Canadian				
oil	5	1,058-2,952	1,648	1,476
wc/d	6	503-1,939	1,386	1,402
SURTEL, Paul (1893-1985) French				
oil	5	1,271-2,855	1,890	1,844
SURVAGE, Leopold (1879-1968) French				
oil	15	1,918-167,307	36,499	20,414
wc/d	42	418-34,000	5,054	1,757
SUSINI, Antonio (?-1624) Italian				
3D	1	127,143	127,143	127,143
SUSS, Johann J (1857-1937) Austrian				
oil	1	2,079	2,079	2,079
SUSSMEIER, Josef (1896-1971) German				
oil	2	702-1,458	1,080	702
SUSTERMANS, Justus (1597-1681) Flemish				
oil	1	40,700	40,700	40,700
SUSTRIS, Lambert (c.1515-1568) Dutch				
oil	2	7,709-451,892	229,800	7,709
SUTA, Romans (1896-1943) Latvian				
oil	1	18,200	18,200	18,200
SUTCLIFFE, Lester (1848-1933) British				
oil	4	435-1,800	1,101	700
SUTHERLAND, David (1883-1973) British				
oil	1	2,941	2,941	2,941
SUTHERLAND, Graham (1903-1980) British				
oil	8	28,320-278,400	108,902	44,880
wc/d	35	456-121,800	19,471	9,048
SUTHERLAND, Robert Lewis (?-1932) British				
oil	1	3,363	3,363	3,363
SUTHERS, Leghe (1855-1924) British				
oil	1	3,747	3,747	3,747
SUTTER, Jules de (1895-1970) Belgian				
oil	2	3,567-5,007	4,287	3,567
SUTTMAN, Paul (20th C) ?				
3D	1	3,600	3,600	3,600
SUTTON, Gerda (1923-2005) British				
oil	11	482-7,836	1,432	723
SUTTON, Harry (jnr) (1897-1984) American				
oil	1	1,200	1,200	1,200
SUTTON, Ivan (1944-) Irish?				
oil	9	1,940-6,793	3,343	3,038
SUTTON, John (1935-) British				
oil	3	1,100-1,300	1,233	1,300
SUTTON, John (19/20th C) British				
oil	9	500-1,628	825	700
wc/d	2	435-528	481	435
SUTTON, Philip (1928-) British				
oil	5	974-10,285	4,641	4,488
SUVERO, Mark di (1933-) American				
wc/d	2	3,200-16,000	9,600	3,200
3D	8	1,900-850,000	147,353	48,552
SUVOROVA, Olga (20th C) Russian				
oil	2	1,424-1,581	1,502	1,424

Name	No.	Price Range	Average	Median
SUYDAM, Edward Howard (1885-1940) American				
oil	1	1,400	1,400	1,400
SUZANNE, Léon (1870-1923) French				
oil	1	5,761	5,761	5,761
SUZOR-COTE, Marc-Aurele de Foy (1869-1937) Canadian				
oil	8	1,237-62,500	26,236	22,156
wc/d	3	618-6,185	4,054	5,360
3D	18	7,009-105,972	19,999	13,118
SUZUKI, James (1933-) Japanese				
oil	1	3,750	3,750	3,750
SUZUKI, Lewis (1920-) American				
wc/d	1	1,500	1,500	1,500
SVANBERG, Max Walter (1912-1995) Swedish				
wc/d	14	620-34,358	4,896	2,445
SVANKMAJEROVA, Eva (1940-2005) Czechoslovakian				
oil	1	5,400	5,400	5,400
SVEDBERG, Lena (1946-1972) Swedish				
wc/d	2	661-3,568	2,114	661
SVEINSDOTTIR, Juliana (1889-1966) Icelandic				
oil	1	4,364	4,364	4,364
SVENDSEN, Svend (1864-1934) Norwegian/American				
oil	6	550-2,000	1,150	1,000
SVENSSON, Christian Fredrik (1834-1909) Swedish				
oil	5	755-6,319	2,395	1,620
SVENSSON, Gunnar (1892-1977) Swedish				
oil	1	2,445	2,445	2,445
SVENSSON, Roland (1910-2003) Swedish				
wc/d	4	549-4,121	1,631	758
SVENSSON-PIEHL, Berta (1892-1963) Swedish				
oil	1	2,926	2,926	2,926
SVERTSCHKOFF, Nicolas Gregorovitch (1817-1898) Russian				
oil	9	6,442-3,567,123	761,809	44,645
SVESHNIKOV, Boris Petrovich (1927-) Russian				
oil	2	27,900-29,760	28,830	27,900
wc/d	2	2,000-3,750	2,875	2,000
SVETLITSKI, Evgeny (20th C) Russian				
oil	1	6,541	6,541	6,541
SVETOSLAVSKY, Sergei Ivanovich (1857-1931) Russian				
oil	3	23,356-93,000	46,810	24,076
SWAGERS, Frans (1756-1836) Dutch				
oil	10	4,241-12,740	7,921	7,644
SWAIN, Edward A (20th C) British				
wc/d	1	1,131	1,131	1,131
SWAIN, Robert (1940-) American				
oil	1	3,500	3,500	3,500
SWAINE, Francis (1740-1782) British				
oil	8	1,309-32,130	10,317	4,425
SWALLOW, Ricky (1974-) Australian				
wc/d	1	7,500	7,500	7,500
SWAMINATHAN, Jagdish (1928-1993) Indian				
oil	4	119,680-700,000	319,345	121,100
wc/d	3	8,000-13,000	10,000	9,000
SWAN, Alice Macallan (1864-1935) British				
oil	1	1,239	1,239	1,239
SWAN, Cuthbert Edmund (1870-1931) British				
oil	1	15,000	15,000	15,000
wc/d	1	1,665	1,665	1,665
SWAN, Douglas (1930-2001) American				
oil	3	1,060-1,671	1,334	1,272
wc/d	6	478-1,012	745	699
SWAN, John (1948-) American				
oil	1	14,000	14,000	14,000
wc/d	1	575	575	575
SWAN, Paul (1956-) British				
oil	1	1,145	1,145	1,145
SWANE, Christine (1876-1960) Danish				
oil	4	1,771-8,890	4,319	2,897
SWANE, Sigurd (1879-1973) Danish				
oil	9	809-3,395	1,728	1,455
SWANEVELT, Herman van (1600-1655) Dutch				
oil	2	5,303-37,380	21,341	5,303

Name	No.	Price Range	Average	Median
SWANSON, Garry R (1941-) American				
oil	4	1,500-7,500	5,500	6,000
SWANSON, Ray (1937-) American				
oil	15	3,000-32,500	11,266	8,500
wc/d	3	3,600-7,000	5,366	5,500
SWANWICK, Harold (1866-1929) British				
wc/d	2	1,566-2,649	2,107	1,566
SWANZY, Mary (1882-1978) Irish				
oil	7	5,449-167,400	52,443	11,781
wc/d	5	637-1,937	1,206	1,262
SWART, Cristianus Hendricus de (1818-1897) Dutch				
oil	1	3,109	3,109	3,109
SWARTZLANDER, Frank (20th C) American				
oil	2	400-2,200	1,300	400
wc/d	1	650	650	650
SWASEY, Henry Street (1864-1954) American				
oil	1	1,000	1,000	1,000
SWATSLEY, John (1937-) American				
oil	1	4,000	4,000	4,000
SWEARINGEN, Johnnie (1908-1993) American				
oil	1	2,900	2,900	2,900
SWEBACH, Bernard Edouard (1800-1870) French				
wc/d	4	1,100-1,580	1,357	1,308
SWEBACH-DESFONTAINES, Jacques François (1769-1823) French				
oil	3	3,637-16,069	9,035	7,400
wc/d	3	476-2,674	1,307	772
SWEELINK, Gerrit Pietersz (1566-1645) Dutch				
oil	1	15,000	15,000	15,000
SWEERTS, Michiel (1618-1664) Flemish				
oil	1	311,400	311,400	311,400
SWEET, Darrell K (1939-) American				
oil	1	4,500	4,500	4,500
SWETT, Moses (fl.1823-1837) American				
oil	1	2,500	2,500	2,500
SWIENTOCHOWSKI, John (1911-2002) American				
oil	1	5,500	5,500	5,500
SWIEYKOWSKI, Alfred (1869-1953) Russian				
oil	1	1,152	1,152	1,152
SWIFT, Clement (1846-1918) American				
oil	2	1,100-1,500	1,300	1,100
SWIFT, Patrick (1927-1983) Irish				
oil	1	7,800	7,800	7,800
SWIMBERGHE, Gilbert (1927-) Belgian				
oil	2	1,798-1,806	1,802	1,798
SWINNERTON, James G (1875-1974) American				
oil	9	425-37,500	6,905	2,750
SWINSTEAD, George Hillyard (1860-1926) British				
oil	1	2,760	2,760	2,760
SWOBODA VON WIKINGEN, Emmerich Alexius (1849-1920) Austrian				
3D	1	7,417	7,417	7,417
SWOBODA, Rudolf (elder) (1819-1859) Austrian				
oil	1	5,890	5,890	5,890
SWOBODA, Rudolf (younger) (1859-1914) Austrian				
oil	1	1,549	1,549	1,549
SWOPE, H Vance (19/20th C) American				
oil	3	850-1,600	1,100	850
SWORD, James Brade (1839-1915) American				
oil	1	3,250	3,250	3,250
wc/d	1	700	700	700
SWYNCOP, Charles (1895-1970) Belgian				
oil	4	467-2,180	1,214	1,090
SWYNCOP, Philippe (1878-1949) Belgian				
oil	5	1,064-4,529	2,105	1,752
SYBERG, Fritz (1862-1939) Danish				
oil	5	1,352-7,938	3,701	2,654
wc/d	5	552-1,304	896	879
SYCHKOV, Feodor Vasilievich (1870-1958) Russian				
oil	5	13,469-136,416	63,633	37,200
wc/d	2	52,080-573,288	312,684	52,080
SYER, John (1815-1885) British				
oil	3	1,197-3,806	2,493	2,478
wc/d	1	828	828	828

Name	No.	Price Range	Average	Median
SYER, John C (1846-1913) British				
oil	1	3,500	3,500	3,500
wc/d	3	470-696	574	557
SYER, John and WELLS, George (19th C) British				
oil	1	1,403	1,403	1,403
SYKES, Henry (1855-1921) British				
wc/d	1	3,480	3,480	3,480
SYKES, John (1859-1934) American				
oil	1	6,500	6,500	6,500
SYKORA, Zdenek (1920-) Czechoslovakian				
oil	1	12,740	12,740	12,740
SYLVESTER, Frederick Oakes (1869-1915) American				
oil	5	3,750-13,000	6,730	5,000
wc/d	2	443-1,900	1,171	443
SYMONS, George Gardner (1863-1930) American				
oil	17	500-16,000	6,870	7,500
SYMONS, William Christian (1845-1911) British				
oil	2	3,988-15,660	9,824	3,988
SYNAVE, Tancrede (1860-?) French				
oil	4	1,089-4,839	2,632	1,215
SYPKENS, Ferdinand Hendrik (1813-1860) Dutch				
oil	1	1,447	1,447	1,447
SYRIEX, Robert Daniel (20th C) French?				
oil	1	1,752	1,752	1,752
SZABO, Lajos (1902-1967) Hungarian				
wc/d	1	1,030	1,030	1,030
SZABO, Vladimir (1905-1991) Hungarian				
oil	1	1,598	1,598	1,598
SZAFRAN, Sam (1930-) French				
wc/d	7	876-471,233	113,083	6,241
SZALAY, Lajos (1919-1995) Argentinian				
wc/d	2	1,500-3,600	2,550	1,500
SZANKOWSKI, Boleslaw von (1873-1953) Polish				
oil	2	2,384-3,600	2,992	2,384
SZANTHO, Maria (1898-1984) Hungarian				
oil	4	1,029-3,330	2,195	1,506
SZAPOCZNIKOW, Alina (1926-1973) Polish				
3D	1	4,214	4,214	4,214
SZASZ, Endre (1926-2003) Hungarian				
oil	7	1,800-4,000	2,492	2,250
SZCZEBLEWSKI, Waclaw Bernard (1888-?) Polish				
3D	1	2,800	2,800	2,800
SZEJSTECKI, Eberhard (1958-) German				
3D	1	2,104	2,104	2,104
SZEKESSY, Zoltan (1899-1968) Hungarian				
3D	1	2,356	2,356	2,356
SZENES, Arpad (1897-1985) French				
oil	14	4,200-108,288	27,497	16,365
wc/d	9	5,066-17,700	9,683	7,304
SZERBAKOW, Fedor (1911-) German?				
oil	5	605-1,875	1,057	994
SZOBOTKA, Imbre (1890-1961) Hungarian				
oil	2	50,658-70,685	60,671	50,658
SZONTAGH, Tibor (1873-1930) Hungarian				
oil	1	2,000	2,000	2,000
SZPINGER, Alexander von (1889-1956) German				
oil	1	1,940	1,940	1,940
SZUKALSKI, Albert (1945-) Belgian				
3D	8	3,356-6,181	4,529	4,555
SZYK, Arthur (1894-1951) Polish				
wc/d	1	2,200	2,200	2,200
SZYMANOWSKA, Lucrynska (?) Polish?				
oil	1	4,000	4,000	4,000
SZYMANSKI, Rolf (1928-) German				
wc/d	1	742	742	742
3D	1	2,577	2,577	2,577
SZYSKOWITZ, Rudolf (1905-1976) Austrian				
wc/d	1	1,168	1,168	1,168
SZYSZLO, Fernando de (1925-) Peruvian				
oil	2	12,000-28,000	20,000	12,000

Name	No.	Price Range	Average	Median
TAAFFE, Philip (1955-) American				
oil	4	6,500-180,000	77,625	14,000
wc/d	3	4,800-100,000	58,266	70,000
TAANMAN, Jacob (1836-1923) Dutch				
oil	1	1,085	1,085	1,085
TABAR, François Germain Leopold (1818-1869) French				
oil	2	1,683-3,250	2,466	1,683
TABARA, Enrique (19/20th C) Ecuadorian				
oil	3	531-1,745	1,011	759
TABENKIN, Lev (1952-) Russian				
oil	1	85,000	85,000	85,000
TABERNER, Luis (19th C) Spanish				
oil	1	2,827	2,827	2,827
TABNER, Len (1936-) British				
oil	1	4,698	4,698	4,698
wc/d	2	2,124-2,832	2,478	2,124
TABUCHI, Yasse (1921-) Japanese				
oil	3	1,401-1,850	1,676	1,778
wc/d	1	1,014	1,014	1,014
TABUENA, Romeo (1921-) Mexican				
oil	5	1,900-2,400	2,160	2,200
wc/d	2	400-550	475	400
TABUSSO, Francesco (1930-) Italian				
oil	3	4,411-17,644	9,738	7,159
wc/d	12	504-4,772	1,481	1,197
TACCA, Pietro (1577-1640) Italian				
3D	1	44,803	44,803	44,803
TACCHI, Cesare (1940-) Italian				
wc/d	3	8,414-38,163	22,553	21,082
TACKE, Andreas (1823-1899) German				
oil	2	7,224-24,082	15,653	7,224
TADEUSZ, Norbert (1940-) German				
oil	3	972-7,633	3,732	2,592
wc/d	1	3,822	3,822	3,822
TADINI, Emilio (1927-2002) Italian				
oil	15	1,001-26,714	8,152	6,214
wc/d	1	2,054	2,054	2,054
TADOLINI, Giulio (1849-1918) Italian				
3D	1	5,000	5,000	5,000
TAELEMANS, Jean François (1851-1931) Belgian				
oil	1	1,293	1,293	1,293
wc/d	1	602	602	602
TAEUBER-ARP, Sophie (1889-1943) Swiss				
wc/d	1	44,582	44,582	44,582
TAEYE, Camille de (1938-) Belgian				
oil	1	1,731	1,731	1,731
TAFURI, Clemente (1903-1971) Italian				
oil	11	1,600-16,829	3,770	2,000
TAFURI, Raffaele (1857-1929) Italian				
oil	2	10,730-10,776	10,753	10,730
TAGGART, Elizabeth (1943-) British				
oil	2	1,566-2,223	1,894	1,566
TAGGER, Siona (1900-1988) Israeli				
oil	6	900-22,000	8,091	4,000
wc/d	6	800-4,200	2,050	1,100
TAGLIABUE, Carlo Costantino (1880-1960) Italian				
oil	2	3,633-8,281	5,957	3,633
TAGLIAFERRO, Aldo (1936-) Italian				
oil	4	3,024-6,361	4,858	4,325
wc/d	1	3,024	3,024	3,024
TAGLIAPIETRA, Maria (19th C) Italian				
oil	1	3,770	3,770	3,770
TAGORE, Abanindranath (1871-1951) Indian				
wc/d	1	6,000	6,000	6,000
TAGTSTROM, David (1894-1981) Swedish				
oil	1	4,396	4,396	4,396
TAHON, Isidore (17/18th C) French				
oil	1	7,007	7,007	7,007
TAIBO GONZALEZ, German (1889-1919) Spanish				
oil	1	5,100	5,100	5,100
TAIKYO, Uda (1899-1977) Japanese				
wc/d	1	4,200	4,200	4,200

Name	No.	Price Range	Average	Median
TAILLANDIER, Yvon (1926-) French				
oil	7	421-1,985	1,009	747
wc/d	4	421-583	480	458
TAIRA, Frank (1913-) American				
oil	1	1,600	1,600	1,600
TAIT, Arthur Fitzwilliam (1819-1905) American				
oil	10	8,000-85,000	26,150	13,000
TAIT, John Robinson (1834-1909) American				
oil	2	8,500-17,000	12,750	8,500
TAIT, Neal (1965-) American?				
oil	1	12,025	12,025	12,025
wc/d	1	2,750	2,750	2,750
TAIT, Renny (1965-) British				
oil	1	5,632	5,632	5,632
TAJAR, Ziona (1900-1988) Israeli				
oil	2	4,600-8,000	6,300	4,600
wc/d	6	440-2,400	1,023	500
TAJIRI, Shinkichi (1923-) American				
wc/d	2	818-1,414	1,116	818
3D	3	4,849-15,315	10,209	10,463
TAKAMATSU, Jiro (1936-1998) Japanese				
oil	1	13,000	13,000	13,000
TAKANEN, Johannes (1849-1885) Finnish				
3D	1	3,631	3,631	3,631
TAKAWIRA, John (1938-1989) Zimbabwean				
3D	2	3,010-4,937	3,973	3,010
TAKIS (1925-) Greek				
oil	1	10,285	10,285	10,285
wc/d	1	597	597	597
3D	18	3,053-27,194	9,880	7,027
TAKKIRUQ, Nelson (1930-) North American				
3D	1	4,893	4,893	4,893
TAKPAUNGAI, Quvianatuliak (1942-) Canadian				
3D	1	3,775	3,775	3,775
TAL COAT (1905-1985) French				
oil	1	2,035	2,035	2,035
TAL COAT, Pierre (1905-1985) French				
oil	21	479-29,223	10,975	9,535
wc/d	17	486-3,214	1,487	1,295
TAL R (1967-) Israeli				
oil	8	2,575-54,727	20,669	15,356
TALBOT, Graham (20th C) British?				
3D	1	10,800	10,800	10,800
TALBOT, Jesse (1806-1879) American				
oil	1	5,000	5,000	5,000
TALICHKIN, Sergey (20th C) ?				
oil	2	803-1,942	1,372	803
TALIRUNILI, Joe (1906-1976) North American				
3D	2	2,531-3,374	2,952	2,531
TALLAL, Chaibia (1929-2004) Moroccan				
oil	1	17,436	17,436	17,436
wc/d	1	9,187	9,187	9,187
TALLENTIRE, Anne (1949-) British				
oil	4	570-870	713	626
wc/d	1	623	623	623
TALLON, Robert (20th C) American				
wc/d	1	3,000	3,000	3,000
TALLONE, Cesare (1853-1919) Italian				
oil	2	597-19,082	9,839	597
TALLONE, Guido (1894-1967) Italian				
oil	4	605-8,326	4,343	3,524
TALMAGE, Algernon (1871-1939) British				
oil	5	1,376-12,000	5,450	6,156
wc/d	1	4,914	4,914	4,914
TALPINO, Enea (c.1558-1626) Italian				
wc/d	1	3,625	3,625	3,625
TAM, Reuben (1916-) American				
oil	3	2,600-6,500	4,566	4,600
TAMAGNINI, Torquato (1886-1965) Italian				
3D	1	1,757	1,757	1,757
TAMARI, Amiram (1913-1981) Israeli				
oil	3	1,000-1,900	1,600	1,900

Name	No.	Price Range	Average	Median
TAMAYO, Rufino (1899-1991) Mexican				
oil	16	32,000-500,000	236,218	140,000
wc/d	12	3,813-75,000	28,234	26,000
3D	1	180,000	180,000	180,000
TAMBURELLA, Paolo (1963-) Italian				
wc/d	1	3,503	3,503	3,503
TAMBURI, Orfeo (1910-1994) Italian				
oil	25	492-25,890	6,708	6,085
wc/d	10	492-1,145	752	611
TAMBURINI, Arnaldo (1843-1901) Italian				
oil	6	950-5,160	2,968	2,600
TAMBURINI, Arnaldo Casella (jnr) (1885-1936) American				
oil	1	1,900	1,900	1,900
TAMBURINI, Jose Maria (1856-1932) Spanish				
oil	1	1,085	1,085	1,085
TAMBURRO, Antonio (1948-) Italian				
oil	2	1,453-1,585	1,519	1,453
wc/d	1	942	942	942
TAMBURRO, Marco (1974-) Italian				
oil	1	2,330	2,330	2,330
wc/d	1	431	431	431
TAMM, Franz Werner (1658-1724) German				
oil	5	9,790-83,040	37,956	39,160
TANABE, Takao (1926-) Canadian				
oil	8	1,097-16,839	7,609	4,848
wc/d	3	810-1,148	977	973
TANAKA, Akira (1918-1982) Japanese				
oil	1	9,351	9,351	9,351
TANAKA, Atsuko (1932-2005) Japanese				
wc/d	1	35,000	35,000	35,000
TANCREDI (1927-1964) Italian				
oil	10	10,177-216,259	74,488	50,884
wc/d	5	1,767-99,224	27,447	9,425
TANEV, Nikola (1864-1928) Bulgarian				
oil	2	3,822-58,603	31,212	3,822
TANG HAIWEN (1929-1991) Chinese				
wc/d	11	816-6,904	3,441	2,510
TANG YIFEN (1778-1853) Chinese				
wc/d	1	1,000	1,000	1,000
TANG ZHIGANG (1959-) Chinese				
oil	2	68,000-85,000	76,500	68,000
TANGUY, Yves (1900-1955) American/French				
oil	1	777,000	777,000	777,000
wc/d	6	9,000-92,500	41,841	33,658
TANK, Heinrich Friedrich (1808-1872) German				
oil	3	1,414-2,003	1,806	2,003
TANNAES, Marie (1854-1939) Norwegian				
oil	1	1,299	1,299	1,299
TANNER, Henry Ossawa (1859-1937) American				
oil	2	50,000-95,000	72,500	50,000
TANNERT, Louis (19th C) German				
oil	1	1,200	1,200	1,200
TANNING, Dorothea (1910-) American				
oil	1	49,192	49,192	49,192
wc/d	3	4,919-7,000	6,217	6,732
TANOBE, Miyuki (1937-) Canadian				
oil	1	5,673	5,673	5,673
wc/d	2	7,493-7,493	7,493	7,493
TANOUX, Adrien Henri (1865-1923) French				
oil	3	3,449-5,178	4,052	3,529
TANSEY, Francis (1959-) Irish				
oil	3	2,422-3,527	3,114	3,395
TANSEY, Mark (1949-) American				
oil	1	20,000	20,000	20,000
TANTARDINI, Antonio (1829-1879) Italian				
3D	1	6,500	6,500	6,500
TAPIA, Alvard (1976-) ?				
oil	1	1,909	1,909	1,909
TAPIES, Antonio (1923-) Spanish				
oil	22	14,055-616,000	176,698	140,800
wc/d	14	1,910-212,055	51,728	24,220
3D	12	2,434-154,880	53,985	31,450

Name	No.	Price Range	Average	Median
TAPIOLA, Marjatta (1951-) Finnish				
oil	1	4,676	4,676	4,676
TAPIRO Y BARO, Jose (1830-1913) Spanish				
wc/d	3	6,027-156,400	63,475	28,000
TAPLIN, Guy (1939-) British				
3D	5	1,850-5,984	3,458	2,655
TAPPER, Kain (1930-2004) Finnish				
oil	1	3,039	3,039	3,039
wc/d	1	659	659	659
3D	3	4,371-6,325	5,517	5,856
TAPPERT, Georg (1880-1957) German				
oil	2	3,239-228,800	116,019	3,239
wc/d	7	486-1,674	754	572
TAQUOY, Maurice (1878-1952) French				
oil	7	589-10,744	2,269	876
wc/d	60	526-7,007	1,803	1,432
TARASENKO, Vladimir (1938-) Russian?				
oil	1	15,930	15,930	15,930
TARASIN, Jan (1926-) Polish				
oil	2	9,737-18,500	14,118	9,737
TARAVAL, Guillaume (1701-1750) French				
oil	1	30,000	30,000	30,000
TARAVAL, Hugues (1729-1785) French				
oil	2	18,123-60,000	39,061	18,123
TARBELL, Edmund C (1862-1938) American				
oil	2	8,000-30,000	19,000	8,000
TARBET, J A Henderson (c.1865-1938) British				
oil	3	2,262-6,018	3,675	2,745
wc/d	1	731	731	731
TARDIA, Enzo (1960-) Italian				
oil	4	471-1,229	695	492
wc/d	1	1,178	1,178	1,178
TARDY, Michel (1939-) French				
3D	2	2,093-4,414	3,253	2,093
TARENGHI, Enrico (1848-1938) Italian				
oil	1	2,572	2,572	2,572
wc/d	5	379-7,560	4,038	3,600
TARKHOFF, Nicolas (1871-1930) Russian				
oil	25	3,708-250,000	40,791	27,195
wc/d	2	2,383-2,719	2,551	2,383
TARRANT, Percy (fl.1881-1930) British				
oil	2	3,325-4,862	4,093	3,325
TASKER, William (1808-1852) British				
oil	2	3,806-4,392	4,099	3,806
TASLITZKY, Boris (1911-) French				
oil	2	1,260-1,890	1,575	1,260
TASSAERT, Octave (1800-1874) French				
oil	1	1,414	1,414	1,414
wc/d	1	707	707	707
TASSI, Matteo (1840-1895) Italian				
oil	1	4,483	4,483	4,483
TASSON, Francois (1811-1890) Belgian				
oil	1	2,506	2,506	2,506
TATAFIORE, Ernesto (1943-) Italian				
oil	3	1,274-4,757	2,933	2,768
wc/d	2	908-1,720	1,314	908
TATAFIORE, Guido (1919-1980) Italian				
wc/d	3	701-2,293	1,550	1,656
TATANIQ, George (1910-) North American				
3D	2	3,881-21,934	12,907	3,881
TATE, Gayle B (1944-) American				
oil	3	600-1,700	1,266	1,500
TATE, William (1748-1806) British				
oil	1	4,200	4,200	4,200
TATHAM, Agnes Clara (1893-?) British				
oil	1	3,514	3,514	3,514
TATIN, Robert (1902-1983) French				
oil	2	1,318-2,760	2,039	1,318
TATLIN, Vladimir (1885-1953) Russian				
3D	1	6,541	6,541	6,541
TATO (1896-1974) Italian				
oil	3	1,230-43,208	24,927	30,345

Name	No.	Price Range	Average	Median
TATOSSIAN, Armand (1948-) Canadian				
oil	24	408-5,730	1,915	1,587
TATTEGRAIN, Francis (1852-1915) French				
oil	2	790-8,038	4,414	790
TAUBE, Eugen (1860-1913) Finnish				
oil	10	1,139-11,314	3,749	3,039
TAUNAY, Nicolas Antoine (1755-1830) French				
oil	4	8,870-66,458	33,987	22,620
TAUREL, Henri (1843-?) French				
oil	2	2,903-8,870	5,886	2,903
TAVARIA, Ardeshir Ruishayee (20th C) Indian				
oil	1	4,928	4,928	4,928
TAVARONE, Lazzaro (1556-1641) Italian				
wc/d	5	911-13,368	4,435	2,917
TAVELLA, Carlo Antonio (1668-1738) Italian				
oil	2	5,946-31,140	18,543	5,946
wc/d	1	1,400	1,400	1,400
TAVENIER, Hendrik (1734-1807) Dutch				
wc/d	1	1,401	1,401	1,401
TAVENRAAT, Johannes (1809-1881) Dutch				
oil	3	1,775-4,849	2,826	1,854
TAVERNIER, Andrea (1858-1932) Italian				
oil	4	7,184-16,973	13,260	13,124
TAVERNIER, Jules (1844-1899) French				
oil	5	4,400-85,000	35,480	22,500
TAVERNIER, Louis de (20th C) Belgian				
oil	1	18,473	18,473	18,473
TAVERNIER, Paul (1852-?) French				
oil	1	7,304	7,304	7,304
TAYLER, Albert Chevallier (1862-1925) British				
oil	2	1,777-1,092,000	546,888	1,777
TAYLER, Norman E (1843-1915) British				
wc/d	1	1,750	1,750	1,750
TAYLOR, Alfred Henry (?-1868) British				
wc/d	1	1,298	1,298	1,298
TAYLOR, Anna Heyward (1879-1956) American				
wc/d	1	1,100	1,100	1,100
TAYLOR, Charles (19th C) British				
oil	1	1,800	1,800	1,800
wc/d	1	1,467	1,467	1,467
TAYLOR, Charles (jnr) (fl.1841-1883) British				
wc/d	6	555-16,530	3,889	1,018
TAYLOR, Charles Andrew (1910-) American				
oil	2	1,100-1,100	1,100	1,100
TAYLOR, D (?) ?				
oil	1	3,400	3,400	3,400
TAYLOR, Edward (?) British				
wc/d	1	3,540	3,540	3,540
TAYLOR, Ernest Archibald (1874-1952) British				
oil	1	8,010	8,010	8,010
wc/d	1	450	450	450
TAYLOR, Frederick Bourchier (1906-1987) Canadian				
oil	11	408-2,952	1,172	611
wc/d	1	410	410	410
TAYLOR, Henry King (fl.1857-1869) British				
oil	3	5,235-10,560	8,101	8,510
TAYLOR, Henry White (1899-1943) American				
oil	1	2,500	2,500	2,500
TAYLOR, Isaac (19th C) American				
oil	1	4,250	4,250	4,250
TAYLOR, John C E (1902-) American				
oil	2	850-2,500	1,675	850
TAYLOR, John D (fl.1880-1900) British				
oil	1	14,160	14,160	14,160
TAYLOR, Julian (1954-) British?				
oil	1	2,937	2,937	2,937
TAYLOR, Leonard Campbell (1874-1963) British				
oil	3	6,000-14,080	8,901	6,624
TAYLOR, Rolla S (1872-1970) American				
oil	6	800-9,000	3,491	2,000

Name	No.	Price Range	Average	Median
TAYLOR, Samuel Connolly (1870-1944) British				
oil	1	2,520	2,520	2,520
wc/d	1	942	942	942
TAYLOR, Stephen (19th C) British				
oil	1	1,701	1,701	1,701
TAYLOR, Walter (1875-1965) British				
oil	1	692	692	692
wc/d	1	504	504	504
TAYLOR, William Francis (1883-1970) American/Canadian				
oil	5	1,400-13,000	7,380	7,000
TAYSON, Lyle (20th C) American				
oil	6	1,700-6,750	2,991	2,100
TCHEKHONINE, Sergei (1878-1936) Russian				
wc/d	2	4,500-14,560	9,530	4,500
TCHELITCHEV, Pavel (1898-1957) American/Russian				
oil	16	3,802-160,000	31,011	20,000
wc/d	71	500-56,960	4,912	2,500
TCHERKESSOFF, Georges (1900-1943) Russian				
oil	3	2,158-2,939	2,539	2,521
TCHERNIAWSKY, Charles (1900-1976) Russian				
oil	4	1,318-3,907	2,094	1,381
TCHISTOVSKI, Lew (1902-1969) Russian				
wc/d	1	1,051	1,051	1,051
TCHORZEWSKI, Jerzy (1928-1999) Polish				
oil	2	12,945-14,144	13,544	12,945
wc/d	1	1,529	1,529	1,529
TCHOUMAKOFF, Theodore (1823-1911) Russian				
oil	4	761-4,841	2,938	1,626
wc/d	2	1,390-2,119	1,754	1,390
TCHOUPRINA, Nikolai (1928-) Russian				
oil	1	2,154	2,154	2,154
TCHUBANOV, Boris (1946-) Russian				
oil	1	6,715	6,715	6,715
TEAGUE, Donald (1897-1991) American				
oil	3	3,500-30,000	14,833	11,000
wc/d	9	925-150,000	28,741	6,000
TEASDALE, Percy Morton (1870-?) British				
oil	1	14,904	14,904	14,904
TEED, Douglas Arthur (1864-1929) American				
oil	5	850-2,900	1,770	2,000
TEEL, Lewis Woods (1883-1948) American				
oil	1	1,400	1,400	1,400
TEELING, Norman (1944-) Irish				
oil	5	997-2,417	1,485	1,211
TEERLINK, Abraham (1776-1857) Dutch				
oil	1	4,671	4,671	4,671
TEGIN, Dmitri Kapitonovich (1914-1988) Russian				
oil	1	5,580	5,580	5,580
TEGNER, Christian Martin (1803-1881) Danish				
oil	1	1,423	1,423	1,423
TEICHERT, Minerva (1889-1976) American				
oil	1	10,000	10,000	10,000
TEICHMANN, Alfred (1903-1980) German				
oil	1	3,748	3,748	3,748
TEINTURIER, Louis Ferdinand Victor (1825-?) French				
oil	1	1,296	1,296	1,296
TEITELBAUM, Mashel Alexander (1921-1985) Canadian				
oil	1	1,402	1,402	1,402
TEIXEIRA LOPES, Antonio (1866-1942) Portuguese				
3D	1	6,960	6,960	6,960
TEIXIDOR, Jordi (1941-) Spanish				
oil	3	1,796-9,643	5,098	3,857
TELARIK, Alois (1884-1961) ?				
oil	1	2,031	2,031	2,031
TELEKI, Andre (1928-1999) Belgian				
oil	1	1,142	1,142	1,142
TELEMAQUE, Herve (1937-) Haitian				
oil	4	23,302-69,694	43,795	23,787
wc/d	3	4,171-11,404	6,594	4,208
TELL, E (19/20th C) Austrian				
3D	2	1,909-20,384	11,146	1,909

Name	No.	Price Range	Average	Median
TELLES, Sergio (1936-) French?				
oil	2	895-1,980	1,437	895
TELLEZ LORIGUILLO, Santiago (20th C) Spanish				
oil	1	1,916	1,916	1,916
TELLIER, Raymond (1897-1985) French				
oil	6	468-10,188	2,626	1,136
TELLUFSEN, Jacob (1969-) Danish?				
oil	1	1,127	1,127	1,127
TELRONI, F (20th C) ?				
3D	1	2,700	2,700	2,700
TEMPESTA, Antonio (1555-1630) Italian				
oil	1	54,687	54,687	54,687
wc/d	1	3,092	3,092	3,092
TEMPLE, Hans (1857-1931) Austrian				
oil	1	1,522	1,522	1,522
TEMPLE, T (19th C) British				
oil	1	1,800	1,800	1,800
TEMPLIN, Victor (1920-1994) Russian				
oil	1	1,451	1,451	1,451
TEMPRA, Quirino (1849-?) Italian				
3D	2	2,003-3,888	2,945	2,003
TEN BERGE, Bernardus Gerardus (1825-1875) Dutch				
oil	1	1,326	1,326	1,326
TEN BRUGGEN KATE, Christiaan (1920-2003) Dutch				
oil	3	836-1,447	1,125	1,093
TEN CATE, Hendrik Gerrit (1803-1856) Dutch				
oil	2	1,463-4,267	2,865	1,463
TEN CATE, Johannes Marinus (1859-1896) Dutch				
oil	2	1,260-4,350	2,805	1,260
wc/d	1	900	900	900
TEN CATE, Siebe Johannes (1858-1908) Dutch				
oil	1	4,425	4,425	4,425
wc/d	5	589-3,529	2,364	2,548
TEN COMPE, Jan (1713-1761) Dutch				
oil	1	33,866	33,866	33,866
TEN HAGEN, Jacob (1820-?) Dutch				
oil	1	2,200	2,200	2,200
TEN HAVE, Jan (1903-1991) Dutch				
oil	1	1,097	1,097	1,097
TEN HOLT, Friso (1921-1997) Dutch				
oil	4	837-3,004	1,981	1,627
TEN KATE, Herman (1822-1891) Dutch				
oil	10	1,400-25,205	7,250	3,250
wc/d	5	665-2,443	1,159	728
TEN KATE, Jan Jacob Lodewijk (1850-1929) Dutch				
wc/d	1	2,667	2,667	2,667
TEN KATE, Johan Mari (1831-1910) Dutch				
oil	10	4,243-36,370	20,643	17,671
wc/d	4	1,012-14,833	8,282	5,163
TENCALLA, Carpoforo (1623-1685) Swiss				
oil	1	15,534	15,534	15,534
TENCH, E G (1885-1942) British				
oil	1	2,263	2,263	2,263
TENCH, Ernest George (1885-1942) British				
oil	2	1,558-2,655	2,106	1,558
TENE, Yoel (1889-1973) Israeli				
oil	1	50,000	50,000	50,000
TENER, René (1846-1925) French				
oil	1	1,860	1,860	1,860
TENERANI, Pietro (1789-1869) Italian				
3D	1	8,918	8,918	8,918
TENGGREN, Gustaf Adolf (1896-1981) Swedish				
wc/d	3	2,000-11,000	5,583	3,750
TENIERS, Abraham (1629-1670) Flemish				
oil	1	4,607	4,607	4,607
TENIERS, David (younger) (1610-1690) Flemish				
oil	16	2,500-709,300	139,982	91,216
wc/d	2	2,076-3,460	2,768	2,076
TENNANT, Dorothy (1855-1926) British				
oil	1	12,000	12,000	12,000
TENNANT, John F (1796-1872) British				
oil	3	846-6,574	3,181	2,124

Name	No.	Price Range	Average	Median
TENNANT, Lady Emma (1943-) British				
wc/d	1	1,122	1,122	1,122
TENRE, Henry (1864-1924) French				
oil	2	1,648-4,158	2,903	1,648
TEPPER, Saul (1899-1987) American				
oil	3	2,500-10,000	5,500	4,000
TER MEULEN, Frans Pieter (1843-1927) Dutch				
oil	1	2,100	2,100	2,100
TERAOKA, Masami (1936-) American				
wc/d	1	4,750	4,750	4,750
TERBOIS, Pierre (1932-) Swiss				
oil	2	1,513-2,573	2,043	1,513
TERCAFS, Jeanne (1898-1944) Belgian				
3D	2	4,195-7,192	5,693	4,195
TERECHKOVITCH, Costia (1902-1978) French				
oil	24	2,900-18,771	7,429	6,650
wc/d	7	760-2,351	1,336	1,199
TERELAK, John (1942-) American				
oil	1	3,000	3,000	3,000
TERESZCZUK, P (20th C) Austrian				
3D	1	3,009	3,009	3,009
TERESZCZUK, Peter (fl.1895-1925) Austrian				
3D	1	2,028	2,028	2,028
TERLEMEZIAN, Panos (1865-1941) Armenian				
oil	1	13,020	13,020	13,020
TERLIKOWSKI, Vladimir de (1873-1951) Polish				
oil	18	518-5,562	1,698	1,276
TERLINK, Abraham (1777-1857) Dutch				
oil	1	5,088	5,088	5,088
wc/d	1	1,215	1,215	1,215
TERLOUW, Kees (1890-1948) Dutch				
oil	6	1,239-2,474	2,119	2,264
TERMOHLEN, Karl E (1863-?) American				
oil	4	1,200-18,000	5,925	1,900
TERNI, A L (?) Italian				
oil	1	3,992	3,992	3,992
TERNO, Nina (1935-) Finnish				
3D	4	6,429-15,429	10,128	6,442
TERPENING, Sonya (1954-) American				
oil	1	2,500	2,500	2,500
TERPNING, Howard A (1927-) American				
oil	5	125,000-1,300,000	680,000	650,000
TERPNING, Susan (1953-) American				
oil	1	7,000	7,000	7,000
TERRAIRE, Clovis (19/20th C) French				
oil	10	720-3,296	1,354	937
TERRIS, John (1865-1914) British				
wc/d	3	465-1,418	1,004	1,131
TERRUELLA, Joaquim (1891-1957) Spanish				
oil	1	4,701	4,701	4,701
TERRUSO, Saverio (1939-2003) Italian				
oil	34	884-4,638	2,403	2,316
TERRY, Emilio (20th C) French?				
wc/d	1	1,296	1,296	1,296
TERRY, Henry (fl.1879-1920) British				
wc/d	5	528-1,476	1,100	1,134
TERRY, Joseph Alfred (1872-1939) British				
oil	3	736-32,130	11,257	905
wc/d	1	515	515	515
TERWESTEN, Augustin (17/18th C) Dutch				
oil	1	14,449	14,449	14,449
TERZI, Aleardo (1870-1943) Italian				
wc/d	2	1,764-1,890	1,827	1,764
TERZIAN, Georges (1935-) French				
oil	1	1,401	1,401	1,401
TERZOLO, Carlo (1904-1975) Italian				
oil	2	2,061-4,671	3,366	2,061
TESCHENDORFF, Emil (1833-1894) German				
oil	1	5,702	5,702	5,702
TESCHNER, Richard (1879-1948) Austrian				
3D	1	23,790	23,790	23,790

Name	No.	Price Range	Average	Median
TESDORPF-EDENS, Ilse (1892-1966) German				
oil	3	546-5,121	2,275	1,158
wc/d	1	837	837	837
TESHIGAHARA, Sofu (1900-1979) Japanese				
3D	1	4,685	4,685	4,685
TESI, Mauro Antonio (1730-1766) Italian				
wc/d	1	1,215	1,215	1,215
TESKEY, Donald (1956-) Irish?				
oil	5	5,691-61,806	28,196	25,027
TESSARI, Romolo (1868-?) Italian				
oil	1	607	607	607
wc/d	1	707	707	707
TESSARI, Vittorio (1860-1947) Italian				
oil	1	2,848	2,848	2,848
wc/d	1	700	700	700
TESSIER, Louis (1719-1781) French				
oil	1	29,000	29,000	29,000
TESSIER, Louis Adolphe (1858-1915) French				
oil	1	2,580	2,580	2,580
TESSON, Louis (19th C) French				
wc/d	2	650-1,798	1,224	650
TESTA, Angelo (20th C) American?				
wc/d	6	600-5,000	2,050	1,500
TESTA, Clorindo (1923-) Italian				
wc/d	1	1,230	1,230	1,230
TESTA, Pietro (1611-1650) Italian				
wc/d	1	8,414	8,414	8,414
TESTAS, Willem de Famars (1834-1896) Dutch				
wc/d	1	5,980	5,980	5,980
TESTU, P (19/20th C) French				
oil	1	3,562	3,562	3,562
TESTU, Pierre (19/20th C) French				
oil	2	1,600-4,607	3,103	1,600
TETAR VAN ELVEN, Jan Baptist (1805-1889) Dutch				
oil	3	605-4,159	2,339	2,253
TETAR VAN ELVEN, Paul Constantin Dominique (1823-1896) Belgian				
oil	1	5,021	5,021	5,021
TETAR VAN ELVEN, Pierre Henri Theodore (1828-1908) Dutch				
oil	4	714-22,932	10,005	737
wc/d	1	1,438	1,438	1,438
TETE, Maurice Louis (1880-1948) French				
wc/d	1	1,193	1,193	1,193
TETSIS, Panayiotis (1925-) Greek				
oil	1	60,480	60,480	60,480
wc/d	1	10,395	10,395	10,395
TEUBER, Hermann (1894-1985) German				
oil	5	942-5,271	4,067	5,036
wc/d	1	4,326	4,326	4,326
TEUNINK, Walter (1941-) Belgian				
oil	1	1,435	1,435	1,435
TEUPKEN, Dirk Antoon (19th C) Dutch				
wc/d	1	1,600	1,600	1,600
TEWES, Robin (1950-) American				
oil	1	3,737	3,737	3,737
TEXIER, Richard (1955-) French				
oil	2	3,236-4,767	4,001	3,236
wc/d	3	983-11,959	5,589	3,827
3D	2	36,521-78,003	57,262	36,521
TEZAK-NEOGY, Edgar (1944-) Austrian				
oil	1	1,808	1,808	1,808
THAL, Sam (1903-1964) American				
oil	1	1,700	1,700	1,700
THALMANN, Peter (1926-) Swiss?				
oil	1	1,679	1,679	1,679
THAMM, Adolf (1859-1925) German				
oil	4	911-6,941	3,298	1,936
THARRATS, Juan Jose (1918-2001) Spanish				
oil	5	455-5,469	1,798	746
wc/d	1	1,205	1,205	1,205
THAUBERGER, David (1948-) Canadian				
wc/d	1	1,540	1,540	1,540

Name	No.	Price Range	Average	Median
THAULOW, Fritz (1847-1906) Norwegian				
oil	9	3,850-42,381	19,860	14,720
THAYAHT, Ernesto (1893-1959) Italian				
wc/d	1	1,405	1,405	1,405
THAYER, Abbott H (1849-1921) American				
oil	1	25,000	25,000	25,000
THEER, Adolf (1811-1868) Austrian				
wc/d	1	1,331	1,331	1,331
THEER, Albert (1815-1902) Austrian				
wc/d	1	1,576	1,576	1,576
THEGERSTROM, Robert (1857-1919) Swedish				
oil	2	6,594-36,768	21,681	6,594
THEIMER, Ivan (1944-) ?				
oil	1	8,870	8,870	8,870
3D	1	4,186	4,186	4,186
THELANDER, Par Gunnar (1936-) Swedish				
oil	3	763-9,797	5,855	7,007
3D	1	1,784	1,784	1,784
THELWELL, Norman (1923-2004) British				
wc/d	2	528-1,691	1,109	528
THENN, G (20th C) Austrian?				
3D	1	3,063	3,063	3,063
THEODOROS (1931-) Greek				
3D	1	3,740	3,740	3,740
THEOFILAKTOPOULOS, Makis (1939-) Greek				
oil	2	7,480-12,320	9,900	7,480
THEOFILOS (c.1867-1934) Greek				
oil	2	96,800-365,400	231,100	96,800
THEPOT, Roger François (1925-) French				
wc/d	1	1,818	1,818	1,818
THERKILDSEN, Michael (1850-1925) Danish				
oil	3	812-1,299	1,051	1,042
THERRIEN, Robert (1947-) American				
oil	1	55,000	55,000	55,000
wc/d	1	6,500	6,500	6,500
3D	4	20,000-60,000	38,500	26,000
THESLEFF, Ellen (1869-1954) Finnish				
oil	3	6,429-39,857	18,857	10,286
wc/d	1	2,186	2,186	2,186
THESSEL, Anton Moritz (1830-1873) German				
oil	1	4,961	4,961	4,961
THEUNERT, Christian (1899-1982) German				
wc/d	1	1,414	1,414	1,414
THEUNISSEN, Charles (1871-1949) Belgian				
oil	1	1,927	1,927	1,927
THEURICH, Josef (19th C) Austrian				
oil	3	1,094-4,861	3,119	3,403
THEVENET, Louis (1874-1930) Belgian				
oil	13	477-12,858	4,681	4,325
THEVENET, Pierre (1870-1937) Belgian				
oil	12	607-6,204	1,637	1,051
wc/d	3	578-1,193	902	935
THEVENIN, Jean Charles Bienvenu Gaspard (1819-1869) Italian				
oil	1	1,784	1,784	1,784
THEYNET, Max (1875-1949) Swiss				
oil	1	1,221	1,221	1,221
THIAN, Jean Baptiste (?-1816) French?				
wc/d	1	38,720	38,720	38,720
THIBESART, Raymond (1874-?) French				
oil	5	1,885-4,671	3,011	2,790
THIBON DE LIBIAN, Valentin (1889-1931) Argentinian				
oil	2	45,000-45,000	45,000	45,000
THIEBAUD, Wayne (1920-) American				
oil	9	135,000-1,800,000	558,888	420,000
wc/d	3	7,000-300,000	195,666	280,000
THIEL, Carl (1835-1900) German				
oil	1	4,633	4,633	4,633
THIELE, Arthur (1841-1919) German				
oil	1	3,646	3,646	3,646
THIELE, Hermann (1867-?) German				
oil	1	1,054	1,054	1,054

Name	No.	Price Range	Average	Median
THIELE, Otto (1870-1955) German				
oil	3	1,219-1,414	1,342	1,394
THIELE, Rudolf (1856-1930) German				
3D	2	3,405-4,560	3,982	3,405
THIELEMANN, Alfred (1883-?) German				
oil	2	606-2,829	1,717	606
THIELEN, Jan Philips van (1618-1667) Flemish				
oil	1	48,440	48,440	48,440
THIELER, Fred (1916-1999) German				
oil	15	2,108-21,205	9,971	10,520
wc/d	7	1,781-11,466	3,930	2,349
THIEM, Paul (1858-1922) German				
oil	4	877-3,514	1,964	1,034
THIEMANN, Carl (1881-1966) German				
oil	1	1,193	1,193	1,193
THIEME, Anthony (1888-1954) American/Dutch				
oil	23	3,250-120,000	20,354	9,500
THIERFELDER, Vivian (1929-) Canadian				
oil	1	1,484	1,484	1,484
wc/d	5	412-4,948	2,602	1,702
THIERRIAT, Augustin Alexandre (1789-1870) French				
oil	2	4,886-14,367	9,626	4,886
THIL, Jeanne (1887-1968) French				
wc/d	1	1,445	1,445	1,445
THIRIAT, Paul (19/20th C) French				
wc/d	2	1,285-1,401	1,343	1,285
THIRION, Victor Charles (1833-1878) French				
oil	1	124,849	124,849	124,849
THIRIOT, Pierre (1904-?) French				
wc/d	1	1,014	1,014	1,014
THIVET, Antoine Auguste (1856-1927) French				
oil	1	3,403	3,403	3,403
THIVET, Yvonne (1888-1972) French				
oil	1	2,922	2,922	2,922
THOLANDER, August (1835-1910) Swedish				
oil	1	1,741	1,741	1,741
THOLEN, Willem Bastiaan (1860-1931) Dutch				
oil	7	3,254-26,671	11,384	10,014
THOM, James Crawford (1835-1898) American				
oil	6	600-15,000	5,236	3,250
THOMA, Hans (1839-1924) German				
oil	12	479-41,759	12,595	8,247
wc/d	5	535-4,123	1,405	701
THOMA, Josef (1828-1899) Austrian				
oil	13	1,265-8,281	3,312	2,832
THOMANN, Adolf (1874-1961) Swiss				
oil	2	992-1,499	1,245	992
THOMAS, Alma Woodsey (1891-1978) American				
oil	3	13,000-43,000	29,333	32,000
wc/d	1	13,000	13,000	13,000
THOMAS, Andy (?) American				
oil	1	17,000	17,000	17,000
THOMAS, Bernard P (1918-) American				
oil	1	1,400	1,400	1,400
THOMAS, Eugene Emile (1817-1882) French				
3D	1	2,027	2,027	2,027
THOMAS, George Housman (1824-1868) British				
oil	1	1,745	1,745	1,745
THOMAS, Gerard (1663-1720) Flemish				
oil	2	4,500-24,000	14,250	4,500
THOMAS, Grosvenor (1856-1923) British				
oil	2	1,152-2,314	1,733	1,152
THOMAS, Henri Joseph (1878-1972) Belgian				
oil	8	1,312-7,827	4,042	3,973
THOMAS, Karl (1948-) American				
oil	6	400-7,000	3,083	2,600
THOMAS, Les (1962-) Canadian				
oil	1	1,216	1,216	1,216
THOMAS, M (?) ?				
oil	1	4,152	4,152	4,152
THOMAS, Margaret (1916-) British				
oil	3	637-3,894	2,808	3,894

Name	No.	Price Range	Average	Median
THOMAS, Norbert (1947-) German				
oil	1	2,930	2,930	2,930
THOMAS, Paul (1859-1910) French				
3D	1	3,889	3,889	3,889
THOMAS, Pieter Hendrik (1814-1866) Dutch				
oil	1	1,878	1,878	1,878
THOMAS, Richard D (1935-) American				
oil	2	9,500-11,000	10,250	9,500
THOMAS, Robert Strickland (1787-1853) British				
oil	3	2,580-9,250	4,943	3,000
THOMAS, Roy (1949-2004) Canadian				
oil	1	2,204	2,204	2,204
THOMAS, Walter (1894-1971) British				
wc/d	1	2,188	2,188	2,188
THOMAS, William Bartol (1877-1947) British				
wc/d	5	452-1,958	1,101	801
THOMASSIN, Desire (1858-1933) Austrian				
oil	18	1,028-6,115	3,058	2,225
THOMASSIN, Louis (18th C) French				
oil	1	1,903	1,903	1,903
THOMASSIN, Renardt (19th C) French				
oil	1	2,289	2,289	2,289
THOME, Verner (1878-1953) Finnish				
oil	4	1,575-5,400	3,415	2,571
wc/d	4	580-30,575	8,179	731
THOMING, Frederik Christian (1802-1873) Danish				
oil	1	2,223	2,223	2,223
THOMKINS, Andre (1930-1985) Swiss				
oil	4	999-3,816	3,111	3,816
wc/d	2	324-3,242	1,783	324
THOMMESEN, Erik (1916-) Danish				
3D	1	37,021	37,021	37,021
THOMON, Thomas de (1754-1813) French				
wc/d	1	1,883	1,883	1,883
THOMOPOULOS, Epaminondas (1878-1974) Greek				
oil	3	4,400-15,660	11,588	14,705
THOMOPOULOS, Thomas (1873-1937) Greek				
3D	1	13,840	13,840	13,840
THOMPSON, Alfred Wordsworth (1840-1896) American				
oil	1	18,000	18,000	18,000
THOMPSON, Bob (1937-1966) American				
oil	2	20,000-55,000	37,500	20,000
wc/d	3	4,000-8,500	6,000	5,500
THOMPSON, Edward H (1879-1949) British				
oil	1	1,196	1,196	1,196
wc/d	52	513-3,917	1,500	1,288
THOMPSON, Estelle (1960-) British				
oil	1	1,062	1,062	1,062
THOMPSON, Gemma (1981-) British				
oil	1	1,964	1,964	1,964
THOMPSON, Jacob (1806-1879) British				
oil	1	3,365	3,365	3,365
THOMPSON, Jerome (1814-1886) American				
oil	5	800-45,000	10,080	1,400
THOMPSON, John (1924-) British				
oil	1	3,024	3,024	3,024
THOMPSON, Michel (1921-) French				
oil	2	957-2,472	1,714	957
THOMPSON, Sydney Lough (1877-1973) New Zealander				
oil	3	5,961-6,319	6,093	6,000
THOMPSON, Tim (1951-) British				
oil	7	1,683-7,308	3,877	3,740
THOMPSON, Wilfred (fl.1884-1894) British				
wc/d	1	1,496	1,496	1,496
THOMPSON, William (19th C) British				
oil	1	6,615	6,615	6,615
THOMSEN, August Carl Wilhelm (1813-1886) Danish				
oil	2	1,042-1,477	1,259	1,042
THOMSEN, Emma Augusta (1822-1897) Danish				
oil	1	2,436	2,436	2,436
THOMSEN, Frederik Gotfred (1819-1891) Danish				
oil	1	1,183	1,183	1,183

Name	No.	Price Range	Average	Median
THOMSEN, Pauline (1858-1931) Danish				
oil	2	679-7,643	4,161	679
THOMSEN, Valdemar (?) ?				
oil	3	1,186-1,543	1,331	1,265
THOMSON OF DUDDINGTON, Rev John (1778-1840) British				
oil	4	510-40,480	12,798	4,862
THOMSON, Adam Bruce (1885-1976) British				
oil	1	1,038	1,038	1,038
wc/d	5	842-1,514	1,116	1,038
THOMSON, Carl Christian Frederik Jakob (1847-1912) Danish				
oil	2	893-3,260	2,076	893
THOMSON, George (1860-1939) British				
oil	1	1,548	1,548	1,548
THOMSON, John Leslie (1851-1929) British				
oil	1	5,671	5,671	5,671
THOMSON, John Murray (1885-1974) British				
oil	3	1,305-17,500	6,761	1,480
wc/d	1	1,500	1,500	1,500
THOMSON, Robert Sinclair (1915-1983) British				
oil	1	2,832	2,832	2,832
wc/d	3	1,682-3,540	2,448	2,124
THOMSON, Tom (1877-1917) Canadian				
oil	3	129,668-324,171	241,469	270,569
wc/d	1	176,303	176,303	176,303
THON, Miltiadis (1875-1945) Greek				
oil	1	1,232	1,232	1,232
THON, William (1916-2000) American				
wc/d	3	425-5,250	2,425	1,600
THONY, Eduard (1866-1950) German				
wc/d	7	647-6,479	1,734	1,060
THONY, Wilhelm (1888-1949) Austrian				
oil	2	51,429-57,857	54,643	51,429
wc/d	6	900-24,101	5,292	1,414
THOR, Walter (1870-1929) German				
oil	1	3,152	3,152	3,152
THORBURN, Archibald (1860-1935) British				
wc/d	52	481-38,720	9,726	6,048
THOREN, Esaias (1901-1981) Swedish				
oil	39	561-38,170	3,726	1,654
wc/d	4	2,775-14,536	8,622	5,286
THOREN, Otto von (1828-1889) Austrian				
oil	4	1,145-10,669	4,902	3,084
THORENFELD, Anton Erik (1839-1907) Danish				
oil	3	1,265-5,973	3,572	3,478
THORESEN, Elsa (1909-) American				
oil	3	566-2,414	1,370	1,132
THORMA, Janos (1870-1937) Hungarian				
oil	1	4,628	4,628	4,628
THORNAM, Emmy (1852-1935) Danish				
oil	1	7,014	7,014	7,014
THORNE, Alfred (1850-1916) Swedish				
oil	11	561-5,609	1,640	992
THORNE, Joan (20th C) ?				
oil	2	500-1,800	1,150	500
THORNE, William (19th C) American				
oil	1	4,000	4,000	4,000
THORNELEY, Charles (fl.1858-1898) British				
oil	1	1,780	1,780	1,780
THORNHILL, Sir James (1675-1734) British				
wc/d	3	700-3,460	1,645	777
THORNING, F (19/20th C) ?				
oil	1	3,853	3,853	3,853
THORNLEY, Georges W (1857-1935) French				
oil	2	1,800-3,588	2,694	1,800
wc/d	4	540-2,188	1,467	1,270
THORNLEY, Hubert (19th C) British				
oil	22	1,325-28,027	6,471	4,224
THORNLEY, Thomas (19th C) British?				
wc/d	1	2,625	2,625	2,625
THORNLEY, William (19/20th C) British				
oil	33	651-13,090	4,538	4,498
wc/d	2	500-650	575	500

Name	No.	Price Range	Average	Median
THORNTON, Herbert (19/20th C) British				
oil	1	8,500	8,500	8,500
THORNYCROFT, Hamo (1850-1925) British				
3D	1	17,010	17,010	17,010
THORPE, David (1972-) ?				
wc/d	2	2,640-10,175	6,407	2,640
THORPE, John (fl.1834-1873) British				
oil	1	1,305	1,305	1,305
THORPE, Mackenzie (20th C) British				
wc/d	2	5,568-6,960	6,264	5,568
THORPE, Thomas Bangs (1815-1878) American				
wc/d	1	3,000	3,000	3,000
THORS, Joseph (fl.1863-1900) British				
oil	35	519-6,195	2,484	2,268
THORSEN, Jens Jorgen (1932-) Scandinavian				
oil	1	4,507	4,507	4,507
THORSEN, Lars (1876-1952) American?				
oil	1	1,850	1,850	1,850
THORVALDSEN, Bertel (1770-1844) Danish				
3D	2	11,545-32,601	22,073	11,545
THRAP, Birte (20th C) Danish				
oil	1	1,137	1,137	1,137
THRASH, Dox (1893-1965) American				
oil	1	5,000	5,000	5,000
wc/d	1	1,700	1,700	1,700
THRASH, Rezalia C (1893-1982) American				
wc/d	1	1,000	1,000	1,000
THUILLIER, Pierre (1799-1858) French				
oil	1	1,543	1,543	1,543
THUILLIER-MORNARD, Louise (1829-?) French				
oil	1	1,546	1,546	1,546
THULDEN, Theodor van (1606-1669) Dutch				
oil	1	58,820	58,820	58,820
THUMANN, Paul (1834-1908) German				
oil	3	487-2,432	1,178	615
THURAU, Friedrich (?-1888) German				
oil	2	519-1,824	1,171	519
THURBER, James Grover (1894-1961) American				
wc/d	1	7,000	7,000	7,000
THURET, C J (19th C) French				
oil	1	4,743	4,743	4,743
THURLO, Frank (1828-1913) American				
wc/d	2	550-1,500	1,025	550
THURNER, Gabriel Edouard (1840-1907) French				
oil	2	8,640-11,931	10,285	8,640
THURSTON, Eugene (1896-1993) American				
oil	3	800-3,500	1,733	900
THYS, Pieter (1624-1677) Flemish				
oil	2	38,000-148,000	93,000	38,000
THYS, Susy Kathy (1936-) Swiss				
oil	4	763-2,165	1,304	791
THYSEBAERT, Émile (1873-1962) Belgian				
oil	5	477-2,167	1,082	800
TIBALDI, Pellegrino (1527-1596) Italian				
wc/d	1	55,500	55,500	55,500
TIBBLE, Geoffrey (1909-1952) British				
oil	2	4,914-6,615	5,764	4,914
TIBON, Cristina Cassy (1937-) Mexican				
oil	1	1,051	1,051	1,051
TICHO, Anna (1894-1980) Israeli				
wc/d	10	700-42,500	12,520	8,000
TICHY, Hans (1861-1925) Austrian				
oil	1	3,879	3,879	3,879
TICULIN, Mario (19/20th C) Italian				
oil	1	1,349	1,349	1,349
TIDEMAND, Adolph (1814-1876) Norwegian				
oil	1	5,557	5,557	5,557
TIEBERT, Hermann (1895-) German				
oil	1	1,649	1,649	1,649

Name	No.	Price Range	Average	Median
TIECHE, Adolf (1877-1957) Swiss				
oil	1	757	757	757
wc/d	4	541-1,832	874	541
TIEDJEN, Willy (1881-1950) German				
oil	7	510-2,309	1,182	849
TIELENS, Alexandre (1868-1959) Belgian				
oil	6	514-3,503	1,712	615
TIEPOLO, Giovanni Battista (1696-1770) Italian				
oil	7	37,479-555,000	250,366	188,108
wc/d	12	12,950-120,000	35,633	31,808
TIEPOLO, Giovanni Domenico (1727-1804) Italian				
oil	3	43,347-380,000	162,917	65,405
wc/d	10	2,941-40,000	18,973	13,000
TIEPOLO, Lorenzo (1736-1776) Italian				
oil	2	3,620-65,000	34,310	3,620
wc/d	1	550	550	550
TIERCE, Jean-Baptiste Antoine (1737-1790) French				
wc/d	1	2,301	2,301	2,301
TIFFANY, Louis Comfort (1848-1933) American				
oil	4	10,000-100,000	38,375	16,000
wc/d	3	17,000-45,000	29,000	25,000
TIGER, Frans Johan (1849-1919) Finnish				
oil	2	1,171-1,741	1,456	1,171
TIGLIO, Marcos (1903-1976) Argentinian				
oil	2	1,905-4,490	3,197	1,905
TIKHMENOV, Efim (19/20th C) Russian				
oil	1	22,360	22,360	22,360
TIKHONOV, Viktor (1955-) Belarussian				
oil	1	1,253	1,253	1,253
TIKTAK, John (1916-1981) North American				
3D	7	2,446-11,810	6,760	8,014
TILBORCH, Gillis van (c.1625-1678) Flemish				
oil	4	9,633-29,195	23,035	26,615
TILL, Johann (jnr) (1827-1894) Austrian				
oil	2	2,166-140,000	71,083	2,166
TILLBERG, Peter (1946-) Swedish				
oil	1	1,781	1,781	1,781
wc/d	1	509	509	509
TILLIER, Paul (1834-?) French				
oil	2	3,739-13,721	8,730	3,739
TILLYER, William (1938-) British				
oil	1	30,940	30,940	30,940
wc/d	2	833-833	833	833
TILPO, Fruls (1960-) Swedish				
oil	7	524-2,643	1,330	1,123
TILSON, Henry (1659-1695) British				
oil	1	3,553	3,553	3,553
TILSON, Joe (1928-) British				
oil	1	50,170	50,170	50,170
wc/d	8	1,219-7,938	4,635	4,919
3D	3	5,340-95,150	41,570	24,220
TIMKOV, Nikolai (1912-1993) Russian				
oil	3	3,440-16,000	8,658	6,536
TIMM, Vassili Fedorovich (1820-1895) Russian				
wc/d	1	4,861	4,861	4,861
TIMMEL, Vito (1886-1949) Austrian				
oil	1	10,286	10,286	10,286
wc/d	1	2,571	2,571	2,571
TIMMERMANS, Henri (1858-1942) Belgian				
oil	1	4,767	4,767	4,767
TIMMERMANS, Jean (1899-1986) Belgian				
oil	2	546-4,767	2,656	546
TIMMERMANS, Louis (1846-1910) French				
oil	2	4,315-6,726	5,520	4,315
wc/d	2	400-1,014	707	400
TIMMONS, Karmel (?) American				
wc/d	2	5,000-6,200	5,600	5,000
TIMPE, Wil (1920-) American				
oil	1	1,500	1,500	1,500
TINDALL, Charles E S (1863-1951) Australian				
wc/d	1	1,380	1,380	1,380

Name	No.	Price Range	Average	Median
TINDLE, David (1932-) British				
oil	10	400-3,762	1,889	1,740
wc/d	2	870-8,905	4,887	870
TING, Walasse (1929-1998) Chinese				
oil	15	1,927-54,727	14,859	14,000
wc/d	15	1,436-33,802	9,691	4,671
TINGLE, Minnie (1874-1926) American				
oil	1	6,000	6,000	6,000
TINGUELY, Jean (1925-1991) Swiss				
oil	7	1,461-14,432	6,823	6,473
wc/d	54	486-32,070	5,043	3,461
3D	16	23,378-699,786	182,412	105,600
TINT, Francine (1943-) American				
oil	1	1,200	1,200	1,200
TINTORE, Simone del (1630-1708) Italian				
oil	1	72,660	72,660	72,660
TINTORETTO, Jacopo (1518-1594) Italian				
oil	3	103,172-290,612	180,594	148,000
wc/d	1	48,100	48,100	48,100
TIPARY, Dezso (1887-?) Hungarian				
oil	1	3,816	3,816	3,816
TIPPETTS, Linda (1944-) American				
oil	1	5,000	5,000	5,000
TIRADO Y CARDONA, Fernando (1862-1907) Spanish				
oil	2	4,750-5,986	5,368	4,750
TIRATELLI, Aurelio (1842-1900) Italian				
oil	1	1,784	1,784	1,784
TIRATELLI, Cesare (1864-1933) Italian				
oil	1	7,120	7,120	7,120
TIRAVANIJA, Rirkrit (1961-) American				
3D	1	40,000	40,000	40,000
TIRELLI, Marco (1956-) Italian				
oil	8	2,827-19,090	9,888	9,159
wc/d	5	1,767-4,071	2,672	2,180
TIREN, Gerda (1858-1928) Swedish				
wc/d	1	5,484	5,484	5,484
TIREN, Johan (1853-1911) Swedish				
wc/d	5	3,022-11,814	6,676	5,083
TIREN, Nils (1885-1935) Swedish				
oil	1	1,488	1,488	1,488
TIRINNANZI, Nino (1923-2002) Italian				
oil	17	1,440-6,943	3,130	2,422
wc/d	8	660-6,062	1,681	1,130
TIRONI, Francesco (?-1800) Italian				
oil	1	51,900	51,900	51,900
TISCHBEIN, Anton Johann (1720-1784) German				
oil	1	15,429	15,429	15,429
TISCHBEIN, August Anton (1805-1867) German				
oil	1	1,135	1,135	1,135
wc/d	1	643	643	643
TISCHBEIN, Johann Heinrich (18th C) German				
oil	1	6,020	6,020	6,020
wc/d	1	529	529	529
TISCHBEIN, Johann Heinrich (elder) (1722-1789) German				
oil	6	6,090-59,069	30,906	29,035
wc/d	2	589-1,060	824	589
TISCHBEIN, Johann Heinrich Wilhelm (1751-1829) German				
oil	1	15,226	15,226	15,226
wc/d	1	4,607	4,607	4,607
TISCHBEIN, Ludwig Philipp (1744-1806) German				
wc/d	1	9,500	9,500	9,500
TISDALL, Hans (1910-1997) British				
oil	1	3,186	3,186	3,186
wc/d	1	2,646	2,646	2,646
TISIO, Benvenuto da Garofalo (1481-1559) Italian				
oil	3	67,315-161,815	103,043	80,000
wc/d	1	64,750	64,750	64,750
TISNIKAR, Joze (1928-1998) ?				
oil	1	1,940	1,940	1,940
TISSOT, James Jacques Joseph (1836-1902) French				
oil	4	2,330-2,835,000	872,943	4,442
wc/d	3	4,224-60,900	23,233	4,576

Name	No.	Price Range	Average	Median
TITCOMB, Mary Bradish (1858-1927) American				
wc/d	1	4,000	4,000	4,000
TITIAN (c.1488-1576) Italian				
oil	2	44,980-800,000	422,490	44,980
TITKOV, Aleksandr (20th C) Russian?				
oil	1	20,020	20,020	20,020
TITO, Ettore (1859-1941) Italian				
oil	2	13,993-33,945	23,969	13,993
TITO, Santi di (1536-1603) Italian				
oil	1	300,000	300,000	300,000
TITOV, Vladimir (?) Russian				
oil	1	3,596	3,596	3,596
TITOV, Vladimir Gerasimovih (fl.1950s) Russian				
oil	1	2,141	2,141	2,141
TITUS-CARMEL, Gerard (1942-) French				
oil	2	876-1,790	1,333	876
wc/d	6	660-1,590	1,070	993
TIVOLI, Serafino de (1826-1892) Italian				
oil	2	18,000-21,626	19,813	18,000
TJUPURRULA, Johnny Warrangula (1932-2001) Australian				
wc/d	1	2,000	2,000	2,000
TKACHEV, Aleksei Petrovich (1922-) Russian				
oil	1	32,490	32,490	32,490
TKACHEV, Aleksei and Sergei (20th C) Russian				
oil	3	16,740-72,240	43,993	43,000
TKACHEV, Sergei Petrovich (1925-) Russian				
oil	1	13,950	13,950	13,950
wc/d	1	3,933	3,933	3,933
TKATCHENKO, Michail (1860-1916) Russian				
oil	2	819-14,880	7,849	819
TOBAS, Christian (1944-) French				
oil	1	2,854	2,854	2,854
wc/d	1	1,331	1,331	1,331
TOBEY, Mark (1890-1976) American				
oil	12	1,142-369,600	60,538	11,572
wc/d	23	522-220,000	18,540	6,500
TOBIASSE, Theo (1927-) Israeli				
oil	31	3,012-29,600	15,910	17,000
wc/d	15	2,600-11,500	6,790	6,577
TOBIESEN, Ally (19th C) ?				
oil	1	2,473	2,473	2,473
TOCHILKIN, Mark (1958-) Ukranian				
oil	2	3,600-8,500	6,050	3,600
TOCQUE, Louis (1696-1772) French				
oil	3	14,000-111,000	74,239	97,718
TODARO, V (19th C) Italian				
oil	1	8,000	8,000	8,000
TODD, Arthur Ralph Middleton (1891-c.1967) British				
oil	1	756	756	756
wc/d	1	552	552	552
TODD, Harold (?) British?				
oil	1	1,178	1,178	1,178
TODD, Henry George (1846-1898) British				
oil	3	708-3,514	2,082	2,024
TODD, Ralph (1856-1932) British				
wc/d	5	979-4,400	2,770	2,992
TODDY, Jimmy (1928-) American				
wc/d	1	1,110	1,110	1,110
TODE, Knut Gustaf Waldemar (1859-1900) Swedish				
oil	2	1,191-2,336	1,763	1,191
TODERI, Grazia (1963-) Italian				
3D	1	2,220	2,220	2,220
TODHUNTER, Francis Augustus (1884-1963) American				
oil	1	2,000	2,000	2,000
TODHUNTER, Henry (20th C) American				
oil	1	1,700	1,700	1,700
TODINI, Lorenzo (17th C) Italian				
wc/d	1	9,500	9,500	9,500
TODO GARCIA, Francisco (1922-) Spanish				
oil	5	1,543-2,238	1,869	1,665
wc/d	1	449	449	449

Name	No.	Price Range	Average	Median
TOECHE, Karl Friedrich (1814-1890) German				
oil	1	10,022	10,022	10,022
TOEFAERT, Albert (1856-1909) Flemish				
oil	1	1,019	1,019	1,019
TOEN, Azumaya (1893-1976) Japanese				
wc/d	1	5,500	5,500	5,500
TOEPUT, Lodewyk (1550-1603) Flemish				
oil	2	44,980-61,817	53,398	44,980
wc/d	3	773-5,550	2,668	1,683
TOFANARI, Sirio (1886-1969) Italian				
3D	2	3,500-8,500	6,000	3,500
TOFANELLI, Stefano (1752-1812) Italian				
oil	1	8,000	8,000	8,000
TOFANO, Edouardo (1838-1920) Italian				
oil	3	1,153-14,640	6,076	2,436
TOFFOLI, Louis (1907-1999) French				
oil	9	1,753-31,129	10,977	7,864
TOFT, Albert (1862-1949) British				
3D	1	1,703	1,703	1,703
TOJETTI, Virgilio (1851-1901) American				
oil	2	3,500-18,000	10,750	3,500
TOJNER, Vibeke (20th C) ?				
oil	1	1,825	1,825	1,825
TOKI, E S (20th C) Oriental				
wc/d	1	5,500	5,500	5,500
TOKMIN, Boris (1933-) Russian				
oil	1	1,151	1,151	1,151
TOL, Claes Jacobsz (17th C) Dutch				
oil	1	5,946	5,946	5,946
TOLEDO, Francisco (1940-) Mexican				
oil	7	11,000-80,000	46,357	37,500
wc/d	14	2,500-120,000	24,789	6,000
TOLER, William Pinkney (1826-1899) American				
oil	1	2,000	2,000	2,000
TOLL, Countess (20th C) German				
oil	1	1,659	1,659	1,659
TOLMAN, Robert (1886-?) American				
oil	2	600-1,800	1,200	600
TOLMER, Roger (?) ?				
oil	1	775	775	775
wc/d	1	894	894	894
TOLOMEO, Carla (1944-) Italian				
oil	1	1,121	1,121	1,121
3D	1	4,099	4,099	4,099
TOLSTEADT, Lowell (20th C) American				
wc/d	2	1,100-1,800	1,450	1,100
TOLSTOI, Count Fiodr Petrovich (1783-1873) Russian				
wc/d	1	30,000	30,000	30,000
TOM, Jan Bedys (1813-1894) Dutch				
oil	3	906-7,360	3,767	3,035
TOM-PETERSEN, Peter (1861-1926) Danish				
oil	2	1,859-9,617	5,738	1,859
TOMA, Giovacchino (1836-1891) Italian				
oil	2	9,709-17,568	13,638	9,709
TOMA, Matthias Rudolf (1792-1869) Austrian				
oil	2	1,555-9,103	5,329	1,555
TOMALTY, Terry (1935-) Canadian?				
oil	5	633-2,624	1,360	1,234
TOMANECK, Joseph (1889-1974) American				
oil	3	1,100-2,400	1,866	2,100
TOMASELLI, Fred (1956-) American?				
oil	2	22,000-84,480	53,240	22,000
wc/d	1	11,000	11,000	11,000
TOMASELLI, Onofrio (1866-1956) Italian				
oil	1	4,531	4,531	4,531
TOMASELLO, Luis (1915-) Argentinian				
3D	5	3,822-26,000	17,058	19,085
TOMASI, Oddone (1884-1929) Italian				
oil	1	1,800	1,800	1,800
TOMASINI, Luis Assencio (1823-1902) Portuguese				
oil	1	7,899	7,899	7,899

Name	No.	Price Range	Average	Median
TOMBA, Casimiro (1857-1929) Italian				
wc/d	2	634-3,185	1,909	634
TOMEA, Fiorenzo (1910-1960) Italian				
oil	10	1,171-17,068	7,577	6,283
wc/d	6	636-4,241	2,544	1,929
TOMEC, Heinrich (1863-1928) Austrian				
oil	2	2,264-3,299	2,781	2,264
TOMGISENY, H (19th C) ?				
oil	1	2,646	2,646	2,646
TOMINZ, Alfredo (1854-1936) Italian				
oil	6	3,254-21,338	8,847	6,181
TOMINZ, Augusto (1818-1883) Italian				
oil	1	2,577	2,577	2,577
TOMIOLO, Eugenio (1911-) Italian				
oil	2	934-1,753	1,343	934
TOMITA, Keisen (1879-1936) Japanese				
wc/d	1	3,000	3,000	3,000
TOMKINS, Margaret (1916-2002) American				
oil	1	9,000	9,000	9,000
TOMLIN, Bradley Walker (1899-1953) American				
oil	1	200,000	200,000	200,000
TOMMASI FERRONI, Riccardo (1934-2000) Italian				
oil	3	1,649-14,531	6,964	4,712
wc/d	3	567-2,296	1,366	1,237
TOMMASI, Adolfo (1851-1933) Italian				
wc/d	2	2,773-3,128	2,950	2,773
TOMMASI, Angiolo (1858-1923) Italian				
oil	1	27,986	27,986	27,986
TOMMASI, Ludovico (1866-1941) Italian				
oil	4	4,159-34,347	17,177	8,381
TOMMASI, Marcello (1928-) Italian				
3D	1	5,878	5,878	5,878
TOMPKINS, Frank H (1847-1922) American				
oil	2	3,800-4,500	4,150	3,800
TOMS, Carl (1927-1999) British				
wc/d	1	12,880	12,880	12,880
TOMSCHICZEK, Peter (1940-) Czechoslovakian				
wc/d	1	3,840	3,840	3,840
TOMSON, Clifton (1775-1828) British				
oil	1	1,620	1,620	1,620
TONDO, Michele (19/20th C) ?				
wc/d	1	3,204	3,204	3,204
TONDU, Andre (1903-1980) French				
oil	1	3,190	3,190	3,190
TONGE, Lammert van der (1871-1937) Dutch				
oil	1	2,049	2,049	2,049
TONGEREN, Jan van (1897-1991) Dutch				
oil	1	10,220	10,220	10,220
TONGERLOO, Frans van (1882-) Belgian				
oil	2	1,001-1,455	1,228	1,001
TONK, Ernest (1889-1968) American				
oil	1	4,250	4,250	4,250
TONKS, Henry (1862-1937) British				
oil	1	3,366	3,366	3,366
wc/d	2	783-1,368	1,075	783
TONKS, Myles Denison Boswell (1890-1960) British				
oil	1	6,960	6,960	6,960
TONNANCOUR, Jacques de (1917-2004) Canadian				
oil	2	9,019-12,341	10,680	9,019
wc/d	2	4,123-4,231	4,177	4,123
TONNEAU, Joseph (19th C) British				
oil	1	4,000	4,000	4,000
TOOBY, Katherine (1916-) American				
oil	1	2,000	2,000	2,000
TOOGOOD, Romeo (1902-1966) British				
oil	1	10,584	10,584	10,584
TOOKER, George (1920-) American				
oil	3	115,000-280,000	198,333	200,000
TOOKTOO, Charlie (1926-) North American				
3D	1	3,543	3,543	3,543

Name	No.	Price Range	Average	Median
TOORENBURGH, Gerrit (1732-1785) Dutch				
oil	1	11,466	11,466	11,466
wc/d	1	1,285	1,285	1,285
TOORENVLIET, Jacob (1635-1719) Dutch				
oil	1	11,678	11,678	11,678
TOOROP, Charley (1891-1955) Dutch				
oil	2	35,068-41,233	38,150	35,068
TOOROP, Jan Th (1858-1928) Dutch				
oil	3	8,836-848,219	353,530	203,537
wc/d	14	468-91,726	10,917	4,071
TOPANARI, S (?) ?				
3D	1	5,780	5,780	5,780
TOPCHEVSKY, Morris (1899-1947) American				
wc/d	1	2,400	2,400	2,400
TOPFFER, Wolfgang Adam (1766-1847) Swiss				
oil	2	1,725-6,105	3,915	1,725
wc/d	5	534-6,105	2,309	1,311
TOPHAM, Francis William (1808-1877) British				
wc/d	3	440-6,555	2,591	779
TOPHAM, Frank William Warwick (1838-1929) British				
oil	1	3,135	3,135	3,135
wc/d	1	766	766	766
TOPHAM, William Thirston (1886-1967) Canadian				
oil	1	1,141	1,141	1,141
TOPOLSKI, Feliks (1907-1989) Polish				
wc/d	10	525-7,000	1,611	900
TOPOR, Roland (1938-1997) French				
oil	1	2,378	2,378	2,378
wc/d	9	908-9,555	3,511	3,279
TOPP, Arnold (1887-1945) German				
oil	2	15,534-203,500	109,517	15,534
wc/d	2	11,651-14,137	12,894	11,651
TOPPELIUS, Woldemar (1858-1933) Russian				
oil	7	1,405-16,365	4,614	2,805
TOPPING, James (1879-1949) American				
oil	1	2,832	2,832	2,832
TORDI, Sinibaldo (1876-1955) Italian				
oil	1	1,640	1,640	1,640
TORELLI, Stefano (1712-1784) Italian				
oil	1	144,300	144,300	144,300
TORGGLER, Erich (1899-1938) Austrian				
oil	1	1,212	1,212	1,212
TORHAMN, Gunnar (1894-1955) Swedish				
oil	6	996-4,552	2,461	1,896
TORLAKSON, Jim (1951-) American				
oil	1	8,000	8,000	8,000
TORMER, Benno Friedrich (1804-1859) German				
oil	1	4,123	4,123	4,123
TORNA, Oscar (1842-1894) Swedish				
oil	5	1,205-30,575	7,444	1,359
TORNAI, Gyula (1861-1928) Hungarian				
oil	6	647-36,800	14,947	10,192
wc/d	1	2,700	2,700	2,700
TORNAU, Karl Wilhelm Gustav (1820-1864) Austrian				
oil	1	1,500	1,500	1,500
TORNEMAN, Axel (1880-1925) Swedish				
oil	3	1,992-18,449	8,722	5,726
wc/d	1	1,786	1,786	1,786
TORNER, Gloria (20th C) Spanish				
oil	1	1,070	1,070	1,070
TORNER, Gustavo (1925-) Spanish				
oil	3	1,405-7,531	3,447	1,405
wc/d	2	9,633-13,597	11,615	9,633
3D	1	18,828	18,828	18,828
TORNING, Erik (1928-) Swedish				
oil	1	774	774	774
wc/d	1	2,728	2,728	2,728
TORNOE, Wenzel (1844-1907) Danish				
oil	4	811-9,033	4,058	2,895
TORNQUIST, Jorrit (1938-) Austrian				
oil	13	642-4,685	2,774	3,045
wc/d	2	589-610	599	589

Name	No.	Price Range	Average	Median
TORO, Attilio (1892-1982) Italian				
oil	3	2,293-4,182	3,092	2,803
TORO, Elias (20th C) Venezuelan?				
3D	2	2,320-9,100	5,710	2,320
TORONI, Niele (1937-) French				
oil	1	18,061	18,061	18,061
TORRALLARDONA, Carlos (1913-1986) Argentinian				
oil	7	1,400-4,300	2,814	2,600
TORRE, Antonio de la (19th C) Italian				
oil	1	3,616	3,616	3,616
TORRE, Carlos de la (1856-1832) Argentinian				
oil	3	2,600-6,500	4,200	3,500
TORRE, Enrico della (1931-) Italian				
oil	3	1,332-1,942	1,719	1,885
TORRE, Giulio del (1856-1932) Italian				
oil	1	3,045	3,045	3,045
TORRES AGUERO (1924-) Argentinian				
oil	1	1,316	1,316	1,316
TORRES AGUERO, Leopoldo (1924-) Argentinian				
oil	3	2,500-10,000	6,833	8,000
wc/d	1	1,200	1,200	1,200
TORRES MARTINEZ, Manuel (1901-1995) Spanish				
3D	1	4,868	4,868	4,868
TORRES, Augusto (1913-1992) Uruguayan				
oil	2	1,800-4,576	3,188	1,800
wc/d	1	2,000	2,000	2,000
TORRES, Horacio (1924-1976) Uruguayan				
oil	4	1,500-3,232	2,408	2,400
TORRES-GARCIA, Joaquin (1874-1949) Uruguayan				
oil	5	70,541-380,000	234,108	240,000
wc/d	8	900-250,000	39,552	7,782
3D	1	110,000	110,000	110,000
TORRESCASSANA, Francisco (1845-1918) Spanish				
oil	1	8,438	8,438	8,438
TORRESINI, Attilio (1884-1961) Italian				
3D	1	2,670	2,670	2,670
TORREY, Elliot Bouton (1867-1949) American				
oil	4	1,000-2,000	1,650	1,750
TORRIGLIA, Giovanni Battista (1858-1937) Italian				
oil	1	120,000	120,000	120,000
TORRINI, E (19th C) Italian				
oil	2	3,240-8,004	5,622	3,240
TORRINI, Pietro (1852-1920) Italian				
oil	2	4,500-22,750	13,625	4,500
TORSCHENKO, Igor (1965-) Russian				
oil	2	1,326-1,558	1,442	1,326
TORSLEFF, August (1884-1968) Danish				
oil	1	6,194	6,194	6,194
TORSLEFF, Martin (1963-) Danish				
oil	2	1,106-1,106	1,106	1,106
TORSSLOW, Harald (1838-1909) Swedish				
oil	1	2,861	2,861	2,861
TOSI, Arturo (1871-1956) Italian				
oil	11	8,650-39,243	16,449	15,288
TOSINI, Michele (1503-1577) Italian				
oil	4	22,500-101,750	52,009	30,272
TOSLAVSKI, P (20th C) Russian?				
oil	1	7,153	7,153	7,153
TOTSIKAS, Thanassis (1951-) Greek				
3D	1	5,610	5,610	5,610
TOUCHAGUES, Louis (1893-1974) French				
oil	1	1,543	1,543	1,543
TOUDOUZE, Edouard (1848-1907) French				
oil	1	5,000	5,000	5,000
TOUDOUZE, Simon Alexandre (1850-1909) French				
oil	1	1,132	1,132	1,132
TOULLEC, Jean Louis le (20th C) French				
oil	4	718-1,520	1,095	883
TOULMAN, Moussia (1903-1997) Israeli				
oil	1	1,200	1,200	1,200
TOULMOUCHE, Auguste (1829-1890) French				
oil	6	2,934-70,000	27,072	22,500

Name	No.	Price Range	Average	Median
TOULOUSE, Roger (1918-1994) French				
oil	2	1,549-3,520	2,534	1,549
TOULOUSE-LAUTREC, Henri de (1864-1901) French				
oil	5	50,959-20,000,000	4,404,191	700,000
wc/d	48	4,253-980,000	55,556	12,390
3D	1	52,800	52,800	52,800
TOURGUENEFF, Pierre Nicolas (1854-1912) Russian/French				
3D	1	3,500	3,500	3,500
TOURNES, Étienne (1857-1931) French				
oil	2	1,500-1,592	1,546	1,500
TOURNIER, George (c.1850-?) French				
oil	1	3,016	3,016	3,016
TOURNIER, Jean Ulrich (?-c.1865) French				
oil	1	3,865	3,865	3,865
TOURNIER, Nicolas (1590-1657) French				
oil	1	101,372	101,372	101,372
TOURNIKIOTIS, Alice (20th C) Greek				
oil	1	1,870	1,870	1,870
TOURRIER, Alfred Holst (1836-1892) British				
oil	1	3,600	3,600	3,600
TOURSKY, Gerard de (19/20th C) ?				
oil	1	3,075	3,075	3,075
TOUSIGNANT, Claude (1932-) Canadian				
oil	3	6,647-12,370	9,087	8,246
wc/d	2	550-687	618	550
TOUSSAINT, Fernand (1873-1956) Belgian				
oil	36	651-52,200	12,970	9,633
wc/d	6	818-5,334	2,126	1,060
TOUSSAINT, Louis (1826-1887) German				
oil	1	3,214	3,214	3,214
TOUSSAINT, Pierre Joseph (1822-1888) Belgian				
oil	2	450-2,275	1,362	450
TOUTENEL, Lodewijk Jan Petrus (1819-1883) Belgian				
oil	1	7,836	7,836	7,836
TOUVIA, Naphtali (20th C) Israeli?				
oil	1	2,000	2,000	2,000
TOVAR, Ivan (1942-) Dominican				
3D	1	2,047	2,047	2,047
TOVEY, John (19th C) British				
oil	1	3,500	3,500	3,500
TOWAR, M (19th C) American				
oil	1	6,000	6,000	6,000
TOWN, Harold Barling (1924-1990) Canadian				
oil	3	2,952-11,521	8,123	9,896
wc/d	7	640-10,635	5,635	6,597
TOWNE, Charles (1763-1840) British				
oil	7	6,048-26,400	17,260	18,000
wc/d	1	8,000	8,000	8,000
TOWNE, Francis (1740-1816) British				
wc/d	1	51,900	51,900	51,900
TOWNSEND, A (20th C) British				
oil	1	1,890	1,890	1,890
TOWNSEND, Harry Everett (1879-1941) American				
oil	1	1,000	1,000	1,000
TOWNSEND, I (19th C) British				
oil	1	21,668	21,668	21,668
TOWNSEND, John R (19th C) British				
oil	1	1,068	1,068	1,068
TOWNSEND, Sarah Thompson (fl.1923-1924) British				
oil	1	2,768	2,768	2,768
TOWNSHEND, James A (?-1949) British				
oil	1	1,003	1,003	1,003
TOWNSLEY, Channel Pickering (1867-1921) American				
oil	1	4,250	4,250	4,250
TOXIC (1965-) American				
oil	4	1,670-16,397	6,144	1,790
wc/d	4	895-1,551	1,163	954
TOYEN (1902-1980) Czechoslovakian				
wc/d	2	597-1,730	1,163	597
TOYEN, Marie Germinova (1902-1980) Czechoslovakian				
oil	3	51,954-102,003	78,519	81,602
wc/d	5	1,730-26,401	7,778	2,730

Name	No.	Price Range	Average	Median
TOYNBEE, Lawrence L (1922-2002) British				
oil	1	1,947	1,947	1,947
TOYOFUKU, Tomonori (1925-) Japanese				
3D	1	9,103	9,103	9,103
TOYOKUNI, Utagawa (1769-1825) Japanese				
wc/d	1	13,000	13,000	13,000
TOZER, H Spernon (1864-c.1938) British				
wc/d	13	660-2,625	1,687	1,567
TOZER, Henry E (fl.1889-1892) British				
wc/d	1	1,075	1,075	1,075
TOZZI, Mario (1895-1979) Italian				
oil	18	20,027-114,490	42,839	32,363
wc/d	5	3,270-23,302	8,529	5,163
TRABALLESI, Francesco (1544-1588) Italian				
oil	1	17,014	17,014	17,014
TRACHEL, Domenico (1830-1897) French				
wc/d	3	730-1,670	1,122	966
TRACHEL, Ercole (1820-1872) French				
oil	1	3,337	3,337	3,337
TRACY, John M (1844-1893) American				
oil	4	6,500-28,000	12,875	7,500
TRAFFELET, Fritz (1897-1954) Swiss				
oil	1	1,679	1,679	1,679
TRAGARDH, Carl (1861-1899) Swedish				
oil	12	812-3,739	2,108	1,870
TRAIN, Edward (1801-1866) British				
oil	5	963-2,610	1,785	1,548
TRAMPEDACH, Kurt (1943-) Danish				
oil	3	10,302-16,901	12,823	11,267
wc/d	2	2,022-2,093	2,057	2,022
TRAN LONG, Mara (1935-) ?				
oil	1	648	648	648
wc/d	1	1,070	1,070	1,070
TRAN VAN TUNG (20th C) Vietnamese				
oil	1	2,667	2,667	2,667
TRAQUANDI, Gerard (1952-) French?				
oil	1	1,253	1,253	1,253
wc/d	4	536-12,114	4,367	1,854
TRAUT, Wolfgang (1486-1520) German				
oil	1	9,926	9,926	9,926
TRAUTMANN, Johann Georg (1713-1769) German				
oil	6	3,588-14,517	6,810	5,271
wc/d	1	777	777	777
TRAUTSCHOLD, Carl Friedrich Wilhelm (1815-1877) German				
oil	1	36,486	36,486	36,486
TRAUTSCHOLD, Manfred (1854-?) German				
oil	1	1,484	1,484	1,484
TRAVERSI, Gaspare (?-1769) Italian				
oil	1	12,975	12,975	12,975
TRAVI, Antonio (1608-1665) Italian				
oil	2	23,108-34,054	28,581	23,108
TRAVIES, Edouard (1809-1870) French				
wc/d	19	1,288-25,767	6,821	4,802
TRAVIESO, Francisco (1942-) Argentinian				
oil	1	2,500	2,500	2,500
TRAVIS, Kathryn Hail (1888-1972) American				
oil	1	8,000	8,000	8,000
TRAVIS, Olin Herman (1888-1975) American				
oil	7	1,600-15,000	5,114	3,000
TRAVIS, Paul Bough (1891-1975) American				
oil	1	4,200	4,200	4,200
wc/d	1	780	780	780
TRAYER, Jules (1824-1908) French				
oil	6	2,259-9,644	6,371	7,176
TRAYLOR, Bill (1854-1947) American				
wc/d	2	45,000-50,000	47,500	45,000
TREACY, Liam (1934-2004) Irish				
oil	20	727-7,068	3,315	3,390
TREBACZ, Maurycy (1861-1941) Polish				
oil	1	7,500	7,500	7,500

Name	No.	Price Range	Average	Median
TRECCANI, Ernesto (1920-1994) Italian				
oil	22	419-2,259	1,321	1,341
wc/d	4	514-719	646	660
TRECCHI, Walter (1964-) Italian				
wc/d	1	1,054	1,054	1,054
TRECK, Jan Janssen (1606-1652) Dutch				
oil	1	25,000	25,000	25,000
TRECOURT, Giacomo (1812-1882) Italian				
oil	1	12,153	12,153	12,153
TREFNY, Frank (1948-) American				
oil	1	2,200	2,200	2,200
TREGO, Jonathan Kirkbridge (1817-1901) American				
oil	1	1,700	1,700	1,700
TREGO, William Brooke Thomas (1859-1909) American				
oil	2	3,250-8,000	5,625	3,250
TREIMAN, Joyce Wahl (1922-1991) American				
oil	1	400	400	400
wc/d	1	4,250	4,250	4,250
TREMBLAY, John (20th C) ?				
oil	1	1,100	1,100	1,100
TREMERIE, Carolus (1858-1945) Belgian				
oil	1	1,023	1,023	1,023
TREMLETT, David (1945-) British				
wc/d	4	2,093-4,451	3,436	3,000
TRENCH, Marianne L (1888-1940) British				
oil	2	748-1,000	874	748
wc/d	1	1,770	1,770	1,770
TRENK, Franz (1899-1960) Austrian				
oil	3	971-1,295	1,105	1,051
TRENTANOVE, Raimondo (1792-1832) Italian				
3D	1	30,000	30,000	30,000
TRETCHIKOFF, Vladimir (1913-) Russian				
oil	1	2,743	2,743	2,743
TREVELYAN, Julian (1910-1989) British				
oil	9	522-32,870	12,663	9,450
wc/d	2	2,805-31,140	16,972	2,805
TREVISANI, Francesco (1656-1746) Italian				
oil	4	12,460-108,367	44,206	17,939
wc/d	1	3,500	3,500	3,500
TRIANDAFYLLIDIS, Theofrastos (1881-1955) Greek				
oil	1	26,180	26,180	26,180
TRICKETT, John (1952-) British				
oil	6	599-2,768	1,961	1,760
TRICKETT, W Wasdell (fl.1921-1939) British				
oil	1	1,672	1,672	1,672
TRIEBEL, Carl (1823-1885) German				
oil	3	1,204-4,671	3,063	3,314
TRIER, Hann (1915-1999) German				
oil	2	6,115-10,014	8,064	6,115
wc/d	4	1,095-3,279	1,976	1,656
TRIGA, Giacomo (?-1746) Italian				
oil	1	25,000	25,000	25,000
TRIGO, Modesto (1960-) Spanish				
oil	7	1,073-4,219	2,079	1,808
TRILLHAASE, Adalbert (20th C) German				
wc/d	2	523-2,342	1,432	523
TRINQUESSE, Louis Rolland (1746-1800) French				
oil	2	2,674-610,500	306,587	2,674
wc/d	2	535-5,550	3,042	535
TRINQUIER, Antonin (1833-?) French				
oil	1	13,000	13,000	13,000
TRISCOTT, Samuel Peter Rolt (1846-1925) American				
wc/d	1	7,000	7,000	7,000
TRIVIGNO, Pat (1922-) American				
wc/d	1	1,400	1,400	1,400
TROCKEL, Rosemarie (1952-) German				
oil	3	3,567-7,040	5,234	5,096
wc/d	10	1,911-155,000	31,744	5,096
3D	3	3,181-3,770	3,455	3,416
TROGER, Paul (1698-1762) Austrian				
oil	1	22,986	22,986	22,986

Name	No.	Price Range	Average	Median
TROIANI, Don (1949-) American				
oil	1	21,000	21,000	21,000
TROKES, Heinz (1913-1997) German				
oil	4	6,184-9,625	8,090	7,633
wc/d	7	586-2,057	970	761
TROMBADORI, Francesco (1886-1961) Italian				
oil	2	2,577-15,265	8,921	2,577
TROMKA, Abram (1896-1954) American				
oil	1	1,100	1,100	1,100
TROMP, Jan Zoetelief (1872-1947) Dutch				
oil	4	8,342-90,925	34,240	15,570
wc/d	1	7,400	7,400	7,400
TROMPIZ, Virgilio (1927-) Venezuelan				
oil	10	580-88,370	9,726	980
TROOSEWYK, Wouter Johannes van (19th C) ?				
oil	1	5,839	5,839	5,839
TROOST, Willem (18/19th C) Dutch				
oil	1	1,168	1,168	1,168
wc/d	1	3,200	3,200	3,200
TROPININ, Vassili (1776-1857) Russian				
oil	1	154,800	154,800	154,800
TROTTER, Newbold Hough (1827-1898) American				
oil	6	1,400-4,800	2,433	2,000
TROTZIG, Ulf (1925-) Norwegian				
oil	5	1,870-28,027	7,509	2,775
TROUBETZKOY, Prince Paolo (1866-1938) Russian				
3D	27	3,720-133,920	31,999	25,000
TROUILLEBERT, Paul Desire (1829-1900) French				
oil	30	787-27,185	10,897	7,476
TROUTOVSKY, Konstantin (1826-1893) Russian				
oil	2	764-44,720	22,742	764
TROUVILLE, Henri-Charles (19th C) French				
oil	1	3,099	3,099	3,099
TROVA, Ernest (1927-) American				
oil	3	1,400-6,500	3,113	1,440
3D	6	1,600-7,000	3,116	2,000
TROWELL, Jonathan (1938-) British				
wc/d	1	1,647	1,647	1,647
TROY, François de (1645-1730) French				
oil	2	11,658-40,000	25,829	11,658
wc/d	1	2,431	2,431	2,431
TROYE, Edward (1808-1874) American				
oil	1	30,000	30,000	30,000
TROYEN, Rombout van (1605-c.1650) Dutch				
oil	2	2,689-6,370	4,529	2,689
TROYER, F (?) ?				
oil	1	6,429	6,429	6,429
TROYER, Prosper de (1880-1961) Belgian				
oil	2	477-2,472	1,474	477
TROYON, Constant (1810-1865) French				
oil	7	1,600-72,500	19,491	8,696
wc/d	3	829-1,717	1,182	1,000
TRUBNER, Wilhelm (1851-1917) German				
oil	11	2,238-19,082	10,585	9,219
wc/d	1	486	486	486
TRUDEAU, Angus (1908-1984) Canadian?				
oil	1	2,788	2,788	2,788
wc/d	1	2,788	2,788	2,788
TRUE, David (1942-) American				
oil	1	1,000	1,000	1,000
TRUE, Virginia (1900-1989) American				
oil	1	2,400	2,400	2,400
TRUEX, Van Day (1904-1979) American				
wc/d	2	2,000-2,800	2,400	2,000
TRUMBULL, John (1756-1843) American				
oil	1	4,000	4,000	4,000
TRUMBULL, John and WEST, Benjamin (18/19th C) American				
oil	1	550,000	550,000	550,000
TRUMPFHELLER, Johann Balthasar (1876-1961) German				
3D	1	3,979	3,979	3,979

Name	No.	Price Range	Average	Median
TRUPHEMUS, Jacques (1922-) French				
oil	2	5,708-8,000	6,854	5,708
wc/d	1	1,320	1,320	1,320
TRUPPE, Karl (1887-1959) Austrian				
oil	2	1,212-5,839	3,525	1,212
wc/d	1	665	665	665
TRUSZ, Ivan (1869-1940) Russian				
oil	2	5,351-16,340	10,845	5,351
TRYGGELIN, Erik (1878-1962) Swedish				
oil	6	784-15,580	5,240	1,122
TRYON, Dwight W (1849-1925) American				
wc/d	1	1,000	1,000	1,000
TSAKALI, Anna Maria (1959-) Greek				
oil	1	4,576	4,576	4,576
TSAROUKHIS, Yannis (1910-1989) Greek				
oil	5	13,050-156,600	66,498	41,760
wc/d	5	5,236-18,900	10,880	8,174
TSCHACBASOV, Nahum (1899-1984) Russian				
oil	2	500-1,600	1,050	500
TSCHAGGENY, Charles Philogene (1815-1894) Belgian				
oil	6	482-33,899	6,797	895
wc/d	1	783	783	783
TSCHAGGENY, Edmond (1818-1873) Belgian				
oil	5	876-20,000	7,013	4,381
TSCHARNER, Johann Wilhelm von (1886-1946) Swiss				
oil	7	446-15,233	3,029	916
TSCHARNER, Theodore (1826-1906) Belgian				
oil	1	1,678	1,678	1,678
TSCHAUTSCH, Albert (1843-?) German				
oil	1	3,646	3,646	3,646
TSCHELAN, Hans (1873-1964) Austrian				
oil	2	1,050-1,576	1,313	1,050
TSCHERNIKOFF, Alexej Filippowitsch (1824-1863) Russian				
wc/d	1	3,440	3,440	3,440
TSCHERNJAWSKI, Alex (20th C) American				
oil	1	6,880	6,880	6,880
TSCHICHOLD, Jan (1902-1974) German				
wc/d	1	1,788	1,788	1,788
TSCHUDI, Lill (1911-2001) German				
oil	3	1,832-1,958	1,916	1,958
TSCHUMI, Otto (1904-1985) Swiss				
oil	1	1,374	1,374	1,374
wc/d	2	4,215-4,961	4,588	4,215
TSELKOV, Oleg (1934-) Russian				
oil	1	70,000	70,000	70,000
TSENG YU-HO (20th C) Chinese				
wc/d	3	400-5,500	2,366	1,200
TSERETELI, Zurab Konstantinovich (1934-) Russian				
oil	1	103,200	103,200	103,200
TSINGOS, Thanos (1914-1965) Greek				
oil	26	1,776-57,420	12,937	8,976
TSIREH, Awa (1895-1955) American				
wc/d	1	1,100	1,100	1,100
TSIRIGOTI, Nikolai Grigorievich (1864-1942) Russian				
oil	1	17,897	17,897	17,897
TSIROGIANIS, Apostolos (1946-) Greek				
oil	3	4,576-15,895	10,603	11,340
TSOCLIS, Costa (1930-) Greek				
oil	1	11,220	11,220	11,220
wc/d	4	6,181-14,960	10,505	10,440
TSUNETOMI, Kitano (1880-1947) Japanese				
wc/d	1	3,700	3,700	3,700
TUAL, Pierre (1941-) French				
3D	2	2,281-5,703	3,992	2,281
TUBBECKE, Paul (1848-1924) German				
oil	2	1,573-2,057	1,815	1,573
TUBKE, Werner (1929-2004) German				
oil	2	15,226-39,435	27,330	15,226
wc/d	3	2,293-6,442	4,183	3,816
TUCKER, Allen (1866-1939) American				
oil	5	6,000-20,000	13,300	15,000

Name	No.	Price Range	Average	Median
TUCKER, James W (1898-1972) British				
oil	1	3,480	3,480	3,480
wc/d	1	626	626	626
TUCKER, Mary B (19th C) American				
wc/d	1	3,750	3,750	3,750
TUCKERMAN, Stephen Salisbury (1830-1904) American				
oil	3	1,100-5,643	2,814	1,700
TUDGAY (19th C) British				
oil	1	1,500	1,500	1,500
TUDGAY, Frederick (1841-1921) British				
oil	1	3,097	3,097	3,097
TUDGAY, Frederick and John (19th C) British				
oil	1	4,537	4,537	4,537
TUDGAY, I (19th C) British				
oil	2	15,930-46,020	30,975	15,930
TUDGAY, J (19th C) British				
oil	1	4,872	4,872	4,872
TUDOR, Joseph (c.1695-1759) Irish				
wc/d	1	126,207	126,207	126,207
TUERENHOUT, Jef van (1926-) Belgian				
wc/d	5	607-5,529	3,436	3,312
TUKE, Henry Scott (1858-1929) British				
oil	3	2,534-325,600	138,544	87,500
wc/d	8	440-33,480	7,719	4,779
TULK, A (fl.1877-1892) British				
oil	1	3,695	3,695	3,695
TULK, Augustus (fl.1877-1897) British				
oil	2	2,852-5,568	4,210	2,852
TULLAT, Luc (1895-?) French				
oil	1	1,850	1,850	1,850
TULLI, Wladimiro (1922-2003) Italian				
oil	6	589-4,295	1,805	1,296
wc/d	3	1,054-1,640	1,338	1,320
3D	1	1,670	1,670	1,670
TUMARKIN, Igael (1933-) Israeli				
oil	6	2,500-10,000	5,383	3,000
wc/d	5	650-7,000	2,530	1,900
3D	1	2,200	2,200	2,200
TUNICA, Hermann August Theodor (1826-1907) German				
oil	5	3,853-60,204	18,470	6,622
TUNICA, Johann Christian Ludwig (1795-1868) German				
oil	1	31,306	31,306	31,306
TUNNARD, John (1900-1971) British				
oil	2	9,735-25,800	17,767	9,735
wc/d	3	540-14,790	5,860	2,250
TUNNICLIFFE, Charles Frederick (1901-1979) British				
oil	5	661-12,006	4,111	2,220
wc/d	33	463-8,415	1,976	1,203
TUNNILLIE, Ovilu (1949-) North American				
3D	1	2,531	2,531	2,531
TUOHY, Patrick (1894-1930) British				
oil	1	1,178	1,178	1,178
TURAN, Selim (1915-) Turkish				
oil	1	17,107	17,107	17,107
TURBA (19/20th C) ?				
oil	1	8,486	8,486	8,486
TURCATO, Giulio (1912-1995) Italian				
oil	68	3,503-114,490	18,309	12,600
wc/d	6	2,054-26,714	8,985	5,088
TURCHANINOV, Kapiton Fedorovich (1823-1900) Russian				
oil	1	189,200	189,200	189,200
TURCHI, Alessandro (1578-1649) Italian				
oil	5	9,993-153,340	50,879	17,581
TURCHIARO, Aldo (1929-) Italian				
oil	5	835-2,356	1,412	1,229
wc/d	1	615	615	615
TURK, Rudolf (1893-1944) Austrian				
oil	1	1,752	1,752	1,752
TURKEN, Henricus (1791-1856) Dutch				
oil	1	5,103	5,103	5,103
TURKI, Yahia (1903-1968) Tunisian				
oil	2	5,722-9,545	7,633	5,722

Name	No.	Price Range	Average	Median
TURKS, G P (20th C) ?				
oil	1	3,250	3,250	3,250
TURMA, Oscar (19th C) ?				
oil	1	3,399	3,399	3,399
TURNBULL, Robert (?) British?				
wc/d	1	1,074	1,074	1,074
TURNBULL, William (1922-) British				
oil	1	100,100	100,100	100,100
3D	5	7,182-26,460	14,968	17,010
TURNER OF OXFORD, William (1789-1862) British				
wc/d	4	478-4,200	1,725	552
TURNER, Arthur W (fl.1898-1900) British				
oil	1	1,305	1,305	1,305
TURNER, Ben (1912-1966) American				
oil	2	3,800-7,500	5,650	3,800
TURNER, Charles E (1883-1965) British				
oil	2	800-5,292	3,046	800
wc/d	2	800-1,400	1,100	800
TURNER, Charles Henry (1848-1908) American				
oil	1	1,900	1,900	1,900
wc/d	1	450	450	450
TURNER, Charles Yardley (1850-1918) American				
oil	2	1,500-2,750	2,125	1,500
TURNER, Daniel (fl.1782-1817) British				
oil	3	3,306-24,570	12,849	10,672
TURNER, Ethel M (fl.1901-1914) British				
wc/d	1	9,250	9,250	9,250
TURNER, Eva Griffin (1872-?) American				
oil	1	2,500	2,500	2,500
TURNER, Frances Calcott (1795-1865) British				
oil	2	2,736-6,160	4,448	2,736
TURNER, Francis Calcraft (c.1782-1846) British				
oil	3	3,520-17,600	9,686	7,938
wc/d	1	473	473	473
TURNER, George (1843-1910) British				
oil	24	800-9,200	3,359	2,944
TURNER, Helen M (1858-1958) American				
oil	1	3,654	3,654	3,654
TURNER, Johann Christoph (c.1690-1744) Bohemian				
oil	1	6,290	6,290	6,290
TURNER, John (20th C) Irish?				
oil	2	974-2,664	1,819	974
TURNER, Joseph Mallord William (1775-1851) British				
oil	2	3,000-32,000,000	16,001,500	3,000
wc/d	17	556-9,672,001	652,880	41,760
TURNER, Kenneth (20th C) American				
oil	1	2,750	2,750	2,750
TURNER, Margaret (?) British				
oil	1	22,000	22,000	22,000
TURNER, Ross Sterling (1847-1915) American				
oil	1	800	800	800
wc/d	6	700-8,000	3,458	1,400
TURNER, W H M (fl.1850-1887) British				
oil	1	4,158	4,158	4,158
TURNER, William (1920-) British				
oil	19	708-9,261	3,441	2,124
TURNER, William Eddowes (c.1820-1885) British				
oil	4	684-3,111	1,499	855
TURNER, William Lakin (1867-1936) British				
oil	8	773-2,116	1,284	1,067
TURNER, Winifred (1903-) British				
3D	1	2,610	2,610	2,610
TURNERELLI, Peter (1774-1839) British				
3D	1	9,633	9,633	9,633
TURPIN DE CRISSE, Lancelot Theodore (1782-1859) French				
	1	75,000	75,000	75,000
TURPIN, Christina Dorothea (18th C) German?				
oil	1	2,038	2,038	2,038
TURRELL, James (1943-) American				
wc/d	2	14,137-47,500	30,818	14,137
TURRI, Mose (1837-1903) Italian				
oil	1	2,634	2,634	2,634

Name	No.	Price Range	Average	Median
TURTIAINEN, Jorma (1936-) Finnish				
oil	2	501-1,640	1,070	501
TURTLE, Arnold E (1892-1954) American/British				
oil	3	550-4,000	1,916	1,200
TURTSCHER, Franz (1953-) Austrian				
oil	1	1,293	1,293	1,293
TURULL, R F (19th C) ?				
oil	1	3,027	3,027	3,027
TURZAK, Charles (1899-1985) American				
oil	1	1,212	1,212	1,212
TUSQUETS Y MAIGNON, Ramon (1839-1904) Italian				
oil	1	23,784	23,784	23,784
wc/d	2	1,205-4,498	2,851	1,205
TUTSWEETOK, Lucy Tasseor (1934-) North American				
3D	7	1,603-28,682	7,845	2,531
TUTTINE, Johann Baptist (1838-1889) German				
oil	1	3,507	3,507	3,507
TUTTLE, Richard (1941-) American				
oil	2	30,960-350,000	190,480	30,960
wc/d	5	2,434-42,000	19,986	16,000
3D	2	40,000-80,000	60,000	40,000
TUTUNDJIAN, Léon (1905-1968) French/Armenian				
oil	3	4,339-32,145	14,994	8,500
wc/d	8	970-5,959	2,737	2,225
TUTUNOV, Andrei Andreevich (1928-) Russian				
oil	1	2,100	2,100	2,100
TUXEN, Laurits (1853-1927) Danish				
oil	36	929-34,779	6,186	4,743
TUYMANS, Luc (1958-) Belgian				
oil	7	105,000-350,000	223,714	180,000
wc/d	4	4,000-22,200	11,175	8,500
TWACHTMAN, John Henry (1853-1902) American				
oil	1	75,000	75,000	75,000
wc/d	2	2,200-32,000	17,100	2,200
TWEED, Coralie (20th C) American				
wc/d	1	2,100	2,100	2,100
TWOMBLY, Alessandro (1959-) Italian				
3D	1	10,603	10,603	10,603
TWOMBLY, Cy (1928-) American				
oil	8	123,200-7,750,000	2,048,742	281,600
wc/d	12	8,000-450,000	139,126	79,200
TWORKOV, Jack (1900-1982) American				
oil	7	5,000-340,000	77,285	16,000
wc/d	2	2,300-8,500	5,400	2,300
TXILLIDA, Pedro (1952-) Spanish				
oil	2	9,633-9,633	9,633	9,633
TYDEN, Nils (1889-1976) Swedish				
oil	5	503-5,286	2,574	2,379
TYLER, Bayard Henry (1855-1931) American				
oil	2	1,200-1,300	1,250	1,200
TYLER, James Gale (1855-1931) American				
oil	18	650-130,000	11,613	2,700
TYLER, W R (19th C) American				
oil	1	1,100	1,100	1,100
TYLER, William R (1825-1896) American				
oil	4	650-4,000	1,812	1,200
TYN, Lambrecht den (1770-1816) Belgian				
oil	1	1,790	1,790	1,790
TYNDALE, Thomas Nicholson (1858-1936) British				
wc/d	1	1,232	1,232	1,232
TYNDALE, Walter (1855-1943) British				
wc/d	12	743-15,000	3,980	2,100
TYRELL, Charles (20th C) ?				
oil	1	9,929	9,929	9,929
TYSHLER, Aleksander (1898-1980) Russian				
wc/d	2	6,000-6,000	6,000	6,000
TYSON, Carroll (1878-1956) American				
oil	4	1,900-10,000	5,975	3,000
TYSON, Keith (1969-) British				
oil	1	38,000	38,000	38,000
wc/d	1	88,000	88,000	88,000

Name	No.	Price Range	Average	Median
TYSON, Nicola (1960-) British				
oil	4	1,600-27,750	13,652	11,100
wc/d	1	3,520	3,520	3,520
TYSSENS, Jan Baptist (c.1665-1723) Flemish				
oil	1	4,500	4,500	4,500
TYSVER, Peter (20th C) American				
oil	1	5,000	5,000	5,000
TYSZBLAT, Michel (1936-) French				
oil	3	1,236-3,535	2,646	3,168
TYTGAT, Edgard (1879-1957) Belgian				
oil	2	12,858-14,833	13,845	12,858
wc/d	14	486-4,767	2,095	1,753
TYTGAT, Medard (1871-1948) Belgian				
oil	1	1,332	1,332	1,332
TZAPOFF, Antoine (20th C) ?				
oil	1	7,500	7,500	7,500
UBAC, Raoul (1910-1985) Belgian				
wc/d	2	2,383-3,343	2,863	2,383
UBEDA, Augustin (1925-) Spanish				
oil	19	958-10,097	4,661	4,400
wc/d	1	1,865	1,865	1,865
UBERTALLI, Romolo (1871-1928) Italian				
oil	1	908	908	908
wc/d	1	2,148	2,148	2,148
UBERTINI, Francesco (1494-1557) Italian				
oil	1	57,857	57,857	57,857
UDALTSOVA, Nadezhda (1886-1961) Russian				
oil	1	80,000	80,000	80,000
UDEN, Lucas van (1595-1672) Flemish				
oil	6	7,120-38,574	20,207	18,000
UDVARY, Geza (1872-1932) Hungarian				
oil	1	1,531	1,531	1,531
UECHTRITZ-STEINKIRCH, Cuno von (1856-1908) German				
3D	1	13,377	13,377	13,377
UECKER, Gunther (1930-) German				
oil	6	760-57,329	28,072	12,740
wc/d	7	692-76,438	25,984	4,712
3D	4	3,440-153,151	43,801	4,477
UELLIGER, Karl (1920-1993) Swiss				
oil	10	648-4,454	2,458	1,943
UFAN, Lee (1936-) Korean				
wc/d	1	1,573	1,573	1,573
UFER, Walter (1876-1936) American				
oil	3	12,000-100,000	45,666	25,000
UFFELEN, Jan van (1921-) Israeli?				
oil	1	1,500	1,500	1,500
UGALDE, Juan (1958-) Spanish				
oil	3	2,631-3,449	3,017	2,973
wc/d	2	753-9,633	5,193	753
UGO, Antonio (1870-?) Italian				
3D	1	3,185	3,185	3,185
UGYUK, Charlie (1931-) North American				
3D	1	2,025	2,025	2,025
UHDE, Fritz von (1848-1911) German				
oil	4	1,029-15,310	5,565	2,342
wc/d	1	5,400	5,400	5,400
UHL, Louis (1860-1902) Austrian				
oil	1	1,332	1,332	1,332
UHLIG, Max (1937-) German				
oil	6	1,874-5,271	3,289	3,180
wc/d	11	511-1,277	757	608
UHLMAN, Fred (1901-1985) British				
oil	10	651-5,760	2,038	851
UHLMANN, Hans (1900-1975) German				
wc/d	12	890-4,325	2,072	1,683
3D	4	4,079-55,973	30,928	11,743
UHRDIN, Sam (1886-1964) Swedish				
oil	6	373-24,205	5,938	1,620
UJVARY, Ignac (1880-1927) Hungarian				
oil	3	400-6,081	2,482	967
UKLANSKI, Piotr (1968-) Polish?				
3D	3	91,520-190,000	133,923	120,250

Name	No.	Price Range	Average	Median
ULFT, Jacob van der (1627-1689) Dutch				
wc/d	2	622-2,281	1,451	622
ULIANOFF, Vsevolod (1880-1940) American?				
wc/d	3	500-2,750	1,383	900
ULIANOV, Nikolai Pavlovich (1875-1949) Russian				
oil	1	2,811	2,811	2,811
ULIBARRI GARCIA, Blanca de (1946-) Spanish				
oil	1	2,735	2,735	2,735
ULLIK, Hugo (1838-1881) Czechoslovakian				
oil	1	6,442	6,442	6,442
ULLIK, Rudolf (20th C) Austrian				
oil	5	1,767-3,982	2,636	2,342
ULLNER-LARSEN (19th C) Scandinavian				
oil	1	2,655	2,655	2,655
ULLULAQ, Judas (1937-1998) North American				
3D	10	3,037-13,498	5,884	3,881
ULNITZ, E C (1856-1933) Danish				
oil	1	1,774	1,774	1,774
ULRICH, Charles Frederic (1858-1908) American				
oil	1	5,500	5,500	5,500
ULRICH, Johann (1798-1877) Swiss				
oil	4	935-3,137	1,681	1,135
ULTVEDT, Per Olof (1927-) Finnish				
3D	2	2,643-26,429	14,536	2,643
ULVING, Even (1863-1952) Norwegian				
oil	2	720-4,362	2,541	720
ULYSSE-ROY, Jean (19th C) French				
oil	1	1,107	1,107	1,107
UMBRICHT, Honore Louis (1860-1943) French				
oil	1	1,646	1,646	1,646
UMLAUF, Charles (1911-1994) American				
3D	1	3,000	3,000	3,000
UMLAUF, Karl (1939-) American				
oil	1	1,600	1,600	1,600
UNBEREIT, Paul (1884-1937) German/Austrian				
oil	3	1,784-3,579	2,433	1,937
UNCETA Y LOPEZ, Marcelino de (1835-1905) Spanish				
oil	2	7,151-23,946	15,548	7,151
UNCINI, Giuseppe (1929-) Italian				
wc/d	6	2,356-5,622	3,440	3,319
3D	8	3,262-102,660	27,182	17,173
UNDERHILL, Frederick Thomas (fl.1868-1896) British				
oil	1	9,720	9,720	9,720
UNDERHILL, William (19th C) British				
oil	3	5,500-13,275	8,274	6,048
UNDERWOOD, Clarence F (1871-1929) American				
wc/d	1	4,750	4,750	4,750
UNGAR, Otto (1901-1945) German?				
wc/d	1	1,973	1,973	1,973
UNGER, Carl (1915-1995) German?				
wc/d	5	1,697-3,857	2,310	1,908
UNGER, Hans (1872-1936) German				
oil	5	1,196-2,038	1,669	1,627
UNGER, Wolfgang Heinz (1929-) German				
oil	3	596-1,640	1,096	1,054
UNGERN, Ragnar (1885-1955) Finnish				
oil	2	2,057-5,143	3,600	2,057
UNGEWITTER, Hugo (1869-c.1944) German				
oil	11	4,795-30,362	17,702	20,640
UNOLD, Max (1885-1964) German				
oil	1	2,356	2,356	2,356
wc/d	1	1,090	1,090	1,090
UNSWORTH, Peter (1937-) British				
oil	2	744-2,379	1,561	744
UNTERBERGER, F R (1838-1902) Belgian				
oil	1	37,297	37,297	37,297
UNTERBERGER, Franz Richard (1838-1902) Belgian				
oil	16	2,336-160,000	43,192	29,440
UNTERBERGER, Michelangelo (1695-1758) Austrian				
oil	1	3,612	3,612	3,612

Name	No.	Price Range	Average	Median
UNTIEDT, Michael Ome (1953-) American				
oil	1	3,000	3,000	3,000
UNTURBE, Jose (1895-1983) Spanish?				
oil	1	1,119	1,119	1,119
UPADHYAY, Chintan (20th C) Indian				
oil	1	7,000	7,000	7,000
wc/d	1	6,000	6,000	6,000
UPHOFF, Carl Emil (1885-1971) German				
oil	1	6,997	6,997	6,997
UPHOFF, Fritz (1890-1966) German				
oil	1	1,252	1,252	1,252
UPRKA, Joza (1861-?) Czechoslovakian				
wc/d	1	2,750	2,750	2,750
URBACH, Josef (1889-1973) German				
oil	1	718	718	718
wc/d	1	7,658	7,658	7,658
URBAHN, Oskar (19/20th C) German				
oil	2	703-1,331	1,017	703
URBAINSKI DE NIECZNJA, F (20th C) European				
oil	1	5,622	5,622	5,622
URBAN, Hermann (1866-1946) German				
oil	3	788-2,068	1,333	1,145
URBIETA, Jesus (1959-1977) Mexican				
oil	1	17,000	17,000	17,000
URCULO, Eduardo (1938-2003) Spanish				
oil	4	11,189-48,163	29,766	17,572
URDIALES-URDE, Jorge (20th C) Latin American				
oil	1	1,000	1,000	1,000
URGELL Y INGLADA, Modesto (1839-1919) Spanish				
oil	2	954-12,884	6,919	954
URI, Aviva (1927-1989) Israeli				
oil	2	2,600-6,500	4,550	2,600
wc/d	7	400-9,500	3,550	3,000
URIA MONZON, Antonio (1929-1996) Spanish				
oil	1	1,784	1,784	1,784
URIARTE, Carlos (1910-) Argentinian				
oil	1	4,500	4,500	4,500
wc/d	1	2,000	2,000	2,000
URIBURU, Nicolas Garcia (1937-) Argentinian				
oil	4	4,500-11,500	7,782	5,040
wc/d	1	851	851	851
URLAUB, Georg Anton (1713-1759) German				
wc/d	1	5,444	5,444	5,444
URQUHART, Murray (1880-1972) British				
oil	6	513-4,956	2,024	570
URQUHART, Tony (1934-) Canadian				
oil	1	2,788	2,788	2,788
wc/d	1	6,559	6,559	6,559
URSELLA, Enrico (1887-1955) Italian				
oil	1	2,571	2,571	2,571
URSULA (1921-) German				
oil	1	1,100	1,100	1,100
URTEIL, Andreas (1933-1963) Austrian				
3D	3	1,818-2,957	2,567	2,928
URY, Lesser (1861-1931) German				
oil	15	11,712-228,800	45,600	25,442
wc/d	12	1,316-99,358	30,017	10,541
USADEL, Max (1880-) German				
oil	2	764-4,234	2,499	764
USELLINI, Gian Filippo (1903-1971) Italian				
oil	2	2,625-6,760	4,692	2,625
USHER, Arland A (fl.1885-1893) British				
oil	1	2,675	2,675	2,675
USLE, Juan (1953-) Spanish				
oil	6	6,654-60,204	28,966	20,660
wc/d	2	500-500	500	500
USSI, Stefano (1822-1901) Italian				
oil	5	3,185-50,884	20,810	12,600
USTINOV, Igor (1956-) ?				
3D	1	2,104	2,104	2,104
UTAMARO, Kitagawa (1753-1806) Japanese				
oil	2	7,030-10,175	8,602	7,030

Name	No.	Price Range	Average	Median
UTH, Max (1863-1914) German				
oil	2	941-1,098	1,019	941
UTRECHT, Adriaen van (1599-1653) Flemish				
oil	1	22,188	22,188	22,188
UTRILLO, Maurice (1883-1955) French				
oil	52	18,000-300,000	116,379	111,000
wc/d	25	9,352-111,000	37,892	30,752
UTTER, Andre (1886-1948) French				
oil	7	605-3,758	1,662	1,553
UTTER, Bror (1913-1933) American				
wc/d	5	400-2,750	1,340	750
UTZON-FRANK, Ejnar (1888-1955) Danish				
3D	4	1,741-15,130	8,085	4,527
UUTINEN, Marianna (1961-) Finnish				
oil	1	4,889	4,889	4,889
UVA, Cesare (1824-1886) Italian				
oil	1	1,405	1,405	1,405
UVAROV, S (19th C) Russian				
wc/d	1	4,816	4,816	4,816
UWINS, Thomas (1782-1857) British				
oil	1	930	930	930
wc/d	2	505-1,018	761	505
UYTEWAEL, Joachim (1566-1638) Dutch				
oil	1	1,072,600	1,072,600	1,072,600
UYTEWAEL, Pieter (1596-1660) Dutch				
oil	1	19,852	19,852	19,852
UYTTENBROECK, Moses van (1590-1648) Dutch				
oil	4	2,253-16,910	6,557	2,436
UZELAC, Milivoy (1897-1950) Yugoslavian				
wc/d	2	1,255-12,643	6,949	1,255
VA, Barry le (1941-) American				
wc/d	1	2,338	2,338	2,338
VAAMONDE, Joaquin (1872-1900) Spanish				
wc/d	1	1,145	1,145	1,145
VAARBERG, H (19/20th C) Dutch				
oil	1	3,814	3,814	3,814
VAARBERG, Johannes Christoffel (1825-1871) Dutch				
oil	2	1,252-5,192	3,222	1,252
VAARULA, Olavi (1927-1989) Finnish				
oil	3	900-3,039	1,781	1,405
wc/d	6	584-1,671	1,120	1,199
VACCARI, Alfredo (1877-1933) Italian				
oil	1	12,945	12,945	12,945
VACCARI, Leandro (1945-) Italian?				
oil	2	1,302-1,581	1,441	1,302
VACCARO, Andrea (c.1598-1670) Italian				
oil	3	11,781-15,130	13,717	14,240
VACCARO, Vincenzo (1858-1929) Italian				
oil	1	7,474	7,474	7,474
VACCHI, Sergio (1925-) Italian				
oil	5	657-2,945	1,952	2,063
wc/d	4	884-1,288	1,090	983
VACHAL, Josef (1884-1969) Czechoslovakian				
oil	1	4,784	4,784	4,784
VACHAROV, A (20th C) Russian				
oil	1	6,668	6,668	6,668
VACHE, Jacques (1895-1919) French				
wc/d	3	2,829-12,857	7,157	5,786
VADASZ, Endre (1901-1944) Hungarian				
oil	1	1,344	1,344	1,344
VADASZ, Miklos (1884-1927) Hungarian				
wc/d	1	2,234	2,234	2,234
VADDER, Frans de (1862-1935) Belgian				
oil	1	3,295	3,295	3,295
VADDER, Lodewyk de (1605-1655) Flemish				
oil	1	23,128	23,128	23,128
wc/d	1	2,803	2,803	2,803
VADER, Hendrik (19/20th C) Belgian				
oil	1	1,753	1,753	1,753
VADILLO, Francisco (20th C) Spanish?				
oil	11	560-4,100	1,693	980

Name	No.	Price Range	Average	Median
VAELTL, Otto (1885-1977) German				
oil	2	482-2,779	1,630	482
VAES, Walter (1882-1958) Belgian				
oil	5	1,243-14,027	5,631	4,841
wc/d	1	1,033	1,033	1,033
VAGAGGINI, Memo (1892-1955) Italian				
oil	3	1,205-3,616	2,008	1,205
VAGH WEINMANN, Nandor (1897-1978) Hungarian				
oil	1	5,469	5,469	5,469
VAGLIERI, Tino (1929-2000) Italian				
oil	7	900-2,428	1,701	1,646
wc/d	5	486-1,800	1,225	1,457
VAGNETTI, Gianni (1898-1956) Italian				
oil	8	485-8,919	2,824	1,560
wc/d	3	558-727	646	655
VAGO, Valentino (1931-) Italian				
oil	11	1,812-3,495	2,564	2,460
VAIKUNTAM, Thotha (1942-) Indian				
oil	1	16,830	16,830	16,830
VAIL, Pegeen (1925-1967) American				
wc/d	1	1,683	1,683	1,683
VAILLANCOURT, Armand (1929-) Canadian				
3D	2	3,146-12,370	7,758	3,146
VAILLANT, Bernard (1632-1698) French				
wc/d	1	5,255	5,255	5,255
VAILLANT, Jacques (1625-1691) Flemish				
oil	5	7,224-15,653	9,337	7,827
wc/d	1	945	945	945
VAILLANT, Louis David (1875-1944) American				
oil	1	2,000	2,000	2,000
VAILLANT, Wallerant (1623-1677) Dutch				
oil	1	6,336	6,336	6,336
VAISMAN, Meyer (1960-) American				
3D	1	11,000	11,000	11,000
VAJDA, Lajos (1908-1941) Hungarian				
wc/d	1	1,669	1,669	1,669
VALADIE, Jean Baptiste (1933-) French				
oil	5	700-2,800	1,527	935
wc/d	2	510-530	520	510
VALADON, Suzanne (1865-1938) French				
oil	7	12,000-60,842	34,827	32,500
wc/d	6	2,322-21,626	8,547	7,200
VALCKERT, Werner van den (1585-c.1655) Dutch				
oil	1	69,200	69,200	69,200
VALDES LEAL, Juan de (1622-1690) Spanish				
oil	3	8,000-140,000	81,000	95,000
wc/d	1	20,000	20,000	20,000
VALDES, Lucas de (1661-1724) Spanish				
oil	1	5,400	5,400	5,400
VALDES, Manuel (1942-) Spanish				
oil	7	160,000-240,816	210,888	222,000
wc/d	1	70,400	70,400	70,400
VALDIVIESO, Antonio (1918-2000) Spanish				
oil	1	2,392	2,392	2,392
wc/d	3	510-1,094	772	714
VALENCIA, Manuel (1856-1935) American				
oil	8	1,300-5,500	2,618	1,800
VALENCIENNES, Pierre Henri de (1750-1819) French				
oil	2	41,760-278,767	160,263	41,760
VALENKAMPH, Theodor Victor Carl (1868-1924) American				
oil	8	500-6,500	2,250	1,600
VALENSI, Henry (1883-1960) French				
oil	3	851-5,712	2,479	876
wc/d	3	1,527-3,394	2,574	2,803
VALENTA, Ludwig (1882-1943) Austrian				
oil	2	700-2,408	1,554	700
VALENTI, Italo (1912-1995) Italian				
oil	5	1,623-6,431	4,245	3,982
wc/d	10	1,669-8,357	3,629	2,759
VALENTIEN, Anna Marie (1862-1947) American				
oil	1	3,000	3,000	3,000

Name	No.	Price Range	Average	Median
VALENTIN, François (1738-1805) ?				
wc/d	1	1,036	1,036	1,036
VALENTIN, J M (19th C) French				
3D	1	2,000	2,000	2,000
VALENTINE, Nelson (1960-) American				
oil	1	2,750	2,750	2,750
VALENTINE-DAINES, Sherree (1956-) British				
oil	2	1,295-1,476	1,385	1,295
VALENTINI, Vanni (20th C) Italian				
3D	1	3,048	3,048	3,048
VALENTINI, Walter (1912-1995) Italian				
oil	3	3,816-4,844	4,457	4,712
wc/d	6	1,937-7,375	4,471	3,982
VALENZUELA LLANOS, Alberto (1869-1923) Chilean				
oil	2	1,796-6,527	4,161	1,796
VALENZUELA, Gustavo (1974-) Chilean				
oil	2	1,900-2,100	2,000	1,900
VALERA, Victor (1927-) Venezuelan				
oil	1	3,720	3,720	3,720
3D	1	4,650	4,650	4,650
VALERI, Ugo (1874-1911) Italian				
wc/d	1	2,428	2,428	2,428
VALERIO, Theodore (1819-1879) French				
oil	1	5,041	5,041	5,041
wc/d	1	818	818	818
VALERY, Paul (1871-1945) French				
oil	1	3,857	3,857	3,857
VALETTE, Adolphe (1861-1942) French				
oil	5	3,009-13,875	8,167	9,072
wc/d	2	522-1,416	969	522
VALETTE, Pierre Adolphe (1876-1942) French				
oil	2	2,262-4,200	3,231	2,262
VALETTE, René (19/20th C) French				
wc/d	2	1,360-30,903	16,131	1,360
VALINOTTI, Domenico (1889-1962) Italian				
oil	2	1,211-1,432	1,321	1,211
VALK, Hendrik Jacobus (1897-1986) Dutch				
oil	2	1,512-2,521	2,016	1,512
VALKENBORCH, Gillis van (c.1570-1622) Flemish				
oil	1	25,950	25,950	25,950
VALKENBORCH, Lucas van (1535-1597) Flemish				
oil	1	59,200	59,200	59,200
VALKENBURG, Dirk (1675-1727) Dutch				
oil	2	15,288-37,380	26,334	15,288
VALKENBURG, Hendrik (1826-1896) Dutch				
oil	2	7,510-12,098	9,804	7,510
wc/d	1	1,200	1,200	1,200
VALLANCE, Jeffrey (20th C) ?				
oil	1	1,700	1,700	1,700
VALLANGCA, Roberto V (1907-1979) American				
oil	1	2,250	2,250	2,250
VALLATI, P (19th C) Italian				
oil	1	2,000	2,000	2,000
VALLAYER-COSTER, Anne (1744-1818) French				
oil	1	6,362	6,362	6,362
VALLAYER-MOUTET, Pauline (19th C) French				
oil	1	1,914	1,914	1,914
VALLEE, Étienne Maxime (19th C) French				
oil	5	1,166-5,260	2,439	1,767
VALLEE, Ludovic (1864-1939) French				
oil	1	2,474	2,474	2,474
VALLEJO, Don Francisco Antonio (fl.1752-1784) Mexican				
oil	1	9,500	9,500	9,500
VALLELY, John B (1941-) British				
oil	3	6,726-32,139	17,380	13,275
wc/d	4	925-2,422	1,885	1,947
VALLET, Edouard (1876-1929) Swiss				
oil	4	1,472-25,184	14,270	11,762
wc/d	5	913-8,372	4,683	5,675
VALLET-BISSON, Frederic (1865-?) French				
wc/d	1	8,522	8,522	8,522

Name	No.	Price Range	Average	Median
VALLET-GILLIARD, Marthe (1888-1918) Swiss				
oil	1	2,283	2,283	2,283
VALLEY, Jonas Joseph la (1858-1930) American				
oil	1	2,100	2,100	2,100
VALLGREN, Ville (1855-1940) French				
3D	7	3,471-13,050	6,793	4,114
VALLIN, Hugo Golli (1921-) Italian				
oil	1	4,758	4,758	4,758
VALLIN, Jacques Antoine (1760-1831) French				
oil	8	2,336-120,000	18,787	2,788
wc/d	1	1,798	1,798	1,798
VALLOIS, Paul Felix (19th C) French				
oil	1	2,922	2,922	2,922
VALLON, Joel (20th C) French				
oil	1	2,569	2,569	2,569
VALLONE, Vincenzo (1938-) Italian				
wc/d	2	3,527-4,474	4,000	3,527
VALLOT, L (20th C) ?				
3D	1	2,107	2,107	2,107
VALLOTTON, Felix (1865-1925) Swiss				
oil	26	17,947-1,858,500	204,103	83,717
wc/d	16	763-37,286	5,511	2,137
VALLS, Dino (1959-) Spanish				
oil	2	11,493-13,320	12,406	11,493
VALLS, Ernesto (1891-1941) ?				
oil	2	4,485-25,780	15,132	4,485
VALLS, Xavier (1923-) Spanish				
oil	3	7,500-18,000	11,000	7,500
wc/d	1	2,400	2,400	2,400
VALMIER, Georges (1885-1937) French				
oil	1	116,892	116,892	116,892
wc/d	12	5,130-21,014	11,992	9,678
VALMON, P (19th C) French				
oil	2	1,297-4,597	2,947	1,297
VALTAT, Louis (1869-1952) French				
oil	89	375-234,421	40,430	30,245
wc/d	25	586-18,000	3,346	1,987
VALTER, Frederick E (1850-1930) British				
oil	1	1,796	1,796	1,796
wc/d	4	555-920	729	708
VALTON, Charles (1851-1918) French				
3D	7	1,911-7,560	5,424	6,233
VALYRAKI, Mina Paptheodorou (1956-) Greek				
oil	1	5,610	5,610	5,610
VANAISE, Gustaaf (1854-1902) Belgian				
oil	2	1,377-1,520	1,448	1,377
VANCE, Karen (20th C) American				
oil	1	16,000	16,000	16,000
VANDENBERG, Philippe (1952-) Belgian?				
oil	3	1,753-2,805	2,328	2,428
VANDENBRANDEN, Guy (1926-) Belgian				
oil	7	468-4,243	1,278	909
wc/d	2	1,455-1,940	1,697	1,455
VANDERBACH, Count (19th C) British				
wc/d	1	1,418	1,418	1,418
VANDERBANK, John (1694-1739) British				
oil	1	9,405	9,405	9,405
VANDERBILT, Gloria (1924-) American				
oil	2	6,500-14,000	10,250	6,500
VANDERCAM, Serge (1924-2005) Danish				
oil	3	3,180-5,733	4,576	4,816
wc/d	1	1,771	1,771	1,771
3D	1	1,870	1,870	1,870
VANDERLICK, Armand (1897-1985) Belgian				
oil	7	764-5,034	2,886	3,273
wc/d	3	1,214-1,821	1,451	1,318
VANDERLYN, John (1775-1852) American				
oil	1	1,000	1,000	1,000
wc/d	2	1,400-4,750	3,075	1,400
VANDERSTEEN, Germain (1925-) French				
oil	2	878-1,200	1,039	878
wc/d	1	628	628	628

Name	No.	Price Range	Average	Median
VANDEVERDONCK, Franz (19th C) Belgian				
oil	1	1,230	1,230	1,230
VANDIERVORT, Louis (1875-1963) Belgian				
oil	1	4,442	4,442	4,442
VANGELLI, Antonio (1917-2004) Italian				
oil	6	453-1,260	731	592
wc/d	2	610-853	731	610
VANGI, Giuliano (1931-) Italian				
wc/d	3	2,395-5,088	3,672	3,534
3D	1	23,425	23,425	23,425
VANKA, Maximilian (1889-1963) Croatian				
oil	1	3,000	3,000	3,000
VANMOUR, Jan Baptiste (1671-1737) Flemish				
oil	2	21,979-23,353	22,666	21,979
VANNI, Francesco (c.1563-1610) Italian				
wc/d	2	1,546-8,500	5,023	1,546
VANNI, Giovanni Battista (1599-1660) Italian				
oil	1	92,500	92,500	92,500
VANNI, Sam (1908-1992) Finnish				
oil	5	760-19,286	6,778	3,343
wc/d	2	1,286-4,685	2,985	1,286
VANNUTELLI, Scipione (1834-1894) Italian				
oil	2	3,185-3,646	3,415	3,185
VANSTON, Dairine (1903-1988) Irish				
oil	1	1,636	1,636	1,636
VANZO, Julio (1901-1966) Argentinian				
oil	2	1,500-5,000	3,250	1,500
wc/d	1	1,200	1,200	1,200
VAQUERO TURCIOS, Joaquin (1933-) Spanish				
oil	2	1,384-3,375	2,379	1,384
wc/d	1	1,178	1,178	1,178
VARDANEGA, Gregorio (1923-) Argentinian				
3D	1	2,649	2,649	2,649
VARDHANA, S Harsha (1958-) Indian				
wc/d	1	12,000	12,000	12,000
VARELA, Emilio (1877-1951) Spanish				
oil	3	1,823-4,664	2,891	2,188
VARESE, Carlo (1903-?) Italian				
oil	4	703-4,500	2,014	973
VARESE, Gerelamo (1860-1935) Italian				
oil	1	1,914	1,914	1,914
VARGARES, S (?) ?				
3D	1	4,000	4,000	4,000
VARGAS, Alberto (1896-1983) American				
wc/d	1	28,000	28,000	28,000
VARGAS, Jo (1957-) French				
oil	1	1,051	1,051	1,051
VARI, Sophie (1940-) Greek				
oil	1	5,178	5,178	5,178
wc/d	1	1,730	1,730	1,730
3D	4	10,283-133,077	56,884	35,084
VARIAN, Dorothy (1895-1985) American				
oil	1	4,500	4,500	4,500
VARLEY, Charles Smith (1811-1888) British				
wc/d	1	1,229	1,229	1,229
VARLEY, Cornelius (1781-1873) British				
wc/d	7	513-27,680	7,465	1,295
VARLEY, Frederick Horsman (1881-1969) Canadian/British				
oil	3	36,076-115,213	85,880	106,351
wc/d	9	902-26,445	8,488	4,919
VARLEY, Illingworth (fl.1901-1909) British				
oil	1	2,394	2,394	2,394
VARLEY, John (1778-1842) British				
oil	2	546-9,450	4,998	546
wc/d	41	433-9,450	2,703	2,088
VARLIN, Willy Guggenheim (1900-1977) Swiss				
oil	7	9,410-34,044	19,003	17,639
wc/d	3	2,548-136,991	47,506	2,980
VARNI, Antonio (c.1840-1908) Italian				
oil	3	974-2,131	1,425	1,171
VARNIER, Charles (19/20th C) French				
wc/d	1	1,018	1,018	1,018

Name	No.	Price Range	Average	Median
VARO, Remedios (1900-1963) Spanish				
oil	2	15,350-300,000	157,675	15,350
wc/d	1	60,000	60,000	60,000
VAROTSOS, Costas (1955-) Greek				
oil	1	10,560	10,560	10,560
VARRAILHON, Anne (20th C) French				
oil	1	1,824	1,824	1,824
VARRONE, Johann (1832-1910) Austrian				
oil	1	1,665	1,665	1,665
VARVARO, Giovanni (1888-1973) Italian				
oil	1	5,438	5,438	5,438
VASA, Velizar (1933-) Yugoslavian				
oil	1	1,300	1,300	1,300
3D	5	3,000-4,250	3,650	3,750
VASARELY, Victor (1908-1997) Hungarian				
oil	103	3,884-250,000	48,319	37,178
wc/d	27	817-60,000	12,847	8,281
3D	16	1,874-60,204	8,939	4,097
VASELLI, Jacob (17/18th C) ?				
wc/d	1	1,914	1,914	1,914
VASILEFF, Ivan (1897-1966) Bulgarian				
oil	1	2,500	2,500	2,500
VASILIEV, Aleksei Sergeievich (1833-1877) Russian				
wc/d	1	19,842	19,842	19,842
VASILOVSKY, Sergei Ivanovich (1854-1917) Russian				
oil	2	17,100-53,940	35,520	17,100
VASNETSOV, Viktor Mikhaelovich (1848-1926) Russian				
oil	1	558,000	558,000	558,000
wc/d	3	840-51,600	17,852	1,116
VASNETZOV, Apollinar M (1856-1933) Russian				
oil	2	46,711-55,040	50,875	46,711
VASQUEZ BRITO, Ramón (1927-) Venezuelan				
oil	4	980-3,955	2,211	1,210
VASQUEZ, Carlos (1869-1944) Spanish				
oil	2	1,414-3,038	2,226	1,414
VASSALLO, Antonio Maria (17th C) Italian				
oil	1	39,973	39,973	39,973
VASSE, Louis Claude (1716-1772) French				
wc/d	1	1,189	1,189	1,189
VASSELON, Marius (19th C) French				
oil	1	2,408	2,408	2,408
VASSILACCHI, Antonio (1556-1629) Italian				
oil	2	14,887-15,429	15,158	14,887
VASSILIEFF, Marie (1894-1955) Russian				
oil	3	12,123-15,000	13,264	12,671
wc/d	6	1,215-37,500	17,233	8,990
VASSILIEFF, Nicolai (1892-1970) American/Russian				
oil	2	7,500-15,000	11,250	7,500
VASSILIEV, Oleg (1931-) Russian				
oil	2	17,670-52,080	34,875	17,670
VASSILIKIOTIS, Aristotelis (1902-1972) Greek				
oil	1	3,366	3,366	3,366
VASSILIOU, Spyros (1902-1984) Greek				
oil	15	4,325-45,240	20,558	16,830
wc/d	1	7,920	7,920	7,920
VASTAGH, Geza (1866-1919) Hungarian				
oil	2	17,000-160,000	88,500	17,000
VASTAGH, Gyorgy (elder) (1834-1922) Hungarian				
oil	1	1,052	1,052	1,052
VASTAGH, Gyorgy (younger) (1868-?) Hungarian				
3D	1	3,822	3,822	3,822
VASTON, Margaret de (19/20th C) Spanish				
oil	1	3,024	3,024	3,024
VASZARY, Janos (1867-1939) Hungarian				
oil	2	1,565-14,684	8,124	1,565
VATANURO, Oscar (?) ?				
oil	1	3,733	3,733	3,733
VAUGHAN, Keith (1912-1974) British				
oil	17	2,610-195,000	43,751	45,000
wc/d	40	463-41,580	10,832	3,294
VAUTHIER, Pierre (1845-1916) French				
oil	1	1,578	1,578	1,578

Name	No.	Price Range	Average	Median
VAUTHRIN, Ernest Germain (1878-1949) French				
oil	1	1,767	1,767	1,767
VAUTIER, Benjamin (elder) (1829-1898) German				
oil	6	3,263-57,819	27,298	16,743
wc/d	2	493-1,138	815	493
VAUTIER, Benjamin (younger) (1895-1974) Swiss				
oil	1	1,526	1,526	1,526
VAUTIER, Otto (1863-1919) Swiss				
oil	3	1,068-9,158	6,207	8,395
wc/d	3	496-5,342	2,404	1,374
VAUZELLE, Jean Lubin (1776-?) French				
wc/d	1	1,197	1,197	1,197
VAWTER, Mary Howey Murray (1871-1950) American				
oil	1	1,500	1,500	1,500
VAYREDA CANADELL, Josep Maria (1932-2001) Spanish				
oil	2	800-1,757	1,278	800
VAZ, Joao (1859-1931) Portuguese				
wc/d	1	1,215	1,215	1,215
VAZ, Oscar (1909-1987) Argentinian				
oil	7	2,200-21,000	10,680	6,500
VAZQUEZ DIAS, Daniel (1881-1969) Spanish				
oil	3	16,685-89,796	44,672	27,537
wc/d	6	599-1,665	986	927
VEAL, George (19th C) British				
oil	1	9,500	9,500	9,500
VEBER, Jean (1868-1928) French				
oil	2	2,384-2,384	2,384	2,384
wc/d	1	972	972	972
VECCHIA, Pietro della (1605-1678) Italian				
oil	2	5,890-102,857	54,373	5,890
VECCHIARINO, Leonardo (1956-) Italian				
oil	1	958	958	958
wc/d	1	1,197	1,197	1,197
VECCHIETTA, Lorenzo di Pietro di Giovanni (1405-1480) Italian				
oil	1	120,000	120,000	120,000
VECELLIO, Francesco (1483-1559) Italian				
oil	1	27,500	27,500	27,500
VECENAJ, Yvan (1920-) Yugoslavian				
oil	1	2,640	2,640	2,640
VEDANI, Michele (1874-?) Italian				
3D	4	1,556-3,884	2,467	1,916
VEDDER, Elihu (1836-1923) American				
oil	2	12,000-24,000	18,000	12,000
VEDEL, Herman (1875-1948) Danish				
oil	3	776-2,608	1,578	1,352
VEDOVA, Emilio (1919-) Italian				
oil	8	21,575-445,238	176,227	63,247
wc/d	15	1,070-38,054	17,943	17,678
3D	1	115,126	115,126	115,126
VEDOVA, Mario della (1958-) Italian				
3D	1	28,320	28,320	28,320
VEDOVE, Antonio delle (1865-?) Italian				
oil	1	7,000	7,000	7,000
VEEL, Armand le (1821-1905) French				
3D	1	8,505	8,505	8,505
VEEN, Otto van (1556-1629) Flemish				
oil	1	3,000	3,000	3,000
VEEN, Stuyvesant van (1910-1977) American				
wc/d	2	800-1,200	1,000	800
VEENFLIET, Richard (19th C) American				
wc/d	1	1,000	1,000	1,000
VEGA Y MARRUGAL, Jose de la (19th C) Spanish				
oil	1	5,890	5,890	5,890
VEGA, Jorge de la (1930-1971) Argentinian				
oil	1	7,000	7,000	7,000
VEILHAN, Xavier (1963-) French				
3D	1	25,103	25,103	25,103
VEILLON, Auguste-Louis (1834-1890) Swiss				
oil	6	2,284-8,609	4,225	3,100
VEIMBERG, Joannes (1918-1982) French				
oil	74	468-8,400	1,520	1,200

Name	No.	Price Range	Average	Median
VEISBERG, Vladimir Grigoryevich (1924-1985) Russian				
oil	2	115,320-120,900	118,110	115,320
wc/d	2	37,200-48,360	42,780	37,200
VEIT, H (19th C) ?				
oil	1	6,969	6,969	6,969
VEKEMANS, Bruno (20th C) Belgian?				
wc/d	3	957-2,472	1,541	1,196
VEKENS, Hugo van der (20th C) Belgian				
3D	1	4,756	4,756	4,756
VELA ZANETTI, Jose (1913-1999) Spanish				
oil	1	22,250	22,250	22,250
wc/d	4	1,373-5,724	2,611	1,647
VELA, Vincenzo (1820-1891) Italian				
3D	3	2,655-27,840	13,315	9,450
VELASCO (1960-) Italian				
oil	11	2,121-22,669	10,124	8,199
wc/d	8	1,214-21,848	5,838	2,054
VELASCO, Jose Maria (1840-1912) Mexican				
oil	1	70,000	70,000	70,000
VELASCO, Leandro (1933-) Colombian				
oil	2	1,200-1,200	1,200	1,200
VELASQUEZ, Diego Rodriguez de Silva y (1599-1660) Spanish				
oil	1	10,680	10,680	10,680
VELASQUEZ, Jose Antonio (1906-1983) Honduran				
oil	2	600-1,750	1,175	600
VELAZQUEZ, Eugenio Lucas (1817-1870) Spanish				
oil	4	3,827-22,595	10,990	8,507
wc/d	2	1,411-3,400	2,405	1,411
VELDE, Adriaen van de (1636-1672) Dutch				
oil	2	24,050-25,950	25,000	24,050
wc/d	3	634-6,423	3,208	2,569
VELDE, Bram van (1895-1981) Dutch				
oil	3	28,027-246,400	103,165	35,068
wc/d	2	1,688-17,810	9,749	1,688
VELDE, Esaias van de (1587-1630) Dutch				
oil	4	22,932-203,500	92,420	43,250
wc/d	1	8,758	8,758	8,758
VELDE, Geer van (1898-c.1977) Dutch				
oil	9	5,000-51,434	22,389	15,780
wc/d	22	1,212-10,062	3,397	2,910
VELDE, Hanny Vander (1883-?) American				
oil	1	1,100	1,100	1,100
VELDE, Henri van de (1896-1969) Dutch				
oil	2	715-1,818	1,266	715
wc/d	2	400-3,575	1,987	400
VELDE, Henry Clemens van de (1863-1957) Belgian				
oil	1	1,224	1,224	1,224
VELDE, Pieter van de (1634-?) Flemish				
oil	6	7,120-30,362	17,651	12,025
VELDE, Willem van de (elder) (1611-1693) Dutch				
wc/d	14	2,768-220,000	82,491	70,000
VELDE, Willem van de (younger) (1633-1707) Dutch				
oil	2	10,192-24,670	17,431	10,192
wc/d	9	550-15,570	7,364	6,000
VELDEN, Adrianus Dirk Blok van der (1913-1980) Dutch				
oil	1	2,314	2,314	2,314
VELDEN, Petrus van der (1837-1915) New Zealander/Dutch				
oil	1	26,000	26,000	26,000
VELDHUYZEN, Willem Frederik (1814-1873) Dutch				
oil	1	1,475	1,475	1,475
VELEZ, Christian (20th C) French				
wc/d	1	3,649	3,649	3,649
VELICKOVIC, Vladimir (1935-) Yugoslavian				
oil	11	722-15,780	7,019	5,562
wc/d	7	409-5,720	2,553	1,868
VELLACOTT, Elizabeth (1905-) British				
wc/d	1	2,492	2,492	2,492
VELLAN, Felice (1889-1976) Italian				
oil	18	716-4,849	2,035	1,386
wc/d	1	606	606	606
VELLUTINI, Pierre (20th C) French?				
oil	3	533-1,598	1,045	1,006
wc/d	1	1,243	1,243	1,243

Name	No.	Price Range	Average	Median
VELMAN, J E (19th C) Dutch				
oil	1	2,751	2,751	2,751
VELSEN, Jacob Jansz van (?-1656) Dutch				
oil	1	11,564	11,564	11,564
VELTEN, Wilhelm (1847-1929) Russian				
oil	20	1,585-16,272	4,448	3,100
VELTZ, Ivan (1866-1926) Russian				
oil	2	42,164-60,200	51,182	42,164
VELZEN, Johannes Petrus van (1816-1853) Dutch				
oil	2	647-1,567	1,107	647
VEN, Paul van der (1892-?) Dutch				
oil	1	2,330	2,330	2,330
VENA, Angel Domingo (1888-1963) Argentinian				
oil	1	2,300	2,300	2,300
VENARD, Claude (1913-1999) French				
oil	46	600-20,760	4,450	3,245
wc/d	2	742-3,461	2,101	742
VENET, Bernar (1941-) French				
oil	2	9,555-11,438	10,496	9,555
wc/d	12	3,200-15,535	8,171	7,249
3D	3	15,196-52,980	30,839	24,342
VENETSIANOV, Alexei Gavrilovich (1780-1847) Russian				
oil	1	4,331,507	4,331,507	4,331,507
VENI, R (19th C) Austrian				
oil	1	2,610	2,610	2,610
VENIOS, Markos (1946-) Greek				
oil	1	1,936	1,936	1,936
VENNA, Lucio (1897-1974) Italian				
oil	1	849	849	849
wc/d	2	1,171-1,874	1,522	1,171
VENNE, Adolf van der (1828-1911) Austrian				
oil	5	1,300-4,000	2,203	2,125
VENNE, Adriaen Pietersz van de (1589-1662) Dutch				
oil	3	18,502-66,247	37,592	28,027
VENNE, Jan van de (1636-?) Dutch				
oil	1	2,661	2,661	2,661
VENNE, Jan van de (?-c.1650) Flemish				
oil	1	6,370	6,370	6,370
VENNEMAN, Charles (1802-1875) Flemish				
oil	1	2,803	2,803	2,803
VENOTTI, M (19th C) Italian				
oil	1	4,576	4,576	4,576
VENT, Hans (1934-) German				
oil	1	789	789	789
wc/d	1	494	494	494
VENTO, Jose (1925-2005) Spanish				
oil	2	951-3,588	2,269	951
VENTO, Vicente (20th C) Argentinian				
oil	2	1,600-2,000	1,800	1,600
VENTRONE, Luciano (1942-) Italian				
oil	1	3,514	3,514	3,514
VENTURA MILLAN, Manuel (1923-1984) Spanish				
oil	2	2,238-3,616	2,927	2,238
VENTURELLI, Gerard (1949-) ?				
oil	1	2,101	2,101	2,101
VENTURI, Osvaldo (20th C) Argentinian				
wc/d	1	3,200	3,200	3,200
VENUS, Albert Franz (1842-1871) German				
oil	2	2,524-4,039	3,281	2,524
wc/d	1	1,532	1,532	1,532
VENUSIO, G (?) Italian				
oil	1	1,764	1,764	1,764
VERA GONZALEZ, Jose (1861-1936) Spanish				
oil	1	3,279	3,279	3,279
VERA, Cristino de (1931-) Spanish				
oil	2	12,721-20,400	16,560	12,721
VERANNEMAN, Emiel (1924-) Belgian				
3D	1	25,286	25,286	25,286
VERBAERE, Herman (1906-1993) Belgian				
wc/d	1	1,073	1,073	1,073
VERBANCK, Geo (1881-1961) Belgian				
3D	1	1,821	1,821	1,821

Name	No.	Price Range	Average	Median
VERBEECK, Cornelis (1590-c.1635) Dutch				
oil	3	12,110-18,685	15,931	17,000
VERBEECK, François Xavier Henri (1686-1755) Flemish				
oil	1	11,444	11,444	11,444
VERBEECK, Frans (?-1570) Flemish				
oil	1	22,794	22,794	22,794
VERBEEK, Gustave A (1867-1937) American				
oil	1	4,200	4,200	4,200
VERBEEK, P (18th C) Dutch				
wc/d	1	8,000	8,000	8,000
VERBEET, Willem (1801-c.1840) Dutch				
wc/d	1	1,052	1,052	1,052
VERBOECKHOVEN, Eugène (1798-1881) Belgian				
oil	32	1,100-138,767	26,421	16,069
wc/d	8	468-2,249	1,034	882
3D	1	3,392	3,392	3,392
VERBOECKHOVEN, Eugène and VERWEE, Louis (19th C) Belgian				
oil	1	11,040	11,040	11,040
VERBOECKHOVEN, Louis (1802-1889) Belgian				
oil	13	2,805-20,469	7,199	7,159
VERBOOM, Adriaen (1628-1670) Dutch				
oil	1	28,524	28,524	28,524
VERBRUGGE, Jean Charles (1756-1831) Flemish				
wc/d	1	2,201	2,201	2,201
VERBRUGGEN, Gaspar Pieter I (1635-1687) Flemish				
oil	1	40,000	40,000	40,000
VERBRUGGEN, Gaspar Pieter II (1664-1730) Flemish				
oil	1	25,950	25,950	25,950
VERBRUGGHE, Charles (1877-1974) Belgian				
oil	4	1,013-1,636	1,317	1,070
VERBRUGGHE, H (1886-1957) Belgian				
oil	2	2,026-2,384	2,205	2,026
VERBURGH, Dionys (1655-1722) Dutch				
oil	2	7,043-11,678	9,360	7,043
VERBURGH, Medard (1886-1957) Belgian				
oil	4	656-5,096	2,920	2,071
wc/d	4	537-954	773	764
VERBURGH, Rutger (1678-1746) Dutch				
oil	1	18,500	18,500	18,500
VERCELLI, Giulio Romano (1871-1951) Italian				
oil	10	637-2,267	1,405	1,323
VERCRUYSSE, Jan (1948-) Dutch?				
3D	1	5,993	5,993	5,993
VERDE RUBIO, Ricardo (1876-1955) Spanish				
oil	2	644-1,399	1,021	644
VERDEGEM, Jos (1897-1957) Belgian				
wc/d	1	6,712	6,712	6,712
VERDET, Andre (20th C) French				
oil	1	1,929	1,929	1,929
VERDI, E (19th C) Italian				
wc/d	1	1,780	1,780	1,780
VERDIER, François (1651-1730) French				
wc/d	2	500-2,977	1,738	500
VERDIER, Jean Louis (1849-1895) French				
oil	2	1,400-1,500	1,450	1,400
VERDIER, Marcel Antoine (1817-1856) French				
oil	1	1,637	1,637	1,637
VERDILHAN, Mathieu (1875-1928) French				
oil	6	1,907-30,993	11,148	6,146
wc/d	3	529-860	668	615
VERDOEL, Adriaan (1620-1695) Dutch				
oil	1	20,384	20,384	20,384
VERDUSSEN, Jan Peeter (1700-1763) Flemish				
oil	1	30,260	30,260	30,260
VERDYEN, Eugène (1836-1903) Belgian				
oil	2	2,221-3,299	2,760	2,221
VERELST, Pieter (c.1618-1668) Dutch				
oil	2	4,625-70,300	37,462	4,625
VERELST, Simon (1644-1721) Dutch				
oil	1	24,220	24,220	24,220
VERENDAEL, Nicolas van (1640-1691) Flemish				
oil	2	25,691-200,000	112,845	25,691

Name	No.	Price Range	Average	Median
VERESMITH, Daniel Albert (1861-1932) German				
oil	1	3,132	3,132	3,132
VERETSHCHAGIN, Piotr (1836-1886) Russian				
oil	4	55,800-1,300,000	435,700	129,000
VERETSHCHAGIN, Vassily Vasilievich (1842-1904) Russian				
oil	1	95,000	95,000	95,000
wc/d	1	5,160	5,160	5,160
VEREYCKEN, Edouard (1893-1967) Belgian				
3D	1	15,600	15,600	15,600
VERGA, Angelo (1933-) Italian				
oil	1	2,957	2,957	2,957
VERGARA GREZ, Ramon (20th C) Chilean				
oil	1	1,200	1,200	1,200
VERGE-SARRAT, Henri (1880-1966) French				
oil	1	1,176	1,176	1,176
VERGHI, Chryssa (1959-) Greek				
oil	1	3,872	3,872	3,872
VERHAECHT, Tobias (1561-1631) Flemish				
oil	2	12,857-76,120	44,488	12,857
VERHAEGEN, Fernand (1884-1976) Belgian				
oil	7	2,071-8,905	4,167	3,612
wc/d	1	1,078	1,078	1,078
VERHAERT, Dirck (17th C) Dutch				
oil	4	3,380-7,032	4,978	4,500
VERHAGEN, Pierre Jean Joseph (1728-1811) Flemish				
oil	2	7,791-33,300	20,545	7,791
VERHAS, Frans (c.1827-1897) Belgian				
oil	4	9,000-99,358	46,991	9,643
VERHAS, Jan Frans (1834-1896) Belgian				
oil	2	3,960-180,000	91,980	3,960
wc/d	1	1,401	1,401	1,401
VERHAS, Theodor (1811-1872) German				
oil	1	4,417	4,417	4,417
wc/d	2	1,010-1,514	1,262	1,010
VERHEYDEN, François (1806-1889) Belgian				
oil	2	865-1,865	1,365	865
VERHEYDEN, Isidore (1848-1905) Belgian				
oil	15	971-65,405	8,341	3,153
VERHEYEN, Bart (1963-) Belgian				
oil	1	2,349	2,349	2,349
VERHEYEN, Jan Hendrik (1778-1846) Dutch				
oil	2	1,752-11,063	6,407	1,752
VERHEYEN, Jef (1932-1984) Belgian				
oil	8	1,638-46,757	14,314	7,510
VERHOEF, Hans (20th C) Dutch				
oil	2	1,295-1,295	1,295	1,295
VERHOEK, Gysbert (1644-1690) Dutch				
wc/d	1	1,781	1,781	1,781
VERHOESEN, A (1806-1881) Dutch				
oil	4	1,874-3,755	2,892	2,788
VERHOESEN, Albertus (1806-1881) Dutch				
oil	21	949-10,305	3,451	2,500
VERHOEVEN, Jan (1870-1941) Dutch				
oil	1	3,497	3,497	3,497
VERHOEVEN-BALL, Adrien Joseph (1824-1882) Belgian				
oil	2	957-1,900	1,428	957
VERKADE, Kees (1941-) Dutch				
3D	9	4,909-21,041	9,476	6,997
VERKERK, Emo (1955-) Dutch				
wc/d	1	5,733	5,733	5,733
VERKOLJE, Jan (1650-1693) Dutch				
oil	1	14,013	14,013	14,013
VERKOLJE, Nicolaes (1673-1746) Dutch				
oil	1	58,389	58,389	58,389
wc/d	1	3,737	3,737	3,737
VERLAT, Charles Michel Maria (1824-1890) Belgian				
oil	7	595-27,435	7,128	3,612
VERLET, Raoul (1857-1923) French				
3D	4	1,885-6,264	4,661	4,281
VERLINDE, Claude (1927-) ?				
oil	2	878-3,000	1,939	878

Name	No.	Price Range	Average	Median
VERLING, Walter (1930-) Irish				
oil	2	848-2,182	1,515	848
VERLON, Andre (1917-1993) Swiss				
oil	2	844-1,286	1,065	844
VERLY, Adelin (1883-1967) Belgian				
oil	1	5,419	5,419	5,419
VERMEER OF HAARLEM, Jan (elder) (1628-1691) Dutch				
oil	1	74,000	74,000	74,000
VERMEER OF HAARLEM, Jan (younger) (1656-1705) Dutch				
wc/d	1	2,102	2,102	2,102
VERMEHREN, Frederik (1822-1910) Danish				
oil	1	1,746	1,746	1,746
VERMEHREN, Sophus (1866-1950) Danish				
oil	2	404-3,952	2,178	404
VERMEIRE, Jules (1885-1977) Dutch				
wc/d	1	1,165	1,165	1,165
3D	6	3,299-10,813	5,909	4,703
VERMEIRE, Paul (1928-) Belgian				
oil	1	1,147	1,147	1,147
VERMEULEN, A (1763-1814) Dutch				
oil	1	2,088	2,088	2,088
VERMEULEN, Andreas Franciscus (1821-1884) Dutch				
oil	1	2,400	2,400	2,400
VERMEULEN, Andries (1763-1814) Dutch				
oil	5	4,944-22,932	13,188	13,840
wc/d	2	467-3,737	2,102	467
VERMEULEN, Marinus Cornelis Thomas (1868-1941) Dutch				
oil	1	1,334	1,334	1,334
VERMI, Arturo (1929-1988) Italian				
oil	8	1,908-6,615	4,365	4,757
wc/d	6	1,229-8,199	3,767	2,090
VERMONT, Nicolae (1886-1932) Rumanian				
oil	1	1,528	1,528	1,528
VERMORCKEN, Frederic Marie (1860-1946) Belgian				
oil	1	2,400	2,400	2,400
VERMOTE, Seraphin Francois (1788-1837) Belgian				
oil	1	2,777	2,777	2,777
VERNA, Claudio (1937-) Italian				
oil	2	2,386-3,034	2,710	2,386
wc/d	1	712	712	712
VERNA, Germaine (1900-1975) French				
oil	10	425-1,800	1,182	1,200
VERNAZZA, Eduardo (1910-1991) South American				
oil	1	1,100	1,100	1,100
VERNER, Elizabeth O'Neill (1884-1979) American				
wc/d	2	18,000-22,000	20,000	18,000
VERNER, Frederick Arthur (1836-1928) Canadian				
oil	2	4,431-13,194	8,812	4,431
wc/d	13	412-14,180	6,907	5,773
VERNET, Carle (1758-1836) French				
wc/d	4	2,000-22,500	7,505	2,022
VERNET, Horace (1789-1863) French				
oil	4	3,591-40,000	17,471	9,955
wc/d	3	450-10,000	4,126	1,929
VERNET, Joseph (1714-1789) French				
oil	5	14,240-184,324	110,925	138,750
wc/d	2	701-9,722	5,211	701
VERNIER, Émile Louis (1829-1887) French				
oil	6	1,068-10,207	4,216	2,510
VERNON, Arthur Langley (fl.1871-1922) British				
oil	2	1,850-6,000	3,925	1,850
VERNON, Emile (19/20th C) British				
oil	4	1,200-140,000	46,471	16,685
wc/d	1	1,634	1,634	1,634
VERNON, Harold (?) British				
oil	1	1,728	1,728	1,728
VERNON, Paul (1796-1875) French				
oil	2	1,767-2,592	2,179	1,767
VERON (19th C) French				
oil	1	4,756	4,756	4,756
VERON, Alexandre René (1826-1897) French				
oil	13	666-13,000	5,446	5,021

Name	No.	Price Range	Average	Median
VERON-FARE, Jules Henri (19th C) French				
oil	1	1,200	1,200	1,200
VERONE (20th C) Swiss				
oil	2	571-2,119	1,345	571
VERONESE, Paolo (1528-1588) Italian				
wc/d	1	32,500	32,500	32,500
VERONESI, Luigi (1908-1998) Italian				
oil	17	3,949-28,479	10,780	10,356
wc/d	12	450-6,008	2,305	1,784
VERONIQUE, Blanche (?) French?				
wc/d	1	3,658	3,658	3,658
VERREYT, Jacob Johan (1807-1872) Belgian				
oil	3	939-2,114	1,421	1,210
VERRIER, Max le (19/20th C) Belgian				
3D	1	3,633	3,633	3,633
VERRYCK, Theodor (1734-1786) Dutch				
wc/d	3	589-3,754	2,070	1,868
VERSCHAEREN, Bart (1888-1946) Belgian				
oil	1	1,430	1,430	1,430
VERSCHAEREN, Theodoor (1874-1937) Belgian				
oil	4	808-2,984	1,561	1,210
VERSCHAFFELT, Edouard (1874-1955) Belgian				
oil	6	1,911-36,821	13,269	7,591
VERSCHOOR, Jan (1943-) Dutch				
3D	1	4,948	4,948	4,948
VERSCHUIER, Lieve (1630-1686) Dutch				
oil	1	34,600	34,600	34,600
VERSCHURING, Hendrik (1627-1690) Dutch				
oil	1	35,000	35,000	35,000
VERSCHUUR, Wouter (jnr) (1841-1936) Dutch				
oil	3	1,462-3,250	2,079	1,526
VERSCHUUR, Wouter (snr) (1812-1874) Dutch				
oil	13	343-110,625	26,799	11,743
wc/d	2	1,678-3,014	2,346	1,678
VERSPRONCK, Jan (1597-1662) Dutch				
oil	1	7,856	7,856	7,856
VERSPUY, Gysbertus Johannes (1823-1862) Dutch				
oil	1	2,238	2,238	2,238
VERSTEEGH, Michiel (1756-1843) Dutch				
oil	2	5,531-14,240	9,885	5,531
VERSTER, Floris (1861-1927) Dutch				
oil	1	12,292	12,292	12,292
VERSTRAETE, Theodore (1850-1907) Belgian				
oil	2	5,007-5,993	5,500	5,007
VERSTRAETEN, Alfred (1858-1936) Belgian				
oil	1	1,001	1,001	1,001
VERSTRAETEN, Edmond (1870-1956) Belgian				
oil	2	1,023-3,507	2,265	1,023
VERSTRALEN, Anthonie (1594-1641) Dutch				
oil	3	10,669-152,877	91,515	111,000
VERTANGEN, Daniel (1598-1684) Dutch				
oil	2	3,857-11,003	7,430	3,857
VERTES, Marcel (1895-1961) French				
oil	10	584-6,838	2,524	1,253
wc/d	4	750-3,400	1,996	834
VERTEVILLE, Christian de la (1949-) French				
wc/d	1	1,607	1,607	1,607
VERTEVILLE, Jean de (20th C) French				
wc/d	2	1,451-1,607	1,529	1,451
VERTIN, Petrus Gerardus (1819-1893) Dutch				
oil	12	712-11,677	4,960	3,527
wc/d	1	2,182	2,182	2,182
VERTUNNI, Achille (1826-1897) Italian				
oil	4	3,000-9,000	5,359	3,360
VERVEER, Mauritz (1817-1903) Dutch				
oil	1	3,004	3,004	3,004
VERVEER, Salomon Leonardus (1813-1876) Dutch				
oil	10	2,397-21,014	11,489	10,672
wc/d	2	648-2,910	1,779	648
VERVIER, J (19th C) ?				
oil	1	2,001	2,001	2,001

Name	No.	Price Range	Average	Median
VERVISCH, Godfried (1930-) Belgian				
oil	1	2,421	2,421	2,421
VERVISCH, Jean (1896-1977) Belgian				
oil	2	964-1,414	1,189	964
VERVLOET, Frans (1795-1872) Dutch				
oil	5	2,102-70,541	27,219	7,562
wc/d	2	1,560-2,160	1,860	1,560
VERVOU, Pierre (1822-1913) Belgian				
oil	1	2,071	2,071	2,071
VERWEE, Alfred Jacques (1838-1895) Belgian				
oil	4	1,517-3,646	2,553	2,411
VERWEE, Charles Louis (?-1882) Belgian				
oil	1	7,644	7,644	7,644
VERWEE, Louis Pierre (1807-1877) Belgian				
oil	6	1,204-40,767	10,338	3,153
VERWEE, Louis Pierre and VERBOECKHOVEN, Eugène (19th C) Belgian				
oil	1	78,261	78,261	78,261
VERWER, Justus (c.1626-c.1688) Dutch				
oil	1	6,938	6,938	6,938
VERWEY, Kees (1900-1995) Dutch				
oil	4	1,764-10,788	4,796	2,879
wc/d	1	2,997	2,997	2,997
VERWILT, François (1620-1691) Dutch				
oil	2	3,196-5,260	4,228	3,196
VERZETTI, Libero (1906-1989) Italian				
oil	4	1,034-1,539	1,205	1,065
VESCOVI, Dani (1969-) Italian				
oil	2	2,421-6,990	4,705	2,421
VESIN, Jaroslav Fr Julius (1859-1915) Bulgarian				
oil	2	10,603-42,500	26,551	10,603
VESNIN, Alexander (1883-1959) Russian				
wc/d	2	6,353-24,180	15,266	6,353
VESPASIANI, Mario (1978-) Italian				
oil	8	671-1,097	796	707
wc/d	1	597	597	597
VESPEIRA (1925-2000) Portuguese				
wc/d	1	3,403	3,403	3,403
VESPIGNANI, Renzo (1924-2001) Italian				
oil	11	2,000-16,386	8,778	9,384
wc/d	8	1,168-11,931	4,676	3,307
VEST, Jim (20th C) Canadian				
oil	1	1,152	1,152	1,152
VESTER, Willem (1824-1895) Dutch				
oil	3	936-5,605	3,737	4,671
VESTIER, Antoine (1740-1824) French				
oil	3	6,082-75,000	29,561	7,603
VETH, Jan (1864-1925) Dutch				
oil	2	1,072-1,649	1,360	1,072
VETSCH, Christian (20th C) Swiss				
oil	3	725-3,263	1,626	892
VETTER, Charles (1858-1936) German				
oil	3	4,600-18,522	9,920	6,640
VETTRIANO, Jack (1954-) British				
oil	22	4,800-504,600	52,491	23,375
VEYRASSAT, J J (1828-1893) French				
oil	1	5,173	5,173	5,173
VEYRASSAT, Jules Jacques (1828-1893) French				
oil	12	1,255-42,500	9,014	4,123
wc/d	3	595-900	736	714
VEZZANI, F (19th C) Italian?				
oil	1	12,055	12,055	12,055
VEZZO, Virginia da (1601-1638) Italian				
oil	1	67,315	67,315	67,315
VIALA, Eugene (1859-1913) French				
wc/d	1	2,589	2,589	2,589
VIALET, Laurent (1967-) French				
oil	1	2,384	2,384	2,384
VIALLAT, Claude (1936-) French				
oil	10	3,748-18,062	9,724	8,365
wc/d	8	537-8,237	1,779	597
VIALOV, Konstantin (1900-1976) Russian				
oil	1	40,920	40,920	40,920

Name	No.	Price Range	Average	Median
VIANELLI, Achille (1803-1894) Italian				
wc/d	5	1,171-4,024	2,360	1,752
VIANELLI, Alberto (1841-1927) Italian				
oil	1	3,758	3,758	3,758
VIANELLO, Cesare (1862-1915) Italian				
oil	3	2,500-6,096	3,754	2,667
VIANI, Alberto (1906-1989) Italian				
wc/d	1	1,272	1,272	1,272
3D	1	8,000	8,000	8,000
VIANI, Antonio Maria (c.1555-1620) Italian				
oil	1	6,336	6,336	6,336
VIANI, Lorenzo (1882-1936) Italian				
oil	4	16,407-76,130	56,552	63,605
wc/d	16	477-12,123	3,132	840
VIAUD, Charles (1920-1975) French				
oil	1	1,578	1,578	1,578
VIAVANT, George L (1872-1925) American				
wc/d	6	9,000-35,000	20,000	10,500
VIAVANT, Ruby (20th C) American				
wc/d	1	2,700	2,700	2,700
VIAZZI, Cesare (1857-1943) Italian				
oil	1	1,640	1,640	1,640
VIBERT, Jean Georges (1840-1902) French				
oil	5	935-160,000	63,487	25,000
wc/d	3	5,000-18,000	10,333	8,000
VICARI, Andrew (1938-) British				
wc/d	1	1,464	1,464	1,464
VICENTE, Eduardo (1909-1968) Spanish				
oil	4	1,688-7,774	3,911	1,808
wc/d	2	559-1,094	826	559
VICENTE, Esteban (1906-2001) American/Spanish				
oil	4	18,000-123,200	66,550	30,000
wc/d	1	19,000	19,000	19,000
VICHI, Ferdinando (19th C) Italian				
3D	7	1,971-40,000	12,083	4,000
VICKERS, A (19th C) British				
oil	1	2,303	2,303	2,303
VICKERS, A H (fl.1853-1907) British				
oil	2	1,239-1,320	1,279	1,239
VICKERS, Alfred (19th C) British				
oil	3	496-905	749	846
wc/d	1	522	522	522
VICKERS, Alfred (snr) (1786-1868) British				
oil	9	552-4,900	2,887	3,250
VICKERS, Alfred Gomersal (1810-1837) British				
wc/d	4	952-5,292	2,642	1,730
VICKERS, Alfred H (fl.1853-1907) British				
oil	12	498-3,366	1,463	945
VICKERS, Emilie E (19/20th C) Irish?				
wc/d	1	1,920	1,920	1,920
VICKERS, Henry Harold (1851-1919) British				
oil	9	690-1,940	1,141	882
VICKINS, A H (20th C) ?				
oil	1	2,805	2,805	2,805
VICKREY, Robert (1926-) American				
oil	8	2,600-18,000	6,550	4,100
VICTOR, L (19th C) American?				
oil	1	1,200	1,200	1,200
VICTORIA, Salvador (1929-1994) Spanish				
oil	2	2,511-2,754	2,632	2,511
wc/d	1	1,492	1,492	1,492
VICTORICA, Miguel Carlos (1884-1955) Argentinian				
oil	1	9,000	9,000	9,000
wc/d	1	2,000	2,000	2,000
VICTORS, Jacobus (1640-1705) Dutch				
oil	1	35,671	35,671	35,671
VICTORS, Jan (1620-1676) Dutch				
oil	5	30,208-101,918	65,016	70,000
VICTORYNS, Anthonie (1612-1655) Flemish				
oil	1	8,035	8,035	8,035
VIDAL, Francisco (1898-1980) Argentinian				
oil	1	9,550	9,550	9,550

Name	No.	Price Range	Average	Median
VIDAL, Francisco (fl.1867-1889) Spanish?				
oil	1	2,800	2,800	2,800
VIDAL, Gustave (1895-1966) French				
oil	9	666-3,810	1,492	1,097
VIDAL, Henri (1864-1918) French				
3D	1	2,088	2,088	2,088
VIDAL, Louis (1754-1807) French				
wc/d	1	7,770	7,770	7,770
VIDAL, Louis (1831-1892) French				
3D	1	3,480	3,480	3,480
VIDAL, Miguel Angel (1928-) Argentinian				
oil	2	3,000-5,500	4,250	3,000
VIDON, Marie (1948-) French				
oil	3	1,080-1,200	1,140	1,140
VIDOVSZKY, Bela (1883-?) Hungarian				
oil	1	1,543	1,543	1,543
VIDROVITCH, Nina (1930-) French				
oil	1	2,686	2,686	2,686
VIE, Gabriel (1888-1973) French				
oil	2	922-1,193	1,057	922
VIEGENER, Eberhard (1890-1969) German				
oil	3	1,401-21,205	8,393	2,574
wc/d	3	2,548-3,038	2,712	2,552
VIEGERS, Bernardus Petrus (1886-1947) Dutch				
oil	8	839-3,299	1,623	1,134
wc/d	1	1,296	1,296	1,296
VIEILLARD, Fabien (1877-1904) French				
oil	2	3,534-6,479	5,006	3,534
VIEILLEVOYE, Barthelemy Josef (1788-1855) Belgian				
oil	1	1,564	1,564	1,564
VIEIRA DA SILVA, Maria Elena (1908-1992) French/Portuguese				
oil	23	15,904-510,400	178,360	160,950
wc/d	15	12,959-457,361	76,156	29,452
VIELRICH, I (?) ?				
oil	1	3,371	3,371	3,371
VIERA, F (18th C) ?				
oil	1	3,781	3,781	3,781
VIERIN, Emmanuel (1869-1954) Belgian				
oil	2	1,139-1,169	1,154	1,139
VIERKANT, Brigitte (1942-) German				
oil	1	3,200	3,200	3,200
VIERRA, Carlos (1876-1937) American				
oil	3	4,500-9,500	7,166	7,500
VIERTHALER, Ludwig (1875-?) German				
3D	1	1,800	1,800	1,800
VIETTI, Nicola (1945-) French				
oil	9	492-1,590	814	712
wc/d	1	553	553	553
VIGAS, Oswaldo (1926-) Venezuelan				
oil	4	1,860-7,210	4,897	5,120
wc/d	2	560-700	630	560
VIGE, Jens (1864-1912) Danish				
oil	1	1,825	1,825	1,825
VIGEE, Louis (1715-1767) French				
wc/d	4	1,901-4,152	3,217	3,270
VIGEE-LEBRUN, Marie Louise Elisabeth (1755-1842) French				
oil	2	2,571-48,163	25,367	2,571
wc/d	1	18,904	18,904	18,904
VIGELIUS, Viktor (19/20th C) ?				
oil	1	2,919	2,919	2,919
VIGER DU VIGNEAU, Jean Louis Victor (1819-1879) French				
oil	1	3,254	3,254	3,254
VIGNALI, Jacopo (1592-1664) Italian				
oil	2	24,920-30,000	27,460	24,920
wc/d	1	2,022	2,022	2,022
VIGNANI, Giuseppe (1932-) Italian				
oil	10	895-2,195	1,342	1,178
VIGNAUD, Jean (1775-1826) French				
oil	1	19,027	19,027	19,027
VIGNE, Emma de (1850-1896) Belgian				
oil	1	1,019	1,019	1,019

Name	No.	Price Range	Average	Median
VIGNOLES, Andre (1920-) French				
oil	13	550-4,250	1,852	1,682
VIGNON, Claude (1593-1670) French				
oil	1	12,945	12,945	12,945
VIGNON, Victor Alfred Paul (1847-1909) French				
oil	8	1,005-20,125	8,342	5,363
wc/d	1	1,401	1,401	1,401
VIGOR, Charles (fl.1882-1917) British				
oil	1	52,920	52,920	52,920
VIGOUREUX, Paul Maurice (1876-?) French				
oil	1	2,016	2,016	2,016
VIGOUREUX, Pierre Octave (1884-?) French				
3D	1	1,764	1,764	1,764
VIGUIER, Fortune (19th C) French				
oil	1	1,451	1,451	1,451
VIKATOS, Spyros (1878-1960) Greek				
oil	3	2,464-5,610	3,626	2,805
VIKSTEN, Hans (1926-1987) Swedish				
oil	3	700-1,718	1,224	1,255
VILA GRAU, Joan (1932-) Spanish				
oil	1	1,176	1,176	1,176
VILA PUIG, Juan (1890-1963) Spanish				
oil	1	1,286	1,286	1,286
VILA Y PRADES, Julio (1873-1930) Spanish				
oil	3	777-1,211	921	777
wc/d	2	668-1,176	922	668
VILAIN, Walter (1938-) Belgian				
oil	1	1,212	1,212	1,212
VILALLONGA, Jesus Carlos de (1927-) Canadian				
oil	7	749-1,814	1,169	1,146
VILAR TORRES, Jose (1828-1904) Spanish				
oil	2	2,649-8,381	5,515	2,649
VILATO, Javier (1921-2000) French				
oil	2	2,425-4,995	3,710	2,425
VILHUNEN, Risto (1945-) Finnish				
oil	1	1,271	1,271	1,271
VILLA, Aleardo (1865-1906) Italian				
wc/d	1	1,539	1,539	1,539
VILLA, Émile (19th C) French				
oil	1	3,250	3,250	3,250
VILLA, Hernando (1881-1952) American				
oil	4	850-3,750	2,462	2,000
wc/d	3	1,000-2,000	1,533	1,600
VILLA-TORO, Antonio (1949-) Spanish				
oil	1	5,272	5,272	5,272
VILLAGRAN, Armando (1945-1995) Mexican				
oil	1	1,350	1,350	1,350
VILLAIN, Ernest le (1834-1916) French				
oil	2	1,430-1,929	1,679	1,430
wc/d	1	2,259	2,259	2,259
VILLAIN, Henri (1878-1938) French				
oil	1	1,295	1,295	1,295
VILLAIN, Henri Georges (19th C) French				
oil	1	2,057	2,057	2,057
VILLALBA, Dario (1939-) Spanish				
oil	2	1,748-21,551	11,649	1,748
VILLALOBOS MASTER (15th C) Spanish				
oil	1	24,050	24,050	24,050
VILLALOBOS, Jose Antonio (1935-) Mexican				
3D	1	2,200	2,200	2,200
VILLAMIL MARRACHI, Bernardo (19th C) Spanish				
oil	1	3,616	3,616	3,616
VILLANI, Gennaro (1885-1948) Italian				
oil	1	1,401	1,401	1,401
VILLANIS, E (19th C) French				
3D	1	1,929	1,929	1,929
VILLANIS, Emmanuele (1880-1920) Italian				
3D	18	1,942-7,864	3,309	3,000
VILLAPAREDES, Esteban (1933-) Venezuelan				
oil	4	1,490-3,255	2,233	1,630
VILLAR, Isabel (1934-) Spanish				
oil	1	2,290	2,290	2,290

Name	No.	Price Range	Average	Median
VILLAR, Jesus (1930-) Spanish				
oil	3	500-1,874	1,162	1,113
VILLARS, P (?) ?				
oil	1	4,295	4,295	4,295
VILLE, Rulletzky E (20th C) ?				
3D	1	2,061	2,061	2,061
VILLE, Vickers de (1856-1925) British				
oil	2	1,300-1,408	1,354	1,300
VILLEBESSEYX, Jenny (1854-?) French				
oil	1	4,005	4,005	4,005
VILLEGAS Y CORDERO, Jose (1848-1922) Spanish				
oil	3	5,400-14,351	10,949	13,098
VILLEGAS Y CORDERO, Ricardo (1852-?) Spanish				
oil	1	12,225	12,225	12,225
VILLEGAS, Armando (1928-) Peruvian				
oil	1	1,200	1,200	1,200
VILLEGAS, Jose (?) Spanish				
oil	1	43,500	43,500	43,500
VILLEGAS, Margarita (20th C) South American				
wc/d	1	1,440	1,440	1,440
VILLEGLE, Jacques de la (1926-) French				
oil	1	8,500	8,500	8,500
wc/d	12	1,109-132,750	26,420	15,901
VILLELIA, Moises (1928-) Spanish				
3D	3	1,916-22,878	9,620	4,066
VILLEON, Eliane de la (1910-1969) French				
oil	1	1,077	1,077	1,077
VILLEON, Emmanuel de la (1858-1944) French				
oil	27	468-16,993	4,106	2,928
wc/d	8	418-2,589	825	589
VILLERET, François Etienne (1800-1866) French				
wc/d	2	1,084-1,415	1,249	1,084
VILLEROY, Maurice de (1844-1914) French				
oil	1	9,900	9,900	9,900
VILLEVALDE, Bogdan Pavlovich (1818-1903) Russian				
oil	1	11,127	11,127	11,127
VILLEVALDE, Count Alexander Bogdanovich (1857-?) Russian				
oil	1	74,409	74,409	74,409
VILLEVIELLE, Léon (1826-1863) French				
oil	2	1,885-3,200	2,542	1,885
VILLIE, Michail (1838-1910) ?				
wc/d	1	3,096	3,096	3,096
VILLODAS DE LA TORRE, Ricardo de (1846-1904) Spanish				
oil	2	598-1,137	867	598
wc/d	1	723	723	723
VILLON, A (19/20th C) French?				
oil	1	4,839	4,839	4,839
VILLON, Eugène (1879-?) French				
wc/d	1	1,178	1,178	1,178
VILLON, Jacques (1875-1963) French				
oil	8	4,091-50,486	22,426	13,000
wc/d	21	450-95,000	6,450	2,000
VINADER, Rafael (1856-1922) Spanish				
oil	1	1,060	1,060	1,060
VINAY, Jean (1907-1978) French				
oil	3	500-1,794	1,294	1,590
VINCENT, François Andre (1746-1816) French				
oil	1	13,548	13,548	13,548
wc/d	3	3,700-28,986	13,407	7,535
VINCENT, George (1796-c.1831) British				
oil	8	500-26,460	9,108	6,000
VINCENT, Harry A (1864-1931) American				
oil	5	460-17,000	6,272	4,000
wc/d	1	900	900	900
VINCENT, William (1939-2004) American				
oil	1	2,500	2,500	2,500
VINCENTE, Esteban (1903-?) American/Spanish				
wc/d	1	1,600	1,600	1,600
VINCENZI, Giorgio de (1884-?) Italian				
oil	1	3,152	3,152	3,152
VINCENZINA, Giuseppe (18th C) Italian				
oil	1	12,460	12,460	12,460

Name	No.	Price Range	Average	Median
VINCHE, Lionel (1936-) Belgian				
oil	5	534-5,088	1,606	849
VINCHON, Auguste Jean Baptiste (1789-1855) French				
oil	2	1,200-2,750	1,975	1,200
VINCK, Joseph (1900-1979) Belgian				
oil	7	935-2,719	1,917	1,854
VINCKEBOONS, David (1576-1629) Flemish				
oil	3	5,838-23,784	15,713	17,517
VINE OF COLCHESTER, John (1809-1867) British				
oil	1	24,500	24,500	24,500
VINE, Stella (1969-) British				
oil	1	2,000	2,000	2,000
VINEA, F (1845-1902) Italian				
oil	1	2,400	2,400	2,400
VINEA, Francesco (1845-1902) Italian				
oil	11	947-12,000	5,405	4,500
wc/d	1	1,218	1,218	1,218
VINELLA, Ray (?) ?				
oil	2	900-1,100	1,000	900
VINER, Giuseppe (1875-1925) Italian				
oil	1	7,572	7,572	7,572
wc/d	1	2,906	2,906	2,906
VINES, Hernando (1904-1993) Spanish				
oil	7	2,990-45,755	20,993	21,087
wc/d	1	3,211	3,211	3,211
VINNE, Jan Vincents van der (1663-1721) Dutch				
oil	1	74,000	74,000	74,000
VINNEN, Carl (1863-1922) German				
oil	4	3,152-18,185	7,599	3,857
VINNEN, Lucienne van der (1925-2001) Belgian				
oil	1	1,553	1,553	1,553
VINOGRADOV, Sergei Arsenevich (1869-1938) Russian				
oil	11	12,858-223,200	65,233	28,027
wc/d	1	2,480	2,480	2,480
VINOGRADOV, Yuri Evegenevich (1926-1995) Russian				
oil	1	2,022	2,022	2,022
VINTON, Frederick Porter (1846-1911) American				
oil	3	700-1,900	1,466	1,800
VIOLA, Bill (1951-) American				
3D	2	85,000-320,000	202,500	85,000
VIOLA, Giuseppe (1933-) Italian				
oil	10	647-7,054	1,616	922
VIOLA, Manuel (1919-1987) Spanish				
oil	34	784-8,429	3,071	2,259
VIOLET, Pierre Noel (1749-1819) French				
wc/d	1	1,750	1,750	1,750
VIOLETTE, Banks (1973-) American				
wc/d	1	27,000	27,000	27,000
VIOLLET LE DUC, Victor (1848-1901) French				
oil	5	817-2,160	1,482	1,808
VIOLLET, Catherine (1955-) French				
oil	1	1,077	1,077	1,077
VIOLLET-LE-DUC, Adolphe Étienne (younger) (1817-1878) French				
oil	1	2,832	2,832	2,832
VIOLLIER, Jean (1896-1985) Swiss				
oil	1	2,186	2,186	2,186
VIONOJA, Veikko (1909-2001) Finnish				
oil	6	1,858-10,286	4,519	2,571
wc/d	2	551-839	695	551
VIOT, Antoine (1817-1886) French				
oil	1	3,034	3,034	3,034
VIRGIN, Gottfrid (1831-1876) Swedish				
oil	1	2,985	2,985	2,985
VIRIGLIO, Riccardo (1897-1951) Italian				
oil	1	1,054	1,054	1,054
VIRNICH, Thomas (1957-) German				
3D	2	2,003-4,123	3,063	2,003
VIRTUE, John (1947-) British				
oil	1	4,956	4,956	4,956
wc/d	1	1,505	1,505	1,505
VIRY, Paul Alphonse (19th C) French				
oil	1	4,000	4,000	4,000

Name	No.	Price Range	Average	Median
VISCONTI MERINO, Julio (1921-) Spanish				
wc/d	6	838-2,682	1,358	1,137
VISCONTI, Adolfo Ferraguti (1850-1924) Italian				
oil	1	3,366	3,366	3,366
VISEUX, Claude (1927-) French				
oil	4	536-1,192	800	596
wc/d	1	894	894	894
VISO, Nicola (18th C) Italian				
oil	1	14,108	14,108	14,108
VISSCHER, Cornelis de (1619-1662) Dutch				
wc/d	1	119,097	119,097	119,097
VISSER, Adrianus de (1762-1837) Dutch				
wc/d	1	1,100	1,100	1,100
VISSER, Carel (1928-) Dutch				
3D	8	7,642-36,122	16,234	14,014
VISSER, Johannes Gesinus (1898-1978) Dutch				
oil	2	1,414-1,414	1,414	1,414
VISSER, S (19/20th C) Dutch				
oil	1	1,798	1,798	1,798
VISSER, Tjipke (1876-1955) Dutch				
3D	1	5,878	5,878	5,878
VISWANADHAN, V (1940-) Indian				
oil	1	6,500	6,500	6,500
VITA, Miguel de (1923-2001) South American				
oil	2	1,400-2,600	2,000	1,400
VITA, P de (19/20th C) Italian				
oil	1	4,531	4,531	4,531
VITAL, Not (1948-) American				
wc/d	1	1,000	1,000	1,000
3D	1	18,165	18,165	18,165
VITALI, Candido (1680-1753) Italian				
oil	1	45,190	45,190	45,190
VITALIS, Macario (1898-1990) Philippino				
oil	1	909	909	909
wc/d	1	440	440	440
VITALONI, Michele (20th C) ?				
3D	1	3,078	3,078	3,078
VITHAL, B (1935-) Indian				
oil	2	11,220-13,000	12,110	11,220
VITI, Giusto (19th C) Italian				
3D	1	1,770	1,770	1,770
VITI, Timoteo (1469-1523) Italian				
oil	1	210,000	210,000	210,000
VITO, Camillo de (19th C) Italian				
wc/d	4	2,498-8,256	4,407	3,026
VITRINGA, Wigerus (1657-1721) Dutch				
oil	3	7,559-18,685	13,938	15,570
wc/d	1	4,844	4,844	4,844
VITTINI, Giulio (1888-1968) Italian				
oil	1	5,069	5,069	5,069
VITTORI, Carlo (1881-1943) Italian				
oil	2	1,200-3,514	2,357	1,200
VITTORINI, Umberto (1890-1970) Italian				
oil	1	1,134	1,134	1,134
VIUDES, Vincente (1916-1984) Spanish				
oil	2	1,300-2,000	1,650	1,300
VIVANCOS, Miguel Garcia (1895-1972) Spanish				
oil	3	1,189-1,440	1,316	1,320
VIVARINI, Antonio (c.1415-c.1484) Italian				
oil	1	284,558	284,558	284,558
VIVARINI, Bartolommeo (c.1432-c.1499) Italian				
oil	1	91,233	91,233	91,233
VIVES-ATSARA, Jose (1919-1988) Mexican				
oil	1	3,750	3,750	3,750
VIVIAN, J (19th C) British				
oil	3	5,046-5,292	5,163	5,152
VIVIAN, John Comley (19th C) British				
oil	1	4,725	4,725	4,725
VIVIAN, Miss Jane (fl.1869-1877) British				
oil	2	9,936-17,300	13,618	9,936
VIVIANI, Raoul (1883-1965) Italian				
oil	4	958-1,676	1,410	1,332

Name	No.	Price Range	Average	Median
VIVIANI, Vanni (1939-) Italian				
oil	1	1,045	1,045	1,045
VIVIEN, Joseph (1657-1735) French				
oil	1	6,306	6,306	6,306
VIVIN, Louis (1861-1936) French				
oil	6	1,000-8,000	3,453	2,270
VIVO, Andres (1955-) Uruguayan				
oil	2	1,100-1,200	1,150	1,100
VIVO, Tommaso de (1790-1884) Italian				
oil	1	19,747	19,747	19,747
VIVOT, Lea (1952-) Canadian/Czech				
3D	2	1,476-2,788	2,132	1,476
VIZZINI, Andrea (?) Italian				
oil	1	851	851	851
wc/d	1	1,337	1,337	1,337
VLADIMIROFF, Ivan Alexeievitch (1869-1947) Russian				
oil	4	3,116-9,460	6,568	5,985
wc/d	1	1,740	1,740	1,740
VLADIMIRSKY, Boris Eremeievich (1878-1950) Russian				
oil	3	1,308-197,466	69,411	9,460
VLAMINCK, Maurice de (1876-1958) French				
oil	66	11,837-3,864,000	268,100	70,000
wc/d	24	2,000-31,140	19,484	18,000
VLIEGER, Simon de (1600-1653) Dutch				
oil	3	44,376-899,600	400,992	259,000
wc/d	4	2,102-22,490	8,353	3,270
VLIET, Willem van der (1584-1642) Dutch				
oil	1	25,000	25,000	25,000
VNODCHENKO, Yuri Fedorovich (1927-) Russian				
oil	1	1,665	1,665	1,665
VOELLMY, Fritz (1863-?) Swiss				
oil	1	1,800	1,800	1,800
VOERMAN, Jan (jnr) (1890-1976) Dutch				
oil	2	4,712-8,970	6,841	4,712
wc/d	1	2,378	2,378	2,378
VOERMAN, Jan (snr) (1857-1941) Dutch				
oil	4	1,585-7,417	5,281	5,455
VOET, Jacob Ferdinand (1639-c.1700) Flemish				
oil	3	16,435-35,288	23,542	18,904
VOGEL VON VOGELSTEIN, Carl Christian (1788-1868) German				
oil	2	23,034-31,521	27,277	23,034
VOGEL, Bernhard (1961-) Austrian				
wc/d	1	2,038	2,038	2,038
VOGEL, Christian Leberecht (1759-1816) German				
oil	1	19,082	19,082	19,082
wc/d	1	954	954	954
VOGEL, Donald Stanley (1917-2004) American				
oil	1	1,400	1,400	1,400
VOGEL, Hugo (1855-1934) German				
oil	2	1,868-2,493	2,180	1,868
VOGEL, Johannes Gysbert (younger) (1828-1915) Dutch				
oil	1	2,225	2,225	2,225
wc/d	2	738-1,189	963	738
VOGEL, Ludwig (1788-1879) Swiss				
oil	3	4,576-19,265	13,230	15,849
wc/d	4	403-2,272	1,355	1,062
VOGEL-JORGENSEN, Age (1888-1964) Danish				
oil	1	1,288	1,288	1,288
VOGELER, Heinrich (1872-1942) German				
oil	1	63,605	63,605	63,605
wc/d	2	1,060-1,940	1,500	1,060
VOGELS, Guillaume (1836-1896) Belgian				
oil	7	895-5,856	2,647	1,762
VOGLER, Adam (1822-1856) Austrian				
oil	1	1,169	1,169	1,169
VOGLER, Georges (20th C) French?				
oil	1	1,285	1,285	1,285
VOGLER, Hermann (1859-?) German				
oil	1	3,273	3,273	3,273
VOGLER, Paul (1852-1904) French				
oil	4	1,752-3,500	2,636	2,378

Name	No.	Price Range	Average	Median
VOGUE, Guy de (1929-) French				
oil	1	1,590	1,590	1,590
VOIGT, Baron Alastair Hans Henning (20th C) German				
wc/d	1	1,083	1,083	1,083
VOIGT, Bruno (1912-1989) German				
wc/d	2	865-4,066	2,465	865
VOIGT, Otto Eduard (19th C) German				
wc/d	1	2,057	2,057	2,057
VOIGT-FOLGER, August (1836-1918) German				
oil	1	2,195	2,195	2,195
VOIGTLANDER, Rudolf von (1854-?) German				
oil	2	2,592-7,658	5,125	2,592
VOILLEMOT, Charles (1823-1893) French				
wc/d	1	1,414	1,414	1,414
VOIRIN, Jules Antoine (1833-1898) French				
oil	1	1,386	1,386	1,386
VOIRIN, Leon-Joseph (1833-1887) French				
oil	4	4,822-100,000	28,955	5,000
VOIRIOT, Guillaume (1713-1799) French				
wc/d	1	2,569	2,569	2,569
VOIS, Arie de (1631-1680) Flemish				
oil	1	15,181	15,181	15,181
VOISARD-MARGERIE, Adrien Gabriel (1867-1954) French				
oil	2	1,403-1,636	1,519	1,403
VOKEY, Sam (1963-) American				
oil	2	600-2,100	1,350	600
VOKOS, Nicolaos (1861-1902) Greek				
oil	2	22,620-26,180	24,400	22,620
VOLAIRE, Pierre Jacques (1729-1802) French				
oil	3	29,167-316,781	127,005	35,068
VOLANG, Jean (1921-2005) Vietnamese				
oil	2	1,671-2,400	2,035	1,671
VOLAUARDS, C (20th C) American				
oil	1	8,000	8,000	8,000
VOLCK, Frederick (1833-1891) German				
3D	1	3,500	3,500	3,500
VOLCKAERT, Piet (1902-1973) Belgian				
oil	12	542-2,860	1,275	941
VOLCKER, Robert (1854-1924) German				
oil	2	1,229-2,694	1,961	1,229
VOLK, B (18th C) ?				
oil	1	2,303	2,303	2,303
VOLK, Douglas (1856-1935) American				
oil	4	400-17,132	5,633	1,000
VOLK, Leonard Wells (1828-1895) American				
3D	1	6,250	6,250	6,250
VOLKEL, Oswald (1873-?) German				
oil	1	1,091	1,091	1,091
VOLKEL, Rudolf (19/20th C) Austrian				
wc/d	1	1,908	1,908	1,908
VOLKER, Wilhelm (19th C) Swiss				
oil	1	12,123	12,123	12,123
VOLKERS, Emil (1831-1905) German				
oil	9	1,868-13,000	4,593	3,440
VOLKERS, Fritz (19/20th C) German				
oil	1	1,865	1,865	1,865
VOLKERS, Karl (1868-1944) German				
oil	3	1,739-9,633	5,476	5,057
VOLKERT, Edward Charles (1871-1935) American				
oil	4	3,500-14,000	7,187	5,500
wc/d	1	550	550	550
VOLKHART, Max (1848-1935) German				
oil	3	814-40,000	17,517	11,739
VOLKHART, Wilhelm (1815-1876) German				
oil	2	2,432-4,576	3,504	2,432
VOLKMANN, Arthur Joseph Wilhelm (1851-1941) German				
3D	1	24,205	24,205	24,205
VOLKMANN, Hans Richard von (1860-1927) German				
oil	10	701-4,839	2,248	2,122
VOLKOV, Alexandre (1886-1957) Russian				
oil	1	350,000	350,000	350,000

Name	No.	Price Range	Average	Median
VOLKOV, Efim Efimovich (1844-1920) Russian				
oil	3	1,520-372,000	125,040	1,600
VOLKOV, Sergei (1956-) Russian				
oil	1	213,900	213,900	213,900
VOLL, Christoph (1897-1939) German				
wc/d	1	546	546	546
3D	1	35,158	35,158	35,158
VOLLERDT, Johann Christian (1708-1769) German				
oil	4	10,888-44,980	22,673	17,027
VOLLET, Jean (20th C) French				
oil	1	3,250	3,250	3,250
VOLLEVENS, Johannes (elder) (1649-1728) Dutch				
oil	2	2,410-8,515	5,462	2,410
VOLLMAR, Ludwig (1842-1884) German				
oil	4	2,420-24,080	8,955	4,120
VOLLMER, Grace Libby (1884-1977) American				
oil	2	2,250-3,750	3,000	2,250
VOLLMERING, Joseph (1810-1887) American				
oil	2	1,500-2,800	2,150	1,500
VOLLON, Alexis (1865-1945) French				
oil	3	3,000-7,500	4,743	3,729
VOLLON, Antoine (1833-1900) French				
oil	9	1,272-49,167	7,655	1,460
VOLMAR, Georg (1770-1831) German				
oil	2	567-2,498	1,532	567
wc/d	1	2,335	2,335	2,335
VOLMAR, Theodor (1847-?) Swiss				
oil	3	605-1,665	1,210	1,362
VOLOORDOM, C (19th C) Belgian				
oil	1	2,870	2,870	2,870
VOLOV, I (19th C) Russian				
oil	1	13,680	13,680	13,680
VOLOVICK, Lazare (1902-1977) Russian				
oil	9	1,788-13,109	5,685	6,181
VOLPE, Alessandro la (1820-1887) Italian				
oil	6	3,092-38,571	23,230	19,982
VOLPE, Vincenzo (1855-1929) Italian				
oil	3	500-12,000	4,566	1,198
VOLPI, Alessandro (1909-) Italian				
oil	1	1,074	1,074	1,074
VOLPI, Alfredo (1896-1988) Brazilian				
oil	3	45,000-160,000	98,333	90,000
VOLPINI, Renato (1934-) Italian				
oil	5	1,060-2,290	1,431	1,295
wc/d	1	595	595	595
VOLTI (1915-1990) French				
wc/d	3	1,288-1,991	1,561	1,405
3D	1	6,473	6,473	6,473
VOLTI, Antoniucci (1915-1990) French				
oil	1	3,827	3,827	3,827
wc/d	14	400-3,480	1,830	1,488
3D	15	4,767-53,507	14,041	10,623
VOLTZ, Friedrich (1817-1886) German				
oil	15	474-23,562	5,508	3,263
wc/d	2	1,483-2,182	1,832	1,483
VOLTZ, Ludwig (1825-1911) German				
oil	3	760-2,510	1,581	1,475
VOLZ, Hermann (1814-1894) German				
oil	2	753-2,611	1,682	753
VONCK, Elias (1605-1652) Dutch				
oil	3	14,449-111,000	54,316	37,500
VONCK, Jan (1630-?) Dutch				
oil	2	2,076-5,993	4,034	2,076
VONNOH, Bessie Potter (1872-1955) American				
3D	3	21,000-47,500	35,833	39,000
VONNOH, Robert (1858-1933) American				
oil	2	10,000-26,000	18,000	10,000
wc/d	1	1,400	1,400	1,400
VONTILLIUS, Jeppe (1915-1994) Danish				
oil	7	485-1,617	1,200	1,212
VOOGD, Hendrik (1766-1839) Dutch				
oil	1	69,200	69,200	69,200

Name	No.	Price Range	Average	Median
VOORDECKER, Henri (1779-1861) Belgian				
oil	1	5,845	5,845	5,845
VOORDEN, August Willem van (1881-1921) Dutch				
oil	3	3,637-11,959	7,219	6,062
VOORT, Frans Anthony van der (1816-1848) Dutch				
oil	1	1,707	1,707	1,707
VOPAVA, Walter (1958-) Austrian				
oil	1	1,334	1,334	1,334
VORDEMBERGE, Friedrich (1897-1980) German				
oil	2	1,784-2,421	2,102	1,784
VORGANG, Paul (1860-1927) German				
oil	1	7,633	7,633	7,633
VOROBIOV, Sokrat Maksimovich (1817-1888) Russian				
oil	1	7,000	7,000	7,000
wc/d	2	13,760-13,760	13,760	13,760
VOROS, Bela (1899-1983) Hungarian				
3D	2	1,731-3,514	2,622	1,731
VOROSHILOV, Sergei Semenovich (19th C) Russian				
oil	2	5,655-13,950	9,802	5,655
VORST, Joseph Paul (1897-1947) American/German				
oil	1	1,200	1,200	1,200
VORST, Tony van de (1946-) Dutch				
3D	1	2,351	2,351	2,351
VOS, Christoffel Albertus (1813-1877) Dutch				
oil	1	1,640	1,640	1,640
VOS, Cornelis de (1585-1651) Flemish				
oil	3	5,575-51,900	35,191	48,100
VOS, Hubert (1855-1935) American				
oil	2	2,000-2,100	2,050	2,000
VOS, Jan de IV (1593-1649) Dutch				
oil	1	20,384	20,384	20,384
VOS, Maria (1824-1906) Dutch				
oil	5	7,375-18,437	11,996	11,743
VOS, Martin de (1532-1603) Flemish				
oil	3	30,000-110,000	69,265	67,797
wc/d	1	3,503	3,503	3,503
VOS, Paul de (1596-1678) Flemish				
oil	1	25,950	25,950	25,950
VOS, Paul de and WILDENS, Jan (17th C) Flemish				
oil	1	144,490	144,490	144,490
VOS, Simon de (1603-1676) Flemish				
oil	4	3,680-141,860	44,190	10,837
VOS, Vincent de (1829-1875) Belgian				
oil	12	504-3,190	1,327	1,009
VOSBERG, Heinrich (1833-1891) German				
oil	1	5,531	5,531	5,531
VOSCHER, Leopold Heinrich (1830-1877) Austrian				
oil	2	2,264-3,822	3,043	2,264
VOSS, Jan (1936-) German				
oil	8	4,944-17,810	9,326	7,644
wc/d	8	655-17,840	6,090	4,203
VOSSEN, Andre van der (1893-1963) Dutch				
oil	1	1,219	1,219	1,219
wc/d	1	909	909	909
VOSTELL, Wolf (1932-1998) German				
3D	4	6,479-16,829	12,477	12,361
VOUET, Simon (1590-1649) French				
wc/d	2	28,000-81,918	54,959	28,000
VOULKOS, Peter (1924-2002) American				
3D	5	3,000-9,500	7,400	8,000
VOULLEMIER, Anne Nicole (1796-1886) French				
wc/d	1	5,096	5,096	5,096
VOURLOUMIS, Andreas (1910-) Greek				
oil	1	5,632	5,632	5,632
VOYATZIS, Charis (1924-1981) Greek				
oil	2	935-1,870	1,402	935
VOYET, Maxime (1896-1985) French				
oil	1	1,028	1,028	1,028
VOYSEY, Charles Francis Annesley (1857-1941) British				
wc/d	1	8,750	8,750	8,750

Name	No.	Price Range	Average	Median
VRANCX, Sebastian (1573-1647) Flemish				
oil	5	14,013-117,808	46,151	30,362
wc/d	1	2,400	2,400	2,400
VREEDENBURGH, C (1880-1946) Dutch				
oil	1	7,481	7,481	7,481
VREEDENBURGH, Cornelis (1880-1946) Dutch				
oil	6	1,499-63,041	17,021	5,563
wc/d	3	482-7,500	3,896	3,708
VREESE, Godefroid (1861-1941) Belgian				
3D	1	3,063	3,063	3,063
VRIELINK, N (?) ?				
oil	1	3,395	3,395	3,395
VRIELINK, Nico (1958-) Dutch				
oil	1	1,136	1,136	1,136
VRIENDT, Juliaan de (1842-1935) Belgian				
oil	2	727-28,800	14,763	727
VRIES, Abraham de (1590-c.1662) Dutch				
oil	1	5,255	5,255	5,255
VRIES, Catharina Julia de (1813-1883) Dutch				
oil	1	1,091	1,091	1,091
VRIES, Emanuel de (1816-1875) Dutch				
oil	1	2,395	2,395	2,395
VRIES, Herman de (1931-) Dutch				
3D	1	6,115	6,115	6,115
VRIES, Roelof van (1631-1681) Dutch				
oil	3	5,839-15,288	9,119	6,230
VROLYK, Jan (1845-1894) Dutch				
oil	4	1,073-3,781	2,189	1,113
VROMAN, Ton (1948-) Dutch				
oil	1	1,553	1,553	1,553
VROOM, Cornelis Hendriksz (1591-1661) Dutch				
oil	2	9,555-69,200	39,377	9,555
VROUTOS, Georgios (1843-1908) Greek				
3D	2	6,500-8,500	7,500	6,500
VRUBEL, Mikhail Alexandrovich (1856-1910) Russian				
wc/d	1	78,473	78,473	78,473
VU CAO DAM (1908-2000) Vietnamese				
oil	8	2,420-21,000	10,827	8,491
VUCHETICH, Evgeniy Viktorovich (1908-1974) Russian				
3D	1	5,005	5,005	5,005
VUCHT, Gerrit van (1610-1699) Dutch				
oil	2	6,938-8,199	7,568	6,938
VUCHT, Jan van der (1603-1637) Dutch				
oil	1	23,514	23,514	23,514
VUILLARD, Edouard (1868-1940) French				
oil	17	27,986-6,624,000	583,442	167,200
wc/d	20	1,100-51,800	12,734	8,919
VUILLERMET, Charles François (1849-1918) Swiss				
oil	1	1,832	1,832	1,832
VULLIAMY, Gerard (1909-2005) French				
oil	6	1,318-3,090	1,905	1,455
wc/d	5	596-3,576	1,595	1,553
VULLIAMY, Lewis (18/19th C) British				
wc/d	1	2,088	2,088	2,088
VULOKH, Igor (1938-) Russian				
oil	2	12,000-15,000	13,500	12,000
VUNDERINK, Ido Pieter (1935-) Dutch				
oil	1	2,121	2,121	2,121
VUUREN, Jan van (1871-1941) Dutch				
oil	1	1,001	1,001	1,001
VYARET, Auguste (19th C) French				
oil	1	1,455	1,455	1,455
VYATKIN, Aleksandr (1922-) Russian				
oil	1	10,620	10,620	10,620
VYLBRIEF, Ernst (1934-) Dutch				
oil	2	763-1,527	1,145	763
VYLDER, C de (19th C) Dutch				
oil	1	3,000	3,000	3,000
VYSEKAL, Edouard Antonin (1890-1939) American				
oil	2	60,000-65,000	62,500	60,000

Name	No.	Price Range	Average	Median
VYTLACIL, Vaclav (1892-1984) American				
oil	2	1,300-10,000	5,650	1,300
wc/d	3	650-3,750	1,683	650
VYZANTIOS, Konstantinos (1924-) Greek				
oil	1	2,431	2,431	2,431
W J (18th C) British				
oil	1	2,250	2,250	2,250
WAAGEN, Adalbert (1833-1898) German				
oil	6	618-7,292	2,441	995
WAAGEN, Arthur (19th C) French				
3D	3	4,500-22,080	11,470	7,830
WAAGSTEIN, Joen (1879-1949) Danish				
oil	1	2,093	2,093	2,093
WAARDEN, Jan van der (1811-1872) Dutch				
oil	2	3,600-30,729	17,164	3,600
WAAY, Nicolaas van der (1855-1936) Dutch				
oil	3	2,428-6,096	4,467	4,877
wc/d	1	732	732	732
WABEL, Henry (1889-1981) Swiss				
oil	6	683-2,125	1,118	941
WACH, Aloys (1892-1940) German				
oil	1	4,204	4,204	4,204
wc/d	4	410-1,985	1,316	1,414
WACHSMUTH, Maximilian (1859-1912) German				
oil	1	3,012	3,012	3,012
WACHTEL, Elmer (1864-1929) American				
oil	4	7,500-35,000	19,125	14,000
wc/d	1	7,000	7,000	7,000
WACHTEL, Marion K (1876-1954) American				
oil	8	3,750-60,000	24,156	17,000
wc/d	4	13,000-35,000	24,500	22,500
WACHTEL, Wilhelm (1875-1942) German				
oil	2	7,500-12,500	10,000	7,500
WACIK, Franz (1883-1938) Austrian				
wc/d	1	1,790	1,790	1,790
WACKER, Nicolas (1897-1987) Russian				
oil	46	516-3,687	1,632	1,598
wc/d	7	492-3,319	1,387	615
WACKER, Rudolf (1893-1939) Austrian				
oil	3	21,848-114,490	77,295	95,548
wc/d	5	1,216-3,180	2,063	2,035
WACKERLE, Joseph (1880-1959) German				
3D	1	3,600	3,600	3,600
WACKERMANN, Hubert (1945-) American				
oil	3	1,300-1,400	1,366	1,400
wc/d	1	1,237	1,237	1,237
WACKERS, Ruud (1941-) Dutch				
3D	1	9,425	9,425	9,425
WACKLIN, Isak (1720-1758) Finnish				
oil	1	36,308	36,308	36,308
WADE, David (20th C) American				
oil	1	12,500	12,500	12,500
WADE, Jonathan (1960-) British				
oil	15	561-2,784	1,210	1,197
WADE, Jonathan (1941-1973) Irish				
oil	1	2,221	2,221	2,221
WADSWORTH, Edward (1889-1949) British				
oil	1	113,400	113,400	113,400
WAEL, Cornelis de (1592-1667) Flemish				
oil	2	3,341-14,240	8,790	3,341
wc/d	1	494	494	494
WAEL, Cornelis de and WILDENS, Jan (16th C) Flemish				
oil	1	14,800	14,800	14,800
WAELE, Rene de (?) French				
wc/d	1	1,149	1,149	1,149
WAENERBERG, Thorsten (1846-1917) Finnish				
oil	7	1,678-45,863	9,411	3,600
WAENTIG, Walter (1881-1962) German				
oil	4	458-2,751	1,356	512
WAERDIGH, Dominicus Gottfried (1700-1789) German				
oil	1	11,217	11,217	11,217

Name	No.	Price Range	Average	Median
WAGEMAEKERS, Victor (1876-1953) Belgian				
oil	11	602-3,330	1,488	1,403
wc/d	7	760-2,026	1,328	1,084
WAGEMAKER, Jaap (1906-1972) Dutch				
wc/d	3	2,548-10,192	7,003	8,269
WAGEMANS, Maurice (1877-1927) Belgian				
oil	4	1,907-3,063	2,596	2,356
WAGENBAUER, Max Josef (1774-1829) German				
oil	4	2,071-9,545	6,930	7,755
wc/d	2	1,067-1,145	1,106	1,067
WAGENSCHOEN, Franz Xaver (1726-1790) Austrian				
oil	2	2,178-5,874	4,026	2,178
WAGNER, Albert (19th C) German?				
oil	1	1,581	1,581	1,581
WAGNER, Carl (1796-1857) German				
wc/d	3	589-2,356	1,435	1,360
WAGNER, Cornelis (1870-1956) German				
oil	1	1,331	1,331	1,331
WAGNER, F (?) ?				
oil	1	4,393	4,393	4,393
WAGNER, Ferdinand (jnr) (1847-1927) German				
oil	7	2,704-26,000	7,688	3,857
WAGNER, Fritz (20th C) German				
oil	13	668-8,604	3,648	2,682
WAGNER, Fritz (1902-1976) German				
oil	1	1,720	1,720	1,720
WAGNER, Fritz (1896-1939) German				
oil	5	2,571-13,336	6,179	3,395
WAGNER, Jacob (1852-1896) American				
oil	3	700-2,500	1,333	800
WAGNER, Johan Georg (1744-1767) German				
wc/d	1	3,534	3,534	3,534
WAGNER, Johann Peter (1730-1809) German				
3D	1	9,600	9,600	9,600
WAGNER, Karl (1839-1923) German				
oil	8	1,215-4,216	2,342	1,945
WAGNER, Karl Ludwig Friedrich (1839-1923) German				
oil	1	1,000	1,000	1,000
WAGNER, Karl Theodor (1856-1921) Austrian				
oil	1	3,036	3,036	3,036
WAGNER, Paul Hermann (1852-1937) German				
oil	2	9,730-11,340	10,535	9,730
WAGNER, Philipp Jakob (1812-1877) German				
oil	1	5,444	5,444	5,444
WAGNER, Rolf (1914-) German				
oil	2	605-1,483	1,044	605
WAGNER, Sigmund von (1759-1835) Swiss				
wc/d	2	1,457-1,457	1,457	1,457
WAGNER, Theodor (19/20th C) ?				
3D	1	2,432	2,432	2,432
WAGNER, Wilhelm (?-1887) German				
oil	1	6,689	6,689	6,689
WAGNER-HOHENBERG, Josef (1870-1939) German				
oil	3	1,940-3,779	3,098	3,575
WAGONER, Harry B (1889-1950) American				
oil	1	1,300	1,300	1,300
wc/d	1	400	400	400
WAGONER, Robert B (1928-) American				
oil	1	1,000	1,000	1,000
wc/d	1	800	800	800
WAGREZ, Jacques Clement (1846-1908) French				
oil	3	1,411-76,028	47,759	65,838
WAHL, Johann Salomon (1689-1765) Danish				
oil	1	24,265	24,265	24,265
WAHLBERG, Alfred (1834-1906) Swedish				
oil	12	373-48,080	6,789	1,923
WAHLBERG, Ulf (1938-) Swedish				
oil	2	1,454-8,143	4,798	1,454
WAHLISS, Ernst (20th C) Austrian				
3D	2	2,816-28,160	15,488	2,816
WAHLQVIST, Ehrnfried (1814-1895) Swedish				
oil	3	550-2,747	1,504	1,216

Name	No.	Price Range	Average	Median
WAHLROOS, Dora (1870-1947) Finnish				
oil	1	1,403	1,403	1,403
WAHLSTROM, Charlotte (1849-1924) Swedish				
oil	11	824-17,171	3,828	1,099
WAILLY, Charles de (1729-1798) French				
wc/d	1	1,070	1,070	1,070
WAIN, Louis (1860-1939) British				
oil	3	1,060-27,840	10,080	1,342
wc/d	53	440-13,050	2,101	1,388
WAINEWRIGHT, Thomas Francis (19th C) British				
oil	1	850	850	850
wc/d	3	450-2,405	1,424	1,418
WAINWRIGHT, John (19th C) British				
oil	2	8,850-21,840	15,345	8,850
WAINWRIGHT, William John (1855-1931) British				
oil	4	2,431-8,550	5,444	3,500
wc/d	8	730-7,832	2,802	1,800
WAITE, Edward Wilkins (fl.1878-1927) British				
oil	2	3,402-3,680	3,541	3,402
WAITE, Harold (19/20th C) British				
oil	1	1,131	1,131	1,131
WAITE, James Clarke (1832-1921) British				
oil	2	2,565-3,000	2,782	2,565
WAITE, Robert Thorne (1842-1935) British				
wc/d	9	727-4,176	2,069	2,036
WAKHEVITCH, Georges (1907-1984) French				
wc/d	4	467-2,993	1,157	584
WALBERER, Richard (1907-1984) German				
oil	1	2,571	2,571	2,571
WALBOURN, Ernest (1872-1927) British				
oil	29	440-11,718	3,616	3,460
WALCH, Charles (1896-1948) French				
oil	2	2,342-2,401	2,371	2,342
wc/d	7	586-3,660	1,856	1,287
WALCH, Paul Johann (1881-1958) German				
oil	4	510-1,818	1,072	666
WALCH, Thomas (1867-1843) Austrian				
oil	1	3,507	3,507	3,507
WALCHEGGER, Franz (1913-1965) Austrian				
oil	1	8,199	8,199	8,199
WALCKIERS, Gustave (1831-1891) Belgian				
oil	2	1,532-2,571	2,051	1,532
WALCOM, J (19th C) American				
oil	1	4,750	4,750	4,750
WALCOT, William (1874-1943) British				
oil	1	1,085	1,085	1,085
wc/d	7	1,044-4,914	2,857	2,590
WALDBERG, Isabelle (1911-1990) Swiss				
3D	1	3,625	3,625	3,625
WALDE, Alfons (1891-1958) Austrian				
oil	19	6,429-188,493	74,001	58,562
wc/d	5	5,539-20,634	12,396	10,603
WALDEN, Kari (1941-) Finnish				
oil	1	1,640	1,640	1,640
WALDEN, Lionel (1861-1933) American				
oil	6	2,500-60,000	25,030	20,180
WALDMULLER, F G (1793-1865) Austrian				
oil	1	10,888	10,888	10,888
WALDMULLER, Ferdinand Georg (1793-1865) Austrian				
oil	4	6,000-1,295,890	362,199	30,345
wc/d	1	156,600	156,600	156,600
WALDO, Samuel Lovett (1783-1861) American				
oil	2	1,500-3,250	2,375	1,500
WALDORP, Antonie (1803-1866) Dutch				
oil	5	2,503-6,062	3,513	3,151
wc/d	2	760-1,512	1,136	760
WALDRUM, Harold Joe (1934-2003) American				
oil	1	9,000	9,000	9,000
WALKER, Dame Ethel (1861-1951) British				
oil	10	512-15,120	4,447	1,830
wc/d	3	680-1,305	927	797

Name	No.	Price Range	Average	Median
WALKER, E (?) British				
wc/d	1	1,823	1,823	1,823
WALKER, Francis S (1848-1916) Irish				
oil	10	957-6,264	3,567	3,480
WALKER, Frederick (1840-1875) British				
oil	1	715	715	715
wc/d	1	102,300	102,300	102,300
WALKER, Horatio (1858-1938) Canadian				
oil	3	4,210-18,555	10,560	8,915
WALKER, Inez Nathaniel (1911-1990) American				
wc/d	5	425-2,350	1,045	600
WALKER, James Alexander (1841-1898) British				
oil	3	880-8,750	3,799	1,767
WALKER, Jeff (20th C) American				
oil	1	4,000	4,000	4,000
WALKER, John Eaton (fl.1855-1866) British				
oil	1	1,900	1,900	1,900
WALKER, John Hanson (1844-1933) British				
oil	2	500-3,200	1,850	500
WALKER, Kara (1969-) American				
wc/d	3	30,000-180,000	85,833	47,500
3D	2	7,770-85,000	46,385	7,770
WALKER, Robert (1607-1658) British				
oil	1	14,175	14,175	14,175
WALKER, William Aiken (1838-1921) American				
oil	20	8,192-250,000	33,359	20,000
wc/d	2	900-3,400	2,150	900
WALKLEY, David B (1849-1934) American				
oil	1	1,800	1,800	1,800
WALKOWITZ, Abraham (1878-1965) American/Russian				
oil	1	3,500	3,500	3,500
wc/d	20	500-4,750	1,548	1,100
WALL, A Bryan (1861-1935) American				
oil	1	1,300	1,300	1,300
WALL, Bernhardt (1872-1956) American				
wc/d	1	1,000	1,000	1,000
WALL, Brian (1931-) British				
3D	2	10,920-14,560	12,740	10,920
WALL, Jeff (1946-) Canadian				
3D	1	300,900	300,900	300,900
WALL, Michael (20th C) British				
wc/d	1	1,040	1,040	1,040
WALL, William Allen (1801-1885) American				
wc/d	1	2,200	2,200	2,200
WALL, William Guy (1792-c.1864) American/Irish				
oil	1	3,500	3,500	3,500
WALLA, August (1936-2001) Austrian				
oil	1	5,400	5,400	5,400
wc/d	3	877-6,370	2,795	1,139
WALLACE, H Frank (1881-1962) British				
oil	1	750	750	750
wc/d	3	519-2,100	1,503	1,890
WALLACE, John (1841-1905) British				
oil	1	1,754	1,754	1,754
WALLANDER, Alf (1862-1914) Swedish				
oil	4	1,246-4,487	2,188	1,511
wc/d	3	893-5,083	3,320	3,984
WALLANDER, Josef Wilhelm (1821-1888) Swedish				
oil	1	2,493	2,493	2,493
WALLAT, Paul (1879-?) German				
oil	1	1,455	1,455	1,455
WALLEN, Gustaf Teodor (1860-1948) Swedish				
oil	3	979-12,464	5,403	2,768
WALLENIUS, Otto (1855-1925) Finnish				
oil	1	2,928	2,928	2,928
WALLER, Frank (1842-1923) American				
oil	1	1,800	1,800	1,800
WALLER, Lucy (fl.1890-1900) British				
oil	2	865-5,000	2,932	865
WALLER, Samuel Edmund (1850-1903) British				
oil	3	14,000-73,710	45,663	49,280

Name	No.	Price Range	Average	Median
WALLET, Albert-Charles (1852-1918) French				
oil	1	2,397	2,397	2,397
WALLET, Taf (1902-2000) Belgian				
oil	10	756-3,637	1,909	1,678
WALLIN, Anders (1953-) Swedish				
wc/d	1	1,718	1,718	1,718
WALLINGER, Mark (1959-) British				
oil	1	120,250	120,250	120,250
3D	1	11,440	11,440	11,440
WALLIS, Alfred (1855-1942) British				
oil	4	26,550-54,600	39,757	33,630
wc/d	2	2,457-3,402	2,929	2,457
WALLNER, Thure (1888-1965) Swedish				
oil	10	738-4,986	2,019	1,305
wc/d	1	794	794	794
WALLS, William (1860-1942) British				
oil	2	1,183-4,400	2,791	1,183
WALMSLEY, James Ulric (1860-1954) British				
oil	2	552-661	606	552
wc/d	2	487-690	588	487
WALRAVEN, J (1827-?) Dutch				
oil	1	2,704	2,704	2,704
WALRAVEN, Jan (1827-?) Dutch				
oil	1	4,290	4,290	4,290
WALRECHT, Ben (1911-1980) Dutch				
oil	1	13,443	13,443	13,443
WALSCAPELLE, Jacob van (1644-1727) Dutch				
oil	2	103,800-171,062	137,431	103,800
WALSCHE, Alphonse de (1828-1912) Belgian				
oil	1	2,057	2,057	2,057
WALSCHE, P G de (19th C) Belgian				
oil	1	6,880	6,880	6,880
WALSER, Karl (1877-1943) Swiss				
oil	1	21,082	21,082	21,082
wc/d	1	878	878	878
WALSH, George Stephen (1911-1988) Irish				
oil	1	1,360	1,360	1,360
WALSH, Lorcan (?) ?				
wc/d	1	2,059	2,059	2,059
WALSH, Owen (1933-) Irish				
oil	2	2,455-3,507	2,981	2,455
wc/d	1	2,104	2,104	2,104
WALSH, Sam (1934-1989) Irish				
oil	2	1,107-1,747	1,427	1,107
WALSH, Wendy (1915-) Irish				
wc/d	1	3,041	3,041	3,041
WALT DISNEY STUDIOS (20th C) American				
wc/d	23	600-11,000	5,221	5,000
3D	77	2,500-52,000	7,918	5,000
WALTE, Johann Georg (1811-1890) German				
oil	1	2,182	2,182	2,182
WALTER, C (?) ?				
oil	1	2,784	2,784	2,784
WALTER, Joseph (1783-1856) British				
oil	3	6,612-44,880	19,408	6,732
WALTER, Karl (1868-?) German				
oil	1	1,196	1,196	1,196
WALTER, Martha (1875-1976) American				
oil	26	600-130,000	11,184	4,200
wc/d	1	9,500	9,500	9,500
WALTER, Otto (1853-1904) Austrian				
oil	1	32,500	32,500	32,500
WALTER, Zoum (1902-1973) Belgian				
oil	77	492-7,129	1,257	860
wc/d	20	492-1,045	617	590
WALTER-KURAU, Johann (1869-1932) German				
oil	1	15,000	15,000	15,000
WALTERS, Curt (1950-) American				
oil	6	1,300-40,000	8,366	2,000
WALTERS, George Stanfield (1838-1924) British				
oil	3	657-5,374	3,277	3,800
wc/d	5	785-2,024	1,238	1,200

Name	No.	Price Range	Average	Median
WALTERS, Miles (1774-1849) British				
oil	1	22,620	22,620	22,620
WALTERS, Samuel (1811-1882) British				
oil	1	7,525	7,525	7,525
WALTHER, Jakob (c.1570-1604) ?				
wc/d	1	42,550	42,550	42,550
WALTHER, Ludwig (1890-1972) German				
3D	2	4,498-5,536	5,017	4,498
WALTNER, Alexander (1967-) Austrian				
oil	1	2,221	2,221	2,221
WALTON, Constance (1865-1960) British				
wc/d	2	2,262-5,600	3,931	2,262
WALTON, Edward Arthur (1860-1922) British				
oil	5	661-37,170	12,677	9,515
WALTON, Frank (1840-1928) British				
oil	3	641-6,960	2,951	1,253
wc/d	3	748-1,113	946	979
WALTON, George (?-1906) British				
oil	2	1,740-5,220	3,480	1,740
WALTON, James Trout (1818-1867) British				
oil	1	5,888	5,888	5,888
WALTON, John W (19th C) British				
oil	1	6,793	6,793	6,793
WALZ, Rolf (1958-) German				
wc/d	1	1,000	1,000	1,000
WANDERER, Georg Wilhelm (1804-1863) German				
oil	1	6,500	6,500	6,500
WANDESFORDE, Juan B (1817-1902) American				
oil	1	4,000	4,000	4,000
WANE, Richard (1852-1904) British				
oil	2	684-726	705	684
wc/d	1	533	533	533
WANG BAO (20th C) Chinese				
wc/d	1	1,518	1,518	1,518
WANG CHUAN (1953-) Chinese				
wc/d	1	8,000	8,000	8,000
WANG DONGLING (1945-) Chinese				
wc/d	1	30,000	30,000	30,000
WANG DU (1959-) ?				
3D	2	27,194-280,000	153,597	27,194
WANG GUANGYI (1957-) Chinese				
oil	8	30,000-240,000	131,946	129,500
WANG JIAO (?) Chinese?				
wc/d	1	1,200	1,200	1,200
WANG JIN (20th C) Chinese				
3D	1	60,000	60,000	60,000
WANG JIQIAN (1907-) Chinese				
wc/d	4	4,000-11,000	8,250	9,000
WANG KEPING (1949-) Chinese				
3D	5	8,329-60,000	33,975	37,656
WANG NAIZHUANG (1929-) Chinese				
wc/d	2	5,000-6,500	5,750	5,000
WANG QINGSONG (1966-) Chinese				
oil	1	29,600	29,600	29,600
WANG WUCIUS (1936-) Chinese				
wc/d	1	22,000	22,000	22,000
WANG YAN CHENG (1960-) Chinese				
oil	1	106,692	106,692	106,692
WANG YUANQI (1642-1715) Chinese				
wc/d	1	90,000	90,000	90,000
WANG YUPING (1962-) Chinese				
oil	1	18,000	18,000	18,000
WANG ZHAO (16th C) Chinese				
wc/d	1	9,000	9,000	9,000
WANG ZHIYUAN (1958-) Chinese				
3D	1	3,330	3,330	3,330
WANG ZIWEI (1963-) Chinese				
oil	1	69,034	69,034	69,034
WANG, Tyrus (20th C) American				
wc/d	1	1,800	1,800	1,800

Name	No.	Price Range	Average	Median
WANING, Cornelis Anthony van (1861-1929) Dutch				
oil	3	707-3,616	1,786	1,036
WANING, Martin van (1889-1972) Dutch				
oil	2	937-1,199	1,068	937
WANN, Michael (20th C) Irish?				
wc/d	2	906-4,043	2,474	906
WARB, Nicolaas (1906-1957) Dutch				
oil	4	715-8,800	4,315	2,979
WARD OF HULL, John (1798-1849) British				
oil	2	7,360-13,275	10,317	7,360
WARD, James (1769-1859) British				
oil	14	524-769,500	76,495	9,500
wc/d	3	528-6,090	2,782	1,730
WARD, John (1917-) British				
oil	1	2,775	2,775	2,775
wc/d	15	452-8,050	1,711	963
WARD, Sir Leslie (1851-1922) British				
wc/d	26	1,584-26,400	4,645	2,640
WARD, Stephen (20th C) British				
wc/d	1	10,395	10,395	10,395
WARD, Vernon (1905-1985) British				
oil	22	558-5,250	1,594	1,131
wc/d	1	546	546	546
WARD, William (fl.1860-1876) British				
wc/d	1	1,010	1,010	1,010
WARD, William H (fl.1850-1882) British				
oil	2	522-2,000	1,261	522
WARDI, Rafael (1928-) Finnish				
oil	3	3,741-21,857	11,104	7,715
WARDLE, Arthur (1864-1947) British				
oil	8	1,320-26,466	9,147	2,592
wc/d	8	515-4,250	2,166	1,625
WARE, Florence Ellen (1891-1971) American				
oil	1	2,250	2,250	2,250
WARGH, Carl (1938-) Finnish				
oil	1	1,139	1,139	1,139
wc/d	1	551	551	551
WARHOL, Andy (1928-1987) American				
oil	57	2,686-8,200,000	932,133	270,000
wc/d	163	661-10,500,000	346,526	43,000
3D	4	4,204-1,100,000	367,551	176,000
WARHOL, Andy and BASQUIAT, Jean Michel (20th C) American				
wc/d	1	345,000	345,000	345,000
WARING, William Henry (19/20th C) British				
oil	1	2,088	2,088	2,088
WARKOV, Esther (1941-) Canadian				
oil	1	1,237	1,237	1,237
WARMINGTON, E A (19th C) British				
wc/d	2	1,325-2,392	1,858	1,325
WARMINGTON, Ebeneezer A (1830-1903) British				
wc/d	2	1,032-1,914	1,473	1,032
WARNDOF, Frederick (20th C) American				
oil	2	1,500-1,500	1,500	1,500
WARNER, Everett L (1877-1963) American				
oil	1	17,000	17,000	17,000
WARNER, Nell Walker (1891-1970) American				
oil	7	1,700-3,500	2,678	3,000
WAROQUIER, Henry de (1881-1970) French				
oil	7	550-15,196	3,590	2,057
wc/d	7	540-1,458	826	720
WARREN, Andrew W (?-1873) American				
oil	1	15,000	15,000	15,000
WARREN, Barbara (1925-) Irish?				
oil	7	1,665-14,905	6,151	4,714
wc/d	1	1,018	1,018	1,018
WARREN, Bonomi Edward (19th C) British				
wc/d	1	3,249	3,249	3,249
WARREN, Don (1935-) American				
oil	1	2,500	2,500	2,500
WARREN, Edmund George (1834-1909) British				
wc/d	1	17,670	17,670	17,670

Name	No.	Price Range	Average	Median
WARREN, Harold Broadfield (1859-1934) American				
wc/d	4	600-1,900	1,334	1,138
WARREN, Knighton (fl.1890's) British				
oil	1	4,250	4,250	4,250
WARREN, Melvin C (1920-1995) American				
oil	2	8,500-31,000	19,750	8,500
wc/d	1	12,000	12,000	12,000
WARREN, William W (c.1832-1912) British				
oil	2	1,305-1,566	1,435	1,305
WARRICK, Keith (20th C) American				
oil	1	2,000	2,000	2,000
WARSHAWSKY, Abel George (1883-1962) American				
oil	7	1,020-26,000	5,695	1,800
WARSHAWSKY, Alexander (1887-1945) American				
oil	2	1,500-2,000	1,750	1,500
WARUN-SEKRET, Eugen von (1896-1963) German				
oil	1	3,520	3,520	3,520
WASASTJERNA, Torsten (1863-1924) Finnish				
oil	1	1,798	1,798	1,798
WASHINGTON, Elizabeth Fisher (1871-1953) American				
oil	2	2,000-32,500	17,250	2,000
WASHINGTON, Georges (1827-1910) French				
oil	19	4,000-239,200	31,456	18,432
WASILEWSKI, Czeslaw (1875-1946) Polish				
oil	3	1,197-2,035	1,482	1,216
WASKE, Erich (1889-?) German				
oil	2	1,030-2,225	1,627	1,030
wc/d	1	1,030	1,030	1,030
WASLEY, Frank (1848-1934) British				
oil	7	1,739-10,304	3,784	3,560
wc/d	19	479-3,256	1,459	1,131
WASMANN, Friedrich (1805-1886) German				
oil	1	3,600	3,600	3,600
WASMER, Erich (1915-1972) Swiss				
oil	2	1,332-1,984	1,658	1,332
WASSMUTH, Ernst Georg H (1872-1949) Swiss				
oil	2	849-1,540	1,194	849
WATELET, Charles Joseph (1867-1954) Belgian				
oil	5	1,721-7,880	4,142	3,529
WATERFORD, Louisa Marchioness of (1818-1891) British				
wc/d	1	1,958	1,958	1,958
WATERHOUSE, John William (1849-1917) British				
oil	3	8,850-234,247	90,132	27,300
wc/d	11	555-21,750	5,239	2,436
WATERLOO, Anthonie (1609-1690) Flemish				
wc/d	4	3,270-8,325	6,607	7,049
WATERLOW, Sir Ernest Albert (1850-1919) British				
oil	5	821-6,090	4,127	4,070
wc/d	1	1,388	1,388	1,388
WATERMAN, Marcus (1834-1914) American				
oil	3	700-4,750	2,550	2,200
WATERS, Billie (1896-1979) British				
oil	3	1,044-1,392	1,276	1,392
WATERS, George W (1832-1912) American				
oil	3	1,100-21,000	8,433	3,200
WATERS, Owen (1916-2004) British				
oil	3	620-1,384	1,023	1,067
WATERS, Susan (1823-1900) American				
oil	2	4,000-31,000	17,500	4,000
WATERS, W R (19th C) British				
oil	1	1,740	1,740	1,740
WATKINS, Franklin Chenault (1894-1972) American				
oil	3	3,500-14,000	7,833	6,000
wc/d	1	900	900	900
WATKINS, John Samuel (1886-1942) Australian				
oil	1	1,488	1,488	1,488
WATKINS, Susan (19th C) British				
oil	1	9,000	9,000	9,000
WATKISS, Gill (1938-) British				
oil	10	458-1,672	791	704
wc/d	1	968	968	968

Name	No.	Price Range	Average	Median
WATMOUGH, Amos (fl.1884-1885) British				
oil	1	9,048	9,048	9,048
WATROUS, Harry W (1857-1940) American				
oil	1	2,250	2,250	2,250
WATSON, Charles Edward (19/20th C) British				
oil	1	4,872	4,872	4,872
WATSON, Colin (?) Irish?				
oil	1	4,425	4,425	4,425
WATSON, Colin Webster (20th C) New Zealander				
3D	1	14,000	14,000	14,000
WATSON, F Hunnun (?) ?				
oil	1	4,914	4,914	4,914
WATSON, Harry (1871-1936) British				
oil	7	484-2,349	1,328	1,556
wc/d	1	824	824	824
WATSON, Homer Ransford (1855-1936) Canadian				
oil	13	1,434-5,739	3,133	2,997
WATSON, James (1851-1936) British				
oil	2	525-1,067	796	525
wc/d	1	450	450	450
WATSON, R (18th C) British				
oil	3	1,850-3,086	2,502	2,571
WATSON, Robert (fl.1877-1920) British				
oil	8	864-8,234	3,575	3,114
WATSON, Robert (1923-2004) American				
oil	5	500-1,900	1,250	1,300
WATSON, Robert (1865-1916) British				
oil	3	1,600-5,310	3,424	3,363
WATSON, Robert F (1815-1885) British				
oil	1	1,838	1,838	1,838
WATSON, Thomas J (1847-1912) British				
oil	1	1,529	1,529	1,529
WATSON, W R C (fl.1890-1898) British				
oil	2	2,478-3,717	3,097	2,478
WATSON, William (19/20th C) British				
oil	2	1,434-4,914	3,174	1,434
wc/d	1	692	692	692
WATSON, William Henry (19/20th C) British				
oil	1	1,274	1,274	1,274
WATSON, William R C (fl.1890-1898) British				
oil	2	2,805-10,380	6,592	2,805
WATT, E J (?) British?				
oil	1	4,375	4,375	4,375
WATT, Elizabeth Mary (1886-1954) British				
oil	1	743	743	743
wc/d	5	956-5,664	3,138	2,784
WATT, Linnie (fl.1874-1908) British				
oil	2	885-5,481	3,183	885
wc/d	1	1,392	1,392	1,392
WATTEAU, Jean Antoine (1684-1721) French				
oil	1	60,000	60,000	60,000
wc/d	2	50,000-164,063	107,031	50,000
WATTER, Josef (1838-1913) German				
oil	2	1,296-1,946	1,621	1,296
WATTS, Beulah (1872-1941) American				
oil	1	1,000	1,000	1,000
WATTS, Ernest (19/20th C) British				
oil	1	1,040	1,040	1,040
WATTS, Frederick William (1800-1862) British				
oil	9	1,218-19,000	8,190	6,423
wc/d	1	1,018	1,018	1,018
WATTS, George Frederick (1817-1904) British				
oil	4	4,450-50,000	18,180	7,350
wc/d	4	875-36,400	10,336	1,325
WATTS, Leonard (1871-1951) British				
oil	1	9,396	9,396	9,396
WATTS, William (1752-1851) British				
wc/d	1	1,800	1,800	1,800
WAUGH, Frederick J (1861-1940) American				
oil	11	1,200-25,000	11,768	9,000
wc/d	1	7,000	7,000	7,000

Name	No.	Price Range	Average	Median
WAUGH, Ida (?-1919) American				
oil	1	1,500	1,500	1,500
WAUTERS, Charles Augustin (1811-1869) Belgian				
oil	1	2,378	2,378	2,378
WAUTERS, Émile Charles (1846-1933) Belgian				
oil	4	895-7,315	3,387	1,812
wc/d	1	1,144	1,144	1,144
WAY, Andrew John Henry (1826-1888) American				
oil	2	800-32,000	16,400	800
WAY, Charles Jones (1834-1919) British				
oil	1	5,303	5,303	5,303
wc/d	15	392-3,626	882	597
WAY, Mary (1769-1833) American				
wc/d	1	11,000	11,000	11,000
WAYNE, Joe (20th C) American				
oil	1	3,000	3,000	3,000
WEATHERBY, Richard (fl.1919-1940) British				
oil	1	2,880	2,880	2,880
WEATHERHEAD, William Harris (1843-1903) British				
oil	3	1,392-6,254	3,208	1,980
wc/d	6	487-1,357	773	531
WEATHERILL, George (1810-1890) British				
wc/d	13	626-9,000	3,529	2,821
WEATHERILL, Mary (1834-1913) British				
oil	1	540	540	540
wc/d	4	696-2,124	1,368	1,062
WEAVER, Herbert Parsons (1872-1945) British				
wc/d	2	978-1,740	1,359	978
WEAVER, Robert (20th C) American				
oil	1	4,750	4,750	4,750
WEAVER, Thomas (1774-1843) British				
oil	3	5,000-19,250	10,300	6,650
WEBB, Archibald (snr) (fl.1825-1866) British				
oil	1	3,520	3,520	3,520
WEBB, Byron (fl.1846-1866) British				
oil	1	1,656	1,656	1,656
WEBB, James (1825-1895) British				
oil	28	915-20,570	5,734	3,514
WEBB, Josephine (?) Irish				
wc/d	1	1,399	1,399	1,399
WEBB, Kenneth (1927-) British				
oil	29	1,682-19,438	8,663	7,633
wc/d	1	4,208	4,208	4,208
WEBB, L M (19/20th C) ?				
oil	1	2,378	2,378	2,378
WEBB, William (1790-1856) British				
oil	1	6,426	6,426	6,426
WEBB, William Edward (1862-1903) British				
oil	6	3,366-12,825	6,700	5,220
wc/d	1	3,806	3,806	3,806
WEBBE, William J (fl.1853-1878) British				
oil	2	30,000-110,400	70,200	30,000
WEBBER, Wesley (1841-1914) American				
oil	17	550-3,250	1,764	1,900
WEBER, Alfred (1859-1936) Swiss				
oil	1	5,444	5,444	5,444
WEBER, Alfred Charles (1862-1922) French				
oil	1	4,208	4,208	4,208
WEBER, August (1817-1873) German				
oil	1	5,473	5,473	5,473
WEBER, C Phillip (1849-1921) American				
oil	4	1,300-3,750	2,675	2,400
WEBER, Carl (1850-1921) American				
oil	5	1,216-7,500	3,313	1,800
wc/d	4	450-1,700	975	800
WEBER, Denise (1929-1992) ?				
wc/d	3	2,752-5,504	4,128	4,128
WEBER, Evarist Adam (1887-1968) German				
oil	1	10,603	10,603	10,603
WEBER, H (1843-1913) German				
oil	1	2,213	2,213	2,213

Name	No.	Price Range	Average	Median
WEBER, Hugo (1918-1971) Swiss				
oil	1	12,000	12,000	12,000
WEBER, Jakob (c.1860-?) Russian				
oil	1	57,414	57,414	57,414
WEBER, Max (1881-1961) American				
oil	2	565-850,000	425,282	565
wc/d	7	600-320,000	57,114	6,500
WEBER, Otis S (19th C) American				
oil	2	850-1,700	1,275	850
WEBER, Paul (1823-1916) American/German				
oil	14	526-7,500	1,935	1,296
wc/d	1	539	539	539
WEBER, Robert (?) ?				
oil	1	1,050	1,050	1,050
WEBER, Rudolf (1872-1949) Austrian				
oil	2	1,216-4,332	2,774	1,216
WEBER, Sarah S Stilwell (1878-1939) American				
wc/d	1	6,000	6,000	6,000
WEBER, Theodore (1838-1907) French				
oil	6	1,392-8,372	4,522	3,041
WEBER, Walter Alois (1865-1905) American				
wc/d	2	850-1,600	1,225	850
WEBER, Werner (1892-1977) Swiss				
oil	5	524-3,044	1,163	763
WEBER, Werner Alois (1925-) Swiss				
3D	1	6,118	6,118	6,118
WEBER-TYROL, Hans Josef (1874-1957) Austrian				
oil	1	5,856	5,856	5,856
wc/d	1	5,455	5,455	5,455
WEBSTER, Daniel (?) American				
oil	1	1,200	1,200	1,200
WEBSTER, George (19th C) British				
oil	4	10,788-38,000	19,475	13,800
WEBSTER, Thomas (1800-1886) British				
oil	15	525-8,352	1,827	1,157
WEBSTER, Walter Ernest (1878-1959) British				
oil	4	885-7,785	4,518	2,500
wc/d	1	6,230	6,230	6,230
WECHBACHER, J (19th C) German				
oil	1	10,726	10,726	10,726
WECKESSER, August (1821-1899) Swiss				
oil	2	1,443-2,588	2,015	1,443
WECZERZICK, Alfred (1864-?) Czechoslovakian				
oil	1	1,294	1,294	1,294
WEDEL, Nils (1897-1967) Swedish				
oil	3	744-7,400	3,348	1,900
wc/d	2	1,454-3,822	2,638	1,454
WEDER, Jakob (1906-) ?				
oil	1	1,582	1,582	1,582
WEEBER, Eduard von (1834-1891) Austrian				
wc/d	1	1,018	1,018	1,018
WEEKES, Catharine (fl.1896-1918) British				
oil	2	1,403-13,275	7,339	1,403
WEEKES, William (fl.1864-1904) British				
oil	10	1,009-11,342	5,639	4,350
WEEKS, Edwin Lord (1849-1903) American				
oil	10	1,800-450,000	64,552	8,000
WEEKS, James (1922-1998) American				
oil	2	850-5,500	3,175	850
WEENIX, Jan (1640-1719) Dutch				
oil	2	13,877-242,200	128,038	13,877
WEENIX, Jan Baptist (1621-1663) Dutch				
oil	2	5,838-37,775	21,806	5,838
WEERT, Anna de (1867-1950) Belgian				
oil	6	1,920-96,680	28,935	7,265
wc/d	1	3,312	3,312	3,312
WEERTS, Jean Joseph (1847-1927) French				
oil	2	1,210-6,685	3,947	1,210
WEGELIN, Émile (1875-1962) French				
oil	1	7,350	7,350	7,350
wc/d	3	468-1,523	895	694

Name	No.	Price Range	Average	Median
WEGENER, Gerda (1885-1940) Danish				
oil	1	8,853	8,853	8,853
wc/d	8	1,204-5,369	2,600	1,324
WEGENER, Theodor (1817-1877) Danish				
oil	1	1,429	1,429	1,429
WEGMAN, William (1942-) American				
oil	3	5,500-13,000	10,100	11,800
wc/d	4	400-5,500	1,975	600
WEGMANN, Bertha (1847-1926) Danish				
oil	4	1,056-19,761	7,060	1,390
WEGMAYR, Sebastian (1776-1857) Austrian				
oil	1	29,189	29,189	29,189
WEGNER, Erich (1899-1980) German				
oil	1	1,854	1,854	1,854
wc/d	2	589-3,461	2,025	589
WEGUELIN, John Reinhard (1849-1927) British				
wc/d	1	1,701	1,701	1,701
WEHN, Randolf (1911-) German				
oil	1	1,332	1,332	1,332
WEI DONG (1968-) Chinese				
oil	1	15,000	15,000	15,000
WEI GUANGQING (1962-) Chinese				
oil	1	20,000	20,000	20,000
WEICHBERGER, Eduard (1843-1913) German				
oil	3	606-1,929	1,334	1,468
wc/d	2	730-4,364	2,547	730
WEIDEMANN, Friedrich Wilhelm (1668-1750) German				
oil	2	6,020-18,061	12,040	6,020
WEIDEMANN, Magnus (1880-1966) German				
oil	1	1,430	1,430	1,430
wc/d	1	825	825	825
WEIDINGER, Franz Xaver (1890-1972) Austrian				
oil	4	599-994	822	784
wc/d	3	514-759	660	707
WEIDL, Seff (1915-1972) ?				
3D	1	2,631	2,631	2,631
WEIDMANN, Ulrich (1840-1892) Swiss				
oil	1	2,289	2,289	2,289
WEIDNER, Joseph (1801-1870) Austrian				
oil	2	1,132-1,211	1,171	1,132
WEIE, Edvard (1879-1943) Danish				
oil	11	1,467-128,770	17,844	7,938
WEIGALL, Arthur Howes (fl.1856-1892) British				
oil	1	1,600	1,600	1,600
WEIGHT, Carel (1908-1997) British				
oil	17	873-28,350	7,132	4,779
wc/d	1	1,253	1,253	1,253
WEIGL, Robert (1851-1902) Austrian				
3D	1	3,214	3,214	3,214
WEILAND, Jaap (1891-1970) Dutch				
oil	1	1,553	1,553	1,553
WEILAND, James G (1872-1968) American				
oil	1	3,750	3,750	3,750
WEILAND, Johannes (1856-1909) Dutch				
oil	5	953-5,845	3,669	3,500
wc/d	1	2,169	2,169	2,169
WEILAND, Johannes (jnr) (1894-1976) Dutch				
oil	1	2,926	2,926	2,926
WEILER, Max (1910-2001) Austrian				
oil	8	12,138-145,655	49,593	29,131
wc/d	6	1,543-9,000	4,672	3,857
WEINBAUM, Abraham (1890-1943) Russian				
oil	4	1,176-3,781	2,165	1,798
wc/d	1	630	630	630
WEINBERG, Elbert (1928-1991) American				
3D	1	5,800	5,800	5,800
WEINER, Lawrence (1942-) American				
wc/d	2	6,000-20,000	13,000	6,000
3D	2	40,000-40,000	40,000	40,000
WEINERT, Mathilde (19th C) German?				
oil	2	2,662-2,926	2,794	2,662

Name	No.	Price Range	Average	Median
WEINGART, Joachim (1895-1942) Polish				
oil	4	2,219-11,744	6,716	2,383
wc/d	2	599-3,503	2,051	599
WEINMANN, Rudolf (1810-1878) Swiss				
oil	1	1,142	1,142	1,142
WEINSHEIMER, Henry William (1875-?) American				
oil	1	1,100	1,100	1,100
WEINSTEIN, Gal (1970-) Israeli				
wc/d	1	6,500	6,500	6,500
WEIR, Harrison William (1824-1906) British				
wc/d	1	1,471	1,471	1,471
WEIR, J Alden (1852-1919) American				
oil	1	50,000	50,000	50,000
wc/d	3	3,800-25,000	11,600	6,000
WEIR, Robert W (1803-1889) American				
oil	4	900-8,500	4,050	1,300
wc/d	1	900	900	900
WEIROTTER, Franz Edmund (1730-1771) Austrian				
oil	1	4,214	4,214	4,214
WEIS, John Ellsworth (1892-?) American				
oil	1	1,300	1,300	1,300
WEISBUCH, Claude (1927-) French				
oil	17	544-15,122	6,009	5,260
wc/d	4	970-2,421	1,583	1,030
WEISCHER, Matthias (1973-) German?				
oil	16	33,300-334,400	157,482	121,027
wc/d	3	2,293-2,464	2,407	2,464
WEISENBORN, Rudolph (1882-1974) American				
oil	2	1,000-4,000	2,500	1,000
WEISKONIG, Werner (1907-1982) Swiss				
oil	1	2,937	2,937	2,937
WEISMAN, Nadav (1969-) Israeli				
oil	1	3,300	3,300	3,300
WEISMANN, Jacques (1878-?) French				
oil	1	1,701	1,701	1,701
WEISS, David (1946-) Swiss				
wc/d	1	6,491	6,491	6,491
WEISS, Emil Rudolf (1875-1942) German				
oil	1	4,370	4,370	4,370
WEISS, Ferdinand Friedrich (1814-1878) German				
oil	2	648-1,989	1,318	648
WEISS, Franz Anton (1729-1784) German				
oil	1	2,041	2,041	2,041
WEISS, Jose (1859-1919) British				
oil	12	531-2,119	1,135	1,004
WEISS, Noah (1842-1907) American				
oil	2	9,500-9,500	9,500	9,500
WEISS, Peter (1916-1982) Swedish				
oil	1	4,453	4,453	4,453
wc/d	5	891-8,143	2,392	954
WEISS, Rudolf Johann (1846-1933) Swiss				
oil	4	609-69,600	31,751	1,798
WEISS, Rudolph (1869-?) Czechoslovakian				
oil	1	9,425	9,425	9,425
WEISS, Wojciech (1875-1950) Polish				
oil	1	1,200	1,200	1,200
WEISSBERG, Léon (1893-1943) Polish				
oil	3	1,259-1,576	1,384	1,318
WEISSE, Henry (?) ?				
3D	1	2,503	2,503	2,503
WEISSENBRUCH, Jan (1822-1880) Dutch				
oil	4	2,330-32,139	15,738	11,743
wc/d	1	975	975	975
WEISSENBRUCH, Jan Hendrik (1824-1903) Dutch				
oil	11	942-95,676	15,823	4,849
wc/d	7	1,001-46,708	12,436	7,500
WEISSENBRUCH, W (1864-1941) Dutch				
oil	1	1,821	1,821	1,821
WEISSENBRUCH, Willem (1864-1941) Dutch				
oil	2	1,199-3,048	2,123	1,199
WEISTLING, Morgan (20th C) American				
oil	1	42,500	42,500	42,500

Name	No.	Price Range	Average	Median
WEISZ, Adolphe (1838-1900) French/Hungarian				
oil	1	32,500	32,500	32,500
WEISZ, Paloma Varga (1966-) German				
3D	1	12,000	12,000	12,000
WEITSCH, Friedrich Georg (1758-1828) German				
oil	1	9,633	9,633	9,633
WEITSCH, Johann Friedrich (1723-1803) German				
oil	1	10,192	10,192	10,192
WELBY, G (19th C) British				
oil	1	4,250	4,250	4,250
WELCH, Denton (1915-1948) British				
oil	2	1,416-2,992	2,204	1,416
wc/d	1	2,431	2,431	2,431
WELCH, Ludmilla P (1867-1925) American				
oil	3	1,400-4,000	2,400	1,800
WELCH, Rosemary Sarah (1946-) British				
oil	2	626-4,048	2,337	626
WELCH, Thaddeus (1844-1919) American				
oil	5	700-7,500	4,640	4,500
wc/d	1	8,000	8,000	8,000
WELDEN, Leo von (1899-1967) ?				
oil	1	1,459	1,459	1,459
WELDON, Charles D (1855-1935) American				
oil	1	8,000	8,000	8,000
WELDON, Henry A (1841-?) American				
oil	1	5,000	5,000	5,000
WELIE, Antoon van (1866-?) Dutch				
oil	1	6,300	6,300	6,300
WELLENS, Charles (1889-1958) Belgian				
oil	2	583-3,879	2,231	583
WELLER, Simona (1940-) Italian				
oil	1	2,417	2,417	2,417
WELLER, Theodor Leopold (1802-1880) German				
wc/d	1	3,800	3,800	3,800
WELLERSHAUS, Paul (1887-1976) German				
oil	1	1,332	1,332	1,332
WELLING, James (1951-) American?				
oil	1	4,750	4,750	4,750
WELLIVER, Neil (1929-2005) American				
oil	1	8,000	8,000	8,000
WELLS, C J (1952-) American				
oil	1	2,000	2,000	2,000
WELLS, Cady (20th C) American?				
wc/d	1	8,500	8,500	8,500
WELLS, Dennis G (1881-1973) British				
oil	1	1,305	1,305	1,305
WELLS, George (fl.1842-1888) British				
oil	2	2,100-7,500	4,800	2,100
WELLS, John (1907-2000) British				
oil	7	8,550-30,940	16,839	15,170
wc/d	8	566-3,784	2,233	2,112
WELLS, Lynton (1940-) American				
oil	6	700-2,250	1,100	900
wc/d	1	600	600	600
WELLS, William (1842-1880) British				
oil	1	3,460	3,460	3,460
WELLS, William Page Atkinson (1871-1923) British				
oil	7	1,840-13,200	5,800	3,553
WELONSKI, Pius (1849-1931) Polish				
3D	1	2,500	2,500	2,500
WELSH, C (19th C) British				
oil	1	7,134	7,134	7,134
WELTI, Albert (1862-1912) Swiss				
oil	1	1,832	1,832	1,832
wc/d	2	1,082-1,998	1,540	1,082
WEMAIRE, Pierre (1913-) Belgian				
oil	5	1,753-3,395	2,673	2,748
wc/d	1	971	971	971
WENBAUM, Albert (c.1880-1943) French/Russian				
oil	1	2,091	2,091	2,091
WENCKE, Sophie (1874-1963) German				
oil	5	775-4,001	1,694	1,212

Name	No.	Price Range	Average	Median
WENCKEBACH, Oswald (1895-1962) Dutch				
3D	1	4,115	4,115	4,115
WENDEL, Theodore (1859-1932) American				
oil	3	25,000-65,000	50,000	60,000
WENDELIN, Martta (1893-1986) Finnish				
oil	1	2,805	2,805	2,805
wc/d	5	701-1,753	1,149	1,052
WENDLER, Friedrich Moritz (1814-1872) German				
oil	2	835-1,821	1,328	835
WENDLING, Gustav (1862-?) German				
oil	1	2,178	2,178	2,178
WENDT, William (1865-1946) American				
oil	10	6,500-65,000	35,550	32,000
WENGENROTH, Stow (1906-1978) American				
wc/d	3	750-1,920	1,456	1,700
WENGI, C (19th C) Swiss				
oil	1	2,447	2,447	2,447
WENGLEIN, Joseph (1845-1919) German				
oil	9	608-12,162	4,906	4,005
WENGLER, Johann Baptist (1815-1889) Austrian				
oil	3	626-2,804	1,397	761
WENK, Albert (1863-1934) German				
oil	4	608-4,295	1,680	816
WENKEBACH, L W R (19/20th C) ?				
oil	1	2,950	2,950	2,950
WENNERBERG, Brynolf (1823-1894) Swedish				
oil	2	1,296-2,592	1,944	1,296
WENNERBERG, Gunnar (1863-1914) Swedish				
oil	1	1,433	1,433	1,433
WENNING, Pieter (1873-1921) South African				
oil	1	3,277	3,277	3,277
WENNING, Ype (1879-1959) Dutch				
oil	3	647-1,767	1,079	825
WENNSTROM, Berndt (1945-) Swedish				
oil	2	786-1,586	1,186	786
WENOR, G (19th C) German?				
oil	1	2,068	2,068	2,068
WENTORF, Carl (1863-1914) Danish				
oil	1	1,429	1,429	1,429
WENTWORTH, Daniel F (1850-1934) American				
oil	2	900-3,000	1,950	900
WENTWORTH, Richard (20th C) ?				
3D	1	6,920	6,920	6,920
WENTZEL, Michael (1792-1866) German				
oil	1	7,500	7,500	7,500
WENZELL, Albert Beck (1864-1917) American				
oil	1	22,500	22,500	22,500
wc/d	2	6,500-8,000	7,250	6,500
WERDEHAUSEN, Hans (1910-1977) German				
oil	4	1,083-2,432	1,737	1,649
wc/d	2	884-942	913	884
WEREFKIN, Marianne von (1870-1938) Russian				
oil	3	18,542-133,745	85,962	105,600
WERFF, Adriaen van der (1659-1722) Dutch				
oil	1	29,195	29,195	29,195
wc/d	2	1,532-3,737	2,634	1,532
WERLEN, Ludwig (1884-1928) Swiss				
oil	1	1,945	1,945	1,945
WERNER, Alexander Friedrich (1827-1908) German				
wc/d	1	3,343	3,343	3,343
WERNER, B (?) ?				
oil	1	2,497	2,497	2,497
WERNER, Bernd (19/20th C) German				
oil	1	1,984	1,984	1,984
WERNER, Carl (1808-1894) German				
oil	1	6,555	6,555	6,555
WERNER, F (19th C) German				
oil	1	3,750	3,750	3,750
WERNER, Gosta (1909-1989) Swedish				
oil	4	755-6,871	3,639	1,586
WERNER, Gotthard (1837-1903) Swedish				
oil	1	2,610	2,610	2,610

Name	No.	Price Range	Average	Median
WERNER, Heinrich Ferdinand (1867-1928) German				
oil	2	1,113-1,360	1,236	1,113
WERNER, Hermann (1816-1905) German				
oil	1	5,000	5,000	5,000
WERNER, Hilding (1880-1944) Swedish				
oil	1	6,869	6,869	6,869
WERNER, Joseph (1818-1887?) Austrian				
wc/d	1	1,414	1,414	1,414
WERNER, Joseph II (1637-1710) Swiss				
wc/d	2	763-46,980	23,871	763
WERNER, Lambert (1900-1983) Swedish				
oil	3	509-1,718	1,251	1,527
WERNER, Theodor (1886-1969) German				
oil	8	927-17,199	6,708	3,461
wc/d	5	771-10,829	3,379	972
WERSIG, Bruno (1882-?) German				
oil	1	1,694	1,694	1,694
WERTHEIMER, Gustave (1847-1904) Austrian				
oil	2	400-3,250	1,825	400
WERTMULLER, Adolf Ulrik (1751-1811) Swedish				
oil	2	23,058-27,000	25,029	23,058
WERY, Albert (1650-?) Flemish				
oil	1	55,000	55,000	55,000
WERZ, Katharina von (1940-) German				
oil	1	1,058	1,058	1,058
WESCOTT, Paul (1904-1970) American				
oil	5	2,000-5,000	3,560	4,200
WESLEY, Frank (?) British?				
oil	1	1,139	1,139	1,139
WESLEY, John (1928-) American				
oil	5	1,100-125,000	54,420	55,000
wc/d	2	30,000-35,000	32,500	30,000
WESSEL, B (19th C) ?				
3D	1	3,131	3,131	3,131
WESSEL, Erich (20th C) German?				
oil	1	1,106	1,106	1,106
WESSEL, John (19/20th C) American				
oil	1	1,100	1,100	1,100
WESSEL-ZUMLOH, Irmgart (1907-) German				
oil	1	1,298	1,298	1,298
WESSELING, Hendrik Jan (1881-1950) Dutch				
oil	1	1,576	1,576	1,576
WESSELMANN, Tom (1931-2004) American				
oil	27	10,548-1,500,000	293,855	120,000
wc/d	48	2,102-222,945	25,338	15,000
3D	10	10,000-270,000	73,673	30,575
WESSMAN, Bjorn (1949-) Swedish				
oil	2	2,545-3,944	3,244	2,545
WESSON, Edward (1910-1983) British				
oil	13	797-2,112	1,155	1,026
wc/d	24	487-4,752	1,290	952
WESSON, Robert Shaw (1907-1967) American				
oil	1	1,900	1,900	1,900
WEST, Benjamin (1738-1820) British/American				
oil	4	10,395-59,850	36,046	23,940
wc/d	4	1,674-5,600	3,368	2,800
WEST, David (1868-1936) British				
oil	1	1,062	1,062	1,062
wc/d	9	1,381-5,696	4,264	4,984
WEST, Edgar (fl.1857-1889) British				
wc/d	2	453-1,750	1,101	453
WEST, Franz (1947-) Austrian				
oil	1	9,632	9,632	9,632
wc/d	2	42,041-100,000	71,020	42,041
3D	6	7,000-16,714	11,375	10,000
WEST, Lowren (1923-) American				
oil	1	1,800	1,800	1,800
wc/d	1	1,000	1,000	1,000
WEST, Michael (1908-1991) American				
oil	2	1,600-7,000	4,300	1,600
WEST, Norman (20th C) American				
oil	1	1,300	1,300	1,300

Name	No.	Price Range	Average	Median
WEST, Reginald (fl.1900-1910) British				
oil	1	2,288	2,288	2,288
WEST, Richard Whately (1848-1905) British				
oil	2	1,020-1,694	1,357	1,020
WEST, Samuel (19th C) British				
oil	1	1,500	1,500	1,500
WEST, Samuel S (fl.1818-1830) American				
oil	1	2,000	2,000	2,000
WESTALL, Richard (1765-1836) British				
oil	2	1,656-8,505	5,080	1,656
wc/d	1	400	400	400
WESTALL, William (1781-1850) British				
wc/d	1	5,180	5,180	5,180
WESTCHILOFF, Constantin (1877-1945) Russian				
oil	24	5,500-35,000	15,350	12,000
wc/d	4	1,150-11,000	4,924	3,548
WESTCOTT, Sarah Melendy (fl.1840-1880) American				
oil	1	6,000	6,000	6,000
WESTENDORP-OSIECK, Betsy (1880-1968) Dutch				
oil	2	853-2,170	1,511	853
WESTERBEEK, Cornelis (1844-1903) Dutch				
oil	4	471-2,003	1,304	1,178
WESTERGREN, Charlotta (1969-) Swedish				
oil	2	2,800-8,500	5,650	2,800
WESTERHOLM, Victor (1860-1919) Finnish				
oil	6	995-23,378	8,309	4,795
WESTERIK, Jacobus (1924-) Dutch				
oil	2	766-1,060	913	766
wc/d	12	1,060-10,014	3,251	2,438
WESTFELT-EGGERTZ, Ingeborg (1855-1936) Swedish				
oil	3	1,496-1,698	1,563	1,496
WESTHOVEN, Huybert van (c.1643-1687) Dutch				
oil	1	7,259	7,259	7,259
WESTIN, Fredrik (1782-1862) Swedish				
oil	1	7,830	7,830	7,830
WESTMACOTT, Richard (younger) (1799-1872) British				
3D	1	148,000	148,000	148,000
WESTMAN, Edvard (1865-1917) Swedish				
oil	4	7,071-50,143	18,762	8,486
WESTMAN, Inge Lise (1945-) Danish				
oil	1	1,161	1,161	1,161
WESTON, William Percy (1879-1967) Canadian				
oil	4	2,109-31,019	10,797	2,362
WESTPFAHL, Conrad (1891-1976) German				
oil	2	775-1,311	1,043	775
wc/d	4	618-2,351	1,347	775
WESTRA, Roelf (1908-1985) Dutch				
oil	1	3,816	3,816	3,816
WESTWOOD, Dennis (1928-) British				
3D	3	1,740-6,426	3,360	1,914
WET, Jacob Jacobsz de (1640-1697) Dutch				
oil	4	2,747-10,137	6,823	4,438
WET, Jacob de (1610-1671) Dutch				
oil	6	2,430-14,000	5,402	3,010
wc/d	1	595	595	595
WETERING DE ROOY, Johann Embrosius van de (1877-1972) Dutch				
oil	3	1,252-9,271	4,107	1,798
WETHERBEE, George Faulkner (1851-1920) American				
oil	3	900-4,350	2,050	900
WETLI, Hugo (1916-1972) Swiss				
oil	3	1,415-3,358	2,557	2,900
wc/d	1	534	534	534
WETS, Hubert (20th C) Belgian				
oil	1	1,080	1,080	1,080
WETZEL, Michael (1966-) American				
oil	1	5,000	5,000	5,000
WEVER, Auguste de (1836-?) Belgian				
3D	4	1,790-11,721	4,377	1,929
WEX, Adalbert (1867-1932) German				
oil	2	589-1,429	1,009	589
WEXLER, Jacob (1912-1994) Israeli				
oil	11	600-2,400	1,231	1,000

Name	No.	Price Range	Average	Median
WEYDEN, Harry van der (1868-?) American				
oil	10	550-2,600	1,377	915
WEYER, Hermann (17th C) German				
wc/d	1	4,055	4,055	4,055
WEYER, Jacob (c.1620-1670) German				
oil	1	4,304	4,304	4,304
wc/d	1	925	925	925
WEYER, Omer van de (1910-) Belgian				
oil	1	954	954	954
wc/d	1	890	890	890
WEYERMAN, Jacob Christoph (1698-1757) Dutch?				
oil	1	12,460	12,460	12,460
WEYHEN, Jacques van der (17th C) Flemish				
oil	1	24,196	24,196	24,196
WEYL, Max (1837-1914) American/German				
oil	3	1,400-3,500	2,466	2,500
WEYLSER, K (19th C) German				
oil	1	5,856	5,856	5,856
WEYNS, Jan Harm (1864-1945) Dutch				
oil	1	1,600	1,600	1,600
WEYNS, Jules (1849-1925) Belgian				
3D	1	7,707	7,707	7,707
WEYSSER, Karl (1833-1904) German				
oil	6	1,767-9,678	5,550	4,477
WEYTS, Petrus Cornelius (1799-1855) Flemish				
oil	1	13,000	13,000	13,000
WHAITE, T (19th C) British				
oil	1	3,750	3,750	3,750
WHALE, Robert Reginald (1805-1887) Canadian				
oil	2	1,939-44,076	23,007	1,939
WHALEY, Harold (20th C) British				
oil	1	2,175	2,175	2,175
WHALLEY, John (20th C) American				
wc/d	2	1,000-1,700	1,350	1,000
WHANKI, Kim (1913-1974) Korean				
wc/d	1	8,500	8,500	8,500
WHARF, John (?) American				
wc/d	1	7,100	7,100	7,100
WHATLEY, Henry (1824-1901) British				
wc/d	1	1,350	1,350	1,350
WHEALE, Ivan Trevor (?) Canadian				
oil	1	1,312	1,312	1,312
WHEATLEY, Francis (1747-1801) British				
oil	4	950-170,100	54,268	2,760
WHEATLEY, G H (20th C) American				
oil	1	1,100	1,100	1,100
WHEATON, Francis (1849-?) American				
oil	1	1,700	1,700	1,700
WHEELER, Alfred (1852-1932) British				
oil	7	1,343-4,900	2,864	2,580
WHEELER, John Arnold (1821-1903) British				
oil	9	540-12,000	5,122	4,862
WHEELER, John Frederick (1875-1930) British				
oil	1	1,218	1,218	1,218
WHEELER, Walter Herbert (1878-1960) British				
oil	1	1,700	1,700	1,700
WHEELWRIGHT, R (1870-1955) British				
oil	1	1,392	1,392	1,392
WHEELWRIGHT, Roland (1870-1955) British				
oil	2	9,744-11,832	10,788	9,744
WHEELWRIGHT, William H (fl.1857-1897) British				
oil	2	1,323-2,655	1,989	1,323
WHELAN, Leo (1892-1956) British				
oil	3	2,418-146,507	52,467	8,476
WHELAN, Michael (1950-) American				
oil	1	1,600	1,600	1,600
WHICHELO, Henry Mayle (snr) (1800-1884) British				
oil	1	2,208	2,208	2,208
WHIPPLE, Charles Ayer (1859-1928) American				
oil	1	1,600	1,600	1,600

Name	No.	Price Range	Average	Median
WHIPPLE, John (19th C) British				
oil	1	828	828	828
wc/d	1	560	560	560
WHISHAW, Anthony (1930-) British				
oil	4	777-4,248	1,803	797
wc/d	1	522	522	522
WHISTLER, James Abbott McNeill (1834-1903) American				
wc/d	3	11,830-200,000	93,943	70,000
WHISTLER, Rex (1905-1944) British				
wc/d	2	777-2,003	1,390	777
WHITAKER, David (1938-) British				
oil	1	1,653	1,653	1,653
WHITAKER, George (1834-1874) British				
wc/d	2	957-2,000	1,478	957
WHITAKER, George William (1841-1916) American				
oil	6	550-2,000	1,266	1,100
WHITAKER, William (1943-) American				
wc/d	1	1,000	1,000	1,000
WHITBY, William R (19th C) British				
oil	1	1,298	1,298	1,298
WHITCOMB, Jon (1906-1988) American				
wc/d	4	350-4,250	2,200	1,600
WHITCOMBE, Thomas (1760-c.1824) British				
oil	9	9,570-103,950	48,747	36,800
WHITE, Arthur (1865-1953) British				
oil	5	1,416-2,655	1,859	1,644
wc/d	6	616-3,520	1,455	1,021
WHITE, Charles J (20th C) American				
oil	1	1,100	1,100	1,100
WHITE, Cherry Ford (19/20th C) American				
oil	1	1,500	1,500	1,500
WHITE, Clarence Scott (1872-1965) American				
oil	1	1,400	1,400	1,400
wc/d	1	475	475	475
WHITE, Edith (1855-1946) American				
oil	5	500-8,500	3,680	3,250
WHITE, Elizabeth (1893-1976) American				
oil	1	15,000	15,000	15,000
WHITE, Ethelbert (1891-1972) British				
oil	6	704-8,256	4,300	1,653
wc/d	6	712-3,740	1,290	740
WHITE, Fritz (1930-) American				
3D	3	2,000-3,700	2,833	2,800
WHITE, Henry Cooke (1861-1952) American				
oil	2	2,000-3,250	2,625	2,000
WHITE, Jessie Aline (1889-1988) American				
wc/d	1	1,000	1,000	1,000
WHITE, John (1851-1933) British				
oil	1	3,872	3,872	3,872
wc/d	12	519-3,717	1,935	1,758
WHITE, Larry (1946-) American?				
oil	1	1,555	1,555	1,555
WHITE, Lieutenant Frederick (19th C) British				
wc/d	1	3,560	3,560	3,560
WHITE, Orrin A (1883-1969) American				
oil	15	3,500-45,000	14,283	7,500
WHITE, Ralph (1921-) American				
oil	1	1,500	1,500	1,500
WHITE, Ruby Zahn (1899-1986) American				
oil	1	2,000	2,000	2,000
WHITE, Valentino (1909-1985) Italian				
oil	2	2,000-3,884	2,942	2,000
WHITEHAND, Michael J (1941-) British				
oil	16	500-15,000	5,310	1,309
WHITEHEAD, Elizabeth (19th C) British				
oil	2	518-1,628	1,073	518
WHITEHEAD, Frederick (1853-1938) British				
oil	5	1,018-3,439	2,200	2,035
wc/d	3	525-760	615	560
WHITEHEAD, Jane Byrd (19/20th C) American				
oil	2	1,500-2,000	1,750	1,500
wc/d	1	375	375	375

Name	No.	Price Range	Average	Median
WHITELEY, John William (fl.1882-1916) British				
oil	2	1,730-3,850	2,790	1,730
WHITEREAD, Rachel (1953-) British				
wc/d	1	18,000	18,000	18,000
3D	6	27,750-444,000	276,975	230,100
WHITESIDE, Frank Reed (1866-1929) American				
oil	3	1,100-1,700	1,466	1,600
wc/d	2	375-1,300	837	375
WHITFORD, Richard (19th C) British				
oil	6	3,250-15,750	9,356	9,100
WHITING, Frederick (1874-1962) British				
oil	1	650	650	650
wc/d	2	515-1,890	1,202	515
WHITING, Henry W (19th C) American				
oil	1	2,500	2,500	2,500
WHITMAN, Sarah Wyman (1842-1904) American				
oil	1	3,250	3,250	3,250
WHITMORE, Coby (1913-1988) American				
oil	4	1,250-3,500	2,587	2,800
wc/d	1	6,500	6,500	6,500
WHITNEY, Edgar Albert (1891-1987) American				
wc/d	2	1,600-2,500	2,050	1,600
WHITTLE, Thomas (jnr) (19th C) British				
oil	3	550-1,496	1,028	1,040
WHITTONUS, Lucas (18th C) British?				
oil	1	3,220	3,220	3,220
WHITTREDGE, W (1820-1910) American				
oil	1	4,700	4,700	4,700
WHITTREDGE, Worthington (1820-1910) American				
oil	8	800-400,000	118,225	36,000
WHOOD, Isaac (1688-1752) British				
oil	2	1,925-34,020	17,972	1,925
WHORF, John (1903-1959) American				
oil	2	4,250-9,300	6,775	4,250
wc/d	46	750-32,000	7,657	4,000
WHORF, Nancy (20th C) American				
oil	2	2,100-4,500	3,300	2,100
WHYBROW, Terry (1932-) British				
oil	2	669-1,593	1,131	669
WHYDALE, Ernest Herbert (1886-1952) British				
oil	1	5,984	5,984	5,984
WHYMPER, Charles (1853-1941) British				
wc/d	6	703-3,168	1,500	739
WHYTE, Duncan McGregor (1866-1953) British				
oil	4	1,392-5,340	4,135	4,498
WIBAULT, Marcel (20th C) French				
oil	1	1,698	1,698	1,698
WIBERG, Gosta (1900-1971) Swedish				
oil	1	3,042	3,042	3,042
WIBERG, Harald (1908-1986) Swedish				
oil	6	1,424-2,894	2,010	1,496
wc/d	8	520-1,506	1,016	1,026
WICART, Nicolaas (1748-1815) Dutch				
wc/d	8	934-4,087	1,910	1,337
WICHERA, Raimund von (1862-1925) Austrian				
oil	1	3,400	3,400	3,400
wc/d	1	1,403	1,403	1,403
WICHGRAF, Fritz (1853-?) German				
oil	1	2,800	2,800	2,800
WICHMAN, Erich (1890-1929) Dutch				
oil	1	5,343	5,343	5,343
WICKENBERG, Per (1812-1846) Swedish				
oil	2	1,321-1,786	1,553	1,321
WICKENDEN, Robert J (1861-1931) American/British				
oil	1	2,468	2,468	2,468
WICKS, Ren (1911-1997) American				
wc/d	2	800-2,700	1,750	800
WICKS, Robert (1902-?) American				
oil	1	1,000	1,000	1,000
WIDDAS, Richard Dodd (1826-1885) British				
oil	1	1,216	1,216	1,216

Name	No.	Price Range	Average	Median
WIDFORSS, Gunnar M (1879-1934) American				
wc/d	10	416-30,000	15,010	14,000
WIDGERY, F J (1861-1942) British				
wc/d	2	496-2,921	1,708	496
WIDGERY, Frederick John (1861-1942) British				
oil	6	669-6,408	3,172	2,301
wc/d	53	460-6,764	1,585	1,044
WIDGERY, William (1822-1893) British				
oil	2	1,584-1,665	1,624	1,584
wc/d	8	450-5,622	1,885	1,125
WIDHOPFF, D O (1867-1933) French				
oil	6	1,764-4,468	2,973	3,073
WIDHOPFF, David Ossipovitch (1867-1933) French				
oil	4	1,558-2,397	2,130	2,170
wc/d	1	1,204	1,204	1,204
WIDLIZKA, Leopold (1870-?) Austrian				
oil	1	7,000	7,000	7,000
WIDMAN, Bruno (1930-) Uruguayan				
oil	2	1,900-2,000	1,950	1,900
WIDOFF, Anders (1953-) Swedish				
oil	6	396-15,904	5,160	2,445
wc/d	3	1,272-2,511	2,098	2,511
WIEDERHOLD, Carl (1865-1961) German				
oil	1	6,622	6,622	6,622
WIEDERHOLD, Sascha (1904-1962) German				
wc/d	1	2,038	2,038	2,038
WIEGAND, Charmion von (1899-1983) American				
wc/d	3	900-40,000	15,216	4,750
WIEGAND, Gustave (1870-1957) American				
oil	15	400-3,200	1,610	1,500
WIEGANDT, Bernhard (1851-1918) German				
wc/d	1	7,440	7,440	7,440
WIEGELE, Franz (1887-1944) Austrian				
oil	1	52,705	52,705	52,705
wc/d	1	788	788	788
WIEGERS, Jan (1893-1959) Dutch				
oil	6	3,312-34,347	15,075	6,361
wc/d	7	1,911-82,687	22,460	10,813
WIEGHORST, Olaf (1899-1988) American				
oil	17	1,200-65,000	28,541	26,000
wc/d	22	500-25,000	4,325	2,200
WIEGMAN, Matthieu (1886-1971) Dutch				
oil	4	1,502-23,562	8,146	3,255
WIEGMAN, Petrus Jacobus Maria (1930-) Dutch				
wc/d	1	2,338	2,338	2,338
WIEHL, Hermann (20th C) German				
oil	1	13,245	13,245	13,245
WIELAND, Hans Beat (1867-1945) Swiss				
oil	9	653-5,881	2,265	1,522
wc/d	2	1,450-1,783	1,616	1,450
WIELAND, Joyce (1931-) Canadian				
wc/d	1	1,280	1,280	1,280
WIELANDT, Manuel (1863-1922) German				
oil	4	1,940-9,864	5,790	4,757
WIEMANS, Andries (1826-?) Dutch				
oil	1	1,627	1,627	1,627
WIEMKEN, Walter Kurt (1907-1940) Swiss				
oil	1	7,216	7,216	7,216
wc/d	1	757	757	757
WIEN, Agathe van (20th C) German?				
oil	1	1,458	1,458	1,458
WIERER, Alois (1878-?) Czechoslovakian				
oil	1	1,767	1,767	1,767
WIERINGEN, Cornelis Claesz van (1580-1633) Dutch				
wc/d	1	22,000	22,000	22,000
WIERTZ, Antonie (1806-1865) Belgian				
oil	2	899-4,529	2,714	899
WIERUSZ-KOWALSKI, Alfred von (1849-1915) Polish				
oil	9	3,039-165,600	36,529	18,400
WIERUSZ-KOWALSKI, Maria (1926-1997) Polish				
3D	2	2,408-3,010	2,709	2,408

Name	No.	Price Range	Average	Median
WIESENTHAL, Franz (1856-1938) Hungarian				
oil	2	1,073-3,770	2,421	1,073
WIESSNER, Conrad (1796-1865) German				
wc/d	2	906-1,100	1,003	906
WIETHASE, Edgard (1881-1965) Belgian				
oil	5	514-3,240	1,361	989
wc/d	1	716	716	716
WIETHUCHTER, Gustav (1873-1946) German				
oil	1	7,644	7,644	7,644
WIGAND, Albert (1890-1978) German				
oil	1	3,956	3,956	3,956
wc/d	6	494-3,090	1,413	1,076
WIGAND, Balthasar (1771-1846) Austrian				
wc/d	3	1,216-15,727	8,873	9,678
WIGERT, Hans (1932-) Swedish				
oil	12	661-9,161	3,206	1,654
WIGGERS, Dirk (1866-1933) Dutch				
oil	2	1,008-2,397	1,702	1,008
WIGGINS, Carleton (1848-1932) American				
oil	8	1,100-9,000	4,147	1,632
WIGGINS, Guy A (1920-) American				
oil	1	4,690	4,690	4,690
WIGGINS, Guy Carleton (1883-1962) American				
oil	30	1,250-320,000	62,493	35,000
wc/d	2	750-1,100	925	750
WIGGINS, Kim Douglas (1960-) American				
oil	6	2,610-7,500	5,076	3,750
WIGGINS, Sydney Miller (1881-1940) American				
oil	1	1,500	1,500	1,500
WIGGLI, Oskar (1927-) Swiss				
3D	1	16,211	16,211	16,211
WIHLBORG, Gerhard (1897-1982) Swedish				
oil	3	373-5,418	2,137	622
WIIG-HANSEN, Svend (1922-1997) Danish				
3D	2	2,451-16,096	9,273	2,451
WIIK, Maria (1853-1928) Finnish				
wc/d	5	1,286-3,273	2,442	2,571
WIJNGAERDT, Piet van (1873-1964) Dutch				
oil	8	844-12,103	3,840	1,219
wc/d	1	2,586	2,586	2,586
WIKSTROM, Bror Anders (1854-1909) American/Swedish				
oil	1	1,500	1,500	1,500
WIKSTROM, Emil (1864-1942) Finnish				
3D	1	8,433	8,433	8,433
WILBERG, Martin (1853-?) German				
oil	1	2,238	2,238	2,238
WILBUR, Lawrence Nelson (1897-1988) American				
oil	1	2,800	2,800	2,800
wc/d	2	800-2,800	1,800	800
WILCOX, Dwayne (?) American				
wc/d	1	2,250	2,250	2,250
WILCOX, Frank Nelson (1887-1964) American				
wc/d	1	1,080	1,080	1,080
WILCOX, James Ralph (1866-1915) American				
wc/d	1	1,200	1,200	1,200
WILCOX, Jim (20th C) American				
oil	2	3,500-14,000	8,750	3,500
WILCOX, Leslie A (1904-1981) British				
oil	3	561-3,000	1,912	2,175
wc/d	1	496	496	496
WILCOX, Ruth (1908-) American				
oil	1	1,500	1,500	1,500
WILCOX, William H (1831-?) American				
oil	1	1,000	1,000	1,000
WILD, Charles (1781-1835) British				
wc/d	1	8,208	8,208	8,208
WILDA, Charles (1854-1907) Austrian				
oil	1	5,670	5,670	5,670
WILDE, August (1882-1950) German				
oil	1	1,211	1,211	1,211
WILDE, Charles (19th C) British				
oil	2	756-1,424	1,090	756

Name	No.	Price Range	Average	Median
WILDE, Frans de (19th C) Belgian				
oil	1	1,100	1,100	1,100
WILDE, John (1919-) American				
oil	2	5,000-5,000	5,000	5,000
WILDE, Samuel de (1748-1832) British				
oil	1	8,000	8,000	8,000
WILDER, Andre (1871-1965) French				
oil	8	1,546-11,000	4,508	3,330
wc/d	1	590	590	590
WILDNER, O (?) ?				
oil	2	2,289-3,100	2,694	2,289
WILDT, Adolfo (1868-1931) Italian				
3D	3	33,833-226,800	104,277	52,200
WILES, Irving Ramsey (1861-1948) American				
oil	2	10,000-90,000	50,000	10,000
WILES, Lemuel (1826-1905) American				
oil	6	1,000-8,500	4,291	3,500
WILEY, Kehinde (1977-) American				
oil	2	28,000-38,000	33,000	28,000
WILFORD, Loran (1892-1972) American				
oil	1	1,250	1,250	1,250
WILHELM, Paul (1886-1965) German				
oil	2	2,472-10,507	6,489	2,472
wc/d	5	658-1,196	1,018	1,051
WILHELMSON, Carl (1866-1928) Swedish				
oil	8	2,742-445,890	70,210	5,495
wc/d	2	2,247-2,267	2,257	2,247
WILHJELM, Johannes (1868-1938) Danish				
oil	4	893-2,445	1,441	1,161
WILKE, Paul Ernst (1894-1972) German				
oil	6	546-1,576	1,050	849
WILKENSON, Michael (20th C) American?				
3D	1	2,800	2,800	2,800
WILKERSON, Jerry (20th C) American				
oil	1	900	900	900
wc/d	1	1,900	1,900	1,900
WILKIE, Paul Brent (20th C) American				
oil	1	2,750	2,750	2,750
WILKIE, Sir David (1785-1841) British				
oil	1	1,381	1,381	1,381
wc/d	7	623-4,836	2,404	1,232
WILKINS, Cleo (1895-1979) American				
oil	1	1,000	1,000	1,000
WILKINSON, John B (19th C) Canadian				
wc/d	1	1,319	1,319	1,319
WILKINSON, Norman (1878-1971) British				
oil	11	743-9,300	3,735	2,835
wc/d	8	570-1,472	826	676
WILKOW, A (?) ?				
oil	1	2,066	2,066	2,066
WILKS, Maurice C (1910-1984) British				
oil	62	1,463-24,740	6,448	5,537
wc/d	10	708-2,680	1,241	1,025
WILKS, Sissa (1956-) British				
oil	1	1,073	1,073	1,073
WILLAERT, Ferdinand (1861-1938) Belgian				
oil	4	1,168-7,151	4,146	2,890
WILLAERTS, Abraham (1603-1669) Dutch				
oil	4	14,270-77,700	44,261	40,700
WILLAERTS, Adam (1577-1669) Dutch				
oil	4	12,370-160,000	84,860	79,486
WILLAERTS, Isaac (1620-1693) Dutch				
oil	2	5,340-28,480	16,910	5,340
WILLARD, Henry (1802-1855) American				
oil	1	2,500	2,500	2,500
WILLE, August von (1829-1887) German				
oil	3	907-7,297	4,324	4,770
WILLE, Fritz von (1860-1941) German				
oil	9	593-15,727	5,143	2,918
WILLE, Johann Georg (1715-1808) German				
oil	1	7,658	7,658	7,658
wc/d	2	3,180-4,834	4,007	3,180

Name	No.	Price Range	Average	Median
WILLE, Pierre-Alexandre (1748-1821) French				
wc/d	4	1,001-18,500	5,597	1,135
WILLEBOIRTS, Thomas (1614-1654) Flemish				
oil	2	5,444-13,308	9,376	5,444
WILLEMS, Florent (1823-1905) Belgian				
oil	7	850-14,384	4,028	2,600
WILLEMS, Jozef (1845-1910) Belgian				
3D	1	2,544	2,544	2,544
WILLEMSENS, Abraham (fl.1627-1672) Flemish?				
oil	2	29,410-42,000	35,705	29,410
WILLENHOUDT, Abraham (1600-1665) Flemish				
oil	1	6,072	6,072	6,072
WILLETO, Charlie (1906-1964) American				
oil	1	3,500	3,500	3,500
WILLIAMS FAMILY (19th C) British				
oil	1	2,450	2,450	2,450
WILLIAMS OF PLYMOUTH, William (1808-1895) British				
oil	2	2,001-7,120	4,560	2,001
WILLIAMS, A K (?) ?				
oil	1	1,994	1,994	1,994
WILLIAMS, Albert (1922-) British				
oil	6	696-2,595	1,654	1,151
WILLIAMS, Alexander (1846-1930) Irish				
oil	19	552-6,360	2,299	1,816
wc/d	8	690-1,937	1,217	848
WILLIAMS, Alfred Walter (1824-1905) British				
oil	3	600-1,980	1,296	1,309
WILLIAMS, Claudia (1933-) British				
oil	1	1,151	1,151	1,151
WILLIAMS, Darren (?) British				
wc/d	2	2,175-2,975	2,575	2,175
WILLIAMS, Don (20th C) American				
oil	2	700-1,000	850	700
wc/d	2	375-800	587	375
WILLIAMS, E C (1807-1881) British				
oil	1	1,144	1,144	1,144
WILLIAMS, Edward (1782-1855) British				
oil	4	708-5,520	2,487	1,125
WILLIAMS, Edward Charles (1807-1881) British				
oil	6	696-45,500	12,402	3,250
WILLIAMS, Frederick (fl.1827) British?				
wc/d	1	5,130	5,130	5,130
WILLIAMS, Frederick Ballard (1871-1956) American				
oil	5	850-3,800	2,380	2,750
WILLIAMS, Frederick Dickenson (1829-1915) American				
oil	1	3,600	3,600	3,600
WILLIAMS, George (20th C) American				
3D	1	2,500	2,500	2,500
WILLIAMS, George Augustus (1814-1901) British				
oil	5	890-3,114	2,399	2,662
WILLIAMS, Glynn (1939-) British				
3D	2	3,458-9,100	6,279	3,458
WILLIAMS, Harry (19th C) British				
oil	1	1,770	1,770	1,770
WILLIAMS, Harry Hughes (?) British				
wc/d	2	1,328-5,040	3,184	1,328
WILLIAMS, Harry J (fl.1885-1886) British				
wc/d	1	1,581	1,581	1,581
WILLIAMS, Henry (1787-1830) American				
oil	1	2,600	2,600	2,600
WILLIAMS, Hugh Grecian (1773-1829) British				
wc/d	6	1,575-14,960	4,173	1,780
WILLIAMS, J W C (19th C) American				
wc/d	1	3,200	3,200	3,200
WILLIAMS, John Haynes (1836-1908) British				
oil	1	2,640	2,640	2,640
WILLIAMS, Kate (?-1939) American				
oil	1	2,400	2,400	2,400
WILLIAMS, Kyffin (1918-) British				
oil	12	8,000-82,080	37,405	32,178
wc/d	18	1,197-12,600	6,949	5,742

Name	No.	Price Range	Average	Median
WILLIAMS, Lt Richard (c.1750-1776) British				
wc/d	7	2,478-290,000	97,231	75,000
WILLIAMS, Marian E (20th C) American				
oil	1	1,000	1,000	1,000
WILLIAMS, Paul A (1934-) American				
oil	1	1,700	1,700	1,700
WILLIAMS, Pauline Bliss (1888-?) American				
oil	1	1,600	1,600	1,600
WILLIAMS, Penry (1798-1885) British				
oil	1	19,500	19,500	19,500
WILLIAMS, Ruth Moore (1911-) American				
oil	1	1,300	1,300	1,300
WILLIAMS, Sheldon S (19th C) British				
oil	1	1,592	1,592	1,592
wc/d	1	1,539	1,539	1,539
WILLIAMS, Sue (1954-) American				
oil	3	35,000-45,000	40,000	40,000
wc/d	2	1,813-22,000	11,906	1,813
WILLIAMS, Terrick (1860-1936) British				
oil	8	1,208-17,915	6,222	3,400
wc/d	1	777	777	777
WILLIAMS, Virgil (1830-1886) American				
oil	1	10,000	10,000	10,000
WILLIAMS, Walter (1920-1998) American				
oil	1	4,750	4,750	4,750
WILLIAMS, Walter (1835-1906) British				
oil	4	519-7,785	3,244	2,249
WILLIAMS, Walter (19th C) British				
oil	1	1,313	1,313	1,313
WILLIAMS, Walter (fl.1841-1876) British				
oil	1	3,480	3,480	3,480
WILLIAMS, Walter Heath (19th C) British				
oil	5	481-3,096	1,789	1,653
WILLIAMS, Warren (1863-1918) British				
oil	1	648	648	648
wc/d	25	494-4,680	1,978	1,739
WILLIAMS, Wheeler (1897-1972) American				
3D	1	6,000	6,000	6,000
WILLIAMS, William (1727-1791) American				
oil	1	5,152	5,152	5,152
WILLIAMS, William (1837-1915) British				
oil	1	3,767	3,767	3,767
WILLIAMS-LYOUNS, Herbert (1863-1933) British				
oil	1	963	963	963
wc/d	1	806	806	806
WILLIAMSON, Frederick (c.1835-1900) British				
wc/d	3	1,408-3,828	2,358	1,838
WILLIAMSON, George (19th C) British				
oil	1	1,068	1,068	1,068
WILLIAMSON, Harold (1898-1972) British				
oil	1	1,512	1,512	1,512
WILLIAMSON, John (1826-1885) American				
oil	2	950-18,000	9,475	950
WILLIAMSON, R (19th C) British?				
oil	1	2,944	2,944	2,944
WILLIAMSON, William Henry (1820-1883) British				
oil	9	673-3,395	1,692	1,044
wc/d	1	443	443	443
WILLICH, Caesar (1825-1886) German				
oil	1	84,000	84,000	84,000
WILLIFORD, Hollis (1940-) American				
3D	1	4,250	4,250	4,250
WILLIKENS, Ben (1939-) German				
wc/d	2	865-2,474	1,669	865
WILLING, Victor (1928-1988) British				
	10	684-14,160	5,277	3,186
WILLINK, Carel (1900-1979) Dutch				
oil	1	19,110	19,110	19,110
wc/d	2	5,611-7,014	6,312	5,611
WILLIOT, Louis Auguste Adolphe (1829-1865) French				
oil	1	1,267	1,267	1,267

Name	No.	Price Range	Average	Median
WILLIS, Charles (20th C) British				
oil	1	1,313	1,313	1,313
WILLIS, Henry Brittan (1810-1884) British				
oil	2	750-3,591	2,170	750
wc/d	2	936-1,068	1,002	936
WILLIS, Thomas (1850-1912) American				
oil	7	900-10,000	4,957	4,500
wc/d	2	1,100-4,000	2,550	1,100
WILLISON, George (1741-1797) British				
oil	1	6,052	6,052	6,052
WILLMOTT, Orson P (19th C) American				
oil	1	1,200	1,200	1,200
WILLMS, Albert (19/20th C) ?				
wc/d	1	1,144	1,144	1,144
WILLOUGHBY, Trevor V (1926-) British				
oil	1	1,044	1,044	1,044
WILLOUGHBY, William (19th C) British?				
oil	1	2,750	2,750	2,750
WILLROIDER, Josef (1838-1915) Austrian				
oil	8	730-20,283	5,714	1,368
wc/d	1	1,331	1,331	1,331
WILLROIDER, Ludwig (1845-1910) German				
oil	9	471-10,216	3,880	3,299
WILLS, Edgar W (f.1874-1893) British				
oil	1	1,056	1,056	1,056
WILLSHER, Brian (1930-) British				
3D	1	2,646	2,646	2,646
WILLUMS, Olaf Abrahamsen (1886-1967) Norwegian				
oil	1	2,432	2,432	2,432
WILLUMSEN, Jens Ferdinand (1863-1958) Danish				
oil	1	33,945	33,945	33,945
wc/d	4	3,380-10,463	6,519	6,117
WILMARTH, Christopher (1943-1987) American				
wc/d	4	5,500-13,000	8,750	5,500
3D	1	80,000	80,000	80,000
WILMS, Albert (?) ?				
wc/d	1	1,731	1,731	1,731
WILSON, A M (19th C) British				
oil	1	4,498	4,498	4,498
WILSON, Benjamin (1721-1788) British				
oil	1	11,340	11,340	11,340
WILSON, Bryan (1927-2002) American				
oil	3	1,500-2,000	1,700	1,600
WILSON, Charles Edward (1854-1941) British				
wc/d	3	2,340-3,520	2,922	2,907
WILSON, Charles Heath (1840-1886) British				
wc/d	1	1,414	1,414	1,414
WILSON, Donald Roller (1938-) American				
oil	1	13,000	13,000	13,000
WILSON, Dora Lynell (1883-1946) Australian				
oil	1	1,044	1,044	1,044
WILSON, Edward Adrian (1872-1912) British				
wc/d	5	910-8,100	4,625	3,916
WILSON, Ellis (1899-1977) American				
oil	6	5,500-32,000	13,416	8,000
wc/d	1	4,000	4,000	4,000
WILSON, Francis (1876-1957) British				
oil	1	1,239	1,239	1,239
WILSON, Frank Avray (1914-) British				
oil	3	2,119-3,000	2,703	2,992
WILSON, Gus (1864-1950) American				
3D	1	140,000	140,000	140,000
WILSON, Hiram G (19th C) American				
oil	1	8,500	8,500	8,500
WILSON, John (1774-1855) British				
oil	4	1,148-7,350	3,729	1,620
WILSON, John James (1818-1875) British				
oil	7	491-5,568	2,758	1,656
WILSON, Mary Loomis (1907-1999) American				
oil	1	5,000	5,000	5,000
WILSON, Matthew Henry (1814-1892) American				
oil	1	1,900	1,900	1,900

Name	No.	Price Range	Average	Median
WILSON, Oscar (1867-1930) British				
oil	1	1,300	1,300	1,300
WILSON, Pat (20th C) French?				
oil	8	549-2,104	1,111	850
WILSON, Patten (1868-1928) British				
oil	1	884	884	884
wc/d	1	1,142	1,142	1,142
WILSON, Richard (1714-1782) British				
oil	2	800-4,250	2,525	800
wc/d	1	6,228	6,228	6,228
WILSON, Robert (1941-) American				
wc/d	6	927-3,131	2,020	2,047
WILSON, Ronald York (1907-1984) Canadian				
oil	6	498-3,526	1,698	1,066
wc/d	2	1,148-1,312	1,230	1,148
WILSON, Ross (1959-) British				
oil	2	3,720-7,440	5,580	3,720
wc/d	4	708-3,009	2,089	2,301
WILSON, Samuel Henry (?) British				
wc/d	1	1,309	1,309	1,309
WILSON, Scottie (1891-1972) British				
wc/d	26	460-8,486	1,495	837
WILSON, Sol (1896-1974) American/Polish				
oil	2	750-1,700	1,225	750
wc/d	1	475	475	475
WILSON, Thomas Walter (19th C) British				
wc/d	1	2,349	2,349	2,349
WILSON, W (18/19th C) British				
oil	1	1,144	1,144	1,144
WILSON, William (1905-1972) British				
oil	1	783	783	783
wc/d	7	1,098-7,434	4,246	4,602
WILSON, William Hardy (1881-1955) Australian				
wc/d	1	1,573	1,573	1,573
WIMMER, Konrad (1844-1905) German				
oil	2	2,761-4,176	3,468	2,761
WIMPERIS, Edmund Morison (1835-1900) British				
oil	4	634-6,612	2,471	1,176
wc/d	10	443-1,110	709	620
WINANT, Alice (1926-1989) Rumanian				
3D	1	2,250	2,250	2,250
WINCHELL, Paul (20th C) American				
oil	2	700-1,425	1,062	700
WINCK, Johann Amandus (1748-1817) German				
oil	4	9,936-22,500	13,523	10,829
WINCK, Johann Christian Thomas (1738-1797) German				
oil	1	53,650	53,650	53,650
WINDHAUSER, H (19/20th C) ?				
oil	1	2,035	2,035	2,035
WINDHEIM, Dorothee von (1945-) German				
oil	2	1,028-1,028	1,028	1,028
WINDLE, J (19th C) British?				
oil	1	28,000	28,000	28,000
WINDMAIER, Anton (1840-1896) German				
oil	3	1,210-2,572	1,804	1,632
WINDRED, E H (?) ?				
oil	1	2,392	2,392	2,392
WINDT, Chris van der (1877-1952) Dutch				
oil	2	2,503-2,719	2,611	2,503
wc/d	3	1,502-2,503	1,877	1,627
WINGATE, Sir James Lawton (1846-1924) British				
oil	10	557-2,958	1,418	1,044
WINGE, Marten Eskil (1825-1896) Swedish				
wc/d	1	1,374	1,374	1,374
WINGER-STEIN, Helene (1884-1945) Austrian				
oil	1	21,848	21,848	21,848
WINGFIELD, James Digman (1809-1872) British				
oil	3	1,057-22,680	8,979	3,200
WINGFIELD, R C (19th C) ?				
oil	1	1,281	1,281	1,281

Name	No.	Price Range	Average	Median
WINGREN, Dan (1923-) American				
oil	2	1,500-4,000	2,750	1,500
wc/d	1	800	800	800
WINKLER-HAGEDORN, Carl Friedrich (19/20th C) German?				
oil	1	1,576	1,576	1,576
WINPENNY, George H (19/20th C) British?				
oil	1	1,116	1,116	1,116
WINSOR, Jackie (1941-) American				
3D	1	50,000	50,000	50,000
WINSTANLEY, Paul (1954-) British				
oil	2	4,440-14,800	9,620	4,440
WINSTEN, Clare (20th C) British?				
oil	1	531	531	531
3D	1	9,680	9,680	9,680
WINT, Peter de (1784-1849) British				
wc/d	14	736-17,400	5,427	2,076
WINTER, Agnes (20th C) ?				
3D	1	2,267	2,267	2,267
WINTER, Andrew (1893-1958) American				
oil	8	2,500-9,500	4,812	4,000
WINTER, Charles Allan (1869-1942) American				
oil	3	500-4,000	2,300	2,400
WINTER, Emi (1973-) Mexican				
oil	1	3,800	3,800	3,800
WINTER, Fritz (1905-1976) German				
oil	38	1,288-140,137	21,105	11,449
wc/d	23	514-13,993	3,307	1,929
WINTER, George (1810-1876) American				
oil	3	3,250-85,000	42,750	40,000
WINTER, Heinrich (1843-1911) German				
oil	1	1,420	1,420	1,420
WINTER, Janus de (1882-1951) Dutch				
oil	1	1,341	1,341	1,341
wc/d	3	1,463-2,572	1,995	1,951
WINTER, Robert A (1953-) American				
oil	1	2,500	2,500	2,500
WINTER, William Arthur (1909-1986) Canadian				
oil	11	820-3,299	1,951	1,898
wc/d	1	436	436	436
WINTERHALTER, Franz Xavier (1806-1873) German				
oil	2	14,000-1,748,000	881,000	14,000
WINTERHALTER, Hermann (1808-1891) German				
oil	1	9,722	9,722	9,722
WINTERLIN, Anton (1805-1894) Swiss				
oil	2	916-5,724	3,320	916
wc/d	1	1,388	1,388	1,388
WINTERS, Terry (1949-) American				
oil	1	60,000	60,000	60,000
wc/d	4	4,800-35,000	21,450	22,000
WINTERSBERGER, Lambert Maria (1941-) German				
oil	3	1,560-6,181	3,610	3,090
wc/d	1	2,803	2,803	2,803
WINTHER, Frederick Julius August (1853-1916) Danish				
oil	4	697-1,630	1,056	949
WINTHER, Poul (1939-) Danish				
oil	2	1,051-1,293	1,172	1,051
WINTHER, Richard (1926-) Danish				
oil	4	889-6,496	3,865	1,610
WINTTER, Joseph Georg (1751-1789) German				
wc/d	2	1,576-2,122	1,849	1,576
WINTZ, Guillaume (1823-1899) French				
oil	1	1,511	1,511	1,511
WINTZ, Raymond (1884-1956) French				
oil	3	631-3,039	1,628	1,215
WIRBEL, Veronique (1950-1990) French				
oil	1	4,122	4,122	4,122
WIRGMAN, Charles (1832-1891) British				
oil	1	14,508	14,508	14,508
wc/d	1	1,850	1,850	1,850
WIRTH, Anna Maria (1846-1922) Russian				
oil	1	6,008	6,008	6,008

Name	No.	Price Range	Average	Median
WIRTH, Henri (1869-1947) French				
oil	1	3,029	3,029	3,029
WIRTH-MILLER, Denis (1915-) British				
oil	1	1,112	1,112	1,112
WISELBERG, Rose (1908-1992) Canadian				
oil	4	734-1,939	1,441	1,386
WISINGER-FLORIAN, Olga (1844-1926) Austrian				
oil	6	5,260-215,280	78,350	14,566
WISLICENUS, Lilli (1872-1939) German				
3D	1	2,395	2,395	2,395
WISSELINGH, Johannes Pieter van (1812-1899) Dutch				
oil	2	1,060-8,429	4,744	1,060
WISSING, Willem (1653-1687) Dutch				
oil	3	5,670-156,531	58,741	14,022
WISTROM, Alfred (1833-1873) Swedish				
oil	1	1,786	1,786	1,786
WISZNIEWSKI, Adrian (1958-) ?				
oil	1	6,960	6,960	6,960
WIT, Jacob de (1695-1754) Dutch				
oil	3	12,098-57,329	27,389	12,740
wc/d	3	1,000-4,253	2,140	1,168
WIT, Prosper Joseph de (c.1862-c.1951) Belgian				
oil	9	514-3,567	1,557	1,092
WITASEK, Emil (1900-?) Austrian				
oil	1	4,841	4,841	4,841
WITDOECK, Petrus Josephus (1803-1840) Flemish				
oil	2	1,520-1,870	1,695	1,520
WITHERINGTON, William Frederick (1785-1865) British				
oil	3	1,040-4,176	2,550	2,436
WITHERS, Edward Oscar (1896-1964) American				
oil	1	3,500	3,500	3,500
WITHERS, Walter (1854-1914) Australian				
oil	1	16,815	16,815	16,815
WITHERSTINE, Donald (1896-1961) American				
oil	1	1,500	1,500	1,500
WITHOOS, Alida (1660-1715) Dutch				
oil	1	9,993	9,993	9,993
WITHOOS, Matthias (1627-1703) Dutch				
oil	2	2,768-15,000	8,884	2,768
WITHOOS, Pieter (1654-1693) Dutch				
wc/d	1	2,544	2,544	2,544
WITJENS, Jacques Stephen (1881-1956) Dutch				
oil	13	2,000-13,000	4,546	4,000
WITJENS, Willem (1884-1962) Dutch				
oil	2	610-1,808	1,209	610
WITKAMP, Ernest Sigismund (1854-1897) Dutch				
oil	2	3,781-3,827	3,804	3,781
WITKOWSKI, Karl (1860-1910) American				
oil	4	3,500-18,000	11,000	7,500
WITSEN, Willem (1860-1923) Dutch				
oil	1	2,158	2,158	2,158
WITTE, Adrien de (1850-1935) Belgian				
oil	1	1,432	1,432	1,432
wc/d	1	2,185	2,185	2,185
WITTE, Emanuel de (1617-1692) Dutch				
oil	1	270,000	270,000	270,000
WITTE, Marthe de (1893-1976) ?				
wc/d	1	4,555	4,555	4,555
WITTEL, Gaspar van (1653-1736) Dutch				
oil	4	362,466-1,656,164	901,320	778,500
WITTEVRONGEL, Roger (1933-) Belgian				
wc/d	1	1,052	1,052	1,052
WITTIG, Hermann (1819-1891) German				
3D	2	3,058-3,185	3,121	3,058
WITTKAMP, Johann Bernhard (1820-1885) German				
oil	1	2,384	2,384	2,384
WITTLER, Heinrich (1918-1979) German				
oil	1	1,051	1,051	1,051
wc/d	2	574-718	646	574
WITTLICH, Josef (1903-1982) German?				
oil	1	4,123	4,123	4,123
wc/d	2	2,127-4,868	3,497	2,127

Name	No.	Price Range	Average	Median
WITTMACK, Edgar Franklin (1894-1956) American				
oil	1	2,200	2,200	2,200
WITTMANN, Karoline (1913-) German				
oil	1	5,040	5,040	5,040
WITZ, C (19th C) ?				
oil	1	7,297	7,297	7,297
WITZ, Johann Benedikt (1709-1780) German				
3D	3	12,000-17,027	14,388	14,137
WIVELL, Abraham (jnr) (fl.1848-1865) British				
wc/d	1	2,340	2,340	2,340
WIX, Henry Otto (1866-1922) American				
oil	1	1,200	1,200	1,200
WLASOFF, Sergej F (1859-1924) Russian				
oil	1	1,798	1,798	1,798
WLERICK, Robert (1882-1944) French				
3D	1	7,169	7,169	7,169
WOCHER, Tiberius Dominikus (1728-1799) Swiss				
wc/d	1	1,767	1,767	1,767
WOELFFER, Emerson (1914-) American				
oil	1	4,000	4,000	4,000
WOERFFEL, Abraham C F (19/20th C) Russian				
3D	1	3,800	3,800	3,800
WOERFFEL, C F (?) Russian?				
3D	1	3,750	3,750	3,750
WOESTIJNE, Gustave van de (1881-1947) Belgian				
oil	3	17,671-48,208	29,421	22,384
wc/d	2	1,944-2,386	2,165	1,944
WOESTIJNE, Maxime van de (1911-2000) Belgian				
oil	2	1,607-2,343	1,975	1,607
wc/d	1	718	718	718
WOHLWILL, Gretchen (1878-1962) German				
wc/d	1	1,967	1,967	1,967
WOICESKE, Ronau William (1887-1953) American				
oil	1	1,700	1,700	1,700
WOLBERS, Hermanus Gerhardus (1856-1926) Dutch				
oil	2	756-2,500	1,628	756
WOLCHONOK, Louis (1898-1973) American				
oil	1	3,000	3,000	3,000
WOLCK, Nikolaus (1887-1950) German				
oil	2	3,484-3,735	3,609	3,484
wc/d	2	995-1,213	1,104	995
WOLCK, Preben (1925-2000) Danish				
oil	2	995-1,127	1,061	995
WOLF, Franz Xaver (1896-1989) Austrian				
oil	5	1,138-6,300	2,996	2,420
WOLF, Georg (1882-1962) German				
oil	12	477-2,057	939	746
wc/d	1	676	676	676
WOLF, Victorine (19th C) German				
oil	1	1,086	1,086	1,086
WOLF, Wallace L de (1854-1930) American				
oil	1	1,200	1,200	1,200
WOLFAERTS, Artus (1581-c.1641) Flemish				
oil	1	21,673	21,673	21,673
WOLFE, Byron B (1904-1973) American				
wc/d	5	550-3,000	2,210	2,750
WOLFE, Edward (1897-1982) British				
oil	5	1,620-14,800	7,260	3,600
wc/d	8	661-2,500	1,578	1,710
WOLFE, Karl (1904-) American				
wc/d	1	3,500	3,500	3,500
WOLFE, Mildred Nungester (1912-) American				
oil	2	1,000-3,250	2,125	1,000
WOLFE, Steve (1955-) American				
3D	1	65,000	65,000	65,000
WOLFE, Wayne E (1945-) American				
oil	1	15,000	15,000	15,000
WOLFERS, Philippe (1858-1929) Belgian				
3D	1	27,986	27,986	27,986
WOLFF, Albert (1814-1892) German				
3D	1	9,031	9,031	9,031

Name	No.	Price Range	Average	Median
WOLFF, Albert Moritz (1854-1923) German				
3D	6	4,841-20,640	11,104	7,440
WOLFF, Balduin (1819-1907) German				
oil	1	1,401	1,401	1,401
WOLFF, Bertha (19th C) German				
oil	1	1,936	1,936	1,936
WOLFF, Cornelis de (1889-1963) Dutch				
oil	1	2,303	2,303	2,303
WOLFF, Eugen (1873-1937) German				
oil	2	650-4,351	2,500	650
WOLFF, Jose (1884-1964) Belgian				
oil	9	607-1,890	1,038	1,011
WOLFF, Moritz (19th C) ?				
3D	2	2,676-4,487	3,581	2,676
WOLFLE, Franz Xavier (1887-1972) German				
oil	9	650-2,832	1,173	850
WOLFLI, Adolf (1864-1930) Swiss				
wc/d	4	7,566-48,947	26,773	13,868
WOLFRATH, Harry (1926-) German				
oil	1	1,168	1,168	1,168
WOLFSEN, Aleijda (1648-1690) Dutch				
oil	1	8,900	8,900	8,900
WOLFSFELD, Erich (19/20th C) ?				
oil	3	542-2,640	1,748	2,062
WOLFTHORN, Julie (1868-?) ?				
oil	3	2,967-4,834	3,754	3,461
WOLFVOET, Victor (1612-1652) Flemish				
oil	1	34,600	34,600	34,600
WOLGA, P (19th C) Russian				
oil	1	1,824	1,824	1,824
WOLGERS, Dan (1955-) Swedish				
oil	1	3,817	3,817	3,817
wc/d	3	5,947-9,670	8,068	8,589
3D	4	2,643-4,625	3,725	3,181
WOLINSKI, Georges (1934-) Tunisian				
wc/d	1	3,201	3,201	3,201
WOLLASTON, John (?-1770) British				
oil	1	65,000	65,000	65,000
WOLLEN, William Barns (1857-1936) British				
wc/d	2	962-1,936	1,449	962
WOLLHEIM, Gert (1894-1974) American/German				
oil	5	1,532-10,014	4,776	4,795
wc/d	2	994-1,178	1,086	994
WOLMANS, Jacques (1919-1991) Belgian				
oil	1	1,106	1,106	1,106
WOLMARK, Alfred (1877-1961) British				
oil	9	703-31,450	6,154	2,379
WOLPERDING, Friedrich Ernst (1815-1888) German				
oil	1	4,849	4,849	4,849
WOLS, Wolfgang (1913-1951) German				
wc/d	9	16,035-52,800	28,564	22,490
WOLSELEY, Garnet (1884-1967) British				
oil	4	1,593-10,395	6,797	5,190
WOLSKI, Ignacy (20th C) ?				
oil	1	1,000	1,000	1,000
WOLSKI, Jan (?) ?				
oil	1	1,400	1,400	1,400
WOLSTENHOLME, Dean (snr) (1757-1837) British				
oil	4	6,688-47,250	26,534	20,520
WOLTER, Hendrik Jan (1873-1952) Dutch				
oil	10	1,318-11,689	5,342	4,425
wc/d	1	1,678	1,678	1,678
WOLTERS, Eugène (1844-1905) Belgian				
oil	2	1,790-4,142	2,966	1,790
WOLTERS, Georg (1866-1943) German				
oil	1	1,463	1,463	1,463
WOLTZE, Berthold (1829-1896) German				
oil	1	12,000	12,000	12,000
WOLVECAMP, Theo (1925-1992) Dutch				
oil	6	1,781-15,774	7,087	3,507
wc/d	4	427-1,929	954	602

Name	No.	Price Range	Average	Median
WOLVENS, Henri Victor (1896-1977) Belgian				
oil	11	1,171-14,651	6,229	5,890
wc/d	1	514	514	514
WONDER, Wolf (1947-) German				
oil	1	15,276	15,276	15,276
WONDRUSCH, Ernst Ferdinand (1949-) Austrian				
oil	1	1,798	1,798	1,798
WONG, Harold (1943-) Chinese				
wc/d	2	1,286-2,829	2,057	1,286
WONNER, Paul (1920-) American				
oil	7	1,400-240,000	72,914	20,000
wc/d	4	2,250-25,000	10,562	4,000
WONTNER, William Clarke (1857-1930) British				
oil	4	31,320-90,000	52,330	38,000
WOO, Jade Fon (1911-1983) American				
wc/d	10	600-7,500	2,320	1,600
WOOD, Alan (1935-) British/Canadian				
oil	1	1,062	1,062	1,062
WOOD, Albert Victor Ormsby (1904-1977) Irish				
oil	1	1,488	1,488	1,488
wc/d	2	957-957	957	957
WOOD, Beatrice (1893-1998) American				
wc/d	1	1,286	1,286	1,286
WOOD, Catherine M (fl.1880-1929) British				
oil	4	890-3,872	2,075	1,593
wc/d	1	443	443	443
WOOD, Christopher (1901-1930) British				
oil	6	493-302,400	150,990	121,100
wc/d	6	1,044-23,270	6,906	3,480
WOOD, Edgar Thomas (1860-1935) British				
oil	1	2,076	2,076	2,076
WOOD, Ella Miriam (1888-1976) American				
oil	1	5,250	5,250	5,250
WOOD, Frank Watson (1862-1953) British				
oil	2	1,754-10,380	6,067	1,754
wc/d	10	502-2,655	1,582	1,406
WOOD, George Bacon (jnr) (1832-1910) American				
oil	2	2,000-2,400	2,200	2,000
WOOD, Grant (1892-1942) American				
oil	2	18,000-6,200,000	3,109,000	18,000
wc/d	1	3,000	3,000	3,000
WOOD, J B (19/20th C) British				
oil	1	17,500	17,500	17,500
WOOD, John T (1845-1919) American				
oil	1	1,200	1,200	1,200
WOOD, John Warrington (1839-1886) British				
3D	1	2,670	2,670	2,670
WOOD, Kate (fl.1912-1927) British				
oil	1	1,200	1,200	1,200
WOOD, Kenneth A (20th C) American?				
wc/d	1	2,400	2,400	2,400
WOOD, Lawson (1878-1957) British				
wc/d	2	704-3,096	1,900	704
WOOD, Lewis John (1813-1901) British				
oil	2	641-2,119	1,380	641
wc/d	3	555-626	579	557
WOOD, Ogden (1851-1912) American				
oil	1	2,250	2,250	2,250
WOOD, Robert E (1926-1999) American				
oil	1	486	486	486
wc/d	1	2,750	2,750	2,750
WOOD, Robert Sydney Rendle (1894-?) British				
wc/d	1	1,225	1,225	1,225
WOOD, Robert W (1889-1979) American				
oil	51	950-12,000	4,896	4,500
wc/d	1	1,000	1,000	1,000
WOOD, Robert William (1901-1977) American				
oil	2	3,750-6,750	5,250	3,750
WOOD, Stanley (1894-1949) American				
wc/d	3	1,600-2,500	2,033	2,000
WOOD, Thomas Peploe (1817-1845) British				
oil	1	4,121	4,121	4,121

Name	No.	Price Range	Average	Median
WOOD, Thomas Waterman (1823-1903) American				
oil	1	10,000	10,000	10,000
WOOD, Watson (1900-1985) British				
wc/d	1	1,056	1,056	1,056
WOOD, William J (20th C) British?				
oil	2	1,216-1,460	1,338	1,216
WOODALL, William (18th C) British				
oil	1	1,607	1,607	1,607
WOODBURY, Charles (1864-1940) American				
oil	13	800-35,000	8,326	4,000
wc/d	3	1,300-3,250	2,183	2,000
WOODBURY, Marcia Oakes (1865-1913) American				
oil	2	2,000-2,750	2,375	2,000
wc/d	1	2,000	2,000	2,000
WOODCOCK, Percy Franklin (1855-1936) Canadian				
oil	1	1,322	1,322	1,322
WOODFORD, David (1938-) British				
oil	3	885-4,320	2,089	1,062
WOODHOUSE, William (1857-1939) British				
oil	5	3,401-17,000	9,099	6,802
wc/d	4	576-2,001	1,052	688
WOODINGTON, William Frederick (1806-1893) British				
oil	1	2,973	2,973	2,973
WOODLOCK, David (1842-1929) British				
wc/d	11	455-5,985	2,030	1,674
WOODROW, Bill (1948-) British				
3D	1	2,800	2,800	2,800
WOODRUFF, Hale (1900-1980) American				
oil	1	36,000	36,000	36,000
WOODRUFF, Jonah ('?) American				
oil	1	4,750	4,750	4,750
WOODRUFF, Porter (20th C) American				
oil	1	2,577	2,577	2,577
WOODS, Clare (1972-) British				
oil	1	14,800	14,800	14,800
WOODS, Henry (1846-1921) British				
oil	3	969-54,560	24,576	18,200
WOODS, Padraic (1893-1991) Irish				
oil	4	1,272-3,720	2,052	1,311
WOODSIDE, Christine A (1946-) British				
oil	1	1,225	1,225	1,225
WOODSIDE, John Archibald (snr) (1781-1852) American				
oil	1	4,000	4,000	4,000
WOODVILLE, Richard Caton (jnr) (1856-1927) British				
oil	1	15,120	15,120	15,120
wc/d	4	493-1,850	1,018	595
WOODWARD, Ellsworth (1861-1939) American				
oil	1	4,250	4,250	4,250
WOODWARD, G Pewstress (19th C) British				
oil	1	3,204	3,204	3,204
WOODWARD, Mabel (1877-1945) American				
oil	23	1,300-49,000	6,186	3,000
wc/d	2	1,300-1,500	1,400	1,300
WOODWARD, Stanley W (1890-1970) American				
oil	5	681-8,000	2,386	900
wc/d	2	375-1,450	912	375
WOODWARD, Thomas (1801-1852) British				
oil	1	1,214	1,214	1,214
WOODWARD, William (1935-) American				
oil	1	1,800	1,800	1,800
WOODWARD, William (1859-1939) American				
oil	1	15,000	15,000	15,000
wc/d	2	1,600-1,800	1,700	1,600
WOOL, Christopher (1955-) American				
oil	16	4,000-1,250,000	283,656	80,000
wc/d	2	38,000-40,000	39,000	38,000
WOOLLETT, Henry (19th C) British				
oil	1	2,249	2,249	2,249
WOOLLETT, Henry A (19th C) British				
oil	1	14,000	14,000	14,000
WOOLLETT, Henry Charles (fl.1851-1872) British				
oil	2	1,488-1,492	1,490	1,488

Name	No.	Price Range	Average	Median
WOOLLEY, W (19th C) British?				
oil	1	3,145	3,145	3,145
WOOLMER, Alfred Joseph (1805-1892) British				
oil	1	1,232	1,232	1,232
WOOLNER, Thomas (1825-1892) British				
3D	2	4,275-5,340	4,807	4,275
WOOLSEY, Clarence (20th C) American				
3D	2	3,500-5,000	4,250	3,500
WOOTTON, Frank (1911-1998) British				
oil	5	1,062-3,738	2,314	2,538
wc/d	1	1,584	1,584	1,584
WOOTTON, John (c.1682-1764) British				
oil	5	11,040-342,000	105,688	68,400
WOPFNER, Joseph (1843-1927) Austrian				
oil	5	3,633-15,000	9,212	8,948
wc/d	1	890	890	890
WORES, Theodore (1859-1939) American				
oil	3	19,000-37,500	26,333	22,500
wc/d	1	2,250	2,250	2,250
WORMS, Gastao (1905-) Brazilian				
oil	1	3,360	3,360	3,360
WORMS, Jules (1832-1924) French				
oil	2	1,052-4,275	2,663	1,052
WORN, Walter (1901-1963) German				
oil	1	5,096	5,096	5,096
wc/d	2	486-1,435	960	486
WORNDLE, Edmund von (1827-1906) Austrian				
oil	2	2,385-7,342	4,863	2,385
WORP, Willem van der (1803-1878) Belgian				
oil	1	2,253	2,253	2,253
WORRALL, Joseph E (1829-1913) British				
oil	2	1,566-5,985	3,775	1,566
WORRALL, Mark (1942-) British				
oil	1	1,368	1,368	1,368
WORSEL, Troels (1950-) Danish				
oil	10	705-3,863	1,907	1,543
wc/d	1	514	514	514
WORSEY, Thomas (1829-1875) British				
oil	6	864-4,928	2,180	1,296
WORTEL, Ans (1929-1996) Dutch				
oil	1	2,128	2,128	2,128
wc/d	3	539-1,908	1,185	1,110
WORTHINGTON, David (20th C) British				
wc/d	1	1,193	1,193	1,193
3D	1	1,790	1,790	1,790
WORTHINGTON, John (19th C) British				
oil	1	2,700	2,700	2,700
WORTLEY, Archibald James Stuart (1847-1905) British				
oil	1	1,032	1,032	1,032
WOTRUBA, Fritz (1907-1975) Austrian				
wc/d	2	2,803-6,069	4,436	2,803
3D	11	1,987-105,411	22,954	3,233
WOU, Claes Claesz (1592-1665) Dutch				
oil	2	8,500-9,570	9,035	8,500
WOUTERMAERTENS, Edouard (1819-1897) Belgian				
oil	7	533-13,368	3,847	2,592
WOUTERS, Frans (1614-1659) Flemish				
oil	2	4,984-19,852	12,418	4,984
WOUTERS, Jean François de (18th C) Dutch?				
oil	1	5,733	5,733	5,733
WOUTERS, Rik (1882-1916) Belgian				
oil	1	2,003	2,003	2,003
wc/d	9	4,326-70,068	20,503	10,520
3D	2	11,181-229,315	120,248	11,181
WOUW, Anton van (1862-1945) South African				
3D	1	20,790	20,790	20,790
WOUWER, Roger van de (1933-) Belgian				
oil	1	1,798	1,798	1,798
WOUWERMAN, Philips (1619-1668) Dutch				
oil	8	27,474-573,500	195,352	95,548
WOYTUK, Peter (?) ?				
3D	1	10,141	10,141	10,141

Name	No.	Price Range	Average	Median
WRAGE, Hans (1921-) German				
oil	1	1,829	1,829	1,829
WRETLING, David (1901-1986) Swedish				
3D	1	1,860	1,860	1,860
WRETMAN, Fredrik (1953-) Swedish?				
3D	1	1,784	1,784	1,784
WRIGHT OF DERBY, Joseph (1734-1797) British				
oil	4	49,140-368,550	204,322	153,900
wc/d	2	20,790-297,600	159,195	20,790
WRIGHT, Charles Lennox (1876-?) American				
oil	1	6,000	6,000	6,000
WRIGHT, Cliff (1963-) British				
wc/d	1	4,400	4,400	4,400
WRIGHT, David (20th C) British				
oil	1	18,000	18,000	18,000
WRIGHT, Ferdinand von (1822-1906) Finnish				
oil	3	7,143-29,281	18,784	19,929
wc/d	2	1,374-1,987	1,680	1,374
WRIGHT, Frank (1932-) American				
oil	1	3,250	3,250	3,250
WRIGHT, Frank Arnold (1874-1930) British				
3D	1	6,048	6,048	6,048
WRIGHT, George (1860-1942) British				
oil	19	557-20,000	7,958	5,670
WRIGHT, George H B (20th C) British				
oil	1	26,400	26,400	26,400
WRIGHT, Gilbert Scott (1880-1958) British				
oil	4	2,500-9,450	5,959	4,158
WRIGHT, H C Seppings (1850-1937) British				
wc/d	2	560-4,576	2,568	560
WRIGHT, James (?-1947) British				
oil	3	550-1,151	750	550
wc/d	2	460-1,903	1,181	460
WRIGHT, Joseph (fl.1880-1927) British				
oil	1	2,200	2,200	2,200
WRIGHT, Magnus von (1805-1868) Finnish				
oil	1	1,019	1,019	1,019
wc/d	3	659-10,775	5,826	6,044
WRIGHT, Richard Henry (1857-1930) British				
wc/d	7	512-2,457	1,105	945
WRIGHT, Robert Murdoch (fl.1889-1902) British				
wc/d	2	968-1,239	1,103	968
WRIGHT, Robert W (fl.1880-1900) British				
oil	1	10,092	10,092	10,092
WRIGHT, Wilhelm von (1810-1887) Finnish				
wc/d	1	30,575	30,575	30,575
WRINCH, Mary Evelyn (1877-1969) Canadian				
oil	5	1,280-3,565	1,936	1,649
WROBLEWSKI, Constantin (1868-1939) Russian				
oil	1	10,320	10,320	10,320
WSSEL DE GUIMBARDA, Manuel (1833-1907) Spanish				
oil	2	18,828-25,000	21,914	18,828
WU HAO (1973-) Chinese				
oil	1	5,021	5,021	5,021
WU MINGZHONG (1963-) Chinese				
oil	1	40,700	40,700	40,700
WU SHANZHUAN (1960-) Chinese				
oil	1	38,000	38,000	38,000
WU WEI (1459-1508) Chinese				
wc/d	1	25,000	25,000	25,000
WUBBELS, Jan (18th C) Dutch				
oil	1	51,800	51,800	51,800
WUCHERER, Fritz (1873-1948) Swiss				
oil	2	1,438-1,678	1,558	1,438
wc/d	3	658-1,001	862	927
WUERMER, Carl (1900-1982) American				
oil	6	4,500-15,000	7,333	5,000
WUIDAR, Léon (1938-) Belgian				
oil	1	1,214	1,214	1,214
WUJCIK, Theo (1936-) American				
oil	1	1,100	1,100	1,100

Name	No.	Price Range	Average	Median
WULFEN, Amelie von (1966-) German?				
wc/d	1	1,800	1,800	1,800
WULFF, Willy (1881-?) Danish				
3D	1	1,610	1,610	1,610
WULFFAERT, Adrien (1804-1873) Belgian				
oil	1	6,072	6,072	6,072
WULFRAET, Mathijs (1648-1727) Dutch				
oil	1	7,013	7,013	7,013
WUNDERLICH, Edmund (1902-1985) Swiss				
oil	1	2,061	2,061	2,061
wc/d	1	1,166	1,166	1,166
WUNDERLICH, Max Julius (1878-1966) Austrian				
oil	1	2,180	2,180	2,180
WUNDERLICH, Paul (1927-) German				
oil	4	1,900-4,919	2,949	2,033
wc/d	7	701-6,592	2,803	2,719
3D	5	1,767-3,836	2,387	2,153
WUNDERWALD, Gustav (1882-1945) German				
oil	3	12,361-23,425	19,737	23,425
wc/d	2	1,145-1,316	1,230	1,145
WURBS, Carl (1807-1876) Czechoslovakian				
oil	1	7,000	7,000	7,000
WURM, Erwin (1954-) Austrian				
wc/d	1	964	964	964
3D	2	1,808-7,283	4,545	1,808
WURTH, Xavier (1869-1933) Belgian				
oil	5	535-832	639	618
wc/d	1	501	501	501
WURTZEN, Carl (1825-1880) Danish				
oil	3	650-6,640	2,957	1,581
WURZEN, Johann (19th C) ?				
oil	1	1,462	1,462	1,462
WUST, Christoffel (1801-?) American				
oil	1	2,425	2,425	2,425
WUST, Johann Heinrich (1741-1821) Swiss				
oil	2	12,938-15,175	14,056	12,938
WUSTLICH, Otto (1818-1886) German				
oil	2	1,566-3,012	2,289	1,566
WUTHRICH, Charles (1875-1967) Swiss				
oil	2	3,263-3,753	3,508	3,263
WUTKY, Michael (1739-1823) Austrian				
oil	1	53,400	53,400	53,400
WUTTKE, Carl (1849-1927) German				
oil	12	726-10,177	2,878	1,829
wc/d	1	1,168	1,168	1,168
WYANT, Alexander H (1836-1892) American				
oil	13	1,100-18,000	5,600	4,250
wc/d	2	500-6,000	3,250	500
WYATT, Benjamin Dean (1775-1850) British				
wc/d	2	2,262-6,615	4,438	2,262
WYATT, Sir Matthew Digby (1820-1877) British				
wc/d	1	1,044	1,044	1,044
WYCK, J van (?) Belgian				
oil	1	1,000	1,000	1,000
WYCK, Jan (1640-1702) Dutch				
oil	1	2,922	2,922	2,922
WYCK, Thomas (1616-1677) Dutch				
oil	7	4,110-37,000	16,277	15,419
WYCKAERT, Maurice (1923-1996) Belgian				
oil	16	1,641-28,603	9,856	8,182
wc/d	2	1,204-4,697	2,950	1,204
WYDEVELD, Arnoud (19th C) Dutch				
oil	3	2,500-5,500	3,666	3,000
WYDOOGEN, N M (19th C) Dutch				
oil	6	1,753-6,466	4,239	3,319
WYETH, Andrew (1917-) American				
oil	1	3,900,000	3,900,000	3,900,000
wc/d	11	4,750-480,000	188,613	170,000
WYETH, Henriette (1907-1997) American				
oil	3	14,000-40,000	24,666	20,000

Name	No.	Price Range	Average	Median
WYETH, James (1946-) American				
oil	1	330,000	330,000	330,000
wc/d	7	450-85,000	36,207	31,000
WYETH, Newell Convers (1882-1945) American				
oil	8	44,000-800,000	228,125	160,000
wc/d	1	2,800	2,800	2,800
WYGANT, Bob (1927-) American				
oil	2	6,500-10,000	8,250	6,500
WYGRZYWALSKI, Feliks (1875-1944) Polish				
oil	1	2,580	2,580	2,580
WYK, Charles van (1875-1917) Dutch				
3D	1	2,338	2,338	2,338
WYK, Henri van (1833-?) Dutch				
oil	1	1,638	1,638	1,638
WYLD, William (1806-1889) British				
oil	3	3,080-24,076	12,681	10,888
wc/d	6	4,576-24,180	10,454	9,570
WYLIE, Kate (1877-1941) British				
oil	7	880-3,784	2,239	1,619
WYLLIE, Charles William (1853-1923) British				
oil	1	6,000	6,000	6,000
WYLLIE, Gordon H (1930-) British				
oil	1	1,298	1,298	1,298
WYLLIE, William Lionel (1851-1931) British				
oil	6	2,992-42,000	12,112	7,080
wc/d	23	525-5,610	1,510	1,218
WYMER, Reginald Augustus (19/20th C) British				
wc/d	2	1,147-1,517	1,332	1,147
WYN, A van der (?) ?				
oil	1	1,991	1,991	1,991
WYNANTS, Ernest (1878-1964) Belgian				
3D	4	2,428-49,140	15,909	3,822
WYNANTS, Jan (1630-1684) Dutch				
oil	2	36,294-62,500	49,397	36,294
wc/d	1	452	452	452
WYNANTSZ, August (1795-1848) Dutch				
oil	2	1,008-2,408	1,708	1,008
WYNDHAM, Richard (1896-1948) British				
oil	1	1,092	1,092	1,092
WYNER, Irv (20th C) American				
wc/d	1	3,500	3,500	3,500
WYNGAARD, L (?) ?				
oil	1	2,342	2,342	2,342
WYNGAERDT, Anthonie Jacobus van (1808-1887) Dutch				
oil	10	1,381-10,448	5,147	4,712
WYNGAERT, Ch van (19th C) ?				
oil	1	2,790	2,790	2,790
WYNN, Kenneth (1922-) British?				
oil	2	4,000-5,000	4,500	4,000
WYNNE, David (1926-) British				
3D	4	3,024-27,000	11,628	4,488
WYNNE, Gladys (1878-1968) Irish				
wc/d	1	1,636	1,636	1,636
WYNNE-JONES, Nancy (1922-) British				
oil	1	1,649	1,649	1,649
wc/d	1	1,216	1,216	1,216
WYNTER, Bryan (1915-1975) British				
oil	2	15,470-15,930	15,700	15,470
wc/d	2	1,074-4,862	2,968	1,074
WYNTRACK, Dirck (1625-1678) Dutch				
oil	1	2,926	2,926	2,926
WYRSCH, Charles (1920-) Swiss				
oil	5	647-2,664	1,348	1,176
WYSMULLER, Jan Hillebrand (1855-1925) Dutch				
oil	4	1,764-3,687	2,771	2,038
wc/d	6	585-2,397	1,735	1,798
WYSOCKI, Charles M (1929-2002) American				
oil	1	4,200	4,200	4,200
WYTSMAN, Juliette (1866-1925) Belgian				
oil	1	1,528	1,528	1,528
WYTSMAN, Rodolphe (1860-1927) Belgian				
oil	8	814-11,192	5,037	3,624

Name	No.	Price Range	Average	Median
WYTTENBACH, Emanuel (1903-) American				
oil	1	2,600	2,600	2,600
WYWIORSKY, Michal (1861-1926) Polish				
oil	7	701-5,021	2,490	1,944
XCERON, Jean (1890-1967) American/Greek				
oil	1	500	500	500
wc/d	3	900-2,300	1,500	1,300
XENOS (1939-) Greek				
oil	1	1,870	1,870	1,870
XENOS, Nicholaos (1908-1984) Greek				
oil	2	655-1,730	1,192	655
XIANG JING (1968-) Chinese				
3D	1	25,000	25,000	25,000
XIAO MOU (18/19th C) Chinese				
wc/d	1	1,051	1,051	1,051
XIMENES, Ettore (1855-1926) Italian				
oil	1	1,352	1,352	1,352
wc/d	2	592-3,568	2,080	592
XIN HAIZHOU (1966-) Chinese				
oil	1	5,019	5,019	5,019
XIONG YU (1975-) Chinese				
oil	1	20,000	20,000	20,000
XU BEIHONG (1895-1953) Chinese				
wc/d	1	7,591	7,591	7,591
XU BING (1955-) Chinese				
wc/d	1	140,000	140,000	140,000
3D	1	350,000	350,000	350,000
XU GU (1824-1896) Chinese				
wc/d	2	5,500-9,500	7,500	5,500
XU GUANGJU (1974-) Chinese				
wc/d	1	16,000	16,000	16,000
XU LEI (1963-) Chinese				
wc/d	1	85,000	85,000	85,000
XU LONGSEN (1956-) Chinese				
wc/d	1	10,000	10,000	10,000
XU WENTAO (1968-) Chinese				
oil	1	5,021	5,021	5,021
XU XIUKAI (1963-) Chinese				
oil	1	8,818	8,818	8,818
XUAREZ, Nicolas Rodriguez (1667-1734) Mexican				
oil	1	32,000	32,000	32,000
XUE SONG (1965-) Chinese				
wc/d	1	22,000	22,000	22,000
XUL SOLAR, Alejandro (1887-1963) Argentinian				
oil	1	20,000	20,000	20,000
XYLANDER, Wilhelm (1840-1913) Danish				
oil	1	7,027	7,027	7,027
YABLONSKA, Tetyana Nilovna (1917-) Russian				
oil	1	65,360	65,360	65,360
YAGHFOURI, Said (1975-) Moroccan				
oil	1	1,495	1,495	1,495
YAKOVLEV, Vladimir (1934-1998) Russian				
wc/d	5	3,162-40,000	16,480	11,160
YAKUNIN, Vladimir Fedorovich (1944-) Russian				
oil	1	13,760	13,760	13,760
YAMAGUCHI, Ai (1977-) Japanese				
oil	1	9,500	9,500	9,500
YAMOU, Abderrahim (1959-) Moroccan				
oil	1	4,131	4,131	4,131
YAN (20th C) ?				
oil	1	8,900	8,900	8,900
YAN LEI (1965-) Chinese				
oil	1	40,000	40,000	40,000
YAN PEI MING (1960-) Chinese				
oil	12	24,547-187,027	95,114	92,500
wc/d	1	18,542	18,542	18,542
YANDELL, Enid (1870-1934) American				
3D	1	2,188	2,188	2,188
YANEZ, Ferrando (fl.1506-1560) Spanish				
oil	1	48,611	48,611	48,611
YANG JIECHANG (1956-) Chinese				
wc/d	2	8,000-20,084	14,042	8,000

Name	No.	Price Range	Average	Median
YANG JINSONG (1971-) Chinese				
oil	1	14,800	14,800	14,800
YANG KIHOON (1843-1897) Korean				
wc/d	1	1,300	1,300	1,300
YANG LIMING (1975-) Chinese				
oil	1	5,933	5,933	5,933
YANG LIU (1982-) Chinese				
oil	1	5,000	5,000	5,000
YANG QIAN (1959-) Chinese				
oil	5	16,000-40,000	28,260	25,900
YANG SHAOBIN (1963-) Chinese				
oil	3	75,000-115,000	91,083	83,250
YANKEL (1920-) French				
wc/d	1	1,753	1,753	1,753
YANKEL, Jacques (1920-) French				
oil	9	643-4,326	1,740	1,178
YANKILEVSKY, Vladimir (1938-) Russian				
oil	1	30,000	30,000	30,000
wc/d	2	15,810-40,920	28,365	15,810
YANN, Robert (1901-1994) French				
oil	3	807-1,286	1,087	1,169
YAO HENG (18/19th C) Chinese				
wc/d	1	2,500	2,500	2,500
YARBER, Robert (1948-) American				
oil	1	16,397	16,397	16,397
YARD, Sydney Janis (1855-1909) American				
oil	1	1,600	1,600	1,600
wc/d	8	850-3,500	2,006	1,000
YARDLEY, Bruce (1962-) British				
oil	2	728-1,274	1,001	728
YARDLEY, John (1933-) British				
oil	4	968-1,079	1,038	1,044
wc/d	5	428-1,295	858	819
YARWOOD, Walter Hawley (1917-1996) Canadian				
3D	1	2,474	2,474	2,474
YARZ, Edmond (19th C) French				
oil	1	10,703	10,703	10,703
YASUYUKI, Suzuki (1911-1980) Japanese				
wc/d	1	5,000	5,000	5,000
YATCHENKO, Youri (1928-) Russian				
oil	1	3,186	3,186	3,186
YATES, Cullen (1866-1945) American				
oil	4	1,200-13,000	4,275	1,300
YATES, Fred (1922-) British				
oil	58	440-10,560	2,295	1,539
wc/d	6	440-1,770	730	493
YATES, Gideon (1790-1837) British				
wc/d	5	2,035-4,524	3,119	2,784
YATES, Harold James (?) British				
oil	1	1,050	1,050	1,050
YBANEZ, Miguel (20th C) ?				
oil	1	1,252	1,252	1,252
YBERTRACHTER, Simon (1694-1772) Austrian				
oil	1	6,181	6,181	6,181
YDSTROM, Gosta (1861-1952) Swedish				
oil	1	1,020	1,020	1,020
YE YONG QING (1958-) Chinese				
oil	2	11,470-12,552	12,011	11,470
YEATS, Anne (1919-2001) Irish				
oil	9	1,359-6,675	3,709	3,892
wc/d	1	2,655	2,655	2,655
YEATS, Jack Butler (1871-1957) Irish/British				
oil	20	35,116-966,027	172,634	93,000
wc/d	23	2,104-130,200	19,904	9,300
YECKLEY, Norman H (1914-1994) American				
oil	1	2,250	2,250	2,250
YEGOROV, Andrei (1878-1954) Russian				
oil	2	509-3,185	1,847	509
wc/d	10	1,496-4,234	2,799	2,790
YELLAND, Raymond D (1848-1900) American				
oil	5	3,500-30,000	10,650	5,000

Name	No.	Price Range	Average	Median
YENCESSE, Hubert (1900-) French				
3D	2	2,514-7,014	4,764	2,514
YENS, Karl Julius Heinrich (1868-1945) American				
oil	4	750-2,750	1,937	2,000
YENTE, Maria Eugenia Crenovich (1905-?) Argentinian				
wc/d	1	26,000	26,000	26,000
YEPEZ ARTEAGA, Jose (1898-?) Ecuadorian				
oil	1	8,270	8,270	8,270
YERMOLOV, Pavel (1971-) Russian				
oil	1	1,145	1,145	1,145
YEROS, Dimitris (1948-) Greek				
oil	1	5,280	5,280	5,280
YEWELL, George Henry (1830-1923) American				
oil	1	14,000	14,000	14,000
YI HAUNG (1820-1898) Korean				
wc/d	1	3,500	3,500	3,500
YIHUA WANG (20th C) Chinese				
oil	1	11,931	11,931	11,931
YKENS, Catharina (1659-?) Flemish				
oil	1	22,200	22,200	22,200
YKENS, Frans (1601-1693) Flemish				
oil	2	6,081-15,570	10,825	6,081
YO LANZ (?) Chinese?				
oil	1	2,957	2,957	2,957
YOAKUM, Joseph E (1886-1973) American				
wc/d	2	1,600-3,400	2,500	1,600
YOCKNEY, Algernon (19/20th C) British				
oil	1	1,056	1,056	1,056
YOHN, Frederick Caffrey (1875-1933) American				
oil	3	750-2,200	1,583	1,800
YOKOI, Teruko (1924-) Japanese				
oil	2	1,221-1,298	1,259	1,221
wc/d	2	1,249-5,342	3,295	1,249
YOKOYAMA, Taikan (1868-1958) Japanese				
wc/d	2	27,750-40,000	33,875	27,750
YOLDJOGLOU, Georges (c.1955-) French				
oil	13	475-1,800	1,146	1,100
YONG, Joe de (1894-1975) American				
oil	1	10,000	10,000	10,000
wc/d	2	1,500-2,500	2,000	1,500
YOO SEUNG HO (1973-) Chinese				
wc/d	1	24,000	24,000	24,000
YORKE, William Gay (1817-1883) American				
oil	3	6,500-55,000	25,166	14,000
YORKE, William Hoard (fl.1858-1903) British				
oil	9	2,028-19,000	7,092	7,480
YOSHIDA, Hiroshi (1876-1950) Japanese				
wc/d	6	700-5,000	2,300	1,850
YOSHIMITSU (19/20th C) Japanese				
3D	1	20,880	20,880	20,880
YOUNG HOON KO (20th C) ?				
oil	1	13,155	13,155	13,155
YOUNG SUN LIM (1958-) Korean				
3D	1	12,000	12,000	12,000
YOUNG, Alexander (1865-1923) British				
oil	4	673-6,688	2,424	769
YOUNG, Bessie Innes (1855-1936) British				
oil	1	3,629	3,629	3,629
YOUNG, Charles Morris (1869-1964) American				
oil	1	18,000	18,000	18,000
wc/d	2	2,200-2,400	2,300	2,200
YOUNG, Edward (1823-1882) Austrian/British				
oil	1	1,574	1,574	1,574
wc/d	1	602	602	602
YOUNG, Florence Upson (1872-1964) American				
oil	2	1,100-3,500	2,300	1,100
YOUNG, Harry Anthony de (1893-1956) American				
oil	3	500-15,000	6,916	5,250
YOUNG, Harvey (1840-1901) American				
oil	4	2,000-7,500	4,500	3,000
YOUNG, Jean (1914-) British				
oil	2	543-2,937	1,740	543

Name	No.	Price Range	Average	Median
YOUNG, Mabel (1889-1974) Irish/British				
oil	9	1,052-5,220	3,611	3,828
YOUNG, Mahonri (1877-1957) American				
3D	1	19,000	19,000	19,000
YOUNG, Purvis (1943-) American				
oil	7	650-1,900	1,057	800
wc/d	1	2,750	2,750	2,750
YOUNG, Robert Clouston (fl.1920s) British				
oil	1	2,768	2,768	2,768
YOUNG, Stephen Scott (1957-) American				
wc/d	1	17,000	17,000	17,000
YOUNG, William (19th C) British				
oil	1	1,427	1,427	1,427
YOUNG, William S (fl.1850-1870) American				
oil	2	2,250-2,750	2,500	2,250
YOUNGERMAN, Jack (1926-) American				
oil	5	547-17,000	5,739	3,400
wc/d	1	1,000	1,000	1,000
3D	1	8,000	8,000	8,000
YOUNGMAN, Paul (1941-) American				
oil	1	2,500	2,500	2,500
YOUON, Konstantin (1875-1958) Russian				
oil	4	7,144-930,000	302,025	34,145
wc/d	1	206,400	206,400	206,400
YOUQUA (19th C) Oriental				
oil	1	42,500	42,500	42,500
YOURIEVITCH, Serge (20th C) French				
3D	1	26,162	26,162	26,162
YPPEN, Grete (1917-) Austrian				
oil	1	4,886	4,886	4,886
YSENDYCK, Anton van (1801-1875) Belgian				
oil	1	4,808	4,808	4,808
YSERN Y ALIE, Pedro (1876-1946) Spanish				
oil	3	1,093-1,532	1,346	1,414
YSSEL, Aart van den (1922-1983) Dutch				
oil	1	589	589	589
wc/d	4	589-1,885	1,030	707
YTURRALDE, Jose Maria (1942-) Spanish				
oil	2	4,071-4,190	4,130	4,071
YU CHENG-YAO (1898-1993) Chinese				
wc/d	2	27,500-32,500	30,000	27,500
YU HONG (1966-) Chinese				
oil	1	50,000	50,000	50,000
YU PENG (1955-) Chinese				
wc/d	1	18,000	18,000	18,000
YUDIN, Lev (1903-1941) Russian				
oil	1	8,650	8,650	8,650
YUE MINJUN (1962-) Chinese				
oil	3	65,000-490,000	318,333	400,000
YUKINOBU, Kiyohara (1643-1682) Japanese				
oil	1	5,000	5,000	5,000
YULE, William James (19th C) British				
oil	1	2,992	2,992	2,992
YUN SHOUPING (1633-1690) Chinese				
wc/d	4	882-3,151	2,048	1,764
YUN XIANG (1586-1655) Chinese				
wc/d	1	22,500	22,500	22,500
YUREVICH, Sergei Aleksandrovich (1876-1969) Russian				
3D	1	5,208	5,208	5,208
YURKIN, Vladimir Aleksandrovich (1931-) Russian				
oil	1	17,300	17,300	17,300
YUSKAVAGE, Lisa (1962-) American				
oil	7	12,000-900,000	209,571	90,000
wc/d	2	14,000-65,000	39,500	14,000
YUZBASIYAN, Arto (1948-) Canadian				
oil	12	410-5,289	2,061	1,814
wc/d	1	1,558	1,558	1,558
YVARAL (1934-2002) French				
oil	32	750-148,649	8,246	3,058
wc/d	1	15,582	15,582	15,582
3D	1	6,829	6,829	6,829

Name	No.	Price Range	Average	Median
YVON, Adolphe (1817-1893) French				
oil	1	1,798	1,798	1,798
wc/d	2	584-2,453	1,518	584
ZAALBERG, Hester Adriana Cornelia (1836-1909) Dutch				
oil	1	1,753	1,753	1,753
ZABALETA, Rafael (1907-1960) Spanish				
oil	2	95,700-147,459	121,579	95,700
ZABEHLITZKY, Alois (1883-1969) Austrian				
oil	7	788-4,487	1,974	1,558
ZABEL, Larry (?) American				
oil	2	10,000-16,000	13,000	10,000
ZABOROV, Boris (1937-) ?				
oil	3	4,477-34,213	16,038	9,425
wc/d	2	1,549-3,535	2,542	1,549
ZACH, Anton Karl (20th C) Austrian?				
wc/d	1	1,452	1,452	1,452
ZACH, Bruno (1891-?) Austrian				
3D	5	2,057-36,540	11,680	3,800
ZACHAREWICZ, A (20th C) Russian				
wc/d	1	1,870	1,870	1,870
ZACHAROFF, A (19/20th C) Russian?				
oil	1	3,000	3,000	3,000
ZACHAROFF, Alexandre (19/20th C) Russian?				
oil	1	2,510	2,510	2,510
ZACHO, Christian (1843-1913) Danish				
oil	20	550-8,150	1,584	1,051
ZACK, Léon (1892-1980) Russian				
oil	33	656-11,125	4,326	3,741
wc/d	7	490-1,784	1,008	803
ZADIKOV, Alexander (1884-1943) German				
3D	1	2,422	2,422	2,422
ZADKINE, Ossip (1890-1967) French				
wc/d	35	417-69,414	11,169	5,178
3D	16	6,500-323,630	75,838	40,000
ZADOUNAISKY, Michel (1903-1983) French				
3D	2	4,200-108,284	56,242	4,200
ZADRAZIL, Franz (1942-) Austrian				
wc/d	1	2,910	2,910	2,910
ZAFAUREK, Gustav (1841-1906) Austrian				
oil	1	25,800	25,800	25,800
ZAGO, Erma (1880-1942) Italian				
oil	10	1,334-3,633	2,549	2,003
ZAGO, Luigi (1894-1952) Italian				
oil	3	1,211-2,592	1,875	1,824
ZAHN, Friedrich (19th C) ?				
oil	1	2,121	2,121	2,121
ZAHND, Johann (1854-1934) Swiss				
oil	3	1,679-13,320	5,863	2,592
ZAHRADNICZEK, Josef (1813-1844) Austrian				
oil	1	3,330	3,330	3,330
ZAHRTMANN, Kristian (1843-1917) Danish				
oil	9	632-15,809	5,286	3,650
ZAINO, Salvador (1853-1942) Argentinian				
oil	2	1,600-2,500	2,050	1,600
ZAIRIS, Emmanuel (1876-1948) Greek				
oil	1	2,595	2,595	2,595
ZAIS, Giuseppe (1709-1784) Italian				
oil	6	8,919-121,040	48,932	33,820
wc/d	1	584	584	584
ZAITSEV, I (20th C) Russian				
oil	1	4,216	4,216	4,216
ZAJICEK, Carl Wenzel (1860-1923) Austrian				
wc/d	8	584-1,927	1,350	1,149
ZAK, Eugène (1884-1926) Polish				
oil	1	55,000	55,000	55,000
wc/d	3	6,055-29,259	14,646	8,626
ZAKANITCH, Robert (1935-) American				
oil	5	700-7,500	4,252	4,000
ZAKARIAN, Zacharie (?-1922) Turkish				
oil	1	3,970	3,970	3,970
ZAKHARIN, Vladimir (1923-) Russian				
oil	1	2,378	2,378	2,378

Name	No.	Price Range	Average	Median
ZALCE, Alfredo (1908-2003) Mexican				
oil	2	4,750-8,500	6,625	4,750
wc/d	1	1,005	1,005	1,005
ZALEZ, Ernesto (20th C) ?				
oil	2	725-1,745	1,235	725
ZALIOUK, Sacha (1887-1971) ?				
oil	1	1,553	1,553	1,553
wc/d	7	606-8,370	4,405	5,351
ZALOPANY, Michele (1955-) American				
wc/d	1	1,000	1,000	1,000
ZAMACOIS Y ZABALA, Eduardo (1842-1871) Spanish				
oil	1	4,822	4,822	4,822
ZAMBELLI, Evaristo (1889-?) Italian				
oil	1	1,211	1,211	1,211
ZAMPETTI, Luca (1966-) Italian				
oil	1	1,291	1,291	1,291
wc/d	1	2,267	2,267	2,267
ZAMPIGI II, Eugenio (1859-1944) Italian				
oil	14	2,492-30,000	16,857	16,000
wc/d	4	2,742-15,660	8,049	6,048
ZANDER, F van der (1947-) Dutch?				
oil	1	2,997	2,997	2,997
ZANDER, Heinz (1939-) German				
oil	2	1,236-1,483	1,359	1,236
wc/d	2	742-742	742	742
ZANDLEVEN, Jan Adam (1868-1923) Dutch				
oil	4	939-2,754	1,490	1,018
ZANDOMENEGHI, Federico (1841-1917) Italian				
oil	3	11,167-339,658	140,366	70,274
wc/d	2	50,959-90,480	70,719	50,959
ZANDT, W van (19th C) American				
oil	1	3,750	3,750	3,750
ZANDT, William C van (19/20th C) American				
oil	1	3,750	3,750	3,750
ZANDT, William van (19th C) American				
oil	1	4,000	4,000	4,000
ZANELLI, Mario (18th C) Italian				
wc/d	1	8,544	8,544	8,544
ZANETTI ZILLA, Vettore (1864-1946) Italian				
oil	1	5,400	5,400	5,400
ZANG FANZHI (1964-) Chinese				
oil	1	85,000	85,000	85,000
ZANG, Genevieve (20th C) ?				
3D	1	3,592	3,592	3,592
ZANGRANDO, Giovanni (1869-1941) Italian				
oil	5	817-2,186	1,348	1,286
wc/d	1	823	823	823
ZANGS, Herbert (1924-2003) German				
oil	4	957-8,000	3,240	1,649
wc/d	6	634-4,712	2,023	823
3D	3	1,885-10,192	4,711	2,057
ZANICHELLI, Bruno (1963-1990) Italian				
oil	1	2,577	2,577	2,577
wc/d	1	1,757	1,757	1,757
ZANIN, Francesco (19th C) Italian				
oil	3	3,884-33,892	22,898	30,919
wc/d	1	2,740	2,740	2,740
ZANKOVSKII, Ilia Nikolaevich (1843-1917) Russian				
oil	5	18,810-94,600	49,610	40,920
ZAO-WOU-KI (1920-) Chinese				
oil	15	14,549-985,600	286,867	192,860
wc/d	9	17,083-72,617	31,441	26,550
ZAOZERSKY, Boris (1934-) Russian				
oil	1	210,139	210,139	210,139
ZAPATA, Pedro León (1929-) Venezuelan				
oil	1	5,100	5,100	5,100
ZAPF, Carl (19th C) German				
wc/d	1	2,976	2,976	2,976
ZARAGOZA, Arsenio Gerardo (1902-?) Spanish				
3D	1	3,134	3,134	3,134
ZARAGOZA, Raymunda Solis (20th C) Mexican				
oil	1	1,900	1,900	1,900

Name	No.	Price Range	Average	Median
ZARDO, Alberto (1876-1959) Italian				
oil	3	1,304-2,059	1,682	1,683
ZARETSKY, Victor I (1925-1978) Russian				
oil	2	15,810-15,810	15,810	15,810
ZARFIN, Faibich Shraga (1900-1975) Russian				
oil	4	865-1,674	1,150	865
ZARING, Louise E (1872-1970) American				
oil	2	1,400-2,750	2,075	1,400
ZARITSKY, Joseph (1891-1985) Israeli				
oil	4	32,000-160,000	94,250	35,000
wc/d	5	600-8,500	3,730	4,250
ZARITZKY, Dan (1939-) Israeli				
3D	1	2,600	2,600	2,600
ZARRAGA, Angel (1886-1946) Mexican				
oil	11	17,341-240,000	65,642	38,271
ZARUBIN, Viktor Ivanovich (1866-1928) Russian				
oil	7	894-43,500	15,200	5,160
ZATZKA, Hans (1859-1949) Austrian				
oil	23	3,096-40,000	15,738	14,000
ZAVERDINOS, Dionissis (1954-) Greek				
oil	1	1,384	1,384	1,384
ZDANEVITCH, Ilia (1894-1975) Russian				
wc/d	1	6,552	6,552	6,552
ZDRAZILA, Adolf (1868-?) Austrian				
oil	1	11,125	11,125	11,125
ZECHYR, Othmar (1938-1996) Austrian				
oil	1	705	705	705
wc/d	4	2,108-3,770	2,689	2,303
ZEE, Jan van der (1898-1988) Dutch				
wc/d	7	1,798-6,479	3,924	3,658
ZEEPEN, Guillyn Peter van der (/-1711) Dutch				
oil	2	6,020-26,490	16,255	6,020
ZEGELAAR, Gerrit (1719-1794) Dutch				
oil	1	9,790	9,790	9,790
ZEISS, Friedrich (19th C) German				
wc/d	1	2,165	2,165	2,165
ZEITLIN, Alexander (1872-?) Russian				
3D	1	10,260	10,260	10,260
ZEKVELD, Jacob (1945-2002) Dutch				
oil	1	3,134	3,134	3,134
ZELENKA, Rudolf (1875-1938) Austrian				
oil	1	2,443	2,443	2,443
ZELGER, Jakob Joseph (1812-1885) Swiss				
oil	1	2,348	2,348	2,348
ZELIKSON, Serge (c.1890-) French				
3D	1	2,400	2,400	2,400
ZELLENBERG, Franz Zeller von (1805-1876) Austrian				
oil	2	3,814-4,562	4,188	3,814
ZELLER, Fred (1912-) French				
oil	1	1,800	1,800	1,800
ZELLER, Friedrich (1817-1896) Austrian				
oil	1	4,066	4,066	4,066
ZELLER, Hans Arnold (1897-1983) Swiss				
oil	9	1,045-19,434	7,452	4,211
ZELLER, Johann Conrad (1807-1856) Swiss				
oil	4	979-5,418	2,431	999
ZELLER, Magnus (1888-1972) German				
oil	1	1,338	1,338	1,338
ZEMSKY, Jessica (1923-) American				
wc/d	1	2,500	2,500	2,500
ZEN, Sergio (1936-) Italian				
oil	6	676-3,625	1,369	884
ZENDEL, Gabriel (1906-1992) French				
oil	3	884-1,260	1,048	1,001
ZENDER, Rudolf (1901-1988) Swiss				
oil	23	416-2,744	1,152	964
wc/d	2	603-2,518	1,560	603
ZENDEROUDI, Hossein (20th C) ?				
oil	1	25,890	25,890	25,890
ZENETZIS, Vasilis (1935-) Greek				
oil	1	2,288	2,288	2,288

Name	No.	Price Range	Average	Median
ZENG HAO (20th C) Chinese				
oil	2	49,950-70,300	60,125	49,950
ZENG MI (1935-) Chinese				
wc/d	1	11,000	11,000	11,000
ZENG XIAOJUN (1954-) Chinese				
wc/d	1	60,000	60,000	60,000
ZENGELIS, Zoe (1937-) Greek				
oil	2	1,557-1,557	1,557	1,557
ZENIL, Nahum B (1947-) Mexican				
wc/d	1	4,000	4,000	4,000
ZENK, Josef (1904-?) American				
oil	1	3,500	3,500	3,500
ZENKER, Flora (1876-?) ?				
oil	1	1,004	1,004	1,004
ZENNSTROM, Petter (1945-) Swedish				
oil	5	1,018-3,181	1,749	1,520
wc/d	1	5,726	5,726	5,726
ZENO, Jorge (1956-) Puerto Rican				
oil	2	11,000-14,000	12,500	11,000
ZENS, Herwig (1943-) Austrian				
oil	2	2,158-3,600	2,879	2,158
ZENTS, Shawn (1965-) American				
oil	1	1,100	1,100	1,100
ZEPPEL-SPERL, Robert (1944-2005) Austrian				
oil	5	1,318-5,733	2,506	1,918
wc/d	4	546-1,641	878	659
ZERBE, Karl (1903-1972) American/German				
oil	3	750-2,400	1,366	950
wc/d	1	550	550	550
ZERGE, Ove (1894-1983) Swedish				
oil	2	1,368-1,368	1,368	1,368
ZERILLI, Francesco (?-1837) Italian				
wc/d	1	6,487	6,487	6,487
ZERMATI, Jules (20th C) Italian				
oil	2	1,678-1,918	1,798	1,678
ZERNOVA, Ekaterina (1900-1976) Russian				
oil	6	476-2,664	1,373	1,142
ZESATTI, Luis Armando (1967-) Mexican				
oil	2	45,000-45,000	45,000	45,000
ZESHIN, Shibata (1807-1891) Japanese				
oil	1	1,700	1,700	1,700
wc/d	3	2,600-2,600	2,600	2,600
ZETSCHE, Eduard (1844-1927) Austrian				
oil	1	13,081	13,081	13,081
wc/d	6	304-2,903	1,736	1,285
ZETTERSTROM, Gunnar (1902-1965) Swedish				
oil	1	1,364	1,364	1,364
ZETTERWALL, Eva H (1941-) Swedish				
oil	1	3,964	3,964	3,964
ZEUNER, Jonas (1727-1814) Dutch				
oil	2	12,162-12,162	12,162	12,162
ZEUTHEN, Ernst (1880-1938) Danish				
oil	1	2,263	2,263	2,263
ZEVENBERGHEN, Georges van (1877-1968) Belgian				
oil	2	526-3,575	2,050	526
wc/d	1	700	700	700
ZEWY, Karl (1855-1929) Austrian				
oil	3	2,264-5,000	3,904	4,450
ZEZZOS, Alessandro (1848-1914) Italian				
oil	1	60,616	60,616	60,616
wc/d	3	2,356-7,120	4,408	3,748
ZHABA, Alfons (1878-1942) Russian				
oil	2	953-114,658	57,805	953
ZHAN WANG (1962-) Chinese				
3D	2	15,063-48,000	31,531	15,063
ZHANG DAQIAN (1899-1983) Chinese				
wc/d	7	3,000-90,000	32,770	10,000
ZHANG FAZHI (1976-) Chinese				
oil	2	6,904-17,000	11,952	6,904
ZHANG HONG TU (1943-) Chinese				
oil	1	55,000	55,000	55,000
wc/d	1	32,000	32,000	32,000

Name	No.	Price Range	Average	Median
ZHANG HONGNIAN (1976-) Chinese				
oil	1	32,000	32,000	32,000
ZHANG HUAN (1965-) Chinese				
3D	2	277,500-350,000	313,750	277,500
ZHANG JIAN (c.1662-1722) Chinese				
oil	1	60,000	60,000	60,000
ZHANG LEI (1968-) Chinese				
oil	2	19,000-27,500	23,250	19,000
ZHANG QIZHENG (1921-1997) Chinese				
oil	1	8,787	8,787	8,787
ZHANG XIAO GANG (1958-) Chinese				
oil	4	360,000-860,000	511,750	407,000
wc/d	1	54,355	54,355	54,355
ZHANG XIAO TAO (1970-) Chinese				
oil	1	20,083	20,083	20,083
ZHANG YIBO (1966-) American?				
oil	1	3,628	3,628	3,628
ZHAO BO (1974-) Chinese				
oil	1	13,000	13,000	13,000
ZHAO CHUNXIANG (1912-1991) Chinese				
wc/d	2	3,583-80,000	41,791	3,583
ZHAO GANG (1961-) Chinese				
oil	1	13,000	13,000	13,000
ZHAO NEN ZHI (1968-) Chinese				
oil	1	14,800	14,800	14,800
ZHAO SHAOANG (1905-1998) Chinese				
wc/d	3	810-6,256	3,105	2,250
ZHAO ZHIQIAN (1829-1884) Chinese				
wc/d	1	8,700	8,700	8,700
ZHENG LI (1964-) Chinese				
wc/d	1	12,000	12,000	12,000
ZHENG WUCHANG (1894-1952) Chinese				
wc/d	1	16,650	16,650	16,650
ZHONG BIAO (1968-) Chinese				
oil	2	27,614-37,500	32,557	27,614
ZHOU CHUNYA (1955-) Chinese				
oil	1	45,000	45,000	45,000
ZHOU TIEHAI (1966-) Chinese				
oil	1	31,000	31,000	31,000
ZHOU YUWEI (1937-) Chinese				
oil	1	9,555	9,555	9,555
ZHU ANGZHI (1764-1842) Chinese				
wc/d	1	1,286	1,286	1,286
ZHU DE-QUN (1922-) Chinese				
oil	3	120,498-296,000	201,592	188,279
ZHU QIZHAN (1892-1996) Chinese				
wc/d	3	1,200-1,700	1,395	1,286
ZHU WEI (1958-) Chinese				
wc/d	1	38,000	38,000	38,000
ZHU XIAOGANG (1954-) American				
wc/d	1	10,000	10,000	10,000
ZHUKOVSKY, Stanislav Yulianovich (1873-1944) Polish				
oil	10	4,816-186,000	54,810	25,800
ZICHY, Count Mihaly von (1827-1906) Hungarian				
wc/d	1	114,658	114,658	114,658
ZICK, Conrad (1773-1836) German				
oil	1	1,635	1,635	1,635
ZICK, Januarius (1730-1797) German				
oil	1	32,510	32,510	32,510
ZICKWOLFF, Fred (20th C) Dutch?				
oil	1	2,631	2,631	2,631
ZIEGLER, Eustace Paul (1881-1969) American				
oil	7	600-35,000	18,371	21,000
ZIEGLER, Henry Bryan (1793-1874) British				
oil	1	1,380	1,380	1,380
wc/d	1	890	890	890
ZIEGLER, Jules Claude (1804-1856) French				
oil	2	9,115-11,040	10,077	9,115
ZIEGLER, Richard (1891-1992) German				
oil	1	3,708	3,708	3,708
wc/d	13	486-1,457	826	728

Name	No.	Price Range	Average	Median
ZIELASCO, Robert (1948-) Austrian				
oil	1	1,297	1,297	1,297
ZIELENKIEWICZ, Kazimierz (1906-1988) Polish				
oil	1	1,100	1,100	1,100
ZIELER, Mogens (1905-1983) Danish				
oil	2	485-13,740	7,112	485
ZIELKE, Julius (1826-1907) German				
wc/d	2	1,135-2,497	1,816	1,135
ZIEM, Felix (1821-1911) French				
oil	34	3,801-118,320	35,771	26,610
wc/d	16	565-4,919	1,904	1,620
ZIER, François Edouard (1856-1924) French				
oil	4	1,214-6,000	2,840	1,900
wc/d	1	817	817	817
ZIESENIS, Johan Georg (1716-1776) Danish				
oil	4	1,767-24,082	13,094	2,445
ZIGAINA, Giuseppe (1924-) Italian				
oil	1	12,138	12,138	12,138
wc/d	7	1,070-15,265	5,879	3,816
ZIGLER, John (c.1827-?) ?				
oil	1	2,873	2,873	2,873
ZILBERSTEIN, Ludwikowi (19/20th C) Polish				
oil	1	1,097	1,097	1,097
ZILLE, Heinrich (1858-1929) German				
wc/d	78	586-30,531	3,809	2,160
ZILLER (?) ?				
oil	2	3,879-5,845	4,862	3,879
ZILOTTI, Domenico Bernardino (1730-1780) Italian				
wc/d	1	1,730	1,730	1,730
ZIMMER, Bernd (1948-) German				
oil	4	4,083-21,205	12,688	10,177
wc/d	4	707-9,370	3,235	1,331
ZIMMER, Hans Peter (1936-1992) German				
oil	4	2,036-30,575	13,498	2,910
wc/d	3	805-1,274	1,117	1,272
ZIMMERMAN, Frederick A (1886-1974) American				
oil	1	1,525	1,525	1,525
ZIMMERMAN, Jan W G (1816-1887) Dutch				
oil	1	3,250	3,250	3,250
ZIMMERMAN, Theodore (20th C) British				
wc/d	11	473-3,680	1,767	1,790
ZIMMERMANN, Albert (1809-1888) German				
oil	5	572-12,846	6,177	3,649
ZIMMERMANN, Alfred (1854-1910) German				
oil	1	1,120	1,120	1,120
ZIMMERMANN, August Albert (1808-1888) German				
oil	6	853-10,041	5,043	5,500
ZIMMERMANN, Carl (1863-1930) German				
oil	3	766-1,694	1,263	1,331
ZIMMERMANN, Ernst Karl Georg (1852-1901) German				
oil	4	574-1,573	1,014	700
ZIMMERMANN, Helmut (1924-) German				
oil	1	3,168	3,168	3,168
ZIMMERMANN, Reinhard Sebastian (1815-1893) German				
oil	2	2,518-4,419	3,468	2,518
wc/d	1	1,824	1,824	1,824
ZIMMERMANN, Richard (1820-1875) German				
oil	3	1,946-4,529	3,187	3,086
ZIMNIK, Reiner (1931-) German/Polish				
wc/d	1	1,120	1,120	1,120
ZINGG, Adrian (1734-1816) Swiss				
wc/d	2	8,834-11,781	10,307	8,834
ZINGG, Jules (1882-1942) French				
oil	13	385-24,913	8,654	7,644
wc/d	4	707-2,603	1,860	1,854
ZINGONI, Aurelio (1853-1922) Italian				
oil	3	2,035-11,571	5,785	3,750
ZINI, Umberto (1878-?) Italian				
oil	1	1,387	1,387	1,387
wc/d	1	468	468	468

Name	No.	Price Range	Average	Median
ZINKEISEN, Anna (1901-1976) British				
oil	7	1,218-7,938	4,207	4,675
wc/d	2	555-1,239	897	555
ZINKEISEN, Doris (1898-1991) British				
oil	18	669-9,568	2,790	2,165
ZITKO, Otto (1959-) Austrian				
oil	1	3,616	3,616	3,616
wc/d	1	1,999	1,999	1,999
ZITMAN, Cornelis (1926-) Dutch/Venezuelan				
oil	1	1,054	1,054	1,054
3D	1	8,818	8,818	8,818
ZIVERI, Alberto (1908-1990) Italian				
oil	3	3,053-41,269	16,409	4,905
wc/d	2	727-954	840	727
ZIX, Benjamin (1772-1811) French				
wc/d	1	1,521	1,521	1,521
ZO, Henri (1873-1933) French				
oil	1	5,888	5,888	5,888
ZOBEL, Fernando (1924-1987) Spanish				
oil	1	19,000	19,000	19,000
wc/d	1	1,286	1,286	1,286
ZOBERNIG, Heimo (1958-) ?				
oil	1	20,384	20,384	20,384
ZOBOLI, Jacopo (1681-1767) Italian				
wc/d	1	3,534	3,534	3,534
ZOCCHI, C (18th C) Italian				
oil	1	47,182	47,182	47,182
ZOCCHI, Cesare (1851-1922) Italian				
3D	1	76,928	76,928	76,928
ZOCCHI, Guglielmo (1874-?) Italian				
oil	4	4,000-35,000	17,950	15,400
ZOFF, Alfred (1852-1927) Austrian				
oil	6	1,526-36,294	11,738	3,884
ZOFFANY, Johann (1733-1810) British				
oil	1	75,600	75,600	75,600
ZOFFOLI, Angelo (fl.1860-1910) Italian				
oil	1	3,500	3,500	3,500
ZOFFOLI, Giacomo (18th C) Italian				
3D	2	7,899-9,115	8,507	7,899
ZOFFOLI, Giacomo and Giovanni (18th C) Italian				
3D	1	25,900	25,900	25,900
ZOI, Dante (20th C) French				
3D	2	3,500-3,879	3,689	3,500
ZOLL, Kilian (1818-1860) Swedish				
oil	2	435-3,572	2,003	435
ZOLLA, Venanzio (1880-1961) Italian				
oil	18	716-2,586	1,534	1,551
ZOLLER, Joseph Anton (1730-1791) Austrian				
wc/d	1	2,408	2,408	2,408
ZOLNHOFER, Fritz (1896-1965) German				
oil	1	2,432	2,432	2,432
ZOMMER, Richard Karlovich (1866-1939) Russian				
oil	24	4,464-407,671	40,409	21,658
wc/d	1	7,440	7,440	7,440
ZONA, Antonio (1813-1892) Italian				
oil	2	350-1,760	1,055	350
ZONARO, Fausto (1854-1929) Italian				
oil	14	2,356-208,800	59,478	36,486
wc/d	4	1,274-2,761	2,282	2,548
ZONGOLOPOULOS, George (1903-2004) Greek				
3D	2	26,400-35,200	30,800	26,400
ZOPF, Carl (1858-1944) German				
oil	1	5,160	5,160	5,160
ZOPF, Julius (1838-1897) Austrian				
oil	1	1,011	1,011	1,011
ZOPPI, Antonio (1860-1926) Italian				
oil	1	1,302	1,302	1,302
ZORACH, Marguerite (1887-1968) American				
oil	1	22,500	22,500	22,500
ZORACH, William (1887-1966) American				
wc/d	24	850-8,500	4,214	4,000
3D	15	2,000-27,500	9,480	7,500

Name	No.	Price Range	Average	Median
ZORIO, Gilberto (1944-) Italian				
wc/d	5	3,170-8,918	6,032	5,966
3D	2	50,884-65,000	57,942	50,884
ZORN, Anders (1860-1920) Swedish				
oil	7	5,096-498,551	262,866	211,884
wc/d	6	2,738-382,192	99,742	14,957
3D	3	13,087-16,826	14,550	13,737
ZORNES, Milford (1908-) American				
oil	4	1,800-19,000	7,137	2,750
wc/d	21	1,000-7,000	2,621	2,000
ZORRILLA Y LUNA, Francisco (1679-1747) Spanish				
oil	1	3,568	3,568	3,568
ZORRILLA, Alfredo (1927-1990) Uruguayan				
oil	1	4,000	4,000	4,000
ZOTL, Aloys (1803-1887) Swiss				
wc/d	3	10,000-43,552	32,368	43,552
ZOTTI, Carmelo (1933-) Italian				
oil	1	1,193	1,193	1,193
ZOUNI, Opy (1941-) Greek				
oil	1	5,632	5,632	5,632
ZOX, Larry (1936-) American				
oil	2	1,300-1,600	1,450	1,300
ZUBER, Henri (1844-1909) French				
wc/d	2	750-1,308	1,029	750
ZUBER, Max (20th C) Swiss?				
oil	1	1,674	1,674	1,674
ZUBER-BUHLER, Fritz (1822-1896) Swiss				
oil	4	2,182-55,000	25,295	8,000
wc/d	2	1,669-3,084	2,376	1,669
ZUBIAURRE, Ramon de (1882-1969) Spanish				
oil	1	9,000	9,000	9,000
ZUBIAURRE, Valentin de (1879-1963) Spanish				
oil	4	3,185-174,000	54,441	13,230
wc/d	6	478-999	637	530
ZUBTSOV, Sergei (1972-) Russian				
oil	1	1,483	1,483	1,483
ZUCCARELLI, Francesco (1702-1788) Italian				
oil	3	38,219-74,000	57,707	60,904
wc/d	4	1,001-55,500	19,647	3,588
ZUCCARO, Federico (1540-1609) Italian				
wc/d	1	25,900	25,900	25,900
ZUCCARO, Taddeo (1529-1566) Italian				
wc/d	1	55,500	55,500	55,500
ZUCCHI, Antonio (1726-1795) Italian				
oil	1	8,500	8,500	8,500
ZUCCHI, Francesco II (1692-1764) Italian				
wc/d	1	5,833	5,833	5,833
ZUCKER, Joe (1941-) American				
oil	2	4,000-6,000	5,000	4,000
wc/d	1	1,000	1,000	1,000
ZUCKERBERG, Stanley (1919-1995) American				
oil	2	550-2,550	1,550	550
ZUCKERKANDL-STEKEL, Gertrud (1895-1981) Austrian				
oil	1	3,534	3,534	3,534
ZUGEL, Heinrich von (1850-1941) German				
oil	13	600-43,589	10,165	6,868
wc/d	1	2,221	2,221	2,221
ZUGEL, Wilhelm (1876-1950) German				
3D	1	3,279	3,279	3,279
ZUHR, Hugo (1895-1971) Swedish				
oil	5	988-2,907	1,871	1,982
ZUIDEMA BROOS, Jan Jacob (1833-1877) Dutch				
oil	1	7,054	7,054	7,054
ZUILL, Abbie Luella (1856-1921) American				
oil	1	3,200	3,200	3,200
ZULLE, Johannes (1841-1938) Swiss				
oil	1	5,881	5,881	5,881
ZULOAGA, Elisa Elvira (1900-1980) South American?				
oil	1	7,440	7,440	7,440
ZULOAGA, Ignacio (1870-1945) Spanish				
oil	1	87,842	87,842	87,842
wc/d	2	727-5,470	3,098	727

Name	No.	Price Range	Average	Median
ZULOW, Franz von (1883-1963) Austrian				
oil	1	16,397	16,397	16,397
wc/d	9	1,558-2,928	2,246	2,338
ZUMBO, Giulio Gaetano (1656-1701) Italian				
3D	1	71,757	71,757	71,757
ZUMBUSCH, Kaspar Clemens Eduard (1830-1915) Austrian				
3D	1	6,689	6,689	6,689
ZUND, Robert (1827-1909) Swiss				
oil	10	9,894-159,823	72,113	76,316
wc/d	6	986-6,868	3,649	3,358
ZUNIGA, Francisco (1913-1998) Costa Rican				
oil	1	6,000	6,000	6,000
wc/d	27	1,500-26,000	7,202	6,000
3D	24	2,395-3,300,000	176,112	22,000
ZURBARAN, Francisco (1598-1664) Spanish				
oil	1	309,189	309,189	309,189
ZURBRIGGEN, Werner (1931-1980) Swiss				
oil	1	3,263	3,263	3,263
ZURN, Hans (younger) (1585-?) Austrian?				
3D	1	5,890	5,890	5,890
ZURN, Jorg (c.1583-1635) Austrian				
3D	1	62,438	62,438	62,438
ZURN, Unica (1916-1970) German				
wc/d	1	2,631	2,631	2,631
ZURZARREN, Cayo (19th C) ?				
oil	1	3,000	3,000	3,000
ZUSH (1946-) Spanish				
oil	5	1,070-7,459	3,212	1,796
wc/d	6	598-4,071	1,815	1,308
ZUYDERHOUDT, Cryn van (c.1704-c.1773) Dutch				
wc/d	1	3,036	3,036	3,036
ZVEREV, Anatoli (1931-1986) Russian				
oil	6	1,523-15,000	6,383	2,356
wc/d	9	896-6,000	2,117	1,005
ZWART, Arie (1903-1981) Dutch				
oil	14	707-4,555	1,668	1,341
ZWART, Willem de (1862-1931) Dutch				
oil	10	964-55,452	12,482	3,134
wc/d	1	2,316	2,316	2,316
ZWEDEN, Johan van (1896-1975) Dutch				
wc/d	1	1,085	1,085	1,085
ZWEEP, Douwe Jan van der (1890-1975) Dutch				
oil	2	1,219-1,463	1,341	1,219
wc/d	1	775	775	775
ZWEIGBERGK, Bo Eison von (1897-1940) Swedish				
wc/d	2	865-1,255	1,060	865
ZWENGAUER, Anton (elder) (1810-1884) German				
oil	1	1,753	1,753	1,753
ZWICKLE, Hubert von (1875-1947) Austrian				
oil	2	1,215-2,671	1,943	1,215
ZWYNEN, Ruud (20th C) Dutch				
oil	1	3,107	3,107	3,107
ZYL, Lambertus (1866-1947) Dutch				
3D	3	2,116-3,527	2,664	2,351